Grade 8

Annotated Teacher's Edition

Prentice Hall
LITERATURE
Timeless Voices, Timeless Themes

SILVER

ISBN 0-13-436018-4

PRENTICE HALL
Upper Saddle River, New Jersey
Glenview, Illinois
7 8 9 10   04 03 02 01   Needham, Massachusetts

Create a fresh enthusiasm for literature while building lifelong communication skills

Program Components

◆ **Student Edition**

◆ **Annotated Teacher's Edition**

◆ **Teaching Resources**

◆ **Assessment Success Kit**

◆ **Writing and Language Transparencies**

◆ **Selection Support Workbook**

◆ **Grammar Practice Workbook**

◆ **Literature Library**

◆ **Humanities Pack**

◆ **Interdisciplinary Units**

◆ **Looking at Literature Videotape/Videodisc**

◆ **Listening to Literature Audiocassettes**

◆ **Formal Assessment/Computer Test Bank CD-ROM**

◆ **Literature CD-ROM Library**

◆ **Interactive Student Tutorial CD-ROM**

◆ **Resource Pro® CD-ROM with Literature Database**

◆ **Prentice Hall *Writer's Solution***
  • **Writing Lab CD-ROM**
  • **Language Lab CD-ROM**
  • **Writers at Work Videotape/Videodisc**

The finest classic and contemporary literature in a flexible organization

A perfect blend of classic and contemporary literature is presented in a table of contents that lets you choose a thematic approach, a genre-based approach, or a combination of the two.

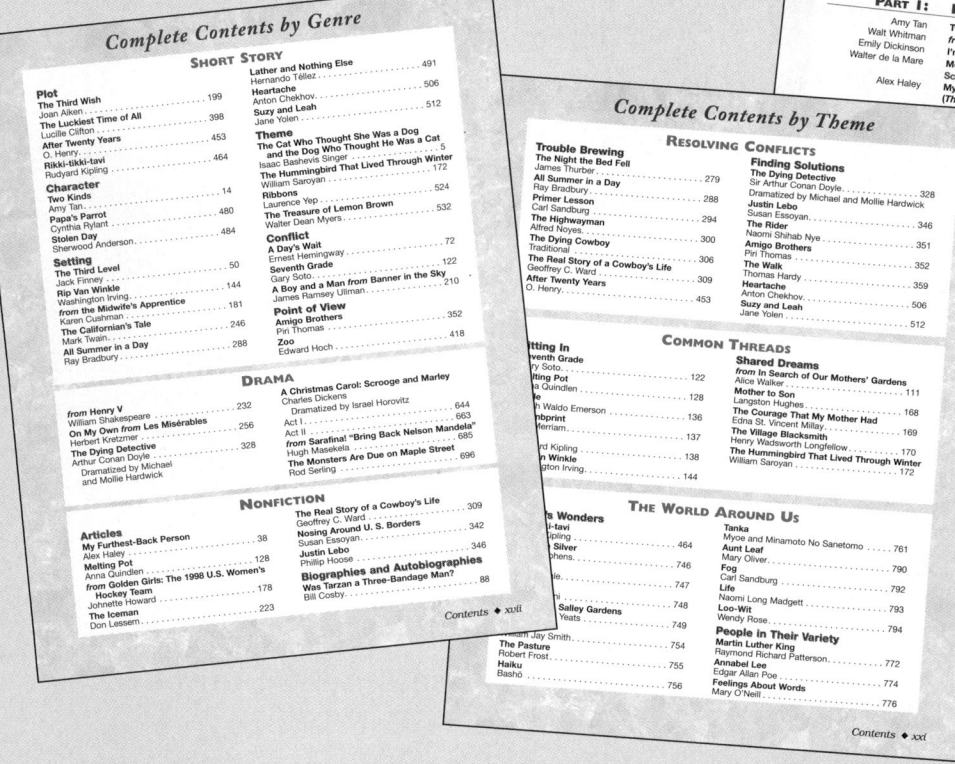

Complete Contents by Genre

SHORT STORY

Plot
The Third Wish 199
Joan Aiken
The Luckiest Time of All 398
Lucille Clifton
After Twenty Years 453
O. Henry
Rikki-tikki-tavi 464
Rudyard Kipling

Character
Two Kinds 14
Amy Tan
Papa's Parrot 480
Cynthia Rylant
Stolen Day 484
Sherwood Anderson

Setting
The Third Level 50
Jack Finney
Rip Van Winkle 144
Washington Irving
from the Midwife's Apprentice 181
Karen Cushman
The Californian's Tale 246
Mark Twain
All Summer in a Day 288
Ray Bradbury

Lather and Nothing Else 491
Hernando Téllez
Heartache 506
Anton Chekhov
Suzy and Leah 512
Jane Yolen

Theme
The Cat Who Thought She Was a Dog
and the Dog Who Thought He Was a Cat 5
Isaac Bashevis Singer
The Hummingbird That Lived Through Winter 172
William Saroyan
Ribbons 524
Laurence Yep
The Treasure of Lemon Brown 532
Walter Dean Myers

Conflict
A Day's Wait 72
Ernest Hemingway
Seventh Grade 122
Gary Soto
A Boy and a Man from Banner in the Sky 210
James Ramsey Ullman

Point of View
Amigo Brothers 352
Piri Thomas
Zoo 418
Edward Hoch

DRAMA

from Henry V 232
William Shakespeare
On My Own from Les Misérables 256
Herbert Kretzmer
The Dying Detective 328
Arthur Conan Doyle
Dramatized by Michael
and Mollie Hardwick

A Christmas Carol: Scrooge and Marley 644
Charles Dickens
Dramatized by Israel Horovitz
Act I 644
Act II 663
from Sarafina! "Bring Back Nelson Mandela" 685
Hugh Masekela
The Monsters Are Due on Maple Street 696
Rod Serling

NONFICTION

Articles
My Furthest-Back Person 38
Alex Haley
Melting Pot 128
Anna Quindlen
from Golden Girls: The 1998 U.S. Women's Hockey Team 178
Johnette Howard
The Iceman 223
Don Lessem

The Real Story of a Cowboy's Life 309
Geoffrey C. Ward
Nosing Around U. S. Borders 342
Susan Essoyan
Justin Lebo 346
Phillip Hoose

Biographies and Autobiographies
Was Tarzan a Three-Bandage Man? 88
Bill Cosby

Contents ◆ xvii

Looking at Universal Themes
Finding Yourself

Unit 1

READING FOR SUCCESS
Isaac Bashevis Singer
Literal Comprehension Strategies ....
The Cat Who Thought She Was a Dog and the Dog Who Thought He Was a Cat .... Short Story 4 5

PART 1: INVENTING YOURSELF
Amy Tan — Two Kinds .... Short Story 14
Walt Whitman — from Song of Myself ....
Emily Dickinson — I'm Nobody .... Poem ....
Walter de la Mare — Me .... Poem 30
Science Connection: Nature's One-of-a-Kind .... Poem ....
Alex Haley — My Furthest-Back Person
(The ...)

Complete Contents by Theme

RESOLVING CONFLICTS

Trouble Brewing
The Night the Bed Fell ....
James Thurber
All Summer in a Day 279
Ray Bradbury
Primer Lesson 288
Carl Sandburg
The Highwayman 294
Alfred Noyes
The Dying Cowboy 300
Traditional
The Real Story of a Cowboy's Life 306
Geoffrey C. Ward
After Twenty Years 309
O. Henry 453

Finding Solutions
The Dying Detective 328
Sir Arthur Conan Doyle
Dramatized by Michael and Mollie Hardwick
Justin Lebo 346
Susan Essoyan
The Rider 346
Naomi Shihab Nye
Amigo Brothers 351
Piri Thomas
The Walk 352
Thomas Hardy
Heartache 359
Anton Chekhov 506
Suzy and Leah 512
Jane Yolen

COMMON THREADS

Fitting In
Seventh Grade ....
Gary Soto
Melting Pot 122
Anna Quindlen
... . 128
... Waldo Emerson 136
...print
... Merriam 137
... Kipling
... Winkle 138
...ington Irving 144

Shared Dreams
from In Search of Our Mothers' Gardens ....
Alice Walker
Mother to Son 111
Langston Hughes
The Courage That My Mother Had 168
Edna St. Vincent Millay
The Village Blacksmith 169
Henry Wadsworth Longfellow
The Hummingbird That Lived Through Winter 170
William Saroyan 172

THE WORLD AROUND US

... Wonders
...i-tavi ....
... Kipling
... Silver 464
...phens 746
... . 747
... Salley Gardens 748
... Yeats 749
...iam Jay Smith
The Pasture 754
Robert Frost
Haiku 755
Bashō 756

Tanka
Myoe and Minamoto No Sanetomo 761
Aunt Leaf 790
Mary Oliver
Fog 792
Carl Sandburg
Life 793
Naomi Long Madgett
Loo-Wit 794
Wendy Rose

People in Their Variety
Martin Luther King 772
Raymond Richard Patterson
Annabel Lee 774
Edgar Allan Poe
Feelings About Words 776
Mary O'Neill

Contents ◆ xxi

Looking at Literary Forms
Nonfiction

Unit 7

READING FOR SUCCESS
James Dickey
Strategies for Reading Nonfiction 556
How to Enjoy Poetry .... Expository Essay 557

PART 1: BIOGRAPHY AND AUTOBIOGRAPHY
Russell Baker — No Gumption .... Autobiography 566
Career Connection: Careers in Journalism 573
CONNECTIONS TO TODAY'S WORLD
Let the Reader Beware: Tips for Verifying Information on the Internet .... Guidelines 574
Reid Goldsborough — The Chase from An American Childhood .... Autobiography 576
Annie Dillard — Winslow Homer: America's Greatest Painter .... Biography 586
H. N. Levitt — Nolan Ryan, Texas Treasure .... Biography 590
William W. Lace — Sports Connection: Baseball—A Game of Records 593
.... 596
Writing Process Workshop: Biographical Report
APPLYING LANGUAGE SKILLS: Documenting Sources 597
Drafting/Revising Application: 598
Editing/Proofreading Application: Avoiding Double Negatives 599
REAL-WORLD READING SKILLS WORKSHOP: Reading for Specific Information 600
GRAMMAR REVIEW: Phrases ....

PART 2: TYPES OF ESSAYS
Charles Kuralt — Independence Hall .... Narrative Essay 604
Marjorie Kinnan Rawlings — Rattlesnake Hunt .... Descriptive Essay 607
Ernesto Galarza — from Barrio Boy .... Personal Essay 611
Community Connection: One School, Many Languages 614
Chief Dan George — I Am a Native of North America .... Reflective Essay 615
Barbara Jordan — All Together Now .... Persuasive Essay 618
CONNECTING LITERATURE TO SOCIAL STUDIES: GEOGRAPHY
Jacqueline Dineen — Tenochtitlán: Inside the Aztec Capital .... Visual Essay 623
.... 630
Writing Process Workshop: Report on a Current Event
APPLYING LANGUAGE SKILLS: 631
Drafting/Revising Application: Use Synonyms for Variety ....
Editing/Proofreading Application: Capitalize Proper Nouns 632
REAL-WORLD READING SKILLS WORKSHOP: 633
Using Headlines and Text Structure in Newspapers 634
GRAMMAR REVIEW: Correct Use of Pronouns 635
SPEAKING, LISTENING, AND VIEWING WORKSHOP: Speaking Persuasively ....
VOCABULARY ADVENTURES WITH RICHARD LEDERER: 636
Idioms From Land, Sea, and Sky ....
EXTENDED READING OPPORTUNITIES 637

Contents ◆ xiii

Real-life connections that engage and motivate

CONNECTIONS TO TODAY'S WORLD

Many people didn't believe that the Wright brothers would ever get a plane off the ground. If those people had looked into the future, they would have seen that the Wright brothers' dream led to airplanes, supersonic jets, and even space travel!

John Glenn was the first American to travel around the Earth in space. On February 20, 1962, he orbited (went around) the Earth three times in the spacecraft *Friendship 7*. His return to space at age seventy-seven makes him the oldest person ever to travel in space. In this on-line interview, he answered questions about his first space journey around the world.

An Astronaut's Answers

John Glenn

The first time you went into space, how did it feel to be all alone except for communication through radio?

In 1962, I looked down from an orbit high above our planet and saw our beautiful Earth and its curved horizon against the vastness of space. I have never forgotten that sight nor the sense of wonder it engendered. Although I was alone in Friendship 7, I did not feel alone in space. I knew that I was supported by my family, my six fellow astronauts, thousands of NASA engineers and employees, and millions of people around the world.

Why did you want to be an astronaut? How did you fly around the Earth three times? Was it hard?

I served as a fighter pilot in World War II and the Korean conflict. After Korea, I graduated from the Naval Test Pilot School and worked as a fighter test pilot. I applied for the astronaut program because I thought it was a logical career step, a challenging opportunity and one in which I could help start a new area of research that would be very valuable to everyone here on Earth. I have always considered myself very fortunate to be selected in the first group of seven astronauts.

An Atlas rocket boosted me into space and I orbited the Earth in my space capsule, the Friendship 7. It certainly was a challenge but one for which I was well prepared. The National Aeronautics and Space Administration (NASA) wanted people who were test pilots and accustomed to working under very unusual

◀ **Critical Viewing** Why do you think John Glenn needs a special suit and helmet for space travel? [Draw Conclusions]

266 ◆ Proving ...

Literature and Your Life feature helps capture student interest by linking literature to life experiences throughout every selection.

Connections to Today's World feature ties contemporary popular writings—including articles, songs, and television scripts—to the classics.

High Interest Visuals hook students' interest as they begin <u>every</u> selection.

The most comprehensive integrated skills instruction

Writing Process Workshops provide detailed step-by-step writing process instruction in all modes of writing.

- Provides 20 opportunities for extended writing projects
- Linked to the end-of-selection Writing Mini-Lesson through the Writing Skills Focus sections; enables students to build on skills they've already learned

Two **Applying Language Skills** mini-lessons accompany each Writing Process Workshop.

Real-World Reading Skills Workshops help students build skills essential to success in careers and in daily life.

- 20 lessons in each book

Speaking, Listening, and Viewing Workshops provide instruction in real-life communication skills.

Grammar Review provides a review of the grammar skills featured in each unit, following a developmental sequence.

What's Behind the Words: Vocabulary Adventures with Richard Lederer will delight students and increase their vocabulary.

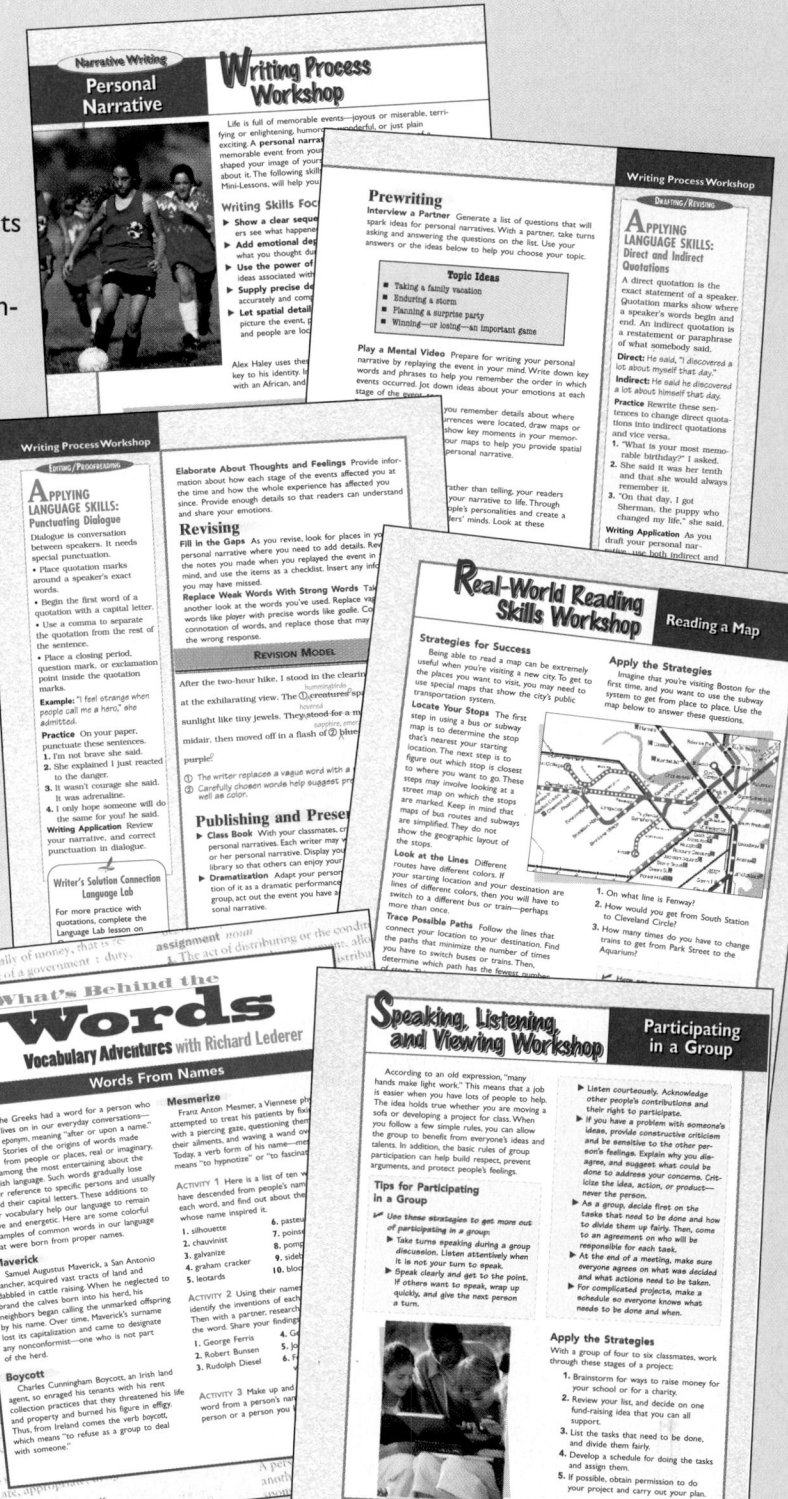

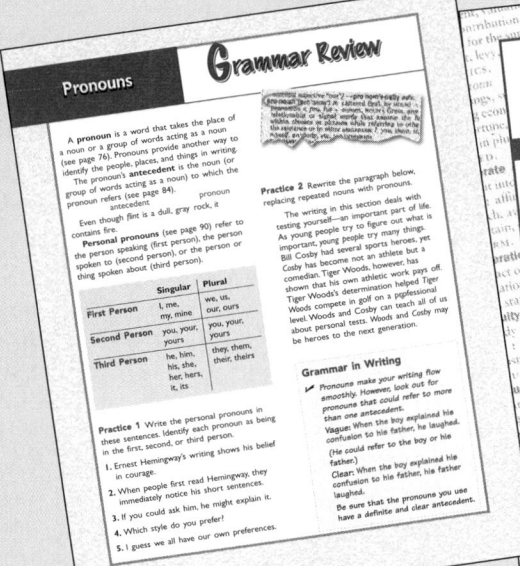

The only literature program to provide complete skills instruction with every selection

Guide for Reading

Meet the Author:

John Steinbeck (1902–1968)
When John Steinbeck received the Nobel Prize for Literature in 1962, it capped a long, successful career in which he established himself as one of our nation's best-loved and most highly regarded writers.

Voice of the Working Class Steinbeck grew up in the Salinas Valley of California, where he became aware of the hard lives of migrant farm workers. After college, he spent five years drifting and writing; he even joined a hobo camp to study the lives of its people. His Pulitzer Prize-winning novel *The Grapes of Wrath* and the novels *Of Mice and Men* and *The Pearl* express sympathy for poor people who are exploited by society.

THE STORY BEHIND THE STORY
Although he had been acclaimed as one of the foremost writers of America's heartland, Steinbeck worried that he had lost touch with the country and its people. He decided to reestablish his ties by driving east to west—from Maine to California—along a northern route. He returned to New York along the southern route, passing through the Mohave Desert, Texas, and the Deep South. Steinbeck published an account of his travels entitled *Travels with Charley,* in 1962. The book's subtitle was "In Search of America."

◆ LITERATURE AND YOUR LIFE

CONNECT YOUR EXPERIENCE
Think for a moment of trips you've taken—to another country, state, or region. Did the people you meet have attitudes, beliefs, or ways of speaking different from your own? In *Travels with Charley,* John Steinbeck sets out to meet people all across the United States and learns about their different views of life in the process.

THEMATIC FOCUS: A Land of Promise
As you follow Steinbeck on his journey, ask yourself what qualities make the United States "a land of promise" for people from all regions of the land.

◆ Background for Understanding

GEOGRAPHY
As Steinbeck travels through the western United States, he finds himself in the Badlands of North Dakota. Located in the western parts of both North and South Dakota, the Badlands are a rugged region of fantastically shaped rock formations separated by valleys. In that barren landscape, there is little vegetation to prevent the erosion of the soft sedimentary rocks. The elevation of the Badlands is between 2,000 and 5,000 feet.

◆ Build Vocabulary

SUFFIXES: -ic
The suffix *-ic* means "like" or "having to do with." The word *diagnostic,* therefore, means "having to do with a diagnosis"—the study of facts.

WORD BANK
Which word from the story do you think might mean "the act of inquiring"? Check the Build Vocabulary box on page 356 to see if you chose correctly.

diagnostic
peripatetic
rigorous
maneuver
inquiry
inexplicable
celestial

◆ from Travels with Charley ◆

◆ Literary Focus

TRAVEL ESSAY
An essay is a short nonfiction work about a particular subject. A **travel essay** focuses on a trip or journey that someone actually made. In it, the writer may include factual information as well as descriptions that reveal how a place looks, sounds, or feels. It is, however, the writer's personal impressions and reflections that make the essay unique.

◆ Reading Strategy

CLARIFY DETAILS
When you don't completely understand a passage in a travel essay or other piece of writing, take time to stop and **clarify** what is not clear. Sometimes, this may simply involve pausing to think about the meaning of a detail. Other times, it may be necessary to reread a portion of the text or read ahead to piece together the meaning of something. Sometimes, it may even be necessary to go outside the text to find out what something means. Fill out a chart like the one below to clarify details as you read.

Detail to Clarify	Meaning of Detail	Strategy Used: Pause, Read Ahead, Read Back, Use Other Source

Before Reading

Engage your students and prepare them to read each selection.

◆ **An extensive author biography** brings the author to life for students.

◆ **Build Vocabulary** previews new words and teaches a vocabulary-building strategy.

◆ **Background for Understanding** provides context related to history, science, culture, and more.

◆ **Reading Strategy** helps students read more critically and with a higher level of comprehension.

◆ **Literary Focus** teaches a literary form or element.

During Reading

Two types of support help students through the selections:

◆ **Reading Strategy** prompts guide students in using the strategy introduced before the selection.

◆ **Literary Focus** prompts help students see how the literary element is illustrated in specific passages.

> ◆ **Reading Strategy**
> Is this a fact or an impression? How do you know?

> ◆ **Literary Focus**
> In what specific ways is this passage typical of a descriptive essay?

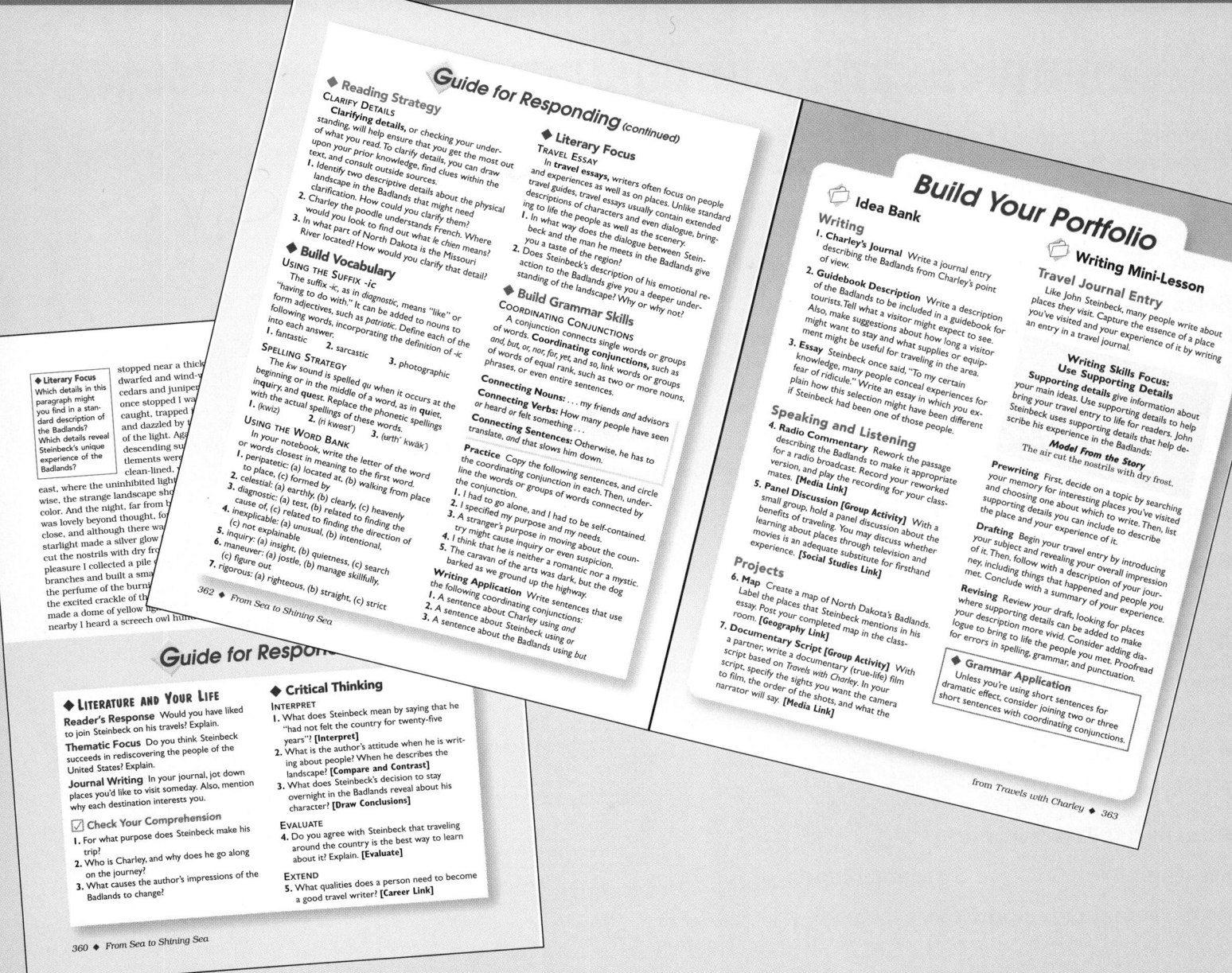

After Reading

Assess students' understanding and **extend** their learning.

✓ **Check Your Comprehension** questions assess students' literal understanding of the selection.

◆ **Critical Thinking** questions assess students' ability to use higher-level thinking skills.

◆ **Reading Strategy** assesses students' mastery of the reading strategy.

◆ **Literary Focus** reinforces students' understanding of the literary element.

◆ **Build Vocabulary** checks students' mastery of both the vocabulary strategy and the words used in the selection. Also includes a Spelling Strategy.

◆ **Build Grammar Skills** provides instruction and practice activities and a writing application.

Build Your Portfolio provides a wealth of activities for students to demonstrate their understanding.

◈ **Idea Bank** provides
- Three writing activities keyed to varying performance levels
- Two speaking and listening activities
- Two projects, often linked to cross-curricular topics

◈ **Writing Mini-Lesson** provides step-by-step writing process instruction.

A complete array of customizable resources.

The Annotated Teacher's Edition provides flexible teaching pathways and customized strategies to meet your curricular goals and your students' individual needs. Plus it organizes the program's wealth of materials for reteaching, extension, and assessment.

Teaching Resources

Selection Support: Skills Development
Practice pages for skills taught with each selection:

◆ **Build Vocabulary**

◆ **Build Spelling Skills**

◆ **Build Grammar Skills**

◆ **Reading Strategy**

◆ **Literary Focus**

Beyond Literature

Daily Language Practice

Art Transparencies

Readings From Social Studies

Formal Assessment
◆ **Selection Tests**

◆ **Unit Tests**

Alternative Assessment

Strategies for Diverse Student Needs

Professional Development Library

Also available on Resource Pro® CD-ROM!

Writing and Language Transparencies

◆ Over 100 transparencies for writing and grammar instruction

Assessment Success Kit

◆ Supports student performance on standardized tests

◆ Includes an Interactive Student Tutorial CD-ROM with standardized test practice

Prentice Hall Literature Library

◆ The only literature library with mini-anthologies featuring writings from specific regions, cultures, and genre

◆ More than 40 titles to choose from

◆ Comprehensive teaching support

◆ Special hardcovers with a beautiful design for attractiveness and durability

◆ Uncut editions so students enjoy complete works

◆ Classic novels by honored writers

◆ Great drama, including additional Shakespeare offerings

Humanities Pack

◆ A unique mini-course in the creative arts

◆ Fine-art transparencies and posters

◆ Audio CDs

◆ Performing arts video

PLUS

Interdisciplinary Units

◆ A complete interdisciplinary exploration for every unit in the literature text

Selection Support Practice Book

◆ Reinforcement for all skills instruction in a consumable format

A wide range of quality technology enhances and extends literature instruction.

Listening to Literature Audiocassettes

Use these complete, unabridged recordings of selections in *Prentice Hall Literature: Timeless Voices, Timeless Themes* to bring the literature to life and to meet the diverse needs and learning styles of your students. Includes <u>all of the selections</u> in the program.

- ◆ Motivate auditory learners
- ◆ Help less proficient readers
- ◆ Aid English language learners

Looking at Literature Videodiscs and Videotapes

Full-motion video segments provide a wide range of support for the literature—from student response to historical context to connections to today's world.

- ◆ Motivate students
- ◆ Build background
- ◆ Establish relevance
- ◆ Encourage class discussion of the literature

Resource Pro and Literature Database CD-ROM

Imagine a complete Teaching Resources, a customizable Lesson Planner, and a wide range of additional literature selections that all fit in one hand! With this CD-ROM, you can customize lesson plans at the touch of a button. You can also review, edit, and print an entire year's worth of blackline masters and other teaching support materials. In addition, more than 100 supplemental literature selections are provided for every grade level.

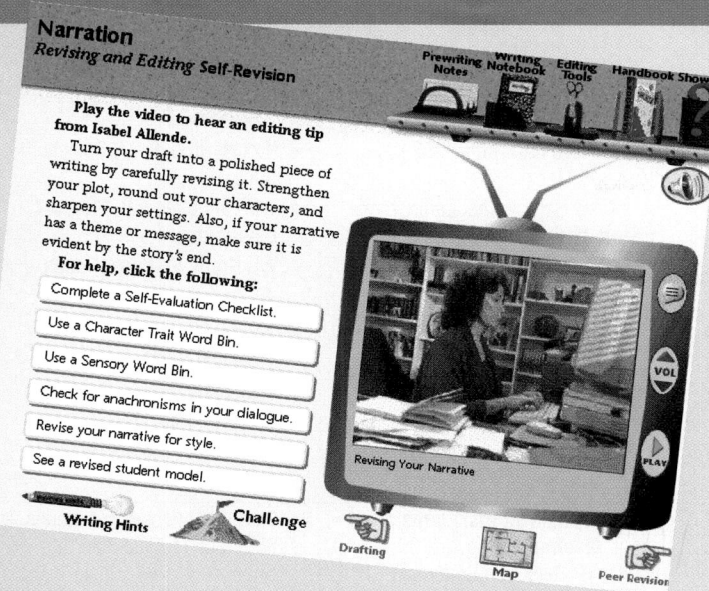

Narration
Revising and Editing Self-Revision

Prewriting Notes / Writing Notebook / Editing Tools / Handbook Show H

Play the video to hear an editing tip from Isabel Allende.

Turn your draft into a polished piece of writing by carefully revising it. Strengthen your plot, round out your characters, and sharpen your settings. Also, if your narrative has a theme or message, make sure it is evident by the story's end.

For help, click the following:

- Complete a Self-Evaluation Checklist.
- Use a Character Trait Word Bin.
- Use a Sensory Word Bin.
- Check for anachronisms in your dialogue.
- Revise your narrative for style.
- See a revised student model.

Writing Hints   Challenge

Drafting   Map   Peer Revision

Revising Your Narrative

Writer's Solution

Writer's Solution, Prentice Hall's award-winning interactive writing instruction program, has been fully integrated into *Prentice Hall Literature: Timeless Voices, Timeless Themes*. Components include

- ◆ Writing Lab CD-ROM—provides interactive tutorials on the major modes of writing, including Response to Literature
- ◆ Language Lab CD-ROM—provides self-directed instruction and practice in grammar, usage, and mechanics
- ◆ Writers at Work videodisc and videotape—to bring real writers into the classroom
- ◆ Writer's Toolkit networked software—provides tools and activities for all stages of writing

Formal Assessment CD-ROM

All selection tests and unit tests are available on software so you can customize assessment for your students. The software enables you to

- ◆ Customize tests to ability levels
- ◆ Customize tests by skills objectives
- ◆ Administer tests on-line in the computer lab

Literature CD-ROM Library

Multimedia presentations; hyperlinks to glossaries, indexes, and encyclopedias; and complete, on-line testing are just some of the outstanding features on these interactive CD-ROMs. Titles include the following:

- ◆ How to Read and Understand Poetry
- ◆ How to Read and Understand Drama
- ◆ The Time, Life, and Works of Shakespeare
- ◆ The History of American Literature, Part 1
- ◆ The History of American Literature, Part 2
- ◆ Greek Myths and Legends
- ◆ Science Fiction and Fantasy
- ◆ Myths of Africa, Arabia, Ireland, and Scandinavia
- ◆ Short Story Writing

Interactive Student Tutorial CD-ROM

A tool designed to help students review and prepare for standardized tests.

Internet Home Page

Visit the Prentice Hall Web site at **phschool.com** for features that support *Prentice Hall Literature: Timeless Voices, Timeless Themes:*

- ◆ Visit literary sites through our updated Links.
- ◆ Share ideas through our Faculty Forum electronic bulletin board.
- ◆ Take part in special events, such as electronic dialogues with notable authors.

PH @school
PRENTICE HALL

www.phlit.phschool.com

Program Planner Unit 1 Coming of Age

Selection	Reading	Literary Elements/Forms	Vocabulary	Grammar
"The Drummer Boy of Shiloh," Ray Bradbury, SE p. 5 Reading level: Average	• Literal Comprehension Strategies, SE pp. 4, 9; TR Selection Support, pp. 4–5 • Paraphrase, TR Str. for Diverse St. Needs, pp. 1–2 • Model Selection, SE pp. 5–8	• Historical Setting, SE pp. 3, 9; TR Selection Support, p. 6	• Word Part: *bene-*, SE pp. 3, 9; TR Selection Support, p. 1 Word Bank: benediction, riveted, p. 5; compounded, resolute, p. 7	• Nouns, SE p. 9; TR Selection Support, p. 3 • WS Language Lab CD-ROM, Using Nouns • WS Gram. Pr. Book, Nouns, pp. 5–7
"Charles," Shirley Jackson, SE p. 15 Reading level: Average	• Break Down Long Sentences, SE pp. 13, 20; TR Selection Support, p. 10 • Reread or Read Ahead, TR Str. for Diverse St. Needs, pp. 3–4	• Point of View, SE pp. 13, 20; TR Selection Support, p. 11	• Word Root: *-cred-*, SE pp. 12, 20; TR Selection Support, p. 7 Word Bank: renounced, insolently, p. 15; simultaneously, p. 16; incredulously, p. 17	• Nouns, SE p. 20; TR Selection Support, p. 9 • WS Language Lab CD-ROM, Using Nouns • WS Gram. Pr. Book, Nouns, p. 7
from ***I Know Why the Caged Bird Sings,*** Maya Angelou, SE p. 24 Reading level: Average	• Reread or Read Ahead, SE pp. 23, 30; TR Selection Support, p. 15 • List Key Ideas, TR Str. for Diverse St. Needs, pp. 5–6	• Memoir, SE pp. 23, 30; TR Selection Support, p. 16	• Related Words: Forms of *tolerate*, SE pp. 22, 30; TR Selection Support, p. 12 Word Bank: fiscal, p. 25; taut, benign, infuse, p. 27; intolerant, couched, p. 28	• Plural and Possessive Nouns, SE p. 30; TR Selection Support, p. 14 • WS Language Lab CD-ROM, Plural and Possessive Nouns
"The Road Not Taken," Robert Frost; **"All But Blind,"** Walter de la Mare; **"The Choice,"** Dorothy Parker, SE pp. 34, 36, 37 Reading levels: Average, Average, Easy	• Paraphrase, SE pp. 33, 38; TR Selection Support, p. 20 • Explain Poetic Phrases, TR Str. for Diverse St. Needs, pp. 7–8	• The Speaker in a Poem, SE pp. 33, 38; TR Selection Support, p. 21	• Word Root: *-verg-*, SE pp. 32, 38; TR Selection Support, p. 17 Word Bank: diverged, p. 34; blunders, smoldering, lilting, p. 36	• General and Specific Nouns, SE p. 38; TR Sel. Sup., p. 19 • WS Language Lab CD-ROM, Using Nouns • WS Gram. Pr. Book, Nouns, pp. 5–7
from **"E-Mail from Bill Gates,"** John Seabrook, SE p. 42 Reading level: Average	• Context Clues, SE pp. 41, 46; TR Selection Support, p. 25 • Summarize Main Ideas, TR Str. for Diverse St. Needs, pp. 9–10	• Magazine Article, SE pp. 41, 46; TR Selection Support, p. 26	• Prefix: *inter-*, SE pp. 40, 46 ; TR Selection Support, p. 22 Word Bank: interaction, misinterpret, intimate, etiquette, p. 43; spontaneously, p. 44	• Concrete and Abstract Nouns, SE p. 46; TR Selection Support, p. 24 • WS Language Lab CD-ROM, Identifying Concrete and Abstract Nouns
"The Girl Who Hunted Rabbits," Zuñi, SE p. 49 Reading level: Average			• TR Selection Support, p. 27 Word Bank: procured, p. 49; sinew, mantle, unwonted, bedraggled, p. 51; voracious, p. 53	
"Christmas Day in the Morning," Pearl S. Buck, SE p. 64 Reading level: Easy	• Identify Sequence of Events, SE pp. 63, 70; TR Selection Support, p. 32 • Relate What You Know, TR Str. for Diverse St. Needs, pp. 11–12	• Flashback, SE pp. 63, 70; TR Selection Support, p. 33	• Related Words: Forms of *Finite,* SE pp. 62, 70; TR Selection Support, p. 29 Word Bank: infinite, p. 65; brisk, loitering, placidly, p. 67; acquiescent, p. 68	• Pronouns and Antecedents, SE p. 70; TR Sel. Sup., p. 31 • WS Language Lab CD-ROM, Pronouns and Antecedents • WS Gram. Pr. Book, Pronouns and Antecedents, p. 8
"The Old Grandfather and His Little Grandson," Leo Tolstoy; **"Grandma,"** Amy Ling; **"Old Man,"** Ricardo Sánchez, SE pp. 74, 75, 76 Reading levels: Easy, Easy, Avg.	• Relate to What You Know, SE pp. 73, 78; TR Selection Support, p. 37 • Read Poetry According to Punctuation, TR Str. for Diverse St. Needs, pp. 13–14	• Sensory Language, SE pp. 73, 78; TR Selection Support, p. 38	• Synonyms for *rivulets,* SE pp. 72, 78; TR Selection Support, p. 34 Word Bank: scolded, sturdy, p. 75; rivulets, furrows, supple, stoic, p. 76	• Personal Pronouns, SE p. 78; TR Selection Support, p. 36 • WS Language Lab CD-ROM, Pronouns • WS Gram. Pr. Book, Pronouns, pp. 8–9
"Shooting Stars," Hal Borland; **"Something From the Sixties,"** Garrison Keillor, SE pp. 82, 84 Reading levels: Challenging, Easy	• Word Identification, SE pp. 81, 86; TR Sel. Sup., p. 42 • Identify Sequence of Events, TR Str. for Diverse St. Needs, pp. 15–16	• First-Person Narrative, SE pp. 81, 86; TR Selection Support, p. 43	• Prefix: *extra-*, SE pp. 80, 86; TR Selection Support, p. 39 Word Bank: orbit, friction, constellation, p. 82; descended, extravagance, p. 85	• Indefinite Pronouns, SE p. 86; TR Selection Support, p. 41 • WS Language Lab CD-ROM, Using Pronouns • WS Gram. Pr. Book, Indefinite Pronouns, p. 10
"Poets to Come," Walt Whitman; **"Winter Moon,"** Langston Hughes; **"Ring Out, Wild Bells,"** Alfred, Lord Tennyson, SE pp. 90, 91, 92 Reading levels: Avg., Easy, Easy	• Read Poetry, SE pp. 89, 94; TR Selection Support, p. 47 • Explain Poetic Phrases, TR Str. for Diverse St. Needs, pp. 17–18	• Repetition, SE pp. 89, 94; TR Selection Support, p. 48	• Suffixes: *-or,* SE pp. 88, 94; TR Selection Support, p. 44 Word Bank: orators, indicative, sauntering, p. 90; strife, p. 92	• Intensive Pronouns, SE p. 94; TR Selection Support, p. 46 • WS Language Lab CD-ROM, Using Pronouns

KEY: SE: Student Edition;   ATE: Annotated Teacher's Edition;   TR: Teaching Resources;   LL: Listening to Literature;   WS: Writer's Solution

Writing	Speaking and Listening Viewing and Representing	Projects	Assessment	Technology
• Diary Entry, Job Manual, News Article, SE p.10 • Mini-Lesson: Letter [Show, Don't Tell], SE p. 10 • Story Illustration, TR Alt. Assess., p. 1	• Retelling, Debate, SE p. 10 • S/L Mini-Lesson, Retelling, ATE, p. 7 • Role Play, TR Alt. Assess., p. 1	• Report on the Civil War, Time Capsule, SE p. 10 • Night Images, TR Alt. Assess., p. 1	• Selection Test, TR Formal Assessment, pp. 1–3; Assess. Res. Software • Desc. Rubric [for Wr. Mini-Lesson], TR Alt. Assess., p. 93 • TR Alt. Assess., p. 1	• "The Drummer Boy of Shiloh," LL Audiocassettes • WS Writing Lab CD-ROM, Description Tutorial
• Description, Letter, Problem-and-Solution Essay, SE p. 21 • Mini-Lesson: Description [Appropriate Tone], SE p. 21 • Dramatization, TR Alt. Assess., p. 2	• Retelling, Panel, SE p. 21 • S/L Mini-Lesson: Advisory Panel, ATE p.15 • V/R Mini-Lesson: Multimedia Display, ATE p. 18 • Book, TR Alt. Assess., p. 2	• Multimedia Display, Comic Strip, SE p. 21 • Baby-sitter's Guide, TR Alt. Assess., p. 2	• Selection Test, TR Formal Assessment, pp. 4–6; Assess. Res. Software • Desc. Rubric [for Wr. Mini-Lesson], TR Alt. Assess., p. 93 • TR Alt. Assess., p. 2	• "Charles," LL Audiocassettes • WS Writing Lab CD-ROM, Description Tutorial
• Journal Entry, Memoir Poem, Analysis, SE p. 31 • Mini-Lesson: Personal Memoir [Elaborate], SE p. 31 • Before-and-After Reading, TR Alt. Assess., p. 3	• Oral Interpretation, Oral Tribute, SE p. 31 • S/L Mini-Lesson: Oral Interpretation, ATE p. 28 • V/R Mini-Lesson: Ad, ATE p. 26 • Letter, TR Alt. Assess., p. 3	• Advertisement, Photo Essay, SE p. 31 • Inventory Chart, TR Alt. Assess., p. 3	• Selection Test, TR Formal Assessment, pp. 7–9; Assess. Res. Software • Pers. Exp. Rubric [for Wr. Mini-Lesson], TR Alt. Assess., p. 92 • TR Alt. Assess., p. 3	• from I Know Why the Caged Bird Sings, LL Audiocassettes • WS Writing Lab CD-ROM, Expression Tutorial
• List, Dialogue, Compare and Contrast, SE p. 39 • Mini-Lesson: Persuasive Essay [Supporting Your Argument], SE p. 39 • Desc., TR Alt. Assess., p. 4	• Scene, Speech, SE p. 39 • S/L Mini-Lesson: Speech, ATE p. 36 • V/R Mini-Lesson: Illustration, ATE p. 35 • Chart, TR Alt. Assess., p. 4	• Final Words, Illustration, SE p. 39 • Dance, TR Alt. Assess., p. 4	• Selection Test, TR Formal Assessment, pp. 10–12; Assess. Res. Software • Persuasion Rub. [for Wr. Mini-Lesson], TR Alt. Assess., p.101 • TR Alt. Assess., p. 4	• "The Road Not Taken"; "All But Blind"; "The Choice," LL Audiocassettes • WS Writing Lab CD-ROM, Persuasion Tutorial
• Letter, Advertisement, Cause-and-Effect Essay, SE p. 47 • Mini-Lesson: Comparison [Transitions That Show Relationships], SE p. 47 • Comp. Art, TR Alt. Assess., p. 5	• Dialogue, Interview, SE p. 47 • S/L Mini-Lesson: Dialogue, ATE p. 43 • Timeline, TR Alt. Assess., p. 5	• Internet Exploration, Diagram, SE p. 47 • Slogan, TR Alt. Assess., p. 5	• Selection Test, TR Formal Assessment, pp. 13–15; Assess. Res. Software • Comparison/Contrast Rubric [for Wr. Mini-Lesson], TR Alt. Assess., p. 99 • TR Alt. Assess., p. 5	• from "E-Mail from Bill Gates," LL Audiocassettes • WS Writing Lab CD-ROM, Exposition Tutorial
• List of Clues, Letter, Cause and Effect, SE p. 55	• Music Connection, SE p. 55 • V/R Mini-Lesson: Illustrated Map, ATE p. 53	• Art, Encyclopedia Entry, SE p. 55	• Selection Test, TR Formal Assessment, pp. 16–17; Assess. Res. Software	• "The Girl Who Hunted Rabbits," LL Audiocassettes
• Letter From Robert, Book-Jacket Copy, Essay, SE p. 71 • Mini-Lesson: Fict. Narr. [Use Transitions], SE p. 71 • Illustration, TR Alt. Assess., p. 6	• Speech, Modern Scene, SE p. 71 • S/L Mini-Lesson: Speech, ATE p. 68 • Personal Essay, TR Alt. Assess., p. 6	• Holiday Spirit, Comic Strip, SE p. 71 • Research Report, TR Alt. Assess., p. 6	• Selection Test, TR Formal Assessment, pp.18–20; Assess. Res. Software • Fict. Narr. Rubric [for Wr. Mini-Lesson], TR Alt. Assess., p. 91 • TR Alt. Assess., p. 6	• "Christmas Day in the Morning," LL Audiocassettes • WS Writing Lab CD-ROM, Narration Tutorial
• Descriptive Close-up, Proposal, Folk Tale, SE p. 79 • Mini-Lesson: Description [Use Precise Language], SE p. 79 • Interview, TR Alt. Assess., p. 7	• Storytelling Circle, Dialogue With Yourself, SE p. 79 • S/L Mini-Lesson: Storytelling Circle, ATE p. 75 • Portrait, TR Alt. Assess., p. 7	• Life Dance, Community-Service Report, SE p. 79 • Oral Interpretation, TR Alt. Assess., p. 7	• Selection Test, TR Formal Assessment, pp. 21–23; Assess. Res. Software • Desc. Rubric [for Wr. Mini-Lesson], TR Alt. Assess., p. 93 • TR Alt. Assess., p. 7	• "The Old Grandfather and His Little Grandson"; "Grandma"; "Old Man," LL Audiocassettes • WS Writing Lab CD-ROM, Description Tutorial
• Thank-You Note, Poem, Essay, SE p. 87 • Mini-Lesson: Extended Definition [Audience], SE p. 87 • Astronomy Notes, TR Alt. Assess., p. 8	• Debate, Monologue, SE p. 87 • S/L Mini-Lesson: Radio Monologue, ATE p. 83 • V/R Mini-Lesson: Decades on Display, ATE p. 84 • Compare-and-Contrast Paragraph, TR Alt. Assess., p. 8	• Social Research, Meteor Presentation, SE p. 87 • Theme Party Plan, TR Alt. Assess., p. 8	• Selection Test, TR Formal Assessment, pp. 24–26; Assess. Res. Software • Definition/Classification Rubric [for Wr. Mini-Lesson], TR Alt. Assess., p. 95 • TR Alt. Assess., p. 8	• "Shooting Stars"; "Something From the Sixties," LL Audiocassettes • WS Writing Lab CD-ROM, Exposition Tutorial
• Description, Poem, Critical Interpretation, SE p. 95 • Mini-Lesson: Script [Use the Right Format], SE p. 95 • Music for the Seasons, TR Alt. Assess., p. 9	• New Year's Speech, Poetry Reading, SE p. 95 • S/L Mini-Lesson: New Year's Speech, ATE p. 92 • Interview, TR Alt. Assess., p. 9	• Multimedia Presentation, Report, SE p. 95 • Art Exhibit Plan, TR Alt. Assess., p. 9	• Selection Test, TR Formal Assessment, pp. 27–30; Assess. Res. Software • TR Alt. Assess., p. 9	• "Poets to Come"; "Winter Moon"; "Ring Out, Wild Bells," LL Audiocassettes • WS Writing Lab CD-ROM, Creative Writing Tutorial

Program Planner   Unit 2 Meeting Challenges

Selection	Reading	Literary Elements/Forms	Vocabulary	Grammar
"Cub Pilot on the Mississippi," Mark Twain, SE p. 109 Reading level: Average	• Interactive Reading Strategies, SE pp. 108, 117; TR Selection Support, pp. 52–53 • Ask Questions, TR Str. for Diverse St. Needs, pp. 19–20 • Model Sel., SE pp. 109–116	• Conflict Between Characters, SE pp. 107, 117; TR Selection Support, p. 54	• Related Words: Forms of *judge,* SE pp. 107, 117; TR Selection Support, p. 49 Word Bank: furtive, p. 110; pretext, p. 113; intimation, judicious, p. 114; emancipated, p. 116	• Verbs and Verb Phrases, SE p. 117; TR Sel. Sup., p. 51 • WS Language Lab CD-ROM, Verb and Verb Phrases • WS Gram. Pr. Book, Verbs, pp. 11–15
"The Secret," Arthur C. Clarke, SE p. 122 Reading level: Average	• Ask Questions, SE pp. 121, 128; TR Selection Support, p. 58 • Ask Questions, TR Str. for Diverse St. Needs, pp. 21–22	• Science Fiction, SE pp. 121, 128; TR Selection Support, p. 59	• Word Part: *micro,* SE pp. 120, 128; TR Sel. Sup., p. 55 Word Bank: receding, p. 122; competent, microbes, hemisphere, radial, heedless, implications, p. 125; looming, p. 126	• Action and Linking Verbs, SE p. 128; TR Sel. Sup., p. 57 • WS Language Lab CD-ROM, Using Verbs • WS Gram. Pr. Book, Using Verbs, pp. 70–76
"Harriet Tubman: Guide to Freedom," Ann Petry, SE p. 132 Reading level: Average	• Set a Purpose for Reading, SE pp. 131, 140 • Set a Purpose for Reading, TR Str. for Diverse St. Needs, pp. 23–24	• Third-Person Narrative, SE pp. 131, 140	• Word Roots: *-fug-,* SE pp. 130, 140 Word Bank: fugitives, p. 133; incentive, disheveled, guttural, p. 135; mutinous, cajoling, indomitable, p. 137; fastidious, p. 139	• Transitive and Intransitive Verbs, SE p. 140 • WS Language Lab CD-ROM, Verbs • WS Gram. Pr. Book, Action Verbs, p. 12
"Columbus," Joaquin Miller; **"Western Wagons,"** Stephen Vincent Benét; **"The Other Pioneers,"** Roberto Félix Salazar, SE pp. 144, 146, 148 Reading levels: Easy, Easy, Avg.	• Relate to What You Know, SE pp. 143, 150; TR Selection Support, p. 68 • Relate to What You Know, TR Str. for Diverse St. Needs, pp. 25–26	• Stanzas in Poetry, SE pp. 143, 150; TR Selection Support, p. 69	• Antonyms: *wan* and *swarthy,* SE pp. 142, 150; TR Selection Support, p. 65 Word Bank: mutinous, wan, swarthy, unfurled, p. 144; stalwart, p. 148	• Commonly Confused Verbs: *lie* and *lay,* SE p. 150; TR Selection Support, p. 67 • WS Gram. Pr. Book, Glossary of Troublesome Verbs, p. 76
"Up the Slide," Jack London, SE p. 154 Reading level: Challenging	• Predict, SE pp. 153, 160; TR Selection Support, p. 73 • Predict, TR Str. for Diverse St. Needs, pp. 27–28	• Conflict With Nature, SE pp. 153, 160; TR Selection Support, p. 74	• Related Words: Forms of *exhaust,* SE pp. 152, 160; TR Selection Support, p. 70 Word Bank: exhausted, thoroughly, p. 155; manifestly, exertion, p. 156; maneuver, ascent, p. 158	• Active/Passive, SE p. 160; TR Selection Support, p. 72 • WS Language Lab CD-ROM, Styling Sentences • WS Gram. Pr. Book, Active and Passive Voice, p. 74
"The Pilgrims' Landing and First Winter," William Bradford, SE p. 163; Reading: Challenging			• TR Selection Support, p. 75	
"The Ninny," Anton Chekhov; **"The Governess,"** Neil Simon, SE pp. 174, 176 Reading levels: Average, Easy	• Question Characters' Actions, SE pp. 173, 182; TR Selection Support, p. 80 • Question Characters' Actions, TR Str. for Diverse St. Needs, pp. 29–30	• Characters' Motives, SE pp. 173, 182; TR Selection Support, p. 81	• Suffixes: *-ment,* SE pp. 172, 182; TR Selection Support, p. 77 Word Bank: bitter, timidly, p. 175; inferior, discrepancies, p. 176; discharged, p. 178; guileless, bafflement, p. 180	• Principal Parts of Regular Verbs, SE p. 182; TR Selection Support, p.79 • WS Language Lab CD-ROM, Using Verbs • WS Gram. Pr. Book, Principal Parts of Regular Verbs, p. 70
"Thank You, M'am," Langston Hughes, SE p. 186 Reading level: Average	• Respond to Characters' Actions, SE pp. 185, 190; TR Selection Support, p. 85 • Respond to Characters' Actions, TR Str. for Diverse St. Needs, pp. 31–32	• Theme, SE pp. 185, 190; TR Selection Support, p. 86	• Suffixes: *-able,* SE pp. 184, 190; TR Selection Support, p. 82 Word Bank: presentable, mistrusted, latching, barren, p. 189	• Principal Parts of Irregular Verbs, SE p. 190; TR Selection Support, p. 84 • WS Gram. Pr. Book, Principal Parts of Verbs, p. 71
"Prospective Immigrants . . . ," Adrienne Rich; **"Much Madness . . . ,"** Emily Dickinson; **"This We Know,"** Chief Seattle; **"Hard Questions,"** Margaret Tsuda, SE pp. 194–198 Reading levels: Average, Challenging, Average, Average	• Use Your Senses, SE pp. 193, 200; TR Selection Support, p. 90 • Use Your Senses, TR Str. for Diverse St. Needs, pp. 33–34	• Imagery, SE pp. 193, 200; TR Selection Support, p. 91	• Forms of *evade,* SE pp. 192, 200; TR Selection Support, p. 87 Word Bank: worthily, evade, discerning, prevail, assent, p. 194; ancestors, p. 197	• Verb Tenses, SE p. 200; TR Selection Support, p. 89 • WS Gram. Pr. Book, Six Tenses of Verbs, p. 72
"Flowers for Algernon," Daniel Keyes, SE p. 204 Reading level: Average	• Summarize, SE pp. 203, 226; TR Selection Support, p. 95 • Summarize, TR Str. for Diverse St. Needs, pp. 35–36	• First-Person Point of View, SE pp. 203, 226; TR Selection Support, p. 96	• Word Roots: *-psych-,* SE pp. 202, 226; TR Selection Support, p. 92 Word Bank: psychology, p. 212; tangible, specter, refute, p. 216; illiteracy, p. 219; obscure, syndromes, introspective, p. 220	• Verbs: Perfect Tenses, SE p. 226; TR Selection Support, p. 94 • WS Gram. Pr. Book, Using Verbs, pp. 70–76

KEY: SE: Student Edition;   ATE: Annotated Teacher's Edition;   TR: Teaching Resources;   LL: Listening to Literature;   WS: Writer's Solution

Writing	Speaking and Listening Viewing and Representing	Projects	Assessment	Technology
• Journal Entry, Character Sketch, Essay, SE p. 118 • Mini-Lesson: Anecdote [Introduction, Body, Conclusion], SE p. 118 • Music, TR Alt. Assess., p. 10	• Dramatic Reading, Talk-Show Interview, SE p. 118 • S/L Mini-Lesson: Dramatic Reading, ATE p. 114 • Great Rivers Show, TR Alt. Assess., p. 10	• Timeline, Transportation Brochure, SE p. 118 • Round Table Discussion, TR Alt. Assess., p. 10	• Selection Test, TR Formal Assessment, pp. 38–40; Assess. Res. Software • Pers. Exp. Narr. [for Wr. Mini-Lesson], TR Alt. Assess., p. 92 • TR Alt. Assess., p. 10	• "Cub Pilot on the Mississippi," LL Audiocassettes • WS Writing Lab CD-ROM, Narration Tutorial
• Advertisement, News Article, Critical Response, SE p. 129 • M/L: Story Continuation [Seq. of Events], SE p. 129 • Role Play, TR Alt. Assess., p. 11	• Telephone Call, Radio Review, SE p. 129 • S/L Mini-Lesson: Radio Review, ATE p. 124 • Debate, TR Alt. Assess., p. 11	• Space Settlement, Comic Book, SE p. 129 • Film Review, TR Alt. Assess., p. 11	• Sel. Test, TR Form. Assess., pp. 41–43; Assess. Res. Software • Fict. Narr. [for Wr. Mini-Lesson], TR Alt. Assess., p. 91 • TR Alt. Assess., p. 11	• "The Secret," LL Audiocassettes • WS Writing Lab CD-ROM, Description Tutorial
• Diary Entry, Biographical Description, Dramatization, SE p. 141 • Mini-Lesson: Introduction [Specific Examples], SE p. 141 • Report, TR Alt. Assess., p. 12	• Speech, Debate, SE p. 141 • S/L Mini-Lesson: Speech, ATE p. 138 • Book Jacket, TR Alt. Assess., p. 12	• Research Project, Fugitive Slave Laws, SE p. 141 • Author Report, TR Alt. Assess., p. 12	• Selection Test, TR Formal Assessment, pp. 44–46; Assess. Res. Software • Persuasion [for Wr. Mini-Lesson], TR Alt. Assess., p. 101 • TR Alt. Assess., p. 12	• "Harriet Tubman: Guide to Freedom," LL Audiocassettes • WS Writing Lab CD-ROM, Persuasion Tutorial
• Letter, Dialogue, Comparison-and-Contrast Essay, SE p. 151 • Mini-Lesson: Speech [Support Ideas], SE p. 151 • Oral Interpretation, TR Alt. Assess., p. 13	• Skit, Oral Presentation, SE p. 151 • S/L Mini-Lesson: Oral Presentation, ATE p. 148 • Corrido Research, TR Alt. Assess., p. 13	• Living History, Book Cover, SE p. 151 • History Report, TR Alt. Assess., p. 13	• Selection Test, TR Formal Assessment, pp. 47–49; Assess. Res. Software • Speaker/Speech [for Wr. Mini-Lesson], TR Alt. Assess., p. 114 • TR Alt. Assess., p. 13	• "Columbus"; "Western Wagons"; "The Other Pioneers," LL Audiocassettes • WS Writing Lab CD-ROM, Persuasion Tutorial
• Diary Entry, Job Description, Modified Story, SE p. 161 • Mini-Lesson: Report [Narrowing a Topic], SE p. 161 • Photo, TR Alt. Assess., p. 14	• Oral Interpretation, Casting Proposal, SE p. 161 • S/L Mini-Lesson: Casting Proposal, ATE p. 158 • Skit, TR Alt. Assess., p. 14	• Multimedia Report, Author Research, SE p. 161 • Report, TR Alt. Assess., p. 14	• Selection Test, TR Formal Assessment, pp. 50–52; Assess. Res. Software • Res. Rep. Rubric [for Wr. Mini-Lesson], TR Alt. Assess., p. 102 • TR Alt. Assess., p. 14	• "Up the Slide," LL Audiocassettes • WS Writing Lab CD-ROM, Reports Tutorial
• Letter, Script, Regulations, SE p. 165	• Discussion, SE p. 165	• Oral Report, Mayflower Illustration, SE p. 165	• Selection Test, TR Formal Assessment, pp. 53–54; Assess. Res. Software	• "The Pilgrims' Landing and First Winter," LL Audiocassettes
• Advertisement, Letter, Interior Monologue, SE p. 183 • Mini-Lesson: Comparison of Stories [Organization], SE p. 183 • Program Notes, TR Alt. Assess., p. 15	• Dramatization, Job Interview, SE p. 183 • S/L Mini-Lesson: Dramatization, ATE p. 180 • A Contemporary Version, TR Alt. Assess., p. 15	• Production Plan, Opinion Poll, SE p. 183 • Comic Strip, TR Alt. Assess., p. 15	• Selection Test, TR Formal Assessment, pp. 55–57; Assess. Res. Software • Comparison/Contrast Rubric [for Wr. Mini-Lesson], TR Alt. Assess., p. 99 • TR Alt. Assess., p. 15	• "The Ninny"; "The Governess," LL Audiocassettes • WS Writing Lab CD-ROM, Exposition Tutorial
• Letter, Sequel, Speech, SE p. 191 • Mini-Lesson: Letter [Give Necessary Background], SE p. 191 • Tribute, TR Alt. Assess., p. 16	• Readers Theatre, Rap Song, SE p. 191 • S/L Mini-Lesson: Readers Theatre, ATE p. 188 • Oral Interpretation, TR Alt. Assess., p. 16	• Multimedia Presentation, Painting or Drawing, SE p. 191 • Author Report, TR Alt. Assess., p. 16	• Selection Test, TR Formal Assessment, pp. 58–60; Assess. Res. Software • Exp. Rubric [for Wr. Mini-Lesson], TR Alt. Assess., p. 90 • TR Alt. Assess., p. 16	• "Thank You, M'am," LL Audiocassettes • WS Writing Lab CD-ROM, Expression Tutorial
• Journal Entry, Letter, Speech Analysis, SE p. 201 • Mini-Lesson: Persuasive Appeal [Clear Purpose], SE p. 201 • Speech, TR Alt. Assess., p. 17	• Committee Discussion, Dramatization, SE p. 201 • S/L Mini-Lesson: Dramatization, ATE p. 198 • Illustration, TR Alt. Assess., p. 17	• Timeline, Sculpture, SE p. 201 • Brochure, TR Alt. Assess., p. 17	• Selection Test, TR Formal Assessment, pp. 61–63; Assess. Res. Software • Persuasion [for Wr. Mini-Lesson], TR Alt. Assess., p. 101 • TR Alt. Assess., p. 17	• "Prospective Immigrants Please Note"; "Much Madness . . ."; "This We Know"; "Hard Questions," LL Audiocassettes • WS Writing Lab CD-ROM, Persuasion Tutorial
• Award Plaque, Explanation, Journal Article, SE p. 227 • Mini-Lesson: Observation Journal [Details to Support Points], SE p. 227 • Debate, TR Alt. Assess., p. 18	• Drama, Debate, SE p. 227 • S/L M/L: ATE pp. 212, 217 • V/R Mini-Lesson: Inkblots, ATE p. 214; Interviews, ATE p. 219; Timeline, ATE p. 224, • Review, TR Alt. Assess., p. 18	• Research Report, Audiovisual Interviews, SE p. 227 • Round Table Discussion, TR Alt. Assess., p. 18	• Selection Test, TR Formal Assessment, pp. 64–66; Assess. Res. Software • Desc. Rubric [for Wr. Mini-Lesson], TR Alt. Assess., p. 93 • TR Alt. Assess., p. 18	• "Flowers for Algernon," LL Audiocassettes • WS Writing Lab CD-ROM, Expression Tutorial

Program Planner   Unit 3 Quest for Justice

Selection	Reading	Literary Elements/Forms	Vocabulary	Grammar
"Brown *vs*. Board of Education," Walter Dean Myers, SE p. 241 Reading level: Challenging	• Strategies for Constructing Meaning, SE pp. 240, 247; TR Selection Support, pp. 100–101 • Make Inferences, TR Str. for Diverse St. Needs, pp. 37–38 • Model Selection, SE pp. 241–246	• Informative Essay, SE pp. 239, 247; TR Selection Support, p. 102	• Prefixes: *in-*, SE pp. 239, 247; TR Selection Support, p. 97 Word Bank: elusive, predominantly, SE p. 241; diligent, p. 243; intangible, unconstitutional, deliberating, oppressed, p. 245	• Adjectives, SE p. 247; TR Selection Support, p. 99 • WS Language Lab CD-ROM, Using Modifiers • WS Gram. Pr. Book, Adjectives as Modifiers, p. 16
"A Retrieved Reformation," O. Henry, SE p. 252 Reading level: Average	• Ask Questions, SE pp. 251, 258; TR Selection Support, p. 106 • Ask Questions, TR Str. for Diverse St. Needs, pp. 39–40	• Surprise Ending, SE pp. 251, 258; TR Selection Support, p. 107	• Word Roots: *-simul-*, SE pp. 250, 258; TR Selection Support, p. 103 Word Bank: assiduously, virtuous, p. 253; retribution, unobtrusively, p. 255; simultaneously, anguish, p.257	• Placement of Adjectives, SE p. 258; TR Selection Support, p. 105 • WS Language Lab CD-ROM, Supporting Sentences • WS Gram. Pr. Book, Adjectives as Modifiers, p. 16
"Emancipation" from ***Lincoln: A Photobiography,*** Russell Freedman; **"O Captain! My Captain!"** Walt Whitman, SE pp. 262, 266 Reading levels: Challenging, Average	• Determine Cause and Effect, SE pp. 261, 268; TR Selection Support, p. 111 • Determine Cause and Effect, TR Str. for Diverse St. Needs, pp. 41–42	• Historical Context, SE pp. 261, 268; TR Selection Support, p. 112	• Suffixes: *-ate*, SE pp. 260, 268; TR Selection Support, p. 108 Word Bank: alienate, compensate, shackles, peril, p. 263; decisive, humiliating, p. 265; exulting, tread, p. 267	• Adverbs, SE p. 268; TR Selection Support, p. 110 • WS Language Lab CD-ROM, Using Modifiers • WS Gram. Pr. Book, Adverbs as Modifiers, p. 22
"Gentleman of Río en Medio," Juan A. A. Sedillo; **"Saving the Wetlands,"** Barbara A. Lewis, SE pp. 272, 276 Reading levels: Average, Easy	• Make Inferences, SE pp. 271, 282; TR Selection Support, p. 116 • Make Inferences, TR Str. for Diverse St. Needs, pp. 43–44	• Resolution of a Conflict, SE pp. 271, 282; TR Selection Support, p. 117	• Word Roots: *-num-*, SE pp. 270, 282; TR Selection Support, p. 113 Word Bank: negotiation, gnarled, innumerable, p. 273; broached, p. 275; petition, wizened, brandishing, p. 279	• Adverbs Modifying Adjectives and Adverbs, SE p. 282; TR Selection Support, p. 115 • WS Language Lab CD-ROM, Persuasion • WS Gram. Pr. Book, Adverbs as Modifiers, p. 21
"Raymond's Run," Toni Cade Bambara, SE p. 292 Reading level: Average	• Predict, SE pp. 291, 300; TR Selection Support, p. 121 • Predict, TR Str. for Diverse St. Needs, pp. 45–46	• Major and Minor Characters, SE pp. 291, 300; TR Selection Support, p. 122	• Word Parts: *scope*, SE pp. 290, 300; TR Selection Support, p. 118 Word Bank: prodigy, signify, ventriloquist, p. 295; periscope, p. 297	• Prepositions, SE p. 300; TR Selection Support, p. 120 • WS Language Lab CD-ROM, Prepositions • WS Gram. Pr. Book, Prepositions, p. 24
"Paul Revere's Ride," Henry Wadsworth Longfellow; **"Barbara Frietchie,"** John Greenleaf Whittier; **"Elizabeth Blackwell,"** Eve Merriam, SE pp. 306, 311, 314 Reading levels: Easy, Average, Easy	• Interpret the Meaning, SE pp. 305, 318; TR Selection Support, p. 126 • Interpret the Meaning, TR Str. for Diverse St. Needs, pp. 47–48	• Heroic Characters, SE pp. 305, 318; TR Selection Support, p. 127	• Word Roots: *-spec-*, SE pp. 304, 318; TR Selection Support, p. 123 Word Bank: stealthy, somber, p. 307; impetuous, spectral, tranquil, aghast, p. 309; horde, p. 311	• Prepositional Phrases, SE p. 318; TR Selection Support, p. 125 • WS Language Lab CD-ROM, Prepositional Phrases • WS Gram. Pr. Book, Prepositions, p. 24
"Young Jefferson Gets Some Advice From Ben Franklin," Thomas Jefferson, SE p. 321 Reading level: Challenging			Word Bank: ire, strictures, abhorrence, p. 321; inscription, amendments, p. 322	
"Always to Remember: The Vision of Maya Ying Lin," Brent Ashabranner, SE p. 326 Reading level: Average	• Identifying Important Ideas, SE pp. 325, 332; TR Selection Support, p. 133 • Identify Important Ideas, TR Str. for Diverse St. Needs, pp. 49–50	• Biographical Profile, SE pp. 325, 332; TR Selection Support, p. 134	• Latin Plural Forms, SE pp. 324, 332; TR Selection Support, p. 130 Word Bank: criteria, registrants, harmonious, p. 328; anonymously, eloquent, unanimous, p. 329; prominent, conception, p. 331	• Prepositional Phrases as Adjectives and Adverbs, SE p. 332; TR Selection Support, p. 132 • WS Language Lab CD-ROM, Preposition Lesson • WS Gram. Pr. Book, Prepositions, p. 24

T16   **KEY:**   SE: Student Edition;   ATE: Annotated Teacher's Edition;   TR: Teaching Resources;   LL: Listening to Literature;   WS: Writer's Solution

Writing	Speaking and Listening Viewing and Representing	Projects	Assessment	Technology
• Letter, Editorial, Biography, SE p. 248 • Mini-Lesson: Personal Essay [Strong Introduction], SE p. 248 • Photo Essay, TR Alt. Assess., p.19	• Drama, Panel Discussion, SE p. 248 • S/L Mini-Lesson: Drama, ATE p. 245 • V/R Mini-Lesson: Collage, ATE p. 243 • Social Studies Report, TR Alt. Assess., p. 19	• Timeline, Collage, SE p. 248 • Round Table Discussion, TR Alt. Assess., p. 19	• Selection Test, TR Formal Assessment, pp. 75–77; Assess. Res. Software • Expression Rubric [for Wr. Mini-Lesson], TR Alt. Assess., p. 90 • TR Alt. Assess., p.19	• "Brown vs. Board of Education," LL Audiocassettes • WS Writing Lab CD-ROM Persuasion Tutorial
• Letter From Billy, Another Surprise Ending, Essay, SE p. 259 • Mini-Lesson: Response to the Story [Support Through Examples], SE p. 259 • Illustration, TR Alt. Assess., p. 20	• Debate, Monologue, SE p. 259 • S/L Mini-Lesson: Monologue, ATE p. 255 • A Sequel in Performance, TR Alt. Assess., p. 20	• Comic Book, Research Report, SE p. 259 • Casting Notes, TR Alt. Assess., p. 20	• Selection Test, TR Formal Assessment, pp. 78–80; Assess. Res. Software • Response to Literature Rubric [for Wr. Mini-Lesson], TR Alt. Assess., p. 106 • TR Alt. Assess., p. 20	• "A Retrieved Reformation," LL Audiocassettes • WS Writing Lab CD-ROM Response to Literature Tutorial
• Epitaph, Poem, Character Profile, SE p. 269 • Mini-Lesson: Letter [Descriptive Details], SE p. 269 • Photo Essay, TR Alt. Assess., p. 21	• Dramatic Reading, Dialogue, SE p. 269 • S/L Mini-Lesson: Dialogue, ATE p. 266 • V/R Mini-Lesson: Lincoln Character Profile, ATE p. 263 • Prize Research, TR Alt. Assess., p. 21	• Multimedia Presentation, Picture Book, SE p. 269 • Music Research, TR Alt. Assess., p. 21	• Selection Test, TR Formal Assessment, pp. 81–83; Assess. Res. Software • Expression Rubric [for Wr. Mini-Lesson], TR Alt. Assess., p. 90 • TR Alt. Assess., p. 21	• "Emancipation" from Lincoln: A Photobiography; "O Captain! My Captain!" LL Audiocassettes • WS Writing Lab CD-ROM Expression Tutorial
• Advertisement, Letter to the Editor, Formula, SE p. 283 • Mini-Lesson: Speech Supporting the Environment [Persuasive Tone], SE p. 283 • Nature Report, TR Alt. Assess., p. 22	• Speech, Debate, SE p. 283 • S/L Mini-Lesson: Debate, ATE p. 280 • Speech, TR Alt. Assess., p. 22	• Artwork, Community Action, SE p. 283 • Round Table Discussion, TR Alt. Assess., p. 22	• Selection Test, TR Formal Assessment, pp. 84–86; Assess. Res. Software • Persuasion Rubric [for Wr. Mini-Lesson], TR Alt. Assess., p. 101 • TR Alt. Assess., p. 22	• "Gentleman of Río en Medio"; "Saving the Wetlands," LL Audiocassettes • WS Writing Lab CD-ROM Persuasion Tutorial
• Letter, Sequel, Essay, SE p. 301 • Mini-Lesson: Script for a Sportscaster [Background Information], SE p. 301 • Poster, TR Alt. Assess., p. 23	• Scene, Telephone Conversation, SE p. 301 • S/L Mini-Lesson: Telephone Conversation, ATE p. 295 • V/R Mini-Lesson: Story Board, ATE p. 298 • Round Table Discussion, TR Alt. Assess., p. 23	• Map of the Setting, Track and Running Bibliography, SE p. 301 • Opinion Poll, TR Alt. Assess., p. 23	• Selection Test, TR Formal Assessment, pp. 87–89; Assess. Res. Software • Drama Rubric [for Wr. Mini-Lesson], TR Alt. Assess., p. 105 • TR Alt. Assess., p. 23	• "Raymond's Run," LL Audiocassettes • WS Writing Lab CD-ROM Creative Writing Tutorial
• Movie Summary, Character Sketch, Report, SE p. 319 • Mini-Lesson: "Eyewitness" Speech [Appeal to Your Audience], SE p. 319 • Tourist Brochure, TR Alt. Assess., p. 24	• Retelling, Dramatic Reading, SE p. 319 • S/L Mini-Lesson: Dramatic Reading, ATE p. 309 • V/R Mini-Lesson: Heroism Award, ATE p. 315 • Oral Interpretation, TR Alt. Assess., p. 24	• Boston Area Map, Folk Ballad, SE p. 319 • Social Studies Report, TR Alt. Assess., p. 24	• Selection Test, TR Formal Assessment, pp. 90–92; Assess. Res. Software • Description Rubric [for Wr. Mini-Lesson], TR Alt. Assess., p. 93 • TR Alt. Assess., p. 24	• "Paul Revere's Ride"; "Barbara Frietchie"; "Elizabeth Blackwell," LL Audiocassettes • WS Writing Lab CD-ROM Description Tutorial
• Letter, Article, Biographical Report, SE p. 323	• Role Play, SE p. 323	• Research, SE p. 323	• Selection Test, TR Formal Assessment, pp. 93–94; Assess. Res. Software	• "Young Jefferson Gets Some Advice From Ben Franklin," LL Audiocassettes
• Letter, Journal Entry, Biographical Profile, SE p. 333 • Mini-Lesson: Tourist Brochure for a Memorial [Persuasive Details], SE p. 333 • Tourist Brochure, TR Alt. Assess., p. 25	• Commencement Address, Oral History, SE p. 333 • S/L Mini-Lesson: Oral History, ATE p. 330 • Sound Track, TR Alt. Assess., p. 25	• Memorial Budget, Multimedia Presentation, SE p. 333 • History Report, TR Alt. Assess., p. 25	• Selection Test, TR Formal Assessment, pp. 95–97; Assess. Res. Software • Persuasion Rubric [for Wr. Mini-Lesson], TR Alt. Assess., p. 101 • TR Alt. Assess., p. 25	• "Always to Remember: The Vision of Maya Ying Lin," LL Audiocassettes • WS Writing Lab CD-ROM Persuasion Tutorial

Program Planner   Unit 4 From Sea to Shining Sea

Selection	Reading	Literary Elements/Forms	Vocabulary	Grammar
from **"The People, Yes,"** Carl Sandburg, SE p. 347 Reading level: Average	• Interactive Reading Strategies, SE pp. 346, 349; TR Selection Support, p. 138–139 • Respond, TR Str. for Diverse St. Needs, pp. 51–52 • Model Selection, SE pp. 347–348	• Oral Tradition, SE pp. 345, 349; TR Selection Support, p. 140	• Suffixes: -eer, SE pp. 345, 349; TR Selection Support, p. 135 Word Bank: mutineers, runt, mosquitoes, flue, SE p. 347	• Subordinating Conjunctions, SE p. 349; TR Selection Support, p. 137 • WS Language Lab CD-ROM, Conjunctions • WS Gram. Pr. Book, Conjunctions, p. 27
from *Travels with Charley,* John Steinbeck, SE p. 354 Reading level: Average	• Clarify Details, SE pp. 353, 362; TR Selection Support, p. 144 • Clarify Details, TR Str. for Diverse St. Needs, pp. 53–54	• Travel Essay, SE pp. 353, 362; TR Selection Support, p. 145	• Suffixes: -ic, SE pp. 352, 362; TR Selection Support, p. 141 Word Bank: diagnostic, p. 355; peripatetic, rigorous, maneuver, inquiry, inexplicable, p. 356; celestial, p. 358	• Coordinating Conjunctions, SE p. 362; TR Selection Support, p. 143 • WS Language Lab CD-ROM, Coordinating Conjunctions • WS Gram. Pr. Book, Conjunctions, p. 26
"The New Colossus," Emma Lazarus; **"Ellis Island,"** Joseph Bruchac; **"Achieving the American Dream,"** Mario Cuomo; **"Choice: A Tribute to Dr. Martin Luther King, Jr.,"** Alice Walker, SE pp. 366, 367, 368, 370 Reading levels: Challenging, Average, Easy, Average	• Summarize, SE pp. 365, 374; TR Selection Support, p. 149 • Summarize, TR Str. for Diverse St. Needs, pp. 55–56	• Epithet, SE pp. 365, 374; TR Selection Support, p. 150	• Related Words: Forms of *migrate,* SE pp. 364, 374; TR Selection Support, p. 146 Word Bank: immigrate, apprehension, immersed, ancestral, p. 369; colossal, conscience, literally, p. 372	• Correlative Conjunctions, SE p. 374; TR Selection Support, p. 148 • WS Language Lab CD-ROM, Transitions • WS Gram. Pr. Book, Correlative Conjunctions, p. 26
"The Man Without a Country," Edward Everett Hale, SE pp. 377 Reading level: Challenging			Word Bank: obscure, p. 377; availed, stilted, swagger, p. 379; blunders, p. 385	
"Sancho," J. Frank Dobie; **"The Closing of the Rodeo,"** William Jay Smith, SE p. 400, 405 Reading levels: Easy, Average	• Envision Setting, SE pp. 399, 406; TR Selection Support, p. 156 • Envision Setting, TR Str. for Diverse St. Needs, pp. 57–58	• Setting in Nonfiction and Poetry, SE pp. 399, 406; TR Selection Support, p. 157	• Word Endings: -ent and -ant, SE pp. 398, 406; TR Selection Support, p. 153 Word Bank: vigorous, yearling, p. 401; persistent, accustomed, p. 403	• Subject and Predicates, SE p. 406; TR Selection Support, p. 155 • WS Language Lab CD-ROM, Subjects and Predicates • WS Gram. Pr. Book, Complete Subjects and Predicates, p. 31
"A Ribbon for Baldy," Jesse Stuart; **"The White Umbrella,"** Gish Jen, SE pp. 410, 414 Reading levels: Easy, Average	• Predict, SE pp. 409, 420; TR Selection Support, p. 161 • Predict, TR Str. for Diverse St. Needs, pp. 59–60	• Character Traits, SE pp. 409, 420; TR Selection Support, p. 162	• Word Roots: -cred-, SE pp. 408, 420; TR Selection Support, p. 158 Word Bank: surveyed, envelop, bargain, p. 411; discreet, credibility, p. 415; constellation, anxiously, p. 416; revelation, p. 419	• Compound Subjects and Verbs, SE p. 420; TR Selection Support, p. 160 • WS Language Lab CD-ROM, Compound Subjects and Compound Verbs • WS Gram. Pr. Book, Compound Subjects and Verbs, p. 32
"Those Winter Sundays," Robert Hayden; **"Taught Me Purple,"** Evelyn Tooley Hunt; **"The City Is So Big,"** Richard García, SE pp. 424, 425, 426 Reading levels: Average, Average, Easy	• Respond, SE pp. 423, 428; TR Selection Support, p. 166 • Respond, TR Str. for Diverse St. Needs, pp. 61–62	• Word Choice, SE pp. 423, 428; TR Selection Support, p. 167	• Word Roots: -chron-, SE pp. 422, 428; TR Selection Support, p. 163 Word Bank: banked, chronic, austere, p. 424; tenement, molding, p. 425; quake, p. 427	• Inverted Sentences, SE p. 428; TR Selection Support, p. 165 • WS Language Lab CD-ROM, Inverted Sentence • WS Gram. Pr. Book, Diagraming Basic Sentence Parts, pp. 43–46

T18   **KEY:**   SE: Student Edition;   ATE: Annotated Teacher's Edition;   TR: Teaching Resources;   LL: Listening to Literature;   WS: Writer's Solution

Writing	Speaking and Listening Viewing and Representing	Projects	Assessment	Technology
• Personal Response, Yarn, Essay, SE p. 350 • Mini-Lesson: Profile of a Legendary Figure [Precise Language], SE p. 350 • Contest Poster, TR Alt. Assess., p. 26	• Memorized Reading, Group Story, SE p. 350 • Sound Track, TR Alt. Assess., p. 26	• Drawing or Painting, Collection of Folk Tales, SE p. 350 • Internet Research, TR Alt. Assess., p. 26	• Selection Test, TR Formal Assessment, pp. 106–108; Assess. Res. Software • Description Rubric [for Wr. Mini-Lesson], TR Alt. Assess., p. 93 • TR Alt. Assess., p. 26	• from "The People, Yes," LL Audiocassettes • WS Writing Lab CD-ROM, Narration Tutorial
• Charley's Journal, Guidebook Description, Essay, SE p. 363 • Mini-Lesson: Travel Journal Entry [Use Supporting Details], SE p. 363 • Round Table Discussion, TR Alt. Assess., p. 27	• Radio Commentray, Panel Discussion, SE p. 363 • S/L Mini-Lesson: Panel Discussion, ATE p. 359 • Author Research, TR Alt. Assess., p. 27	• Map, Documentary Script, SE p. 363 • Travel Brochure, TR Alt. Assess., p. 27	• Selection Test, TR Formal Assessment, pp. 109–111; Assess. Res. Software • Description Rubric [for Wr. Mini-Lesson], TR Alt. Assess., p. 93 • TR Alt. Assess., p. 27	• from Travels With Charley, LL Audiocassettes • WS Writing Lab CD-ROM, Description Tutorial
• Postcard, Journal, Essay, SE p. 375 • Mini-Lesson: Tribute [Transitions], SE p. 375 • Museum Profile, TR Alt. Assess., p. 28	• Address, Dramatization, SE p. 375 • S/L Mini-Lesson: Address, ATE p. 371 • V/R Mini-Lesson: The Immigrant Experience, ATE p. 368 • History Oral Report, TR Alt. Assess., p. 28	• Multimedia Report, Monument, SE p. 375 • Immigration Research, TR Alt. Assess., p. 28	• Selection Test, TR Formal Assessment, pp. 112–114; Assess. Res. Software • Expression Rubric [for Wr. Mini-Lesson], TR Alt. Assess., p. 90 • TR Alt. Assess., p. 28	• "The New Colossus"; "Ellis Island"; "Achieving the American Dream"; "Choice: A Tribute to Dr. Martin Luther King, Jr.," LL Audiocassettes • WS Writing Lab CD-ROM, Expression Tutorial
• Letter, Newspaper Account, Persuasive Essay, SE p. 391	• Conversation, Oral Report, SE p. 391 • S/L Mini-Lesson: Conversation, ATE p. 383 • V/R Mini-Lesson: Symbols, ATE p. 387	• Illustrated Scene, SE p. 391	• Selection Test, TR Formal Assessment, pp. 115–116; Assess. Res. Software • Selection Test, TR Formal Assessment, pp. 117–119; Assess. Res. Software	• "The Man Without a Country," LL Audiocassettes
• Letter, Character Profile, Persuasive Essay, SE p. 407 • Mini-Lesson: Report [Elaborate With Factual Details], SE p. 407 • Illustrated Report, TR Alt. Assess., p. 29	• Oral Presentation, Tour Guide Speech, SE p. 407 • S/L Mini-Lesson: Tour Guide Speech, ATE p. 404 • Rodeo Roundup, TR Alt. Assess., p. 29	• Poster, Historic Newspaper, SE p. 407 • Cowboy Songs, TR Alt. Assess., p. 29	• Research Report/Paper Rubric [for Wr. Mini-Lesson], TR Alt. Assess., p. 102 • TR Alt. Assess., p. 29 • Selection Test, TR Formal Assessment, pp. 120–122; Assess. Res. Software	• "Sancho"; "The Closing of the Rodeo," LL Audiocassettes • WS Writing Lab CD-ROM, Reports Tutorial
• Newspaper Article, Diary Entry, Compare and Contrast, SE p. 421 • Mini-Lesson: Recommendation [Support Points], SE p. 421 • Story Cover, TR Alt. Assess., p. 30	• Dramatic Scene, Work Song, SE p. 421 • S/L Mini-Lesson: Work Song, ATE p. 413 • V/R Mini-Lesson: White Umbrella, ATE p. 417 • Science Project Report, TR Alt. Assess., p. 30	• History of the Piano, Kentucky Farm Report, SE p. 421 • TV Adaptation, TR Alt. Assess., p. 30	• Persuasion Rubric [for Wr. Mini-Lesson], TR Alt. Assess., p. 101 • TR Alt. Assess., p. 30 • Selection Test, TR Formal Assessment, pp. 123–125; Assess. Res. Software	• "A Ribbon for Baldy"; "The White Umbrella," LL Audiocassettes • WS Writing Lab CD-ROM, Persuasion Tutorial
• Book Jacket, Word Analysis, Comparison of Poems, SE p. 429 • Mini-Lesson: Response to Poems [Compare-and-Contrast Organization], SE p. 429 • Greeting Card Design, TR Alt. Assess., p. 31	• Choral Reading, Telephone Conversation, SE p. 429 • S/L Mini-Lesson: Choral Reading, ATE p. 426 • Sound Track, TR Alt. Assess., p. 31	• Poetry Display, City Life Magazine, SE p. 429 • Round Table Discussion, TR Alt. Assess., p. 31	• Response to Literature Rubric [for Wr. Mini-Lesson], TR Alt. Assess., p. 106 • TR Alt. Assess., p. 31	• "Those Winter Sundays"; "Taught Me Purple"; "The City Is So Big," LL Audiocassettes • WS Writing Lab CD-ROM, Response to Literature Tutorial

Program Planner   Unit 5 Extraordinary Occurrences

Selection	Reading	Literary Elements/Forms	Vocabulary	Grammar
"Lights in the Night" from *An American Childhood,* Annie Dillard, SE p. 443 Reading level: Average	• Strategies for Reading Critically, SE pp. 442, 447; TR Selection Support, p. 171–172 • Recognize the Author's Purpose, TR Str. for Diverse St. Needs, pp.63–64 • Model Selection, SE pp. 443–446	• Vignette, SE pp. 441, 447; TR Selection Support, p. 173	• Word Roots: *-lum-,* SE pp. 441, 447; TR Selection Support, p. 168 Word Bank: luminous, ascent, membrane, contiguous, p. 444; conceivably, coincidental, elongate, p. 446	• Direct Objects, SE p. 447; TR Selection Support, p. 170 • WS Gram. Pr. Book, Direct Objects, pp. 35–37
"What Stumped the Blue Jays," Mark Twain; **"Why Leaves Turn Color in the Fall,"** Diane Ackerman, SE pp. 452, 458 Reading levels: Average, Challenging	• Recognize the Author's Purpose, SE pp. 451, 462; TR Selection Support, p. 177 • Recognize the Author's Purpose, TR Str. for Diverse St. Needs, pp. 65–66	• Observation, SE pp. 451, 462; TR Selection Support, p. 178	• Word Roots: *-grat-,* SE pp. 450, 462; TR Selection Support, p. 174 Word Bank: gratification, countenance, p. 455; singular, guffawed, p. 457; macabre, camouflage, predisposed, p. 459; capricious, p. 460	• Indirect Objects, SE p. 462; TR Selection Support, p. 176 • WS Gram. Pr. Book, Indirect Objects, pp. 38–39
"Southbound on the Freeway," May Swenson; **"The Story-Teller,"** Mark Van Doren; **"Los New Yorks,"** Victor Hernández Cruz, SE pp. 466, 467, 468 Reading levels: Easy, Easy, Average	• Understand the Author's Bias, SE pp. 465, 470; TR Selection Support, p. 182 • Understand the Author's Bias, TR Str. for Diverse St. Needs, pp. 67–68	• Free Verse, SE pp. 465, 470; TR Selection Support, p. 183	• Prefixes: *trans-,* SE pp. 464, 470; TR Selection Support, p. 179 Word Bank: transparent, p. 466; galore, tropical, romp, p. 469	• Predicate Adjectives, SE p. 470; TR Selection Support, p. 181
"The Adventure of the Speckled Band," Sir Arthur Conan Doyle, SE p. 474 Reading level: Average	• Identify the Evidence, SE pp. 473, 492; TR Selection Support, p. 187 • Identify the Evidence, TR Str. for Diverse St. Needs, pp. 69–70	• Mystery Story, SE pp. 473, 492; TR Selection Support, p. 188	• Related Words: Forms of *convulse,* SE pp. 472, 492; TR Selection Support, p. 184 Word Bank: defray, manifold, morose, p. 477; convulsed, p. 479; imperturbably, p. 482; reverie, tangible, p. 487	• Predicate Nouns, SE p. 492; TR Selection Support, p. 186
"A Glow in the Dark" from *Woodsong,* Gary Paulsen; **"Mushrooms,"** Sylvia Plath; **"Southern Mansion,"** Arna Bontemps; **"The Bat,"** Theodore Roethke, SE pp. 504, 508, 510, 511 Reading levels: Easy, Average, Average, Easy	• Make Inferences, SE pp. 503, 512; TR Selection Support, p. 192 • Make Inferences, TR Str. for Diverse St. Needs, pp. 71–72	• Tone, SE pp. 503, 512; TR Selection Support, p. 193	• Prefixes: *a-,* SE pp. 502, 512; TR Selection Support, p. 189 Word Bank: diffused, p. 507; discreetly, acquire, p. 508; amiss, p. 511	• Appositive Phrases, SE p. 512; TR Selection Support, p. 191 • WS Gram. Pr. Book, Appositives in Phrases, p. 48
"A Horseman in the Sky," Ambrose Bierce, SE p. 515 Reading level: Challenging			Word Bank: configuration, p. 515; sentinel, languor, equestrian, eminence, p. 517; sublimity, mandate, impetuous, p. 519	

KEY: SE: Student Edition;   ATE: Annotated Teacher's Edition;   TR: Teaching Resources;   LL: Listening to Literature;   WS: Writer's Solution

Writing	Speaking and Listening Viewing and Representing	Projects	Assessment	Technology
• Annotated List, Letter, Summary, SE p. 448 • Mini-Lesson: Childhood Remembrance [Identify Your Purpose], SE p. 448 • Oral Performance, TR Alt. Assess., p. 32	• Oral Interpretation, Role Play, SE p. 448 • S/L Mini-Lesson: Role Play, ATE p. 444 • V/R Mini-Lesson: Research Report, ATE p. 445 • Round Table Discussion, TR Alt. Assess., p. 32	• Diagram and Caption, Research Report, SE p. 448 • Illustration, TR Alt. Assess., p. 32	• Selection Test, TR Formal Assessment, pp. 134–135; Assess. Res. Software • Narrative Based on Personal Experience, Rubric [for Wr. Mini-Lesson], TR Alt. Assess., p. 92 • TR Alt. Assess., p. 32	• "Lights in the Night" from *An American Childhood*, LL Audiocassettes • WS Writing Lab CD-ROM, Description Tutorial
• Descriptive Letter, Editor's Foreword, Science Magazine, SE p. 463 • Mini-Lesson: Observational Essay [Writing to the Audience], SE p. 463 • Foliage Guide, TR Alt. Assess., p. 33	• Oral Interpretation, Author's Chat, SE p. 463 • S/L Mini-Lesson: Oral Interpretation, ATE p. 454 • V/R Mini-Lesson: Local Trees, ATE p. 459 • Internet Research, TR Alt. Assess., p. 33	• Research, Botanical Drawing, SE p. 463 • Field Guide Entry, TR Alt. Assess., p. 33	• Selection Test, TR Formal Assessment, pp. 137–139; Assess. Res. Software • Observational Essay: Narrative Based on Personal Experience, or Research/ Report Paper Rubric [for Wr. Mini-Lesson], TR Alt. Assess., p. 92, 102 • TR Alt. Assess., p. 33	• "What Stumped the Blue Jays"; "Why Leaves Turn Color in the Fall," LL Audiocassettes • WS Writing Lab CD-ROM, Description Tutorial
• Travel Advertisement, City Poem, Analysis, SE p. 471 • Mini-Lesson: Poem About a Person or Place [Using Appropriate Tone], SE p. 471 • Oral Reading, TR Alt. Assess., p. 34	• Talk-Show Appearance, Storyteller, SE p. 471 • S/L Mini-Lesson: Talk-Show Appearance, ATE p. 468 • Book Jacket, TR Alt. Assess., p. 34	• Multimedia Report, Painting, SE p. 471 • Internet Research, TR Alt. Assess., p. 34	• Selection Test, TR Formal Assessment, pp. 140–142; Assess. Res. Software • Poetry Rubric [for Wr. Mini-Lesson], TR Alt. Assess., p. 104 • TR Alt. Assess., p. 34	• "Southbound on the Freeway"; "The Story-Teller"; "Los New Yorks," LL Audiocassettes • WS Writing Lab CD-ROM, Creative Writing Tutorial
• Advertisement, Action Plan, Personal Essay, SE p. 493 • Mini-Lesson: Letter of Recommendation [Support Your Points], SE p. 493 • Illustration, TR Alt. Assess., p. 35	• Talk Show, Radio Play, SE p. 493 • S/L Mini-Lesson: Radio Play, ATE p. 488 • V/R Mini-Lesson: Set Design, ATE p. 485 • Science Report, TR Alt. Assess., p. 35	• Classroom Mystery, Collage, SE p. 493 • Literature Report, TR Alt. Assess., p. 35	• Selection Test, TR Formal Assessment, pp. 143–145; Assess. Res. Software • Description Rubric [for Wr. Mini-Lesson], TR Alt. Assess., p. 93 • TR Alt. Assess., p. 35	• "The Adventure of the Speckled Band," LL Audiocassettes • WS Writing Lab CD-ROM, Expression Tutorial
• List, News Story, Essay, SE p. 513 • Mini-Lesson: I-Search Paper [State Your Main Points Clearly], SE p. 513 • Internet Research, TR Alt. Assess., p. 36	• Monologue, Oral Presentation, SE p. 513 • S/L Mini-Lesson: Monologue, ATE p. 510 • V/R Mini-Lesson: Science Article, ATE p. 508 • Oral Performance, TR Alt. Assess., p. 36	• Science Article, Story Illustration, SE p. 513 • Internet Research, TR Alt. Assess., p. 36	• Selection Test, TR Formal Assessment, pp. 146–148; Assess. Res. Software • Research/Report Paper Rubric [for Wr. Mini-Lesson], TR Alt. Assess., p. 102 • TR Alt. Assess., p. 36	• "A Glow in the Dark" from *Woodsong*; "Mushrooms"; "Southern Mansion"; "The Bat," LL Audiocassettes • WS Writing Lab CD-ROM, Reports Tutorial
• Diary Entry, Prequel, Reflective Essay, SE p. 521	• Retelling, Debate, SE p. 521 • S/L Mini-Lesson: Retelling, ATE p. 519 • V/R Mini-Lesson: Multimedia Presentation, ATE p. 518	• Multimedia Presentation, SE p. 521	• Selection Test, TR Formal Assessment, pp. 149–150; Assess. Res. Software	• "A Horseman in the Sky," LL Audiocassettes

Program Planner   Unit 6 Short Stories

Selection	Reading	Literary Elements/Forms	Vocabulary	Grammar
"The Dinner Party," Mona Gardner, SE p. 535 Reading level: Average	• Strategies for Reading Fiction, SE pp. 534, 537; TR Selection Support, pp. 199–200 • Make Inferences, TR Str. for Diverse St. Needs, pp. 73–74 • Model Selection, SE pp. 535–536	• Plot, SE pp. 533, 537; TR Selection Support, p. 201	• Word Roots: *-spir-*, SE pp. 532, 537; TR Selection Support, p. 196 Word Bank: naturalist, spirited, p. 535; arresting, sobers, p. 536	• Clauses, SE p. 537; TR Selection Support, p. 198 • WS Language Lab CD-ROM, Independent Clauses and Subordinate Clauses • WS Gram. Pr. Book, Clarifying Sentences by Structure, pp. 59–60
"The Tell-Tale Heart," Edgar Allan Poe, SE p. 542 Reading level: Challenging	• Predict, SE pp. 541, 548; TR Selection Support, p. 205 • Predict, TR Str. for Diverse St. Needs, pp. 75–76	• Suspense in a Plot, SE pp. 541, 548; TR Selection Support, p. 206	• Wood Roots: *-found-*, SE pp. 540, 548; TR Selection Support, p. 202 Word Bank: acute, dissimulation, profound, sagacity, p. 543; crevice, p. 544; gesticulations, derision, p. 546	• Adverb Clauses, SE p. 548; TR Selection Support, p. 204 • WS Language Lab CD-ROM, Adverb Clauses • WS Gram. Pr. Book, Adverb Clauses, p. 57
"An Episode of War," Stephen Crane, SE p. 551 Reading level: Challenging			Word Bank: precipitate, aggregation, inscrutable, p. 553	
"The Day I Got Lost," Isaac Bashevis Singer; **"Hamadi,"** Naomi Shihab Nye, SE pp. 558, 562 Reading levels: Easy, Average	• Identify With a Character, SE pp. 557, 570; TR Selection Support, p. 212 • Identify With the Characters, TR Str. for Diverse St. Needs, pp. 77–78	• Characterization, SE pp. 557, 570; TR Selection Support, p. 213	• Word Roots: *-chol-*, SE pp. 556, 570; TR Selection Support, p. 209 Word Bank: forsaken, pandemonium, p. 560; brittle, p. 562; lavish, p. 565; refugees, melancholy, p. 569	• Adjective Clauses, SE p. 570; TR Selection Support, p. 211 • WS Language Lab CD-ROM, Clauses in Sentence Errors • WS Gram. Pr. Book, Adjective Clauses, p. 55
"The Finish of Patsy Barnes," Paul Laurence Dunbar; **"Tears of Autumn,"** Yoshiko Uchida, SE pp. 580, 586 Reading levels: Average, Average	• Ask Questions, SE pp. 579, 592; TR Selection Support, p. 217 • Ask Questions, TR Str. for Diverse St. Needs, pp. 79–80	• Setting, SE pp. 579, 592; TR Selection Support, p. 218	• Word Roots: *-flu-*, SE pp. 578, 592; TR Selection Support, p. 214 Word Bank: compulsory, meager, p. 581; obdurate, diplomatic, p. 583; turbulent, affluence, p. 587; degrading, p. 590	• Simple and Compound Sentences, SE pp. 592; TR Selection Support, p. 216 • WS Language Lab CD-ROM, Simple and Compound Sentences • WS Gram. Pr. Book, Classifying Sentences by Structure, p. 59
"The Story-Teller," Saki (H. H. Munro); **"The Medicine Bag,"** Virginia Driving Hawk Sneve, SE pp. 596, 602 Reading levels: Average, Easy	• Make Inferences, SE pp. 595, 610; TR Selection Support, p. 222 • Make Inferences, TR Str. for Diverse St. Needs, pp. 81–82	• Theme, SE pp. 595, 610; TR Selection Support, p. 223	• Suffixes: *-less,* SE pp. 594, 610; TR Selection Support, p. 219 Word Bank: bachelor, p. 597; resolute, listlessly, p. 599; authentic, procession, p. 603	• Complex Sentences, SE p. 610; TR Selection Support, p. 221 • WS Language Lab CD-ROM, Complex Sentences • WS Gram. Pr. Book, Classifying Sentences by Structure, p. 60

Writing	Speaking and Listening Viewing and Representing	Projects	Assessment	Technology
• Research Plan, Diary Entry, Sequel, SE p. 538 • Mini-Lesson: Interior Monologue [Use Details to Reveal Character], SE p. 538 • Internet Research, TR Alt. Assess., p.37	• Scene, Dinner Speech, SE p. 538 • S/L Mini-Lesson: Scene, ATE p. 535 • Snake Poison, TR Alt. Assess., p. 37	• Reality Check, Film Treatment, SE p. 538 • Illustration, TR Alt. Assess., p. 37	• Selection Test, TR Formal Assessment, pp. 159–161; Assess. Res. Software • Expression Rubric [for Wr. Mini-Lesson], TR Alt. Assess., p. 90 • TR Alt. Assess., p. 37	• "The Dinner Party," LL Audiocassettes • WS Writing Lab CD-ROM, Creative Writing Tutorial
• Prediction, Police Report, Comparative Essay, SE p. 549 • Mini-Lesson: Suspenseful Anecdote [Create Suspense], SE p. 549 • Readers Theatre, TR Alt. Assess., p. 38	• News Interview, Opening Argument, SE p. 549 • S/L Mini-Lesson: News Interview, ATE p. 546 • V/R Mini-Lesson: Suspense, ATE p. 545 • Film Proposal, TR Alt. Assess., p. 38	• Movie Review, Literary Panel, SE p. 549 • Set Design, TR Alt. Assess., p. 38	• Selection Test, TR Formal Assessment, pp. 162–164; Assess. Res. Software • Expression Rubric [for Wr. Mini-Lesson], TR Alt. Assess., p. 90 • TR Alt. Assess., p. 38	• "The Tell-Tale Heart," LL Audiocassettes • WS Writing Lab CD-ROM, Expression Tutorial
• Journal Entry, Official Report, Essay, SE p. 555	• Role Play, SE p. 555 • S/L Mini-Lesson: Role Play, ATE p. 553	• Report, Drawings, SE p. 555	• Selection Test, TR Formal Assessment, pp. 165–166; Assess. Res. Software	• "An Episode of War," LL Audiocassettes
• Missing-Person Bulletin, Self-Portrait, Episode, SE p. 571 • Mini-Lesson: Dialogue [Create Realistic Dialogue], SE p. 571 • Photo Essay, TR Alt. Assess., p. 39	• Monologue, Role Play, SE p. 571 • S/L Mini-Lesson: Monologue, ATE p. 568 • V/R Mini-Lesson: Book Jacket, ATE p. 561 • Holiday Time, TR Alt. Assess., p. 39	• Report on Kahlil Gibran, Wise Fools and Tricksters, SE p. 571 • Folk Tale Presentation, TR Alt. Assess., p. 39	• Selection Test, TR Formal Assessment, pp. 167–169; Assess. Res. Software • Drama Rubric [for Wr. Mini-Lesson], TR Alt. Assess., p. 105 • TR Alt. Assess., p. 39	• "The Day I Got Lost"; "Hamadi," LL Audiocassettes • WS Writing Lab CD-ROM, Creative Writing Tutorial
• Description, Personal Letter, Critical Review, SE p. 593 • Mini-Lesson: Comparison and Contrast [Clear and Logical Organization], SE p. 593 • History Report, TR Alt. Assess., p. 40	• Monologue, Sportscast, SE p. 593 • S/L Mini-Lesson: Monologue, ATE p. 588 • Oral Interpretation, TR Alt. Assess., p. 40	• Museum Display, Set Design, SE p. 593 • Round Table Discussion, TR Alt. Assess., p. 40	• Selection Test, TR Formal Assessment, pp. 170–172; Assess. Res. Software • Comparison/Contrast Rubric [for Wr. Mini-Lesson], TR Alt. Assess., p. 99 • TR Alt. Assess., p. 40	• "The Finish of Patsy Barnes"; "Tears of Autumn," LL Audiocassettes • WS Writing Lab CD-ROM Exposition: Making Connections Tutorial
• List, Compare and Contrast, Analysis and Evaluation, SE p. 611 • Mini-Lesson: Book Jacket [Supporting Details], SE p. 611 • Photo Essay, TR Alt. Assess., p. 41	• Storytelling, DJ's Rap, SE p. 611 • S/L Mini-Lesson: Storytelling, ATE p. 601 • V/R Mini-Lesson: Remembering an Elder, ATE p. 605 • Illustration, TR Alt. Assess., p. 41	• Space Capsule, Travel Itinerary, SE p. 611 • Readers Theatre, TR Alt. Assess., p. 41	• Selection Test, TR Formal Assessment, pp. 173–175; Assess. Res. Software • Response to Literature Rubric [for Wr. Mini-Lesson], TR Alt. Assess., p. 106 • TR Alt. Assess., p. 41	• "The Story-Teller"; "The Medicine Bag," LL Audiocassettes • WS Writing Lab CD-ROM, Description Tutorial

Program Planner   Unit 7 Nonfiction

Selection	Reading	Literary Elements/Forms	Vocabulary	Grammar
"Animal Craftsmen," Bruce Brooks, SE p. 625 Reading level: Average	• Strategies for Reading Nonfiction, SE pp. 624, 629; TR Selection Support, pp. 227–228 • Identify the Author's Main Points, TR Str. for Diverse St. Needs, pp. 83–84 • Model Selection, SE pp. 625–628	• Reflective Essay, SE pp. 623, 629; TR Selection Support, p. 229	• Related Words: Forms of *habitable,* SE pp. 623, 629; TR Selection Support, p. 224 Word Bank: subtle, p. 625; infusion, habitable, empathy, p. 627	• Subjective Case Pronouns, SE p. 629; TR Selection Support, p. 226 • WS Language Lab CD-ROM, Pronouns
from **"One Writer's Beginnings,"** Eudora Welty; **"Baseball,"** Lionel García, SE pp. 634, 636 Reading levels: Average, Average	• Understand the Author's Purpose, SE pp. 633, 640; TR Selection Support, p. 233 • Understand the Author's Purpose, TR Str. for Diverse St. Needs, pp. 85–86	• Autobiography, SE pp. 633, 640; TR Selection Support, p. 234	• Word Roots: *-vis-,* SE pp. 632, 640; TR Selection Support, p. 230 Word Bank: visible, reigning, respectively, constellations, eclipses, p. 634; devices, p. 637; evaded, p. 638	• Objective Case Pronouns, SE p. 640; TR Selection Support, p. 232 • WS Language Lab CD-ROM, Objective Case Pronouns
from **"The United States *vs.* Susan B. Anthony,"** Margaret Truman, SE p. 643 Reading level: Challenging			• TR Selection Support, p. 235 Word Bank: unremitting, p. 643; abridge, oratory, inadvertently, intimidated, p. 644; retrospect, p. 647; consternation, futile, p. 648	
"Hokusai: The Old Man Mad About Drawing," Stephen Longstreet; **"Not to Go With the Others,"** John Hersey, SE pp. 654, 656 Reading levels: Easy, Average	• Identify the Author's Main Points, SE pp. 653, 660; TR Selection Support, p. 240 • Identify the Author's Main Points, TR Str. for Diverse St. Needs, pp. 87–88	• Biography, SE pp. 653, 660; TR Selection Support, p. 241	• Prefixes: *en-,* SE pp. 652, 660; TR Selection Support, p. 237 Word Bank: apprenticed, engulfing, mania, p. 655; feigned, ensued, dispatched, pretense, p. 657; immersed, p. 658	• Using *who* and *whom,* SE p. 660; TR Selection Support, p. 239 • WS Language Lab CD-ROM, Use of *who* and *whom* • WS Gram. Pr. Book, Cases of *who* and *whom,* p. 80
"Debbie," James Herriot; **"Forest Fire,"** Anaïs Nin; **"How to Be Polite Online"** from *Netiquette,* Virginia Shea, SE pp. 670, 675, 678 Reading levels: Average, Average, Average	• Set a Purpose for Reading, SE pp. 669, 682; TR Selection Support, p. 245 • Set a Purpose for Reading, TR Str. for Diverse St. Needs, pp. 89–90	• Essay, SE pp. 669, 682; TR Selection Support, p. 246	• Word Roots: *-vac-,* SE pp. 668, 682; TR Selection Support, p. 242 Word Bank: privations, p. 673; evacuees, p. 675; tenacious, dissolution, ravaging, p. 676; implemented, encompasses, p. 679	• Pronoun and Antecedent Agreement, SE pp. 682; TR Selection Support, p. 244 • WS Language Lab CD-ROM, Pronoun and Antecedent Agreement • WS Gram. Pr. Book, Agreement Between Pronouns and Antecedents, p. 85
"The Trouble With Television," Robert MacNeil; **"The American Dream,"** Martin Luther King, Jr., SE pp. 686, 689 Reading levels: Average, Average	• Identify Persuasive Techniques, SE pp. 685, 692; TR Selection Support, p. 250 • Identify Persuasive Techniques, TR Str. for Diverse St. Needs, pp. 91–92	• Persuasive Essay, SE pp. 685, 692; TR Selection Support, p. 251	• Prefixes: *anti-,* SE pp. 684, 692; TR Selection Support, p. 247 Word Bank: diverts, usurps, august, pervading, p. 687; antithesis, paradoxes, devoid, p. 690	• Pronoun Agreement With Indefinite Subjects, SE p. 692; TR Selection Support, p. 249 • WS Language Lab CD-ROM, Subject-Verb Agreement • WS Gram. Pr. Book, Agreement Between Pronouns and Antecedents, p. 85

Writing	Speaking and Listening Viewing and Representing	Projects	Assessment	Technology
• Fan Letter, Nature Poem, Essay, SE p. 630 • Mini-Lesson: Article for the School Newspaper [Appropriate Tone], SE p. 630 • Illustration, TR Alt. Assess., p. 42	• Discussion, Dramatic Reading, SE p. 630 • S/L Mini-Lesson: Discussion, ATE p. 627 • Science Report, TR Alt. Assess., p. 42	• Animal Poster, Mud Wasps' Nest, SE p. 630 • Health Report, TR Alt. Assess., p. 42	• Selection Test, TR Formal Assessment, pp. 184–186; Assess. Res. Software • Research Report/Paper Rubric [for Wr. Mini-Lesson], TR Alt. Assess., p. 102 • TR Alt. Assess., p. 42	• "Animal Craftsmen," LL Audiocassettes • WS Writing Lab CD-ROM, Exposition: Making Connections Tutorial
• Glossary, Autobiography, Report, SE p. 641 • Mini-Lesson: Rule Book [Clarity], SE p. 641 • Onomatopoeia Bee, TR Alt. Assess., p. 43	• Sports Radio, Monologue, SE p. 641 • S/L Mini-Lesson: Sports Radio, ATE p. 638 • Team Role, TR Alt. Assess., p. 43	• Plan for a Baseball Field, Moon Chart, SE p. 641 • Rule Book, TR Alt. Assess., p. 43	• Selection Test, TR Formal Assessment, pp. 187–189; Assess. Res. Software • Definition/Classification Rubric [for Wr. Mini-Lesson], TR Alt. Assess., p. 95 • TR Alt. Assess., p. 43	• from "One Writer's Beginnings"; "Baseball," LL Audiocassettes • WS Writing Lab CD-ROM, Exposition: Giving Information Tutorial
• Journal Entry, Dialogue, Editorial, SE p. 651	• Legal Arguments, SE p. 651 • S/L Mini-Lesson: Legal Arguments, ATE p. 647 • V/R Mini-Lesson: Commemorative Coins, ATE p. 649	• Timeline of the Woman Suffrage Movement, SE p. 651	• Selection Test, TR Formal Assessment, pp. 190–191; Assess. Res. Software	• from "The United States *vs.* Susan B. Anthony," LL Audiocassettes
• Advice Letters, Casting Memo, Biography, SE p. 661 • Mini-Lesson: Testimonial [Support With Examples], SE p. 661 • Round Table Discussion, TR Alt. Assess., p. 44	• Radio Play, Dialogue, SE p. 661 • S/L Mini-Lesson: Radio Play, ATE p. 657 • Arts Report, TR Alt. Assess., p. 44	• Holocaust Exhibit, Art Catalog, SE p. 661 • Museum Brochure, TR Alt. Assess., p. 44	• Selection Test, TR Formal Assessment, pp. 192–194; Assess. Res. Software • Expression Rubric [for Wr. Mini-Lesson], TR Alt. Assess., p. 90 • TR Alt. Assess., p. 44	• "Hokusai: The Old Man Mad About Drawing"; "Not to Go With the Others," LL Audiocassettes • WS Writing Lab CD-ROM, Reports Tutorial
• Computer Checklist, Essay, Analysis, SE p. 683 • Mini-Lesson: Interview [Using Quotation Marks], SE p. 683 • Round Table Discussion, TR Alt. Assess., p. 45	• Role Play, Oral Interpretation, SE p. 683 • S/L Mini-Lesson: Role Play, ATE p. 676 • V/R Mini-Lesson: Computer Symbol Imagery, ATE p. 680 • Interview, TR Alt. Assess., p. 45	• Survey and Analysis, Firefighting Report, SE p. 683 • Illustration, TR Alt. Assess., p. 45	• Selection Test, TR Formal Assessment, pp. 195–197; Assess. Res. Software • Research Report/Paper Rubric [for Wr. Mini-Lesson], TR Alt. Assess., p. 102 • TR Alt. Assess., p. 45	• "Debbie"; "Forest Fire"; "How to Be Polite Online" from *Netiquette,* LL Audiocassettes • WS Writing Lab CD-ROM, Reports Tutorial
• List, Business Letter, News Analysis, SE p. 693 • Mini-Lesson: Persuasive Speech [Strong Beginning and Ending], SE p. 693 • Television News Review, TR Alt. Assess., p. 46	• Speech, Dialogue, SE p. 693 • S/L Mini-Lesson: Speech, ATE p. 690 • Postcard, TR Alt. Assess., p. 46	• Civil Rights Exhibit, Multimedia Presentation, SE p. 693 • Round Table Discussion, TR Alt. Assess., p. 46	• Selection Test, TR Formal Assessment, pp. 198–200; Assess. Res. Software • Persuasion Rubric [for Wr. Mini-Lesson], TR Alt. Assess., p. 101 • TR Alt. Assess., p. 46	• "The Trouble With Television"; "The American Dream," LL Audiocassettes • WS Writing Lab CD-ROM, Persuasion Tutorial

Program Planner   Unit 8 Drama

Selection	Reading	Literary Elements/Forms	Vocabulary	Grammar
The Diary of Anne Frank, Act I, SE p. 712 Reading level: Average	• Be Aware of Historical Context, SE pp. 711, 745; TR Selection Support, p. 255 • Summarize, TR Str. for Diverse St. Needs, pp. 93–94	• Staging, SE pp. 711, 745; TR Selection Support, p. 256	• Prefixes: *un-* and *in-*, SE pp. 708, 745; TR Selection Support, p. 252 Word Bank: conspicuous, p. 715; mercurial, leisure, p. 716; unabashed, p. 719; insufferable, p. 725; meticulous, p. 731; fatalist, p. 737; ostentatiously, p. 740	• Subject and Verb Agreement, SE p. 745; TR Selection Support, p. 254 • WS Gram. Pr. Book, Agreement Between Subjects and Verbs, p. 81
The Diary of Anne Frank, Act II, SE p. 749 Reading level: Average	• Envision, SE pp. 747, 770; TR Selection Support, p. 260 • Envision, TR Str. for Diverse St. Needs, pp. 95–96	• Characterization and Theme in Drama, SE pp. 747, 770; TR Selection Support, p. 261	• Related Words: Forms of *effect,* SE pp. 747, 770; TR Selection Support, p. 257 Word Bank: inarticulate, p. 750; apprehension, p. 752; intuition, p. 757; sarcastic, indignant, p. 758; stealthily, p. 761; ineffectually, p. 766	• Verb Agreement With Indefinite Pronouns, SE p. 770; TR Selection Support, p. 259 • WS Language Lab CD-ROM, Agreement With Indefinite Pronouns • WS Gram. Pr. Book, Special Problems With Subject-Verb Agreement, p. 84
from **A Walk in the Woods,** Lee Blessing, SE p. 773 Reading level: Average			• TR Selection Support, p. 262	
from **A Midsummer Night's Dream, Act III, scene ii;** from **Much Ado About Nothing, Act II, scene iii;** from **The Life and Death of King Richard III, Act I, scene i,** William Shakespeare, SE pp. 784, 790, 792 Reading levels: Challenging, Challenging, Challenging	• Summarize, SE pp. 783, 794; TR Selection Support, p. 267 • Summarize, TR Str. for Diverse St. Needs, pp. 97–98	• Scenes and Soliloquies, SE pp. 783, 794; TR Selection Support, p. 268	• Suffix: *-ous,* SE pp. 782, 794; TR Selection Support, p. 264 Word Bank: apprehension, confederacy, p. 785; officious, p. 789; discourse, censured, p. 791; adversaries, p. 793	• Subject and Verb Agreement in Inverted Sentences, SE p. 794; TR Selection Support p. 266 • WS Language Lab CD-ROM, Special Problems in Agreement 1 and 2 • WS Gram. Pr. Book, Special Problems With Subject-Verb Agreement, p. 84

KEY: SE: Student Edition;   ATE: Annotated Teacher's Edition;   TR: Teaching Resources;   LL: Listening to Literature;   WS: Writer's Solution

Writing	Speaking and Listening Viewing and Representing	Projects	Assessment	Technology
• Letter, Program Notes, SE p. 745 • Diary, TR Alt. Assess., p. 47	• Dramatic Reading, SE p. 745 • S/L Mini-Lesson: Reading, ATE p. 741 • V/R Mini-Lesson: Commemorative Stamps, ATE p. 743 • V/R Mini-Lesson: Design Stage Set, ATE p. 719 • Hannukkah Song, TR Alt. Assess., p. 47	• Design, TR Alt. Assess., p. 47	• Selection Test, TR Formal Assessment, pp. 209–211; Assess. Res. Software • TR Alt. Assess., p. 47	• *The Diary of Anne Frank,* LL Audiocassettes
• Timeline, Diary Entry, Essay, SE p. 771 • Mini-Lesson: Scene With Dialogue [Script Format], SE p. 771 • Stage Set Model, TR Alt. Assess., p.48	• Scene, Dramatic Monologue, SE p. 771 • S/L Mini-Lesson: Dramatic Monologue, ATE p. 751 • V/R Mini-Lesson: Decorated Wall, ATE p. 755 • Research Report, TR Alt. Assess., p. 48	• Book Club, Holocaust Research, SE p. 771 • Tourist Brochure, TR Alt. Assess., p. 48	• Selection Test, TR Formal Assessment, pp. 212–214; Assess. Res. Software • Drama Rubric [for Wr. Mini-Lesson], TR Alt. Assess., p. 105 • TR Alt. Assess., p. 48	• *The Diary of Anne Frank,* LL Audiocassettes • WS Writing Lab CD-ROM Creative Writing Tutorial
• Description, Reporter's Questions, Official Report, SE p. 775	• Dramatic Reading, SE p. 775	• Maps, SE p. 775	• Selection Test, TR Formal Assessment, pp. 215–216; Assess. Res. Software	• from *A Walk in the Woods,* LL Audiocassettes
• Summary, Casting Advice, Comparison-and-Contrast Essay, SE p. 795 • Mini-Lesson: Biographical Report [Narrowing Your Topic], SE p. 795 • Dramatic Performance, TR Alt. Assess., p. 49	• Shakespeare Recitation, Radio Drama, SE p. 795 • S/L Mini-Lesson: Radio Drama, ATE p. 788 • V/R Mini-Lesson: Shakespearean Comic Book, ATE p. 791 • Sound Effects Script, TR Alt. Assess., p. 49	• Comic Book, Historical Soliloquy, SE p. 795 • Production Research, TR Alt. Assess., p. 49	• Selection Test, TR Formal Assessment, pp. 217–219; Assess. Res. Software • Research Report/Paper Rubric [for Wr. Mini-Lesson], TR Alt. Assess., p. 102 • TR Alt. Assess., p. 49	• from *A Midsummer Night's Dream,* Act III, scene ii; from *Much Ado About Nothing,* Act II, scene iii; from *The Life and Death of King Richard III,* Act I, scene i, LL Audiocassettes • WS Writing Lab CD-ROM Creative Writing Tutorial

Program Planner   Unit 9 Poetry

Selection	Reading	Literary Elements/Forms	Vocabulary	Grammar
"The Secret Heart," Robert P. Tristram Coffin, SE p. 809 Reading level: Easy	• Strategies for Reading Poetry, SE pp. 808, 811; TR Selection Support, p. 272 • Use Your Senses, TR Str. for Diverse St. Needs, pp. 99–100 • Model Selection, SE pp. 809–810	• Symbols, SE pp. 807, 811; TR Selection Support, p. 273	• Word Roots: -semble-, SE pp. 807, 811; TR Selection Support, p. 269 Word Bank: kindled, semblance, p. 810	• Comparison of Modifiers, SE p. 811; TR Selection Support, p. 271 • WS Language Lab CD-ROM • WS Gram. Pr. Book, Adverbs, p. 21
"The Wreck of the Hesperus," Henry Wadsworth Longfellow; **"The Centaur,"** May Swenson, SE pp. 816, 820 Reading levels: Average, Average	• Read Lines According to Punctuation, SE pp. 815, 824; TR Selection Support, p. 277 • Read Lines According to Punctuation, TR Str. for Diverse St. Needs, pp. 101–102	• Narrative Poetry, SE pp. 815, 824; TR Selection Support, p. 278	• Suffixes: -ful, SE pp. 814, 824; TR Selection Support, p. 274 Word Bank: scornful, gale, p. 817; breakers, p. 818; cinched, canter, p. 820; negligent, p. 822	• Comparisons With more and most, SE p. 824; TR Selection Support, p. 276 • WS Language Lab CD-ROM, Using Modifiers • WS Gram. Pr. Book, Using Comparative and Superlative Degrees, p. 88
"Harlem Night Song," Langston Hughes; **"Blow, Blow, Thou Winter Wind,"** William Shakespeare; **"love is a place,"** E. E. Cummings; **"The Freedom of the Moon,"** Robert Frost, SE pp. 828, 829, 830, 831 Reading levels: Average, Average, Challenging, Easy	• Identify the Speaker, SE pp. 827, 832; TR Selection Support, p. 282 • Identify the Speaker, TR Str. for Diverse St. Needs, pp. 103–104	• Lyric Poetry, SE pp. 827, 832; TR Selection Support, p. 283	• Word Roots: -lus-, SE pp. 826, 832; TR Selection Support, p. 279 Word Bank: roam, keen, feigning, p. 828; breadth, luster, p. 831	• Irregular Comparisons of Modifiers, SE p. 832; TR Selection Support, p. 281 • WS Language Lab CD-ROM, Troublesome Adjectives and Adverbs • WS Gram. Pr. Book, Irregular Adjectives and Adverbs, p. 87
"January," John Updike; **Two Haiku,** Bashō and Moritake; **"Identity,"** Julio Noboa Polanco; **"400-Meter Free Style,"** Maxine Kumin, SE pp. 836, 837, 838, 839 Reading levels: Easy, Easy, Average, Average	• Paraphrase Lines, SE pp. 835, 842; TR Selection Support, p. 287 • Paraphrase Lines, TR Str. for Diverse St. Needs, pp. 105–106	• Poetic Form, SE pp. 835, 842; TR Selection Support, p. 288	• Related Words: Forms of fertile, SE pp. 834, 842; TR Selection Support, p. 284 Word Bank: harnessed, abyss, shunned, fertile, catapults, p. 838; cunningly, extravagance, nurtures, p. 840	• Coordinate Adjectives, SE p. 842; TR Selection Support, p. 286 • WS Language Lab CD-ROM, Using Modifiers
"Wahbegan," Jim Northrup, SE p. 845 Reading level: Average			• TR Selection Support, p. 289 Word Bank: casualty, p. 846	
"Silver," Walter de la Mare; **"Forgotten Language,"** Shel Silverstein; **"Drum Song,"** Wendy Rose; **"If I can stop one Heart from breaking,"** Emily Dickinson, SE pp. 856–859 Reading levels: Average, Easy, Average, Easy	• Make Inferences, SE pp. 855, 860; TR Selection Support, p. 294 • Make Inferences, TR Str. for Diverse St. Needs, pp. 107–108	• Sound Devices, SE pp. 855, 860; TR Selection Support, p. 295	• Word Pairs, SE pp. 854, 860; TR Selection Support, p. 291 Word Bank: vertical, burrow, gourds, p. 858	• Correct Use of Adjectives and Adverbs, SE p. 860; TR Selection Support p. 293 • WS Language Lab CD-ROM, Problems With Modifiers • WS Gram. Pr. Book, Adjectives and Adverbs, pp. 16–23
"New World," N. Scott Momaday; **"One Time,"** William Stafford; **"Lyric 17,"** José Garcia Villa; **"For My Sister Molly Who in the Fifties,"** Alice Walker, SE pp. 864, 866, 867, 868 Reading levels: Average, Average, Average, Average	• Use Your Senses, SE pp. 863, 870; TR Selection Support, p. 299 • Use Your Senses, TR Str. for Diverse St. Needs, pp. 109–110	• Imagery, SE pp. 863, 870; TR Selection Support, p. 300	• Word Roots: -cede-, SE pp. 862, 870; TR Selection Support, p. 296 Word Bank: glistens, borne, low, hover, recede, p. 865; luminance, p. 867	• Pronouns in Comparisons With than or as, SE p. 870; TR Selection Support, p. 298 • WS Language Lab CD-ROM, Using Pronouns • WS Gram. Pr. Book, Using Pronouns, pp. 77–80
"The Dark Hills," Edwin Arlington Robinson; **"Solar,"** Philip Larkin; **"Incident in a Rose Garden,"** Donald Justice, SE pp. 876, 877, 878 Reading levels: Average, Challenging, Average	• Respond, SE pp. 875, 880; TR Selection Support, p. 304 • Respond, TR Str. for Diverse St. Needs, pp. 111–112	• Figurative Language, SE pp. 875, 880; TR Selection Support, p. 305	• Commonly Confused Words: continuously and continually, SE pp. 874, 880; TR Selection Support, p. 301 Word Bank: hovers, legions, unrecompensed, continuously, p. 876; scythe, beckoned, gestures, p. 879	• Correct Use of like and as, SE p. 880; TR Selection Support, p. 303 • WS Language Lab CD-ROM, Special Problems With Pronouns • WS Gram. Pr. Book, Common Usage Problems, p. 92

T28   **KEY:**   SE: Student Edition;   ATE: Annotated Teacher's Edition;   TR: Teaching Resources;   LL: Listening to Literature;   WS: Writer's Solution

Writing	Speaking and Listening Viewing and Representing	Projects	Assessment	Technology
• List, Poem, Essay, SE p. 812 • Mini-Lesson: Explanation of a Symbol [Give Reasons], SE p. 812 • Illustration, TR Alt. Assess., p. 50	• Love Song, Poetry Reading, SE p. 812 • Round Table Discussion, TR Alt. Assess., p. 50	• Salute to the Poet, Musical Archives, SE p. 812 • Research Report, TR Alt. Assess., p. 50	• Selection Test, TR Formal Assessment, pp. 228–230; Assess. Res. Software • Rubric [for Wr. Mini-Lesson], TR Alt. Assess., p. 106 • TR Alt. Assess., p. 50	• "The Secret Heart," LL Audiocassettes • WS Writing Lab CD-ROM, Tutorial
• Continue the Poem, News Story, Character Study, SE p. 825 • Mini-Lesson: Response to a Poem [Support Points], SE p. 825 • Oral Reading, TR Alt. Assess., p. 51	• "Fireside" Reading, Anecdotes, SE p. 825 • S/L Mini-Lesson: Anecdotes, ATE p. 820 • V/R Mini-Lesson: Imagery, ATE p. 821 • Author Report, TR Alt. Assess., p. 51	• Weather Report, Mythical Creatures Poster, SE p. 825 • Artist Report, TR Alt. Assess., p. 51	• Selection Test, TR Formal Assessment, pp. 231–233; Assess. Res. Software • Response to Literature Rubric [for Wr. Mini-Lesson], TR Alt. Assess., p. • TR Alt. Assess., p. 51	• "The Wreck of the Hesperus"; "The Centaur," LL Audiocassettes • WS Writing Lab CD-ROM, Response to Literature Tutorial
• Invitation, Paraphrase, Essay, SE p. 833 • Mini-Lesson: Retelling of a Poem in Prose [Use an Appropriate Tone], SE p. 833 • Oral Interpretation, TR Alt. Assess., p. 52	• Monologue, Discussion, SE p. 833 • S/L Mini-Lesson: Monologue, ATE p. 830 • Poet Profile, TR Alt. Assess., p. 52	• Music of the 1920's, Constellations Poster, SE p. 833 • Science Report, TR Alt. Assess., p. 52	• Selection Test, TR Formal Assessment, pp. 234–236; Assess. Res. Software • Summary Rubric [for Wr. Mini-Lesson], TR Alt. Assess., p. 94 • TR Alt. Assess., p. 52	• "Harlem Night Song"; "Blow, Blow, Thou Winter Wind"; "love is a place"; "The Freedom of the Moon," LL Audiocassettes • WS Writing Lab CD-ROM, Creative Writing Tutorial
• Glossary, Concrete Poem, Essay, SE p. 843 • Mini-Lesson: Description of Yourself With a Comparison [Elaborate With Supporting Details], SE p. 843 • Round Table Discussion, TR Alt. Assess., p. 53	• Rebuttal, Dramatic Reading, SE p. 843 • S/L Mini-Lesson: Dramatic Reading, ATE p. 839 • V/R Mini-Lesson: Swimming Poem, ATE p. 840 • Book Jacket, TR Alt. Assess., p. 53	• Multimedia Presentation, Glossary of Terms, SE p. 843 • Tanka Research, TR Alt. Assess., p. 53.	• Selection Test, TR Formal Assessment, pp. 237–239; Assess. Res. Software • Comparison/Contrast Rubric [for Wr. Mini-Lesson], TR Alt. Assess., p. 99 • TR Alt. Assess., p. 53	• "January"; Two Haiku; "Identity"; "400-Meter Free Style," LL Audiocassettes • WS Writing Lab CD-ROM, Description Tutorial
• Letter Home, Response to a Poem, Persuasive Essay, SE p. 847	• Discussion, SE p. 847	• Art, Encyclopedia Entry, SE p. 847	• Selection Test, TR Formal Assessment, pp. 240–241; Assess. Res. Software	• "Wahbegan," LL Audiocassettes
• Stanza of Poetry, Public-Service Announcement, Inference About an Author, SE p. 861 • Mini-Lesson: Song Lyrics [Use Effective Repetition], SE p. 861 • Science Report, TR Alt. Assess., p. 54	• Reading, Poem With Drums, SE p. 861 • S/L Mini-Lesson: Reading, ATE p. 857 • Mood Music, TR Alt. Assess., p. 54	• Sound Devices in Speeches, Report on Animal Communication, SE p. 861 • Dickinson Festival, TR Alt. Assess., p. 54	• Selection Test, TR Formal Assessment, pp. 242–244; Assess. Res. Software • Poetry Rubric [for Wr. Mini-Lesson], TR Alt. Assess., p. 104 • TR Alt. Assess. p. 54	• "Silver"; "Forgotten Language"; "Drum Song"; "If I can stop one Heart from breaking," LL Audiocassettes • WS Writing Lab CD-ROM, Creative Writing Tutorial
• Description, License-Plate Proposal, Essay, SE p. 871 • Mini-Lesson: Free-Verse Poem [Dominant Image], SE p. 871 • Poetic Tribute, TR Alt. Assess., p. 55	• Choral Reading, Tribute, SE p. 871 • S/L Mini-Lesson: Choral Reading, ATE p. 867 • V/R Mini-Lesson: Class Bulletin Board Display, ATE p. 868 • Report, TR Alt. Assess., p. 55	• Presentation, Captioned Picture, SE p. 871 • Shot List, TR Alt. Assess., p. 55	• Selection Test, TR Formal Assessment, pp. 245–247; Assess. Res. Software • Poetry Rubric [for Wr. Mini-Lesson], TR Alt. Assess., p. 104 • TR Alt. Assess. p. 55	• "New World"; "One Time"; "Lyric 17"; "For My Sister Molly Who in the Fifties," LL Audiocassettes • WS Writing Lab CD-ROM, Creative Writing Tutorial
• Personification, Report, Figurative Definition, SE p. 881 • Mini-Lesson: Dialogue [Use Figurative Language], SE p. 881 • Science Report, TR Alt. Assess., p. 56	• Readers Theatre, Oral Interpretation, SE p. 881 • S/L Mini-Lesson: Readers Theatre, ATE p. 878 • Poetry Symposium, TR Alt. Assess., p. 56	• Presentation and Discussion, Personification in Art, SE p. 881 • Landscaping Report, TR Alt. Assess., p. 56	• Selection Test, TR Formal Assessment, pp. 248–250; Assess. Res. Software • Fictional Narrative Rubric [for Wr. Mini-Lesson], TR Alt. Assess., p. 91 • TR Alt. Assess. p. 56	• "The Dark Hills"; "Solar"; "Incident in a Rose Garden," LL Audiocassettes • WS Writing Lab CD-ROM, Creative Writing Tutorial

Program Planner   Unit 10 The American Tradition

Selection	Reading	Literary Elements/Forms	Vocabulary	Grammar
"Johnny Appleseed," Rosemary Carr Benét, SE p. 895 Reading level: Easy	• Strategies for Reading Folk Literature, SE pp. 894, 897; TR Selection Support, p. 309 • Recognize the Storyteller's Purpose, TR Str. for Diverse St. Needs, pp. 113–114 • Model Selection, SE pp. 895–896	• Oral Tradition, SE pp. 893, 897; TR Selection Support, p. 310	• Related Words: Forms of *encumber,* SE pp. 893, 897; TR Selection Support, p. 306 Word Bank: gnarled, ruddy, encumber, tendril, p. 895; stalking, lair, p. 896	• Unnecessary Commas, SE p. 897; TR Selection Support, p. 308 • WS Language Lab CD-ROM, Punctuation • WS Gram. Pr. Book, Commas That Set Off Added Elements, pp. 106–108
"Coyote Steals the Sun and Moon," Zuñi, retold by Richard Erdoes and Alfonso Ortiz; **"The Spirit Chief Names the Animal People,"** Mourning Dove, SE pp. 902, 905 Reading levels: Average, Average	• Understand the Cultural Context, SE pp. 901, 908; TR Selection Support, p. 315 • Understand the Cultural Context, TR Str. for Diverse St. Needs, pp. 115–116	• Myth, SE pp. 901, 908; TR Selection Support, p. 316	• Suffixes: *-ify,* SE pp. 900, 908; TR Selection Support, p. 312 Word Bank: shriveled, pursuit, p. 904; arouse, purify, p. 906	• Commas in Compound Sentences, SE p. 908; TR Selection Support, p. 314 • WS Language Lab CD-ROM, Commas
"Chicoria," José Griego y Maestas and Rudolfo A. Anaya; **"Brer Possum's Dilemma,"** Jackie Torrence; **"Why the Waves Have Whitecaps,"** Zora Neale Hurston, SE pp. 912, 915, 918 Reading levels: Average, Average, Average	• Recognize the Storyteller's Purpose, SE pp. 911, 920; TR Selection Support, p. 320 • Recognize the Storyteller's Purpose, TR Str. for Diverse St. Needs, pp. 117–118	• Folk Tale, SE pp. 911, 920; TR Selection Support, p. 321	• Synonyms, SE pp. 910, 920; TR Selection Support, p. 317 Word Bank: cordially, haughty, p. 913; commenced, p. 915; pitiful, p. 917	• Commas in a Series, SE p. 920; TR Selection Support, p. 319 • WS Language Lab CD-ROM, Commas • WS Gram. Pr. Book, Commas That Separate Basic Elements, p. 105
from ***The Right Stuff,*** Tom Wolfe, SE p. 923 Reading level: Average			• TR Selection Support, p. 322 Word Bank: aerobatic, p. 924	
"Hammerman," Adrien Stoutenburg; **"John Henry,"** Traditional; **"Paul Bunyan of the North Woods,"** Carl Sandburg; **"Pecos Bill: The Cyclone,"** Harold W. Felton; **"Davy Crockett's Dream,"** Davy Crockett, SE pp. 934, 940, 944, 946, 952 Reading levels: Average, Average, Average, Average, Average	• Predict, SE p. 933, 954; TR Selection Support, p. 327 • Predict, TR Str. for Diverse St. Needs, pp. 119–120	• Tall Tale, SE pp. 933, 954; TR Selection Support, p. 328	• Related Words: Forms of *skeptic,* SE pp. 932, 954; TR Selection Support, p. 324 Word Bank: hefted, p. 936; granite, commotion, p. 945; usurped, invincible, futile, inexplicable, p. 949; skeptics, p. 950	• Variety in Sentence Beginnings, SE p. 954; TR Selection Support, p. 326 • WS Language Lab CD-ROM, Varying Sentence Structure • WS Gram. Pr. Book, Using a Variety of Sentences, p. 125

KEY: SE: Student Edition;   ATE: Annotated Teacher's Edition;   TR: Teaching Resources;   LL: Listening to Literature;   WS: Writer's Solution

Writing	Speaking and Listening Viewing and Representing	Projects	Assessment	Technology
• Epitaph, Folk Ballad, Essay, SE p. 898 • Mini-Lesson: Legendary Story [Show, Don't Tell], SE p. 898 • Oral Performance, TR Alt. Assess., p. 57	• Interview, Musical Setting, SE p. 898 • Portrait Illustration, TR Alt. Assess., p. 57	• Apple Poster, How-to Booklet, SE p. 898 • Round Table Discussion, TR Alt. Assess., p. 57	• Selection Test, TR Formal Assessment, pp. 259–261; **Assess. Res. Software** • Fictional Narrative Rubric [for Wr. Mini-Lesson], TR Alt. Assess., p. 91 • TR Alt. Assess., p. 57	• "Johnny Appleseed," LL Audiocassettes • WS Writing Lab CD-ROM, Creative Writing Tutorial
• Letter, Newspaper Story, Essay, SE p. 909 • Mini-Lesson: Report on an Animal [Give Visual Support], SE p. 909 • Internet Research, TR Alt. Assess., p. 58	• Coyote's Trial, Dramatic Reading, SE p. 909 • S/L Mini-Lesson: Coyote's Trial, ATE p. 904 • V/R Mini-Lesson: Myths, ATE p. 906 • Dramatic Performance, TR Alt. Assess., p. 58	• Multimedia Report, Collection of Story Summaries, SE p. 909 • Myth Report, TR Alt. Assess., p. 58	• Selection Test, TR Formal Assessment, pp. 262–264; **Assess. Res. Software** • Multimedia Report Rubric [for Wr. Mini-Lesson], TR Alt. Assess., p. 103 • TR Alt. Assess., p. 58	• "Coyote Steals the Sun and Moon"; "The Spirit Chief Names the Animal People," LL Audiocassettes • WS Writing Lab CD-ROM, Reports Tutorial
• List, Retelling, Essay, SE p. 921 • Mini-Lesson: Persuasive Advertisement [Use an Effective Format], SE p. 921 • Oral Reading, TR Alt. Assess., p. 59	• Skit, Oral Tale, SE p. 921 • S/L Mini-Lesson: Oral Tale, ATE p. 916 • Book Jacket, TR Alt. Assess., p. 59	• Folk-Tale Collection, Illustration of a Story, SE p. 921 • Folk Melody Report, TR Alt. Assess., p. 59	• Selection Test, TR Formal Assessment, pp. 265–267; **Assess. Res. Software** • Persuasion Rubric [for Wr. Mini-Lesson], TR Alt. Assess., p. 101 • TR Alt. Assess., p. 59	• "Chicoria"; "Brer Possum's Dilemma"; "Why the Waves Have Whitecaps," LL Audiocassettes • WS Writing Lab CD-ROM, Persuasion Tutorial
• Journal Entry, News Article, Essay, SE p. 925	• Dialogue, Speech, SE p. 925	• Report, Illustration, SE p. 925	• Selection Test, TR Formal Assessment, pp. 268–269; **Assess. Res. Software**	• from *The Right Stuff,* LL Audiocassettes
• Journal Entry, Tall Tale, Analysis, SE p. 955 • Mini-Lesson: Nomination for Hero of the Year [Use Only Important Details], SE p. 955 • Cartoon, TR Alt. Assess., p. 60	• Performance, Oral Storytelling, SE p. 955 • S/L Mini-Lesson: Oral Storytelling, ATE p. 946 • V/R Mini-Lesson: Folk Hero Illustration, ATE p. 948 • Science Report, TR Alt. Assess., p. 60	• Collage, Report, SE p. 955 • Poster, TR Alt. Assess., p. 60	• Selection Test, TR Formal Assessment, pp. 270–272; **Assess. Res. Software** • Persuasion Rubric [for Wr. Mini-Lesson], TR Alt. Assess., p. 101 • TR Alt. Assess., p. 60	• "Hammerman"; "John Henry"; "Paul Bunyan of the North Woods"; "Pecos Bill: The Cyclone"; "Davy Crockett's Dream," LL Audiocassettes • WS Writing Lab CD-ROM, Persuasion Tutorial

Skills Workshops

Unit	Writing Process Workshops	Applying Language Skills	Real-World Reading Workshops	Speaking and Listening Workshops
Coming of Age	Personal Narrative, p. 56 Description, p. 96	Writing Realistic Dialogue; Common and Proper Nouns, pp. 57, 58 Using Sensory Words; Avoiding Fragments, pp. 97, 98	Understanding an Author's Purpose, p. 59 Adjusting Your Reading Rate, p. 99	Participating in a Group, p. 101
Meeting Challenges	Historical Cause-and-Effect Essay, p. 166 Problem-and-Solution Essay, p. 228	Using Correct Verb Forms; Using Active Voice, pp. 167, 168 Avoiding Run-on Sentences; Combining Sentences, pp. 229, 230	Reading to Find Specific Information, p. 169 Challenging the Text, p. 231	Expressing Disagreement, p. 233
Quest for Justice	Letter to the Editor, p. 284 Persuasive Essay, p. 334	Degrees of Comparison; Using Commas With Coordinate Adjectives, pp. 285, 286 Placing Adverbs; Commas in a Series, pp. 335, 336	Analyzing a Position, p. 287 Evaluating Persuasive Techniques, p. 337	Presenting Persuasively, p. 339
From Sea to Shining Sea	Summary, p. 392 Consumer Report, p. 430	Verb Phrases With *have*; Correcting Run-on Sentences, pp. 393, 394 Using Precise Adjectives; Avoiding Jargon, pp. 431, 432	Identifying Main Ideas in Articles, p. 395 Making Inferences, p. 433	Telephone Communications, p. 435
Extraordinary Occurrences	Business Letter, p. 496 How-to Essay, p. 522	Using Informal and Formal English; Correctly Writing Company Names, pp. 497, 498 Using Transitions to Indicate Time; Using Commas After Introductory Transitions, pp. 523, 524	Reading Product Labels, p. 499 Reading Manuals, p. 525	Delivering a Speech, p. 527
Short Stories	Fictional Narrative, p. 572 Literary Analysis, p. 612	Varying Tag Words; Consistency in Verb Tense, pp. 573, 574 Avoiding Wordiness; Writing Titles Correctly, pp. 613, 614	Reading Novels and Other Extended Works, p. 575 Recognizing Bias, p. 615	Interviewing, p. 617
Nonfiction	Public-Service Announcement, p. 662 Research Paper, p. 696	Using Appositives; Using *Who*, *That*, and *Which* Correctly, pp. 663, 664 Varying Sentence Structure; Citing Your Sources, pp. 697, 698	Evaluating Advertisements, p. 665 Evaluating Sources of Information, p. 699	Resisting Persuasion, p. 701
Drama	Video Script, p. 776 Critical Review, p. 796	Using Pronouns Correctly; Avoiding Double Negatives, pp. 777, 778 Direct and Indirect Quotations; Using *good* and *well* Correctly, pp. 797, 798	Reading Visuals, p. 779 Distinguishing Between Important and Unimportant Details, p. 799	Debating, p. 801
Poetry	Comparison-and-Contrast Essay, p. 848 Poem, p. 882	Varying Sentence Beginnings; Avoiding Double Comparisons, pp. 849, 850 Avoiding Clichés; Choosing the Correct Homophone, pp. 883, 884	Extend Cultural Understanding, p. 851 Breaking Down Difficult Texts, p. 885	Critically Viewing TV Messages, p. 887
The American Folk Tradition	Multimedia Presentation, p. 926 Internet Web Page, p. 956	Creating Unity; Using Commas in Compound Sentences, pp. 927, 928 Commonly Confused Words; Capitalization of Proper Nouns, pp. 957, 958	Using Headings and Text Structure, p. 929 Using an Internet Web Page,	Conducting Business, p. 961

Prentice Hall

LITERATURE
Timeless Voices, Timeless Themes

Copper

Bronze

Silver

Gold

Platinum

The American Experience

The British Tradition

SERIES AUTHORS

The series authors guided the direction and the philosophy of Prentice Hall Literature: Timeless Voices, Timeless Themes. *Working closely with the development team, they contributed to the pedagogical integrity of the program and to its relevance for today's teachers and students.*

Heidi Hayes Jacobs
Department of Curriculum and Teaching
Teachers College
Columbia University
New York, New York
Heidi Hayes Jacobs has served as an educational consultant to over 1,000 schools nationally and internationally. A frequent contributor to professional journals, she has published two best-selling books through ASCD: Interdisciplinary Curriculum: Design and Implementation *and* Mapping the Big Picture: Integrating Curriculum and Assessment K–12. *She has been on the faculty of Teachers College, Columbia University, since 1981, and her years as a teacher of high-school, middle-school, and elementary-school students in Utah, Massachusetts, and New York provide the fundamental background of her experience.*

Richard Lederer
Author, speaker, columnist, and teacher
San Diego, California
Richard Lederer celebrates the English language as the best-selling author of more than ten books, including Anguished English *and* The Miracle of Language. *He writes a syndicated weekly column, "Looking at Language," and he is the* Grammar Grappler *for* Writer's Digest. *His work has also appeared in publications such as* The New York Times, Sports Illustrated, National Review, *and* Reader's Digest. *Well-known as a speaker and a presenter, Lederer has entertained and informed a wide variety of audiences, including the National Council of Teachers of English. For many years, he taught English at St. Paul's School in Concord, New Hampshire.*

Sharon Sorensen
Author, speaker, and consultant
Mt. Vernon, Indiana
An educator with more than thirty years of classroom experience, Sharon Sorensen has taught both secondary language arts and language arts methods at the university level. She has also published over eighty articles and has authored or co-authored more than twenty-five books on writing, writing process, and the teaching of writing, including How to Write Short Stories, How to Write Research Papers, *and* Webster's New World Student Writing Handbook. *She and her husband live in a self-created wildlife sanctuary in rural Indiana, where they are active in the National Audubon Society.*

PROGRAM ADVISORS

The program advisors provided ongoing input throughout the development of Prentice Hall Literature: Timeless Voices, Timeless Themes. *Their valuable insights ensure that the perspectives of teachers throughout the country are represented within this literature series.*

Diane Cappillo
Language Arts Department Chair
Barbara Goleman Senior High School
Miami, Florida
Past President of the Dade County Council of Teachers of English.

Anita Clay
English Instructor
Gateway Institute of Technology
St. Louis, Missouri
Former Middle School Team Leader; Former Chair, High School English Department.

Mary Curfman
Teacher of English
Clark County School District
Las Vegas, Nevada

Ellen Eberly
Teacher of Language Arts
Catholic Memorial
West Roxbury, Massachusetts

Nancy M. Fahner
Language Arts Instructor
Ingham Intermediate School District
Mason, Michigan
Recipient of Charlotte, Michigan, Teacher of the Year Award, 1992. Curriculum Coordinator for School-to-Work Program.

Terri Fields
Language Arts and Communication Arts Teacher, Author
Sunnyslope High School
Phoenix, Arizona
Recipient of Arizona Teacher of the Year and U.S. WEST Outstanding Arizona Teacher awards.

Susan J. Goldberg
Teacher of English
Westlake Middle School
Thornwood, New York
President, Westchester Council of English Educators. President-Elect, New York State English Council.

Prentice Hall
LITERATURE
Timeless Voices, Timeless Themes

SILVER

PRENTICE HALL
Upper Saddle River, New Jersey
Needham, Massachusetts

ISBN 0-13-435295-5

2 3 4 5 6 7 8 9 10   03 02 01 00 99

ACKNOWLEDGMENTS

Grateful acknowledgment is made to the following for permission to reprint copyrighted material:

Albion Books "How to Be Polite Online" from *Netiquette:* by Virginia Shea. Copyright © 1994 by Virginia Shea. Used Courtesy of Albion.com (www.albion.com).

Arte Público Press "Baseball" by Lionel G. García from *I Can Hear the Cowbells Ring* (Houston: Arte Público Press— University of Houston, 1994). "Old Man" by Ricardo Sánchez from *Selected Poems* (Houston: Arte Público Press—University of Houston, 1985). Reprinted by permission of the publisher.

Brent Ashabranner "The Vision of Maya Ying Lin" by Brent Ashabranner from *Always to Remember.* Copyright © 1988 by Brent Ashabranner. Reprinted by permission of the author.

The Estate of Yoshiko Uchida "Tears of Autumn" from *The Forbidden Stitch* by Yoshiko Uchida. Copyright © 1989 by Yoshiko Uchida. Reprinted by permission of the author's estate.

Borden Publishing Company From "Hokusai: The Old Man Mad About Drawing," reproduced by permission of the publisher, from *The Drawings of Hokusai* by Stephen Longstreet, published by Borden Publishing Co., Alhambra, California.

Brandt & Brandt Literary Agents, Inc. "Western Wagons" by Stephen Vincent Benét, from *A Book of Americans* by Rosemary and Stephen Vincent Benét (Holt, Rinehart & Winston, Inc.). Copyright © 1937 by Rosemary and Stephen Vincent Benét. Copyright renewed © 1964 by Thomas C. Benét, Stephanie B. Mahin, and Rachel Benét Lewis. "Johnny Appleseed" by Stephen Vincent Benét, from *A Book of Americans* by Rosemary and Stephen Vincent Benét (Holt, Rinehart & Winston, Inc.). Copyright © 1933 by Rosemary and Stephen Vincent Benét. Copyright renewed © 1961 by Rosemary Carr Benét. Reprinted by permission of Brandt & Brandt Literary Agents, Inc.

Clarion Books/Houghton Mifflin Company Excerpt from "Emancipation" from *Lincoln: A Photobiography.* Copyright © 1987 by Russell Freedman. Reprinted by permission of Clarion Books/Houghton Mifflin Company. All rights reserved.

Frances Collin, Literary Agent "Shooting Stars" from *This World of Wonder* by Hal Borland (J.B. Lippincott), copyright © 1972, 1973 by Hal Borland. Reprinted by permission of Frances Collin, Literary Agent.

Don Congdon Associates, Inc. "The Drummer Boy of Shiloh" by Ray Bradbury. Copyright © 1960 by Curtis Publishing Co., renewed 1988 by Ray Bradbury. Reprinted by permission of Don Congdon Associates, Inc.

Doubleday, a division of Bantam Doubleday Dell Publishing Group Inc. "The Bat," copyright 1938 by Theodore Roethke, from *The Collected Poems of Theodore Roethke* by Theodore Roethke. Used by permission of Doubleday, a division of Bantam Doubleday Dell Publishing Group Inc. "A Retrieved Refor-mation" from *Roads of Destiny* by O. Henry.

Dutton Signet, a division of Penguin Putnam Inc. "A Horseman in the Sky" by Ambrose Bierce, from *In the Midst of Life* by Ambrose Bierce, afterword by Morris Cunliffe. Copyright © 1961 by the New American Library of World Literature, Inc. From *A Walk In the Woods* by Lee Blessing. Copyright © 1986 by Lee Blessing. Used by permission of Dutton Signet, a division of Penguin Putnam Inc.

Farrar, Straus & Giroux, Inc. "Charles" from *The Lottery* by Shirley Jackson. Copyright © 1948, 1949 by Shirley Jackson, and copyright renewed © 1976, 1977 by Laurence Hyman, Barry Hyman, Mrs. Sarah Webster and Mrs. Joanne Schnurer. Excerpt from *The Right Stuff* by Tom Wolfe. Copyright © 1979 by Tom Wolfe. "Animal Craftsmen" from *Nature by Design* by Bruce Brooks. Copyright © 1992 by Educational Broadcasting Corporation and Bruce Brooks. "The Day I Got Lost" from *Stories for Children* by Isaac Bashevis Singer. Copyright © 1984 by Isaac Bashevis Singer. Used by permission of Farrar, Straus & Giroux, Inc. Reprinted by permission of Farrar, Straus & Giroux, Inc.

Farrar, Straus & Giroux, Inc., and Faber and Faber "Solar" from *Collected Poems* by Philip Larkin. Copyright © 1988, 1989 by the Estate of Philip Larkin. Reprinted by permission.

Free Spirit Publishing Inc. "Saving the Wetlands" excerpted from *Kids With Courage,* by Barbara A. Lewis, © 1992. Used with permission from Free Spirit Publishing Inc., Minneapolis, MN; 1-800-735-7323; www.freespirit.com. All Rights Reserved.

Chris Granstrom From "How to Tell a Good Story" by Chris Granstrom featured in *Country Journal,* Nov/Dec 1997. © Chris Granstrom. Used by permission of the author.

Graywolf Press "One Time," copyright 1982, 1998 by the Estate of William Stafford. Reprinted from *The Way It Is: New & Selected Poems* by William Stafford with the permission of Graywolf Press, Saint Paul, Minnesota.

(Acknowledgments continue on page 1027.)

READING FOR SUCCESS Literal Comprehension Strategies. 4
Ray Bradbury **The Drummer Boy of Shiloh** . . . . Short Story 5

PART 1: ARRIVING AT UNDERSTANDING

Shirley Jackson **Charles** . . . . Short Story 14
● Connections to Today's World
Bill Watterson **Calvin and Hobbes** . . . . Cartoon 19
Maya Angelou *from* **I Know Why the Caged Bird Sings**. . . . . . Nonfiction. 24
Robert Frost **The Road Not Taken** . . . . Poem 34
Walter de la Mare **All But Blind** . . . . Poem 36
Dorothy Parker **The Choice** . . . . Poem 37
John Seabrook *from* **E-Mail from Bill Gates** . . . . Nonfiction. 42
Science Connection: How E-Mail Works 45
Connecting Literature to Social Studies: The First Americans
Zuñi Legend **The Girl Who Hunted Rabbits**. . . . . Legend. 49
Writing Process Workshop: Personal Narrative. 56
Applying Language Skills:
Drafting/Revising Application: Writing Realistic Dialogue. 57
Editing/Proofreading Application: Common and Proper Nouns. 58
Real-World Reading Skills Workshop: Understanding an Author's Purpose 59
Grammar Review: Nouns. 60

PART 2: SEASONS AND CYCLES

Pearl S. Buck **Christmas Day in the Morning** . . . . Short Story 64
Leo Tolstoy **The Old Grandfather and His Little Grandson** . . Folk Tale. 74
Amy Ling **Grandma** . . . . Poem 75
Ricardo Sánchez **Old Man**. . . . . Poem 76
Social Studies Connection: Caring for the Elderly 77
Hal Borland **Shooting Stars** . . . . Nonfiction. 82
Science Connection: The Hubble Telescope 83
Garrison Keillor **Something From the Sixties** . . . . Nonfiction. 84
Walt Whitman **Poets to Come** . . . . Poem 90
Langston Hughes **Winter Moon** . . . . Poem 91
Alfred, Lord Tennyson **Ring Out, Wild Bells** . . . . Poem 92
Writing Process Workshop: Description 96
Applying Language Skills:
Drafting/Revising Application: Using Sensory Words 97
Editing/Proofreading Application: Avoiding Fragments. 98
Real-World Reading Skills Workshop: Adjusting Your Reading Rate 99
Grammar Review: Pronouns. 100
Speaking, Listening, and Viewing Workshop: Participating in a Group 101
Vocabulary Adventures With Richard Lederer: Origins of Calendar Words 102
Extended Reading Opportunities 103

Unit 2

Looking at Universal Themes

Meeting Challenges

READING FOR SUCCESS	**Interactive Reading Strategies** 108
Mark Twain	**Cub Pilot on the Mississippi**. . . . . Nonfiction 109
	Science Connection: River Navigation 116

PART 1:   BLAZING TRAILS

Arthur C. Clarke	**The Secret**. . . . . Short Story 122
	● Connections to Today's World
David Bowie	**Space Oddity** . . . . Song 127
Ann Petry	**Harriet Tubman: Guide to Freedom** . . . . . . Nonfiction 132
Joaquin Miller	**Columbus** . . . . Poem 144
Stephen Vincent Benét	**Western Wagons**. . . . . Poem 146
Roberto Félix Salazar	**The Other Pioneers**. . . . . Poem 148
Jack London	**Up the Slide** . . . . Short Story 154
	Social Studies Connection: The Klondike Gold Rush 159
	Connecting Literature to Social Studies: The Colonial Era
William Bradford	**The Pilgrims' Landing and First Winter** . . . Nonfiction 163
	Writing Process Workshop: Historical Cause-and-Effect Essay 166
	Applying Language Skills:
	Drafting/Revising Application: Using Correct Verb Forms 167
	Editing/Proofreading Application: Using Active Voice. 168
	Real-World Reading Skills Workshop: Reading to Find Specific Information. . . . 169
	Grammar Review: Verbs 170

PART 2:   FACING HARD QUESTIONS

Anton Chekhov	**The Ninny** . . . . Short Story 174
Neil Simon	**The Governess** . . . . Drama 176
Langston Hughes	**Thank You, M'am** . . . . Short Story 186
Adrienne Rich	**Prospective Immigrants Please Note**. . . . . Poem 194
Emily Dickinson	**Much Madness is divinest Sense—** . . . . . . Poem 195
Chief Seattle	**This We Know**. . . . . Nonfiction 196
	Social Studies Connection: History of Our National Parks 197
Margaret Tsuda	**Hard Questions**. . . . . Poem 198
Daniel Keyes	**Flowers for Algernon** . . . . Short Story 204
	Writing Process Workshop: Problem-and-Solution Essay. 228
	Applying Language Skills:
	Drafting/Revising Application: Avoiding Run-on Sentences 229
	Editing/Proofreading Application: Combining Sentences. 230
	Real-World Reading Skills Workshop: Challenging the Text. 231
	Grammar Review: Principal Parts and Verb Tenses. 232
	Speaking, Listening, and Viewing Workshop: Expressing Disagreement. 233
	Vocabulary Adventures With Richard Lederer:
	Words Borrowed From Native Americans. 234
	Extended Reading Opportunities 235

Looking at Universal Themes

Quest for Justice

READING FOR SUCCESS	**Strategies for Constructing Meaning**		240
Walter Dean Myers	**Brown vs. Board of Education**	Nonfiction	241
	Social Studies Connection: The Role of the Supreme Court		246

PART 1: TAKING A STAND

O. Henry	**A Retrieved Reformation**	Short Story	252
Russell Freedman	**Emancipation** *from* **Lincoln: A Photobiography**	Nonfiction	262
Walt Whitman	**O Captain! My Captain!**	Poem	266
Juan A.A. Sedillo	**Gentleman of Río en Medio**	Short Story	272
Barbara A. Lewis	**Saving the Wetlands**	Nonfiction	276
	Science Connection: Saving the Earth		

Writing Process Workshop: Letter to the Editor 284
Applying Language Skills:
Drafting/Revising Application: Degrees of Comparison 285
Editing/Proofreading Application: Using Commas With Coordinate Adjectives . . 286
Real-World Reading Skills Workshop: Analyzing a Position 287
Grammar Review: Adjectives and Adverbs 288

PART 2: LEADING THE WAY

Toni Cade Bambara	**Raymond's Run**	Short Story	292
	● Connections to Today's World		
Special Olympics	**There Is No Off-Season**	Brochure	302
Henry Wadsworth Longfellow	**Paul Revere's Ride**	Poem	306
John Greenleaf Whittier	**Barbara Frietchie**	Poem	311
Eve Merriam	**Elizabeth Blackwell**	Poem	314
	Career Connection: Facts About Women in Medicine		317
	Connecting Literature to Social Studies: The Revolutionary Period		
Thomas Jefferson	**Young Jefferson Gets Some Advice From Ben Franklin**	Nonfiction	321
Brent Ashabranner	**Always to Remember: The Vision of Maya Ying Lin**	Nonfiction	326

Writing Process Workshop: Persuasive Essay 334
Applying Language Skills:
Drafting/Revising Application: Placing Adverbs 335
Editing/Proofreading Application: Commas in a Series 336
Real-World Reading Skills Workshop: Evaluating Persuasive Techniques 337
Grammar Review: Prepositions and Prepositional Phrases 338
Speaking, Listening, and Viewing Workshop: Presenting Persuasively 339
Vocabulary Adventures With Richard Lederer:
Vocabulary From Government and Politics 340
Extended Reading Opportunities 341

Unit

4

Looking at Universal Themes

From Sea to Shining Sea

READING FOR SUCCESS   **Interactive Reading Strategies** 346

Carl Sandburg   *from* **The People, Yes** . . . . Poem 347

PART 1:   A LAND OF PROMISE

John Steinbeck   *from* **Travels with Charley** . . . . Nonfiction 354

 Connections to Today's World

Jamie Jensen   *from* **Road Trip U.S.A.** . . . . Travel Article 361

Emma Lazarus   **The New Colossus** . . . . Poem 366

Joseph Bruchac   **Ellis Island** . . . . Poem 367

Mario Cuomo   **Achieving the American Dream** . . . . Nonfiction 368

Alice Walker   **Choice:**
        A Tribute to Dr. Martin Luther King, Jr. . Nonfiction 370

        Social Studies Connection: March on Washington 373
        Connecting Literature to Social Studies: A Young Nation

Edward Everett Hale   **The Man Without a Country** . . . . Short Story 377

    Writing Process Workshop: Summary 392
    Applying Language Skills:
    Drafting/Revising Application: Verb Phrases With *Have* 393
    Editing/Proofreading Application: Correcting Run-on Sentences 394
    Real-World Reading Skills Workshop: Identifying Main Ideas in Articles 395
    Grammar Review: Conjunctions 396

PART 2:   AN ALBUM OF STORIES

J. Frank Dobie   **Sancho** . . . . Nonfiction 400

William Jay Smith   **The Closing of the Rodeo** . . . . Poem 405

        Science Connection: Animal Imprinting 405

Jesse Stuart   **A Ribbon for Baldy** . . . . Short Story 410

        Science Connection: Corn Crops 413

Gish Jen   **The White Umbrella** . . . . Short Story 414

Robert Hayden   **Those Winter Sundays** . . . . Poem 424

Evelyn Tooley Hunt   **Taught Me Purple** . . . . Poem 425

Richard García   **The City Is So Big** . . . . Poem 426

    Writing Process Workshop: Consumer Report 430
    Applying Language Skills:
    Drafting/Revising Application: Using Precise Adjectives 431
    Editing/Proofreading Application: Avoiding Jargon 432
    Real-World Reading Skills Workshop: Making Inferences 433
    Grammar Review: Subjects and Predicates 434
    Speaking, Listening, and Viewing Workshop: Telephone Communications 435
    Vocabulary Adventures With Richard Lederer:
    Newspaper and Magazine Vocabulary 436
    Extended Reading Opportunities 437

READING FOR SUCCESS	**Strategies for Reading Critically**		442
Annie Dillard	**Lights in the Night** *from* **An American Childhood**	Nonfiction	443

PART 1: THE EXTRAORDINARY IN THE ORDINARY

Mark Twain	**What Stumped the Blue Jays**	Short Story	452
	Science Connection: Birds		457
Diane Ackerman	**Why Leaves Turn Color in the Fall**	Nonfiction	458
May Swenson	**Southbound on the Freeway**	Poem	466
Mark Van Doren	**The Story-Teller**	Poem	467
Victor Hernández Cruz	**Los New Yorks**	Poem	468
	Social Studies Connection: Puerto Rico		469
Sir Arthur Conan Doyle	**The Adventure of the Speckled Band**	Short Story	474
	Connections to Today's World		
California Commission	**Crime-Solving Procedures for the Modern Detective**	Manual	494

Writing Process Workshop: Business Letter		496
Applying Language Skills:		
Drafting/Revising Application: Using Informal and Formal English		497
Editing/Proofreading Application: Correctly Writing Company Names		498
Real-World Reading Skills Workshop: Reading Product Labels		499
Grammar Review: Complements		500

PART 2: STRANGE DOINGS

Gary Paulsen	**A Glow in the Dark** *from* **Woodsong**	Nonfiction	504
Sylvia Plath	**Mushrooms**	Poem	508
	Science Connection: Mushrooms		509
Arna Bontemps	**Southern Mansion**	Poem	510
Theodore Roethke	**The Bat**	Poem	511
	Connecting Literature to Social Studies: The Civil War: Families Torn Apart		
Ambrose Bierce	**A Horseman in the Sky**	Short Story	515

Writing Process Workshop: How-to Essay		522
Applying Language Skills:		
Drafting/Revising Application: Using Transitions to Indicate Time		523
Editing/Proofreading Application: Using Commas After Introductory Transitions		524
Real-World Reading Skills Workshop: Reading Manuals		525
Grammar Review: Phrases		526
Speaking, Listening, and Viewing Workshop: Delivering a Speech		527
Vocabulary Adventures With Richard Lederer:		
Mystery and Detective Vocabulary		528
Extended Reading Opportunities		529

Looking at Literary Forms

Short Stories

READING FOR SUCCESS	**Strategies for Reading Fiction**		534
Mona Gardner	**The Dinner Party** . . . . Plot		535

PART 1: PLOT AND CHARACTER

Edgar Allan Poe	**The Tell-Tale Heart** . . . . Plot		542
	Connecting Literature to Social Studies: The Civil War: Battles		
Stephen Crane	**An Episode of War** . . . . Short Story		551
Isaac Bashevis Singer	**The Day I Got Lost** . . . . Character		558
Naomi Shihab Nye	**Hamadi** . . . . Character		562
	Social Studies Connection: Jerusalem		569
	Writing Process Workshop: Fictional Narrative		572
	Applying Language Skills:		
	Drafting/Revising Application: Varying Tag Words		573
	Editing/Proofreading Application: Consistency in Verb Tense.		574
	Real-World Reading Skills Workshop:		
	Reading Novels and Other Extended Works		575
	Grammar Review: Clauses.		576

PART 2: SETTING AND THEME

Paul Laurence Dunbar	**The Finish of Patsy Barnes**. . . . . Setting		580
	Career Connection: Horse Trainer		585
Yoshiko Uchida	**Tears of Autumn** . . . . Setting		586
Saki (H. H. Munro)	**The Story-Teller**. . . . . Theme		596
	● Connections to Today's World		
Chris Granstrom	**How to Tell a Good Story** . . . . Article.		601
Virginia Driving Hawk Sneve	**The Medicine Bag**. Theme		602
	Cultural Connection: The Sioux.		609
	Writing Process Workshop: Literary Analysis		612
	Applying Language Skills:		
	Drafting/Revising Application: Avoiding Wordiness		613
	Editing/Proofreading Application: Writing Titles Correctly		614
	Real-World Reading Skills Workshop: Recognizing Bias.		615
	Grammar Review: Sentence Structure.		616
	Speaking, Listening, and Viewing Workshop: Interviewing		617
	Vocabulary Adventures With Richard Lederer: Phobia Words		618
	Extended Reading Opportunities		619

Looking at Literary Forms

Nonfiction

Unit 7

READING FOR SUCCESS
Bruce Brooks

Strategies for Reading Nonfiction 624
Animal Craftsmen . . . . Reflective Essay . . . 625

PART 1: PERSONAL ACCOUNTS AND BIOGRAPHIES

Eudora Welty   *from* **One Writer's Beginnings** . . . . Autobiography 634
Lionel G. García   **Baseball** . . . . Autobiography . . . 636
Sports Connection: Little League Baseball 639
Connecting Literature to Social Studies: The Suffragist Movement
Margaret Truman   *from* **The United States vs.
Susan B. Anthony** . . . . Biography 643
Stephen Longstreet   **Hokusai: The Old Man Mad About Drawing** . . Biography 654
John Hersey   **Not to Go With the Others** . . . . Biography 656
Social Studies Connection: Axis vs. Allies 659
Writing Process Workshop: Public-Service Announcement 662
Applying Language Skills:
Drafting/Revising Application: Using Appositives 663
Editing/Proofreading Application: Using *Who, That,* and *Which* Correctly 664
Real-World Reading Skills Workshop:
Evaluating Advertisements 665
Grammar Review: Correct Pronoun Use 666

PART 2: ESSAYS AND SPEECHES

James Herriot   **Debbie** . . . . Narrative Essay 670
Anaïs Nin   **Forest Fire** . . . . Descriptive Essay . . 675
Virginia Shea   **How to Be Polite Online** *from* **Netiquette** . . . . Expository Essay . . . 678
Robert MacNeil   **The Trouble with Television** . . . . Persuasive Essay . . 686
Martin Luther King, Jr.   **The American Dream** . . . . Speech 689
Social Studies Connection: The Nobel Prize 691
Connections to Today's World
Colin Powell   *from* **Sharing the American Dream** . . . . Speech 694
Writing Process Workshop: Research Paper 696
Applying Language Skills:
Drafting/Revising Application: Varying Sentence Structure 697
Editing/Proofreading Application: Citing Your Sources 698
Real-World Reading Skills Workshop:
Evaluating Sources of Information 699
Grammar Review: Pronoun and Antecedent Agreement 700
Speaking, Listening, and Viewing Workshop: Resisting Persuasion 701
Vocabulary Adventures With Richard Lederer: Sportspeak 702
Extended Reading Opportunities 703

Looking at Literary Forms

Drama

READING FOR SUCCESS   **Strategies for Reading Drama** 706

PART 1:   **MODERN DRAMA**

Frances Goodrich
and Albert Hackett   **The Diary of Anne Frank, Act I** . . . . Drama 712

     Social Studies Connection: Broadway Theaters 744

🌐 **Connections to Today's World**
Anne Frank . . . On Broadway . . . . Playbill 746

The Diary of Anne Frank, Act II 748

     Connecting Literature to Social Studies: The Cold War

Lee Blessing   *from* **A Walk in the Woods** . . . . Drama 773

Writing Process Workshop: Video Script 776
Applying Language Skills:
Drafting/Revising Application: Using Pronouns Correctly. 777
Editing/Proofreading Application: Avoiding Double Negatives 778
Real-World Reading Skills Workshop: Reading Visuals 779
Grammar Review: Subject and Verb Agreement 780

PART 2:   **SCENES AND SOLILOQUIES**

William Shakespeare   **Introduction to Shakespeare**

from **A Midsummer Night's Dream**
     from **Act III, scene ii** . . . . Scene 784

from **Much Ado About Nothing**
     from **Act II, scene iii** . . . . Soliloquy 790

from **The Life and Death of King Richard III**
     from **Act I, scene i** . . . . Soliloquy 792

Writing Process Workshop: Critical Review 796
Applying Language Skills:
Drafting/Revising Application: Direct and Indirect Quotations 797
Editing/Proofreading Application: Using *good* and *well* Correctly 798
Real-World Reading Skills Workshop:
Distinguishing Between Important and Unimportant Details 799
Grammar Review: Subject and Verb Agreement 800
Speaking, Listening, and Viewing Workshop: Debating 801
Vocabulary Adventures With Richard Lederer: Movie Vocabulary 802
Extended Reading Opportunities 803

Looking at Literary Forms

Poetry

READING FOR SUCCESS   **Strategies for Reading Poetry** 808
Robert P. Tristram Coffin   **The Secret Heart**. . . . . Elements of Poetry. . . 809

PART I: TYPES OF POETRY

Henry Wadsworth Longfellow   **The Wreck of the Hesperus** . . . . Narrative Poem 816
May Swenson   **The Centaur** . . . . Narrative Poem 820
     Humanities Connection: The Centaur 823
Langston Hughes   **Harlem Night Song** . . . . Lyric Poem 828
William Shakespeare   **Blow, Blow, Thou Winter Wind** . . . . Lyric Poem 829
E. E. Cummings   **love is a place** . . . . Lyric Poem 830
Robert Frost   **The Freedom of the Moon** . . . . Lyric Poem 831
John Updike   **January** . . . . Poetic Form 836
Bashō and Moritake   **Two Haiku** . . . . Poetic Form 837
Julio Noboa Polanco   **Identity** . . . . Poetic Form 838
Maxine Kumin   **400-Meter Free Style** . . . . Poetic Form 839
     Sports Connection: Freestyle Swimming 841
     Connecting Literature to Social Studies: The Vietnam War
Jim Northrup   **Wahbegan** . . . . Poem 845

Writing Process Workshop: Comparison-and-Contrast Essay 848
Applying Language Skills:
Drafting/Revising Application: Varying Sentence Beginnings 849
Editing/Proofreading Application: Avoiding Double Comparisons 850
Real-World Reading Skills Workshop: Extend Cultural Understanding 851
Grammar Review: Correct Use of Modifiers 852

PART 2: ELEMENTS OF POETRY

Walter de la Mare   **Silver** . . . . Sound Devices 856
Shel Silverstein   **Forgotten Language** . . . . Sound Devices 857
Wendy Rose   **Drum Song** . . . . Sound Devices 858
Emily Dickinson   **If I can stop one Heart from breaking** . . . . Sound Devices 859
N. Scott Momaday   **New World**. . . . . Imagery 864
William Stafford   **One Time**. . . . . Imagery 866
     Science Connection: Braille 866
José Garcia Villa   **Lyric 17** . . . . Imagery 867
Alice Walker   **For My Sister Molly Who in the Fifties** . . . . Imagery 868
   Connections to Today's World
Larry Henley and Jeff Silbar   **The Wind Beneath My Wings** . . . . Song 872
Edwin Arlington Robinson   **The Dark Hills** . . . . Figurative Language . . 876
Philip Larkin   **Solar** . . . . Figurative Language . . 877
Donald Justice   **Incident in a Rose Garden** . . . . Figurative Language . . 878

Writing Process Workshop: Poem 882
Applying Language Skills:
Drafting/Revising Application: Avoiding Clichés 883
Editing/Proofreading Application: Choosing the Correct Homophone 884
Real-World Reading Skills Workshop: Breaking Down Difficult Texts 885
Grammar Review: Usage Problems 886
Speaking, Listening, and Viewing Workshop: Critically Viewing TV Messages . . 887
Vocabulary Adventures With Richard Lederer: Analogies 888
Extended Reading Opportunities 889

Contents ◆ *xv*

READING FOR SUCCESS   **Strategies for Reading Folk Literature** 894
Rosemary Carr Benét   **Johnny Appleseed** .... Poem 895

PART 1:   A SAMPLING OF STORIES

Zuñi, Retold by Richard
Erdoes and Alfonso Ortiz   **Coyote Steals the Sun and Moon** ... Native American Myth 902
    Cultural Connection: Coyote the Trickster 904

Mourning Dove   **The Spirit Chief Names
the Animal People** .... Native American Myth 905

José Griego y Maestas
and Rudolfo A. Anaya   **Chicoria.** .... Mexican American Cuento . . 912
    Social Studies Connection: The Mexican-American War 914

Jackie Torrence   **Brer Possum's Dilemma.** .... African American Tale 915
Zora Neale Hurston   **Why the Waves Have Whitecaps** .... African American Tale 918
    Connecting Literature to Social Studies: The Space Age: Pushing the Frontier

Tom Wolfe   *from* **The Right Stuff.** .... Nonfiction 923

Writing Process Workshop: Multimedia Presentation 926
Applying Language Skills:
Drafting/Revising Application: Creating Unity. 927
Editing/Proofreading Application: Using Commas in Compound Sentences.... 928
Real-World Reading Skills Workshop: Using Headings and Text Structure..... 929
Grammar Review: Commas 930

PART 2:   TALES OF AMERICAN HEROES

Adrien Stoutenburg   **Hammerman.** .... Legend 934
Traditional   **John Henry** .... Ballad 940
    Science Connection: Development of the Locomotive 943

Carl Sandburg   **Paul Bunyan of the North Woods.** ... Tall Tale. 944
Harold W. Felton   **Pecos Bill: The Cyclone** .... Tall Tale. 946

    Connections to Today's World
    Superman Online .... Internet Home Page....... 951
Davy Crockett   **Davy Crockett's Dream** .... Tall Tale. 952

Writing Process Workshop: Internet Web Page. 956
Applying Language Skills:
Drafting/Revising Application: Commonly Confused Words 957
Editing/Proofreading Application: Capitalization of Proper Nouns 958
Real-World Reading Skills Workshop: Using an Internet Web Page 959
Grammar Review: Variety in Sentence Beginnings 960
Speaking, Listening, and Viewing Workshop: Conducting Business 961
Vocabulary Adventures With Richard Lederer: Regional Vocabulary 962
Extended Reading Opportunities 963

      ACCESS GUIDE TO VOCABULARY. 964
      LITERARY TERMS HANDBOOK 966
      WRITING HANDBOOK. 974
      GRAMMAR AND MECHANICS HANDBOOK 978
      SPEAKING, LISTENING, AND VIEWING HANDBOOK. 985
      INDEX OF AUTHORS AND TITLES 987
      INDEX OF SKILLS 989
      ACKNOWLEDGMENTS (CONTINUED). 995

Complete Contents by Genre

SHORT STORY

Plot

Christmas Day in the Morning
Pearl S. Buck 64

Up the Slide
Jack London 154

A Retrieved Reformation
O. Henry 252

Gentleman of Río en Medio
Juan A.A. Sedillo 272

The Dinner Party
Mona Gardner 535

The Tell-Tale Heart
Edgar Allan Poe 542

Character

The Ninny
Anton Chekhov 174

Raymond's Run
Toni Cade Bambara 292

A Ribbon for Baldy
Jesse Stuart 410

The White Umbrella
Gish Jen 414

The Day I Got Lost
Isaac Bashevis Singer 558

Hamadi
Naomi Shihab Nye 562

Setting

The Drummer Boy of Shiloh
Ray Bradbury 5

An Episode of War
Stephen Crane 551

The Finish of Patsy Barnes
Paul Laurence Dunbar 580

Tears of Autumn
Yoshiko Uchida 586

Theme

Thank You, M'am
Langston Hughes 186

The Man Without a Country
Edward Everett Hale 377

A Horseman in the Sky
Ambrose Bierce 515

The Story-Teller
Saki (H. H. Munro) 596

The Medicine Bag
Virginia Driving Hawk Sneve 602

Point of View

Charles
Shirley Jackson 14

Flowers for Algernon
Daniel Keyes 204

What Stumped the Blue Jays
Mark Twain 452

Types

The Secret
Arthur C. Clarke 122

The Adventure of the Speckled Band
Sir Arthur Conan Doyle 474

NONFICTION

Essays

from **E-Mail from Bill Gates**
John Seabrook 42

Shooting Stars
Hal Borland 82

Something From the Sixties
Garrison Keillor 84

The Pilgrims' Landing and First Winter
William Bradford 163

Brown *vs.* Board of Education
Walter Dean Myers 241

Saving the Wetlands
Barbara A. Lewis 276

from **Travels with Charley**
John Steinbeck 354

Achieving the American Dream
Mario Cuomo 368

Sancho
J. Frank Dobie 400

Why Leaves Turn Color in the Fall
Diane Ackerman 458

A Glow in the Dark
Gary Paulsen 504

How to Tell a Good Story
Chris Granstrom 601

Animal Craftsmen
Bruce Brooks 625

Debbie
James Herriot 670

Forest Fire
Anaïs Nin 675

How to Be Polite Online *from* Netiquette
Virginia Shea 678

The Trouble with Television
Robert MacNeil 686

Speeches

This We Know
Chief Seattle 196

The American Dream
Martin Luther King, Jr. 689

from **Sharing the American Dream**
Colin Powell 694

Complete Contents by Genre

NONFICTION (CONTINUED)

Autobiographies
from **I Know Why the Caged Bird Sings**
Maya Angelou 24
Cub Pilot on the Mississippi
Mark Twain. 109
Young Jefferson Gets Some Advice . . .
Thomas Jefferson. 321
Lights in the Night *from* **An American Childhood**
Annie Dillard. 443
from **One Writer's Beginnings**
Eudora Welty 634
Baseball
Lionel G. García 636

Biographies
Harriet Tubman: Guide to Freedom
Ann Petry. 132

Emancipation *from* **Lincoln: A Photobiography**
Russell Freedman. 262
Always to Remember: The Vision of Maya Ying Lin
Brent Ashabranner 326
Choice: A Tribute to Dr. Martin Luther King, Jr.
Alice Walker 370
The United States *vs.* **Susan B. Anthony**
Margaret Truman 643
Hokusai: The Old Man Mad About Drawing
Stephen Longstreet 654
Not to Go With the Others
John Hersey. 656
from **The Right Stuff**
Tom Wolfe 923

DRAMA

The Governess
Neil Simon 176
The Diary of Anne Frank
Frances Goodrich and Albert Hackett. . . . 712
from **A Walk in the Woods**
Lee Blessing. 773

from **A Midsummer Night's Dream**
William Shakespeare 784
from **Much Ado About Nothing**
William Shakespeare 790
from **The Life and Death of King Richard III**
William Shakespeare 792

POETRY

Narrative
Paul Revere's Ride
Henry Wadsworth Longfellow 306
Barbara Frietchie
John Greenleaf Whittier 311
Elizabeth Blackwell
Eve Merriam. 314
The Wreck of the Hesperus
Henry Wadsworth Longfellow 816
The Centaur
May Swenson 820
Johnny Appleseed
Rosemary Carr Benét 895

Lyric
The Bat
Theodore Roethke 511
Harlem Night Song
Langston Hughes. 828
Blow, Blow, Thou Winter Wind
William Shakespeare 829
love is a place
E. E. Cummings 830
The Freedom of the Moon
Robert Frost. 831

Poetic Form
Columbus
Joaquin Miller. 144
Western Wagons
Stephen Vincent Benét. 146
The Other Pioneers
Roberto Félix Salazar 148
Southbound on the Freeway
May Swenson 466
The Story-Teller
Mark Van Doren 467
Los New Yorks
Victor Hernández Cruz 468
January
John Updike. 836
Two Haiku
Bashō and Moritake 837
Identity
Julio Noboa Polanco 838
400-Meter Free Style
Maxine Kumin 839
Wahbegan
Jim Northrup 845

Sound Devices
Poets to Come
Walt Whitman. 90

Complete Contents by Genre

POETRY (CONTINUED)

Winter Moon
Langston Hughes 91

Ring Out, Wild Bells
Alfred, Lord Tennyson 92

Mushrooms
Sylvia Plath 508

Silver
Walter de la Mare 856

Forgotten Language
Shel Silverstein 857

Drum Song
Wendy Rose 858

If I can stop one Heart from breaking
Emily Dickinson 859

Imagery
Grandma
Amy Ling 75

Old Man
Ricardo Sánchez 76

Prospective Immigrants Please Note
Adrienne Rich 194

Much Madness is divinest Sense—
Emily Dickinson 195

Hard Questions
Margaret Tsuda 198

from **The People, Yes**
Carl Sandburg 347

The Closing of the Rodeo
William Jay Smith 405

Those Winter Sundays
Robert Hayden 424

Taught Me Purple
Evelyn Tooley Hunt 425

The City Is So Big
Richard García 426

Southern Mansion
Arna Bontemps 510

New World
N. Scott Momaday 864

One Time
William Stafford 866

Lyric 17
José Garcia Villa 867

For My Sister Molly Who in the Fifties
Alice Walker 868

Figurative Language
O Captain! My Captain!
Walt Whitman 266

The New Colossus
Emma Lazarus 366

Ellis Island
Joseph Bruchac 367

The Secret Heart
Robert P. Tristram Coffin 809

The Dark Hills
Edwin Arlington Robinson 876

Solar
Philip Larkin 877

Incident in a Rose Garden
Donald Justice 878

Speaker in Poetry
The Road Not Taken
Robert Frost 34

All But Blind
Walter de la Mare 36

The Choice
Dorothy Parker 37

MYTHS, TALES, AND LEGENDS

Myths
Coyote Steals the Sun and Moon
Richard Erdoes and Alfonso Ortiz 902

The Spirit Chief Names the Animal People
Mourning Dove 905

Tales
The Old Grandfather and His Little Grandson
Leo Tolstoy 74

Chicoria
Maestas and Anaya 912

Brer Possum's Dilemma
Jackie Torrence 915

Why the Waves Have Whitecaps
Zora Neale Hurston 918

Paul Bunyan of the North Woods
Carl Sandburg 944

Pecos Bill: The Cyclone
Harold W. Felton 946

Davy Crockett's Dream
Davy Crockett 952

Legends
The Girl Who Hunted Rabbits
Zuñi Legend 49

Hammerman
Adrien Stoutenburg 934

John Henry
Traditional 940

Complete Contents by Theme

COMING OF AGE

Arriving at Understanding
The Drummer Boy of Shiloh
Ray Bradbury........................ 5
Charles
Shirley Jackson 14
from **I Know Why the Caged Bird Sings**
Maya Angelou 24
The Road Not Taken
Robert Frost....................... 34
All But Blind
Walter de la Mare.................. 36
The Choice
Dorothy Parker..................... 37
from **E-Mail from Bill Gates**
John Seabrook...................... 42
The Girl Who Hunted Rabbits
Zuñi Legend........................ 49

Seasons and Cycles
Christmas Day in the Morning
Pearl S. Buck 64
The Old Grandfather and His Little Grandson
Leo Tolstoy........................ 74
Grandma
Amy Ling 75
Old Man
Ricardo Sánchez 76
Shooting Stars
Hal Borland 82
Something From the Sixties
Garrison Keillor 84
Poets to Come
Walt Whitman....................... 90
Winter Moon
Langston Hughes.................... 91
Ring Out, Wild Bells
Alfred, Lord Tennyson.............. 92

MEETING CHALLENGES

Blazing Trails
The Secret
Arthur C. Clarke 122
Harriet Tubman: Guide to Freedom
Ann Petry.......................... 132
Columbus
Joaquin Miller..................... 144
Western Wagons
Stephen Vincent Benét.............. 146
The Other Pioneers
Roberto Félix Salazar 148
Up the Slide
Jack London 154
The Pilgrims' Landing and First Winter
William Bradford................... 163

Facing Hard Questions
Cub Pilot on the Mississippi
Mark Twain......................... 109

The Ninny
Anton Chekhov...................... 174
The Governess
Neil Simon 176
Thank You, M'am
Langston Hughes.................... 186
Prospective Immigrants Please Note
Adrienne Rich...................... 194
Much Madness is divinest Sense—
Emily Dickinson 195
This We Know
Chief Seattle...................... 196
Hard Questions
Margaret Tsuda 198
Flowers for Algernon
Daniel Keyes 204
The Trouble with Television
Robert MacNeil 686
The American Dream
Martin Luther King, Jr. 689

QUEST FOR JUSTICE

Taking a Stand
Brown *vs.* Board of Education
Walter Dean Myers.................. 241
A Retrieved Reformation
O. Henry........................... 252
Emancipation *from* Lincoln: A Photobiography
Russell Freedman................... 262
O Captain! My Captain!
Walt Whitman....................... 266
Gentleman of Río en Medio
Juan A.A. Sedillo 272

Saving the Wetlands
Barbara A. Lewis 276

Leading the Way
Raymond's Run
Toni Cade Bambara 292
Paul Revere's Ride
Henry Wadsworth Longfellow......... 306
Barbara Frietchie
John Greenleaf Whittier 311
Elizabeth Blackwell
Eve Merriam........................ 314

Complete Contents by Theme

QUEST FOR JUSTICE (CONTINUED)

Young Jefferson Gets Some Advice
Thomas Jefferson 321

Always to Remember
Brent Ashabranner 326

FROM SEA TO SHINING SEA

A Land of Promise
from Travels with Charley
John Steinbeck 354

The New Colossus
Emma Lazarus 366

Ellis Island
Joseph Bruchac 367

Achieving the American Dream
Mario Cuomo 368

Choice: A Tribute to Dr. Martin Luther King, Jr.
Alice Walker 370

The Man Without a Country
Edward Everett Hale 377

An Album of Stories
from The People, Yes
Carl Sandburg 347

Sancho
J. Frank Dobie 400

The Closing of the Rodeo
William Jay Smith 405

A Ribbon for Baldy
Jesse Stuart 410

The White Umbrella
Gish Jen 414

Those Winter Sundays
Robert Hayden 424

Taught Me Purple
Evelyn Tooley Hunt 425

The City Is So Big
Richard García 426

EXTRAORDINARY OCCURRENCES

The Extraordinary in the Ordinary
Lights in the Night
Annie Dillard 443

What Stumped the Blue Jays
Mark Twain 452

Why Leaves Turn Color in the Fall
Diane Ackerman 458

Southbound on the Freeway
May Swenson 466

The Story-Teller
Mark Van Doren 467

Los New Yorks
Victor Hernández Cruz 468

The Adventure of the Speckled Band
Sir Arthur Conan Doyle 474

Strange Doings
A Glow in the Dark
Gary Paulsen 504

Mushrooms
Sylvia Plath 508

Southern Mansion
Arna Bontemps 510

The Bat
Theodore Roethke 511

A Horseman in the Sky
Ambrose Bierce 515

The Tell-Tale Heart
Edgar Allan Poe 542

THE ENVIRONMENT AND YOU

Respecting Nature
Animal Craftsmen
Bruce Brooks 625

The Wreck of the Hesperus
Henry Wadsworth Longfellow 816

The Centaur
May Swenson 820

Harlem Night Song
Langston Hughes 828

Blow, Blow, Thou Winter Wind
William Shakespeare 829

love is a place
E. E. Cummings 830

The Freedom of the Moon
Robert Frost 831

January
John Updike 836

Two Haiku
Bashō and Moritake 837

Identity
Julio Noboa Polanco 838

400-Meter Free Style
Maxine Kumin 839

The Dark Hills
Edwin Arlington Robinson 876

Solar
Philip Larkin 877

Complete Contents by Theme

THE ENVIRONMENT AND YOU (CONTINUED)

Incident in a Rose Garden
Donald Justice 878

Coyote Steals the Sun and Moon
Richard Erdoes and Alfonso Ortiz 902

The Spirit Chief Names the Animal People
Mourning Dove 905

Living Each Day
from One Writer's Beginnings
Eudora Welty 634

Baseball
Lionel G. García 636

Debbie
James Herriot 670

Forest Fire
Anaïs Nin 675

How to Be Polite Online
Virginia Shea 678

A WORLD OF PEOPLE

Relationships
from A Midsummer Night's Dream
William Shakespeare 784

from Much Ado About Nothing
William Shakespeare 790

from The Life and Death of King Richard III
William Shakespeare 792

Silver
Walter de la Mare 856

Forgotten Language
Shel Silverstein 857

Drum Song
Wendy Rose 858

If I can stop one Heart from breaking
Emily Dickinson 859

New World
N. Scott Momaday 864

One Time
William Stafford 866

Lyric 17
José Garcia Villa 867

For My Sister Molly Who in the Fifties
Alice Walker 868

Chicoria
Maestas and Anaya 912

Brer Possum's Dilemma
Jackie Torrence 915

Why the Waves Have Whitecaps
Zora Neale Hurston 918

Appreciating Others
The Day I Got Lost
Isaac Bashevis Singer 558

Hamadi
Naomi Shihab Nye 562

The Story-Teller
Saki (H. H. Munro) 596

The Medicine Bag
Virginia Driving Hawk Sneve 602

The Secret Heart
Robert P. Tristram Coffin 809

HEROES AND ADVENTURES

Heroes
An Episode of War
Stephen Crane 551

from The United States *vs.* Susan B. Anthony
Margaret Truman 643

Hokusai: The Old Man Mad About Drawing
Stephen Longstreet 654

Not to Go With the Others
John Hersey 656

The Diary of Anne Frank
Frances Goodrich and Albert Hackett 712

Johnny Appleseed
Rosemary Carr Benét 895

from The Right Stuff
Tom Wolfe 923

Hammerman
Adrien Stoutenburg 934

John Henry
Traditional 940

Paul Bunyan of the North Woods
Carl Sandburg 944

Pecos Bill: The Cyclone
Harold W. Felton 946

Davy Crockett's Dream
Davy Crockett 952

Conflicts and Challenges
The Dinner Party
Mona Gardner 535

The Finish of Patsy Barnes
Paul Laurence Dunbar 580

Tears of Autumn
Yoshiko Uchida 586

from A Walk in the Woods
Lee Blessing 773

Wahbegan
Jim Northrup 845

LITERATURE
Timeless Voices, Timeless Themes

Planning Instruction and Assessment

Unit Objectives

1. To read selections in different genres that develop the theme of "Coming of Age"
2. To apply a variety of reading strategies, particularly strategies for literal comprehension, appropriate for reading these selections
3. To recognize literary elements used in these selections
4. To increase vocabulary
5. To learn elements of grammar and usage
6. To write in a variety of modes about situations based on the selections
7. To develop speaking and listening skills by completing activities
8. To view images critically and to create visual representations

Meeting the Objectives Each selection provides instructional material and portfolio opportunities by which students can meet unit objectives. You will find additional practice pages for reading strategies, literary elements, vocabulary, and grammar in the **Selection Support** booklet in the **Teaching Resources** box.

Setting Goals Work with your students to set goals for unit outcomes. Plan skills concepts and match instruction and activities according to students' performance levels or learning modalities.

Portfolios Students may keep portfolios of their completed work or of their work in progress. The Build Your Portfolio page of each selection provides opportunities for students to apply the concepts presented.

 Humanities: Art

The Cat, by Robert Vickrey
    Robert Vickrey uses a process called egg tempera. It takes about 6 months for the paint to harden, then it is polished with cloth to produce a shine. Vickrey's work is detailed and realistic, as shown in *The Cat.* His paintings often show images casting shadows, viewed from above.
1. Why does the artist use this perspective? *Looking down gives the viewer a "all-seeing" perspective.*
2. What details depict "Coming of Age"? *The bike shows the girl's life journey; shadows indicate change in sunlight, showing her life is changing.*

The Cat, Robert Vickrey, Licensed by VAGA, New York

Art Transparencies

The **Art Transparencies** booklet in the **Teaching Resources** box offers fine art to help students make connections to other curriculum areas and high-interest topics.

Beyond Literature

Each unit presents Beyond Literature features that lead students into an exploration of careers, communities and other subject areas. In this unit, students will find out how e-mail works, look into caring for the elderly, and make a science connection with the Hubble Telescope. In addition, the **Teaching Resources** box contains a **Beyond Literature** booklet of activities. Using literature as a springboard, these activity pages offer students opportunities to connect literature to other curriculum areas and to the workplace and careers, community, media, and humanities.

Coming of Age

Laughter, tears, failure, and triumph are part of every life. These experiences are part of growing up and part of growing older. Along with the characters and authors in this unit, experience what it's like to travel on the road of life—finding adventure and friendship, and gaining insights about life along the way.

◆ 1

Assessing Student Progress

The tools that are available to measure the degree to which students meet the unit objectives are listed below.

Informal Assessment

The questions in the Guide for Responding sections are a first level of responses to the concepts and skills presented with the selection. As a brief, informal measure of students' grasp of the material, these responses indicate where further instruction and practice are needed. The practice pages in the **Selection Support** booklet provide for this type of instruction and practice.

You will also find literature and reading guides in the **Alternative Assessment** booklet, which students can use for informal assessment of their individual performances.

Formal Assessment

The **Formal Assessment** booklet contains Selection Tests and Unit Tests.

Selection Tests measure comprehension and skills acquisition for each selection or group of selections.

Each Unit Test provides students with 30 multiple-choice questions and 5 essay questions designed to assess students' knowledge of the literature and skills taught in the unit.

Each Alternative Unit Test: Standardized-Test Practice provides 15 multiple-choice questions and 3 essay questions based on two new literature selections not contained in the student book. The questions on the Alternative Unit Test are designed to assess students' ability to compare and contrast selections, applying skills taught in the unit.

Alternative Assessment

For portfolio and alternative assessment, the **Alternative Assessment** booklet contains Scoring Rubrics, Assessment sheets, and Learning Modalities activities.

Scoring Rubrics provide writing modes that can be applied to Writing activities, Writing Mini-Lessons, and Writing Process Workshop lessons.

Assessment sheets for speaking and listening activities provide peer and self-assessment direction.

Learning Modalities activities appeal to different learning styles. Use these as an alternative measurement of students' growth.

Connections

Within this unit, you will find selections and activities that make connections beyond literature. Use these selections to connect students' understanding and appreciation of literature beyond the traditional literature and language arts curriculum.

Encourage students to connect literature to other curriculum areas. You may wish to coordinate with teachers in other curriculum areas to determine ways to team teach and further extend instruction.

Connections to Today's World

Use these selections to guide students to recognize the relevance of literature to contemporary writings. In this unit, students can appreciate the humor of a Calvin and Hobbes cartoon that connects to a Shirley Jackson short story.

Connecting Literature to Social Studies

Each unit contains a selection that connects literature to social studies. In this unit, students will read a Native American legend, "The Girl Who Hunted Rabbits."

Guide for Reading

OBJECTIVES

1. To read, comprehend, and interpret a short story
2. To relate a short story to personal experience
3. To apply literal comprehension reading strategies
4. To analyze a historical setting
5. To build vocabulary in context and learn the word part *bene-*
6. To recognize and use nouns
7. To write a letter that includes vivid descriptions of feelings and events
8. To respond to the story through writing, speaking and listening, and projects

SKILLS INSTRUCTION

Vocabulary:
Word Part: *bene-*

Spelling:
Adding *-ed* to Two-Syllable Words

Grammar:
Nouns

Reading for Success:
Literal Comprehension Strategies

Literary Focus:
Historical Setting

Writing:
Show, Don't Tell

Speaking and Listening:
Retelling (Teacher Edition)

Critical Viewing:
Assess

PORTFOLIO OPPORTUNITIES

Writing: Diary Entry; Job Manual; News Article

Writing Mini-Lesson: Letter Home From a Soldier

Speaking and Listening: Retelling; Debate

Projects: Report on the Civil War; Time Capsule

More About the Author

Ray Bradbury was writing his own stories on butcher paper at age 11. Bradbury's parents encouraged his interest in writing by giving him a six-dollar typewriter, on which he began to write tales of space travel. Although he is best known for his science-fiction stories and novels, Bradbury has published both long and short fiction, children's books, stage plays, screenplays, television scripts, poems, and essays. His nonliterary accomplishments include conceiving the idea for Spaceship Earth at EPCOT, Disney World, and helping to develop ideas for the Orbitron space ride at Euro-Disney.

Meet the Author:

Ray Bradbury (1920–   )

Ray Bradbury grew up in Waukegan, Illinois, and later moved with his family to California. As a teenager, he read science-fiction stories and soon began writing his own.

The young writer eventually became an award-winning science-fiction author, known for such works as *The Martian Chronicles*.

Time Travel Bradbury often travels to the future in his stories, setting them on Mars or Venus. Occasionally, however, he shifts his time-travel machine into reverse and heads for the past. This story, for instance, takes place in Shiloh, Tennessee, on the eve of a great Civil War battle.

Timeless Themes Although Bradbury travels in time to find his stories, his themes are timeless. His themes include the need to be true to oneself and the importance of accepting others. "The Drummer Boy of Shiloh" deals with growing up during a crisis.

THE STORY BEHIND THE STORY

This story began with the poetic words of its title. Many years ago, Bradbury read the death notice of an actor whose grandfather had been "the drummer boy of Shiloh." This phrase inspired him to write his tale. Before he began to write, he went to the Los Angeles library to look up the weather conditions during the Battle of Shiloh.

◆ *Coming of Age*

◆ LITERATURE AND YOUR LIFE

CONNECT YOUR EXPERIENCE

Everyone has felt the last-minute jitters. You're about to take the big test, step up to the plate with runners on base, or go on a first date. Your heart is racing and your breathing is shallow. You've survived these moments. However, suppose you were about to risk your life in battle. In this story, you'll discover how the jitters feel when your life is at stake.

THEMATIC FOCUS: Arriving at Understanding

Often, the most trying experiences teach us valuable lessons. As you read, note what, if anything, the character learns from going into battle.

◆ Background for Understanding

HISTORY

This story is about a Civil War drummer boy. Drummer boys went with troops into battle, pacing their drumbeats to the speed of the attack. They didn't carry rifles or other weapons. The boy in the story is fourteen, and at least one real-life drummer boy was only thirteen. There was no age requirement for drummer boys because the job supposedly didn't involve combat. In reality, it involved great risk. Because few parents allowed their children to take that risk, drummer boys were usually orphans or runaways.

2

 Prentice Hall Literature Program Resources

REINFORCE / RETEACH / EXTEND

Selection Support Pages
Build Vocabulary: Word Part: *bene-*, p. 1
Build Spelling Skills, p. 2
Build Grammar Skills: Nouns, p. 3
Reading for Success: Literal Comprehension Strategies, pp. 4–5
Literary Focus: Historical Setting, p. 6

Strategies for Diverse Student Needs, pp. 1–2

Beyond Literature Cross-Curricular Connection: Social Studies, p. 1

Formal Assessment Selection Test, pp. 1–3, Assessment Resources Software

Alternative Assessment, p. 1

Writing and Language Transparencies Series of Events Chain, p. 57; Main Idea and Supporting Details, p. 61; Sensory Language Chart, p. 69

Resource Pro CD-ROM

Art Transparencies Art Transparency 11, pp. 47–50

 Listening to Literature Audiocassettes "The Drummer Boy of Shiloh"

The Drummer Boy of Shiloh

Drummer Boy, Julian Scott, N.S. Mayer

◆ Literary Focus

HISTORICAL SETTING

You study the past, but your history books probably don't give you a true sense of what it was actually like to *live* in an earlier era. In a story with a **historical setting,** however, you can see places and events from history through the eyes of fictional characters. As you share their experiences, you'll discover what it might have been like to live through the events yourself.

In this story, you'll keep watch with a boy on the eve of his first Civil War battle. You'll feel his fear and see the "familiar shadows" of soldiers lying exhausted around him.

◆ Build Vocabulary

WORD PART: *bene-*

Bradbury writes that for many Civil War soldiers, their youth was their "benediction." This word, which means "blessing," contains the word parts *bene-,* meaning "well" or "good," and *diction,* which means "saying."

WORD BANK

Look over these words from the story. Which word means "fastened or made firm"? Check the Build Vocabulary box on page 5 to see if you chose correctly.

benediction
riveted
compounded
resolute

Guide for Reading ◆ 3

Interest Grabber To give a sense of the story's setting, use Art Transparency II in **Art Transparencies,** pp. 47–50. Show students Winslow Homer's *Home Sweet Home* and invite them to share their impressions of the Civil War scene. Ask how they might feel if they were a long way from home, staying in a camp like the one shown. Tell students that the main character of the story is in a similar camp the night before a major battle. What thoughts might he be having?

◆ Build Grammar Skills

Nouns If you wish to introduce the grammar concept for this selection before students read, refer to the instruction on p. 9.

Customize for
Less Proficient Readers

Listening to the recording may help students understand the complex imagery of Bradbury's descriptions. Encourage them to think about the senses to which he is appealing with phrases such as the *sound* of peach blossoms which "lit with rustling taps," the *sight* of "bayonets fixed like eternal lightning," and the *touch* of "a peach blossom."

 Listening to Literature Audiocassettes

Customize for
More Advanced Students

Have students note and organize examples of descriptions on the Sensory Language Chart in **Writing and Language Transparencies,** p. 69. Have them rewrite the first paragraph with descriptions that appeal to the same senses and evoke similar images.

Humanities: Art

Drummer Boy, by Julian Scott

The artist Julian Scott was a Vermont veteran of the Civil War. His paintings are a visual record of the people and events of that time. In this portrait, the dark blue of the boy's uniform indicates he was a member of the Union army. Confederate soldiers wore gray uniforms.

What clues to the historical setting of the Civil War are found in this painting? *It shows the clothes soldiers wore and the housing of army camps.*

 Preparing for Standardized Tests

Reading Using context clues is one of the Literal Comprehension Strategies introduced in this unit. This strategy can improve students' performance on standardized tests that require them to identify the correct meaning of a word in a given sentence. Write this example on the board: "Another army was strewn helter-skelter. . . ." The context clue *helter-skelter,* meaning "haphazardly," helps define *strewn* as "scattered carelessly about." Write this sample test item on the board:

The soldiers, tired and without shelter, were <u>vulnerable</u> in the battle.

In this sentence, *vulnerable* means—

(A) protected   (C) sleeping
(B) open to attack   (D) victorious

Help students analyze the answer choices in relation to the context clues of the sentence, including *tired, without shelter,* and *in the battle* to eliminate (A) *protected* and (D) *victorious,* because they do not describe tired and shelterless soldiers, and (C) *sleeping,* because the soldiers are fighting a battle. (B) *open to attack* describes the soldiers' weak position in the battle.

3

The Reading for Success page in each unit presents a set of problem-solving strategies to help readers understand authors' words and ideas on multiple levels. Good readers develop a bank of strategies from which they can draw as needed.

Unit I introduces strategies for literal comprehension. Students must understand a work on its literal level before they apply higher-level critical thinking strategies. Literal comprehension strategies help readers attack text on a surface level—understanding vocabulary, sentence structure, and sometimes complex language.

These strategies for literal comprehension are modeled with "The Drummer Boy of Shiloh." Each green box shows an example of the thinking process involved in applying one of these strategies. Additional notes provide support for applying these strategies throughout the selection.

How to Use the Reading for Success Page

• Introduce the literal comprehension strategies, presenting each as a problem-solving procedure.

• Before students read the story, have them preview it, looking at the annotations in the green boxes that model the strategies.

• To reinforce these strategies after students have read the story, have them do the Reading for Success, pp. 4–5, in **Selection Support**. These pages give students an opportunity to read a selection and practice literal comprehension strategies by writing their own annotations.

Reading Strategies: Support and Reinforcement
Using Boxed Annotations and Prompts

Throughout the unit, the notes in green, red, and maroon boxes are intended to help students apply reading strategies, understand the literary focus, and make a connection with their lives. You may use boxed material in these ways:

• Have students pause at each box and respond to its prompt before they continue reading.

• Urge students to read through the selection, ignoring the boxes. After they complete the selection, they may go back and review the text, responding to the prompts.

Reading for Success

Literal Comprehension Strategies

When you watch television, you can put your brain to bed, leave your finger on the remote, and channel-surf. Reading is different. It's more rewarding than television, but it's also more work. These strategies will help you train your mind to connect with the page.

Break down long sentences.
▶ Read long sentences in meaningful groups of words, not word by word. Often punctuation will guide you to words that work together as a unit. Notice, for example, how the words before the first comma combine to answer the question *when*:

> In the April night, more than once, blossoms fell from the orchard trees. . . .

▶ Read through the sentence quickly to find the subject—the person, place, thing, or idea that the sentence is discussing. Then, decide what the sentence is saying about the subject.

Use context clues.
Use the context, or the surroundings, of an unfamiliar word to find clues to its meaning. As the passage below indicates, words similar or opposite in meaning can help you understand the unfamiliar word:

> . . . forty thousand men, exhausted by nervous expectation, unable to sleep for romantic dreams of battles yet unfought, lay crazily askew in their uniforms.

The word *askew* may be unfamiliar to you, but the word *crazily* suggests something "crooked" or "out of order." Men lying askew must therefore be lying "in a crooked way."

Reread or read ahead.
▶ Reread passages that confuse you until you understand them.
▶ If rereading doesn't clarify a passage, read ahead. You may find the answer in the next few sentences or paragraphs.

Paraphrase.
▶ Restate a sentence or paragraph in your own words to be sure you understand it.

As you read Ray Bradbury's "The Drummer Boy of Shiloh," look at the notes in the boxes. The notes demonstrate how to apply these strategies to a work of literature.

Model a Reading Strategy: Paraphrase
Tell students that when they read, it may help to paraphrase long or difficult sentences—a strategy they can use to check their understanding of what they read. Model paraphrasing for students:

When I read the sentence that begins at the bottom of the first column on the first page of the story, there are many images and unfamiliar words, such as "strewn helter-skelter" and "blind plunge." I think I may have missed the author's meaning, so I restate the sentence in my own words:

"The enemy soldiers were lying on the ground a mile away. They imagine how they will charge into battle with lots of energy."

You may wish to write the sentence from the selection and your paraphrased model on the board. Point out to students that there are other ways to restate the sentence and they should use their own words when they paraphrase. Then, invite students to paraphrase the original sentence in their notebooks.

THE DRUMMER BOY of SHILOH

Ray Bradbury

★ ★ ★ ★ ★ ★ ★ ★ ★ ★ ★ ★

In the April night, more than once, blossoms fell from the orchard trees and lit with rustling taps on the drumskin. At midnight a peach stone left miraculously on a branch through winter, flicked by a bird, fell swift and unseen, struck once, like panic, which jerked the boy upright. In silence he listened to his own heart ruffle away, away—at last gone from his ears and back in his chest again.

❶

After that, he turned the drum on its side, where its great lunar face peered at him whenever he opened his eyes.

His face, alert or at rest, was solemn. It was indeed a solemn time and a solemn night for a boy just turned fourteen in the peach field near the Owl Creek not far from the church at Shiloh.[1]

❷

"... thirty-one, thirty-two, thirty-three ..." Unable to see, he stopped counting.

> **Break down this long sentence** and you'll discover that its subject is "forty thousand men." The sentence tells you how these men lay.

Beyond the thirty-three familiar shadows, forty thousand men, exhausted by nervous expectation, unable to sleep for romantic dreams of battles yet unfought, lay crazily askew in their uniforms. A mile yet farther on, another army was strewn helter-skelter,

1. **Shiloh** (shī´ lō): Site of a Civil War battle in 1862; now a national military park in southwest Tennessee.

turning slow, basting themselves[2] with the thought of what they would do when the time came: a leap, a yell, a blind plunge their strategy, raw youth their protection and <u>benediction</u>.

Now and again the boy heard a vast wind come up, that gently stirred the air. But he knew what it was—the army here, the army there, whispering to itself in the dark. Some men talking to others, others murmuring to themselves, and all so quiet it was like a natural element arisen from South or North with the motion of the earth toward dawn.

❸

What the men whispered the boy could only guess, and he guessed that it was: "Me, I'm the one, I'm the one of all the rest who won't die. I'll live through it. I'll go home. The band will play. And I'll be there to hear it."

Yes, thought the boy, that's all very well for them, they can give as good as they get!

For with the careless bones of the young men harvested by night and bindled[3] around campfires were the similarly strewn steel bones of their rifles, with bayonets fixed like eternal lightning lost in the orchard grass.

Me, thought the boy, I got only a drum, two sticks to beat it, and no shield.

There wasn't a man-boy on this ground tonight who did not have a shield he cast, <u>riveted</u> or carved himself on his way to his

---

2. **basting themselves:** Here, letting their thoughts pour over them as they turn in their sleep.
3. **bindled** (bin´ dəld) *adj.*: Bedded.

◆ **Build Vocabulary**

benediction (ben´ ə dik´ shən) *n.*: Blessing
riveted (riv´ it əd) *adj.*: Fastened or made firm

★ ★ ★ ★ ★ ★ ★ ★ ★ ★ ★ ★ ★ ★ ★ ★ ★ *The Drummer Boy of Shiloh* ◆ 5

►Critical Viewing◄

① Assess *Most students will say that the drummer boy in this photograph seems prepared to go into battle and do his job, so he may have gotten past wanting "to hide inside himself."*

◆Reading for Success

② Use Context Clues Ask students to use context clues to determine the author's meaning of *flicked*. *The boy mistakes the blossom for a moth. A moth's touch is light and rapid; therefore, flicked means "touched lightly and quickly."*

◆Reading for Success

③ Read Ahead Encourage students to read ahead to learn who it is that the boy recognizes. Clues in the passage ahead are "brass buttons" and the person being like "all fathers," indicating that the boy is talking to the general.

◆Critical Thinking

④ Interpret Help students review story details that give meaning to this sentence. *The boy is near a peach tree. His cheek is covered with fuzz "off the tree overhead" because he is too young to grow a beard.*

Customize for
English Language Learners
Point out and explain the descriptive phrases (metaphors and similes) in this story. For example, on p. 5, "its great lunar face" means the surface of the boy's drum is large, bright, and round like the moon; "bayonets fixed like eternal lightning" means that the blades are shiny and sharp.

Customize for
Visual/Spatial Learners
Have students preview the illustrations on pp. 3, 5, and 6. Encourage them to use these images of Civil War drummer boys as they imagine the setting and characters of the story.

① ▲ **Critical Viewing** Does the drummer boy in this photograph seem to want to "hide inside himself"? Explain. **[Assess]**

first attack, <u>compounded</u> of remote but nonetheless <u>firm</u> and fiery family devotion, flag-blown patriotism and cocksure immortality strengthened by the touchstone of very real gunpowder, ramrod, Minié ball[4] and flint. But without these last, the boy felt his family move yet farther off away in the dark, as if one of those great prairie-burning trains had chanted them away never to return—leaving him with this drum which was worse than a toy in the game to be played tomorrow or some day much too soon.

② The boy turned on his side. A moth brushed his face, but it was a peach blossom. A peach blossom flicked him, but it was a moth. Nothing stayed put. Nothing had a name. Nothing was as it once was.

If he lay very still, when the dawn came up and the soldiers put on their bravery with their caps, perhaps they might go away, the war with them, and not notice him lying small here, no more than a toy himself.

"Well, now," said a voice.

The boy shut up his eyes, to hide inside

---

4. **Minié** (min´ ē) **ball:** Cone-shaped rifle bullet that expands when fired.

himself, but it was too late. Someone, walking by in the night, stood over him.

"Well," said the voice quietly, "here's a soldier crying *before* the fight. Good. Get it over. Won't be time once it all starts."

And the voice was about to move on when the boy, startled, touched the drum at his elbow. The man above, hearing this, stopped. The boy could feel his eyes, sense him slowly bending near. A hand must have come down out of the night, for there was a little *rat-tat* as the fingernails brushed and the man's breath fanned his face.

"Why, it's the drummer boy, isn't it?"

The boy nodded, not knowing if his nod was seen. "Sir, is that *you*?" he said.

"I assume it is." The man's knees cracked as he bent still closer.

③ He smelled as all fathers should smell, of salt sweat, ginger tobacco, horse and boot leather, and the earth he walked upon. He had many eyes. No, not eyes—brass buttons that watched the boy.

He could only be, and was, the general.

"What's your name, boy?" he asked.

"Joby," whispered the boy, starting to sit up.

"All right, Joby, don't stir." A hand pressed his chest gently, and the boy relaxed. "How long you been with us, Joby?"

"Three weeks, sir."

"Run off from home or joined legitimately, boy?"

Silence.

"Fool question," said the general. "Do you shave yet, boy? Even more of a fool. There's your cheek, fell right

> Use **context clues** to see that *legitimately* means "lawfully." The words "run off from home" provide a clue.

④ off the tree overhead. And the others here not much older. Raw, raw, the lot of you. You ready for tomorrow or the next day, Joby?"

"I think so, sir."

"You want to cry some more, go on ahead. I did the same last night."

"*You*, sir?"

Cultural Connection

Battle Drums From earliest history, the sound of drums has been an important part of many cultures. Drums were used in sacred settings until musical instruments introduced sacred music. Then, drums found a new place on the battlefield, because the beat of a drum could energize soldiers. Early war drums were often kettledrums, which produced a low booming sound that carried for miles and could frighten the enemy. Because these drums were large, they were usually carried into battle on horses or camels and even on elephants in India. As smaller drums became more popular for battle, rhythmic patterns were developed to communicate information among groups, such as signaling soldiers to march or charge. Typically, it was considered dishonorable to wound or kill a drummer, although capturing the enemy's drums was a celebrated achievement. During the Revolutionary War, the American drummers learned and used the drum signals of the British. Those same signals have developed into the basic drumming rudiments, or patterns, that drummers in modern times use as they march in parades or improvise in a rock band.

"It's the truth. Thinking of everything ahead. Both sides figuring the other side will just give up, and soon, and the war done in weeks, and us all home. Well, that's not how it's going to be. And maybe that's why I cried."

"Yes, sir," said Joby.

The general must have taken out a cigar now, for the dark was suddenly filled with the smell of tobacco unlit as yet, but chewed as the man thought what next to say.

"It's going to be a crazy time," said the general. "Counting both sides, there's a hundred thousand men, give or take a few thousand out there tonight, not one as can spit a sparrow off a tree, or knows a horse clod from a Minié ball. Stand up, bare the breast, ask to be a target, thank them and sit down, that's us, that's them. We should turn tail and train four months, they should do the same. But here we are, taken with spring fever and thinking it ❺ blood lust, taking our sulfur with cannons instead of with molasses, as it should be, going to be a hero, going to live forever. And I can see all of them over there nodding agreement, save the other way around. It's wrong, boy, it's wrong as a head put on hindside front and a man marching backward through life. More innocents will get shot out of pure enthusiasm than ever got shot before. Owl Creek was full of boys splashing around in the noonday sun just a few hours ago. I fear it will be full of boys again, just floating, at sundown tomorrow, not caring where the tide takes them."

> **Read ahead** to find out what the general means when he says "It's going to be a crazy time."

The general stopped and made a little pile of winter leaves and twigs in the darkness, as if he might at any moment strike fire to them to see his way through the coming days when the sun might not show its face because of what was happening here and just beyond.

◆ **Build Vocabulary**

compounded (käm pound´ əd) *adj.*: Mixed or combined

resolute (rez´ ə lōōt´) *adj.*: Showing a firm purpose; determined

The boy watched the hand stirring the leaves and opened his lips to say something, but did not say it. The general heard the boy's breath and spoke himself.

"Why am I telling you this? That's what you wanted to ask, eh? Well, when you got a bunch of wild horses on a loose rein somewhere, somehow you got to bring order, rein them in. These lads, fresh out of the milkshed, don't know what I know, and I can't tell them: men actually die, in war. So each is his own army. I got to make *one* army of them. And for that, boy, I need you."

"Me!" The boy's lips barely twitched.

"Now, boy," said the general quietly, "you are the heart of the army. Think of that. You're the heart of the army. Listen, now."

And, lying there, Joby listened. And the general spoke on.

If he, Joby, beat slow tomorrow, the heart would beat slow in the men. They would lag by the wayside. They would drowse in the fields on their muskets. They would sleep forever, after that, in those same fields—their hearts slowed by a drummer boy and stopped by enemy lead. ❻

But if he beat a sure, steady, ever faster rhythm, then, then their knees would come up in a long line down over that hill, one knee after the other, like a wave on the ocean shore! Had he seen the ocean ever? Seen the waves rolling in like a well-ordered cavalry charge to the sand? Well, that was it, that's what he

> **Paraphrase** the general's description of what will happen if Joby beats a sure rhythm.

wanted, that's what was needed! Joby was his right hand and his left. He gave the orders, but Joby set the pace!

So bring the right knee up and the right foot out and the left knee up and the left foot out. One following the other in good time, in brisk time. Move the blood up the body and make the head proud and the spine stiff and the jaw resolute. Focus the eye and set the teeth, flare ❼ the nostrils and tighten the hands, put steel armor all over the men, for blood moving fast in them does indeed make men feel as if they'd put on steel. He must keep at it, at it! Long and steady, steady and long! Then, even

---

Clarification

❺ During the nineteenth century, a teaspoon of molasses mixed with sulfur was a home remedy commonly used to cure a nonspecific ailment referred to as spring fever. In this passage, the general is comparing that remedy with the use of sulfur in gunpowder for cannons.

◆Build Grammar Skills

❻ **Nouns** Tell students that a noun is a word that names a person, animal, place, thing, or idea. Have students read these sentences and identify three nouns and tell what they name. *Possible nouns include* Joby, *a person;* fields, *a place;* muskets, *things.*

◆ LITERATURE AND YOUR LIFE

❼ Point out that the general is coaching Joby about what he should do during the next day's battle. Ask students how this type of instruction can help a person deal with fear. *Students may suggest that it takes away some of the mystery of a difficult or overwhelming task that lies ahead.*

Customize for
Musical/Rhythmic Learners
To demonstrate the power of a drumbeat, invite students to march around the room, or in place, as you or another student beat a steady rhythm. First, use a slow beat like the beat of a resting heart (70–80 beats per minute). Then, pick up the tempo to 100–120 beats per minute. Ask students to describe how the different speeds affected their marching, as well as their overall attitude. How might the difference between a slow and a fast beat affect the attitude of soldiers marching into battle?

Customize for
Bodily/Kinesthetic Learners
Have partners act out the first interaction between the boy and the general to demonstrate the boy's anxious feelings and the gentle way in which the general responds to him. Encourage students to use what they discover to describe how Joby views his role as drummer boy.

Speaking and Listening Mini-Lesson

Retelling
This mini-lesson supports the Speaking and Listening activity in the Idea Bank, p. 10.

Introduce Discuss with students how retelling a story can offer new insights into characters, events, and setting. Often, we notice more details or perceive events from a different perspective when telling or listening to a story. A reteller chooses which details and events to emphasize.

Develop Have students review the order of events in the selection and identify the main idea and details. The Series of Events Chain and the

Main Idea and Supporting Details Organizer in **Writing and Language Transparencies,** pp. 57 and 61, may help organize the information.

Apply Pair students to practice retelling. Then have volunteers retell the story for the entire class.

Assess Evaluate students' retellings based on their understanding of the sequence of events and important details, as well as their presentation. You may also want to have students use the Peer-Assessment: Oral Interpretation form in **Alternative Assessment,** p. 115.

7

◆ Build Vocabulary

❶ Word Part: *bene-* Ask students to tell what the general gives to the boy by saying these words. You may want to review Build Vocabulary, p. 3, and guide them to use one of the words from the Word Bank in their answer. *He gives the boy a benediction.*

Reinforce and Extend

Answers

◆ LITERATURE AND YOUR LIFE

Reader's Response Some students may feel that war is dangerous, and he is too young for such responsibility. Others may say that times were different, and he may be old enough to make such a decision.

Thematic Focus Joby understands the importance and responsibility of his role as drummer boy.

☑ Check Your Comprehension

1. Joby is 14 years old.
2. He is worrying about what it will be like to go into battle.
3. He has only a drum and no weapons to protect himself.
4. He cried because he knows neither side will give up and many soldiers will die.
5. He needs Joby to use his drum to set a pace so the men will fight with a strong spirit.

◆ Critical Thinking

1. Like the others, Joby is anxious about the coming battle. Unlike them, he carries a drum but no weapon, so he may feel more nervous than they do.
2. The general is checking on all of the army or something about Joby catches the general's attention.
3. His drumbeat is like a heartbeat for all of the soldiers.
4. Joby seems to feel better, because he is able to settle himself for the night.
5. Some students will agree with the general's words, while others may suggest that he exaggerates in order to build up Joby's sense of importance and confidence.
6. Most students will realize that Joby is still fearful but displays courage by controlling his fear in order to do his job. They should also identify the general as a man who is in control of his fears.

8

---

though shot or torn, those wounds got in hot blood—in blood he'd helped stir—would feel less pain. If their blood was cold, it would be more than slaughter, it would be murderous nightmare and pain best not told and no one to guess.

The general spoke and stopped, letting his breath slack off. Then, after a moment, he said, "So there you are, that's it. Will you do that, boy? Do you know now you're general of the army when the general's left behind?"

The boy nodded mutely.

"You'll run them through for me then, boy?"

"Yes, sir."

❶ "Good. And, maybe, many nights from tonight, many years from now, when you're as old or far much older than me, when they ask you what you did in this awful time, you will tell them—one part humble and one part proud—'I was the drummer boy at the battle of Owl Creek,' or the Tennessee River, or maybe they'll just name it after the church there. 'I was the drummer boy at Shiloh.' Good grief, that has a beat and sound to it fitting for Mr. Longfellow. 'I was the drummer boy at Shiloh.' Who will ever hear those words and not know you, boy, or what you thought this night, or what you'll think tomorrow or the next day when we must get up on our legs and *move!*"

The general stood up. "Well, then. Bless you, boy. Good night."

"Good night, sir." And tobacco, brass, boot polish, salt sweat and leather, the man moved away through the grass.

Joby lay for a moment, staring but unable to see where the man had gone. He swallowed. He wiped his eyes. He cleared his throat. He settled himself. Then, at last, very slowly and firmly, he turned the drum so that it faced up toward the sky.

He lay next to it, his arm around it, feeling the tremor, the touch, the muted thunder as, all the rest of the April night in the year 1862, near the Tennessee River, not far from the Owl Creek, very close to the church named Shiloh, the peach blossoms fell on the drum.

Guide for Responding

◆ LITERATURE AND YOUR LIFE

Reader's Response Do you think Joby should have enlisted as a drummer boy? Why or why not?

Thematic Focus What new understanding of himself and his role does Joby get from the general?

☑ Check Your Comprehension

1. How old is the drummer boy?
2. What is the boy thinking about as he lies in the orchard?
3. What frightens him about the coming battle?
4. Why did the general cry the night before?
5. Why does the general say he needs Joby?

◆ Critical Thinking

INTERPRET

1. In what ways is Joby like and unlike the other soldiers? **[Compare and Contrast]**
2. Why do you think the general stops to talk to Joby? **[Infer]**
3. In what way is Joby "the heart of the army"? **[Interpret]**
4. How do you think Joby feels after his talk with the general? Explain. **[Draw Conclusions]**

EVALUATE

5. Is the role of the drummer boy as crucial as the general says? Explain. **[Evaluate]**

APPLY

6. The writer Mark Twain once said, "Courage is resistance to fear, mastery of fear—not absence of fear." How does this quotation apply to the story? **[Apply]**

8 ◆ *Coming of Age*

 Beyond the Selection

FURTHER READING

Other Works by Ray Bradbury
The Martian Chronicles
The Illustrated Man

Other Works With the Theme of Arriving at Understanding
Snow in August, Pete Hamill
The Giver, Lois Lowry
Honor to the Hills, Eileen Charbonneau

Other Works About the Civil War
Reluctant Witnesses, Emmy E. Werner (ed.)

INTERNET

We suggest the following Internet sites (all Web sites are subject to change).

For more information about Ray Bradbury:
http://www.brookingsbook.com/bradbury/bradbury.htm

For links to information about the Civil War:
http://www.cwc.lsu.edu/links/cwinfo.htm

We *strongly recommend* that you preview these sites before you send students to them.

Guide for Responding (continued)

◆ Reading for Success

LITERAL COMPREHENSION STRATEGIES

Review the reading strategies and the notes that show how to understand a writer's words and messages. Then, apply the strategies to answer the following:

1. Break down the sentence on page 8 that begins, "And, maybe, many nights . . ." What is the subject? What key words tell what the subject will do?
2. Use context clues to find the meaning of *tremor* on page 8. Explain how you figured out the meaning.
3. Paraphrase the paragraph on page 7 that begins, "'Why am I telling you . . .'" What is the paragraph's basic meaning?

◆ Build Vocabulary

USING THE WORD PART *bene-*

In your notebook, explain how the word part *bene-* ("well" or "good") contributes its upbeat meaning to each italicized word:

The general showed Joby the *benefit* that the soldiers would receive from his drumming. In that sense, the general's visit to Joby was more than *beneficial*. It was a *benediction*.

SPELLING STRATEGY

When adding *-ed* to a two-syllable word, don't double the final consonant if the stress is on the first syllable:

riv′ et + -ed = riveted

On your paper, add *-ed* to the following verbs:

1. travel   2. hinder   3. label

USING THE WORD BANK

On your paper, write the word closest in meaning to that of the first word.

1. benediction: (a) curse, (b) wealth, (c) blessing
2. riveted: (a) fastened, (b) drilled, (c) split
3. compounded: (a) flattened, (b) complicated, (c) mixed
4. resolute: (a) determined, (b) absolute, (c) calm

◆ Literary Focus

HISTORICAL SETTING

Bradbury creates a **historical setting,** a place and time from history, by using such diverse details as peach blossoms and bayonets. However, it takes more than details—even accurate ones—to bring the past to life. The real emotions of made-up characters give added truth to the story.

1. Identify three additional details from the Civil War era. Then, explain your choices.
2. The general blesses Joby as he leaves. How does this expression of feeling give added truth to the details of the general's appearance?

◆ Build Grammar Skills

NOUNS

Nouns are words that name a person, animal, place, thing, or idea. In just the first three paragraphs of "The Drummer Boy of Shiloh," Bradbury uses nouns that name each.

Person	boy	Thing	branch
Animal	bird	Idea	silence
Place	field		

Practice   On your paper, rewrite each sentence, underlining the nouns. Then, tell whether each noun is a person, animal, place, thing, or idea.

1. The young drummer boy felt solemn.
2. The soldiers camped in a field near the Owl Creek.
3. A moth brushed his face and landed on a branch.
4. The soldiers dreamed of battles.
5. Raw youth was their protection.

Writing Application   Rewrite each sentence, replacing the italicized nouns with nouns of the same kind. For example, replace a person with a person and a thing with a thing. Be sure the new sentence makes sense.

1. The *boy* was camped near the *creek*.
2. The *blossom* fell onto the *drum*.
3. How could the *moth* understand the boy's *nervousness*?

Writing Application
Possible responses:
1. The girl was camped near the river.
2. The branch fell onto the log.
3. How could the dog understand the boy's fear?

✎ Writer's Solution

For additional instruction and practice, use the lesson in the *Writer's Solution Language Lab CD-ROM* on Using Nouns. You may also use the practice pages on Nouns, pp. 5–7, in the *Writer's Solution Grammar Practice Book.*

Answers
Reading for Success

1. The subject is *you*. The key words are "will tell them . . .'I was the drummer boy at Shiloh.'"
2. *Tremor* means "slight trembling." Nearby words that seem to mean the same are *touch* and *muted thunder.* All these terms describe the effect produced when falling peach blossoms strike the drum face.
3. Possible response: The general tells him all this because the soldiers are untrained and wild, and Joby's drumming can help keep them in order and mold them into an army. He wants to ease the boy's fears.

◆ Build Vocabulary

Using the Word Part *bene-*
A *benefit* is something good. Something that's *beneficial* brings good. A *benediction* is a prayer that requests some good for someone.

Spelling Strategy
1. traveled; 2. hindered; 3. labeled

Using the Word Bank
1. blessing
2. fastened
3. complicated
4. determined

◆ Literary Focus

1. Students should explain how their choices are specific to the Civil War era. Possible responses: gunpowder, ramrod, Minié ball, the general smelling of horse, cannon smelling of sulfur, muskets, role of drummer boy in battle, reference to Longfellow as a current poet.
2. The blessing demonstrates both kindness and authority. This supports the details that suggest the general is both a leader of men and a father figure.

◆ Build Grammar Skills

Practice
1. The young drummer <u>boy</u> felt solemn. (person)
2. The <u>soldiers</u> camped in a <u>field</u> near the <u>Owl Creek</u>. (persons; place; place)
3. A <u>moth</u> brushed his <u>face</u> and landed on a <u>branch</u>. (animal [insect]; thing; thing)
4. The <u>soldiers</u> dreamed of <u>battles</u>. (persons; idea)
5. Raw <u>youth</u> was their <u>protection</u>. (idea; idea)

Idea Bank

Following are suggestions for matching the Idea Bank topics with your students' performance levels and learning modalities:

Customize for
Performance Levels
Less Advanced Students: 1, 7
Average Students: 3, 4, 5, 6, 7
More Advanced Students: 2, 4, 5, 6, 7

Customize for
Learning Modalities
Verbal/Linguistic: 1, 2, 3, 4, 5, 6
Interpersonal: 4, 5, 7
Logical/Mathematical: 2, 6, 7

Writing Mini-Lesson

Refer students to the Writing Handbook in the back of the book for instruction on the writing process and for further information on description. Have students use the Sensory Language Chart in **Writing and Language Transparencies,** p. 69, to arrange their prewriting examples.

Writer's Solution

Writing Lab CD-ROM
Have students complete their letter home from a soldier by using the tutorial on Description. Follow these steps:

1. Have students use the audio annotated writing models to learn how to make descriptions more vivid.
2. Students can then use the Descriptive Word Bin to add more precise language while revising.
3. Have students use the Interactive Models of Revision to learn how to replace vague language.

Writer's Solution Sourcebook
Have students use Chapter 2, "Description," pp. 33–69, for additional support. This chapter includes in-depth instruction on using vivid descriptions.

Build Your Portfolio

Idea Bank

Writing

1. **Diary Entry** As Joby, write a diary entry in which you respond to what the general has just said to you.

2. **Job Manual** Review the general's description of a drummer boy's duties. Then, write a brief manual that will teach new drummer boys how to perform their job. Divide your information into categories, such as *duties* and *qualifications*. **[Career Link]**

3. **News Article** You're a reporter for a newspaper and have overheard the general speaking to Joby. Write an article about this scene that will appeal to your readers. **[Career Link]**

Speaking and Listening

4. **Retelling** Imagine you're Joby as an old man. Tell your grandchildren the story of what happened to you on the night before the Battle of Shiloh. Perform this retelling for the class. **[Social Studies Link; Performing Arts Link]**

5. **Debate [Group Activity]** Form two groups and debate this proposition: that the age of enlistment in the armed forces should be lowered to sixteen. Have a panel of students judge the outcome based on the content of the argument and the skill of the presentation. **[Social Studies Link]**

Projects

6. **Report on the Civil War** Write a report for your classmates on the roles that teenagers played in the Civil War—as drummer boys, bugle boys, and soldiers. **[Social Studies Link]**

7. **Time Capsule [Group Activity]** With a group, prepare a time capsule to be opened in a hundred years. List items you'd include to give people of the future a picture of our time. Also, write brief explanations to go with each of the items. **[Social Studies Link]**

Writing Mini-Lesson

Letter Home From a Soldier

Some soldiers camping near Joby that night must have been writing letters home. Step into the shoes of one of those soldiers and write a letter home to your anxious family. Combine your deep feelings with accurate historical details to give your letter the ring of truth.

Writing Skills Focus: Show, Don't Tell
Make your letter lively by **showing** feelings and events, not just telling about them. Notice how Bradbury doesn't tell you that the boy is nervous. Instead, he shows you the boy's nervous behavior:

Model From the Story
At midnight a peach stone left miraculously on a branch through winter, flicked by a bird . . . struck once, like panic, which jerked the boy upright.

Prewriting Imagine yourself as a soldier in camp on the eve of a Civil War battle. Jot down what you might be thinking, seeing, hearing, smelling, tasting, and touching. Also, jot down ideas and feelings to tell your parents.

Drafting Put yourself in the time and place described in "The Drummer Boy of Shiloh," and begin drafting. Use vivid descriptions and stories to show your parents what's happening at camp and how much you miss them.

> ◆ **Grammar Application**
> Circle the nouns in your letter. Where appropriate, replace general nouns with more specific ones.

Revising Reread your draft critically. Take out references to items, like appliances, that wouldn't have existed in 1862. Find passages in which you just tell your parents what's happening or how you feel. Revise these passages by adding examples or stories to show what you mean.

✓ ASSESSMENT OPTIONS

Formal Assessment, Selection Test, pp. 1–3, and Assessment Resources Software. The selection test is designed so that it can easily be customized to the performance levels of your students.

Alternative Assessment, p. 1, includes options for less advanced students, more advanced students, visual/spatial learners, interpersonal learners, and verbal/linguistic learners.

PORTFOLIO ASSESSMENT
Use the following rubrics in the **Alternative Assessment** booklet to assess students' writing:
Diary Entry: Expression, p. 90
Job Manual: How-to/Process Explanation, p. 96
News Article: Description, p. 93
Writing Mini-Lesson: Description, p. 93

PART 1

Arriving at Understanding

Untitled, Jim Lang, Stockworks

Arriving at Understanding ◆ 11

 Humanities: Art

Untitled, by Jim Lang

The artist's use of color and lines helps the viewer see individual elements of the painting separately and together at the same time. Point out to students that the word *path* means "a trodden way," as well as "a way of life or conduct." Encourage them to keep this in mind as they view the picture.

1. Where does the path in the picture lead? Why? *The path leads to an open door. It may be an opportunity for the man to gain knowledge or understanding.*

2. Are the man in profile and the man running one and the same? Why? *Yes. The man runs on a path that leads through the mind—he seeks knowledge or understanding; or, the running man represents what the man in profile is thinking.*

3. What do the clouds represent? *Students may say that they represent thoughts.*

4. Are there two parts to this painting? If so, what do they represent? *Color and lines set off the left and right sections, which may represent competing choices or aspects of character.*

One-Minute Planning Guide

The selections in this part provide insights on how to better understand ourselves and others and the choices we face in life. In the humorous short story "Charles," a mother gains an understanding of her little boy's behavior; the story is paired with a *Calvin and Hobbes* comic strip. A more serious note is struck in the excerpt from *I Know Why the Caged Bird Sings,* in which a withdrawn girl learns to appreciate herself through the guidance of a caring woman. Three poems, "The Road Not Taken," "All But Blind," and "The Choice," explore the idea of the choices we make in life. The informative article "E-Mail from Bill Gates" helps readers understand the importance of e-mail in our lives. The legend of "The Girl Who Hunted Rabbits," tells of a young Zuñi girl who comes to understand her world and her place in it.

Customize for
Varying Student Needs
When assigning the selections in this part, keep in mind these factors:

"Charles"
- Dialogue is useful for students who benefit from role play
- Humorous, appealing plot

Calvin and Hobbes
- Less proficient readers may need help with the punch line

from *I Know Why the Caged Bird Sings*
- Short, personal memoir
- Setting in the South provides historical and cultural connections

"The Road Not Taken"
- Some students may need help to rephrase
- Effective use of metaphor

"All But Blind"
- Short, accessible poem
- Effective use of metaphor

"The Choice"
- Humorous, accessible poem

from "E-Mail from Bill Gates"
- Computer-related subject matter may be of high interest
- Jargon may need explaining

"The Girl Who Hunted Rabbits"
- Early Native American legend
- Opportunities for social studies and cultural connections

11

Guide for Reading

OBJECTIVES

1. To read, comprehend, and interpret a story
2. To relate a story to personal experience
3. To break down long sentences
4. To identify point of view
5. To build vocabulary in context and learn the word root *-cred-*
6. To recognize common and proper nouns
7. To write a humorous description
8. To respond to the story through writing, speaking and listening, and projects

SKILLS INSTRUCTION

Vocabulary:
Word Roots: *-cred-*

Spelling:
Words With *-ly*

Grammar:
Common and Proper Nouns

Reading Strategy:
Break Down Long Sentences

Literary Focus:
Point of View

Writing:
Appropriate Tone

Speaking and Listening:
Advisory Panel (Teacher Edition)

Viewing and Representing:
Multimedia Display (Teacher Edition)

Critical Viewing:
Connect

PORTFOLIO OPPORTUNITIES

Writing: Description; Letter; Problem-and-Solution Essay

Writing Mini-Lesson: Humorous Description

Speaking and Listening: Retelling; Advisory Panel

Projects: Multimedia Display; Comic Strip

More About the Author
Shirley Jackson was born in San Francisco and spent most of her childhood writing poetry rather than playing with neighborhood children. She became more devoted to writing while studying at Syracuse University in New York State, where she began "The Spectre," a campus magazine, with her future husband and fellow classmate Stanley Edgar Hyman. Her chilling short story "The Lottery" gained her fame when it was published in *The New Yorker* in 1948. Many of her works were adapted for broadcast on radio and television. Part of Jackson's appeal as a writer is her ability to ground both her horror stories and humorous narratives in everyday events.

Meet the Author:

Shirley Jackson (1919–1965)

As the mother of four energetic children, Shirley Jackson once said that she wrote because "It's the only chance I get to sit down." As a writer, she produced mainly two types of stories—spine-tingling tales of supernatural events and hilarious stories about daily life. She made a joking reference to her contrasting styles by giving her family stories titles that sound as if they were horror tales: *Life Among the Savages* and *Raising Demons*.

From Family Stories to Horror Stories In all, Jackson wrote fifty-five short stories, several articles and other nonfiction works, two family books, a play, seven novels, and some poetry. Among her novels are the horror and suspense classics *The Haunting of Hill House* (1959) and *We Have Always Lived in the Castle* (1962). Author Dorothy Parker once wryly commented that Jackson "restores my faith in terror and dread."

THE STORY BEHIND THE STORY
Many fictional stories enlarge real characters and events. Often the characters and events come from the writer's own life. Shirley Jackson collected countless ideas from her four children. The main character in "Charles" is patterned after Jackson's son Laurie.

◆ LITERATURE AND YOUR LIFE

CONNECT YOUR EXPERIENCE
"The dog did it!" "Not me—my invisible twin!" You have probably heard the amazing excuses children use to cover up bad behavior. What outrageous excuses have you given or heard? In "Charles," you'll read about a young boy who comes up with a unique way to cover for his bad behavior.

THEMATIC FOCUS: Arriving at Understanding
As you read "Charles," ask yourself who's learned more—Laurie, the main character, or his parents.

◆ Background for Understanding

SCIENCE
School can be a place of fun as well as a place of learning, as the photograph at right suggests. Laurie, the boy in "Charles," is just beginning kindergarten, adjusting to a new school environment. Some experts believe that children's play—both make-believe and group-oriented—can help children adjust to such new situations. In "Charles," you'll meet a boy who focuses on just one type of play and causes mayhem in the classroom.

◆ Build Vocabulary

WORD ROOTS: -cred-
The word root *-cred-* means "believe." With the prefix *in-*, which makes what follows negative or opposite, the word *incredulous* means "not willing to believe." Adding the suffix *-ly* creates the adverb *incredulously*.

WORD BANK
Which words on the list might describe how something is done? Check the Build Vocabulary boxes on pages 15 and 17 to see if you chose correctly.

renounced
insolently
elaborately
simultaneously
incredulously

Prentice Hall Literature Program Resources

REINFORCE / RETEACH / EXTEND
Selection Support Pages
Build Vocabulary: Word Roots: *-cred-*, p. 7
Build Spelling Skills, p. 8
Build Grammar Skills: Common and Proper Nouns p. 9
Reading Strategy: Break Down Long Sentences p. 10
Literary Focus: Point of View, p. 11
Strategies for Diverse Student Needs, pp. 3–4
Beyond Literature Career Connection: School Counselor, p. 2

Formal Assessment Selection Test, pp. 4–6
Assessment Resources Software
Alternative Assessment, p. 2
Writing and Language Transparencies
Series of Events Chain, p. 57
Resource Pro CD-ROM
"Charles"—includes all resource material and customizable lesson plan
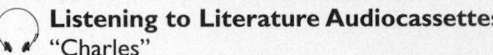 **Listening to Literature Audiocassettes**
"Charles"

◆ Charles ◆

Interest Grabber Challenge students to think back to kindergarten, when they were about 5 years old. Ask them to freewrite about the activities they remember, who their friends were, what the first day of school was like, and whatever else comes to mind. Then, open a discussion about students' impressions of kindergarten as they look back. Is it hard for them to remember being that age? Was the first day of middle school like the first day of kindergarten? Tell students the main character in the story they will read is a young boy who is creative and mischievous about starting kindergarten.

◆ Build Grammar Skills

Common and Proper Nouns If you wish to introduce the grammar concept before students read, you may use the instruction on p. 20.

Customize for
Less Proficient Readers
Students may benefit from organizing the story's events to help them follow the action. Display the Series of Events Chain from **Writing and Language Transparencies,** p. 57. Fill in the first box with the following text: "Laurie starts kindergarten." In the second box, write "Laurie tells about meeting Charles, who got a spanking at school." Encourage students to continue noting events.

Customize for
More Advanced Students
Have students identify the character traits of Laurie and "Charles." Form groups of students, and have one group create a character web for Laurie and one group create a web for Charles.

◆ Literary Focus

POINT OF VIEW

Every story is told by someone—either by a narrator outside the story or by a character in the story. The vantage point or perspective from which a story is told is referred to as its **point of view.** "Charles" is told from the point of view of a character in the story, the main character's mother.

◆ Reading Strategy

BREAK DOWN LONG SENTENCES

Have you ever gotten lost in the middle of a sentence? When you come across a long sentence, it can be helpful to **break it down**. Begin by reading the sentence in meaningful sections, not word by word. Look for natural breaks, signaled by punctuation. Then, look for main parts in each section of a long sentence.

You can use a chart like this one:

What is the sentence about?	What does the sentence say about the subject?
Laurie (her son)	Started kindergarten Renounced overalls Began wearing jeans

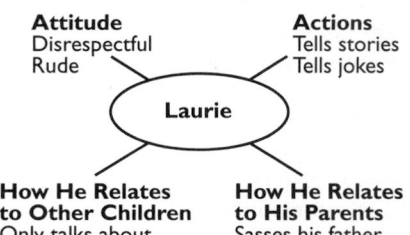

Attitude
Disrespectful
Rude

Actions
Tells stories
Tells jokes

Laurie

How He Relates to Other Children
Only talks about Charles

How He Relates to His Parents
Sasses his father
Is offhand with his mother

After they finish reading, ask the groups to compare character webs to see how the traits indicate that Laurie and Charles are one and the same.

Preparing for Standardized Tests

Vocabulary General vocabulary questions on standardized tests may evaluate students' knowledge of word roots, including Latin roots, such as the word root *-cred-* (the vocabulary skill for this selection), which comes from the Latin word *credere*, meaning "to believe." If someone says, "Laurie's mother thought Charles's behavior was *incredibly* bad" students can use their knowledge of *-cred-* to understand that *incredibly* means *unbelievably*.

Write this sample test item on the board:

Laurie's parents gave credit to the stories about Charles's behavior.

In this sentence, *credit* means

(A) doubt about details
(B) belief in the truth
(C) questions about accuracy
(D) opinions about the truth

Guide students to use their knowledge of the word root *-cred-* to determine that *(B) belief in the truth* is the correct answer. Although the other answers could fit in the sentence, knowing that the meaning of *credit* has to do with "believe" allows for correct understanding of the sentence.

13

Develop Understanding

One-Minute Insight It is with mixed emotions of sadness and pride that Laurie's mother sends him off for his first day at kindergarten. When Laurie returns home, he reports to his parents about a boy named Charles who got a spanking on the very first day of school. As the days go by and the stories about Charles's bad behavior continue, Laurie's parents become concerned about the influence that this ill-mannered child is having on their son. The mother eagerly attends a parent meeting at school, anxious to see what kind of mother Charles has. With the story's surprising conclusion, the mother arrives at an unexpected understanding about her son and herself.

Customize for
English Language Learners

To help students understand the precise wording Jackson uses to describe her characters, you may want to pantomime descriptive words or phrases for students. For example, after reading the first paragraph, you might pantomime a person walking and then compare this action with that of a person *swaggering*. Similarly, after students read the third paragraph, you can compare speaking in a pleasant manner with speaking *insolently*. Invite more-proficient English speakers to help you pantomime for English language learners.

Customize for
Visual/Spatial Learners

Invite students to look at the photograph on p. 14 and to speculate about the child's personality, based on visual clues. As they read, encourage students to imagine that the smiling face belongs to Laurie. After they read the story, have them study the picture again and decide whether they think it is a good representation of Laurie. Invite them to create their own representation of Laurie by drawing or finding another picture that fits their impression of the main character.

 Block Scheduling Strategies

Consider these suggestions to take advantage of extended class time:

- Focus on the Reading Strategy. As students read, have them listen to the audiocassette of the story, noting how the speaker reads long sentences. When they finish, have students work in pairs to answer the Reading Strategy questions on p. 20. For additional practice, they can use **Selection Support,** p. 10.

- After students read the selection, form groups to answer the Critical Thinking questions on p. 19 and to complete the questions for the

Connections to Today's World feature on p. 19, comparing their answers. Regroup students and have them work together to complete the Comic Strip project in the Idea Bank on p. 21.

- If students have access to technology, ask them to work in pairs using the tutorial on Description in the *Writer's Solution Writing Lab CD-ROM* to complete the Writing Mini-Lesson on p. 21.

 Listening to Literature Audiocassettes

Charles

Shirley Jackson

❶ The day my son Laurie started kindergarten he renounced corduroy overalls with bibs and began wearing blue jeans with a belt; I watched him go off the first morning with the older girl next door, seeing clearly that an era of my life was ended, my sweet-voiced nursery-school tot replaced by a long-trousered, swaggering[1] character who forgot to stop at the corner and wave good-bye to me.

❷ He came home the same way, the front door slamming open, his cap on the floor, and the voice suddenly become raucous[2] shouting, "Isn't anybody *here*?"

At lunch he spoke insolently to his father, spilled his baby sister's milk, and remarked that his teacher said we were not to take the name of the Lord in vain.

❸ "How *was* school today?" I asked, elaborately casual.

"All right," he said.

"Did you learn anything?" his father asked.

Laurie regarded his father coldly. "I didn't learn nothing," he said.

"Anything," I said. "Didn't learn anything."

---

1. **swaggering** (swag´ ər iŋ) *v.*: Strutting; walking with a bold step.
2. **raucous** (rô´ kəs) *adj.*: Boisterous; disorderly.

"The teacher spanked a boy, though," Laurie said, addressing his bread and butter. "For being fresh," he added, with his mouth full.

❹ "What did he do?" I asked. "Who was it?"

Laurie thought. "It was Charles," he said. "He was fresh. The teacher spanked him and made him stand in a corner. He was awfully fresh."

"What did he do?" I asked again, but Laurie slid off his chair, took a cookie, and left, while his father was still saying, "See here, young man."

The next day Laurie remarked at lunch, as soon as he sat down, "Well, Charles was bad again today." He grinned enormously and said, "Today Charles hit the teacher."

❺ "Good heavens," I said, mindful of the Lord's name, "I suppose he got spanked again?"

"He sure did," Laurie said. "Look up," he said to his father.

"What?" his father said, looking up.

◆ Build Vocabulary

renounced (ri nounst´) *v.*: Gave up

insolently (in´ sə lənt lē) *adv.*: Boldly disrespectful in speech or behavior

Charles ◆ 15

◆Reading Strategy

❶ Break Down Long Sentences Point out that the first paragraph is a single, long sentence. Model the process of breaking down long sentences by reading the paragraph aloud, pausing to discuss how you identify each meaningful section. You may want to write the sentence on the board to illustrate the process. Guide students to look for natural pauses in the sentence, which are often signaled by punctuation. In this sentence, call attention to the semicolon that breaks two longer thoughts: Laurie deciding to change his choice of clothing, and his mother watching him go. The comma after "girl next door" introduces the reader to the mother's inner thoughts.

◆Critical Thinking

❷ Infer Ask students what they can infer about Laurie from this description. *Laurie seems to be behaving badly, or with little respect for his family.*

◆Literary Focus

❸ Point of View Ask students to identify who "I" is. Who is telling the story? *Students should establish that "I" refers to Laurie's mother, and she is telling the story.*

Clarification

❹ Tell students that *fresh* used in this context refers to someone who is bold or cocky and disregards the feelings of others.

◆Critical Thinking

❺ Analyze Ask students why Laurie "grinned enormously" when remarking about Charles's behavior. *Students may say that Laurie is amused by Charles's behavior and that Laurie may look up to Charles.*

 Speaking and Listening Mini-Lesson

Advisory Panel

This mini-lesson supports the Speaking and Listening activity on p. 21.

Introduce Tell students that a *panel* is a group of people who are selected to advise, often in front of an audience. Effective communication skills address the need to provide appropriate information—in this case, advice—to an audience. Point out that a panel format is useful in situations where differing expert opinions may be held. Students may have seen TV talk shows that use advisory

panels; discuss their impressions of this method of presenting information.

Develop Form groups of 3–4 students. Have them brainstorm for a list of types of misbehavior in children. Then, ask them to use personal experience and observations to come up with practical ways to deal with each type of behavior. After students have developed a bank of information on the subject of dealing with children's misbehavior, have them practice answering questions within their groups.

Apply Have each group sit as a panel in front of the class and answer questions from classmates. Panels can discuss answers among themselves in order to elaborate on the information they provide for the audience.

Assess Evaluate students on the thoroughness of their preparation, their ability to field questions, and their interaction as a panel. Have students use the Peer Assessment: Speaker/Speech form, p. 114, in **Alternative Assessment,** adapting the criteria so as to evaluate each panel as a "speaker."

◆Reading Strategy

❶ Break Down Long Sentences
Read this sentence aloud to the class, animating the voice of Laurie. Explain that this sentence is long because the writer is trying to make Laurie's dialogue seem real, like the language of a kindergartner who runs all his thoughts together without stopping. Guide students to identify words that help the reader know where to break this sentence. *Students should recognize that the transitions "but," "so," and "and" help the reader identify separate actions in the sentence.*

◆Critical Thinking

❷ Analyze Ask students to analyze the relationship between Laurie and his parents based on his actions and the way he speaks to them. *Laurie makes fun of his parents, but his parents do not attempt to stop him or seem to notice.*

◆Critical Thinking

❸ Draw Conclusions Ask students why they think Laurie's mother and father both assume that the friend of the teacher who came to school was Charles's mother. *Students may respond that Laurie's parents are thinking that the teacher must be getting fed up and has called Charles's mother in to see how badly her son behaves.*

Comprehension Check ☑

❹ You may want to help students recognize the author's clues to the surprise ending that is coming. Has Laurie ever described his own behavior at school? Why does he know all of the details of Charles's behavior? *Students may recognize the fact that because Laurie only describes Charles's behavior and knows exactly what has happened with Charles are clues that Charles may in fact be Laurie.*

"Look down," Laurie said. "Look at my thumb. Gee, you're dumb." He began to laugh insanely.

"Why did Charles hit the teacher?" I asked quickly.

❶ "Because she tried to make him color with red crayons," Laurie said. "Charles wanted to color with green crayons so he hit the teacher and she spanked him and said nobody play with Charles but everybody did."

The third day—it was Wednesday of the first week—Charles bounced a see-saw on to the head of a little girl and made her bleed, and the teacher made him stay inside all during recess. Thursday Charles had to stand in a corner during story-time because he kept pounding his feet on the floor. Friday Charles was deprived of blackboard privileges because he threw chalk.

On Saturday I remarked to my husband, "Do you think kindergarten is too unsettling for Laurie? All this toughness, and bad grammar, and this Charles boy sounds like such a bad influence."

"It'll be all right," my husband said reassuringly. "Bound to be people like Charles in the world. Might as well meet them now as later."

On Monday Laurie came home late, full of news. "Charles," he shouted as he came up the hill; I was waiting anxiously on the front steps. "Charles," Laurie yelled all the way up the hill, "Charles was bad again."

"Come right in," I said, as soon as he came close enough. "Lunch is waiting."

❷ "You know what Charles did?" he demanded, following me through the door. "Charles yelled so in school they sent a boy in from first grade to tell the teacher she had to make Charles keep quiet, and so Charles had to stay after school. And so all the children stayed to watch him."

"What did he do?" I asked.

"He just sat there," Laurie said, climbing into his chair at the table. "Hi, Pop, y'old dust mop."

"Charles had to stay after school today," I told my husband. "Everyone stayed with him."

"What does this Charles look like?" my husband asked Laurie. "What's his other name?"

"He's bigger than me," Laurie said. "And he doesn't have any rubbers and he doesn't ever wear a jacket."

Monday night was the first Parent-Teachers meeting, and only the fact that the baby had a cold kept me from going; I wanted passionately to meet Charles's mother. On Tuesday Laurie remarked suddenly, "Our teacher had a friend come to see her in school today."

❸ "Charles's mother?" my husband and I asked simultaneously.

"Naaah," Laurie said scornfully. "It was a man who came and made us do exercises, we had to touch our toes. Look." He climbed down from his chair and squatted down and touched his toes. "Like this," he said. He got solemnly back into his chair and said, picking up his fork, "Charles didn't even *do* exercises."

"That's fine," I said heartily. "Didn't Charles want to do exercises?"

"Naaah," Laurie said. "Charles was so fresh to the teacher's friend he wasn't *let* do exercises."

"Fresh again?" I said.

"He kicked the teacher's friend," Laurie said. "The teacher's friend told Charles to touch his toes like I just did and Charles kicked him."

❹ "What are they going to do about Charles, do you suppose?" Laurie's father asked him.

Laurie shrugged elaborately. "Throw him out of school, I guess," he said.

Wednesday and Thursday were routine; Charles yelled during story hour and hit a boy in the stomach and made him cry. On Friday Charles stayed after school again and

◆ Build Vocabulary

simultaneously (sī′ məl tā′ nē əs lē) *adv.*: At the same time

16 ◆ *Coming of Age*

 Beyond the Classroom

Career Connection

Careers in Early Education In this story, readers observe some of the difficulties of teaching. Primary teachers have many responsibilities besides teaching, such as creating a safe environment and introducing young children to new experiences. Teachers must show children how they are expected to behave in the classroom.

Invite students to interview a primary teacher about his or her job. Why did he or she choose this field? What kind of education and training does it require? What are the challenges and rewards?

Community Connection

Parent-Teacher Associations Parent-Teacher Associations, or PTAs, are programs designed to help parents, teachers, school officials, and community leaders work together to ensure the highest quality education for students. PTA meetings are held to discuss needs of students, promote fundraising events and activities for schools, and help educate parents as to what they can do about legislation that affects schools, teachers, and students. Encourage students to investigate and discuss the activities of your school's parent-teacher organization.

▲ Critical Viewing Examine the expressions on these children's faces. Which of them might have a personality like that of Charles? **[Connect]**

so did all the other children.

With the third week of kindergarten Charles was an institution in our family; the baby was being a Charles when she cried all afternoon; Laurie did a Charles when he filled his wagon full of mud and pulled it through the kitchen; even my husband, when he caught his elbow in the telephone cord and pulled the telephone, ashtray, and a bowl of flowers off the table, said, after the first minute, "Looks like Charles."

 ♦ Reading Strategy Break down this long sentence into sections. What is each section about?

During the third and fourth weeks it looked like a reformation in Charles; Laurie reported grimly at lunch on Thursday of the third week, "Charles was so good today the teacher gave him an apple."

"What?" I said, and my husband added warily, "You mean Charles?"

"Charles," Laurie said. "He gave the crayons around and he picked up the books afterward and the teacher said he was her helper."

"What happened?" I asked incredulously.

♦ Build Vocabulary

incredulously (in krej′ oo ləs lē) *adv.*: With doubt or disbelief

Charles ◆ 17

►Critical Viewing◄

❺ Connect Students may suggest that the girl on the left with the bow in her hair might be like Charles because her facial expression is more animated than the rest of the children's.

◆Reading Strategy

❻ Break Down Long Sentences *The first section describes what Charles represents in the family; the other sections are about the way in which each family member's behavior reflects Charles's behavior.*

◆Build Grammar Skills

❼ Common and Proper Nouns Proper nouns name a particular person, place, or thing; whereas common nouns name people, places, or things in general. Point out that when Charles's name is used by the family to name examples of unacceptable or careless behavior, the word is treated as a proper noun and the capital letter is used because it is a particular behavior.

◆Critical Thinking

❽ Speculate Ask students why Laurie reported Charles's good behavior *grimly,* while he had delighted in telling about Charles's bad behavior. *Students should recognize that, for some reason, Laurie is not happy with the turn of events.*

◆Literary Focus

❾ Point of View Draw students' attention to how the narrator's point of view allows readers to observe a heightened contrast in Charles's behavior. How would the change in Charles seem different if the story were being told from the teacher's point of view? *Guide students to recognize that the change would probably seem more gradual because the narrator would be observing schoolroom events firsthand.*

Humanities: Photography

Photo Illustrations Photographs of children are used to illustrate this story. The photograph on this page shows a group of kindergarten children during the 1940's, around the time Jackson was first sending her children to school. Have students refer to the photograph as they answer the following questions:

1. How does this photograph help you imagine what it must have been like in Laurie's kindergarten class? *It shows how children might have looked and acted in the classroom at the*

time the story was written. The facial expressions show the variety of reactions children have toward school.

2. What details in this photograph give clues about the time period during which the story was set? *Clothing styles are different from those today.*

3. What impressions do you get about kindergarten-aged children from looking at this photograph? *Many students will say that they think the children look sweet and innocent.*

◆ Reading Strategy

1 Break Down Long Sentences
Have students break down this sentence to find four separate ideas. *He told a little girl to say a word / she said it / the teacher washed her mouth out with soap / Charles laughed.*

◆ Critical Thinking

2 Analyze Ask students why Charles might have gone back to his old ways. *Charles likes the attention he gets and probably wanted to get caught for telling the little girl to say a bad word. When she got in trouble and he didn't, he decided to act in a way to assure he would get attention.*

◆ Literary Focus

3 Point of View *Students may have figured out that the mother, who is telling the story, is the only person at the meeting who knows anything about Charles.*

Comprehension Check ☑

4 Who is Charles? *Students probably have put the clues together along with the mother to determine that Charles is really Laurie.*

◆ LITERATURE AND YOUR LIFE

5 Have you ever read another story or seen TV programs or movies about a fictitious character who takes the blame? How did the situation turn out? *Students may give examples of trickster tales or TV programs they have watched. Encourage them to identify similarities in the scenarios.*

"He was her helper, that's all," Laurie said, and shrugged.

"Can this be true, about Charles?" I asked my husband that night. "Can something like this happen?"

"Wait and see," my husband said cynically.[3] "When you've got a Charles to deal with, this may mean he's only plotting." He seemed to be wrong. For over a week Charles was the teacher's helper; each day he handed things out and he picked things up; no one had to stay after school.

"The PTA meeting's next week again," I told my husband one evening. "I'm going to find Charles's mother there."

"Ask her what happened to Charles," my husband said. "I'd like to know."

"I'd like to know myself," I said. On Friday of that week things were back to normal. "You know what Charles did today?" Laurie demanded at the lunch table, in a voice slightly awed. **1** "He told a little girl to say a word and she said it and the teacher washed her mouth out with soap and Charles laughed."

"What word?" his father asked unwisely, and Laurie said, "I'll have to whisper it to you, it's so bad." He got down off his chair and went around to his father. His father bent his head down and Laurie whispered joyfully. His father's eyes widened.

"Did Charles tell the little girl to say *that*?" he asked respectfully.

"She said it *twice*," Laurie said. "Charles told her to say it *twice*."

"What happened to Charles?" my husband asked.

"Nothing," Laurie said. "He was passing out the crayons."

2 Monday morning Charles abandoned the little girl and said the evil word himself three or four times, getting his mouth washed out with soap each time. He also threw chalk.

My husband came to the door with me that evening as I set out for the PTA

---

3. **cynically** (sin´ i klē) *adv.*: With disbelief as to the sincerity of people's intentions or actions.

---

meeting. "Invite her over for a cup of tea after the meeting," he said. "I want to get a look at her."

"If only she's there," I said prayerfully.

"She'll be there," my husband said. I don't see how they could hold a PTA meeting without Charles's mother."

At the meeting I sat restlessly, scanning each comfortable matronly face, trying to determine which one hid the secret of Charles. None of them looked to me haggard enough. No one stood up in the meeting and apologized for the way her son had been acting. No one mentioned Charles.

After the meeting I identified and sought out Laurie's kindergarten teacher. She had a plate with a cup of tea and a piece of chocolate cake; I had a plate with a cup of tea and a piece of marshmallow cake. We maneuvered[4] up to one another cautiously, and smiled.

"I've been so anxious to meet you," I said. "I'm Laurie's mother."

"We're all so interested in Laurie," she said.

"Well, he certainly likes kindergarten," I said. "He talks about it all the time."

"We had a little trouble adjusting, the first week or so," she said primly, "but now he's a fine little helper. With occasional lapses, of course."

"Laurie usually adjusts very quickly," I said. "I suppose this time it's Charles's influence."

"Charles?"

"Yes," I said, laughing, "you must have your hands full in that kindergarten, with Charles."

"Charles?" she said. "We don't have any Charles in the kindergarten." **5**

> ◆ **Literary Focus**
> Why do you think no one mentions Charles at the PTA meeting? **3**

4

---

4. **maneuvered** (mə nōō´ vərd) *v.*: Moved in a planned way.

---

18 ◆ *Coming of Age*

Viewing and Representing Mini-Lesson

Multimedia Display

This mini-lesson supports the Multimedia Display Idea Bank project on p. 21.

Introduce Tell students that in order to create a display of childhood memories that communicates strongly, they will need to do more than just collect pictures. Have them brainstorm for a list of important childhood activities they have experienced. Then, have them form groups and share their lists.

Develop Encourage students to consider these points:

• How will they represent their childhood stories? Will they display a group of photos or videotapes, or will they re-create a childhood scene and videotape it?

• Will each student provide a story, or should the group concentrate on a few?

• How will they organize the childhood stories they have chosen? Will they focus on medium, theme, or some other aspect?

Apply Have groups assign responsibilities. Provide art materials such as posterboard and markers or videotape equipment for

students to create their displays.

Assess When all of the displays have been presented, discuss each multimedia display. Encourage students to tell what they would do differently if assigned a similar group project. Assess students' group interaction and involvement in preparations. In addition, you may want to use the Creative Thinking, Decision Making, Problem Solving, and Seeing Things in the Mind's Eye portions of the Work Readiness Skills: Teacher Observation form in **Alternative Assessment,** p. 122.

CONNECTIONS TO TODAY'S WORLD

School experiences like those in "Charles" are often funny and memorable. In Bill Watterson's popular comic strip, he often uses Calvin's school experiences as humorous subject matter.

Calvin and Hobbes   by Bill Watterson

CALVIN AND HOBBES ©Watterson. Dist. by UNIVERSAL PRESS SYNDICATE. Reprinted with permission. All rights reserved.

1. Why do you think the substitute teacher went home at noon?
2. In what ways is Calvin, the boy in the cartoon, similar to Laurie, the boy in "Charles"?

Guide for Responding

◆ LITERATURE AND YOUR LIFE

Reader's Response Were you surprised to learn that Charles and Laurie were the same person? Why or why not?

Thematic Focus What lesson do you think the narrator learns about her son?

☑ Check Your Comprehension

1. Why does Charles become a well-known character to the family?
2. Give three examples of Charles's bad behavior at school.
3. Give three examples of Laurie's bad behavior at home.
4. What does Laurie's mother discover about her son at the PTA meeting?

◆ Critical Thinking

INTERPRET

1. How do you think Laurie feels when he starts kindergarten? **[Infer]**
2. How is Charles's behavior at school similar to Laurie's at home? **[Compare and Contrast]**
3. Why do you think Laurie invented Charles? **[Draw Conclusions]**
4. How do you think Laurie will react after his parents learn his secret? **[Infer]**

EVALUATE

5. Does Laurie deserve to be punished, or has he learned his lesson? **[Make a Judgment]**

APPLY

6. How would this story be different if Laurie were entering high school? **[Hypothesize]**

Charles ◆ 19

Beyond the Selection

FURTHER READING

Other Works by Shirley Jackson
The Haunting of Hill House
The Road Through the Wall
We Have Always Lived in the Castle

Other Works on the Theme of Coming of Age
The Pigman, Paul Zindel
Secret Diary of Adrian Mole, Age 13
Tangerine, Edward Bloor

INTERNET

We suggest the following site on the Internet (all Web sites are subject to change).

For information on Shirley Jackson:
http://www.salonmagazine.com/jan97/jackson970106.html

We *strongly recommend* that you preview the site before you send students to it.

Connections to Today's World

About *Calvin and Hobbes*
Calvin and Hobbes is a series of cartoon strips about an engaging 6-year-old (Calvin) and his stuffed tiger (Hobbes). Created by Bill Watterson, the cartoon was first syndicated in 1985. *Calvin and Hobbes* ceased publication in 1996 when Watterson retired.

Like "Charles," this strip is about the difficult job of teaching.

1. *The students may have misbehaved and the teacher couldn't take it.*
2. *He thinks that any type of behavior is acceptable in school.*

Reinforce and Extend

Answers
◆ LITERATURE AND YOUR LIFE

Reader's Response Some students may have been surprised because Laurie's descriptions were so realistic; others may have noticed that Laurie didn't describe his own behavior, so he must be Charles.

Thematic Focus Possible response: She learns that her son is not as innocent as she thinks.

☑ Check Your Comprehension

1. Laurie describes all of Charles's actions.
2. Examples include being fresh, hitting the teacher, bouncing the seesaw on a classmate's head, throwing chalk, and using bad words.
3. Examples include door-slamming, shouting, and speaking rudely.
4. She discovers that Charles does not exist; Laurie made him up.

◆ Critical Thinking

1. Students may say Laurie feels older and more grown up.
2. Both Charles and Laurie are rude and need a lot of attention.
3. Some students will say Laurie invented Charles because he doesn't want his parents to know that he is the bad student, or he is proud of his bad behavior.
4. Students may say that Laurie will be sorry for his behavior or he may try to make up another story.
5. Many students will say that Laurie should be punished; others may say that the teacher has helped him learn his lesson.
6. Students may say that his misbehavior would be more serious and probably be punished quicker.

◆ Reading Strategy

1. Charles was the teacher's helper; Charles/he handed things out and picked things up; Charles was a helper/no one stayed after school; Charles didn't get into trouble.

2. We had a little trouble adjusting; the teacher and Laurie/she said primly; she is a prim person/now he's a fine little helper; being a helper allowed Laurie to adjust.

◆ Build Vocabulary

Using the Word Root -cred-
1. unbelievable;   2. believable;
3. believability

Spelling Strategy
1. closely; 2. regally; 3. fortunately;
4. jealously

Using the Word Bank
1. incredulously
2. renounced
3. insolently
4. simultaneously

◆ Literary Focus

1. Laurie has told his parents about Charles and what he does at school; then, when his mother talks to the teacher, she discovers that there is no Charles in Laurie's class.

2. Charles's identity would be known throughout the story.

3. The mother's point of view allows for the surprise ending because the reader is surprised when the mother is surprised.

◆ Build Grammar Skills

Practice
1. Laurie (proper); father (common)
2. Charles (proper); husband (common); Laurie (proper)
3. Friday (proper); week (common); things (common)
4. He (common); chair (common); father (common)
5. No one (common); meeting (common); way (common); son (common)

Writing Application
1. Edward is to begin kindergarten.
2. Listen to the crossing guard's directions.
3. On Tuesday, we're going on a field trip.

Guide for Responding (continued)

◆ Reading Strategy

BREAK DOWN LONG SENTENCES

Like many stories, "Charles" contains some long, difficult sentences. It's helpful to **break down the sentences** to identify basic parts. Once you've done that, you can reread to get the full picture.

Divide each long sentence into sections. Tell what each section is about (the subject) and what the rest of the section says about the subject.

1. For over a week Charles was the teacher's helper; each day he handed things out and he picked things up; no one had to stay after school.

2. "We had a little trouble adjusting, the first week or so," she said primly, "but now he's a fine little helper."

◆ Build Vocabulary

USING THE WORD ROOT -cred-

Jackson uses the adverb *incredulously* to show the narrator's disbelief: "'What happened?' I asked incredulously." Use the meaning of the word root *-cred-* to define these words. Use a dictionary to check your definitions.

1. incredible   2. credible   3. credence

SPELLING STRATEGY

You can change most adjectives to adverbs by adding *-ly*. When you add *-ly,* do not change the spelling of the adjective.

vicious → viciously   absolute → absolutely
ideal → ideally   respectful → respectfully

Copy each adjective. Then write the adverb form.
1. close   2. regal   3. fortunate   4. jealous

USING THE WORD BANK

On your paper, complete the paragraph sensibly, using the Word Bank. Use each word only once.

Tia's teacher, Mr. Acevedo, stared at her paper ____?____. The page was covered with drawings but no words. "I have ____?____ language in favor of Art," Tia declared. Mr. Acevedo laughed, but he refused to accept the paper. Tia stamped her foot ____?____ and ____?____ started to pout.

◆ Literary Focus

POINT OF VIEW

"Charles" is told from the **point of view** of Laurie's mother. It is through her eyes that the story unfolds; we learn information only as Laurie's mother learns it.

1. How does Laurie's mother learn about Charles and his doings?
2. How would "Charles" be different if it were told from Laurie's point of view?
3. Explain how the point of view from which "Charles" is told helps contribute to the surprise ending.

◆ Build Grammar Skills

COMMON AND PROPER NOUNS

Nouns may be common or proper. **Common nouns** name any person, place, thing, or idea. **Proper nouns** name a particular person, place, thing, or idea. Capitalize proper nouns wherever they appear. Do not capitalize common nouns unless they begin a sentence.

Example: Charles bounced a see-saw on to the head of a little girl. . . .

Practice Write the sentences on your paper. Underline common nouns and circle proper nouns.
1. Laurie regarded his father coldly.
2. "What does this Charles look like?" my husband asked Laurie.
3. On Friday of that week things were back to normal.
4. He got down off his chair and went around to his father.
5. No one stood up in the meeting and apologized for the way her son had been acting.

Writing Application Rewrite each sentence, fixing capitalization in common and proper nouns.
1. Edward is to begin Kindergarten.
2. Listen to the Crossing Guard's directions.
3. On tuesday, we're going on a field trip.

✎ Writer's Solution

For additional instruction and practice, use the lesson in the *Writer's Solution Language Lab CD-ROM* on Using Nouns and the practice page on Common and Proper Nouns, p. 7, in the *Writer's Solution Grammar Practice Book.*

Build Your Portfolio

Idea Bank

Writing

1. **Description** Using details from the story, write a description of Charles and his behavior at school.

2. **Letter** Write a letter from Laurie's teacher to his family, describing his behavior at school. Describe Laurie's actions, and tell how they affect the class.

3. **Problem-and-Solution Essay** Laurie's naughty behavior poses a problem to his teacher and his parents. Write a problem-and-solution essay in which you lay out steps they could take in handling the situation.

Speaking and Listening

4. **Retelling** Imagine that you are Laurie several years after the story takes place. Now you are in the eighth grade, telling a story about your own childhood. Tell the story of "Charles" from your new point of view. **[Performing Arts Link]**

5. **Advisory Panel [Group Activity]** With a group of classmates, form an advisory panel to discuss how to deal with children who misbehave, like Charles. Hold your discussion in front of the class.

Projects

6. **Multimedia Display [Group Activity]** With a group, collect kindergarten stories and pictures from classmates and peers. Working together, design and assemble the stories into a multimedia display about childhood memories. **[Media Link]**

7. **Comic Strip** Create a comic strip featuring Charles as a main character. What humorous activities might you show Charles doing? Use speech balloons to indicate dialogue. **[Art Link]**

Writing Mini-Lesson

Humorous Description

If this story were true, Laurie's parents would probably have plenty of stories to tell about their son's mischief. Think back to your own childhood, and write a humorous description of a childhood event. Include details that will bring the description to life for your readers. As you develop your description, focus on creating a light and humorous tone.

Writing Skills Focus: Appropriate Tone

Tone refers to a writer's attitude toward his or her subject. Choose words carefully, and use exaggeration to create a humorous **tone** for your description. In the following example, words were changed and one detail was exaggerated to change the tone from neutral to humorous.

Neutral Tone: He swallowed the uncooked pasta.

Humorous Tone: He downed the entire box of macaroni.

Prewriting Decide on the childhood event you will describe. List the characters involved; jot down notes about who they are and their actions and responses. You may also plan out the series of events you're going to describe.

Drafting Begin your draft by telling the story. Be sure that you set the scene, and include all the characters and events from your Prewriting notes.

Revising Review your draft to be sure that the characters are fully described and that the events are clear. Read it aloud, and listen for comic words and rhythms. You can often change the tone of a passage by replacing one or two words.

◆ **Grammar Application**

Reread your draft to be sure that you've capitalized proper nouns but not common nouns.

Charles ◆ 21

Idea Bank

Following are suggestions for matching the Idea Bank topics with your student's performance levels and learning modalities:

Customize for
Performance Levels
Less Advanced Students: 1, 4, 6
Average Students: 2, 4, 5, 6
More Advanced Students: 3, 5, 7

Customize for
Learning Modalities
Verbal/Linguistic: 2, 3, 4, 5
Interpersonal: 5, 6
Visual/Spatial: 6, 7
Logical/Mathematical: 3
Intrapersonal: 1, 2, 3, 7
Bodily/Kinesthetic: 4, 5

Writing Mini-Lesson

Refer students to the Writing Handbook in the back of the book for instruction on the writing process and for further information on description.

✎ **Writer's Solution**

Writing Lab CD-ROM
Have students complete the tutorial on Description. Follow these steps:
1. Have students view the video clip from *Star Trek* which illustrates the concept of audience.
2. Have students use the Interactive Instruction on Ordering Details.
3. Have students draft on computer.
4. Have students use the Revision Checklist when revising.

Writer's Solution Sourcebook
Have students use Chapter 2, "Description," pp. 32–69, for additional support. This chapter includes in-depth instruction on using vivid and precise verbs, pp. 62–64.

✓ **ASSESSMENT OPTIONS**

Formal Assessment, Selection Test, pp. 4–6, and Assessment Resources Software. The selection test is designed so that it can easily be customized to the performance levels of your students.

Alternative Assessment, p. 2, includes options for less advanced students, more advanced students, interpersonal learners, bodily/kinesthetic learners, musical/rhythmic learners, and verbal/linguistic learners.

PORTFOLIO ASSESSMENT
Use the following rubrics in the **Alternative Assessment** booklet to assess student writing:
Description: Description, p. 93
Letter: Expression, p. 90
Problem-and-Solution: Problem-Solution, p. 97
Writing Mini-Lesson: Description, p. 93.

Guide for Reading

More About the Author
Maya Angelou graduated first in her eighth-grade class in Stamps, Arkansas. She attended high school in California, graduating in 1945. The early influence of Bertha Flowers, "the aristocrat of Black Stamps," gave Angelou a love of language and culture that has lasted a lifetime. Angelou began writing about her life. *I Know Why the Caged Bird Sings,* published in 1970, is the first in a series of five autobiographical works. The little girl who would not speak has since become a major voice in modern American literature.

Meet the Author:

Maya Angelou (1928–)

Born Marguerite Johnson in St. Louis, Missouri, Maya Angelou received her unusual first name from her brother, Bailey, who referred to her as "mya sister." Maya and Bailey were raised by their grandmother, who owned a country store in rural Arkansas.

Overcoming Obstacles Growing up in the segregated South did not prevent Maya Angelou from breaking through the barriers of racism and poverty to remarkable achievements in many areas. She has been a streetcar conductor in San Francisco, a journalist, an actor, a civil rights worker, a teacher, and a poet.

A Presidential Commission In 1992, Maya Angelou was asked by President-elect Bill Clinton to write a poem for his inauguration. In January 1993, Angelou read "On the Pulse of Morning" for an appreciative President and an admiring nation.

THE STORY BEHIND THE STORY

I Know Why the Caged Bird Sings is a true account of Maya Angelou's humble beginnings. The excerpt included here tells how her life was influenced by a remarkable woman named Mrs. Flowers.

The publication *I Know Why the Caged Bird Sings* places Angelou among the first African American women to hit the bestseller list. Her story later became a screenplay that aired as a television special.

◆ **LITERATURE AND YOUR LIFE**

CONNECT YOUR EXPERIENCE
In this true-life story, a young girl is taken under the wing of a very special person. Perhaps you, too, have received guidance from a special person—a parent, sibling, coach, or friend—who helped you to develop self-esteem.

THEMATIC FOCUS: Arriving at Understanding
As you read, take note of how Mrs. Flowers, a friend of Angelou's family, helped Angelou to appreciate her own abilities.

◆ **Background for Understanding**

HISTORY
When Angelou was growing up in Arkansas in the 1930's and 1940's, blacks and whites lived apart and attended separate schools. In addition, blacks were excluded from many social facilities and barred from all-white restaurants. As an African American woman, Angelou experienced both racial and gender discrimination, yet with the help of Mrs. Flowers, she learned to rise above it.

◆ **Build Vocabulary**

RELATED WORDS: FORMS OF *tolerate*
The verb *tolerate* means "to accept." Other forms of *tolerate* include *tolerance, tolerable,* and *intolerant,* which is used in the story and means "not accepting others' ideas."

WORD BANK
Which words from the list do you think are adjectives? Why? Check the Build Vocabulary boxes on pages 25, 27, and 28 to see if you chose correctly.

fiscal
taut
benign
infuse
intolerant
couched

22 ◆ *Coming of Age*

 Prentice Hall Literature Program Resources

REINFORCE / RETEACH / EXTEND
Selection Support Pages
Build Vocabulary: Related Words: Forms of *tolerate,* p. 12
Build Spelling Skills, p. 13
Build Grammar Skills: Plural and Possessive Nouns, p. 14
Reading Strategy: Reread or Read Ahead, p. 15
Literary Focus: Memoir, p. 16
Strategies for Diverse Student Needs, pp. 5–6
Beyond Literature Community Connection: Learning From Elders, p. 3

Formal Assessment Selection Test, pp. 7–9, Assessment Resources Software
Alternative Assessment, p. 3
Writing and Language Transparencies
Series of Events Chain, p. 57; Main Idea and Supporting Details Organizer, p. 61
Resource Pro CD-ROM
"from *I Know Why the Caged Bird Sings*"—includes all resource material and customizable lesson plan
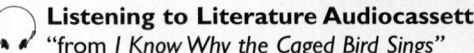 **Listening to Literature Audiocassettes**
"from *I Know Why the Caged Bird Sings*"

from I Know Why the Caged Bird Sings

1936 JULY 1936
SUN MON TUE WED THU FRI SAT
1 2 3 4
5 6 7 8 9 10 11
12 13 14 15 16 17 18
19 20 21 22 23 24 25
26 27 28 29 30 31

Interest Grabber Ask students to think of a person who was important to them. Was there a time or an experience in which someone helped them in a special way? Was he or she there for a turning point in their lives? Use a talk-show format for students to share important experiences. Have two students play the roles of announcer and host. Invite two or three students to be guests on the talk show. Encourage students to use what they have observed from television talk shows to play the parts of the announcer and host. Instruct the "guests" to discuss important events in their lives. Tell students that the memoir they will read describes a time in a girl's life when a special person helped change how she thought about herself.

◆ Build Grammar Skills

Plural and Possessive Nouns If you wish to introduce the grammar concept before students read, refer to the instruction on p. 30.

◆ Literary Focus

MEMOIR

A **memoir** is a form of autobiographical writing—true writing from a person's own life—that deals with the writer's memory of someone or of a significant event. In this excerpt from *I Know Why the Caged Bird Sings*, Angelou writes about her memories of working in the family store, like the one in the photograph.

◆ Reading Strategy

REREAD OR READ AHEAD

Reading can be a many-step process. On a first reading, you may miss details or have questions about what's happening. It makes sense, then, to go back and **reread** a passage to clarify details. Sometimes you may need to **read ahead** to find answers to questions or to understand why an author is presenting certain information.

A chart like the one below can help you note when to reread or read ahead to find an answer.

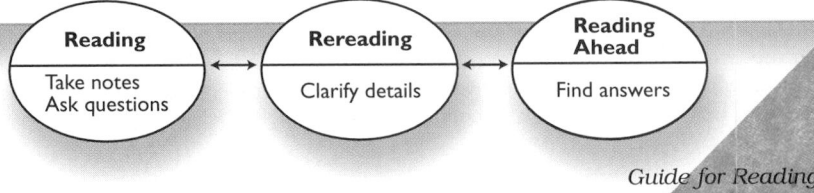

Reading	Rereading	Reading Ahead
Take notes / Ask questions	Clarify details	Find answers

Guide for Reading ◆ 23

Customize for *Less Proficient Readers*

Tell students that the main idea in this story is change in the author's view of herself when she is befriended by someone special. Then, display the Main Idea and Supporting Details Organizer in **Writing and Language Transparencies,** p. 61. Help students use this chart during reading to record details of the author's life that support the main idea. For example, have them record the details the author provides about her thoughts before and after her encounter with Mrs. Flowers. Students can review the chart after reading to study how the main idea is supported by details.

Customize for *More Advanced Students*

Have students take notes as they read in order to prepare a brief oral or written biographical sketch of the author as a young girl, focusing on the changes in her life. Suggest that students use the Series of Events Chain, p. 57, in **Writing and Language Transparencies** to help them note events that lead to the changes in Maya Angelou's life.

Preparing for Standardized Tests

Grammar The grammar concept for this selection is plural and possessive nouns. Explain to students that while both plural nouns and possessive nouns may end with s, possessive nouns include an apostrophe. "Word's mean more than what is set down on paper." The meaning of the sentence is unclear because the possessive noun *Word's* is incorrectly used instead of the plural noun *Words*.

Grammar, usage, and mechanics portions of standardized tests may require students to complete sentences by selecting correct plural or possessive nouns. Choose the correct noun to

complete this sentence:

Mrs. Flowers read the _____ first sentence.

(A) book   (C) books'
(B) books   (D) book's

Guide students to see that *(A) book* and *(B) books* are wrong because the "first sentence" must be part of something being read; therefore, a possessive noun is required. Only one sentence is being read, so the plural possessive *(C) books'* is incorrect. *(D) book's*, a singular possessive noun, is the only word that correctly completes the sentence.

One-Minute Insight This excerpt from Maya Angelou's autobiography describes a turning point in her life. Born Marguerite Johnson, the author lives with her grandmother, uncle, and brother in a small Arkansas town. She enjoys the delicious world of her grandmother's general store and the companionship of her brother, Bailey. Around the age of ten, though, Marguerite becomes withdrawn and stops speaking. Mrs. Bertha Flowers, a woman who is admired in the community, takes an interest in the girl. Building on Marguerite's love of reading, Mrs. Flowers encourages her to read aloud. Mrs. Flowers's interest in Marguerite as a unique individual makes a lasting impression. This excerpt points out the power of language and the influence of others in unlocking doors to personal understanding.

Team Teaching Strategy

The setting of the memoir—a small town in the South during the time of segregation—provides an opportunity to explore a historical and cultural setting of African Americans in the late 1930's. You may want to work with a social studies teacher to coordinate ways of extending instruction.

Customize for
English Language Learners

Have peer tutors help English language learners understand the meanings of unfamiliar expressions as they read the selection. For example, to help students understand the meaning of "Don't you try to make your profit offa me," suggest that peer tutors paraphrase the statement as "Don't give me less than I'm paying for." Have them explain that *offa* derives from *off of,* which in this case means "at my expense."

Customize for
Verbal/Linguistic Learners

Maya Angelou writes about the power of language in her memoir. She exercises this power in her writing through her use of vivid descriptions. Have students note words and phrases from the selection that especially appeal to them. Encourage them to write original sentences using these words.

---

from I Know Why the Caged Bird Sings

Maya Angelou

1 We lived with our grandmother and uncle in the rear of the Store (it was always spoken of with a capital s), which she had owned some twenty-five years.

Early in the century, Momma (we soon stopped calling her Grandmother) sold lunches to the sawmen in the lumberyard (east Stamps) and the seedmen at the cotton gin (west Stamps). Her crisp meat pies and **2** cool lemonade, when joined to her miraculous ability to be in two places at the same time, assured her business success. From being a mobile lunch counter, she set up a stand between the two points of <u>fiscal</u> interest and supplied the workers' needs for a few years. Then she had the Store built in the heart of

the Negro area. Over the years it became the lay center of activities in town. On Saturdays, barbers sat their customers in the shade on the porch of the Store, and troubadours[1] on their ceaseless crawlings through the South leaned across its benches and sang their sad songs of The Brazos[2] while they played juice harps[3] and cigar-box guitars.

The formal name of the Store was the Wm. Johnson General Merchandise Store. Customers could find food staples, a good variety of colored thread, mash for hogs, corn for

---

1. **troubadours** (trōo′ bə dôrz′) *n.*: Traveling singers.
2. **The Brazos** (brä′ əs): Area in central Texas near the Brazos River.
3. **juice** (jōos) **harps:** Small musical instruments held between the teeth and played by plucking.

24 ◆ Coming of Age

 Block Scheduling Strategies

Consider these suggestions to take advantage of extended class time:

• After using the Interest Grabber to draw students into the selection, play the audiocassette "from *I Know Why the Caged Bird Sings*" as students read along. Follow with a class discussion about how the reading enhances the presentation of the story.

• As an alternative, have students read the selection independently. Then, reinforce and extend the selection skills by having students work together in small groups to discuss and com-

plete the Guide for Responding questions, pp. 29–30. Encourage students to take turns reading questions and writing responses.

• Have students work on the *Writer's Solution Language Lab CD-ROM* and *Writer's Solution Writing Lab CD-ROM* to prepare for and complete all or part of the Writing Mini-Lesson. Refer to the teaching suggestions on p. 31 to guide students through the process.

Listening to Literature Audiocassettes

3 ▲ Critical Viewing The town in this painting is similar to the town of Stamps, as described by Angelou. What might it be like to grow up in a town like this? **[Speculate]**

◆Critical Thinking

1 Infer Ask students what they think the author means by "[My grandmother's store] was always spoken of with a capital *s*." *Students should draw on their knowledge of capitalization rules for proper nouns to conclude that when people refer to "the Store," they mean a specific (and important) place, not any store in general.*

Clarification

2 Explain to students that because of segregation in the South, blacks and whites led separate lives within the same town and community. Opportunities that were available to whites often were denied to blacks. The civil rights movement, in which African Americans and others struggled to end such discrimination, was just beginning at the time Angelou lived with her grandmother.

►Critical Viewing◄

3 Speculate Encourage students who are familiar with small-town life to draw on their own experience to add to the details of the painting. *Students may respond that a person living in a town like this may know everyone who lives there; it is also possible to know every place and what each store sells; there is not a lot of traffic; getting from one place to another doesn't take very long.*

◆Reading Strategy

4 Reread or Read Ahead Instruct students to reread the beginning of the excerpt, which implies that *we* refers to the author and another person or persons who share the same grandmother and uncle. Point out that students can combine this information with what they learned in Meet the Author on p. 22 to answer the question. *We refers to the author and her brother, Bailey.*

◆Literary Focus

5 Memoir What do these sentences reveal about the author as a young girl? *Possible responses: She held herself to high standards; she was overly harsh with herself when she made a mistake.*

chickens, coal oil for lamps, light bulbs for the wealthy, shoestrings, hair dressing, balloons, and flower seeds. Anything not visible had only to be ordered.

◆ Reading Strategy
4 Who is meant by the pronoun *we*? Reread to find out.

Until we became familiar enough to belong to the Store and it to us, we were locked up in a Fun House of Things where the attendant had gone home for life. . . .

Weighing the half-pounds of flour, excluding the scoop, and depositing them dust-free into the thin paper sacks held a simple kind of adventure for me. I developed an eye for measuring how full a silver-looking ladle of flour, mash, meal, sugar or corn had to be to push the scale indicator over to eight ounces or one

pound. When I was absolutely accurate our appreciative customers used to admire: "Sister Henderson sure got some smart grandchildrens." If I was off in the Store's favor, the eagle-eyed women would say, "Put some more in that sack, child. Don't you try to make your profit offa me."

Then I would quietly but persistently punish myself. For every bad judgment, the fine was no silver-wrapped kisses, the sweet chocolate drops that I loved more than anything in the world, except Bailey. And maybe canned pineapples. My obsession with pineapples nearly drove me mad. I dreamt of the **5**

◆ Build Vocabulary
fiscal (fis´ kəl) *adj.*: Having to do with finances

from *I Know Why the Caged Bird Sings* ◆ 25

Humanities: Art

Parkville, Main Street (Missouri), 1933, by Gale Stockwell

The painting on this page of a small Midwestern town in 1933 evokes the time and place of the selection's setting. Invite students to study the picture to discover clues that provide information about the place it portrays.

1. What details in the painting tell you that this is not a modern scene? *The cars are old; there is an old-fashioned street lamp; there are no illuminated signs in the stores.*

2. Describe other characteristics of this town,

and explain how you came to your conclusions. *The town is on a hill, but it is probably in a valley because of the mountains in the background; the few pedestrians, cars, and trucks indicate a small population; there is a train crossing, but no station is visible.*

3. How does the scene in the painting differ from the setting of the story? *The town seems more prosperous; the storefronts do not have porches, instead they have display windows; there are more stores and businesses; there are fewer people and activities.*

❶ Draw Conclusions Ask students why they think the Store was the author's favorite place to be. *The Store was a center of activity in the community; the sights and smells were exciting; there were good treats; and it was a part of her home.*

Clarification

❷ *Y'all* is a contraction of *you* and *all*, meaning "you jointly." The expression has been widely used in the southern United States for many years. Many people incorrectly believe that southerners use *you-all* to mean one person. In fact, it should only be addressed to individuals when they are thought of as representatives of a group, as when asking a supermarket clerk "Do y'all sell beans?"

◆LITERATURE AND YOUR LIFE

❸ The author states that she has always admired Bertha Flowers. Invite students to list some of the qualities of Mrs. Flowers that the author admires. Then, have them describe the qualities of a person they admire and respect. Encourage students to be specific and to give examples. List these qualities on the board, and help students determine which qualities are universally admired.

◆Reading Strategy

❹ Reread or Read Ahead The meaning of this paragraph may be unclear to students. Suggest that they read ahead through the next page to learn why Momma and Mrs. Flowers exchange knowing looks. *From reading ahead, students will learn that Mrs. Flowers knows what Marguerite's teachers have reported and that she and Momma have discussed Marguerite's reading habits.*

---

days when I would be grown and able to buy a whole carton for myself alone.

Although the syrupy golden rings sat in their exotic cans on our shelves year round, we only tasted them during Christmas. Momma used the juice to make almost-black fruit cakes. Then she lined heavy soot-encrusted iron skillets with the pine-apple rings for rich upside-down cakes. Bailey and I received one slice each, and I carried mine around for hours, shredding off the fruit until nothing was left except the perfume on my fingers. I'd like to think that my desire for pineapples was so sacred that I wouldn't allow myself to steal a can (which was possible) and eat it alone out in the garden, but I'm certain that I must have weighed the possibility of the scent exposing me and didn't have the nerve to attempt it.

❶ Until I was thirteen and left Arkansas for good, the Store was my favorite place to be. Alone and empty in the mornings, it looked like an unopened present from a stranger. Opening the front doors was pulling the ribbon off the unexpected gift. The light would come in softly (we faced north), easing itself over the shelves of mackerel, salmon, tobacco, thread. It fell flat on the big vat of lard and by noontime during the summer the grease had softened to a thick soup. Whenever I walked into the Store in the afternoon, I sensed that it was tired. I alone could hear the slow pulse of its job half done. But just before bedtime, after numerous people had walked in and out, had argued over their bills, or joked about their neighbors, or just dropped in "to give **❷** Sister Henderson a 'Hi y'all,'" the promise of magic mornings returned to the Store and spread itself over the family in washed life waves. . . .

When Maya was about ten years old, she returned to Stamps from a visit to St. Louis with her mother. She had become depressed and withdrawn.

For nearly a year, I sopped around the house, the Store, the school and the church, like an old biscuit, dirty and inedible. Then I met, or rather got to know, the lady who threw me my first lifeline.

Mrs. Bertha Flowers was the aristocrat[4] of Black Stamps. She had the grace of control to appear warm in the coldest weather, and on the Arkansas summer days it seemed she had a private breeze which swirled around, cooling her. She was thin without the <u>taut</u> look of wiry people, and her printed voile[5] dresses and flowered hats were as right for her as denim overalls for a farmer. She was our side's answer to the richest white woman in town.

Her skin was a rich black that would have peeled like a plum if snagged, but then no one would have thought of getting close enough to Mrs. Flowers to ruffle her dress, let alone snag her skin. She didn't encourage familiarity. She wore gloves too.

I don't think I ever saw Mrs. Flowers laugh, but she smiled often. A slow widening of her thin black lips to show even, small white teeth, then the slow effortless closing. When she chose to smile on me, I always wanted to thank her. The action was so graceful and inclusively <u>benign</u>.

❸ She was one of the few gentlewomen I have ever known, and has remained throughout my life the measure of what a human being can be. . . .

One summer afternoon, sweet-milk fresh in my memory, she stopped at the Store to buy provisions. Another Negro woman of her health and age would have been expected to carry the paper sacks home in one hand, but Momma said, "Sister Flowers, I'll send Bailey up to your house with these things."

❹ She smiled that slow dragging smile, "Thank you, Mrs. Henderson. I'd prefer Marguerite, though." My name was beautiful when she said it. "I've been meaning to talk to her, anyway." They gave each other age-group looks.

---

4. **aristocrat** (ə ris´ tə krat) *n.*: Person belonging to the upper class.
5. **voile** (voil) *n.*: Light cotton fabric.

Viewing and Representing Mini-Lesson

Advertisement

This mini-lesson supports the Advertisement project in the Idea Bank on p. 31.

Introduce Explain that students will create posters that advertise merchandise sold in the Wm. Johnson General Merchandise Store. Have students work with partners to list the merchandise mentioned in the selection.

Develop Have groups of students discuss elements which should be included in a printed advertisement for a general store,

such as its name, location, hours of operation, items for sale or services provided, special sales or discounts, and special qualities such as friendly service or guarantees. To generate design ideas, provide students with newspaper or flyer advertisements for stores in their community.

Apply Ask students to use markers or stencils to create their individual posters, remembering to fulfill the project's requirements: a drawing of the store, the merchandise it sells, and its importance as a center

of activity. Have students display their posters to the class. Encourage them to discuss the basis for the design and the information they want to emphasize.

Assess Evaluate students' work based on their inclusion of the project requirements and selection's information about the store, as well as how clearly and effectively the information is presented and explained. You may write a checklist on the board based on these criteria and have students use the checklist to assess their own work.

Momma said, "Well, that's all right then. Sister, go and change your dress. You going to Sister Flowers's. . . ."

There was a little path beside the rocky road, and Mrs. Flowers walked in front swinging her arms and picking her way over the stones.

She said, without turning her head, to me, "I hear you're doing very good school work, Marguerite, but that it's all written. The teachers report that they have trouble getting you to talk in class." We passed the triangular farm on our left and the path widened to allow us to walk together. I hung back in the separate unasked and unanswerable questions.

"Come and walk along with me, Marguerite." I couldn't have refused even if I wanted to. She pronounced my name so nicely. Or more correctly, she spoke each word with such clarity that I was certain a foreigner who didn't understand English could have understood her.

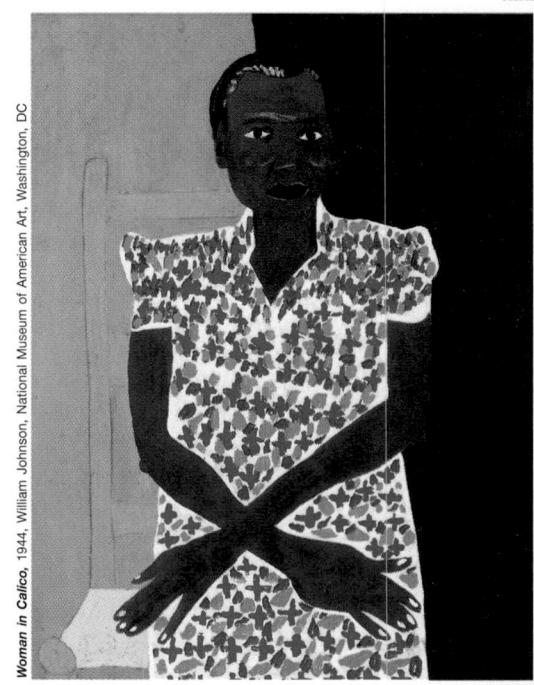

Woman in Calico, 1944, William Johnson, National Museum of American Art, Washington, DC

> ◆ **Literary Focus**
> **5** What does this passage reveal about Angelou's personality?

"Now no one is going to make you talk—possibly no one can. But bear in mind, language is man's way of communicating with his fellow man and it is language alone which separates him from the lower animals." That was a totally new idea to me, and I would need time to think about it.

"Your grandmother says you read a lot. Every chance you get. That's good, but not good enough. Words mean more than what is set down on paper. It takes the human **7** voice to <u>infuse</u> them with the shades of deeper meaning."

I memorized the part about the human voice infusing words. It seemed so valid and poetic.

She said she was going to give me some books and that I not only must read them, I must read them aloud. She suggested that I

◆ **Build Vocabulary**
taut (tôt) *adj.*: Tightly stretched
benign (bi nīn´) *adj.*: Kindly
infuse (in fyo͞oz´) *v.*: Put into

▲ **Critical Viewing** Reread the description of Mrs. Flowers on page 26. How well does this **8** painting capture her essence? Explain. **[Assess]**

try to make a sentence sound in as many different ways as possible.

"I'll accept no excuse if you return a book to me that has been badly handled." My imagination boggled at the punishment I would deserve if in fact I did abuse a book of Mrs. Flowers'. Death would be too kind and brief.

The odors in the house surprised me. Somehow I had never connected Mrs. Flowers with food or eating or any other common experience of common people. There must have been an outhouse, too, **9** but my mind never recorded it.

The sweet scent of vanilla had met us as she opened the door.

"I made tea cookies this morning. You see, I had planned to invite you for cookies and lemonade so we could have this little chat. The lemonade is in the icebox."

from *I Know Why the Caged Bird Sings* ◆ 27

◆**Literary Focus**
5 **Memoir** Ask students to reread the passage to discover what Angelou reveals about herself. Suggest that students reach more than one conclusion about the author. *Students should see that Angelou already has a love of language, because she appreciates the clear pronunciation used by Mrs. Flowers. Angelou also reveals that she is open to new ideas, because she recognizes a new concept and decides to consider its truth.*

Comprehension Check
6 Ask students to explain why Mrs. Flowers says this to Marguerite. *She knows that Marguerite is withdrawn, and she wants her to start talking to people.*

◆**Critical Thinking**
7 **Infer** Ask students to explain this statement by Mrs. Flowers. *The human voice adds meaning to spoken words through variations in loudness and pitch, the amount of emphasis placed on different syllables in a word, pauses for effect, the tone or mood of speech, and so on.*

▶**Critical Viewing**◀
8 **Assess** *The woman in the painting sits very properly in her chair, which reflects Mrs. Flowers's proper attitude. She is also dressed neatly and looks friendly like Mrs. Flowers. The painting captures a calm, serene manner that Mrs. Flowers always seems to have.*

◆**Critical Thinking**
9 **Predict** Ask students to predict what Mrs. Flowers and Marguerite will do during the rest of the visit. *Based on the exchange so far, Mrs. Flowers will probably offer more advice and Marguerite will continue to listen quietly, while appreciating both Mrs. Flowers's words and attention.*

Customize for
Verbal/Linguistic Learners
Have students make a list of the foods described by Maya Angelou on these two pages. Ask students to describe to a partner some of their own "food memories" from childhood.

Humanities: Art

Woman in Calico, by William Johnson
William Johnson (1901–1970) is known for paintings that depict the African American experience in the United States. Like Angelou, Johnson was raised in the segregated South. Explain that *Woman in Calico* is among a series of portraits of family members and friends in his native South Carolina. Johnson uses flat, geometric shapes and patterns to show a woman seated calmly in a chair. Connect the artwork to the selection by leading students to see that Angelou has also created a portrait of Mrs. Flowers, but with words.

1. How does the simple style of the painting reflect its subject? *The style may show that the woman is uncomplicated; others may say it invites the viewer to consider the woman's hidden qualities.*
2. In what ways does the woman in this painting resemble Mrs. Flowers? *The woman seems confident and poised.*
3. Describe a portrait of Marguerite by the same artist. *The painting might show a 10-year-old girl in a dress, seated quietly in a chair, looking shy but curious. Students may also describe Marguerite engaged in another activity from the story.*

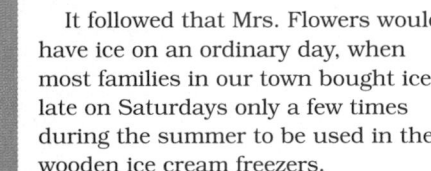

◆ Critical Thinking

❶ Relate As a young girl, Angelou feels that everything about Mrs. Flowers is perfect. Have students discuss whether her judgment is accurate. Ask students if they have ever thought an older person was perfect and whether their opinion ever changed. *Students should realize that no one is perfect, but that Mrs. Flowers is perfect for Marguerite's needs. Students should relate the motives for Marguerite's opinion to people and events in their own lives.*

Comprehension Check ☑

❷ When Mrs. Flowers begins reading aloud from the novel, Angelou writes, "I heard poetry for the first time in my life." What does the author mean by this? *The sound and rhythm of Mrs. Flowers's voice was musical, as though she were reading a poem.*

◆ Reading Strategy

❸ Reread or Read Ahead Ask students to reread to explain what Angelou means by "On that first day . . ." *Students should conclude that the story describes only the first of many visits, which is also supported by the sentence on p. 28 that begins, "As I ate she began the first of what we later called 'my lessons in living,'" and the sentence near the end of the same page that begins, "Next time you pay me a visit . . ."*

◆ Literary Focus

❹ Memoir Review with students that a memoir is the writer's remembrance of an important person or event from the writer's life. Ask students to explain why Marguerite feels good about her visit with Mrs. Flowers. *The attention given by Mrs. Flowers proves that she likes Marguerite, and this makes the withdrawn girl feel good about herself.*

It followed that Mrs. Flowers would have ice on an ordinary day, when most families in our town bought ice late on Saturdays only a few times during the summer to be used in the wooden ice cream freezers.

She took the bags from me and disappeared through the kitchen door. I looked around the room that I had never in my wildest fantasies imagined I would see. Browned photographs leered or threatened from the walls and the white, freshly done curtains pushed against themselves and against the wind. I wanted to gobble up the room entire and take it to Bailey, who would help me analyze and enjoy it.

"Have a seat, Marguerite. Over there by the table." She carried a platter covered with a tea towel. Although she warned that she hadn't tried her hand at baking sweets for some time, I was certain that like **❶** everything else about her the cookies would be perfect.

They were flat round wafers, slightly browned on the edges and butter-yellow in the center. With the cold lemonade they were sufficient for childhood's lifelong diet. Remembering my manners, I took nice little ladylike bites off the edges. She said she had made them expressly for me and that she had a few in the kitchen that I could take home to my brother. So I jammed one whole cake in my mouth and the rough crumbs scratched the insides of my jaws, and if I hadn't had to swallow, it would have been a dream come true.

As I ate she began the first of what we later called "my lessons in living." She said that I must always be <u>intolerant</u> of ignorance but understanding of illiteracy. That some people, unable to go to school, were more educated and even more intelligent than college professors. She

encouraged me to listen carefully to what country people called mother wit. That in those homely sayings was <u>couched</u> the collective wisdom of generations.

When I finished the cookies she brushed off the table and brought a thick, small book from the bookcase. I had read *A Tale of Two Cities* and found it up to my standards as a romantic novel. She opened the first page and I heard poetry for the first **❷** time in my life.

"It was the best of times and the worst of times . . ." Her voice slid in and curved down through and over the words. She was nearly singing. I wanted to look at the pages. Were they the same that I had read? Or were there notes, music, lined on the pages, as in a hymn book? Her sounds began cascading gently. I knew from listening to a thousand preachers that she was nearing the end of her reading, and I hadn't really heard, heard to understand, a single word.

"How do you like that?"

It occurred to me that she expected a response. The sweet vanilla flavor was still on my tongue and her reading was a wonder in my ears. I had to speak.

I said, "Yes, ma'am." It was the least I could do, but it was the most also.

"There's one more thing. Take this book of poems and memorize one for me. Next time you pay me a visit, I want you to recite."

I have tried often to search behind the sophistication of years for the enchantment I so easily found in those

◆ Build Vocabulary

intolerant (in täl´ ər ənt) *adj.*: Not able or willing to accept

couched (koucht) *v.*: Put into words; expressed

◆◆ Speaking and Listening Mini-Lesson

Oral Interpretation

This mini-lesson supports the Speaking and Listening activity in the Idea Bank on p. 31.

Introduce Explain that through oral interpretation a reader can communicate the meaning of a passage through volume, pitch, speed, pronunciation, and tone of voice. Write the sentence "I like those cookies" on the board. Demonstrate different interpretations of the sentence by using a serious tone, an incredulous tone, or an exclamation of surprise; stressing different words;

or speaking loudly, softly, or in singsong.

Develop Have students form groups and choose a passage from the selection. Then, direct students to develop their own oral interpretations of that passage. To prepare, students should follow steps 3 through 6 in the Peer Assessment: Oral Interpretation form in **Alternative Assessment,** p. 115. Explain that each interpretation should be true to the author's intent, but each student should make his or her delivery different from the rest of the group.

Apply Have students give their oral interpretations for the class. After each group's readings, have the class discuss variations among the interpretations.

Assess Evaluate each student's performance based on the introduction, prepared script, overall impression, and audience rapport. Students may use another copy of the Peer Assessment: Oral Interpretation form, p. 115, in **Alternative Assessment** to evaluate each group's performance.

gifts. The essence escapes but its aura[6] remains. To be allowed, no, invited, into the private lives of strangers, and to share their joys and fears, was a chance to exchange the Southern bitter wormwood[7] for a cup of mead with Beowulf[8] or a hot cup of tea and milk with Oliver Twist. When I said aloud, "It is a far far better thing that I do, than I have ever done . . ."[9] tears of love filled my eyes at my selflessness.

---

6. **aura** (ôr′ ə) *n.*: Atmosphere or quality.
7. **wormwood** (wʉrm′ wŏŏd′) *n.*: Plant that produces a bitter oil.
8. **Beowulf** (bā′ ə wŏŏlf′): Hero of an old Anglo-Saxon epic. People in this poem drink mead, (mēd), a drink made with honey and water.
9. **"It is . . . than I have ever done":** Speech from *A Tale of Two Cities* by Charles Dickens.

On that first day, I ran down the hill and into the road (few cars ever came along it) and had the good sense to stop running before I reached the Store.

I was liked, and what a difference it made. I was respected not as Mrs. Henderson's grandchild or Bailey's sister but for just being Marguerite Johnson.

Childhood's logic never asks to be proved (all conclusions are absolute). I didn't question why Mrs. Flowers had singled me out for attention, nor did it occur to me that Momma might have asked her to give me a little talking to. All I cared about was that she had made tea cookies for *me* and read to *me* from her favorite book. It was enough to prove that she liked me.

Guide for Responding

◆ LITERATURE AND YOUR LIFE

Reader's Response Does Mrs. Flowers remind you of anyone you know? Explain.

Thematic Focus What does Maya learn about herself as a result of her visit with Mrs. Flowers?

Thank-You Note As the character Marguerite, write a thank-you note to Mrs. Flowers following the visit.

☑ Check Your Comprehension

1. Describe how the "Store" came into existence.
2. According to Mrs. Flowers, for what two reasons is language important?
3. Although Marguerite reads a great deal, what does she not do?
4. What does Mrs. Flowers tell Marguerite in the first of her "lessons in living"?
5. Mrs. Flowers makes cookies and reads to Marguerite. What do these actions prove to Marguerite?

◆ Critical Thinking

INTERPRET
1. What can you tell about Marguerite's character from her actions at the Store? **[Infer]**
2. Why does Mrs. Flowers tell Marguerite to read aloud and in as many different ways as possible? **[Interpret]**
3. How do you think Marguerite changes as a result of her meetings with Mrs. Flowers? **[Draw Conclusions]**
4. Why has Mrs. Flowers remained "the measure of what a human being can be"? **[Interpret]**

APPLY
5. Mrs. Flowers throws Marguerite a "lifeline" by talking and reading with her. In what other ways do people offer "lifelines"? **[Relate]**

EXTEND
6. Angelou's memoir takes place during a time in which segregation laws governed most of the South. How might Angelou's self-esteem have been affected by those laws? **[Social Studies Link]**

from I Know Why the Caged Bird Sings ◆ 29

Beyond the Selection

FURTHER READING
Other Works by Maya Angelou
All God's Children Need Traveling Shoes
"On the Pulse of Morning"
I Know Why the Caged Bird Sings—If you wish to recommend this book (the longer work from which the selection is excerpted) to students, please be aware that it contains sensitive issues that may be upsetting or difficult for some students.

INTERNET
We suggest the following sites on the Internet (all Web sites are subject to change).

For additional information about Maya Angelou:
http://hs1.hst.msu.edu/~cal/caleb/angelou.html

For more information about the artist William Johnson and views of his art:
http://www.nku.edu/~diesmanj/whjohnson.html

We *strongly recommend* that you preview these sites before you send students to them.

Answers

◆ Reading Strategy

1. Students may mention details such as why Marguerite, instead of Bailey, carried Mrs. Flowers's purchases home and questions such as what Angelou means by the literary references in the third-to-last paragraph of the selection.
2. Students may mention information such as the reasons Mrs. Flowers took an interest in Marguerite.

◆ Build Vocabulary

Using Forms of *tolerate*
1. tolerance; intolerant
2. tolerable; tolerant

Spelling Strategy
1. design; 2. assign; 3. sign

Using the Word Bank
1. taut
2. fiscal
3. infuse
4. benign
5. couched
6. intolerant

◆ Literary Focus

1. The people in the Store are not as well-spoken or refined as Mrs. Flowers. The sharp contrast in her demeanor and appearance indicate that something new and important is about to happen.
2. Angelou sees Mrs. Flowers as graceful, intelligent, and kind—as someone to look up to. Marguerite describes her as thin, well-dressed, with beautiful skin, somewhat distant, and a gentlewoman.
3. It is the first time Angelou realizes that she is liked and respected for herself and not in relation to others.

◆ Build Grammar Skills

1. *Mrs. Flowers's:* possessive
2. *pictures':* possessive
3. *Marguerite's:* possessive
4. *words:* plural
5. *poems:* plural

 **Writer's Solution**

For additional instruction and practice, use the lesson in the *Writer's Solution Language Lab CD-ROM* on Plural and Possessive Nouns in the Using Nouns section.

Guide for Responding (continued)

◆ Reading Strategy

REREAD OR READ AHEAD

Rereading can help you answer questions or clear up confusing issues. Another strategy for clearing up confusion or piecing together meaning is to **read ahead** with a specific purpose in mind.
1. Give two questions or details that you clarified by rereading.
2. What question or piece of information made sense to you after you read ahead?

◆ Build Vocabulary

USING FORMS OF *tolerate*

Knowing that *tolerate* means "to recognize someone else's beliefs or actions," you can determine the meaning of its related forms. Complete the following sentences with an appropriate related word.

intolerant tolerance tolerable tolerant
1. Mrs. Flowers suggested that Marguerite show _____?_____ toward people who are illiterate, but to always be _____?_____ of ignorance.
2. Marguerite's working at the store was _____?_____, but Mrs. Flowers was _____?_____ and helped her realize that she was special.

SPELLING STRATEGY

In some words, like *benign*, the īn sound is spelled *ign*, with a silent *g*. Complete each of the following with an *ign* word that fits the definition.
1. A pattern or arrangement of parts: _____?_____
2. To give out as a task, such as homework: _____?_____
3. A publicly displayed board: _____?_____

USING THE WORD BANK

In your notebook, write the word from the Word Bank that best completes each sentence.
1. The rope was pulled _____?_____ to secure the boxes of goods.
2. For _____?_____ reasons, the Store was open late.
3. Mrs. Flowers used lemons to _____?_____ her tea.
4. Although stern, Mrs. Flowers was also _____?_____.
5. Her voice was _____?_____ with wisdom.
6. Marguerite learned not to be _____?_____ of those who are unschooled.

◆ Literary Focus

MEMOIR

This **memoir** focuses on a significant person and a significant event in Maya Angelou's life—Mrs. Flowers and her positive influence on young Marguerite.
1. Why is Angelou's description of life at the Store important to the introduction of Mrs. Flowers?
2. Why is Angelou so impressed with Mrs. Flowers? How does she describe her?
3. Why does the visit to Mrs. Flowers's house remain so memorable to Angelou?

◆ Build Grammar Skills

PLURAL AND POSSESSIVE NOUNS

Plural and possessive nouns are sometimes confused. A **plural noun** indicates more than one person, place, thing, or idea. Most plural nouns end with the letter *-s*.

Plural Nouns: On *Saturdays, barbers* sat their *customers* in the shade on the porch. . . .

A **possessive noun** shows ownership, belonging, or other close relationship. A possessive noun can be **singular,** ending in *-'s,* or **plural,** usually ending in *-s'.*

Singular Possessive: If I was off in the *Store's* favor, the eagle-eyed woman would . . .

Plural Possessive: "[S]he . . . supplied the *workers'* needs for a few years."

Practice In your notebook, identify whether each italicized noun is plural or possessive.
1. *Mrs. Flowers's* home smelled like vanilla.
2. The *pictures'* torn edges and fading colors made their appearance threatening.
3. *Marguerite's* shyness showed when she first visited Mrs. Flowers.
4. The only *words* she uttered during her visit were "yes, ma'am."
5. Take this book of *poems* and memorize one.

Writing Application Write a paragraph using the plural of the nouns *store, owner,* and *customer.* Then, write a paragraph making these nouns plural and possessive.

Build Your Portfolio

Idea Bank

Writing

1. **Journal Entry** Write a journal entry that Maya Angelou might have written after her visit with Mrs. Flowers. Include a description of how she felt during and after the visit.

2. **Memoir Poem** Choose a significant event in your life to describe in a poem. Choose details that express emotion as well as tell your story.

3. **Analysis** Write a brief analysis. In it, point out which details about Mrs. Flowers's home and her treatment of Angleou indicate the writer's feeling about that fateful visit.

Speaking and Listening

4. **Oral Interpretation [Group Activity]** Mrs. Flowers says that the way in which words are spoken can help determine their meaning. Working with a group of classmates, choose a passage from the story to read aloud. Each member should read the passage to the class, stressing different words.

5. **Oral Tribute** Put yourself in Angelou's shoes, and deliver an oral tribute about Mrs. Flowers to your class. Use details from the story to help you to describe her. **[Performing Arts Link]**

Projects

6. **Advertisement** Create a poster advertising the Wm. Johnson General Merchandise Store. List the merchandise mentioned in the selection, and emphasize its importance as a center of activity for this rural town in Arkansas. **[Art Link]**

7. **Photo Essay [Group Activity]** With a group, compile a photo essay of the rural South in the 1930's and 1940's. Photocopy the photographs, and write explanatory captions for them. Display your photo essay in the classroom. **[Social Studies Link]**

Writing Mini-Lesson

Personal Memoir About a Turning Point

Angelou's visit with Mrs. Flowers was a turning point in her life—one that changed her outlook and future behavior. Cast your thoughts back to a time when you experienced a turning point of some kind. Then, write a memoir that describes the event. Personalize the memoir by choosing details that infuse the writing with your personality.

Writing Skills Focus: Elaborate to Make Writing Personal

Include details that explain why the event you're describing was so significant. For example, in the following passage, Angelou makes her writing personal by describing why her visit with Mrs. Flowers was a turning point.

Model From the Story

I was liked, and what a difference it made. I was respected not as Mrs. Henderson's grandchild or Bailey's sister but for just being Marguerite Johnson.

Prewriting List specific details that describe your turning point. Include explanations of how events and people made you feel and why. Then, organize the details into a sequence.

Drafting Use your organized list as the basis for drafting your memoir. As you write, include transitions, such as *after that* and *to our surprise,* that make connections between ideas clear.

Revising Revise your personal memoir by looking for places where adding personal details will help you reveal your feelings and emotions at the time of the event.

> ◆ **Grammar Application**
> Check all words that end in *-s.* Do not use apostrophes to make a word plural. Use apostrophes only to show possession.

from I Know Why the Caged Bird Sings ◆ 31

Idea Bank

Following are suggestions for matching the Idea Bank topics with your students' performance levels and learning modalities:

Customize for *Performance Levels*
Less Advanced Students: 1, 4
Average Students: 3, 4, 5, 6
More Advanced Students: 2, 5, 7

Customize for *Learning Modalities*
Verbal/Linguistic: 1, 2, 3, 4, 5, 7
Musical/Rhythmic: 5
Visual/Spatial: 6
Logical/Mathematical: 7
Interpersonal: 4
Intrapersonal: 2

Writing Mini-Lesson

Refer students to the Writing Handbook in the back of the book for instruction on the writing process and for further information on personal narrative. Have students use the Series of Events Chain in **Writing and Language Transparencies,** p. 57, to arrange their prewriting examples.

✎ Writer's Solution

Writing Lab CD-ROM
Have students complete the tutorial on Expression. Follow these steps:
1. Have students use the Writing Hints on recalling personal experience or the personal memoir Inspirations for Expression to generate topic ideas.
2. For drafting on the computer, have students review the audio-annotated organization models and Student Model of a personal memoir.
3. Have students use the Self-Evaluation Checklist on Expression in the Revising section for help with their revisions.

Writer's Solution Sourcebook
Have students use Chapter 1, "Expression," pp. 1–31, for additional support. This chapter includes in-depth instruction on gathering personal details, p. 19.

✓ ASSESSMENT OPTIONS

Formal Assessment, Selection Test, pp. 7–9, and Assessment Resources Software. The selection test is designed so that it can be customized easily to the performance levels of your students.

Alternative Assessment, p. 3, includes options for less advanced students, more advanced students, visual/spatial learners, interpersonal learners, and verbal/linguistic learners.

PORTFOLIO ASSESSMENT
Use the following rubrics in the **Alternative Assessment** booklet to assess student writing:
Journal Entry: Narrative Based on Personal Experience, p. 92
Memoir Poem: Poetry, p. 104
Letter: Expression, p. 90
Writing Mini-Lesson: Narrative Based on Personal Experience, p. 92

Guide for Reading

OBJECTIVES

1. To read, comprehend, and interpret three poems
2. To relate poetry to personal experience
3. To paraphrase lines of poetry
4. To identify the speaker in a poem
5. To build vocabulary in context and use the word root *-verg-*
6. To recognize general and specific nouns
7. To write a persuasive essay
8. To respond to the poems through writing, speaking and listening, and projects

SKILLS INSTRUCTION

Vocabulary:
Word Roots: *-verg-*

Spelling:
Adding *-ing* to a Verb

Grammar:
General and Specific Nouns

Reading Strategy:
Paraphrase

Literary Focus:
The Speaker in a Poem

Writing:
Supporting Your Argument

Speaking and Listening:
Speech (Teacher Edition)

Viewing and Representing:
Illustration (Teacher Edition)

PORTFOLIO OPPORTUNITIES

Writing: List; Dialogue; Compare and Contrast
Writing Mini-Lesson: Persuasive Essay
Speaking and Listening: Dramatic Scene; Speech
Projects: Final Words; Illustration

More About the Authors

Robert Frost tried for almost 12 years to get his poetry published, then it received critical acclaim, and he went on to win four Pulitzer Prizes. Congress gave him a medal to recognize his poetry's enrichment of U.S. culture and the world's philosophy.

Walter de la Mare lived most of his life near London, England. When he received a yearly pension from the British government, he devoted himself to writing. His literary talent made him a successful poet, novelist, and editor of poetry anthologies.

Dorothy Parker began her literary career in 1916 as a magazine writer. For several years, she was the regular book reviewer for *The New Yorker*. Today, she is best remembered for her stories and poems, which are known for their wit and sarcasm.

Meet the Authors:

Robert Frost (1874–1963)

One of the high points for poetry in the twentieth century was Robert Frost's reading of his poem "The Gift Outright" at the inauguration of President John F. Kennedy. Many of Frost's poems are set in or are about some aspect of rural New England, and they contain the same rhythms as everyday spoken English.

Walter de la Mare (1873–1956)

British poet and novelist Walter de la Mare has been called the "last poet of the Romantic tradition." De la Mare believed that the world beyond human experience could best be understood through the imagination. His poetry has a sense of magic about it, with subject matter that includes childhood, nature, dreams, and the uncanny.

Dorothy Parker (1893–1967)

A poet, short-story writer, and famed wit, Dorothy Parker has written many poems that comment on departed and departing love and various kinds of suitors. In New York literary circles, Parker was known as a member of the Algonquin Round Table. This group of writers lunched regularly at the Algonquin Hotel in the 1920's, trading brilliant insults and witty observations.

◆ LITERATURE AND YOUR LIFE

CONNECT YOUR EXPERIENCE

Making simple decisions, like choosing a fork in the road like the one in this photograph, may inspire you to think about life—where you've been, the choices you've made, and what the future holds. In these poems, the speakers reflect upon their lives and how they've chosen to live them.

THEMATIC FOCUS: Arriving at Understanding

As you read, think about the lessons people learn from important life decisions.

◆ Background for Understanding

SCIENCE

In "All But Blind," the speaker compares himself to creatures that are blind or have poor vision: moles, bats, and barn owls. Moles are small furry blind animals who live underground. Bats, although not blind, have very poor eyesight. Barn owls have eyes that are much smaller than those of other types of owls, leading some to believe that they lack adequate vision.

◆ Build Vocabulary

WORD ROOTS: -verg-

The word root *-verg-* means "to bend or turn." When preceded by the prefix *di-* from *dis-*, meaning "apart," you can figure out that *diverged*, as used in "The Road Not Taken," means "bending apart."

WORD BANK

Which word from the list might mean "burning without flame"? Check the Build Vocabulary box on page 36 to see if you chose correctly.

diverged
blunders
smoldering
lilting

Prentice Hall Literature Program Resources

REINFORCE / RETEACH / EXTEND

Selection Support Pages
Build Vocabulary: Word Roots: *-verg-*, p. 17
Build Spelling Skills, p. 18
Build Grammar Skills: General and Specific Nouns, p. 19
Reading Strategy: Paraphrase, p. 20
Literary Focus: The Speaker in a Poem, p. 21

Strategies for Diverse Student Needs, pp. 7–8

Beyond Literature Workplace Skills: Decision Making, p. 4

Formal Assessment Selection Test, pp. 10–12, Assessment Resources Software

Alternative Assessment, p. 4

Writing and Language Transparencies
Main Idea and Supporting Details Organizer, p. 61

Resource Pro CD-ROM
"The Road Not Taken"; "All But Blind"; "The Choice"

 **Listening to Literature Audiocassettes**
"The Road Not Taken"; "All But Blind"; "The Choice"

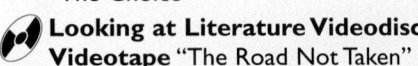 **Looking at Literature Videodisc/ Videotape** "The Road Not Taken"

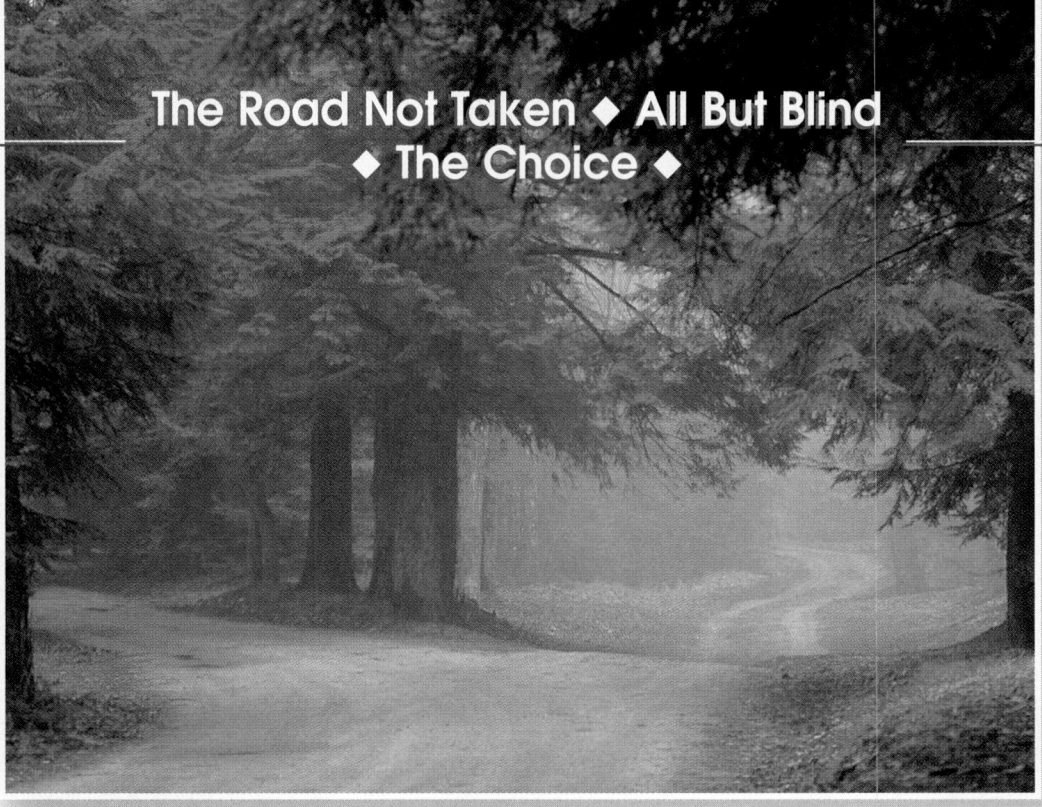

The Road Not Taken ◆ All But Blind
◆ The Choice ◆

◆ Literary Focus
THE SPEAKER IN A POEM

The **speaker in a poem** is the voice assumed by the writer of the poem. Sometimes the speaker is the poet; sometimes the speaker is a character the poet has created. This character may not even be human. It could be a lamp, a butterfly, a princess in disguise, or a tree. Don't be fooled by the use of the pronoun "I" in a poem: This does not always mean that the poem's speaker is the author.

◆ Reading Strategy
PARAPHRASE

Most poems contain language unlike everyday speech. To better understand poetry, **paraphrase,** or restate the lines in your own words.

Original: All but blind/In his chambered hole/Gropes for worms/The four-clawed Mole.

Paraphrase: The nearly blind mole searches for worms in his underground cave.

Apply this technique to other lines in the poems, filling out a chart like the one below.

Poem Title	Original Lines	Paraphrased Lines
The Road Not Taken	as just as fair	just as nice
All But Blind		
The Choice		

 Discuss with students that life is full of choices, and many times choices cause regret. Invite them to think about whether they have ever asked themselves, "What if?" For instance, "What if I had studied for my math test instead of going to the concert?" or "What if I had saved my money for a CD instead of spending it on gum and magazines?" Then, lead students into the poems by explaining that each poem describes a choice. What if the speakers of the poems had chosen differently?

◆ Build Grammar Skills

General and Specific Nouns If you wish to introduce the grammar concept before students read, refer to the instruction on p. 38.

Customize for
Less Proficient Readers
Students may benefit from listening to the recording of the poems prior to reading. Encourage them to listen not only to the words but also for the tone of each poem. The manner in which the poems are read can offer clues to help them decide whether the speaker is satisfied with his or her choice.

Listening to Literature Audiocassettes

Customize for
More Advanced Students
After students read the three poems, invite them to write a brief description or poem that answers the question, "What if the speaker had chosen differently?" In "The Road Not Taken," what if the speaker had gone the other way? In "All But Blind," what if the speaker had not been blind to someone? And in "The Choice," what if the speaker had chosen the other man? Encourage them to share their responses with the class.

Customize for
English Language Learners
Use body language as you read the poems aloud. For instance, as you read the beginning of "The Road Not Taken," indicate two choices and indecision by pointing and shrugging; in "All But Blind," you can pantomime groping; and in "The Choice," use facial expressions to indicate the speaker's regretful attitude toward the choice she didn't make.

 Preparing for Standardized Tests

Grammar and Analogies Understanding the relationship between general and specific nouns may help students complete analogy portions of standardized tests. Write the following analogy on the board, and tell students it is read "bird is to barn owl as gem is to what?" The analogy can be completed with a specific noun, such as ruby, emerald, diamond, and so forth.

bird : barn owl :: gem : _____
Completing an analogy requires determining the relationship between the first two items and then finding a word that applies to the second item

that satisfies the same relationship. Standardized tests may offer a choice of words to complete an analogy.

writer : poet :: house : _____
    (A) building   (C) mansion
    (B) apartment   (D) people

Point out to students that they must select the best answer to complete an analogy. In this sample analogy, "writer" is a general noun and "poet" is a specific noun, so the best answer will be a specific noun that relates to "house" as a general noun: *(C) mansion.*

One-Minute Insight

On the surface, "The Road Not Taken" is about a walk in the woods. On a deeper level, it is about what to do when faced with life's important decisions. The speaker must decide which path to follow—which way to live his or her life—knowing that whichever decision is made, he or she is bound to wonder if it is the right one. As the speaker comes to the understanding that there is no way to know which is the right decision, the less traveled road becomes the right choice simply because it is the road taken.

◆ Literary Focus

❶ Speaker in a Poem Have students speculate about the identity of the speaker in the poem. *Most students will say that the "I" in the poem refers to the poet himself because the poem seems to come from personal experience.*

◆ Critical Thinking

❷ Infer Ask students why the speaker "looked down one as far as I could." *Students may say he is trying to make a judgment as to which road to follow and he thinks the more he can see of the road, the more he will have to judge by.*

◆ Reading Strategy

❸ Paraphrase Have students restate the meaning of lines 6–8 in their own words. *Students may say the speaker took the second path, which was just as good as the first—maybe even better since it was covered with fresh grass and less worn.*

Looking at Literature Videodisc/Videotape

To capture students' interest and motivate them to read "The Road Not Taken," play Chapter One of the videodisc. The segment begins with a presentation of "The Road Not Taken," followed by one student's response to the poem. Ask students to compare and contrast their responses with the response of the student.

Chapter 1

34

The Road
Robert Frost

Two roads diverged in a yellow wood, ❶
And sorry I could not travel both
And be one traveler, long I stood
And looked down one as far as I could ❷
5 To where it bent in the undergrowth;

Then took the other, as just as fair,
And having perhaps the better claim, ❸
Because it was grassy and wanted wear;
Though as for that, the passing there
10 Had worn them really about the same,

And both that morning equally lay
In leaves no step had trodden black.
Oh, I kept the first for another day!
Yet knowing how way leads on to way, ❹
15 I doubted if I should ever come back.

I shall be telling this with a sigh
Somewhere ages and ages hence: ❺
Two roads diverged in a wood, and I—
I took the one less traveled by,
20 And that has made all the difference.

◆ Build Vocabulary
diverged (dī vʉrjd´) *v.*: Branched off

Block Scheduling Strategies

Consider these suggestions to take advantage of extended class time:

- After students read independently, have them work in pairs to paraphrase and discuss the poems. Then, have them answer the questions on pp. 35 and 37.
- To prepare students for the Writing Mini-Lesson on p. 39, suggest a two-sided issue such as year-round school. Divide students into two groups, based on which side of the issue they support. Have each group brainstorm for reasons, facts, and examples to support their arguments.

- Focus on the grammar concept by having students complete Build Grammar Skills on p. 38. You may wish to reinforce the concept by using **Selection Support,** p. 19. Encourage them to use specific nouns in their Persuasive Essay.
- Play the videodisc chapter about "The Road Not Taken" for students to view and respond to, and then have them answer the questions on p. 35.

 Looking at Literature Videodisc/ Videotape "The Road Not Taken"

Not Taken

Guide for Responding

◆ LITERATURE AND YOUR LIFE

Reader's Response Do you think the speaker made a wise choice? Explain.

Thematic Focus At what understanding did the speaker arrive?

Journal Writing In your journal, write about a time you made a decision like the one the speaker made.

☑ Check Your Comprehension

1. Where is the speaker standing when he has to make his decision?
2. In what way are the roads similar and different?
3. Which road did the speaker choose to take?
4. What reason does the speaker give for choosing one road over the other?

◆ Critical Thinking

INTERPRET

1. What can you determine about the speaker's character in the first five lines of the poem? **[Infer]**
2. Find two details suggesting that the speaker feels his decision is significant. **[Connect]**
3. What do the two roads symbolize, or stand for? **[Interpret]**
4. Explain the message or theme of the poem. **[Analyze]**

EVALUATE

5. The poem's speaker senses that his decision was important. Do you agree? Explain. **[Make a Judgment]**

APPLY

6. An old proverb states that opportunity never knocks twice. How does this saying relate to the poem? **[Apply]**

The Road Not Taken ◆ 35

◆ LITERATURE AND YOUR LIFE

❹ Have you ever meant to do something and just never got around to it? What prevented you? *Students may cite examples such as not going to a museum because other activities kept them busy or not reading a particular book because TV distracted them.*

◆ Critical Thinking

❺ **Interpret** Ask students why the speaker is "telling this with a sigh" and then pauses at the end of line 18. *The speaker still wonders about the other path; he knows the decision was significant and is proud of his choice.*

Reinforce and Extend

Answers
◆ LITERATURE AND YOUR LIFE

Reader's Response Students may say the speaker chose wisely because he took the road less used; others may say it would be safer to take the more traveled road.

Thematic Response The speaker understands that whichever road, he will always wonder what would have happened if he had taken the other.

☑ Check Your Comprehension

1. He is standing at a fork in the road.
2. Both paths are fair and covered in leaves; one path is grassier.
3. He decides to take the grassy road.
4. The road seems to need someone to travel it.

Interpret

1. The speaker is hesitant and thoughtful; he does not want to make any rash decisions, but to choose carefully.
2. He is sorry he can't travel both roads; he knows his decision has "made all the difference."
3. The roads stand for directions the speaker can take with his life.
4. Most students will say the theme of the poem is that small decisions change your life and lead you in a certain direction.
5. Some students may agree because the speaker explained why it was a significant decision; others may disagree because the speaker was not trying to get anywhere, so it didn't matter which road he took.
6. The speaker admits, "I doubted if I should ever come back," so the choice won't ever be made again.

Viewing and Representing Mini-Lesson

Illustration
This mini-lesson supports the Illustration project in the Idea Bank on p. 39.

Introduce Discuss illustrations that students have seen and liked. Have them suggest types of media they might use to create their own illustrations, such as paints, charcoal, pastels, or collage.

Develop Point out that illustrations can show objects and background in a literal representation or they can use line, shape, and color in a way that expresses the mood of the scene they are representing: Sharp shapes and jagged lines

show uneasiness or power, and soft shapes and curved lines express a relaxed tone.

Apply Provide materials and supplies, and have each student create an illustration and write a descriptive caption.

Assess Invite students to display their illustrations and explain the relationship to one of the poems. Evaluate illustrations based on students' explanations and captions. You may wish to follow up with an individual conference to assess whether they achieved what they were trying to represent.

35

In "All But Blind," the speaker describes three animals that are hindered by their limited sight, but also successfully exist in their environments. Then, he realizes that they are unaware that they can't see and he, too, may be blind to someone without realizing it.

The speaker in "The Choice" compares her two suitors and what they have to offer. One offers her riches; the other, only a song. In the end, she questions her attraction to romance over wealth.

◆Reading Strategy

❶ Paraphrase Help students paraphrase these lines by leading them to see that the subject, "the four-clawed mole," is placed uncharacteristically at the end of the sentence.

◆Critical Thinking

❷ Speculate Ask students if, based on the poet's description in this passage, they think the bat is hindered by its blindness. *Most students will say the description "twirls softly by" shows the bat may be blind but is also graceful.*

◆Build Grammar Skills

❸ General and Specific Nouns Tell students that a general noun conveys broad information, while a specific noun conveys more precise information. Ask students why the poet used the specific noun, *Barn-Owl*. *Students may know, or can use context to determine, that the barn-owl is a bird with limited eyesight, so this specific bird's actions are an example of the poet's idea of creatures' blindness.*

◆Literary Focus

❹ Speaker in a Poem Ask students to identify who they think the speaker of the poem is and explain why. *Students may say they think the speaker in the poem is the poet because he calls himself "I."*

All But Blind
Walter de la Mare

All but blind
   In his chambered hole
Gropes for worms
   The four-clawed Mole.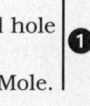

5 All but blind
   In the evening sky
The hooded Bat
   Twirls softly by.

All but blind
10 In the burning day
The Barn-Owl blunders
   On her way.

And blind as are
   These three to me,
15 So, blind to Some-One
   I must be.

◆ Build Vocabulary

blunders (blun´ dərz) *v.*: Moves clumsily or carelessly

smoldering (smōl´ dər iŋ) *adj.*: Burning or smoking without flame

lilting (lilt´ iŋ) *adj.*: Singing or speaking with a light, graceful rhythm

Speaking and Listening Mini-Lesson

Speech

This mini-lesson supports the Speaking and Listening activity in the Idea Bank on p. 39.

Introduce A persuasive speech convinces the audience to accept a certain position on an issue. Students will assume the role of the speaker in "The Road Not Taken" and will attempt to persuade the audience that the correct decision was made.

Develop Discuss techniques that speakers use to persuade an audience, such as restating key points and supporting their position with facts and examples. Then, have the class list reasons the speaker

takes the road less traveled. For example, he does not want to follow the crowd and he sees the potential in trying something new.

Apply Encourage students to develop ideas gathered from discussion as they prepare their speeches. Students can organize their ideas on note cards and refer to them as they speak.

Assess Evaluate each speech on overall persuasiveness, specific arguments, and clarity of presentation. Alternatively, use the Peer Assessment: Speech/Speaker form, p. 114, in **Alternative Assessment.**

The Choice
Dorothy Parker

He'd have given me rolling lands, |
   Houses of marble, and billowing farms,
Pearls, to trickle between my hands,
   Smoldering rubies, to circle my arms.
5   You—you'd only a lilting song.
   Only a melody, happy and high,
You were sudden and swift and strong,—
   Never a thought for another had I.

He'd have given me laces rare,
10   Dresses that glimmered with frosty sheen,
Shining ribbons to wrap my hair,
   Horses to draw me, as fine as a queen.
You—you'd only to whistle low,
   Gaily I followed wherever you led.
15 I took you, and I let him go,—
   Somebody ought to examine my head! | 6

Guide for Responding

◆ LITERATURE AND YOUR LIFE

Reader's Response With which poem's speaker would you rather converse? Why?

Thematic Focus Describe the understanding arrived at by each of the speakers.

☑ Check Your Comprehension

1. In "All But Blind," to what three animals does the speaker compare himself?
2. (a) In "The Choice," what are the two choices the speaker had? (b) What choice did the speaker make?
3. What evidence is there that the speaker in "The Choice" is not sure she made the right decision?

◆ Critical Thinking

INTERPRET

1. (a) Who might be the "Some-One" referred to in line 15 of "All But Blind"? (b) What does the reference reveal about the speaker's world view? **[Interpret]**
2. What do the details in "The Choice" reveal about the speaker's personality? **[Infer]**
3. What might have happened to make her question her decision? **[Speculate]**

COMPARE LITERARY WORKS

4. Examine the last lines in "The Road Not Taken" and in "The Choice." How would the emotional impact of each poem differ if the last lines were switched? **[Hypothesize]**

All But Blind/The Choice ◆ 37

Beyond the Selection

FURTHER READING

Other Works by the Authors
Selected Poems, Robert Frost
The Listeners and Other Poems, Walter de la Mare
Enough Rope, Dorothy Parker

INTERNET
We suggest the following sites on the Internet (all Web sites are subject to change).
   To learn more about Robert Frost, go to:
http://www.poets.org/lit/poet/rfrosfst.htm
   For more on Walter de la Mare:
http://www.lib.udel.edu/ud/spec/findaids/delamare.htm
   For Dorothy Parker, try:
http://www.levity.com/corduroy/parker.htm
   We *strongly recommend* that you preview these sites before you send students to them.

Answers

◆ Reading Strategy

1. Possible response: Verse 1:
   (a) I came to a fork in the road and looked down both ways as far as I could, wishing I could somehow go both directions. (b) The speaker's careful consideration of his or her choices became evident.
2. Possible response: Verse 2: (a) Although bats are nearly blind, they fly gracefully through the air. (b) Limited eyesight doesn't hold back bats.

◆ Build Grammar Skills

Practice

GENERAL NOUNS	SPECIFIC NOUNS
planet	Jupiter, Mercury
flower	daisy, rose
car	sedan, convertible
holiday	Thanksgiving
musician	cellist, guitarist

Writing Application

Possible responses:
1. They served *soft drinks* at the dance.
2. The *oak* will be chopped down.
3. For her eighteenth birthday party, she wore her grandmother's *bracelet.*
4. *Mosquitoes* are annoyingly persistent.
5. She listens to *rap* all day.

 **Writer's Solution**

For additional instruction and practice, use the lesson in the *Writer's Solution Language Lab CD-ROM* on Using Nouns. You may also use the Nouns practice pages, pp. 5–7, in the *Writer's Solution Grammar Practice Book.*

◆ Literary Focus

1. The speaker realizes he must make a decision and that there will be no turning back, but he is content.
2. The speaker implies that he only knows what he observes and realizes that there is plenty about life that he may not know. It gives the poem meaning because he shows what he observes, but then says someone could observe a similar blindness in him.
3. Some students will say that she values love and romance because she chose the charming suitor. Others will say that she values material wealth most because she thinks her choice may have been crazy.

Guide for Responding *(continued)*

◆ Reading Strategy

PARAPHRASE

This **paraphrase,** or restatement, of lines 5–8 from "The Choice" may lead you to recognize the main, or key, idea in the passage.

Original: You—you'd only a lilting song./Only a melody, happy and high,/You were sudden and swift and strong,—/Never a thought for another had I.

Paraphrase: The only thing you had was your joyous attitude. You were like a whirlwind that drove thoughts of all other boyfriends out of my head.

1. (a) Paraphrase any passage of "The Road Not Taken." (b) What important ideas were you able to identify through paraphrasing?
2. (a) Paraphrase any passage of "All But Blind." (b) What is the passage about (the subject)? What does it say about the subject?

◆ Build Grammar Skills

GENERAL AND SPECIFIC NOUNS

Nouns name people, places, things, or ideas. **General nouns,** like *tree* and *flower,* convey broad information. **Specific nouns,** like *elm* and *willow* or *daisy* and *violet,* convey more precise information. Although it's not necessary to use only specific nouns in your writing, you should recognize that they give writing clarity.

Practice Divide your paper into two columns. Write the general nouns in one column and the corresponding specific nouns in the other.

planet, flower, car, daisy, sedan, Jupiter, holiday, musician, rose, convertible, Thanksgiving, cellist, Mercury, guitarist

Writing Application On your paper, revise each sentence, replacing the italicized general noun with a more specific noun.

1. They served *beverages* at the dance.
2. The *tree* will be chopped down.
3. For her eighteenth birthday party, she wore her grandmother's *jewelry.*
4. *Insects* are annoyingly persistent.
5. She listens to *music* all day.

◆ Literary Focus

THE SPEAKER IN A POEM

When you read poetry, be alert to the **speaker,** the character or voice assumed by the poet. The thoughts, attitude, and character of the speaker give meaning to a poem.

1. Describe the speaker's attitude or philosophy in "The Road Not Taken."
2. In "All But Blind," the speaker reveals his view of life. Describe his view, and explain how it gives the poem its meaning.
3. If you assume that the speaker of "The Choice" is Dorothy Parker herself, what do you think she values most?

◆ Build Vocabulary

USING THE WORD ROOT -verg-

The word root *-verg-,* meaning "to bend or turn" and found in *diverged,* also appears in *converge,* the opposite of *diverge.* The prefix *con-* means "together." What does *converge* mean?

Complete the following sentences using a form of *converge* or *diverge.*

1. The two groups plan to _____?_____ at noon.
2. Because of the boulder, the stream _____?_____.

SPELLING STRATEGY

When adding *-ing* to a verb to make an adjective, keep this in mind: If a verb has more than one syllable, ends in a consonant, and is not accented on the last syllable, just add *-ing.*

    smolder + -ing = smoldering

On your paper, add *-ing* to the following.

1. travel 2. gallop 3. billow 4. administer

USING THE WORD BANK

On your paper, replace each italicized word or phrase with the correct Word Bank word.

1. Through the *smoking* pile of leaves a bear *stumbles.*
2. On the tree branch that *curved in two directions,* a robin ceased her *melodic* song.

◆ Build Vocabulary

Using the Word Root -verg-
1. converge; 2. diverged

Spelling Strategy
1. traveling; 2. galloping; 3. billowing;
4. administering

Using the Word Bank
1. smoldering, blunders
2. diverged, lilting

Build Your Portfolio

Idea Bank

Writing

1. **List** List the qualities of each suitor in "The Choice." You might have to "read between the lines" of the poem to determine the character of each suitor.

2. **Dialogue** Imagine that you are hiking with the speaker of "The Road Not Taken." You have just come to the place described in the poem. Write the dialogue you might have with the speaker about which road to take.

3. **Compare and Contrast** The speakers of these poems have distinct personalities and attitudes. Choose two of the poems, and write an essay in which you compare and contrast the poems and the speakers.

Speaking and Listening

4. **Dramatic Scene [Group Activity]** The speaker of "The Road Not Taken" is satisfied with his life choice, whereas the speaker in "The Choice" is not so sure she chose wisely. With a classmate, prepare and present a scene in which the two speakers discuss their feelings. **[Performing Arts Link]**

5. **Speech** In "The Road Not Taken," the speaker is convinced that he made a sound decision in choosing a path. Transform the poem into a persuasive speech, and deliver it to the class. **[Performing Arts Link]**

Projects

6. **Final Words** An obituary is a notice of someone's death that includes a brief biography. With two classmates, write obituary notices for each poem's speaker. Tailor the notices to the speakers' personalities as closely as possible.

7. **Illustration** Illustrate a scene from one of the poems. Write a caption for your art, as if it were appearing in a book or being displayed on a museum wall. Display your work in class. **[Art Link]**

Writing Mini-Lesson

Persuasive Essay

Like the speakers in "The Road Not Taken" and "The Choice," you make decisions every day. Although some decisions affect only yourself, sometimes you need the cooperation of others in order to make a change or take a step. Think about a path you'd like to take that involves the agreement of others. Then, write a persuasive essay to convince them to support you.

Writing Skills Focus: Supporting Your Argument

Persuasive writing usually contains an argument, a set of reasons for doing or believing something. To make your argument forceful, **support it** by giving reasons why one particular choice is better than another.

Here, the speaker in Frost's poem explains why he chose one path over another.

Model From the Poem
Then took the other, as just as fair,
And having perhaps the better claim,
Because it was grassy and wanted wear;

Prewriting Choose a two-sided issue about which you feel strongly. Jot down arguments that support your position on the issue.

Drafting Begin your persuasive essay by stating what you want to do and why you deserve your readers' support. Then, develop and support your argument by giving reasons, facts, and examples.

Revising Look for places in which your argument can be strengthened. For example, you may want to add facts and details or choose more powerful words.

> ◆ **Grammar Application**
> Read through your draft, underlining general nouns and circling specific nouns. Consider whether you can strengthen your argument by replacing some general nouns with specific ones.

The Road Not Taken/All But Blind/The Choice ◆ 39

Idea Bank

Following are suggestions for matching the Idea Bank topics with your students' performance levels and learning modalities:

Customize for *Performance Levels*
Less Advanced Students: 1, 4, 7
Average Students: 2, 4, 5, 6, 7
More Advanced Students: 3, 5, 6

Customize for *Learning Modalities*
Verbal/Linguistic: 2, 3, 4, 6
Interpersonal: 4
Visual/Spatial: 7
Intrapersonal: 1, 2, 3, 6, 7

Writing Mini-Lesson

Refer students to the Writing Handbook in the back of the book for instruction on the writing process and for further information on persuasion. Have students use the Main Idea and Supporting Details Organizer in **Writing and Language Transparencies,** p. 61, to arrange their prewriting examples.

Writer's Solution

Writing Lab CD-ROM
Have students complete the tutorial on Persuasion. Follow these steps:
1. Have students use audioannotated models of persuasive essays.
2. Have students draft on computer.
3. Suggest that students use the interactive instruction on avoiding faulty reasoning.
4. Encourage students to use the revision checker for sentence openers to help them make sure they have variety.

Writer's Solution Sourcebook
Have students use Chapter 6, "Persuasion," pp. 166–199. This chapter includes in-depth instruction on eliminating unnecessary words and using active and passive voice, pp. 195–198.

✓ ASSESSMENT OPTIONS

Formal Assessment, Selection Test, pp. 10–12, and Assessment Resources Software. The selection test is designed so that it can easily be customized to the performance levels of your students.

Alternative Assessment, p. 4, includes options for less advanced students, more advanced students, visual/spatial learners, logical/mathematical learners, and bodily/kinesthetic or interpersonal learners.

PORTFOLIO ASSESSMENT
Use the following rubrics in the **Alternative Assessment** booklet to assess student writing:
List: Summary, p. 94
Dialogue: Fictional Narrative, p. 91
Compare and Contrast: Comparison/Contrast, p. 99
Writing Mini-Lesson: Persuasion, p. 101

Guide for Reading

OBJECTIVES

1. To read, comprehend, and interpret a magazine article
2. To relate a magazine article to personal experience
3. To use context clues to determine word meaning
4. To analyze a magazine article
5. To build vocabulary in context and use the prefix *inter-*
6. To recognize concrete and abstract nouns
7. To write a comparison essay using transitions that show relationships
8. To respond to the story through writing, speaking and listening, and projects

SKILLS INSTRUCTION

Vocabulary:
Prefixes: *inter-*
Spelling:
Words With *-tion*
Grammar:
Concrete and Abstract Nouns
Reading Strategy:
Context Clues
Literary Focus:
Magazine Article

Writing:
Transitions That Show Relationships
Speaking and Listening:
Dialogue (Teacher Edition)

PORTFOLIO OPPORTUNITIES

Writing: Letter to the Author; Advertisement; Cause-and-Effect Essay
Writing Mini-Lesson: Comparison of Forms of Communication
Speaking and Listening: Dialogue; Interview
Projects: Internet Exploration; Diagram

More About the Author
John Seabrook discussed his job at *The New Yorker* in an on-line interview with *People Magazine,* saying that he created his job of on-line specialist. "No one else wanted it. It didn't exist before I did it." He says that writing on-line has given him valuable practice in putting things into words and he likes the way it reduces the distance between writer and reader.

Meet the Author:

John Seabrook (1959–   )

John Seabrook grew up in the tomato farm community of Salem, New Jersey. Years later, he was to write an article about a new industry, biotechnology, and the process scientists used to develop a new supermarket tomato. Almost as an afterthought, he included some comments on his boyhood connection to tomatoes. The positive reaction to that article helped Seabrook realize that science writers need to tell their audiences why they are interested in a subject and show how it affects them.

THE STORY BEHIND THE STORY

Bill Gates (1955–   ) is the chief executive officer and co-founder of Microsoft Corporation, the world's largest computer software company. His phenomenal success and astounding wealth have made him a legendary figure in the business world. When John Seabrook began writing this article for *The New Yorker,* he attempted to contact Gates by e-mail, not knowing whether or not he'd get a response. To his surprise, he got an immediate reply and was able to conduct the interview almost entirely through e-mail correspondence.

40 ◆ Coming of Age

◆ LITERATURE AND YOUR LIFE

CONNECT YOUR EXPERIENCE

Although virtually everyone loves getting cards and letters in the mail, many people don't write letters, preferring the quickness of making phone calls. Recently, however, letter writing has undergone a renewed popularity due to the emergence of e-mail—electronic mail.

THEMATIC FOCUS: Arriving at Understanding

In "E-Mail from Bill Gates," John Seabrook interviews the computer industry's biggest player, Bill Gates, in an effort to understand e-mail and its impact on our lives.

◆ Background for Understanding

TECHNOLOGY

In "E-Mail from Bill Gates," John Seabrook conducts an interview with Bill Gates, head of Microsoft Corporation, via e-mail. E-mail stands for electronic mail, which is relayed through telephone lines. Messages that used to take weeks to arrive by traditional mail can now be sent round the world in minutes. This new technology also allows for attachments of files, making it possible for many people to work from their homes.

◆ Build Vocabulary

PREFIXES: *inter-*

The prefix *inter-*, meaning "between," appears in the word *interaction*, which means "actions that have an effect on each other."

WORD BANK

Which word from the list means "in a spontaneous way"? Check the Build Vocabulary box on page 44 to see if you chose correctly.

interaction
misinterpret
intimate
etiquette
spontaneously

Prentice Hall Literature Program Resources

REINFORCE / RETEACH / EXTEND
Selection Support Pages
Build Vocabulary: Prefixes: *inter-*, p. 22
Build Spelling Skills, p. 23
Build Grammar Skills: Concrete and Abstract Nouns, p. 24
Reading Strategy: Context Clues, p. 25
Literary Focus: Magazine Article, p. 26
Strategies for Diverse Student Needs, pp. 9–10
Beyond Literature Study Skills: Using the Internet, p. 5

Formal Assessment Selection Test, pp. 13–15, Assessment Resources Software
Alternative Assessment, p. 5
Writing and Language Transparencies
Venn Diagram, p. 77
Resource Pro CD-R✍M
from "E-mail from Bill Gates"—includes all resource material and customizable lesson plan
🎧 **Listening to Literature Audiocassettes**
from "E-mail from Bill Gates"

from E-Mail from Bill Gates

Interest Grabber Draw the following symbols on the board, and ask students to explain or speculate about what they mean:

frowning	oh!	winking
:-(	:-O	;-)
what?	laughing	crying
%-(	:-D	:'(

These symbols are called "smileys" or "emoticons" and are used to express the tone of a comment in e-mail. Lead students into the article by telling them that they will read the e-mail of one of the giants of the computer industry and gain insight into the art of e-mailing.

◆ Build Grammar Skills

Concrete and Abstract Nouns
If you wish to introduce the grammar concept before students read, refer to the instruction on p. 46.

Customize for
Less Proficient Readers
Students may better understand the article's information if you help them summarize each e-mail. Use a graphic organizer to record the main ideas.

Seabrook Wrote	Then Gates Wrote	Then Seabrook Wrote
I am writing an article about you. What is special about e-mail?		

Customize for
More Advanced Students
As students read, have them consider the effect of e-mail messages being printed in the article. Ask them how the article would differ if Seabrook had summarized each message rather than sharing excerpts, as he did.

◆ Literary Focus
MAGAZINE ARTICLE

A **magazine article** is a short work of nonfiction that gives information. Some articles are human-interest stories that give insights on interesting people and their accomplishments. Other articles explain or investigate specific subjects, like the behavior of bees or a new technology.

This magazine article by John Seabrook does both: It profiles a fascinating person who is at the cutting edge of the new technology, and, at the same time, it provides knowledge on a scientific subject.

◆ Reading Strategy
CONTEXT CLUES

While reading, you may occasionally encounter unfamiliar words. By using **context clues,** examining the surrounding text, you may be able to make an informed guess about the meaning of words new to you.

As you read, use a chart like the one below to record unknown words and guess at their meanings. When you've finished reading, use a dictionary to see if you were on target.

Word	Clue	Predicted Meaning
nevertheless	wasting money/logged on again	"anyway" or "in spite of"

Guide for Reading ◆ 41

Preparing for Standardized Tests

Vocabulary Students' knowledge of affixes may be evaluated on standardized tests. Using the prefix *inter-* (the vocabulary skill with this selection) will help them develop their ability to apply affixes in a test format.

Write this sentence on the board: "E-mail is not a good way to get mad at someone because you can't interact." Guide them to identify the base word *act* and point out that knowing *inter-* means "between" will help students determine that *interact* means "to act between." Then, write the following sample test question on the board:

E-mail has greatly improved the speed of <u>international</u> communication.

In the sentence above, *international* means
(A) overseas   (C) between cities
(B) between countries   (D) within the nation

Help students assess the answer choices. Neither (A) nor (D) apply the prefix *inter-*, and (C) is incorrect because *cities* does not relate to the base word *national*. (B) *between countries* applies the affix *inter-*, meaning "between," to the base word *national*, which relates to countries.

Humanities: Art

Montage of Computer, Phone, and Globe, by Michael Agliolo

A montage combines several different images. Ask students what message they think the artist wanted to express with this montage. Discuss how this art is appropriate for an article about e-mail. *The combined elements of technological communication and the globe show the power of worldwide communication via the World Wide Web.*

One-Minute Insight

In this excerpt, John Seabrook describes his contact with Bill Gates via e-mail while gathering information for a magazine article that Seabrook was writing. Ongoing correspondence between the two provides Seabrook with insights into Gates's personality and philosophy about technology. The text of these e-mail letters provides readers with a sense of who Bill Gates is. It also reveals the type of communication that is possible using electronic correspondence.

Clarification

1 Share with students that advances in technology occur regularly and rapidly. Since this article was written, much of what Seabrook described as possible in the future has become commonplace. People can transmit real-time sound and video images from their computers to other computers around the world.

Customize for
English Language Learners

Before they read, students may benefit from a demonstration of sending and receiving e-mail messages. As you identify and describe parts of the process (send, open, date, subject, and so on), write symbols, jargon, and technical terms on the board and demonstrate correct pronunciation.

Customize for
Verbal/Linguistic Learners

Have students make notes about their response to Gates's e-mail as they read. Then, ask them to write and send an e-mail to Bill Gates, stating what they think of his ideas.

E-MAIL

| ADDRESS | SEND | REPLY | DELETE |

JOHN SEABROOK

from E-Mail from Bill Gates

At the moment, the best way to communicate with another person on the information highway[1] is to exchange electronic mail: to write a message on a computer and send it through the telephone lines into someone else's computer. In the future, people will send each other sound and pictures as well as text, and do it in real time,[2] and improved technology will make it possible to have rich, human electronic exchanges, but at present E-mail is the closest thing we have to that. Even now, E-mail allows you to meet and communicate with people in a way that would be impossible on the phone, through the regular mail, or face to face, as I discovered while I was working on this story. Sitting at my computer one day, I realized that I could try to communicate with Bill Gates, the chairman and co-founder of the software giant Microsoft, on the information highway. At least, I could send E-mail to his electronic address, which is widely available, not tell anyone at Microsoft I was doing it, and see what happened. I wrote:

---

1. **information highway:** Network of computers and file servers that allows for the rapid exchange of electronic information.
2. **real time:** Accessing of information or exchange of data that requires no downloading of files.

---

42 ◆ *Coming of Age*

Dear Bill,

I am the guy who is writing the article about you for The New Yorker. It occurs to me that we ought to be able to do some of the work through e-mail. Which raises this fascinating question—What kind of understanding of another person can e-mail give you? . . .

You could begin by telling me what you think is unique about e-mail as a form of communication.

John

I hit "return," and the computer said, "mail sent." I walked out to the kitchen to get a drink of water and played with the cat for a while, then came back and sat at my computer. Thinking that I was probably wasting money, I nevertheless logged on again and entered my password. "You have mail," the computer said.

I typed "get mail," and the computer got the following:

From: Bill Gates <billg@microsoft.com>
Ok, let me know if you get this email.

According to my computer, eighteen minutes had passed between the time I E-mailed Bill and he E-mailed me back. His message said:

E-mail is a unique communication

Block Scheduling Strategies

Consider these suggestions to take advantage of extended class time:

- Invite students to read the selection in small groups, exploring the literary focus for the selection. Have them stop occasionally to discuss information that the magazine article provides about technology and Bill Gates.

- Have students work with partners to complete the Literary Focus activity on p. 46. Have them use their answers as a basis for completing the Speaking and Listening Mini-Lesson (Dialogue) on p. 43 of the Teacher Edition.

- If you have access to technology, have students use the *Writer's Solution Writing Lab CD-ROM* to organize their drafts and revise their essays for the Writing Mini-Lesson, p. 47. Refer to the suggestions on p. 47 to help you structure class time.

vehicle for a lot of reasons. However email is not a substitute for direct interaction. . . .

There are people who I have corresponded with on email for months before actually meeting them—people at work and otherwise. If someone isn't saying something of interest its easier to not respond to their mail than it is not to answer the phone. In fact I give out my home phone number to almost no one but my email address is known very broadly. I am the only person who reads my email so no one has to worry about embarrassing themselves or going around people when they send a message. Our email is completely secure. . . .

Email helps out with other types of communication. It allows you to exchange a lot of information in advance of a meeting and make the meeting far far more valuable. . . .

❷ Email is not a good way to get mad at someone since you can't interact. You can send friendly messages very easily since those are harder to misinterpret.

❸ We began to E-mail each other three or four times a week. I would have a question about something and say to myself, "I'm going to E-mail Bill about that," and I'd write him a message and get a one- or two-page message back within twenty-four hours, sometimes much sooner. At the beginning of our electronic relationship, I would wake up in the middle of the night and lie in bed wondering if I had E-mail from Bill. Generally, he seemed to write messages at night, sleep (maybe), then send them the next morning. We were

◆ Build Vocabulary

interaction (in´ tər ak´ shən) *n.*: Actions that affect each other

misinterpret (mis´ in tur´ prit) *v.*: To understand or explain incorrectly

intimate (in´ tə mət) *adj.*: Private or personal

etiquette (et´ i kit) *n.*: Rules for behavior

intimate in a curious way, in the sense of being wired into each other's minds, but our contact was elaborately stylized, like ballroom dancing.

In some ways, my E-mail relationship with Bill was like an ongoing, monthlong conversation, except that there was a pause after each response to think; it was like football players huddling up after each play. There was no beginning or end to Gates' messages—no time wasted on stuff like "Dear" and "Yours"—and I quickly corrected this etiquette breach in my own messages. Nor were there any fifth-grade-composition-book standards like "It may have come to your attention that" and "Looking forward to hearing from you." Social niceties are not what Bill Gates is about. Good spelling is not what Bill Gates is about, either. He never signed his messages to me, but sometimes he put an "&" at the end, which, I learned, means "Write back" in E-mail language. After a while, he stopped putting the "&," but I wrote back anyway. He never addressed me by name. Instead of a letterhead, there was this:

❹

> Sender: billg@microsoft.com
> Received: from netmail.microsoft.com by dub-img-2.compuserve.com (5.67/5.930129sam) id AA03768; Wed, 6 Oct 93 14:00:51-0400
> Received: by netmail.microsoft.com (5.65/25—eef) id AA27745; Fri, 8 Oct 93 10:56:01-0700
> Message-Id: <9310081756.AA27745@netmail.microsoft.com>
> X-Msmail-Message-Id: 15305A55
> X-Msmail-Conversation-Id: 15305A55
> From: Bill Gates <billg@microsoft.com>
> To: 73124.1524@CompuServe.COM

I sometimes felt that this correspondence was a game I was playing with Gates through the computer, or maybe a game I was playing against a computer. What is the right move? What question will get me past the dragon and into the wizard's star

❺
> ◆ **Reading Strategy**
> What context clues point to the meaning of the term "letterhead"?

❻

from E-Mail from Bill Gates ◆ 43

Speaking and Listening Mini-Lesson

Dialogue

This mini-lesson supports the Speaking and Listening activity in the Idea Bank on p. 47.

Introduce Dialogue is often thought of as an oral conversation or a written version of a spoken conversation. Dialogue is also the exchange of ideas and opinions, such as the e-mail correspondence between Seabrook and Gates.

Develop Have pairs of students discuss how to convert the e-mail into a traditional conversation:
- What is the attitude of each writer?
- What is the relationship between the writers?

- Does the relationship change over time?

Apply Have students develop the conversation, referring to the e-mail to make sure they include all pertinent information. Encourage them to interpret mood and attitude.

Assess Have students present their dialogues to the class. Discuss variations among the presentations. Evaluate students' work based on clarity of expression, creativity, and thoroughness of preparation, or use the Peer Assessment Dramatic Performance form, p. 116, in **Alternative Assessment.**

❶ Context Clues Lead students to see that the context clue *jumped from topic to topic* helps them define *random* as "having no clear pattern."

◆ Build Grammar Skills

❷ Concrete and Abstract Nouns Concrete nouns name something that can be perceived with the senses, whereas abstract nouns name something that cannot be touched. Point out that whether a noun is concrete or abstract may depend on how it is used in a sentence. Have students identify two concrete nouns and one abstract noun in this sentence. *The concrete nouns are people and wound, and the abstract noun is loss.*

◆ Literary Focus

❸ Magazine Article Ask students to describe the insight about Bill Gates they can gain from this paragraph. *Possible response: He likes helping people and enjoys being directly involved in technology development.*

◆ Critical Thinking

❹ Compare and Contrast Point out that the information in this e-mail is a response to the questions posed by Seabrook in the preceding message. Ask students to discuss how a conversation carried on in this way is similar to and different from face-to-face conversations. *Students should suggest similarities such as informal tone and an exchange of information and differences such as a lack of spontaneous give-and-take when using e-mail.*

Customize for
Intrapersonal Learners

Have students independently research the history of e-mail. You may want to direct or supervise their research on the Internet. In addition, suggest that they use the *Readers' Guide to Periodical Literature* to find Seabrook's complete magazine article, as well as other magazine articles that have chronicled the development of e-mail communication.

44

---

chamber, where the rich information is stored? I had no idea where Gates was when he wrote to me, except that once he told me he was on a "think week" at his family's summer place on Hood Canal. I could not tell whether he was impatient or bored with my questions and was merely answering them because it served his interest. Because we couldn't talk at the same time, there was little chance for the conversation to move spontaneously. On the other hand, his answers meant more, in a certain way, being written, than answers I would have received on the phone. ❶ I worried that he might think I was being "random" (a big putdown at Microsoft) because I jumped from topic to topic. I sometimes wondered if I was actually communicating with Bill Gates. How hard would it be for an assistant to write these messages? Or for an intelligent agent to do it?

I wrote a message titled "What motivates you?":

You love to compete, right? Is that where your energy comes from—love of the game? I wonder how it feels to win on your level. How much do you fear losing? How about immortality—being remembered for a thousand years after you're dead—does that excite you? How strong is your desire to improve people's lives (by providing them with better tools for thinking and communicating)? Some ❷ driven people are trying to heal a wound or to recover a loss. Is that the case with you?

Gates wrote back:

Its easy to understand why I think I have the best job around because of day to day enjoyment rather than some grand long term deep psychological explanation. It's a lot of fun to work with very smart people in a competitive environment. . . . We get to hire the best people coming out of school and give them challenging jobs. We get to try and figure

44 ◆ *Coming of Age*

---

out how to sell software in every part of the world. Sometimes our ideas work very well and sometimes they work very poorly. As long as we stay in the feedback loop and keep trying it's a lot of fun.

It is pretty cool that the products we work on empower individuals and make their jobs more interesting. It helps a lot ❸ in inventing new software ideas that I will be one of the users of the software so I can model what's important. . . .

Just thinking of things as winning is a terrible approach. Success comes from focusing in on what you really like and ❹ are good at—not challenging every random thing. My original vision of a personal computer on every desk and every home will take more than 15 years to achieve so there will have been more than 30 years since I first got excited about that goal. My work is not like sports where you actually win a game and its over after a short period of time.

Besides a lot of luck, a high energy level and perhaps some IQ I think having an ability to deal with things at a very detailed level and a very broad level and synthesize[3] between them is probably the thing that helps me the most. This allows someone to take deep technical understanding and figure out a business strategy that fits together with it.

It's ridiculous to consider how things will be remembered after you are dead. The pioneers of personal computers including Jobs, Kapor, Lampson, Roberts, Kaye,[4] are all great people but I don't think any of us will merit an entry in a history book.

---

3. synthesize: To form by bringing together separate parts.
4. Jobs, . . . Kaye: Pioneers in technology.

◆ Build Vocabulary
spontaneously (spän tā′ nē əs lē) *adv.*: Resulting from a natural feeling

---

Beyond the Classroom

Career Connection
The Right Job Personal satisfaction is an important consideration of job opportunities. Emphasize to students that enjoyable work tasks and a sense of accomplishment provide the basis for a long and rewarding career.

Review with students the reasons Bill Gates likes his job, including day-to-day enjoyment, working with able people, a competitive environment, challenging tasks, and providing what others need. Lead a discussion about job attributes that students consider to be important. Ask them

to give reasons to support their opinions, and write a list on the board. Have students make their own personal list by choosing attributes from those proposed by the class.

Arrange students in small groups and ask them to brainstorm for a list of jobs they think are interesting. Have them discuss whether each job on the list provides some or all of the attributes they would each like to find in a job. Based on the discussion, invite students to research the requirements and training needed for each career that may interest them.

I don't remember being wounded or losing something big so I don't think that is driving me. I have wonderful parents and great siblings. I live in the same neighborhood I grew up in (although I will be moving across the lake when my new house is done). I can't remember any major disappointments. I did figure out at one point that if I pursued pure mathematics it would be hard to make a major contribution and there were a few girls who turned me down when I asked them out.

At the end of one message, I wrote:

This reporting via e-mail is really fascinating and I think you are going to come across in an attractive way, in case you weren't sure of that.

Gates wrote:

❺ I comb my hair everytime before I send email hoping to appear attractive. I try and use punctuation in a friendly way also. I send :) and never :(.

Beyond Literature

Science Connection

How E-Mail Works:
1. Your computer translates e-mail messages into a binary code made up of 1's and 0's.
2. To send the message, you log onto the worldwide computer network called the Internet. Basically, your computer calls another computer on the telephone.
3. When you click Send, your e-mail message is transferred through telephone lines from your computer to a file server on the Internet. That server reads the e-mail address and routes the message.

Cross-Curricular Activity
Class Debate Organize a class debate on this resolution: "E-mail is faster and easier to use than traditional mail. Our government should replace traditional mail with e-mail."

Guide for Responding

◆ LITERATURE AND YOUR LIFE

Reader's Response Would you like to meet Bill Gates? Why or why not?

Thematic Focus What did you learn about both e-mail and Bill Gates from reading this article?

☑ **Check Your Comprehension**

1. Who are the two people exchanging e-mail messages in this article?
2. What does Seabrook learn about the etiquette of sending and receiving e-mail?
3. What does Gates say about his motivation for success that might help other people achieve their goals?

◆ Critical Thinking

INTERPRET

1. What does Seabrook accomplish by letting Gates speak for himself? **[Analyze]**
2. How do Seabrook's and Gates's e-mail messages change over time? **[Analyze]**
3. Does the author learn what he had hoped to learn about Bill Gates? **[Draw Conclusions]**
4. Would you include Gates in a history book? **[Make a Judgment]**

EXTEND

5. What skills do you think are needed by people who work in the computer field? **[Career Link]**

from *E-Mail from Bill Gates* ◆ 45

Beyond the Selection

FURTHER READING

Other Works by Seabrook and Gates
Deeper: My Two-Year Odyssey in Cyberspace, John Seabrook
The Road Ahead, Bill Gates

INTERNET
We suggest the following Internet sites (all Web sites are subject to change).

For more information about Bill Gates:
http://www.microsoft.com/BillGates/bio.htm

To send an e-mail message to Bill Gates:
http://www.microsoft.com/BillGates/email.htm

For information about creating and sending e-mail:
http://www.webfoot.com/advice/email.top.html?yahoo

We *strongly recommend* that you preview these sites before you send students to them.

◆ **Critical Thinking**

❺ **Interpret** Review the symbols from the Interest Grabber, p. 41. Then, ask students to rewrite the sentence using words instead of the symbols. *Students should recognize that the two symbols are abbreviated versions of the emoticons used in the Interest Grabber: I send a smile and never a frown.*

Beyond Literature

As students organize the debate, remind them that they should take a position for or against the proposition and research facts that support their position for their arguments.

Reinforce and Extend

Answers

◆ LITERATURE AND YOUR LIFE

Reader's Response Students should support their responses with details. For example, students might like to meet Gates to learn about the challenges of his job.

Thematic Focus Some students may say they came to a better understanding of e-mail. Others may say that they gained insight into Bill Gates's philosophy and personality.

☑ **Check Your Comprehension**

1. John Seabrook, a magazine writer, and Bill Gates, the chairman of Microsoft, exchange e-mail.
2. E-mail etiquette is different from conventional letter-writing and composition standards.
3. "Success comes from focusing in on what you really like and are good at."

◆ Critical Thinking

1. He lets the reader make his or her own judgments about Bill Gates; he gives an example of e-mail correspondence.
2. The messages become less formal and more frequent.
3. Yes, he learns how Gates uses e-mail, what motivates Gates, and Gates's plans for the future.
4. Students may say that Gates should be in a history book because his products change world communication and productivity.
5. Students should suggest skills such as mathematics, computer technology, and an ability to envision what people might want or need.

◆ Reading Strategy

1. The words *ballroom dancing* indicate that *elaborately stylized* refers to something that conforms to a certain complex pattern or style.
2. (a) Students may suggest e-mail terms or unfamiliar vocabulary. (b) Students' answers should indicate correct use of context clues such as surrounding text to figure out meaning.

◆ Build Vocabulary

Using the Prefix *inter-*
1. interconnection
2. international
3. interstate

Spelling Strategy
1. creation; 2. connection; 3. designation; 4. reflection

Using the Word Bank
1. understand; 2. independence; 3. incorrectness; 4. hesitantly; 5. public

◆ Literary Focus

1. Possible responses: It is sent over telephone wires; the rules for writing e-mail are different from those for letters.
2. Possible responses: To prove he really got e-mail from Gates; to show e-mail interaction.
3. Answers will vary but should be supported with reasons. Most students will say the article is informative because it provides facts about e-mail and about Bill Gates.

◆ Build Grammar Skills

Practice
1. I had a <u>question</u> about <u>something</u>.
2. In the <u>future</u>, <u>people</u> will send each other <u>sound</u> and <u>pictures</u>.
3. <u>E-mail</u> is not a good <u>way</u> to get mad at <u>someone</u>.
4. How strong is your <u>desire</u> to improve people's <u>lives</u>?
5. I can't remember any major <u>disappointments</u>.

Writing Application
Students' paragraphs should have concrete and abstract nouns correctly identified.

Guide for Responding (continued)

◆ Reading Strategy

CONTEXT CLUES
When reading a science article like "E-Mail from Bill Gates," it's helpful to identify **context clues,** clues in the surrounding text, to figure out the meaning of unfamiliar words.
1. What context clues help you understand the italicized term in this passage? "[O]ur contact was *elaborately stylized,* like ballroom dancing."
2. (a) With which words or phrases in the article were you unfamiliar? (b) What context clues helped you guess at their meanings?

◆ Build Vocabulary

USING THE PREFIX *inter-*
The prefix *inter-* means "between." Write the word that should appear in each blank by adding *inter-* to these words: state, connection, national.
1. E-mail can help you establish an ____?____ with faraway friends.
2. Instead of airmail, you can send an ____?____ e-mail.
3. To get from Texas to Arizona, take the ____?____ highway.

SPELLING STRATEGY
The suffix sound *shun* is often spelled *-tion.* Before adding the suffix, you will probably have to drop the final letter of the base word.

interact + -tion = interaction

On your paper, add *-tion* to the following verbs.
1. create 2. connect 3. designate 4. reflect

USING THE WORD BANK
On your paper, write the antonym, or opposite, of each first word.
1. misinterpret: (a) understand, (b) explain, (c) true
2. interaction: (a) play, (b) independence, (c) collaboration
3. etiquette: (a) program, (b) rules, (c) incorrectness
4. spontaneously: (a) quickly, (b) hesitantly, (c) accidentally
5. intimate: (a) close, (b) personal, (c) public

◆ Literary Focus

MAGAZINE ARTICLE
Magazine articles are short nonfiction works meant to inform and entertain. In "E-Mail from Bill Gates," John Seabrook does both: He publishes the actual e-mail messages that he received from Bill Gates to make his point about e-mail as a communications tool.
1. List two facts you learned about e-mail.
2. Why do you think Seabrook printed the e-mail identification you see on page 43?
3. Would you describe this article as more informative or more entertaining? Why?

◆ Build Grammar Skills

CONCRETE AND ABSTRACT NOUNS
In his article, Seabrook often gives information about technology by using concrete nouns. A **concrete noun** names a place or thing that you can perceive with your senses. You can touch a *computer* and type a *message.* An **abstract noun** names an idea, concept, belief, or quality—something that can't be touched. When Seabrook talks about ideas or relationships, he often uses abstract nouns, such as *understanding.*

Practice Copy the following sentences. Decide whether the nouns in italics are concrete or abstract. Underline each concrete noun. Draw two lines under each abstract noun.
1. I had a *question* about *something.*
2. In the *future, people* will send each other *sound* and *pictures.*
3. *E-mail* is not a good *way* to get mad at *someone.*
4. How strong is your *desire* to improve people's *lives?*
5. I can't remember any major *disappointments.*

Writing Application Write a paragraph about technology using both concrete and abstract nouns. Underline concrete nouns and circle abstract nouns.

46 ◆ *Coming of Age*

✎ **Writer's Solution**

For additional instruction and practice, use the lesson in the *Writer's Solution Language Lab CD-ROM* on identifying concrete and abstract nouns in the Using Nouns section.

Build Your Portfolio

 Idea Bank

Writing

1. **Letter to the Author** In a letter to John Seabrook, tell him why you appreciated "E-Mail from Bill Gates." Include any questions about technology or Bill Gates that you would like him to answer.

2. **Advertisement** Write an advertisement that might have appeared to introduce a technological product such as the telephone or the radio when it was first made available to the public. **[Science Link]**

3. **Cause-and-Effect Essay** In this article, Seabrook and Gates discuss the impact of technology on our lives. Choose one technological breakthrough and write a cause-and-effect essay in which you examine its effect on daily life.

Speaking and Listening

4. **Dialogue [Group Activity]** With a classmate, convert the series of e-mail letters between Bill Gates and John Seabrook into a traditional conversation. Perform their dialogue for the class. **[Performing Arts Link]**

5. **Interview** Interview a science teacher to learn how technology has changed and will change our lives. Publish both your questions and the teacher's answers.

Projects

6. **Internet Exploration** Write a report on how to send and receive e-mail, how to download files sent by e-mail, and how to create an e-mail address book. Present your information to the class. If possible, use a computer to demonstrate your knowledge. **[Science Link]**

7. **Diagram** Do research to find out how e-mail is relayed from one computer to another. Make a diagram, with explanatory captions to show how the system works.

 Writing Mini-Lesson

Comparison of Forms of Communication

In this article, John Seabrook uses comparisons and contrasts to show how e-mail is similar to and different from other forms of communication. Choose two forms of communication, such as the telephone and e-mail, and write a short essay comparing and contrasting them.

Writing Skills Focus: Transitions That Show Relationships

Help make your essay clear by using **transitions that show relationships.** Transitions such as *similarly, in addition, too,* and *likewise* signal that things are alike. Transitions such as *whereas, despite,* and *however* signal differences. Notice how Seabrook uses a transitional phrase to show relationships.

Model From the Article
[T]here was little chance for the conversation to move spontaneously. *On the other hand,* his answers meant more, in a certain way. . . .

Prewriting Choose the two forms of communication you will compare and contrast. List the ways in which your subjects are alike and different.

Drafting Organize your essay in a way that is easy to follow. You might want to discuss each type of communication separately, or you might want to discuss each similarity and difference in turn. As you draft the body, be specific about the ways in which your subjects are alike and different.

Revising Reread your draft carefully. Look for passages that are confusing or weak, and revise them. Add transitions to make sense out of confusing passages.

◆ **Grammar Application**
Look for places where adding a concrete noun would clarify your comparisons.

 Idea Bank

Following are suggestions for matching the Idea Bank topics with your students' performance levels and learning modalities:

Customize for
Performance Levels
Less Advanced Students: 1, 4, 7
Average Students: 2, 4, 5, 7
More Advanced Students: 3, 4, 6

Customize for
Learning Modalities
Verbal/Linguistic: 1, 2, 3, 4, 5, 6
Interpersonal: 4, 5, 6, 7
Logical/Mathematical: 6, 7
Visual/Spatial: 7
Intrapersonal: 1, 3

 Writing Mini-Lesson

Refer students to the Writing Handbook in the back of the book for instruction on the writing process and for further information on comparison-and-contrast essays. Have students use the Venn Diagram in **Writing and Language Transparencies,** p. 77, to arrange their prewriting examples.

 Writer's Solution

Writing Lab CD-ROM
Have students complete their Comparison of Forms of Communication essay by using the tutorial on Exposition: Making Connections. Follow these steps:
1. Use the purpose checklist in Considering Your Audience and Considering Your Purpose to help students clearly define their purpose for writing.
2. Develop clear comparisons by using the Venn diagram on details.
3. Draft on the computer, using the Transition Word Bin to generate words that show relationships.
4. Use the Writing Hint on revising to improve the written draft.

Allow about 90 minutes to complete these steps.

Writer's Solution Sourcebook
Have students use Chapter 5, "Expositions: Making Connections," pp. 137–165, for additional support. The chapter includes in-depth instruction on organizing a comparison-and-contrast essay.

from *E-Mail from Bill Gates* ◆ 47

✓ ASSESSMENT OPTIONS

Formal Assessment, Selection Test, pp. 13–15, and Assessment Resources Software. The selection test is designed so that it can easily be customized to the performance levels of your students.

Alternative Assessment, p. 5, includes options for less advanced students, more advanced students, visual/spatial learners, logical/mathematical learners, and verbal/linguistic learners.

PORTFOLIO ASSESSMENT
Use the following rubrics in the **Alternative Assessment** booklet to assess student writing:
Letter to an Author: Expression, p. 90
Advertisement: Persuasion, p. 101
Cause and Effect: Cause-Effect, p. 98
Writing Mini-Lesision: Comparison/Contrast, p. 99

OBJECTIVES

1. To read, comprehend, and interpret a legend that has a social studies focus
2. To relate a legend with a social studies focus to personal experience
3. To connect literature to social studies
4. To respond to Social Studies Guiding Questions
5. To respond to the legend through writing, speaking and listening, and projects

SOCIAL STUDIES GUIDING QUESTIONS

Reading a Zuñi legend and learning more about their culture will help students explore these Social Studies Guiding Questions:

- What ways of life did Native Americans follow?
- What beliefs did Native American groups hold?

Interest Grabber Have students freewrite about their reactions to being told "You can't do that." Invite them to share what they wrote and discuss how they handled situations where they were told they couldn't or shouldn't follow through with something about which they felt strongly. Encourage them to consider the consequences of going ahead with their plans despite opposition. Then, explain that the main character of this legend is a girl who is told she shouldn't go hunting. When she goes anyway, she faces the consequences of her decision—some bad and some good.

Map Study

Historical Maps Connecting geography to history can help students understand the development of certain cultures. The map on this page shows that the Zuñis are part of the group of Native Americans who live in the Southwest, which is a region of plains, deserts, and mountains. Knowing where the Zuñis live may help students picture the differing terrains that are described in the story. Have students read this page to understand more about Zuñi history.

CONNECTING LITERATURE TO SOCIAL STUDIES

THE FIRST AMERICANS

The Girl Who Hunted Rabbits *Zuñi Legend*

Understanding the World Growing up and learning about the world go hand in hand. From continent to continent, throughout the centuries, folk tales and songs have chronicled the achievements, hopes, and dreams of the young. Many wonderful tales of youth come to us from Native American literature.

Native Americans Native American civilizations provide the longest continuous record of human habitation on the North American continent. Evidence of native peoples dates back 5,000 years to Bat Cave, New Mexico.

The Zuñi From the tenth century to the present, the Zuñi have lived in the Four Corners area, where the states of Colorado, Utah, New Mexico, and Arizona now meet. A story is told of a Spanish explorer who first sighted a Zuñi pueblo village and thought he had found the fabled Seven Cities of Cibola. In fact, the explorer may have interrupted an important ceremony; he was killed by the Zuñi.

Voices of the Past "The Girl Who Hunted Rabbits" is a legend, a story passed down orally from generation to generation and partially based on truth. It tells of a Zuñi girl who goes out alone to hunt. The girl's courage and bravery embody the qualities held in admiration by those of the Zuñi culture.

Native American Culture Areas

```
0        500      1000 Miles
0    500    1000 Kilometers
```

 Prentice Hall Literature Program Resources

REINFORCE / RETEACH / EXTEND

Selection Support Pages
Build Vocabulary, p. 27
Connect Literature to Social Studies, p. 28

Formal Assessment Selection Test, pp. 16–17
Assessment Resources Software

Readings From Social Studies

Writing and Language Transparencies
Series of Events Chain, p. 57

Resource Pro CD-ROM
"The Girl Who Hunted Rabbits"

Listening to Literature Audiocassettes
"The Girl Who Hunted Rabbits"

Connection to Prentice Hall The American Nation *Independence Through 1914*—Ch. 2, Section 1, "The First Americans"

The Girl Who Hunted Rabbits

Zuñi Legend

It was long ago, in the days of the ancients, that a poor maiden lived at "Little Gateway of Zuñi River." You know there are black stone walls of houses standing there on the tops of the cliffs of lava, above the narrow place through which the river runs, to this day.

In one of these houses there lived this poor maiden alone with her feeble old father and her aged mother. She was unmarried, and her brothers had all been killed in wars, or had died gently; so the family lived there helplessly, so far as many things were concerned, from the lack of men in their house.

It is true that in making the gardens—the little plantings of beans, pumpkins, squashes, melons, and corn—the maiden was able to do very well; and thus mainly on the products of these things the family were supported. But, as in those days of our ancients we had neither sheep nor cattle, the hunt was depended upon to supply the meat; or sometimes it was procured by barter of the products of the fields to those who hunted mostly. Of these things this little family had barely enough for their own subsistence; hence, they could not

Connecting Literature to Social Studies
Which details supply information about the value and importance of land cultivation in relation to hunting?

procure their supplies of meat in this way.

Long before, it had been a great house, for many were the brave and strong young men who had lived in it; but the rooms were now empty, or at best contained only the leavings of those who had lived there, much used and worn out.

One autumn day, near wintertime, snow fell, and it became very cold. The maiden had gathered brush and firewood in abundance, and it was piled along the roof of the house and down underneath the ladder which descended from the top. She saw the young men issue forth the next morning in great numbers, their feet protected by long stockings of deerskin, the fur turned inward, and they carried on their shoulders and stuck in their belts stone axes and rabbit sticks. As she gazed at them from the roof, she said to herself, "O that I were a man and could go forth, as do these young men, hunting rabbits! Then my poor old mother and father would not lack for flesh with which to duly season their food and nourish their lean bodies." Thus ran her thoughts, and before night, as she saw these same young men coming in, one after another, some of them bringing long strings

◆ **Build Vocabulary**

procured (prō kyoord´) v.: Obtained by some effort

Links Across Time

❶ Zuñi men were responsible for providing food for families by farming and hunting. As farmers, they created a sophisticated system of floodwater irrigation to compensate for the region's lack of water. Hunting was conducted in large groups. In the desert close to the village, small game such as mice and rabbits were plentiful. Rabbits were hunted with rabbit sticks that were flung like boomerangs. Larger game, such as bear, deer, and elk, were found farther away in the woods and mountains. Deer were usually corralled or trapped in pits for easy killing. The men also fished and snared birds such as ducks, eagles, hawks, and crows, using a special trap for each kind of bird.

CONNECTING LITERATURE TO SOCIAL STUDIES

❷ Infer Have students reread the parents' response and use what they know about gender roles to answer the question. *Because the parents do not want the girl to go hunting and are afraid for her—even though young men go hunting every day—hunting must not be a job for women.*

Customize for
More Advanced Students

Review with students that a legend is a story that people hand down by word of mouth, generation to generation. Like myths, legends sometimes include supernatural elements, but legends usually are based more on historical facts. Invite students, as they read, to list elements that could be true and those that indicate it is a legend. They may use a chart like the following:

Real	Fantasy
The girl hunts with rabbit sticks.	The girl is rescued by two war-gods.

Guide students to determine that without the fantastical elements, the story seems factual.

Customize for
English Language Learners

This story has many words describing a character's way of moving that may be unfamiliar to students, such as *quavered, hobbled, crouching,* and *shuddering.* Have students read with a proficient partner who can pantomime these movements where they appear in the legend.

50

CONNECTING LITERATURE TO SOCIAL STUDIES

of rabbits, others short ones, but none of them empty-handed, she decided that she would set forth on the morrow to try what luck she might find in the killing of rabbits herself.

It may seem strange that, although this maiden was beautiful and young, the youths did not give her some of their rabbits. But their feelings were not friendly, for no one of them would she accept as a husband, although one after another of them had offered himself for marriage.

Fully resolved, the girl that evening sat down by the fireplace, and turning toward her aged parents, said, "O my mother and father, I see that the snow has fallen, whereby easily rabbits are tracked, and the young men who went out this morning returned long before evening heavily laden with strings of this game. Behold, in the other rooms of our house are many rabbit sticks, and there hang on the walls stone axes, and with these I might per-chance strike down a rabbit on his trail, or, **❶** if he runs into a log, split the log and dig him out. So I have thought during the day, and have decided to go tomorrow and try my for-tunes in the hunt."

"*Naiya*, my daughter," quavered the feeble, old mother, "you would surely be very cold, or you would lose your way, or grow so tired that you could not re-turn before night, and you must not go out to hunt rabbits."

> **Connecting Literature to Social Studies**
> **❷** What does the parents' reaction to the girl's wish to go hunting tell us about the gender roles of the Zuñi Indians?

"Why, certainly not," insisted the old man, rubbing his lean knees and shaking his head over the days that were gone. "No, no; let us live in poverty rather than that you should run such risks as these, O my daughter."

But, say what they would, the girl was de-termined. And the old man said at last, "Very well! You will not be turned from your course. Therefore, O daughter, I will help you as best I may." He hobbled into another room, and found there some old deerskins covered thickly with fur; and drawing them out, he

moistened and carefully softened them, and cut out for the maiden long stockings, which he sewed up with <u>sinew</u> and the fiber of the yucca[1] leaf. Then he selected for her from among the old possessions of his brothers and sons, who had been killed or perished other-wise, a number of rabbit sticks and a fine, heavy stone ax. Meanwhile, the old woman busied herself in preparing a lunch for the girl, which was composed of little cakes of cornmeal, spiced with pepper and wild onions, pierced through the middle, and baked in the ashes. When she had made a long string of these by threading them like beads on a rope of yucca fiber, she laid them down not far from the ladder on a little bench, with the rabbit sticks, the stone ax, and the deerskin stockings.

That night the maiden planned and planned, and early on the following morning, even before the young men had gone out from the town, she had put on a warm, short-skirted dress, knotted a <u>mantle</u> over her shoulder and thrown another and larger one over her back, drawn on the deerskin stock-ings, had thrown the string of corncakes over her shoulder, stuck the rabbit sticks in her belt, and carrying the stone ax in her hand sallied[2] forth eastward through the Gateway of Zuñi and into the plain of the valley beyond, called the Plain of the Burnt River, on account of the black, roasted-looking rocks along some parts of its sides. Dazzlingly white the snow stretched out before her—not deep, but un-broken—and when she came near the cliffs with many little canyons in them, along the northern side of the valley, she saw many a trail of rabbits running out and in among the rocks and between the bushes.

Warm and excited by her <u>unwonted</u> exer-cise, she did not heed a coming snowstorm, but ran about from one place to another, fol-lowing the trails of the rabbits, sometimes up into the canyons where the forests of pine and

---

1. **yucca** (yuk´ ə) *n.*: Desert plant with stiff leaves and white flowers.
2. **sallied** (sal´ ēd) *v.*: Set out energetically.

50 ◆ Coming of Age

Block Scheduling Strategies

Consider these suggestions to take advantage of extended class time:

- Have students record events of the girl's journey, using the Series of Events Chain in **Writing and Language Transparencies,** p. 57. The information can be used to complete the Viewing and Representing Mini-Lesson, p. 53.
- Have students read the selection independently. Then, reinforce and extend their understanding by having them work in small groups to complete the Guide for Responding questions, p. 54. Encourage students to take turns reading

questions and writing responses.

- Have students use the Gathering Information, Organizing Details, Drafting, and the Revising and Editing sections of the tutorial on Exposition, Making Connections, of the *Writer's Solution Writing Lab CD-ROM,* to complete all or part of the Letter or Cause and Effect writing activities in the Idea Bank on p. 55.
- Use *The American Nation: Independence Through 1914,* Chapter 2, Section 1, "The First Americans," to team teach or to further con-nect literature to social studies.

cedar stood, and where here and there she had the good fortune sometimes to run two, three, or four rabbits into a single hollow log. It was little work to split these logs, for they were small, as you know, and to dig out the rabbits and slay them by a blow of the hand on the nape of the neck, back of the ears; and as she killed each rabbit she raised it reverently to her lips, and breathed from its nostrils its expiring breath[3] and, tying its legs together, placed it on the string, which after a while began to grow heavy on her shoulders. Still she kept on, little heeding the snow which was falling fast; nor did she notice that it was growing darker and darker, so intent was she on the hunt, and so glad was she to capture so many rabbits. Indeed, she followed the trails until they were no longer visible, as the snow fell all around her, thinking all the while, "How happy will be my poor old father and mother that they shall now have flesh to eat! How strong will they grow! And when this meat is gone, that which is dried and preserved of it also, lo! another snowstorm will no doubt come, and I can go out hunting again."

At last the twilight came, and, looking around, she found that the snow had fallen deeply, there was no trail, and that she had lost her way.

❸ True, she turned about and started in the direction of her home, as she supposed, walking as fast as she could through the soft, deep snow. Yet she reckoned not rightly, for instead of going eastward along the valley, she went southward across it, and entering the mouth of the Descending Plain of the Pines, she went

---

3. **expiring** (ik spīr′ iŋ) **breath:** Dying breath.

◆ **Build Vocabulary**

sinew (sin′ yo͞o) *n.:* Tendon; band of fibrous tissue that connects muscles to bones or other parts and can also be used as thread for sewing

mantle (man′ təl) *n.:* Sleeveless cloak or cape

unwonted (un wän′ tid) *adj.:* Not usual

bedraggled (bi drag′ əld) *adj.:* Dirty and wet

---

on and on, thinking she was going homeward, until at last it grew dark and she knew not which way to turn.

"What harm," thought she, "if I find a sheltered place among the rocks? What harm if I remain all night, and go home in the morning when the snow has ceased falling, and by the light I shall know my way?"

❹ So she turned about to some rocks which appeared, black and dim, a short distance away. Fortunately, among these rocks is the cave which is known as Taiuma's[4] Cave. This she came to, and peering into that black hole, she saw in it, back some distance, a little glowing light. "Ha, ha!" thought she, "perhaps some rabbit hunters like myself, belated yesterday, passed the night here and left the fire burning. If so, this is greater good fortune than I could have looked for." So, lowering the string of rabbits which she carried on her shoulder, and throwing off her mantle, she crawled in, peering well into the darkness, for fear of wild beasts; then, returning, she drew in the string of rabbits and the mantle.

Behold! there was a bed of hot coals buried in the ashes in the very middle of the cave, and piled up on one side were fragments of broken wood. The girl, happy in her good fortune, issued forth and gathered more sticks ❺ from the cliffside, where dead pines are found in great numbers, and bringing them in little armfuls one after another, she finally succeeded in gathering a store sufficient to keep the fire burning brightly all the night through. Then she drew off her snow-covered stockings of deerskin and the bedraggled mantles, and, ❻ building a fire, hung them up to dry and sat down to rest herself. The fire burned up and glowed brightly, so that the whole cave was as light as a room at night when a dance is being celebrated. By and by, after her clothing had dried, she spread a mantle on the floor of the cave by the side of the fire, and, sitting down, dressed one of her rabbits and roasted it, and, untying the string of corncakes her mother

---

4. **Taiuma's** (tī o͞o′ məz)

The Girl Who Hunted Rabbits ◆ 51

CONNECTING LITERATURE TO SOCIAL STUDIES *(side tab)*

CONNECTING LITERATURE TO SOCIAL STUDIES

❸ **Draw Conclusions** Have students explain why the girl makes a wrong turn as she tries to get home. *She had never been hunting before, so she was unfamiliar with the territory; she could not see as well, because it was darker than when she started; there was no trail to follow, because the snow had covered it.*

Comprehension Check ☑

❹ Ask students to tell why the girl turns toward the rocks. *She hopes to find shelter from the snowstorm and a place to spend the night.*

◆ **LITERATURE AND YOUR LIFE**

❺ Invite students to offer an opinion, and support it, as to whether the girl should be happy at this point. *Some students may say she should be happy, because she feels safe—she is able to find shelter and start a fire to keep warm. Others may say she should be unhappy, because she is lost and alone.*

Links Across Time

❻ In this passage, the girl takes off her deerskin stockings and her mantles, or cloaks, to dry. The Zuñis used both cotton fabric and animal skins for clothing. Deerskin and antelope hides were used for footwear and men's leggings. The women's cotton clothing included blouses, cloaks, blankets, sashes, and skirts, and the men wore shirts, cloaks, blankets, sashes, and aprons that covered their leggings. Point out to students that this is similar to men wearing pants and women wearing dresses in European cultures of the same period. The Zuñis' cotton clothing was dyed in bright colors and featured embroidery done in geometric designs.

Cultural Connection

Women's Roles Zuñi society was, by and large, matriarchal. When a Zuñi male was married, he left his home to join the household of his new wife, whereas the daughter remained with her family of birth. This family structure established the role of women as leaders in their families. The oldest woman in the household organized the family workload, and the plots of clan farmland were distributed (to use, not to own) by the clan heads, who also were female.

Gender played a role in the workload division, as well. Men were responsible for the major farming; made jewelry, baskets, tools, and utensils; and wove cotton into cloth. Women were in charge of preparing and preserving the food, keeping small gardens, gathering wild plants for medicinal use, maintaining the interior walls of the adobe house, and keeping the household fire burning. Men gathered the wood for that fire.

Hold a class discussion to help students understand how lifestyles and beliefs affect cultural differences. Guide them to see that legends such as this Zuñi story represent historical changes as well as cultural differences.

◆ LITERATURE AND YOUR LIFE

❶ Invite students to express their opinion of the girl's actions in this passage. *Some students may approve of her actions because she seems to have a good heart and is trying to help another lost person. Others may say she is too reckless; since she is all alone, she should be more cautious.*

◆ CONNECTING LITERATURE TO SOCIAL STUDIES

❷ Draw Conclusions Ask students to explain how the girl knows that it is a demon who has cried out to her. *In addition to crying and shouting, she hears "the clatter of an enormous rattle."*

▶ Critical Viewing ◀

❸ Interpret *The girl in the painting seems to be about the age of the maiden; students may feel that she looks independent, like the girl who goes out to hunt rabbits. Others may think that she looks timid and scared, which are not qualities we see in the maiden before the old Demon arrives.*

Comprehension Check ☑

❹ Ask students to tell you why the Demon does not get the rabbit himself. *He is too big to get past the entrance of the cave.*

◆ CONNECTING LITERATURE TO SOCIAL STUDIES

❺ Infer Have students explain why the Demon demands the girl's overshoes. *He is a Cannibal Demon, so he eats meat. He wants the girl but can not get to her, so he settles for rabbits. When she runs out of rabbits, he asks for what must be the next best thing, her deerskin overshoes.*

Customize for
Verbal/Linguistic Learners

Invite students to work in groups of three to read aloud the three paragraphs beginning with "The old Demon. . . ." Have one be the narrator, another the Demon, and the third the girl. As they read, encourage them to reflect the drama and emotion of each part in order to capture the suspense, danger, and terror the writer imparts.

had made for her, feasted on the roasted meat and cakes.

She had just finished her evening meal, and was about to recline and watch the fire for awhile, when she heard away off in the distance a long, low cry of distress—*"Ho-o-o-o thlaia-a!"*

❶ "Ah!" thought the girl, "someone, more belated than myself, is lost; doubtless one of the rabbit-hunters." She got up, and went nearer to the entrance of the cavern.

"Ho-o-o-o thlaia-a!" sounded the cry, nearer this time. She ran out, and, as it was repeated again, she placed her hand to her mouth, and cried, as loudly as possible, *"Li-i- thlaia-a!"* ("Here!")

❷ The cry was repeated near at hand, and presently the maiden, listening first, and then shouting, and listening again, heard the clatter of an enormous rattle. In dismay and terror she threw her hands into the air, and,

❸ ▼ Critical Viewing Does the girl in the painting seem to have the same qualities as the maiden in the story? Explain. [Interpret]

Indian Girl, Robert Henri, Indianapolis Museum of Art

crouching down, rushed into the cave and retreated to its farthest limits, where she sat shuddering with fear, for she knew that one of the Cannibal Demons of those days, perhaps the renowned Atahsaia[5] of the east, had seen the light of her fire through the cave entrance, with his terrible staring eyes, and assuming it to be a lost wanderer, had cried out, and so led her to guide him to her place of concealment.

On came the Demon, snapping the twigs under his feet and shouting in a hoarse, loud voice, *"Ho lithlsh tâ ime!"* ("Ho, there! So you are in here, are you?") *Kothl!* clanged his rattle, while, almost fainting with terror, closer to the rock crouched the maiden.

The old Demon came to the entrance of the cave and bawled out, "I am cold, I am hungry! Let me in!" Without further ado, he stooped and tried to get in; but, behold! the entrance was too small for his giant shoulders to pass. Then he pretended to be wonderfully civil, and said, "Come out, and bring me something to eat."

"I have nothing for you," cried the maiden. "I have eaten my food."

"Have you no rabbits?"

"Yes."

"Come out and bring me some of them."

But the maiden was so terrified that she dared not move toward the entrance.

❹ "Throw me a rabbit!" shouted the old Demon.

The maiden threw him one of her precious rabbits at last, when she could rise and go to it. He clutched it with his long, horny hand, gave one gulp and swallowed it. Then he cried out, "Throw me another!" She threw him another, which he also immediately swallowed; and so on until the poor maiden had thrown all the rabbits to the voracious old monster. Every one she threw him he caught in his huge, yellow-tusked mouth, and swallowed, hair and all, at one gulp.

"Throw me another!" cried he, when the last

5. **Atahsaia** (ah´ tə si´ ə)

52 ◆ *Coming of Age*

Humanities: Art

Indian Girl, 1917, by Robert Henri
Robert Henri (1865–1929) was born in Cincinnati, Ohio, received his art education at the Pennsylvania Academy of Fine Arts in Philadelphia, furthered his education in Paris, then settled in New York City to teach. Henri was one of eight artists who made up the Ashcan School, which championed the portrayal of city life in all its dimensions, from rich to poor.

This painting is one of many portraits of Pueblo Indians made by Henri on trips to the Southwest. He was more interested in the character of his subjects than in the environment in which they lived. Through bold brushwork and deep colors, Henri hoped to capture the Southwest's beauty as embodied in its individual people.

1. What details in this painting remind you of the girl in the story? *The painting shows a young Native American girl; she is wearing a mantle like the one described in the story; the girl seems to be thoughtful and strong like the girl in the story.*

2. Why do you think the artist included the pattern in the background? *It is similar to the geometric designs of Pueblo arts and crafts.*

had already been thrown to him.

So the poor maiden was forced to say, "I have no more."

5 | "Throw me your overshoes!" cried he.

She threw the overshoes of deerskin, and these like the rabbits he speedily <u>devoured</u>. Then he called for her moccasins, and she threw them; for her belt, and she threw it; and finally, wonderful to tell, she threw even her mantle, and blanket, and her overdress, until, behold, she had nothing left!

Now, with all he had eaten, the old Demon was swollen hugely at the stomach, and, though he tried and tried to squeeze himself through the mouth of the cave, he could not by any means succeed. Finally, lifting his great flint ax, he began to shatter the rock about the entrance to the cave, and slowly but surely he enlarged the hole and the maiden now knew that as soon as he could get in he would devour her also, and she almost fainted at the sickening thought. Pound, pound, pound, pound, went the great ax of the Demon as he struck the rocks.

> **Connecting Literature to Social Studies**
> **6** What details reveal the maiden's belief in folklore?

In the distance the two war-gods were sitting in their home at the Shrine amid the Bushes beyond Thunder Mountain, and though far off, they heard thus in the middle of the night the pounding of the Demon's hammer ax against the rocks. And of course they knew at once that a poor maiden, for the sake of her father and mother, had been out hunting—that she had lost her way and, finding a cave where there was a little fire, entered it, rebuilt the fire, and rested herself; that, attracted by the light of her fire, the Cannibal Demon had come and besieged her retreat,[6] and only a little time hence would he so enlarge the entrance to the cave that he could squeeze even his great overfilled paunch through it and come at the maiden to destroy her. So, catching up their wonderful weapons,

---

6. **besieged** (bi sējd´) **her retreat:** Attacked her place of refuge.

these two war-gods flew away into the darkness and in no time they were approaching the Descending Plain of the Pines.

Just as the Demon was about to enter the cavern, and the maiden had fainted at seeing his huge face and gray shock of hair and staring eyes, his yellow, protruding tusks, and his horny, taloned hand, they came upon the old beast. Each one hitting him a blow with his war club, they "ended his daylight," and then hauled him forth into the open space. They opened his huge paunch and withdrew from it the maiden's garments, and even the rabbits which had been slain. The rabbits they cast away among the soap-weed plants that grew on the slope at the foot of the cliff. The garments they spread out on the snow, and cleansed and made them perfect, even more perfect than they had been before. Then, flinging the huge body of the giant Demon down into the depths of the canyon, they turned them about and, calling out gentle words to the maiden, entered and restored her. She, seeing in them not their usual ugly persons, but handsome youths, was greatly comforted; and bending low, and breathing upon their hands, thanked them over and over for the rescue they had brought her. But she crouched herself low with shame that her garments were but few, when, behold! the youths went out and brought in to her the garments they had cleaned, restoring them to her.

Then, spreading their mantles by the door of the cave, they slept there that night, in order to protect the maiden, and on the morrow wakened her. They told her many things, and showed her many things which she had not known before, and counseled her thus, "It is not fearful that a maiden should marry; therefore, O maiden, return unto thy people in the Village of the Gateway of the River of Zuñi.

7

8

◆ **Build Vocabulary**

voracious (vô rā´ shəs) *adj.*: Eager to devour large quantities of food

devoured (di voȯrd´) *v.*: Ate greedily

The Girl Who Hunted Rabbits ◆ 53

CONNECTING LITERATURE TO SOCIAL STUDIES

6 **Analyze** Have students reread the paragraph to find folklore details. *A real demon threatens the girl; the Demon shatters rock with an ax so he can enter the cave; there are two war-gods who live in a shrine, know everything, and can fly.*

CONNECTING LITERATURE TO SOCIAL STUDIES

7 **Speculate** Invite students to speculate about the things the war-gods tell the girl. *Answers will vary, but some students may say they teach her about hunting; others may say they teach her about the spirit world; still others may say they teach her about her duties to her people. Accept all reasonable responses.*

Links Across Time

8 Have students recall that the girl had refused to get married. Then, explain that in Zuñi society, young girls were expected to marry young. After a decision to marry, the girl would consult her mother to see if the family approved of the marriage. Then the couple would determine whether they were compatible; if not, either the man or the woman could choose to call off the marriage.

 Viewing and Representing Mini-Lesson

Illustrated Map

This mini-lesson supports the Art project in the Idea Bank on p. 55.

Introduce Explain that students will create an illustrated map showing the journey made by the girl and the other places and landscapes described in the legend.

Develop Have students work with a partner, using the Series of Events Chain in **Writing and Language Transparencies,** p. 57, to understand the girl's trip in the proper sequence. Then, have them review the story to list other places, such as Thunder Mountain, where the war-gods live. They may want to research maps of the area to find out more about the topographical features and specific places, such as the Descending Plain of the Pines. Have students make a short note for each scene describing the illustration they will use for their maps. Tell students that the illustrations may be symbolic, rather than elaborate scenes.

Apply Have students use craft paper and markers or pencils to create their maps.

Remind them that the information on their maps should reflect the route described in the story and show that the journey starts and ends at the village. Before combining the maps in a class atlas, invite students to form small groups and retell the legend by pointing to the places shown on their maps.

Assess Evaluate students' work based on whether they have depicted the principal points of the journey in correct sequence. Illustrations should clearly relate to events and geographical features.

CONNECTING LITERATURE TO SOCIAL STUDIES

① Draw Conclusions *The girl returns with many more rabbits than the men could ever catch. They believe she is a much greater hunter than they are even though she is a girl—she is beyond comparison.*

Reinforce and Extend

Answers
◆ LITERATURE AND YOUR LIFE

Reader's Response Some students may admire the girl because she bravely sets out to help her family despite her inexperience and the social taboos. Others may say that the girl behaves rashly, placing herself in unnecessary danger.

Thematic Focus The girl learns that there is a lot she does not know about the world and that she must be prepared to venture out where she has not been before.

☑ **Check Your Comprehension**

1. She wants to provide meat for her family's survival because there are no young men in her family to help.
2. Hunting is not a woman's job; they are afraid she might get lost or become tired and cold.
3. Two war-gods save her from the Demon and take her home.
4. The girl is treated with awe and respect.

◆ Critical Thinking

1. They see that she will go with or without their permission, so they at least try to make sure she will be as safe as possible and have what she needs for a safe trip.
2. They want to save the girl because she has a good heart—she was only trying to help her parents.
3. Students may answer that the war-gods appear that way in order not to frighten the girl; others may say the girl sees them that way because they are her rescuers.
4. She learns many new things, including that she should not be afraid to marry.
5. Some students will say that it was wise, because she needed shelter; others will say it was unwise, because she had no way to escape in case of danger.

This morning we will slay rabbits unnumbered for you, and start you on your way, guarding you down the snow-covered valley. When you are in sight of your home we will leave you, telling you our names."

So, early in the morning the two gods went forth, flinging their sticks among the soap-weed plants. Behold! as though the soap-weed plants were rabbits, so many lay killed on the snow before these mighty hunters. And they gathered together great numbers of these rabbits, a string for each one of the party. When the Sun had risen clearer in the sky, and his light sparkled on the snow around them, they took the rabbits to the maiden and presented them, saying, "We will carry each one of us a string of these rabbits." Then taking her hand, they led her out of the cave and down the valley, until, beyond on the high black mesas[7] at the Gateway of the River of Zuñi, she saw the smoke rise from the houses of her village.

---

7. **mesas** (mā′ sez) *n.*: Small mountains with flat tops and steep sides.

Then turned the two war-gods to her, and they told her their names. And again she bent low, and breathed on their hands. Then, dropping the strings of rabbits which they had carried close beside the maiden, they swiftly disappeared.

Thinking much of all she had learned, she continued her way to the home of her father and mother. As she went into the town, staggering under her load of rabbits, the young men and the old men and women and children beheld her with wonder; and no hunter in that town thought of comparing himself with the Maiden Hunter of Zuñi River. The old man and the old woman, who had mourned the night through and sat up anxiously watching, were overcome with happiness when they saw their daughter had returned.

> **Connecting Literature to Social Studies**
> What conclusion can you draw from the fact that the huntsmen of the town would not compare themselves with the Maiden Hunter? ①

Guide for Responding

◆ LITERATURE AND YOUR LIFE

Reader's Response Do you admire the actions of the girl in the story? Why or why not?

Thematic Focus What does the girl in the story learn about herself and the world?

☑ **Check Your Comprehension**

1. For what reasons does the girl go hunting?
2. Why do the girl's parents at first resist her plans?
3. How is the girl rescued?
4. How do the villagers regard the girl when she returns?

◆ Critical Thinking

INTERPRET

1. Why do the girl's parents help her when they really do not want her to go hunting? **[Speculate]**
2. For what reason do the war gods help the girl? **[Connect]**
3. Why does the girl see the two war gods as handsome youths? **[Draw Conclusions]**
4. What does the girl learn from the war gods? **[Interpret]**

EVALUATE

5. Was the girl's decision to spend the night in a cave a wise one or a foolish one? Explain. **[Make a Judgment]**

54 ◆ *Coming of Age*

Beyond the Selection

FURTHER READING
Other Works About First Americans
The Zuñi, Nancy Bonvillain
American Indians of the Southwest, Bertha P. Dutton
Cherokee Animal Tales, George F. Scheer (ed.)
Many Winters, Nancy C. Wood
Native American Stories, Joseph Bruchac

INTERNET
We suggest the following Internet site for information about the Zuñis (all Web sites are subject to change):
http://thememall.com/tribes/zuni.htm
We *strongly recommend* that you preview the site before you send students to it.

CONNECTING LITERATURE TO SOCIAL STUDIES

"The Girl Who Hunted Rabbits" gives insights into the culture of the Zuñi Native Americans from the Southwest. For example, the girl who hunts rabbits displays attitudes and behaviors that are valued by the Zuñi, such as courage, skill at hunting, and strength of purpose.

1. Judging from "The Girl Who Hunted Rabbits," what can you learn about the place of women in Zuñi culture?
2. What can you determine about the climate and terrain of Zuñi territory?
3. What might the Demon represent in "The Girl Who Hunted Rabbits"?

 ## Idea Bank

Writing

1. **List of Clues** Read through "The Girl Who Hunted Rabbits," and make a list of the clues in the story that give information about Zuñi society and culture.

2. **Letter** Write a letter to the girl in "The Girl Who Hunted Rabbits." Explain how the legends and heroes of your ancestors are similar to and different from those of the Zuñi. You may want to include a chart that shows how categories such as clothing and food differ between your culture and that of the Zuñis.

3. **Cause and Effect** Analyze Zuñi traditions using clues in "The Girl Who Hunted Rabbits." Then, write a cause-and-effect essay showing how Zuñi traditions, such as hunting, cause the girl in the story to take certain actions.

Speaking and Listening

4. **Music Connection** Find several pieces of music that enhance "The Girl Who Hunted Rabbits." Play the music for the class as you read the story aloud.

Projects

5. **Art** Make an illustrated map of the landscape described and places named in "The Girl Who Hunted Rabbits." Indicate the maiden's path, and illustrate scenes along the way. **[Art Link]**

6. **Encyclopedia Entry** With a group of students, do research about the Zuñi people. Create an illustrated encyclopedia entry, giving information about where they live (then and now), their beliefs and social structure, and their customs. **[Social Studies Link]**

Further Reading, Listening, and Viewing

- *Gluskabe Stories,* Audio Edition, by Joseph Bruchac
- *The Apaches* by Virginia Driving Hawk Sneve
- *A Narrative of the Captivity and Restoration of Mrs. Mary Rowlandson* by Mary Rowlandson

 ## Idea Bank

Following are suggestions for matching the Idea Bank topics with your students' performance levels and learning modalities:

Customize for *Performance Levels*
Less Advanced Students: 1, 6
Average Students: 2, 4, 5, 6
More Advanced Students: 3, 5, 6

Customize for *Learning Modalities*
Verbal/Linguistic: 2, 3, 4
Visual/Spatial: 5, 6
Interpersonal: 6
Logical/Mathematical: 2, 3, 5, 6
Musical/Rhythmic: 4

Answers *(continued)*
CONNECTING LITERATURE TO SOCIAL STUDIES

1. Women have a defined role in Zuñi society, but typically they do not hunt and they are not forced to marry.
2. The climate and terrain are varied, ranging from forested mountains to desert mesas. Autumn and winter are mentioned in the story, so the seasons vary.
3. The Demon may represent qualities like greed, selfishness, and evil. He may also represent the unknown.

✓ ASSESSMENT OPTIONS

Formal Assessment, Selection Test, pp. 16–17, and Assessment Resources Software. The selection test is designed so that it can be customized easily to the performance levels of your students.

PORTFOLIO ASSESSMENT
Use the following rubrics in the **Alternative Assessment** booklet to assess student writing:
Clues to Culture: Definition/Classification, p. 95
Letter: Comparison/Contrast, p. 99
Cause and Effect: Cause-Effect, p. 98

Prepare and Engage

Establish Writing Guidelines
Review the following key characteristics of a personal narrative:

- A personal narrative relates a true story about a memorable experience.
- The writer's thoughts or insights about the event help to re-create the experience.

You may want to distribute the Scoring Rubric for Narrative Based on Personal Experience, p. 92 in **Alternative Assessment,** to make students aware of the criteria on which they will be evaluated. See the suggestions on p. 58 for how you can customize the rubric to this workshop.

Refer students to the Writing Handbook in the back of the book for instruction on the writing process and for further information on narrative writing.

 Writer's Solution

Writers at Work Videodisc
To introduce students to the key elements of narration and show how Rudolfo Anaya uses the elements of personal narrative as he writes, play the videodisc segment on Narration (Ch. 3). Have students respond to Anaya's insights into narrative writing.

Play frames 21977 to 31219

Writing Lab CD-ROM
If you have access to computers, you may want to have students work in the tutorial on Narration to complete all or part of their personal narratives. Follow these steps:

1. Students can view a model from literature of a personal narrative.
2. Have students view the video clip to learn from Eudora Welty's tips for writing about what they already know.
3. Students can draft on the computer.
4. Have students use the interactive models for tips on using dialogue.

Writer's Solution Sourcebook
Students can find additional support, including instruction on Creating a Beginning, pp. 91–92, in the chapter on Narration, pp. 70–103.

Connect to Literature Unit 7, "Nonfiction," includes an example of a personal narrative: an excerpt from Annie Dillard's *An American Childhood.*

Personal Narrative

Writing Process Workshop

Like the writers in this unit, you are a storyteller. When you tell a friend about what happened to you on your vacation or describe the time you won a T-ball competition, you're telling a **personal narrative,** a story that relates a real-life experience from your point of view. Personal narratives bring past events to life through action, description, and dialogue. Write a personal narrative about an important experience you've had.

The following skills, introduced in this section's Writing Mini-Lessons, will help you write your personal narrative.

Writing Skills Focus

▶ **Use an appropriate tone** to describe the people and events in your narrative. (See p. 21.)
▶ **Elaborate to make writing personal.** Include details that reveal your ideas about people, places, and events. (See p. 31.)
▶ Connect the events in your narrative using **transitions.** (See p. 47.)

MODEL FROM LITERATURE

from *I Know Why the Caged Bird Sings* by Maya Angelou

Weighing the half-pounds of flour, excluding the scoop, and depositing them dust-free into the thin paper sacks held a simple kind of adventure for me. ① I developed an eye for measuring how full a silver-looking ladle of flour, mash, meal, sugar or corn had to be to push the scale indicator over to eight ounces or one pound. When I was absolutely accurate ② our appreciative customers used to admire: "Sister Henderson sure got some smart grandchildrens." ③

① Specific incidents bring Angelou's personal experience to life.
② The transition word when makes the logical connection clear.
③ This line of dialogue gives the narrative a warm, homey tone.

56 ◆ *Coming of Age*

 Cultural Connection

Storytelling Long before people recorded stories in written form, they shared them orally. For example, in some African cultures, oral historians called *griots* have always been responsible for passing down the history of tribes through music and words.

Have students research storytelling around the world and throughout history. Divide the class into groups, and have each group research a particular culture or time period. Next, ask groups to summarize the methods of storytelling that they discovered. Then, discuss with the class the differences between oral storytelling and written personal narratives.

Ask students what place storytelling has in society today. Point out that every time they tell someone about their day or describe an event, they are telling a story. Writing these kinds of stories on paper is the bridge to a written personal narrative.

Encourage students to think of details they would include and gestures they would use if they were telling their personal narratives aloud to an audience. They may want to incorporate some or all of these storytelling techniques in their writing.

Prewriting

Choose a Topic Your memory is probably the best place to search for a topic for your personal narrative. Recall holidays, birthdays, school trips, or even what you did this morning to find an experience to describe in a personal narrative. You may also select from among these topic ideas:

> ### Topic Ideas
> - A misunderstanding between you and a friend
> - The best vacation ever
> - Getting a pet

Create a Timeline Make a chronological list of events you want to include in your story by filling in a timeline like this one:

Arrived at school. → Met Johnny for lunch. → Spilled pudding. → Slipped in spill. → Missed bus home.

Drafting

Tell the Story As you draft, check off events on your timeline. By doing this, you'll be sure to include all the specific incidents of the narrative.

Elaborate to Personalize Your Writing Consider how you would describe the events of your narrative to a close friend. Elaborate on the events with specific details and personal observations. Personalizing your narrative in this way will bring your reader closer to the events as you experienced them.

Choose an Appropriate Tone One way to make your personal narrative memorable is to give it an appropriate tone, or to convey your attitude about the event. To do this, choose words and phrasing that support or mirror the emotional impact of the scene you're describing.

Serious Tone: His face fell when I said I have to move to another town.

Humorous Tone: His jaw hit the floor when I said "I'm outta here."

APPLYING LANGUAGE SKILLS: Writing Realistic Dialogue

Realistic dialogue captures the way people really speak. In casual speech, people use informal language and contractions rather than phrasing that would be expected in formal writing.

Formal Phrasing
"I will buy you some french-fried potatoes."

Realistic Dialogue
"I'll get you some fries."

Practice For each statement below, write a line of dialogue.

1. Filip tells you after class that he can't come to the meeting after school today.
2. Mother asked Alonso to bring home a gallon of milk from the store.
3. Stan asked Wendy why she wasn't at the Fun Fair on Saturday.

Writing Application As you edit, revise your dialogue to make it realistic.

> ### Writer's Solution Connection Writing Lab
>
> To learn more about realistic dialogue, see the interactive models on improving dialogue in the Revising and Editing section of the Narration tutorial.

Develop Student Writing

Prewriting
After students have replayed their experiences in their mind and gathered details, you may want them to use the Cluster Organizer from **Writing and Language Transparencies,** p. 73, to help them organize events and details for drafting.

Customize for *English Language Learners*
Pair students with native speakers, and have them review each other's Timeline and Cluster Organizer. Have students take turns verbally describing the events of their narratives. Encourage students to tell what they like about the descriptions and offer suggestions about information that isn't clear to them.

Customize for *Visual/Spatial Learners*
Invite students to sketch parts of their stories before they write. They may sketch a character, a scene, or a series of scenes. Suggest that they add details to their drawings, which will provide additional details for their written narratives. Point out that vivid words and sensory details help readers "see" the story events.

Drafting
You may want to have students work with peers. Readers should note what tone the narrative has and offer clues to writers as to where information is unclear, where the order of events is confusing, or where more elaboration would help. Have students review their dialogue, making sure it sounds realistic—peers may help by reading dialogue aloud and offering suggestions about the way people really speak.

> ### ✎ Writer's Solution
>
> **Writing Lab CD-ROM**
> Students can develop strategies for writing their drafts by viewing video clips on story beginnings in the Drafting section of the tutorial on Narration. Using the Transitional Word Phrase Bin activity will help them gather words and phrases to develop and organize narrative events in time order.

Applying Language Skills
Writing Realistic Dialogue Remind students that dialogue brings to life certain events and creates a way for readers to see the characters. The way a character speaks and what a character says reveal a lot about that character.

Answers
Suggested responses:
1. Filip came up to me after class and said, "I won't make it to the meeting after school today."
2. Mom reminded Alonso, "Don't forget to get some milk when you go to the store."
3. Stan asked, "Wendy, where were you on Saturday? Why weren't you at the Fun Fair?"

> ###  Writer's Solution
>
> For additional practice and instruction, use the *Writer's Solution Language Lab CD-ROM* Writing Dialogue lesson in the Composing unit.

Revising

When revising, have students consider whether they have included enough details to create a vivid setting.

 Writer's Solution

Writing Lab CD-ROM

In the tutorial on Narration, have students use the Self-Evaluation Checklist to think about ways to revise narrative elements. The revision checker for language variety will allow them to highlight words used three or more times in their narratives.

Publishing

Encourage students to include a drawing, photograph, or collage to accompany their narratives.

Reinforce and Extend

Review the Writing Guidelines
After students complete their writing, review the characteristics of a personal narrative.

Applying Language Skills
Common and Proper Nouns
Point out to students that the capitalization of proper nouns is a sign to readers that the noun is specific.

Answers
1. The Pueblo peoples lived in the area of the country now known as the Four Corners.
2. I remember my family's trip to the Grand Canyon.
3. Stories of the exchange student from Turkey taught us a lot about our life in the United States.
4. Moving to Indiana changed Melanie's life.

 Writer's Solution

For additional practice, complete Common and Proper Nouns, p. 7, of the *Writer's Solution Grammar Practice Book*.

Writing Process Workshop

EDITING/PROOFREADING

APPLYING LANGUAGE SKILLS:
Common and Proper Nouns

Proper nouns name specific people, places, and things; they should be capitalized. Common nouns, which name general people, places, and things, are not capitalized unless they begin a sentence.

Common Nouns
state, store, girl

Proper Nouns
Arkansas, Marguerite

Practice Rewrite the following, correcting capitalization as needed.

1. The pueblo peoples live in the area of the country now known as the four corners.
2. I remember my family's trip to the grand canyon.
3. Stories of the exchange student from turkey taught us a lot about our life in the united states.
4. Moving to indiana changed melanie's life.

Writing Application Check your draft to be sure you've capitalized proper nouns but not common nouns.

Writer's Solution Connection
Language Lab

For more practice with proper nouns, complete the Language Lab lesson Proper Nouns in the Capitalization unit.

---

58 ◆ Coming of Age

Revising

Make Connections Look over your draft. Have you described events so they are clear and detailed? Have you used transitions to indicate how events are related?

Transitions Showing Time Order: *first, then, next, now, after, before, while, during, when*

Transitions Showing Importance: *although, however, yet, despite, even though*

Add Dialogue to Make Characters Memorable In the real-life event you're describing, conversation probably took place. Instead of telling what people said, bring their actual words to life by adding dialogue.

Telling: Mike promised he'd never go there again.

Dialogue: "I'll never, ever go there again!" Mike sobbed.

REVISION MODEL

Working after school at the library made a big difference in my life. I learned to smile at people and look them in ① *My cheery "How can I help you?" usually won me smiles at the kids' corner.* the eye as I helped them locate and check out books. I ② *most of all* learned to work quickly and efficiently to keep the check- ③ *My least favorite* out line moving. The yuckiest part of the job was stocking shelves at the end of the day, but knowing that was the last thing to do before I could go home made even that part tolerable.

① I added dialogue to help make events more personal.
② Adding a transition connects ideas in my narrative.
③ I changed the beginning of this sentence to match the tone of the rest of the piece.

Publishing and Presenting

▶ **Classroom** One way to share your personal narrative is to read it aloud to your classmates. You may want to work with fellow classmates to arrange a reading of your personal narratives to a class of younger students.

▶ **E-mail** Share your narrative by e-mailing it to a close friend or relative.

Real-World Reading Skills Workshop

Understanding an Author's Purpose

Strategies for Success

In a typical week, you probably skim through magazines or news articles, glance at posters and advertisements, and read through menus or sales catalogs. You probably won't be tested on the meaning of these pieces of writing. You will, however, benefit by learning to recognize the author's purpose behind each piece and to read appropriately. The tips at the right will help you identify an author's purpose.

These wool-lined leather mountain boots are a "must-have" for serious hikers. Lovingly crafted from all-natural materials, these boots cradle your feet while allowing them to breathe.
Skid resistant and waterproof.
Available in Butter, Toffee, and Mocha colors.
Specify size when ordering.

Men's Boots: $89.99 plus tax and shipping
Women's Boots: $79.99 plus tax and shipping

How to Read Magazine and News Articles

Most magazine and news articles are meant to inform, to entertain, or to persuade. Look at the title of the article, and skim the first paragraph to get a hint about the author's purpose. Once you've determined the author's purpose, adjust your reading accordingly. For example, if the article is meant to entertain, you can read quickly for enjoyment. If, however, the author wants to convince you of something, read critically, questioning his or her ideas.

How to Read Advertisements, Brochures, Catalogs, and Menus

Writers of advertisements, brochures, catalogs, and menus want you to buy their products or services. If you're an interested customer, read carefully and critically before buying. For example, in a catalog description of an item, separate factual details, such as "solid oak" or "$1.99 plus tax," from persuasive details, such as "lovely" or "inexpensive."

How to Read Posters and Flyers

Most posters and flyers are meant to inform or persuade. If the poster or flyer is meant to inform, skim it to find such important information as dates, times, and maps. If the poster or flyer is persuasive, read it more critically, questioning the information that is given.

Apply the Strategies

Read the catalog entry at the left, and answer the following questions.
1. What is the author's purpose?
2. Should you read this piece carefully and critically, or should you read for enjoyment? Explain why.

Introduce the Strategies

Some writers make a career writing novels or plays, others write newspaper or magazine articles, and others write technical instructions or sales brochures. Suggest to students that, as they read, they imagine the writer behind the scenes. Encourage students to ask themselves, "What is the writer trying to tell me?"

Customize for *English Language Learners*

Students may be able to recognize important information in a catalog description, such as size and price, but be unfamiliar with terms that provide more detailed information about an item they want to buy. Help them develop a list of words to get a clearer picture of descriptions, such as color names and descriptions, including mocha (brown), grape (purple), and sage (green); fabric names and descriptions, including nylon, rayon, spandex, natural, and waterproof; and information about garment construction, including fully lined and generous fit. Discuss strategies for determining the meanings of unfamiliar descriptions, such as using pictures and context clues. You may wish to have students who are native speakers help you gather examples of catalogs and review the descriptions with English language learners to help them understand unfamiliar terms.

Apply the Strategies

Discuss with students approaches to reading critically. Have students brainstorm for a list of questions they can apply to help them read critically:
- Can I verify the information through another source?
- Does the author seem to be leaving out details or important information?
- Does any of the information seem to be contradictory?

Answers

1. The author wants to persuade the reader to purchase the boots.
2. You should read this piece critically to determine whether the boots are something you need to buy and if they are worth the price.

◆Build Grammar Skills

Reviewing Nouns

The selections in Part 1 include instruction on the following:

- Common and Proper Nouns
- Plural and Possessive Nouns
- General and Specific Nouns
- Concrete and Abstract Nouns

This information is reinforced with the Build Grammar Skills practice pages in **Selection Support,** pp. 9, 14, 19, and 24.

As you review nouns, you may wish to include the following:

- Collective Nouns

Collective nouns name a group of individual people, animals, or things. Some examples are *family, group, audience, crowd, herd, flock, bundle, set, bouquet,* and *stack.*

- Compound Nouns

A compound noun is made up of two or more words that function as a single noun. Compound nouns may be written as one word, separate words, or hyphenated words; for example, *barbell, middle school, great-uncle.*

Using charts such as the following, invite students to suggest words for each category.

Collective Nouns

People	Animals	Things
band	swarm	fleet

Compound Nouns

One Word	Separate Words	Hyphenated Words
taxpayer	seat belt	half-moon

Customize for
Less Proficient Readers

Suggest that students note troublesome nouns as they read by recording them on charts similar to those above. They can use charts to compare common and proper nouns, concrete and abstract nouns, and plural and possessive nouns.

 **Writer's Solution**

For additional practice and support in Using Nouns, use the practice pages on Nouns in the *Writer's Solution Grammar Practice Book,* pp. 5–7.

Nouns | Grammar Review

Nouns are words that refer to people, places, things, and ideas or qualities. They are the building blocks of nearly everything we say.

Person	general, teacher, Bill Gates
Place	home, kindergarten, Texas
Thing	drum, pearl, e-mail
Idea or quality	fear, childhood, communication

You can put nouns into these categories:

Common	uniform, store, computer (See p. 20.)
Proper	Shiloh, Charles, Macintosh (See p. 20.)
Concrete	peach, woods, rabbit (See p. 46.)
Abstract	taste, imagination, technology (See p. 46.)
Plural	drums, desks, lunches, cookies (See p. 30.)
Possessive Singular	the general's coat (See p. 30.)
Possessive Plural	the armies' strategies (See p. 30.)

Practice 1 On your paper, write the nouns in each sentence that follows. Label each as common or proper; then label them as concrete or abstract.

1. How did the students respond to the story set during the Civil War?

2. On Fridays, her sister helped out in the grocery store.

3. The little boy has great concentration.

4. The kindergarten students went to see bats and monkeys at the Harris Zoo.

5. When do you think Senator Lee will talk about progress?

Practice 2 Create plurals and possessives of the given nouns according to the directions after each word.

1. march (plural)

2. building (possessive, singular)

3. teacher (possessive, plural)

4. brother (possessive, plural)

5. dress (possessive, plural)

Grammar in Writing

✔ *Nouns can sharpen your writing. Whenever possible, choose nouns that are specific.*

General: The gym teacher loved *sports.*

Specific: The gym teacher loved *soccer, tennis,* and *baseball.*

✔ *Be careful not to use apostrophes when you make nouns plural. Use apostrophes only when you make nouns possessive.*

Answers
Practice 1

1. students (common; concrete); story (common; concrete); Civil War (proper; concrete)
2. Fridays (proper; concrete); sister (common; concrete); grocery store (common; concrete)
3. boy (common; concrete); concentration (common; abstract)
4. kindergarten students (common; concrete); bats (common; concrete); monkeys (common; concrete); Harris Zoo (proper; concrete)
5. Senator Lee (proper; concrete); progress (common; abstract)

Practice 2

1. marches
2. building's
3. teachers'
4. brothers'
5. dresses'

PART *2*

Seasons and Cycles

Late September Afternoon, Viola's Field, 1997, Jim Schantz, Pucker Gallery

Seasons and Cycles ◆ 61

 Humanities: Art

Late September Afternoon, Viola's Field,
1997, by Jim Schantz

Jim Schantz works in pastel and usually depicts landscapes from the Berkshires in western Massachusetts. Pastel is an art medium in which chalky sticks like crayons are used to draw on paper. Working in pastel produces light, creamy colors and texture, which Schantz uses to show gradations of color, light, and shadow.

Use the following discussion questions to help students relate the art to the theme "Seasons and Cycles":

1. **What season is depicted in this picture?**
   Students should be able to tell from the title and the color of the field that it is late summer.

2. **What time of day is shown in this picture?**
   Both the title of the painting and the light of the setting sun should tell students that the light and landscape show late afternoon.

3. **How do the time of year and time of day presented here relate to the concept of cycles?**
   The end of a season and of a day indicate that a change will take place soon, and the changes of seasons and from day to night are cyclic.

⏱ **One-Minute**
Planning Guide

The selections in this part explore coming of age as reflected in both the changing seasons and cycles of the world around us and in our individual lives. In the short story "Christmas Day in the Morning," a grandfather remembers an important day from his youth. A short tale, "The Old Grandfather and His Little Grandson," and two poems, "Grandma" and "Old Man," each tackle a relationship between grandparents and their children or grandchildren. The first-person narratives "Shooting Stars" and "Something From the Sixties" deal with the comforting effect of cyclic events. The poems "Poets to Come," "Winter Moon," and "Ring Out, Wild Bells" embrace both single moments in time and visions of the future.

Customize for
Varying Student Needs
When assigning the selections in this part, keep in mind these factors:

"Christmas Day in the Morning"
• Good example of flashback
• Easily accessible to most students

"The Old Grandfather and His Little Grandson"
• Simple tale with a clear moral

"Grandma"
• Cultural connection

"Old Man"
• Non-capitalization of proper nouns may need explaining

"Shooting Stars"
• Science connection
• Special appeal for logical/ mathematical learners

"Something From the Sixties"
• Humorous and heartwarming

"Poets to Come"
• Whitman's perspective on poetry

"Winter Moon"
• Seemingly simple poem merits deeper examination

"Ring Out, Wild Bells"
• Repetition and rhyme make this poem accessible to students

61

Guide for Reading

More About the Author

Pearl Sydenstriker Buck was born in West Virginia while her parents were in America on leave from their missionary work in China. She grew up speaking both English and Chinese. By the time of her death, Buck had published over 70 books: novels, story collections, biography and autobiography, poetry, drama, children's literature, and translations from the Chinese.

Pearl Buck's passionate interest in true and lasting Asian-American understanding led her to establish Welcome House, the first international, interracial adoption agency. She formed it in 1949 in response to the prejudice against adopting Asian and mixed-race children.

Meet the Author:

Pearl S. Buck (1892–1973)

The first woman ever to win both the Pulitzer Prize and the Nobel Prize, Pearl S. Buck grew up in China, where her parents were missionaries. Like many of her books, Buck's Pulitzer Prize-winning novel, *The Good Earth*, is set in China. However, Buck also wrote novels, short stories, and essays that are set in the United States. "Christmas Day in the Morning," for example, takes place on a small American dairy farm.

At Home in Two Cultures Following her childhood in China, Buck attended college in the United States. She later went back to China to teach. Eventually, Buck returned to American shores, finally settling in Bucks County, Pennsylvania. There she became active in promoting women's rights and child welfare, and in condemning racism.

THE STORY BEHIND THE STORY

Like the main character in "Christmas Day in the Morning," Buck, too, had an experience of giving the gift of love at Christmas. When she was fifteen years old and living in China, that country experienced a terrible famine. Rather than spending money on a holiday feast for themselves, Buck's family bought rice for the starving peasants. They spent all of Christmas Day feeding hungry families.

◆ LITERATURE AND YOUR LIFE

CONNECT YOUR EXPERIENCE

Not all gifts come in brightly wrapped packages, like those in the photograph at right. Some gifts come in the form of kindness and caring. Take a moment to recall the best gift you ever gave and the best one you ever received. In "Christmas Day in the Morning," you'll learn about a precious gift that one boy gives to his dad.

THEMATIC FOCUS: Seasons and Cycles

As you read this story, look for ways in which the Christmas season—a time of gift giving—comes to hold special meaning for the main character.

◆ Background for Understanding

SOCIAL STUDIES

Small family dairy farms, like the one in "Christmas Day in the Morning," once were commonplace in America. Because they were not automated, as most dairy farms are today, all chores had to be done by hand. Not only did the cows have to be milked, they had to be moved from pasture to pasture and cared for when ill.

◆ Build Vocabulary

RELATED WORDS: FORMS OF *finite*

Pearl Buck describes the main character's children as showing "infinite gentleness." The word *infinite* is a form of the word *finite*, which means "having a beginning and an end." Coupled with the prefix *-in,* meaning "without" or "not," it means "having no limits or end."

WORD BANK

Preview these words from the selection. Which word do you think means "calmly"? Check the Build Vocabulary box on page 67 to see if you chose correctly.

infinite
brisk
loitering
placidly
acquiescent

◆ Christmas Day in the Morning ◆

◆ Literary Focus

FLASHBACK

A **flashback** is a scene within a story that interrupts the sequence of events to relate events that occurred in the past. Flashbacks allow writers to present two different time frames simultaneously, enabling readers to compare and contrast the present and the past. In "Christmas Day in the Morning," Pearl Buck uses a flashback to show why the main character, Robert, who is now a grandfather, has had special feelings about Christmas since he was fifteen years old.

◆ Reading Strategy

IDENTIFY SEQUENCE OF EVENTS

The **sequence of events** in a story is the order in which things happen. Authors use time-order words like *first, before, later,* and *eventually* to let you know which events happened first, next, and last. These signal words are especially important in stories that shift backward or forward in time.

To keep track of the story events, create a timeline like the one below. Chart the key events that happen in the present time and in the flashback.

Timeline

Flashback

Rob wakes. → _____ [_____ → _____] → _____

 By this time in their lives, most students have given and received a variety of gifts. Divide the class into discussion groups to brainstorm for qualities they believe would describe an ideal gift. Challenge them to focus on generalizations about gifts, not on specific items. For instance, students might say that an ideal gift is appropriate for the recipient, shows that the giver took time and care selecting it, or reflects the relationship between the giver and receiver. Then lead students to the story by guiding them through the Literature and Your Life feature, p. 62.

◆ Build Grammar Skills

Pronouns and Antecedents If you wish to introduce the grammar concept for this selection before students read, refer to the instruction on p. 70.

Customize for
Less Proficient Readers

Because this story has an old-fashioned flavor and is narrated by an older character, some students may have difficulty sustaining solo reading. Consider dividing the class into groups of four, with each student reading aloud one page of the story to the others.

Customize for
More Advanced Students

Challenge students to find evidence of the affect of cycles and seasons in this story. Direct them by writing the expression "A gift that keeps on giving . . ." on the board and asking them to think about how this phrase applies to the story.

Customize for
English Language Learners

Students from non-Christian families, or whose Christmas traditions differ from what is described in the story, may not grasp some holiday terms, details, and expectations. For example, they may not understand the excitement Christmas morning holds for Robert; they may not know what it means to "trim the tree." Invite knowledgeable students to clarify the terms and traditions, or retell the details of the Christmas story.

 Preparing for Standardized Tests

Reading This selection presents the reading strategy of identifying sequence of events to help students as they read. Standardized tests may evaluate students' understanding of events and their sequence to analyze cause-and-effect relationships in a story or passage. To help prepare them for test items, present the following sample question, based on the story:

What did the adult Robert do first to prepare for this Christmas morning?

(A) He quietly milked the cows.
(B) He wrote a love letter to his wife.
(C) He bought his father a tie.
(D) He decorated the tree.

Students should understand the sequence of events in the story, which has a flashback to Robert's youth—Robert has milked cows (A) and bought his father a tie (C) in the past. He has already written a card to his wife when he decorates the tree (D), but in the sequence of story events, he has not yet written the love letter. The correct answer is (B). For further practice, use Reading Strategy: Identify Sequence of Events, p. 32, in **Selection Support.**

One-Minute Insight

"Christmas Day in the Morning" conveys the belief that receiving love enables a person to give love. In an extended flashback, Robert recalls how, as a boy, his father would wake him very early to help with the milking. Robert then recalls the Christmas Eve when he was 15 and overheard his father express his love for him. Young Rob decided then to give his dad a gift of love along with the usual tie. On that morning long ago, Rob arose even earlier and milked the cows himself. When his father saw what Rob had done, he recognized the true worth of the gift; father and son for the first time acknowledged their mutual love. Now, on an early Christmas morning 50 years later, the cycle repeats: Robert's fond memory leads him to give his wife a similar heartfelt gift— a love letter she can cherish forever.

Customize for
Intrapersonal Learners

Have students create a reader's response journal as they read the story. Ask them to focus their observations and reactions on the details that reveal Robert's growing realization that his father loves him and on the change in Rob's behavior that results. Encourage students to respond personally to the insecurity Robert feels about his father's love and the importance to him of feeling loved. Challenge students to explain why it can be so hard for people to express their deepest feelings.

Humanities: Art

Christmas Snow, 1984, by David Armstrong

In this watercolor, the artist creates a rural winter scene set at Christmas time. Discuss these questions:

1. What clues does the artist give to suggest a fresh snowfall? *There are neither footprints nor paths shoveled clear; the horses have snow on their backs; the sky is still gray.*
2. In what ways does the scene suggest the very first Christmas? *The wreath on the barn signals Christmas. According to the Gospel of St. Luke in the New Testament in the Bible, Jesus was born in a stable— a barn; like then, animals are nearby.*

Christmas Day

64 ◆ *Coming of Age*

Block Scheduling Strategies

Consider these suggestions to take advantage of extended class time:

- Introduce the story with the Interest Grabber activity, p. 63, in the Teacher Edition and the Literature and Your Life feature, p. 62, in the Student Edition.
- In small groups, have students read the story or listen to it on audiocassette. Discuss the Literary Focus, p. 63, of flashback to help students plan for the Writing Mini-Lesson, p. 71.
- Peer groups can discuss the Guide for Responding to questions on pp. 69–70, and

work on related **Selection Support** pages as needed.

- Set aside class time for students to develop their portfolios by working on one of the projects or writing activities in the Idea Bank on p. 71, or by completing the Writing Mini-Lesson, p. 71. For additional instruction, direct students to Developing Narrative Elements in the chapter on Narration, pp. 88–89 of *The Writer's Solution Sourcebook*.

in the Morning
Pearl S. Buck

H e woke suddenly and completely. It was four o'clock, the hour at which his father had always called him to get up and help with the milking. Strange how the habits of his youth clung to him still! Fifty years ago, and his father had been dead for thirty years, and yet he waked at four o'clock in the morning. He had trained himself to turn over and go to sleep, but this morning, because it was Christmas, he did not try to sleep.

Yet what was the magic of Christmas now? His childhood and youth were long past, and his own children had grown up and gone. Some of them lived only a few miles away but they had their own families, and though they would come in as usual toward the end of the day, they had explained with <u>infinite</u> gentleness that they wanted their children to build Christmas memories about *their* houses, not his. He was left alone with his wife.

Yesterday she had said, "It isn't worthwhile, perhaps—"

And he had said, "Oh, yes, Alice, even if there are only the two of us, let's have a Christmas of our own."

Then she had said, "Let's not trim the tree until tomorrow, Robert—just so it's ready when the children come. I'm tired."

He had agreed, and the tree was still out in the back entry.

Why did he feel so awake tonight? For it was still night, a clear and starry night. No moon, of course, but the stars were extraordinary! Now that he thought of it, the stars seemed always large and clear before the dawn of Christmas Day. There was one star now that was certainly larger and brighter than any of the others. He could even imagine it moving, as it had seemed to him to move one night long ago.

He slipped back in time, as he did so easily nowadays. He was fifteen years old and still on his father's farm. He loved his father. He had not known it until one day a few days before Christmas, when he had overheard what his father was saying to his mother.

◆ Build Vocabulary

infinite (in′ fə nit) *adj.*: Extending beyond measure or comprehension

◀ **Critical Viewing** What in this painting creates a feeling of expectation? [Interpret]

Christmas Day in the Morning ◆ 65

Christmas Snow, 1984, David Armstrong, North Mountain Press, Inc.

Cultural Connection

Holiday Gifts In diverse cultures all over the world, people show their love and affection for one another at holiday times through the giving and receiving of gifts that are more important for their symbolic value than for their monetary worth, as in this story. In China, children bow to their elders at the first stroke of the New Year and get small red envelopes of lucky coins in return. On the second day of the New Year, the Chinese visit friends to offer New Year's cards and sometimes baskets of fruit. The Greek Orthodox celebrate Easter by visiting friends and exchanging gifts of elaborately decorated eggs.

On Durga Puja, the Feast of the Divine Mother, Hindu children in India honor their mothers with small gifts.

Have students select a culture to research. Have them find answers to these questions, and share results with the class:

- What important holidays in the culture involve gifts?
- What is the significance of the gifts?
- What kinds of gifts are given, and to whom?

Use the image of the boy in the painting on this page to spark a discussion about the character of Rob in the story.

Humanities: Art

Albert's Son, 1959, by Andrew Wyeth

American artist Andrew Newell Wyeth (b. 1917) is best known for his realistic and sometimes enigmatic pictures of people and places in rural Pennsylvania and Maine. He made portraits of real people, especially his family and neighbors. The son of illustrator and muralist N. C. Wyeth, Andrew Wyeth held his first solo art show at the age of twenty. In 1963, he won the U.S. Presidential Medal of Freedom, and in 1970 he became the first living artist to have an art exhibition in the White House.

Tell students that this is a tempera painting. The word *tempera* refers to a technique in which egg yolk is added to paint other than oil paint. Tempera paint dries quickly, so the brush strokes do not blend easily. In a tempera painting, most shapes are sharp and clear. Tones are bright and details are exact and strong. Guide students to notice Wyeth's remarkable precision in using a tempera brush to show the countless numbers of hairs on the boy's head and the individual straws of hay in the loft. Use these questions for discussion:

1. What feelings do you detect in the boy's eyes, in his stance, and in his facial expression? *Possible answer: He seems faraway in thought, a bit sad, unsure what to do, and longing for something.*

2. Do you think the painting is an appropriate illustration for this story? Explain. *Students may say that it fits the story because the boy's face and stance suggest reflection and recollection. Others may disagree, having imagined Rob as older, stronger, or happier.*

66 ◆ *Coming of Age*

Beyond the Classroom

Community Connection
Civic Outreach This story is about one person giving a special gift to another. Giving can also be done on a larger scale—within communities. Have students survey the ways in which people in your area give to the community through donations of time, service, money, or goods.

Suggest that students find out about groups such as voter registration groups, animal rescue teams, organizations that collect and distribute clothing, or agencies that bring hot meals to the homebound. Students can contact a leader of one of these groups or someone who participates in the giving. Students can informally interview the person that they contact and ask about reasons to get involved, the work required, and the rewards of giving. If possible, they might contact someone who receives help from one of these groups—perhaps a homebound person who receives meals. Students can work in pairs to conduct their research and prepare a presentation for the class, including informative pamphlets from the groups, and sharing what they learned from the people with whom they talked.

❶ "Mary, I hate to call Rob in the mornings. He's growing so fast and he needs his sleep. If you could see how he sleeps when I go in to wake him up! I wish I could manage alone."

"Well, you can't, Adam." His mother's voice was <u>brisk</u>. "Besides, he isn't a child anymore. It's time he took his turn."

"Yes," his father said slowly. "But I sure do hate to wake him."

When he heard these words, something in him woke: his father loved him! He had never thought of it before, taking for granted the tie of their blood. Neither his father nor his mother talked about loving their children—they had no time for such things. There was always so much to do on a farm.

◆ Reading Strategy
❷ Which signal words in this paragraph indicate the sequence of events?

Now that he knew his father loved him, there would be no more <u>loitering</u> in the mornings and having to be called again. He got up after that, stumbling blind with sleep, and pulled on his clothes, his eyes tight shut, but he got up.

And then on the night before Christmas, that year when he was fifteen, he lay for a few minutes thinking about the next day. They were poor, and most of the excitement was in the turkey they had raised themselves and in the mince pies his mother made. His sisters sewed presents and his mother and father always bought something he needed, not only a warm jacket, maybe, but something more, such as a book. And he saved and bought them each something, too.

He wished, that Christmas he was fifteen, he had a better present for his father. As usual he had gone to the ten-cent store and bought a tie.

◆ Build Vocabulary
brisk (brisk) *adj.:* Quick in manner
loitering (loit´ ər in) *n.:* Lingering in an aimless way
placidly (plas´ id lē) *adv.:* In a calm way

◀ **Critical Viewing** How would you describe the boy's mood? In what way does it resemble young Rob's mood in the days before Christmas? [Analyze]

Opposite page: *Albert's Son,* Andrew Wyeth, Nasjonalgalleriet

It had seemed nice enough until he lay thinking the night before Christmas, and then he wished that he had heard his father and mother talking in time for him to save for something better.

❸ He lay on his side, his head supported by his elbow, and looked out of his attic window. The stars were bright, much brighter than he ever remembered seeing them, and one star in particular was so bright that he wondered if it were really the Star of Bethlehem.

"Dad," he had once asked when he was a little boy, "what is a stable?"

❺ "It's just a barn," his father had replied, "like ours."

Then Jesus had been born in a barn, and to a barn the shepherds and the Wise Men had come, bringing their Christmas gifts!

The thought struck him like a silver dagger. Why should he not give his father a special gift too, out there in the barn? He could get up early, earlier than four o'clock, and he could creep into the barn and get all the milking done. He'd do it alone, milk and clean up, and then when his father went in to start the milking, he'd see it all done. And he would know who had done it.

He laughed to himself as he gazed at the stars. It was what he would do, and he mustn't sleep too sound.

He must have waked twenty times, scratching a match each time to look at his old watch—midnight, and half past one, and then two o'clock.

At a quarter to three he got up and put on his clothes. He crept downstairs, careful of the creaky boards, and let himself out. The big star hung lower over the barn roof, a reddish gold. The cows looked at him, sleepy and surprised. It was early for them too.

"So, boss," he whispered. They accepted him <u>placidly</u> and he fetched some hay for each cow and then got the milking pail and the big milk cans.

He had never milked all alone before, but it seemed almost easy. He kept thinking about his father's surprise. His father would come in and call him, saying that he would get things started while Rob was getting dressed. He'd go to the barn, open the door, and then he'd go to get the

Christmas Day in the Morning ◆ 67

◆ Literary Focus
❶ Flashback Guide students to realize that because we are now within a flashback, Mary and Adam are the parents of "Rob," who is the "he" from the opening of the story. Ask students to examine the exchange between Rob's mother and father to infer something about the character of each parent. *Students may say that Mary is a down-to-earth, no-nonsense mother who has no time for sentimentality; Adam has a soft spot toward his son, although he knows he needs Rob's help to manage the chores.*

◆ Reading Strategy
❷ Identify Sequence of Events *Students should recognize that "now" means in the time of the flashback, and refers to the moment, long ago, when Rob realized that his father loved him. The "after that" means after the realization.*

◆ Critical Thinking
❸ Connect Discuss with students why Rob is so disappointed in the gift he has already chosen for his father. Guide them to understand that although the family is poor and the modest gift was chosen with care, such an ordinary, routine gift no longer seems enough, for it doesn't express his deep love for his father.

▶ Critical Viewing ◀
❹ Analyze *Possible response: The boy seems to have something on his mind and appears to be in a serious mood. Perhaps, like young Rob, he is in the barn thinking of how he might manage a better gift for his dad.*

Clarification
❺ If students are unfamiliar with the traditional Christmas story, you or a volunteer may wish to explain that, according to the Gospel of St. Matthew in the New Testament, three Wise Men, visitors from the East, followed a guiding star to Bethlehem, where Jesus was born, to bring gifts to honor the child. That story about Christmas, a barn, and gifts gives Rob the idea for his father's special gift. Bring in the Thematic Focus, pointing to how the cycle and season of the ancient story repeat to give young Rob his special gift idea.

Beyond the Classroom

Workplace Skills
Self-Discipline The main character in this story, while still a boy, demonstrates a strong sense of self-discipline. He decides what he wants to accomplish and, with no help or prodding from others, follows through. In so doing, he creates a unique and meaningful surprise gift for his father.

In any workplace, employees are expected to show the self-discipline to complete tasks, initiate action as needed, and work without constant supervision. This is true in jobs for young people, such as baby-sitting or doing homework, right on

up through high-level management or professional jobs. Have groups of students brainstorm for examples of self-discipline in their lives so far. For example, they may cite how they always walk a dog before breakfast without being told, or always make their bed before leaving for school. Then have them identify characters in films, TV shows, or in books who show—or lack—self-discipline in the workplace. Conclude by discussing how people can develop and improve self-discipline.

◆Critical Thinking

❶ Interpret Challenge students to explain how a task Rob has done so many times before can seem so much easier this morning. *Students may say that as the task of milking was transformed from a routine chore to an act of loving kindness and giving, it became a pleasure for the boy to do; he knew the joy and satisfaction it would bring his father.*

◆Literary Focus

❷ Flashback Have students predict how Rob's father will react to the gift. *Most students will expect Rob's dad to be surprised and pleased.*

◆Reading Strategy

❸ Identify Sequence of Events Guide students to notice that Rob's gift enables his father to receive yet another unexpected gift that day. Talk about what happens. Because Rob has finished the milking, his father can enjoy the pleasure of seeing his children's excited faces as they first see the Christmas tree, an experience that milking cows has kept him from enjoying. Discuss with students ways in which both the father and the son will be affected by the other's expressions of love. *Both will feel cherished and special, knowing that each is highly valued by the other.*

◆Literary Focus

❹ Flashback *"Now that his father was dead . . . had made his first gift of true love" signals a return to the present time in Robert's adult life.*

Thematic Focus

❺ Seasons and Cycles Robert thinks that being able to love is life's true joy. Ask students to explain why they think Robert believes this. Then have them suggest the ways that Robert's present feelings reflect how he felt so many years before. *His father's love for him made a difference in Robert's life, enabling him, in turn, to love and be loved by his wife. He recalls the powerful impact of his gift of love and how it changed his relationship with his father and with himself, and wants to offer that kind of powerful gift of love again—to his wife.*

two big empty milk cans. But they wouldn't be waiting or empty; they'd be standing in the milk-house, filled.

"What the—" he could hear his father exclaiming.

He smiled and milked steadily, two strong streams rushing into the pail, frothing and fragrant. The cows were still surprised but acquiescent. For once they were behaving well, as though they knew it was Christmas.

❶ The task went more easily than he had ever known it to before. Milking for once was not a chore. It was something else, a gift to his father who loved him. He finished, the two milk cans were full, and he covered them and closed the milkhouse door carefully, making sure of the latch. He put the stool in its place by the door and hung up the clean milk pail. Then he went out of the barn and barred the door behind him.

Back in his room he had only a minute to pull off his clothes in the darkness and jump into bed, for he heard his father up. He put the covers over his head to silence his quick breath-
❷ ing. The door opened.

"Rob!" his father called. "We have to get up, son, even if it is Christmas."

"Aw-right," he said sleepily.

"I'll go on out," his father said. "I'll get things started."

The door closed and he lay still, laughing to himself. In just a few minutes his father would know. His dancing heart was ready to jump from his body.

The minutes were endless—ten, fifteen, he did not know how many—and he heard his father's footsteps again. The door opened and he lay still.

"Rob!"

"Yes, Dad—"

"You son of a—" His father was laughing, a queer sobbing sort of a laugh. "Thought you'd fool me, did you?" His father was standing beside his bed, feeling for him, pulling away the cover.

◆ **Build Vocabulary**

acquiescent (ak´ wē es´ ənt) *adj.*: Agreeing without protest

"It's for Christmas, Dad!"

He found his father and clutched him in a great hug. He felt his father's arms go around him. It was dark and they could not see each other's faces.

"Son, I thank you. Nobody ever did a nicer thing—"

"Oh, Dad, I want you to know—I do want to be good!" The words broke from him of their own will. He did not know what to say. His heart was bursting with love.

❸ "Well, I reckon I can go back to bed and sleep," his father said after a moment. "No, hark—the little ones are waked up. Come to think of it, son, I've never seen you children when you first saw the Christmas tree. I was always in the barn. Come on!"

He got up and pulled on his clothes again and they went down to the Christmas tree, and soon the sun was creeping up to where the star had been. Oh, what a Christmas, and how his heart had nearly burst again with shyness and pride as his father told his mother and made the younger children listen about how he, Rob, had got up all by himself.

"The best Christmas gift I ever had, and I'll remember it, son, every year on Christmas morning, so long as I live."

❹ They had both remembered it, and now that his father was dead he remembered it alone: that blessed Christmas dawn when,

◆ **Literary Focus**
How do you know that this is the end of the flashback?

alone with the cows in the barn, he had made his first gift of true love.

Outside the window now the great star slowly sank. He got up out of bed and put on his slippers and bathrobe and went softly upstairs to the attic and found the box of Christmas-tree decorations. He took them downstairs into the living room. Then he brought in the tree. It was a little one—they had not had a big tree since the children went away—but he set it in the holder and put it in the middle of the long table under the window. Then carefully he began to trim it.

It was done very soon, the time passing as quickly as it had that morning long ago in the barn. He went to his library and fetched the

Speaking and Listening Mini-Lesson

Speech

This mini-lesson supports the Speaking and Listening activity in the Idea Bank on p. 71.

Introduce Discuss the elements of a good speech, such as a clear theme, a strong introduction and conclusion, and details that support the main idea. For inspiration, you might recite or play a recording of a famous speech, such as Lincoln's Gettysburg Address.

Develop Explain that students must write and deliver the speech from Rob's point of view. They may choose whether to act as young Rob or as

the adult Robert. Have them write a draft of the speech, then deliver it to a partner who times it so it can be edited for length, as needed.

Apply Have students deliver the speeches before the entire class or for small groups.

Assess Evaluate speeches on how accurately students reflect the attitudes the character would be likely to express, and how well the speech conforms to the required length and topic. Or use the Peer Assessment: Dramatic Performance form, p. 116, in **Alternative Assessment.**

little box that contained his special gift to his wife, a star of diamonds, not large but dainty in design. He had written the card for it the day before. He tied the gift on the tree and then stood back. It was pretty, very pretty, and she would be surprised.

But he was not satisfied. He wanted to tell her—to tell her how much he loved her. It had been a long time since he had really told her, although he loved her in a very special way, much more than he ever had when they were young.

He had been fortunate that she had loved him—and how fortunate that he had been able to love! Ah, that was the true joy of life, the ability to love! For he was quite sure that some people were genuinely unable to love anyone. But love was alive in him, it still was.

It occurred to him suddenly that it was alive because long ago it had been born in him when he knew his father loved him. That was it: love alone could waken love.

And he could give the gift again and again. This morning, this blessed Christmas morning, he would give it to his beloved wife. He could write it down in a letter for her to read and keep forever. He went to his desk and began his love letter to his wife: *My dearest love . . .*

When it was finished he sealed it and tied it on the tree where she would see it the first thing when she came into the room. She would read it, surprised and then moved, and realize how very much he loved her.

He put out the light and went tiptoeing up the stairs. The star in the sky was gone, and the first rays of the sun were gleaming in the sky. Such a happy, happy Christmas!

Guide for Responding

◆ LITERATURE AND YOUR LIFE

Reader's Response What do you think of Rob's gift to his father?

Thematic Focus In what way does "Christmas Day in the Morning" reveal cycles of life?

Group Discussion With a group of classmates, explore the saying "It is better to give than to receive." Use events in the story as examples.

☑ Check Your Comprehension

1. Why does young Rob's father wake him every morning at four o'clock?
2. What happens to make Rob realize that he loves his father?
3. What gift does young Rob first plan to give his father? Why does he alter his plan?
4. How does Rob's father show his gratitude for Rob's gift?
5. What gift does Robert, as an adult, first plan to give his wife? What does he do to enhance his gift?

◆ Critical Thinking

INTERPRET

1. What is special about the gift young Rob gives his father? How does giving it make Rob feel? **[Connect]**
2. How are Rob's feelings about the gift similar to his father's feelings? How are they different? **[Compare and Contrast]**
3. At the beginning of the story, the adult Robert wakes up and wonders what happened to the magic of Christmas. (a) How do his feelings change by the end of the story? (b) What has brought about the change? **[Draw Conclusions]**
4. In what ways other than by giving gifts does Robert show his "ability to love"? Explain. **[Interpret]**

EVALUATE

5. Do you agree with the statement "Love alone could waken love"? **[Criticize]**

APPLY

6. What are "gifts of true love," such as the ones Robert gives? **[Define]**

Christmas Day in the Morning ◆ 69

Beyond the Selection

FURTHER READING
Other Works by Pearl S. Buck
The Good Earth
Sons
A House Divided
Other Works With Flashbacks
"The Invalid's Story," Mark Twain
"Incident at Owl Creek Bridge," Ambrose Bierce
Pincher Martin, William Golding

INTERNET
We suggest the following site on the Internet (all Web sites are subject to change).
For more information about Pearl Buck:
http://www.pearl-s-buck.org
We *strongly recommend* that you preview the site before you send students to it.

◆ Literary Focus

6 Flashback Challenge students to link this passage with the message of the flashback. *Just as he kept the gift of his father's love with him always, he wants to give a gift of love to his wife that she can keep.*

Reinforce and Extend

Answers
◆ LITERATURE AND YOUR LIFE

Reader's Response Students should support their ideas with details from the story.

Thematic Focus It shows that a meaningful act can repeat itself; it shows that people can hold love in their hearts for their whole lives and pass the feelings on to others.

☑ Check Your Comprehension

1. Rob's father needs help milking the cows.
2. Rob overhears his father saying how much he regrets having to wake his son so early each day.
3. His first gift is a tie. He changes his plan because the tie doesn't seem sufficient to express his feelings.
4. He hugs Rob and tells Rob and the rest of the family that the gift is the best he has ever received.
5. He first plans to give her a star of diamonds; he writes a letter that his wife will find hanging on the tree in the morning.

◆ Critical Thinking

1. It is special because it is a gift of time, love, and caring that makes Rob feel grown up and loving.
2. The gift pleases both of them and moves them to tears. Rob feels the love in his heart; his father wants to share it with the family.
3. (a) Robert finds the missing magic by remembering an evening from long ago. (b) Robert realizes the importance of expressing love to the ones you care about the most.
4. He loves his wife and family; he finds pleasure in simple things and knows that love is the greatest gift of all. He cherishes his memories and keeps beloved traditions alive.
5. Most students will agree; others may say that one cannot give love without receiving it in return.
6. Possible responses include care, help, loyalty, kindness, support, commitment, devotion, affection, and tenderness.

69

Answers

◆ Literary Focus

1. It begins in paragraph 8: "He slipped back in time . . ."
2. There is an obvious shift from the past back to the present: ". . . and now that his father was dead, he remembered it alone."
3. Readers grasp Robert's feelings about Christmas, his father, and what he learned about love as a boy. We understand what motivates him to write a love letter to his wife.

◆ Build Vocabulary

Using Forms of *finite*
1. infinite/finite; 2. infinitesimal;
3. infinitely; 4. infinity

Spelling Strategy
1. acquaintance; 2. acquit;
3. acquire

Using the Word Bank
1. (c) 2. (b) 3. (c) 4. (c) 5. (a)

◆ Reading Strategy

1. past; 2. present; 3. present;
4. past

◆ Build Grammar Skills

Practice
1. pronoun: *his*; antecedent: *Adam*
2. pronouns: *he, his*; antecedent: *Rob*
3. pronoun: *their*; antecedent: *cows*
4. pronoun: *it*; antecedent: *tree*
5. pronoun: *she*; antecedent: *wife*

Writing Application
1. Adam and Mary discussed what to do about the chores on their farm.
2. Rob remembered that on that past Christmas he gave his father a special gift.
3. Because Alice didn't feel well, Robert wanted to surprise her by trimming the tree.

Writer's Solution

For additional instruction and practice, use the lesson in the Language Lab CD-ROM on pronouns and antecedents, and the practice page on pronouns and antecedents, p. 8, in the *Writer's Solution Grammar Practice Book.*

Guide for Responding *(continued)*

◆ Literary Focus

FLASHBACK

Flashbacks, which interrupt story events to reveal events that happened in the past, may help you gain insight into a story. They can give you a broader view of the story's events or help you understand a character's actions.
1. When does the flashback begin in "Christmas Day in the Morning"?
2. How do you know when the flashback is over?
3. What insights about Robert do you gain from the flashback?

◆ Build Vocabulary

USING FORMS OF *finite*

The adjective *finite*, meaning "with a beginning and end," can stand alone or combine with prefixes and suffixes to make related words. On your paper, write the form(s) of *finite* that answers each question.

infinity infinitesimal infinite finite infinitely
1. Which two words are antonyms, or opposites?
2. Which word means "too small to be measured"?
3. Which word is an adverb?
4. Which noun means "the state of being infinite"?

SPELLING STRATEGY

The letter combination *qu* usually makes the *kw* sound. In words like *acquiescent,* the *c* preceding the *qu* is sometimes mistakenly dropped because it is unvoiced. On your paper, fill in the following, using words that begin with the letters *acqu.*
1. Someone you've met is an _____?_____.
2. When a defendant is not guilty, you _____?_____ him or her.
3. When you buy something, you _____?_____ it.

USING THE WORD BANK

On your paper, write the word that is opposite in meaning to the first word.
1. brisk: (a) clever, (b) curt, (c) slow
2. infinite: (a) endless, (b) limited, (c) tiny
3. loitering: (a) littering, (b) dawdling, (c) moving
4. acquiescent: (a) watery, (b) dull, (c) argumentative
5. placidly: (a) turbulently, (b) nicely, (c) meanly

◆ Reading Strategy

IDENTIFY SEQUENCE OF EVENTS

Sometimes an author will interrupt a story's regular **sequence of events** to tell about something that happened before the story began. As you read, look for clues, like "He slipped back in time," that indicate a time change.

Tell whether each event takes place in the past, in the flashback, or in the present.
1. Rob realizes his father loves him.
2. Rob writes a love letter to his wife.
3. Rob remembers his gift to his father.
4. Rob decides to get up early and milk the cows.

◆ Build Grammar Skills

PRONOUNS AND ANTECEDENTS

A **pronoun** takes the place of a noun or another pronoun. Some common pronouns are *we, you, he, she, it, we, they, us, mine, their,* and *who.* An **antecedent** is the word or group of words that a pronoun replaces. In these sentences from the story, the pronoun *he* replaces the antecedent *Rob.*

I hate to call *Rob* in the mornings. *He's* growing so fast and *he* needs his sleep.

Practice Copy the following sentences. Underline each pronoun and draw an arrow to its antecedent.
1. Adam hated to wake his son.
2. When Rob heard his father's words, he became filled with love.
3. The cows were in their stalls.
4. When the tree was trimmed, it glistened.
5. When she saw the gift, Robert's wife cried.

Writing Application Rewrite the following sentences, replacing repeated nouns with pronouns.
1. Adam and Mary discussed what to do about the chores on Adam and Mary's farm.
2. Rob remembered that on that past Christmas Rob gave his father a special gift.
3. Because Alice didn't feel well, Robert wanted to surprise Alice by trimming the tree.

Build Your Portfolio

 ## Idea Bank

Writing

1. **Letter From Robert** Write a letter from Robert to his children, expressing his thoughts on the night before Christmas.

2. **Book-Jacket Copy** Write an attention-grabbing summary of "Christmas Day in the Morning" for a book jacket. Don't give away the whole story, but provide enough information to interest potential readers.

3. **Essay** How would "Christmas Day in the Morning" be different if it had contained no flashback but told the story of Rob from his youth to old age? Explain your ideas in an essay. Use details from the story to support your ideas.

Speaking and Listening

4. **Speech** As Rob, prepare a one-minute speech about the meaning of the Christmas season. Practice reading your speech aloud before presenting it to the class.

5. **Modern Scene [Group Activity]** With a group, create a script for a dramatic scene based on events from "Christmas Day in the Morning" but set in a modern setting of your choice. Rehearse your scene, and then perform it for the class. **[Performing Arts Link]**

Projects

6. **Holiday Spirit [Group Activity]** Work with a group of classmates to create a multimedia presentation about various holidays celebrated by diverse cultures. For example, you might compare and contrast Christmas, Hanuka, and Kwanzaa. **[Social Studies Link]**

7. **Comic Strip** Create a comic strip about an important event in a character's life. In your comic strip, include a flashback scene. You may want to refer to actual comic strips to get ideas about formatting. **[Art Link]**

 ## Writing Mini-Lesson

Fictional Narrative Containing a Flashback

In "Christmas Day in the Morning," Robert lets his thoughts wander back to a memorable Christmas on which he gave a very special gift. Write a story of your own, containing a flashback in which your main character relives an incident from the past.

Writing Skills Focus: Use Transitions

Use **transitions** like *after a while, before,* and *earlier* to show what happens first, next, and last. Also, use transitions to indicate to readers where the flashback begins, as Pearl Buck does in the following example.

Model From the Story
He slipped back in time, as he did so easily nowadays. He was fifteen years old and still on his father's farm.

Prewriting Sketch out the form your narrative will take—who the characters are and what happens. Make a timeline showing the order of events and where you will insert the flashback.

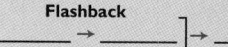

Drafting Now, write the story, weaving together plot events and developing your characters. Use transitions as you write, indicating the sequence of story events.

Revising Where necessary, add description to your narrative to strengthen characters and setting. Insert transitions wherever the time order of plot events is unclear. Also, be sure that you've begun your flashback with a transition.

> ◆ **Grammar Application**
> If you've used a particular noun repeatedly, replace the noun with a pronoun.

 ## Idea Bank

Following are suggestions for matching the Idea Bank topics with your students' performance levels and learning modalities:

Customize for
Performance Levels
Less Advanced Students: 2, 4, 7
Average Students: 1, 5, 6, 7
More Advanced Students: 3, 6, 7

Customize for
Learning Modalities
Verbal/Linguistic: 1, 2, 3, 4, 5, 6
Visual/Spatial: 2, 6, 7
Bodily/Kinesthetic: 4, 5
Interpersonal: 5, 6
Intrapersonal: 1, 3, 7

 ## Writing Mini-Lesson

Refer students to the Writing Handbook in the back of the book for instructions on the writing process and for further information on fictional narrative and flashbacks.

✎ Writer's Solution

Writing Lab CD-ROM
Have students complete the tutorial on Narration. Follow these steps:

1. Have students focus on the Developing Narrative Elements parts of the Prewriting section.
2. Have students draft on computer.
3. Suggest use of the Transition Word and Phrase Bin.
4. Have students use interactive guides on strengthening characters and improving dialogue, as needed.

Allow about 75 minutes of class time to complete these steps.

Writer's Solution Sourcebook
Have students use Chapter 3, "Narration," pp. 70–103, for more support. The chapter includes in-depth instruction on introducing and developing characters, pp. 90–91.

✓ ASSESSMENT OPTIONS

Formal Assessment, Selection Test, pp. 18–20, and Assessment Resources Software. The selection test is designed so that it can be easily customized to the performance levels of your students.

Alternative Assessment, p. 6, includes options for less advanced students, more advanced students, interpersonal learners, visual/spatial learners, intrapersonal learners, verbal/linguistic learners, and logical/mathematical learners.

PORTFOLIO ASSESSMENT
Use the following rubrics in the **Alternative Assessment** booklet to assess student writing:
Letter From Robert: Expression, p. 90
Book-Jacket Copy: Description, p. 93
Essay: Comparison/Contrast, p. 99
Writing Mini-Lesson: Fictional Narrative, p. 91

OBJECTIVES

1. To read, comprehend, and interpret a short story and two poems
2. To relate sensory language to personal experience
3. To relate characters and situations to what you know
4. To appreciate sensory language
5. To build vocabulary in context and learn synonyms for *rivulets*
6. To develop skill in using personal pronouns
7. To write a description of an older person
8. To respond to a short story and two poems through writing, speaking and listening, and projects

SKILLS INSTRUCTION

Vocabulary:
Synonyms
for *rivulets*

Spelling:
Doubling Middle
Consonants in
Two-syllable
Words

Grammar:
Personal Pronouns

Reading Strategy:
Relate to What
You Know

Literary Focus:
Sensory Language

Writing:
Use Precise
Language

Speaking and Listening:
Storyteller's Circle
(Teacher Edition)

Critical Viewing:
Interpret; Compare and Contrast; Make a Judgment

PORTFOLIO OPPORTUNITIES

Writing: Descriptive Close-Up; Proposal for a Reunion; Folk Tale
Writing Mini-Lesson: Description of an Older Person
Speaking and Listening: Storyteller's Circle; Dialogue With Yourself
Projects: Life Dance; Community Service Report

More About the Author
Leo Tolstoy started a small publishing company in 1884 to put out inexpensive booklets of stories based on traditional tales and legends. Tolstoy's short stories convey moral lessons reflecting his own beliefs.

Amy Ling is a professor of Asian-American studies and has edited books of Asian-American writings.

Ricardo Sánchez grew up in a rough section of El Paso. There he developed a "street-wise" mind to go with his deep intellectual curiosity and love for books. He has been a librarian, professor, columnist, poet-in-residence, and political activist.

Guide for Reading

Meet the Authors:

Leo Tolstoy (1828–1910)

Leo Tolstoy, a Russian writer, is regarded by many experts to be one of the world's finest novelists. He developed a taste for literature as a boy, when he discovered the joys of reading the folk tales of his native land, poems about Russian heroes, and stories from the Bible.

THE STORY BEHIND THE STORY

In "The Old Grandfather and His Little Grandson," Tolstoy stresses the importance of providing care and showing respect for the elderly. Because Tolstoy lost both parents to illness when he was still a boy, he probably felt very strongly that parents were to be valued and loved.

Amy Ling (1939–   )

Amy Ling is fascinated by China. She was born in that country and spent six years there before coming with her family to the United States. In the 1960's, she visited her grandmother in Taiwan, an island off the coast of China. She describes the dramatic meeting in "Grandma."

Ricardo Sánchez (1941–1995)

Born in El Paso, Texas, Ricardo Sánchez had roots in Spanish Mexican, North American, and Native American cultures. Most of his work, including "Old Man," is an exploration and celebration of his rich heritage. That's why he often used both English and Spanish words in his writing.

◆ LITERATURE AND YOUR LIFE

CONNECT YOUR EXPERIENCE

The painting at the right might be described as showing a circle of life in which people old and young dance together. In the world around you, what might symbolize a circle of life? The writers in this section focus on their relatives and ancestors—and how those people contributed to their lives.

THEMATIC FOCUS: Seasons and Cycles

What do these writers suggest about the gifts that people from different stages in life can give to one another?

◆ Background for Understanding

SOCIAL STUDIES

In "Grandma," the poem's speaker tells of visiting her grandmother in Taiwan. Taiwan, formed by islands off the coast of China, has a rich and interesting history. Over the centuries, it has been occupied by Portugal, China, Holland, and Japan. Today, it is an independent nation inhabited largely by people who fled from mainland China when the communist forces won control of the Chinese government.

◆ Build Vocabulary

SYNONYMS FOR *rivulets*

English is rich in synonyms—words that express the same meaning in slightly different ways. For example, *rivulets* ("little streams") has the synonyms *brooks, streams,* and *creeks.*

WORD BANK

Which word from the list might describe a well-made table? Check the Build Vocabulary box on page 75 to see if you chose correctly.

scolded
sturdy
rivulets
furrows
supple
stoic

 Prentice Hall Literature Program Resources

REINFORCE / RETEACH / EXTEND

Selection Support Pages
Build Vocabulary: Synonyms for *rivulets*, p. 34
Build Spelling Skills, p. 35
Build Grammar Skills: Personal Pronouns, p. 36
Reading Strategy: Relate to What You Know, p. 37
Literary Focus: Sensory Language, p. 38

Strategies for Diverse Student Needs,
p. 13–14

Beyond Literature Cultural Connection: Attitudes Toward Old Age, p. 7

Formal Assessment Selection Test, pp. 21–23
Assessment Resources Software

Alternative Assessment, p. 7

Writing and Language Transparencies
Sensory Language Chart, p. 69

Resource Pro CD-ROM
"The Old Grandfather and His Little Grandson";
"Grandma"; "Old Man"

Listening to Literature Audiocassettes
"The Old Grandfather and His Little Grandson"; "Grandma"; "Old Man"

The Old Grandfather and His Little Grandson
Grandma ◆ Old Man

Second Circle Dance, Phoebe Beasley

◆ Literary Focus
SENSORY LANGUAGE

Reading a work of literature can allow you to step through a door into a new world. Writers enable you to picture this new world clearly by using **sensory language**—language that captures sights, sounds, smells, tastes, and sensations of touch. As you read these works, take full advantage of the sensory language by reading them with your senses as well as with your mind. For example, use Tolstoy's description of the grandfather to see him sitting at the table, "old" and blind and "toothless."

◆ Reading Strategy
RELATE TO WHAT YOU KNOW

Your own memories and observations help you to appreciate the sensory language in a literary work. Similarly, you can better understand the characters and situations if you **relate them to what you know.** Consider what you've learned through experience, as well as the knowledge you've gained from school and other sources. Use a reader's journal like this one to help you make connections to these selections.

Passage	⟶	What I Know
The grandfather had become very old. His legs would not carry him....		My grandfather recently fell and broke his hip.

Guide for Reading ◆ 73

Interest Grabber
Before you begin this selection, have students ask grandparents or someone older for one important piece of advice. Have students share this advice in class and discuss what life experience they believe influenced that point of view. Talk about the stories or attitudes students typically associate with their grandparents or older people they know. Explain that each selection they will read offers a view of grandparents.

◆ Build Grammar Skills

Personal Pronouns If you wish to introduce the grammar concept for this selection before students read, refer to the instruction on p. 78.

Customize for
Less Proficient Readers
Some expressions in the poems may elude students. For example, in "Grandma," explain the idea behind digging to China by saying that people sometimes say that if they dig a hole deep enough they will eventually come out in China. For "Old Man," explain that "... our blood was here" (line 29) refers to the speaker's ancestors who died here. In line 44, "gone into dust" means the man died and has been buried in the earth.

Customize for
More Advanced Students
These selections contain examples of sensory language. Have students use the Sensory Language Chart, p. 69, in **Writing and Language Transparencies,** to record examples of language that address sight, sound, smell, taste, and touch.

Humanities: Art

Second Circle Dance, by Phoebe Beasley

Phoebe Beasley often paints real characters who represent aspects of family history.
1. How does this work make you think of seasons and cycles? *The people are of all ages—the cycle of life; the chain starts and ends outside the scene—the cycle is ongoing.*
2. What sensory impressions does the work give? *The colors appeal to sight; rhythmic movements of the dancers depict sound and touch.*

Preparing for Standardized Tests

Writing Standardized tests may assess students' descriptive writing skills. Precise language is an important element of good descriptive writing. The Writing Mini-Lesson on p. 79 will help students prepare for writing assessments.

Writing prompts requires that criteria for a particular type of writing be met. A descriptive writing prompt probably will ask students to describe the physical characteristics of a person, place, or thing. As a writer, they should picture their subject and identify important features. Next the features must be organized. When students

are working in a timed, test situation, basic organization such as spatial order may be the best choice for responding quickly and efficiently.

Present the writing activity in the Idea Bank on p. 79 as a descriptive writing prompt:

> Think about the face of a person you know well. Describe what his or her face looks like so that someone who has not seen this person can picture him or her.

To further prepare students, refer to the instruction on p. 79 of the Teacher Edition.

73

74

The Old Grandfather and His Little Grandson

Leo Tolstoy

Remembrance (Erinnerung), ca. 1918, Marc Chagall, Solomon R. Guggenheim Museum

The grandfather had become very old. His legs would not carry him, his eyes could not see, his ears could not hear, and he was toothless. When he ate, bits of food sometimes dropped out of his mouth. His son and his son's wife no longer allowed him to eat with them at the table. He had to eat his meals in the corner near the stove. ❶

One day they gave him his food in a bowl. He tried to move the bowl closer; it fell to the floor and broke. His daughter-in-law <u>scolded</u> him. She told him that he spoiled everything in the house and broke their dishes, and she said that from now on he would get his food in a wooden dish. The old man sighed and said nothing. ❷

A few days later, the old man's son and his wife were sitting in their hut, resting and watching their little boy playing on the floor. They saw him putting together something out of small pieces of wood. His father asked him, "What are you making, Misha?" ❸

The little grandson said, "I'm making a wooden bucket. When you and Mamma get old, I'll feed you out of this wooden dish."

The young peasant and his wife looked at each other, and tears filled their eyes. They were ashamed because they had treated the old grandfather so meanly, and from that day they again let the old man eat with them at the table and took better care of him. ❹

◄ **Critical Viewing** How do the details in this painting symbolize, or represent, the story's message? [Interpret] ❺

74 ◆ *Coming of Age*

 Humanities: Art

Remembrance (Erinnerung), ca. 1918, by Marc Chagall

Marc Chagall (1887–1985) first studied painting in his native Russia. Seeking knowledge and greater artistic freedom, he left his homeland in 1910 to study and live in Paris, where he spent much of his artistic life. Despite the many artistic trends in Europe during his lifetime, Chagall developed a fiercely independent style that blended images of dreams and memories in a colorful, personal way. Chagall created this India ink and pencil work at the end of World War I.

1. How would you describe the look on the old man's face? *He seems sad and downtrodden.*
2. Why do you think Chagall shows him bent over, carrying a house on his back? *Students should note the female figure in the doorway and may infer that she stands for the man's wife, mother, or family—the man carries the house because he shoulders responsibilities for his home and family. The title of the work may lead students to say that the artist shows memories of family and home we always carry with us—these memories may be a painful, heavy burden.*

Woman with White Kerchief (Uygur), Lunda Hoyle Gill

◀ **Critical Viewing** Compare and contrast the woman in this painting with Grandma, as described in the poem. **[Compare and Contrast]** ❻

Grandma

Amy Ling

If you dig that hole deep enough
you'll reach China, they used to tell me,
a child in a backyard, Allentown, Pa.
Not strong enough to dig that hole,
5   I waited twenty years
then sailed back
half way around the world. ❼

In Taiwan I first met Grandma.
Before she came to view I heard
10   her slippered feet softly measure
the tatami[1] floor with even step.
The aqua paper door slid open
and there, breathless, I faced
my five foot height, my <u>sturdy</u> legs and feet,
15   my square forehead, high cheeks, and wide-set eyes.
My image stood before me
acted on by fifty years;
here in my past was my future. ❾ ❽

She smiled, stretched her arms
20   to take to heart the eldest daughter
of her youngest son a quarter century away.
She spoke a tongue I knew no word of
and I was sad I could not understand,
but I could hug her.

◆ **Build Vocabulary**

scolded (skōld´ əd) v.: Criticized harshly

sturdy (stʉr´ dē) adj.: Firm; strong

---

1. **tatami** (tə tä´ mē) adj.: Woven of rice straw.

The Old Grandfather and His Little Grandson/Grandma ◆ 75

One-Minute Insight

A young woman travels to China to meet her maternal grandmother. Although the two women cannot communicate in words, they form an immediate, deep connection based on family ties and physical resemblance.

▶ **Critical Viewing** ◀

❻ **Compare and Contrast**
Students may say that Grandma and the woman in the painting are both Chinese, have "high cheeks and wide-set eyes," and smiles. The woman in the painting seems more modern than grandma in the poem.

Clarification

❼ Tell students that Amy Ling was born in China and spent some of her earliest years there, but never went back until she was an adult. This poem conveys her impression of her meeting there.

◆ **Reading Strategy**

❽ **Relate to What You Know**
Have students describe in their own words what the speaker notices when she first sees her grandmother. *The speaker notices the strong family resemblance, and understands that in her grandmother she gets a glimpse into how she herself may look as she ages.*

Comprehension Check ☑

❾ Ask students to explain the meaning of line 18: "here in the past was my future." *In her native country of China ("here in the past"), the speaker sees her grandmother, whose physical features suggest how she may look as she ages ("was my future").*

 Humanities: Art

Woman With White Kerchief (Uygur), 1990, by Lunda Hoyle Gill
Some of Lunda Hoyle Gill's paintings can be found in the book *Portraits of China,* by Colin Mackerras. Discuss with students the kind of information an artist can convey in a portrait. *Students may say that a portrait can convey a sense of the person, much like a photograph can capture a moment in a person's life. Some portraits allow an audience to infer social or family status, health, age, and attitudes the person has toward life or toward the surroundings.*

One-Minute Insight

The speaker shows deep respect and appreciation for his grandfather, who has died. He notes that the old man's qualities and traits live on in himself.

◆ Reading Strategy

❶ Relate to What You Know Discuss with students the ways in which a shepherd's life could be "lived freely." *Shepherds follow sheep, who wander and graze wherever they find food and water. A shepherd is not bound by schedules and modern routines, but by cycles of nature.*

◆ Reading Strategy

❷ Relate to What You Know Discuss with students aspects of life that can make a person grow "wise with time," and how life experiences can shape someone's physical and emotional traits. *Students may say that the old man has seen a lot in his life; his experiences point out what to value.*

◆ Literary Focus

❸ Sensory Language Challenge students to use other sensory words to describe the old man's face. *Students may say that his face is rugged, craggy, leathery, rough, or creased.*

► Critical Viewing ◄

❹ Make a Judgment *Students may say that this old man shows their idea of the old man in the poem because his face is wrinkled and leathery, and seems to reflect the cares of a long, hard life.*

◆ Critical Thinking

❺ Interpret Until the last line of the poem, no other words in the poem, including place names and the beginnings of lines, start with capital letters. Ask students to interpret the poet's decision to capitalize *Old Man*. *He may want to summarize or emphasize his respect for his grandfather, so he capitalizes the words Old Man.*

Customize for *Less Proficient Readers*

This poem is written with sentence fragments that are easy to read, but their meaning may be hard to grasp. Model how to insert "missing" words, paraphrase lines or phrases, and read this work as a stream-of-consciousness remembrance.

Old Man

Ricardo Sánchez

remembrance (smiles/hurts sweetly)
October 8, 1972

old man
with brown skin
talking of past
   when being shepherd ❶
5   in utah, nevada, colorado and
     new mexico
was life lived freely;

old man,
  grandfather,
wise with time ❷
10 running <u>rivulets</u> on face, ❸
deep, rich <u>furrows</u>,
   each one a legacy,
deep, rich memories
of life . . .
15   "you are indio,[1]

---

1. **indio** (ēn´ dyō) *n.*: Indian; Native American.

◆ Build Vocabulary

rivulets (riv´ yōō lits) *n.*: Little streams
furrows (fur´ ōz) *n.*: Deep wrinkles
supple (sup´ əl) *adj.*: Flexible and pliant
stoic (stō´ ik) *adj.*: Calm and unbothered in spite of suffering

76 ◆ *Coming of Age*

El Pan Nuestro (Our Daily Bread), c. 1905, Ramon Frade, Instituto de Cultura Puertorriqueña, San Juan

▲ **Critical Viewing** Does this painting effectively convey an old man "wise with time"? Explain. [Make a Judgment] ❹

   among other things,"
he would tell me
   during nights spent
so long ago
20   amidst familial gatherings
   in albuquerque . . .

old man, loved and respected,
he would speak sometimes
of pueblos,[2]
25   san juan, santa clara,
   and even santo domingo,
and his family, he would say,
came from there:
   some of our blood was here,
30 he would say,
   before the coming of coronado,[3]

---

2. **pueblos** (pweb´ lōz) *n.*: Here, Native American towns in central and northern New Mexico.
3. **coronado** (kô rô nä´ dô): Coronado explored what is today the American Southwest.

 Humanities: Art

El Pan Nuestro (Our Daily Bread), c. 1905, by Ramon Frade

In this painting, done around 1905, the artist creates a portrait of an old man bringing home supplies for his family. Encourage students to note his demeanor and expression. Then have students study the portrait, and then use these questions for discussion:

1. What might the title, *Our Daily Bread* mean? *Students may suggest that it refers to the man's responsibility of feeding his family; it echoes a line from The Lord's Prayer ("give us this day our daily bread"), which suggests that the man holds spiritual or religious beliefs.*

2. What clues can you find in the painting to show that this painting is set in a Southwest or Central American environment? *There's a palm tree in the background, the man wears a straw hat to protect him from the sun; he carries plantains or some other type of tropical plant.*

3. Why might the artist have painted this figure alone? *Possibly to show that the man bears the responsibility on his own; it heightens the dramatic effect of the painting's simplicity..*

other of our blood
    came with los españoles,[4]
and the mixture
35 was rich,
    though often painful . . .
old man,
who knew earth
    by its awesome aromas
40 and who felt
the heated sweetness
    of chile verde [5]
by his supple touch,
gone into dust is your body
45   with its stoic look and resolution,
but your reality, old man, lives on
in a mindsoul touched by you . . .

5 | Old Man . . .

---

4. **los españoles** (lōs es pä nyōl′ es) *n.:* The Spaniards.
5. **chile verde** (chē′ le vehr′ dē) *n.:* Green pepper.

Beyond Literature

Social Studies Connection

Caring for the Elderly Social scientists study aging trends to help us plan for the future. The average human life span has greatly increased due to advances in medical care and living conditions. It will take careful economic and social planning to ensure that we are able to care for the large numbers of elderly citizens living in our society.

Cross-Curricular Activity
Science Do research on average life expectancy rates from the 1700's onward. Create a chart showing the average life span for men and women throughout the years.

Beyond Literature

Most almanacs provide the type of information students need to complete the Science Activity. Be aware that almanacs may present data by ethnic groups, which can present sensitive political and social issues and questions.

Reinforce and Extend

Answers
◆LITERATURE AND YOUR LIFE

Reader's Response Be sure students support their responses with details from the works.

Thematic Focus They suggest a special bond: a grandson is more sensitive to his grandfather's emotions than adults are; a grandmother and grandchild haven't met and can barely communicate, but feel an instant bond; a poet acknowledges the great influences of his grandfather.

✓ Check Your Comprehension

1. They don't like how he eats, so they make him eat in the corner.
2. Their son's response shames them into showing the old man more kindness and understanding.
3. The poet hears her grandmother coming before she sees her, then sees their physical resemblance. They embrace and feel connected, although they cannot communicate.
4. He addresses his grandfather, who is no longer alive.
5. The old man taught him the importance of their combined Native American and Spanish heritage.

◆Critical Thinking

1. When the parents realize that they, too, will be old some day, and subject to similar bad treatment, they feel pity for the old man.
2. The meeting is important because Ling's grandmother represents her Chinese heritage that she has heard about, but had not experienced firsthand.
3. These lines say that the traits and qualities of the old man will always live on in his grandson.
4. Students can share experiences that support their responses.
5. Both emphasize the value of older people and represent the family's links with the past and its traditions.

Guide for Responding

◆ LITERATURE AND YOUR LIFE

Reader's Response Which person in these works do you admire most? Why?

Thematic Focus What do these works suggest about the bond between a grandparent and a grandchild?

✓ Check Your Comprehension

1. How do the old man's son and his wife treat the grandfather in "The Old Grandfather . . ."?
2. Describe how and why the couple changes their behavior at the end of "The Old Grandfather . . ."
3. Describe the meeting between Ling and her grandmother in "Grandma."
4. To whom does Sánchez address his poem?
5. What did the old man teach Sánchez about their shared heritage?

◆ Critical Thinking

INTERPRET
1. Why does the boy's response to his father's question in "The Old Grandfather . . ." make his parents feel "ashamed"? **[Interpret]**
2. Why is Ling's meeting with her grandmother so important to her? **[Draw Conclusions]**
3. In what way do lines 46–47 sum up the meaning of "Old Man"? **[Analyze]**

EVALUATE
4. Can children in real life teach grown-ups, as the grandson does in "The Old Grandfather . . ."? Why or why not? **[Make a Judgment]**

COMPARE LITERARY WORKS
5. What similar attitudes toward older people do "The Old Grandfather . . ." and "Grandma" express? **[Compare and Contrast]**

Old Man ◆ 77

 Beyond the Selection

FURTHER READING
Other Works by Leo Tolstoy
"The Kreutzer Sonata"
"The Cossacks"

Other Works Edited Amy Ling
Imagining America: Stories From the Promised Land
Between Worlds: Women Writers of Chinese Ancestry

Other Works by Ricardo Sánchez
The Liberation of a Chicano Mind Soul (Canto y grito mi liberación)
The Loves of Ricardo Sanchez

INTERNET
We suggest the following sites on the Internet (all Web sites are subject to change).
    For information about Leo Tolstoy:
http://www.tolstoy.org/index.html
    For more on Ricardo Sanchez, including photos:
http://www.dr-ricardo-sanchez.com
    We *strongly recommend* that you preview these sites before you send students to them.

Answers

◆ **Reading Strategy**

Students' answers will vary with their experiences. However, insist that they relate the themes to their own observations, encounters, and life lessons.

◆ **Build Vocabulary**

Using Synonyms for *rivulets*

1. brook; a brook is a more lively body of water, so it might make a sound as it flows.
2. creek; a brook is probably too small to swim across.
3. stream; it would be impossible to row a boat down a tiny rivulet.

Spelling Strategy

1. furrow; 2. (correct); 3. little; 4. better

Using the Word Bank

1. (b)   2. (a)   3. (c)   4. (a)
5. (b)   6. (c)

◆ **Literary Focus**

1. sight: in line 20, the grandmother smiles and stretches out her arms; touch: in line 24, the speaker hugs her grandmother
2. smell and touch: in lines 38–42, the old man recognizes earth scents, and his touch discerns the quality of green chiles.

◆ **Build Grammar Skills**

Practice

1. His/him   4. You/he/me
2. She/him/he/their 5. your/its
3. she/I/her

Writing Application

Sample answers:
1. They seated the grandfather at the head of the table.
2. Your smile is so much like mine.
3. Our family is from Guatemala.

Writer's Solution

For additional instruction and practice, use the lessons in the *Writer's Solution Language Lab CD-ROM* on pronouns, and the practice pages on pronouns, pp. 8–9 in the *Writer's Solution Grammar Practice Book*.

Guide for Responding (continued)

◆ **Reading Strategy**

RELATE WHAT YOU KNOW

By **relating what you know** to these works, you brought the gift of your own life to the writers' words. Describe an experience of your own that helped you understand each of these situations:

1. "The Old Grandfather . . .": adults learning from a child
2. "Grandma": seeing yourself in an older relative
3. "Old Man": feeling grateful to an older person

◆ **Build Vocabulary**

USING SYNONYMS FOR *rivulets*

Synonyms express different shades of the same basic meaning. For example, although *rivulets, brooks, streams,* and *creeks* are synonyms, streams are larger than creeks, which are larger than both rivulets and brooks. Also, *brook* suggests a more lively body of water than *rivulet* does.

On your paper, choose one synonym to complete each sentence. Then, explain your choice.

1. All day, he listened to the babbling (rivulet, brook).
2. He liked to swim across the (creek, brook).
3. Row, row, row your boat, gently down the (rivulet, stream).

SPELLING STRATEGY

When spelling most two-syllable words with a consonant sound in the middle after a short vowel sound, double the middle consonant:

supple: (short *u* sound followed by *p* sound)
brittle: (short *i* sound followed by *t* sound)

On your paper, correct any misspelled words.

1. furow   2. battle   3. litle   4. beter

USING THE WORD BANK

On your paper, write the word closest in meaning to the first word.

1. scolded: (a) praised, (b) criticized, (c) scalded
2. sturdy: (a) strong, (b) flimsy, (c) intelligent
3. rivulets: (a) oceans, (b) fasteners, (c) brooks
4. furrows: (a) wrinkles, (b) creeks, (c) holes
5. stoic: (a) pained, (b) unbothered, (c) unconscious
6. supple: (a) rigid, (b) tasty, (c) flexible

◆ **Literary Focus**

SENSORY LANGUAGE

In these works, the **sensory language**—language appealing to the senses—helps you experience what the writers describe. In "Grandma," for example, you can hear the grandmother approach before you actually see her: "her slippered feet softly measure/the tatami floor with even step."

1. Find two more sensory details in "Grandma," one appealing to sight and one to touch.
2. Explain how details appealing to the senses of smell and touch enhance "Old Man."

◆ **Build Grammar Skills**

PERSONAL PRONOUNS

Speakers or writers use **personal pronouns** to refer to themselves (first person), the person spoken to (second person), or the person spoken about (third person).

	Singular	Plural
First Person	I, me, my, mine	we, us, our, ours
Second Person	you, your, yours	you, your, yours
Third Person	he, him, his, she, her, hers, it, its	they, them, their, theirs

Practice On your paper, identify the personal pronouns in these sentences.

1. His legs would not carry him.
2. She told him that he spoiled everything in the house and broke their dishes.
3. Before she came into view, I heard her slippered feet.
4. "You are indio, among other things," he would tell me.
5. Gone into dust is your body with its stoic look.

Writing Application Write sentences that include the personal pronoun in the form indicated.

1. A description of a family having dinner with an older relative (third-person plural)
2. Something a granddaughter might say to her grandmother (second-person singular)
3. A statement a grandfather might make to describe his family (first-person plural)

Build Your Portfolio

Idea Bank

Writing

1. **Descriptive Close-up** Focus on the hands or face of a person who is dear to you. Then, use sensory details to describe your close-up picture for a reader.

2. **Proposal for a Reunion** In a letter to family members, propose a family reunion that they can attend. Suggest a place, ways to get there, and activities that everyone would enjoy.

3. **Folk Tale** Write a brief tale like Tolstoy's, focusing on an elderly person. Make sure that the characters and plot of the tale teach a lesson about growing older or about the relationships between different generations.

Speaking and Listening

4. **Storytelling Circle [Group Activity]** With several classmates, exchange stories in front of the class about older family members or friends who have inspired you. Include details to help listeners visualize the person you are describing.

5. **Dialogue With Yourself** Imagine that you could travel forward in time and meet yourself as an older person. Act out both sides of that dialogue for your classmates, playing yourself as you are now and yourself as you will become. **[Performing Arts Link]**

Projects

6. **Life Dance [Group Activity]** With several classmates, create and perform a dance illustrating the different stages of life. Show through movement what it's like to be a child, a teenager, an adult, and an elder. **[Performing Arts Link]**

7. **Community-Service Report** Volunteer to help out at a home for older people in your community. Then, give an oral report on your experiences to the class. You may want to explain the training and skills required in caring for the elderly. **[Social Studies Link]**

Writing Mini-Lesson

Description of an Older Person

All the authors in this group paint a portrait of an older person. Follow their lead by writing your own description of a senior citizen. Your subject can be someone you know well, someone you've observed from a distance, or a character from a novel. Whether your subject is real or fictional, describe this person as an individual and not as a "typical" older person.

Writing Skills Focus: Use Precise Language

Use **precise language,** terms that convey a detailed impression, to describe your subject. For example, notice how precise Amy Ling is in her self-description in "Grandma:"

> **Model From the Poem**
> my five foot height, my sturdy legs and feet,
> my square forehead, high cheeks, and wide-set eyes.

Prewriting Once you've chosen your subject, gather details that describe his or her appearance, habits, and qualities.

Drafting Begin your description by showing your subject in action, or hook readers by revealing an intriguing or mysterious aspect of your subject. As you draft, refer to the descriptive details you gathered in Prewriting.

Revising Replace general terms with precise language that describes your subject as an individual. For example, instead of calling a man *pleasant,* you might say that he has *an amused glint in his eye.*

> ◆ **Grammar Application**
> In reviewing your draft, make sure readers can tell to whom each personal pronoun refers.

The Old Grandfather and His Little Grandson/Grandma/Old Man ◆ 79

Idea Bank

Following are suggestions for matching the Idea Bank topics with your students' performance levels and learning modalities:

Customize for
Performance Levels
Less Advanced Students: 1, 4, 6
Average Students: 2, 4, 5, 6, 7
More Advanced Students: 3, 4, 5, 6, 7

Customize for
Learning Modalities
Verbal/Linguistic: 1, 2, 3, 4, 7
Bodily/Kinesthetic: 5, 6
Logical/Mathematical: 2, 7
Musical/Rhythmic: 6
Interpersonal: 2, 4, 6
Intrapersonal: 1, 3, 4, 5

Writing Mini-Lesson

Refer students to the Writing Handbook in the back of the book for instructions on the writing process and for further information on using descriptive writing.

 Writer's Solution

Writers at Work Videodisc
Have students view the videodisc segment on Description (Ch. 2), featuring Rosie McNulty, to get her opinion on the importance of using precise words. Have students discuss her technique of hunting down repeated adjectives.

Play frames 24265 to 27473

Writing Lab CD-ROM
Have students complete the tutorial on Description. Follow these steps:
1. Introduce Descriptive Writing and types of description.
2. Have students draft on computer.
3. Have students use a Sensory Details Chart and the Descriptive Word Bin Revision Checker.

Allow about 70 minutes of class time to complete these steps.

Writer's Solution Sourcebook
Have students use Chapter 2, "Description," pp. 32–69, for further support. The chapter includes in-depth instruction on using vivid and precise verbs, pp. 62–64.

✓ ASSESSMENT OPTIONS

ASSESSMENT OPTIONS
Formal Assessment, Selection Test, pp. 21–23, and Assessment Resources Software. The selection test is designed so that it can be easily customized to the performance levels of your students.

Alternative Assessment, p. 7, includes options for less advanced students, more advanced students, interpersonal learners, verbal/linguistic learners, intrapersonal learners, visual/spatial learners, and musical/rhythmic learners.

PORTFOLIO ASSESSMENT
Use the following rubrics in the **Alternative Assessment** booklet to assess student writing:
Descriptive Close-Up: Description, p. 93
Proposal for a Reunion: How-To/Process Explanation, p. 96
Folk Tale: Fictional Narrative, p. 91
Writing Mini-Lesson: Description, p. 93

OBJECTIVES

1. To read, comprehend, and interpret a first-person narrative
2. To relate a first-person narrative to personal experience
3. To apply word identification
4. To appreciate a first-person narrative
5. To build vocabulary in context and learn the prefix *extra-*
6. To develop skill in using indefinite pronouns
7. To write an extended definition
8. To respond to the narratives through writing, speaking and listening, and projects

SKILLS INSTRUCTION

Vocabulary:
Prefixes: *extra-*

Spelling: s Sound Spelled *sc*

Grammar:
Indefinite Pronoun

Reading Strategy:
Word Identification

Literary Focus:
First-Person Narrative

Writing:
Considering Your Audience

Speaking and Listening:
Radio Monologue (Teacher Edition)

Viewing and Representing:
Decades on Display (Teacher Edition)

Critical Viewing:
Interpret

PORTFOLIO OPPORTUNITIES

Writing: Thank-You Note; Poem; Essay
Writing Mini-Lesson: Extended Definition
Speaking and Listening: Debate; Radio Monologue
Projects: Social Research; Meteor Presentation

More About the Author

Hal Borland broke his first bronco at the age of 5 in Colorado, where he lived near the homeland of the Ute Indians. As a young man, Borland learned about nature from the Utes. In addition to several short stories and other works of fiction, Borland wrote 350 nonfiction articles for leading magazines.

Garrison Keillor is a humorist, writer, and performer whose thoughtful and clever social commentary entertains his public radio listeners. In addition to hosting *A Prairie Home Companion,* Keillor hosts *The Writer's Almanac,* a daily 5-minute radio program about poetry and history.

Guide for Reading

Meet the Authors:
Hal Borland (1900–1978)

Born in Sterling, Nebraska, Hal Borland became a naturalist, a person who studies animals and plants. Borland loved and respected the outdoors. He once said that "if you would know strength and patience, welcome the company of trees." The National Audubon Society honored him by creating the Hal Borland Trail in Connecticut.

As a writer, Borland wore many hats: He wrote documentary film scripts, radio scripts, and other pieces of nonfiction. He also worked as a reporter for the *Denver Post* and the *Brooklyn Times*. "Shooting Stars" blends his fascination with nature and his ability to report facts in a clear, appealing way.

Garrison Keillor (1942–   )

Every Saturday night, more than two million public radio listeners tune in to Garrison Keillor's show, "A Prairie Home Companion." The variety show includes music, comedy sketches, and Keillor's dryly amusing monologue, "The News From Lake Wobegon." A member of the Radio Hall of Fame and author of several books of humorous and insightful commentary, Keillor often focuses on life in the imaginary yet universal midwestern town of Lake Wobegon.

80 ◆ Coming of Age

◆ LITERATURE AND YOUR LIFE

CONNECT YOUR EXPERIENCE

From Halley's Comet to clothing styles, virtually everything in the universe fits into a season or cycle. Chances are, a style considered "out" now will be "in" again soon. In these essays, two writers observe two very different kinds of cycles.

THEMATIC FOCUS: Seasons and Cycles

As you read, ask: Why are seasons and cycles reassuring or comforting to people?

◆ Background for Understanding

CULTURE

Decades are often given a "personality" in hindsight. For example, the sixties are remembered as a time of social and political change. During this turbulent decade, a strong youth movement rebelled against established social rules and staged protests on college campuses across the nation. Many aspects of culture—from fashion and music to film and writing—also departed from traditional formats and styles. In "Something From the Sixties," Garrison Keillor offers a glimpse of what sixties clothing styles were like.

◆ Build Vocabulary

PREFIXES: *extra-*

In his essay, Keillor describes the extravagance of an outfit. Notice how the prefix *extra-*, meaning "outside" or "beyond," combines with the root *vagant*, meaning "to wander," to create a term meaning "to go outside the norm."

WORD BANK

Which word from the list means "to circle an orb"? Check the Build Vocabulary box on page 82 to see if you chose correctly.

orbit
friction
constellation
descended
extravagance

Prentice Hall Literature Program Resources

REINFORCE / RETEACH / EXTEND

Selection Support Pages
Build Vocabulary: Prefixes: *extra-*, p. 39
Build Spelling Skills, p. 40
Build Grammar Skills: Indefinite Pronouns, p. 41
Reading Strategy: Word Identification, p. 42
Literary Focus: First-Person Narrative, p. 43

Strategies for Diverse Student Needs, pp. 15–16

Beyond Literature Career Connection: Costume Designer, p. 8

Formal Assessment Selection Test, pp. 24–26
Assessment Resources Software

Alternative Assessment, p. 8

Writing and Language Transparencies
KWL Organizer, p. 49

Resource Pro CD-ROM "Shooting Stars"; "Something From the Sixties"—includes all resource material and customizable lesson plan

 Listening to Literature Audiocassettes
"Shooting Stars"; "Something From the Sixties"

Shooting Stars
◆ Something From the Sixties ◆

◆ Literary Focus
FIRST-PERSON NARRATIVE

A **first-person narrative** is an account of a writer's own experience. It is written in the first person, which is signaled by the narrator's use of the pronoun "I." In a first-person narrative, the author gives his reactions to and reflections on the meaning of an event, often revealing his or her personal viewpoint, as Hal Borland does in this statement:

> I once watched the August Perseids with an astronomer on a hilltop in open country, and in two hours we counted almost a thousand meteors.

Unfamiliar Word	Word Parts	My Definition

◆ Reading Strategy
WORD IDENTIFICATION

Narratives by people with different backgrounds from your own are likely to include unfamiliar words. When you encounter an unfamiliar word, you can apply **word identification** to unlock its meaning. Break the word into its syllables or parts, and look for something familiar in it.

Unfamiliar Word:	periodically
Familiar Word Part:	period
Possible Definition:	happening at different periods

Use a chart like the one to the left to identify word meanings as you read.

Guide for Reading ◆ 81

Preparing for Standardized Tests

Vocabulary Comprehension test questions on standardized tests often necessitate students' applying word identification to figure out the meaning of unfamiliar words. Present the following statement:

> By using a fake English accent, wearing clothes from the 60's, and singing Beatles songs, the boy showed that he idolized the Beatles.

Based on this sentence, which statement best defines *idolized*?

(A) The boy was friends with the Beatles.
(B) The boy imitated the Beatles perfectly.
(C) The boy was really much older than he appeared to be.
(D) The boy worshipped the Beatles.

Students can determine that (D) is the best answer because the unfamiliar word *idolized* contains the familiar word part *idol,* which can mean "an object of worship." Also, students will recognize that the context of the sentence indicates the boy's strong interest in the Beatles. For further practice with word identification, use the Reading Strategy page in **Selection Support,** p. 42.

Interest Grabber Write the well-worn saying "What goes around comes around" on the board. Invite students to respond to it by citing examples of ideas, fads, events, and fashions that appear to be cyclical—keep coming back. As needed, provide examples to get them started: from astronomy, the appearance of Halley's Comet; from pop culture, hula hoops, bell-bottoms, and yoyos. Invite students to predict which of today's styles or pursuits will fade away only to reappear at another time, for a new generation. Then tell students that they will read about how cyclical events can provide comfort as they connect us with our past.

◆ Build Grammar Skills

Indefinite Pronouns If you wish to introduce the grammar concept for this selection before students read, refer to the instruction on p. 86.

Customize for
Less Proficient Readers

Students may not bring a general knowledge of basic science or of the observation process to their reading. Guide them to stop and list their questions as they read. They can organize their questions, using the KWL Organizer in **Writing and Language Transparencies,** p. 49.

Customize for
More Advanced Students

As students read the selections, suggest that they think about cycles of life, either positive or negative, that capture the mind. What about cyclical events is reassuring? What is depressing about them? Invite students to share their thoughts with classmates.

Customize for
English Language Learners

The first selection contains scientific terms and the second selection presents 1960's slang and pop culture references. Some of these words and expressions may be unfamiliar to students. Help them understand the unfamiliar language by bringing in representative pictures or objects. For example, show a photo of a meteorite or of Meteor Crater, or display the *Sgt. Pepper's Lonely Hearts Club Band* album cover.

81

One-Minute Insight

In this first-person narrative, Hal Borland provides readers with an overview of what shooting stars are, and defines and describes meteors, meteorites, comets, and constellations. In so doing, he presents the cyclical nature of some celestial events, pointing out that we can see the same exciting celestial shows people have enjoyed for centuries.

◆ Critical Thinking

❶ Connect Discuss the title of the essay with students, pointing out the distinction between its literal meaning (white-hot meteors streaking across the sky) and the metaphorical meaning it can have (a person who quickly rises to fame and then falls into obscurity just as rapidly).

Thematic Focus

❷ Seasons and Cycles Ask students to name constellations they know and can recognize. Ask them to explain how knowing about and being able to spot constellations links us with the past. *Students may say that learning how ancient peoples described and explained the constellations and other celestial bodies and events tells us a great deal about those cultures and civilizations and, also, about ourselves as humans.*

◆ Literary Focus

❸ First-Person Narrative Point out this example of the narrator's personal touch. Guide students to appreciate that the detail about the mosquitoes is a joke, but that the meteor count is meant to be accurate.

Customize for
Verbal/Linguistic Learners
Guide students, as they read these pieces, to look for indications that each is a first-person narrative, that each contains descriptions of real events, all filtered through the eyes of the story teller.

❶ SHOOTING STARS

Hal Borland

Most clear, dark nights you can see a shooting star, as we call it, if you keep looking. Those shooting stars are meteors. They are points of light that suddenly appear in the sky, like distant stars, race across the darkness, usually toward the horizon, and disappear.

For a long time nobody knew what a meteor was. But finally those who study stars and the sky decided that a meteor is a piece of a comet that exploded long ago. Those pieces are still wandering about the universe in huge, looping paths that follow the original comet's <u>orbit</u>. There are uncounted pieces of such comets out there in the depths of space. Periodically clusters of them come close to the earth's orbit, or path around the sun. Most meteors are small, probably only a few inches in diameter, but when they enter the earth's atmosphere the <u>friction</u> makes them white-hot. Then they look big as stars streaking across the darkness.

 There are half a dozen meteor showers each year. Each is named after the <u>constellation</u> from which it appears to come. The biggest of all, the Perseids, named for the constellation of Perseus, occurs on the 10th, 11th, and 12th of August. The next largest, the Leonids, named for the constellation of Leo, comes on the nights of November 14, 15, and 16. Another, the Andromedids, which is not quite so big, comes from November 17 through 23. There are other meteor showers in December, January, April, May, and July, but none of them is as big as those in August and November.

Most people watching meteors will be satisfied if they see ten or twenty in an hour of watching. On special occasions, however, the meteors seem to come in droves. The most remarkable meteor shower I ever heard of was seen by a distinguished astronomer, Professor Denison Olmstead, of New Haven,

Connecticut, on the night of November 12, 1833. He was watching the Leonids, which seem to come from directly overhead and race downward toward the horizon in all directions. He reported that meteors fell "like flakes of snow." He estimated that he saw 240,000 meteors in nine hours that night. He said they ranged in size from mere streaks of light to "globes of the moon's diameter." If he had not been a notable astronomer whose accuracy was beyond question, such statements would seem ridiculous. But there is no reason to doubt what he reported. He had seen one of the most unusual meteor showers ever reported. What he watched should be called a meteor storm rather than a shower.

I once watched the August Perseids with an astronomer on a hilltop in open country, and in two hours we counted almost a thousand meteors. That was the most I ever saw at one time. And we were bitten by one mosquito for every meteor we saw. After that I tried watching for meteors in November, when there were no mosquitoes. But the most I ever saw in November was about one hundred meteors in two hours of watching. ❸

The amazing thing about these meteor showers is that they come year after year. Professor Olmstead saw all those Leonids in November of 1833, but if you watch for meteors this year you almost certainly will see them on the same nights he saw them. They will come

◆ Build Vocabulary

orbit (ôr´ bit) *n.*: Path a planet or other celestial body takes moving around another celestial body

friction (frik´ shən) *n.*: Rubbing of one object against another

constellation (kän´ stə lā´ shən) *n.*: Collection of stars

◆ Block Scheduling Strategies

Consider these suggestions to take advantage of extended class time:

- Use the Interest Grabber, p. 81, to familiarize students with nature of cyclical ideas and events.
- Discuss the Literary Focus concept: First-Person Narrative, p. 81. Guide students to look for examples of how each narrative in the selection is colored by the narrator's personal reactions and reflections.
- Devote class time to having students work in small groups on the Projects in the Idea Bank

on p. 87, or have them plan the cross-curricular activity for the Science Connection in Beyond Literature, p. 83.
- Use class time to help students prepare for and do the Speaking and Listening activities, p. 87.
- To help students prepare for the Writing Mini-Lesson: Extended Definition on p. 87, review the elements of expository writing, using *Writer's Solution Sourcebook*, Chapter 4, Exposition: Giving Information.

next year, the year after that, and for countless years more. Your grandfather saw them, and your grandchildren will see them if they look for them.

Occasionally a meteor reaches the earth. Then it is called a meteorite and it is valued as a sample of the vast mystery of the deep space in the sky. Scientists examine it, try to guess what it was to begin with, where it came from, what it is like out there. Nobody ever learned very much from the meteorites except that they often contain a great deal of nickel and iron.

Only a few large meteorites have struck the earth. The largest we know about fell in Arizona many centuries ago and made what is now called Meteor Crater, a hole about a mile across and 600 feet deep. Some Indian legends of the Southwest tell of a big fire that fell from the sky and ate a huge hole in the earth, so this big meteorite may have fallen since man first arrived in America, perhaps twenty-five thousand years ago.

Other big meteorites have fallen, in ancient times, in Texas, in Argentina, in northern Siberia, in South-West Africa, and in Greenland. A meteorite weighing more than thirty-six tons was found in Greenland and now can be seen in the Hayden Planetarium in New York City. Millions of meteors have flashed across the night sky, but only a few large meteorites have ever reached the earth. Never in all the centuries of written history has there been a report of anyone being struck by a meteorite.

Beyond Literature

Science Connection

The Hubble Telescope In the 1600's, Galileo invented the first telescope, which created magnified views of celestial bodies. Throughout the years, telescopes have improved, becoming more accurate and powerful. In 1990, the Hubble Space Telescope was launched by the space shuttle *Discovery*. Because it is outside our atmosphere, it can collect undistorted light. The Hubble broadcasts the clearest pictures of the universe yet seen.

Cross-Curricular Activity
Science Create an astral journal by viewing the night sky and making specific observations about its appearance.

Guide for Responding

◆ LITERATURE AND YOUR LIFE

Reader's Response What do you think is the most beautiful part of the night sky?

Thematic Focus In what way does the idea of seasons and cycles apply to meteor showers?

☑ **Check Your Comprehension**

1. What are meteors?
2. Why are meteorites valued so highly?
3. What was the effect of the largest meteorite that fell to Earth?

◆ Critical Thinking

INTERPRET
1. Why do scientists observe meteors? **[Interpret]**
2. What might be learned from studying meteorites? **[Speculate]**
3. What does Borland say to encourage his readers to become amateur observers? **[Analyze]**

APPLY
4. Will astronomers 100 years from today still study meteors? Explain. **[Speculate]**

EXTEND
5. What characteristics do you think a professional astronomer should have? **[Science Link]**

Shooting Stars ◆ 83

Speaking and Listening Mini-Lesson

Radio Monologue
This mini-lesson supports the Speaking and Listening activity in the Idea Bank on p. 87.

Introduce Discuss with students what a monologue is. Then play an example of one of Garrison Keillor's radio monologues. Discuss its features, tone, and how his delivery enhances his message.

Develop Have students plan and write their monologues. Guide them to choose and narrow their topic, and then to draft and revise the monologue so it is as effective and as entertaining as they wish it to be. Students should practice their deliveries. With the help of peer reviewers, they can fine-tune the content and their presentations.

Apply Have students tape record their monologues. Play them for the class. One or more students might act as radio hosts to introduce the pieces and to begin and end the program.

Assess Have students respond to what they enjoyed about the monologues. Evaluate performances based on the topics, the personal viewpoints expressed, as well as delivery. Or, use the Peer Assessment: Dramatic Performance form, p. 116, in **Alternative Assessment.**

Clarification

❹ Meteor Crater is located 35 miles east of Flagstaff just off Interstate 40. The crater, which is large enough to hold 20 football fields, was formed by a meteorite that weighed millions of tons and fell to Earth at a speed of nearly 45,000 mph. It had an explosive force equal to 15 million tons of TNT. Because of its lunar-like terrain, it has been one of NASA's official training sites for Apollo astronauts.

Beyond Literature

Students can use the Internet for information from the Hubble Space Telescope. To see pictures from Mars:
http://oposite.stsci.edu/pubinfo/ PR/97/23.html
For telescope links:
http:// www.nationalgeographic. com/stars/telescope/index.html
We *strongly recommend* that you preview these sites before sending students to them.

Reinforce and Extend

Answers
◆ LITERATURE AND YOUR LIFE

Reader's Response Have students explain their choices.

Thematic Focus Meteor showers are cyclical. They appear at the same time of year, every year.

☑ **Check Your Comprehension**

1. They are pieces of comets that exploded long ago.
2. Meteorites are valued as samples from space. Scientists use them to find answers to questions.
3. It made a huge crater in the Earth's surface.

◆ Critical Thinking

1. Scientists observe meteors to understand more about the motions of objects in space.
2. Meteorites provide information about the composition of planets, moons, and other celestial objects.
3. He describes viewing meteors as an accessible, intriguing, and an ongoing human activity.
4. Students may say that with more space information, scientists will have new reasons to study meteors.
5. Charactersitics include patience, curiosity, and ability to conduct careful, thorough observations.

To provide his son with an outfit from the 1960's to wear to a party, Garrison Keillor roots through his attic for clothes he once wore. In the course of finding what he was looking for and through what results from the search, he learns much about himself and his son.

Clarification

① When we refer to "the 60's" as the time when people dressed like those in the photo do, we refer to a time period that began not in 1960, but in the mid-to-late 1960's. In the early 1960's, people dressed much more conservatively; men wore crew cuts; no one in America had heard of the Beatles (their first concert in America was in 1964); and the conflict in Vietnam had not yet escalated into an undeclared war

◆ LITERATURE AND YOUR LIFE

② Here, Keillor recognizes that he and his son share a trait: no sense of time. Have students think about and then tell what traits they may share with their parents. As a homework assignment, have students get their parents' opinions on this issue.

►Critical Viewing◄

③ Interpret *Students may say that if the clothing was fanciful, colorful, and wild, then the era must have been one of openness in thought and expression. Or they may observe that it must have been fashionable to show off and "be different."*

◆Literary Focus

④ **First-Person Narrative** Point out to students that these people were television figures of Keillor's youth, all of whom wore distinctive and elaborate clothes not usually worn by conventional people.

Customize for
Less Proficient Readers

Students may have more success reading aloud with a partner or listening to the recording in order to more fully understand long sentences and better appreciate Keillor's dry humor.

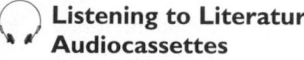
Listening to Literature Audiocassettes

Something From the Sixties

Garrison Keillor

About five o'clock last Sunday evening, my son burst into the kitchen and said, "I didn't know it was so late!" He was due at a party immediately—a sixties party, he said—and he needed something from the sixties to wear. My son is almost fifteen years old, the size of a grown man, and when he bursts into a room glassware rattles and the cat on your lap grabs on to your knees and leaps from the starting block. I used to think the phrase "burst into the room" was only for detective fiction, until my son got his growth. He can burst in a way that, done by an older fellow, would mean that angels had <u>descended</u> into the front yard and were eating apples off the tree, and he does it whenever he's late—as being my son, he often is. I have so little sense of time that when he said he needed something from the sixties it took me a moment to place that decade. It's the one he was born toward the end of.

I asked, "What sort of stuff you want to wear?"

He said, "I don't know. Whatever they wore then."

We went up to the attic, into a long, low room under the eaves where I've squirreled away some boxes of old stuff; I dug into one box, and the first thing I hauled out was the

▲ **Critical Viewing** What can you learn of the sixties by studying the fashions of the time? [Interpret] **③**

very thing he wanted. A thigh-length leather vest covered with fringe and studded with silver, it dates from around 1967, a fanciful time in college-boy fashions. Like many boys, I grew up in nice clothes my mother bought, but was meanwhile admiring Roy Rogers, Sergeant Rock, the Cisco Kid, and other sharp dressers, so when I left home I was ready to step out and be somebody. Military Surplus was the basic style then—olive drab, and navy-blue pea jackets—with a touch of Common Man in the work boots and blue work shirts, but if you showed up in Riverboat Gambler or Spanish Peasant or Rodeo King nobody blinked, nobody laughed. I haven't worn the vest in ten years, but a few weeks ago, seeing a picture of Michael Jackson wearing a fancy band jacket like the ones the Beatles wore on the cover of "Sgt. Pepper," I missed the fun I used to have getting dressed in the morning. Pull on the jeans, a shirt with

---

Viewing and Representing Mini-Lesson

Decades on Display

This mini-lesson supports the Thematic Focus: Seasons and Cycles.

Introduce Each decade has its own unique character, shaped by political, social, economic, and scientific events. Discuss how the photo on p. 84 captures a moment from the 60's, and how pictures can also represent other decades. Discuss music, dance steps, foods, and the many other things that can also identify a decade.

Develop Have students form groups, each responsible for a recent decade, and research

characteristic features of life that set their time period apart from others. The representations might include showing photos, preparing foods, giving examples of slang or jargon, or playing or performing a song from that time. Have students ask their elders about their memories of specific time periods when gathering information.

Apply Have groups make their presentations to the class.

Assess Evaluate groups according to the variety and accuracy of their choices and whether they captured the essence of their decades.

brilliant-red roses, a pair of Red Wing boots. A denim jacket. Rose-tinted glasses. A cowboy hat. Or an engineer's cap. Or, instead of jeans, bib overalls. Or white trousers with blue stripes. Take off the denim jacket, take off the rose shirt, try the neon-green bowling shirt with "Moose" stitched on the pocket, the black dinner jacket. Now the dark-green Chinese Army cap. And an orange tie with hula dancers and palm trees.

Then—presto!—I pulled the rose shirt out. He put it on, and the vest, which weighs about fifteen pounds, and by then I had found him a hat—a broad-brimmed panama that ought to make you think of a cotton planter enjoying a Sazerac on a veranda in New Orleans. I followed him down to his bedroom, where he admired himself in a full-length mirror.

"Who wore this?" he asked.

I said that I did.

"Did you really? This? You?"

⑤ Yes, I really did. After he was born, in 1969, I wore it less and less, finally settling down

with what I think of as the Dad look, and now I would no sooner wear my old fringed vest in public than walk around in a taffeta tutu. I loved the fact that it fitted him so well, though, and his pleasure at the heft and <u>extravagance</u> of the thing, the poses he struck in front of the mirror. Later, when he got home and reported that his costume was a big hit and that all his friends had tried on the vest, it made me happy again. You squirrel away old stuff on the principle of its being useful and interesting someday; it's wonderful when the day finally arrives. That vest was waiting for a boy to come along—a boy who has a flair for the dramatic, who bursts into rooms—and to jump right into the part. I'm happy to be the audience. **⑥**

⑤

◆ Build Vocabulary

descended (dē send´ id) *v.*: Came down

extravagance (ek strav´ ə gəns) *n.*: A spending of more than is necessary; wastefulness

◆ Literary Focus

⑤ First-Person Narrative What does this list of reminiscences tell about the father? *Students may say that although he now dresses like "a dad," his attic reveals that he once was very much a part of that fanciful time.*

◆ Literary Focus

⑥ First-Person Narrative Discuss with students how the narrator happily revisits his past by sharing it with his son. When he sees how naturally his son wears the old outfit, he glimpses himself at that age.

Reinforce and Extend

Answers

◆ LITERATURE AND YOUR LIFE

Reader's Response Some students wouldn't wear it for fear of looking foolish. Others, who are more outgoing or individualistic, may find the idea intriguing.

Thematic Focus Students may respond that clothing styles come back for nostalgic reasons and because they hold the same appeal that they originally had.

✓ Check Your Comprehension

1. He needs the clothes for a 60's party.
2. They find a vest and a rose shirt and other examples of fanciful clothing from the 60's.
3. His costume is a big hit.

◆ Critical Thinking

1. He is amused by it and nostalgic for the youthful fun he had wearing the unusual outfits.
2. He had only seen his father wearing "dad clothes."
3. It suggests that he is content to pass the baton to his son, to allow him the pleasure of exploring unusual and playful ways of dressing.
4. Students might say that he would sympathize with his son's motivation to express himself through his clothing.
5. The first essay describes the yearly cycles of meteor showers; the second, the cycles of fashion and aging. Meteor showers are more predictable, but no less inevitable than the cycles of life.

Guide for Responding

◆ LITERATURE AND YOUR LIFE

Reader's Response Would you like to wear the vest described in "Something From the Sixties"? Why or why not?

Thematic Focus Why do you think old clothing styles come back in fashion?

Sketch Make a sketch of the vest described in the story.

✓ Check Your Comprehension

1. Why does the narrator's son want to borrow some clothing?
2. What clothing do the father and son find in the attic?
3. How successful is the son's costume at the party?

◆ Critical Thinking

INTERPRET

1. What is the narrator's attitude toward his past style of dress? **[Interpret]**
2. Why is the narrator's son surprised that his father wore such dramatic clothing? **[Infer]**
3. What does the final sentence reveal about the narrator's current attitude toward fashion? **[Draw Conclusions]**

APPLY

4. How might the narrator respond if his son began wearing extravagant clothing? **[Hypothesize]**

COMPARE LITERARY WORKS

5. How does the idea of cycles of events connect these two essays? Are the cycles described in both predictable? **[Interpret]**

Something From the Sixties ◆ 85

Beyond the Selection

FURTHER READING

Other Works by Hal Borland
When the Legends Die
"An American Year"
"Creed"

Other Works by Garrison Keillor
Lake Wobegon Days
Happy to Be Here

INTERNET

We suggest the following sites on the Internet (all Web sites are subject to change).

For some quotations by Hal Borland:
http://www.bemorecreative.com/one/324.htm
For an interview with Garrison Keillor:
http://www.aclu.org/about/transcripts/Keillor.html
For more about Keillor and "The Writer's Almanac":
http://almanac.mpr.org
We *strongly recommend* that you preview the sites before you send students to them.

Answers

◆ Reading Strategy

1. *astro*; it identifies a connection to stars.
2. (a) glass + ware = an article made of glass; (b) fancy + ful = full of fancy; (c) no + body = no one

◆ Build Vocabulary

Using the Prefix *extra-*

1. beyond ordinary; more than ordinary
2. outside of the regular curriculum
3. from beyond Earth
4. beyond the ability to be sensed

Spelling Strategy

1. scientist, ascent; 2. scene, crescent; 3. scented

Using the Word Bank

1. descended; 2. extravagance;
3. constellation; 4. orbit;
5. friction

◆ Literary Focus

1. Possible response: when Borland describes the most remarkable meteor shower he'd ever heard of
2. (a) Borland's; (b) Keillor's; it focuses on an episode in Keillor's life and is more like a memoir or personal anecdote than an essay.
3. Keillor's piece would change most because it relies heavily on opinions and humor.

◆ Build Grammar Skills

Practice

1. everything; 2. few; 3. most;
4. something; 5. many

Writing Application

Possible responses:

1. Many people in the late 60's wore fanciful clothing.
2. Several wore brightly colored shirts and pants and elaborate vests.
3. No one was surprised by something someone was wearing.
4. Most of the clothing in the attic would be worn by few today.

✐ Writer's Solution

For additional instruction and practice, use the lesson in the *Writer's Solution Language Lab CD-ROM* on Using Pronouns, and the practice page on indefinite pronouns, p. 10, in the *Writer's Solution Grammar Practice Book.*

Guide for Responding *(continued)*

◆ Reading Strategy

WORD IDENTIFICATION

Apply **word identification** to unlock the meaning of unfamiliar words. Break unfamiliar words into parts, looking for familiar words or word parts within them that will help you determine the word's meaning.

1. Which word part in the word *astronomer* gives a clue to its meaning?
2. Explain how you would use word identification to make sense of these words:
   a. glassware   **b.** fanciful   **c.** nobody

◆ Build Vocabulary

USING THE PREFIX *extra-*

Knowing that the prefix *extra-* means "outside" or "beyond," figure out the meaning of each word. Then, use a dictionary to check your definitions.

1. extraordinary   3. extraterrestrial
2. extracurricular   4. extrasensory

SPELLING STRATEGY

The *s* sound is sometimes spelled *sc*, as in *descended*. On your paper, write the words in each sentence that use the *sc* spelling for the *s* sound.

1. The scientist studied the ascent of the missile.
2. The scene was lit by a crescent moon.
3. Scented candles were popular in the sixties.

USING THE WORD BANK

Write the word from the Word Bank that best completes each sentence. Use each word only once.

1. The sun _____?_____ behind the hills.
2. The _____?_____ of the colorful display seemed almost overdone.
3. Can you identify the _____?_____ of Orion?
4. The moon's _____?_____ circles the Earth.
5. While entering the atmosphere, _____?_____ eroded the surface of the meteorite.

◆ Literary Focus

FIRST-PERSON NARRATIVE

Both essays in this section are **first-person narratives,** accounts of events from the authors' lives. They are told from the first-person point of view. Some first-person narrators act as on-the-scene reporters, sticking to the facts, whereas others reveal their personal reactions to the events.

1. At what point in "Shooting Stars" does it become clear that it is a first-person narrative and not a purely factual report? Explain.
2. (a) Which narrative is primarily reporting? (b) Which is primarily a personal recounting of a true-life event? How can you tell?
3. Which piece would be more greatly altered if it were rewritten to be a newspaper report? Why?

◆ Build Grammar Skills

INDEFINITE PRONOUNS

An **indefinite pronoun** refers to a person, place, or thing that is not specifically named. Indefinite pronouns are singular or plural.

Singular: *another, anyone, anything, each, either, everyone, everything, much, neither, no one, nothing, one, someone, something*

Plural: *both, few, several, many*

Singular or Plural: *all, any, most, none, some*

Practice Write each sentence on your paper. Then, circle each indefinite pronoun.

1. Everything is ready for the meteor watch.
2. Few appear in March.
3. In August and November, most of the meteors fall.
4. Something unexpected often happens.
5. The spectacular sight surprised many of us.

Writing Application Write four sentences about "Something From the Sixties." Include at least one indefinite pronoun in each sentence.

Build Your Portfolio

 Idea Bank

Writing

1. **Thank-You Note** Imagine that you are the son in "Something From the Sixties." Write a thank-you note to your father for letting you borrow his old clothing.

2. **Poem** Write a poem about shooting stars or some other element of the night sky. Create word images to represent the pictures that you see in your mind's eye.

3. **Essay** Write an essay in which you explore a cycle or season. For example, you might describe the phases of the moon, a comet's orbit, or the northern lights. **[Science Link]**

Speaking and Listening

4. **Debate [Group Activity]** Hold a class debate about the idea that "clothes make the man." Appoint a moderator to make sure that the debate rules are followed and that everyone has a turn to voice an opinion.

5. **Radio Monologue** Garrison Keillor's essay is like a written version of his radio monologues—oral narratives about his life. Write a radio monologue of your own. Then, record and play it for the class. **[Performing Arts Link]**

Projects

6. **Social Research** Conduct research to find out about events like the civil rights marches and the moon landing that took place during the sixties. Consider how this period of history affected the decades that followed. **[Social Studies Link]**

7. **Meteor Presentation [Group Activity]** Work in a group to create a presentation on meteors. You might focus on the Perseids, Leonids, and the Andromedids, or you might focus on meteorites that have hit the Earth. Create charts and illustrations to make your presentation visually interesting. **[Science Link]**

 Writing Mini-Lesson

Extended Definition

Hal Borland's "Shooting Stars" is an extended definition of the title topic—meteors. An extended definition is a full exploration of a single topic. Choose a topic to explore fully in an extended definition. You might write about a scientific term, such as *supernova* or *black hole,* or a fashionable item, such as *high tops.*

Writing Skills Focus: Audience

Always consider the **audience** for whom you are writing. You need to provide information and speak in language that's appropriate for their level of understanding.

Model From "Shooting Stars"

But finally those who study stars and the sky decided that a meteor is a piece of a comet that exploded long ago. Those pieces are still wandering about the universe in huge, looping paths that follow the original comet's orbit.

Prewriting Conduct research in a variety of sources to gather information about your topic. Think about who your audience is and what information they'll need to know. Jot down examples, and draw diagrams they'll find useful.

Drafting Begin with a basic definition of the term. Then, extend your definition by describing a different aspect of your main topic in each paragraph.

Revising Test your writing on an audience by reading your draft aloud to a partner. Have him or her identify the points that need to be made more clear or expanded upon.

> ◆ **Grammar Application**
> If you've used indefinite pronouns, be sure that your audience will understand to what they refer.

Shooting Stars / Something From the Sixties ◆ 87

 Idea Bank

Following are suggestions for matching the Idea Bank topics with your students' performance levels and learning modalities:

Customize for
Performance Levels
Less Advanced Students: 1, 4
Average Students: 2, 3, 4, 5, 7
More Advanced Students: 2, 3, 5, 6, 7

Customize for
Learning Modalities
Verbal/Linguistic: 1, 2, 3, 4, 5, 6, 7
Visual/Spatial: 7
Logical/Mathematical: 3, 4, 6, 7
Musical/Rhythmic: 5
Interpersonal: 5, 6, 7
Intrapersonal: 1, 2

 Writing Mini-Lesson

Refer students to the Writing Handbook in the back of the book for instructions on the writing process and for further information on extended definitions.

 **Writer's Solution**

Writers at Work Videodisc
Have students view the videodisc segment on Exposition (Ch. 4), to see how Gary Matsumoto uses "outside eyes" to help revise his news stories. This may affect how students work with peers to revise their definitions.

Play frames 42272 to 43065

Writing Lab CD-ROM
Have students complete the Tutorial on Exposition: Giving Information. Follow these steps:
1. Students can do an Audience Profile to identify their audience.
2. Guide students to use note cards when gathering information.
3. Have students draft on computer.
4. Have students consult the Peer Editing Guidelines and Checklist before revising with partners.

Allow about 75 minutes of class time to complete these steps.

Writer's Solution Sourcebook
Have students use Chapter 4, "Exposition: Giving Information," pp. 105–136, for additional support. The chapter includes in-depth instruction on gathering and organizing details, p. 124.

✓ **ASSESSMENT OPTIONS**

Formal Assessment, Selection Test, pp. 24–26, and Assessment Resources Software. The selection test is designed so that it can be easily customized to the performance levels of your students.
Alternative Assessment, p. 8, includes options for less advanced students, more advanced students, verbal/linguistic learners, logical/mathematical learners, visual/spatial learners, and musical/rhythmic learners.

PORTFOLIO ASSESSMENT
Use the following rubrics in the **Alternative Assessment** booklet to assess student writing:
Thank-You Note: Expression, p. 90
Poem: Poetry, p. 104
Essay: Description, p. 93
Writing Mini-Lesson: Definition/Classification, p. 95

Guide for Reading

OBJECTIVES

1. To read, comprehend, and interpret poetry
2. To relate repetition in poetry to personal experience
3. To read poetry according to punctuation
4. To recognize repetition in poetry
5. To build vocabulary in context and learn the suffix -or
6. To develop skill in using intensive pronouns
7. To write a script for a time-capsule video
8. To respond to poetry through writing, speaking and listening, and projects

SKILLS INSTRUCTION

Vocabulary:
Suffixes: -or
Spelling:
Adding Suffixes to Words Ending in e
Grammar:
Intensive Pronouns
Reading Strategy:
Read Poetry According to Punctuation

Literary Focus:
Repetition in Poetry
Writing:
Use the Right Format
Speaking and Listening:
New Year's Speech (Teacher Edition)
Critical Viewing:
Interpret

PORTFOLIO OPPORTUNITIES

Writing: Description; Pattern Poem; Critical Interpretation
Writing Mini-Lesson: Script for a Time-Capsule Video
Speaking and Listening: New Year's Speech; Poetry Reading
Projects: Multimedia Presentation; Report

More About the Authors

Walt Whitman expresses his ideas about true poets in his preface to *Leaves of Grass.* "Poets to Come" may seem to be written by an older, experienced poet, but it appeared in the first edition of *Leaves of Grass,* when Whitman was in his 30's.

Langston Hughes was the first African American to devote his life to a literary career. He held a variety of jobs—teacher, ranch hand, farmer, seaman, and cook in a night club, among others. Hughes drew on all these experiences for his writing.

Alfred, Lord Tennyson served as Poet Laureate of England and he worked hard to perfect his craft as a poet. His shorter poems show inspired word choice, metrical mastery, and powerful imagery.

Meet the Authors:

Walt Whitman (1819–1892)

American poetry was born with Walt Whitman's *Leaves of Grass* (1855). Whitman, a New Yorker who worked at a variety of jobs, created bold new poems to suit a new country. He discarded the regular rhythms and rhymes of British poetry in favor of his own invented rhythms and unrhymed lines.

Langston Hughes (1902–1967)

Langston Hughes was the first African American to get the rhythm and feel of "blues" music into his poems. He came of age during the Harlem Renaissance of the 1920's. This renaissance, "rebirth," was a flowering of African American writers, musicians, and painters in New York City's Harlem.

Alfred, Lord Tennyson (1809–1892)

Born in rural England, Tennyson left home as a teenager to attend Cambridge University. While at Cambridge, Tennyson won a university prize for poetry, his first step on the way to becoming a famous poet. In 1850, Queen Victoria appointed him Poet Laureate of England.

THE STORY BEHIND THE POEM

"Ring Out, Wild Bells" is part of the long poem "In Memoriam, A.H.H." This poem's title means "In Memory," and Tennyson wrote it in memory of his close friend Arthur Henry Hallam, who died in 1833. The section "Ring Out, Wild Bells" marks the third New Year's holiday after his friend's death.

◆ LITERATURE AND YOUR LIFE

CONNECT YOUR EXPERIENCE

Just as the moon has cycles or phases, so does life itself. Think for a moment about various cycles you've observed. For example, think about the seasons, the school year, birthdays, and so on. In these poems, the speakers all make observations about life's patterns.

THEMATIC FOCUS: Seasons and Cycles

As you read, compare each speaker's thoughts about life's patterns to your own observations.

◆ Background for Understanding

CULTURE

"Ring Out, Wild Bells" captures the English tradition of ringing bells to express New Year's hopes. Here are other customs for welcoming the New Year:

- Scandinavia—skiing with torches
- Southern India—boiling new rice
- Bangladesh—worshiping the river Ganges
- Southern United States—eating black-eyed peas
- China—going to theatrical performances

◆ Build Vocabulary

SUFFIXES: -or

The prefix -or signals that a word means "a person or thing that does something." In "Poets to Come," Whitman addresses future *orators,* "people who give public speeches." *Orators* combines *orate,* "to give a speech," and *-or.*

WORD BANK

Which word from the list is often paired with *trouble* and has a similar meaning? Check the Build Vocabulary box on page 92 to see if you chose correctly.

orators
indicative
sauntering
strife

 Prentice Hall Literature Program Resources

REINFORCE / RETEACH / EXTEND

Selection Support Pages
Build Vocabulary: Suffixes: -or, p. 44
Build Spelling Skills, p. 45
Build Grammar Skills: Intensive Pronouns, p. 46
Reading Strategy: Read Poetry According to Punctuation, p. 47
Literary Focus: Repetition, p. 48
Strategies for Diverse Student Needs, pp. 17–18
Beyond Literature Cross-Curricular Connection: Science, p. 9

Formal Assessment Selection Test, pp. 27–29, Assessment Resources Software
Alternative Assessment, p. 9
Resource Pro CD-ROM "Poets to Come"; "Winter Moon"; "Ring Out, Wild Bells"—includes all resource material and customizable lesson plan
🎧 **Listening to Literature Audiocassettes** "Poets to Come"; "Winter Moon"; "Ring Out, Wild Bells"

Poets to Come ◆ Winter Moon
◆ Ring Out, Wild Bells ◆

◆ Literary Focus
REPETITION IN POETRY

Songwriters and poets hate to waste good words. That's why they use **repetition** in their works, returning again and again to a haunting word or phrase with a special meaning. Repetition is also an excellent way of tying a poem together. The familiar phrase is like a melody that keeps reappearing.

Pay special attention to repeated words and phrases in these poems. Notice their sounds and rhythms as well as their meanings. Then, ask yourself how these repetitions capture, in a tiny space, a whole world of thought and feeling.

◆ Reading Strategy
READ POETRY ACCORDING TO PUNCTUATION

Every poem comes equipped with a set of instructions on how to read it. Those instructions are its **punctuation** marks. You don't automatically stop at the ends of lines, but you do pause briefly for commas and stop for end marks like periods and exclamation points.

As you read, make sure you're clear about the poet's reading instructions. Copy a poem on your paper, and put little Post-it reminders near punctuation marks. Here's an example:

Poets to come! Orators, singers, musicians to come!

Guide for Reading ◆ 89

Play for students the final 2–3 minutes of Tchaikovsky's *1812 Festival Overture*, opus 49. Have them respond to the sounds of cannons and bells, and tell what feelings the music evokes. Tell them that this Russian composer wrote the piece in 1880 to commemorate and celebrate the 1812 defeat of Napoleon's army and a new beginning for the Russian people. Then tell students that the pieces in the selection are about life's transitions, its moments of passage, and its new beginnings.

◆ Build Grammar Skills

Intensive Pronouns If you wish to introduce the grammar concept for this selection before students read, refer to the instruction on p. 94.

Customize for
Less Proficient Readers
The Whitman and Tennyson poems are the most challenging of the three; have students listen to them on tape as they read along silently.

 Listening to Literature Audiocassettes

Customize for
More Advanced Students
Challenge students to read the poems more deeply to attempt to ascertain the poets' tone or mood. Have them justify their opinions by referring to lines in the poems. For instance, students may say that Whitman is deferential, that he modestly expects new generations to take his ideas further (lines 3, 5, 8, and 9 of "Poets to Come"). More perceptive students may sense the desperation of Tennyson's calls for change in "Ring Out, Wild Bells."

Customize for
English Language Learners
These poems contain phrases and exclamations rather then declarative sentences. Model understanding by providing similar exclamations, such as "How deep the snow!" or "How bright the stars!" To help students better interpret the Whitman poem, define the following words as the poet intends them: *continental* (well-traveled); *arouse* (stir to action); *justify* (show proof of value); *wheel* (turn around); and *averts* (turns away).

Preparing for Standardized Tests

Grammar The grammar concept for this selection is intensive pronouns. Standardized tests may include questions that test students' understanding of the correct use of these pronouns.

Point out that intensive pronouns either emphasize a person's role or indicate that a person performs an action alone. Present the following sample test question:

Identify the sentence that contains an intensive pronoun that emphasizes a person's role.

(A) I've resigned myself to the fact that I'll never be a great poet.

(B) I myself will be responsible for publishing the work.

(C) He outdid himself that time!

(D) She is her own favorite poet.

The intensive pronoun *myself* in (B) emphasizes the speaker's role. The pronouns in (A) and (C) refer to the subject and are needed to complete the sentence, but do not emphasize the subject's role. The last sentence (D) does not contain a pronoun with the *-self* or *-selves* suffix. For additional practice, use Build Grammar Skills in **Selection Support,** p. 46.

One-Minute Insight With modesty and optimism, Whitman exhorts artists of future generations to complete the work he has begun.

Thematic Focus

❶ Seasons and Cycles Ask students to explain where, according to this poem, Whitman places himself in the continuum of ideas and artistic achievement. *Students may say that he sees himself as one who merely observes the world around him and then presents his thoughts for shaping it. He urges the next generation to judge his ideas and then take them further.*

◆ Literary Focus

❷ Repetition Guide students to appreciate that the repetition of "I" at the beginning of lines serves to reinforce the poet's modesty.

◆ Reading Strategy

❸ Read Poetry According to Punctuation Have students listen to the recording of "Poets to Come" to hear how the reader uses punctuation to follow Whitman's reading instructions. Encourage them to review the punctuation on their own and then work in pairs to experience reading the poem aloud according to punctuation.

🎧 **Listening to Literature Audiocassettes**

Customize for
Bodily/Kinesthetic Learners
Invite students to act out how they'd deliver the lines from each poem to best get across the poem's tone and the poet's message.

POETS TO COME
Walt Whitman

Poets to come! <u>orators</u>, singers, musicians to come!
Not to-day is to justify me and answer what I am for,
❶ But you, a new brood, native, athletic, continental,
    greater than before known,
Arouse! for you must justify me.

5 I myself but write one or two <u>indicative</u> words for
    the future,
❷ I but advance a moment only to wheel and hurry
    back in the darkness.

I am a man who, <u>sauntering</u> along without fully
    stopping, turns a casual look upon you and then
    averts his face,
❸ Leaving it to you to prove and define it,
Expecting the main things from you.

◆ Build Vocabulary
orators (ôr´ ət ərz) *n.*: Public speakers
indicative (in dik´ ə tiv) *adj.*: Giving a suggestion; showing
sauntering (sân´ tər iŋ) *v.*: Walking slowly and confidently

 Block Scheduling Strategies

Consider these suggestions to take advantage of extended class time:

• Review the Reading Strategy, p. 89, to prepare students to be able to read the poems the way the poets intended them to be read. Play the Listening to Literature Audiocassettes for the selection.

• Devote class time to having students work in small groups on the Projects in the Idea Bank, p. 95. Allow time for groups to share their multimedia presentations and to give their reports on moon phases. Also invite volunteers to read aloud their pattern poems and New Year's speeches.

• To help students prepare for the Writing Mini-Lesson, refer them to *Writer's Solution Sourcebook,* Ch. 8, which includes tips for gathering details about setting and characters, and pointers for writing dialogue, and using stage directions.

• If possible, invite students not only to share video scripts, but to create and show actual videos based on them.

WINTER MOON ④
Langston Hughes

How thin and sharp is the moon tonight! ⑤
How thin and sharp and ghostly white
Is the slim curved crook of the moon tonight!

The speaker gives his response to a crescent moon that might appear on a winter's night.

◆Critical Thinking

④ **Classify** Discuss with students why "Winter Moon" should still be considered a poem even though it is so short. *Students may say that it's a poem because, like others they've read, it uses language that is concise and rhythmic. They may say that the quality of a poem is not measured by its length, but by its language, rhythm, and emotional content.*

◆Literary Focus

⑤ **Repetition in Poetry** What is the effect of the repeated phrase of the first two lines of the poem? *Students may say that it establishes how the poet sees the moon he about which he is writing.*

Reinforce and Extend

Answers
◆LITERATURE AND YOUR LIFE

Reader's Response Possible response: Students may say that they are; Whitman exhorts them to carry on the work of the artist, and Hughes asks them to respond to his depiction of the moon he sees.

Thematic Focus Possible response: Whitman makes a moment special by using it to address future poets and artists. Hughes does so by focusing on a fairly ordinary image from nature that evokes a deep emotional response.

Speech Students' speeches will vary, but should respond to Whitman's plea to examine his ideas about the future and then take them further.

☑ Check Your Comprehension

1. He addresses poets, orators, singers, and musicians of the future.
2. He asks them to justify, prove, and define the future.
3. He describes himself as one who saunters along, notes a thing or two about the world around him, and then casually passes the baton to the next generation to take it to the next level.
4. The sight is that of a thin, curved moon on a winter night.

Guide for Responding

◆ LITERATURE AND YOUR LIFE

Reader's Response Do you feel that Whitman and Hughes are speaking directly to you in their poems? Why or why not?

Thematic Focus How does each poet mark the present moment as special?

Speech Make up and deliver a brief speech in which you respond to the message that Whitman delivers to you.

☑ Check Your Comprehension

1. Whom is Whitman addressing in "Poets to Come"?
2. What is Whitman asking his audience to do?
3. How does Whitman describe himself?
4. Describe the sight that catches Hughes's eye in "Winter Moon."

◆ Critical Thinking

INTERPRET
1. What does Whitman mean in "Poets to Come" when he asks future poets to "justify" him? **[Draw Conclusions]**
2. What does the phrase "hurry back in the darkness" mean? **[Interpret]**
3. (a) In "Winter Moon," what phrase is repeated? (b) To what effect? **[Interpret]**
4. What qualities of the moon appeal to Hughes? **[Connect]**

EVALUATE
5. In "Poets to Come," Whitman directly addresses future readers. Is this device effective? Why or why not? **[Criticize]**

COMPARE LITERARY WORKS
6. Does "Winter Moon" reveal that Hughes was one of the "poets to come" who listened to Whitman? Explain. **[Connect]**

Poets to Come/Winter Moon ◆ 91

◆Critical Thinking

1. He asks them to prove the merit of his observations and contributions, to confirm what he has said about life and art.
2. Students may say that it means that he refuses to proclaim his own fame; that, like most other people, he knows that he does not have all the answers to life; he, too, is "in the dark."
3. (a) The phrase "how thin and sharp" is repeated. (b) Students may say that the effect is emphasis, amazement at nature's powerful beauty, and, perhaps, a feeling of mystery.

4. They may say that its shape, color, and size appeal to him. They may also say that the speaker is impressed by the moon's power to move him so.
5. Students should support their opinions by pointing to lines from the poem that affected or moved them.
6. Some students will say that Hughes did listen because his poem's musical free verse suggests that he emulated Whitman, the founder of American free verse.

In this poem, which celebrates the new year, Tennyson optimistically expresses his hopes that the future will improve upon the past.

Comprehension Check

❶ When is this poem set? *It takes place on New Year's Eve.*

◆Critical Thinking

❷ **Modify** Ask students to restate this wish in their own words. *Students may say that the poet says we should no longer drag ourselves down in sadness by grieving for those who've died.*

Thematic Focus

❸ **Seasons and Cycles** Discuss with students that the resolutions people make on New Year's are generally of a personal nature. Have them add to Tennyson's wishes to create a list of resolutions that are not about personal goals but rather about goals for the betterment of the entire world.

▶Critical Viewing◀

❹ **Interpret** *Students may say that the celebratory fireworks display in the sky above this ski resort captures the spirit of renewal, and that the torchlight parade symbolizes both a reverence for the past and hope for the future.*

Customize for
Musical/Rhythmic Learners

Discuss with students the meter and rhyme scheme of this poem. Guide them to understand that it uses iambic (one unaccented syllable followed by one accented one) tetrameter (four feet [eight beats] per line) with an ABBA rhyme scheme.

Ring Out, Wild Bells

Alfred, Lord Tennyson

❶
Ring out, wild bells, to the wild sky,
 The flying cloud, the frosty light:
 The year is dying in the night;
Ring out, wild bells, and let him die.

5 Ring out the old, ring in the new,
 Ring, happy bells, across the snow:
 The year is going, let him go;
Ring out the false, ring in the true.

Ring out the grief that saps[1] the mind,
10 For those that here we see no more;
❷ Ring out the feud of rich and poor,
Ring in redress[2] to all mankind.

Ring out a slowly dying cause,
 And ancient forms of party <u>strife</u>;
15 Ring in the nobler modes[3] of life,
With sweeter manners, purer laws.

Ring out the want, the care, the sin,
 The faithless coldness of the times;
 Ring out, ring out thy mournful rhymes,
20 But ring the fuller minstrel[4] in.

❸
Ring out false pride in place and blood,
 The civic[5] slander and the spite;
 Ring in the love of truth and right,
Ring in the common love of good.

25 Ring out old shapes of foul disease;
 Ring out the narrowing lust of gold;
 Ring out the thousand wars of old,
Ring in the thousand years of peace.

92 ◆ *Coming of Age*

◆ Build Vocabulary
strife (strīf) *n.*: Conflict

1. **saps** (saps) *v.*: Drains; exhausts.
2. **redress** (ri dres´) *n.*: The righting of wrongs.
3. **modes** (mōdz) *n.*: Ways; forms.
4. **fuller minstrel** (min´ strəl) *n.*: Singer of the highest rank.
5. **civic** (siv´ ik) *adj.*: Of a city.

Speaking and Listening Mini-Lesson

New Year's Speech
This mini-lesson supports the Speaking and Listening activity in the Idea Bank on p. 95.

Introduce Discuss the customs of making New Year's resolutions and of wishing others well for the upcoming year. Next, brainstorm for a list of broad topics into which hopes for the new year would fall. For example, in the category of "peace," students might offer hope for peace in countries around the world.

Develop Have students work in groups. Encourage them to be serious about issues that are serious, but to use wit and humor, as fitting, as they plan and write. They may find discussion within their group helpful to get ideas for their speeches.

Apply Have students plan, compose, edit, and practice the speeches within their groups and then present them in front of the class.

Assess Evaluate students' speeches on thoughtfulness of content, clarity of expression, poignancy and/or wit, and quality of the presentation. Or, use the Peer Assessment: Speaker/Speech form, p. 114, in **Alternative Assessment.**

Guide for Responding

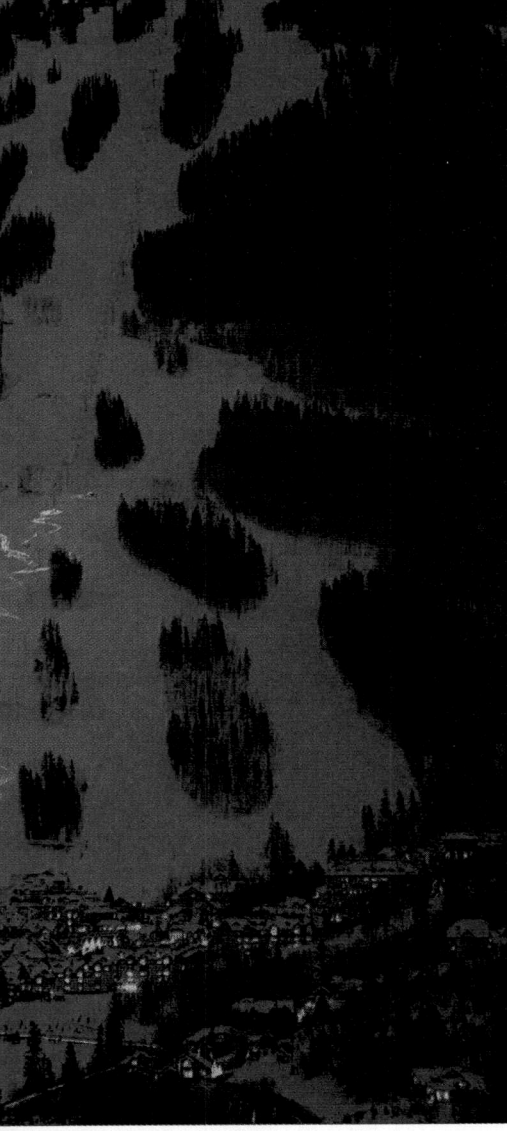

▲ Critical Viewing In what ways does this photograph capture the spirit of the poem? **[Interpret]**

4

◆ LITERATURE AND YOUR LIFE

Reader's Response What is a New Year's hope that you have expressed?

Thematic Focus Why is New Year's Eve a time when people focus on the past and the future?

New Year's Ceremony With several classmates, create a New Year's ceremony that would help people feel good about the coming year.

Journal Writing Jot down in your journal some New Year's resolutions you've made over the years.

☑ Check Your Comprehension

1. List five things the poet wants to "ring out."
2. Name five things that the poet wants to "ring in."

◆ Critical Thinking

INTERPRET

1. How does the poet seem to feel about the past? **[Infer]**
2. Explain what the poet hopes the future will bring. **[Interpret]**
3. In what way is this poem about more than the passing of the old year? **[Draw Conclusions]**

EVALUATE

4. Would it be appropriate to read this poem aloud at a modern New Year's Eve celebration? Why or why not? **[Make a Judgment]**

EXTEND

5. What do you think would bring a "thousand years of peace" to today's world? Explain. **[Social Studies Link]**

COMPARING LITERARY WORKS

6. How are the messages or themes of "Poets to Come" and "Ring Out, Wild Bells" similar and different? **[Compare and Contrast]**

Ring Out, Wild Bells ◆ 93

 Beyond the Selection

FURTHER READING

Other Works by Walt Whitman
Leaves of Grass
Specimen Days

Other Works by Langston Hughes
The Weary Blues
The Best of Simple

Other Works by Alfred, Lord Tennyson
Idylls of the King

INTERNET
We suggest the following sites on the Internet (all Web sites are subject to change).
For more information about Whitman: **http://www.liglobal.com/walt**
For more information about Hughes: **http://www.technoir.net/Jazz/hughes.html**
For more about Tennyson: **http:// charon.sfsu.edu/TENNYSON/tennyson.html**
We *strongly recommend* that you preview these sites before you send students to them.

◆ Reading Strategy

1. Pause at the ends of lines 21–23, which end with either a comma or a semicolon; stop at the end of line 24, where there is a period.

2. Hughes's poem stops after the first and last lines, but neither pauses nor stops after the second line.

3. There are four brief pauses because there are four commas.

◆ Build Vocabulary

Using the Suffix *-or*

1. A *Terminator* might be a person who ends people's lives

2. An *Eliminator* might be someone who eliminates, or wipes out, people

3. A *Hesitator* would be a person who delays.

4. A *projector* is a device that projects movies onto a screen.

5. An *operator* is a person who operates a telephone.

Spelling Strategy

1. creator;   2. facial;   3. senator;
4. machinist

Using the Word Bank

1. true; a good public speaker is a formidable opponent in a debate.

2. false; a jogger isn't walking slowly and confidently.

3. true; red usually signals danger or warning.

4. false; strife is conflict, what war is about.

◆ Literary Focus

1. The repetition of *I* and *you* suggests the idea of the poem: what "I," the poet, have begun, "you," the next generation, will finish. *I* appears first in the poem, and *you* is the final, stressed word.

2. Possible responses may include repetition of the words "How thin and sharp" along with students' own descriptions of a winter crescent moon.

3. Possible response: The first stanza speaks only of what will be rung out; the second stanza devotes two lines to what is rung out; the third devotes three lines to what is rung out and one to what is rung in; the fourth devotes equal time to both; and so on. Students may say that the variation in repetition keeps readers interested.

Guide for Responding (continued)

◆ Reading Strategy

READ POETRY ACCORDING TO PUNCTUATION

By **reading according to punctuation,** you used commas and end marks in these poems as guides to pauses and stops. In line 3 of "Ring Out, Wild Bells," each comma and semicolon signals a pause. The colon, however, that ends line 2 and the period that ends line 4 signal stops.

1. Explain where you would pause and where you would stop in lines 21–24 of "Ring Out, Wild Bells."

2. Which of these poems calls for no pauses and just two stops? Explain.

3. How many brief pauses are there in the final stanza of "Poets to Come"? How do you know?

◆ Build Vocabulary

USING THE SUFFIX *-or*

Use your knowledge of the suffix *-or* ("the person or thing that does something") to explain the meaning of the italicized words:

A new movie featured a fight among the *Terminator*, the *Eliminator*, and the *Hesitator*. While the Hesitator was waiting, the first two guys destroyed each other. Then the movie *projector* caught on fire. I had to stop applauding to dial the emergency *operator*.

SPELLING STRATEGY

When adding a suffix beginning with a vowel to words ending in e, drop the e in the new word:

advise + -or = advisor   race + -ial = racial

On your paper, spell the word that results from combining these words and suffixes:

1. create + -or   3. senate + -or
2. face + -ial   4. machine + -ist

USING THE WORD BANK

On your paper, answer these true-or-false questions. Then, explain your answers.

1. The best *orators* usually win debates.

2. A jogger in action is an example of *sauntering*.

3. The color red on a sign is usually *indicative* of a warning.

4. *Strife* is what ends when a war begins.

◆ Literary Focus

REPETITION IN POETRY

Repetition makes poems easy to remember by adding to the verbal "music," linking the different sections of a poem, and revealing key ideas.

1. In "Poets to Come," how does the repetition of the pronouns *I* and *you* tie the poem together and emphasize its meaning?

2. Extend "Winter Moon" by two lines, repeating and adding to what Hughes says. Help readers see and feel a winter moon.

3. Explain how stanzas in "Ring Out, Wild Bells" use repetition in different ways.

◆ Build Grammar Skills

INTENSIVE PRONOUNS

Intensive pronouns are formed by combining the personal pronoun and the suffix *-self* or *-selves*:

myself; ourselves; yourself, yourselves; herself, himself, itself; themselves

Intensive pronouns emphasize the person's role or indicate that a person performs an action alone:

Emphasizes Person: "I *myself* but write one or two . . ."

Indicates Person Acts Alone: I'll do it *myself*, thanks.

Practice On your paper, identify the intensive pronoun in each sentence. Then, indicate whether it stresses the person performing the act or the idea that the person performs the action alone.

1. I myself read "Poets to Come."

2. Did you yourself see the winter moon?

3. They themselves heard the New Year's bells.

4. Whitman himself addresses future poets, without a backup chorus of voices.

5. Should we ourselves ring those bells?

Writing Application On your paper, fill in each blank with a suitable intensive pronoun.

1. I ____?____ was born on January fifth.

2. Have you ____?____ seen a crescent moon?

3. They made the poetry book ____?____.

◆ Build Grammar Skills

Practice

1. myself; emphasizes person
2. yourself; emphasizes person
3. themselves; emphasizes people
4. himself; person performs alone
5. ourselves; person performs alone

Writing Application

Possible responses:

1. myself;   2. yourself;   3. themselves

✎ Writer's Solution

For additional instruction and practice, use the lesson in the *Writer's Solution Language Lab CD-ROM* on Using Pronouns.

Build Your Portfolio

Idea Bank

Writing

1. **Description** As Hughes does in "Winter Moon," write a brief sentence describing something. Then, in a follow-up sentence, repeat your description and add to it.

2. **Pattern Poem** Write a poem expressing your wishes for the New Year. Follow the pattern in Tennyson's poem, telling the bells to "ring out" some things and "ring in" others.

3. **Critical Interpretation** Interpret the lyrics of your favorite song, explaining the message they contain. Show how the songwriter has used repetition to convey important thoughts and feelings.

Speaking and Listening

4. **New Year's Speech** As a class, imagine you are having dinner with a group of friends on New Year's Eve. Give a brief speech expressing your good wishes for your friends and your hopes for the new year.

5. **Poetry Reading** Read these poems aloud for your classmates. Before reading, prepare rehearsal copies of the poems by marking where you will pause, stop, or emphasize a key word. **[Performing Arts Link]**

Projects

6. **Multimedia Presentation** Choose a holiday that marks an anniversary or a change in seasons. Then, give a presentation explaining how the same type of holiday is celebrated in different cultures. If possible, include photographs, film clips, diagrams, recorded interviews, and samples of food. **[Social Studies Link; Media Link]**

7. **Report [Group Activity]** Work with a group to prepare a multimedia report on the phases of the moon. You may create a chart showing the monthly changes in the moon's appearance—from new moon to full moon. You may also want to explore the moon's effect on the tides. **[Science Link]**

Writing Mini-Lesson

Script for a Time-Capsule Video

"Poets to Come" is like a time-capsule message to people living in the future. Suppose you could write the script for a video that would be placed into a time capsule. Your purpose would be to give teenagers living a hundred years from now a sense of our life today.

> #### Writing Skills Focus: Use the Right Format
>
> When writing a script, **use the right format** to set up dialogue, directions, and camera shots:
> - To show dialogue, capitalize the character's name, put a period after it, and then write the character's words.
> TEENAGER. Let me tell you about our music. . . .
>
> - To show directions and camera shots, use brackets and put text in italics.
> TEENAGER. [*Standing in CD store*] [*Long shot down the aisle*] Let me tell you about our music. . . .

Prewriting Think what teenagers of the future will want to know, and outline the topics you'll cover, like sports or music. Also, decide on the order in which you'll present these topics.

Drafting Convey as much information as possible through images and sequences of images. Use dialogue or voice-over, a person speaking off camera, to enhance and summarize the visual "story."

> #### ◆ Grammar Application
>
> Use intensive pronouns in the camera directions to indicate that someone performs an action alone.

Revising Add information that future teenagers would want to know. Wherever necessary, add directions for characters and the camera. Review the formatting guidelines to be sure your script conforms.

Poets to Come/Winter Moon/Ring Out, Wild Bells ◆ 95

Idea Bank

Following are suggestions for matching the Idea Bank topics with your students' performance levels and learning modalities:

Customize for
Performance Levels
Less Advanced Students: 1, 6
Average Students: 2, 4, 6, 7
More Advanced Students: 3, 5, 6, 7

Customize for
Learning Modalities
Verbal/Linguistic: 1, 2, 3, 4, 5, 6, 7
Visual/Spatial: 6, 7
Logical/Mathematical: 4, 6, 7
Musical/Rhythmic: 3, 5, 6
Interpersonal: 4, 5, 6, 7
Intrapersonal: 2, 3

Writing Mini-Lesson

Refer students to the Writing Handbook in the back of the book for instructions on the writing process and for further information on scriptwriting and on the format for scripts.

Writer's Solution

Writing Lab CD-ROM
Have students complete the tutorial on Creative Writing. Follow these steps:

1. Refer students to the Writing Hints for making dialogue sound realistic and believable, for showing dialect and accent, and for formatting and punctuating a script.
2. Have students do the Character Trait Word Bin activity.
3. Have them use the video clip on setting and stage directions.
4. Have students draft on computer.
5. Have them use the Self-Evaluation Checklist for plays.

Allow about 80 minutes of class time to complete these steps.

Writer's Solution Sourcebook
Have students use Chapter 8, "Creative Writing," pp. 235–266, for additional support. The chapter includes tips for gathering details about characters and about setting, p. 254, and pointers for drafting a play, for writing dialogue, and for using stage directions, p. 258.

✓ ASSESSMENT OPTIONS

Formal Assessment, Selection Test, pp. 27–29, and Assessment Resources Software. The selection test is designed so that it can be easily customized to the performance levels of your students.

Alternative Assessment, p. 9, includes options for less advanced students, more advanced students, musical/rhythmic learners, interpersonal learners, verbal/linguistic learners, and visual/spatial learners.

PORTFOLIO ASSESSMENT
Use the following rubrics in the **Alternative Assessment** booklet to assess student writing:
Description: Description, p. 93
Pattern Poem: Poetry, p. 104
Critical Interpretation: Literary Analysis/Interpretation, p. 108
Script for a Time-Capsule Video: Drama, p. 105

Establish Writing Guidelines
Before students begin, review the following characteristics of a description:

- A description creates a vivid picture of a character or event that makes the reader feel as though they have actually met the person or experienced the event.

- A description uses sensory details to create a single main impression of the subject.

You may wish to distribute the scoring rubric for Description, p. 93, in **Alternative Assessment** to inform students of the criteria on which they will be evaluated. See p. 98 for suggestions on customizing the rubric to this workshop.

Refer students to the Writing Handbook in the back of the book for instruction on the writing process and for further information on descriptive writing.

 Writer's Solution

Writers at Work Videodisc
Show how food critic Rosie McNulty uses these elements in her descriptive writing, by playing the videodisc segment on Description. Have students discuss what McNulty does to make sure she writes the best descriptions she can for her reviews.

Play frames 20832 to 29640

Writing Lab CD-ROM
Have students use the tutorial on Description to develop their writing. Follow these steps:
1. Have students use the video clip of Eudora Welty for topic advice.
2. Students can use the interactive writing models to see how the intended audience affects writing.
3. Have students draft on computer.
4. The interactive Models of Revision offer examples of replacing vague language with precise language.

Writer's Solution Sourcebook
For additional support, have students use the chapter on Description, pp. 33–69.

Connect to Literature Examples of description can be found throughout "from *I Know Why the Caged Bird Sings*" by Maya Angelou, p. 24, a personal memoir that uses precise details.

Descriptive Writing
Description

Writing Process Workshop

In this unit, the writers use descriptive language to bring to life a meteor shower, a special Christmas, and a hopeful New Year's Eve. Descriptive writing can appear in any type of writing—from poetry to essays—but no matter where it is used, it conveys vivid impressions through sensory details. Think about a person, place, thing, or experience that calls to mind vivid memories, and share those vivid impressions by writing a piece of description.

Use the skills in the Writing Mini-Lessons introduced in this section to help you.

Writing Skills Focus

▶ **Use transitional words** and phrases to weave together your description. (See p. 71.)
▶ **Use precise language** to create a main impression of your topic. (See p. 79.)
▶ Use details and language that **your audience** will understand and appreciate. (See p. 87.)

Garrison Keillor uses these skills in "Something From the Sixties."

MODEL FROM LITERATURE

from "Something From the Sixties" by Garrison Keillor

About five o'clock last Sunday evening, ① my son burst into the kitchen and said, "I didn't know it was so late!" He was due at a party immediately—a sixties party, he said—and he needed something from the sixties to wear. My son is almost fifteen years old, the size of a grown man, ② and when he bursts into a room glassware rattles and the cat on your lap grabs on to your knees and leaps from the starting block. ③

① This transitional phrase leads into the story.
② Precise details like these give necessary information about the son.
③ This colorful example amuses the audience.

 Beyond the Classroom

Career Connection
Naturalist Explain to students that a naturalist is a student of natural history, the study of natural objects in the field. Point out the many careers that are linked to natural history, such as zoologists who study animals, botanists who study plants, and geologists who study rocks. Then explain the need in each of these fields for mastery of descriptive writing: The observations of natural phenomena must be detailed, focused, and accurate, both to enhance learning and to enable others to share the experience.

Discuss that *naturalist* and *natural history* are sometimes used to refer to nature observers who write from an amateur or popular point of view, but whose observations are as valid as a formally trained scientist. For example, Henry David Thoreau (1817–1862) was a great naturalist as well as a great writer. His observations of the flora and fauna of Concord, Massachusetts are among the most complete for any American locale.

Have students research other naturalists who have observed and recorded nature, such as Ansel Adams and John Audubon.

Prewriting

Choose a Topic Spend some time jotting down observations about things, people, events, and ideas. Circle three or four you like. Jot down a one- or two-word impression for each. Then, choose the one that would make the best topic for a description.

Make a Sunburst Diagram Collect precise details about your topic using a sunburst diagram.

Identify Your Audience Who will read your description? Jot down notes about your readers' familiarity with your subject and the style of language they'll respond to and enjoy. For example, will they better appreciate humor or sincerity? Will technical descriptions or slang confuse them?

Description Writing Tip Try closing your eyes to re-create an image in your mind. Imagine or recall the sight, sound, scent, taste, and feel of your topic before you write about it.

Drafting

Create a Main Impression As you draft, focus on capturing the essence, or most important quality, of your subject.

Write for Your Audience Draft your description using words and a writing style that will interest and appeal to your readers.

Use Transitional Words Connect your thoughts and ideas by using transitional words and phrases like *first, not only,* and *before you knew it.*

DRAFTING/REVISING

APPLYING LANGUAGE SKILLS: Using Sensory Words

Using words that appeal to the five senses will make your description more interesting.

Neutral Words:

I like summer.

Sensory Words:

I like the *smell of cook-outs,* the *sounds of cardinals,* and the *taste of fresh strawberries* that summer brings.

Notice how the sentence with sensory details captures the smell, sound, and taste of a summer day.

Practice On your paper, rewrite each sentence, providing sensory descriptive words for the sense in parentheses.

1. There was an odor coming from the trunk. (smell)
2. We sat in the attic, listening to the rain. (sound)
3. Hank lifted out the vest. (touch)

Writing Application As you draft, use sensory words to make your description more alive and realistic.

Writer's Solution Connection Writing Lab

For help with sensory words, use the Sensory Word Bin in the Prewriting sections of the Description tutorial.

Writing Process Workshop ◆ 97

Prewriting

Suggest that when students choose a topic for their description, they choose one that both excites them and brings many details to mind. Suggest that they also make a list of the sensory words used in the Model From Literature, p. 96, to learn how precise details enhance the reader's connection to the description.

Customize for *Less Proficient Writers*

Suggest that students use the Main Idea and Supporting Details graphic organizer, p. 74, in **Writing and Language Transparencies** to help focus on the main impression they want to create.

Customize for *English Language Learners*

Students can acquire additional vocabulary by using the Sensory Language Chart graphic organizer, p. 82 in **Writing and Language Transparencies.** To help generate sensory words to add to the chart, have students use picture magazines. Guide students to think of sensory words they know that are appropriate to the magazine photos, such as *cold, sour, rough, dark,* or *whisper.* Then have students refer to the chart as they write their descriptions.

Drafting

Encourage students to write down their main impression and some details that support it to refer to as they write their drafts. When considering their audience, advise students to focus on the use of formal or informal language, whether to include basic details, and which details would be most interesting. Also suggest that they stop at each new sentence to determine whether transitional words or phrases are needed.

 **Writer's Solution**

Writing Lab CD-ROM

To help students draft their descriptions, have them use the video tip from Rosie McNulty in the Drafting section of the tutorial on Description for advice on how to draft a description and avoid writer's block.

Applying Language Skills

Using Sensory Words Explain to students the importance of using sensory words in their descriptions: Sensory words and phrases appeal to the five senses. People use these senses to experience the real world around them. To enable readers to experience a character or event on the same level as the writer, details must include words that relate to the same senses people use in their real experiences.

Answers
Practice
Answers will vary, but should reflect smell, sound, and touch. Examples are:

1. There was a foul smell coming from the musty trunk.
2. We sat in the hushed attic, listening to the pounding rain.
3. Hank lifted out the soft satin vest.

Writer's Solution

For additional instruction and practice, have students complete the practice page on Choosing Precise Words in the *Writer's Solution Grammar Practice Book,* p. 121.

Revising

Have students work in pairs to revise by using the Peer Conferencing Notes: Writer form in **Alternative Assessment,** pp. 81–82.

Writer's Solution

Writing Lab CD-ROM
Students may use the Revision Checker and the Descriptive Word Bin to evaluate and revise their descriptions.

Publishing

Suggest that students save their descriptions in their portfolios to use in a longer piece of writing.

Reinforce and Extend

Review the Writing Guidelines
After students complete their writing, review the criteria for writing a description.

Applying Language Skills

Avoiding Fragments Suggest that students identify incomplete sentences by reading their finished work aloud. Reading aloud is a good way of telling whether a sentence "sounds right."

Answers

Possible answers:
1. The small island is surrounded by water.
2. The lifeguards were riding their rafts in on the tide.
3. Our trip to the Grand Canyon was the best vacation ever.

Writer's Solution

For additional practice, have students complete the practice page on Avoiding Fragments in the *Writer's Solution Grammar Practice Book,* p. 63.

Writing Process Workshop

EDITING/PROOFREADING

APPLYING LANGUAGE SKILLS: Avoiding Fragments

A fragment is a group of words, written as a sentence, that does not express a complete thought. Avoid fragments in your writing. Correct them by adding words to make a complete thought.

Fragment:
A slight twig over the expanding tide

Complete Thought:
The bridge looked like a slight twig over the expanding tide.

Practice On your paper, rewrite these fragments as complete thoughts.
1. The small island surrounded by water.
2. Riding their rafts in on the tide.
3. Dolphins in the sea.
4. Each evening, clambakes.
5. Was the best vacation ever.

Writing Application Review your description, and correct any sentence fragments.

> **Writer's Solution Connection**
> **Language Lab**
> For help identifying and correcting fragments, complete the lesson on Sentence Fragments in the Sentence Errors unit.

98 ◆ *Coming of Age*

Revising

Read Your Description Aloud Listening to your words read aloud can help you to identify unwanted repetition, bland words, mistakes, sentence fragments, and other errors.

Use a Checklist Go back to the Writing Skills Focus on the first page of this lesson, and use the items as a checklist to evaluate and revise your description.
► Have I used precise language? *Overuse of adjectives and adverbs may indicate that you need to choose a more precise noun or verb.*
► Do transitions connect the thoughts and ideas within the description? *Review each paragraph in your description. Be sure that you've linked your thoughts by using transitions to lead into and out of each paragraph.*
► Have I chosen details and a style that are appropriate for my audience? *Read your description aloud to someone who represents your audience. Ask him or her to point out confusing or dull passages so that you may revise them.*

REVISION MODEL

I didn't even notice the bridge because the neap tide was ①
In a way, though, the ②
out. The bridge is interesting. It's wooden, short, and plain
connects two sand dunes. ③
and just goes over some sand. The tide began coming in,
spectacular
and it was really neat. No cars can cross that bridge until

the tide goes back out!

① The writer deleted this term because it's not important and might confuse the audience.
② This transitional phrase leads into the main idea of the sentence.
③ The vague phrase "just goes over some sand" was replaced with a more precise description.

Publishing and Presenting

► **Classroom** Illustrate your description with your own drawing or design, or with a picture you've found. Display your description in the classroom.
► **E-mail** Consider e-mailing your description to a relative or friend.

✓ ASSESSMENT		4	3	2	1
PORTFOLIO ASSESSMENT Use the rubric on Narrative Based on Personal Experience in the **Alternative Assessment** booklet, p. 93, to assess the students' writing. Add these criteria to customize this rubric to this assignment.	**Avoiding Fragments**	The writer consistently uses complete sentences.	The writer uses complete sentences, but some do not express complete thoughts.	The writer includes many sentences that do not express complete thoughts.	The writing is difficult to understand because of the numerous sentence fragments.
	Use Sensory Words	The writer uses many vivid and precise sensory words to help readers visualize the subject.	The writer uses sensory words, but some of the description is general.	The writer does not use enough sensory words to make the description alive and realistic.	The writer uses few or no sensory words and the description is general.

Real-World Reading Skills Workshop

Adjusting Your Reading Rate

Strategies for Success

You may have noticed that when you read things out of idle curiosity or for pleasure, you skim the text quickly. When you read things to find specific information that you will be tested on, however, you read slowly and carefully. This is called adjusting your reading rate, and you can use this strategy to help you read different kinds of texts.

The following strategies will help you adjust your reading rate according to your purpose and the level of difficulty of the writing.

▶ **Identify Your Reading Goals** If you are reading for entertainment, you don't need to read carefully and slowly. If, however, you're reading in order to learn something, you should read more slowly and carefully.

▶ **Preview Headings and Captions** Headings, subheads, and captions will give you clues about the subject matter of the writing.

▶ **Skim a Text for Difficulty** Quickly skim the text of the writing, looking for the types of words used. If the text appears to have technical or sophisticated ideas, read it slowly. If the text contains simple language and ideas, you can read it more quickly.

✔ *Here are other situations in which you adjust your reading rate for the situation:*
- ▶ *Selecting a suitable book for a friend*
- ▶ *Reading a long reference article*
- ▶ *Searching through Web sites on the World Wide Web*

Apply the Strategies

1. How would you read the following article "Great Pastas," judging from the headings you see?

2. Skim the text. How would you describe the level of difficulty of this article?

3. If you came across this article in a magazine, how would you read it if:

   a. You had little interest in cooking

   b. You were writing a report for school about Italian foods

   c. You planned to make pasta that evening

Great Pastas

Pasta is one of the easiest, most nutritious meals you can make. With sauces ranging from oil and garlic to meat and vegetable, you can eat pasta every day of the week and not become bored.

Following are some popular pasta types:

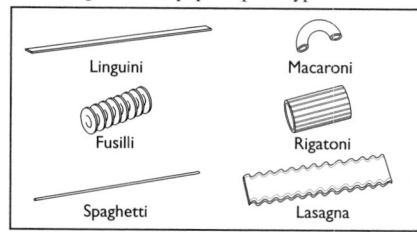

Linguini	Macaroni
Fusilli	Rigatoni
Spaghetti	Lasagna

Basic Cooking Instructions

For each pound of pasta, bring two quarts of water to a rolling boil in a covered pot. If desired, add a teaspoon of vegetable oil and a pinch of salt to the water. Add dry pasta and allow pasta to boil uncovered, stirring occasionally. After approximately 8 to 10 minutes, test pasta for doneness. When done, pour into colander and strain out the water. Toss pasta with your favorite sauce.

◆ Build Grammar Skills

Pronouns

The selections in Part 2 include instruction on the following:

- Pronouns and Antecedents
- Personal Pronouns
- Indefinite Pronouns
- Intensive Pronouns

This information is reinforced with the Build Grammar Skills practice pages in **Selection Support**, pp. 31, 36, 41, and 46.

As you review pronouns, you may wish to include the following:

- Demonstrative Pronouns

Demonstrative pronouns direct attention to specific nouns. They are located before or after their antecedents.

Demonstrative Pronouns	
Singular	**Plural**
this, that	these, those

- Reflexive Pronouns

Pronouns that end in *-self* or *-selves* are either reflexive pronouns or intensive pronouns. A reflexive pronoun adds information by referring to a noun ear-lier in the sentence. An intensive pronoun simply adds emphasis to a noun or pronoun in the same sentence.

A reflexive pronoun always adds information to a sentence; it cannot be left out without changing meaning.

Reflexive and Intensive Pronouns		
	Singular	**Plural**
First Person	myself	ourselves
Second Person	yourself	yourselves
Third Person	himself, herself, itself	themselves

Reflexive:

He taught *himself* to identify the constellations.

An intensive pronoun emphasizes its antecedent but does not add infor-mation to a sentence. If an intensive pronoun is removed, a sentence will have the same meaning.

Intensive:

The astronomer *himself* was amazed by the meteor shower.

Customize for
Less Proficient Readers

Suggest that students review each pronoun they have used in their writ-ing and ask themselves "What could this pronoun possibly refer to?" If it can refer to more than one noun, they should revise the sentence so that the antecedent, if any, of the pro-noun is clear.

100

Pronouns

Grammar Review

Pronouns are words that take the place of nouns or groups of words acting as nouns. They are used in order to avoid repetition of nouns. The word or group of words a pronoun replaces is called its **antecedent.**

> **antecedent**
> *Andrea* attended night-school classes.
> **pronoun**
> During the day, *she* worked.

Personal pronouns refer to the person speaking (first person), the person spoken to (second person), and the person spoken about (third person).

	Singular	**Plural**
First Person	I, me, my, mine	we, us, our, ours
Second Person	you, your, yours	you, your, yours
Third Person	he, him, his, she, her, hers, it, its	they, them, their, theirs

Indefinite pronouns—such as *another, anybody, neither, each, everything, several,* and *many*—refer to people, places, or things in general. Some indefinite pronouns are used without antecedents.

With Antecedent: Of the candidates, *none* was qualified.

Without Antecedent: *Everyone* was nice.

Grammar in Writing

✔ *Use pronouns to avoid repeating nouns unnecessarily. Be sure each pronoun has a clear antecedent.*

✔ *Add emphasis to a noun by using an intensive pronoun within the same sentence.*

100 ◆ *Coming of Age*

An **intensive pronoun** ends in *-self* or *-selves* and adds emphasis to a noun or pronoun in the same sentence.

Example: I, *myself,* prefer to stand.

Practice 1 Locate the pronouns in each sentence, and label each as a personal pronoun, an indefinite pronoun, or an intensive pronoun.

1. She preferred watching shooting stars herself.

2. Both Bill and Rita enjoy the holidays.

3. They went to a costume party together.

4. Do your grandparents live nearby?

5. Our New Year's Eve celebration was a hit.

6. Nothing in memory was more fun.

7. He, himself, said he will visit soon.

Practice 2 Rewrite this paragraph, replacing repeated nouns with an appropriate pronoun.

In the nineteenth century, few people owned cameras. Cameras were too costly. Not many people could go to photographers because photographers charged too much. During the Civil War, young soldiers wanted to be photographed in uniform. Some merchants knew this. Merchants sold inexpensive copies of photographs of soldiers. A private with little cash would buy a picture of someone who looked like the private. Then, the private sent this picture home.

Answers

Practice I

In the nineteenth century few people owned cameras. *They* were too costly. Not *everyone* could go to photographers, because they charged too much. Young soldiers wanted to be photographed in uniform. Some merchants knew this. They sold inexpensive copies of pho-tographs of *them*. A private with little cash would buy a picture of someone who looked like *him*.

Then *he* sent *it* home. *His* parents were thrilled to receive the photograph. *It* was then put in the family album.

Practice 2

1. she (personal); herself (intensive)
2. both (indefinite)
3. they (personal)
4. your (personal)
5. our (personal)
6. nothing (indefinite)
7. he (personal); himself (intensive); he (personal)

 **Writer's Solution**

For additional practice and sup-port in using pronouns, use the practice pages on pronouns in the *Writer's Solution Grammar Practice Book,* pp. 8–10.

Speaking, Listening, and Viewing Workshop

Participating in a Group

Sometimes problems and tasks are more easily solved or accomplished by a group of people working together than by an individual tackling them alone. Often, you will find that talking out ideas with others helps you think more clearly, just as your response to other people's ideas can help them organize their thoughts. For a group to work effectively, though, there are certain ground rules that should be observed. Following are suggestions that will help you work effectively in a group.

- **Clearly state the group's purpose.** Once you have a purpose, you can keep the discussion focused.
- **Take turns speaking while others listen.** If everyone speaks at once, no one is heard and no progress is made toward reaching an understanding.
- **Record ideas as they are stated.** Assign one person to be responsible for taking notes as ideas are discussed.
- **Be sure everyone is heard.** A moderator, or discussion leader, can ensure that everyone's ideas are heard. No one person should be allowed to dominate the discussion.
- **Make a contribution.** It's your responsibility as a group member to voice your ideas. Don't let others do the work.

- **Respond to what others say.** Politely voice your agreements and disagreements to what others say. Sometimes solutions come out of conflict.

Apply the Strategies

Form groups of three or more to address one of the following tasks. Then, use the checklist that follows to assess your group's performance.

1. A hospital or nursing home in your community is in need of student volunteers. Devise a recruitment plan that will persuade students to donate their free time.

2. The boys' and girls' soccer teams are arguing over who gets to use the school's playing field. With the group, come up with a compromise plan.

Use a Checklist

✔ *When your group has completed its task, complete a checklist such as the following to decide whether you have worked effectively as a group.*

▶ *Did we define our task clearly?*
▶ *Was attention given to each speaker?*
▶ *Did we keep a record of the ideas presented?*
▶ *Was everyone given a chance to contribute?*
▶ *Did we complete our task successfully?*

Speaking, Listening, and Viewing Workshop ◆ 101

 Beyond the Classroom

Community Connection

Community Goals Point out to students that there are many local community projects for which people must cooperate to achieve common goals. Have students brainstorm for a list of community events that require participation in a group, such as getting a traffic light installed, organizing a fund drive, or holding a parade.

Discuss with students group methods that can be used to achieve these common goals. Guide students to see that some activities may be accomplished by a committee, while others may require the cooperation of the entire community. Encourage them also to discuss how compromises are reached when different parts of a community disagree on a particular issue.

Invite students to form groups and discuss how a group might plan a local street fair. Goals might include choosing a date, assigning tasks, obtaining permits, and publicizing the event.

Introduce the Strategies

Invite students to describe times when they made a group decision or participated in an activity with family or friends, such as deciding which video to rent or organizing a softball game. Point out that these are all examples of participating in a group. Effective group participation requires that all members contribute and cooperate to achieve a common goal. What is best for one person is less important than what works best for the group.

Apply the Strategies

Encourage students to remain focused on the goal of the task they chose as they voice their ideas and opinions. You may want to suggest some positive ways to state differing opinions, such as "I understand what you are saying, but I think ..." and "You may be right, but we also could ..."

Assessment
Evaluate students' performance based on both their individual contribution and the group's success in completing its task. Students may use the checklist on this page to assess their group's performance and the Self-Assessment: Speaking and Listening Progress form in **Alternative Assessment,** pp. 118–119, to evaluate their own participation.

Customize for
Bodily/Kinesthetic Learners
Students may observe body language that indicates the speakers' reluctance to contribute or disagreement with decisions. Encourage them to communicate what they see to other members of the group. You may want to suggest positive ways for them to share their observations and elicit ideas from their peers, such as "I think Sharon may have an idea" and "Mario, do you agree?"

Customize for
Logical/Mathematical Learners
Encourage students to record the points and decisions made in the group's discussion and then organize the notes into an outline or chart that the group can use to carry out the plan.

What's Behind the Words

To research words about time, students can use dictionaries or other reference books that explain etymology, such as the *Dictionary of Word and Phrase Origins,* by William Morris and Mary Morris.

Answers
Activity 1

- January: From *Januarius,* the month named for Janus, god of gates and doors and of beginnings and endings
- February: From *februarius mensis,* meaning "month of purification or atonement"
- March: From *Martius mensis,* meaning "month of Mars," god of war
- April: From *Aprilis,* the month dedicated to Venus, goddess of love and beauty
- May: From *Majus,* the month named for Maia, goddess of plant growth
- June: From *Junius,* the month named for Juno, wife of Jupiter, queen of heaven, and goddess of light, birth, women, and marriage
- July: From *Julius,* the month named for the Roman general Gaius Julius Caesar, who was born in this month
- August: From *Augustus,* the month named for the first Roman emperor, Augustus Caesar; *augustus* means "majestic" in Latin
- September: From *septem,* meaning "seven" (7th month of the ancient Roman 10-month calendar)
- October: From *octo,* meaning "eight" (8th month of the ancient Roman 10-month calendar)
- November: From *noven,* meaning "nine" (9th month of the ancient Roman 10-month calendar)
- December: From *decem,* meaning "ten" (10th month of the ancient Roman 10-month calendar)

Activity 2

Students' essays should include the following information: The word *fall* comes from the Old English word *feallan;* its use in the sense of autumn dates to 1664 as a shortening of the phrase *fall of the leaf.* The word *autumn* comes from the Latin word *autumnus.* The word *winter* is from the Old English *wintar,* meaning "fourth season of the year." The word *spring* is from the Old English *springan,* meaning "move suddenly; leap; jump." Around 1398, it came to

also mean "the season when plants spring up." The word *summer* comes from the Old English word *sumor.*

Activity 3

1. From English *chronology* + *-ic* and *-al; chronology* is from the Greek *chronos:* time
2. From the Greek *kyklo:* circle, ring, wheel.
3. From the Greek *aion:* age, lifetime
4. From the Greek *epoche:* stoppage, fixed point of time; from e*pechein:* to stop, take up a fixed position
5. From the Latin *sationem:* a sowing

What's Behind the Words
Vocabulary Adventures With Richard Lederer

Origins of Calendar Words

Long before we humans knew that time was a way of measuring the Earth's circle around the sun—back in the days when we believed that the Earth was flat and the sun moved across its face—we became filled with fear as the days grew short.

As the winter darkness engulfed our lives, we invoked the ancient gods with bonfires, feasts, and dances in the hope of charming the sun back to Earth. Slowly, over time, we learned that the sun always does return to warm the face of the Earth, and we grew to understand that time is a tide that ebbs and flows like the sea.

The First Calendar

It wasn't long before units of time, like the year, became standard. A year is about 365 days, 5 hours, 48 minutes, and 46 seconds. The word *calendar,* used to mark years, comes from the Latin, in which the first day of each Roman month was called the *kalends.* Interest on loans was due on the first day of each month, and the record of interest days was called a *calendarium.*

People throughout the years have adapted and used the calendarium to track the passage of years. When the Anglo Saxons, from whose language English is descended, wanted names for their days, they substituted their own gods for the Roman ones.

ACTIVITY 1 Unlike the days of our week, the names of our months descend directly from Latin. Create a chart like the one below to explain how each month got its name.

ACTIVITY 2 Write an essay explaining how the four seasons acquired their names.

ACTIVITY 3 Our word *day* comes from an Indo-European base *dhegwh-,* meaning "the time when the sun shines." *Month* comes to us through the Old English *mona,* meaning both "a measure of time" and "moon." What is the source or origin of each of the following words that describe time?

1. chronological
2. cycle
3. eon
4. epoch
5. season
6. solstice
7. temporal
8. week

January

☀ Sunday	Monday	Tuesday	Wednesday	Thursday	Friday	Saturday
Sunday is "sun's day." In Old English, it is *Sunnan daeg,* taken from the Latin *Dies solis.*	**Monday** is "moon's day," from *Monan daeg,* the Old English translation of the Latin *Lunae dies,* "day of the moon."	**Tuesday** is "Tiw's day," honoring Tiw, an Anglo-Saxon god of war and a son of Woden.	**Wednesday** is "Woden's day," dedicated to Tiw's father, Woden, who was chief of the Anglo-Saxon gods.	**Thursday** is "Thunor's day." Thunor, another of Woden's sons, also known by his Norse name of Thor, was the Anglo-Saxon god of thunder.	**Friday** is "Frig's day." Frig was the wife of Woden and the Anglo-Saxon goddess of marriage.	**Saturday** is from the Latin "Saturn's day," the only day of our week not fashioned from an Anglo-Saxon word or god. Saturn (*Cronus* in Greek) was the father of Jove (*Zeus* in Greek).

6. From the Latin s*olstitium:* a point at which the sun seems to stand still; from *sol:* sun + *-stitium*
7. From the Latin *temporalis:* of time, temporary; from *tempus:* time, season, proper time or season
8. From the Old English *wice*

Please note that more than one reference book may provide differing information regarding word origins, so you may want to have students list their sources for you to review their answers.

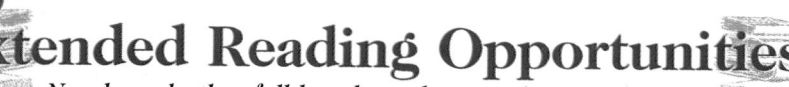

Extended Reading Opportunities

Novels and other full-length works sometimes explore "coming of age"—what it's like to grow up or to arrive at some new understanding about the world or yourself. Following are a few possibilities for extending your exploration of this theme.

Suggested Titles

Johnny Tremain
Esther Forbes

Johnny Tremain is set in pre-Revolutionary New England, and it is an example of historical fiction. Following a serious accident, a young apprentice silversmith, Johnny Tremain, is swept up into the colonists' rebellion against the British. Tremain participates in the Boston Tea Party and the Battle of Lexington—events that prompted the Revolutionary War. During his escapades, Tremain meets such notable figures as Paul Revere, Samuel Adams, and John Hancock.

A Gathering of Days
Joan W. Blos

This story is told through the entries of a young girl's journal. Born to the rigors of life on a small New Hampshire farm, thirteen-year-old Catherine Hall is keeping house for her widowed father and younger sister as she begins her journal in 1830. Her father's remarriage introduces a new mother and brother into her home, the plight of a runaway slave opens her eyes to injustice, and the death of her best friend through illness introduces her to grief.

M.C. Higgins, the Great
Virginia Hamilton

This story revolves around fifteen-year-old M.C., eldest boy of the Higgins family. M.C. longs to move from Sarah Mountain because their property is threatened by a sliding spoil heap left over from a strip mine, but M.C.'s father won't move from the land of his ancestors. By the story's end, M.C. convinces his father to take action about the spoil heap. In doing so, M.C. brings together the Higgins family and the neighboring Killburn family, from whom they had always been estranged.

Other Possibilities

Dicey's Song	Cynthia Voight
Picture Bride	Yoshiko Uchida
Dogsong	Gary Paulsen

Planning Students' Extended Reading

All of the works listed on this page are good choices for extending the theme "Coming of Age." The following information may help you choose which to teach.

Customize for
Varying Student Needs

When assigning these extended reading selections to your students, keep in mind the following factors:

- *Johnny Tremain* is a popular historical novel with a strong social studies connection and a high interest level. However, it does have some sensitivity issues, as listed below.

- *A Gathering of Days* is a novel written in diary form. A Newbery Award winner, the narrator's diary entries tell of a year in the life of a young woman in 19th century New England. Students will relate to the change, loss, and leave-taking she experiences. See below for sensitivity issues.

- *M. C. Higgins, the Great* is an accessible novel in which a boy comes to terms with his own identity and his family heritage.

Sensitive Issues
The depiction of battles and killing in *Johnny Tremain* may be difficult for some students to read about. However, the novel provides an opportunity for a discussion of war's effect on young people.

A Gathering of Days explores the issues of death and a parent's remarriage. You may wish to use caution when recommending this book to readers who are vulnerable regarding these issues. However, students also may benefit from reading literature about issues that have touched their own lives.

Literature Study Guides
Literature study guides are available for *Johnny Tremain* and *M. C. Higgins, the Great.* These guides include section summaries, discussion questions, and activities.

Planning Instruction and Assessment

Unit Objectives

1. To read selections in different genres that develop the theme of "Meeting Challenges"
2. To apply a variety of reading strategies, particularly strategies for interactive reading appropriate for reading these selections
3. To recognize literary elements used in these selections
4. To increase vocabulary
5. To learn elements of grammar and usage
6. To write in a variety of modes about situations based on the selections
7. To develop speaking and listening skills by completing activities
8. To view images critically and create visual representations

Meeting the Objectives Each selection provides instructional material and portfolio opportunities by which students can meet unit objectives. You will find additional practice pages for reading strategies, literary elements, vocabulary, and grammar in the **Selection Support** booklet in the **Teaching Resources** box.

Setting Goals Work with your students at the beginning of the unit to set goals for unit outcomes. Plan what skills and concepts you wish students to acquire. You may match instruction and activities according to students' performance levels or learning modalities.

Portfolios Students may keep portfolios of their completed work or of their work in progress. The Build Your Portfolio page of each selection provides opportunities for students to apply the concepts presented.

 Humanities: Art

The Idleness of Sisyphus, 1981, by Sandro Chia

Sandro Chia created large, splashy paintings in the 1980's. In Greek mythology, Sisyphus was condemned to the unending task of pushing a stone up a hill, only to have it roll back down once he got it to the top.

1. Why does Sisyphus's task look hard? *The hill is large and steep, the ball seems almost as large as he is.*
2. Do you think Sisyphus "meets his challenge"? *Students may say yes because he keeps trying.*

The Idleness of Sisyphus, 1981, Sandro Chia, Museum of Modern Art

Art Transparencies

The **Art Transparencies** booklet in the **Teaching Resources** box offers fine art to help students make connections to other curriculum areas and high-interest topics.

To connect to the theme of "Meeting Challenges," use Art Transparency 8, p. 35, *Lewis and Clark with Sacajewea at the Great Falls on the Missouri* by O. C. Seltzer. The historical characters in this painting—as all explorers do—are blazing trails. Use one of the booklet's activities to help students explore the art through discussion, a writing activity, or a photo essay.

Beyond Literature

Each unit presents Beyond Literature features that lead students into an exploration of careers, communities, and other subject areas. In this unit, students will explore river navigation and make social studies connections with the Klondike Gold Rush and the history of national parks. In addition, the **Teaching Resources** box contains a **Beyond Literature** booklet of activities. Using literature as a springboard, these activity pages offer students opportunities to connect literature to other curriculum areas and to the workplace and careers, community, media, and humanities.

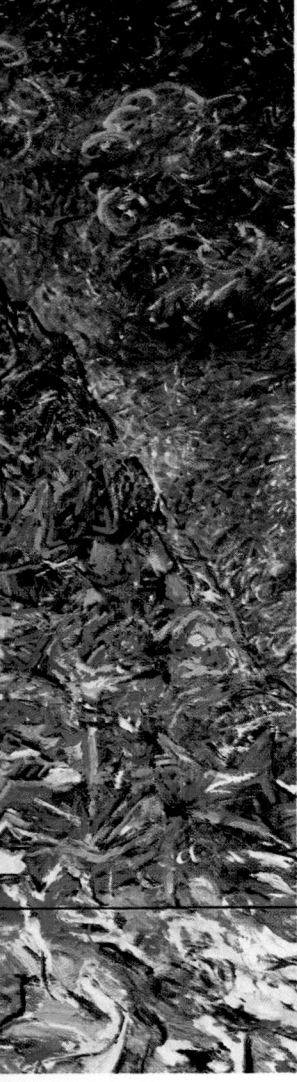

2

Meeting Challenges

From taking your first steps, to learning to ride a two-wheeled bicycle, to graduating with honors, to curing cancer or eliminating world hunger—challenges occur throughout life. Some challenges make headlines; others are personal. In these stories, poems, and essays, you'll meet people who encounter challenges of all types and meet them head on.

◆ 105

Assessing Student Progress

The tools that are available to measure the degree to which students meet the unit objectives are listed below.

Informal Assessment

The questions in the Guide for Responding sections are a first level of response to the concepts and skills presented with the selection. As a brief, informal measure of students' grasp of the material, these responses indicate where further instruction and practice are needed. The practice pages in the **Selection Support** booklet provide for this type of instruction and practice.

You will also find literature and reading guides in the **Alternative Assessment** booklet, which students can use for informal assessment of their individual performances.

Formal Assessment

The **Formal Assessment** booklet contains Selection Tests and Unit Tests.

Selection Tests measure comprehension and skills acquisition for each selection or group of selections.

Each Unit Test provides students with 30 multiple-choice questions and 5 essay questions designed to assess students' knowledge of the literature and skills taught in the unit.

Each Alternative Unit Test: Standardized-Test Practice provides 15 multiple-choice questions and 3 essay questions based on two new literature selections not contained in the student book. The questions on the Alternative Unit Test are designed to assess students' ability to compare and contrast selections, applying skills taught in the unit.

Alternative Assessment

For portfolio and alternative assessment, the **Alternative Assessment** booklet contains Scoring Rubrics, Assessment sheets, and Learning Modalities activities.

Scoring Rubrics provide writing modes that can be applied to Writing activities, Writing Mini-Lessons, and Writing Process Workshop lessons.

Assessment sheets for speaking and listening activities provide peer and self-assessment direction.

Learning Modalities activities appeal to different learning styles. Use these as an alternative measurement of students' growth.

Connections

Within this unit, you will find selections and activities that make connections beyond literature. Use these selections to connect students' understanding and appreciation of literature beyond the traditional literature and language arts curriculum.

Encourage students to connect literature to other curriculum areas. You may wish to coordinate with teachers in other curriculum areas to determine ways to team teach and further extend instruction.

Connections to Today's World

Use these selections to guide students to recognize the relevance of literature to contemporary writings. In this unit, students will find the science fiction genre presented in song lyrics by David Bowie.

Connecting Literature to Social Studies

Each unit contains a selection that connects literature to social studies. In this unit, students will read about the challenge of coming to a "New World," in "The Pilgrims' Landing and First Winter."

Guide for Reading

OBJECTIVES

1. To read, comprehend, and interpret a story
2. To relate a story to personal experience
3. To apply interactive reading strategies
4. To identify conflict between characters
5. To build vocabulary in context and learn forms of *judge*
6. To recognize verbs and verb phrases
7. To write an anecdote using introduction, body, and conclusion
8. To respond to the story through writing, speaking and listening, and projects

SKILLS INSTRUCTION

Vocabulary:
Using Forms of *judge*

Spelling:
Spelling the *shus*
Sound at the End
of Words as *cious*

Grammar:
Verbs and Verb
Phrases

**Reading for
Success:**
Interactive Reading
Strategies

Literary Focus:
Conflict Between
Characters

Writing:
Introduction, Body,
Conclusion

**Speaking and
Listening:**
Dramatic Reading
(Teacher Edition)

Critical Viewing:
Analyze; Assess

PORTFOLIO OPPORTUNITIES

Writing: Journal Entry; Character Sketch; Essay on Humor

Writing Mini-Lesson: Anecdote

Speaking and Listening: Dramatic Reading; Talk-Show Interview

Projects: Timeline; Transportation Brochure

More About the Author

Mark Twain first gained recognition as a writer in 1865 when he published "The Celebrated Jumping Frog of Calaveras County." Even though he was a major American author and published many well-known works, he received very little formal education. He did not attend college or even high school. Just as he learned to be a riverboat pilot as an apprentice, he received his writing training on the job in print shops and newspapers. His down-to-earth and humorous writing style has remained popular for many years worldwide and is often quoted and studied.

Meet the Author:

Mark Twain (1835–1910)

As a boy growing up in Hannibal, Missouri, Mark Twain was enchanted by the Mississippi River, which ran through town. Born Samuel Langhorne Clemens, he took his pen name from a riverman's call, "By the mark—twain," which means "the water is two fathoms (twelve feet) deep."

Real-Life Inspirations Although Twain traveled all over the United States and worked as a printer, prospector, reporter, editor, and lecturer, his boyhood experiences on the Mississippi River were the strongest influences on his most memorable writing. In *The Adventures of Tom Sawyer,* Twain draws on his early life in Hannibal to write a coming-of-age story about a boy in a small Missouri town. In his novel *The Adventures of Huckleberry Finn,* Twain tells about a boy and a runaway slave who travel down the Mississippi together.

THE STORY BEHIND THE STORY

At age twenty-two, Twain became an apprentice riverboat pilot. Being an apprentice involved on-the-job training, learning a skill or trade from someone practicing the skill or trade. Sometimes apprentices were badly treated by their masters. In "Cub Pilot on the Mississippi," Twain tells the true story of how he dealt with the cruel treatment he received from Pilot Brown, a master riverboat pilot.

106 ◆ *Meeting Challenges*

◆ LITERATURE AND YOUR LIFE

CONNECT YOUR EXPERIENCE

At one time or another, most people face a conflict with another person. Have you ever encountered a schoolyard bully or someone whose behavior was impossible to ignore? What did you do about the situation? In "Cub Pilot on the Mississippi," you'll find out how young Mark Twain dealt with an ill-tempered boss.

THEMATIC FOCUS: Meeting Challenges

Mark Twain meets the challenge of dealing with a bully while learning to become a riverboat pilot. What might be difficult about both of these challenges?

◆ Background for Understanding

SOCIAL STUDIES

In "Cub Pilot on the Mississippi," Mark Twain shares his memories of being an apprentice pilot on a Mississippi steamboat. In the 1800's, steamboats like the ones shown on the facing page appeared on the nation's waterways, carrying goods and people from port to port. Especially on the wide, long Mississippi River, people could travel quickly and sometimes luxuriously. However, there were also dangers. Fires broke out, boilers burst, hidden rocks had to be avoided, and ever-changing currents had to be negotiated.

Prentice Hall Literature Program Resources

REINFORCE / RETEACH / EXTEND

Selection Support Pages
Build Vocabulary: Forms of *judge* p. 49
Build Spelling Skills, p. 50
Build Grammar Skills: Verbs and Verb Phrases, p. 51
Reading for Success: Interactive Reading Strategies, pp. 52–53
Literary Focus: Conflict Between Characters, p. 54

Strategies for Diverse Student Needs, pp. 19–20

Beyond Literature Workplace Skills: Problem Solving, p. 10

Formal Assessment Selection Test, pp. 38–40, Assessment Resources Software

Alternative Assessment, p. 10

Writing and Language Transparencies Cluster Organizer, p. 73

Resource Pro CD-ROM
"Cub Pilot on the Mississippi"—includes all resource material and customizable lesson plan

 Listening to Literature Audiocassettes, "Cub Pilot on the Mississippi"

◆ Cub Pilot on the Mississippi ◆

The Champions of the Mississippi, Currier & Ives

◆ Literary Focus

CONFLICT BETWEEN CHARACTERS

Like short stories, many pieces of nonfiction involve a **conflict,** or struggle between opposing forces. Sometimes the conflict is between two characters and may be caused by a difference in ideas or personalities. In "Cub Pilot on the Mississippi," Twain describes the conflict between himself and Pilot Brown, the steamboat pilot for whom he works. As you read, list the differences that develop the conflict between Twain and Brown.

DIFFERENCES	
Twain	**Brown**
Young; inexperienced	Older; experienced

◆ Build Vocabulary

RELATED WORDS: FORMS OF *judge*

In this story, you'll encounter the word *judicious,* which is part of a word family related to *judge.* The root is an important clue to the meaning of *judicious,* which is "having or showing good judgment."

WORD BANK

Which word on this list has a beginning sound like *hint* and means "hint"? Check the Build Vocabulary box on page 114 to see if you chose correctly.

furtive
pretext
intimation
judicious
indulgent
emancipated

Guide for Reading ◆ 107

Preparing for Standardized Tests

Reading Strategies Standardized tests often assess students' reading comprehension and ability to apply reading strategies to a passage. After students have read "Cub Pilot on the Mississippi," review the interactive reading strategies on p. 108. Then give students this sample test item:

"Brown was at the wheel. I paused in the middle of the room, all fixed to make my bow, but Brown did not look around."

If you don't know why Brown is acting this way, which of these reading strategies will help you understand his behavior?

(A) Form a question and read on to find the answer.
(B) Set a purpose for reading.
(C) Respond to characters and situations.
(D) Use prior knowledge to figure it out.

Discuss the possible answers, then guide students to understand that (A), forming a question and reading to find the answer, is the strategy that would be most helpful in this case. For further practice, use **Selection Support** Pages, Reading for Success: Interactive Reading Strategies, pp. 52–53.

Interest Grabber Ask students to offer nautical terms that they know. Then write the following phrases on the board:
   "Pull her down"
   "Meet her"
   "Round her to"
   "Snatch her"
   Ask students to guess what these orders given to a young river boat pilot may mean. Lead students into the story by explaining that Mark Twain is learning to be a riverboat pilot in "Cub Pilot on the Mississippi" from a very mean and impatient teacher.

◆Build Grammar Skills

Verbs and Verb Phrases If you wish to introduce the grammar concept for this selection before students read, refer to the instruction on p. 117.

Customize for
Less Proficient Readers

To help students understand and appreciate Twain's use of dialect in the story, have them listen to the recording of the selection. Alternatively, have student pairs read sections of dialogue, stopping as necessary to discuss meaning.

🎧 **Listening to Literature Audiocassettes**

Customize for
More Advanced Students

Challenge students to retell the story from Brown's point of view. Encourage students to think about how Brown really feels about teaching young, inexperienced pilots to navigate the dangerous river currents. Then discuss how this retelling changes the description of the conflict between the characters.

 Humanities: Art

The Champions of the Mississippi, by Currier and Ives
   Printmakers Nathaniel Currier (1813–1888) and James Merrit Ives (1824–1895) created affordable lithograph artworks illustrating life in post-Civil War America. Ask students what they can learn about steamboats and about the story's time and place from studying this print.

The Reading for Success page in each unit presents a set of problem-solving strategies to help readers understand authors' words and ideas on multiple levels. Good readers develop a bank of strategies from which they can draw as needed.

Unit 2 introduces interactive reading strategies. Students must be able to interact with a work before they apply higher-level critical thinking strategies. These strategies for interactive reading give readers an array of approaches for mastering a text: set a purpose, use prior knowledge, ask questions and respond.

These interactive reading strategies are modeled with "Cub Pilot on the Mississippi." Each green box shows an example of the thinking process involved in applying one of these strategies. Additional notes provide support for applying these strategies throughout the selection.

How to Use the Reading for Success Page

- Introduce the interactive reading strategies, presenting each as a problem-solving procedure.

- Before students read the story, have them preview it, looking at the annotations in the green boxes that model the strategies.

- To reinforce these strategies after students have read the story, have them use Reading for Success, pp. 52–53, in **Selection Support.** These pages give students an opportunity to read a selection and practice interactive comprehension strategies by writing their own annotations.

Reading Strategies: Support and Reinforcement
Using Boxed Annotations and Prompts

Throughout the unit, the notes in green, red, and maroon are intended to help students apply reading strategies, understand the literary focus, and make a connection with their lives. You may use boxed material in these ways:

- Have students pause at each box and respond to its prompt before they continue reading.

- Urge students to read through the selection, ignoring the boxes. After they complete the selection, they may go back and review the text, responding to the prompts.

108

Reading for Success

Interactive Reading Strategies

You get more out of life when you really live it—laughing with friends, standing up for what you believe in, learning something new. The same is true when you read. The more you read interactively—questioning, comparing, reading for specifics, and responding—the more you'll enjoy and remember your reading. Use these strategies to interact with your reading.

Set a purpose.
Decide what you want to get from a piece of literature before you begin to read. Then, look for details that help you meet this purpose. For example, you might read "Cub Pilot on the Mississippi" to find out about life as a riverboat pilot. To achieve this purpose, look for details that describe Twain's experiences on the job.

Purpose	Details
To learn about being a riverboat pilot	Apprenticeships last for years

Use your prior knowledge.
Your prior knowledge is what you already know. As you read, apply this knowledge to make connections with what the author is saying.

Ask questions.
Don't blindly accept characters' actions and statements. Question their motives and judgment. Question why the writer gives you certain information. Then, read on to find out what happens.

Story Text: I still remember the first time I ever entered the presence of that man.
Question: Why is the encounter so memorable?

Respond.
Allow yourself to respond to characters and situations. Become angry, become amazed, become enthralled. Root for your hero, and hiss at the villain. Then, examine why each character provokes a specific emotional response from you. You may want to keep a reader's response journal, in which you record your reactions to characters, events, and ideas.

As you read "Cub Pilot on the Mississippi," look at the notes in the boxes along the sides of the pages. The notes demonstrate how to apply these strategies to a work of literature.

Model a Reading Strategy: Ask Questions
Tell students that as they read, they should ask questions, think carefully about what they are reading, and then read to find the answers. Have students read the following description:

"He was a middle-aged, long, slim, bony, smooth-shaven, horse-faced, ignorant, stingy, malicious, snarling, fault-hunting, mote magnifying tyrant. I early got the habit of coming on watch with dread at my heart."

Demonstrate how to ask questions as you read by modeling your thinking for students.

As I read this description from the story, I asked myself:
- Why does Mark Twain describe Brown this way?
- Does Twain's choice of words accurately describe Brown?
- Does Mark Twain like Brown?
- Will the cub pilot and Brown be able to get along with each other?
- Do I believe everything in this description or is some of it exaggerated?

Asking questions helps clarify the author's meanings as well as increasing the reader's appreciation and enjoyment.

The Great Mississippi Steamboat Race, 1870, Currier & Ives

❶ ▲ **Critical Viewing** What do the details in this painting reveal about steamboat travel? **[Analyze]**

CUB PILOT ON THE MISSISSIPPI

◆—— Mark Twain ——◆

During the two or two and a half years of my apprenticeship[1] I served under many pilots, and had experience of many kinds of steamboatmen and many varieties of steamboats. I am to this day profiting somewhat by that experience; for in that brief, sharp schooling, I got personally and familiarly acquainted with about all the different types of human nature that are to be found in fiction, biography, or history.

The fact is daily borne in upon me that the average shore-employment requires as much as forty years to equip a man with this sort of an education. When I say I am still profiting by this thing, I do not

mean that it has constituted me a judge of men—no, it has not done that, for judges of men are born, not made. My profit is various in kind and degree, but the feature of it which I value most is the zest which that early experience has given to my later reading. When I find a well-drawn character in fiction or biography I generally take a warm personal interest in him, for the reason that I have known him before—met him on the river.

> Your **purpose** for reading this may be to discover what characters Twain has "met . . . on the river."

The figure that comes before me oftenest, out of the shadows of that vanished time, is that of Brown, of the steamer *Pennsylvania.* He was a middle-aged, long, slim, bony,

---

1. **apprenticeship** (ə prenˊ tis ship) *n.*: Time a person spends working for a master craftsperson in a craft or trade in return for instruction.

Cub Pilot on the Mississippi ◆ 109

 Block Scheduling Strategies

Consider these suggestions to make use of extended class time.

- Discuss the Reading for Success strategies, p. 108. Encourage students to be aware of these strategies as they read. Suggest that they jot down their questions and then check them off as they find answers in their reading.
- Have students read the selection independently
- After students read the story, expand the Interest Grabber on p. 107 and have students pair off and attempt to guide a blindfolded

partner across the room without bumping into furniture and obstacles.

- Have students join small groups to discuss Literature and Your Life, Check Your Comprehension, and Critical Thinking questions, p. 116.
- Invite students to complete the Transportation Brochure project in the Idea Bank, p. 118.
- To prepare students for the Writing Mini-Lesson, have them review the Using Verbs section of the *Writer's Solution Language Lab CD-ROM.*

Develop Understanding

One-Minute Insight

Recalling real-life characters he met while working as an apprentice riverboat pilot on the Mississippi River, Twain describes his experience working for Pilot Brown, a mean and intolerant man. Although young Twain tries hard to please his boss, nothing works. Pushed to the breaking point, Twain finally turns on Brown and gives him a beating. Much to Twain's surprise, Brown backs down and the riverboat captain secretly commends him. The story illustrates that challenges can sometimes be met in unconventional ways.

▶Critical Viewing◀

❶ **Analyze** *People can walk around the boat or relax on different balcony levels. Steamboat travel was probably an elegant and luxurious way to travel quickly.*

Customize for *English Language Learners*

When reading this selection, students will find both dialect and words seldom used in modern, everyday English. You may want to have students read the story aloud, stopping to address troublesome phrases or passages. Help students understand these by restating the material in more familiar language.

Humanities: Art

The Great Mississippi Steamboat Race, 1870, by Currier and Ives

In this lithograph print, Currier and Ives show a scene from the July 1870 race between two steamboats, the *Robert E. Lee* and the *Natchez.* Covering a distance of 1210 miles, the race began in New Orleans and ended in St. Louis. The riverboat race was won by the *Robert E. Lee,* with a time of 3 days, 18 hours, and 30 minutes. Ask students to study the print and decide where they think the riverboat pilots stand as they steer the boat. *They stand in the small white structure on the top level near the front of the boat, because it gives them a view for steering the boat down the river.*

109

◆Literary Focus

❶ Conflict Between Characters
Ask students what they can tell from this description of Brown and about the conflict that might arise with the young cub pilot. *Brown seems rude, mean and indifferent. Although the cub pilot seems optimistic and eager to please, he might become discouraged and find it hard to please Brown.*

Clarification

❷ Explain that "removed his countenance" means that he turned his face away from the boy. Ask students how they would feel if someone stared at them for a length of time and then deliberately turned away. *Most students will say it would make them feel embarrassed, scared, or nervous.*

►Critical Viewing◄

❸ Analyze *The riverboat might be dropping off passengers, mail and needed supplies and picking up materials or products to ship to other locations to sell for the townspeople. Riverboats provided an important way for small towns along the river to be connected to the larger world. The arrival of a riverboat was an exciting event in the life of a river town.*

Customize for
Visual/Spatial Learners
Encourage students to preview and study the selection artwork. Have them use details from the artwork to help them understand the setting and action of the story.

smooth-shaven, horse-faced, ignorant, stingy, malicious, snarling, fault-hunting, mote-[2] magnifying tyrant. I early got the habit of coming on watch with dread at my heart. No

❶ | This statement prompts the question "Why does he dread coming on watch?"

matter how good a time I might have been having with the off-watch below, and no matter how high my spirits might be when I started aloft, my soul became lead in my body the moment I approached the pilothouse.

I still remember the first time I ever entered the presence of that man. The boat had backed out from St. Louis and was "straightening down." I ascended to the pilothouse in high feather, and very proud to be semiofficially a member of the executive family of so fast and famous a boat. Brown was at the wheel. I paused in the middle of the room, all fixed to make my bow, but Brown did not look around. I thought he took a <u>furtive</u> glance at me out of the corner of his eye, but as not even this notice was repeated, I judged I had been mistaken. By this time he was picking his way among some dangerous "breaks" abreast the wood-yards; therefore it would not be proper to interrupt him; so I stepped softly to the high bench and took a seat.

There was silence for ten minutes; then my new boss turned and inspected me deliberately and painstakingly from head to heel for about—as it seemed to me—a quar-❷ ter of an hour. After which he removed his countenance[3] and I saw it no more for some seconds; then it came around once more, and this question greeted me: "Are you Horace Bigsby's cub?"[4]

---
2. **mote** (mōt) *n.*: Speck of dust.
3. **countenance** (koun´ tə nəns) *n.*: Face.
4. **cub** (kub) *n.*: Beginner.

▲ **Critical Viewing** Imagine the activity that might be occurring in this scene. Why were riverboats important to the life of Mississippi towns like this? **[Analyze]** ❸

"Yes, sir."

After this there was a pause and another inspection. Then: "What's your name?"

I told him. He repeated it after me. It was probably the only thing he ever forgot; for although I was with him many months he never addressed himself to me in any other way than "Here!" and then his command followed.

"Where was you born?"

"In Florida, Missouri."

A pause. Then: "Dern sight better stayed there!"

By means of a dozen or so of pretty direct questions, he pumped my family history out of me.

◆ Build Vocabulary

furtive (fur´ tiv) *adj.*: Sly or done in secret

 Humanities: Art

Looking Down the Mississippi River at Hannibal, MO, 1868, by George L. Crosby
  George Crosby (1833–1877), a native of Massachusetts, was commissioned by the Hannibal and St. Joseph Railroad to paint views of the area around Hannibal, Missouri. He moved to Hannibal, married, and started a framing and art business. The tragic and untimely death of Crosby and his family in a drowning accident shocked the small community. Two of the works Crosby completed, including this one, now hang in the Mark Twain Home and Museum in Hannibal. Help students

connect the painting to the story by asking questions such as these:
1. What does the painting tell you about the area where Mark Twain grew up? *It was on the river; there were hills and trees around the town; the town was small, with only a few large buildings; riverboats sometimes docked there to bring supplies and passengers.*
2. Why do you think this painting was chosen to hang in the Mark Twain museum? *It shows what the area looked like during the time Twain lived and worked there.*

Looking down the Mississippi River at Hannibal, MO, George L. Crosby, Mark Twain Home and Museum

round upon me again—and then what a change! It was as red as fire, and every muscle in it was working. Now came this shriek: "Here! You going to set there all day?" **⑥**

I lit in the middle of the floor, shot there by the electric suddenness of the surprise. As soon as I could get my voice I said apologetically: "I have had no orders, sir."

"You've had no *orders*! My, what a fine bird we are! We must have *orders*! Our father was a *gentleman*—and *we've* been to *school*. Yes, *we* are a gentleman, *too*, and got to have *orders*! ORDERS, is it? ORDERS is what you want! Dod dern my skin, *I'll* learn you to swell yourself up and blow around *here* about your dod-derned *orders*! G'way from the wheel!" (I had approached it without knowing it.)

I moved back a step or two and stood as in a dream, all my senses stupefied by this frantic assault.

"What you standing there for? Take that ice-pitcher down to the texas-tender![7] Come, move along, and don't you be all day about it!"

The moment I got back to the pilothouse Brown said: "Here! What was you doing down there all this time?"

"I couldn't find the texas-tender; I had to go all the way to the pantry."

"Derned likely story! Fill up the stove."

I proceeded to do so. He watched me like a cat. Presently he shouted: "Put down that shovel! Derndest

The leads[5] were going now in the first crossing. This interrupted the inquest.[6] When the leads had been laid in he resumed:

"How long you been on the river?"
I told him. After a pause:
❹ "Where'd you get them shoes?"
I gave him the information.
"Hold up your foot!"

I did so. He stepped back, examined the shoe minutely and contemptuously, scratching his head thoughtfully, tilting his high sugar-loaf hat well forward to facilitate the operation, then ejaculated, "Well, I'll be **❺** dod derned!" and returned to his wheel.

What occasion there was to be dod derned about it is a thing which is still as much of a mystery to me now as it was then. It must have been all of fifteen minutes—fifteen minutes of dull, homesick silence—before that long horse-face swung

---

> Footnotes are useful if you have no **prior knowledge** about a particular reference.

5. **leads** (ledz) *n.*: Weights that were lowered to test the depth of the river.
6. **inquest** (in´ kwest) *n.*: Investigation.

7. **texas-tender:** The waiter in the officers' quarters. On Mississippi steamboats, rooms were named after the states. The officers' area, which was the largest, was named after what was then the largest state, Texas.

Cub Pilot on the Mississippi ◆ 111

Cross-Curricular Connection: Geography

The Mississippi River The third-longest river system in the world (the Amazon and Nile rivers are longer), the Mississippi River system stretches 3,860 miles and has about 15,000 miles of navigable waterways. Long before Europeans explored the Mississippi, it was important to the lives of the native peoples who lived nearby. In fact, the name *Mississippi* evolved from the Ojibwa (Chippewa) name *Messipi,* which means "big river."

The Mississippi River provided the fastest way for native peoples and early settlers to travel long distances. Later it was used for transporting raw materials and manufactured products to and from cities along and near the Mississippi. As railroads became more popular and available, people along the river came to rely more on fishing and farming than on shipping for their livelihoods.

Today, shipping on the river has regained popularity as a relatively inexpensive method of transport. Ships can enter the river at its mouth near New Orleans, Louisiana, and travel the length of the river to Chicago, Illinois, and from there into the system of Great Lakes.

1 ▲ Critical Viewing Put yourself in the place of this pilot. What challenges does the river pose? [Assess]

numskull I ever saw—ain't even got sense enough to load up a stove."

All through the watch this sort of thing went on. Yes, and the subsequent watches were much like it during a stretch of months. As I have said, I soon got the habit of coming on duty with dread. The moment I was in the presence, even in the darkest night, I could feel those yellow eyes upon me, and knew their owner was watching for a pretext to spit out some venom on me. Preliminarily he would say: "Here! Take the wheel."

> The examples of Brown's behavior support your **purpose** of learning about characters met on the river.

Two minutes later: "*Where* in the nation you going to? Pull her down! pull her down!"

After another moment: "Say! You going to hold her all day? Let her go—meet her! meet her!"

Then he would jump from the bench, snatch the wheel from me, and meet her himself, pouring out wrath upon me all the time.

George Ritchie was the other pilot's cub. He was having good times now; for his boss, George Ealer, was as kind-hearted as Brown wasn't. Ritchie had steered for Brown the season before; consequently, he knew exactly how to entertain himself and plague me, all by the one operation. Whenever I took the wheel for a moment on Ealer's watch, Ritchie would sit back on the bench and play Brown, with continual ejaculations of "Snatch her! Snatch her! Derndest mudcat I ever saw!" "Here! Where are you going *now*? Going to run over that snag?" "Pull her *down*! Don't you hear me? Pull her *down*!" "There she goes! *Just* as I expected! I *told* you not to cramp that reef. G'way from the wheel!"

Humanities: Art

Book Illustrations Book illustrations are used for a variety of reasons. Some illustrations are used to portray what might be difficult to explain in words. Others are included to enhance readers' enjoyment or draw their interest. The drawing on this page is an illustration from a book called *The Great South*, by Edward W. King, originally published in 1875. This detailed black-and-white drawing gives the reader a sense of being inside the pilot house of a riverboat. Use the following questions for discussion:

1. Why do you think this illustration was included in a book entitled *The Great South*? *The Mississippi River and riverboats were important to the culture and economy of the South.*
2. Why do you think the drawing was chosen to illustrate this selection? *It illustrates a riverboat pilot house where much of the action in the story takes place.*
3. Would you want to steer a riverboat like this one? *Some might think it would be exciting, others might find the responsibility frightening.*

So I always had a rough time of it, no matter whose watch it was; and sometimes it seemed to me that Ritchie's good-natured badgering was pretty nearly as aggravating as Brown's dead-earnest nagging.

I often wanted to kill Brown, but this would not answer. A cub had to take everything his boss gave, in the way of vigorous comment and criticism; and we all believed that there was a United States law making it a penitentiary offense to strike or threaten a pilot who was on duty.

However, I could *imagine* myself killing Brown; there was no law against that; and that was the thing I used always to do the moment I was abed. Instead of going over my river in my mind, as was my duty, I threw business aside for pleasure, and killed Brown. I killed Brown every night for months; not in old, stale, commonplace ways, but in new and picturesque ones—ways that were sometimes surprising for freshness of design and ghastliness of situation and environment.

> Ask why Twain provides this information about killing Brown. Watch for a connection to the action later on.

Brown was *always* watching for a pretext to find fault; and if he could find no plausible pretext, he would invent one. He would scold you for shaving a shore, and for not shaving it; for hugging a bar, and for not hugging it; for "pulling down" when not invited, and for *not* pulling down when not invited; for firing up without orders, and *for* waiting for orders. In a word, it was his invariable rule to find fault with *everything* you did and another invariable rule of his was to throw all his remarks (to you) into the form of an insult.

One day we were approaching New Madrid, bound down and heavily laden. Brown was at one side of the wheel, steering; I was at the other, standing by to "pull down" or "shove up." He cast a furtive glance at me every now and then. I had long ago learned what that meant; viz., he was trying to invent a trap for me. I wondered what shape it was going to take. By and by he stepped back from the wheel and said in his usual snarly way:

"Here! See if you've got gumption enough to round her to."

This was simply *bound* to be a success; nothing could prevent it; for he had never allowed me to round the boat to before; consequently, no matter how I might do the thing, he could find free fault with it. He stood back there with his greedy eye on me, and the result was what might have been foreseen: I lost my head in a quarter of a minute, and didn't know what I was about; I started too early to bring the boat around, but detected a green gleam of joy in Brown's eye, and corrected my mistake. I started around once more while too high up, but corrected myself again in time. I made other false moves, and still managed to save myself; but at last I grew so confused and anxious that I tumbled into the very worst blunder of all—I got too far *down* before beginning to fetch the boat around. Brown's chance was come.

His face turned red with passion; he made one bound, hurled me across the house with a sweep of his arm, spun the wheel down, and began to pour out a stream of vituperation[8] upon me which lasted till he was out of breath. In the course of this speech he called me all the different kinds of hard names he could think of, and once or twice I thought he was even going to swear—but he had never done that, and he didn't this time. "Dod dern" was the nearest he ventured to the luxury of swearing.

Two trips later I got into serious trouble. Brown was steering; I was "pulling down." My younger brother Henry appeared on the hurricane deck, and shouted to Brown to

---

8. **vituperation** (vĭ tōō′ pə rā′ shən) *n.*: Abusive language.

◆ **Build Vocabulary**

pretext (prē′ tekst) *n.*: False reason or motive used to hide a real intention

Cub Pilot on the Mississippi ◆ 113

◆**Critical Thinking**

❺ **Infer** Ask students to explain why Ritchie teased the other cub pilot. *Ritchie had already experienced all the difficulties the cub pilot is now enduring at the hands of Brown. He enjoys pointing out the many ways in which the cub pilot's life is more miserable than his own.*

Clarification

❻ Explain that *viz.* is an abbreviation for *videlicet,* which means "that is to say" or "namely."

◆**LITERATURE AND YOUR LIFE**

❼ Have students think of a time when they have been so nervous about performing that they wound up making mistakes. Ask them how their own experience helps them understand what the cub pilot is going through. Encourage volunteers to share their experiences with the class and to connect them to the selection.

Humanities: Art

Lithograph Prints Lithography is a printmaking process which was used by the firm of Currier and Ives in the 1800's because prints—with and without color—could be made and reproduced at a reasonable cost. People across the United States used these prints to bring art and color to the walls of their homes.

Making lithograph prints is an artistic printing process based on the principle that grease and water do not mix, following these steps:

• Draw a design with grease on a prepared stone surface, often limestone.
• Treat the grease drawing with chemicals and then water.
• Apply a greasy ink to the drawing which sticks to the grease drawing, but not the water.
• Press and roll a sheet of paper against the inked drawing on the stone leaving the inked impression.

As students study the Currier and Ives illustrations on pp. 107 and 109, they will notice that they are printed with more than one color. To make a multi-colored print, the printing steps are followed more than once. New stones are prepared and the paper is put through the printing process for each color. For example, a lithography print of a red flower with green stem and leaves requires 2 drawings and 2 printing processes—one for red and one for green. Multiple color lithograph print making is an intricate process, but still more practical than applying color to individual pieces of art.

Clarification

❶ Explain that Twain uses humor by explaining his decision not to speak because he has only one head, so that it can be interpreted two ways. Ask students to identify both meanings. *If he had two heads, the cub pilot would have been smart enough to have spoken. If he had two heads, he could afford to lose the one that Brown might knock off his shoulders.*

◆ Critical Thinking

❷ Connect Ask students to connect this statement to earlier comments about striking or threatening a pilot on duty. *On p. 113, the cub pilot says that "we all believed that there was a United States law making it a penitentiary offense to strike or threaten a pilot who was on duty." At this point, Twain believes that he has committed a serious offense.*

◆ Literary Focus

❸ Conflict Between Characters Ask students to explain the pilot's behavior in getting up and rushing to the wheel. Encourage them to discuss what this reveals about the conflict between the pilot and the cub pilot. *He rushed to the wheel for two reasons: to keep the boat safely on course and to avoid facing the cub pilot, who has shocked Brown by refusing to be bullied. By standing up to Brown, the cub pilot has become the more-powerful character.*

---

stop at some landing or other, a mile or so below. Brown gave no <u>intimation</u> that he had heard anything. But that was his way: he never condescended to take notice of an underclerk. The wind was blowing; Brown was deaf (although he always pretended he wasn't), and I very much doubted if he had heard the order. If I had had two heads, I would have spoken; but as I had only one, it seemed <u>judicious</u> to take care of it; so I kept still.

Presently, sure enough, we went sailing by that plantation. Captain Klinefelter appeared on the deck, and said: "Let her come around, sir, let her come around. Didn't Henry tell you to land here?"

"*No*, sir!"

"I sent him up to do it."

"He *did* come up; and that's all the good it done, the dod-derned fool. He never said anything."

"Didn't *you* hear him?" asked the captain of me.

Of course I didn't want to be mixed up in this business, but there was no way to avoid it; so I said: "Yes, sir."

I knew what Brown's next remark would be, before he uttered it. It was: "Shut your mouth! You never heard anything of the kind."

I closed my mouth, according to instructions. An hour later Henry entered the pilot-house, unaware of what had been going on. He was a thoroughly inoffensive boy, and I was sorry to see him come, for I knew Brown would have no pity on him. Brown began, straightway: "Here! Why didn't you tell me we'd got to land at that plantation?"

"I did tell you, Mr. Brown."

"It's a lie!"

I said: "You lie, yourself. He did tell you."

◆ Build Vocabulary

intimation (in´ tə mā´ shən) *n.*: Hint or suggestion

judicious (jōō dish´ əs) *adj.*: Showing sound judgment; wise and careful

indulgent (in dul´ jənt) *adj.*: Very mild and tolerant; not strict or critical

114 ◆ *Meeting Challenges*

Brown glared at me in unaffected surprise; and for as much as a moment he was entirely speechless; then he shouted to me: "I'll attend to your case in a half a minute!" then to Henry, "And you leave the pilothouse; out with you!"

Respond to Twain's answer to Brown. Did you expect Twain to stand his ground?

It was pilot law, and must be obeyed. The boy started out, and even had his foot on the upper step outside the door, when Brown, with a sudden access of fury, picked up a ten-pound lump of coal and sprang after him; but I was between, with a heavy stool, and I hit Brown a good honest blow which stretched him out.

I had committed the crime of crimes—I had lifted my hand against a pilot on duty! I supposed I was booked for the penitentiary sure, and couldn't be booked any surer if I went on and squared my long account with this person while I had the chance; consequently I stuck to him and pounded him with my fists a considerable time. I do not know how long, the pleasure of it probably made it seem longer than it really was; but in the end he struggled free and jumped up and sprang to the wheel: a very natural solicitude, for, all this time, here was this steamboat tearing down the river at the rate of fifteen miles an hour and nobody at the helm! However, Eagle Bend was two miles wide at this bank-full stage, and correspondingly long and deep: and the boat was steering herself straight down the middle and taking no chances. Still, that was only luck—a body *might* have found her charging into the woods.

Perceiving at a glance that the *Pennsylvania* was in no danger, Brown gathered up the big spyglass, war-club fashion, and ordered me out of the pilothouse with more than ordinary bluster. But I was not afraid of him now; so, instead of going, I tarried, and criticized his grammar. I reformed his ferocious speeches for him, and put them into good English, calling his attention to the advantage of pure English over the

---

Speaking and Listening Mini-Lesson

Dramatic Reading

This lesson supports the Speaking and Listening activity on p. 118.

Introduce Point out that Twain's use of colorful dialogue makes this story good material for a dramatic reading.

Develop As students prepare, have them consider how many people will be required to present the reading. Most groups will consist of three people—one to read the narration and two to read the dialogue. Suggest that they select an interesting passage to read, for example the first

meeting between Brown and the cub pilot or the meeting between the cub pilot and the captain. Finally, have groups decide on the mood and emotions they want to express in the reading.

Apply Allow time for groups to practice their dramatic reading. Then invite groups to perform their reading for the class.

Assess Evaluate each group's presentation based on preparation and appropriateness of mood and emotions projected. You may want students use the Peer Assessment, Dramatic Performance form, p. 116, in **Alternative Assessment.**

dialect of the collieries[9] whence he was extracted. He could have done his part to admiration in a crossfire of mere vituperation, of course; but he was not equipped for this species of controversy; so he presently laid aside his glass and took the wheel, muttering and shaking his head; and I retired to the bench. The racket had brought everybody to the hurricane deck, and I trembled when I saw the old captain looking up from amid the crowd. I said to myself, "Now I *am* done for!" for al-

> You might be **asking** what the captain will do to Twain.

though, as a rule, he was so fatherly and indulgent toward the boat's family, and so patient of minor shortcomings, he could be stern enough when the fault was worth it.

I tried to imagine what he *would* do to a cub pilot who had been guilty of such a crime as mine, committed on a boat guard-deep[10] with costly freight and alive with passengers. Our watch was nearly ended.

> Use your **prior knowledge** or experience to understand Twain's nervousness when confronted with a figure of authority.

I thought I would go and hide somewhere till I got a chance to slide ashore. So I slipped out of the pilothouse, and down the steps, and around to the texas-door, and was in the act of gliding within, when the captain confronted me! I dropped my head, and he stood over me in silence a moment or two, then said impressively: "Follow me."

❺ I dropped into his wake; he led the way to his parlor in the forward end of the texas. We were alone now. He closed the afterdoor, then moved slowly to the forward one and closed that. He sat down; I stood before him. He looked at me some little time, then said: "So you have been fighting Mr. Brown?"

I answered meekly: "Yes, sir."

"Do you know that that is a very serious matter?"

---

9. **collieries** (käl´ yər ēz) *n.*: Coal mines.
10. **guard-deep:** Here, a wooden frame protecting the paddle wheel.

"Yes, sir."

"Are you aware that this boat was plowing down the river fully five minutes with no one at the wheel?"

"Yes, sir."

"Did you strike him first?"

"Yes, sir."

"What with?"

"A stool, sir."

"Hard?"

"Middling, sir."

"Did it knock him down?"

"He—he fell, sir."

"Did you follow it up? Did you do anything further?"

"Yes, sir."

"What did you do?"

"Pounded him, sir."

"Pounded him?"

"Yes, sir."

"Did you pound him much? that is, severely?"

"One might call it that, sir, maybe."

"I'm deuced glad of it! Hark ye, never mention that I said that. You have been guilty of a great crime; and don't you ever be guilty of it again, on this boat. *But*—lay for him ashore! Give him a good sound thrashing, do you hear? I'll pay the expenses. Now go—and mind you, not a word of this to anybody. Clear out with you! You've been guilty of a great crime, you whelp!"[11]

I slid out, happy with the sense of a close shave and a mighty deliverance; and I heard him laughing to himself and slapping his fat thighs after I had closed his door.

When Brown came off watch he went straight to the captain, who was talking with some passengers on the boiler deck, and demanded that I be put ashore in New Orleans—and added: "I'll never turn a wheel on this boat again while that cub stays."

The captain said: "But he needn't come round when you are on watch, Mr. Brown."

"I won't even stay on the same boat with him. One of us has got to go ashore."

---

11. **whelp** (hwelp) *n.*: Here, a disrespectful young man.

Cub Pilot on the Mississippi ◆ 115

Beyond Literature

Interested students might research the locations of other rivers in the United States that are navigable and have been used for transportation and trade. Suggest that they create a map to illustrate their findings.

Reinforce and Extend

Answers

◆ LITERATURE AND YOUR LIFE

Reader's Response Most students will believe Twain dealt with a bully in the best way he knew how.

Thematic Focus Steamboat pilots face challenges presented by nature and the river.

☑ Check Your Comprehension

1. He is about 22 years old.
2. He is learning to become a pilot.
3. Twain defends his younger brother, Henry.
4. He feels free because he no longer has to put up with Brown's controlling and bullying behavior.

◆ Critical Thinking

1. Brown ignored Twain, asked him to do impossible tasks, criticized him, and spoke in mean and disrespectful ways.
2. George Ritchie's teasing indicates that he knows from personal experience how Brown is treating Twain.
3. The captain does not like Brown. He is happy with Twain for thrashing him; he encourages Brown to quit.
4. Twain is an honest and respectful young man.
5. Twain will make a good riverboat captain because he has the qualities of a good leader—honesty, courage, and a sense of what is right.
6. Riverboat pilots must be physically strong and skilled in reading danger signs in the river; they must know how the riverboat will respond in various conditions.

"Very well," said the captain, "let it be yourself," and resumed his talk with the passengers.

During the brief remainder of the trip I knew how an <u>emancipated</u> slave feels, for I was an emancipated slave myself. While we lay at landings I listened to George Ealer's flute, or to his readings from his two Bibles, that is to say, Goldsmith and Shakespeare, or I played chess with him—and would have beaten him sometimes, only he always took back his last move and ran the game out differently.

◆ Build Vocabulary

emancipated (i man´ sə pā´ təd) v.: Freed from the control or power of another

---

Beyond Literature

Science Connection

River Navigation In the early nineteenth century, the Mississippi River was navigable by small boats only. They faced dangerous rapids, rocks, and snags. Snags are submerged trees that are not always visible from the surface.

Steamboats could not use this major waterway until it was cleared of snags. In the 1820's, riverboat builder Henry Shreve invented a boat to pull up and remove snags. The boat had two hulls, with a heavy iron wedge between them. To remove a snag, the boat rammed the wedge into the submerged tree. The powerful boat engine operated lifting machinery that hoisted the large, sodden trunks. By 1830, the snag boats, called "Uncle Sam's Tooth Pullers," had cleared the Mississippi River for navigation.

Cross-Curricular Activity
Boat Diagram Use reference sources to find out about the snag boats that cleared the Mississippi. Then, create a diagram that shows how the boats worked. Label the parts of your diagram.

116 ◆ Meeting Challenges

Guide for Responding

◆ LITERATURE AND YOUR LIFE

Reader's Response Do you think that Mark Twain could have resolved the conflict with Brown in another way? Why or why not?

Thematic Focus What challenges does a steamboat pilot face?

Role Play With a partner, role-play a conversation between Mark Twain and his brother Henry about Mr. Brown.

☑ Check Your Comprehension

1. About how old is Twain at the time the story takes place?
2. Why is Twain in the pilothouse with Mr. Brown?
3. Whom does Twain try to defend when he hits Brown?
4. Why does Twain feel like "an emancipated slave" at the end?

◆ Critical Thinking

INTERPRET

1. In what ways was Brown's treatment of the young Twain unfair? **[Support]**
2. How do you know that Brown treated other cub pilots the same way he treated Twain? **[Deduce]**
3. How does the captain feel about Mr. Brown? What evidence supports your answer? **[Draw Conclusions]**
4. What do Twain's answers to the captain suggest about Twain's character? **[Infer]**

EVALUATE

5. From what you learn about him in the story, do you think Twain will make a good riverboat captain? **[Evaluate]**

EXTEND

6. What kinds of skills do you think would be necessary to pilot a riverboat? **[Career Link]**

 Beyond the Selection

FURTHER READING
Other Works by Mark Twain
A Connecticut Yankee in King Arthur's Court
The Celebrated Jumping Frog of Calaveras County, and Other Sketches

Other Books About Meeting Challenges
Dancing on the Edge, Han Nolan
Parrot in the Oven: Mi Vida: A Novel, Victor Martinez
The Thief, Megan Whalen Turner

INTERNET
We suggest the following site on the Internet (all Web sites are subject to change).
For more information about Mark Twain:
http://marktwain.miningco.com/msub5.htm
We *strongly recommend* that you preview the site before you send students to it.

Guide for Responding (continued)

◆ Reading for Success

INTERACTIVE READING STRATEGIES

Review the reading strategies on page 108 and notes that show how to interact with the text. Then, apply them to answer these questions.

1. (a) What was your purpose for reading? (b) What details in the text helped you fulfill your purpose?
2. (a) What was your response to Twain's method of resolving the conflict with Brown? (b) Was the captain's reaction to Twain's confession what you expected? Explain.
3. Using your own experience with bullies as a guide, advise Twain on how to deal with them in the future.

◆ Build Vocabulary

USING FORMS OF _judge_

The word family that includes _judicious, judgment,_ and _judicial_ descends from the verb _judge,_ meaning "to decide [in a court of law]." Correctly complete each sentence, using _judicious, judgment,_ or _judicial._

1. I wouldn't want to make a ____?____ about that.
2. She was a ____?____ referee.
3. The Supreme Court is a ____?____ branch of government.

SPELLING STRATEGY

The _shus_ sound at the end of a word may be spelled in different ways. One way to spell it is _cious,_ as in _judicious._

Rewrite these words to end in the _shus_ sound.

1. lush   2. grace   3. malice

USING THE WORD BANK

On your paper, write the word closest in meaning to the Word Bank word.

1. pretext: (a) pretend, (b) excuse, (c) scholarly
2. indulgent: (a) soft, (b) greedy, (c) tolerant
3. judicious: (a) wise, (b) critical, (c) lawful
4. emancipated: (a) fled, (b) freed, (c) tied
5. furtive: (a) random, (b) curious, (c) secretive
6. intimation: (a) hint, (b) caution, (c) mild

◆ Literary Focus

CONFLICT BETWEEN CHARACTERS

The **conflict between characters** in this story propels the plot, or the story's action. The struggle between Twain and Brown escalates until it is finally resolved at the story's conclusion.

1. List three occasions in the story during which Twain and Mr. Brown are involved in conflict.
2. (a) Why does Twain always come to the pilot-house with "dread at my heart"? (b) Why doesn't Twain, the cub pilot, defy Mr. Brown sooner?
3. How is the conflict between Twain and Mr. Brown finally resolved?

◆ Build Grammar Skills

VERBS AND VERB PHRASES

A **verb** is a word that expresses an action or the fact that something exists.

> I _closed_ my mouth, according to instructions.
> My profit _is_ various in kind and degree.

A **verb phrase** consists of a main verb and its helping verbs. In the following sentence, _closed_ is the main verb; _had_ is the helping verb.

> I _had closed_ my mouth.

Common Helping Verbs:

be, been, am, are, is, was, were, do, does, did, have, has, had, can, could, will, would, may, might, shall, should, must

Practice Copy the following passages from the story. Circle the verb phrases. Then, underline each helping verb once and each main verb twice.

1. Then he would jump from the bench . . .
2. The racket had brought everybody to the hurricane deck . . .
3. He would scold you for shaving a shore . . .
4. I had long ago learned what that meant . . .
5. I could feel those yellow eyes upon me . . .

Writing Application Write a paragraph about what it might have been like to be a riverboat pilot. In the paragraph, use the verbs _concentrate_ and _steer,_ along with the helping verbs _would_ and _have._

Cub Pilot on the Mississippi ◆ 117

◆ Build Grammar Skills

1. Then he (would jump) from the bench . . .

2. The racket (had brought) everybody to the hurricane deck . . .

3. He (would scold) you for shaving a shore . . .

4. I (had learned) what that meant . . .

5. I (could feel) those yellow eyes upon me . . .

Writing Application
Paragraphs will vary, check to see that students have followed the directions given and used the verbs *concentrate* and *steer,* and the helping verbs *would* and *have.*

Answers
Reading for Success

1. (a) To find out why Brown was such a tyrant. (b) Details about Brown's abusive and mean-spirited behavior toward Twain and others helped fulfill this purpose.
2. (a) I was happy and relieved when Twain turned on Brown. (b) The captain's reaction was unexpected. The reader is led to believe that striking a pilot is always a punishable offense.
3. Stand up to bullies from the beginning, because they usually pick on those they believe are weak.

◆ Build Vocabulary

Using forms of _judge_

1. judgment   3. judicial
2. judicious

Spelling Strategy

1. luscious   3. malicious
2. gracious

Using the Word Bank

1. (b) excuse   4. (b) freed
2. (c) tolerant   5. (c) secretive
3. (a) wise   6. (a) hint

◆ Literary Focus

1. The two are involved in conflict at their first meeting; when Brown forced Twain to round the boat; when Twain protected Henry by attacking Brown.
2. (a) Twain knows that Brown will make him miserable. (b) Twain is respectful of authority and wants to obey the laws of the land and the rules of the ship.
3. Twain finally stands up to Brown and when Brown demands that the captain remove Twain from the boat, the captain fires Brown instead.

Writer's Solution

For additional instruction and practice, use the lesson in the *Writer's Solution Language Lab CD-ROM* on Verbs and Verb Phrases. You may also use practice pages on Verbs, pp. 11–15 in the *Writer's Solution Grammar Practice Book.*

117

Idea Bank

Following are suggestions for matching the Idea Bank topics with your students' performance levels and learning modalities:

Customize for
Performance Levels
Less Advanced Students: 1, 5, 7
Average Students: 2, 4, 5, 6, 7
More Advanced Students: 3, 4, 5, 6, 7

Customize for
Learning Modalities
Verbal/Linguistic: 1, 2, 3, 4, 5, 7
Interpersonal: 4, 5
Visual/Spatial: 6, 7
Intrapersonal: 1, 2, 3, 6, 7
Logical/Mathematical: 6

 Writing Mini-Lesson

Refer students to the Writing Handbook in the back of the book for instructions on the writing process and for further information on writing guidelines. Have students use the Cluster Organizer in **Writing and Language Transparencies,** p. 73, to arrange their prewriting examples.

 Writer's Solution

Writers at Work Videodisc
Have students view the videodisc segment (Ch. 3) featuring Rudolfo Anaya to see how he uses the revision process in his writing.

Play frames 29630 to 31179

Writing Lab CD-ROM
Have students complete the tutorial on Narration. Follow these steps:
1. Have students use the Inspirations for Narration to stimulate topic ideas.
2. Suggest that students use the Plot Outline to help them organize their introduction, body, and conclusion.
3. Have students draft on computer.
4. Students can use the Checklist to revise and evaluate their anecdotes.
You will need approximately 75 minutes of class time to complete these steps.

Writer's Solution Sourcebook
Have students use Chapter 3, "Narration," pp. 70–103, for additional support. This chapter includes in-depth instruction on anecdotes, p. 83.

118

Build Your Portfolio

 Idea Bank

Writing

1. **Journal Entry** Write a journal entry that Mark Twain might have written about the outcome of his conflict. The journal entry should be dated the night of Twain's conversation with the captain.
2. **Character Sketch** Write a character sketch of Mark Twain, cub pilot, based on his actions and comments within the story.
3. **Essay on Humor** In an essay, write about Mark Twain's use of humor in "Cub Pilot on the Mississippi." Discuss his use of dialogue and dialect, and explain how he uses humor to engage the reader in this story.

Speaking and Listening

4. **Dramatic Reading [Group Activity]** With several classmates, prepare and deliver a dramatic reading of part of the story. Use the tone, volume, and inflection of your voices to highlight changes in character or mood. **[Performing Arts Link]**
5. **Talk-Show Interview [Group Activity]** With a group, produce a talk show on the subject of fighting, featuring Mark Twain as a guest. The talk-show host should interview Twain and find out his views on fighting as a means of solving a conflict. Choose several other characters to participate in the talk show to offer views that are different from Twain's. **[Media Link]**

Projects

6. **Timeline** Research Twain's life and achievements. Then, create an illustrated timeline of his life. Post your finished product in the classroom. **[Literature Link; Art Link]**
7. **Transportation Brochure** Create a brochure that encourages people to travel on the Mississippi steamboats of the 1800's. Do research to make your brochure seem authentic. Display your brochure in the classroom. **[Social Studies Link]**

Writing Mini-Lesson

Anecdote

Like Mark Twain, we all have stories to tell about our lives. Choose a memorable experience, and write an **anecdote,** a brief true account of something meaningful that happened to you. The following may help you organize your anecdote.

Writing Skills Focus:
Introduction, Body, Conclusion

Using an **introduction, body,** and **conclusion** will give your anecdote structure and shape. In his introduction, Twain reveals that he learned a lesson about human character when he was a cub pilot. In the body of the story, he relates events that illustrate that lesson. In the conclusion, Twain wraps up the story, revealing his feelings about the incident.

Prewriting Take notes about the most dramatic aspects and colorful details of the event you've chosen. Jot down bits of dialogue you might include in your anecdote.

Drafting Capture readers' interest in the introduction, tell your story in the body, and describe what you learned or how you changed in the conclusion. Consider using dialogue to make the people and situations in your anecdote come alive.

> ◆ **Grammar Application**
> Choose a paragraph of your narrative. In each sentence, identify the verb or verb phrases.

Revising Reread your draft, and make sure it has a beginning, a middle, and an ending. Revise by adding details about characters or events that will make the importance of the story more clear. Proofread to correct errors in grammar, spelling, and punctuation.

✓ ASSESSMENT OPTIONS

Formal Assessment, Selection Test, pp. 38–40, and Assessment Resources Software. The selection test is designed so that it can easily be customized to the performance levels of your students.

Alternative Assessment, p. 10, includes options for less-advanced students, more advanced students, verbal/linguistic learners, musical/rhythmic learners, visual/spatial learners, and interpersonal learners.

PORTFOLIO ASSESSMENT
Use the following rubrics in the **Alternative Assessment** booklet to assess student writing:
Journal Entry: Expression, p. 90
Character Sketch: Description, p. 93
Essay on Humor: Critical Review, p. 107
Writing Mini-Lesson: Narrative Based on Personal Experience Rubric, p. 92

PART 1

Blazing Trails

The Parkman Outfit-Henry Chatillon, Guide and Hunter N.C. Wyeth, Wells Fargo & Co.

Blazing Trails ◆ 119

The selections in this section focus on the theme of blazing trails. "The Secret" is a futuristic science fiction story about a new development that a reporter discovers. "Harriet Tubman: Guide to Freedom" details Harriet Tubman's journey to bring eleven slaves to freedom. A grouping of the poems "Columbus," "Western Wagons," and "The Other Pioneers" uses the language and structure of poetry to tell the stories of settlers and explorers. "Up the Slide" is Jack London's story of a boy's courageous adventure in the Yukon.

Customize for
Varying Student Needs
When assigning the selections to your students, keep in mind the following factors:

"The Secret"
• Short science fiction story

"Harriet Tubman: Guide to Freedom"
• Excerpt from the biography *Harriet Tubman: Conductor of the Underground Railroad*
• Good example of third-person narrative

"Columbus"
• Rhyming poem
• Students may need help with vocabulary

"Western Wagons"
• Rhyming poem about American settlers

"The Other Pioneers"
• Presents Hispanic culture and Texas history
• Students may need help with pronunciation of Spanish names

"Up the Slide"
• Classic short story by Jack London
• Provides an opportunity for Beyond Literature study of the Gold Rush

"The Pilgrims' Landing and First Winter"
• Provides an opportunity for connecting literature to social studies
• Students may need help with antiquated language

 Humanities: Art

The Parkman Outfit—Henry Chatillon, Guide and Hunter, by N.C. Wyeth

N.C. Wyeth (1882–1945) was one of America's most noted illustrators and painters. Among the books he illustrated were *Treasure Island, Robin Hood,* and *The Yearling.* Wyeth also painted murals for hotels, churches, and banks, and landscape scenes of rural life in Maine and Pennsylvania. His son Andrew Wyeth, was his pupil, and also an accomplished painter.

"The Parkman Outfit" refers to Francis Parkman, a Harvard graduate, who set out to explore the western U. S. with Henry Chatillon, who was illiterate, but an experienced guide. Chatillon grew up on the prairies and was knowledgeable in hunting, fishing, and trading. Parkman published diaries of these explorations in *The Oregon Trail,* for which Wyeth did this illustration.

Have students study the illustration and then ask them how the men in the picture seem to be "blazing trails." *Students may say that the men look as though they are peering into an unknown landscape. The man on the white horse seems to be the leader because he is at the head of the group.*

119

Guide for Reading

1. To read, comprehend, and interpret science fiction
2. To relate science fiction to personal experience
3. To ask questions
4. To appreciate science fiction
5. To build vocabulary in context and learn the word part *micro*
6. To develop skill in using action verbs and linking verbs
7. To write a story continuation
8. To respond to science fiction through writing, speaking and listening, and projects

SKILLS INSTRUCTION

Vocabulary:
Word Part: *micro*

Literary Focus:
Science Fiction

Spelling:
Add *-ing* to Words
That End With *-cede*

Writing:
Sequence of
Events

Grammar:
Action Verbs and
Linking Verbs

**Speaking and
Listening:**
Radio Review
(Teacher Edition)

Reading Strategy:
Ask Questions

PORTFOLIO OPPORTUNITIES

Writing: Advertisement; News Article; Critical Response

Writing Mini-Lesson: Sequence of Events

Speaking and Listening: Telephone Call; Radio Review

Projects: Space Settlement; Comic Book

More About the Author
Arthur C. Clarke wrote his first science-fiction stories when he served in the Royal Air Force during World War II. Born in Somerset, England, today he lives in Sri Lanka, a small island country off the southeast coast of India. For a time, Clarke had the only television in Sri Lanka, with a special dish antenna on loan from India and the United States as a reward for originating the concept of satellite communication. Clarke keeps up with world events by subscribing to many scientific journals, by listening to the news on radio, and by using the modem on his computer.

Meet the Author:

Arthur C. Clarke (1917–)
This writer has always been ahead of his time. As a twenty-eight-year-old scientist, Clarke outlined ideas for a worldwide satellite system. Today, we rely on satellites to transmit radio and television communication signals. One common satellite orbit is even named in Clarke's honor.

From Scientist to Author Clarke built on his career as a scientist by writing science fiction. The author of more than seventy books, he has presented many versions of what our future might hold. Many of his stories have inspired motion pictures. The most famous is *2001: A Space Odyssey.*

Clarke has said that his curiosity about the future keeps him going. How would he like to be remembered? He suggests this simple epitaph: "He never grew up; but he never stopped growing."

THE STORY BEHIND THE STORY
"The Secret" is set in a human colony on the moon. Clarke believes that with efficient research, human colonies in space will someday be an affordable reality. He says, "There's no reason why, in the next century, it should cost more to go to the Moon than it costs to fly around the world today."

◆ LITERATURE AND YOUR LIFE
CONNECT YOUR EXPERIENCE
You might keep a personal diary or mark a letter "confidential." Most people feel the need to keep some things private. Yet many journalists believe that all information should be accessible to the public. In "The Secret," a character struggles over whether or not to publish an intriguing discovery.

THEMATIC FOCUS: Blazing Trails
What are the advantages of being the first person to discover something? What are possible disadvantages?

◆ Background for Understanding
SCIENCE
"The Secret" takes place in a colony on the moon. Although it may be hard to believe, the idea of living in a space colony is not as far-fetched as it might seem. In fact, for years, astronauts like the one in the photograph have conducted ongoing experiments to learn about living in space. For example, they evaluate how the human body adapts to extreme changes in atmosphere and gravity. Information collected in space is then analyzed on Earth; the results help scientists develop new strategies for survival in space.

◆ Build Vocabulary
WORD PART: *micro*
The word *microbes*, meaning "small form of life" or "tiny organism," contains the word parts *micro*, meaning "small," and *bio* (*be*), meaning "life."

WORD BANK
Which word from this list means "radiating or branching out from the center"? Check the Build Vocabulary box on page 125 to see if you chose correctly.

receding
competent
microbes
hemisphere
radial
heedless
implications
looming

Prentice Hall Literature Program Resources

REINFORCE / RETEACH / EXTEND

Selection Support Pages
Build Vocabulary: Word Part: *micro*, p. 55
Build Spelling Skills, p. 56
Build Grammar Skills: Action Verbs and Linking Verbs, p. 57
Reading Strategy: Ask Questions, p. 58
Literary Focus: Science Fiction, p. 59

Strategies for Diverse Student Needs, pp. 21–22

Beyond Literature Workplace Skills: Acting Responsibly, p. 11

Formal Assessment Selection Test, pp. 41–43, Assessment Resources Software

Alternative Assessment, p. 11

Resource Pro CD-ROM
"The Secret"—includes all resource material and customizable lesson plan

Listening to Literature Audiocassettes
"The Secret"

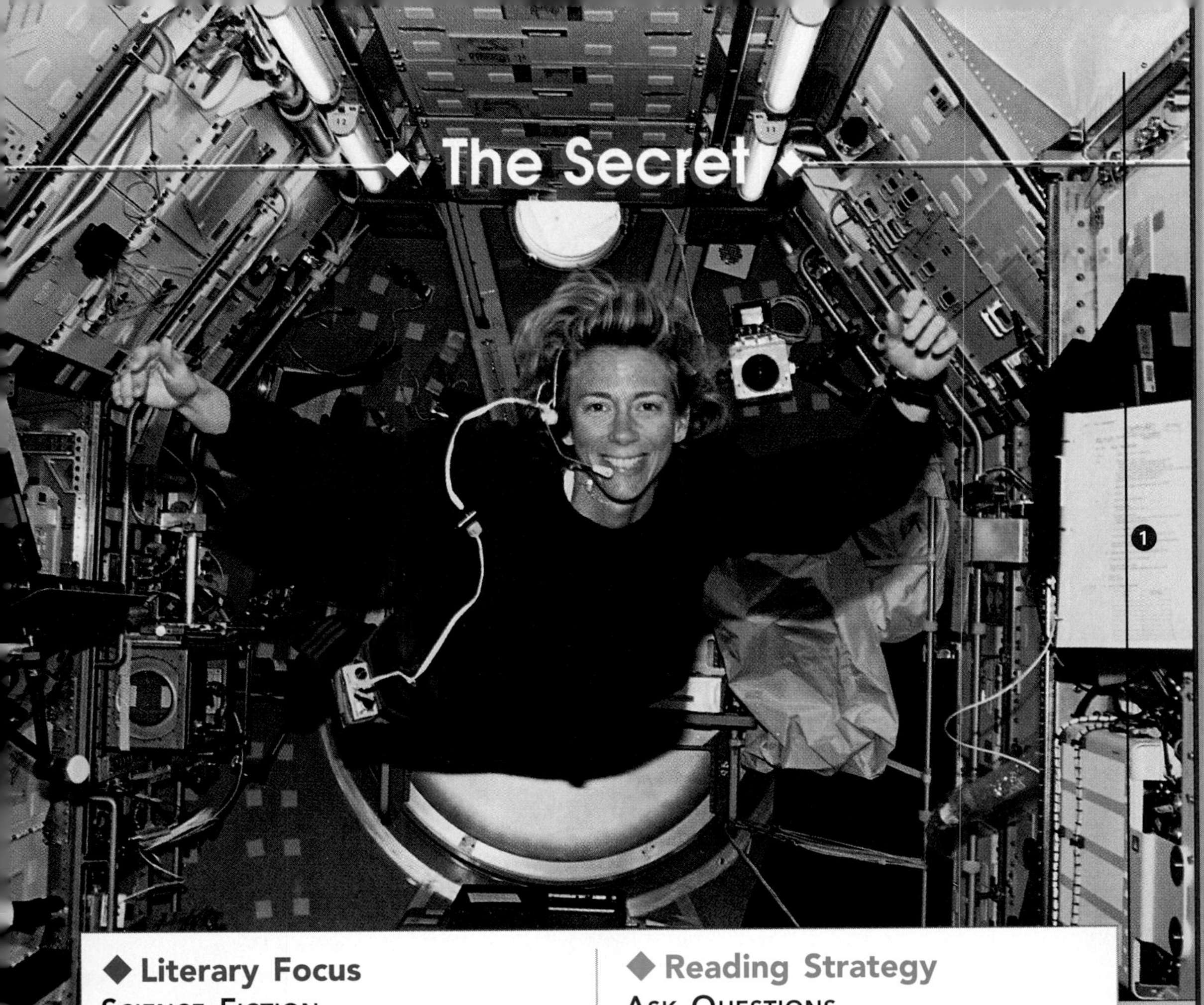

◆ The Secret ◆

① Support

◆ Literary Focus
SCIENCE FICTION

Science fiction combines elements of fiction and fantasy with scientific fact. This type of writing is most effective when the writer creates a believable setting and characters, and balances new ideas with familiar details. Arthur C. Clarke has said that "the only way of discovering the limits of the possible is to venture a little way past them into the impossible." As you read "The Secret," think about which elements are "possible" and which approach the "impossible."

◆ Reading Strategy
ASK QUESTIONS

Most writers don't spell out everything for readers. It's up to you to **ask questions** about characters' actions, the meaning of events, and why certain details are included. For example, consider this opening sentence:

> Henry Cooper had been on the Moon for almost two weeks before he discovered that something was wrong.

After reading this, you might ask: "Who's Henry Cooper? What's he doing on the moon?" As you read, record questions and answers in a chart like this one.

Questions	Answers
Who is Henry Cooper? Why is he on the moon?	He's a journalist.

Guide for Reading ◆ 121

One-Minute Insight
In this futuristic story, journalist Henry Cooper visits a space colony on the Moon. Sensing that people, particularly the Medical Research staff, have started trying to hide things from him, he presses the Inspector General for information. Henry learns that confidential medical research estimates life expectancy for humans living on the Moon at over 200 years. Since the Moon can only sustain 100,000 people, Henry must decide how—or whether—to reveal the startling information to the six billion people on an overpopulated Earth.

Team Teaching Strategy

You may want to coordinate with a science teacher to come up with ideas for extending instruction. For example, the science teacher might focus on the scientific facts of life on the moon and the likely effects of actual lunar conditions on human beings and other earthly life forms.

Customize for
English Language Learners

Science fiction may use technical terms and science jargon that is unfamiliar to students acquiring English. You may wish to prepare a glossary with terms such as *air lock, interplanetary, lunar,* and *gravity.*

Customize for
Interpersonal Learners

Have students find evidence in the story that can help them imagine what life might be like for a lunar colonist. Challenge them to answer questions such as: What aspects make life there inviting? What is unappealing? What problems are likely to arise? What solutions are possible—or unavailable?

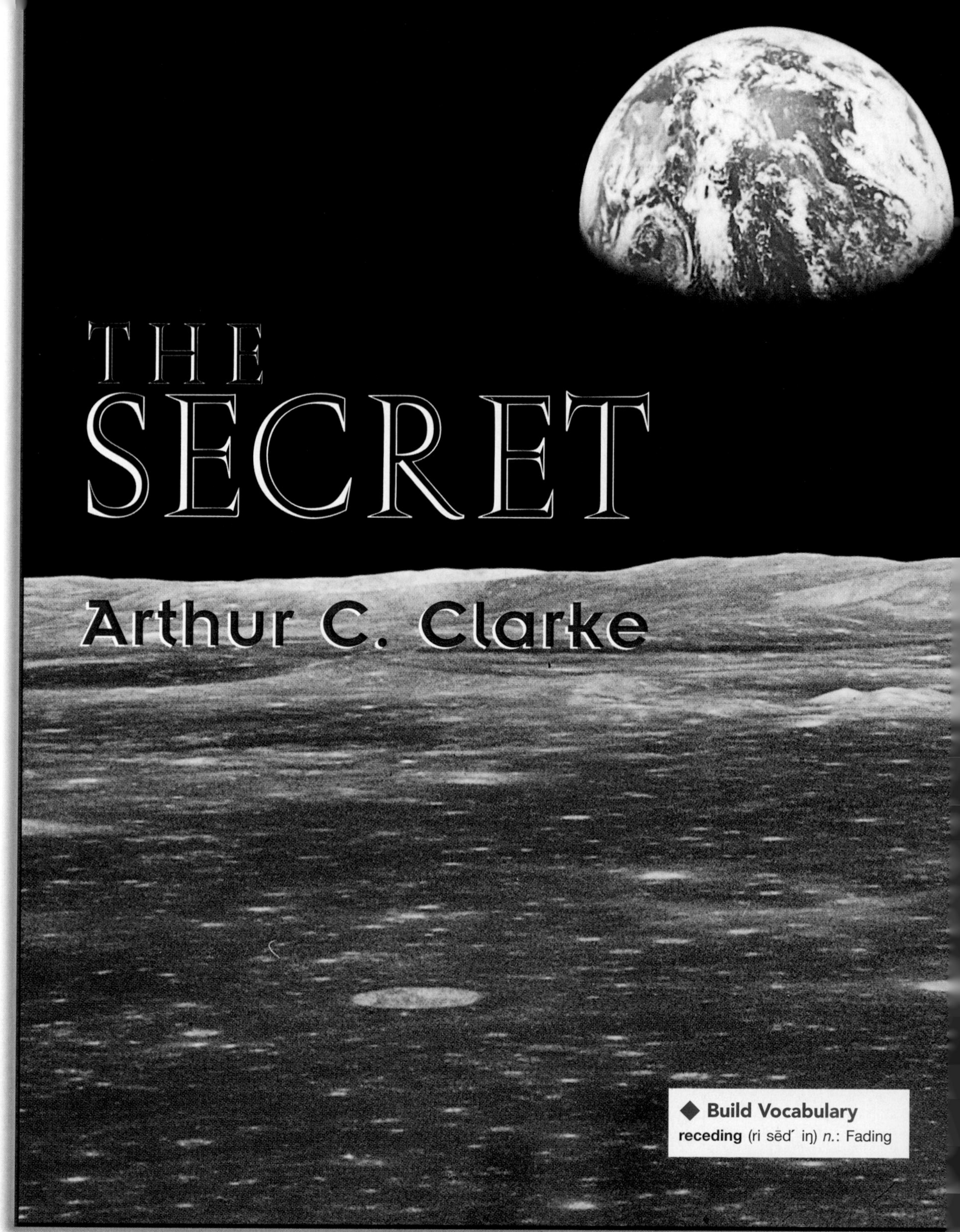

THE SECRET

Arthur C. Clarke

◆ **Build Vocabulary**
receding (ri sēd´ iŋ) *n.*: Fading

Block Scheduling Strategies

Consider these suggestions to take advantage of extended class time:

• Prepare students for reading science fiction by discussing the Background for Understanding, p. 120, and Literary Focus, p. 121, features.

• To help students prepare for the Writing Mini-Lesson, use the News Article and Critical Response activities in the Idea Bank on p. 129.

• Have students read the selection independently, then work in peer groups to discuss and answer the Guide for Responding questions on p. 126.

• Use the Connections to Today's World selection, p. 127, to present another example of science fiction, this time written in the form of a song lyric. Play a recording of the song, if possible.

Henry Cooper had been on the Moon for almost two weeks before he discovered that something was wrong. At first it was only an ill-defined suspicion, the sort of hunch that a hard-headed science reporter would not take too seriously. He had come here, after all, at the United Nations Space Administration's own request. UNSA had always been hot on public relations—especially just before budget time, when an overcrowded world was screaming for more roads and schools and sea farms, and complaining about the billions being poured into space.

So here he was, doing the lunar circuit for the second time, and beaming back two thousand words of copy a day. Although the novelty had worn off, there still remained the wonder and mystery of a world as big as Africa, thoroughly mapped, yet almost completely unexplored. A stone's throw away from the pressure domes, the labs, the spaceports, was a yawning emptiness that would challenge humankind for centuries to come.

Some parts of the Moon were almost too familiar, of course. Who had not seen that dusty scar on the Mare Imbrium, with its gleaming metal pylon and the plaque that announced in the three official languages of Earth:

ON THIS SPOT
AT 2001 UT
13 SEPTEMBER 1959
THE FIRST MAN-MADE OBJECT
REACHED ANOTHER WORLD

Cooper had visited the grave of Lunik II—and the more famous tomb of the men who had come after it. But these things belonged to the past; already, like Columbus and the Wright brothers,[1] they were receding into history. What concerned him now was the future.

When he had landed at Archimedes Spaceport, the Chief Administrator had been obviously glad to see him, and had shown a personal interest in his tour. Transportation, accommodation, and official guide were all

arranged. He could go anywhere he liked, ask any questions he pleased. UNSA trusted him, for his stories had always been accurate, his attitudes friendly. Yet the tour had gone sour; he did not know why, but he was going to find out.

He reached for the phone and said: "Operator? . . . Please get me the Police Department. I want to speak to the Inspector General."

Presumably Chandra Coomaraswamy possessed a uniform, but Cooper had never seen him wearing it. They met, as arranged, at the entrance to the little park that was Plato City's chief pride and joy. At this time in the morning of the artificial twenty-four-hour "day" it was almost deserted, and they could talk without interruption.

As they walked along the narrow gravel paths, they chatted about old times, the friends they had known at college together, the latest developments in interplanetary politics. They had reached the middle of the park, under the exact center of the great blue-painted dome, when Cooper came to the point.

"You know everything that's happening on the Moon, Chandra," he said. "And you know that I'm here to do a series for UNSA—hope to make a book out of it when I get back to Earth. So why should people be trying to hide things from me?"

It was impossible to hurry Chandra. He always took his time to answer questions, and his few words escaped with difficulty around the stem of his hand-carved Bavarian[2] pipe.

"What people?" he asked at length.

"You've really no idea?"

The Inspector General shook his head.

"Not the faintest," he answered; and Cooper knew that he was telling the truth. Chandra might be silent, but he would not lie.

"I was afraid you'd say that. Well, if you don't know any more than I do, here's the only clue I have—and it frightens me. Medical Research is trying to keep me at arm's length."

"Hmmm," replied Chandra, taking his pipe from his mouth and looking at it thoughtfully.

---

1. **Columbus . . . Wright brothers:** Christopher Columbus (16th c. Italian navigator) and Orville and Wilbur Wright (19th c. American inventors of the airplane) were great explorers, the former of land and the latter of air.

2. **Bavarian** (bə ver´ ē ən) adj.: Of or related to Bavaria, a region in Germany.

The Secret ◆ 123

Beyond the Classroom

Career Connection

Journalist In this story, Henry Cooper is a journalist who specializes in science reporting. Journalism is a broad field with practitioners who work in print, radio, and television. They write news stories, opinion columns, analytical pieces, and critical essays based on their findings. Journalists sometimes specialize in certain areas, such as science reporting, politics, medicine, law, sports, or environmental issues, to name a few.

Have students brainstorm for a list of qualities that any good journalist should possess. Examples include strong writing skills, an ability to interview people and encourage them to share information, accurate information-gathering skills, and a sense of how to interpret what people say—or don't say—to determine the many sides of an issue. You might have students support their ideas by naming famous journalists who exemplify these traits.

◆ Reading Strategy

❶ Ask Questions *Possible answers: They may not trust Cooper; they may have discovered something so incredible or radical that they do not want to reveal it yet; they fear that their discovery may be stolen by others.*

◆ Reading Strategy

❷ Ask Questions Have students ask what this revelation tells them about Chandra and his role in the intrigue. *Students may say that Chandra knows more than he lets on, but has not been forced to face it until Henry starts snooping around.*

◆ Literary Focus

❸ Science Fiction Ask students what Chandra means when he predicts that the "morning shower's due in five minutes." Help them to interpret this as an example of a detail of the planned environment of the Moon station. It doesn't rain on the Moon, and even if it did, it would probably be as difficult to predict it there as it is on Earth. Chandra knows that a daily rain shower is part of the artificial environment of Plato City.

◆ Critical Thinking

❹ Infer Challenge students to explain what the author is trying to say here about the human need to explore. *Students may say that Clarke suggests that people are drawn to mysteries and feel compelled to try to explain them, even if the journey brings them to unlikely or inhospitable places.*

◆ Reading Strategy

❺ Ask Questions This passage will generate many questions. Some students may wonder: What would be found in an even more remote place on an already remote outpost? Why are there such tight transportation and security issues? What kinds of labs exist there? What can be so secret? Encourage students to jot down questions to answer as they read on.

"Is that all you have to say?"

"You haven't given me much to work on. Remember, I'm only a cop; I lack your vivid journalistic imagination."

"All I can tell you is that the higher I get in Medical Research, the colder the atmosphere becomes. Last time I was here, everyone was very friendly, and gave me some fine stories. But now, I can't even meet the Director. He's always too busy, or on the other side of the Moon. Anyway, what sort of man is he?"

"Dr. Hastings? Prickly little character. Very competent, but not easy to work with."

"What could he be trying to hide?"

"Knowing you, I'm sure you have some interesting theories."

> **◆ Reading Strategy**
> Ask yourself: "What other reasons might Medical Research have for trying to avoid Cooper?"

"Oh, I thought of narcotics, and fraud, and political conspiracies—but they don't make sense, in these days. So what's left scares the heck out of me."

Chandra's eyebrows signaled a silent question mark.

"Interplanetary plague," said Cooper bluntly.

"I thought that was impossible."

"Yes—I've written articles myself proving that the life forms of other planets have such alien chemistries that they can't react with us, and that all our microbes and bugs took millions of years to adapt to our bodies. But I've always wondered if it was true. Suppose a ship has come back from Mars, say, with something *really* vicious—and the doctors can't cope with it?"

There was a long silence. Then Chandra said: "I'll start investigating. *I* don't like it, either, for here's an item you probably don't know. There were three nervous breakdowns in the Medical Division last month—and that's very, very unusual."

He glanced at his watch, then at the false sky, which seemed so distant, yet was only two hundred feet above their heads.

"We'd better get moving," he said. "The morning shower's due in five minutes."

The call came two weeks later in the middle of the night—the real lunar night. By Plato City time, it was Sunday morning.

"Henry? . . . Chandra here. Can you meet me in half an hour at air lock five? . . . Good. I'll see you."

This was it, Cooper knew. Air lock five meant they were going outside the dome. Chandra had found something.

The presence of the police driver restricted conversation as the tractor moved away from the city along the road roughly bulldozed across the ash and pumice. Low in the south, Earth was almost full, casting a brilliant blue-green light over the infernal landscape. However hard one tried, Cooper told himself, it was difficult to make the Moon appear glamorous. But nature guards her greatest secrets well; to such places men must come to find them.

The multiple domes of the city dropped below the sharply curved horizon. Presently, the tractor turned aside from the main road to follow a scarcely visible trail. Ten minutes later, Cooper saw a single glittering hemisphere ahead of them, standing on an isolated ridge of rock. Another vehicle, bearing a red cross, was parked beside the entrance. It seemed that they were not the only visitors.

Nor were they unexpected. As they drew up to the dome, the flexible tube of the air-lock coupling groped out toward them and snapped into place against their tractor's outer hull. There was a brief hissing as pressures equalized. Then Cooper followed Chandra into the building.

The air-lock operator led them along curving corridors and radial passageways toward the center of the dome. Sometimes they caught glimpses of laboratories, scientific instruments, computers—all perfectly ordinary, and all deserted on this Sunday morning. They must have reached the heart of the building, Cooper told himself, when their guide ushered them into a large circular chamber and shut the door softly behind them.

It was a small zoo. All around them were cages, tanks, jars containing a wide selection of the fauna and flora of Earth. Waiting at its center was a short, gray-haired man, looking very

Speaking and Listening Mini-Lesson

Radio Review

This mini-lesson supports the Speaking and Listening activity in the Idea Bank on p. 129.

Introduce Ask students whether they have ever heard a radio review of any form of entertainment: a film, a television show, a book, an album, a play, a concert, or an art show. Discuss the characteristics of any good review, and how these must be adapted for radio delivery. For instance, examples cannot be shown but must be described; tone of voice can suggest the reviewer's opinions and affect listeners' attitudes.

Develop Have students compose their radio reviews, then practice aloud with a peer, who can critique them for length, interest level, accuracy of detail, and overall effectiveness of delivery.

Apply Have students deliver the radio reviews "live" or by making tapes of them.

Assess Evaluate radio reviews in terms of delivery, accuracy of detail, ability to attract readers to "The Secret," and the effectiveness of any analytical information students include. Or use the Peer Assessment: Dramatic Performance form, p. 116, in **Alternative Assessment**.

worried, and very unhappy.

"Dr. Hastings," said Coomaraswamy, "meet Mr. Cooper." The Inspector General turned to his companion and added, "I've convinced the Doctor that there's only one way to keep you quiet—and that's to tell you everything."

"Frankly," said Hastings, "I'm not sure if I care anymore." His voice was unsteady, barely under control, and Cooper thought, Hello! There's another breakdown on the way.

The scientist wasted no time on such formalities as shaking hands. He walked to one of the cages, took out a small bundle of fur, and held it toward Cooper.

"Do you know what this is?" he asked abruptly.

"Of course. A hamster—the commonest lab animal."

"Yes," said Hastings. "A perfectly ordinary golden hamster. Except that this one is five years old—like all the others in this cage."

"Well? What's odd about that?"

"Oh, nothing, nothing at all . . . except for the fact that hamsters live for only two years. And we have some here that are getting on for ten."

For a moment no one spoke; but the room was not silent. It was full of rustlings and slitherings and scratchings, of faint whimpers and tiny animal cries. Then Cooper whispered, "My God—you've found a way of prolonging life!"

"No," retorted Hastings. "We've not found it. The Moon has given it to us . . . as we might have expected, if we'd looked in front of our noses." He seemed to have gained control over his emotions—as if he was once more the pure scientist, fascinated by a discovery for its own sake and <u>heedless</u> of its <u>implications</u>.

"On Earth," he said, "we spend our whole lives fighting gravity. It wears down our muscles, pulls our stomachs out of shape. In seventy years, how many tons of blood does the heart lift through how many miles? And all that work, all that strain is reduced to a sixth here on the Moon, where a one-hundred-and-eighty-pound human weighs only thirty pounds?"

"I see," said Cooper slowly.

> ◆ **Literary Focus**
> How does Clarke use facts to make his science-fiction story believable?

> ◆ **Build Vocabulary**
> **competent** (käm´ pə tənt) *adj.*: Well qualified and capable
>
> **microbes** (mī´ krōbes´) *n.*: Extremely small organisms
>
> **hemisphere** (hem´ i sfir´) *n.*: Half of a sphere; dome
>
> **radial** (rā´ dē əl) *adj.*: Branching out in all directions from a common center
>
> **heedless** (hēd´ lis) *adj.*: Unmindfully careless
>
> **implications** (im´ pli kā´ shəns) *n.*: Possible conclusions

The Secret ◆ 125

◆**Reading Strategy**

❻ **Ask Questions** In this passage, Chandra tells Dr. Hastings to stop avoiding Cooper, and share with him the awesome secret. Ask students how, since Cooper is a journalist, this tactic could ensure continued privacy. *Students may say that, as a journalist, Cooper will weigh the public's right to know with the other issues that surround this secret. Chandra trusts Cooper to have good enough judgment to grasp the seriousness of the issue, whatever it is.*

◆**Literary Focus**

❼ **Science Fiction** Point out the realistic details of the scientific laboratory that are included here. How does this set the stage for something fantastic to happen in the story? *Students should realize that the factual aspects of the setting make the fantastic events more believable.*

◆**Reading Strategy**

❽ **Ask Questions** Guide students to ask themselves whether it makes sense to them that reduced gravitational pull would lead to increased life span. *Whether or not they have enough scientific knowledge to support or refute the idea, they can read on to find out how the author explains this surprising idea.*

◆**Literary Focus**

❾ **Science Fiction** *Students may cite Clarke's use of some known effects of gravity to suggest a radical possibility. He plays with humanity's questions about immortality by hinting that an alternative might actually exist.*

Customize for
Visual/Spatial Learners
Have students review Clarke's description of the route that Cooper and Chandra take from air lock five of the city to reach the dome where the Doctor is waiting for them. Using the visual image that Clarke creates, suggest that students map or draw this fictional colony on the moon. Like Clarke, they may choose to use science-fiction elements to create a visual representation, or instead they may want to rely on realistic visual elements to represent the setting of this futuristic story.

Cultural Connection

Philosophy/Ethics Ethics is the study of what is morally good and bad or right and wrong. Though considered a branch or philosophy, ethics is closely associated with other fields, such as sociology and economics. (It is also called *moral philosophy*.) Science fiction may present ethical issues that the present-day world has not yet faced, but that might arise in the future.

In "The Secret," a journalist faces an ethical question: Does he reveal or withhold highly sensitive, very important information? Variations of this ethical question occur daily, and may have presented themselves to students. For instance, if you see a friend stealing, do you betray the friendship to reveal the truth? If you withhold the knowledge, are you morally guilty, too?

Have students form groups to consider the ethics of real-life questions like these. Or broaden the discussion to consider the ethics of secret agencies, of keeping state secrets, of securing classified documents, or of confidentiality in general. Conclude the discussion by taking suggestions about ethical principles students can live by.

❶ Ask students whether they would choose to trade an ordinary life span on Earth for one three times longer in a Moon colony.

Reinforce and Extend

Answers
♦ **LITERATURE AND YOUR LIFE**

Reader's Response Some may think that Cooper's job is to report news, despite the consequences. Others may believe that the impact of this news would cause such chaos on Earth that he should withhold it, at least for now.

Thematic Focus Moon residents will have to plan for extended lives, considering how to use their time.

✓ Check Your Comprehension

1. He is there to report on the lunar colony for UNSA.
2. His sources, who previously spoke with him freely, now seem to avoid him and may be hiding something.
3. He presses his friend for help, and then visits the remote laboratories on a Sunday, to speak with Dr. Hastings about his research.
4. He learns that lab hamsters living on the moon have lived extended lives—8 years more than their typical 2-year life span.

♦ Critical Thinking

1. Since a journalist's job is to investigate and then reveal what he learns, his profession will force him to face a difficult decision.
2. He knows that the startling news will create havoc, that the moon can't support all the people who will want to live longer.
3. It's good news to know how to extend life, but it's bad news that there's no simple way to inform the public and make extended life available to anyone who wants it.
4. He must decide whether to defer to the scientist's concerns or to stand by his journalistic obligations.
5. Possible answers: Good reporters investigate the story, but must consider the positive and negative effects of their stories. Cooper possesses the skills, but we never learn about his judgment.
6. Students should use story details to support their opinions.

"Ten years for a hamster—and how long for a man?"

"It's not a simple law," answered Hastings. "It varies with the sex and the species. Even a month ago, we weren't certain. But now we're quite sure of this: on the Moon, the span of human life will be at least two hundred years."

"And you've been trying to keep this a secret!"

"You fool! Don't you understand?"

"Take it easy, Doctor—take it easy," said Chandra softly.

With an obvious effort of will, Hastings got control of himself again. He began to speak with such icy calm that his words sank like freezing raindrops into Cooper's mind.

"Think of them up there," he said, pointing to the roof, to the invisible Earth, whose looming presence no one on the Moon could forget. "Six billion of them, packing all the continents to the edges—and now crowding over into the sea beds. And here—" he pointed to the ground—

"only a hundred thousand of *us*, on an almost empty world. But a world where we need miracles of technology and engineering merely to exist, where a man with an IQ of only a hundred and fifty can't even get a job.

"And now we find that we can live for two hundred years. Imagine how they're going to react to that news! This is your problem now, Mister Journalist; you've asked for it, and you've got it. Tell me this, please—I'd really be interested to know—*just how are you going to break it to them?*"

He waited, and waited. Cooper opened his mouth, then closed it again, unable to think of anything to say.

In the far corner of the room, a baby monkey started to cry.

♦ Build Vocabulary

looming (lōōm´ iŋ) *adj.*: Ominous and awe-inspiring

Guide for Responding

♦ LITERATURE AND YOUR LIFE

Reader's Response Do you think Cooper should write about the secret or hide this information from people on Earth? Why?

Thematic Focus How will this situation affect the new residents of the moon?

Journal Writing Jot down in your journal notes that Cooper may have taken while investigating "the secret."

✓ Check Your Comprehension

1. Why is Cooper on the moon?
2. What makes Cooper suspect that something is wrong?
3. How does Cooper investigate his hunch?
4. What secret does Cooper discover when he meets with Dr. Hastings?

♦ Critical Thinking

INTERPRET
1. How is Cooper's profession important to the story? **[Connect]**
2. Why is Dr. Hastings discouraged? **[Infer]**
3. How can the secret be interpreted as both good news and bad news? **[Interpret]**
4. What hard question does Cooper face once he learns the secret? **[Speculate]**

EVALUATE
5. What makes a good reporter? Judging from details in the story, do you think that Cooper is a good reporter? Explain. **[Assess]**

APPLY
6. Do you think this story supports or discourages the idea of human colonies in space? Explain. **[Generalize]**

126 ♦ *Meeting Challenges*

Beyond the Selection

FURTHER READING
Other Works by Arthur C. Clarke
The Other Side of the Sky
Childhood's End
"Crime on Mars"

Other Science Fiction Works
I, Robot, Isaac Asimov
The Martian Chronicles, Ray Bradbury
This Star Shall Abide, Sylvia Louise Engdahl

INTERNET
We suggest the following sites on the Internet (all Web sites are subject to change).

For more on Arthur C. Clarke and links to Internet resources about the film *2001: A Space Odyssey:*
http://www.lsi.usp.br/~rbianchi/clarke/

For an exclusive interview with Clarke just before his 80th birthday:
http://www.news.lk/Arthur.html

We *strongly recommend* that you preview the sites before you send students to them.

CONNECTIONS TO TODAY'S WORLD

For more than a century, ideas about space travel have inspired writers of novels, scripts, poems, and songs. Arthur C. Clarke writes often about everyday life set on other planets or on our moon. In this song, rock star David Bowie explores another aspect of space travel—its very real dangers.

1. What message does the song convey?
2. In what ways does Major Tom blaze a trail?
3. Would you describe this song as science fiction or realistic? Explain.

SPACE ODDITY
David Bowie

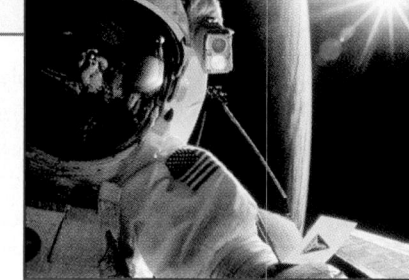

Ground Control to Major Tom,
Ground Control to Major Tom,
Take your protein pills and put
   your helmet on.
Ten
5 Ground Control to Major Tom
   Nine, Eight, Seven
Commencing countdown, engines
   on *Six, Five, Four*
Check ignition and may God's love
   be with you *Three, Two, One*
Liftoff

This is Ground Control to Major Tom,
10 You've really made the grade
And the papers want to know whose
   shirts you wear
Now it's time to leave the capsule if
   you dare.

"This is Major Tom to Ground Control
I'm stepping through the door
15 And I'm floating in a most peculiar
   way
And the stars look very different
   today.

For here
Am I sitting in a tin can
Far above the world,
20 Planet Earth is blue
And there's nothing I can do.

Though I'm past one hundred
   thousand miles,
I'm feeling very still,
And I think my spaceship knows
   which way to go.
25 Tell my wife I love her very much
   she knows."

Ground Control to Major Tom
Your circuit's dead, there's
   something wrong.
Can you hear me, Major Tom?
Can you hear me, Major Tom?
30 Can you hear me, Major Tom?
Can you . . .

"Here I am floating round my tin can,
Far above the Moon,
Planet Earth is blue
35 And there's nothing I can do."

SPACE ODDITY, Words and Music by David Bowie. © Copyright 1969 (Renewed) Onward Music Ltd., London, England. TRO-Essex Music International, Inc., New York, New York controls all publication rights for the U.S.A. and Canada. Used by permission.

More About the Author
Born **David Robert Jones** in London in 1947, musician, actor, and pop star David Bowie released his song "Space Oddity" in the United Kingdom in 1969. The release coincided with the American lunar expedition that resulted in Neil Armstrong's first moonwalk, but it wasn't until 1975 that "Space Oddity" became an American hit. For more on David Bowie, students can go to **http://www.bowieart.com**
   We *strongly recommend* that you preview this site before you send students to it.

Develop Understanding

One-Minute Insight
The lyrics of this moody song tell of a pioneering astronaut who finds his trip into space to be so hypnotic and compelling that he decides to stay aloft rather than return to Earth.

Clarification
❷ Help students recognize the pun that links this song's title to the Arthur C. Clarke story adapted for film—*2001: A Space Odyssey.*

Thematic Focus
❸ **Blazing Trails** This song lyric is a work of creative writing, but it addresses a truth about any trail blazing: Pioneering is dangerous. Discuss the dangers the song addresses, which include a mental breakdown as well as a physical one.

Comprehension Check ☑
❹ Ask students to summarize what happens to Major Tom. *He makes a space walk, which moves him so deeply that he has no interest in returning to Earth. When Ground Control loses connection to Major Tom's craft, he's really lost in space.*

Reinforce and Extend
Answers
1. The song conveys the message that space travel is risky, heroic, hypnotic, and ultimately dangerous.
2. He is the first to do a space walk; he shares observations of Earth from space in ways that other men have not yet done.
3. The song has elements of realism (the countdown, Ground Control, helmet, capsule, no gravity) along with a feeling of mystery and unreality. Major Tom is resigned to his fate and perhaps embraces it.

Answers

◆ Reading Strategy

1. The title suggests that the secret may remain unknown for the good of Earth. Sample titles: The Journalist's Decision; Lunacy on the Moon; Life Span.
2. Chandra believes that Cooper is smart enough to realize the strategic value of keeping this explosive information quiet.
3. Students may say that Dr. Hastings had little choice, or that he wanted to get the reaction of someone outside the secret world of the moon lab.

◆ Build Vocabulary

Using the Word Part *micro-*

1. "scopic" relates to view; a microscopic gives a view of something small
2. "wave" refers to a scientific cycle of movement; a microwave is a very short wave
3. "film" is light-sensitive material used to take pictures; microfilm gives reduced-size images

Spelling Strategy

1. preceding
2. acceding
3. conceding

Using the Word Bank

1. c
2. c
3. a
4. a
5. c
6. c
7. b
8. b

◆ Literary Focus

1. Possible examples: space travel; science reporting; billions of dollars spent of space research; Mare Imbrium; Columbus and the Wright brothers; medical research; political conspiracies; lunar night; ash and pumice; blue-green Earth; isolated ridge of rock; computers; gravity; lab animals; overcrowding on Earth
2. Answers include: colonization of the Moon; regular travel between Earth and the lunar colonies; research into the relationship between gravity and life span.
3. Students may say that science fiction is most convincing when it presents "regular" characters readers can identify with.

Guide for Responding (continued)

◆ Reading Strategy

ASK QUESTIONS

After reading a story, think about the **questions** you asked and answered while reading. If any questions remain unanswered, piece together details from the story to find answers.

1. Why do you think Clarke chose to title his story "The Secret"? What other titles might you suggest for this story?
2. Why does Chandra help Cooper?
3. Why do you think Dr. Hastings revealed the secret to Cooper?

◆ Build Vocabulary

USING THE WORD PART *micro*

Many words combine *micro* with various word parts. Determine the meanings of the following words by analyzing the word parts.

1. microscopic   2. microwave   3. microfilm

SPELLING STRATEGY

When adding *-ing* to words that end with *-cede*, drop the e and then add the ending.

recede + -ing = receding

On your paper, add *-ing* to the following words.

1. precede   2. accede   3. concede

USING THE WORD BANK

In your notebook, write the letter of the word or phrase that is most nearly the same in meaning as the Word Bank word.

1. competent: (a) simple, (b) attractive, (c) able
2. receding: (a) tiring, (b) surging, (c) decreasing
3. heedless: (a) unmindful, (b) cautious, (c) sly
4. implications: (a) possible effects, (b) facts, (c) styles
5. hemisphere: (a) pyramid, (b) cube, (c) dome
6. radial: (a) from outside to inside, (b) from outer space, (c) from a central point
7. microbes: (a) scientists, (b) tiny forms of life, (c) substances
8. looming: (a) glowing, (b) appearing, (c) building

◆ Literary Focus

SCIENCE FICTION

"The Secret" is a **science-fiction** story set in the distant future. Like many science-fiction stories, it combines scientific fact with familiar details to make this future believable.

1. List elements in the story that are based on scientific fact.
2. What changes does Clarke suggest will happen between the present and the time of the story?
3. Do you think the story would be as effective if all the characters were from other planets? Explain.

◆ Build Grammar Skills

ACTION VERBS AND LINKING VERBS

An **action verb** expresses action:

> He *walked* to one of the cages.
> He *waited*, and *waited*.

A **linking verb** expresses a state of being. Linking verbs include forms of the verb *to be* as well as *seem, appear, look, feel, become, sound, stay, remain,* and *grow*. To determine whether a verb is an action or a linking verb, replace it with a form of *to be*. If the sentence still makes sense, it is a linking verb.

> I thought that *was* impossible.

Practice Copy the following sentences. Underline each verb. Above each verb, write *AV* if it is an action verb and *LV* if it is a linking verb.

1. The space colony orbits Mars.
2. Last year was the settlement's first anniversary.
3. Radiation shields protected the inhabitants.
4. Life became routine for the colonists.
5. They remain optimistic about their future.

Writing Application Follow the directions for each item.

1. Use two action verbs in a sentence about a space colony.
2. Use a linking verb in a sentence about a planet.
3. Use an action verb to describe an action performed by Cooper.

◆ Build Grammar Skills

Practice

1. orbits: AV;   2. was: LV;   3. protected: AV;
4. became: LV;   5. remain: LV

Writing Application

Possible responses:

1. On a space colony, scientists study life forms and report back to Earth.
2. Mercury is closest to the sun.
3. Cooper pressed for details.

✎ Writer's Solution

For more instruction and practice, use the lesson in the *Writer's Solution Language Lab CD-ROM* on Using Verbs, and the practice pages on Using Verbs, pp. 70–76 in the *Writer's Solution Grammar Practice Book*.

Build Your Portfolio

 ## Idea Bank

Writing

1. **Advertisement** Create an advertisement to attract new colonists to the moon settlement. Use information from the story to describe the colony.

2. **News Article** Imagine that you are Cooper. Write an article informing people on Earth about the discovery at the moon colony.

3. **Critical Response** Write a response to the story in which you examine how effectively Clarke has developed the story's characters and setting.

Speaking and Listening

4. **Telephone Call** Imagine that Cooper calls a friend on Earth using a satellite phone. Role-play the conversation between the two characters. Will Cooper reveal the secret? **[Performing Arts Link]**

5. **Radio Review** Prepare a brief radio review of "The Secret." Provide enough information to interest listeners in the story, but don't give away too much. **[Media Link]**

Projects

6. **Space Settlement [Group Activity]** With a small group, design your own space settlement. Present your drawings, ideas, and plans to the class. You may want to visit this Web site to get information and ideas: http://science.nas.nasa.gov/Services/Education/SpaceSettlement/index.html. **[Science Link]**

7. **Comic Book** Work with a team to create a comic book based on "The Secret." Each team member should have a specific job, such as artist, author, or colorist. First, work together to outline your ideas. Decide how many pages your comic will contain and how many frames will appear on each page. Display the finished product in the classroom. **[Art Link]**

 ## Writing Mini-Lesson

Story Continuation

What might happen after "the secret" is revealed? What if "the secret" is never revealed? Write a continuation of the story. In your story, include science-fiction elements of scientific fact and fantasy.

Writing Skills Focus: Sequence of Events

Stories contain a sequence of events, the order in which things happen. In this passage from "The Secret," transitions make the sequence of events clear.

Model From the Story
Presently, the tractor turned aside from the main road to follow a scarcely visible trail. *Ten minutes later,* Cooper saw a single glittering hemisphere ahead of them. . . .

Prewriting Reread the story, and decide what will happen next. Use a story chart like the one below to organize your ideas.

Characters:
Setting:
Events:
Outcome:

Drafting Use your story chart to describe what happens after "The Secret" ends. Keep the original story nearby, and use it to help you with characters and details. Create a sequence of events, and use transitions to show the order in which things happen.

Revising Will readers be able to follow your new ending? Make sure you have used transitions to make the sequence of events clear. Look for places where the addition of science-fiction details will make the futuristic setting more vivid.

> ◆ **Grammar Application**
> Replace some linking verbs with action verbs to make your story more dramatic.

The Secret ◆ 129

 ## Idea Bank

Following are suggestions for matching the Idea Bank topics with your students' performance levels and learning modalities:

Customize for
Performance Levels
Less Advanced Students: 1, 4, 7
Average Students: 2 4, 5, 6, 7
More Advanced Students: 3, 5

Customize for
Learning Modalities
Verbal/Linguistic: 1, 2, 3, 4, 5, 7
Visual/Spatial: 1, 6, 7
Bodily/Kinesthetic: 4
Logical/Mathematical: 6
Interpersonal: 4, 6, 7
Intrapersonal: 1, 2, 3, 5

Writing Mini-Lesson

Refer students to the Writing Handbook in the back of the book for instructions on the writing process and for further information on using transitional words to indicate sequence of events.

Writing Lab CD-ROM
Have students complete the tutorial on Description. Follow these steps:
1. Have students use the Topic Web to narrow the focus of the story continuation.
2. Have students draft on computer.
3. Refer students to the Descriptive Word Bin to add more precise language to their writing.
Allow about 70 minutes of class time to complete these steps.

Writer's Solution Sourcebook
Have students use Chapter 2, "Description," pp. 32–69, for further support. The chapter includes in-depth instruction on Using Vivid and Precise Verbs, pp. 62–64.

✓ ASSESSMENT OPTIONS

Formal Assessment, Selection Test, pp. 41–43, and Assessment Resources Software. The selection test is designed so that it can be easily customized to the performance levels of your students.

Alternative Assessment, p. 11, includes options for less advanced students, more advanced students, verbal/linguistic learners, bodily/kinesthetic learners, and logical/mathematical learners.

PORTFOLIO ASSESSMENT
Use the following rubrics in the **Alternative Assessment** booklet to assess student writing:
Advertisement: Persuasion, p. 101
News Article: Summary, p. 94
Critical Response: Response to Literature, p. 106
Writing Mini-Lesson: Fictional Narrative, p. 91

OBJECTIVES

1. To read, comprehend, and interpret biographical narrative
2. To relate biographical narrative to personal experience
3. To set a purpose for reading
4. To understand third-person narrative
5. To build vocabulary in context and learn the wood root *-fug-*
6. To develop skill in using transitive and intransitive verbs
7. To write a spoken introduction
8. To respond to biographical narrative through writing, speaking and listening, and projects

SKILLS INSTRUCTION

Vocabulary:
Using the Word Roots: *-fug-*

Spelling:
Spelling the *s* Sound With *c*

Grammar:
Transitive and Intransitive Verbs

Reading Strategy:
Set a Purpose for Reading

Literary Focus:
Third-Person Narrative

Writing:
Give Specific Examples

Speaking and Listening:
Speech (Teacher Edition)

Critical Viewing:
Draw Conclusions; Infer

PORTFOLIO OPPORTUNITIES

Writing: Diary Entry; Biographical Description; Dramatization

Writing Mini-Lesson: Spoken Introduction

Speaking and Listening: Speech; Debate

Projects: Research Project; Fugitive Slave Laws

More About the Author

Ann Lane Petry encountered hostile treatment when she was 7 years old, although her family tried to shield her from racial prejudice. Her mother tried to counteract this bad experience by telling young Ann tales of her ancestors who fought racial oppression. These stories led to Petry's love of reading, writing, and narrative. When she turned her full attention to writing, she began to explore the links between gender, race, and class, and tried to depict the humanity and complexity of African Americans in a natural style.

Meet the Author:

Ann Petry (1912–1997)

Growing up in Old Saybrook, Connecticut, in a predominantly white community, Ann Petry sometimes encountered racism during her childhood. Her family, however, provided her with a caring and protective environment, and Petry became inspired by tales told to her by her mother of the strength and courage of her ancestors.

A Writer's Life Petry began writing while in high school, but she went on to get a degree as a pharmacist. Following her marriage to George D. Petry, a mystery writer, Petry herself refocused her attention and energy on writing. She became a reporter for the New York City newspapers *The Amsterdam News* and the *People's Voice* before she went on to write novels and short stories. Her first novel, *The Street*, was set in New York's Harlem.

THE STORY BEHIND THE STORY

Petry believed that it is impossible to understand the present without a knowledge of the past. Harriet Tubman, a historical hero, became a particular object of Petry's admiration. She pays tribute to Tubman in the biography *Harriet Tubman: Conductor of the Underground Railroad*, from which this selection is taken.

◆ LITERATURE AND YOUR LIFE

CONNECT YOUR EXPERIENCE

Climbing on the roof to get a Frisbee is taking a foolish risk, but is climbing on the roof to rescue a kitten as foolish? Think about risks you've taken and whether or not taking those risks was justified. In the following story, you'll read about Harriet Tubman, a woman who broke the law and risked her life—but for a worthy cause.

THEMATIC FOCUS: Blazing Trails

As you read the story, identify the trails that Tubman blazed and the risks she took.

◆ Background for Understanding

HISTORY

The narrative you're about to read tells the story of Harriet Tubman. She was one of the leading forces behind the Underground Railroad, a network of people who helped enslaved Africans escape from the South in the mid-1800's. Led by abolitionists—people against slavery—the Underground Railroad hid, fed, and sometimes supplied money to runaway slaves. Tubman made nineteen trips on this "railroad," during which she brought 300 people North to freedom.

◆ Build Vocabulary

WORD ROOTS: *-fug-*

In "Harriet Tubman: Guide to Freedom," you'll learn how Tubman guided *fugitives* to freedom. The word *fugitives,* meaning "persons running from the law," is built on the word root *-fug-*, meaning "to flee."

WORD BANK

Which word from the list means "rebellious" or "engaged in mutiny"? Check the Build Vocabulary box on page 137 to see if you chose correctly.

fugitives
incentive
disheveled
guttural
mutinous
cajoling
indomitable
fastidious

 Prentice Hall Literature Program Resources

REINFORCE / RETEACH / EXTEND

Selection Support Pages
Build Vocabulary: Word Roots: *-fug-*, p. 60
Build Spelling Skills, p. 61
Build Grammar Skills: Transitive and Intransitive Verbs, p. 62
Reading Strategy: Set a Purpose for Reading, p. 63
Literary Focus: Third-Person Narrative, p. 64

Strategies for Diverse Student Needs, p. 23

Beyond Literature Humanities Connection: Personal Courage, p. 12

Formal Assessment Selection Test, pp. 44–46, Assessment Resources Software

Alternative Assessment, p. 12

Resource Pro CD-R∅M
"Harriet Tubman: Guide to Freedom"

Art Transparencies Art Transparency 10, pp. 43–46

 **Listening to Literature Audiocassettes**
"Harriet Tubman: Guide to Freedom"

 Looking at Literature Videodisc/Videotape
"Harriet Tubman: Guide to Freedom"

Harriet Tubman: Guide to Freedom

Harriet Tubman Quilt made by the Negro History Club of Marin City and Sausalito, designed by Ben Irvin, Atlanta University Center, Robert W. Woodruff Library

◆ Literary Focus

THIRD-PERSON NARRATIVE

A narrative is a story. All narratives, both fiction and nonfiction, have narrators who describe the action. When the narrator is outside the story, the story is a **third-person narrative.** The narrator uses third-person pronouns to refer to the character. Although not part of the action, the narrator can provide details, dialogue, and even sometimes the characters' thoughts, as if he or she were there, to bring the characters' experiences to life.

◆ Reading Strategy

SET A PURPOSE FOR READING

Just as you have reasons for seeing a movie—to be entertained, to be scared, to learn something—you should have a reason, or **purpose,** for reading literature. For example, your purpose in reading this selection might be to learn about Harriet Tubman. To further define this purpose, you might ask *who, what, when, where, why,* and *how* questions like the ones in the chart below. You can then fill in answers to these questions as you read.

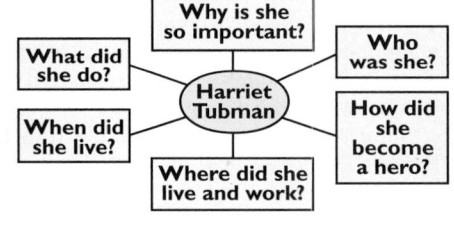

Guide for Reading ◆ 131

Interest Grabber Divide students into groups to discuss and explain these sayings: "out of the frying pan—into the fire," and "go from bad to worse." As groups share their ideas, challenge them to imagine actual situations that these sayings might represent. For example, a student might say that it's bad enough to have a big report due tomorrow, but then the computer crashes and corrupts the file. Guide students to the selection by telling them that they will read about slaves, who already suffered terrible conditions, but who made the decision to risk their lives to try for freedom.

◆ Build Grammar Skills

Transitive and Intransitive Verbs
If you wish to introduce the grammar concept for this selection before students read, refer to the instruction on p. 140.

Customize for
Less Proficient Readers
To help students follow the story, use the Series of Events Chain, p. 73, in **Writing and Language Transparencies.** Students can record major incidents and get a better picture of the risks and dangers the escaping slaves faced, even under Harriet Tubman's solid leadership.

Customize for
More Advanced Students
Have students keep a response journal as they read. Ask them to observe details that reveal Tubman's personality and show her to be the "Moses" of her people. Have them respond to the obstacles she and her band of fugitives face on their flight to freedom. Invite students to respond to Tubman's style, manner, courage, and beliefs.

Preparing for Standardized Tests

Writing The Writing Mini-Lesson on p. 141 focuses on giving specific examples. Many types of writing require specific examples. For instance, persuasive writing, which often is assessed on standardized tests requires specific examples in order to adequately support an argument.

Write the following sentences on the board:

Harriet Tubman was a great leader because she helped people.

Harriet Tubman was a great leader because she help enslaved Africans escape from the South in the mid-1800's.

Ask students to compare and contrast the two sentences, and guide them to see that the specific example of how Harriet Tubman helped people makes the statement about her stronger. Then, ask them to add specific examples to the following sentence:

Harriet Tubman traveled the Underground Railroad.

Invite students to share their sentences that include specific examples. For more practice with writing assessment, use p. 150 of *Writer's Solution Grammar Practice Book.*

Humanities: Art

Harriet Tubman Quilt, 1951, by the Negro History Club of Marin City and Sausalito, California

Discuss the visual symbols in this quilt. Ask students what they can infer about who Harriet Tubman was. *The owl may stand for wisdom; the star a compass; the people behind her show she's a leader; her bag suggests travel.*

One-Minute Insight

In this excerpt from a longer biography, readers follow Harriet Tubman from the fall of 1851 through the spring of 1852 as she leads eleven frightened, weary slaves on the dangerous journey from Maryland to freedom in Canada on the Underground Railroad. Tubman defies the Fugitive Slave laws to "conduct" her group because she believes that those laws are immoral, and she does all she can to help runaway slaves escape safely.

Team Teaching Strategy

You may want to coordinate with a social studies teacher to extend instruction about the Underground Railroad.

Clarification

1 According to the Bible, Moses was the leader who challenged the powerful Pharaoh, led the Israelites out of slavery in Egypt, and delivered them to the Promised Land.

◆ Reading Strategy

2 Set a Purpose for Reading
Students may say that this passage suggests some of the things Harriet Tubman did. She had to do a lot of planning in order to lead a group of fugitive slaves to safety.

Customize for
English Language Learners

Students not from the United States may be unfamiliar with details of slavery in this country. Provide some general background of the time by showing pertinent videos, art, or by telling stories. Also, help students prepare a glossary of terms related to slavery that they will find in the piece, such as *abolition, quarters, freedom, slave-hunters,* and so on.

Customize for
Logical/Mathematical Learners

Have students refer to maps of the eastern United States and Canada as they read to visualize the route Tubman and her group followed to freedom. Have them estimate the total distance the group traveled and the time their journey probably took.

Harriet Tubman Quilt made by the Negro History Club of Marin City and Sausalito (detail), Designed by Ben Irvin, Atlanta University Center, Robert W. Woodruff Library

HARRIET TUBMAN:
Guide to Freedom
ANN PETRY

Along the Eastern Shore of Maryland, in Dorchester County, in Caroline County, the masters kept hearing whispers about the man named Moses, who **1** was running off slaves. At first they did not believe in his existence. The stories about him were fantastic, unbelievable. Yet they watched for him. They offered rewards for his capture.

They never saw him. Now and then they heard whispered rumors to the effect that he was in the neighborhood. The woods were searched. The roads were watched. There was never anything to indicate his whereabouts. But a few days afterward, a goodly number of slaves would be gone from the plantation. Neither the master nor the overseer had heard or seen anything unusual in the quarter. Sometimes one or the other would vaguely remember having heard a whippoorwill call somewhere in the woods, close by, late at night. Though it was the wrong season for whippoorwills.

Sometimes the masters thought they had heard the cry of a hoot owl, repeated, and would remember having thought that the intervals between the low moaning cry were wrong, that it had been repeated four times in succession instead of three. There was

never anything more than that to suggest that all was not well in the quarter. Yet when morning came, they invariably discovered that a group of the finest slaves had taken to their heels.

Unfortunately, the discovery was almost always made on a Sunday. Thus a whole day was lost before the machinery of pursuit could be set in motion. The posters offering rewards for the <u>fugitives</u> could not be printed until Monday. The men who made a living hunting for runaway slaves were out of reach, off in the woods with their dogs and their guns, in pursuit of four-footed game, or they were in camp meetings[1] saying their prayers with their wives and families beside them.

Harriet Tubman could have told them that there was far more involved in this matter of running off slaves than signaling the would-be runaways by imitating the call of a whippoorwill, or a hoot owl, far more involved than a matter of waiting for a clear night when the North Star was visible.

◆ Reading Strategy
How do these details help you achieve your purpose? **2**

---

1. **camp meetings:** Religious meetings held outdoors or in a tent.

Block Scheduling Strategies

Consider these suggestions to take advantage of extended class time:

- Help students with the Reading Strategy: Set a Purpose for Reading by opening with the Guide for Reading features, pp. 130–131. Have students preview the illustrations that go with the piece to stimulate their curiosity.

- Have students read independently or in small groups and answer the Guide for Responding questions, pp. 139–140.

- To help students prepare to write spoken introductions in the Writing Mini-Lesson, use the Speaking and Listening Mini-Lesson on p. 141 of the Teacher Edition, and/or the Biographical Description or Debate activities in the Idea Bank, p. 141.

- Use the Build Grammar Skills: Transitive and Intransitive Verbs, p. 62, of **Selection Support,** to reinforce and extend instruction on p. 140.

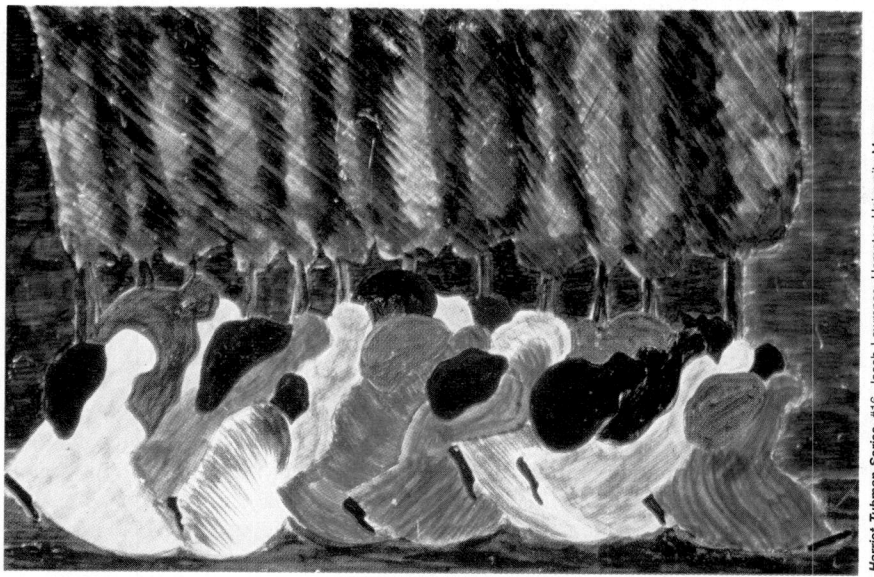

Harriet Tubman Series, #16, Jacob Lawrence, Hampton University Museum

In December 1851, when she started out with the band of fugitives that she planned to take to Canada, she had been in the vicinity of the plantation for days, planning the trip, carefully selecting the slaves that she would take with her.

She had announced her arrival in the quarter by singing the forbidden spiritual[2]—"Go down, Moses, 'way down to Egypt Land"—singing it softly outside the door of a slave cabin, late at night. The husky voice was beautiful even when it was barely more than a murmur borne on the wind.

Once she had made her presence known, word of her coming spread from cabin to cabin. The slaves whispered to each other, ear to mouth, mouth to ear, "Moses is here." "Moses has come." "Get ready. Moses is back again." The ones who had agreed to

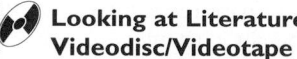
▲ **Critical Viewing** This painting depicts fugitive slaves fleeing north. Why might the artist have chosen not to include details showing faces and clothing? [Draw Conclusions] ④

go North with her put ashcake and salt herring in an old bandanna, hastily tied it into a bundle, and then waited patiently for the signal that meant it was time to start.

There were eleven in this party, including one of her brothers and his wife. It was the largest group that she had ever conducted, but she was determined that more and more slaves should know what freedom was like.

She had to take them all the way to Canada. The Fugitive Slave Law[3] was no longer a great many incomprehensible ⑤

---

3. **Fugitive Slave Law:** This part of the Compromise of 1850 held that escaped slaves, even if found in free states, could be returned to their masters. As a result, fugitives were not safe until they reached Canada.

◆ **Build Vocabulary**

fugitives (fyo͞o′ ji tivs′) *n.*: People fleeing

---

2. **forbidden spiritual:** In 1831, a slave named Nat Turner encouraged an unsuccessful slave uprising in Virginia by talking about the biblical story of the Israelites' escape from Egypt. Afterwards, the singing of certain spirituals was forbidden, for fear of encouraging more uprisings.

Harriet Tubman: Guide to Freedom ◆ 133

Humanities: Art

Harriet Tubman Series, #16, by Jacob Lawrence
Painter, professor, and illustrator-author Jacob Lawrence was born in 1917, the son of migrant laborers from the South, and grew up in Harlem during the Depression. He admired and regarded the story of Harriet Tubman as a perfect example of a person's ability to rise from any depth. Lawrence created the Tubman series of paintings, from 1939–1940, to honor her life as the most famous and successful organizer of the Underground Railroad.

1. What part of the story does this painting best represent? *It shows the difficulties of traveling at night.*
2. In what ways does the artist use the element of repetition? *Lawrence repeats the shapes of trees, bags, and how the people stand; and he reuses a few colors.*
3. What message does repetition convey about the flight to freedom? *The running seems to never end; safety is rare; they had to keep moving at a steady pace; the routines of the long journey were the same for weeks.*

133

◆ Literary Focus

① Third-Person Narrative In this passage, what qualities does the author reveal about Tubman? *She is brave; she feels responsible for the slaves in her care; she knows how important it is to keep up their spirits and hopes.*

◆ Literary Focus

② Third-Person Narrative *The narrator reveals that Tubman depends on her past experiences to keep on, although she senses fear.*

◆ Build Grammar Skills

③ Transitive and Intransitive Verbs The distinction between a transitive verb and an intransitive verb is whether the verb expresses an action directed toward a person or thing (has a direct object and sometimes an indirect object as well). Here, the verb *turned* is intransitive because it conveys no action to a receiver; *had promised* has the direct objects *food, rest* and *warmth* and is transitive. Have students find other examples of transitive and intransitive verbs as they read.

◆ Literary Focus

④ Third-Person Narrative Guide students to recognize that these details, which provide readers with Tubman's feelings and thoughts, are subjective. In third-person narrative, an all-knowing narrator may express subjective details in an effort to give a broader picture of the subject.

◆ Critical Thinking

⑤ Infer Ask students what challenge Harriet Tubman faces in this passage. *She must not let her group lose hope, and must urge them on, though she knows that they are hungry, tired, and frightened; so is she, but she can't let her personal feelings show.*

◆ Critical Thinking

⑥ Analyze In this passage, Harriet Tubman shows an understanding of human nature that guides her actions. Ask students to explain why Tubman wants to make the slaves afraid as well as encouraged. *Tubman believes that if the slaves lose heart, they won't press on; yet if they don't feel some fear, they may get a false sense of safety and let down their guard.*

---

words written down on the country's law-books. The new law had become a reality. It was Thomas Sims, a boy, picked up on the streets of Boston at night and shipped back to Georgia. It was Jerry and Shadrach, arrested and jailed with no warning.

She had never been in Canada. The route beyond Philadelphia was strange to her. But she could not let the runaways who accompanied her know this. As they walked along she told them stories of her own first flight, she kept painting vivid word pictures of what it would be like to be free.

But there were so many of them this time. She knew moments of doubt when she was half-afraid, and kept looking back over her shoulder, imagining that she heard the sound of pursuit. They would certainly be pursued. Eleven of them. Eleven thousand dollars' worth of flesh and bone and muscle that belonged to Maryland planters. If they were caught, the eleven runaways would be whipped and sold South, but she—she would probably be hanged.

◆ **Literary Focus**
What insight into Tubman's thoughts does the narrator provide?

They tried to sleep during the day but they never could wholly relax into sleep. She could tell by the positions they assumed, by their restless movements. And they walked at night. Their progress was slow. It took them three nights of walking to reach the first stop. She had told them about the place where they would stay, promising warmth and good food, holding these things out to them as an <u>incentive</u> to keep going.

When she knocked on the door of a farmhouse, a place where she and her parties of runaways had always been welcome, always been given shelter and plenty to eat, there was no answer. She knocked again, softly. A voice from within said, "Who is it?" There was fear in the voice.

She knew instantly from the sound of the voice that there was something wrong. She said, "A friend with friends," the password on the Underground Railroad.

The door opened, slowly. The man who stood in the doorway looked at her coldly, looked with unconcealed astonishment and fear at the eleven <u>disheveled</u> runaways who were standing near her. Then he shouted, "Too many, too many. It's not safe. My place was searched last week. It's not safe!" and slammed the door in her face.

She turned away from the house, frowning. She had promised her passengers food and rest and warmth, and instead of that, there would be hunger and cold and more walking over the frozen ground. Somehow she would have to instill courage into these eleven people, most of them strangers, would have to feed them on hope and bright dreams of freedom instead of the fried pork and corn bread and milk she had promised them.

They stumbled along behind her, half-dead for sleep, and she urged them on, though she was as tired and as discouraged as they were. She had never been in Canada but she kept painting wondrous word pictures of what it would be like. She managed to dispel their fear of pursuit, so that they would not become hysterical, panic-stricken. Then she had to bring some of the fear back, so that they would stay awake and keep walking though they drooped with sleep.

Yet during the day, when they lay down deep in a thicket, they never really slept, because if a twig snapped or the wind sighed in the branches of a pine tree, they jumped to their feet, afraid of their own shadows, shivering and shaking. It was very cold, but they dared not make fires because someone would see the smoke and wonder about it.

She kept thinking, eleven of them. Eleven thousand dollars' worth of slaves. And she had to take them all the way to Canada.

134 ◆ *Meeting Challenges*

▨ Cross-Curricular Connection: Social Studies

Liberia Many white Americans anticipated the struggles over slavery that the Compromise of 1850 brought on, and the American Colonization Society was founded in 1816, aided in its efforts by President James Monroe. In 1824 the Society set up an African colony for freed slaves. Liberia's main settlement was called Monrovia. Instead of expecting an immediate end to slavery, the Society offered to pay slave owners who freed their slaves.

This experiment in colonization was controversial from the beginning. Abolitionist William Lloyd Garrison, the publisher of the *Liberator*, supported colonization at first but then turned against it. African Americans were divided in their opinions. Some emigrated; others denounced the plan as white society's attempt to end the "Negro problem" by expelling them. By the 1850's, immigration to Liberia had diminished.

Liberia declared its independence in 1847 under the leadership of Joseph Jenkins Roberts, the first non-white governor. Despite political problems (including a civil war as recently as 1990), Liberia remains Africa's oldest republic. The official language has always been English.

Sometimes she told them about Thomas Garrett, in Wilmington. She said he was their friend even though he did not know them. He was the friend of all fugitives. He called them God's poor. He was a Quaker and his speech was a little different from that of other people. His clothing was different, too. He wore the wide-brimmed hat that the Quakers wear.

She said that he had thick white hair, soft, almost like a baby's, and the kindest eyes she had ever seen. He was a big man and strong, but he had never used his strength to harm anyone, always to help people. He would give all of them a new pair of shoes. Everybody. He always did. Once they reached his house in Wilmington, they would be safe. He would see to it that they were.

She described the house where he lived, told them about the store where he sold shoes. She said he kept a pail of milk and a loaf of bread in the drawer of his desk so that he would have food ready at hand for any of God's poor who should suddenly appear before him, fainting with hunger. There was a hidden room in the store. A whole wall swung open, and behind it was a room where he could hide fugitives. On the wall there were shelves filled with small boxes—boxes of shoes—so that you would never guess that the wall actually opened.

While she talked, she kept watching them. They did not believe her. She could tell by their expressions. They were thinking. New shoes, Thomas Garrett, Quaker, Wilmington—what foolishness was this? Who knew if she told the truth? Where was she taking them anyway?

That night they reached the next stop—a farm that belonged to a German. She made the runaways take shelter behind trees at the edge of the fields before she knocked at the door. She hesitated before she approached the door, thinking, suppose that he, too,

should refuse shelter, suppose—Then she thought, Lord, I'm going to hold steady on to You and You've got to see me through—and knocked softly.

She heard the familiar <u>guttural</u> voice say, "Who's there?"

She answered quickly, "A friend with friends."

He opened the door and greeted her warmly. "How many this time?" he asked.

"Eleven," she said and waited, doubting, wondering.

He said, "Good. Bring them in."

He and his wife fed them in the lamplit kitchen, their faces glowing, as they offered food and more food, urging them to eat, saying there was plenty for everybody, have more milk, have more bread, have more meat.

They spent the night in the warm kitchen. They really slept, all that night and until dusk the next day. When they left, it was with reluctance. They had all been warm and safe and well-fed. It was hard to exchange the security offered by that clean, warm kitchen for the darkness and the cold of a December night.

Harriet had found it hard to leave the warmth and friendliness, too. But she urged them on. For a while, as they walked, they seemed to carry in them a measure of contentment; some of the serenity and the cleanliness of that big warm kitchen lingered on inside them. But

> ◆ Literature
> and Your Life
> The fugitives find it hard to leave the safe warmth for the cold December night. Have you ever experienced a similar feeling? Explain.

◆ **Build Vocabulary**

incentive (in sent´ iv) *n.*: Something that stimulates one to action; encouragement

disheveled (di shev´ əld) *adj.*: Untidy; messy

guttural (gut´ ər əl) *adj.*: Made in back of the throat

Harriet Tubman: Guide to Freedom ◆ 135

Clarification
❼ The Quakers, or Society of Friends, are a sect whose beliefs include pacifism, a duty toward righteous action, and a ban on slavery. In the pre–Civil War period, Quakers often took part in active resistance to slavery, raised money to support freed slaves, and set up schools where former slaves could learn to read and write.

◆**Critical Thinking**
❽ **Infer** At this point, the slaves do not believe Harriet Tubman. Ask students why the fugitives would continue to follow Tubman if they were so suspicious of her. *Students may say that a life of slavery is so bad that taking a life-or-death risk is better than staying where they are. Have students read on to see how the piece answers this question.*

◆**LITERATURE AND YOUR LIFE**
❾ Invite students to share their responses. Then challenge them to generalize from the experiences.

Customize for
Interpersonal Learners
Discuss with students the leadership skills that Harriet Tubman uses to keep the group motivated and moving. Can she be their friend? Can she be sympathetic to their discomforts and anxieties? Can she indulge their desire to rest? Encourage students to consider the isolation that a person in a leadership role may experience in an effort to successfully guide a group to achieve a goal.

Cross-Curricular Connection: Science

Celestial Navigation Most slaves were not allowed to learn to read or write, but many developed other important skills that they drew on to help them make dangerous journeys to freedom. One such skill was observing the nighttime sky for relative positions of the stars and planets. Without maps, compasses, or any other standard navigational tools, people the world over have used the positions of celestial bodies to determine their positions on earth.

The positions of planets and stars vary throughout the calendar year and also according to the earth's daily rotation. To navigate by celestial positions, one must know these variations.

Have interested students investigate the basic principles of celestial navigation: how to recognize and use planets, stars, and constellations to determine direction, time, and other key information. Invite volunteers to share with classmates some of the tips or techniques they learn.

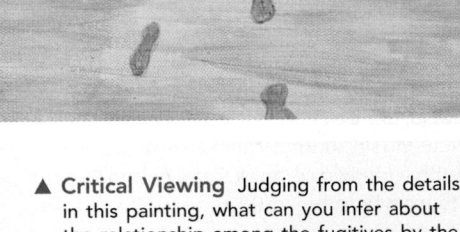

Harriet Tubman Series, #20, Jacob Lawrence, Hampton University Museum, Hampton, Virginia

as they walked farther and farther away from the warmth and the light, the cold and the darkness entered into them. They fell silent, sullen, suspicious. She waited for the moment when some one of them would turn <u>mutinous</u>. It did not happen that night.

1 Two nights later she was aware that the feet behind her were moving slower and slower. She heard the irritability in their voices, knew that soon someone would refuse to go on.

She started talking about William Still and the Philadelphia Vigilance Committee.[4] No one commented. No one asked any questions. She told them the story of William and Ellen Craft and how they escaped from Georgia. Ellen was so fair that she looked as though she were white, and so she dressed up in a man's clothing and she looked like a wealthy young planter. Her husband, William, who was dark, played the role of her slave. Thus they traveled **2** from Macon, Georgia, to Philadelphia, riding on the trains, staying at the finest ho- **3** tels. Ellen pretended to be very ill— her right arm was in a sling, and her right hand was bandaged, because she was supposed to have rheumatism. Thus she avoided having to sign the register at the hotels for she could not read or write. They finally arrived safely in Philadelphia, and then went on to Boston.

4 No one said anything. Not one of them seemed to have heard her.

---

4. Philadelphia Vigilance Committee: Group of citizens who helped escaped slaves. Its secretary was a free black man named William Still.

▲ **Critical Viewing** Judging from the details in this painting, what can you infer about **5** the relationship among the fugitives by the

She told them about Frederick Douglass, the most famous of the escaped slaves, of his eloquence, of his magnificent appearance. Then she told them of her own first vain effort at running away, evoking the memory of that miserable life she had led as a child, reliving it for a moment in the telling.

But they had been tired too long, hungry too long, afraid too long, footsore too long. One of them suddenly cried out in despair, "Let me go back. It is better to be a slave than to suffer like this in order to be free."

She carried a gun with her on these

 Humanities: Art

Harriet Tubman Series, #20, by Jacob Lawrence

In this piece from the Harriet Tubman series, Lawrence presents a stark winter scene that suggests another aspect of the dangerous escape to freedom. Use these questions for discussion:

1. What do you think is happening in this scene? *An adult carries two children who are too small to trudge through the deep snow; or, fugitives move in a single-file line, each one stepping in the footprints of the person before to leave fewer tracks.*

2. What details in the picture suggest isolation and loneliness? *Possible answers: a single set of footprints; two bare trees; a dark sky without stars*

3. What details in the story support a winter scene? *The fugitives travel in December, a winter month; they head north to Canada.*

trips. She had never used it—except as a threat. Now as she aimed it, she experienced a feeling of guilt, remembering that time, years ago, when she had prayed for the death of Edward Brodas, the Master, and then not too long afterward had heard that great wailing cry that came from the throats of the field hands, and knew from the sound that the Master was dead.

One of the runaways said, again, "Let me go back. Let me go back," and stood still, and then turned around and said, over his shoulder, "I am going back."

She lifted the gun, aimed it at the despairing slave. She said, "Go on with us or die." The husky low-pitched voice was grim.

He hesitated for a moment and then he joined the others. They started walking again. She tried to explain to them why none of them could go back to the plantation. If a runaway returned, he would turn traitor, the master and the overseer would force him to turn traitor. The returned slave would disclose the stopping places, the hiding places, the cornstacks they had used with the full knowledge of the owner of the farm, the name of the German farmer who had fed them and sheltered them. These people who had risked their own security to help runaways would be ruined, fined, imprisoned. She said, "We got to go free or die. And freedom's not bought with dust."

This time she told them about the long agony of the Middle Passage on the old slave ships, about the black horror of the holds, about the chains and the whips. They too knew these stories. But she wanted to remind them of the long hard way they had come, about the long hard way they had yet to go. She told them about Thomas Sims, the boy picked up on the streets of Boston and sent back to Georgia. She said when they got him back to Savannah, got him in prison there, they whipped him until a doctor who was

standing by watching said, "You will kill him if you strike him again!" His master said, "Let him die!"

Thus she forced them to go on. Sometimes she thought she had become nothing but a voice speaking in the darkness, cajoling, urging, threatening. Sometimes she told them things to make them laugh, sometimes she sang to them, and heard the eleven voices behind her blending softly with hers, and then she knew that for the moment all was well with them.

She gave the impression of being a short, muscular, indomitable woman who could never be defeated. Yet at any moment she was liable to be seized by one of those curious fits of sleep, which might last for a few minutes or for hours.[5]

Even on this trip, she suddenly fell asleep in the woods. The runaways, ragged, dirty, hungry, cold, did not steal the gun as they might have, and set off by themselves, or turn back. They sat on the ground near her and waited patiently until she awakened. They had come to trust her implicitly, totally. They, too, had come to believe her repeated statement, "We got to go free or die." She was leading them into freedom, and so they waited until she was ready to go on.

Finally, they reached Thomas Garrett's house in Wilmington, Delaware. Just as Harriet had promised, Garrett gave them all new shoes, and provided carriages to take them on to the next stop.

---

5. **sleep . . . hours:** When she was about 13, Harriet accidentally received a severe blow on the head. Afterwards, she often lost consciousness and could not be awakened until the episode was over.

◆ Build Vocabulary

mutinous (myōōt′ ən əs) *adj.*: Rebellious

cajoling (kə jōl′ iŋ) *v.*: Coaxing or persuading gently

indomitable (in däm′ it ə bəl) *adj.*: Not easily discouraged

 Cross-Curricular Connection: Music

Songs Some spirituals, work songs, and popular tunes that plantation slaves sang, such as "Follow the Drinking Gourd," "Go Down, Moses," and "Oh, Susanna," contained lyrics with double meanings. Play recordings of the songs for students and challenge them to discover the secret messages they contain. For example, the "drinking gourd" is the Big Dipper constellation, which indicated the way north for runaway slaves.

Another musical approach to this selection might be to obtain a recording of the song "Harriet Tubman" by Walter Robinson and play it

for students. This song is included on the 1983 album *Lifeline* by Holly Near and Ronnie Gilbert. The album title echoes a line in this song: "Come on up, I got a lifeline," which is Tubman urging runaway slaves to join her "train."

Or, invite interested students to research other spirituals that were used by travelers on the Underground Railroad.

◆ Literary Focus

❶ Third-Person Narrative Guide students to understand that in a third-person narrative, the narrator can include quotations. The narrator maintains the third-person distance even when including a quotation, such as this one, that is written in the first person.

◆ Reading Strategy

❷ *Students may say that this is some evidence that Tubman had a life beyond the Underground Railroad.*

Thematic Focus

❸ Blazing Trails Harriet Tubman is widely known for conducting fugitive slaves to freedom. However, it is less known that her work did not end at the Canadian border. Discuss how Tubman's trail-blazing efforts went beyond the journey itself.

Clarification

❹ Point out that slaves in the United States enjoyed none of these rights.

Customize for
Intrapersonal Learners

Invite students to place themselves in Harriet Tubman's place on the day she arrives in Canada. Encourage them to think about her reaction to the group's safe arrival and her thoughts about past and future journeys. You may wish to have them use the Diary Entry writing activity in the Idea Bank on p. 141.

By slow stages they reached Philadelphia, where William Still hastily recorded their names, and the plantations whence they had come, and something of the life they had led in slavery. Then he carefully hid what he had written, for fear it might be discovered. In 1872 he published this record in book form and called it *The Underground Railroad.* In the foreword to his book he said: "While I knew the danger of keeping strict records, and while I did not then dream that in my day slavery would be blotted out, or that the time would come when I could publish these records, it used to afford me great satisfaction to take them down, fresh from the lips of fugitives on the way to freedom, and to preserve them as they had given them."

William Still, who was familiar with all the station stops on the Underground Railroad, supplied Harriet with money and sent her and her eleven fugitives on to Burlington, New Jersey.

Harriet felt safer now, though there were danger spots ahead. But the biggest part of her job was over. As they went farther and farther north, it grew colder; she was aware of the wind on the Jersey ferry and aware of the cold damp in New York. From New York they went on to Syracuse, where the temperature was even lower.

> ◆ Reading Strategy
> What do you learn about Tubman in this passage?

In Syracuse she met the Reverend J.W. Loguen, known as "Jarm" Loguen. This was the beginning of a lifelong friendship. Both Harriet and Jarm Loguen were to become friends and supporters of Old John Brown.[6]

From Syracuse they went north again, into a colder, snowier city—Rochester. Here they almost certainly stayed with Frederick Douglass, for he wrote in his autobiography:

---

6. John Brown: White abolitionist (1800–1859) who was hanged for leading a raid on the arsenal at Harpers Ferry, Virginia, as part of a slave uprising.

"On one occasion I had eleven fugitives at the same time under my roof, and it was necessary for them to remain with me until I could collect sufficient money to get them to Canada. It was the largest number I ever had at any one time, and I had some difficulty in providing so many with food and shelter, but, as may well be imagined, they were not very <u>fastidious</u> in either direction, and were well content with very plain food, and a strip of carpet on the floor for a bed, or a place on the straw in the barnloft."

Late in December 1851, Harriet arrived in St. Catharines, Canada West (now Ontario), with the eleven fugitives. It had taken almost a month to complete this journey; most of the time had been spent getting out of Maryland.

That first winter in St. Catharines was a terrible one. Canada was a strange frozen land, snow everywhere, ice everywhere, and a bone-biting cold the like of which none of them had ever experienced before. Harriet rented a small frame house in the town and set to work to make a home. The fugitives boarded with her. They worked in the forests, felling trees, and so did she. Sometimes she took other jobs, cooking or cleaning house for people in the town. She cheered on these newly arrived fugitives, working herself, finding work for them, finding food for them, praying for them, sometimes begging for them.

Often she found herself thinking of the beauty of Maryland, the mellowness of the soil, the richness of the plant life there. The climate itself made for an ease of living that could never be duplicated in this bleak, barren countryside.

In spite of the severe cold, the hard work, she came to love St. Catharines, and the other towns and cities in Canada where black men lived. She discovered that freedom meant more than the right to change jobs at will, more than the right to keep the money that one earned. It was the right to vote and to sit on juries. It was the right to

---

Speaking and Listening Mini-Lesson

Speech

This mini-lesson supports the Speaking and Listening activity in the Idea Bank on p. 141.

Introduce Discuss the elements of a good speech and the qualities that memorable public speakers share. For example, students might cite a strong opening remark or anecdote to capture listeners' attention, or a spirited or rhythmic style of delivery that holds their interest.

Develop A speech, like any kind of persuasion, needs an introduction, a body, and a conclusion. The speaker uses details to support his or her viewpoint, presented in a logical, effective order. Have students work in pairs to research, write, and rehearse their speeches.

Apply Suggest that students memorize their speeches, or know the material well enough to make eye contact with the audience. Have students deliver their speeches to the class.

Assess Evaluate speeches on the completeness and accuracy of supporting details, on structure, organization, delivery, and overall effectiveness. Or use the Peer Assessment: Speaker/Speech form, p. 114, in **Alternative Assessment.**

④ be elected to office. In Canada there were black men who were county officials and members of school boards. St. Catharines had a large colony of ex-slaves, and they owned their own homes, kept them neat and clean and in good repair. They lived in whatever part of town they chose and sent their children to the schools.

When spring came she decided that she would make this small Canadian city her home—as much as any place could be said to be home to a woman who traveled from Canada to the Eastern Shore of Maryland as often as she did.

In the spring of 1852, she went back to Cape May, New Jersey. She spent the summer there, cooking in a hotel. That fall she returned, as usual, to Dorchester County, and brought out nine more slaves,

conducting them all the way to St. Catharines, in Canada West, to the bone-biting cold, the snow-covered forests—and freedom.

She continued to live in this fashion, spending the winter in Canada, and the spring and summer working in Cape May, New Jersey, or in Philadelphia. She made two trips a year into slave territory, one in the fall and another in the spring. She now had a definite crystallized purpose, and in carrying it out, her life fell into a pattern which remained unchanged for the next six years.

⑤

◆ Build Vocabulary

fastidious (fas tid′ ē əs) *adj.*: Refined in an oversensitive way, so as to be easily disgusted or displeased

◇ Guide for Responding

◆ LITERATURE AND YOUR LIFE

Reader's Response Would you have trusted Harriet Tubman to take you on a long, difficult journey? Why or why not?

Thematic Focus What aspects of Harriet Tubman's character might inspire a young person to follow a difficult path today?

Journal Writing Write a journal entry in which you list the main concerns that Harriet Tubman might have had in conducting a group north on the Underground Railroad.

☑ Check Your Comprehension

1. What part does Tubman play in the Underground Railroad?
2. How does Harriet Tubman announce her arrival in the headquarters late at night?
3. Summarize the general sequence of events in traveling on the Underground Railroad.
4. Why was no fugitive allowed to turn back?

◆ Critical Thinking

INTERPRET

1. (a) What kinds of stories does Tubman tell the fugitives? (b) Why does she tell them these stories? **[Analyze]**
2. Why did Tubman never admit she was afraid? **[Draw Conclusions]**
3. Explain one of the several possible meanings of Tubman's statement "We live free or die." **[Interpret]**

EVALUATE

4. Is Harriet Tubman justified in threatening to take the life of the man who wants to turn back? Explain. **[Make a Judgment]**

EXTEND

5. What modern figures share qualities with Harriet Tubman? Explain. **[Social Studies Link]**

Harriet Tubman: Guide to Freedom ◆ 139

Beyond the Selection

FURTHER READING

Other Works by Ann Petry
Harriet Tubman: Conductor of the Underground Railroad
Tituba of Salem Village

Other Works About Fugitive Slaves
I Was Born a Slave: The Story of Harriet Jacobs, Jennifer Fleischner, illustrated by Melanie Reim
Anthony Burns: The Defeat and Triumph of a Fugitive Slave, Virginia Hamilton
To Be a Slave, Julius Lester

INTERNET
We suggest the following sites on the Internet (all Web sites are subject to change).
For more on author Ann Petry: **http://www. english.cla.umn.edu/lkd/vfg/Authors/AnnPetry**
For information about Harriet Tubman: **http://www. acusd.edu/~jdesmet/tubman.html**
We *strongly recommend* that you preview the sites before you send students to them.

◆ Reading Strategy

❺ **Set a Purpose for Reading**
Though this excerpt ends, the quilt on p. 131 shows that Harriet Tubman lived until 1913. Challenge students to set a purpose for reading more about Tubman by discussing questions they might like answered, such as: Was Tubman ever caught, arrested, or tried for her actions? How did she spend the later years of her life?

Reinforce and Extend

Answers
◆ LITERATURE AND YOUR LIFE

Reader's Response Encourage students to cite references from this piece to support their views.

Thematic Focus Possible answers: her courage; her ability to make quick decisions; her ability to evaluate people; her desire to help others

☑ Check Your Comprehension

1. She guides fugitive slaves on a secret route north and finds places for them to stay until they reach Canada.
2. She uses the password: "A friend with friends."
3. Slaves sneak away from their plantation; travel north by night; seek shelter and food at Underground Railroad "safe houses"; cross the border into Canada.
4. They might be forced to reveal the secrets of their escape, which would jeopardize other fugitives and their helpers.

◆ Critical Thinking

1. (a) She tells them stories about the Middle Passage; about the success and failure of other slave escapes; about what Quakers are like and why they are willing to help. (b) She wants to educate and inspire them and give them hope.
2. She had a reputation to live up to; she inspired courage by showing courage.
3. Possible answer: Living in slavery is no life at all, so we'd rather die trying to get our freedom.
4. Possible response: She is willing to shoot a slave who wants to return to slavery because one slave's life is less important than keeping the secret escape paths safe for many.
5. Possible figures: Raoul Wallenberg, Nelson Mandela, Cesar Chavez

139

Answers

◆ Reading Strategy

1. Most students will say that they read to learn more about Harriet Tubman and to find out how she led so many fugitives to freedom. Students may say that they read more actively. Have them support responses with examples from the story.
2. Students may say that they learned about Tubman's success with this group of fugitives; they learned about the difficulties of achieving freedom; or they discovered that they want to learn more about Harriet Tubman or the Underground Railroad.

◆ Build Vocabulary

Using the Word Root -fug-

1. *Subter* means secretly, so a subterfuge is a secret plan used to help an escape.
2. *Re* means back, so a refuge is a safe place that someone can flee to.
3. *Centri-* refers to the center, so centrifugal force causes objects to flee, or move away from, the center.

Spelling Strategy

Sample sentences:

1. The most recent book I read was a science fiction thriller.
2. Mario makes fairly decent pizza.
3. One hundred years is a century.

Using the Word Bank

1. b	5. f
2. g	6. h
3. e	7. c
4. a	8. d

◆ Literary Focus

1. Examples include "How many this time?" he asked. "Eleven," she said and waited, doubting, wondering.
2. Examples include p. 133, where Harriet is determined that more slaves should know what freedom is like; p. 134, when she hides from the fugitives the truth that she had never been to Canada; p. 136, when Harriet predicts that someone will eventually refuse to go on.
3. Possible response: It might be more immediate and include that fugitive's observations and feelings, but it might lack the broad background about Harriet and about the stories of other fugitive slaves.

140

Guide for Responding (continued)

◆ Reading Strategy

SET A PURPOSE FOR READING

Setting a purpose helps you focus your reading to find information or note particular kinds of details. With your purpose in mind—to learn about Harriet Tubman—answer the following.

1. How did having a purpose focus your reading?
2. List three things you learned from the story that helped you to achieve your purpose.

◆ Build Vocabulary

USING THE WORD ROOT -fug-

Write a sentence explaining how the word root -fug- contributes to the meaning of each word. Use a dictionary to help you.

1. subterfuge
2. refuge
3. centrifugal

SPELLING STRATEGY

In the word *incentive,* the s sound is spelled with a c. Because there is no rule that tells you when to spell the s sound with a c, try remembering this little tip: An *incentive* to work might involve *cents.*

Other words in which the s sound is spelled c include *recent, decent,* and *century.* Use each of these words in a sentence to practice spelling the s sound with a c.

USING THE WORD BANK

On your paper, match each Word Bank word with the word closest in meaning.

1. guttural	a. escapees
2. disheveled	b. gruntlike
3. incentive	c. unconquerable
4. fugitives	d. picky
5. mutinous	e. encouragement
6. cajoling	f. rebellious
7. indomitable	g. messy
8. fastidious	h. coaxing

◆ Literary Focus

THIRD-PERSON NARRATIVE

In a **third-person narrative,** the narrator tells the story but does not participate in it. Most biographies, like the one from which this true-life story comes, are third-person narratives. To make third-person narratives interesting, many biographers, like Petry, use dialogue and reveal the thoughts of the subject.

1. Cite an example of dialogue within the narrative.
2. Locate a passage in which Petry reveals the inner thoughts of Harriet Tubman.
3. How would this story be different if it were written by someone whom Tubman led on the Underground Railroad?

◆ Build Grammar Skills

TRANSITIVE AND INTRANSITIVE VERBS

A verb is **transitive** when it expresses an action directed toward a person or thing; the action passes from the doer to the receiver of the action. The person or thing receiving the action is the object of the verb.

Transitive: They never *saw* him.
(verb → *saw*; object → him)

A verb is **intransitive** when it expresses action (or tells something about the subject) without passing the action to the receiver.

Intransitive: They *did* not *believe* in his existence.

Practice Identify each verb as transitive or intransitive in your notebook. If the verb is transitive, identify its object.

1. At night she guided the fugitives.
2. She knocked on the farmhouse door.
3. One fugitive pleaded to go back.
4. They arrived safely in Philadelphia.
5. The abolitionist gave them food and money.

Writing Application Write sentences that contain transitive and intransitive verbs, as indicated.

1. *run,* intransitive
2. *hide,* transitive
3. *whistle,* transitive
4. *arrive,* intransitive

◆ Build Grammar Skills

Practice

1. guided (transitive); fugitives
2. knocked (intransitive)
3. pleaded (intransitive)
4. arrived (intransitive)
5. gave (transitive); food, money

Writing Application

Possible responses:

1. We must run before sunrise.
2. Thomas Garrett will hide them.
3. Tell Harriet to whistle if all is clear.
4. We arrive in Philadelphia tonight.

✎ Writer's Solution

For additional instruction and practice, use the lesson in the *Writer's Solution Language Lab CD-ROM* on Verbs, and the practice page on Action Verbs, p. 12 in the *Writer's Solution Grammar Practice Book.*

Build Your Portfolio

 Idea Bank

Writing

1. **Diary Entry** Write a diary entry that Harriet Tubman might have recorded on the day she arrived in Canada with her group of fugitives.

2. **Biographical Description** Write a short biographical description of Harriet Tubman, using information revealed in this selection. **[Social Studies Link]**

3. **Dramatization** Write a dramatic scene based on the selection. Describe the setting, and create dialogue and stage directions actors could use to perform the scene. **[Performing Arts Link]**

Speaking and Listening

4. **Speech** Write and deliver a speech in which you praise Harriet Tubman and others associated with running the Underground Railroad. You may do research to gather details for your speech.

5. **Debate [Group Activity]** Form two teams to debate the following issue: Harriet Tubman was taking part in an illegal activity. Were her actions justified? You may appoint a classmate to act as moderator, who times the teams' responses and ensures that rules of debate are followed.

Projects

6. **Research Project [Group Activity]** Work with a group to create a map showing the Underground Railroad routes, the approximate location of safe houses, final destinations, and other relevant information. Display your map in the classroom. **[Social Studies Link]**

7. **Fugitive Slave Laws** Do research to find out about the Fugitive Slave Laws—when they were passed, who supported them, and who opposed them. Then, report to your class on your findings. **[Social Studies Link]**

 Writing Mini-Lesson

Spoken Introduction

Heroes like Harriet Tubman deserve awards, tributes, and banquets to honor their work. Imagine that you are a speaker at an awards banquet and your role is to acknowledge the achievements of Harriet Tubman. In your speech, let the audience know why she's such an inspiration to you.

Writing Skills Focus: Give Specific Examples

An introduction that includes **specific examples** has more meaning than one that consists of generalizations—broad, vague statements.

General: "She is an extraordinary person."

Specific: "Harriet Tubman's extraordinary efforts to help escaped Africans find a new life in the North deserve admiration."

Prewriting Gather details about Harriet Tubman that you'd like to include in your acknowledgment. Include biographical information as well as specific examples of how she influenced your own life.

Drafting Begin with an attention-grabbing statement. You might pose a question, state a fact, or cite a stunning statistic. Use specific examples to support statements you make about Tubman. Conclude by "introducing" her to your audience.

Revising Read your draft to a classmate, and ask for suggestions about how to make it more interesting and clear. Add specific examples wherever your draft is vague. Proofread carefully to eliminate errors in grammar, punctuation, and spelling.

◆ **Grammar Application**
Read through your speech. Circle transitive verbs and underline intransitive verbs.

 Idea Bank

Following are suggestions for matching the Idea Bank topics with your students' performance levels and learning modalities:

Customize for *Performance Levels*
Less Advanced Students: 2, 4
Average Students: 3, 4, 5, 6
More Advanced Students: 1, 5, 6, 7

Customize for *Learning Modalities*
Verbal/Linguistic: 1, 2, 3, 4, 5, 7
Visual/Spatial: 6
Bodily/Kinesthetic: 4, 5
Logical/Mathematical: 5, 7
Interpersonal: 5, 6, 7
Intrapersonal: 1, 2, 4

 Writing Mini-Lesson

Refer students to the Writing Handbook in the back of the book for instructions on the writing process and for further information on writing a persuasive speech.

 Writer's Solution

Writing Lab CD-ROM
Have students complete the tutorial on Persuasion. Follow these steps:

1. Have students work through the About Persuasion section to learn more about persuasive writing.
2. Assign the Considering Audience and Purpose and Gathering Details segments.
3. Have students draft on computer.
4. Suggest use of the instruction on word choice to show how to improve sentences with more precise words or words with strong connotations.

Allow about 60 minutes of class time to complete these steps.

Writer's Solution Sourcebook
Have students use Chapter 6, "Persuasion," pp. 166–199, for additional support. The chapter includes in-depth instruction on writing an effective introduction, body, and conclusion, pp. 188–189.

✓ ASSESSMENT OPTIONS

Formal Assessment, Selection Test, pp. 44–46, and Assessment Resources Software. The selection test is designed so that it can be easily customized to the performance levels of your students.
Alternative Assessment, p. 12, includes options for less advanced students, more advanced students, interpersonal learners, musical/rhythmic learners, visual/spatial learners, intrapersonal learners, and verbal/linguistic learners.

PORTFOLIO ASSESSMENT
Use the following rubrics in the **Alternative Assessment** booklet to assess student writing:
Diary Entry: Fictional Narrative, p. 91
Biographical Description: Description, p. 93
Dramatization: Drama, p. 105
Writing Mini-Lesson: Persuasion, p. 101

OBJECTIVES

1. To read, comprehend, and interepret three poems
2. To relate poems to personal experience
3. To relate poetry to what you know
4. To analyze stanzas in poetry
5. To build vocabulary in context and learn the antonyms *wan* and *swarthy*
6. To distinguish between the commonly confused verbs *lie* and *lay*
7. To write a speech, supporting ideas with reasons
8. To respond to the poems through writing, speaking and listening, and projects

SKILLS INSTRUCTION

Vocabulary:
Antonyms: *wan* and *swarthy*

Spelling:
Suffixes: *-ous*

Grammar:
Commonly Confused Verbs: *lie* and *lay*

Reading Strategy:
Relate to What You Know

Literary Focus:
Stanzas in Poetry

Writing:
Support Ideas with Reasons

Speaking and Listening:
Oral Presentation (Teacher Edition)

Critical Viewing:
Compare and Contrast; Infer

PORTFOLIO OPPORTUNITIES

Writing: Letter; Dialogue; Comparison-and-Contrast Essay

Writing Mini-Lesson: Speech

Speaking and Listening: Skit; Oral Presentation

Projects: Living History; Book Cover

More About the Authors

Joaquin Miller's poetry reflects his adventurous life in Oregon, where he practiced law, mined for gold, taught, and edited. He achieved fame in London, where he published his *Songs of the Sierras* in 1871. There, he wore cowboy boots and a sombrero and behaved as the English imagined American westerners should.

Stephen Vincent Benét spent his childhood in army posts, following the movements of his military father and listening to poetry, read aloud by his father. Benét's works were—and are—quite popular, becoming the basis for plays, operas, and films.

Roberto Félix Salazar links his cultural past to the present by using poetry to describe features of the American southwest—like its missions—that can still be viewed today.

Guide for Reading

Meet the Authors:

Joaquin Miller (1839–1913)

Joaquin Miller was born near Liberty, Indiana, though he once claimed that his cradle was "a covered wagon pointed West." A man of vision and energy, Miller is credited with helping to establish a pony express route between Idaho and Washington. Later in life, as a tribute to Mexican bandit Joaquin Murrietta, Miller changed his given name, Cincinnatus Hiner Miller, to Joaquin Miller.

Stephen Vincent Benét (1898–1943)

A poet, short-story writer, and dramatist, Stephen Vincent Benét had his first collection of poetry published when he was only seventeen years old. *John Brown's Body,* his epic poem, won the Pulitzer Prize in 1928.

Roberto Félix Salazar

In his writing, Roberto Félix Salazar aims to dramatize his Mexican American heritage as well as challenge his readers' assumptions about the nation's beginnings.

THE STORY BEHIND "THE OTHER PIONEERS"

According to Philip Ortego, a professor of Chicano Studies, "The Other Pioneers" was written to remind Mexican Americans and others that the first pioneers to settle the Southwest had Spanish names—and that their descendants still do, although they are American citizens.

142 ◆ Meeting Challenges

◆ LITERATURE AND YOUR LIFE

CONNECT YOUR EXPERIENCE

If you've ever moved to a new home, changed schools, or traveled to new places, you understand the thrill of going someplace you've never been before. The poems that follow celebrate those who took risks to explore and settle a new land.

THEMATIC FOCUS: Blazing Trails

As you read these poems, imagine what it was like to be an explorer or early pioneer.

◆ Background for Understanding

SOCIAL STUDIES

"Columbus," "Western Wagons," and "The Other Pioneers" celebrate the discovery and settlement of what is now the West Indies and North America. The map on the facing page shows trails to the West that were used by pioneers described in "Western Wagons." Also shown is the Republic of Texas, where the "other pioneers" described by Roberto Félix Salazar settle after crossing the Rio Grande from Mexico.

◆ Build Vocabulary

ANTONYMS: *wan* AND *swarthy*

In "Columbus," Joaquin Miller uses antonyms, words that have opposite meanings. *Wan* means "pale and sickly," and its antonym *swarthy* means "being of a dark color or complexion."

WORD BANK

Look over these words from the poems. They are all descriptive words. Which word do you think describes something coming unfolded? How do you know? Check the Build Vocabulary box on page 144 to see if you chose correctly.

mutinous
wan
swarthy
unfurled
stalwart

Prentice Hall Literature Program Resources

REINFORCE / RETEACH / EXTEND

Selection Support Pages
Build Vocabulary: Antonyms: *wan* and *swarthy*, p. 65
Build Spelling Skills, p. 66
Building Grammar Skills: Commonly Confused Verbs: *lie* and *lay*, p. 67
Reading Strategy: Relate to What You Know, p. 68
Literary Focus: Stanzas in Poetry, p. 69

Strategies for Diverse Student Needs, pp. 25–26

Beyond Literature Media Connection: Documentary Film, p. 13

Formal Assessment Selection Test, pp. 47–49, Assessment Resources Software

Alternative Assessment, p. 13

Writing and Language Transparencies Cluster Organizer, p. 73

Resource Pro CD-ROM
"Columbus"; "Western Wagons"; "The Other Pioneers"

◯ Listening to Literature Audiocassettes
"Columbus"; "Western Wagons"; "The Other Pioneers"

Columbus ◆ Western Wagons ◆ The Other Pioneers ◆

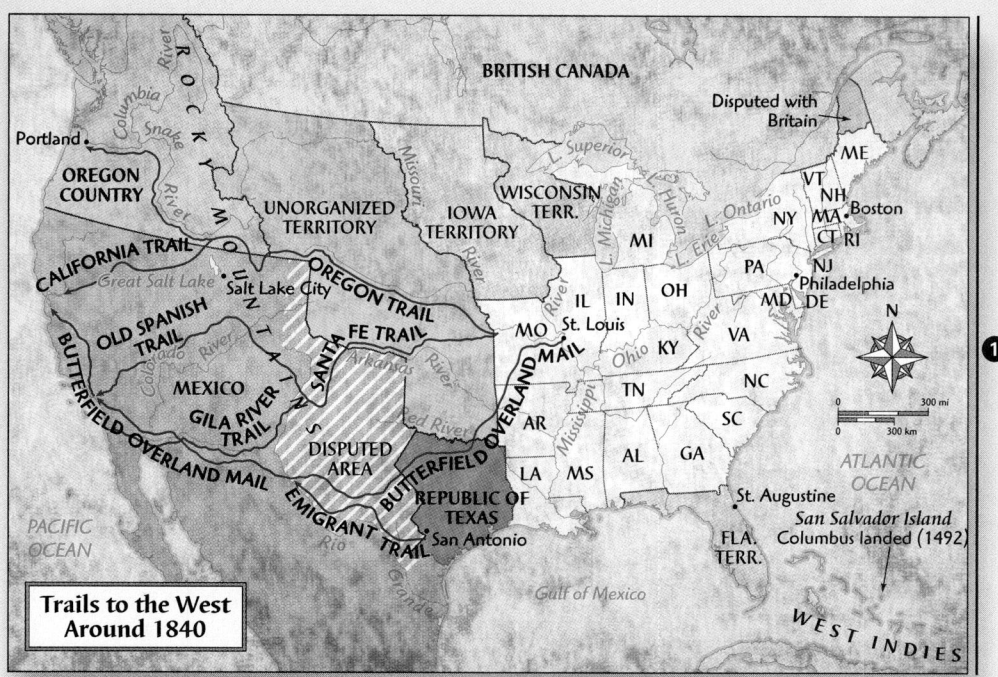

Trails to the West Around 1840

◆ Literary Focus

STANZAS IN POETRY

These poems are organized in **stanzas,** groups of lines that form units in a poem, just as paragraphs form units of prose. The stanzas in a poem are separated by spaces. Some poems have stanzas of matching length, rhythms, and rhyme schemes, and some poems have stanzas that do not match at all. Stanzas often focus on a single topic. As you read these poems, fill out a chart like this one to keep track of the stanzas.

Poem	Number of Stanzas	Number of Lines in Each	Rhyming Words
Columbus			
Western Wagons			
The Other Pioneers			

◆ Reading Strategy

RELATE TO WHAT YOU KNOW

One way to understand a poem is to **relate** what the poet is saying to what you know.

In "Columbus," Joaquin Miller describes Columbus's voyage of discovery. You may know that Columbus sailed for America in the late 1400's. Knowing the dangers of sea voyages during that time period, you can better understand the courage and determination of Columbus and the fear of the crew.

As you read these poems, relate what the poets are saying to what you already know about history and human nature.

Guide for Reading ◆ 143

143

"Columbus" recreates the sea journey of Christopher Columbus. Alternating between the voices of Columbus and his first mate, the poem shows the explorer's determined leadership and his mate's fearful doubts. Columbus's refrain—"sail on"—characterizes this historical figure.

Team Teaching Strategy

You might team teach these poems with a social studies teacher, focusing on exploration and 19th-century America.

◆ Build Vocabulary

❶ **Antonyms: *wan* and *swarthy***
Have one volunteer read aloud lines 10–12 as another explains the definitions of *wan* and *swarthy*. Then, using their understanding of antonyms, ask them to describe the stout mate and his sailors. *The sailors are pale and ill from the long journey, while the stout mate still shows his natural dark skin and is therefore tolerating the trip.*

◆ Literary Focus

❷ **Stanzas in Poetry** Ask students to read aloud the last lines of each stanza and explain their similarities. How does the refrain contribute to the poem's meaning? *Students should note that each stanza ends with a form of the refrain, "sail on," emphasizing Columbus's confidence and determination; it also links the stanzas, each of which describes a portion of the journey.*

Customize for
Visual/Spatial Learners

Have students locate the Azores and the Strait of Gibraltar on a globe or world map. Ask them to find a route for Columbus from this region to the Caribbean, where he landed in the Bahamas group. Urge students to calculate the journey's mileage.

Customize for
English Language Learners

Make sure students understand that "Adm'r'l" is a contraction for "Admiral." Poets may use contractions to suggest how a word should be spoken and to adjust the syllable count to fit the rhythm.

Columbus
Joaquin Miller

Behind him lay the gray Azores,[1]
Behind the Gates of Hercules;[2]
Before him not the ghost of shores;
Before him only shoreless seas.
5 The good mate said: "Now must we pray,
For lo! the very stars are gone.
Brave Adm'r'l, speak; what shall I say?"
"Why, say: 'Sail on! sail on! and on!'"

"My men grow <u>mutinous</u> day by day;
10 My men grow ghastly <u>wan</u> and weak."
❶ The stout mate thought of home; a spray
Of salt wave washed his <u>swarthy</u> cheek.
"What shall I say, brave Adm'r'l, say,
If we sight naught[3] but seas at dawn?"
15 "Why, you shall say at break of day:
'Sail on! sail on! sail on! and on!'"

They sailed and sailed, as winds might blow,
Until at last the blanched mate said:
"Why, now not even God would know
20 Should I and all my men fall dead.
These very winds forget their way,
For God from these dread seas is gone.
Now speak, brave Adm'r'l; speak and say—"
❷ He said: "Sail on! sail on! and on!"

25 They sailed. They sailed. Then spake[4] the mate:
"This mad sea shows his teeth to-night.
❸ He curls his lip, he lies in wait,
With lifted teeth, as if to bite!
Brave Adm'r'l, say but one good word:
30 What shall we do when hope is gone?"
The words leapt like a leaping sword:
"Sail on! sail on! sail on! and on!"

Then, pale and worn, he kept his deck,
And peered through darkness. Ah, that night
35 Of all dark nights! And then a speck—
A light! A light! A light! A light!
It grew, a starlit flag unfurled!
It grew to be Time's burst of dawn.
He gained a world; he gave that world
40 Its grandest lesson: "On! sail on!"

1. **Azores** (ā´ zôrz):
Group of Portuguese islands in the North Atlantic west of Portugal.

2. **Gates of Hercules** (gāts uv hʉr´ kyə lēz´): Entrance to the Strait of Gibraltar, between Spain and Africa.

3. **naught** (nôt) *n.*: Nothing.

4. **spake** (spāk) *v.*: Old-fashioned word for "spoke."

◆ Build Vocabulary

mutinous (myōōt´ ən əs) *adj.*: Rebellio
wan (wän) *adj.*: Pale
swarthy (swôr´ thē) *adj.*: Having a dar
unfurled (un fʉrld´) *adj.*: Unfolded

Block Scheduling Strategies

Consider these suggestions to take advantage of extended class time:

- Link the reading strategy to the poetry's historical context. Review Background for Understanding, p. 142, and the map, p. 143, and have students scan the fine art for data. Then invite students to read the selection, noting what they know about each topic in a journal or with a reading partner. Use the Reading Strategy, p. 143, to expand students' understanding. Extend the connection with **Selection Support,** p. 68; Travel List, p. 147; and Dialogue, p. 151.

- Alternatively, focus on how the poems sound. Play the audiocassette, stopping after each poe for small groups to discuss the Critical Thinki questions. Then, use Literary Focus, p. 150, to address the poems' structures. Urge students to consider rhythm as they complete the Writing Mini-Lesson, p. 151.

- Organize the lesson as a multi-media present tion. After students read independently, invite them to present the Skit or Oral Presentatio or Speech, Book Cover, or Living History, fro the activities on p. 151.

The Landing of Columbus, 1876, Currier & Ives, Museum of the City of New York

▲ **Critical Viewing** What qualities of Columbus depicted in the poem are revealed or suggested by the figure of Columbus, standing at the front of the boat in this painting? What qualities are not shown? **[Compare and Contrast]**

④

Guide for Responding

◆ LITERATURE AND YOUR LIFE

Reader's Response Would you like to have been on Columbus's voyage? Explain.

Thematic Focus What personal qualities of Columbus are suited to a trailblazer?

Journal Writing As the first mate, write a journal entry about the voyage to the "New World."

☑ Check Your Comprehension

1. In "Columbus," who is the "Brave Adm'r'l"? What does he say each time to the mate?
2. What seems to frighten the mate in each of the first four stanzas?

◆ Critical Thinking

INTERPRET

1. (a) To what does Miller compare the sea in lines 26–28 of "Columbus"? (b) What is the effect of the comparison? **[Interpret]**
2. What is the light sighted in the last stanza of "Columbus"? **[Interpret]**
3. What is the "grandest lesson"? **[Interpret]**
4. Compare and contrast the mate and Adm'r'l in "Columbus." **[Compare and Contrast]**
5. In what ways is this poem about the value of determination and courage? **[Analyze]**

EVALUATE

6. In "Columbus," is the explorer portrayed as brave or stubborn? Explain. **[Evaluate]**

Columbus ◆ 145

◆**Build Grammar Skills**

❸ **Commonly Confused Verbs: lie and lay** Ask students to identify the basic form of the second verb Miller uses in line 27. Ask them why he uses this verb. *The verb is lie; he uses this verb because the wave is reclining, waiting to rise up and strike.* Remind students that *lie* means "to rest or recline" and is intransitive, while *lay* means "to put or set something down," is transitive, and therefore always takes an object.

▶**Critical Viewing**◀

❹ **Compare and Contrast**
Students may say that the print shows Columbus's eagerness, courage, and self-assurance. They might notice that neither Columbus nor his men show any evidence of the hardship of their voyage. Also, standing in a small landing boat does not show much seafaring experience.

Humanities: Art

The Landing of Columbus, by Currier and Ives, 1876
Nathanial Currier and James Merritt Ives were well-known 19th-century New York City printmakers who depicted all kinds of events. Their more than 7,000 prints were used to decorate walls inexpensively, and sold in the U. S. and London for between 5¢ and $3, depending upon size, subject, and number of colors.
Created as part of a series celebrating America's 1876 centennial, this print shows Columbus about to step onto land in the Caribbean, carrying Spain's flag onto new lands.
How does the print show Columbus's entire journey? *The open sea and ship, rocky shore and landing boat, and tropical land with Indians indicate the complete span of the journey.*

Reinforce and Extend

Answers
◆**LITERATURE AND YOUR LIFE**

Reader's Response Make sure that students justify their opinions with citations from the poem.

Thematic Focus Students may note Columbus' determination, courage, and confidence as trailblazer qualities.

Journal Writing Students' entries should reflect the first mate's reservations about Columbus's determination.

☑ **Check Your Comprehension**
1. He is Christopher Columbus. He says, "Sail on," each time to the mate.
2. The Admiral's silence and the open, endless seas frighten him.

◆**Critical Thinking**
1. (a) He compares it to an angry animal (b) It suggests the sailors' vulnerability but has no effect on Columbus.
2. The light is the dawn.
3. The lesson is either that the world is round or that perseverance pays off.

4. Students may say that Columbus is a determined leader, brave, silent, and confident, while the mate is fearful, talkative, and doubtful.
5. Students may say this poem shows determination and courage as important values because these prove successful.
6. Students may say that the explorer appears both brave and stubborn—brave because he keeps going in the face of doubt, stubborn because he's risking men's lives despite their fear.

Develop Understanding

One-Minute Insight

"Western Wagons" follows a journey of exploration across America's West. Stephen Vincent Benét celebrates the adventurous and restless spirit of America's westward pioneers, recognizing that these explorers need not to be crowded and have no time for fear or weakness.

◆ Reading Strategy

1 Relate to What You Know To help students appreciate the descriptions of where the pioneers were headed and what they encountered, have students share information about California, Nebraska, Wyoming, and Iowa. *Students may note gold discoveries in California that could make someone rich, conflict over land rights in the plains states that could make it a "wild" place, and Iowa's farmlands.*

Clarification

2 Tell students that "Ioway" is "Iowa" spoken in dialect and used to make the rhyme work.

◆ Build Vocabulary

3 Antonyms Remind students that antonyms are words with opposite meanings. Then ask them to describe westward pioneers, using antonyms to *cowards* and *weak* as a starting point. *Students should say pioneers were "brave and strong."*

Customize for
Visual/Spatial Learners

Have students skim the poem for place names. Return together to the map on p. 143 to locate these places and note how far each is from the safety of the settled East. Have students study the painting on p. 147 as they imagine the westward journey.

Customize for
Musical/Rhythmic Learners

Point out lines 3–4, which allude to the folk song "Oh, Susanna." Play, or present the lyrics to students and then compare them to the version in the poem. What information does the poem offer about the lives of westward pioneers? *Students should note that the lyrics suggest an almost light-hearted acceptance of danger.*

146

Western Wagons

Stephen Vincent Benét

They went with axe and rifle, when the trail was
    still to blaze,
They went with wife and children, in the prairie-
    schooner days,
With banjo and with frying pan—Susanna, don't
    you cry!
For I'm off to California to get rich out there or die!

5   We've broken land and cleared it, but we're tired
    of where we are.
They say that wild Nebraska is a better place
    by far.
There's gold in far Wyoming, there's black earth
    in Ioway,
So pack up the kids and blankets, for we're moving
    out today!

The cowards never started and the weak died on
    the road,
10   And all across the continent the endless campfires
    glowed.
We'd taken land and settled—but a traveler
    passed by—
And we're going West tomorrow—Lordy, never ask
    us why!

We're going West tomorrow, where the promises
    can't fail.
O'er the hills in legions, boys, and crowd the
    dusty trail!
15   We shall starve and freeze and suffer. We shall die,
    and tame the lands.
But we're going West tomorrow, with our fortune
    in our hands.

146 ◆ Meeting Challenges

Cross-Curricular Connection: Social Studies

The Louisiana Purchase In 1803 the size of the U. S. was doubled to include what is now part or all of Louisiana, Missouri, Arkansas, Oklahoma, Kansas, Nebraska, Iowa, Minnesota, and North and South Dakota. Before long, Americans were heading west to settle that land. As they moved westward, settlers spilled into lands still held by Great Britain, Mexico, and later, the Republic of Texas. The United States ultimately took over these additional lands by treaty, war, or annexation.

In the Southwest, long-standing Mexican and Spanish settlements strongly influenced the region's culture, even for newcomers from America's East Coast. Places like Santa Fe, which Spanish settlers founded in 1610, were sites of missions that were centers of Hispanic Roman Catholic culture. That Hispanic culture remains vibrant today.

Have students consult an atlas or national zip code directory to find place names from America's West and Southwest. What cultural influences do these names suggest? *Students should find Hispanic influences in the Southwest, French influences in the upper Midwest and along the Canadian border, and Indian names scattered through the entire West.*

A New Beginning, Duane Bryers, Courtesy of the artist

▲ **Critical Viewing** What do the expressions on the faces of the couple in the painting reveal about their emotions? [Infer]

Guide for Responding

◆ **LITERATURE AND YOUR LIFE**

Reader's Response Does the life of a westward pioneer appeal to you? Explain.

Thematic Focus Would you describe these pioneers as trailblazers or adventure seekers—or both?

Travel List Imagine that you're about to embark on a journey west in a covered wagon. Make a list of the supplies you'd need to take along.

☑ **Check Your Comprehension**

1. With what items did these pioneers travel?
2. What are the destinations of the people in "Western Wagons"?

◆ **Critical Thinking**

INTERPRET

1. What is meant by the phrase "when the trail was still to blaze"? [Interpret]
2. What circumstances might have prompted the pioneers to seek a better life? [Speculate]
3. Is the thrill of blazing trails or the need for a better home the driving force in the pioneers' lives? [Draw Conclusions]

EVALUATE

4. Are these pioneers foolish in their quest for riches and adventure? Explain. [Make a Judgment]

COMPARE LITERARY WORKS

5. Compare and contrast the motivation and character of Columbus with that of the pioneers in "Western Wagons." [Compare and Contrast]

One-Minute Insight

In "The Other Pioneers," Roberto Félix Salazar traces the history of his Mexican American ancestors as they settled in America's Southwest. He describes the communities they founded, the culture they planted, and the dreams they fostered for the future.

◆ **Reading Strategy**

❶ **Relate to What You Know**
Most students will know that Native Americans inhabited what is now the American Southwest before the Spanish arrived on the continent. Discuss the importance that Salazar attributes to the Hispanic Americans' coming to the Southwest before the settlers with Northern European backgrounds. Help students use what they know to recognize that much of the character and appearance of the American Southwest derives from the language, culture, and architecture of the Mexicans who settled there—a source of pride.

◆ **Literary Focus**

❷ **Stanzas in Poetry** The middle stanza is longer than the others. Have students identify other ways that Salazar's stanzas are unique to this poem. *Salazar's poem has just a few stanzas which vary in length.*

Clarification

❸ Salazar honors his ancestors and their modern descendants by listing names that reflect Spanish heritage. Some highly accomplished Hispanic Americans bear these names. For example, Dr. Clotilde García overcame obstacles facing both women and Mexican Americans to become a doctor. Her brother, Hector, became a U.S. Ambassador and earned the Medal of Freedom for his activism on behalf of Hispanics.

Customize for
Interpersonal Learners
Have students interview older family or community members to learn what they hope to pass on to future generations. Invite students to contemplate and describe what they would hope to establish in a new community. Encourage them to use the poem's details that suggest hopes.

148

The Other Pioneers

Roberto Félix Salazar

❶ Now I must write
Of those of mine who rode these plains
Long years before the Saxon[1] and the Irish came.
Of those who plowed the land and built the towns
5   And gave the towns soft-woven Spanish names.
Of those who moved across the Rio Grande
Toward the hiss of Texas snake and Indian yell.
Of men who from the earth made thick-walled homes
And from the earth raised churches to their God.
10 And of the wives who bore them sons
And smiled with knowing joy.

They saw the Texas sun rise golden-red with
promised wealth
And saw the Texas sun sink golden yet, with
wealth unspent.
"Here," they said. "Here to live and here to love."
15 "Here is the land for our sons and the sons of
our sons."
❷ And they sang the songs of ancient Spain
And they made new songs to fit new needs.
They cleared the brush and planted the corn
And saw green stalks turn black from lack of rain.
20 They roamed the plains behind the herds
And stood the Indian's cruel attacks.
There was dust and there was sweat.
And there were tears and the women prayed.

And the years moved on.
25 Those who were first placed in graves
Beside the broad mesquite[2] and the tall nopal.[3]
Gentle mothers left their graces and their arts
And <u>stalwart</u> fathers pride and manly strength.
Salinas, de la Garza, Sánchez, García,
30 Uribe, González, Martinez, de León:[4]
❸ Such were the names of the fathers.
Salinas, de la Garza, Sánchez, García,
Uribe, González, Martinez, de León:
Such are the names of the sons.

1. **Saxon** (sak´ sən) *n.*: English.

2. **mesquite** (mes kēt´) *n.*: Thorny tree or shrub common in the southwestern United States and Mexico.
3. **nopal** (nō´ pəl) *n.*: Cactus with red flowers.
4. **Salinas** (sä lē´ näs), **de la Garza** (dā lä gär´sä), **Sánchez** (sän´ chäs), **García** (Gär sē´ ä), **Uribe** (ōō rē´ bā) **Gonzáles** (gōn sä´ läs), **Martinez** (mär tē´ näs), **de León** (dā lā ōn´)

◆ **Build Vocabulary**

stalwart (stôl´ wərt) *adj.*: Resolute; firm; unyielding

Speaking and Listening Mini-Lesson

Oral Presentation
This mini-lesson supports the Speaking and Listening activity in the Idea Bank on p. 151.

Introduce Oral presentations offer a way to share information. They can be interactive to create a dialogue between speaker and audience.

Develop Give students these tips:
• Narrow the topic geographically or by content: "The Rio Grande" or "Spanish Missions in Texas."
• Organize the presentation in chunks—allow for mental breaks and audience contributions.

• Engage audience interest with audiovisual or hands-on elements.
• Acknowledge audience reaction.

Apply Allow time for research and preparation. Have groups practice as presenter and audience. Urge students to plan for audience participation.

Assess Evaluate students' presentations on organization and preparation, fluency, and audience interaction. Have students use Self-Assessment: Speech, p. 113, and Peer Assessment: Speaker/Speech, p. 118, in **Alternative Assessment** to evaluate their efforts.

East Side Main Plaza, San Antonio, Texas, 1844, William G.M. Samuel, Courtesy of Bexar County and the Witte Museum, San Antonio, Texas

▲ **Critical Viewing** This painting depicts San Antonio, Texas, in the mid 1800's. What does the painting reveal about the climate and living conditions there? [Infer] **4**

Guide for Responding

◆ LITERATURE AND YOUR LIFE

Reader's Response What feelings toward the pioneers does the poem evoke in you? Why?

Thematic Focus In what ways did these "other pioneers" blaze trails?

Letter Write a letter to one of the "other pioneers." In it, ask questions about their experiences in settling the region that is now Texas.

☑ Check Your Comprehension

1. Who are the "other pioneers"?
2. When did they ride the plains?
3. What did they accomplish?

◆ Critical Thinking

INTERPRET

1. From what country did the "other pioneers" come? [Interpret]
2. Why might the pioneers have chosen to settle in a new land? [Infer]
3. What does the repetition of family names in the final lines of the poem signify? [Analyze]

EVALUATE

4. How would you describe the speaker's attitude toward his ancestors? [Assess]

APPLY

5. The poem describes the pioneers' legacy to their children. What do you think is the most valuable thing a parent can leave to a child? [Generalize]

The Other Pioneers ◆ 149

Beyond the Selection

FURTHER READING

Other Works by the Authors
Songs of the Sierra, Joaquin Miller
John Brown's Body, Stephen Vincent Benét

Other Works About Trailblazers
I, Columbus; My Journal 1492–3, ed. by Peter and Connie Roop
Our Tejano Heroes by Sammye Munson
Buffalo Gals: Women of the Old West, by Brandon Marie Miller

INTERNET

We suggest the following sites on the Internet (all Web sites are subject to change). For information on Columbus:
http://sunsite.unc.edu/expo/1492.exhibit/c-columbus/columbus.html

For information on life as a pioneer:
http://ourworld.compuserve.com/homepages/trailofthe49ers/index.htm

Learn about Hispanic history at
http//www. santafe.org/hispanic.html

We *strongly recommend* that you preview these sites before you send your students to them.

Answers

◆ Reading Strategy

1. Students may say the poem shows more of Columbus's idealism.
2. They knew they faced tasks such as clearing a trail and dangers such as hostile Indians and wild animals.
3. Texas was once part of Mexico and still has a large Hispanic population.

◆ Build Vocabulary

1. wan 2. swarthy

Spelling Strategy

1. joyous   4. beauteous
2. victorious   5. glorious
3. larcenous   6. bounteous

Using the Word Bank

1. c
2. a
3. c
4. a
5. b

◆ Literary Focus

1. Both have 8 lines, similar rhyme patterns, and a refrain based on "Sail on." The first contains dialogue, which the last lacks.
2. (a) There are four. (b) Yes, all have an AABB rhyming pattern.
3. Stanza 1: My Spanish ancestors are worth remembering. Stanza 2: They faced many challenges with courage and vision. Stanza 3: They left a valuable and vibrant culture behind.

◆ Build Grammar Skills

Practice

1. lie; 2. laid; 3. lay; 4. laid;
5. lain

Writing Application
Possible sentences:

1. Columbus laid his hand on the helm.
2. The pioneer lay in the wagon.

 **Writer's Solution**

For additional instruction and practice, use the Glossary of Troublesome Verbs page, p. 76, in the *Writer's Solution Grammar Practice Book.*

Guide for Responding (continued)

◆ Reading Strategy

RELATE TO WHAT YOU KNOW

Relating to what you know helps you understand literature. Use your own experience and knowledge to answer the following:

1. How does your previous knowledge of Christopher Columbus compare with the way he's described in "Columbus"?
2. Why might the pioneers in "Western Wagons" have traveled with an axe and a rifle?
3. What do you know about Texas that makes "The Other Pioneers" easier to understand?

◆ Build Vocabulary

USING THE ANTONYMS *wan* AND *swarthy*

Joaquin Miller uses the antonyms *wan* and *swarthy* in "Columbus." If you know that *wan* means "pale," you can guess that *swarthy* means "having a dark complexion."

Copy the following sentences on your paper. Fill in each blank with *wan* or *swarthy*.

1. The sickly child looked pale and ____?____.
2. The old sailor had a ____?____ complexion because of years spent in the sun and wind.

SPELLING STRATEGY

When adding *-ous* to a word that ends in *y,* follow these rules. Drop the *y* if the sound it represents disappears: mutiny + -ous = mutinous

Keep the *y* or change it to *e* or *i* if the sound it represents remains: harmony + -ous = harmonious

On your paper, add *-ous* to these words.

1. joy   3. larceny   5. glory
2. victory   4. beauty   6. bounty

USING THE WORD BANK

On your paper, write the letter of the word that has the opposite meaning of the Word Bank word.

1. mutinous: (a) silly, (b) rebellious, (c) obedient
2. wan: (a) swarthy, (b) pale, (c) wanting
3. swarthy: (a) true, (b) complicated, (c) wan
4. unfurled: (a) folded, (b) opened, (c) hidden
5. stalwart: (a) strong, (b) weak, (c) heavy

◆ Literary Focus

STANZAS IN POETRY

Stanzas are groupings of two or more lines in poetry. In some poems, each stanza has the same line length, rhythm, and rhyme pattern. In "Columbus," for example, each stanza has eight lines and a repeated rhyme pattern (the last word in every other line rhymes). Like paragraphs in prose, stanzas in poetry mark changes in thought or emphasis.

1. Compare the first and last stanzas of "Columbus." What is alike about them, and what is different?
2. (a) How many stanzas are in "Western Wagons"? (b) Do they repeat a rhyme pattern?
3. Examine the stanzas in "The Other Pioneers." Explain the main thought in each.

◆ Build Grammar Skills

COMMONLY CONFUSED VERBS: *lie* AND *lay*

The verbs *lie* and *lay* are often confused, especially in speech. *Lie* means "to rest or recline." Its forms are *lie, lay,* and (*have* or *had*) *lain. Lie* is intransitive; it does not pass action to a receiver: The sailors *lie* in their bunks.

Lay means "to put or set something down." Its forms are *lay, laid,* and (*have* or *had*) *laid.* The verb *lay* is transitive: It always passes its action to a receiver: Please *lay* the supplies in the wagon.

These words are frequently confused because the past of *lie* is the same as the present of *lay.* Miller uses the past form of *lie* in this line from "Columbus": Behind him *lay* the great Azores . . .

Practice Copy the following sentences. Choose the correct form of the verb.

1. The tired traveler wanted to (lie, lay) down.
2. First, she (lay, laid) the baby down for a nap.
3. She had to (lie, lay) a blanket over the baby.
4. She had (lain, laid) her head on the pillow for only five minutes before she fell asleep.
5. After she had (lain, laid) down, she felt better.

Writing Application Complete the following.

1. Write a sentence using the past tense of *lay.*
2. Write a sentence using the past tense of *lie.*

Build Your Portfolio

 Idea Bank

Writing

1. **Letter** Put yourself in the place of a pioneer described in "Western Wagons" or "The Other Pioneers." Write a letter to someone you had to leave behind as you traveled to another area. Tell about your adventures along the way.

2. **Dialogue** Imagine that you are one of the sailors growing "mutinous day by day" in "Columbus." Write the dialogue you might have with another sailor about the voyage.

3. **Comparison-and-Contrast Essay** In a brief essay, compare and contrast the reasons or motives behind Columbus's exploration and the westward pioneers' travels. Use lines from the poems for support.

Speaking and Listening

4. **Skit** With a classmate, take on the roles of Columbus and the first mate. Using "Columbus" as a guide, write and perform a skit for the class. **[Performing Arts Link]**

5. **Oral Presentation** Find out about the early settlement of any area named in "Western Wagons" or "The Other Pioneers." Make an oral presentation to your class on one aspect of this settlement that interests you. **[Social Studies Link]**

Projects

6. **Living History [Group Activity]** With a group of classmates, reenact a scene that might have taken place during the early settlement of the Americas. Use props to make your scene come to life. Each group member should be responsible for a different task, such as checking historical accuracy, obtaining props, or writing dialogue. **[Social Studies Link]**

7. **Book Cover** Design and create a book cover for a collection of poems in which "Columbus," "Western Wagons, " and "The Other Pioneers" might appear. **[Art Link]**

 Writing Mini-Lesson

Speech

The characters in these poems are courageous trailblazers. (Some of them are named in history books, and some remain nameless, yet all are worthy of remembrance.) One way we remember such people is by naming places, such as schools and parks, after them. Write a speech in which you give reasons for naming a place after an explorer or a hero.

Writing Skills Focus: Support Ideas With Reasons

Your goal is to convince your audience of something. To make your speech persuasive, **support your ideas with reasons.** To do this, find facts through library research and on-line sources. In the following, Stephen Vincent Benét gives reasons why the pioneers were admirable.

Model From "Western Wagons"
We shall starve and freeze and suffer. We shall die, /and tame the lands.

Prewriting Decide which hero or explorer you would like to honor. Gather facts about that person's achievements.

Drafting Begin by naming the place and the person whom you want to honor. Develop and support your ideas by giving facts about the person's life. Conclude by restating your main points.

> ◆ **Grammar Application**
> In your speech, use the verb *lie* or *lay*. Make sure you have used it correctly.

Revising Deliver your speech to a classmate. Ask him or her to point out places where additional facts would strengthen your argument. Add information to support your ideas.

Columbus/Western Wagons/The Other Pioneers ◆ 151

 Idea Bank

Following are suggestions for matching the Idea Bank topics with your students' performance levels and learning modalities:

Customize for
Performance Levels
Less Advanced Students: 1, 6
Average Students: 2, 4, 6, 7
More Advanced Students: 3, 5, 6, 7

Customize for
Learning Modalities
Verbal/Linguistic: 1, 2, 3, 5
Interpersonal: 4, 5, 6
Visual/Spatial: 1, 6, 7
Bodily/Kinesthetic: 4, 5, 6
Logical/Mathematical: 3, 5
Intrapersonal: 3, 7

 Writing Mini-Lesson

Refer students to the Writing Handbook for instruction on the writing process and further information on speeches. Have students use the Cluster Organizer, in **Writing and Language Transparencies,** p. 73, to arrange their prewriting facts.

> ✒ **Writer's Solution**

Writing Lab CD-ROM
Have students complete the tutorial on Persuasion. Follow these steps:
1. Have students use the Considering Audience and Purpose section to help explore ways to gear their speeches to the intended audience.
2. Students can view the *Star Trek* video clip to hear examples of giving details.
3. The Publishing and Presenting section of the tutorial includes tips for giving a speech.

Writer's Solution Sourcebook
Have students use Chapter 6, "Persuasion," pp. 166–199 for additional support. This chapter includes in-depth instruction on persuasive speeches, pp. 181 and 183.

✓ ASSESSMENT OPTIONS

Formal Assessment, Selection Test, pp. 47–49, and Assessment Resources Software. The selection test is designed so that it can be easily customized to the performance levels of your students.

Alternative Assessment, p. 13, includes options for less advanced students, more advanced students, verbal/linguistic learners, musical/rhythmic learners, interpersonal learners, and visual/spatial learners.

PORTFOLIO ASSESSMENT
Use the following rubrics and assessment form in the **Alternative Assessment** booklet to assess student writing:
Letter: Expression: p. 90
Dialogue: Fictional Narrative, p. 91
Comparison-and-Contrast Essay: Comparison/Contrast, p. 99
Writing Mini-Lesson: Peer Assessment: Speaker/Speech, p. 114

Objectives

1. To read, comprehend, and interpret a short story
2. To relate a conflict with nature to personal experience
3. To make predictions
4. To understand conflict between a character and nature
5. To build vocabulary in context and learn forms of *exhaust*
6. To develop skill in using active voice and passive voice
7. To write a report on the Yukon
8. To respond to the story through writing, speaking and listening, and projects

Skills Instruction

Vocabulary:
Related Words: Forms of *exhaust*

Spelling:
Using *ough* for the Long *o* Sound

Grammar:
Active and Passive Voice

Reading Strategy:
Predict

Literary Focus:
Conflict With Nature

Writing:
Narrowing a Topic

Speaking and Listening:
Casting Proposal (Teacher Edition)

Critical Viewing:
Connect

Portfolio Opportunities

Writing: Diary Entry; Job Description; Modified Story

Writing Mini-Lesson: Report on the Yukon

Speaking and Listening: Oral Interpretation; Casting Proposal

Projects: Multimedia Report; Author Research

More About the Author

Jack London's friends said that during his lifetime the stories he told were even better than those he wrote. London, whose real name was John Griffith London, certainly could draw upon a wealth of first-hand experiences. By the time he sold his first story in 1899, he had had a series of adventures, including a march across the country to protest unemployment. These adventures provided material for the collection of stories he published only a year later, *The Son of the Wolf* (1900). London has always been admired for his compassion for the downtrodden of the world and his belief in the will to survive.

Guide for Reading

Meet the Author:

Jack London (1876–1916)

Jack London was the highest paid, most popular novelist and short-story writer of his day. His exciting tales of adventure and courage were inspired by his own challenging experiences. At age seventeen, London sailed with a seal-hunting ship to Japan and Siberia. On his return, he became involved with a band of oyster thieves. When caught, he worked with the local coastal patrol to catch other such outlaws.

Capturing Adventures in Print At the age of nineteen, London returned to high school and vowed to become a writer. He eventually wrote more than fifty books, including novels, short stories, and nonfiction. His best-known works create vivid pictures of strong characters facing the challenges of nature—from Buck the dog in *Call of the Wild* to the ruthless Wolf Larson of *The Sea Wolf*.

The Story Behind the Story

London spent the winter of 1897 in the Yukon Territory of northwest Canada. Along with thousands of others, he journeyed to the Klondike region of the Yukon in search of gold. Although he did not find the valuable mineral, he did find an important source of inspiration. The cold, stark climate of the Yukon became the backdrop for many of his stories, including "Up the Slide."

◆ Literature and Your Life

Connect Your Experience

Think about times you've gotten in over your head. For example, you may have taken a bike ride that turned into a marathon after you got lost, or you may have gone swimming in the ocean and gotten caught in the undertow. In "Up the Slide," a young man sets out to do something simple that turns into a hair-raising, life-threatening adventure.

Thematic Focus: Blazing Trails

The young man in London's story was one of many prospectors who blazed a trail into Canada's frigid Yukon Territory in search of gold. What risks might these trailblazers have faced?

◆ Background for Understanding

Geography

The Yukon Territory is in the northwestern corner of Canada, just beside Alaska. The climate there is one of the most challenging on Earth. It is part of the subarctic climate zone, where temperatures have been known to plunge to -80°F. Because of its northern position on the globe, daylight hours vary greatly—from more than twenty hours a day in summer to only a few hours in winter.

◆ Build Vocabulary

Related Words: Forms of *exhaust*

The main character in "Up the Slide" becomes *exhausted* by his struggles against the elements. *Exhausted* is a form of the verb *exhaust*, meaning "to tire completely." Related forms are *exhaustion* (noun) and *exhausting* (adjective).

Word Bank

Which words from the story might have opposite meanings? Check the Build Vocabulary box on page 158 to see if you chose correctly.

exhausted
thoroughly
manifestly
exertion
maneuver
ascent
descent

Prentice Hall Literature Program Resources

REINFORCE / RETEACH / EXTEND

Selection Support Pages
Build Vocabulary: Related Words: Forms of *exhaust*, p. 70
Build Spelling Skills, p. 71
Build Grammar Skills: Active Voice and Passive Voice, p. 72
Reading Strategy: Predict, p. 73
Literary Focus: Conflict with Nature, p. 74

Strategies for Diverse Student Needs, pp. 27–28

Beyond Literature Cross-Curricular Connection: Physical Education, p. 14

Formal Assessment Selection Test, pp. 50–52, Assessment Resources Software

Alternative Assessment, p. 14

Writing and Language Transparencies Series of Events Chain, p. 57

Resource Pro CD-ROM "Up the Slide"—includes all resource material and customizable lesson plan

Listening to Literature Audiocassettes "Up the Slide"

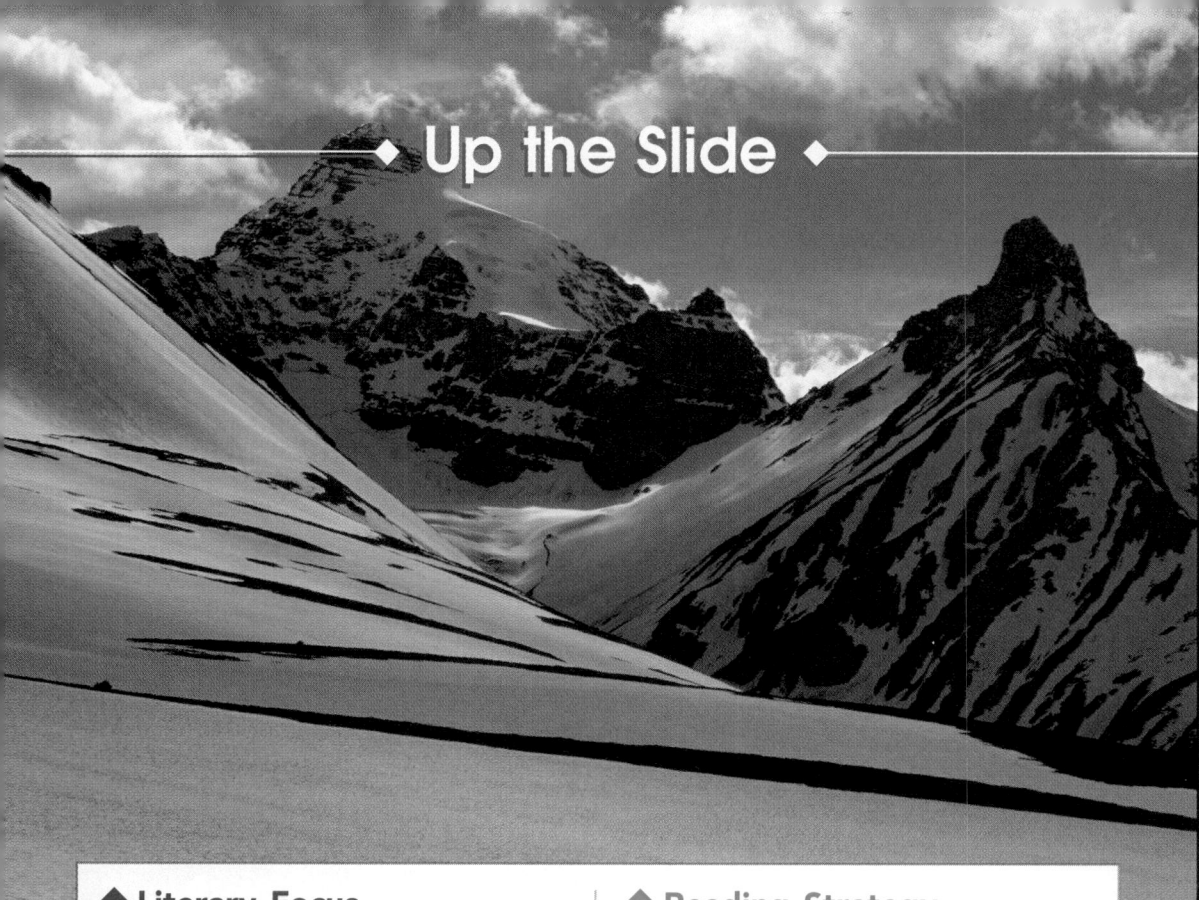

◆ Up the Slide ◆

◆ Literary Focus

CONFLICT WITH NATURE

A **conflict** is a struggle between opposing forces. In literature, a conflict may be between characters, within a character's mind, or between a character and some force of nature. In "Up the Slide," the primary conflict is between a character, Clay Dilham, and nature—the cold, icy conditions of the Yukon. You can get an idea of what Clay faces from this photograph of Yukon wilderness.

◆ Reading Strategy

PREDICT

As you read an adventure story like "Up the Slide," you keep wondering what will happen. You can **predict,** or make educated guesses about, story events based on clues in the story that suggest a certain outcome. You might also base a prediction on your own experience in a similar situation. After you make a prediction, read on to see how your prediction matches the actual outcome. Use a chart like this one to record your ideas.

Story Event or Clue	Prediction	Actual Outcome
Each step became more difficult and perilous, and he was faint from exertion and from lack of Swanson's dinner.	He will collapse and have to be rescued.	

Guide for Reading ◆ 153

Interest Grabber

Write the common statement "Be back in a minute" on the board. Ask students to explain what they think or expect when they hear someone say that. Then present a few simple multi-step tasks all students will understand, such as buying a pair of sneakers, shopping for food, completing all their homework, or taking out a certain book from the library. Ask them to predict how long each task will take, from start to finish. Compare estimates. Talk about what can make a task take more or less time than estimated. Then tell students that in the story they are about to read, a young prospector sets out to do something he says will take only half an hour.

◆ Build Grammar Skills

Active Voice and Passive Voice

If you wish to introduce the grammar concept for this selection before students read, refer to the instruction on p. 160.

Customize for
Less Proficient Readers

Students may have trouble visualizing the terrain and the obstacles Clay faces. Help them picture what he does to overcome them, both on his ascent to the tree and on his attempt to return his sled and dogs. Advise students to reread the confusing portions of the adventure and, within a group, go over what Clay faces, how he responds, and what results from his efforts. It may help students to sketch the mountainside as described or to keep track of Clay's climb using a graphic organizer, such as Series of Events Chain, p. 57, of **Writing and Language Transparencies.**

Customize for
More Advanced Students

Seventeen-year-old Clay faces challenges he had not anticipated and then manages to overcome them, obstacle by obstacle. Guide students to think about which youthful traits get him in over his head in the first place, and which ones serve to help him get through the ordeal in the end.

Preparing for Standardized Tests

Vocabulary Knowledge of related forms of a word may help students as they read in general, and with analogy sections of standardized tests. The object of an analogy question is to determine the relationship between two items and then to apply that same relationship to fill in the missing part of another.

    Jack London : adventure stories ::
    Emily Dickinson : poetry

Most standardized tests offer a choice of words to complete an analogy. Present the following sample test question:

Rock climbing : exhaustion : _____ : relaxation.

  (A) snow shoveling   (C) refreshing
  (B) jogging   (D) TV watching

Point out to students that more than one answer may complete an analogy, but they should select the best answer. *(B) jogging* completes the analogy, but *(D) TV watching* is the better answer since, for most people, TV watching is the activity more likely to lead to relaxation. For further practice, use Build Vocabulary in **Selection Support,** p. 70.

One-Minute Insight

"Up the Slide" is set in the harsh Yukon landscape. Clay Dilham, an over-confident 17-year-old, sets out on his dog-sled to get firewood. He leaves his traveling partner, Swanson, behind, cooking dinner. Although his youthful exuberance causes him to underestimate the challenge of scaling an icy, snow-covered cliff, Clay's agility, strength, and instinctive survival skills enable him to do this and get through an unexpected avalanche. He also discovers a new source of firewood.

Team Teaching Strategy

You may want to coordinate with a social studies teacher to come up with ideas for extending instruction to cover the historical period of the Yukon Gold Rush.

Clarification

1 A cord is a 128-cubic-foot measure of wood cut for use as fuel, and arranged in a pile 8 feet long, 4 feet wide, and 4 feet high.

◆ Reading Strategy

2 Predict Ask students to consider reasons other than those Clay gives for why other prospectors in need of firewood had left that particular tree alone. Students may say that more experienced miners saw the tree, recognized the dangers in getting to it, and knew better than to try to make the attempt.

Customize for
Logical/Mathematical Learners

Students may note the unusual title, "Up the Slide." Guide them to keep that idea in mind as they read, and to make diagrams to try to follow the route and logic of Clay's climb. He does a 20-foot perpendicular rock climb, zigzags up a slide to the tree, and then climbs higher up the slide to eventually make his way back down to the camp using an easier route. As needed, review the mathematical terms London uses, including *perpendicular, angle,* and *slope.* To help them appreciate the difficulty of Clay's ascent through snow and ice, draw a large 30° angle on the board or model one.

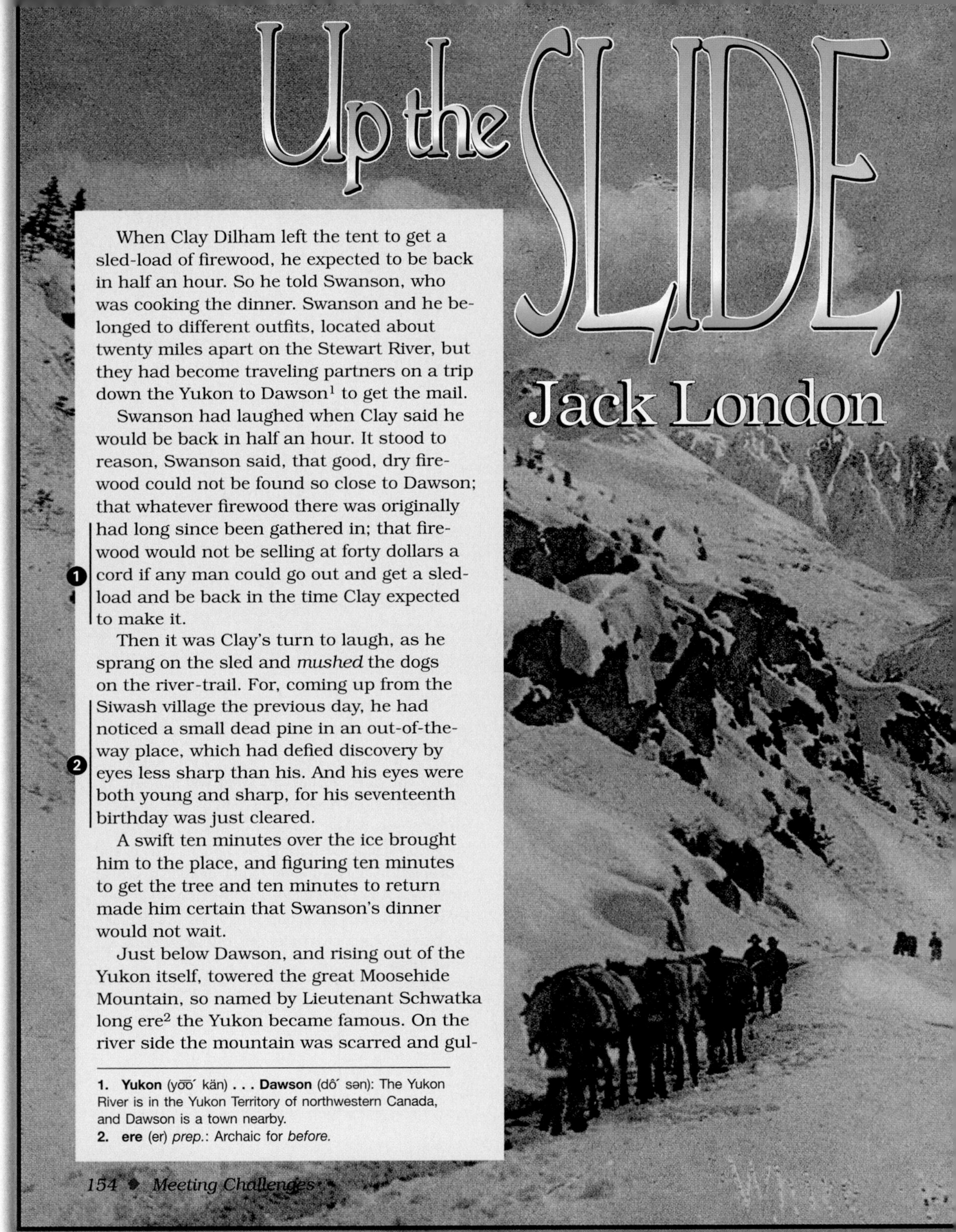

154

Up the SLIDE
Jack London

When Clay Dilham left the tent to get a sled-load of firewood, he expected to be back in half an hour. So he told Swanson, who was cooking the dinner. Swanson and he belonged to different outfits, located about twenty miles apart on the Stewart River, but they had become traveling partners on a trip down the Yukon to Dawson[1] to get the mail.

Swanson had laughed when Clay said he would be back in half an hour. It stood to reason, Swanson said, that good, dry firewood could not be found so close to Dawson; that whatever firewood there was originally had long since been gathered in; that firewood would not be selling at forty dollars a **1** cord if any man could go out and get a sled-load and be back in the time Clay expected to make it.

Then it was Clay's turn to laugh, as he sprang on the sled and *mushed* the dogs on the river-trail. For, coming up from the Siwash village the previous day, he had noticed a small dead pine in an out-of-the-way place, which had defied discovery by **2** eyes less sharp than his. And his eyes were both young and sharp, for his seventeenth birthday was just cleared.

A swift ten minutes over the ice brought him to the place, and figuring ten minutes to get the tree and ten minutes to return made him certain that Swanson's dinner would not wait.

Just below Dawson, and rising out of the Yukon itself, towered the great Moosehide Mountain, so named by Lieutenant Schwatka long ere[2] the Yukon became famous. On the river side the mountain was scarred and gul-

1. **Yukon** (yōō´ kän) . . . **Dawson** (dô´ sən): The Yukon River is in the Yukon Territory of northwestern Canada, and Dawson is a town nearby.
2. **ere** (er) *prep.*: Archaic for *before.*

154 ◆ *Meeting Challenges*

Block Scheduling Strategies

Consider these suggestions to take advantage of extended class time:

- Provide time for students to discuss the Literature and Your Life ideas, p. 152, to motivate them to read the story.
- To help students prepare for the Writing Mini-Lesson, refer them to Chapter 7, Reports, p. 201, in *Writer's Solution Sourcebook.* If you have access to technology, use the About Reports section of the Reports tutorial on the *Writer's Solution Writing Lab CD-ROM.*

- To provide students with portfolio opportunities, devote class time to having them work in small groups on the Projects in the Idea Bank on p. 161, or to research the Klondike Gold Rush for the Social Studies Connection in Beyond Literature on p. 159. Refer students to the Web site given on the bottom of that page. That site, which includes photographs of the miners, the camps, and the terrain, will be of use to those doing the Multimedia Report project in the Idea Bank on p. 161.

lied and gored; and it was up one of these gores or gullies that Clay had seen the tree.

Halting his dogs beneath, on the river ice, he looked up, and after some searching, rediscovered it. Being dead, its weatherbeaten gray so blended with the gray wall of rock that a thousand men could pass by and never notice it. Taking root in a cranny, it had grown up, <u>exhausted</u> its bit of soil, and perished. Beneath it the wall fell sheer for a hundred feet to the river. All one had to do was to sink an ax into the dry trunk a dozen times and it would fall to the ice, and most probably smash conveniently to pieces. This Clay had figured on when confidently limiting the trip to half an hour.

He studied the cliff <u>thoroughly</u> before attempting it. So far as he was concerned, the longest way round was the shortest way to the tree. Twenty feet of nearly perpendicular climbing would bring him to where a slide sloped more gently in. By making a long zigzag across the face of this slide and back again, he would arrive at the pine.

Fastening his ax across his shoulders so that it would not interfere with his movements, he clawed up the broken rock, hand and foot, like a cat, till the twenty feet were cleared and he could draw breath on the edge of the slide.

The slide was steep and its snow-covered surface slippery. Further, the heelless, walrus-hide shoes of his *muclucs* were polished by much ice travel, and by his second step he realized how little he could depend upon them for clinging purposes. A slip at that point meant a plunge over the edge and a twenty-foot fall to the ice. A hundred feet farther along, and a slip would mean a fifty-foot fall.

He thrust his mittened hand through the snow to the earth to steady himself, and went on. But he was forced to exercise such care that the first zigzag consumed five minutes. Then, returning across the face of the slide toward the pine, he met with a new difficulty. The slope steepened considerably, so that little snow collected, while bent flat

◆ **Build Vocabulary**

exhausted (eg zôst′ əd) *v.*: Used up; expended completely

thoroughly (thŭr′ ō lē) *adv.*: Accurately and with regard to detail

Up the Slide ◆ 155

Humanities: Film

Gold Rush Like any great North American adventure, the Yukon Gold Rush has often been the subject of Hollywood's attention. Among the many movies made, one stands out: Charlie Chaplin's *The Gold Rush*. Made in 1925, this silent classic pits the Little Tramp against a brawny prospector and the rigors of the Yukon itself. Finding something to laugh about, somehow, in the grim Klondike experience, Chaplin includes the unforgettable scenes of the starving tramp

eating a leather shoe, his flirtation with a dancehall girl, and his scuffle with the prospector in a cabin that teeters on the edge of a cliff.

Invite students to rent and watch this film, featuring Chaplin at his best, or obtain and show it to the class if time permits. There are two versions of this film on videotape, the original 82-minute silent version and a 72-minute version that Chaplin prepared in 1942 with his own narration on the soundtrack.

◆**Critical Thinking**

❸ **Deduce** Tell students that the background picture on these pages is an old photograph of people in White Pass during the Yukon Gold Rush. Discuss what the photo reveals about the Yukon terrain and climate and the challenges that the landscape must have presented to the many inexperienced gold seekers who entered it. *Students may say that the terrain appears to be harsh, unforgiving, cold, and rugged. They may say that it looks like a place where food, shelter, and services would be inadequate at best, where comforts would be few, and where travel would be very hard.*

◆**Literary Focus**

❹ **Conflict With Nature** Guide students to appreciate that even nature itself is in conflict; the hearty pine tree used up the meager soil that once nourished it and has died.

◆**Literary Focus**

❺ **Conflict With Nature** From here on, London describes in vivid detail Clay's hazardous climb both to the tree and then back to safety. His plan and movements may be difficult for students to follow. Have students reread passages, as needed, to keep pace with Clay's adventure on the slope.

Customize for
English Language Learners
"Up the Slide" is full of geographical terms and terms from nature that may be unfamiliar to students. Make available a geography text or other resource that would provide pictures and/or vivid descriptions of the words that note landscape features such as *gully, gore, weather-beaten, cranny, slide, buttresses, pitch, avalanche, rock outcroppings, gravel, basin, timber, barren rock, crest,* and *flank.* Encourage students to keep a glossary of these terms.

Customize for
Visual/Spatial Learners
Refer students to a map of North America or one showing northwestern Canada and Alaska, to have them locate the Yukon region and the town of Dawson. From the maps, students can imagine the distance and difficulty of the miners' journey there from the ports of the Pacific Northwest, such as Seattle.

◆ Literary Focus

❶ Conflict with Nature *Students may say that while Clay struggles to climb upwards, the slide and the slippery, loose footing it presents often force him in the opposite direction.*

◆ Reading Strategy

❷ Predict Clay is now safe for the moment. Do you think his luck will hold out? *Students may predict that if it did, the story would end quickly; they might say that since he faced danger on the way up, he is likely to encounter more of the same on the way back down.*

Comprehension Check ☑

❸ Ask students what happens to the tree after Clay chops it down. *Clay's chopping down the tree propels it over the edge, down to where the dogs wait. He calls to them because they are frightened by the tree's unexpected crash to the ground.*

◆ Literary Focus

❹ Conflict with Nature Guide students to visualize Clay's predicament. Students can appreciate, perhaps from their own experience, that whether they find themselves on a slippery mountain slope, high up in a tree, or in other high spots, it is harder and more frightening to climb down than it was to climb up.

---

beneath this thin covering were long, dry last-year's grasses.

> **◆ Literary Focus**
> **❶** In what ways is the slide an opposing force to Clay?

The surface they presented was as glassy as that of his muclucs, and when both surfaces came together his feet shot out, and he fell on his face, sliding downward and convulsively clutching for something to stay himself.

❷ This he succeeded in doing, although he lay quiet for a couple of minutes to get back his nerve. He would have taken off his muclucs and gone at it in his socks, only the cold was thirty below zero, and at such temperature his feet would quickly freeze. So he went on, and after ten minutes of risky work made the safe and solid rock where stood the pine.

❸ A few strokes of the ax felled it into the chasm, and peeping over the edge, he indulged a laugh at the startled dogs. They were on the verge of bolting when he called aloud to them, soothingly, and they were reassured.

Then he turned about for the trip back. Going down, he knew, was even more dangerous than coming up, but how dangerous he did not realize till he had slipped half a dozen times, and each time saved himself by what appeared to him a miracle. Time and again he ventured upon the slide, and time and again he was balked when he came to the grasses.

He sat down and looked at the treacherous snow-covered slope. It was <u>manifestly</u> impossi-**❹**ble for him to make it with a whole body, and he did not wish to arrive at the bottom shattered like the pine tree.

But while he sat inactive the frost was stealing in on him, and the quick chilling of his body warned him that he could not delay. He must be doing something to keep his blood circulating. If he could not get down by going down, there only remained to him to get down

> **◆ Build Vocabulary**
> **manifestly** (man´ ə fest´ lē) *adv.*: Clearly
> **exertion** (eg zʉr´ shən) *n.*: Energetic activity; effort

156 ◆ *Meeting Challenges*

 Cross-Curricular Connection: Science

Winter Activity Discuss with students that the rising popularity of winter outdoor activities, such as skiing, ice skating, and mountain and rock climbing, has led to a rise in cold-weather ailments and accidents. Frostbite is one result of prolonged exposure to extremely low temperatures, and so is hypothermia, or subnormal body temperature. The most obvious signs of frostbite are progressive—painful loss of feeling, leading to numbness, skin discoloration, and then loss of function. Hypothermia causes confusion, drowsiness, difficulty in moving, and, if not treated properly, death.

Ask students to find out about precautions people who plan to spend time in subfreezing temperatures can take to prevent these severe problems. Have them learn what first-aid steps to follow if frostbite or hypothermia occur.

⑤ by going up. It was a herculean task, but it was the only way out of the predicament.

From where he was he could not see the top of the cliff, but he reasoned that the gully in which lay the slide must give inward more and more as it approached the top. From what little he could see, the gully displayed this tendency; and he noticed, also, that the slide extended for many hundreds of feet upward, and that where it ended the rock was well broken up and favorable for climbing. . . .

So instead of taking the zigzag which led downward, he made a new one leading upward and crossing the slide at an angle of thirty degrees. The grasses gave him much trouble, and made him long for soft-tanned moosehide moccasins, which could make his feet cling like a second pair of hands.

◆ **Reading Strategy**
Clay encounters problem after problem. What do you predict will happen?

⑥ He soon found that thrusting his mittened hands through the snow and clutching the grass roots was uncertain and unsafe. His mittens were too thick for him to be sure of his grip, so he took them off. But this brought with it new trouble. When he held on to a bunch of roots the snow, coming in contact with his bare warm hand, was melted, so that his hands and the wristbands of his woolen shirt were dripping with water. This the frost was quick to attack, and his fingers were numbed and made worthless.

Then he was forced to seek good footing, where he could stand erect unsupported, to put on his mittens, and to thrash his hands against his sides until the heat came back into them.

⑦ This constant numbing of his fingers made his progress very slow; but the zigzag came to an end finally, where the side of the slide was buttressed by a perpendicular rock, and he turned back and upward again. As he climbed higher and higher, he found that the slide was wedge-shaped, its rocky buttresses pinching it away as it reared its upper end. Each step increased the depth which seemed to yawn for him.

While beating his hands against his sides he turned and looked down the long slippery slope, and figured, in case he slipped, that he would be flying with the speed of an express train ere he took the final plunge into the icy bed of the Yukon.

He passed the first outcropping rock, and the second, and at the end of an hour found himself above the third, and fully five hundred feet above the river. And here, with the end nearly two hundred feet above him, the pitch of the slide was increasing.

Each step became more difficult and perilous, and he was faint from exertion and from lack of Swanson's dinner. Three or four times he slipped slightly and recovered himself; but, growing careless from exhaustion and the long tension on his nerves, he tried to continue with too great haste, and was rewarded by a double slip of each foot, which tore him loose and started him down the slope.

On account of the steepness there was little snow; but what little there was was displaced by his body, so that he became the nucleus of a young avalanche. He clawed desperately with his hands, but there was little to cling to, and he sped downward faster and faster.

The first and second outcroppings were below him, but he knew that the first was almost out of line, and pinned his hope on the second. Yet the first was just enough in line to catch one of his feet and to whirl him over and head downward on his back.

The shock of this was severe in itself, and the fine snow enveloped him in a blinding, maddening cloud; but he was thinking quickly and clearly of what would happen if he brought up head first against the outcropping. He twisted himself over on his stomach, thrust both hands out to one side, and pressed them heavily against the flying surface.

This had the effect of a brake, drawing his head and shoulders to the side. In this position he rolled over and over a couple of times, and then, with a quick jerk at the right moment, he got his body the rest of the way round.

And none too soon, for the next moment his feet drove into the outcropping, his legs doubled up, and the wind was driven from his stomach with the abruptness of the stop.

There was much snow down his neck and up his sleeves. At once and with unconcern he

Up the Slide ◆ 157

Clarification

⑤ The mythical Greek figure Hercules was known for his great strength and for performing a series of twelve challenging tasks. So, a herculean task is one that is extraordinarily difficult. Provide and discuss the meaning of other common adjectives that come from mythology, such as *narcissistic*, *Promethean*, and *volcanic*. Invite students to suggest others.

◆ **Reading Strategy**

⑥ Predict *Students' predictions will vary. Those who have read London's story "To Build a Fire" may predict the worst for Clay. Those who know White Fang may expect a happy ending.*

◆ **Build Grammar Skills**

⑦ Active and Passive Voice
Explain to students that a verb is in the active voice when the subject performs the action and in the passive voice when the subject receives the action. The passive voice uses a form of the helping verb *be*. Ask students to identify examples of both voices in this passage. *Possible responses: ". . . the slide was buttressed by a perpendicular rock . . ." is in passive voice and ". . . he turned back . . ." is in active voice.*

Customize for
Bodily/Kinesthetic Learners
Suggest that students recall a time that they exerted a tremendous amount of physical energy, such as running a long-distance race or playing a fast-paced game of basketball. Discuss with them the bodily sensations they associate with physical exertion, including fast heart rate and breathing, tight muscles, perspiration, and heightened physical awareness. Encourage them to keep these sensations in mind as they continue reading about Clay's efforts to make it up the slope.

Cultural Connection

Inuit People The Inuit or Eskimo people have survived in the far northern regions of Canada for centuries. Because the frozen environment in which they hunted game like caribou and marine mammals discouraged visitors, the Inuit were able to keep largely to themselves and to continue their way of life while other Native American groups were losing theirs.

Invite students to investigate aspects of Inuit life, culture, and history to discover how the Inuit have managed to make a life in such a hostile place and how they have satisfied the basic needs of food, shelter, and clothing in the past and now. How does their life in northern Canada today differ from that of generations past? Have students present their findings to classmates.

You may wish to show or suggest that students see the video *Nanook of the North,* a pioneering 55-minute documentary of Inuit life made in 1922. Note that although the film has come under some criticism for containing staged scenes, students are likely to find viewing it informational and helpful in understanding the environmental conditions of London's story.

❶ Predict In what way do you think the ax will come in handy? *Students may suggest that Clay will use the ax much like a rock climber uses a piton—to wedge it into the climbing surface and use it to grab onto and pull himself up.*

Comprehension Check ☑

❷ Ask students to explain what has happened here. *Finally, Clay has reached a part of the mountain's slope, near its top, where the land flattens somewhat and the footing is much improved. He is safe again.*

▶ Critical Viewing ◀

❸ Connect *Students may say that among the hardships they faced was the need to carry heavy loads of gear and supplies up steep hills.*

Customize for
Visual/Spatial Learners

Call students' attention to the slope of the mountain in the photograph on this page. Discuss with them the elements depicted that would make reaching the top of the mountain difficult, such as snow and incline. Ask them how they might feel when they reached the top. Then have them review the details of Clay's ascent.

Beyond Literature

Have students research to compare this gold rush to the one that took place half a century earlier in California. They might compare statistics, nationalities, personalities, and expectations of the participants, the mining methods, the towns, and the length of time each event lasted.

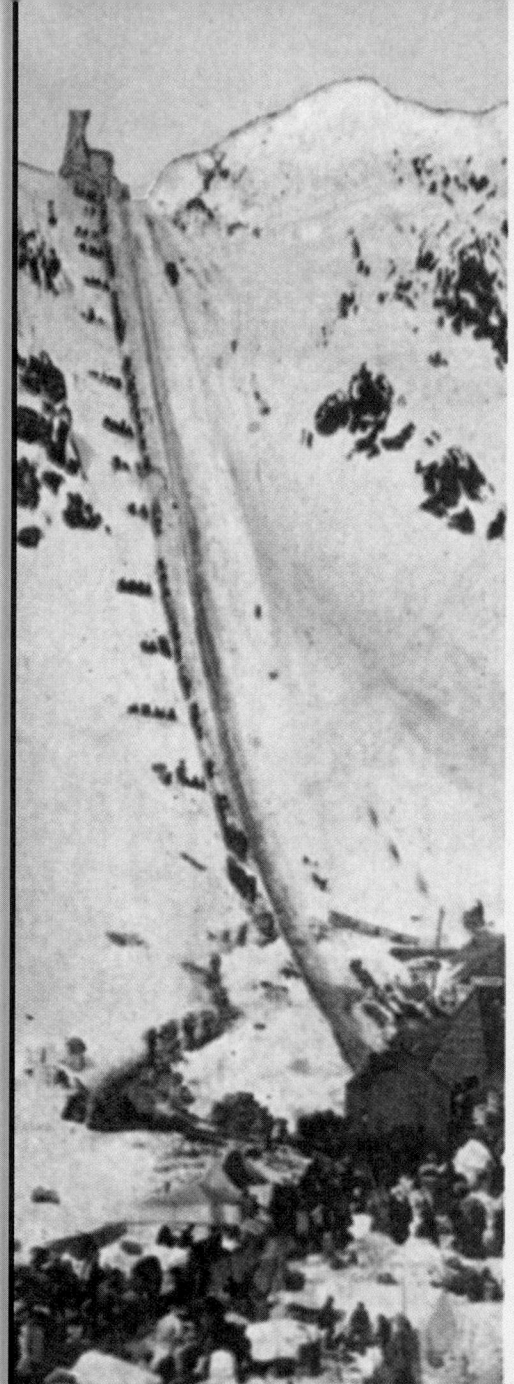

shook this out, only to discover, when he looked up to where he must climb again, that he had lost his nerve. He was shaking as if with a palsy, and sick and faint from a frightful nausea.

Fully ten minutes passed ere he could master these sensations and summon sufficient strength for the weary climb. His legs hurt him and he was limping, and he was conscious of a sore place in his back, where he had fallen on the ax.   **❶**

In an hour he had regained the point of his tumble, and was contemplating the slide, which so suddenly steepened. It was plain to him that he could not go up with his hands and feet alone, and he was beginning to lose his nerve again when he remembered the ax.

Reaching upward the distance of a step, he brushed away the snow, and in the frozen gravel and crumbled rock of the slide chopped a shallow resting place for his foot. Then he came up a step, reached forward, and repeated the <u>maneuver</u>. And so, step by step, foot-hole by foot-hole, a tiny speck of toiling life poised like a fly on the face of Moosehide Mountain, he fought his upward way.

Twilight was beginning to fall when he gained the head of the slide and drew himself into the rocky bottom of the gully. At this point the shoulder of the mountain began to bend back toward the crest, and   **❷** in addition to its being less steep, the rocks afforded better handhold and foothold. The worst was over, and the best yet to come!

The gully opened out into a miniature basin, in which a floor of soil had been deposited, out of which, in turn, a tiny grove of pines had sprung. The trees were all dead, dry and seasoned, having long since exhausted the thin skin of earth.

Clay ran his experienced eye over the timber, and estimated that it would chop up into fifty cords at least. Beyond, the gully closed in and became barren rock again. On every hand was barren rock, so the wonder was small that the trees had escaped the eyes

◀ **Critical Viewing** What does this photograph reveal about the hardships endured by gold prospectors in the Yukon? [Connect]   **❸**

◆ Build Vocabulary

maneuver (mə noo′ vər) *n*.: Series of planned steps

ascent (ə sent′) *n*.: The act of climbing or rising

descent (dē sent′) *n*.: The act of climbing down

Speaking and Listening Mini-Lesson

Casting Proposal

This mini-lesson supports the Speaking and Listening activity in the Idea Bank on p. 161.

Introduce Discuss with students the kinds of issues to consider when choosing an actor to play a role in a movie. Compare and contrast issues that are important to the filmmaker (or author or screenwriter) and those of value to the film's producers.

Develop Have students form groups. Guide each to brainstorm for a list of characteristics, both mental and physical, that

describe Clay Dilham. Then ask each group to list actors they would consider for the role. Guide them to make the lists long and then narrow them down. Invite students to discuss the pros and cons for each actor and eliminate all but a final few. Groups should then prepare a written explanation for the choice of each actor who remains on their lists. They should prepare to argue their cases before the class (the producers).

Apply Have groups present their casting decisions. Keep a class list of the choices.

Then have all students vote to determine their first, second, and third choices. If you or anyone in your class has access to a casting agent or film critic, invite that person to give a professional opinion.

Assess Evaluate casting decisions according to how strong a case students can make for the actor based upon their accurate characterizations of Clay. Assess students' abilities to make their cases clearly and convincingly. Or, use the scoring rubric for Persuasion, p. 101, in **Alternative Assessment**.

of men. They were only to be discovered as he had discovered them—by climbing after them.

He continued the ascent, and the white moon greeted him when he came out upon the crest of Mooseshide Mountain. At his feet, a thousand feet below, sparkled the lights of Dawson.

But the descent was precipitate and dangerous in the uncertain moonlight, and he elected to go down the mountain by its gentler northern flank. In a couple of hours he reached the Yukon at the Siwash village, and took the river-trail back to where he had left the dogs. There he found Swanson, with a fire going, waiting for him to come down.

④ And although Swanson had a hearty laugh at his expense, nevertheless, a week or so later, in Dawson, there were fifty cords of wood sold at forty dollars a cord, and it was he and Swanson who sold them.

Beyond Literature

Social Studies Connection

The Klondike Gold Rush History's largest gold discovery took place in August 1896 near a remote Klondike river, Dawson's Creek. News of the discovery didn't reach the world until the spring of 1897, when a Seattle newspaper headline trumpeted the discovery of "more than a ton of gold," divided among 68 miners!

The news triggered the last great gold rush. An estimated 100,000 people began the trek, but only about 30,000 actually made it to Dawson's Creek. Once there, few of the prospectors found gold, and the few who did often lost their fortunes as quickly.

Cross-Curricular Activity
Historic Newspaper What might a newspaper of the time have said about the Gold Rush in the spring of 1898? Work with a team to create a historic newspaper that focuses on the Klondike Gold Rush.

Guide for Responding

◆ LITERATURE AND YOUR LIFE

Reader's Response Do you think the risks that Clay took were reasonable or foolish? Why?

Thematic Focus Is it more important for trailblazers to be lucky or skillful? Explain.

Group Activity With a few classmates, jot down some ways in which you would adjust to life in the harsh and frozen Yukon.

☑ Check Your Comprehension

1. Why is Clay so confident at the beginning of his journey?
2. What events reduce his confidence?
3. How does Clay escape his difficult position?
4. What surprise does Clay discover at the end of his adventure?

◆ Critical Thinking

INTERPRET
1. Why does London begin the story with a description of Clay and Swanson's disagreement? **[Speculate]**
2. How is Clay's age reflected in his actions? **[Deduce]**
3. Identify three specific skills Clay possesses that aid his survival. **[Infer]**

EVALUATE
4. Based on his actions in the story, for what specific jobs do you think Clay is suited? **[Assess]**

APPLY
5. How would this story be different if it were set in the jungle? **[Modify]**
6. What lesson does this story hold for readers who will never visit the Yukon? **[Generalize]**

Thematic Focus

④ **Blazing Trails** Discuss with students that although the results were mostly unintentional, Clay braved a number of risks to blaze a trail not only to the shoulder of that mountain, but to unexpected wealth in firewood.

Reinforce and Extend

Answers
◆ LITERATURE AND YOUR LIFE

Reader's Response Possible response: They were foolish, since his goal was a small batch of firewood, not enough to risk his life for.

Thematic Focus Students may say that success in trailblazing requires skill and luck in equal amounts, but that since most trailblazers must possess some amount of skill already, it is luck that may put them over the top.

☑ Check Your Comprehension

1. He alone had seen the small dead pine.
2. He realizes that the tree would be hard to climb to and that he is not dressed or equipped for the climb.
3. He climbs rather than descends, using every climbing technique he knows.
4. Clay discovers more firewood in a hidden gully.

◆ Critical Thinking

1. Possible response: It provides tension; it implies that Clay's undertaking will be eventful.
2. The exuberance of his youth causes him to attempt a task older, more experienced prospectors would avoid.
3. He knows how to climb rocks and slides; he has a good sense of direction; he knows the lay of the land.
4. Possible responses: forest ranger; mountain climbing guide; entrepreneur; stuntman; logger.
5. Clay might have to rely on his ability to find food, to avoid danger from animals, to swim, and to keep his sense of direction.
6. Possible response: You should take chances, as long as you carefully weigh each choice you make and are prepared to give your best effort.

Beyond the Selection

FURTHER READING
Other Works by Jack London
Call of the Wild
White Fang

Other Works About Survival Against the Forces of Nature
"To Build a Fire," Jack London
Bearstone, Will Hobbs

INTERNET
We suggest the following sites on the Internet (all Web sites are subject to change).

For biographical information, images of Jack London, documents, some writings, a bibliography, and research aids:
http://sunsite.berkeley.edu/London/

For comprehensive information on the Yukon Gold Rush, including photos and personal recollections:
http://www.gold-rush.org

We *strongly recommend* that you preview the sites before you send students to them.

Answers

◆ Reading Strategy

1. Students may have predicted that he wouldn't survive, that in his inexperience, he underestimates the challenge he faces, that he gets more tired with each step, and that his extremities will go numb and he'll freeze.

2. Students may predict that Clay will find success eventually because he demonstrates a willingness to take chances, a knack for thinking on his feet, and an eye for opportunity.

◆ Build Vocabulary

Using the forms of exhaust
1. exhausted
2. exhaustible
3. exhaustion

Spelling Strategy
1. thoroughly
2. Although
3. dough

Using the Word Bank
1. thoroughly
2. ascent
3. exertion
4. exhausted
5. descent
6. maneuver
7. manifestly

◆ Literary Focus

1. In his effort to find firewood, Clay faces a steep and treacherous slope, wetness from the snow and ice, and freezing temperatures.

2. Clay uses his self-confidence, his abilities to understand the terrain and make good decisions at each point of crisis, and the tools he has to meet the challenges nature places in his path. He eventually reaches safety on the mountain's shoulder.

3. Possible response: Yes, the Yukon, with its menacing climate and terrain, the needs it creates, and the demands it presents, causes great conflict. It affects the story and Clay as much as a human character might.

Guide for Responding (continued)

◆ Reading Strategy

PREDICT

Predicting while you read keeps you involved in what you're reading. For example, in "Up the Slide," your predictions may become less optimistic with each challenge Clay faces. Uncertainty about Clay's fate increases your interest in the story.

1. Did you predict that Clay would survive? On what clues did you base your prediction?

2. What prediction would you make about Clay's future? Describe the story clues that support this prediction.

◆ Build Vocabulary

USING FORMS OF exhaust

Add forms of the word exhaust to your vocabulary. Copy the following sentences on your paper. Then, fill in each blank sensibly by adding -ion, -ible, and -ed to exhaust.

1. He was ____?____ when he reached the top.
2. Because they had no wells, their water supply was ____?____.
3. The hiker collapsed from ____?____.

SPELLING STRATEGY

The long o sound is occasionally spelled ough, as in thoroughly, dough, and though. Copy the following sentences on your paper. Fill in the blank with a long o word from the words listed above.

1. We were ____?____ exhausted by the journey.
2. ____?____ it was still light, we went to bed.
3. He formed the ____?____ into a loaf.

USING THE WORD BANK

Write the word from the Word Bank that best matches the meaning of the italicized word(s).

1. He felt *completely* ready for the climb.
2. His *upward journey* began at dawn.
3. Trembling from *effort*, he collapsed.
4. By noon, he felt surprisingly *tired*.
5. The *downward journey* was even more difficult.
6. Eventually, he devised a new *strategy* that he called "controlled sliding."
7. The strategy was *clearly* successful as he arrived back feeling alert and not at all tired.

160 ◆ Meeting Challenges

◆ Literary Focus

CONFLICT WITH NATURE

The central **conflict,** or struggle, in "Up the Slide" occurs between Clay and an element of nature. As Clay struggles against the icy, rocky terrain and the bitter cold, his fate becomes uncertain and the suspense builds.

1. Explain how elements of nature oppose Clay's efforts to find firewood.

2. How is the conflict resolved?

3. Critics sometimes say that a story's setting is like another character. Do you think this idea applies to "Up the Slide"? Explain.

◆ Build Grammar Skills

ACTIVE AND PASSIVE VOICE

A verb is in the **active voice** when the subject of the sentence performs the action. It is in the **passive voice** when the subject receives the action. The passive voice uses a form of the helping verb *be*.

> **Active Voice:** Clay *threw* the ax.
> **Passive Voice:** The ax *was thrown* by Clay.

Practice In your notebook, indicate whether each verb is in the active or the passive voice.

1. Clay climbed the steep mountain.
2. The thin crust of ice was broken by his heavy feet.
3. In the moonlight, the icy surface glistened like crystal.
4. After the landslide, the snow settled in a large heap at the bottom of the basin.
5. Swanson was surprised by Clay.

Writing Application Rewrite the following passage, changing the passive voice to the active voice. Verbs in the passive voice are italicized.

The mountain *was climbed* by Clay. Although the parka covered Clay, the icy air *was felt* by him. The frigid temperature chilled his fingers and toes. Suddenly, the thin crust of ice *was broken* by his feet. A distant shout *was heard* faintly by the numbed climber. He *had been found* by the rescue party!

◆ Build Grammar Skills

Practice
1. active; 2. passive; 3. active; 4. active
5. passive

Writing Application

Possible response:

Clay climbed the mountain. Although the parka covered him, Clay felt the icy air. The frigid temperature chilled his fingers and toes. Suddenly, his feet broke the thin crust of ice. The numbed climber faintly heard a distant shout. The rescue party had found him!

✒ Writer's Solution

For additional instruction and practice, use the lesson in the *Writer's Solution Language Lab CD-ROM* on Styling Sentences, and the practice page on Active and Passive Voice, p. 74 in the *Writer's Solution Grammar Practice Book.*

160

Build Your Portfolio

 ## Idea Bank

Writing

1. Diary Entry Write a diary entry that Clay might have composed after his difficult journey. Include details that show his feelings.

2. Job Description Write a job description for a gold prospector. Describe the skills necessary, as well as the types of challenges prospectors are likely to face. **[Career Link]**

3. Modified Story Rewrite "Up the Slide" using a different extreme climate, such as a desert or tropical rain forest. Keep the character of Clay the same, and describe a similar adventure.

Speaking and Listening

4. Oral Interpretation Choose an exciting part of "Up the Slide," and read it aloud. Change the speed, volume, and tone of your reading to create varied effects. Perform your reading for classmates. **[Performing Arts Link]**

5. Casting Proposal Choose an actor that you think should portray Clay Dilham in a film version of "Up the Slide." Imagine that your classmates are the film's producers. Make a speech to them about why this actor is perfect for the role. **[Media Link]**

Projects

6. Multimedia Report [Group Activity] Work with a group to create an exhibit highlighting the climate of the Yukon. Use visuals and texts that help your audience experience this unusual climate. **[Geography Link]**

7. Author Research Find out more about Jack London's life and works. Consult biographies, Internet sources, and London's own writings, such as the autobiographical novel *Martin Eden* or stories in "Tales of the Fish Patrol." Share your findings with the class, and identify the sources you used. **[Literature Link]**

 ## Writing Mini-Lesson

Report on the Yukon

The Yukon is a vast and fascinating region that inspired Jack London to write many of his best-known works. Write a research report about the Yukon, focusing on one specific topic that interests you. Use several reference sources to gain factual details for your report.

Writing Skills Focus: Narrowing a Topic

Narrow a broad topic like the Yukon by dividing it into subtopics. Reading in a general reference source, like an encyclopedia, can help you find different subtopics to consider.

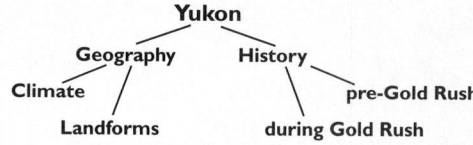

Prewriting Identify a specific topic that addresses a single key feature of the Yukon. Use a variety of sources, including nonfiction books, encyclopedias, and Internet sites to gather details.

Drafting Begin your research report with a clear statement of your topic. Present your facts in a logical order, and conclude with a brief summary or an appropriate conclusion.

Revising Check the facts in your report for accuracy. Wherever passages are unclear, reorganize the facts and edit out unnecessary words. Be sure that you've begun your report with a topic statement and ended with a conclusion that sums up the facts.

> ◆ **Grammar Application**
>
> Wherever you can, change statements in the passive voice to the active voice to give your report more impact.

 ## Idea Bank

Following are suggestions for matching the Idea Bank topics with your students' performance levels and learning modalities:

Customize for *Performance Levels*
Less Advanced Students: 1, 5
Average Students: 2, 4, 5, 6
More Advanced Students: 3, 6, 7

Customize for *Learning Modalities*
Verbal/Linguistic: 1, 2, 3, 4, 5, 6, 7
Visual/Spatial: 6
Bodily/Kinesthetic: 4
Logical/Mathematical: 2, 4
Musical/Rhythmic: 4
Interpersonal: 2, 5, 6
Intrapersonal: 1, 7

 ## Writing Mini-Lesson

Refer students to the Writing Handbook in the back of the book for instructions on the writing process and for further information on reports.

 ### Writer's Solution

Writers at Work Videodisc
Have students view the videodisc segment on Reports (Ch. 7), featuring Virginia Hamilton, to hear what approach she uses to narrow her topic.

Play frames 18484 to 19340

Writing Lab CD-ROM
Have students complete the tutorial on Reports. Follow these steps:
1. Have students use a Topic Web and Word Bin to focus their ideas.
2. Have students use the Guidelines for Taking Notes, which presents the use of notecard stationery, and the Organizing Information section to help them arrange their notes so readers can follow their thinking.
3. Have students draft on computer, using audio-annotated writing models to learn about quotations and a bibliography.
4. Have students use the revision checker.
Allow about 75 minutes of class time to complete these steps.

Writer's Solution Sourcebook
Have students use Chapter 7, "Reports," pp. 201–233, for additional support. The chapter includes suggestions for narrowing a topic, p. 218.

✓ ASSESSMENT OPTIONS

Formal Assessment, Selection Test, pp. 50–52, and Assessment Resources Software. The selection test is designed so that it can be easily customized to the performance levels of your students.
Alternative Assessment, p. 14, includes options for less advanced students, more advanced students, interpersonal learners, visual/spatial learners, verbal/linguistic learners, bodily/kinesthetic learners, and logical/mathematical learners.

PORTFOLIO ASSESSMENT
Use the following rubrics in the **Alternative Assessment** booklet to assess student writing:
Diary Entry: Expression, p. 90
Job Description: Technical Description, p. 111
Modified Story: Fictional Narrative, p. 91
Writing Mini-Lesson: Research Report, p. 102

CONNECTING LITERATURE TO SOCIAL STUDIES
THE COLONIAL ERA

The Pilgrims' Landing and First Winter *by William Bradford*

OBJECTIVES

1. To read, comprehend, and interpret a selection that has a social studies focus
2. To relate a selection with a social studies focus to personal experience
3. To connect literature to social studies
4. To respond to Social Studies Guiding Questions
5. To respond to the selection through writing, speaking and listening, and projects

SOCIAL STUDIES GUIDING QUESTIONS

Reading about the earliest experiences of Pilgrims arriving in New England will help students discover answers to these Social Studies Guiding Questions:

• How have historical events affected the cultures of the United States?

• How has physical geography affected the cultures of the United States?

Interest Grabber Invite students to recall activities from the first day of school, focusing especially on how they familiarized themselves with new classmates and surroundings. Explain that this selection describes some settlers' first view of a place they'd never been and their first encounter with its inhabitants. Help students link their own "first day" emotions to the selection as they read.

Map Study

Historical/Route Maps Visualizing the location of existing cultures and the routes of new arrivals can help students understand historical journeys. For example, students can use the map on this page to follow the Pilgrims' 1620 route to their first landing and then discern that the exploratory party probably saw members of either the Wampanoag or Narragansett peoples.

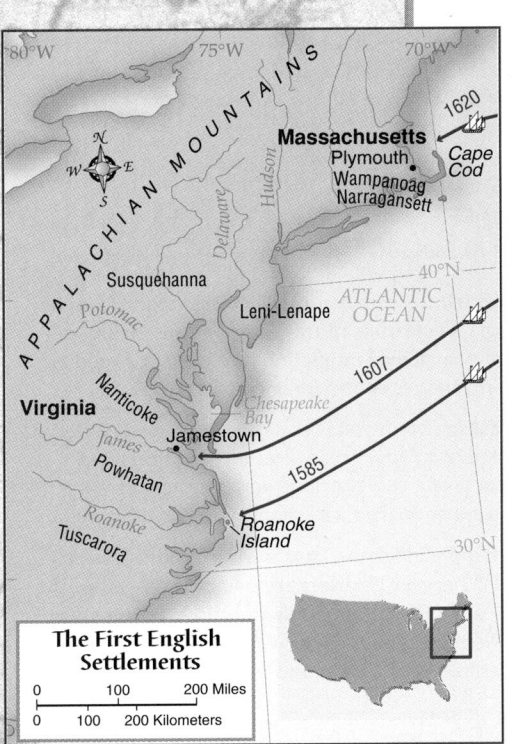

The First English Settlements

0   100   200 Miles
0 100   200 Kilometers

THE PILGRIMS Once the "New World" was discovered, it wasn't long before groups of Europeans braved the crossing of the Atlantic to settle on Roanoke Island, Jamestown, and Plymouth. Among the earliest English groups to settle in America were the Pilgrims. Many of the Pilgrims were members of the Puritan sect, a religious group unpopular in England because of their beliefs. They left England for Holland, hoping to be allowed to practice their religion freely in that country. However, things weren't much better for them in Holland, so they set sail for America.

The *Mayflower* Their ship, the *Mayflower,* arrived at Plymouth, Massachusetts, in November 1620. It had been a long, hard journey across the Atlantic. Many passengers died during the voyage, including the wife of William Bradford. Bradford became the first governor of Plymouth, the settlement formed by the Puritans. He wrote a book called *History of Plymouth Plantation*, from which this selection comes. This book is the source of most of what we know about the early Puritan settlement.

The Challenge of the New World The Puritans came to the "New World" so they could practice their religion freely. They expected life in America to be hard, but they did not realize how difficult it would be. The area they called New England was not very good for farming. The winter weather was much more fierce than weather in England or in Holland. They had left behind not only family and friends, but such necessities as medical care, housing supplies, and food. In addition, some of the natives—Indians—feared and distrusted these strangers, and there was the constant danger of fights. In this selection, William Bradford tells about some of the challenges the Puritans met when they first arrived on shore.

162 ◆ *Meeting Challenges*

Prentice Hall Literature Program Resources

REINFORCE / RETEACH / EXTEND
Selection Support Pages
Build Vocabulary, p. 75
Theme, p. 76
Formal Assessment Selection Test, pp. 53–54, Assessment Resources Software
Readings From Social Studies
Writing and Language Transparencies
Sunburst Organizer, p. 85

Resource Pro CD-ROM
"The Pilgrims' Landing and First Winter"—includes all resource material and customizable lesson plan
Listening to Literature Audiocassettes "The Pilgrims' Landing and First Winter"
Connection to Prentice Hall *The American Nation,* Ch. 3, "The 13 English Colonies"

Pilgrims Going to Church, George Henry Boughton, Collection of The New-York Historical Society

▲ **Critical Viewing** What can you learn from this painting about the Pilgrims' first winter? [Analyze] ❶

The Pilgrims' Landing and First Winter

William Bradford

Being thus arrived at Cape Cod the 11th of November, and necessity called them to look out a place for habitation (as well as the master's and mariners' importunity[1]); they having brought a large shallop[2] with them out of England, stowed in quarters in the ship, they now got her out and set their carpenters to work to trim her up; but being much bruised and shattered in the ship with foul weather, they saw she would be long in mending. Whereupon a few of them tendered themselves to go by land and discover those nearest places, whilst the shallop was in mending; and the rather because as they went into that harbor there seemed to be an opening some two or three leagues off, which the master judged to be a river. It was conceived there might be some danger in the attempt, yet seeing them resolute, they were permitted to go, being sixteen of them well armed under the conduct of Captain Standish, having such instructions given them as was thought meet.[3] They set forth the 15th of November; and when they had marched about the space of a mile by the seaside, they espied five or six persons with a dog coming towards them, who were savages; but they fled from them and ran up into the woods, and the English followed them, partly to see if they could speak with them, and partly to discover if there might not be

1. **importunity** (im pôr tōōn′ i tē) *n.*: Urgent demands.
2. **shallop** (shal′ əp) *n.*: Small open boat.
3. **meet** (mēt) *adj.*: Old English word meaning "proper" or "fit."

The Pilgrims' Landing and First Winter ◆ 163

⏱ One-Minute Insight

"The Pilgrims' Landing ..." recounts the discoveries of the first Puritan settlers arriving on what is now Cape Cod, Massachusetts. A small landing party looks for a safe harbor and fresh water, encounters some Native Americans, and spends its first night on American soil. Through William Bradford's detailed narrative, we experience the wonder—and fear—of exploring a totally unfamiliar place.

Team Teaching Strategy

Team taught with a social studies teacher, "The Pilgrim's Landing ..." is well-suited to a cross-curricular unit on America's colonial period.

▶**Critical Viewing**◀

❶ *The snowy landscape, heavy clothing, and lack of buildings indicate a difficult winter.*

Customize for
Less Proficient Readers

Urge students to reread the information on p. 162 and use the painting on this page to picture the setting. Then, read the text aloud in thought groups, including punctuation. Pause after each thought group to clarify meaning and allow students to picture the landing party's progress. Help students paraphrase as they construct a personal text summary.

Customize for
More Advanced Students

As they read, have students use a log to note the emotions that the landing party members might have experienced.

🎼 Humanities: Art

Pilgrims Going to Church, by George Henry Boughton, 1867
    This is British painter George Henry Boughton's most famous work. In an attached inscription, Boughton describes the scene as a small band of Pilgrims headed for church through a dangerous wilderness.
    What does the scene suggest about the group's comfort in the woods? *The guns, close-knit group, and watchful eyes suggest the Pilgrims' concern.*

✎ Preparing for Standardized Tests

Social Studies Reading Selections When reading standardized test passages from other curriculum areas, students may encounter unfamiliar or technical words. Context can help them infer meanings for these words. Remind students that context includes the words and phrases around an unfamiliar word. Clues can include synonyms, examples, or definitions. To practice, ask students to choose the answer that best defines the underlined word:

Whereupon a few of them <u>tendered</u> themselves to go by land and discover those

nearest places ...

(A) offered   (C) built
(B) distressed   (D) omitted

After a student reads aloud the question, review the answer choices. Point out that while all the alternatives describe actions, *(A) offered* is the only response that makes sense with the journey's purpose to *discover*. For more practice, have students incorporate this strategy into their paraphrasing efforts in Customize for Less Proficient Readers, on p. 163 and English Language Learners, p. 164.

❶ The Wampanoag people, who lived on Cape Cod when the Puritans arrived, are an Algonquin group. Village dwellers, the Wampanoag probably lived in wigwams. Corn was a main food, along with hunted game and fish.

Two Wampanoags were important to early Pilgrims—Squanto and Samoset. Both helped Captain Standish's group survive their first New England winter. Eventually, however, the Wampanoag began to resist European desire for land. In 1675, they attacked colonial villages.

Customize for
English Language Learners
Help English Language Learners work through the text, defining difficult words and breaking down lengthy sentences. Then they can paraphrase portions of text and, as a group, summarize the selection.

Reinforce and Extend

Answers
◆ LITERATURE AND YOUR LIFE

Reader's Response Students may say "yes," as how else can Pilgrims discover their surroundings or "no," as the wilderness contains many dangers.

Thematic Focus They faced the challenges of finding safe harbor, food, water, shelter, and supplies.

☑ Check Your Comprehension

1. The shallop needed repair.
2. They wanted to speak with the Indians and see if any lay in ambush.
3. They found old and new cornfields, graves, the remains of a house, and baskets of corn.

More About the Author
On the 1620 journey to New England, **William Bradford** (1590–1657) helped draft the *Mayflower Compact*. This document outlined a dramatic plan for a community in which everyone shares responsibilities and also led to democratic institutions such as the town meeting (still used today in many New England communities). Reelected 30 times as Plymouth's governor, Bradford was a well-read and open-minded man—he welcomed people of any, or no, religion!

164

CONNECTING LITERATURE TO SOCIAL STUDIES

❶ more of them lying in ambush. But the Indians seeing themselves thus followed, they again forsook[4] the woods and ran away on the sands as hard as they could, so as they could not come near them but followed them by the track of their feet sundry miles and saw that they had come the same way. So, night coming on, they made their rendezvous and set out their sentinels,[5] and rested in quiet that night; and the next morning followed their track till they had headed a great creek and so left the sands, and turned another way into the woods. But they still followed them by guess, hoping to find their dwellings; but they soon lost both them and themselves, falling into such thickets as were ready to tear their clothes and armor in pieces; but were most distressed for want of drink. But at length they found water and refreshed themselves. . . .

Afterwards they directed their course to come to the other shore, for they knew it was a neck of land they were to cross over, and so at length got to the seaside and marched to this supposed river, and by the way found a pond of clear, fresh water, and shortly after a good quantity of clear ground where the Indians had formerly set corn, and some of their graves. And proceeding further they saw new stubble where corn had been set the same year; also they found where lately a house had been, where some planks and a great kettle was remaining, and heaps of sand newly paddled with their hands. Which, they digging up,

---

4. **forsook** (fôr sook´) *v.*: Abandoned.
5. **sentinels** (sen´ ti nəls) *n.*: Guards.
6. **divers** (dī´ vərz) *adj.*: Diverse.

---

found in them divers[6] fair Indian baskets filled with corn, and some in ears, fair and good, of divers colours, which seemed to them a very goodly sight (having never seen any such before). This was near the place of that supposed river they came to seek, unto which they went and found it to open itself into two arms with a high cliff of sand in the entrance but more like to be creeks of salt water than any fresh, for aught[7] they saw; and that there was good harborage for their shallop, leaving it further to be discovered by their shallop, when she was ready. So, their time limited them being expired, they returned to the ship lest they should be in fear of their safety; and took with them part of the corn and buried up the rest. And so, like the men from Eshcol, carried with them the fruits of the land and showed their brethren; of which, and their return, they were marvelously glad and their hearts encouraged.

After this, the shallop being got ready, they set out again for the better discovery of this place, and the master of the ship desired to go himself. So there went some thirty men but found it to be no harbor for ships but only for boats. There was also found two of their houses covered with mats, and sundry of their implements in them, but the people were run away and could not be seen. Also there was found more of their corn and of their beans of various colours; the corn and beans they brought away, purposing to give them full satisfaction when they should meet with any of them as, about some six months afterward they did, to their good content.

---

7. **aught** (ôt) *n.*: Anything.

Guide for Responding

◆ LITERATURE AND YOUR LIFE
Reader's Response Do you find the Puritans' actions sensible? Explain.

Thematic Focus What challenges did the Puritans face when they arrived in America?

☑ Check Your Comprehension
1. Why did several men volunteer to explore the land, instead of using the shallop?
2. What two reasons did the men have for following the Indians into the woods?
3. What items did the men find when they reached the Indian village?

164 ◆ Meeting Challenges

Block Scheduling Strategies

Consider these suggestions to take advantage of extended class time:

• After students read the text on p. 162, use the accompanying map to clarify the Pilgrims' route. Invite students to share their own knowledge of early colonial history. They can note this data on a Sunburst organizer, p. 85, in **Writing and Language Transparencies,** when researching their Oral Report, p. 165. Have student pairs read the selection. Then, discuss Critical Thinking, p. 165, as a class, polling students on Reader's Response.

• Before students read, review the Idea Bank activities on p. 165 and help students determine graphic organizers that they might use to complete the activities. Encourage them to use the graphic organizer(s) they select to record data as volunteers read the selection aloud or as they listen to the recording. After students present their scripts, debate their Regulations, display their Illustrations from p. 165, or discuss the Thematic Focus on p. 164.

 **Listening to Literature Audiocassettes**

◆ Critical Thinking

INTERPRET

1. What do the Puritans assume to be true about the Indians before the two groups have even met? [Infer]
2. How can you tell that the Indians were a civilized group of people? [Draw Conclusions]

3. What might the Puritans have done to keep the Indians from running away from them? [Make a Judgment]

EXTEND

4. What part or parts of this account might have inspired European readers to follow the Puritans to America? [Social Studies Link]

CONNECTING LITERATURE TO SOCIAL STUDIES

One reason people study history is to learn how the modern world got to be the way it is. For example, Americans often state that they prefer to depend on themselves, without help from government or other institutions. This is an attitude the Puritans brought with them from Europe.

1. What parts of Bradford's story show that the Puritans have admirable qualities?
2. What parts show that they have qualities that are not so admirable?
3. Which of these two sets of qualities have you seen in present-day Americans?

📁 Idea Bank

Writing

1. **Letter** As a passenger on the *Mayflower,* write a letter to a friend or relative in England. Describe your first few days in New England.
2. **Script** Imagine that one of the Puritans and one of the Indians can speak the same language. Write a script for a conversation that might take place when the two meet for the first time.
3. **Regulations** As an assistant to Governor Bradford, write a series of regulations showing the settlers how they must behave toward the Indians, who lived there before the Puritans arrived.

Speaking and Listening

4. **Discussion [Group Activity]** Role-play a discussion between one settler who wants to live peacefully with the Indians and one who wants to drive them away and use their land.

Projects

5. **Oral Report** Use encyclopedias and other reference works to learn details about how the Puritans lived. Present the information you find to the class in an oral report.
6. *Mayflower* **Illustration** Do research on the *Mayflower,* the Pilgrims' ship. Then, draw a realistic illustration of it and post it in the classroom. [Art Link]

Further Reading, Listening, and Viewing

- Gary D. Schmidt's *William Bradford, Plymouth's Faithful Pilgrim* is a biography of Bradford.
- Henri Nouwen's *A Pilgrim's Report* is an audio book about Pilgrim life.
- Lucille Recht Penner's *Eating the Plates: A Pilgrim Book of Food and Manners* gives information about the daily lives of the Pilgrims.

The Pilgrims' Landing and First Winter ◆ 165

 Beyond the Selection

FURTHER READING

Other Works by William Bradford
The Mayflower Compact
Mourt's Relation

Other Works About Colonial America
Colonial America: English Colonies, ed. by Margaret Fisher and Mary J. Fowler
Encyclopedia of Native American Tribes, ed. by Carl Waldman
Cobblestone Magazine, "Jamestown," 4/94; "Pilgrims to a New World," 11/89

INTERNET

We suggest the following Internet sites (all Web sites are subject to change).

For a virtual tour of the first permanent European settlement:

http://www.plimoth.org/1627.htm

For links to sites about the Mayflower:

http://members.aol.com/calebj/mayflower.htm

We *strongly recommend* that you preview these sites before you send your students to them.

 Idea Bank

Following are suggestions for matching the Idea Bank topics with your students' performance levels and learning modalities.

Customize for
Performance Levels
Less Advanced Students: 1, 4, 6
Average Students: 2, 4, 5
More Advanced Students: 3, 5, 6

Customize for
Learning Modalities
Verbal/Linguistic: 1, 2, 3, 4, 5
Verbal/Spatial: 6
Bodily/Kinesthetic: 4
Interpersonal: 2, 3, 4
Intrapersonal: 1
Logical/Mathematical: 3

Answers (continued)
◆ Critical Thinking

1. The Puritans assume the Indians are savages.
2. Students may cite details from the abandoned village as evidence.
3. If the Puritans hadn't followed them, the Indians might not have fled.
4. Students may mention the wealth of apparently open land and new crops.

CONNECTING LITERATURE TO SOCIAL STUDIES

1. The opening shows the Puritans' bravery and willingness to work hard, the middle shows their endurance, while the end shows their curiosity.
2. The middle shows their prejudice and snobbery, while the end shows them taking others' belongings.
3. Students may say they have seen both sets of qualities. Americans are adventurous and resourceful, but sometimes closed-minded.

ASSESSMENT OPTIONS

Formal Assessment, Selection Test, pp. 53–54, and Assessment Resources Software. The selection test is designed so that it can be customized to the performance levels of your students.

PORTFOLIO ASSESSMENT
Use the following rubrics in the **Alternative Assessment** booklet to assess student writing:
Letter: Expression, p. 90
Script: Fictional Narrative, p. 91
Regulations: Definition/Classification, p. 95

Establish Writing Guidelines

Before students begin, review the characteristics of a historical cause-and-effect essay:

- A historical cause-and-effect essay explains the cause of a historical event.
- A historical cause-and-effect essay includes solid facts and details.

You may want to distribute the scoring rubric for Cause-Effect, p. 99 in **Alternative Assessment,** to make students aware before they begin of the criteria on which they will be evaluated. See the suggestions on p. 168 for how you can customize the rubric to this workshop.

Refer students to the Writing Handbook in the back of the book for instruction on the writing process and for further information on expository writing.

Writer's Solution

Writers at Work Videodisc

Students can find out how Bruce Brooks answers the question *What is exposition?* by viewing the videodisc segment on Exposition: Making Connections (Ch. 5).

Play frames 43069 to 51462

Writing Lab CD-ROM

If your students have access to computers, you may want to have them use the tutorial on Exposition: Making Connections to complete all or part of their historical cause-and-effect essays. Follow these steps:

1. Students can use the Cluster Diagram to help narrow their topics.
2. Suggest that students view the Interactive Writing Hint about gathering details.
3. Have students draft on computer.
4. Have students use the Proofreading Checklist to find usage errors.

Writer's Solution Sourcebook

Students can find additional support, including in-depth instruction on using modifiers, p. 163, in the chapter on Exposition: Making Connections, pp. 136–165.

Connect to Literature Unit 5,

"Extraordinary Occurrences," includes an example of a cause-and-effect essay: Diane Ackerman's "Why Leaves Turn Color in the Fall."

166

Expository Writing
Historical Cause-and-Effect Essay

Writing Process Workshop

Harriet Tubman Series, #28, Jacob Lawrence, Hampton University Museum

Many of the selections in this section take place in the past, during various periods of history. Often the events of history, such as the Yukon Gold Rush or the westward movement by settlers, cause other events to happen. When you write a **historical cause-and-effect essay,** you investigate a situation or event and then explore how and why that event occurred. The challenge is to find the causes behind the events.

Which puzzles of history interest you? Write a historical cause-and-effect essay that investigates one of them. Use the skills introduced in the Writing Mini-Lessons in this section to help you.

Writing Skills Focus

▶ **Narrow your topic** so that your cause-and-effect essay will be focused. (See p. 161.)

▶ **Create an introduction, body, and conclusion** that will state your topic in a captivating way, build a body of important details, and bring your essay to a satisfying close. (See p. 118.)

▶ **Follow a logical sequence of events** to help your readers see how one action or event is related to the next. (See p. 129.)

▶ **Support your statements with reasons.** (See p. 151.)

Ann Petry uses these skills in her account of Harriet Tubman.

MODEL FROM LITERATURE

from Harriet Tubman: Guide to Freedom by Ann Petry

① But there were so many of them this time. She knew moments of doubt when she was half-afraid, and kept looking back over her shoulder, imagining that she heard the sound of pursuit. ② They would certainly be pursued. Eleven of them. Eleven thousand dollars' worth of flesh and bone and muscle that belonged to Maryland planters. ③ If they were caught, the eleven runaways would be whipped and sold South, but she—she would probably be hanged. ④

① This essay's topic is narrow. It focuses on Tubman's role in the Underground Railroad.

② In the body of her account, Petry provides important details.

③ Petry gives the reason (cause) the runaway slaves will be pursued.

④ Using a logical sequence of events, Petry clearly points out what will happen if they're caught.

166 ◆ Meeting Challenges

Cross-Curricular Connection: Social Studies

Historical Essays Explain to students that historical essays help enhance statements of fact to make important historical events more accessible. By clearly explaining causes and effects of events, writers can help readers appreciate and understand the movement of time and the progress of culture.

Suggest that students do preliminary research for ideas of events and people that have influenced history. There are several good books that compile brief annotations of events, such as

Herstory: Women Who Changed the World, Ruth Ashby and Deborah Gore Ohm, eds.; *100 Artists Who Shaped World History,* by Barbara Krystal; and *100 Inventions That Shaped World History,* by Bill Yenne. Suggest that students do further research on an event or person from one of these books. Have students compile a bibliography of sources on their proposed topic. Create a class pamphlet of bibliographies and suggest that students refer to them when doing research for their social studies classes.

Prewriting

Choose a Topic Why did the American colonies allow slavery in their new country? Which was more important—the discovery of penicillin or the computer chip? Which historical questions puzzle you? Choose one to investigate, and explain it in a cause-and-effect essay.

Review the Literary Selections to Find a Topic Think of the theme *blazing a trail*. Are there others who have blazed a trail you'd like to follow back to its source, perhaps colonists who went to Rhode Island or to Jamestown, Virginia?

Narrow Your Topic Once you've selected a topic, make sure it's narrow enough for you to cover in depth. Take time to jot down subtopics. Then, consider using one of the subtopics as your main topic. You may want to create a Topic Web like this:

Make a Cause-and-Effect Chain to Find Support A cause-and-effect chain will help you identify the support you'll need for your essay. Write the historical event at the end of a chain, then write the causes that led up to it.

History Writing Tip If you're writing about a different culture or era, don't assume that the people of that time or place had the same values and ideas that you have today. Try to put yourself in their shoes.

Drafting

Create an Introduction, Body, and Conclusion As you draft, structure your essay with an introduction, in which you introduce your topic. Then, write the body, in which you develop your ideas. In the conclusion, restate your main points.

Follow a Logical Organization Use an organization that will allow you to present your facts in the most effective way. A chronological organization will allow you to trace how each cause triggered each effect. Another possible organization is to pinpoint a major event (effect) and then examine the various causes that contributed to it.

Proceed Slowly and Carefully This is nonfiction—factual writing. You don't need to write quickly to get your ideas on paper. Follow your organization plan, and check off your notes as you include them in your first draft.

DRAFTING/REVISING

APPLYING LANGUAGE SKILLS: Using Correct Verb Forms

Some verb forms require the use of a helping verb, such as *will* or *had*. Be sure to include a helping verb with the past participle of a verb. Do not use a helping verb with the past form.

Incorrect:
He <u>had saw</u> the play.
He <u>seen</u> the play.

Correct:
He <u>saw</u> the play.
He <u>had seen</u> the play.

Practice On your paper, re-write this paragraph. Correct the verb forms of the under-lined verbs, if necessary.

After blasting off for the moon, Cooper <u>seen</u> something unusual. He <u>had knew</u> that the trip was risky, but never <u>guessed</u> it would be so dangerous.

Writing Application Review your essay to be sure you've correctly used verb forms.

Writer's Solution Connection
Language Lab

For more practice with verb tenses, complete the lesson Using the Correct Verb Tense in the Using Verbs unit.

Prewriting

Have students consider if they have a favorite event or person from history that they want to know more about. Suggest that students think of inventors, historical battles, or famous court cases. Encourage students to flip through history books or magazines for topic ideas.

Customize for
Less Proficient Writers

Suggest that students consider topics that they have already studied in their social studies classes. They may be able to write a more effective essay if they can begin their research with their history book or other books recommended to them by their social studies teacher.

Drafting

Remind students that their introductions should clearly state the topic of their essays. Students will want to have a smooth transition from the introduction to the body of the paper, by letting readers know what to expect.

✒ Writer's Solution

Suggest that students use the Transition Word Bin in the Drafting section of the tutorial on Exposition: Making Connections, to select words and phrases they can use to connect ideas in their essays.

Applying Language Skills
Using Correct Verb Forms Explain to students that helping verbs are added to other verbs to make a verb phrase. They help add meaning to other verbs.

Answers
After blasting off for the moon, Cooper <u>saw</u> something unusual. He <u>knew</u> that the trip was risky, but he never <u>guessed</u> it would be so dangerous.

✒ Writer's Solution

For additional practice and instruction, use the practice page on The Progressive Forms of Verbs, p. 73 in the *Writer's Solution Grammar Practice Book*.

Revising

Suggest that students consider using peer reviewers who may know something of the topic the students wrote about. If reviewers are familiar with the topic, they may be able to offer more support.

 Writer's Solution

Suggest that students use the Peer Revision worksheet activity in the Revising section of the tutorial on Exposition: Making Connections to have their partners help them with suggestions for revision.

Publishing

Students might give oral presentations of their historical cause-and-effect essays. Encourage them to use visuals such as illustrations, photographs, or maps to enhance their presentations.

Applying Language Skills

Using Active Voice Explain to students that the form of the verb alters when changing from the active to the passive voice. Passive verbs are always made from a form of *be* and the past participle of a transitive verb, as in *was helped, have been chosen,* or *was being beaten.*

Answers

1. The family sent the flowers.
2. The lab developed the photos.
3. The President signed the letter.
4. The hungry cat ate the meal.

 Writer's Solution

For additional practice and support, complete the practice pages on Active and Passive Voice, pp. 74–75, in the *Writer's Solution Grammar Practice Book.*

Writing Process Workshop

EDITING/PROOFREADING

APPLYING LANGUAGE SKILLS: Using Active Voice

When the subject of a sentence performs the action of the verb, the verb is in the active voice. When the action is performed on the subject, the verb is in the passive voice. In your writing, use the active voice whenever possible. It is crisper and more direct than the passive voice.

Active Voice:
Harriet knocked on the door.

Passive Voice:
The door was knocked on by Harriet.

Practice Rewrite these sentences. Change passive voice to active voice.

1. The flowers were sent by the family.
2. The photos were developed by the lab.
3. The letter was signed by the President.
4. The meal was eaten by the hungry cat.

Writing Application As you draft, use the active voice where possible.

Writer's Solution Connection
Writing Lab

For more practice with the active voice, see the Revising section of the Narration tutorial.

Revising

Consult With a Peer Reviewer Ask a peer to review your essay and answer questions such as these:

▶ Is the essay logical and interesting?
▶ Do the cause-and-effect statements make sense? Is the connection between the cause(s) and effect(s) clear?
▶ Are there factual errors?

Use your reviewers' responses to help you revise.

Use a Checklist Use the Writing Skills Focus points on the first page of this lesson as a checklist to evaluate and revise your essay.

Review Your Organizational Strategy Reread your essay, paying close attention to its organization. Add transitions where necessary to link your ideas. Change the order of details that seem to be "out of place."

Delete Unnecessary Details As you review your draft, remove details that do not contribute to the main points in your essay.

REVISION MODEL

Harriet Tubman was a great person. ① who helped bring slavery to its knees with her work on the Underground Railroad. Because of her work, ② escaped herself, found a route to Canada, and helped many others escape. many slaves were freed. She found a route to help escaped slaves to Canada and she escaped herself. ③ Her work will never be forgotten.

① The writer adds reasons to support her statements.
② These facts are presented in chronological order.
③ This added sentence makes the essay's conclusion more satisfying.

Publishing and Presenting

▶ **Classroom** Display your historical cause-and-effect essays on a timeline.
▶ **Social Studies Classroom** Read your historical essay to your social studies class.
▶ **Internet** Post your essay on a Web site devoted to the same historical period.

✓ ASSESSMENT		4	3	2	1
PORTFOLIO ASSESSMENT Use the rubric on Cause-and-Effect Essay in the **Alternative Assessment** booklet, p. 99, to assess the students' writing. Add these criteria to customize this rubric to this assignment.	**Using Correct Verb Forms**	All verbs in the essay are in the correct form.	Most verbs in the essay are in the correct form.	Some verbs in the essay are in the correct form.	None of the verbs in the essay are in the correct form.
	Using Active Voice	Whenever possible, the writer has used the active voice.	In most cases, the writer has used the active voice.	In some cases, the writer has used the active voice.	In most cases, the writer has used the passive voice.

Real-World Reading Skills Workshop

Reading to Find Specific Information

Strategies for Success

Suppose you want to find information about a historical figure, such as Benjamin Rush, in your social studies book. Use the following strategies to conduct a quick and effective search for specific information.

Check the Index A book's index provides a specific listing of information found in it. If any information about your topic is in the book, it will be listed in the index.

Look for Related Topics You may find specific information about your topic by looking under related headings in the table of contents. For example, you might find information about Benjamin Rush under the related topic Revolutionary Figures.

Skim Subheads Subheads usually appear in boldface type. They reveal the main point of a book's section or chapter. Skim subheads to see if any of the material is related to your topic.

Scan Maps Maps provide many types of specific information, such as geographical features, population density, place names and locations, distances between points, and so on. Scan maps to see what kind of information they offer.

Apply the Strategies

Examine the sample table of contents, and answer these questions:

1. If you wanted to find out whether Benjamin Rush was a signer of the Declaration of Independence, which chapter would you turn to?

2. Which chapter might give you more in-depth information about Benjamin Rush? How can you tell?

3. If you wanted to find out whether Benjamin Rush's portrait appears in the book, where would you look? Why?

Table Of Contents

Unit I The Revolutionary Period

Chapter 1 Early Battles

Chapter 2 The Declaration of Independence— Who Signed the Document?

Chapter 3 Profiles of Founding Fathers

Chapter 4 Women in War

Index

Rough Riders, 621, 633, photo 636

Rush, Benjamin, 187, 194, photo 196

Russia, map 1041; immigrants from, 502; revolution, 499

✔ *You may also find specific information in*
- ▶ *Guide books for historic sites*
- ▶ *Biographical dictionaries*
- ▶ *Magazines*

Introduce the Strategies

Explain to students that reading for specific information is important for schoolwork and research as well as for many other daily activities. Tell students that if they have ever consulted manuals for operating computer software, looked through a movie database to select a film, or checked a rule book to learn how to play a new game, they have probably read for specific information. For example, if they wanted to find a movie directed by Woody Allen, they might consult the director index in a movie guide, usually found in the back of the book.

Customize for
Less Proficient Learners

Explain to students that most indices include categorical entries, under which more specific entries may be listed. In a science textbook, for example, an entry for *Humans* may include subentries such as *history of, physical characteristics of,* and *population of.* Such entries are usually indented under the main entry. Encourage students to think of possible categories under which information on their topic may be found.

Apply the Strategies

Remind students that another key to reading for specific information is identifying how sources are formatted. Some books have more than one index on different topics. Some books may include a list of maps or illustrations. Remind students that in an index, an italicized entry may be the title of a movie, play, or book. People's names are usually indexed last name first.

Answers

1. Chapter 2
2. Chapter 3, Profiles of Founding Fathers, because of the title.
3. You would look in the index, under the entry for Rush, Benjamin, because the index lists pages with photos.

◆ Build Grammar Skills

Reviewing Verbs

The selections in Part 1 include instruction on the following:

- Verbs and Verb Phrases
- Action and Linking Verbs
- Transitive and Intransitive Verbs
- Commonly Confused Verbs: *lie* and *lay*
- Active and Passive Voice

This instruction is reinforced with the Build Grammar Skills practice pages in **Selection Support,** pp. 41, 46, and 51.

As you review verbs, you may wish to include the following:

- Progressive Forms of Verbs

Each of the six tenses of verbs has a progressive form, which shows action in progress. Each progressive form of a verb uses the present participle. For example, the progressive forms of *talk* are listed in the table below:

Tense	Progressive Form
Present	I am talking
Past	I was talking
Future	I will be talking
Present Perfect	I have been talking
Past Perfect	I had been talking
Future Perfect	I will have been talking

✒ Writer's Solution

For additional practice and support using verbs, use the practice pages on Verbs, pp. 11–15, and 70–74 in the *Writer's Solution Grammar Practice Book.* If students have access to computers, have them complete the Using Verbs unit in the *Writer's Solution Language Lab CD-ROM.*

Verbs | Grammar Review

A **verb** is a word used to express action or a state of being. A verb may appear in a **verb phrase,** which consists of a main verb and at least one helping verb. The following chart gives the characteristics of verbs.

verb (vurb) *n.* a word that shows action or a condition of being: some verbs are used to link a subject with words that tell about the subject, or to help other verbs show special features [In "The children ate early" and "Cactuses grow slowly," the words "ate" and "grow" are *verbs.* In "He is asleep," the word "is" is a linking *verb.* In "Where have you gone?", the word "have" ...

Action Verbs (see p. 128)	Express action: I *moved* quickly.
Linking Verbs (see p. 128)	Express a state of being: She *became* suspicious.
Transitive Verbs (see p. 140)	Express action directed toward a person or thing: She *caught him* as he stumbled.
Intransitive Verbs (see p. 140)	Express action without passing the action to a receiver: Tubman *whistled* softly.
Active Voice (see p. 160)	The subject of the sentence performs the action: *Columbus sailed* the ocean.
Passive Voice (see p. 160)	The subject of the sentence receives the action: *America was discovered* by Columbus.

Practice 1 On your paper, identify the verb or verb phrase in each sentence. Tell whether the verb is an action or a linking verb. For each action verb, tell if it's transitive or intransitive.

1. She was trained to survive subzero conditions.
2. He climbed the icy mountain.
3. They crawled slowly in the darkness.
4. They grew confident because of success.
5. They called to one another with joy.

Practice 2 Rewrite the following paragraph, changing passive voice verbs to active voice wherever appropriate.

The reporter was awakened by the telephone's ring. The telephone was answered by him. The person on the other end was upset and scared. "Is it true?" was asked by the caller. "Is what true?" the reporter asked wearily. "Is it true that you can live forever on the moon?" The bed was collapsed on by the stunned reporter. "Who told?" he thought.

Grammar in Writing

✔ Use the active voice when you write. Reserve the use of passive voice for emphasizing the receiver of the action rather than the performer of the action or when the doer of the action is unknown.

✔ Use *lie* and *lay* correctly. Lay means "to put something down." Lie means "to place yourself in a horizontal position."

Answers

Practice 1
1. was trained, linking verb
2. climbed, action verb, transitive
3. crawled, action verb, intransitive
4. grew confident, linking verb
5. called, action verb, intransitive

Practice 2
The telephone's ring awakened the reporter. He answered the telephone. The person on the other end was upset and scared. "Is it true?" the caller asked. "Is what true?" the reporter asked wearily. "Is it true that you can live forever on the moon?" The stunned reporter collapsed on the bed. "Who told?" he thought.

PART 2   *Facing Hard Questions*

The Letter, Tim Solliday, Courtesy of the artist

The selections in this section focus on the theme of "Facing Hard Questions." "The Ninny" and "The Governess" are different tellings—one a dramatization—of the same story about the unfair treatment of a governess. In "Thank You M'am," a young thief is caught in the act by his intended victim. "Prospective Immigrants Please Note" and "Much Madness Is divinest Sense" are two poems about the importance of individuality. "This We Know" is a historical speech by Chief Seattle. "Hard Questions" is a poem about the importance of nature. In "Flowers for Algernon," Daniel Keyes presents the issues and questions surrounding artificially creating intelligence.

Customize for
Varying Student Needs

When assigning the selections to your students, keep in mind the following factors:

"The Ninny"
• Short short story by Chekhov

"The Governess"
• Chekhov's story, dramatized by Neil Simon
• Opportunity for comparing and contrasting style and format

"Thank You, Ma'm"
• A short story by Langston Hughes

"Prospective Immigrants Please Note"
• Short poem about immigrants
• Students may need background on immigration

"Much Madness Is divinest Sense"
• Short poem
• Presents Dickinson's poetic style

"This We Know"
• Historical speech by Native American leader
• Provides an opportunity for Beyond Literature Social Studies connection

"Hard Questions"
• Short poem about nature

"Flowers for Algernon"
• Long story (22 pp.)
• Students may need help understanding the written version of one of the character's speech patterns

---

Humanities: Art

The Letter, by Tim Solliday

Tim Solliday grew up in Iowa and was influenced by his father, a technical illustrator. Solliday attended the Lukits Academy of Fine Arts in Los Angeles, California. He is an accomplished painter of figures, still life, and open air landscapes. Solliday is an active member of the California Art Club.

1. What expression does the girl have on her face? *Most students will perceive her expression as unhappy, or serious and thoughtful.*

2. What do the painting's details show about the type of day it is? *Students should note details*

such as the sunlight, the potted plant, rose bushes indicating summertime, and the girl is wearing a summer dress.

3. Ask students to tell a brief story that connects the title of the painting—*The Letter*—with the theme of this unit part—Facing Hard Questions. *Possible response: The girl in the painting has just received a letter telling her that her fiancé has found a job in California. She lives in Idaho with her sick mother. Now she must decide whether she can leave her mother to join her fiancé, or if she must seek some other solution.*

171

OBJECTIVES

1. To read, comprehend, and interpret a short story and a play
2. To relate a short story and a play to personal experience
3. To question characters' actions
4. To look for clues to characters' motives
5. To build vocabulary in context and learn the suffix: -ment
6. To develop skill in using the principal parts of regular verbs
7. To write a comparison of stories using clear and effective organization
8. To respond to a play and a story through writing, speaking and listening, and projects

SKILLS INSTRUCTION

Vocabulary:
Suffixes: -ment

Spelling:
Plurals of Nouns Ending in y

Grammar:
Principal Parts of Regular Verbs

Reading Strategy:
Question Characters' Actions

Literary Focus:
Characters' Motives

Writing:
Organization

Speaking and Listening:
Dramatization (Teacher Edition)

Critical Viewing:
Draw Conclusions; Interpret

PORTFOLIO OPPORTUNITIES

Writing: Advertisement; Letter of Resignation; Interior Monologue

Writing Mini-Lesson: Comparison of Stories

Speaking and Listening: Dramatization; Job Interview

Projects: Production Plan; Opinion Poll

More About the Authors
Anton Chekhov's grandfather was a serf who had purchased his freedom. Many of Chekhov's stories concern the sadness that results from the inability of people to respond to one another or even communicate successfully, and the lives of poor people and their struggles. Checkhov is Russia's most highly regarded playwright.

Neil Simon began as a comedy script writer in the early days of television. In addition to his plays, Simon has written several successful screenplays. He is the most commercially successful playwright in Broadway history.

Guide for Reading

Meet the Authors:

Anton Chekhov (1860–1904)

Chekhov's short stories and plays present such a detailed and precise view of Russian life that some critics believe they contain more information than nonfiction works.

Chekhov was trained as a doctor, and many reviewers feel that his medical training greatly influenced his writing. Although his ideas are sharply analytical, his tone is always compassionate. Chekhov's understanding of people is reflected in the humor and emotion of "The Ninny."

Neil Simon (1927–   )

Neil Simon has entertained millions of people with his plays and films. His ability to depict human frailty with hilarious one-line gags has brought him tremendous success.

Simon grew up in Washington Heights, a section of New York City. Many of his plays, from "The Odd Couple" to "Broadway Bound," take place in his chaotic and crazy version of New York.

"The Governess" is taken from *The Good Doctor*, a collection of Simon's adaptations of Chekhov's stories.

◆ LITERATURE AND YOUR LIFE

CONNECT YOUR EXPERIENCE

An old expression says that "the squeaky wheel gets the grease." People use it to stress the importance of speaking up for yourself. Think of situations in which you've either spoken up for yourself, or decided it was wiser to stay silent.

In "The Ninny" and "The Governess," a retelling of "The Ninny," you'll learn how a governess reacts to unfair treatment from her employer.

THEMATIC FOCUS: Facing Hard Questions

As you read, ask yourself if you would have reacted as the governess did when faced with hard questions.

◆ Background for Understanding

HISTORY

In nineteenth-century Europe, most upper-class families hired governesses for their children. Governesses taught lessons, monitored safety, and provided moral instruction. The life of a governess was often lonely because she belonged to neither the servant class nor the upper class. "The Ninny" and "The Governess" are two works about one particular governess.

◆ Build Vocabulary

SUFFIXES: -ment

The suffix -ment can be added to some verbs to create nouns. For example, the verb *baffle* means "to confuse." The noun *bafflement* means "a state of confusion."

WORD BANK

Which word from the list is the opposite of *superior*? Check the Build Vocabulary box on page 176 to see if you chose correctly.

bitter
timidly
inferior
discrepancies
discharged
guileless
bafflement

 Prentice Hall Literature Program Resources

REINFORCE / RETEACH / EXTEND
Selection Support Pages
Build Vocabulary: Suffixes: -ment, p. 77
Build Spelling Skills, p. 78
Build Grammar Skills: Principal Parts of Regular Verbs, p. 79
Reading Strategy: Question Characters' Actions, p. 80
Literary Focus: Characters' Motives, p. 81
Strategies for Diverse Student Needs, pp. 29–30

Beyond Literature Career Connection: Working With Children, p. 15
Formal Assessment Selection Test, pp. 55–57
Assessment Resources Software
Alternative Assessment, p. 15
Resource Pro CD-R⊘M "The Ninny"; "The Governess"—includes all resource material and customizable lesson plan
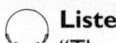 **Listening to Literature Audiocassettes** "The Ninny"; "The Governess"

The Ninny ◆ The Governess

The Rev. and Mrs. Palmer-Lovell with their daughters Georgina and Christina, Augustus Egg, Phillips, the International Fine Art Auctioneers, UK

◆ Literary Focus
CHARACTERS' MOTIVES

People in real life rarely act without a cause or reason. The same is true in literature. **Characters' motives** are the reasons behind their actions. Some motives are obvious. For example, a character's motive for scolding a child is that the child misbehaved. Sometimes, however, motives are hidden and must be guessed at by the reader.

As you read "The Ninny" and "The Governess," look for clues to the employer's motives.

◆ Reading Strategy
QUESTION CHARACTERS' ACTIONS

Characters in literature usually act and react as real people do. To get a deeper understanding of characters, **question their actions**—what the characters do and say. For example, after an important event, ask yourself, "Why did the character do this?" Your answers can help you to understand a character's motives.

Character	What the Character Said or Did	Why?
The Mistress	She calls Julia.	To review her salary

Guide for Reading ◆ 173

Preparing for Standardized Tests

Reading The reading strategy of questioning characters' actions will help students with comprehension items on standardized tests.

Present the following sample test question after students have read the selection:

Julia's mistress tells her to "look straight at my face and look hard . . ." Why does she say this?

(A) She wants Julia to see what she looks like.
(B) She wants to intimidate Julia, to make her agree with what she is saying.

(C) She thinks Julia has poor hearing.
(D) She wants to jog Julia's memory of a discussion the two once had.

Discuss the characters' actions to help students see that *(B)* is the best answer because Julia's employer tells her to look her in the eye as a way of commanding Julia to agree with something she, the mistress, knows is false. Point out that *(D)* is wrong because the mistress has no reason to think that Julia has forgotten anything. For further practice, use Reading Strategy: Question Characters' Actions in **Selection Support**, p. 80.

One-Minute Insight

A man calls in his children's governess to settle her pay, and lists deductions he is making from her salary; she sadly accepts his list. In fact, he is testing her to see if she'll stand up for her rights—he thinks he is teaching her a lesson. After paying her correct salary in full and explaining what he was doing, he can't understand why she continues to act meekly. In fact, he doesn't seem to grasp the effect of their class difference upon their relationship. The girl, who needs her job and is no stranger to unfair treatment, behaves as she feels she must.

Clarification

❶ A *ninny* is a fool. The term may derive from the word *innocent*.

◆Reading Strategy

❷ Question Characters' Actions Why does Yulia blush and fiddle with her dress? *Students may say that she is uncomfortable in the situation; or she knows what her boss is saying is wrong.*

◆Critical Thinking

❸ Make a Judgment Ask students whether any of these charges are legitimate deductions to Yulia's wages. *Students are likely to say that most, if not all, are not legitimate reasons for reducing her salary.*

►Critical Viewing◄

❹ Draw Conclusions *Students may say her downcast expression suggests resignation and perhaps unhappiness.*

◆Literary Focus

❺ Characters' Motives Why is the employer treating Yulia in this manner? *Possible response: as her employer, he can treat her as he likes, and even fire her.*

Customize for
English Language Learners

Students may be familiar with the English words for numbers but not recognize them in their written form. Help them create a chart with the digits and numbers. In addition, you may want to clarify that a *ruble* is a denomination of Russian money.

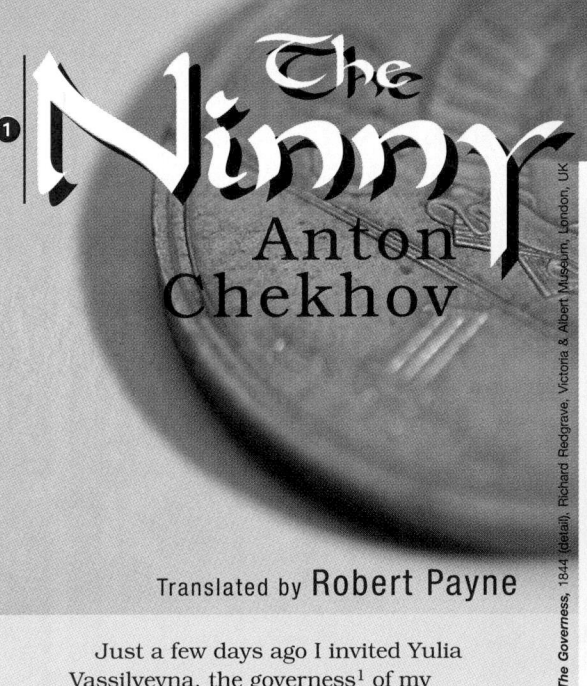

❶ The Ninny
Anton Chekhov

The Governess, 1844 (detail), Richard Redgrave, Victoria & Albert Museum, London, UK

Translated by **Robert Payne**

Just a few days ago I invited Yulia Vassilyevna, the governess[1] of my children, to come to my study. I wanted to settle my account with her.

"Sit down, Yulia Vassilyevna," I said to her. "Let's get our accounts settled. I'm sure you need some money, but you keep standing on ceremony and never ask for it. Let me see. We agreed to give you thirty rubles a month, didn't we?"

"Forty."

"No, thirty. I made a note of it. I always pay the governess thirty. Now, let me see. You have been with us for two months?"

"Two months and five days."

"Two months exactly. I made a note of it. So you have sixty rubles coming to you. Subtract nine Sundays. You know you don't tutor Kolya on Sundays, you just go out for a walk. And then the three holidays . . ."

❷ Yulia Vassilyevna blushed and picked at the trimmings of her dress, but said not a word.

❸ "Three holidays. So we take off twelve rubles. Kolya was sick for four days—those days you didn't look after him. You looked

---

1. **governess** (guv′ ər nis) *n.*: Woman employed in a private home to train and teach a child or children.

174 ◆ Meeting Challenges

▲ **Critical Viewing** Judging by the expression on the governess's face, do you think her life is a happy one? **[Draw Conclusions]** **❹**

after Vanya, only Vanya. Then there were the three days you had toothache, when my wife gave you permission to stay away from the children after dinner. Twelve and seven makes nineteen. Subtract. . . . That leaves . . . hm . . . forty-one rubles. Correct?" **❸**

Yulia Vassilyevna's left eye reddened and filled with tears. Her chin trembled. She began to cough nervously, blew her nose, and said nothing.

"Then around New Year's Day you broke a cup and saucer. Subtract two rubles. The cup cost more than that—it was an heirloom, but we won't bother about that. We're the ones who pay. Another matter. Due to your carelessness Kolya climbed a tree and tore his coat. Subtract ten. Also, due to your carelessness the chambermaid ran off with Vanya's boots. You ought to have kept your eyes open. You get a good salary. So we dock off five more. . . . On the tenth of January you took ten rubles from me." **❺**

Block Scheduling Strategies

Consider these suggestions to take advantage of extended class time:

• Discuss the Background for Understanding, p. 172, to prepare students for the nature of the employer/governess relationship.

• When students have finished reading the story, before they read the play, have them discuss and answer the Guide for Responding questions on p. 175. Use the Guide for Responding questions on p. 181 to help them compare and contrast the two treatments of the same story.

• Devote class time to having students work on and present advertisements, letters of resignation, or interior monologues for the portfolio opportunities for writing in the Idea Bank on p. 183. Provide time for groups to work on the Projects in the Idea Bank on p. 183.

• To help students prepare for the Writing Mini-Lesson, refer them to the Organizing Details section of Chapter 5, Exposition: Making Connections, pp. 154–155, in *Writer's Solution Sourcebook*.

"I didn't," Yulia Vassilyevna whispered. "But I made a note of it."

"Well, yes—perhaps . . ."

"From forty-one we take twenty-seven. That leaves fourteen."

Her eyes filled with tears, and her thin, pretty little nose was shining with perspiration. Poor little child!

"I only took money once," she said in a trembling voice. "I took three rubles from your wife . . . never anything more."

"Did you now? You see, I never made a note of it. Take three from fourteen. That leaves eleven. Here's your money, my dear. Three, three, three . . . one and one. Take it, my dear."

I gave her the eleven rubles. With trembling fingers she took them and slipped them into her pocket.

"*Merci*," she whispered.

 I jumped up, and began pacing up and down the room. I was in a furious temper.

"Why did you say '*merci*'?" I asked.

"For the money."

"Don't you realize I've been cheating you? I steal your money, and all you can say is '*merci*'!"

"In my other places they gave me nothing."

"They gave you nothing! Well, no wonder! I was playing a trick on you—a dirty trick. . . . I'll give you your eighty rubles, they are all here in an envelope made out for you. Is it possible for anyone to be such a nitwit? Why didn't you protest? Why did you keep your mouth shut? Is it possible that there is anyone in this world who is so spineless? Why are you such a ninny?"

She gave me a bitter little smile. On her face I read the words: "Yes, it is possible."

I apologized for having played this cruel trick on her, and to her great surprise gave her the eighty rubles. And then she said "*merci*" again several times, always timidly, and went out. I gazed after her, thinking how very easy it is in this world to be strong.

◆ **Build Vocabulary**

bitter (bit′ ər) *adj.*: Showing discomfort, sorrow, or pain

timidly (tim′ id lē) *adv.*: In a shy manner

Guide for Responding

◆ **LITERATURE AND YOUR LIFE**

Reader's Response What advice would you like to give the governess?

Thematic Focus Do you think that the governess answered the narrator's questions wisely? Explain.

Journal Writing Taking on the character of the governess, write a journal entry she might have written following this interview with her employer.

☑ **Check Your Comprehension**

1. Who narrates "The Ninny"?
2. How does the governess respond to each question?
3. What trick does the narrator reveal at the end of the story?

◆ **Critical Thinking**

INTERPRET

1. What strategies does the narrator use to decrease the governess's salary? **[Classify]**
2. Why does the narrator decide to play this trick? **[Infer]**
3. What does the governess's response to the trick suggest about her? **[Interpret]**

EVALUATE

4. Which character do you admire more at the end of the story? Why? **[Make a Judgment]**

APPLY

5. Suppose the narrator decided to give this story a moral. What moral might he have chosen? **[Generalize]**

The Ninny ◆ 175

Humanities: Art

The Governess, 1844, by Richard Redgrave
Richard Redgrave (1804–1888) was among the first British painters to address realistic social issues. Guide students to observe the clothing, facial expression, and body language of the governess in the forefront of the painting with those of the other young women in the painting.

1. How would you describe the governess as she appears in this painting? *Students may say that she seems reserved and shy because she is looking downward. Some students may say that she looks unhappy.*

2. Do you think this is how she always looks? *Students may realize that she is "on duty" in the scene that is portrayed. They may realize that she has a life of her own besides her employment.*

3. Might this governess respond to her employer the same or differently than Yulia does? *Students should realize that although the title of the story implies that the Yulia may be somewhat foolish, she and the governess in the picture are probably glad that they have a position and will behave as they think they must to keep that position.*

One-Minute Insight Neil Simon's play retells the Chekhov story, with a few changes. But the essence remains the same: an employer tries to teach a meek employee a lesson about assertiveness. Here, as in Chekhov's version, an employer discovers that people can indeed be timid. And here again, the mistress does not understand the reasons for the governess's behavior.

◆ Critical Thinking

❶ Compare and Contrast Guide students, as they read, to notice what in this play is the same as the Chekhov story and what is changed. *Possible answers: The employer is now a woman; Yulia is now Julia; Julia is somewhat more assertive in the play than in the story; the stage directions allow readers to visualize characters' actions and appearances.*

◆ Reading Strategy

❷ Question Characters' Actions Explain the distinction between feeling inferior and acting in a deferential manner. Point out that the Mistress and Julia are from different social classes, and that it would be customary for Julia to show courteous respect for one in a higher position. Keeping her head down may be Julia's way of showing that she understands her social rank. (Remind students that the play takes place at a time of rigid class distinctions.)

Comprehension Check ☑

❸ What book does the Mistress point to? *The book is a ledger of some kind, in which the Mistress records her household expenses.*

Customize for
Visual/Spatial Learners
Students will notice that a play looks different from a story. Point out and discuss the conventions of script writing, including the use of capitalization, different type faces, and punctuation. For instance, point out that ellipses (. . .) are used to indicate a pause in conversation and that a dash indicates that a character's speech is interrupted by the next line. Or discuss the meaning of information given in italics within brackets (stage directions).

176

---

❶ The Governess
Neil Simon

MISTRESS. Julia! [*Calls again*] Julia!

[*A young governess,* JULIA, *comes rushing in. She stops before the desk and curtsies.*]

JULIA. [*Head down*] Yes, madame?

❷ MISTRESS. Look at me, child. Pick your head up. I like to see your eyes when I speak to you.

JULIA. [*Lifts her head up*] Yes, madame. [*But her head has a habit of slowly drifting down again*]

MISTRESS. And how are the children coming along with their French lessons?

JULIA. They're very bright children, madame.

MISTRESS. Eyes up . . . They're bright, you say. Well, why not? And mathematics? They're doing well in mathematics, I assume?

JULIA. Yes, madame. Especially Vanya.

MISTRESS. Certainly. I knew it. I excelled in mathematics. He gets that from his mother, wouldn't you say?

JULIA. Yes, madame.

MISTRESS. Head up . . .

[*She lifts head up*]

That's it. Don't be afraid to look people in the eyes, my dear. If you think of yourself as <u>inferior</u>, that's exactly how people will treat you.

JULIA. Yes, ma'am.

MISTRESS. A quiet girl, aren't you? . . . Now then, let's settle our accounts. I imagine you must need money, although you never ask me for it yourself. Let's see now, we agreed on thirty rubles[1] a month, did we not?

JULIA. [*Surprised*] Forty, ma'am.

❸ MISTRESS. No, no, thirty. I made a note of it. [*Points to the book*] I always pay my governess thirty . . . Who told you forty?

JULIA. You did, ma'am. I spoke to no one else concerning money . . .

MISTRESS. Impossible. Maybe you *thought* you heard forty when I said thirty. If you kept your head up, that would never happen. Look at me again and I'll say it clearly. *Thirty rubles a month.*

JULIA. If you say so, ma'am.

1. rubles (rōō´ bəlz) *n.*: Basic monetary unit of Russia.

◆ Build Vocabulary

inferior (in fir´ ē ər) *adj.*: Lower in status, order, or rank

discrepancies (di skrep´ ən sēz) *n.*: Differences; inconsistencies; lack of agreement

176 ◆ *Meeting Challenges*

Beyond the Classroom

Workplace Skills

Management Various work situations call for effective management skills. Discuss students' views on the management styles of the employers in both pieces in this selection. Ask students to judge those employers' methods for getting the most from their employees.

Point out to students that in certain work situations, it may fall upon them to manage or be responsible for the work and well-being of others.

Discuss that knowing how to encourage the best efforts and support from employees and co-workers is a key issue not only for executives, but also for store managers, office supervisors, team leaders, and many others. Have groups brainstorm for a list of jobs that require management skills. Then have them develop a "Manager's Do's and Don'ts" memo that outlines behaviors they believe will be effective with workers. Have groups present and compare their documents.

Woman in Chair, John Collier, Courtesy of the artist.

4 Interpret *Students may say that, like the governess in the play, this woman appears to be respectful and meek. They may point to the fact that she sits in the corner, her hands clasped in her lap, with a deferential look on her face. She appears to be looking away.*

◆**Reading Strategy**

5 Questioning Characters' Actions Discuss this interaction between Julia and the Mistress with students. Ask them to tell what they can infer about the relationship between the two. *Students may say that the Mistress uses her position to bully Julia, who defers and never argues, even when she knows her mistress is wrong. Students may note that it's not clear—at this point, anyway—who is right.*

Customize for
Interpersonal Learners
Discuss with students how the circumstance of unequal relationships can influence and even dictate behavior. To help them understand this idea, provide examples of unequal relationships with which students are familiar, such as coach/athlete, principal/student, tutor/tutee, clergy member/congregant, and so on. Invite students to explain how being in one of these relationships guides ones' behavior.

4 ▲ **Critical Viewing** Do you think that, like the governess in the play, this woman is "afraid to look people in the eyes"? Explain. [Interpret]

MISTRESS. Settled. Thirty a month it is . . . Now then, you've been here two months exactly.

JULIA. Two months and five days.

MISTRESS. No, no. Exactly two months. I made a note of it. You should keep books the way I do so there wouldn't be these discrepancies. So—we have two months at thirty rubles a month . . . comes to sixty rubles. Correct?

JULIA. [*Curtsies*] Yes, ma'am. Thank you, ma'am.

MISTRESS. Subtract nine Sundays . . . We did agree to subtract Sundays, didn't we?

JULIA. No, ma'am.

MISTRESS. Eyes! Eyes! . . . Certainly we did. I've always subtracted Sundays. I didn't bother making a note of it because I always do it. Don't you recall when I said we will subtract Sundays?

5

◆ **Reading Strategy**
Wy doesn't Julia stand up for herself?

5

The Governess ◆ 177

 Humanities: Art

Woman in Chair, by John Collier
John Collier (1850–1934) had an aristocratic background. He was a popular portrait painter of members of the British upper class. His subjects included Rudyard Kipling and Aldous Huxley. His paintings have been used as illustrations of fiction that deals with both the British and American upper classes. Use these questions for discussion:
1. What details in this painting provide clues to its time and place, and to who the woman might be? *Students may realize the style of the woman's elegant, old-fashioned dress and her elaborate*

necklace place her in a time period of about a hundred years ago; the chair, rug, and wall painting are indications of an upper-class home; her composed, proper way of sitting is a sign that she's been taught the good manners of the time—she probably is a member of a wealthy family.

2. How would you describe the expression on the woman's face? *Students may say that she is either deep in thought or is perhaps distracted by something. Some may say that they see fear, sadness, or apprehension in her face and in her stiff posture.*

178

Literary Focus

❶ Characters' Motives Point out that the Mistress demands that Julia look straight at her face so that she'll remember what the Mistress wants her to remember. Ask students whether they think that this technique encourages memory. Students may say that it is not a memory technique, only another way for the Mistress to intimidate Julia. The Mistress's demand makes it clear that she wants and expects Julia to agree with her, which Julia says she does.

Reading Strategy

❷ Questioning Characters' Actions Discuss with students that it now becomes clear that the Mistress is trying to take advantage of Julia, and that the governess seems to tell the truth, but won't press a point. Help students interpret this behavior as Julia's awareness of her status as a servant: she knows the Mistress is taking advantage, but she doesn't know how to prevent it.

Literary Focus

❸ Characters' Motives *Since students have already read Checkhov's story, they will know that the Mistress is pressing Julia to see what it will take to get a reaction out of her. Otherwise, students might say she is being cheap and manipulative.*

JULIA. No, ma'am.

MISTRESS. Think.

JULIA. [*Thinks*] No, ma'am.

❶ MISTRESS. You weren't thinking. Your eyes were wandering. Look straight at my face and look hard . . . Do you remember now?

JULIA. [*Softly*] Yes, ma'am.

MISTRESS. I didn't hear you, Julia.

JULIA. [*Louder*] Yes, ma'am.

MISTRESS. Good. I was sure you'd remember . . . Plus three holidays. Correct?

JULIA. Two, ma'am. Christmas and New Year's.

MISTRESS. And your birthday. That's three.

JULIA. I worked on my birthday, ma'am.

MISTRESS. You did? There was no need to. My governesses never worked on their birthdays . . .

❷ JULIA. But I did work, ma'am.

MISTRESS. But that's not the question, Julia. We're discussing financial matters now. I will, however, only count two holidays if you insist . . . Do you insist?

JULIA. I did work, ma'am.

MISTRESS. Then you *do* insist.

JULIA. No, ma'am.

MISTRESS. Very well. That's three holidays, therefore we take off twelve rubles. Now then, four days little Kolya was sick, and there were no lessons.

JULIA. But I gave lessons to Vanya.

MISTRESS. True. But I engaged you to teach two children, not one. Shall I pay you in full for doing only half the work?

JULIA. No, ma'am.

MISTRESS. So we'll deduct it . . . Now, three days you had a toothache and my husband gave you permission not to work after lunch. Correct?

JULIA. After four. I worked until four.

MISTRESS. [*Looks in the book*] I have here: "Did not work after lunch." We have lunch at one and are finished at two, not at four, correct?

JULIA. Yes, ma'am. But I—

MISTRESS. That's another seven rubles . . . Seven and twelve is nineteen . . . Subtract . . . that leaves . . . forty-one rubles . . . Correct?

JULIA. Yes, ma'am. Thank you, ma'am.

MISTRESS. Now then, on January fourth you broke a teacup and saucer, is that true?

178 ◆ Meeting Challenges

◆ Literary Focus **❸**
What might be the Mistress's motive for deducting the money from Julia's salary?

◆ Build Vocabulary
discharged (dis chärjd´) *v.*: Relieved or released from something; fired

---

 Beyond the Classroom

Career Connection
Private Child Care Discuss with students that the job of governess did not go out with the end of the Victorian age. Private, live-in child-care exists in a variety of forms today. Families with parents who must be away from home for work or other reasons may hire nannies or other live-in helpers to look after and instruct their children.

Some hire au pairs—girls from other countries who are hired to do housework or supervise children in return for room and board and an opportunity to learn the family's language and culture. In most cases this is a satisfactory arrangment for both the au pair and the family.

Suggest that students interview a nanny, an au pair, or a family that employs one or the other, to find out the pros and cons of the jobs, including pay, accommodations, work hours, and responsibilities. Have them find out about the qualifications and on-the-job skills these positions demand.

Discuss students' findings with the class. Although child-care is a demanding job, the unfairness that the characters of this play and story experienced is less likely to occur today.

JULIA. Just the saucer, ma'am.

4 ┃ **MISTRESS.** What good is a teacup without a saucer, eh? . . . That's two rubles. The saucer was an heirloom. It cost much more, but let it go. I'm used to taking losses.

JULIA. Thank you, ma'am.

MISTRESS. Now then, January ninth, Kolya climbed a tree and tore his jacket.

JULIA. I forbid him to do so, ma'am.

MISTRESS. But he didn't listen, did he? . . . Ten rubles . . . January fourteenth, Vanya's shoes were stolen . . .

JULIA. But the maid, ma'am. You discharged her yourself.

MISTRESS. But you get paid good money to watch everything. I explained that in our first meeting. Perhaps you weren't listening. Were you listening that day, Julia, or was your head in the clouds?

JULIA. Yes, ma'am.

MISTRESS. Yes, your head was in the clouds?

JULIA. No, ma'am. I was listening.

MISTRESS. Good girl. So that means another five rubles off [*Looks in the book*] . . . Ah, yes . . . The sixteenth of January I gave you ten rubles.

JULIA. You didn't.

MISTRESS. But I made a note of it. Why would I make a note of it if I didn't give it to you?

JULIA. I don't know, ma'am.

MISTRESS. That's not a satisfactory answer, Julia . . . Why would I make a note of giving you ten rubles if I did not in fact give it to you, eh? . . . No answer? . . . Then I must have given it to you, mustn't I?

JULIA. Yes, ma'am. If you say so, ma'am.

MISTRESS. Well, certainly I say so. That's the point of this little talk. To clear these matters up. Take twenty-seven from forty-one, that leaves . . . fourteen, correct?

Woman Standing at Highboy, John Collier, Courtesy of the artist

▲ **Critical Viewing** The subject of this painting has her back turned to the viewer. In what way is the effect created suited for depicting "the governess"? [Interpret] **5**

The Governess ◆ 179

◆**Reading Strategy**

4 Question Characters' Actions
Encourage students to question the logic the Mistress uses here. Is it true that a teacup is no good without a saucer? Is the tear in Kolya's jacket really Julia's fault? Then have students read Julia's response to these charges. Ask them to say how they would respond to the Mistress's accusations if they were Julia. Remind them that Julia would maintain a polite and deferential tone. *Responses will vary, but students should recognize that they would have to be respectful and express a clear viewpoint that calmly addresses each of the Mistress's claims.*

▶**Critical Viewing**◀

5 Interpret *Students may suggest that with her back turned, perhaps away from an accusing employer, the governess can privately show her true feelings.*

 Humanities: Art

Woman Standing at Highboy, by John Collier
This painting is by the same artist as the portrait on p. 179. Call students' attention to the similarity in style: subdued colors, shadows and play of light and dark and shading. Encourage them to study both paintings, and then use these questions for discussion:

1. Compare and contrast this painting with the other Collier work on p. 179. *They both show young well-dressed women, both apparently deep in thought, in rooms of nice homes. Both paintings show a time that is many years ago.*

2. What lines from "The Governess" might make good captions for this painting and for the painting on p. 179? Explain your choices. *Possible reponses: p. 179: "Don't be afraid to look people in the eyes, my dear," or "Your eyes were wandering. Look straight at my face and look hard . . . "; this page: "Yes, ma'am. [She turns away, softly crying]. Students may select the first caption because they can see from the woman's face that her eyes are turned away. They may choose the second caption because the woman's back is to the viewer—she is turned away.*

179

Comprehension Check ☑

❶ Why is Julia crying? *Students may say that she cries out of a sense of frustration, with anger at being taken advantage of, or in fear that she is trapped with no way out.*

◆ **Literary Focus**

❷ Characters' Motives Why does Julia say that there's no need to count the coins? *Students may say that she thinks that counting the money might offend her mistress by showing distrust. (They are not likely to know that it was considered "good form" for servants not to look at money when it was handed to them.) They may say that even if the count is wrong, she would be powerless to do anything about it.*

◆ **Literary Focus**

❸ Characters' Motives What is Julia's motive for thanking her employer, even after she has been swindled? *Students may say that she is demoralized and feels hopeless to do anything about her circumstance, so she falls back on the politeness of her rank.*

◆ **Critical Thinking**

❹ Predict Do you think this version of the story will end as the first one did? Explain. *Students may predict that it will, since the gist of the story and play is the same to this point.*

◆ **LITERATURE AND YOUR LIFE**

❺ Ask students to tell whether they think the Mistress's tactics have amounted to a "little joke," as she claims they have. Is her way a good way to teach a lesson? *Students may say that her approach is too cruel to be a joke and that tricking people is a poor way to teach them because they may also learn mistrust and anger for the "teacher."*

180

---

❶ JULIA. Yes, ma'am. [*She turns away, softly crying*]

MISTRESS. What's this? Tears? Are you crying? Has something made you unhappy, Julia? Please tell me. It pains me to see you like this. I'm so sensitive to tears. What is it?

JULIA. Only once since I've been here have I ever been given any money and that was by your husband. On my birthday he gave me three rubles.

❷ MISTRESS. Really? There's no note of it in my book. I'll put it down now. [*She writes in the book.*] Three rubles. Thank you for telling me. Sometimes I'm a little lax with my accounts . . . Always short-changing myself. So then, we take three more from fourteen . . . leaves eleven . . . Do you wish to check my figures?

JULIA. There's no need to, ma'am.

MISTRESS. Then we're all settled. Here's your salary for two months, dear. Eleven rubles. [*She puts the pile of coins on the desk.*] Count it.

JULIA. It's not necessary, ma'am.

MISTRESS. Come, come. Let's keep the records straight. Count it.

JULIA. [*Reluctantly counts it*] One, two, three, four, five, six, seven, eight, nine, ten . . . ? There's only ten, ma'am.

MISTRESS. Are you sure? Possibly you dropped one . . . Look on the floor, see if there's a coin there.

JULIA. I didn't drop any, ma'am. I'm quite sure.

MISTRESS. Well, it's not here on my desk, and I *know* I gave you eleven rubles. Look on the floor.

JULIA. It's all right, ma'am. Ten rubles will be fine.

MISTRESS. Well, keep the ten for now. And if we don't find it on the floor later, we'll discuss it again next month.

JULIA. Yes, ma'am. Thank you, ma'am. You're very kind, ma'am.

[*She curtsies and then starts to leave.*]

MISTRESS. Julia!

[JULIA *stops, turns.*]

❸ Come back here.

[*She goes back to the desk and curtsies again.*]

Why did you thank me?

JULIA. For the money, ma'am.

❹ MISTRESS. For the money? . . . But don't you realize what I've done? I've cheated you . . . *Robbed* you! I have no such notes in my book. I made up whatever came into my mind. Instead of the eighty rubles which I owe you, I gave you only ten. I have actually stolen from you and you still thank me . . . Why?

JULIA. In the other places that I've worked, they didn't give me anything at all.

180 ◆ *Meeting Challenges*

◆ **Build Vocabulary**

guileless (gīl′ lis) *adj.*: Without deceit, slyness, or trickery

bafflement (baf′ əl mənt) *n.*: State of confusion or puzzlement

---

Speaking and Listening Mini-Lesson

Dramatization

This mini-lesson supports the Speaking and Listening activity in the Idea Bank on p. 183.

Introduce Discuss with students the elements of an effective play-reading, such as understanding of the characters, and strong and clear delivery of lines. As needed, review the conventions of scripts. Discuss proper audience behavior, such as quiet listening and attentiveness.

Develop Have pairs choose their roles and practice them. You might have students work in groups of three, in which one of the three acts as director or acting coach.

Apply Hold the performances. Remind the class that those not performing need to act as audience members and therefore have their own set of responsibilities.

Assess Evaluate performances on how accurately students interpret the personalities of the characters and the key elements of the drama. Or, use the Peer Assessment: Dramatic Performance form, p. 116, in **Alternative Assessment**.

MISTRESS. Then they cheated you even worse than I did . . . I was playing a little joke on you. A cruel lesson just to teach you. You're much too trusting, and in this world that's very dangerous ❺ . . . I'm going to give you the entire eighty rubles. [*Hands her an envelope*] It's all ready for you. The rest is in this envelope. Here, take it.

JULIA. As you wish, ma'am. [*She curtsies and starts to go again.*] ❻

MISTRESS. Julia!

[JULIA *stops.*]

Is it possible to be so spineless? Why don't you protest? Why don't you speak up? Why don't you cry out against this cruel and unjust treatment? Is it really possible to be so <u>guileless</u>, so innocent, such a—pardon me for being so blunt—such a simpleton? ❼

JULIA. [*The faintest trace of a smile on her lips*] Yes, ma'am . . . it's possible.

[*She curtsies again and runs off. The* MISTRESS *looks after her a moment, a look of complete <u>bafflement</u> on her face. The lights fade.*]

◆ Literature
and Your Life
Have you ever met someone who didn't stand up for himself or herself? Explain. ❽

◇Guide for Responding

◆ LITERATURE AND YOUR LIFE

Reader's Response What did you think of the Mistress's behavior?

Thematic Focus How do people use questions to get the answers they want to hear?

Letter of Advice Write a letter to the governess in which you give her advice on how to stand up for herself.

✓ Check Your Comprehension

1. How are Julia and the Mistress related?
2. What happens to Julia's salary during the meeting?
3. How does Julia respond to the Mistress's actions?

◆ Critical Thinking

INTERPRET
1. How are the Mistress and Julia different? **[Compare and Contrast]**
2. In what way does the Mistress try to provoke a reaction from Julia? **[Infer]**
3. Do you think the Mistress is satisfied with her trick? **[Speculate]**
4. How does Neil Simon create humor in this situation? **[Analyze]**

APPLY
5. How can people learn to stand up for their rights? **[Apply]**

COMPARE LITERARY WORKS
6. Which version of this story do you think is more successful? Why? **[Assess]**

The Governess ◆ 181

Beyond the Selection

FURTHER READING
Other Works by Anton Chekhov
The Seagull
Uncle Vanya
Other Works by Neil Simon
Barefoot in the Park
Biloxi Blues

INTERNET
We suggest the following sites on the Internet (all Web sites are subject to change).
For more information about Anton Chekhov:
http://eldred.ne.mediaone.net/ac/chekhov.html
For more on Neil Simon:
http://kennedy-center.org/honors/1995/neisim.html
We *strongly recommend* that you preview these sites before you send students to them.

◆Critical Thinking

❻ **Interpret** Why is Julia's response so brief and agreeable? *She doesn't want to reveal her true feelings.*

◆Critical Thinking

❼ **Compare and Contrast** Ask students to compare the employer's final statement in each selection. How are they alike? How do they differ? *Students may say the employer in the Chekhov story accuses Yulia of being a "nitwit" and being "spineless"; in Simon's play, the accusations are slightly gentler. Julia is accused of being "guileless" and "innocent" and her employer asks her pardon before calling her a "simpleton."*

◆LITERATURE AND YOUR LIFE

❽ *Students may also remember examples from films or television dramas.*

Reinforce and Extend

Answers
◆LITERATURE AND YOUR LIFE

Reader's Response Students should support their views with examples from the selection.

Thematic Focus Students may say that people get the answers they want by phrasing questions in a way that makes disagreement difficult.

✓ Check Your Comprehension

1. Julia is the Mistress's governess; she is employed to takes care of the Mistress's children.
2. The Mistress keeps deducting from it for various reasons.
3. She is deferential and agreeable at all times.

◆Critical Thinking

1. The Mistress is confident and assertive; Julia is meek and deferential.
2. She uses increasingly preposterous excuses for lowering her salary.
3. Possible response: She is not satisfied since she never gets Julia to speak up for herself.
4. Students may say that the humor stems from the far-fetched reasons the Mistress finds for reducing Julia's salary.
5. Possible response: They can learn by trying it once or twice.
6. Students should support their opinions with details from the story and play.

Answers

◆ Reading Strategy

1. He loses his temper.
2. Possible response: The employer, because of his lofty position, is able to speak up for himself. But he is too narrow-minded to understand the actions of others less fortunate than himself.
3. Her body language indicates that she is meek and shy.

◆ Build Vocabulary

Using the Suffix -ment
1. judgment
2. encouragement

Spelling Strategy
1. opportunities
2. alloys
3. monkeys
4. mercies

Using the Word Bank
1. c
2. b
3. a
4. f
5. d
6. g
7. e

◆ Literary Focus

1. Students should support their choices with examples from the selection.
2. She says that she does so in thanks for the money; she claims that other employers paid her nothing.
3. Possible responses: The smile may be one of relief that she has received all the money owed to her. Also, it could indicate some pleasure at having frustrated her employer for a moment.

◆ Build Grammar Skills

Practice
1. look, looked, looking, looked
2. invite, invited, inviting, invited
3. subtract, subtracted, subtracting, subtracted
4. trap, trapped, trapping, trapped
5. compel, compelled, compelling, compelled

Writing Application
Possible responses:
1. The employer stared coldly at the governess.
2. The governess had to listen to each ridiculous reason.
3. The governess was longing for the conversation to end.
4. The conversation had finally ended with the employer still not understanding the governess.

Guide for Responding (continued)

◆ Reading Strategy

QUESTION CHARACTERS' ACTIONS
Questioning characters' actions while reading can lead you to understand story events and characters' motives.
1. How does the narrator of "The Ninny" react when the governess says, "*merci*"?
2. Why might the narrator of "The Ninny" have chosen to act so unreasonably toward the governess?
3. In "The Governess," what does Julia's body language—her posture and movements—tell you about her character?

◆ Build Vocabulary

USING THE SUFFIX -ment
The suffix -ment can be added to verbs such as *entertain* to form nouns such as *entertainment*. On your paper, fill in the blank in the second sentence by adding -ment to a word from the first.
1. The mistress judged Julia. She passed ____?____.
2. Julia is not encouraged. She needs ____?____.

SPELLING STRATEGY
If a noun ends in a consonant and *y*, form the plural by changing the *y* to *i* and adding -es:

discrepancy → discrepancies

If a noun ends in a vowel and *y*, form the plural by adding -s.

buoy → buoys   Saturday → Saturdays

On your paper, write the plural of each noun.
1. opportunity   3. monkey
2. alloy   4. mercy

USING THE WORD BANK
In your notebook, match each Word Bank word with the word opposite in meaning.
1. bitter   a. boldly
2. discrepancies   b. similarities
3. timidly   c. happy
4. bafflement   d. hired
5. discharged   e. superior
6. guileless   f. understanding
7. inferior   g. sly

◆ Literary Focus

CHARACTERS' MOTIVES
You can understand **characters' motives**—the reasons for their actions—by reviewing what the characters say and do. In both versions of this story, the employer tricks the governess.
1. Who do you think is trickier, the narrator in "The Ninny" or the Mistress in "The Governess"? Why?
2. What motive does the governess give for saying "*merci*" in "The Ninny"?
3. What is the governess's motive for smiling at the end of each story?

◆ Build Grammar Skills

PRINCIPAL PARTS OF REGULAR VERBS
Every verb has four **principal parts**. A **regular verb** forms its past and past participle by adding -d or -ed to the base form. The following chart explains the principal parts of regular verbs.

Principal Part	Description	Examples
Base Form:	basic form	listen, care
Past:	adds -ed or -d	listened, cared
Present Participle:	adds -ing	listening, caring
Past Participle:	adds -ed or -d	listened, cared

Some spellings change when forming principal parts. You may need to drop the final *e* when adding -ing: *dare, dared, daring, dared*. Sometimes you need to double the final consonant when you add -ed or -ing: *wrap, wrapped, wrapping, wrapped*.

Practice On your paper, write the principal parts of each verb.
1. look 2. invite 3. subtract 4. trap 5. compel

Writing Application On your paper, write sentences about the story, using each verb in the principal part indicated. You will need a helping verb with present and past participles.
1. (*stare*; past)
2. (*listen*; base)
3. (*long*; present participle)
4. (*end*; past participle)

✒ Writer's Solution

For additional instruction and practice, use the lesson in the *Writer's Solution Language Lab CD-ROM* on Using Verbs, and the practice page on the principal parts of regular verbs, p. 70 in the *Writer's Solution Grammar Practice Book*.

Build Your Portfolio

 ## Idea Bank

Writing

1. **Advertisement** Write an advertisement seeking a governess. Identify the job duties and list the qualities that a good governess should have.

2. **Letter of Resignation** Imagine that you are a governess who has decided to leave your current employer. Write a letter explaining why you are leaving.

3. **Interior Monologue** An interior monologue is a speech in which a character reveals his or her thoughts. Imagine what the governess is thinking during the scene you've just read, and write an interior monologue. **[Performing Arts Link]**

Speaking and Listening

4. **Dramatization** Work with a partner to perform "The Governess." First, rehearse to develop effective readings of each line. Then, present a script-in-hand performance for your class. **[Performing Arts Link]**

5. **Job Interview** Role-play the part of the narrator in "The Ninny" and interview several classmates for the job of governess. Then, explain which governess you would hire and why. **[Career Link]**

Projects

6. **Production Plan [Group Activity]** Working with a group of classmates, create a complete production plan for a stage version of "The Governess." Include casting suggestions, set designs, rehearsal schedule, as well as a poster and publicity materials. Each group member should be responsible for preparing one aspect of the production plan. **[Performing Arts Link]**

7. **Opinion Poll** Design and conduct a survey about work attitudes in your community. Ask questions, such as when, if ever, is it appropriate to speak up to your boss. Summarize your findings, and share the results with the class.

 ## Writing Mini-Lesson

Comparison of Stories

Neil Simon adapted Chekhov's short story "The Ninny" for the stage. He made several changes to the original story. Think about the alterations he made, and consider why he made each of them. Then, write an essay in which you compare and contrast the two versions of this story.

Writing Skills Focus: Organization

Organize your comparison-and-contrast essay clearly and effectively. For example, you might present all of the similarities in one section and describe all of the differences in another section. Another strategy is to focus each paragraph on one aspect of your subject, pointing out both similarities and differences.

Prewriting Gather details about each version of the story. Use a Venn diagram like the one below to record similarities and differences.

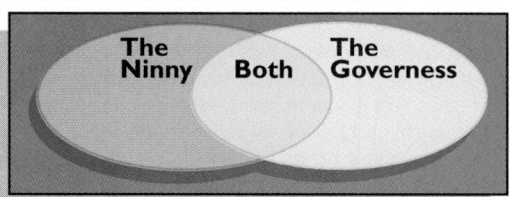

Drafting Follow your organizational plan. While drafting, refer to information you recorded in your Venn diagram. Use transitions, such as *in contrast, both, neither,* and *although,* to help readers follow your ideas.

Revising Give your paper to a writing partner to review. Ask for feedback on the clarity of your organization. Correct any errors in grammar and spelling.

> ◆ **Grammar Application**
> Make sure that you have formed principal parts of regular verbs correctly.

 ## Idea Bank

Following are suggestions for matching the Idea Bank topics with your students' performance levels and learning modalities:

Customize for
Performance Levels
Less Advanced Students: 1, 4
Average Students: 2, 4, 5, 7
More Advanced Students: 3, 4, 5, 6, 7

Customize for
Learning Modalities
Verbal/Linguistic: 1, 2, 3, 4, 5, 6, 7
Visual/Spatial: 6
Bodily/Kinesthetic: 4
Logical/Mathematical: 1, 2, 5, 7
Interpersonal: 4, 5, 6, 7
Intrapersonal: 2, 3

 ## Writing Mini-Lesson

Refer students to the Writing Handbook in the back of the book for instructions on the writing process and for further information on compare and contrast essays.

✐ Writer's Solution

Writing Lab CD-ROM
Have students complete the tutorial on Exposition: Making Connections. Follow these steps:

1. Have students use the Gathering Information section to see an annotated model on details for comparison and contrast.
2. Have them use the Organizing Details section for suggestions on ways to logically organize a compare-and-contrast essay.
3. Have students draft on computer.
4. Have students use Self-Evaluation Checklists to help them revise.

Allow about 70 minutes of class time to complete these steps.

Writer's Solution Sourcebook
Have students use Chapter 5, "Exposition: Making Connections," pp. 137–166, for additional support. The chapter includes in-depth instruction on how to organize a comparison-and-contrast paper, pp. 154–155.

✓ ASSESSMENT OPTIONS

Formal Assessment, Selection Test, pp. 55–57, and Assessment Resources Software. The selection test is designed so that it can be easily customized to the performance levels of your students.

Alternative Assessment, p. 15, includes options for less advanced students, more advanced students, interpersonal learners, verbal/linguistic learners, logical/mathematical learners, visual/spatial learners, and bodily/kinesthetic learners.

PORTFOLIO ASSESSMENT
Use the following rubrics in the **Alternative Assessment** booklet to assess student writing:
Advertisement: Definition/Classification, p. 95
Letter of Resignation: Cause-Effect, p. 98
Interior Monologue: Expression, p. 90
Writing Mini-Lesson: Comparison/Contrast, p. 99

Guide for Reading

OBJECTIVES

1. To read, comprehend, and interpret a story
2. To relate a story to personal experience
3. To respond to characters' actions
4. To determine the story's theme
5. To build vocabulary in context and learn the suffix *-able*
6. To identify principal parts of irregular verbs
7. To write a letter of guidance giving necessary background
8. To respond to the story through writing, speaking and listening, and projects

SKILLS INSTRUCTION

Vocabulary:
Suffixes: *-able*

Spelling:
Adding *mis-* to the beginning of a word

Grammar:
Principal Parts of Irregular Verbs

Reading Strategy:
Respond to Characters' Actions

Literary Focus:
Theme

Writing:
Give Necessary Background

Speaking and Listening:
Readers Theater (Teacher's Edition)

Critical Viewing:
Make a Judgment

PORTFOLIO OPPORTUNITIES

Writing: Letter; Sequel; Speech
Writing Mini-Lesson: Letter of Guidance
Speaking and Listening: Readers Theater; Rap Song
Projects: Multimedia Presentation; Painting or Drawing

More About the Author
Langston Hughes spent a year in Mexico and then traveled as a merchant seaman to Africa and Europe, after leaving college. While working as a bus boy in a hotel restaurant, Hughes placed a packet of his poems on the table of the famous poet Vachel Lindsay. Lindsay left with the poems and later read them before an audience, giving Hughes his first public reading. Using Lindsay's support as a spring-board, Hughes soon achieved success as a writer. Following his death in 1967, Hughes's Harlem home was given landmark status by the New York City Preservation Commission.

Meet the Author:

Langston Hughes (1902–1967)

Famed writer Langston Hughes was born in Joplin, Missouri. As a boy, his favorite destination was the library. He began writing poetry as a way of coping with an ever-changing home address and the difficulties of being a young African American in the early 1900's. His grandmother's stories about slavery and freedom, in which "always life moved, moved heroically toward an end," encouraged his love of words and understanding of African American history.

Literary Success Hughes attended Columbia University for a year. In 1926, he published his first collection of poetry, *The Weary Blues*. By 1930, he had become an internationally famous poet. Hughes was also a novelist, essayist, and dramatist, and he was awarded numerous prizes and grants. "Thank You, M'am" is one of Hughes's many stories about city life for African Americans.

THE STORY BEHIND THE STORY

Hughes felt it was important to write about the African American experience. In "Thank You, M'am," he writes about the dignity of the common people against the backdrop of Harlem. The characters in the story speak in urban dialect, using everyday speech and expressions.

184 ◆ Meeting Challenges

◆ LITERATURE AND YOUR LIFE

CONNECT YOUR EXPERIENCE

Have you ever been surprised by someone's act of kindness and trust? Perhaps it came at a particularly significant point in your life and made a profound difference in the way you viewed the world. In "Thank You, M'am," a young boy is taught a lesson in kindness and trust by a woman he meant to rob.

THEMATIC FOCUS: Facing Hard Questions

As you read this story, think about the hard questions both the young boy and the woman must face.

◆ Background for Understanding

CULTURE

"Thank You, M'am" is set in Harlem, a community in New York City that became the center of African American intellectual and artistic life in the 1920's. As more and more people moved to Harlem, many single-family buildings were converted into small apartments to create more housing. The character Mrs. Jones lives in a "bedsit," or "kitchenette," which is even smaller than an apartment. It usually had just one room for both sleeping and living, plus a bath.

◆ Build Vocabulary

SUFFIXES: *-able*

The suffix *-able* means "capable of" or "like." When combined with the verb *present*, it forms a word meaning "good enough to be present in company."

WORD BANK

Which word on the list means the opposite of *trusted*? Check the Build Vocabulary box on page 189 to see if you chose correctly.

presentable
mistrusted
latching
barren
barely

Prentice Hall Literature Program Resources

REINFORCE / RETEACH / EXTEND
Selection Support Pages
Build Vocabulary: Suffixes: *-able,* p. 82
Build Spelling Skills, p. 83
Build Grammar Skills: Principal Parts of Irregular Verbs, p. 84
Reading Strategy: Respond to Characters' Actions, p. 85
Literary Focus: Theme, p. 86
Strategies for Diverse Student Needs, pp. 31–32

Beyond Literature Cross-Curricular Connection: Math, p. 16
Formal Assessment Selection Test, pp. 58–60, Assessment Resources Software
Alternative Assessment, p. 16
Writing and Language Transparencies, Open Mind Organizer, p. 81
Daily Language Practice p. 52
Resource Pro CD-ROM "Thank You, M'am"
 Listening to Literature Audiocassettes "Thank You, M'am"

◆ Thank You, M'am ◆

Empire State, Tom Christopher, Vicki Morgan Associates

◆ Literary Focus

THEME

The **theme** of a literary work is the underlying message or insight about life that it communicates. Although a theme may be stated directly in the text, it is more often presented indirectly. You can determine a story's theme by noticing details about the characters, the story's events and setting, and asking, "What aspect of life does the author want me to think about?"

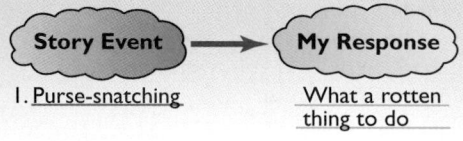

Story Event	My Response
1. Purse-snatching	What a rotten thing to do

◆ Reading Strategy

RESPOND TO CHARACTERS' ACTIONS

Reading stories is much more rewarding when you get involved. One way to do this is to **respond to the characters' actions** as you read. You may start rooting for one character or wishing another one would stop behaving in a certain way. You can ask questions like these to help you respond to a character's actions.

- Why does the character take this action?
- If I put myself in the character's shoes, what actions might I take?
- Does the character do or say anything that I can apply to my own life?

As you read, fill out a chart like the one to the left.

Guide for Reading ◆ 185

Preparing for Standardized Tests

Grammar The grammar concept for this story is principal parts of irregular verbs. Standardized tests may include questions that test students' ability to correctly use irregular verbs. Remind students that irregular verbs do not add *-ed* to the base verb to form the past or past participle. Review the present, past, and past participle of several irregular verbs, such as *go, went, gone; see, saw, seen; sleep, slept, slept*. Have students suggest other examples of irregular verbs and discuss their forms. Then write this sample test question on the board:

Identify the sentence that correctly uses an irregular verb.

(A) Mrs. Jones weared a large purse on her arm.
(B) She catched Roger trying to steal it.
(C) Then Mrs. Jones took him home with her.
(D) Later they eated dinner together.

Have students identify the verb in each sentence (wear, catch, take, eat). They should recognize that only (C) has the correct form of the irregular verb. For additional practice, use **Selection Support,** p. 84, on Principal Parts of Irregular Verbs.

One-Minute Insight In "Thank You, M'am," Mrs. Luella Bates Washington Jones is walking home when a boy tries to steal her large purse. As he turns to flee, the boy falls down and the woman is able to grab him by the shirt. She gives him a stern lecture, and then marches him off to her home. Mrs. Jones asks the boy about himself and learns that his name is Roger and he tried to steal her money to buy blue suede shoes. She prepares dinner for the two of them. After they have eaten, Mrs. Jones gives Roger $10 to buy his shoes. As she warns him to behave, the reader is left to think about the ways in which each character responded to a difficult question.

◆ Reading Strategy

❶ Respond to Characters' Actions Suggest that students also respond to the boy's actions. *Some students will be glad she is a strong and confident person and stood up for herself instead of screaming and running away. Some will think that the boy needs to be taught a lesson.*

◆ Critical Thinking

❷ Infer Ask students why the boy tells the truth now. *He tells the truth because he knows the woman will recognize a lie.*

Customize for
English Language Learners
Before students read, discuss examples of dialect in the selection, such as *Yes'm* (Yes, m'am, or madam); *You a lie* (You are a liar); *ain't* (are not); *got a great mind to* (think I will); *No'm* (No, madam); *could of* (could have); *come by devilish* (get in a dishonest way). You may want to write some of these, along with their standard English translations, on the board for students to refer to as they read.

Thank You, M'am

LANGSTON HUGHES

She was a large woman with a large purse that had everything in it but hammer and nails. It had a long strap and she carried it slung across her shoulder. It was about eleven o'clock at night, and she was walking alone, when a boy ran up behind her and tried to snatch her purse. The strap broke with the single tug the boy gave it from behind. But the boy's weight, and the weight of the purse combined caused him to lose his balance. Instead of taking off full blast as he had hoped, the boy fell on his back on the sidewalk, and his legs flew up. The large woman simply turned around and kicked him right square in his blue-jeaned sitter. Then she reached down, picked the boy up by his shirt front, and shook him until his teeth rattled.

After that the woman said, "Pick up my pocketbook, boy, and give it here."

She still held him. But she bent down enough to permit him to stoop and pick up her purse. Then she said, "Now ain't you ashamed of yourself?"

Firmly gripped by his shirt front, the boy said, "Yes'm."

The woman said, "What did you want to do it for?"

The boy said, "I didn't aim to."

She said, "You a lie!"

By that time two or three people passed, stopped, turned to look, and some stood watching.

"If I turn you loose, will you run?" asked the woman.

"Yes'm," said the boy.

❶ **◆ Reading Strategy**
What is your response to the woman's actions?

186 ◆ *Meeting Challenges*

Block Scheduling Strategies

Consider these suggestions to take advantage of extended class time:

- Have students read the selection independently. Then have students work in groups to discuss and complete the Guide for Responding questions, pp. 189–190. Have students take turns reading questions and writing responses.
- You may wish to have students use activities from the **Daily Language Practice**, p. 52.
- If you have access to technology, have students work on the *Writer's Solution Language Lab*

CD-ROM and *Writer's Solution Writing Lab CD-ROM* to prepare for and complete the Writing Mini-Lesson. Refer to the teaching suggestions on p. 191 to guide students through the process.

- After discussing the Reading Strategy, play the audiocassette of the selection and have students follow along in their books. Initiate a class discussion so that students can explore their reactions to the specific actions of each character.

Listening to Literature Audiocassettes

"Then I won't turn you loose," said the woman. She did not release him.

"Lady, I'm sorry," whispered the boy.

"Um-hum! Your face is dirty. I got a great mind to wash your face for you. Ain't you got nobody home to tell you to wash your face?"

❸ "No'm," said the boy.

"Then it will get washed this evening," said the large woman starting up the street, dragging the frightened boy behind her.

He looked as if he were four-
❹ teen or fifteen, frail and willow-
wild, in tennis shoes and blue jeans.

The woman said, "You ought to be my son. I would teach you right from wrong. Least I can do right now is to wash your face. Are you hungry?"

"No'm," said the being-dragged boy. "I just want you to turn me loose."

"Was I bothering *you* when I
❺ turned that corner?" asked the woman.

"No'm."

"But you put yourself in contact with *me*," said the woman. "If you think that that contact is not going to last awhile, you got another thought coming. When I get through with you, sir, you are going to remember Mrs. Luella Bates Washington Jones."

Sweat popped out on the boy's face and he began to struggle. Mrs. Jones stopped, jerked him around in front of her, put a half nelson[1] about his neck, and continued to drag him up the street. When she got to her door, she dragged the boy inside, down a hall, and into a large kitchenette-

---

1. **half nelson:** Wrestling hold using one arm.

furnished room at the rear of the house. She switched on the light and left the door open. The boy could hear other roomers laughing and talking in the large house. Some of their ❻ doors were open, too, so he knew he and the woman were not alone. The woman still had him by the neck in the middle of her room.

She said, "What is your name?"

▼ Critical Viewing Does the woman in the painting resemble Mrs. Jones as described in the story? ❼
Explain. **[Make a Judgment]**

Minnie, 1930, William Johnson, National Museum of American Art, Washington, DC

Thank You, M'am ◆ 187

◆ **Literary Focus**

❸ **Theme** Ask students what aspect of life the author wants the reader to think about. *Caring families teach children right from wrong. Adult friends, relatives, teachers, or even a stranger can help teach children how to act.*

◆ **Critical Thinking**

❹ **Infer** Ask students what this description reveals about the boy. *He is scared of what Mrs. Jones will do, and he wants to get away. He might have been treated badly by adults in the past.*

◆ **Reading Strategy**

❺ **Respond to Characters' Actions** Suggest that students reread Mrs. Jones' conversation with the young thief on the street. What does it reveal about her character? *Mrs. Jones is a very strong and confident woman. She is obviously concerned about children and the behavior of a boy like this one. She wants to make sure that he understands what he did was wrong and help him to behave better.*

◆ **Critical Thinking**

❻ **Speculate** Discuss Mrs. Jones's reason for leaving the door open. *She saw that the boy was frightened, and she wanted him to know that there were other people nearby and that she meant him no harm. She was also allowing him to escape if he didn't want her help.*

▶**Critical Viewing**◀

❼ **Make a Judgment** *The story describes Mrs. Jones as a large woman, and the woman in the painting appears to have a sturdy build. The woman's face in the painting has a warm and caring expression, which you would expect to see on the face of a woman like Mrs. Jones.*

◈ **Humanities: Art**

Minnie, 1930, by William Johnson
Overcoming poverty and lack of education, William Johnson left his home in Florence, South Carolina, for New York at age 17. He worked at various jobs to earn enough money to pay for classes at the National Academy of Design. Later he went to Europe, where he worked and lived for 10 years. After returning to the United States, he changed his style radically, rejecting the formal techniques of his training. His later paintings use broad, flat shapes to show his favorite subjects: the African Americans within his family and

community. Connect this painting to the selection by asking questions such as these:
1. What can you tell about the woman from her expression? *She has a kind smile. She looks a little sad. One eyebrow arched higher than the other and the knowing expression indicate thoughtfulness.*
2. What might the woman be thinking? *She is wondering why the boy would try to steal her purse. She is thinking about how she can teach the boy a lesson and help him learn right from wrong.*

◆ Critical Thinking

❶ Assess Ask students why Roger might have chosen to stay. *Most students will see that Mrs. Jones is not to be feared and has a kind heart. Since Roger has nowhere to go and no one at home, he has no reason to leave and he may be curious to see what Mrs. Jones is going to do.*

◆ Literary Focus

❷ Theme Discuss how this response by Mrs. Jones helps to build the underlying message in the story. *Her response reinforces her belief that there are right ways and wrong ways to get what you want in life.*

◆ Critical Thinking

❸ Interpret Ask students why Mrs. Jones shares these details about her life with Roger. *She wants him to know that they are not so different. Roger can see that people can make mistakes and still go on to lead happy and productive lives.*

◆ Reading Strategy

❹ Respond to Characters' Actions Ask students how they think Roger feels about Mrs. Jones's conversation. *He is probably relieved that he does not have to answer questions about himself. He may or may not recognize that she is being kind in talking only about herself.*

Customize for
Logical/Mathematical Learners

Discuss with students the effect of inflation on the price of products. For example, a movie ticket that cost $1 in the past might cost $7 or more today. Tell students to pretend, for the sake of the activity, that this story took place in 1960 and that the average annual rate of inflation has been 5 percent each year since. Challenge them to calculate how much $10 in the story would be worth today. Ask them what effect, if any, this calculation has on their understanding of the story.

188

"Roger," answered the boy.

"Then, Roger, you go to that sink and wash your face," said the woman, whereupon she ❶ turned him loose—at last. Roger looked at the door—looked at the woman—looked at the door—*and went to the sink.*

"Let the water run until it gets warm," she said. "Here's a clean towel."

"You gonna take me to jail?" asked the boy, bending over the sink.

"Not with that face, I would not take you nowhere," said the woman. "Here I am trying to get home to cook me a bite to eat and you snatch my pocketbook! Maybe you ain't been to your supper either, late as it be. Have you?"

"There's nobody home at my house," said the boy.

"Then we'll eat," said the woman. "I believe you're hungry—or been hungry—to try to snatch my pocketbook."

"I wanted a pair of blue suede shoes," said the boy.

"Well, you didn't have to snatch *my* pocket- ❷ book to get some suede shoes," said Mrs. Luella Bates Washington Jones. "You could of asked me."

"M'am?"

The water dripping from his face, the boy looked at her. There was a long pause. A very long pause. After he had dried his face and not knowing what else to do dried it again, the boy turned around, wondering what next. The door was open. He could make a dash for it down the hall. He could run, run, run, run, *run!*

The woman was sitting on the day bed. Af- ❸ ter awhile she said, "I were young once and I wanted things I could not get."

There was another long pause. The boy's mouth opened. Then he frowned, but not knowing he frowned.

The woman said, "Um-hum! You thought I was going to say *but,* didn't you? You thought I was going to say, *but I didn't snatch people's pocketbooks.* Well, I wasn't going to say that." Pause. Silence. "I have done things,

188 ◆ Meeting Challenges

---

too, which I would not tell you, son—neither tell God, if He didn't already know. So you set down while I fix us something to eat. You might run that comb through your hair so you will look presentable."

In another corner of the room behind a screen was a gas plate and an icebox. Mrs. Jones got up and went behind the screen. The woman did not watch the boy to see if he was going to run now, nor did she watch her purse which she left behind her on the day bed. But the boy took care to sit on the far side of the room where he thought she could easily see him out of the corner of her eye, if she wanted to. He did not trust the woman *not* to trust him. And he did not want to be mistrusted now.

"Do you need somebody to go to the store," asked the boy, "maybe to get some milk or something?"

"Don't believe I do," said the woman, "unless you just want sweet milk yourself. I was going to make cocoa out of this canned milk I got here."

"That will be fine," said the boy.

She heated some lima beans and ham she had in the icebox, made the cocoa, and set the table. The woman did not ask the boy any- ❹ thing about where he lived, or his folks, or anything else that would embarrass him. Instead, as they ate, she told him about her job in a hotel beauty shop that stayed open late, what the work was like, and how all kinds of women came in and out, blondes, redheads, and brunettes. Then she cut him a half of her ten-cent cake.

"Eat some more, son," she said.

When they were finished eating she got up and said, "Now, here, take this ten dollars and buy yourself some blue suede shoes. And next time, do not make the mistake of latching onto *my* pocketbook *nor nobody else's*—because shoes come by devilish like that will burn your feet. I got to get my rest now. But from here on in, son, I hope you will behave yourself."

Speaking and Listening Mini-Lesson

Readers Theater

This mini-lesson supports the Speaking and Listening activity in the Idea Bank on p. 191.

Introduce Explain that Readers Theater is a dramatic reading of a story. Since readers remain seated and do not show what is happening by acting out the parts, expressive use of the voice when reading is necessary to convey meaning.

Develop Arrange students in groups of three. Have each group write a script that will help listeners see what is happening in the story. The script will contain parts for Mrs. Jones, Roger,

and a narrator. Allow students to choose whether or not to use dialect in the scripts. As groups practice reading their scripts, remind them to be expressive in their delivery.

Apply Have students present their reading for the class. After each presentation, have the class discuss the scripts and manner of delivery.

Assess Evaluate each group's performance based on level of preparation, expressiveness of delivery, and audience response. Alternatively, have students complete the Peer Assessment: Dramatic Performance form, p. 116, in **Alternative Assessment.**

◆ **Literary Focus**
With what message does Mrs. Jones leave Roger? How does that contribute to the story's theme?

5 **Theme** *Mrs. Jones leaves Roger with the message, "Behave yourself, boy." Her remark contributes to the story's theme by showing that Mrs. Jones feels Roger is basically a good boy and can be trusted to do better.*

She led him down the hall to the front door and opened it. "Goodnight! Behave yourself, boy!" she said, looking out into the street.

The boy wanted to say something other than, "Thank you, m'am," to Mrs. Luella Bates Washington Jones, but although his lips moved, he couldn't even say that as he turned at the foot of the <u>barren</u> stoop and looked up at the large woman in the door. Then she shut the door.

◆ **Build Vocabulary**
presentable (prē zent′ ə bəl) *adj.*: In proper order for being seen, met, etc., by others
mistrusted (mis′ trust′ əd) *v.*: Doubted
latching (lach′ iŋ) *v.*: Grasping or attaching oneself to
barren (bar′ ən) *adj.*: Sterile; empty

Reinforce and Extend

Answers

◆ **LITERATURE AND YOUR LIFE**

Reader's Response Some will think she behaved wisely, because she motivated Roger to act in a trustworthy way.

Thematic Focus Mrs. Jones might have asked herself if Roger was dangerous. Roger might have asked why he tried to steal from someone who was so kind and generous.

☑ **Check Your Comprehension**
1. She grabs him and takes him home with her.
2. She would teach him right from wrong.
3. Roger says he wanted to buy blue suede shoes. She asks him why he did not just ask her for the money.
4. She gives him $10 to buy the shoes he wants so badly.

Guide for Responding

◆ LITERATURE AND YOUR LIFE

Reader's Response Do you think Mrs. Jones is wise or foolish to trust Roger? Why?

Thematic Focus If you were Mrs. Jones, what is the hardest question you would have asked yourself about Roger? What is the main question Roger might have asked himself about his own actions?

☑ **Check Your Comprehension**
1. What does Mrs. Jones do when Roger tries to steal her purse?
2. What does she say she would teach Roger if he were her son?
3. What reason does Roger give for trying to steal her purse? How does Mrs. Jones respond to this reason?
4. Why does Mrs. Jones give Roger ten dollars?

◆ Critical Thinking

INTERPRET
1. Why doesn't Roger run away from Mrs. Jones's apartment at the first opportunity? **[Analyze]**
2. What does the following tell about Roger: "He did not trust the woman *not* to trust him. And he did not want to be mistrusted now." **[Infer]**
3. Why does Mrs. Jones trust Roger to sit alone with her purse? **[Deduce]**
4. At the end of the story, why does Roger want to say more than just "Thank you, m'am"? **[Interpret]**

EVALUATE
5. Do you think that Mrs. Jones did Roger a favor by not turning him over to the police? Explain. **[Make a Judgment]**

APPLY
6. Can you change someone's behavior through kindness and understanding? Explain. **[Generalize]**

Thank You, M'am ◆ 189

◆ Critical Thinking
1. He realizes that Mrs. Jones is not going to hurt him, and he has no where else to go.
2. He wants to be better than his thieving showed him to be. He would like to prove to Mrs. Jones that he can be trustworthy.
3. Mrs. Jones wants to make Roger see that he is a good person.
4. He feels she gave him self-respect, and simple words can't express his gratitude for such a gift.
5. By showing him kindness instead of turning him over to the police, she made it possible for him to start over.
6. Yes, you can give them examples of the right way to behave toward others.

 Beyond the Selection

FURTHER READING
Other Works by Langston Hughes
The Big Sea: An Autobiography
Not Without Laughter (Introduction by Maya Angelou)
Short Stories
Other Works About Facing Hard Questions
Holes, Louis Sachar
Stay True: Short Stories for Strong Girls, Marilyn Singer (Compiler)
Dancing on the Edge, Han Nolan

INTERNET
We suggest the following sites on the Internet (all Web sites are subject to change).
For information about Langston Hughes:
http://myhero.com/poets/hughes.asp
We *strongly recommend* that you preview this site before you send students to it.

Answers

◆ Reading Strategy

1. I learned from Mrs. Jones that lessons can sometimes be taught more effectively with kindness than with punishment.
2. I liked and respected Mrs. Jones. I felt sorry for Roger and hoped that he could turn his life around.

◆ Build Vocabulary

Using the Suffix -able
1. disagreeable
2. reasonable

Spelling Strategy
1. misspeak
2. mistake
3. misfortune
4. mistrust
5. misstep

Using the Word Bank
1. barren
2. mistrusted
3. presentable
4. latching
5. barely

◆ Literary Focus

1. Responding with kindness rather than punishment when someone tries to hurt you can bring about good results. The theme was not directly stated.
2. Mrs. Jones expresses the theme by helping Roger understand the errors in his behavior.
3. People use their own experiences to help them interpret a story, and since experiences differ, so will the lessons learned.

◆ Build Grammar Skills

Practice
1. risen
2. bought
3. spoke
4. chosen
5. stole

Writing Application
Possible Response: Mrs. Jones had not <u>seen</u> the boy walking behind her. After he fell, Roger <u>heard</u> Mrs. Jones telling him to get up. It is good that Mrs. Jones <u>chose</u> not to turn Roger into the police. Maybe Roger <u>wrote</u> her a thank-you note.

Guide for Responding (continued)

◆ Reading Strategy

RESPOND TO CHARACTERS' ACTIONS
   Responding to characters' actions involves you in a story and increases your appreciation of the story's characters, plot events, and theme.
1. What did you learn from a character in the story? Explain.
2. Describe your feelings about Mrs. Jones and Roger at the end of the story.

◆ Build Vocabulary

USING THE SUFFIX -able
   The suffix -able can be added to some verbs, such as present, to form adjectives (descriptive words), like presentable. On your paper, complete these sentences sensibly by adding -able to one of the following words: disagree, reason
1. A _____?_____ encounter turned out well for both characters.
2. Roger's _____?_____ behavior once he was in the house surprised me.

SPELLING STRATEGY
   The miss sound at the beginning of a word is spelled "mis." When adding mis- to a word, do not change the original spelling of the word:
   mis- + spell = misspell
   On your paper, add mis- to the following words.
1. speak   2. take   3. fortune   4. trust   5. step

USING THE WORD BANK
   On your paper, rewrite the following sentences. Replace the italicized word or phrase with the appropriate word from the Word Bank.
1. The kitchenette was empty of furniture.
2. The boy was suspicious of kindness from adults.
3. After combing her hair and changing her shoes, she felt she could go out in public.
4. She felt someone grasping onto her arm to prevent her from stumbling.
5. There was so much clutter in the attic that there was hardly room to stand.

◆ Literary Focus

THEME
   The **theme** of a story is its message about life or human nature. Often a character's actions and experiences will convey the story's theme.
1. How would you state the theme of "Thank You, M'am"? Is the theme stated directly or indirectly?
2. Which character expresses the theme? By what means?
3. Why is it possible that different readers may learn different lessons from the story?

◆ Build Grammar Skills

PRINCIPAL PARTS OF IRREGULAR VERBS
   A verb's **principal parts** are the basic forms of a verb. An **irregular verb** forms its past and past participle in some other way than by adding -ed to the present or base form of the verb.
   Below are listed some commonly used irregular verbs and their principal parts.

Present	Past	Past Participle
eat	ate	eaten
have	had	had
drink	drank	drunk
grow	grew	grown

Practice On your paper, replace each verb in parentheses with the correct form of the verb. Use the past participle after a helping verb.
1. By the time he awoke, the sun had (rise).
2. He (buy) a pair of blue suede shoes.
3. Mrs. Jones (speak) calmly but with authority.
4. She had (choose) to ignore his excuses.
5. He (steal) the purse to buy some shoes.

Writing Application Write a paragraph about the story using various principal parts of these irregular verbs: see, hear, write, choose.

 Writer's Solution

For additional instruction and practice, use The Principal Parts of Verbs page, p. 71, in the Writer's Solution Grammar Practice Book.

Build Your Portfolio

 Idea Bank

Writing

1. **Letter** Write a letter from Mrs. Jones to an advice columnist, asking if she did the right thing in her treatment of Roger. Include specific questions in your letter.

2. **Sequel** Write a sequel to "Thank You, M'am," telling what happens when Roger and Mrs. Jones meet again.

3. **Speech** Imagine that Mrs. Jones has been invited to give a speech on the health and education of children at her local community center. Write a brief speech in which Mrs. Jones expresses her beliefs about how children should be treated.

Speaking and Listening

4. **Readers Theater [Group Activity]** With classmates, prepare and present a Readers Theatre version of "Thank You, M'am." Write a script and practice reading, putting emphasis on oral interpretation of the characters and their actions. **[Performing Arts Link]**

5. **Rap Song** Compose and perform a rap song that is inspired by your response to the story "Thank You, M'am." **[Music Link]**

Projects

6. **Multimedia Presentation [Group Activity]** Work with several classmates to create a multimedia presentation about Langston Hughes and his role in the Harlem Renaissance. Include photographs, music recordings, examples of art, and readings of poems and texts. Share your findings with the class.

7. **Painting or Drawing** Chose your favorite visual medium, and re-create a scene or a character from "Thank You, M'am." Give your finished work a title. Then, reveal to your class the feeling you tried to convey in your artwork. **[Art Link]**

 Writing Mini-Lesson

Letter of Guidance

Imagine that you are Roger twenty years after the story took place. Write a letter to a young relative who needs guidance and direction. In your letter, tell about your encounter with Mrs. Jones, sharing what you learned from it.

Writing Skills Focus: Give Necessary Background

In your letter, supply the **necessary background** about what happened to you in the past. For example, explain who you are, what you did, and how it affected you.

Model

When I was about your age, I tried to rob an older woman who taught me a valuable lesson about life.

Prewriting Begin by jotting down the advice you plan to give in the letter. Also, think about how Roger might have changed through the years and what he has made of his life.

Drafting Take on Roger's personality as you write the letter to your relative. Whenever necessary, give background information to support your points. Use the standard format for informal letters: Include a greeting, body, and closing.

Revising Review your letter, looking for places where you can add background information that will support your impression of Mrs. Jones or yourself as a young boy. Check your letter to be sure it's free of spelling, punctuation, and grammar errors.

> ◆ **Grammar Application**
>
> Look at the irregular verbs you have used. Make sure that you have written the correct verb form and used the correct spelling.

 Thank You, M'am ◆ 191

 Idea Bank

Following are suggestions for matching the Idea Bank topics with your students' performance levels and learning modalities:

Customize for
Performance Levels
Less Advanced Students: 1, 4, 6
Average Students: 2, 4, 6, 7
More Advanced Students: 3, 5, 6, 7

Customize for
Learning Modalities
Verbal/Linguistic: 1, 2, 3, 4
Musical/Rhythmic: 5
Visual/Spatial: 6, 7
Interpersonal: 4, 6
Intrapersonal: 1, 2, 3, 7

 Writing Mini-Lesson

Refer students to the Writing Handbook in the back of the book for instruction on the writing process and for further information on personal letters. Have students use the Open Mind Organizer in **Writing and Language Transparencies,** p. 81, to arrange their prewriting examples.

 Writer's Solution

Writing Lab CD-ROM
Have students complete the tutorial on Expression. Follow these steps:
1. Have students complete the Audience Profile activity.
2. Students can use the audio-annotated audience models to find out how each model was written to fit a specific audience.
3. Students can draft on computer.
4. Have students use the Proofreading Checklist to check punctuation, spelling, and grammar

Writer's Solution Sourcebook
Have students use Chapter 1, "Expression," pp. 1–31, for additional support. This chapter includes instruction on writing letters, pp. 18–19.

✓ ASSESSMENT OPTIONS

Formal Assessment, Selection Test, pp. 58–60, and Assessment Resources Software. The selection test is designed so that it can easily be customized to the performance levels of your students.

Alternative Assessment, p. 16, includes options for less advanced students, more advanced students intrapersonal learners, verbal/linguistic learners, musical/rhythmic learners, visual/spatial learners, and interpersonal learners.

PORTFOLIO ASSESSMENT
Use the following rubrics in the **Alternative Assessment** booklet to assess student writing:
Letter: Expression, p. 90
Sequel: Fictional Narrative, p. 91
Speech: Persuasion, p. 101
Writing Mini-Lesson: Expression, p. 90

Guide for Reading

OBJECTIVES

1. To read, comprehend, and interpret three poems and a speech
2. To relate poetry and a speech to personal experience
3. To use your senses to appreciate a writer's imagery
4. To explore the use of imagery in writing
5. To build vocabulary in context and use forms of *evade*
6. To develop skill in using verb tenses
7. To write a persuasive appeal that reflects a clear purpose
8. To respond to the poems and speech through writing, speaking and listening, and projects

SKILLS INSTRUCTION

Vocabulary:
Using Forms of *evade*
Spelling:
The Suffix *-or*
Grammar:
Verb Tenses
Reading Strategy:
Use Your Senses
Literary Focus:
Imagery

Writing:
Clear Purpose
Speaking and Listening:
Dramatization (Teacher Edition)
Critical Viewing:
Speculate

PORTFOLIO OPPORTUNITIES

Writing: Journal Entry; Letter; Speech Analysis
Writing Mini-Lesson: Persuasive Appeal
Speaking and Listening: Committee Discussion; Dramatization
Projects: Timeline; Sculpture

More About the Authors
Adrienne Rich has published more than fifteen volumes of poetry in the past forty years. Her recent poems explore the theme of democracy.

Emily Dickinson published only ten poems during her lifetime. She used simple images from nature and daily life as metaphors for love, pain, and faith.

Chief Seattle was a chief of the Suquamish and Duwamish Indians in the Puget Sound area.

Margaret Tsuda has published a collection of poetry, *Cry Love Aloud,* which celebrate nature—she illustrated the book as well as writing the poems.

Meet the Authors:

Adrienne Rich (1929–)

Born in Baltimore, Maryland, Adrienne Rich was educated at Radcliffe College. Her first volume of poetry, *A Change of World,* was published in 1951. Today, she is a widely published poet and essayist. She lives in California.

Emily Dickinson (1830–1886)

Known by her neighbors as the "moth of Amherst," Emily Dickinson dressed only in white after 1862. A recluse, she observed the life of Amherst, Massachusetts, her birthplace, from her upstairs bedroom window. After her death, nearly 1,800 of her poems, tied neatly in packets, were found in the house by her sister and later published.

Chief Seattle (1786?–1866)

Chief Seattle, whose ancestors came from several tribes in the Pacific Northwest, was born into Native American nobility. A warrior, Seattle led his last attack when he was almost sixty years old. He later became a diplomat and speaker.

Margaret Tsuda (1921–)

Margaret Tsuda, who obtained a degree in art history from the City University of New York, has written several essays on art. An admirer of Walt Whitman, Tsuda strives to find the "unusual in common, ordinary things" in her own poetry.

192 ◆ Meeting Challenges

◆ LITERATURE AND YOUR LIFE

CONNECT YOUR EXPERIENCE

Society has a great impact on our lives—from where and how we live to how we're regarded as individuals. In these selections, four writers voice their concerns about modern society. Two of the writers focus on maintaining individuality. The other two writers present heartfelt pleas about the importance of preserving nature's bounty in an increasingly developed world.

THEMATIC FOCUS: Facing Hard Questions

As you read these selections, think about what the speakers have to say about society and the individual.

◆ Background for Understanding

HISTORY

In 1854, when he met with the first governor of Washington Territory (now Washington State), Chief Seattle delivered the speech "This We Know." It has since become famous. Chief Seattle's purpose was to make a statement about Indian lands and traditions. The speech is now frequently quoted by environmentalists and Native American leaders.

◆ Build Vocabulary

RELATED WORDS: FORMS OF *evade*

The word *evade* means "to avoid something by cleverness or trickery." Knowing this, you can figure out the meaning of related words, like *evasion, evasive, evasively,* and *evasiveness.*

WORD BANK

Review this list. Find a word embedded in *worthily* that suggests its meaning. Check the Build Vocabulary box on page 194 to see if you guessed correctly.

worthily
evade
discerning
prevail
assent
ancestors

 Prentice Hall Literature Program Resources

REINFORCE / RETEACH / EXTEND

Selection Support Pages
Build Vocabulary: Forms of *evade*, p. 87
Build Spelling Skills, p. 88
Build Grammar Skills: Verb Tenses, p. 89
Reading Strategy: Use Your Senses, p. 90
Literary Focus: Imagery, p. 91
Strategies for Diverse Student Needs, pp. 33–34
Beyond Literature Community Connection: Land Development, p. 17
Formal Assessment Selection Test, pp. 61–63,

Assessment Resources Software
Alternative Assessment, p. 17
Writing and Language Transparencies
Sunburst Organizer, p. 85; Main Idea and Supporting Details Organizer, p. 61
Resource Pro CD-ROM "Prospective Immigrants Please Note"; "Much Madness is divinest Sense"; "This We Know"; "Hard Questions"

 Listening to Literature Audiocassettes
"Prospective Immigrants Please Note"; "Much Madness is divinest Sense"; "This We Know"; "Hard Questions"

Prospective Immigrants Please Note
◆ Much Madness is divinest Sense— ◆
This We Know ◆ Hard Questions

1955, M.C. Escher, Cordon Art B.V.–Baarn-Holland

◆ Literary Focus

IMAGERY

Imagery refers to words and phrases that appeal to one or more of the five senses. The following line from "This We Know" includes images that appeal to the sense of sound.

> The water's murmur is the voice of my father's father.

Through vivid images, a writer draws you into a work of literature and enables you to see, hear, touch, taste, and smell what the characters are experiencing.

◆ Reading Strategy

USE YOUR SENSES

To appreciate the imagery in a poem, essay, or story, **use your senses** as you read. When a writer is describing the appearance of something, for example, see it in your mind. Then, close your eyes and imagine the smells, sounds, and other sensations that the writer describes. Draw from your own experiences to fill in details the writer may not have mentioned.

Keep track of the sensory images in these works by filling out a chart like the one below.

	Sight	Sound	Touch	Taste	Smell
Prospective Immigrants ...					
Much Madness ...					
This We Know					
Hard Questions					

Preparing for Standardized Tests

Reading The Literary Focus for this selection is imagery. Explain to students that writers often use vivid word pictures, or imagery, to help readers experience descriptions through one or more senses. Open-ended assessments in the Reading portion of standardized tests may require students to demonstrate an understanding of techniques the author uses to convey meaning. Have students read "Hard Questions," p. 199. Then ask them to cite two examples of imagery in the poem and tell what senses the images appeal to.

Students may mention images such as "neat rectangles/squares and clover leafs" and "bands of roads" as appealing to the sense of sight. For further practice, have students identify imagery used in the other selections.

Point out to students that tests that assess their writing abilities may give them a descriptive prompt, which requires them to describe the physical characteristics of a place or thing. A written description requires basic information and clear organization, but a well-written description also includes sensory details that create vivid images.

Write the column headings "Individual" and "Society" on the board. Ask students to consider what individuals owe themselves and society. List their responses under the "Individual" column. Then ask students to name things that society owes the individual. List responses under the "Society" column. Next, work together as a class to write a brief compact, or agreement, between individuals and the society in which they live, based on the ideas in the columns.

◆ Build Grammar Skills

Articles If you wish to introduce the grammar concept for this selection before students read, refer to the instruction on p. 200.

Customize for
Less Proficient Readers
Have students read the poems and speech aloud with partners and discuss the meaning of each work. Then instruct partners to work together to record the main idea and supporting details for each work on a Sunburst Organizer, p. 85, in **Writing and Language Transparencies.** Encourage partners to share and discuss their organizers with other student pairs.

Customize for
More Advanced Students
As students explore what the speakers in the selections have to say about society and the individual, encourage them to jot down ideas that are sparked by their reading. Then invite students to use these ideas to write poems about rights and responsibilities of society and individuals. Challenge students to use vivid images in their poems.

Humanities: Art

Rind, by M. C. Escher
Dutch graphic artist M. C. Escher (1898–1970) is known for artworks that challenge the mind and delight the imagination. Have students speculate about what Escher is saying in this image. *He might be saying that a person's outer appearance—like a fruit rind—is just a covering for the important substance that lies within.*

One-Minute Insight The speaker in "Prospective Immigrants Please Note" offers two choices, each of which carries risks: Do you pass through the door to face a new life, new customs, and perhaps even a new name, or do you choose not go through the door and avoid the challenges of a new life? Adrienne Rich's caution is addressed to anyone on the threshold of a change—not just those settling in a new country.

►Critical Viewing◄

❶ Speculate *Possible responses: The people in the photograph may be wondering what their new life will be like. To Rich's words of caution, the people might say they are willing to face risks and uncertainties for the chance at a new life.*

◆ Literary Focus

❷ Imagery What image do you picture in your mind as you read lines 7–9? *Students may say that they have an image of someone being stared at for being different, as people with dual identities might be. The person being stared at looks back proudly.*

◆ Build Vocabulary

❸ Using Forms of *evade* Ask students to think about the meaning of *evade* in the context of lines 16–18. Then have them use their understanding of *evade* to paraphrase these lines. *Students may say that the lines mean that a person could miss opportunities to learn and grow by not going through the door.*

Customize for
English Language Learners
Help students understand the poems and the speech and relate them to their own experiences. Have students listen to the works in this selection. Then have students work with partners proficient in English to discuss the meanings of the poems and speech and to demonstrate through words or pantomime how the works relate to students' own experiences.

🎧 **Listening to Literature Audiocassettes**

PROSPECTIVE IMMIGRANTS PLEASE NOTE

A d r i e n n e   R i c h

▲ **Critical Viewing** What might the people in the photograph be thinking about? How might they respond to Rich's words of caution? [Speculate]

◆ Build Vocabulary

worthily (wʉr´ thə lē) *adv.*: With merit; well
evade (i vād´) *v.*: Escape
discerning (di sʉrn´ iŋ) *adj.*: Having keen perception or judgment
prevail (prē vāl´) *v.*: Win; triumph
assent (a sent´) *v.*: Consent

194 ◆ Meeting Challenges

Either you will
go through this door
or you will not go through.

If you go through
5 there is always the risk
of remembering your name.

Things look at you doubly[1]   **❷**
and you must look back
and let them happen.

10 If you do not go through
it is possible
to live <u>worthily</u>

to maintain your attitudes
to hold your position
15 to die bravely

but much will blind you,   **❸**
much will <u>evade</u> you,
at what cost who knows?

The door itself
20 makes no promises.
It is only a door.

---

1. **doubly** *adv.*: Twice; having more than one perspective.

Block Scheduling Strategies

Consider these suggestions to take advantage of extended class time:

• Have students complete the Journal Writing activity in Literature and Your Life, p. 195. Then have them work with partners to answer Critical Thinking questions on pp. 195 and 199.

• Have students complete Build Vocabulary and Build Grammar Skills, p. 200. You may wish to reinforce the concepts by using **Selection Support**, pp. 87 and 89. Then have students read the poems and speech independently.

• Have students use the *Writer's Solution Writing*

Lab CD-ROM as they draft their persuasive appeals for the Writing Mini-Lesson, p. 201. Follow the instructional suggestions listed on p. 201 of the Teacher Edition.

• Guide students in a discussion of the Literary Focus and Reading Strategy, p. 193. Then have students listen to the poems and speech on audiocassette. As students listen, encourage them to complete the graphic organizer on p. 193.

🎧 **Listening to Literature Audiocassettes**

Much Madness is divinest Sense—

Emily Dickinson

Much Madness is divinest Sense—
To a discerning Eye—
❹ Much Sense—the starkest Madness—
'Tis[1] the Majority
5   In this, as All, prevail—
Assent—and you are sane—
❺ Demur—you're straightway dangerous—
And handled with a Chain—

1. **'tis** (tiz): It is.

In "Much Madness is divinest Sense," Emily Dickinson also proposes two choices: going one's own way or living according to the will of "the Majority." Choosing what the world calls sense can produce boredom or emptiness, which is madness to a sensitive person. Choosing one's own values can produce an intense life, which is madness to the majority.

◆ Critical Thinking

❹ **Interpret** What kind of "Sense" does the speaker refer to in line 3? *She refers to the majority's standards for personal values and conduct.*

◆ Literary Focus

❺ **Imagery** What image in the last two lines makes the speaker's suffering seem real and intense? What sense or senses does the image appeal to? *The image of someone in chains highlights the speaker's suffering. This image appeals to the senses of sight and sound.*

Reinforce and Extend

Answers
◆ LITERATURE AND YOUR LIFE

Reader's Response Students may define madness variously as "originality," "daring," "creativity," "irresponsibility," or "insanity."

Thematic Focus Both questions are general, and both suggest that taking the greater risk may offer greater personal rewards. The question in "Prospective Immigrants" is about moving forward or staying where you are; the question in "Much Madness" is about being true to yourself or bending to society's will.

☑ Check Your Comprehension

1. The choices are to go through the door to a new life or stay where you are.
2. They are considered dangerous and are shunned or locked away from society.

Guide for Responding

◆ LITERATURE AND YOUR LIFE

Reader's Response Dickinson defines madness as "divinest sense." How would you define it?

Thematic Focus In what ways are the hard questions faced in these two poems similar? How are they different?

Journal Writing In your journal, jot down your thoughts on the importance of maintaining one's individuality.

☑ Check Your Comprehension

1. What are the two choices in "Prospective Immigrants Please Note"?
2. In "Much Madness is divinest Sense—," what does the poet say happens to those who don't go along with the majority?

◆ Critical Thinking

INTERPRET

1. Other than immigrants, to whom might the poem "Prospective Immigrants Please Note" be addressed? **[Speculate]**
2. Explain the meaning of line 21—that the door "is only a door"? **[Interpret]**
3. Compare and contrast the potential results of the two possible choices in "Prospective Immigrants . . ." **[Compare and Contrast]**
4. What kind of behavior is considered insane, according to the speaker in "Much Madness . . ." **[Analyze Causes and Effects]**

EVALUATE

5. Do you agree with the speaker's ideas in "Prospective Immigrants Please Note"? Explain. **[Make a Judgment]**

Prospective Immigrants Please Note/Much Madness is divinest Sense— ◆ 195

◆ Critical Thinking

1. Students may say that the poem might be addressed to someone on the brink of any important decision, such as whether to go to college, start a new career, or move to a new town.
2. The act of going through the door offers no guarantees; people must take personal responsibility for choosing a new life.
3. Going through the door offers opportunities to learn and grow. By not going through the door, a person can remain safe but stagnant.

4. According to the speaker, going against the majority is considered insane.
5. Students should support their responses with observations from their own experiences or ideas. Students who are actual immigrants may agree that in spite of the risks, they have benefited from going through the door.

Develop Understanding

One-Minute Insight

"This We Know" is based on a speech by Chief Seattle, who was known for his natural eloquence. The words of the speech affirm the sacredness of the sky, land, and water and warn that these precious treasures could be lost in the zeal to possess and develop the land. A classic and inspiring message, "This We Know" has been the basis of ecological movements around the world.

Clarification

❶ At the time Chief Seattle made his speech, Governor Isaac Stevens, Commissioner of Indian Affairs for the Washington Territory, had offered Native Americans in the Puget Sound area a treaty that provided for the sale of 2 million acres of their land to the federal government.

◆ Reading Strategy

❷ **Use Your Senses** *The imagery appeals to the senses of sight, touch, taste, and smell.*

◆ LITERATURE AND YOUR LIFE

❸ Have students name several specific things a person might do to show kindness toward a river. *Students might name acts such as helping to create and pass legislation to ensure that the river is not polluted by chemicals or sewage, or helping to restrict development near the river.*

◆ Critical Thinking

❹ **Interpret** What do you think Chief Seattle means when he asks the government to keep the land "apart and sacred"? *Students may say that he wants the government to keep the land wild and undeveloped, in the way that national parks and forests are preserved.*

Customize for
Visual/Spatial Learners

Have students view the photograph while a volunteer reads aloud the paragraphs on this page. Discuss with students ways that the photograph enhances the description of the natural resources.

Chief Seattle
This We Know

The President in Washington sends word that he wishes to buy our land. But how can you buy or sell the sky? The land? The idea is strange to us. If we do not own the freshness of the air and the sparkle of the water, how can you buy them?

Every part of this earth is sacred to my people. Every shining pine needle, every sandy shore, every mist in the dark woods, every meadow, every humming insect. All are holy in the memory and experience of my people.

We know the sap which courses through the trees as we know the blood that courses through our veins. We are part of the earth and it is part of us. The perfumed flowers are our sisters. The bear, the deer, the great eagle, these are our brothers. The rocky crests, the juices in the meadow, the body heat of the pony, and man, all belong to the same family.

◆ **Reading Strategy**
To what senses does the imagery in this paragraph appeal?

The shining water that moves in the streams and rivers is not just water, but the blood of our <u>ancestors</u>. If we sell you our land, you must remember that it is sacred. Each ghostly reflection in the clear water of the lakes tells of events and memories in the life of my people. The water's murmur is the voice of my father's father.

The rivers are our brothers. They quench our thirst. They carry our canoes and feed our children. So you must give to the rivers the kindness you would give any brother.

If we sell you our land, remember that the air is precious to us, that the air shares its spirit with all the life it supports. The wind that gave our grandfather his first breath also receives his last sigh. The wind also gives our children the spirit of life. So if we sell you our land, you must keep it apart and sacred, as a place where man can go to taste the wind that is sweetened by the meadow flowers.

Will you teach your children what we have

 Cross-Curricular Connection: Social Studies

Chief Seattle's Speech According to the Suquamish Museum, in Suquamish, Washington, the more credible version of Chief Seattle's speech was published by Dr. Henry Smith, an interpreter between the government and the Suquamish and Duwamish groups during treaty negotiations in the 1850's. "This We Know" is an adaptation of Chief Seattle's message. It was written by screenwriter Ted Perry for a 1972 film about ecology.

If possible, obtain a copy of the speech translated by Henry Smith (available through the Suquamish Museum, P.O. Box 498, Suquamish, WA 98392). Have students read the speech and compare its content with that in "This We Know." You may want to discuss the following points:

• What are some ways that ideas and information changed in translations or tellings?

• Can stereotypes be favorable as well as unfavorable? Do you think the perception of Native Americans as natural-born conservators is a stereotype? Explain.

Guide students to understand how different perspectives and objectives affect the presentation of material such as Chief Seattle's speech.

196

taught our children? That the earth is our mother? What befalls the earth, befalls all the sons of the earth.

This we know: The earth does not belong to man, man belongs to the earth. All things are connected like the blood which unites us all. Man did not weave the web of life, he is merely a strand in it. Whatever he does to the web, he does to himself.

One thing we know: Our god is also your god. The earth is precious to him and to harm the earth is to heap contempt on its creator.

Your destiny is a mystery to us. What will happen when the buffalo are all slaughtered? The wild horses tamed? What will happen when the secret corners of the forest are heavy with the scent of many men and the view of the ripe hills is blotted by talking wires? Where will the thicket be? Gone! Where will the eagle be? Gone! And what is it to say good-bye to the swift pony and the hunt? The end of living and the beginning of survival.

When the last Red Man has vanished with his wilderness and his memory is only the shadow of a cloud moving across the prairie, will these shores and forests still be here? Will there be any of the spirit of my people left?

We love this earth as a newborn loves its mother's heartbeat. So, if we sell you our land, love it as we have loved it. Care for it as we have cared for it. Hold in your mind the memory of the land as it is when you receive it. Preserve the land for all children and love it, as God loves us all.

As we are part of the land, you too are part of the land. This earth is precious to us. It is also precious to you. One thing we know: There is only one God. No man, be he Red Man or White Man, can be apart. We *are* brothers after all.

◆ **Build Vocabulary**

ancestors (an′ ses′ tərs) *n.*: People from whom one is descended

---

Beyond Literature

Social Studies Connection

History of Our National Parks
Artist and traveler George Catlin was one of the first people to envision a national park to protect America's wilderness. He hoped for "A nation's park, containing man and beast, in all the wild and freshness of their nature's beauty!" His dream became reality in 1872, when Congress created Yellowstone National Park.

In 1903, President Theodore Roosevelt established a Florida island as the first national wildlife refuge. The President asked his advisors, "Is there any law that will prevent me from declaring Pelican Island a Federal Bird Reservation?" When no law was discovered, he said, "Very well, then I so declare it." He also doubled the number of current national parks. The new additions included Mesa Verde, Colorado, and Crater Lake, Oregon.

In 1916, President Woodrow Wilson signed the Organic Act, which created the National Park Service. Today, the system of parks and refuges includes 376 areas covering a total of more than 83 million acres of protected land.

Cross-Curricular Activity
Parks Tour Use an atlas of the United States to plan a tour of at least three National Parks. Your itinerary should describe the parks you will visit, how you will explore them, and how long it will take to travel from one location to another. You may wish to work with a partner or team to plan a practical and efficient itinerary.

◆ **Literary Focus**

❺ **Imagery** Explore the image of a "web of life" with students. For example, have students imagine the intricacy of a spider's web, in which a drop of rain on the web sends a vibration through the delicate strands to all other parts of the web. Have students suggest other images that help show the interrelatedness of life on Earth.

Clarification

❻ Native Americans living in the Pacific Northwest were unfamiliar with buffalo, because these animals did not roam west of the Cascades. Pacific Coast Native Americans were salmon fishers who traveled by canoe, rather than overland. Explain that mention of buffalo and hunts on the prairie were probably added in later versions of Chief Seattle's original speech.

◆ **Critical Thinking**

❼ **Infer** Why do you think Chief Seattle fears that his people will vanish, along with the wilderness? *Students may say that Chief Seattle has probably witnessed enough changes brought by the government and by white pioneers to justify his sense that the disappearance of his people and the land is inevitable.*

Beyond Literature

Provide students with travel guides and other sources of information on national parks in the United States. Have students describe at least one attraction to see at each park they will visit. Ask students to create a visual representation of their itinerary. Make materials such as construction paper or stickers in geometric shapes available for them to use to create their visuals.

 Cultural Connection

Native Americans of the Northwest Coast
Native Americans, such as Chief Seattle, have lived along the shores of what are now Alaska and Washington State for thousands of years. The area is known for its mild climate, vast resources, and constant supplies of food—especially salmon. Many different cultural groups make up Northwest Coast Native Americans: Tlingit, Haida, Tsimshian, Coast Salish. Each culture has developed its own artistic style, myths, and ceremonies.

Have students conduct research more about the various Northwest Coast cultural groups.

Suggest that they focus their research on a specific cultural group or on one of these topics:
- What types of artworks are Northwest Coast Native Americans known for?
- What aspects of the Northwest Coast were conducive to the development of these artworks?

You may wish to discuss how artwork can be symbolic of cultures. In addition, you might discuss the symbolic nature of "This We Know"—exploring how this version of Chief Seattle's speech may have been symbolic of the entire Native American experience of that time.

One-Minute Insight The speaker in "Hard Questions" offers the reader images of geometric parcels of land on which sit the cuboid structures in which humans live and work, contrasted with images of wildlife and the wild lands that nourish the human heart. Through "Hard Questions," Adrienne Rich reminds us of the price that humans pay for developing the land.

◆ Literary Focus

❶ Imagery Ask students what they see in their mind's eye as they read lines 1–10. *Some students may say that they picture areas of their town that match this description. Others may picture a similar scene from high in an airplane. Other students may say they picture the rectangles of a board game, on which tiny replicas of houses and hotels are crowded.*

◆ Critical Thinking

❷ Interpret Ask students what "silence fraught with living" means to them. *Students may say that away from a bustling city, the sounds from a swamp or a forest are as calming or refreshing as silence.*

Customize for
Musical/Rhythmic Learners
Bring to class recordings of popular songs with ecological themes, such as "Mercy Mercy Me (The Ecology)," by Marvin Gaye, "Big Yellow Taxi," by Joni Mitchell, and "Conviction of the Heart," by Kenny Loggins. As you play the recordings for students, encourage them to make notes on the messages in the lyrics. Have students determine whether there is a common message or theme among the songs and, if so, to connect the theme to the message in "Hard Questions."

HARD QUESTIONS
Margaret Tsuda

 Speaking and Listening Mini-Lesson

Dramatization
This mini-lesson supports the Dramatization activity in the Idea Bank, p. 201.

Introduce Explain to students that a dramatization involves a performance of one or more events in a story, or an imagined event inspired by a story.

Develop Have student pairs discuss possible scenarios in which two people disagree about their readiness to make a big life change. Encourage students to make notes based on their discussion. As students plan their dramatiza-

tions, remind them to convey ideas with gestures and facial expressions as well as words.

Apply Have each student pair prepare a script. Encourage students to rehearse the performance at least once, offering suggestions to each other about how to improve the performance.

Assess Invite pairs to present their dramatizations. Evaluate students' work based on their preparation and the effectiveness of their performances. Or, have students use the Peer Assessment: Dramatic Performance form, p. 116, in **Alternative Assessment.**

Why not mark out the land
into neat rectangles
squares and clover leafs?

❶ Put on them cubes of
5   varying sizes
according to use—
dwellings
    singles/multiples
complexes
10   commercial/industrial.

Bale them together with
bands of roads.

What if a child shall cry
"I have never known spring!
15 I have never seen autumn!"

What if a man shall say
"I have never heard
❷ silence fraught with living as
in swamp or forest!"
20 What if the eye shall never see
marsh birds and muskrats?

Does not the heart need
wildness?
Does not the thought need
25 something
to rest upon
not self-made by man,
a bosom
not his own?

Guide for Responding

◆ LITERATURE AND YOUR LIFE

Reader's Response Are the issues raised in Chief Seattle's speech still being raised today? Explain.

Thematic Focus In your opinion, who poses the harder questions—Chief Seattle or Margaret Tsuda? Explain.

☑ Check Your Comprehension

1. In "This We Know," what does Chief Seattle want the white settlers to do with the land?
2. What does Chief Seattle say is the relationship between people and the Earth?
3. In "Hard Questions," what is the poet's attitude about the development of wild land for human use?

◆ Critical Thinking

1. What does the speaker in "This We Know" think will happen to his people? **[Interpret]**
2. "This We Know" is generally regarded as a defense of Indian traditions and an argument in favor of environmentalism. Support this view with specific examples from the speech. **[Support]**
3. What does the speaker in "Hard Questions" mean when she asks "Does not the heart need wildness?" **[Interpret]**
4. How can lines 13–29 in "Hard Questions" be seen as the answers to the question in lines 1–3? **[Interpret]**

APPLY

5. What if the speaker in "Hard Questions" were to meet a city planner who was considering the development of a large tract of homes on a wild hillside? What advice do you think the speaker would give to the city planner? **[Hypothesize]**

COMPARE LITERARY WORKS

6. Find lines in "This We Know" that convey the same feelings and ideas as lines 13–29 in "Hard Questions." Explain your choice. **[Connect]**

Hard Questions ◆ *199*

Reinforce and Extend

Answers
◆ LITERATURE AND YOUR LIFE

Reader's Response The environmental issues that Chief Seattle's speech addresses—caring for the air, water, and land—are still being raised today.

Thematic Focus Some students may say that Chief Seattle poses harder questions because the questions deal with survival. Others may say that both Chief Seattle and Tsuda pose equally hard questions about the future of the planet.

☑ Check Your Comprehension

1. He wants them to carefully preserve the land.
2. He says that people belong to the Earth, rather than the Earth belonging to people.
3. She feels that the development of wild land deprives people of the comfort and delights of "wildness."

◆ Critical Thinking

1. He thinks that his people and their way of life will disappear.
2. Examples include Chief Seattle's statements and supporting evidence that the Indians are "part of the earth and it is part of us" and that "to harm the earth is to heap contempt on its creator."
3. She means that people need to feel close to nature.
4. Lines 13–29 suggest what people will lose if all the land is developed as described in lines 1–3.
5. The speaker would probably advise the planner not to put homes on the hillside and instead to leave it wild for people to enjoy.
6. Students may suggest lines such as "The wind also gives our children the spirit of life," which relates to lines 13–15 in "Hard Questions," and "What will happen when the secret corners of the forest are heavy with the scent of many men . . . ," which relates to lines 20 and 21.

Beyond the Selection

FURTHER READING
Other Works by the Authors
The Fact of a Doorframe: Poems Selected and New, 1950–1984, Adrienne Rich
Final Harvest: Emily Dickinson's Poems, T. H. Johnson (ed.)

INTERNET
We suggest the following sites on the Internet (all Web sites are subject to change).
    To learn more about Adrienne Rich:
http://www.poetry.books.com/nrich.htm
    For Emily Dickinson:
http://www.planet.net/pkrisxle/emily/dickinson.html
    For Chief Seattle and Northwest Coast Native American culture:
http://www.chiefseattle.com/history/NWCoast/northwes.htm
    We *strongly recommend* that you preview these sites before you send students to them.

◆ Reading Strategy

1. Students may name words and phrases such as these: "sparkle of the water" (sight), "humming insect" (sound), "body heat of the pony" (touch), "wind that is sweetened by the meadow flowers" (taste), "perfumed flowers" (smell).
2. Possible response: For the image in the sentence "The water's murmur . . .," students may describe a hiking or camping experience near a river or stream.
3. "Hard Questions" appeals equally to the senses of sight and sound.

◆ Build Grammar Skills

Practice
1. courses
2. will happen
3. quenched
4. harm
5. will belong

Writing Application
Students' paragraphs should include these verb forms:
will achieve, will grow, will succeed

◆ Literary Focus

Possible responses:
1. (a) "The wind also gives our children the spirit of life." (b) "The shining water. . . is not just water, but the blood of our ancestors."
2. The images of the sky, air, land, water, and the living things on Earth combine to create an image of a wondrous and fragile world.

◆ Build Vocabulary

Using Forms of *evade*
1. His evasive maneuvers helped him escape.
2. Modern technology makes evasion difficult.
3. Her evasiveness makes her seem mysterious.

Spelling Strategy
1. operator
2. governor
3. inventor
4. percolator

Using the Word Bank
1. e
2. b
3. c
4. d
5. f
6. a

Guide for Responding (continued)

◆ Reading Strategy

USE YOUR SENSES
To appreciate writer's imagery, **use your senses** as you read. Draw upon the details the writer provides, along with your own memories and associations, to picture in your mind what the writer is describing.
1. From "This We Know," list a word or phrase that appeals to each of the five senses.
2. Explain how personal experiences or things you've observed in the movies or on television helped you picture one or more of the images in Chief Seattle's speech.
3. Which poem appeals equally to the senses of sight and sound?

◆ Build Grammar Skills

VERB TENSES
The **tense** of a verb shows the time of action or the condition expressed by the verb. The three main verb tenses are present, past, and future. Here are the forms of the regular verb *own*. Other regular verbs use the same endings or helping words.

Present Tense: I own; you own; he, she, or it owns; we own; you own; they own

Past Tense: I owned; you owned; he, she, or it owned; we owned; you owned; they owned

Future Tense: I will own; you will own; he, she, or it will own; we will own; you will own; they will own

Practice Copy these sentences, writing the tense of the verb indicated in parentheses.
1. Now the sap (*course*, present) through the trees.
2. Tomorrow, what (*happen*, future) to the eagle?
3. Yesterday, the rivers (*quench*, past) our thirst.
4. Today, some people (*harm*, present) the Earth.
5. Next year, we still (*belong*, future) to the Earth.

Writing Application Write a paragraph about your high-school years. Use the future tense of the verbs *achieve, grow,* and *succeed*.

◆ Literary Focus

IMAGERY
Through **imagery,** writers paint vivid word pictures, making their writing interesting and memorable. In "This We Know," for example, Chief Seattle's imagery brings the beauty of nature to life for the reader.
1. (a) In "This We Know," find an example of imagery that indicates that the air itself is sacred. (b) Find an example of imagery that emphasizes the importance of natural bodies of water.
2. Explain how the individual images in "Hard Questions" combine to create one dominant image.

◆ Build Vocabulary

USING FORMS OF *evade*
Copy these sentences on your paper, filling in the blank with a form of *evade*, which means "to avoid."
evasion   evasive   evasiveness
1. His _____?_____ maneuvers helped him escape.
2. Modern technology makes _____?_____ difficult.
3. Her _____?_____ makes her seem mysterious.

SPELLING STRATEGY
Ancestors has an *-or* suffix, which indicates that the word refers to a person who is or does something. Add *-or* to these verbs to create nouns that refer to persons or things that perform the action of the verb.
- If the root ends in a silent e, drop it before adding *-or*: imitate + -or = imitator
- If the root ends in a consonant, simply add *-or*: act + -or = actor

On your paper, add *-or* to these words.
1. operate   2. govern   3. invent   4. percolate

USING THE WORD BANK
On your paper, write the letter of the word or phrase closest in meaning to each Word Bank word.
1. discerning   a. forebears
2. prevail   b. succeed
3. assent   c. agree
4. worthily   d. well
5. evade   e. showing good judgment
6. ancestors   f. escape

 Writer's Solution

For additional instruction and practice, use The Six Tenses of Verbs, p. 72, in the *Writer's Solution Grammar Practice Book*.

Build Your Portfolio

Idea Bank

Writing

1. **Journal Entry** Put yourself in the place of the speaker in "Much Madness is divinest Sense—." Write a journal entry in which you elaborate on what is "sanity" in the world and what is "madness."

2. **Letter** Imagine that you have gone through the door described in "Prospective Immigrants Please Note." Write a letter to someone you left behind about how your life has changed.

3. **Speech Analysis** News commentators frequently summarize and analyze the speeches of political figures and discuss their impact. Prepare a news commentary on Chief Seattle's speech "This We Know" for a television audience. **[Media Link]**

Speaking and Listening

4. **Committee Discussion [Group Activity]** As a group, take on the role of a committee that approves or disapproves of the land development projects described in "Hard Questions." Stage a working discussion on the subject.

5. **Dramatization** With a partner, act out a scene that might take place between two relatives or close friends, one of whom wants to go through a door—or make a big change in his or her life—whereas the other does not. **[Performing Arts Link]**

Projects

6. **Timeline** Create a timeline of the life of Chief Seattle. On the timeline, note his accomplishments. You may also want to display portraits of him at various stages of the timeline and show on a map where he lived. **[Media Link]**

7. **Sculpture** Design and create a clay or papier-mâché sculpture to represent any image or idea from "Much Madness is divinest Sense—," "Prospective Immigrants Please Note," "This We Know," or "Hard Questions." **[Art Link]**

Writing Mini-Lesson

Persuasive Appeal

The writers in this section all make persuasive appeals on issues about which they feel strongly. Choose a topic you have strong opinions about, and write a persuasive appeal. Your appeal should be in prose.

Writing Skills Focus: Clear Purpose

Always have a **clear purpose** in mind as you write. Because you will be writing a persuasive appeal, your purpose will be to persuade someone to agree with your thinking. To do so, give several examples that support your ideas. In the following passage, Chief Seattle gives an example to support his purpose:

> **Model From "This We Know"**
> What befalls the earth, befalls all the sons of the earth.

Prewriting Decide on an issue or problem that you feel needs to be addressed. Jot down reasons why you think as you do.

Drafting Begin your appeal with a dramatic statement that calls attention to the issue or problem about which you're writing. Then, develop and support your ideas with facts that inform or alert the reader about the situation.

Revising Reread to be sure your purpose is clear. Also, check to make sure you've clearly and effectively given examples that support the points you're making. Proofread carefully to correct errors in spelling, punctuation, and grammar.

> ◆ **Grammar Application**
> Reread your written advice to be sure that you have used appropriate verb tenses.

Prospective Immigrants . . . /Much Madness . . . /This We Know/Hard Questions ◆ 201

Idea Bank

Following are suggestions for matching the Idea Bank topics with your students' performance levels and learning modalities:

Customize for
Performance Levels
Less Advanced Students: 1, 5
Average Students: 2, 4, 5, 6
More Advanced Students: 3, 4, 6, 7

Customize for
Learning Modalities
Verbal/Linguistic: 1, 2, 3
Visual/Spatial: 6, 7
Bodily/Kinesthetic: 5
Logical/Mathematical: 6
Intrapersonal: 1, 7
Interpersonal: 4, 5

Writing Mini-Lesson

Refer students to the Writing Handbook in the back of the book for instruction on the writing process and for further information on persuasion. Have students use the Main Idea and Supporting Details Organizer in **Writing and Language Transparencies,** p. 61, to arrange their prewriting ideas.

Writer's Solution

Writing Lab CD-ROM
Have students complete the tutorial on Persuasion. Follow these steps:
1. Have students view the video clip on Considering Audience and Purpose.
2. Have students ues the Active Verb Bin to find active verbs to use in their persuasive appeal.
3. Students can draft on computer.
4. Have students use the Proofreading Checklist to check their writing for errors in spelling, punctuation, and grammar.

Writer's Solution Sourcebook
Have students use Chapter 6, "Persuasion," pp. 166–199, for additional support. This chapter includes in-depth instruction on purpose, p. 185.

✓ ASSESSMENT OPTIONS

Formal Assessment, Selection Test, pp. 61–63, and Assessment Resources Software. The selection test is designed so that it can be easily customized to the performance levels of your students.
Alternative Assessment, p. 17, includes options for less advanced students, more advanced students, musical/rhythmic learners, bodily/kinesthetic learners, visual/spatial learners, and interpersonal learners.

PORTFOLIO ASSESSMENT
Use the following rubrics in the **Alternative Assessment** booklet to assess student writing:
Journal Entry: Narrative Based on Personal Experience, p. 92
Letter: Expression, p. 90
Speech Analysis: Literary Analysis/Interpretation, p. 108
Writing Mini-Lesson: Persuasion, p. 101

OBJECTIVES

1. To read, comprehend, and interpret a story
2. To relate a story to personal experience
3. To summarize sections of a story
4. To analyze the use of a first-person point of view
5. To build vocabulary in context and learn the word root -psych-
6. To develop skill in using the perfect tenses of verbs
7. To write an observation journal using details to support points
8. To respond to the story through writing, speaking and listening, and projects

SKILLS INSTRUCTION

Vocabulary:
Word Roots: -psych-
Spelling:
Spelling the s Sound With ps and the k Sound With ch
Grammar:
Verbs: Perfect Tenses
Reading Strategy:
Summarize
Literary Focus:
First-Person Point of View
Writing:
Use Details to Support Points

Critical Viewing:
Infer; Compare and Contrast; Interpret; Analyze; Support
Speaking and Listening:
Dramatization; Debate (Teacher Edition)
Viewing and Representing:
Inkblots; Audiovisual Interviews; Timeline Project (Teacher Edition)

PORTFOLIO OPPORTUNITIES

Writing: Award Plaque; Explanation; Journal Article

Writing Mini-Lesson: Observation Journal

Speaking and Listening: Dramatization; Debate

Projects: Research Report; Audiovisual Interviews

Guide for Reading

Meet the Author:

Daniel Keyes (1927–)

Daniel Keyes was raised in Brooklyn, New York. He has been a photographer, merchant seaman, and editor. His many works of fiction include the novels *The Touch* (1968) and *The Fifth Sally* (1980). Keyes has also written several nonfiction books, including *The Minds of Billy Milligan,* an in-depth portrait of a man with multiple-personality disorder. A sequel, *The Milligan Wars,* continues the harrowing account.

An Award-Winning Story "Flowers for Algernon," Keyes's best-known story, won the Hugo Award of the Science Fiction Writers of America in 1959. Inspired by its success, Keyes later expanded the story into a novel. Actor Cliff Robertson won an Academy Award for his portrayal of the title character in the film adaptation, *Charly.* The story was also adapted as a Broadway musical, *Charlie and Algernon.*

THE STORY BEHIND THE STORY

The idea for "Flowers for Algernon" came to Keyes after he met a mentally disadvantaged young man. Keyes began to wonder what would happen "if it were possible to increase human intelligence artificially." He points out that "Charlie Gordon (the main character in the story) is not real, nor is he based on a real person: he is imagined or invented, probably a composite of many people I know—including a little bit of me."

◆ LITERATURE AND YOUR LIFE

CONNECT YOUR EXPERIENCE

At some point or another in your life, you may have unfairly judged someone because he or she was different from you. In "Flowers for Algernon," the main character is unfairly judged and taunted by those around him. He decides to subject himself to scientific experimentation in an effort to become "like everyone else."

THEMATIC FOCUS: Facing Hard Questions

Shown at right is an EEG, a brain scan, that helps doctors understand how the brain works. How far should science go in "fixing" human capabilities and intelligence?

◆ Background for Understanding

SCIENCE

The story focuses on an experiment aimed at increasing a character's intelligence level. The most common measure of intelligence is the IQ (intelligence quotient). A person's IQ is determined by a test first developed at the turn of the twentieth century. An IQ of 100 is considered average. Recently, people have come to recognize that one test cannot accurately measure intelligence, and that people may have different types of ability.

◆ Build Vocabulary

WORD ROOTS: -psych-

The word root -psych- comes from the Greek word meaning "soul." In English word combinations, -psych- usually refers to the mind. For example, *psychology* is "the science of the mind."

WORD BANK

Which two words on the list contain the same root? What might the root mean? Check the Build Vocabulary boxes on pages 216 and 220 to see if you chose correctly.

psychology
tangible
specter
refute
illiteracy
obscure
syndromes
introspecti[

More About the Author
Daniel Keyes majored in psychology in college—most of his works deal with psychology and science. The novel version of *Flowers for Algernon,* published in 1966, combines both topics. Charlie's story is studied in schools around the world.

As he began writing "Flowers for Algernon," Keyes had many false starts. Then he had Charlie write his Progress Reports and was able to finish the story.

Prentice Hall Literature Program Resources

REINFORCE / RETEACH / EXTEND
Selection Support Pages
Build Vocabulary: Word Roots: -psych-, p. 92
Build Spelling Skills, p. 93
Build Grammar Skills: Verbs: Perfect Tenses, p. 94
Reading Strategies: Summarize, p. 95
Literary Focus: First-Person Point of View, p. 96
Strategies for Diverse Student Needs, pp. 35–36
Beyond Literature Cross-Curricular Connection: Science, p. 18

Formal Assessment Selection Test, pp. 64–66
Alternative Assessment, p. 18
Writing and Language Transparencies
Sunburst Organizer, p. 85; Timeline, p. 65.
Resource Pro CD-ROM "Flowers for Algernon"—includes all resource material and customizable lesson plan
Listening to Literature Audiocassettes
"Flowers for Algernon"

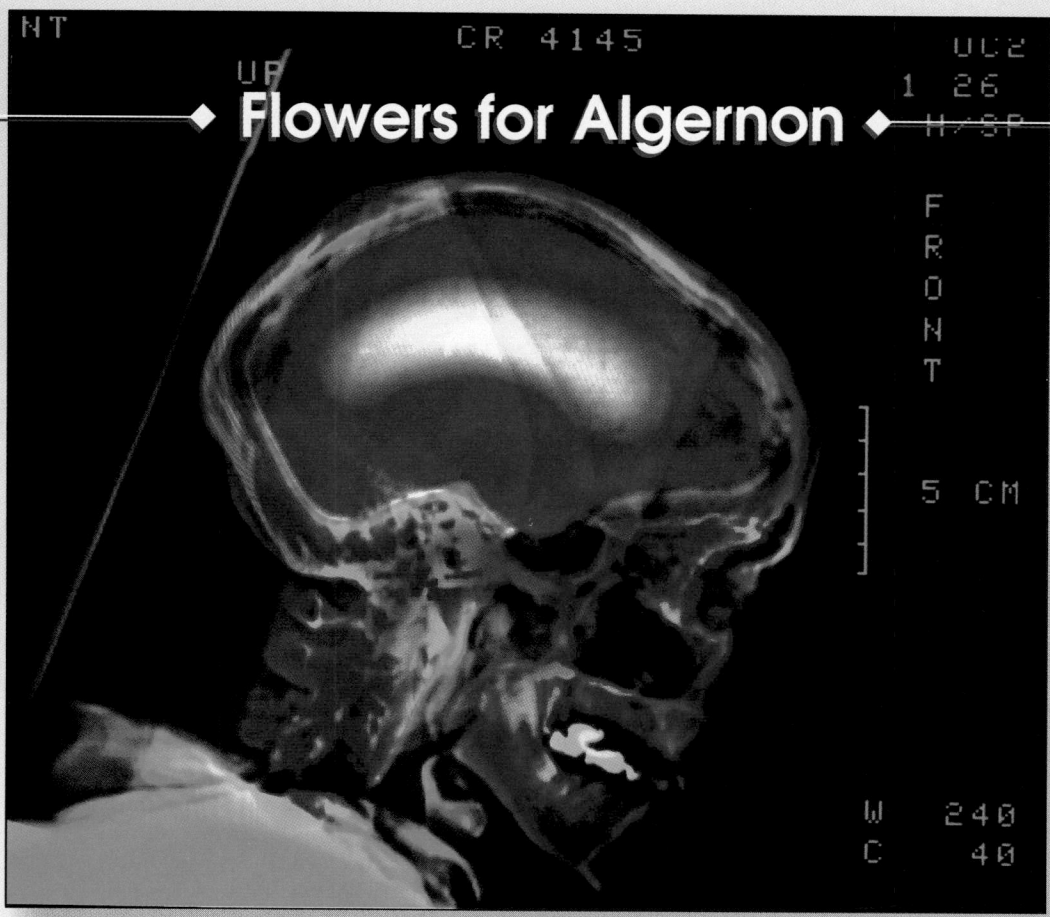

◆ Flowers for Algernon ◆

```
NT              CR 4145                UC2
     UP                                 1 26
                                        H/SP
                                    F
                                    R
                                    O
                                    N
                                    T

                                    5 CM

                                    W  240
                                    C   40
```

◆ Literary Focus

FIRST-PERSON POINT OF VIEW

Point of view refers to the vantage point from which a story is told. A story with a **first-person point of view** is told from the perspective of one of the characters, who uses the first-person pronoun "I." In "Flowers for Algernon," you'll learn about a fascinating scientific experiment through the eyes of the experiment's subject, Charlie Gordon. What he can tell you is limited to the things that he sees, feels, and thinks. For example, you will learn about other characters through Charlie's eyes.

◆ Reading Strategy

SUMMARIZE

When you **summarize,** you state in your own words the key ideas and details of a piece of writing. Summarizing sections of a story as you read will help you clarify and remember story events. As you read Charlie's progress reports in "Flowers for Algernon," summarize each report or each set of reports. Use a chart like the one below to keep track of your summaries.

Section of Story	Summary
Progress Report 1	Says he wants to be smart. He gives his name and age.

Guide for Reading ◆ 203

Interest Grabber

To help students appreciate Charlie's experiences, invite students to imagine that they have moved to a foreign country and have only begun to learn the language of that country. During the first week in school, they are barely able to communicate with the other students. When they approach a group of other students who are talking and laughing, the group falls silent. Individual students make excuses and avoid conversation with them and move away quickly. Worst of all, they sense that the other students are saying things to them that are insulting—but it's impossible to understand what they are actually saying.

◆ Build Grammar Skills

Verbs: Perfect Tenses If you wish to introduce the grammar concept for this selection before students read, refer to the instruction on p. 226.

Customize for
Less Proficient Readers

In "Flowers for Algernon," readers learn about events from Charlie's journal writings. Encourage students to notice that Charlie may be confused about what is actually going on at times. Point out that they can follow the events by paying attention to the dates of the reports.

Customize for
More Advanced Students

Encourage students to think about how this story might have developed if it had been written from another character's point of view. Invite students to choose a section of the story and write it in the words of Miss Kinnian, Burt, or Dr. Strauss.

Humanities: Visual Art

While the image shown on this page comes from a brain scan, it can still be viewed as a photograph or other visual art work. Invite students to comment on their feelings when looking at the picture. Do they relate the image to their own skulls? Do they believe their brains "look" like this one?

Preparing for Standardized Tests

Vocabulary General vocabulary questions on standardized tests may evaluate students' knowledge of word roots, such as *-psych-*, which comes from the Greek word meaning "soul." In English *-psych-* refers to the mind. If someone says she is taking a psychology course, students can use their knowledge of *-psych-* to understand that *psychology* meaning *science of the mind.*

Write this sample test item on the board:

Since the patient had no obvious symptoms of physical disease, the doctor suggested that psychotherapy might help.

In this sentence, *psychotherapy* means—

(A) soaking the head in warm water
(B) psychological testing
(C) treatment by psychological means
(D) brain surgery

Guide students to use their knowledge of the word root *-psych-* to determine that *(C)* is the correct answer. Although the other answers make sense in the sentence, *psycho-* has to do with "mind" and *therapy* means "treatment," which allows for correct understanding of the sentence.

Develop Understanding

⏱ One-Minute Insight

In "Flowers for Algernon," Charlie, a 37-year old man with a low IQ, is the subject of a scientific experiment to triple a person's IQ. Both Charlie and a white mouse named Algernon undergo the experiment. Charlie grows rapidly more intelligent and discovers that his "friends" at work have been ridiculing his slowness of mind. He soon becomes more knowledgeable than the doctors involved in the experiment. His co-workers turn against him—now because they resent his intelligence. Charlie observes Algernon's reversal and death. Charlie, with his new brilliance, is able to discover the flaws in the experiment and to predict his own fate. As the story closes, Charlie knows from two sides the hostility that the mentally disadvantaged suffer.

◆ Literary Focus

❶ First-Person Point of View
Students may say that the character telling the story uses the pronoun I.

Customize for
English Language Learners
The unusual spelling at the beginning of the story may pose a problem for English language learners. Explain that the writing is incorrect on purpose, in order to show that Charlie has trouble reading and writing. Have students listen to at least the first half of the story on audiocassette.

🎧 **Listening to Literature Audiocassettes**

Customize for
Verbal/Linguistic Learners
Daniel Keyes uses nonstandard English to reveal Charlie's abilities and feelings. Have students analyze the nonstandard elements, taking small sections and correcting the spelling and punctuation.

Flowers for ALGERNON

Daniel Keyes

progris riport 1—martch 5 1965

Dr. Strauss says I shud rite down what I think and evrey thing that happins to me from now on. I dont know why but he says its importint so they will see if they will use me. I hope they use me. Miss Kinnian says maybe they can make me smart. I want to be smart. My name is Charlie Gordon. I am 37 years old and 2 weeks ago was my brithday. I have nuthing more to rite now so I will close for today.

> ◆ **Literary Focus**
> ❶ How can you tell this story is told from a first-person point of view?

progris riport 2—martch 6

I had a test today. I think I faled it. and I think that maybe now they wont use me. What happind is a nice young man was in the room and he had some white cards with ink spilled all over them. He sed Charlie what do you see on this card. I was very skared even tho I had my rabits foot in my pockit because when I was a kid I always faled tests in school and I spilled ink to.

Edited for this edition.

204 ◆ Meeting Challenges

I told him I saw a inkblot. He said yes and it made me feel good. I thot that was all but when I got up to go he stopped me. He said now sit down Charlie we are not thru yet. Then I dont remember so good but he wantid me to say what was in the ink. I dint see nuthing in the ink but he said there was picturs there other pepul saw some picturs. I coudnt see any picturs. I reely tryed to see. I held the card close up and then far away. Then I said if I had my glases I coud see better I usally only ware my glases in the movies or TV but I said they are in the closit in the hall. I got them. Then I said let me see that card agen I bet Ill find it now.

I tryed hard but I still coudnt find the picturs I only saw the ink. I told him maybe I need new glases. He rote somthing down on a paper and I got skared of faling the test. I told him it was a very nice inkblot with littel points all around the eges. He looked very sad so that wasnt it. I said please let me try agen. Ill get it in a few minits becaus Im not so fast

---

 Block Scheduling Strategies

Consider these suggestions to take advantage of extended class time:

- Ask students to write a brief journal entry on the subject in Literature and Your Life on p. 202. Invite students to comment on this topic in a class discussion.
- Have students read the story independently. You may wish to assign the story as homework. Then have students meet in groups to discuss the effects of the first-person narrative. Ask

them to complete the Literary Focus on p. 226.

- Have students work in groups to create a scene from the story to perform, based on the Speaking and Listening activity on p. 227. Further support for this dramatization activity is provided on p. 217 of the Teacher Edition.
- If you have access to technology, have students use the *Writer's Solution Writing Lab CD-ROM* to prepare for and complete the Writing Mini-Lesson.

◀ **Critical Viewing** What impression of Charlie Gordon do you get from this scene from the movie? [Infer] ❷

somtimes. Im a slow reeder too in Miss Kinnians class for slow adults but I'm trying very hard.

He gave me a chance with another card that had 2 kinds of ink spilled on it red and blue.

He was very nice and talked slow like Miss Kinnian does and he explained it to me that it was a *raw shok*.[1] He said pepul see things in the ink. I said show me where. He said think. I told him I think a inkblot but that wasnt rite eather. He said what does it remind you—pretend somthing. I closd my eyes for a long time to pretend. I told him I pretned a fowntan pen with ink leeking all over a table cloth. Then he got up and went out.

I dont think I passd the *raw shok* test.

progris report 3—martch 7

Dr Strauss and Dr Nemur say it dont matter about the inkblots. I told them I dint spill the ink on the cards and I coudnt see anything in the ink. They said that maybe they will still use me. I said Miss Kinnian never gave me tests like that one only spelling and reading. They said Miss Kinnian told that I was her bestist pupil in the adult nite scool becaus I tryed the hardist and I reely wantid to lern. They said how come you went to the adult nite scool all by yourself Charlie. How did you find it. I said I askd pepul and sumbody told me where I shud go to lern to read and spell good. They said why did you want to. I told them becaus all my life I wantid to be smart and not dumb. But its very hard to be smart. They said you know it will probly be tempirery. I said yes. Miss Kinnian told me. I dont care if it herts.

Later I had more crazy tests today. The nice lady who gave it me told me the name and I

---

1. **raw shok:** Misspelling of Rorschach (rôr´ shäk) test, a psychological test involving inkblots that the subject describes.

▶Critical Viewing◀

❷ **Infer** *Charlie's expression and body language show he enjoys the seesaw as much as the children do. He appears childlike and unsophisticated.*

◆ Critical Thinking

❸ **Analyze** Ask students why Charlie tries so hard to find the pictures in the inkblots. *He is afraid of failing a test, as he did in school. He also wants to pass the test so he can become smart.*

◆ Reading Strategy

❹ **Summarize** Have students summarize what they learn about Charlie in his account of his conversation with Dr. Strauss and Dr. Nemur. *Students may say that Charlie tries hard and wants to learn. He attends night school on his own because he wants to be smart.*

◆ Literary Focus

❺ **First-Person Point of View** Ask students if they think Charlie knows what "temporary" means. Do they think he understands the possible effects of the experiment? *Students may say that he appears not to fully understand what will happen. He responds to the idea that the change may be temporary by saying he doesn't care if it hurts. He may not realize that he may get to "be smart" for only a short period of time.*

Cross-Curricular Connection: Science

Rorschach Test A psychologist administers a Rorschach test, asking a person to view ink blots and describe what he or she sees. Based on the person's response, psychologists can learn something about how the test subject's brain processes visual information.

The Rorschach test was introduced by the Swiss psychiatrist Hermann Rorschach in 1921. Dr. Rorschach was interested in the field of psychoanalysis, which is a procedure for investigating the unconscious mental processes. However,

Rorschach was not the first scientist to experiment with inkblot interpretation. One of his forerunners was Leonardo da Vinci!

While pictures of inkblots are not available to the general public, students can find approximations of inkblots in the second Web site listed on p. 225 (Teacher Edition). You will want to preview this site before you send students to it. After viewing the inkblots, students can e-mail their interpretations to the site and read what other middle grade students saw in the inkblots.

◆ Critical Thinking

❶ Infer Ask students what they learn about Charlie based on his reaction to the Thematic Apperception Test. *They may say that Charlie cannot see the difference between making up a story and lying. He apparently has had a bad experience with telling lies. Also, he cannot see the point in making up a story about the picture.*

◆ Literary Focus

❷ First-Person Point of View What is Charlie's interpretation of being timed while doing the maze? Do you think his interpretation is correct? *Charlie thinks the scientist is trying to hide the stopwatch, which makes Charlie even more nervous. The scientist may indeed have tried to hide the watch because he didn't want to make Charlie nervous.*

◆ Reading Strategy

❸ Summarize Students should try to organize the events in this entry in their own words. *Possible response: Charlie is very happy at being chosen to have the operation. He learns, however, that Dr. Nemur has doubts about using him. Dr. Strauss convinces his co-worker by praising Charlie's motivation, good nature, and the fact that he is eager to please. When Dr. Nemur agrees, Charlie promises to try hard to be smart after the operation.*

Comprehension Check ☑

❹ Why is cheese Algernon's motivation? What traits show Charlie's motivation? *The mouse gets to eat cheese when he finishes the maze. Charlie's motivation comes through in his determination to improve his reading and writing skills.*

---

asked her how do you spellit so I can rite it in my progris riport. THEMATIC APPERCEPTION TEST.[2] I dont know the frist 2 words but I know what *test* means. You got to pass it or you get bad marks. This test lookd easy becaus I coud see the picturs. Only this time she dint want me to tell her the picturs. That mixd me up. I said the man yesterday said I shoud tell him what I saw in the ink she said that dont make no difrence. She said make up storys about the pepul in the picturs.

❶

I told her how can you tell storys about pepul you never met. I said why shud I make up lies. I never tell lies any more becaus I always get caut.

She told me this test and the other one the raw-shok was for getting personalty. I laffed so hard. I said how can you get that thing from inkblots and fotos. She got sore and put her picturs away. I dont care. It was sily. I gess I faled that test too.

Later some men in white coats took me to a difernt part of the hospitil and gave me a game to play. It was like a race with a white mouse. They called the mouse Algernon. Algernon was in a box with a lot of twists and turns like all kinds of walls and they gave me a pencil and a paper with lines and lots of boxes. On one side it said START and on the other end it said FINISH. They said it was *amazed*[3] and that Algernon and me had the same *amazed* to do. I dint see how we could have the same *amazed* if Algernon had a box and I had a paper but I dint say nothing. Anyway there wasnt time because the race started.

❷

One of the men had a watch he was trying to hide so I woudnt see it so I tryed not to look and that made me nervus.

Anyway that test made me feel worser than

---

2. **THEMATIC** (thē mat′ ik) **APPERCEPTION** (ap′ ər sep′ shən) **TEST:** Personality test in which the subject makes up stories about a series of pictures.
3. **amazed:** A maze, or confusing series of paths. Often, the intelligence of animals is assessed by how fast they go through a maze.

---

all the others because they did it over 10 times with difernt *amazeds* and Algernon won every time. I dint know that mice were so smart. Maybe thats because Algernon is a white mouse. Maybe white mice are smarter than other mice.

progris riport 4——Mar 8

Their going to use me! Im so exited I can hardly write. Dr Nemur and Dr Strauss had a argament about it first. Dr Nemur was in the office when Dr Strauss brot me in. Dr Nemur was worried about using me but Dr Strauss told him Miss Kinnian rekemmended me the best from all the pepul who she was teaching. I like Miss Kinnian becaus shes a very smart teacher. And she said Charlie your going to have a second chance. If you volenteer for this experament you mite get smart. They dont know if it will be perminint but theirs a chance. Thats why I said ok even when I was scared because she said it was an operashun. She said dont be scared Charlie you done so much with so little I think you deserv it most of all.

So I got scaird when Dr Nemur and Dr Strauss argud about it. Dr Strauss said I had something that was very good. He said I had a good *motor-vation*.[4] I never even knew I had that. I felt proud when he said that not every body with an *eye-q*[5] of 68 had that thing. I dont know what it is or where I got it but he said Algernon had it too. Algernons *motor-vation* is the cheese they put in his box. But it cant be that because I didnt eat any cheese this week.

Then he told Dr Nemur something I dint understand so while they were talking I

◆ Reading Strategy
How would you summarize this entry of Charlie's progress report?

❸

❹

---

4. **motor-vation:** Motivation, or desire to work hard and achieve a goal.
5. **eye-q:** IQ, or intelligence quotient. A way of measuring human intelligence.

Cross-Curricular Connection: Science

Psychological Testing Psychologists give the Rorschach test and the Thematic Apperception Test to help determine traits of a subject's personality. These tests are based on the idea of *projection*. In psychological terms, projection means that a person tends to believe that other people have his or her feelings or are motivated by the same impulses. The person *projects* his own feelings or characteristics onto another

person because they are painful to recognize in himself or herself. In these tests, a subject projects his own interpretations onto abstract designs or pictures.

Personality is a person's pattern of thought, feeling, and behavior. The personality may determine how someone will act or react to different circumstances.

wrote down some of the words.

He said Dr Nemur I know Charlie is not what you had in mind as the first of your new brede of intelek** (coudnt get the word) super-man. But most people of his low ment** are host** and uncoop** they are usualy dull apath** and hard to reach. He has a good natcher hes intristed and eager to please.

Dr Nemur said remember he will be the first human beeng ever to have his intelijence trippled by surgicle meens.

Dr Strauss said exakly. Look at how well hes lerned to read and write for his low mentel age its as grate an acheve** as you and I lerning einstines therey of **vity without help. That shows the intenss motorvation. Its comparat** a tremen** achev** I say we use Charlie.

I dint get all the words and they were talking to fast but it sounded like Dr Strauss was on my side and like the other one wasnt.

Then Dr Nemur nodded he said all right maybe your right. We will use Charlie. When he said that I got so exited I jumped up and shook his hand for being so good to me. I told him thank you doc you wont be sorry for giving me a second chance. And I mean it like I told him. After the operashun Im gonna try to be smart. Im gonna try awful hard.

progris ript 5—Mar 10

❺ Im skared. Lots of people who work here and the nurses and the people who gave me the tests came to bring me candy and wish me luck. I hope I have luck. I got my rabits foot and my lucky penny and my horse shoe. Only a black cat crossed me when I was comming

to the hospitil. Dr Strauss says dont be super-sitis Charlie this is sience. Anyway Im keeping my rabits foot with me. ❺

I asked Dr Strauss if Ill beat Algernon in the race after the operashun and he said maybe. If the operashun works Ill show that mouse I can be as smart as he is. Maybe smarter. Then Ill be abel to read better and spell the words

▲ **Critical Viewing** In what ways are Charlie and Algernon alike? [Compare and Contrast] ❻

good and know lots of things and be like other people. I want to be smart like other people. If it works perminint they will make everybody smart all over the wurld.

They dint give me anything to eat this morning. I dont know what that eating has to do with getting smart. Im very hungry and Dr Nemur took away my box of candy. That Dr Nemur is a grouch. Dr Strauss says I can have it back after the operashun. You cant eat befor a operashun . . .

Flowers for Algernon ◆ 207

◆ **Critical Thinking**

❺ **Compare and Contrast** How does Charlie's idea of luck compare and contrast with Dr. Strauss's idea of science? *Charlie believes his charms will help him, and is worried about seeing an unlucky black cat. Dr. Strauss believes that superstition has no place in science.*

▶**Critical Viewing**◀

❻ **Compare and Contrast** *They are both subjects of an experiment. Neither of them understands the consequences of the operation. Although Charlie consented to it, he does not truly understand what may happen to him.*

Customize for
English Language Learners
Students may have difficulty following the conversation. Read aloud the paragraphs that include the incomplete words, filling in the whole words. Encourage students to figure out the meanings from context clues. Write the correct spellings on the board and have students look up the definitions in the dictionary if they need to.

Customize for
Logical/Mathematical Learners
Ask students to determine what Charlie's IQ will be after the operation. A person with an IQ of 140 or above is considered a genius. Have students speculate on how this change will affect Charlie's ability to learn. They will quickly calculate that Charlie's IQ should be around 204, which means that he may be able to learn very advanced material.

 Beyond the Classroom

Workplace Skills

Motivation Ask for a volunteer to explain why Dr. Strauss wanted Charlie to be the subject of the experiment: Elicit that Charlie has intense motivation. Have students discuss why motivation is an important characteristic for someone in Charlie's situation. Be sure to include the large amount of new knowledge he will be able to acquire, based on his increased mental capacity—since Charlie has shown that he can work hard to learn even with his IQ of 68, Dr. Strauss expects that he will want to learn more when

his IQ is increased.

Invite students to list reasons why having motivation is a good workplace skill. Help them recognize that a motivated person will try to do a good job on any task. Then have students write journal entries in two parts. In the first, students describe a household chore that they feel motivated to do, and explain why. Next, students describe a career in which they feel they would be motivated. Remind them to support their ideas with reasons.

◆ Critical Thinking

❶ Analyze Why is Charlie surprised to find out that the operation did not hurt? *He had not realized that he would be asleep during the operation.*

◆ Literary Focus

❷ First-Person Point of View Why is Charlie angry in his Progress Report 7? *Students may say he is disappointed that he cannot yet beat Algernon in the maze race. He is uncomfortable with the psychological tests, too. He is trying to think, since Dr. Strauss told him to, but he doesn't know what to think about. Charlie also feels lonely. He may be increasing in intelligence but does not realize it.*

◆ Reading Strategy

❸ Summarize Ask students to summarize the events Charlie records in Progress Report 8. What is Charlie going to do? What does he learn about the experiment? *Charlie is going to return to his job and come to the lab in the evenings. He learns that Algernon also had the operation, and that the development of intelligence takes time.*

◆ LITERATURE AND YOUR LIFE

❹ *Students will probably say that they have seen people making fun of someone who is different in some way.* **Ask them to discuss how the "picked on" person may feel. Encourage students to discuss what to do if they witness this kind of cruelty.** *They may say that the person may not realize he is being laughed at, like Charlie, or be puzzled at certain remarks, as Charlie is about the expression "pull a Charlie Gordon." Many students may say that the person feels sad and wants to be accepted by the others. They might suggest that being friendly to the person would make him or her feel better and perhaps discourage other people from making fun of the person.*

Progress Report 6—Mar 15

❶ The operashun dint hurt. He did it while I was sleeping. They took off the bandijis from my eyes and my head today so I can make a PROGRESS REPORT. Dr Nemur who looked at some of my other ones says I spell PROGRESS wrong and he told me how to spell it and REPORT too. I got to try and remember that.

I have a very bad memary for spelling. Dr Strauss says its ok to tell about all the things that happin to me but he says I shoud tell more about what I feel and what I think. When I told him I dont know how to think he said try. All the time when the bandijis were on my eyes I tryed to think. Nothing happened. I dont know what to think about. Maybe if I ask him he will tell me how I can think now that Im suppose to get smart. What do smart people think about. Fancy things I suppose. I wish I knew some fancy things alredy.

Progress Report 7—Mar 19

Nothing is happining. I had lots of tests and different kinds of races with Algernon. I hate that mouse. He always beats me. Dr Strauss said I got to play those games. And he said some time I got to take those tests over again. Thse inkblots are stupid. And those pictures ❷ are stupid too. I like to draw a picture of a man and a woman but I wont make up lies about people.

I got a headache from trying to think so much. I thot Dr Strauss was my frend but he dont help me. He dont tell me what to think or when Ill get smart. Miss Kinnian dint come to see me. I think writing these progress reports are stupid too.

Progress Report 8—Mar 23

Im going back to work at the factery. They said it was better I shud go back to work but ❸ I cant tell anyone what the operashun was for and I have to come to the hospitil for an hour evry night after work. They are gonna pay me mony every month for lerning to be smart.

Im glad Im going back to work because I miss my job and all my frends and all the fun we have there.

Dr Strauss says I shud keep writing things down but I dont have to do it every day just when I think of something or something speshul happins. He says dont get discoridged because it takes time and it happins slow. He ❸ says it took a long time with Algernon before he got 3 times smarter then he was before. Thats why Algernon beats me all the time because he had that operashun too. That makes me feel better. I coud probly do that *amazed* faster than a reglar mouse. Maybe some day

Ill beat Algernon. Boy that would be something. So far Algernon looks like he mite be smart perminent.

Mar 25 (I dont have to write PROGRESS REPORT on top any more just when I hand it in once a week for Dr Nemur to read. I just have to put the date on. That saves time)

We had a lot of fun at the factery today. Joe Carp said hey look where Charlie had his operashun what did they do Charlie put some brains in. I was going to tell him but I remembered Dr Strauss said no. Then Frank Reilly said what did you do Charlie forget your key and open your door the hard way. That made me laff. Their really my friends and they like me.

Sometimes somebody will say hey look at Joe or Frank or George he really pulled a Charlie Gordon. I dont know why they say that but they always laff. This morning Amos Borg who is the 4 man at Donnegans used my name when he shouted at Ernie the office boy. Ernie lost a packige. He said Ernie what are you trying to be a Charlie Gordon. I dont understand why he said that. I never lost any packiges.

> ◆ **Literature and Your Life**
> Have you ever witnessed cruel behavior like this? ❹

Cross-Curricular Connection: Science

Nature Versus Nurture Scientists who study how animals behave are divided into two main groups. Ethnologists believe that much of what animals know is instinctive. Behaviorists believe that most animal behavior is learned. Ethnology supports the idea that animals learn their behavior naturally. Behaviorism supports the idea that animals nurture, or help and teach, their young. The debate between the two groups is sometimes called "nature versus nurture."

Have students work in pairs or small group to debate nature versus nurture. Encourage them to

think of pets, birds, and insects they have observed. Do they think the behavior was learned or instinctive?

Suggest that students fold a sheet of notebook paper lengthwise, forming two columns. In one column they can list reasons to agree with ethnologists. In the other column they can list reasons that behaviorism makes sense. Each group can report on its conclusions.

Nature	Nurture

Mar 28 Dr Straus came to my room tonight to see why I dint come in like I was suppose to. I told him I dont like to race with Algernon any more. He said I dont have to for a while but I shud come in. He had a present for me only it wasnt a present but just for lend. I thot it was a little television but it wasnt. He said I got to turn it on when I go to sleep. I said your kidding why shud I turn it on when Im going to sleep. Who ever herd of a thing like that. But he said if I want to get smart I got to do what he says. I told him I dint think I was going to get smart and he put his hand on my sholder and said Charlie you dont know it yet but your getting smarter all the time. You wont notice for a while. I think he was just being nice to make me feel good because I dont look any smarter.

Oh yes I almost forgot. I asked him when I can go back to the class at Miss Kinnians school. He said I wont go their. He said that soon Miss Kinnian will come to the hospitil to start and teach me speshul. I was mad at her for not comming to see me when I got the operashun but I like her so maybe we will be frends again.

Mar 29 That crazy TV kept me up all night. How can I sleep with something yelling crazy things all night in my ears. And the nutty pictures. Wow. I dont know what it says when Im up so how am I going to know when Im sleeping.

Dr Strauss says its ok. He says my brains are lerning when I sleep and that will help me when Miss Kinnian starts my lessons in the hospitl only I found out it isnt a hospitil its a labatory. I think its all crazy. If you can get smart when your sleeping why do people go to school. That thing I dont think will work. I use to watch the late show and the late late show on TV all the time and it never made me smart. Maybe you have to sleep while you watch it.

PROGRESS REPORT 9—April 3

Dr Strauss showed me how to keep the TV turned low so now I can sleep. I don't hear a thing. And I still dont understand what it says. A few times I play it over in the morning to find out what I lerned when I was sleeping and I dont think so. Miss Kinnian says Maybe its another langwidge or something. But most times it sounds american. It talks so fast faster then even Miss Gold who was my teacher in 6 grade and I remember she talked so fast I coudnt understand her.

I told Dr Strauss what good is it to get smart in my sleep. I want to be smart when Im awake. He says its the same thing and I have two minds. Theres the *subconscious* and the *conscious* (thats how you spell it). And one dont tell the other one what its doing. They dont even talk to each other. Thats why I dream. And boy have I been having crazy dreams. Wow. Ever since that night TV. The late late late late late show.

I forgot to ask him if it was only me or if everybody had those two minds.

(I just looked up the word in the dictionary Dr Strauss gave me. The word is *subconscious. adj. Of the nature of mental operations yet not present in consciousness; as, subconscious conflict of desires.*) There's more but I still dont know what it means. This isnt a very good dictionary for dumb people like me.

Anyway the headache is from the party. My frends from the factery Joe Carp and Frank Reilly invited me to go with them to Muggsys Saloon for some drinks. I dont like to drink but they said we will have lots of fun. I had a good time.

Joe Carp said I shoud show the girls how I mop out the toilet in the factory and he got me a mop. I showed them and everyone laffed when I told that Mr Donnegan said I was the best janiter he ever had because I like my job and do it good and never come late or miss a day except for my operashun.

Flowers for Algernon ◆ 209

Cross-Curricular Connection: Science

Psychological Terms The Viennese doctor Sigmund Freud (1856–1939) developed a theory of zones of activity in the mind. The terms he used to describe them are conscious, preconscious, and unconscious. According to Freud, a person is immediately aware of ideas in the conscious mind. In the preconscious, or subconscious, mind are ideas that a person does not immediately notice but may be able to recognize simply by paying attention to them. The unconscious contains ideas from the past that a person cannot become aware of because they are hidden too deeply.

Let students know that while these theories cannot be proven and contemporary psychologists have explored these ideas in many different ways, Freud has had a great influence on psychology. Ask students how this view of the mind may affect the way the psychologist Dr. Nemur viewed the experiment.

◆ **LITERATURE AND YOUR LIFE**

❶ Why do Joe and Frank invite Charlie to go to Muggsy's Saloon with them and then send him out for coffee? *Students may say that the co-workers like to make fun of Charlie, especially since Charlie doesn't realize that he is being laughed at. Joe and Frank may like to trick Charlie since he is no threat to them.*

◆ **Critical Thinking**

❷ **Cause and Effect** Why have Charlie's feelings toward Algernon changed? *Students may say that Charlie likes the mouse better after beating Algernon in the race. Also, Charlie is beginning to be more aware of his surroundings. He feels a comradeship with Algernon because they are both subjects of the experiment. He can see that the treatment of the mouse is not fair.*

Customize for
Interpersonal Learners
Students can work in groups and examine Charlie's progress reports through April 9. Have students look for clues that may help them predict what will happen in the story. Draw their attention to the comments made by Miss Kinnian and Dr. Strauss that the operation may not be permanent, as well as Charlie's observation that Algernon is still smart "so far." Each group can report its findings to the class.

Customize for
Visual/Spatial Learners
Have students create mazes for others to try to complete. If possible, make copies of the mazes and let students race each other.

I said Miss Kinnian always said Charlie be proud of your job because you do it good.

Everybody laffed and we had a good time and they gave me lots of drinks and Joe said Charlie is a card when hes potted. I dont know what that means but everybody likes me and we have fun. I cant wait to be smart like my best frends Joe Carp and Frank Reilly.

❶ I dont remember how the party was over but I think I went out to buy a newspaper and coffe for Joe and Frank and when I came back there was no one their. I looked for them all over till late. Then I dont remember so good but I think I got sleepy or sick. A nice cop brot me back home. Thats what my landlady Mrs Flynn says.

But I got a headache and a big lump on my head and black and blue all over. I think maybe I fell. Anyway I got a bad headache and Im sick and hurt all over. I dont think Ill drink anymore.

April 6 I beat Algernon! I dint even know I beat him until Burt the tester told me. Then the second time I lost because I got so exited I fell off the chair before I finished. But after that I beat him 8 more times. I must be getting smart to beat a smart mouse like Algernon. ❷ But I dont *feel* smarter.

I wanted to race Algernon some more but Burt said thats enough for one day. They let me hold him for a minit. Hes not so bad. Hes soft like a ball of cotton. He blinks and when he opens his eyes their black and pink on the eges.

I said can I feed him because I felt bad to beat him and I wanted to be nice and make frends. Burt said no Algernon is a very spec-shul mouse with an operashun like mine, and he was the first of all the animals to stay smart so long. He told me Algernon is so smart that every day he has to solve a test to get his food. Its a thing like a lock on a door that changes every time Algernon goes in to eat so he has to lern something new to get his food. That made me sad because if he coudnt

lern he woud be hungry.

I dont think its right to make you pass a test to eat. How woud Dr Nemur like it to have to pass a test every time he wants to eat. I think Ill be frends with Algernon.

April 9 Tonight after work Miss Kinnian was at the laboratory. She looked like she was glad to see me but scared. I told her dont worry Miss Kinnian Im not smart yet and she laffed. She said I have confidence in you Charlie the way you struggled so hard to read and right better than all the others. At werst you will have it for a littel wile and your doing something for sience.

We are reading a very hard book. I never read such a hard book before. Its called *Robinson Crusoe*[6] about a man who gets merooned on a dessert Iland. Hes smart and figers out all kinds of things so he can have a house and food and hes a good swimmer. Only I feel sorry because hes all alone and has no frends. But I think their must be somebody else on the iland because theres a picture with his funny umbrella looking at footprints. I hope he gets a frend and not be lonly.

April 10 Miss Kinnian teaches me to spell better. She says look at a word and close your eyes and say it over and over until you remember. I have lots of truble with *through* that you say *threw* and *enough* and *tough* that you dont say *enew* and *tew*. You got to say *enuff* and *tuff*. Thats how I use to write it before I started to get smart. Im confused but Miss Kinnian says theres no reason in spelling.

Apr 14 Finished Robinson Crusoe. I want to find out more about what happens to him but Miss Kinnian says thats all there is. *Why*

Apr 15 Miss Kinnian says Im lerning fast. She read some of the Progress Reports and she

---

6. **Robinson Crusoe** (krōō′ sō): Novel written in 1719 by Daniel Defoe, a British author.

 Cross-Curricular Connection: Science

Behaviorism In the study of animal behavior, behaviorism includes classical conditioning and operant conditioning. Ivan Pavlov, a 19th-century Russian scientist, originated classical conditioning. He discovered that dogs salivate when offered food. By ringing a bell whenever he served the dogs food, Pavlov found that eventually the dogs would salivate when they heard the bell, even when they were not being fed.

Operant conditioning works on the principle of reward and punishment and is based on trial and error learning. A rat in a cage is "taught" to press a bar to receive food. When it does the right thing, it gets to eat. Discuss with students that the rat is subject to operant conditioning, since it is rewarded with a piece of cheese when it solves a test.

▲ **Critical Viewing** Compare and contrast your vision of Charlie as described in the story with these photographs showing the actor's portrayal of the character. [Compare and Contrast] ❹

looked at me kind of funny. She says Im a fine person and Ill show them all. I asked her why. She said never mind but I shoudnt feel bad if I find out that everybody isnt nice like I think. She said for a person who god gave so little to you done more then a lot of people with brains they never even used. I said all my frends are smart people but there good. They like me and they never did anything that wasnt nice. Then she got something in her eye and she had to run out to the ladys room. ❸

Apr 16 Today, I lerned, the *comma*, this is a comma (,) a period, with a tail, Miss Kinnian, says its importent, because, it makes writing, better, she said, somebody, coud lose, a lot of money, if a comma, isnt, in the, right place, I dont have, any money, and I dont see, how a comma, keeps you, from losing it,

But she says, everybody, uses commas, so Ill use, them too,

Apr 17 I used the comma wrong. Its punctuation. Miss Kinnian told me to look up long words in the dictionary to lern to spell them. I said whats the difference if you can read it anyway. She said its part of your education so now on Ill look up all the words Im not sure how to spell. It takes a long time to write that way but I think Im remembering. I only have to look up once and after that I get it right. Anyway thats how come I got the word *punctuation* right. (Its that way in the dictionary). ❺

Flowers for Algernon ◆ 211

◆ **LITERATURE AND YOUR LIFE**
❸ Why does Miss Kinnian look at Charlie "kind of funny" after reading his progress reports? Why is she concerned about Charlie and his co-workers? *Students may say that she realizes Charlie will soon understand that he is being laughed at. She knows he is a good person and she is worried that he will feel bad the more he learns about people.*

▶**Critical Viewing**◀
❹ **Compare and Contrast**
Students may say that they viewed Charlie as sweet and earnest, always trying to learn but always being unable to understand very much. He thinks everyone he knows is smart and he wants to be, too. The photographs show these qualities, as well as how he is beginning to get along with Algernon. The top photograph shows how he admires Miss Kinnian.

◆ **Literary Focus**
❺ **First-Person Point of View**
What does the reader learn about Charlie from his April 17 report that he does not yet recognize in himself? *Students may say that Charlie has advanced to the point that he can use a dictionary and remember how to spell a word after looking it up just once.*

Customize for
Logical/Mathematical Learners
Invite students to write a series of rules for using the comma that would make sense to Charlie at this stage in his development.

Humanities: Literature

Robinson Crusoe, by Daniel Defoe

Daniel Defoe (1660–1731) was one of the first British writers of realistic fiction. Like *Robinson Crusoe*, his books *Moll Flanders* and *Colonel Jack* are adventure novels with realistic physical and psychological details. The main characters are self-reliant, resourceful individuals.

Defoe wrote *Robinson Crusoe* after hearing of the true experience of a marooned sailor, Alexander Selkirk. In the novel, Crusoe is shipwrecked and lives alone on a deserted island for many years. He learns to survive, building shelter, planting crops, and domesticating wild goats. After he rescues a man from a nearby island from cannibals, Crusoe finally has a companion.

Ask students why they think the author Daniel Keyes shows Charlie reading *Robinson Crusoe*. Have students write journal entries on this idea now, and again when they finish reading the story.

◆ Literary Focus

❶ First-Person Point of View
Ask students if they have noticed bits of humor in Charlie's progress reports, such as his mention of the business letter. Remind them of other funny comments, such as his reaction to the Thematic Apperception Test and to the TV Dr. Strauss brought him. Do students think Charlie intended to be humorous? *Some students may see his humor as unknowing; that is, humor intended by the author for the reader. Others may see it as a sign that he is getting smarter.*

◆ Critical Thinking

❷ Compare and Contrast How is the progress report of April 18 different from the previous reports? *Students may say that this is the first report with almost no mistakes. Suddenly Charlie is writing with correct spelling and sentence structure. He also learned about punctuation by reading a whole grammar book during the night.*

◆ Literary Focus

❸ First-Person Point of View
Students may say that the other people do not realize that Charlie is changing and that he may notice they are making fun of him. These characters may be surprised that he behaves in a different way.

◆ LITERATURE AND YOUR LIFE

❹ Why is it so much harder for Charlie now that he understands his co-workers have always been making fun of him? *Students may say that as long as he didn't know, Charlie enjoyed being with the group of friends. Once he knows, he cannot feel the same about them or himself.*

Miss Kinnian says a period is punctuation too, and there are lots of other marks to lern. I told her I thot all the periods had to have tails but she said no.

You got to mix them up, she showed? me" how. to mix! them(up,. and now; I can! mix up all kinds" of punctuation, in! my writing? There, are lots! of rules? to lern; but Im get-tin'g them in my head.

❶ One thing I? like about, Dear Miss Kinnian: (thats the way it goes in a business letter if I ever go into business) is she, always gives me' a reason" when—I ask. She's a gen'ius! I wish! I cou'd be smart" like, her;

(Punctuation, is; fun!)

April 18 What a dope I am! I didn't even understand what she was talking about. I read the grammar book last night and it explanes the whole thing. Then I saw it was the same way as Miss Kinnian was trying to tell me, but I didn't get it. I got up in the middle of the night, and the whole thing straightened out in my mind.

Miss Kinnian said that the TV working in my sleep helped out. She said I reached a plateau. Thats like the flat top of a hill.

❷ After I figgered out how punctuation worked, I read over all my old Progress Reports from the beginning. Boy, did I have crazy spelling and punctuation! I told Miss Kinnian I ought to go over the pages and fix all the mistakes but she said, "No, Charlie, Dr. Nemur wants them just as they are. That's why he let you keep them after they were photostated, to see your own progress. You're coming along fast, Charlie."

That made me feel good. After the lesson I went down and played with Algernon. We don't race any more.

April 20 I feel sick inside. Not sick like for a doctor, but inside my chest it feels empty like getting punched and a heartburn at the same time.

I wasn't going to write about it, but I guess I got to, because its important. Today was the first time I ever stayed home from work.

Last night Joe Carp and Frank Reilly invited me to a party. There were lots of girls and some men from the factory. I remembered how sick I got last time I drank too much, so I told Joe I didn't want anything to drink. He gave me a plain coke instead. It tasted funny, but I thought it was just a bad taste in my mouth.

We had a lot of fun for a while. Joe said I should dance with Ellen and she would teach me the steps. I fell a few times and I couldn't understand why because no one else was dancing besides Ellen and me. And all the time I was tripping because somebody's foot was always sticking out.

Then when I got up I saw the look on Joe's face and it gave me a funny feeling in my stomack. "He's a scream," one of the girls said. Everybody was laughing.

Frank said, "I ain't laughed so much since we sent him off for the newspaper that night at Muggsy's and ditched him."

"Look at him. His face is red."

"He's blushing. Charlie is blushing."

"Hey, Ellen, what'd you do to Charlie? I never saw him act like that before."

I didn't know what to do or where to turn. Everyone was looking at me and laughing and I felt naked. I wanted to hide myself. I ran out into the street and I threw up. Then I walked home. It's a funny thing I never knew that Joe and Frank and the others liked to have me around all the time to make fun of me.

Now I know what it means when they say

> ◆ **Literary Focus**
> Explain how this episode would differ if it were told from someone else's point of view.
>
> ❸

> ❹

◆ Build Vocabulary

psychology (sī käl′ ə jē) *n.*: Science dealing with the mind and with mental and emotional processes

212 ◆ Meeting Challenges

Speaking and Listening Mini-Lesson

Debate
This mini-lesson supports the Speaking and Listening activity on p. 227.

Introduce Share the information about IQ in the Cross-Curricular Connection box on p. 213 (Teacher Edition). Also have students read Charlie's April 21 entry on p. 213. Tell students they will be debating the topic of using IQ tests to measure intelligence.

Develop Have students choose teams for or against the topic. Point out that in addition to

their own opinions, they will have to support their statements with specific details.

Apply Have two teams debate before a student panel of judges. Then another two teams can debate on another day.

Assess The panel will pick the winner based on the logic of the generalizations and the supporting details. Evaluate each student in terms of preparation, speaking, and composure. Panel members can use the Listening: Self-Assessment form, p. 117, in **Alternative Assessment**.

4 "to pull a Charlie Gordon."
I'm ashamed.

PROGRESS REPORT 11

April 21 Still didn't go into the factory. I told Mrs. Flynn my landlady to call and tell Mr. Donnegan I was sick. Mrs. Flynn looks at me very funny lately like she's scared of me.

I think it's a good thing about finding out how everybody laughs at me. I thought about it a lot. It's because I'm so dumb and I don't even know when I'm doing something dumb. People think it's funny when a dumb person can't do things the same way they can.

5 Anyway, now I know I'm getting smarter every day. I know punctuation and I can spell good. I like to look up all the hard words in the dictionary and I remember them. I'm reading a lot now, and Miss Kinnian says I read very fast. Sometimes I even understand what I'm reading about, and it stays in my mind. There are times when I can close my eyes and think of a page and it all comes back like a picture.

Besides history, geography and arithmetic, Miss Kinnian said I should start to learn a few foreign languages. Dr. Strauss gave me some more tapes to play while I sleep. I still don't understand how that conscious and unconscious mind works, but Dr. Strauss says not to worry yet. He asked me to promise that when I start learning college subjects next week I wouldn't read any books on psychology—that is, until he gives me permission.

6 I feel a lot better today, but I guess I'm still a little angry that all the time people were laughing and making fun of me because I wasn't so smart. When I become intelligent like Dr. Strauss says, with three times my I.Q. of 68, then maybe I'll be like everyone else and people will like me and be friendly.

I'm not sure what an I.Q. is. Dr. Nemur said it was something that measured how intelligent you were—like a scale in the drugstore weighs

pounds. But Dr. Strauss had a big arguement with him and said an I.Q. didn't weigh intelligence at all. He said an I.Q. showed how much intelligence you could get, like the numbers on the outside of a measuring cup. You still had to fill the cup up with stuff.

Then when I asked Burt, who gives me my intelligence tests and works with Algernon, he said that both of them were wrong (only I had to promise not to tell them he said so). Burt says that the I.Q. measures a lot of different things including some of the things you learned already, and it really isn't any good at all.

So I still don't know what I.Q. is except that mine is going to be over 200 soon. I didn't want to say anything, but I don't see how if they don't know *what* it is, or *where* it is—I don't see how they know *how much* of it you've got. **7**

Dr. Nemur says I have to take a *Rorshach Test* tomorrow. I wonder what *that* is.

April 22 I found out what a *Rorshach* is. It's the test I took before the operation—the one with the inkblots on the pieces of cardboard. The man who gave me the test was the same one.

I was scared to death of those inkblots. I knew he was going to ask me to find the pictures and I knew I wouldn't be able to. I was thinking to myself, if only there was some way of knowing what kind of pictures were hidden there. Maybe there weren't any pictures at all. Maybe it was just a trick to see if I was dumb enough too look for something that wasn't there. Just thinking about that made me sore at him.

"All right, Charlie," he said, "you've seen these cards before, remember?"

"Of course I remember."

The way I said it, he knew I was angry, and he looked surprised. "Yes, of course. Now I want you to look at this one. What might this be? What do you see on this card? People see

Flowers for Algernon ◆ *213*

◆ **Literary Focus**
5 First-Person Point of View
Charlie says that he knows he's getting smarter now. What clues does he give that he is suddenly getting smarter even faster than he seems to realize? *Students may say that he now enjoys looking up words in the dictionary, and can remember them. He reads very fast, and can remember a whole page after reading.*

◆ **LITERATURE AND YOUR LIFE**
6 Ask students if they think Charlie will be like everyone else when his IQ is tripled? Will people accept him as a friend when that happens? *Students may say that Charlie will not be like anyone else when he has such a high IQ. He may feel lonely, because he will still be different.*

◆ **Critical Thinking**
7 Evaluate Charlie is questioning the information he's received from the scientists. How does this differ from his earlier view of the doctors? How might this affect the experiment? *Students may say that earlier Charlie considered the doctors very intelligent and never questioned them. Now he is able to form his own opinions. This may affect the experiment because the subject of the experiment may be smarter that the scientists running the experiment.*

Customize for
More Advanced Students
Have students explain why they think Dr. Strauss asked Charlie not to read any psychology books without the doctor's permission. Ask them to find hints in Charlie's journal entries that show he is undergoing some psychological effects from the changes in his existence.

Cross-Curricular Connection: Science

Intelligence Quotient French psychologist Alfred Binet designed the IQ test around 1900. This test was intended to measure children's intelligence so that educators could learn the students' weaknesses, and tutor them accordingly. It has been used in the United States to rank students, and is the basis upon which standardized tests were developed. However, many contemporary educators believe that humans possess several different kinds of intelligences, or learning styles, making the IQ test invalid.

In traditional terms, Charlie's IQ of 68 would mean that he could perform all ordinary human tasks, but that he would need special teaching and extra studying in order to learn in academic courses. Discuss with students the ways that Charlie uses his intelligence before he has the operation.

◆ Literary Focus

❶ First-Person Point of View
Charlie is not sure whether the man giving him the Rorschach test is telling him the truth. Ask students if they think the man treated Charlie differently the first time, or if Charlie just understands the directions better this time. *Some students may think the man treated Charlie differently when his IQ was lower, possibly not expecting him to understand the directions. Others may say that the man probably used the same words, which Charlie is now able to understand.*

◆ Critical Thinking

❷ Make a Judgment Charlie saves his boss $10,000 a year. Do you think Mr. Donnegan is fair in giving Charlie a $25 bonus? Why do you think he chooses this amount? *Students may say that $25 is too small an amount. They may think Mr. Donnegan believes Charlie will be happy just to receive the bonus.*

◆ LITERATURE AND YOUR LIFE

❸ Point out to students that Charlie had hoped to be like everyone else when he became more intelligent. Instead, how do his co-workers react to him? How does this make Charlie feel? *They are now nervous around Charlie because he is obviously getting smarter. Charlie is lonelier now, because his former friends cannot act the same way with him any longer.*

◆ Reading Strategy

❹ Summarize What is the conflict between Dr. Nemur and Dr. Strauss? *They argue over who has contributed more to the experiment and over how soon they should publish the results.*

---

all sorts of things in these inkblots. Tell me what it might be for you—what it makes you think of."

I was shocked. That wasn't what I had expected him to say at all. "You mean there are no pictures hidden in those inkblots?"

He frowned and took off his glasses. "What?"

❶ "Pictures. Hidden in the inkblots. Last time you told me that everyone could see them and you wanted me to find them too."

He explained to me that the last time he had used almost the exact same words he was using now. I didn't believe it, and I still have the suspicion that he misled me at the time just for the fun of it. Unless—I don't know any more—could I have been *that* feeble-minded?

We went through the cards slowly. One of them looked like a pair of bats tugging at some thing. Another one looked like two men fencing with swords. I imagined all sorts of things. I guess I got carried away. But I didn't trust him any more, and I kept turning them around and even looking on the back to see if there was anything there I was supposed to catch. While he was making his notes, I peeked out of the corner of my eye to read it. But it was all in code that looked like this:

WF + A DdF-Ad orig. WF-A

SF + obj

The test still doesn't make sense to me. It seems to me that anyone could make up lies about things that they didn't really see. How could he know I wasn't making a fool of him by mentioning things that I didn't really imagine? Maybe I'll understand it when Dr. Strauss lets me read up on psychology.

❷ ❸ **April 25** I figured out a new way to line up the machines in the factory, and Mr. Donnegan says it will save him ten thousand dollars a year in labor and increased production. He gave me a $25 bonus.

I wanted to take Joe Carp and Frank Reilly out to lunch to celebrate, but Joe said he had to buy some things for his wife, and Frank

said he was meeting his cousin for lunch. I guess it'll take a little time for them to get used to the changes in me. Everybody seems to be frightened of me. When I went over to Amos Borg and tapped him on the shoulder, he jumped up in the air.

People don't talk to me much any more or kid around the way they used to. It makes the job kind of lonely.

April 27 I got up the nerve today to ask Miss Kinnian to have dinner with me tomorrow night to celebrate my bonus.

At first she wasn't sure it was right, but I asked Dr. Strauss and he said it was okay. Dr. Strauss and Dr. Nemur don't seem to be getting along so well. They're arguing all the time. This evening when I came in to ask Dr. Strauss about having dinner with Miss Kinnian, I heard them shouting. Dr. Nemur was saying that it was *his* experiment and *his* research, and Dr. Strauss was shouting back that he contributed just as much, because he found me through Miss Kinnian and he performed the operation. Dr. Strauss said that someday thousands of neurosurgeons[7] might be using his technique all over the world.

❹ Dr. Nemur wanted to publish the results of the experiment at the end of this month. Dr. Strauss wanted to wait a while longer to be sure. Dr. Strauss said that Dr. Nemur was more interested in the Chair[8] of Psychology at Princeton than he was in the experiment. Dr. Nemur said that Dr. Strauss was nothing but an opportunist who was trying to ride to glory on *his* coattails.

When I left afterwards, I found myself trembling. I don't know why for sure, but it was as if I'd seen both men clearly for the first time. I remember hearing Burt say that Dr. Nemur had a shrew of a wife who was pushing

---

7. **neurosurgeons** (noo' rō sur' jənz) *n*.: Doctors who operate on the nervous system, including the brain and spine.

8. **chair:** Professorship.

 Viewing and Representing Mini-Lesson

Inkblots

In this mini-lesson, students will use their imaginations to create and interpret inkblots.

Introduce Tell students they will be creating their own inkblots and testing one another, in order to share Charlie's experience taking the Rorschach test.

Develop Have students make inkblots on large index cards at home. They may make abstract designs using markers, or create shapes using tempera paints or watercolors.

Apply Students can work in pairs, showing one another the inkblots and recording results. Have students change partners and repeat several times. Each student writes a report on the reactions to his or her inkblot, noting similarities and differences in the responses.

Assess Students may present their findings to the class. Encourage discussion comparing and contrasting the different inkblots and responses. Evaluate students on the critical thinking in their written reports and class discussion participation.

him all the time to get things published so that he could become famous. Burt said that the dream of her life was to have a big shot husband.

Was Dr. Strauss really trying to ride on his coattails?

April 28 I don't understand why I never noticed how beautiful Miss Kinnian really is. She has brown eyes and feathery brown hair that comes to the top of her neck. She's only thirty-four! I think from the beginning I had the feeling that she was an unreachable genius—and very, very old. Now, every time I see her she grows younger and more lovely.

We had dinner and a long talk. When she said that I was coming along so fast that soon I'd be leaving her behind, I laughed.

"It's true, Charlie. You're already a better reader than I am. You can read a whole page at a glance while I can take

in only a few lines at a time. And you remember every single thing you read. I'm lucky if I can recall the main thoughts and the general meaning."

"I don't feel intelligent. There are so many things I don't understand."

She took out a cigarette and I lit it for her.

"You've got to be a *little* patient. You're accomplishing in days and weeks what it takes normal people to do in half a lifetime. That's what makes it so amazing. You're like a giant sponge now, soaking things in. Facts, figures, general knowledge. And soon you'll begin to

◄ **Critical Viewing** Does Charlie seem to have made progress, judging from the details in this photograph? Explain. [Interpret] ❻

Flowers for Algernon ◆ 215

❺ **First-Person Point of View** How is Charlie continuing to change? What do you predict is going to happen? *He is beginning to see people he knows from a different point of view. Now he sees Miss Kinnian as a beautiful woman younger than himself, whereas before he thought she was a wise, older person. Students may predict that Charlie will fall in love with his teacher.*

▶**Critical Viewing**◄

❻ **Interpret** *Charlie's face and body language are very different now. He looks intelligent and thoughtful, and has a more natural way of moving. He seems to be an adult now, rather than a childlike person.*

Customize for
English Language Learners
Students may need assistance understanding English expressions, such as "big shot" and "to ride on his coattails." Explain that a big shot means an important person. Riding on someone's coattails means using another person's ability or talent to help yourself get credit for doing something.

Customize for
Bodily/Kinesthetic Learners
Invite students to work in groups and use pantomime to show conflicts between characters. Students might show Charlie with Joe Carp and Frank Reilly or Dr. Nemur and Dr. Strauss, for example.

Beyond the Classroom

Career Connection
Literacy Education for Adults In this story, Miss Kinnian teaches reading and writing to adults. Like Charlie, some of her other students may have learning disabilities. Others may never have had the opportunity to learn to read and write as children. In some adult education situations, teachers work with people who speak a language other than English. Although these students may be learning the same literacy skills as children, their interest and motivation levels, like Charlie's, are often very high.

Teachers of adults work at community centers, community colleges, and at private schools. They may work with adult students on an individual basis or train volunteers to help tutor students one-on-one. Teaching adults can be a rewarding experience because often it offers students a second chance to obtain an education.

Invite students to interview a literacy teacher at a local college or community center about his or her job. Why did he or she choose this field? What kind of education and training does it require? What are the rewards and challenges?

◆ Literary Focus

❶ First-Person Point of View
What do you think Charlie and Miss Kinnian are thinking about? *They are considering the possibility that Charlie's intelligence may be only temporary.*

◆ Critical Thinking

❷ Interpret Why do you think Fanny tells Charlie that "it's not right" for him to have become smart so suddenly? *Students may say that the change in Charlie scares his co-workers. They know a person could not naturally become intelligent so rapidly. Since Charlie could not tell them what his operation was, they do not know about the experiment.*

◆ Reading Strategy

❸ Summarize *As part of an experiment on increasing intelligence, Charlie has an operation and his IQ rises. He gradually learns to read and write better, then he quickly becomes able to learn many complicated subjects. He has also become more aware of the world around him, first realizing that people had been making fun of him, and later falling in love with Miss Kinnian. Though he wanted to become smart, he is now lonely because his former friends are afraid of him.*

Customize for
Less Proficient Readers
Students may find it easier to summarize the story up to this point by using the Timeline, p. 65, in **Writing and Language Transparencies.** On this timeline they can record the events that happened to Charlie and the dates.

Customize for
Visual/Spatial Learners
Discuss Miss Kinnian's ladder metaphor for branches of knowledge with the class. Then have students draw charts or create 3-dimensional figures showing how the branches of their own knowledge are related.

---

connect them, too. You'll see how the different branches of learning are related. There are many levels, Charlie, like steps on a giant ladder that take you up higher and higher to see more and more of the world around you.

"I can see only a little bit of that, Charlie, and I won't go much higher than I am now, but you'll keep climbing up and up, and see more and more, and each step will open new worlds that you never even knew existed." She frowned. "I hope . . . I just hope to God—"

"What?"

"Never mind, Charles. I just hope I wasn't wrong to advise you to go into this in the first place."

❶ I laughed. "How could that be? It worked, didn't it? Even Algernon is still smart."

We sat there silently for a while and I knew what she was thinking about as she watched me toying with the chain of my rabbit's foot and my keys. I didn't want to think of that possibility any more than elderly people want to think of death. I *knew* that this was only the beginning. I knew what she meant about levels because I'd seen some of them already. The thought of leaving her behind made me sad.

I'm in love with Miss Kinnian.

PROGRESS REPORT 12

April 30 I've quit my job with Donnegan's Plastic Box Company. Mr. Donnegan insisted that it would be better for all concerned if I left. What did I do to make them hate me so?

The first I knew of it was when Mr. Donnegan showed me the petition. Eight hundred

◆ Build Vocabulary

tangible (tan´ jə bəl) *adj.*: That can be understood; definite; objective

specter (spek´ tər) *n.*: Disturbing thoughts

refute (ri fyo͞ot´) *v.*: Prove (an argument or statement) to be false by argument or evidence

and forty names, everyone connected with the factory, except Fanny Girden. Scanning the list quickly, I saw at once that hers was the only missing name. All the rest demanded that I be fired.

Joe Carp and Frank Reilly wouldn't talk to me about it. No one else would either, except Fanny. She was one of the few people I'd known who set her mind to something and believed it no matter what the rest of the world proved, said or did—and Fanny did not believe that I should have been fired. She had been against the petition on principle and despite the pressure and threats she'd held out.

"Which don't mean to say," she remarked, "that I don't think there's something mighty strange about you, Charlie. Them changes. I don't know. You used to be a good, dependable, ordinary man—not too bright maybe, but honest. Who knows what you done to yourself to get so smart all of a sudden. Like everybody around here's been saying, Charlie, it's not right." **❷**

"But how can you say that, Fanny? What's wrong with a man becoming intelligent and wanting to acquire knowledge and understanding of the world around him?"

She stared down at her work, and I turned to leave. Without looking at me, she said: "It was evil when Eve listened to the snake and ate from the tree of knowledge. It was evil when she saw that she was naked. If not for that none of us would ever have to grow old and sick, and die."

Once again now I have the feeling of shame burning inside me. This intelligence has driven a wedge between me and all the people I once knew and loved. Before, they laughed at me and despised me for my ignorance and dullness; now, they hate me for my knowledge and understanding. What do they want of me?

> **◆ Reading Strategy**
> Summarize Charlie's progress up to this point of the story. **❸**

They've driven me out of the factory. Now I'm more alone than ever before . . .

May 15 Dr. Strauss is very angry at me for not having written any progress reports in two weeks. He's justified because the lab is now paying me a regular salary. I told him I was too busy thinking and reading. When I pointed out that writing was such a slow process that it made me impatient with my poor hand writing, he suggested that I learn to type. It's much easier to write now because I can type nearly seventy-five words a minute. Dr. Strauss continually reminds me of the need to speak and write simply so that people will be able to understand me.

I'll try to review all the things that happened to me during the last two weeks. Algernon and I were presented to the American Psychological Association sitting in convention with the World Psychological Association last Tuesday. We created quite a sensation. Dr. Nemur and Dr. Strauss were proud of us.

I suspect that Dr. Nemur, who is sixty—ten years older than Dr. Strauss—finds it necessary to see <u>tangible</u> results of his work. Undoubtedly the result of pressure by Mrs. Nemur.

Contrary to my earlier impressions of him, I realize that Dr. Nemur is not at all a genius. He has a very good mind, but it struggles under the <u>specter</u> of self-doubt. He wants people to take him for a genius. Therefore, it is important for him to feel that his work is accepted by the world. I believe that Dr. Nemur was afraid of further delay because he worried that someone else might make a discovery along these lines and take the credit from him.

Dr. Strauss on the other hand might be called a genius, although I feel that his areas of knowledge are too limited. He was educated in the tradition of narrow specialization; the broader aspects of background were neglected far more than necessary—even for a neurosurgeon.

I was shocked to learn that the only ancient languages he could read were Latin, Greek and Hebrew, and that he knows almost nothing of mathematics beyond the elementary levels of the calculus of variations. When he admitted this to me, I found myself almost annoyed. It was as if he'd hidden this part of himself in order to deceive me, pretending—as do many people I've discovered—to be what he is not. No one I've ever known is what he appears to be on the surface.

Dr. Nemur appears to be uncomfortable around me. Sometimes when I try to talk to him, he just looks at me strangely and turns away. I was angry at first when Dr. Strauss told me I was giving Dr. Nemur an inferiority complex. I thought he was mocking me and I'm oversensitive at being made fun of.

How was I to know that a highly respected psychoexperimentalist like Nemur was unacquainted with Hindustani[9] and Chinese? It's absurd when you consider the work that is being done in India and China today in the very field of his study.

I asked Dr. Strauss how Nemur could <u>refute</u> Rahajamati's attack on his method and results if Nemur couldn't even read them in the first place. That strange look on Dr. Strauss' face can mean only one of two things. Either he doesn't want to tell Nemur what they're saying in India, or else—and this worries me—Dr. Strauss doesn't know either. I must be careful to speak and write clearly and simply so that people won't laugh.

May 18 I am very disturbed. I saw Miss Kinnian last night for the first time in over a week. I tried to avoid all discussions of intellectual concepts and to keep the conversation on a simple, everyday level, but she just stared at me blankly and asked me what I meant about the mathematical variance equivalent in Dorbermann's *Fifth Concerto*.

When I tried to explain she stopped me and

---

9. **Hindustani** (hin´ dōō stä´ nē) *n.:* A language of northern India.

Flowers for Algernon ◆ 217

◆ **Critical Thinking**

4 Compare and Contrast Compare Dr. Strauss's reminder to speak and write simply with the way Charlie was speaking and writing one month earlier. *A month ago Charlie was struggling to look up words in the dictionary and learning how to use punctuation. Now he is so much smarter than other people that they cannot understand him.*

◆ **Reading Strategy**

5 Summarize Ask students to summarize Charlie's impressions of Dr. Nemur and Dr. Strauss. *Charlie thinks that Dr. Nemur, while intelligent, would like to be a genius and feels insecure. Charlie thinks Dr. Strauss is a genius but has had too limiting an education.*

◆ **Critical Thinking**

6 Speculate Why is it important to Charlie that Dr. Nemur and Dr. Strauss know what Rahajamati is writing about their experiment? *Since the Indian scientist is attacking the method and results of the experiment, he may have discovered an error in the process that Dr. Nemur and Dr. Strauss have missed. If there is a mistake, it affects Charlie as well as the scientists' careers.*

Customize for
Intrapersonal Learners
Point out that several times on this page Charlie mentions his concern that people cannot understand him or that they may make fun of him. Have students review these statements. Then have each pretend to be a psychologist writing a progress report on Charlie's emotional condition.

Speaking and Listening Mini-Lesson

Dramatization
This mini-lesson supports the Speaking and Listening activity on p. 227.

Introduce Show the class a drama script as an example of how dialogue and stage directions are written. Ask students to form groups and discuss how they imagine some of the scenes they have read.

Develop Each group will choose an episode from the story to dramatize. Suggest that they choose one that tells a main point about Charlie's experience.

Apply Students in each group write out the dialogue and stage directions, select roles, rehearse, and perform the scene.

Assess Ask the class to tell each group what they liked about the performance. Evaluate students' work based on the writing of their script and effectiveness of preparation. Have students use the Peer Assessment: Dramatic Performance form, p. 116, in **Alternative Assessment.**

◆ Critical Thinking

1 Assess Ask students if they think Charlie will be able to talk with Miss Kinnian better if he reviews Vrostadt's equations. Why or why not? *Students may say that reviewing the equations will not help Charlie communicate. He is so intelligent that he thinks differently from other people now.*

◆ Literary Focus

2 First-Person Point of View Point out that Charlie writes several paragraphs describing this scene. Ask students what they think is going to happen. *Students may say that the boy may be mentally disabled, and Charlie will recognize his former self.*

▶ Critical Viewing ◀

3 Analyze *Charlie's posture and expression indicate intelligence. He looks like he is thinking about something important. The lab equipment and the assistant show he is doing serious scientific work.*

Customize for
Musical/Rhythmic Learners

If you have access to a tape or CD player, invite students to choose a piece of music that Charlie might have listened to alone in his room at Mrs. Flynn's boarding house. Ask students to play the music for the class, then explain why they think Charlie would have enjoyed it.

▲ **Critical Viewing**
Which details in the photograph reveal that Charlie has increased intelligence? **[Analyze]**

laughed. I guess I got angry, but I suspect I'm approaching her on the wrong level. No matter what I try to discuss with her, I am unable to communicate. I must review Vrostadt's equations on *Levels of Semantic Progression.* I find that I don't communicate with people much any more. Thank God for books and music and things I can think about. I am alone in my apartment at Mrs. Flynn's boarding house most of the time and seldom speak to anyone.

May 20 I would not have noticed the new dishwasher, a boy of about sixteen, at the corner diner where I take my evening meals if not for the incident of the broken dishes.

They crashed to the floor, shattering and sending bits of white china under the tables.

The boy stood there, dazed and frightened, holding the empty tray in his hand. The whistles and catcalls from the customers (the cries of "hey, there go the profits!" . . . "*Mazeltov!*" . . . and "well, *he* didn't work here very long . . ." which invariably seems to follow the breaking of glass or dishware in a public restaurant) all seemed to confuse him.

When the owner came to see what the excitement was about, the boy cowered as if he expected to be struck and threw up his arms as if to ward off the blow.

"All right! All right, you dope," shouted the owner, "don't just stand there! Get the broom and sweep that mess up. A broom . . . a broom, you idiot! It's in the kitchen. Sweep up all the pieces."

The boy saw that he was not going to be punished. His frightened expression disappeared and he smiled and hummed as he came back with the broom to sweep the floor. A few of the rowdier customers kept up the remarks, amusing themselves at his expense.

"Here, sonny, over here there's a nice piece behind you . . ."

"C'mon, do it again . . ."

"He's not so dumb. It's easier to break 'em than to wash 'em . . ."

As his vacant eyes moved across the crowd of amused onlookers, he slowly mirrored their smiles and finally broke into an uncertain

218 ◆ *Meeting Challenges*

Humanities: Film

Film Portrayals Ask students to look back at each of the photographs that accompany the story. Discuss what they notice about the progression of movie stills, eliciting Charlie has changed during the course of the movie. Have students identify ways that the actor looks different with each step in Charlie's development, such as facial expressions, ways of holding his body, ways of dressing. Encourage students to describe how these acting and costuming techniques portray the character's changes. Ask students whether the changes reflect their own images

that they have from reading the text. Do the actor's portrayals seem to fit the author's descriptions?

Invite a drama teacher, director, or actor to visit the classroom to talk about or demonstrate how an actor prepares for and performs a part like this. Ask students to brainstorm for a list of questions in advance to ask the speaker after he or she finishes talking.

Have students form groups and try some of the acting techniques in role-play activities based on scenes from the story.

grin at the joke which he obviously did not understand.

I felt sick inside as I looked at his dull, vacuous smile, the wide, bright eyes of a child, uncertain but eager to please. They were laughing at him because he was mentally retarded.

And I had been laughing at him too.

4 Suddenly, I was furious at myself and all those who were smirking at him. I jumped up and shouted, "Shut up! Leave him alone! It's not his fault he can't understand! He can't help what he is! But . . . he's still a human being!"

The room grew silent. I cursed myself for losing control and creating a scene. I tried not to look at the boy as I paid my check and walked out without touching my food. I felt ashamed for both of us.

5 How strange it is that people of honest feelings and sensibility, who would not take advantage of a man born without arms or legs or eyes—how such people think nothing of abusing a man born with low intelligence. It infuriated me to think that not too long ago I, like this boy, had foolishly played the clown.

And I had almost forgotten.

I'd hidden the picture of the old Charlie Gordon from myself because now that I was intelligent it was something that had to be pushed out of my mind. But today in looking at that boy, for the first time I saw what I had been. *I was just like him!*

Only a short time ago, I learned that people laughed at me. Now I can see that unknowingly I joined with them in laughing at myself. That hurts most of all.

I have often reread my progress reports and seen the <u>illiteracy</u>, the childish naïvete,[10] the mind of low intelligence peering from a dark room, through the keyhole, at the dazzling light outside. I see that even in my dullness I knew that I was inferior, and that other people had something I lacked—something denied

me. In my mental blindness, I thought that it was somehow connected with the ability to read and write, and I was sure that if I could get those skills I would automatically have intelligence too.

Even a feeble-minded man wants to be like other men.

A child may not know how to feed itself, or what to eat, yet it knows of hunger.

This then is what I was like. I never knew. Even with my gift of intellectual awareness, I never really knew.

This day was good for me. Seeing the past more clearly, I have decided to use my knowledge and skills to work in the field of increasing human intelligence levels. Who is better equipped for this work? Who else has lived in both worlds? These are my people. Let me use my gift to do something for them.

Tomorrow, I will discuss with Dr. Strauss the manner in which I can work in this area. I may be able to help him work out the problems of widespread use of the technique which **6** was used on me. I have several good ideas of my own.

There is so much that might be done with this technique. If I could be made into a genius, what about thousands of others like myself? What fantastic levels might be achieved by using this technique on normal people? On *geniuses*?

There are so many doors to open. I am impatient to begin.

PROGRESS REPORT 13

May 23 It happened today. Algernon bit me. I visited the lab to see him as I do occasionally, and when I took him out of his cage, he snapped at my hand. I put him back and watched him for a while. He was unusually disturbed and vicious.

◆ **Build Vocabulary**

illiteracy (il lit´ ər ə sē) *n.*: Inability to read or write

---

10. **naïvete** (nä ēv tā´) *n.*: Simplicity.

Flowers for Algernon ◆ 219

◆ Critical Thinking

❶ Infer What does it mean to Charlie if Algernon changes? Why? *Since Algernon had the operation before Charlie did, whatever happens to Algernon as a result may also happen to Charlie.*

◆ Literary Focus

❷ First-Person Point of View Why does Charlie say that time is suddenly very important to him? *He is aware that he may soon lose his intelligence, as Algernon apparently has. Charlie believes he is the only person who can find a solution to this problem, if one exists.*

◆ Critical Thinking

❸ Analyze What does Charlie mean by saying that studying intelligence is the problem he has been concerned with all his life? *Before the operation, Charlie always tried hard to improve his reading and writing skills, hoping this ability would make him smarter and more like other people. Now he is working hard to hold onto his intelligence, which he is aware he may lose.*

◆ Critical Thinking

❹ Interpret Based on Charlie's letter, what conclusion do you think he makes in his report? Why? *Since Charlie refers to a failed experiment, students may predict that the report concludes he will regress as Algernon has.*

Customize for
Interpersonal Learners
Have students meet in groups to discuss how Dr. Nemur and Dr. Strauss may be reacting to the change in Algernon. Students can brainstorm to come up with ideas, then write a conversation between the two doctors.

---

❶ May 24 Burt, who is in charge of the experimental animals, tells me that Algernon is changing. He is less cooperative; he refuses to run the maze any more; general motivation has decreased. And he hasn't been eating. Everyone is upset about what this may mean.

May 25 They've been feeding Algernon, who now refuses to work the shifting-lock problem. Everyone identifies me with Algernon. In a way we're both the first of our kind. They're all pretending that Algernon's behavior is not necessarily significant for me. But it's hard to hide the fact that some of the other animals who were used in this experiment are showing strange behavior.

Dr. Strauss and Dr. Nemur have asked me not to come to the lab any more. I know what they're thinking but I can't accept it. I am going ahead with my plans to carry their research forward. With all due respect to both of these fine scientists, I am well aware of their **❷** limitations. If there is an answer, I'll have to find it out for myself. Suddenly, time has become very important to me.

May 29 I have been given a lab of my own and permission to go ahead with the research. I'm on to something. Working day and night. I've had a cot moved into the lab. Most of my writing time is spent on the notes which I keep in a separate folder, but from time to time I feel it necessary to put down my moods and my thoughts out of sheer habit.

❸ I find the *calculus of intelligence* to be a fascinating study. Here is the place for the

◆ Build Vocabulary

obscure (əb skyoor´) *v.:* Conceal or hide

syndromes (sin´ drōmz´) *n.:* A number of symptoms occurring together and characterizing a specific disease or condition

introspective (in´ trō spekt´ iv) *adj.:* Inward looking; thoughtful

220 ◆ Meeting Challenges

---

application of all the knowledge I have acquired. In a sense it's the problem I've been **❸** concerned with all my life.

May 31 Dr. Strauss thinks I'm working too hard. Dr. Nemur says I'm trying to cram a lifetime of research and thought into a few weeks. I know I should rest, but I'm driven on by something inside that won't let me stop. I've got to find the reason for the sharp regression in Algernon. I've got to know *if* and *when* it will happen to me.

June 4

LETTER TO DR. STRAUSS (*copy*)
Dear Dr. Strauss:
Under separate cover I am sending you a copy of my report entitled, "The Algernon-Gordon Effect: A Study of Structure and Function of Increased Intelligence," which I would like to have you read and have published.

As you see, my experiments are completed. I have included in my report all of my formulae, as well as mathematical analysis in the appendix. Of course, these should be verified.

Because of its importance to both you and Dr. Nemur (and need I say to myself, too?) I have checked and rechecked my results a dozen times in the hope of finding an error. I **❹** am sorry to say the results must stand. Yet for the sake of science, I am grateful for the little bit that I here add to the knowledge of the function of the human mind and of the laws governing the artificial increase of human intelligence.

I recall your once saying to me that an experimental *failure* or the *disproving* of a theory was as important to the advancement of learning as a success would be. I know now that this is true. I am sorry, however, that my own contribution to the field must rest upon the ashes of the work of two men I regard so highly.

Yours truly,
Charles Gordon

encl.: rept.

Beyond the Classroom

Career Connection
Laboratory Assistant In "Flowers for Algernon," Burt works as a laboratory assistant for Dr. Nemur and Dr. Strauss. Burt takes care of the experimental animals and gives them tests, such as having Algernon run through a maze. He also tests Charlie as part of the experiment.

Students who enjoy science may be interested in learning about this kind of job. Often college students studying science may work as lab assistants. They may help a professor by setting up lab experiments for science courses. Assistants in a research lab may help set up experiments, run tests, or do whatever tasks the scientists train them to do. Being a lab assistant is a good way for students to find out if they want to have a career as a research scientist.

Ask students to brainstorm for a list of skills that a lab assistant needs to have, such as attention to detail, ability to follow directions, patience in dealing with animals, ability to get along with others. Write their ideas on the board.

June 5 I must not become emotional. The facts and the results of my experiments are clear, and the more sensational aspects of my own rapid climb cannot obscure the fact that the tripling of intelligence by the surgical technique developed by Drs. Strauss and Nemur must be viewed as having little or no practical applicability (at the present time) to the increase of human intelligence.

As I review the records and data on Algernon, I see that although he is still in his physical infancy, he has regressed mentally. Motor activity[11] is impaired; there is a general reduction of glandular activity; there is an accelerated loss of coordination.

There are also strong indications of progressive amnesia.

As will be seen by my report, these and other physical and mental deterioration syndromes can be predicted with statistically significant results by the application of my formula.

The surgical stimulus to which we were both subjected has resulted in an intensification and acceleration of all mental processes. The unforeseen development, which I have taken the liberty of calling the "Algernon-Gordon Effect," is the logical extension of the entire intelligence speedup. The hypothesis here proven may be described simply in the following terms: Artificially increased intelligence deteriorates at a rate of time directly proportional to the quantity of the increase.

I feel that this, in itself, is an important discovery.

As long as I am able to write, I will continue to record my thoughts in these progress reports. It is one of my few pleasures. However, by all indications, my own mental deterioration will be very rapid.

> **◆ Reading Strategy**
> How would you summarize this paragraph?

---

11. **motor activity:** Movement; physical coordination.

I have already begun to notice signs of emotional instability and forgetfulness, the first symptoms of the burnout.

June 10 Deterioration progressing. I have become absent-minded. Algernon died two days ago. Dissection shows my predictions were right. His brain had decreased in weight and there was a general smoothing out of cerebral convolutions as well as a deepening and broadening of brain fissures.

I guess the same thing is or will soon be happening to me. Now that it's definite, I don't want it to happen.

I put Algernon's body in a cheese box and buried him in the back yard. I cried.

June 15 Dr. Strauss came to see me again. I wouldn't open the door and I told him to go away. I want to be left to myself. I have become touchy and irritable. I feel the darkness closing in. I keep telling myself how important this introspective journal will be.

It's a strange sensation to pick up a book that you've read and enjoyed just a few months ago and discover that you don't remember it. I remembered how great I thought John Milton[12] was, but when I picked up *Paradise Lost* I couldn't understand it at all. I got so angry I threw the book across the room.

I've got to try to hold on to some of it. Some of the things I've learned. Oh, God, please don't take it all away.

June 19 Sometimes, at night, I go out for a walk. Last night I couldn't remember where I lived. A policeman took me home. I have the strange feeling that this has all happened to me before—a long time ago. I keep telling myself I'm the only person in the world who can describe what's happening to me.

---

12. **John Milton:** British poet (1608–1674) who wrote *Paradise Lost*.

Flowers for Algernon ◆ 221

◆ Literary Focus

❺ First-Person Point of View
Why does Charlie tell himself not to become "emotional"? *Faced with the evidence that the experiment has failed, he is telling himself to stay calm.*

◆ Reading Strategy

❻ Summarize *Students may say that, as a result of the operation, the subjects' intelligence levels go down as dramatically and quickly as they went up.*

◆ Critical Thinking

❼ Speculate If Charlie is experiencing signs of deterioration similar to Algernon's, what else is likely to happen to him? *He may soon die, as Algernon did.*

◆ Critical Thinking

❽ Connect How does Charlie's reference to the "darkness closing in" connect to his description of his former self on page 219? *Students may say that he describes his former self as being in a dark room looking out at the light. Now he can feel the darkness returning.*

🎵 Humanities: Literature

Paradise Lost by John Milton
John Milton (1608–1674) was an English poet and writer with interests in both politics and religion. *Paradise Lost* is a long poem in twelve sections that tells the Christian story of the first humans, Adam and Eve. The poem includes the origin of Satan as God's opponent, an account of how the world was created, and the narrative of how Adam and Eve were forced to leave the paradise in which they first lived.

Milton became blind in 1652 and wrote his major long works despite this disability. The lines of the poem are unrhymed. At the beginning of *Paradise Lost*, Milton includes a note that rejects rhyme as a necessary part of poetry and declares that it can hinder expression.

Discuss why Keyes may have had Charlie reading *Paradise Lost*. Help students recognize the connection between this book and the reason Fanny gave for Charlie's change being "not right."

June 21 Why can't I remember? I've got to fight. I lie in bed for days and I don't know who or where I am. Then it all comes back to me in a flash. Fugues of amnesia.[13] Symptoms of senility—second childhood. I can watch them coming on. It's so cruelly logical. I learned so much and so fast. Now my mind is deteriorating rapidly. I won't let it happen. I'll fight it. I can't help thinking of the boy in the restaurant, the blank expression, the silly smile, the people laughing at him. No—please—not that again . . .

June 22 I'm forgetting things that I learned recently. It seems to be following the classic pattern—the last things learned are the first things forgotten. Or is that the pattern? I'd better look it up again . . .

I reread my paper on the "Algernon-Gordon Effect" and I get the strange feeling that it was written by someone else. There are parts I don't even understand.

Motor activity impaired. I keep tripping over things, and it becomes increasingly difficult to type.

June 23 I've given up using the typewriter completely. My coordination is bad. I feel that I'm moving slower and slower. Had a terrible shock today. I picked up a copy of an article I used in my research, Krueger's "Uber psychische Ganzheit," to see if it would help me understand what I had done. First I thought there was something wrong with my eyes. Then I realized I could no longer read German. I tested myself in other languages. All gone.

June 30 A week since I dared to write again. It's slipping away like sand through my fingers. Most of the books I have are too hard for me now. I get angry with them because I know that I read and understood them just a few weeks ago.

---

13. **Fugues** (fyoogz) **of amnesia** (am ne′ zhe): Periods of loss of memory.

222 ◆ *Meeting Challenges*

I keep telling myself I must keep writing these reports so that somebody will know what is happening to me. But it gets harder to form the words and remember spellings. I have to look up even simple words in the dictionary now and it makes me impatient with myself.

Dr. Strauss comes around almost every day, but I told him I wouldn't see or speak to anybody. He feels guilty. They all do. But I don't blame anyone. I knew what might happen. But how it hurts.

July 7 I don't know where the week went. Todays Sunday I know because I can see through my window people going to church. I think I stayed in bed all week but I remember Mrs. Flynn bringing food to me a few times. I keep saying over and over Ive got to do something but then I forget or maybe its just easier not to do what I say Im going to do.

I think of my mother and father a lot these days. I found a picture of them with me taken at a beach. My father has a big ball under his arm and my mother is holding me by the hand. I dont remember them the way they are in the picture. All I remember is my father arguing with mom about money.

He never shaved much and he used to scratch my face when he hugged me. He said he was going to take me to see cows on a farm once but he never did. He never kept his promises . . .

July 10 My landlady Mrs Flynn is very worried about me. She said she doesnt like loafers. If Im sick its one thing, but if Im a loafer thats another thing and she wont have it. I told her I think Im sick.

I try to read a little bit every day, mostly stories, but sometimes I have to read the same thing over and over again because I dont know what it means. And its hard to write. I know I should look up all the words in the dictionary but its so hard and Im so tired all the time.

Cross-Curricular Connection: Science

Psychiatric Terms In psychiatry, a fugue of amnesia is a period during which a person suffers a loss of memory and may begin a new life. When he or she recovers, the person remembers nothing of the period of amnesia. A state of amnesia may be the result of a serious head injury or a severe shock. Amnesia is a normal condition during infancy because the brain has not yet developed the ability to hold on to messages in the order that they occurred. That is why most people don't remember anything about being a baby.

The medical term for what Charlie calls senility is dementia. This describes symptoms that show a person's deterioration from his or her previous level of functioning. Dementia impairs memory, language, judgment, spatial perception, behavior, and personality. Older people suffer from dementia more often than younger people, because it may be caused by Alzheimer's disease or a stroke. Since the symptoms may make the patient seem childlike, sometimes the person is said to be going through a second childhood.

Critical Viewing

❺ Charlie's boss says "Charlie Gordon, you got guts." How does this scene illustrate his comment? [Support]

◆ **Critical Thinking**

❻ **Infer** Ask students why they think Charlie puts flowers on Algernon's grave. *Students may say that Charlie feels a connection with Algernon and this is his way of showing that the mouse has not been forgotten. It may also be Charlie's way of hoping that he himself won't be forgotten.*

◆ **Literary Focus**

❼ **First-Person Point of View** Ask students to give reasons why Charlie will accept help from Mrs. Flynn when he has refused to see Dr. Strauss. *Students may say that Charlie has known Mrs. Flynn longer. He may feel more comfortable with her since she was not connected with the experiment. She is apparently a compassionate woman who helps Charlie with the necessities of life.*

Then I got the idea that I would only use the easy words instead of the long hard ones. That saves time. I put flowers on Algernons grave about once a week. Mrs. Flynn thinks Im crazy to put flowers on a mouses grave but I told her that Algernon was special. ❻

July 14 Its sunday again. I dont have anything to do to keep me busy now because my television set is broke and I dont have any money to get it fixed. (I think I lost this months check from the lab. I dont remember)

I get awful headaches and asperin doesnt help me much. Mrs. Flynn knows Im really sick and she feels very sorry for me. Shes a wonderful woman whenever someone is sick.

July 22 Mrs. Flynn called a strange doctor to see me. She was afraid I was going to die. I told the doctor I wasnt too sick and that I only forget sometimes. He asked me did I have any friends or relatives and I said no I dont have ❼

Flowers for Algernon ◆ 223

 Humanities: Film

Movie Stills Remind students that each photographic illustration with this story comes from a scene in the movie version of "Flowers for Algernon." These excerpts from the film adaptation of the story are referred to as movie stills (because the pictures aren't moving). Have students look at these movie stills in the order they appear in the story. Encourage them to review the progress reports they accompany. Then discuss the following questions:

1. In which still does Charlie look happiest?
2. In which still does Charlie show the beginnings of change?
3. In which still can you see Charlie at the height of his intelligence?
4. What impression do you have of Charlie based on the photograph on this page?

After students formulate responses to the questions, have them summarize Charlie's experience by writing captions for each movie still.

◆ LITERATURE AND YOUR LIFE

1 Encourage students to discuss how Charlie's fear of being laughed at is a theme throughout the story. When does he first begin to show this fear? How has his reaction to people's cruelty changed as he has changed? *Students may note that he first showed this fear when he became smart enough to realize that his co-workers were laughing at him. He remains sensitive, even thinking Dr. Strauss is making fun of him when he tells Charlie that Dr. Nemur feels inferior to him. Finally he defends the dishwasher. Now he still has enough awareness to know when people are making fun of him, and it makes him angry.*

◆ Critical Thinking

2 Analyze Why does Miss Kinnian respond to Charlie in this way? *She cares for Charlie and is sad at what has happened; she may feel guilty for having encouraged him to have the operation and feel responsible for his experience.*

◆ Literary Focus

3 First-Person Point of View Is Charlie's view of his co-workers accurate? Why or why not? *Students may say that Charlie is right to remind himself that his co-workers are not so smart; others may agree with Charlie that the co-workers really are his friends, even if they did laugh at him; others may say that if people make fun of someone, they are not true friends.*

◆ LITERATURE AND YOUR LIFE

4 Ask students if they think Joe and Frank are Charlie's friends. *Students may say they are, since they seem to realize what Charlie has gone through.*

◆ Literary Focus

5 First-Person Point of View How does this report show Charlie's return to his former personality? *Charlie is less sensitive to being laughed at; he can admit he made a mistake.*

Customize for
Verbal/Linguistic Learners

Ask students to think about what might happen to Charlie next. Have them write their own endings using information from the story. Remind them that this is science fiction, so they are free to bring in new "scientific" information in their endings.

---

any. I told him I had a friend called Algernon once but he was a mouse and we used to run races together. He looked at me kind of funny like he thought I was crazy.

He smiled when I told him I used to be a genius. He talked to me like I was a baby and he winked at Mrs Flynn. I got mad and chased him out because he was making fun of me the way they all used to.

July 24 I have no more money and Mrs Flynn says I got to go to work somewhere and pay the rent because I havent paid for over two months. I dont know any work but the job I used to have at Donnegans Plastic Box Company. I dont want to go back there because they all knew me when I was smart and maybe they'll laugh at me. But I dont know what else to do to get money.

July 25 I was looking at some of my old progress reports and its very funny but I cant read what I wrote. I can make out some of the words but they dont make sense.

Miss Kinnian came to the door but I said go away I dont want to see you. She cried and I cried too but I wouldnt let her in because I didnt want her to laugh at me. I told her I didn't like her any more. I told her I didn't want to be smart any more. Thats not true. I still love her and I still want to be smart but I had to say that so shed go away. She gave Mrs. Flynn money to pay the rent. I dont want that. I got to get a job.

Please . . . please let me not forget how to read and write . . .

July 27 Mr. Donnegan was very nice when I came back and asked him for my old job of janitor. First he was very suspicious but I told him what happened to me then he looked very sad and put his hand on my shoulder and said Charlie Gordon you got guts.

Everybody looked at me when I came downstairs and started working in the toilet sweeping it out like I used to. I told myself Charlie if they make fun of you dont get sore because

you remember their not so smart as you once thot they were. And besides they were once your friends and if they laughed at you that doesnt mean anything because they liked you too.

One of the new men who came to work there after I went away made a nasty crack he said hey Charlie I hear your a very smart fella a real quiz kid. Say something intelligent. I felt bad but Joe Carp came over and grabbed him by the shirt and said leave him alone or Ill break your neck. I didnt expect Joe to take my part so I guess hes really my friend.

Later Frank Reilly came over and said Charlie if anybody bothers you or trys to take advantage you call me or Joe and we will set em straight. I said thanks Frank and I got choked up so I had to turn around and go into the supply room so he wouldnt see me cry. Its good to have friends.

July 28 I did a dumb thing today I forgot I wasnt in Miss Kinnians class at the adult center any more like I use to be. I went in and sat down in my old seat in the back of the room and she looked at me funny and she said Charles. I dint remember she ever called me that before only Charlie so I said hello Miss Kinnian Im ready for my lesin today only I lost my reader that we was using. She startid to cry and run out of the room and everybody looked at me and I saw they wasnt the same pepul who use to be in my class.

Then all of a suddin I rememberd some things about the operashun and me getting smart and I said holy smoke I reely pulled a Charlie Gordon that time. I went away before she come back to the room.

Thats why Im going away from New York for good. I dont want to do nothing like that agen. I dont want Miss Kinnian to feel sorry for me. Evry body feels sorry at the factery and I dont want that eather so Im going someplace where nobody knows that Charlie Gordon was once a genus and now he cant even reed a book or rite good.

224 ◆ Meeting Challenges

Viewing and Representing Mini-Lesson

Timeline Project
In this mini-lesson students will extend their understanding of Charlie's experience by charting his changes over time.

Introduce Ask students to look back at the beginning of the story to see at what date Charlie begins his progress reports. Then have them check this page to see when he makes his last entry. They will see that the whole story takes place in less than five months.

Develop Have students work in groups to list

the most important events in Charlie's story. Then ask them to brainstorm ways to visually represent the events. For example, they might draw pictures of Charlie climbing one flight of stairs and then going down another.

Apply Let each group work cooperatively to create their timeline projects and present them to the class.

Assess Evaluate students on their grasp of key events, the originality of the projects, and their presentations to the class.

Im taking a cuple of books along and even if I cant reed them Ill practise hard and maybe I wont forget every thing I lerned. If I try reel hard maybe Ill be a littel bit smarter then I was before the operashun. I got my rabits foot and my luky penny and maybe they will help me.

If you ever reed this Miss Kinnian dont be sorry for me Im glad I got a second chanse to be smart becaus I lerned a lot of things that I never even new were in this world and Im grateful that I saw it all for a littel bit. I dont know why Im dumb agen or what I did wrong maybe its becaus I dint try hard enuff. But if I try and practis very hard maybe Ill get a littl smarter and know what all the words are. I remember a littel bit how nice I had a feeling with the blue book that has the torn cover

when I red it. Thats why Im gonna keep trying to get smart so I can have that feeling agen. Its a good feeling to know things and be smart. I wish I had it rite now if I did I woud sit down and reed all the time. Anyway I bet Im the first dumb person in the world who ever found out somthing importent for sience. I remember I did somthing but I dont remember what. So I gess its like I did it for all the dumb pepul like me.

Goodbye Miss Kinnian and Dr Strauss and evreybody. And P.S. please tell Dr Nemur not to be such a grouch when pepul laff at him and he woud have more frends. Its easy to make frends if you let pepul laff at you. Im going to have lots of frends where I go.

P.P.S. Please if you get a chanse put some flowrs on Algernons grave in the bak yard . . .

Guide for Responding

◆ LITERATURE AND YOUR LIFE

Reader's Response Was being part of the experiment good for Charlie? Explain.

Thematic Focus What difficult questions does Charlie face in this story?

☑ Check Your Comprehension

1. Why is Charlie keeping a journal?
2. Why does Miss Kinnian believe that Charlie should take part in this experiment?
3. (a) Why does Charlie believe he failed the Rorschach test? (b) What does he come to learn about the Rorschach test?
4. (a) How do Charlie's co-workers treat him after he becomes smart? (b) Why does Charlie leave his job?
5. Why does Charlie decide to leave New York?

◆ Critical Thinking

INTERPRET
1. Explain how Charlie's development parallels Algernon's. **[Compare and Contrast]**
2. How do the spelling, punctuation, and grammar in Charlie's reports contribute to your view of his progress? **[Infer]**
3. How is Charlie at the end of the story different from the way he was at the beginning? **[Compare and Contrast]**

EVALUATE
4. Do you think that Charlie was a good subject for this experiment? Explain. **[Make a Judgment]**

APPLY
5. As Charlie grows smarter, he asks questions. Explain why the ability to ask questions is an important part of intelligence. **[Apply]**

Flowers for Algernon ◆ 225

Beyond the Selection

FURTHER READING
Other Works by Daniel Keyes
Flowers for Algernon (novel version)
The Touch
The Fifth Sally
Other Related Science Fiction Works
The Island of Dr. Moreau by H. G. Wells
The Invisible Man by H. G. Wells
Dr. Jekyll and Mr. Hyde by Robert Louis Stevenson

INTERNET
We suggest the following sites on the Internet (all Web sites are subject to change).
For "Flowers for Algernon" and Daniel Keyes:
http://in.flite.net/~dkeyes/index.html
For additional information about science fiction:
http://www.scifi.com
We *strongly recommend* that you preview these sites before you send students to them.

◆ Reading Strategy

1. Students should briefly describe Charlie's experience taking the Rorschach Test.
2. Summaries should outline the experiment and its initial outcome, with hints of further development.

◆ Build Vocabulary

Using the Root Word -psych

1. a method for investigating mental and emotional processes
2. sensitive to mental, nonphysical forces
3. a person who treats mental or emotional problems

Spelling Strategy

1. pseudonym; chaos
2. chorus; psychology

Using the Word Bank

1. psychology
2. specter
3. tangible
4. refute
5. obscure
6. introspective
7. illiteracy
8. syndromes

◆ Literary Focus

1. Charlie's writing clearly shows his openness, his eagerness to learn, and his frustration with his own performance.
2. He becomes smarter until he is a genius, then he loses his intelligence again.
3. Using Charlie as the narrator allows the reader to experience the experiment directly and emotionally.

◆ Build Grammar Skills

Practice

1. have started (present perfect)
2. has ended (present perfect)
3. will have published (future perfect)
4. had arrived (past perfect)
5. has taught (present perfect)

Writing Application

Check that students have used the verb improve in the present perfect, past perfect, and future perfect tenses.

Guide for Responding (continued)

◆ Reading Strategy

SUMMARIZE

When you **summarize,** you restate key ideas and details in your own words. An effective written summary is brief and omits less significant details.
1. Summarize the progress report of March 6.
2. Write a summary of "Flowers for Algernon" to put on a book jacket.

◆ Build Vocabulary

USING THE WORD ROOT -psych-

When used in English words, the word root -psych- usually refers to the mind. Speculate about the meaning of each word below. Then, use a dictionary to check your definitions.
1. psychoanalysis   **2.** psychic   **3.** psychotherapist

SPELLING STRATEGY

In -psych-, the s sound is spelled ps and the k sound is spelled ch. Identify the words in these sentences that follow one of the two rules.
1. She used a pseudonym on her essay about chaos.
2. The chorus sang at the psychology convention.

USING THE WORD BANK

Write the word from the Word Bank that best completes each sentence. Use each word only once.
1. The doctor taught a _____?_____ course about common mental disorders.
2. In one case study, a man was haunted by the _____?_____ of growing older.
3. The doctor achieved concrete, _____?_____ results using psychotherapy.
4. No one could _____?_____ the success of the treatment.
5. No longer would rivals describe his studies and experiments as being _____?_____.
6. Another case was about a quiet, thoughtful _____?_____ woman.
7. She was troubled by her _____?_____, or inability to read and write.
8. Her condition did not exactly match any of the mental _____?_____ described in the textbooks.

◆ Literary Focus

FIRST-PERSON POINT OF VIEW

"Flowers for Algernon" is told from the **first-person point of view.** Charlie, the story's main character, serves as narrator. What you learn about people and events in the story is filtered through Charlie's eyes and mind.
1. What do you learn about Charlie's personality through his writing?
2. How does Charlie's condition change as the story progresses?
3. Why did Keyes use a first-person narrator rather than one who is not a story character?

◆ Build Grammar Skills

VERBS: PERFECT TENSES

In addition to the simple present, past, and future tenses, verbs have **perfect tenses.** Perfect verb tenses use have, has, or had with the past participle.

The **present perfect** tense shows an action that began in the past and continues into the present:

They *have wondered* about it for centuries.

The **past perfect** tense shows a past action that ended before another past action began:

The show *had ended* before we arrived.

The **future perfect** shows a future action that will have ended before another begins. This tense uses the helping verbs will have:

In ten years, they *will have finished* their work.

Practice Classify the verbs in each sentence as present perfect, past perfect, or future perfect:
1. We have started the experiment.
2. Last week's experiment has ended.
3. By next year, the scientists will have published the results.
4. Our publication had arrived before the experiment began.
5. It has taught readers throughout the world.

Writing Application Write a paragraph about the story, using the present perfect, past perfect, and future perfect tenses of the verb *improve*.

✎ Writer's Solution

For additional instruction and practice, use the Using Verbs pages, pp. 70–76, in *Writer's Solution Grammar Practice Handbook.*

Build Your Portfolio

 ## Idea Bank

Writing

1. **Award Plaque** Create an award plaque for Charlie Gordon, honoring his contribution to science. Explain why he deserves to be remembered.

2. **Explanation** Write an essay explaining whether or not "Flowers for Algernon" is an appropriate and effective title.

3. **Journal Article** Imagine that you are Dr. Strauss or Dr. Nemur. Write an article about the experiment with Charlie. Describe the predicted and the actual outcomes, as well as what you have learned.

Speaking and Listening

4. **Dramatization [Group Activity]** Work with a group to dramatize a scene from the story. Develop dialogue and stage directions for your scene. Assign roles, rehearse, and perform your scene for the class. **[Performing Arts Link]**

5. **Debate** Hold a class debate on the topic of using IQ tests to measure intelligence. Choose teams for and against the topic. In your arguments, use specific details and support your generalizations. Present your arguments in front of a panel of student judges. **[Science Link]**

Projects

6. **Research Report** Use reference sources to find out about intelligence and how it is measured. Share your findings with the class, and talk about Charlie's intellectual growth and decline throughout the story. **[Science Link]**

7. **Audiovisual Interviews** Work with a partner and "hold" three interviews with Charlie. Choose three specific dates in the story on which a reporter might have interviewed Charlie. Practice your interviews, and record them on audio- or videotape. Play the results for the class. **[Media Link]**

 ## Writing Mini-Lesson

Observation Journal

Imagine that you are Miss Kinnian, observing Charlie's progress. Write several entries in her observation journal to describe the events from her point of view.

Writing Skills Focus: Details to Support Points

As you write, support your observations with specific **details.** Choose a variety of details to help readers understand each important event, as in this passage from the story.

Model From the Story
It happened today. Algernon bit me. I visited the lab to see him as I do occasionally, and when I took him out of his cage, he snapped at my hand. I put him back and watched him for a while. He was unusually disturbed and vicious.

Prewriting Choose a specific day or period of days to write about. Review Charlie's version in his progress reports. Then, jot down ideas about how Miss Kinnian's point of view would differ.

Drafting Begin each day's entry with a day and date. Start each paragraph with a simple description of an event. Then, expand the description with specific details that Miss Kinnian might observe and find significant.

Revising Read your entries to a classmate. Look for inconsistencies in point of view, as well as unsupported details. Does each journal entry have a main point that is supported by details?

> ◆ **Grammar Application**
> Check that your verb tenses are correct. Form present perfect, past perfect, and future perfect tenses using *has, had,* or *have* and the past participle of the verb.

Flowers for Algernon ◆ 227

 ## Idea Bank

Following are suggestions for matching the Idea Bank topics with your students' performance levels and learning modalities:

Customize for *Performance Levels*
Less Advanced Students: 1, 4
Average Students: 2, 4, 5
More Advanced Students: 3, 4, 5, 6

Customize for *Learning Modalities*
Verbal/Linguistic: 2, 3, 4, 5, 6, 7
Logical/Mathematical: 6
Visual/Spatial: 1
Bodily/Kinesthetic: 4
Interpersonal: 4, 5, 7
Intrapersonal: 6
Refer students to the Writing

 ## Writing Mini-Lesson

Handbook at the back of the book for instruction on the writing process and for further information on expression.

✎ Writer's Solution

Writers at Work Videodisc
Have students view the segment in which Gish Jen talks about the way she records her experiences and observations.

Play frames 2571 to 4400

Writing Lab CD-ROM
Have students complete their Observation Journal entries by using the tutorial on Expression. Follow these steps:
1. Students can use the Interactive Writing Hints on linking format, audience, and purpose to find out more about audiences and purposes related to those formats.
2. Have students use the Sunburst Diagram activity to list details.
3. Have students draft on computer
4. Students can use the Self-Evaluation Checklist on Expression.

Writer's Solution Sourcebook
Have students use Chapter 1, "Expression," pp. 1–31, for additional support. The chapter includes in-depth instruction on gathering details.

✓ ASSESSMENT OPTIONS

Formal Assessment, Selection Test, pp. 64–66, and Assessment Resources Software. The selection test is designed so that it can easily be customized to the performance levels of your students.

Alternative Assessment, p. 18, includes options for less advanced students, more advanced students, verbal/linguistic learners, logical/mathematical learners, interpersonal learners, and visual/spatial learners.

PORTFOLIO ASSESSMENT
Use the following rubrics in the **Alternative Assessment** booklet to assess student writing:
Award Plaque: Definition/Classification, p. 95
Explanation: How To/Process Explanation, p. 96
Journal Article: Comparison/Contrast, p. 99
Writing Mini-Lesson: Description, p. 93

Establish Writing Guidelines

Review the following key characteristics of a problem-and-solution essay:

- A problem-and-solution essay focuses on a problem and offers one or more possible solutions.
- A problem-and-solution essay must be well-organized and the solution must be supported with facts and/or examples.

You may want to distribute the scoring rubric for Problem-and-Solution Essay, p. 98 in **Alternative Assessment,** to make students aware of the criteria on which they will be evaluated. See the suggestions on p. 230 for how you can customize the rubric to this workshop.

Refer students to the Writing Handbook in the back of the book for instruction on the writing process and further information on exposition.

 Writer's Solution

Writers at Work Videodisc

To introduce students to expository writing and to have them hear Bruce Brooks's ideas on exposition, play the videodisc segment on Exposition: Making Connections (Ch. 5). Have students discuss how Brooks finds writing topics.

Play frames 43069 to 51462

Writing Lab CD-ROM

If your students have access to computers, you may want to have them work in the tutorial on Exposition: Making Connections to complete all or part of their problem-and-solution essays. Follow these steps:

1. Have students view the interactive model of a problem-and-solution essay.
2. Suggest that students use the Topic Wheel of problems and people to come up with topic ideas.
3. Allow students to draft on computer.
4. Have students view the audio-annotated student model to find explanations for certain revisions.

Writer's Solution Sourcebook

Students can find additional support, including in-depth instruction on unity and coherence in paragraphs, p. 162, in the chapter on Exposition: Making Connections, pp. 134–165.

Expository Writing
Problem-and-Solution Essay

Writing Process Workshop

The selections in this part all deal with facing hard questions—when to speak up for oneself, what should be done to preserve our identities and the environment, and how far science should go in "fixing" what nature has given us. Very often the best way to face a hard question—and find an answer to it—is to set it down on paper. Write an essay that poses a problem and provides a solution to a hard question.

Use the skills in the Writing Mini-Lessons introduced in this section to help you.

Writing Skills Focus

▶ **Use an organizational strategy** that presents your problem and solution clearly. (See p. 183.)

▶ **Provide the necessary background** of your problem so all aspects of the situation are clear and the solution makes sense. (See p. 191.)

▶ Use relevant details to **support your points,** enabling your readers to see the depth of your problem and the logic of your solution. (See p. 227.)

WRITING MODEL

We were approaching bear country and needed to know what to do if we met a bear. We had a problem, though. ① Each guidebook offered different advice about bears: stay away from them altogether *or* it's okay to get close to bears as long as you don't separate the mother from its cub *or* make lots of noise near bears *or* be quiet. ② We were confused and a little scared. Our solutions seemed to be to skip the wilderness altogether or try to find a better guidebook. Then we heard a voice behind us, "Why not ask an expert?" ③ There sat the solution to our problem, a tanned and smiling park ranger. He stretched out and began, "Let me tell you about bears. . . ."

① The writer provides background information about the problem.

② These details support the statement that advice about bears was contradictory.

③ The essay is organized logically, identifying the problem first, giving possible solutions next, and then identifying the best solution.

 Beyond the Classroom

Workplace Skills

Problem-and-Solution Essays Explain to students that one of the responsibilities of a job is to propose solutions to potential or current problems. A police officer may suggest a way to keep citizens safe, an office worker may suggest a way to improve communication among co-workers, a delivery person may suggest a more efficient route. Tell students that in many cases, possible solutions are offered in memorandums, or memos, circulated to fellow workers and officials in charge. Explain that a memo is a formal but abbreviated style of letter.

Have students work in groups and choose a career field, for which they will create a problem-solution scenario. You may wish to provide professional publications to help students find ideas for topics. After students have identified a problem, encourage them to discuss the issues and possible solutions. Then guide them to outline steps for a solution. Ask them to draft written solutions to the problems as a memo. Invite volunteers to read their group's memo to the rest of the class.

Prewriting

Choose a Topic Your problem-and-solution essay might deal with a personal, local, or universal problem. For a personal topic, consider how you have mastered different situations. Look for a local topic in the editorial pages of your school and town newspapers. For a universal problem, listen to special reports on the evening news.

Make a Problem-and-Solution Diagram Create a diagram that shows the relationship between a problem and possible solutions.

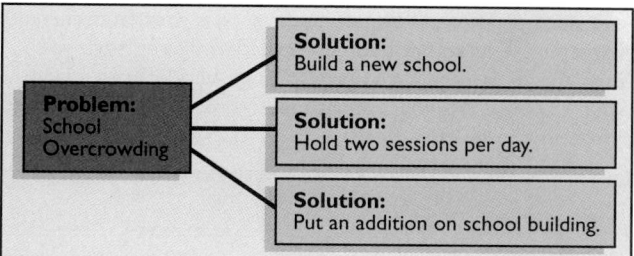

Choose an Organizational Plan Once you've gathered details for your problem-and-solution essay, decide on the best way to present them. Chronological, or time, order will be effective if your solution has many steps. Use order-of-importance organization if you're presenting several possible solutions and want to save the best for last. Use point-by-point organization if you want to discuss a problem that is complicated and has several separate solutions.

Drafting

Refer to Your Prewriting Notes and Diagrams As you draft, be sure you're on track by referring to the details you have gathered.

Begin by Providing Background Be sure your readers will be able to follow what you say by providing necessary background as you draft. You may want to place an asterisk beside words you'll need to define. When finished drafting, go back and insert definitions for those terms.

Support Your Points As you draft, include details that support the points you're making.

DRAFTING/REVISING

APPLYING LANGUAGE SKILLS: Avoiding Run-on Sentences

A run-on sentence is two or more complete sentences that are not properly joined or separated. You can correct run-on sentences by separating complete thoughts with a period (not a comma) or with a comma and conjunction such as *and, or, for, so, yet,* and *but.*

Run-on:

He hesitated a moment, he finally joined the others.

Correct:

He hesitated a moment, but he finally joined the others.

Practice On your paper, correct the run-on sentences.

1. She didn't know the way, she was determined to go on.
2. Harriet's challenge was great she had to get eleven slaves to Canada.
3. There were many dangers lurking everywhere, there were great friends along the way.

Writing Application Review your essay and correct run-on sentences.

Writer's Solution Connection Writing Lab

For help choosing a topic, use the Inspirations for Writing in the tutorial for Exposition: Making Connections.

Develop Student Writing

Prewriting

To stimulate topic ideas, hold a class discussion with students about current issues and problems in the school or local community. You may want to bring in a copy of a community newspaper and read articles from the editorial section. Encourage students to take notes on possible topic ideas.

Customize for *More Advanced Writers*

Suggest that students choose a problem-and-solution essay from a local newspaper. Have them identify the problem, and then have them offer an alternative solution to the one in the essay. Encourage them to include references to the newspaper article, and to point out why they prefer their own solution.

Drafting

Remind students that good organization is an essential part of a well-written essay. Suggest that they use chronological order to give step-by-step instructions or when describing a series of events. You may want students to use the Series of Events Chain in **Writing and Language Transparencies,** p. 57, to help them organize their essays.

Writer's Solution

Writing Lab CD-ROM
In the drafting section of the tutorial on Exposition: Making Connections, have students view audio-annotated models of introductions, bodies, and conclusions to develop strategies for writing their own drafts.

Applying Language Skills
Avoid Run-on Sentences Point out to students that run-on sentences are usually the result of carelessness and haste. Suggest that they avoid them by rereading their work, listening for the natural stops that indicate where the sentences end. It may be helpful to read aloud in order to hear the natural stops.

Answers
Possible responses:
1. She didn't know the way, yet she was determined to go on.
2. Harriet's challenge was great. She had to get eleven slaves to Canada.
3. There were many dangers lurking everywhere, but there were great friends along the way.

Writer's Solution

For additional practice and support, use the practice pages on Avoiding Run-ons, pp. 65–66, in the *Writer's Solution Grammar Practice Book.* If students have access to technology, have them use the Run-On Sentences lesson in the unit on Problems With Sentences in the *Writer's Solution Language Lab CD-ROM.*

229

Revising

Students might work with peers to revise their drafts. Reviewers can use the checklist for the writing skills focus on p. 228 to guide their review.

 Writer's Solution

Writing Lab CD-ROM

In the tutorial on Exposition: Making Connections, students can use the Revision Checker for sentence length to revise for sentence variation.

Publishing

Suggest that students submit their problem-and-solution essays to the editorial section of a newspaper.

Reinforce and Extend

Review the Writing Guidelines

After students have completed their papers, review the characteristics of a problem-and-solution essay.

Applying Language Skills

Combining Sentences Short sentences can sometimes be useful, but too many short sentences can make writing seem choppy. To preserve the strength of short sentences, they need to be set off by longer ones.

Answers

1. There were eleven fugitives who all wanted to flee north.
2. The slaves had nothing to eat and nowhere to sleep.
3. They had to reach Canada because they faced death if they were captured in the United States.

 Writer's Solution

For additional practice and support, use the practice page on Expanding Short Sentences, p. 123, in the *Writer's Solution Grammar Practice Book*.

Writing Process Workshop

EDITING / PROOFREADING

APPLYING LANGUAGE SKILLS: Combining Sentences

Combine short, choppy sentences to make your writing smooth and clear. Use connecting words and phrases such as *in order, because,* and *who* to connect your sentences.

Short Sentences: Harriet Tubman risked her life. She wanted to save many slaves.

Combined Sentence: Harriet Tubman risked her life in order to save many slaves.

Practice On your paper, combine the short sentences into a longer, more logical and fluid one. Use the word provided to combine the sentences.

1. There were eleven fugitives. They all wanted to flee north. (*who*)
2. The slaves had nothing to eat. They had nowhere to sleep. (*and*)
3. They had to reach Canada. They faced death if they were captured in the United States. (*because*)

Writing Application As you draft, combine short choppy sentences.

Writer's Solution Connection Language Lab

For more practice combining sentences, complete the Combining Sentences lesson in the Styling Sentences unit.

---

230 ◆ *Meeting Challenges*

Revising

Add Details Reread your draft critically. Add details wherever necessary to support your main points.

Do an Organization Check Read your paper critically. Circle or highlight in blue all the points that refer to the problem. Then, circle or highlight in red all the solution points. Make sure your points are all in the right places.

Use a Checklist Go back to the Writing Skills Focus on page 228, and use the items as a checklist to evaluate and revise your essay.

Do a Fact Check Have you used strong, undeniable facts and not opinions and/or assumptions? Are your facts current? For example, if you've quoted population figures, have you used the most recent census? Do your facts actually support your solution? Do you need to add more or different facts to make your essay stronger?

REVISION MODEL

① We wanted to learn about wolves in the wilderness, but we didn't want to be in any danger.
This time we went straight to the Park Service. We learned more about wolves than we ever could on our own. There was a program all about wolves as well as a guided hike.
③ It was called "Wolves: Myths and Realities," and it included a presentation about the wolves' lives. Then, we went by truck up into the mountains and hiked with the ranger near areas that wolves frequent. We saw a timber wolf.

① This sentence was added to provide necessary background.
② For better organization, this sentence was moved to the end to summarize the solution.
③ These details were added to support the main point.

Publishing and Presenting

▶ **Classroom** Share your problem-and-solution essays in class by reading them aloud.
▶ **Library** With your classmates, bind your essays together. Display a copy in your school library.
▶ **Letter** Enclose your problem-and-solution essay in a letter to a friend or relative.

Real-World Reading Skills Workshop

Challenging the Text

Strategies for Success

"All that glitters is not gold." This saying warns you to avoid accepting things at face value. This also holds true for things you read. Magazine and newspaper advertisements, political pamphlets, editorials, and even help-wanted advertisements may be deceptive in their wording. Rather than accepting everything you read as truth, challenge texts to determine whether they are unbiased and truthful.

Use Your Common Sense Give advertisements, editorials, and political pledges the reality test. Ask yourself: "Does this make sense? Have I ever heard of an offer this good or a promise so wonderful?" If the answer is no, beware.

Consider Motivation Think about why someone is paying for an ad or writing an editorial. What is it he or she is trying to accomplish? Is the writer working for your benefit or the employer's?

Look for Details Remember the first time you got a toy and expected it to do something, but all it did was lie in the box? Then, you learned it needed batteries to run. Details are like batteries—they are necessary. Make sure the details about the promise or the advertisement are included!

Check References Ask other people for their opinions about the product, candidate, or issue. Find out whether past promises or claims turned out to be true. You may also want to contact the Better Business Bureau to find out whether customers have lodged complaints about the company.

KIDS – Earn BIG BUCKS!!
Lots of money and not much work!
Choose your hours.
No experience needed.
Call Pat at 878-2367 Today!!!
Must be strong, healthy, and willing to follow directions.

Apply the Strategies

Read the advertisement above carefully. Then, answer the questions below.

1. What are the wages for this job?
2. What will you do to earn your money?
3. What is written in smaller print? Why, do you think, is it written this way?
4. What actual facts and details does this advertisement provide?
5. Using your common sense as a guide, is this a good job to have? Why or why not?

✔ Here are other situations in which challenging the text is important:
▶ Reading a campaign flyer
▶ Reading a newspaper editorial
▶ Reading a scientific report

Answers

1. The wages are identified as "Big Bucks" and "lots of money."
2. "Not much work."
3. In smaller print, "Must be strong, healthy, and willing to follow directions" appears. The words *strong* and *healthy* may mean that the job requires some kind of physical labor. "Willing to follow directions" may mean they want people who will not question authority and will do exactly as they are told.
4. Other than the name, Pat, and the phone number, there are no real facts on the advertisement. If someone applied for the job, they may be able to figure out if "Choose your hours" and "No experience needed" are true claims.
5. Most students will say there is no way to know whether this is a good job to have because there is no job description, and the job requirements of being "strong, healthy, and willing to follow directions" could apply to many types of jobs, some of which might not be good jobs to have.

Reviewing Principal Parts and Verb Tenses

The selections in Part 2 include instruction on the following:

• Principal Parts of Regular Verbs
• Verb Tenses (simple)
• Principal Parts of Irregular Verbs
• Verb Tenses: Perfect Tenses

This instruction is reinforced with the Build Grammar Skills practice pages in **Selection Support,** pp. 79, 84, 89, and 94

Writer's Solution

For additional practice and support using principal parts and verb tenses, use the Using Verbs practice pages, pp. 70–72 in the *Writer's Solution Grammar Practice Book.* If students have access to technology, they can use the Using Verbs lesson in the *Writer's Solution Writing Lab CD-ROM.*

Answers
Practice 1

1. Has she *gotten* up yet?
2. She had *run* to the North before.
3. The fugitives *sang* while fleeing.
4. The doorbell had already *rang* twice before it was answered.
5. She must have *grown* tired waiting.
6. She will be *remembered* for all time.
7. I *think* of her as a hero.

Practice 2

1. Her employer *surprised* the governess with the news.
2. The governess *remained* silent.
3. She may have *wondered* why her employer was being mean.
4. Charlie is *worried* about the tests.
5. Algernon *died* during the experiment.

Principal Parts and Verb Tenses

Grammar Review

tense (tens) *n.* any of the forms of a verb that show the time of the action or condition [The present tense of the verb "talk" is "talk" or "talks"; the past tense is "talked"; the future *tense* is "will talk."] [This word comes to us, through Old French, from Latin *tempus,* meaning "time."]

A **verb** is a word that shows action or being. Verbs have four basic forms called the **principal parts.** The principal parts are the present (or base form), the present participle, the past, and the past participle.

A regular verb forms its past and past participle by adding *-ed* or *-d* to the present form (see p. 182). Irregular verbs form their past and past participle in different ways (see p. 190).

Present	Present Participle	Past	Past Participle
walk	walking	walked	(have) walked
draw	drawing	drew	(have) drawn

Verb Tense The **tense** of a verb shows the time of the action or condition expressed by the verb. You form the verb tenses by using the principal parts and helping verbs (see p. 200).

Present:	I walk
Past:	I walked
Future:	I will walk
Present Perfect:	I have walked
Past Perfect:	I had walked
Future Perfect:	I will have walked

Practice 1 For each of the following sentences, choose the correct verb from the choices in parentheses and write it on your paper.

1. Has she (got, gotten) up yet?
2. She had (run, ran) to the North before.
3. The fugitives (sang, sung) while fleeing.
4. The doorbell had already (rung, rang) twice before it was answered.
5. She must have (grown, grew) tired waiting.
6. She will be (remember, remembered) for all time.
7. I have always (thought, think) of her as a hero.

Practice 2 On your paper, write the required form of the verb in parentheses for the following sentences.

1. Her employer (surprise, past) the governess with the news.
2. The governess (remain, past) silent.
3. She may have (wonder, past participle) why her employer was being mean.
4. Charlie is (worry, present participle) about the tests.
5. Algernon (die, past) during the experiment.

Speaking, Listening, and Viewing Workshop

Expressing Disagreement

Strategies for Success

How dull it would be if everyone had the same opinions, or if they liked the same color, the same dog, the same ice cream. People disagree; it's natural, normal, and can often be a useful tool for change and improvement. Problems arise, however, when disagreements lead to anger, disrespect, and resentment. Your task is to disagree reasonably, in an intelligent and mature way.

Listen Thoughtfully Many people are so eager to express their own opinions that they ignore what others are saying. *Before* you express your disagreement, listen thoughtfully.

Listen to Agree, Not to Disagree Listen to find points on which you agree. First, this will put you in a cooperative state of mind. Second, it will help you find a common ground, an idea on which you both agree.

Think Before You Speak This strategy helps you to order your thoughts so that when you do speak, your arguments are easier to follow, and it allows you time to collect your feelings. If you're angry or insulted, it allows you time to cool down.

Speak Slowly and in a Low Voice

Nothing inflames a disagreement more than a loud, rapid-fire, high-pitched verbal attack. Speak in a way that encourages people to trust your judgment.

Use Common Sense and Facts Argue from a position of knowledge. Give reasons, and back up your reasons with facts. Make it clear why your opinion makes sense.

Inappropriate: That's a stupid idea.

Better: If you do it that way, it will cause other problems.

Apply the Strategies

With a partner, role-play these situations. Express your disagreement reasonably and maturely.

1. You believe that Ned doesn't do his share of the work in your science group, which makes you feel you have to do extra work. What would you say to express your opinion?

2. Each year, your class does a community service project. You and your friends want to work in the community food pantry. Kylee and her friends want to clean up the park. How would you express your disagreement?

Tips for Expressing Disagreement

- ▶ Before you disagree, listen.
- ▶ Never disagree in anger. Think before you speak.
- ▶ Never shout. Speak in a calm, confident, low-pitched voice.
- ▶ Disagree from a position of knowledge.
- ▶ Use common sense and facts.

Speaking, Listening, and Viewing Workshop ◆ 233

Introduce the Strategies

Ask students to consider reasons why disagreement can be beneficial. Guide them to see that if two people are discussing whether they like a movie and they disagree, they can learn from the other person why they have made the choice they have. Disagreements, when handled conscientiously, can further a person's interest by providing perspective on other sides of an issue.

Customize for
Less Proficient Readers

Invite students to describe disagreements they have observed in TV shows or in movies. Help them discuss and distill both sides of the disagreement and the responses that may have ensued. Encourage them to explain how and what resolutions were reached.

Apply the Strategies

Encourage students to videotape their role plays and then play them for the rest of the class. Discuss effective techniques that were used, as well as places that could benefit from improvement. If possible, compare different role plays of the same situation and have students determine which aspects of each are the most successful.

 Beyond the Classroom

Workplace Skills

Working Together Explain to students that jobs often require working together for some or all parts of tasks. Learning to appropriately express disagreement can help smooth out potentially volatile and unproductive situations in the workplace.

Have students form groups of three or four. Have each group choose a career and then help them decide on a project for that career to complete. For example, students who pick catering as a career can choose catering a wedding banquet as

their project. Or, students who pick architecture as a career can choose building a new gymnasium for the school as a project. Next have students invent an issue on which to have a disagreement between the workers. Encourage students to predict what problems that disagreement may lead to and what steps can be taken to solve it. Have students script a brief scenario. Then suggest they perform or role-play it for the rest of the class. Have them introduce the situation before they begin, and hold a class discussion about effective means of resolving the differences following each presentation.

What's Behind the Words?
Explain to students that historians estimate the number of distinct Indian languages in both North and South America at one point was between 1,000 and 2,000.

Customize for
More Advanced Learners
Suggest that students research Native American groups to provide background for the rest of the class. You may wish to have them research individual tribes of Native Americans to find out where they lived and when colonists first arrived and how the tribe maintains its culture today.

Answers
Practice 1
1. opossum
2. woodchuck
3. raccoon
4. reindeer
5. skunk

Activity 2
1. Squash is the name of several related fruits that grow on vines or small bushes. Their skins can be white, yellow, tan, or green. Common types of squash include pumpkin, zucchini, and buttercup.
2. Pecan is a nut tree of the walnut family, related to the hickory.
3. Hominy is whole or ground corn from which the bran and grain have been removed. Hominy is what grits are made of.
4. Pone is a baked or fried bread made of cornmeal.
5. Pemmican is a small, pressed caked of shredded dried meat mixed with fat and dried fruits or berries.
6. Succotash is a cooked dish of kernels of corn mixed with shell beans, especially lima beans.

Activity 3
Suggest that students use the Internet as another place to do research. One good site, designed especially for K–12 classrooms, is the Native American History Archive at **http://www.ilt.columbia.edu/k12/naha/index.html**

We *strongly recommend* you preview this site before sending students to it. In addition, keep in mind that all Web sites are subject to change.

What's Behind the
Words

Vocabulary Adventures With Richard Lederer

Words Borrowed From Native Americans

The North American Indians, or Native Americans, were here long before any other group of people who are now living in the United States. The early colonists began borrowing words almost from the moment of first contact, and many of those words have remained in our everyday language. Native American names for animals (*moose*), plants (*hickory*), and Indian life (*tomahawk*) started to appear in our language soon after the colonists landed.

A Native Way of Life

Many Native American terms offer insight into the people and way of life of North American Indians:

People: *sachem* (Narraganset), *squaw* (Massachuset), *papoose* (Narraganset), *mugwump* (Natick)
Native American life: *moccasin* (Chippewa), *toboggan* (Algonquian), *wigwam* (Abenaki), *tepee* (Dakota), *pow-wow* (Narraganset), *wampum* (Massachuset), *hogan* (Navajo), *hickory* (Algonquian), *kayak* (Inuit)

ACTIVITY 1 Pronouncing many of the Native American words was difficult for the early explorers and settlers. In many instances, they shortened and simplified the names. Given the Native American names, identify the following animals:
1. apossoun (Don't play dead now.)
2. wuchak (How much wood?)
3. rahaugcum (Ring around the tail)

4. khalibu (Rudolph is one.)
5. seganku (What's black and white and stinks all over?)

ACTIVITY 2 The following food names originated as Native American words. Find out what kind of food each one is.

1. squash (Natick)
2. pecan (Algonquian)
3. hominy (Algonquian)
4. pone (Algonquian)
5. pemmican (Cree)
6. succotash (Narraganset)

The Poetry of Place Names

If you look at a map of the United States, you will realize how freely settlers used words of Indian origin to name states, cities, towns, mountains, lakes, rivers, ponds, and creeks. The people of Webster, Massachusetts (especially those who sell postcards), continue to take pride in a local lake named *Chargoggagogg-manchauggauggagoggchaubunagungamaugg*, Nipmuck for "You fish on your side, I fish on my side, and nobody fish in the middle."

ACTIVITY 3 With help from an encyclopedia, find out which Native American tribes lived in your part of the country. Have their languages survived in many place names? Pick out five names of places in your state—cities, towns, mountains, or bodies of water—that have Native American names. Try to find their exact origins. What can you find out about the history of your state that will help explain why these names were chosen?

234 ◆ *Meeting Challenges*

Extended Reading Opportunities

The many challenges that life brings and the struggles of those who must confront them are the basis for the works of literature in this unit. To further explore the theme of meeting challenges, choose from the following works.

Suggested Titles

The Double Life of Pocahontas
Jean Fritz

Biographer Jean Fritz dispels the romantic stories surrounding Pocahontas. A Powhatan Indian, she befriended settler Captain John Smith and made him part of her tribe. She was permitted to move freely between the settlers and her tribe. When relations between the tribe and the settlers became tense, she was kidnapped in an attempt to negotiate peace. This biography portrays Pocahontas as a pawn between two worlds, a woman who pays a high price for keeping peace.

Across Five Aprils
Irene Hunt

Jethro Creighton lives on a farm in southern Illinois, a border state, during the Civil War. Although Jethro's town supports the Union, his family has divided loyalties—two of his brothers fight for the North and one fights for the South. When Jethro's father passes away, he must run the farm and take care of his family. Watching his family and country torn apart by war, Jethro grows too rapidly from boy to man.

Shark Beneath the Reef
Jean Craighead George

Fourteen-year-old Tomás Torres dreams of catching a great shark in the Sea of Cortez. He aspires to become a marine biologist, and his family supports this decision. When Tomás finds out that his family is having financial troubles, he wants to help them. Tomás is then confronted with deciding between going to high school or becoming a fisherman. His battle with a shark and voyage to self-discovery help him come to his decision.

Other Possibilities

Lyddie	Katherine Paterson
Among the Volcanoes	Omar Castenda
Lupita Mañana	Patricia Beatty

Planning Students' Extended Reading

All of the works listed on this page are good choices for extending the theme "Facing Hard Questions." Following is some information that may help you choose which to teach.

Customize for
Varying Student Needs

When assigning the selections in this part to your students, keep in mind the following factors.

- *The Double Life of Pocahontas* is a short biography (96 pp.) of this legendary character. Students may appreciate Jean Fritz's treatment of Pocahontas as a historical figure, because she relies on journals and diaries for accuracy to bring her subject out of myth and into reality.

- *Across Five Aprils* is a novel that uses a young boy's growing-up experiences in dealing with issues of slavery and secession at the time of the Civil War. This book would be a good choice to read in conjunction with a social studies unit on the Civil War.

- *Shark Beneath the Reef* is a novel by Jean Craighead George, author of the award-winning book *Julie of the Wolves*. Students interested in fishing or marine biology may especially like this book.

Literature Study Guides

A literature study guide is available for *Shark Beneath the Reef*. The guide includes section summaries, discussion questions, and activities.

Planning Instruction and Assessment

Unit Objectives

1. To read selections in different genres that develop the theme of "Quest for Justice"
2. To apply a variety of reading strategies, particularly strategies for constructing meaning, appropriate for reading these selections
3. To recognize literary elements used in these selections
4. To increase vocabulary
5. To learn elements of grammar and usage
6. To write in a variety of modes about situations based on the selections
7. To develop speaking and listening skills, by completing activities
8. To view images critically and create visual representations

Meeting the Objectives Each selection provides instructional material and portfolio opportunities by which students can meet unit objectives. You will find additional practice pages for reading strategies, literary elements, vocabulary, and grammar in the **Selection Support** booklet in the **Teaching Resources** box.

Setting Goals Work with your students to set unit goals. Plan what skills and concepts you wish students to acquire. Match instruction and activities according to students' performance levels or learning modalities.

Portfolios Students may keep portfolios of their completed work or of their work in progress. The Build Your Portfolio page of each selection provides opportunities for students to apply the concepts presented.

 Humanities: Art

Trial by Jury, 1964, by Thomas Hart Benton

Thomas Hart Benton (1889–1975) painted American subjects, especially portraits of rural life in the South and Midwest. His experiences as an architectural draftsman in World War I influenced his regionalist ideas.

1. Who are the characters in the painting? *The judge, jury, the lawyers, clients, and maybe a court reporter.*
2. What are the characters doing? *Students may cite one lawyer as trying to persuade the jury, the judge as listening patiently, and one lawyer waiting his turn to talk to the jury.*

236

Trial by Jury, 1964, Thomas Hart Benton, Nelson-Atkins Museum of Art, Kansas City, Missouri; © T.H. Benton and R.P. Benton Testamentary Trusts/Licensed by VAGA, New York, NY

◆ 236

Art Transparencies

The **Art Transparencies** booklet in the **Teaching Resources** box offers fine art to help students make connections to other curriculum areas and high-interest topics.

Beyond Literature

Each unit presents Beyond Literature features that lead students into an exploration of careers, communities and other subject areas. In this unit, students will find out about the Supreme Court and find out about women in medicine. In addition, the **Teaching Resources** box contains a **Beyond Literature** booklet of activities. Using literature as a springboard, these activity pages offer students opportunities to connect literature to other curriculum areas and to the workplace and careers, community, media, and humanities.

UNIT 3

Quest for Justice

I t's human nature to fight for what we believe is right. The quest for justice occurs in many forms and in many places—courtroom battles, drawing attention to world hunger, solving a dispute among friends. The selections in this unit explore the various ways in which people join the search for justice.

♦ 237

Assessing Student Progress

The tools that are available to measure the degree to which students meet the unit objectives are listed below.

Informal Assessment

The questions in the Guide for Responding sections are a first level of response to the concepts and skills presented with the selection. As a brief, informal measure of students' grasp of the material, these responses indicate where further instruction and practice are needed. The practice pages in the **Selection Support** booklet provide for this type of instruction and practice.

You will also find literature and reading guides in the **Alternative Assessment** booklet, which students can use for informal assessment of their individual performances.

Formal Assessment

The **Formal Assessment** booklet contains Selection Tests and Unit Tests.

Selection Tests measure comprehension and skills acquisition for each selection or group of selections.

Each Unit Test provides students with 30 multiple-choice questions and 5 essay questions designed to assess students' knowledge of the literature and skills taught in the unit.

Each Alternative Unit Test: Standardized-Test Practice provides 15 multiple-choice questions and 3 essay questions based on two new literature selections not contained in the student book. The questions on the Alternative Unit Test are designed to assess students' ability to compare and contrast selections, applying skills taught in the unit.

Alternative Assessment

For portfolio and alternative assessment, the **Alternative Assessment** booklet contains Scoring Rubrics, Assessment sheets, and Learning Modalities activities.

Scoring Rubrics provide writing modes that can be applied to Writing activities, Writing Mini-Lessons, and Writing Process Workshop lessons.

Assessment sheets for speaking and listening activities provide peer and self-assessment direction.

Learning Modalities activities appeal to different learning styles. Use these as an alternative measurement of students' growth.

Connections

Within this unit, you will find selections and activities that make connections beyond literature. Use these selections to connect students' understanding and appreciation of literature beyond the traditional literature and language arts curriculum.

Encourage students to connect literature to other curriculum areas. You may wish to coordinate with teachers in other curriculum areas to determine ways to team teach and further extend instruction.

Connections to Today's World

Use these selections to guide students to recognize the relevance of literature to contemporary writings. In this unit, students will read about the Special Olympics in "There Is No Off-season."

Connecting Literature to Social Studies

Each unit contains a selection that connects literature to social studies. In this unit, students will read advice that Thomas Jefferson received from Benjamin Franklin during the process of the revision of the Declaration of Independence.

237

Guide for Reading

OBJECTIVES

1. To read, comprehend, and interpret an informative essay
2. To relate an informative essay to personal experience
3. To apply reading strategies for constructing meaning
4. To analyze an informative essay
5. To build vocabulary in context and learn the prefix *in-*
6. To develop skill in using adjectives
7. To write a personal essay that has a strong introduction
8. To respond to an informative essay through writing, speaking and listening, and projects

SKILLS INSTRUCTION

Vocabulary:
Prefixes: *in-*

Spelling:
Adding *-ed* to Form the Past Tense of a Verb

Grammar:
Adjectives

Reading for Success:
Strategies for Constructing Meaning

Literary Focus:
Informative Essay

Writing:
Strong Introduction

Speaking and Listening:
Drama (Teacher Edition)

Viewing and Representing:
Collage (Teacher Edition)

Critical Viewing:
Connect; Interpret

PORTFOLIO OPPORTUNITIES

Writing: Letter; Editorial; Biography
Writing Mini-Lesson: Personal Essay
Speaking and Listening: Drama; Panel Discussion
Projects: Timeline; Collage

More About the Author
Walter Dean Myers developed a love of reading and writing at a young age. He was not always a writer, however. After serving in the army, Myers worked for the New York State Department of Labor, the U.S. Post Office, a rehabilitation center, and a transformer company. He didn't earn his college degree until 1984, when he was well into his forties. In addition to writing, he does volunteer work at schools in Jersey City, New Jersey, where he lives.

Meet the Author:

Walter Dean Myers (1937–   )

"I've got more ideas than I'll ever have time to write," says Walter Dean Myers. A native of West Virginia, Myers was raised in Harlem, an African American community in New York City. His foster parents, the Deans, encouraged him to read widely, and from them he developed a lifelong love of books.

Early Inspiration Early in his life, Myers realized the importance of quality education. The combination of education and love of words led young Myers to see writing as a way to overcome a serious childhood speech problem and his painful shyness. Langston Hughes, the renowned African American poet, encouraged Myers to try writing poetry.

Skill and Chance Myers's career as an author began almost by chance in 1969 when he entered a contest for minority writers. His story won the $500 prize. Since then, Myers has published more than forty works for young people, and he has won four Coretta Scott King Awards and two Newbery Honor Awards.

THE STORY BEHIND THE STORY

Long interested in and concerned by the injustices suffered by African Americans, Walter Dean Myers has focused much of his writing on their experiences. In "Brown *vs.* Board of Education," Myers writes about the historic Supreme Court decision and its effect on the nation.

238 ◆ Quest for Justice

◆ LITERATURE AND YOUR LIFE

CONNECT YOUR EXPERIENCE

When treated unfairly, you are likely to feel hurt and angry. Like the people in this essay, however, you can also take a positive step and work to change the situation.

THEMATIC FOCUS: Quest for Justice

The African American struggle for justice and racial equality has affected generations of Americans—from the schoolchildren who integrated the Little Rock, Arkansas, schools, shown on the facing page, to people of all ages, races, and economic backgrounds.

◆ Background for Understanding

HISTORY

Following the Civil War, Congress passed several laws protecting the civil rights of African Americans. However, those laws were often disregarded. In 1883, for example, the Supreme Court ruled that congressional acts to prevent racial discrimination were unconstitutional. The often-cited 1896 case of *Plessy* v. *Ferguson* upheld a law requiring "separate but equal" accommodations in railroad cars. For fifty years, that ruling was applied to segregate the races in transportation, hotels, restaurants, and even in the public schools. It wasn't until 1954, in *Brown* v. *Board of Education of Topeka,* that segregation in public schools was declared unconstitutional. Eventually, this decision broke down the "separate but equal" doctrine.

Prentice Hall Literature Program Resources

REINFORCE / RETEACH / EXTEND
Selection Support Pages
Build Vocabulary: Prefixes: *in-*, p. 97
Build Spelling Skills, p. 98
Build Grammar Skills: Adjectives, p. 99
Reading for Success: Strategies for Constructing Meaning, pp. 100–101
Literary Focus: Informative Essay, p. 102
Strategies for Diverse Student Needs, pp. 37–38
Beyond Literature Study Skills: Using a Graphic Organizer, p. 19

Formal Assessment Selection Test, pp. 75–77, Assessment Resources Software
Alternative Assessment, p. 19
Writing and Language Transparencies
Main Idea and Support Details Graphic Organizer, p. 61
Resource Pro CD-ROM "Brown *vs.* Board of Education"—includes all resource material and customizable lesson plan

🎧 **Listening to Literature Audiocassettes**
"Brown *vs.* Board of Education"

◆ Brown *vs.* Board of Education ◆

Interest Grabber Obtain a video of the civil rights documentary "Eyes on the Prize." Play the section that shows archival film of the first black students entering a previously all-white high school in Little Rock, Arkansas. In addition, have students study the photograph on p. 239. Ask students to note the range of expressions on the faces of the participants, such as fear, anger, courage, and determination. Introduce the essay by explaining to students that they will read about the important legal decision that opened a door in African Americans' struggle for justice and racial equality.

◆ Build Grammar Skills

Adjectives If you wish to introduce the grammar concept or skill for this selection before students read, refer to the instruction on p. 247.

Customize for
Less Proficient Readers
This essay has different sections, and presents information out of time sequence. Identify the rows of asterisks that form visual separators between sections and discuss how this graphic feature helps organize the information in the text. Point out that students can use this organization tool to help them outline the essay. As they read, help students summarize the important ideas of each part of the essay: I. background on segregation in America, II. Thurgood Marshall's early life, III. facts about the case, and IV. memories of a key participant. Encourage them to reread and list details on their outlines.

Customize for
More Advanced Students
Discuss with students that when reading an informative essay, it is a good idea to vary reading rate. For instance, to get a broad idea of the essay, they can skim, or read it quickly. To grasp complex ideas, they need to read—and reread—slowly, pausing to clarify ideas or to look up difficult terms. To locate specific details to answer a question, they might scan, or quickly review, the essay.

◆ Literary Focus

INFORMATIVE ESSAY

An **informative essay** is a short nonfiction piece that gives information about a topic, including facts, examples, and details. It may also present the writer's point of view or opinion about the topic. "Brown *vs.* Board of Education" informs us about the long struggle to desegregate public schools. Use an outline like the one below to record the information in the essay.

> I. History of School Segregation
>   A.
>   B.
>   C.
> II. Thurgood Marshall's Life
>   A.
>   B.
>   C.
> III. The *Brown vs. Board of Education* Decision
>   A.
>   B.
>   C.

◆ Build Vocabulary

PREFIXES: *in-*

In "Brown *vs.* Board of Education," attorney Thurgood Marshall argued that "there were *intangible* factors" which made segregated education unequal. In the word *intangible,* the prefix *in-* means "not." The word *intangible* is a combination of *in-*, "not," and *tangible*, "able to be touched or felt." Therefore, *intangible* means "cannot be touched or defined."

WORD BANK

Look over these words from the essay. Which one is something a jury might be doing? Check the Build Vocabulary box on page 245 to see if you chose correctly.

> elusive
> predominantly
> diligent
> intangible
> unconstitutional
> deliberating
> oppressed

Brown vs. *Board of Education* ◆ 239

 Preparing for Standardized Tests

Reading Standardized tests often evaluate students' ability to interpret what they read by asking them to restate an idea or to explain the importance of what an author says. Present the following sample test question:

In "Brown *vs.* Board of Education," the author writes: "The law was one thing, but most Southern whites felt just as strongly about their customs as they did the law." Which statement is the best interpretation of what Myers means?

(A) It is customary to follow laws, and it is lawful to follow customs.

(B) Passing laws won't necessarily make people give up their unlawful attitudes.

(C) Civil rights laws were not customary at the time of *Brown* vs. *Board of Education*.

(D) Customs and laws applied only to whites in the South.

Discuss the answer choices and help students interpret the statements in relation to the question. Help them recognize that *(B)* does the best job of restating the author's meaning. For further practice, use Reading for Success Skills in **Selection Support,** pp. 100–101.

The Reading for Success page in each unit presents a set of problem-solving strategies to help readers understand authors' words and ideas on multiple levels. Good readers develop a bank of strategies from which they can draw as needed.

Unit 3 introduces strategies for constructing meaning. Students must be able to construct meaning before they apply higher-level critical thinking strategies. These strategies give readers an array of approaches for mastering a text: make inferences, determine cause and effect, identify important ideas, and interpret what you read.

These reading strategies are modeled with "Brown *vs.* Board of Education." Each green box shows an example of the thinking process involved in applying one of these strategies. Additional notes provide support for applying these strategies throughout the selection.

How to Use the Reading for Success Page

• Introduce the strategies for constructing meaning, presenting each as a problem-solving procedure.

• Before students read the selection, have them preview it, looking at the annotations in the green boxes that model the strategies.

• To reinforce the strategies after students read the essay, have them use Reading for Success, pp. 100–101, in **Selection Support.** These pages give students an opportunity to read a selection and practice constructing meaning by writing their own annotations.

Reading Strategies: Support and Reinforcement
Using Boxed Annotations and Prompts
Throughout the unit, the notes in green, red, and maroon are intended to help students apply reading strategies, understand the literary focus, and make a connection with their lives. You may use boxed material in these ways:

• Have students pause at each box and respond to its prompt before they continue reading.

• Urge students to read through the selection, ignoring the boxes. After they complete the selection, they may go back and review the text, responding to the prompts.

Reading for Success

Strategies for Constructing Meaning

To understand a piece of writing fully—especially nonfiction—you must put words and ideas together in your own mind, so that they have meaning for you. Use these strategies to help you construct meaning:

Make inferences.
Writers don't always tell you everything directly. Sometimes you must "read between the lines," or make inferences, to arrive at ideas the writer suggests but doesn't say. This includes looking beyond the literal meaning of the words to get a full picture of what the author means.
▶ Make an inference by considering the details that the writer includes or doesn't include.
▶ Think about what this choice of details tells you about the author's opinions or purpose in writing.

Determine cause and effect.
To better understand the information presented to you, look for relationships among ideas. Cause and effect is one kind of relationship. A *cause* makes something happen. An *effect* is what happens—the result. You will read in this selection that segregation caused black children to feel inferior to white children. The cause is segregation. The effect is a feeling of inferiority.

Identify important ideas.
In many nonfiction pieces, most paragraphs have a main idea that is either stated or implied. Main ideas are general statements supported by facts, examples, and details. To discover the important, or main, ideas, try these strategies:
▶ Answer the question, "What is the author's point?"
▶ Identify the supporting details for each main idea.

Interpret what you read.
Interpreting what you read will help make the information your own. To interpret, follow these steps:
▶ Restate in your own words what the author has written.
▶ Explain the importance of what the author is saying.

As you read "Brown *vs.* Board of Education," look at the notes in the boxes. They show you how to apply these strategies to your reading.

Model a Reading Strategy: Interpret What You Read
Tell students they should interpret what they read to make information their own. Ask them to read a paragraph from "Brown *vs.* Board of Education":

"I didn't understand why I couldn't go to school with my playmates. I lived in an integrated neighborhood and played with children of all nationalities, but when school started they went to a school only four blocks from my home and I was sent to school across town."

Demonstrate how to interpret what you read by modeling your thinking for students:

To understand this passage from the essay, I restate what the speaker is saying in my own words. "The speaker felt left out and different because she was not allowed to go to school with her friends. Instead she was sent to a separate school far away." As I restate the meaning of the paragraph in my own mind, I see that this was a serious problem for the speaker because she could not understand and this explains her feeling of being left out.

Point out to students that there are many ways to interpret information—they should use their own words and ideas to interpret information.

BROWN vs. BOARD OF EDUCATION

MODEL

Walter Dean Myers

There was a time when the meaning of freedom was easily understood. For an African crouched in the darkness of a tossing ship, wrists chained, men with guns standing on the decks above him, freedom was a physical thing, the ability to move away from his captors, to follow the dictates of his own heart, to listen to the voices within him that defined his values and showed him the truth of his own path. The plantation owners wanted to make the Africans feel helpless, inferior. They denied them images of themselves as Africans and told them that they were without beauty. They segregated them and told them they were without value.

> You can **infer** from the images here that Myers believes the problems caused by slavery continued long after slavery had been abolished.

Slowly, surely, the meaning of freedom changed to an <u>elusive</u> thing that even the strongest people could not hold in their hands. There were no chains on black wrists, but there were the shadows of chains, stretching for hundreds of years back through time, across black minds.

* * *

❷ From the end of the Civil War in 1865 to the early 1950's, many public schools in both the North and South were segregated. Segregation was different in the different sections of the country. In the North most of the schools were segregated *de facto*;[1] that is, the law allowed

---
1. *de facto* (dē fak´ tō): Latin for "existing in actual fact."

blacks and whites to go to school together, but they did not actually always attend the same schools. Since a school is generally attended by children living in its neighborhood, wherever there were <u>predominantly</u> African-American neighborhoods there were, "in fact," segregated schools. In many parts of the country, however, and especially in the South, the segregation was *de jure*,[2] meaning that there were laws which forbade blacks to attend the same schools as whites.

❷

> This is an **important idea**—that segregation in schools was occurring in both the North and the South.

The states with segregated schools relied upon the ruling of the Supreme Court in the 1896 *Plessy* vs. *Ferguson* case for legal justification: Facilities that were "separate but equal" were legal.

In the early 1950's the National Association for the Advancement of Colored People (N.A.A.C.P.) sponsored five cases that eventually reached the Supreme Court. One of the cases involved the school board of Topeka, Kansas.

Thirteen families sued the Topeka school board, claiming that to segregate the children ▼

---
2. *de jure* (dē jur´ ə): Latin for "by right or legal establishment."

◆ Build Vocabulary

elusive (i lōō´ siv) *adj.*: Hard to grasp or retain mentally

predominantly (pri däm´ ə nənt lē) *adj.*: Mainly; most noticeably

★ ★ ★   *Brown* vs. *Board of Education* ◆ 241

Develop Understanding

One-Minute Insight "Brown vs. Board of Education" explores the nature of segregation in America in the century after the Civil War, and the start of its legal downfall. Led by Thurgood Marshall, who would later become a Supreme Court Justice, a dedicated legal team for the N.A.A.C.P. successfully challenged the "separate but equal" doctrine as it applied to segregated schools. This landmark case, on which the Supreme Court ruled in 1954, brought the nation closer to full legal equality and demonstrated that the American legal system could be used in the struggle for civil rights and racial equality.

Team Teaching Strategy
You might wish to coordinate with a social studies teacher to provide further background that will put "Brown vs. Board of Education" in its proper historical and social context.

Clarification
❶ Legal cases are named by identifying the plaintiff (*Brown;* the person who files suit in court), followed by versus (abbreviated as vs.) and the name of the defendant (*Board of Education;* the person or group being sued).

Comprehension Check ☑
❷ What is segregation? What is the difference between *de jure* and *de facto* segregation? *Segregation is an action meant to keep African Americans separate. De jure segregation is separation based on laws; de facto segregation is separation that occurs by custom or practice, not because of specific laws.*

Customize for
English Language Learners
Students will come across a number of historical and legal terms in this essay. Suggest that they create a set of index cards for new terms or ideas they encounter. On each card, students can copy down a word or expression, and on the back they can define, clarify, or explain it in their own words.

Block Scheduling Strategies

Consider these suggestions to take advantage of extended class time:

- Build background on the constitutional issues involved in "Brown vs. Board of Education" and the history of segregation in America by teaming with a social studies teacher; stimulate interest with the Interest Grabber activity, p. 239.

- Introduce the Reading for Success strategies on p. 240 before students read the essay. Then, read together, reviewing the annotations in the side notes. Students can work on their own to apply the strategies to annotate the Reading

for Success practice selection in **Selection Support,** pp. 100–101.

- Use the Speaking and Listening Mini-Lesson on p. 245 or Viewing and Representing Mini-Lesson on p. 243 to help prepare students for some of the Idea Bank activities on p. 248.

- Devote class time to having students work on the Projects in the Idea Bank, p. 248, to research the Biography or Timeline ideas, or to focus on the Social Studies Connection in Beyond Literature on p. 246. You may wish to assign the Writing Mini-Lesson as a homework activity.

❶ Connect *The classroom seems old, shabby, poorly supplied, and crowded.*

Clarification

❷ The Fourteenth Amendment to the U. S. Constitution addresses the rights of American citizens and grants these rights to former slaves. In addition, it contains the due process and equal protection clauses, which protect basic civil rights.

Comprehension Check ☑

❸ Ask students what the words of Linda Brown reveal. *Even though she experienced racial integration in her own neighborhood, she wasn't allowed to go to school with her friends. Seeing the pain of segregation through the eyes of a young child makes the civil rights struggle seem more real.*

Reading for Success

❹ Identify Important Ideas
Discuss with students what important ideas the flashback to the life of young Thurgood Marshall reveals. *Students should note that Marshall himself experienced racial injustice and did not like it; he worked hard and respected his family; he had a deep sense of right and wrong.*

Customize for
Visual/Spatial Learners

Suggest that interested students use a map to locate Topeka, Kansas, where the lawsuit was filed, and Baltimore, Maryland, where Thurgood Marshall grew up.

❶ ▲ **Critical Viewing** What details in this photograph reveal that segregated education was "separate but not equal"? [Connect]

❷ was harmful to the children and, therefore, a violation of the equal protection clause of the Fourteenth Amendment. The names on the Topeka case were listed in alphabetical order, with the father of seven-year-old Linda Brown listed first.

❸ "I didn't understand why I couldn't go to school with my playmates. I lived in an integrated neighborhood and played with children of all nationalities, but when school started they went to a school only four blocks from my home and I was sent to school across town," she says.

For young Linda the case was one of convenience and of being made to feel different, but for African-American parents it had been a long, hard struggle to get a good education for their children. It was also a struggle waged by lawyers who had worked for years to overcome segregation. The head of the legal team who presented the school cases was Thurgood Marshall.

* * *

The city was Baltimore, Maryland, and the year was 1921. Thirteen-year-old Thurgood Marshall struggled to balance the packages he was carrying with one hand while he tried to get his bus fare out of his pocket with the other. It was almost Easter, and the part-time job he had would provide money for flowers for his mother. Suddenly he felt a violent tug at his right arm that spun him around, sending his packages sprawling over the floor of the bus.

❹ "Nigguh, don't you never push in front of no white lady again!" an angry voice spat in his ear.

Thurgood turned and threw a punch into the face of the name caller. The man charged

242 ◆ *Quest for Justice*

★ ★ ★

 Cross-Curricular Connection: Social Studies

U. S. Constitution Our nation's rule book is the U. S. Constitution. This brief but vital document sets forth the basic principles on which American government is based, and describes the structure, procedures, powers, and limits of government. Suggest that students learn more about the Constitution and how it has been updated over time.

To grasp the concepts of the lawsuit *Brown* vs. *Board of Education,* it is necessary to have an understanding of the Fourteenth Amendment. One of the so-called Civil War Amendments, its subjects are citizenship, due process, and equal protection. Have study groups locate a copy of the Constitution to read and discuss. Suggest that they read Section 1 of the amendment. Then, help them restate the legal terms in familiar English. Challenge students to give concrete examples of how the issues discussed in the Fourteenth Amendment apply to their own lives. For instance, a student who lives in Florida but who was born in Jamaica is not an American or Florida citizen until she becomes naturalized.

into Thurgood, throwing punches that mostly missed, and tried to wrestle the slim boy to the ground. A policeman broke up the fight, grabbing Thurgood with one huge black hand and pushing him against the side of the bus. Within minutes they were in the local courthouse.

Thurgood was not the first of his family to get into a good fight. His father's father had joined the Union Army during the Civil War, taking the names Thorough Good to add to the one name he had in bondage. His grandfather on his mother's side was a man brought from Africa and, according to Marshall's biography, "so ornery that his owner wouldn't sell him out of pity for the people who might buy him, but gave him his freedom instead and told him to clear out of the county."

Thurgood's frequent scrapes earned him a reputation as a young boy who couldn't be trusted to get along with white folks.

His father, Will Marshall, was a steward at the Gibson Island Yacht Club near Baltimore, and his mother, Norma, taught in a segregated school. The elder Marshall felt he could have done more with his life if his education had been better, but there had been few opportunities available for African Americans when he had been a young man. When it was time for the Marshall boys to go to college, he was more than willing to make the sacrifices necessary to send them.

Young people of color from all over the world came to the United States to study at Lincoln University, a predominantly black institution in southeastern Pennsylvania. Here Marshall

majored in predentistry, which he found boring, and joined the Debating Club, which he found interesting. By the time he was graduated at the age of twenty-one, he had decided to give up dentistry for the law. Three years later he was graduated, first in his class, from Howard University Law School.

At Howard there was a law professor, Charles Hamilton Houston, who would affect the lives of many African-American lawyers and who would influence the legal aspects of the civil rights movement. Houston was a

> This passage shows a **cause and effect.** Marshall became a lawyer as a result of his boredom with predentistry and his interest in debating.

▲ **Critical Viewing** In this photograph, a woman explains the significance of the ruling to her young daughter. What does the newspaper the woman is holding tell you about the impact of the ruling? [Connect] ❼

great teacher, one who demanded that his students be not just good lawyers but great lawyers. If they were going to help their people—and for Houston the only reason for African Americans to become lawyers was to do just that—they would have to have absolute understanding of the law, and be diligent in the preparation of their cases. At the time, Houston was an attorney for the

Reading for Success

❺ **Make Inferences** Based on this passage, what can students infer about the values that the Marshall family held? *Mr. and Mrs. Marshall valued hard work and education; understood how segregation had kept them from fulfilling their highest potential; and were willing to make sacrifices for their children.*

◆ Literary Focus

❻ **Informative Essay** Although it is not the main idea of this essay, the author provides insight into Thurgood Marshall's character by explaining how one teacher influenced and inspired him. Discuss how this passage both informs and conveys opinions and challenge students to give examples of each. *It is a fact that Charles Hamilton Houston was a demanding professor at Howard University, where Marshall studied law. It is an opinion that Houston was a great teacher.*

▶ Critical Viewing ◀

❼ **Connect** *It must have been very big news because the paper gave it a banner sized headline.*

Comprehension Check ☑

❽ Why did Houston believe it was important for African Americans to become lawyers? *He believed that the legal system could influence civil rights and that by becoming excellent lawyers, African Americans could help their people.*

🔍 Viewing and Representing Mini-Lesson

Collage

This mini-lesson supports the Collage project in the Idea Bank on p. 248.

Introduce Review the art form known as collage. Point out that a collage can use pictures, objects, text, fabric, or any other items that convey ideas or emotions. At first glance, collages may seem like random collections. The best collages highlight a central theme and can evoke strong feelings.

Develop Form groups of 2–4 students. Help them to determine a unifying theme

for their collage, and have them begin searching for images, objects, and quotations that would work together to convey the struggle to gain civil rights. If you have access to equipment such as digital scanners or copy machines, help students use them. Students might wish to create their collages with computer software.

Apply Allow time for students to collect materials and complete their collages. For news media materials, help them access your school's library or media center or the

periodical archives at your local library. Schedule time to use technological equipment and provide art materials such as posterboard or craft paper, scissors, and glue. Display the completed collages around the classroom.

Assess Give students time to view one another's works. Assess their collages in terms of visual composition, content, and impact of imagery. You may wish to have students write critiques in which they evaluate their own and other students' works.

❶ Interpret *The President of the United States is there; everyone is wearing dress-up clothes; people have serious looks on their faces, and Thurgood Marshall is taking an official oath.*

Reading for Success

❷ Make Inferences Thurgood Marshall was just 32 years old when he became the N.A.A.C.P.'s chief legal counsel. Ask students what they can infer about him as a lawyer and as a citizen. *He was smart, well educated, dedicated to social change, righteous, and willing to take on a challenge.*

Comprehension Check ☑

❸ What was the importance of winning a legal case about school segregation? *If school segregation could be ended, then other aspects of society could eventually become free of segregation, too.*

Customize for
Logical/Mathematical
Learners

Challenge students to evaluate the logic used to argue the *Brown* vs. *Board of Education* case. Have them offer support or present examples based on their experience with and interpretation of segregation, and the concept of "separate but equal."

❶ ▲ **Critical Viewing** Thurgood Marshall is being sworn in as a Supreme Court justice as President Johnson looks on. What details show that this is a solemn, historic occasion? **[Interpret]**

N.A.A.C.P. and fought against discrimination in housing and in jobs.

After graduation, Thurgood Marshall began to do some work for the N.A.A.C.P., trying the difficult civil rights cases. He not only knew about the effects of discrimination by reading about it, he was still living it when he was graduated from law school in 1933. In 1936 Marshall began working full-time for the N.A.A.C.P., and in 1940 became its chief counsel.

It was Thurgood Marshall and a battery of N.A.A.C.P. attorneys who began to challenge segregation throughout the country. These men and women were warriors in the cause of freedom for African Americans, taking their battles into courtrooms across the country. They understood the process of American justice and the power of the Constitution.

Based on the words he uses, such as *warriors, cause,* and *battles*, you can **infer** that Myers considers Marshall and the other attorneys to be engaged in a heroic struggle.

In *Brown* vs. *Board of Education of Topeka,* Marshall argued that segregation was a violation of the Fourteenth Amendment—that even if the facilities and all other "tangibles" were equal, which was the heart of the case in *Plessy* vs. *Ferguson,* a violation still existed. There were intangible factors, he argued, that made the education unequal.

Everyone involved understood the significance of the case: that it was much more than whether black children could go to school with white children. If segregation in the schools was declared unconstitutional, then all segregation in public places could be declared unconstitutional.

Southerners who argued against ending school segregation were caught up, as then-

Beyond the Classroom

Career Connection There are many jobs available for people who want to bring about social or political change. Some require higher education; all demand strong communication skills and commitment. Lawyers and politicians can effect legal and political change. Journalists and essayists can encourage change with the power of their persuasive writing. Cartoonists can have influence with their drawings; graphic designers can get ideas across visually. Songwriters, with their powerful lyrics, can inspire change. And of course, community activists, social workers, teachers, and clergy members can bring about change as they work within their communities.

Discuss with students what all those jobs or careers have in common—an interest in reaching out to the larger world and in making the world a better place for everyone. Invite students to write essays in support of a career of their choice that they believe could lead to positive social change.

Congressman Brooks Hays of Arkansas put it, in "a lifetime of adventures in that gap between law and custom." The law was one thing, but most Southern whites felt just as strongly about their customs as they did the law.

Dr. Kenneth B. Clark, an African-American psychologist, testified for the N.A.A.C.P. He presented clear evidence that the effect of segregation was harmful to African-American children. Describing studies conducted by black and white psychologists over a twenty-year period, he showed that black children felt inferior to white children. In a particularly dramatic study that he had supervised, four dolls, two white and two black, were presented to African-American children. From the responses of the children to the dolls, identical in every way except color, it was clear that the children were rejecting the black dolls. African-American children did not just feel separated from white children, they felt that the separation was based on their inferiority.

> This paragraph discusses a **cause-and-effect** relationship. Segregation was the cause of feelings of inferiority in African American children.

Dr. Clark understood fully the principles and ideas of those people who had held Africans in bondage and had tried to make slaves of captives. By isolating people of African descent, by barring them from certain actions or places, they could make them feel inferior. The social scientists who testified at *Brown* vs. *Board of Education* showed that children who felt inferior also performed poorly.

❺
> The **main idea** of this paragraph—that Marshall and the N.A.A.C.P. won their case—is supported by such details as the Court's looking beyond the intentions of the Fourteenth Amendment and overturning *Plessy* vs. *Ferguson*.

The Justice Department argued that racial segregation was objectionable to the Eisenhower Administration and hurt our relationships with other nations.

* * *

On May 17, 1954, after deliberating for nearly a year and a half, the Supreme Court made its ruling. The Court stated that it could not use the intentions of 1868, when the Fourteenth Amendment was passed, as a guide to its ruling, or even those of 1896, when the decision in *Plessy* vs. *Ferguson* was handed down. Chief Justice Earl Warren wrote:

> We must consider public education in the light of its full development and its present place in American life throughout the nation. We must look instead to the effect of segregation itself on public education.

The Court went on to say that "modern authority" supported the idea that segregation deprived African Americans of equal opportunity. "Modern authority" referred to Dr. Kenneth B. Clark and the weight of evidence that he and the other social scientists had presented.

❻

The high court's decision in *Brown* vs. *Board of Education* signaled an important change in the struggle for civil rights. It signaled clearly that the legal prohibitions that oppressed African Americans would have to fall. Equally important was the idea that the nature of the fight for equality would change. Ibrahima, Cinqué, Nat Turner, and George Latimer had struggled for freedom by fighting against their captors or fleeing from them. The 54th had fought for African freedom on the battlefields of the Civil War. Ida B. Wells had fought for equality with her pen. Lewis H. Latimer and Meta Vaux Warrick had tried to earn equality with their work. In *Brown* vs. *Board of Education* Thurgood Marshall, Kenneth B. Clark, and the lawyers and social scientists, both black and white, who helped them had

❼

❽

◆ Build Vocabulary

intangible (in tan′ jə bəl) *adj.*: Not able to be touched or grasped

unconstitutional (un′ kän stə tōō′ shə nəl) *adj.*: Not in accordance with or permitted by the U.S. Constitution

deliberating (di lib′ ə rā tin) *v.*: Thinking or considering very carefully and fully

oppressed (ə prest′) *adj.*: Kept down by cruel or unjust use of power

★ ★ ★   *Brown* vs. *Board of Education* ◆ 245

Speaking and Listening Mini-Lesson

Drama

This mini-lesson supports the Speaking and Listening activity in the Idea Bank on p. 248.

Introduce Many of the events in Thurgood Marshall's life were full of natural drama. Direct students to identify, either from this essay or from their research, an event that they can present in the form of a skit.

Develop Form groups to research, write a script, rehearse, and perform a brief dramatic scene. This task will take several days to prepare, and may involve library or Internet research

time. Advise groups to keep props, costumes, and scenery to a minimum, but focus on the event itself and the people involved.

Apply Have groups perform their dramatic scenes for the class. Invite audience members to ask questions of the cast after their presentation.

Assess Evaluate the dramas based on students' understanding of the event represented and its important details, as well as the quality of their preparation and presentation. Or, have students use the Peer Assessment: Dramatic Performance form in **Alternative Assessment,** p. 116.

Beyond Literature

The Supreme Court opens its annual season on the first Monday in October. Invite students to examine newspapers or magazines from that time period to find articles about the kinds of cases the Court will hear.

Reinforce and Extend

Answers

◆ LITERATURE AND YOUR LIFE

Reader's Response Students may cite schools, hospitals, or restaurants they are familiar with that would not have been integrated before 1954.

Thematic Focus He took part in a landmark case that had a profound effect on our society, and rose to hold a position on the highest court in the land.

☑ Check Your Comprehension

1. They claimed that segregation harmed children, and therefore violated the 14th Amendment.
2. They realized that if school segregation was declared unconstitutional, then all public segregation could be ended.
3. It proved that the Constitution could be used to win moral battles, and that laws against African Americans could be changed.

◆ Critical Thinking

1. People knew that children need good education, but segregation was depriving African American children.
2. He means that the history of slavery lingers in their memory.
3. The author wants to show that Brown now appreciates the importance of an act she barely understood as a child.
4. Students may say that it caused a major shift in civil rights and equality for all Americans.
5. Students may say that because African Americans were looked down on, they had to work even harder, and that the cases they would try would need to demonstrate "great" legal skills in order to ensure that African American lawyers would be looked at favorably.

---

won for African Americans a victory that would bring them closer to full equality than they had ever been in North America. There would still be legal battles to be won, but the major struggle would be in the hearts and minds of people and "in that gap between law and custom."

> You can **interpret** this appointment to mean that Marshall had a successful law career.

In 1967 Thurgood Marshall was appointed by President Lyndon B. Johnson as an associate justice of the U.S. Supreme Court. He retired in 1991.

* * *

"I didn't think of my father or the other parents as being heroic at the time," Linda Brown says. "I was only seven. But as I grew older and realized how far-reaching the case was and how it changed the complexion of the history of this country, I was just thrilled that my father and the others here in Topeka were involved."

Beyond Literature

Social Studies Connection

The Role of the Supreme Court
Why was the Supreme Court of the United States charged with making a decision in the case of *Brown* vs. *Board of Education of Topeka*? Article III of the Constitution gives the Supreme Court the right to decide cases concerning constitutional issues, such as whether racially "separate but equal" schools are constitutionally legal. The Supreme Court also has the right of judicial review—the right to strike down a law made by Congress, a state, or a local government if that law violates the Constitution.

Cross-Curricular Activity
The Judges Supreme Court justices are appointed by the President of the United States. Find out who the current justices are and which President appointed each one.

246 ◆ Quest for Justice

Guide for Responding

◆ LITERATURE AND YOUR LIFE

Reader's Response How do you think the Supreme Court's decision in *Brown* vs. *Board of Education* has affected your life?

Thematic Focus In what ways was Marshall's quest for justice fulfilled?

Journal Writing Jot down in your journal some ways in which you have joined in a quest for justice.

☑ Check Your Comprehension

1. What were the main claims made by parents in the lawsuit against the Topeka school board?
2. Why were some people concerned about the *Brown* vs. *Board of Education* case, although these people had nothing to do with schools?
3. Name two significant changes in the nature of the African American struggle following *Brown* vs. *Board of Education*.

◆ Critical Thinking

INTERPRET
1. Why were so many people willing to fight against segregation in the schools? **[Analyze]**
2. What does Myers mean when he refers to "shadows of chains" in black minds? **[Interpret]**
3. What is the author's purpose in concluding with Linda Brown's comments about the impact of this case? **[Speculate]**

APPLY
4. Why is this Supreme Court case so important in American history? **[Apply]**

EVALUATE
5. Charles Hamilton Houston thought it was important for his students to become "great" lawyers. Do you agree or disagree? Explain. **[Make a Judgment]**

 **Beyond the Selection**

FURTHER READING
Other Works by Walter Dean Myers
Now Is Your Time: The African American Struggle for Freedom
Other Works About the Quest for Justice
Thurgood Marshall: The Fight for Equal Justice, Debra Hess
The Courage of Their Convictions, Peter Irons
Cesar Chavez, Consuelo Rodriguez
The Fighting Ground, Avi

INTERNET
We suggest the following sites on the Internet (all Web sites are subject to change).
For more about Walter Dean Myers:
http://www.bdd.com/teachers/myer.html
For Thurgood Marshall and a link to the case of *Brown* vs. *Board of Education* of Topeka and the opinion delivered by Chief Justice Warren:
http://www.law.ab.umd.edu/marshall/thurbio.htm
We *strongly recommend* that you preview these sites before you send students to them.

Guide for Responding (continued)

◆ Reading for Success

STRATEGIES FOR CONSTRUCTING MEANING

Review the reading strategies and the notes showing how to construct meaning. Then, apply them to answer the following.

1. What can you infer about Myers's opinion of Thurgood Marshall? Support your answer.
2. Identify three important ideas in this essay.
3. Interpret Myers's statement that the future "struggle would be in the hearts and minds of people and 'in that gap between law and custom.'" Do you agree with his opinion? Explain.

◆ Build Vocabulary Skills

USING THE PREFIX in-

The prefix in- usually means "not." On a sheet of paper, form words by adding in- to the following. Then, write a definition of each new word.

1. appropriate   2. capable   3. tolerant

SPELLING STRATEGY

You may have to drop or change a letter before adding -ed to form the past tense of a verb. When a verb ends in silent e, drop the e before adding -ed: escape + -ed = escaped. When a verb ends in a consonant and y, change the y to i and add -ed: solidify + -ed = solidified.

Add -ed to these verbs to form their past tense.

1. release   2. beautify   3. exchange   4. qualify

USING THE WORD BANK

On your paper, write the word that is closest in meaning to the Word Bank word.

1. elusive: (a) outstanding, (b) ungraspable, (c) frightening
2. predominantly: (a) mainly, (b) quickly, (c) unfairly
3. diligent: (a) respectful, (b) lazy, (c) hardworking
4. intangible: (a) weak, (b) concrete, (c) not solid
5. unconstitutional: (a) legal, (b) illegal, (c) illogical
6. deliberating: (a) considering, (b) noting, (c) waiting
7. oppressed: (a) cleansed, (b) beaten down, (c) hurried

◆ Literary Focus

INFORMATIVE ESSAY

An **informative essay** is a short nonfiction work that explains or gives information about a topic. The writer may also express a point of view or an opinion about the topic of the essay.

1. What are three main ideas that Myers wants his readers to know about the *Brown* vs. *Board of Education* decision?
2. How important does Myers think the *Brown* vs. *Board of Education* decision is? Find three examples that are evidence of his opinion.

◆ Build Grammar Skills

ADJECTIVES

Adjectives are words that modify, or describe, nouns or pronouns. They tell more about the nouns or pronouns they modify by answering the questions *which, what kind, how many,* or *how much*. In the following sentence, Myers uses adjectives to tell *what kind* of tug he felt and on *which* arm:

> Suddenly he felt a *violent* tug at his *right* arm . . .

Practice Copy these sentences. Underline each adjective, and draw an arrow to the word it modifies. Then, tell what question it answers.

1. His mother taught in a segregated school.
2. Thurgood's frequent scrapes earned him a reputation.
3. Marshall graduated first in his law class.
4. Four dolls were presented to African American children.
5. The decision signaled an important change.

Writing Application On your paper, write this paragraph, replacing the blanks with adjectives.

The _____?_____ child showed _____?_____ interest in going to the _____?_____ school. Her _____?_____ friends went to the _____?_____ school. A _____?_____ counselor eased the _____?_____ child's fears.

Brown vs. *Board of Education* ◆ 247

◆ Build Grammar Skills

Practice

1. segregated modifies school
2. frequent modifies scrapes
3. law modifies class
4. Four modifies dolls; African American modifies children
5. important modifies change

Writing Application

Possible responses:
minority; deep; best; neighborhood; nearby; guidance; frightened

 Writer's Solution

For additional instruction and practice, use the Using Modifiers lesson in the *Writer's Solution Language Lab CD-ROM,* and the practice page on Adjectives as Modifiers, p. 16 in the *Writer's Solution Grammar Practice Book.*

Answers
Reading for Success

1. You know that Myers admires Marshall because he includes inspiring stories about Marshall's life and applauds his career.
2. Possible answers: Segregation was an intentional policy to keep African Americans feeling inferior; there were two kinds of segregation: *de jure* and *de facto;* Thurgood Marshall and his team won a case that changed society; laws cannot change attitudes.
3. Students may agree that laws might not force people to let go of outdated customs or unfair values, therefore people must be re-educated.

◆ Build Vocabulary

Using the Prefix in-

1. inappropriate: not suitable, not proper
2. incapable: not able, powerless
3. intolerant: not accepting, biased

Spelling Strategy

1. released
2. beautified
3. exchanged
4. qualified

Using the Word Bank

1. b
2. a
3. c
4. c
5. b
6. a
7. b

◆ Literary Focus

1. Possible answers: It changed American society; it was a long battle; it involved people who knew it would be a struggle; it changed how leaders approached civil rights struggles.
2. Myers thinks that the decision is very important. You can tell by the dramatic way he begins the essay, his portrayal of Thurgood Marshall as an inspiring figure, and the links he presents between legal freedom fighters and other freedom fighters in African American history.

Idea Bank

Following are suggestions for matching the Idea Bank topics with your students' performance levels and learning modalities:

Customize for
Performance Levels
Less Advanced Students: 1, 4, 7
Average Students: 2, 4, 5, 6, 7
More Advanced Students: 3, 4, 5, 6

Customize for
Learning Modalities
Verbal/Linguistic: 1, 2, 3, 4, 5
Visual/Spatial: 6, 7
Bodily/Kinesthetic: 4
Logical/Mathematical: 6
Interpersonal: 4, 5
Intrapersonal: 1, 2, 3, 6, 7

 Writing Mini-Lesson

Refer students to the Writing Handbook in the back of the book for instruction on the writing process and for further information on writing a strong introduction. Have students use the Main Idea and Supporting Details Graphic Organizer in **Writing and Language Transparencies,** p. 61, to organize main ideas and supporting details.

  *Writer's Solution*

Writer's at Work Videodisc
Have students view the videodisc segment on Persuasion (Ch. 6), featuring Kate Mitchell, to see how she uses a "hook" to start an essay.

Play frames 5312 to 6086

Writing Lab CD-ROM
Have students complete the tutorial on Persuasion. Follow these steps:
1. Have students study the interactive models that show the different parts of a draft.
2. Have students draft on computer.
3. Have students use the Revision Checker for sentence openers.

Writer's Solution Sourcebook
Have students use Chapter 6, "Persuasion," pp. 166–199, for more support. The chapter includes in-depth instruction on drafting a strong introduction, body, and conclusion, pp. 188–189.

Build Your Portfolio

 Idea Bank

Writing

1. **Letter** Compose a letter to Linda Brown that expresses your feelings about what she and her family accomplished.
2. **Editorial** Write an editorial for your school newspaper in which you reveal your thoughts about a current issue in your community. **[Community Link]**
3. **Biography** Write a brief biography of Thurgood Marshall, Kenneth B. Clark, or another civil rights leader who was involved in the legal battle to end segregation in the public schools.

Speaking and Listening

4. **Drama [Group Activity]** Work with a small group to dramatize one event in Thurgood Marshall's life. You might choose the occurrence at the bus stop, his argument before the Supreme Court in "Brown vs. Board of Education," or another event you learn about through research. Allow each group member to play a part in your dramatization. **[Performing Arts Link]**
5. **Panel Discussion [Group Activity]** With a small group, prepare and present a panel discussion on the current status of the civil rights movement in the United States. Conduct research to learn about differing positions and views, and present your findings in your panel discussion. **[Social Studies Link]**

Projects

6. **Timeline** Research the history of the civil rights movement in the United States. Create an illustrated timeline of key events in the movement. **[Social Studies Link]**
7. **Collage** Photocopy photographs, news headlines, and magazine articles, and with them, create a collage that captures the essence of the civil rights movement. **[Art Link]**

Writing Mini-Lesson

Personal Essay

"Brown vs. Board of Education" is an informative essay that conveys information, but it also expresses Myers's personal views. Write an essay that tells about your personal views on a topic that is currently in the news.

Writing Skills Focus:
Strong Introduction

Use a **strong introduction** to grab your readers' interest. You might begin with a quotation, a question, a startling fact, or a brief story. Walter Dean Myers uses a startling image to capture his readers' attention:

Model From the Essay
There was a time when the meaning of freedom was easily understood. For an African crouched in the darkness of a tossing ship, wrists chained, men with guns stand on the decks above him, freedom was a physical thing, . . .

Prewriting Outline the most important ideas you want to communicate in your essay. Then, list a few details that will support each main idea.

Drafting Follow your outline to write your first draft. Begin with a strong introduction. Then, present your main points one by one. Remember that a personal essay is about your ideas and feelings. Make it personal and reflective of *you*.

Revising Review your introduction to be sure you opened in an interesting way. Will it make the reader want to continue reading?

◆ **Grammar Application**
Add adjectives to your personal essay to create greater detail and add interest.

✓ ASSESSMENT OPTIONS

Formal Assessment, Selection Test, pp. 75–77, and Assessment Resources Software. The selection test is designed so that it can be easily customized to the performance levels of your students.

Alternative Assessment, p. 19, includes options for less advanced students, more advanced students, interpersonal learners, visual/spatial learners, verbal/linguistic learners, and logical/mathematical learners.

PORTFOLIO ASSESSMENT
Use the following rubrics in the **Alternative Assessment** booklet to assess student writing:
Letter: Expression, p. 90
Editorial: Persuasion, p. 101
Biography: Research Report/Paper, p. 102
Writing Mini-Lesson: Expression, p. 90

PART **1**

Taking a Stand

We Demand, Joe Jones, Butler Institute of American Art, Youngstown, Ohio

Taking a Stand ◆ 249

The selections in this section focus on the theme of "Taking a Stand." "A Retrieved Reformation" tells the story of a former robber who tries to redeem himself. "Emancipation" is an excerpt from a photobiography on Lincoln, detailing his difficult position on what stand to take and when in the Civil War. "O Captain! My Captain!" is Walt Whitman's tribute to Lincoln. In "Gentleman of Rio en Medio," the main character stands firm on his beliefs in regard to a legal agreement. Finally, "Saving the Wetlands" tells the story of a young boy's pursuit to save the wetlands in his hometown.

Customize for
Varying Student Needs
When assigning the selections in this section, keep in mind the following factors:

"A Retrieved Reformation"
• Short story by O. Henry
• Students may need help with vocabulary
• Stories with a surprise ending

"Emancipation"
• An excerpt from *Lincoln: A Photobiography* detailing Lincoln's difficult decision about abolition during the Civil War

"O Captain! My Captain!"
• A famous poem by Walt Whitman
• Literature written in a historical context
• Students may need help with Whitman's language

"Gentleman of Rio en Medio"
• Short story based on an actual legal case
• Students may need help with vocabulary

"Saving the Wetlands"
• A short story about a boy's efforts to save the wetlands
• May serve as an inspiration for students to learn how they can make a difference

 Humanities: Art

We Demand, by Joe Jones
   Joe Jones (1909–1963) was born in St. Louis, Missouri, where he first began painting Midwestern scenes. He became interested in the social protest movements of the labor force at the time of the Great Depression. In 1953, he moved to New York where his social activities and art made him the leading social protest artist until after World War II.
   Explain to students that due to economic difficulties, many industrial workers protested for labor reform during the Great Depression.

1. Why do you think the painting is titled *We Demand? Students may say that the people are demanding better working conditions or more pay for their work.*
2. Why do you think the artist made the hand on the lead protestor so large? *Students may say the hand serves to represent the determination and force behind the protestors.*
2. How does this painting relate to the theme "Taking a Stand"? *Students may say that the workers are taking a stand against the hardships they are facing. They are demanding reform.*

249

Guide for Reading

OBJECTIVES

1. To read, comprehend, and interpret a short story
2. To relate a surprise ending to personal experience
3. To ask questions
4. To anticipate a surprise ending
5. To build vocabulary in context and learn the word root -simul-
6. To develop understanding of the placement of adjectives
7. To write a response to the story, with support through examples
8. To respond to a short story through writing, speaking and listening, and projects

SKILLS INSTRUCTION

Vocabulary:
Word Roots: -simul-
Spelling:
Adding -ion to Verbs That End in -te
Grammar:
Placement of Adjectives
Reading Strategy:
Ask Questions
Literary Focus:

Surprise Ending
Writing:
Support Through Examples
Speaking and Listening:
Monologue (Teacher Edition)
Critical Viewing:
Connect; Deduce; Connect

PORTFOLIO OPPORTUNITIES

Writing: Letter From Billy; Another Surprise Ending; Essay
Writing Mini-Lesson: Response to the Story
Speaking and Listening: Debate; Monologue
Projects: Comic Book; Research Report

More About the Author
William Sydney Porter, alias **O. Henry,** moved to New York City in 1902, where he wrote short stories at a rapid pace. He used mainly the language of ordinary conversation and explored how coincidence effects characters in their routines as they seek romance, adventure, and fulfillment. Many of his stories, including perhaps his most famous, "The Gift of the Magi," were inspired by his observations of the lives and losses of ordinary people in New York.

Meet the Author:

O. Henry (1862–1910)

O. Henry, who became one of America's best-known short-story writers, was born William Sydney Porter. His gift for storytelling was nurtured by his sister Evelina, who developed a game in which she would begin to tell a story and her brother would finish it. After his childhood in Greensboro, North Carolina, Porter moved to Texas in 1882. There, he worked as a ranch hand, a bank teller, a writer and publisher of a humor magazine, and a reporter for the *Houston Post*.

A Difficult Start O. Henry's career as a short-story writer did not start off well—in fact, it began in prison. In 1896, he was sent to jail for embezzling bank funds. During his three years in prison, he began to write short stories. Upon his release, William Sydney Porter adopted the pen name O. Henry. His stories, which show a keen understanding of human nature and often feature surprise endings, became very popular with magazine readers.

THE STORY BEHIND THE STORY

O. Henry spent much of his time in prison observing people and developing story lines. It was there that he heard of a bank robber and a safe cracker who inspired the character of Jimmy Valentine, the hero of "A Retrieved Reformation."

250 ◆ Quest for Justice

◆ LITERATURE AND YOUR LIFE

CONNECT YOUR EXPERIENCE

You may know, or have heard about, a person who has changed his or her life in a major way. A character in this story, caught in an unforeseen situation, decides to turn his life around completely.

THEMATIC FOCUS: Taking a Stand

In this story, a character takes a surprising stand and prepares to accept the consequences of his actions.

◆ Background for Understanding

HISTORY

"A Retrieved Reformation" takes place around the turn of the twentieth century in a town like the one on the facing page. The main character breaks into bank safes to steal money. At the time of the story, the locks, dials, and levers of most safes were located on the outside. Safe crackers developed special tools and techniques to punch out these parts. Today, safes are built with their locks and bolts on the inside, making them much harder to break into.

◆ Build Vocabulary

WORD ROOTS: -simul-

In this story, you'll encounter the word *simultaneously*. It contains the word root -simul-, which means "same." Therefore, events that happen simultaneously happen at the same time.

WORD BANK

Which word from the story means "full of virtue or goodness"? Check the Build Vocabulary box on page 253 to see if you chose correctly.

assiduously
virtuous
retribution
unobtrusively
simultaneously
anguish

Prentice Hall Literature Program Resources

REINFORCE / RETEACH / EXTEND
Selection Support Pages
Build Vocabulary: Word Roots: -simul-, p. 103
Build Spelling Skills, p. 104
Build Grammar Skills: Placement of Adjectives, p. 105
Reading Strategy: Ask Questions, p. 106
Literary Focus: Surprise Ending, p. 107
Strategies for Diverse Student Needs, pp. 39–40
Beyond Literature Cross-Curricular Connection: Science, p. 20

Formal Assessment Selection Test, pp. 78–80
Assessment Resources Software
Alternative Assessment, p. 20
Writing and Language Transparencies
Sunburst Organizer, p. 85
Daily Language Practice, p. 10
Resource Pro CD-ROM "A Retrieved Reformation"—includes all resource material and customizable lesson plan

 Listening to Literature Audiocassettes
"A Retrieved Reformation"

♦ A Retrieved Reformation ♦

Young of the Town, 1933, Gerrit V. Sinclair, Williams American Art Galleries, Tennessee

♦ Literary Focus

SURPRISE ENDING

O. Henry is known for startling his readers with surprise endings. A **surprise ending** is one that's different from what the writer leads you to expect. Even though you often can't predict a surprise ending, writers make them believable by dropping a few hints about the ending without giving it away.

♦ Reading Strategy

ASK QUESTIONS

You will get a better understanding of what you read if you **ask questions** about the characters and events. You might ask why a character behaves in a certain way or what an action really means. Then, read on to find answers to your questions. Use a chart like the one below to list your questions and the answers you find as you read "A Retrieved Reformation."

Questions	Answers
What will Jimmy do when he gets out of prison?	

Guide for Reading ♦ 251

Preparing for Standardized Tests

Grammar Students are often required to demonstrate their knowledge and understanding of grammar concepts, such as placement of adjectives (the concept for this selection), in order to answer standardized test questions. Point out to students that an *adjective* is a word used to describe a noun or pronoun—it *modifies* the noun or pronoun.

The story was *intriguing*.

Use the following sample test item:
The famous writer, O. Henry, penned an exciting story that is well-known.
In this sentence, *famous* modifies—

(A) O. Henry   (C) writer
(B) penned   (D) story

Tell students that an adjective may be placed before the word that it modifies, after the word it modifies, or after a linking verb (you may wish to use the Build Grammar Skills instruction on p. 258). Guide them to understand that *famous* is not specifically related to *penned* in this sentence; that *story* is modified by *exciting,* and although O. Henry is *famous*, the adjective modifies *writer*. Therefore, (*C*) *writer* is the correct answers. For further practice, use **Selection Support,** p. 105.

Write the words *retrieve* and *reformation* on the board. Have individuals or pairs of students look up the words in the dictionary and jot down the definitions. Then tell them that the title of the short story they will read is "A Retrieved Reformation." Challenge students to brainstorm for what the title might mean and what the story might be about. Allow students to glance at the illustrations that accompany the story if you wish. Record students' predictions, which you can refer to after they finish reading.

♦ Build Grammar Skills

Placement of Adjectives If you wish to introduce the grammar concept for this selection before students read, refer to the instruction on p. 258.

Customize for
Less Proficient Readers
Students will encounter many long sentences in this selection, which may present problems. Suggest that students break down long sentences into shorter parts.

Customize for
More Advanced Students
O. Henry often uses irony in his stories. For instance, he calls a jailed prisoner a "compulsory guest." Have students look for other examples of irony in this story, and record the examples in a two-column chart:

Ironic Phrase	Real Meaning
compulsory guest	*prisoner*

Humanities: Art

Young of the Town, 1933, by Gerrit V. Sinclair

This painting offers a glimpse into small-town America of the past. Discuss with students the mood of the scene, and what it suggests about the story to come. *The scene is peaceful, calm, safe, and homey. Students may predict that the story is set in a small town, or that young people play a significant part.*

"A Retrieved Reformation" tells of Jimmy Valentine, a convicted safe cracker who gets out of prison, commits some more robberies, falls in love, and then "goes straight." Under the alias Ralph Spencer, he begins to lead a respectable life as a shoe retailer engaged to the daughter of the local bank owner. One day "Ralph" is forced to use his crime skills to rescue a child locked in a safe. Ben Price, the police officer who is after Jimmy, sees him crack the vault. Since Jimmy acts out of love and without regard for the possible trouble he could bring upon himself, Price decides to believe in Jimmy's reformation.

◆ Reading Strategy

❶ **Ask Questions** Guide students to make inferences into the character of Jimmy Valentine by answering the question, "How might it affect Jimmy to have so many 'friends on the outside'"? *Students may say that he knows people who can "pull strings" for him to shorten his sentence or make his prison stay easier.*

◆ Reading Strategy

❷ **Ask Questions** Students may learn more about Jimmy by answering the question, "Why is the warden so sarcastic?" *The warden knows that Jimmy is guilty, but expects criminals to deny their guilt.*

►Critical Viewing◄

❸ **Connect** *The subject's clothing, hair style, and waxed moustache are old-fashioned; the formal pose was fashionable in photography in the past.*

Customize for
English Language Learners
This story has many idiomatic expressions that may elude students acquiring English. Pair these students with peer tutors who can paraphrase or pantomime the idioms. For example, "she colored slightly" means that she blushed, or turned red in the face. Peer tutors can pantomime this.

A Retrieved Reformation
O. HENRY

❶ A guard came to the prison shoe-shop, where Jimmy Valentine was <u>assiduously</u> stitching uppers, and escorted him to the front office. There the warden handed Jimmy his pardon, which had been signed that morning by the governor. Jimmy took it in a tired kind of way. He had served nearly ten months of a four-year sentence. He had expected to stay only about three months, at the longest. When a man with as many friends on the outside as Jimmy Valentine had is received in the "stir" it is hardly worthwhile to cut his hair.

"Now, Valentine," said the warden, "you'll go out in the morning. Brace up, and make a man of yourself. You're not a bad fellow at heart. Stop cracking safes, and live straight."

"Me?" said Jimmy, in surprise. "Why, I never cracked a safe in my life."

"Oh, no," laughed the warden. "Of course not. Let's see, now. How was it you happened to get sent up on that Springfield job? Was it because you ❷ wouldn't prove an alibi for fear of compromising somebody in extremely high-toned society? Or was it simply a case of a mean old jury that had it in for you? It's always one or the other with you innocent victims."

"Me?" said Jimmy, still blankly <u>virtuous</u>. "Why, warden, I never was in Springfield in my life!"

"Take him back, Cronin," smiled the warden, "and fix him up with outgoing clothes. Unlock him at seven in the morning, and let him come to the

▲ **Critical Viewing** What details in this photograph reveal that it was taken long ago? [Connect] ❸

bullpen.[1] Better think over my advice, Valentine."

At a quarter past seven on the next morning Jimmy stood in the warden's outer office. He had on a suit of the villainously fitting, ready-made clothes and a pair of the stiff, squeaky shoes that the state furnishes to its discharged compulsory guests.

The clerk handed him a railroad ticket and the five-dollar bill with which the law expected him to rehabilitate himself into good citizenship and prosperity. The

---
1. **bullpen** *n.*: Barred room in a jail, where prisoners are kept temporarily.

Block Scheduling Strategies

Consider these suggestions to take advantage of extended class time:

- Begin instruction with the **Daily Language Practice,** p. 10. Or you may wish to begin with the Build Vocabulary feature on p. 250.
- Use Reading Strategy: Ask Questions, p. 251, to help students develop ways to examine the text. Have them read in pairs, applying the strategy as they go. When they have finished reading, have them review the Reading Strategy exercise on p. 258 to reinforce their concept of asking questions as they read.

- Alternatively, have students read on their own, then meet in small groups to discuss the Guide for Responding, p. 257, and the Literary Focus, p. 258. Encourage them to share their reactions to the story's surprise ending.
- Have students select portfolio opportunities from the Idea Bank activities, p. 259. You might use the Speaking and Listening Mini-lesson, p. 259, to prepare students for the Monologue.
- Conclude with the Cross-Curricular Connection: Literature, p. 254, or Beyond the Classroom: Workplace Skills, p. 253.

warden gave him a cigar, and shook hands. Valentine, 9762, was chronicled on the books "Pardoned by Governor," and Mr. James Valentine walked out into the sunshine.

Disregarding the song of the birds, the waving green trees, and the smell of the flowers, Jimmy headed straight for a restaurant. There he tasted the first sweet joys of liberty in the shape of a chicken dinner. From there he proceeded leisurely to the depot and boarded his train. Three hours set him down in a little town near the state line. He went to the café of one Mike Dolan and shook hands with Mike, who was alone behind the bar.

"Sorry we couldn't make it sooner, Jimmy, me boy," said Mike. "But we had that protest from Springfield to buck against, and the governor nearly balked. Feeling all right?"

"Fine," said Jimmy. "Got my key?"

He got his key and went upstairs, unlocking the door of a room at the rear. Everything was just as he had left it. There on the floor was still Ben Price's collar-button that had been torn from that eminent detective's shirt-band when they had overpowered Jimmy to arrest him.

◆ Reading Strategy
What is Valentine planning to do with the burglar's tools?

Pulling out from the wall a folding-bed, Jimmy slid back a panel in the wall and dragged out a dust-covered suitcase. He opened this and gazed fondly at the finest set of burglar's tools in the East. It was a complete set, made of specially tempered steel, the latest designs in drills, punches, braces and bits, jimmies, clamps, and augers,[2] with two or three novelties invented by Jimmy himself, in which he took pride. Over nine hundred dollars they had cost him to have made at —, a place where they make such things for the profession.

In half an hour Jimmy went downstairs and through the café. He was now dressed in tasteful and well-fitting clothes, and carried his dusted and cleaned suitcase in his hand.

"Got anything on?" asked Mike Dolan, genially.

___

2. **drills . . . augers** (ô′ gərz) n.: Tools used in metalwork.

"Me?" said Jimmy, in a puzzled tone. "I don't understand. I'm representing the New York Amalgamated Short Snap Biscuit Cracker and Frazzled Wheat Company."

This statement delighted Mike to such an extent that Jimmy had to take a seltzer-and-milk on the spot. He never touched "hard" drinks.

A week after the release of Valentine, 9762, there was a neat job of safe-burglary done in Richmond, Indiana, with no clue to the author. A scant eight hundred dollars was all that was secured. Two weeks after that a patented, improved, burglar-proof safe in Logansport was opened like a cheese to the tune of fifteen hundred dollars, currency; securities and silver untouched. That began to interest the rogue-catchers.[3] Then an old-fashioned bank-safe in Jefferson City became active and threw out of its crater an eruption of bank-notes amounting to five thousand dollars. The losses were now high enough to bring the matter up into Ben Price's class of work. By comparing notes, a remarkable similarity in the methods of the burglaries was noticed. Ben Price investigated the scenes of the robberies, and was heard to remark:

"That's Dandy Jim Valentine's autograph. He's resumed business. Look at that combination knob—jerked out as easy as pulling up a radish in wet weather. He's got the only clamps that can do it. And look how clean those tumblers were punched out! Jimmy never has to drill but one hole. Yes, I guess I want Mr. Valentine. He'll do his bit next time without any short-time or clemency foolishness."

Ben Price knew Jimmy's habits. He had learned them while working up the Springfield case. Long jumps, quick getaways, no confederates,[4] and a taste for good society—these

___

3. **rogue-catchers** n.: Police.
4. **confederates** (kən fed′ ər its) n.: Accomplices.

◆ Build Vocabulary

assiduously (ə sij′ oo wəs lē) adv.: Carefully and busily

virtuous (vʉr′ choo wəs) adj.: Moral; upright

A Retrieved Reformation ◆ 253

◆ **Reading Strategy**
④ Ask Questions *He is probably planning more bank robberies.*

◆ **Literary Focus**

⑤ Surprise Endings Guide students to note the detail with which O. Henry describes Jimmy's tools and his pride in them. Ask them to predict how or if the tools will play a part in the story's ending. *Most students will expect at least one more bank robbery, although they may not predict the circumstances of the surprise ending.*

Comprehension Check ☑

⑥ Ask students what Mike is asking Jimmy? Does Jimmy have something in mind? *He is asking whether Jimmy has plans for another bank robbery. Jimmy ducks the issue with a joke.*

Customize for
Logical/Mathematical Learners

Students may or may not think that $900 for tools and robbery takes of $800, $1500, and $5000 sound like a lot of money. Remind them that the story is set nearly a hundred years ago, when $1500 could buy a house. Have students do research to determine how much these amounts would be worth at today's buying power. An Internet tool, at **http://www.westegg.com/inflation** is an inflation calculator, which allows users to get rough estimates of the value of those amounts today. We *strongly recommend* that you preview this site before you send students to it.

Customize for
Interpersonal Learners

This story has many ethical turning points where a character must make a decision about what to do. Have groups discuss rights and wrongs in this story, and how extenuating circumstances affect the characters. Challenge students to decide when—or whether—Jimmy redeems himself.

___

Beyond the Classroom

Career Connection
Careers in Security In this story, Jimmy Valentine eludes security to commit a crime. However, the "rogue-catcher," Ben Price, is able to track Valentine. In addition to being a police officer, there are many jobs for people interested in security, such as off-hours guards, drivers of armored vehicles, personal bodyguards, undercover store detectives, and members of the U.S. Secret Service, an agency charged with protecting the President and other public officials.

Invite interested students to list the traits people who work in the field of security might need, such as courage, a sense of duty, and the desire to protect. Then have them research the requirements and responsibilities for one or more security positions. They may want to include personal interviews in their research. To extend students' explorations into careers in security, encourage them to use information they obtained from researching to compare and contrast to another field of work, such as medicine or business.

ways had helped Mr. Valentine to become noted as a successful dodger of <u>retribution</u>. It was given out that Ben Price had taken up the trail of the elusive cracksman, and other people with burglar-proof safes felt more at ease.

One afternoon, Jimmy Valentine and his suitcase climbed out of the mail hack[5] in Elmore, a little town five miles off the railroad down in the blackjack country of Arkansas. Jimmy, looking like an athletic young senior just home from college, went down the board sidewalk toward the hotel.

A young lady crossed the street, passed him at the corner and entered a door over which was the sign "The Elmore Bank." Jimmy Valentine looked into her eyes, forgot what he was, and became another man. She lowered her eyes and colored slightly. Young men of Jimmy's style and looks were scarce in Elmore.

▲ **Critical Viewing** What would appeal to Jimmy Valentine about this town? [Deduce]

Jimmy collared a boy that was loafing on the steps of the bank as if he were one of the stockholders, and began to ask him questions about the town, feeding him dimes at intervals. By and by the young lady came out, looking royally unconscious of the young man with the suitcase, and went her way.

"Isn't that young lady Miss Polly Simpson?" asked Jimmy, with specious guile.[6]

"Naw," said the boy. "She's Annabel Adams. Her pa owns this bank. What'd you come to Elmore for? Is that a gold watch chain? I'm going to get a bulldog. Got any more dimes?"

5. mail hack *n.*: Horse and carriage used to deliver mail.
6. specious guile (spē´ shəs gīl´) *n.*: Crafty, indirect way of obtaining information.

Jimmy went to the Planters' Hotel, registered as Ralph D. Spencer, and engaged a room. He leaned on the desk and declared his platform[7] to the clerk. He said he had come to Elmore to look for a location to go into business. How was the shoe business, now, in the town? He had thought of the shoe business. Was there an opening?

The clerk was impressed by the clothes and manner of Jimmy. He, himself, was something of a pattern of fashion to the thinly gilded[8] youth of Elmore, but he now perceived his shortcomings. While trying to figure out Jimmy's manner of tying his four-in-hand,[9] he cordially gave information.

Yes, there ought to be a good opening in the shoe line. There wasn't an exclusive shoe store in the place. The dry-goods and general stores handled them. Business in all lines was fairly good. Hoped Mr. Spencer would decide to locate in Elmore. He would find it a pleasant town to live in, and the people very sociable.

Mr. Spencer thought he would stop over in the town a few days and look over the situation. No, the clerk needn't call the boy. He would carry up his suitcase, himself: it was rather heavy.

Mr. Ralph Spencer, the phoenix[10] that arose

7. platform *n.*: Here, a statement of intention.
8. thinly gilded *adj.*: Coated with a thin layer of gold; here, appearing well dressed.
9. four-in-hand *n.*: Necktie.
10. phoenix (fē´ niks) *n.*: In Egyptian mythology, a beautiful bird that lived for about 600 years and then burst into flames. A new bird arose from its ashes.

Cross-Curricular Connection: Social Studies

Rehabilitation The shoe shop that Jimmy Valentine worked in when he was in prison was a contemporary type of prisoner rehabilitation—generally considered one of the four main reasons for prisons (the others are retribution, incapacitation, and deterrence).

The practice of rehabilitation began at the Elmira Reformatory in New York in 1876, a correctional institution for younger offenders. The directors encouraged prisoners to prepare themselves for life outside, and they sought early parole for prisoners who demonstrated good behavior.

The theory behind rehabilitation, which has always been controversial, is that prisoners should participate in activities designed to change them into law-abiding citizens for eventual release. These activities often include taking educational courses and learning job skills. At the time that O. Henry's story takes place, the emphasis was on manual skills and crafts. Today, many disciplines are taught, including computer studies and law. In some prisons, inmates are paid to provide incentive. Some prisons have work-release programs in which inmates leave prison during the day for outside jobs.

from Jimmy Valentine's ashes—ashes left by the flame of a sudden and alterative attack of love—remained in Elmore, and prospered. He opened a shoe store and secured a good run of trade.

Socially he was also a success, and made many friends. And he accomplished the wish of his heart. He met Miss Annabel Adams, and became more and more captivated by her charms.

At the end of a year the situation of Mr. Ralph Spencer was this: he had won the respect of the community, his shoe store was flourishing, and he and Annabel were engaged to be married in two weeks. Mr. Adams, the typical, plodding, country banker, approved of Spencer. Annabel's pride in him almost equaled her affection. He was as much at home in the family of Mr. Adams and that of Annabel's married sister as if he were already a member.

One day Jimmy sat down in his room and wrote this letter, which he mailed to the safe address of one of his old friends in St. Louis:

Dear Old Pal:

I want you to be at Sullivan's place, in Little Rock, next Wednesday night, at nine o'clock. I want you to wind up some little matters for me. And, also, I want to make you a present of my kit of tools. I know you'll be glad to get them—you couldn't duplicate the lot for a thousand dollars. Say, Billy, I've quit the old business—a year ago. I've got a nice store. I'm making an honest living, and I'm going to marry the finest girl on earth two weeks from now. It's the only life, Billy—the straight one. I wouldn't touch a dollar of another man's money now for a million. After I get married I'm going to sell out and go West, where there won't be so much danger of having old scores brought up against me. I tell you, Billy, she's an angel. She believes in me; and I wouldn't do another crooked thing for the whole world. Be sure to be at Sully's, for I must see you. I'll bring along the tools with me.

Your old friend,
Jimmy.

On the Monday night after Jimmy wrote this letter, Ben Price jogged unobtrusively into Elmore in a livery buggy.[11] He lounged about town in his quiet way until he found out what

he wanted to know. From the drugstore across the street from Spencer's shoe store he got a good look at Ralph D. Spencer.

"Going to marry the banker's daughter are you, Jimmy?" said Ben to himself, softly. "Well, I don't know!"

The next morning Jimmy took breakfast at the Adamses. He was going to Little Rock that day to order his wedding suit and buy something nice for Annabel. That would be the first time he had left town since he came to Elmore. It had been more than a year now since those last professional "jobs," and he thought he could safely venture out.

After breakfast quite a family party went downtown together—Mr. Adams, Annabel, Jimmy, and Annabel's married sister with her two little girls, aged five and nine. They came by the hotel where Jimmy still boarded, and he ran up to his room and brought along his suitcase. Then they went on to the bank. There stood Jimmy's horse and buggy and Dolph Gibson, who was going to drive him over to the railroad station.

All went inside the high, carved oak railings into the banking-room—Jimmy included, for Mr. Adams's future son-in-law was welcome anywhere. The clerks were pleased to be greeted by the good-looking, agreeable young man who was going to marry Miss Annabel. Jimmy set his suitcase down. Annabel, whose heart was bubbling with happiness and lively youth, put on Jimmy's hat, and picked up the suitcase. "Wouldn't I make a nice drummer?"[12] said Annabel. "My! Ralph, how heavy it is! Feels like it was full of gold bricks."

"Lot of nickel-plated shoehorns in there," said Jimmy, coolly, "that I'm going to return. Thought I'd save express charges by taking them up. I'm getting awfully economical."

---

11. **livery buggy** *n.*: Horse and carriage for hire.
12. **drummer** *n.*: Traveling salesman.

◆ Build Vocabulary

retribution (re′ trə byoo′ shən) *n.*: Punishment for wrong-doing

unobtrusively (un′ əb troo′ siv lē) *adv.*: Without calling attention to oneself

255

◆ Literary Focus

6 Surprise Endings Ask students whether they believe that love has the power to reform a person. Do they believe that Ralph Spencer is a new man? *Some students may say that love can make people want to become something different than they were before. Challenge them to predict what may happen, and then read on to verify their predictions.*

Spelling

7 With this selection's Build Vocabulary excercise, p. 258, students learn to drop the silent e in action verbs that end in *te* before adding *-ion* to make the noun form. Ask students how they would alter the spelling of the word *duplicate* to create the noun form. *Drop the e, add -ion to spell duplication.*

◆ Reading Strategy

8 Ask Questions Ask students to explain what Ben means when he questions himself about whether Jimmy will marry the banker's daughter. *Ben hints that the wedding may not take place because he will arrest Ralph Spencer, who is really ex-convict Jimmy Valentine.*

Speaking and Listening Mini-Lesson

Monologue

This mini-lesson supports the Speaking and Listening activity in the Idea Bank on p. 259.

Introduce Review with students what a monologue is; how a monologue differs from a dialogue; and how a monologue can convey feelings and thoughts without narrative description.

Develop Have students work in pairs or small groups to determine the kinds of responses Annabel would be likely to give. Remind them to be true to the character of Annabel and to the nature of her relationship with Ralph/Jimmy.

Students can use the Sunburst Organizer in **Writing and Language Transparencies,** p. 85, to organize their ideas. Then, have them plan their monologues.

Apply Have students perform the monologues live for the class, or on videotape, if equipment is available.

Assess Evaluate students based on how well their monologues reflect the character of Annabel. In addition, students might use the Peer Assessment: Dramatic Performance form, p. 116, in **Alternative Assessment.**

►Critical Viewing◄

❶ Connect *Like Annabel, the woman in the photo is young, beautiful, wealthy, romantic, and she holds a rose.*

◆ Critical Thinking

❷ Speculate As Mr. Adams explains the workings of the lock, why would Spencer show "a courteous but not too intelligent interest"? *Jimmy, an experienced safe cracker, would probably be very interested to know how a modern time lock works. But he doesn't want to seem too interested for fear of revealing his hidden past.*

◆ Literary Focus

❸ Surprise Endings Students already know that this story has a surprise ending; they've made some predictions about it. At this point, ask them where they think this plot line is going. *Students may expect Jimmy to use his tools to crack open the safe to free the child and in so doing expose his identity to Ben Price.*

Thematic Focus

❹ Taking a Stand What stand does Jimmy take? What does he risk by doing this? *He knows that he must use his crime skills to rescue Agatha, although it will make him look bad in front of Annabel, and will bring up all kinds of uncomfortable questions he will have to answer.*

▲ **Critical Viewing** Does the woman in this photograph share any qualitites with Annabel, as described in the story? Explain. **[Connect]**

The Elmore Bank had just put in a new safe and vault. Mr. Adams was very proud of it, and insisted on an inspection by everyone. The vault was a small one, but it had a new, patented door. It fastened with three solid steel bolts thrown <u>simultaneously</u> with a single handle, and had a time lock. Mr. Adams beamingly explained its workings to Mr. Spencer, who showed a courteous but not too intelligent interest. The two children, May and Agatha, were delighted by the shining metal and funny clock and knobs.

While they were thus engaged Ben Price sauntered in and leaned on his elbow, looking casually inside between the railings. He told

the teller that he didn't want anything; he was just waiting for a man he knew.

Suddenly there was a scream or two from the women, and a commotion. Unperceived by the elders, May, the nine-year-old girl, in a spirit of play, had shut Agatha in the vault. She had then shot the bolts and turned the knob of the combination as she had seen Mr. Adams do.

The old banker sprang to the handle and tugged at it for a moment. "The door can't be opened," he groaned. "The clock hasn't been wound nor the combination set."

Agatha's mother screamed again, hysterically.

"Hush!" said Mr. Adams, raising his trembling hand. "All be quiet for a moment. Agatha!" he called as loudly as he could. "Listen to me." During the following silence they could just hear the faint sound of the child wildly shrieking in the dark vault in a panic of terror.

"My precious darling!" wailed the mother. "She will die of fright! Open the door! Oh, break it open! Can't you men do something?"

"There isn't a man nearer than Little Rock who can open that door," said Mr. Adams, in a shaky voice. "My God! Spencer, what shall we do? That child—she can't stand it long in there. There isn't enough air, and, besides, she'll go into convulsions from fright."

Agatha's mother, frantic now, beat the door of the vault with her hands. Somebody wildly suggested dynamite. Annabel turned to Jimmy, her large eyes full of <u>anguish</u>, but not yet despairing. To a woman nothing seems quite impossible to the powers of the man she worships.

"Can't you do something, Ralph—*try*, won't you?"

He looked at her with a queer, soft smile on his lips and in his keen eyes.

◆ **Beyond the Classroom**

Workplace Skills

Accepting Consequences At the end of this story, Jimmy Valentine, who once denied doing anything wrong, prepares to accept the consequences of demonstrating his safe-cracking skills. People who accept the outcome of their actions exhibit a sense of maturity, honesty, and respect for others. These traits are highly valued by employers.

Have students discuss the kinds of hard choices people might have to make in their jobs, such as admitting to a costly error, missing a deadline,

losing something of value, or accidentally passing on faulty information. Although making mistakes is human, facing them forthrightly can be painful. Invite pairs of students to role-play job situations in which someone admits an error in judgment to his or her boss, and a boss reacts to the admission. Help them develop their scenarios and then encourage them to try several approaches to the situations. When they feel they have achieved the most successful way of handling the situation, ask them to share their role-plays with their classmates.

"Annabel," he said, "give me that rose you are wearing, will you?"

Hardly believing that she heard him aright, she unpinned the bud from the bosom of her dress, and placed it in his hand. Jimmy stuffed it into his vest pocket, threw off his coat and pulled up his shirt sleeves. With that act Ralph D. Spencer passed away and Jimmy Valentine took his place.

"Get away from the door, all of you," he commanded, shortly.

He set his suitcase on the table, and opened it out flat. From that time on he seemed to be unconscious of the presence of anyone else. He laid out the shining, queer implements swiftly and orderly, whistling softly to himself as he always did when at work. In a deep silence and immovable, the others watched him as if under a spell.

In a minute Jimmy's pet drill was biting smoothly into the steel door. In ten minutes—breaking his own burglarious record—he threw back the bolts and opened the door.

Agatha, almost collapsed, but safe, was gathered into her mother's arms.

Jimmy Valentine put on his coat, and walked outside the railings toward the front door. As he went he thought he heard a far-away voice that he once knew call "Ralph!" But he never hesitated.

At the door a big man stood somewhat in his way.

"Hello, Ben!" said Jimmy, still with his strange smile. "Got around at last, have you? Well, let's go. I don't know that it makes much difference, now."

And then Ben Price acted rather strangely.

"Guess you're mistaken, Mr. Spencer," he said. "Don't believe I recognize you. Your buggy's waiting for you, ain't it?"

And Ben Price turned and strolled down the street.

◆ **Literary Focus**
In what way is this ending surprising? **5**

◆ **Build Vocabulary**

simultaneously (sī´ məl tā´ nē əs lē) *adv.*: Occurring at the same time

anguish (aŋ´ gwish) *n.*: Great suffering from worry

Guide for Responding

◆ LITERATURE AND YOUR LIFE

Reader's Response Would you have done what Ben Price did? Explain.

Thematic Focus Why does Valentine take a stand that could alter the course of his life?

☑ Check Your Comprehension

1. Why is Jimmy Valentine in prison?
2. How does Valentine support himself after his release from prison?
3. Who is Ben Price?
4. At what point in the story does Valentine have a change of heart? What causes this change?

◆ Critical Thinking

INTERPRET
1. Find at least two details in the story that prove Valentine has really changed. **[Support]**
2. Why does Ben Price pretend not to know Valentine at the bank? **[Infer]**
3. In your opinion, does Price do the right thing? Explain. **[Draw Conclusions]**
4. Explain the meaning of the story's title. **[Interpret]**

APPLY
5. What message does this story suggest about life in general? **[Synthesize]**

A Retrieved Reformation ◆ 257

Beyond the Selection

FURTHER READING
Other Works by O. Henry
"The Gift of the Magi"
"The Ransom of Red Chief"
"After Twenty Years"
Other Works with Surprise Endings
"The Californian's Tale," Mark Twain
"The Necklace," Guy de Maupassant
"The Dying Detective," Arthur Conan Doyle

INTERNET
We suggest the following site on the Internet (all Web sites are subject to change).
For more about the O. Henry Museum in Austin, Texas, with a virtual walking tour of O. Henry sites:

http://www.ci.austin.tx.us/parks/ohenry.htm
We *strongly recommend* that you preview this site before you send students to it.

257

Answers

◆ Reading Strategy

1. Students may cite Jimmy's love for Annabel and his desire for a future with her, as well as his letter offering to give away his old tools, as evidence that his new life would last.

2. It shows the unpredictability of life, O. Henry's belief that people can change, and that forgiveness and mercy exist.

◆ Build Vocabulary

Using the Word Root -simul-
1. b   2. a   3. c

Spelling Strategy
1. rehabilitation;   2. relation;
3. stimulation;   4. promotion

Using the Word Bank
1. assiduously
2. virtuous
3. retribution
4. unobtrusively
5. simultaneously
6. anguish

◆ Literary Focus

1. (a) Students will probably say that they expected another bank robbery. (b) The clues that may have led them to this belief include Jimmy getting his old crime tools and plotting to meet the banker's daughter.

2. (a) It ended with Price's decision not to recognize Jimmy. (b) O. Henry says that Jimmy "forgot who he was, and became another man." He describes Ralph as a "phoenix that arose from Jimmy Valentine's ashes." Ralph (Jimmy) says that he's "getting economical." Jimmy is ready to accept the consequences of his actions.

◆ Build Grammar Skills

Practice
1. adjective: innocent; modified noun: victims
2. adjective: young; modified noun: men; adjective: scarce; modified noun: men
3. adjective: all; modified noun: lines; adjective: good; modified noun: business
4. adjectives: typical, plodding; modified noun: Mr. Adams; adjective: country; modified noun: banker
5. adjective: pet; modified noun: drill; adjective: steel; modified noun: door

---

Guide for Responding (continued)

◆ Reading Strategy

ASK QUESTIONS

Asking questions and then answering them helps you to remember details about a story's plot and its characters.

1. You may have questioned whether Jimmy's "new life" in Elmore would last. What details in the story led to your answer?

2. How does answering "Why does Ben Price let Jimmy go?" help you to understand the story?

◆ Build Vocabulary

USING THE WORD ROOT -simul-

Keeping in mind that the word root -simul-, as in simultaneously, means "same," match each word with its definition.

1. simulcast   a. to look or act the same
2. simulate   b. broadcast at the same time on radio and television
3. simulation   c. an imitation

SPELLING STRATEGY

When you add -ion to verbs that end in te, you drop the e before adding -ion:

contribute + -ion = contribution

On a piece of paper, write the noun forms of these verbs by adding the -ion suffix.

1. rehabilitate   3. stimulate
2. relate   4. promote

USING THE WORD BANK

On your paper, complete each sentence with one of the words in the Word Bank.

1. If you are studying _____?_____, you are studying carefully.
2. Jimmy earned respect in Elmore by living a _____?_____ life.
3. Detention is a type of _____?_____.
4. An elephant cannot move _____?_____.
5. Two things that occur at the same time happen _____?_____.
6. Tears can be a sign of _____?_____.

◆ Literary Focus

SURPRISE ENDING

To make a **surprise ending** believable, an author includes hints in the story that point to the ending without giving it away.

1. (a) How did you think the story would end? (b) Which clues led you to expect this ending?
2. (a) How did the story really end? (b) What clues did the author plant, leading to this ending?

◆ Build Grammar Skills

PLACEMENT OF ADJECTIVES

Adjectives make nouns and pronouns more vivid and precise by telling *what kind, which one,* or *how many.* An adjective may occupy one of several positions in relation to the word it modifies:

Before the modified word: The *dusty* case contained *expensive* tools.

After the modified word: The thief, *skilled* and *clever,* escaped with the money.

After a linking verb: The clerk thought the suitcase was *heavy.*

Practice Copy the following sentences. Underline each adjective, and draw an arrow to the noun it modifies.

1. "It's always one or the other with you innocent victims."
2. Young men of Jimmy's style and looks were scarce in Elmore.
3. Business in all lines was fairly good.
4. Mr. Adams, the typical, plodding, country banker, approved of Spencer.
5. In a minute Jimmy's pet drill was biting smoothly into the steel door.

Writing Application Write pairs of sentences in your notebook. In the first sentence, place the adjective before a noun it modifies. In the second sentence, use a linking verb and place the adjective after the noun or pronoun it modifies.

1. popular 2. honest 3. responsible 4. hilarious

Writing Application
Possible responses:

1. This popular story has a surprise ending. This story is popular for its surprise ending.
2. A bank job needs an honest worker. He is an honest worker.
3. She is a responsible mom. Moms are responsible for their kids.
4. Hilarious comments are an O. Henry specialty. That comment was truly hilarious.

 Writer's Solution

For additional instruction and practice, use the lesson in the *Writer's Solution Language Lab CD-ROM* on Supporting Sentences. You may also use Adjectives as Modifiers, p. 16, in the *Writer's Solution Grammar Practice Book.*

Build Your Portfolio

 ## Idea Bank

Writing

1. **Letter From Billy** Answer the letter that Jimmy Valentine sends to his "Old Pal" Billy in St. Louis.

2. **Another Surprise Ending** Write a new ending for "A Retrieved Reformation." You might change the existing ending or continue the story by adding another episode that tells what happens next.

3. **Essay** Write a brief essay in which you identify the story's theme and explain how the theme is revealed. Use details from the story to support your points.

Speaking and Listening

4. **Debate** [Group Activity] Form two teams to debate the pros and cons of Ben Price's decision not to recognize Jimmy Valentine in the bank. Meet with your team to prepare your argument before conducting the debate.

5. **Monologue** If you were Annabel, how would you feel about Jimmy at the end of the story? Deliver a monologue, a dramatic speech, to share Annabel's inner thoughts and feelings with the class. [Performing Arts Link]

Projects

6. **Comic Book** Retell the story of Jimmy Valentine in comic-strip form. Draw cartoon frames with captions and speech balloons to re-create the most important events from the story. [Art Link]

7. **Research Report** Research the history of banks in the United States. Find answers to these questions: What services did the first banks provide? How was money stored? How are banks different today? Share your findings with your class. [Social Studies Link]

 ## Writing Mini-Lesson

Response to the Story

Do you agree that Ben Price should have let Jimmy go free at the end of the story? Write a response to the story in which you present your opinion of Price's action.

Writing Skills Focus: Support Through Examples

Strengthen your writing by **supporting your ideas with examples.** Notice how O. Henry gives specific examples to support his statement that Jimmy's tools are "the finest set of burglar's tools in the East."

Model From the Story

It was a complete set made of specially tempered steel, the latest designs in drills, punches, braces and bits, jimmies, clamps, and augers, with two or three novelties invented by Jimmy himself . . .

Prewriting Decide whether or not you think Ben Price should have let Jimmy go free. In your notebook, write three reasons for your opinion. Next to each reason, write an example from the story that supports it.

Drafting Begin by stating your position, either for or against Ben Price's action. Then, list your reasons, and give support for those reasons. You might present your strongest reason first or you might save it for last.

Revising Make sure you've supported your ideas with examples. If necessary, go back through the story to find additional examples. Proofread carefully to correct errors in grammar, spelling, and punctuation.

> ◆ **Grammar Application**
> Look for places where changing the placement of adjectives will add variety to your sentences.

A Retrieved Reformation ◆ 259

 ## Idea Bank

Following are suggestions for matching the Idea Bank topics with your students' performance levels and learning modalities:

Customize for
Performance Levels
Less Advanced Students: 1, 4, 6
Average Students: 2, 4, 5, 6, 7
More Advanced Students: 3, 4, 5, 6, 7

Customize for
Learning Modalities
Verbal/Linguistic: 1, 2, 3, 4, 5, 7
Visual/Spatial: 6
Bodily/Kinesthetic: 5
Logical/Mathematical: 4, 7
Interpersonal: 4
Intrapersonal: 1, 2, 3, 6, 7

 ## Writing Mini-Lesson

Refer students to the Writing Handbook in the back of the book for instruction on the writing process and for further information on writing a response to literature.

 ### Writer's Solution

Writers at Work Videodisc
Have students view the videodisc segment on response to literature (Ch. 9), featuring Marilyn Stasio, to get ideas on how to write a literary response. Have students discuss the writing techniques that she shares.

Play frames 30102 to 39013

Writing Lab CD-ROM
Have students complete the tutorial on Response to Literature. Follow these steps:

1. Have students work through the Choosing Your Topic section, with audio clips to suggest ideas and techniques for the response.

2. Assign the Gathering Details section, which includes a character personality profile and an audio-annotated model on details that support an opinion.

3. Have students draft on computer.

4. Have students revise using use the Proofreading Checklist.

Writer's Solution Sourcebook
Have students use Chapter 9, "Response to Literature," pp. 266–295, for further support. The chapter includes in-depth instruction on varying sentence length and structure, p. 294.

✓ ASSESSMENT OPTIONS

Formal Assessment, Selection Test, pp. 78–80, and Assessment Resources Software. The selection test is designed so that it can be easily customized to the performance levels of your students.
Alternative Assessment, p. 20, includes options for less advanced students, more advanced students, interpersonal learners, visual/spatial learners, verbal/linguistic learners, bodily/kinesthetic learners, musical/rhythmic learners, and logical/mathematical learners.

PORTFOLIO ASSESSMENT
Use the following rubrics in the **Alternative Assessment** booklet to assess student writing:
Letter From Billy: Expression, p. 90
Another Surprise Ending: Fictional Narrative, p. 91
Essay: Critical Review, p. 107
Writing Mini-Lesson: Response to Literature, p. 106

Guide for Reading

OBJECTIVES

1. To read, comprehend, and interpret an essay and a poem
2. To relate historical context to personal experience
3. To determine cause and effect
4. To appreciate historical context
5. To build vocabulary in context and learn the suffix -ate
6. To develop skill in using adverbs
7. To write a letter using descriptive details
8. To respond to the selection through writing, speaking and listening, and projects

SKILLS INSTRUCTION

Vocabulary:
Suffixes: -ate

Spelling:
Words With the egz Sound Spelled ex

Grammar:
Adverbs

Reading Strategy:
Determine Cause and Effect

Literary Focus:
Historical Context

Writing:
Descriptive Details

Speaking and Listening:
Dialogue (Teacher Edition)

Viewing and Representing:
Lincoln Character Profile (Teacher Edition)

Critical Viewing:
Connect; Make a Judgment; Defend; Interpret

PORTFOLIO OPPORTUNITIES

Writing: Epitaph; Poem; Character Profile

Writing Mini-Lesson: Letter

Speaking and Listening: Dramatic Reading; Dialogue

Projects: Multimedia Presentation; Picture Book

More About the Authors
Russell Freedman visited major Lincoln historical sites while researching *Lincoln: A Photobiography.* The book not only won the Newbery Medal but was named the *School Library Journal's* Book of the Year.

Walt Whitman, while living in Washington, saw Lincoln almost every day—a fact he notes in *Specimen Days.* Whenever the president passed Whitman on his return from the Soldier's Home, they exchanged "cordial bows." Whitman was close enough on several occasions to describe the President's "sad" face. Whitman wrote that no artists or photographers had been able to capture this, Lincoln's true expression.

Meet the Authors:

Russell Freedman (1929–)

If you like to read biographies, you may be familiar with the work of Russell Freedman. His critically acclaimed non-fiction books for young people focus on great figures in American history, such as the Wright brothers and Eleanor Roosevelt.

Freedman was born and grew up in San Francisco, California. After his discharge from the army, he worked as a reporter and writer for the Associated Press. He published his first book in 1961 and has been a full-time writer ever since. *Lincoln: A Photobiography* won a Newbery Medal in 1988.

Walt Whitman (1819–1892)

Walt Whitman, one of America's greatest poets, began his career as a printer and journalist in New York City. During the Civil War, he worked in military hospitals in Washington, D.C. Although he never met President Lincoln, he often saw the President at a distance in Washington. Lincoln's death moved Whitman to compose two famous poems, "O Captain! My Captain!" and "When Lilacs Last in the Dooryard Bloom'd." Whitman became widely recognized as a poet who loved democracy and who championed the individual.

◆ LITERATURE AND YOUR LIFE

CONNECT YOUR EXPERIENCE

Think of a leader you admire, someone who has the capacity to change the world for the better. This is the kind of leader Abraham Lincoln was. Lincoln, the subject of these two selections, is considered by many people to be among the greatest leaders of all time.

THEMATIC FOCUS: Taking a Stand

Doing what is right can be challenging. President Lincoln, for example, had to make an important decision about slavery. As you read "Emancipation," notice all the factors he had to consider in making his decision.

◆ Background for Understanding

HISTORY

Although President Lincoln is remembered as a great leader, he did not always have the full support of the American people. One reason is that Lincoln opposed slavery while many southern landowners supported it. A month after Lincoln's inauguration in 1861, eleven southern states left the Union to form their own Confederacy. Civil war broke out between the Union and the Confederacy. Slavery was one of the key issues of the war.

◆ Build Vocabulary

SUFFIXES: -ate

Lincoln feared that his decision might "alienate" certain people. The word *alienate* is derived from *alien,* an adjective meaning "opposed." The suffix -ate means "to make or apply." When you add -ate to *alien,* it becomes a verb meaning "to make unfriendly or opposed."

WORD BANK

Which word from the list is related to the verb *humiliate*? Check the Build Vocabulary box on page 265 to see if you chose correctly.

alienate
compensate
shackles
peril
decisive
humiliating
exulting
tread

Prentice Hall Literature Program Resources

REINFORCE / RETEACH / EXTEND
Selection Support Pages
Build Vocabulary: Suffixes: -ate, p. 108
Build Spelling Skills, p. 109
Build Grammar Skills: Adverbs, p. 110
Reading Strategy: Cause and Effect, p. 111
Literary Focus: Historical Context, p. 112

Strategies for Diverse Student Needs,
pp. 41–42

Beyond Literature Workplace Skills: Decision Making, p. 21

Formal Assessment Selection Test, pp. 81–83, Assessment Resources Software

Alternative Assessment, p. 21

Daily Language Practice, p. 48

Resource Pro CD-ROM "Emancipation"; "O Captain! My Captain!"—includes all resource material and customizable lesson plan

Listening to Literature Audiocassettes "Emancipation"; "O Captain! My Captain!"

◆ Emancipation ◆
O Captain! My Captain!

Abraham Lincoln, George Peter Alexander Healy, In the Collection of The Corcoran Gallery of Art, Washington, DC

◆ Reading Strategy

DETERMINE CAUSE AND EFFECT

A **cause** is an action, event, or situation that makes something happen. An **effect** is the result produced by a cause. Historians agree that slavery was one of several causes of the Civil War. In "Emancipation," President Lincoln debates with himself whether he should abolish slavery and, if so, what the effect of his decision would be. As you read, look for cause-and-effect relationships among events.

◆ Literary Focus

HISTORICAL CONTEXT

The **historical context** of a literary work is the time period about which it is written or during which it is set. Knowing the events and issues of a period in history can help you understand references and ideas in a work of literature. For example, "O Captain! My Captain!" was inspired by the tragic death of President Lincoln and reflects the pain Americans experienced during the Civil War.

The timeline below shows events you will read about in these selections.

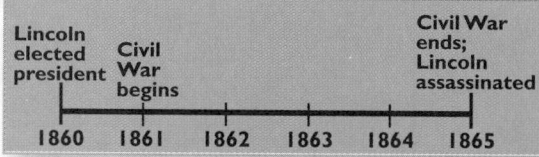

	Lincoln elected president	Civil War begins				Civil War ends; Lincoln assassinated	
	1860	1861	1862	1863	1864	1865	

Guide for Reading ◆ 261

Abraham Lincoln was the first American President extensively photographed throughout his political career—the physical effects of the job's heavy responsibility were captured on film. Show students two photos of Lincoln: one taken when he first took office in 1861, and the final portrait, by Alexander Gardner, which was taken 4 days before the assassination. Ask students to respond to the photos. Then lead them into the selection by having them examine the images of Lincoln in their books.

◆ Build Grammar Skills

Adverbs If you wish to introduce the grammar concept or skill for this selection before students read, refer to the instruction on p. 268.

Customize for
Less Proficient Readers

Give students geograhical information to understand the issues in 1862. Identify the settings of the essay, and use a map of the divided country (p. 514). Use any U.S. map to show the two streams that were sites of major battles, Bull Run (Manassas, VA) and Antietam Creek (Sharpsburg, MD).

Customize for
More Advanced Students

Have students use a chart to record the issues and likely responses to Lincoln's questions or decisions:

Lincoln	Abolitionists	Abolition Opponents
Free slaves?	Yes, at once	No; free black in North will take our jobs

Humanities: Art

Abraham Lincoln, by George Peter Alexander Healy

Healy was a leading American portrait painter of the mid-nineteenth century. He studied and painted in France and then returned to the U.S. to paint prominent business leaders and statesmen. Ask students to speculate about when this portrait of Lincoln was done. *Lincoln's youth and clean-shaven face suggest that he sat for the portrait before he became President.*

Preparing for Standardized Tests

Reading Standardized tests often include reading selections that require students to think critically about various curriculum areas. The test format may call for students to evaluate all possible answers in order to identify the best one. To offer students practice in thinking critically, have them read p. 264. Give them the following set of answers to the boxed Reading Strategy prompt:

(A) The fall is a good time for proclamations to have a strong effect.

(B) A proclamation is more effective when it is delivered from a position of strength.

(C) For a proclamation to be effective, it needs to be threatening to political enemies.

(D) Proclamations are more effective when they're issued after a battle, not before.

Discuss Seward's argument to show that *(B)* is the best answer. Guide students to understand that *(D)* is a weaker choice because that statement is true only in certain circumstances; if the battle is lost, then the losing side's proclamation is likely to be less effective. *(C)* is a weak choice, because a threat might stiffen resistance to a proclamation.

261

One-Minute Insight

In "Emancipation," Russell Freedman describes some of the difficult decisions Lincoln had to make in the process of trying to restore the Union. The piece shows that making the emancipation decree was risky militarily and politically, and the proclamation was both hailed and hated. It shows also that Lincoln understood the historical implications of his actions.

Clarification

❶ Discuss with students that "emancipation" is the act of releasing someone from bondage or servitude.

Thematic Focus

❷ **Taking a Stand** Tell students that Frederick Douglass was a former slave and one of the most eloquent abolitionists of his time. Ask them to explain what stand Douglass believed was essential for the government to take. *Douglass believed that the freeing of the slaves should be the punishment for the treason of the Southern states.*

◆ Literary Focus

❸ **Historical Context** Discuss with students that not all northerners were antislavery, that a vocal minority were abolitionists, and that not all southerners owned slaves or wanted to leave the Union.

▶ Critical Viewing ◀

❹ **Connect** *Students may point to the heavy load each carries and to the long shadows, indicating that they have worked a long day.*

Customize for
English Language Learners
To help students better understand the issues, events, and views expressed in this essay, have them make a 3-column chart and fill it in with related, but opposing, ideas and people.

	Opposites	
Union	←→	Confederacy
North	←→	South

Emancipation
from Lincoln: A Photobiography
Russell Freedman

❧

President Abraham Lincoln was leading the country in 1862 during the Civil War. He was challenged to find the best means for preserving the Union. His troops had just been beaten in fierce battles in Virginia. He had tough military and political decisions to make.

The toughest decision facing Lincoln . . . was the one he had to make about slavery. Early in the war, he was still willing to leave slavery alone in the South, if only he could restore the Union. Once the rebellion was crushed, slavery would be confined to the Southern states, where it would gradually die out. "We didn't go into the war to put down slavery, but to put the flag back," Lincoln said. "To act differently at this moment would, I have no doubt, not only weaken our cause, but smack of bad faith."

Abolitionists were demanding that the president free the slaves at once, by means of a wartime proclamation. "Teach the rebels and traitors that the price they are to pay for the attempt to abolish this Government must be the abolition of slavery," said Frederick Douglass, the famous black editor and reformer. "Let the war cry be down with treason, and down with slavery, the cause of treason!"

But Lincoln hesitated. He was afrald to <u>alienate</u> the large numbers of Northerners who supported the Union but opposed emancipation. And he worried about the loyal, slaveholding border states—Kentucky, Missouri, Maryland, and Delaware—that had refused to join the Confederacy. Lincoln feared

◀ **Critical Viewing** This photograph shows enslaved African Americans bringing in cotton from the fields. How can you tell theirs was a life of hardship? **[Connect]**

◆ Block Scheduling Strategies

Consider these suggestions to take advantage of extended class time:
- Before students read the selection, have them read both Meet the Authors and Background for Understanding, p. 260.
- Have students read the essay and the poem independently and then consider the Reader's Response and Thematic Focus on p. 267. Form small groups for the Discus-sion activity on p. 267. Encourage students to discuss their feelings about each—have them imagine themselves both in Lincoln's place and then in Whitman's.

- Invite volunteers to prepare a Dramatic Reading of the poem in the Speaking and Listening activities, p. 269.
- Set aside class time for students to complete their research for the Speaking and Listening Mini Lesson: Dialogue, and for the Multimedia Presentation and Picture Book activities on p. 269. Allow time for presentations.
- Provide time for students to conduct their research in order to complete their letters for the Writing Mini-Lesson, p. 269.

that emancipation might drive those states into the arms of the South.

Yet slavery was the issue that had divided the country, and the president was under mounting pressure to do something about it. At first he supported a voluntary plan that would free the slaves gradually and compensate their owners with money from the federal treasury. Emancipation would begin in the loyal border states and be extended into the South as the rebel states were conquered. Perhaps then the liberated slaves could be resettled in Africa or Central America.

⑤

Lincoln pleaded with the border-state congressmen to accept his plan, but they turned him down. They would not part with their slave property or willingly change their way of life. "Emancipation in the cotton states is simply an absurdity," said a Kentucky congressman. "There is not enough power in the world to compel it to be done."

⑥
> ◆ **Literary Focus**
> Which details in this paragraph reveal historical context?

Lincoln came to realize that if he wanted to attack slavery, he would have to act more boldly. A group of powerful Republican senators had been urging him to act. It was absurd, they argued, to fight the war without destroying the institution that had caused it. Slaves provided a vast pool of labor that was crucial to the South's war effort. If Lincoln freed the slaves, he could cripple the Confederacy and hasten the end of the war. If he did not free them, then the war would settle nothing. Even if the South agreed to return to the Union, it would start another war as soon as slavery was threatened again.

⑦

Besides, enslaved blacks were eager to throw off their shackles and fight for their own freedom. Thousands of slaves had already escaped from behind Southern lines. Thousands more were ready to enlist in the Union armies. "You need more men," Senator Charles Sumner told Lincoln, "not only at the North, but at the South, in the rear of the rebels. You need the slaves."

⑧

▲ **Critical Viewing** Here, an overseer watches over cotton-picking. Who do you think has an easier job—the overseer or the cotton pickers? [Make a Judgment] **⑨**

All along, Lincoln had questioned his authority as president to abolish slavery in those states where it was protected by law. His Republican advisors argued that in time of war, with the nation in peril, the president *did* have the power to outlaw slavery. He could do it in his capacity as commander in chief of the armed forces. Such an act would be justified

◆ **Build Vocabulary**

alienate (āl´ yən āt´) *v.*: To make unfriendly; estrange

compensate (käm´ pən sāt´) *v.*: To repay

shackles (shak´ əls) *n.*: Metal fastenings, usually a linked pair for the wrists or ankles of a prisoner

peril (per´ əl) *n.*: Exposure to harm or injury; danger

Emancipation ◆ 263

◆ **Literary Focus**

⑤ Historical Context In 1862, the idea of resettling liberated slaves overseas did not seem as inappropriate as it does today. It was a plan favored by many northerners, who wanted to free the slaves but felt that allowing them to remain as permanent residents would create social problems. As early as 1822, President James Monroe aided in the establishment of Liberia for the colonization of free African Americans in Africa.

◆ **Literary Focus**

⑥ Historical Context *Freeing the slaves was seen not only as a political or philosophical issue, but as a military one, too: ending slavery would damage the Confederate war effort.*

◆ **Build Grammar Skills**

⑦ Adverbs Discuss with students that adverbs answer the question to what extent about the adjectives and adverbs they modify. Tell them that when adverbs describe other modifiers, they are called intensifiers. Then, ask students to identify the adverbs and the words they modify in this sentence. *Boldly modifies* act; more *modifies* boldly.

◆ **Reading Strategy**

⑧ Determine Cause and Effect Ask students what Sumner, an abolitionist Republican from Massachusetts, said would happen if the slaves were freed. *Sumner said that many would immediately join the Union army and that the Confederacy would have to contend with former slaves who remained in the South.*

▶ **Critical Viewing** ◀

⑨ Make a Judgment *Most students will respond that the overseer had the easier job.*

Viewing and Representing Mini-Lesson

Lincoln Character Profile

This lesson supports the Character Profile writing activity in the Idea Bank on p. 269.

Introduce Have students brainstorm for ways of creating a character sketch or profile of a famous person, such as a great leader, without relying on language. Discuss how the essence of Lincoln's greatness might be captured with, for example, a collage, a mural, a diorama, a banner, a dance, or a performance piece.

Develop Begin by having students list ideas, qualities, events, and images that capture Lincoln's

stature. Then have students select their interpretive vehicle and begin gathering what they need to create their character sketches. You might enlist the aid of an art teacher or a drama teacher.

Apply Invite students to present their completed works, either by displaying them or performing them.

Assess Judge students' character profiles by how effective each is in terms of wordlessly expressing the essence of Lincoln. Judge them on their complexity, originality, and also on how well they get their message across to other students.

1 Defend *The Emancipation Proclamation changed the focus of the war and the course of history.*

Thematic Focus

2 Taking a Stand In what way was Lincoln's stand a compromise with slaveholders? *Although Lincoln was against slavery, he did not want to alienate citizens and slaveholders in the border states. To keep those states loyal to the Union, he treated slavery there differently.*

◆ Reading Strategy

3 Determine Cause and Effect *Seward claimed that for the proclamation to be effective, it had to come from a position of strength; a victory on the battlefield was needed.*

Clarification

4 The battle of Antietam, near the hamlet of Sharpsburg, Maryland, was not only the bloodiest day of the Civil War, but the bloodiest single day ever for Americans in any war in history. The day resulted in more than 23,000 casualties.

as a necessary war measure, because it would weaken the enemy. If Lincoln really wanted to save the Union, Senator Sumner told him, he must act now. He must wipe out slavery.

The war had become an endless nightmare of bloodshed and bungling generals. Lincoln doubted if the Union could survive without

The First Reading of the Emancipation Proclamation before the Cabinet, Courtesy of the Library of Congress

▲ **Critical Viewing** This painting depicts President Lincoln presenting the Emancipation Proclamation to his Cabinet. Why is this occasion worthy of capturing in art? [Defend]

bold and drastic measures. By the summer of 1862, he had worked out a plan that would hold the loyal slave states in the Union, while striking at the enemies of the Union.

On July 22, 1862, he revealed his plan to his cabinet. He had decided, he told them, that emancipation was "a military necessity, absolutely essential to the preservation of the Union." For that reason, he intended to issue a proclamation freeing all the slaves in rebel states that had not returned to the Union by January 1, 1863. The proclamation would be aimed at the Confederate South only. In the loyal border states, he would continue to push for gradual, compensated emancipation.

Some cabinet members warned that the country wasn't ready to accept emancipation.

But most of them nodded their approval, and in any case, Lincoln had made up his mind. He did listen to the objection of William H. Seward, his secretary of state. If Lincoln published his proclamation now, Seward argued, when Union armies had just been defeated in Virginia, it would seem like an act of desperation, "the last shriek on our retreat." The president must wait until the Union had won a decisive military victory in the East. Then he could issue his proclamation from a position of strength. Lincoln agreed. For the time being, he filed the document away in his desk.

◆ **Reading Strategy** According to William H. Seward, how would the timing of the proclamation change its effect?

A month later, in the war's second battle at Bull Run, Union forces commanded by General John Pope suffered another humiliating defeat. "We are whipped again," Lincoln moaned. He feared now that the war was lost. Rebel troops under Robert E. Lee were driving north. Early in September, Lee invaded Maryland and advanced toward Pennsylvania.

Lincoln again turned to General George McClellan—Who else do I have? he asked—and ordered him to repel the invasion. The two armies met at Antietam Creek in Maryland on September 17 in the bloodiest single engagement of the war. Lee was forced to retreat back to Virginia. But McClellan, cautious as ever, held his position and failed to pursue the defeated rebel army. It wasn't the decisive victory Lincoln had hoped for, but it would have to do.

On September 22, Lincoln read the final wording of his Emancipation Proclamation to his cabinet. If the rebels did not return to the Union by January 1, the president would free "thenceforward and forever" all the slaves everywhere in the Confederacy. Emancipation would become a Union war objective. As Union armies smashed their way into rebel territory, they would annihilate slavery once and for all.

The next day, the proclamation was released to the press. Throughout the North, opponents of slavery hailed the measure, and black people rejoiced. Frederick Douglass, the black abolitionist, had criticized Lincoln

 Beyond the Classroom

Workplace Skills

Leadership Abraham Lincoln exhibited leadership skills that were second to none. Facing issues as tough as any President will ever have to face, he guided the government successfully through his ability to make hard decisions, to respect the opinions of others, to compromise, and to show endless patience with subordinates.

Though few people will ever have the kind of leadership challenges that Lincoln did, all leaders must make decisions and deal with their consequences. Leaders must understand the impor-

tance of assuming responsibility for other peoples' welfare. These considerations apply to all leaders, from scoutmasters to political leaders.

Have students discuss why successful leaders on any level and in any context need these qualities. Then, ask them to add other qualities leaders should have to this list. Then, have students describe professional positions for which leadership skills are essential. Students should support their ideas with hypothetical situations in which a particular kind of leader might find himself or herself. Invite them to act out these situations.

severely in the past. But he said now: "We shout for joy that we live to record this righteous decree."

When Lincoln delivered his annual message to Congress on December 1, he asked support for his program of military emancipation:

"Fellow citizens, *we* cannot escape history. We of this Congress and this administration, will be remembered in spite of ourselves. . . . In *giving* freedom to the *slave*, we *assure* freedom to the *free*—honorable alike in what we give, and what we preserve."

On New Year's Day, after a fitful night's sleep, Lincoln sat at his White House desk and put the finishing touches on his historic decree. From this day forward, all slaves in the rebel states were "forever free." Blacks who wished to could now enlist in the Union army and sail on Union ships. Several all-black regiments were formed immediately. By the end of the war, more than 180,000 blacks—a majority of them emancipated slaves—had volunteered for the Union forces. They manned military garrisons and served as front-line combat troops in every theatre of the war.

The traditional New Year's reception was held in the White House that morning. Mary appeared at an official gathering for the first time since Willie's death[1], wearing garlands in her hair and a black shawl about her head.

During the reception, Lincoln slipped away and retired to his office with several cabinet members and other officials for the formal signing of the proclamation. He looked tired. He had been shaking hands all morning, and now his hand trembled as he picked up a gold pen to sign his name.

Ordinarily he signed "A. Lincoln." But today, as he put pen to paper, he carefully wrote out his full name. "If my name ever goes into history," he said then, "it will be for this act." ❺

---

1. **Mary appeared . . . Willie's death:** Mary Todd Lincoln was the President's wife. The couple's son William died in 1861 at the age of eleven.

◆ **Build Vocabulary**

decisive (di sī' siv) *adj.*: Having the power to settle a question or dispute

humiliating (hyoo mil' ē āt' iŋ) *adj.*: Embarrassing; undignified

◆ **Literary Focus**

❺ **Historical Context** Discuss with students that during this time of unprecedented events, Lincoln and the Congress knew that they were making history. They knew that they were dealing with ideas essential to the preservation of democracy and the future well-being of the nation.

Reinforce and Extend

Answers

◆ **LITERATURE AND YOUR LIFE**

Reader's Response Some students may respond that if Lincoln had not ended slavery, thereby helping the North to win the war, we would be two countries now, not one, and slavery would have gone on longer.

Thematic Focus Students may say that he was a good leader because he was able to act, but was also able to compromise and show patience.

☑ **Check Your Comprehension**

1. The hardest decision was the one Lincoln had to make about slavery.
2. Lincoln was afraid to alienate the northerners who supported the Union but opposed emancipation.
3. Lincoln recognized that freeing the slaves would help the Union war effort, and he understood that as commander-in-chief, he had the power to act.

◆ **Critical Thinking**

1. He feared that these states would join the Confederacy if he alienated them with anti-slavery measures.
2. Students may say that freeing the slaves would become a Union war objective and help the North win.
3. Lincoln wanted to jump-start the Northern war effort by making ending slavery the goal of the war. The battle of Antietam, a limited victory that followed several defeats, was the chance he had been waiting for.
4. Many students will choose issues involving civil rights; others may suggest that legal reform, education, international diplomacy, improvements in roads and transportation, and scientific endeavors would interest him. Some might say that Lincoln's compromises would be universally respected; others might say that people would find him wishy-washy.

Guide for Responding

◆ **LITERATURE AND YOUR LIFE**

Reader's Response Did Lincoln end slavery at the right time? Support your answer.

Thematic Focus Does Freedman present Abraham Lincoln as a good leader? Explain.

☑ **Check Your Comprehension**

1. During the Civil War, what was the toughest decision facing Abraham Lincoln?
2. What consequences did he anticipate from certain northerners?
3. Name two reasons that Lincoln decided to attack the issue of slavery boldly.

◆ **Critical Thinking**

INTERPRET

1. Why did Lincoln worry about Kentucky, Missouri, Maryland, and Delaware? **[Infer]**
2. Explain Lincoln's reasoning when he finally decided to issue the Emancipation Proclamation. **[Infer]**
3. Why did Lincoln choose to end slavery after the battle of Antietam Creek? **[Speculate]**

EXTEND

4. If Lincoln were President today, what issues would he bring to national attention? Would they earn him national respect? **[Social Studies Link]**

Emancipation ◆ 265

◆ **Cross-Curricular Connection: Social Studies**

African Americans in the War Free blacks, freed slaves, and slaves had a considerable effect on the outcome of the Civil War. There were slaves who supported the Confederate armies by working behind the lines, producing what the armies needed. There were the runaways and freed slaves who attached themselves to Union armies and worked behind northern lines. They were known as the "contraband of war." Then there were the free blacks who joined Union regiments or formed their own, and fought in several battles. The most famous of these was the 54th Massachusetts Regiment.

Have students learn more about the role of African Americans in the Civil War. In what engagements did they participate? How did they acquit themselves? How were they treated by the U.S. Army? By the Confederates? Were they equipped and paid like other troops? What, exactly, did those working behind the lines do in the North? In the South? Interested students should form research teams to find out the answers to these questions. Have them present their findings.

One-Minute Insight

"O Captain! My Captain!" is Walt Whitman's eulogy to Abraham Lincoln. In this famous poem of praise, Whitman compares Lincoln to a captain of a ship and our country to a ship.

◆ **Literary Focus**

❶ Historical Context Discuss with students that the "fearful trip" is the Civil War, the "ship" is the United States, and that the "prize" and the "port" refer to peace. Guide them to understand that the poem takes place at a time when the war has just ended. As needed, tell students that Lincoln was shot just days after Lee surrendered to Grant.

◆ **Critical Thinking**

❷ Draw Conclusions How do the poet and the nation feel about Lincoln's death? *Students may say that at first the people were in disbelief or shock, as if they had lost a father. For the poet, that disbelief will turn to mourning.*

▶ **Critical Viewing** ◀

❸ Interpret *Students may point to his calm and reassuring demeanor and the knowing look on his intelligent face as indications of his leadership qualities.*

Customize for
English Language Learners
Students may not be familiar with the nautical terms used in the poem. Guide them to look up the meanings of *port, vessel, deck,* and *anchor.* Point out that a ship of state is a metaphor for our country.

Customize for
More Advanced Students
Students who know Whitman's poetry may observe that "O Captain! My Captain!" is nothing like the unrhymed free verse of most of his poems. Guide them to see that Whitman reverted to more traditional forms so that a larger reading public might understand, share, and remember his grief over Lincoln's death. Also, he probably wanted to make the poem easy to memorize. Encourage interested students to memorize the poem.

266

O Captain! My Captain!

Walt Whitman

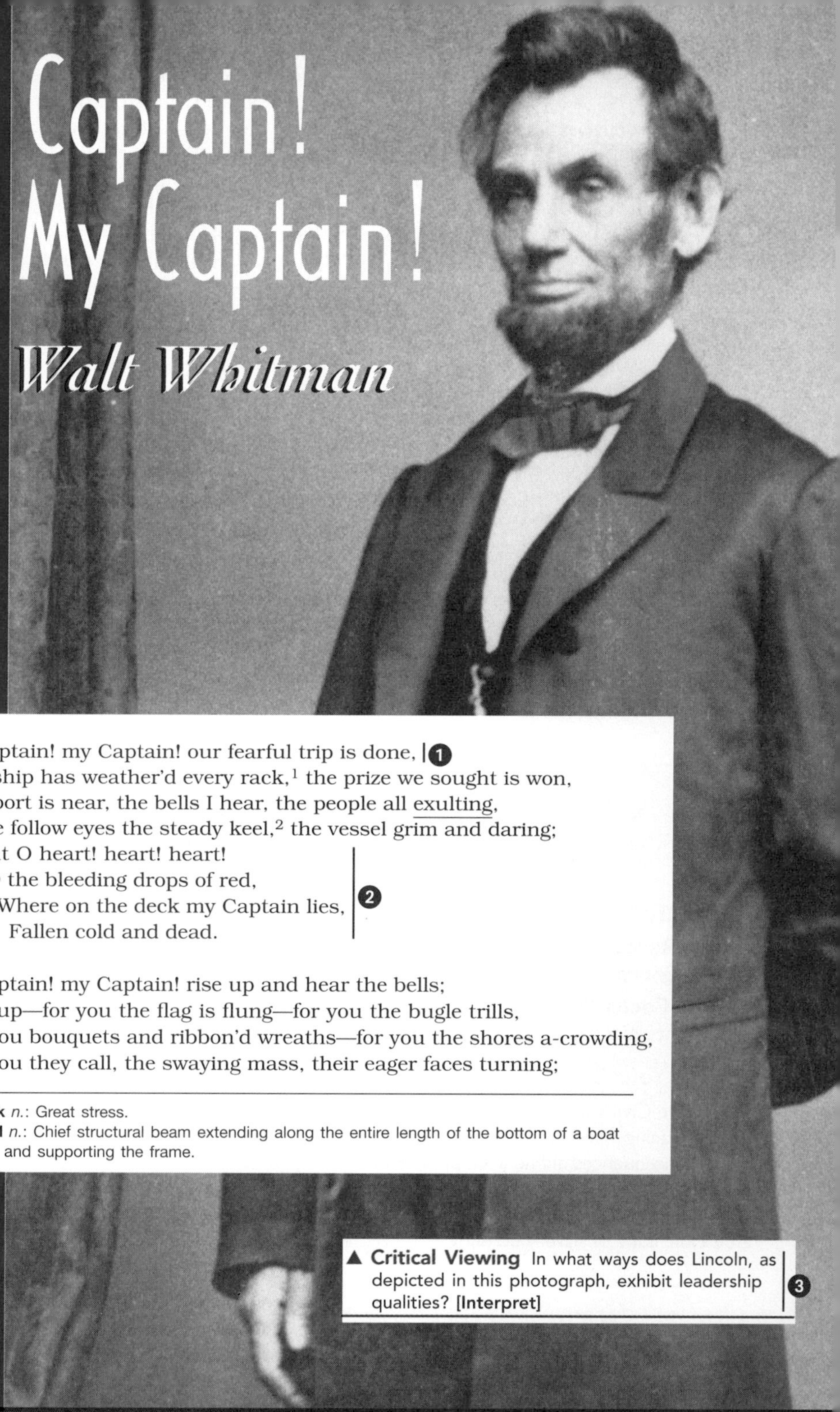

O Captain! my Captain! our fearful trip is done, **❶**
The ship has weather'd every rack,[1] the prize we sought is won,
The port is near, the bells I hear, the people all <u>exulting</u>,
While follow eyes the steady keel,[2] the vessel grim and daring;
5   But O heart! heart! heart!
    O the bleeding drops of red,
      Where on the deck my Captain lies,
      Fallen cold and dead.

O Captain! my Captain! rise up and hear the bells;
10 Rise up—for you the flag is flung—for you the bugle trills,
For you bouquets and ribbon'd wreaths—for you the shores a-crowding,
For you they call, the swaying mass, their eager faces turning;

___

1. **rack** *n.*: Great stress.
2. **keel** *n.*: Chief structural beam extending along the entire length of the bottom of a boat or ship and supporting the frame.

▲ **Critical Viewing** In what ways does Lincoln, as depicted in this photograph, exhibit leadership qualities? [Interpret] **❸**

Speaking and Listening Mini-Lesson

Dialogue
This mini-lesson supports the Speaking and Listening activity in the Idea Bank on p. 269.

Introduce Review with students the gist of what Seward advised Lincoln to do and how the President responded (p. 264). Review what dialogues are and how to format and punctuate them.

Develop Have small groups of students use the library to gather more information on this issue. Point out that general Civil War sources aimed at a broad audience, like Bruce Catton's *American Heritage Picture History of the Civil War,* are better

resources than encyclopedias. Once they have their information, students should write, revise, and practice their dialogues.

Apply Have teams present their dialogues. One way is for one student to narrate, another to speak Lincoln's lines, and a third to speak Seward's.

Assess Judge students' dialogues by the accuracy of their interpretations of key issues and views and by the quality of the performances. Or, use any of the following Peer Assessments: Dramatic Performance, p. 116; Speaker/Speech, p. 114; or Oral Interpretation, p. 115; in **Alternative Assessment.**

Here Captain! dear father!
  This arm beneath your head!
15   It is some dream that on the deck,
      You've fallen cold and dead.

My Captain does not answer, his lips are pale and still,
My father does not feel my arm, he has no pulse nor will,
The ship is anchor'd safe and sound, its voyage closed and done,
20 From fearful trip the victor ship comes in with object won;
    Exult O shores, and ring O bells! |**④**
      But I with mournful <u>tread</u>,
        Walk the deck my Captain lies,
          Fallen cold and dead.

◆ **Build Vocabulary**

exulting (ig zult´ iŋ) *v.*: Rejoicing
tread (tred) *n.*: Step

Guide for Responding

◆ **LITERATURE AND YOUR LIFE**

Reader's Response How does this poem affect you?

Thematic Focus "O Captain! My Captain!" mourns the death of President Lincoln. What kind of leader does Whitman consider Lincoln?

Discussion With a small group, create a list of the qualities that make a good leader. How close does Lincoln come to your standard?

☑ **Check Your Comprehension**

1. What has happened to the Captain? Why is this event unfortunate?
2. What is the other name the poet calls the Captain?

◆ **Critical Thinking**

INTERPRET
1. What pronoun does the poet use to modify the word *captain*? What is the significance of the pronoun? **[Interpret]**
2. In what ways does Lincoln's leadership of the country resemble a captain's role on a ship? **[Compare and Contrast]**
3. What is the mood of the poem? **[Interpret]**

EVALUATE
4. Do you think that the fate of a nation ever rests entirely on one person? Explain your answer. **[Make a Judgment]**

COMPARE LITERARY WORKS
5. Compare and contrast the portrayal of President Lincoln in these two selections. **[Compare and Contrast]**

O Captain! My Captain! ◆ 267

 Beyond the Selection

FURTHER READING
Other Works by Russell Freedman
Children of the Wild West
Eleanor Roosevelt: A Life of Discovery
Kids at Work: Lewis Hine and the Crusade Against Child Labor
Other Works by Walt Whitman
Specimen Days
Leaves of Grass

INTERNET
We suggest the following sites on the Internet (all Web sites are subject to change).
    For more information about Walt Whitman
http://www.liglobal.com/walt
    For links to sites about Abraham Lincoln:
http://deil/lang.uiuc.edu/web.pages/holidays/Lincoln.html/
    We *strongly recommend* that you preview these sites before you send students to them.

Answers

◆ Reading Strategy

1. They advised him that it would help the Union war effort and cripple that of the Confederacy.
2. He was waiting for a Union victory in battle.
3. The battle of Antietam, which ended Lee's invasion of the North, gave Lincoln cause to issue the proclamation.

◆ Build Vocabulary

Using the Suffix -ate
1. salivate; 2. vaccinate

Spelling Strategy
1. exhibit; 2. exert; 3. exact

Using the Word Bank
1. f
2. e
3. g
4. h
5. d
6. c
7. a
8. b

◆ Literary Focus

1. He felt pressure to preserve the Union, to both end and keep slavery, and to win the war.
2. Freeing the slaves would deprive the South of its behind-the-lines support system and it would provide troops for the Union armies. For these and moral reasons, Lincoln wanted to emancipate the slaves.
3. It was a tragedy because the nation lost a leader whose main interest was in preserving the Union and reuniting the country as painlessly as possible.

◆ Build Grammar Skills

Practice
1. adverb: differently; modifies *act*
2. adverb: already; modifies *had escaped*
3. adverb: carefully; modifies *wrote*
4. adverb: Yesterday; modifies *read*
5. adverb: more; modifies *moving*

Writing Application
Possible responses:
1. Lincoln was very cautious about freeing the slaves too soon.
2. Many firmly believed that slavery had caused the division between the North and the South.
3. Others expressed fear that the South would eventually begin another war if Lincoln ended slavery.

Guide for Responding (continued)

◆ Reading Strategy

DETERMINE CAUSE AND EFFECT

A **cause** produces a result. An **effect** is the result of the cause. To identify an effect, ask yourself, "What happened?" To identify a cause, ask, "Why?"
1. What did Lincoln's Republican advisors say would be the effect if Lincoln ended slavery?
2. What caused Lincoln's delay in issuing the Emancipation Proclamation?
3. What event caused Lincoln to believe it was time to issue the Emancipation Proclamation?

◆ Build Vocabulary Skills

USING THE SUFFIX -ate

The suffix -ate is usually used to form verbs. Often it is added to a root word that cannot stand alone as an English word: *compensate, emancipate.* Sometimes it is added to a noun or adjective: alien + -ate = alienate. Complete these sentences by adding the suffix -ate to the word in parentheses.
1. The smell of food can make a hungry person ____?____. (saliva)
2. Doctors ____?____ children against measles and other diseases. (vaccine)

SPELLING STRATEGY

The egz sound at the beginning of some words, like *exult,* is spelled ex. Write the word that begins with ex that fits each of the following definitions.

    exhibit   exert   exact

1. to present: ____?____
2. to put forth great effort: ____?____
3. very accurate: ____?____

USING THE WORD BANK

On your paper, match each Word Bank word to its closest definition.
1. compensate		a. great rejoicing
2. peril		b. make unfriendly
3. decisive		c. step
4. humiliating		d. restraints
5. shackles		e. danger
6. tread		f. repay
7. exulting		g. crucial
8. alienate		h. hurtful to one's pride

◆ Literary Focus

HISTORICAL CONTEXT

The **historical context** is the time period about which a literary work is written or during which it is set. Besides historical people and events, historical context refers to attitudes and beliefs common during the time.
1. What political pressures did Lincoln feel during the Civil War?
2. Why was emancipation important not just morally, but politically as well? How does knowing this help you to understand Lincoln's action?
3. Why was Lincoln's death a tragedy for both the North and the South?

◆ Build Grammar Skills

ADVERBS

An **adverb** is a word that modifies, or describes, a verb, an adjective, or another adverb. Adverbs answer the questions *when, where, in what manner,* and *to what extent.* This example from "Emancipation" shows how adverbs can add detail and clarity to writing:

> "If Lincoln *really* wanted to save the Union, . . . he must act *now.*"
>
> (*Really* tells to what extent he wanted; *now* tells when he must act.)

Practice On your paper, copy the following sentences. Underline the adverb in each sentence, and draw an arrow to the word it modifies.
1. "To act differently at this moment would . . . smack of bad faith."
2. Thousands of slaves had already escaped. . . .
3. Lincoln carefully wrote out his full name.
4. Yesterday I read a poem by Walt Whitman.
5. It was more moving than another poem I read.

Writing Application Copy the sentences below. Add at least one adverb to each sentence.
1. Lincoln was cautious about freeing the slaves.
2. Many believed that slavery had caused the division between the North and the South.
3. Others expressed fear that the South would begin another war if Lincoln ended slavery.

 Writer's Solution

For additional instruction and practice, use the lesson in the *Writer's Solution Language Lab CD-ROM* on Using Modifiers. You may also use Adverbs as Modifiers, p. 22, in the *Writer's Solution Grammar Practice Book.*

Build Your Portfolio

 Idea Bank

Writing

1. **Epitaph** An epitaph is an inscription on a tomb. Write an epitaph for Lincoln's grave that tells what he did for his country.

2. **Poem** "O Captain! My Captain!" mourns a leader for whom the poet had great respect. Write a poem honoring a leader whom you admire.

3. **Character Profile** Write a short profile of Lincoln, describing the qualities he possessed that made him a great leader.

Speaking and Listening

4. **Dramatic Reading** Give a dramatic reading of the poem "O Captain! My Captain!" Use your voice and gestures to convey the emotion of the poem. **[Performing Arts Link]**

5. **Dialogue [Group Activity]** With a partner, write and perform a dialogue between Lincoln and Seward about when to issue the Emancipation Proclamation. Before you write, conduct library research to find out what the issues were. **[Social Studies Link]**

Projects

6. **Multimedia Presentation** Dramatize the life of Walt Whitman or Abraham Lincoln in a multimedia presentation. Research the individual's life, collecting pictures, quotations, and relevant maps and timelines. Then, weave these materials into a script, and present the biography to your class. **[Social Studies Link; Media Link]**

7. **Picture Book [Group Activity]** As a class, create an illustrated book about the Civil War period, with small groups responsible for each chapter. The book should provide background information and illustrations. It may include the following: interviews with soldiers, enslaved people, citizens, and political leaders; reports about battles; and information on home life. **[Social Studies Link]**

 Writing Mini-Lesson

Letter

Before telephones and e-mail were invented, people communicated by writing letters. Imagine that you are someone who has just been freed by the Emancipation Proclamation. Write a letter to a friend describing your feelings.

Writing Skills Focus: Descriptive Details

Express your deepest feelings by using **descriptive details** that convey your emotions. For example, saying "joyful tears flooded my face" does more to indicate happiness than "I cried." Notice how Freedman conveys Lincoln's tension and exhaustion in this detail:

Model From the Selection
". . . now his hand trembled as he picked up a gold pen to sign his name."

Prewriting Imagine that you are someone who was born into slavery. List the thoughts you might have had upon learning that you are now free. Jot down phrases that express your emotions. To add authenticity to your letter, conduct research to find out what life was like for enslaved people before and after the Emancipation Proclamation. Take notes on what you learn.

Drafting Use your notes to draft your letter. Reread your writing, and add vivid details to give emphasis to your emotions. Order events chronologically to create clarity.

Revising Make sure that your letter includes a heading, a salutation, body, closing, and signature. If you aren't sure about standard letter form, refer to the Writing Process Workshop on p. 285.

> ◆ **Grammar Application**
> Look for places where you can use adverbs to make a description more precise.

Emancipation/O Captain! My Captain! ◆ 269

 Idea Bank

Following are suggestions for matching the Idea Bank topics with your students' performance levels and learning modalities:

Customize for *Performance Levels*
Less Advanced Students: 1, 4
Average Students: 2, 4, 5
More Advanced Students: 3, 5, 6, 7

Customize for *Learning Modalities*
Verbal/Linguistic: 1, 2, 3, 4, 5, 6, 7
Visual/Spatial: 6, 7
Bodily/Kinesthetic: 4, 5
Logical/Mathematical: 1, 3, 5, 6
Musical/Rhythmic: 2, 4
Interpersonal: 5, 6, 7
Intrapersonal: 2, 4

 Writing Mini-Lesson

Refer students to the Writing Handbook in the back of the book for instruction on the writing process and for further information on using descriptive details in letter writing.

 Writer's Solution

Writing Lab CD-ROM
Have students complete the tutorial on Expression. Follow these steps:
1. Have students use a Sunburst Diagram to gather details. Encourage them to use the Descriptive Word Bin to help them find words that express thoughts and details vividly.
2. Have students draft on the computer.
3. Have students use Revision Checklist when revising to strengthen their choice of adverbs by replacing weak ones.

Writer's Solution Sourcebook
Have students use Chapter 1, "Expression," pp. 1–31, for additional support. The chapter includes in-depth instruction on writing a personal letter, p. 7.

✓ ASSESSMENT OPTIONS

Formal Assessment, Selection Test, pp. 81–83, and Assessment Resources Software. The selection test is designed so that it can be easily customized to the performance levels of your students.

Alternative Assessment, p. 21, includes options for less advanced students, more advanced students, visual/spatial learners, intrapersonal learners, verbal/linguistic learners, logical/ mathematical learners, and musical/rhythmic learners.

PORTFOLIO ASSESSMENT
Use the following rubrics in the **Alternative Assessment** booklet to assess student writing:
Epitaph: Description, p. 93
Poem: Poetry, p. 104
Character Profile: Research Report/Paper, p. 102
Writing Mini-Lesson: Expression, p. 90

Guide for Reading

OBJECTIVES

1. To read, comprehend, and interpret a story and an essay
2. To relate a story and an essay to personal experience
3. To make inferences
4. To identify the resolution of a conflict
5. To build vocabulary in context and learn the word root -num-
6. To develop skill using adverbs to modify adjectives and adverbs
7. To write a persuasive speech supporting the environment
8. To respond to a story and an essay through writing, speaking and listening, and projects

SKILLS INSTRUCTION

Vocabulary:
Word Roots: -num-
Spelling:
Words With Silent g Before n
Grammar:
Adverbs Modifying Adjectives and Adverbs
Reading Strategy:
Make Inferences
Literary Focus:
Resolution of a Conflict

Writing:
Persuasive Tone
Speaking and Listening:
Debate (Teacher Edition)
Critical Viewing:
Infer; Evaluate; Speculate; Draw Conclusions; Compare and Contrast; Classify

PORTFOLIO OPPORTUNITIES

Writing: Advertisement; Letter to the Editor; Formula
Writing Mini-Lesson: Speech Supporting the Environment
Speaking and Listening: Speech; Debate
Projects: Artwork; Community Action

More About the Authors

Juan A. A. Sedillo held a deep love and regard for the Southwest where he and his ancestors lived. In writing this story, Sedillo made use of his legal background and understanding of people.

Barbara A. Lewis has won national acclaim for her work as an author and teacher. Lewis strongly believes in guiding young people to learn to think and solve real community and environmental problems in the world around them. To this end, she has appeared on television and has written many magazine articles and books.

Meet the Authors:

Juan A. A. Sedillo (1902–1982)

A native of New Mexico, Juan A. A. Sedillo was a descendant of early Spanish colonists of the Southwest. In addition to being a writer, Sedillo served as a lawyer and judge, and held a number of public offices.

THE STORY BEHIND THE STORY

"Gentleman of Río en Medio" is based on an actual legal case that arose from a conflict over the value of a piece of property. Sedillo turned this case into a gentle tale that reveals the attitudes and culture of the people he knew so well.

Barbara A. Lewis (1943–   )

Barbara Lewis never expected to be a writer. While teaching sixth grade in her home state of Utah, her class began a campaign to get rid of a hazardous waste site. Lewis was so impressed by her students' efforts that she decided to write about them.

Inspiration Lewis believes that when it comes to taking social action, age doesn't matter. She wants young people to know that they can make a difference. To demonstrate this belief, she wrote *Kids With Courage,* a book that tells the stories of eighteen young people who spoke up for what they believed in.

◆ LITERATURE AND YOUR LIFE

CONNECT YOUR EXPERIENCE

Something that you find valuable may not be valuable to someone else. Each of these selections focuses on a person who finds value in nature—a value that is not shared by everyone.

THEMATIC FOCUS: Taking a Stand

As you read these selections, think about the different ways in which people can take a stand.

◆ Background for Understanding

SCIENCE

Wetlands are areas of land where the water level remains near or above the surface of the ground for most of the year. Types of wetlands include bogs, fens, marshes, and swamps. Wetlands are home to many types of plants and animals, including several endangered species. They also help control flooding by retaining large amounts of water. Although wetlands in the United States are protected by the Federal Clean Water Act and by various state and local laws, many environmentalists are asking for stronger laws to protect them.

◆ Build Vocabulary

WORD ROOTS: -num-

The old man in "Gentleman of Río en Medio" has *innumerable* kin. The word root -num- tells you that the meaning of this word is related to *number*. *Innumerable* means "too many to be counted."

WORD BANK

If you needed to reach an agreement or negotiate, which word from the list indicates something you might take part in? Check the Build Vocabulary box on page 273 to see if you chose correctly.

negotiation
gnarled
innumerable
broached
petition
wizened
brandishing

Prentice Hall Literature Program Resources

REINFORCE / RETEACH / EXTEND
Selection Support Pages
Build Vocabulary: Word Roots: -num-, p. 113
Build Spelling Skills, p. 114
Build Grammar Skills: Adverbs Modifying Adjectives and Adverbs, p. 115
Reading Strategy: Make Inferences, p. 116
Literary Focus: Resolution of a Conflict, p. 117
Strategies for Diverse Student Needs, pp. 43–44
Beyond Literature Cross-Curricular Connection: Math, p. 22

Formal Assessment Selection Test, pp. 84–86
Assessment Resources Software
Alternative Assessment, p. 22
Writing and Language Transparencies
Sunburst Organizer, p. 85; Timeline, p. 65; Main Idea and Supporting Details Organizer, p. 61
Resource Pro CD-ROM "Gentleman of Rio en Medio"; "Saving the Wetlands"
Listening to Literature Audiocassettes "Gentleman of Rio en Medio"; "Saving the Wetlands"

Gentleman of Río en Medio
◆ Saving the Wetlands ◆

Interest Grabber Write on the board: "What makes someone a gentleman?" Have groups brainstorm for qualities or traits they believe gentlemen have. They can record ideas in a Sunburst Organizer in **Writing and Language Transparencies,** p. 85, or in a basic character web. Then, tell students that as they read about Don Anselmo, they can look for ways in which he fits the qualities, and find others they had not considered.

◆ Build Grammar Skills

Adverbs Modifying Adjectives and Adverbs If you wish to introduce the grammar concept for this selection before students read, refer to the instruction on p. 282.

Customize for
Less Proficient Readers
This story is mostly narration, but the few lines of dialogue reveal a great deal about Don Anselmo, especially when read aloud. Have trios of students locate parts of the story that contain dialogue, and then read them aloud. One student can read the narration, another can be Don Anselmo, and a third can read the narrator's responses.

Customize for
More Advanced Students
Challenge students to find deeper levels of meaning as they make inferences about characters or situations. They can adapt the chart on p. 271 by adding a third column, in which they list subtle or hidden meanings. For instance, they can infer from the detail about Don Anselmo's umbrella that he is poor. On a deeper level, they might infer that a walking stick befits a proud gentleman, or that it serves as a link to the past.

◆ Literary Focus
RESOLUTION OF A CONFLICT
In literature, as in life, a **conflict** is a struggle between opposing forces or a problem that must be solved. The **resolution** is the way that the conflict is solved, the final outcome. As you read, think about how the conflicts in these selections might be resolved. When you finish, ask yourself if each resolution satisfies you.

◆ Reading Strategy
MAKE INFERENCES
An **inference** is a reasonable conclusion you can draw from given facts or clues. Noticing details a writer shares with you helps you "read between the lines," or make inferences, about a character, a situation, or the way in which a conflict might be resolved. Use a chart like the one below to list details in the selections and the inferences you draw from them.

Detail	Inference
Don Anselmo carries a broken umbrella instead of a cane.	He has little money, or he is thrifty.

Guide for Reading ◆ 271

Customize for
English Language Learners
Tell students from non-Spanish-speaking backgrounds that the Don in Don Anselmo is a title of respect used before a man's first name—generally used before a man's last name in Spanish is Señor, the equivalent of the English "Mr." Help students make an analogy between these titles of respect and similar titles in English and in their own languages.

Preparing for Standardized Tests

Reading In general, students who can make inferences get more from what they read. They can use this strategy to answer certain items on standardized tests. Standardized tests may evaluate how well students "read between the lines," combining information from the text with their own experience in order to draw reasonable conclusions from given details. Present the following sample test question:

The author describes the young man who accompanies Don Anselmo as having "eyes like a gazelle." So, he is probably—

(A) a close relative
(B) a fast runner
(C) alert to danger
(D) gentle and tall

Students can draw on prior knowledge that a gazelle is a deer-like animal whose key traits are great speed, agility, and ability to escape danger. Someone with "eyes like a gazelle" might run fast (B), but a better answer is (C), one who is alert to danger, which fits the situation. For additional practice, use Reading Strategy: Make Inferences in **Selection Support,** p. 116.

271

One-Minute Insight

In "Gentleman of Rio en Medio," old traditions conflict with new ways. The central issue is the sale of Don Anselmo's land, and what is—and is not—included in the deal. The new owners discover that Don Anselmo's property is twice as large as he has claimed, and they offer to double their payment. Don Anselmo says that his honor dictates that he accept their original offer. After the new owners take possession, the neighborhood children, many of whom are descendants of Don Anselmo, continue to play in his orchard. When they complain, the new tenants discover that the trees actually belong to the neighbors and they must purchase each tree from its owner. Don Anselmo may be old-fashioned, but his sense of tradition results in a new understanding on the part of the buyers.

Customize for
Interpersonal Learners

Have groups explore Don Anselmo's view that moral obligations outweigh legal terms. He feels that it is more important to let the children play under the trees he planted for them than to force them off the land he sold to the Americans. Extend by having students brainstorm for situations they can imagine in which there may be a discrepancy between moral values and legal ones.

Customize for
Visual/Spatial Learners

The paintings that accompany this story can help students understand its setting and characters. Encourage them to use these visual aids to help them picture the characters' actions.

GENTLEMAN OF
Río en Medio
Juan A. A. Sedillo

The Sacristan of Trampas (detail), ca. 1915, Paul Burlin Museum of Fine Arts, New Mexico

272 ◆ *Quest for Justice*

Block Scheduling Strategies

Consider these suggestions to take advantage of extended class time:

• Use the Literary Focus: Resolution of a Conflict, p. 271, to stimulate discussion and to introduce the essays. Augment this with Selection Support, p. 117.

• Have students read the story and essay and work in peer groups to discuss the Guide for Responding questions, pp. 275 and 281, before completing written responses.

• To prepare students for the Writing Mini-Lesson, teach the Speaking and Listening Mini-Lesson, p. 280, and/or guide students to use the *Writer's Solution Writing Lab CD-ROM* tutorial on Persuasion.

• Present one or more of the Beyond the Classroom activities, pp. 276–278, to reinforce the theme of taking a stand.

• Have individuals or small groups work on a project in the Idea Bank, p. 283, or plan for the Cross-Curricular Science Activity suggested on p. 281.

*I*t took months of negotiation to come to an understanding with the old man. He was in no hurry. What he had the most of was time. He lived up in Río en Medio,[1] where his people had been for hundreds of years. He tilled the same land they had tilled. His house was small and wretched, but quaint. The little creek ran through his land. His orchard was gnarled and beautiful.

The day of the sale he came into the office. His coat was old, green and faded. I thought of Senator Catron,[2] who had been such a power with these people up there in the mountains. Perhaps it was one of his old Prince Alberts.[3] He also wore gloves. They were old and torn and his fingertips showed through them. He carried a cane, but it was only the skeleton of a worn-out umbrella. Behind him walked one of his innumerable kin—a dark young man with eyes like a gazelle.

The old man bowed to all of us in the room. Then he removed his hat and gloves, slowly and carefully. Chaplin[4] once did that in a picture, in a bank—he was the janitor. Then he handed his things to the boy, who stood obediently behind the old man's chair.

There was a great deal of conversation, about rain and about his family. He was very proud of his large family. Finally we got down to business. Yes, he would sell, as he had agreed, for twelve hundred dollars, in cash. We would buy, and the money was ready. "Don[5] Anselmo," I said to him in Spanish, "we have made a discovery. You remember that we sent that surveyor, that engineer, up there to

1. **Río en Medio** (rē´ ō en mä´ dē ō)
2. **Senator Catron:** Thomas Benton Catron, senator from New Mexico, 1912–1917.
3. **Prince Alberts:** Long, double-breasted coats.
4. **Chaplin:** Charlie Chaplin (1889–1977), actor and producer of silent films in the United States.
5. **don:** Spanish title of respect, similar to *sir* in English.

◄ **Critical Viewing** Does the man in this painting look like someone who would "bow to all of us in the room"? Why or why not? [Infer]

survey your land so as to make the deed. Well, he finds that you own more than eight acres. He tells us that your land extends across the river and that you own almost twice as much as you thought." He didn't know that. "And now, Don Anselmo," I added, "these Americans are *buena gente*,[6] they are good people, and they are willing to pay you for the additional land as well, at the same rate per acre, so that instead of twelve hundred dollars you will get almost twice as much, and the money is here for you."

The old man hung his head for a moment in thought. Then he stood up and stared at me. "Friend," he said, "I do not like to have you speak to me in that manner." I kept still and let him have his say. "I know these Americans are good people, and that is why I have agreed to sell to them. But I do not care to be insulted. I have agreed to sell my house and land for twelve hundred dollars and that is the price."

I argued with him but it was useless. Finally he signed the deed and took the money but refused to take more than the amount agreed upon. Then he shook hands all around, put on his ragged gloves, took his stick and walked out with the boy behind him.

◆ **Reading Strategy**
What inference can you draw about Don Anselmo based on his refusal to accept more money?

A month later my friends had moved into Río en Medio. They had replastered the old adobe house, pruned the trees, patched the fence, and moved in for the summer. One day they came back to the office to complain. The children of the village were overrunning their

6. *buena gente* (bwā´ nä hen´ tā): Spanish for "good people."

◆ **Build Vocabulary**

negotiation (ni gō´ shē ā´ shən) *n.*: Discussion to reach an agreement

gnarled (närld) *adj.*: Knotty and twisted

innumerable (i noo´ mər ə bəl) *adj.*: Too many to be counted

Humanities: Art

The Sacristan of Trampas (detail), ca. 1915, by Paul Burlin

Paul Burlin (1886–1969) studied at the National Academy of Design in New York City and in England and Paris. He was an early Santa Fe School painter, painting Indian portraits and landscapes. He applied personal approaches to color and distortion that were not approved of or understood by his colleagues in Santa Fe.

Before you discuss tthe painting, explain the meaning of its title to students. A sacristan is an

official in charge of the room in a church where sacred vessels are kept.

1. Does the person in this painting remind you of Don Anselmo? *Students may say that Don Anselmo isn't a sacristan, but he observes a sacred duty to his descendants. They may also say that of the story's descriptions Don Anselmo match the look of the "gentleman" in the painting.*

2. In what ways does the sacristan resemble Don Anselmo? *Both are old, with worn faces, and both dress carefully.*

❶ Evaluate *Students may have different opinions about the appearance of the orchard, but most will agree that the trees are beautiful; some are gnarled.*

◆ Literary Focus

❷ Resolution of a Conflict *He tries to appeal to Don Anselmo as village elder, one who commands respect in his community. The narrator hopes that words from Don Anselmo will keep the children away, which would end the conflict without a law suit.*

◆ LITERATURE AND YOUR LIFE

❸ *Students might cite natural wonders, parks, or historic sites.*

◆ Reading Strategy

❹ Make Inferences Have students make inferences about the buyers' decision to find and make separate deals with each child's family. *They wanted to do right and were willing to go out of their way to buy the privacy they hoped for in the first place.*

◆ Critical Thinking

❺ Compare and Contrast In what ways do the children's families differ from Don Anselmo? *They are practical people; they may share a respect for tradition and family, but are willing to part with the trees for other reasons.*

---

property. They came every day and played under the trees, built little play fences around them, and took blossoms. When they were spoken to they only laughed and talked back good-naturedly in Spanish.

I sent a messenger up to the mountains for Don Anselmo. It took a week to arrange another meeting. When he arrived he repeated his previous preliminary performance. He wore the same faded cutaway,[7] carried the same stick and was accompanied by the boy again. He shook hands all around, sat down

---

7. **cutaway** (kut′ ə wā′) *n.*: Coat worn by men for formal daytime occasions.

---

with the boy behind his chair, and talked about the weather. Finally I <u>broached</u> the subject. "Don Anselmo, about the ranch you sold to these people. They are good people and want to be your friends and neighbors always. When you sold to them you signed a document, a deed, and in that deed you agreed to several things. One thing was that they were to have the complete possession of the property. Now, Don Anselmo, it seems that every day the children of the village overrun the orchard and spend most of their time there. We would like to know if

◆ **Literary Focus**
Why does the narrator try to resolve the conflict in this way?

❷

Springtime. c. 1928–29, Victor Higgins. Private collection, photo courtesy of the Gerald Peters Gallery, Santa Fe, NM.

 ▲ **Critical Viewing** Does this orchard seem "gnarled and beautiful" to you? [Evaluate]

274 ◆ *Quest for Justice*

Humanities: Art

Springtime, c. 1928–29, by Victor Higgins
 William Victor Higgins (1884–1949) loved the land and architecture of the Southwest. He first visited New Mexico in 1913, where he found inspiration in the strong light and bold colors. This painting uses colors typical of the area: pink adobe building and blossoms, deep red ground, and bright blue sky.
 Have students study the painting and then use these questions for discussion:

1. Do you think Higgins painted this home exactly as he saw it? How might he have changed the scene? *For dramatic effect, he might have varied the size or shapes of the trees, the proportion of trees to the house, or the intensity of colors.*

2. In what ways does this scene suggest Rio en Medio? *Both are set in the Southwest and have flowering trees and adobe houses, although Don Anselmo's house may have been more modest.*

you, as the most respected man in the village, could not stop them from doing so in order that these people may enjoy their new home more in peace."

Don Anselmo stood up. "We have all learned to love these Americans," he said, "because they are good people and good neighbors. I sold them my property because I knew they were good people, but I did not sell them the trees in the orchard."

This was bad. "Don Anselmo," I pleaded, "when one signs a deed and sells real property one sells also everything that grows on the land, and those trees, every one of them, are on the land and inside the boundaries of what you sold."

"Yes, I admit that," he said. "You know," he added, "I am the oldest man in the village. Almost everyone there is my relative and all the children of Río en Medio are my *sobrinos* and *nietos*,[8] my descendants. Every time a child

---

8. ***sobrinos*** (sō brē′ nōs) **and *nietos*** (nyä′ tōs): Spanish for "nieces and nephews" and "grandchildren."

has been born in Río en Medio since I took possession of that house from my mother I have planted a tree for that child. The trees in that orchard are not mine, *Señor,* they belong to the children of the village. Every person in Río en Medio born since the railroad came to Santa Fe owns a tree in that orchard. I did not sell the trees because I could not. They are not mine."

There was nothing we could do. Legally we owned the trees but the old man had been so generous, refusing what amounted to a fortune for him. It took most of the following winter to buy the trees, individually, from the descendants of Don Anselmo in the valley of Río en Medio.

> ◆ **Literature and Your Life**
>
> Is there anything in your hometown that belongs to "the people," as trees do in Río en Medio? Explain.

❸

❹

❺

◆ **Build Vocabulary**

broached (brōcht) *v.:* Started a discussion about a topic

Guide for Responding

◆ LITERATURE AND YOUR LIFE

Reader's Response If you had bought Don Anselmo's land, would you be satisfied with the way things turned out? Why or why not?

Thematic Focus Don Anselmo stands up for his beliefs, even though he loses money. Do you think he is foolish or admirable? Why?

✓ Check Your Comprehension

1. Why is Don Anselmo in no hurry to do things?
2. Why do the Americans want to pay more than originally agreed upon for the land?
3. Why does Don Anselmo refuse to accept more money?
4. According to Don Anselmo, who owns the trees?

◆ Critical Thinking

INTERPRET

1. (a) What is the role of the narrator in this story? (b) How does his behavior affect the outcome? **[Analyze]**
2. Don Anselmo talks about other topics before getting down to business. What does this tell you about him? **[Infer]**
3. Compare the attitudes of Don Anselmo and the Americans toward money and what it can buy. **[Compare and Contrast]**
4. What makes Don Anselmo the "Gentleman of Río en Medio"? **[Infer]**

APPLY

5. Put yourself in the Americans' place. How would you have solved their problem? **[Relate]**

Gentleman of Río en Medio ◆ 275

Cultural Connection

Trees The practice of planting trees to mark an occasion is an ancient and widespread custom with many groups of people.

Arbor Day is a special celebration of tree-planting, celebrated at different times throughout the year. The holiday is always commemorated by tree planting.

Many cultures regard trees as symbols of life and of the cycle of rebirth. Trees might be planted, as in the story, to celebrate the birth of a child, to remember lost lives, or to mark the site of historical events. The ancient Hebrews planted

a cedar tree for each baby boy born; the birth of a girl was marked by planting a cypress. This custom is still practiced by some modern Jews.

Invite students to investigate within their own cultures and community to learn about the role of planting trees. You may want to suggest that they find out when Arbor Day is celebrated in your area, and what community activities are held to plant trees. Some students might find out whether there are memorial groves, arboretums, or forests in your area, and what events prompted the creation of those areas.

275

Saving the Wetlands

Barbara A. Lewis

One day in 1987, Andy Holleman's family received a letter from a land developer. The letter announced the developer's plans to build 180 condominium[1] units near the Hollemans' home in Chelmsford, Massachusetts.

Twelve-year-old Andy snatched the letter and shouted, "He can't do that! He's talking about building right on top of the wetlands!"

Andy knew that several species living on that land were either endangered or on the Special Concern list of animals whose numbers are shrinking. He had spent much of his

---

1. **condominium** (kän′ də min′ ē əm) *n.*: Group of living units joined together; each unit is separately owned.

276 ◆ Quest for Justice

▲ **Critical Viewing** What might happen to deer like these if wetlands were to disappear? [Speculate] ❷

free time roaming the area, watching great blue herons bend their long, delicate legs in marshy waters, seeing blue-spotted salamanders slither past shy wood turtles, and hearing the red-tailed hawk's lonely call—*cree, cree.* He often ripped off his baseball cap and waved to salute their graceful flight.

"Mom, you've got to take me to the library," Andy insisted. "I need to find out everything I can about the land. We've got to fight this." ❸

Cheryl Holleman, a school nurse, dropped her son off at the library. There Andy examined the master plan for their town. He dug

Beyond the Classroom

Career Connection

Environmentalist Many people claim to love the outdoors and nature, but young Andy Holleman stood up for his beliefs and made a difference. The world's natural environments need ongoing help from people who share his values.

Have groups of students brainstorm for a list of jobs that benefit the environment. Students might list work in national, state, or county parks and with environmental agencies. Other areas included wildlife science, animal rescue, land

or water management, trail maintenance, pollution control, and waste clean-up. Related fields are farming, forestry, or working for environmental advocacy groups, such as the Sierra Club or the Appalachian Mountain Club. Invite interested students to investigate courses in environmental studies that are offered in local high schools, extension programs, or colleges, to get a sense of the issues to explore. Other students might contact local environmental agencies to find out how community members can volunteer to help.

276

into the Annotated Laws[2] for the state. And he discovered that the condos would take up 16.3 acres of land, one-half of which would cover and destroy the wetlands. A new sewage treatment plant, oil from driveways, and fertilizer runoff could all pollute the water system or penetrate the soil, contaminating both water and land.

Andy also learned that the proposed development sat on a stream which led into Russell Mill Pond. The pond fed into town wells. So it was possible that Chelmsford's drinking water could be contaminated, too. "Our drinking water was already terrible enough," Andy says, grinning.

He had his ammunition, and he had to do *something*. He thought of all the living things whose habitats would be destroyed by the condos: the ladyslippers, mountain laurels, fringed gentians, foxes, and snakes. And he knew he could count on his parents' support. They had always encouraged him to respect the environment.

Even now, when Cheryl needs Andy to do a chore, she doesn't bother looking for him in front of the TV. She knows she'll find him sprawled half off his bed or stretched across the floor, reading. Andy devours Audubon books about wildlife. He loves author Gerald Durrell's *The Drunken Forest* and *Birds, Beasts, and Other Relatives*. Sometimes, of course, he sneaks in a Stephen King thriller.

Andy and his family have taken many nature walks in the wooded area

◆ **Reading Strategy**
What kind of relationship does Andy have with his family?

▲ **Critical Viewing** Why might salamanders like these depend on water for survival? [Draw Conclusions]

by Russell Mill Pond. It's something they enjoy doing together—Andy, Cheryl, his dad, David, and his younger brother and sister, Nicholas and Elizabeth.

Andy remembers sitting on the glacial rocks by the stream in the middle of winter, eating baloney sandwiches. In the warmer months, he and Nicholas and Elizabeth played tag in the stream, jumping on the slippery rocks, soaking their shoes, socks, and jeans. When fall came, they gathered brilliant red leaves from swamp maples and golden oak, while their mother picked dried grape vines for wreaths. The children took their leaves home, pressed them between waxed paper, ironed them flat, then hung them on doorknobs and from picture frames.

The wetlands area where the developer wanted to build held other memories for Andy. Sometimes he ice-skated on the pond. Sometimes he made important discoveries.

"Once I brought home a huge baby crow," he says. "A baby crow is called a 'fledgling,' and this one was just learning to fly. It had fallen out of the nest. So I fed him popcorn and water that night, and built him a perch.

"Mom wouldn't let me keep him in the house while I was at school. But that was okay. He was able to fly away the next day to return to his home in the swamp."

When Andy was eleven, he found a skunk caught in a steel-jaw trap, the kind that rips animals' legs apart. Since he had been swimming with a friend, Andy was wearing only his swim trunks and tattered sneakers—luckily, as it turned out.

He put on a diving mask, sneaked up

---

2. **Annotated** (an ō tāt′ əd) **Laws:** Laws with explanatory notes.

Saving the Wetlands ◆ 277

Thematic Focus
❹ **Taking a Stand** Discuss with students what they think a twelve-year-old boy could possibly do to stop a major development plan. *Students may say that he can write letters, make phone calls, raise money, or otherwise use his energy to support what he believes in.*

▶**Critical Viewing**◀
❺ **Draw Conclusions** *Salamanders are amphibians, whose thin skin offers little protection against drying. They need a habitat in which water is always available.*

◆**Reading Strategy**
❻ **Make Inferences** *They share an interest in nature, and they like doing things together.*

◆**Critical Thinking**
❼ **Evaluate** How does a description such as this help bring Andy to life? *By including everyday details about Andy and his family, the author shows that he is much like any kid.*

Customize for
Interpersonal Learners
This essay suits interpersonal learners well because so much of Andy's success came from his work with other people. Suggest that students identify Andy's interpersonal skills and list the most important ones.

◈ **Beyond the Classroom**

Workplace Skills
Public Speaking In this essay, Andy Holleman fights his nerves to speak at a town meeting. Public speaking is a skill that many job situations demand. Some people fear public speaking, but most can learn to overcome that fear by improving their speaking skills.

One of the fundamental skills necessary for public speaking is using the voice to express meaning and feeling. Four techniques for using the voice that are usually emphasized are: quality, or the way and degree to which the voice conveys attitudes; pausing, one of the ways to vary the rate of speech to emphasize a point or give the audience an opportunity to think about what is being said; stress, the force with which a word is spoken; and pitch, or the rise and fall of the voice to give variety to speech.

Have groups discuss these and other aspects of public speaking that are challenging, and how to make public speaking easier on the speaker and more effective for the audience. Conclude by having students apply their ideas and suggestions as they complete the Writing Mini-Lesson, p. 283.

❶ The Pied Piper is a character from German folklore who agrees to play his magic flute to rid the town of Hamelin of rats. When the mayor refuses to pay the piper, he plays his flute again, this time luring away all the town's children.

▶Critical Viewing◀

❷ Compare and Contrast *All share the wetlands habitat; the skunk is a mammal, the snake and turtle are reptiles; the skunk and turtle have four legs, the snake has no legs.*

◆Reading Strategy

❸ Make Inferences *Andy hopes that the people who attend the meeting will learn about the developer's plans and be prompted to join his fight to save the wetlands.*

◆Reading Strategy

❹ Make Inferences How would Andy know about the town meeting? *The developer was probably required to make his plans public.*

◆Literary Focus

❺ Resolution of a Conflict Who is Andy's petition for? How is a petition a democratic action? *Andy's petition is probably aimed at the town council or other governmental agency that has the power to affect public policy. It is an act of democracy because citizens who sign petitions are exercising their right to free speech and to openly share their criticisms.*

---

behind the skunk, pressed the release button on the trap, and grabbed the startled skunk by the tail. Then he carried him upside-down for a quarter of a mile—all the way to his house. He knew that skunks can't spray when held by the tail.

Small children trailed behind him, holding their noses and giggling. A neighbor telephoned Andy's mother and said, "Go outside and watch. And shut your windows and doors behind you. Don't ask me to explain. Just do it."

By the time Andy arrived home, he was leading twenty dancing, squealing children, like the Pied Piper. The skunk dangled from his hand at arm's length.

"This is one animal you're not going to keep, Andrew," his mom called in a shrill voice.

His father, who was home from his job as a medical technologist, phoned the local animal shelter for advice.

"They said we could either let the skunk go in the woods, or bring it in to the shelter," David Holleman told his son. "You'd better let him go and let nature take its course. There is no way you're putting that animal in my car, and you certainly can't hold him out the window by his tail the whole way to the shelter."

"I let him go," Andy recalls. "His leg wasn't too bad, so it would probably heal by itself. Everyone thought I smelled pretty skunky, though. I bathed in vinegar, which smelled just as

▲ **Critical Viewing** In what way are the animals pictured on these two pages alike? How are they different? [Compare and Contrast]

awful as the skunk to me. I finally came clean, but we had to throw my sneakers away."

Crows and skunks aren't the only creatures Andy has brought home from the wetlands. "My mother remembers an eighteen-inch snapping turtle which went to the bathroom all over the kitchen linoleum." He laughs. "I fed him raw hamburger."

Often Andy just wandered through the woods to think or to write a poem. Sometimes he sat quietly for hours, studying animal behavior. He spotted deer and red foxes. He captured salamanders, snakes, mice, and moles; after learning all he could from observing each animal, Andy carefully carried it back to its home in the woods.

◆ **Reading Strategy** Infer why Andy wants people to come to the meeting.

The wetlands were too important to cover with concrete and steel. Andy couldn't allow Pontiacs and Toyotas to replace blue herons and shy wood turtles. He couldn't permit blaring car horns to muffle the *cree* of the red-tailed hawk.

"So I drafted a petition for the residents to sign to try to stop the developer from building," Andy says. "I walked around the neighborhood and collected 180 signatures. I told everyone to come to the public town meeting scheduled with the developer. I also collected about fifty signatures from students in the neighborhood and at McCarthy Middle School."

◆◆◆ **Beyond the Classroom**

Community Connection

Taking a Stand Every community has needs and issues that can be addressed by the efforts of interested citizens. Work with students to identify problems in your community that young people their age can work to solve. Talk about realistic courses of action for eighth graders, and how they might gather support from neighbors, business people, and political leaders. For example, students might publish a newsletter, draft and circulate a petition, or write opinion letters to the editors of local newspapers or radio stations.

They might find out when public meetings are held to address certain community issues, and plan to attend. Students can explore how particular skills and talents can be applied to solve the problem. Students who resist public speaking can make posters or pass out flyers; those who speak languages other than English can serve as translators to communicate concerns to others in the community; those with strong persuasive skills can make calls to persuade people to join their effort; and those with strong organization skills can help plan and maintain the project efforts.

Only one or two people refused to sign the petition. "They acted like they thought I was too young, like I didn't know what I was doing. But almost everybody was really supportive."

Often Andy carried his petition around for an hour and collected only a few signatures—not because people didn't want to sign, but because they wanted to talk. They'd offer Andy a Coke and invite him in to discuss the problem. Andy spent a lot of time conversing with his neighbors.

An elderly lady named Agatha answered her door with long, bony fingers. Although she was <u>wizened</u> and thin with wild, white hair, Andy's enthusiasm breathed new life into her. She attended over forty meetings and became a real activist.

Once, on the way back from carrying his petition, Andy decided to detour through the swamp. He kicked up his heels with too much energy and tripped over a rotted log. He snatched helplessly at the pages of his petition as they tumbled into a muddy stream, but he managed to salvage them.

"It took a while for the pages to dry out," he recalls with a grin, "and then my mom had to iron them out flat. That's the last time I ever went through the swamp with something that wasn't waterproofed."

Andy sent copies of his petition to the Board of Selectmen,[3] the Conservation Commission, the Zoning Board of Appeals,[4] the Board of Health, and the land developer. He wrote letters to senators, representatives, and a TV anchorwoman. Although he received letters of support in return, no one did anything to help.

---

3. **Board of Selectmen:** Group of persons elected to manage town affairs.
4. **Zoning Board of Appeals:** Group of persons who review problems dealing with construction in business and residential areas.

"When I called the Massachusetts Audubon Society and told them my problem with the wetlands and that no one was really helping me, the woman gave me no sympathy," Andy says. "She just told me, 'That's no excuse for *you*,' and went right on giving information. I learned that when you really believe in something, you have to stand up for it no matter how old you are."

Slowly, Andy's neighbors joined in, neighbors he had contacted with his petition. They organized into the Concord Neighborhood Association and raised $16,000 to hire a lawyer and an environmental consultant to fight the development of the wetlands.

On the night of the town meeting with the developer, over 250 people showed up. The meeting had to be moved to the basement of the Town Hall to make room for the crowd. And when the developer stood up and announced that *he* was the one who had invited everyone, the residents disagreed, saying, "No, it was Andy Holleman who invited us here."

Andy had prepared a speech to give at the meeting. When it was time for him to speak, his stomach flipped, but he walked to the front of the room anyway, <u>brandishing</u> the brown shell of a wood turtle.

"You call yourself the Russell Mill Pond Realty Trust, Inc.," Andy began. "I don't understand how you can call yourself this when you're essentially polluting your own name."

◆ Build Vocabulary

petition (pə tish´ ən) *n.*: A formal document that makes a request, addressed to a person or group and often signed by a number of people

wizened (wiz´ ənd) *adj.*: Shriveled or withered

brandishing (bran´ dish iŋ) *v.*: Waving or exhibiting in a challenging way

Saving the Wetlands ◆ 279

Thematic Focus

6 Taking a Stand In what ways can conversing with neighbors help Andy take his stand? *By talking with people, Andy can express his point of view, share information with them, and urge them to consider ways to join him in his fight to defeat the development.*

◆ Critical Thinking

7 Distinguish Andy gets letters of support, but he says that nobody did anything. Ask students to explain the distinction between letters of support and true help. *Letters of support may say that someone agrees with Andy's position, which is a start. Andy needs people who are willing to take action.*

◆ LITERATURE AND YOUR LIFE

8 Ask students to think back on times in their own lives when, like Andy, they felt really nervous about something they had to do. What physical symptoms did they experience? Did they perspire? Did their stomachs flip? Invite volunteers to share memories with the class.

Customize for
Less Proficient Readers
It might help students keep track of events in Andy's story if they made a time line that includes what they read about and what probably took place before the story began. Provide copies of the Timeline from **Writing and Language Transparencies,** p. 65.

Humanities: Photography

Nature and Wildlife Photographs

All the photographs that accompany this essay were taken by Dr. E. R. Degginger. Nature photography appears frequently in magazines and in many books. Degginger's photos that appear in the Student Edition show animals and plants that live in or near water habitats.

Have students review and study the photographs and then use these questions to spark discussion:

1. What traits or skills might nature photographers need in order to take pictures of wild animals? *They should like the outdoors, respect nature, be patient, and have a good visual sense.*

2. Do you think photographs are more effective than paintings or other types of art would be for this essay? Explain. *Students may say that photos make the facts of the essay seem more realistic; animals shown in their natural habitats help readers visualize the wetlands as Andy does.*

❶ Have students summarize the events leading up to the 10 months of meetings. Then ask what they think was discussed in the meetings and who took part in them. *Students may say that the meetings were a way to publicly debate saving the wetlands versus building condominiums, with any interested parties such as lawyers, neighbors, scientists, engineers, business people, and community leaders taking part.*

◆ **Literary Focus**

❷ Resolution of a Conflict
Students may say that this is the best way to resolve the conflict, because it will give an objective scientific measure, not just another opinion.

◆ **Reading Strategy**

❸ Make Inferences Why is Andy so happy? *He knows that the results of the test strongly support his stand.*

◆ **Reading Strategy**

❹ Make Inferences Challenge students to make inferences about the developer's intent. Why would he have pushed ahead all these months if the developer thought the land might not support the buildings? *Students may say that the developer's goal is to build and sell the condos, make a profit, and then let the new owners worry about any problems that might arise.*

◆ **Literary Focus**

❺ Resolution of a Conflict In some debates between developers and environmentalists, the developers complain that the environmentalists would oppose any development. How does this passage show that Andy never held that extreme a position? *He came up with an alternative site idea early on, which proves that he was not against condos in general, he just didn't want them built at the expense of the wetlands.*

▶ **Critical Viewing** ◀

❻ Classify *It has strong talons, a powerful beak, sharp eyesight, and strength to fly and hunt for great lengths of time. But it would become powerless if its habitat were ruined, or if its natural food supply were to disappear.*

280

The residents responded with thunderous applause. White-haired Agatha winked at him and motioned a thumbs-up.

Andy continued. "We need the wetlands to prevent flooding and to purify the water through the mud," he said. "We need the plants and the creatures living there."

Nobody won that night's debate. In fact, the meetings continued for ten months. There were at least two meetings every week and sometimes more. Andy and either his mom or his dad attended every meeting—and Andy *still* got high grades in school. He spoke at most of the meetings.

In one meeting with the Board of Health, the developer arose and announced, "I'm not going to argue hydro-geological[5] facts with a thirteen-year-old!" Andy's parents were angry, but Andy just shrugged his shoulders.

◆ **Literary Focus**
Is this a good way to resolve the conflict? Why or why not?

Nine months after the first meeting, an important test called a "deep-hole test" was conducted in the swamp. The purpose of the test was to find out how quickly a hole dug in the swamp would fill up with water. If it filled up very fast, that would be a sign that the land was not suitable for building.

The developer, members of the Concord Neighborhood Association, and state environmental officials gathered to observe the test. The hole was dug—and it filled with water almost immediately. Andy grinned clear around his head.

The developer tried to withdraw his application to build on the wetlands, but the Zoning Board of Appeals wouldn't let him. Legally, that wouldn't have solved the problem. Someone else could have applied for the same kind of project, and Andy and his neighbors would have had to start fighting all over again. Instead, the Board totally denied the application. Their refusal prevented anyone from trying to build a big development on the wetlands.

5. **hydro-geological** (hī´ drō jē ä lä´ jə kəl) *adj.*: Related to water and to the science of the nature and history of the Earth.

280 ◆ Quest for Justice

When they got the news, Andy and the Concord Neighborhood Association cheered. Their battle was over! And the wetlands were safe from large developers.

Soon after, the developer started building condos on an old drive-in movie lot—an acceptable site Andy had suggested in the beginning.

What did all of this mean to Andy? He became a celebrity. Even though he is modest and shy, he accepted invitations to speak at schools, community groups, and organizations. He received many awards, including the Young Giraffe Award for young people who "stick their necks out" for the good of others. His award was a free trip to the Soviet Union in July, 1990.

And what is Andy doing now? He's planning to go to college in a few years, where he'd like to study environmental law. Meanwhile, he's setting up a non-profit, tax-exempt fund to purchase the wetlands and any surrounding threatened land to preserve it forever. Then he can always wander by Russell Mill Pond, gathering autumn leaves from crimson swamp maples and golden oaks. He can watch the blue herons bend their long, delicate legs in marshy waters, and see blue-spotted salamanders slither safely past shy wood turtles. And he can hear the lonely *cree* of the red-tailed hawk as it soars freely, high above the pond, dipping its wings as if in salute to him. To Andy.

Speaking and Listening Mini-Lesson

Debate

This mini-lesson supports the Speaking and Listening activity in the Idea Bank on p. 283.

Introduce A formal debate follows clearly defined rules and its outcome is determined by which side most effectively argues its point of view in accordance with the rules. In this debate, students will play the roles of Andy and the developer who wants to build on the wetlands.

Develop Discuss techniques debaters use to persuade audiences, such as restating key points, and supporting their position with examples,

facts, and expert testimony. Then, divide the class into pairs. Have students select roles, research, plan their arguments, and practice the debate.

Apply Encourage students to develop their debate strategies using the essay's details. Suggest that they use note cards to organize their information and refer to during the debate. Visual aids may be helpful as they present their arguments.

Assess Evaluate each debate on overall persuasiveness, specific arguments, and clarity of presentation. Or, use the Peer Assessment: Speaker/ Speech form, p. 114, in **Alternative Assessment**.

◀ **Critical Viewing** In what way is a red-tailed hawk like this strong? In what ways is it fragile? [Classify]

Beyond Literature

Science Connection

Saving the Earth Would you like to see a new swimming pool or baseball diamond or even a new school built in your community? It's not always so easy. Throughout the United States, the presence of wetlands affects whether undeveloped land may be developed. Wetlands—swamps, marshes, and some forests—are protected by law on both public and private property. We now recognize how vital they are to preserving the ecology. Their importance was not widely known, however, until the 1970's. By then, more than half of the nation's wetlands had been destroyed, resulting in erosion and flooding in many places. The decrease in wetlands has also decreased populations of waterfowl, fish, and shellfish. Protecting the remaining wetlands has become a critical national priority.

Cross-Curricular Activity
Observing Animal Life in Wetlands
If possible, visit wetlands located near you with a group of classmates. Watch closely to track the types of animal life you observe. Take notes so that you can make a chart or poster to show the animals you saw. If there are no wetlands close by, research wetlands to learn about the species that live in this environment in your state. Create a chart or poster based on your findings.

Guide for Responding

◆ LITERATURE AND YOUR LIFE

Reader's Response What part of the environment do you care about most? Would you mount a campaign to save it?

Thematic Focus Can you think of other instances when people have joined together to save something worth saving?

Brainstorm List some things in the natural environment near your home that are important to you.

☑ Check Your Comprehension

1. Why did Andy want to save the wetlands?
2. What was the first thing Andy did in his struggle against the developer?
3. What did Andy ask his neighbors to do?
4. In the end, were the developers able to build condominiums?

◆ Critical Thinking

INTERPRET
1. How does Andy transform his sense of outrage about the plan to build condominiums into action? [Connect]
2. Why does the author tell so much about Andy's experiences with the animals? [Analyze]
3. Do you think Andy's age worked for or against him in his campaign to stop the developers? Explain. [Analyze]

APPLY
4. Suppose Andy had lost his fight. What would have happened to the wildlife and the wetlands? [Hypothesize]

EXTEND
5. Andy learned a great deal in his campaign to save the wetlands. Identify several careers he might pursue using the knowledge and skills he gained. [Career Link]

Saving the Wetlands ◆ 281

Beyond Literature

Introduce the term *limnology*, which is the scientific study of the features of inland fresh water. Limnologists examine the many interrelated factors that affect a wetland habitat, so they consider biology, chemistry, physics, geography, weather, and climate. Direct students to field guides on pond life, or other limnological resources, to learn the difference between ponds, lakes, streams, bogs, fens, swamps, and so on.

Reinforce and Extend

Answers
◆ LITERATURE AND YOUR LIFE

Reader's Response Encourage students to support their views. If they are unsure how they might react in a situation such as Andy's, you might ask questions to help them decide.

Thematic Focus Students might cite examples such as community groups working to save historic old buildings, to stop developers from paving over national battlefield sites, or to save local natural treasures.

☑ Check Your Comprehension
1. He cared about the animals that lived there; he liked spending time there; he learned the value of wetlands in the web of life.
2. He researched the issue.
3. He asked them to sign a petition and to attend a town meeting.
4. They built condos, but on an old drive-in movie lot.

◆ Critical Thinking
1. He educates himself and rallies the community . He redirects his anger to fuel positive action.
2. She wants to show Andy as a nature lover, which builds support for him and engages readers.
3. Students may say that his age worked against him at first, when people thought he couldn't understand such "adult" issues. But his age may have helped with publicity for his cause.
4. The wildlife population in the remaining wetland would change and eventually decrease. The water supply might become fouled, and flooding might occur.
5. He might pursue a career in law, politics, public relations, or environmental science.

 Beyond the Selection

FURTHER READING
Other Works by Barbara A. Lewis
The Kid's Guide to Service Projects
What Do You Stand For?
The Kid's Guide to Social Action
Other Works About Taking a Stand
Come Back, Salmon, Molly Cone
Shades of Gray, Carolyn Rieder
Cesar Chavez, Consuelo Rodriguez
Crusade for Kindness: Henry Hergh and the ASPCA,
John J. Loeper

INTERNET
We suggest the following site on the Internet (all Web sites are subject to change).
    For more information on the Wetlands:
http://www.eswr.com
http://www.nwi.fws.gov
    We *strongly recommend* that you preview this site before you send students to it.

Answers

◆ Reading Strategy

1. The Americans are fair-minded; they don't want to cheat Don Anselmo.
2. The narrator is a lawyer, maybe also a translator, for the buyers. He speaks Spanish, knows law, and respects the local people and customs.
3. He is diligent, dedicated to things he believes in, and self-assured.

◆ Build Vocabulary

Using the Word Root *-num-*
1. innumerable
2. numerator
3. enumerate

Spelling Strategy
1. gnaw; to bite at bit by bit
2. gnat; a small insect
3. gnash; to grind together
4. gnome; a dwarflike being

Using the Word Bank
1. a
2. c
3. a
4. a
5. a
6. b
7. a

◆ Literary Focus

1. Don Anselmo expects the Americans to behave as he would. He expects that they will see things as he does, and will behave politely, respectfully, and honorably.
2. He sees deep conflicts of interest between the developer and those who value the wetlands.
3. In "Gentleman of Rio en Medio" everyone wins: the Americans get a good deal on the property and do the right thing, the villagers are treated as "owners" of the trees, and Don Anselmo keeps his word. In "Saving the Wetlands," Andy wins by stopping current and future development of the wetlands. The developers lose the chance to build on that site, but do build elsewhere.

Guide for Responding (continued)

◆ Reading Strategy

MAKE INFERENCES
An **inference** is an educated guess you make based on details in a story, essay, or article.

1. What can you infer about the Americans based on the fact that they offer more money for Don Anselmo's land?
2. Who is the narrator of "Gentleman of Río en Medio"? How can you tell?
3. List three inferences you can make about Andy based on his actions in "Saving the Wetlands."

◆ Build Vocabulary

USING THE WORD ROOT *-num-*
Words that contain the word root *-num-,* as in *innumerable,* are related in meaning to the word *number.* On a sheet of paper, write the word from the list below that best completes each sentence.

   enumerate   numerator   innumerable

1. The sky was dotted with _____?_____ stars.
2. The _____?_____ is the top number in a simple fraction.
3. The teacher will _____?_____ the rules of the classroom.

SPELLING STRATEGY
The *n* sound you hear in *gnarled* is spelled with a silent g preceding the *n.* Unscramble these *gn* words. Then, refer to a dictionary to write a definition for each one.
1. wagn   2. tnag   3. hnags   4. mogen

USING THE WORD BANK
On your paper, write the word that is closest in meaning to the Word Bank word.

1. negotiation: (a) discussion, (b) argument, (c) opinion
2. gnarled: (a) angry, (b) intelligent, (c) twisted
3. innumerable: (a) countless, (b) difficult, (c) impossible
4. broached: (a) mentioned, (b) bejeweled, (c) followed
5. petition: (a) request, (b) reply, (c) complaint
6. wizened: (a) wise, (b) shriveled, (c) empty
7. brandishing: (a) waving, (b) bragging, (c) swaying

◆ Literary Focus

RESOLUTION OF A CONFLICT
The characters in these selections **resolve conflicts** over land use and ownership in very different ways. In each selection, the resolution depends on the attitudes of the key people and on the way in which their communities respond to them.

1. In "Gentleman of Río en Medio," how does Don Anselmo expect the Americans to behave when conflicts arise?
2. In "Saving the Wetlands," why does Andy assume from the start that there will be a conflict?
3. Identify winners and losers in each selection. Tell what each has gained or lost.

◆ Build Grammar Skills

ADVERBS MODIFYING ADJECTIVES AND ADVERBS
An **adverb** is a word that modifies or describes a verb. It can also modify an adjective or another adverb. The following adverbs are commonly used to modify adjectives and other adverbs: *too, so, very, quite, much, more, rather, usually, almost.*

> . . . the old man had been *so* generous (*How generous?*)
> Our drinking water was *already* terrible (*When was it terrible?*)

Practice On your paper, write each adverb, and tell whether the word it modifies is an adjective or an adverb.
1. Don Anselmo spoke very slowly.
2. Andy was an unusually persistent boy.
3. The developers were quite angry.
4. Andy's family rather consistently supported his efforts.
5. The developers were very aggressive.

Writing Application Copy the following sentences. Fill in each blank with an appropriate adverb.
1. Don Anselmo arrived _____?_____ late.
2. Andy thought the developers were _____?_____ unfair.
3. The Americans were _____?_____ patient.

◆ Build Grammar Skills

Practice
1. *very* modifies the adverb *slowly*
2. *unusually* modifies the adjective *persistent*
3. *quite* modifies the adjective *angry*
4. *rather* modifies the adverb *consistently;* both modify the verb *supported*
5. *very* modifies the adjective *aggressive*

Writing Application
Possible responses:
1. unusually, too
2. remarkably, very
3. always, quite

✎ Writer's Solution

For further instruction and practice, use the lesson in the *Writer's Solution Language Lab CD-ROM* on Persuasion. You may also use Adverbs and Modifiers, p. 21, in the *Writer's Solution Grammar Practice Book.*

Build Your Portfolio

 ## Idea Bank

Writing

1. **Advertisement** Write a real estate advertisement for the condominiums that the developers would have built on the wetlands if they had not been stopped.

2. **Letter to the Editor** Write a letter that Andy Holleman might have written to his local newspaper. Explain the threat to the wetlands, and ask people for help in the fight to stop the developers.

3. **Formula** If the Americans in Río en Medio came to you for advice about how much they should pay for each tree, what formula would you develop? Write a paragraph explaining the formula and why you think it is fair to all parties. **[Math Link]**

Speaking and Listening

4. **Speech** Imagine you live in Río en Medio. Deliver a speech to your "neighbors," praising Don Anselmo for his contributions to the village. Tape-record your speech so you can listen to it afterward. **[Performing Arts Link]**

5. **Debate [Group Activity]** With another classmate, research the subject of wetlands and environmental protection laws. Stage a debate with one of you playing the role of Andy Holleman and the other playing the role of a developer.

Projects

6. **Artwork** Draw or paint a portrait of Don Anselmo or a landscape showing the house and orchard the Americans bought from him. **[Art Link]**

7. **Community Action [Group Activity]** Identify an environmental problem in your community. With several classmates, work out a plan for solving the problem. Consult with your teacher or other adults about putting the plan into action. **[Science Link; Career Link]**

 ## Writing Mini-Lesson

Speech Supporting the Environment

When Andy Holleman gave his first speech at a town meeting, he spoke persuasively about an issue that meant a lot to him—saving the wetlands. Choose an environmental issue you care about, and write a short speech supporting that issue.

Writing Skills Focus: Persuasive Tone

The **tone** of a piece of writing is the writer's attitude toward his or her subject. As you write, choose words that will persuade your audience that the subject of your speech is important. Notice the tone that Andy's words convey at the town meeting:

> **Model From the Selection**
> "You call yourself the Russell Mill Pond Realty Trust, Inc.," Andy began. "I don't understand how you can call yourself this when you're essentially polluting your own name."

Prewriting Conduct research to learn the facts about both sides of your issue. Look for details, statistics, and quotations that support your position. Take careful notes on what you learn.

Drafting Begin by stating the issue and your position. Then, support your position with details you uncovered in your research. Use language that conveys the importance of your cause.

Revising Read your speech aloud to a friend to find out if your arguments are clear and convincing. If not, look for places where replacing a word or adding a fact will strengthen the persuasive tone of your speech.

> ◆ **Grammar Application**
> Make your writing more vivid and precise by adding adverbs to modify adjectives and other adverbs.

Gentleman of Río en Medio/Saving the Wetlands ◆ 283

 ## Idea Bank

Following are suggestions for matching the Idea Bank topics with your students' performance levels and learning modalities:

Customize for *Performance Levels*
Less Advanced Students: 1, 4, 6, 7
Average Students: 2, 4, 5, 6, 7
More Advanced Students: 3, 4, 5, 7

Customize for *Learning Modalities*
Verbal/Linguistic: 1, 2, 3, 4, 5, 7
Visual/Spatial: 1, 6
Logical/Mathematical: 3, 5
Interpersonal: 4, 5, 7
Intrapersonal: 1, 2, 3, 6

 ## Writing Mini-Lesson

Refer students to the Writing Handbook in the back of the book for instruction on the writing process and for further information on persuasive speeches. Have students use the Main Idea and Supporting Details Organizer in **Writing and Language Transparencies,** p. 61, to organize their statements on issues.

 ## Writer's Solution

Writers at Work Videodisc
Have students view the video segment, featuring environmental writer Kate Mitchell, to see how she develops persuasive arguments. Students can discuss the importance of knowing one's audience to help them focus the tone of their speeches.

Play frames 3 to 7453

Writing Lab CD-ROM
Have students complete the tutorial on Persuasion. Follow these steps:
1. Have students browse through the Inspirations for Persuasion to select a topic.
2. Have students draft on computer, paying particular attention to how they organize the evidence they have gathered for the piece.
3. Have students use the Revision Checker for sentence openers.

Writer's Solution Sourcebook
Have students use Chapter 6, "Persuasion," pp. 166–199, for more support. The chapter includes an annotated literature model of a persuasive essay on an environmental topic, p. 199.

✓ ASSESSMENT OPTIONS

Formal Assessment, Selection Test, pp. 84–86, and Assessment Resources Software. The selection test is designed so that it can be easily customized to the performance levels of your students.

Alternative Assessment, p. 22, includes options for less advanced students, more advanced students, logical/mathematical learners, verbal/linguistic learners, bodily/kinesthetic learners, and interpersonal learners.

PORTFOLIO ASSESSMENT
Use the following rubrics in the **Alternative Assessment** booklet to assess student writing:
Advertisement: Description, p. 93
Letter to the Editor: Persuasion, p. 101
Formula: Technical Description/Explanation, p. 111
Writing Mini-Lesson: Persuasion, p. 101

Establish Writing Guidelines

Review the following key characteristics of a letter to an editor:

- A letter to an editor is a reader's response to an article or editorial in a magazine or newspaper.
- A letter to an editor intends to argue a point or persuade others.
- A letter to an editor supports the point with facts, details, and/or examples.

You may want to distribute the scoring rubric for Persuasion, p. 102, in **Alternative Assessment** to make students aware of the criteria on which they will be evaluated. See the suggestions on p. 286 for how you can customize the rubric to this workshop.

Refer students to the Writing Handbook in the back of the book for instruction on the writing process and further information on persuasive writing.

Writer's Solution

Writer's at Work Videodisc

To introduce students to expository writing, and to show them what Kate Mitchell says about "hooking" her readers, play the videodisc segment on Persuasion (Ch. 6).

Play frames 3 to 7453

Writing Lab CD-ROM

If your students have access to computers, you may want to have them use the tutorial on Persuasion to complete all or part of their letters to an editor. Follow these steps:

1. Have students view the interactive model of a letter to the editor.
2. Suggest that students use the Pros-and-Cons chart to evaluate the arguments for and against their opinions.
3. Allow students to draft on computer.
4. When revising, have students use the Revision Checker for sentence openers.

Writer's Solution Sourcebook

Students can find additional support, including in-depth instruction on eliminating unnecessary words, pp. 195–196, in the chapter on Persuasion, pp. 166–199.

Persuasive Writing

Letter to the Editor

Writing Process Workshop

One way newspaper and magazine readers can take a stand is by writing a **letter to the editor.** In this type of letter, you agree or disagree with an article or editorial and try to persuade others to do the same. Write a letter to the editor, responding to an issue about which you feel strongly. The following skills, introduced in this section's Writing Mini-Lessons, will help you.

Writing Skills Focus

▶ **Begin with a strong opening** to grab your readers' attention. (See p. 248.)

▶ **Support your points with examples, facts, statistics, and quotations** to strengthen your arguments. (See p. 259.)

▶ **Use descriptive details** that will help readers to see things from your point of view. (See p. 269.)

▶ **Adopt a persuasive tone** by using positive, emotionally charged language. (See p. 283.)

In this passage from a letter to the editor, the writer uses these skills to persuade readers to accept a particular point of view.

WRITING MODEL

Dear Editor:

Don't call me lazy! ① In a May 19 article "The Trouble With Teens," the writer stated that, "typical teenagers do nothing but skateboard and hang out at the mall." I strongly disagree, and here's why. In a survey conducted by eighth graders at Hanover Middle School, 65% of the students said that they participate in an after-school club or play on a sports team. ② . . . More importantly though, there is no "typical teenager," just as there is no "typical" adult. We are all individual and unique—just like you. ③

① The writer's strong beginning makes you want to read more.

② This statistic supports the writer's opinion with a fact.

③ The writer adopts a persuasive tone by comparing teenagers with adults.

284 ◆ Quest for Justice

 Beyond the Classroom

Career Connection

Editor Explain to students that editors of magazines and newspapers are in charge of deciding which articles will go to print as well as the scope and content of those articles. In addition, they decide which editorials and letters to the editor to print. Sometimes, they may write short responses to these letters.

Suggest that students browse through magazines or newspapers, paying special attention to the letters to the editor sections. Have them choose a letter they think has particularly good points to make. Then, have the students find and read the article to which the letter refers. Suggest that students pretend that they are the editor of that magazine or newspaper and have them write a response to the letter. Encourage them to address each of the letter's points in their responses. Have students present their letters and responses to the rest of the class.

Prewriting

Choose a Topic Choose an issue of current concern to focus on in your letter. For ideas, scan newspapers and magazines, watch television news shows, and talk to people in your community.

Gather Facts and Details Once you've decided on a topic, conduct research in the library or on the Internet to gather facts, details, statistics, and quotations that support your position. Take careful notes on what you learn.

Brainstorm for "Forceful Language" Jot down a list of forceful words, like those in this list, that you can use to make your argument persuasive and effective:

Weak	Forceful
should	must
probably	certainly
ask	implore
necessary	crucial

Drafting

Use the Correct Letter Form A letter to the editor follows the form of a business letter:

[Return Address ➡]	Your street address City, State, and Zip Code Date
Editor Title of publication Publication street address City, State, and Zip Code	**[◀— Address of Editor at Publication]**
Dear Editor: Body of your letter	**[◀— Greeting]**
[Closing ➡]	Sincerely, Your signature Your name

Write a Strong Opening Hook your readers right from the start by beginning your letter with a clever statement, a thought-provoking question, or a powerful quotation.

Adopt a Persuasive Tone Readers can be put off by a negative approach. If you make a criticism, state it fairly and simply. Then, explain an alternative, using positive, persuasive language.

APPLYING LANGUAGE SKILLS: Degrees of Comparison

The **comparative form** compares two items. It is formed by adding the ending -er or by beginning with the word *more*. The **superlative form** compares three or more items. It is formed by adding the ending -est or by beginning with the word *most*.

Comparative: Champ is the faster of the two horses, but Star is the more intelligent.

Superlative: Champ is the fastest horse I've ever seen, and Star is the most intelligent.

Practice On your paper, write the correct form of the adjective in parentheses.

1. Of all the kids on the team, Jen is the (strong).
2. Patrick probably throws (hard) than Stephen.
3. Chiara is (graceful) on the ice than Cerise.
4. Ana is the (fast) runner on the team.

Writing Application As you draft, be sure to use the correct degree of comparison.

Writer's Solution Connection Writing Lab

For more help using degrees of comparison, see the Proofreading section of the Exposition: Making Connections tutorial.

Prewriting

Explain to students that they will want to decide on a method of organization for the details in their letter. They may want to organize their details in order of importance, or they may want to show the pros and cons of their argument, explaining why the reasons for their opinions are stronger than the ones against it.

Customize for
Less Proficient Writers
Students may want to simplify the organization of their letter by using main ideas and details. Suggest that students use the Main Idea and Supporting Details Organizer in **Writing and Language Transparencies,** p. 61 to help them with their arguments. Explain that each main idea should be a reason for their opinion.

 **Writer's Solution**

In the Prewriting section of the tutorial on Exposition: Giving Information, have students view the audio-annotated writing models to see different types of organization methods.

Drafting

Suggest to students that they use quotations from the article or editorial to which they are responding in their letter. They may also want to use quotations from people they may have interviewed during their research. Remind students to use quotation marks when quoting directly.

Applying Language Skills

Degrees of Comparison Explain to students that most adjectives and adverbs have different forms to show degrees of comparison. These include the positive, the comparative, and the superlative.

Answers
1. strongest
2. harder
3. more graceful
4. fastest

Writer's Solution

For additional instruction and practice, have students use the practice page on Using Comparative and Superlative Degrees, p. 88 in the *Writer's Solution Grammar Practice Book.* Or, they can use the Forms of Comparison lesson in the Using Modifiers section in the *Writer's Solution Language Lab CD-ROM.*

Revising

Have peer reviewers consider if the topic of the letter has two definite sides and if there is enough evidence to support the writer's opinion.

 Writer's Solution

Writing Lab CD-ROM

Encourage students to use the Proofreading Checklist in the Revising and Editing section of the tutorial on Persuasion.

Publishing

Students can e-mail their letters to the editors of an appropriate publication.

Reinforce and Extend

Review the Writing Guidelines

After students have completed their papers, review the characteristics of a letter to an editor.

Applying Language Skills

Using Commas with Coordinate Adjectives To determine if adjectives in a sentence are of equal rank, students can see if the sentence keeps the same meaning when *and* is inserted between the adjectives.

Answers

1. It was a terribly hot, humid, stormy day.
2. A huge, old, hungry alligator crawled out of the swamp.
3. The child played with his red and black tin soldiers.
4. The students pulled the screaming, sobbing, frightened child to safety.

 **Writer's Solution**

For practice, use p. 105, Commas That Separate Basic Elements, in *Writer's Solution Grammar Practice Book*.

Writing Process Workshop

EDITING/PROOFREADING

APPLYING LANGUAGE SKILLS: Using Commas With Coordinate Adjectives

Coordinate adjectives are adjectives of equal rank that separately modify the noun they precede. The order of coordinate adjectives can be switched without changing the meaning of a sentence. Coordinate adjectives should be separated by commas.

Incorrect: The honest kind intelligent student was popular.

Correct: The honest, kind, intelligent student was popular.

Practice On your paper, add commas where necessary. Some sentences may be correct.

1. It was a terribly hot humid stormy day.
2. A huge old hungry alligator crawled out of the swamp.
3. The child played with his red and black tin soldiers.
4. The student pulled the screaming sobbing frightened child to safety.

Writing Application Review your letter, and make sure you've used commas correctly with coordinate adjectives.

Writer's Solution Connection Language Lab

For more practice in using commas correctly, refer to the lesson on Commas in the unit on Punctuation.

Revising

Work With a Peer Reviewer Ask a classmate to read and evaluate your letter, using the following checklist:
▶ What is the writer's position?
▶ Does the letter have a strong beginning?
▶ What descriptive details support the writer's position?
▶ Are ideas supported with facts, statistics, and examples?
▶ Does the language help persuade you to adopt the writer's point of view?

Use your reviewer's responses to these questions to help you improve your letter to the editor.

Verify the Format Before submitting your letter to the editor, check to be sure you've followed standard letter format.

Proofread Check your letter carefully to be sure it's free of errors in grammar, spelling, and punctuation.

REVISION MODEL

① *desperately*
Our schools need more money for the Performing Arts
② *over 500*
and Music departments. Last year, many students signed
② *more than half*
up for drama, band, and orchestra classes, but a lot had

to be turned away because there weren't enough classes
③ *due to a shortage of teachers and classrooms*
available. Please support us.
④ *We matter. We are the future. Support us now!*

① Adding a forceful word increases the impact of this statement.
② The writer adds facts and statistics to support the argument.
③ This descriptive detail helps emphasize the writer's position.
④ This sentence was rewritten to convey a more persuasive, positive message.

Publishing and Presenting

▶ **Newspaper** Submit your letter to the editor for publication in your local newspaper.
▶ **School** Read your letter at a school meeting or assembly. If others agree with you, ask them to write their own letters to the editor in support of your position.

Real-World Reading Skills Workshop

Analyzing a Position

Strategies for Success

In a newspaper or magazine, you'll sometimes come across an editorial, which expresses the writer's point of view on an issue. Analyze the writer's position before you agree or disagree with it.

Identify an Editorial Sometimes editorials are not identified as such. You must determine whether an article is news—fact, not opinion—or an editorial—primarily opinion.

Determine the Writer's Position Usually an editorial writer will quickly identify the subject and explain his or her position on it. Sometimes the writer will suggest a course of action that the reader should take.

Recognize the Writer's Bias A *bias* is a leaning toward a certain position; for example, a lawyer writing about unfair treatment of lawyers may be writing from a bias. Be aware of subtle forms of bias. Notice clues such as quotations from "my friends" or "my colleagues," or statements such as "Most thinking people agree . . ."

Separate Facts From Opinions Facts can be checked. When a writer uses vague generalizations, they often indicate opinions rather than facts.

Consider Opposing Positions Sometimes a writer will include an opposing idea in an editorial and then refute it. If the writer doesn't do this, the job is yours. Think of the opposing position, and decide whether the writer has dealt with it fairly. For example, did he or she include current and important facts?

Apply the Strategies

Read "Fireworks for Us." Then, analyze the writer's position by answering these questions:

1. Is this a news article or an editorial? What evidence do you have?
2. Explain the writer's position. Be specific.
3. Does the writer have a bias? Explain.
4. What facts does the writer present? Do you think they're reliable? Where might you check them?
5. Does the writer present an opposing view? If so, how does he deal with it?
6. Do you agree or disagree with the writer? Why?

✔ Here are other situations in which analyzing a position is important:
▶ Reading a letter to the editor
▶ Reading the text of a political speech
▶ Reading a petition you are asked to sign

Fireworks for Us
by Dale Croyle

All the other states in the USA are allowed to have fireworks except us, and, frankly, I think that stinks! We should be allowed to have fireworks too. On special occasions like the Fourth of July, our towns and cities have to pay professional companies to come and set off fireworks. My friend's father says that costs a lot of money. If individuals and minors were allowed to own and discharge fireworks, we'd save the state plenty. You may argue that people get hurt using fireworks. That's like saying skis aren't safe because some people have accidents. I say "Fireworks for Us," and so should YOU!

Dale Croyle is an eighth grader at Biegly Junior High.

◆ Build Grammar Skills

Reviewing Adjectives and Adverbs

The selections in Part 1 include instruction on the following:

- Adjectives
- Placement of Adjectives
- Adverbs
- Adverbs Modifying Adjectives and Adverbs

This instruction is reinforced with the Build Grammar Skills practice pages in **Selection Support,** pp. 99, 105, 110, and 115.

As you review adjectives and adverbs, you may wish to include the following:

- Proper Adjectives

A proper adjective is either a proper noun used as an adjective, as in *Connecticut* doctor, or, an adjective formed from a proper noun, as in *Petrarchan* sonnet. Like regular adjectives, they answer the questions "What kind?" or "Which?"

- Nouns as Adjectives

Nouns become adjectives when they modify other nouns and answer the question "What kind?" or "Which one?" For example, in the phrase *chocolate* cake, *chocolate* is a noun used as an adjective to answer the question "What kind of cake?"

- Adjective or Adverb?

Sometimes the same word can be used as either an adjective or adverb, depending on its use in the sentence. For example, in the sentence *They worked hard on the building,* the word *hard* is an adverb modifying the verb *worked.* But in the following sentence, *hard* is used as an adjective modifying the noun *bed: They slept poorly on the hard bed.*

✎ Writer's Solution

For additional practice and support using adjectives and adverbs, have students use the practice pages on adjectives and adverbs in the *Writer's Solution Grammar Practice Book,* pp. 16–23.

Adjectives and Adverbs | Grammar Review

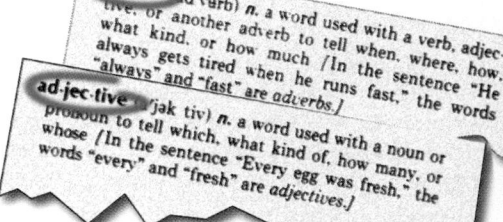

An **adjective** modifies or describes a noun or pronoun. Adjectives answer questions such as *which, what kind, how many,* or *how much.* (See page 247.)

Question	Example
Which?	*That* lawyer argued brilliantly.
What kind?	Lincoln was an *effective* president.
How many?	*Several* wetlands animals were endangered.
How much?	There was *enough* land for everyone.

Adjectives are located most commonly before the word they modify or after a linking verb. (See page 258.)

> *Three* egrets stood in the *shallow* water.
> Those birds are *beautiful.*

Question	Example
How?	The students felt *strongly* about ending segregation.
When?	I read the selection *yesterday.*
Where?	Jimmy Valentine put his tools *there.*
To what extent?	He *hardly* noticed that everyone was watching.

An **adverb** modifies a verb, an adjective, or another adverb. Adverbs answer the questions *how, when, where,* and *to what extent.* (See pages 268 and 282.)

Practice 1 Copy these sentences. Underline each adjective once and each adverb twice. Draw arrows from the adjectives and adverbs to the words they modify.

1. Marshall, well-spoken and intelligent, happily joined the Debating Club.

2. The students enthusiastically supported the Supreme Court's decision.

3. Many of his stories have surprise endings.

4. The next morning, Lincoln delivered his proclamation.

5. We were very worried about the wetlands.

Practice 2 Rewrite this paragraph, filling in the blanks with adjectives or adverbs.

The __(adjective)__ detective returned to his office. He sat __(adverb)__ at his desk, feeling __(adverb)__ __(adjective)__ with himself. "I did a __(adjective)__ thing today," he said __(adverb)__ .

Grammar in Writing

✔ A proper adjective is formed from a proper noun: American author. A proper adjective begins with a capital letter.

✔ Many adverbs are formed by adding *-ly* to an adjective; for example, happily carefully, strangely.

Answers
Practice 1

1. Marshall, well-spoken and intelligent, happily joined the Debating Club.

2. The students enthusiastically supported the Supreme Court's decision.

3. Many of his stories have surprise endings.

4. The next morning, Lincoln delivered his proclamation.

5. We were very worried about the wetlands.

Practice 2
Possible responses:
The determined detective returned to his office. He sat quietly at his desk, feeling unhappy with himself. "I did a crummy thing today," he said sadly.

PART **2**

Leading the Way

Lightning Bolt, Paul Colon

The selections in this section focus on the theme of "Leading the Way." "Raymond's Run" is the story of a girl's passion for running and her love for her special brother. "Paul Revere's Ride" details the famous man's efforts to save his country. "Barbara Frietchie" shows the strength of an older woman and her loyalty to her country. "Elizabeth Blackwell" details the struggle and ambition of the first woman doctor. Finally, "Young Jefferson Gets Advice from Ben Franklin" is a true account of the writing of the Declaration of Independence.

Customize for
Varying Students Needs
When assigning the selections in this section, keep in mind the following factors:

"Raymond's Run"
• Short story focusing on the theme of respect and winning
• Offers students ideas about the value and alternatives to winning

"Paul Revere's Ride"
• A classic poem by Henry Wadsworth Longfellow
• Students may need help with vocabulary

"Barbara Frietchie"
• A narrative poem set during the Battle of Fredericksburg
• Students may need help with the poem's theme

"Elizabeth Blackwell"
• A narrative poem about Elizabeth Blackwell's life goal to be a doctor at a time when women were not allowed to go to medical school
• Includes a Beyond Literature Career Connection

"Young Jefferson Gets Some Advice from Ben Franklin"
• True account by Thomas Jefferson of the revising of the Declaration of Independence
• Provides an opportunity for connecting literature with social studies
• Students may need help with vocabulary

 Humanities: Art

Lightning Bolt, by Paul Colon
This painting reflects part of the surrealistic art movement, which first came into popularity in the 1920's. A group of artists and writers sought to revolutionize art by opposing traditional style and subject matter. Surrealism uses images from dreams, the subconscious mind, and fantasy—it preceded abstract expressionism, the first internationally recognized style of American painting.

1. What do you think is the significance of the man's position in the painting? *Students may say the man is standing in the sky, possibly empowered*

by flashes of lightning, and seemingly pushing the world through the sky.

2. How do the painting's colors affect your impression of the subject matter? *Students may say the bright colors show strength, capture the viewer's attention, or reinforce the lightning bolts.*

3. Do you think this painting depicts someone "Leading the Way?" *Some students may say yes because the man is pushing open the dark, thunderstorm sky to reveal a blue sky with clouds, as if he is finding a new way. Others may say they would prefer a more realisitic painting.*

Guide for Reading

OBJECTIVES

1. To read, comprehend, and interpret a short story
2. To relate major and minor events to personal experience
3. To use prediction as a reading strategy
4. To recognize major and minor characters
5. To build vocabulary in context and use the word part *scope*
6. To develop skill in using prepositions
7. To write a script for a sportscaster that includes background information
8. To respond to a short story through writing, speaking and listening, and projects

SKILLS INSTRUCTION

Vocabulary:
Using the Word Part *scope*

Spelling:
Words That End in *-gy*

Grammar:
Prepositions

Reading Strategy:
Predict

Literary Focus:
Major and Minor Characters

Writing:
Background Information

Speaking and Listening:
Telephone Conversation (Teacher Edition)

Viewing and Representing:
Story Board (Teacher Edition)

Critical Viewing:
Generalize; Speculate; Define

PORTFOLIO OPPORTUNITIES

Writing: Letter; Sequel; Essay

Writing Mini-Lesson: Script for a Sportscaster

Speaking and Listening: Scene; Telephone Conversation

Projects: Map of the Setting; Track and Running Bibliography

More About the Author
Toni Cade Bambara was not only a writer, filmmaker, and educator, she was also a feminist and political activist who felt that art and the ongoing struggles for civil rights and social change belonged together. She felt her writing might help someone else see issues more clearly. She published her first short story, "Sweet Town," in 1959; her last work, *Deep Sightings and Rescue Missions,* a collection of fiction, essays, and conversations, was published after her death.

Meet the Author:

Toni Cade Bambara (1939–1995)

Reading the work of Toni Cade Bambara, you can't help noticing the writer's interest in African American heritage and her concern for other people. As one critic noted, "Bambara tells me more about being black through her quiet, proud, silly, tender, hip, acute, loving stories than any amount of literary [discussion] could hope to do.... All of her stories share the affection that their narrator feels for the subject ... "

Teacher and Writer A New York City native, Bambara was educated in Europe and the United States. She worked as a teacher, with pupils ranging from preschoolers to college students. She also wrote two collections of short stories—*Gorilla, My Love,* in which "Raymond's Run" appears, and *The Sea Birds Are Still Alive*—as well as a novel, *The Salt Eaters.*

THE STORY BEHIND THE STORY

In 1971, Bambara edited a collection of stories called *Tales and Stories for Black Folks.* In the preface to the book, she urges readers to take the stories "seriously as valuable lessons in human behavior and examples of living history." "Raymond's Run," about a young runner, appears in the section of the book entitled "Stories I Wish I Had Read Growing Up."

290 ◆ Quest for Justice

◆ LITERATURE AND YOUR LIFE

CONNECT YOUR EXPERIENCE

Have you ever competed in an athletic event or an academic contest that you just *had* to win? Squeaky, the main character in "Raymond's Run," always wants to come out on top. In this story, she learns an important lesson about what being a winner really means.

THEMATIC FOCUS: Leading the Way

In "Raymond's Run," notice how a sister leads the way for her brother.

◆ Background for Understanding

PHYSICAL EDUCATION

Runners, like Squeaky in "Raymond's Run," get a number of benefits from their running. Squeaky trains by doing breathing exercises and prancing and trotting to keep her legs strong. The more a runner trains, the stronger he or she becomes. Running strengthens the heart and the leg muscles and increases the circulation of oxygen through the bloodstream to the body's organs and tissues.

◆ Build Vocabulary

WORD PARTS: *scope*

In the story, Mr. Pearson "looks around the park for Gretchen like a periscope in a submarine movie." The word part *scope* means "an instrument for seeing." A periscope is an instrument used to see above the water from a submerged submarine.

WORD BANK

Which word from the story means "to show or make known, as by a sign"? Check the Build Vocabulary box on page 295 to see if you guessed correctly.

prodigy
signify
ventriloquist
periscope

Prentice Hall Literature Program Resources

REINFORCE / RETEACH / EXTEND

Selection Support Pages
Build Vocabulary: Using the Word Part *scope,* p. 118
Build Spelling Skills, p. 119
Build Grammar Skills: Prepositions, p. 120
Reading Strategy: Predict, p. 121
Literary Focus: Major and Minor Characters, p. 122
Strategies for Diverse Student Needs, pp. 45–46
Beyond Literature Career Connection: Athletic Coach, p. 23

Formal Assessment Selection Test, pp. 87–89, Assessment Resources Software
Alternative Assessment, p. 23
Writing and Language Transparencies
Cluster Organizer, p. 73; Sunburst Organizer, p. 85
Daily Language Practice, p. 12
Resource Pro CD-ROM "Raymond's Run"
Art Transparencies Art Transparency 19, pp. 79–82

Listening to Literature Audiocassettes "Raymond's Run"

◆ Raymond's Run ◆

Interest Grabber Draw a 2-column chart on the board with the following headings:

Winning	Losing

Ask students to work individually or in groups to brainstorm for ideas and fill in the chart with words, phrases, sensory images, or sayings. Allow about five minutes for this activity. Then invite volunteers to share their ideas. Discuss with the class how good sportsmanship relates to winning and losing. Introduce the story by telling them that the main character is a sassy young girl who has a talent for running and likes very much to win races.

◆ Build Grammar Skills

Prepositions If you wish to introduce the grammar concept for this selection before students read, refer to the instruction on p. 300.

Customize for
Less Proficient Readers

In this story, students will encounter long passages that may be harder to follow than shorter, unified ones that start with a topic sentence followed by supporting details. Discuss some strategies that may enhance the reading process. For example, suggest that students read more slowly in order to digest all the details, or read long passages aloud, as if the character is speaking to them.

Customize for
More Advanced Learners

To help focus students on aspects of major and minor characters, have them keep a double-entry response log as they read. In one column, have them list Squeaky's perceptions of minor characters; in the other, impressions they can gather about those same characters from other details in the selection.

◆ Literary Focus

MAJOR AND MINOR CHARACTERS

Characters are the people (or sometimes animals) who take part in a literary work. Most stories have both major and minor characters. A **major character** is the most important character in the story. This person often changes in a significant way as the story unfolds. **Minor characters** play lesser roles in the story's events but are necessary for the story to develop. In "Raymond's Run," Squeaky, the major character, tells the story.

◆ Reading Strategy

PREDICT

As you read a story, you may find yourself wondering what's going to happen. You can often **predict** the story events by paying attention to details the author provides. Your prediction is an informed guess based on story details. In "Raymond's Run," two characters compete in an important race. Keep track of details the author gives you about each character to see if you can predict what will happen. Use a chart like the one below to help you make predictions.

Story Text	Prediction
"I'm the fastest thing on two feet."	She will meet her match.

Guide for Reading ◆ 291

Preparing for Standardized Tests

Reading Students who use prediction as a reading strategy notice details the author gives, and then use those details to determine what is most likely to happen. This ability will help students as they read in general, and as they answer comprehension items on standardized tests. Use the following sample question, based on "Raymond's Run":

Predict what Cynthia would be most likely to say about an original poem she wrote:

(A) "I revised this five times until I was happy with it."

(B) "This poem was hard for me to write."
(C) "I'd like you to hear to my latest poem."
(D) "This poem came to me in a flash."

Discuss with students that (A) and (B) may reflect what Cynthia really did and felt, but it goes against her character. She likes to act as though things come easily to her, when in reality she works very hard. For the best answer, students should pick (D), which is consistent with what is known about Cynthia's personality and the observations Squeaky has made. For further practice with prediction, use p. 121 in **Selection Support**.

One-Minute Insight

"Raymond's Run" is a story about respect and the many ways there are to earn it. Squeaky, the fastest runner in her class, cares for her "not quite right" big brother Raymond, whom she protects with fierce loyalty. During the annual May Day races, Squeaky learns valuable lessons about herself, about Gretchen, her nearest competitor, and, most important, about Raymond and his need for respect and pride.

Customize for
English Language Learners

In this story, students will encounter words spelled as they sound in casual speech rather than as they would appear in Standard English. Examples include *lotta* (a lot of), *cause* (because), *ole* (old), and *sayin* (saying). Pair students with native English speakers who can help them recognize informal spellings and link them with conventional ones.

Customize for
Intrapersonal Learners

Have students consider how they would act or react in situations like the ones that Squeaky experiences: at the start of a big race or contest, in an uncomfortable confrontation, or when doing an unpleasant chore. Ask students to draw conclusions about Squeaky's character by comparing and contrasting how she acts with how they might act.

Customize for
Bodily/Kinesthetic Learners

Invite students to focus on the many physical events described in this story. Have them imitate Squeaky's training regimen, Raymond's fantasy walking, or the way minor characters move or act, to gain a deeper sense of who they are.

RAYMOND'S RUN

Toni Cade Bambara

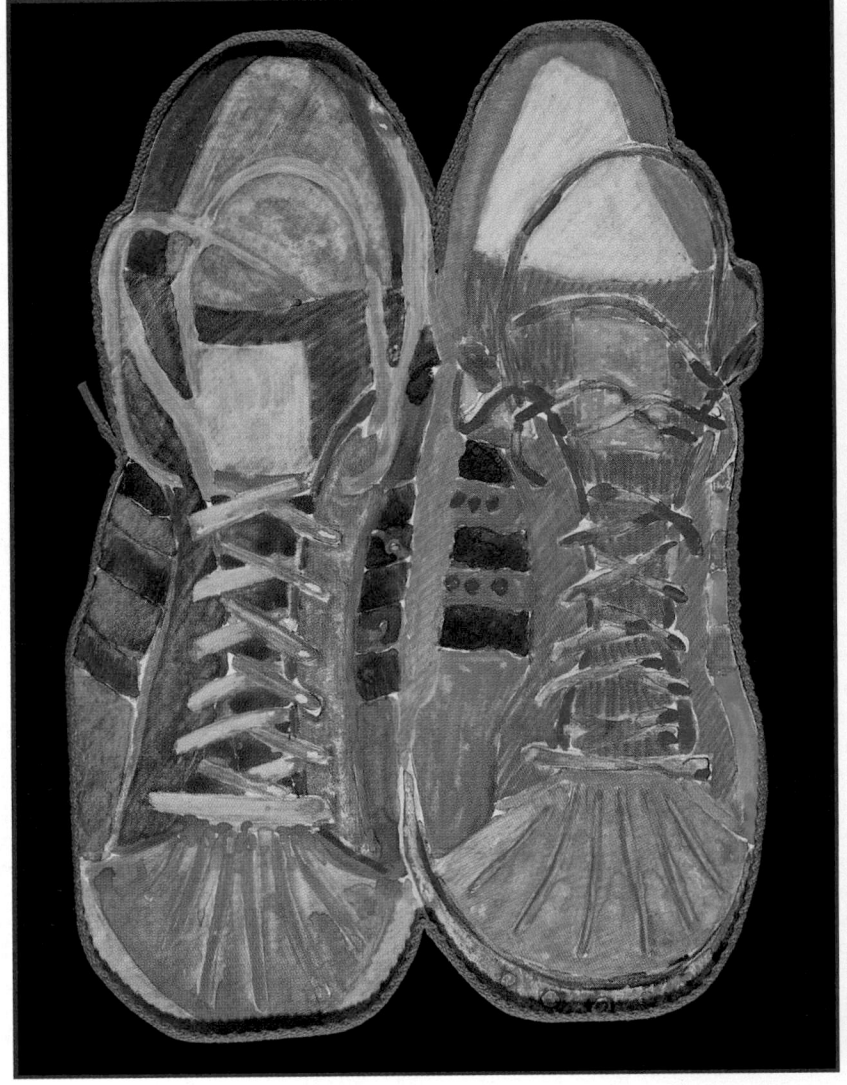

Shoe Series, #2, Marilee Whitehouse-Holm

292 ◆ *Quest for Justice*

 Humanities: Art

Shoe Series, #2, 1982–83, by Marilee Whitehouse-Holm

Marilee Whitehouse-Holm (born 1949) was born in Walla Walla, Washington. She earned a degree in fine arts, and has worked with American artists Jacob Lawrence, R. C. Jones, and Alden Mason. In addition to working in oil, watercolor, and acrylic paint, Whitehouse-Holm has also explored collage, gouache, colored pencil, mixed media, fabric design, ceramics, and lamp building.

1. What aspects of the work are realistic? *The shoes have the basic shape and look of athletic shoes, but the vibrant colors and mismatched designs are unrealistic.*

2. What messages might the artist want to convey with this boldly colored pair of shoes? *Students may say that she enjoys running or that sports attracts diverse individuals. She might be using the shoes to represent action or opportunities to leap forward.*

I don't have much work to do around the house like some girls. My mother does that. And I don't have to earn my pocket money by hustling; George runs errands for the big boys and sells Christmas cards. And anything else that's got to get done, my father does. All I have to do in life is mind my brother Raymond, which is enough.

Sometimes I slip and say my little brother Raymond. But as any fool can see he's much bigger and he's older too. But a lot of people call him my little brother cause he needs looking after cause he's not quite right. And a lot of smart mouths got lots to say about that too, especially when George was minding him. But now, if anybody has anything to say to Raymond, anything to say about his big head, they have to come by me. And I don't play the dozens[1] or believe in standing around with somebody in my face doing a lot of talking. I much rather just knock you down and take my chances even if I am a little girl with skinny arms and a squeaky voice, which is how I got the name Squeaky. And if things get too rough, I run. And as anybody can tell you, I'm the fastest thing on two feet.

There is no track meet that I don't win the first place medal. I used to win the twenty-yard dash when I was a little kid in kindergarten. Nowadays, it's the fifty-yard dash. And tomorrow I'm subject to run the quarter-meter relay all by myself and come in first, second, and third. The big kids call me Mercury[2] cause I'm the swiftest thing in the neighborhood. Everybody knows that—except two people who know better, my father and me.

He can beat me to Amsterdam Avenue with me having a two fire-hydrant headstart and him running with his hands in his pockets and whistling. But that's private information. Cause can you imagine some thirty-five-year-

---

1. **the dozens:** Game in which the players insult one another; the first to show anger loses.
2. **Mercury:** In Roman mythology, the messenger of the gods, known for great speed.

◀ **Critical Viewing** Most young people, not just athletes, wear athletic shoes. What do athletic shoes symbolize to you? [Generalize]

old man stuffing himself into PAL[3] shorts to race little kids? So as far as everyone's concerned, I'm the fastest and that goes for Gretchen, too, who has put out the tale that she is going to win the first-place medal this year. Ridiculous. In the second place, she's got short legs. In the third place, she's got freckles. In the first place, no one can beat me and that's all there is to it.

I'm standing on the corner admiring the weather and about to take a stroll down Broadway so I can practice my breathing exercises, and I've got Raymond walking on the inside close to the buildings, cause he's subject to fits of fantasy and starts thinking he's a circus performer and that the curb is a tightrope strung high in the air. And sometimes after a rain he likes to step down off his tightrope right into the gutter and slosh around getting his shoes and cuffs wet. Or sometimes if you don't watch him he'll dash across traffic to the island in the middle of Broadway and give the pigeons a fit. Then I have to go behind him apologizing to all the old people sitting around trying to get some sun and getting all upset with the pigeons fluttering around them, scattering their newspapers and upsetting the waxpaper lunches in their laps. So I keep Raymond on the inside of me, and he plays like he's driving a stage coach, which is O.K. by me so long as he doesn't run me over or interrupt my breathing exercises, which I have to do on account of I'm serious about my running, and I don't care who knows it.

Now some people like to act like things come easy to them, won't let on that they practice. Not me. I'll high prance down 34th Street like a rodeo pony to keep my knees strong even if it does get my mother uptight so that she walks ahead like she's not with me, don't know me, is all by herself on a shopping trip, and I am somebody else's crazy child.

Now you take Cynthia Procter for instance. She's just the opposite. If there's a test tomorrow, she'll say something like, "Oh, I guess I'll play handball this afternoon and watch television tonight," just to let you know she ain't

---

3. **PAL:** Police Athletic League.

Raymond's Run ◆ 293

Comprehension Check ☑

① What details do you know about the narrator and her brother? *The narrator is younger than her brother Raymond. He is bigger than she is but is developmentally challenged. She looks after him, which is a big job.*

◆ Literary Focus

② Major and Minor Characters Have students explain how they know that Squeaky is a major character in this story. *She is the narrator; all characters and details are seen through her eyes and explained from her viewpoint.*

◆ Reading Strategy

③ Predict Ask students to use the "private information" to predict what may happen to Squeaky later in the story. *Squeaky admits that she isn't really "the fastest thing on two feet" because her father can outrace her. This detail might lead students to predict that she might lose an upcoming race.*

▶ Critical Viewing ◀

④ Generalize *Students may say that athletic shoes symbolize fun, speed, power, freedom, and opportunity.*

◆ Literary Focus

⑤ Major and Minor Characters Ask students whether they see Raymond as a major or minor character. *Some may see him as a major character, because his name is in the title and he has a big influence on Squeaky's life. Others may say that he is minor because Squeaky seems to be the center of the story so far.*

◆ Critical Thinking

⑥ Draw Conclusions What is Squeaky's attitude toward Raymond, and what does this attitude say about her? *She cheerfully takes full responsibility for caring for Raymond and always looks out for him. She must be confident, patient, and strong to be so loyal to such a demanding and sometimes embarrassing job.*

Block Scheduling Strategies

Consider these suggestions to take advantage of extended class time:

- Begin and end with activities from the **Daily Language Practice**, p. 12.
- Discuss the role that sports, physical education, and athletics can play in life, including both positive and negative impacts. Focus on the Background for Understanding, p. 290. You may wish to have students research the roles of female runners as suggested in the Customize for Bodily/Kinesthetic Learners note on p. 296.

- Have students read the story independently, then prepare answers to the Guide for Responding questions on pp. 299–300. Have students form discussion groups to share and discuss their answers.
- Present the Speaking and Listening Mini-Lesson, p. 295, before assigning the Writing Mini-Lesson p. 301.
- Have students work in groups on a project you assign or they select from the Portfolio Opportunities in the Idea Bank, p. 301.

◆ **Critical Thinking**

❶ **Compare and Contrast** Ask students to discuss Cynthia and Squeaky's attitudes and approaches to excellence. *Cynthia likes people to think that things come very easily to her when, in fact, she works hard at what she does. Squeaky is proud of how hard she works to achieve excellence and is not ashamed to admit that she works hard.*

▶**Critical Viewing**◀

❷ **Speculate** *Students may say that the runner on the right seems to love running as Squeaky does; they may think that the others seem less involved in the race.*

◆ **LITERATURE AND YOUR LIFE**

❸ When Squeaky says that Rosie "can't afford to throw stones," she is referring to the saying, "People who live in glass houses shouldn't throw stones." Ask students to explain what they think the saying means, and how they think it fits this selection. Then, suggest that they think of a time in their own lives when someone they know was teased or ridiculed. Have volunteers share strategies for solving the problem of teasing and unnecessary remarks.

◆ **Reading Strategy**

❹ **Predict** Have students predict what may happen in the encounter Squeaky is about to have with Gretchen and her pals. *Students may predict a verbal or physical fight.*

Comprehension Check ☑

❺ Why doesn't Squeaky duck into the candy store and avoid a confrontation with the other girls? *She does not want to get a reputation as being afraid or chicken.*

thinking about the test. Or like last week when she won the spelling bee for the millionth time, "A good thing you got 'receive,' Squeaky, cause I would have got it wrong. I completely forgot about the spelling bee." And she'll clutch the lace on her blouse like it was a narrow escape. Oh, brother.

But of course when I pass her house on my early morning trots around the block, she is practicing the scales on the piano over and over and over and over. Then in music class she always lets herself get bumped around so she falls accidently on purpose onto the piano stool and is so surprised to find herself sitting there that she decides just for fun to try out the ole keys and what do you know—Chopin's[4] waltzes just spring out of her fingertips and she's the most surprised thing in the world. A regular <u>prodigy</u>. I could kill people like that.

I stay up all night studying the words for the spelling bee. And you can see me any time of day practicing running. I never walk if I can trot, and shame on Raymond if he can't keep up. But of course he does, cause if he hangs back someone's liable to walk up to him and get smart, or take his allowance from him, or ask him where he got that great big pumpkin head. People are so stupid sometimes.

So I'm strolling down Broadway breathing

4. **Chopin** (shō pan'): Frédéric François Chopin (1810–1849), Polish composer and pianist.

294 ◆ *Quest for Justice*

▲ **Critical Viewing** Do you think the runners in this photograph love to race as much as Squeaky does? Why or why not? [Speculate]

out and breathing in on counts of seven, which is my lucky number, and here comes Gretchen and her sidekicks—Mary Louise who used to be a friend of mine when she first moved to Harlem from Baltimore and got beat up by everybody till I took up for her on account of her mother and my mother used to sing in the same choir when they were young girls, but people ain't grateful, so now she hangs out with the new girl Gretchen and talks about me like a dog; and Rosie who is as fat as I am skinny and has a big mouth where Raymond is concerned and is too stupid to know that there is not a big deal of difference between herself and Raymond and that she can't afford to throw stones. So they are steady coming up Broadway and I see right away that it's going to be one of those Dodge City[5] scenes cause the street ain't that big and they're close to the buildings just as we are. First I think I'll step into the candy store and look over the new comics and let them pass. But that's chicken and I've got a reputation to consider. So then I think I'll just walk straight

5. **Dodge City:** Location of the television program *Gunsmoke*, which often presented a gunfight between the sheriff and an outlaw.

Cross-Curricular Connection: Math

Shoe Survey More and more people use athletic shoes—running shoes, basketball shoes, cross-trainers, hiking boots—for everyday wear.

Have interested students work in small groups to conduct a shoe survey in your class, grade, or school. Have the students consider the following as they plan and conduct their survey:

• Determine what data they wish to gather and analyze. For example: type of shoe, size, material, color, type of closure (laces, Velcro, buckles), tread design, degree of wear, intended purpose.

• Plan a questionnaire they can use to gather that data.

• Gather the data.

• Use the raw data and determine the best way to display it in graphic form.

• Prepare a written summary that includes a statistical analysis of the data.

Have students share their findings with the class in a visual display or oral report.

on through them or even over them if necessary. But as they get to me, they slow down. I'm ready to fight, cause like I said I don't feature a whole lot of chit-chat, I much prefer to just knock you down right from the jump and save everybody a lotta precious time.

❻ "You signing up for the May Day races?" smiles Mary Louise, only it's not a smile at all.

A dumb question like that doesn't deserve an answer. Besides, there's just me and Gretchen standing there really, so no use wasting my breath talking to shadows.

◆ **Literary Focus**
What do you learn about the major character, Squeaky, through her conversation with the minor characters Mary Louise, Gretchen, and Rosie?

❼

"I don't think you're going to win this time," says Rosie, trying to signify with her hands on her hips all salty, completely forgetting that I have whupped her many times for less salt than that.

"I always win cause I'm the best," I say straight at Gretchen who is, as far as I'm concerned, the only one talking in this ventriloquist-dummy routine.

Gretchen smiles, but it's not a smile, and I'm thinking that girls never really smile at each other because they don't know how and don't want to know how and there's probably no one to teach us how cause grown-up girls don't know either. Then they all look at Raymond who has just brought his mule team to a standstill. And they're about to see what trouble they can get into through him.

"What grade you in now, Raymond?"

"You got anything to say to my brother, you say it to me, Mary Louise Williams of Raggedy Town, Baltimore."

"What are you, his mother?" sasses Rosie.

"That's right, Fatso. And the next word out

◆ **Build Vocabulary**

prodigy (präd´ ə jē) *n.*: A wonder; an unusually talented person

signify (sig´ nə fī) *v.*: To show or make known, as by a sign, words, etc.

ventriloquist (ven tril´ ə kwist) *n.*: Someone who speaks through a puppet or dummy

of anybody and I'll be *their* mother too." So they just stand there and Gretchen shifts from one leg to the other and so do they. Then Gretchen puts her hands on her hips and is about to say something with her freckle-face self but doesn't. Then she walks around me looking me up and down but keeps walking up Broadway, and her sidekicks follow her. So me and Raymond smile at each other and he says, "Gidyap" to his team and I continue with my breathing exercises, strolling down Broadway toward the ice man on 145th with not a care in the world cause I am Miss Quicksilver herself.

❽

I take my time getting to the park on May Day because the track meet is the last thing on the program. The biggest thing on the program is the May Pole dancing, which I can do without, thank you, even if my mother thinks it's a shame I don't take part and act like a girl for a change. You'd think my mother'd be grateful not to have to make me a white organdy dress with a big satin sash and buy me new white baby-doll shoes that can't be taken out of the box till the big day. You'd think she'd be glad her daughter ain't out there prancing around a May Pole getting the new clothes all dirty and sweaty and trying to act like a fairy or a flower or whatever you're supposed to be when you should be trying to be yourself, whatever that is, which is, as far as I am concerned, a poor black girl who really can't afford to buy shoes and a new dress you only wear once a lifetime cause it won't fit next year.

❾

❿

I was once a strawberry in a Hansel and Gretel pageant when I was in nursery school and didn't have no better sense than to dance on tiptoe with my arms in a circle over my head doing umbrella steps and being a perfect fool just so my mother and father could come dressed up and clap. You'd think they'd know better than to encourage that kind of nonsense. I am not a strawberry. I do not dance on my toes. I run. That is what I am all about. So I always come late to the May Day program, just in time to get my number pinned on and lay in the grass till they announce the fifty-yard dash.

Raymond's Run ◆ *295*

◆ **LITERATURE AND YOUR LIFE**
❻ Discuss with students how the coming of spring is noted in your community. Suggest that students think of activities that aren't related to a specific holiday celebration, but nevertheless celebrate the end of winter and the beginning of warm weather, such as digging a new garden, planting flowers, wearing spring clothes, and playing outdoor sports.

◆ **Literary Focus**
❼ Major and Minor Characters
Students may say that Squeaky shows that she is direct, confident, and strongly opinionated.

◆ **Reading Strategy**
❽ Predict Have students predict whether they believe Squeaky and Gretchen and her followers will have another confrontation at a later time. *Many students will believe that the conflict between the girls will continue until something resolves it. Some may predict another verbal confrontation or a physical fight, while others may predict that a contest, such as the May Day race, will end their conflict.*

Clarification
❾ A May Pole dance moves around a tall pole with long colorful ribbons strung from the top. Dancers weave over and under each other, holding the ends of long ribbons to make an intricate ribbon design on the pole.

◆ **Critical Thinking**
❿ Assess Ask students to react to Squeaky's matter-of-fact self-analysis, and assess how they feel about her, based on this passage. *Students may admire Squeaky's independent and realistic approach toward something she sees as foolish; or feel she is overly critical.*

Speaking and Listening Mini-Lesson

Telephone Conversation
This mini-lesson supports the Speaking and Listening activity in the Idea Bank on p. 301.

Introduce Review the concept of improvisation—making something up as you go along. Explain that improvisation is used in the performing arts. "Improv" is a classic technique used in drama classes to encourage students to think on their feet and to stay in character and keep going no matter what happens. Musicians also improvise, creating new and different sounds and motifs.

Develop Divide the class into pairs—each student taking the role of one of the girls. Suggest that students prepare for their conversations by discussing the character traits of each girl. Then they can begin to plan their conversations by jotting down notes about what each girl would likely say, her general attitude and tone of voice, and the goals of the conversation. Urge them not to practice the actual conversations, however, until they are present, in order to keep the improvisation "fresh" and lively.

Apply Have pairs present their improvised conversations to small groups or to the entire class. You might videotape their conversations if you have access to the appropriate equipment.

Assess Evaluate improvised conversations on how well students keep the conversation moving, how accurately they portray Squeaky and Gretchen, and how believable the conversations are. Or, use the Peer Assessment: Dramatic Performance form, p. 116, in **Alternative Assessment**.

I put Raymond in the little swings, which is a tight squeeze this year and will be impossible next year. Then I look around for Mr. Pearson, who pins the numbers on. I'm really looking for Gretchen if you want to know the truth, but she's not around. The park is jam-packed. Parents in hats and corsages and breast-pocket handkerchiefs peeking up. Kids in white dresses and light-blue suits. The parkees unfolding chairs and chasing the rowdy kids from Lenox as if they had no right to be there. The big guys with their caps on backwards, leaning against the fence swirling the basketballs on the tips of their fingers, waiting for all these crazy people to clear out the park so they can play. Most of the kids in my class are carrying bass drums and glockenspiels[6] and flutes. You'd think they'd put in a few bongos or something for real like that.

Then here comes Mr. Pearson with his clipboard and his cards and pencils and whistles and safety pins and fifty million other things he's always dropping all over the place with his clumsy self. He sticks out in a crowd because he's on stilts. We used to call him Jack and the Beanstalk to get him mad. But I'm the only one that can outrun him and get away, and I'm too grown for that silliness now.

"Well, Squeaky," he says, checking my name off the list and handing me number seven and two pins. And I'm thinking he's got no right to call me Squeaky, if I can't call him Beanstalk.

"Hazel Elizabeth Deborah Parker," I correct him and tell him to write it down on his board.

"Well, Hazel Elizabeth Deborah Parker, going to give someone else a break this year?" I squint at him real hard to see if he is seriously thinking I should lose the race on purpose just to give someone else a break. "Only six girls running this time," he continues, shaking his head sadly like it's my fault all of New York didn't turn out in sneakers. "That new girl should give you a run for your money." He looks around the park for Gretchen like a periscope in a submarine movie. "Wouldn't it be a nice gesture if you were . . . to ahhh . . ."

I give him such a look he couldn't finish putting that idea into words. Grownups got a lot of nerve sometimes. I pin number seven to myself and stomp away, I'm so burnt. And I go straight for the track and stretch out on the grass while the band winds up with "Oh, the Monkey Wrapped His Tail Around the Flag Pole," which my teacher calls by some other name. The man on the loudspeaker is calling everyone over to the track and I'm on my back looking at the sky, trying to pretend I'm in the country, but I can't, because even grass in the city feels hard as sidewalk, and there's just no pretending you are anywhere but in a "concrete jungle" as my grandfather says.

The twenty-yard dash takes all of two minutes cause most of the little kids don't know no better than to run off the track or run the wrong way or run smack into the fence and fall down and cry. One little kid, though, has got the good sense to run straight for the white ribbon up ahead, so he wins. Then the second-graders line up for the thirty-yard dash and I don't even bother to turn my head to watch cause Raphael Perez always wins. He wins before he even begins by psyching[7] the runners, telling them they're going to trip on their shoelaces and fall on their faces or lose their shorts or something, which he doesn't really have to do since he is very fast, almost as fast as I am. After that is the forty-yard dash which I use to run when I was in first grade. Raymond is hollering from the swings cause he knows I'm about to do my thing cause the man on the loudspeaker has just announced the fifty-yard dash, although he

◆ **Reading Strategy**
Predict what will happen in the race. On what details in the story do you base your prediction?

---

6. **glockenspiels** (gläk´ ən spēlz) *n.*: Musical instruments with flat metal bars that make bell-like tones when struck with small hammers.

7. **psyching** (sīk´ iŋ) *v.*: Slang for playing on a person's mental state.

296 ◆ *Quest for Justice*

◆ **Reading Strategy**

❺ **Predict** Squeaky, who always looks out for Raymond, is now in a race and can't stay with him. Point out that she worries about him even as she prepares to bolt from the starting line. Ask students to predict what will happen to Raymond, who now looks as if he, too, is preparing to race. *Students may predict that Raymond will race along the other side of the fence.*

◆ **LITERATURE AND YOUR LIFE**

❻ *Students may express feelings of anxiety, nervousness, excitement, worry, or fear.*

◆ **LITERATURE AND YOUR LIFE**

❼ Explain to students that many athletes use visualization to help them compete and win. Point out that what Squeaky does in this passage resembles techniques that world-class athletes actually use. Have students reread the passage and discuss how visualization can work. Invite student athletes who go through similar routines to share with the class what they do and how it helps. Have students think about and suggest other activities besides athletic competition where visualization would benefit students.

▶ **Critical Viewing** ◀

❽ **Define** *On the most obvious level, success in a race means beating all other contestants. On another level, a successful race can be one that a runner finishes despite obstacles, or one in which a runner takes part to show his or her courage and desire to compete. Students may realize that Raymond took part in the race to be part of the fun and excitement, not because he thought he would win.*

might just as well be giving a recipe for angel food cake cause you can hardly make out what he's saying for the static. I get up and slip off my sweat pants and then I see Gretchen standing at the starting line, kicking her legs out like a pro. Then as I get into place I see that ole Raymond is on line on the other side of the fence, bending down with his fingers on the ground just like he knew what he was doing. I was going to yell at him but then I didn't. It burns up your energy to holler.

Every time, just before I take off in a race, I always feel like I'm in a dream, the kind of dream you have when you're sick with fever and feel all hot and weightless. I dream I'm flying over a sandy beach in the early morning sun, kissing the leaves of the trees as I fly by. And there's always the smell of apples, just like in the country when I was little and used to think I was a choo-choo train, running through the fields of corn and chugging up the

> ◆ **Literature and Your Life**
> How do you feel right before you compete?

▲ **Critical Viewing** What constitutes success in a race? Is the winner the only one who succeeds? Explain. [Define] ❽

hill to the orchard. And all the time I'm dreaming this, I get lighter and lighter until I'm flying over the beach again, getting blown through the sky like a feather that weighs nothing at all. But once I spread my fingers in the dirt and crouch over the Get on Your Mark, the dream goes and I am solid again and am telling myself, Squeaky you must win, you must win, you are the fastest thing in the world, you can even beat your father up Amsterdam if you really try. And then I feel my weight coming back just behind my knees then down to my feet then into the earth and the pistol shot explodes in my blood and I am

◆ **Build Vocabulary**

periscope (per′ ə skōp) *n.*: An instrument containing mirrors and lenses, used to see objects not in a direct line from the viewer; often used in submarines to see objects above the water

Raymond's Run ◆ 297

 Cultural Connection

Good Luck Habits During Squeaky's pre-race routine, she visualizes the same things she always thinks of whenever she runs. Point out to students that athletes in many sports go through various pre-performance rituals, such as a set number of "good-luck bounces" basketball players take before making foul shots, or the actions batters take before a baseball game and before stepping up to the plate in a baseball game. Have students look for routines like these as they watch sporting events on television. Invite them to interview high school athletes or coaches to learn more

about what is behind these habits, and why players believe so strongly in them.

Suggest that students extend the activity to observe habits or patterns that people follow to insure success in many activities of everyday life. For example, have them think about what they do before an important test: get a good night's sleep, sharpen a certain number of pencils, eat a special food for breakfast. Some cooks won't bake bread if the weather conditions are not just right, or gardeners won't plant potatoes if the moon is in a certain phase.

Thematic Focus

❶ Leading the Way Raymond, who Squeaky has described as "not quite right," is running, too. Discuss with students why he runs, and why this is such a big moment for him. *For maybe the first time, Raymond participates in something others are doing— a real event, not a fantasy. Students may say that Raymond's run is important because it suggests that running may be something he is good at, something in which he can lead the way and belong to the group.*

►Critical Viewing◄

❷ Speculate *She probably feels glad, excited, proud, relieved, and tired.*

◆ Literary Focus

❸ Major and Minor Characters *She realizes that Raymond may be a fine runner, and that no matter who won this race, which is unclear to her at the moment, she can help Raymond become a runner. She is a major character because she matures significantly through the course of the story.*

Customize for
Verbal/Linguistic Learners

Squeaky uses many idioms and slang expressions that were common among New York City kids at the time that Toni Cade Bambara wrote this story. Ask students which idioms and expressions are still in use. Help them substitute current idioms or slang for outdated ones. Suggest that they create a dictionary of slang terms and definitions to explain the words to an adult or share with a learner who is new to the English language.

▲ **Critical Viewing** Put yourself in the place of this race's winner. How must she feel? [Speculate] ❷

off and weightless again, flying past the other runners, my arms pumping up and down and the whole world is quiet except for the crunch as I zoom over the gravel in the track. I glance to my left and there is no one. To the right a blurred Gretchen, who's got her chin jutting out as if it would win the race all by itself. And on the other side of the fence is Raymond with his arms down to his side and the palms tucked up behind him, running in his very own style, and it's the first time I ever saw that and I almost stop to watch my brother Raymond on his first run. But the white ribbon is bouncing toward me and I tear past it, racing into the distance till my feet with a mind of their own start digging up footfuls of dirt and brake me short. Then all the kids standing on the side pile on me, banging me on the back and slapping my head with their May Day programs, for I have won again and everybody on 151st Street can walk tall for another year.

"In first place . . ." the man on the loudspeaker is clear as a bell now. But then he pauses and the loudspeaker starts to whine. Then static. And I lean down to catch my breath and here comes Gretchen walking back, for she's overshot the finish line too, huffing and puffing with her hands on her hips taking it slow, breathing in steady time like a real pro and I sort of like her a little for the first time. "In first place . . ." and then

three or four voices get all mixed up on the loudspeaker and I dig my sneaker into the grass and stare at Gretchen who's staring back, we both wondering just who did win. I can hear old Beanstalk arguing with the man on the loudspeaker and then a few others running their mouths about what the stopwatches say. Then I hear Raymond yanking at the fence to call me and I wave to shush him, but he keeps rattling the fence like a gorilla in a cage like in them gorilla movies, but then like a dancer or something he starts climbing up nice and easy but very fast. And it occurs to me, watching how smoothly he climbs hand over hand and remembering how he looked running with his arms down to his side and with the wind pulling his mouth back and his teeth showing and all, it occurred to me that Raymond would make a very fine runner. Doesn't he always keep up with me on my trots? And he surely knows how to breathe in counts of seven cause he's always doing it at the dinner table, which drives my brother George up the wall. And I'm smiling to beat the band cause if I've lost this race, or if me and Gretchen tied, or

◆ **Literary Focus** What realization has Squeaky come to? How does this show that she is a major character? ❸

298 ◆ *Quest for Justice*

Viewing and Representing Mini-Lesson

Story Board

In this mini-lesson, students will analyze the visual image of Raymond's run, and create a story board to visually portray it.

Introduce Review Raymond's run on p. 298, using the Cluster Organizer, p. 73, in **Writing and Language Transparencies** to help students organize words and phrases that give a visual image of Raymond running alongside Squeaky's race.

Develop Discuss examples of strong visual images students have seen represented on

TV and in movies. They may suggest a variety of images, but ask them to describe the scene in detail—pinpointing film or video techniques and special effects, such as slow motion, computer enhanced images, background music or sounds, costuming or makeup. Just as writers use words to create images in readers minds, the creators of TV and films use visual effects to create images.

Apply Create groups of 3 or 4 students, and have each group use the Cluster Organizer as a basis to create a storyboard

that indicates a series of visual images for Raymond's run. For instance, begin with an image of the race; move to a close-up of Squeaky's face, with sounds of cheering. As Squeaky sees Raymond running, slow the frames and use background music.

Assess Have students present their storyboards and explain what techniques are intended for the filmed version of their storyboards. Evaluate students on group participation, analysis of the story's descriptions, and understanding of the characters.

even if I've won, I can always retire as a runner and begin a whole new career as a coach with Raymond as my champion. After all, with a little more study I can beat Cynthia and her phony self at the spelling bee. And if I bugged my mother, I could get piano lessons and become a star. And I have a big rep as the baddest thing around. And I've got a roomful of ribbons and medals and awards. But what has Raymond got to call his own?

So I stand there with my new plans, laughing out loud by this time as Raymond jumps down from the fence and runs over with his teeth showing and his arms down to the side, which no one before him has quite mastered as a running style. And by the time he comes over I'm jumping up and down so glad to see him—my brother Raymond, a great runner in the family tradition. But of course everyone thinks I'm jumping up and down because the

men on the loudspeaker have finally gotten themselves together and compared notes and are announcing "In first place—Miss Hazel Elizabeth Deborah Parker." (Dig that.) "In second place—Miss Gretchen P. Lewis." And I look over at Gretchen wondering what the "P" stands for. And I smile. Cause she's good, no doubt about it. Maybe she'd like to help me coach Raymond; she obviously is serious about running, as any fool can see. And she nods to congratulate me and then she smiles. And I smile. We stand there with this big smile of respect between us. It's about as real a smile as girls can do for each other, considering we don't practice real smiling every day, you know, cause maybe we too busy being flowers or fairies or strawberries instead of something honest and worthy of respect . . . you know . . . like being people.

❹

Thematic Focus

❹ **Leading the Way** Though they are opponents, Gretchen and Squeaky come to respect one another. How do these girls lead the way? *Both appreciate and respect athletic talent. They are leaders because they are true to their talents and show pride—marks of maturity and confidence.*

Reinforce and Extend

Answers

◆ LITERATURE AND YOUR LIFE

Reader's Response She might feel discouraged, but, seeing how well Raymond did and how much mutual respect she and Gretchen shared, she might take it in stride.

Thematic Focus She is true to herself and stands up for what she believes, she demands respect for herself and for her brother, and she refuses to play silly games.

☑ Check Your Comprehension

1. Her nickname comes from her squeaky voice. She is also called Mercury because she is a fast runner. Mercury was the Roman god with winged heels who swiftly delivered messages.
2. He asks her to let Gretchen win.
3. She feels like she's in a dream, visualizing images that will help her run as fast as she can.
4. (a) She realizes that she respects Gretchen. (b) She realizes that Raymond may have the makings of a fine runner.

◆ Critical Thinking

1. Squeaky loves her brother and doesn't mind looking out for him—she makes him walk on the inside so he won't drift into the street.
2. She is aggressive, direct, proud, and somewhat immature.
3. She doesn't think Mary Louise and Rosie are important enough to acknowledge. She thinks Cynthia is a phony. She's unsure of Gretchen, who is new to the group.
4. The smile shows their mutual respect for each other as good athletes.
5. Most students will say that it is, because Raymond shows progress that nobody expected from him.
6. Some students may say girls like Mary Louise don't earn respect; or girls like Squeaky are loyal and worthy of great respect.

◇ Guide for Responding

◆ LITERATURE AND YOUR LIFE

Reader's Response If you were Squeaky, how would you feel if you had lost the race?

Thematic Focus In what way does Squeaky show that she is "leading the way"?

Journal Writing Briefly write about a time when helping someone made you feel good.

☑ Check Your Comprehension

1. How did Squeaky get her nickname? Why is she also called Mercury?
2. What does Mr. Pearson want Squeaky to do in the race?
3. How does Squeaky feel before each race?
4. (a) What does Squeaky realize about herself at the end of the race? (b) What does she realize about Raymond?

◆ Critical Thinking

INTERPRET
1. How does Squeaky feel about taking care of Raymond? Support your answer. **[Analyze]**
2. What does Squeaky's behavior toward people who "talk smart" to her suggest about her? **[Interpret]**
3. How does Squeaky feel about the other girls in her class? Explain. **[Analyze]**
4. Explain the significance of the smile that Squeaky and Gretchen share. **[Interpret]**

EVALUATE
5. Is "Raymond's Run" a good title for this story? Explain. **[Assess]**

APPLY
6. Squeaky suggests that it is difficult for girls in our society to be "something honest and worthy of respect." Explain why you agree or disagree with her opinion. **[Relate]**

Raymond's Run ◆ 299

Beyond the Selection

FURTHER READING
Other Works by Toni Cade Bambara
Gorilla, My Love
The Sea Birds Are Still Alive
Deep Sightings and Rescue Missions
Other Works About Overcoming Obstacles
Tears of the Sea, Olive Senior
Winners, Mary-Ellen Lang Collura
"Mother to Son," Langston Hughes

INTERNET
We suggest the following sites on the Internet (all Web sites are subject to change).
For biographical information on Toni Cade Bambara:
http://www.public.asu.edu/~metro/aflit/bambara/bio.html
For a poetic eulogy to Toni Cade Bambara:
http://www.inmotionmagazine.com/bambara.html
We *strongly recommend* that you preview the sites before you send students to them.

Answers

◆ Reading Strategy

1. Students may recall that in the confrontation between Squeaky and her classmates, Gretchen didn't make any remarks and seemed friendly.
2. Students may say that he will keep running, as Squeaky does.

◆ Build Vocabulary

Using the Word Part *scope*

1. optical tool with lenses and mirrors used to see over things
2. optical tool that makes distant objects seem nearer and larger
3. optical tool for looking at tiny objects

Spelling Strategy

1. apology; 2. strategy; 3. psychology

Using the Word Bank

1. c 2. d 3. a 4. b

◆ Literary Focus

1. At first she is aggressive, and defensive. She grows more tolerant of others as she realizes that she can help Raymond become a runner.
2. She is a minor character who challenges Squeaky in the race.
3. Raymond is a major character, but not as fully developed as Squeaky, and we don't have the benefit of knowing how he feels.

◆ Build Grammar Skills

Practice

1. for; 2. on; 3. by; 4. on; 5. with

Writing Application

Possible responses:
The racers ran behind the fence.
The racers ran over the fence.
The racers ran into the fence.

 Writer's Solution

For further instruction and practice, use the lesson in the *Writer's Solution Language Lab CD-ROM* on Prepositions. You may also use the Preposition page, p. 24, in the *Writer's Solution Grammar Practice Book.*

300

Guide for Responding *(continued)*

◆ Reading Strategy

PREDICT

When you **predict,** you look ahead to what will happen in a story, using details the author shares with you.
1. What details might lead you to predict that Squeaky and Gretchen would share a friendly moment at the end of the story?
2. Do you predict that Raymond will become a runner like Squeaky? Explain your answer.

◆ Build Vocabulary

USING THE WORD PART *scope*

The word part *scope* combines with other word parts to form nouns that name instruments for seeing. Use a dictionary to find the definitions of these words. What other *scope* words do you know?
1. periscope   2. telescope   3. microscope

SPELLING STRATEGY

In most words that end in *gy,* the vowel that precedes *gy* is *o.* Examples include *biology, physiology,* and *anthropology.*

However, in a few words, like *prodigy,* another vowel precedes *gy.* It is best to memorize these exceptions to the rule.

strat**e**gy   el**e**gy   eff**i**gy

On your paper, complete each sentence with the correct *gy* word.

strategy   apology   psychology

1. I made an _____?_____ for my mistake.
2. My winning _____?_____ is to act like a pro.
3. I'll study _____?_____ when I get to high school.

USING THE WORD BANK

On your paper, match each word with its definition.
1. prodigy   a. person who speaks through a puppet or dummy
2. signify   b. instrument for seeing from a submarine
3. ventriloquist   c. child genius
4. periscope   d. show or make known

◆ Literary Focus

MAJOR AND MINOR CHARACTERS

In literature, the **major character** is the one who plays the largest role in the story and the one who changes the most. The **minor characters** have less significant roles. In "Raymond's Run," you see Squeaky, the major character, grow and change when she recognizes that her brother is a natural runner.
1. What changes do you see in Squeaky as the story progresses?
2. What role does Gretchen play in this story?
3. How is Raymond's role in the story different from Squeaky's role?

◆ Build Grammar Skills

PREPOSITIONS

A **preposition** is a word that relates the noun or pronoun that follows it to another word in the sentence. Prepositions often show relationships of time (*before, after*) and space (*beyond, behind*).

Here are some other common prepositions:

about   above   across   around   as   behind
below   beside   between   down   for   from   in
near   of   on   over   toward   under   up   with

Some prepositions, like the following, consist of more than one word: *according to, ahead of, as of, because of, in front of,* and *instead of.*

Toni Cade Bambara uses the preposition *in* to relate the word *neighborhood* to *the swiftest thing:*

. . . I'm the swiftest thing *in* the neighborhood.

Practice On your paper, underline the preposition in each sentence.
1. George runs errands for the big boys.
2. I'm standing on the corner.
3. Raymond was walking close by the wall.
4. Gretchen puts her hands on her hips.
5. Here comes Mr. Peabody with his clipboard.

Writing Application Copy this sentence three times, completing each version with a different preposition. Notice how the meaning of the sentence changes.

The racers ran _____?_____ the fence.

Build Your Portfolio

 ## Idea Bank

Writing

1. **Letter** Write a letter from Gretchen to a friend. Describe Squeaky's victory in the race, along with your reaction.

2. **Sequel** A sequel is a continuation of a story. Write a sequel to "Raymond's Run" that tells what happens to Squeaky and Raymond in the weeks following the race.

3. **Essay** In an essay, trace the changes the main character, Squeaky, undergoes during the course of the story.

Speaking and Listening

4. **Scene [Group Activity]** In a small group, choose a scene from "Raymond's Run" to perform. Different group members can be responsible for writing dialogue, supplying or creating props and costumes, providing background music, and so on. Practice the scene before performing it for the class. **[Performing Arts Link]**

5. **Telephone Conversation [Group Activity]** With a partner, improvise a telephone conversation in which Squeaky asks Gretchen to help coach Raymond. **[Performing Arts Link]**

Projects

6. **Map of the Setting [Group Activity]** In a small group, create a map that shows where the events in "Raymond's Run" take place. You may wish to consult a map of New York City. You may also wish to add to your map any details mentioned in the story that would not be on a city map. **[Social Studies Link]**

7. **Track and Running Bibliography** Research to create a bibliography or listing of track and running magazines, books, and Web sites. Share your bibliography with the class. **[Technology Link; Sports Link]**

 ## Writing Mini-Lesson

Script for a Sportscaster

Squeaky's description of the May Day race makes you feel as if you were there—just as a good sportscast vividly captures the excitement of an athletic event. Write a script for a sportscaster. It can be about any sport you choose, but it should bring an athletic event to life for your audience.

Writing Skill Focus: Background Information

Include **background information,** such as facts, statistics, and interesting or unusual details, to bring the event to life. In this example from the story, Squeaky provides information that is both factual and amusing:

> ##### Model From the Story
> The twenty-yard dash takes all of two minutes cause most of the little kids don't know no better than to run off the track . . .

Prewriting Recall a sports event that you have seen. List, in chronological order, the events that took place. Make notes about the human emotions that you observed. Research background information that your audience needs to know or that will enliven your script.

Drafting As you draft, include only the most interesting background information. Use a lively tone that conveys the excitement of the event.

> ◆ **Grammar Application**
> Use prepositions to add details to your sportscast script.

Revising Imagine that you are a sportscaster, and read your script aloud to a peer. Ask whether you have provided enough background information and if your sportscast is interesting and exciting. Revise according to the feedback you receive.

Raymond's Run ◆ 301

Connections to Today's World

For over thirty years, athletes like Raymond, who have weaknesses, handicaps or disabilities, have gained pride and satisfaction from taking part in the Special Olympics.

Thematic Focus

❶ Leading the Way Experience may have inspired Eunice Kennedy Shriver, sister of 35th president John F. Kennedy, to lead the way on the Special Olympics. Her older sister, Rosemary, was diagnosed as "mentally retarded" and spent much of her life in an institution.

◆ Critical Thinking

❷ Interpret Ask students to explain the meaning of this slogan. Students may say that the year-round time frame of the Special Olympics allows people who are mentally and/or physically challenged to train whenever they can.

Clarification

❸ This quotation is taken directly from the mission statement of the Special Olympics.

Customize for
Visual/Spatial Learners

Have students examine the photographs that accompany this selection to determine the level of intensity and dedication Special Olympians seem to demonstrate. In addition, you may wish to use Art Transparency 19 in **Art Transparencies,** pp. 79–82, and draw on the Humanities Note and learning options to extend students' understanding of the Special Olympics.

CONNECTIONS TO TODAY'S WORLD

❶ In 1963, Eunice Kennedy Shriver organized an athletic tournament for mentally challenged young people. In 1968, that tournament became the Special Olympics. Today, thousands of Special Olympians, ages eight and up, compete in the World Summer and Winter Games.

❷ The Special Olympics organization likes to say that it is "training for life." In fact, increased confidence, self-esteem, and social skills are the real gains—even more important to participants than the development of athletic skills.

THERE IS NO OFF-SEASON.

Special Olympics

❸ *"To provide year-round sports training and athletic competition in a variety of Olympic-type sports for individuals with mental retardation by giving them continuing opportunities to develop physical fitness, demonstrate courage, experience joy and participate in a sharing of gifts, skills and friendship with their families, other Special Olympics athletes and the community."*

482
SPORT. SPIRIT. SPLENDOR.

302 ◆ *Quest for Justice*

Beyond the Classroom

Career Connection

Sports Reporting Sporting events are big news. People with an interest in sports and a flair for public speaking or writing may want to pursue careers in sports reporting. Invite students to talk about the kinds of sports reporting they have had experience with: TV sports commentary, newspaper or magazine sports articles, biographies of great athletes, or inspirational books based on athletic accomplishments. Still others who love sports might become involved as statisticians or in team public relations.

Invite interested students to try their hand at informal sports reporting by focusing on local sporting events, school sports, or individual athletes in the area. They can prepare mock TV or radio reports or do write-ups of games or events to get a sense of the kinds of things actual sports reporting might involve.

Special Olympics is "training for life."

You may have thought that Special Olympics was just a few days of games once or twice a year. But in reality, the training for competition is as important as the competition itself. Special Olympics involves individuals of all ages and ability levels—from people with low motor abilities to highly-skilled athletes who can compete in a higher level of sports both in and out of Special Olympics. To accommodate this range of skill levels, Special Olympics offers a wide variety of programs so athletes may choose those best suited to their abilities and interests.

Special Olympics is a year-round program, a lifetime of learning through sport. The mission of the Special Olympics movement has remained constant since Eunice Kennedy Shriver began the program and organized the first games in 1968.

1. What are the positive and negative outcomes from participation in competitive athletic programs? Do you think the outcomes are the same for mentally challenged people? Explain.
2. What does Special Olympics mean by the phrase "training for life"?
3. Do you think Raymond in "Raymond's Run" would benefit from a program like Special Olympics? Why or why not?

Special Olympics ◆ 303

Thematic Focus

4 Leading the Way In "Raymond's Run," Squeaky led the way for her brother to experience the thrill of running. Because athletes understand aspects of sports that others must learn, they can provide motivation and model appropriate behaviors. Talk with students about the ways in which athletes can coach and motivate people with mental and physical challenges.

Comprehension Check ☑

5 How does the Special Olympics organization reach all ages and skill levels? *They provide a wide variety of programs suited to many levels and ages of participants.*

Answers

1. Positive outcomes of competitive athletics may include improved fitness or motor skills, greater self-confidence, positive self-image, and better ability to concentrate; negative outcomes may include injury or frustration. Most students will believe that the positive and negative outcomes are probably the same for mentally challenged people.
2. It means that the true goal is to prepare people for life, not just to compete in a physical event.
3. Students may say that Raymond would benefit, because he would get the support of caring people who could nurture his abilities while being aware of his deficits. He would be able to participate and enjoy the thrill of being a part of the competition and the fun.

 Beyond the Selection

FURTHER READING
Other Works About the Special Olympics
Hearts of Gold: A Celebration of Special Olympics and Its Heroes, Sheila Dinn
Brave in the Attempt, Vicki Cobb
Heroes of a Special Kind, Mary Frances Froese

INTERNET
We suggest the following site on the Internet (all Web sites are subject to change).
For more information about Special Olympics:
http://www.specialolympics.org
We *strongly recommend* that you preview the site before you send students to it.

Guide for Reading

OBJECTIVES

1. To read, comprehend, and interpret three poems
2. To relate poems to personal experience
3. To interpret the meaning behind poets' words
4. To appreciate the heroic qualities of characters
5. To build vocabulary in context and learn the word root: -spec-
6. To develop skill in using prepositional phrases
7. To write an "eyewitness" speech that appeals to an audience
8. To respond to poetry through writing, speaking and listening, and projects

SKILLS INSTRUCTION

Vocabulary:
Word Roots: -spec-
Spelling:
Words With the Hard g Sound Spelled gh
Grammar:
Prepositional Phrases
Reading Strategy:
Interpret the Meaning
Literary Focus:
Heroic Characters

Writing:
Appeal to Your Audience
Speaking and Listening:
Dramatic Reading (Teacher Edition)
Viewing and Representing:
Heroism Award (Teacher Edition)
Critical Viewing:
Analyze; Connect; Assess; Deduce; Speculate

PORTFOLIO OPPORTUNITIES

Writing: Movie Summary; Character Sketch; Report
Writing Mini-Lesson: "Eyewitness" Speech
Speaking and Listening: Retelling; Dramatic Reading
Projects: Boston Area Map; Folk Ballad

More About the Authors
Henry Wadsworth Longfellow studied European cultures, but chose American subjects for his poetry. He was drawn to American heroes like Paul Revere.

John Greenleaf Whittier became acquainted with poetry at an early age. His favorite poet was John Milton, whose views on freedom he greatly admired and imitated.

Eve Merriam wrote poems and prose for both adults and younger readers. She thought that poetry was the "most immediate and richest form of communication."

Meet the Authors:

Henry Wadsworth Longfellow (1807–1882)

Henry Wadsworth Longfellow's talents as a poet were recognized when he published a poem at the age of thirteen. Many of his long narrative poems, including "Paul Revere's Ride," idealize America's early history and democratic values. Longfellow became known as one of the "fireside poets," whose works were frequently read by families who gathered around the fireplace. [For more about Longfellow, see p. 814.]

John Greenleaf Whittier (1807–1892)

Another "fireside poet," John Greenleaf Whittier had a Quaker upbringing that inspired in him a strong belief in hard work and simplicity. Born in poverty and raised on a farm in Massachusetts, he received no formal education. His works express his political views, such as his opposition to slavery, and also present the simple pleasures of country life.

Eve Merriam (1916–1992)

Eve Merriam's family was interested in books and reading. As a young girl in Philadelphia, she became fascinated with poetry. "I remember being enthralled by the sound of words, by their musicality . . . ," she has said. Merriam is known for her award-winning collections of poetry, as well as for her fiction, nonfiction, and drama.

◆ LITERATURE AND YOUR LIFE

CONNECT YOUR EXPERIENCE

Sometimes ordinary people perform extraordinary acts. You probably read about or hear about these "everyday heroes" in newspapers, magazines, and on television. In these poems, you'll meet three people who became unlikely heroes.

THEMATIC FOCUS: Leading the Way

During the Revolutionary War, Paul Revere, pictured on the opposite page, risked his life to warn fellow colonists about the approaching British army. Think about what might inspire someone to lead the way—even if it means facing danger.

◆ Background for Understanding

HISTORY

Elizabeth Blackwell, the subject of the poem by Eve Merriam, was one woman who led the way for other women. In the nineteenth century, it was uncommon for women to consider a career in medicine. In fact, until little more than 150 years ago, no American medical college would admit female students. However, in 1847, Elizabeth Blackwell entered medical school. She graduated with high honors to become the first female medical doctor in the United States.

◆ Build Vocabulary

WORD ROOTS: -spec-

The word *spectral* in "Paul Revere's Ride" contains the word root -spec-, which is related to appearances. *Spectral* means "appearing ghostly."

WORD BANK

Which word from the poems might describe someone who steals into a room? Check the Build Vocabulary box on page 307 to see if you chose correctly.

stealthy
somber
impetuo[us]
spectral
tranquil
aghast
horde

 Prentice Hall Literature Program Resources

REINFORCE / RETEACH / EXTEND
Selection Support Pages
Build Vocabulary: Word Roots: -spec-, p. 123
Build Spelling Skills, p. 124
Build Grammar Skills: Prepositional Phrases, p. 125
Reading Strategy: Interpret the Meaning, p. 126
Literary Focus: Heroic Characters, p. 127
Strategies for Diverse Student Needs, pp. 47–48
Beyond Literature Cultural Connection: Heroes, p. 24
Formal Assessment Selection Test, pp. 90–92
Assessment Resources Software

Alternative Assessment, p. 24
Writing and Language Transparencies Series of Events Chain, p. 57
Daily Language Practice, pp. 44, 46
Resource Pro CD-ROM "Paul Revere's Ride;" "Barbara Frietchie;" "Elizabeth Blackwell"—includes all resource material and customizable lesson plan

Listening to Literature Audiocassettes
"Paul Revere's Ride"; "Barbara Frietchie"; "Elizabeth Blackwell"

Paul Revere's Ride ◆ Barbara Frietchie ◆ Elizabeth Blackwell ◆

◆ Literary Focus

HEROIC CHARACTERS

A man risks his life for the good of his country. A woman braves danger to express her patriotism. A girl stubbornly refuses to give up her dream of helping others. These characters are **heroes** because their actions are inspiring and noble. They bravely struggle to overcome the obstacles and problems that stand in their way. As you read about these characters, keep track of their heroic qualities and actions on character wheels like the one below.

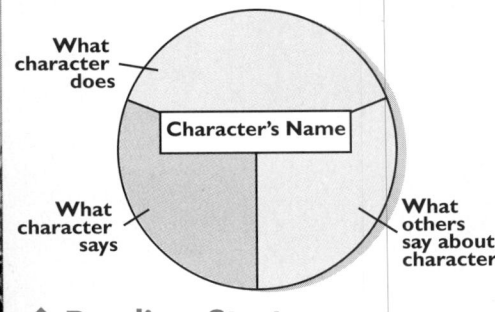

What character does

Character's Name

What character says

What others say about character

◆ Reading Strategy

INTERPRET THE MEANING

The characters in these poems all perform heroic deeds. You'll better understand the significance of their actions if you **interpret the meaning** behind the poets' words. First, use the images the poet includes to form a picture in your mind of what is being described. Next, ask yourself why the poet has chosen these specific images. Finally, explain the meaning and importance of these images.

Guide for Reading ◆ 305

Interest Grabber Have groups of students brainstorm for a list of the most heroic people that come to mind. Then, have groups pool their choices to create a class top ten list of heroes. Once the list has been established, have students discuss the qualities that their "pantheon" of heroes shares. Then, lead students to the selection by asking them to consider, as they read the poems, whether any of the heroes celebrated in these poems should be added to their list.

◆ Build Grammar Skills

Prepositional Phrases If you wish to introduce the grammar concept or skill for this selection before students read, refer to the instruction on p. 318.

Customize for
Less Proficient Readers
Play the recording of the poems in this selection to emphasize the excitement or drama in the stories they tell and to highlight the heroism of their characters.

🎧 **Listening to Literature Audiocassettes**

Customize for
More Advanced Students
The poems in this selection are narrative poems because each tells a story. Review the narrative elements: plot, character, setting, and point of view. Ask students, when they read, to think about ways that narrative poems differ from narrative prose.

Customize for
English Language Learners
Each of the poems in the selection is a narrative poem. To help students get the gist of the story each tells, suggest that they use a Series of Events Chain, p. 57, in **Writing and Language Transparencies,** to record events in the order in which they occur.

Preparing for Standardized Tests

Vocabulary Vocabulary test questions on standardized tests often evaluate students' knowledge and understanding of word roots. Students can develop the ability to decode unfamiliar words if they understand the meanings of different word roots. For example, if they know the meaning of the root -*spec*-, they may be able to figure out the meaning of words like *inspector* and *spectacular.*

Present the following sample test question:

Choose the word or phrase that means "wearing a pair of eyeglasses."

(A) near-sighted   (C) spectacled
(B) glassed   (D) goggle-eyed

Knowing that -*spec*- means "related to appearances or something seen" will help students choose the correct answer, *(C) spectacled.* For further practice, use Build Vocabulary Skills in **Selection Support,** p. 123.

Point out to students that when they are taking tests, if they know the material and read the questions carefully, the first answer that they think is correct is probably the best choice for them to select for the test item.

One-Minute Insight

In 1775, on a spring night in Boston, Massachusetts, an ordinary man did a brave and patriotic thing. On that night, Paul Revere became a hero. Upon a signal from another patriot at North Church, Revere rode his horse from town to town, alerting citizens that British soldiers were on the move and that they were traveling by river. Thanks to Longfellow's poem "Paul Revere's Ride," this earnest patriot became an American hero for the ages.

Team Teaching Strategy

You may want to coordinate with a social studies teacher to come up with ideas for extending instruction to address related Revolutionary War, Civil War, and feminist issues.

Clarification

❶ Paul Revere, unlike such colonial leaders as John Adams and John Hancock, was a tradesman, not a patrician. He was Colonial America's finest silversmith. He was also one of several riders who rode from colony to colony, spreading news and carrying messages. The purpose of Revere's April 18 ride was to warn colonists of when the British were leaving Boston to seize cannon and other military supplies stored in Concord. That ride, although it was his most famous, was not his first. Among his earlier trips was an 11-day winter ride from Boston to New York and Philadelphia, and back.

Customize for
Visual/Spatial Learners

Invite students to flip through the selection to look at the paintings and photographs. Ask them to explain what they can determine about the period in which the action in the poems took place and what the poems are about, just from examining the accompanying illustrations.

❶ *Paul Revere's Ride*

Henry Wadsworth Longfellow

306 ◆ *Quest for Justice*

Block Scheduling Strategies

Consider these suggestions to take advantage of extended class time:

- Have students read and discuss the Background for Understanding, p. 304. In addition, invite students to research and then report to classmates on what actually happened in Massachusetts on April 18, 1775 (see Projects on p. 319), and in Frederick, Maryland, when Jackson's army occupied it in early September of 1862.

- Have students read the poems independently and then discuss them and their answers to the Guide for Responding questions in groups.

- Assign the Speaking and Listening activities, p. 319. Devote class time to one or two students' retellings of the Barbara Frietchie tale and to one or two dramatic readings of lines 111–130 from "Paul Revere's Ride."

- To help students prepare for the Writing Mini-Lesson, review features of eyewitness reports and descriptive writing, using the *Writer's Solution Writing Lab CD-ROM*. Invite volunteers to imagine and then present eyewitness accounts of Paul Revere's ride and of Barbara Frietchie's flag-waving.

Listen, my children, and you shall hear
Of the midnight ride of Paul Revere,
On the eighteenth of April, in Seventy-five;
Hardly a man is now alive
5 Who remembers that famous day and year.

He said to his friend, "If the British march
By land or sea from the town to-night,
Hang a lantern aloft in the belfry arch[1]
Of the North Church tower as a signal light,—
10 One, if by land, and two, if by sea;
And I on the opposite shore will be,
Ready to ride and spread the alarm
Through every Middlesex[2] village and farm,
For the country folk to be up and to arm."

15 Then he said, "Good night!" and with muffled oar
Silently rowed to the Charlestown[3] shore,
Just as the moon rose over the bay,
Where swinging wide at her moorings[4] lay
The *Somerset*, British man-of-war;[5]
20 A phantom ship, with each mast and spar[6]
Across the moon like a prison bar,
And a huge black hulk, that was magnified
By its own reflection in the tide.

Meanwhile, his friend, through alley and street,
25 Wanders and watches with eager ears,
Till in the silence around him he hears
The muster[7] of men at the barrack door,
The sound of arms, and the tramp of feet,
And the measured tread of the grenadiers,[8]
30 Marching down to their boats on the shore.

Then he climbed the tower of the Old
   North Church,
By the wooden stairs, with <u>stealthy</u> tread,
To the belfry-chamber overhead,
And startled the pigeons from their perch
35 On the <u>somber</u> rafters,[9] that round him made

◄ **Critical Viewing** How does this painting reinforce the legendary nature of Paul Revere's ride? **[Analyze]**

1. **belfry arch** (bel´ frē ärch): Curved top of a tower or steeple that holds the bells.

2. **Middlesex** (mid´ əl seks´): A county in Massachusetts.

3. **Charlestown**: Part of Boston on the harbor.
4. **moorings** (moor´ iŋs) n.: Lines, cables, or chains that hold a ship to the shore.
5. **man-of-war**: Armed naval vessel; warship.
6. **mast and spar**: Poles used to support sails.

7. **muster** n.: An assembly of troops summoned for inspection, roll call, or service.
8. **grenadiers** (gren´ ə dirz´) n.: Members of a special regiment or corps.
9. **rafters** n.: Beams that slope from the ridge of a roof to the eaves and serve to support the roof.

◆ **Build Vocabulary**

stealthy (stel´ thē) *adj.*: Artfully sly and secretive

somber (säm´ bər) *adj.*: Dark and gloomy

Paul Revere's Ride ◆ 307

◆ **Literary Focus**

❷ **Heroic Characters** Guide students to notice how the opening line of the poem is reminiscent of the oral story-telling tradition. Discuss how it leads readers to expect to read about something of importance.

◆ **Reading Strategy**

❸ **Interpret the Meaning** Inform students that "Seventy-five" is 1775, and that Longfellow published the poem in 1863. Ask them to predict how writing 88 years after an event can affect the interpretation. *Students may say that elapsed time can give an event legendary status or that time provides the benefit of perspective and a better understanding of past events.*

◆ **Literary Focus**

❹ **Heroic Characters** Have students summarize Revere's heroic plan. Tell them that the friend and accomplice was 23-year-old Robert Newman, the sexton of North Church.

◆ **Reading Strategy**

❺ **Interpret the Meaning** How does this stanza help to build tension? *Students may say that the fact that Revere had to muffle his oar indicates that he knew he was in danger. They may point to the images of doom presented by the "black hulk" of the "phantom ship" that he had to row past in the moonlight, as well as the "prison bar" effect created by the silhouette of the ship's poles.*

Comprehension Check ☑

❻ What is Revere's friend watching for? What signal will he give? Why? He needs to find out whether the British will leave Boston by land or by sea. When he sees and hears them walking to the boats in the dock, he knows to signal Revere by hanging two lanterns.

▶**Critical Viewing**◀

❼ **Analyze** *The painting presents an idealized view of a colonial village that lights up as he passes through.*

🎵 **Humanities: Art**

The Midnight Ride of Paul Revere, 1931, by Grant Wood

Grant Wood (1892–1942) was best known for his scenes of rural American life, but he also painted simplified, childlike depictions of American history, of which this painting is an example. Discuss with students how the painting takes on the effect of an illustration. Use these questions:

1. What is the effect of the contrast between the huge, bright church and the well-lit road that dominate the scene, with the small, dark figure of Revere on his horse? *The smallness of the lone, dark horseman makes him look even braver as he gallops through the night.*

2. Why do you think the artist chose to make Revere so small and the buildings so large? *Students may suggest that had Revere and his horse been the largest figures, the focus of the painting would have been on him and not on his historic night journey.*

◆ **Reading Strategy**

❶ **Interpret the Meaning** What mood is created here for the night of Revere's ride? *Students might say that the atmosphere is tense and foreboding.*

◆ **Literary Focus**

❷ **Heroic Characters** How would you describe Paul Revere's frame of mind at this point? *Students may say that he is eager, nervous, and tense as he paces and stomps about, awaiting his signal from the church belfry.*

Comprehension Check ☑

❸ What signal does Revere receive? What does it tell him? *Two lanterns have been hung in the belfry, indicating that the British are coming by sea.*

Masses and moving shapes of shade,—
By the trembling ladder, steep and tall,
To the highest window in the wall,
Where he paused to listen and look down
40 A moment on the roofs of the town,
And the moonlight flowing over all.

Beneath, in the churchyard, lay the dead,
In their night-encampment on the hill,
Wrapped in silence so deep and still
45 That he could hear, like a sentinel's[10] tread,
 The watchful night-wind, as it went
Creeping along from tent to tent,
And seeming to whisper, "All is well!"
A moment only he feels the spell
50 Of the place and the hour, and the secret dread
Of the lonely belfry and the dead;
For suddenly all his thoughts are bent
On a shadowy something far away,
Where the river widens to meet the bay,—
55 A line of black that bends and floats
On the rising tide, like a bridge of boats.

Meanwhile, impatient to mount and ride,
Booted and spurred, with a heavy stride
On the opposite shore walked Paul Revere.
60 Now he patted his horse's side,
Now gazed at the landscape far and near,
❷ Then, <u>impetuous</u>, stamped the earth,
And turned and tightened his saddle-girth;[11]
But mostly he watched with eager search
65 The belfry-tower of the Old North Church,
As it rose above the graves on the hill,
Lonely and <u>spectral</u> and somber and still.
And lo! as he looks, on the belfry's height
❸ A glimmer, and then a gleam of light!
70 He springs to the saddle, the bridle[12] he turns,
But lingers and gazes, till full on his sight
A second lamp in the belfry burns!

A hurry of hoofs in a village street,

---

10. sentinel (sen′ ti nəl) *n.*: Guard.
11. girth (gɤrth) *n.*: A band put around the belly of a horse for holding a saddle.
12. bridle (brid′ əl) *n.*: A head harness for guiding a horse.

 Cross-Curricular Connection: Social Studies

Revolutionary Societies While the British occupied Boston, patriotic activity continued there and elsewhere in the colonies. The Sons of Liberty—Paul Revere was a member—was an intercolonial resistance organization. This group formed during the Stamp Act crisis to protest British policies. Women set up their own group, the Daughters of Liberty. Throughout the colonies, these groups placed lanterns in large trees. Gathering around these Liberty Trees, as they were called, they hanged British officials in effigy to intimidate British tax collectors. Merchants were pressured not to sell British goods. In Boston, they met secretly in a tavern near Revere's home.

Invite students to find out more about the history, composition, interests, and activities of the Sons of Liberty or Daughters of Liberty, including their campaigns against the Stamp Act and the Townshend Acts. They can research protest activities of the Daughters of Liberty and other groups of colonial women. What, for instance, was the Edenton Ladies' Tea Party? Enlist the help of a social studies teacher, as needed, to guide students in their research.

◄ **Critical Viewing** Why would a church steeple like this one be ideal for a signal? [Connect]

❹

75 A shape in the moonlight, a bulk in the dark,
And beneath, from the pebbles, in passing,
    a spark
Struck out by a steed flying fearless and fleet:
That was all! And yet, through the gloom and
    the light,
The fate of a nation was riding that night;
And the spark struck out by that steed[13]
    in his flight,

❺

80 Kindled the land into flame with its heat.
He has left the village and mounted the steep,[14]
And beneath him, tranquil and broad and deep,
Is the Mystic,[15] meeting the ocean tides;
And under the alders[16] that skirt its edge,
85 Now soft on the sand, now loud on the ledge,
Is heard the tramp of his steed as he rides.

❻

It was twelve by the village clock,
When he crossed the bridge into Medford[17] town.
He heard the crowing of the cock,
90 And the barking of the farmer's dog,
And felt the damp of the river fog,
That rises after the sun goes down.

It was one by the village clock,
When he galloped into Lexington.[18]
95 He saw the gilded weathercock[19]
Swim in the moonlight as he passed,
And the meeting-house windows, blank and bare,
Gaze at him with a spectral glare,
As if they already stood aghast
100 At the bloody work they would look upon.

❼

It was two by the village clock,
When he came to the bridge in Concord[20] town.
He heard the bleating[21] of the flock,

◆ **Build Vocabulary**

impetuous (im pech´ oo əs) *adj.*: Done suddenly with little thought

spectral (spek´ trəl) *adj.*: Phantomlike; ghostly

tranquil (tran´ kwil) *adj.*: Quiet or motionless; peaceful

aghast (ə gäst´) *adj.*: Feeling great horror or dismay

---

13. **steed** *n.*: Horse, especially a high-spirited riding horse.
14. **steep** *n.*: Slope or incline having a sharp rise.
15. **Mystic** (mis´ tik): A river in Massachusetts.
16. **alders** (ôl´ dərz) *n.*: Trees and shrubs of the birch family.
17. **Medford**: A town outside Boston.
18. **Lexington**: A town in eastern Massachusetts, outside Boston.
19. **weathercock** (weth´ ər käk´) *n.*: Weathervane in the form of a rooster.
20. **Concord**: A town in eastern Massachusetts. The first battles of the Revolutionary War (April 19, 1775) were fought in Lexington and Concord.
21. **bleating** (blēt´ iŋ) *n.*: Sound made by sheep.

Paul Revere's Ride ◆ 309

Thematic Focus

❺ **Leading the Way** What was the "spark" struck by the horse that night? *Students may say that the spark, in a narrow sense, might have been caused by the horse's shoes striking cobblestones. In a larger sense, the spark was the spark of freedom and rebellion.*

◆ Literary Focus

❻ **Heroic Characters** Guide students to notice the sensory images here—what Revere sees, hears, and feels. Discuss how these details put the reader in the saddle, on the way to Medford, with Paul Revere.

◆ Reading Strategy

❼ **Interpret the Meaning** What future events do these lines foreshadow? *Students can note that they foreshadow the coming bloodshed of revolution and, more precisely, the first firings of guns at Lexington and at Concord.*

Speaking and Listening Mini-Lesson

Dramatic Reading

This mini-lesson supports the Speaking and Listening activity in the Idea Bank on p. 319.

Introduce Review the elements of a dramatic reading. Discuss with students that lines 111–118 describe the events following the battle of Concord, and that the last stanza gives an overview of Revere's ride and presents the lasting historic impact of that event. Emphasize Longfellow's rhythmic pacing of the lines in these final stanzas and point out how they recall and evoke the pacing of Revere's ride on his horse.

Develop Encourage students to practice by taping and then listening to their readings to hear whether they are expressing the heroic excitement of these lines, as well as the rhythmic pace. Encourage students to listen to one another and to make suggestions for improvement.

Apply Have students present their dramatic readings for classmates.

Assess Judge students' performances on how vividly they capture the poet's intent, or use the Peer Assessment: Dramatic Performance form, p. 116, in **Alternative Assessment.**

◆ Critical Thinking

❶ Defend Why do you think the poet tells the story of Paul Revere's ride in such detail but then skims over the dramatic and important events of the following days? *Students may suggest that Longfellow wanted to focus exclusively on Revere's ride to establish his heroic role in the beginning of the American Revolution.*

Thematic Focus

❷ Leading the Way Discuss with students that here Longfellow is making the point that, in crisis, Americans will rise to the occasion; that Revere's act symbolizes American spirit and courage.

Reinforce and Extend

Answers

◆ LITERATURE AND YOUR LIFE

Reader's Response Many students will think that the poem does capture the excitement of the ride. Have all students support their views with details from the poem.

Thematic Focus Students may suggest that Revere was brave, decisive, thoughtful, and tireless.

☑ Check Your Comprehension

1. He made his ride on the night of April 18, 1775.
2. If the British march by land, Revere will be signaled by one lantern; if they move by sea, two lanterns will be the signal.
3. He rides through several villages and alerts the people that the British are on the move.
4. Yes, he awakens colonists, who respond immediately to his call.

◆ Critical Thinking

1. (a) The ship is compared to a ghost, and its masts and spars to prison bars. (b) The description creates an ominous effect.
2. The poet claims that Revere's ride sparked the colonial rebellion against the British.
3. Students may say that Revere was careful, thorough, brave, determined, and tireless.
4. The poem has the narrative elements of a short story: plot, characters, setting, and point of view, but also has stanzas, rhythm, and rhyme.

---

105 And the twitter of birds among the trees,
And felt the breath of the morning breeze
Blowing over the meadows brown.
And one was safe and asleep in his bed
Who at the bridge would be first to fall,
Who that day would be lying dead,
110 Pierced by a British musket-ball.

You know the rest. In the books you
have read,
How the British Regulars fired and fled,—
How the farmers gave them ball for ball,
❶ From behind each fence and farm-yard wall,
115 Chasing the red-coats down the lane,
Then crossing the fields to emerge again
Under the trees at the turn of the road,
And only pausing to fire and load.

So through the night rode Paul Revere;
120 And so through the night went his cry
of alarm
To every Middlesex village and farm,—
A cry of defiance and not of fear,
A voice in the darkness, a knock at the door,
❷ And a word that shall echo forevermore!
125 For, borne on the night-wind of the Past,
Through all our history, to the last,
In the hour of darkness and peril and need,
The people will waken and listen to hear
The hurrying hoof-beats of that steed,
130 And the midnight message of Paul Revere.

---

5. Yes. He, too, played a key role by spying on the British and then conveying the information in a timely and accurate manner.
6. Students may say that that night the colonists would show whether or not they could respond to a crisis.

◆ LITERATURE AND YOUR LIFE

Reader's Response Does this poem capture the excitement of Revere's ride? Explain.

Thematic Focus List three qualities of leadership that Paul Revere shows.

Journal Writing In your journal, jot down some thoughts or feelings Revere may have had during his midnight ride.

☑ Check Your Comprehension

1. When does Paul Revere make his ride?
2. Explain the meaning of the signals used to communicate to Revere.
3. What does Revere do after seeing the signals?
4. Does Revere accomplish his purpose?

◆ Critical Thinking

INTERPRET

1. (a) To what is the *Somerset* compared in lines 15–23? (b) What is the effect of this image? **[Interpret]**
2. How do lines 78 through 80 express the importance the poet places on the ride? **[Analyze]**
3. Describe Paul Revere's character. **[Analyze]**
4. In what ways is this poem similar to and different from a short story? **[Compare and Contrast]**

EVALUATE

5. Do you think Revere's friend is also a hero? Explain. **[Make a Judgment]**

EXTEND

6. What does Longfellow mean when he says, "The fate of a nation was riding that night"? **[Social Studies Link]**

Barbara Frietchie

John Greenleaf Whittier

The Battle of Fredericksburg, 1862, Frederic Cavada, The Historical Society of Pennsylvania

Up from the meadows rich with corn,
Clear in the cool September morn,

The clustered spires of Frederick[1] stand
Green-walled by the hills of Maryland.

5 Round about them orchards sweep,
Apple and peach tree fruited deep,

Fair as the garden of the Lord
To the eyes of the famished rebel horde,

▲ Critical Viewing This painting depicts the Battle of Fredericksburg. Does this painting help you understand what it was like to fight in such a battle? Why or why not? [Assess]

1. **Frederick** (fred′ rik): A town in Maryland.

◆ **Build Vocabulary**

horde (hôrd) *n.*: Large, moving group

Barbara Frietchie ◆ 311

◆ Build Grammar Skills

❶ Prepositional Phrases This stanza has three prepositional phrases, groups of words that begin with a preposition and end with the noun or pronoun that is the object of the preposition. Prepositional phrases may also include words that modify the noun or pronoun. Help students identify the three phrases and the preposition and object of the preposition in each. *On that pleasant morn: on, morn; of the early fall: of, fall; over the mountain wall: over, wall*

Clarification

❷ The Confederate flag is known as the "Stars and Bars." It consists of two crossing blue lines that divide a red background into four triangles. There are thirteen stars on those blue lines: four sets of three stars and one in the center, where the lines cross. Show students a picture of the flag.

◆ Literary Focus

❸ Heroic Characters What marks of heroism do you find in these lines? *Students may say that it is brave of Barbara Frietchie to pick up the flag after it's been fired upon and then to refer to it as "your country's flag," knowing that the invading troops wouldn't see it that way.*

◆ Reading Strategy

❹ Interpret the Meaning What is the poet saying about the general's character? *The poet makes the point that Jackson is a man of honor who respects the heroism of the old woman and shows it by ordering his men not to fire again.*

---

❶ On that pleasant morn of the early fall
10 When Lee[2] marched over the mountain wall;

Over the mountains winding down,
Horse and foot, into Frederick town.

❷ Forty flags with their silver stars,
Forty flags with their crimson bars,

15 Flapped in the morning wind: the sun
Of noon looked down, and saw not one.

Up rose old Barbara Frietchie then,
Bowed with her fourscore[3] years and ten;

Bravest of all in Frederick town,
20 She took up the flag the men hauled down

❸ In her attic window the staff she set,
To show that one heart was loyal yet.

Up the street came the rebel tread,
Stonewall Jackson[4] riding ahead.

25 Under his slouched hat left and right
He glanced; the old flag met his sight.

"Halt!"—the dust-brown ranks stood fast.
"Fire!"—out blazed the rifle-blast.

It shivered the window, pane and sash;[5]
30 It rent the banner with seam and gash.

Quick, as it fell, from the broken staff
Dame Barbara snatched the silken scarf.

She leaned far out on the window-sill,
And shook it forth with a royal will.

35 "Shoot, if you must, this old gray head,
But spare your country's flag," she said.

A shade of sadness, a blush of shame,
Over the face of the leader came;

❹ The nobler nature within him stirred
40 To life at that woman's deed and word;

"Who touches a hair of yon gray head
Dies like a dog! March on!" he said.

312 ◆ Quest for Justice

---

2. Lee: Robert E. Lee, Commander in Chief of the Confederate army in the Civil War.

3. fourscore (fôr´ skôr´) *adj.*: Four times twenty; eighty.

4. Stonewall Jackson: Nickname of Thomas Jonathan Jackson, Confederate general in the Civil War.

5. sash (sash) *n.*: The frame holding the glass panes of a window.

 Cultural Connection

Flags Discuss with students the function of flags as symbols of nations or organizations. Point out that the elements on a flag are themselves symbolic. For example, the fifty stars on the American flag represent the fifty states; the thirteen stars on the original Stars and Stripes stood for the American colonies.

Similarly, on New Zealand's flag, four stars stand for the Southern Cross constellation, a blue field for the Pacific Ocean, and the Union Jack for the country's one-time British rulers.

Invite students to research and report on various flags of interest to them and on the symbols used in their designs. Ask them to identify and find more information about flags that symbolize groups and events other than individual nations, such as those for the United Nations or for the Olympic Games. They may also be interested in tracing changes in flags—like the number of stars on the U. S. flag—throughout the years. Suggest that students begin their search for flags in an almanac or encyclopedia.

All day long through Frederick street
Sounded the tread of marching feet:

45 All day long that free flag tost[6]
Over the heads of the rebel host.[7]

⑤ Ever its torn folds rose and fell
On the loyal winds that loved it well;

And through the hill-gaps sunset light
50 Shone over it with a warm good-night.

Barbara Frietchie's work is o'er,
And the Rebel rides on his raids no more.

⑥ Honor to her! and let a tear
Fall, for her sake, on Stonewall's bier.[8]

55 Over Barbara Frietchie's grave,
Flag of Freedom and Union, wave!

Peace and order and beauty draw
Round thy symbol of light and law;

And ever the stars above look down
60 On thy stars below in Frederick town!

6. **tost** (tôst) v.: Old-fashioned form of *tossed*.
7. **host** (hōst) n.: An army; a multitude or great number.

8. **bier** (bir) n.: A coffin and its supporting platform.

Guide for Responding

◆ LITERATURE AND YOUR LIFE

Reader's Response Would you have done what Barbara Frietchie did? Why or why not?

Thematic Focus In the poem, Barbara Frietchie acts alone—no one follows her actions. Do you consider her a leader? Why or why not?

✓ Check Your Comprehension

1. Describe the time and place of the poem.
2. What does Frietchie do before the soldiers arrive in town?
3. How does Frietchie meet Stonewall Jackson?
4. What is Jackson's response to Frietchie's actions?

◆ Critical Thinking

INTERPRET
1. Why does Barbara Frietchie do what she does? **[Analyze]**
2. Why do you think Stonewall Jackson orders his soldiers to fire on the flag? **[Speculate]**
3. What is the meaning of the last two lines of the poem? **[Interpret]**

EVALUATE
4. Was Jackson a good leader? Explain. **[Assess]**

COMPARE LITERARY WORKS
5. Compare and contrast the ways in which Paul Revere and Barbara Frietchie show their patriotism. **[Compare and Contrast]**

Barbara Frietchie ◆ 313

◆ Beyond the Classroom

Community Connection

Memorials Refer students to the statue of Paul Revere (p. 305) that stands in Boston's North End. Ask students to describe monuments, statues, and memorials with which they are familiar. Discuss the reasons why we honor our heroes in this manner. Talk about the value to us today of statues and monuments to events and people of the past. Discuss what features all these statues and monuments share and cite ways in which they differ.

Have students list the ways your community honors heroes or heroic historic events, besides naming parks, streets, or buildings in their honor. Suggest that they think about holidays that honor individuals with parades or other events.

Invite students to choose monuments or statues, and photograph or draw them. They might visit a local monument for their research or find a monument in the encylopedia, almanac, or on the Internet. Have students present the monument to the class and report on its location, size, message, and other key attributes. Encourage them to explain why they selected the monument, and express their personal response to it.

313

One-Minute Insight

In 1849, Elizabeth Blackwell graduated with a degree in medicine, becoming the first American woman to do so. In the poem "Elizabeth Blackwell," Eve Merriam recounts the obstacles to Blackwell's path to medical school and the prejudice she endured during her time as a medical student (which included the disapproval of members of her own sex), and describes the heroic, determined effort it took for her to achieve her goal—to be a doctor.

◆ Reading Strategy

❶ Interpret the Meaning Whom is the poet addressing here? Why doesn't she mention that person by name? *Students may say that the poet addresses all women of the 19th century, all of whom faced obstacles if they wished to be other than seamstresses.*

◆ Critical Thinking

❷ Evaluate How do you react to these views about women? How do you think these perceptions influenced the behavior and attitudes of both men and women of that time? *Students are likely to take issue with the limitations placed on women. They may say that the low expectations were shared by both men and women, and that they held back women who might have done more with their abilities.*

◆ Literary Focus

❸ Heroic Characters In what ways does Elizabeth Blackwell begin to challenge the boundaries women faced? *Her rebellion is gentle, but surefooted; she rejects the career paths open to women and chooses to train in a profession previously closed to them: medicine.*

►Critical Viewing◄

❹ Deduce *The oval picture, ruffled collar, plain dress, and stern hairstyle reveal that Blackwell lived in 19th-century Victorian times.*

Elizabeth Blackwell

Eve Merriam

1 What will you do when you grow up,
nineteenth-century-young-lady?
Will you sew a fine seam and spoon dappled cream
under an apple tree shady?

5 Or will you be a teacher
in a dames' school
and train the little dears
by the scientific rule
that mental activity
10 may strain
the delicate female brain;
therefore let
the curriculum stress music, French,
    and especially
2 etiquette:[1]
15 teach how to set
a truly refined banquet.
Question One:
What kind of sauce
for the fish dish,
20 and pickle or lemon fork?
Quickly, students,
which should it be?

Now Elizabeth Blackwell, how about you?
Seamstress or teacher, which of the two?
25 You know there's not much else that a girl can do.
3 Don't mumble, Elizabeth. Learn to raise your head.
"I'm not very nimble with a needle and thread.
I could teach music—if I had to," she said,
"But I think I'd rather be a doctor instead."

30 "Is this some kind of joke?"
asked the proper menfolk.
"A woman be a doctor?

---

1. **etiquette** (et′ i kət) *n.*: Forms, manners, and ceremonies considered to be acceptable means of behavior.

▲ **Critical Viewing** What do the details in this photograph of Blackwell reveal about the time in which she lived? [Deduce] **4**

Beyond the Classroom

Community Connection

Equal Employment From reading this poem, students know that Elizabeth Blackwell struggled against the odds to become the first American woman with a medical degree. Blackwell was remarkable for what she achieved for herself and for all women, but she was not alone in the struggle. The first woman to be a pilot or the president of a labor union deserves our admiration and thanks, as does the first woman judge or the first woman to edit a major magazine.

Have students research women who broke the gender barrier and thus paved the way for women to contribute in ways previously denied to them. They can write brief reports that highlight both the achievement and the struggle(s) that the woman or women faced. Invite students to post their reports in a bulletin-board display of women's firsts. Encourage students to read one another's reports.

A useful source is *The Book of Women's Firsts* by Phyllis J. Read and Bernard L. Witlieb, 1992.

Not in our respectable day!
A doctor? An M.D.! Did you hear what she said?
35 She's clearly and indubitably[2] out of her head!"
"Indeed, indeed, we are thoroughly agreed,"
⑤ hissed the ladies of society all laced in and prim,
"it's a scientific fact a doctor has to be a him.
Yes, sir,
40 'twould be against nature
if a doctor were a her."

hibble hobble bibble bobble
widdle waddle wag
tsk tsk
45   twit twit
        flip flap flutter
            mitter matter mutter
⑥ moan groan wail and rail
        Indecorous![3]
50   Revolting!!
            A *scandal*
                A SIN
their voices pierced the air like a jabbing hat-pin.
But little miss Elizabeth wouldn't give in.

55 To medical schools she applied.
In vain.
And applied again
and again
and again
60 and one rejection offered this plan:
why not disguise herself as a man?
If she pulled her hair back, put on boots
    and pants,
she might attend medical lectures in France.
❼ Although she wouldn't earn a degree,
65 they'd let her study anatomy.

Elizabeth refused to hide
her feminine pride.
She drew herself up tall
(all five feet one of her!)
70 and tried again.
And denied again.
The letters answering no
mounted like winter snow.

---

2. **indubitably** (in doo′ bi tə blē) *adv.*: That cannot be
doubted; unquestionably.
3. **indecorous** (in dek′ ə rəs) *adj.*: Improper; in poor taste.

▲ Critical Viewing This
is an Elizabeth Blackwell
Award, awarded by the
American Medical
Women's Association.
On whom might such
an award be bestowed?
[Speculate] **⑧**

Elizabeth Blackwell ◆ 315

◆ **Critical Thinking**

⑤ Deduce Why do you think other
women had these anti-woman attitudes? *Students may suggest that these
women needed to justify their own lives
and career paths.*

◆ **Reading Strategy**

⑥ Interpret the Meaning Why
does the poet insert these nonsense
words here? *Students may say that she
is implying that all the objections to
Elizabeth Blackwell's plans were nonsensical.*

◆ **Literary Focus**

❼ Heroic Characters What do
Elizabeth Blackwell's actions reveal
about her character? Why didn't she
take the advice about disguising herself? *Students may respond that she
was both proud of her goals and proud
of her feminism.*

► **Critical Viewing** ◄

⑧ Speculate *Students may guess
that the award is for women who excel
as doctors or in medical research, or for
women who break certain gender barriers in medicine.*

Customize for
More Advanced Students
Guide students to notice that although
this poem has rhyme, its form varies.
Have them consider reasons that
might explain the poet's shift from
long stanzas to shorter ones, or from
long lines to short ones. Ask them to
try to justify why some lines are staggered and why some entire stanzas
have only lower-case letters.

Viewing and Representing Mini-Lesson

Heroism Award
This lesson supports the Report writing activity
in the Idea Bank on p. 319.

Introduce Tell students to imagine that they
have entered a contest to design something to
honor the efforts and achievements of Elizabeth
Blackwell. Tell them that their designs will be for
a final product that is a medal, trophy, certificate,
or badge.

Develop Have students work individually or in
pairs. Direct them first to review the elements of
Blackwell's character and heroism that will be the
focus of their design. Then, have them choose
how they will honor Blackwell and complete
their designs for that symbol. Guide them to
come up with more than one saying or phrase,
pick the best one, and revise and edit it until it
works just right.

Apply Invite students to present their designs
for medals, badges, certificates, and trophies.
Have them explain any writings or other design
elements.

Assess Judge students' efforts by how effectively
and uniquely each honors the recipient.

Comprehension Check ☑

1 **What has happened?** *Blackwell's many efforts to study medicine have come to a successful conclusion; she has been accepted to a school in Geneva, New York.*

◆ Critical Thinking

2 **Draw Conclusions** Why did the women of Geneva treat Elizabeth so rudely? *They did not approve of her career choice; they did not think women should be doctors.*

◆ Literary Focus

3 **Heroic Characters** What aspects of heroism are revealed here? *Despite the cold reception she received from townspeople and the fact that she was far from home and lonely, Elizabeth Blackwell displayed a heroic desire to succeed in her studies and then pursue her chosen life path—to help those in pain.*

◆ Reading Strategy

4 **Interpret the Meaning** What does the poet think the world is waiting for? *Some students may say that she thinks the world was waiting for a woman to be successful in the field of medicine. Others may say that she thinks that it was the world's sick who awaited Blackwell.*

Beyond Literature

At the time of the Civil War, nursing services were desperately needed but in short supply. Women took the lead in establishing associations to provide nursing care for the soldiers and in establishing training programs for nurses. Have students find out what role Dr. Elizabeth Blackwell played in organizing these efforts.

75 Until the day
when her ramrod will
finally had its way.
After the twenty-ninth try,
there came from Geneva, New York
the reply
80 of a blessed
Yes!

1 Geneva,
Geneva,
how sweet the sound;
85 Geneva,
Geneva,
sweet sanctuary found . . .

2 . . . and the ladies of Geneva
passing by her in the street
90 drew back their hoopskirts[4]
so they wouldn't have to meet.

Psst, psst,
hiss, hiss
the sinister scarlet miss.
95 Avoid her, the hoyden,[5] the hussy,
lest we all be contaminated!
If your glove so much as touch her, my dear,
best to get it fumigated!

When Elizabeth came to table,
100 their talking all would halt;
wouldn't so much as ask her
please to pass the salt.

3 In between classes
without a kind word,
105 Elizabeth dwelt
like a pale gray bird.

In a bare attic room
cold as stone,
far from her family,
110 huddled alone

studying, studying
throughout the night

warming herself
with an inner light:

115 don't let it darken
the spark of fire;
keep it aglow,
that heart's desire:

the will to serve, **3**
120 to help those in pain—
flickered and flared
and flickered again—

until
like a fairy tale
125 (except it was true!)
Elizabeth received
her honored due.

The perfect happy ending
came to pass:
130 Elizabeth graduated . . .
. . . at the head of her class.

And the ladies of Geneva
all rushed forward now to greet
that clever, dear Elizabeth,
135 so talented, so sweet!

Wasn't it glorious
she'd won first prize?

Elizabeth smiled
with cool gray eyes

140 and she wrapped her shawl
against the praise:

how soon there might come
more chilling days.

Turned to leave
145 without hesitating.

She was ready now,
and the world was waiting. **4**

---

4. **hoopskirts** *n.*: Skirt worn over a framework of hoops or rings, to make it spread out.
5. **hoyden** (hoi′ dən) *n.*: Tomboy.

Beyond the Classroom

Career Connection
Placement Counselors and Other Brokers
When Elizabeth Blackwell wanted to earn an M.D., she applied to many colleges until one accepted her. Today, when students are ready to choose a college or any other school, there are placement counselors who can guide them through a seemingly endless number of options. These advisors can be of great help by narrowing down choices to match institutions with students' interests and skills.

People turn to brokers when they face other important choices. That's why employment agents, real estate agents, insurance agents, investment advisors, and other kinds of brokers make up a growing part of today's labor force. Have students brainstorm for a list of all the jobs they can think of that fit the category of brokering. Invite them to debate the usefulness of each. Then, invite interested students to find out more about the ups, downs, and training needed for any of the jobs that appeal to them.

Beyond Literature

Career Connection

Facts About Women in Medicine
A century ago, it was almost impossible for a woman to be accepted into a medical school in the United States. In the 1930's, only one hospital in ten would accept a female doctor to its staff. Forty years ago, people still found it difficult to imagine a female surgeon. Times have changed. Today, about one fifth of all doctors practicing medicine in the United States, more than 100,000, are women. By 2010, women are expected to make up about one third of the total number of physicians in practice.

Cross-Curricular Activity
Becoming a Doctor Find out what kind of education and training a person must have to prepare for a medical career. Research the qualifications for admission to medical school and the number of years of training it takes to become a physician. Share your findings with your class.

Guide for Responding

◆ LITERATURE AND YOUR LIFE

Reader's Response What would you like to say to the people who mistreated and misjudged Elizabeth Blackwell?

Thematic Focus What might have happened to Blackwell if she had been a follower rather than a leader?

Journal Writing Jot down a list of women who, like Blackwell, integrated what were previously male-dominated professions.

☑ Check Your Comprehension

1. What special purpose does Elizabeth Blackwell set for herself?
2. How do people respond when they know of Blackwell's ambitions?
3. What happens when Blackwell applies to medical school?
4. How do people treat Blackwell after she graduates from medical school?

◆ Critical Thinking

INTERPRET
1. Do you think Elizabeth Blackwell was a person easily discouraged? Explain. **[Support]**
2. What personality traits helped Blackwell to reach her goal? **[Analyze]**
3. What effect did people's opinions seem to have on Blackwell? **[Speculate]**
4. Explain what the following lines from "Elizabeth Blackwell" may mean: "and she wrapped her shawl/against the praise:/how soon there might come/more chilling days." **[Interpret]**

EVALUATE
5. Do you think Elizabeth Blackwell had the qualities necessary to become a successful doctor? Why or why not? **[Assess]**

APPLY
6. How have society's expectations changed for "twentieth-century-young-ladies"? **[Apply]**

Elizabeth Blackwell ◆ 317

Beyond the Selection

FURTHER READING
Other Works by Henry Wadsworth Longfellow
Evangeline and Selected Tales and Ballads
Other Works by John Greenleaf Whittier
Legends of New England, Snow-Bound
Other Works by Eve Merriam
It Doesn't Always Have to Rhyme
Other Works About Paul Revere
Paul Revere and the World He Lived In, Esther Forbes

INTERNET
We suggest the following sites on the Internet (all Web sites are subject to change).
For information on Henry Wadsworth Longfellow:
http://www.auburn.edu/~vestmon/longfellow_bio.html
For the Longfellow National Historical Site (in Cambridge, MA) home page:
http://www.nps.gov/long/index.htm
For biographical data on John Greenleaf Whittier:
http://home.erols.com/kfraser/whittier.html
We *strongly recommend* that you preview these sites before you send students to them.

Answers
◆ LITERATURE AND YOUR LIFE

Reader's Response It is most likely that students will want to tell those people that their behavior was old-fashioned, prejudiced, short-sighted, and counterproductive.

Thematic Focus Students may say that she would have become a nurse or that she might never have achieved her goals because it takes bold leadership to effect change in a society.

☑ Check Your Comprehension

1. She wants to be a doctor.
2. They try to dissuade her; some mock her.
3. She has to apply many times and deal with constant rejection; she considers, then rejects, an alternate plan.
4. When she graduates at the head of her class, Elizabeth Blackwell gets the respect due her.

◆ Critical Thinking

1. No, she was not easily discouraged. The proof is that she withstood so many rejections at first, and then studied hard and achieved success despite the lack of support.
2. Blackwell was an independent thinker who was goal-oriented, persistent, hard-working, optimistic, confident, and thick-skinned.
3. Blackwell seemed to take others' opinions in stride; she followed her own conscience despite the lack of support from others.
4. Blackwell knew that she had to brace herself for the future obstacles and disappointments that she would surely face as a woman doctor.
5. Students may say that Blackwell had many good qualities, including the most important one: she wanted to help those in pain.
6. Students may say that although prejudices still exist, women face fewer obstacles today, no matter what career path they choose.

Answers

◆ Reading Strategy

1. Revere is nervous, impatient, and excited as he awaits the signal from the church. He shows his feelings by the way he paces and stomps, keeps looking at the church, and springs into action once he gets his signal. The image of the lonely, somber church steeple reflects the seriousness of his act and the dangers he'll face.

2. Frietchie's character is reflected in her setting out the flag to defy the passing soldiers, shaking the tattered flag after it had been shot down, and challenging the general to shoot her.

3. Like the "nineteenth-century-young-lady," Blackwell is modest and respectful. But unlike her, Blackwell is independent, bold, broadminded, interested in things other than sewing and music, and willing to set off in a new direction.

◆ Build Vocabulary

Using the word root: -spec-
1. c 2. a 3. b

Spelling Strategy
1. ghost; 2. ghoul; 3. spaghetti

Using the Word Bank
1. c 2. f 3. e 4. g 5. a 6. d 7. b

◆ Literary Focus

1. Revere risked his life to lead resistance to the British. He was brave, but careful, too, muffling his oars as he passed the man-of-war in the river.

2. Frietchie was heroic by defying an army with her actions and by putting herself at risk with her patriotism.

3. Blackwell is heroic because she blazes new ground for women and does so despite many obstacles, including the disapproval of other women.

◆ Build Grammar Skills

Practice
1. . . . in the silence around him he hears/The muster of men at the barrack door
2. Then he climbed the tower of the Old North Church, . . .
3. He heard the bleating of the flock, . . .
4. And felt the breath of the morning breeze/Blowing over the meadows brown.
5. So through the night rode Paul Revere

Guide for Responding (continued)

◆ Reading Strategy

INTERPRET THE MEANING

One way to **interpret the meanings** of these poems about heroic characters is to analyze the images in them.
1. Describe how Paul Revere feels in lines 57–72 of "Paul Revere's Ride." What words and images convey this feeling?
2. List three images in "Barbara Frietchie" that convey Frietchie's character.
3. Compare and contrast Elizabeth Blackwell with the image of the "nineteenth-century-young-lady" described at the beginning of the poem.

◆ Build Vocabulary

USING THE WORD ROOT -spec-

The word root -spec- in *spectral* means "related to appearances or something seen." On your paper, match the words with their definitions.
1. spectacle   a. colors in a series
2. spectrum   b. look carefully at
3. inspect   c. an unusual sight

SPELLING STRATEGY

Sometimes the hard g sound is spelled *gh,* as in *aghast.* On your paper, fill in the blanks to write words that contain *gh,* pronounced as a hard g.
1. gh_s t
2. _ _oul
3. spa_ _etti

USING THE WORD BANK

On your paper, match each Word Bank word in Column A with a synonym in Column B.

Column A	Column B
1. stealthy	a. calm
2. somber	b. crowd
3. impetuous	c. secret
4. spectral	d. horrified
5. tranquil	e. impulsive
6. aghast	f. gloomy
7. horde	g. ghostly

◆ Literary Focus

HEROIC CHARACTERS

The subjects of these poems are all **heroic characters.** Their actions in the face of great obstacles are inspiring and noble.
1. What heroic traits does Paul Revere possess? Support your answer.
2. Why was Barbara Frietchie's action heroic?
3. Elizabeth Blackwell does not risk her life, but she is heroic nonetheless. Explain why.

◆ Build Grammar Skills

PREPOSITIONAL PHRASES

A **prepositional phrase** is a group of words beginning with a preposition and ending with a noun or a pronoun. A preposition is a word like *of, between,* or *from* that shows a relationship. The noun or pronoun in the phrase is called the object of the preposition. In this example from "Paul Revere's Ride," there are two prepositional phrases, each beginning with the preposition *of.* The two objects of the preposition are *midnight ride* and *Paul Revere.*

> Listen, my children, and you shall hear
> *of the midnight ride of Paul Revere,*

Practice Copy the following passages on your paper. Underline each prepositional phrase.
1. . . . in the silence around him he hears/The muster of men at the barrack door, . . .
2. Then he climbed the tower of the Old North Church, . . .
3. He heard the bleating of the flock, . . .
4. And felt the breath of the morning breeze/Blowing over the meadows brown.
5. So through the night rode Paul Revere; . . .

Writing Application Write two sentences about Paul Revere's ride that contain at least three of the following prepositions:

on, across, until, during, of, like, at

Writing Application
Possible responses:
1. During the night he rowed across the river, passing the guns of the *Somerset,* until he arrived on the other shore.
2. He looked across the river at the church until he saw his signal.

 Writer's Solution

For additional instruction and practice, use the lesson in the *Writer's Solution Language Lab CD-ROM* on Prepositional Phrases. You may also use Prepositions, p. 24, and Prepositional Phrases, p. 470., in the *Writer's Solution Grammar Practice Book.*

Build Your Portfolio

 Idea Bank

Writing

1. **Movie Summary** Write a brief summary of "The Elizabeth Blackwell Story" for the back of a videocassette box.

2. **Character Sketch** Who was Paul Revere's friend and partner? Use your imagination to write a character sketch of this person.

3. **Report** Research one of the heroes in the poems, and write a report on his or her contributions to history. **[Social Studies Link]**

Speaking and Listening

4. **Retelling** Imagine that you are a Confederate soldier marching into Frederick, Maryland. Retell to the class the story of Barbara Frietchie from your point of view. **[Performing Arts Link]**

5. **Dramatic Reading** Prepare a dramatic reading of lines 111–130 from "Paul Revere's Ride." Use a tape recorder to practice reading rhythmically, to imitate the pace of the horse. Read the poem aloud to your class. **[Performing Arts Link]**

Projects

6. **Boston Area Map [Group Activity]** Work with a small group to research what actually happened on the night of April 18, 1775, and on the following day. Draw a map of Boston and the surrounding area, tracing the route of Paul Revere's ride and locating landmarks and places mentioned in the poem. **[Social Studies Link; Art Link]**

7. **Folk Ballad [Group Activity]** Set the words of "Barbara Frietchie" to music. Work with a partner to compose or to find a melody. Select the stanzas to include in your song. If possible, record the song for others to hear. **[Music Link]**

 Writing Mini-Lesson

"Eyewitness" Speech

Each of these poems gives a detailed report about an important event in American history. Write a speech that gives an "eyewitness" account of an important current event.

Writing Skills Focus: Appeal to Your Audience

A successful speech keeps the audience on the edge of their seats, waiting eagerly to hear more. To **appeal to your audience,** use words and phrases that will arouse people's emotions, amuse them, or cause them to think. Notice how these lines from "Barbara Frietchie" make you want to keep reading to find out what happens next:

Model From the Poem
"Shoot, if you must, this old gray head,
But spare your country's flag," she said.

Prewriting Choose a current event that interests you. Then, check newspapers, magazines, television news shows, and the Internet to find details about the setting, who was there, and what happened. Make an outline of your findings.

Drafting Using your outline, write your speech as if you were an on-the-scene observer of the events taking place. Include words and phrases that convey emotional impact, to hook your audience and hold their interest.

> ◆ **Grammar Application**
> Use prepositional phrases to add precise details and interest to your speech.

Revising Deliver your speech to several classmates. Ask if they feel as if they were present at the event you are describing. Revise any sections that your audience found dull or confusing.

 Idea Bank

Following are suggestions for matching the Idea Bank topics with your students' performance levels and learning modalities:

Customize for
Performance Levels
Less Advanced Students: 1, 4
Average Students: 2, 4, 5, 7
More Advanced Students: 3, 5, 6, 7

Customize for
Learning Modalities
Verbal/Linguistic: 1, 2, 3, 4, 5, 6, 7
Visual/Spatial: 6
Logical/Mathematical: 2, 3, 4, 6
Musical/Rhythmic: 5, 7
Interpersonal: 2, 4, 6, 7
Intrapersonal: 4, 5

 Writing Mini-Lesson

Refer students to the Writing Handbook in the back of the book for instruction on the writing process and for further information on eyewitness accounts. Have students use the Series of Events Chain in **Writing and Language Transparencies,** p. 57, to organize their eyewitness speeches.

 Writer's Solution

Writers at Work Videodisc
Have students view the videodisc segment on Description (Ch. 2), featuring Rosie McNulty, to see how she organizes events chronologically.

Play frames 30697 to 31490

Writing Lab CD-ROM
Have students complete the tutorial on Description. Follow these steps:
1. Have students view the *Star Trek* video clip, which illustrates the concept of audience, and then do the Considering Audience and Purpose section.
2. Have students draft on computer.
3. Have students use the Revision Checker to highlight any vague adjectives they have used.

Writer's Solution Sourcebook
Have students use Chapter 2, "Description," for additional prewriting support. The chapter includes in-depth instruction on organizing details, pp. 54–55.

✓ ASSESSMENT OPTIONS

Formal Assessment, Selection Test, pp. 90–92, and Assessment Resources Software. The selection test is designed so that it can be easily customized to the performance levels of your students.

Alternative Assessment, p. 24, includes options for less advanced students, more advanced students, visual/spatial learners, verbal/linguistic learners, musical/rhythmic learners, and bodily/kinesthetic learners.

PORTFOLIO ASSESSMENT
Use the following rubrics in the **Alternative Assessment** booklet to assess student writing:
Movie Summary: Summary, p. 94
Character Sketch: Description, p. 93
Report: Research Report, p. 102
Writing Mini-Lesson: Description, p. 93

Prepare and Engage

OBJECTIVES

1. To read, comprehend, and interpret a selection that has a social studies focus
2. To relate a selection with a social studies focus to personal experience
3. To connect literature to social studies
4. To respond to Social Studies Guiding Questions
5. To respond to the selection through writing, speaking and listening, and projects

SOCIAL STUDIES GUIDING QUESTIONS

Reading about the people who drafted the Declaration of Independence will help students discover answers to these Social Studies Guiding Questions.

- How have historical events affected the culture of the United States?
- What factors helped shape the founding of the United States government?

 **Interest Grabber** Post the exact wording of a school, community, or classroom policy on the chalkboard. Ask students to comment on how the policy is worded. Might it offend anyone? Is it too harsh or too lenient? Invite suggestions for rewording the policy. After some discussion, note that students have role-played a process similar to that of the Declaration of Independence writers.

Map Study

Historical Maps Visualizing geographic elements can help students understand why events occurred in a particular historical time. For example, students might understand why the Continental Congress delegates had divergent ideas by noting the distance between the colonies. Without e-mail, telephone, or even trains to link the colonies, these men came from very different communities.

CONNECTING LITERATURE TO SOCIAL STUDIES
THE REVOLUTIONARY PERIOD

Young Jefferson Gets Some Advice From Ben Franklin *by Thomas Jefferson*

The Thirteen Original States

AMERICA AS A COLONY To many people, the American Revolutionary period brings to mind a British government forcing Americans to live by laws that treated them unjustly. It's easy to forget that the people we think of as Americans were actually British citizens living in a British colony. Until the Revolutionary War, the British government had a legal right to pass laws that governed its citizens in America.

The Movement Toward Independence Some American colonists were talking about independence from England as early as the 1730's. However, for a long time after that, most colonists did not want to break away from England. They would have preferred to see the British government give more attention to their complaints about unfair treatment. It took many years to get most colonists to favor independence. Even in 1776, many were still opposed to the idea.

The Declaration of Independence In 1776, the Second Continental Congress met in Philadelphia to resolve the issue of independence. Thomas Jefferson, a delegate from Virginia, was chosen to write a declaration of independence, a document which would state the colonies' reasons for proclaiming their freedom from Britain. Once presented to the Congress, the document underwent many revisions at the suggestion and demand of various delegates. Jefferson was, understandably, upset at the amount of revision made to the document he wrote. In the passage that follows, Thomas Jefferson recalls advice that he received from elder statesman Benjamin Franklin during the process of the Declaration's revision.

320 ◆ *Quest for Justice*

 Prentice Hall Literature Program Resources

REINFORCE / RETEACH / EXTEND
Selection Support Pages
Build Vocabulary, p. 128
Theme, p. 128
Formal Assessment Selection Test, pp. 93–94, Assessment Resources Software
Writing and Language Transparencies KWL Organizer, p. 49
Resource Pro CD-ROM "Young Jefferson Gets Some Advice From Ben Franklin"—includes all resource material and customizable lesson plan

Listening to Literature Audiocassettes "Young Jefferson Gets Some Advice From Ben Franklin"

Connection to Prentice Hall World Explorer *Western Hemisphere* Ch. 7, "The United States and Canada: Shaped by History"
Connection to Prentice Hall American Nation *American Nation* Ch. 5, "Creating a Republic"

Young Jefferson Gets Some Advice From Ben Franklin

THOMAS JEFFERSON

Thomas Jefferson, 3rd President of the United States, Museum of the City of New York

Benjamin Franklin (1706-1790), 19th century colored engraving

W hen the Declaration of Independence was under the consideration of Congress, there were two or three unlucky expressions in it which gave offense to some members. The words "Scotch and other foreign auxiliaries" excited the <u>ire</u> of a gentleman or two of that country. Severe <u>strictures</u> on the conduct of the British king, in negativing[1] our repeated repeals of the law which permitted the importation of slaves, were disapproved by some Southern gentlemen, whose reflections were not yet matured to the full <u>abhorrence</u> of that traffic.

❶ **Connecting Literature to Social Studies** What does this suggest about Jefferson's attitude toward laws allowing slavery?

1. **negativing** (neg´ ə tiv´ iŋ) *n.*: Vetoing; rejecting.

▲ **Critical Viewing** Name a character trait that you can infer about each of these men from these portraits. [Infer] ❷

Altho' the offensive expressions were immediately yielded, these gentlemen continued their depredations[2] on other parts of the instrument. I was sitting by Dr. Franklin, who perceived that I was not insensible to these mutilations. "I have made it a rule," said he,

2. **depredations** (dep´ rə dā´ shəns) *n.*: Here, extremely harsh and destructive criticism.

◆ **Build Vocabulary**
ire (īr) *n.*: Anger; wrath
strictures (strik´ chərs) *n.*: Criticisms
abhorrence (əb hôr´ əns) *n.*: Loathing; disgust

Young Jefferson Gets Some Advice From Ben Franklin ◆ 321

Reinforce and Extend

Answers

◆ LITERATURE AND YOUR LIFE

Reader's Response Students may say yes, a simple and funny anecdote often reaches listeners better than a serious lecture.

Thematic Focus Students may note that Franklin renders advice without making Jefferson feel he's being ordered around.

☑ Check Your Comprehension

1. Negative references to the Scotch; disagreement over slave trade laws.
2. He sees that Jefferson is distressed by the changes being made to the Declaration.
3. Each comment takes out text that the reader believes is redundant or obvious.

More About the Author

Thomas Jefferson (1743–1826) In addition to serving as America's third president, Thomas Jefferson was an accomplished and respected architect (designing, for example, the campus and buildings of the University of Virginia). He also contributed with excellence as a sciencist, musician, philosopher, lawyer, and inventor. As U.S. President, Jefferson completed the Louisiana Purchase to double the nation's size and supported Lewis and Clark's mapping expedition. Born of a wealthy Virginia family, Jefferson spent his adult life in politics and civic affairs, early on deciding the colonies needed greater independence from Britain. He was the main writer of the Declaration of Independence, and later advocated for the Constitution and Bill of Rights.

CONNECTING LITERATURE TO SOCIAL STUDIES

"whenever in my power, to avoid becoming the draughtsman[3] of papers to be reviewed by a public body. I took my lesson from an incident which I will relate to you. When I was journeyman[4] printer, one of my companions, an apprentice Hatter, having served out his time, was about to open shop for himself. His first concern was to have a handsome signboard, with a proper inscription. He composed it in these words 'John Thomson, Hatter, makes and sells hats for ready money,' with a figure of a hat subjoined. But he thought he would submit it to his friends for their amendments. The first he showed it to thought the word 'Hatter,' tautologous,[5] because followed by the words 'makes hats' which show he was a Hatter. It was struck out. The next observed that the word 'makes' might as well be omitted, because his customer would not care who made the hats. If good and to their mind, they would buy, by whomsoever made. He struck it out. A third said he thought the words 'for ready money' were useless as it was not the custom of the place to sell on credit. Every one who purchased expected to pay. They were parted with, and the inscription now stood 'John Thomson sells hats.' 'Sells hats' says his next friend? Why nobody will expect you to give them away. What then is the use of that word? It was stricken out, and 'hats' followed it, as there was one painted on the board. So his inscription was reduced ultimately to 'John Thomson' with the figure of a hat."

---

3. **draughtsman** (dräfts′ mən): Person who draws up legal documents, speeches, etc.
4. **journeyman:** Worker who has served his apprenticeship and thus qualifies to work at his trade.
5. **tautologous** (tô täl′ ə gəs) *adj.*: Redundant; repetitious.

◆ Build Vocabulary

inscription (in skrip′ shən) *n.*: Something written or engraved onto a surface

amendments (ə mend′ mənts) *n.*: Corrections of errors, faults, etc.

*G*uide for Responding

◆ LITERATURE AND YOUR LIFE

Reader's Response Do you think Franklin chooses an effective way to get his point across to Jefferson? Explain your answer.

Thematic Focus How does Franklin's advice show Franklin to be a leader?

☑ Check Your Comprehension

1. Name two complaints about the Declaration that Jefferson had to address.
2. Why does Franklin offer advice to Jefferson?
3. How does each comment reduce the content of John Thomson's sign?

◆ Critical Thinking

INTERPRET
1. Why were people from Scotland offended by a phrase in the Declaration of Independence? **[Infer]**
2. What is Jefferson's opinion of people who want to continue importing slaves into America? **[Infer]**

APPLY
3. What does Franklin's story suggest about the role of leaders in situations similar to the one faced by the colonists in 1776? **[Apply]**

Block Scheduling Strategies

Consider these suggestions to take advantage of extended class time:

• Use the Interest Grabber to introduce students to the Continental Congress's interactive discussions. Read the text as a class, then group students to perform the Role Play, first as Franklin and then as Jefferson.

• You might structure the lesson around historical context, having students use the KWL Organizer, p. 49, in **Writing and Language Transparencies** to identify questions and organize information that they can use for the

Biographical Report or Research activities in the Idea Bank on p. 323.

• Use *World Explorer* and *The American Nation* to further connect literature to social studies.

• After students read the background on p. 320, play the recording. Then, have student pairs discuss and answer the Critical Thinking and Connecting to Social Studies questions.

Listening to Literature Audiocassettes "Young Jefferson Gets Some Advice From Ben Franklin"

CONNECTING LITERATURE TO SOCIAL STUDIES

Because most members of the Continental Congress considered Thomas Jefferson very intelligent, they chose him to write the first draft of the statement declaring the colonies' independence from England. When he had finished his draft, the Congress made several changes, most of which were meant to soften the language of the Declaration. Even though the members of the Congress were declaring the colonies independent, they were worried about offending the king and other members of the British government. Many years later, Jefferson wrote in his autobiography that these changes reflected the "pusillanimous [cowardly] idea that we had friends in England worth keeping terms with. . . ."

1. What does the disagreement about the Declaration's wording reveal about the group of men usually referred to as "the founding fathers"?
2. Explain why you believe Benjamin Franklin would or would not have approved of the changes made by the members of the Continental Congress.

Idea Bank

Writing

1. **Letter** Pretend that you are John Thomson. Write a letter describing the sign you put outside your store. Explain why you did or did not accept the advice of your various friends.

2. **Article** As a newspaper reporter, write an article about the making of the Declaration of Independence.

3. **Biographical Report** Using various resources, research the life of Thomas Jefferson or Benjamin Franklin. Include your findings in a biographical report. You may also want to list in the report the various accomplishments of your subject.

Speaking and Listening

4. **Role Play** Prepare the story told by Benjamin Franklin so that you can deliver it to the class. Pretend that you are Franklin, and share the advice with another classmate who plays the role of Jefferson.

Project

5. **Research** Read the Declaration of Independence in an encyclopedia or a history book. Note the list of offenses that led the colonists to separate from England. Select two offenses, and explain how the king and his supporters would have reacted to the statement of these offenses.

Further Reading, Listening, and Viewing

- Margaret Cousins's *Ben Franklin of Old Philadelphia* (1987) tells about the amazing life of Benjamin Franklin.
- *1776* by Peter Stone is a movie musical that brings the actions of the Second Continental Congress to life.
- Richard Conrad Stein's *The Declaration of Independence* (1995) provides an in-depth look at this important document.

Young Jefferson Gets Some Advice From Ben Franklin ◆ 323

Beyond the Selection

FURTHER READING
Other Works by Thomas Jefferson
The Portable Thomas Jefferson, ed. Merrill D. Peterson
Jefferson Readers, ed. Francis Coleman Rosenberger
Other Works About Revolutionary America
Who Were the Founding Fathers?, Steven H. Jaffe
The Young Oxford Companion to the Presidency of the United States, Richard M. Pious
The American Revolutionarie: A History in Their Own Words, Milton Meltzer

INTERNET
We suggest the following Internet sites (all Web sites are subject to change).
Visit the PBS site on Thomas Jefferson at **http://www.pbs.org/jefferson/**
Learn more about Jefferson at **http://www.lido.com/americana/presidents/Jefferson-Thomas.html**
We *strongly recommend* that you preview these sites before you send your students to them.

Idea Bank

Following are suggestions for matching the Idea Bank topics with your students' performance levels and learning modalities.

Customize for *Performance Levels*
Less Advanced Students: 1, 4
Average Students: 2, 4
More Advanced Students: 3, 5

Customize for *Learning Modalities*
Verbal/Linguistic: 1, 2, 3, 4, 5
Interpersonal: 1, 4
Logical/Mathematical: 1, 5
Intrapersonal: 1
Bodily/Kinesthetic: 4

Answers (continued)
◆ Critical Thinking

1. They believed the reference to Scotland was insulting to their native land.
2. Jefferson believes they don't understand the horror of the slave trade.
3. Students should note that leaders in such a situation face difficult tasks, such as getting people of many different backgrounds and viewpoints to compromise.

CONNECTING LITERATURE TO SOCIAL STUDIES

1. Despite their great foresight, education, and ingenuity, they were also ordinary men with differing views and some petty concerns.
2. Franklin would probably have understood why and how the changes came about. He might have declined to offer his approval or disapproval.

ASSESSMENT OPTIONS

Formal Assessment, Selection Test, pp. 93–94, and Assessment Resources Software. The selection test is designed so that it can be easily customized to the performance levels of your students.
Portfolio Assessment
Use the following rubrics in the **Alternative Assessment** booklet to assess student writing:
Letter: Expression, p. 90
Article: Fictional Narrative, p. 91
Biographical Report: Research Report/Paper p. 102

Guide for Reading

OBJECTIVES

1. To read, comprehend, and interpret a biographical profile
2. To relate a biographical profile to personal experience
3. To identify important ideas
4. To understand a biographical profile
5. To build vocabulary in context and learn Latin plural forms
6. To develop skill in using prepositional phrases as adjectives and adverbs
7. To write a tourist brochure for a memorial, including persuasive details
8. To respond to a biographical profile through writing, speaking and listening, and projects

SKILLS INSTRUCTION

Vocabulary:
Using Latin Plural Forms

Spelling:
-ant and -ent Endings

Grammar:
Prepositional Phrases as Adjectives and Adverbs

Reading Strategy:
Identify Important Ideas

Literary Focus:
Biographical Profile

Writing:
Persuasive Details

Speaking and Listening:
Oral History (Teacher Edition)

Critical Viewing:
Draw Conclusions; Analyze; Defend; Speculate

PORTFOLIO OPPORTUNITIES

Writing: Letter; Journal Entry; Biographical Profile

Writing Mini-Lesson: Tourist Brochure for a Memorial

Speaking and Listening: Commencement Address; Oral History

Projects: Memorial Budget; Multimedia Presentation

More About the Author

When he was in high school, **Brent Ashabranner** won fourth prize in a short story writing contest—and never stopped writing! He believes that his many years living outside of the United States helped him become a better observer of his own country. For Ashabranner, writing is often a family affair. His wife helps him with research. One of his daughters is a professional photographer whose work appears in at least six of her father's books. His other daughter is a newspaper editor and writer who has collaborated with her dad on two of his books.

324

Meet the Author:

Brent Ashabranner (1921–   )

Brent Ashabranner knows what it's like to have good friends die in battle. He served in the military during World War II. That experience was one of the things that drew him to the story of the Vietnam Veterans Memorial.

Cultural and Social Issues Ashabranner found his creative voice when he began writing about places he knew and things he cared about. Born and raised in Oklahoma, he worked for a number of years as an advisor to the Peace Corps. Many of his books grew out of his experiences living in Africa, India, the Philippines, and Indonesia. In addition to writing about other cultures, Ashabranner writes about complex social issues, explaining them in ways young readers can understand. He has won acclaim for his books on migrant farm workers, Native Americans, and immigration policy.

THE STORY BEHIND THE STORY

Ashabranner, who lives in Washington, D.C., wanted to write about the Vietnam Veterans Memorial because "It will make us remember that war—any war, any time, any place . . . is about sacrifice and sorrow, not about glory and reward."

324 ◆ Quest for Justice

◆ LITERATURE AND YOUR LIFE

CONNECT YOUR EXPERIENCE

Maya Ying Lin designed the Vietnam Veterans Memorial, which honors the memory of every American killed or missing in the Vietnam War. Think of a person or group you would like to honor with a memorial. What would the memorial look like?

THEMATIC FOCUS: Leading the Way

The Vietnam Veterans Memorial might not exist if Jan Scruggs hadn't led the way—and rallied others, like Maya Ying Lin, to turn his dream into reality.

◆ Background for Understanding

HISTORY

In 1961, President John F. Kennedy sent 400 military advisors to help the South Vietnamese government fight against communist rebels supported by North Vietnam. By 1968, the U.S. had more than 500,000 troops in Vietnam. In the United States, the war sparked massive protests. When the war ended, the soldiers returned to a nation bitterly divided between those who supported the war and those who opposed it.

◆ Build Vocabulary

LATIN PLURAL FORMS

Before the Vietnam Veterans Memorial could be built, *criteria* for its design were established. *Criteria* is the plural form of *criterion*, which means "a standard by which something can be judged."

WORD BANK

Which word from the selection means "people who register"? Check the Build Vocabulary box on page 328 to see if you chose correctly.

| criteria |
| registrants |
| harmonious |
| anonymously |
| eloquent |
| unanimous |
| prominent |
| conception |

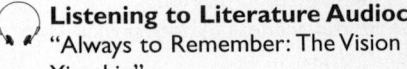

Prentice Hall Literature Program Resources

REINFORCE / RETEACH / EXTEND

Selection Support Pages
Build Vocabulary: Latin Plural Forms, p. 130
Build Spelling Skills, p. 131
Build Grammar Skills: Prepositional Phrases as Adjectives and Adverbs, p. 132
Reading Strategy: Identify Important Ideas, p. 133
Literary Focus: Biographical Profile, p. 134
Strategies for Diverse Student Needs, pp. 49–50
Beyond Literature: Humanities Connection: Fine Art, p. 25

Formal Assessment Selection Test, pp. 95–97, Assessment Resources Software
Alternative Assessment, p. 25
Writing and Language Transparencies
KWL Organizer; Sunburst Organizer, p. 85
Resource Pro CD-ROM "Always to Remember: The Vision of Maya Ying Lin"—includes all resource material and customizable lesson plan

Listening to Literature Audiocassettes
"Always to Remember: The Vision of Maya Ying Lin"

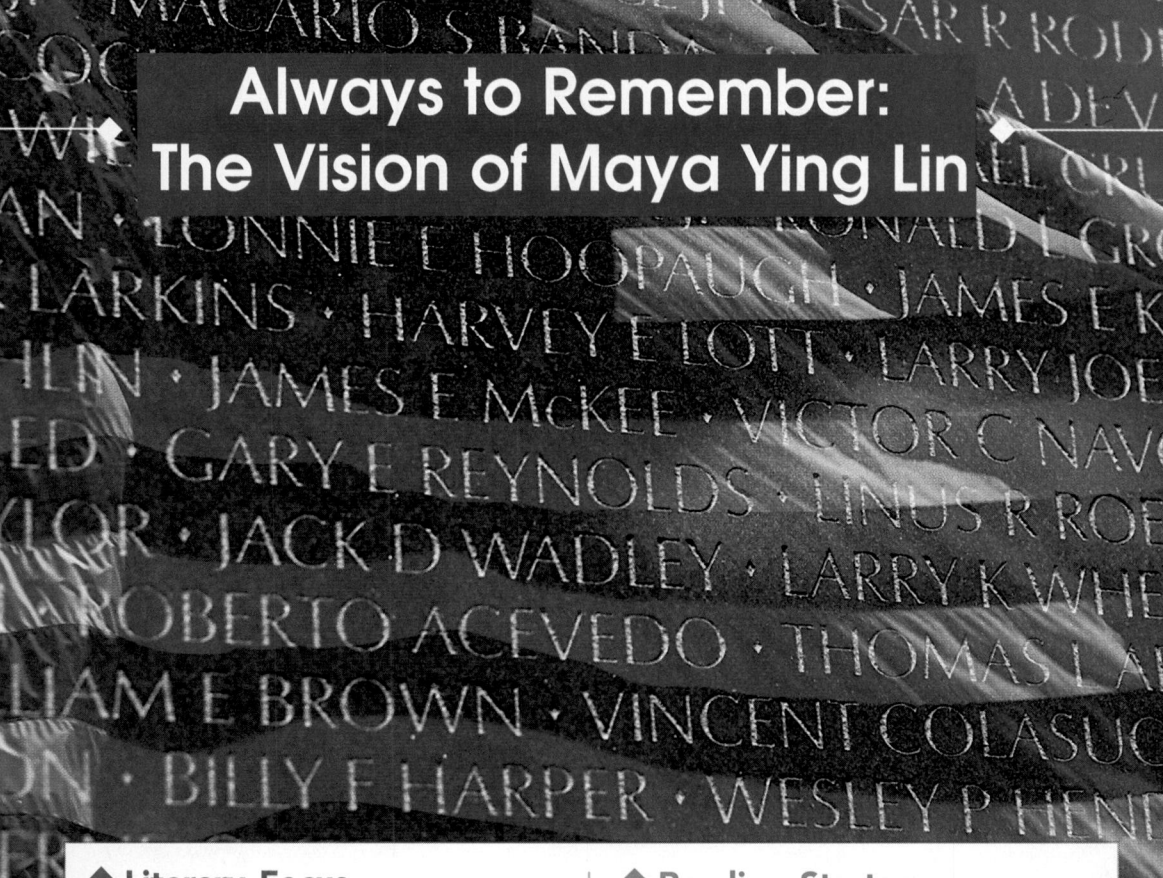

Always to Remember: The Vision of Maya Ying Lin

Interest Grabber Write the word *memorial* on the board. Then ask student groups to discuss these concepts:

- What is the purpose of a memorial?
- What should a memorial evoke?
- How do memorials move people?

Invite volunteers to describe memorials they have seen. If anyone mentions the Vietnam Veterans Memorial in Washington, D.C., use the opportunity to guide them to the selection by telling them that the person who designed the memorial was five or six years older than they are now.

◆ **Build Grammar Skills**

Prepositional Phrases as Adjectives and Adverbs If you wish to introduce the grammar concept or skill for this selection before students read, refer to the instruction on p. 332.

Customize for
Less Proficient Readers
Provide copies of the KWL Organizer, p. 49 in **Writing and Language Transparencies,** to help students read and respond to this selection.

◆ Literary Focus

BIOGRAPHICAL PROFILE

A biography tells the full story of a person's life. A **biographical profile** is a shorter version, often focusing on one important event or achievement. "Always to Remember" is a profile that concentrates on aspects of architect Maya Lin's life that led to her design of the Vietnam Veterans Memorial. After reading a profile, you may want to learn more about the person by reading a full biography.

◆ Reading Strategy

IDENTIFY IMPORTANT IDEAS

When you read nonfiction, **identify the important ideas** by asking questions such as: Who is the subject of this selection? Why did this event occur? What points does the author want to make? Your answers will help you focus on the main ideas of the piece. Copy this chart. Then, as you read, jot down the most important information in each category.

Customize for
More Advanced Students
This profile includes terms that students may not know, but whose meanings are essential for them to identify important ideas. Have them make a glossary of terms in a simple two-column chart like this one:

Term	Synonym
durable	long-lasting

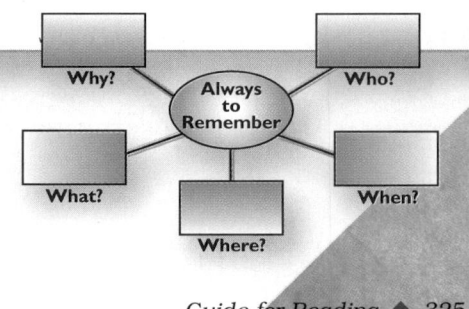

Why? — Always to Remember — Who?
What? — Where? — When?

Guide for Reading ◆ 325

 Humanities: Art

Vietnam Veterans Memorial, by Maya Ying Lin

This is a close-up of part of the memorial that Maya Lin designed, with an American flag reflected against its facade. "The Wall" is panels of black granite cut into a hillside and inscribed with names of Americans who died or were missing in action in the Vietnam War. Talk about the impact of seeing so many names engraved in stone. *Students may say that it reminds them that soldiers were real men and women who lived—and died—serving their country. Their loss deserves honor.*

 Preparing for Standardized Tests

Vocabulary This selection presents eight words in the Word Bank that will help students broaden their vocabulary, which may help them as they answer reading comprehension items on standardized tests. One of the words students will learn in this piece is *anonymously*. Present the following sample test question, in which students must select the answer that best completes the statement:

All design entries were displayed anonymously. This means that judges—

(A) did not wear name tags
(B) had no idea who created each entry

(C) could not make a fair decision
(D) had to vote secretly

Students who know that anonymously means "with the name withheld" can select (B) as the correct answer. When entries are displayed anonymously, judges cannot be influenced by background information. For further practice, use Build Vocabulary Skills in **Selection Support,** p. 130.

Tell students that when they take a standardized test they should use their time wisely by responding to all of the questions they are sure of and then returning to those that take longer.

One-Minute Insight

Youth and inexperience do not necessarily stop someone from making a major contribution to society. In "Always to Remember: The Vision of Maya Ying Lin," the author describes the design contest held for a memorial in Washington, D.C., to honor Vietnam War veterans, and presents a brief biographical sketch of the remarkable young college student whose eloquent design became a great monument.

Clarification

❶ Be sure students understand that the term "Armed Forces" includes all branches of the military: Air Force, Army, Navy, Marine Corps, and all special units, such as Green Berets.

Customize for
English Language Learners

Provide basic background material to help students appreciate this essay: the capital of our nation, Washington, D.C., is the site of America's most important national symbols, such as the Washington Monument and the Lincoln Memorial. Use maps, guidebooks, or videos of Washington, D.C., to help students visualize the Mall and the layout of sites mentioned.

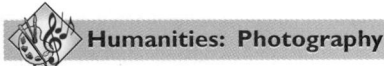

Humanities: Photography

Grieving Vet, by Catherine Ursillo

Be sure students realize that the picture of Maya Ying Lin is a separate image from the one of visitors to the Vietnam Veterans Memorial. Discuss these questions:

1. Except for the central figure, everyone in this photo is seen as a reflection on the wall. What message does this suggest? *The man's inner thoughts and feelings are his alone, so he physically stands apart from the others, lost in his memories.*

2. Contrast the attitude of the man leaning on the wall with that of the other people. *He appears sad and absorbed; the others seem to be more casual observers.*

3. Why might the man be touching the wall? *He may be overcome with the emotions that the wall evokes, or he may be touching the name of someone who was important to him.*

Always to Remember: The Vision of Maya Ying Lin

Brent Ashabranner

> "in honor and recognition of the men and women of the Armed Forces of the United States who served in the Vietnam War." ❶

Block Scheduling Strategies

Consider these suggestions to take advantage of extended class time:

• Build curiosity for the selection by using the Interest Grabber on p. 325 of the Teacher Edition, and by having students preview the photos in the Student Edition that support the essay. You can use the Humanities features on pp. 325 and 328 of the Teacher Edition to guide discussion.

• Have students read the biographical profile independently. They can answer the Guide for Responding questions, pp. 331–332, orally or in

written form, and share them in discussion groups. Also use the Reading Strategy: Identify Important Ideas in **Selection Support,** p. 133, for additional assistance.

• Add historical context with the Cross-Curricular Connection: Social Studies activity, p. 327, and by assigning the Oral History Speaking and Listening activity or the Multimedia Presentation project, p. 333.

• If possible, display some actual travel brochures to help students focus on the Writing Mini-Lesson, p. 333.

In the 1960's and 1970's, the United States was involved in a war in Vietnam. Because many people opposed the war, Vietnam veterans were not honored as veterans of other wars had been. Jan Scruggs, a Vietnam veteran, thought that the 58,000 U.S. servicemen and women killed or reported missing in Vietnam should be honored with a memorial. With the help of lawyers Robert Doubek and John Wheeler, Scruggs worked to gain support for his idea. In 1980, Congress authorized the building of the Vietnam Veterans Memorial in Washington, D.C., between the Washington Monument and the Lincoln Memorial.

The memorial had been authorized by Congress "in honor and recognition of the men and women of the Armed Forces of the United States who served in the Vietnam War." The law, however, said not a word about what the memorial should be or what it should look like. That was left up to the Vietnam Veterans Memorial Fund, but the law did state that the memorial design and plans would have to be approved by the Secretary of the Interior, the Commission of Fine Arts, and the National Capital Planning Commission.

What would the memorial be? What should it look like? Who would design it? Scruggs, Doubek, and Wheeler didn't know, but they were determined that the memorial should help bring closer together a nation still bitterly divided by the Vietnam War. It couldn't be something like the Marine Corps Memorial showing American troops planting a flag on enemy soil at Iwo Jima. It couldn't be a giant dove with an olive branch of peace in its beak. It had to soothe passions, not stir them up. But there was one thing Jan Scruggs insisted on: The memorial, whatever it turned out to be, would have to show the name of every man and woman killed or missing in the war.

The answer, they decided, was to hold a national design competition open to all Americans. The winning design would receive a prize of $20,000, but the real prize would be the

---

◀ **Critical Viewing** What does the pictured veteran's reaction to the memorial tell you about its effectiveness? [Draw Conclusions] ❹

Always to Remember: The Vision of Maya Ying Lin ◆ 327

Thematic Focus
❷ **Leading the Way** Tell students that, as the war in Vietnam went on, a sharp division grew among Americans: one group believed that the war was morally wrong and should be brought to an immediate end, and the other group believed that anyone opposed to the war was unpatriotic. Ask students why they think it took the efforts of a Vietnam veteran to lead the way for this project. *Students may say that a veteran would have highly personal and deep feelings about the war, a great need to bring closure to the nation's pain, and might be persuasive in taking the lead.*

◆ **Reading Strategy**

❸ **Identify Important Ideas** According to Jan Scruggs, what was the main purpose of the monument? *He believed that it was crucial for it to soothe, not stir, passions.*

▶ **Critical Viewing** ◀

❹ **Draw Conclusions** *The memorial must be effective because this man is clearly moved.*

Customize for
Intrapersonal Learners
The experience of visiting a memorial is both public and private. Have students keep a reader's log of feelings and responses to this essay.

 Cross-Curricular Connection: Social Studies

Vietnam Tell students that Vietnam was a colony of France from the mid-19th century until the end of World War II, when Vietnamese forces rebelled to seek independence. Despite American support, the French were defeated in 1954. Vietnam was then divided: North Vietnam had a Communist government, and South Vietnam was ruled by a series of U.S.-backed weak regimes. When North Vietnam tried to take over South Vietnam in the 1960's, the United States sent increasing numbers

of armed forces, until the total reached well into the hundreds of thousands. Finally, in 1975, United States troops left the country, which was reunited under the leadership of the North Vietnamese.

American sentiment was divided as to whether or not U.S. troops should remain in Vietnam. Invite interested groups of students to research the issues involved, discuss the pros and cons for each side, and interview people who recall that period of American history.

winner's knowledge that the memorial would become a part of American history on the Mall in Washington, D.C. Although fund raising was only well started at this point, the choosing of a memorial design could not be delayed if the memorial was to be built by Veterans Day, 1982. H. Ross Perot contributed the $160,000 necessary to hold the competition, and a panel of distinguished architects, landscape architects, sculptors, and design specialists was chosen to decide the winner.

Announcement of the competition in October, 1980, brought an astonishing response. The Vietnam Veterans Memorial Fund received over five thousand inquiries. They came from every state in the nation and from every field of design; as expected, architects and sculptors were particularly interested. Everyone who inquired received a booklet explaining the <u>criteria</u>. Among the most important: The memorial could not make a political statement about the war; it must contain the names of all persons killed or missing in action in the war; it must be in harmony with its location on the Mall.

A total of 2,573 individuals and teams registered for the competition. They were sent photographs of the memorial site, maps of the area around the site and of the entire Mall, and other technical design information. The competitors had three months to prepare their designs, which had to be received by March 31, 1981.

▲ **Critical Viewing** What impact does the listing of names have on the viewer? **[Analyze]**

Of the 2,573 <u>registrants</u>, 1,421 submitted designs, a record number for such a design competition. When the designs were spread out for jury selection, they filled a large airplane hangar. The jury's task was to select the design which, in their judgment, was the best in meeting these criteria:

• a design that honored the memory of those Americans who served and died in the Vietnam War.
• a design of high artistic merit.
• a design which would be <u>harmonious</u> with its site, including visual harmony with the Lincoln Memorial and the Washington Monument.
• a design that could take its place in the "historic continuity" of America's national art.
• a design that would be buildable, durable, and not too hard to maintain.

The designs were displayed without any indication of the designer's name so that they could be judged <u>anonymously</u>, on their design merits alone. The jury spent one week reviewing all the designs in the airplane hangar. On May 1 it made its report to the

◆ Build Vocabulary

criteria (krī tir´ ē ə) *n.:* Standards or tests by which something can be judged

registrants (rej´ is trənts) *n.:* People who register to participate in something

harmonious (här mō´ nē əs) *adj.:* Combined in a pleasing, orderly arrangement

Humanities: Photography

Grieving Vet in a Wheelchair, by Paul Conklin

The powerful impact of the Vietnam Veterans Memorial extends to photographs that are taken of it. Have students study each of the photos that accompanies this essay. Then ask students to compare and contrast the photograph on this page with the one shown on p. 326. Use these questions for discussion:

1. What common themes link the two men? *Each is the central focus of the shot; both bow their heads in pain or reflection; both seem to feel deep emotions as they touch the wall; both pictures show other people, but only as reflections on the memorial's surface.*

2. Why do both scenes show other visitors keeping away from the grieving men? *The photographers want to highlight the responses of the men who seem deeply touched by being at the wall; other spectators keep their distance not to intrude on the men's grief.*

Vietnam Veterans Memorial Fund; the experts declared Entry Number 1,026 the winner. The report called it "the finest and most appropriate" of all submitted and said it was "superbly harmonious" with the site on the Mall. Remarking upon the "simple and forthright" materials needed to build the winning entry, the report concludes:

This memorial, with its wall of names, becomes a place of quiet reflection, and a tribute to those who served their nation in difficult times. All who come here can find it a place of healing. This will be a quiet memorial, one that achieves an excellent relationship with both the Lincoln Memorial and Washington Monument, and relates the visitor to them. It is uniquely horizontal, entering the earth rather than piercing the sky.

This is very much a memorial of our own times, one that could not have been achieved in another time and place. The designer has created an <u>eloquent</u> place where the simple meeting of earth, sky and remembered names contain messages for all who will know this place.

The eight jurors signed their names to the

▲ **Critical Viewing** What word would you use to describe the effect of this photograph? Explain your choice. **[Defend]**

◆ **Reading Strategy**
How does this passage convey the importance of the memorial to the American people?

report, a <u>unanimous</u> decision. When the name of the winner was revealed, the art and architecture worlds were stunned. It was not the name of a nationally famous architect or sculptor, as most people had been sure it would be. The creator of Entry Number 1,026 was a twenty-one-year-old student at Yale University. Her name—unknown as yet in any field of art or architecture—was Maya Ying Lin.

How could this be? How could an undergraduate student win one of the most important design competitions ever held? How could she beat out some of the top names in American art and architecture? Who was Maya Ying Lin?

The answer to that question provided some of the other answers, at least in part. Maya Lin, reporters soon discovered, was a Chinese-American girl who had been born and raised in the small midwestern city of Athens, Ohio. Her father, Henry Huan Lin, was a ceramicist of considerable reputation and dean of fine arts at Ohio University in Athens. Her mother, Julia C. Lin, was a poet and professor of

◆ **Build Vocabulary**

anonymously (ə nän′ ə məs lē) *adv.*: With the name withheld or secret

eloquent (el′ ə kwənt) *adj.*: Fluent, forceful, and persuasive

unanimous (yo͞o nan′ ə məs) *adj.*: Agreeing completely; united in opinion

Always to Remember: The Vision of Maya Ying Lin ◆ 329

►**Critical Viewing**◄
6 Defend *Students might use words such as* heroic, uplifting, patriotic, respectful, *and* memorable.

◆►**Reading Strategy**
7 Identify Important Ideas As this passage summarizes the intended effects of the memorial, it offers hope that the American people will be moved and healed when they see it, as the judges were when they chose it as the winning entry.

◆ **Build Grammar Skills**
8 Prepositional Phrases as Adjectives and Adverbs Tell students that a prepositional phrase is a group of words that begins with a preposition and ends with a noun or pronoun. Prepositional phrases can function as adjectives that tell *what kind* or *how much;* or as adverbs that tell *when, where,* and *how.* Help students identify each prepositional phrase in this passage and determine its function. "In the small midwestern city of Athens, Ohio" is a prepositional phrase serving as an adverb to tell where Lin was born and raised. "Of considerable reputation" and "of fine arts at Ohio University in Athens" are prepositional phrases that act as adjectives to modify *ceramist* and *dean,* answering *what kind.*

 Beyond the Classroom

Workplace Skills

Industriousness Explain to students that Maya Ying Lin was talented and had the advantage of design training, but she would never have entered nor won the design competition if she had not been industrious, or willing to work hard. Review with students some of the efforts she put forth in order to do a better job on her assignment. Lin traveled from Connecticut to Washington to examine the site where the memorial would be built. After building her clay model, she spent six weeks working on the design drawings. Ask students

to suggest other areas in which talent is supported by hard work. Students may say that talented dancers or musicians must practice; the best athletes maintain a training regimen; and the smartest students must study and do homework.

Industriousness is highly regarded in the workplace, no matter what kind of job a person has. Challenge students to apply the notion of industriousness to jobs they know about or have observed that require it. You might have them evaluate their own levels of industriousness and consider what factors, if any, influence how industrious they can be.

►Critical Viewing◄

❶ Speculate *He might be touching a name that has significance to him—a friend, family member, or someone that shares his own name—or he might just be making contact with the wall, as many are moved to do.*

◆ Literary Focus

❷ Biographical Profile *Students may say that some details about a subject's family background are usually given in a biographical piece. Here, the author also reveals that Maya Lin's family valued art.*

◆ Literary Focus

❸ Biographical Profile Ask students to tell what this detail reveals about Lin herself. *She is practical and down-to-earth.*

◆ LITERATURE AND YOUR LIFE

❹ Ask students to share their own views of cemeteries, and to discuss how they think they would feel about using a cemetery as a park. *Some students may say that cemeteries are too sacred to be used casually; others may feel uncomfortable in cemeteries and would prefer not to spend any more time there than necessary.*

◆ LITERATURE AND YOUR LIFE

❺ *Students might share times when they got the perfect idea for a gift, for a school project, for the name of a pet, for a costume, and so on.*

❶ ▲ Critical Viewing What might this visitor to the memorial be doing? **[Speculate]**

Oriental and English literature. Maya Lin's parents were born to culturally <u>prominent</u> families in China. When the Communists came to power in China in the 1940's, Henry and Julia Lin left the country and in time made their way to the United States.

Maya Lin grew up in an environment of art and literature. She was interested in sculpture and made both small and large sculptural figures, one cast in bronze. She learned silversmithing and made jewelry. She was surrounded by books and read a great deal, especially fantasies such as *The Hobbit* and *Lord of the Rings*.[1]

But she also found time to work at McDonald's. "It was about the only way to make money in the summer," she said.

A covaledictorian at high school graduation,

◆ Literary Focus
❷ Why does the author tell you about Maya Lin's parents?

Maya Lin went to Yale without a clear notion of what she wanted to study and eventually decided to major in Yale's undergraduate program in architecture. During her junior year she studied in Europe and found herself increasingly interested in cemetery architecture. "In Europe there's very little space, so graveyards are used as parks," she said. "Cemeteries are cities of the dead in European countries, but they are also living gardens."

In France, Maya Lin was deeply moved by the war memorial to those who died in the Somme offensive in 1916 during World War I.[2] The great arch by architect Sir Edwin Lutyens is considered one of the world's most outstanding war memorials.

Back at Yale for her senior year, Maya Lin enrolled in Professor Andrus Burr's course in funerary (burial) architecture. The Vietnam Veterans Memorial competition had recently been announced, and although the memorial would be a cenotaph—a monument in honor of persons buried someplace else—Professor Burr thought that having his students prepare

---

1. ***The Hobbit*** and ***Lord of the Rings***: Mythical novels by the English author and scholar J.R.R. Tolkien (1892–1973), chronicling the struggle between various good and evil kingdoms for possession of a magical ring that can shift the balance of power in the world.

2. **Somme offensive** . . . : A costly and largely unsuccessful Allied offensive during World War I that sustained roughly 615,000 casualties of British and French troops.

Speaking and Listening Mini-Lesson

Oral History

This mini-lesson supports the Speaking and Listening activity in the Idea Bank on p. 333.

Introduce Tell students that although they were not yet born during the Vietnam war, many adults remember those times from personal experience in the military or because they knew someone who served in Vietnam. Help students identify family members, friends, neighbors, or teachers who might be interviewed.

Develop Encourage students to prepare a list of questions for their interviews. Discuss suitable interview protocol, reasonable time limits, ways to record details, and appropriate follow-up. Suggest that students take notes, or use an audio or video tape recorder, if they have access to the equipment and if the subject agrees.

Apply Allow time for students to contact interviewees, set up appointments, conduct interviews, summarize, and prepare a presentation for the class.

Assess Evaluate oral summaries on students' preparation and the quality of information presented. Or, use the Peer Assessment: Oral Interpretation, p. 115, in **Alternative Assessment.**

a design of the memorial would be a worthwhile course assignment.

Surely, no classroom exercise ever had such spectacular results.

After receiving the assignment, Maya Lin and two of her classmates decided to make the day's journey from New Haven, Connecticut, to Washington to look at the site where the memorial would be built. On the day of their visit, Maya Lin remembers, Constitution Gardens was awash with a late November sun; the park was full of light, alive with joggers and people walking beside the lake.

"It was while I was at the site that I designed it," Maya Lin said later in an interview about the memorial with *Washington Post* writer Phil McCombs. "I just sort of visualized it. It just popped into my head. Some people were playing Frisbee. It was a beautiful park. I didn't want to destroy a living park. You use the landscape. You don't fight with it. You absorb the landscape. . . . When I looked at the site I just

❺

◆ Literature and Your Life
Have you ever had a great idea that "just popped into your head"? Explain.

knew I wanted something horizontal that took you in, that made you feel safe within the park, yet at the same time reminding you of the dead. So I just imagined opening up the earth. . . ."

When Maya Lin returned to Yale, she made a clay model of the vision that had come to her in Constitution Gardens. She showed it to Professor Burr; he liked her <u>conception</u> and encouraged her to enter the memorial competition. She put her design on paper, a task that took six weeks, and mailed it to Washington barely in time to meet the March 31 deadline.

A month and a day later, Maya Lin was attending class. Her roommate slipped into the classroom and handed her a note. Washington was calling and would call back in fifteen minutes. Maya Lin hurried to her room. The call came. She had won the memorial competition.

❻

◆ **Build Vocabulary**

prominent (präm´ ə nənt) *adj.*: Widely and favorably known

conception (kən sep´ shən) *n.*: An original idea, design, plan, etc.

◆ Literary Focus

❻ **Biographical Profile** Ask students to think about other information or details about Lin they would like to know here. For instance, they might wonder who made the call, what was said, how Lin reacted, or whom she told of the news. Or, have students imagine a movie depicting the story of Lin's winning the design contest. How would they visualize the scene in which she learns that she won? *Visualizations should include an emotional response such as joy, excitement, or surprise, maybe even shock or disbelief.*

Reinforce and Extend

Answers
◆ LITERATURE AND YOUR LIFE

Reader's Response Responses may include a new understanding that a great deal of care and thought goes into the creation of a memorial.

Thematic Focus Students may say that had Scruggs not come forward, someone else eventually would have.

☑ Check Your Comprehension

1. Vietnam veterans had not yet been honored, although the veterans of other wars had been.
2. It was an assignment given in one of her classes. Her teacher was so impressed with her design that he encouraged her to enter the actual competition.
3. It fit the all criteria that the committee had set forth, and did so in an eloquent, modern way.

◆ Critical Thinking

1. Experienced architects or sculptors were expected to submit more noble and worthy ideas than a college student with little real design experience.
2. It soothes, it presents the names of every veteran lost in the war, and it is in harmony with its site.
3. Possible responses: You are never too young to try to reach a goal; hard work and diligence pay off; life's experiences contribute to creativity and originality.
4. Possible responses: Students might not have known that architects design anything other than buildings; they might not have realized how many elements an architect must consider to create a design.

𝒢uide for Responding

◆ LITERATURE AND YOUR LIFE

Reader's Response How has this essay changed the way you think about memorials?

Thematic Focus Would there be a Vietnam Memorial today if Vietnam veteran Jan Scruggs had not spoken out? Why or why not?

☑ Check Your Comprehension

1. Why did people think that a Vietnam veterans memorial was needed?
2. Why did Maya Lin enter the design competition?
3. Give two reasons why her design won.

◆ Critical Thinking

INTERPRET
1. Why was it surprising that a twenty-one-year-old student beat architects and sculptors in the design competition? **[Draw Conclusions]**
2. In what ways does Maya Lin's design fit the criteria set forth by Scruggs, Doubeck, and Wheeler? **[Connect]**

APPLY
3. What lessons can Maya Lin's experience teach others about reaching for a goal? **[Apply]**

EXTEND
4. What are some things that architects do that you learned about from reading this article? **[Career Link]**

Always to Remember: The Vision of Maya Ying Lin ◆ 331

Beyond the Selection

FURTHER READING
Other Works by Brent Ashabranner
Dark Harvest: Migrant Farmworkers in America
Our Beckoning Borders: Illegal Immigration to America

Other Works About Maya Ying Lin
Maya Lin: Architect and Artist, Mary Malone
Maya Lin: Public/Private, Sarah Rogers
Images of Commitment: Maya Ying Lin, Diane D. Kordich, Stevie Mack, Jennifer Fiore

INTERNET
We suggest the following sites on the Internet (all Web sites are subject to change).
For more information on Brent Ashabranner:
http://www.childrensbookguild.org/Ashabranner.html
For information about the Vietnam Memorial:
http://www.greatbuildings.com/gbc/buildings/Vietnam_War_Memorial.html
We *strongly recommend* that you preview these sites before you send students to them.

Answers

◆ Reading Strategy

1. The memorial must honor Vietnam vets; it must bring the nation together; it must show the name of every American killed or missing in action during the war. Students may say that these requirements show that Scruggs wanted to help the nation heal.

2. She became interested in cemetery architecture, was moved by cemeteries and war memorials in Europe, and took a course in the subject at Yale, which led to her entering the contest. This shows that what begins as an interest can turn out to become one's work.

◆ Build Vocabulary

Using Latin Plural Forms
1. media; 2. criteria; 3. data

Spelling Strategy
1. eloquent; 2. registrant; 3. prominent

Using the Word Bank
1. g	3. f	5. d	7. e
2. c	4. a	6. b	8. h

◆ Literary Focus

1. (a) He tells about Lin making sculptures and jewelry, and reading books of fantasy. (b) This reveals an artistic, imaginative, creative person, one who could be able to think about a familiar topic in a new way.

2. She saw cemeteries as living gardens and evocative memorials, which led to an interest in funerary architecture.

3. She comes to life as a real person when he presents her words. No one else could express so clearly how Lin felt when she visited the site.

◆ Build Grammar Skills

Practice
1. returned from the war; adverb
2. stands between two monuments; adverb
3. Announcement of the competition; adjective
4. judged by a committee; adverb
5. arrived near the deadline; adverb

Writing Application
Possible response:
The Vietnam Veterans Memorial on the Mall in Washington, D.C. [adverb], is a symbol of remembrance and healing [adjective].

Guide for Responding (continued)

◆ Reading Strategy

IDENTIFY IMPORTANT IDEAS

The **important ideas** in "Always to Remember" reflect the deep feelings of the people involved.
1. Identify three ideas that were important to Jan Scruggs in his campaign to build a memorial. What did you learn from his requirements?
2. Identify two ideas that influenced Maya Lin in the creation of her design. What did you learn about creative expression from her?

◆ Build Vocabulary

USING LATIN PLURAL FORMS

Some words in English, such as *criterion,* retain their Latin plural forms. Change -*on* to -*a* to form the plural of *criterion.* Change -*um* to -*a* to form the plural of other Latin words. On your paper, write the plural form of each of the words below. Refer to a dictionary if you need help.
1. medium   2. criterion   3. datum

SPELLING STRATEGY

Some word endings like *ant* and *ent* sound alike but are spelled differently. Because there is no rule about these spellings, it is best to memorize the correct spelling. On your paper, complete the following words with *ant* or *ent,* using a dictionary to help you.
1. The president's speech was eloqu_____?_____.
2. The registr_____?_____ looked forward to voting for the first time.
3. Her promin_____?_____ facial features were memorable.

USING THE WORD BANK

Match each Word Bank word in the left column with its definition on the right.

1. unanimous	**a.** without giving a name
2. criteria	**b.** vividly expressive
3. prominent	**c.** standards
4. anonymously	**d.** people who register
5. registrants	**e.** pleasing musical tones
6. eloquent	**f.** noticeable
7. harmonious	**g.** agreeing completely
8. conception	**h.** idea

◆ Literary Focus

BIOGRAPHICAL PROFILE

A **biographical profile** is a short biography. The author focuses on one or two important aspects of the subject's life.
1. (a) What does Ashabranner tell you about Maya Lin's childhood? (b) How does this information relate to her designing the memorial?
2. How do Maya Lin's studies in Europe affect her as an artist?
3. Why does Ashabranner use Maya Lin's own words to tell about her visit to the site of the memorial?

◆ Build Grammar Skills

PREPOSITIONAL PHRASES AS ADJECTIVES AND ADVERBS

A **prepositional phrase** is a group of words that begins with a preposition and ends with a noun or pronoun. Prepositional phrases function as adjectives or adverbs.

Adjective: The memorial could not make a political statement *about the war.* (Modifies *statement* and tells *what kind.*)

Adverb: This is very much a memorial . . . that could not have been achieved *in another time and place.* (Modifies *could have been achieved* and tells *when* and *where.*)

Practice Copy the following sentences. Underline each prepositional phrase, and draw an arrow to the word it modifies. Then, tell whether the phrase is acting as an adjective or an adverb.
1. American soldiers returned from the war.
2. The memorial stands between two monuments.
3. Announcement of the competition brought an astonishing response.
4. Designs were judged by a committee.
5. Maya Lin's design arrived near the deadline.

Writing Application Add two prepositional phrases to the following sentence. Tell whether they function as adjectives or adverbs.
    The Vietnam Veterans Memorial is a symbol.

 Writer's Solution

For additional instruction and practice, use the Preposition lesson in the *Writer's Solution Language Lab CD-ROM.* You may also use the page on Prepositions, p. 24, in the *Writer's Solution Grammar Practice Book.*

Build Your Portfolio

 Idea Bank

Writing

1. **Letter** Write a letter that Jan Scruggs might have written, asking Congress for funds to build the Vietnam Veterans Memorial.

2. **Journal Entry** Imagine that you visit the memorial and find the name of a friend or relative carved on the wall. Write a journal entry describing your feelings about the experience.

3. **Biographical Profile** Research Maya Lin's life. Write a short profile telling what she has done since designing the Vietnam Veterans Memorial.

Speaking and Listening

4. **Commencement Address** Pretend that you are Maya Lin. Deliver an address to a high-school graduating class, advising the class members about finding their own creative voices.

5. **Oral History** Interview several people who lived through the Vietnam War era. Find out what they thought about the war, how their views may have changed, and what they think about the importance of the Vietnam Veterans Memorial. Share an oral summary of your interviews with the class. **[Social Studies Link; Media Link]**

Projects

6. **Memorial Budget** Design your own memorial for a person or group you admire. Draw the design to "scale." For instance, one inch might represent ten feet. Decide on the materials you would use, and find out how much they cost. Then, calculate the total cost of your monument. **[Math Link; Art Link]**

7. **Multimedia Presentation [Group Activity]** With a group of classmates, create a multimedia presentation about the Vietnam era. Try to capture the sensitivities of the political turmoil and discord of the times. **[Social Studies Link; Media Link]**

 Writing Mini-Lesson

Tourist Brochure for a Memorial

A good tourist brochure for a memorial enriches the visitors' trip. It presents background, history, and facts in a way that helps visitors understand why the memorial is important. Write your own brochure that gives information about a memorial.

Writing Skills Focus: Persuasive Details

Besides giving information, a tourist brochure uses **persuasive details** to emphasize the importance of a particular place. Look at this description of the Vietnam Veterans Memorial:

Model From the Selection
This memorial . . . becomes a place of quiet reflection, and a tribute to those who served their nation in difficult times. All who come here can find it a place of healing.

Persuasive details such as *quiet reflection* and *place of healing* make you see why the memorial is important and special.

Prewriting Research why, when, and how your memorial was built. Visit the memorial, or study photographs of it. Then, make an outline, organizing your information into different topics.

Drafting Write a separate, catchy heading for each topic in your outline. Under each heading, use persuasive details to describe the memorial, its setting, and why it is an important place to visit.

> ◆ **Grammar Application**
> Use prepositional phrases as both adjectives and adverbs in your tourist brochure.

Revising If you were a visitor to the memorial, would this brochure be helpful? Do the headings draw you in? Add persuasive details to make your brochure more interesting.

 Idea Bank

Following are suggestions for matching the Idea Bank topics with your students' performance levels and learning modalities:

Customize for *Performance Levels*
Less Advanced Students: 1, 5
Average Students: 3, 5, 6, 7
More Advanced Students: 2, 4, 5, 6, 7

Customize for *Learning Modalities*
Verbal/Linguistic: 1, 2, 3, 4, 5
Visual/Spatial: 6, 7
Bodily/Kinesthetic: 4
Logical/Mathematical: 6
Musical/Rhythmic: 7
Interpersonal: 4, 5, 7
Intrapersonal: 1, 2, 3, 6

 Writing Mini-Lesson

Refer students to the Writing Handbook in the back of the book for instruction on the writing process and for further information on persuasion. Have students use the Sunburst Organizer in **Writing and Language Transparencies,** p. 85, to organize their persuasive details on each topic of their outline.

 Writer's Solution

Writers at Work Videodisc
Have students view the videodisc segment on Persuasion (Ch. 6), featuring Kate Mitchell, to see how she does her research. Help them apply her ideas as they research and write their tourist brochures.

Play frames 2689 to 3883

Writing Lab CD-ROM
Have students complete the tutorial on Persuasion. Follow these steps:
1. Have students view the video clip about audience and purpose.
2. Have students spend time on the Organizing Evidence section.
3. Have students draft on computer.
4. Have students use Self-Evaluation Checklist when revising.

Writer's Solution Sourcebook
Have students use Chapter 6, "Persuasion," pp. 166–199, for more support. The chapter includes in-depth instruction on eliminating unnecessary words, pp. 195–196.

✓ ASSESSMENT OPTIONS

Formal Assessment, Selection Test, pp. 95–97, and Assessment Resources Software. The selection test is designed so that it can be easily customized to the performance levels of your students.

Alternative Assessment, p. 25, includes options for less advanced students, more advanced students, visual/spatial learners, verbal/linguistic learners, musical/rhythmic learners, and logical/mathematical learners.

PORTFOLIO ASSESSMENT
Use the following rubrics in the **Alternative Assessment** booklet to assess student writing:
Letter: Persuasion, p. 101
Journal Entry: Fictional Narrative, p. 91
Biographical Profile: Research Report/Paper, p. 102
Writing Mini-Lesson: Persuasion, p. 101

Establish Writing Guidelines
Review the following key characteristics of a persuasive essay:

- A persuasive essay attempts to get the reader to take action or believe a position on an issue.
- A persuasive essay must include logical information to back up the writer's opinion.

You may want to distribute the scoring rubric for Persuasion, p. 102 in **Alternative Assessment,** to make students aware of the criteria on which they will be evaluated. See the suggestions on p. 336 for customizing the rubric to this workshop.

Refer students to the Writing Handbook in the back of the book for instruction on the writing process and further information on persuasion.

Writer's Solution

Writers at Work Videodisc
To introduce students to persuasive writing and to have them see what Kate Mitchell thinks about persuasive writing, play the videodisc segment on Persuasion (Ch. 6). Have students discuss what Mitchell says about "hooking" her readers.

Play frames 3 to 7453

Writing Lab CD-ROM
If your students have access to computers, you may want to have them work in the tutorial on Persuasion to complete all or part of their persuasive essays. Follow these steps:
1. Have students view the interactive model of a persuasive essay.
2. Suggest that students use the Brainstormer activity to spark topic ideas.
3. Allow students to draft on the computer.
4. Have students use the Interactive instruction in word choice when revising.

Writer's Solution Sourcebook
Students can find additional support, including in-depth instruction on eliminating unnecessary words, pp. 195–196, in the chapter on Persuasion, pp. 166–199.

Connect to Literature Unit 7, "Nonfiction," includes an example of a persuasive essay: Robert MacNeil's "The Trouble With Television."

Persuasive Writing
Persuasive Essay

Writing Process Workshop

In this section, a young narrator convinces you that she is the fastest runner in her neighborhood, three poets help you to see the subjects of their poems as heroes, and Benjamin Franklin influences Thomas Jefferson by telling him a story. In all of these selections, the writers use persuasion. Persuasion is a type of writing that attempts to convince an audience to think or act in a certain way.

Lead the way by writing a **persuasive essay** that influences your audience to agree with your position or to take a certain action. The following skills, introduced in this section's Writing Mini-Lessons, will help you.

Writing Skills Focus

▶ **Provide relevant background** to help your readers understand your topic and to convince them that your arguments are sound. (See p. 301.)

▶ **Appeal to your audience** by addressing their concerns, stirring their emotions, or making them think. (See p. 319.)

▶ **Include persuasive details** to hook your audience and make them want to see things your way. (See p. 333.)

Notice how Toni Cade Bambara uses these skills in this passage from "Raymond's Run."

MODEL FROM LITERATURE

from "Raymond's Run" by Toni Cade Bambara

So as far as everyone's concerned, I'm the fastest ① and that goes for Gretchen, too, who has put out the tale that she is going to win the first-place medal this year. Ridiculous. ② In the second place, she's got short legs. In the third place, she's got freckles. In the first place, no one can beat me and that's all there is to it. ③

① The narrator provides relevant background—she is considered the fastest runner in town.

② The narrator's friendly, casual tone will appeal to her audience.

③ These details support the narrator's claim that she will win the race.

334 ◆ *Quest for Justice*

Beyond the Classroom

Community Connection
Newspapers and Magazines Tell students that community newspapers and magazines are good forums for persuasive writing. Explain that people who write persuasively include newspaper editors and columnists, movie, music, and book reviewers, restaurant critics, advertisers, local politicians, and concerned citizens. In addition to using local newspapers and magazines, people write persuasive messages on posters, billboards, television and radio commercials, the Internet, and as mailers.

Have students form groups and analyze a local publication for persuasive issues. Suggest that students create a chart identifying the topic of the article, the section of the newspaper where the article appears, and the audience the article is trying to address. Then, have students break down the writer's argument. They may find it helpful to use the Main Idea and Supporting Details in **Writing and Language Transparencies,** p. 61. Have them consider whether they think the article is convincing. If not, have them make suggestions for improvement.

Prewriting

Choose a Topic Think of an issue that is important to you. For inspiration, check national and local news stories or ask friends and family members about topics that concern them. Jot down all the ideas you get, and choose the one you like best.

Know Your Audience In order to appeal to your audience, you have to know who they are. Is your persuasive essay directed toward your classmates? Your neighbors? An elected official? Knowing your audience will help you choose the writing style and details that will be most effective. Create an audience profile to help focus your writing:

Audience Profile

My Readers: eighth-grade teachers and the principal at my school

Language: I will use friendly but polite language, good grammar, a respectful tone.

Audience's Knowledge

About My Topic: I am suggesting a class trip to the Vietnam Veterans Memorial. My audience is familiar with my topic, but they may not realize how many students are interested in visiting the memorial.

Audience's Interests: My audience wants class trips to be interesting, educational, affordable, and safe.

Conduct Research If you know your topic well, you should be able to provide good support for your position. To develop the strongest argument possible, however, conduct research for additional background information and persuasive details.

Drafting

Write a Strong Introduction The introduction is the first thing your readers will see. Compare these introductions to see how powerful language can hook an audience right from the start:

Weak Introduction: The Vietnam Veterans Memorial would be a great place to visit on the eighth-grade class trip.

Strong Introduction: It's moving. It's historically important. It's a place no visitor will ever forget. The Vietnam Veterans Memorial should be the destination of this year's eighth-grade trip.

Consider Opposing Arguments Some members of your audience may disagree with your point of view—at least at first. Consider opposing arguments that readers might have, and address them in your essay. You may want to conduct additional research to strengthen your argument further.

APPLYING LANGUAGE SKILLS: Placing Adverbs

Adverbs that modify verbs can often be placed in more than one position in a sentence without changing the meaning.

Example: We visited the memorial yesterday.

Example: Yesterday, we visited the memorial.

Adverbs that modify adjectives or other adverbs come right before the word they modify and cannot be moved.

Example: I am very interested in U.S. history.

Practice On your paper, place the indicated adverbs in these sentences.

1. We return to Washington, D.C. [frequently]
2. I was moved by the monument. [very]
3. The trip passed quickly. [rather]

Writing Application As you draft, place adverbs effectively—next to the words they modify—or vary placement to give variety to your sentences.

Writer's Solution Connection Language Lab

For more practice with adverbs, complete the lesson on Using Modifiers in the Using Modifiers unit.

Develop Student Writing

Prewriting

Tell students that after they choose a topic they must make sure they can develop it into an effective persuasive essay. Have them consider whether they can come up with evidence to support their position and if the topic is debatable.

Writer's Solution

To help students evaluate their topics, suggest they use the Pros-and-Cons chart, p. 184, in the *Writer's Solution Sourcebook,* or, in the Prewriting section of the *Writer's Solution Writing Lab CD-ROM.* If students can only fill one side of the column with arguments, the topic they have chosen isn't controversial enough.

Customize for
Less Proficient Writers
Some students may benefit from using the Main Idea and Supporting Details Organizer in **Writing and Language Transparencies,** p. 61. Once they have chosen a position on an issue, they can record it in the space marked Main Idea. Then, they will have to identify three details or facts to support their position. If students cannot come up with supporting details, they may want to change their topic.

Drafting

Remind students that their introduction should clearly state the position of their essay, as well as capturing the attention of their readers.

Applying Language Skills

Placing Adverbs Remind students that adverbs are words which modify verbs, adjectives, or other adverbs. Adverbs answer the questions *Where? When? In what manner?* or *To what extent?*

Writer's Solution

For additional practice and support, have students use the lesson on Misplaced Modifiers in the Problems with Sentences unit in the *Writer's Solution Language Lab CD-ROM.*

Answers

1. We frequently return to Washington D.C.
   or Frequently, we return to Washington D.C.
   or We return frequently to Washington D.C.
   or We return to Washington D.C. frequently.
2. I was very moved by the monument.
3. The trip passed rather quickly.

Revising

Tell students to also consider: Are their opinion and purpose clearly stated? Have they considered opposing arguments? Are transitions used to help readers follow the ideas of the essay?

Publishing

Suggest that students submit their essays to a school or local newspaper.

Review the Writing Guidelines
After students have completed their papers, review the characteristics of a persuasive essay.

Applying Language Skills

Commas in a Series Remind students the adjectives in some sentences must stay in a specific order.

Answers

1. We walked to the Washington Monument, then we visited the Vietnam Memorial, and finally we climbed the Lincoln Memorial.
2. Annie met visitors from Japan, Indonesia, Cambodia, England, Scotland, and Hungary.
3. The parks were filled with thoughtful tourists, determined joggers, and playful toddlers.

Writing Process Workshop

EDITING/PROOFREADING

APPLYING LANGUAGE SKILLS: Commas in a Series

Use commas to separate words, phrases, or clauses in a series.

Series of Words: *Visitors leave flowers, letters, mementos, and candles as tributes.*

Series of Phrases: *We drove to the store, to the bank, and to the library.*

Practice: On your paper, insert commas correctly.

1. We walked to the Washington Monument then we visited the Vietnam Memorial and finally we climbed the Lincoln Memorial.
2. Annie met visitors from Japan Indonesia Cambodia England Scotland and Hungary.
3. The parks were filled with thoughtful tourists determined joggers and playful toddlers.

Writing Application Review your essay, and correct any mistakes with commas in a series.

Writer's Solution Connection Writing Lab

For help revising your persuasive essay, use the Revision Checker for sentence openers in the Self-Revision section of the Persuasion tutorial.

336 ◆ Quest for Justice

Revising

Use a Checklist Go back to the Writing Skills Focus on page 334, and use the items as a checklist to evaluate and revise your essay.

▶ Have I appealed to my audience?
Are the language and tone appropriate for my audience? Have I appealed to their interests?

▶ Do I provide relevant background?
Do I tell my audience what they need to know in order to fully understand my argument? Have I avoided telling my readers things they already know? What language and details can I add that will make my essay more appropriate for my audience?

▶ Have I used persuasive details?
Do I need to add facts, statistics, examples, reasons, or other evidence? How can I strengthen my evidence?

REVISION MODEL

A trip to the Vietnam Veterans Memorial would be good. ① *a valuable educational experience*
② *Of twenty students polled, fourteen said they* Many students want to visit the memorial. ③ *The memorial was designed by Maya Ying Lin, who at the time was a college student at Yale.*

① This detail will appeal to the intended audience of teachers and the school principal.
② This statistic provides background information and also helps to strengthen the writer's persuasive argument.
③ To provide relevant background, this sentence was added.

Publishing and Presenting

Speech Share your opinion by delivering a persuasive speech. You can present your speech "live" or prerecorded on videotape or audiotape. Here are some tips:

▶ Practice several times on your own.
▶ Mark places in your essay that you want to emphasize.
▶ Speak slowly and clearly.
▶ Allow your voice to rise and fall naturally.
▶ Speak loudly enough to be heard.
▶ Look at your audience or at the camera.
▶ Try looking in a mirror or, if possible, ask a friend to serve as your audience.

✓ ASSESSMENT		4	3	2	1
PORTFOLIO ASSESSMENT Use the rubric on Persuasion in the **Alternative Assessment** booklet, p. 102, to assess the students' writing. Add these criteria to customize this rubric to this assignment.	**Persuasive Elements**	The argument convincingly appeals to the reader's emotions and reasons are supported with facts.	The argument is effective but not without questions. Most of the argument is supported with facts.	The argument has some holes in it, but some of the reasons are supported with facts.	The argument is not supported with facts, but relies on opinions of the writer.
	Placement of Adverbs	All adverbs are placed correctly in sentences.	Most adverbs are placed correctly in sentences.	Some adverbs are placed correctly in sentences.	None of the adverbs are placed correctly in sentences.

Real-World Reading Skills Workshop

Evaluating Persuasive Techniques

Strategies for Success

Persuasive techniques are the methods used by advertisers to try to convince you to buy products. These techniques work by making claims such as these:

▶ This product will make you feel smarter, more attractive, stronger, faster, cleaner, or more popular than you are now.

▶ Without this product, you will be less popular, attractive, intelligent, athletic, acceptable, or happy than you could be.

▶ You are smart to buy this product.

▶ You are foolish not to buy this product.

Find the Real Message Determine what is being sold in an advertisement—sneakers, shampoo, cereal. Almost everything else in the advertisement is a persuasive technique.

Identify Your Response People often respond because of how they *feel* rather than what they *think*. An advertisement can make you feel excited or curious. Before you know it, you smile to yourself and say, "I'll buy SuperStar Shampoo." Recognize your emotional response to an advertisement.

Identify Reality Remember that most of the people in advertisements are models or actors using persuasive techniques to sell products. Real athletes practice long hours and have great coaches. Real A students study hard. Before you believe all the claims in an advertisement, conduct a "reality check."

Make an Informed Decision Consider the product—not what is being said about it. Think about yourself and what you want and need. Base your decision on how well you and the product match.

Apply the Strategies

Read the advertisement below that appeared in the *Middle School News,* and analyze the persuasive techniques employed in it.

**Hey, Math Students—
Go to the head of class!**

Feeling bad about low grades in math? Now your troubles are over. The **Techtronix 2000** calculator is all you need to breeze through your homework and ace your next test.

Get the 10% discount for all Jefferson Middle School students. Quantities are limited, so HURRY!

1. What persuasive claims does this advertisement make?

2. What is the real message?

3. How might this advertisement make you feel? Explain.

4. How does "reality" match the picture painted by this advertisement? Explain.

5. Would you buy this product? Why or why not?

✔ Here are other situations in which evaluating persuasive techniques is important:
▶ Reading an editorial
▶ Reading a request for a donation
▶ Reading the text of a political speech

Reviewing Prepositions and Prepositional Phrases

The selections in Part 2 include instruction on the following:

- Prepositions
- Prepositional Phrases
- Prepositional Phrases as Adjectives and Adverbs

This instruction is reinforced with the Build Grammar Skills practice pages in **Selection Support,** pp. 120, 125, and 132.

As you review prepositions and prepositional phrases, you may wish to include the following:

- Adverb or Preposition?

Explain to students that some words can be used as either an adverb or a preposition. Remind students that prepositions always have objects and adverbs do not. For example, the word *down* can be used as an adverb in the sentence *She fell down.* However, it can also be used as a preposi- tional phrase, as in the sentence *The dog trotted down the path.*

Customize for
Less Proficient Readers

To help students identify prepositions and prepositional phrases, have them first identify the subject and verb of the sentence. Then, have students consider what information the rest of the words in the sentence pro- vide. If the words show a relationship of time or space, they may be a prepositional phrase.

Writer's Solution

For additional practice and support using prepositions and prepositional phrases, use the practice pages, pp. 24 and 47 in the *Writer's Solution Grammar Practice Book.* If students have access to technology, they can use the Prepositional Phrases lesson in the Using Modifiers unit of the *Writers' Solution Writing Lab CD-ROM.*

Prepositions and Prepositional Phrases

Grammar Review

A **preposition** is a word that relates a noun or a pronoun to another word in the sentence. It often shows relationships of time (*after, before*) or space (*over, under*). Here are some common prepositions:

Common Prepositions

about	behind	from	over
above	below	in	since
across	beneath	inside	through
after	beside	into	till
against	between	like	to
along	beyond	near	toward
among	by	of	under
around	down	off	until
as	during	on	up
at	except	out	upon
before	for	outside	with

A **prepositional phrase** is a group of words that begins with a preposition and ends with a noun or pronoun, called the object of the preposition. Prepositional phrases can act as adjectives or adverbs.

Adjective: Frietchie displayed the flag *outside her window.*
Adverb: Squeaky practiced *before the race.*

Practice 1 Copy these sentences, underlining each prepositional phrase once and each object of the preposition twice. Draw an arrow from the prepositional phrase to the word it modifies. Then, tell whether the prepositional phrase acts as an adjective or an adverb.

1. Squeaky stood near Gretchen in the line.

2. Revere saw a lamp in the window.

3. Elizabeth Blackwell graduated at the top of her class.

4. Jefferson spoke to Benjamin Franklin about the Declaration of Independence.

5. The memorial stands between two monuments in Washington, D.C.

Practice 2 Write a paragraph about someone who has led the way. Include at least three of the following prepositional phrases.

according to historians	from the beginning
like no other	before anyone else
during this time	with others
until the end	for everyone

Grammar in Writing

✔ *In most instances, it is better not to end a sentence with a preposition:*

Incorrect: A preposition is not a word you should end a sentence with.

Certain expressions, however, sound better when you break this rule:

Awkward: About what are you talking?

Better: What are you talking about?

Sometimes you can rewrite a sentence to avoid this situation:

Reworded sentence: What are you discussing?

338 ◆ *Quest for Justice*

Answers
Practice 1

1. Squeaky stood near Gretchen in the line.

2. Revere saw a lamp in the window.

3. Elizabeth Blackwell graduated at the top of her class.

4. Jefferson spoke to Benjamin Franklin about the Declaration of Independence.

5. The memorial stands between two monuments in Washington D.C.

Speaking, Listening, and Viewing Workshop

Presenting Persuasively

When someone skillfully presents an idea—whether in a classroom report or in a political speech—it can be a powerful experience for the audience. Remember these tips the next time you give an oral presentation:

Write It Out A few people can deliver a presentation "off the cuff," without preparation, but most people must write out their ideas first. Prepare for an oral presentation by putting your ideas on paper. To present your ideas persuasively, state your major points early and repeat them at least once in the middle and again in the summary. Use strong, colorful words to catch your audience's attention. Using a rhetorical question (in which you ask a question you answer yourself) is another good technique. Allow your sense of humor and personality to show; you will communicate better with your audience.

Practice You don't have to memorize your speech, but practice it several times to become comfortable giving it. Listen to yourself, and change the tone, volume, and pace of your voice to provide variety. Speak loudly and clearly. Stress important points with your voice and with gestures. Stand straight and tall, and hold your arms in a relaxed manner. Watch yourself in a mirror as you practice. Before you make your presentation, ask a friend to critique your delivery—your voice, stance, and movements.

Apply the Strategies

Take turns with a partner role-playing and critiquing the following situations. Then, present one to the rest of your class, and ask them for feedback.

1. You want to join an after-school club that focuses on a hobby or interest of yours. Deliver a brief presentation in which you explain why you'd be an asset to the club.
2. You're a television newscaster delivering a report on an issue of local concern in your community.
3. You're the captain of the school team. Tomorrow is the game with your arch rival, and your best player is out with an injury. Talk to your teammates to convince them they can win without the star.

Tips for Presenting Persuasively
▶ Be confident about your speech and the way you deliver it.
▶ Stand straight and tall with your arms relaxed.
▶ Establish eye contact with your audience.
▶ Take your time.
▶ Smile. If you aren't having fun speaking, pretend you are. Soon, you'll convince yourself and your audience.

Speaking, Listening, and Viewing Workshop ◆ 339

 Beyond the Classroom

Career Connection
Careers in Sales Explain to students that the ability to speak persuasively is one of the most important skills a good salesperson can possess. A salesperson must be able to convince the customer that the item for sale is essential, practical, important, and a good value. Have students brainstorm for a list of different kinds of salespeople. Some suggestions to get them started include a car salesperson, a clothing salesperson in a department store, or an insurance salesperson.

Then, suggest that students create a scenario with a possible client, an item for sale, and a salesperson's attempt to make the client buy the item. Ask for volunteers to play the salesperson and the client. As they act out the scene in front of the class, have students participate by suggesting techniques the salesperson can use or ways for the client to make the salesperson's job more difficult. If there is time, role-play several different scenarios.

Introduce the Strategies
Explain to students that when they try to convince their parents to let them stay out beyond their curfew or when they try to persuade their friends to see a new movie, they are speaking persuasively. Remind them that they are most successful when they present clear reasons for their position and when they speak confidently. These same elements are important when addressing a more formal audience.

Customize for
English Language Learners
You may want to have students pair up when working on their speeches. Encourage partners to suggest alternate word choices, to note where body language is used effectively, and to monitor whether speakers are going too fast or not speaking loudly enough.

Apply the Strategies
Suggest to students that they videotape or audiotape their presentations. They can then review the tapes as a class and open up class to discussion about the speaker's tone, posture, and body language. Have students suggest places for improvement, as well as note places where the speaker has done a good job.

◆ Build Vocabulary

What's Behind the Words?

To clarify meaning for students, provide them with definitions of the following words used on this page: politics = the science or art of government; democracy = government by the people; candidate = a person who seeks an office; election = the selection of a person or persons for office by vote. Suggest that students refer to dictionaries or encyclopedias to find the origins of words.

Answers
Activity 1

1. capital/capitol — *capital* comes from the Latin word *capital(is)* meaning "of the head." *Capital* means the city or town that is the official seat of the government in a city, state, etc. The Capitol refers to the building in Washington, D.C., where the U.S. Congress holds its sessions. The Latin word *capitol(ium)* refers to the temple of Jupiter on Capitoline hill in Rome.

2. congress — *congress* is from the Latin word *congress(us)* which means a coming together. *Congress* means the national legislative body of the U.S., consisting of the Senate and the House of Representatives.

3. conservative — from the Latin *conserv(are)* to preserve, to watch over. *Conservative* means disposed to preserve existing conditions, institutions, and to resist change.

4. legislator — from the Latin *legis lator,* a law's bringer or proposer. *Legislator* means a person who gives or makes laws.

5. liberal — from the Latin *liberal,* meaning of freedom, befitting the free. *Liberal* means favorable to progress or reform, as in political affairs.

6. senator — from the Latin *senatus,* the council of elders. *Senator* is a member of the Senate, the upper house of the legislature of the United States.

What's Behind the
Words

Vocabulary Adventures With Richard Lederer

Vocabulary From Government and Politics

From the ancient Greeks and Romans, we have inherited our system of democracy. From those same people, we have also gained many fascinating and colorful words that describe our form of government.

Government by the People

The word *politics* itself issues from the Greek word *polites,* which means "citizen." We also discover people in the word *democracy,* made from two Greek word parts—*demos,* "common people," and *kratos,* "rule by."

In a democracy, we have elections to pick out the candidates we prefer for office. In Latin, *e* means "out" and *lectus,* "pick" or "choose."

Before elections, candidates conduct campaigns. The first campaigns were carried out on battlefields, and *campaign* derives from the Latin *campus,* or "field." A military campaign is a series of operations mounted to achieve a particular wartime goal. A political campaign is an all-out effort to secure the election of a candidate to office.

Glowing Candidates

The word *candidate* has a shining history. When he went to the Forum in ancient Roman times, a candidate for office wore a bleached white toga to symbolize his humility, honesty, and purity of motive. The original Latin word, *candidarus,* meant "one who wears white," from the belief that white was the color of purity.

The Ship of State

President derives from the Latin *praesidio,* "to preside; sit in front of; protect." Presidents preside over our government and are sometimes likened to a captain steering the ship of state. That metaphor turns out to be quite accurate. The Greek word *kybernao* meant "to direct a ship." The Romans borrowed the word as *guberno,* and, ultimately, it crossed the Channel to England as *governor,* originally designating a steersman.

ACTIVITY 1 Research and report on the origins of these terms relating to politics and government:

1. capital/capitol   3. conservative   5. liberal
2. congress   4. legislator   6. senator

ACTIVITY 2 In ancient Rome, an *augur* was a kind of fortuneteller who made predictions based on the way that birds were flying.

The augurs would tell a general whether to do battle, and the general would take the advice seriously. From that custom, we get the word *inauguration,* a ceremony that marks the start of the term of a president or other official.

Now that you know the story behind *inaugurate* and *inauguration,* find out the origins of two other animal-related terms in politics:
1. dark horse
2. lame duck

340 ◆ *Quest for Justice*

Activity 2

1. dark horse — a dark horse is a race horse about whom little is known or who unexpectedly wins. In politics, it means a person who is unexpectedly nominated in a political convention.

2. lame duck — a lame duck is an elected official who is completing his term in office after an election in which he has failed to be reelected. The Twentieth Amendment is called the Lame Duck Amendment because it shortened the time from the elections in November until the newly elected leaders took office. Now they are inaugurated in January; previously they were inaugurated in March.

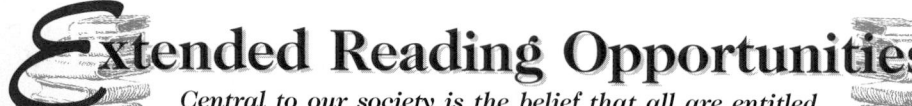
Extended Reading Opportunities

Central to our society is the belief that all are entitled to justice. The following novels explore the quest for fairness and understanding in a world filled with injustices.

Suggested Titles

The House of Dies Drear
Virginia Hamilton

The house of Dies Drear is not just a new home for the Small family, but an important part of the nation's history. The house, a stop on the Underground Railroad, was built by the abolitionist Dies Drear. Thirteen-year-old Thomas Small finds the house full of mystery. He encounters secret passageways, finds bizarre symbols left by an intruder, and flees in fear from an old man living in the forest. The novel traces Thomas and his family's steps in solving the mystery surrounding their new home.

The Pearl
John Steinbeck

The inability to see what is truly valuable in life when one's vision is clouded by the promise of material possessions is the focus of this novel. When he finds a magnificent pearl, the poverty-stricken Kino believes that he has found good fortune that will enable him to provide for his family. His wife, Juana, immediately sees how the pearl might change their lives and begs Kino for her sake and for the welfare of their son to throw it back into the ocean. Kino refuses, and the tragic events that follow change their lives forever.

my brother Sam is dead
James Lincoln Collier and Christopher Collier

Ten-year-old Tim Meeker lives in Redding Ridge, Connecticut, during the Revolutionary War. Tim's father is a British loyalist, while Tim's sixteen-year-old brother Sam has run off to join the Patriots in their fight for freedom. Throughout the novel, Tim struggles to understand both sides and to respect both his father's and his brother's beliefs. Through Tim's eyes, we are able to see the sacrifices made by ordinary people during the war.

Other Possibilities

The Slave Dancer	Paula Fox
April Morning	Howard Fast
Children of the River	Linda Crew
Farewell to Manzanar	Jeanne W. Houston and James D. Houston

Planning Students' Extended Reading

All of the works listed on this page are good choices for extending the theme "Quest for Justice." Following is some information that may help you choose which to teach.

Customize for *Varying Student Needs*

When assigning the selections in this part to your students, keep in mind the following factors:

- *The House of Dies Drear* is a longer novel (279 pp.), full of mystery and intrigue. It provides a good opportunity for a connection to social studies and history.

- *The Pearl* is a short but classic novel by John Steinbeck. Students may need help getting at the theme.

- *my brother Sam is dead* is another historical novel. It could be taught along with a social studies unit on the Revolutionary War.

Literature Study Guides

A literature study guide is available for *The House of Dies Drear*. The guide includes section summaries, discussion questions, and activities.

Planning Instruction and Assessment

Unit Objectives

1. To read nonfiction selections
2. To apply a variety of reading strategies, particularly strategies for reading nonfiction, appropriate for reading these selections
3. To recognize literary elements used in these selections
4. To increase vocabulary
5. To learn elements of grammar and usage
6. To write in a variety of modes about situations based on the selections
7. To develop speaking and listening skills, by completing activities
8. To view images critically and create visual representations

Meeting the Objectives Each selection provides instructional material and portfolio opportunities by which students can meet unit objectives. You will find additional practice pages for reading strategies, literary elements, vocabulary, and grammar in the **Selection Support** booklet in the **Teaching Resources** box.

Setting Goals Work with your students to set goals for unit outcomes. Plan what skills and concepts you wish students to acquire. You may match instruction and activities according to students' performance levels or learning modalities.

Portfolios Students may keep portfolios of their completed work or of their work in progress. The Build Your Portfolio page of each selection provides opportunities for students to apply the concepts presented.

 Humanities: Art

From Sea to Shining Sea, 1990, by Jacqueline Paton

Quilting is the craft of stitching layers of fabric together, usually with a layer of stuffing between. Art quilts use the same basic technique as traditional quilts, but the result is an artistic image for viewing.

How does the quilt represent the idea of the United States as a melting pot? *Students may say that the quilt is made up of pieces of fabric, each with a different pattern, like the different kinds of people who live in the U. S. Also, the quilt includes an image of the country, the flag. The wavy lines may represent different landscapes across the nation.*

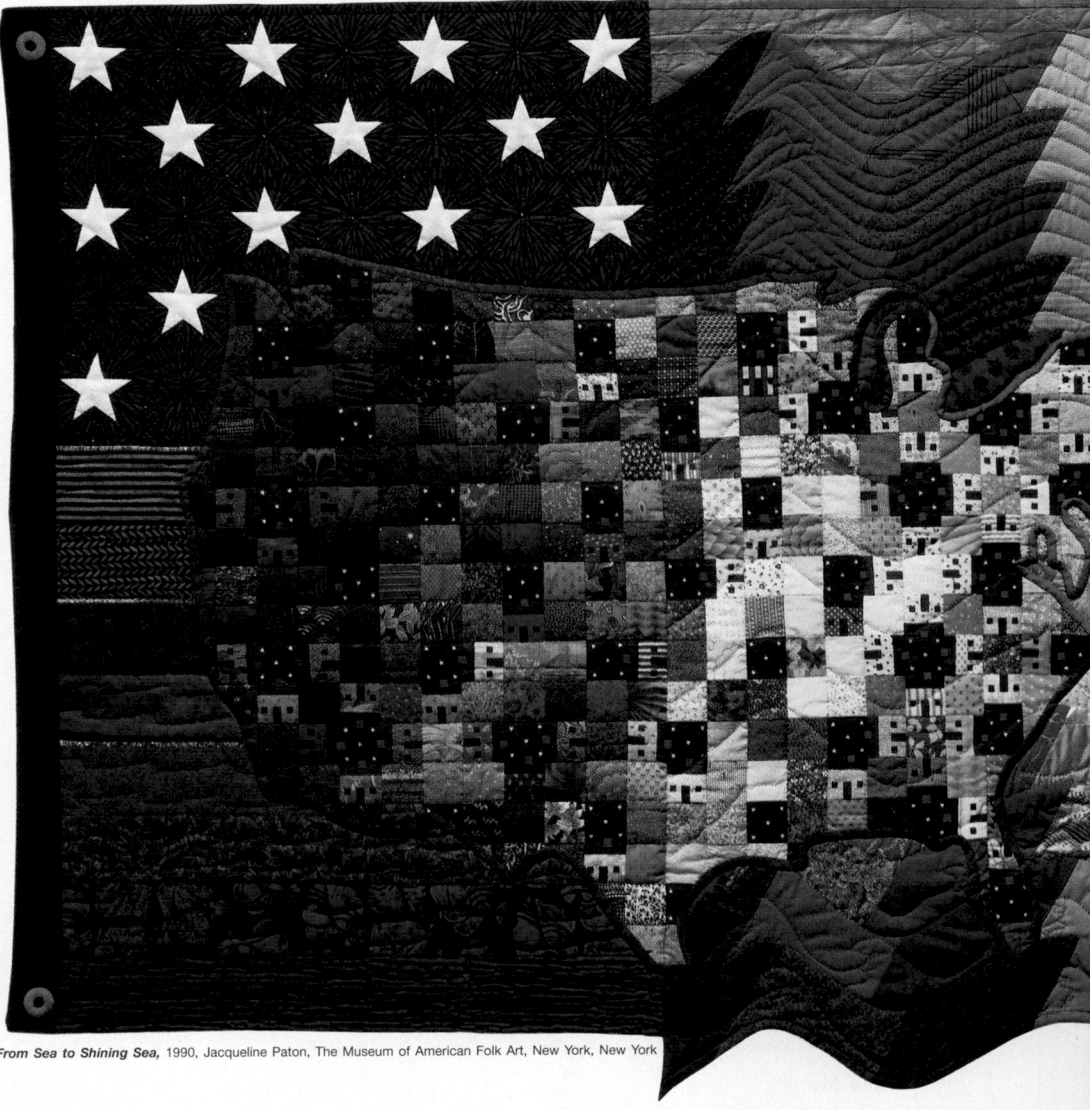

From Sea to Shining Sea, 1990, Jacqueline Paton, The Museum of American Folk Art, New York, New York

Art Transparencies

The **Art Transparencies** booklet in the **Teaching Resources** box offers fine art to help students make connections to other curriculum areas and high-interest topics.

To connect to Unit 4's theme, "From Sea to Shining Sea," use Art Transparency 1, p. 7, *Lotto: The American Dream* by Luis Cruz Azaceta. Like the quilt art on this page, Azaceta's colorful art uses symbols to portray American images. Use one of the booklet's activities to help students explore the art through discussion, writing, or creating their own design of a dream car.

Beyond Literature

Each unit presents Beyond Literature features that lead students into an exploration of careers, communities, and other subject areas. In this unit, students will find out about The March on Washington —a pivotal event of the Civil Rights Movement, explore animal imprinting, and make a science connection. In addition, the **Teaching Resources** box contains a **Beyond Literature** booklet of activities. Using literature as a springboard, these activity pages offer students opportunities to connect literature to other curriculum areas and to the workplace and careers, community, media, and humanities.

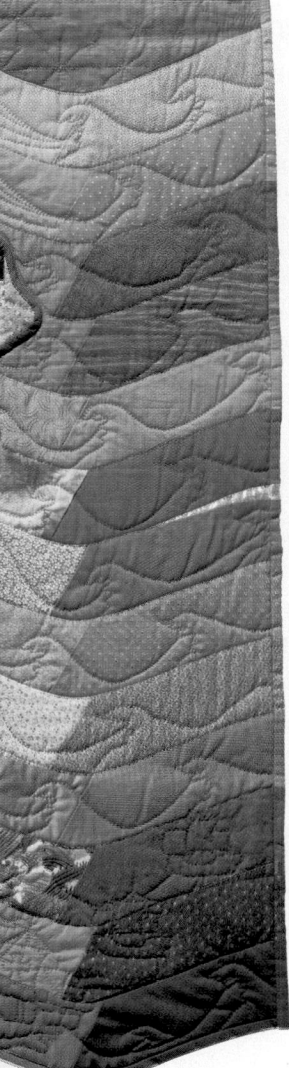

From Sea to Shining Sea

Some people describe the United States as a melting pot, in which people from all cultures blend to become American. Others prefer the image of the United States as a mosaic, in which people retain their original cultural heritage and pride, while sharing the values and beliefs that unite all Americans. No matter whether you choose to celebrate Americans' likenesses or differences, there's no disputing the fact that the United States is a rich nation—both in its people and in its geography and resources. The selections in this unit explore what it means to live in this vast and diverse nation.

◆ 343

Connections

Within this unit, you will find selections and activities that make connections beyond literature. Use these selections to connect students' understanding and appreciation of literature beyond the traditional literature and language arts curriculum.

Encourage students to connect literature to other curriculum areas. You may wish to coordinate with teachers in other curriculum areas to determine ways to team teach and further extend instruction.

Connections to Today's World

Use these selections to guide students to recognize the relevance of literature to contemporary writings. In this unit, students will connect John Steinbeck's Travels With Charley to another writer's observations while traveling the U. S.—from Road Trip USA.

Connecting Literature to Social Studies

Each unit contains a selection that connects Literature to Social Studies. In this unit, students will read about patriotism in the 1800's in the short story, "The Man Without a Country."

Assessing Student Progress

The tools that are available to measure the degree to which students meet the unit objectives are listed below.

Informal Assessment

The questions in the Guide for Responding sections are a first level of response to the concepts and skills presented with the selection. As a brief, informal measure of students' grasp of the material, these responses indicate where further instruction and practice are needed. The practice pages in the **Selection Support** booklet provide for this type of instruction and practice.

You will also find literature and reading guides in the **Alternative Assessment** booklet, which students can use for informal assessment of their individual performances.

Formal Assessment

The **Formal Assessment** booklet contains Selection Tests and Unit Tests.

Selection Tests measure comprehension and skills acquisition for each selection or group of selections.

Each Unit Test provides students with 30 multiple-choice questions and 5 essay questions designed to assess students' knowledge of the literature and skills taught in the unit.

Each Alternative Unit Test: Standardized-Test Practice provides 15 multiple-choice questions and 3 essay questions based on two new literature selections not contained in the student book. The questions on the Alternative Unit Test are designed to assess students' ability to compare and contrast selections, applying skills taught in the unit.

Alternative Assessment

For portfolio and alternative assessment, the **Alternative Assessment** booklet contains Scoring Rubrics, Assessment sheets, and Learning Modalities activities.

Scoring Rubrics provide writing modes that can be applied to Writing activities, Writing Mini-Lessons, and Writing Process Workshop lessons.

Assessment sheets for speaking and listening activities provide peer and self-assessment direction.

Learning Modalities activities appeal to different learning styles. Use these as an alternative measurement of students' growth.

OBJECTIVES

1. To read, comprehend, and interpret a poem
2. To relate oral tradition to personal experience
3. To apply interactive reading strategies
4. To appreciate oral tradition
5. To build vocabulary in context and learn the suffix -eer
6. To develop skill using subordinating conjunctions
7. To write a profile of a legendary figure, using precise language
8. To respond to a poem through writing, speaking and listening, and projects

SKILLS INSTRUCTION

Vocabulary:
Using the Suffix -eer

Spelling:
Plurals of Nouns That End in o

Grammar:
Subordinating Conjunctions

Reading for Success:
Interactive Reading Strategies

Literary Focus:
Oral Tradition

Writing:
Precise Language

Critical Viewing:
Interpret

PORTFOLIO OPPORTUNITIES

Writing: Personal Response; Yarn; Essay

Writing Mini-Lesson: Profile of a Legendary Figure

Speaking and Listening: Memorized Reading; Group Story

Projects: Drawing or Painting; Collection of Folk Tales

More About the Author
Carl Sandburg liked to take walks, watch movies, and collect, compose, and sing folk songs in his deep voice. He was a public figure who knew presidents and the legendary actress Marilyn Monroe, who sent him copies of her poetry. Among Sandburg's many awards was one from the NAACP, citing his civil rights work and naming him a lifetime member. Perhaps his most cherished honor, however, was to have had more than two dozen schools named after him.

Guide for Reading

Meet the Author:
Carl Sandburg (1878–1967)

Born in Galesburg, Illinois, Carl Sandburg became one of the best-known American poets. He often wrote about the lives of ordinary citizens, and his tone was generally upbeat.

A Man of Many Talents Besides being a poet, Sandburg was also a journalist, an author of children's books, and a historian. He won the Pulitzer Prize in 1940 for his six-volume biography of Abraham Lincoln, and he won it again in 1950 for his *Complete Poems*.

THE STORY BEHIND THE POEM

Sandburg's epic poem "The People, Yes" was published in 1936. At that time, the United States was experiencing the Great Depression, a time of economic struggle that began in 1929 and continued until World War II. Like many of Sandburg's other poems, "The People, Yes" celebrates the common people and their courage in facing hard times. Sandburg said of Americans during the Depression, "The people will live on, the people so peculiar in renewal and comeback."

◆ LITERATURE AND YOUR LIFE
CONNECT YOUR EXPERIENCE

Campfires seem to inspire the storyteller in us all. Often, the stories told around a campfire blend reality and fantasy; the listener happily puts reality aside and waits eagerly to find out what will happen. Think about some stories you've told or heard around a campfire or in a similar setting. In "The People, Yes," Carl Sandburg celebrates the tradition of tall tales and legends like those told around a campfire.

THEMATIC FOCUS: From Sea to Shining Sea

"The People, Yes" celebrates the American landscape and people. What characteristics does Sandburg emphasize?

◆ Background for Understanding
CULTURE

In this section of "The People, Yes," Carl Sandburg summarizes the story lines of many different yarns. A yarn is a long, made-up story filled with exaggeration. By describing characteristics or actions that the listener knows are impossible but that are fun to imagine, the teller of a yarn creates humor. Yarns became especially popular during America's pioneer days. People amused each other with yarns that reflected the accomplishments and obstacles faced as they settled an unknown land.

344 ◆ *From Sea to Shining Sea*

 Prentice Hall Literature Program Resources

REINFORCE / RETEACH / EXTEND
Selection Support Pages
Build Vocabulary: Using the Suffix -eer, p. 135
Build Spelling Skills, p. 136
Build Grammar Skills: Subordinating Conjunctions, p. 137
Reading for Success: Interactive Reading Strategies, pp. 138–139
Literary Focus: Oral Tradition, p. 140
Strategies for Diverse Student Needs, pp. 51–52
Beyond Literature Career Connection: How Jobs Change, p. 26

Formal Assessment Selection Test, pp. 106–108
Assessment Resources Software
Alternative Assessment, p. 26
Writing and Language Transparencies
Sensory Language Chart, p. 69
Resource Pro CD-ROM
from "The People, Yes"—includes all resource material and customizable lesson plan

Listening to Literature Audiocassettes
from "The People, Yes"

from The People, Yes

◆ Literary Focus

ORAL TRADITION

The **oral tradition** is the passing of stories, poems, and songs from generation to generation by word of mouth. Most folklore—including yarns, tall tales, and legends—existed long before anyone captured it in writing. In "The People, Yes," Carl Sandburg celebrates the American oral tradition, making reference to many of our nation's best-known and most-loved tales.

◆ Build Vocabulary

SUFFIXES: *-eer*

One of the tales Sandburg describes involves a railroad engineer; another is about mutineers on a ship. Both words contain the suffix *-eer,* which means "a person who makes" or "a person who has to do with." *Engineer* means "someone who operates an engine," and *mutineer* means "one who mutinies, or rebels."

WORD BANK

Which of these words from the poem names summertime pests? Check the Build Vocabulary box on page 347 to see if you chose correctly.

mutineers
runt
mosquitoes
flue

Guide for Reading ◆ 345

Write the word *exaggeration* on the board and tell students that it is an ancient form of humor. Distribute blank index cards to each member of the class. Have each student write the beginning of a sentence that could be completed with exaggeration, such as "He's so happy, . . ." (. . .he's walking on air) or "I'm so musical that . . ." (. . . I snore in 4-part harmony). Collect the cards, mix them up, and redistribute them. Have students complete the sentence starters they get, exaggerating for humorous effect. Introduce the poem by explaining that Carl Sandburg uses well-known American folklore for a humorous and exaggerated effect in the selection they will read.

◆ Build Grammar Skills

Subordinating Conjunctions If you wish to introduce the grammar concept for this selection before students read, refer to the instruction on p. 349.

Customize for
Less Proficient Readers
Point out to students that although this poem may seem long and hard, nearly every line begins with "Of . . ." and is a short example of an exaggerated yarn. Suggest that students jot down a word to capture the essence of each yarn, such as: It's about: speed, size, hunger, or nature.

Customize for
More Advanced Students
Folklore yarns certainly entertain, but they may be told for other purposes as well. Have students think of reasons besides humor for a storyteller to use exaggeration, such as to teach, warn, or emphasize. Challenge students to select lines from the poem to use as examples.

Customize for
English Language Learners
The images in this poem represent a wide range of American landscapes. Help students understand and better appreciate some of the images by showing photos of the actual places or things mentioned. Examples include the Mississippi River, the Rocky Mountains, a redwood forest, a cyclone, or rattlesnakes.

Preparing for Standardized Tests

Reading The interactive reading strategies presented with this selection may help students to answer reading comprehension items on standardized tests. One strategy reminds students to envision what the writer is saying to gain understanding. Suggest that students use this strategy to answer the following sample test question, based on the excerpt from "The People, Yes":
Read and picture this line:

"Of the old man's whiskers: 'When the wind was with him his whiskers arrived a day before he did . . .' "

The poet means that the old man:

(A) braided his whiskers
(B) enjoyed walking on windy days
(C) had an extremely long beard
(D) mailed his whiskers to the next town

Students might envision this scene to see that the old man has such long whiskers that when it was windy, the wind makes them sail out ahead of him like a long banner. Therefore, *(C)* is the best answer. For further practice, use Reading for Success: Interactive Reading Strategies in **Selection Support,** pp. 138–139.

The Reading for Success page in each unit presents a set of problem-solving strategies to help readers understand authors' words and ideas on multiple levels. Good readers develop a bank of strategies from which they can draw as needed.

Unit 4 introduces interactive reading strategies. Students must interact with a work before they apply higher-level critical thinking strategies. These strategies for interactive reading give readers an array of approaches for mastering a text: Envision what the writer is saying, use your prior knowledge, clarify, and respond.

These interactive reading strategies are modeled with an excerpt from "The People, Yes." Each green box shows an example of the thinking process involved in applying one of these strategies. Additional notes provide support for applying these strategies throughout the selection.

How to Use the Reading for Success Page

- Introduce the interactive reading strategies, presenting each as a problem-solving procedure.

- Before students read the selection, have them preview it, looking at the annotations in the green boxes that model the strategies.

- To reinforce these strategies after students have read the selection, have them use Reading for Success, pp. 138–139, in **Selection Support.** These pages give students an opportunity to read a selection and practice interactive reading strategies by writing their own annotations.

Reading Strategies: Support and Reinforcement

Using Boxed Annotations and Prompts

Throughout the unit, the notes in green, red, and maroon are intended to help students apply reading strategies, understand the literary focus, and make a connection with their lives. You may use boxed material in these ways:

- Have students pause at each box and respond to its prompt before they continue reading.

- Urge students to read through the selection, ignoring the boxes. After they complete the selection, they may go back and review the text, responding to the prompts.

346

Reading for Success

Interactive Reading Strategies

Interactive computer games are fun because you take a real role in the proceedings. Interactive reading is similar: When you participate in your reading, the experience becomes fuller, richer, and more fun. Use these reading strategies to help you interact with your reading:

Envision what the writer is saying.

Use the details a writer provides, along with your own imagination and experience, to picture in your mind the people, places, objects, and events the writer describes. To help you do so, be on the lookout for sensory details—details that capture sights, sounds, tastes, smells, or physical sensations.

Use your prior knowledge.

Draw from your own knowledge and experience as you read. For example, you might use what you've learned about history to help you understand a story with a historical setting. Similarly, your knowledge of geography might help you appreciate the magnitude of one of the amazing accomplishments described in Sandburg's poem.

Passage:	**My Knowledge:**
Of the man who drove a swarm of bees across the Rocky Mountains . . .	The Rocky Mountain range is the tallest in the continental United States.

Clarify.

It's not unusual to come across confusing passages or words in your reading. Take time to clarify the details or information through the following strategies:
- Reread the passage slowly and carefully.
- Draw on prior knowledge to help you puzzle out the confusing section.
- Read ahead to see whether information there will clarify the confusion.

Respond.

Allow yourself to respond to what's happening or being described. Question the characters' actions, react to settings, and experience suspense or joy as the story, essay, or poem unfolds.

As you read this section from "The People, Yes," look at the notes in the boxes on each page. The notes demonstrate how to apply these strategies to a work of literature.

Model a Reading Strategy: Ask Questions

Tell students that as they read, they should use the writer's descriptions to envision events, characters, and settings in their own minds. Details that provide sensory clues, students' own personal experiences and prior knowledge, along with creativity, will help them picture what the writer is describing with words. Ask students to read the first two lines of the selection from "The People, Yes." Demonstrate how to envision what the writer is saying by modeling the process for students.

As I read these lines from the poem, I imagine the tallest building I've ever seen—the World Trade Center in New York City. I picture it with hinges like a draw bridge to raise and lower the top to let the moon pass over it (I also picture the moon crashing into the top of the World Trade Center and getting stuck because the moon couldn't get past).

Point out to students that when they envision what the writer is saying, they should use their own imagination and experience to help picture the writer's descriptions. In this selection, picturing details will increase their appreciation and enjoyment of the humorous exaggeration used by Carl Sandburg.

from THE PEOPLE, YES

MODEL

Carl Sandburg

❶ They have yarns
Of a skyscraper so tall they had to put hinges
On the two top stories so to let the moon go by,
Of one corn crop in Missouri when the roots
❷ 5   Went so deep and drew off so much water
The Mississippi riverbed that year was dry,
Of pancakes so thin they had only one side,
Of "a fog so thick we shingled the barn and six feet
    out on the fog,"
Of Pecos Pete straddling a cyclone in Texas and
    riding it to the west coast where "it rained out
    under him,"
10   Of the man who drove a swarm of bees across
    the Rocky Mountains and the Desert "and didn't
    lose a bee,"
Of a mountain railroad curve where the engineer
    in his cab can touch the caboose and spit in the
    conductor's eye,
Of the boy who climbed a cornstalk growing so fast
    he would have starved to death if they hadn't
    shot biscuits up to him,
Of the old man's whiskers: "When
    the wind was with him his whiskers
    arrived a day before he did,"
Of the hen laying a square egg and
    cackling, "Ouch!" and of hens laying
    eggs with the dates printed on them,
15   Of the ship captain's shadow: it froze to the deck
    one cold winter night,
Of mutineers on that same ship put to chipping
    rust with rubber hammers,
Of the sheep counter who was fast
    and accurate: "I just count their feet
    and divide by four,"
Of the man so tall he must climb a
    ladder to shave himself,
Of the runt so teeny-weeny it takes
    two men and a boy to see him,
20   Of mosquitoes: one can kill a dog, two of them
    a man,
Of a cyclone that sucked cookstoves out of
    the kitchen, up the chimney flue, and on to
    the next town,

> To enjoy the humor in this passage, **envision** the wind blowing the old man's whiskers.

> To **clarify** the meaning of this passage, **reread** it or use your **prior knowledge** of division.

Paul Bunyan, Rockwell Kent

▲ **Critical Viewing** Which aspects of this illustration of Paul Bunyan are realistic? Which aspects are exaggerated? [Interpret] **❸**

◆ Build Vocabulary

mutineers (my$\overline{oo}t'$ ən irz′) *n.*: People on a ship who revolt against their officers

runt (runt) *n.*: The smallest animal in a litter

mosquitoes (mə skēt′ ōz) *n.*: Insects having two wings, the females of which extract blood from animals and people

flue (fl$\overline{oo}$) *n.*: The pipe in a chimney that leads the smoke outside

from The People, Yes ◆ 347

Develop Understanding

One-Minute Insight

In this excerpt from "The People, Yes," poet Carl Sandburg affirms his love for America as a land of variety. Using folktales and yarns as varied as its people, the poem lists some of the exploits of well-known characters from American folklore, such as Pecos Pete, Paul Bunyan, and John Henry. Sandburg also uses other humorous exaggerations.

◆ Literary Focus

❶ Oral Tradition The excerpt opens with the words, "They have yarns . . ." Ask students whom *they* refers to. *They* are storytellers—people who passed along yarns by word of mouth or *they* are the American people who listen to the storytellers.

Reading for Success

❷ Clarify Students can better grasp the boastful nature of this image if they clarify the relationship between Missouri and the Mississippi River, which forms the state's eastern border. Corn roots deep enough to dry the Mississippi (a very wide and long river) would be incredibly long.

▶ Critical Viewing ◀

❸ Interpret Bunyan looks and dresses like a logger, and holds an ax as a logger realistically would. But, he is enormously big, compared with the landscape, the people, the houses, and the trees in the scene.

Customize for *Bodily/Kinesthetic Learners*

Invite students to read this excerpt aloud, using suitable gestures and vocal or facial expressions that highlight the boastful humor and exaggeration of the yarns.

Customize for *Logical/Mathematical Learners*

Have students study a map of the United States to locate the places Carl Sandburg mentions in his poem. For example: the Rocky Mountains, the states of Missouri, Texas, California, Nebraska, and the Dakotas, and the Mississippi River.

 Humanities: Art

Paul Bunyan, 1941, by Rockwell Kent
  American painter and graphic artist Rockwell Kent (1882–1971) began his career doing architectural drafting, but soon changed to fine art. His works use powerful imagery, masses of color, and striking lines in a highly stylized fashion. Point out to students the style elements in this picture that indicate the artist had a drafting background, such as the clean lines and angles, the chiseled effect of the hatched shading, and stark white background of the sky. Use the following questions for discussion:

1. Based on this picture, what is your impression of Paul Bunyan? *Students may say that his stance, massive neck and hands, and facial expression show determination and strength.*
2. What clues does Kent give about Paul's size? *He is standing above normal-sized men in the valley; the comparison of these figures to Paul shows that he is very large.*
3. Ask students to read line 30 of the poem, which refers to Paul Bunyan. What character is missing from the illustration? *Paul Bunyan's big blue ox, Babe.*

347

1 Use Your Prior Knowledge

Students may know that California redwoods are the largest trees that grow in North America. Those who have been to Yosemite National Park or have seen pictures of it may know that early visitors cut tunnels in the trunks of some giant redwoods so wagons could pass through them. Knowing this can help students appreciate the humor of line 26: Redwoods are big, but not big enough to swallow up a herd of cattle.

Reinforce and Extend

Answers

◆ LITERATURE AND YOUR LIFE

Reader's Response Students may list individuals, such as Pecos Pete, Paul Bunyan, and John Henry, or events, such as cyclones or swarms of bees.

Thematic Focus Like the United States itself, the poem features a variety of characters and events in a bold, lively, energetic, and ever-changing world.

☑ Check Your Comprehension

1. Its subject is yarns about America and American folk heroes.
2. Examples of exaggerated height are the skyscraper and the man who climbed a ladder to shave. Examples of fantastic speed are the fast-growing cornstalk, and trains that reach stations before their whistles do.

◆ Critical Thinking

1. They are characters that are exaggerated.
2. The hammer swing forms a shape like that of a rainbow.
3. They were imaginative, had a sense of humor, and laughed in the face of possible disasters.
4. It's entertaining to tell a good story; it is empowering to make fun of the aspects of life that can, in reality, be deadly.
5. Possible answer: Those areas are less populated, so stories about them could be wildly exaggerated.

Your prior knowledge of geography will help you to appreciate the humor created by the exaggerated distance.

Of the same cyclone picking up wagontracks in Nebraska and dropping them over in the Dakotas,

Of the hook-and-eye snake[1] unlocking itself into forty pieces, each piece two inches long, then in nine seconds flat snapping itself together again,

Of the watch swallowed by the cow—when they butchered her a year later the watch was running and had the correct time,

25 Of horned snakes, hoop snakes that roll themselves where they want to go, and rattlesnakes carrying bells instead of rattles on their tails,

1 Of the herd of cattle in California getting lost in a giant redwood tree that had hollowed out,

Of the man who killed a snake by putting its tail in its mouth so it swallowed itself,

Of railroad trains whizzing along so fast they reach the station before the whistle,

You may respond to this line with a chuckle or a groan.

Of pigs so thin the farmer had to tie knots in their tails to keep them from crawling through the cracks in their pens,

30 Of Paul Bunyan's big blue ox, Babe, measuring between the eyes forty-two ax-handles and a plug of Star tobacco exactly,

Of John Henry's hammer and the curve of its swing and his singing of it as "a rainbow round my shoulder."

1. hook-and-eye snake: Here, a snake that is fastened together with metal hooks.

Guide for Responding

◆ LITERATURE AND YOUR LIFE

Reader's Response Which of the subjects in the tall tales that Sandburg mentions would you like to hear more about? Why?

Thematic Focus In what way does this poem reveal the character of the people of the United States?

☑ Check Your Comprehension

1. How would you describe the subject matter of "The People, Yes"?
2. Identify two yarns that involve exaggerated heights and two yarns that involve fantastic speed.

◆ Critical Thinking

INTERPRET
1. What characteristics do the people, animals, and things in these yarns share? **[Connect]**
2. What does John Henry mean when he describes the swing of his hammer as "a rainbow round my shoulder"? **[Interpret]**
3. What do the yarns suggest about the people who told them? **[Infer]**

APPLY
4. Why do you think people take pleasure in spinning yarns? **[Speculate]**

EXTEND
5. Why do you think most of these yarns are set in the Midwest and West? **[Social Studies Link]**

348 ◆ From Sea to Shining Sea

 Beyond the Selection

FURTHER READING
Other Works by Carl Sandburg
Paul Bunyan of the North Woods
The Complete Poems of Carl Sandburg
Other Tall Tales
Pecos Bill: The Cyclone, Harold W. Felton
Hammerman, Adrien Stoutenburg
Tussle With a Bear, Davy Crockett

INTERNET
We suggest the following site on the Internet (all Web sites are subject to change).
    For more information about Carl Sandburg:
http://alexia.lis.uiuc.edu/~roberts/carlpage.htm
    We *strongly recommend* that you preview the site before you send students to it.

Guide for Responding (continued)

◆ Reading for Success

INTERACTIVE READING STRATEGIES

Review the reading strategies and the notes that show how to interact with your reading. Then, answer these questions:

1. Name one detail from the selection that you clarified.
2. How does your prior knowledge of trains help you understand the passage about the mountain railroad curve?
3. To which passage did you have the strongest response? Why?

◆ Build Vocabulary

USING THE SUFFIX -eer

The suffix -eer can be added to words to form nouns like *engineer*. Add the suffix -eer to these words. Then, use each of the words you created in a sentence.

1. ballad   2. musket   3. profit

SPELLING STRATEGY

Follow these rules to make plurals of nouns that end in o:

- For most nouns ending in an o that follows a vowel, add -s:

  radio + -s = radios   rodeo + -s = rodeos

- For most nouns ending in an o that follows a consonant, add -es:

  mosquito + -es = mosquitoes

- To form plurals of musical terms, add -s:

  piano + -s = pianos   solo + -s = solos

On your paper, write the plurals of the following:

1. potato   2. studio   3. zero   4. concerto

USING THE WORD BANK

On your paper, write the word from the Word Bank that best completes each statement.

1. A chimney _____?_____ can become clogged.
2. The bites of some _____?_____ can cause disease.
3. The puppy was the _____?_____ of the litter.
4. _____?_____ are people who disobey a captain's orders.

◆ Literary Focus

ORAL TRADITION

In the **oral tradition,** stories are passed from one generation to another by word of mouth. In "The People, Yes," Carl Sandburg summarizes stories from the American oral tradition, many of which are based on real events, like settling the frontier or encountering strange new animals.

1. In the yarn about corn crops, would it make a difference if the storyteller substituted the Missouri River for the Mississippi? Explain.
2. In the yarn about cyclones, what elements do you think are true? Which are invented?
3. Find two yarns that reveal the dangers of nature. Find two that reveal the need for hard work.

◆ Build Grammar Skills

SUBORDINATING CONJUNCTIONS

A conjunction connects words or groups of words. A **subordinating conjunction** connects two ideas by making one dependent on the other.

Although the mountain lion was strong, it was not as strong as Paul Bunyan.

Common Subordinating Conjunctions:
after, although, as, because, before, if, since, when, where, whenever, wherever, while, unless, until

Practice Rewrite these sentences, underlining the subordinating conjunctions.

1. The boy would have starved to death if they hadn't shot biscuits up to him.
2. The cattle kept running until they reached California.
3. The horse couldn't keep up with Bill although it tried.
4. The herd got lost because the tree was hollow.
5. People stared whenever they saw Babe.

Writing Application On your paper, join each pair of sentences with a subordinating conjunction.

1. The snake hissed. It heard the wind.
2. He played the guitar. The rabbit fell asleep.
3. He pulled on his boots. He waded into the river.

from *The People, Yes* ◆ 349

✎ Writer's Solution

For additional instruction and practice, use the lesson in the *Writer's Solution Language Lab CD-ROM* on conjunctions. You may also use The Conjunction page, p. 27 in the *Writer's Solution Grammar Practice Book*.

Answers

◆ Reading Strategy

1. Students might list cyclones, chipping rust with rubber hammers, or killer mosquitoes.
2. Train tracks had to curve or switch back to allow slow, heavy trains to make it up and over steep mountains.
3. Students might respond to the passage about snakes, or to the exaggerated natural facts, such as hens laying square eggs, and extremely thin pigs.

◆ Build Vocabulary

Using the Suffix -eer
1. balladeer; Carl Sandburg was an American balladeer.
2. musketeer; Some Civil War soldiers were crack musketeers.
3. profiteer; The greedy profiteer tripled prices after the flood.

Spelling Strategy
1. potatoes; 2. studios; 3. zeroes; 4. concertos

Using the Word Bank
1. flue; 2. mosquitoes; 3. runt; 4. mutineers

◆ Literary Focus

1. No; the idea of corn stalk roots draining a major river is ridiculous, no matter which river is named.
2. Nebraska really has cyclones, but they cannot pick up wagontracks or suck stoves out the small chimney flue.
3. Natural dangers include: thick fog, cyclones, swarms of bees, cold winter nights, and snakes; yarns about hard work include the ones about the mutineers, the sheep counter, and farming.

◆ Build Grammar Skills

Practice
1. if; 2. until; 3. although; 4. because; 5. whenever

Writing Application
Possible responses:
1. The snake hissed whenever it heard the wind.
2. He played the guitar after the rabbit fell asleep.
3. He pulled on his boots before he waded into the river.

Idea Bank

Following are suggestions for matching the Idea Bank topics with your students' performance levels and learning modalities:

Customize for
Performance Levels
Less Advanced Students: 1, 4, 5, 6
Average Students: 2, 4, 5, 6, 7
More Advanced Students: 3, 4, 5, 6, 7

Customize for
Learning Modalities
Verbal/Linguistic: 1, 2, 3, 4, 5, 7
Visual/Spatial: 6, 7
Bodily/Kinesthetic: 4
Musical/Rhythmic: 4
Interpersonal: 4, 5, 7
Intrapersonal: 1, 2, 3, 6

Writing Mini-Lesson

Refer students to the Writing Handbook in the back of the book for instruction on the writing process and for further information on using precise language. Have students use the Sensory Language Chart, p. 69 in **Writing and Language Transparencies,** to organize vivid images.

Writer's Solution

Writers at Work Videodisc
Have students view the videodisc segment on Description (Ch. 2), featuring Rosie McNulty, to see how she develops sensory details.

Play frames 24273 to 26446

Writing Lab CD-ROM
Have students complete the tutorial on Narration. Follow these steps:
1. Play the introduction to narrative writing to help students see narrative writing as a form of storytelling.
2. Have students work through the prewriting section that develops narrative elements.
3. Have them draft on computer.
4. Have students use the interactive guide on strengthening character and the revision checker for language variety as they edit.

Writer's Solution Sourcebook
Have students use Chapter 3, "Narration," pp. 70–103, for more support. The chapter includes in-depth instruction on using vivid adjectives and adverbs, pp. 97–98.

Build Your Portfolio

Idea Bank

Writing

1. **Personal Response** Write a journal entry in which you share your reactions to this poem—what you liked and disliked about it. Use details from the poem to support your responses.

2. **Yarn** Choose a passage from "The People, Yes" that presents a situation that you find especially interesting. Then, use your imagination to develop a complete yarn that tells a story based on the details Sandburg describes.

3. **Essay** Write a brief essay in which you explain what Sandburg's poem suggests about the United States and its people. Use details from the poem for support.

Speaking and Listening

4. **Memorized Reading** Memorize a passage from the poem, and recite it to the class using gestures and inflections suitable to the poem. You may wish to work with a classmate, with each of you memorizing parts of the poem. **[Performing Arts Link]**

5. **Group Story [Group Activity]** Sit in a circle with two classmates and tape-record a tall tale that you create. One person should begin the tale, and the next should add to it. The last person should complete the story. Play the recording for the class. **[Media Link]**

Projects

6. **Drawing or Painting** Use one or more images from the poem as an inspiration for a drawing or painting. In your artwork, convey the folk quality of a tall tale, yarn, or legend. **[Art Link]**

7. **Collection of Folk Tales [Group Activity]** With a group, brainstorm for tall tales like those told of Paul Bunyan and John Henry. Each group member can locate copies of the tall tales and photocopy them. Collect the tales in a book, and display it for the class to read.

Writing Mini-Lesson

Profile of a Legendary Figure

If a legendary figure like Pecos Pete or John Henry were alive today, you'd probably read profiles about him or her in magazines. A profile is an article that offers a close-up look at an interesting personality. It usually includes biographical information and interesting stories about the person's life.

Write a profile of a legendary figure—either a real person, such as Michael Jordan, or a fictional character, such as John Henry.

**Writing Skills Focus:
Precise Language**

Use **precise language** to create a vivid picture of your subject for your readers. Carl Sandburg includes precise language in this description of Pecos Pete:

Model From the Poem
Of Pecos Pete straddling a cyclone in Texas and riding it to the west coast where "it rained out under him."

Prewriting To find out about a fictional subject's background, read stories and poems about him or her. If it's a real person, jot down information about his or her life. Then, focus your profile by deciding on one aspect of the person's life to cover.

Drafting First, introduce your subject to your readers. In the body, include anecdotes, quotations, and details about what makes your person legendary. End with a summary statement that reinforces the focus of the profile.

◆ **Grammar Application**
Use subordinating conjunctions to join sentences in which one idea is dependent on the other.

Revising As you revise, replace general statements and descriptions with precise language that presents a vivid portrait of your subject.

✓ ASSESSMENT OPTIONS

Formal Assessment, Selection Test, pp. 106–108, and Assessment Resources Software. The selection test is designed so that it can be easily customized to the performance levels of your students.

Alternative Assessment, p. 26, includes options for less advanced students, more advanced students, visual/spatial learners, interpersonal learners, musical/rhythmic learners, logical/mathematical learners, and verbal/linguistic learners.

PORTFOLIO ASSESSMENT
Use the following rubrics in the **Alternative Assessment** booklet to assess student writing:
Personal Response: Response to Literature, p. 106
Yarn: Fictional Narrative, p. 91
Essay: Literary Analysis/Interpretation, p. 108
Writing Mini-Lesson: Description, p. 93

PART **1**   *A Land of Promise*

July Hay, 1942, Thomas Hart Benton, The Metropolitan Museum of Art, New York, NY/© T. H. Benton and R. P. Benton Testamentary Trusts/Licensed by VAGA, New York, NY.

A Land of Promise ◆ 351

One-Minute
Planning Guide

The selections in this section explore "A Land of Promise." "Travels with Charley" details John Steinbeck's rediscovery of America. "The New Colossus" is a poem about the promises America offers to immigrants. In the poem "Ellis Island," Joseph Bruchac tells the story of his immigrant parents. Former governor Mario Cuomo describes the journey of his parents' immigration in "Achieving the American Dream." Alice Walker honors an American hero and relates the story of her ancestors in "Choice: A Tribute to Martin Luther King, Jr." Finally, "The Man Without a Country" is a short story that examines patriotism.

Customize for
Varying Student Needs

When assigning the selections in this section to your students, keep in mind the following factors:

"Travels with Charley"
• An excerpt from a travel essay by John Steinbeck
• Students may need help with vocabulary

"The New Colossus"
• Famous sonnet whose lines are inscribed on the Statue of Liberty
• Students may need help with language

"Ellis Island"
• Short poem by Joseph Bruchac
• Gives voice to the poet's Slovak parents as well as the Native American viewpoint

"Achieving the American Dream"
• Mario Cuomo's story of his parents' immigration and his definition of the American dream

"A Tribute to Dr. Martin Luther King, Jr."
• A speech made by Alice Walker commemorating the civil rights movement and Martin Luther King, Jr.
• Includes a Beyond Literature social studies connection about the Civil Rights Movement

"The Man Without a Country"
• Longer story (13 pp.)
• Provides an opportunity for connecting literature to social studies

 Humanities: Art

July Hay, 1942, by Thomas Hart Benton
     Thomas Hart Benton (1899–1975) was one of America's leading Regionalist painters. Born in Missouri, Benton studied at the Art Institute of Chicago, and later, in Paris. In World War II, he served as an architectural draftsman and made several trips through the South and Midwest. The sketches he made on those trips served as the foundation for his later paintings. Most of Benton's subjects are characters from rural towns, exploring the dramatization of American themes. Benton is famous for being the teacher

of abstract expressionist painter Jackson Pollack.
     Have students study the painting and then ask the following questions:
1. What are the men in this painting doing? *The men are cutting hay with scythes.*
2. What does this painting show you about "A Land of Promise"? *Some students may say that the painting shows an American landscape—farmers working on the land; the work of harvesting is full of promise because it is the result of the farmer's planting earlier in the year and provides food.*

351

Guide for Reading

OBJECTIVES

1. To read, comprehend, and interpret a travel essay
2. To relate a travel essay to personal experience
3. To clarify details
4. To appreciate a travel essay
5. To build vocabulary in context and learn the suffix *-ic*
6. To develop skill in using coordinating conjunctions
7. To write a travel journal entry, using supporting details
8. To respond to an essay through writing, speaking and listening, and projects

SKILLS INSTRUCTION

Vocabulary:
Suffixes: *-ic*

Spelling:
qu Spelling of *kw* Sound

Grammar:
Coordinating Conjunctions

Reading Strategy:
Clarify Details

Literary Focus:
Travel Essay

Writing:
Use Supporting Details

Speaking and Listening:
Panel Discussion (Teacher Edition)

Critical Viewing:
Relate; Analyze

PORTFOLIO OPPORTUNITIES

Writing: Charley's Journal; Guidebook Description; Essay

Writing Mini-Lesson: Travel Journal Entry

Speaking and Listening: Radio Commentary; Panel Discussion

Projects: Map; Documentary Script

More About the Author
John Steinbeck wrote about subjects other than social injustice, although he is best known for his sympathetic novels and stories about the downtrodden. During World War II, he was a war correspondent and also wrote several pieces of government propaganda, including *The Moon is Down,* a novel about Nazi-occupied Norway. Steinbeck also wrote movie scripts, of which *Viva Zapata!* is an example.

Meet the Author:

John Steinbeck (1902–1968)

When John Steinbeck received the Nobel Prize for Literature in 1962, it capped a long, successful career in which he established himself as one of our nation's best-loved and most highly regarded writers.

Voice of the Working Class Steinbeck grew up in the Salinas Valley of California, where he became aware of the hard lives of migrant farm workers. After college, he spent five years drifting and writing; he even joined a hobo camp to study the lives of its people. His Pulitzer Prize-winning novel *The Grapes of Wrath* and the novels *Of Mice and Men* and *The Pearl* express sympathy for poor people who are exploited by society.

THE STORY BEHIND THE STORY

Although he had been acclaimed as one of the foremost writers of America's heartland, Steinbeck worried that he had lost touch with the country and its people. He decided to reestablish his ties by driving east to west—from Maine to California—along a northern route. He returned to New York along the southern route, passing through the Mohave Desert, Texas, and the Deep South. Steinbeck published an account of his travels entitled *Travels with Charley,* in 1962. The book's subtitle was "In Search of America."

352 ◆ *From Sea to Shining Sea*

◆ LITERATURE AND YOUR LIFE

CONNECT YOUR EXPERIENCE

Think for a moment of trips you've taken—to another country, state, or region. Did the people you meet have attitudes, beliefs, or ways of speaking different from your own? In *Travels with Charley,* John Steinbeck sets out to meet people all across the United States and learns about their different views of life in the process.

THEMATIC FOCUS: A Land of Promise

As you follow Steinbeck on his journey, ask yourself what qualities make the United States "a land of promise" for people from all regions of the land.

◆ Background for Understanding

GEOGRAPHY

As Steinbeck travels through the western United States, he finds himself in the Badlands of North Dakota. Located in the western parts of both North and South Dakota, the Badlands are a rugged region of fantastically shaped rock formations separated by valleys. In that barren landscape, there is little vegetation to prevent the erosion of the soft sedimentary rocks. The elevation of the Badlands is between 2,000 and 5,000 feet.

◆ Build Vocabulary

SUFFIXES: *-ic*

The suffix *-ic* means "like" or "having to do with." The word *diagnostic,* therefore, means "having to do with a diagnosis"—the study of facts.

WORD BANK

Which word from the story do you think might mean "the act of inquiring"? Check the Build Vocabulary box on page 356 to see if you chose correctly.

Word Bank
diagnostic
peripatetic
rigorous
maneuver
inquiry
inexplicable
celestial

 Prentice Hall Literature Program Resources

REINFORCE / RETEACH / EXTEND
Selection Support Pages
Build Vocabulary: Suffixes: *-ic,* p. 141
Build Spelling Skills, p. 142
Build Grammar Skills: Coordinating Conjunctions, p. 143
Reading Strategy: Clarify Details, p. 144
Literary Focus: Travel Essay, p. 145
Strategies for Diverse Student Needs, pp. 53–54
Beyond Literature Career Connection: Travel Writer, p. 27

Formal Assessment Selection Test, pp. 109–111, Assessment Resources Software
Alternative Assessment, p. 27
Writing and Language Transparencies, Main Idea and Supporting Details Organizer, p. 61
Resource Pro CD-R⊘M
from *Travels with Charley*—includes all resource material and customizable lesson plan

🎧 **Listening to Literature Audiocassettes** from *Travels with Charley*

from Travels with Charley

Interest Grabber Ask students the following question: *If you were going to take a long car trip, what kind of traveling companion would you enjoy having?* Have students list characteristics of a good companion, for example: doesn't talk too much and likes adventure. Give students time to create a newspaper want ad for a travel companion. Invite volunteers to read their ads aloud, or post the ads in the classroom. Invite students to read the selection to see how—or if—Charley fills the bill.

◆ Build Grammar Skills

Coordinating Conjunctions If you wish to introduce the grammar concept for this selection before students read, refer to the instruction on p. 362.

Customize for
Less Proficient Readers
The selection has quite a few long or complicated sentences, some of which contain grammatical complexities, such as subordinate clauses. Many of the sentences contain intermediate punctuation, such as commas, dashes, and semicolons. Encourage students to reread any confusing sentences, and to break apart long ones for ease of understanding.

Customize for
More Advanced Students
Have students look for evidence that this selection is the work of a legendary American writer, and not a typical travel brochure or essay on travel. Guide them to notice the author's use of descriptive language, personification, ordinary language used in unexpected combinations and contexts, and rich, humorous descriptions and comparisons.

◆ Literary Focus
TRAVEL ESSAY
An essay is a short nonfiction work about a particular subject. A **travel essay** focuses on a trip or journey that someone actually made. In it, the writer may include factual information as well as descriptions that reveal how a place looks, sounds, or feels. It is, however, the writer's personal impressions and reflections that make the essay unique.

◆ Reading Strategy
CLARIFY DETAILS
When you don't completely understand a passage in a travel essay or other piece of writing, take time to stop and **clarify** what is not clear. Sometimes, this may simply involve pausing to think about the meaning of a detail. Other times, it may be necessary to reread a portion of the text or read ahead to piece together the meaning of something. Sometimes, it may even be necessary to go outside the text to find out what something means. Fill out a chart like the one below to clarify details as you read.

Detail to Clarify	Meaning of Detail	Strategy Used: Pause, Read Ahead, Read Back, Use Other Source

Guide for Reading ◆ 353

Preparing for Standardized Tests

Reading This selection presents suggestions for clarifying details (a strategy for interactive reading) that will help students with all of their reading, and as they answer reading comprehension items on standardized tests. Students may need to find clues within text and use prior knowledge in order to decide whether a statement is true or not. After they read the excerpt from *Travels with Charley*, present this sample test question:

According to the selection, which of the following statements is not true?

(A) Bringing the fishing and hunting equipment turned out to be an unnecessary precaution.

(B) Steinbeck was inspired by the views of Mount Rushmore in the late afternoon.

(C) Some of the people Steinbeck and Charley met in the Badlands were talkative.

(D) Nobody recognized Steinbeck, or at least none of them let on if they did.

Review the statements and have students reread and clarify details to determine that the statements in *(A), (C),* and *(D)* are true, so *(B)* is the best answer to the question—this excerpt does not state that Steinbeck visited Mount Rushmore. Point out the negative format of this question (which . . . is *not* . . . ?) which can sometimes be confusing. It is a good idea to reread negative questions to be sure of choosing correct answers. For more practice, use Reading Strategy in **Selection Support,** p. 144.

353

One-Minute Insight

The author outfits a truck, takes his dog, and sets out on a driving journey to rediscover America and the American people. In this first-person excerpt from John Steinbeck's *Travels with Charley,* the author describes the very beginning of his trip, including his mental and physical preparations. The selection then describes the portion of the travels that took the traveler and his companion through the Badlands of North Dakota.

Team Teaching Strategy

The geographical and travel aspects of this essay provide an opportunity for connections to the social studies curriculum. You may want to coordinate with a social studies teacher to extend instruction.

Customize for
English Language Learners

This selection contains several examples of common words used in uncommon ways or in unexpected combinations. Examples include "monster land" and "rabbity wind." Encourage students to work with partners to find other examples of uncommon usage and discuss the meanings.

Customize for
Visual/Spatial Learners

Invite students to scan the selection and study the photos of the landscape. Have them respond to these images; students can express the feelings the vistas evoke, or they can make inferences about the topic or tone of the piece. Later, students can think about what impact the illustrations have on what they are reading.

from Travels with Charley

John Steinbeck

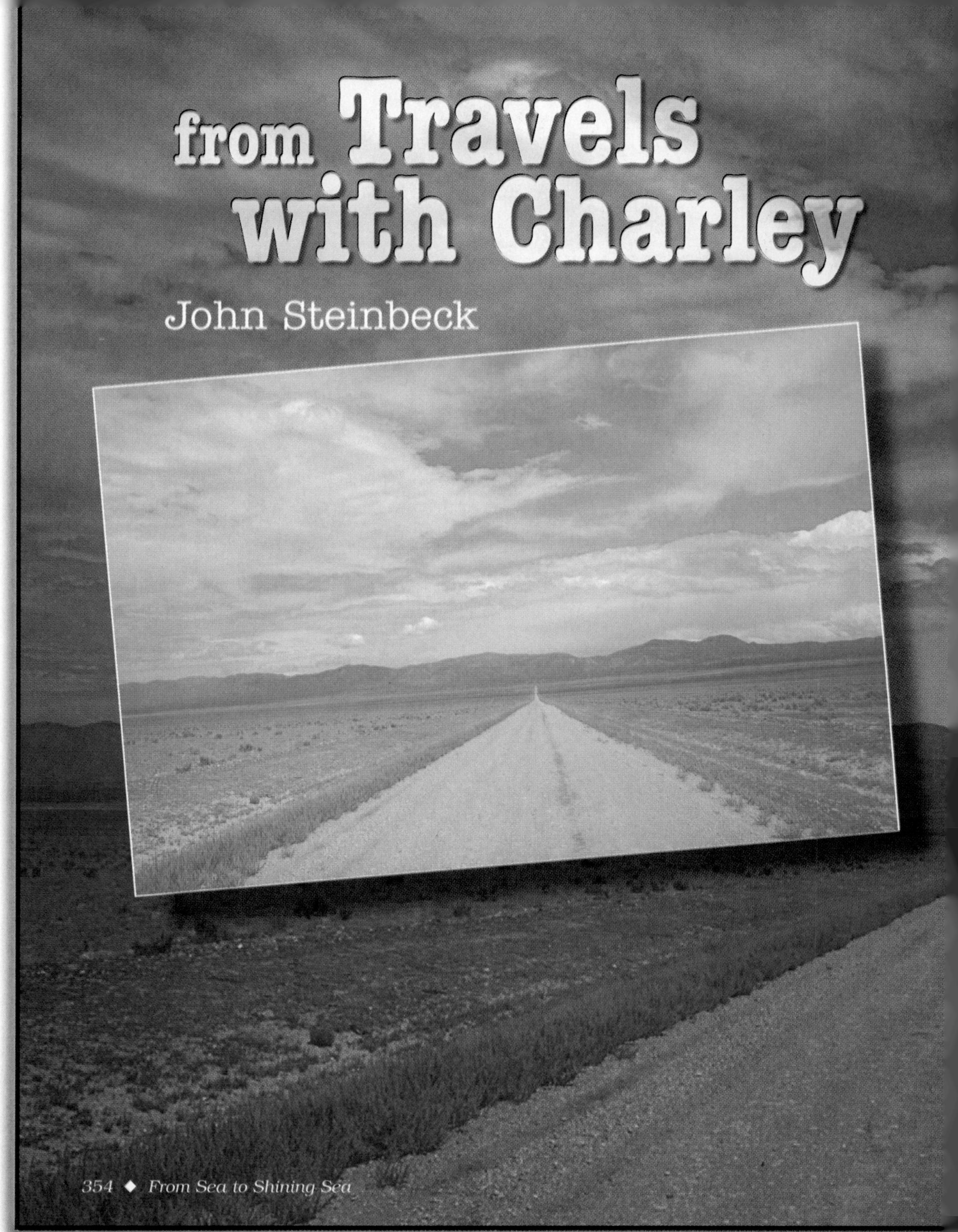

354 ◆ From Sea to Shining Sea

 Block Scheduling Strategies

Consider these suggestions to take advantage of extended class time:

- Before students read, have them complete the Connect Your Experience activity in Literature and Your Life on p. 352. Then discuss the Thematic Focus question about the United States as a land of promise. Then review the Background for Understanding feature on p. 352, using a map, as needed, for clarification.

- Have students read the selection independently, including the Connections to Today's World on p. 361. Have them discuss their answers to the Guide to Responding questions on pp. 360 and 362. Invite students who have had the opportunity to visit either Mount Rushmore, the Badlands, or Carhenge to describe their reactions to those places.

- After students have completed any or all of the portfolio activities on p. 363, encourage them to share their work with the class: They might read aloud their Travel Journal Entries, present Radio Commentaries, hold Panel Discussions, or examine the Maps and Guidebook Descriptions that they created.

My plan was clear, concise, and reasonable, I think. For many years I have traveled in many parts of the world. In America I live in New York, or dip into Chicago or San Francisco. But New York is no more America than Paris is France or London is England. Thus I discovered that I did not know my own country. I, an American writer, writing about America, was working from memory, and the memory is at best a faulty, warpy reservoir. I had not heard the speech of America, smelled the grass and trees and sewage, seen its hills and water, its color and quality of light. I knew the changes only from books and newspapers. But more than this, I had not felt the country for twenty-five years. In short, I was writing of something I did not know about, and it seems to me that in a so-called writer this is criminal. My memories were distorted by twenty-five intervening years.

Once I traveled about in an old bakery wagon, double-doored rattler with a mattress on its floor. I stopped where people stopped or gathered, I listened and looked and felt, and in the process had a picture of my country the accuracy of which was impaired only by my own shortcomings.

So it was that I determined to look again, to try to rediscover this monster land. Otherwise, in writing, I could not tell the small <u>diagnostic</u> truths which are the foundations of the larger truth. One sharp difficulty presented itself. In the intervening twenty-five years my name had become reasonably well known. And it has been my experience that when people have heard of you, favorably or not, they change; they become, through shyness or the other qualities that publicity inspires, something they are not under ordinary

---

◀ **Critical Viewing** Put yourself in the traveler's place. What feeling do you experience as you approach the mountains? [Relate]

◆ **Build Vocabulary**

diagnostic (dī´ əg näs´ tik) *adj.*: Providing a distinguishing sign or characteristic as evidence

from *Travels with Charley* ◆ 355

◆ **Beyond the Classroom**

Career Connection

Careers in the Travel Industry Students who enjoy travel will find a wide range of travel-related career opportunities available. Travel agents help people plan trips, hotel or resort workers help people enjoy their vacations, and travel guide writers provide people with opportunities to read about travel destinations.

There are also many kinds of jobs that require travel. Although these jobs are not actually part of the travel industry, flight attendants, salespeople, pilots, and truckers travel a great deal.

Invite students to brainstorm for a list of jobs in the travel industry or which require travel. Then encourage them to look into the jobs that interest them—they might interview someone who has the job, and research on the Internet or in the library to learn more about job qualifications and requirements. In addition, discuss with them the kinds of personality traits and workplace skills that they think might be necessary. For instance, a travel agent works with many different kinds of people, spends many hours on the telephone, and must have good computer skills.

circumstances. This being so, my trip demanded that I leave my name and my identity at home. I had to be peripatetic eyes and ears, a kind of moving gelatin plate.[1] I could not sign hotel registers, meet people I knew, interview others, or even ask searching questions. Furthermore, two or more people disturb the ecologic complex of an area. I had to go alone and I had to be self-contained, a kind of casual turtle carrying his house on his back.

With all this in mind I wrote to the head office of a great corporation which manufactures trucks. I specified my purpose and my needs. I wanted a three-quarter-ton pick-up truck, capable of going anywhere under possibly rigorous conditions, and on this truck I wanted a little house built like the cabin of a small boat. A trailer is difficult to maneuver on mountain roads, is impossible and often illegal to park, and is subject to many restrictions. In due time, specifications came through, for a tough, fast, comfortable vehicle, mounting a camper top—a little house with double bed, a four-burner stove, a heater, refrigerator and lights operating on butane, a chemical toilet, closet space, storage space, windows screened against insects—exactly what I wanted. It was delivered in the summer to my little fishing place at Sag Harbor near the end of Long Island. Although I didn't want to start before Labor Day, when the nation settles back to normal living, I did want to get used to my

---

1. **gelatin plate:** Sensitive glass plate used to reproduce pictures.

◆ Build Vocabulary

peripatetic (per´ i pə tet´ ik) *adj.*: Moving from place to place; walking about

rigorous (rig´ ər əs) *adj.*: Very strict or harsh

maneuver (mə n$\overline{oo}$´ vər) *v.*: To manage; lead; control

inquiry (in´ kwə rē) *n.*: An investigation or examination; questioning

inexplicable (in eks´ pli kə bəl) *adj.*: That cannot be explained or understood

---

turtle shell, to equip it and learn it. It arrived in August, a beautiful thing, powerful and yet lithe. It was almost as easy to handle as a passenger car. And because my planned trip had aroused some satiric remarks among my friends, I named it Rocinante, which you will remember was the name of Don Quixote's[2] horse.

Since I made no secret of my project, a number of controversies arose among my friends and advisers. (A projected journey spawns advisers in schools.) I was told that since my photograph was as widely distributed as my publisher could make it, I would find it impossible to move about without being recognized. Let me say in advance that in over ten thousand miles, in thirty-four states, I was not recognized even once. I believe that people identify things only in context. Even those people who might have known me against a background I am supposed to have, in no case identified me in Rocinante.

I was advised that the name Rocinante painted on the side of my truck in sixteenth-century Spanish script would cause curiosity and inquiry in some places. I do not know how many people recognized the name, but surely no one ever asked about it.

Next, I was told that a stranger's purpose in moving about the country might cause inquiry or even suspicion. For this reason I racked a shotgun, two rifles, and a couple of fishing rods in my truck, for it is my experience that if a man is going hunting or fishing his purpose is understood and even applauded. Actually, my hunting days are over. I no longer kill or catch anything I cannot get into a frying pan; I am too old for sport killing. This stage setting turned out to be unnecessary.

---

2. **Don Quixote** (dän´ kē hōt´ ē): Hero of an early 17th-century satirical romance by Cervantes, who tries in a chivalrous but unrealistic way to rescue the oppressed and fight evil.

It was said that my New York license plates would arouse interest and perhaps questions, since they were the only outward identifying marks I had. And so they did—perhaps twenty or thirty times in the whole trip. But such contacts followed an invariable pattern, somewhat as follows:

Local man: "New York, huh?"

Me: "Yep."

Local man: "I was there in nineteen thirty-eight—or was it thirty-nine? Alice, was it thirty-eight or thirty-nine we went to New York?"

Alice: "It was thirty-six. I remember because it was the year Alfred died."

Local man: "Anyway, I hated it. Wouldn't live there if you paid me."

There was some genuine worry about my traveling alone, open to attack, robbery, assault. It is well known that our roads are dangerous. And here I admit I had senseless qualms. It is some years since I have been alone, nameless, friendless, without any of the safety one gets from family, friends, and accomplices. There is no reality in the danger. It's just a very lonely, helpless feeling at first—a kind of desolate feeling. For this reason I took one companion on my journey—an old French gentleman poodle known as Charley. Actually his name is Charles le Chien.[3] He was born in Bercy on the outskirts of Paris and trained in France, and while he knows a little poodle-English, he responds quickly only to **➏** commands in French. Otherwise he has to translate, and that slows him down. He is a very big poodle, of a color called *bleu,* and he is blue when he is clean. Charley is a born diplomat. He prefers negotiation to fighting, and properly so, since he is very bad at fighting. Only once in his ten years has he been in trouble—when he met a dog who refused to negotiate. Charley lost a piece of his right ear that time. But he is a good watch dog—has a roar like a lion, designed to conceal from night-wandering strangers the fact that he couldn't bite his way out of a *cornet de papier.*[4] He is a good friend and traveling companion, **➐** and would rather travel about than anything **➏** he can imagine. If he occurs at length in this account, it is because he contributed much to the trip. A dog, particularly an exotic like Charley, is a bond between strangers. Many conversations en route began with "What degree of a dog is that?"

The techniques of opening conversation are universal. I knew long ago and rediscovered **➑** that the best way to attract attention, help, and conversation is to be lost.

* * *

The night was loaded with omens. The grieving sky turned the little water to a dangerous metal and then the wind got up—not **➒** the gusty, rabbity wind of the seacoasts I know but a great bursting sweep of wind with nothing to inhibit it for a thousand miles in any direction. Because it was a wind strange to me, and therefore mysterious, it set up mysterious responses in me. In terms of reason, it was strange only because I found it so. But a goodly part of our experience which we find inexplicable must be like that. To my certain knowledge, many people conceal experiences for fear of ridicule. How many people have seen or heard or felt something which so out- **➓** raged their sense of what should be that the whole thing was brushed quickly away like dirt under a rug?

For myself, I try to keep the line open even for things I can't understand or explain, but it is difficult in this frightened time. At this moment in North Dakota I had a reluctance to drive on that amounted to fear. At the same

---

3. **Charles le Chien** (shärl' lə shē un'): French for "Charles the dog."

4. *cornet de papier* (kôr nā' də pá pyā'): French for "paper bag."

from *Travels with Charley* ◆ 357

Humanities: Film

Many of John Steinbeck's writings have been made into movies—some more than once. The best known, perhaps, is John Ford's unforgettable 1940 version of *The Grapes of Wrath.* Steinbeck's *Of Mice and Men, Cannery Row,* and *East of Eden* were made into films, as were *Tortilla Flat, The Pearl,* and *The Red Pony.*

Interested students may wish to plan a Steinbeck film festival, in which they watch one of the films as a homework project and then report on it to the class. If time permits, have students read the novel on which the film is based prior to viewing the movie and compare the two.

You might use these questions to spark a classroom discussion:

1. Why do you suppose there has been no movie made of *Travels with Charley?*
2. If someone were planning to make one, who would you choose to play the narrator? Explain your choice.

◆ **Critical Thinking**

➏ **Analyze** Have students reread Steinbeck's description of his traveling companion Charley. What can they learn about Charley from the details he includes? *Steinbeck has probably owned Charley for a long time and they are good friends. Charley is a small dog, not very aggressive or mean, but he has a loud bark that sounds threatening.*

◆ **Build Grammar Skills**

➐ **Coordinating Conjunctions** Words that link words or groups of words of equal rank are called coordinating conjunctions. In this sentence, the conjunction *and* links the nouns *friend* and *companion.*

Thematic Focus

➑ **A Land of Promise** How does this technique show that Steinbeck views America as a land of promise? *Americans are usually friendly and helpful, and are willing and eager to assist those in need.*

Comprehension Check ☑

➒ Why did the "great bursting sweep of wind" make Steinbeck feel uneasy? *It was a mysterious sound that was unfamiliar to him and therefore frightened him a little. He explained that he was more used to "rabbity wind" near the ocean.*

◆ **LITERATURE AND YOUR LIFE**

➓ Steinbeck indicates that some experiences cause people to brush them "quickly away like dirt under a rug." Challenge students to think of a time in their own experience when they tried to keep something a secret because they were afraid of being ridiculed. Invite volunteers to share what it was that they tried to hide and why.

① **Travel Essay** Steinbeck, like other writers, explores different perspectives of an issue by having the main character bounce ideas off of another character. Who is the narrator talking to while he is deciding whether to go or to stay? *He is having a one-sided "conversation" with Charley.*

Comprehension Check ☑

② How does Steinbeck describe the boundary between the eastern and western landscapes? *When he crosses the Missouri River at Bismarck, North Dakota, he compares the green grassy east with the brown and dry west. He observed that the map should be folded at exactly that place.*

◆ Reading Strategy

③ **Clarify Details** Using a dictionary can help students clarify words and better imagine the unusual and rugged setting. Have them look up "troglodytes" and "trolls." What kind of landscape is Steinbeck describing? *He is describing a landscape of craggy rock formations and cave-like features.*

Customize for
Visual/Spatial Learners

Challenge students to use information in the selection and the information contained on p. 352 in the Story Behind the Story to trace John Steinbeck's travels across the United States on a map. Suggest that interested students make a visual display to share with others in the class illustrating the route they believe he may have taken. If they wish, they may select highways as well.

---

time, Charley wanted to go—in fact, made such a commotion about going that I tried to reason with him.

"Listen to me, dog. I have a strong impulse to stay amounting to <u>celestial</u> command. If I should overcome it and go and a great snow should close in on us, I would recognize it as a warning disregarded. If we stay and a big snow should come I would be certain I had a pipeline to prophecy."

① Charley sneezed and paced restlessly. "All right, *mon cur,*[5] let's take your side of it. You want to go on. Suppose we do, and in the night a tree should crash down right where we are presently standing. It would be you who have the attention of the gods. And there is always that chance. I could tell you many stories about faithful animals who saved their masters, but I think you are just bored and I'm not going to flatter you." Charley leveled at me his most cynical eye. I think he is neither a romantic nor a mystic. "I know what you mean. If we go, and no tree crashes down, or stay and no snow falls—what then? I'll tell you what then. We forget the whole episode and the field of prophecy is in no way injured. I vote to stay. You vote to go. But being nearer the pinnacle of creation than you, and also president, I cast the deciding vote."

We stayed and it didn't snow and no tree fell, so naturally we forgot the whole thing and are wide open for more mystic feelings when they come. And in the early morning swept clean of clouds and telescopically clear, we crunched around on the thick white ground cover of frost and got under way. The caravan of the arts was dark but the dog barked as we

---

5. ***mon cur*** (mōn kŭr′): French slang for "my dear mutt."

ground up to the highway.

② Someone must have told me about the Missouri River at Bismarck, North Dakota, or I must have read about it. In either case, I hadn't paid attention. I came on it in amazement. Here is where the map should fold. Here is the boundary between east and west. On the Bismarck side it is eastern landscape, eastern grass, with the look and smell of eastern America. Across the Missouri on the Mandan side, it is pure west, with brown grass and water scorings and small outcrops. The two sides of the river might well be a thousand miles apart. As I was not prepared for the Missouri boundary, so I was not prepared for the Bad Lands. They deserve this name. They are like the work of an evil child. Such a place the Fallen Angels might have built as a spite to Heaven, dry and sharp, desolate and dangerous, and for me filled with foreboding. A sense comes from it that it does not like or welcome humans. But humans being what they are, and I being human, I turned off the highway on a shaley road and headed in among the buttes, but with a shyness as though I crashed a party. The road surface tore viciously at my tires and made Rocinante's overloaded springs cry with anguish. What a place for a colony of troglodytes, or better, of trolls. **③** And here's an odd thing. Just as I felt unwanted in this land, so do I feel a reluctance in writing about it.

Presently I saw a man leaning on a two-strand barbed-wire fence, the wires fixed not to posts but to crooked tree limbs stuck in the

◆ Build Vocabulary
celestial (sə les′ chəl) *adj.*: Of heaven; divine

Cross-Curricular Connection: Social Studies

Place Names Write Badlands, Grand Canyon, Monument Valley, Los Angeles, Seattle, Red River, Jamestown, Des Moines, Phoenix, and Colorado on the board. Ask students to explain, hypothesize, or speculate on how each of these locations was named.

Use this activity to begin a discussion of the variety of ways in which places are named, and why some are renamed at a later time. Talk about how places in your community got their names. Discuss why, occasionally, there is more than one name for the same place.

Invite students to choose a region of interest to them in the United States. Have them research the place names of that region. For example, a student might choose Yosemite National Park and find out how and when names were chosen for the valley itself, and its peaks, falls, lakes, and trails. Or they might choose the state of Ohio to learn how counties and towns were named and who selected the names. Students might create a map with captioned explanations of the place names, or a chart that relates places to the origins of their names.

▲ Critical Viewing Why is the name "Badlands" appropriate for the region pictured here? [Analyze]

ground. The man wore a dark hat, and jeans and long jacket washed palest blue with lighter places at knees and elbows. His pale eyes were frosted with sun glare and his lips scaly as snakeskin. A .22 rifle leaned against the fence beside him and on the ground lay a little heap of fur and feathers—rabbits and small birds. I pulled up to speak to him, saw his eyes wash over Rocinante, sweep up the details, and then retire into their sockets. And I found I had nothing to say to him. The "Looks like an early winter," or "Any good fishing hereabouts?" didn't seem to apply. And so we simply brooded at each other.

"Afternoon!"

"Yes, sir," he said.

"Any place nearby where I can buy some eggs?"

"Not real close by 'less you want to go as far as Galva or up to Beach."[6]

"I was set for some scratch-hen eggs."

"Powdered," he said. "My Mrs. gets powdered."

"Lived here long?"

"Yep."

I waited for him to ask something or to say something so we could go on, but he didn't. And as the silence continued, it became more and more impossible to think of something to say. I made one more try. "Does it get very cold here winters?"

"Fairly."

"You talk too much."

───────────────

6. **Galva . . . Beach:** Cities in western North Dakota near the border of Montana.

He grinned. "That's what my Mrs. says."

"So long," I said, and put the car in gear and moved along. And in my rear-view mirror I couldn't see that he looked after me. He may not be a typical Badlander, but he's one of the few I caught.

A little farther along I stopped at a small house, a section of war-surplus barracks, it looked, but painted white with yellow trim, and with the dying vestiges of a garden, frosted-down geraniums and a few clusters of chrysanthemums, little button things yellow and red-brown. I walked up the path with the certainty that I was being regarded from behind the white window curtains. An old woman answered my knock and gave me the drink of water I asked for and nearly talked my arm off. She was hungry to talk, frantic to talk, about her relatives, her friends, and how she wasn't used to this. For she was not a native and she didn't rightly belong here. Her native clime was a land of milk and honey and had its share of apes and ivory and peacocks. Her voice rattled on as though she was terrified of the silence that would settle when I was gone. As she talked it came to me that she was afraid of this place and, further, that so was I. I felt I wouldn't like to have the night catch me here.

I went into a state of flight, running to get away from the unearthly landscape. And then the late afternoon changed everything. As the sun angled, the buttes and coulees, the cliffs and sculptured hills and ravines lost their burned and dreadful look and glowed with yellow and rich browns and a hundred variations of red and silver gray, all picked out by streaks of coal black. It was so beautiful that I

from Travels with Charley ◆ 359

▶ Critical Viewing ◀

❹ Analyze *Students may note the rugged, forbidding, treeless terrain, and the gray-brown jagged formations as good reasons for the name "Badlands."*

◆ **Literary Focus**

❺ Travel Essay Why do you think this man might not be much of a conversationalist? What can you infer about life in the Badlands from this brief encounter? *Students may suggest that the Badlands are very sparsely populated and that life there is lonely. They may say that this kind of environment might attract self-sufficient people who don't mind the solitude and who aren't accustomed to conversation.*

◆ **Critical Thinking**

❻ Compare and Contrast Have students compare the personalities of the two people the author meets in the Badlands. *While the man was satisfied with a very brief meeting, the woman seemed starved for company and eager to chat.*

◆ **LITERATURE AND YOUR LIFE**

❼ Students may have noticed the pleasing effects of sunlight in the late afternoon and in the early morning. At those times, when the sun is lower in the sky, shadows emerge, and colors of the landscape become more vivid. Invite students to describe times when all it took was a change in the time of day to alter their impression of the appearance of a place.

Speaking and Listening Mini-Lesson

Panel Discussion

This mini-lesson supports the Speaking and Listening activity in the Idea Bank on p. 363.

Introduce Present two statements, one that supports travel as a way to learn about different places, and another that asserts that watching TV shows or movies about travel destinations provides the same benefits as going there in person. Form groups of 3–4 students and tell them that they will address these views within the format of a

panel discussion; they will choose one view or the other to support. Review the fundamentals of panel discussions, emphasizing the need to listen to one another, follow agreed-upon rules for speaking, and address the given topic.

Develop Have students formulate their arguments and gather supporting information. Invite them to practice their statements. Urge them to try to predict questions and to prepare persuasive responses.

Apply Hold the panel discussions, with volunteers acting as moderators. Non-participants can be audience members and can ask questions of panelists during that stage of the activity.

Assess Judge participation on the persuasiveness of arguments and on students' ability to listen respectfully and abide by the rules of the panel discussion. Or, use the Peer Assessment: Speaker/Speech form, p. 114, in **Alternative Assessment**.

◆ Literary Focus

① Travel Essay Details about the landscape and the names of flowers and animals could be found in any travel article about the Badlands. Challenge students to tell how Steinbeck's essay is different. *He adds colorful descriptions, fresh metaphors, personification, and his personal and emotional responses to the environment.*

Reinforce and Extend

Answers

◆ LITERATURE AND YOUR LIFE

Reader's Response Students might say that they would have enjoyed traveling with Steinbeck because of his appreciation of the world around him.

Thematic Focus Although only two encounters with people are described in this excerpt, Steinbeck probably talked with many more.

☑ Check Your Comprehension

1. He wants to get back in touch with America and American people.
2. Charley is Steinbeck's pet poodle. Steinbeck takes Charley along for companionship and to make meeting people easier.
3. When the light changes toward day's end, it makes the land beautiful and colorful.

◆ Critical Thinking

1. In not traveling across the country for so long, he had lost touch with America and American people.
2. When writing about the people, his tone is humorous. When he describes the land, he does so with reverence and uses descriptive language to express its beauty and power.
3. He reveals that he pays attention to his gut feelings, even though he can't fully explain them.
4. Most students will agree that experiencing a place provides a richer understanding of it than does just reading about it.
5. Students may say that a good travel writer should be observant, open-minded, and neither shy nor timid.

360

◆ Literary Focus

① Which details in this paragraph might you find in a standard description of the Badlands? Which details reveal Steinbeck's unique experience of the Badlands?

stopped near a thicket of dwarfed and wind-warped cedars and junipers, and once stopped I was caught, trapped in color and dazzled by the clarity of the light. Against the descending sun the battlements were dark and clean-lined, while to the east, where the uninhibited light poured slant-wise, the strange landscape shouted with color. And the night, far from being frightful, was lovely beyond thought, for the stars were close, and although there was no moon the starlight made a silver glow in the sky. The air cut the nostrils with dry frost. And for pure pleasure I collected a pile of dry dead cedar branches and built a small fire just to smell the perfume of the burning wood and to hear the excited crackle of the branches. My fire made a dome of yellow light over me, and nearby I heard a screech owl hunting and a barking of coyotes, not howling but the short chuckling bark of the dark of the moon. This is one of the few places I have ever seen where the night was friendlier than the day. And I can easily see how people are driven back to the Bad Lands.

Before I slept I spread a map on my bed, a Charley-tromped map. Beach was not far away, and that would be the end of North Dakota. And coming up would be Montana, where I had never been. That night was so cold that I put on my insulated underwear for pajamas, and when Charley had done his duties and had his biscuits and consumed his usual gallon of water and finally curled up in his place under the bed, I dug out an extra blanket and covered him—all except the tip of his nose—and he sighed and wriggled and gave a great groan of pure ecstatic comfort. And I thought how every safe generality I gathered in my travels was canceled by another. In the night the Bad Lands had become Good Lands. I can't explain it. That's how it was.

Guide for Responding

◆ LITERATURE AND YOUR LIFE

Reader's Response Would you have liked to join Steinbeck on his travels? Explain.

Thematic Focus Do you think Steinbeck succeeds in rediscovering the people of the United States? Explain.

Journal Writing In your journal, jot down places you'd like to visit someday. Also, mention why each destination interests you.

☑ Check Your Comprehension

1. For what purpose does Steinbeck make his trip?
2. Who is Charley, and why does he go along on the journey?
3. What causes the author's impressions of the Badlands to change?

◆ Critical Thinking

INTERPRET

1. What does Steinbeck mean by saying that he "had not felt the country for twenty-five years"? **[Interpret]**
2. What is the author's attitude when he is writing about people? When he describes the landscape? **[Compare and Contrast]**
3. What does Steinbeck's decision to stay overnight in the Badlands reveal about his character? **[Draw Conclusions]**

EVALUATE

4. Do you agree with Steinbeck that traveling around the country is the best way to learn about it? Explain. **[Evaluate]**

EXTEND

5. What qualities does a person need to become a good travel writer? **[Career Link]**

Beyond the Selection

FURTHER READING

Other Works by John Steinbeck
The Grapes of Wrath
The Pearl
Of Mice and Men

Other Works by Jamie Jenson
Rough Guide to California
Rough Guide to the USA

Other Works About American Travel
Great Plains, Ian Frazier
Blue Highways, William Least Heat Moon

INTERNET

We suggest the following sites on the Internet (all Web sites are subject to change).

To contact the Center for Steinbeck Studies:
http://www.sjsu.edu/depts/steinbec/srchome.html

For more information about Badlands National Park:
http://www.nps.gov/badl/exp/home.htm

For information about the Badlands:
http://www.nps.gov/badl/exp/home.htm

We *strongly recommend* that you preview these sites before you send students to them.

CONNECTIONS TO TODAY'S WORLD

In *Travels with Charley,* Steinbeck takes off in a van to reexplore the United States and strengthen his emotional ties with its people. Tourism of the United States and its sites is still a popular vacation activity for many people. In *Road Trip USA* by Jamie Jensen, the author tells about two very interesting and unique tourist sites in the United States.

from ROAD TRIP USA

by Jamie Jensen
Mount Rushmore and Carhenge

Two of the nation's most distinctive outdoor sculptures stand along US-385 within a manageable drive from US-20. One is perhaps the best-known artwork in the U.S., the giant presidential memorial at Mount Rushmore. Roughly 100 miles north from Chadron, at the far eastern side of the beautiful Black Hills, Mount Rushmore is graced by the 60-foot heads of four U.S. Presidents—Washington, Jefferson, Lincoln, and Teddy Roosevelt—carved into a granite peak. It's equal parts impressive monument and kitschy Americana, and one of those places you really have to see to believe.

Another newer, less famous monument to America sits in a flat field along US-385 outside the town of Alliance, 62 miles south of Chadron. Built in 1987 as part of a local family reunion, Carhenge is a giant-sized replica of the famous Druidical ruin, Stonehenge; this one, however, is built entirely out of three dozen late-model American cars, stacked on top of one another to form a semi-circular temple.

1. What kind of information is revealed in this travel article?
2. Which travel destination—Mt. Rushmore or Carhenge—is more traditional? Which is more offbeat? Why might Jensen have chosen to include both types of tourist sites within one article?
3. Would John Steinbeck have enjoyed visiting these sites? Why or why not?

from *Road Trip USA* ◆ 361

Connections to Today's World

Students can learn more about Mount Rushmore, Stonehenge, and Carhenge by visiting the Internet sites listed on p. 360. Alternatively, they may wish to find information in library and travel book resources.

Customize for *Logical/Mathematical Learners*

Have students find US-385 and these two travel destinations on a map of South Dakota. Suggest that students who do the Map project on p. 363 include these sites on their maps.

Customize for *Verbal/Linguistic Learners*

Suggest that interested students write a brief description for a travel guide of a place nearby in your area. Suggest that they select a location that travelers might find interesting, for example, a museum, park, or building. Remind students that they should give location information and use interesting details that will intrigue readers and make them want to visit. Collect the descriptions for a local classroom travel brochure.

Answers

1. The article reveals basic tourist information about two huge sculptures—the presidential heads on Mount Rushmore, and the unusual sculpture called Carhenge. It describes where each is in relation to US-20 and US-385.
2. Of the two, Mount Rushmore is more traditional and Carhenge is more offbeat. Both are included here because they are near one another and therefore might be visited on the same trip.
3. Steinbeck probably would have enjoyed the playful aspects of the sculptures and the reactions of visitors.

Cross-Curricular Connection: Social Studies

Stonehenge, in southern England, is one of the many puzzles left for us by ancient peoples. What we do know is that about 3,800 years ago, early inhabitants of the area began to build this huge circle of 82 giant stones. We know that the stones were quarried in Wales and then brought to where they stand. What we don't know is what purpose Stonehenge served for its builders. Was it an ancient calendar used to predict eclipses? Was it a temple or a palace? Or was it a fortress?

Invite students to find out more about Stonehenge. They can do research on the Internet, perhaps with the help of a social studies teacher, to learn the most current views on its history. They can examine photos of the ancient monument in order to make their own guesses as to what purpose it served. Suggest that interested students compare the information they found on Stonehenge to the whimsical Carhenge replica in South Dakota. Have students report their findings and their views to the class.

◆ Reading Strategy

1. *home for troglodytes and trolls:* consult outside source; *buttes and coulees:* consult outside source or prior knowledge
2. You might consult a French/English dictionary.
3. It enters the state in the northwestern part, near Williston, flows in a southeasterly direction, passes through Bismarck, and exits the state due south of the capital. Clarify by using a map.

◆ Build Vocabulary

Using the Suffix -ic

1. fantastic: having to do with fantasy
2. sarcastic: having to do with sarcasm
3. photographic: having to do with photography

Spelling Strategy

1. quiz
2. request
3. earthquake

Using the Word Bank

1. b
2. c
3. b
4. c
5. c
6. b
7. c

◆ Literary Focus

1. It may show students that only a few people live there and those that do spend a lot of time by themselves.
2. From personal experience, some students may realize the power of a dramatic landscape to affect them emotionally.

◆ Build Grammar Skills

Practice

1. I had to go home alone, (and) I had to be self-contained.
2. I specified my purpose (and) my needs.
3. A stranger's purpose in moving about the country might cause inquiry (or) even suspicion.
4. I think that he is neither a romantic (nor) a mystic.
5. The caravan of the arts was dark, (but) the dog barked as we ground up the highway.

◆ *Guide for Responding* (continued)

◆ Reading Strategy

CLARIFY DETAILS

Clarifying details, or checking your understanding, will help ensure that you get the most out of what you read. To clarify details, you can draw upon your prior knowledge, find clues within the text, and consult outside sources.

1. Identify two descriptive details about the physical landscape in the Badlands that might need clarification. How could you clarify them?
2. Charley the poodle understands French. Where would you look to find out what *le chien* means?
3. In what part of North Dakota is the Missouri River located? How would you clarify that detail?

◆ Build Vocabulary

USING THE SUFFIX -ic

The suffix *-ic,* as in *diagnostic,* means "like" or "having to do with." It can be added to nouns to form adjectives, such as *patriotic.* Define each of the following words, incorporating the definition of *-ic* into each answer.

1. fantastic   2. sarcastic   3. photographic

SPELLING STRATEGY

The *kw* sound is spelled *qu* when it occurs at the beginning or in the middle of a word, as in **qu**iet, in**qu**iry, and **qu**est. Replace the phonetic spellings with the actual spellings of these words.

1. (kwiz)   2. (ri kwest´)   3. (ᵾrth´ kwāk´)

USING THE WORD BANK

In your notebook, write the letter of the word or words closest in meaning to the first word.

1. peripatetic: (a) located at, (b) walking from place to place, (c) formed by
2. celestial: (a) earthly, (b) clearly, (c) heavenly
3. diagnostic: (a) test, (b) related to finding the cause of, (c) related to finding the direction of
4. inexplicable: (a) unusual, (b) intentional, (c) not explainable
5. inquiry: (a) insight, (b) quietness, (c) search
6. maneuver: (a) jostle, (b) manage skillfully, (c) figure out
7. rigorous: (a) righteous, (b) straight, (c) strict

362 ◆ *From Sea to Shining Sea*

◆ Literary Focus

TRAVEL ESSAY

In **travel essays,** writers often focus on people and experiences as well as on places. Unlike standard travel guides, travel essays usually contain extended descriptions of characters and even dialogue, bringing to life the people as well as the scenery.

1. In what way does the dialogue between Steinbeck and the man he meets in the Badlands give you a taste of the region?
2. Does Steinbeck's description of his emotional reaction to the Badlands give you a deeper understanding of the landscape? Why or why not?

◆ Build Grammar Skills

COORDINATING CONJUNCTIONS

A conjunction connects single words or groups of words. **Coordinating conjunctions,** such as *and, but, or, nor, for, yet,* and *so,* link words or groups of words of equal rank, such as two or more nouns, phrases, or even entire sentences.

Connecting Nouns: . . . my friends *and* advisors

Connecting Verbs: How many people have seen *or* heard *or* felt something . . .

Connecting Sentences: Otherwise, he has to translate, *and* that slows him down.

Practice Copy the following sentences, and circle the coordinating conjunction in each. Then, underline the words or groups of words connected by the conjunction.

1. I had to go alone, and I had to be self-contained.
2. I specified my purpose and my needs.
3. A stranger's purpose in moving about the country might cause inquiry or even suspicion.
4. I think that he is neither a romantic nor a mystic.
5. The caravan of the arts was dark, but the dog barked as we ground up the highway.

Writing Application Write sentences that use the following coordinating conjunctions:

1. A sentence about Charley using *and*
2. A sentence about Steinbeck using *or*
3. A sentence about the Badlands using *but*

Writing Application
Possible responses:

1. Charley was a dog and a traveling companion.
2. Steinbeck wanted to pretend he was fishing or hunting.
3. The Badlands are depressing at midday, but magnificent at sunset.

✎ Writer's Solution

For additional instruction and practice, use the lesson in the *Writer's Solution Language Lab CD-ROM* on coordinating conjunctions. You may also use The Conjunction page, p. 26, in the *Writer's Solution Grammar Practice Book.*

Build Your Portfolio

 Idea Bank

Writing

1. **Charley's Journal** Write a journal entry describing the Badlands from Charley's point of view.

2. **Guidebook Description** Write a description of the Badlands to be included in a guidebook for tourists. Tell what a visitor might expect to see. Also, make suggestions about how long a visitor might want to stay and what supplies or equipment might be useful for traveling in the area.

3. **Essay** Steinbeck once said, "To my certain knowledge, many people conceal experiences for fear of ridicule." Write an essay in which you explain how this selection might have been different if Steinbeck had been one of those people.

Speaking and Listening

4. **Radio Commentary** Rework the passage describing the Badlands to make it appropriate for a radio broadcast. Record your reworked version, and play the recording for your classmates. **[Media Link]**

5. **Panel Discussion [Group Activity]** With a small group, hold a panel discussion about the benefits of traveling. You may discuss whether learning about places through television and movies is an adequate substitute for firsthand experience. **[Social Studies Link]**

Projects

6. **Map** Create a map of North Dakota's Badlands. Label the places that Steinbeck mentions in his essay. Post your completed map in the classroom. **[Geography Link]**

7. **Documentary Script [Group Activity]** With a partner, write a documentary (true-life) film script based on *Travels with Charley*. In your script, specify the sights you want the camera to film, the order of the shots, and what the narrator will say. **[Media Link]**

 Writing Mini-Lesson

Travel Journal Entry

Like John Steinbeck, many people write about places they visit. Capture the essence of a place you've visited and your experience of it by writing an entry in a travel journal.

Writing Skills Focus: Use Supporting Details

Supporting details give information about your main ideas. Use supporting details to help bring your travel entry to life for readers. John Steinbeck uses supporting details that help describe his experience in the Badlands:

Model From the Story
The air cut the nostrils with dry frost.

Prewriting First, decide on a topic by searching your memory for interesting places you've visited and choosing one about which to write. Then, list supporting details you can include to describe the place and your experience of it.

Drafting Begin your travel entry by introducing your subject and revealing your overall impression of it. Then, follow with a description of your journey, including things that happened and people you met. Conclude with a summary of your experience.

Revising Review your draft, looking for places where supporting details can be added to make your description more vivid. Consider adding dialogue to bring to life the people you met. Proofread for errors in spelling, grammar, and punctuation.

> ◆ **Grammar Application**
>
> Unless you're using short sentences for dramatic effect, consider joining two or three short sentences with coordinating conjunctions.

from Travels with Charley ◆ 363

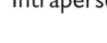 **Idea Bank**

Following are suggestions for matching the Idea Bank topics with your students' performance levels and learning modalities:

Customize for *Performance Levels*
Less Advanced Students: 1, 5
Average Students: 2, 4, 5, 6
More Advanced Students: 3, 4, 5, 6, 7

Customize for *Learning Modalities*
Verbal/Linguistic: 1, 2, 3, 4, 5, 7
Visual/Spatial: 2, 5, 6, 7
Logical/Mathematical: 2, 5, 6, 7
Musical/Rhythmic: 4, 7
Interpersonal: 4, 5
Intrapersonal: 1, 3, 7

 Writing Mini-Lesson

Refer students to the Writing Handbook in the back of the book for instruction on the writing process and for further information on travel journals. Have students use the Main Idea and Supporting Details Organizer in **Writing and Language Transparencies,** p. 61, to organize the supporting details that describe the place and their experience there.

 **Writer's Solution**

Writers at Work Videodisc
Have students view the videodisc segment on note-taking methods (Ch. 3), featuring Rosie McNulty, to see how she develops sensory details.

Play frames 24273 to 26446

Writing Lab CD-ROM
Have students complete the tutorial on Description. Follow these steps:
1. Have students use a Topic Web Graphic Organizer to help them narrow their topics.
2. Students can use a Sensory Word Bin activity to help them gather details that appeal to the senses.
3. Have students draft on computer.
4. Have students use a Descriptive Word Bin to add more precise language to their writing.

Writer's Solution Sourcebook
Have students use Chapter 2, "Description," pp. 33–70, for additional support. The chapter includes in-depth instruction on organizing details, pp. 54–55.

✓ ASSESSMENT OPTIONS

Formal Assessment, Selection Test, pp. 109–111, and Assessment Resources Software. The selection test is designed so that it can be easily customized to the performance levels of your students.

Alternative Assessment, p. 27, includes options for less advanced students, more advanced students, verbal/linguistic learners, logical/mathematical learners, interpersonal learners, and visual/spatial learners.

PORTFOLIO ASSESSMENT
Use the following rubrics in the **Alternative Assessment** booklet to assess student writing:
Charley's Journal: Expression, p. 90
Guidebook Description: Description, p. 93
Essay: Cause-Effect, p. 98
Writing Mini-Lesson: Description, p. 93

OBJECTIVES

1. To read, comprehend, and interpret two poems and two essays
2. To relate two poems and two essays to personal experience
3. To summarize
4. To identify an epithet
5. To build vocabulary in context and learn forms of *migrate*
6. To develop skill using correlative conjunctions
7. To write a tribute that includes smooth transitions
8. To respond to two poems and two essays through writing, speaking and listening, and projects

SKILLS INSTRUCTION

Vocabulary:
Using Forms of *migrate*

Spelling:
Small Words in Longer Ones

Grammar:
Correlative Conjunctions

Reading Strategy:
Summarize

Literary Focus:
Epithet

Writing:
Transitions

Speaking and Listening:
Address (Teacher Edition)

Viewing and Representing:
The Immigrant Experience (Teacher Edition)

Critical Viewing:
Analyze; Deduce; Infer

PORTFOLIO OPPORTUNITIES

Writing: Postcard; Journal; Essay
Writing Mini-Lesson: Tribute
Speaking and Listening: Address; Dramatization
Projects: Multimedia Report; Monument

More About the Authors

Emma Lazarus wrote "The New Colossus" for an auction to raise money to build the pedestal of the Statue of Liberty.

Joseph Bruchac believes that people need poetry and storytelling to give them a sense of wholeness. He believes that understanding others teaches people about themselves.

Mario Cuomo, a lawyer who has held office, is only one generation removed from the rural Italian home where his mother lived without electricity or running water.

Alice Walker kept a journal and wrote poems from the age of 8. In the 1950's, she was active in the civil rights movement.

Guide for Reading

Meet the Authors:

Emma Lazarus (1849–1887)

Born in New York City, Emma Lazarus began writing poetry in her teens. Enraged by the Russian massacre of Jews in 1882, she changed the focus of her writing to meet her new purpose: to defend and glorify the Jewish people. She is most famous for her sonnet "The New Colossus" (1883), the last lines of which are inscribed below the Statue of Liberty.

Joseph Bruchac (1942–   )

Joseph Bruchac is the son of an Abenaki Indian mother and a Czechoslovakian father. He grew up in the foothills of New York's Adirondacks. In addition to juggling careers as a writer, storyteller, editor, and lecturer, he is an avid gardener and holds a black belt in Pentjak Silat, the martial art of Indonesia.

Mario Cuomo (1932–   )

Mario Cuomo was the governor of New York from 1983 to 1995. He was widely regarded as one of the Democratic party's foremost thinkers. His main concern is that rich and poor Americans should work together to solve the country's problems.

Alice Walker (1944–   )

One of today's best-known and most highly regarded writers, Alice Walker produces fiction, poetry, and essays that focus mainly on social injustice. She received the Pulitzer Prize for her novel *The Color Purple* (1982), which was made into a movie in 1985.

364 ◆ From Sea to Shining Sea

◆ LITERATURE AND YOUR LIFE

CONNECT YOUR EXPERIENCE

Unless you are a Native American, you or your ancestors came from a culture that is based outside the United States. The selections you're about to read give voice to the hopes and dreams that prompted millions of people—possibly including your ancestors—to leave their native lands and come to America to forge a new life.

THEMATIC FOCUS: A Land of Promise

How do the visions of America in these selections compare with your own vision?

◆ Background for Understanding

HISTORY

The photograph opposite was taken at Ellis Island, the chief immigration station of the eastern United States from 1892 to 1954. Between 1892 and 1924, more than 12,000,000 immigrants entered the United States through Ellis Island, hoping to find a better life. Three of these selections are about immigrants coming through Ellis Island.

◆ Build Vocabulary

RELATED WORDS: FORMS OF *migrate*

The word *immigrate* includes the root *migrate*, which means "to move from one place to another." Other words related to *migrate* include *immigration, emigrate, migrant,* and *migratory.*

WORD BANK

Which word from the selections means "of or belonging to ancestors"? Check the Build Vocabulary box on page 369 to see if you chose correctly.

immigrate
apprehension
immersed
ancestral
colossal
conscience
literally

Prentice Hall Literature Program Resources

REINFORCE / RETEACH / EXTEND
Selection Support Pages
Build Vocabulary: Forms of *migrate*, p. 146
Build Spelling Skills, p. 147
Build Grammar Skills, p. 148
Reading Strategy: Summarize, p. 149
Literary Focus: Epithet, p. 150
Strategies for Diverse Student Needs, pp. 55–56
Beyond Literature Cross-Curricular Connection: Math, p. 28
Formal Assessment Selection Test, pp. 112–114, Assessment Resources Software

Alternative Assessment, p. 28
Writing and Language Transparencies, Open Mind Organizer, p. 81; Sunburst Organizer, p. 85
Resource Pro CD-R⊘M "The New Colossus"; "Ellis Island"; "Achieving the American Dream"; "Choice: A Tribute to Dr. Martin Luther King, Jr."
Listening to Literature Audiocassettes "The New Colossus"; "Ellis Island"; "Achieving the American Dream"; "Choice: A Tribute to Dr. Martin Luther King, Jr."
Looking at Literature Videodisc/ Videotape "Ellis Island"

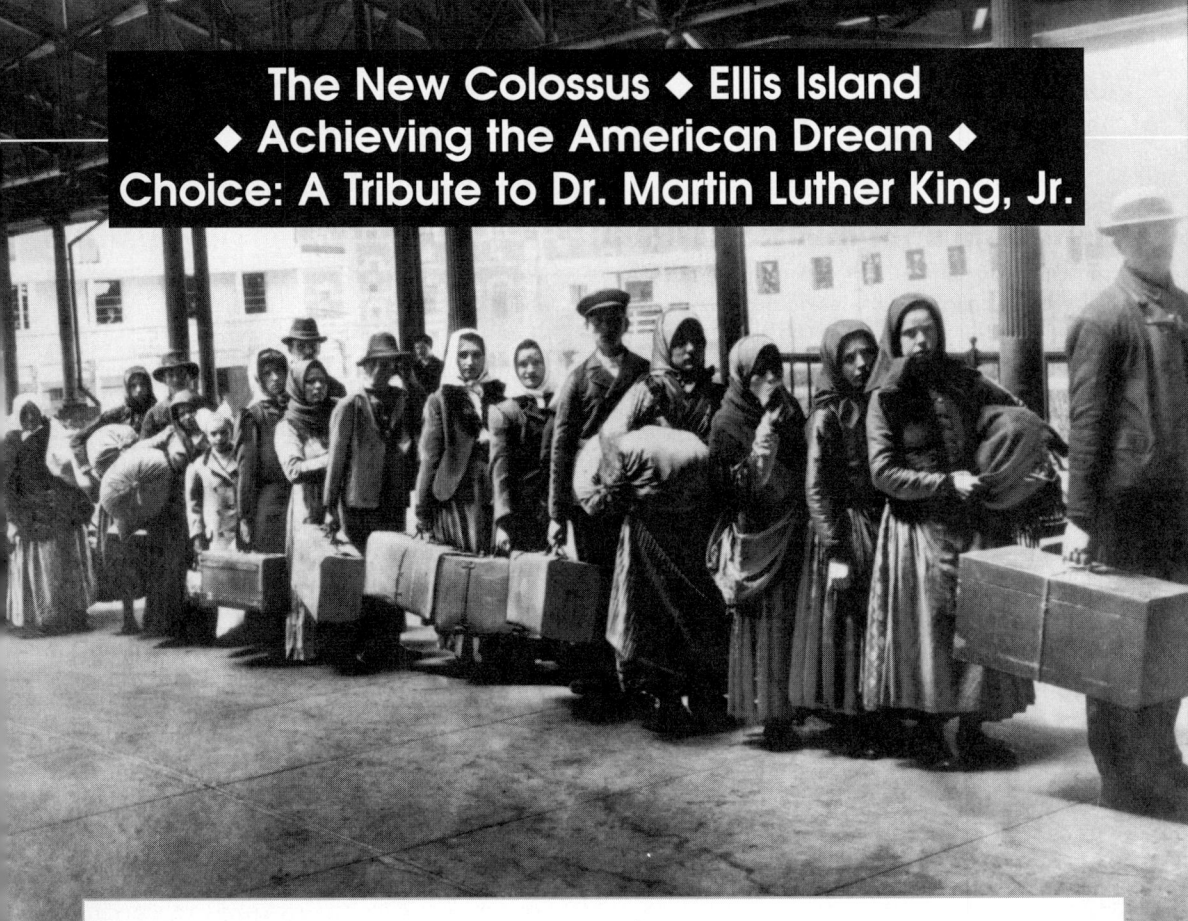

The New Colossus ◆ Ellis Island
◆ Achieving the American Dream ◆
Choice: A Tribute to Dr. Martin Luther King, Jr.

◆ Literary Focus

EPITHET

An **epithet** is a phrase used to point out a characteristic of a person or thing. For example, the "Milky Way" is an epithet for our galaxy, the "Big Apple" is a popular epithet for New York City, and "Honest Abe" is an epithet for Abraham Lincoln. Look for epithets in these selections, and note how they shape your impression of the people and things they describe.

◆ Reading Strategy

SUMMARIZE

When you read a group of selections such as these with related themes, or when you read a longer piece, it's helpful to pause every now and then to **summarize.** When you summarize, you restate in your own words the main points and key details of a piece or a section of a piece.

As you read these selections, summarize each section by filling out a chart like the one below.

Title	Section	Summary
"The New Colossus"	lines 10–14	Welcome to all immigrants.

Guide for Reading ◆ 365

Interest Grabber

Display a picture of the Statue of Liberty. Without any preliminary discussion, ask students to freewrite about that image for three minutes. Then invite them to share some of their thoughts in groups or with the whole class. Lead them to the selection by connecting the symbolism of that famed statue with the hope immigrants feel when they enter a land of promise.

◆ Build Grammar Skills

Correlative Conjunctions If you wish to introduce the grammar concept or skill for this selection before students read, refer to the instruction on p. 374.

Customize for
Less Proficient Readers

An author's message is not always apparent in one reading, especially in poems. Encourage students to reread sections of the works in this set as many times as necessary to determine the author's meaning.

Customize for
More Advanced Students

Each piece in this set reflects certain aspects of the writer's heritage and viewpoint. Provide copies of the Open Mind Organizer, in **Writing and Language Transparencies,** p. 81. Have students use it to jot down impressions of each writer based on his or her words, images, and ideas.

Humanities: Photography

Historical Photos This turn-of-the-century photograph shows newly arrived immigrants waiting to be processed at Ellis Island, in New York Harbor. Direct students to examine the looks on the people's faces.

1. What ideas or feelings might be going through their minds? *Students may cite fear, excitement, fatigue, curiosity, and hope.*

2. What ideas or feelings might go through your own mind if you were waiting in this line? *Students may say that they'd be excited about coming to America or they may say that they would be scared about coming to a new and different place.*

Preparing for Standardized Tests

Reading Summarizing (the reading strategy featured with this selection) will help students answer some reading comprehension items on standardized tests. Summarizing is the restating of key ideas or details in someone's own words. Readers who can summarize show that they have grasped the important points. Use the following sample test question, based on Mario Cuomo's essay "Achieving the American Dream":

On p. 368, Cuomo lovingly describes his parents' grocery store: the sights, smells, tastes, and the customers.

Which statement best summarizes that section?

(A) The store was open 24 hours a day.
(B) The shop offered a glimpse into Italy.
(C) Customers bought cheese and bread.
(D) Jamaica is in the borough of Queens.

Statements *(A), (C),* and *(D)* are all true, and come from that passage, but only *(B)* offers a summary. For further practice, use Reading Strategy: Summarize in **Selection Support,** p. 149.

365

One-Minute Insight In "The New Colossus," the poet expresses her belief in the United States as a sanctuary for immigrants who long for the fresh air of democracy in a land of promise.

Team Teaching Strategy

You might coordinate with a social studies teacher to determine ways to extend instruction. The Beyond Literature feature on p. 373, or the Connections on pp. 367 and 372 of the Teacher Edition are both spring-boards for team teaching.

 Looking at Literature Videodisc/ Videotape

To provide the historical background on Ellis Island and Angel Island, play Chapter 4 of the videodisc. This segment features historical photos and information on immigrants who flocked to Ellis Island and Angel Island in the late 1800's and early 1900's. Discuss why so many people immigrated to the United States during this time in history.

Chapter 4

◆ Literary Focus

❶ Epithet Point out that "The New Colossus" is not only the title of this poem, but is an epithet that Lazarus created for the Statue of Liberty.

▶Critical Viewing◀

❷ Analyze *Students may cite her raised torch, whose light shines over the water and is visible from afar; the sunny rays that flow from her crown; and the protective look on her calm face.*

Customize for
English Language Learners

Five of the words in this sonnet are probably unfamiliar to students acquiring English, but are essential to their grasp of the poem: *beacon, yearning, wretched, refuse, teeming.* You might preview these words with ESL students and invite them to present definitions, synonyms, or examples to classmates.

❶ # THE NEW COLOSSUS
Emma Lazarus

Not like the brazen giant of Greek fame,[1]
With conquering limbs astride from land to land;
Here at our sea-washed, sunset gates shall stand
A mighty woman with a torch, whose flame
5 Is the imprisoned lightning, and her name
Mother of Exiles. From her beacon-hand
Glows world-wide welcome; her mild eyes command
The air-bridged harbor that twin cities frame.
"Keep, ancient lands, your storied pomp!" cries she
10 With silent lips. "Give me your tired, your poor,
Your huddled masses yearning to breathe free,
The wretched refuse of your teeming shore.
Send these, the homeless, tempest-tost[2] to me,
I lift my lamp beside the golden door!"

1. **brazen giant of Greek fame:** The Colossus of Rhodes, one of the Seven Wonders of the World, is a huge bronze statue built at the harbor of Rhodes in commemoration of the siege of Rhodes (305–304 B.C.).
2. **tempest-tost** (tĕm′ pĭst tôst): Here, having suffered a turbulent ocean journey.

▲ **Critical Viewing** In what ways does the Statue of Liberty seem like a welcoming figure? [Analyze]

366 ◆ *From Sea to Shining Sea*

 Block Scheduling Strategies

Consider these suggestions to take advantage of extended class time:

• Spark students' interest by teaching the Viewing and Representing Mini-Lesson, p. 368 of the Teacher Edition, or by using the Interest Grabber, p. 365 of the Teacher Edition.

• Form four groups, one for each work. Appoint a discussion leader for each selection who can facilitate reading, discussing, and sharing answers to the related Guide for Responding

Questions, pp. 367, 369, 373, and 374. Students can move among leaders to have a chance to read and discuss all four pieces.

• Devote class time to having students work in groups on the Projects in the Idea Bank on p. 375, to research the cross-curricular activity in the Social Studies Connection in Beyond Literature on p. 373, to focus on the Speaking and Listening activities on p. 375, or to complete one of the writing activities.

ELLIS ISLAND
Joseph Bruchac

Beyond the red brick of Ellis Island
where the two Slovak children
who became my grandparents
waited the long days of quarantine,[1]
5   after leaving the sickness,
the old Empires of Europe,
a Circle Line ship slips easily
on its way to the island
❸ of the tall woman, green
10 as dreams of forests and meadows
waiting for those who'd worked
a thousand years
yet never owned their own.

Like millions of others,
15 I too come to this island,
nine decades the answerer
of dreams.

Yet only one part of my blood loves
        that memory.
Another voice speaks
20 of native lands
within this nation.
Lands invaded
when the earth became owned.
Lands of those who followed
25 the changing Moon,
❹ knowledge of the seasons
in their veins.

---

1. **quarantine** (kwôr´ ən tēn) *n.*: Period, originally
40 days, during which an arriving vessel suspected
of carrying contagious disease is detained in port
in strict isolation to prevent any diseases from
spreading.

Guide for Responding

◆ LITERATURE AND YOUR LIFE

Reader's Response Which symbol of the United States do you find more moving—the Statue of Liberty or Ellis Island? Explain.

Thematic Focus Which poem has a more optimistic vision of immigrants fulfilling their dreams? Explain.

☑ Check Your Comprehension

1. In "The New Colossus," who is the "mighty woman with a torch," called the "Mother of Exiles"?
2. What does the Colossus "say"?
3. In "Ellis Island," where does the speaker say his grandparents came from?
4. What is "the island of the tall woman" in lines 8 and 9?

◆ Critical Thinking

INTERPRET
1. According to Emma Lazarus's poem, what is the difference between the old Colossus "of Greek fame" and the new Colossus, the Statue of Liberty? **[Compare and Contrast]**
2. What is the attitude of the Colossus toward the immigrants? **[Infer]**
3. What does the speaker in "Ellis Island" mean by the phrase "native lands within this nation"? **[Interpret]**
4. In "Ellis Island," the attitude of the immigrants is different from that of the Native Americans concerning land ownership. Explain the difference. **[Compare and Contrast]**

APPLY
5. Why might people from other countries have viewed the United States as "a land of promise"? **[Apply]**

The New Colossus/Ellis Island ◆ 367

◆ Reading Strategy

❸ **Summarize** Ask students to summarize what the speaker is doing. *As a tourist, he is sailing past the Statue of Liberty to Ellis Island.*

Spelling

❹ The spelling strategy on p. 374 is to find small words in longer ones. Guide students to notice that *knowledge* contains the word *know.*

Reinforce and Extend

Answers
◆ LITERATURE AND YOUR LIFE

Reader's Response Some students may respond to the powerful symbolism of the Statue of Liberty; others may respond to the historic site where people came into the country.

Thematic Focus Most students will say "The New Colossus" because it welcomes people to promise and hope. "Ellis Island" reflects the conflict or discomfort that many people feel about immigration.

☑ Check Your Comprehension
1. She is the Statue of Liberty.
2. She welcomes the "huddled masses yearning to breathe free."
3. They came from Czechoslovakia.
4. It is Liberty Island.

◆ Critical Thinking
1. The old Colossus was a conquering giant; the new Colossus is a motherly figure who welcomes the needy.
2. She wants to take them in.
3. He refers to Native American sacred or tribal lands within the political boundaries of the U.S.
4. Native Americans do not believe that people can own land, but that all beings share the bounties of earth and take what they need. By contrast, European traditions of ownership and title led to conflicts between the groups.
5. The United States may have seemed like a place where good things could happen.

Cross-Curricular Connection: Social Studies

Ellis Island/Angel Island Part of the drama new immigrants faced as they entered America was going through the unsettling stage of being examined by immigration workers. The workers decided to let the newcomers into the country or to turn them away if they were ill, unfit, or lacked proper documents. The sight of the Statue of Liberty was both a welcome and a reminder of yet another step before newcomers could truly be free.

Many late nineteenth- and early twentieth-century immigrants who entered the United States through New York Harbor passed through Ellis Island for processing. Immigrants to the west coast who entered through San Francisco passed through Angel Island. Still other immigrants came into the U. S. through Boston. Have students contact the U.S. Parks Department to gather information on these two sites when they were active immigration centers, and as they are today, as national historic sites. Other students might research the history of "Liberty Enlightening the World," as the Statue of Liberty is officially named.

"Achieving
the American
Dream" was
written by the first-generation son
of hard-working Italian immigrants.
He sees the beauty and promise of
America as a nation of immigrants,
a view that affirms the present while
embracing diverse traditions.

◆ Literary Focus

❶ Epithet Point out the epithet
"Lady Liberty" as another nickname
for the Statue of Liberty. Ask students
what impression this particular epithet
evokes. *Students may say that "Lady
Liberty" suggests respect or honor.*

Comprehension Check ☑

❷ Why would Mr. Cuomo sell Italian
items in his New York City grocery
store? *He sells Italian items because he
is familiar with them and he wants to
keep alive a connection between his
new country and his homeland. He
knows that other Italian immigrants
appreciate their availability.*

►Critical Viewing◄

❸ Deduce *Students may mention
Immaculata's stern look, or her hands on
her son's shoulders, as if guiding him or
showing him off with pride. Young Mario
looks serious, perhaps determined.*

Customize for
Verbal/Linguistic Learners
This story works well read aloud,
as if it were a speech. Have students
deliver it at a deliberate pace, pausing
for laughter or applause.

Achieving the American Dream
Mario Cuomo

In the Provincia di Salerno[1] just outside the Italian city of Naples, a
laborer named Andrea Cuomo asked
Immaculata Giordano to marry him. The
young woman accepted under one condition:
that the couple immigrate to the far-off land of
her dreams—America. Andrea Cuomo agreed,
and after marrying, the Cuomos made the long
voyage to New York Harbor in the late 1920s.
The young couple left the life, the language,
the land, the family, and the friends they
knew, arriving in Lady Liberty's shadow with
no money, unable to speak English, and without any education. They were filled with both
hope and apprehension.

All that my parents brought to their new
home was their burning desire to climb out of
poverty on the strength of their labor. They
believed that hard work would bring them and
their children better lives and help them
achieve the American Dream.

1. **Provincia di Salerno** (prō vin´ sē ə dē sə lär´ nō):
Region surrounding Salerno, a seaport in southern Italy.

368 ◆ From Sea to Shining Sea

At first, my
father went to work in
Jersey City, New Jersey, as
a ditchdigger. After Momma and
Poppa had three children, Poppa
realized he needed to earn more to support his growing family. So he opened a
small Italian American grocery store in South
Jamaica, in the New York City borough
of Queens.

By the time I was born in 1932, the store
was open 24 hours a day, and it seemed as if
Momma and Poppa were working there all the
time. I can still see them waiting on customers
and stocking shelves. And I can still smell and
see and almost taste the food that brought in
the customers: the provolone, the Genoa
salami, the prosciutto,[2] the fresh bread, the

2. **prosciutto** (prə shōōt´ ō) n.: Spicy Italian ham.

▲ **Critical Viewing** Do the facial expressions of the
Cuomos pictured here reveal their determination
to prosper in the United States? Why or why not?
[Deduce]

Viewing and Representing Mini-Lesson

The Immigrant Experience
This mini-lesson supports the Thematic
Focus, "A Land of Promise," as students
empathize with the immigrant experience.

Introduce Have students imagine what
they might feel if they knew they would
leave their homeland forever and move to
a strange new country where they knew
no one, did not speak the language, and had
no idea what life would be like. Remind students that most poor immigrants never had
a chance to return to their homelands, and

many never again saw old friends and family
members. Students who may be recent
immigrants themselves might be willing to
share their own feelings.

Develop Pose this situation to students:
Suppose you could bring only ten things
(not counting clothes) with you as you
immigrate to a new land. What would you
bring, and why? Have students ponder this
challenge, make their selections, and bring
the ten items (or facsimiles of them) to
school in a suitcase or backpack.

Apply Provide display space for each student's array of items. Have students set out
the items with labels identifying what each
is and its significance to them. Allow students'
classmates time to peruse the displays and
to ask questions.

Assess Evaluate students on how well their
displays represent and capture what is important to them. Assess students also on the
explanations they give for what the items
represent and how well they answer their
classmates' questions.

❷ fruits and vegetables. Our store gave our neighbors a delicious taste of Italy in New York.

My parents lacked the education to help us much with our schoolwork. But they taught us every single day, just by being who they were, about the values of family, hard work, honesty, and caring about others. These were not just Italian values, or American ones, but universal values that everyone can embrace.

From my earliest days, I felt <u>immersed</u> in the culture and traditions of my parents' homeland. I grew up speaking Italian. I heard story after story from my parents and relatives about life in the Old Country.

❹ Though not an immigrant myself, I saw the hardships Italian immigrants had to endure. I saw their struggle to make themselves understood in an alien language, their struggle to rise out of poverty, and their struggle to overcome the prejudices of people who felt superior because they or their ancestors had arrived earlier on this nation's shores.

As an Italian American, I grew up believing that America is the greatest country on earth, and thankful that I was born here. But at the same time, I have always been intensely proud that I am the son of Italian immigrants and

that my Italian heritage helped make me the man I am.

The beauty of America is that I don't have to deny my past to affirm my present. No one does. We can love this nation like a parent and still embrace our <u>ancestral</u> home like cherished grandparents.

I like to tell the story of Andrea and Immaculata Cuomo because it tells us what America is about. Their story is the story not just of my parents, or of Italian immigrants at the beginning of this century, but of all immigrants. Our nation is renewed and strengthened by the infusion³ of new Americans from around the world. **❺**

---

3. **infusion** (in fyōō' zhən) *n.*: Addition.

◆ **Build Vocabulary**

immigrate (im' ə grāt) *v.*: Come into a foreign country to make a new home

apprehension (ap' rə hen' shən) *n.*: Fear; anxiety that something bad will happen

immersed (i mʉrst') *adj.*: Deeply involved in

ancestral (an ses' trəl) *adj.*: Of or inherited from one's forefathers or ancestors

Guide for Responding

◆ **LITERATURE AND YOUR LIFE**

Reader's Response What is your reaction to hearing about the experiences of Cuomo's parents? Why?

Thematic Focus Would you say that Cuomo's parents fulfilled the "American Dream"? Explain.

☑ **Check Your Comprehension**

1. Why do Cuomo's parents move to the United States?
2. How do his parents make a living once they arrive in the United States?

◆ **Critical Thinking**

INTERPRET

1. What does Cuomo mean when he says that "I don't have to deny my past to affirm my present"? **[Analyze]**
2. Based on what he says about his own parents, what character traits do you think Mario Cuomo values? **[Deduce]**
3. (a) What is "the American Dream"? (b) How do Mario Cuomo's parents achieve it? **[Infer]**

APPLY

4. In what ways can Mario Cuomo's parents, as described in "Achieving the American Dream," be role models for everyone—not just for immigrants? **[Generalize]**

Achieving the American Dream ◆ 369

Beyond the Classroom

Workplace Skills

Resourcefulness Like many immigrants, the Cuomos started their new life with few possessions and no money. To survive, then to prosper, they had to make do with little, and manage in new surroundings. This ability, known as resourcefulness, is not only a key survival skill, but is also useful at work and in many facets of life.

Resourceful people are creative with what they have; they use items in more than one way. Resourceful people respond to the old saying,

"If life gives you lemons, make lemonade." Have students role-play situations in which resourceful workers make a difference. For example, how might a resourceful coach without a tennis court have her students practice serving? How might a resourceful babysitter without art supplies provide an activity to delight young children? How might a resourceful decorator with a tiny budget brighten up a dull apartment? Conclude by having students envision ways that adults they know are resourceful at their jobs.

Thematic Focus

❹ A Land of Promise Discuss with students the ways in which the promises of America are difficult for immigrants to achieve, regardless of their culture or heritage. *Most immigrants face language barriers, financial strains, the strangeness of new customs and social situations, and the sting of prejudice.*

◆ **Reading Strategy**

❺ Summarize Ask students to summarize the key point of the closing paragraph. *Cuomo sees universal truths in his own parents' experience; he takes pride in knowing how they and other immigrants add to the fabric of America.*

Reinforce and Extend

Answers

◆ **LITERATURE AND YOUR LIFE**

Reader's Response Students may find it inspiring to learn how far the Cuomos came from such humble beginnings.

Thematic Focus Most students will say that they did, because they made a better life for themselves and their family. Despite hardships and obstacles, they found opportunity in America.

☑ **Check Your Comprehension**

1. They want to escape poverty, and they are willing to work hard.
2. Mr. Cuomo works at first digging ditches, then he opens and runs a grocery store with his wife.

◆ **Critical Thinking**

1. He can enjoy his Italian heritage while being a proud American.
2. He values hard work, freedom, honesty, and caring for others.
3. (a) It is the chance to seek your dreams in a land of promise and freedom. (b) Although they start with nothing, through hard work they make a successful new life.
4. They show that anyone who is willing to work hard, to make sacrifices, and to respect others can have the chance to succeed in America.

In "Choice: A Tribute to Dr. Martin Luther King, Jr.," Alice Walker makes the case that King not only achieved success for civil rights on a national level, but his actions and beliefs inspired African Americans to appreciate their heritage.

Comprehension Check ☑

❶ Why is it significant for Dr. King's speech to be given in this particular restaurant? *The accomplishments of the Civil Rights Movement made it possible for people of color to eat in restaurants, go places, and enjoy rights as Americans that had previously been denied to them.*

◆ Reading Strategy

❷ **Summarize** Ask students to summarize the details that lead Walker to make this statement. *She has described the cemetery near her family church, where many of her relatives lie.*

Thematic Focus

❸ **A Land of Promise** In what ways were the hopes of America as "a land of promise" out of reach for African Americans before the gains of the civil rights movement? *Segregation and prejudice kept most African Americans from being able to reap the benefits of freedom.*

►Critical Viewing◄

❹ **Infer** *Students may say that he was an inspiring speaker to have drawn such a large crowd; his ideas must have appealed to many.*

Choice: A Tribute to Dr. Martin Luther King, Jr.

Alice Walker

❶ *This address was made in 1972 at a Jackson, Mississippi, restaurant that refused to serve people of color until forced to do so by the Civil Rights Movement a few years before.*

My great-great-great-grandmother walked as a slave from Virginia to Eatonton, Georgia—which passes for the Walker ancestral home—with two babies on her hips. She lived to be a hundred and twenty-five years old and my own father knew her as a boy. (It is in memory of this walk that I choose to keep and to embrace my "maiden" name, Walker.)

There is a cemetery near our family church where she is buried; but because her marker was made of wood and rotted years ago, it is impossible to tell exactly where her body lies. In the same cemetery are most of my mother's people, who have lived in Georgia for so long nobody even remembers when they came. And all of my great-aunts and -uncles are there, and my grandfather and grandmother, and, very recently, my own father.

❷ If it is true that land does not belong to anyone until they have buried a body in it, then the land of my birthplace belongs to me,

dozens of times over. Yet the history of my family, like that of all black Southerners, is a history of dispossession. We loved the land and worked the land, but we never owned it; and even if we bought land, as my great-grandfather did after the Civil War, it was always in danger of being taken away, as his was, during the period following Reconstruction.[1]

My father inherited nothing of material value from his father, and when I came of age in the early sixties I awoke to the bitter knowledge that in order just to continue to love the land of my birth, I was expected to leave it. For black people—including my parents—had learned a long time ago that to stay willingly in a beloved but brutal place is to risk losing the love and being forced to acknowledge only the brutality.

It is a part of the black Southern sensibility that we treasure memories; for such a long **❸**

---

1. Reconstruction: Period following the American Civil War (1867–1877) when the South was rebuilt and reestablished as part of the Union.

► **Critical Viewing** Judging from the size of the crowd, what can you infer about Dr. Martin Luther King, Jr.? [Infer] **❹**

🎵 Humanities: Music

American Music American music has benefited from the diverse musical styles that immigrants have brought to this country. For instance, jazz, the most American of all music, can trace its roots to Afro-Caribbean rhythms and Eastern European klezmer music. Some of America's great composers, such as George Gershwin, explored ways to combine varied elements and styles of these musical heritages to create fresh, memorable music that represents the diverse nature of the people of the United States. Jazz

musicians play music that has the same unique American influence.

Invite students to focus on an American composer, musical style, or body of music whose roots are elsewhere. Some examples are gospel music, Cajun music, and reggae. You might wish to work with a music teacher to help students find ideas, information, and musical examples. Students can present multimedia reports, play recordings, perform music, or prepare written reports to share the music that they research.

Choice: A Tribute to Dr. Martin Luther King, Jr. ◆ 371

Customize for
English Language Learners
This selection contains a number of English words with which students may not be familiar. They also may encounter unfamiliar forms of words, such as *inherited* and *disinherit,* or *brutal* and *brutality.* Provide self-stick note pads so that students can identify unfamiliar words as they read. Then meet with them in a group or pair them with native speakers to clarify how these words are used in Walker's tribute.

Customize for
Visual/Spatial Learners
Have students examine the composition of the crowd in the photograph on this page. Discuss what conclusions they can draw about Dr. Martin Luther King, Jr.'s, views, based on what they see. Guide them to notice the diversity in age and clothing and to notice that the group is not entirely African American, indicating that Dr. King's ideas spoke to different kinds of people. You may wish to point out the microphones and photographers that show that King was a newsworthy public speaker.

Customize for
Musical/Rhythmic Learners
Dr. Martin Luther King, Jr., was known for his dynamic speeches. One aspect of his public speaking was the musical delivery of his words. He used pitch, pauses, and phrasing to emphasize his spoken ideas. Encourage students to find and listen to a recording of this speech or another of King's famous speeches to hear the musical quality of his speaking.

◈ Speaking and Listening Mini-Lesson

Address
This mini-lesson supports the Speaking and Listening activity in the Idea Bank on p. 375.

Introduce Tell students that an address can be a formal or informal speech, and can be delivered to a small group or an enormous crowd. No matter what the particulars, any good address will engage listeners. In this activity, the address is already written; students will prepare it for oral presentation.

Develop Determine whether students will deliver the address from memory, or be allowed to refer to the text. Encourage them to work on the piece with a partner or peer coach who can make helpful suggestions, such as aiding them to pronounce difficult terms, or finding the best pace.

Apply Have students deliver the address to a small group sitting at a table, as they might sit in a restaurant. Remind audience members to apply appropriate listening skills and respectful behavior.

Assess Evaluate students on how effectively and persuasively they deliver Walker's address, or use the Peer Assessment: Dramatic Performance form, p. 116, in **Alternative Assessment.**

371

◆ **Reading Strategy**

❶ **Summarize** Ask students to summarize the impact on young Alice Walker of seeing Dr. King get arrested that day in 1960. *He was a role model to her, someone who stood up for his rights even at the risk of getting arrested. This had a powerful influence on young Alice, who vowed to fight for what she felt was hers.*

◆ **Literary Focus**

❷ **Epithet** Epithets for Dr. King are The One, The Hero, and The One Fearless Person. All these epithets stress his unique power and his ability to lead and inspire.

Clarification

❸ Ebeneezer Baptist Church is in Atlanta, Georgia, and was where Dr. King regularly preached.

◆ **Reading Strategy**

❹ **Summarize** Discuss with students what Walker means by saying that King "gave us back our heritage." *By championing civil rights for all, King enabled African Americans to gain a sense of belonging to the land where they had long worked and lived, but that had never really been theirs. His pride inspired other African Americans to feel proud and to take their rightful place as full citizens.*

time, that is all of our homeland those of us who at one time or another were forced away from it have been allowed to have.

I watched my brothers, one by one, leave our home and leave the South. I watched my sisters do the same. This was not unusual; abandonment, except for memories, was the common thing, except for those who "could not do any better," or those whose strength or stubbornness was so <u>colossal</u> they took the risk that others could not bear.

In 1960, my mother bought a television set, and each day after school I watched Hamilton Holmes and Charlayne Hunter[2] as they struggled to integrate—fair-skinned as they were—the University of Georgia. And then, one day, there appeared the face of Dr. Martin Luther King, Jr. What a funny name, I thought. At the moment I first saw him, he was being handcuffed and shoved into a police truck. He had dared to claim his rights as a native son, and had been arrested. He displayed no fear, but ❶ seemed calm and serene, unaware of his own extraordinary courage. His whole body, like his <u>conscience</u>, was at peace.

At the moment I saw his resistance I knew I would never be able to live in this country without resisting everything that sought to disinherit me, and I would never be forced away from the land of my birth without a fight.

He was The One, The Hero, The One Fearless Person for whom we had waited. I hadn't even realized before that we *had* been waiting for Martin Luther King, Jr., but we had. And I knew it for sure when my mother added his name to the list of people she prayed for every night.

I sometimes think that it was <u>literally</u> the prayers of people like my mother and father, who had bowed down in the struggle for such a long time, that kept Dr. King alive until five

> ◆ **Literary Focus**
> ❷ What epithets can you find in this paragraph? What impression do they convey?

2. **Hamilton Holmes and Charlayne Hunter:** Hamilton Holmes and Charlayne Hunter made history in January 1961 by becoming the first two African Americans to attend the University of Georgia.

years ago.[3] For years we went to bed praying for his life, and awoke with the question "Is the 'Lord' still here?"

The public acts of Dr. King you know. They are visible all around you. His voice you would recognize sooner than any other voice you have heard in this century—this in spite of the fact that certain municipal libraries, like the one in downtown Jackson, do not carry recordings of his speeches, and the librarians chuckle cruelly when asked why they do not.

You know, if you have read his books, that his is a complex and revolutionary philosophy that few people are capable of understanding fully or have the patience to embody in themselves. Which is our weakness, which is our loss.

And if you know anything about good Baptist preaching, you can imagine what you ❸ missed if you never had a chance to hear Martin Luther King, Jr., preach at Ebeneezer Baptist Church.

You know of the prizes and awards that he tended to think very little of. And you know of his concern for the disinherited: the American Indian, the Mexican-American, and the poor American white—for whom he cared much.

You know that this very room, in this very restaurant, was closed to people of color not more than five years ago. And that we eat here together tonight largely through his efforts and his blood. We accept the common pleasures of life, assuredly, in his name.

But add to all of these things the one thing that seems to me second to none in importance: He gave us back our heritage. He gave us ❹ back our homeland; the bones and dust of our

3. **until five years ago:** Dr. Martin Luther King, Jr. (b. 1929); U.S. clergyman and leader in the civil rights movement from the mid-1950's until his death by assassination on April 4, 1968.

◆ **Build Vocabulary**

colossal (kə läs′ əl) *adj.*: Astonishingly great; extraordinary

conscience (kän′ shəns) *n.*: Knowledge or sense of right and wrong; inner thoughts and feelings

literally (lit′ ər əl ē) *adv.*: Actually; in fact

 Cultural Connection

Immigration When people think of events that changed the demographics of America, many cite waves of European and Asian immigration in the 19th and 20th centuries, or the Gold Rush and land rushes that lured thousands west. One of the most significant American demographic changes was called the Great Migration. This refers to a population shift of millions of African Americans from the rural South to the industrial centers of the Northeast and Midwest. The single

largest wave of the Great Migration took place during World War I, when half a million African Americans moved north.

Have students find out more about this wave of "internal immigration." They can find out what caused this phenomenon, why so many African Americans were willing to uproot themselves, and what impact these demographic changes had on individuals, on communities, and on the fabric of American society.

ancestors, who may now sleep within our caring *and* our hearing. He gave us the blueness of the Georgia sky in autumn as in summer; the colors of the Southern winter as well as glimpses of the green of vacation-time spring. Those of our relatives we used to invite for a visit we now can ask to stay. . . . He gave us full-time use of our woods, and restored our memories to those of us who were forced to run away, as realities we might each day enjoy and leave for our children.

He gave us continuity of place, without which community is ephemeral. He gave us home.

1973

Beyond Literature

Social Studies Connection

March on Washington Until the 1960's, in many places African Americans were prevented from using public facilities, such as drinking fountains, restaurants, buses, and schools. On August 28, 1963, civil rights leader Martin Luther King, Jr., and more than 200,000 other people demonstrated to the world the importance of confronting and solving the racial problems of the United States. They peacefully gathered at the Lincoln Memorial to demand equal justice for all the citizens of the nation. The people were inspired by King's famous "I Have a Dream" speech, which emphasized his vision of a nation where all people would be free. The March on Washington had a strong effect on the country and led to the Civil Rights Act of 1964, which enforced desegregation and outlawed discrimination.

Cross-Curricular Activity

Martin Luther King, Jr., was awarded the Nobel Prize for Peace in 1964. Do some research on King, to achieve a better understanding of his career, his writings, and his important contributions to society. Share your findings with your class.

Guide for Responding

◆ LITERATURE AND YOUR LIFE

Reader's Response Would you have liked to be present when Walker delivered this address? Why or why not?

Thematic Focus How did Dr. Martin Luther King, Jr., help to ensure that America was a land of promise for all its citizens?

Journal Writing Jot down in your journal the names of some people you admire. Note their accomplishments and how they made the world a better place.

☑ Check Your Comprehension

1. Why does Walker say she kept her maiden name?
2. Whom does Walker describe as "The One, The Hero, The One Fearless Person"?
3. What does Alice Walker say is the greatest thing King did?

◆ Critical Thinking

INTERPRET
1. What does Walker mean when she says that the history of her family is one of dispossession? **[Interpret]**
2. Why did Walker and her brothers feel it necessary to leave the place of their birth? **[Analyze]**
3. With what qualities of King's was Walker impressed? **[Connect]**

APPLY
4. What might the atmosphere of the room have been like when Walker delivered this address? **[Speculate]**

COMPARE LITERARY WORKS
5. How does the black southern experience described by Alice Walker compare with that of the Italian immigrant experience described by Mario Cuomo? **[Compare and Contrast]**

Choice: A Tribute to Dr. Martin Luther King, Jr. ◆ 373

Beyond Literature

Students who wish to read the full text of King's speech can find it, with annotations, on the Internet at:

http://douglass.speech.nwu.edu/king_b12.htm

Keep in mind that all Web sites are subject to change. We *strongly recommend* that you preview this site before you send students to it.

Reinforce and Extend

Answers
◆ LITERATURE AND YOUR LIFE

Reader's Response Students may say that they would have liked to hear the address given in the author's own voice, and would have enjoyed asking her questions.

Thematic Focus By devoting his life to end racial segregation and discrimination, he tried to ensure that the promise of this nation would be available to everyone.

☑ Check Your Comprehension

1. She says she kept it to honor her great-great-great-grandmother, who walked to freedom.
2. She refers to Dr. Martin Luther King, Jr.
3. She says that he gave African Americans back their heritage.

◆ Critical Thinking

1. She refers to her people not really owning the land on which they lived and worked.
2. They felt that they had no chance to succeed there, so they had to try their luck elsewhere.
3. His calm serenity moved her.
4. Students might guess that the mood was solemn, respectful, sad, grateful, and proud.
5. Both groups experienced prejudice. But the Cuomo family just had to work hard to make a new life. By contrast, Walker suggests that racial prejudice made it hard for Southern blacks to succeed no matter how hard they worked.

Beyond the Selection

FURTHER READING
Other Works by the Authors
Poems and Translations, Emma Lazarus
Near the Mountains, Joseph Bruchac
Reason to Believe, Mario Cuomo
Horses Make a Landscape Look More Beautiful, Alice Walker
Other Works About the American Dream
"I Have a Dream," Martin Luther King, Jr.
Typical American, Gish Jen
Martin Dressler, Steven Millhauser

INTERNET
We suggest the following sites on the Internet.
For details on the life of Emma Lazarus:
http://www.soros.org/emma/html/emma_.html
For information about Joseph Bruchac:
http://nativeauthors.com/search/bio/biobruchac.html
For biographical information on Mario Cuomo:
http://www.phoenixat.com/~vnn2/MarioC.htm
For more on Alice Walker:
http://www.luminarium.org/contemporary/alicew/
We *strongly recommend* that you preview the sites before you send students to them.

Answers

◆ Reading Strategy

1. On a Circle Line boat sailing past the Statue of Liberty to Ellis Island, the speaker imagines his grandparents entering America.
2. (a) Many of Walker's relatives lie buried in a cemetery near land they loved but never owned. She is grateful to the efforts of Dr. Martin Luther King, Jr., who gave her a sense of place and home. (b) It helps you focus on the most important ideas.

◆ Build Vocabulary

Using Forms of *migrate*

1. migrant
2. immigration
3. migratory

Spelling Strategy

1. ball
2. ear
3. pie
4. pal
5. to + get + her
6. loss

Using the Word Bank

1. g
2. e
3. b
4. c
5. d
6. a
7. f

◆ Literary Focus

1. (a) The New Colossus; Mother of Exiles; (b) Lady Liberty
2. (a) The One, The Hero, The One Fearless Person; (b) They focus on his role as courageous leader.

◆ Build Grammar Skills

Practice

1. neither . . . nor
2. both . . . and
3. not just . . . but
4. either . . . or
5. not only . . . but

Writing Application

Possible responses:

1. The Statue of Liberty is not only an American symbol, but also a symbol of freedom to the world.
2. Dr. Martin Luther King, Jr., was both a scholar and a dynamic leader.

Guide for Responding (continued)

◆ Reading Strategy

SUMMARIZE

Summarizing what you have read is a good way to check your understanding. A summary should restate in your own words the most important points of the original.

1. Summarize the first stanza, or group of lines, in "Ellis Island."
2. (a) List the main points of "Choice: A Tribute to Dr. Martin Luther King, Jr." (b) How can summarizing help you to identify the main points?

◆ Build Vocabulary

USING FORMS OF *migrate*

Remember that *migrate* means "to move from one place to another," and that this meaning is included in its related words. Copy these sentences on your paper. Complete them with one of these forms of *migrate: immigration, migrant,* or *migratory.*

1. The _____?_____ workers picked tomatoes.
2. Most countries control _____?_____.
3. What are the _____?_____ patterns of whales?

SPELLING STRATEGY

One way to master the spelling of a word is to remember smaller words within it. For example, if you remember that the word *loss* appears in the center of *colossal,* you will not be confused about which consonants are doubled.

Identify a smaller word in each word that might help you spell it.

1. balloon   3. piece   5. together
2. early   4. principal   6. glossy

USING THE WORD BANK

Match each Word Bank word with the word or phrase closest in meaning.

1. immigrate   a. inner voice
2. apprehension   b. dipped
3. immersed   c. inherited from ancestors
4. ancestral   d. huge
5. colossal   e. fear
6. conscience   f. actually
7. literally   g. move into a country

◆ Literary Focus

EPITHET

An **epithet** is a phrase that captures an essential quality of a person or thing. For example, an epithet often applied to the Statue of Liberty is "The Lady in the Harbor." Epithets help to make writing and speech colorful and memorable.

1. (a) What are two epithets for the Statue of Liberty in "The New Colossus"? (b) In "Achieving the American Dream," what epithet describes the Statue of Liberty?
2. (a) In "Choice: A Tribute . . .," what three epithets describe Dr. King? (b) On what qualities or characteristics do these epithets focus?

◆ Build Grammar Skills

CORRELATIVE CONJUNCTIONS

Correlative conjunctions, like all conjunctions, are used to join words or series of words. Unlike other conjunctions, correlative conjunctions always appear in pairs. The most commonly used correlative conjunctions are *both . . . and, either . . . or, neither . . . nor,* and *not only . . . but also.*

> This story is *not just* of my parents, *but* of all immigrants.

Practice Rewrite these pairs of sentences, and underline the correlative conjunctions.

1. Neither Andrea nor Immaculata knew what to expect when they set sail for the United States.
2. They were filled with both hope and apprehension.
3. These were not just Italian values, or American ones, but universal values that everyone can embrace.
4. To be an American either you have to be born here or you have to take a citizenship oath.
5. America is not only renewed by new Americans, but also strengthened by them.

Writing Application Write sentences about the following that contain correlative conjunctions.

1. A sentence about the Statue of Liberty
2. A sentence about Martin Luther King, Jr.

✒ Writer's Solution

For additional instruction and practice, use the lesson in the *Writer's Solution Language Lab CD-ROM* on transitions. You may also use the Correlative Conjunction page, p. 26, in the *Writer's Solution Grammar Practice Book.*

Build Your Portfolio

 ## Idea Bank

Writing

1. **Postcard** Put yourself in the place of one of the Slovak children described in "Ellis Island." Write a postcard to the folks back home telling them of your first impressions of the United States.

2. **Journal** Imagine that the Statue of Liberty has come to life. She remembers a typical day when immigrants came through Ellis Island. Write her journal entry for that day. **[Social Studies Link]**

3. **Essay** Write a brief essay in which you describe the qualities that you believe people must possess in order to leave their homeland to emigrate to the United States. If possible, quote lines from one or more selections.

Speaking and Listening

4. **Address** "Choice: A Tribute to Dr. Martin Luther King, Jr.," is an address, or speech, originally given by Alice Walker. Rehearse and deliver this address to your class.

5. **Dramatization [Group Activity]** With a partner, act out a scene between a person who wants to emigrate to the United States and a parent who wants that person to stay home. **[Performing Arts Link]**

Projects

6. **Multimedia Report** Report on the life of Dr. Martin Luther King, Jr. Gather photos, news clippings, and, if possible, video- and audiotapes. Write text to explain and connect the pieces you gather. Then, present the report to the class. **[Media Link; Social Studies Link]**

7. **Monument [Group Activity]** Work with a group to design and build a model of a monument to honor past and future immigrants. Also, plan where you would like your monument to be erected. Finally, work together to write a poem that will be placed on the monument. **[Art Link]**

 ## Writing Mini-Lesson

Tribute

A **tribute** is something, such as a gift or a service, that is given to show respect, affection, or gratitude. In Alice Walker's case, the tribute she gives to Dr. Martin Luther King, Jr., is in the form of a public address, or speech, in his honor. Like Alice Walker, write a tribute to someone to show your respect, admiration, or gratitude—or to show all three of those feelings.

Writing Skills Focus: Transitions
Your writing will flow more easily if you use **transitions**—words and groups of words that connect one idea to another.

Model From
"Achieving the American Dream"
At first, my father went to work in Jersey City, New Jersey, as a ditchdigger. *After* Momma and Poppa had three children, Poppa realized he needed to earn more to support his growing family. *So* he opened a small Italian American grocery store. . . .

Prewriting Choose a person to whom you would like to pay tribute. Jot down admirable qualities that the person possesses, and note good deeds he or she has done. Then, decide on the organization that best fits the details you've gathered.

Drafting As you draft, refer to the notes you've taken to include all the details you planned to use. Use transitions to make connections among your ideas.

> ◆ **Grammar Application**
> As you write, use correlative conjunctions in places where they will help show connections.

Revising Look for places to add transitions to make the connections between ideas clearer. Also, add details wherever appropriate to strengthen the portrait of your subject.

 ## Idea Bank

Following are suggestions for matching the Idea Bank topics with your students' performance levels and learning modalities:

Customize for
Performance Levels
Less Advanced Students: 1, 4, 5, 7
Average Students: 2, 4, 5, 6, 7
More Advanced Students: 3, 4, 5, 6, 7

Customize for
Learning Modalities
Verbal/Linguistic: 1, 2, 3, 4, 5, 6, 7
Visual/Spatial: 6, 7
Bodily/Kinesthetic: 4, 5
Logical/Mathematical: 7
Interpersonal: 5, 6, 7
Intrapersonal: 1, 2, 3

Writing Mini-Lesson

Refer students to the Writing Handbook in the back of the book for instruction on the writing process and for further information on expressive writing. Have students use the Sunburst Organizer, p. 85 in **Writing and Language Transparencies,** to gather details.

 ## Writer's Solution

Writing Lab CD-ROM
Have students complete the tutorial on Expression. Follow these steps:
1. Use the About Expression section to introduce this mode of writing.
2. Use Gathering Details to guide students through prewriting.
3. Have students draft on computer.
4. Have students revise using the Proofreading Checklist.

Writer's Solution Sourcebook
Have students use Chapter 1, "Expression," pp. 1–31, for further support. The chapter includes in-depth instruction on addressing different audiences, p. 18.

✓ ASSESSMENT OPTIONS

Formal Assessment, Selection Test, pp. 112–114, and Assessment Resources Software. The selection test is designed so that it can be easily customized to the performance levels of your students.

Alternative Assessment, p. 28, includes options for less advanced students, more advanced students, visual/spatial learners, logical/ mathematical learners, interpersonal learners, verbal/linguistic learners.

PORTFOLIO ASSESSMENT
Use the following rubrics in the **Alternative Assessment** booklet to assess student writing:
Postcard: Fictional Narrative, p. 91
Journal: Description, p. 93
Essay: Response to Literature, p. 106
Writing Mini-Lesson: Expression, p. 90

OBJECTIVES

1. To read, comprehend, and interpret a selection that has a social studies focus
2. To relate a selection with a social studies focus to personal experience
3. To connect literature to social studies
4. To respond to Social Studies Guiding Questions
5. To respond to the selection through writing, speaking and listening, and projects

SOCIAL STUDIES GUIDING QUESTIONS

Reading about the legend of King Arthur will help students discover answers to these Social Studies Guiding Questions:

• How have historical events affected the culture of the United States?

• What are some ways that citizens define loyalty to their nation?

Interest Grabber Invite students to write or draw words and images they connect to the United States. Circulate or post examples. Ask students to imagine that they have been banished from the United States—they can never return, contact loved ones, or hear news of home. (Be aware of and sensitive to the fact that some students may have had similar experiences with their native homes.) How would they feel? Can they imagine a crime deserving of this punishment? What attitude would they adopt in order to survive?

Map Study

Historical Maps, Legends, and Route Maps Historical maps can help students understand geographical changes occurring over time, and thereby place events from literature in a more vivid context. For example, the map on this page depicts the United States as defined in 1807, when the selection story begins. Students can use the map as they read to understand Philip Nolan's image of his country. Additionally, the route maps indicated on the map and its legends help explain how the nation changed over time.

CONNECTING LITERATURE TO SOCIAL STUDIES
A YOUNG NATION

The Man Without a Country *by Edward Everett Hale*

The United States in 1803

United States (1802)	Lewis and Clark 1804–1806
Louisiana Purchase (1803)	Pike 1805–1806
	Pike 1806–1807

376 ◆ From Sea to Shining Sea

THE NATION TAKES SHAPE Following the Revolutionary War, the United States went through a sometimes difficult process of establishing itself as a nation. As the system of government was put in place, political leaders came into conflict about the balance of power between the central government and individual states. At the same time, the country was rapidly expanding—the Louisiana Purchase (1803) doubled the size of the United States—and differences between the northern and southern states began to take on increasing importance.

Aaron Burr "The Man Without a Country" is set during this turbulent time. The main character is tried for treason after aligning himself with Aaron Burr, a key political figure of the late 1700's and early 1800's, whose career ended in disgrace. A lawyer and career politician, Burr ran for President in 1800. He received the same number of votes as Thomas Jefferson, and the U.S. House of Representatives had to vote to break the tie, making Jefferson President and Burr Vice President. Alexander Hamilton, who was Secretary of the Treasury, cast one of the votes that defeated Burr in the House. He later opposed Burr in his bid for governor of New York. Following Burr's loss, Burr challenged Hamilton to a duel, fatally wounding Hamilton with one shot. Following that incident, Burr's career declined. He was accused of planning to invade Mexico to establish a separate government there. He was tried for treason in 1807 but was acquitted of the charges.

A Story With a Moral Edward Everett Hale was a strong supporter of patriotism. He wrote "The Man Without a Country" as a way of getting his views across. Although the story is fictional, Hale wove many historical facts into the story, giving it the flavor of a nonfiction piece.

Prentice Hall Literature Program Resources

REINFORCE / RETEACH / EXTEND
Selection Support Pages
Build Vocabulary, p. 151
Connect Literature to Social Studies, p. 152
Formal Assessment Selection Test, pp. 115–116
Assessment Resources Software
Readings From Social Studies
Writing and Language Transparencies
Series of Events Chain, p. 57

Resource Pro CD-ROM "The Man Without a Country"—includes all resource material and customizable lesson plan

Listening to Literature Audiocassettes "The Man Without a Country"
Connection to Prentice Hall World Explorer *Western Hemisphere*—Ch. 7, "The United States and Canada: Shaped by History"
Connection to Prentice Hall The American Nation—Ch. 8, "The Age of Jefferson"

The Man Without a Country

Edward Everett Hale

I suppose that very few casual readers of the *New York Herald* of August 13, 1863, observed, in an <u>obscure</u> corner, among the "Deaths," the announcement:

NOLAN. Died, on board U.S. Corvette *Levant*, Lat. 2° 11' S., Long. 131° W., on the 11th of May, PHILIP NOLAN.

Hundreds of readers would have paused at the announcement had it read thus: "Died, May 11, THE MAN WITHOUT A COUNTRY." For it was as "The Man Without a Country" that poor Philip Nolan had generally been known by the officers who had him in charge during some fifty years, as, indeed, by all the men who sailed under them.

There can now be no possible harm in telling this poor creature's story. Reason enough there has been till now for very strict secrecy, the secrecy of honor itself, among the gentlemen of the Navy who have had Nolan in charge. And certainly it speaks well for the profession and the personal honor of its members that to the press this man's story has been wholly unknown—and, I think, to the country at large also. This I do know, that no naval officer has mentioned Nolan in his report of a cruise.

But there is no need for secrecy any longer. Now the poor creature is dead, it seems to me worthwhile to tell a little of his story, by way of showing young Americans of today what it is to be "A Man Without a Country."

Philip Nolan was as fine a young officer as there was in the "Legion of the West," as the Western division of our army was then called.

◆ Build Vocabulary

obscure (äb skyoor')
adj: Hidden; not obvious

The Man Without a Country ◆ 377

Links Across Time

❶ Aaron Burr Explain that Aaron Burr traveled through the American West recruiting men for what many believed was his plan to invade Mexico. It was also suspected that Burr was scheming to detach part of the Southwest from the United States.

Clarification

❷ Explain that people serving in the armed forces are subject to military, or martial, law. This law differs from the civil and criminal laws governing ordinary citizens. Thus, if a soldier is accused of breaking the law, he or she is tried by a military court in a proceeding called a *court-martial*.

CONNECTING LITERATURE TO SOCIAL STUDIES

❸ Loyalties Ask students what they think Burr had accomplished with Nolan. Why was Nolan now loyal to Burr? What does this suggest about how political loyalties may be formed? *Burr had succeeded in shifting Nolan's loyalty from the U.S. to Burr personally. Nolan was loyal to Burr because of the leader's special attention to him. Students may infer that political loyalties often arise from personal loyalties.*

Customize for
English Language Learners

This story contains references to military procedure and U.S. history which may be unfamiliar to students. Assign a proficient partner to draw, explain, or pantomime confusing elements, using the selection illustrations where these are helpful.

Customize for
More Advanced Students

Review with students that this story is fictional, though peppered with realistic historical details. Invite students, as they read, to list details or events they believe to be factual. Have them research to prove or disprove their belief and then record their findings. They might use a chart like the following:

Detail	Real/ Fictional	History
Aaron Burr's journey	real	part of Burr's supposed recruiting trip

Guide students to recognize how the factual details make the story seem real and thus increase its impact.

378

 When Aaron Burr[1] made his first dashing expedition down to New Orleans in 1805, he met this gay, dashing, bright young fellow. Burr marked[2] him, talked to him, walked with him, took him a day or two's voyage in his flatboat,[3] and, in short, fascinated him. For the next year, barrack life was very tame to poor Nolan. He occasionally <u>availed</u> himself of the permission the great man had given him to write to him. Long, <u>stilted</u> letters the poor boy wrote and rewrote and copied. But never a line did he have in reply. The other boys in the garrison[4] sneered at him, because he lost the fun which they found in shooting or rowing while he was working away on these grand letters to his grand friend. But before long the young fellow had his revenge. For this time His Excellency, the Honorable Aaron Burr, appeared again under a very different aspect. There were rumors that he had an army behind him and an empire before him. At that time the youngsters all envied him. Burr had not been talking twenty minutes with the commander before he asked him to send for Lieutenant Nolan. Then, after a little talk, he asked Nolan if he could show him something of the great river and the plans for the new post. He asked Nolan to take him out in

his skiff to show him a canebrake[5] or a cottonwood tree, as he said—really to win him over; and by the time the sail was over, Nolan was enlisted body and soul. From that time, though he did not yet know it, he lived as a man without a country.

What Burr meant to do I know no more than you. It is none of our business just now. Only, when the grand catastrophe came—Burr's great treason trial at Richmond—some of the lesser fry at Fort Adams[6] got up a string of court-martials on the officers there. One and another of the colonels and majors were tried, and, to fill out the list, little Nolan, against whom there was evidence enough that he was sick of the service, had been willing to be false to it, and would have obeyed any order to march anywhere had the order been signed "By command of His Exc. A. Burr." The courts dragged on. The big flies[7] escaped—rightly, for all I know. Nolan was proved guilty enough, yet you and I would never have heard of him but that, when the president of the court asked him at the close whether he wished to say anything to show that he had always been faithful to the United States, he cried

---

1. **Aaron Burr:** American political leader (1756–1836). Burr was U.S. Vice President from 1801 to 1805. He was believed to have plotted to build an empire in the Southwest.
2. **marked** *v.*: Here, paid attention to.
3. **flatboat** *n.*: Boat with a flat bottom.
4. **garrison** (gar′ ə sən) *n.*: Military post or station.

5. **canebrake** (kān′ brāk′) *n.*: Dense area of cane plants.
6. **Fort Adams:** Fort at which Nolan was stationed.
7. **big flies:** Burr and the other important men who may have been involved in his scheme.

▲ **Critical Viewing** This is a portrait of Aaron Burr. In it, is he depicted as a distinguished statesman or as a disgraced traitor? Explain. **[Make a Judgment]**

378 ◆ From Sea to Shining Sea

 Block Scheduling Strategies

Consider these suggestions to take advantage of extended class time:

- Have students record key events of Nolan's sentence using the Series of Events Chain, p. 57, in **Writing and Language Transparencies.** The information can form background for the Letter or Oral Report in the Idea Bank, p. 391.
- Preview the selection with students, using the text and map on p. 376 and the selection illustrations. Then, as students read, pause to discuss background. Pair students to answer the end-of-selection questions, pp. 390–391.

- Play the audiocassette of "The Man Without a Country" to establish the story's mood. Use the chapters of *World Explorer* and *The American Nation,* as noted in Program Resources on p. 48. If you have access to technology, use video and CD-ROM components such as *Prentice Hall United States History Video Collection* and *American Heritage History of the United States CD-ROM* to broaden students' grasp of the historical context for this story.

Listening to Literature Audiocassettes

out, in a fit of frenzy:

"Damn the United States! I wish I may never hear of the United States again!"

4 I suppose he did not know how the words shocked old Colonel Morgan, who was holding the court. Half the officers who sat in it had served through the Revolution, and their lives had been risked for the very idea which he cursed in his madness. He, on his part, had grown up in the West of those days. He had been educated on a plantation where the finest company was a Spanish officer or a French merchant from Orleans. His education had been perfected in commercial expeditions to Vera Cruz, and I think he told me his father once hired an Englishman to be a private tutor for a winter on the plantation. He had spent half his youth with an older brother, hunting horses in Texas; and to him "United States" was scarcely a reality. I do not excuse Nolan; I only explain to the reader why he cursed his country and wished he might never hear her name again.

> **Connecting Literature to Social Studies**
> What does Hale suggest about how the term "United States" changed in meaning between 1776 and 1863?

5

6 Old Morgan, as I said, was terribly shocked. If Nolan had compared George Washington to Benedict Arnold, or had cried, "God save King George," Morgan would not have felt worse. He called the court into his private room, and returned in fifteen minutes, with a face like a sheet, to say: "Prisoner, hear the sentence of the Court! The Court decides, subject to the approval of the President, that you never hear the name of the United States again."

Nolan laughed. But nobody else laughed. Old Morgan was too solemn, and the whole room was hushed dead as night for a minute. Even Nolan lost his <u>swagger</u> in a moment. Then Morgan added: "Mr. Marshal, take the prisoner to Orleans in an armed boat, and deliver him to the naval commander there."

The marshal gave his orders and the prisoner was taken out of court.

"Mr. Marshal," continued old Morgan, "see that no one mentions the United States to the prisoner. Mr. Marshal, make my respects to Lieutenant Mitchell at Orleans, and request him to order that no one shall mention the United States to the prisoner while he is on board ship. You will receive your written orders from the officer on duty here this evening. The court is adjourned."

Before the *Nautilus*[8] got round from New Orleans to the Northern Atlantic coast with the prisoner on board, the sentence had been approved, and he was a man without a country.

The plan then adopted was substantially the same which was necessarily followed ever after. The Secretary of the Navy was requested to put Nolan on board a government vessel bound on a long cruise, and to direct that he should be only so far confined there as to make it certain that he never saw or heard of the country. We had few long cruises then, and I do not know certainly what his first cruise was. But the commander to whom he was entrusted regulated the etiquette and the precautions of the affair, and according to his scheme they were carried out till Nolan died.

When I was second officer of the *Intrepid*, some thirty years after, I saw the original paper of instructions. I have been sorry ever since that I did not copy the whole of it. It ran, however, much in this way:

> Washington (with a date, which must have been late in 1807).
>
> Sir:
>
> You will receive from Lieutenant Neale the person of Philip Nolan, late a lieutenant in the United States Army.
>
> This person on his trial by court-

---

8. ***Nautilus:*** Naval ship to which Nolan was assigned.

◆ **Build Vocabulary**

availed (ə vāld´) *v.*: Made use of

stilted (stil´ təd) *adj.*: Unnatural; very formal

swagger (swag´ ər) *n.*: Arrogance or boastfulness

The Man Without a Country ◆ 379

CONNECTING LITERATURE TO SOCIAL STUDIES

4 **National Unity** Explain that during the nation's early decades, many American citizens identified more strongly with their state or region. Some wanted to increase state loyalty by limiting national government's powers. This debate contributed to the Civil War, in which Southerners fought in part for regional independence. Ask students to compare Colonel Morgan's view of the United States with that of Philip Nolan. *Nolan's loyalty was probably to Texas or the western region; the United States was a far-away and abstract entity to Nolan, rather than the precious ideal it was to Morgan.*

CONNECTING LITERATURE TO SOCIAL STUDIES

5 **Infer** Remind students that the story opens with Nolan's 1863 death announcement, printed in a New York newspaper. *If the death of a Texan is now printed in a New York newspaper, perhaps the "United States" is more united in 1863 than in 1807.*

Links Across Time

6 Benedict Arnold was an American revolutionary who switched sides to fight for the British. The oath to King George of England was typically used by British subjects. The narrator uses these examples to describe Nolan's traitorous words.

Customize for
Visual/Spatial Learners
Point out that Nolan's journey begins at New Orleans. After locating this city on a current world map, have students begin their own map to trace Nolan's journey.

Customize for
More Advanced Students
Provide students with the following background: In 1807, to establish neutrality in the conflicts raging between France and Great Britain, President Jefferson passed the Embargo Act forbidding American imports or exports. Challenge students to speculate on how this might affect the U.S. Navy and its ships. Urge them to explore how other real political changes (such as those identified for students in *The Nation Takes Shape* on p. 376) at home might have affected Philip Nolan's life.

 Cultural Connection

Patriotism and Cultural Loyalty "The Man Without a Cause" stresses the importance of patriotism. In a society as culturally diverse as ours, however, patriotism often coexists with other loyalties. For many Americans, their style of dress is one way to express those other loyalties. African Americans may wear kente cloth, a traditional African fabric, to show pride in their heritage. Members of religious groups, such as Hasidic Jews, Sikhs, and the Amish, wear distinctive styles of dress. Even "the wearing o' the green" on St. Patrick's Day was originally a statement of Irish pride.

Invite students to conduct interviews with classmates, family, or friends, asking what patriotism and cultural loyalty mean to them. Identify some ways they express these feelings in daily life. Have students present their findings.

1 Remind students of, and if necessary explain, the saying "Be careful what you wish for because you may get it." Then ask them to recall times they have wished for something, only to regret that wish later. Invite volunteers to share their memories.

CONNECTING LITERATURE TO SOCIAL STUDIES

2 **Personal Identity** Note with students that the men didn't like to eat with Nolan because they couldn't discuss life in the U.S. Discuss how sharing experiences and a common cultural background both contribute to an individual's identity and also brings that individual into a community.

Customize for
Musical/Rhythmic Learners

Read aloud or play a recording of the song "America the Beautiful." Play recordings of "Freedom" and "The Only Home I Know Of" from the musical *Shenandoah*. Examine with students the patriotism and love for country that inspired each of these works. Discuss how these themes relate to Hale's story.

Customize for
Logical/Mathematical Learners

Have students reread the terms of Nolan's sentence. Ask them to analyze the problems that might arise in enforcing such a sentence. Urge them, as they read, to look for any inconsistencies in the sentence and also for ways that Nolan evades it.

Customize for
Visual/Spatial Learners

Invite students to draw a uniform front, first with ordinary and then with "plain" buttons. Discuss what other visual changes might need to be made on a naval boat in order to distance Nolan from any symbols of the United States.

---

martial expressed, with an oath, the wish that he might "never hear of the United States again."

The court sentenced him to have his wish fulfilled.

For the present, the execution of the order is entrusted by the President to this department.

You will take the prisoner on board your ship, and keep him there with such precautions as shall prevent his escape.

You will provide him with such quarters, rations, and clothing as would be proper for an officer of his late rank, if he were a passenger on your vessel on the business of his government.

The gentlemen on board will make any arrangements agreeable to themselves regarding his society. He is to be exposed to no indignity of any kind, nor is he ever unnecessarily to be reminded that he is a prisoner.

But under no circumstances is he ever to hear of his country or to see any information regarding it; and you will especially caution all the officers under your command to take care that this rule, in which his punishment is involved, shall not be broken.

It is the intention of the government that he shall never again see the country which he has disowned. Before the end of your cruise you will receive orders which will give effect to this intention.

> Respectfully yours,
> W. Southard,
> for the Secretary of the Navy.

The rule adopted on board the ships on which I have met "the man without a country" was, I think, transmitted from the beginning. No mess[9] liked to have him permanently, because his presence cut off all talk of home or of the prospect of return, of politics or letters, of peace or of war—cut off

---

9. **mess** *n.*: Here, a group of people who routinely have their meals together.

---

more than half the talk men liked to have at sea. But it was always thought too hard that he should never meet the rest of us, except to touch hats, and we finally sank into one system. He was not permitted to talk with the men, unless an officer was by. With officers he had unrestrained intercourse, as far as they and he chose. But he grew shy, though he had favorites: I was one. Then the captain always asked him to dinner on Monday. Every mess in succession took up the invitation in its turn. According to the size of the ship, you had him at your mess more or less often at dinner. His breakfast he ate in his own stateroom. Whatever else he ate or drank, he ate or drank alone. Sometimes, when the marines or sailors had any special jollification,[10] they were permitted to invite "Plain Buttons," as they called him. Then Nolan was sent with some officer, and the men were forbidden to speak of home while he was there. I believe the theory was that the sight of his punishment did them good. They called him "Plain Buttons," because, while he always chose to wear a regulation army uniform, he was not permitted to wear the army button, for the reason that it bore either the initials or the insignia of the country he had disowned.

I remember, soon after I joined the Navy, I was on shore with some of the older officers from our ship and some of the gentlemen fell to talking about Nolan. Someone told of the

---

10. **jollification** (jäl´ ə fi kā´ shən) *n.*: Merry-making.

 Beyond the Classroom

Career Connection
Military Service The sailors who are Nolan's companions may have spent years at sea. Today, U.S. military personnel are stationed all over the world, both on ships and land. They can sometimes interact with the cultures they visit—for example, learning languages. Though technology such as e-mail has expanded their ability to communicate, these servicemen and women may feel isolated from community and family. Unlike the sailors of Nolan's day, however, they have the capability of returning before the ship does.

Community Connection
Military Bases Families of servicemen or women may live on U.S. military bases, or accompany their family member to live on U.S. bases abroad. In both cases, a community of people supports one another through on-base services such as child care, schools, and medical facilities.

Invite students to interview a soldier or a member of a military family. What does he or she regard as the advantages and disadvantages of military service? How does the military community provide support?

system which was adopted from the first about his books and other reading. As he was almost never permitted to go on shore, even though the vessel lay in port for months, his time at the best hung heavy. Everybody

USS Constitution and HMS Guerriere (Aug. 19, 1812), Thomas Birch, U.S. Naval Academy Museum

3 ▲ **Critical Viewing** What might Nolan's life have been like, spent aboard ships like this? [Speculate]

was permitted to lend him books, if they were not published in America and made no allusion to it. These were common enough in the old days. He had almost all the foreign papers that came into the ship, sooner or later; only somebody must go over them first, and cut out any advertisement or stray paragraph that referred to America. This was a little cruel sometimes, when the back of what was cut out might be innocent. Right in the midst of one of Napoleon's battles poor Nolan would

find a great hole, because on the back of the page of that paper there had been an advertisement of a packet[11] for New York, or a scrap from the President's message. This was the first time I ever heard of this plan. I remember it, because poor Phillips, who was of the party, told a story of something which happened at the Cape of Good Hope on Nolan's first voyage. They had touched at the Cape, paid their respects to the English Admiral and the fleet, and then Phillips had borrowed a lot of English books from an officer. Among them was *The Lay of the Last Minstrel*,[12] which they had all of them heard of, but which most of them had never seen. I think it could not have been published long. Well, nobody thought there could be any risk of anything national in that. So Nolan was permitted to join the circle one afternoon when a lot of them sat on deck reading aloud. In his turn, Nolan took the book and read to the others; and he read very well. Nobody in the circle knew a line of the poem, only it was all magic and chivalry, and was ten thousand years ago. Poor Nolan read steadily through the fifth canto,[13] stopped a minute and drank something, and then began, without a thought of what was coming:

Breathes there the man, with soul so dead
Who never to himself hath said,—

It seems impossible to us that anybody ever heard this for the first time; but all these fellows did then, and poor Nolan himself

---

11. **packet** *n.*: Boat that carries passengers, freight, and mail along a regular route.
12. ***The Lay of the Last Minstrel:*** Narrative poem by Sir Walter Scott, Scottish poet and novelist (1771–1832).
13. **canto** (kan´ tō) *n.*: A main division of certain long poems.

The Man Without a Country ◆ 381

▶**Critical Viewing**◀

3 **Speculate** *Students should note the isolation, cramped quarters, exposure to storms, and battle dangers—as well as adventures—of life spent on ship.*

Links Across Time

4 In the early 1800s, France was led by Napoleon I. A brilliant military leader, Napoleon won repeated victories over Austria, Britain, and Russia and largely redrew the map of Europe. In 1812, Napoleon invaded Russia but was caught by the Russian winter. This disaster helped turn the tide against him, and in 1814, Napoleon was defeated. People around the world were greatly interested in his activities throughout the rise and fall of his power.

CONNECTING LITERATURE TO SOCIAL STUDIES

5 **Draw Conclusions** After looking at an atlas, have students explain something of Philip Nolan's experiences on this particular journey. *Students should conclude that the journey was long, as the Cape of Good Hope is at the southern tip of Africa. Explain also that in 1814, the British seized the Cape as a territory.*

Customize for
Bodily/Kinesthetic Learners
Give students a newspaper and some scissors. Tell them to highlight and then remove all mentions, in both text and advertising, of a particular entity (your community or state, for example). When students are done, link the activity to the story by discussing the emotions the task inspired. Emphasize the lengths Nolan's guards went to in enforcing his sentence and guide students in recognizing the resentment sailors may have felt about the inconveniences his presence caused.

Humanities: Art

USS *Constitution* **and HMS** *Guerriere,* (August 19, 1812), by Thomas Birch
Thomas Birch (1779–1851) emigrated to the United States from England in 1793. A boat trip down the Delaware River sparked Birch's interest in the sea and ships.
During the War of 1812 between the U.S. and Great Britain, Birch painted a series of historical views of American naval victories. This painting, *U.S.S. Constitution and H.M.S. Guerriere* (Aug. 19, 1812), is from this series. The painting is a glorified impression of the encounter between the two ships.

1. Based on this painting, describe a typical sea battle. *Students may suggest that a sea battle is messy, smoky, and very dangerous.*
2. What features shown in the painting suggest the vulnerability of these ships? *Students may note the ships' small size, high masts causing instability, fabric sails, and wooden hulls, as opposed to the metal warships that are built today.*
3. Which side do you think is winning? How can you tell? *The U.S. appears to be winning, as several American flags fly high in prominent positions while the British ship with its flags is floundering.*

1 Infer Discuss with students why this line is so significant to Nolan—he has been cut off from his native land and cannot even say its name. Extend the discussion by telling students that the word *native* comes from the root *natus,* meaning "to be born." Remind them, however, that for many Americans throughout our history, America has been "home" without being the land of their birth. Discuss what makes a place feel like home.

Clarification

2 The Cape of Good Hope, from which Nolan's ship has journeyed, is at the southern tip of Africa, while the Windward Islands lie just east of the Caribbean Sea.

►Critical Viewing◄

3 Connect *They are attached by ankle shackles to a bar. Also, their expressions suggest hopelessness.*

Customize for
Verbal/Linguistic
Invite students to read aloud the poem from the text. Ask them to explain its effect on Nolan. Suggest that they analyze the specific words used in the poem, as well as the overall connotative or emotional impact of the language. Invite students to share their analysis with the class.

Customize for
Visual/Spatial Learners
Have students use a world map to trace the ship's route from the Cape of Good Hope to the Windward Islands. Then have them trace the second ship's route from that site of rendezvous and exchange to the Mediterranean. Discuss what it might feel like to Nolan to be crisscrossing the sea in this manner. Have them add the routes to their ongoing map.

---

went on, still unconsciously or mechanically:

1 | This is my own, my native land!

Then they all saw that something was to pay; but he expected to get through, I suppose, turned a little pale, but plunged on:

> Whose heart hath ne'er within him
> burned,
> As home his footsteps he hath turned
> From wandering on a foreign strand?—
> If such there breathe, go, mark him well,—

By this time the men were all beside themselves, wishing there was any way to make him turn over two pages; but he had not quite presence of mind for that; he gagged a little, colored crimson, and staggered on:

> For him no minstrel raptures swell;
> High though his titles, proud his name,
> Boundless his wealth as wish can claim,
> Despite these titles, power, and pelf,[14]
> The wretch, concentered all in self,—

and here the poor fellow choked, could not go on, but started up, swung the book into the sea, vanished into his stateroom, "And by Jove," said Phillips, "we did not see him for two months again. And I had to make up some beggarly story to that English surgeon why I did not return his Walter Scott to him."

That story shows about the time when Nolan's braggadocio[15] must have broken down. At first, they said, he took a very high tone, considered his imprisonment a mere farce, affected to enjoy the voyage, and all that; but Phillips said that after he came out of his stateroom he never was the same man again. He never read aloud again, unless it was the Bible or Shakespeare, or something else he was sure of. But it was not that merely. He never entered in with the other young men exactly as a companion again. He was always shy afterwards, when I knew him—very seldom spoke unless he was spoken to, except to a very few friends.

---

14. **pelf** *n.*: Ill-gotten wealth.
15. **braggadocio** (brag´ ə dō´ shē ō) *n.*: Here, pretense of bravery; Nolan acts as if he does not mind his imprisonment.

Generally he had the nervous, tired look of a heart-wounded man.

When Captain Shaw was coming home, rather to the surprise of everybody they made one of the Windward Islands, and lay off and on for nearly a week. The boys said the officers were sick of salt-junk,[16] and meant to have turtle-soup before they came home. But

▲ **Critical Viewing** What details in this drawing reveal that these men are prisoners? [Connect] **3**

after several days the *Warren* came to the same rendezvous;[17] they exchanged signals; she told them she was outward bound, perhaps to the Mediterranean, and took poor Nolan and his traps[18] on the boat to try his second cruise. He looked very blank when he was told to get ready to join her. He had known enough of the signs of the sky to know that till that moment he was going **4**

---

16. **salt-junk** *n.*: Hard salted meat.
17. **rendezvous** (rän´ dā vōō) *n.*: Meeting place.
18. **traps** *n.*: Here, bags or luggage.

Cultural Connection

Exiles Remind students of the poem "The Lay of the Last Minstrel," which Nolan reads, and discuss patriotism, or the love of one's country. Explain that many people throughout history have been punished by being sent into exile. Perhaps the most famous of these was Napoleon (about whom Nolan tries to read), who was exiled to the small Mediterranean island of Elba. Other famous patriots have fought for their countries' independence, such as Gandhi in India, Nasser in Egypt, and Mandela in South Africa. In all these examples, patriotism sometimes meant risking one's life and often meant standing at odds with popularly held opinions or policies.

Have students research and read about one or more of these patriots or another famous patriot. Then ask them to write their definition of a patriot. What qualities should a patriot have? Does being a patriot always mean agreeing with the policies of your country?

"home." But this was a distinct evidence of something he had not thought of, perhaps—that there was no going home for him, even to a prison. And this was the first of some twenty such transfers, which brought him sooner or later into half our best vessels, but which kept him all his life at least some hundred miles from the country he had hoped he might never

Prisoners, from Iconographic Encyclopedia, drawn by G. Heck, eng. by Henry Winkles, Collection of The New-York Historical Society

❹ I hear of again.

It may have been on that second cruise—it was once when he was up the Mediterranean—that Mrs. Graff, the celebrated Southern beauty of those days, danced with him. The ship had been lying a long time in the Bay of Naples, and the officers were very intimate in the English fleet, and there had been great festivities, and our men thought they must give a great ball on board the ship. They wanted to use Nolan's stateroom for something, and they hated to do it without asking him to the ball; so the captain said they might ask him, if they would be responsible that he did not talk with the wrong

❺

people, "who would give him intelligence."[19] So the dance went on. For ladies they had the family of the American consul, one or two travelers who had adventured so far, and a nice bevy of English girls and matrons.

Well, different officers relieved each other in standing and talking with Nolan in a friendly way, so as to be sure that nobody else spoke to him. The dancing went on with spirit, and after a while even the fellows who took this honorary guard of Nolan ceased to fear any trouble.

As the dancing went on, Nolan and our fellows all got at ease—so much so, that it seemed quite natural for him to bow to that splendid Mrs. Graff, and say, "I hope you have not forgotten me, Miss Rutledge. Shall I have the honor of dancing?"

He did it so quickly, that Fellows, who was with him, could not hinder him. She laughed and said, "I am not Miss Rutledge any longer, Mr. Nolan; but I will dance all the same." She nodded to Fellows, as if to say he must leave Mr. Nolan to her, and led him off to the place where the dance was forming.

Nolan thought he had got his chance. He had known her at Philadelphia, and at other places had met her. He began with her travels, and Europe, and then he said boldly—a little pale, she said, as she told me the story years after—"And what do you hear from home, Mrs. Graff?"

And that splendid creature looked through him. How she must have looked through him!

"Home! Mr. Nolan! I thought you were the man who never wanted to hear of home again!"—and she walked directly up the deck to her husband, and left poor Nolan alone. He did not dance again.

A happier story than either of these I have told is of the war.[20] That came along soon after. I have heard this affair told in three or four ways—and, indeed, it may have

> **Connecting Literature to Social Studies**
> Why would a song called "The Old Thirteen" be something that could not be mentioned in front of Nolan?

❻

---

19. **intelligence** *n.*: Here, news about his country.
20. **the war:** The War of 1812 between the United States and Great Britain.

The Man Without a Country ◆ 383

CONNECTING LITERATURE TO SOCIAL STUDIES

❹ Interpret Ask students how Nolan could tell he was getting close to home. What might he have felt every time he got close to his home shore? *Nolan knew how to track his position by the stars, and he may have recognized landmarks such as specific islands. He probably felt both elated to be getting close to home and saddened to realize that he'd never get there.*

CONNECTING LITERATURE TO SOCIAL STUDIES

❺ Point out the Bay of Naples (at the southern end of Italy's west coast) on a world map or globe. Have Visual/Spatial Learners add this location to the map they began on p. 379.

CONNECTING LITERATURE TO SOCIAL STUDIES

❻ Connect *It refers to the thirteen original U.S. colonies.*

Customize for
Less Proficient Readers

Help students orient themselves to the story's progress through predictions. Remind them of Nolan's sentence. Then ask them what they think Nolan will ask Mrs. Graff and what her response will be. If necessary, guide students to predict that Nolan will ask Mrs. Graff about home and she will refuse to answer.

 Humanities: Art

Prisoners, drawn by G. Heck, engraved by Henry Winkles
From *Heck's Iconographic Encyclopedia,* a 19th century collection of engravings. This image shows two prisoners in their cell. The artist strove to depict the scene as realistically and in as much detail as possible.

How does the prison sentence of these men compare and contrast with that of Philip Nolan? *Nolan was neither shackled nor confined to a room; however, his emotional experience would probably be similar to the hopelessness these men display.*

Speaking and Listening Mini-Lesson

Conversation
This mini-lesson supports the Speaking and Listening activity in the Idea Bank on p. 391.

Introduce Discuss with students how conversation provides the opportunity for two or more people to exchange ideas and share experiences.

Develop Have pairs of students discuss the emotions sailors accompanying Nolan might have:
• How does Nolan's presence affect them?
• Would they find the sentence harsh or fair?

• Might they sympathize with or resent Nolan?
• What fears and hopes might these sailors share, even if they disagree about Nolan?

Apply Based on their discussions, have students develop their conversations. Encourage them to include gestures and attitude, and try to use words that are true to the sailors' likely emotions.

Assess Have students present their conversations to the class. Evaluate students' work for expression, creativity, and plausibility, or use the Peer Assessment: Dramatic Performance form, p. 116, in **Alternative Assessment.**

① **Infer** *The war was bloody, terrifying, messy, with many wounded and dead.*

◆ **Critical Thinking**

② **Analyze** Ask students how they think Nolan, who was a fairly junior officer back in New Orleans, gained the ability to lead with authority. *Students may note that Nolan has matured throughout his sentence or that he has always had natural leadership abilities.*

CONNECTING LITERATURE TO SOCIAL STUDIES

③ Ask students to describe Nolan's behavior during the War of 1812. What did he do to save his ship? Why did he do it? *Nolan leads the frightened and disorganized soldiers in battle, at his own risk, because he now loves his country and wants to defend it.*

◆ **LITERATURE AND YOUR LIFE**

④ Invite students to tell whether they were surprised that Nolan wasn't pardoned. Do they think he should have been? *Many students will say his bravery and loyalty should have earned him a pardon, others will say it was "too little, too late."*

CONNECTING LITERATURE TO SOCIAL STUDIES

⑤ **Infer** Ask students why they think Nolan always went aloft (up to the crow's nest). What was he hoping to see? *Perhaps a glimpse of his homeland.*

384

---

happened more than once. In one of the great frigate[21] duels with the English, in which the navy was really baptized, it happened that a round-shot[22] from the enemy entered one of our ports[23] square, and took right down the officer of the gun himself, and almost every man of the gun's crew. Now you may say what you choose about courage, but that is not a nice thing to see. But, as the men who were not killed picked themselves up, and as

> **Connecting Literature to Social Studies**
> ① From the details in this paragraph, what can you learn about the War of 1812?

they and the surgeon's people were carrying off the bodies, there appeared Nolan in his shirt sleeves, with the rammer in his hand, and, just as if he had been the officer, told them off with authority—who should go to the cockpit with the wounded men, who should stay with him—perfectly cheery, and with that way which makes men feel sure all is right and is going to be right. And he finished loading the gun with his own hands, aimed it, and bade the men fire. And there he stayed, captain of that gun, keeping those fellows in spirits, till the enemy struck[24]—sitting on the carriage while the gun was cooling, though he was exposed all the time—showing them easier ways to handle heavy shot—making the raw hands laugh at their own <u>blunders</u>—and when the gun cooled again, getting it loaded and fired twice as often as any other gun on the ship. The captain walked forward by way of encouraging the men, and Nolan touched his hat and said, "I am showing them how we do this in the artillery, sir."

And this is the part of the story where all the legends agree; the commodore said, "I see you do, and I thank you, sir; and I shall never forget this day, sir, and you never shall, sir."

And after the whole thing was over, and the commodore had the Englishman's

---

21. **frigate** (frig´ it) *n.*: Fast-sailing warship equipped with guns.
22. **round-shot:** Cannonball.
23. **ports** *n.*: Here, portholes or openings for cannons.
24. **struck** *v.*: Lowered their flag to admit defeat.

---

sword[25] in the midst of the state and ceremony of the quarter-deck, he said, "Where is Mr. Nolan? Ask Mr. Nolan to come here."

And when Nolan came, he said, "Mr. Nolan, we are all very grateful to you today; you are one of us today; you will be named in the dispatches."

And then the old man took off his own sword of ceremony, gave it to Nolan, and made him put it on. The man told me this who saw it. Nolan cried like a baby, and well he might. He had not worn a sword since that infernal day at Fort Adams. But always afterwards on occasions of ceremony, he wore that quaint old French sword of the commodore's.

The captain did mention him in the dispatches. It was always said he asked that Nolan might be pardoned. He wrote a special letter to the Secretary of War, but nothing ever came of it.

All that was nearly fifty years ago. If Nolan was thirty then, he must have been near eighty when he died. He looked sixty when he was forty. But he never seemed to me to change a hair afterwards. As I imagine his life, from what I have seen and heard of it, he must have been in every sea, and yet almost never on land. Till he grew very old, he went aloft a great deal. He always kept up his exercise, and I never heard that he was ill. If any other man was ill, he was the kindest nurse in the world; and he knew more than half the surgeons do. Then if anybody was sick or

---

25. **the Englishman's sword:** A defeated commander would turn over his sword to the victor.

 Cross-Curricular Connection: History

War of 1812 By 1812, the United States and Great Britain had been headed toward war for years. First, during the years of its conflict with France, the British had attacked U.S. ships and impressed Americans (forcing them to serve on British boats). Then the British supplied weapons to Native Americans fighting U.S. settlers on the frontier. Many Americans favored war, for these and other reasons. In June of 1812, they persuaded Congress to declare war on the British.

During the War of 1812, the British Navy blockaded American ports, keeping both military and trading ships from passing in or out. The U.S. Navy, which was quite limited due to former President Jefferson's belief in a small Federal government, was unprepared for war. It had few boats and even fewer trained soldiers. Volunteers often quickly deserted. Still, U.S. ships won battles such as the one pictured on pp. 380–381.

Point out that Nolan's presence at an 1812 battle suggests he was fairly close to U.S. shores. Have students research other key events in U.S. naval history between 1807–1863 to learn about other events Nolan might have witnessed.

died, or if the captain wanted him to, on any other occasion, he was always ready to read prayers. I have said that he read beautifully.

My own acquaintance with Philip Nolan began six or eight years after the English war, on my first voyage after I was appointed a midshipman. From the time I joined, I thought Nolan was a sort of lay chaplain—a chaplain

Row of Cannon, from Iconographic Encyclopedia, drawn by G. Heck, eng. by Henry Winkles, Collection of The New-York Historical Society

⑥ ▲ Critical Viewing Judging from the details in this etching, what type of ship is this? [Interpret]

with a blue coat. I never asked about him. Everything in the ship was strange to me. I knew it was green to ask questions, and I suppose I thought there was a "Plain Buttons" on every ship. We had him to dine in our mess once a week, and the caution was given that on that day nothing was to be said about home. But if they had told us not to say anything about the planet Mars or the Book of Deuteronomy,[26] I should not have asked why; there were a great many things which seemed to me to have as little reason. I first came to

26. **Book of Deuteronomy** (dōōt′ ər än′ ə mē): Fifth book of the Bible.

understand anything about "The Man Without a Country" one day when we overhauled a dirty little schooner which had slaves[27] on board. An officer named Vaughan was sent to take charge of her, and after a few minutes, he sent back his boat to ask that someone might be sent to him who could speak Portuguese. None of the officers did; and just as the captain was sending forward to ask if any of the people could, Nolan stepped out and said he should be glad to interpret, if the captain wished, as he understood the language. The captain thanked him, fitted out another boat with him, and in this boat it was my luck to go.

When we got there, it was such a scene as you seldom see, and never want to. Nastiness beyond account, and chaos run loose in the midst of the nastiness. There were not a great many of the Negroes; but by way of making what there were understand that they were free, Vaughan had had their handcuffs and anklecuffs knocked off. The Negroes were, most of them, out of the hold and swarming all round the dirty deck, with a central throng surrounding Vaughan and addressing him in every dialect.

As we came on deck, Vaughan looked down from a hogshead,[28] which he had mounted in desperation, and said, "Is there anybody who can make these people understand something?"

Nolan said he could speak Portuguese, and one or two fine-looking Kroomen who had

---

27. **slaves:** In 1808, it became illegal to bring slaves into the United States. In 1842, the U.S. and Great Britain agreed to use ships to patrol the African coast, to prevent slaves from being taken.

28. **hogshead** (hôgz′ hed′) *n.*: Large barrel or cask.

◆ **Build Vocabulary**

blunders (blun′ dərs) *n.*: Foolish or careless mistakes

The Man Without a Country ◆ 385

▶**Critical Viewing**◀

⑥ Interpret *The guns and uniformed men suggest that it is a military ship.*

CONNECTING LITERATURE TO SOCIAL STUDIES

⑦ Recall for students that Nolan had considered going with Aaron Burr, who was believed to be headed for Mexico. Ask students what, if anything, they can infer from Nolan's history and shipboard experiences in order to explain his ability to speak Portuguese. *Students may infer that Nolan speaks Spanish, or was in general highly educated and therefore potentially useful to Burr in Mexico. Certainly, students can infer from Nolan's sentence so far that he's had ample opportunity to educate himself.*

Customize for
English Language Learners
Point out the phrase "I knew it was green to ask questions, . . ." and help students understand that *green* in this context means "inexperienced." Guide students to understand the concept of following orders without questioning in order to appreciate the narrator's comment, "But if they had told us not to say anything about the Planet Mars or the Book of Deuteronomy, I should not have asked why."

Customize for
Less Proficient Readers
Help students summarize the story to this point and predict what will happen to Nolan. *You may want to model a summary for them: After showing loyalty to Aaron Burr, Lieutenant Nolan is court-martialled. In the courtroom, he calls out his wish to never hear of the United States again. His wish is granted as a life sentence aboard a series of U.S. boats at sea. During the sentence, Nolan begins to grasp the error of his thoughts and words. In an 1812 battle at sea, he shows great courage and loyalty, as well as leadership on behalf of the United States. Students may predict that he'll be pardoned for his courage.*

♫ **Humanities: Art**

Row of Cannon, drawn by G. Heck, engraved by Henry Winkles

This 19th-century engraving from *Heck's Iconographic Encyclopedia* presents a highly realistic and detailed image of the placement of cannons on a ship. Point out that the cannons do not seem to have much maneuverability, and aiming them would depend on the direction the ship was facing. Encourage students to study the details of the painting, such as the cannon balls in the lower right-hand corner and the chains that hold the cannons in place.

1. Judging from the image of the cannons in this engraving, what was the weaponry like on ships of this period? *Students may note that the cannons seem heavy and powerful, but may infer that accurate aim was limited and the cannons could only fire once before being reloaded.*

2. What would the atmosphere in this area of the ship be like during a battle? *Possible responses: the enclosed area would be smoky and the noise of the cannons firing would be deafening in this type of space; fires might start because of the wooden floors and walls.*

CONNECTING LITERATURE TO SOCIAL STUDIES

1 Liberia Use a world map or globe to point out Cape Palmas on the west coast of Liberia. Ask students why the Africans might not wish to go to Liberia. *Africa is a large continent and Liberia might be a huge distance from the Africans' home.*

CONNECTING LITERATURE TO SOCIAL STUDIES

2 Connect *One of the main issues over which the Civil War was fought was slavery, still integral to the South's economy but despised by the North.*

CONNECTING LITERATURE TO SOCIAL STUDIES

3 Draw Conclusions Ask students what statement they think the author might be making about slavery. As this story was written during the Civil War, which side would they say the author was on? *He seems to be saying slavery is horribly wrong and was therefore probably on the side of the North.*

►Critical Viewing◄

4 Draw Conclusions *Some students may say that it looks well-run because things look "shipshape"—neat and well-cared-for. Others may note the casual attitude of the figures in the illustration and conclude that there is a casual approach to running the ship.*

◆ LITERATURE AND YOUR LIFE

5 Invite students to think privately about conflicts they have had with family or community. Is it easier to see home as an ideal place when you're far away from it than when you live there?

Customize for
Intrapersonal Learners
Discuss with students why they think Nolan's speech to Vaughan is difficult for him. Ask students to write a diary entry about this encounter as seen through Philip Nolan's eyes. Urge them to record the feelings this incident might inspire in Nolan.

worked for the Portuguese on the coast were dragged out.

"Tell them they are free," said Vaughan.

Nolan explained it in such Portuguese as the Kroomen could understand, and they in turn to such of the Negroes as could understand them. Then there was a yell of delight, clenching of fists, and leaping and dancing by way of celebration.

"Tell them," said Vaughan, well pleased, "that I will take them all to Cape Palmas."

This did not answer so well. Cape Palmas was practically as far from the homes of most of them as New Orleans or Rio de Janeiro was; that is, they would be eternally separated from home there. And their interpreters, as we could understand, instantly said, "*Ah, non Palmas,*" and began to protest volubly. Vaughan was rather disappointed at this result of his liberality, and asked Nolan eagerly what they said. The drops stood on poor Nolan's white forehead, as he hushed the men down, and said, "He says, 'Not Palmas.' He says, 'Take us home; take us to our own country; take us to our own house; take us to our own children and our own women.' He says he has an old father and mother who will die if they do not see him. And this one says he left his people all sick, and paddled down to Fernando to beg the white doctor to come and help them, and that these devils caught him in the bay just in sight of home, and that he has never seen anybody from home since then. And this one says," choked out Nolan, "that he has not heard a word from his home in six months."

Vaughan always said he grew gray himself while Nolan struggled through this interpretation. I, who did not understand anything of the passion involved in it, saw that the very elements were melting with fervent heat and that something was to pay somewhere. Even the Negroes themselves stopped howling, as they saw Nolan's agony and Vaughan's

almost equal agony of sympathy. As quick as he could get words, Vaughan said, "Tell them yes, yes, yes; tell them they shall go to the Mountains of the Moon, if they will. If I sail the schooner through the Great White Desert, they shall go home!"

And after some fashion Nolan said so. And then they all fell to kissing him again.

Officer of the Watch on the Horseblock, Heck's Iconographic Encyclopedia, 1851, Collection of The New-York Historical Society

▲ **Critical Viewing** Would you say that the ship in this illustration was well-run? Why or why not? [Draw Conclusions]

But he could not stand it long; and getting Vaughan to say he might go back, he beckoned me down into our boat. As we started back he said to me, "Youngster, let that show you what it is to be without a family, without a home, and without a country. And if you are ever tempted to say a word or to do a thing that shall put a bar between you and your family, your home, and your country, pray God in His mercy to take you that instant home to His own heaven. Think of your home, boy; write and send, and talk about it. Let it be nearer and nearer to your thought the

386 ◆ *From Sea to Shining Sea*

 Humanities: Art

Officer of the Watch on the Horseblock,
1851, from *Heck's Iconographic Encyclopedia*

The collection of engravings in which this image appears covers many aspects of 19th-century life, including science, literature, and art. J.G. Heck arranged the nearly 12,000 engravings in volumes according to subject matter. Each showed a piece of life in these times.

Before photographs, etchings were used to represent people, places, and things realistically. This engraving shows a typical naval scene. Without the elaborate navigational and tracking

equipment now available, sailors had to take turns on a ship watching for changes in weather conditions, for other ships, and for enemy attacks.

1. How is this engraving like a photograph? *Like a photo, the edges between elements are cleanly drawn; there are many details included.*
2. What do you learn about life aboard a 19th-century ship from this picture? *Men stood around a lot, either watching or talking. They wore elaborate and probably not very comfortable uniforms. They had only very simple tools such as a looking glass.*

farther you have to travel from it, and rush back to it when you are free, as that poor slave is doing now. And for your country, boy" and the words rattled in his throat, "and for that flag," and he pointed to the ship, "never dream a dream but of serving her as she bids you, though the service carry you through a thousand hells. No matter what happens to you,

no matter who flatters you or who abuses you, never look at another flag, never let a night pass but you pray God to bless that flag. Remember, boy, that behind all these men you have to do with, behind officers, and government, and people even, there is the Country herself, your Country, and **❻** that you belong to her as you belong to your own mother. Stand by her, boy, as you would stand by your mother!"

❻ I was frightened to death by his calm, hard passion; but I blundered out that I would, by all that was holy, and that I had never thought of doing anything else. He hardly seemed to hear me; but he did, almost in a whisper, say, "Oh, if anybody had said so to me when I was of your age!"

I think it was this half-confidence of his, which I never abused, that afterward made us great friends. He was very kind to me. Often he sat up, or even got up, at night, to walk the deck with me, when it was my watch. He explained to me a great deal of my mathematics, and I owe to him my taste for mathematics. He

lent me books and helped me about my reading. He never referred so directly to his story again; but from one and another officer I have learned, in thirty years, what I am telling.

After that cruise I never saw Nolan again. The other men tell me that in those fifteen years he aged very fast, but he was still the same gentle, uncomplaining, silent sufferer that he ever was, bearing as best he could his self-appointed punishment. And now it seems the dear old fellow is dead. He has found a home at last, and a country.

Since writing this, and while considering whether or not I would print it, as a warning to the young Nolans of today of what it is to throw away a country, I have received from Danforth, who is on board the *Levant*, a letter which gives an account of Nolan's last hours. It removes all my doubts about telling this story.

Here is the letter:

Dear Fred,

I try to find heart and life to tell you that it is all over with dear old Nolan. I have been with him on this voyage more than I ever was, and I can understand wholly now the way in which you used to speak of the dear old fellow. I could see that he was not strong, but I had no idea the end was so near. The doctor has been watching him very carefully, and yesterday morning came to me and told me that Nolan was not so well, and had not left his stateroom—a thing I never remember before. He had let the doctor come and see him as he lay there—the first time the doctor had been in the stateroom—and he said he should like to see me. Do you remember the mysteries we boys used to invent about his room in the old *Intrepid* days? Well, I went in, and there, to be sure, the poor fellow lay in his berth, smiling pleasantly as he gave me his hand, but looking very frail. I could not help a glance round, which showed me what a little shrine he had made of the box he was lying in. The Stars and Stripes were draped up above

The Man Without a Country ◆ *387*

CONNECTING LITERATURE TO SOCIAL STUDIES

❻ Compare and Contrast Ask students how Nolan's life might have been different if someone had taught him what it means to belong to a country. How did he learn that lesson? *He wouldn't have become loyal to Aaron Burr and certainly wouldn't have spoken so rashly at his trial, and thus would not have been exiled from home. He learned the lesson through his exile.*

CONNECTING LITERATURE TO SOCIAL STUDIES

❼ Interpret Ask students what they think the author means by these lines. Why can Philip Nolan find a home only in death? *Nolan can go home to the U.S. now that he is dead; also, Hale may be suggesting that now Nolan will have a home in Heaven.*

Customize for
Visual/Spatial Learners
Show students the image on p. 377 and ask them to visualize an unending expanse of water. Urge those students who have no personal experience with oceans to view photographs or films. Then have students sketch or draw the view from Nolan's stateroom. Ask them to consider what emotions they think the image should evoke.

Customize for
Less Proficient Readers
Help students rewrite the text from "No matter what happens . . ." to ". . . as you belong to your own mother" in traditional lines for easier reading. Also clarify that in this context, *Country* is capitalized because Nolan experiences his country almost as a separate person or character. Finally, remind students again that, despite many realistic historical details, the letter shown on this page is fictional.

Viewing and Representing Mini-Lesson

Symbols

In this mini-lesson students will extend their grasp of Nolan's experiences by creating story symbols.

Introduce Explain that a symbol is an object, action, or idea that stands for something other than itself. For example, the U. S. flag is a symbol of the ideas on which the nation was founded. Have students share familiar symbols.

Develop Point out that symbols may be used to express an author's ideas or to convey a story's central idea. Help students relate the following symbols to Nolan's feelings for his country:

• Nolan's plain buttons
• the sword Nolan receives after the 1812 battle
• the Stars and Stripes draped in Nolan's stateroom

Apply Provide materials and supplies, and have each student adapt versions of the story symbols or create a new symbol for the United States.

Assess Have students work together to create an exhibit of the symbols. Let each student explain his or her symbol to the class. Evaluate students on their explanations of the symbols.

and around a picture of Washington and he had painted a majestic eagle, with lightning blazing from his beak and his foot just clasping the whole globe, which his wings overshadowed. The dear old boy saw my glance, and said, with a sad smile, "Here, you see I have a country!" And then he pointed to the foot of his bed, where I had not seen before a great map of the United States, as he had drawn it from memory, and which he had there to look upon as he lay. Quaint, queer old names were on it, in large letters: "Indiana Territory," "Mississippi Territory," and "Louisiana Territory," as I suppose our fathers learned such things: but the old fellow had patched in Texas, too: he had carried his western boundary all the way to the Pacific, but on that shore he had defined nothing.

"O Captain," he said, "I know I am dying. I cannot get home. Surely you will tell me something now?— Stop! stop! Do not speak till I say what I am sure you know, that there is not in this ship, that there is not in America a more loyal man than I. There cannot be a man who loves the old flag as I do, or prays for it as I do, or hopes for it as I do. There are thirty-four stars in it now, Danforth, though I do not know what their names are. There has never been one taken away. I know by that that there has never been any successful Burr. O Danforth, Danforth," he sighed out, "how like a wretched night's dream a boy's idea of personal fame or of separate sovereignty seems, when one looks back on it after such a life as mine! But tell me—tell me something—tell me

everything, Danforth, before I die!"

I swear to you that I felt like a monster that I had not told him everything before. "Mr. Nolan," said I, "I will tell you everything you ask about. Only, where shall I begin?"

Ship Plans, from Iconographic Encyclopedia, drawn by G. Heck, eng. by Henry Winkles, Collection of The New-York Historical Society

▲ **Critical Viewing** This diagram shows various parts and features of a ship. Why do you think so much effort was put into ship-building design in the 1800's? **[Speculate]**

Oh, the blessed smile that crept over his white face! He pressed my hand and said, "Bless you! Tell me their names," and he pointed to the stars on the flag. "The last I know is Ohio. My father lived in Kentucky. But I have guessed Michigan and Indiana and Mississippi—that was where Fort Adams was—they make

Humanities: Plans

Ship Plans, drawn by G. Heck, engraved by Henry Winkles.

Heck's Iconographic Encyclopedia, from which this engraving comes, contained information on many different topics. Four volumes grouped related topics—for example, military sciences, naval sciences, and geography. Though these ship plans were probably not for building purposes, they could be used to itemize the parts of a 19th-century ship. Some images are from above, a view called a plan. Others, such as Fig. 3, are from the side, a view called an elevation. Some are cut, or sectioned, for partial views. Many show small details at a larger scale for easier visibility. Each element is labelled with a figure number for reference in accompanying text.

1. Which view of a plan do you find easiest to read? Which is most difficult? *Most students will say that an elevation is easiest and a section is most difficult.*

2. What details about Philip Nolan's experiences do these plans suggest to you? *Students should note from the plans how small 19th-century ships were and thus how confining Nolan's sentence was.*

twenty. But where are your other four-teen? You have not cut up any of the old ones, I hope?"

Well, that was not a bad text, and I told him the names in as good order as I could, and he bade me take down his beautiful map and draw them in as I best could with my pencil. He was wild with delight about Texas, told me how his cousin died there; he had marked a gold cross near where he supposed his grave was; and he had guessed at Texas. Then he was delighted as he saw California and Oregon;—that, he said, he had suspected partly, because he had never been permitted to land on that shore, though the ships were there so much. Then he asked whether Burr ever tried again—and he ground his teeth with the only passion he showed. But in a moment that was over. He asked about the old war—told me the story of his serving the gun the day we took the *Java*. Then he settled down more quietly, and very happily, to hear me tell in an hour the history of fifty years.

How I wished it had been somebody who knew something! But I did as well as I could. I told him of the English war. I told him about Fulton[29] and the steamboat beginning. I told him about old Scott,[30] and Jackson:[31] told him all I could think of about the Mississippi, and New Orleans, and Texas, and his own old Kentucky.

I tell you, it was a hard thing to condense the history of half a century into that talk with a sick man. And I do not now know what I told him—of emigration,

---

29. **Fulton:** Robert Fulton (1765–1815), who invented the steamboat.
30. **Scott:** General Winfield Scott (1786–1866), who served in the War of 1812 and the Mexican War.
31. **Jackson:** Andrew Jackson (1767–1845), seventh President of the United States (1829–1837) and a general in the War of 1812.

and the means of it—of steamboats, and railroads, and telegraphs—of inventions, and books, and literature—of the colleges, and West Point, and the Naval School—but with the queerest interruptions that ever you heard. You see it was Robinson Crusoe asking all the accumulated questions of fifty-six years!

I remember he asked, all of a sudden, who was President now; and when I told him, he asked if Old Abe was General Benjamin Lincoln's son. He said he met old General Lincoln, when he was quite a boy himself, at some Indian treaty. I said no, that Old Abe was a Kentuckian like himself, but I could not tell him of what family; he had worked up from the ranks. "Good for him!" cried Nolan; "I am glad of that." Then I got talking about my visit to Washington. I told him about the Smithsonian, and the Capitol. I told him everything I could think of that would show the grandeur of his country and its prosperity.

And he drank it in and enjoyed it as I cannot tell you. He grew more and more silent, yet I never thought he was tired or faint. I gave him a glass of water, but he just wet his lips, and told me not to go away. Then he asked me to bring the Presbyterian Book of Public Prayer which lay there, and said, with a smile, that it would open at the right place—and so it did. There was his double red mark down the page; and I knelt down and read, and he repeated with me:

For ourselves and our country, O gracious God, we thank Thee, that, notwithstanding our manifold transgressions of Thy holy laws, Thou hast continued to us Thy marvelous kindness . . . and so to the end of that thanksgiving.

Then he turned to the end of the same book, and I read the words more familiar to me:

Most heartily we beseech Thee with Thy favor to behold and bless Thy servant, the President of the United States, and all others in authority.

The Man Without a Country ◆ *389*

5 Connect Ask students what Philip Nolan thinks of Burr now and how his feelings compare to those of the story's beginning. *Students should infer that Nolan now despises Burr with intense passion. They should recall that earlier he had admired Burr.*

Links Across Time

6 Railroads and telegraphs were just two of the many inventions that changed American life during the 19th century. Some of these include the mowing machine, automatic revolver, Morse code, and refrigerator. The Industrial Revolution, begun in the late 18th century, also brought factories and machine production to America. Many more people moved to cities. Education was changing, though not at the two military schools—West Point and the Naval School—that the narrator mentions. By the late 1800s, some colleges were accepting women.

Clarification

7 Robinson Crusoe was a character created by author Daniel Defoe in 1719. Crusoe was marooned on a desert island, removed from news of the world, for twenty-eight years.

Links Across Time

8 Abraham Lincoln was President in 1863. He'd come from a simple Kentucky family and spent his early years in the now-famous log cabin. He was largely self-taught and later worked as a rail-splitter and postmaster, among other jobs, before becoming a lawyer.

CONNECTING LITERATURE TO SOCIAL STUDIES

9 Interpret Ask students how these prayers have acted as Nolan's penance for his crime. *Students may say that by saying these prayers, Nolan reminded himself of how much he valued his country and therefore of how grave was his mistake.*

Cross-Curricular Connection: History

Westward Expansion During the years of Philip Nolan's sentence (1807–1863), his nation expanded dramatically. As the map on p. 376 shows, several parts of the Midwest were still in large territories rather than the many smaller states of today. The Louisiana Purchase had just been completed in 1803, doubling the nation's size. In 1845, the U.S. annexed Texas (leading to the Mexican War). As victor over Mexico, the U.S. also obtained California and lands in today's Southwest. Britain soon peacefully turned over the Pacific Northwest. Thus, by 1863, though the U.S. was torn apart by its Civil War, its land holdings now reached completely to the Pacific Ocean.

One cause for the constant westward expansion was an idea called Manifest Destiny, which said that white Americans were meant to take these lands. Unfortunately, this belief system included displacing those already living on new lands—both Native Americans and Mexicans. Have interested students research to learn about life on 19th century America's ever-moving western frontier.

CONNECTING LITERATURE TO SOCIAL STUDIES

1 Interpret Ask students why they think Nolan wants a tombstone even though he will be buried at sea. What does this suggest about how he views his home? *Possible responses: Nolan wants a tombstone so he and his lesson will be remembered; he'll go "home" if only in name.; home is terribly important and now includes the sea.*

Reinforce and Extend

Answers

◆ LITERATURE AND YOUR LIFE

Reader's Response Possible responses: Yes, because he betrayed his country without hesitation; No, because he didn't really mean what he said.

Thematic Focus It became more industrialized and much larger; it fought a civil war.

☑ Check Your Comprehension

1. The narrator is a man who served with Nolan on a ship. He tells the story to show young Americans what it means to be without a country.
2. Nolan is tried for his participation in subversive activities with Aaron Burr.
3. Nolan says, "Damn the United States! I wish I may never hear of the United States again!" The judge is shocked and grants Nolan his wish as a punishment.
4. Nolan's sentence is to "never hear the name of the United States again." The sentence will be carried out by assigning Nolan to different ships for the rest of his life. The sailors are told not to mention home to Nolan, and his reading material is censored.
5. Nolan's last wish is that he be buried at sea but that a tombstone be erected for him on land.

More About the Author

Edward Everett Hale (1822–1909) may have recalled his famous ancestor Nathan Hale when writing "The Man Without a Country." The earlier Hale, who was hanged as a spy by the British in 1776, said "I only regret that I have but one life to give for my country." Though Hale's character Philip Nolan gives his life in a different way, he comes to much the same conclusion.

"Danforth," said he, "I have repeated those prayers night and morning—it is now fifty-five years." And then he said he would go to sleep. He bent me down over him and kissed me; and he said, "Look in my Bible, Captain, when I am gone." And I went away.

But I had no thought it was the end. I thought he was tired and would sleep. I knew he was happy, and I wanted him to be alone.

But in an hour, when the doctor went in gently, he found Nolan had breathed his life away with a smile.

We looked in his Bible, and there was a slip of paper at the place where he had marked the text:

They desire a country, even a heavenly: where God is not ashamed to be called their God: for He hath prepared for them a city.[32]

On this slip of paper he had written:

Bury me in the sea; it has been my home, and I love it. But will not someone set up a stone for my memory at Fort Adams or at Orleans, that my disgrace may not be more than I ought to bear? Say on it:

In Memory of
PHILIP NOLAN,
*Lieutenant in the Army
of the United States.*
He loved his country as no other
man has loved her; but no man
deserved less at her hands.

---

32. They desire . . . a city: A passage from the Bible, Hebrews 11:16.

Meet the Author

Edward Everett Hale (1822–1909) was a clergyman, a teacher, and the author of several books. He was also a distant relative of Nathan Hale, one of the heroes of the American Revolution. Hale began writing stories when he was a boy. He later published his own newspaper.

After graduating from Harvard University and becoming a Unitarian minister, Hale continued writing short stories, essays, and novels. "The Man Without a Country" may be viewed as one of Hale's sermons, in which he passionately offers his views on patriotism.

390 ◆ *From Sea to Shining Sea*

Guide for Responding

◆ LITERATURE AND YOUR LIFE

Reader's Response Did Nolan deserve the punishment he was given? Explain.

Thematic Focus In what way did the United States change during the years when Nolan was a prisoner?

Journal Writing Take on the character of Nolan and write a journal entry he might have written about his first week of exile.

☑ Check Your Comprehension

1. Who is the narrator of the story?
2. Why is Nolan brought to trial?
3. What rash words does Nolan utter when the judge asks him if he wishes to say anything?
4. What is Nolan's sentence?
5. What is Nolan's last wish?

◆ Critical Thinking

INTERPRET

1. How is it that Aaron Burr is able to win Nolan over so easily? **[Interpret]**
2. How does the narrator feel about Nolan's punishment? **[Draw Conclusions]**
3. How does Nolan change during the course of the story? **[Analyze]**

EVALUATE

4. Do you think the government should have pardoned Nolan years after the trial was over? Why or why not? **[Make a Judgment]**

APPLY

5. What epitaph, or gravestone inscription, would you write for Nolan? **[Relate]**

Beyond the Selection

FURTHER READING
Other Works by Edward Everett Hale
A New England Boyhood
"My Double, and How He Undid Me"
In His Name
Other Works About 19th Century America
Bull Run, Paul Fleischman
The Call of the Wild, Jack London
Little Women, Louisa May Alcott

INTERNET
We suggest the following Internet sites (all Web sites are subject to change).
For a tour of 19th century history, visit
http:// www.timeship.com
To learn about U.S. Naval history, visit
http:// www.history.navy.mil/index.html
We *strongly recommend* that you preview these sites before you send your students to them.

CONNECTING LITERATURE TO SOCIAL STUDIES

Edward Everett Hale used historical facts to make "The Man Without a Country" realistic. He did his job well. When the story first appeared in a magazine in 1863, many readers believed it was true. In fact, decades after the story first appeared, it was still accepted as true by many people.

1. What details in the story might have led readers to believe it had really happened?
2. What can you learn about the United States Navy by reading this story?
3. What might have been the inspiration for this tale about traitors and patriotism?
4. What do the characters and events from the story tell you about "the young nation"?

Idea Bank

Writing

1. **Letter** Write a letter from Philip Nolan to a friend or relative telling them about the sentence he has received.
2. **Newspaper Account** As a reporter present at Philip Nolan's trial, write a newspaper story describing the charges against Nolan and the sentence he received.
3. **Persuasive Essay** Write an essay either condemning Nolan's actions or excusing them. Use details from the story as support.

Speaking and Listening

4. **Conversation** Role-play a conversation between two sailors on one of the ships that kept Nolan imprisoned. Assume that the sailors know of his crimes and his sentence but are not clear about how the sentence is to be carried out. **[Performing Arts Link]**

5. **Oral Report** Choose a historical figure or event mentioned in the story to research for a report. Use an encyclopedia and other sources to find out about the person or event. Share your findings with the class in an oral report. **[Social Studies Link]**

Project

6. **Illustrated Scene** Do some research on the kind of ships on which Nolan was kept prisoner. Then, find out about the uniforms worn by members of the navy at the time the story takes place. Use this information to illustrate any scene from the story. Here are some scenes you might consider:
   • Nolan is sentenced.
   • Nolan talks to the people captured as slaves.
   • Nolan shows his stateroom to Danforth.
   [Art Link]

Further Reading, Listening, and Viewing

• Ken Burns and Dayton Duncan's documentary film *Lewis and Clarke: The Journey of the Corps of Discovery* gives an in-depth view of the expanding American frontier.
• Edward Everett Hale's *A New England Boyhood* tells of life in the early 1800's.
• Roger Brun's *Thomas Jefferson: World Leaders Past and Present* is about the third president of the United States, under whom Aaron Burr served as vice president.

The Man Without a Country ◆ 391

✓ ASSESSMENT OPTIONS

Formal Assessment, Selection Test, pp. 115–116, and Assessment Resources Software. The selection test is designed so that it can be easily customized to the performance levels of your students.

PORTFOLIO ASSESSMENT
Use the following rubrics in the **Alternative Assessment** booklet to assess student writing:
Letter: Expression, p. 90
Newspaper Account: Fictional Narrative, p. 91
Persuasive Essay: Persuasion, p. 101

Idea Bank

Following are suggestions for matching the Idea Bank topics with your students' performance levels and learning modalities.

Customize for
Performance Levels
Less Advanced Students: 1, 4
Average Students: 2, 4, 5
More Advanced Students: 3, 5, 6

Customize for
Learning Modalities
Verbal/Linguistic: 1, 2, 3, 4, 5
Interpersonal: 4
Logical/Mathematical: 3
Intrapersonal: 1
Visual/Spatial: 6
Bodily/Kinesthetic: 4, 6

Answers (continued)
◆ Critical Thinking

1. Burr impresses Nolan and courts him, singling him out as a guide to local sights so that barracks life seems boring to Nolan by comparison.
2. The narrator believes the punishment is overly harsh.
3. He has changed from a brash, swaggering young officer to a humble, uncomplaining servant of his fellow men.
4. Possible response: Yes, because he had clearly learned his lesson; No, because his sentence was also serving as an example to others.
5. Possible response: Epitaphs should show that in the final analysis, Nolan did serve his country well.

CONNECTING LITERATURE TO SOCIAL STUDIES

1. Possible details: The opening obituary, the battle from the War of 1812, the seizing of a slave ship, letters to and from naval officers.
2. Possible response: The Navy had many ships and had a presence around the world.
3. Possible response: The Civil War, which was tearing apart the nation, or the real-life trial of Aaron Burr, may have both inspired Hale.
4. Possible response: The young nation was changing rapidly, but still held dearly to its founding principles.

Establish Writing Guidelines

Review the following key characteristics of a summary:

- A summary is an account that provides only the most important details.

- A summary should recount events in chronological order, and use transitions to clarify the order of events.

- A summary should include only facts, not opinions or comments.

You may want to distribute the scoring rubric for Summary, p. 94 in **Alternative Assessment,** to make students aware of the criteria on which they will be evaluated. See the suggestions on p. 394 for customizing the rubric to this workshop.

Refer students to the Writing Handbook in the back of the book for instruction on the writing process and further information on expository writing.

Writer's Solution

Writers at Work Videodisc

To introduce students to expository writing, and show them how professional journalist Gary Matsumoto answers the question *What is expository writing?* play the videodisc segment on Exposition: Giving Information (Ch. 4).

Play frames 33108 to 41558

Writing Lab CD-ROM

If your students have access to computers, you may want to have them work in the tutorial on Exposition to complete all or part of their summaries. Follow these steps:

1. Have students use the Sunburst Diagram for summaries to come up with topic ideas.

2. Encourage students to use the Timeline Activity to arrange events of their summaries in chronological order.

3. Students can draft on computer.

4. When revising, have students use the Revision Checker to find transition words.

Writer's Solution Sourcebook

Students can find additional support, including in-depth instruction on building paragraphs, pp. 132–133, in the chapter on Exposition: Giving Information, pp. 104–135.

Expository Writing
Summary

Writing Process Workshop

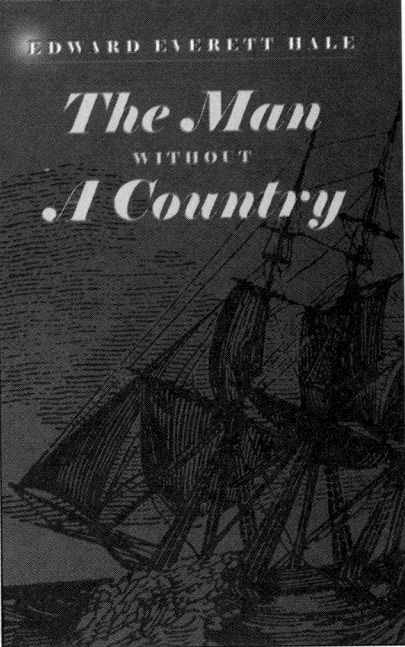

You probably summarize things constantly—books, movies, television programs, sporting events. As a reader or a writer, you'll find summaries extremely useful. They present the most important elements of an item or event in a concise, detailed way. You can summarize stories, political or historical events, movies, plays, poems, or time periods. A summary doesn't attempt to capture the tone or style of the original piece—just what the piece is about. Write a summary of an article or a story you've recently read, or summarize a real-life event.

The following skills from this section's Writing Mini-Lessons will help you write your summary:

Writing Skills Focus

▶ **Use precise language** to make your summary accurate and exact. (See p. 350.)

▶ **Choose supporting details** to convey the main ideas of the original piece. (See p. 363.)

▶ **Use transitions** to make connections and relationships among the details clear and easy to follow. (See p. 375.)

MODEL FROM LITERATURE

On the death of Philip Nolan, who was known as "The Man Without a Country," the narrator decides that it is time to tell the exiled man's story. Nolan started out as a promising young officer stationed ① in New Orleans, but became infatuated with Aaron Burr's teachings and political schemes. ② When Burr was tried for treason, Nolan was court-martialed. At his trial, ③ he blurted out that he wished he would "never hear of the United States again." The outraged judge sentenced him to "have his wish fulfilled," and for the next fifty-six years, Nolan lived on U.S. government ships but was never again allowed to see, hear, or read about his country.

① Precise language like this gives the summary clarity.

② This detail is an important part of the original story.

③ Transitions like this one connect ideas.

392 ◆ *From Sea to Shining Sea*

 Beyond the Classroom

Community Connection

Day-to-Day Summaries Explain to students that they probably encounter a wide variety of summaries in everyday life. For example, if students check television listings, they may see summaries for upcoming movies or television specials. Likewise, students may read summaries on the back of videotape cases at the video store. Local newspapers may summarize upcoming community events such as public meetings, poetry readings, and conferences.

Encourage students to spend some time gathering samples of local listings which summarize important information. Then have students work in groups to create their own listings calendar of upcoming events. They may want to come up with ideas for events that do not yet exist, or work with school or local events already planned. Remind students to include only the most important details of the events. Have the groups share their listings calendar with the rest of the class.

Prewriting

Choose a Topic Summarize something you've seen, heard, or experienced that you'd like to share with a friend. Perhaps you've read a thriller, or seen an exciting movie or television documentary, or listened to a great concert that you want to tell your friends about. Any of those ideas would work, or you can use one of the topics in the box below.

> ### Topic Ideas
> - The last minutes of a significant ballgame
> - A lecture by a park ranger on wildlife
> - The biography of your personal hero

Choose Important Details Gather details for your summary. If you're writing a summary of a published work, reread the original, and jot down the most important details. If you're summarizing an event, re-create it in your mind. Then, write down the most exciting or significant details.

Use Precise Language Your summary should be to the point; each word should be exact and precise. To achieve that style, use specific nouns and active verbs.

Vague Noun: He told the *man* to leave.

Specific Noun: He told the *police officer* to leave.

Set Up a Chain of Events List the events to include in your summary, and organize the events chronologically. Use this chain of events as a model.

Nolan falls in with Burr. → Nolan tried and found guilty. → Nolan says he wished he would never hear of the U.S. again

Drafting

Use an Introduction, Body, and Conclusion Give your summary an introduction, in which you reveal what you'll be summarizing; a body, which contains the essence of the summary; and a conclusion, in which you wrap up the summary with your personal views or insights.

Avoid Listing Events As you draft, don't simply list events. Instead, reweave the essential points in an interesting and entertaining way. Remember that this is a summary, not a list.

Use Transitions to Make Connections Transitional words offer guideposts to your reader; they connect your ideas. As you draft, include transitional words and phrases like *next, as a result,* and *surprisingly,* to keep your readers on track.

DRAFTING/REVISING

APPLYING LANGUAGE SKILLS: Verb Phrases With *Have*

When writing verb phrases or contractions containing the word *have,* avoid the common mistake of using the word *of* in place of *have.*

Incorrect:
He *should of* called first.

Correct:
He *should have* called first.

Correct:
He *should've* called first.

Practice Make contractions of each italicized verb phrase.

1. We *would have* traveled across the United States.
2. We *should have* checked the gas tank before we left.
3. We *could have* flown, but driving was cheaper and more fun.

Writing Application As you write your summary, be sure you write verb phrases and contractions containing *have* correctly.

Writer's Solution Connection Writing Lab

You may want to use the Cause-and-Effect Chain in the Exposition: Giving Information tutorial.

Writing Process Workshop ◆ 393

Prewriting

Remind students that, when they gather information for a summary, they should include only the most important details. Any questions, observations, or opinions about the topic should be left out.

Customize for *Less Proficient Writers*

Explain to students that they may need to narrow their topic to write an efficient summary. Suggest that students use the Cluster Organizer, p. 73 in **Writing and Language Transparencies,** to organize their topic into subtopics and supporting details. Students may then want to consider writing their summary on one of the subtopics rather than the whole main topic.

 Writer's Solution

Writing Lab CD-ROM

For additional help on narrowing topics, suggest that students view the Writing Hints on narrowing summary topics and the Interactive models on narrowing topics for summaries in the Prewriting section of the tutorial on Exposition: Giving Information in the *Writer's Solution Writing Lab CD-ROM.*

Drafting

Explain to students that their introduction should clearly state the topic of the summary as well as grab the reader's interest.

Writer's Solution

Writing Lab CD-ROM

Students can develop strategies for writing their drafts by using the interactive models of introductions, bodies, and conclusions in the drafting section of the tutorial on Exposition: Giving Information.

Applying Language Skills

Verb Phrases With *Have* Explain to students that they may make the mistake of using the word *of* in place of *have* because in spoken English, the two words sound alike.

Writer's Solution

For additional instruction and practice, have students use the practice page on The Six Tenses of Verbs, p. 72, in the *Writer's Solution Grammar Practice Book.*

Answers

Suggested responses:
1. We *would've* traveled across the United States.
2. We *should've* checked the gas tanks before we left.
3. We *could've* flown, but driving was cheaper and more fun.

Revising

Students might work with a peer editor to revise. Suggest that partners take turns reading their drafts aloud to each other and making suggestions for improvement.

Writing Lab CD-ROM

In the tutorial on Exposition: Giving Information, have students use the interactive guide on negative feedback to help them work with peer editors.

Publishing

Students might place their summaries in the school library or media center.

Reinforce and Extend

Review the Writing Guidelines
After students have finished writing, review characteristics of a summary.

Applying Language Skills
Correcting Run-on Sentences
Explain to students that some run-on sentences have no punctuation, while others use punctuation incorrectly when combining sentences.

Answers
Possible responses:
1. We saw six whales and we learned about ocean mammals.
2. Some kids got seasick but I did not get sick.
3. A newborn whale weighs over five tons and it drinks about 130 gallons of its mother's milk a day.

For additional instruction, have students use the lesson on Run-on Sentences in the unit on Problems With Sentences in the *Writer's Solution Language Lab CD-ROM.*

Writing Process Workshop

EDITING/PROOFREADING

APPLYING LANGUAGE SKILLS:
Correcting Run-on Sentences

Run-on sentences occur when two or more sentences are written or punctuated as one. To correct, create separate sentences or combine the sentences with a conjunction.

Run-on: *The whale watch was very exciting, we saw a mother and her two calves.*

Correct: *The whale watch was very exciting. We saw a mother and her two calves.*

Correct: *The whale watch was very exciting because we saw a mother and her two calves.*

Practice On your paper, correct the run-on sentences.

1. We saw six whales we learned about ocean mammals.
2. Some kids got seasick I did not get sick.
3. A newborn whale weighs over five tons it drinks about 130 gallons of its mother's milk a day.

Writing Application Correct any run-on sentences you find in your draft.

> **Writer's Solution Connection**
> **Language Lab**
>
> For more practice correcting run-on sentences, complete the Run-on Sentences lesson in the Sentence Errors unit.

394 ◆ *From Sea to Shining Sea*

Revising

Use Transitions Review your draft. Have you clearly shown how major points are related to one another? Add transitions to make connections clear.

Time Order: *first, finally, next, then, after, when, following, while, during, meanwhile, immediately*

Logical Relationship: *therefore, consequently, for this reason, as a result of, since*

Concluding: *in short, to sum up, that is, therefore, in other words, in conclusion*

Review Writing Focus Points Review the Writing Skills Focus points on page 392, to make sure you've taken them into consideration in your summary.

Publishing and Presenting

Library Collect story summaries your classmates have written. Post them in the library for others to read.

Web Site Post your summary on a Web site that is dedicated to the topic of your summary.

REVISION MODEL

> *tells the story*
> In this summary of "The Gift of the Magi," ① ~~I'll tell you about~~
> ~~the story.~~ Della is the girl in the story, and she's married to
> ②
> Jim. ~~She is very friendly.~~ It's Christmas, and they don't have
> enough money to buy each other presents. Della decides to
> *beautiful, long*   ③ *a chain*   *pocket*
> cut her hair and sell it to buy ~~this thing~~ for Jim's watch.
> ④ *Meanwhile,*   ⑤ *pawns*
> Jim does something with his watch to buy Della combs
> ⑥ *ironic*
> for her hair. It's ~~funny~~ that they give up what they each
> treasured most for each other.

① Eliminate useless language; be concise.
② Delete unimportant details like this.
③ Include important details to make the meaning clear.
④ This time transition word connects ideas.
⑤ *Pawn* is more exact than *does something with.*
⑥ The exact word *ironic* conveys more than *funny* does.

	ASSESSMENT	4	3	2	1
PORTFOLIO ASSESSMENT Use the rubric on Summary in the **Alternative Assessment** booklet, p. 94, to assess the students' writing. Add these criteria to customize this rubric to this assignment.	**Using Transitions**	The writer has creatively used transitions to connect ideas in the summary.	The writer has used transitions, but there are one or two places a transition may be needed.	The writer has used some transitions, but some are redundant and there are places where transitions are needed.	The writer rarely uses transitions, making the writing hard to follow.
	Avoid Run-on Sentences	There are no run-on sentences in the summary.	There are one or two run-on sentences in the summary.	There are several run-on sentences in the suumary.	Most of the sentences in the summary are run-on sentences.

Real-World Reading Skills Workshop

Identifying Main Ideas in Articles

Strategies for Success

Identifying the main idea of an article will help you understand how the details work together to convey a single message. The main idea may be stated directly or implied. Use the following strategies to help you identify the main idea:

Check the Lead Sentence In an article, each paragraph may contain its own main idea, which is often stated in the lead sentence—or the first sentence—of the paragraph. As you read, you'll find details to support the main idea.

Look for Implied Main Ideas If the main idea is not directly stated, it will be implied. To identify implied main ideas, pause after you read each section and ask yourself these questions:

▶ What was that section about?
▶ Why did the writer include these details?
▶ How can I state the main idea of this section in one sentence?

Review the End of the Article The end of an article sometimes summarizes the main idea. If you find previously mentioned ideas repeated in this final paragraph, they are probably the main ideas of the article.

✔ *Here are situations in which finding the main idea is helpful:*
▶ *Reading a news story in a newspaper*
▶ *Reading a scientific article*
▶ *Reading an information sheet about a club*

Apply the Strategies

Read the article "Symbols of Freedom," and answer the questions that follow.

Symbols of Freedom

Ellis Island and the Statue of Liberty are two of the most important historical sites in our country. Ellis Island was used as an immigration center for over 60 years. More than 12 million people first entered the United States this way. These 12 million immigrants were greeted by the sight of the Statue of Liberty as they pulled into New York Harbor.

Imagine how breathtaking the sight of our Lady of Liberty must have been for those who risked everything to come to America. She represented to them the reasons they packed up their belongings, sold everything they had, and left their families. The opportunities that freedom entitled them to here could not be surpassed anywhere else on Earth!

1. In the first paragraph, is the main idea implied or stated directly? Explain.
2. Do any of the paragraphs have a lead sentence that states the main idea? If so, which one?
3. Use questions to determine the implied main idea of the second paragraph.

Real-World Reading Skills Workshop ◆ 395

◆ Build Grammar Skills

Reviewing Conjunctions

The selections in Part 1 include instruction on the following:
- Subordinating Conjunctions
- Coordinating Conjunctions
- Correlative Conjunctions

This instruction is reinforced with the Build Grammar Skills practice pages in **Selection Support,** pp. 105, 110, 115, and 120.

As you review conjunctions, you may wish to include the following:
- Conjunction, Preposition, or Adverb?

Point out to students that some subordinating conjunctions can also be prepositions or adverbs. The words *after, before, since, till,* and *until* can be used as subordinating conjunctions or prepositions. *After, before,* and *since* can also be adverbs. *When* and *where* can be used as subordinating conjunctions or adverbs. Show students the following examples of the word *before* used in three different ways.

Subordinating Conjunction: She went to the park *before* she came home from school.

Preposition: Greg went to the gym *before* dinner.

Adverb: Have you ever been here *before*?

Remind students that conjunctions connect complete ideas.

Answers
Practice 1
1. Not only . . . but also—correlative conjunction; and—coordinating conjunction
2. Although—subordinating conjunction
3. and—coordinating conjunction
4. but—coordinating conjunction
5. As—subordinating conjunction; and—coordinating conjunction

Practice 2
1. The Badlands were more comfortable after the sun went down.
2. Both Martin Luther King, Jr., and King's followers did not approve of violence.
3. The land of the United States belongs to all people but many believe that it has not been divided fairly.

Conjunctions | Grammar Review

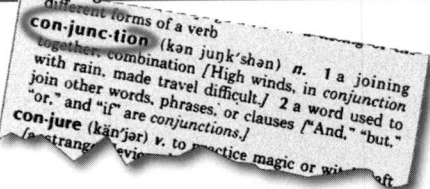

A **conjunction** joins words or groups of words. There are three types of conjunctions: **coordinating, correlative,** and **subordinating.**

Type	Examples	Use
Coordinating Conjunctions link words, phrases, or clauses that have the same function in a sentence (p. 362).	and, but, or, nor, for, yet, so	. . . I listened *and* felt *and* in the process had a picture of my country . . .
Correlative Conjunctions are used in pairs (p. 374). They link words, phrases, or clauses that have the same function.	both . . . and, either . . . or, neither . . . nor, not only . . . but also, whether . . . or	These were *not* just Italian values, or American, *but* universal values. . .
Subordinating Conjunctions connect two ideas by making one dependent on the other (p. 349).	after, although, as, because, before, if, since, when, where, while, unless, until	According to legend, *when* the weather was frigid, a ship captain and his daughter froze.

Practice 1 On your paper, write each conjunction. Then, label it as coordinating, correlative, or subordinating.

1. Not only was Sandburg a great poet, but he was also a journalist and historian.

2. Although yarns have always been told, they were especially popular during pioneer days.

3. Steinbeck and his dog Charley visited the Badlands of North Dakota.

4. "He displayed no fear, but seemed calm and serene. . . ."

5. "As an Italian American, I grew up believing that America is the greatest country on earth, and thankful that I was born here."

Practice 2 On your paper, join the sentences using the type of conjunction specified.

1. The sun went down. The Badlands were more comfortable. (subordinating)

2. Martin Luther King, Jr., did not approve of violence. King's followers did not approve of violence. (correlative)

3. The land of the United States belongs to all people. Many believe that it has not been divided fairly. (coordinating)

Grammar in Writing

✔ Decide on the relationship between or among ideas before choosing a conjunction.

✔ Avoid stringing together too many ideas or sentences with *and.*

Part 2 *An Album of Stories*

High Noon, New York, 1986, Chen Chi, The Butler Institute of American Art, Youngstown, Ohio

An Album of Stories ◆ 397

The selections in this section are "An Album of Stories." "Sancho" is the story of an abandoned bull calf with a unique personality. "A Ribbon for Baldy" tells of a young student's ambitious science project. In "The White Umbrella," the narrator learns to question the white umbrella she so strongly desires. "Those Winter Sundays" is a poem about the poet's hardworking father. "Taught Me Purple" is a poem commemorating the poet's mother. "The City Is So Big" shares with readers a sense of New York City.

Customize for
Varying Students Needs

When assigning the selections in this section to your students, keep in mind the following factors:

"Sancho"
- A short story with geographic elements of Texas and cowboy life
- Includes a Beyond Literature Science Connection

"The Closing of the Rodeo"
- A short rhyming poem

"A Ribbon for Baldy"
- A short story about a young person's struggle to fit in
- Includes a Beyond Literature Science Connection

"The White Umbrella"
- A short story whose main characters are a family of Chinese immigrants
- Explores the main character's desires and pride

"Those Winter Sundays"
- A poem about a man's growing understanding of his father

"Taught Me Purple"
- A poem praising the poet's mother and questioning life

"The City Is So Big"
- A short poem about New York City

 Humanities: Art

High Noon, New York, 1986, Chen Chi

Chen Chi (born 1912) was born near Shanghai, China. His first job was in an oil-pressing factory at the age of 14. He enrolled in an art school that emphasized Western techniques rather than traditional Chinese painting. This influenced his work greatly. Before moving to the United States in 1947, Chen Chi taught painting at a girls' high school in China. Most of his paintings focus on urban landscapes of New York City. Though this painting is not a typical cityscape, the crowd of people and street signs clearly indicte a city setting.

Have students study the painting and then ask the following questions.
1. Describe what you see in the painting. *Most students note flags on the buildings, yellow taxi cabs in the street, crowds of people walking down the sidewalks; it looks cold and windy.*
2. What stories might the people in this painting have? *Encourage students to describe the possible activities of people on a city street, such as being on their way to work, shopping, appointments, to meet friends, and so forth.*

OBJECTIVES

1. To read, comprehend, and interpret a narrative and a poem
2. To relate a narrative and a poem to personal experience
3. To envision setting
4. To appreciate the role of setting in narratives and in poems
5. To build vocabulary in context and learn the word endings: -ent and -ant
6. To develop skill in using subjects and predicates
7. To write a factually detailed report
8. To respond to a narrative and a poem through writing, speaking and listening, and projects

SKILLS INSTRUCTION

Vocabulary:
Word Endings: -ent and -ant

Spelling:
Using acc to Make ak or aks Sounds

Grammar:
Subjects and Predicates

Reading Strategy:
Envision Setting

Literary Focus:
Setting in Nonfiction and Poetry

Writing:
Elaborate With Factual Details

Speaking and Listening:
Tour Guide Speech (Teacher Edition)

Critical Viewing:
Draw Conclusions; Analyze; Speculate

PORTFOLIO OPPORTUNITIES

Writing: Letter; Character Profile; Persuasive Essay

Writing Mini-Lesson: Report

Speaking and Listening: Oral Presentation; Tour Guide Speech

Projects: Poster; Historic Newspaper

More About the Authors
J. Frank Dobie grew up in the brush country of southwest Texas. In *The Longhorns*, he tells the tales of some memorable Texas steers, including Sancho. As a folklorist, Dobie appreciated the impact that the animals of the region had on the people and the legends.

William Jay Smith has produced more than 50 volumes of writing. Among his works is "Indian Removal," a seven-part series of poems about the forced removal of Indian tribes from the southeastern part of the United States.

Guide for Reading

Meet the Authors:

J. Frank Dobie (1888–1964)

Texan J. Frank Dobie devoted himself to writing and teaching about the folklore and history of his native state. He described himself as "a historian of the longhorns, the mustangs, the coyote, and the other characters of the West." In 1964, President Johnson presented Dobie with the United States' highest civilian award, the Medal of Freedom, for his contributions to historic preservation and regional pride.

THE STORY BEHIND THE STORY

Dobie interviewed many Texans to gather stories for his collection *The Longhorns,* which tells amazing tales about these legendary Texas steers. "Sancho" is one of these tales. Dobie based the story of Sancho on a tale he heard from John Rigby, a trail boss on the Texas Range.

William Jay Smith (1918–   )

William Jay Smith wears many hats as a writer. The author of more than thirty books, he is a successful poet, critic, and translator. In his poetry, Smith vividly captures distinctively American settings. From 1968 to 1970, Smith served as Poet Laureate of the United States, sponsoring programs to promote reading and literature.

398 ◆ *From Sea to Shining Sea*

◆ LITERATURE AND YOUR LIFE

CONNECT YOUR EXPERIENCE

Homesickness strikes almost all of us at some point. Whether you're away for a night, for a week, or even for years, thoughts of home, with its comforting smells, sounds, and routines, sometimes overtake you. In "Sancho," you'll read about a very special animal who cures his homesickness in a unique and courageous way.

THEMATIC FOCUS: An Album of Stories

The story of "Sancho" was told to Dobie by someone who had heard the story. Ask yourself as you read: Why is "Sancho" worth telling over and over?

◆ Background for Understanding

SOCIAL STUDIES

"Sancho" takes place in the southwestern United States. Because most of the region is very dry, much of the vegetation is low to the ground and blooms only briefly. Dobie includes some of this unique vegetation in "Sancho." The spicy chiltipiquin peppers, the guajilla bush, and the fresh green mesquite bushes of spring play an important role in this story.

◆ Build Vocabulary

WORD ENDINGS: -ent AND -ant

The word endings -ent and -ant can be added to verbs to create adjectives. For example, -ent, added to the verb *persist,* which means "to refuse to give up," creates *persistent,* which means "in a stubborn way."

WORD BANK

Which word from the list means "an animal between one and two years old"? Check the Build Vocabulary box on page 401 to see if you chose correctly.

Word Bank
vigorous
yearling
persistent
accustomed

◆ Sancho ◆
The Closing of the Rodeo

Stampeded by Lightning, Frederic Remington

◆ Literary Focus

SETTING IN NONFICTION AND POETRY

As in a fictional short story, **setting** can play a key role in works of nonfiction that tell a story. For example, in "Sancho," the southwestern setting gives the piece its overall flavor and drives the events that occur. Similarly, in poetry, the setting can play a key role, especially in poems that tell a story or capture a moment in time.

◆ Reading Strategy

ENVISION SETTING

When you **envision a setting** while reading, picture it in your mind, like a movie. As you read details that describe setting in "Sancho" and "The Closing of the Rodeo," envision the time and place being described. You can use a sensory web like this one to help you use all of your senses as you envision a setting.

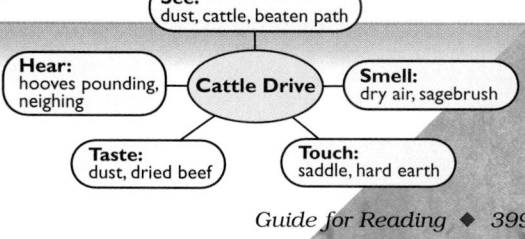

See: dust, cattle, beaten path

Hear: hooves pounding, neighing

Cattle Drive

Smell: dry air, sagebrush

Taste: dust, dried beef

Touch: saddle, hard earth

Guide for Reading ◆ 399

Interest Grabber Tell students that the story they are about to read takes place in Texas and in the Great Plains during the late nineteenth century. Ask them to freewrite words, names, and phrases they associate with that time and those places. Invite students to share what they have written.

◆ Build Grammar Skills

Subjects and Predicates If you wish to introduce the grammar concept or skill for this selection before students read, refer to the instruction on p. 406.

Customize for
Less Proficient Readers

The selection contains many terms associated with cowboys, ranches, cattle drives, and the terrain of the cattle country of the Old West. Words such as chuck wagons, mustangs, branding, lariat, brush corral, and line riders may be unfamiliar to students. To help them learn these new terms, students can develop cowboy-talk glossaries.

Customize for
More Advanced Students

In the story, Sancho is taken on a cattle drive north to Wyoming. Have students predict what will happen to him. Tell them to look for clues about his fate as they read.

Humanities: Art

Stamped by Lightning, by Frederick Remington

Remington (1861–1909) was an artist-historian of the vanishing frontier. He is considered the best and most popular painter of the Old West. For him, the West symbolized adventure and excitement. Use these questions for discussion:

1. Why do you think this image of the cowboy might have been appealing to the public? *Students might point to its energy and action, and to the way the cowboy appears larger than life.*

2. What part of the story does this painting suggest? *It shows a cowboy in action during the cattle drive, perhaps herding Sancho back in the right direction.*

Preparing for Standardized Tests

Grammar The grammar concept for this selection is subjects and predicates. Standardized tests may include questions that evaluate students' understanding of complete sentences. Explain that the subject of a sentence tells who or what the sentence is about and the predicate tells what the subject does or is. Discuss that the main noun in the subject is the simple subject and that the verb or verb phrase in the predicate is the simple predicate. Use this sample test question:

Identify the group of words that is a complete sentence with a subject and a predicate.

(A) Sancho walking back to the ranch in Texas.
(B) Rides along the riverbed to the town.
(C) Arrived just before sunset, their trip made longer by the stampede.
(D) The thunder surprised the cows.

Sentence *(A)* lacks a predicate, while *(B)* and *(C)* need subjects. Sentence *(D)* has both a subject and a predicate and therefore is a complete sentence. For further practice with subjects and predicates, use Build Grammar Skills in **Selection Support,** p. 155.

One-Minute Insight

"Sancho" is based on a true story of the life of a remarkable steer in Texas of the 1880's. It retells how Sancho, who was raised on a ranch, became more domesticated than other steers, both in his habits and in his taste in foods. Sancho became so comfortable in his lifestyle that, while on a cattle drive, he managed to elude trail riders and escape his fate as steak. Alone, he returned hundreds of miles to his familiar home on the ranch.

◆ **Literary Focus**

❶ **Setting in Nonfiction and Poetry** What do the place names tell you about the land on which Kerr has his ranch? *The creek, town, and county have Spanish names, indicating the proximity to Mexico. Until about 1850, the area was, in fact, part of Mexico.*

▶**Critical Viewing**◀

❷ **Draw Conclusions** *Students may say that the job of herding required a watchful eye, caution, anticipation, and a good understanding of the terrain, as these men had to herd thousands of cattle long distances over rugged land and across rivers. They may suggest that the men were alone much of the day and exposed to the elements.*

Customize for
English Language Learners
"Sancho" contains a number of Spanish words and place names. Ask Spanish speakers to help other English language learners with pronunciation and meaning by saying and interpreting names such as Esperanza Creek, Frio County, and words such as tamale and piloncillo.

Customize for
Visual/Spatial Learners
Provide students with a map of Texas and the states north of Texas, so that they can appreciate the great distance the cows are taken (and from which Sancho returns). Have them identify the states, rivers, and towns along the cattle drive route.

Sancho

J. Frank Dobie

The Wagon Boss, Charles M. Russell

❶ **A** man by the name of Kerr had a little ranch on Esperanza Creek in Frio County, in the mesquite lands[1] south of San Antonio. He owned several good cow ponies, a few cattle, and a little bunch of goats that a dog guarded by day. At night they were shut up in a brush corral near the house. Three or four acres of land, fenced in with brush and poles, grew corn, watermelons and "kershaws"—except when the season was too drouthy.[2] A hand-dug well equipped with pulley wheel, rope and bucket furnished water for the establishment.

1. **mesquite** (mes kēt´) **lands** *n.*: Areas in which certain thorny trees and shrubs grow.
2. **drouthy** (drouth´ ē) *adj.*: Dried up due to drought—a lack of rain.

▲ **Critical Viewing** Based on the details in this painting, what can you tell about the job of herding cattle on a trail? [Draw Conclusions] ❷

Kerr's wife was named María. They had no children. She was clean, thrifty, cheerful, always making pets of animals. She usually milked three or four cows and sometimes made cheese out of goat's milk.

Late in the winter of 1877, Kerr while riding over on the San Miguel found one of his cows dead in a bog-hole. Beside the cow was a mud-plastered little black-and-white paint bull calf less than a week old. It was too weak to run; perhaps other cattle had saved it from the coyotes. Kerr pitched his rope over its head, drew it up across the saddle in front of him, carried it home, and turned it over to María.

400 ◆ From Sea to Shining Sea

 Block Scheduling Strategies

Consider these suggestions to take advantage of extended class time:
- Discuss the Background for Understanding on p. 398 and the Reading Strategy on p. 399. Invite students to share prior knowledge of the terrain and lifestyle of southern Texas and of the nature and history of cattle drives.
- Have students read the story and poem independently. They can use a map to find the places mentioned in the story. Then ask them to compare and discuss answers to the Guide to Responding questions on pp. 404, 405, and 406.

- Have students answer the Literary Focus questions on p. 406. Then, before they complete the Writing Mini-Lesson to write a report on p. 407, discuss techniques to help them gather factual details that will help readers envision the setting.
- Devote class time to having students develop their portfolios by having them work in small groups on the Projects and independently on the Speaking and Listening activities in the Idea Bank on p. 407. Provide time for students to share their Speaking and Listening presentation or speech.

She had raised many dogie calves[3] and numerous colts captured from mustang mares. The first thing she did now was to pour milk from a bottle down the orphan's throat. With warm water she washed the caked mud off its body. But hand-raising a calf is no end of trouble. The next day Kerr rode around until he found a thrifty brown cow with a young calf. He drove them to the pen. By tying this cow's head up close to a post and hobbling her hind legs, Kerr and María forced her to let the orphan suckle. She did not give a cup of milk at this first sucking. Her calf was kept in the pen next day, and the poor thing bawled herself hoarse. María began feeding her some prickly pear[4] with the thorns singed off. After being tied up twice daily for a month, she adopted the orphan as a twin to her own offspring.

Now she was one of the household cows. Spring weeds came up plentifully and the guajilla brush put out in full leaf. When the brown cow came in about sundown and her two calves were released for their supper, it was a cheering sight to see them wiggle their tails while they guzzled milk.

The dogie was a vigorous little brute, and before long he was getting more milk than the brown cow's own calf. María called him Sancho, a Mexican name meaning "pet." She was especially fond of Sancho, and he grew to be especially fond of her.

She would give him the shucks wrapped around tamales. Then she began treating him to whole tamales, which are made of ground corn rolled around a core of chopped-up meat, this banana-shaped roll, done up in a shuck, then being steam-boiled. Sancho seemed not to mind the meat. As everybody who has eaten them knows, Mexican tamales are highly seasoned with pepper. Sancho seemed to like the seasoning.

In southern Texas the little chiltipiquin peppers,[5] red when ripe, grow wild in low, shaded places. Cattle never eat them, leaving them for the wild turkeys, mockingbirds and blue quail to pick off. Sometimes in the early fall wild turkeys used to gorge on them so avidly that their flesh became too peppery for human consumption. By eating tamales Sancho developed a taste for the little red peppers growing in the thickets along Esperanza Creek. In fact, he became a kind of chiltipiquin addict. He would hunt for the peppers.

Furthermore, the tamales gave him a tooth for corn in the ear. The summer after he became a yearling he began breaking through the brush fence that enclosed Kerr's corn patch. A forked stick had to be tied around his neck to prevent his getting through the fence. He had been branded and turned into a steer, but he was as strong as any young bull. Like many other pets, he was something of a nuisance. When he could not steal corn or was not humored with tamales, he was enormously contented with grass, mixed in summertime with the sweet mesquite beans. Now and then María gave him a lump of the brown *piloncillo* sugar,[6] from Mexico, that all the border country used.

Every night Sancho came to the ranch pen to sleep. His bed ground was near a certain mesquite tree just outside the gate. He spent hours every summer day in the shade of this mesquite. When it rained and other cattle drifted off, hunting fresh pasturage, Sancho stayed at home and drank at the well. He was strictly a home creature.

In the spring of 1880 Sancho was three years old and past, white of horn and as blocky of build as a long-legged Texas steer ever grew. Kerr's ranch lay in a big unfenced range grazed by the Shiner brothers. That spring they had a contract to deliver three herds of steers, each to number 2500 head, in Wyoming. Kerr was helping the Shiners

---

6. **piloncillo** (pē lōn´ sē yō) **sugar** n.: Unrefined sugar.

◆ **Build Vocabulary**

vigorous (vig´ ər əs) *adj.*: Strong and energetic

yearling (yir´ liŋ) n.: An animal that is between one and two years old

---

3. **dogie** (dō´ gē) **calves** n.: Motherless calves or strays.
4. **prickly pear**: A cactus plant with large flat oval stems, which bears pear-shaped fruit.
5. **chiltipiquin** (chil´ tē pē´ kwin) **peppers**: Peppers that are characterized by their hot and spicy flavor.

Sancho ◆ 401

◆ **Critical Thinking**

❸ **Infer** What does this passage tell you about an animal's inclination to adopt young not her own? *The ranchers had to force the cow to mother the calf. This indicates that they knew she would not have cared for it voluntarily.*

◆ **Reading Strategy**

❹ **Envision Setting** Students can use their senses of sight, smell, sound, and taste to envision the flora and fauna in the thickets by Esperanza Creek.

Clarification

❺ Tell students that branding was burning a mark with a hot iron on the skin of cattle to show ownership. Different brands were used to distinguish which cattle belonged to which owners. Clarify that a bull is an adult male cow and that a steer is a bull that has been castrated.

◆ **Build Grammar Skills**

❻ **Subjects and Predicates** Discuss the distinction between a complete subject and a simple subject, and between a complete predicate and a simple predicate. Then ask students to identify the simple subject and simple predicate in each of the sentences of this paragraph: *Sancho, came; ground, was; He, spent; Sancho, stayed, drank.*

Humanities: Art

The Wagon Boss, by Charles M. Russell

Russell, who was born in St. Louis, moved to Montana at the age of 15 to become a cowboy. He never left. By 1893, when he was 29, he had become a professional artist. Throughout his career, he created more than 3,000 paintings, drawings, and sculptures which captured the essence and splendor of the American West. He is considered to be among the most authentic of the western painters. Encourage students to study the details and the overall effect of the painting. Then, use these questions for discussion:

1. How would you describe the terrain through which these cattle are being moved? *Students may suggest words such as rugged, hilly, rocky, empty to describe what they see in the painting; they may also note that there are rivers for the cattle to cross.*

2. What might the rider in the foreground of the painting be looking at? What do you notice about his attitude? *Students may notice that he is looking back intently at the herd or something near it—perhaps another animal; they also may notice that the rider's hand is on his rifle.*

401

Cattle Stampede, Olaf C. Seltzer

❶ | ▲ Critical Viewing What is the main impression conveyed in this painting of a cattle drive? [Analyze]

gather cattle, and, along with various other ranchers, sold them what steers he had.

Sancho was included. One day late in March the Shiner men road-branded him *7 Z* and put him in the first herd headed north. The other herds were to follow two or three days apart.

It was late in the afternoon when the "shaping up" of the herd was completed. It was watered and thrown out on open prairie ground to be bedded down. But Sancho had no disposition to lie down—there. He wanted to go **❷** back to that mesquite just outside the pen gate at the Kerr place on the Esperanza where he had without variation slept every night since he had been weaned. Perhaps he had in mind an evening tamale. He stood and roamed about on the south side of the herd. A dozen times during the night the men on guard had to drive him back. As reliefs were changed, word passed to keep an eye on that paint steer on the lower side.

When the herd started on next morning,

Sancho was at the tail end of it, often stopping and looking back. It took constant attention from one of the drag drivers to keep him moving. By the time the second night arrived, every **❸** hand in the outfit knew Sancho, by name and sight, as being the stubbornest and gentlest steer of the lot. About dark one of them pitched a loop over his horns and staked him to a bush. This saved bothering with his <u>persistent</u> efforts to walk off.

Daily when the herd was halted to graze, spreading out like a fan, the steers all eating their way northward, Sancho invariably pointed himself south. In his lazy way he grabbed many a mouthful of grass while the herd was moving. Finally, in some brush up on the Llano, after ten days of trailing, he dodged into freedom. On the second day following, one **❹** of the point men of the second Shiner herd saw him walking south, saw his *7 Z* road brand, rounded him in, and set him traveling north again. He became the chief drag animal of this

402 ◆ *From Sea to Shining Sea*

 Humanities: Art

Cattle Stampede, by Olaf C. Seltzer
  Olaf C. Seltzer (1877–1957) was born in Denmark, but moved to Montana at a young age. He worked as a cowboy and then for the railroad. He met and became friends with Charles Russell, who influenced his work. Seltzer did not become a full-time painter until he was 44 years old, but was still considered an important western painter. Have students compare and contrast the the style of this painting with the others that accompany the story. Then use these questions for discussion of Seltzer's painting:

1. What is happening in this scene? What may have caused the actions of the cattle and riders? *Cowboys are frantically trying to get control of a stampeding herd. It is during a downpour; the cows might have been spooked by thunder or lightning, or perhaps the driving rain.*

2. What impression of a cattle drive does the painting create? *Students may talk about the difficult and dangerous work of cattle drivers and the massive, almost unmanageable size of a herd of cattle; they may also note that the artist has conveyed the challenge of a cattle drive.*

herd. Somewhere north of the Colorado there was a run one night, and when morning came Sancho was missing. The other steers had held together; probably Sancho had not run at all. But he was picked up again, by the third Shiner herd coming on behind.

He took his accustomed place in the drag and continued to require special driving. He picked up in weight. He chewed his cud peacefully and slept soundly, but whenever he looked southward, which was often, he raised his head as if memory and expectation were stirring. The boys were all personally acquainted with him, and every night one of them would stake him.

One day the cattle balked and milled at a bank-full river. "Rope Old Sancho and lead him in," the boss ordered, "and we'll point the other cattle after him." Sancho led like a horse. The herd followed. As soon as he was released, he dropped back to the rear. After this, however, he was always led to the front when there was high water to cross.

By the time the herd got into No Man's Land, beyond Red River, the sand-hill plums and the low-running possum grapes were turning ripe. Pausing now and then to pick a little of the fruit, Sancho's driver saw the pet steer following his example.

Meantime the cattle were trailing, trailing, always north. For five hundred miles across Texas, counting the windings to find water and keep out of breaks, they had come. After getting into the Indian Territory, they snailed on across the Wichita, the South Canadian, the North Canadian, and the Cimarron. On into Kansas they trailed and across the Arkansas, around Dodge City, cowboy capital of the world, out of Kansas into Nebraska, over the wide, wide Platte, past the roaring cow town of Ogallala, up the North Platte, under the Black Hills, and then against the Big Horn Mountains. For two thousand miles, making ten or twelve miles a day, the Shiner herds trailed. They "walked with the grass." Slow, slow, they

moved. "Oh, it was a long and lonesome go"— as slow as the long drawn-out notes of "The Texas Lullaby," as slow as the night herder's song on a slow-walking horse:

> It's a whoop and a yea, get along my little
> dogies,
> For camp is far away.
> It's a whoop and a yea and a-driving the
> dogies,
> For Wyoming may be your new home.

When, finally, after listening for months, day and night, to the slow song of their motion, the "dogies" reached their "new home," Sancho was still halting every now and then to sniff southward for a whiff of the Mexican Gulf. The farther he got away from home, the less he seemed to like the change. He had never felt frost in September before. The Mexican peppers on the Esperanza were red ripe now.

The Wyoming outfit received the cattle. Then for a week the Texas men helped brand *C R* on their long sides before turning them loose on the new range. When Sancho's time came to be branded in the chute,[7] one of the Texans yelled out, "There goes my pet. Stamp that *C R* brand on him good and deep." Another one said, "The line riders had better watch for his tracks."

And now the Shiner men turned south, taking back with them their saddle horses and chuck wagons—and leaving Sancho behind. They made good time, but a blue norther was whistling at their backs when they turned the remuda[8] loose on the Frio River. After the "Cowboys' Christmas Ball" most of them settled down for a few weeks of winter sleep. They could rub tobacco juice in their eyes during the summer when they needed something in addition to night rides and runs to keep them awake.

Spring comes early down on the Esperanza. The mesquites were all in new leaf with that green so fresh and tender that the color seems to emanate into the sky. The bluebonnets and the pink phlox were sprinkling every hill and

---

7. **chute** (shoōt) *n.*: Narrow, high-walled device used to restrain cattle.
8. **remuda** (rə moō´ də) *n.*: Group of extra saddle horses kept as a supply of remounts.

◆ **Build Vocabulary**

persistent (pər sist´ ənt) *adj.*: Stubborn; persevering
accustomed (ə kus´ təmd) *adj.*: Customary; usual

Sancho ◆ 403

❺ **Setting in Nonfiction and Poetry** Have students locate these states, rivers, and towns on a map to follow the route of the drive. Discuss that crossing rivers was challenging, that breaks were dangerous interruptions or gaps in the trail, and that cow towns were towns from which cows were shipped to army posts, mining boom towns, and east to big cities. You might wish to provide an opportunity for students to view cow towns like Ogallala, what the terrain of the land was like, and what river crossings involved, by watching parts of the TV miniseries "Lonesome Dove."

◆ **Reading Strategy**

❻ **Envision Setting** Ask students to explain why cowboys sang songs like this one. *Cowboys sang to pass the time and, more important, to soothe the cows in an attempt to avoid stampedes.*

◆ **Reading Strategy**

❼ **Envision Setting** How do Sancho's senses tell him that he's far from home? *He no longer smells the Mexican Gulf waters or the peppers; he feels the cold of the north for the first time.*

Comprehension Check ☑

❽ Ask students what they think a "blue norther" is. *It is a strong, cold north wind.*

◆ **Reading Strategy**

❾ **Envision Setting** Guide students to appreciate the way the author identifies the early spring by its fresh colors and fragrances.

Cultural Connection

Chilis and Spices Sancho develops a taste for chili peppers, a staple of Southwest cooking. Diets in most hot climates feature hot peppers because they cool people by making them perspire. Also, using chilis in food preparation can delay spoilage. Worldwide, there are more than 1,000 different kinds of hot peppers, although not all are fiery enough to make a person (or steer) sweat. Peppers come in many degrees of hotness; for instance, the habañero (Scotch Bonnet) is about 1,000 times hotter than the jalapeño.

Tex-Mex cooking is not the only cuisine to use hot peppers liberally. Invite students to investigate the use of peppers in the foods of India, China, Thailand, the Caribbean, Ethiopia, and other regions. For those with brave palates, try a class taste test—either in prepared food or simply by comparing the taste of actual peppers. Or, students can find out about the Scoville scale that ranks by heat, and learn how some of their favorite hot peppers stack up against the hottest.

403

◆ Literary Focus

❶ Setting in Nonfiction and Poetry Discuss with students how the examples of cowboy expressions in the dialogue between Rigby and Kerr evoke a particular time and place.

Answers

◆ LITERATURE AND YOUR LIFE

Reader's Response Some students may think that the many challenges, discomforts, and hazards of a cattle drive would make the experience an unappealing one; others may be intrigued by the adventure.

Thematic Focus Students may say that life is full of amazing stories.

☑ Check Your Comprehension

1. Kerr brought the calf home to her care; Maria had a history of caring for calves and colts.
2. Sancho, who eats tamales and hot peppers, reveals that he is more domesticated than most steers.
3. Eventually, he makes his way back to Kerr's ranch, and Joe Shiner says he isn't going to drive him back to Wyoming.

◆ Critical Thinking

1. Sancho is more domesticated than other steers, he eats foods they don't eat, and he makes an incredible journey back to the ranch on which he was raised.
2. He eats tamales, hot peppers, and sugar, he stays at the ranch while other cattle drift off, and he manages to make his way back to the ranch from a great distance away.
3. He may have liked the story because it was true, amusing, and showed one steer's remarkable humanlike qualities.
4. Writers may give animals human characteristics to make them seem real and believable and so that readers can imagine the world from an animal's perspective.
5. Life on a ranch might have been lonely and often tedious. A pet might give Maria a diversion, companionship, and affection.

---

draw. The prickly pear was studded with waxy blossoms, and the glades were heavy with the perfume of white brush. It was a good season, and tallow weed and grass were coming together. It was time for the spring cow hunts and the putting up of herds for the annual drive north. The Shiners were at work.

"We were close to Kerr's cabin on Esperanza Creek," John Rigby told me, "when I looked across a pear flat and saw something that made me rub my eyes. I was riding with Joe Shiner, and we both stopped our horses."

"Do you see what I see?" John Rigby asked.

"Yes, but before I say, I'm going to read the brand," Joe Shiner answered.

They rode over. "You can hang me for a horse thief," John Rigby will tell, "if it wasn't that Sancho paint steer, four years old now, the Shiner *7 Z* road brand and the Wyoming *C R* range brand both showing on him as plain as boxcar letters."

The men rode on down to Kerr's.

"Yes," Kerr said, "Old Sancho got in about six weeks ago. His hoofs were worn mighty nigh down to the hair, but he wasn't lame. I thought Maria was going out of her senses, she was so glad to see him. She actually hugged him and she cried and then she begun feeding him hot tamales. She's made a batch of them nearly every day since, just to pet that steer. When she's not feeding him tamales, she's giving him *piloncillo*."

Sancho was slicking off and certainly did seem contented. He was coming up every night and sleeping at the gate, Maria said. She was nervous over the prospect of losing her pet, but Joe Shiner said that if that steer loved his home enough to walk back to it all the way from Wyoming, he wasn't going to drive him off again, even if he was putting up another herd for the *C R* owners.

As far as I can find out, Old Sancho lived right there on the Esperanza, now and then getting a tamale, tickling his palate with chili peppers in season, and generally staying fat on mesquite grass, until he died a natural death. He was one of the "walking Texas Longhorns."

◆Guide for Responding

◆ LITERATURE AND YOUR LIFE

Reader's Response Would you have enjoyed going on a cattle drive? Explain.

Thematic Focus What does the story of "Sancho" reveal about life in the United States?

Journal Writing In your journal, jot down your impressions of what it must have been like to go on a cattle drive.

☑ Check Your Comprehension

1. Why does María adopt Sancho as a pet?
2. What unusual traits does Sancho reveal while living on the ranch?
3. What finally happens to Sancho? Why does Joe Shiner agree to this decision?

◆ Critical Thinking

INTERPRET

1. How is Sancho different from other steer? **[Compare and Contrast]**
2. Find three examples of Sancho's humanlike personality. **[Connect]**
3. Dobie said that Sancho's story was the best range story he ever heard. Why do you think he liked the story so much? **[Interpret]**

EVALUATE

4. Why do you think writers often assign animals human characteristics? **[Assess]**

APPLY

5. Considering María's daily life, why would a pet be important to her? **[Hypothesize]**

404 ◆ From Sea to Shining Sea

Speaking and Listening Mini-Lesson

Tour Guide Speech

This mini-lesson supports the Speaking and Listening activity in the Idea Bank on p. 407.

Introduce Discuss the importance of knowing one's audience when preparing and delivering a speech. Then, direct students to research in order to be knowledgeable tour guides—able to describe ranch life and answer questions about it.

Develop Have students practice their speeches, revising them as needed so that they are both informative and effective. Invite students to tape themselves to listen to the quality of their presentation. Some students may wish to use pictures of ranch life for their speeches. They might place the pictures so that they can walk listeners from station to station, giving a "guided tour."

Apply Have students deliver their speeches to groups of classmates. Provide time for question-and-answer sessions.

Assess Evaluate students on the quality and organization of their research and how successfully they address the intended audience. Or, use the Peer Assessment: Speaker/Speech form, p. 114, in **Alternative Assessment.**

The Closing of the Rodeo

William Jay Smith

▲ **Critical Viewing** This photograph shows a cowboy swinging a lasso. What skills do you think a cowboy should have to be qualified for the job? **[Speculate]**

The lariat[1] snaps; the cowboy rolls
　　His pack, and mounts and rides away.
Back to the land the cowboy goes.

Plumes of smoke from the factory sway
5　　In the setting sun. The curtain falls,
A train in the darkness pulls away.

Good-by, says the rain on the iron roofs.
　　Good-by, say the barber poles.
Dark drum the vanishing horses' hooves.

---

1. **lariat** (lar′ ē it) *n.*: Rope used for tying or catching horses.

Guide for Responding

◆ LITERATURE AND YOUR LIFE

Reader's Response Which image in the poem affects you most strongly?

Thematic Focus Why do you think Smith selected this topic for a poem?

☑ Check Your Comprehension

1. What event is described in the poem?
2. Where has the rodeo been?
3. Where does the cowboy go?

◆ Critical Thinking

INTERPRET
1. Will the rodeo come back to the town? **[Speculate]**
2. Personification is assigning human feelings to nonhuman things. How does Smith use this technique? **[Classify]**

COMPARE LITERARY WORKS
3. Do you think that J. Frank Dobie would have enjoyed reading "The Closing of the Rodeo"? Why or why not? **[Speculate]**

The Closing of the Rodeo ◆ 405

⬥ Beyond the Selection

FURTHER READING
Other Works by J. Frank Dobie
Tales of Old-Time Texas
Legends of Texas
I'll Tell You a Tale
Other Works by William Jay Smith
The World Below the Window
Dark Valentine
"Indian Removal"
Other Works About Cattle Drives
Lonesome Dove, Larry McMurtry
The Last Cattle Drive, Robert Day

INTERNET
We suggest the following sites on the Internet (all Web sites are subject to change).
　For J. Frank Dobie's *Guide to Life and Literature of the Southwest:*
http://ftp.sunet.se/ftp/pub/etext/gutenberg/ etext95/swest10.txt
　For information on William Jay Smith:
http://www.english.upenn.edu/~afilreis/88/ smith-epigrams.html
　We *strongly recommend* that you preview these sites before you send students to them.

Develop Understanding

One-Minute Insight "The Closing of the Rodeo" is a poem that describes that melancholy time when the rodeo packs up and leaves town. Even the rain and the barber poles are sad to see it leave.

►Critical Viewing◄

❷ **Speculate** *Students are likely to say that, above all, he needs superb riding skills and a good understanding of the behavior of horses and cows. Some may say that a cowboy should also have good balance, flexibility, strength, and endurance.*

Beyond Literature

Scientists who raise endangered birds, like condors, in captivity know that birds will imprint on them. To ensure that the birds don't, so they will be better able to cope with being released, scientists trick them. Scientists use a mother bird hand puppet to feed young birds.

Reinforce and Extend

Answers
◆ LITERATURE AND YOUR LIFE

Reader's Response Some students may say the train pulling away into the setting sun; or the image of the barber poles saying good-bye.

Thematic Focus Students may say he selected this topic because of his personal interest in rodeos.

☑ Check Your Comprehension

1. A rodeo is closing and the performers are leaving town.
2. The rodeo has been in a factory town.
3. The cowboy goes back to the ranch.

◆ Critical Thinking

1. Students may speculate that it will, but not for a long time.
2. He personifies the rain and the barber poles, imagining that they can say goodbye to the cowboys.
3. Responses will vary; some students will say that Dobie would appreciate its poignant look at an aspect of today's West.

Answers

◆ Reading Strategy

1. Settings include the Kerr ranch and the route of the cattle drive. Students should cite details such as peppers, tamales, mesquites, prickly pear cacti, rivers, windings, and breaks, and the brands on the cows.
2. Students might choose images from the poem, such as a lariat snapping, a cowboy packing to leave town, a train pulling out, a barber pole, and a factory. They might film in any city or town with a clear western flavor, such as Casper, Wyoming or Prescott, Arizona.

◆ Build Vocabulary

Using the Word Endings -ent and -ant
1. resistant; 2. existent; 3. defendant; 4. attendant

Spelling Strategy
1. accommodate; 2. accepted; 3. accustomed

Using the Word Bank
1. a   2. b   3. c   4. d

◆ Literary Focus

1. (a) It is set in the West, first on a ranch in Texas and then on a cattle trail heading north to Wyoming. (b) The setting can be identified by the cacti and other plants, by the descriptions of the grasses and flowers of the prairie, and by the names of the rivers crossed.
2. (a) In a different place, it might involve a different kind of animal. (b) In modern times, someone might find the lost animal and, using its brand to know where it is from, call the ranch. That person might drive or ship it back.
3. (a) That it has a rodeo at all means it is likely that the town is in the West; the factory smoke may indicate that it is an industrial town of some size. (b) Students may say that the end of the rodeo recalls the end of the vision of the cowboy riding the open prairie.

406

Guide for Responding (continued)

◆ Reading Strategy

ENVISION SETTING

When you **envision the setting** of a story or poem, you use your senses to put yourself in the time and place in which the events occur.
1. Describe two major settings presented in "Sancho." What details bring these settings to life?
2. If you were to make a short film to accompany a reading of "The Closing of the Rodeo," what images would you choose? Where would you film?

◆ Build Grammar Skills

SUBJECTS AND PREDICATES

The **subject** of a sentence tells who or what the sentence is about. The **predicate** tells what the subject is or does.

> S   P
> A man by the name of Kerr | had a little ranch on Esperanza Creek. . . .

The **simple subject** is the main noun or pronoun in the complete subject. The **simple predicate** is the verb or verb phrase in the predicate.

> SS   SP
> The Wyoming outfit | received the cattle.

Practice Copy the following sentences on your paper. Underline each subject once and each predicate twice. Circle each simple subject and simple predicate.
1. The steer arrived in Wyoming after the long trek.
2. Late that night, I heard a loud noise.
3. One of the new arrivals had escaped.
4. Our moonlit chase continued for an hour.
5. Finally, we cornered the frightened animal.

Writing Application Complete each sentence by adding the element shown in parentheses.
1. The old steer ____?____. (predicate)
2. ____?____ arrived at our ranch. (subject)
3. Then, ____?____ bought a steer. (simple subject)
4. He ____?____ the steer home in an open truck. (simple predicate)

◆ Literary Focus

SETTING IN NONFICTION AND POETRY

A setting is the time and place in which a literary work takes place. In each of these works, the **setting** plays an important role. As in a short story, the setting can have a huge impact on the events described and the mood or atmosphere of the work.
1. (a) Identify the setting of "Sancho." (b) Describe three details that helped you to identify the setting.
2. (a) How would "Sancho" be different if it were set in a different place? (b) If it were set in modern times?
3. (a) Which details in "The Closing of the Rodeo" reveal its setting? (b) In what ways does the setting support the meaning of the poem?

◆ Build Vocabulary

USING THE WORD ENDINGS -ent AND -ant

The word endings -ent and -ant can be added to verbs to create adjectives. Change each of these verbs to an adjective by adding -ant or -ent. Use a dictionary to check which spelling to use.
1. resist   2. exist   3. defend   3. attend

SPELLING STRATEGY

Accustomed and *accept* begin with *acc*, which can have the sound of *ak* or *aks*. Rearrange the letters at the end of each sentence to make a word beginning with *acc* that completes the sentence.
1. It was difficult to ____?____ all of the steers on the drive. (c a d m a o t m c o e)
2. The rancher ____?____ the job reluctantly. (e c t a d e c p)
3. The steers were ____?____ to living on a ranch. (a e s m c o d u t c)

USING THE WORD BANK

On your paper, match the Word Bank words in Column A with the words and phrases in Column B that are most nearly the same in meaning.

Column A	Column B
1. vigorous	a. strong and lively
2. yearling	b. young animal
3. persistent	c. without giving up
4. accustomed	d. used to

◆ Build Grammar Skills

Practice
1. The (steer) (arrived) in Wyoming after the long trek.
2. Late that night (I) (heard) a loud noise.
3. (One) of the new arrivals (had escaped).
4. Our moonlit (chase) (continued) for an hour.
5. Finally, (we) (cornered) the frightened animal.

Writing Application
Possible responses:
1. The old steer slept under a tree.
2. A new hand arrived at our ranch.
3. Then, Ed bought a steer.
4. He drove the steer home in an open truck.

Writer's Solution

For additional instruction and practice, use the lesson in the *Writer's Solution Language Lab CD-ROM* on Subjects and Predicates. You may also use the page on Complete Subjects and Predicates, p. 31 in the *Writer's Solution Grammar Practice Book.*

Build Your Portfolio

 ## Idea Bank

Writing

1. **Letter** Imagine that you are María in "Sancho." Then, write a letter to a friend describing Sancho's return.

2. **Character Profile** Write a character profile of Sancho in which you describe his main characteristics. Support your points with details from the selection.

3. **Persuasive Essay** "Sancho" is said to be a true story. In a brief persuasive essay, explain whether you believe the story to be true. Use story details to support your views.

Speaking and Listening

4. **Oral Presentation** Memorize "The Closing of the Rodeo" and practice reciting it. You may wish to use a tape recorder to record your practice and refine your delivery. When you are ready, present the poem to your class. **[Performing Arts Link]**

5. **Tour Guide Speech** Imagine that you are a tour guide at a Texas ranch. Prepare a brief introduction that you would provide to give visitors an idea of ranch life. You may want to research ranches and Texas livestock. Present your speech to the class, and answer questions at the end. **[Career Link]**

Projects

6. **Poster** Create a poster advertising the opening of a new rodeo. Include specific details that will attract customers. **[Art Link]**

7. **Historic Newspaper [Group Activity]** Work with a team to create a newspaper from 1880, the year in which Sancho returned home. Some team members should act as reporters who find stories from 1880 to write about, including Sancho's tale. Other team members can edit and lay out the newspaper. **[Social Studies Link]**

 ## Writing Mini-Lesson

Report

The settings of "Sancho" and "The Closing of the Rodeo" make a great start to a research project. Do research about cattle drives or rodeos, and write a report to share your findings with the class.

Writing Skills Focus: Elaborate With Factual Details

The key to a successful report is the careful choice of **factual details** that convey a complete and accurate picture of the subject. Notice the details italicized in this example:

Model

Cattle drives were *long* and *grueling journeys. Most drives began in Texas* and *ended in the Midwest,* covering sometimes as much as *2,000 miles* of rugged terrain. A drive commonly took more than *six months.*

Prewriting Choose your topic. Then, gather information about your topic from a variety of sources, including nonfiction books, historic journals, encyclopedias, and Web sites. Organize your notes into an outline before you begin to write.

Drafting Follow your outline or refer to your notes as you draft. Then, weave together the facts you've gathered during your research.

Revising Work with a classmate to evaluate your draft. Ask your partner to identify unclear or vague sentences, as well as statements that should be elaborated with additional facts.

> ◆ **Grammar Application**
>
> Make sure that each sentence has both a subject and a predicate. If a sentence is missing one part, you have a sentence error—a fragment.

Sancho/The Closing of the Rodeo ◆ 407

 ## Idea Bank

Following are suggestions for matching the Idea Bank topics with your students' performance levels and learning modalities:

Customize for *Performance Levels*
Less Advanced Students: 1, 4, 6
Average Students: 2, 4, 5, 6,
More Advanced Students: 3, 5, 7

Customize for *Learning Modalities*
Verbal/Linguistic: 1, 2, 3, 4, 5, 6, 7
Visual/Spatial: 6
Logical/Mathematical: 2, 3, 5, 7
Musical/Rhythmic: 4
Interpersonal: 4, 5, 6, 7
Intrapersonal: 1

 ## Writing Mini-Lesson

Refer students to the Writing Handbook in the back of the book for instruction on the writing process and for further information on writing reports. Have students use the Main Idea and Supporting Details Organizer in **Writing and Language Transparencies,** p. 61, to organize their reports.

 ### Writer's Solution

Writers at Work Videodisc
Have students view the videodisc segment on Gathering Information (Ch. 7), featuring Virginia Hamilton, to see how she uses interviews in her research process.

Play frames 9916 to 11013

Writing Lab CD-ROM
Have students complete the tutorial on Reports. Follow these steps:
1. Have students use the Gathering Information section for ideas on using library resources and for guidelines on note-taking.
2. Have students use the Organizing Information section for examples of notes organized according to different plans.
3. Have students draft on computer.
4. Have students use the Revision Checker for coherence and unity within and between paragraphs.

Writer's Solution Sourcebook
Have students use Chapter 7, "Reports," pp. 201–233, for additional support. The chapter includes in-depth instruction on gathering information, pp. 220–221.

✓ ASSESSMENT OPTIONS

Formal Assessment, Selection Test, pp. 117–119, and Assessment Resources Software. The selection test is designed so that it can be easily customized to the performance levels of your students.

Alternative Assessment, p. 29, includes options for less advanced students, more advanced students, visual/spatial learners, verbal/linguistic learners, interpersonal learners, bodily/kinesthetic learners, and musical/rhythmic learners.

PORTFOLIO ASSESSMENT
Use the following rubrics in the **Alternative Assessment** booklet to assess student writing:
Letter: Description, p. 93
Character Profile: Description, p. 93
Persuasive Essay: Persuasion, p. 101
Writing Mini-Lesson: Research Report/Paper, p. 102

OBJECTIVES

1. To read, comprehend, and interpret two short stories
2. To relate two short stories to personal experience
3. To predict
4. To identify character traits
5. To build vocabulary in context and learn the word root *-cred-*
6. To develop skill using compound subjects and verbs
7. To write a recommendation that includes supporting points
8. To respond to two short stories through writing, speaking and listening, and projects

SKILLS INSTRUCTION

Vocabulary:
Using the Word Root *-cred-*

Spelling:
Use *xi* to Spell *ksh* Sounds

Grammar:
Compound Subjects and Verbs

Reading Strategy:
Predict

Literary Focus:
Character Traits

Writing:
Support Points

Speaking and Listening:
Work Song (Teacher Edition)

Viewing and Representing:
White Umbrella (Teacher Edition)

Critical Viewing:
Draw Conclusions; Deduce; Infer; Make a Judgment

PORTFOLIO OPPORTUNITIES

Writing: Newspaper Article; Diary Entry; Compare and Contrast

Writing Mini-Lesson: Recommendation

Speaking and Listening: Dramatic Scene; Work Song

Projects: History of the Piano; Kentucky Farm Report

More About the Authors

Jesse Hilton Stuart published more than sixty books, thousands of poems, and over 3,000 articles during his lifetime. Kentucky's former poet laureate was also a dedicated educator. A 733-acre nature preserve in Greenup County—the place where he was born and raised, and later lived and taught—was named in his memory.

Gish Jen's given first name is Lillian, but she took her nickname from the actress Lillian Gish. To prove herself as a writer rather than an "ethnic writer," her early works did not include Asian American characters.

Guide for Reading

Meet the Authors:

Jesse Stuart (1906–1984)

Poet and novelist Jesse Stuart grew up in rural surroundings in eastern Kentucky. After high school, he worked for a circus and a steel mill before attending college. He then became a teacher and school superintendent. Stuart is known for his children's books, including *The Red Mule*. Although he received many awards and honors in his lifetime, he was most proud of being a teacher. "First, last, always, I am a school teacher," he said. "I love the firing line of the classroom."

Gish Jen (1956–)

The daughter of Chinese immigrants, Gish Jen grew up in Yonkers and Scarsdale, New York, communities that had very few Asian Americans. Jen began writing fiction as an undergraduate at Harvard. After teaching English in China, she entered the University of Iowa writing program, where she wrote "The White Umbrella." Her first novel, *Typical American,* was published in 1991, and her second, *Mona in the Promised Land,* in 1996. Both of these novels deal with the clash of cultures that Asian Americans face in the United States.

◆ LITERATURE AND YOUR LIFE

CONNECT YOUR EXPERIENCE

Some accomplishments are rewarded with trophies. Others are more personal, bringing only a smile to the face of the person who's achieved something. Think for a moment about something special you accomplished and how it made you feel. In the following stories, you'll learn of two young people who strive to succeed at different things.

THEMATIC FOCUS: An Album of Stories

As you read these stories, think about what they reveal about people's needs to achieve success.

◆ Background for Understanding

SCIENCE

In "A Ribbon for Baldy," the main character plants corn for his school science project. On a small farm like the one in the story, planting and harvesting were done by hand rather than by machines. To prepare for planting, the land is cleared to a depth of about eight inches, plowed, and fertilized. Corn seeds are planted in early spring, most often in long rows. The growing season is four to six months, so the narrator's corn, planted in April, would be ready to harvest in August.

◆ Build Vocabulary

WORD ROOTS: -cred-

The narrator of "The White Umbrella" tries to convince her piano teacher of "the credibility of [her] lie." The word *credibility* comes from the root *-cred-*, which means "believe." Understanding the meaning of the root will help you figure out that *credibility* means "believability."

WORD BANK

Which word from the list is an adverb? Check the Build Vocabulary box on page 416 to see if you chose correctly.

surveyed
envelop
bargain
discreet
credibility
constellation
anxiously
revelation

Prentice Hall Literature Program Resources

REINFORCE / RETEACH / EXTEND

Selection Support Pages

Build Vocabulary: Word Roots: *-cred-*, p. 158
Build Spelling Skills, p. 159
Build Grammar Skills: Compound Sentences and Verbs, p. 160
Reading Strategy: Predict, p. 161
Literary Focus: Character Traits, p. 162
Strategies for Diverse Student Needs, pp. 59–60
Beyond Literature Cross-Curriculum Connection: Science, p. 30

Formal Assessment Selection Test, pp. 120–122, Assessment Resources Software
Alternative Assessment, p. 30
Writing and Language Transparencies
Sunburst Organizer, p. 85
Resource Pro CD-ROM "A Ribbon for Baldy"; "The White Umbrella"—includes all resource material and customizable lesson plan

🎧 **Listening to Literature Audiocassettes**
"A Ribbon for Baldy"; "The White Umbrella"

408

A Ribbon for Baldy ◆ The White Umbrella

◆ Literary Focus

CHARACTER TRAITS

Character traits are the qualities that make up a character's personality. For example, a character may be generous, clever, or stubborn. Writers reveal characters' traits through their actions, dialogue, and other characters' descriptions of and reactions to them. In "A Ribbon for Baldy," for example, this statement reveals the main character's trait of determination: "Every day I thought about my project for the General Science class."

◆ Reading Strategy

PREDICT

Understanding a character's traits can help you make **predictions,** or educated guesses, about what will happen in a story. Your predictions may also be guided by your own experiences in similar situations or by hints that the author provides. Predicting gets you involved in a story. As you read these two stories, compare your predictions with the actual outcomes. Fill out a chart like the one below to record your predictions and the actual outcomes.

Prediction	Based on	Outcome
The girls will find out where their mother works. →	"For weeks we wondered what kind of work she was doing." →	

Guide for Reading ◆ 409

 **Interest Grabber** Most people strive for success, pride, and recognition at one time or another. One's motivations to strive can vary widely. Challenge students to complete one or more of these statements in a private journal:

- I feel successful when I . . .
- I want to be acknowledged for . . .
- I hope ___ notices my ability to . . .

Invite volunteers to share their statements, if they are comfortable doing so. Guide students to the stories by telling them that each is about a young person with a strong desire to excel.

◆ Build Grammar Skills

Compound Subjects and Verbs
If you wish to introduce the grammar concept for this selection before students read, refer to the instruction on p. 420.

Customize for
Less Proficient Readers
Both stories in this set are told in the first person. To help students better grasp the Literary Focus, suggest that, as they read, students list traits they can attribute to each narrator. They can ascertain these traits by trying to ascribe a deeper meaning to what the narrator says or does.

Customize for
More Advanced Students
Each story in this set uses symbols, things that represent something else. Symbols, such as the umbrella in "The White Umbrella," convey abstract ideas or deeper issues. Have students chart the symbols they find in the stories, as follows:

Symbol	Represents
fat pork sandwich	*poverty, humiliation*

Customize for
English Language Learners
Help students understand the tools and farming terms mentioned in "A Ribbon for Baldy." You might use pictures to illustrate items such as *windlass, barnlot, crosscut, corn row, handspike,* and *rod pole.* You can amplify students' understanding of the terms by pantomiming actions such as planting, plowing, or using any of the tools.

 Preparing for Standardized Tests

Reading The literary focus in this set—character traits—will help students as they read in general, and as they answer some reading comprehension items on standardized tests.

Tests may evaluate students' grasp of character traits by asking them to summarize a character based on analyzing something that he or she says or does. Use the following sample test question:

In "The White Umbrella," Miss Crosman offers to give Mona and her sister a ride home when Mrs. Lee is late. This shows that MissCrosman—

(A) likes to drive
(B) is considerate and thoughtful
(C) doesn't trust Mrs. Lee's driving skill
(D) wants to get rid of the girls

Students may consider that she might enjoy driving *(A),* or mistrust Mrs. Lee's driving skill *(C),* but the best answer is based on her character trait of being helpful and kind—she offers to drive the girls home in order to make them feel comfortable, and to get them home out of the rain *(B).* For more practice, use Literary Focus: Character Traits, in **Selection Support,** p. 162.

410

A Ribbon for Baldy

Jesse Stuart

❶ The day Professor Herbert started talking about a project for each member of our General Science class, I was more excited than I had ever been. I wanted to have an outstanding project. I wanted it to be greater, to be more unusual than those of my classmates. I wanted to do something worthwhile, and something to make them respect me.

❷ I'd made the best grade in my class in General Science. I'd made more yardage, more tackles and carried the football across the goal line more times than any player on my team. But making good grades and playing rugged football hadn't made them forget that I rode a mule to school, that I had worn my mother's shoes the first year and that I slipped away at the noon hour so no one would see me eat fat pork between slices of corn bread.

Every day I thought about my project for the General Science class. We had to have our project by the end of the school year and it was now January.

❸ In the classroom, in study hall and when I did odd jobs on my father's 50 acres, I thought about my project. But it wouldn't come to me like an algebra problem or memorizing a poem. I couldn't think of a project that would help my father and mother to support us. One ❸ that would be good and useful.

"If you set your mind on something and keep on thinking about it, the idea will eventually come," Professor Herbert told us when Bascom Wythe complained about how hard it was to find a project.

One morning in February I left home in a white cloud that had settled over the deep valleys. I could not see an object ten feet in front of me in this mist. I crossed the pasture into the orchard and the mist began to thin. When I reached the ridge road, the light thin air was clear of mist. I looked over the sea of rolling white clouds. The tops of the dark winter hills jutted up like little islands.

I have to ride a mule, but not one of my classmates lives in a prettier place, I thought, as I surveyed my world. Look at Little Baldy! What a pretty island in the sea of clouds. A thin ribbon of cloud seemed to envelop cone-shaped Little Baldy from bottom to top like the new rope Pa had just bought for the windlass[1] over our well.

Then, like a flash—the idea for my project ❹ came to me. And what an idea it was! I'd not

---

1. **windlass** (wind′ləs) *n.*: Device for raising and lowering a bucket on a rope.

410 ◆ From Sea to Shining Sea

tell anybody about it! I wouldn't even
tell my father, but I knew he'd be for it.
Little Baldy wrapped in the white coils
of mist had given me the idea for it.

I was so happy I didn't care who
laughed at me, what anyone said or who watched me eat fat meat on corn bread for my lunch. I had an idea and I knew it was a wonderful one.

◆ Literary Focus
What does this passage reveal about the boy's personality?

"I've got something to talk over with you," I told Pa when I got home. "Look over there at that broom-sedge[2] and the scattered pines on Little Baldy. I'd like to burn the broom-sedge and briers and cut the pines and farm that this summer."

We stood in our barnlot and looked at Little Baldy.

"Yes, I've been thinkin' about clearin' that hill up someday," Pa said.

"Pa, I'll clear up all this south side and you clear up the other side," I said. "And I'll plow all of it and we'll get it in corn this year."

"Now this will be some undertakin'," he said. "I can't clear that land up and work six days a week on the railroad section. But if you will clear up the south side, I'll hire Bob Lavender to do the other side."

"That's a bargain," I said.

That night while the wind was still and the broom-sedge and leaves were dry, my father and I set fire all the way around the base. Next morning Little Baldy was a dark hill jutting high into February's cold, windy sky.

Pa hired Bob Lavender to clear one portion and I started working on the other. I worked early of mornings before I went to school. I hurried home and worked into the night.

Finn, my ten-year-old brother, was big enough to help me saw down the scattered

▲ **Critical Viewing** How much effort do you think it would take to plant and harvest a cornfield like this one? [Draw Conclusions] ⑦

◆ **Build Vocabulary**

surveyed (sǝr vād´) v.: Looked over in a careful way; examined; inspected

envelop (en vel´ ǝp) v.: To wrap up; cover completely

bargain (bär´ gǝn) n.: Something bought, offered, or sold at a price favorable to the buyer

A Ribbon for Baldy ◆ 411

---

2. **broom-sedge** (bro͞om´ sej) n.: Coarse grass used in making brooms.

◆ **LITERATURE AND YOUR LIFE**

④ When the boy gets what he believes is a great idea, he makes a point of keeping it to himself. Ask students what they would do in his place, and to explain their decision. *Students may say they would keep an idea secret so nobody would mock them, copy them, or talk them out of it.*

◆ **Literary Focus**

⑤ **Character Traits** *The boy has enough self-confidence to know that his idea is terrific and that it should accomplish all that he hopes it will.*

◆ **Build Grammar Skills**

⑥ **Compound Subjects and Verbs** A sentence with a compound verb has two or more verbs that share the same subject and are linked by a coordinating conjunction such as *and* or *or*. This sentence is one such example. Help students identify the subject and the compound verb: *We; stood* and *looked.*

▶**Critical Viewing**◀

⑦ **Draw Conclusions** *Students will likely say that it would take great effort, experience, and the right equipment or tools.*

Customize for
English Language Learners
The author replaces the final *g* with an apostrophe in words like *thinkin'* and *clearin'*. Tell students that this is done to make words sound more like casual speech. Have students find similar examples in the story. Suggest that they confer, as needed, with English-speaking classmates when the meaning of a word is unclear because of atypical spelling.

Customize for
Visual/Spatial Learners
The images for these two stories are varied yet have a common theme. Invite students to begin with the photos on p. 409 and study them and the other images to predict what the stories will be about. Guide students to see that the people in the photos on p. 409 are achieving something: They may predict that the stories are about accomplishments that make a person stand out among peers. The other images may give students ideas about what the accomplishments are.

 Cross-Curricular Connection: Math

Area In this story, the boy's farm has fifty acres. Discuss with students whether they think that this is a small or large farm. Then, have them investigate the area of an acre. An acre measures 160 square rods or 43,560 square feet. Next, challenge students to express the approximate size of the boy's farm in terms of familiar benchmarks, such as a ballfield, parking lot, or swimming pool. Then, have students estimate the size of your school's property in acres. Help them research the appropriate information for this with your school's administration.

Students can create charts to show the relative sizes of an acre and one or more of the other areas. Help them determine ratios in order to accurately represent each area. They might use visual representation techniques, such as color and labeling, to enhance their charts. If you have access to technology, students might use computers to create their charts. Have students present their charts and describe their impressions of the areas they represented. Relate their descriptions back to the original discussion of whether the boy's farm is "small" or "large."

▶Critical Viewing◀

❶ Deduce *Students may say that the brownish wedge of land that comes in from the right is cleared for planting because no green shows on it. Its furrows indicate that the land has been turned and plowed.*

◆ Reading Strategy

❷ Predict *Students may say that the boy has so much determination that he must succeed.*

Comprehension Check ☑

❸ What has the boy done? *He has secretly worked to prepare the land on Little Baldy in one long corkscrew furrow, and has planted corn each night for three nights.*

◆ Literary Focus

❹ Character Traits The boy gives his father a very brief answer. Ask students to tell what they can infer about his character by his response. *He is a proud and private person; his project is important to him, yet he keeps his plans to himself. Ask a volunteer to give the father a more elaborate answer. Answers should include details on how the boy feels about his classmates and his need to impress them with a spectacular science project.*

❶ ▲ Critical Viewing Which area of this terrain is cleared for planting? How can you tell? [Deduce]

pines with a crosscut.[3] With a handspike I started the logs rolling and they rolled to the base of Little Baldy.

By middle March, I had my side cleared. Bob Lavender had finished his too. We burned the brush and I was ready to start plowing.

By April 15th I had plowed all of Little Baldy. My grades in school had fallen off some. Bascom Wythe made the highest mark in General Science and he had always wanted to pass me in this subject. But I let him make the grades.

> **❷ ◆ Reading Strategy** Predict whether or not the boy's plan will succeed.

---

3. **crosscut** (krôs′ kut) *n.:* Saw that cuts across the grain of wood.

412 ◆ *From Sea to Shining Sea*

If my father had known what I was up to, he might not have let me do it. But he was going early to work on the railway section and he never got home until nearly dark. So when I laid Little Baldy off to plant him in corn, I started at the bottom and went around and around this high cone-shaped hill like a corkscrew. I was three days reaching the top. Then, with a hand planter, I planted the corn on moonlit nights.

When I showed my father what I'd done, he looked strangely at me. Then he said, "What made you do a thing like this? What's behind all of this?"

"I'm going to have the longest corn row in the world," I said. "How long do you think it is, Pa?"

Beyond the Classroom

Workplace Skills

Persistence Tell students that persistence, or the ability to see something through to completion, is important to many jobs. In order to succeed and earn recognition for a job well done, employees must develop skills to keep going with tasks, despite problems that may arise. Persistent workers will find ways to:

• Start over if something goes wrong
• Juggle a complicated schedule
• Take the time to solve a tricky problem

• Ask questions more than once
• Listen to others' suggestions more than once

Have students brainstorm for a list of careers. Then have them discuss the responsibilities of that career, and how persistence can help workers succeed. Help students think of work scenarios that demand persistence, or would benefit from persistence. Discuss possible results when the worker persists, and when the worker gives up. Students might role-play the scenarios both ways to compare and contrast outcomes.

"That row is over 20 miles," Pa said, laughing.

Finn and I measured the corn row with a rod pole and it was 23.5 miles long.

When it came time to report on our projects and I stood up in class and said I had a row of corn on our hill farm 23.5 miles long, everybody laughed. But when I told how I got the idea and how I had worked to accomplish my project, everybody was silent.

Professor Herbert and the General Science class hiked to my home on a Saturday in early May when the young corn was pretty and green in the long row. Two newspapermen from a neighboring town came too, and a photographer took pictures of Little Baldy and his ribbon of corn. He took pictures of me, of my home and parents and also of Professor Herbert and my classmates.

When the article and pictures were published, a few of my classmates got a little jealous of me but not one of them ever laughed at me again. And my father and mother were the proudest two parents any son could ever hope to have.

Beyond Literature

Science Connection

Corn Crops Corn is a type of grass similar to wheat, rice, oats, and barley. Most varieties of corn grow in rich, dry soil. The crops are planted when the soil temperature is about 55 degrees Fahrenheit—which occurs around April or May, although states with warmer climates, such as Texas, may plant earlier. Harvesting begins when the water content of a mature kernel has dropped to 28 percent. Corn production in the United States provides two fifths of the world's corn supply.

Cross-Curricular Activity
Look at various food products in your kitchen. Create a list of every product that lists corn as an ingredient. Compare your list with those of other students.

Guide for Responding

◆ LITERATURE AND YOUR LIFE

Reader's Response What did you admire about the boy in this story?

Thematic Focus To whom would you recommend this story? Why?

Journal Writing Describe any contests you've entered in a brief journal entry.

☑ Check Your Comprehension

1. What does the boy have to decide at the beginning of the story?
2. Who or what is Little Baldy?
3. What kinds of preparations does the boy have to make in order to begin his project?
4. Does the boy succeed in his project?

◆ Critical Thinking

INTERPRET
1. Why does the boy feel he has to win the respect of his classmates? **[Analyze]**
2. Why does the boy keep his project a secret from his father? **[Infer]**
3. When the boy explains his project to the class, why are they silent? **[Draw Conclusions]**

EVALUATE
4. Were the boy's efforts to complete the project worth it? **[Make a Judgment]**

APPLY
5. What do you think the boy might have done if weather conditions had ruined the corn he planted? **[Hypothesize]**

A Ribbon for Baldy ◆ 413

◆ Critical Thinking

❺ **Speculate** Ask students to explain why the other students laughed and then fell silent. *They laughed at first because they thought the boy just had a long row of corn on his farm, but that it couldn't possibly be so long. They stopped laughing when they realized that he planned the project and carried it all out himself, and that his unusual technique did indeed produce a row more than 23 miles long.*

Beyond Literature

As students delve into this activity, you might suggest that they investigate the many varieties of corn; the use of corn cobs, husks, or corn silk in byproducts; and the impact of corn allergies on people's food choices.

Reinforce and Extend

Answers
◆ LITERATURE AND YOUR LIFE
Reader's Response Students may admire the boy's determination to help both his family and himself.

Thematic Focus Students might recommend this story to anyone who feels under-appreciated by his or her peers, or to those who enjoy reading about a challenge.

☑ Check Your Comprehension
1. He has to select a science project.
2. Little Baldy is a cone-shaped hill on the family farm.
3. He must clear the land, plow the rows, and plant the corn.
4. Yes; his spectacular science project has impressed his peers and will also help his family.

◆ Critical Thinking
1. He feels he must turn their focus from his poor "hayseed" image to his respectable accomplishments.
2. He fears that his father would not approve, or would prevent him from doing it.
3. They are amazed at the planning and effort he put into his project.
4. Students may say that they were, because the boy achieved both of his original goals.
5. Students might guess that he would have presented his plans and hopes for the project with an explanation of its failure.

Speaking and Listening Mini-Lesson

Work Song
This mini-lesson supports the Speaking and Listening activity in the Idea Bank on p. 421.

Introduce Tell students that work songs are one of the oldest forms of folk music. People often sang as they worked to pass the time, to keep up a rhythm for physical tasks, and to express hopes for the future.

Develop Students may work independently or in pairs to create their work songs. Suggest that they first determine a rhythmic pattern for the song, then a chorus that repeats, and verses that

tell a story or provide details. Students may wish to accompany themselves with a guitar, or percussion instruments.

Apply Have students practice their songs to prepare for performing them. They can sing the song live or prepare a tape of it to play for the class.

Assess Evaluate songs on how well they convey a sense of work, how vividly they relate details, and how clearly students present and explain their project to classmates. Or, use a variation of the Peer Assessment: Dramatic Performance form, p. 116 in **Alternative Assessment.**

One-Minute Insight

The narrator of "The White Umbrella" is a Chinese American girl who struggles with deceit and longing. At last she realizes how much she loves and respects her mother and her Chinese ways. She absolves herself of guilt over a regrettable comment by discarding the gift of an umbrella, an item she once coveted but that came to represent her misdirected feelings.

◆ Literary Focus

① Character Traits The story opens with the narrator's statement that her mother took a job without discussing it with her or her sister, Mona. Have students evaluate the narrator's character, based on this detail, and the nature of the conflict that has been set up between the mother and her daughters. *The daughter expects to be consulted in family decisions, and wishes that her family would be more like American families. The conflict seems to be about a clash of expectations for mothers in American families and in Chinese ones.*

◆ Literary Focus

② Character Traits Ask students to suggest why the narrator doesn't just ask her mother about her job. *Students may say that the girl knows that her mother views it as shameful to have to work and so does not want to embarrass her mother by asking about the job.*

Comprehension Check ☑

③ What is the meaning of Mona's comment about her mother when the narrator guesses that the mother might be delivering roses? *Mona implies that their mother is an accident-prone driver.*

►Critical Viewing◄

④ Infer *Students may say that the girl looks longingly from the car, as if she hopes for a different path in life; the story may have something to do with riding in a car, with longing, or with being part of a neighborhood or community.*

The White Umbrella

Gish Jen

Girl in Car Window, Winson Trang, Courtesy of the artist

When I was twelve, my mother went to work without telling me or my little sister.

"Not that we need the second income." The lilt of her accent drifted from the kitchen up to the top of the stairs, where Mona and I were listening.

"No," said my father, in a barely audible voice. "Not like the Lee family."

The Lees were the only other Chinese family in town. I remembered how sorry my parents had felt for Mrs. Lee when she started waitressing downtown the year before; and so when my mother began coming home late, I didn't say anything, and tried to keep Mona from saying anything either.

"But why shouldn't I?" she argued. "Lots of people's mothers work."

"Those are American people," I said.

"So what do you think we are? I can do the pledge of allegiance with my eyes closed." **①**

Nevertheless, she tried to be <u>discreet</u>; and if my mother wasn't home by 5:30, we would start cooking by ourselves, to make sure dinner would be on time. Mona would wash the vegetables and put on the rice; I would chop.

For weeks we wondered what kind of work she was doing. I imagined that she was selling perfume, testing dessert recipes for the local newspaper. Or maybe she was working for the florist. Now that she had learned to drive, she might be delivering boxes of roses to people. **②**

"I don't think so," said Mona as we walked to our piano lesson after school. "She would've hit something by now." **③**

A gust of wind littered the street with leaves.

▲ **Critical Viewing** What inferences might you make about this story based on the painting above? [Infer] **④**

🎵 Humanities: Art

Girl in Car Window, by Winson Trang

Painter Winson Trang has illustrated many books. This painting shows an Asian American girl looking out a car window. Point out the visual effect of reflection in this painting—cultural aspects of the story, the author, and the painter are visible in these reflections. In addition, direct students' attention to how color enhances the reflective aspects of the painting. Then, use these questions to spark discussion:

1. What ideas do the reflections evoke that fit the story? *Possible answer: They suggest a mix of Chinese and American imagery in an urban setting, which echoes part of the conflict in the story.*
2. Suppose that the girl in the car is the narrator of "The White Umbrella." What might she be thinking? *Possible answer: She might be worrying about her mother's driving, or thinking about how to solve conflicts between her American views and those of her Chinese heritage.*

"Maybe we better hurry up," she went on, looking at the sky. "It's going to pour."

"But we're too early." Her lesson didn't begin until 4:00, mine until 4:30, so we usually tried to walk as slowly as we could. "And anyway, those aren't the kind of clouds that rain. Those are cumulus clouds."[1]

We arrived out of breath and wet.

"Oh, you poor, poor dears," said old Miss Crosman. "Why don't you call me the next time it's like this out? If your mother won't drive you, I can come pick you up."

"No, that's okay," I answered. Mona wrung her hair out on Miss Crosman's rug. "We just couldn't get the roof of our car to close, is all. We took it to the beach last summer and got sand in the mechanism." I pronounced this last word carefully, as if the credibility of my lie depended on its middle syllable. "It's never been the same." I thought for a second. "It's a convertible."

"Well then make yourselves at home." She exchanged looks with Eugenie Roberts, whose lesson we were interrupting. Eugenie smiled good-naturedly. "The towels are in the closet across from the bathroom."

Huddling at the end of Miss Crosman's nine-foot leatherette couch, Mona and I watched Eugenie play. She was a grade ahead of me and, according to school rumor, had a boyfriend in high school. I believed it. . . . She had auburn hair, blue eyes, and, I noted with a particular pang, a pure white folding umbrella.

"I can't see," whispered Mona.

"So clean your glasses."

"My glasses *are* clean. You're in the way."

I looked at her. "They look dirty to me."

"That's because *your* glasses are dirty."

Eugenie came bouncing to the end of her piece.

"Oh! Just stupendous!" Miss Crosman hugged her, then looked up as Eugenie's mother walked in. "Stupendous!" she said again. "Oh! Mrs. Roberts! Your daughter has a gift, a real gift. It's an honor to teach her."

1. **cumulus** (kyōō´ myōō ləs) **clouds** n.: Fluffy, white clouds that usually indicate fair weather.

Mrs. Roberts, radiant with pride, swept her daughter out of the room as if she were royalty, born to the piano bench. Watching the way Eugenie carried herself, I sat up, and concentrated so hard on sucking in my stomach that I did not realize until the Robertses were gone that Eugenie had left her umbrella. As Mona began to play, I jumped up and ran to the window, meaning to call to them—only to see their brake lights flash then fade at the stop sign at the corner. As if to allow them passage, the rain had let up; a quivering sun lit their way.

The umbrella glowed like a scepter on the blue carpet while Mona, slumping over the keyboard, managed to eke out[2] a fair rendition of a catfight. At the end of the piece, Miss Crosman asked her to stand up.

"Stay right there," she said, then came back a minute later with a towel to cover the bench. "You must be cold," she continued. "Shall I call your mother and have her bring over some dry clothes?"

"No," answered Mona. "She won't come because she . . ."

"She's too busy," I broke in from the back of the room.

"I see." Miss Crosman sighed and shook her head a little. "Your glasses are filthy, honey," she said to Mona. "Shall I clean them for you?"

Sisterly embarrassment seized me. Why hadn't Mona wiped her lenses when I told her to? As she resumed abuse of the piano, I stared at the umbrella. I wanted to open it, twirl it around by its slender silver handle; I wanted to dangle it from my wrist on the way to school the way the

◆ **Literary Focus**
What does this passage reveal about the narrator's character traits?

2. **eke** (ēk) **out:** Barely manage to play.

◆ **Build Vocabulary**

discreet (di skrēt´) *adj.*: Careful about what one says or does; prudent

credibility (kred´ ə bil´ ə tē) *n.*: Believability

The White Umbrella ◆ 415

◆ **Build Grammar Skills**

❺ **Compound Subjects and Verbs** In this passage, one sentence has a compound subject, and another has a compound verb. Help students identify these elements. *The first sentence has the compound subject Mona and I; the second sentence has the compound verb was and had.*

◆ **Literary Focus**

❻ **Character Traits** Ask students to respond to Miss Crosman's reaction to Mona's playing. Guide them to notice that rather than criticize, the teacher focuses on Mona's comfort. What does this reveal about her character? *She is considerate and kind, and realizes that Mona's physical condition may affect her ability to play well.*

◆ **Literary Focus**

❼ **Character Traits** *Students may say that the narrator is easily embarrassed by her sister, and, when she feels that way, she seeks to escape from the embarrassment.*

Customize for
Less Proficient Readers
Help students recognize that although the narrator may say one thing, she feels or knows something else. For example, she tells a lie about the car's broken convertible top to get Miss Crosman to think that her family is well-off. Students might make a chart to compare what the narrator says with the truth:

Statement	Reality
Car top jammed	They don't have a convertible

Customize for
Verbal/Linguistic Learners
Have students note concrete nouns, such as *scepter* and *keyboard*; vivid verbs, such as *glower, slumping,* and *eke*; and figurative language, such as *glowed like a scepter* and *fair rendition of a catfight*. Discuss how such language makes a story interesting to read by appealing to readers' senses. Urge students to look for other uses of figurative and precise language as they read.

Beyond the Classroom

Community Connection
In this story, the Lee sisters take private music lessons. But many communities provide public outlets for musical or artistic people to explore, perform, or participate in music, dance, theater, and fine arts. Some communities sponsor local museums, open-air dances, art exhibits, civic theater, and more.

Have students investigate the music and arts opportunities available in your community. Students might present their findings in the form of a community music and arts calendar, a directory of music or arts associations or agencies, or a list of phone numbers or Web sites that can direct people to the music or arts activity of their choice.

❶ Predict Point out the power the umbrella seems to have over the narrator. Ask students to predict what she may do, with respect to the umbrella. *Students may predict that she will steal it or pretend that it is really hers in the first place.*

Comprehension Check ☑

❷ Ask students what the narrator means by saying, "An entire constellation rose in my heart." *She is so thrilled by Miss Crosman's reaction that she glows with delight.*

◆ **Literary Focus**

❸ Character Traits Ask students to draw conclusions about the narrator, based on this passage. Discuss what motivates her to stretch the truth and tell outright lies. *She is eager to please her teacher and wants her approval. She'd like her teacher to know more about her real accomplishments, but she'll stretch the truth or lie to make Miss Crosman think better of her, and to make herself seem more important.*

◆ **LITERATURE AND YOUR LIFE**

❹ *Some students would accept the ride as a way to end the awkward situation; others would insist on waiting, as the narrator does, out of stubborn pride.*

◆ **Literary Focus**

❺ Character Traits In what ways does Miss Crosman show that she cares for the sisters' well-being, yet respects their wishes? *She offers to drive them home herself, calls their mother, invites them to wait inside, and asks them to dinner. But she does not press any of the points because she senses that the girls must have their reasons for refusing her many kindnesses.*

---

other girls did. I wondered what Miss Crosman would say if I offered to bring it to Eugenie at school tomorrow. She would be impressed with my consideration for others; Eugenie would be pleased to have it back; and I would have possession of the umbrella for an entire night. I looked at it again, toying with the idea of asking for one for Christmas. I knew, however, how my mother would react.

"Things," she would say. "What's the matter with a raincoat? All you want is things, just like an American."

Sitting down for my lesson, I was careful to keep the towel under me and sit up straight.

"I'll bet you can't see a thing either," said Miss Crosman, reaching for my glasses. "And you can relax, you poor dear." She touched my chest, in an area where she never would have touched Eugenie Roberts. "This isn't a boot camp."[3]

When Miss Crosman finally allowed me to start playing I played extra well, as well as I possibly could. See, I told her with my fingers. You don't have to feel sorry for me.

"That was wonderful," said Miss Crosman. "Oh! Just wonderful."

An entire <u>constellation</u> rose in my heart.

"And guess what," I announced proudly. "I have a surprise for you."

Then I played a second piece for her, a much more difficult one that she had not assigned.

"Oh! That was stupendous," she said without hugging me. "Stupendous! You are a genius, young lady. If your mother had started you younger, you'd be playing like Eugenie Roberts by now!"

I looked at the keyboard, wishing that I had still a third, even more difficult piece to play for her. I wanted to tell her that I was the school spelling bee champion, that I wasn't ticklish, that I could do karate.

"My mother is a concert pianist," I said.

She looked at me for a long moment, then finally, without saying anything, hugged me. I

---

3. **boot camp:** Place where soldiers receive basic training and are disciplined severely.

---

didn't say anything about bringing the umbrella to Eugenie at school.

The steps were dry when Mona and I sat down to wait for my mother.

"Do you want to wait inside?" Miss Crosman looked <u>anxiously</u> at the sky.

"No," I said. "Our mother will be here any minute."

"In a while," said Mona.

"Any minute," I said again, even though my mother had been at least twenty minutes late every week since she started working.

According to the church clock across the street we had been waiting twenty-five minutes when Miss Crosman came out again.

"Shall I give you ladies a ride home?"

"No," I said. "Our mother is coming any minute."

"Shall I at least give her a call and remind her you're here? Maybe she forgot about you."

"I don't think she *forgot*," said Mona.

"Shall I give her a call anyway? Just to be safe?"

"I bet she already left," I said. "How could she forget about us?"

Miss Crosman went in to call.

"There's no answer," she said, coming back out.

"See, she's on her way," I said.

"Are you sure you wouldn't like to come in?"

"No," said Mona.

"Yes," I said. I pointed at my sister. "She meant yes too. She meant no, she wouldn't like to go in."

Miss Crosman looked at her watch. "It's 5:30 now, ladies. My pot roast will be coming

---

◆ **Literature and Your Life**

❹ If you were in the narrator's position, would you have accepted a ride from Miss Crosman? Why or why not?

◆ **Build Vocabulary**

constellation (kän′ stə lā′ shən) *n.:* Group of stars named after, and thought to resemble, an object, an animal, or a mythological character in outline

anxiously (aŋk′ shəs lē) *adv.:* In a worried way

---

5 out in fifteen minutes. Maybe you'd like to come in and have some then?"

"My mother's almost here," I said. "She's on her way."

We watched and watched the street. I tried to imagine what my mother was doing; I tried to imagine her writing messages in the sky, even though I knew she was afraid of planes. I watched as the branches of Miss Crosman's big willow tree started to sway; they had all been trimmed to exactly the same height off the ground, so that they looked beautiful, like hair in the wind.

It started to rain.

"Miss Crosman is coming out again," said Mona.

"Don't let her talk you into going inside," I whispered.

"Why not?"

"Because that would mean Mom isn't really coming any minute."

"But she isn't," said Mona. "She's *working*."

"Shhh! Miss Crosman is going to hear you."

6 "She's working! She's working! She's working!"

I put my hand over her mouth, but she licked it, and so I was wiping my hand on my wet dress when the front door opened.

"We're getting even *wetter*," said Mona right away. "Wetter and wetter."

"Shall we all go in?" Miss Crosman pulled Mona to her feet. "Before you young ladies catch pneumonia? You've been out here an hour already."

"We're *freezing*." Mona looked up at Miss Crosman. "Do you have any hot chocolate? We're going to catch *pneumonia*."

"I'm not going in," I said. "My mother's coming any minute."

"Come on," said Mona. "Use your *noggin*."[4]

"Any minute."

"Come on, Mona," Miss Crosman opened the door. "Shall we get you inside first?" 6

"See you in the hospital," said Mona as she went in. "See you in the hospital with pneumonia."

I stared out into the empty street. The rain was pricking me all over; I was cold; I wanted to go inside. I wanted to be able to let myself go inside. If Miss Crosman came out again, I decided, I would go in.

She came out with a blanket and the white umbrella.

I could not believe that I was actually holding the umbrella, opening it. It sprang up by itself as if it were alive, as if that were what it wanted to do—as if it belonged in my hands, above my head. I stared up at the network of silver spokes, then spun the umbrella around and around and around. It was so clean and white that it seemed to glow, to illuminate everything around it. 8

"It's beautiful," I said.

Miss Crosman sat down next to me, on one end of the blanket. I moved the umbrella over so that it covered that too. I could feel the rain on my left shoulder and shivered. She put her arm around me.

"You poor, poor dear."

7 ▲ **Critical Viewing** Are the girls in the photograph playing the piano in earnest or just having fun? Explain. **[Make a Judgment]**

4. **Use your *noggin*** (näg´ in): Informal expression for "use your head" or "think."

◆ Literary Focus

6 Character Traits Ask students to evaluate the conflict between the sisters. Have them try to explain why each girl acts as she does. *Mona is not ashamed of the reason their mother is late, and is glad to accept Miss Crosman's kindness. The narrator, however, believes that it's important not to reveal that their mother works. She tries to stop Mona before she blurts out the truth, which the narrator fears may make Miss Crosman feel sorry for the family or think less of them.*

▶Critical Viewing◀

7 Make a Judgment *Most students will say that the girls may be having fun. Some may say that the serious looks on their faces suggest that they are playing in earnest, or are at least thinking hard about what they are doing.*

◆ Reading Strategy

8 Predict Have students predict what the narrator will do with the white umbrella, or what impact it will have on her. *Students might predict that she will ask to have it, or that she will fall under its "spell" and become more "American."*

Customize for *Verbal/Linguistic Learners*

On p. 416, the narrator tells Miss Crosman that her mother will arrive "any minute." Brainstorm with students for a list of expressions that suggest the passing of time, such *as in a flash, just a second, one of these days, in a heartbeat,* or *a bit later.* Then have them classify expressions by whether they suggest a long or short time, and show the results in a table or chart. Extend by having students create original expressions that mean "any minute now" or "in a little while."

Viewing and Representing Mini-Lesson

White Umbrella

In this mini-lesson students will extend their understanding of the white umbrella as a symbol.

Introduce Discuss with students the importance of the white umbrella, eliciting that its function is secondary to what it represents for the narrator. Then, discuss where and how students have seen umbrellas used as symbols, for instance as a company logo or to represent protection.

Develop Have students review the writer's description of the white umbrella in this story, encouraging them to look for sensory details. Then, ask them how they picture the white umbrella in their own minds.

Apply Provide students with a variety of art materials, such as paints, markers, tissue paper, and glitter to create a white umbrella. Allow time for students to develop their representations.

Assess Have students display their white umbrellas for the class, explaining their choices of art medium and why the narrator might or might not appreciate their represenations. Evaluate students on their explanations and understanding of the white umbrella's meaning to the narrator.

❶ Invite students to respond to the narrator's internal conflict of not wanting others to feel sorry for her although she feels sorry for herself. Or, discuss their responses to the idea of not wanting others to be nice to you when you need their kindness but feel bad about accepting it.

◆ **Reading Strategy**

❷ Predict *Students may think that she will get to keep the umbrella she covets so much. Others may predict that her mother or sister will persuade her not to accept the gift.*

Comprehension Check ☑

❸ How does the narrator's eagerness to please her piano teacher set up a new conflict? Why does the narrator immediately feel bad? *The girl feels disloyal to her mother because, in an effort to please her teacher, she blurts out something she doesn't really mean.*

◆ **Literary Focus**

❹ Character Traits Ask students to interpret the narrator's motivation for concealing the umbrella. *Students may say that the narrator hides the umbrella because she knows her mother will disapprove of it. Also, in light of the inappropriate comment she made to Miss Crosman, she may feel awkward about having the gift at all.*

◆ **Critical Thinking**

❺ Compare and Contrast Have students compare how the two sisters respond to the news about their mother's job. *Disappointed to learn that her mother's job is dull, Mona still finds something positive to say. By contrast, the narrator says she wishes that her mother would quit her job.*

---

❶ I knew that I was in store for another bolt of sympathy, and braced myself by staring up into the umbrella.

"You know, I very much wanted to have children when I was younger," she continued.

"You did?"

She stared at me a minute. Her face looked dry and crusty, like day-old frosting.

"I did. But then I never got married."

I twirled the umbrella around again.

"This is the most beautiful umbrella I have ever seen," I said. "Ever, in my whole life."

"Do you have an umbrella?"

◆ **Reading Strategy**
❷ Do you think the narrator will get to keep the umbrella? Why or why not?

"No. But my mother's going to get me one just like this for Christmas."

"Is she? I tell you what. You don't have to wait until Christmas. You can have this one."

"But this one belongs to Eugenie Roberts," I protested. "I have to give it back to her tomorrow in school."

"Who told you it belongs to Eugenie? It's not Eugenie's. It's mine. And now I'm giving it to you, so it's yours."

"It is?"

She hugged me tighter. "That's right. It's all yours."

"It's mine?" I didn't know what to say. "Mine?" Suddenly I was jumping up and down in the rain. "It's beautiful! Oh! It's beautiful!" I laughed.

Miss Crosman laughed too, even though she was getting all wet.

❸ "Thank you, Miss Crosman. Thank you very much. Thanks a zillion. It's beautiful. It's *stupendous!*"

"You're quite welcome," she said.

"Thank you," I said again, but that didn't seem like enough. Suddenly I knew just what she wanted to hear. "I wish you were my mother."

Right away I felt bad.

"You shouldn't say that," she said, but her face was opening into a huge smile as the lights of my mother's car cautiously turned the corner. I quickly collapsed the umbrella **❹** and put it up my skirt, holding onto it from the outside, through the material. **❹**

"Mona!" I shouted into the house. "Mona! Hurry up! Mom's here! I told you she was coming!"

Then I ran away from Miss Crosman, down to the curb. Mona came tearing up to my side as my mother neared the house. We both backed up a few feet, so that in case she went onto the curb, she wouldn't run us over.

"But why didn't you go inside with Mona?" my mother asked on the way home. She had taken off her own coat to put over me, and had the heat on high.

"She wasn't using her noggin," said Mona, next to me in the back seat.

"I should call next time," said my mother. "I just don't like to say where I am."

That was when she finally told us that she was working as a check-out clerk in the A&P. She was supposed to be on the day shift, but the other employees were unreliable, and her boss had promised her a promotion if she would stay until the evening shift filled in.

For a moment no one said anything. Even Mona seemed to find the revelation disappointing.

"A promotion already!" she said, finally.

I listened to the windshield wipers.

"You're so quiet." My mother looked at me in the rear view mirror. "What's the matter?"

"I wish you would quit," I said after a moment.

She sighed. "The Chinese have a saying: one beam cannot hold the roof up."

"But Eugenie Roberts's father supports their family."

She sighed once more. "Eugenie Roberts's father is Eugenie Roberts's father," she said.

As we entered the downtown area, Mona started leaning hard against me every time the car turned right, trying to push me over. Remembering what I had said to Miss Crosman, I tried to maneuver the umbrella under my leg so she wouldn't feel it.

"What's under your skirt?" Mona wanted to know as we came to a traffic light. My mother, watching us in the rear view mirror again, rolled slowly to a stop.

"What's the matter?" she asked.

❺

418 ◆ From Sea to Shining Sea

 Beyond the Classroom

Career Connection

Teacher/Tutor Many people with skills to share do so by taking on private students in tutorial settings. Ask students what they think of Miss Crosman as a teacher. Suggest that one quality of being a good teacher is to enjoy young people and to be understanding of the pressures and problems they face. Another quality is interest in or love for a subject or skill. Students whose strengths include compassion and talent in a particular skill might consider a teaching career. They can think about classroom teaching or teaching in out-of-classroom settings, such as private music teaching, software training, or exercise coaching. Students who share these interests could form a group to find out more about careers in teaching, such as the training and skills needed, the variety of possible workplaces, and the types of challenges they can expect to face. Encourage them to interview teachers as a source of information.

"There's something under her skirt!" said Mona, pulling at me.

"Under her skirt?"

Meanwhile, a man crossing the street started to yell at us. "Who do you think you are, lady?" he said. "You're blocking the whole crosswalk."

We all froze. Other people walking by stopped to watch.

"Didn't you hear me?" he went on, starting to thump on the hood with his fist. "Don't you speak English?"

6 My mother began to back up, but the car behind us honked. Luckily, the light turned green right after that. She sighed in relief.

"What were you saying, Mona?" she asked.

We wouldn't have hit the car behind us that hard if he hadn't been moving too, but as it was our car bucked violently, throwing us all first back and then forward.

"Uh oh," said Mona when we stopped. "*Another* accident."

I was relieved to have attention diverted from the umbrella. Then I noticed my mother's head, tilted back onto the seat. Her eyes were closed.

"Mom!" I screamed. "Mom! Wake up!"

She opened her eyes. "Please don't yell," she said. "Enough people are going to yell already."

"I thought you were dead," I said, starting to cry. "I thought you were dead."

She turned around, looked at me intently, then put her hand to my forehead.

"Sick," she confirmed. "Some kind of sick is giving you crazy ideas."

As the man from the car behind us started tapping on the window, I moved the umbrella away from my leg. Then Mona and my mother were getting out of the car. I got out after **7** them; and while everyone else was inspecting the damage we'd done, I threw the umbrella down a sewer.

◆ Build Vocabulary

revelation (rev′ ə lā′ shən) *n*: Something revealed; a disclosure of something not previously known or realized

---

Guide for Responding

◆ Literature and Your Life

Reader's Response Were you surprised when the narrator threw away the umbrella at the end of the story? Why or why not?

Thematic Focus What points does this story make about being an American?

Journal Writing Have you ever wanted something, like a white umbrella, that you thought would transform you? Jot down your thoughts in your journal.

☑ Check Your Comprehension

1. What excuse does the narrator give for arriving at the piano lesson soaking wet?

2. Why is the narrator's mother always late to pick up the sisters?

◆ Critical Thinking

INTERPRET

1. In what ways are the personalities of the sisters different? **[Compare and Contrast]**

2. What does the white umbrella represent to the narrator? **[Analyze]**

3. Why does the narrator have mixed feelings about going back into Miss Crossman's house to get out of the rain? **[Infer]**

4. Why does the narrator throw the umbrella away at the end of the story? **[Draw Conclusions]**

EVALUATE

5. Do you think that the narrator learned an important lesson that will change her behavior in the future? Explain. **[Evaluate]**

APPLY

6. The narrator believes that her mother's response to her desire for an umbrella will be "All you want is things, just like an American." The narrator disagrees. Choose either the narrator's or her mother's point of view to defend. **[Defend]**

The White Umbrella ◆ 419

Comprehension Check ☑

6 Ask students what happened at the intersection. Mrs. Lee, who had blocked the crosswalk, backed up and bumped into the car behind her.

◆ Reading Strategy

7 Predict Ask students whether they think the narrator will ever tell anyone about the white umbrella and what she did with it. *Some students may predict that she will always keep the fate of the white umbrella to herself; others may recognize that the author, herself, may have had the experience of the white umbrella, or something similar, and predict that the tendency is to eventually talk about this type of experience.*

Reinforce and Extend

Answers

◆ Literature and Your Life

Reader's Response Most students will say that the narrator's action surprised them in light of how much she had coveted the umbrella.

Thematic Focus Possible responses: Americans are materialistic; they favor finances over family.

☑ Check Your Comprehension

1. She lies that the family's convertible car top is broken.
2. She cannot come to get them until she is done at her job.

◆ Critical Thinking

1. The narrator seems dissatisfied with life, while Mona seems more upbeat and accepting.
2. The white umbrella represents being a successful American girl.
3. She wants Miss Crosman's approval, but not her pity.
4. The girl comes to see the white umbrella as a symbol of the regrettable remark she made to Miss Crosman, and of frivolous, external things, when what is truly important is her family.
5. Students may say that she did learn a lesson for now, but until she really accepts the values that her family supports, she may behave the same way again.
6. Responses will vary, but should express each student's personal view and support it with details.

 Beyond the Selection

FURTHER READING

Other Works by Jesse Stuart
The Thread That Runs So True
Men of the Mountains
Harvest of Youth

Other Works by Gish Jen
The Water Faucet Vision
Mona in the Promised Land

Other Works About Belonging
American Eyes, Lori M. Carlson
An Island Like You, Judith Ortiz Cofer

INTERNET

We suggest the following sites on the Internet (all Web sites are subject to change).

For links to information on Jesse Stuart:
http://www.English.eku.edu/services/kylit/default.htm

For links to information about Gish Jen:
http://www.hope.edu/academic/english/creatwrit/visitwrit/jen.html

We *strongly recommend* that you preview these sites before you send students to them.

419

Answers

◆ Reading Strategy

1. Students may predict that the project has something to do with the hill and corn.
2. (a) Students may have predicted that the mother would be late. (b) The narrator knew that their mother had to come from work.

◆ Build Vocabulary

Using the word Root -cred-
1. credit; 2. incredibly; 3. credibility

Spelling Strategy
1. noxious; 2. complexion; 3. obnoxious; 4. anxiously

Using the Word Bank
1. constellation; 2. surveyed; 3. anxiously; 4. credibility; 5. envelop; 6. revelation; 7. discreet; 8. bargain

◆ Literary Focus

1. He has already known success, but wants to achieve even more.
2. The narrator is impatient; Mona is accepting and calm.
3. She exaggerates or lies.

◆ Build Grammar Skills

Practice
1. We took/got
2. Mona/I watched
3. I could feel/shivered
4. Father/I set
5. I hurried/worked

Writing Application
Possible responses:
1. Mona and I take piano lessons from Miss Crosman.
2. The boy cleared the land and planted the corn.

 **Writer's Solution**

For additional instruction and practice, use the lesson in the *Writer's Solution Language Lab CD-ROM* on Compound Subjects and Compound Verbs. You may also use the Compound Subjects and Verbs page, p. 32 in the *Writer's Solution Grammar Practice Book*.

420

◆ Guide for Responding (continued)

◆ Reading Strategy

PREDICT

When you **predict,** you build on information the author gives you to determine what will happen next. Predicting helps keep you involved in a story, as you read on to see if your predictions came true.

1. When the narrator of "A Ribbon for Baldy" says, "Then, like a flash—the idea for my project came to me," what did you predict the project would be?
2. (a) What did you predict when the narrator in "The White Umbrella" said that her mother would pick them up "any minute"? (b) What led you to make that prediction?

◆ Build Vocabulary

USING THE WORD ROOT -cred-

The words below each contain the word root -cred-, meaning "believe." Rewrite the sentences, filling in the blank with the correct word from this list:

    a. incredibly   **b.** credit   **c.** credibility

1. She earned _____?_____ for taking piano lessons.
2. Planting miles of corn was _____?_____ difficult.
3. She told so many fibs that she didn't have much _____?_____ with her friends.

SPELLING STRATEGY

The *ksh* sound in *anxious* and in some other words is spelled *xi*. Write the following words, spelling the *sh* sound with the letters *xi.*

1. no__ous
2. comple__on
3. obno__ous
4. an__ously

USING THE WORD BANK

On your paper, write the word from the Word Bank that best completes each sentence.

1. The _____?_____ of Orion was visible in the sky.
2. He _____?_____ the land before building a fence.
3. They waited _____?_____ for their mom to arrive.
4. The story was so fantastic it had no _____?_____.
5. At dusk, the fog would _____?_____ the hilltop, making it invisible.
6. After his _____?_____, he solved the problem.
7. She was _____?_____, telling no one about her job.
8. At the sale, she got a _____?_____ on piano music.

420 ◆ From Sea to Shining Sea

◆ Literary Focus

CHARACTER TRAITS

Character traits are the qualities of a character's personality. These traits are revealed by a character's actions, words, and thoughts, as well as by what other characters say about him or her.

1. What does the first paragraph of "A Ribbon for Baldy" reveal about the narrator's character traits?
2. In "The White Umbrella," which sister is impatient? Which sister is accepting and calm?
3. Which character trait of the narrator's is revealed when she tells Miss Crosman, "my mother is a concert pianist"?

◆ Build Grammar Skills

COMPOUND SUBJECTS AND VERBS

Sentences may have more than one subject or verb. A **compound subject** is two or more subjects that have the same verb and are linked by a coordinating conjunction such as *and* or *or:*

Mona and I were listening.

A **compound verb** is two or more verbs that have the same subject and are linked by a coordinating conjunction such as *and* or *or:*

Mona *would wash* the vegetables and *put* on the rice.

Practice On your paper, underline each compound subject once and each compound verb twice.

1. We took it to the beach last summer and got sand in the mechanism.
2. Mona and I watched Eugenie play.
3. I could feel the rain on my left shoulder and shivered.
4. My father and I set fire all the way around the base.
5. I hurried home and worked into the night.

Writing Application Write a sentence about "The White Umbrella" that contains a compound subject. Then, write a sentence about "A Ribbon for Baldy" that contains a compound verb.

Build Your Portfolio

Idea Bank

Writing

1. **Newspaper Article** Imagine that you are one of the students who visited the narrator's corn row with Professor Herbert's General Science class. Write an article for your school newspaper describing the boy's accomplishment.

2. **Diary Entry** Write a diary entry that Mona might have written on the night following the events in "The White Umbrella."

3. **Compare and Contrast** Write an essay in which you compare and contrast the personality traits of the main characters in "A Ribbon for Baldy" and "The White Umbrella." Use passages from both stories for support.

Speaking and Listening

4. **Dramatic Scene [Group Activity]** With several classmates, act out a scene from "The White Umbrella." As you write the script for your scene, show the character traits of each of the people you will portray. Present your scene to the class. **[Performing Arts Link]**

5. **Work Song** Write a song that the narrator in "A Ribbon for Baldy" might have made up and sung as he planted "the longest corn row in the world." When you have finished, sing the song for your class or make copies of the song lyrics to distribute to your classmates. **[Music Link]**

Projects

6. **History of the Piano** Write a short history of the piano. Give information about when it came into being and how it is played. Also, list famous composers of piano music. **[Music Link]**

7. **Kentucky Farm Report [Group Activity]** With a group, find out about the agriculture and livestock that are grown and raised in Kentucky. Present your findings in a report that might appear in a local magazine. Look for maps, photographs, and charts that you can include in your report. **[Social Studies Link; Science Link]**

Writing Mini-Lesson

Recommendation

A recommendation is a written statement about someone's abilities or accomplishments. Recommendations are often written by teachers to call attention to the student's suitability for advancement. Imagine that you are a teacher of either the boy in "A Ribbon for Baldy" or the narrator in "The White Umbrella." Then, write a recommendation for that character, suggesting whether or not the pupil should advance a level.

Writing Skills Focus: Support Points

In your recommendation, give specific examples to **support** the statements you make. For example, if your character is a good student, give examples of his or her progress and accomplishments.

Prewriting Decide which character you will write about. Then, take notes about the qualities or accomplishments you will mention in your recommendation.

Drafting Begin your recommendation by stating who you are, your relationship to the student, and why you are recommending him or her. Continue by introducing each of your main points in a separate paragraph. End with a restatement of the main points of your recommendation.

Revising When you revise, make sure you have included at least two facts or details to support each point you make about the person. Check to see that the overall impression you give about the student is positive and supportive. Proofread to correct errors in grammar, spelling, and punctuation.

> ◆ **Grammar Application**
> Look for sentences in your draft that could be combined by making a compound subject or a compound verb.

A Ribbon for Baldy/The White Umbrella ◆ 421

Idea Bank

Following are suggestions for matching the Idea Bank topics with your students' performance levels and learning modalities:

Customize for
Performance Levels
Less Advanced Students: 2, 5, 7
Average Students: 1, 4, 5, 6, 7
More Advanced Students: 3, 4, 5, 6, 7

Customize for
Learning Modalities
Verbal/Linguistic: 1, 2, 3, 4, 5, 6, 7
Visual/Spatial: 7
Bodily/Kinesthetic: 4, 5
Logical/Mathematical: 3, 5, 6
Musical/Rhythmic: 5
Interpersonal: 4, 7
Intrapersonal: 1, 2, 3, 5, 6

Writing Mini-Lesson

Refer students to the Writing Handbook in the back of the book for instruction on the writing process and for further information on persuasion. Have students use the Sunburst Organizer in **Writing and Language Transparencies,** p. 85, to organize their supporting points.

Writer's Solution

Writers at Work Videodisc
Have students view the videodisc segment on Expression (Ch. 1), which features Gish Jen, to learn more about the author of "The White Umbrella" and her views on the writing process.

Play frames 323 to 9443

Writing Lab CD-ROM
Have students complete the tutorial on Persuasion. Follow these steps:

1. Have students work through the Prewriting parts, which focus on evaluating topics, considering audience and purpose, gathering and organizing evidence.
2. Have students draft on computer.
3. Have them use the interactive instruction in word choice and the Transition Word Bin when revising.

Writer's Solution Sourcebook
Have students use Chapter 6, "Persuasion," pp. 166–199, for additional support. The chapter includes in-depth instruction on writing a strong introduction, body, and conclusion, pp. 188–189.

✓ ASSESSMENT OPTIONS

Formal Assessment, Selection Test, pp. 120–122, and Assessment Resources Software. The selection test is designed so that it can be easily customized to the performance levels of your students.

Alternative Assessment, p. 30, includes options for less advanced students, more advanced students, visual/spatial learners, interpersonal learners, verbal/linguistic learners, and logical/mathematical learners.

PORTFOLIO ASSESSMENT
Use the following rubrics in the **Alternative Assessment** booklet to assess student writing:
Newspaper Article: Description, p. 93
Diary Entry: Fictional Narrative, p. 91
Compare and Contrast: Comparison/Contrast, p. 99
Writing Mini-Lesson: Persuasion, p. 101

Guide for Reading

More About the Authors
Robert Hayden was born Asa Bundy Sheffey. As a boy, his eyesight kept him from playing sports, but not from immersing himself in books. Hayden spent much of his life as a college teacher. He also worked as a publisher and edited a collection of African American literature.

Evelyn Tooley Hunt graduated from William Smith College in Geneva, New York, where she edited the school's literary magazine. In 1982, she was listed in the International *Who's Who of Poetry.*

Some of **Richard García**'s works, including *My Aunt Otilia's Spirits,* have been published in bilingual editions (English and Spanish).

Meet the Authors:

Robert Hayden (1913–1980)

Raised in a poor Detroit neighborhood, Robert Hayden became the first African American poet to be appointed as Consultant of Poetry to the Library of Congress. His poetry covers a wide range of subjects—from personal remembrances to celebrations of the history and achievements of African Americans.

Evelyn Tooley Hunt (1904–   )

In 1961, Evelyn Tooley Hunt won the Sidney Lanier Memorial Award for her first collection of poems, *Look Again, Adam.* Her poems demonstrate a keen interest in other cultures. "I like to write from the inside of some culture other than my own," she says. She is best known for her variations of haiku, a type of Asian poetry, which she writes under the pen name of Tao-Li.

Richard García (1941–   )

Richard García writes poetry for adults and children. He has published *Selected Poems* (1973) and a contemporary folk tale for children, *My Aunt Otilia's Spirits* (1978). García is the director of the Poets in Schools program in Marin, California. Born in San Francisco, he has also lived in Mexico and Israel.

◆ LITERATURE AND YOUR LIFE

CONNECT YOUR EXPERIENCE

Think for a moment about people and places you see every day and how they influence you. In two of the poems that follow, you'll meet very special people who have influenced the poets. In the third poem, you'll learn of a special place.

THEMATIC FOCUS: An Album of Stories

As you read, think about how these poems would fit into a scrapbook of someone's life.

◆ Background for Understanding

SOCIAL STUDIES

"Taught Me Purple" tells of a tenement in which the speaker and her mother lived. Tenements are buildings that provide housing for low-income families in urban environments. Conditions in many tenements are crowded and even dangerously substandard. They reflect one of the challenges of urban living—how to provide safe housing for millions of people living within a few square miles of one another.

◆ Build Vocabulary

WORD ROOTS: *-chron-*

The word root *-chron-* comes from the Greek word for time. Knowing this, you can figure out that *chronic* means "continuing for a long period of time."

WORD BANK

Which word from the list might be related to the noun *earthquake*? Check the Build Vocabulary box on page 427 to see if you chose correctly.

banked
chronic
austere
tenement
molding
quake

◆ Those Winter Sundays ◆
Taught Me Purple ◆ The City Is So Big

Interest Grabber Write the following question on the board: "How do we learn lessons about life?" Divide the class into small groups to talk about it. Invite volunteers to share some of their responses, which may include learning by example, by imitation, by trial-and-error, or by study. Then, ask students to complete this statement: "I used to think that ___, but now I realize that ___." Tell students that the speakers in each poem in this set consider life's lessons, and realize that there is much to learn from others.

◆ Build Grammar Skills

Inverted Sentences If you wish to introduce the grammar concept for this selection before students read, refer to the instruction on p. 428.

Customize for
Less Proficient Readers
The poems in this set use simple words to convey rich ideas and deeper levels of meaning. For instance, "The city is so big" conveys the obvious idea of a large, densely populated place with tall buildings, but it also evokes a feeling of being overwhelmed and unable to describe any other aspects of it. Have students use a Cluster Organizer or Sunburst Organizer, pp. 73 and 85 in **Writing and Language Transparencies,** to explore deeper meanings in the simple language.

Customize for
More Advanced Students
Two of the poems in this set are examples of *free verse.* Free verse departs from the forms of traditional poetry, but it is not prose. Challenge students, as they read, to think about elements that characterize free verse, such as irregular rhyme and varied line length, and elements that distinguish it from prose. Give them copies of the Venn Diagram, p. 77 in **Writing and Language Transparencies.**

◆ Literary Focus
WORD CHOICE

Because poems tend to be brief, **word choice**—the specific decisions a poet makes about which words to use to present each idea and detail—is especially important. As you read poetry, pay careful attention to the words chosen by the poet. For example, in "Those Winter Sundays," Robert Hayden describes the cold as "blueblack." His choice of the word *blueblack* makes you both see and feel the cold. Blue is a color you associate with cold (people are said to turn blue from too much exposure to the cold), and black is the color of the cold night sky.

◆ Reading Strategy
RESPOND

Whenever you read a poem or other work of literature, you **respond** to it in a personal way. The work might please you, or you might connect it with an experience the writer is presenting, or you might totally disagree with the writer's view of something. You respond the way you do because you bring your own experiences and memories to everything you read.

Use a chart like the one below to record your responses to these poems.

Those Winter Sundays

Lines	Response
Lines 1—5	I felt cold and shivery. I felt sorry for his father.

Guide for Reading ◆ 423

Preparing for Standardized Tests

Vocabulary This selection presents the word root *-chron-*. Students can determine meanings of derivatives by applying their knowledge of word roots, which will help them with their reading comprehension and as they answer comprehension and vocabulary items on standardized tests.

Standardized test vocabulary questions may ask students to select a synonym for a given word. Present the following sample test question:

In "Those Winter Sundays," the poet tells that however hard his father worked for his family, he experienced a chronic lack of

appreciation. Another word for *chronic* is—

(A) constant
(B) lonely
(C) strict
(D) surprising

Students who know that the word root *-chron-* comes from the Greek word for time can determine that *chronic* means "lasting over time." Thus, (A) is the best synonym. For further practice, use Build Vocabulary in **Selection Support,** p. 163.

One-Minute Insight

"Those Winter Sundays" expresses the speaker's realization, in looking back at his youth, that his father had worked tirelessly and struggled without thanks to care for his family.

In "Taught Me Purple," the speaker sadly honors her mother, who also struggled and who taught her daughter to appreciate the world's beauty, although she died without experiencing it herself.

◆ Reading Strategy

❶ Respond Ask students to respond to life in the speaker's home, as they imagine it from the ideas he expresses. What can they infer about the prevailing emotions? *Students may say that frustration, poverty, fatigue, and ingratitude set off tensions among family members.*

◆ Literary Focus

❷ Word Choice Discuss with students the poet's choice of words in lines 13–14. Why does he ask a question of himself, and why does he repeat the question? *Students may say that he questions himself in amazement because he now realizes how much escaped his awareness when he was younger; he repeats the question out of remorse.*

►Critical Viewing◄

❸ Make a Judgment *A fire that has been banked has dirt heaped around it for protection, and is arranged to burn low and last longer. This fire is blazing, so it has not been banked.*

Customize for
English Language Learners
Poetic word choice can challenge students acquiring English. The poems use words students may know in one sense, but whose meaning in context varies. For example, students may know *offices* as rooms where people work. But in "Those Winter Sundays," *offices* are services performed for others. Before students read, present words like *circle, quake,* and *bank.* Help students build on their knowledge of the literal or common meanings to grasp the specific meanings that fit the context of the poems.

424

Those Winter Sundays

Robert Hayden

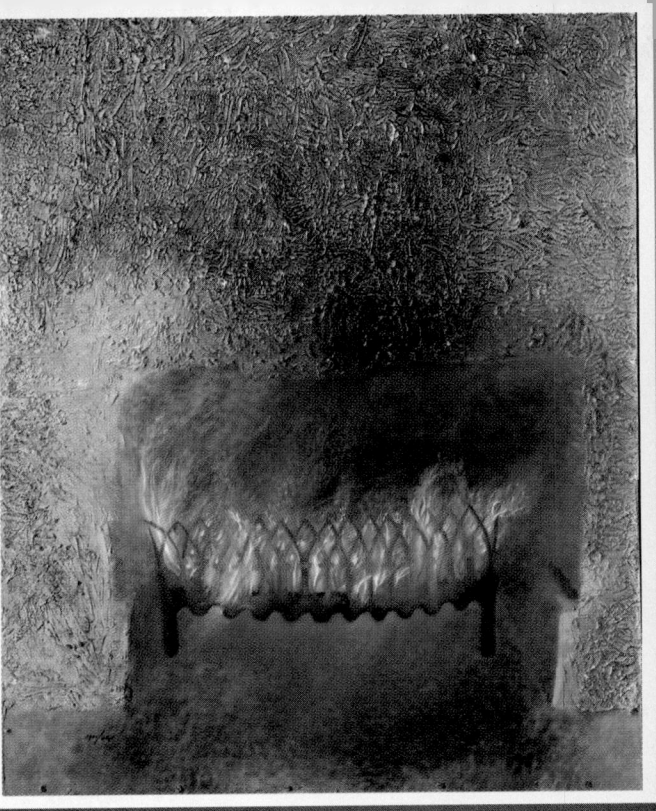

Hearth, 1957. Loren MacIver. The Metropolitan Museum of Art

Sundays too my father got up early
and put his clothes on in the blueblack cold,
then with cracked hands that ached
from labor in the weekday weather made
5 banked fires blaze. No one ever thanked him.

I'd wake and hear the cold splintering, breaking.
When the rooms were warm, he'd call,
and slowly I would rise and dress,
fearing the chronic angers of that house,

10 Speaking indifferently to him,
who had driven out the cold
and polished my good shoes as well.
What did I know, what did I know
of love's austere and lonely offices?

▲ **Critical Viewing** Would you say that this fire has been banked? Explain. [Make a Judgment] **❸**

◆ Build Vocabulary
banked (baŋt) *adj.:* Adjusted to burn slowly and long

chronic (krän´ ik) *adj.:* Continuing indefinitely; perpetual; constant

austere (ô stir´) *adj.:* Showing strict self-discipline; severe

424 ◆ *From Sea to Shining Sea*

Block Scheduling Strategies

Consider these suggestions to take advantage of extended class time:

• To prepare students for the Writing Mini-Lesson, group them by which poems they want to respond to so they clarify their ideas by talking with peers. Students who would benefit from extra guidance might work through all or part of the tutorial on Response to Literature in the *Writing Lab CD-ROM,* or Ch. 9 in the Writer's Solution Sourcebook.

• For project-oriented instruction, have students read independently, then work in pairs or groups

to complete one or more of the Idea Bank activities or projects on p. 429.

• Emphasize the literary focus and reading strategy. First, have students listen to the recording of the poems. Have them note how certain words leap out, and give their first reactions. Next, have them read in pairs and answer the questions in the Literary Focus and Reading Strategy features on p. 428. To reinforce the concepts, use **Selection Support,** pp. 166–167.

 **Listening to Literature Audiocassettes**

Taught Me Purple

Evelyn Tooley Hunt

My mother taught me purple
  Although she never wore it.
Wash-gray was her circle,
  The <u>tenement</u> her orbit.

5 My mother taught me golden ❹
  And held me up to see it,
Above the broken <u>molding</u>,
  Beyond the filthy street.

  My mother reached for beauty ❺
10 And for its lack she died,
Who knew so much of duty
  She could not teach me pride.

◆ **Literary Focus**

❹ **Word Choice** Ask students to explain what they think the word "golden" refers to or implies. *Students may say that it refers to money or jewels, or that it implies wealth or precious things to strive for.*

◆ **Critical Thinking**

❺ **Speculate** Ask students to imagine how the mother conveyed a love of beauty to her daughter. *Students may guess that she inspired a love of beauty by introducing her child to lovely things, although she couldn't afford them herself. Or, maybe she supported her daughter's dreams.*

Reinforce and Extend

Answers

◆ **LITERATURE AND YOUR LIFE**

Reader's Response Students may find them admirable because they sacrificed and worked hard so that their children could benefit.

Thematic Focus Responses will vary; students might cite examples of selfless deeds family members did for others, dramatic events, or moments of tenderness or insight.

☑ **Check Your Comprehension**

1. He rose early, dressed, made a fire to warm the house, and shined his son's good shoes.
2. The speaker was indifferent.
3. The mother taught her purple and golden.
4. She dies from a lack of beauty.

◆ **Critical Thinking**

1. As the fire grew, warmth replaced the cold.
2. He now admires his father's actions and recognizes the love in them.
3. She loves and respects her mother, but regrets that her life was cut short without a chance to enjoy the marvels she taught her daughter to love.
4. The mother was so busy coping in tough circumstances that she had no chance to develop pride. So, she couldn't teach it to her daughter.
5. Both speakers express love for a parent and realize that the parent sacrificed. One poet recalls the problems a parent and child have communicating, while the other explores how a parent can inspire a child.

Guide for Responding

◆ **LITERATURE AND YOUR LIFE**

Reader's Response In what way are the father and mother in these poems admirable?

Thematic Focus What story about growing up would you like to tell in a poem?

☑ **Check Your Comprehension**

1. In "Those Winter Sundays," what did the speaker's father do on Sunday mornings?
2. How did the speaker respond to his father at the time?
3. What two things does the speaker in "Taught Me Purple" say her mother taught her?
4. What causes the speaker's mother's death?

◆ **Critical Thinking**

INTERPRET
1. In "Those Winter Sundays," what does the speaker mean when he says he could "hear the cold splintering, breaking"? **[Interpret]**
2. How have the speaker's feelings about his father changed since he was young? **[Infer]**
3. How does the speaker of "Taught Me Purple" feel about her mother? **[Infer]**
4. Why couldn't the mother teach her daughter pride? **[Draw Conclusions]**

COMPARE LITERARY WORKS
5. What are the similarities and differences in the feelings the two speakers describe? **[Compare]**

Those Winter Sundays/Taught Me Purple ◆ 425

🎵 Humanities: Art

Hearth, 1957, by Loren MacIver
  Much of the work of the imaginative Loren MacIver (1909–1998) is characterized by symbolism and mystery. Discuss with students the literal image in this painting and their own experiences with hearths. Point out the colors that the artist chose to represent the fire and heat of the hearth. Encourage them to view the painting with the poet's phrase in line 5, "banked fires blaze on p. 424." Then, use these questions to help students think about the symbol of a hearth and the hearth in this painting specifically:

1. What might a hearth represent? *Students may suggest that a hearth usually represents home, family, warmth, comfort, safety, and security; they may also realize that historically a hearth was the place where most of a family's food was prepared.*
2. What about this hearth is mysterious or unsettling? *Students may say that the iron grate looks like teeth in a mocking smile, that the recessed fireplace seems to lure viewers into it, or that the hot flames are in stark contrast to the cold gray walls.*

Develop Understanding

One-Minute Insight In "The City Is So Big," the poet expresses how intimidated he feels by the images of an urban night.

◆ Literary Focus

❶ Word Choice Talk with students about the poet's choice of the words "so big" to describe the city. Is this the best choice? What responses do these words evoke in readers? *Students may say that the words "so big" sound like something a child might say; it implies feeling small or being overwhelmed.*

◆ Reading Strategy

❷ Respond Invite students to share their reactions to the figurative language the poet uses to describe bridges, trains, and city occurrences. If necessary, review personification (lines 2, 6–7) and simile (line 6).

Customize for
Visual/Spatial Learners

Have students examine this photograph of New York City. The shot, taken from Brooklyn looking across the East River to Manhattan, shows the twin towers of the World Trade Center in the background behind the Brooklyn Bridge, whose twin gothic arches are visible in the moonlight. Discuss the impressions that this image evokes about night in the city.

THE CITY IS SO BIG

❶

Richard García

426 ◆ *From Sea to Shining Sea*

🎙 Speaking and Listening Mini-Lesson

Choral Reading

This mini-lesson supports the Speaking and Listening activity in the Idea Bank on p. 429.

Introduce Tell students that, in this sense, choral means recited together by a group, or chorus. Choral reading is like choral singing—but without melody. As in choral singing, the object is to present a unified, cohesive sound, which requires rehearsal and may rely on a conductor.

Develop Form three groups, one for each poem. Each group should be prepared to interpret the poem. Help them with their interpretations by giving them questions to consider:

• What feelings or moods do we convey?
• How fast will it go? How soft or loud?
• What words will we emphasize?
• Which, if any, should be solo lines?

Based on their responses to these questions, have students prepare a script for their choral reading. Groups may find it helpful to have one student act as a conductor who guides them through their interpretations. As students practice, remind them to deliver the words slowly and clearly so an audience can hear what they are saying.

Apply When students feel prepared, have them present their choral readings.

Assess Evaluate choral readings on how well the groups perform as a group, how well they interpret the poem, and how interesting they make the words. Or, use the Peer Assessment: Oral Interpretation form, p. 115 in **Alternative Assessment.**

426

The city is so big
Its bridges quake with fear
I know, I have seen at night

The lights sliding from house to house
5   And trains pass with windows shining
Like a smile full of teeth

I have seen machines eating houses
And stairways walk all by themselves
And elevator doors opening and closing
10   And people disappear.

◄ **Critical Viewing** What images from the poem does this photograph of New York City convey or suggest? **[Apply]**

◆ **Build Vocabulary**

quake (kwāk) *v.*: To tremble or shake; to shudder or shiver, as from fear or cold

Guide for Responding

◆ LITERATURE AND YOUR LIFE

Reader's Response Would you like to visit the city described in the poem? Why or why not?

Thematic Focus To whom might you recommend this poem? Why?

Journal Writing In your journal, jot down your impressions of a city—either one in which you live or one that you have visited. How do your impressions compare with García's?

☑ Check Your Comprehension

1. What is the setting of this poem?
2. What has the speaker seen the bridges doing?
3. What do the passing trains resemble?

◆ Critical Thinking

INTERPRET

1. Describe the mood or overall atmosphere of this poem. Find five details that help create this mood. **[Analyze]**
2. Explain how each of the events described in the final four lines of the poem is possible. **[Interpret]**
3. How does the title of the poem relate to its main theme or message? **[Connect]**

APPLY

4. This poem presents one side of living in a big city. Discuss with your classmates the pros and cons of city living. **[Relate]**

EVALUATE

5. How well has García captured the essence of a big city? Use details from the poem to support your opinion. **[Evaluate]**

The City Is So Big ◆ 427

Beyond the Selection

FURTHER READING
Other Works by the Poets
Words in the Mourning Time, Robert Hayden
Toad Song, Evelyn Tooley Hunt
The Flying Garcías, Richard García
Other Poems About Cities
"Four Songs of the City," Charles Reznikoff
"Chicago," Carl Sandburg

INTERNET
We suggest the following sites on the Internet (all Web sites are subject to change).
    For more information about Robert Hayden:
http://www.poets.org/LIT/POET/rhayden.htm
    For ever-changing images of Manhattan:
http://www.realtech.com/webcam/index.htm
    We *strongly recommend* that you preview these sites before you send students to them.

❸ What do these lines really describe?
They describe the demolition of a building (line 7), escalators (line 8), and automated doors (lines 9–10).

►Critical Viewing◄

❹ **Apply** *It captures the bridge, the sliding lights, and "windows shining like a smile full of teeth."*

Reinforce and Extend

Answers
◆ LITERATURE AND YOUR LIFE

Reader's Response Students will probably say that they would like to visit the city because they'd like to see it for themselves and form their own impressions.

Thematic Focus You might recommend it to someone who fears the city, so they know that someone else shares their view. Or you might recommend it to people who have never been to a large city so they can get someone else's impression.

☑ Check Your Comprehension

1. It is set in a big city.
2. He has seen the bridges quake.
3. Their windows look like toothy smiles.

◆ Critical Thinking

1. The mood conveys apprehension and fear. Supporting details are "bridges quake with fear," "like a smile full of teeth," "machines eating houses," "stairways that walk by themselves," and "people disappearing behind elevator doors."
2. Demolition equipment may look like it is "eating houses"; escalators are moving stairways; people who enter an elevator "disappear" as the elevator takes them to another floor.
3. It emphasizes the overwhelming size of the city, which can have a dehumanizing effect. The poem then presents images of fear, threat, and inhumanity.
4. Responses will vary. Pros may include excitement, diversity, opportunity, and a thrilling pace. Cons may include crowds, costs, crime, and lack of open space.
5. Students who agree that the big city is scary can point to images of fear in García's poem. Those who like the city will disagree with the poem's message.

427

◆ Reading Strategy

1. Students may say that they feel badly that the father was not acknowledged.
2. Students may cite a relative or friend who worked hard for the family.
3. Students should list specific words and justify their responses.

◆ Build Vocabulary

Using the Word Root -chron-
1. historic record of events that took place over time
2. in time order
3. instrument that measures time

Spelling Strategy
1. reference; 2. element; 3. independence

Using the Word Bank
1. tenement; 2. austere; 3. chronic; 4. banked; 5. quake; 6. molding

◆ Literary Focus

1. It refers to family tensions that upset the speaker when he was a boy.
2. Possible answers might include: harsh, severe, rigid, lonesome, solitary, remote, or forlorn.
3. He repeats the word *and,* perhaps to emphasize the overwhelming nature of the city. He accumulates details and joins them by *and.*

◆ Build Grammar Skills

Practice
1. father went (inverted)
2. mother was (inverted)
3. parents walked (standard)
4. snow fell (standard)
5. cloud are (inverted)

Writing Application
Sample responses:
1. My mother worked so hard!; So hard worked my mother!
2. There are many bridges in New York; Many bridges are in New York.
3. The coals glow in the grate; Glow the coals in the grate.

Writer's Solution

For additional instruction and practice, use the lesson in the *Writer's Solution Language Lab CD-ROM* on Inverted Sentences. You may also use the pages on Diagraming Basic Sentence Parts, pp. 43–46, in the *Writer's Solution Grammar Practice Book.*

Guide for Responding (continued)

◆ Reading Strategy

RESPOND

When you **respond** to a poem, you bring your own feelings and reactions to it.
1. In "Those Winter Sundays," the speaker says that "No one ever thanked" his father. How did you respond to this information?
2. Do you know anyone who is like the mother in "Taught Me Purple"? Explain.
3. What words would you use to describe your response to "The City Is So Big"?

◆ Build Vocabulary

USING THE WORD ROOT -chron-

The word root -chron- comes from the Greek word for time. Apply that information to suggest a meaning for each of the words below. Then, use a dictionary to check your definitions.
1. chronicle   2. chronological   3. chronometer

SPELLING STRATEGY

Some words, like *tenement* and *cemetery,* are spelled with three e's. To remember how to spell these words, think of the three e's in the word *remember!* Find the misspelled word in each sentence, and write it correctly on your paper.
1. I found the poet's age in a refirence book.
2. There is an elament of suspense in her poetry.
3. Her work clearly declares independance.

USING THE WORD BANK

Write the word from the Word Bank that best completes each sentence.
1. The ____?____ was built to house the poor.
2. The room was so bare that it looked ____?____ and forbidding.
3. The ____?____ problem with the heat kept the rooms from ever getting warm enough.
4. A ____?____ fire will burn through the night.
5. When the radiator came on, the pipes would quiver and the floors would ____?____.
6. The ____?____ around the door is decorative.

◆ Literary Focus

WORD CHOICE

Word choice is especially important in poetry. In fact, poets often labor over a single word. Sometimes they come up with unusual word choices to surprise readers and lead them to view things in new ways. For example, in "Taught Me Purple," the poet writes that the tenement was "her orbit." The word *orbit* draws the reader's attention to the mother's narrowly defined life.
1. What does Hayden mean by "the chronic angers of that house" in "Those Winter Sundays"?
2. Hayden uses the adjectives *austere* and *lonely* in the final line of his poem. What similar words might he have considered instead of these words? How would the choice of one of these other words have affected the poem's meaning?
3. What word appears at the beginning of four lines in "The City Is So Big"? Why might García have chosen to repeat that word?

◆ Build Grammar Skills

INVERTED SENTENCES

In most English sentences, the subject comes first, followed by the verb. Poets sometimes **invert** this order, placing the verb or some part of the predicate before the subject. For example, Evelyn Tooley Hunt writes:

> Wash-gray was her circle, . . .

In standard English, you would say "Her circle was wash-gray." Poets may invert sentences to create a particular rhythm, a rhyme, or a poetic sound.

Practice Identify the subject and the verb in each sentence. Then, label each as standard or inverted.
1. Bounding down the street went my father.
2. There on the corner was my mother.
3. My parents walked in the park.
4. The snow gently fell outside my window.
5. There are no clouds in the sky today.

Writing Application Write three sentences in standard order. Then, rewrite the sentences, inverting the subject and verb order.

428 ◆ *From Sea to Shining Sea*

Build Your Portfolio

 Idea Bank

Writing

1. **Book Jacket** Create a book title and jacket description for a collection of poems that includes "Those Winter Sundays," "Taught Me Purple," and "The City Is So Big." Describe the collection in a way that will attract readers. Mention each of the poems you've just read.

2. **Word Analysis** Find a word in one of the poems that is critical to the poem's overall meaning. Then, write a brief essay in which you discuss why the writer chose this word and how the word relates to the poem's message.

3. **Comparison of Poems** Compare and contrast "Those Winter Sundays" and "Taught Me Purple" in a brief essay. Use passages from the poems to support your points.

Speaking and Listening

4. **Choral Reading [Group Activity]** Prepare a choral reading of one of the poems with a group of classmates. Choose lines to read together and lines to read individually. Make sure everyone in your group has a specified role.

5. **Telephone Conversation [Group Activity]** With a partner, improvise for the class a telephone conversation between the speaker of "Taught Me Purple" and the speaker of "Those Winter Sundays." [Performing Arts Link]

Projects

6. **Poetry Display** Find more poems written by Hayden, Hunt, and García. Photocopy them, and create a colorful display that includes not only the poems but also related photographs and illustrations.

7. **City Life Magazine [Group Activity]** With a group, create a magazine that describes city life. Group members can contribute and edit articles, select illustrations, and write headlines. Display a copy of your magazine in your classroom or school library. [Social Studies Link]

 Writing Mini-Lesson

Response to Poems

When you respond to literature, you react on a personal level to what you've read. Choose two of the poems from this section, and share how they affected you by writing a response to them.

> **Writing Skills Focus:**
> **Compare-and-Contrast Organization**
> Use **comparison-and-contrast organization** in your response to the two poems. You might decide to write about one poem first and then write about the other poem, or you might discuss similarities in your responses in one paragraph and differences in the next paragraph.
>
> ### Model
> I had different reactions to the last lines of each poem. The final line of "Those Winter Sundays" made me feel regret and sympathy, and the final line of "The City Is So Big" made me feel tense and frightened.

Prewriting Reread the poems about which you're writing, and jot down notes about your response to each. List how your responses to the two poems are similar and different.

Drafting Organize your notes to compare and contrast your responses. As you draft, support the points you make by citing passages from the poems.

> ◆ **Grammar Application**
> If inverted sentences appear in the poems, you may want to describe your response to their effect.

Revising Check your notes to see whether you have included all of your points in your essay. Review your organization to be sure that it's consistent and that your ideas are clearly presented.

 Idea Bank

Following are suggestions for matching the Idea Bank topics with your students' performance levels and learning modalities:

Customize for
Performance Levels
Less Advanced Students: 1, 4, 6
Average Students: 2, 4, 5, 6, 7
More Advanced Students: 3, 5, 7

Customize for
Learning Modalities
Verbal/Linguistic: 1, 2, 3, 5, 7
Visual/Spatial: 1, 6, 7
Bodily/Kinesthetic: 4, 5
Logical/Mathematical: 3
Musical/Rhythmic: 4
Interpersonal: 4, 5, 7
Intrapersonal: 1, 2, 3

 Writing Mini-Lesson

Refer students to the Writing Handbook in the back of the book for instruction on the writing process and for further information on responding to literature. Students might use the Venn Diagram, p. 77 in **Writing and Language Transparencies,** to organize their responses.

Writer's Solution

Writers at Work Videodisc
Have students view the videodisc segment on Response to Literature (Ch. 9), featuring Marilyn Stasio, as a springboard for a class discussion on responding to poetry.

Play frames 30102 to 39013

Writing Lab CD-ROM
Have students complete the tutorial on Response to Literature. Follow these steps:

1. Direct students to the prewriting segments on focusing your response and gathering details about a poem.
2. Have students draft on computer.
3. Refer students to the interactive model on using quotations.
4. Have students use the revision checker for language variety.

Writer's Solution Sourcebook
Have students use Chapter 9, "Response to Literature," pp. 266–295, for more support. The chapter includes in-depth instruction on using quotations, p. 292.

✓ ASSESSMENT OPTIONS

Formal Assessment, Selection Test, pp. 123–125, and Assessment Resources Software. The selection test is designed so that it can be easily customized to the performance levels of your students.

Alternative Assessment, p. 31, includes options for less advanced students, more advanced students, visual/spatial learners, interpersonal learners, musical/rhythmic learners, verbal/linguistic learners, and logical/mathematical learners.

PORTFOLIO ASSESSMENT

Use the following rubrics in the **Alternative Assessment** booklet to assess student writing:
Book Jacket: Summary, p. 94
Word Analysis: Literary Analysis/Interpretation, p. 108
Comparison of Poems: Comparison/Contrast, p. 99
Writing Mini-Lesson: Response to Literature, p. 106

Establish Writing Guidelines
Review the following key characteristics of a consumer report:

- A consumer report is an objective report on a product, including information on cost, ratings, and statistics.

- A consumer report reveals both the strengths and weaknesses of a product.

You may want to distribute the scoring rubric for Technical Description/ Explanation, p. III in **Alternative Assessment,** to make students aware of the criteria on which they will be evaluated. See the suggestions on p. 432 for how you can customize the rubric to this workshop.

Refer students to the Writing Handbook in the back of the book for instruction on the writing process and further information on expository writing.

 **Writer's Solution**

Writers at Work Videodisc
To introduce students to expository writing, and to show them how writer Bruce Brooks answers the question "What is expository writing?" play the videodisc segment on Exposition: Making Connections (Ch. 5).

Play frames 43069 to 51462

Writing Lab CD-ROM
If your students have access to computers, you may want to have them work in the tutorial on Exposition: Making Connections to complete all or part of their consumer reports. Follow these steps:

1. Have students use the Cluster Diagram to collect details related to their topic.
2. Suggest that students view the audio-annotated model for details of an evaluation.
3. Allow students to draft on computer.
4. When revising, have students use the revision checker for sentence length.

Writer's Solution Sourcebook
Students can find additional support, including in-depth instruction on using modifiers, pp. 163–164, in the chapter on Exposition: Making Connections, pp. 136–165.

430

Expository Writing
Consumer Report

Writing Process Workshop

If Sancho were a person and not a steer, he would probably offer some great advice on what goes into excellent southwestern food. Whenever you need advice on purchasing a product, it's helpful to turn to a consumer report that will reveal the strengths and weaknesses of different products and the advantages of using one over another. A consumer report is objective; it presents facts, statistical data, product ratings, and recommendations. Write your own consumer report about a product that interests you.

The skills introduced in this section's Writing Mini-Lessons will help you write your consumer report.

Writing Skills Focus

▶ In your consumer report, **elaborate with factual details.** (See p. 407.)

▶ **Use supporting points** to back up your recommendations. (See p. 421.)

▶ **Use a comparison-and-contrast organization** to develop your consumer report. (See p. 429.)

MODEL

① The stick umbrella is easy to use and opens when a push button is pressed. ② Because of its size and strength, it offers protection from rain and wind without turning inside out. Prices vary from about $15 to $80 and above for a high-fashion design.

① Folding umbrellas ② are smaller; the smallest is about 8 inches long. They do not offer as much protection as the stick umbrella, and they are not as durable. Since they are so inexpensive— from $6 to $30—and easy to carry, many people keep them handy for protection from a sudden shower.

All in all, I recommend the folding umbrella. ③ For the difference in price and the ease of use, it's worth it.

① The writer uses a comparison-and-contrast organization to develop her consumer report.

② Factual details about umbrella size, strength, and cost are used to elaborate.

③ These supporting points back up the writer's recommendation.

430 ◆ *From Sea to Shining Sea*

 Beyond the Classroom

Workplace Skills
Analyzing Consumer Reports Explain to students that being able to understand, analyze, and create consumer reports can be a skill important in a variety of workplaces. For example, a cleaning company may want to consult a consumer report on vacuum cleaners to decide which product to purchase for their intended clients. Or, a group of employees may want to consult a consumer report on health care providers to make recommendations to their employer about the kind of health plan they think will suit their needs.

Have students form groups and choose a career. Then have them consider what type of products they may need for jobs in that field. For example, students who choose a career as a video editor may need recording equipment, televisions, and high-quality video tape; a groundskeeper may need lawnmowers, rakes, and fertilizer. Then, have students find consumer reports and use them to decide which products they would choose to use. Have them annotate their lists of equipment with information from the report and their reasons for their choices and decisions.

Prewriting

Choose a Topic Television and magazine advertisements are great sources for products to use in your report. If those fail you, consider the ideas in the box below:

Topic Ideas

- A big purchase your family has made
- Popular food products and their nutritional claims
- Personal products that target the teen market

Limit Your Items A consumer report should focus only on a few items within one topic: three different brands of in-line skates, for example, rather than all in-line skates. Choose a category, such as *best known* or *least known* or a certain price range, to help you limit the items you're comparing.

Elaborate With Factual Details As you research the products you plan to discuss in your consumer report, write down factual details that will help you present your findings in an objective, unbiased way.

Use a Venn Diagram Use a Venn diagram like the one below to gather and organize details according to similarities and differences among the products in your report.

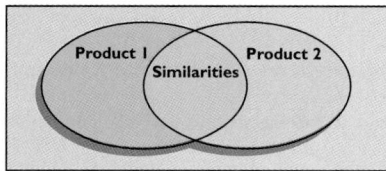

Use Comparison-and-Contrast Organization You can develop your paragraphs subject by subject or point by point. In other words, you can completely cover one item and then the next, or you can cover the cost of both, durability of both, and so on.

Drafting

Review Your Notes Before you begin drafting your consumer report, review your notes to keep fresh in your mind the points you'll be discussing and the order in which you plan to discuss them.

Write the Body First Write the body of your consumer report first. Then, create an introduction that leads into it and a conclusion in which you make your recommendation.

DRAFTING/REVISING

Applying Language Skills: Using Precise Adjectives

Adjectives are words that point out, describe, and limit; *collie* dog, *white* dog, *six* dogs. Precise, exact adjectives present a clear picture to readers.

Vague Adjectives:
There were some people on the old boat.

Precise Adjectives:
There were four tired, frightened people on the dilapidated boat.

Notice how the precise adjectives *four*, *tired*, *frightened*, and *dilapidated* paint a much clearer picture than *some* and *old*.

Practice Replace the vague adjectives or add precise ones to these sentences:

1. They got into the car.
2. The boys went on a trip.
3. After seeing the show, they had some dinner.
4. The dog chased the cat.
5. Last year, I donated books to the flea market.

Writing Application As you edit your consumer report, include precise adjectives.

Writer's Solution Connection Writing Lab

For help using precise adjectives, use the Revision Checker in the Revising section of the Description tutorial.

Develop Student Writing

Prewriting

Explain to students that when comparing two products, they want to make sure they evaluate both products on the same criteria. For example, comparing two umbrellas means evaluating each umbrella on durability, cost, protection, and portability.

✒ Writer's Solution

Writing Lab CD-ROM
Students may want to use the Venn Diagram on details in the Prewriting section of the tutorial on Exposition: Making Connections to help them develop clear comparisons.

Customize for
Less Proficient Writers
Some students may do better working with a partner on their consumer reports. After they choose a product or products to write about, they can confer to develop a list of criteria on which the products should be judged. Explain to students that they should spend some time examining each product in order to come to a conclusion about their recommendations.

Drafting

Explain to students that they may want to use an order-of-importance organization plan to build their reports. Tell students that they can begin with the most important details and end with the least important, or they can work the other way around.

✒ Writer's Solution

Writing Lab CD-ROM
In the Drafting section of the tutorial on Exposition: Making Connections, suggest to students that they use the Transitional Word Bin to select transitional words and phrases to connect their ideas.

Applying Language Skills

Using Precise Adjectives Read the following list of adjectives to students: big, huge, nice, small, slow. Then read the following list: gigantic, generous, petite, cautious. Explain that the adjectives in the second list are more precise and more specific than the ones in the first list. They present the reader with a clearer idea.

Answers

Suggested responses:
1. They got into the red convertible car.
2. The boys went on a cross-country skiing trip.
3. After seeing the photography show, they had a five-course dinner.
4. The aging dog chased the striped cat.
5. Last year, I donated twenty books to the flea market.

✒ Writer's Solution

For additional instruction and practice, have students use the practice page on Choosing Precise Words, p. 121, in the *Writer's Solution Grammar Practice Book.*

Revising

Have students take turns reading their drafts aloud, with peer editors making constructive comments.

Writer's Solution

Writing Lab CD-ROM
Students can view the video demonstrating how to add visuals to a report.

Publishing

Students might create a class anthology of consumer reports with photographs, illustrations, or charts.

Reinforce and Extend

Review the Writing Guidelines
After students have completed their papers, review the characteristics of a consumer report.

Applying Language Skills

Avoiding Jargon Explain to students that their consumer reports are for a general audience, and therefore should avoid using specialized vocabulary, jargon.

Answers

Possible responses:
1. Tiara said, "I want the information on her."
2. The editor asked her friend, "Will you take a look at this for me?"
3. I'll write out a prescription for you this evening," the doctor assured him.

Writer's Solution

For additional instruction, use Looking at Reports, p. 136, and Writing a Report, p. 137, in the *Writer's Solution Grammar Practice Book*, pp. 65–66.

Writing Process Workshop

EDITING/PROOFREADING

APPLYING LANGUAGE SKILLS:
Avoiding Jargon

Jargon is a specialized language used by people in a certain group, such as actors, lawyers, bicyclists, or football fans. Jargon often confuses and excludes others. In your writing, use straightforward language that all readers will understand.

Jargon:
There was road rash on Pete's legs and arms.

Specific Language:
Pete's arms and legs were covered with cuts and scratches.

Practice Replace the jargon (defined in parentheses) in these sentences.

1. Tiara said, "I want the *411* on her." (information)
2. The editor asked her friend, "Will you *eyeball* this for me?" (look at)
3. "I'll write out a *scrip* for you this evening," the doctor assured him. (prescription)

Writing Application Check your draft to eliminate any jargon.

Writer's Solution Connection
Language Lab

For more practice using formal and informal language, complete the lesson in Formal and Informal English Idioms.

Revising

Add or Delete Details Look over your draft. If your point lacks support, add factual details. If you've included opinions, you may want to delete them to keep your report objective.

Improve Your Word Choice and Language Review your report to find vague adjectives and/or jargon. Replace them with precise, straightforward statements and descriptions.

Review Your Organization Make sure you maintained a subject-by-subject or a point-by-point organization as you developed your comparison-and-contrast consumer report.

REVISION MODEL

Both Jackson Airlines and Air Delight fly the same route from Calgary to Branston. Jackson flies small commuter jets and old DC9s. The basic flight costs about $150, and they serve ① *coffee, soft drinks, and peanuts.* food and drink. ② Air Delight serves honey-coated cashews. Their on-time record is ③ *82 percent.* good. They don't post their accident record.

The basic flight on Air Delight costs more, but they use newer planes. Air Delight has an 88 percent on-time record and had only one minor accident in the last six years. ④ *I'd recommend* It's hard *Air Delight based on its on-time record.* to tell which is better.

① These factual details were added to present a clear picture.
② The sentence about Air Delight was eliminated because it weakens the organization of the paper.
③ This detail supports the writer's point.
④ The recommendation was reworded to be more specific.

Publishing and Presenting

On Line Share your consumer reports either through e-mail or on your school's Web page.

Bulletin Board Post your consumer report in an area where interested individuals can read it. For example, a report on running shoes might be posted in the gym.

Real-World Reading Skills Workshop

Making Inferences

Strategies for Success

Writers don't always tell you everything directly. You have to make inferences to arrive at ideas authors suggest but don't say. You make inferences by considering the details a writer includes or doesn't include. Making a series of inferences will help you draw conclusions about what you read.

Read Between the Lines Look beyond the literal meaning of the words to understand a writer's attitude or purpose for writing.

Example Passage: For those who like salmon, this entree is quite interesting.

Possible Inference: The writer doesn't like salmon, so his or her opinion may be biased.

Question One way to make inferences is to question the text. Ask the following as you read:

▶ Why did the writer include these details?
▶ Why did the writer exclude information?

Draw Conclusions Using the inferences you have made about a writer's choice of details, draw conclusions about what you read.

✔ Here are other situations in which making inferences is helpful:
▶ Reading a menu
▶ Reading an editorial
▶ Reading a news article
▶ Reading a poster

Apply the Strategies

Read the passage from a sports article. Then, make inferences about the text to answer the questions that follow:

> **Indoor Rock Climbing**
> A new sport is sweeping the nation: indoor rock climbing. The equipment—shoes, helmet, harness—are usually provided at the clubs at a low daily rental charge. Club memberships are also usually available, but if you'd like to test out the sport first, entrance fees average about $6 per day. Lessons range from $25 to $35 an hour.
> Most indoor climbing clubs offer walls to challenge various levels of climber—from beginner to expert. Some walls are restricted: You have to take a test to prove that you have the ability to climb it safely.
> Most rock-climbing clubs offer special deals for birthday parties and school outings. Parents, however, are required by law to sign a release form permitting children under the age of 17 to climb.

1. Is this an established sport, or might it be a fad?

2. What can you infer about the overall cost of participating in this sport?

3. Is this sport challenging—one you can grow in? How can you tell?

4. What might you infer about this sport, knowing that parents are required by law to sign a release form for minors?

Introduce the Strategies

Explain to students that an inference is a form of reasoning, like making an educated guess based on the information given. When reading, this includes considering what information is left out as well as the information the author includes. Tell students to ask themselves what the author's choices tell about his/her purpose for writing.

Customize for
Less Proficient Readers

Explain to students that making an inference is like making an educated guess. Suggest that as students read, they first consider the literal meaning. Then, they should consider what they already know about the topic. The combination of information in the text and prior knowledge can lead students to make good inferences.

Apply the Strategies

As students read, remind them to look for details that are clues to the main idea of the passage. Once they have drawn inferences, have them consider whether these inferences follow logically from the information given.

Answers

1. This may be a fad, since it is so new and needs special equipment which is usually rented.
2. Overall, the sport is fairly expensive because you have to pay entrance fees, fees for equipment rental, and fees for lessons.
3. This sport is challenging because there are various levels, from beginner to expert.
4. You can infer that this sport may be dangerous because parents are required to sign a release form for minors. The clubs don't want to be liable for any injuries.

◆ Build Grammar Skills

Reviewing Subjects and Predicates

The selections in Part 2 include instruction on the following:

- Subjects and Predicates (simple and complete)
- Compound Subjects and Predicates
- Inverted Sentences

This instruction is reinforced with the Build Grammar Skills practice pages in **Selection Support**, pp. 155, 160, and 165.

As you review subjects and predicates, you may wish to include the following:

- Four Kinds of Sentences

Explain to students that sentences can be classified by their function. The four functions of sentences are *declarative, interrogative, imperative,* or *exclamatory.* A declarative sentence states an idea and ends with a period. An interrogative sentence asks a question and ends with a question mark. An imperative sentences gives a command or an order and ends in either a period or an exclamation point. An exclamatory sentence conveys strong emotion and ends with an exclamation point. Give students the following examples:

| **Declarative:** She went to the store. |
| **Interrogative:** Did she go to the store? |
| **Imperative:** Go to the store. |
| **Exclamatory:** The store is burning! |

For further practice, use The Four Functions of Sentences page, p. 42, in the *Writer's Solution Grammar Practice Handbook.*

Answers
Practice 1

1. <u>Mona and I</u> <u>watched Eugene play.</u> (Circle *Mona, I,* and *watched.*) Mona and *I* is a compound subject. Standard sentence
2. Next morning <u>Little Baldy</u> <u>was a dark hill jutting high into February's cold, windy, sky.</u> (Circle *Little Baldy, was.*) Standard sentence
3. <u>Wash-gray was</u> <u>her circle.</u> (Circle *circle, wash-gray.*) Inverted sentence
4. <u>He</u> <u>stood and roamed about on the south side of the herd.</u> (Circle *He, stood and roamed. Stood* and *roamed* is a compound verb.) Standard sentence
5. <u>Dark drum</u> the vanishing horses' hooves. (Circle *hooves* and *drum.*) Inverted sentence

434

Subjects and Predicates | Grammar Review

A sentence is a group of words that expresses a complete thought. Every sentence consists of two parts: the subject and the predicate. The **subject** states whom or what the sentence is about. The **predicate** tells what the subject is or does.

> subject   predicate
> Every night Sancho | came to the ranch pen to sleep.

Simple Subject and Simple Predicate Each complete subject and predicate contains a simple subject and a simple predicate. **The simple subject** is the main noun or pronoun in the complete subject, and the **simple predicate** is the verb or verb phrase in the predicate.

> simple   simple
> subject   predicate
> Every night *Sancho* | *came* to the ranch pen to sleep.

Compound Subject and Compound Verb Some sentences may have more than one subject or verb. A **compound subject** is two or more subjects that have the same verb and are linked by a coordinating conjunction, such as *and* or *or.* A **compound verb** is two or more verbs that have the same subject and are linked by a coordinating conjunction, such as *and* or *or.*

> **Compound Subject:** The *bluebonnets and pink phlox* were sprinkling every hill. . . .
> **Compound Verb:** We *stood* in our barnlot *and looked* at Little Baldy.

Inverted Order In standard sentences, the subject comes before the verb. Writers sometimes **invert** this order, placing the verb or some part of the predicate before the subject.

>   subject   verb
> **Standard:** The *herd* of cattle *moved* slowly.
>   verb   subject
> **Inverted:** Slowly *moved* the *herd* of cattle.

sen-tence (sen'təns) *n.* 1 a group of words that is used to tell, ask, command, or exclaim something, usually having a subject and a predicate: a sentence begins with a capital letter and ends with a period, question mark, or exclamation point

Practice 1 Copy each sentence into your notebook. Underline the complete subject once and the complete predicate twice. Then, circle the simple subject and simple verb, and label those that are compound. Finally, identify each sentence as standard or inverted.

1. Mona and I watched Eugenie play.
2. Next morning Little Baldy was a dark hill jutting high into February's cold, windy sky.
3. Wash-gray was her circle . . .
4. He stood and roamed about on the south side of the herd.
5. Dark drum the vanishing horses' hooves.

Practice 2 Retell a story that has been told and retold about a family member. As you write, use two sentences with compound subjects, two with compound verbs, and two in inverted order.

Grammar in Writing

✔ *Avoid wordiness and repetition by combining sentences to use compound subjects and verbs.*

     Repetitive: Mona took piano lessons. I also took piano lessons.

     Revised: Mona and I took piano lessons.

Speaking, Listening, and Viewing Workshop

Telephone Communications

Talking with friends, calling for help, ordering a pizza, carrying on business—for all these reasons and more, the telephone is an essential part of our lives. Your telephone transaction will go smoothly if you use good sense and good manners.

Get Off to a Good Start When you're making a personal or professional call, begin by introducing yourself and stating your purpose. "Hello, my name is Carolyn Keller. I'm calling in response to your advertisement for a baby sitter." "Hi, Mrs. Fagan, this is Darren. Is Dan at home?"

When calling for information or to order a product, it is not necessary to introduce yourself. If you're ordering something, you will be asked for personal information at the appropriate time.

Speak Clearly If your listeners keep asking you to repeat yourself, it's a good sign that you need to speak more clearly. Speak slowly and distinctly. Remember that the person on the other end of the phone is relying completely on your voice to receive information.

Say It Again Repeating information ensures that you have heard the other person correctly. When you are receiving phone numbers, addresses, directions, name spellings, or the date and time of appointments, repeat them to verify their accuracy.

Manners Count Be courteous when communicating on the phone. Say "please" and "thank you" when asking for and receiving information. End your call on a good note by saying "thank you." Confirm any future contact. "Thanks for calling, Scott. I'll speak with you again on Tuesday."

Apply the Strategies

Role-play the following telephone conversations with a classmate:

1. You see an injured dog on the street in front of your house. Call a veterinarian for help.

2. You want to apply for a baby-sitting job you saw advertised in Sunday's paper.

3. Call your father at work and leave a message for him to pick you up at 5:30 at Pat Kelly's house at 206 Waverly Ave.

4. You have to find out if your sister is visiting her friend Eliza or her friend Rachel and tell her to come home early.

Tips for Telephone Conversations

▶ Speak loudly and clearly.
▶ Greet your listener pleasantly.
▶ Identify yourself and your purpose for calling.
▶ Repeat important information.

Introduce the Strategies

Ask students to volunteer any confusing experiences they may have had using the telephone. Remind them of any incidents involving wrong numbers or perhaps times when they had a bad connection. Explain to students that even the way you hold the phone near your mouth can make a big difference on how the person on the other end hears you. Tell students that if they use cordless phones, they should be careful not to move around too much and cause the phone to go out of range.

Customize for
Bodily/Kinesthetic Learners

Ask volunteers to act out their telephone conversations in front of the class. To emphasize the strategies for effective telephone communications, suggest that students prepare two different scripts for one of the scenarios; one in which the communication goes smoothly, and one in which the speaker is unclear.

Apply the Strategies

Students may want to script out their conversations before they role-play with their partners. The following answers indicate information that should be given when making the telephone calls.

1. "Hello, my name is Dave Kendall. I found an injured dog on the corner of Maple Avenue and Clark Street. I can't see any blood but his leg seems to be broken. What should I do?" The speaker should identify himself and his reason for calling immediately.

Then he should identify where he is and what condition the dog seems to be in. Finally, he should ask a question and let the veterinarian's office give him advice.

2. "Hello, my name is Carlos Sanchez. I'm calling about the baby-sitting job advertised in Sunday's paper." The speaker should identify himself and his purpose immediately, explaining where he saw the advertisement.

3. "Hi, Dad, it's Cindy. I need you to pick me up at 5:30 at Pat Kelly's house, 206 Waverly Avenue. That's 206 Waverly Avenue at 5:30. Thanks." The speaker can be informal, but

must include all the information and may want to repeat the information since it may be hard to hear on the message.

4. "Hello, this is Jamie's sister, Lacey. Is Jamie there? Can you tell her to come home early?" The speaker may have to make more than one phone call to determine where her sister is. She should identify herself by her relationship to her sister.

◆ Build Vocabulary

What's Behind the Words Ask students to discuss what newspapers, if any, they or their families subscribe to. Then, ask students which section of the newspaper is their favorite, and why.

Answers
Activity 1

1. The banner is a prominent head-line in large type; it may be the name of the newspaper itself.
2. A byline is the name of the per-son who has written the article.
3. A headline is the title of an article, in large type.
4. An editorial is a special article in the newspaper, sometimes written by the editor, which expresses an opinion.
5. The classified section is the part of the paper that has advertise-ments classed by different head-ings, such as type of firm for help wanted advertisements, or by specific area for real estate advertisements.
6. The masthead is the printed matter in the newspaper that gives the title and pertinent details of ownership, advertising rates, and subscription rates.
7. The nameplate is the line of type across the front page containing the name of the publication.
8. A review is a critical account of a new book, film, show, etc. for newspapers and other periodicals.
9. An opinion article is an article which expresses an opinion rather than facts.
10. A feature article is a prominent article in the newspaper. Sometimes a feature may consist of several articles.

What's Behind the
Words
Vocabulary Adventures With Richard Lederer

Newspaper and Magazine Vocabulary

The United States is a newspaper nation. Because our country was the first great modern democracy, the free press was born here. Today, about one fifth of the newspapers around the globe are printed in our land.

America Reads the Newspaper

Americans are great newspaper readers. Because of our high literacy rate, about 20 percent of the world's news readers live here, even though we have only 6 or 7 percent of the Earth's population. Nearly 90 percent of American homes have newspapers in them, and four of five adults read a newspaper regularly.

Journalistic Words

Journalism—the writing, editing, and publishing of news—is borrowed from the French *journal*, "a daily record." Words dealing with newspapers and magazines have interest-ing origins:

advertisement: In Latin, *advertere* meant "to turn toward." The later French word, *advertir,* meant "to tell about or warn." An *advertisen* in early English was a notice about something, similar to the meaning of the word *advertisement* today.

article: In Latin, *articulus* was the word for "joint" or "knuckle." Articles were joined together to create a whole work.

cartoon: From the Latin *charta,* "a piece of paper," descends the Italian word *cartone,* meaning "pasteboard." The first cartoons were drawn on such large pieces of heavy paper.

column: Through the Greek *kolōnós* ("hill") to the Latin *columna* ("pillar or post"), the word *column* has taken on the additional meaning of "the vertical part of a page."

editor: This word is a combination of the Latin *e* ("out") and *dere* ("to give"). The meaning became "one who gives out, who publishes."

reporter: This word is a combination of Latin word parts, and you can figure out their meanings. *Re-*, as in *rework* and *repeat,* means "again." *Port* (from the Latin *portare*), as in *transport* and *porter,* means "to carry." In time, *reporter* came to mean "one who carries the news."

ACTIVITY 1 Define and show an example of the following parts of a newspaper:

1. banner	6. masthead
2. byline	7. nameplate
3. headline	8. review
4. editorial	9. opinion article
5. classified section	10. feature article

ACTIVITY 2 Headline writers must say a lot in a small space. They need to know many short words to replace the longer ones used in the stories themselves. These shortcuts are called headline words. What longer words do the following headline verbs replace?

1. bar	3. nab	5. quiz	7. top	9. urge
2. curb	4. OK	6. seek	8. up	10. vow

ACTIVITY 3 Newspapers are full of lines, including *bylines, deadlines,* and *headlines.* Report on the meanings and origins of these three words.

436 ◆ *From Sea to Shining Sea*

Activity 2
Possible responses:
1. exclude, rule out, forbid
2. restrain, hold back, keep under control
3. seize, catch in the act of wrong-doing
4. approve, agree
5. ask questions, interrogate
6. undertake, attempt
7. exceed, outdo, come in first
8. increase, raise, boost
9. pressure, insist
10. promise, guarantee, pledge

Activity 3
Deadline means the time after which copy is not accepted for an issue of a publication. The original meaning of *deadline* was a line drawn within or around a prison that a prisoner crosses at the risk of being shot.
Byline is the line giving the writer's name at the beginning of a news story.
Headline refers to the head of a newspaper story, usually printed in large type, giving the gist of the story or article that follows.

Extended Reading Opportunities

A land as vast as the United States poses all kinds of challenges. The following novels describe some of the challenges that humans and animals must overcome to live harmoniously with nature.

Suggested Titles

The Call of the Wild
Jack London

This novel follows the trail of Buck, a domestic dog who is kidnapped to be trained as a sled dog during the Alaskan Gold Rush. Buck reverts back to his primitive nature and undertakes a journey in which he abandons the safety of his domestic world for that of the wild. He becomes a hero when he is transformed into the legendary "Ghost Dog" of the Klondike.

Where the Lilies Bloom
Vera and Bill Cleaver

The saga of the Luther family is set in the Trial Valley between two fictional peaks of the Smoky Mountains on the Tennessee border of western North Carolina. The members of the Luther family are share-croppers on land belonging to Kiser Pease and his sister. The story vividly describes the will of the Luther children to overcome their poverty, meet the challenges of nature, and find comfort in each other—all under the direction of fourteen-year-old Mary Call Luther.

The Yearling
Marjorie Kinnan Rawlings

The characters of this story focus on their daily struggle to earn a living in an isolated and harsh environment. Set in northcentral Florida in the years following the Civil War, the book follows the life of Jody Baxter, a boy on the verge of adulthood. Life on the farm becomes less grim for Jody when he adopts a fawn and names her Flag. Jody is then forced to make a painful decision, which helps him cross the border into manhood.

Other Possibilities

A Day No Pigs Would Die   Robert Newton Peck

Prairie Songs   Pamela Conrad

When the Legends Die   Hal Borland

Little Women   Louisa May Alcott

Planning Students' Extended Reading

All of the works listed on this page are good choices for extending the theme "From Sea to Shining Sea." Following is some information that may help you choose which to teach:

Customize for
Varying Student Needs

When assigning the selections in this part to your students, keep in mind the following factors:

- *The Call of the Wild* is considered Jack London's masterpiece novel, based on the author's own experiences in the Alaskan Gold Rush in 1897.

- *Where the Lilies Bloom* is set in Appalachia in the 1940's and narrated by a fourteen-year-old girl. Her struggle through hardships to save her family after the deaths of her parents may instill empathy in students.

- *The Yearling* is Pulitzer prize-winning novel based on the author's own experiences in backwoods Florida. However, it does have some sensitivity issues, listed below.

Sensitive Issues
The Yearling describes the killing of animals, which may not be appropriate for some students. You may wish to use caution when assigning this book to readers for whom violence to animals is a personally sensitive issue. However, this book may also provide excellent discussion opportunities about the realities of animal death and the laws of nature.

Literature Study Guides

Literature study guides are available for *The Call of the Wild, Where the Lilies Bloom,* and *The Yearling.* The guides include section summaries, discussion questions, and activities.

437

Planning Instruction and Assessment

Unit Objectives

1. To read nonfiction selections
2. To apply a variety of reading strategies, particularly strategies for reading nonfiction, appropriate for reading these selections
3. To recognize literary elements used in these selections
4. To increase vocabulary
5. To learn elements of grammar and usage
6. To write in a variety of modes about situations based on the selections
7. To develop speaking and listening skills, by completing activities
8. To view images critically and create visual representations

Meeting the Objectives Each selection provides instructional material and portfolio opportunities by which students can meet unit objectives. You will find additional practice pages for reading strategies, literary elements, vocabulary, and grammar in the **Selection Support** booklet in the **Teaching Resources** box.

Setting Goals Work with your students at the beginning of the unit to set goals for unit outcomes. Plan what skills and concepts you wish students to acquire. You may match instruction and activities according to students' performance levels or learning modalities.

Portfolios Students may keep portfolios of their completed work or of their work in progress. The Build Your Portfolio page of each selection provides opportunities for students to apply the concepts presented.

 Humanities: Art

Les Mémoires d'un saint (The Memories of a Saint), 1950, by René Magritte

René Magritte (1898–1967) was one of the leading Surrealist painters of the twentieth century. Born in Belgium, Magritte studied at the Academy of Fine Arts in Brussels. He lived briefly in Paris from 1927 to 1930, where he met the French surrealists.

What is extraordinary about the painting? Students may say that the curtain seems to be freestanding and rather than opening onto a stage it opens onto an outdoor scene.

Les Memoires d'un saint, (The Memories of a Saint), 1960, René Magritte, The Menil Collection

Art Transparencies
The **Art Transparencies** booklet in the **Teaching Resources** box offers fine art to help students make connections to other curriculum areas and high-interest topics.

Beyond Literature
Each unit presents Beyond Literature features that lead students into an exploration of careers, communities, and other subject areas. In this unit, students will make science and social studies connections. In addition, the **Teaching Resources** box contains a **Beyond Literature** booklet of activities. Using literature as a springboard, these activity pages offer students opportunities to connect literature to other curriculum areas and to the workplace and careers, community, media, and humanities.

Extraordinary Occurrences

Life is full of surprises, big and small. For example, on a "typical" day, you might be surprised by the strange behavior of birds, a spooky deserted mansion, or a frightening apparition that turned out to be nothing more than headlights through a window. As you read the selections in this unit, be prepared to encounter some extraordinary occurrences of all kinds.

◆ *439*

Connections

Within this unit, you will find selections and activities that make connections beyond literature. Use these selections to connect students' understanding and appreciation of literature beyond the traditional literature and language arts curriculum.

Encourage students to connect literature to other curriculum areas. You may wish to coordinate with teachers in other curriculum areas to determine ways to team-teach and further extend instruction.

Connections to Today's World

Use these selections to guide students to recognize the relevance of literature to contemporary writings. In this unit, students will connect contemporary detectives to Sherlock Holmes by reading "Crime-Solving Procedures for the Modern Detective."

Connecting Literature to Social Studies

Each unit contains a selection that connects Literature to Social Studies. In this unit, students will read a story about the Civil War, "A Horseman in the Sky."

Assessing Student Progress

The tools that are available to measure the degree to which students meet the unit objectives are listed below.

Informal Assessment

The questions in the Guide for Responding sections are a first level of response to the concepts and skills presented with the selection. As a brief, informal measure of students' grasp of the material, these responses indicate where further instruction and practice are needed. The practice pages in the **Selection Support** booklet provide for this type of instruction and practice.

You will also find literature and reading guides in the **Alternative Assessment** booklet, which students can use for informal assessment of their individual performances.

Formal Assessment

The **Formal Assessment** booklet contains Selection Tests and Unit Tests.

Selection Tests measure comprehension and skills acquisition for each selection or group of selections.

Each Unit Test provides students with 30 multiple-choice questions and 5 essay questions designed to assess students' knowledge of the literature and skills taught in the unit.

Each Alternative Unit Test: Standardized-Test Practice provides 15 multiple-choice questions and 3 essay questions based on two new literature selections not contained in the student book. The questions on the Alternative Unit Test are designed to assess students' ability to compare and contrast selections, applying skills taught in the unit.

Alternative Assessment

For portfolio and alternative assessment, the **Alternative Assessment** booklet contains Scoring Rubrics, Assessment sheets, and Learning Modalities activities.

Scoring Rubrics provide writing modes that can be applied to Writing activities, Writing Mini-Lessons, and Writing Process Workshop lessons.

Assessment sheets for speaking and listening activities provide peer and self-assessment direction.

Learning Modalities activities appeal to different learning styles. Use these as an alternative measurement of students' growth.

OBJECTIVES

1. To read, comprehend, and interpret a vignette
2. To relate a vignette to personal experience
3. To apply strategies for reading critically
4. To analyze a vignette
5. To build vocabulary in context and learn the word root -lum-
6. To develop skill in recognizing and using direct objects
7. To write a childhood remembrance, identifying your purpose
8. To respond to the vignette through writing, speaking and listening, and projects

SKILLS INSTRUCTION

Vocabulary:
Word Roots: -lum-

Spelling:
Words With ie or ei

Grammar:
Direct Objects

Reading for Success:
Strategies for Reading Critically

Literary Focus:
Vignette

Writing:
Identify Your Purpose

Speaking and Listening:
Role Play
(Teacher Edition)

Viewing and Representing:
Research Report
(Teacher Edition)

Critical Viewing:
Interpret; Relate

PORTFOLIO OPPORTUNITIES

Writing: Annotated List; Letter; Summary

Writing Mini-Lesson: Childhood Remembrance

Speaking and Listening: Oral Interpretation; Role Play

Projects: Diagram and Caption; Research Report

More About the Author
Annie Dillard advises young people who want to be writers to develop their own prose style because whatever one writes becomes their own. Dillard admits that writing can be hard work—you have to keep trying and find out later whether you've reached a dead end or found a subject that can be real to you. She has been successful in her own writing efforts. Her first book, *Pilgrim at Tinker Creek,* won the Pulitzer Prize in 1974.

Guide for Reading

Meet the Author:

Annie Dillard (1945–   )

An intense, creative writer, Annie Dillard spends as many as sixteen hours a day choosing and refining her words. Inspired partly by Henry David Thoreau's *Life on Walden Pond,* she spent four seasons living in a remote area. There, she kept a journal in which she recorded her observations of nature and humanity. She edited the journal material to create *Pilgrim at Tinker Creek,* which won the 1974 Pulitzer Prize for general nonfiction.

Early Fame Dillard was not always comfortable with the attention gained by winning this prestigious prize at the age of twenty-nine. Somewhat suspicious of the literary world and its influences, she moved to a small, isolated island in Puget Sound. Later, she relocated to Connecticut, where she is currently a professor and writer in residence at Wesleyan University. She also tours the country as a speaker and reader.

THE STORY BEHIND THE STORY

"Lights in the Night" is from *An American Childhood,* Dillard's memoir about growing up. In it, she describes how her parents fostered her eagerness to explore the world. She also discusses the importance of books in her early life, emphasizing the relationship between reading and life.

◆ **LITERATURE AND YOUR LIFE**

CONNECT YOUR EXPERIENCE

A shadowy figure in the back of the closet, an odd noise coming from downstairs, a feeling that you're being watched—these are all common experiences, especially in childhood, when you're most impressionable. Annie Dillard, a celebrated author, shares an eerie childhood episode in "Lights in the Night," a passage from *An American Childhood.*

THEMATIC FOCUS: Extraordinary Occurrences

As you read this true account, look for an ordinary explanation behind what appears to be an extraordinary occurrence.

◆ **Background for Understanding**

SCIENCE

In "Lights in the Night," Annie Dillard tells of the mysterious appearance of moving lights in her childhood bedroom at night.

Light has unique properties. It is a form of electromagnetic radiation, and it travels in waves. Light waves are affected by objects. Some objects block light. For example, when you are outside in sunlight, your body blocks the light waves from the sun and creates a shadow. Some objects, such as a mirror, reflect, or bounce, rays of light in another direction. Other objects refract, or bend, light waves. For example, a prism bends light waves and creates a rainbow of color.

 Prentice Hall Literature Program Resources

REINFORCE / RETEACH / EXTEND
Selection Support Pages
Build Vocabulary: Word Roots: -lum-, p. 168
Build Spelling Skills, p. 169
Build Grammar Skills: Direct Objects, p. 170
Reading for Success: Strategies for Reading Critically, pp. 171–172
Literary Focus: Vignette, p. 173
Strategies for Diverse Student Needs, pp. 63–64

Beyond Literature Cultural Connection: Shadow Puppets, p. 32
Formal Assessment Selection Test, pp. 134–136
Alternative Assessment, p. 32
Resource Pro CD-ROM "Lights in the Night"—includes all resource material and customizable lesson plan

🎧 **Listening to Literature Audiocassettes** "Lights in the Night"

◆ Lights in the Night ◆

◆ Literary Focus

VIGNETTE

Writers sometimes describe carefully observed events in their lives in vignettes. A **vignette** is a sketch or brief narrative of a memorable scene. You might think of a vignette as a close-up inspection of an event or feeling. It contains enough details to provide you with a complete understanding and vivid feeling for the incident being described. In "Lights in the Night," look for details and insights that characterize the piece as a vignette.

◆ Build Vocabulary

WORD ROOTS: -lum-

English words that come from the Latin root -lum- include the meaning "light." Something that is *luminous* reflects or produces a steady, glowing light.

WORD BANK

Look over these words from the selection. Which word might mean "long and narrow"? How did you guess? Check the Build Vocabulary box on page 446 to see if you chose correctly.

| luminous |
| ascent |
| membrane |
| contiguous |
| conceivably |
| coincidental |
| elongate |

Guide for Reading ◆ 441

◆ Build Grammar Skills

Direct Objects If you wish to introduce the grammar concept for this selection before students read, refer to the instruction on p. 447.

Customize for
Less Proficient Readers

Students may have difficulty following the detailed description of the mysterious light. Have them work in groups to discuss how they think the light is moving around the room. Some students may want to draw pictures; others may understand best by walking through the light's path in a room. Let each group report to the class, and see if the class can reach a consensus.

Customize for
More Advanced Students

Invite students to make their own studies of a natural phenomenon they have observed. They might explore the way the sun is in different parts of the sky in different seasons or why the moon rises at a different time each night (or day). Have them write what they have observed and explain the process they went through to discover the reason behind the phenomenon. Let them know they can model their writing on "Light in the Night."

Preparing for Standardized Tests

Reading Evaluating the author's message is one of the strategies for reading critically in this unit. Standardized tests may include passages for students to read and determine the author's main point or idea. The test format requires students to evaluate all possible answers in order to identify the one best answer.

Have students read the first paragraph of the vignette on p. 443. Then write the following question on the board:

Which is the best statement of the main idea in this paragraph?

(A) Annie Dillard grew up in Pittsburgh in the 1950's.
(B) Annie Dillard hated to go to bed when she was five years old.
(C) Annie Dillard's life was threatened.
(D) Annie Dillard did not want to go to bed because she was afraid of something.

Guide students to evaluate the author's message and see that although (C) summarizes the last two sentences of the paragraph, (D) is the best answer to the question because it states the overall message of the paragraph.

The Reading for Success page in each unit presents a set of problem-solving strategies to help readers understand authors' words and ideas on multiple levels. Good readers develop a bank of strategies from which they can draw as needed.

Unit 5 introduces strategies for reading critically. Students must examine and question the author's ideas, statements, and message. Strategies for reading critically help readers evaluate information the author includes as support and form judgments about the content and quality of the work.

These strategies for reading critically are modeled with "Lights in the Night." Each green box shows an example of the thinking process involved in applying one of these strategies. Additional notes provide support for applying these strategies throughout the selection.

How to Use the Reading for Success Page

- Introduce the strategies for reading critically, presenting each as a problem-solving procedure.

- Before students read the vignette, have them preview it, looking at the annotations in the green boxes that model the strategies.

- To reinforce these strategies after students have read the story, have them do the Reading for Success, pp. 171–172, in **Selection Support.** These pages give students an opportunity to read a selection and practice critical reading strategies by writing their own annotations.

Reading Strategies: Support and Reinforcement

Using Boxed Annotations and Prompts

Throughout the unit, the notes in green, red, and maroon boxes are intended to help students apply reading strategies, understand the literary focus, and make a connection with their lives. You may use boxed material in these ways:

- Have students pause at each box and respond to its prompt before they continue reading.

- Urge students to read through the selection, ignoring the boxes. After they complete the selection, they may go back and review the text, responding to the prompts.

Reading for Success

Strategies for Reading Critically

Whenever you read a work that contains an author's ideas or opinions, it is wise to read the work critically. When you read critically, you examine and question the author's ideas, statements, and message. You also evaluate information the author includes as support and form a judgment about the content and quality of the work. Use the following strategies to help you read critically:

Recognize the author's purpose.

An author's purpose is his or her reason for writing. An author's purpose may be obvious; for instance, a how-to essay is probably written to teach. Sometimes, however, an author's purpose is more subtle; for example, a how-to essay might also try to persuade you to buy a certain product.

Make inferences.

To make an inference, you use details from a literary work to arrive at a conclusion. In other words, you make an educated guess about characters, events, or an author's message, based on the details given.

> **Detail:** All night long she slept smoothly in a series of pleasant and serene, if artificial-looking, positions . . .
>
> **Inference:** The author is slightly jealous of her baby sister.

Understand the author's bias.

Bias is a strong feeling for or against something. An author's experience and background may sometimes bias his or her writing. For example, the attitude toward war of a victim of war will almost certainly differ from a career soldier's attitude toward war.

Evaluate the author's message.

An author's message is the main point or idea that he or she wants to convey to the reader. Evaluating involves making a critical judgment. Evaluate or judge the author's message according to how well it's presented and supported. You may also evaluate its originality and timeliness.

As you read "Lights in the Night," look at the notes and ideas in the boxes. The notes demonstrate how to apply these strategies to a work of literature.

Model a Reading Strategy: Recognize the Author's Purpose

Good readers read critically to try to understand the author's reason for writing a certain work. Demonstrate how to recognize the author's purpose in the first two paragraphs of the vignette by modeling your thinking for students.

> The author tells us that this thing would "kill" her if she told anyone about it, so she keeps it private. I remember that feeling as a child, believing I could not speak about something. I know that a fear like that is

very important to a child, but it actually is not life threatening. The author describes lying in the dark being too afraid to breathe.

Again, I remember that feeling of being afraid of something in the dark and holding my breath. I think the author is reminding us how serious a fear can be to a child, and insisting that we don't take it lightly. Since I know about these fears, I can understand why the author describes them so vividly—they must be important to her message.

Lights in the Night

from An American Childhood
Annie Dillard

When I was five, growing up in Pittsburgh in 1950, I would not go to bed willingly because something came into my room. This was a private matter between me and it. If I spoke of it, it would kill me.

Who could breathe as this thing searched for me over the very corners of the room? Who could ever breathe freely again? I lay in the dark.

1 My sister Amy, two years old, was asleep in the other bed. What did she know? She was innocent of evil. Even at two she composed herself attractively for sleep. She folded the top sheet tidily under her prettily outstretched arm; she laid her perfect head

▲ **Critical Viewing** Which word best describes this photograph of lights in the night: threatening, comforting, or useful? Explain. **[Interpret]** **2**

lightly on an unwrinkled pillow, where her thick curls spread evenly in rays like petals. All night long she slept smoothly in a series of pleasant and serene, if artificial-looking, positions, a faint smile on her closed lips, as if she were posing for an ad for sheets. There was no messiness in her, no roughness for things to cling to, only a charming and charmed innocence that seemed then to protect her, an innocence I needed but couldn't muster. Since Amy was asleep, furthermore,

Lights in the Night ◆ 443

Develop Understanding

One-Minute Insight

In "Lights in the Night," Annie Dillard tells of a childhood experience that scares her each night: a streetlight reflecting off a passing car's windshield flashes through her bedroom. She thinks it is a presence that will harm her if it reaches her. Dillard describes how she figures out the light is caused by a car and makes the startling realization that the inside world and the outside world are connected.

Team Teaching Strategy

The movement pattern of the reflected light offers a strong connection to physics and the study of light. You may want to coordinate with a science teacher to plan ways to extend instruction.

Reading for Success

1 Make Inferences What does the author imply by saying that her sister is "innocent of evil"? *The narrator believes the thing that comes into her room is evil, and wishes she, too, could be innocent.*

▶Critical Viewing◀

2 Interpret *Some students may find the lights threatening, since the viewer is level with the cars. Others may say the lights are comforting, as night is falling; still others may say they are useful, allowing the drivers to see one another.*

Customize for
English Language Learners
Students may find it easier to follow Dillard's descriptions if they read the vignette while listening to the audiocassette. As they listen, encourage them to visualize the descriptions of the sleeping little sister, the path of the light, and the narrator's walk "in her mind" from her room to the outside of her house.

🎧 **Listening to Literature Audiocassettes**

Block Scheduling Strategies

Consider these suggestions to take advantage of extended class time:
- Have students work with partners and tell each other childhood memories. By telling their stories out loud, they may discover the subject they want to write about.
- Have students present their Oral Interpretations from the Speaking and Listening activity on p. 448.

Encourage the audience members to evaluate the interpretation.
- Have students use the *Writer's Solution Writing Lab CD-ROM* to complete all or part of the Writing Mini-Lesson.
- To reinforce the critical reading strategies, have students complete the Reading for Success pages in **Selection Support,** pp. 171–172.

and since when I needed someone most I was afraid to stir enough to wake her, she was useless.

❶ I lay alone and was almost asleep when the thing entered the room by flattening itself against the open door and sliding in. It was a transparent, <u>luminous</u> oblong. I could see the door whiten at its touch; I could see the blue wall turn pale where it raced over it, and see the maple headboard of Amy's bed glow. It was a swift spirit; it was an awareness. It made noise. It had two joined parts, a head and a tail, like a Chinese dragon. It found the door, wall, and headboard; and it swiped them, charging them with its luminous glance. After its fleet, searching passage, things looked the same, but weren't.

❷ I dared not blink or breathe; I tried to hush my whooping blood. If it found another awareness, it would destroy it.

> The author's purpose may be to keep the reader in suspense.

Every night before it got to me it gave up. It hit my wall's corner and couldn't get past. It shrank completely into itself and vanished like a cobra down a hole. I heard the rising roar it made when it died or left. I still couldn't breathe. I knew—it was the worst fact I knew, a very hard fact—that it could return again alive that same night.

Sometimes it came back, sometimes it didn't. Most often, restless, it came back. The light stripe slipped in the door, ran searching over Amy's wall, stopped, stretched lunatic at the first corner, raced wailing toward my wall, and vanished into the second corner with a cry. So I wouldn't go to bed.

❸ It was a passing car whose windshield reflected the corner streetlight outside. I figured it out one night.

Figuring it out was as memorable as the oblong itself. Figuring it out was a long and forced <u>ascent</u> to the very rim of being, to the <u>membrane</u> of skin that both separates and connects the inner life and the

> Here, you can **infer** that the author enjoys intellectual activity.

▶ **Critical Viewing** Why might a light like this, casting shadows in a room at night, have caused the narrator anxiety? [Relate] ❹

outer world. I climbed deliberately from the depths like a diver who releases the monster in his arms and hauls himself hand over hand up an anchor chain till he meets the ocean's sparkling membrane and bursts through it; he sights the sunlit, becalmed hull of his boat, which had bulked so ominously from below.

I recognized the noise it made when it left. That is, the noise it made called to mind, at last, my daytime sensations when a car passed—the sight and noise together. A car came roaring down hushed Edgerton Avenue in front of our house, stopped at the corner stop sign, and passed on shrieking as its engine shifted up the gears. What, precisely, came into the bedroom? A reflection from the car's oblong windshield. Why did it travel in two parts? The window sash split the light and cast a shadow.

❺ Night after night I labored up the same long chain of reasoning, as night after night the thing burst into the room where I lay awake and Amy slept prettily and my loud heart thrashed and I froze.

There was a world outside my window and <u>contiguous</u> to it. If I was so all-fired bright, as my parents, who had patently no basis for comparison, seemed to think, why did I have to keep learning this same thing over and over? For I had learned it a summer ago, when men with jackhammers broke up Edgerton Avenue. I had watched them from the yard; the street came up in jagged slabs like floes. When I lay to nap, I listened. One restless afternoon I connected the new noise in my

◆ Build Vocabulary

luminous (loo′ mə nəs) *adj.*: Giving off light; shining; bright

ascent (ə sent′) *n.*: The act of rising or climbing

membrane (mem′ brān) *n.*: A thin, soft sheet or layer serving as a covering

contiguous (kən tig′ yoo əs) *adj.*: In physical contact; near or next to

444 ◆ *Extraordinary Occurrences*

Speaking and Listening Mini-Lesson

Role Play
This mini-lesson supports the Speaking and Listening activity in the Idea Bank, p. 448.

Introduce Students can work in groups of three to role-play the girl telling her parents why she doesn't want to go to bed. Discuss with students that role-playing this scene can help them understand the narrator's feelings.

Develop Students in each group choose their roles and work together to write a script for the scene. Encourage them to refer to the vignette

to learn about the character of the child and the parents. They should try to make the scene as realistic as possible.

Apply Have the groups practice their scenes, then present them to the class.

Assessment Evaluate students in terms of the script, their speaking, and their connection with their characters. Or, have student audience members use the Peer Assessment: Dramatic Performance form, p. 116 in **Alternative Assessment.**

Customize for
Logical/Mathematical Learners

Students can create a step-by-step diagram, to trace the author's realization that the light comes from a car. They might start with the following example, then continue with her realization about the connection between indoors and outdoors.

She hears the sound the light makes.	→	She connects the noise with the sound of a car.
(indoors)	→	(outdoors)
	→	

Customize for
Bodily/Kinesthetic Learners

Students can work in pairs or small groups to create a pantomime or dance of the narrator's experience. Encourage students to be creative in their approach. For example, one student could act out the child's reaction when the light enters the room, while another student acts out the movement of the light itself. The person acting as the light could assume a terrifying presence. A third student could provide narration, perhaps describing the scene from the girl's point of view.

Customize for
Visual/Spatial Learners

Have students study the photograph and let their imaginations take flight. Ask them to visualize the room the door opens into, and then the room on the other side of the door. What does the house look like? Encourage students to describe the door and its surroundings in writing, by drawing or painting, or by making a model.

Viewing and Representing Mini-Lesson

Research Report

Introduce This mini-lesson supports the Project activity in the Idea Bank on p. 448.

Develop Tell students that they will be researching scientific information about light. Let them know that they will need to read material and explain what they've learned to an audience of non-scientists. Suggest that they decide on ways to share the research and reporting.

Apply Suggest to groups that they research one of these topics:

- reflection and refraction
- lasers
- the speed of light and the effect of black holes on light in space

Encourage students to create diagrams or illustrations showing properties of light.

Assess Have each group present its report. Evaluate students on their group work, preparation, and presentations. Invite other students to express whether the material was presented in a clear and understandable fashion.

Reading for Success

❶ Recognize the Author's Purpose How does this paragraph sum up the author's purpose in writing this vignette? *The narrator comes to the conclusion that she is not the center of the world, based on what she's learned about the connection between the inside and outside worlds. She realizes her fear comes from her feelings, not from the light itself, and that she may be able to control her feelings to some extent.*

◆ Literary Focus

❷ Vignette How does this paragraph illustrate the importance of this event in the author's life? *Figuring out the cause of the light is as important to her as the feeling of fear. In this paragraph she combines the two feelings.*

Reinforce and Extend

Answers

◆ LITERATURE AND YOUR LIFE

Reader's Response Students may admit that they had similar fears, so they can understand Dillard's fear.

Thematic Focus She describes its effects from a child's point of view.

☑ **Check Your Comprehension**

1. She saw a mysterious oblong of light that traveled across her room.
2. She was frightened of the light and afraid to tell anyone about it.
3. The light was reflected by the windshields of passing cars.

◆ Critical Thinking

1. Amy is only two and is unaware of the fear that Dillard attaches to the light. She is too "innocent" to be afraid.
2. She believes the "thing" will kill her if she tells anyone about it. In her fear, she believes the mysterious light is evil.
3. She realizes that she is not the center of the world. The events of the world are not all related directly to her and her life.
4. She teases herself with the fear, knowing she can stop it. Once she knows the source of the light, she can enjoy the fear.
5. Students may say that childhood events can have a big impact on a person's life.

---

bedroom with the jack-hammer men I had been seeing outside. I understood abruptly that these worlds met, the outside and the inside. I traveled the route in my mind: You walked downstairs from here, and outside from downstairs. "Outside," then, was <u>conceivably</u> just beyond my windows. It was the same world I reached by going out the front or the back door. I forced my imagination yet again over this route.

The world did not have me in mind; it had no mind. It was a <u>coincidental</u> collection of things and people, of items, and I myself was one such item—a child walking up the sidewalk, whom anyone could see or ignore. The things in the world did not necessarily cause my overwhelming feelings; the feelings were inside me, beneath my skin, behind my ribs, within my skull. They were even, to some extent, under my control.

I could be connected to the outer world by reason, if I chose, or I could yield to what

amounted to a narrative fiction, to a tale of terror whispered to me by the blood in my ears, a show in light projected on the room's blue walls. As time passed, I learned to amuse myself in bed in the darkened room by entering the fiction deliberately and replacing it by reason deliberately.

When the low roar drew nigh and the oblong slid in the door, I threw my own switches for pleasure. It's coming after me; it's a car outside. It's after me. It's a car. It raced over the wall, lighting it blue wherever it ran; it bumped over Amy's maple headboard in a rush, paused, slithered <u>elongate</u> over the corner, shrank, flew my way, and vanished into itself with a wail. It was a car.

◆ Build Vocabulary

conceivably (kən sē′ və blē) *adv.*: Possibly

coincidental (kō in′ sə dent′ əl) *adj.*: Occurring at the same time or place

elongate (i lôn′ gāt) *adj.*: Long and narrow

Guide for Responding

◆ LITERATURE AND YOUR LIFE

Reader's Response Do you find Dillard's childhood fears understandable? Explain.

Thematic Focus How does Dillard make the ordinary event of a car passing in the street seem extraordinary?

Journal Writing Write a journal entry that Dillard might have written when she first saw the mysterious lights in the night.

☑ **Check Your Comprehension**

1. What did Dillard see in her room each night when she was five?
2. How did she feel about the event?
3. What did she finally figure out was the source of the event?

◆ Critical Thinking

INTERPRET

1. Why doesn't Dillard's sister, Amy, react to the event in the same way? **[Compare and Contrast]**
2. Why doesn't Dillard confide her fears to her parents? **[Draw Conclusions]**
3. What realization does Dillard come to after understanding the source of the mystery? **[Analyze]**
4. After she figures out the mystery, Dillard sometimes pretends that she does not know the solution. Why? **[Infer]**

EXTEND

5. Why do many writers draw on childhood experiences? Explain. **[Career Link]**

446 ◆ *Extraordinary Occurrences*

 Beyond the Selection

FURTHER READING
Other Nonfiction Works by Annie Dillard
Teaching a Stone to Talk
The Living
Living by Fiction
The Writing Life
Poetry by Annie Dillard
Mornings Like This: Found Poems
Tickets for a Prayer Wheel

INTERNET
For more information on Annie Dillard visit the following sites on the Internet (all Web sites are subject to change):
http://www.yale.edu/herald/archive/xxii/10.4.96/ae/dillard.html
http://www.english.upenn.edu/~afilreis/88/dillard.html
http://www.amherst.edu/~makligma/ee.html
We *strongly recommend* that you preview these sites before you send students to them.

Guide for Responding (continued)

◆ Reading for Success

STRATEGIES FOR READING CRITICALLY

Review the strategies and the notes showing how to read critically. Then, answer the following questions:

1. (a) What is one inference you made about the author's personality? (b) Give details from the story to support your inference.
2. (a) What is Dillard's purpose in writing "Lights in the Night"? (b) How do you know?
3. (a) What details from the story led you to identify the author's message? (b) Give your evaluation of the message.

◆ Build Vocabulary

USING THE WORD ROOT -lum-

The word root -lum- in luminous comes from a Latin word meaning "light." You will find -lum- in the words that follow. Predict the meaning of each word. Then, use a dictionary to check your definitions.

1. luminescence   2. illuminate   3. luminary

SPELLING STRATEGY

When deciding whether to spell the long e sound ie or ei in a word like conceivable, remember this helpful rule: Use i before e except after c.

Find the spelling error or errors in each sentence, and rewrite the sentences correctly on your paper.

1. The child was deceived by the fictional feind.
2. She will receive a peice of cake.
3. She perceived a feild of roses in her dream.

USING THE WORD BANK

Decide how each word pair is related. On your paper, write synonyms for words similar in meaning and antonyms for words having opposite meanings.

1. luminous, dark
2. ascent, rise
3. membrane, layer
4. contiguous, separated
5. conceivably, impossibly
6. coincidental, intentional
7. elongate, narrow

◆ Literary Focus

VIGNETTE

Annie Dillard describes a vivid childhood memory in a short **vignette,** a sketch or brief narrative of a memorable scene. She carefully chooses words and images that bring the episode to life for the reader.

1. How does the opening line of Dillard's story grab a reader's interest?
2. Describe three details Dillard uses to describe the nightly event.
3. What does Dillard find most memorable about this event from her childhood?

◆ Build Grammar Skills

DIRECT OBJECTS

A **direct object** is a noun or a pronoun that receives the action of a verb. You can determine if a word is a direct object by asking whom or what following an action verb. For example, in this sentence, the direct object answers the question: "She heard what?"

I heard the rising *roar* it made when it died or left.

In the following example, the direct objects answer the questions "Split what?" and "Cast what?"

The window sash split the *light* and cast a *shadow.*

Practice Write these passages on your paper, and underline the direct object(s) in each.

1. She folded the top sheet tidily. . . .
2. She laid her perfect head lightly on an unwrinkled pillow. . . .
3. It found the door, wall, and headboard; . . .
4. It hit my wall's corner and couldn't get past.
5. I traveled the route in my mind: . . .

Writing Application On your paper, write sentences according to the following directions.

1. Write a sentence about light containing the direct object *wall.*
2. Write a sentence about Dillard containing the direct object *book.*

Lights in the Night ◆ 447

Idea Bank

Following are suggestions for matching the Idea Bank topics with your students' performance levels and learning modalities:

Customize for
Performance Levels
Less Advanced Students: 1, 5
Average Students: 3, 4, 5, 6, 7
More Advanced Students: 2, 4, 5, 6, 7

Customize for
Learning Modalities
Verbal/Linguistic: 1, 2, 3, 4, 6, 7
Logical/Mathematical: 7
Visual/Spatial: 6
Bodily/Kinesthetic: 5
Interpersonal: 5, 7
Intrapersonal: 1, 6

Writing Mini-Lesson

Refer students to the Writing Handbook at the back of the book for instruction on the writing process and for further information on identifying your purpose.

Writer's Solution

Writers at Work Videodisc
To help students prepare to write their remembrances, play the segment in which Rosie McNulty speaks about her method for reenvisioning a past experience as she sits at her desk to begin work.

Play frames 29643 to 30695

Writing Lab CD-ROM
Have students complete the tutorial on Description. Follow these steps:
1. Have students use the Annotated Models of Description to learn more about remembrances.
2. Students can use the Narrowing Your Topic section to evaluate whether or not their topics are narrow enough.
3. Have students draft on computer.
4. Students can use the audio tips on Peer Revision to learn about approaches to peer revision.

Writer's Solution Sourcebook
Have students use Chapter 2, "Description," pp. 32–69, for additional support. This chapter includes instruction on writing remembrances.

Build Your Portfolio

Idea Bank

Writing

1. **Annotated List** Write a list of at least three common childhood fears, and describe how you might help a child overcome each of the fears.

2. **Letter** Imagine that you are Annie Dillard. Write a letter to your best friend, in which you describe the night you finally figured out the source of the mysterious light.

3. **Summary** Write a short summary of this story that might appear on the back of the book's jacket. Grab the interest of the reader without giving away too much of the story.

Speaking and Listening

4. **Oral Interpretation** Read the final two paragraphs of "Lights in the Night" aloud. Use your voice to project the excitement Dillard feels when she pretends that the light is a mysterious force. Indicate the feelings of tension and release by varying your tone and pitch.

5. **Role Play [Group Activity]** With two classmates, re-create a scene in which five-year-old Annie tells her parents about her fears. Show how her parents react to the frightened child's news. **[Performing Arts Link]**

Projects

6. **Diagram and Caption** Create a diagram or series of diagrams showing how reflected light created the illusion in Annie Dillard's bedroom. Write a detailed caption explaining the path of the light and the resulting image. **[Science Link]**

7. **Research Report [Group Activity]** With a group of classmates, find out more about the qualities of light. Write a report that includes charts and illustrations to show light's various properties. You may also want to research and report on the speed at which light travels. **[Science Link]**

Writing Mini-Lesson

Childhood Remembrance

Your own childhood is a rich source of inspiration for writing. Almost any memory can become the subject of an interesting story—so long as it interests you to begin with. When you choose a particularly vivid memory, your enthusiasm will come through in your writing. Write a short remembrance explaining why a childhood memory is important to you.

Writing Skills Focus:
Identify Your Purpose

Before you begin writing, **identify the purpose** of your remembrance. How do you want your audience to feel? Do you want them to laugh or to cry? Your purpose will guide your choice of details and words. Notice how Dillard amuses the reader with her re-creation of a child's overly serious attitude.

Model From the Story
This was a private matter between me and it. If I spoke of it, it would kill me.

Prewriting Make a list of memories, and choose the memory that interests you most. Then, use a cluster diagram to generate details and words for your remembrance. Decide on your purpose for writing, and select details that will help you achieve your purpose.

Drafting Put yourself in the time and place of the memory, and begin drafting.

Revising Read your remembrance aloud to a partner, and ask for feedback. Does your partner recognize your purpose? Incorporate changes that will help you to achieve your goal.

◆ **Grammar Application**
In your draft, circle each direct object and underline the verb it completes.

✓ ASSESSMENT OPTIONS

Formal Assessment, Selection Test, pp. 134–136, and Assessment Resources Software. The selection test is designed so that it can easily be customized to the performance levels of your students.
Alternative Assessment, p. 32, includes options for less advanced students, more advanced students, verbal/linguistic learners, musical/rhythmic learners, interpersonal learners, and visual/spatial learners.

PORTFOLIO ASSESSMENT
Use the following rubrics in the **Alternative Assessment** booklet to assess student writing:
Annotated List: How-to/Process Explanation, p. 100
Letter: Description, p. 93
Summary: Summary, p. 94
Writing Mini-Lesson: Narrative Based on Personal Experience, p. 92

PART **1**

The Extraordinary in the Ordinary

Spring, ©1922, Georgia O'Keeffe, Frances Lehman Loeb Art Center, Vassar College, Poughkeepsie, New York

The Extraordinary in the Ordinary ◆ 449

 Humanities: Art

Spring, 1922, by Georgia O'Keeffe
Georgia O'Keeffe (1887–1986) is one of America's best known female painters. Her subject matters are taken from nature: flowers, rocks, bones, clouds. She was influenced by Expressionism, but her art shows an abstraction of the forms of nature, often by using close-up or unusual viewpoints.

Born in Wisconsin, O'Keeffe grew up painting watercolors as a child. She studied at both the Art Institute of Chicago and the Art Students

League in New York City, where she painted her first landscapes of the East River.
1. Do the colors of the painting strike you as ordinary or extraordinary? Why? *Students will probably note the intensity of the colors and tend to classify them as extraordinary.*
2. Is a spring day ordinary or extraordinary? Explain your answer. *Most students will respond that the warmth, light, and colors of spring feel extraordinary after winter.*

The selections in this section focus on the theme of the extraordinary in the ordinary. "What Stumped the Blue Jays" is a classic Mark Twain tale about a blue jay and a mysterious hole he encounters. "Why Leaves Turn Color in the Fall" is a detailed observation and scientific explanation for the leaves changing colors in autumn. "Southbound on the Freeway" examines how an alien might view a traffic jam on the highway. "The Story-Teller" is a short poem about the power of stories and the imagination. "Los New Yorks" describes the scenery of New York with images of a tropical paradise. In "The Adventure of the Speckled Band," readers will accompany Sherlock Holmes as he solves a murder mystery.

Customize for
Varying Student Needs
When assigning the selections in this section to your students, keep in mind the following factors:

"What Stumped the Blue Jays"
• Mark Twain story
• Students may need help with language
• Includes a Beyond Literature Science Connection

"Why Leaves Turn Color in the Fall"
• A observational essay about leaves changing in autumn
• Students may need help with scientific vocabulary

"Southbound on the Freeway"
• Short poem which introduces students to the theme of technology and how it advances and hinders society

"The Story-Teller"
• Short, rhyming poem

"Los New Yorks"
• Students may need help with Spanish words in the poem
• Includes a Beyond Literature Social Studies Connection

"The Adventure of the Speckled Band"
• A longer selection (18 pp.)
• A classic mystery story by Sir Arthur Conan Doyle

449

Guide for Reading

OBJECTIVES

1. To read, comprehend, and interpret a story and an essay

2. To relate a story and an essay to personal experience

3. To recognize the author's purpose in a story or an essay

4. To recognize and analyze the use of observation in a literary work

5. To build vocabulary in context and learn the word root -grat-

6. To develop skill in using indirect objects

7. To write an observational essay using details and tone to appeal to your audience

8. To respond to the story and essay through writing, speaking and listening, and projects

SKILLS INSTRUCTION

Vocabulary:
Word Roots: -grat-

Spelling:
Words Ending With ar

Grammar:
Indirect Objects

Reading Strategy:
Recognize the Author's Purpose

Literary Focus:
Observation

Writing:
Writing to the Audience

Speaking and Listening:
Oral Interpretation (Teacher Edition)

Viewing and Representing:
Local Trees (Teacher Edition)

Critical Viewing:
Draw Conclusions; Compare and Contrast; Connect

PORTFOLIO OPPORTUNITIES

Writing: Descriptive Letter; Editor's Foreword; Science Magazine

Writing Mini-Lesson: Observational Essay

Speaking and Listening: Oral Interpretation; Author's Chat

Projects: Research; Botanical Drawing

More About the Authors
Mark Twain, born Samuel Langhorne Clemens, left school at the age of twelve to go to work. He piloted a steamboat on the Mississippi River, prospected for gold in California, and was briefly a soldier during the Civil War. He took his pen name from an expression used by pilots to note safe places for boats in the river.

Diane Ackerman has traveled widely to observe the subjects of her writing, such as icebergs in Antarctica, bats in Mexico, and whales off of Maui.

Meet the Authors:

Mark Twain (1835–1910)

Mark Twain wrote books that have become American classics, such as *The Adventures of Tom Sawyer* and *The Adventures of Huckle-berry Finn.* Many of Twain's short stories and yarns are prized for his humorous, sometimes outrageous, style.

A Frequent Traveler
Although Twain was born near Hannibal, Missouri, and is most often associated with his books that center on the Mississippi River, his days as a reporter took him all across the country. "What Stumped the Blue Jays" combines Twain's humor with one of his favorite settings—the West. [For more on Mark Twain, see page 106.]

Diane Ackerman (1948–   )

A native of Waukegan, Illinois, nature writer Diane Ackerman studied psychology, physiology, and English in college, eventually earning two master's degrees and a Ph.D. at Cornell University. She has published five books of poems and five books of nonfiction, including *A Natural History of the Senses.* Her literary skills and scientific training enable her to describe the natural world in a captivating way.

450 ◆ *Extraordinary Occurrences*

◆ LITERATURE AND YOUR LIFE

CONNECT YOUR EXPERIENCE

Observing the natural world can be a source of pleasure and, often, surprise. Even if you don't think of yourself as a nature-lover, you have probably observed remarkable things in nature, such as birds migrating or mosquitoes swarming on a summer night. In the following selections, you'll read about two of nature's wonders—blues jays and the color changes of leaves in the fall.

THEMATIC FOCUS: The Extraordinary in the Ordinary

Which fascinates you more—the behavior of blue jays or the seasonal changes that autumn brings?

◆ Background for Understanding

SCIENCE

With their blue-gray crests and large size (about a foot long), blue jays are easy to spot. Their diet consists largely of nuts and seeds, although they sometimes steal eggs from other birds' nests. They are also easy to hear. Their voices are loud and harsh, like those of their relatives the crows and the magpies. Some people describe the sound blue jays make as a shriek.

◆ Build Vocabulary

WORD ROOTS: -grat-

The word *gratification* contains the root -grat-, which means "pleasing" or "satisfying." Knowing the meaning of -grat- will help you figure out that *gratification* is "the condition of being pleased or satisfied."

WORD BANK

Which word from the list means "single" or "unique"? Check the Build Vocabulary box on page 457 to see if you chose correctly.

gratification
countenance
singular
guffawed
macabre
camouflage
predisposed
capricious

Prentice Hall Literature Program Resources

REINFORCE / RETEACH / EXTEND
Selection Support Pages
Build Vocabulary: Word Roots: -grat-, p. 174
Build Spelling Skills, p. 175
Build Grammar Skills: Indirect Objects, p. 176
Reading Strategies: Recognize the Author's Purpose, p. 177
Literary Focus: Observation, p. 178
Strategies for Diverse Student Needs, pp. 65–66
Beyond Literature Community Connection: Community Action, p. 33
Formal Assessment Selection Test, pp. 137–139

Alternative Assessment, p. 33
Writing and Language Transparencies
Sensory Language Chart, p. 69; Series of Events Chain, p. 69
Resource Pro CD-ROM
"What Stumped the Blue Jays"; "Why Leaves Turn Color in the Fall"—includes all resource material and customizable lesson plan
Listening to Literature Audiocassettes
"What Stumped the Blue Jays"; "Why Leaves Turn Color in the Fall"

◆ What Stumped the Blue Jays ◆
Why Leaves Turn Color in the Fall

Interest Grabber Stimulate students' interest in these selections by having them record their observations of the natural world. Have students spend ten to fifteen minutes in a park, their own backyards, or another place with some element of nature present. Each student can record elements of sight, sound, smell, and touch with journal writing and sketches or by using the Sensory Language Chart in **Writing and Language Transparencies,** p. 81. (They should not complete the "taste" section of the chart.) Students may choose to observe one tree, animal, or bird, or describe the whole scene. Invite students to share with the class their observations—particularly of any unexpected occurrences—before reading the story and essay.

◆ Build Grammar Skills

Indirect Objects If you wish to introduce the grammar concept for this selection before students read, refer to the instruction on p. 462.

Customize for
Less Proficient Readers
Students may be puzzled about who is speaking in "What Stumped the Blue Jays." Tell them that this is a story within a story. The narrator begins, describing the setting and the character Jim Baker. Then Jim Baker tells the story about what the blue jays did.

Customize for
More Advanced Students
The storyteller in "What Stumped the Blue Jays" says that some animals and birds talk fluently with a large vocabulary, while others use only simple words and phrases. Have students choose pets or other animals and describe the kind of "talkers" they are, based on the animals' behavior that students observe. Students may write descriptions of how the animals talk or invent conversations between the animals.

◆ Literary Focus

OBSERVATION

An **observation** is a writer's eyewitness account of an event that he or she has studied over a period of time. The writer re-creates the event for the reader with precise details and vivid language. Ackerman's essay about why leaves turn color is an example of an observation.

◆ Reading Strategy

RECOGNIZE THE AUTHOR'S PURPOSE

An **author's purpose** is his or her reason for writing. Most authors have a broad purpose, such as to teach or to convince you of something. Sometimes, in addition to a broad purpose, an author will have a more specific purpose, such as to create suspense or to provoke laughter. As you read, use a chart like the one below to determine the author's purpose or purposes.

Details From Text	My Response	Possible Purpose
"Animals talk to each other, of course."	Silly comment	To make me laugh

Guide for Reading ◆ 451

Preparing for Standardized Tests

Vocabulary General vocabulary questions on standardized tests may evaluate students' knowledge of word roots, such as *-grat-,* which means "pleasing" or "satisfying." For example, if someone makes the statement, "The blue jay seemed *gratified* by the size and location of the knot hole," students can use their knowledge of the word root *-grat-* to understand that gratified means *pleased* or *satisfied.*

Write this sample test item on the board:

Jim Baker felt gratification at being able to understand the blue jays' speech.

In this sentence, *gratification* means—

  (A) thankfulness   (C) satisfaction
  (B) amazement   (D) confidence

Guide students to use their knowledge of the word root *-grat-* to determine that *(C) satisfaction* is the correct answer. Although the other answers could fit in the sentence, knowing that the meaning of *gratification* has to do with "satisfying" allows for correct understanding of the sentence. For more practice with the word root *-grat-,* use the Vocabulary page of **Selection Support,** p. 174.

One-Minute Insight In "What Stumped the Blue Jays," a storyteller makes the ordinary extraordinary by "translating" what some blue jays said during an event he observed. He relates the story to prove that blue jays have a highly developed command of language. The birds act surprisingly human. One blue jay thinks he has found a good hole in which to store acorns. After working hard to fill it up, he cannot see any of the acorns that should be inside the hole. Other jays join the first one, and try to figure out what is wrong with the hole. Finally an older jay discovers that the hole is in the roof of an empty log cabin, and that the first blue jay has been dropping acorns into the house. All the blue jays have a good laugh, proving they are not only articulate but have a great sense of humor.

Team Teaching Strategy

The focus on observing nature offers a strong connection to scientific observation. You may want to coordinate with a science teacher to find ways to extend instruction.

Customize for
English Language Learners

English language learners may have difficulty understanding some of the "folk" expressions that the storyteller Jim Baker uses in "What Stumped the Blue Jays." Have peer tutors help students by rephrasing or defining the terms "commonplace," "book-talk," "bristling," and other words or phrases.

Customize for
Visual/Spatial Learners

Encourage students to pay attention to details that describe the blue jays' movements on and around the cabin. Have students create a diagram showing where the birds were located at different times in the story.

Customize for
Bodily/Kinesthetic Learners

Point out this photograph and the one on p. 451, and have students look for descriptions in the story about how the blue jays move. Have students act out or pantomime the birds' movements.

452

What Stumped the BLUE JAYS

Mark Twain

452 ◆ *Extraordinary Occurrences*

Block Scheduling Strategies

Consider these suggestions to take advantage of extended class time:

• Discuss the reading strategy for these selections, which is to recognize the author's purpose. As they read, have students respond to the questions on pp. 457 and 461. Then have students complete the Reading Strategy questions on p. 462.

• After students read "What Stumped the Blue Jays," have them work with partners to prepare

the Oral Interpretation activity on p. 463. See suggestions in the Speaking and Listening Mini-Lesson on p. 454 of the Teacher's Edition.

• Prior to class, have students make notes on the subject of their observational essays for the Writing Mini-Lesson on p. 463. Allow class time for students to begin writing the first draft.

• If you have access to technology, have students work on the *Writer's Solution Writing Lab CD-ROM* to help with the Writing Mini-Lesson.

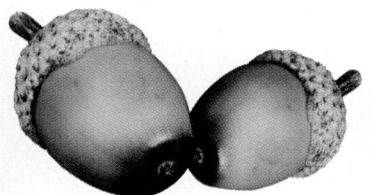

Animals talk to each other, of course. There can be no question about that; but I suppose there are very few people who can understand them. I never knew but one man who could. I knew he could, however, because he told me so himself. He was a middle-aged, simple-hearted miner who had lived in a lonely corner of California, among the woods and mountains, a good many years, and had studied the ways of his only neighbors, the beasts and the birds, until he believed he could accurately translate any remark which they made. This was Jim Baker. According to Jim Baker, some animals have only a limited education, and use only very simple words, and scarcely ever a comparison or a flowery figure; whereas, certain other animals have a large vocabulary, a fine command of language and a ready and fluent delivery; consequently these latter talk a great deal; they like it; they are conscious of their talent, and enjoy "showing off." Baker said, that after long and careful observation, he had come to the conclusion that the blue jays were the best talkers he had found among birds and beasts. Said he:—

"There's more *to* a blue jay than any other creature. He has got more moods, and more different kinds of feelings than any other creature; and mind you, whatever a blue jay feels, he can put into language. And no mere commonplace language, either, but rattling, out-and-out book-talk—and bristling with

◀ **Critical Viewing** Based on this photograph, what "personality" might a blue jay have? [Draw Conclusions]

metaphor, too—just bristling! And as for command of language—why *you* never see a blue jay get stuck for a word. No man ever did. They just boil out of him! And another thing: I've noticed a good deal, and there's no bird, or cow, or anything that uses as good grammar as a blue jay. You may say a cat uses good grammar. Well, a cat does—but you let a cat get excited once; you let a cat get to pulling fur with another cat on a shed, nights, and you'll hear grammar that will give you the lockjaw. Ignorant people think it's the *noise* which fighting cats make that is so aggravating, but it ain't so; it's the sickening grammar they use. Now I've never heard a jay use bad grammar but very seldom; and when they do, they are as ashamed as a human; they shut right down and leave.

> ◆ **Reading Strategy**
> What details in this passage indicate the author's purpose?

"When I first begun to understand jay language correctly, there was a little incident happened here. Seven years ago, the last man in this region but me, moved away. There stands his house,—been empty ever since; a log house, with a plank roof—just one big room, and no more; no ceiling—nothing between the rafters and the floor. Well, one Sunday morning I was sitting out here in front of my cabin, with my cat, taking the sun, and looking at the blue hills, and listening to the leaves rustling so lonely in the trees, and thinking of the home away yonder in the States, and I hadn't heard from in thirteen years, when a blue jay lit on that house, with an acorn in his mouth, and says, 'Hello, I reckon I've struck something.' When he spoke, the acorn dropped out of his mouth and rolled

What Stumped the Blue Jays ◆ 453

◆ **Reading Strategy**

❶ **Recognize the Author's Purpose** Why does Mark Twain describe the miner and his environment in this way? *He is showing that the man, who has lived alone in the country for many years, may only imagine that he understands animals' speech.*

◆ **LITERATURE AND YOUR LIFE**

❷ Ask students to write journal entries about any animals or birds they have ever observed "showing off."

▶**Critical Viewing**◀

❸ **Draw Conclusions** *The blue jay looks alert, sharp-eyed, and quick, as if he may notice other birds and animals to be prepared to take action.*

◆ **Reading Strategy**

❹ **Recognize the Author's Purpose** *The author entertains by describing the blue jays' language as expressing feeling, "bristling with metaphor," and correct in grammar. However, the description is based on the behavior of jays, known for their variety of noisy calls and cries and their aggressiveness.*

◆ **Critical Thinking**

❺ **Infer** Where is Jim Baker when he tells the story? *He is in front of his cabin, looking at the empty cabin nearby, just where he was sitting when he observed the blue jay incident.*

 Humanities: Photography

Nature Photography The photographs on pp. 451 and 452 fall into the category of nature or wildlife photography. Students can find more examples of this kind of photography in magazines such as *National Geographic, Audubon,* and *Backpacker.* Have students bring in magazines and books with wildlife photographs to compare and contrast to the photos that accompany this essay. Encourage them to think about the photos from both artistic and scientific perspectives. After students have studied all of the photographs, use the following questions for discussion:

1. What can you learn from a nature or wildlife photograph? *Students may suggest that you learn about an animal or environment, or just appreciate the beauty or unusual viewpoint.*

2. How do you think photographers are able to take these pictures? *Students may say they have to wait quietly in one place for a long time.*

3. Is it a nature photograph if a human or human-made object is present in the photograph? *Let students know this is a debate among photographers. The Photographic Society of America rules require that nothing human can be present.*

◆ Literary Focus

❶ Observation How can you tell the author has observed blue jays? *He describes the movements, appearance, and behavior of the blue jay.*

Comprehension Check ☑

❷ Why is the blue jay so happy that he has found a hole? *The bird can store acorns in the hole to have for food in the future.*

Customize for
Visual/Spatial Learners
Have students look at the photograph and check details in the story. Ask them whether or not the story could take place in the time of year shown in the photograph. Have them give their reasons.

Customize for
English Language Learners
Students may have difficulty following the storytelling style. Listening to the oral interpretation may help them comprehend the details of the story. Play the audiocassette and let students follow the printed words as they listen. Have them discuss the reader's interpretation of the storytelling.

🎧 **Listening to Literature Audiocassettes**

down the roof, of course, but he didn't care; his mind was all on the thing he had struck. It was a knothole in the roof. He cocked his head to one side, shut one eye and put the other one to the hole, like a 'possum looking down a jug; then he glanced up with his bright eyes, gave a wink or two with his wings,—which signifies <u>gratification</u>, you understand,—and says, 'It looks like a hole, it's located like a hole,—blamed if I don't believe it *is* a hole!'

"Then he cocked his head down and took another look; he glances up perfectly joyful,

454 ◆ *Extraordinary Occurrences*

🎙 Speaking and Listening Mini-Lesson

Oral Interpretation
This mini-lesson supports the Speaking and Listening activity in the Idea Bank on p. 463.

Introduce For this oral interpretation activity, each student will be acting as a storyteller. Explain that storytellers usually speak directly to the audience.

Develop Give students these tips for preparing their presentations:

• They may want to develop different voices to use when speaking as the narrator and as the blue jays.

• They should keep in mind the author's purpose, which includes entertaining and comparing the birds' behavior with that of humans.

Apply Have students choose short sections of the story to present to the class. Instruct students, as audience members, to listen carefully and to take notes during the performances.

Assess Evaluate students' performances in terms of preparation, interpretation, eye contact, and body language. Audience members can use the Peer Assessment: Oral Interpretation form, p. 119 in **Alternative Assessment.**

454

this time; winks his wings and his tail both, and says, 'O, no, this ain't no fat thing, I reckon! If I ain't in luck!—why it's a perfectly elegant hole!' So he flew down and got that acorn, and fetched it up and dropped it in, and was just tilting his head back, with the heavenliest smile on his face, when all of a sudden he was paralyzed into a listening attitude and that smile faded gradually out of his <u>countenance</u> like breath off 'n a razor, and the queerest look of surprise took its place. Then he says, 'Why, I didn't hear it fall!' He cocked his eye at the hole again, and took a long look; raised up and shook his head; stepped around to the other side of the hole and took another look from that side; shook his head again. He studied a while, then he just went into the *de*-tails—walked round and round the hole and spied into it from every point of the compass. No use. Now he took a thinking attitude on the comb of the roof and scratched the back of his head with his right foot a minute, and finally says, 'Well, it's too many for *me*, that's certain; must be a mighty long hole; however, I ain't got no time to fool around here, I got to 'tend to business; I reckon it's all right—chance it, anyway.'

"So he flew off and fetched another acorn and dropped it in, and tried to flirt his eye to the hole quick enough to see what become of it, but he was too late. He held his eye there as much as a minute; then he raised up and sighed, and says, 'Consound it, I don't seem to understand this thing, no way; however, I'll tackle her again.' He fetched another acorn, and done his level best to see what become of it, but he couldn't. He says, 'Well, *I* never struck no such a hole as this, be-fore; I'm of the opinion it's a totally new kind of a hole.' Then he begun to get mad. He held in for a spell, walking up and down the comb

◆ **Build Vocabulary**

gratification (grat´ ə fi kā´ shən) *n*.: Satisfaction

countenance (koun´ tə nəns) *n*.: The look on a person's face that shows his or her nature or feeling

▲ Critical Viewing What features does this log house have in common with the log house described on page 453? [Compare and Contrast]
3

What Stumped the Blue Jays ◆ 455

►Critical Viewing◄

3 **Compare and Contrast**
Students may say that the pictured log house resembles the one in the story in that it is simply built, probably has just one room, and may have no ceiling under the roof. However, this log cabin does not appear to be in as isolated a location as the one described in the story.

◆ **Literary Focus**

4 **Observation** Which descriptions in this paragraph may be taken from the author's actual observation of blue jays? *Students may mention the movement of the bird's head, tail, and wings; his dropping the acorn down the hole; and the jay's listening attitude as evidence that the author has observed jays.*

Customize for
Verbal/Linguistic Learners
Ask students to notice how the storyteller mixes folk expressions with more sophisticated language. These may appear together within a sentence or phrase, such as "when all of a sudden he was paralyzed into a listening attitude and that smile faded gradually out of his countenance like breath off 'n a razor." Have students write descriptions that mix contemporary expressions with more formal written language. They can share their writing with partners and discuss the effect this technique creates.

🎵 **Humanities: Literature**

Storytelling To give students an idea of how ancient an art storytelling is, let them know that in the eighth century B.C. the Greek poet Homer created *The Iliad* and *The Odyssey*. These epics describe Greek heroes who fought in the Trojan War, which took place in the twelfth century B.C. Homer based his works on traditional stories and songs told or sung long before he was born. The telling of stories was important because the people of Homer's time did not have a written language.

Mark Twain also draws on a storytelling back-ground, but his characters come from American folk tradition. Based on his observations of human nature and people's idiosyncracies, he describes ordinary people acting in extraordinary ways rather than heroes performing great deeds. Like Homer, Twain gives each character in a story his or her own voice. In "What Stumped the Blue Jays," his narrator uses the language spoken by people in rural areas of America in the 1800's.

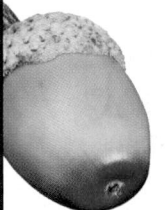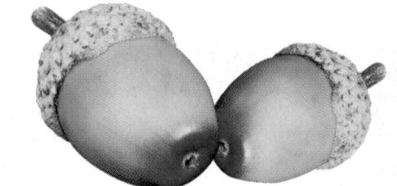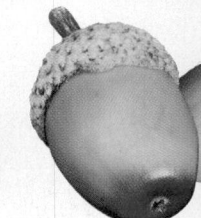

◆ Critical Thinking

① Analyze Why is the jay determined to fill the hole with acorns? *Students may say the bird is being stubborn, trying to make this knothole fit his own idea of what a hole should be. Students who have observed birds' behavior will know that they can be very persistent in a task, even if it isn't accomplishing what they expect, like some humans.*

◆ Reading Strategy

② Recognize the Author's Purpose Ask students to picture the position the blue jay has taken—leaning his back against the chimney. Why does the author have the bird take this unrealistic posture? *Students may say the author is trying to be humorous, by making the bird act like a human.*

◆ Reading Strategy

③ Recognize the Author's Purpose Ask students why the author compares the blue jays to humans. *Students may say that the point of the story is that the birds act like humans; or, Jim Baker is so lonely that he imagines the birds are acting like humans. Either way, the story shows how silly humans can act at times.*

◆ LITERATURE AND YOUR LIFE

④ Let volunteers describe the experience of seeing a huge flock of birds, including details of sights and sounds.

Customize for
Less Proficient Readers
Students may find it useful to trace the story's events. Have them use the Series of Events Chain, p. 69, of **Writing and Language Transparencies,** or create their own record of the series of events that lead to the final outcome.

Series of Events Chain
Beginning Event

Jim Baker tells of observing blue jays.

↓

A blue jay finds a knothole in a cabin roof and tries to fill it with acorns.

↓

Other blue jays come to try to find out what is wrong with the hole.

Final Outcome

One jay discovers that the hole opens into a house, and all the birds are amused.

of the roof and shaking his head and muttering to himself; but his feelings got the upper hand of him, presently, and he broke loose and cussed himself black in the face. I never see a bird take on so about a little thing. When he got through he walks to the hole and looks in again for half a minute; then he says, 'Well, you're a long hole, and a deep hole, and a mighty <u>singular</u> hole altogether— but I've started in to fill you, if it takes a hundred years!'

①

"And with that, away he went. You never see a bird work so since you was born. He laid into his work, and the way he hove acorns into that hole for about two hours and a half was one of the most exciting and astonishing spectacles I ever struck. He never stopped to take a look any more—he just hove 'em in and went for more. Well at last he could hardly flop his wings, he was so tuckered out. He comes a drooping down, once more, sweating like an ice-pitcher, drops his acorn in and says, '*Now* I guess I've got the bulge on you by this time!' So he bent down for a look. If you'll believe me, when his head come up again he was just pale with rage. He says, 'I've shoveled acorns enough in there to keep the family thirty years, and if I can see a sign of one of 'em I wish I may land in a museum with a belly full of sawdust in two minutes!'

② "He just had strength enough to crawl up on to the comb and lean his back agin the chimbly, and then he collected his impressions and begun to free his mind.

③ "Another jay was going by, and stops to inquire what was up. The sufferer told him the whole circumstance, and says, 'Now yonder's the hole, and if you don't believe me, go and look for yourself.' So this fellow went and

looked, and comes back and says, 'How many did you say you put in there?' 'Not any less than two tons,' says the sufferer. The other jay went and looked again. He couldn't seem to make it out, so he raised a yell, and three more jays come. They all examined the hole, they all made the sufferer tell it over again, then they all discussed it, and got off as many leather-headed opinions about it as an average crowd of humans could have done.

③

"They called in more jays; then more and more, till pretty soon this whole region 'peared to have a blue flush about it. There must have been five thousand of them; and such another jawing and disputing and ripping and cussing, you never heard. Every jay in the whole lot put his eye to the hole and delivered a more chuckle-headed opinion about the

> ◆ **Literature and Your Life**
> Have you ever seen a huge flock of birds like the one described here? If so, describe the experience.

④

mystery than the jay that went there before him. They examined the house all over, too. The door was standing half open, and at last one old jay happened to go and light on it and look in. Of course that knocked the mystery galley-west in a second. There lay the acorns, scattered all over the floor. He flopped his wings and raised a whoop. 'Come here!' he says, 'Come here, everybody; hang'd if this fool hasn't been trying to fill up a house with acorns!' They all came a-swooping down like a blue cloud, and as each fellow lit on the door and took a glance, the whole absurdity of the contract that that first jay had tackled hit him home and he fell over backwards suffocating with laughter, and the next jay took his place and done the same.

456 ◆ Extraordinary Occurrences

◆ **Beyond the Classroom**

Community Connection
Bird Watching There may be a group of bird watchers in your area. Encourage students to locate a group by looking in the telephone directory, calling the community newspaper, searching on the Internet, or asking people they know. Have students invite a bird watcher to visit the class and tell about bird behavior, calls, and habitats. What contributions do bird watchers make to the community and the environment? Students may want to ask the speaker to describe his or her observations of blue jays.

If possible, arrange for the class to participate in a bird watching session. Before going, discuss important qualities of bird watchers, such as
- the ability to be quiet and still
- the ability to be observant and notice details
- the ability to take notes on observations

You may want to point out that bird watchers find early morning hours the best time to observe birds. After bird watching, have students record their experiences, including sketches and descriptions of the birds they saw.

456

"Well, sir, they roosted around here on the house-top and the trees for an hour, and guffawed over that thing like human beings. It ain't any use to tell me a blue jay hasn't got a sense of humor, because I know better. And memory, too. They brought jays here from all over the United States to look down that hole, every summer for three years. Other birds, too. And they could all see the point, except an owl that come from Nova Scotia to visit the Yosemite and he took this thing in on his way back. He said he couldn't see anything funny in it. But then he was a good deal disappointed about Yosemite too."

❺

◆ **Build Vocabulary**

singular (sin´ gyə lər) *adj.*: Unique; exceptional; extraordinary

guffawed (gə fôd´) *v.*: Laughed in a loud and coarse manner

Beyond Literature

Science Connection

Birds Vertebrates (animals with backbones) are divided into eight classes. Birds form the class Aves. Within Aves, birds are classified into twenty-eight orders, based largely on internal features. Blue jays are members of the order Passeriformes, which are perching birds. Within this order are about 60 families, including broadbill, manakin, and all songbirds. The blue jay is a member of the songbird family.

Cross-Curricular Activity
Research bird orders, and create a wall chart that includes illustrations and descriptions of various bird orders and families.

Guide for Responding

◆ LITERATURE AND YOUR LIFE

Reader's Response Would you have liked to witness the scene described in the story? Why or why not?

Thematic Focus Which aspects of blue jay behavior do you most appreciate?

☑ Check Your Comprehension

1. Who tells the story?
2. According to him, what is so special about blue Jays?
3. Why can't the blue jay hear the nut when it drops?
4. Why are all the blue jays laughing at the end of the story?

◆ Critical Thinking

INTERPRET
1. Why does Jim Baker admire blue jays? Give examples to support your opinion. **[Infer]**
2. What facts about blue jays are probably true? **[Distinguish]**
3. What human characteristics does Twain give to blue jays? **[Analyze]**
4. Why do the blue jays keep coming back for years to look at the hole in the roof? **[Draw Conclusions]**

APPLY
5. What message for readers might Twain hint at by including the passage about the owl at the end of the story? **[Speculate]**
6. Tales such as "What Stumped the Blue Jays" were often told on the American frontier to counteract loneliness, to entertain others, and to enliven a hardworking existence. What forms of entertainment today serve the same purpose? **[Relate]**

◆ **Critical Thinking**
❺ **Relate** Ask students what kind of person the owl may represent. *Students may say that the owl is like a tourist who doesn't enjoy any of the sights he or she sees. People who aren't impressed by Yosemite will not be impressed by any natural site.*

Beyond Literature

Have students work in groups and choose the orders and families to portray on the chart. They may do research in bird identification books or the encyclopedia.

Reinforce and Extend

Answers
◆ **LITERATURE AND YOUR LIFE**

Reader's Response Some may say they would have liked to witness the scene to see how much of it really happened; others may say the scene derived its humor and insight from Jim Baker's imagination and they prefer the story.

Thematic Focus Some students may appreciate the first blue jay's determination, others may say the human-like behavior of all the jays.

☑ Check Your Comprehension

1. The narrator introduces Jim Baker, who tells the story.
2. The blue jays are the best talkers among the birds and beasts.
3. It lands inside the house, so far down the bird can't hear it.
4. They realize the bird was trying to fill up a whole house with acorns, and this seems hilarious to them.

◆ **Critical Thinking**

1. They can put their feelings into words, have a remarkable command of language, and use good grammar.
2. They gather acorns, are noisy, and make a lot of different sounds.
3. The birds can talk, reason, get angry, be stubborn, and laugh.
4. They think it is so funny that a bird would have tried to fill up the whole house with acorns.
5. If readers don't think the story is funny, they are like the owl who wasn't even impressed with Yosemite, which is a national park in the Sierra Nevada mountains in California.
6. Students may mention television and movies.

One-Minute Insight

Diane Ackerman describes fall foliage and explains the natural process that causes the leaves to turn each year. Along with her observations she muses on life and death, the change of seasons, and the human enjoyment of seeing things move through the air—whether they are balloons, birds, or autumn leaves.

Team Teaching Strategy

The explanation of why leaves change colors offers a strong connection to science. You may want to coordinate with a science teacher to find ways to extend instruction.

◆ LITERATURE AND YOUR LIFE

1 Ask students if they have ever had the experience the author describes: that of suddenly realizing the fall has arrived. Have students discuss why this season or any other may take us by surprise.

◆ Reading Strategy

2 Recognize the Author's Purpose What clue do you have of the author's purpose? *Students may say that the question lets them know the author is going to explain why the leaves change colors.*

Comprehension Check ☑

3 Ask students to explain in their own words why we can see red, yellow, and other colors in the leaves as they begin to turn. *The colors are always there in the leaves, but cannot be seen because the green produced by chlorophyll hides them.*

WHY LEAVES TURN COLOR IN THE FALL
Diane Ackerman

1 The stealth of autumn catches one unaware. Was that a goldfinch perching in the early September woods, or just the first turning leaf? A red-winged blackbird or a sugar maple closing up shop for the winter? Keen-eyed as leopards, we stand still and squint hard, looking for signs of movement. Early-morning frost sits heavily on the grass, and turns barbed wire into a string of stars. On a distant hill, a small square of yellow appears to be a lighted stage. At last the truth dawns on us: Fall is staggering in, right on schedule, with its baggage of chilly nights, <u>macabre</u> holidays, and spectacular, heart-stoppingly beautiful leaves. Soon the leaves will start cringing on the trees, and roll up in clenched fists before they actually fall off. Dry seedpods will rattle like tiny gourds. But first there will be weeks of gushing color so bright, so pastel, so confettilike, that people will travel up and down the East Coast just to stare at it—a whole season of leaves.

2 Where do the colors come from? Sunlight rules most living things with its golden edicts.[1] When the days begin to shorten, soon after the summer solstice on June 21, a tree reconsiders its leaves. All summer it feeds them so they can process sunlight, but in the dog days of summer the tree begins pulling nutrients back into its trunk and roots, pares down, and gradually chokes off its leaves. A corky layer of cells forms at the leaves' slender petioles,[2] then scars over. Undernourished, the leaves stop producing the pigment chlorophyll,[3] and photosynthesis[4] ceases. Animals can migrate, hibernate, or store food to prepare for winter. But where can a tree go? It survives by dropping its leaves, and by the end of autumn only a few fragile threads of fluid-carrying xylem[5] hold leaves to their stems.

A turning leaf stays partly green at first, then reveals splotches of yellow and red as the chlorophyll gradually breaks down. Dark green seems to stay longest in the veins, outlining and defining them. During the summer, chlorophyll dissolves in the heat and light, but it is also being steadily replaced. In the fall, on the other hand, no new pigment is produced, and so we notice the other colors that were always there, right in the leaf, although chlorophyll's shocking green hid them from view. With their <u>camouflage</u> gone, we see these colors for the first time all year, and marvel, but they were always there, hidden

---

1. **edicts** (ē´ dikts´) *n.*: Authority; order.

2. **petioles** (pet´ ē ōlz´) *n.*: Stalks of leaves.
3. **chlorophyll** (klôr´ ə fil´) *n.*: Green pigment found in cellplants. It is essential for the photosynthetic process.
4. **photosynthesis** (fōt´ ō sin´ thə sis) *n.*: The production of organic substances; the transformation of radiant or light energy into chemical form.
5. **xylem** (zī´ ləm) *n.*: Woody tissue of a plant that carries water and minerals in the stems, roots, and leaves, giving support to softer tissues.

Cross-Curricular Connection: Science

Photosynthesis Students may need to review their knowledge of photosynthesis in order to understand how it affects the autumn leaves. Photosynthesis is the food-making process of a plant. Some plant cells contain the pigment chlorophyll, which has the ability to capture the energy in sunlight to make food. In addition to sunlight and chlorophyll, a plant needs water and carbon dioxide in order to have photosynthesis. When all of these ingredients are in place, the plant creates a simple sugar for its food and oxygen as its waste product. The sugar remains in the plant, but the oxygen exits.

Have a group of students create a poster illustrating photosynthesis in a deciduous tree. These students can explain photosynthesis in a presentation to the class. Encourage volunteers to explain how photosynthesis relates to the turning leaves, based on the information in the essay. Then invite questions from the rest of the class.

like a vivid secret beneath the hot glowing greens of summer.

The most spectacular range of fall foliage occurs in the northeastern United States and in eastern China, where the leaves are robustly colored thanks in part to a rich climate. European maples don't achieve the same flaming reds as their American relatives, which thrive on cold nights and sunny days. In Europe, the warm, humid weather turns the leaves brown or mildly yellow. Anthocyanin, the pigment that gives apples their red and turns leaves red or red-violet, is produced by sugars that remain in the leaf after the supply of nutrients dwindles. Unlike the carotenoids, which color carrots, squash, and corn, and turn leaves orange and yellow, anthocyanin varies from year to year, depending on the temperature and amount of sunlight. The fiercest colors occur in years when the fall sunlight is strongest and the nights are cool and dry (a state of grace scientists find vexing to forecast). This is also why leaves appear dizzyingly bright and clear on a sunny fall day: The anthocyanin flashes like a marquee.

❹

Not all leaves turn the same color. Elms, weeping willows, and the ancient ginkgo all grow radiant yellow, along with hickories, aspens, bottlebrush buckeyes, cottonweeds, and tall, keening poplars. Basswood turns bronze, birches bright gold. Water-loving maples put on a symphonic display of scarlets. Sumacs turn red, too, as do flowering dogwoods, black gums, and sweet gums. Though some oaks yellow, most turn a pinkish brown. The farmlands also change color, as tepees of cornstalks and bales of shredded-wheat-textured hay stand drying in the fields. In some spots, one slope of a hill may be green and the other already in bright color, because the hillside facing south gets more sun and heat than the northern one.

❺
◆ Literary Focus
What vivid details does the author observe?

An odd feature of the colors is that they don't seem to have any special purpose. We are predisposed to respond to their beauty, of course. They shimmer with the colors of sunset, spring flowers, the tawny[6] buff of a colt's pretty rump, the shuddering pink of a blush. Animals and flowers color for a reason—adaptation to their environment—but there is no adaptive reason for leaves to color so beautifully in the fall any more than there is for the sky or ocean to be blue. It's just one of the haphazard marvels the planet bestows every year. We find the sizzling colors thrilling, and in a sense they dupe us. Colored like living things, they signal death and disintegration. In time, they will become fragile and, like the body, return to dust. They are as we hope our own fate will be when we die; not to vanish, just to sublime from one beautiful state into another. Though leaves lose their green life, they bloom with urgent colors, as the woods grow mummified day by day, and Nature becomes more carnal, mute, and radiant.

❻

We call the season "fall," from the Old English *feallan*, to fall, which leads back through time to the Indo-European *phol*, which also means to fall. So the word and the idea are both extremely ancient, and haven't really changed since the first of our kind needed a name for fall's leafy abundance. As we say the word, we're reminded of that other Fall, in the Garden of Eden, when fig leaves never withered and scales fell from our eyes. Fall is the time when leaves fall from the trees, just as spring is when flowers spring up, summer is when we simmer, and winter is when we whine from the cold.

Children love to play in piles of leaves, hurling them into the air like confetti, leaping into

---

6. **tawny** (tô′ nē) *adj.*: Brownish-yellow; tan.

◆ **Build Vocabulary**

macabre (mə käb′ rə) *adj.*: Gruesome; grim and horrible

camouflage (kam′ ə fläzh′) *n.*: Disguise or concealment

predisposed (prē′ dis pōzd′) *adj.*: Inclined; willing

Why Leaves Turn Color in the Fall ◆ 459

◆ **Critical Thinking**

❹ Compare and Contrast Have students compare the two pigments anthocyanin and carotenoid, explaining how each affects the changing leaves in the fall. Ask students to comment on how these pigments had an effect on nearby trees during the fall. *Anthocyanin colors apples red and leaves red or red-violet. Carotenoids color carrots, squash, and corn and turn leaves orange or yellow. Anthocyanin depends on sunlight and temperature, varying each year. Students may point out which trees had which pigment, and tell how the weather affected the brightness of the colors this year.*

◆ **Literary Focus**

❺ Observation Point out to students that the author describes the different colors that different trees have, as well as explaining why neighboring areas may change color at varying times.

◆ **Reading Strategy**

❻ Recognize the Author's Purpose Ask students what the author means by saying that the changing colors of the leaves "dupe" us. *Students may say that the colors are so bright and beautiful that we forget they are dying.*

Customize for
Verbal/Linguistic Learners
In the essay, the author says there is apparently no "special purpose" for the beautiful colors of the leaves. Students can work in groups to create myths that explain why the leaves turn in the fall. Encourage students to use their imaginations and base their stories on myths they have read. Let each group present its myth to the class as a group story or any other method the students choose.

◆ **Viewing and Representing Mini-Lesson**

Local Trees

In this mini-lesson students will study and learn to identify trees in your area.

Introduce Point out the paragraph in which the author names several kinds of trees. Ask students to think of ways they can find out what kinds of trees grow in and around their community. They may suggest using guidebooks or asking people who work in parks or gardens.

Develop Students can work with partners and choose a local tree to study. They may observe the tree, read information about it, take photographs of it, and/or draw it. They should take note of its leaves, bark, flowers, fruit, and whether it loses its leaves in the fall.

Apply Each pair of students decides how to illustrate the tree, by making a model, drawing it, or photographing it, and how to present the information, such as writing captions or making diagrams.

Assess Have each pair present the project to the class. Evaluate students on their partner work, research, and presentations.

❶ Connect *Students may respond that people travel to see this scenery because it is beautiful and it happens only once a year. Some people may go view the leaves as a ritual of fall, a "last outing" before the difficult weather of winter. Students may recognize that the autumn is ordinary, in that it is an annual event, yet people respond to the colors as an extraordinary occasion.*

◆ Reading Strategy

❷ Recognize the Author's Purpose *The author combines her scientific explanations with her sense of the beauty of the leaves as they turn colors and fall.*

Customize for
Bodily/Kinesthetic Learners
Encourage students to pantomime reactions to fall and the other seasons. Have them brainstorm for a list of seasonal occurrences or events, whether natural or social. Then have them take turns pantomiming the reactions.

Customize for
Intrapersonal Learners
Invite students to write journal entries describing their personal responses to autumn. They may want to include sketches as well. If they enjoy writing this entry, encourage students to explore their feelings about all the seasons.

▲ **Critical Viewing** Why might people "travel up and down the East Coast" to stare at this scenery? [Connect]

soft unruly mattresses of them. For children, leaf fall is just one of the odder figments of Nature, like hailstones or snowflakes. Walk down a lane overhung with trees in the never-never land of autumn, and you will forget about time and death, lost in the sheer delicious spill of color. . . .

◆ Build Vocabulary

capricious (kə prē´ shəs) *adj.*: Tending to change abruptly and without apparent reason

But how do the colored leaves fall? As a leaf ages, the growth hormone, auxin, fades, and cells at the base of the petiole divide. Two or three rows of small cells, lying at right angles to the axis of the petiole, react with water, then come apart, leaving the petioles hanging on by only a few threads of xylem. A light breeze, and the leaves are airborne. They glide and swoop, rocking in invisible cradles. They are all

◆ **Reading Strategy**
This passage suggests the author's purpose for writing. What might it be?

Beyond the Classroom

Workplace Skills
Attention to Details Ask students to explain why the author's observations make the autumn scene so realistic. Elicit that it is because she uses precise details in her descriptions. She includes details of how humans react to fall as well as details of the natural effects of autumn. She also provides particular scientific facts about the leaves.

Encourage students to brainstorm how paying attention to details is an important workplace

skill. They may suggest it is necessary for doing any job well, whether as an office assistant making copies or as a chef cooking in a restaurant. They may also suggest that paying attention to co-workers may also be important in being able to work well with other people.

Ask students to choose a job or profession and to write a paragraph about why a person holding that position needs to pay attention to detail.

wing and may flutter from yard to yard on small whirlwinds or updrafts, swiveling as they go. Firmly tethered to earth, we love to see things rise up and fly—soap bubbles, balloons, birds, fall leaves. They remind us that the end of a season is <u>capricious</u>, as is the end of life. We especially like the way leaves rock, careen, and swoop as they fall. Everyone knows the motion. Pilots sometimes do a maneuver called a "falling leaf," in which the plane loses altitude quickly and on purpose, by slipping first to the right, then to the left. The machine weighs a ton or more, but in one pilot's mind it is a weightless thing, a falling leaf. She has seen the motion before, in the Vermont woods where she played as a child. Below her the trees radiate gold, copper, and red. Leaves are falling, although she can't see them fall, as she falls, swooping down for a closer view.

At last the leaves leave. But first they turn color and thrill us for weeks on end. Then they crunch and crackle underfoot. The *shush*, as children drag their small feet through leaves heaped along the curb. Dark, slimy mats of leaves cling to one's heels after a rain.

A damp, stuccolike mortar of semidecayed leaves protects the tender shoots with a roof until spring, and makes a rich humus. An occasional bulge or ripple in the leafy mounds signals a shrew or a field mouse tunneling out of sight. Sometimes one finds in fossil stones the imprint of a leaf, long since disintegrated, whose outlines remind us how detailed, vibrant, and alive are the things of this earth that perish.

❸

◆ **Reading Strategy**

❸ **Recognize the Author's Purpose** How does the author connect the fallen leaves to future seasons? *The leaves protect new life until spring comes, and make humus that fertilizes the earth for more life.*

Reinforce and Extend

Answers
◆ **LITERATURE AND YOUR LIFE**

Reader's Response Students should cite facts that they found interesting or specific descriptive details that impressed them.

Thematic Focus Some students may say that the explanation makes them appreciate the autumn leaves more, because they understand what is happening. Others may say the essay does not change their reactions to autumn—there may be no practical scientific reason for the leaves to turn such brilliant colors.

☑ **Check Your Comprehension**

1. They change color in the fall.
2. They are most spectacular in the northeastern United States and in eastern China.
3. It makes them lose their green color and reveal their other colors.
4. As a leaf gets old, the growth hormone fades and cells react with water and come apart, which leaves the leaf hanging by a thread. Then a light breeze can make it fall.

◆ **Critical Thinking**

1. They are both keen-eyed and must wait patiently to notice nature.
2. She could observe many things, but probably would have to research specific facts about chlorophyll, photosynthesis, anthocyanin, carotenoids, and other details.
3. The phenomenon seems to have a larger meaning. She relates changing and falling leaves to ideas of life and death; she discusses the origin of the word *fall* and the meaning of a leaf's fossil imprint.
4. Most people are aware of the seasonal changes; this essay might help them to picture it.
5. Twain achieved his purpose of writing an entertaining story by using details to describe birds, therefore exposing human behavior. Ackerman informed by explaining why leaves change colors in autumn.

◇ Guide for Responding

◆ LITERATURE AND YOUR LIFE

Reader's Response Which interested you more—the science details or the author's descriptions and language?

Thematic Focus Does a scientific explanation diminish the wonder of the color changes of the leaves in autumn? Explain.

Art Make a drawing or painting of an autumn scene that you've observed in your region of the country.

☑ **Check Your Comprehension**

1. When do leaves change color?
2. According to the author, in what two countries are the changing colors of the leaves most spectacular?
3. How does undernourishment affect leaves?
4. Why do leaves fall off trees?

◆ Critical Thinking

INTERPRET
1. What connection does Ackerman make between being a nature writer and a leopard? **[Connect]**
2. Do you think Ackerman's scientific knowledge about leaves comes from observation or research? Explain. **[Speculate]**
3. Do the coloring and falling of leaves have a larger meaning for Ackerman, or is she just writing a nature story? Explain. **[Draw Conclusions]**

APPLY
4. What appeal would this essay have for people who have never witnessed seasonal changes? **[Generalize]**

COMPARE LITERARY WORKS
5. How well did Twain and Ackerman achieve their purposes for writing? Explain. **[Evaluate]**

Why Leaves Turn Color in the Fall ◆ 461

Beyond the Selection

FURTHER READING
Other Works by Mark Twain
The Prince and the Pauper
A Connecticut Yankee in King Arthur's Court
Life on the Mississippi
Pudd'nhead Wilson

Other Works by Diane Ackerman
The Curious Naturalist
Bats: Shadows in the Night
The Moon by Whale Light and Other Adventures Among Bats, Penguins, Crocodilians, and Whales
The Rarest of the Rare: Vanishing Animals, Timeless Worlds

INTERNET
We suggest the following sites on the Internet (all Web sites are subject to change).
For Mark Twain:
www.tarleton.edu/activities/pages/facultypages/schmidt/Mark_Twain.html
For additional information about birds:
birdsource.cornell.edu
For nature photography:
www.geocities.com/~greyhawk_1/home.html
We *strongly recommend* that you preview these sites before you send students to them.

Answers

◆ Reading Strategy

1. (a) Twain's purpose is to entertain.
   (b) The blue jays not only talk, they act like humans.
2. She provides scientific information and records detailed observations.

◆ Build Vocabulary

Using the Word Root -grat-
1. gratified; 2. gratitude;
3. ungrateful

Spelling Strategy
1. Blue jays are more muscular birds than hummingbirds.
2. Mark Twain was a popular speaker as well as a famous writer.
3. Autumn leaves sometimes fall in circular patterns.
4. The calendar doesn't always predict when leaves change colors.

Using the Word Bank
1. c 2. a 3. b 4. b 5. a
6. b 7. b 8. c

◆ Literary Focus

1. He describes blue jays' behaviors, calls, and cries with the authority that comes with observation.
2. "Soon the leaves will start cringing on the trees, and roll up in clenched fists before they actually fall off." "Water-loving maples put on a symphonic display of scarlets."
3. She compare trees to other living things. She writes that animals can migrate or hibernate for the winter, but a tree survives by "dropping its leaves."

◆ Build Grammar Skills

Practice
1. i.o.: trees; d.o.: look
2. i.o.: us; d.o.: message
3. i.o.: readers; d.o.: insights
4. i.o.: people; d.o.: insights
5. i.o.: lovers; d.o.: opportunity

Writing Application
Check that students have written nouns or pronouns that answer *to whom, for whom, to what,* or *for what.* Possible answers: 1. me; 2. tourists; 3. us

 Writer's Solution

For additional instruction and practice, use the Indirect Objects pages, pp. 38–39, in the *Writer's Solution Grammar Practice Book.*

Guide for Responding (continued)

◆ Reading Strategy

RECOGNIZE THE AUTHOR'S PURPOSE
An **author's purpose** may be to inform, entertain, or persuade. In these selections, the writing style and content help reveal the authors' purposes. For example, the serious style of Ackerman's essay supports her purpose of informing the reader.
1. (a) What is the purpose of Twain's story? (b) What story details support your conclusion?
2. Describe two ways in which Ackerman fulfills her purpose of informing the reader.

◆ Build Vocabulary

USING THE WORD ROOT -grat-
The root -grat- in *gratification* means "pleasing" or "satisfying." On your paper, write the following sentences, filling in the blank with the appropriate word containing -grat- from this list:
    gratitude   ungrateful   gratified
1. Jim Baker was _____?_____ that the blue jays used correct grammar.
2. The blue jay was filled with _____?_____ for having discovered such a wonderful hole.
3. Only the owl was _____?_____ for the privilege of viewing the site of the historic house.

SPELLING STRATEGY
The *er* sound at the end of *singular* is spelled *ar.* Sometimes, this sound at the end of a word may be spelled *er* (manner) or *or* (actor). Learn the following words that end in *ar.* On your paper, write a sentence using each of these words.
1. muscular 2. popular 3. circular 4. calendar

USING THE WORD BANK
On your paper, write the word whose meaning is closest to that of the Word Bank word.
1. camouflage: (a) costume, (b) forest, (c) disguise
2. countenance: (a) look, (b) composure, (c) stature
3. predisposed: (a) wasted, (b) receptive, (c) changed
4. guffawed: (a) groped, (b) laughed, (c) smiled
5. capricious: (a) changeable, (b) easy, (c) flimsy
6. macabre: (a) sad, (b) grim, (c) mediocre
7. gratification: (a) honor, (b) satisfaction, (c) tip
8. singular: (a) alone, (b) chosen, (c) unique

◆ Literary Focus

OBSERVATION
In an **observation,** a writer gives details about an event that he or she has witnessed firsthand. Writers use precise words and vivid language to make readers feel that they are "in the picture."
1. Although Twain's story is told by a fictional narrator, what clues in the story point toward Twain's familiarity with blue jay behavior?
2. Give two examples of vivid language Ackerman uses to share her observations about leaves.
3. How does Ackerman use comparisons to help you understand the scientific facts in her story? Give an example.

◆ Build Grammar Skills

INDIRECT OBJECTS
An **indirect object** is a noun or pronoun that answers *to whom, for whom, to what,* or *for what* after an action verb. All sentences with an indirect object also have a direct object:

           I.O.   D.O.
The leaves showed *her* their <u>colors</u>. (Showed colors to whom? *her*)

                I.O.   D.O.
Ackerman offers *readers* scientific <u>information</u>. (Offered information to whom? *readers*)

Practice In your notebook, identify the indirect object and the direct object in each sentence.
1. The colors give the trees a festive look.
2. Autumn's foliage sends us a message.
3. Ackerman gives readers insights.
4. She brings people fresh insights about the seasons.
5. Fall offers lovers of beauty a unique opportunity.

Writing Application In your notebook, copy the sentences, and insert an indirect object between each action verb and direct object.
1. The bird-watcher gave _____?_____ her binoculars.
2. Motels offer _____?_____ special foliage season rates.
3. The scientist showed _____?_____ examples of seasonal changes.

462 ◆ *Extraordinary Occurrences*

Build Your Portfolio

 Idea Bank

Writing

1. **Descriptive Letter** Imagine that you are in the northeastern United States during fall foliage season. Write a letter to a friend that includes your observations of the changing leaves.

2. **Editor's Foreword** As the editor of an anthology of nature stories, write the foreword to the book, explaining why you included "What Stumped the Blue Jays" and "Why Leaves Turn Color in the Fall." Describe the unique qualities of each story.

3. **Science Magazine** As a writer for a science magazine, revise Twain's story to make it an article suited for your readers. [Science Link]

Speaking and Listening

4. **Oral Interpretation** In "What Stumped the Blue Jays" you can hear the blue jay's frantic effort to fill the hole. Read this story passage aloud, beginning with "Then he cocked his head down and took another look." Perform your reading for the class. [Performing Arts Link]

5. **Author's Chat [Group Activity]** In a group of three, stage a televised author's chat show with invited guests Mark Twain and Diane Ackerman. One of you will be the host and the others will be the guests. [Performing Arts Link]

Projects

6. **Research** Use various resources to find out about distinctive bird calls or songs and what they communicate. Share your findings with classmates by imitating the sounds and telling what you have learned about the birds. [Science Link]

7. **Botanical Drawing** Research trees and the distinguishing shapes and colors of their leaves. Then, make a botanical drawing of two or more kinds of leaves. On your completed drawing, identify the type of tree the leaf is from, and label its parts. [Art Link]

 Writing Mini-Lesson

Observational Essay

Diane Ackerman's observations are more scientific than those presented in "What Stumped the Blue Jays," but both authors give sharp details about nature. Choose a natural event that interests you, observe it, and then share your observations in an essay for your classmates.

Writing Skills Focus: Writing to the Audience

When you write, choose details and a tone or attitude that will appeal to your **audience**. In the following example, Ackerman uses colorful language to appeal to the senses of her readers, who are the general public.

Model From the Essay

The fiercest colors occur in years when the fall sunlight is strongest and the nights are cool and dry. . . . This is also why leaves appear dizzyingly bright and clear on a sunny fall day.

Prewriting Choose a subject that you can observe firsthand. Make detailed notes as you observe your subject. Organize your notes so that you can follow them as you write.

Drafting Introduce the subject of your essay, and follow with a detailed description of your observations. Keep your audience in mind, and find ways to connect with your audience's own experiences.

Revising Review your essay to be sure you've included details appropriate for your audience. Rearrange any details that disrupt the organizational flow. Proofread carefully for errors.

> ◆ **Grammar Application**
>
> You may be able to replace a prepositional phrase beginning with *to* or *for* with an indirect object. **Phrase:** The dog brought the bone to me. **Indirect Object:** The dog brought me the bone.

 Idea Bank

Following are suggestions for matching the Idea Bank topics with your students' performance levels and learning modalities:

Customize for
Performance Levels
Less Advanced Students: 1, 4
Average Students: 2, 4, 5, 7
More Advanced Students: 3, 5, 6, 7

Customize for
Learning Modalities
Verbal/Linguistic: 1, 2, 3, 4, 5
Visual/Spatial: 7
Musical/Rhythmic: 6
Bodily/Kinesthetic: 4, 5
Interpersonal: 4, 5
Intrapersonal: 5, 6, 7

 Writing Mini-Lesson

Refer students to the Writing Handbook at the back of the book for instruction on the writing process and for further information on expression.

 Writer's Solution

Writing Lab CD-ROM
Have students complete the tutorial on Description. Follow these steps:

1. Students can use the Interactive Instruction on Ordering Details to preview ways to organize details.

2. Before students draft, have them use the Interactive Writing Models to learn how to add a description by describing something from an unusual perspective.

3. Have students draft on computer.

4. Students can use the Publishing and Presenting section to find suggestions about creating a multimedia presentation based on their Observational Essays.

Writer's Solution Sourcebook
Have students use Chapter 2, "Description," pp. 32–69, for additional support. This chapter includes instruction on an Observation of a Natural Event, p. 47.

✓ ASSESSMENT OPTIONS

Formal Assessment, Selection Test, pp. 137–139, and Assessment Resources Software. The selection test is designed so that it can easily be customized to the performance levels of your students.

Alternative Assessment, p. 33, includes options for less advanced students, more advanced students, visual/spatial learners, logical/mathematical learners, verbal/linguistic learners, and musical/rhythmic learners.

PORTFOLIO ASSESSMENT
Use the following rubrics in the **Alternative Assessment** booklet to assess student writing:
Descriptive Letter: Description, p. 93
Editor's Foreword: Definition/Classification, p. 95
Science Magazine: Technical Description/Explanation, p. 111
Writing Mini-Lesson: Observational Essay: Narrative Based on Personal Experience, p. 92, or Research/Report Paper, p. 102

Guide for Reading

OBJECTIVES

1. To read, comprehend, and interpret three poems
2. To relate poems to personal experience
3. To understand the author's bias when reading poems
4. To recognize free verse in poetry
5. To build vocabulary in context and learn the prefix *trans-*
6. To develop skill in using predicate adjectives
7. To write a poem about a person or place using appropriate tone
8. To respond to the poems through writing, speaking and listening, and projects

SKILLS INSTRUCTION

Vocabulary:
Prefixes: *trans-*
Spelling:
Words Ending in *cal* and *cle*
Grammar:
Predicate Adjectives
Reading Strategy:
Understand the Author's Bias
Literary Focus:
Free Verse

Writing:
Using Appropriate Tone
Speaking and Listening:
Talk-Show Appearance (Teacher Edition)
Critical Viewing:
Infer; Evaluate; Assess

PORTFOLIO OPPORTUNITIES

Writing: Travel Advertisement; City Poem; Analysis

Writing Mini-Lesson: Poem About a Person or Place

Speaking and Listening: Talk-Show Appearance; Storyteller

Projects: Multimedia Report; Painting

More About the Authors
May Swenson published more than a dozen books. Her poems are often humorous, involve word play, and use unique imagery.

Mark Van Doren was born in Hope, Illinois, and moved to New York City as an adult. In addition to poetry, he wrote novels, short stories, plays, and children's books.

Victor Hernández Cruz writes of the rhythms, colors, and textures of his native Puerto Rico and the Lower East Side in New York City, where he grew up. He says when he writes he tries to see the connection between everything, including himself and history.

Meet the Authors:

May Swenson (1919–1989)

May Swenson was born and educated in Utah. After completing college, she moved to New York City, where she worked as an editor and as a university lecturer. Swenson believed that poetry is based on the desire to see things as they are, rather than as they appear. In "Southbound on the Freeway," however, she portrays how our culture might appear to visiting aliens. [For more on May Swenson, see page 814.]

Mark Van Doren (1894–1972)

Mark Van Doren is best known as the winner of the 1940 Pulitzer Prize for Poetry for his *Collected Poems 1922–38*. An English professor at Columbia University, he also wrote critical studies of major writers, including William Shakespeare, Henry David Thoreau, and Nathaniel Hawthorne. Among his collections of poetry are *Spring Thunder and Other Poems* and *A Winter Diary and Other Poems*.

Victor Hernández Cruz (1949–   )

Known as a "Nuyorican poet" (for "New York Puerto Rican"), Victor Hernández Cruz began publishing his poetry in the San Francisco Bay Area in the 1970's. His poetry often reads like music, in which the syllables act as chords and notes, producing catchy rhythms.

◆ LITERATURE AND YOUR LIFE

CONNECT YOUR EXPERIENCE

Is the glass half full or half empty? Is a test an obstacle or a chance to show what you know? Your answers to these questions reveal something about your perceptions—how you view the world. In the following poems, the perceptions of the speakers change ordinary people, places, and things into extraordinary ones.

THEMATIC FOCUS: The Extraordinary in the Ordinary

As you read these poems, look for unusual perceptions that make them unique.

◆ Background for Understanding

SOCIAL STUDIES

"Southbound on the Freeway" contains an unusual viewpoint about cars. Little more than a hundred years ago, cars as we know them did not exist. Yet today, much of our culture is based on cars. Because of cars, highways crisscross the country and the economy is based on oil. Collectors restore old cars, and mechanics maintain new ones. Try to imagine life without cars. How would your daily life change?

◆ Build Vocabulary

PREFIXES: *trans-*

In "Southbound on the Freeway," May Swenson uses the word *transparent*. The prefix *trans-*, which means "through" or "across," is a key to the meaning of *transparent*, which means "clear enough to see through."

WORD BANK

Which word from the list relates to the tropics and suggests heat and humidity? Check the Build Vocabulary box on page 469 to see if you chose correctly.

| transparent |
| galore |
| tropical |
| romp |

Prentice Hall Literature Program Resources

REINFORCE / RETEACH / EXTEND
Selection Support Pages
Build Vocabulary: Prefixes: *trans-*, p. 179
Build Spelling Skills, p. 180
Build Grammar Skills: Predicate Adjectives, p. 181
Reading Strategies: Understand the Author's Bias, p. 182
Literary Focus: Free Verse, p. 183
Strategies for Diverse Student Needs, pp. 67–68

Beyond Literature Cross-Curricular Connection: Math, p. 34
Formal Assessment Selection Test, pp. 140–142
Alternative Assessment, p. 34
Resource Pro CD-R⊘M "Southbound on the Freeway"; "The Story-Teller"; "Los New Yorks"— includes all resource material and customizable lesson plan
 Listening to Literature Audiocassettes "Southbound on the Freeway"; "The Story-Teller"; "Los New Yorks"

Southbound on the Freeway ◆ The Story-Teller ◆ Los New Yorks ◆

◆ Literary Focus

FREE VERSE

Free verse is "free" of the traditional structures of poetry. It may contain irregular rhythms and varied line lengths. If it uses rhymes, they are loose and also irregular. Free verse poetry sounds more like conversational speech than other types of poetry.

A poem written in free verse may be long or short, and it may or may not have stanzas. Sometimes, however, as in "Southbound on the Freeway," the stanzas are regular. In general, the lines in free verse flow according to the poet's thoughts, ideas, and images.

◆ Reading Strategy

UNDERSTAND THE AUTHOR'S BIAS

Writers may, intentionally or not, present ideas through their own bias—their own likes and dislikes and particular viewpoint. **Understanding the author's bias** helps you understand his or her world. For example, if you know that Victor Hernández Cruz has a Puerto Rican heritage, you can understand that he is biased toward a tropical environment:

> I present you the tall skyscrapers/as merely huge palm trees with lights . . .

As you read these selections, fill out a chart like the one below.

Poet	Passage	Bias
Swenson	The creatures of this star/are made of metal and glass.	She may feel that cars have taken over the Earth.

Guide for Reading ◆ 465

Interest Grabber Stimulate students' interest in the poems by having them write descriptions of familiar objects from the point of view of a visitor from outer space. Have students exchange papers and see if they can guess the objects being described.

◆ Build Grammar Skills

Predicate Adjectives If you wish to introduce the grammar concept for this selection before students read, refer to the instruction on p. 470.

Customize for
Less Proficient Readers
Students may be confused between the literal and figurative meanings of the poems. Let students know that Swenson and Cruz are describing ordinary scenes as they see them in their imaginations. Van Doren describes a scene that a listener might imagine while hearing the storyteller.

Customize for
More Advanced Students
Encourage students to write a brief essay comparing free verse and more traditionally structured poems. They may use "Southbound on the Freeway" and "The Story-Teller" as models for the two different types of poems. Have them consider these questions as they write: What do they like about free verse? What do they like about poems with regular rhythm and rhyme? Which type of poem would they prefer to read aloud?

Customize for
English Language Learners
Have students work in pairs to interpret the images in "Southbound on the Freeway." Encourage students to study one couplet at a time and determine which part of a car is being described. For example, "Through the transparent parts/you can see their guts" refers to seeing through the windows to the inside of the car.

Preparing for Standardized Tests

Vocabulary Students' knowledge of affixes may be evaluated on standardized tests. Using the prefix *trans-* will help them develop their ability to apply affixes.

Remind students that the prefix *trans-* means "through" or "across." Discuss the connection between *transparent* and *transform. Transparent* means "clear enough to see through" and *transform* means "to go through a change in form." Then write the following sample test question on the board:

> The light from the airplane *transilluminated* the clouds.

In this sentence, transilluminated means—

(A) eliminated
(B) disappeared
(C) changed the color of
(D) shined through

Help students assess the answer choices. Guide them to identify the base word *illuminate,* meaning "to light," and point out that knowing *trans-* means "through" or "across" will help students determine that *transilluminated* means (D) shined through. For more practice, use **Selection Support,** p. 179.

One-Minute Insight

An alien visiting Earth sees a traffic jam on the freeway and assumes that cars are this planet's inhabitants. The poem's curious speaker describes cars on the road from an unusual perspective, which includes believing a police car is a special creature that has a red eye on the top of his head.

◆ Critical Thinking

❶ **Speculate** What is the "star" that the speaker refers to? Why does the poet use this word? *The star is the planet Earth. The poet may use star to add to the feeling that the speaker is from outer space.*

◆ Literary Focus

❷ **Free Verse** Have students write out lines 7–10 as a sentence. Ask them if they have a different impression reading the sentence as opposed to reading the verses in the poem. Why? *Students may say that they pay more attention to the words and images in the verse.*

▶Critical Viewing◀

❸ **Infer** *The cars are the only moving things in sight, which may make them look like living things. Also, the headlights resemble eyes.*

◆ Reading Strategy

❹ **Understand the Author's Bias** How does the last verse show the author's bias against cars? *She wonders whether the humans are driving the cars (the brains) or just being carried along by them (the guts).*

Customize for
Bodily/Kinesthetic Learners

Ask students if they have ever been in a traffic jam. Have students act out a traffic jam by lining up in four "lanes" going in two opposite directions. Tell the leaders to move very, very slowly. Explain to students that they cannot touch each other or they will cause an "accident." Encourage students to discuss the experience.

SOUTHBOUND ON THE FREEWAY

May Swenson

A tourist came in from Orbitville,
parked in the air, and said:

❶
The creatures of this star
are made of metal and glass.

5   Through the <u>transparent</u> parts
you can see their guts.

❷
Their feet are round and roll
on diagrams—or long

measuring tapes—dark
10   with white lines.

They have four eyes.
The two in the back are red.

Sometimes you can see a five-eyed
one, with a red eye turning

15   on the top of his head.
He must be special—

the others respect him,
and go slow,

when he passes, winding
20   among them from behind.

They all hiss as they glide,
like inches, down the marked

tapes. Those soft shapes,
shadowy inside

25   the hard bodies—are they
their guts or their brains? ❹

◆ Build Vocabulary

transparent (trans par′ ənt) *adj.*: Capable of being seen through; clear

▶ **Critical Viewing** Judging from the painting, why might an alien mistake cars for Earth's inhabitants? [Infer]

Where to? What For? #3, Nancie B. Warner, Courtesy of the artist

Block Scheduling Strategies

Consider these suggestions to take advantage of extended class time.

• Set up a writers' workshop to support students in the poetry writing activities on p. 471. Students may bring in poems they have written. Small groups can discuss one another's poems, giving constructive criticism. Another way to approach the workshop is to have students work with partners or in small groups to freewrite on the topics of the assignments. They may use their ideas to write individual or collaborative poems.

• Arrange for students to bring in materials for the Multimedia Report activity from the Idea Bank on p. 471. Have groups of students work together to prepare and present the report to the class.

• Students can explore the literary focus on free verse by listening to the recording. Encourage students to discuss the difference in sound between the free verse and the formal verse poems. Then have students try reading the poems aloud.

 Listening to Literature Audiocassettes

THE STORY-TELLER

Mark Van Doren

He talked, and as he talked
Wallpaper came alive;
Suddenly ghosts walked,
And four doors were five;

5 Calendars ran backward,
And maps had mouths;
Ships went tackward[1]
In a great drowse;[2]

Trains climbed trees,
10 And soon dripped down
Like honey of bees
On the cold brick town.

He had wakened a worm
In the world's brain,
15 And nothing stood firm
Until day again.

Inspiration, Daniel Nevins

▲ **Critical Viewing** Does this painting capture the magical quality of the story-teller? Why or why not? **[Evaluate]** ❼

1. **tackward** (tak´ wərd) *adv.*: Against the wind.
2. **drowse** (drouz) *n.*: Sluggishness; doze.

Guide for Responding

◆ LITERATURE AND YOUR LIFE

Reader's Response Which images in "The Story-Teller" appealed to you most? Why?

Thematic Focus Which poem do you find more extraordinary? Explain.

☑ Check Your Comprehension

1. Who is the speaker in "Southbound on the Freeway"?
2. In "Southbound on the Freeway," what is the tourist describing?
3. Name seven magical things that the story-teller can do.
4. According to "The Story-Teller," when will things be back to normal?

◆ Critical Thinking

INTERPRET
1. Compare and contrast the different kinds of creatures described in "Southbound on the Freeway." **[Compare and Contrast]**
2. How would you answer the tourist's question? **[Interpret]**
3. (a) In "The Story-Teller," what is the "worm" referred to in line 13? (b) What is the "world's brain" in line 14? **[Interpret]**
4. What is the message or theme of "The Story-Teller"? **[Analyze]**

APPLY
5. How might the tourist in "Southbound on the Freeway" "see" a drive-through window at a fast-food restaurant? **[Relate]**

◆ Critical Thinking

1. Most of the cars have two eyes in front and two in back, but the police car has a fifth eye on the top of its head. The "soft shapes" inside the cars are really humans.
2. Some students may say they are the brains, since they drive the cars. Others may say they are the guts, since they are carried by the cars.

3. Students may say that the "worm" is imagination and the "world's brain" is the thoughts of the people hearing the story.
4. A good storyteller can bring language alive and expand the listeners' imaginations.
5. The tourist might believe he was looking into the guts of a very large inhabitant of Earth.

Develop Understanding

One-Minute Insight A listener describes how the storyteller creates a magical world with his tales, making the images come alive.

◆ Critical Thinking

❺ **Speculate** What do these images mean? *A calendar running backward may mean that the story takes place in the past. "Maps had mouths" may mean that the storyteller told of faraway places.*

◆ Reading Strategy

❻ **Understand the Author's Bias** What is the poet's opinion about storytelling? Why do you think a poet feels this way? *He believes a good storyteller can share a special world with other people. A poet probably believes in the power of language.*

► Critical Viewing ◄

❼ **Evaluate** *Students may say that the figure appears to be floating in an unknown world, as if it is in a dream.*

Answers

Reinforce and Extend

◆ LITERATURE AND YOUR LIFE

Reader's Response Students will need to explain the appeal of their favorite images.

Thematic Focus Students may find the odd perspective of ordinary objects extraordinary; or they may feel the bizarre images in "The Story-Teller" are more unusual.

☑ Check Your Comprehension

1. The speaker is a visitor from "Orbitville," or outer space.
2. The tourist is describing a traffic jam of cars on the freeway.
3. Students may say that he makes wallpaper come alive, ghosts walk, time run backward, maps talk, ships go gently against the wind. He can create a door that isn't there, make trains climb trees and then drip down like honey.
4. Things will be normal again the next morning.

467

One-Minute Insight

The speaker hears echoes of his Puerto Rican homeland as he stands on a New York City street corner. He compares buildings to palm trees and trains to a dance. He feels homesick, yet he enjoys the urban excitement.

►Critical Viewing◄

❶ Assess *The city in the picture seems so busy that "everything will pass you by."*

◆Reading Strategy

❷ Understand the Author's Bias Why does the poet use a Spanish word here? *He is thinking of his native Puerto Rico, where Spanish is spoken.*

◆Critical Thinking

❸ Analyze Why does the speaker compare the skyscrapers to palm trees? *He may be trying to make the buildings seem less foreign or more friendly to himself.*

◆Reading Strategy

❹ Understand the Author's Bias

New York	Puerto Rico
skyscrapers	*palm trees*
trains roaring	*guaguanco*

What do the last three lines reveal about how the author views living in New York? *His memories of Puerto Rico are always with him, making New York a strange version of Puerto Rico.*

Customize for *Verbal/Linguistic Learners*

Discuss with students the free verse elements of this poem. They may note its lack of rhyme, its irregular rhythm, and the different lengths of both stanzas and lines. Encourage students to explain why free verse does or doesn't suit this poem.

Customize for *Visual/Spatial Learners*

Have students make a chart with two columns, one for New York and one for Puerto Rico. Then ask them to list the elements of each place that the speaker mentions in the poem.

Los New Yorks

Victor Hernández Cruz

New York City—Bird's Eye View, 1920, Joaquín Torres-García, Yale University Art Gallery

❶ ▲ **Critical Viewing** Do you have the feeling that in the world of this painting "Everything will pass you by"? Explain. [Assess]

In the news that sails through the air
Like the shaking seeds of maracas[1]
I find you out

 Suena[2]

5   You don't have to move here
Just stand on the corner
Everything will pass you by
Like a merry-go-round the red
bricks will swing past your eyes
10   They will melt
So   old
will move out by themselves

Suena

15 I present you the tall skyscrapers
as merely huge palm trees with lights ❸

Suena

The roaring of the trains is a fast
guaguanco[3]
dance of the ages

20 Suena

Snow falls
Coconut chips galore
Take the train to Caguas[4]
and the bus is only ten cents
25   to Aguas Buenas[5]

---

1. **maracas** (mə rä´ kəs) *n.*: Percussion instruments consisting of a rattle with loose pebbles in it, which are shaken.
2. **Suena** (swā´ nə): Spanish for "It echoes."

3. **guaguanco** (gwə gwän´ kō): Rumba, a dance with a complex rhythm.
4. **Caguas** (kä´ gwäs): City in the east-central region of Puerto Rico.
5. **Aguas Buenas** (ä´ gwäs bwä´ nəs): City in Puerto Rico, northwest of Caguas.

Speaking and Listening Mini-Lesson

Talk-Show Appearance

This mini-lesson supports the Speaking and Listening activity in the Idea Bank on p. 471.

Introduce Discuss the idea that if we did find life on another planet, we might not understand it. The alien tourist believes he understands Earthlings, but he has actually made his own interpretation.

Develop Have students work in pairs to act out the roles of talk-show host and traveler. Have them consider:

• What do inhabitants of Orbitville look like?
• What is a talk show like in Orbitville?

Apply Have partners write out a script to follow for the talk-show interview. They may want to create costumes for their roles.

Assess Evaluate students in terms of the script, their speaking, composure, eye contact, and body language. Or, have student audience members use the Peer Assessment: Dramatic Performance form, p. 116 in **Alternative Assessment.**

Suena

A _tropical_ wave settled here
And it is pulling the sun
with a _romp_
30　No one knows what to do

Suena

I am going home now
I am settled there with my fruits
Everything tastes good today
35　Even the ones that are grown here
Taste like they're from outer space
Walk y Suena[6]
❹ Do it strange
Los New Yorks.

---

6. **y suena** (ē swā′ nə): Spanish for "With the rhythm of the echoes."

◆ **Build Vocabulary**

galore (gə lôr′) _adj._: In abundance; plentiful
tropical (träp′ ə kəl) _adj._: Very hot; sultry
romp (rämp) _n._: Lively play or frolic

Social Studies Connection

Puerto Rico In "Los New Yorks," Victor Hernández Cruz compares the tropical atmosphere of Puerto Rico, a commonwealth of the United States, with metropolitan New York. Puerto Rico is an island located about 1,000 miles southeast of Florida. It has a pleasant climate, largely influenced by the warm waters of the Caribbean. Most of the region's land is mountainous, but a walk along the coast provides picturesque views of beaches and rows of flourishing palm trees, which provide the meat and sweet milk of the coconut.

Cross-Curricular Activity

Do further research on the climate and geography of Puerto Rico. Combine your findings into a multimedia report to present to your class.

Guide for Responding

◆ LITERATURE AND YOUR LIFE

Reader's Response Based on the details in this poem, would you like to visit "Los New Yorks"? Explain.

Thematic Focus What is extraordinary about New York? What about New York is ordinary?

Sketch Draw a sketch of New York based on the description provided in "Los New Yorks."

☑ **Check Your Comprehension**

1. Where is the speaker?
2. What two places is the speaker comparing?

◆ Critical Thinking

INTERPRET

1. What evidence is there that the speaker has strong memories of another place? **[Support]**
2. When the speaker says that he is going home, where is he going? **[Draw Conclusions]**
3. What effect does the repetition of the Spanish word _suena_ have on the poem? **[Interpret]**

COMPARE LITERARY WORKS

4. Compare the rhythms, rhymes, and stanza lengths of "The Story-Teller," "Southbound on the Freeway," and "Los New Yorks." How does each style contribute to the feel and effect of the poem? **[Compare and Contrast]**

Los New Yorks ◆ 469

Beyond the Selection

FURTHER READING
Other Works by the Authors
The Complete Poems to Solve, May Swenson
In Other Words, May Swenson
Mortal Summer, Mark Van Doren
Red Beans; Poems, Victor Hernández Cruz

INTERNET
We suggest the following sites on the Internet (all Web sites are subject to change).
　To find additional poems by May Swenson, go to:
http://www.geocities.com/SoHo/9375/retromxs.html
　To find another poem by Mark Van Doren, go to:
http://www.okcom.net/~ggao.html
　To find additional poems by Victor Hernández Cruz, go to:
http://www.wnet.org/archive/lol/cruz.html
　We _strongly recommend_ that you preview these sites before you send students to them.

Students may find information in the encyclopedia, on the Internet, and at travel agencies. Let them know there are two small nearby islands that are part of Puerto Rico, Vieques and Culebra. Students may want to make a three-dimensional model of Puerto Rico to show its varied terrain.

Reinforce and Extend

Answers
◆ **LITERATURE AND YOUR LIFE**

Reader's Response Some might find it too busy; others might find it appealing because it seems to be both New York and Puerto Rico.

Thematic Focus An extraordinary aspect of New York is the "everything" the poet mentions—the buildings, the many people, the roaring trains. The ordinary side is that it is a place where people live, work, and buy fruit.

☑ **Check Your Comprehension**

1. The speaker is in New York City.
2. He is comparing New York and Puerto Rico.

◆ Critical Thinking

1. Evidence includes the repetition of _suena,_ comparisons of the buildings and trains to trees and dances in Puerto Rico, and the way the speaker slips back and forth between them in his imagination.
2. He is going to his home in New York City.
3. The repetition of _suena_ creates an echo in the poem, reminding readers that the speaker is always thinking of his former home.
4. "The Story-Teller" has a regular rhythm and rhyme scheme, and its stanzas are all the same length. "Southbound on the Freeway" has irregular rhythm and no rhyme, but all the stanzas are two lines long. "Los New Yorks" has irregular rhythm, no rhyme, and stanzas of uneven length. "The Story-Teller" has a formal tone because of its structure. "Southbound" sounds more like conversational speech, but the stanzas create a certain order or rhythm. The repetition of _suena_ in "Los New Yorks" gives the poem a rhythm similar to a chant.

469

Answers

◆ Reading Strategy

1. She believes we are too dependent on cars and that they are too important in our lives.
2. He believes it is a great art that encourages imagination.
3. He prefers Puerto Rico to New York.

◆ Build Vocabulary

Using the Prefix trans-
1. transform;   2. transcontinental;
3. transplant;   4. transatlantic

Spelling Strategy
1. tropical;   2. icicle;   3. bicycle;
4. medical;   5. historical;
6. musical

Using the Word Bank
1. d   2. c   3. b   4. a

◆ Literary Focus

1. It has a regular rhythm, a pattern of rhymes at the end of the lines, and the stanzas are each four lines long.
2. The stanzas vary in number of lines and the lines are different lengths.
3. The poet can create his or her own sense of rhythm, or may allow the language to sound conversational. The poet is not bound by certain patterns of rhyme or rhythm, so he or she has more freedom.

◆ Build Grammar Skills

Practice
1. magical; storyteller
2. strange; aliens
3. red; bricks
4. huge; palm trees
5. good; fruit

Writing Application
Check that students place the predicate adjective after the linking verb. It should be clear that the predicate adjective refers to and describes the subject.

Possible responses:
1. Mark Van Doren must have been very talkative.
2. My eyes were red with fatigue.
3. The three-eyed Earthlings were special.
4. The interiors of the cars were shadowy.
5. The buildings were tall.
6. The tropical fruit was sweet.

470

Guide for Responding (continued)

◆ Reading Strategy

UNDERSTAND THE AUTHOR'S BIAS

If you **understand the author's bias,** you recognize his or her tendency to be for or against something.
1. What is May Swenson's attitude toward cars and their importance in our lives?
2. How does Mark Van Doren feel about the art of storytelling?
3. What does "Los New Yorks" reveal about Victor Hernández Cruz's bias concerning New York?

◆ Build Vocabulary

USING THE PREFIX trans-

The prefix *trans-* in *transparent* means "through" or "across." Determine the meaning of the following words with the prefix *trans-.* Then, on your paper, complete the sentences with one of these words: *transatlantic, transcontinental, transform, transplant.*

1. Soon the ugly duckling will ____?____ into a graceful swan.
2. We took a ____?____ road trip.
3. Should we ____?____ this tree in the back yard?
4. Our ____?____ cruise took more than a week.

SPELLING STRATEGY

The ending *cal* usually indicates an adjective; *cle* is always a noun ending.
On your paper, write the word in each pair that is spelled correctly.
1. tropical, tropicle
2. icical, icicle
3. bicycal, bicycle
4. medical, medicle
5. historical, historicle
6. musical, musicle

USING THE WORD BANK

On your paper, write the letter of the definition that matches the numbered word from the Word Bank.
1. galore
2. romp
3. transparent
4. tropical

a. hot and humid
b. may be seen through
c. noisy play
d. in great amounts

◆ Literary Focus

FREE VERSE

Poetry that has irregular rhythms, rhymes, and stanzas is called **free verse.** You will notice that "Southbound on the Freeway" and "Los New Yorks," which are written in free verse, sound more like everyday speech than "The Story-Teller" does.
1. Explain why "The Story-Teller" does not fit the definition of free verse.
2. How do the stanzas of "Los New Yorks" illustrate free verse form?
3. What does a poet accomplish by using free verse rather than traditional forms?

◆ Build Grammar Skills

PREDICATE ADJECTIVES

A **predicate adjective** is an adjective that comes after a linking verb and refers to the subject, describing it.

Their feet are *round.* . . . (The adjective *round* describes the subject *feet.*)

He must be *special.* . . . (The adjective *special* describes the subject *he.*)

Practice Write these sentences on your paper, and underline the predicate adjective in each. Circle the subject to which it refers.
1. The storyteller is almost magical.
2. The aliens were strange.
3. The bricks are red.
4. The palm trees seem huge.
5. The fruit tastes good.

Writing Application On your paper, write a sentence that uses the idea in each phrase. Make the adjective in each phrase a predicate adjective in the sentence.
1. talkative storyteller
2. red eyes
3. special creature
4. shadowy shapes
5. tall skyscrapers
6. sweet peaches

Build Your Portfolio

 ## Idea Bank

Writing

1. **Travel Advertisement** Imagine that you are a travel agent from Orbitville. You are trying to interest tourists on your planet in travel to Earth. Write a travel advertisement, telling them what they might find if they make the trip. **[Career Link]**

2. **City Poem** The speaker in "Los New Yorks" describes New York City. Write your own description of a major city in the form of a free verse poem. **[Social Studies Link]**

3. **Analysis** Write a paper in which you analyze the images in one of these poems. Describe the poet's choice of words, the originality of the images, and their overall effectiveness. Cite lines from the poem to support your ideas.

Speaking and Listening

4. **Talk-Show Appearance [Group Activity]** With a partner, act out an episode of a talk show on Orbitville for the class. One of you is the host, and the other has just returned from a trip to Earth. **[Media Link]**

5. **Storyteller** Perform a story for your class. You may make up a story or tell one you know. Try to make your storytelling a magical experience, like the one described in Van Doren's poem. **[Performing Arts Link]**

Projects

6. **Multimedia Report** Put together a multimedia report on New York City. Gather photos, magazine and newspaper clippings, and, if possible, souvenirs and videotapes. Write your text, and present the report to the class. **[Social Studies Link]**

7. **Painting** Bring "Southbound on the Freeway" to life in a painting. Show Earthlings as seen by the poem's speaker. Display your painting for the class. **[Art Link]**

 ## Writing Mini-Lesson

Poem About a Person or Place

In these poems, you get the poet's attitude toward a person, place, or thing. To create their unique attitudes, the poets chose words to create very specific images. Write a poem about a person or place, and bring it to life through your word choice.

Writing Skills Focus: Using Appropriate Tone

Decide on your attitude toward your subject. Your attitude will help you develop an **appropriate tone,** which is achieved through word choice. In this example, the tone is somewhat distanced and unemotional, like that of a reporter.

Model From "Southbound on the Freeway"

> The creatures of this star
> are made of metal and glass.
>
> Through the transparent parts
> you can see their guts.

Prewriting Choose a subject for your poem. Decide on a tone, and choose details to use in your poem. Also, decide whether you will use free verse or a more traditional form that will require rhyme and specific line and stanza breaks.

Drafting Begin drafting. If you're writing free verse, break stanzas when you change a thought. If you're writing within a traditional poetic form, follow the appropriate structure and rhyme scheme.

> ◆ **Grammar Application**
> Make your predicate adjectives, like all adjectives, vivid and precise.

Revising Look for places where more precise words will make your subject more vivid. Replace words and phrases that do not contribute to the tone you've chosen. Proofread your poem to correct errors.

 ## Idea Bank

Following are suggestions for matching the Idea Bank topics with your students' performance levels and learning modalities:

Customize for *Performance Levels*
Less Advanced Students: 1, 4, 6, 7
Average Students: 2, 4, 5, 6, 7
More Advanced Students: 3, 4, 5, 7

Customize for *Learning Modalities*
Verbal/Linguistic: 1, 2, 3, 4, 5, 6
Visual/Spatial: 1, 6, 7
Bodily/Kinesthetic: 4
Interpersonal: 4
Intrapersonal: 2, 7

 ## Writing Mini-Lesson

Refer students to the Writing Handbook at the back of the book for instruction on the writing process and for further information on expression.

 ## Writer's Solution

Writing Lab CD-ROM
Have students complete the tutorial on Creative Writing. Follow these steps:

1. To stimulate creativity and explore possible topics, have students use *Poem Written* in the Inspirations for Creative Writing.
2. Students can use the Image Bin, Emotion Word Bin, or Character Trait Word Bin activities to help them choose the best words to create the appropriate tone and create specific images.
3. Have students use the Models From Literature poems in the Drafting section to help them draft.
4. Students can use the Audio-annotated Student Models of poems to see changes made to poems when they are proofread and the reasons for each change.

Writer's Solution Sourcebook
Have students use Chapter 8, "Creative Writing," pp. 234–265, for additional support. The chapter includes in-depth instruction on various types of poetry to help students use an appropriate tone and make word choices.

✓ ASSESSMENT OPTIONS

Formal Assessment, Selection Test, pp. 140–142, and Assessment Resources Software. The selection test is designed so that it can easily be customized to the performance levels of your students.

Alternative Assessment, p. 134, includes options for less advanced students, more advanced students, musical/rhythmic learners, bodily/kinesthetic learners, visual/spatial learners, interpersonal learners, logical/mathematical learners, and verbal/linguistic learners.

PORTFOLIO ASSESSMENT
Use the following rubrics in the **Alternative Assessment** booklet to assess student writing:
Travel Advertisement: Description, p. 93
City Poem: Poetry, p. 104
Analysis: Response to Literature, p. 106
Writing Mini-Lesson: Poetry, p. 104

One-Minute Insight

In "The Adventure of the Speckled Band," Dr. Watson describes how Sherlock Holmes takes a case regarding a mysterious death that happened two years earlier. The setting is an ancient manor house in ruinous disrepair, occupied by a young woman, her ill-tempered stepfather, and his "pets," a baboon and a cheetah. Through ingenious deductions and by staying awake all night in an unlit room, Holmes solves the mystery and prevents a second murder from taking place.

◆ Literary Focus

❶ Mystery Story Who is narrating the story? What important details do you learn about Holmes from the beginning of his narration? *Watson is narrating. We learn that he has studied Holmes for the last eight years, during which time the detective has had seventy cases. Also, we learn that Holmes does his work because he enjoys it, not to make money. He prefers unusual cases.*

◆ Critical Thinking

❷ Infer What clue does the narration give to Watson's personality? *He may resent a change in his regular routine.*

◆ Literary Focus

❸ Mystery Story Dr. Watson provides some information about the case, but at this point in the story the reader cannot know what it means.

Customize for
English Language Learners

Initiate a dialogue journal with any student who may be struggling with the 19th-century style of writing. Have the student write entries about the selection as he or she reads. Respond to each entry with your comments, focusing on the reading comprehension rather than writing skills for this activity.

THE ADVENTURE of the SPECKLED BAND

Sir Arthur Conan Doyle

On glancing over my notes of the seventy odd cases in which I have during the last eight years studied the methods of my friend Sherlock Holmes, I find many tragic, some comic, a large number merely strange, but none commonplace; for, working as he did rather for the love of his art than for the acquirement of wealth, he refused to associate himself with any investigation which did not tend towards the unusual, and even the fantastic. Of all these varied cases, however, I cannot recall any which presented more singular features than that which was associated with the well-known Surrey family of the Roylotts of Stoke Moran. The events in question occurred in the early days of my association with Holmes when we were sharing rooms as bachelors in Baker Street. It is possible that I might have placed them upon record before but a promise of secrecy was made at the time, from which I have only been freed during the last month by the untimely death of the lady to whom the pledge was given. It is perhaps as well that the facts should now come to light, for I have reasons to know that there are widespread rumors as to the death of Dr. Grimesby Roylott which tend to make the matter even more terrible than the truth.

It was early in April in the year 1883 that I woke one morning to find Sherlock Holmes standing, fully dressed, by the side of my bed. He was a late riser, as a rule, and as the clock on the mantelpiece showed me that it was only a quarter past seven, I blinked up at him in some surprise, and perhaps just a little resentment, for I was myself regular in my habits.

"Very sorry to wake you up, Watson," said he, "but it's the common lot this morning. Mrs. Hudson has been awakened, she retorted upon me, and I on you."

"What is it, then—a fire?"

"No; a client. It seems that a young lady has arrived in a considerable state of excitement who insists upon seeing me. She is waiting now in the sitting room. Now, when young ladies wander about the metropolis at this hour of the morning, and get sleepy people up out of their beds, I presume that it is something very pressing which they have to communicate. Should it prove to be an interesting case, you would, I am sure, wish to follow it from the outset. I thought, at any rate, that I should call you and give you the chance."

"My dear fellow, I would not miss it for anything."

I had no keener pleasure than in following Holmes in his professional

474 ◆ Extraordinary Occurrences

Block Scheduling Strategies

Consider these suggestions to take advantage of extended class time:

- To introduce this Sherlock Holmes mystery, begin with **Daily Language Practice,** p. 8. Then have students read the mystery story in groups, recording details in their evidence charts. Encourage group members to stop and discuss clues as they go along.

- Have students form groups to work on the Classroom Mystery activity on p. 493 supported by the Viewing and Representing Mini-Lesson on p. 485 (Teacher Edition).

- If you have access to technology, have students use the *Writer's Solution Writing Lab CD-ROM* to prepare for and complete the Writing Mini-Lesson.

- To prepare for the Radio Play activity on p. 493 (and supported by the Speaking and Listening Mini-Lesson on p. 488), have students listen to the recording of "The Adventure of the Speckled Band." Students can create their own dialogue and develop each character's voice.

 Listening to Literature Audiocassettes

investigations, and in admiring the rapid deductions, as swift as intuitions, and yet always founded on a logical basis, with which he unraveled the problems which were submitted to him. I rapidly threw on my clothes and was ready in a few minutes to accompany my friend down to the sitting room. A lady dressed in black and heavily veiled, who had been sitting in the window, rose as we entered.

"Good morning, madam," said Holmes cheerily. "My name is Sherlock Holmes. This is my intimate friend and associate, Dr. Watson, before whom you can speak as freely as before myself. Ha! I am glad to see that Mrs. Hudson has had the good sense to light the fire. Pray draw up to it, and I shall order you a cup of hot coffee, for I observe that you are shivering."

"It is not cold which makes me shiver," said the woman in a low voice, changing her seat as requested.

◆ Literature and Your Life
Does this introduction to Sherlock Holmes fit the picture you have of him through film and television portrayals?

"What, then?"

"It is fear, Mr. Holmes. It is terror." She raised her veil as she spoke, and we could see that she was indeed in a pitiable state of agitation, her face all drawn and gray, with restless, frightened eyes, like those of some hunted animal. Her features and figure were those of a woman of thirty, but her hair was shot with premature gray, and her expression was weary and haggard. Sherlock Holmes ran her over with one of his quick, all-comprehensive glances.

"You must not fear," said he soothingly, bending forward and patting her forearm.

"We shall soon set matters right, I have no doubt. You have come in by train this morning, I see."

"You know me, then?"

"No, but I observe the second half of a return ticket in the palm of your left glove. You must have started early, and yet you had a good drive in a dogcart[1] along heavy roads, before you reached the station."

▲ Critical Viewing What can you tell about the characters of Helen Stoner, Holmes, and Watson based on this illustration? [Infer] ❼

The lady gave a violent start and stared in bewilderment at my companion.

"There is no mystery, my dear madam," said he, smiling. "The left arm of your jacket is spattered with mud in no less than seven places. The marks are perfectly fresh. There is no vehicle save a dogcart which throws up mud in that way, and then only when you sit on the left-hand side of the driver."

"Whatever your reasons may be, you are perfectly correct," said she. "I started from home before six, reached Leatherhead at twenty past, and came in by the

---
1. **dogcart:** Small horse-drawn carriage with seats arranged back-to-back.

The Adventure of the Speckled Band ◆ 475

◆ Literary Focus
❹ Mystery Story Watson explains how Sherlock Holmes solves mysteries. As you read, see if you can follow Holmes's reasoning when he makes deductions.

◆ LITERATURE AND YOUR LIFE
❺ *Students' responses will depend on which portrayals of Holmes they have seen. Encourage them to explain their answers.*

◆ Reading Strategy
❻ Identify the Evidence Ask students to explain how Holmes knows the woman came in by train. Then ask them to guess his reasoning for saying she rode in a dogcart before taking the train. *He knows she came by train because he observes the return ticket in her glove. Students will find Holmes's reasoning for his dogcart assumption in his next quotation.*

▶Critical Viewing◀
❼ Infer *Students may say that Helen Stoner appears upset or nervous and Holmes seems attentive. Watson stays in the background, but is also listening closely.*

Customize for
Verbal/Linguistic Learners
Invite students to try an oral interpretation of Dr. Watson's opening paragraphs and the conversation between the doctor and Sherlock Holmes. Point out that the language is somewhat formal and that each sentence is full of details. Encourage them to speak the way they imagine Englishmen would have sounded one hundred years ago.

✦ **Humanities: Literature**

Sherlock Holmes Sir Arthur Conan Doyle first created the character of Sherlock Holmes in an attempt to organize the fascinating concept of a fictional detective (based on his own boyhood reading) into an exact science. Doyle drew on his medical training, interest in neatly woven plots, experience as a ship's doctor, and an actual surgeon he had known to create Sherlock Holmes. The result was the best known detective in literature.

The name, Sherlock Holmes, was derived from Dr. Oliver Wendell Holmes and a famous cricketeer. Holmes's character shares many traits with the surgeon who was not only medically talented, but skilled in diagnosing occupation and character along with disease.

Doyle was never a dedicated doctor. As his stories about the adventures of Sherlock Holmes quickly became popular, Doyle gave up his career in medicine. His scientific knowledge and technique, however, appears over and over as Holmes believably solves crimes. Sherlock Holmes, in fact, has been so believable that readers have been known to visit Baker Street in London, looking for his fictional address.

Clarification

❶ At this time in England, it was the custom for young women who had an inheritance to receive the money only when they married.

◆ Literary Focus

❷ Mystery Story It was a common device in Sherlock Holmes stories to refer to a previous case that the detective had solved.

◆ Literary Focus

❸ Mystery Story Based on what the young woman is saying, do you think she is a reliable speaker? *Some students may say she seems too nervous and confused, and may be lying; others may believe she is scared, but truthful.*

Clarification

❹ The Regency (1811–1820) was a brief but tumultuous period in British history. In 1811, King George III was declared insane and his son was named Prince Regent. When the king died in 1820, the prince became King George IV. Great Britain and its allies triumphed over Napoleon in 1815. The period was characterized by much extravagance among the privileged classes, which included gambling and prodigal spending.

◆ Reading Strategy

❺ Identify the Evidence If students began keeping the evidence chart on p. 473, they may note that Helen Stoner's stepfather is portrayed as a violent man.

Customize for
Logical/Mathematical Learners

Encourage students to continue filling in the evidence chart they began on p. 473 as they read Helen Stoner's story. Invite them to make predictions about the mystery as it unfolds.

476

---

first train to Waterloo. Sir, I can stand this strain no longer; I shall go mad if it continues. I have no one to turn to—none, save only one, who cares for me, and he, poor fellow, can be of little aid. I have heard of you, Mr. Holmes. I have heard of you from Mrs. Farintosh, whom you helped in the hour of her sore need. It was from her that I had your address. Oh, sir, do you not think that you could help me, too, and at least throw a little light through the dense darkness which surrounds me? At present it is out of my power to reward you for your service, but in a month or six weeks I shall be married, with the control of my own income, and then at least you shall not find me ungrateful."

Holmes turned to his desk and, unlocking it, drew out a small case book, which he consulted.

"Farintosh," said he. "Ah yes, I recall the case; it was concerned with an opal tiara. I think it was before your time, Watson. I can only say, madam, that I shall be happy to devote the same care to your case as I did to that of your friend. As to reward, my profession is its own reward; but you are at liberty to <u>defray</u> whatever expenses I may be put to, at the time which suits you best. And now I beg that you will lay before us everything that may help us in forming an opinion upon the matter."

"Alas!" replied our visitor, "the very horror of my situation lies in the fact that my fears are so vague, and my suspicions depend so entirely upon small points, which might seem trivial to another, that even he to whom of all others I have a right to look for help and advice looks upon all that I tell him about it as fancy. He does not say so, but I can read it from his soothing answers and averted eyes. But I have heard, Mr. Holmes, that you can see deeply into the <u>manifold</u> wickedness of the human heart. You may advise me how to walk amid the dangers which encompass me."

"I am all attention, madam."

"My name is Helen Stoner, and I am living with my stepfather, who is the last survivor of one of the oldest Saxon families in England: the Roylotts of Stoke Moran, on the western border of Surrey."

Holmes nodded his head. "The name is familiar to me," said he.

"The family was at one time among the richest in England, and the estates extended over the borders into Berkshire in the north, and Hampshire in the west. In the last century, however, four successive heirs were of a dissolute and wasteful disposition, and the family ruin was eventually completed by a gambler in the days of the Regency. Nothing was left save a few acres of ground, and the two-hundred-year-old house, which is itself crushed under a heavy mortgage. The last squire dragged out his existence there, living the horrible life of an aristocratic pauper; but his only son, my stepfather, seeing that he must adapt himself to the new conditions, obtained an advance from a relative, which enabled him to take a medical degree and went out to Calcutta, where, by his professional skill and his force of character, he established a large practice. In a fit of anger, however, caused by some robberies which had been perpetrated in the house, he beat his native butler to death and narrowly escaped a capital sentence. As it was, he suffered a long term of imprisonment and afterwards returned to England a <u>morose</u> and disappointed man.

"When Dr. Roylott was in India he married my mother, Mrs. Stoner, the young widow of Major-General Stoner, of the Bengal Artillery. My sister Julia and I were twins, and we were only two years old at the time of my mother's remarriage. She had a considerable sum of money—not less than £1000 a year[2]—and this she bequeathed to Dr. Roylott entirely while we resided with him, with a provision that a certain annual sum should be allowed to

---

2. **£1000:** One thousand pounds; £ is the symbol for pound or pounds, the British unit of money.

✂ Cross-Curricular Connection: Social Studies

India and England During the late 1800's, when this story takes place, Britain had control over India, and many British people traveled there to live and work.

British interest in India dates back to 1600, when the English East India Company was formed to conduct trade. Gradually British financial strength in India grew into political power, and by the mid-1700's, England ruled India.

In 1857, the First War of Indian Independence broke out. While the Indians were defeated in

this effort, they continued to fight the British throughout a series of wars. Finally, in 1947, India won independence from England.

In Conan Doyle's time, many British viewed India as an exotic, mysterious, and somewhat dangerous land. Those with financial means to travel, or military and political reasons to go to India, often visited for months at a time. It was considered unhealthy to live there for a long time, as Europeans often contracted typhoid fever, a disease that affects the intestines.

each of us in the event of our marriage. Shortly after our return to England my mother died—she was killed eight years ago in a railway accident near Crewe. Dr. Roylott then abandoned his attempts to establish himself in practice in London and took us to live with him in the old ancestral house at Stoke Moran. The money which my mother had left was enough for all our wants, and there seemed to be no obstacle to our happiness.

"But a terrible change came over our stepfather about this time. Instead of making friends and exchanging visits with our neighbors, who had at first been overjoyed to see a Roylott of Stoke Moran back in the old family seat, he shut himself up in his house and seldom came out save to indulge in ferocious quarrels with whoever might cross his path. Violence of temper approaching to mania has been hereditary in the men of the family, and in my stepfather's case it had, I believe, been intensified by his long residence in the tropics. A series of disgraceful brawls took place, two of which ended in the police court, until at last he became the terror of the village, and the folks would fly at his approach, for he is a man of immense strength, and absolutely uncontrollable in his anger.

"Last week he hurled the local blacksmith over a parapet into a stream, and it was only by paying over all the money which I could gather together that I was able to avert another public exposure. He had no friends at all save the wandering gypsies, and he would give these vagabonds leave to encamp upon the few acres of bramble-covered land which represent

▲ **Critical Viewing** Which event in Roylott's life does this illustration depict? [Connect] **8**

the family estate, and would accept in return the hospitality of their tents, wandering away with them sometimes for weeks on end. He has a passion also for Indian animals, which are sent over to him by a correspondent, and he has at this moment a cheetah and a baboon, which wander freely over his grounds and are feared by the villagers almost as much as is their master.

◆ **Build Vocabulary**

defray (di frā´) v.: To pay or furnish the money for

manifold (man´ ə fōld´) adj.: Many and varied

morose (mə rōs´) adj.: Gloomy; ill-tempered; sullen

The Adventure of the Speckled Band ◆ 477

Clarification

6 When Helen's mother died, she left money to her husband, Dr. Roylott. However, according to her will, each daughter would receive a certain amount of that money when she got married.

◆ **Critical Thinking**

7 Cause and Effect What reasons does Helen give for her stepfather's violent temper? *It is a hereditary trait, which was worsened by his residence in India.*

▶**Critical Viewing**◀

8 Connect *He is throwing the blacksmith over the parapet, or low wall, into the stream.*

◆ **Reading Strategy**

9 Identify the Evidence What do you learn about Dr. Roylott in this passage? *He travels with the gypsies and he has a baboon and a cheetah for pets.*

Customize for
Logical/Mathematical Learners

Encourage students to look over their evidence charts. Elicit that they have learned several things about Dr. Roylott: He is dead, he had a violent temper and great strength, he was friends with gypsies, and he had a pet baboon and cheetah.

Cultural Connection

Family Estate Aristocratic families in England often owned the same land that had been passed down from ancestors for many generations. The estate would consist of a large house or mansion and the land surrounding it. Usually there was a village nearby, which contained a few shops and perhaps an inn.

This arrangement dates from the feudal system in medieval times. Then the lord of the manor often owned the village as well as the estate and controlled the peasants who worked the land.

By the late 1800's, the workers were no longer tied to the estate, but the villagers may have felt some connection to the family that owned the manor. Maintaining a large estate was a costly venture because of the extensive acreage, large house, and accompanying buildings. As happened with the Roylotts of Stoke Moran, some aristocrats were unable to support their estates and lived in poverty despite being property owners.

❶ **Mystery Story** What details in this passage describe the difficult life of the sisters? *They seldom met anyone of their own age or social position, and they were only allowed brief visits to their aunt.*

◆ **Reading Strategy**

❷ **Identify the Evidence** What do you learn that may explain why Helen is so afraid? *She is soon to be married; her sister died within two weeks (a fortnight) of her own wedding.*

◆ **Reading Strategy**

❸ **Identify the Evidence** Encourage students to make predictions as to the cause of the whistle. Later they may determine whether or not they were correct.

◆ **Reading Strategy**

❹ **Identify the Evidence** Why does Holmes ask this question? *Students may say it is unusual for people to lock themselves in their rooms unless they feel threatened. It also means no one could enter the sister's room.*

Customize for
English Language Learners
Students may have difficulty following Helen Stoner's narrative and description. Have two students read together, paraphrasing each paragraph or quotation as they read.

❶ "You can imagine from what I say that my poor sister Julia and I had no great pleasure in our lives. No servant would stay with us, and for a long time we did all the work of the house. She was but thirty at the time of her death, and yet her hair had already begun to whiten, even as mine has."

"Your sister is dead, then?"

"She died just two years ago, and it is of her death that I wish to speak to you. You can understand that, living the life which I have described, we were little likely to see anyone of our own age and position. We had, however, an aunt, my mother's ❷ maiden sister, Miss Honoria Westphail, who lives near Harrow, and we were occasionally allowed to pay short visits at this lady's house. Julia went there at Christmas two years ago, and met there a major in the Marines, to whom she became engaged. My stepfather learned of the engagement when my sister returned and offered no objection to the marriage; but within a fortnight of the day which had been fixed for the wedding, the terrible event occurred which has deprived me of my only companion."

Sherlock Holmes had been leaning back in his chair with his eyes closed and his head sunk in a cushion, but he half opened his lids now and glanced across at his visitor.

"Pray be precise as to details," said he.

"It is easy for me to be so, for every event of that dreadful time is seared into my memory. The manor house is, as I have already said, very old, and only one wing is now inhabited. The bedrooms in this wing are on the ground floor, the sitting rooms being in the central block of the buildings. Of these bedrooms the first is Dr. Roylott's, the second my sister's, and the third my own. There is no communication between them, but they all open out into the same corridor. Do I make myself plain?"

"Perfectly so."

"The windows of the three rooms open out upon the lawn. That fatal night Dr. Roylott had gone to his room early, though we knew that he had not retired to rest, for my sister was troubled by the smell of the strong Indian cigars which it was his custom to smoke. She left her room, therefore, and came into mine, where she sat for some time, chatting about her approaching wedding. At eleven o'clock she rose to leave me, but she paused at the door and looked back.

"'Tell me, Helen,' said she, 'have you ever heard anyone whistle in the dead of the night?'

"'Never,' said I.

"'I suppose that you could not possibly whistle, yourself, in your sleep?'

"'Certainly not. But why?'

"'Because during the last few nights I have always, about three in the morning, heard a low, clear whistle. I am a light sleeper, and it has awakened me. I cannot tell where it came from—perhaps from the next room, perhaps from the lawn. I ❸ thought that I would just ask you whether you had heard it.'

"'No, I have not. It must be the gypsies in the plantation.'

"'Very likely. And yet if it were on the lawn, I wonder that you did not hear it also.'

"'Ah, but I sleep more heavily than you.'

"'Well, it is of no great consequence, at any rate.' She smiled back at me, closed my door, and a few moments later I heard her key turn in the lock."

"Indeed," said Holmes. "Was it your cus- ❹ tom always to lock yourselves in at night?"

"Always."

"And why?"

"I think that I mentioned to you that the doctor kept a cheetah and a baboon. We had no feeling of security unless our doors were locked."

"Quite so. Pray proceed with your statement."

"I could not sleep that night. A vague feeling of impending misfortune impressed me. My sister and I, you will recollect, were

 Cultural Connection

Gypsies Gypsies have always been viewed with suspicion and dislike. They were often thought to be kidnappers and assassins. Their nomadic ways give them a kind of exotic glamour. In England, Gypsies have traditionally been viewed as being beyond the usual moral constraints. People who associated with them were viewed as rebellious or even dangerous.

Gypsies are a nomadic people who originated in northern India but live all over the world today, principally in Europe. Gypsies first appeared in western Europe in the 1400's. True Gypsies refer to themselves by one name, Rom, and most of them speak Romany—a language that combines the language they brought from India with the local languages of the countries where they live.

Gypsies have managed to maintain their itinerant existence by pursuing occupations that allow them to migrate. The men have been livestock traders, animal trainers, tinkers, and musicians; the women, fortune tellers and entertainers.

The word *Gypsy* is a corruption of *Egyptian*. Many people thought the Gypsies were from Egypt before their Indian origin was known.

twins, and you know how subtle are the links which bind two souls which are so closely allied. It was a wild night. The wind was howling outside, and the rain was beating and splashing against the windows. Suddenly, amid all the hubbub of the gale, there burst forth the wild scream of a terrified woman. I knew that it was my sister's voice. I sprang from my bed, wrapped a shawl round me, and rushed into the corridor. As I opened my door I seemed to hear a low whistle, such as my sister described, and a few moments later a clanging sound, as if a mass of metal had fallen. As I ran down the passage, my sister's door was unlocked, and revolved slowly upon its hinges. I stared at it horror-stricken, not knowing what was about to issue from it. By the light of the corridor lamp I saw my sister appear at the opening, her face blanched with terror, her hands groping for help, her whole figure swaying to and fro like that of a drunkard. I ran to her and threw my arms round her, but at that moment her knees seemed to give way and she fell to the ground. She writhed as one who is in terrible pain, and her limbs were dreadfully <u>convulsed</u>. At first I thought that she had not recognized me, but as I bent over her she suddenly shrieked out in a voice which I shall never forget, 'Oh, Helen! It was the band! The speckled band!' There was something else which she would fain have said, and she stabbed with her finger into the air in the direction of the doctor's room, but a fresh convulsion

seized her and choked her words. I rushed out, calling loudly for my stepfather, and I met him hastening from his room in his dressing gown. When he reached my sister's side she was unconscious, and though he poured brandy down her throat and sent for medical aid from the village, all efforts were in vain, for she slowly sank and died without having recovered her consciousness. Such was the dreadful end of my beloved sister."

"One moment," said Holmes; "are you sure about this whistle and metallic sound? Could you swear to it?"

"That was what the county coroner asked me at the inquiry. It is my strong impression that I heard it, and yet, among the crash of the gale and the creaking of an old house, I may possibly have been deceived."

"Was your sister dressed?"

"No, she was in her nightdress. In her right hand was found the charred stump of a match, and in her left a matchbox."

"Showing that she had struck a light and looked about her when the alarm took place. That is important. And what conclusions did the coroner come to?"

"He investigated the case with great care, for Dr. Roylott's conduct had long been notorious in the county, but he was unable to find any satisfactory cause of

▲ **Critical Viewing** How well does this illustration convey Julia Stoner's face, "blanched with terror"? [Evaluate]

◆ **Build Vocabulary**

convulsed (kən vulst´) *adj.*: Taken over by violent, involuntary spasms

The Adventure of the Speckled Band ◆ 479

◆ **Literary Focus**

⑤ Mystery Story In what way is this scene a cliché in a mystery story? *Students may say the howling wind, the beating rain, and the screaming woman might be expected in a mystery.*

◆ **Reading Strategy**

⑥ Identify the Evidence What aspects of Helen's story might be evidence toward solving the mystery? Why? *The whistle and the clanging sound were unusual for the middle of the night.*

◆ **Reading Strategy**

⑦ Identify the Evidence What do you think the speckled band is? *Students may make guesses.*

▶**Critical Viewing**◀

⑧ Evaluate Students may need to check the definition of "blanched," which means *made pale,* or *drained of color.* *Her face is pale and her expression shows she is terrified.*

Thematic Focus

⑨ Why does Holmes say it is important to know that Julia held a match and a matchbox when she died? *It means she was striking a light in order to see something in her room.*

Beyond the Classroom

Workplace Skills
Careful Listening Point out to students that Sherlock Holmes listens carefully to Helen Stoner. He pays attention to all the details she mentions, encourages her to continue, and asks questions. Then tell students that listening skills are essential for a wide variety of jobs.

Discuss with students the qualities that make a good listener, such as paying attention, visualizing what is being described, encouraging the speaker to provide details, and asking questions to verify comprehension and elicit more details.

Invite students to brainstorm for a list of jobs that require good listening skills. Possibilities include nurse, physical therapist, newspaper/television reporter, personnel manager, lawyer, teacher, and psychotherapist.

Have students work with partners and choose one of these careers. Each pair of students will role-play a situation in that career in which the worker needs to listen carefully. They can take turns acting the parts of speaker and listener. Encourage students to discuss their experiences as they concentrated on listening.

Reading Strategy

1 Identify the Evidence Help students clarify the location of Julia's room in relation to the hallway, the other bedrooms, and the lawn. It appears that there was no entrance to her room from the outside. Ask students to come up with theories on how Julia may have been murdered.

Literary Focus

2 Mystery Story *Students may say Dr. Roylott or the gypsies are the primary suspects; however, some may believe these are too obvious and look for another suspect.*

Critical Thinking

3 Speculate Why do you think Holmes says, "These are very deep waters"? What does he mean by this expression? *Students may say he is finding too much evidence, or that the situation seems very mysterious and possibly evil.*

Reading Strategy

4 Identify the Evidence What are the parallel events in Helen's and Julia's situation? *Helen becomes engaged and the stepfather offers no objection, just as in Julia's case. Now Helen is forced to sleep in Julia's former room, and hears the same whistle that Julia heard before she died.*

Literary Focus

5 Mystery Story Why does Helen Stoner try to keep it a secret that her stepfather has hurt her hand? *Students may say that she is concerned with appearances, as when she wanted to prevent public exposure of the incident with the blacksmith.*

Customize for
Visual/Spatial Learners
Have students make a sketch or simple model showing the relationship of the rooms in the wing of the manor house. They may include the different entrances to the rooms as described by Helen Stoner.

death. My evidence showed that the door had been fastened upon the inner side, and the windows were blocked by old-fashioned shutters with broad iron bars, which were secured every night. The walls were carefully sounded, and were shown to be quite solid all round, and the flooring was also thoroughly examined, with the same result. The chimney is wide, but is barred up by four large staples. It is certain, therefore, that my sister was quite alone when she met her end. Besides, there were no marks of any violence upon her."

◆ **Literary Focus**
What character would you say is the primary suspect in the death of Julia Stoner?

"How about poison?"
"The doctors examined her for it, but without success."
"What do you think that this unfortunate lady died of, then?"
"It is my belief that she died of pure fear and nervous shock, though what it was that frightened her I cannot imagine."
"Were there gypsies in the plantation at the time?"
"Yes, there are nearly always some there."
"Ah, and what did you gather from this allusion to a band—a speckled band?"
"Sometimes I have thought that it was merely the wild talk of delirium, sometimes that it may have referred to some band of people, perhaps to these very gypsies in the plantation. I do not know whether the spotted handkerchiefs which so many of them wear over their heads might have suggested the strange adjective which she used."

Holmes shook his head like a man who is far from being satisfied.

"These are very deep waters," said he; "pray go on with your narrative."

"Two years have passed since then, and my life has been until lately lonelier than ever. A month ago, however, a dear friend, whom I have known for many years, has done me the honor to ask my hand in marriage. His name is Armitage—Percy Armitage—the second son of Mr.

Armitage, of Crane Water, near Reading. My stepfather has offered no opposition to the match, and we are to be married in the course of the spring. Two days ago some repairs were started in the west wing of the building, and my bedroom wall has been pierced, so that I have had to move into the chamber in which my sister died, and to sleep in the very bed in which she slept. Imagine, then, my thrill of terror when last night, as I lay awake, thinking over her terrible fate, I suddenly heard in the silence of the night the low whistle which had been the herald of her own death. I sprang up and lit the lamp, but nothing was to be seen in the room. I was too shaken to go to bed again, however, so I dressed, and as soon as it was daylight I slipped down, got a dogcart at the Crown Inn, which is opposite, and drove to Leatherhead, from whence I have come on this morning with the one object of seeing you and asking your advice."

"You have done wisely," said my friend. "But have you told me all?"
"Yes, all."
"Miss Roylott, you have not. You are screening your stepfather."
"Why, what do you mean?"
For answer Holmes pushed back the frill of black lace which fringed the hand that lay upon our visitor's knee. Five little livid spots, the marks of four fingers and a thumb, were printed upon the white wrist.
"You have been cruelly used," said Holmes.
The lady colored deeply and covered over her injured wrist. "He is a hard man," she said, "and perhaps he hardly knows his own strength."
There was a long silence, during which Holmes leaned his chin upon his hands and stared into the crackling fire.
"This is a very deep business," he said at last. "There are a thousand details which I should desire to know before I decide upon our course of action. Yet we have not a moment to lose. If we were to come to Stoke Moran today, would it be possible for us to

480 ◆ *Extraordinary Occurrences*

Cross-Curricular Connection: Science

Poison Substances that cause harm when swallowed, inhaled, absorbed by the skin, or injected into the human body are known as poisons. The scientific study of poisons—their effect, antidote, and detection—is called toxicology.

Toxins are produced by living organisms such as snakes, poison ivy, or mushrooms. Many powerful poisons are found only in laboratories where their use is strictly controlled. Most illnesses and deaths caused by poisoning occur from weaker poisons found in common household products. Some poisons, however, are used as medicines.

Each year more than a million people in the U. S. are poisoned and over 5000 die. Many poisonings result from failure to carefully read and follow the directions on product labels. Because accidents occur, and results may be quick and fatal, many communities provide a poison control center to give emergency advice over the telephone. Toxicologists can give advice about the best antidote for a specific poison. Interested students may wish to find out more about poisons, particularly those that Sherlock Holmes encounters in his adventures.

▲ **Critical Viewing** Which figure in the illustration is Dr. Roylott? How do you know? [Deduce]

6

look over these rooms without the knowledge of your stepfather?"

"As it happens, he spoke of coming into town today upon some most important business. It is probable that he will be away all day and that there would be nothing to disturb you. We have a housekeeper now, but I could easily get her out of the way."

7

"Excellent. You are not averse to this trip, Watson?"

"By no means."

"Then we shall both come. What are you going to do yourself?"

"I have one or two things which I would wish to do now that I am in town. But I shall return by the twelve o'clock train, so as to be there in time for your coming."

"And you may expect us early in the afternoon. I have myself some small business matters to attend to. Will you not wait and breakfast?"

8

"No, I must go. My heart is lightened already since I have confided my trouble to you. I shall look forward to seeing you again this afternoon." She dropped her thick black veil over her face and glided from the room.

"And what do you think of it all, Watson?" asked Sherlock Holmes, leaning back in his chair.

"It seems to me to be a most dark and sinister business."

"Dark enough and sinister enough."

"Yet if the lady is correct in saying that the flooring and walls are sound, and that the door, window, and chimney are impassable, then her sister must have been undoubtedly alone when she met her mysterious end."

"What becomes, then, of these nocturnal whistles, and what of the very peculiar words of the dying woman?"

"I cannot think."

"When you combine the ideas of whistles at night, the presence of a band of gypsies who are on intimate terms with this old doctor, the fact that we have every reason to believe that the doctor has an interest in preventing his stepdaughter's marriage, the dying allusion to a band, and, finally, the fact that Miss Helen Stoner heard a metallic clang, which might have been caused by one of those metal bars that secured the shutters, falling back into its place, I think that there is good ground to think that the mystery may be cleared along those lines."

9

"But what, then, did the gypsies do?"

"I cannot imagine."

The Adventure of the Speckled Band ◆ 481

►**Critical Viewing**◄

6 Deduce *Dr. Roylott is the large, angry man in the doorway, matching the description in the story. He is a new character to be shown in the illustrations, as Holmes and Watson have been present in earlier pictures.*

◆**Build Spelling Skills**

7 The word *disturb* is an example of the spelling skill, in which an *er* sound may be spelled either *ur* or *er*. Invite students to look for other examples of words containing this sound in the text.

◆**Critical Thinking**

8 Speculate What do you think are Holmes's small business matters? Do you think they relate to the mystery? *Students may assume he plans to follow up an idea he has that may solve the mystery.*

◆**Reading Strategy**

9 Identify the Evidence Point out to students that here Holmes makes a summation of the evidence as he knows it at this time in the story. Encourage students to make judgments about these details. Ask them to consider if some might be included to mislead the reader, and if so, which ones.

 Humanities: Art

Illustrations Have students review the illustrations of the story. Encourage them to discuss their impressions of the illustrations in relation the portion of the story that they have read so far. You might use these question to direct their thinking and guide the discussion:

• Do the drawings show the characters' action, reaction, and emotions?

• What difference do you notice between the portrayals of characters and the backgrounds?

• What do you learn about Holmes, Watson, Helen, and Dr. Roylott from these illustrations?

• What do you learn about the story's events?

Have students write captions for each illustration up to this point in the story. Their captions should identify the character(s), and they might use quotations, summarize, or comment on the action that is pictured. Encourage them to use brevity when writing their captions, but to accurately and adequtely explain the illustrations.

1 Students may have to reread sections that show conversation without designating each speaker. To make sure that students are following the conversation, ask them who is speaking this sentence. *Dr. Watson is speaking.*

◆ **Critical Thinking**

2 Infer Who is the man standing in the doorway? *Students may infer that it is Dr. Roylott.*

◆ **Critical Thinking**

3 Interpret What does Holmes mean by the expression, "you have the advantage of me"? *He is politely saying that the stranger has not introduced himself.*

◆ **Critical Thinking**

4 Interpret Why is Holmes responding to Dr. Roylott with comments on the weather? *Holmes is refusing to answer the man's questions; however, he is avoiding a direct confrontation.*

◆ **Literary Focus**

5 Mystery Story What does Holmes's action prove about the detective? *He is as strong as the threatening Dr. Roylott, though he does not show his strength to the other man.*

◆ **Critical Thinking**

6 Connect Holmes appears to be offended at Dr. Roylott's assumption that the detective is part of Scotland Yard, the London police department. What do you learn about Holmes earlier in the story that might explain this reaction? *At the beginning of the story, Watson described Holmes as investigating only for "love of his art," and refusing to take cases that were not unusual.*

---

1 "I see many objections to any such theory."

"And so do I. It is precisely for that reason that we are going to Stoke Moran this day. I want to see whether the objections are fatal, or if they may be explained away. But what in the name of the devil!"

2 The ejaculation had been drawn from my companion by the fact that our door had been suddenly dashed open, and that a huge man had framed himself in the aperture. His costume was a peculiar mixture of the professional and of the agricultural, having a black top hat, a long frock coat, and a pair of high gaiters,[3] with a hunting crop swinging in his hand. So tall was he that his hat actually brushed the crossbar of the doorway, and his breadth seemed to span it across from side to side. A large face, seared with a thousand wrinkles, burned yellow with the sun, and marked with every evil passion, was turned from one to the other of us, while his deep-set, bile-shot eyes, and his high, thin, fleshless nose, gave him somewhat the resemblance to a fierce old bird of prey.

"Which of you is Holmes?" asked this apparition.

3 "My name, sir; but you have the advantage of me," said my companion quietly.

"I am Dr. Grimesby Roylott, of Stoke Moran."

"Indeed, Doctor," said Holmes blandly. "Pray take a seat."

"I will do nothing of the kind. My stepdaughter has been here. I have traced her. What has she been saying to you?"

4 "It is a little cold for the time of the year," said Holmes.

"What has she been saying to you?" screamed the old man furiously.

---

3. **gaiters** (gāt′ ərz) *n.*: Cloth or leather coverings for the ankles and calves of legs.

◆ **Build Vocabulary**

imperturbably (im′ pər tur′ bə blē) *adv.*: Unexcitedly; impassively

---

4 "But I have heard that the crocuses promise well," continued my companion imperturbably.

"Ha! You put me off, do you?" said our new visitor, taking a step forward and shaking his hunting crop. "I know you, you scoundrel! I have heard of you before. You are Holmes, the meddler."

My friend smiled.

"Holmes, the busybody!"

His smile broadened.

"Holmes, the Scotland Yard Jack-in-office!"

Holmes chuckled heartily. "Your conversation is most entertaining," said he. "When you go out close the door, for there is a decided draft."

"I will go when I have said my say. Don't you dare to meddle with my affairs. I know that Miss Stoner has been here. I traced her! I am a dangerous man to fall foul of! See here." He stepped swiftly forward, seized the poker, and bent it into a curve with his huge brown hands.

"See that you keep yourself out of my grip," he snarled, and hurling the twisted poker into the fireplace he strode out of the room.

5 "He seems a very amiable person," said Holmes, laughing. "I am not quite so bulky, but if he had remained I might have shown him that my grip was not much more feeble than his own." As he spoke he picked up the steel poker and, with a sudden effort, straightened it out again.

6 "Fancy his having the insolence to confound me with[4] the official detective force! This incident gives zest to our investigation, however, and I only trust that our little friend will not suffer from her imprudence in allowing this brute to trace her. And now, Watson, we shall order breakfast, and afterwards I shall walk down to Doctors' Commons, where I hope to get some data which may help us in this matter."

It was nearly one o'clock when Sherlock Holmes returned from his excursion. He

---

4. **confound . . . with:** Mistake me for.

Humanities: Literature

Background Information Scholars and fans of Sherlock Holmes have used information about Doyle's stories and characters to research and gather details on the lives of the fictional Holmes and Watson. These details appear and reappear in various stories. Here are a few tidbits:

• Holmes studied fencing when he was about fourteen years old.

• Holmes was an actor when he was in his 20's. He appeared in Shakespeare's *Hamlet* in London and traveled to the U. S. with a touring company.

• Watson spent his childhood in Australia, though his family returned to England for his teenage years. After he received his doctor of medicine degree, he sailed to India.

• Watson was injured in 1880 in one of the Indian wars and returned to England.

• Holmes and Watson met in 1881 and took up residence in the rooms on Baker Street.

• In addition to his other scientific knowledge, Holmes was an expert beekeeper.

• Holmes was an accomplished violinist.

held in his hand a sheet of blue paper, scrawled over with notes and figures.

"I have seen the will of the deceased wife," said he. "To determine its exact meaning I have been obliged to work out the present prices of the investments with which it is concerned. The total income, which at the time of the wife's death was little short of £1100, is now, through the fall in agricultural prices, not more than £750. Each daughter can claim an income of £250, in case of marriage. It is evident, therefore, that if both girls had married, this beauty would have had a mere pittance,[5] while even one of them would cripple him to a very serious extent. My morning's work has not been wasted, since it has proved that he has the very strongest motives for standing in the way of anything of the sort. And now, Watson, this is too serious for dawdling, especially as the old man is aware that we are interesting ourselves in his affairs; so if you are ready, we shall call a cab and drive to Waterloo. I should be very much obliged if you would slip your revolver into your pocket. An Eley's No. 2 is an excellent argument with gentlemen who can twist steel pokers into knots. That and a toothbrush are, I think, all that we need."

At Waterloo we were fortunate in catching a train for Leatherhead, where we hired a trap at the station inn and drove for four or five miles through the lovely Surrey lanes. It was a perfect day, with a bright sun and a few fleecy clouds in the heavens. The trees and wayside hedges were just throwing out their first green shoots, and the air was full of the pleasant smell of the moist earth. To me at least there was a strange contrast between the sweet promise of the spring and this sinister quest upon which we were engaged. My companion sat in the front of the trap, his arms folded, his hat pulled down over his eyes, and his chin sunk upon his breast, buried in the deepest

---

5. **pittance** (pit′ əns) *n.*: Small or barely sufficient allowance of money.

thought. Suddenly, however, he started, tapped me on the shoulder, and pointed over the meadows.

"Look there!" said he.

A heavily timbered park stretched up in a gentle slope, thickening into a grove at the highest point. From amid the branches there jutted out the gray gables and high rooftop of a very old mansion.

"Stoke Moran?" said he.

"Yes, sir, that be the house of Dr. Grimesby Roylott," remarked the driver.

"There is some building going on there," said Holmes; "that is where we are going."

"There's the village," said the driver, pointing to a cluster of roofs some distance to the left; "but if you want to get to the house, you'll find it shorter to get over this stile, and so by the footpath over the fields. There it is, where the lady is walking."

"And the lady, I fancy, is Miss Stoner," observed Holmes, shading his eyes. "Yes, I think we had better do as you suggest."

We got off, paid our fare, and the trap rattled back on its way to Leatherhead.

"I thought it as well," said Holmes as we climbed the stile, "that this fellow should think we had come here as architects, or on some definite business. It may stop his gossip. Good afternoon, Miss Stoner. You see that we have been as good as our word."

Our client of the morning had hurried forward to meet us with a face which spoke her joy. "I have been waiting so eagerly for you," she cried, shaking hands with us warmly. "All has turned out splendidly. Dr. Roylott has gone to town, and it is unlikely that he will be back before evening."

"We have had the pleasure of making the doctor's acquaintance," said Holmes, and in a few words he sketched out what had occurred. Miss Stoner turned white to the lips as she listened.

"Good heavens!" she cried, "he has followed me, then."

"So it appears."

"He is so cunning that I never know

The Adventure of the Speckled Band ◆ 483

Cross-Curricular Connection: Social Studies

Transportation Sherlock Holmes uses his detective skills to deduce that Helen Stoner has used the train and a dog cart for transportation.

Until the first stage coach line started in Paris during the 1660's, transportation changed little from the time of the Middle Ages. Poor roads and uncomfortable wagons without springs caused the traveler to regret the time it took to get from one place to another by coach or wagon. Due to the expense, most travelers walked or rode horses. Distances of 5 to 10 miles were considered a long trip. When the English and French developed a

system of paved roads for the first time since the Romans in the 1700's, the improved roads and suspension systems added to the design of horse-drawn vehicles improved the slow, bumpy ride.

In 1825, England pioneered the first successful steam-powered locomotive, which eventually provided travel at up to 60 mph and faster.

Have interested students research the development of various modes of transportation. They can focus on the transportation used in this story, or expand their research to encompass the history of modern transportation.

◆ Literary Focus

❶ **Mystery Story** How does the author create suspense in this passage? *Holmes, Watson, and Helen do not really know when Dr. Roylott may return. Since he is violent and strong, his sudden reappearance could be dangerous to them.*

◆ Literary Focus

❷ **Mystery Story** How does this description make the manor house a good setting for a mystery? *Students may say that its wings, like the "claws of a crab," give the house a sinister feeling. The boarded-up windows and the caved-in roof give the house an atmosphere of ruin and sadness.*

◆ Critical Thinking

❸ **Speculate** Ask students why Helen Stoner moves into her sister's room, despite feeling her stepfather is a danger to herself. *Students may say that she is under his control, and that she cannot be free of him until she marries.*

►Critical Viewing◄

❹ **Draw Conclusions** *Students may say this illustration portrays the scene in which Holmes and Watson meet Helen Stoner at Stoke Moran.*

◆ Reading Strategy

❺ **Identify the Evidence** Why does Holmes inspect the windows so carefully? *Students may say that he appears to suspect that someone or something entered Julia's room through the window on the night of her death.*

when I am safe from him. What will he say when he returns?"

"He must guard himself, for he may find that there is someone more cunning than himself upon his track. You must lock ❶ yourself up from him tonight. If he is violent, we shall take you away to your aunt's at Harrow. Now, we must make the best use of our time, so kindly take us at once to the rooms which we are to examine."

The building was of gray, lichen-blotched[6] stone, with a high central portion and two curving wings, like the claws of ❷ a crab, thrown out on each side. In one of these wings the windows were broken and blocked with wooden boards, while the roof was partly caved in, a picture of ruin. The central portion was in little better repair, but the right-hand block was comparatively modern, and the blinds in the windows, with the blue smoke curling up from the chimneys, showed that this was where the family resided. Some scaffolding had been erected against the end wall, and the stonework had been broken into, but there were no signs of any workmen at the moment of our visit. Holmes walked slowly up and down the ill-trimmed lawn and examined with deep attention the outsides of the windows.

"This, I take it, belongs to the room in which you used to sleep, the center one to your sister's, and the one next to the main building to Dr. Roylott's chamber?"

❸ "Exactly so. But I am now sleeping in the middle one."

"Pending the alterations, as I understand. By the way, there does not seem to

---

6. **lichen-blotched** (lī´ kən blächt) *adj.*: Covered with patches of fungus.

▲ **Critical Viewing** Judging from the gestures and facial expressions in this illustration, what seems to be happening? [Draw Conclusions] ❹

---

be any very pressing need for repairs at that end wall."

"There were none. I believe that it was ❸ an excuse to move me from my room."

"Ah! that is suggestive. Now, on the other side of this narrow wing runs the corridor from which these three rooms open. There are windows in it, of course?"

"Yes, but very small ones. Too narrow for anyone to pass through."

"As you both locked your doors at night, ❺ your rooms were unapproachable from that side. Now, would you have the kindness to go into your room and bar your shutters?"

 Cultural Connection

Mysteries People are consistently fascinated with trying to solve mysteries—to understand something beyond apparent understanding. The mystery genre exists in all areas of the arts, including literature, film, TV, and opera. Parties are planned around the entertainment concept of a mystery, sometimes expanding to weekend excursions and cruises. A treasure hunt is a mystery to be solved. Research shows that students are more interested in learning when the subject matter has an obvious mystery premise. Scientists, historians, and archaeologists solve the mysteries of their fields of study.

From the mystery of "where's my other shoe?" to the cases that real-life detectives and Sherlock Holmes and other fictional characters routinely solve, mysteries are a part of life.

Discuss with students what they think the fascination with mysteries is all about. Encourage them to express their own thoughts and ideas about mysteries, and draw conclusions about the general interest in solving a mystery.

Miss Stoner did so, and Holmes, after a careful examination through the open window, endeavored in every way to force the shutter open, but without success. There was no slit through which a knife could be passed to raise the bar. Then with his lens he tested the hinges, but they were of solid iron, built firmly into the massive masonry. "Hum!" said he, scratching his chin in some perplexity. "My theory certainly presents some difficulties. No one could pass through these shutters if they were bolted. Well, we shall see if the inside throws any light upon the matter."

A small side door led into the white-washed corridor from which the three bedrooms opened. Holmes refused to examine the third chamber, so we passed at once to the second, that in which Miss Stoner was now sleeping, and in which her sister had met with her fate. It was a homely little room, with a low ceiling and a gaping fireplace, after the fashion of old country houses. A brown chest of drawers stood in one corner, a narrow white-counterpaned bed in another, and a dressing table on the left-hand side of the window. These articles, with two small wickerwork chairs, made up all the furniture in the room save for a square of Wilton carpet in the center. The boards round and the paneling of the walls were of brown, worm-eaten oak, so old and discolored that it may have dated from the original building of the house. Holmes drew one of the chairs into a corner and sat silent, while his eyes traveled round and round and up and down, taking in every detail of the apartment.

"Where does that bell communicate with?" he asked at last, pointing to a thick bell-rope which hung down beside the bed, the tassel actually lying upon the pillow.

"It goes to the housekeeper's room."

"It looks newer than the other things?"

"Yes, it was only put there a couple of years ago."

"Your sister asked for it, I suppose?"

"No, I never heard of her using it. We used always to get what we wanted for ourselves."

"Indeed, it seemed unnecessary to put so nice a bell-pull there. You will excuse me for a few minutes while I satisfy myself as to this floor." He threw himself down upon his face with his lens in his hand and crawled swiftly backward and forward, examining minutely the cracks between the boards. Then he did the same with the woodwork with which the chamber was paneled. Finally he walked over to the bed and spent some time in staring at it and in running his eye up and down the wall. Finally he took the bell-rope in his hand and gave it a brisk tug.

"Why, it's a dummy," said he.

"Won't it ring?"

"No, it is not even attached to a wire. This is very interesting. You can see now that it is fastened to a hook just above where the little opening for the ventilator is."

"How very absurd! I never noticed that before!"

"Very strange!" muttered Holmes, pulling at the rope. "There are one or two very singular points about this room. For example, what a fool a builder must be to open a ventilator into another room, when, with the same trouble, he might have communicated with the outside air!"

"That is also quite modern," said the lady.

"Done about the same time as the bell-rope?" remarked Holmes.

"Yes, there were several little changes carried out about that time."

"They seem to have been of a most interesting character—dummy bell-ropes, and ventilators which do not ventilate. With your permission, Miss Stoner, we shall now carry our researches into the inner apartment."

Dr. Grimesby Roylott's chamber was larger than that of his stepdaughter, but was as plainly furnished. A camp bed, a small wooden shelf full of books, mostly of a technical character, an armchair beside

The Adventure of the Speckled Band ◆ 485

◆ **Reading Strategy**

❻ **Identify the Evidence** What do you think Holmes's theory was, and why does the condition of the window appear to change his mind? *Students may say that Holmes seemed to suspect that the gypsies somehow entered the room from the lawn on the night of Julia's death. However, this seems improbable, since no one could pass through the bolted shutters.*

◆ **Literary Focus**

❼ **Mystery Story** How does Holmes investigate the room? *He sits in a chair and lets his eyes travel around the room to gather evidence.*

◆ **Reading Strategy**

❽ **Identify the Evidence** What does Holmes discover about the bell-rope? *It is a dummy and hangs from a hook just above the opening for the ventilator.*

Thematic Focus

❾ What is unusual about the ventilator in the middle bedroom? *It opens into another room rather than to the outside hall, where fresh air might circulate.*

Customize for
Bodily/Kinesthetic Learners
Encourage students to discuss Holmes's movements as he studies the window from the outside, sits in the chair in the bedroom, and examines the floor and walls of the room. Have students read the passages carefully and talk about how Holmes moves—or doesn't move. He may appear to prefer sitting and thinking, yet he can be almost acrobatic when he needs to be in the course of an investigation.

Viewing and Representing Mini-Lesson

Set Design

This mini-lesson will provide students with a visual means of understanding Doyle's verbal descriptions.

Introduce Discuss with students why Holmes is studying the rooms in the house so carefully. Point out the relationship of one room to another and specific placement of furniture, windows, and doors. Then encourage them to review the description of the rooms' layout, taking notes and making sketches, to help them orient themselves.

Develop Have students work individually or in pairs to create a set design that might be used for the staged or filmed scene where Holmes, Watson, and Helen Stoner examine the rooms.

Apply Have students draw (they might use an overhead perspective) or build a model of the rooms, as indicated by Doyle's descriptions. Provide materials, as needed, and help them with scale.

Assess Evaluate students' work based on their planning, the logic of their layout, and their ability to produce a representative design.

◆ **Reading Strategy**

❶ Identify the Evidence *Students may say that the saucer of milk is important evidence, since it is an unusual item to have in the room. Students may suggest it is connected to a cat or other animal.*

Thematic Focus

❷ Why do you think Holmes is examining the seat of the wooden chair? *Students may say that he seems to find some evidence there. They may guess that he can tell that someone or something has been on the chair.*

◆ **Literary Focus**

❸ Mystery Story What does this statement by Holmes tell you about his philosophy toward his work? *He is aware of the evil in the world, and the danger of clever criminals. That may be one reason he is a detective, in order to fight that evil.*

◆ **Literary Focus**

❹ Mystery Story What is Sherlock Holmes's plan? Why do you think he is taking such an action that very night? *The plan is for Holmes and Watson to stay in the middle bedroom, unknown to Dr. Roylott. Helen will pretend to sleep in the middle room, but will actually withdraw to her old room. Holmes appears to believe he must be present in order to investigate the noise. He may feel the situation is very dangerous, since he is doing this right away.*

Customize for
Logical/Mathematical Learners

Have students itemize the evidence Holmes discovers in Dr. Roylott's room. Encourage them to list these details in the order of importance as pieces of evidence. Students will find their own order for the iron safe, the saucer of milk, the chair seat, and the dog lash.

---

the bed, a plain wooden chair against the wall, a round table, and a large iron safe were the principal things which met the eye. Holmes walked slowly round and examined each and all of them with the keenest interest.

"What's in here?" he asked, tapping the safe.

"My stepfather's business papers."

"Oh! you have seen inside, then?"

"Only once, some years ago. I remember that it was full of papers."

"There isn't a cat in it, for example?"

◆ **Reading Strategy**
Do you think the saucer of milk is an important piece of evidence? What conclusion might you draw from its presence?

"No. What a strange idea!"

"Well, look at this!" He took up a small saucer of milk which stood on the top of it.

"No; we don't keep a cat. But there is a cheetah and a baboon."

"Ah, yes, of course! Well, a cheetah is just a big cat, and yet a saucer of milk does not go very far in satisfying its wants, I daresay. There is one point which I should wish to determine." He squatted down in front of the wooden chair and examined the seat of it with the greatest attention.

"Thank you. That is quite settled," said he, rising and putting his lens in his pocket. "Hello! Here is something interesting!"

The object which had caught his eye was a small dog lash hung on one corner of the bed. The lash, however, was curled upon itself and tied so as to make a loop of whipcord.

"What do you make of that, Watson?"

"It's a common enough lash. But I don't know why it should be tied."

"That is not quite so common, is it? Ah, me! it's a wicked world, and when a clever man turns his brains to crime it is the worst of all. I think that I have seen enough now, Miss Stoner, and with your permission we shall walk out upon the lawn."

I had never seen my friend's face so grim or his brow so dark as it was when

we turned from the scene of this investigation. We had walked several times up and down the lawn, neither Miss Stoner nor myself liking to break in upon his thoughts before he roused himself from his reverie.

"It is very essential, Miss Stoner," said he, "that you should absolutely follow my advice in every respect."

"I shall most certainly do so."

"The matter is too serious for any hesitation. Your life may depend upon your compliance."[7]

"I assure you that I am in your hands."

"In the first place, both my friend and I must spend the night in your room."

Both Miss Stoner and I gazed at him in astonishment.

"Yes, it must be so. Let me explain. I believe that that is the village inn over there?"

"Yes, that is the Crown."

"Very good. Your windows would be visible from there?"

"Certainly."

"You must confine yourself to your room, on pretense of a headache, when your stepfather comes back. Then when you hear him retire for the night, you must open the shutters of your window, undo the hasp,[8] put your lamp there as a signal to us, and then withdraw quietly with everything which you are likely to want into the room which you used to occupy. I have no doubt that, in spite of the repairs, you could manage there for one night."

"Oh, yes, easily."

"The rest you will leave in our hands."

"But what will you do?"

"We shall spend the night in your room, and we shall investigate the cause of this noise which has disturbed you."

"I believe, Mr. Holmes, that you have already made up your mind," said Miss

---

7. **compliance** (kəm plī′ əns) *n.*: Agreement to a request.
8. **hasp** *n.*: Hinged metal fastening of a window.

486 ◆ *Extraordinary Occurrences*

Beyond the Classroom

Career Connection

Mystery Writer If you enjoy reading mysteries, you might like to try writing mystery fiction. When you read, see if you can notice certain rules that most mystery writers observe. Some of these are:

• The reader must have equal opportunity with the detective to solve the mystery. The writer cannot allow the detective to learn something without telling the reader.

• The writer should not play tricks on the reader, unless she or he also plays them on the detective.

• The mystery must be solved by logical deduction, not by accident or coincidence.

• The solution should not be so complicated that it will need a long and involved technical explanation at the end.

• Here's a tip toward becoming a mystery writer: Have some adventures so you have more to write about. Sir Arthur Conan Doyle worked as a doctor on an Arctic whaling ship and on a West African steamer. He was a war correspondent, traveled up the Nile River, and served in a hospital in South Africa.

Stoner, laying her hand upon my companion's sleeve.

"Perhaps I have."

"Then, for pity's sake, tell me what was the cause of my sister's death."

❺ "I should prefer to have clearer proofs before I speak."

"You can at least tell me whether my own thought is correct, and if she died from some sudden fright."

"No, I do not think so. I think that there was probably some more tangible cause. And now, Miss Stoner, we must leave you, for if Dr. Roylott returned and saw us our journey would be in vain. Goodbye, and be brave, for if you will do what I have told you, you may rest assured that we shall soon drive away the dangers that threaten you."

Sherlock Holmes and I had no difficulty in engaging a bedroom and sitting room at the Crown Inn. They were on the upper floor, and from our window we could command a view of the avenue gate, and of the inhabited wing of Stoke Moran Manor House. At dusk we saw Dr. Grimesby Roylott drive past, his huge form looming up beside the little figure of the lad who drove him. The boy had some slight difficulty in undoing the heavy iron gates, and we heard the hoarse roar of the doctor's voice and saw the fury with which he shook his clinched fists at him. The trap drove on,
❻ and a few minutes later we saw a sudden light spring up among the trees as the lamp was lit in one of the sitting rooms.

"Do you know, Watson," said Holmes as we sat together in the gathering darkness, "I have really some scruples as to taking you tonight. There is a distinct element
❼ of danger."

"Can I be of assistance?"

"Your presence might be invaluable."

"Then I shall certainly come."

"It is very kind of you."

"You speak of danger. You have evidently seen more in these rooms than was visible to me."

"No, but I fancy that I may have deduced a little more. I imagine that you saw all that I did."

"I saw nothing remarkable save the bell-rope, and what purpose that could answer I confess is more than I can imagine."

"You saw the ventilator, too?"

"Yes, but I do not think that it is such a very unusual thing to have a small opening between two rooms. It was so small that a rat could hardly pass through."

"I knew that we should find a ventilator before ever we came to Stoke Moran."

"My dear Holmes!"

"Oh, yes, I did. You remember in her statement she said that her sister could smell Dr. Roylott's cigar. Now, of course that suggested at once that there must be a communication between the two rooms. It could only be a small one, or it would have been remarked upon at the coroner's inquiry. I deduced a ventilator."

"But what harm can there be in that?"

❽ "Well, there is at least a curious coincidence of dates. A ventilator is made, a cord is hung, and a lady who sleeps in the bed dies. Does not that strike you?"

"I cannot as yet see any connection."

"Did you observe anything very peculiar about that bed?"

"No."

❾ "It was clamped to the floor. Did you ever see a bed fastened like that before?"

"I cannot say that I have."

"The lady could not move her bed. It must always be in the same relative position to the ventilator and to the rope—or so we may call it, since it was clearly never meant for a bell-pull."

"Holmes," I cried, "I seem to see dimly what you are hinting at. We are only just in time to prevent some subtle and horrible crime."

◆ Build Vocabulary

reverie (rev´ ər ē) *n.*: Daydream

tangible (tan´ jə bəl) *adj.*: Having form and substance; that can be touched or felt by touch

The Adventure of the Speckled Band ◆ 487

◆ Literary Focus

❺ **Mystery Story** Let students know that it is part of Sherlock Holmes's character to be very confident of his ability to solve a mystery yet to be reluctant to tell others his full ideas until he can prove them.

Comprehension Check ☑

❻ **What is the light Holmes and Watson see from the inn?** *It is a lamp in one of the sitting rooms—not the lamp that Helen is to place in her window as a signal to the men that her stepfather has gone to his room for the night.*

◆ Critical Thinking

❼ **Deduce** Do you think Holmes is really hesitant about asking Watson to come with him? Do you think Watson would consider not coming with Holmes? *Students may say that Holmes may have just wanted to warn Watson. They may say that Watson probably would never want to miss the adventure, despite the danger.*

◆ Reading Strategy

❽ **Identify the Evidence** Holmes is showing that the order of events is important in solving a mystery. He notes that the rope and ventilator were added to Julia's room shortly before she died.

◆ Reading Strategy

❾ **Identify the Evidence** What new evidence about Julia's room does the reader just now learn? *The bed is fastened to the floor and cannot be moved.*

 Humanities: Literature

"Sidekick" Characters Many stories include secondary characters such as Watson. Although Sherlock Holmes clearly is the main character whose actions and character traits are the basis for Doyle's mystery stories, Holmes's believability and appeal would be limited without Watson.

Encourage students to think about why Doyle includes Watson. Lead them to see that Watson asks questions that readers might have; he sets up many of Holmes's deductions by asking questions or not making the keen observations that Holmes does; he provides a genial and agreeable companion for Holmes; and he serves as the story's narrator.

TV sidekicks are sometimes called "second bananas," filling the same type of role that Watson does for Holmes. Have students brainstorm for a list of sidekicks from stories and TV. Then have them create a list of these characters' shared qualities. Point out the similarities of characters' roles in a TV serial format, and in literature that reuses the same characters.

Encourage students to speculate about the success of Sherlock Holmes without Watson.

◆ Critical Thinking

1 Assess Do you agree with Sherlock Holmes's statement that doctors who "go wrong" become expert criminals? Why or why not? *Students should support their opinions with reasons.*

Clarification

2 Sir Arthur Conan Doyle often blended events and people from real life into his writing. William Palmer (1825–1856) and Edward Pritchard (1825–1865) were British doctors who were hanged for the crime of poisoning. Both men's medical knowledge made it possible for them to carry out the crimes. Palmer's motive was always money, mostly insurance and death benefits. Pritchard's motives were never explained.

◆ Literary Focus

3 Mystery Story Point out to students that this is the first time Holmes has appeared flustered. How does Watson show that Holmes is as startled as he is? *Watson describes Holmes's grip on his wrist as "like a vise."*

◆ Literary Focus

4 Mystery Story How does this statement by Holmes create a feeling of suspense? *Students may say that the word "fatal" is frightening. Also, the reader does not know Holmes's plan, so there is suspense about what will happen.*

◆ LITERATURE AND YOUR LIFE

5 Ask students if they have ever been in complete darkness, unable to see any hint of light. How did they feel? Invite students to describe their experiences.

Customize for
Verbal/Linguistic Learners
Invite pairs of students to give oral readings of the description on this page, beginning when Holmes and Watson leave the inn and finishing as they begin their vigil. The partners might take turns reading paragraphs, or one could be Holmes and the other Watson.

1
2 "Subtle enough and horrible enough. When a doctor does go wrong he is the first of criminals. He has nerve and he has knowledge. Palmer and Pritchard were among the heads of their profession. This man strikes even deeper, but I think, Watson, that we shall be able to strike deeper still. But we shall have horrors enough before the night is over; for goodness' sake let us have a quiet pipe and turn our minds for a few hours to something more cheerful."

About nine o'clock the light among the trees was extinguished, and all was dark in the direction of the Manor House. Two hours passed slowly away, and then, suddenly, just at the stroke of eleven, a single bright light shone out right in front of us.

"That is our signal," said Holmes, springing to his feet; "it comes from the middle window."

As we passed out he exchanged a few words with the landlord, explaining that we were going on a late visit to an acquaintance, and that it was possible that we might spend the night there. A moment later we were out on the dark road, a chill wind blowing in our faces, and one yellow light twinkling in front of us through the gloom to guide us on our somber errand.

There was little difficulty in entering the grounds; for unrepaired breaches gaped in the old park wall. Making our way among the trees, we reached the lawn, crossed it, and were about to enter through the window when out from a clump of laurel bushes there darted what seemed to be a hideous and distorted child, who threw itself upon the grass with writhing limbs and then ran swiftly across the lawn into the darkness.

"My God!" I whispered; "did you see it?"

Holmes was for the moment as startled
3 as I. His hand closed like a vise upon my wrist in his agitation. Then he broke into a low laugh and put his lips to my ear.

"It is a nice household," he murmured. "That is the baboon."

488 ◆ Extraordinary Occurrences

I had forgotten the strange pets which the doctor affected. There was a cheetah, too; perhaps we might find it upon our shoulders at any moment. I confess that I felt easier in my mind when, after following Holmes's example and slipping off my shoes, I found myself inside the bedroom. My companion noiselessly closed the shutters, moved the lamp onto the table, and cast his eyes round the room. All was as we had seen it in the daytime. Then creeping up to me and making a trumpet of his hand, he whispered into my ear again so gently that it was all that I could do to distinguish the words:

"The least sound would be fatal to our **4** plans."

I nodded to show that I had heard.

"We must sit without light. He would see it through the ventilator."

I nodded again.

"Do not go asleep; your very life may depend upon it. Have your pistol ready in case we should need it. I will sit on the side of the bed, and you in that chair."

I took out my revolver and laid it on the corner of the table.

Holmes had brought up a long thin cane, and this he placed upon the bed beside him. By it he laid the box of matches and the stump of a candle. Then he turned down the lamp, and we were left in darkness.

How shall I ever forget that dreadful vigil? I could not hear a sound, not even the drawing of a breath, and yet I knew that my companion sat open-eyed, within a few feet of me, in the same state of nervous tension in which I was myself. The shutters cut off the least ray of light, and **5** we waited in absolute darkness. From outside came the occasional cry of a night bird, and once at our very window a long-drawn catlike whine, which told us that the cheetah was indeed at liberty. Far away we could hear the deep tones of the parish clock, which boomed out every quarter of an hour. How long they seemed, those quarters! Twelve struck, and one

---

Speaking and Listening Mini-Lesson

Radio Play
This mini-lesson supports the Speaking and Listening activity in the Idea Bank, p. 493.

Introduce Discuss with students that radio drama depends on the actors' verbal expression, the dialogue, narration, and sound effects. It may be harder for the actor to reveal the character's personality because only the voice is heard.

Develop Have students work in groups of 3 to 4 students. Each group will write a radio script that includes both dialogue and narration. Students may use excerpts of "The Adventure of the

Speckled Band" in the script. Have students choose a director, cast roles, and pick sound engineers to create sound effects.

Apply Give groups time to plan, prepare, and rehearse their plays. Each group can audiotape their radio dramas, then play them for the class.

Assess Evaluate students on their group work, script preparation, presentation of dialogue, narration, and choice of sound effects. Have students evaluate their classmates' presentations, using the Peer Assessment: Dramatic Performance form in **Alternative Assessment,** p. 116.

▲ **Critical Viewing** Does this illustration effectively bring to life the story's climax? Why or why not? [Make a Judgment] **6**

and two and three, and still we sat waiting silently for whatever might befall.

Suddenly there was the momentary gleam of a light up in the direction of the ventilator, which vanished immediately, but was succeeded by a strong smell of burning oil and heated metal. Someone in the next room had lit a dark lantern.[9] I heard a gentle sound of movement, and then all was silent once more, though the smell grew stronger. For half an hour I sat with straining ears. Then suddenly another sound became audible—a very gentle, soothing sound, like that of a small jet of steam escaping continually from a kettle. The instant that we heard it, Holmes sprang from the bed, struck a match, and lashed furiously with his cane at the bell-pull.

9. **dark lantern:** Lantern with a shutter that can hide the light.

"You see it, Watson?" he yelled. "You see it?"

But I saw nothing. At the moment when Holmes struck the light I heard a low, clear whistle, but the sudden glare flashing into my weary eyes made it impossible for me to tell what it was at which my friend lashed so savagely. I could, however, see that his face was deadly pale and filled with horror and loathing.

He had ceased to strike and was gazing up at the ventilator when suddenly there broke from the silence of the night the most horrible cry to which I have ever listened. It swelled up louder and louder, a hoarse yell of pain and fear and anger all mingled in the one dreadful shriek. They say that away down in the village, and even in the distant parsonage, that cry raised the sleepers from their beds. It struck cold to our hearts, and I stood gazing at Holmes, and he at me, until the last echoes of it had died away into the silence from which it rose. **7**

"What can it mean?" I gasped.

"It means that it is all over," Holmes answered. "And perhaps, after all, it is for the best. Take your pistol, and we will enter Dr. Roylott's room."

With a grave face he lit the lamp and led the way down the corridor. Twice he struck at the chamber door without any reply from within. Then he turned the handle and entered, I at his heels, with the cocked pistol in my hand.

It was a singular sight which met our eyes. On the table stood a dark lantern with the shutter half open, throwing a brilliant beam of light upon the iron safe, the door of which was ajar. Beside this table, on the wooden chair, sat Dr. Grimesby Roylott, clad in a long gray dressing gown, his bare ankles protruding beneath, and his feet thrust into red **8**

The Adventure of the Speckled Band ◆ 489

▶**Critical Viewing**◀

6 Make a Judgment *Some students may feel that Holmes's dramatic gesture illustrates the climax; others may feel the drawing is not detailed enough. Students should support their opinions with reasons.*

◆ **LITERATURE AND YOUR LIFE**

7 How does this description of the scream make you feel? *Students may say the description is dramatic, scary, and perhaps makes them sorry for the screamer.*

◆ **Reading Strategy**

8 Identify the Evidence What do you think had been inside the safe? *Students may make guesses.*

Customize for
Logical/Mathematical Learners

Ask students to list the details that occurred from the lighting of the dark lantern in Dr. Roylott's room to the horrible shriek. Write these details on the board as students bring them up: the gleam of light as the lantern is lit; the sound of movement next door; the hissing sound; Holmes's springing up, striking a match, and hitting the rope with his cane; the whistle; the horrible cry. Have students make sure the events are in the right order. Then ask them to speculate on what may have been happening. Record their responses so that after they finish the story students will know whether or not their predictions were correct.

Beyond the Classroom

Workplace Skills

Combining Interests and Skills Point out to students that Sir Arthur Conan Doyle was obviously interested in science—as evidenced by his medical training and general knowledge of science, which he applied to his detective stories.

Many people combine interests and skills in their career choices. Like Doyle, writers may use a specific interest to guide their choices of what to write; an artist who is interested in computer technology may design books, animated film segments, or computer games; a person interested

in a specific type of product may find a career in selling that product; and some people choose their fields of interest to teach.

Being interested in one's job is a key to being successful. Discovering an interest in a particular area is a clue as to what type of job to look for. Encourage students to talk to a career counselor or someone who works in a field in which they are interested to explore what types of skills they can develop to further enhance their job potential in that area. Students with shared interests might work together to investigate job possibilities.

Comprehension Check ☑

1 What is the speckled band? *It is a snake with a diamond shaped head and a puffed neck.*

◆ Literary Focus

2 Mystery Story Here, again, Holmes presents his view of the criminal world. Ask students what they think he means. *A person who is violent may have violence directed against him; a person who plans to hurt someone may end up in his own trap.*

◆ Critical Thinking

3 Connect Have students refer back to Watson's mention of Dr. Roylott's death on p. 474. Ask them why there may have been rumors about the doctor's death "which tend to make the matter even more terrible than the truth." What do they think the rumors may have been? *Students may say that since the official inquiry was not accurate, people may have suspected some information was withheld. Some people may have thought that Helen Stoner killed her stepfather.*

◆ Literary Focus

4 Mystery Story Encourage students to discuss the points that Holmes clears up for them in his summary of the case.

Customize for
Intrapersonal Learners

Invite students to write a conversation in which Helen Stoner tells her fiancé what happened. Remind students that she did not witness all the events, so she may describe only what she actually saw.

---

heelless Turkish slippers. Across his lap lay the short stock with the long lash which we had noticed during the day. His chin was cocked upward and his eyes were fixed in a dreadful, rigid stare at the corner of the ceiling. Round his brow he had a peculiar yellow band, with brownish speckles, which seemed to be bound tightly round his head. As we entered he made neither sound nor motion.

"The band! the speckled band!" whispered Holmes.

1 I took a step forward. In an instant his strange headgear began to move, and there reared itself from among his hair the squat diamond-shaped head and puffed neck of a loathsome serpent.

2 "It is a swamp adder!" cried Holmes; "the deadliest snake in India. He has died within ten seconds of being bitten. Violence does, in truth, recoil upon the violent, and the schemer falls into the pit which he digs for another. Let us thrust this creature back into its den, and we can then remove Miss Stoner to some place of shelter and let the county police know what has happened."

As he spoke he drew the dog whip swiftly from the dead man's lap, and throwing the noose round the reptile's neck he drew it from its horrid perch and, carrying it at arm's length, threw it into the iron safe, which he closed upon it.

Such are the true facts of the death of Dr. Grimesby Roylott, of Stoke Moran. It is not necessary that I should prolong a narrative which has already run to too great a length by telling how we broke the sad news to the terrified girl, how we conveyed her by the morning train to the care of her good aunt at Harrow, of how the slow **3** process of official inquiry came to the conclusion that the doctor met his fate while indiscreetly playing with a dangerous pet. The little which I had yet to learn of the case was told me by Sherlock Holmes as we traveled back next day.

"I had," said he, "come to an entirely erroneous conclusion which shows, my dear Watson, how dangerous it always is to reason from insufficient data. The presence of the gypsies, and the use of the word *band*, which was used by the poor girl, no doubt to explain the appearance which she had caught a hurried glimpse of by the light of her match, were sufficient to put me upon an entirely wrong scent. I can only claim the merit that I instantly reconsidered my position when, however, it became clear to me that whatever danger threatened an occupant of the room could not come either from the window or the door. My attention was speedily drawn, as I have already remarked to you, to this ventilator, and to the bell-rope which hung down to the bed. The discovery that this was a dummy, and that the bed was clamped to the floor, instantly gave rise to the suspicion that the rope was there as a bridge for something passing through the hole and coming to the bed. The idea of a snake instantly occurred to me, and when I coupled it with my knowledge that the doctor was furnished with a supply of creatures from India, I felt that I was probably on the right track. The idea of using a form of poison which could not possibly be discovered by any chemical test was just such a one as would occur to a clever and ruthless man who had had an Eastern training. The rapidity with which such a poison would take effect would also, from his point of view, be an advantage. It would be a sharp-eyed coroner, indeed, who could distinguish the two little dark punctures which would show where the poison fangs had done their work. Then I thought of the whistle. Of course he must recall the snake before the morning light revealed it to the victim. He had trained it, probably by the use of the milk which we saw, to return to him when summoned. He would put it through this ventilator at the hour that he

◆ **Literary Focus**
Mysteries often end with a wrap-up. Notice how Holmes leads you step by step through his reasoning process. **4**

490 ◆ *Extraordinary Occurrences*

Cross-Curricular Connection: Science

Swamp Adder The swamp adder—the "speckled band"—was apparently an invention of Sir Arthur Conan Doyle's, as no snake by that name exists in India. The description of the "speckled band," however, matches that of the Banded Krait. Kraits are extremely poisonous snakes that are common in parts of Asia.

The Banded Krait has alternating bands of yellow and black across its back. Each band may be one to one and a half inches wide. While this krait is very beautiful, it is also very deadly. Its venom is said to be sixteen times as powerful as that of the cobra.

Like the swamp adder in "The Adventure of the Speckled Band," this snake contains teeth-like fangs that are connected to its poison glands. When the fangs puncture the skin of the victim, the venom enters the victim's body immediately.

thought best, with the certainty that it would crawl down the rope and land on the bed. It might or might not bite the occupant, perhaps she might escape every night for a week, but sooner or later she must fall a victim.

"I had come to these conclusions before ever I had entered his room. An inspection of his chair showed me that he had been in the habit of standing on it, which of course would be necessary in order that he should reach the ventilator. The sight of the safe, the saucer of milk, and the loop of whipcord were enough to finally dispel any doubts which may have remained. The metallic clang heard by Miss Stoner was obviously caused by her stepfather hastily closing the door of his

safe upon its terrible occupant. Having once made up my mind, you know the steps which I took in order to put the matter to the proof. I heard the creature hiss as I have no doubt that you did also, and I instantly lit the light and attacked it."

"With the result of driving it through the ventilator."

"And also with the result of causing it to turn upon its master at the other side. Some of the blows of my cane came home and roused its snakish temper, so that it flew upon the first person it saw. In this way I am no doubt indirectly responsible for Dr. Grimesby Roylott's death, and I cannot say that it is likely to weigh very heavily upon my conscience."

❺

❺ **Make a Judgment** Do you think Holmes is responsible for Dr. Roylott's death? Do you agree that such a deed should not weigh on his conscience? Why or why not? *Students may say that Holmes is responsible because he caused the snake to bite Roylott; others may say that Holmes is innocent because he was protecting Helen and didn't intend for Roylott to die.*

Reinforce and Extend

Answers

◆ **LITERATURE AND YOUR LIFE**

Reader's Response Students may say it would be fun to be Holmes's partner and share his adventures; or, they might not like the idea of being a sidekick exposed to danger.

Thematic Focus Holmes is ordinary in that he likes to sleep late; he is extraordinary in his powers of deduction and his courage.

☑ **Check Your Comprehension**

1. She is afraid her life is at danger.
2. Helen hears a whistle, then a metallic clanging sound. Her sister's last words were, "It was the band! The speckled band!"
3. Dr. Roylott follows Helen to Holmes, then warns the detective to stay out of his affairs.
4. They climb through the window to spend the night in Helen's room in total quiet and darkness.
5. It is a poisonous snake called a swamp adder.

◆ **Critical Thinking**

1. Like Julia, Helen is getting married soon. Helen is sleeping in her sister's room and hears the same whistling sound that Julia heard shortly before her death.
2. Dr. Roylott's motive is to maintain control over the money left by Helen's mother. He is required to give the women a certain amount of money when they marry.
3. Instead of biting and killing Helen, the snake bites and kills Dr. Roylott.
4. She would probably have been killed.
5. Students may suggest trying to remember details they see or hear, paying attention to routines, and taking notes to remind themselves of events they witness.
6. Students may describe tests that evaluate an applicant's powers of observation and logical reasoning.

Guide for Responding

◆ **LITERATURE AND YOUR LIFE**

Reader's Response Would you have liked to be Sherlock Holmes's partner? Why or why not?

Thematic Focus In what ways is Holmes ordinary? In what ways is he extraordinary?

Journal Writing Write a journal entry from Watson's point of view about working on this case with Holmes.

☑ **Check Your Comprehension**

1. Why does Helen Stoner come to see Holmes?
2. What two sounds did Helen hear after she was awakened by her sister's scream? What did her sister then say?
3. Why does Dr. Roylott pay a visit to Holmes?
4. How do Holmes and Watson spend the night at Stoke Moran?
5. What is the speckled band?

◆ **Critical Thinking**

INTERPRET

1. Name three ways in which Helen's situation when she comes to Holmes is similar to Julia's just before Julia's death. **[Compare and Contrast]**
2. What is Dr. Roylott's motive for the crimes? **[Infer]**
3. How does Dr. Roylott's plan backfire? **[Analyze]**
4. What do you think would have happened if Helen had not consulted Holmes? **[Speculate]**

EXTEND

5. Sherlock Holmes uses his powers of observation well. Name three ways to improve your own powers of observation. **[Relate]**

APPLY

6. How would you test an applicant who wants to enter a school for detectives? What tests could you invent that would determine whether someone has the necessary natural skills? **[Career Link]**

The Adventure of the Speckled Band ◆ 491

 Beyond the Selection

FURTHER READING

Other Works by Sir Arthur Conan Doyle

The Mysterious Adventures of Sherlock Holmes

The Great Adventures of Sherlock Holmes

Mysteries About Another Genius Detective, Nero Wolfe

Fer-de-Lance by Rex Stout

Black Orchids by Rex Stout

Too Many Cooks by Rex Stout

INTERNET

We suggest the following site on the Internet (all Web sites are subject to change).

For more information about Sir Arthur Conan Doyle and Sherlock Holmes, and to download Sherlock Holmes stories:

http://www.geocities.com/Athens/Delphi/4040/ sherlock.html

We *strongly recommend* that you preview this site before you send students to it.

◆ Reading Strategy

1. The dummy bell-rope allowed the snake to crawl down to reach the victim; the ventilator allowed the snake to crawl from Dr. Roylott's room into Julia's room; the bed was bolted to the floor so it couldn't be moved and the victim would be forced to sleep next to the bell-rope, where the snake could reach her.

2. Holmes knew Dr. Roylott had lived in India and had an interest in Indian animals. The detective also knew the doctor's inheritance from his deceased wife had to be shared with the stepdaughters when they married.

3. (a) At first Holmes thought the speckled band referred to the band of gypsies in the area.
(b) Her words led the detective and the reader to suppose the gypsies were involved in the murder.

◆ Build Vocabulary

Using Forms of *convulse*
1. convulsive;   2. convulsions;
3. convulse

Spelling Strategy
1. She returned after curfew.
2. Do these clues pertain to this murder case?
3. The culprit hid under the curtain.

Using the Word Bank
1. f   2. e   3. a   4. g   5. b
6. c   7. d

◆ Literary Focus

1. Dr. Roylott commits the crime.
2. He plans a murder that is very difficult to detect, and trains a snake in order to accomplish this crime.
3. Holmes uses his powers of observation and deduction to figure out Dr. Roylott's plan before it can succeed a second time.
4. Watson narrates the adventure, describing and explaining how Holmes solves the mystery.
5. Some students might like an open ending that they could solve themselves; others might feel a mystery with no solution would be unfinished and not enjoyable to read.

Guide for Responding (continued)

◆ Reading Strategy

IDENTIFY EVIDENCE
Holmes solved the mystery of the speckled band by analyzing all pieces of **evidence** and drawing a conclusion. Did you recognize the evidence as it was revealed? Review your clue chart as you answer these questions.
1. Explain the significance of each of these clues: the dummy bell-rope, the ventilator, and the bed anchored to the floor in Julia's room.
2. How did background information about Dr. Roylott help Holmes solve the mystery?
3. (a) What had Holmes thought was the significance of Julia's last words? (b) In what way could her words be considered a misleading clue?

◆ Build Vocabulary

USING FORMS OF *convulse*
Convulse means "shake violently." Write the form of *convulse* that best completes each sentence.
convulse   convulsions   convulsive
1. The victim's arm made one ____?____ twitch.
2. The frightening ____?____ will stop when the poison takes effect.
3. Some poisons cause their victims to ____?____.

SPELLING STRATEGY
The *er* sound can be spelled *ur* and *er*. Notice that *perturb* includes both spellings of the sound. Rewrite each sentence, correcting any misspellings.
1. She reterned after cerfew.
2. Do these clues purtain to this murdur case?
3. The culprit hid undur the certain.

USING THE WORD BANK
On your paper, match the Word Bank words in Column A with their synonyms in Column B.

Column A	Column B
1. defray	a. gloomy
2. manifold	b. calmly
3. morose	c. daydream
4. convulsed	d. solid
5. imperturbably	e. numerous
6. reverie	f. pay
7. tangible	g. twitched

◆ Literary Focus

MYSTERY STORY
A **mystery story** usually contains a conflict between a detective and someone who has committed a crime. The detective uses evidence to discover the criminal; the criminal tries to remain undiscovered. The conflict is resolved when the detective proves the identity of the criminal.
1. Who commits the crime in "The Adventure of the Speckled Band"?
2. In what ways does the criminal display cleverness?
3. How does Holmes outwit the criminal?
4. What role does Watson play in the story?
5. Do you think a mystery would be satisfying if it included all of the clues but left the solution up to the reader?

◆ Build Grammar Skills

PREDICATE NOUNS
A **predicate noun** appears after a linking verb and renames, identifies, or explains the subject of the sentence.

My name is *Sherlock Holmes*, . . . (*Sherlock Holmes* is a predicate noun that renames the subject, *name*.)

He seems a very amiable *person*. (*Person* is a predicate noun that identifies the subject, *he*.)

Practice On your paper, write the subject and predicate noun in each sentence.
1. He was a late riser, as a rule. . . .
2. "Which of you is Holmes?" asked this apparition.
3. I am a dangerous man to fall foul of!
4. . . . my profession is its own reward; . . .
5. It was a singular sight which met our eyes.

Writing Application On your paper, write a sentence with a linking verb and predicate noun that renames each subject below.
1. Holmes   3. Roylott
2. Helen   4. snake

◆ Build Grammar Skills

Practice
1. subject: he; predicate noun: riser
2. subject: which; predicate noun: Holmes
3. subject: I; predicate noun: man
4. subject: profession; predicate noun: reward
5. subject: It; predicate noun: sight

Writing Application
Check that students have used a predicate noun that renames the subject and is connected by a linking verb. Possible answers:
1. Holmes was the detective chosen by Miss Stoner.
2. Helen was the first name of Miss Stoner.
3. Roylott was a well-known Surrey family name.
4. The snake was an adder.

Build Your Portfolio

 ## Idea Bank

Writing

1. **Advertisement** Write an advertisement for his services that Sherlock Holmes might have placed in a newspaper or magazine. Include appropriate drawings, as well as detailed descriptions of the services he offers.

2. **Action Plan** Choose a modern mystery, such as an unsolved crime described in a newspaper article, and write an action plan describing the steps you think Sherlock Holmes would take to find a solution.

3. **Personal Essay** Write a personal essay describing how you used logic or observation to solve a problem.

Speaking and Listening

4. **Talk Show [Group Activity]** Imagine that Holmes, Watson, and Helen Stoner are guests on a talk show, where they describe how Dr. Roylott was captured. With classmates, take the parts of the characters and the talk-show host, and improvise the discussion for your class.

5. **Radio Play [Group Activity]** With a group, create a radio drama based on "The Adventure of the Speckled Band." Plan the dialogue, sound effects, and narration. Cast the parts, choose a director, and select sound engineers to produce the effects. Record your drama, and play it for the class. **[Performing Arts Link]**

Projects

6. **Classroom Mystery [Group Activity]** Work with a team to create a mystery for others to solve. Invent a crime, and leave at least three clues that point to the culprit. Challenge your classmates to solve the mystery.

7. **Collage** Research the time period and place in which Sherlock Holmes "lived." Then, create a collage that brings that time and place to life. Display your work for the class. **[Art Link]**

 ## Writing Mini-Lesson

Letter of Recommendation

A letter of recommendation is written by a client or customer to speak favorably of someone's services. For example, satisfied homeowners might write a letter of recommendation for the builder of their home. The builder could show the letter to prospective customers. Imagine that you are a client of Sherlock Holmes, such as Helen Stoner. Write a letter recommending Holmes's services.

Writing Skills Focus: Support Your Points

Support your recommendation by giving specific examples to illustrate the point you are making.

Model
Holmes's powers of observation are amazing. Within minutes of my arrival, he had deduced that I traveled by train and then dogcart. He drew these correct conclusions simply by looking at me carefully.

Prewriting Choose a character from whose point of view you will write. You can choose Helen Stoner or make up another character who has used Holmes's services. Make a list of Holmes's qualities you want to emphasize in your letter.

Drafting Begin your letter with a general opening, such as "To Whom It May Concern." Then, draft your recommendation. Support your points with precise details.

> ◆ **Grammar Application**
> Use predicate nouns in some of your statements about Sherlock Holmes. For example: Mr. Holmes is a highly analytical detective.

Revising Ask a partner whether your letter is effective. You may need to add support for the points you've made.

The Adventure of the Speckled Band ◆ 493

 ## Idea Bank

Following are suggestions for matching the Idea Bank topics with your students' performance levels and learning modalities:

Customize for *Performance Levels*
Less Advanced Students: 1, 4, 7
Average Students: 3, 4, 5, 6, 7
More Advanced Students: 2, 4, 5, 6, 7

Customize for *Learning Modalities*
Verbal/Linguistic: 1, 2, 3, 4, 5
Logical/Mathematical: 2, 6
Visual/Spatial: 1, 7
Musical/Rhythmic: 5
Bodily/Kinesthetic: 4
Interpersonal: 4, 5, 6
Intrapersonal: 1, 2, 3, 7

Writing Mini-Lesson

Refer students to the Writing Handbook at the back of the book for instruction on the writing process and for further information on expression.

 ## Writer's Solution

Writing Lab CD-ROM
Have students complete the tutorial on Expression. Follow these steps:
1. Using the Audio-annotated audience models, students can select passages from three personal letters on the same subject to find out how each was written to fit a specific audience.
2. Have students use the Personal letter template to ensure correct form when drafting their letters.
3. Students can use the Interactive examples and Word Bins for expressive word revision to see how their letters can be revised to use more precise details.
4. Have students use the Writing Hints on peer editing.

Writer's Solution Sourcebook
Have students use Chapter 1, "Expression," pp. 1–31, for additional support. This chapter includes instruction on writing letters for personal reasons.

✓ ASSESSMENT OPTIONS

Formal Assessment, Selection Test, pp. 143–145, and Assessment Resources Software. The selection test is designed so that it can easily be customized to the performance levels of your students.
Alternative Assessment, p. 35, includes options for less advanced students, more advanced students, interpersonal learners, visual/spatial learners, verbal/linguistic learners, and logical/mathematical learners.

PORTFOLIO ASSESSMENT
Use the following rubrics in the **Alternative Assessment** booklet to assess student writing:
Advertisement: Persuasion, p. 101
Action Plan: How-to/Process Explanation, p. 96
Personal Essay: Problem-Solution, p. 97
Writing Mini-Lesson: Description, p. 93

Just as the fictional Sherlock Holmes made observations, asked questions, inferred, deduced, and drew conclusions, real-life crime-solvers have always followed procedures to get to the bottom of the mysteries of crime.

Clarification

❶ Communities across the country have police departments, law enforcement agencies, and other organizations that provide training for those who provide law enforcement services. Training in procedures is an ongoing process for these people.

Thematic Connection

❷ How does solving crimes find the "extraordinary in the ordinary" in today's world? *Students may say that the advances in science give people extraordinary means to solve ordinary crimes.*

◆ Critical Thinking

❸ **Infer** Why might physical evidence not be used in solving or prosecuting crimes? *Students may suggest that evidence may be gathered improperly, "tainted," or inappropriate to the crime that is being prosecuted.*

Customize for
Less Proficient Readers

Guide students through the technical language of this nonfiction piece. You may want to pair them with more proficient readers in order for them to read this informational article together.

Customize for
Logical/Mathematical Learners

Suggest that students create a chart that details the crime-solving procedures presented in this article. They might categorize the information by types of crimes or types of evidence, include visual representations, research real-life examples of the different procedures, and so forth. Invite them to present their chart to the class and offer information that extends the article's facts.

494

ONNECTIONS TO TODAY'S WORLD

Although Sherlock Holmes is a fictional character, his crime-solving procedures are still in use today. Over the years, detectives' tools have become more sophisticated, but basic observational skills—like Holmes's— are still all-important, as you'll see in the article that follows.

CRIME-SOLVING PROCEDURES
for the MODERN DETECTIVE

❶ *This information was adapted from the workbook of the California Commission on Peace Officer Standards and Training for the "Forensic Technology for Law Enforcement" Telecourse presented on May 13, 1993.*

* * *

❷ The purpose of crime scene investigation is to help establish what happened (crime scene reconstruction) and to identify the responsible person. This is done by carefully documenting the conditions at a crime scene and recognizing all relevant physical evidence. The ability to recognize and properly collect physical evidence is oftentimes critical to both solving and prosecuting violent crimes. It is no exaggeration to say that in the majority of cases, the law enforcement officer who protects and searches a crime scene plays a critical role in determining whether physical evidence will be used in solving or prosecuting violent crimes.

❸ Despite Hollywood's portrayal, crime scene investigation is a difficult and time-consuming job. There is no substitute for a careful and thoughtful approach. An investigator must not leap to an immediate conclusion as to what happened based upon limited information but must generate several different theories of the crime,

keeping the ones that are not eliminated by incoming information at the scene. Reasonable inferences[1] about what happened are produced from the scene appearance and information from witnesses. These theories will help guide the investigator to document specific conditions and recognize valuable evidence.

Documenting crime scene conditions can include immediately recording transient[2] details such as lighting (on/off), drapes (open/closed), weather, or furniture moved by medical teams. Certain evidence such as shoeprints or gunshot residue is fragile and if not collected immediately can easily be destroyed or lost. The scope of the investigation also extends to considerations of arguments which might be generated in this case and documenting conditions which would support or refute these arguments.

In addition, it is important to be able to recognize what should be present at a scene but is not (victim's vehicle/wallet) and objects which appear to be out of

---

1. **inferences:** Conclusions arrived at through reason.
2. **transient** (tran´ sē ənt) *adj.*: Temporary.

494 ◆ *Extraordinary Occurrences*

Beyond the Classroom

Career Connection

Law Enforcement There are a broad range of jobs available in the area of law enforcement. Aside from the colorful and outgoing fictional characters that students may be familiar with, such as Sherlock Holmes and various TV detectives, there are jobs that suit many different personalities and workskills.

Have students brainstorm for a list of law enforcement jobs, including city police officers, forensic scientists, security officers, and so forth. Have each student research a job to determine

responsibilities and requirements. Then have students explain the nature of the jobs. As a class, discuss skills and qualities that would benefit a person in each job. List students' ideas on the board, including values such as service, respect, cooperation, teamwork, pride, contribution, innovation, communication, and decision-making.

After students are aware of practical aspects of law enforcement jobs, you may wish to lead a discussion so that they can compare and contrast real-life jobs in law enforcement with the jobs that fictional characters seem to hold.

place (ski mask) and might have been left by the assailant. It is also important to determine the full extent of a crime scene. A crime scene is not merely the immediate area where a body is located or where an assailant concentrated his activities but can also encompass a vehicle and access/escape routes.

Although there are common items which are frequently collected as evidence (fingerprints, shoeprints, or bloodstains), literally any object can be physical evidence. Anything which can be used to connect a victim to a suspect or a suspect to a victim or crime scene is relevant physical evidence. Using the "shopping list" approach (collecting bloodstains, hairs, or shoeprints) will probably not result in recognizing the best evidence. For example, collecting bloodstains under a victim's body or shoeprints from emergency personnel will rarely answer important questions. Conversely, a single matchstick (usually not mentioned as physical evidence) recovered on the floor near a victim's body can be excellent physical evidence since it can be directly tied to a matchbook found in a suspect's pocket.

Since a weapon or burglar tool is easily recognized as significant physical evidence, it is frequently destroyed by the perpetrator.[3] Sometimes the only remaining evidence is microscopic evidence consisting of hairs, fibers, or other small traces the assailant unknowingly leaves behind or takes with him. Although this evidence is effectively collected when the clothing of the victim or suspect is taken, protocols (involving tape lifts) should be in place so as not to lose this fragile evidence.

---

3. **perpetrator** (pûr′ pə trāt ər) *n.*: One who commits a crime.

---

1. According to the article, what is the basic purpose of a crime-scene investigation?
2. Which common items are often collected as evidence?
3. In what ways does the modern detective resemble Sherlock Holmes?

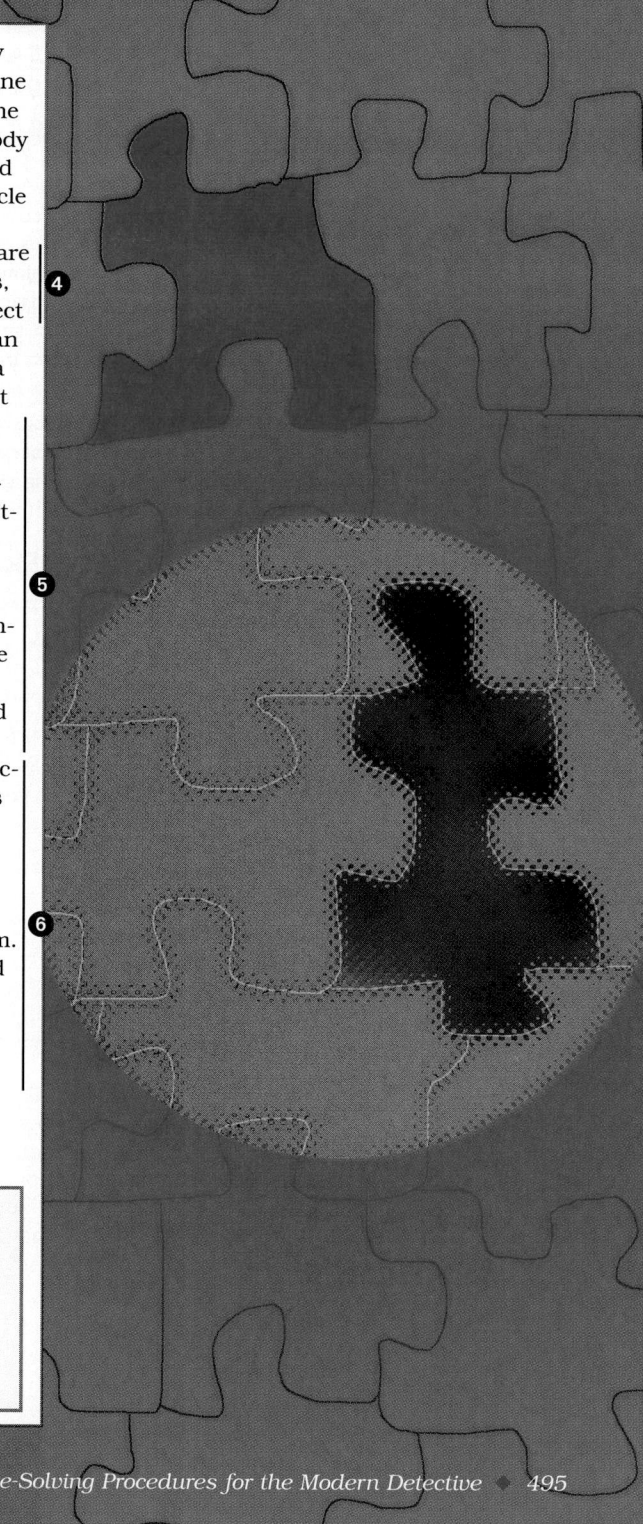

Crime-Solving Procedures for the Modern Detective ◆ 495

Clarification

❹ As DNA forensics becomes more sophisticated and usable as proof, the importance of skin, hair, blood, and saliva are increasing as conclusive evidence to convict criminals. Like all evidence gathered at the scene of a crime, it is essential that officers use proper procedure in gathering these samples.

◆ Critical Thinking

❺ **Infer** Ask students why the "shopping list" approach to gathering evidence might be good despite the article's point that it may cause a person to overlook an important piece of evidence? *Students should recognize the thoroughness that following a list of items provides under many circumstances.*

◆ LITERATURE AND YOUR LIFE

❻ After students have finished reading the article, discuss with them the procedures they use in their lives to solve problems, such as observation and analysis.

Answers

1. The purpose of a crime-scene investigation is to help establish what happened at the scene of the crime in order to identify the responsible person.
2. Fingerprints, shoeprints, and bloodstains are often collected as evidence.
3. Students may say that, like Sherlock Holmes, a modern detective gathers evidence, makes observations, ask questions, and analyzes information.

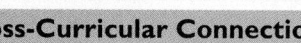

Cross-Curricular Connection: Science

Forensic Science Applying scientific and medical knowledge to legal matters, or crime investigation, is known as forensics. One of the first major developments of forensic science was the 19th-century discovery of fingerprint detection—the key being that no two individuals have the same fingerprints. Like DNA evidence, however, fingerprints can identify a criminal only when there is a record of his or her DNA or fingerprints on file.

There are other scientific techniques available to forensic scientists. Inorganic materials such as glass, paper, and paint can also provide information in solving crimes. Microscopic or chemical analysis is used to obtain information from crime scene samples. Pieces or particles of glass may be carefully measured to determine when it was manufactured so that it can be traced—for instance, in the case of a hit-and-run automobile accident.

Forensic scientists often use computer databases that may be networked across the country or around the world to pool information so that it is available to other law enforcement groups. Encourage interested students to research specific forensic scientific techniques.

Establish Writing Guidelines
Review the following key characteristics of a business letter:

- A business letter is a formal letter whose purpose may be to make a request or place an order; to lodge a complaint; to apply for a position; or to express an opinion.

- A business letter should be clear and direct.

- A business letter should follow an appropriate format and include a heading, date, inside address, salutation, closing, and signature.

You may want to distribute the scoring rubric for Business Letter/Memo, p. 109 in **Alternative Assessment,** to make students aware of the criteria on which they will be evaluated. See the suggestions on p. 498 for how you can customize the rubric to this workshop.

Refer students to the Writing Handbook in the back of the book for instruction on the writing process and further information on workplace writing.

Writer's Solution

Writers at Work Videodisc
Explain to students that a business letter may use persuasive techniques to make a point. To introduce students to persuasion and to show them how Kate Mitchell thinks about writing persuasively, play the videodisc segment on Persuasion (Ch. 5).

Play frames 3 to 7453

Writing Lab CD-ROM
If your students have access to computers, you may want to have them work in the tutorial on Persuasion to complete all or part of their business letters. Follow these steps:

1. Have students view the interactive model of a letter to the editor.
2. Encourage students to use the Topic questionnaire to determine if their topic is suitable.
3. Allow students to draft on computer.
4. When revising, have students use the Proofreading Checklist.

Writer's Solution Sourcebook
For additional support, including in-depth instruction on eliminating unnecessary words, p. 195, use the chapter on Persuasion, pp. 166–199.

Workplace Writing
Business Letter

Writing Process Workshop

In this section, we found Sherlock Holmes conducting business as usual in "The Adventure of the Speckled Band." Although Holmes conducts his business in person, often business transactions are conducted through letters. Whenever you write to get information or advice, to express satisfaction or dissatisfaction with a product, or to propose an idea, you are writing a business letter.

Write a business letter to obtain information about a product or service or to seek the advice of a professional. The following skills, introduced in this section's Writing Mini-Lessons, will help you.

Writing Skills Focus

▶ Your **purpose** will guide you in your choice of details. (See p. 448.)

▶ The level of language and the information that you include should be appropriate for your **audience.** (See p. 463.)

▶ **Use an appropriate tone.** Clarify your attitude toward the subject of your letter. (See p. 471.)

▶ **Support your points** with specific facts and examples. (See p. 493.)

Notice how these skills are used in the following model:

WRITING MODEL

To Whom It May Concern:
   I am writing to inquire about the behavior of blue jays. ① I know that as an expert for the Audubon Society, you can provide me with information about their nesting habits. ② I have several blue jays living in my yard, and I am interested in whether or not they will return next spring. ③

① This letter begins with a statement of purpose. The formal word *inquire* gives the letter a serious tone.

② The writer directly addresses her audience. She knows that an expert will be able to answer her questions.

③ These specific details support the writer's interest in the nesting habits of blue jays.

496 ◆ *Extraordinary Occurrences*

 Beyond the Classroom

Workplace Skills
Writing and Responding to Business Letters Explain to students that part of many office jobs is writing and responding to business letters. A response to a business letter should be just as clear and direct as the letter received. For example, a summer camp receives a letter asking for information on dates and fees. The person at the camp's office who receives the letter might respond by sending the letter writer a camp brochure, and a brief letter introducing himself.

Have students form groups and choose a career field or company that they can simulate representing. Encourage them to discuss what the business goals of someone in that field or at the company might have. Then one or two students can draft a business letter asking for information and the other two students can respond in a business letter. Suggest that students do some investigatory work on the Internet to find a business that interests them. Make sure students use the correct business letter format.

Prewriting

Choose a Topic Think of a product or a service that you are curious about. Write a letter requesting information or asking for an expert's advice. You may want to use one of the following ideas:

Topic Ideas

- Football camp
- Dance lessons
- Value of a classic comic book

Identify Your Audience Knowing your audience will help you determine what information you need to include in your letter. For example, if you are writing to a computer expert about a problem, chances are you need not include much background. If you are writing to a complaint department, you will have to include detailed information about your problem.

Drafting

Keep to a Format A business letter must follow an appropriate format. Follow this model as you prepare your business letter:

Heading: *(the address of the writer)*

_____
_____
_____

Date:_____

Inside Address: *(the address of the recipient)*

_____
_____

Salutation: *(to whom the letter is addressed)*

_____:

Body: *(the main part of the letter)*

_____
_____

Closing: _____,
Signature: _____

APPLYING LANGUAGE SKILLS: Using Informal and Formal English

Informal English is the language of everyday speech. Formal English is the standard language of written communication, formal speeches, and presentations. Use formal English in your business letter.

Informal English:	Formal English:
• Allows contractions	• Does not allow contractions
• Accepts some slang	• Does not accept slang
• May contain incomplete sentences	• Adheres to grammatical standards

Informal English:
Can you give me a break on the next CD I buy?

Formal English:
Can you discount the price of the next CD I purchase?

Writing Application As you draft your business letter, use complete sentences, a formal tone, and avoid slang.

Writer's Solution Connection Writing Lab

For more help with choosing the right words, use the Audience Profile in the Writer's Toolkit.

Develop Student Writing

Prewriting

Explain to students that their first consideration when writing a business letter is purpose. A business letter should be clear and to the point. A letter of complaint may require more information than a letter requesting information. Encourage students to question what information they need to include in their letter to make the reader understand their intent.

Customize for *Less Proficient Writers*

Some students may have difficulty deciding what information to include about themselves when writing a business letter. Suggest that students use a two-column chart like the one below to identify their position and the information they want to know.

Who I Am	What I Need

Explain that a mother requesting information on summer camps for her daughter may write a different type of letter than a prospective counselor or camper.

Drafting

Explain to students that they should state their specific request for information in the first or second sentence of the letter. Then, they can go on to explain their reasons for the request in the body of the letter.

Applying Language Skills
Using Informal and Formal English

Explain to students that when they write personal letters to their friends or relatives, they may use informal English. When writing a business letter, using informal English may be confusing or disrespectful.

Writer's Solution

For additional instruction and practice have students use the practice page on Two Levels of Standard English, p. 69, in the *Writer's Solution Grammar Practice Book*. If students have access technology, they can use the lesson on Formal and Informal English in the Choosing Words unit on the *Writer's Solution Language Lab CD-ROM*.

Revising

Have students work with partners to revise. Readers should note whether the letter is direct, clear, and comprehensive.

 Writer's Solution

Writing Lab CD-ROM

In the Writer's Toolkit, have students use the Self-Evaluation Checklist to help them revise their letters.

Publishing

To help students find the correct e-mail address for their letters, suggest that they do a search for the company's name on the Internet. Usually a company's home page will provide information about how to contact them through the Web.

Reinforce and Extend

Review the Writing Guidelines

After students have finished writing, review business letter characteristics.

Applying Language Skills

Correctly Writing Company Names Company names may be spelled nontraditionally as a way of making them stand out. Students should spell a company's name the way the company spells it.

Answers

1. If you want telephone service, call AT&T.
2. Do you ever shop at K-Mart?
3. UPS can deliver your package the next day.

 Writer's Solution

For additional instruction, use the practice pages on letters, pp. 148–149 in the *Writer's Solution Grammar Practice Book*.

EDITING/PROOFREADING

APPLYING LANGUAGE SKILLS: Correctly Writing Company Names

Find out the exact name of the company to which you are writing, so that you can write it accurately. Pay attention to details of spelling, abbreviations, and completeness. For example, notice the variety among these companies' names:

Acme Lamprey Co.

International Business Machines, Inc.

Simon & Schuster, Inc.

Practice Use a telephone book to check and correct the company names in these sentences.

1. If you want telephone service, call A, T, and T.
2. Do you ever shop at KMart?
3. Ups can deliver your package the next day.

Writing Application In addition to checking company names, verify the title of the person with whom you're corresponding.

Writer's Solution Connection Language Lab

For more practice with capitalization, complete the Proper Nouns lesson in the Capitalization unit.

Revising

Use a Checklist Use the following checklist and tips to help you revise your letter:

▶ **Have you stated your purpose?** Did you include a statement of purpose? If not, include a sentence that clearly lets the reader know why you are writing.

▶ **Did you write to the audience?** If your audience is an expert on rare comic books, you may not have to provide as much information as you might for a clerk in a comic-book store. Review your letter, and either add or delete information, depending on your audience.

▶ **Is the tone of the letter appropriate?** Did you choose words that reflect your attitude: serious, dissatisfied, interested? If not, add words that are more descriptive of your tone.

▶ **Did you support your points?** Did you include specific, concrete facts and examples that support your purpose? For example, if you are dissatisfied with a product, provide concrete examples that will enable your audience to understand your problem.

REVISION MODEL

① I am writing to find out how to identify blue jays' nests.
I have noticed that the blue jays' nests are not as tidy as
② very loose and
other birds' nests, but instead are loose. They use many
twigs. Some blue jays' nests appear in shrubs. Could you
③ interesting
please send me information about those crazy birds?

① The writer adds a statement of purpose.
② This sentence was deleted because an expert on blue jays would already know.
③ The word *interesting* replaces the word *crazy* to maintain a formal tone for a business letter.

Publishing and Presenting

E-Mail Instead of sending your business letter through the mail, send it through e-mail. Use the Internet, or check the packaging of a product to find the address. Using e-mail often provides you with a faster reply.

✓ ASSESSMENT		4	3	2	1
PORTFOLIO ASSESSMENT Use the rubric on Business Letter/Memo in the **Alternative Assessment** booklet, p. 109, to assess the students' writing. Add these criteria to customize this rubric to this assignment.	**Parts of a Letter**	The letter includes a return address, date, greeting, body, and closing. All parts are in the right place and punctuated correctly.	The letter includes a return address, date, greeting, body, and closing. Most parts are in the right place and punctuated correctly.	The letter is missing one part (return address, date, greeting, body, or closing.)	The letter is missing more than one part (return address, date, greeting, body, or closing) and some parts may be in the wrong place.
	Formal Language	The letter is written consistently in formal language.	Most of the letter is written consistently in formal language.	Some of the letter is written consistently in formal language.	The letter is written with informal language.

Real-World Reading Skills Workshop

Reading Product Labels

Strategies for Success

To make an informed decision about any purchase—food, clothes, games, software—you must read and understand the information printed on the packaging.

Identify the Types of Information Identify the kinds of information you are reading—ingredients, care instructions, safety warnings, nutritional information, or directions for use. Classifying information will help you focus your reading.

Read Carefully To use information on product labels to your advantage, read carefully, applying these strategies:

▶ Study the order of ingredients listed on food products; it appears in order of greatest volume.

▶ Use headings and labels to understand chart data.

▶ Consider how required care—"hand wash only," for example—might influence your use of this product.

▶ Note addresses or phone numbers for assistance or questions.

▶ Check for warnings about who should not use the product. The label might offer important information about side effects as well. For example, many cold medications warn about drowsiness or slowed reaction times.

Apply the Strategies

Your health teacher has assigned you to find a nutritious cookie for a class party. Examine

✔ Here are other situations in which it is important to read labels:
▶ Care labels for clothing
▶ Allergy notations on health and beauty aids
▶ Warnings on medications

this label and decide whether this product meets your criteria—can be eaten by everyone, contains small amounts of sugar and fat, and has vitamins and minerals.

1. (a) What is the serving size? (b) How many calories are in one cookie? (c) How much sugar is in one cookie?

2. Are there any vitamins or minerals in the cookie?

3. Could students who are allergic to nuts eat these cookies? Where can you find that information?

4. In your opinion, would these cookies be a nutritious choice?

Julia's Cookies

Nutrition Facts
Serving Size: 1 cookie (23g)
Servings Per Container: about 15

Amount Per Serving
Calories 110   Calories from fat 40

	% Daily Value **
Total Fat 4.5g	7%
Saturated Fat 1g	5%
Cholesterol 0mg	0%
Sodium 55mg	2%
Total Carbohydrates 16g	5%
Dietary Fiber 0g	
Sugars 9g	
Protein 1g	

Vitamin A 0%	•	Vitamin C 0%
Calcium 0%	•	Iron 4%

* Percent Daily Values are based on a 2,000 calorie diet. Your daily values may be higher or lower depending on your calorie needs:

	Calories:	2,000	2,500
Total Fat	Less than	65g	80g
Sat. Fat	Less than	20g	25g
Cholesterol	Less than	300mg	300mg
Sodium	Less than	2,400mg	2,400mg
Total Carbohydrates		375g	375g
Dietary Fiber		25g	30g

Calories per gram:
Fat 9 • Carbohydrate 4 • Protein 4

INGREDIENTS: ENRICHED FLOUR (WHEAT FLOUR, NIACIN, REDUCED IRON, THIAMINE MONONITRATE, RIBOFLAVIN, FOLIC ACID), VEGETABLE OIL, SHORTENING (PARTIALLY HYDROGENATED SOYBEAN AND COTTONSEED OILS, BHA AND BHT (AS PRESERVATIVES)], POWDERED SUGAR, SUGAR, COCOA (PROCESSED WITH ALKALI), CHOCOLATE LIQUOR, CORN STARCH, LEAVENING (SODIUM BICARBONATE, AMMONIUM BICARBONATE, SODIUM ACID PYROPHOSPHATE, MONOCALCIUM PHOSPHATE, CALCIUM SULFATE), SALT, SOYBEAN LECITHIN (AN EMULSIFIER), CARAMEL COLOR, ARTIFICIAL FLAVOR.

MAY CONTAIN TRACES OF PEANUTS AND/OR NUTS.

PACKED FOR JULIA'S COOKIES
CEDAR GROVE, NJ 07009
© 1999

Introduce the Strategies

If possible, bring in a can of soda, juice, or food to show students an example of a product label. You may want to have more than one example so you can compare and contrast how the information is presented. Ask students to identify the different types of information included on each label. If there is writing on the product which is not informational, ask students to identify what the purpose of the writing is.

Customize for
Less Proficient Readers

Students may not recognize technical words used on some labels. Suggest that students use a dictionary to find out what unfamiliar words mean.

Customize for
English Language Learners

Explain to students that many products include information written in different languages. Many times, products come with pamphlets which may have the directions or information written out several times in different languages. Suggest that students try to read the English first, but if they have difficulty to check with their native language.

Customize for
More Advanced Students

Suggest that students write their own product labels. Encourage them to be creative and write labels for unusual products, such as their goldfish, or their big brother. Have them share their labels with the rest of the class.

Apply the Strategies

Answers

1. (a) The serving size is 1 cookie. (b) There are 110 calories in one cookie. (c) One cookie contains 9g of sugar.
2. There is Vitamin A, Vitamin C, Calcium, and Iron in the cookie.
3. Students who are allergic to nuts can eat these cookies. You can find this out by looking at the list of ingredients and making sure nuts are not listed.
4. These cookies may not be considered nutritious because they supply very small amounts of vitamins and minerals, and for one cookie they have a considerable amount of calories which come from fat.

499

◆ Build Grammar

Reviewing Complements

The selections in Part 1 include instruction on the following:

- Direct Objects
- Indirect Objects
- Predicate Adjectives
- Predicate Nouns

This instruction is reinforced with the Build Grammar Skills practice pages in **Selection Support,** pp. 170, 176, 181, and 186.

As you review complements, you may wish to include the following:

- Compound Objects and Complements

Any complement can be compound. A compound direct object occurs when an action verb directs action toward more than one object, as in the following sentence:

The shoemaker fixed the soles and heels of the boots. The compound direct object is *soles* and *heels*.

Answers
Practice 1

1. "I recognized the noise. . . ." (noise is a direct object)
2. "My sister Amy, two years old, was asleep. . . ." (asleep is a predicate adjective)
3. "Everything tastes good today." (good is a predicate adjective)
4. "I present you the tall skyscrapers/as merely huge palm trees with lights." (skyscrapers is a direct object; you is an indirect object)
5. "It is terror." (terror is a predicate noun)

Practice 2
Possible responses:
1. The trees are colorful.
2. Holmes gave her an answer.
3. The noise was heaven.
4. The blue jay dropped an acorn.
5. The shadow grew tall.

Complements   Grammar Review

A **complement** is a word or a group of words that completes the meaning of a verb. There are four kinds of complements:

> A **direct object** receives the action of the verb or shows the result of the action. It answers the questions *whom* or *what*. (See p. 447.)
>
>   A.V.   D.O.
> I ordered you a *cup* of cocoa.
>
> An **indirect object** follows an action verb and tells *to whom* or *what* or *for whom* or *what* the action of the verb is performed. (See p. 462.)
>
>   A.V.   I.O.
> I ordered *you* a cup of cocoa.
>
> A **predicate noun** is a noun that follows a linking verb and renames the subject. (See p. 492.)
>
>   L.V.   P.N.
> "I am *Dr. Grimesby Roylott,* of Stoke Moran."
>
> A **predicate adjective** is an adjective that follows a linking verb and describes the subject. (See p. 470.)
>
>   L.V.   P.A.
> "The marks are perfectly fresh."

Some verbs, such as those that relate to the senses—*sound, look, taste, feel, smell, appear*—or those that express a condition or placement—*remain, grow, seem, stay, become*—can function either as linking verbs or action verbs. Notice the differences in these two sentences:

                         L.V.   P.A.
The blue jay's song *sounds* delightful.
                A.V.   D.O.
The captain *sounded* the horn that signaled the boats to return to the dock.

com·ple·ment (käm′plə mənt) *n.* **1** something that completes a whole or makes perfect *[The sharp cheese was a delicious* complement *to the apple pie.]* **2** the word or words that complete a predicate *[In "We made her our captain," "our captain" is a* complement.*]*

Practice 1 Copy the following sentences into your notebook. Then, underline verbs and label the complements.

1. "I recognized the noise. . . ."
2. "My sister Amy, two years old, was asleep . . ."
3. "Everything tastes good today."
4. "I present you the tall skyscrapers/as merely huge palm trees with lights."
5. "It is terror."

Practice 2 Use the following subjects and verbs to create sentences that include the type of complement indicated.

1. **Subject:** trees **Verb:** are (predicate adjective)
2. **Subject:** Holmes **Verb:** gave (indirect object, direct object)
3. **Subject:** noise **Verb:** was (predicate noun)
4. **Subject:** blue jay **Verb:** dropped (direct object)
5. **Subject:** shadow **Verb:** grew (predicate adjective)

Grammar in Writing

✔ When writing a sentence with a predicate noun or a predicate adjective, choose the most exact noun or precise adjective to complete your thought.

PART 2

Strange Doings

The Blank Signature (Carte Blanche), 1965, René Magritte, National Gallery of Art, Washington, D.C.

One-Minute Planning Guide

The selections in this section focus on the theme of "Strange Doings." "A Glow in the Dark" is an essay by Gary Paulsen about a strange encounter in the woods. "Mushrooms" is a poem by Sylvia Plath personifying the mushrooms as they push through the earth overnight. "Southern Mansion" and "The Bat" explore the strangeness of each of their subjects, respectively. In "A Horseman in the Sky" a Civil War soldier struggles with loyalty.

Customize for
Varying Student Needs
When assigning the selections in this section to your students, keep in mind the following factors:

"A Glow in the Dark"
- An excerpt from Gary Paulsen's novel *Woodsong*

"Mushrooms"
- A short poem about mushrooms
- Includes a Beyond Literature Science Connection

"A Southern Mansion"
- A short poem about an old plantation

"The Bat"
- A short, rhyming poem about a bat

"A Horseman in the Sky"
- A short story set at the time of the Civil War
- Students may need help with long sentences and complex vocabulary
- Provides an opportunity for connecting literature with social studies

 Humanities: Art

The Blank Signature (Carte Blanche), 1965, by René Magritte

René Magritte (1898–1967) was one of the most famous Surrealist painters of the 20th century. His method of transforming images by juxtaposing them with objects with which they have no natural connection, or by changing them in scale, provides a shock to the viewer.

Magritte was born in Belgium and lived in France for a period of 3 years where he met the other French Surrealists, including the writer André Breton.

1. What is ordinary about this scene? *Students may note that the person and the horse look realistic and ordinary, as do the trees, or that riding through the woods is an ordinary activity.*

2. What is strange about the scene of this painting? *Students may describe the interwoven aspects of the trees with the horse and rider— foreground and background in different ways.*

3. Would you call the scene ordinary or strange? Explain your answer. *Most students will perceive the painting as strange. Encourage them to articulate their reasons for their reaction to the scene.*

501

OBJECTIVES

1. To read, comprehend, and interpret non-fiction and poetry
2. To relate nonfiction and poetry to personal experience
3. To make inferences when reading nonfiction and poetry
4. To analyze tone in nonfiction and poetry
5. To build vocabulary in context and learn the prefix *a-*
6. To develop skill in using appositive phrases
7. To write an I-Search paper stating your main points clearly
8. To respond to nonfiction and poetry through writing, speaking and listening, and projects

SKILLS INSTRUCTION

Vocabulary:
Prefixes: *a-*
Spelling:
Words With the *ak* Sound Spelled *acq* or *aq*
Grammar:
Appositive Phrases
Reading Strategy:
Make Inferences
Writing:
State Your Main Points Clearly

Speaking and Listening:
Monologue (Teacher Edition)
Viewing and Representing:
Science Article (Teacher Edition)
Critical Viewing:
Relate; Speculate; Classify; Deduce
Literary Focus:
Tone

PORTFOLIO OPPORTUNITIES

Writing: List; News Story; Essay
Writing Mini-Lesson: I-Search Paper
Speaking and Listening: Monologue; Oral Presentation
Projects: Science Article; Story Illustration

More About the Authors
Gary Paulsen writes more about his dog-sledding experiences in *Dog Song*, which describes the Iditarod, the 1,049-mile race across Alaska.

Sylvia Plath wrote about experiences that were deeply personal to her. Her poetry reveals a great capacity to experience emotion.

Arna Bontemps wrote perhaps the most important record of African American life in the South during the depression: *The Old South*, a collection of short stories that combines fiction and personal reminiscense.

Theodore Roethke's poetry may be straightforward, witty, and use strict poetic forms, or mysterious, with bizarre imagery, and in free verse.

Guide for Reading

Meet the Authors:

Gary Paulsen (1939–   )
Gary Paulsen has won three Newbery Honor awards—for his books *Hatchet, Dog Song,* and *The Winter Room.* With his more than sixty books in print around the world, it is astonishing to learn that the books were all written within a ten-year period.

Sylvia Plath (1932–1963)
Sylvia Plath was born in Boston. She developed an early interest in writing and published her first poems at the age of seventeen. Her *Collected Poems* won the Pulitzer Prize for Poetry in 1982.

Arna Bontemps (1902–1973)
Born in Louisiana and educated at the University of Chicago, Arna Bontemps was a college professor for more than twenty years. In addition to teaching, Bontemps had a career as an editor, writer, librarian, and literary critic.

Theodore Roethke (1908–1963)
The son of a florist, young Theodore Roethke loved to play in and around the family greenhouse, where he developed a kinship with nature that he never lost. Roethke's poetry earned him the Bollingen Prize, the Pulitzer Prize, and the National Book Award.

502 ◆ *Extraordinary Occurrences*

◆ LITERATURE AND YOUR LIFE

CONNECT YOUR EXPERIENCE
A flower bed of pansies seems like faces looking up at you. A sunset reminds you that the world can be a beautiful place. A meal in a restaurant makes you think of a vacation taken last year. Everyday objects and occurrences often inspire thoughts that, on the surface, may appear unrelated.

THEMATIC FOCUS: Strange Doings
The essay and poems that follow present everyday objects in an unusual light. What is strange or haunting about the way the writers describe them?

◆ Background for Understanding

SCIENCE
Roethke's poem "The Bat" describes the behavior of a bat. Though bats fly, they are not birds. A bat is a mammal, meaning that the young are born live, not hatched, and get milk from their mothers. Using a process called echolocation, bats can fly around in the dark without bumping into obstacles. As they fly, they emit high-pitched cries that humans can't hear. These sounds are reflected by all obstacles in the bat's path, echoing back to its sensitive ears. The bat responds to the signal and avoids the obstacles.

◆ Build Vocabulary

PREFIXES: *a-*
Amiss, which means "wrongly placed" contains the prefix *a-,* which can mean "on" or "in." Other words containing this prefix include *asleep, amid,* and *ashore.*

WORD BANK
Which word from the list describes how someone might whisper to another? Check the Build Vocabulary box on page 508 to see if you guessed correctly.

diffused
discreetly
acquire
amiss

Prentice Hall Literature Program Resources

REINFORCE / RETEACH / EXTEND
Selection Support Pages
Build Vocabulary: Prefixes: *a-,* p. 189
Build Spelling Skills, p. 190
Build Grammar Skills: Appositive Phrases, p. 191
Reading Strategies: Make Inferences, p. 192
Literary Focus: Tone, p. 193
Strategies for Diverse Student Needs, pp. 71–72
Beyond Literature Cross-Curricular Connection: Science, p. 36

Formal Assessment Selection Test, pp. 146–148
Alternative Assessment, p. 36
Resource Pro CD-ROM
"A Glow in the Dark"; "Mushrooms"; "Southern Mansion"; "The Bat"

 Listening to Literature Audiocassettes
"A Glow in the Dark"; "Mushrooms"; "Southern Mansion"; "The Bat"

 Looking at Literature Videodisc/Videotape
"The Bat"

A Glow in the Dark ◆ Mushrooms
Southern Mansion ◆ The Bat

Interest Grabber To spark student interest, describe the phenomenon of the will-o'-the-wisp. The will-o'-the-wisp is a flickering light that sometimes appears at night in swampy areas. It often takes a globular shape and floats slowly above the ground. Until it was scientifically explained as a combustion of swamp gas, the will-o'-the-wisp was feared by many people as something supernatural and evil. The jack-o'-lantern may be a representation of the will-o'-the-wisp. Tell students that they are about to read about Gary Paulsen's encounter with a strange light in the night—but he is nowhere near a swamp. What do they think it could be?

◆ **Build Grammar Skills**

Appositive Phrases If you wish to introduce the grammar concept for this selection before students read, refer to the instruction on p. 512.

Customize for
Less Proficient Readers
Students may have trouble making inferences. Let them practice by going through the process in reverse. Have them look for clues in "A Glow in the Dark" that imply that Paulsen is an experienced dog-sledder. Clues may include his care for the young dogs, his ability to fix the cart, and his testing of the head lamp. Then, point out sections of the essay and ask students what they infer. For example, if you mention Paulsen's willingness to run without a head lamp, students may say this action implies that he is reckless or lets his dogs have their way more than he should.

Customize for
More Advanced Students
Challenge students to write a description of an action they have done, such as riding a bike, taking a train, or visiting a new place. Have them include details and their reactions to events, as Gary Paulsen does in the essay.

◆ **Literary Focus**

TONE

The **tone** of a literary work is the writer's attitude toward the subject and the audience. Tone can often be described in a single word, such as *formal, informal, serious,* or *humorous.* Tone is revealed in the writer's choice of subject, choice of words, and even sentence structure. For example, in these lines from "Mushrooms," the poet's word choice and style create a mysterious tone:

> We are shelves, we are/Tables, we are
> meek,/We are edible.

◆ **Reading Strategy**

MAKE INFERENCES

In most literary works, writers do not tell you everything directly; instead, they imply, or hint at, meanings or ideas. Therefore, you may have to **make inferences,** or use clues from the text, to determine the writer's message or a line's meaning. For example, in "A Glow in the Dark," you can infer from Paulsen's actions that he is an experienced dog-sledder.

As you read, fill out a chart like the one below to help you to make inferences.

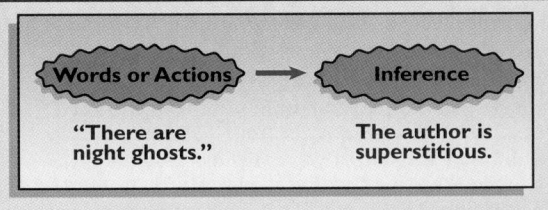

Words or Actions ➝ Inference

"There are night ghosts."

The author is superstitious.

Preparing for Standardized Tests

Vocabulary The vocabulary skill for this story is using the prefix *a-*. Students can use knowledge of prefixes and affixes to analyze and identify unfamiliar words. Vocabulary sections of standardized tests may have multiple-choice questions that test students' knowledge of suffixes. The prefix *a-* adds the meaning "on," "in," or "to" to the root word. Ask students to give the definitions of the following words: *asleep, amid,* and *ashore.* Help them respond that *asleep* means "in a state of sleep, or sleeping." *Amid* means "in the middle"

and *ashore* means "on the shore." Then write this sample test question on the board:

> Paulsen put his sled aside when he set up camp.

In this sentence, *aside* means

  (A) inside   (C) outside
  (B) to one side   (D) on its side

The correct answer is *(B).* Help students understand that in addition to applying their knowledge of the prefix *a-,* they also need to be aware of the context of the sentence.

One-Minute Insight Gary Paulsen describes a frightening light he sees in the forest in the middle of the night while he is practicing a dog-sled run. Both he and his dogs are taken aback by the sight, which he feels compelled to investigate. Though it appears to be a ghostly form, Paulsen forces himself to get close enough to find out what it really is—a tree stump glowing from phosphorus.

Team Teaching Strategy

The source of this mysterious light, phosphorus, is poisonous, combustible, and luminous in the dark. You may want to coordinate with a science teacher to help students learn more about this element.

◆ Literary Focus

❶ Tone How does the author reveal his attitude toward the subject of this essay in the first paragraph? *He is honest about having been afraid and appears to want to share his emotions with the reader.*

◆ Reading Strategy

❷ Make Inferences How does this sentence let you know that Paulsen was not familiar with this logging trail? *He says he had tried to find new places to run the dogs and that this trail was one place they had not run.*

►Critical Viewing◄

❸ Relate *Students may say they would be scared, awed, curious, or have any number of emotions. Ask them to explain their reactions.*

Customize for
English Language Learners
The descriptive details in this essay may be hard for some students to follow. Encourage them to read the essay while listening to the audiocassette of "A Glow in the Dark."

A Glow in the Dark
from Woodsong
Gary Paulsen

❶ There are night ghosts. Some people say that we can understand all things if we can know them, but there came a dark night in the fall when I thought that was wrong, and so did the dogs.

We had been running all morning and were tired; some of the dogs were young and could not sustain a long run. So we stopped in the middle of the afternoon when they seemed to want to rest. I made a fire, set up a gentle, peaceful camp, and went to sleep for four hours.

It hadn't snowed yet so we had been running with a three-wheel cart, which meant we had to run on logging roads and open areas. I had been hard pressed to find new country to run in to keep the young dogs from becoming bored and this logging trail was one we hadn't run. It had been rough going, with a lot of ruts and mud and the cart was a mess so I spent some time fixing it after I awakened, carving off the dried mud. The end result was we didn't get going again until close to one in the morning. This did not pose a problem except that as soon as I hooked the dogs up and got them lined out—I was running an eight-dog team—my head lamp went out. I replaced the bulb and tried a new battery, but that didn't help—the internal wiring was bad. I thought briefly of sleeping again until daylight but the dogs were slamming into the harnesses, screaming to run, so I shrugged and

❷

> ► **Critical Viewing** If you came upon this sight while alone in a dark forest, how would you react? [Relate]

❸

504 ◆ *Extraordinary Occurrences*

Brittle Willow, Brooklyn, 1992, Anders Knutsson, Courtesy of the artist

---

Block Scheduling Strategies

Consider these suggestions to take advantage of extended class time.

- After using the Interest Grabber to draw students into the essay, play the audiocassette of "A Glow in the Dark" as students read along. Follow with a class discussion of how the reading enhances the presentation of the essay.
- Emphasize the Literary Focus as students read the poems aloud. Encourage the class to discuss the atmosphere that the poets create in each poem.

- Have students work in pairs to rehearse their already-written monologues. Students may make suggestions for revisions in their partner's monologue. Some students may give their performances during the extended class time.
- To spark students' interest in "The Bat" and provide a visual reference for the poem, show the video segment for the poem.

Looking at Literature Videodisc/Videotape

A Glow in the Dark ◆ 505

❹ Strange Doings How does this ordinary object, a tree, become terrifying when observed in extraordinary circumstances? *Students may respond that anything may be frightening if it is taken out of its normal situation.*

Customize for
Verbal/Linguistic Learners
Challenge students to make up stories based on the picture of the tree. Students may work in groups and develop a story that they tell together, or they may work individually, writing a story to tell orally. Encourage them to use their imaginations and make up a fantasy, science fiction, or realistic story about the tree. They may use what they've read of "A Glow in the Dark" as a starting place for the story.

Customize for
Visual/Spatial Learners
Encourage students to use the glowing tree in this painting and other visuals that accompany the selections to appreciate the writers' tone and messages.

Beyond the Classroom

Community Connection
Research Community Groups Gary Paulsen spends time in wilderness areas and writes about his experiences. Many people enjoy being in nature while participating in sports. Cross-country skiing and snow-shoeing are popular in northern areas of the country. Hiking, biking, and fishing are other recreational activities that let you enjoy nature. In urban areas, people often visit pockets of nature, such as parks and waterfronts. Often there are local groups of people who get together to take part in these activities.

Some community groups work to protect the environment. Members of these groups may meet to clean up areas, maintain hiking trails, or plan ways to keep natural areas free of development.

Encourage students to investigate community nature groups. They may find information in the local newspaper, in the telephone directory, on the Internet, at the local library, or at other community service locations. Have students locate an organization or group, find out what the group does, and participate if possible. Students can share their findings with the class.

506

jumped on the rig and untied it. Certainly, I thought, running without a head lamp would not be the worst thing I had ever done.

Immediately we blew into the darkness and the ride was madness. Without a lamp I could not tell when the rig was going to hit a rut or a puddle. It was cloudy and fairly warm—close to fifty—and had rained the night before. Without the moon or even starlight I had no idea where the puddles were until they splashed me—largely in the face—so I was soon dripping wet. Coupled with that, tree limbs I couldn't see hit at me as we passed, almost tearing me off the back of the rig. Inside an hour I wasn't sure if I was up, down, or sideways.

And the dogs stopped.

They weren't tired, not even a little, judging by the way they had been ripping through the night, but they stopped dead.

◆ **Literary Focus**
What is the author's tone? How can you tell?

I had just taken a limb in the face and was temporarily blinded. All I knew was that they had stopped suddenly and that I had to jam down on the brakes to keep from running over them. It took me a couple of seconds to clear my eyes and when I did, I saw the light.

In the first seconds I thought it was another person coming toward me. The light had an eerie green-yellow glow. It was quite bright and filled a whole part of the dark night ahead, down the trail. It seemed to be moving. I was in deep woods and couldn't think what a person would be doing there—there are no other teams where I train—but I was glad to

▲ **Critical Viewing** Why might dog-sledding be popular with naturalists like Paulsen? [Speculate]

see the light. At first. Then I realized the light was strange. It glowed and ebbed and seemed to fill too much space to be a regular light source. It was low to the ground, and wide.

I was still not frightened, and would probably not have become frightened except that the dogs suddenly started to sing.

I have already talked about some of their songs. Rain songs and first-snow songs and meat songs and come-back-and-stay-with-us songs and even puppy-training songs, but I had heard this song only once, when an old dog had died in the kennel. It was a death song.

And that frightened me.

They all sat. I could see them quite well in the glow from the light—the soft glow, the green glow, the ghost glow. It crept into my thinking without my knowing it: the ghost glow. Against my wishes I started thinking of all the things in my life that had scared me.

Ghosts and goblins and dark nights and snakes under the bed and sounds I didn't know and bodies I had found and graveyards under covered pale moons and death, death, death . . .

And they sang and sang. The cold song in the strange light. For a time I could do nothing but stand on the back of the wheeled rig and stare at the light with old, dusty terror.

But curiosity was stronger. My legs moved without my wanting them to move and my body followed them, alongside the team in the dark, holding to each dog like a security blanket until I reached the next one, moving

506 ◆ *Extraordinary Occurrences*

🏴 **Cross-Curricular Connection: Social Studies**

Dog–sledding The history of dog-sledding goes back more than 1,000 years. Indigenous people of the Far North have long used sled dogs, not only for transportation but for protection, hunting, and companionship. More recent visitors and inhabitants of the area have benefited by adopting dog-sledding. In the early 1900's, explorers at both the North and South Poles traveled by dog sled. The Royal Canadian Mounted Police patrolled the frontier on dog sled teams until 1969. Dog teams were also used to deliver mail in remote parts of Alaska and Canada.

Gary Paulsen is practicing for dog-sled racing in "A Glow in the Dark"—a sport that has become quite popular. A team of dogs is usually harnessed in pairs, possibly with a lead dog. The human driver, known as a musher, stands on long runners at the rear of the sled. The musher may also pedal with one foot, like a skateboarder, or run holding onto the sled's handle bar. Dog teams may travel 20 miles an hour while racing. The longer races can take up to 2 weeks and cover over 1,000 miles. For these races, the dog sled may carry up to 600 pounds of food and equipment.

closer to the light until I was at the front and there were no more dogs to hold.

The light had gotten brighter, seemed to pulse and flood back and forth, but I still could not see the source. I took another step, then another, trying to look around the corner, deeply feeling the distance from the dogs, the aloneness.

Two more steps, then one more, leaning to see around the corner and at last I saw it and when I did it was worse.

It was a form. Not human. A large, standing form glowing in the dark. The light came from within it, a cold-glowing green light with yellow edges that <u>diffused</u> the shape, making it change and grow as I watched.

I felt my heart slam up into my throat.

I couldn't move. I stared at the upright form and was sure it was a ghost, a being from the dead sent for me. I could not move and might not have ever moved except that the dogs had followed me, pulling the rig quietly until they were around my legs, peering ahead, and I looked down at them and had to laugh.

They were caught in the green light, curved around my legs staring at the standing form, ears cocked and heads turned sideways while they studied it. I took another short step forward and they all followed me, then another, and they stayed with me until we were right next to the form.

It was a stump.

A six-foot-tall, old rotten stump with the bark knocked off, glowing in the dark with a bright green glow. Impossible. I stood there with the dogs around my legs, smelling the stump and touching it with their noses. I found out later that it glowed because it had sucked phosphorus[1] from the ground up into the wood and held the light from day all night.

But that was later. There in the night I did not know this. Touching the stump, and feeling the cold light, I could not quite get rid of the fear until a black-and-white dog named Fonzie came up, smelled the stump, snorted, and relieved himself on it.

So much for ghosts. | ❽

---

1. **phosphorus** (fäs´ fə rəs) *n.*: Substance that gives off light after exposure to radiant energy.

◆ Build Vocabulary

diffused (di fyo͞ozd´) *v.*: Spread out widely into different directions

Guide for Responding

◆ LITERATURE AND YOUR LIFE

Reader's Response What would you have thought you were seeing if you saw the "green-yellow glow"?

Thematic Focus In what way is the story about a "strange doing"?

☑ Check Your Comprehension

1. Describe where and why Paulsen and the dogs are running.
2. Why did the dogs stop suddenly when they were running through the night?
3. What did the author think he saw? What did he actually see?

◆ Critical Thinking

INTERPRET
1. How would you describe the author's personality? Give examples. [Analyze]
2. How does Paulsen show respect for the dogs? How do the dogs show they trust Paulsen? [Connect]
3. Why isn't the company of dogs enough to make Paulsen feel less alone in the story? [Interpret]

APPLY
4. Would you call Paulsen courageous? Explain. [Make a Judgment]

A Glow in the Dark ◆ 507

◆ Critical Thinking

1. Students may say he attends to details, as shown by the care he takes in his equipment and of the dogs. He is also brave, willing to continue running without a light, despite getting hit by branches. He is also willing to admit when he is afraid, as in his description of seeing the light.
2. Paulsen shows he respects the dogs because he stops when he feels the dogs are tired; he tries to find new trails so the young dogs are not bored; and he goes on in the dark because he knows the dogs want to run. The dogs show they trust Paulsen when they follow him to investigate the light.
3. The light seems supernatural to him, in which case the company of dogs or other humans might not be enough to comfort him.
4. Paulsen is courageous for sledding in the dark and investigating the strange light.

◆ **Reading Strategy**

❻ **Make Inferences** Why does Paulsen hold on to each dog as he makes his way toward the light? *He is reassuring the dogs but he also feels less afraid if he can touch the dogs.*

◆ **Reading Strategy**

❼ **Make Inferences** How do the dogs save Paulsen from his fear? *The dogs are also curious, and come forward to investigate the light, pulling the sled. They look so comic in the light with their ears cocked and their heads turned that he laughs, breaking the tension.*

◆ **Critical Thinking**

❽ **Connect** In the beginning of the essay Paulsen says, "There are night ghosts." Now, at the end of the essay, he says, "So much for ghosts." Ask students how they feel about the concluding sentence. Is Paulsen being fair to the reader? *Some students may say that since he believed he was seeing a ghost at the time, his first statement was accurate and his last statement acknowledged that he had been scared and mistaken. Other readers may feel they were misled.*

Reinforce and Extend

Answers

◆ **LITERATURE AND YOUR LIFE**

Reader's Response Some students may have known the light was caused by some natural phenomenon; others may say they would have been afraid or curious.

Thematic Focus Seeing the unearthly light in the forest in the middle of the night is a strange experience. Even though Paulsen later learns there is a scientific explanation for the light, the memory remains haunting.

☑ Check Your Comprehension

1. Paulsen and the dogs were running on a logging trail in a forest, practicing their dog-sledding skills.
2. The dogs stop because they see a strange light.
3. He thought he saw a ghost that had come for him. It was actually a tree that had absorbed phosphorus from the ground so that it glowed in the dark.

In "Mushrooms," Sylvia Plath describes the fungi as silently taking over an area, despite being "bland-mannered." In this poem the quiet and voiceless mushrooms shove their way to the surface, multiplying. They appear unassuming and humble, but they are everywhere.

◆ **Reading Strategy**

❶ **Make Inferences** What is happening in this sentence? *The mushrooms are moving up through the soil to reach the air.*

◆ **Critical Thinking**

❷ **Distinguish** Why does nobody see the mushrooms? *They are quiet and discreet so they are not noticed.*

◆ **Literary Focus**

❸ **Tone** How does the poet show her attitude toward the mushrooms in this stanza? *She recognizes that despite their softness they are determined to push their way up.*

▶ **Critical Viewing** ◀

❹ **Classify** *Students may find young mushrooms, mature ones, and the big ones slightly past their prime.*

Customize for
Verbal/Linguistic Learners

Have students read the poem aloud and analyze the sounds. You might ask questions to help students notice certain qualities in the poem. For example:

- What sounds are repeated within a stanza?

- Can you read this poem quickly? Why or why not?

- Why do you think the seventh stanza is longer than the others?

Students may notice that the long *i* sound is repeated in the first stanza; the long *o* sound is repeated in the second stanza. They may discover that the rhythm of the words makes it hard to read the poem quickly. The seventh stanza tells why mushrooms proliferate and there's also a repeated line.

MUSHROOMS

SYLVIA PLATH

Overnight, very
Whitely, discreetly,
Very quietly

❶

Our toes, our noses
5   Take hold on the loam,[1]
Acquire the air.

❷ Nobody sees us,
Stops us, betrays us;
The small grains make room.

10 Soft fists insist on
❸ Heaving the needles,
The leafy bedding.

Even the paving.
Our hammers, our rams,
15 Earless and eyeless,

1. **loam** (lōm) *n.*: Any rich, dark soil.

▲ Critical Viewing What different stages of growth can you observe in the mushrooms on these pages? [Classify]

◆ **Build Vocabulary**

discreetly (dis krēt´ lē) *adv.*: Carefully; silently

acquire (ə kwīr´) *v.*: To get; come to have as one's own

508 ◆ Extraordinary Occurrences

Viewing and Representing Mini-Lesson

Science Article

This mini-lesson supports the Project in the Idea Bank on p. 513.

Introduce Have students read the Science Connection on p. 509 for an overview about mushrooms.

Develop Students choose partners and begin researching mushrooms. They may find information in encyclopedias, library books, magazines, or a science museum. Cookbooks, gourmet magazines, and newspaper food sections may also have material.

Apply Students can choose a few mushrooms to report on, then write the article. Encourage them to be creative in their display; for example, they might include a sample of a recipe or create a three-dimensional model of a type of mushroom.

Assess Evaluate students on their writing by using the Writing Scoring Rubrics on Description, p. 93, and Definition/Classification, p. 95, in **Alternative Assessment.** Evaluate the display items for their originality and thoroughness.

◆ **Reading Strategy**

⑤ Make Inferences What two contradictory characteristics of the mushrooms do you learn about in this stanza? *They are "bland-mannered," asking for almost nothing, yet they have power because there are so many of them.*

Perfectly voiceless,
Widen the crannies,
Shoulder through holes. We

Diet on water,
20 On crumbs of shadow,
Bland-mannered, asking ⑤
Little or nothing.
So many of us!
So many of us!

25 We are shelves, we are
Tables, we are meek,
We are edible,

Nudgers and shovers
In spite of ourselves. ⑥
30 Our kind multiplies:

We shall by morning
Inherit the earth.
Our foot's in the door. ⑦

Beyond Literature

Science Connection

Mushrooms In "Mushrooms," Sylvia Plath depicts mushrooms as a silent army that constantly multiply and will one day "inherit the earth." Mushrooms are a type of fungus that grows in arcs or rings. When a spore from a mushroom falls on a suitable spot on the ground, it produces tiny strands that grow out in all directions and eventually emerge as stalks and caps of mushrooms. As long as nourishment, adequate temperature, and moisture are provided, mushrooms can live and multiply for hundreds of years.

Cross-Curricular Activity
Many mushrooms are edible, but there are more than seventy kinds of mushrooms that are poisonous and sometimes fatal. Do research about mushrooms, and create an illustrated poster of poisonous mushrooms. List the regions in which each type of poisonous mushroom is commonly found.

◆ **Literary Focus**

⑥ Tone What is the poet's attitude toward the mushrooms in this stanza? *She may be saying that the mushrooms are only "nudgers and shovers" because they multiply so rapidly, or she may be saying that the mushrooms are just pretending to be so meek.*

◆ **Critical Thinking**

⑦ Connect How does the last line connect with lines 4 and 5? *In lines 4 and 5 the mushrooms' toes are taking hold on the loam. Now their whole foot is in the door.*

Beyond Literature

Students can research by looking in a reference book on wild plants or by interviewing people who gather mushrooms. It is difficult to tell whether a mushroom found in the wild is poisonous. Many types of mushrooms resemble one another, which makes tasting wild mushrooms extremely dangerous. There are so many kinds of mushrooms, students may need to restrict their research to certain types or to certain geographical regions.

Reinforce and Extend

Answers
◆ **LITERATURE AND YOUR LIFE**

Reader's Response Students should describe their previous ideas about mushrooms and explain how the poem affected their perception of them.

Thematic Focus The mushrooms see themselves as quiet and bland, yet they are pushing their way up and taking over the earth.

Guide for Responding

◆ **LITERATURE AND YOUR LIFE**

Reader's Response Have your ideas about mushrooms changed since reading this poem? Why or why not?

Thematic Focus What is strange about what the mushrooms are doing and how they see themselves?

☑ **Check Your Comprehension**

1. What are the mushrooms doing at night?
2. How do the mushrooms overcome the obstacles in their way?
3. Why does no one notice what the mushrooms are doing?

◆ **Critical Thinking**

INTERPRET
1. What seems to be the goal or purpose of the mushrooms? **[Infer]**
2. What demands, if any, do the mushrooms make on their surroundings? **[Interpret]**
3. What quality of the mushrooms will enable them to "Inherit the earth"? **[Deduce]**

APPLY
4. "Blessed are the meek: for they shall inherit the earth" is a well-known quotation. How does it apply to "Mushrooms"? **[Apply]**

Mushrooms ◆ 509

☑ **Check Your Comprehension**

1. They are growing out of the ground.
2. They heave the needles in the loam aside, widen the crannies, and shoulder their way through holes. In other words, they do whatever they have to do to get ahead.
3. No one notices the mushrooms because they are quiet, discreet, voiceless, bland-mannered, and meek.

◆ **Critical Thinking**

1. Their purpose is to grow and multiply without being noticed or stopped.
2. They ask only for water and "crumbs of shadow."
3. Their meekness, combined with quiet determination and the ability to multiply, will enable them to "inherit the earth."
4. The mushrooms are humble and underprivileged; yet, despite being voiceless and meek, they quietly multiply and take their place in the world.

One-Minute Insight

In "Southern Mansion," Arna Bontemps tells of the ghosts of a pre-Civil War plantation house, describing how the tinkling of slaves' chains mixes with music coming from the owner's house. The spirit of the days of slavery, the poet seems to say, still haunts us.

◆ Reading Strategy

❶ Make Inferences What image do you have of the people walking in the shade and standing on the steps? *Despite being ghosts, they give off a sense of leisure and privilege. They walk in the shade rather than in the hot sun. They stand on marble steps.*

◆ Literary Focus

❷ Tone Why does the poet mention the bondmen in the second stanza instead of at the beginning? How does this arrangement affect the tone of the poem? *The poet contrasts the hard life of the African American slaves with the leisurely life of the owners. This contrast makes us feel the cruelty more strongly.*

◆ Reading Strategy

❸ Make Inferences Why does the poet use the sound image "an iron clank"? *The clank refers to the sound of a chain. It could also refer to a gate shutting, enclosing the enslaved people.*

◆ Critical Thinking

❹ Connect The first and last lines of the poem are the same sentence. How is the last line different from the first? *In the first line, the reader assumes the "still as death" image is there because of the ghosts. In the last line, the same image could apply to slavery.*

▶ Critical Viewing ◀

❺ Deduce *Students may say that the mansion appears to be inhabited, because the grounds are beautifully kept and the exterior is well-maintained.*

Southern Mansion

Arna Bontemps

| Poplars[1] are standing there still as death
| And ghosts of dead men
❶ | Meet their ladies walking
| Two by two beneath the shade
5 | And standing on the marble steps.

| There is a sound of music echoing
| Through the open door
❷ | And in the field there is
| Another sound tinkling in the cotton:
10 | Chains of bondmen[2] dragging on the ground.

❸ | The years go back with an iron clank,
| A hand is on the gate,
| A dry leaf trembles on the wall.
| Ghosts are walking.
15 | They have broken roses down
❹ | And poplars stand there still as death.

---

1. **Poplars** (päp′ lərz) *n.*: Trees of the willow family, with soft wood and flowers.
2. **bondmen** (bänd′ mən) *n.*: Slaves.

510 ◆ *Extraordinary Occurrences*

▲ **Critical Viewing** Does this southern mansion appear to be deserted or inhabited? How can you tell? [Deduce] **❺**

 Speaking and Listening Mini-Lesson

Monologue

This mini-lesson supports the Speaking and Listening activity in the Idea Bank on p. 513.

Introduce Let students know that a monologue is a talk by a single speaker, who acknowledges the audience or pretends to be talking to himself or herself. In this activity the speaker may be sharing his or her thoughts about the mansion.

Develop Encourage students to begin their monologues by freewriting to develop and discover their ideas. As they write, ask them to consider these questions:

• What does the mansion represent to you?
• How does what happened in the past affect the present?
• How can you communicate the time frame?

Apply Have pairs of students practice before performing their monologues for the whole class.

Assess Evaluate students on ideas expressed, delivery, use of vocal effects, and gestures and movements. Have students in the audience use the Peer Assessment: Dramatic Performance form, p. 116, in **Alternative Assessment.**

THE BAT

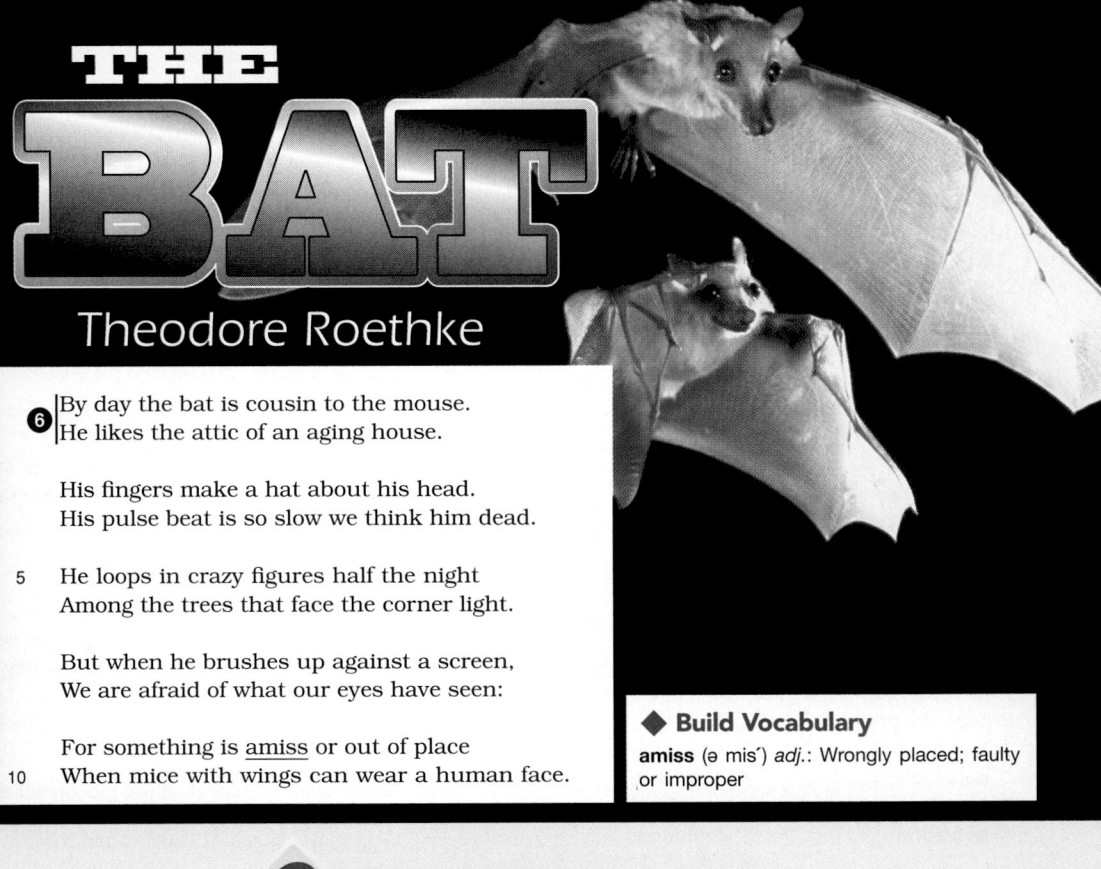

Theodore Roethke

6 By day the bat is cousin to the mouse.
He likes the attic of an aging house.

His fingers make a hat about his head.
His pulse beat is so slow we think him dead.

5   He loops in crazy figures half the night
Among the trees that face the corner light.

But when he brushes up against a screen,
We are afraid of what our eyes have seen:

For something is <u>amiss</u> or out of place
10 When mice with wings can wear a human face.

◆ Build Vocabulary

amiss (ə mis´) *adj.*: Wrongly placed; faulty or improper

Develop Understanding

One-Minute Insight "The Bat" contrasts the bat by day with its behavior at night, explaining why humans find these mammals scary.

◆ Reading Strategy

6 Make Inferences How is the bat like a mouse? *Students may say that the bat not only looks a little like a mouse, but it is a mammal, as is a mouse.*

Looking at Literature Videodisc/Videotape

To provide background information and motivate students to read "The Bat," play Chapter 5 of the videodisc. This chapter presents facts and clears up myths about this mammal. Discuss how bats help humans.

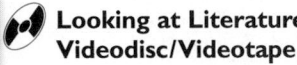

Chapter 5

Guide for Responding

◆ LITERATURE AND YOUR LIFE

Reader's Response With which poet would you rather have a conversation? Why?

Thematic Focus What is strange and extraordinary about the scene Arna Bontemps describes in "Southern Mansion"?

☑ Check Your Comprehension

1. In "Southern Mansion," who are the people mentioned in the poem?
2. What two sounds are mentioned in "Southern Mansion"?
3. In "The Bat," Roethke compares the bat to two other creatures. Name them.

◆ Critical Thinking

INTERPRET
1. What is the effect of the repetition of line 1 at the end of "Southern Mansion"? **[Interpret]**
2. What do the "roses" in the last stanza of "Southern Mansion" represent? **[Interpret]**
3. Compare the daytime and nighttime activities of the bat in "The Bat." **[Compare and Contrast]**
4. What details in line 10 make the picture that Roethke paints so strange? **[Interpret]**

COMPARE LITERARY WORKS
5. In these poems, living things that are normally not threatening to humans are presented in a frightening way. Identify the language each poet uses to accomplish this effect. **[Connect]**

Southern Mansion/The Bat ◆ 511

Beyond the Selection

FURTHER READING
Other Works by the Authors
The Island, Gary Paulsen
The Monument, Gary Paulsen
The Voyage of the Frog, Gary Paulsen
The Old South, Arna Bontemps
Ariel, Sylvia Plath (poems)
I Am! Says the Lamb, Theodore Roethke (nonsense poems)

INTERNET
We suggest the following sites on the Internet (all Web sites are subject to change).
   For Gary Paulsen:
http://www.bdd.com/bin/forums/garypaulsen
   For Sylvia Plath:
http://www.kirjasto.sci.fi/splath.htm
   For Arna Bontemps:
http://falcon.jmu.edu/~ramseyil/bontemps.htm
   For Theodore Roethke:
http://www.thebrothers.com/eraaz/roethke1.html

Reinforce and Extend

Answers
◆ LITERATURE AND YOUR LIFE

Reader's Response Responses and opinions should be supported.

Thematic Focus The scene is strange because it contains ghosts that reveal a historical era.

☑ Check Your Comprehension

1. They are the owners of the plantation and the enslaved workers.
2. The sounds are the music and the chains of the enslaved people.
3. He compares the bat to mice and humans.

◆ Critical Thinking

1. The repetition emphasizes the idea of death.
2. The roses may represent new life in the South, which is threatened by ghosts of the past.
3. In the day the bat has a slow pulse and hangs in an attic. At night it flies in crazy loops outside.
4. A mouse with wings and a human face is a strange image.
5. Bontemps describes the poplars as "still as death." Roethke makes bats resemble humans—which may mean we resemble bats.

511

Answers

◆ Reading Strategy

1. He is resourceful and prepared.
2. The mushrooms do not need much to survive.
3. The speaker is nostalgic about the old South but understands that slavery was a terrible injustice.

◆ Build Vocabulary

1. aboard — on board
2. afire — on fire
3. aside — to one side
4. ashore — on shore

Spelling Strategy

1. acquisition   4. aquamarine
2. acquainted   5. acquit
3. aquarium   6. aqualung

Using the Word Bank

1. amiss   3. acquire
2. discreetly   4. diffused

◆ Literary Focus

1. The tone is serious, because the author takes the subject of dog-sledding and being in nature seriously. However, it is also slightly humorous, because the author is amused—in hindsight—at his fear.
2. In the first three stanzas the tone is playful, as if describing a cute animal. In the final two stanzas, the tone changes to threatening, as the poet describes the bat as something "amiss."

◆ Build Grammar Skills

Practice

1. a cold-glowing green light with yellow edges
2. a death song
3. Nudgers and shovers
4. a crumbling ruin
5. a noise undetectable by humans

Writing Application

Check that students have used appositive phrases to explain or identify a noun or pronoun.

Writer's Solution

For additional instruction and practice, use the practice page on Appositives in Phrases, p. 48, in the *Writer's Solution Grammar Practice Book*.

Guide for Responding (continued)

◆ Reading Strategy

MAKE INFERENCES

When you **make inferences,** you look beyond what the words state to what they imply.

1. Paulsen says that he "replaced the bulb and tried a new battery" when his headlamp blew out. What can you infer about him from this action?
2. What can you infer from these lines from "Mushrooms": "We / Diet on water, / On crumbs of shadow"?
3. In "Southern Mansion," what inference can you make about the speaker's attitude toward slavery in the South?

◆ Build Vocabulary

USING THE PREFIX *a-*

The prefix *a-,* as in *amiss,* means "on" or "in." On your paper, complete these word equations that include the prefix *a-*. Then, define each word.

1. a- + board = ____?____   3. a- + side = ____?____
   definition: ____?____   definition: ____?____
2. a- + fire = ____?____   4. a- + shore = ____?____
   definition: ____?____   definition: ____?____

SPELLING STRATEGY

The sound *ak* can be spelled *acq,* as in *acquire,* or *aq,* as in *aqua.* Words having to do with water are usually spelled with *aq.*

On your paper, complete the following words by adding *acq* or *aq* in the blank.

1. ___?___uisition   4. ___?___uamarine
2. ___?___uainted   5. ___?___uit
3. ___?___uarium   6. ___?___ualung

USING THE WORD BANK

On your paper, complete each sentence with a word from the Word Bank.

1. We knew something was ____?____ when the cat raced across the room.
2. We disposed of the broken lamp ____?____ to avoid upsetting Mom.
3. We must ____?____ a new lamp immediately.
4. The filter ____?____ the ray of light, scattering it around the room.

◆ Literary Focus

TONE

The **tone** of a literary work is the attitude the writer has toward the subject and toward the audience. For example, when Arna Bontemps uses the phrase "still as death," you know the tone of "Southern Mansion" is serious.

1. How would you describe the tone of "A Glow in the Dark"? Explain.
2. The tone in "The Bat" seems to change. Explain the difference in tone between the first three stanzas and the last two stanzas.

◆ Build Grammar Skills

APPOSITIVE PHRASES

An appositive is a noun or pronoun placed near another noun or pronoun to explain or identify it. An **appositive phrase** includes the appositive and its modifiers and complements. Appositive phrases are often set off by commas or dashes.

> I could see them quite well in the glow from the light—*the soft glow, the green glow, the ghost glow.* (The italicized words all further identify the first noun *glow.*)

Practice On your paper, write the appositive phrases in each of the following.

1. The light came from within it, a cold-glowing green light with yellow edges. . . .
2. The dogs' song—a death song—echoed eerily.
3. We are edible, / Nudgers and shovers / In spite of ourselves.
4. The mansion, a crumbling ruin, was outside Savannah.
5. A bat's screech, a noise undetectable by humans, helps it navigate in darkness.

Writing Application Write sentences, using appositive phrases to further describe each noun below:

1. sled dogs   4. mansion
2. tree trunk   5. bat
3. mushrooms   6. mice

Build Your Portfolio

Idea Bank

Writing

1. **List** Make a list of supplies that would be necessary to have with you while dog-sledding in the wilderness.

2. **News Story** Imagine that the mushrooms described in "Mushrooms" have taken over a large area. Write the newspaper story that might cover that event. Include the five W's: *who, what, when, where,* and *why.* **[Media Link]**

3. **Essay** Choose one of the pieces in this group. Write an essay in which you explain how the tone of the work contributes to its meaning.

Speaking and Listening

4. **Monologue** Imagine that you are walking on the grounds described in "Southern Mansion." You can be in the present time, or you can be in the time when the mansion was new. What thoughts go through your head? Write, rehearse, and perform a monologue on this subject for the class. **[Social Studies Link]**

5. **Oral Presentation** Prepare a presentation on bats, giving information about their method of navigation, their habitats, and their diet. Present the information to your classmates. **[Science Link]**

Projects

6. **Science Article [Group Activity]** With a partner, prepare a science article about mushrooms. Include information about the different types of mushrooms, methods of growing and collecting them, how to distinguish edible mushrooms from poisonous ones, and recipes that use mushrooms. Add photos and art to your written text, and display your article in the classroom. **[Science Link]**

7. **Story Illustration** Create a series of drawings that brings to life Gary Paulsen's experience in "A Glow in the Dark." **[Art Link]**

Writing Mini-Lesson

I-Search Paper

The selections in this group cover a variety of topics—from dog-sledding and phosphorescent trees to bats and mushrooms. Choose a topic from these selections that interests you, and prepare an I-Search paper, a self-directed research project. Publish your findings in written form.

Writing Skills Focus:
State Your Main Points Clearly

Your writing will make more sense if you **state your main points clearly.**

Model

Vague: Bats have a special ability to navigate in darkness.

Clear: To navigate in darkness, bats use echolocation, which operates like sonar in a submarine.

Prewriting Decide on a topic for your I-Search, and gather information. Carefully note details as you find them. Also, jot down the source from which they came.

Drafting Begin your I-Search paper with an introduction, in which you reveal the subject you've researched. Develop your findings in the body of the paper, and summarize your findings in the conclusion. Be sure to state clearly the points you're making.

◆ **Grammar Application**

As you write, use appositive phrases to insert additional information about nouns or pronouns in your sentences.

Revising Rephrase unclear or vague passages to make them more clear. Add details where necessary, and delete details that are beside the point. Proofread carefully for errors in grammar, spelling, and punctuation.

A Glow in the Dark/Mushrooms/Southern Mansion/The Bat ◆ 513

Idea Bank

Following are suggestions for matching the Idea Bank topics with your students' performance levels and learning modalities:

Customize for *Performance Levels*
Less Advanced Students: 1, 7
Average Students: 2, 4, 5, 7
More Advanced Students: 3, 4, 5, 6

Customize for *Learning Modalities*
Verbal/Linguistic: 1, 2, 3, 4, 5, 6
Logical/Mathematical: 5, 6
Visual/Spatial: 6, 7
Interpersonal: 6
Intrapersonal: 4, 7

Writing Mini-Lesson

Refer students to the Writing Handbook at the back of the book for instruction on the writing process and for further information on writing reports.

Writers at Work Videodisc
Have students view the videodisc segment in which Virginia Hamilton explains why she sees writing a factual report as a creative process.

Play frames 14517 to 15675

Writing Lab CD-ROM
Have students complete the tutorial on Reports. Follow these steps:

1. Have students use the interactive examples of ways to narrow a topic.
2. Students can use annotated instruction on using library resources to learn how to research at the library and get tips for using various types of resources.
3. Have students draft on computer.
4. Have students use the audio-annotated student models to see revised drafts and hear why writers made revisions to an I-search report.

Writer's Solution Sourcebook
Have students use Chapter 7, "Reports," pp. 200–233, for additional support. The chapter includes in-depth instruction on I-Search Reports, p. 208.

✓ **ASSESSMENT OPTIONS**

Formal Assessment, Selection Test, pp. 146–148, and Assessment Resources Software. The selection test is designed so that it can easily be customized to the performance levels of your students.

Alternative Assessment, p. 36, includes options for less advanced students, more advanced students, verbal/linguistic learners, logical/mathematical learners, musical/rhythmic learners, and bodily/kinesthetic learners.

PORTFOLIO ASSESSMENT
Use the following rubrics in the **Alternative Assessment** booklet to assess student writing:
List: How-to/Process Explanation, p. 96
News Story: Description, p. 93
Essay: Literary Analysis/Interpretation, p. 108
Writing Mini-Lesson: Research Report/Paper, p. 102

OBJECTIVES

1. To read, comprehend, and interpret a story that has a social studies focus
2. To relate a story with a social studies focus to personal experience
3. To connect literature to social studies
4. To respond to Social Studies Guiding Questions
5. To respond to the story through writing, speaking and listening, and projects

SOCIAL STUDIES GUIDING QUESTIONS

Reading historical fiction about the Civil War will help students discover answers to these Social Studies Guiding Questions:

- How did the Civil War affect the culture and society of the United States?
- How did the Civil War affect individual families?

Interest Grabber

Ask students if they have ever disagreed with their parents or family members about a political or social issue. They may have discussed or argued over the issue. They may have agreed to disagree. Or their parents may have insisted on conformity. Now ask students to imagine that they disagree with family members on a life-and-death issue—a war between two parts of the United States. Encourage students to discuss what that experience might be like. Let them know that "A Horseman in the Sky" focuses on a family that split during the Civil War.

Map Study

Historical Maps The connection between history and geography is often a key to understanding why events happened. When the Civil War divided the United States, people in the states along the boundary between North and South faced an extraordinary hardship. Some families were divided in their loyalties. The fictional family in "A Horseman in the Sky" lives in Virginia, where many families were divided between supporters of the North and the South.

CONNECTING LITERATURE TO SOCIAL STUDIES
THE CIVIL WAR: FAMILIES TORN APART

A Horseman in the Sky *by Ambrose Bierce*

A SHADOW FALLS A family is eating a meal when suddenly a shadow falls across the table. The shadow divides the family in half, brother from brother and parent from child. This image doesn't come from a science-fiction story. It symbolizes what happened to real families during the Civil War—and to the fictional family in "A Horseman in the Sky."

A Divided Country A symbolic shadow fell across the U.S. map when war broke out between the northern and southern states in 1861. An issue dividing the industrialized North and the agricultural South was slavery. The South believed its economy depended on slaves, but many in the North opposed slavery. In some cases, this dispute between states divided families.

A War Between Brothers One of the shadowed and divided households was that of the Terrills of Virginia. When Virginia seceded from the Union, James Terrill joined the Confederate army. His brother William, a West Point officer, decided to fight for the Union. William's father angrily told him, "Your name shall be stricken from the family records."

"God Alone Knows" Both Terrills fought bravely, both were made generals, and both died in combat. In its grief, the Terrill family carved these words on the monument it created for the fallen brothers: "God Alone Knows Which Was Right." Like the Terrills, the Virginia family in this story by Ambrose Bierce is shadowed by division and death.

West Virginia separated from Virginia in 1861 and was admitted to the Union in 1863.

Choosing Sides in the Civil War

- Union states
- Confederate states
- Border states that stayed in the Union
- States that joined the Confederacy after April 1861

514 ◆ *Extraordinary Occurrences*

Prentice Hall Literature Program Resources

REINFORCE / RETEACH / EXTEND
Selection Support Pages
Build Vocabulary, p. 194
Connecting Literature to Social Studies, p. 194
Formal Assessment Selection Test, pp. 149–150
Readings From Social Studies
Writing and Language Transparencies
Sunburst Graphic Organizer, p. 97

Resource Pro CD-ROM
"A Horseman in the Sky"—includes all resource material and customizable lesson plan
Listening to Literature Audiocassettes
"A Horseman in the Sky"
Connection to Prentice Hall The American Nation *Independence Through 1914*—Chapter 15, "The Civil War," pp. 374–403

A Horseman in the Sky

Ambrose Bierce

One sunny afternoon in the autumn of the year 1861[1] a soldier lay in a clump of laurel by the side of a road in western Virginia. He lay at full length upon his stomach, his feet resting upon the toes, his head upon the left forearm. His extended right hand loosely grasped his rifle. But for the somewhat methodical disposition of his limbs and a slight rhythmic movement of the cartridge-box at the back of his belt he might have been thought to be dead. He was asleep at his post of duty. But if detected he would be dead shortly afterward, death being the just and legal penalty of his crime.

The clump of laurel in which the criminal lay was in the angle of a road which after ascending southward a steep acclivity[2] to that point turned sharply to the west, running along the summit for perhaps one hundred yards. There it turned southward again and went zigzagging downward through the forest. At the salient of that second angle[3] was a large flat rock, jutting out northward, overlooking the deep valley from which the road ascended. The rock capped a high cliff; a stone dropped from its outer edge would have fallen sheer downward one thousand feet to the tops of the pines. The angle where the soldier lay was on another spur of the same cliff. Had he been awake he would have commanded a view, not only of the short arm of the road and the jutting rock, but of the entire profile of the cliff below it. It might well have made him giddy to look.

The country was wooded everywhere except at the bottom of the valley to the northward, where there was a small natural meadow, through which flowed a stream scarcely visible from the valley's rim. This open ground looked hardly larger than an ordinary door-yard, but was really several acres in extent. Its green was more vivid than that of the inclosing forest. Away beyond it rose a line of giant cliffs similar to those upon which we are supposed to stand in our survey of the savage scene, and through which the road had somehow made its climb to the summit. The configuration of the valley, indeed, was such that from this point of observation it seemed entirely shut in, and one could but have wondered how the road which found a way out of it had found a way into it, and

---

1. **1861:** Marks the beginning of the American Civil War (1861–1865) between the North (the Union) and the South (the Confederacy).
2. **acclivity** (ə kliv´ ə tē) *n.*: Upward slope of the ground.
3. **salient** (sāl´ lē ənt) **of that second angle:** Referring to the point where the summit projects or points outward.

◆ **Build Vocabulary**

configuration (kən fig´ yoo rā´ shən) *n.*: Structure; arrangement

A Horseman in the Sky ◆ 515

---

❶ Infer *The infantry could march unseen since the countryside is full of hills or mountains and valleys.*

Clarification

❷ Be sure students understand that the Northern army is referred to as the Union or Federal army. The Southern army can be called the Confederate army.

Links Across Time

❸ Carter Druse was not unusual. In western Virginia many people supported the Union. When Virginia seceded, or left the Union, the residents in the western part of the state formed their own government. West Virginia became a state in the Union in 1863.

CONNECTING LITERATURE TO SOCIAL STUDIES

❹ *The bitterness of this family division is revealed in the word "traitor."*

Customize for
English Language Learners

Students may have difficulty following the description of the landscape. First, have them look at the picture on this page to get an idea of the countryside. Then have them check the meanings of geographical words, such as *summit, cliff,* and *ridge.* Have students read with a partner and paraphrase the descriptive passages.

Album of Virginia "Rockfish Gap and Mountain House," Edward Beyer, The Library of Virginia

CONNECTING LITERATURE TO SOCIAL STUDIES

▲ **Critical Viewing** Why would countryside like this be ideal for advancing troops in secret? [Infer] **❶**

whence came and whither went the waters of the stream that parted the meadow more than a thousand feet below.

No country is so wild and difficult but men will make it a theater of war; concealed in the forest at the bottom of that military rat-trap, in which half a hundred men in possession of the exits might have starved an army to submission, lay five regiments of Federal **❷** infantry.[4] They had marched all the previous day and night and were resting. At nightfall they would take to the road again, climb to the place where their unfaithful <u>sentinel</u> now slept, and descending the other slope of the ridge fall upon a camp of the enemy at about midnight. Their hope was to surprise it, for the road led to the rear of it. In case of failure, their position would be perilous in the extreme; and fail they surely would should accident or vigilance apprise the enemy of the movement.

4. **Federal infantry:** Foot-soldiers of the Federal Union, or the North.

The sleeping sentinel in the clump of laurel was a young Virginian named Carter Druse. He was the son of wealthy parents, an only child, and had known such ease and cultivation and high living as wealth and taste were able to command in the mountain country of western Virginia. His home was but a few miles from where he now lay. One morning he had risen from the breakfast-table and said, quietly but gravely: "Father, a Union regiment has arrived at Grafton. I am going to join it." **❸**

The father lifted his leonine[5] head, looked at the son a moment in silence, and replied: "Well, go, sir, and whatever may occur do what you conceive to be your duty. Virginia, to which you are a traitor, must get on without you. Should we both live to the end of the war, we will speak further of the matter. Your mother, as the physician has informed you, is in a most

> **Connecting Literature to Social Studies** **❹**
> What word in the father's speech suggests the bitterness of this family division?

❺

5. **leonine** (lē´ ə nin´) *adj.*: Characteristic of, or like a lion.

 Block Scheduling Strategies

Consider these suggestions to take advantage of extended class time:

• Have students read independently, then meet in groups to discuss the story. Use the annotations in the Teacher Edition to help students connect literature to social studies: Make sure they understand the importance of the landscape to the plot, and challenge them to explain the sight of the horseman in the sky. Conclude by having them answer the Guide for Responding questions on p. 520, and discussing Connecting Literature to Social Studies on p. 521.

• Have students build their portfolios by working in pairs either on the Speaking and Listening Retelling activity or on writing the Prequel activity in the Idea Bank on p. 521.

• Partners can work together to make the Multimedia Presentation in the Idea Bank on p. 521. You may want to arrange a trip to the library during an extended class period.

• Use *The American Nation: Independence Through 1914*—Chapter 15, "The Civil War," pp. 374–403— to team teach or to further connect literature to social studies.

critical condition; at the best she cannot be with us longer than a few weeks, but that time is precious. It would be better not to disturb her."

So Carter Druse, bowing reverently to his father, who returned the salute with a stately courtesy that masked a breaking heart, left the home of his childhood to go soldiering. By conscience and courage, by deeds of devotion and daring, he soon commended himself to his fellows and his officers; and it was to these qualities and to some knowledge of the country that he owed his selection for his present perilous duty at the extreme outpost. Nevertheless, fatigue had been stronger than resolution and he had fallen asleep. What good or bad angel came in a dream to rouse him from his state of crime, who shall say? Without a movement, without a sound, in the profound silence and the <u>languor</u> of the late afternoon, some invisible messenger of fate touched with unsealing finger the eyes of his consciousness—whispered into the ear of his spirit the mysterious awakening word which no human lips ever have spoken, no human memory ever has recalled. He quietly raised his forehead from his arm and looked between the masking stems of the laurels, instinctively closing his right hand about the stock of his rifle.

His first feeling was a keen artistic delight. On a colossal pedestal, the cliff,—motionless at the extreme edge of the capping rock and sharply outlined against the sky,—was an <u>equestrian</u> statue of impressive dignity. The figure of the man sat the figure of the horse, straight and soldierly, but with the repose of a Grecian god carved in the marble which limits the suggestion of activity. The gray costume harmonized with its aerial background; the metal of accoutrement and caparison[6] was softened and subdued by the shadow; the animal's skin had no points of high light.

---

6. **accoutrement** (ə kōō′ trə mənt) **and caparison** (kə par′ i sən): The clothing or dress of the man and the ornamented covering of the horse.

A carbine[7] strikingly foreshortened lay across the pommel of the saddle, kept in place by the right hand grasping it at the "grip"; the left hand, holding the bridle rein, was invisible. In silhouette against the sky the profile of the horse was cut with the sharpness of a cameo; it looked across the heights of air to the confronting cliffs beyond. The face of the rider, turned slightly away, showed only an outline of temple and beard; he was looking downward to the bottom of the valley. Magnified by its lift against the sky and by the soldier's testifying sense of the formidableness of a near enemy the group appeared of heroic, almost colossal, size.

For an instant Druse had a strange, half-defined feeling that he had slept to the end of the war and was looking upon a noble work of art reared upon that <u>eminence</u> to commemorate the deeds of an heroic past of which he had been an inglorious part. The feeling was dispelled by a slight movement of the group: the horse, without moving its feet, had drawn its body slightly backward from the verge; the man remained immobile as before. Broad awake and keenly alive to the significance of the situation, Druse now brought the butt of his rifle against his cheek by cautiously pushing the barrel forward through the bushes, cocked the piece, and glancing through the sights covered a vital spot of the horseman's breast. A touch upon the trigger and all would have been well with Carter Druse. At that instant the horseman turned his head and looked in the direction of his concealed foeman—seemed to look into his

---

7. **carbine** (cär′ bïn′) *n*.: Rifle with a short barrel.

◆ **Build Vocabulary**

sentinel (sen′ ti nəl) *n*.: Guard

languor (laŋ′ gər) *n*.: Listlessness; indifference

equestrian (ē kwes′ trē ən) *adj*.: On horseback, or so represented

eminence (em′ i nəns) *n*.: High or lofty place

A Horseman in the Sky ◆ 517

CONNECTING LITERATURE TO SOCIAL STUDIES

❺ How do father and son show respect for each other despite being on opposing sides in the war? *The son bows "reverently" to his father, who is courteous to his son as he says goodbye.*

◆ **Critical Thinking**

❻ **Infer** What do you learn about the horseman from this passage? *He is dignified, sits up straight on the horse, and has a bearing like a statue of a Greek god. He is also a Confederate soldier, as the reader can tell from the gray uniform.*

CONNECTING LITERATURE TO SOCIAL STUDIES

❼ How does the setting of the Civil War affect Carter's perception of the man on horseback? *The soldier reminds Carter that the enemy is very near. Since the man and horse are standing high on a cliff with only the sky behind them, they look heroic and huge, making the idea of the enemy more frightening.*

Comprehension Check ☑

❽ What is the significance of the situation? What is Carter preparing to do? *The significance is that the Confederate soldier may see the Union army and ruin the surprise attack. Carter is getting ready to shoot the horseman.*

◆ **LITERATURE AND YOUR LIFE**

❾ Ask students to discuss how they would feel if they had to shoot someone at such close range, especially someone whose sight had impressed them. Encourage them to try to think of alternatives to killing the soldier.

Cross-Curricular Connection: History

Strategies of the North and the South
When the Civil War began in the summer of 1861, each side believed in its own quick and easy victory. By the time of this story, the autumn of 1861, it was clear that a long, bitter struggle lay ahead.

The Union's strategy was twofold. It planned to use its navy to blockade Southern ports. This would cripple the Confederate economy since Southerners would be unable to trade with other countries. At the same time, the Union

intended to invade Southern territory. In "A Horseman in the Sky," the Union army is in the process of invading Virginia, a Southern state.

The South's strategy at the beginning of the war was simpler. The Confederate army would fight a defensive war until the Northerners got tired of fighting. The Southerners also expected to receive money and supplies from Europeans with whom they traded. The textile industry in England and other countries depended on the cotton grown in the South.

CONNECTING LITERATURE TO SOCIAL STUDIES

❶ Why is the horseman more dangerous for what he knows than the Southern army is for its size? *If the horseman reports to his camp with the news of the Union army near-by, the Union army not only cannot make a surprise attack, but it may be trapped in the valley and destroyed.*

◆ Critical Thinking

❷ Deduce Why is Carter Druse, usually known for his courage, so upset at the thought of killing the horseman? *Students should give reasons for their responses.*

▶ Critical Viewing ◀

❸ Deduce *Students may say warfare was still mostly a man-to-man struggle. This cavalry soldier has the advantage of speed over an infantry soldier, but he and his horse are unprotected from enemy gunfire. Also, his only offensive weapon shown is his rifle. (His sword would have been on the other side, if he wore one.) The huge number of casualties in the war was caused by improvements in weaponry with no changes in tactics or new means of self-protection.*

Links Across Time

❹ When the Union commander allows his soldiers to water the horses within sight of surrounding summits, he is endangering the whole army. The Confederate horseman may see them and carry the news back to his camp. Encourage students to discuss how this particular landscape may have affected events of the war. Include in the discussion how the fact that the armies were dependent on horses for transporting goods and equipment may have shaped the nature of the warfare.

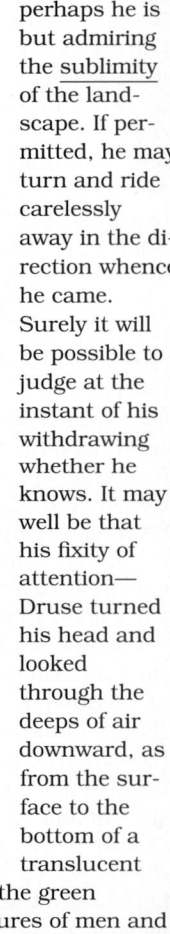

very face, into his eyes, into his brave, compassionate heart.

Is it then so terrible to kill an enemy in war—an enemy who has surprised a secret vital to the safety of one's self and comrades—an enemy more formidable for his knowledge than all his army for its numbers? Carter Druse grew pale; he shook in every limb, turned faint, and saw the statuesque group before him as black figures, rising, falling, moving unsteadily in arcs of circles in a fiery sky. His hand fell away from his weapon, his head slowly dropped until his face rested on the leaves in which he lay. This courageous gentleman and hardy soldier was near swooning from intensity of emotion.

It was not for long; in another moment his face was raised from earth, his hands resumed their places on the rifle, his forefinger sought the trigger; mind, heart, and eyes were clear, conscience and reason sound. He could not hope to capture that enemy; to alarm him would but send him dashing to his camp with his fatal news. The duty of the soldier was plain: the man

 ▲ **Critical Viewing** What does this illustration reveal about warfare during the Civil War? **[Deduce]**

must be shot dead from ambush—without warning, without a moment's spiritual preparation, with never so much as an unspoken prayer, he must be sent to his account. But no—there is a hope; he may have discovered nothing—perhaps he is but admiring the sublimity of the landscape. If permitted, he may turn and ride carelessly away in the direction whence he came. Surely it will be possible to judge at the instant of his withdrawing whether he knows. It may well be that his fixity of attention—Druse turned his head and looked through the deeps of air downward, as from the surface to the bottom of a translucent sea. He saw creeping across the green meadow a sinuous line of figures of men and horses—some foolish commander was permitting the soldiers of his escort to water their beasts in the open, in plain view from a dozen summits!

Druse withdrew his eyes from the valley

518 ◆ *Extraordinary Occurrences*

🎓 Viewing and Representing Mini-Lesson

Multimedia Presentation

This mini-lesson supports the Project in the Idea Bank on p. 521.

Introduce Explain to students that they will be creating a presentation of families who were divided by the Civil War.

Develop Have students choose partners to work with. They will need to do research to locate materials for their presentation. To find letters, diaries, and photographs, students might search on the Internet, look for library books,

and locate articles in magazines and journals. To find film clips and recordings of songs, students should begin at the library.

Apply Students should collect their materials and decide how to present them. Since it is a multimedia presentation, they will need to combine explanatory writing with the other materials.

Assess Evaluate students on their partner work, research, and presentation. You may also use Scoring Rubric: Multimedia Report, p. 103 in **Alternative Assessment**.

and fixed them again upon the group of man and horse in the sky, and again it was through the sights of his rifle. But this time his aim **⑤** was at the horse. In his memory, as if they were a divine <u>mandate</u>, rang the words of his father at their parting: "Whatever may occur, do what you conceive to be your duty." He was calm now. His teeth were firmly but not rigidly closed; his nerves were as tranquil as a sleeping babe's—not a tremor affected any muscle of his body; his breathing, until suspended in the act of taking aim, was regular and slow. Duty had conquered; the spirit had said to the body: "Peace, be still." He fired.

An officer of the Federal force, who in a spirit of adventure or in quest of knowledge had left the hidden *bivouac*[8] in the valley, and with aimless feet, had made his way to the lower edge of a small open space near the foot of the cliff, was considering what he had to gain by pushing his exploration further. At a distance of a quarter-mile before him, but **⑥** apparently at a stone's throw, rose from its fringe of pines the gigantic face of rock, towering to so great a height above him that it made him giddy to look up to where its edge cut a sharp, rugged line against the sky. At some distance to his right it presented a clean, vertical profile against a background of blue sky to a point half the way down, and of distant hills, hardly less blue, thence to the tops of the trees at its base. Lifting his eyes to the dizzy altitude of its summit the officer saw an astonishing sight—a man on horseback riding down into the valley through the air!

Straight upright sat the rider, in military fashion, with a firm seat in the saddle, a strong clutch upon the rein to hold his charger from too <u>impetuous</u> a plunge. From his bare head his long hair streamed upward, waving like a plume. His hands were concealed in the cloud of the horse's lifted mane. The animal's body was as level as if every

---

8. **bivouac** (biv´ wak´) *n.*: Temporary encampment.

hoof-stroke encountered the resistant earth. Its motions were those of a wild gallop, but even as the officer looked they ceased, with all the legs thrown sharply forward as in the act of alighting from a leap. But this was a flight!

Filled with amazement and terror by this apparition of a horseman in the sky—half believing himself the chosen scribe of some new Apocalypse,[9] the officer was overcome by the intensity of his emotions; his legs failed him and he fell. Almost at the same instant he heard a crashing sound in the trees—a sound that died without an echo—and all was still.

The officer rose to his feet, trembling. The familiar sensation of an abraded shin recalled his dazed faculties. Pulling himself together he ran rapidly obliquely away from the cliff to a point distant from its foot; thereabout he expected to find his man; and thereabout he naturally failed. In the fleeting instant of his vision his imagination had been so wrought upon by the apparent grace and ease and intention of the marvelous performance that it did not occur to him that the line of march of aerial cavalry is directly downward, and that he could find the objects of his search at the very foot of the cliff. A half-hour later he returned to camp. **⑦**

This officer was a wise man; he knew better than to tell an incredible truth. He said nothing of what he had seen. But when the commander asked him if in his scout he had learned anything of advantage to the expedition he answered:

---

9. **Apocalypse** (ə päk´ ə lips´): A disclosure regarded as prophetic; revelation.

◆ **Build Vocabulary**

sublimity (sə blim´ ə tē) *n.*: The state or quality of being majestic; noble

mandate (man´ dāt´) *n.*: Order or command

impetuous (im pech´ oo əs) *adj.*: Moving with great force or violence

A Horseman in the Sky ◆ 519

◆ **Critical Thinking**

⑤ Infer How does remembering his father's words help Carter make his decision to shoot the soldier? How is this ironic? *His father advised him to do whatever he conceived of as his duty; killing the soldier is a necessary act to save the Union army. This is ironic because Carter is using the advice to help his own side against his father's side.*

◆ **Critical Thinking**

⑥ Analyze Why does the Federal officer see the horseman falling through the sky like this? *The horse and rider fall this way because Carter shot the horse instead of the man.*

Comprehension Check ☑

⑦ What mistake did the Federal officer make when he looked for the horse and rider? *He was so upset by the sight that he failed to realize that the fall would leave the horse and soldier directly below, at the bottom of the cliff.*

Customize for
Visual/Spatial Learners
Some students may have trouble following the description of the horseman's fall. Invite students to explain the event as they visualize it. Let the class discuss this, as it may be easily interpreted in different ways.

Customize for
Logical/Mathematical Learners
Have students use the Sunburst graphic organizer, p. 85 in **Writing and Language Transparencies,** to identify the various people connected to Carter Druse. At this point in the story, students may fill in the father, the horseman, the commander who let the soldiers water the horses, and the officer. They may find further characters to include by the end of the story.

Speaking and Listening Mini-Lesson

Retelling
This mini-lesson supports the Speaking and Listening activity in the Idea Bank on p. 521.

Introduce Explain to students that they will take on the role of the officer who saw the horseman fall and describe the sight.

Develop First have students reread the passage to make sure they understand what the officer saw. Students might sketch the scene or draw a diagram; others may be more comfortable tracing the action with words. Then have students work individually to decide how to describe the sight.

Encourage them to expand on the possible audience. Perhaps the officer tells this story to his grandchildren years later.

Apply Each student can practice retelling his or her own version of the story with a partner. Have students perform for the class, clarifying who their audience is.

Assess Evaluate students on their attention to detail, quality of speaking, and audience connection. Or, use the Peer Assessment form: Oral Interpretation form, p. 119, in **Alternative Assessment**.

❶ *Students may say that family members fighting against one another symbolizes citizens of the same country fighting against one another.*

Reinforce and Extend

Answers

◆ LITERATURE AND YOUR LIFE

Reader's Response Students may exhibit either sympathy or disgust at what Druse did.

Thematic Focus Druse did an ordinary act for a sentinel in time of war; that he was forced to kill his father is extraordinary.

☑ Check Your Comprehension

1. It is set in western Virginia in 1861, during the Civil War.
2. Carter tells his father he is joining the union army. His father tells him he is a traitor to Virginia.
3. Since he shoots the horse, he causes the animal to fall off the cliff, carrying the soldier as if he were riding the horse through the air.
4. The surprise is that the horseman Druse kills is his own father.

More About the Author

Ambrose Bierce was most famous in his lifetime as a witty newspaper columnist, but his considerable literary talents were recognized by such writers as Mark Twain and Bret Harte. He had a particular talent for creating an atmosphere of horror through a combination of realistic and suggestive detail. One of his most famous stories is "An Occurrence at Owl Creek Bridge," which describes the last-minute visions of escape by a man who is condemned to be hanged as a spy by Union soldiers.

520

"Yes, sir; there is no road leading down into this valley from the southward."

The commander, knowing better, smiled.

After firing his shot, Private Carter Druse reloaded his rifle and resumed his watch. Ten minutes had hardly passed when a Federal sergeant crept cautiously to him on his hands and knees. Druse neither turned his head nor looked at him, but lay without motion or sign of recognition.

"Did you fire?" the sergeant whispered.

"Yes."

"At what?"

"A horse. It was standing on yonder rock—pretty far out. You see it is no longer there. It went over the cliff."

The man's face was white, but he showed no other sign of emotion. Having answered, he turned away his eyes and said no more. The sergeant did not understand.

"See here, Druse," he said, after a moment's silence, "it's no use making a mystery. I order you to report. Was there anybody on the horse?"

> **❶ Connecting Literature to Social Studies**
> How does the tragedy of the Druse family dramatize the nation's experience in the Civil War?

"Yes."

"Well?"

"My father."

The sergeant rose to his feet and walked away. "Good God!" he said.

Meet the Author

Ambrose Bierce (1842–1914?) served as a Union officer in the Civil War. This experience helped determine the bleak view of the world he expressed in his writing.

After the Civil War, Bierce settled in San Francisco as a journalist. His bitter but lively writing, together with his personal charm, won him great popularity. In 1891, he published *Tales of Soldiers and Civilians,* from which this story comes.

Despite his literary success, Bierce's life was tragic. His marriage ended in divorce, and his two sons died at an early age. In 1913, he traveled to Mexico and never returned. The circumstances of his death are still a mystery.

Guide for Responding

◆ LITERATURE AND YOUR LIFE

Reader's Response What would you have said to Druse if he had told you what he had done?

Thematic Focus In what way is this story ordinary and extraordinary?

Role Play With a classmate, reenact the scene between Carter and his father at the breakfast table.

☑ Check Your Comprehension

1. Briefly describe the time and place in which the story is set.
2. What disagreement did Druse and his father have at the breakfast table?
3. How does Druse's decision produce a remarkable sight?
4. What is the surprise at the end of the story?

◆ Critical Thinking

INTERPRET

1. Why is the description of the landscape so important to understanding Druse's decision about whether to shoot? **[Connect]**
2. What is strange or unexpected about the fact that Druse is a "criminal" for sleeping but a good soldier for killing his father? **[Analyze]**
3. How do the title of the story and the image it describes suggest a total devotion to duty? **[Draw Conclusions]**

APPLY

4. E. M. Forster wrote that he'd rather betray his country than his friend. What do you think Forster would have said about Carter Druse? Explain. **[Apply]**

Beyond the Selection

FURTHER READING

Other Works by Ambrose Bierce
The Civil War Stories of Ambrose Bierce, compiled by Ernest Jerome Hopkins
In the Midst of Life
Can Such Things Be?
The Moonlit Road and Other Ghost and Horror Stories

Other Works About the Civil War
The Red Badge of Courage, Stephen Crane
Voices from the Civil War, Milton Meltzer
Shiloh, Shelby Foote

INTERNET

We suggest the following sites on the Internet (all Web sites are subject to change).

For more information on Ambrose Bierce:
http://idt.net/~damone/gbierce.html

For links to Civil War sites:
http://www.cwc.lsu.edu/civlink.htm

We *strongly recommend* that you preview these sites before you send students to them.

CONNECTING LITERATURE TO SOCIAL STUDIES

Abraham Lincoln said, "A house divided against itself cannot stand." He was referring to a divided country—part based on slavery and part free. Here's how the two sides looked in 1861:

Category	North	South
Railroad track	21,847 miles	8,947 miles
Factories	119,500	20,600
Population	22,340,000	9,103,000 (3,954,000 slaves)

Bierce puts a human face on these numbers. His story shows how the nation's divided house, and the war it led to, affects a single household.

Also, as the true story of the Terrills indicates, Bierce's fictional family is based on reality.

Besides focusing on a single household, Bierce zooms in on a moment of truth: A son who is a Union soldier must decide whether to kill his Confederate father in order to protect Union soldiers. The son's ordeal reflects the nation's.

1. What does the story suggest about the cost of duty and of victory in a civil war?
2. In what way does the sergeant's "Good God!" sum up the horror of Druse's choice and of the whole war?
3. Does the chart at left suggest which side might win the war? Explain.

 Idea Bank

Writing

1. **Diary Entry** As Carter Druse, write a diary entry for the day described in "A Horseman in the Sky."
2. **Prequel** Write an introductory episode to the story, explaining what led to the division in the Druse family. Be sure that the facts you make up are consistent with the ones in the story.
3. **Reflective Essay** Write an essay expressing your thoughts on the conflict that Carter Druse faces and the way in which he resolves it. Support your points with your own experience and insights from stories you've read or viewed.

Speaking and Listening

4. **Retelling** As the federal officer who saw the horseman fall, tell your best friend about this remarkable sight.
5. **Debate [Group Activity]** With several classmates, debate the pros and cons of this resolution: Druse was right to follow his military duty.

Project

6. **Multimedia Presentation [Group Activity]** With a partner, give a presentation on families divided by the Civil War. Weave together excerpts from letters and diaries, photographs, film clips, and recordings of Civil War songs.

Further Reading, Listening, and Viewing

- *War Between Brothers* (New York: Time-Life Books, 1996) is a fascinating illustrated account of the Civil War.
- *In the Midst of Life: Tales of Soldiers and Civilians* (New York: Boni, 1924) is the book by Ambrose Bierce that contains "A Horseman in the Sky" and other Civil War stories.
- *The Civil War* (1990), directed by Ken Burns, is an award-winning documentary about the American Civil War.
- Irene Hunt's *Across Five Aprils* is a young-adult novel about a divided family.

A Horseman in the Sky ◆ 521

 Idea Bank

Following are suggestions for matching the Idea Bank topics with your students' performance levels and learning modalities:

Customize for
Performance Levels
Less Advanced Students: 1, 5
Average Students: 2, 4, 5, 6
More Advanced Students: 3, 4, 5, 6

Customize for
Learning Modalities
Verbal/Linguistic: 1, 2, 3, 4
Visual/Spatial: 6
Interpersonal: 5, 6
Intrapersonal: 3

Answers (continued)
◆ **Critical Thinking**

1. The reader needs to understand that the Union army is camped in a location where all the men could be trapped if they were discovered. Also, the Union army plans a surprise attack on the Confederates camped nearby; if the Union soldiers are seen they cannot win the battle. Druse must shoot the horseman in order to protect his fellow soldiers from discovery.
2. The duties seem contrary to common sense, which may be symbolic of the author's view of war.
3. The father, who is devoted to duty and has instilled this value in his son, is seen as a heroic figure on horseback.
4. Students may say that Forster may have been more devoted to friends than to family members. He may have said that he found Carter Druse overly dutiful.

CONNECTING LITERATURE TO SOCIAL STUDIES

1. Soldiers who fought on opposite sides from family members probably had mixed feelings about their duty to their side as well as about victory, since either could harm their family members.
2. His reaction is suitable to the idea of a nation fighting against itself.
3. The North appears to have a stronger economy than the South, as well as a much larger population, which suggests the North might win.

521

Review the following key characteristics of a how-to essay:

- A how-to essay tells the reader how to do or make something.
- A how-to essay states main points clearly and in a logical order.

You may want to distribute the scoring rubric for How-to/Process Explanation, p. 96 in **Alternative Assessment,** to make students aware of the criteria on which they will be evaluated. See the suggestions on p. 524 for how you can customize the rubric to this workshop.

Refer students to the Writing Handbook in the back of the book for instruction on the writing process and further information on expository writing.

Writer's Solution

Writers at Work Videodisc

To introduce students to expository writing and to show how professional journalist Gary Matsumoto what expository writing is. Play the videodisc segment on Exposition: Giving Information (Ch. 4).

Play frames 33108 to 41558

Writing Lab CD-ROM

If your students have access to computers, have them work in the tutorial on Exposition: Giving Information to complete all or part of their how-to essays. Follow these steps:

1. Have students view the interactive model of a how-to composition.
2. Students can use the Chain of Events Activity to see if they need to further narrow their topics.
3. Allow students to draft on computer.
4. When revising, have students use the Self-Evaluation Checklist for explanation of procedures or instructions.

Writer's Solution Sourcebook

Students can find additional support, including in-depth instruction on building paragraphs, pp. 132–133, in Chapter 4, "Exposition: Giving Information," pp. 104–135.

Connect to Literature Unit 7, "Nonfiction," includes an example of a how-to essay: Virginia Shea's "How to Be Polite Online" from *Netiquette.*

Expository Writing
How-to Essay

Writing Process Workshop

Variation IV, Wassily Kandinsky, Russian Bauhaus Archive

If writer Gary Paulsen had a how-to guide for identifying the mysteries of nature, he may not have been so terrified by the mysterious green glow of the tree stump. How-to guides or essays provide instructions for accomplishing a specific task or meeting a goal, such as putting together a bicycle or identifying a natural event.

Write a how-to essay about a subject on which you are an expert. The following skills will help you.

Writing Skills Focus

▶ **State your main points clearly** so your readers know exactly what they must do to accomplish the task. (See p. 513.)

▶ **Elaborate** to provide necessary details and explanations for each step of instruction.

▶ **Use transitions** to show the relationships between ideas.

Read the following how-to guide on how to evaluate a work of abstract art:

WRITING MODEL

Evaluating Abstract Art

When evaluating abstract art, follow this formula: First, give it a gut reaction. ① Decide if you like it and why. ② Then, think it over. Look at the title and the work to try to determine the artist's purpose for creating the work. After you have appreciated the work personally and objectively, you can evaluate it. ③ Decide whether the artist accomplishes what you believe was his or her purpose. Also, ask yourself whether the work has long-standing appeal or is a work only "today's" audience would appreciate.

① The writer's first instruction is stated clearly.

② This detail elaborates by explaining a gut reaction.

③ The transitional word *after* lets you know when this step should be completed.

522 ◆ *Extraordinary Occurrences*

Beyond the Classroom

Career Connection

How-to Writer Many areas of life require instructions, as found in a computer manual, a cookbook that gives directions for preparing foods, and the introductory pages of a dictionary, describing how to use the book. Most public libraries contain a section of how-to guides.

Instructions must be prepared so that a user can understand and follow a process. How-to information may come in the form of a pamphlet, a book or part of a book, a computer "read me" file, and in any type of print, electronic, audio, or visual material. Writers who prepare how-to material may be called technical writers. They must understand the process themselves in order to write clear instructions for others to use. In the case of video or audio instructions, the writer prepares a script that explains the process.

Have students brainstorm for a list of how-to areas that might interest them—encourage them to consider the myriad of possibilities. Then have students investigate technical writing courses in your area and what is required to become a writer of the type of material that interests them.

Prewriting

Choose a Topic For your how-to essay, pick a subject about which you know a great deal. Here are more suggestions:

> ### Topic Ideas
> - Playing a sport or game
> - Taking care of a pet
> - Preparing food
> - Getting used to a new school

Develop Details by Anticipating Questions Jot down some questions that readers might ask, and gather information that will answer them. For example, if you are explaining how to play the guitar, provide answers to questions like these:
- ▶ What kind of guitar is best for a beginner?
- ▶ Do you need anything besides a guitar to start?
- ▶ Where do you get sheet music?

Create an Organizer Use a graphic organizer like the following to map out the steps of the procedure you are describing:

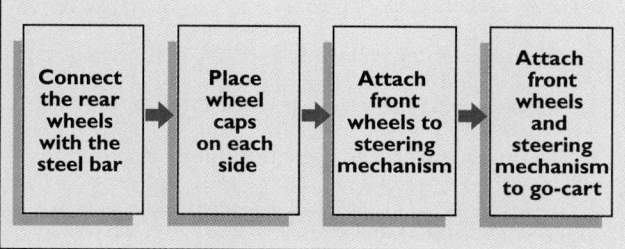

Drafting

State Your Main Points Clearly Too much descriptive detail can cause readers to miss the main point. Before adding details, clearly state instructions in order. Present the most important information first. Then, add any supporting information.

Use Transitions Use words that indicate cause-and-effect relationships—*since, therefore, as a result, because, for that reason, due to, consequently, so,* and *for.* As you draft your paper, use these words to show relationships among ideas, such as steps in programming a VCR or the importance of preheating the oven before starting a recipe.

DRAFTING/REVISING

APPLYING LANGUAGE SKILLS: Using Transitions to Indicate Time

Transitions help your reader connect ideas. Here are some transitions that indicate a time relationship:

> after, as soon as, at last, at the same time, before, during, earlier, eventually, finally, first, later, meanwhile, next, now, second, soon, then

Practice Copy each sentence below into your notebook. Then, fill in the blanks with an appropriate time transition.

1. Preheat the oven to 450°.
   _____?_____, grease and flour a 9" round pan.
2. _____?_____ mixing the ingredients, pour them into a dish.
3. One hour will pass _____?_____ the edges will turn brown.
4. _____?_____, let it cool.
5. _____?_____, enjoy the soufflé!

Writing Application As you write your essay, add transitions to show the order in which steps must be followed.

> ### Writer's Solution Connection Writing Lab
>
> For more help, use the Transitions Word Bin in the Drafting section of the Exposition: Making Connections tutorial.

Applying Language Skills
Using Transitions to Indicate Time Explain to students that they will want to vary the transitions they use in their essays to show differences in time as well as to avoid repetitiveness.

Answers
Suggested responses:
1. Preheat the oven to 450°. Then, grease and flour a 9" round pan.
2. After mixing the ingredients, pour it into a dish.
3. One hour will pass until the edges will turn brown.
4. Then, let it cool.
5. Finally, enjoy the soufflé!

Writer's Solution

For additional instruction and practice have students use lessons in the Sentence Style unit of the *Writer's Solution Language Lab CD-ROM.*

Develop Student Writing

Prewriting
Explain to students that when gathering details for their how-to essays, they should not include unnecessary details that may complicate the procedure and possibly confuse a reader. Rather, they should concentrate on the details that cover the important steps in the procedure.

Writer's Solution

Writing Lab CD-ROM
In the tutorial on Exposition, the audio-annotated models for chronological order in The Organizing Details section may give students guidance as they organize details for their own essays.

Customize for
Less Proficient Writers
Some students may do better working with a partner on their how-to essays. Pair students and have them verbally explain the topics of their essays. As they go through their verbal explanations, partners can ask questions when the explanation is unclear. Encourage students to keep notes during their conversation and to refer to these notes when drafting.

Drafting
Remind students that they will want to include introductions which clearly state what their essays will describe. The body of their essays should include the full range of the topic. The conclusions sum up what the essays showed readers how to do. Students may also want to include information about why knowing how to do their activities is useful.

Writer's Solution

Writing Lab CD-ROM
In the Drafting section of the tutorial on Exposition: Giving Information, suggest that students view the Writing Hints to help them draft in one sitting.

Revising

As students reread their drafts, suggest they visualize the process they are explaining to determine whether any steps are in the wrong order.

Writer's Solution

Writing Lab CD-ROM
In the tutorial on Exposition: Giving Information, have students use the revision checker for transition words.

Publishing

Suggest that students publish their how-to essays in a brochure or mini-booklet with a snazzy cover page and illustrations or other visual aids.

Reinforce and Extend

Review the Writing Guidelines
After students have finished, review the characteristics of a how-to essay.

Applying Language Skills
Using Commas After Introductory Transitions Explain that commas help separate the introductory word, phrase, or clause from the rest of the sentence.

Answers
1. First, gather the materials you need.
2. After that, find one mushroom near your house.
3. Then, check your field guide.
4. Now, identify whether the mushroom is poisonous.
5. Next, repeat steps two through four.

Writer's Solution

For additional instruction, use the practice page on Commas That Set Off Added Elements in the *Writer's Solution Grammar Practice Book,* p. 106.

Writing Process Workshop

EDITING/PROOFREADING

Applying Language Skills: Using Commas After Introductory Transitions

Transitions are used to signal relationships between sentences. When a transition begins a sentence, it is usually set off from the rest of the sentence by a comma:

<u>First</u>, make sure you have matches and newspapers.

<u>Meanwhile</u>, gather dry pinecones, twigs, and bark.

Practice Copy the following sentences into your notebook. Set off introductory transitions with commas.

1. First gather the materials you need.
2. After that find one mushroom near your house.
3. Then check your field guide.
4. Now identify whether the mushroom is poisonous.
5. Next repeat steps two through four.

Writing Application Insert commas following transitions in your how-to essay.

Writer's Solution Connection
Language Lab

For more about commas, see the Commas lesson in the Punctuation unit.

Create Visual Aids Create graphs, diagrams, and charts to convey complex information in an easy-to-understand form. For example, diagrams can sometimes convey assembly instructions better than a bulleted list.

Revising

Do a Test Run Ask a classmate to use your instructions to accomplish the task. Your classmate should use these questions for reviewing your directions:
- ▶ Are the steps clearly stated?
- ▶ Does background information help in understanding the task or does it cause confusion?
- ▶ Are relationships among ideas indicated by transitional words?

REVISION MODEL

My favorite cookies are chocolate chip. Here is my recipe:
① 2 c. flour, 2 T. baking soda, 2 sticks of butter, 2 eggs, 1 T. of vanilla, 2 c. of sugar, 3/4 c. of chocolate chips
~~Gather flower and baking soda and put them to the side.~~

~~Then get butter, eggs, 1 tablespoon of vanilla, two cups of sugar, and chocolate chips.~~

② First,   then
1. Soften the butter and whip it.

       ③ to prevent cookies from sticking.
2. Grease a cookie sheet

3. Mix butter, sugar, and eggs. Beat until smooth.

① The writer replaced his list of ingredients with a precise list of ingredients and measurements.
② Adding the transitions *first* and *then* indicates the order in which the steps must be completed.
③ The writer elaborated with this detail to let readers know why this step is important.

Publishing and Presenting

Classroom Turn your essay into a 5- to 10-minute talk. Demonstrate your instructions for your class.

School Create a step-by-step poster that illustrates your how-to essay. Post your work in school.

Fair Organize a fair at which class members can teach one another the procedures they have written about. Ask classmates to distribute copies at the fair.

524 ◆ *Extraordinary Occurrences*

✓ ASSESSMENT		4	3	2	I
PORTFOLIO ASSESSMENT Use the rubric on How To/ Process Explanation in the **Alternative Assessment** booklet, p. 96, to assess the students' writing. Add these criteria to customize this rubric to this assignment.	**Using Transitions**	The writer has creatively used transitions to connect ideas in the essay.	The writer has effectively used transitions to connect ideas in most of the essay.	The writer has used some transitions to connect ideas, but more are needed.	The writer rarely uses transitions, making the essay hard to follow.
	Using Commas	The writer correctly uses commas after introductory transitions.	The writer uses commas after most introductory transitions.	The writer uses commas after some introductory transitions.	The writer fails to use commas after introductory transitions.

Real-World Reading Skills Workshop

Reading Manuals

Strategies for Success

Whether you are installing a new computer game or putting together a bicycle, you'll be more successful if you read the directions. The owner's manual that comes with new products includes detailed directions and important information that will help you put together and use a product correctly.

Skim the Manual Get acquainted with the organization of the manual. Review the table of contents to see what topics are covered in the manual—what the product does and how information is organized. Read the introduction for a general overview of the product.

Check the Manual for Parts Before you completely unpack the shipping crate or box, find the list of parts you should have for assembling the item. Check off the parts one by one as you unpack them. Sometimes special tools or connections are necessary. Make sure you have those before you proceed.

Read Specific Sections Carefully Your preview will help you determine what parts of the manual you want to read. You will probably read through most of the beginning sections of the manual, but you can put off reading the supplementary material until a later time.

Read to Solve Problems Keep the manual for reference in case you have a problem with the product. A troubleshooting section, providing solutions for common problems, is included in most manuals. You can use the index to locate specific details that pertain to your problem.

Apply the Strategies

You recently purchased a computer program that makes greeting cards. You would like to start preparing cards for the upcoming holiday.

Use the manual's table of contents, shown below, to answer the following questions:

1. Where would you find information on installing the program?
2. Describe the information found in each of the four sections.
3. Which section would you use if you wanted the time and day to be displayed on your screen?
4. Which section would you read first? Why?

Keller's Holiday Cardmaker

Introduction 1

I. Getting Started
Installation 3
Main Menu 6

II. Graphics
Finding Graphics 10
Choosing Graphics 15
Saving Graphics 20

III. Cardmaker
Choosing a Style 25
Importing Graphics 28

IV. Customizing Holiday Cardmaker
Display Preferences 30
Print Preferences 33

Troubleshooting 35
Index 38

✔ *Here are other situations in which you should read the manuals:*
- ► *Using a new word-processing program*
- ► *Assembling a bicycle*
- ► *Setting up an audio system*

Reviewing Phrases

The selections in Part 2 include instruction on the following:

- Appositive Phrases

This instruction is reinforced with the Build Grammar Skills practice pages in **Selection Support**, p. 191.

As you review phrases, you may wish to include the following:

- Infinitive Phrases

An infinitive is a form of a verb that generally appears with the word *to* and can act as a noun, adjective, or adverb. Examples of infinitives include *to understand, to cooperate, to resist.* An infinitive phrase is an infinitive with modifiers, complements, or a subject, all acting together as a single part of speech. Following are some examples of infinitives and other parts of speech combined into an infinitive phrase:

> **With an Adverb Phrase:** They like *to sleep late on the weekends.*
>
> **With a Direct Object:** Emma likes *to watch television.*
>
> **With a Subject:** *To finish the project* requires patience and determination.

✐ Writer's Solution

For additional practice and support, have students complete the practice pages on different types of phrases, pp. 47–54 in the *Writer's Solution Grammar Practice Book.*

Phrases — Grammar Review

A **phrase** is a group of words that usually serves as a single part of speech and does not contain a subject or a verb. Two types of phrases are participial phrases and appositive phrases.

Participial Phrases A **participial phrase** functions as an adjective. It contains a participle, a verb form ending in *-ing* or *-ed,* and all the participle's modifiers and complements.

> "Even Tommy Wright, *wedged between his parents in the front seat,* was subdued."

The participial phrase, *wedged between his parents in the front seat*, modifies Tommy Wright.

Appositive Phrases An **appositive phrase** contains an appositive, a noun or pronoun placed near another noun or pronoun to explain or identify it, and all its modifiers and complements. Appositive phrases are often set off by commas or dashes.

> Gary Paulsen, a nature writer, creates suspense in "A Glow in the Dark."

The appositive phrase "a nature writer" identifies the sentence's subject, Gary Paulsen.

Practice 1 Copy these passages into your notebook. Underline and label any participial or appositive phrases.

1. "A large, standing form glowing in the dark"

2. "Touching the stump, and feeling the cold light, I could not quite get rid of the fear until a black and white dog named Fonzie came up. . . ."

3. Fonzie, a dog that ran with the pack, confronted the glowing stump.

4. Some mushrooms, a fungus, are highly prized by chefs.

5. Bats often fly at night, circling in the sky and looking for prey.

Practice 2 In your notebook, combine each pair of sentences into one sentence that includes the type of phrase indicated.

1. The mushrooms covered the ground. The mushrooms are a kind of fungus. (appositive phrase)

2. The abandoned mansion was swaying in the strong wind. It looked unstable. (participial phrase)

3. The tree stump was glowing with a green tint. The stump frightened the dogs. (participial phrase)

4. The bat likes the attic of an aging house. The bat is a cousin to the mouse. (appositive)

5. The ancient house was hidden by overgrown trees. It was crumbling from decay. (participial phrase)

Grammar in Writing

✔ *Use appositive phrases to insert additional information into sentences.*

✔ *To vary your sentence beginnings, start some sentences with participial phrases.*

Answers

Practice 1
1. "A large, standing form <u>glowing in the dark</u>" (participial phrase)
2. "<u>Touching the stump, and feeling the cold light,</u> I could not quite get rid of the fear until a black and white dog named Fonzie came up. . . ." (participial phrases)
3. Fonzie, <u>a dog that ran with the pack,</u> confronted the glowing stump. (appositive phrase)
4. Some mushrooms, <u>a fungus,</u> are highly prized by chefs. (appositive phrase)
5. Bats often fly at night, <u>circling in the sky and looking for prey.</u> (participial phrase)

Practice 2
Possible responses:
1. The mushrooms, a kind of fungus, covered the ground.
2. The abandoned mansion looked unstable, swaying in the strong wind.
3. The tree stump, glowing with a green tint, frightened the dogs.
4. The bat, a cousin to the mouse, likes the attic of an aging house.
5. The ancient house, crumbling from decay, was hidden by overgrown trees.

Speaking, Listening, and Viewing Workshop

Delivering a Speech

Now that you have chosen a topic, completed your research, and written a final draft of your speech, it is time to deliver it in a way that will accomplish your purpose. Whether your purpose is to inform young children about safety rules or to persuade your classmates to vote for you in an upcoming school election, you must capture the attention of your audience and hold it. The way you deliver information is just as important as what you have to say.

Engage Your Audience Capture the attention of your audience by beginning with a humorous story, a thought-provoking question, or a firm statement of belief that relates to your topic.

Tips for Delivering a Speech

✔ If you want to make a good impression and seem like a professional, follow these strategies:

▶ Look directly at your audience.
▶ Use appropriate gestures and tone of voice.
▶ Speak loudly and clearly.

Look at Your Audience To keep your audience's attention, maintain eye contact. If you simply read from your notes, your audience won't feel that you are speaking to them and may lose interest. Practice your speech so you are comfortable looking up from your notes.

Keep Your Audience's Attention Using your voice emphatically to show enthusiasm about your topic will help keep the attention of your audience. Don't stand stiffly or appear to be simply reading your speech. Instead, use gestures to emphasize important points—raising your hand, tapping the lectern, or pointing to a chart or graph.

Apply the Strategies

Prepare and deliver speeches for the following situations. Then, invite your classmates to share feedback on your effectiveness.

1. Your school is having a Club Fair. You have been chosen by your club, The Ecology Crowd, to give a speech describing the purpose of the club, what you do, and how often you meet.

2. As a member of the student council, you have been asked to introduce the new principal to the student body. You have met the principal and really like her, and you want to communicate that to the student body.

3. You do volunteer work at an animal shelter. Give a brief talk to classmates. Explain the benefits of your work, and try to get others to volunteer.

Introduce the Strategies

Ask students to describe speeches they have attended or seen on television. Encourage them to explain what they liked and disliked about the speeches. Explain to students that their goals in delivering a speech should include capturing the listeners' interest, and keeping that interest throughout the duration of the speech.

Customize for
Bodily/Kinesthetic Learners
Ask students with drama experience to share any tips they may know of from acting in plays or skits. Encourage students to describe how an actor tries to keep the attention of the audience, or how actors may work off each other to create a dramatic scene. Explain to students that just as actors perform for their audience, so should speechmakers "perform" for their listeners.

Apply the Strategies

Encourage students to work in groups on their speeches. First, have them consider whether the purpose of the speech is to persuade or to inform. Then have students write a brief outline of the points they will need to touch on in their speech. Finally, have them practice giving the speech, using the techniques described in this lesson.

 Cross-Curricular Connection: Social Studies

Delivering a Speech Ask students if they have ever been asked to give an oral presentation or speech to their social studies classes. Explain that sometimes when students have done research in a specialized area, the most effective way to transmit the information they have learned is to present it in a speech for the rest of the class.

Ask students to come up with a list of topics which they have studied or are currently studying in their social studies classes. Then have them narrow their topics so they can easily be covered in a short speech. Encourage students to use

their social studies textbooks to begin their research. Students may benefit from working in pairs on a specific topic. They might cover their shared topics in a longer speech.

Explain to students that their purpose is to inform the rest of the class about topics in which they are interested. They will want to include some information that the rest of the class cannot easily find. Have students give their speeches and encourage the rest of the class to take notes on the main topics of the speeches. Then discuss which speeches were most effective and why.

◆ Build Vocabulary

What's Behind the Words

Before students begin this lesson, ask them to brainstorm for a list of mystery or detective-related words they may have encountered in books or movies or on TV. Explain that this vocabulary lesson will describe the origins of many of these words.

Answers

Activity 1

1. genre means a kind, style, or category. In the context of the sentence, ". . . Poe launched the literary genre of the mystery story," genre refers to a category or type of literature.

2. dastardly means of or like a bully, or a coward who is brutal when there is no risk to himself. In the sentence, "The detective's mission is to uncover a villain, a plot, or dastardly deed," students should be able to infer that dastardly means something harmful, suspicious, or foul.

3. labyrinth is a network of winding paths or roads through which it is difficult to find one's way without help. The word labyrinth appears in one sentence, followed by a sentence using the word maze to describe the same structure, just as the word monster in the first sentence is followed by the word beast, both words referring to the Minotaur.

4. perplexing means puzzling or bewildering. The word perplexing is used in the sentence describing the meaning of the word clue, therefore leading the reader to understand that the perplexing situation must be something confusing for which a clue is needed.

Activity 2

1. auto = self, by oneself, independently
2. chron = time
3. dict = word
4. phon = sound
5. tract = drawing

What's Behind the Words

Vocabulary Adventures With Richard Lederer

Mystery and Detective Vocabulary

With his short story "The Murders in the Rue Morgue," in 1841, American author Edgar Allan Poe launched the literary genre of the mystery story. The mystery of the word *mystery* takes us back to the Greek *mysterion*, a secret religious ceremony in which one was "to have closed eyes and lips." Later, the word came to mean anything that was not understood.

Making a Case for Detectives

Poe's detective, named Monsieur C. Auguste Dupin, became a model for many other private investigators, including Sherlock Holmes. Detectives derive their title from the Latin *detectus*, "uncover" (*de*, "from," and *tegere*, "to cover"). The detective's mission is to uncover a villain, a plot, or a dastardly deed.

A detective is sometimes called a sleuth. The word *sleuth* is a shortening of *sleuthhound*, a Scottish bloodhound noted for its dogged pursuit of game, suspects, and fugitives.

Detectives are also known as private eyes. The famous Pinkerton Detective Agency had the motto "We never sleep." The motto was printed on cards, posters, and stationery over a drawing of an open eye, and their detectives became known as private eyes.

Threading Your Way Through Clues

Detectives uncover clues to *deduce* (Latin *deducere*, "lead from") the solutions to mysteries. *Clue* is a native English word, but its origin lies in Greek mythology. The Minotaur, a dreaded monster that was half man and half bull, prowled a labyrinth, on the island of Crete. The hero Theseus offered to enter the maze and kill the beast. Ariadne, daughter of the King of Crete, was in love with Theseus and gave him a thread—in Middle English, a *clewe*—to guide him out of the labyrinth after he had slain the monster. From this story, the word *clewe*, now *clue*, came to mean anything that guides us through a perplexing situation, such as a crime.

ACTIVITY 1 You can be a word detective by using *context* (Latin *contexere*, "to weave together") as a powerful clue to learning new words. When you meet an unknown word, you can infer its meaning from its context by taking account of the surrounding words and the situation being taught or written about. From their contexts on this page, infer the meanings of the words *genre, dastardly, labyrinth,* and *perplexing*.

ACTIVITY 2 Word detectives dig down to the roots of words. They know that words are often related to each other by roots—basic units of language that convey important meanings. As an exercise in root detection, examine each three-word cluster, and then deduce the meaning of each root:

1. autobiography, autograph, automatic
   auto = _____?_____
2. chronic, chronology, synchronize
   chron = _____?_____
3. contradict, dictionary, predict
   dict = _____?_____
4. microphone, phonics, telephone
   phon = _____?_____
5. extract, intractable, tractor
   tract = _____?_____

528 ◆ *Extraordinary Occurrences*

Extended Reading Opportunities

The world is full of unusual and extraordinary occurrences that bewilder and fascinate. The following novels explore amazing worlds of mystery and fantasy.

Suggested Titles

The Man Who Was Poe
Avi
Young Edmund finds himself alone in the city. His mother is gone, his father is missing, and his twin sister has disappeared. Edmund is being followed by a mysterious stranger who turns out to be Edgar Allan Poe. Poe offers to help Edmund solve the mystery surrounding the disappearance of his family in exchange for the boy's help with his own mission. The thriller follows their adventures through the shadowy city of Providence, Rhode Island, in 1848.

Twenty Thousand Leagues Under the Sea
Jules Verne
A ship hunting a deadly seamonster is destroyed in an explosion, and a French scientist, his sidekick, and a Canadian harpoonist are the only survivors. They are then swallowed up by a technological monster—a submarine. The men take part in an underwater odyssey commanded by the madman Captain Nemo. The novel, written in 1870, lays the foundation for much of today's science fiction in its accurate prediction of twentieth-century technological advances.

The Hobbit
J.R.R. Tolkien
Bilbo Baggins, a middle-aged hobbit, is about to have the adventure of his life. With a wizard named Gandalf and thirteen dwarves, Bilbo is headed for Lonely Mountain to confront a dragon that is hoarding treasure. The novel, although set in a world of fantasy, echoes much of the history of the Middle Ages, with knights, warfare, castles, and armies. Having confronted evil and overcome hardship, Bilbo returns from his quest a hero.

Other Possibilities

The Lord of the Rings	J.R.R. Tolkein
Canyons	Gary Paulsen
Invitation to the Game	Monica Hughes

Planning Students' Extended Reading
All of the works listed on this page are good choices for extending the theme "Extraordinary Occurrences." Following is some information that may help you choose which to teach:

Customize for
Varying Student Needs
When assigning the selections in this part to your students, keep in mind the following factors:

- *The Man Who Was Poe* is a short novel of historical fiction set in the 1800's. The main character, Edmund, is alone and followed by the mysterious Edgar Allan Poe, who helps him find Edmund's missing twin sister.

- *Twenty Thousand Leagues Under the Sea* is a classic novel by Jules Verne featuring one of the most horrible literary villains, Captain Nemo. This is a good choice for students interested in science fiction and technology.

- *The Hobbit* is the precursor to J.R.R. Tolkien's classic trilogy *The Lord of the Rings*. With its likable but unlikely hero, Bilbo Baggins, *The Hobbit* is a great novel for students interested in fantasy literature.

Literature Study Guides
A literature study guide is available for *The Hobbit*. The guide includes section summaries, discussion questions, and activities.

Planning Instruction and Assessment

Unit Objectives

1. To read nonfiction selections
2. To apply a variety of reading strategies, particularly strategies for reading nonfiction, appropriate for reading these selections
3. To recognize literary elements used in these selections
4. To increase vocabulary
5. To learn elements of grammar and usage
6. To write in a variety of modes about situations based on the selections
7. To develop speaking and listening skills by completing activities
8. To view images critically and create visual representations

Meeting the Objectives Each selection provides instructional material and portfolio opportunities by which students can meet unit objectives. You will find additional practice pages for reading strategies, literary elements, vocabulary, and grammar in the **Selection Support** booklet in the **Teaching Resources** box.

Setting Goals Work with your students at the beginning of the unit to set goals for unit outcomes. Plan what skills and concepts you wish students to acquire. You may match instruction and activities according to students' performance levels or learning modalities.

Portfolios Students may keep portfolios of their completed work or of their work in progress. The Build Your Portfolio page of each selection provides opportunities for students to apply the concepts presented.

 ## Humanities: Art

Mrs. Cushman's House, 1942, by N.C. Wyeth

N.C. Wyeth (1882–1945) was an American illustrator and painter, most famous for his illustrations of juvenile literary classics such as *Treasure Island* and *Robin Hood*. Wyeth was killed in an automobile accident in 1945.

What kind of stories could be told about this house? *Students may say the house is a good setting for stories because it looks like a family's house; over the years, there may be stories to tell— maybe more than one family has lived there so there may be stories of different generations and different times.*

Mrs. Cushman's House, 1942, N.C. Wyeth, New Britain Museum of American Art, Connecticut

Art Transparencies

The **Art Transparencies** booklet in the **Teaching Resources** box offers fine art to help students make connections to other curriculum areas and high-interest topics.

Beyond Literature

Each unit presents Beyond Literature features that lead students into an exploration of careers, communities and other subject areas. In this unit, students will take a look at Jerusalem—past and present—the career of horse trainer, and make a cultural connection to the Sioux. In addition, the **Teaching Resources** box contains a **Beyond Literature** booklet of activities. Using literature as a springboard, these activity pages offer students opportunities to connect literature to other curriculum areas and to the workplace and careers, community, media, and humanities.

6

Short Stories

Short stories take you on a quick trip to other worlds and into other people's lives. Within the pages of a short story, you may encounter anything—from deadly cobras to absent-minded professors to deranged criminals. Despite their varied content, almost all short stories have the following elements in common:

- **Plot:** the sequence of events that catches your interest and takes you through the story.

- **Characters:** the people, animals, or other beings that take part in the story's action.

- **Setting:** the time and place in which the story takes place.

- **Theme:** the message about life that the story conveys.

This unit highlights the elements of the short story while it shows the power and variety of the form.

◆ 531

Assessing Student Progress

The tools that are available to measure the degree to which students meet the unit objectives are listed below.

Informal Assessment

The questions in the Guide for Responding sections are a first level of response to the concepts and skills presented with the selection. As a brief, informal measure of students' grasp of the material, these responses indicate where further instruction and practice are needed. The practice pages in the **Selection Support** booklet provide for this type of instruction and practice.

You will also find literature and reading guides in the **Alternative Assessment** booklet, which students can use for informal assessment of their individual performances.

Formal Assessment

The **Formal Assessment** booklet contains Selection Tests and Unit Tests.

Selection Tests measure comprehension and skills acquisition for each selection or group of selections.

Each Unit Test provides students with 30 multiple-choice questions and 5 essay questions designed to assess students' knowledge of the literature and skills taught in the unit.

Each Alternative Unit Test: Standardized-Test Practice provides 15 multiple-choice questions and 3 essay questions based on two new literature selections not contained in the student book. The questions on the Alternative Unit Test are designed to assess students' ability to compare and contrast selections, applying skills taught in the unit.

Alternative Assessment

For portfolio and alternative assessment, the **Alternative Assessment** booklet contains Scoring Rubrics, Assessment sheets, and Learning Modalities activities.

Scoring Rubrics provide writing modes that can be applied to Writing activities, Writing Mini-Lessons, and Writing Process Workshop lessons.

Assessment sheets for speaking and listening activities provide peer and self-assessment direction.

Learning Modalities activities appeal to different learning styles. Use these as an alternative measurement of students' growth.

Connections

Within this unit, you will find selections and activities that make connections beyond literature. Use these selections to connect students' understanding and appreciation of literature beyond the traditional literature and language arts curriculum.

Encourage students to connect literature to other curriculum areas. You may wish to coordinate with teachers in other curriculum areas to determine ways to team teach and further extend instruction.

Connecting Literature to Social Studies

Each unit contains a selection that connects literature to social studies. In this unit, students will connect to the Civil War with Stephen Crane's realistic short story, "An Episode of War."

Guide for Reading

OBJECTIVES

1. To read, comprehend, and interpret a short story
2. To relate a short story to personal experience
3. To apply strategies for reading fiction
4. To analyze plot
5. To build vocabulary in context and learn the word root *-spir-*
6. To identify independent and subordinate clauses
7. To write an interior monologue with details that reveal character
8. To respond to the story through writing, speaking and listening, and projects

SKILLS INSTRUCTION

Vocabulary:
Word Roots: *-spir-*

Spelling:
Medial Consonants in Two-Syllable Words With Long Vowels in the First Syllable

Grammar:
Clauses

Reading for Success:
Strategies for Reading Fiction

Literary Focus:
Plot

Writing:
Use Details to Reveal Character

Speaking and Listening:
Scene (Teacher Edition)

Critical Viewing:
Connect

PORTFOLIO OPPORTUNITIES

Writing: Research Plan; Diary Entry; Sequel
Writing Mini-Lesson: Interior Monologue
Speaking and Listening: Scene; Dinner Speech
Projects: Reality Check; Film Treatment

More About the Author
Mona Gardner's story first appeared in *The Saturday Review*, which was originally a literary journal. Later, it widened its focus to include reviews, essays, fiction, and poetry relating to all areas of contemporary life. "The Dinner Party" was published just after the United States had entered World War II, when women were working in jobs formerly done only by men, and facing new challenges in many areas of modern life.

Meet the Author:

Mona Gardner (1900–1982)
Mona Gardner was born in Seattle, Washington, and graduated from California's Stanford University.

Asian Interests Being a West Coast resident may have given Gardner a special interest in Asia, which lies across the Pacific. One of her best-known works, for example, is the historical novel *Hong Kong* (1958). This novel tells about the founding of the Chinese city of Hong Kong.

Writing Career In her long writing career, Gardner contributed stories and articles to such well-known magazines as *The New Yorker, The Atlantic,* and *The Saturday Evening Post.*

THE STORY BEHIND THE STORY
"The Dinner Party" was first published in *The Saturday Review* on January 31, 1942. The story is set in India, which was then a British colony. Most of the guests at the story's dinner party are British officials who control India on behalf of Britain.

◆ LITERATURE AND YOUR LIFE

CONNECT YOUR EXPERIENCE
Life is full of surprises. In "The Dinner Party," a cobra, a deadly snake, intrudes upon an elegant dinner party like the one shown in the painting. Think about unexpected things that have happened in your life. How did you handle the surprise?

THEMATIC FOCUS: Conflicts and Challenges
Think about the different types of challenges people face as you read "The Dinner Party."

◆ Background for Understanding

SCIENCE
In this story, you'll meet with a snake native to India that invades a dinner party. The Indian cobra, which averages 5.5 feet in length and displays a neck "hood" as a warning, kills a few thousand people every year. (Cobra venom is fatal to humans in one out of ten cases.) These deaths usually result from a cobra's twilight visit to a house in search of rats.

◆ Build Vocabulary

WORD ROOTS: *-spir-*
The word root *-spir-*, from a Latin word meaning "breath," breathes its life into a whole family of words. In this story, for instance, a young girl is described as *spirited,* which means "filled with life; lively."

WORD BANK
Which of these words from the list describes someone who studies nature? Check the Build Vocabulary box on page 535 to see if you chose correctly.

naturalist
spirited
arresting
sobers

Prentice Hall Literature Program Resources

REINFORCE / RETEACH / EXTEND
Selection Support Pages
Build Vocabulary: Word Roots: *-spir-*, p. 196
Build Spelling Skills, p. 197
Build Grammar Skills: Clauses, p. 198
Reading for Success: Strategies for Reading Fiction, pp. 199–200
Literary Focus: Plot, p. 201
Strategies for Diverse Student Needs, pp. 73–74
Beyond Literature Cultural Connection: Women's Roles, p. 37

Formal Assessment Selection Test, pp. 159–161, Assessment Resources Software
Alternative Assessment, p. 37
Writing and Language Transparencies
Series of Events Chain, p. 57
Resource Pro CD-ROM
"The Dinner Party" —includes all resource material and customizable lesson plan.

 Listening to Literature Audiocassettes
"The Dinner Party"

The Dinner Party

Dinner at Haddo House, Alfred Edward Emslie, National Portrait Gallery, London

◆ Literary Focus

PLOT

A story's **plot** is a sequence of events in which each event results from a previous one and causes the next. The plot centers on a **conflict**, a struggle between opposing forces. This struggle, explained in the **exposition**, builds in the **rising action** and reaches its point of greatest tension at the **climax**. Afterward, in the **falling action**, the conflict is **resolved**.

As you read "The Dinner Party," use this chart to follow the roller-coaster ride of its plot:

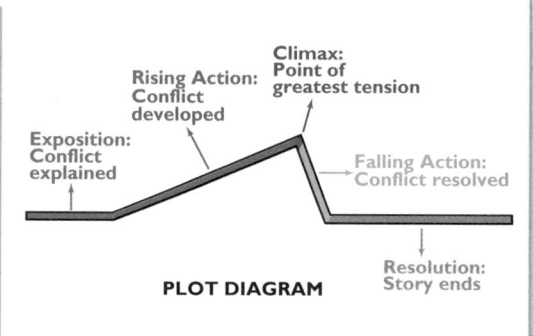

Exposition: Conflict explained

Rising Action: Conflict developed

Climax: Point of greatest tension

Falling Action: Conflict resolved

Resolution: Story ends

PLOT DIAGRAM

Guide for Reading ◆ 533

Interest Grabber
Divide the class into groups. In each, appoint a student to role-play the host of a radio call-in show, and another to be timekeeper. Then, write this statement on the board: "Men are better in a crisis than women." Have group members "call" the host and respond to the assertion in 30 seconds or less. After students have had a chance to voice their opinions, link this activity to the story by saying that at a dinner party guests heatedly debated this very issue—and the results were quite unexpected.

◆ Build Grammar Skills

Clauses If you wish to introduce the grammar concept for this selection before students read, refer to the instruction on p. 537.

Customize for
Less Proficient Readers
To help students follow the story's plot, provide them with the Series of Events Chain, p. 57, in **Writing and Language Transparencies.** Students can list plot events and then refer to the chain to identify the conflict, rising action, climax, falling action, and resolution.

Customize for
More Advanced Students
Challenge students to keep each of these questions in mind as they read, and make inferences about the story:

- Why is it told in present tense?
- Why do most characters lack names?
- Why is a central character an American and a naturalist?

 Humanities: Art

Dinner at Haddo House, by Alfred Edward Emslie
London-born Emslie (1848–1917) was best known for his watercolors and for the two-page illustrations he often created for the *London News*. Ask students what clues they find that this is an elegant dinner party. *Guests wear formal attire and jewels; the table includes crystal, candles, and flowers; a man plays music in the background.*

 Preparing for Standardized Tests

Reading The Reading for Success strategies featured with this selection help students as they read any fiction, and as they answer certain comprehension items on standardized tests.

Tests may evaluate students' ability to infer. Inferences are conclusions based on evidence or details that the writer includes. Use the following sample test question, based on "The Dinner Party":

The scientist sees the hostess's anxious look. He sees a servant set out a bowl of milk, which he knows is "bait for a snake." From this detail, he can reasonably infer that—

(A) there is a snake in the room
(B) the hostess thinks there's a snake in the room
(C) servants usually feed snakes milk
(D) hostesses always expect the worst

The scientist knows that milk lures snakes from places where they are unwanted. He sees the hostess's concern and the bowl of milk. It is reasonable to conclude that she thinks there is a snake in the room (B). For more practice, use Reading for Success: Strategies for Reading Fiction in **Selection Support,** pp. 199–200.

The Reading for Success page in each unit presents a set of problem-solving strategies to help readers understand authors' words and ideas on multiple levels. Good readers develop a bank of strategies from which they can draw as needed.

Unit 6 introduces strategies for reading fiction. Good readers become involved in what they read by predicting what may happen in the story, putting themselves in the characters' situations, asking questions about why things happen, and making inferences.

These strategies for reading fiction are modeled with "The Dinner Party." Each green box shows an example of the thinking process involved in applying one of these strategies. Additional notes provide support for applying these strategies throughout the selection.

How to Use the Reading for Success Page

• Introduce the strategies for reading fiction, presenting each as problem-solving procedure.

• Before students read the short story, have them preview it, looking at the annotations in the green boxes that model the strategies.

• To reinforce these strategies after students have read the story, use the Reading for Success, pp. 199–200, in **Selection Support.** These pages give students an opportunity to read a selection and practice critical reading strategies by writing their own annotations.

Reading Strategies: Support and Reinforcement
Using Boxed Annotations and Prompts

Throughout this unit, the notes in green, red, and maroon boxes are intended to help students apply reading strategies, understand the literary focus, and make a connection with their lives. You may use boxed material in these ways:

• Have students pause at each box and respond to its prompt before they continue reading.

• Urge students to read through the selection, ignoring the boxes. After they complete the selection, they may go back and review the text, responding to the prompts.

Reading for Success

Strategies for Reading Fiction

Reading fiction isn't like reading a how-to article. You need to pack a few extra things in your reading kit besides your brain—for example, your feeling for other people, your imagination, and your willingness to enter and live in a made-up world. Following are strategies for reading fiction, which will help you as you explore the new worlds revealed in these short stories.

Identify with a character or situation.

Enter into the characters' lives, sharing their thoughts and feelings, and rooting for or against them. Relate their experiences and the events that occur to situations you have experienced.

Predict what will happen.

▶ When story characters make broad statements, predict whether or not those statements will prove true.
▶ As story events unfold, predict what will happen.

Ask questions about plot, characters, and theme.

Your questions are worth asking. Question what is happening in a story. Ask why characters do what they do or why the author includes certain details. Here's a sample question:

Passage	Question
. . . a spirited discussion springs up between a young girl and a colonel.	Why does the author bring up this discussion?

Make inferences about what you read.

Writers don't always tell you everything directly. You have to make inferences to arrive at ideas that writers suggest but don't say. Inferences are conclusions based on evidence or the details that the writer includes.

Passage	Inference
The American scientist does not join in the argument, but sits watching the faces of the other guests.	The American is a thoughtful person.

As you read "The Dinner Party," look at the notes along the sides of the pages. The notes demonstrate how to apply these strategies to a work of literature.

Model a Reading Strategy: Predict What Will Happen

Good readers pay attention to where a story is heading and notice how the author is developing the characters and plot. Demonstrate how to predict as you read the 3rd and 4th paragraphs of the story by modeling your thinking for students.

I've noticed that this story is less than two pages long, so the author doesn't have space to go very far beyond the basic plot. The conversation between the colonel and the young girl must be the exposition. He sug-

gests that men have more control in crises than women do. My guess is that something will happen to prove he's right or wrong.

The American scientist, who's not talking, notices the hostess is silent too, but she is rigid with attention. She whispers instructions to the servant boy next to her, and he quickly leaves the room to place a bowl of milk on the verandah floor. I can predict that something remarkable will happen shortly and that it will probably be a crisis that shows how men and women react to it.

The DINNER Party

Mona Gardner

The country is India. A large dinner party is being given in an up-country station by a colonial official and his wife. The guests are army officers and government attachés and their wives, and an American <u>naturalist</u>. ❶

At one side of the long table a <u>spirited</u> discussion springs up between a young girl and a colonel. The girl insists women have long outgrown the jumping-on-a-chair-at-sight-of-a-mouse era, that they are not as fluttery as their grandmothers. The colonel says they are, explaining that women haven't the actual nerve control of men. The other men at the table agree with him.

> Identify with one side or the other in this argument.

"A woman's unfailing reaction in any crisis," the colonel says, "is to scream. And while a man may feel like it, yet he has that ounce more of control than a woman has. And that last ounce is what counts!"

> You can predict that a woman will prove the colonel wrong.

The American scientist does not join in the argument, but sits watching the faces of the other guests. As he looks, he sees a strange expression come over the face of the hostess. ❷

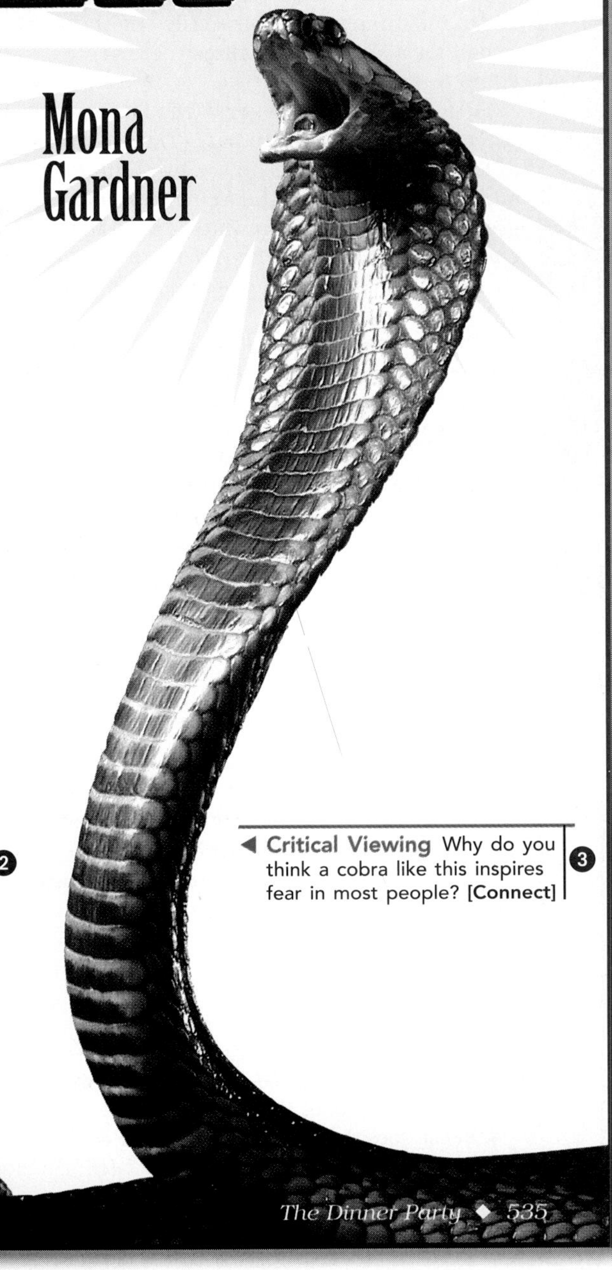

◆ Build Vocabulary

naturalist (nach´ ər əl ist) *n.*: One who studies nature

spirited (spir´ it id) *adj.*: Lively; energetic

◀ **Critical Viewing** Why do you think a cobra like this inspires fear in most people? [Connect] ❸

The Dinner Party ◆ 535

Develop Understanding

One-Minute Insight At "The Dinner Party," a group of British colonial officials and women in India debate whether men or women react better in a crisis. A colonel insists that women have no control over their nerves. The only non-British guest, an American naturalist, realizes that their hostess is directing her servants to lure a cobra from under the table. The guests are unaware of what is going on as the naturalist helps her. When the snake is gone, the host congratulates the naturalist on his nerve. The naturalist then elicits from the iron-nerved hostess that the snake was lying on her foot.

Reading for Success

❶ **Ask Questions** Guide students to begin asking questions to help clarify the setting. They might ask, "What is an 'up-country station'?" "Why is an American naturalist in the group?" *Students who answer these questions will know that the dinner party takes place in a remote area where nature may be a factor, and that the American's skill as a naturalist may come into play.*

Reading for Success

❷ **Predict** Ask students to predict what they think the meaning of the strange expression on the hostess's face may suggest. *Students may predict that she notices something wrong but doesn't want to alarm her guests.*

▶ Critical Viewing ◀

❸ **Connect** *Students may say that most people fear snakes, especially cobras, who rise up to face their enemies and expand their hoods to appear even more fearsome.*

Speaking and Listening Mini-Lesson

Scene
This mini-lesson supports the Speaking and Listening activity in the Idea Bank on p. 538.

Introduce Review the definition, form, and characteristics of dialogue. Good dialogues match words, phrases, and tone with the characters saying them.

Develop Have students brainstorm for ideas or feelings the characters might express in "The Dinner Party." They can begin by reviewing the story's dialogue and then improvising to see what comes to mind that would fit a script.

Have students write the dialogue and practice delivering it with dramatic feeling and clarity.

Apply Have students present the scenes to classmates. Encourage others to listen for evidence that the dialogue captures the action of the story, and the words fit the characters saying them.

Assess Evaluate scenes on how well they use details to reveal character and how clearly they follow the chain of events of the plot. Or, use the Peer Assessment: Dramatic Performance form, p. 116, in **Alternative Assessment.**

Customize for
English Language Learners
Help students understand the premise of the debate by inviting a volunteer to pantomime "jumping-on-a-chair-at-sight-of-a-mouse" women vs. those who are "not as fluttery as their grandmothers." Volunteers can also act out how the hostess, the servant, the naturalist, and the guests act to help students grasp the subject of the debate.

❶ Identify With a Character or Situation Guide students to notice how the hostess and the naturalist react: both are calm, clear-headed, and decisive. Why is it so important that they act quickly and quietly? *Both know that the situation could turn deadly; their chances of preventing death are better if the guests don't panic.*

Reading for Success

❷ Make Inferences Ask students to infer the author's position on the original debate based on the name she gives the hostess—Mrs. Wynnes (wins)—and on the details of her ordeal. *Students may infer that the author rejects the idea that women only scream in a crisis; she supports the belief that women can act with great control in a crisis.*

Reinforce and Extend

Answers

◆ LITERATURE AND YOUR LIFE

Reader's Response Students may say that they hope they might have reacted calmly and quickly, as both Mrs. Wynnes and the naturalist did.

Thematic Focus Both were alert, calm, and decisive. Both kept the well-being of the other guests in mind and acted in ways they hoped would let the situation end safely. They cooperated without planning.

☑ Check Your Comprehension

1. It takes place in a home in a remote part of India.
2. They argue over whether men or women behave better in a crisis.
3. He plays a "game" meant to keep the guests calm and quiet.
4. She reveals that the cobra was lying across her foot.

◆ Critical Thinking

1. He fears that if they knew the real reason for his game they would panic, endangering everyone.
2. He assumes that the naturalist is the only one who knew of the cobra's presence.
3. It shows that a woman faced the greatest danger of all, yet she was calm and acted with control.
4. In most cultures, women are considered capable and courageous.

536

She is staring straight ahead, the muscles of her face contracting slightly. With a small gesture she summons the native boy standing behind her chair. She whispers to him. The boy's eyes widen: he turns quickly and leaves the room. No one else sees this, nor the boy when he puts a bowl of milk on the verandah[1] outside the glass doors.

The American comes to with a start. In India, milk in a bowl means only one thing. It is bait for a snake. He realizes there is a cobra in the room.

He looks up at the rafters—the likeliest place—and sees they are bare. Three corners of the room, which he can see by shifting only slightly, are empty. In the fourth corner a group of servants stand, waiting until the next course can be served. The American realizes there is only one place left—under the table.

His first impulse is to jump back and warn the others. But he knows the commotion will frighten the cobra and it will strike. He speaks quickly, the quality of his voice so <u>arresting</u> that it <u>sobers</u> everyone.

"I want to know just what control everyone at this table has. I will count three hundred—that's five minutes—and not one of you is to

---

1. **verandah** (və ran′ də) *n.*: Open porch.

---

move a single muscle. The persons who move will forfeit 50 rupees.[2] Now! Ready!"

The 20 people sit like stone images while he counts. He is saying ". . . two hundred and eighty . . ." when, out of the corner of his eye, he sees the cobra emerge and make for the bowl of milk. Four or five screams ring out as he jumps to slam shut the verandah doors.

❶ "You certainly were right, Colonel!" the host says. "A man has just shown us an example of real control."

"Just a minute," the American says, turning to his hostess, "there's one thing I'd like to know. Mrs. Wynnes, how did you know that cobra was in the room?"

A faint smile lights up the woman's face as she replies. "Because it was lying across my foot." ❷

---

2. **rupees** (rōō′ pēs) *n.*: Basic monetary unit of India.

◆ Build Vocabulary

arresting (ə rest′ iŋ) *adj.*: Attracting attention; striking

sobers (sō′ bərz) *v.*: Calms; sedates

> **Ask** yourself why the American suddenly begins a game.

> **You can infer** that the host has not seen what the American has.

Guide for Responding

◆ LITERATURE AND YOUR LIFE

Reader's Response How would you have solved the "problem" of the cobra?

Thematic Focus In what ways did the hostess and the American deal with the conflict presented by the cobra?

☑ Check Your Comprehension

1. Where does the story take place?
2. Explain the argument that springs up between the colonel and the young woman.
3. What action does the American take?
4. What does the hostess reveal at the end?

◆ Critical Thinking

INTERPRET

1. Why does the American have everyone play at sitting still without telling them why? **[Infer]**
2. What is the host assuming when he makes his remark about the colonel's being right? **[Infer]**
3. In what way is the final sentence of the story a response to the colonel's argument? **[Connect]**

APPLY

4. How have attitudes toward women changed since the time of this story? **[Relate]**

📖 Beyond the Selection

FURTHER READING
Other Works by Mona Gardner
Shanghai Item and *Other Tales of the Orient*
Middle Heaven
Other Works About Conflicts and Challenges
The House of Dies Drear, Virginia Hamilton
"The Captain and His Horse," Beryl Markham
"Tears of Autumn," Yoshiko Uchida

INTERNET
We suggest the following sites on the Internet (all Web sites are subject to change).
For facts about cobras:
http://cobras.org
For further information on colonial India:
http://www.thatlantic.com/unbound/flashbk/india.htm
We *strongly recommend* that you preview the sites before you send students to them.

Guide for Responding (continued)

◆ Reading for Success

STRATEGIES FOR READING FICTION

Review the strategies and the notes showing how to read fiction. Then, answer these questions about your experience with the story.

1. With which character did you most identify? Why?
2. Note a prediction you made, explain what you based it on, and tell whether it proved accurate.
3. Tell how you answered a question you asked while reading.
4. Explain how you made an inference based on a passage.

◆ Build Vocabulary

USING THE WORD ROOT -spir-

Spirited contains the word root *-spir-*, meaning "breath." Fill in each blank with a *-spir-* word.

   perspire   spirited   inspire

The naturalist wanted to _____?_____ the guests to sit still and hardly _____?_____. When the danger was over, their conversation became very _____?_____.

SPELLING STRATEGY

In a two-syllable word, if the first syllable has a long vowel sound, the consonant that follows is not doubled:

   sobers   (long *o*, followed by single *b*)

On your paper, choose the correct spelling.

1. I'll see you (later, latter).
2. This is your (final, finnal) notice.
3. The (motor, mottor) wouldn't start.
4. I couldn't read the (label, labbel).

USING THE WORD BANK

On your paper, write sentences using the words from the Word Bank as directed.

1. Describe an outdoor scene using the word *naturalist*.
2. Describe an argument using the word *spirited*.
3. Describe a strange sight using the word *arresting*.
4. Describe a newscast using the word *sobers*.

◆ Literary Focus

PLOT

A real dinner party might consist of a series of unrelated conversations and small happenings. However, the story entitled "The Dinner Party" contains a tightly woven **plot** in which one event flows out of another and all the events are related.

1. Summarize the plot, showing how one event flows from another.
2. Diagram the story on your paper, showing the exposition, rising action, climax, and falling action (see p. 533).

◆ Build Grammar Skills

CLAUSES

A **clause** is a group of words with its own subject and verb:

       S   V
   The country is India

An **independent clause** (main clause) has a subject and a verb and can stand by itself as a complete sentence. A **subordinate clause** has a subject and a verb but cannot stand by itself as a complete sentence.

Independent Clause	Subordinate Clause
S V	S V

The 20 people sit like stone images|while he counts.

Practice On your paper, identify the independent clause and the subordinate clause, if any, in each sentence. Also, identify the subject and verb in each clause.

1. The persons who move will forfeit 50 rupees.
2. The American comes to with a start.
3. The corners of the room, which he can see, are empty.
4. As he jumps up to shut the door, screams ring out.
5. A smile lights up her face as she replies.

Writing Application On your paper, write three sentences. Each sentence should contain a main clause and a subordinate clause.

The Dinner Party ◆ 537

◆ Build Grammar Skills

Practice

Subordinate clauses are italicized; S and V follow the word they identify.

1. The persons (S) *who move will forfeit* (V) 50 rupees.
2. The American (S) comes (V) to with a start.
3. The corners (S) of the room, *which he (S) can see (V),* are (V) empty.
4. *As he (S) jumps (V) up to shut the door,* screams (S) ring (V) out.
5. A smile (S) lights (V) up her face *as she (S) replies (V).*

Writing Application

Evaluate students' sentences for their understanding of main clauses and subordinate clauses.

 **Writer's Solution**

For additional instruction and practice, use the lesson in the *Writer's Solution Language Lab CD-ROM* on Independent Clauses and Subordinate Clauses. You may also use the practice pages on Classifying Sentences by Structure, pp. 59–60, in the *Writer's Solution Grammar Practice Book*.

R Answers
Reading for Success

1. Most students will identify with the naturalist, who seems to be the prime mover in the story.
2. Students should clarify the bases for their predictions.
3. Explanations should include the part of the story that prompted the question, how the student found an answer, and how the answer affected understanding of the story.
4. Students might use a flow chart or other kind of diagram to track the logic of their thinking.

◆ Build Vocabulary

Using the Word Root -spir-
inspire; perspire; spirited

Spelling Strategy
1. later; 2. final; 3. motor; 4. label

Using the Word Bank
Possible responses:

1. The naturalist didn't mind wading through the swamp to study snakes.
2. The debate included a spirited argument about feminism.
3. The sight of a double rainbow was so arresting that cars pulled off the highway for a better look.
4. News of the devastation caused by the hurricane sobers listeners around the world.

◆ Literary Focus

1. At a dinner party, guests debate whether men or women react better in a crisis. Soon, the hostess quietly asks her servant to put a bowl of milk on the verandah. The naturalist concludes that this is to lure a cobra from the room. When he can't see the cobra, he guesses it's under the dining table and makes up a calming game for the unknowing guests to play. Someone finally sees the cobra leave the room, and all are relieved. At last, the hostess reveals that the cobra was on her foot.

2. **Climax:** Screams ring out when the guests realize what is happening.

Rising Action: Hostess and naturalist work quietly to get rid of the snake.

Falling Action: Naturalist asks hostess how she knew about the snake.

Exposition: Dinner guests debate women's reactions to crisis.

PLOT DIAGRAM

Resolution: Hostess reveals that the snake was lying on her foot.

Idea Bank

Following are suggestions for matching the Idea Bank topics with your students' performance levels and learning modalities:

Customize for
Performance Levels
Less Advanced Students: 2, 4, 7
Average Students: 1, 4, 5, 6, 7
More Advanced Students: 3, 4, 5, 6, 7

Customize for
Learning Modalities
Verbal/Linguistic: 1, 2, 3, 4, 5, 6, 7
Visual/Spatial: 6, 7
Bodily/Kinesthetic: 4, 5
Logical/Mathematical: 1, 6
Interpersonal: 4, 7
Intrapersonal: 1, 2, 3, 5

Writing Mini-Lesson

Refer students to the Writing Handbook in the back of the book for instruction on the writing process and for further information on monologues. Students can use the Series of Events Chain in **Writing and Language Transparencies,** p. 57, to organize the plot events to react to in the interior monologue.

Writer's Solution

Writing Lab CD-ROM
Have students do the tutorial on Creative Writing. Follow these steps:

1. Have students view the literature model of a monologue.
2. Have them use the Concrete Image Bin activity to gather details for the five senses.
3. Have students draft on computer.
4. Have students revise with the Self-Evaluation checklist.

Writer's Solution Sourcebook
Have students use Chapter 8, "Creative Writing," pp. 234–265, for additional support. The chapter includes in-depth instruction on using figurative language, p. 264.

Build Your Portfolio

Idea Bank

Writing

1. **Research Plan** Jot down two questions that you have after reading "The Dinner Party." Then, explain how you will go about answering these questions. Name specific sources that you'd use to investigate the answers to your questions.

2. **Diary Entry** Take on the role of the colonel in the story. From his point of view, write a diary entry recording his thoughts and feelings about the dinner party.

3. **Sequel** Write a sequel to "The Dinner Party." In it, explore how two or more of the characters reacted to the evening's remarkable events. In your sequel, stay true to the characters as described in the original version.

Speaking and Listening

4. **Scene [Group Activity]** With several classmates, rewrite "The Dinner Party" in script form. Assign parts, and rehearse the dialogue you create. Present your scene for your classmates. **[Performing Arts Link]**

5. **Dinner Speech** As the naturalist, speak to the group around the dinner table. Summarize the evening's events, and explain how they relate to the colonel's statement about women. **[Performing Arts Link]**

Projects

6. **Reality Check** Learn about the habits and behavior of the Indian cobra. Then, use what you've learned to determine whether or not the events of the story could really have occurred. Report your findings to the class. **[Science Link]**

7. **Film Treatment [Group Activity]** With a few classmates, write a memo showing how you would turn this story into a film. Indicate passages where you might insert extra dialogue, include ideas for camera shots, and suggest actors to play the main roles. **[Media Link]**

Writing Mini-Lesson

Interior Monologue

Perhaps you wondered what the hostess was thinking during the story. Write an interior monologue—a speech revealing a character's inner thoughts—that captures the flow of ideas, feelings, and images in the hostess's mind. You may include a few incomplete sentences to give the monologue the flavor of real thought. Be sure your writing is clear enough for readers to follow.

Writing Skills Focus:
Use Details to Reveal Character
Use details that reveal the personality of the hostess. These details are the words that she uses and the thoughts and feelings that she expresses in reaction to events. To express the hostess's frustration with her husband at the end of the story, you might write this:

Model
. . . He doesn't see. Doesn't understand how brave I've been.

Prewriting Outline the events of the plot. Then, beside each item in the outline, jot down the hostess's reactions to it.

Drafting Refer to your annotated outline as you write. However, if you have a new inspiration about her reactions to events, don't hesitate to include it.

> ◆ **Grammar Application**
> Write some sentences containing both independent and subordinate clauses. Put the more important idea in the independent clause and less important ideas in subordinate clauses.

Revising As you read your draft, follow the plot outline to be sure that the character is reacting to events in the right sequence. Also, be sure that her reactions are in keeping with her personality.

✓ ASSESSMENT OPTIONS

Formal Assessment, Selection Test, pp. 159–161, and Assessment Resources Software. The selection test is designed so that it can be easily customized to the performance levels of your students.
Alternative Assessment, p. 37, includes options for less advanced students, more advanced students, verbal/linguistic learners, visual/spatial learners, and interpersonal learners.

PORTFOLIO ASSESSMENT
Use the following rubrics in the **Alternative Assessment** booklet to assess student writing:
Research Plan: Technical Description/Explanation, p. 111
Diary Entry: Fictional Narrative, p. 91
Sequel: Description, p. 93
Writing Mini-Lesson: Expression, p. 90

PART **1** $\quad$ *Plot and Character*

Fisherman's Family, B.J.O. Nordfeldt, Amon Carter Museum, Fort Worth, Texas

The selections in this section focus on the theme of a land of promise. "The Tell-Tale Heart" is a classic Poe story about a man's insanity and his struggle to hide the truth. "An Episode of War" is a short story by Stephen Crane about a lieutenant's plight in the Civil War. In his familiar storytelling style, I. B. Singer's narrator of "The Day I Got Lost" tells a humorous story about his problems finding his way home. "Hamadi" is a short story about a young girl's interest in an old immigrant from Jerusalem.

Customize for
Varying Student Needs
When assigning the selections in this section to your students, keep in mind the following factors:

"The Tell-Tale Heart"
• Classic story by Edgar Allan Poe
• Students may need help with language

"An Episode of War"
• Students may need help with vocabulary
• Provides an opportunity for connecting literature with social studies

"The Day I Got Lost"
• Short story by Isaac Bashevis Singer
• Introduces the character of an absent-minded professor

"Hamadi"
• Introduces a cultural character (Arabic)
• Includes a Beyond Literature Social Studies Connection

 Humanities: Art

Fisherman's Family, by B.J.O. Nordfeldt
   B.J.O. (Bror Julius Olsson) Nordfeldt (1878–1955) was born in Sweden and came to America, where he lived in Minnesota. His paintings often have an abstract geometric quality and focus on the designs found in nature.
   Have students study the painting and then ask the following questions:
1. If you were to create a story about the people in the painting what details would you include? *Students may say that they would include details about how the woman seems to be protecting the*

baby and how the girl looks angry or upset. The story may be more about the father and the girl because they are in the forefront of the painting. The houses or buildings in the background might provide the setting. The man's hat and jacket may mean that the people are on their way to an event.

2. What does the title of the painting tell you about the characters? *Some students may say that the title confirms the notion that this is a painting of a family. Also, from the title we learn that the father is a fisherman, which probably means they live in a fishing village.*

539

Guide for Reading

OBJECTIVES

1. To read, comprehend, and interpret a short story
2. To relate a short story to personal experience
3. To predict what will happen next
4. To appreciate suspense
5. To build vocabulary in context and learn the word root -found-
6. To identify adverb clauses
7. To write a suspenseful anecdote by creating suspense
8. To respond to the story through writing, speaking and listening, and projects

SKILLS INSTRUCTION

Vocabulary:
Word Roots: -found-
Spelling:
Words With the *zhun* Sound Spelled *sion*
Grammar:
Adverb Clauses
Reading Strategy:
Predict
Literary Focus:
Suspense in a Plot

Writing:
Create Suspense
Speaking and Listening:
News Interview (Teacher Edition)
Viewing and Representing:
Suspense (Teacher Edition)
Critical Viewing:
Connect; Assess

PORTFOLIO OPPORTUNITIES

Writing: Prediction; Police Report; Comparative Essay
Writing Mini-Lesson: Suspenseful Anecdote
Speaking and Listening: News Interview; Opening Argument
Projects: Movie Review; Literary Panel

More About the Author
Edgar Allan Poe, one of the first American writers to try to support himself wholly through his writing, is the acknowledged inventor of the detective story. Although Poe's own personal tragedies influenced his writing, his life was, in fact, taking a turn for the better when he unexpectedly died. How he died remains a mystery, but recent scholarship proposes that he was a victim of an unfortunate election-year practice of the time—he was drugged by a voting gang so that he would cast his ballot again and again.

Meet the Author:

Edgar Allan Poe (1809–1849)

If Poe's stories and poems deal with sorrow, crime, and horror, it's because his own life was so troubled. He was born in Boston, Massachusetts, to a family of impoverished traveling actors. While Poe was still a young child, his father deserted the family. Shortly afterward, his mother died.

A Family Rift Poe was raised, but never formally adopted, by Mr. and Mrs. John Allan of Richmond, Virginia. As he grew up, Poe quarreled with his adoptive father. Often their disputes focused on Poe's spending and his increasing debts.

Famed, but Poor Poe achieved early recognition when his story "MS. found in a bottle" won a literary contest in 1833. His stories and poems continued to attract notice, but they did not gain him financial success. In 1849, two years after the death of his wife, Virginia, Poe died penniless and alone.

THE STORY BEHIND THE STORY

While reading an 1830 pamphlet about a real murder, Poe found many of the details he used in "The Tell-Tale Heart." Here are passages from this pamphlet: "Deep sleep had fallen on the destined victim. . . . A healthful old man . . . The assassin enters, and beholds his victim before him. . . ."

◆ LITERATURE AND YOUR LIFE

CONNECT YOUR EXPERIENCE

You're lying in bed, trying to fall asleep, but a leaky faucet won't stop dripping. It's not a loud noise, really, but it seems to become louder and louder, filling the house. Anxiously, you wait for every drop. This common experience shows that, at times, your imagination may exaggerate what you hear or see. In this story, Poe uses this type of experience to create terror.

THEMATIC FOCUS: Strange Doings

How does Poe's choice of a storyteller make this tale even stranger and more frightening?

◆ Background for Understanding

LITERATURE

Poe's great contribution to American literature was to make the short story into an art form. He believed that in a brief story, a writer could create a "unity of effect." By this he meant that every element—from sentence rhythm to a character's personality—would help create a single impression. In "The Tell-Tale Heart" and many of his stories, that impression is one of horror.

◆ Build Vocabulary

WORD ROOTS: -found-

The word root -found- means "bottom." When the narrator of this story suggests that an old man isn't "profound" enough to understand a killer's deceptions, he means the old man is not "able to get to the bottom of things."

WORD BANK

Which word from the list means "ability of a sage" or "wisdom"? Check the Build Vocabulary box on page 543 to see if you chose correctly.

acute
dissimulation
profound
sagacity
crevice
gesticulations
derision

 Prentice Hall Literature Program Resources

REINFORCE / RETEACH / EXTEND

Selection Support Pages
Build Vocabulary: Word Roots: -found-, p. 202
Build Spelling Skills, p. 203
Build Grammar Skills: Adverb Clauses, p. 204
Reading Strategy: Predict, p. 205
Literary Focus: Suspense, p. 206
Strategies for Diverse Student Needs, pp. 75–76
Beyond Literature Career Connection: Set Designer, p. 38

Formal Assessment Selection Test, pp. 162–164, Assessment Resources Software
Alternative Assessment, p. 38
Resource Pro CD-ROM
"The Tell-Tale Heart"—includes all resource material and customizable lesson plan
Listening to Literature Audiocassettes
"The Tell-Tale Heart"

The Tell-Tale Heart

M.C. Escher "Self-Portrait" © 1998 Cordon Art B.V. Baarn-Holland

◆ Literary Focus

SUSPENSE IN A PLOT

Suspense is a feeling of uncertainty about the outcome of events, which keeps you interested in a story's plot. Writers create suspense by hinting at an outcome or by delaying an event that you know is coming. In other words, suspense is a kind of game that writers play with you, showing you some things and hiding others.

To follow Poe's game of suspense in "The Tell-Tale Heart," take notice of the details the narrator gives you and those he holds back.

◆ Reading Strategy

PREDICT

You'll enjoy the suspense in a plot if you continually **predict** what will happen next. This kind of guessing is what involves you in the story. It's not important to be right every time, but it is important to keep predicting and to base your predictions on details found in the story.

Use a diagram like the one below to play the "suspense game" with Poe:

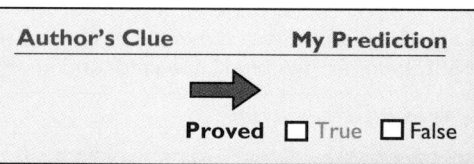

Author's Clue		My Prediction
	Proved ☐ True	☐ False

Guide for Reading ◆ 541

Interest Grabber Ask students to hold in their hands a pencil, or something about that size, and to stand up. Challenge them to see how long they can stay on their feet, completely motionless, holding that object in the same position. Time them. After a minute or two, stop the activity and let students relax. Ask them to predict how much longer they could have held their position. Then, lead them to the story by telling them that the narrator is, among other things, able to stand stock-still for a whole hour.

◆ Build Grammar Skills

Adverb Clauses If you wish to introduce the grammar concept for this selection before students read, refer to the instruction on p. 548.

Customize for
Less Proficient Readers
"The Tell-Tale Heart" contains many lengthy and complicated sentences. Help students break these down into short, simple sentences in order to interpret their meanings.

Customize for
More Advanced Students
The narrator of the story claims to suffer from an "overacuteness of the senses." Have students look for evidence of how this condition ties the story together and creates what Poe called a "unity of effect."

Humanities: Art

Self-Portrait, by M. C. Escher Maurits Cornelis Escher (1898–1972) was born in the Netherlands and lived in Italy, Switzerland, and Belgium. He is known for his use of mathematical forms in his sketches, woodcuts, lithographs, and watercolors—tessellations and transformations create ever-changing visual patterns.
1. Do you think this face represents the narrator or the old man? Why? *Students may say that because of its intense, focused stare, the face suggests the narrator.*
2. How would you describe the look on this man's face? *Students may say that it expresses concentration, understanding, and even a hint of amusement.*

Preparing for Standardized Tests

Grammar The grammar concept for this story is adverb clauses. Standardized tests may test students' understanding of the function of this type of clause by expecting them to use adverb clauses properly in their writing, or by asking them to identify adverb clauses. Point out that adverb clauses are subordinate clauses that function as adverbs, and answer the questions *when, where, how, why, to what extent,* or *under what conditions.* Then present the following sample test question:

Identify the sentence that contains an adverb clause.

(A) He buried the body parts under the floor.
(B) He stood, and they sat on chairs.
(C) Until the suspect cried out, the police had been fooled entirely.
(D) His own heart, which must have been beating rapidly, is what the suspect heard.

Students should recognize that only (C) contains an adverb clause. *Until the suspect cried out* is a subordinate clause that answers the question *when.* (D) contains a subordinate clause, but it functions as an adjective.

One-Minute Insight

"The Tell-Tale Heart" is told by a murderer, who explains his behavior by claiming that he suffers from an "overacuteness of the senses." He explains his obsession with the eye of an old man and describes his nightly visits during which he looked in on the man as he slept. Ironically, it is the overacuteness of his senses that causes the narrator not only to kill but to admit his guilt.

◆ Reading Strategy

❶ **Predict** Draw students' attention to the title of the story. Ask them to explain what "tell-tale" means. Then, ask them to predict, from the title, what the story will be about. *"Tell-tale" means revealing what is meant to be kept secret. Students familiar with the work of Poe may guess that in some way a heart gives away a crime.*

Clarification

❷ Make certain that students understand that by *mad* the narrator here means "crazy" or "insane," not the common modern meaning, "angry."

Thematic Focus

❸ **Strange Doings** Discuss with students their impression of the narrator. Ask them to describe the kind of story they think he is about to tell. *Students may say that they find the narrator unnerving and peculiar. Some may question why he insists right off that he is not mad. They may predict that the story will be an eerie, unsettling one.*

◆ Literary Focus

❹ **Suspense** *Students may say that Poe will keep the reader in suspense about when and how the murder will occur and about how or if the murderer gets caught.*

Customize for
English Language Learners

This selection contains several words or expressions that may be new to students or used in a way unfamiliar to them, but that are neither defined nor included in the Build Vocabulary section. Help students create a visual glossary for words such as *vulture, lantern, evil eye, pitch,* and *shutters.*

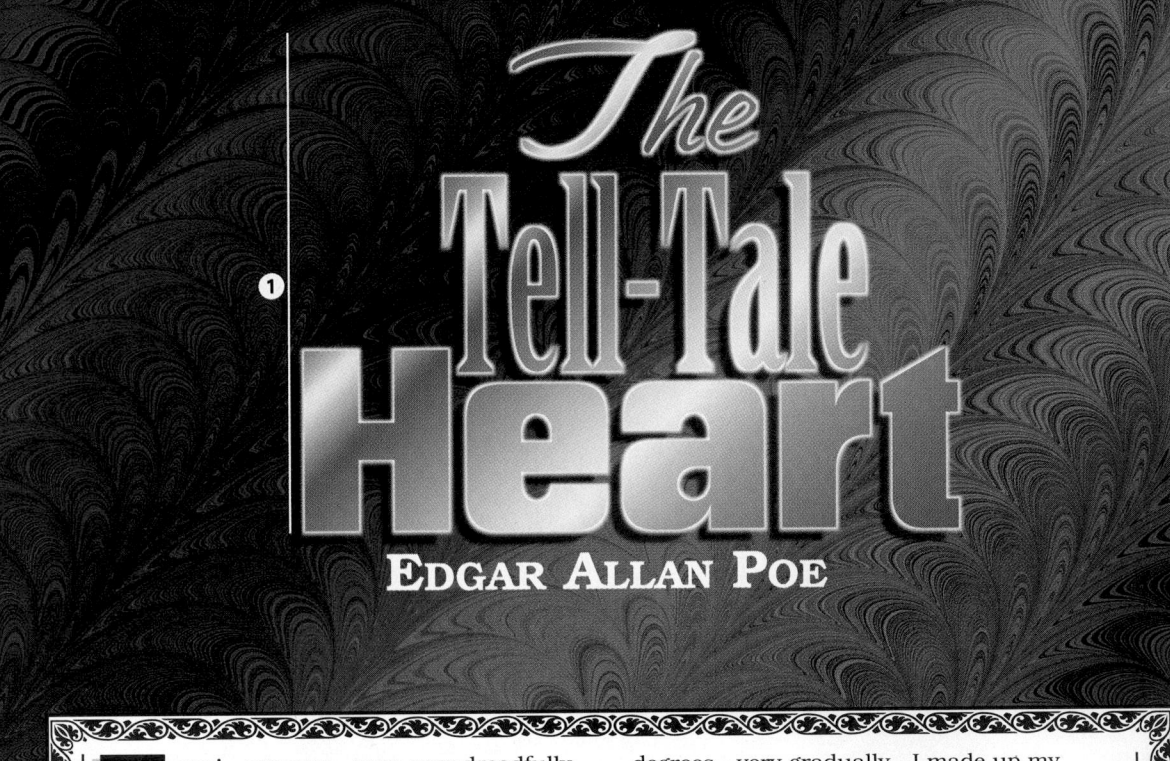

The Tell-Tale Heart
EDGAR ALLAN POE

True!—nervous—very, very dreadfully nervous I had been and am; but why *will* you say that I am mad? The disease had sharpened my senses—not destroyed—not dulled them. Above all was the sense of hearing acute. I heard all things in the heaven and in the earth. I heard many things in hell. How, then, am I mad? Hearken![1] and observe how healthily—how calmly I can tell you the whole story.

It is impossible to say how first the idea entered my brain; but once conceived, it haunted me day and night. Object there was none. Passion there was none. I loved the old man. He had never wronged me. He had never given me insult. For his gold I had no desire. I think it was his eye! yes, it was this! One of his eyes resembled that of a vulture— a pale blue eye, with a film over it. Whenever it fell upon me, my blood ran cold; and so by degrees—very gradually—I made up my mind to take the life of the old man, and thus rid myself of the eye forever.

Now this is the point. You fancy me mad. Madmen know nothing. But you should have seen *me.* You should have seen how wisely I proceeded—with what caution— with what foresight—with what dissimulation I went to work! I was never kinder to the old man than during the whole week before I killed him. And every night, about midnight, I turned the latch of his door and opened it—oh, so gently! And then, when I had made an opening sufficient for my head, I put in a dark lantern, all closed, closed, so that no light shone out, and then I thrust in my head. Oh, you would have laughed to see how cunningly I thrust it in! I moved it slowly—very, very slowly, so that I might not disturb the old man's sleep. It took me an

◆ Literary Focus
How do you think Poe will keep you in suspense about a murder that you know already has occurred?

---
1. **Hearken** (här´ kən) *v.*: Listen.

542 ◆ Short Stories

Block Scheduling Strategies

Consider these suggestions to take advantage of extended class time:

• Introduce the concepts of strange doings and of suspense by discussing the Thematic Focus, p. 540, and the Literary Focus, p. 541.

• Have students read independently. Guide them to look for indications of the strangeness of the storyteller. Have them take notice of details Poe shows as well as those he hides.

• To help students prepare for the Writing Mini-Lesson, refer them to Chapter 1, "Expression," in Writer's Solution.

• Provide time for students who do the Movie Review project on p. 549 to read the stories upon which the chosen films are based. Devote class time to having those students present their reviews.

• Play the audiocassette of the story. Invite discussion of the reading. Have students discuss how it affects their views of the narrator and their interpretations of the tale.

🎧 **Listening to Literature Audiocassettes**

A scene from "The Tell-Tale Heart," a U.P.A. short based on the Edgar Allan Poe story distributed by Columbia Pictures

Thematic Focus

❺ Strange Doings What does the term "vulture eye" suggest? What does the narrator's obsession with it suggest about him? *Students may say that a "vulture eye" suggests a beast of prey awaiting its next victim. They may say that the narrator's obsession with the eye is very odd, suggesting that he is mad and dangerous. They may also say that people are often revolted by abnormal physical features and Poe is using this to induce some reader identification with the narrator.*

Comprehension Check ☑

❻ What has been going on in that house, night after night? *Every night, at midnight, the narrator looks in on the old man and shines a ray of light on his closed eye as he sleeps.*

►Critical Viewing◄

❼ Connect *Students may note that the eye in the picture is large and droopy, but not one they would necessarily associate with a bird of prey.*

Customize for
Intrapersonal Learners
Invite students to keep a response journal as they read the story. Encourage them to respond personally to descriptive details that create the story's mood of horror. Invite them to include words or descriptions of their own that they think would add to the atmosphere of the tale.

hour to place my whole head within the opening so far that I could see him as he lay upon his bed. Ha!—would a madman have been so wise as this? And then, when my head was well in the room, I undid the lantern cautiously—oh, so cautiously—cautiously (for the hinges creaked)—I undid it just so much that a single thin ray fell upon the vulture eye. And this I did for seven long nights—every night just at midnight—but I found the eye always closed; and so it was impossible to do the work; for it was not the old man who vexed me, but his evil eye. And every morning, when the day broke, I went boldly into the chamber, and spoke courageously to him, calling him by name in a hearty tone, and inquiring how he had passed the night. So you see he would have been a very <u>profound</u> old man, indeed, to suspect that every night, just at twelve, I looked in upon him while he slept.

Upon the eighth night I was more than usually cautious in opening the door. A watch's minute hand moves more quickly than did

▲ **Critical Viewing** Does the man in this drawing seem to have a "vulture eye," as described in the beginning of the story? Explain. [Connect] ⑦

mine. Never, before that night, had I *felt* the extent of my own powers—of my <u>sagacity</u>. I could scarcely contain my feelings of triumph. To think that there I was, opening the door, little by little, and he not even to dream of my secret deeds or thoughts. I fairly chuckled at the idea; and perhaps he heard me; for he moved on the bed suddenly, as if startled. Now you may think that I drew back—but no. His room was as black as pitch with the thick

◆ Build Vocabulary

acute (ə kyōōt´) *adj.*: Sensitive

dissimulation (di sim´ yə lā´ shən) *n.*: Hiding of one's feelings or purposes

profound (prō found´) *adj.*: Intellectually deep; getting to the bottom of the matter

sagacity (sə gas´ ə tē) *n.*: High intelligence and sound judgment

The Tell-Tale Heart ◆ 543

Humanities: Art

Still Photography The images on this page and pp. 545 and 546 are still photographs from a black-and-white animated film version of "The Tell-Tale Heart." Point out that a still photo presents "stopped" action from an ongoing scene. Obviously a still does not represent the scene that is taking place in the same manner as the film, but the image can give viewers a sense of character, setting, and plot. Have students study the images and locate text that corresponds to the stills. Then, use these questions for discussion:

1. Does this man look like the one described in the story? *Students may say that he appears old and frail, but alert, and lives in a large, eccentric house—since the narrator's views are not to be trusted, this man could easily be the one described.*

2. What clues do the stills give about the time and setting of the story? *The clothes worn point to the nineteenth century, as do the furnishings and details of the house. The eerie shadows and appearances of the men indicate mystery and strange and evil doings.*

Thematic Focus

❶ Strange Doings Ask students to explain what the feat tells about the narrator. *Students may say that it gives another indication of his control and, more so, of his instability.*

◆ Literary Focus

❷ Suspense Have students analyze how Poe adds to the suspense with this passage. *First, he describes the moment-by-moment terror that the old man is experiencing (as seen by the narrator). Then, he personifies death, and in so doing, uses words like "stalking," "black shadow," "mournful," and "victim" to create a sense of horror and foreboding.*

Comprehension Check ☑

❸ How does the narrator react to the sight of the eye and the beating of the old man's heart? *Both the sight of the eye and the sound of the heart infuriate and stimulate him.*

Clarification

❹ Point out to students that a *tattoo*, in this case, is a noise, a continuous drumming or rapping. You can connect this word to "rat-tat-tat," which may be familiar.

◆ LITERATURE AND YOUR LIFE

❺ *Most students will remember some occasion when their imaginations got the better of them. Invite them to share these experiences.*

---

darkness (for the shutters were close fastened, through fear of robbers), and so I knew that he could not see the opening of the door, and I kept pushing it on steadily, steadily.

I had my head in, and was about to open the lantern, when my thumb slipped upon the tin fastening, and the old man sprang up in the bed, crying out—"Who's there?"

I kept quite still and said nothing. For a whole hour I did not move a muscle, and in the meantime I did not hear him lie down. He was still sitting up in the bed, listening;—just as I have done, night after night, hearkening to the deathwatches² in the wall.

Presently I heard a slight groan, and I knew it was the groan of mortal terror. It was not a groan of pain or of grief—oh, no!—it was the low stifled sound that arises from the bottom of the soul when overcharged with awe. I knew the sound well. Many a night, just at midnight, when all the world slept, it has welled up from my own bosom, deepening, with its dreadful echo, the terrors that distracted me. I say I knew it well. I knew what the old man felt, and pitied him, although I chuckled at heart. I knew that he had been lying awake ever since the first slight noise, when he had turned in the bed. His fears had been ever since growing upon him. He had been trying to fancy them causeless, but could not. He had been saying to himself— "It is nothing but the wind in the chimney— it is only a mouse crossing the floor," or "it is merely a cricket which has made a single chirp." Yes, he has been trying to comfort himself with these suppositions: but he had found all in vain. *All in vain;* because Death, in approaching him, had stalked with his black shadow before him, and enveloped the victim. And it was the mournful influence of the unperceived shadow that caused him to feel—although he neither saw nor heard—to *feel* the presence of my head within the room.

---

2. **deathwatches** (deth′ woch′ əz) *n.:* Wood-boring beetles whose heads make a tapping sound superstitiously regarded as an omen of death.

When I had waited a long time, very patiently, without hearing him lie down, I resolved to open a little—a very, very little crevice in the lantern. So I opened it—you cannot imagine how stealthily, stealthily— until, at length, a single dim ray, like the thread of the spider, shot from out the crevice and fell upon the vulture eye.

It was open—wide, wide open—and I grew furious as I gazed upon it. I saw it with perfect distinctness—all a dull blue, with a hideous veil over it that chilled the very marrow in my bones; but I could see nothing else of the old man's face or person for I had directed the ray as if by instinct, precisely upon the spot.

And now—have I not told you that what you mistake for madness is but overacuteness of the senses?—now, I say, there came to my ears a low, dull, quick sound, such as a watch makes when enveloped in cotton. I knew *that* sound well, too. It was the beating of the old man's heart. It increased my fury, as the beating of a drum stimulates the soldier into courage.

But even yet I refrained and kept still. I scarcely breathed. I held the lantern motionless. I tried how steadily I could maintain the ray upon the eye. Meantime the hellish tattoo of the heart increased. It grew quicker and quicker, and louder and louder every instant. The old man's terror *must* have been extreme! It grew louder, I say, louder every moment!—do you mark me well? I have told you that I am nervous: so I am. And now at the dead hour of the night, amid the dreadful silence of that old house, so strange a noise as this excited me to uncontrollable terror. Yet, for some minutes longer I refrained and stood still. But the beating grew

◆ Literature and Your Life

Perhaps he's hearing his own heart. In any case, has your imagination ever exaggerated what you heard or saw? Explain.

◆ Build Vocabulary

crevice (krev′ is) *n.:* A narrow opening

louder, louder! I thought the heart must burst. And now a new anxiety seized me—the sound would be heard by a neighbor! The old man's hour had come! With a loud yell, I threw open the lantern and leaped into the room. He shrieked once—once only. In an instant I dragged him to the floor, and pulled the heavy bed over him. I then smiled gaily, to find the deed so far done. But, for many minutes, the heart beat on with a muffled sound. This, however, did not vex me; it would not be heard through the wall. At length it ceased. The old man was dead. I removed the bed and examined the corpse. Yes, he was stone, stone dead. I placed my hand upon the heart and held it there many minutes. There was no pulsation. He was stone dead. His eye would trouble me no more.

If still you think me mad, you will think so no longer when I describe the wise precautions I took for the concealment of the body. The night waned, and I worked hastily, but in silence. First of all I dismembered the corpse. I cut off the head and the arms and the legs.

I then took up three planks from the flooring of the chamber, and deposited all between the scantlings.[3] I then replaced the boards so cleverly, so cunningly, that no human eye—not even *his*—could have detected anything wrong. There was nothing to wash out—no stain of any kind— no blood-spot whatever. I had been too wary for that. A tub had caught all—ha! ha!

When I had made an end of these labors, it was four o'clock—still dark as midnight. As the bell sounded the hour, there came a knocking at the street door. I went down to open it with a light heart—for what had I *now* to fear? There entered three men, who introduced themselves, with perfect suavity, as officers of the police. A shriek had been heard by a neighbor during the

---

3. **scantlings** (skant´ liŋz) *n.*: Small beams or timbers.

▶ **Critical Viewing** This drawing depicts the two policemen sent to search the house. What do they know or what can they infer about the situation to make them cautious? [Assess]

A scene from "The Tell-Tale Heart," a U.P.A. short based on the Edgar Allan Poe story distributed by Columbia Pictures

The Tell-Tale Heart ◆ 545

◆ **Reading Strategy**

6 Predict Ask students to summarize what has just happened and to predict what will happen next. Will the narrator get caught? *Students may say that the narrator, disturbed by the sound of the man's (or his own) beating heart, fell upon him and killed him. They may guess that the man's screams were heard and that the killer will eventually get caught. Some may predict that the narrator will be able to cover up the crime but will be "done in" by his madness.*

◆ **Critical Thinking**

7 Make a Judgment Ask students to tell whether they still think the narrator is mad, even after they have read about his careful precautions in concealing the body. *Most students will say that the narrator was mad to have been infatuated with the man's eye and heartbeat, and to have killed him. They are not likely to view the careful steps he took after the murder as reasons to change their minds.*

▶ **Critical Viewing** ◀

8 Assess *Students may say that nothing in the drawing would cause the police to be suspicious, except perhaps that this is a large, creepy-looking house. Some might say that the police might still be concerned about that shriek heard in the night.*

Viewing and Representing Mini-Lesson

Suspense

This mini-lesson will extend students understanding of suspense.

Introduce Invite students to explain why a suspenseful book or movie may have "spooked" them. Writers such as Poe and Stephen King use characters and settings in their "eerie" writing just as movie-makers such as Alfred Hitchcock do. Movies, however, have the advantage of special effects.

Develop Group students in threes or fours and have them brainstorm for ideas about what "spooks" people. Then, have each group create a

visual representation of suspense. They may choose to use a scene from "The Tell-Tale Heart" as a basis or simply as inspiration. Encourage them to be creative, but monitor them so that they do not digress with clichéd representations.

Apply Provide a variety of art materials for students to use to create 2-dimensional represenations. Suggest that they might want to explore shadow and shading for suspenseful effects.

Assess Evaluate students on their group work and the suspenseful intent that is evidenced in their representations.

◆ Reading Strategy

❶ Predict *Some students may predict that it will be the narrator's madness, not police work, that will do him in.*

Thematic Focus

❷ Strange Doings Ask students to assess the narrator's behavior with the police officers in this scene. Why is he acting this way? *He invites them in to rest and chat exactly where the crime was committed and above where the body is buried because he thinks they could never detect his crime. He may be right, but he is showing excess pride and overconfidence here and setting himself up for a fall.*

►Critical Viewing◄

❸ Connect *The drawing illustrates the point in the story at which the police arrive at the house and are about to enter the old man's room.*

◆ Literary Focus

❹ Suspense Discuss with students that Poe's tales are exciting because they emphasize sensual experience. *They describe sights and sounds and force readers to feel emotional events unfolding. Guide students to look for passages like this one, in which seeing or hearing is a key element in creating suspense.*

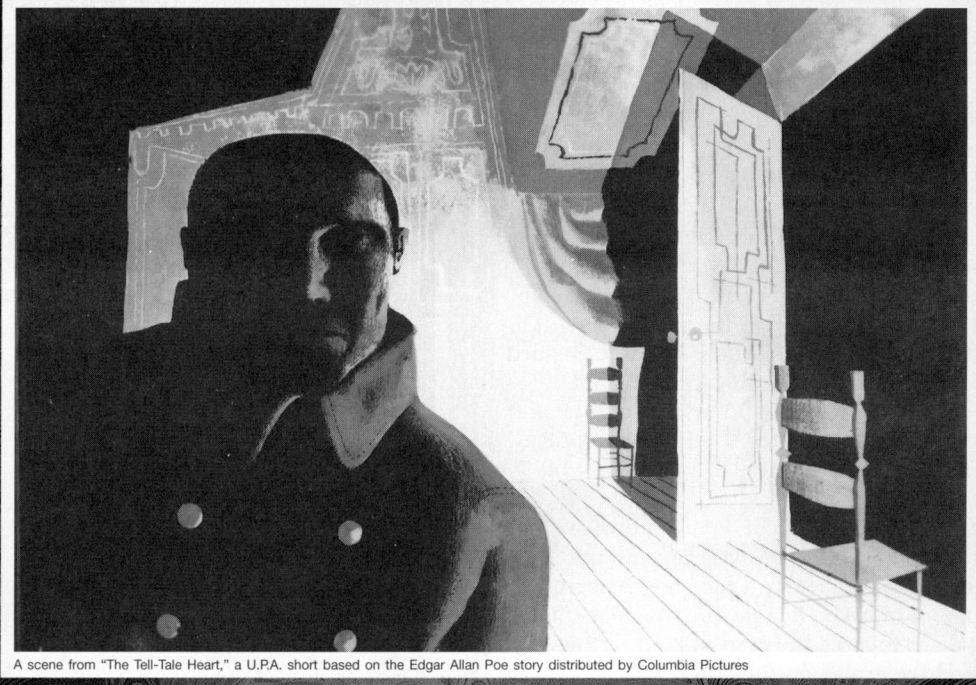

A scene from "The Tell-Tale Heart," a U.P.A. short based on the Edgar Allan Poe story distributed by Columbia Pictures

night; suspicion of foul play had been aroused; information had been lodged at the police office, and they (the officers) had been deputed to search the premises.

◆ **Reading Strategy**
Will the police officers discover the crime? Explain.

I smiled—for *what* had I to fear? I bade the gentlemen welcome. The shriek, I said, was my own in a dream. The old man, I mentioned, was absent in the country. I took my visitors all over the house. I bade them search—search *well.* I led them, at length, to *his* chamber. I showed them his treasures, secure, undisturbed. In the enthusiasm of my confidence, I brought chairs into the room, and desired them *here* to rest from their fatigues, while I myself, in the wild audacity of my perfect triumph, placed my own seat upon the very spot beneath which reposed the corpse of the victim.

The officers were satisfied. My *manner* had convinced them. I was singularly at ease.

▲ **Critical Viewing** What point in the story does this drawing illustrate? **[Connect]** ❸

They sat, and while I answered cheerily, they chatted of familiar things. But, ere long, I felt myself getting pale and wished them gone. My head ached, and I fancied a ringing in my ears: but still they sat and still they chatted. The ringing became more distinct:—it continued and became more distinct: I talked more freely to get rid of the feeling: but it continued and gained definitiveness—until, at length, I found that the noise was *not* within my ears.

No doubt I now grew *very* pale—but I talked more fluently, and with a heightened voice. Yet the sound increased—and what could I do? It was a *low, dull, quick sound*— ❹

◆ **Build Vocabulary**

gesticulations (jes tik′ yŌŌ lā′ shənz) *n.:* Energetic hand or arm movements

derision (di rizh′ ən) *n.:* Contempt; ridicule

546 ◆ Short Stories

Speaking and Listening Mini-Lesson

News Interview

This mini-lesson supports the Speaking and Listening activity in the Idea Bank on p. 549.

Introduce Have students talk about the kinds of questions a reporter might ask a suspect awaiting trial, and the kinds of responses they might get.

Develop Have students choose whether they will be a reporter or a suspect. Students might also be defense attorneys who work with the suspect to answer all questions. Then, have the reporters meet in the "news room" to brainstorm for a list of questions to ask. Have all sus-

pects (and attorneys) meet in the "jail" to go over their responses to questions they anticipate.

Apply If you have access to audio- or videotape equipment, record the interviews.

Assess Evaluate reporters on how their questions reflect the facts of the case, including unknowns, and how well they deduce, infer, or predict details. Evaluate suspects and attorneys on how accurately their answers reflect the case's details and the personality of the narrator. Or, use the Peer Assessment: Dramatic Performance form, p. 116, in **Alternative Assessment.**

much such a sound as a watch makes when enveloped in cotton. I gasped for breath—and yet the officers heard it not. I talked more quickly—more vehemently; but the noise steadily increased. I arose and argued about trifles, in a high key and with violent <u>gesticulations</u>; but the noise steadily increased. Why *would* they not be gone? I paced the floor to and fro with heavy strides, as if excited to fury by the observations of the men—but the noise steadily increased. Oh! what *could* I do? I foamed—I raved—I swore! I swung the chair upon which I had been sitting, and grated it upon the boards, but the noise arose over all, and continually increased. It grew louder—louder—*louder!* And still the men chatted pleasantly, and smiled.

Was it possible they heard not?— no, no! They heard!—they suspected!— they *knew!* —they were making a mockery of my horror!—this I thought, and this I think. But anything was better than this agony! Anything was more tolerable than this <u>derision</u>! I could bear those hypocritical smiles no longer! I felt that I must scream or die!—and now again! hark! louder! louder! louder! *louder!*—

"Villains!" I shrieked, "dissemble[4] no more! I admit the deed!—tear up the planks!—here, here!—it is the beating of his hideous heart!"

---

4. **dissemble** (di sem′ bəl) *v.:* Conceal under a false appearance; to conceal the truth of one's true feelings or motives.

Guide for Responding

◆ LITERATURE AND YOUR LIFE

Reader's Response What are your thoughts about the narrator of this story?

Thematic Focus Would this tale seem less strange if it were told by a police officer? Explain.

Tableau Think of a scene between the old man and the narrator that best conveys the effect of the story. Then, "pose" with a partner to create a tableau of this scene. Don't speak. Convey feelings through body language and facial expression.

☑ Check Your Comprehension

1. Why does the narrator kill the old man?
2. Summarize the steps of his plan.
3. Why do the police arrive?
4. What sound drives the narrator to confess to the crime?

◆ Critical Thinking

INTERPRET

1. In what way is the narrator careful about the means he uses and careless about whether his act is justified? **[Analyze]**
2. Do you think that the narrator feels guilty for his crime? Why or why not? **[Interpret]**
3. At the end, do you think anyone but the narrator hears the beating of the old man's heart? Explain. **[Infer]**

EVALUATE

4. Do the narrator's cleverness and carefulness prove he isn't "mad"? Explain. **[Make a Judgment]**

APPLY

5. Why do you think people like to read tales of terror, such as this one? **[Speculate]**

The Tell-Tale Heart ◆ 547

Beyond the Selection

FURTHER READING
Other Works by Edgar Allan Poe
"The Cask of Amontillado"
"The Fall of the House of Usher"
"The Black Cat"
"The Pit and the Pendulum"
Other Horror Stories
Dracula, Bram Stoker
Frankenstein or the Modern Prometheus,
Mary Wollstonecraft Shelley
The Shining, Stephen King

INTERNET
We suggest the following site on the Internet (all Web sites are subject to change).
For more information about Edgar Allen Poe:
http://www.gothic.net.poe
We *strongly recommend* that you preview the site before you send students to it.

◆ Critical Thinking

5 Hypothesize Ask students to tell what they think is making the beating sound. *Some students may say that the narrator hears his own heart pounding; others may suggest that in his madness, he thinks he hears the beating heart of the dead man; still others may say that the old man's heart is actually beating, because somehow, he is alive.*

Reinforce and Extend

Answers
◆ LITERATURE AND YOUR LIFE

Reader's Response Students can discuss their definitions of insanity and apply them to the narrator.

Thematic Focus Students may say that a police officer's emphasis on nothing but the facts would not capture the suspense and mystery.

☑ Check Your Comprehension

1. He killed him because he could not tolerate the old man's eye, which he thought resembled that of a vulture.
2. The narrator's plan, as far as it goes, seems to be to gain the old man's trust and then practice entering the room while he is asleep to kill him in his sleep. Since the old man wakes up, it's impossible to say if things work out as planned.
3. The police arrived because a neighbor hears the old man's scream.
4. The sound of a heart beating causes the narrator to confess.

◆ Critical Thinking

1. The narrator plans and carries out a near-perfect crime. Although he got on well with the man, he killed him simply because his eye was annoying.
2. Students are likely to think that he didn't feel guilt, only fear that the police could hear the beating sound and that he would be caught.
3. No. The narrator is mad. The heart is not beating; he just imagines that it is, and fears, unjustifiably, that the police can hear it, too.
4. His carefulness and cleverness, as well as his powers of concentration, don't prove he isn't mad, they just make him more dangerous.
5. Students might say that people like being scared, that horror stories are a form of escapism, a way to leave everyday cares behind.

◆ Reading Strategy

1. Students may predict that he will kill the man because he appears to be mad enough to do it.
2. Possible response: Students may predict that the narrator's care and cunning will fool the police.
3. Possible response: Students may not have predicted that the narrator would cause himself to get caught.

◆ Build Vocabulary

Using the Word Root -found-

1. In laying the foundation, Poe introduced the prototype, the basic fundamentals, of the detective story.
2. He knew tales from top to bottom.
3. The critics think that Poe, among others, started a literary movement others built upon.

Spelling Strategy

1. precision;   2. revision
3. collision

Using the Word Bank

1. b   3. c   5. a   7. a
2. a   4. c   6. b

◆ Literary Focus

1. Students might cite the slow entries into the old man's room or the passage in which the narrator begins to hear the heart beating in the presence of the police.
2. Students may say that the suspense is partially a product of what the murderer will do or say under those circumstances.

◆ Build Grammar Skills

Practice

1. When the day broke; when
2. as he lay upon the bed; under what conditions, or where
3. since the first slight noise; to what extent, or when
4. When I had made an end of these labors; when
5. because he acted strangely; why

Writing Application

Possible responses:
1. He might be found innocent because he was insane.
2. Although he pleaded insanity, the murderer was found guilty.
3. As he awaited the verdict, he squirmed in his seat.

Guide for Responding (continued)

◆ Reading Strategy

PREDICT

When you **predict,** you use information the author provides to guess what will happen.
1. When the narrator says that he "made up his mind to take the life of the old man," did you predict he really would kill him? Why or why not?
2. Give one of your predictions and the evidence on which it was based.
3. Was there an event you didn't predict? Explain.

◆ Build Vocabulary

USING THE WORD ROOT -found-

Profound contains the word root -found-, meaning "bottom." Show how each -found- word relates to starting from, or getting to, the "bottom."
1. Poe laid the *foundation* for the detective story.
2. He was *profound* in his knowledge of tales.
3. Critics regard him as one of the *founders* of American literature.

SPELLING STRATEGY

The *zhun* sound at the end of a word, as in *derision,* is usually spelled *sion*. On your paper, fill in each blank with a word ending in a *zhun* sound.
1. The noun form of the adjective *precise*: _____?_____
2. The noun form of the verb *revise*: _____?_____
3. The noun form of the verb *collide*: _____?_____

USING THE WORD BANK

On your paper, write the letter of the word or words opposite in meaning to the Word Bank word.
1. acute: (a) pretty, (b) dull, (c) crooked
2. dissimulation: (a) honesty, (b) frown, (c) imitation
3. profound: (a) lost, (b) unfounded, (c) shallow
4. sagacity: (a) wisdom, (b) stiffness, (c) stupidity
5. crevice: (a) wide opening, (b) small opening, (c) deep hole
6. gesticulations: (a) food, (b) graceful gestures, (c) cramps
7. derision: (a) praise, (b) mockery, (c) revision

◆ Literary Focus

SUSPENSE IN A PLOT

Poe creates **suspense,** a feeling of uncertainty, by having his narrator confess his crime right away but then give a slow, detailed account of the crime. He forces you to experience, instant by instant, every detail of the murder. Also, he leaves you wondering about the sanity of the narrator and whether or not he'll be caught.
1. Cite a passage from the story that shows how Poe creates suspense by slowing the action to a crawl.
2. How does not knowing the police officers' real thoughts increase the suspense at the story's end?

◆ Build Grammar Skills

ADVERB CLAUSES

An **adverb clause** is a subordinate clause that functions as an adverb; that is, it modifies a verb, an adjective, or another adverb and answers the questions *when, where, how, why, to what extent,* or *under what conditions.* Adverb clauses begin with subordinating conjunctions like *after, as, although, because, if, since, when, unless,* and *until.* In this example, the adverb clause is italicized:

> *As the bell sounded the hour,* there came a knocking at the street door. (The adverb clause modifies *came* and answers the question *when.*)

Practice On your paper, identify the adverb clause in each sentence. Then, tell what question it answers.
1. When the day broke, I went boldly into the chamber.
2. I could see him as he lay upon his bed.
3. He had been lying awake since the first slight noise.
4. When I had made an end of these labors, it was four o'clock.
5. The police suspected the narrator because he acted strangely.

Writing Application Write three sentences about the narrator's trial for murder, using an adverb clause in each.

✎ Writer's Solution

For additional instruction and practice, use the lesson in the *Writer's Solution Language Lab CD-ROM* on Adverb Clauses. You may also use the practice page on Adverb Clauses, p. 57, in the *Writer's Solution Grammar Practice Book.*

Build Your Portfolio

 Idea Bank

Writing

1. Prediction Write a prediction explaining what happens to the narrator of the story after he confesses to the crime.

2. Police Report As one of the officers who interviewed the narrator, write a police report on the arrest. Include what the narrator said and did and when you realized he was the murderer. Also, note the time and place of the arrest, the charge, and the police precinct to which you took the accused.

3. Comparative Essay In an essay, compare and contrast the techniques Poe uses to create suspense with those used by filmmakers: suspenseful music, camera shots that slowly explore a dangerous environment, and sudden close-ups. **[Media Link]**

Speaking and Listening

4. News Interview [Group Activity] With a classmate, stage an interview between the narrator, awaiting trial for murder, and a reporter for a newspaper. **[Career Link; Performing Arts Link]**

5. Opening Argument The narrator is being tried for murder. As his attorney, address the jury (your classmates) at the beginning of the trial and introduce your case—not guilty by reason of insanity. **[Career Link; Performing Arts Link]**

Projects

6. Movie Review View a film version of a Poe story—for example, *The Fall of the House of Usher* (1960) or *The Masque of the Red Death* (1964). In a report to the class, compare the story to the film version and give the film a thumbs-up or a thumbs-down. **[Media Link]**

7. Literary Panel [Group Activity] With several classmates, stage a panel discussion on Poe for the class. Each panelist should research and present a different aspect of this author: his life, his poetry, his tales of horror, and his influence on other writers.

 Writing Mini-Lesson

Suspenseful Anecdote

Poe involves you in his tale by keeping you guessing until the end. You use the same device when you tell an anecdote—a brief story about a remarkable or humorous event you've experienced. Write down such an anecdote as if you were telling it to a friend in a personal letter.

Writing Skills Focus: Create Suspense

Hook the reader by **creating suspense,** a feeling of uncertainty about the outcome. Here are two strategies to heighten suspense:

- Tease the reader with hints that suggest, but don't give away, the final outcome. For example, introduce an idea that seems important to the outcome, but don't let readers know for sure.

- Tell what will happen, but keep the reader wondering *how* and *when* it will happen. Poe uses this approach in his slow-motion account of the murderer's movements.

Prewriting Choose an event you've experienced that is remarkable or funny and that has a clear beginning, middle, and end. Create suspense by hiding, and hinting at, the ending or by revealing it and keeping the *when* and *how* uncertain.

Drafting Write as if you were playing a teasing game with your friend: Give some details and hold back others.

◆ **Grammar Application**

Use adverb clauses to give information about *when, how, why,* and *to what extent.*

Revising Have several classmates read your suspenseful anecdote. If it doesn't keep them on the edge of their seats, include some details that hint at the outcome, so your readers will experience suspense.

The Tell-Tale Heart ◆ 549

 Idea Bank

Following are suggestions for matching the Idea Bank topics with your students' performance levels and learning modalities:

Customize for
Performance Levels
Less Advanced Students: 1, 4
Average Students: 2, 4, 5, 6
More Advanced Students: 3, 4, 5, 6, 7

Customize for
Learning Modalities
Verbal/Linguistic: 1, 2, 3, 4, 5, 6, 7
Visual/Spatial: 6
Logical/Mathematical: 2, 4, 5, 7
Interpersonal: 4, 5, 7
Intrapersonal: 1

 Writing Mini-Lesson

Refer students to the Writing Handbook in the back of the book for instruction on the writing process and for further information on anecdotes.

 **Writer's Solution**

Writers at Work Videodisc
Have students view the videodisc segment on Expression (Ch. 1), featuring Gish Jen, to see how she records her experiences and observations. Have students discuss ways they can collect their suspenseful details.

Play frames 2571 to 4400

Writing Lab CD-ROM
Have students complete the tutorial on Expression. Follow these steps:

1. Have students view the video to learn a technique for drafting expressive writing.
2. Suggest that students use the Chain of Events and Notecard Activities to organize details logically.
3. Have students draft on computer.
4. Have students use the Self-Evaluation Checklist for expression and a revision checker for sentence-opener variety.

Writer's Solution Sourcebook
Have students use Chapter 1, "Expression," pp. 1–31, for additional support. The chapter includes in-depth instruction on organizing drafts, p. 20.

✓ **ASSESSMENT OPTIONS**

Formal Assessment, Selection Test, pp. 162–164, and Assessment Resources Software. The selection test is designed so that it can be easily customized to the performance levels of your students.

Alternative Assessment, p. 38, includes options for less advanced students, more advanced students, verbal/linguistic learners, bodily/kinesthetic learners, logical/mathematical learners, and visual/spatial learners.

PORTFOLIO ASSESSMENT
Use the following rubrics in the **Alternative Assessment** booklet to assess student writing:
Prediction: Expression, p. 90
Police Report: Description, p. 93
Comparative Essay: Comparison/Contrast, p. 99
Writing Mini-Lesson: Expression, p. 90

OBJECTIVES

1. To read, comprehend, and interpret a selection that has a social studies focus
2. To relate a selection with a social studies focus to personal experience
3. To connect literature to social studies
4. To respond to social studies guiding questions
5. To respond to the story through writing, speaking and listening, and projects

SOCIAL STUDIES GUIDING QUESTIONS

Reading a story that takes place during a Civil War battle will help students discover answers to these social studies questions:

• What was it like to participate in a large Civil War battle?

• What was it like to be wounded during the Civil War?

 **Interest Grabber** Ask students to imagine being seriously injured in a battle. Instead of going by ambulance to a modern, well-equipped hospital, they are carried to a small tent near a battlefield by their fellow soldiers. The tent is crowded with injured and dying soldiers and only a few doctors and nurses. Outside, cannons and guns are being fired, the air is smoky, and the hospital tent is hot and dirty. Doctors have few medicines, and infections, amputation, and death are common. Tell students that in the selection they are about to read, an injured soldier must visit such a makeshift field hospital.

Map Study

Historical Maps The connection between geography and history is often a key to understanding why events happened. The map on this page shows key battles between the Federal Army of the Potomac, and the Confederate Army of Northern Virginia. Help students understand the 2 armies' movements: the map shows 2 Confederate invasions of the North: one in 1862, ending with the battle of Antietam in Maryland; another about a year later, ending at Gettysburg, Pennsylvania. Guide students to see how close the fighting was to Washington, D.C.

CONNECTING LITERATURE TO SOCIAL STUDIES

THE CIVIL WAR: BATTLES

An Episode of War *by Stephen Crane*

CIVIL WAR BATTLES In 1861, six southern states seceded from the United States and formed the Confederate States of America. When the Confederates fired on Fort Sumter, a U.S. Army post, Union soldiers defended the fort, and the country found itself in a Civil War. Fighting during the Civil War took place in three major areas: the East, the West, and at sea. The Union planned an offensive strategy: They would blockade southern ports, stop the South from using the Mississippi to move supplies, and capture the Confederate government headquartered in Richmond, Virginia. The South originally planned to stay at home and fight a defensive war. Northerners, they believed, would quickly tire of fighting.

Destruction in the Civil War The fighting, it turns out, did not end quickly: The Civil War raged from 1861–1865. One million Americans died in the conflict—more than in any other war the country has ever fought. It has been called the first modern war because land mines and other modern weapons were used. When the war was over, most Americans remembered the destruction with horror; very few thought of it as a heroic period in American history.

Stephen Crane's War Stories Although Stephen Crane was not born until five years after the Civil War ended, he wrote stories about the war that were known for their realism. In "An Episode of War," Crane takes you to the battlefield's edge and vividly depicts the unexpected, severe wounding of an army lieutenant.

The Civil War in the East, 1861–1863

— Union troops
— Confederate troops
✪ Union victories
✪ Confederate victories

550 ◆ Short Stories

Prentice Hall Literature Program Resources

REINFORCE / RETEACH / EXTEND
Selection Support Pages
Build Vocabulary, p. 207
Connect Literature to Social Studies, p. 208
Formal Assessment Selection Test, pp. 165–166, Assessment Resources Software
Readings From Social Studies
Writing and Language Transparencies
Series of Events Chain, p. 57; Venn Diagram, p. 77

Resource Pro CD-ROM
"An Episode of War"—includes all resource material and customizable lesson plan

 Listening to Literature Audiocassettes "An Episode of War"

 Looking at Literature Videodisc "An Episode of War"

Connection to Prentice Hall The American Nation *Independence Through 1914*
Ch. 15, "The Civil War," pp. 374–403

An Episode of War

Stephen Crane

◀ **Critical Viewing** How does this photograph correspond to Crane's description of the wounded lieutenant's being helped by his men? **[Connect]** ❶

The lieutenant's rubber blanket lay on the ground, and upon it he had poured the company's supply of coffee. Corporals and other representatives of the grimy and hot-throated men who lined the breast-work[1] had come for each squad's portion.

The lieutenant was frowning and serious at this task of division. His lips pursed as he drew with his sword various crevices in the heap, until brown squares of coffee, astoundingly equal in size, appeared on the blanket. He was on the verge of a great triumph in mathematics, and the corporals were thronging forward, each to reap a little square, when suddenly the lieutenant cried out and looked quickly at a man near him as if he suspected it was a case of personal assault. The others cried out also when they saw blood upon the lieutenant's sleeve.

He had winced like a man stung, swayed dangerously, and then straightened. The sound of his hoarse breathing was plainly audible. He looked sadly, mystically, over the breast-work at the green face of a wood, where now were many little puffs of white smoke. During this moment the men about him gazed statuelike and silent, astonished and awed by this catastrophe which happened when catastrophes were not expected—when they had leisure to observe it. ❷

As the lieutenant stared at the wood, they too swung their heads, so that for another instant all hands, still silent, contemplated the distant forest as if their minds were fixed upon the mystery of a bullet's journey.

The officer had, of course, been compelled to take his sword into his left hand. He did not hold it by the hilt. He gripped it at the middle of the blade, awkwardly. Turning his eyes from the hostile wood, he looked at the sword as he held it there, and seemed puzzled as to what to do with it, where to put it. In short, this weapon had of a sudden become a strange thing to him. He looked at it in a kind of stupefaction, as if he had been endowed with a trident, a sceptre, or a spade.[2]

---

1. **breast-work:** Low wall put up quickly as a defense in battle.

2. **a trident, a sceptre, or a spade** (trid′ ənt; sep′ tər): Symbols of royal authority.

An Episode of War ◆ 551

Preparing for Standardized Tests

Social Studies and Reading Selections
Historical literature, such as this selection, may be used as subject matter for reading comprehension portions of standardized tests. Sometimes the test format directs students to read a passage and identify its main idea. Have students practice this skill by reading the paragraph on p. 552 that begins, "There were others who . . ." Then, write this sample test item with answer choices on the board:

Choose the main idea that best fits the paragraph.

(A) The lieutenant was glad to be wounded.
(B) The lieutenant knew he had a disease.
(C) The lieutenant knew he had been shot and walked toward the rear.
(D) The wounded lieutenant was stunned and felt helpless.

Review the information in the paragraph with students. Help them recognize that (D) best states the main idea. Discuss that (C) presents some of the details, but not the main idea. For further practice, have students identify main ideas of other paragraphs in the story.

Develop Understanding

One-Minute Insight When a company of Civil War soldiers is on the front line of a battle, during a lull in the fighting, their lieutenant unexpectedly receives a bullet wound in his arm. "An Episode of War" gives readers a glimpse into what a Civil War battle was like, how it felt to be injured, and how soldiers reacted to the casualties around them.

Team Teaching Strategy
"An Episode of War" offers an opportunity to team teach with a social studies teacher, creating a cross-curricular unit on the Civil War.

▶Critical Viewing◀
❶ **Connect** *Students may say that, like the men in the story, the soldier in the photo stands next to, but does not touch his wounded comrade.*

Comprehension Check ☑
❷ Ask students to describe what happened to the lieutenant and explain what the "little puffs of white smoke" are. *The lieutenant was surprised to have been shot in the arm during a lull in the fighting. The puffs of smoke are descriptions of what enemy gunfire looks like.*

Customize for *Less Proficient Readers*
In this story, not only will the setting be unfamiliar to students, the characters are not named. To help readers better understand the story, have students read it more than once. Have them use the Series of Events Chain, p. 57 in **Writing and Language Transparencies,** to organize details about what has happened to the lieutenant, what he does, where he goes, what the other soldiers do, and what the surgeon does.

Customize for *More Advanced Students*
Some details or elements of the selection are specific to the Civil War, while other details are timeless and universal to war in general. Challenge students to use the Venn Diagram, p. 77 in **Writing and Language Transparencies,** to analyze the similarities and differences of the battle and war details to historical aspects of war.

552

Finally he tried to sheathe it. To sheathe a sword held by the left hand, at the middle of the blade, in a scabbard hung at the left hip, is a feat worthy of a sawdust ring.[3] This wounded officer engaged in a desperate struggle with the sword and the wobbling scabbard, and during the time of it breathed like a wrestler.

But at this instant the men, the spectators, awoke from their stone-like poses and crowded forward sympathetically. The orderly-sergeant took the sword and tenderly placed it in the scabbard. At the time, he leaned nervously backward, and did not allow even his finger to brush the body of the lieutenant.

▲ **Critical Viewing** This is an actual photograph of a temporary Civil War hospital. What quality of treatment do you think the soldiers received there? On what details do you base your answer? [Assess]

A wound gives strange dignity to him who bears it. Well men shy from his new and terrible majesty. It is as if the wounded man's hand is upon the curtain which hangs before the revelations of all existence—the meaning of ants, potentates,[4] wars, cities, sunshine, snow, a feather dropped from a bird's wing; and the power of it sheds radiance upon a bloody form, and makes the other men understand sometimes that they are little. His comrades look at him with large eyes thoughtfully. Moreover, they fear vaguely

that the weight of a finger upon him might send him headlong, <u>precipitate</u> the tragedy, hurl him at once into the dim, grey unknown. And so the orderly-sergeant, while sheathing the sword, leaned nervously backward.

There were others who proffered assistance. One timidly presented his shoulder and asked the lieutenant if he cared to lean upon it, but the latter waved him away mournfully. He wore the look of one who knows he is the victim of a terrible disease and understands his helplessness. He again stared over the breast-work at the forest, and then, turning, went slowly rearward. He held his right wrist tenderly in his left hand as if the wounded arm was made of very brittle glass.

And the men in silence stared at the wood, then at the departing lieutenant; then at the wood, then at the lieutenant.

As the wounded officer passed from the line of battle, he was enabled to see many things which as a participant in the fight were unknown to him. He saw a general on a black horse gazing over the lines of blue infantry at the green woods which veiled his problems. An aide galloped furiously, dragged his horse suddenly to a halt, saluted, and presented a paper. It was, for a wonder, precisely like a historical painting.

To the rear of the general and his staff a group, composed of a bugler, two or three orderlies, and the bearer of the corps

---

3. **sawdust ring:** Ring in which circus acts are performed.
4. **potentates** (pōt′ ən tāts): *n.:* Rulers; powerful people.

standard,[5] all upon maniacal horses, were working like slaves to hold their ground, preserve their respectful interval, while the shells boomed in the air about them, and caused their chargers to make furious quivering leaps.

A battery, a tumultuous and shining mass, was swirling toward the right. The wild thud of hoofs, the cries of the riders shouting blame and praise, menace and encouragement, and, last, the roar of the wheels, the slant of the glistening guns, brought the lieutenant to an intent pause. The battery swept in curves that stirred the heart; it made halts as dramatic as the crash of a wave on the rocks, and when it fled onward this aggregation of wheels, levers, motors had a beautiful unity, as if it were a missile. The sound of it was a war-chorus that reached into the depths of man's emotion.

The lieutenant, still holding his arm as if it were of glass, stood watching this battery until all detail of it was lost, save the figures of the riders, which rose and fell and waved lashes over the black mass.

Later, he turned his eyes toward the battle, where the shooting sometimes crackled like bush-fires, sometimes sputtered with exasperating irregularity, and sometimes reverberated like the thunder. He saw the smoke rolling upward and saw crowds of men who ran and cheered, or stood and blazed away at the inscrutable distance.

He came upon some stragglers, and they told him how to find the field hospital. They described its exact location. In fact, these men, no longer having part in the battle, knew more of it than others. They told the performance of every corps, every division, the opinion of every general. The lieutenant, carrying his wounded arm rearward, looked upon them with wonder.

---

5. **corps standard** (kôr): Flag or banner representing a military unit.

At the roadside a brigade was making coffee and buzzing with talk like a girls' boarding-school. Several officers came out to him and inquired concerning things of which he knew nothing. One, seeing his arm, began to scold. "Why, man, that's no way to do. You want to fix that thing." He appropriated the lieutenant and the lieutenant's wound. He cut the sleeve and laid bare the arm, every nerve of which softly fluttered under his touch. He bound his handkerchief over the wound, scolding away in the meantime. His tone allowed one to think that he was in the habit of being wounded every day. The lieutenant hung his head, feeling, in this presence, that he did not know how to be correctly wounded.

The low white tents of the hospital were grouped around an old schoolhouse. There was here a singular commotion. In the foreground two ambulances interlocked wheels in the deep mud. The drivers were tossing the blame of it back and forth, gesticulating and berating, while from the ambulances, both crammed with wounded, there came an occasional groan. An interminable crowd of bandaged men were coming and going. Great numbers sat under the trees nursing heads or arms or legs. There was a dispute of some kind raging on the steps of the schoolhouse. Sitting with his back against a tree a man with a face as grey as a new army blanket was serenely smoking a corncob pipe. The lieutenant wished to rush forward and inform him that he was dying.

A busy surgeon was passing near the

◆ Build Vocabulary

precipitate (prē sip´ ə tāt´) *v*.: Cause to happen before expected or desired

aggregation (ag´ grə gā´ shən) *n*.: Group or mass of distinct objects or individuals

inscrutable (in skrōōt´ ə bəl) *adj*.: Impossible to see or understand

An Episode of War ◆ 553

CONNECTING LITERATURE TO SOCIAL STUDIES

eral men. Teams of horses pulled the guns and the *caissons* (wagons designed to hold ammunition) to where they were needed on the battlefield.

CONNECTING LITERATURE TO SOCIAL STUDIES

7 Compare and Contrast Guide students to understand that many different things were going on simultaneously during a battle. While it may be calm enough behind one breastwork for a company to make coffee, there might be intense fighting close by. Help students picture the contrast between chaos and calm. Ask them to imagine smoke-filled fields and forests, thousands of men and horses, the sounds of cannons, guns firing, and men yelling; and to picture soldiers quietly hunkering down in a trench or behind a stone wall drinking coffee.

◆ LITERATURE AND YOUR LIFE

8 Ask students to think about the lieutenant's behavior after being wounded and relate it to their own brave efforts at acting as if all is well when they know it is not. How are their actions the same or different?

Links Across Time

9 In addition to helping create the profession of nursing, the Civil War produced several innovations in army medical practice. The establishment of a special ambulance corps was one such improvement. The trained Federal ambulance corps gave first-aid treatment to the wounded and evacuated them to field hospitals and surgeons' stations. It was a model for armies through World War I.

Looking at Literature Videodisc

To provide students with historical background for "An Episode of War," play Chapter Six of the videodisc. This segment provides images and information about soldiers' lives during the Civil War. Have students discuss the hardships faced by soldiers during the Civil War.

Chapter 6

---

1 *Students may say that the medical care was compassionate, but less than adequate.*

Links Across Time

2 The bullets used in the Civil War were large and their velocity was slow. Therefore, bullets usually stayed in the body and the wounds they caused were ghastly. Stomach wounds were fatal. Wounds to arms and legs often required amputation because bones were shattered and doctors knew of no other way to try to prevent tissue decay or bone infections.

Reinforce and Extend

Answers

◆ LITERATURE AND YOUR LIFE

Reader's Response Invite students to share their experiences, which are likely to vary widely.

Thematic Focus Students may say that, like all soldiers wounded in combat, he is a hero.

☑ Check Your Comprehension

1. A lieutenant is wounded in the arm while drinking coffee behind the battle lines.
2. Soldiers honored and supported wounded soldiers, but kept their hands off.
3. The surgeon lies to him, telling him that amputation is "nonsense."

More About the Author

Stephen Crane never experienced military combat, but he was obsessed by war. Before writing about the Civil War, he interviewed veterans of that war and studied photographs, battle plans, and biographical accounts. In his writing, he depicted characters —like the lieutenant—whose lives were shaped by forces they could neither control nor comprehend. Crane died from tuberculosis.

Connecting Literature to Social Studies
What does this incident suggest about the kind of medical care Civil War soldiers received?

lieutenant. "Good-morning," he said, with a friendly smile. Then he caught sight of the lieutenant's arm, and his face at once changed. "Well, let's have a look at it." He seemed possessed suddenly of a great contempt for the lieutenant. This wound evidently placed the latter on a very low social plane. The doctor cried out impatiently, "What mutton-head had tied it up that way anyhow?" The lieutenant answered, "Oh, a man."

When the wound was disclosed the doctor fingered it disdainfully. "Humph," he said. "You come along with me and I'll 'tend to you." His voice contained the same scorn as if he were saying: "You will have to go to jail."

The lieutenant had been very meek, but now his face flushed, and he looked into the doctor's eyes. "I guess I won't have it amputated," he said.

"Nonsense, man! Nonsense! Nonsense!" cried the doctor. "Come along, now. I won't **2** amputate it. Come along. Don't be a baby."

"Let go of me," said the lieutenant, holding back wrathfully, his glance fixed upon the door of the old schoolhouse, as sinister to him as the portals of death.

And this is the story of how the lieutenant lost his arm. When he reached home, his sisters, his mother, his wife, sobbed for a long time at the sight of the flat sleeve. "Oh, well," he said, standing shamefaced amid these tears, "I don't suppose it matters so much as all that."

Meet the Author

Stephen Crane (1871–1900)
The son of a minister, Crane grew up in New Jersey and attended Syracuse University. After playing baseball in college, Crane seriously considered becoming a shortstop in the newly formed National League. He decided instead that he wanted to be a writer. He became internationally famous as a writer of stories so realistic that they seemed to be true. His novel *The Red Badge of Courage* is considered one of the best war novels ever written by an American.

Guide for Responding

◆ LITERATURE AND YOUR LIFE

Reader's Response Think of a time when you or someone you know was seriously hurt. Did people treat you or the other person differently because of what had happened?

Thematic Focus Would you describe the lieutenant as a hero? Why or why not?

☑ Check Your Comprehension

1. Who gets wounded? Where is he wounded?
2. What makes the soldiers act differently toward the lieutenant after he has been shot?
3. How does the surgeon react when the lieutenant asks if his arm will have to be amputated?

◆ Critical Thinking

INTERPRET

1. Compare and contrast the lieutenant's and the other soldiers' reactions to the wound. **[Compare and Contrast]**
2. How do the lieutenant's last words in the story relate to his earlier attitude toward his wound? **[Compare and Contrast]**
3. What details in the story suggest Crane's attitude that war is ugly and impersonal? **[Support]**

APPLY

4. Imagine a veteran from the Union army and a veteran from the Confederate army as readers of this story. Would their reactions to the story be similar or different? Explain your reasoning. **[Speculate]**

Beyond the Selection

FURTHER READING
Other Works by Stephen Crane
The Red Badge of Courage
War Is Kind
"The Open Boat"
Other Works About Soldiers' Civil War Experience
The Life of Johnny Reb, Bell I. Wiley
The Life of Billy Yank, Bell I. Wiley
All for the Union: The Civil War Diary and Letters of Elisha Hunt Rhodes, edited by Robert Hunt Rhodes

INTERNET
We suggest the following site on the Internet (all Web sites are subject to change).
For more information about Stephen Crane:
http://www.cwrl.utexas.edu/~mmaynard/crane/crane.html
We *strongly recommend* that you preview the site before you send students to it.

CONNECTING LITERATURE TO SOCIAL STUDIES

"An Episode of War" vividly captures an incident that changes a soldier's life forever. The character's experience was one shared by thousands of real soldiers who fought in the Civil War. Through his brief account of one soldier's experience, Stephen Crane brings to life the tragic impact that the Civil War had on those who were caught up in the conflict. He finds, however, that the realities of war are very different from what he encountered in books.

1. Why do you think Crane did not give names to any of his characters in this story?
2. Why doesn't Crane specify whether the soldiers in the story are in the Union or the Confederate army?
3. How do you learn about the conditions of the Civil War by reading this story?
4. How do the lieutenant's final words relate to the point Crane is making about war?

 ## Idea Bank

Writing

1. **Journal Entry** Imagine that you were one of the corporals waiting for a supply of coffee when the lieutenant was shot. Write an entry in your journal describing the incident.
2. **Official Report** As the surgeon who examined the lieutenant's wound, write a report of your examination for the records you keep of your daily activities.
3. **Essay** Write an essay to explain the main message, or theme, that Crane conveys in "An Episode of War." Support your idea with details from the story.

Speaking and Listening

4. **Role Play [Group Activity]** Role-play a conversation between two of the corporals who were near the lieutenant when he was shot.

Projects

5. **Report** Using various sources, find information about the daily lives of soldiers in either or both of the armies in the Civil War. Report to the class on what you learn.
6. **Drawings [Group Activity]** Form teams to create drawings of Civil War soldiers. Use encyclopedias, books of photographs taken by Mathew Brady, and the pictures that accompany "An Episode of War" as guides.

Further Reading, Listening, and Viewing

- Stephen Crane's novel *The Red Badge of Courage* is a realistic account of the experiences of a young soldier during the Civil War.
- *Behind the Lines: A Sourcebook on the Civil War* by C. Carter Smith is an illustrated history of the Civil War.
- Ken Burns's *The Civil War* is an award-winning documentary film on the Civil War.

An Episode of War ◆ 555

 ## Idea Bank

Following are suggestions for matching the Idea Bank topics with your students' performance levels and learning modalities:

Customize for
Performance Levels
Less Advanced Students: 1, 4, 6
Average Students: 2, 4, 5, 6
More Advanced Students: 3, 4, 5, 6

Customize for
Learning Modalities
Verbal/Linguistic: 1, 2, 3, 4, 5
Visual/Spatial: 6
Bodily/Kinesthetic: 4
Logical/Mathematical: 2, 3, 5
Interpersonal: 4, 6
Intrapersonal: 1

Answers *(continued)*
◆ **Critical Thinking**

1. The lieutenant is stunned and calm. His troops gather around him in awe.
2. At first, he feels dignified by the wound. His last words indicate that he has become resigned to it.
3. The lieutenant is shot unexpectedly, during an apparent lull in the fighting, and he never sees who it is that shoots him. At the field hospital he is treated by an overworked doctor.
4. Students may say that veterans on both sides would sympathize with any wounded soldier. Any war veteran would understand the horrors the men faced, no matter which side they fought on.

CONNECTING LITERATURE TO SOCIAL STUDIES

1. Many soldiers shared the experience of war. Death and casualties were all around and loss was universal. Therefore, the story could have been about any unnamed soldier.
2. The experience of being wounded and of losing comrades was shared by soldiers in both armies.
3. You learn about the random nature of injury and of the helplessness in the face of it. You learn about the state of medical care and of the chaos and great size of battles.
4. The lieutenant's last words indicate that the horrors of war are unimaginable and that his wound is negligible when compared with how others have suffered and died.

555

Guide for Reading

1. To read, comprehend, and interpret two short stories
2. To relate the stories to personal experience
3. To identify with a character
4. To understand direct and indirect characterization
5. To build vocabulary in context and learn the word root *-chol-*
6. To develop skill with adjective clauses
7. To write realistic dialogue
8. To respond to the stories through writing, speaking and listening, and projects

SKILLS INSTRUCTION

Vocabulary:
Word Roots: *-chol-*

Spelling:
Words That End in *-ttle, -ggle, -ffle*

Grammar:
Adjective Clauses

Reading Strategy:
Identify With a Character

Literary Focus:
Direct and Indirect Characterization

Writing:
Create Realistic Dialogue

Speaking and Listening:
Monologue (Teacher Edition)

Viewing and Representing:
Book Jacket (Teacher Edition)

Critical Viewing:
Summarize; Assess; Draw Conclusions; Make a Judgment; Compare and Contrast; Speculate

PORTFOLIO OPPORTUNITIES

Writing: Missing-Person Bulletin; Self-Portrait; Episode

Writing Mini-Lesson: Dialogue

Speaking and Listening: Monologue; Role Play

Projects: Report on Kahlil Gibran; Wise Fools and Tricksters

More About the Authors

Isaac Bashevis Singer was once called "a walking museum of Jewish life in Eastern Europe." He was fascinated by the stories he heard from visitors who came to his father's rabbinical court for advice. Critic Leslie Fiedler saw Singer as "the last of those who will be able to reach a mass audience and still be utterly at home in the Yiddish culture."

Naomi Shihab Nye was steeped in Palestinian folklore as a child. She has been a visiting writer for the Arts America Program, which sends American writers to schools all over the world to share their works with diverse student audiences.

Meet the Authors:

Isaac Bashevis Singer (1904–1991)

Isaac Bashevis Singer came from a family of Jewish religious leaders in Poland. He grew up in Warsaw, Poland's capital, and received a Jewish education. However, Singer decided to become a writer instead of a religious leader.

A Rediscovered Home In 1935, Singer left his home and moved to the United States. However, he rediscovered his lost home in the many Yiddish stories he wrote about Poland's Jews. Translated from Yiddish into English and other languages, these stories won him the Nobel Prize for Literature in 1978.

Naomi Shihab Nye (1952–   )

A poet and fiction writer, Naomi Shihab Nye is concerned with "paying attention to the world." Perhaps her travels and the richness of her heritage inspired her to "pay attention." She grew up in St. Louis as the daughter of a Palestinian father and an American mother. However, she has also lived in Jerusalem and Texas. The poems in *The Words Under the Words* (1995) and the story "Hamadi" show that her imagination is well traveled too.

◆ LITERATURE AND YOUR LIFE

CONNECT YOUR EXPERIENCE

In today's busy world, people tend to rush through their daily routines. They race from home to school or the office, back home, through dinner, and out again to various social functions. However, these stories hint that sometimes it's the people who march to their own drummer—who are "outside" the norm—who find wisdom and peace.

THEMATIC FOCUS: Appreciating Others

As you read these stories, look for ways in which the story characters display their individuality.

◆ Background for Understanding

LITERATURE

Both these stories use a type of character from folk tales known as the wise fool. This character is a fool because he may forget his address, speak strangely, or wear unfashionable clothes. Yet this "fool" turns out to be wiser than the characters who seem to know where they're going.

◆ Build Vocabulary

WORD ROOTS: *-chol-*

People once believed that health depended on the balance of bodily fluids. One of these, bile (*chole* in Greek), was thought to make people feel low. Words with the root *-chol-* still relate to a problem in physical or mental health. For example, the word *melancholy* in "Hamadi" means "sad."

WORD BANK

Which of these words from the stories is associated with a lot of noisy demons? Check the Build Vocabulary box on page 560 to see if you chose correctly.

forsaken
pandemonium
brittle
lavish
refugees
melancholy

Prentice Hall Literature Program Resources

REINFORCE / RETEACH / EXTEND
Selection Support Pages
Build Vocabulary: Word Roots: *-chol-*, p. 209
Build Spelling Skills, p. 210
Build Grammar Skills: Adjective Clauses, p. 211
Reading Strategy: Identify With a Character, p. 212
Literary Focus: Characterization, p. 213
Strategies for Diverse Student Needs,
pp. 77–78
Beyond Literature Study Skills: Map Reading, p. 39

Formal Assessment Selection Test, pp. 167–169, Assessment Resources Software
Alternative Assessment, p. 39
Daily Language Practice, p. 14
Resource Pro CD-ROM "The Day I Got Lost"; "Hamadi"—includes all resource material and customizable lesson plan

 Listening to Literature Audiocassettes
"The Day I Got Lost"; "Hamadi"

The Day I Got Lost ◆ Hamadi

Transfer to the #6, Kathy Ruttenberg, Gallery Henoch

◆ Literary Focus

CHARACTERIZATION

The characters you meet in stories can be so memorable that they become friends for life. The process by which authors create memorable characters is called **characterization.** Authors use **direct characterization** when they tell you what a character is like. They use **indirect characterization** when they reveal a character's personality through his or her appearance, words, actions, and effects on others.

◆ Reading Strategy

IDENTIFY WITH A CHARACTER

If you want to fully understand literary characters, you must read with your heart as well as your head. When you **identify** with a character, you experience that character's joys and sorrows as if they were your own. You may also compare the situations in which characters find themselves with similar situations from your own life.

As you read each story, identify with a character by creating an organizer like the one below:

Story Event: Getting lost

Character's Reaction: Anxiety

My Reaction: Frustration

Guide for Reading ◆ 557

Interest Grabber Ask students to list identifying facts about themselves they can't imagine ever forgetting. For example: their address, name, age, or hair color. Explain that they will read a humorous story about an absent-minded professor who forgets where he lives and ends up lost in his own city. Challenge pairs to brainstorm for strategies the professor might use to find his way home. Then, have students read the story to see whether the lost professor tries any of their suggestions.

◆ Build Grammar Skills

Adjective Clauses If you wish to introduce the grammar concept for this selection before students read, refer to the instruction on p. 570.

Customize for
Less Proficient Readers
The main character in "The Day I Got Lost" is a *wise fool.* He acts foolishly, but possesses an underlying wisdom. Students may better appreciate this aspect of his character by jotting down examples of both kinds of actions:

Foolish Acts	Acts of Wisdom

Customize for
More Advanced Students
In a *caricature,* one or more aspects of someone's character are exaggerated, often for humorous effect. As students explore the characterization in this story, challenge them to look for ways in which Professor Schlemiel is portrayed as a caricature.

 Humanities: Art

Transfer to the #6, by Kathy Ruttenberg
Chicago-born Kathy Ruttenberg has painted many scenes of life in New York City. In this one, subway riders climb the stairs of a subway station.
1. What about these characters can you identify with? *Students may notice ordinary clothing, as if they are off to school or work; a mix of people; or a sense of being on the move.*
2. How does this scene suggest indirect characterization? *You only see people's backs and not their faces.*

 Preparing for Standardized Tests

Reading The Reading Strategy for this selection will help students as they read in general, and as they answer certain items on standardized tests. An ability to identify with characters helps a reader understand reactions. Present the following sample test question, based on "Hamadi":

Which phrase best completes the passage?

Saleh Hamadi is excited by the invitation to go caroling. He insists on taking the bus to Susan's home rather than have her parents pick him up. This shows that he:

(A) cannot drive alone
(B) needs time to practice his music
(C) is independent
(D) does not like cars

Readers may recognize and identify with Hamadi's desire to be independent and not to inconvenience his host. This would lead them to select *(C)* as the best answer. For further practice, use Reading Strategy: Identify With a Character, in **Selection Support,** p. 212.

In "The Day I Got Lost," the absent-minded Professor Shlemiel narrates a day in his life that is filled with misfortune. His gentle and self-effacing humor shows that a character can be both foolish and wise, forgetful and unforgettable.

►Critical Viewing◄

❶ Summarize *Students may say that the buildings look very much alike, and offer few identifying clues.*

Customize for
English Language Learners

The author uses opposites to help convey humor. Help students understand sets of opposites from the story, such as: *uptown–downtown* or *top floor–basement* by drawing simple sketches. For example, model how students can sketch a compass rose on which to indicate *east–west*.

Customize for
Verbal/Linguistic Learners

Singer's brand of humor relies on exaggerating one realistic detail after another until the total picture is unbelievable. In a way, Singer's technique could be called "deadpan." Challenge students to think of stand-up comics they know who specialize in deadpan delivery, and imagine them narrating the story.

Customize for
Logical/Mathematical Learners

When Professor Shlemiel cannot remember his address, the cab driver suggests looking it up in the telephone book. Have interested students suggest other ways to solve the problem of being lost, and methods the absent-minded professor's family might use to be sure he won't get lost again.

The Day I Got Lost

Isaac Bashevis Singer

▶ **Critical Viewing** Explain the ways a person might get lost in a setting like the one shown in the painting. **[Summarize]**

Windows, 1951, Charles Sheeler, Collection, Hirschl & Adler Galleries

558 ◆ *Short Stories*

Block Scheduling Strategies

Consider these suggestions to take advantage of extended class time:

• Begin class or signal breaks between instructional activities with the **Daily Language Practice** tasks, p. 14.

• Discuss the Literary Focus and Reading Strategy, p. 557. As students read each story, have them find examples of characterization and where they can identify with a character. Have them work in groups to discuss and answer the Guide for Responding questions, p. 561 and pp. 569–570.

• Use the Viewing and Representing Mini-Lesson, p. 561, to gauge students' response to "The Day I Got Lost."

• Have students work in small groups to research the Social Studies Connection in Beyond Literature, p. 569. As a class, discuss their findings.

• Prepare students for the Writing Mini-Lesson by first having them complete the Episode, Monologue, or Role Play activities in the Idea Bank, p. 571.

It is easy to recognize me. See a man in the street wearing a too long coat, too large shoes, a crumpled hat with a wide brim, spectacles with one lens missing, and carrying an umbrella though the sun is shining, and that man will be me, Professor Shlemiel.[1] There are other unmistakable clues to my identity. My pockets are always bulging with newspapers, magazines, and just papers. I carry an overstuffed briefcase, and I'm forever making mistakes. I've been living in New York City for over forty years, yet whenever I want to go uptown, I find myself walking downtown, and when I want to go east, I go west. I'm always late and I never recognize anybody.

I'm always misplacing things. A hundred times a day I ask myself, Where is my pen? Where is my money? Where is my handkerchief? Where is my address book? I am what is known as an absentminded professor.

◆ Literary Focus
In this paragraph, what does the narrator tell you directly about himself?

For many years I have been teaching philosophy in the same university, and I still have difficulty in locating my classrooms. Elevators play strange tricks on me. I want to go to the top floor and I land in the basement. Hardly a day passes when an elevator door doesn't close on me. Elevator doors are my worst enemies.

In addition to my constant blundering and losing things, I'm forgetful. I enter a coffee shop, hang up my coat, and leave without it. By the time I remember to go back for it, I've forgotten where I've been. I lose hats, books, umbrellas, rubbers, and above all manuscripts. Sometimes I even forget my own address. One evening I took a taxi because I was in a hurry to get home. The taxi driver said, "Where to?" And I could not remember where I lived.

"Home!" I said.

"Where is home?" he asked in astonishment.

"I don't remember," I replied.

"What is your name?"

"Professor Shlemiel."

"Professor," the driver said, "I'll get you to a telephone booth. Look in the telephone book and you'll find your address."

He drove me to the nearest drugstore with a telephone booth in it, but he refused to wait. I was about to enter the store when I realized I had left my briefcase behind. I ran after the taxi, shouting, "My briefcase, my briefcase!" But the taxi was already out of earshot.

In the drugstore, I found a telephone book, but when I looked under S, I saw to my horror that though there were a number of Shlemiels listed, I was not among them. At that moment I recalled that several months before, Mrs. Shlemiel had decided that we should have an unlisted telephone number. The reason was that my students thought nothing of calling me in the middle of the night and waking me up. It also happened quite frequently that someone wanted to call another Shlemiel and got me by mistake. That was all very well—but how was I going to get home?

I usually had some letters addressed to me in my breast pocket. But just that day I had decided to clean out my pockets. It was my birthday and my wife had invited friends in for the evening. She had baked a huge cake and decorated it with birthday candles. I could see my friends sitting in our living room, waiting to wish me a happy birthday. And here I stood in

---

1. **Shlemiel** (shlə mēl´): Version of the slang word *schlemiel*, an ineffectual, bungling person.

▲ Critical Viewing Does the man in the photograph look confused and absent-minded? Explain. **[Assess]**

◆ **Critical Thinking**
❷ **Analyze** In this passage, what can students determine about Professor Shlemiel's character? *He admits to making many mistakes, being late, and not recognizing people. He also gives clues to his character when he catalogues the things in his pockets.*

◆ **Literary Focus**
❸ **Characterization** *He directly tells that he is a philosophy professor and often gets lost at the university.*

◆ **Critical Thinking**
❹ **Interpret** Does the cab driver have good problem-solving skills when he suggests that Professor Shlemiel look up his address in the telephone book? *Most students will believe that the cab driver is better able to solve the problem of the professor being lost than the professor is himself.*

◆ **LITERATURE AND YOUR LIFE**
❺ Suggest that students think of a time when they were lost and unable to find their way. How did others help them or what were they able to do to help themselves? What kind of advice can they offer to the professor to help him so that he won't absent-mindedly lose his way again? Invite volunteers to share their ideas with the class.

▶**Critical Viewing**◀
❻ **Assess** *Students may say that his wrinkled brow makes him look puzzled or curious. His distant stare might represent absentmindedness.*

Humanities: Art

Windows, 1952, by Charles Sheeler
American painter and photographer Charles Sheeler (1883–1965) was described as a precisionist—the clean lines of the buildings and their shadows demonstrate precision. It was Sheeler's style to combine naturalism and abstraction to depict hard-edged industrial or urban scenes. In "Windows," p. 558, he superimposed skyscraper shapes to create a cityscape. Use questions such as these for discussion:

1. Explain where the scene leads the viewer's eye? *The tall structures create a sense of upward motion; the staggered repeating shapes suggest vibration or sideways motion.*

2. What statement might Sheeler be trying to make with a cityscape like this? *He may be suggesting that cities are bold, tall, and powerful, but also impersonal, as he includes no living things in the scene. The repeated shapes may suggest that the city is an energetic, vibrant, crowded place.*

◆ Reading Strategy

❶ Identify With a Character *He probably feels frustrated, embarrassed, and somewhat ashamed of his absent-mindedness.*

◆ Build Grammar Skills

❷ Adjective Clauses An adjective clause is a subordinate clause that modifies a noun or pronoun. Most adjective clauses begin with a relative pronoun, such as *who, whom, which, that,* or *whose.* Help students locate the adjective clause in this passage and tell what noun or pronoun it modifies—"whose telephone numbers I happened to think of" is an adjective clause that modifies the pronoun *those.*

Thematic Focus

❸ Appreciating Others Until now, Professor Shlemiel has mostly demonstrated the bungling, absent-minded side of his personality. What other traits does he show? *He shows wisdom and inner strength to be able to calm himself by turning his thoughts to philosophy, and by forcing himself to use his head to solve his problem.*

◆ Literary Focus

❹ Characterization Have students explore this passage for hints of indirect characterization. *Students may notice that Shlemiel cares about creatures less fortunate than himself. He is kind to the dog and decides to look after it, although he is miserable and wet himself.*

---

some drugstore, for the life of me not able to remember where I lived.

Then I recalled the telephone number of a friend of mine, Dr. Motherhead, and I decided to call him for help. I dialed and a young girl's voice answered.

"Is Dr. Motherhead at home?"

"No," she replied.

"Is his wife at home?"

"They're both out," the girl said.

"Perhaps you can tell me where they can be reached?" I said.

"I'm only the babysitter, but I think they went to a party at Professor Shlemiel's. Would you like to leave a message?" she said. "Who shall I say called, please?"

"Professor Shlemiel," I said.

"They left for your house about an hour ago," the girl said.

"Can you tell me where they went?" I asked.

"I've just told you," she said. "They went to your house."

> ◆ **Reading Strategy**
> Identify with Professor Shlemiel. How do you think he feels at this moment?

"But where do I live?"

"You must be kidding!" the girl said, and hung up.

I tried to call a number of friends (those whose telephone numbers I happened to think of), but wherever I called, I got the same reply: "They've gone to a party at Professor Shlemiel's."

As I stood in the street wondering what to do, it began to rain. "Where's my umbrella?" I said to myself. And I knew the answer at once. I'd left it—somewhere. I got under a nearby canopy. It was now raining cats and dogs. It lightninged and thundered. All day it had been sunny and warm, but now that I was lost and my umbrella was lost, it had to storm. And it looked as if it would go on for the rest of the night.

To distract myself, I began to ponder the ancient philosophical problem. A mother chicken lays an egg, I thought to myself, and when it hatches, there is a chicken. That's how it has always been. Every chicken comes from an egg and every egg comes from a chicken. But was there a chicken first? Or an egg first? No philosopher has ever been able to solve this eternal question. Just the same, there must be an answer. Perhaps I, Shlemiel, am destined to stumble on it.

It continued to pour buckets. My feet were getting wet and I was chilled. I began to sneeze and I wanted to wipe my nose, but my handkerchief, too, was gone.

At that moment I saw a big black dog. He was standing in the rain getting soaked and looking at me with sad eyes. I knew immediately what the trouble was. The dog was lost. He, too, had forgotten his address. I felt a great love for that innocent animal. I called to him and he came running to me. I talked to him as if he were human. "Fellow, we're in the same boat," I said. "I'm a man shlemiel and you're a dog shlemiel. Perhaps it's also your birthday, and there's a party for you, too. And here you stand shivering and <u>forsaken</u> in the rain, while your loving master is searching for you everywhere. You're probably just as hungry as I am."

I patted the dog on his wet head and he wagged his tail. "Whatever happens to me will happen to you," I said. "I'll keep you with me until we both find our homes. If we don't find your master, you'll stay with me. Give me your paw," I said. The dog lifted his right paw. There was no question that he understood.

A taxi drove by and splattered us both. Suddenly it stopped and I heard someone shouting, "Shlemiel! Shlemiel!" I looked up and saw the taxi door open, and the head of a friend of mine appeared. "Shlemiel," he called. "What are you doing here? Who are you waiting for?"

"Where are you going?" I asked.

"To your house, of course. I'm sorry I'm late, but I was detained. Anyhow, better late than never. But why aren't you at home? And whose dog is that?"

"Only God could have sent you!" I exclaimed. "What a night! I've forgotten my

◆ Build Vocabulary

forsaken (fər sā´ kən) *adj.*: Abandoned; desolate

pandemonium (pan´ də mō´ nē əm) *n.*: A scene of wild disorder

---

Cross-Curricular Connection: Art

Caricature Artists have many techniques for exploring characterization in their work. Portrait artists can choose to include significant objects, colors, backgrounds, or symbols that reveal information about the subject. Caricature is a form of drawing that reveals character and personality by exaggerating certain physical features. For instance, caricatures of late-night TV star Jay Leno exaggerate his pointed chin. Students may have seen drawings by well known caricaturists such as Abe Hirschfeld or Thomas Nast.

Invite interested students to find examples of caricatures in magazines or newspapers (political cartoons are a good source), or in anthologies in the library. Have them determine the subject's character traits based on the visual clues given in the caricature drawing. Artistic students may wish to create original caricatures of people they know.

address, I've left my briefcase in a taxi, I've lost my umbrella, and I don't know where my rubbers are."

"Shlemiel," my friend said, "if there was ever an absentminded professor, you're it!"

When I rang the bell of my apartment, my wife opened the door. "Shlemiel!" she shrieked. "Everybody is waiting for you. Where have you been? Where is your briefcase? Your umbrella? Your rubbers? And who is this dog?"

Our friends surrounded me. "Where have you been?" they cried. "We were so worried. We thought surely something had happened to you!"

"Who is this dog?" my wife kept repeating.

"I don't know," I said finally. "I found him in the street. Let's just call him Bow Wow for the time being."

"Bow Wow, indeed!" my wife scolded. "You know our cat hates dogs. And what about the parakeets? He'll scare them to death."

"He's a quiet dog," I said. "He'll make friends with the cat. I'm sure he loves parakeets. I could not leave him shivering in the rain. He's a good soul."

The moment I said this the dog let out a bloodcurdling howl. The cat ran into the room. When she saw the dog, she arched her back and spat at him, ready to scratch out his eyes. The parakeets in their cage began flapping their wings and screeching. Everybody started talking at once. There was <u>pandemonium</u>.

Would you like to know how it all ended?

Bow Wow still lives with us. He and the cat are great friends. The parakeets have learned to ride on his back as if he were a horse. As for my wife, she loves Bow Wow even more than I do. Whenever I take the dog out, she says, "Now, don't forget your address, both of you."

I never did find my briefcase, or my umbrella, or my rubbers. Like many philosophers before me, I've given up trying to solve the riddle of which came first, the chicken or the egg. Instead, I've started writing a book called *The Memoirs of Shlemiel*. If I don't forget the manuscript in a taxi, or a restaurant, or on a bench in the park, you may read them someday. In the meantime, here is a sample chapter.

❺

❻

*G*uide for Responding

◆ LITERATURE AND YOUR LIFE

Reader's Response Have you ever known anyone who was a little like Professor Shlemiel? Explain.

Thematic Focus What good qualities does the professor exhibit?

☑ Check Your Comprehension

1. Tell how the professor tries to find out his own address.
2. Why can't he get in touch with anyone he knows?
3. How does the professor get home, and what does he bring with him?

◆ Critical Thinking

INTERPRET

1. How does the professor's behavior illustrate the meaning of his name—"a bungler or incompetent person"? **[Support]**
2. How are the professor and the dog alike? **[Connect]**
3. How does the professor seem to be rewarded for his kindness to the dog? **[Interpret]**
4. In what way is the professor a fool who stumbles into wisdom? **[Draw Conclusions]**

EVALUATE

5. Could a person really be as absent-minded as Professor Shlemiel? Why or why not? **[Assess]**

The Day I Got Lost ◆ 561

Viewing and Representing Mini-Lesson

Book Jacket

This mini-lesson expands the Self-Portrait writing activity in the Idea Bank on p. 571.

Introduce Display several hard-cover books so students can see the kinds of information typically included on a book jacket. Discuss the genre of memoir with the students.

Develop Have students create an original book jacket for the upcoming book, *The Memoirs of Shlemiel.* Suggest that they include an "About the Author" insert excerpted from the Self-Portrait writing activity, illustrations, quotations from the

book, reviewers' comments, and any other images or words that would enhance the book jacket and interest potential readers. Students can create the book jacket out of construction paper, or use a computer graphics software program.

Apply Have students display their book jackets and explain why each element of the book jacket design would attract readers.

Assess Evaluate book jackets on how well they capture the essence of the would-be memoir, how appealing they are, and how accurately they reflect the elements typically included on a book jacket.

◆ Reading Strategy

❺ Identify With a Character
Guide students to realize that as Shlemiel describes the dog, he indirectly describes himself. Ask them how they respond to that description. *Students may find it touching that Shlemiel identifies with and defends the dog.*

◆ Critical Thinking

❻ Make a Judgment Discuss with students whether Shlemiel is likely to finish his book. *Some students may say he'll never finish it because he'd lose the manuscript, forget the stories, or simply put it out of his mind. Others may say that, as a professor of words and ideas, he may see it as an assignment, to work on it in bits until it is done.*

Reinforce and Extend

Answers
◆ LITERATURE AND YOUR LIFE

Reader's Response Students might share anecdotes concerning family members, friends, or other acquaintances.

Thematic Focus He is kindhearted, polite, smart, dedicated to his work, has many friends, and can laugh at himself.

☑ Check Your Comprehension

1. He tries to look himself up in the telephone book; then he calls a friend whose number he recalls.
2. His friends are all at his house for his birthday party.
3. A friend in a taxi takes him home; he brings a stray dog with him.

◆ Critical Thinking

1. His absent-mindedness and disorganization make him seem incompetent.
2. Both are good souls who are lost.
3. A friend passing by in a taxi stops to give him a ride.
4. Even though he is disorganized and clumsy, his wisdom shows through his caring heart and goodness.
5. Some students will agree that some people focus on concepts and ideas rather than on the details of life, but most people don't forget their address.

One-Minute Insight "Hamadi" explores how Susan, a Palestinian American high school girl, comes to value Saleh Hamadi, an eccentric family friend, as a kind of surrogate grandparent. As she wrestles with questions about life and growing up, she appreciates his wisdom, his kind heart, and the link he represents to her Lebanese ancestors.

◆ Critical Thinking

❶ Analyze Ask students to analyze Susan's opinion of the brittle women in the counselor's office and determine what it reveals about her values. *She balks at their rigid views of life, and longs for adults who show more understanding and compassion.*

◆ Literary Focus

❷ Characterization *It is an example of direct characterization because the author explicitly tells what Susan is like.*

▶ Critical Viewing ◀

❸ Draw Conclusions *Students may say that his headwear suggests that he grew up in the Middle East, where such garments are commonly worn.*

Customize for
Less Proficient Readers
Because this is a long story, allow students extra time to read it. Break it into parts, with frequent comprehension checks. Also, clarify vocabulary, such as *glum, tedious, purified,* and *expansive.*

Customize for
English Language Learners
Help familiarize students with American holiday traditions, such as the Christmas caroling that is an activity in this story. Explore other holiday traditions, such as spinning the dreydl on Hanukkah, sending cards and flowers on Valentine's Day, or having fireworks and picnics on the Fourth of July.

Hamadi

Naomi Shihab Nye

Susan didn't really feel interested in Saleh Hamadi until she was a freshman in high school carrying a thousand questions around. Why this way? Why not another way? Who said so and why can't I say something else? Those <u>brittle</u> women at school in the counselor's office treated the world as if it were a yardstick and they had tight hold of both ends.

Sometimes Susan felt polite with them, sorting attendance cards during her free period, listening to them gab about fingernail polish and television. And other times she felt she could run out of the building yelling. That's when she daydreamed about Saleh Hamadi, who had nothing to do with any of it. Maybe she thought of him as escape, the way she used to think about the Sphinx at Giza[1] when she was younger. She would picture the golden Sphinx sitting quietly in the desert with sand blowing around its face, never changing its expression. She would think of its wry, slightly crooked mouth and how her grandmother looked a little like that as she waited

> **◆ Literary Focus**
> Why is this an example of direct characterization?

---

1. **Sphinx** (sfiŋks) **at Giza** (gē´ zə): Huge statue with the head of a man and the body of a lion, located near Cario in northern Egypt.

◆ Build Vocabulary

brittle (brit´ əl) *adj*.: Stiff and unbending in manner; lacking warmth

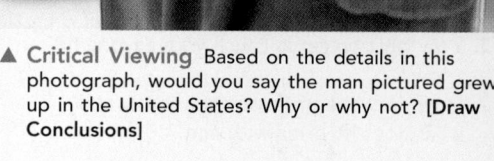

▲ **Critical Viewing** Based on the details in this photograph, would you say the man pictured grew up in the United States? Why or why not? [Draw Conclusions] **❸**

562 ◆ *Short Stories*

Cultural Connection

Elders Many cultures place elders in positions of respect. Discuss with students why this is so, leading them to recognize that in some cultures, elders are respected because the ethical codes of the culture demand it. Ask students to describe how elders are treated in their family. Elders are living resources who can explain traditions, legends, and stories to the next generations. They represent a link to the past, and can offer a voice of wisdom and experience to younger people.

Invite students to explore the roles of elders in your community or their own culture, or in a culture they wish to examine. Have them interview an elder to find out what special roles that person plays in his or her family and culture, what thoughts and ideas the person would like to share, and how the person wishes to be remembered by future generations. Present the findings in terms of a multimedia report or invite the elders to address the class.

for her bread to bake in the old village north of Jerusalem. Susan's family had lived in Jerusalem for three years before she was ten and drove out to see her grandmother every weekend. They would find her patting fresh dough between her hands, or pressing cakes of dough onto the black rocks in the *taboon*, the rounded old oven outdoors. Sometimes she moved her lips as she worked. Was she praying? Singing a secret song? Susan had never seen her grandmother rushing.

Now that she was fourteen, she took long walks in America with her father down by the drainage ditch at the end of their street. Pecan trees shaded the path. She tried to get him to tell stories about his childhood in Palestine. She didn't want him to forget anything. She helped her American mother complete tedious kitchen tasks without complaining—rolling grape leaves around their lemony rice stuffing, scrubbing carrots for the roaring juicer. Some evenings when the soft Texas twilight pulled them all outside, she thought of her far-away grandmother and said, "Let's go see Saleh Hamadi. Wouldn't he like some of that cheese pie Mom made?" And they would wrap a slice of pie and drive downtown. Somehow he felt like a good substitute for a grandmother, even though he was a man.

Usually Hamadi was wearing a white shirt, shiny black tie, and a jacket that reminded Susan of the earth's surface just above the treeline on a mountain—thin, somehow purified. He would raise his hands high before giving advice.

"It is good to drink a tall glass of water every morning upon arising!" If anyone doubted this, he would shake his head. "Oh Susan, Susan, Susan," he would say.

He did not like to sit down, but he wanted everyone else to sit down. He made Susan sit on the wobbly chair beside the desk and he

> ## "It is good to drink a tall glass of water every morning upon arising!"

made her father or mother sit in the saggy center of the bed. He told them people should eat six small meals a day.

They visited him on the sixth floor of the Traveler's Hotel, where he had lived so long nobody could remember him ever traveling. Susan's father used to remind him of the apartments available over the Victory Cleaners, next to the park with the fizzy pink fountain, but Hamadi would shake his head, pinching kisses at his spartan room. "A white handkerchief spread across a tabletop, my two extra shoes lined by the wall, this spells 'home' to me, this says 'mi casa.' What more do I need?"

Hamadi liked to use Spanish words. They made him feel expansive, worldly. He'd learned them when he worked at the fruits and vegetables warehouse on Zarzamora Street, marking off crates of apples and avocados on a long white pad. Occasionally he would speak Arabic, his own first language, with Susan's father and uncles, but he said it made him feel too sad, as if his mother might step into the room at any minute, her arms laden with fresh mint leaves.

He had come to the United States on a boat when he was eighteen years old and he had never been married. "I married books," he said. "I married the wide horizon."

"What is he to us?" Susan used to ask her father. "He's not a relative, right? How did we meet him to begin with?"

Susan's father couldn't remember. "I think we just drifted together. Maybe we met at your uncle Hani's house. Maybe that old Maronite priest who used to cry after every service introduced us. The priest once shared an apartment with Kahlil Gibran[2] in New York—so he said. And Saleh always says he stayed

---

2. **Kahlil Gibran** (kä lēl´ ji brän´): Lebanese novelist, poet, and artist who lived from 1883 to 1931; his most famous book is *The Prophet*.

Hamadi ◆ 563

563

with Gibran when he first got off the boat. I'll bet that popular guy Gibran has had a lot of roommates he doesn't even know about."

"Susan said, "Dad, he's dead.""

"I know, I know," her father said.

Later Susan said, "Mr. Hamadi, did you really meet Kahlil Gibran? He's one of my favorite writers." Hamadi walked slowly to the window of his room and stared out. There wasn't much to look at down on the street—a bedraggled[3] flower shop, a boarded-up tavern with a hand-lettered sign tacked to the front, GONE TO FIND JESUS. Susan's father said the owners had really gone to Alabama.

THE PROPHET

KAHLIL GIBRAN

GIBRAN'S MASTERPIECE

Hamadi spoke patiently. "Yes, I met brother Gibran. And I meet him in my heart every day. When I was a young man—shocked by all the visions of the new world—the tall buildings—the wild traffic—the young people without shame—the proud mailboxes in their blue uniforms—I met him. And he has stayed with me every day of my life."

"But did you really meet him, like in person, or just in a book?"

He turned dramatically. "Make no such distinctions, my friend. Or your life will be a pod with only dried-up beans inside. Believe anything can happen."

---

3. **bedraggled** (bē drag′ əld) *adj.*: Limp and dirty, as if dragged through mud.

Susan's father looked irritated, but Susan smiled. "I do," she said. "I believe that. I want fat beans. If I imagine something, it's true, too. Just a different kind of true."

Susan's father was twiddling with the knobs on the old-fashioned sink. "Don't they even give you hot water here? You don't mean to tell me you've been living without hot water?"

On Hamadi's rickety desk lay a row of different "Love" stamps issued by the post office.

"You must write a lot of letters," Susan said.

"No, no, I'm just focusing on that word," Hamadi said. "I particularly like the globe in the shape of a heart," he added.

"Why don't you take a trip back to his village in Lebanon?" Susan's father asked. "Maybe you still have relatives living there."

Hamadi looked pained. "'Remembrance is a form of meeting,' my brother Gibran says, and I do believe I meet with my cousins every day."

"But aren't you curious? You've been gone so long! Wouldn't you like to find out what has happened to everybody and everything you knew as a boy?" Susan's father traveled back to Jerusalem once every year to see his family.

▲ **Critical Viewing** Would you like to read *The Prophet*, judging by its cover? Why or why not? [Make a Judgment] ❺

🎵 Humanities: Literature

Kahlil Gibran The essayist, philosopher, artist, and mystic poet Kahlil Gibran (1883–1931) was born in Lebanon, but came to America with his parents in 1895. After returning to Beirut to study, he finally settled in New York City, where he devoted himself to writing and art. His deeply spiritual works have been translated into more than twenty languages and his drawings and paintings have been exhibited around the world.

Invite students to read some or all of *The Prophet*, a book of twenty-six poetic essays that was first published in 1923. The essays are about a man who boards a ship to go home after a dozen years in a foreign city. Before he departs, some of the city's people ask him to share what he knows about the mysteries of life.

Interested students can prepare selections from the book as oral interpretations. Alternatively, they may wish to give their reactions to Gibran's ideas and philosophies by writing an essay, or through a small group discussion.

"I would not. In fact, I already know. It is there and it is not there. Would you like to share an orange with me?"

His long fingers, tenderly peeling. Once when Susan was younger, he'd given her a <u>lavish</u> ribbon off a holiday fruit basket and expected her to wear it on her head. In the car, Susan's father said, "Riddles. He talks in riddles. I don't know why I have patience with him." Susan stared at the people talking and laughing in the next car. She did not even exist in their world.

Susan carried *The Prophet* around on top of her English textbook and her Texas history. She and her friend Tracy read it out loud to one another at lunch. Tracy was a junior—they'd met at the literary magazine meeting where Susan, the only freshman on the staff, got assigned to do proofreading. They never ate in the cafeteria; they sat outside at picnic tables with sack lunches, whole wheat crackers and fresh peaches. Both of them had given up meat.

Tracy's eyes looked steamy. "You know that place where Gibran says, 'Hate is a dead thing. Who of you would be a tomb?'"

Susan nodded. Tracy continued. "Well, I hate someone. I'm trying not to, but I can't help it. I hate Debbie for liking Eddie and it's driving me nuts."

"Why shouldn't Debbie like Eddie?" Susan said. "*You* do."

Tracy put her head down on her arms. A gang of cheerleaders walked by giggling. One of them flicked her finger in greeting.

"In fact, we *all* like Eddie," Susan said. "Remember, here in this book—wait and I'll find it—where Gibran says that loving teaches us the secrets of our hearts and that's the way we connect to all of Life's heart? You're not talking about liking or loving, you're talking about owning."

Tracy looked glum. "Sometimes you remind me of a minister."

Susan said, "Well, just talk to me someday when *I'm* depressed."

Susan didn't want a boyfriend. Everyone who had boyfriends or girlfriends all seemed to have troubles. Susan told people she had a boyfriend far away, on a farm in Missouri, but the truth was, boys still seemed like cousins to her. Or brothers. Or even girls.

A squirrel sat in the crook of a tree, eyeing their sandwiches. When the end-of-lunch bell blared, Susan and Tracy jumped—it always seemed too soon. Squirrels were lucky; they didn't have to go to school.

Susan's father said her idea was ridiculous: to invite Saleh Hamadi to go Christmas caroling with the English Club. "His English is archaic,[4] for one thing, and he won't know any of the songs."

"How could you live in America for years and not know 'Joy to the World' or 'Away in a Manger'?"

"Listen, I grew up right down the road from 'Oh Little Town of Bethlehem' and I still don't know a single verse."

"I want him. We need him. It's boring being with the same bunch of people all the time."

So they called Saleh and he said he would come—"thrilled" was the word he used. He wanted to ride the bus to their house, he didn't want anyone to pick him up. Her father muttered, "He'll probably forget to get off." Saleh thought "caroling" meant they were

> "Everyone who had boyfriends or girlfriends all seemed to have troubles."

◆ **Reading Strategy**
If you were Susan, what would you be feeling toward your father right now? Why?

---

4. **archaic** (är kā′ ik) *adj.*: Old-fashioned; out-of-date.

◆ **Build Vocabulary**
lavish (lav′ ish) *adj.*: Showy; more than enough

Hamadi ◆ 565

🎼 **Humanities: Music**

Carols Strolling singers caroling in the street is a tradition that extends far back into history. During the Middle Ages, beggars roamed the streets during the holidays singing carols in exchange for money or food and drink. Later in England, carol singers known as Waits were invited inside to warm up with a cup of wassail. Today, groups of carolers often share their holiday musical spirit with friends and neighbors or nursing homes and hospitals.

The term "carol" originated from *choraulein*, a Greek circle dance performed with a flute accompaniment—not sung at all. These songs and dances were often a popular part of festivals and celebrations on many different occasions throughout the year. When the French replaced the flute accompaniment with singing, words were added. As time passed, Christmas became the main celebration for carol singing. Although some of the early carols were written down, many were passed down orally like folk tales and folk songs, and later set down on paper as written music.

Interested students might research the backgrounds of various carols, play the carols for the class, and share what they learned.

◆ Literary Focus

❶ Characterization Have students use this statement, an example of indirect characterization, to gain insight into Susan. *She sees TV and those who spend time watching it as being dull and uninteresting. She looks for a person with substance and originality.*

Comprehension Check ☑

❷ Why are Susan's parents doing this? *They are looking for warm clothing and flashlights to bring with them when they go caroling with Susan and her friends.*

◆ Critical Thinking

❸ Analyze How does Hamadi feel about going caroling? *Hamadi is excited and anxious to go, because he arrives on time with flushed cheeks.*

◆ LITERATURE AND YOUR LIFE

❹ Challenge students to think of a new holiday they might establish, if they could, and to explain or describe what it would commemorate and how they would choose to celebrate it.

◆ Reading Strategy

❺ Identify With a Character Have students summarize the caroling experience so far, from Susan's point of view. *Susan is delighted to see her parents, Hamadi, and her friends all singing together, each in his or her unique way.*

---

going out with a woman named Carol. He said, "Holiday spirit—I was just reading about it in the newspaper."

Susan said, "Dress warm."

Saleh replied, "Friend, my heart is warmed simply to hear your voice."

All that evening Susan felt light and bouncy. She decorated the coffee can they would use to collect donations to be sent to the children's hospital in Bethlehem. She had started doing this last year in middle school, when a singing group collected $100 and the hospital responded on exotic onion-skin stationery that they were "eternally grateful."

Her father shook his head. "You get something into your mind and it really takes over," he said. "Why do you like Hamadi so much all of a sudden? You could show half as much interest in your own uncles."

 Susan laughed. Her uncles were dull. Her uncles shopped at the mall and watched TV. "Anyone who watches TV more than twelve minutes a week is uninteresting," she said.

Her father lifted an eyebrow.

"He's my surrogate grandmother," she said. "He says interesting things. He makes me think. Remember when I was little and he called me The Thinker? We have a connection." She added, "Listen, do you want to go too? It is not a big deal. And Mom has a *great* voice, why don't you both come?"

A minute later her mother was digging in the closet for neck scarves, and her father was digging in the drawer for flashlight batteries.

Saleh Hamadi arrived precisely on time, with flushed red cheeks and a sack of dates stuffed in his pocket. "We may need sustenance on our journey." Susan thought the older people seemed quite giddy as they drove down to the high school to meet the rest of the carolers. Strands of winking lights wrapped around their neighbors' drainpipes and trees. A giant Santa tipped his hat on Dr. Garcia's roof.

Her friends stood gathered in front of the school. Some were smoothing out song sheets that had been crammed in a drawer or cabinet for a whole year. Susan thought holidays were strange; they came, and you were supposed to

feel ready for them. What if you could make up your own holidays as you went along? She had read about a woman who used to have parties to celebrate the arrival of fresh asparagus in the local market. Susan's friends might make holidays called Eddie Looked at Me Today and Smiled.

Two people were alleluia-ing in harmony. Saleh Hamadi went around the group formally introducing himself to each person and shaking hands. A few people laughed behind their hands when his back was turned. He had stepped out of a painting, or a newscast, with his outdated long overcoat, his clunky old men's shoes and elegant manners.

Susan spoke more loudly than usual. "I'm honored to introduce you to one of my best friends, Mr. Hamadi."

"Good evening to you," he pronounced musically, bowing a bit from the waist.

What could you say back but "Good evening, sir." His old-fashioned manners were contagious.

They sang at three houses which never opened their doors. They sang "We Wish You a Merry Christmas" each time they moved on. Lisa had a fine, clear soprano. Tracy could find the alto harmony to any line. Cameron and Elliot had more enthusiasm than accuracy. Lily, Rita, and Jeannette laughed every time they said a wrong word and fumbled to find their places again. Susan loved to see how her mother knew every word of every verse without looking at the paper, and her father kept his hands in his pockets and seemed more interested in examining people's mailboxes or yard displays than in trying to sing. And Saleh Hamadi—what language was he singing in? He didn't even seem to be pronouncing words, but humming deeply from his throat. Was he saying, "Om?" Speaking Arabic? Once he caught her looking and whispered, "That was an Aramaic word that just drifted into my mouth—the true language of the Bible, you know, the language Jesus Christ himself spoke."

By the fourth block their voices felt tuned up and friendly people came outside to listen. Trays of cookies were passed around and

566 ◆ Short Stories

Cross-Curricular Connection: Social Studies

Celebrations All cultures have unique holidays and celebrations, many of which appeal to people outside of the culture. For instance, in America, one need not be a Christian to know about some of the customs of the Christmas season. In "Hamadi," Susan and Tracy muse about celebrating "Eddie Looked at Me and Smiled" Day.

In fact, there are hundreds of annual celebrations and special-event days with modest or humorous origins that are treated as holidays. For instance,

do you celebrate Save a Spider Day (March 14)? How about Dictionary Day (October 16) to honor the birthday of American lexicographer Noah Webster?

Introduce students to the book *Chase's Calendar of Events,* an annual day-by-day directory of special days, weeks, and months celebrated around the world. Invite them to browse through it to compile a calendar of unusual celebrations or off-beat holidays to share with classmates.

dollar bills stuffed into the little can. Thank you, thank you. Out of the dark from down the block, Susan noticed Eddie sprinting toward them with his coat flapping, unbuttoned. She shot a glance at Tracy, who pretended not to notice. "Hey, guys!" shouted Eddie. "The first time in my life I'm late and everyone else is on time! You could at least have left a note about which way you were going." Someone slapped him on the back. Saleh Hamadi, whom he had never seen before, was the only one who managed a reply. "Welcome, welcome to our cheery group!"

Eddie looked mystified. "Who is this guy?"

Susan whispered, "My friend."

Eddie approached Tracy, who read her song sheet intently

▲ Critical Viewing Do the girls in the photograph seem to share qualities with Susan and Tracy? Explain. [Compare and Contrast] **⑦**

just then, and stuck his face over her shoulder to whisper, "Hi." Tracy stared straight ahead into the air and whispered "Hi" vaguely, glumly. Susan shook her head. Couldn't Tracy act more cheerful at least?

They were walking again. They passed a string of blinking reindeer and a wooden snowman holding a painted candle. Ridiculous!

Eddie fell into step beside Tracy, murmuring so Susan couldn't hear him anymore. Saleh Hamadi was flinging his arms up high as he strode. Was he power walking? Did he even know what power walking was? Between

houses, Susan's mother hummed obscure songs people never remembered: "What Child Is This?" and "The Friendly Beasts."

Lisa moved over to Eddie's other side. "I'm so *excited* about you and Debbie!" she said loudly. "Why didn't she come tonight?"

Eddie said, "She has a sore throat."

Tracy shrank up inside her coat. **⑧**

Lisa chattered on. "James said we should make our reservations *now* for dinner at the

Hamadi ◆ 567

⑥

Cross-Curricular Connection: Math

Language Tally Just as Hamadi spoke another language, many students are exposed to another language in their homes, neighborhood, or in the media. Have students conduct a survey to determine the number of different languages spoken in the homes of, or by family members of, students in your class.

Depending on their level of mathematical experience, students can conduct a simple survey of just the class, grade, or school; or, they may be able to apply sampling techniques to make statistical

projections for the neighborhood or community, based on the data they gather. They may wish to expand the survey to include informational questions concerning how and when the language was learned and how many years it has been spoken.

Students can present their findings in the form of a graph or chart, along with a written report that analyzes and interprets the results for an understanding of how it applies to their lives and the community. Encourage students to consult with their math teacher for additional guidance.

◆ Reading Strategy

❶ Identify With a Character Discuss with students why Susan's father feels "doomed to live in two places at once." *He retains memories of his childhood in Palestine, although he has lived most of his life in America.*

◆ Critical Thinking

❷ Interpret Challenge students to suggest why Susan might find immigrants bigger and melancholy. *Students may say that Susan has some familiarity with the immigrant experience and can appreciate how immigrants can feel torn between their old ways and their new life.*

▶ Critical Viewing ◀

❸ Speculate *He'd be much older, but since this is a diverse group, he would fit in fine. He'd probably do his best to participate fully and enjoy himself.*

Spelling

❹ The strategy for this selection focuses on spelling the unstressed *el* sound at the end of words as *–le* when that sound follows double *f, g,* or *t.* Point out the word *shuffle,* which observes this pattern.

Thematic Focus

❺ Appreciating Others Ask students to explain what Tracy's behavior implies about Hamadi. *Students may say that Tracy presses her face into Hamadi's coat because she senses that he is a kind, caring person who can empathize with her pain.*

Tower after the Sweetheart Dance, can you believe it? In December, making a reservation for February? But otherwise it might get booked up!"

Saleh Hamadi tuned into this conversation with interest; the Tower was downtown, in his neighborhood. He said, "This sounds like significant preliminary planning! Maybe you can be an international advisor someday." Susan's mother bellowed, "Joy to the World!" and voices followed her, stretching for notes. Susan's father was gazing off into the sky. Maybe he thought about all the <u>refugees</u> in camps in Palestine far from doorbells and shutters. Maybe he thought about the horizon beyond Jerusalem when he was a boy, how it seemed to be inviting him, "Come over, come over." Well, he'd come all the way to the other side of the world, and now he was doomed to live in two places at once. To Susan, immigrants seemed bigger than other people, and

▲ **Critical Viewing** How would Saleh Hamadi fit in with this group of carolers? What might he say or do? [Speculate] ❸

always slightly <u>melancholy</u>. They also seemed doubly interesting. Maybe someday Susan would meet one her own age.

Two thin streams of tears rolled down Tracy's face. Eddie had drifted to the other side of the group and was clowning with Cameron, doing a tap dance shuffle. "While fields and floods, rocks hills and plains, repeat the sounding joy, repeat the sounding joy . . ." Susan and Saleh Hamadi noticed her. Hamadi peered into Tracy's face, inquiring, "Why? Is it pain? Is it gratitude? We are such mysterious creatures, human beings!"

Tracy turned to him, pressing her face against the old wool of his coat, and wailed. The song ended. All eyes on Tracy, and this tall, courteous stranger who would never in a thousand years have felt comfortable stroking

568 ◆ Short Stories

Speaking and Listening Mini-Lesson

Monologue

This mini-lesson supports the Speaking and Listening activity in the Idea Bank on p. 571.

Introduce Review the characteristics of a monologue and point out that it can be serious, educational, suspenseful, or humorous, as long as it fits the character who delivers it.

Develop Have students list character traits for Shlemiel or Hamadi, based on direct or indirect story information. Students can use the lists to create monologues that introduce the characters and convey uniqueness. Set a reasonable time limit

for the final delivery of the monologue, such as 2 minutes. Encourage students to rehearse with a partner who can help them fine-tune it for accuracy of detail and general interest.

Apply Have students deliver the monologues, alternating Shlemiels and Hamadis. Challenge the audience to listen for details that support the written story, and for insights into the characters.

Assess Evaluate students on how well their monologues capture the character. Or, use Peer Assessment: Dramatic Performance, p. 116, in **Alternative Assessment.**

her hair. But he let her stand there, crying as Susan stepped up to stand firmly on the other side of Tracy, putting her arms around her friend. Hamadi said something Susan would remember years later, whenever she was sad herself, even after college, a creaky anthem sneaking back into her ear, "We go on. On and on. We don't stop where it hurts. We turn a corner. It is the reason why we are living. To turn a corner. Come, let's move."

Above them, in the heavens, stars lived out their lonely lives. People whispered, "What happened? What's wrong?" Half of them were already walking down the street.

⑤

◆ Literature and Your Life
What words of wisdom have you thought about long after you heard them said? Why?

⑥

◆ Build Vocabulary

refugees (ref´ yōō jēz´) *n.*: People who flee from their homes in a time of trouble

melancholy (mel´ ən käl´ ē) *adj.*: Sad; depressed

Beyond Literature

Social Studies Connection

Jerusalem Susan's father in "Hamadi" is originally from Jerusalem, an ancient city in the Middle East. "Jerusalem is a golden basin filled with scorpions," an Arab philosopher observed centuries ago. Today, Jerusalem is still a place of religious treasures and dangerous conflicts. This ancient city is a holy place to Jews, Christians, and Muslims. In the past, all three groups have fought for control of Jerusalem. During the Crusades, Christians conquered the city and controlled it for a time until the Muslims recaptured it. In modern times, Israel gained control of the city after several wars with Arab neighbors.

Cross-Curricular Activity
Research the Middle East, and draw a map showing current boundaries of its countries.

Guide for Responding

◆ LITERATURE AND YOUR LIFE

Reader's Response Would you like to know someone like Hamadi? Why or why not?

Thematic Focus In what ways is Hamadi a good friend?

✓ Check Your Comprehension

1. When does Susan first become interested in Hamadi?
2. Briefly describe Hamadi's background, where he lives now, and the type of things he says.
3. How do Susan and Tracy differ in the way they think about Eddie?
4. Why doesn't Susan want a boyfriend?
5. Summarize what occurs during the caroling.

◆ Critical Thinking

INTERPRET
1. Why do you think Susan feels Hamadi is a "surrogate grandmother"? **[Infer]**
2. What does Hamadi mean when he says, "I married the wide horizon"? **[Interpret]**
3. What does Susan see in Hamadi that her father and most of her friends don't? **[Analyze]**
4. Why do Hamadi's words and actions at the end of the story become so important to Susan? **[Draw Conclusions]**

COMPARE LITERARY WORKS
5. In what ways are Professor Shlemiel and Hamadi different and alike? **[Compare and Contrast]**

Hamadi ◆ 569

Beyond the Selection

FURTHER READING
Other Works by Isaac Bashevis Singer
Gimpel the Fool and Other Stories
The Magician of Lublin
Other Works by Naomi Shihab Nye
Hugging the Jukebox
Sitti's Secrets
Other Works About Appreciating Others
The Smallest Dragonboy, Anne McCaffrey
When Heaven and Earth Changed Places,
Le Ly Hayslip

INTERNET
We suggest the following sites on the Internet (all Web sites are subject to change).
For an informative article on Isaac Bashevis Singer:
http://www.boston.com/globe/search/stories/nobel/1985/1985ag.html
For an interview with Naomi Shihab Nye:
http://scholar.lib.vt.edu/ejournals/ALAN/spring95/Nye.html
We *strongly recommend* that you preview the sites before you send students to them.

◆ LITERATURE AND YOUR LIFE

⑥ Encourage students to share their responses. Students who prefer to keep such ideas private may record their thoughts in a reader's response journal.

Beyond Literature

Ask whether any of your students have visited Jerusalem, or if they know someone who has. Invite travelers to tell the class about their experiences and to share photographs, souvenirs, and recollections.

Reinforce and Extend

Answers
◆ LITERATURE AND YOUR LIFE

Reader's Response Students may say they would like to have someone in their lives who is as kind, thoughtful, interesting, and supportive as Hamadi.

Thematic Focus He is enthusiastic, caring, and represents a link to Susan's past.

✓ Check Your Comprehension

1. She develops an interest when she is a freshman in high school.
2. Originally from Lebanon, he now lives in a shabby motel room in Texas. He loves ideas and life, and tries to experience everything he can.
3. They both like Eddie, but Tracy has a crush on him.
4. She thinks that it's too much trouble to have a boyfriend.
5. When Eddie joins the caroling group and Tracy gets upset, she turns to Hamadi for comfort.

◆ Critical Thinking

1. He is kindly and reminds her of her relatives in Palestine.
2. He chose an unconventional life, rather than to settle down to marry.
3. She sees a man who appreciates ideas, experiences, and independence.
4. They become a source of inspiration and philosophy of life for her.
5. Both are men of ideas and values with many friends. Shlemiel has a more conventional life as a college professor, while Hamadi leads a more unusual life.

Answers

◆ Reading Strategy

1. He felt both foolish and relieved.
2. She wanted to comfort her friend.

◆ Build Vocabulary

Using the Word Root -chol-

1. b   2. c   3. a

Spelling Strategy

1. rattle; 2. (correct); 3. baffle;
4. (correct)

Using the Word Bank

1. Yes; a forsaken dog is abandoned.
2. Yes; pandemonium is wild disorder.
3. No; brittle people are unbending.
4. Yes; lavish garments are showy.
5. No; refugees usually have to rebuild their lives.
6. Yes; melancholy describes sadness or depression.

◆ Literary Focus

1. Shlemiel's wife has invited lots of people over to celebrate his birthday, which suggests that he is a well-liked person.
2. It is direct characterization to tell that Susan never eats in the cafeteria and is a vegetarian. When Susan remarks that people who watch TV are uninteresting, it is an example of indirect characterization because the comment reveals one of Susan's attitudes without stating it directly.

◆ Build Grammar Skills

Practice

1. *who watches TV more than twelve minutes a week* modifies *Anyone*
2. *who used to have parties to celebrate the arrival of fresh asparagus* modifies *woman*
3. *which never opened their doors* modifies *houses*
4. *that reminded her of the earth's surface* modifies *jacket*
5. *that just drifted into my mouth* modifies *word*

Writing Application

Sample responses:

1. Shlemiel is a professor who specializes in philosophy.
2. Hamadi lived in an apartment that would be too small for me.
3. Hamadi left behind many friends and family members whose lives were very different.

Guide for Responding (continued)

◆ Reading Strategy

IDENTIFY WITH A CHARACTER

By **identifying with characters,** you think and feel with them. In this way, you experience stories as a participant rather than as an onlooker.

1. In "The Day I Got Lost," how might the professor have felt as he finally rang the bell of his apartment?
2. What may have compelled Susan to put her arms around Tracy at the end of "Hamadi"?

◆ Build Vocabulary

USING THE WORD ROOT -chol-

Words with *-chol-*, as in *melancholy*, reflect an old medical idea about the bad effects of bile. On your paper, match each *-chol-* word in the first column with its meaning in the second column.

1. melancholy
2. cholesterol
3. cholera

   a. a disease of the intestines
   b. deep sadness
   c. a fatty substance that can clog arteries

SPELLING STRATEGY

In final, unstressed syllables, the letters *f, g,* and *t* are usually followed by *le* rather than *el*:

   brittle   giggle   raffle

Determine which of the following words are misspelled. Write each misspelled word correctly on your paper.

1. rattel   2. tattle   3. baffel   4. haggle

USING THE WORD BANK

Answer each question yes or no. Then, explain your answer.

1. Might you see a *forsaken* dog wandering in the streets?
2. Can a scene of *pandemonium* make you hold your ears?
3. Are *brittle* people usually open to new ideas?
4. Might you be noticed if you wore something *lavish*?
5. Do *refugees* usually live in fancy houses?
6. Does loss often create a feeling of *melancholy*?

◆ Literary Focus

DIRECT AND INDIRECT CHARACTERIZATION

These authors tell you **directly** what characters are like. They also show you **indirectly** what characters are like through their words, actions, and effects on others. The professor himself tells the story in "The Day I Got Lost," and his self-descriptions are direct characterization. However, you learn of his kindness indirectly through his rescue of the dog.

1. Find another example of indirect characterization in "The Day I Got Lost." Explain what you learn.
2. Locate one example each of direct and indirect characterization in "Hamadi." Explain how they differ.

◆ Build Grammar Skills

ADJECTIVE CLAUSES

An **adjective clause** is a subordinate clause that functions as an adjective; that is, it modifies a noun or a pronoun. Adjective clauses usually begin with a relative pronoun that relates the clause to the word it modifies. Relative pronouns are *who, whom, which, that,* and *whose.*

Adjective Clause

Everyone *who had boyfriends or girlfriends* all seemed to have troubles. (The adjective clause modifies *everyone.*)

Practice Identify the adjective clause in each sentence and the noun or pronoun it modifies.

1. Anyone who watches TV more than twelve minutes a week is uninteresting.
2. She had read about a woman who used to have parties to celebrate the arrival of fresh asparagus.
3. They sang at three houses which never opened their doors.
4. Hamadi had a jacket that reminded her of the earth's surface.
5. That was an Aramaic word that just drifted into my mouth.

Writing Application Use three sentences to describe Shlemiel or Hamadi, and include an adjective clause in each.

570 ◆ Short Stories

✎ Writer's Solution

For further instruction and practice, use the lesson in the *Writer's Solution Language Lab CD-ROM* on Clauses in Sentence Errors. You may also use the Adjective Clauses page, p. 55, in the *Writer's Solution Grammar Practice Book.*

Build Your Portfolio

 Idea Bank

Writing

1. **Missing-Person Bulletin** Professor Shlemiel is wandering around town again. Give the police a brief description that will help them locate him.

2. **Self-Portrait** As Shlemiel or Hamadi, create a written self-portrait. Include your outstanding traits, your likes and dislikes, and a description of your appearance.

3. **Episode** Write about another episode in the life of Professor Shlemiel or Hamadi. Be sure that your character is consistent with Singer's or Nye's. Also, use both direct and indirect characterization to portray the person.

Speaking and Listening

4. **Monologue** As Shlemiel or Hamadi, step out of your story and onto the stage. In a speech, tell an audience who you are and why you're special. **[Performing Arts Link]**

5. **Role Play [Group Activity]** With a partner, role-play a meeting between Shlemiel and Hamadi. As you make up your scene, keep in mind how each of these characters acts and speaks in his story. **[Performing Arts Link]**

Projects

6. **Report on Kahlil Gibran** In "Hamadi," Susan mentions and quotes from the Lebanese poet Kahlil Gibran. Read aloud to your classmates some of Gibran's poems from *The Prophet*. Also, tell them about Gibran's life. **[Literature Link]**

7. **Wise Fools and Tricksters** Find folk tales about wise fools and tricksters. Examples include the wise fool Djuha in the Arabic tradition and the trickster Anansi in African stories. Retell some of these stories to your class. Then, comment on the similarities and differences among the wise fools and tricksters. **[Social Studies Link; Literature Link]**

 Writing Mini-Lesson

Dialogue

One way in which Singer and Nye reveal character is through dialogue, a conversation between two or more people. Write a dialogue between two fictional characters. Use what they say to reveal their personalities indirectly. Also, reveal their personalities, and incorporate action into your dialogue by describing their gestures, actions, and expressions as they talk.

Writing Skills Focus: Create Realistic Dialogue

To **create realistic dialogue,** imitate the informal way in which people usually speak. This informality includes the use of sentence fragments. Here's an example from "Hamadi":

> **Model From the Story**
> Eddie looked mystified. "Who is this guy?"
> Susan whispered, "My friend."

Prewriting Create the framework for your dialogue by inventing two characters and a situation that causes them to meet. Also, jot down a profile of each character. Then, think about how their personalities will influence their speech.

Drafting Refer to your Prewriting notes for ideas. As you write your dialogue, say it aloud to make sure it sounds realistic and natural. Remember that dialogue works by cause and effect—characters respond to what they've just heard.

> ◆ **Grammar Application**
> In your dialogue, use adjective clauses to provide further information about nouns or pronouns.

Revising Have two classmates act out your dialogue. Whenever it sounds unrealistic, have the speaker improvise a more natural way of saying the same thing. Then, incorporate the improvisation into your dialogue.

The Day I Got Lost/Hamadi ◆ 571

 Idea Bank

Following are suggestions for matching the Idea Bank topics with your students' performance levels and learning modalities:

Customize for *Performance Levels*
Less Advanced Students: 1, 4, 7
Average Students: 2, 4, 5, 7
More Advanced Students: 3, 5, 6, 7

Customize for *Learning Modalities*
Verbal/Linguistic: 1, 2, 3, 4, 5, 6, 7
Visual/Spatial: 1, 2
Bodily/Kinesthetic: 4, 5
Logical/Mathematical: 6, 7
Interpersonal: 5, 6, 7
Intrapersonal: 1, 2, 3

Writing Mini-Lesson

Refer students to the Writing Handbook in the back of the book for instruction on the writing process and for further information on creating realistic dialogue.

 Writer's Solution

Writing Lab CD-ROM
Have students do the tutorial on Creative Writing. Follow these steps:
1. Have students examine the Dialogue Model from Literature.
2. Direct students to the Writing Hints on dialogue.
3. Have students draft on computer.
4. Have them edit with the Revision Checklist for dialogue.

Writer's Solution Sourcebook
Have students use Chapter 8, "Creative Writing," pp. 234–265, for additional support. The chapter includes in-depth instruction on punctuating and formatting dialogue, p. 263.

✓ **ASSESSMENT OPTIONS**

Formal Assessment, Selection Test, pp. 167–169, and Assessment Resources Software. The selection test is designed so that it can be easily customized to the performance levels of your students.

Alternative Assessment, p. 39, includes options for less advanced students, more advanced students, interpersonal learners, visual/spatial learners, musical/rhythmic learners, bodily/kinesthetic learners, and verbal/linguistic learners.

PORTFOLIO ASSESSMENT
Use the following rubrics in the Alternative Assessment booklet to assess student writing:
Missing-Person Bulletin: Description, p. 93
Self-Portrait: Description, p. 93
Episode: Fictional Narrative, p. 91
Writing Mini-Lesson: Drama, p. 105

Establish Writing Guidelines
Review the following key characteristics of a fictional narrative:

- Most fictional narratives include a main character who faces a conflict. The climax of the story comes when the conflict is resolved.

- A narrator tells a fictional narrative as someone who is part of the story, has witnessed the story, or describes the story as an outsider.

You may want to distribute the scoring rubric for a Fictional Narrative, p. 91 in **Alternative Assessment,** to make students aware of the criteria on which they will be evaluated. See the suggestions on p. 574 for customizing the rubric to this workshop.

Refer students to the Writing Handbook in the back of the book for instruction on the writing process and more information on narrative writing.

 **Writer's Solution**

Writers at Work Videodisc
To show students how author Rudolfo Anaya discovers story ideas, play the videodisc segment on Narrative Writing (Ch. 3).

Play frames 21977 to 31219

Writing Lab CD-ROM
If your students have access to computers, you may want to have them work in the tutorial on Narration to complete all or part of their fictional narratives. Follow these steps:
1. For topic ideas, have students use the Conflict Wheel activity.
2. Students can use the Character Profile Word Bin activity to describe characters' traits.
3. Have students draft on computer.
4. Students can use the interactive guide on strengthening characters.

Writer's Solution Sourcebook
For additional support, including in-depth instruction on using the correct verb tense, p. 99, use the chapter on Narration, pp. 70–103.

Connect to Literature Units 1–6 include examples of fictional narratives, such as "Charles" by Shirley Jackson and "Christmas Day in the Morning" by Pearl S. Buck.

Narrative Writing
Fictional Narrative

Writing Process Workshop

The Tell-Tale Heart, 1883, Odilon Redon, Santa Barbara Museum of Art

The tales of suspense, emotion, and achievement in this unit are all **fictional narratives.** The writers create events and characters that make you want to keep reading. A fictional narrative can be amusing, sad, or spine-chilling. It can be told by a character in the story or by an observer.

Although fictional narratives can be very different, they contain the same elements: They are made up, and they all have characters that face a conflict or a problem that is resolved by the end. Keeping these elements in mind, write your own fictional narrative.

The following skills, introduced in the Writing Mini-Lessons in this section, will help you plan and write your fictional narrative.

Writing Skills Focus

▶ **Create details that reveal character** and to make your plot believable. (See p. 538.)

▶ **Use suspense** to keep the reader guessing and to move the plot toward the climax and resolution. (See p. 549.)

▶ **Create realistic dialogue.** (See p. 571.)

MODEL FROM LITERATURE

from "The Tell-Tale Heart" by Edgar Allan Poe

I had my head in, and was about to open the lantern, when my thumb slipped upon the tin fastening, and the old man sprang up in the bed, crying out—"Who's there?" ①

I kept quite still and said nothing. For a whole hour, I did not move a muscle, ② and in the meantime I did not hear him lie down. He was still sitting up in the bed listening;—just as I have done, night after night, hearkening to the deathwatches in the wall. ③

① Poe uses realistic dialogue to portray the old man's fear.
② This detail reveals the main character's determination not to be seen or heard.
③ This final sentence creates suspense.

572 ◆ Short Stories

 Beyond the Classroom

Career Connection
Television or Film Writer Remind students that in addition to creating fictional narratives and writing novels for a living, writers may also develop scripts for television and film. Explain to students that most writers for television work together in groups to brainstorm for story ideas and to discuss how characters should act and how the story should progress. Writers in the film industry usually work alone or with one other person developing a script that they can then sell to a movie production house.

Have students work in groups to come up with an idea for a film or a new television show. Make sure students include a reference to indicate what audience the film or program is intended for. Explain that they do not have to create a complete story, but they do have to have all the basic elements developed—a "treatment." When students are finished, have them "pitch" their ideas to the rest of the class. Follow with a discussion in which students offer constructive comments about the ideas that appealed most, and why.

Prewriting

Choose an Idea Find an idea for a story by wondering *what if?* What if all the schools were suddenly closed? Where would kids go? Would they have to work? Use this questioning technique to come up with an idea, or try one of the following suggestions.

> ### Story Ideas
> - A teenager travels to another planet
> - A friendly bear cub appears in your yard
> - A contest
> - A championship game

Make a Timeline or Storyboard In simple terms, any narrative is a series of events. To plan your story's plot, simply list the events you will include as they will occur or—if you like to draw—create a storyboard that shows what events will occur.

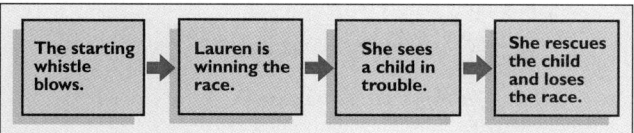

The starting whistle blows. → Lauren is winning the race. → She sees a child in trouble. → She rescues the child and loses the race.

Drafting

Use Dialogue As you tell your story, incorporate dialogue. Instead of simply telling the events, let them unravel through conversation. Keep in mind that in ordinary speech, people often don't use complete sentences and may pause between thoughts. The use of contractions and even nonstandard English is also common in ordinary conversation.

Description: Lauren became emotional when she was given a "hero" award.

Dialogue: Award giver: "Lauren, we would like to present you with this award for unselfishness and bravery."

Lauren replied, with her voice cracking: "Tha-ank you. Winning a race," Lauren wiped away her tears, "could never be as important as helping someone else."

Build Suspense Let your story move toward one moment of high tension—the turning point. Include hints or clues to increase your readers' sense of curiosity or anxiety about the outcome of the events.

APPLYING LANGUAGE SKILLS: Varying Tag Words

Tag words are the phrases, such as *he said* or *she said*, in dialogue. They show who is speaking and how the words are being said. For example:

"Villains!" I shrieked, "dissemble no more!" (Edgar Allan Poe)

"Climb up here," I whispered to Brooke.

"You like pickled broccoli?" I teased.

Practice Copy the following sentences into your notebook, replacing the tag words with more descriptive ones.

1. "Lincoln!" I said, "Come here this instant!"
2. "I'm very sorry," Molly said.
3. My mother said, "Why is your hair green?"
4. "Hamadi," she said, "be careful!"
5. "There was a cobra lying on her foot," he said.

Writing Application As you write dialogue for your fictional narrative, use descriptive tag words to help readers understand how the speaker is feeling.

> ### Writer's Solution Connection
> **Writing Lab**
>
> For more help with story ideas, use the Storyboard Activity in the Narration tutorial.

Writing Process Workshop ◆ 573

Prewriting

When considering topic ideas for a fictional narrative, remind students to write about something with which they are familiar. Even though the story should be of their creation, they may want to look to places and people they know as possible models for characters and settings. Remind students that although they are creating a work of fiction, they want it to be believable.

✒ Writer's Solution

Writing Lab CD-ROM
To help students come up with topic ideas, suggest they browse through the Inspirations for Narration in the Prewriting section of the tutorial on Narration.

Customize for
Visual/Spatial Learners
Encourage students to think of their stories visually—as drawings or pictures. Have them consider what details they would include if they were drawing a picture of the event they are going to write about. Suggest that students stimulate ideas and details by creating a drawing or painting of the event in their story, or perhaps, a character or the setting.

Drafting

Tell students that one of the best ways to check the realism of their dialogue is to read the dialogue out loud. If words sound awkward or stiff when heard aloud, they can usually be changed to seem more realistic.

✒ Writer's Solution

Writing Lab CD-ROM
Students can use the Transition Word and Phrase Bin activity in the Drafting section of the tutorial on Narration to help them select words and phrases to develop the flow of events in their narratives.

Applying Language Skills
Varying Tag Words Suggest that students review a fictional narrative they have read to gather ideas for different tag words.

✒ Writer's Solution

For additional instruction and practice, have students use the *Writer's Solution Language Lab CD-ROM* Writing Dialogue lesson in the Composing unit.

Answers
Suggested responses:
1. "Lincoln!" I exclaimed, "Come here this instant!"
2. "I'm very sorry," Molly whispered.
3. My mother screamed, "Why is your hair green?"
4. "Hamadi," she shouted, "be careful!"
5. "There was a cobra lying on her foot," he stated.

Revising

As students revise their drafts, suggest that they look for places to add details to strengthen descriptions. They may want to swap their narratives with partners and have their partners make suggestions for revisions.

 Writer's Solution

Writing Lab CD-ROM
In the tutorial on Narration, have students use the interactive guide on strengthening characters to help them with character development.

Publishing

Students might collect their stories in a class anthology. Encourage them to illustrate their stories in some way.

Reinforce and Extend

Review the Writing Guidelines
After students have completed their papers, review the characteristics of a fictional narrative.

Applying Language Skills
Consistency in Verb Tense Remind students to avoid shifts of tense when using compound verbs in a sentence. A sentence with a compound verb should have both verbs in the same tense.

Answers
1. The boys ran across the lot. They left their bikes behind.
2. A full moon rises. The Big Dipper hangs above our heads.
3. Lightning flashed. Thunder rumbled. Rain pelted our faces.

 Writer's Solution

For additional support, complete the Using Verbs practice pages in the *Writer's Solution Grammar Practice Book*, pp. 70–76.

Writing Process Workshop

EDITING/PROOFREADING

APPLYING LANGUAGE SKILLS:
Consistency in Verb Tense

When writing a fictional narrative, use verbs in the same tense to express events occurring at the same time. If you shift tenses when no shift is necessary, your meaning will become unclear.

Unnecessary Shifts:
Edgar *pulled* back the curtain. He *screams*—and shut the window just in time.

Consistent Tense:
Edgar *pulls* back the curtain. He *screams*—and *shuts* the window just in time.

Practice Rewrite the following pairs of sentences so they are in the same tense.

1. The boys ran across the lot. They leave their bikes behind.
2. A full moon rises. The Big Dipper hung above our heads.
3. Lightning flashed. Thunder rumbled. Rain pelts our faces.

Writer's Solution Connection Language Lab

For more help with consistent tense, see the Avoiding Shifts in Tense lesson in the Using Verbs unit.

574 ◆ Short Stories

Revising

Follow These Tips for Revising Use the following tips to help revise your narrative.
- ▶ **Characters** Give a boring character an endearing habit to make him or her more interesting.
- ▶ **Dialogue** Make sure that dialogue is realistic. The use of contractions and incomplete statements is acceptable in realistic dialogue. Read dialogue aloud to be sure that it sounds like natural speech.
- ▶ **Suspense** Examine plot events to ensure that they make sense and build suspense. Double-check your hints and clues to make sure they don't reveal too much before the climax.

REVISION MODEL

① , but this noise was moving.
Normally, Quinn was not very frightened of strange noises.
② Having been an Eagle Scout, the wonders of the outdoors were not a mystery, but
He was completely unprepared for the large disc flying
③ "Help! He-e-e-lp!" he stammered as he attempted to defend himself.
directly at his head.

① The writer adds this clause to create suspense and make the reader wonder what was moving toward Quinn.
② This detail provides more background about Quinn's personality. If he was fearful of the object, then it must have been especially frightening.
③ This dialogue reveals Quinn's feelings of fear.

Publishing and Presenting

Classroom Have classmates sit in a circle, and take turns telling or reading your stories. After each, ask listeners to tell what details in the story they liked or remembered most.

Magazines and Journals Submit your story for possible publication. Ask your librarian to help you find magazines for young people that accept unsolicited manuscripts, and send them your fictional narrative.

E-Mail Use e-mail to send your narrative to friends and family who live far away from you.

✓ ASSESSMENT		4	3	2	1
PORTFOLIO ASSESSMENT Use the rubric on Fictional Narrative in the **Alternative Assessment** booklet, p. 91, to assess the students' writing. Add these criteria to customize this rubric to this assignment.	**Details That Reveal Character**	The narrative includes many rich details that make characters understandable and believable.	The narrative includes many details but some do not contribute to the characters' believability.	The narrative includes details but not enough to make the characters believable.	The narrative includes few, if any, details.
	Consistency in Verb Tense	The narrative uses the same verb tense throughout.	The narrative uses the same verb tense, but shifts once or twice.	The narrative shifts verb tenses enough to make meaning unclear in places.	The narrative consistently shifts verb tense, making meaning unclear.

Real-World Reading Skills Workshop

Reading Novels and Other Extended Works

Strategies for Success

Reading a novel, a biography, or a full-length play differs from reading a short story or a poem. Reading an extended work can take several days or several weeks. Longer works usually involve more complex settings and characters than shorter works do. As a result, you need to approach longer works differently from shorter works.

Make a Plan Before beginning an extended work, establish a reading plan. Set goals for the amount you must read at each sitting, based on the time you have. Don't rush through the book, or you may miss important details.

Get an Overview Find out about the work before you begin reading. For a novel, scan the chapter titles to see how the book is divided. Titles of chapters or sections hint at the novel's plot and setting. For nonfiction, look at the table of contents to see how the book is divided. Also, preview any maps or illustrations that are included in the work.

Pause and Reflect Stop periodically to review what you have read. Reflecting on a chapter's main idea or a character's actions will help you better understand the rest of the work. Also, review any changes that have occurred. Has time passed? Has the setting changed? What major events have occurred? Jot down major changes in your journal. Then, refresh your memory by reviewing these details before reading new sections.

Appreciate Details A novelist or biographer has time and space to provide thorough descriptions. As you read, take time to enjoy descriptive passages. These details may help you better understand an upcoming twist in the plot or an action of the subject of a biography.

Apply the Strategies

Use the table of contents for the first part of *Shark Beneath the Reef* to answer the questions that follow.

Shark Beneath the Reef by Jean Craighead George

1.	A Round, Black Eye	1
2.	A Black Cross in the Sky	16
3.	The Reef Sends a Warning	27
4.	Griselda	35
5.	Ships and Sharks and Factory Boats	47

1. Which chapters are the shortest? Which are the longest chapters?

2. About how many pages a day would you have to read in order to finish the first four chapters in three days?

3. What can you tell about the setting of the book from the listing of chapter titles? What can you tell about the plot?

> ✔ Here are some other extended works that you can read strategically:
> ▶ Biographies
> ▶ Autobiographies
> ▶ Full-length plays

Real-World Reading Skills Workshop ◆ 575

◆ Build Grammar Skills

Reviewing Clauses

The selections in Part I include instruction on the following:

- Clauses (independent and subordinate)
- Adverb Clauses
- Adjective Clauses

This instruction is reinforced with the Build Grammar Skills practice pages in **Selection Support,** pp. 198, 204, and 211.

As you review clauses, you may wish to include the following:

- Clause Fragments

A common type of sentence error is using a subordinate clause as a complete sentence. A subordinate clause should not be punctuated and capitalized as a sentence. It should be connected to an independent clause or supplied with the missing parts. See the following examples:

Adjective Clause Fragment: Which he had recommended	Sentence: I enjoyed the book which he had recommended.
Adverb Clause Fragment: When I went home.	Sentence: I went to sleep when I went home.

 **Writer's Solution**

For additional practice and support using clauses, use the practice pages on Clauses, pp. 55–61 in the *Writer's Solution Grammar Practice Book.*

Answers
Practice I

1. Susan didn't really feel interested in Saleh Hamadi <u>until she was a freshman in high school . . .</u> (adverb clause modifies *feel interested*)
2. I swung the chair <u>upon which I had been sitting . . .</u> (adjective clause modifies *chair*)
3. "And <u>here you stand shivering and forsaken in the rain, while your loving master is searching for you everywhere."</u> (adverb clause modifies *stand*)
4. <u>I tried to call a number of friends, those whose telephone numbers I knew.</u> (adjective clause modifies *friends*)
5. <u>When all were sleeping, it came to me.</u> (adverb clause modifies *came*)

Clauses | Grammar Review

A **clause** is a group of words that contains a subject and a verb. There are two kinds of clauses—independent and subordinate. (See page 537.) An **independent clause** can stand alone as a complete sentence. A **subordinate clause** is dependent on an independent, or main, clause to express a complete thought. Subordinate clauses can act as adjectives or adverbs in a sentence.

An **adjective clause** begins with a relative pronoun and modifies a noun or a pronoun. It answers the questions *what kind* or *which one.* (See page 570.)

Relative Pronouns

that, which, who, whom, whose

Maybe that old Maronite priest *who used to cry after every service* introduced us.

An **adverb clause** begins with a subordinating conjunction and usually modifies a verb, an adjective, or an adverb in another clause. It answers the questions *when, where, how, why,* and *to what extent.* (See page 548.)

Common Subordinating Conjunctions

after, although, as, because, before, if, since, though, unless, until, when, where

When she saw the dog, she arched her back and spat at him, ready to scratch his eyes out.

Practice 1 Write each sentence in your notebook. Underline the independent clauses once and the subordinate clauses twice. Label the subordinate clauses as adjective or adverb. Tell what word each modifies.

1. Susan didn't really feel interested in Saleh Hamadi until she was a freshman in high school . . .

2. I swung the chair upon which I had been sitting. . . .
3. "And here you stand shivering and forsaken in the rain, while your loving master is searching for you everywhere."
4. I tried to call a number of friends, those whose telephone numbers I knew.
5. When all were sleeping, it came to me.

Practice 2 Combine the following pairs of sentences into one sentence. Make one of the clauses a subordinate clause as indicated.

1. Edgar Allan Poe wrote many tales of terror. He wrote "A Tell-Tale Heart." (adjective clause beginning with *who*)
2. Professor Shlemiel left his briefcase in the taxi. It might have contained his address. (adjective clause beginning with *which*)
3. The old man shrieked in terror. I entered the room. (adverb clause beginning with *when*)
4. The lady had screamed. This could have caused a cobra attack. (adverb clause beginning with *if*)

Grammar in Writing

✔ A subordinate clause can never stand alone. A clause standing alone is a sentence error called a fragment.

Practice 2
1. Edgar Allan Poe, who wrote many tales of terror, wrote "A Tell-Tale Heart."
2. Professor Shlemiel left his briefcase, which might have contained his address, in the taxi.
3. The old man shrieked with terror when I entered the room.
4. If the lady had screamed, this could have caused a cobra attack.

PART *2* # *Setting and Theme*

Moonwalk, 1987, Andy Warhol, ©1999 Andy Warhol Foundation for the Visual Arts/Ronald Feldman Fine Arts

Setting and Theme ◆ 577

One-Minute
Planning Guide

The selections in this section focus on setting and theme in short stories. "The Finish of Patsy Barnes" is the story of a young boy's struggle to save his dying mother and resolve his feelings about his father's death. "Tears of Autumn" describes a young Japanese woman's first journey to America to meet her husband-to-be. In "The Story-Teller," a traveler on a train entertains children with a story. "The Medicine Bag" details a boy's divided feelings toward his Native American grandfather.

Customize for
Varying Student Needs
When assigning the selections in this section to your students, keep in mind the following factors:

"The Finish of Patsy Barnes"
• A short story which may be of special interest to students who like horses
• Students may need help with dialect
• Includes a Beyond Literature Career Connection

"Tears of Autumn"
• A short story about the harsh realities of immigration in the early twentieth century
• Presents elements of Japanese culture

"The Story-Teller"
• A short story with an ironic twist

"The Medicine Bag"
• A short story about the lessons a boy learns from his Sioux grandfather
• Provides an opportunity for a Beyond Literature Cultural Connection

 Humanities: Art

Moonwalk, 1987, by Andy Warhol
Andy Warhol (1928–1987) was born in Pittsburgh and graduated from the Carnegie Institute of Technology in 1949 with a degree in pictorial design. In the 1950's, Warhol moved to New York City, where he became a succesful fashion illustrator. He is most famous, however, for his pop art series paintings, many produced on silkscreens, focusing on celebrities as well as popular household goods, such as the Campbell's soup can.

Andy Warhol is also associated with other aspects of twentieth-century pop culture. *Moonwalk* is from his last exhibited series, "The History of Television."

As a contrast to the realistic setting of *Moonwalk,* use Art Transparency 18, p. 77, in Art Transparencies. Joan Miró's *Dog Barking at the Moon* provides a fantasy landscape that incorporates the moon.

Have students study *Moonwalk*. Then discuss the following questions:

1. What is the setting and theme of *Moonwalk? Most students will recognize this picture as an astronaut walking on the moon; they may identify a theme as new discoveries or first steps.*

2. What kind of character(s) might you find in this setting? What sequence of events might take place? *Students may base their suggestions of characters and events on the realistic aspects of scientific space travel or on the fantastic elements of "other worlds."*

Guide for Reading

OBJECTIVES

1. To read, comprehend, and interpret two short stories
2. To relate short stories to personal experience
3. To ask questions
4. To appreciate setting
5. To build vocabulary in context and learn the word root: *-flu-*
6. To develop skill in using simple and compound sentences
7. To write a comparison and contrast essay that has clear and logical organization
8. To respond to short stories through writing, speaking and listening, and projects

SKILLS INSTRUCTION

Vocabulary:
Word Roots: *-flu-*
Spelling:
Use *ea* to Spell the Long e Sound
Grammar:
Simple and Compound Sentences
Reading Strategy:
Ask Questions
Literary Focus:
Setting

Writing:
Clear and Logical Organization
Speaking and Listening:
Monologue (Teacher Edition)
Critical Viewing:
Make a Decision; Draw Conclusions; Infer; Interpret

PORTFOLIO OPPORTUNITIES

Writing: Description; Personal Letter; Critical Review

Writing Mini-Lesson: Comparison and Contrast Essay

Speaking and Listening: Monologue; Sportscast

Projects: Museum Display; Set Design

More About the Authors
Paul Laurence Dunbar mowed lawns, raked leaves, and shoveled snow to earn money to go to school. In Central High School in Dayton, Ohio, Dunbar's friendliness and way with words made him popular with his classmates. In 1975, a U.S. postage stamp was issued in his honor.

Yoshiko Uchida experienced discrimination firsthand—during World War II, her family spent a year in Topaz, Utah in an internment camp for Japanese Americans. She was the first woman to write children's books about that internment experience.

Meet the Authors:

Paul Laurence Dunbar (1872–1906)

The first African American to support himself as an author, Dunbar wrote poems, novels, and short stories. He was born in Dayton, Ohio, the son of former slaves.

An Influential Poet
At an early age, Dunbar won recognition for his poetry. Written both in dialect and in standard English, his poems have continued to influence many writers. The title of Maya Angelou's autobiography, *I Know Why the Caged Bird Sings*, comes from Dunbar's poem "Sympathy."

THE STORY BEHIND THE STORY

Like Patsy Barnes, Dunbar was raised by a mother who "had come North from Kentucky." Patsy loves horses, and Dunbar was riding horses in Colorado when he wrote the story. He had moved there in 1899 for his health.

Yoshiko Uchida (1921–1992)

Uchida's twenty-seven children's books include *Picture Bride, Journey to Topaz,* and *Desert Exile.* In addition to works of fiction, she wrote books on Japanese American history and Japanese folklore. She said of her writing, "I hope to give young Asian Americans a sense of their past and to reinforce their self-esteem and self-knowledge."

◆ LITERATURE AND YOUR LIFE

CONNECT YOUR EXPERIENCE

You are rich in worlds. First, you have the everyday world in which you live. Then, you have the places that open out for you on television screens, movie screens, and the pages of books. These two stories will add to your wealth of worlds. They'll take you back in time a hundred years—to a thrilling horse race and to a ship sailing to California on a rough sea.

THEMATIC FOCUS: Conflicts and Challenges

The main characters in each of these stories take risks. In what ways do they display courage?

◆ Background for Understanding

SOCIAL STUDIES

"Tears of Autumn" takes place about a century ago, a time when most Japanese families arranged marriages for their children. An older relative or family friend would help set up these unions. Before reaching an agreement, each family had to be satisfied that the other was worthy. When the bride and groom lived far apart, they often exchanged pictures before meeting.

◆ Build Vocabulary

WORD ROOTS: *-flu-*

The root *-flu-*, meaning "flow," appears in words dealing with flow or movement. For example, the word *affluence* means "wealth." Wealth is a flow of goods to someone or something: *af-* ("to") + *-fluence* ("flow").

WORD BANK

Which word from the list means "one who practices diplomacy, the art of dealing with people"? Check the Build Vocabulary box on page 583 to see if you chose correctly.

compulsory
meager
obdurate
diplomatic
turbulent
affluence
degrading

The Finish of Patsy Barnes ◆ Tears of Autumn

The Jockey, Toulouse Lautrec

◆ Reading Strategy

ASK QUESTIONS

Because a story introduces you to a new world, you'll have questions as you read. To become more comfortable in a story's world, learn how to **ask questions** and answer them. Let yourself wonder about everything—from why a street has a certain name to what a puzzling sentence means. You can find the answers by rereading the passage, looking in a reference book for factual information, or simply reading the rest of the story to see how all the pieces fit together.

◆ Literary Focus

SETTING

The picture on this page takes you into a world of horses and riders. In the same way, a story takes you into the world of its **setting,** the time and place of its action. The setting consists of *all* the details of a place and time—anything from a galloping horse to a rainstorm to a marriage ceremony.

Use a chart like the one below to capture the settings of these stories (some details have been filled in for you).

"The Finish of Patsy Barnes"			
Time	**Place**	**Weather Conditions**	**Attitudes and Beliefs**
Early 1900's	"Little Africa"; racetrack	Not mentioned	Prejudice

Guide for Reading ◆ 579

◆ Build Grammar Skills

Simple and Compound Sentences If you wish to introduce the grammar concept for this selection, refer to the instruction on p. 592.

Customize for
Less Proficient Readers
To help students use the reading strategy of asking questions, have them use a chart for each story.

Who?	
What?	
When?	
Where?	
Why?	

Customize for
More Advanced Students
As they read, have students think about how the lives and actions of both Patsy and Hana are controlled by the setting in which they find themselves. Ask students to describe how each rises above the limitations of his or her circumstances and environment.

Preparing for Standardized Tests

Grammar The grammar concept for this selection is simple and compound sentences. Standardized tests may evaluate students' understanding of the distinction between these two types of sentences. Tell students that a simple sentence is one independent clause and that a compound sentence consists of two or more independent clauses linked by a coordinating conjunction. Remind students that *and, but, or, nor, for, so,* and *yet* are coordinating conjunctions. Present the following sample test question:

Identify the compound sentence.

(A) Hana came to America and married Taro.
(B) Patsy won the race, so his mother got the medical care she needed.
(C) Patsy handled the horse well, despite the fact that he was not really a jockey.
(D) Bringing needed medicine with him, the new doctor treated Eliza's sickness.

Students should note that (B) is the only compound sentence. Choice (A) has a coordinating conjunction, but one independent clause, and (C) has a subordinate clause and is therefore a complex sentence.

Humanities: Art

The Jockey, by Henri Toulouse-Lautrec

Toulouse-Lautrec (1864–1901) was known for his perceptive and moving paintings of Parisian personalities and nightlife. His work was also influenced by Japanese prints he had seen. Ask students to describe the elements of horseracing the artist captures in this painting. *Students may mention the horses' power and speed, the jockeys, and the colorfulness of the racing scene.*

One-Minute Insight "The Finish of Patsy Barnes" chronicles a few weeks in the life of a young boy with a serious problem—a sick mother who needs medical care she can't afford. To solve his problem, the boy uses his skill with horses. In so doing, he courageously confronts his past and takes a large risk. Fortunately, taking the risk pays off.

Clarification

❶ Patsy, an African American boy, may have an Irish name because his parents had been slaves for an Irish family and slaves often used the names of their owners.

◆ LITERATURE AND YOUR LIFE

❷ Point out the terms *colored* and *Negro*, noting that each was commonly used at the end of the nineteenth century to refer to people of African American descent, and that neither term had negative connotations at that time. Ask students to think of names or nicknames that they have used or been called that they may have wished to change over the years. Volunteers may wish to share their observations with the class.

◆ Literary Focus

❸ **Setting** *Students may say that they learn that the story takes place in the past. They can also deduce that Patsy is probably the son of former slaves, and that he and his mother live in an African American neighborhood with other former slaves or their descendants.*

▶ Critical Viewing ◀

❹ **Make a Decision** *The horse appears to be wild and spirited and they would approach it with caution.*

Customize for
English Language Learners
Some of the language in this story is from another era. Students are likely to be unfamiliar with expressions like "actuated by the idea," (excited by the idea) or "comparatively meager appointments" (shabby). Help students appreciate the meanings of these expressions and others they come across.

580

THE FINISH of PATSY BARNES

Paul Laurence Dunbar

His name was Patsy Barnes, and he was a denizen of Little Africa.[1] In fact, he lived on Douglass Street. By all the laws governing the relations between people and their names, he should have been Irish—but he was not. He was colored, and very much so. That was the reason he lived on Douglass Street. The Negro has very strong within him the instinct of colonization and it was in accordance with this that Patsy's mother had found her way to Little Africa when she had come North from Kentucky.

Patsy was incorrigible. Even into the confines of Little Africa had penetrated the truant officer and the terrible penalty of the

---
1. **denizen of Little Africa:** Someone who lives in an area heavily populated by African Americans.

◆ **Literary Focus**
What do you learn about the setting from this first paragraph? **❷**

❸

▲ **Critical Viewing** Would you approach the pictured horse with eagerness or caution? Explain. **[Make a Decision]** **❹**

 **Block Scheduling Strategies**

Consider these suggestions to take advantage of extended class time:

• Introduce the selections with the Interest Grabber. Have students discuss reasons why they do or do not consider themselves risk takers.

• Discuss the Literary Focus: Setting p. 579. Guide students to keep in mind how setting influences the actions of the main characters and causes them to become risk takers.

• To help students prepare for the Writing

Mini-Lesson, refer students to Chapter 5 of *Writer's Solution,* which is about writing expository essays that make connections.

• Devote class time to having students work in small groups on the Projects in the Idea Bank on p. 593. Invite volunteers to read aloud their monologues or sportscasts from p. 593.

• To help students understand the dialect of "The Finish of Patsy Barnes," have them listen to the recording.

 Listening to Literature Audiocassettes

compulsory education law. Time and time again had poor Eliza Barnes been brought up on account of the shortcomings of that son of hers. She was a hard-working, honest woman, and day by day bent over her tub, scrubbing away to keep Patsy in shoes and jackets, that would wear out so much faster than they could be bought. But she never murmured, for she loved the boy with a deep affection, though his misdeeds were a sore thorn in her side.

She wanted him to go to school. She wanted him to learn. She had the notion that he might become something better, something higher than she had been. But for him school had no charms; his school was the cool stalls in the big livery stable[2] near at hand; the arena of his pursuits its sawdust floor; the height of his ambition, to be a horseman. Either here or in the racing stables at the Fair-grounds he spent his truant hours. It was a school that taught much, and Patsy was as apt a pupil as he was a constant attendant. He learned strange things about horses, and fine, sonorous oaths that sounded eerie on his young lips, for he had only turned into his fourteenth year.

A man goes where he is appreciated; then could this slim black boy be blamed for doing the same thing? He was a great favorite with the horsemen, and picked up many a dime or nickel for dancing or singing, or even a quarter for warming up a horse for its owner. He was not to be blamed for this, for, first of all, he was born in Kentucky, and had spent the very days of his infancy about the paddocks[3] near Lexington, where his father had sacrificed his life on account of his love for horses. The little fellow had shed no tears when he looked at his father's bleeding body, bruised and broken by the fiery young two-year-old he was trying to subdue. Patsy did not sob or whimper, though his heart ached, for over all the feeling of his grief was a mad, burning desire to ride that horse.

His tears were shed, however, when, actu-

ated by the idea that times would be easier up North, they moved to Dalesford. Then, when he learned that he must leave his old friends, the horses and their masters, whom he had known, he wept. The comparatively meager appointments of the Fair-grounds at Dalesford proved a poor compensation for all these. For the first few weeks Patsy had dreams of running away—back to Kentucky and the horses and stables. Then after a while he settled himself with heroic resolution to make the best of what he had, and with a mighty effort took up the burden of life away from his beloved home.

Eliza Barnes, older and more experienced though she was, took up her burden with a less cheerful philosophy than her son. She worked hard, and made a scanty livelihood, it is true, but she did not make the best of what she had. Her complainings were loud in the land, and her wailings for her old home smote the ears of any who would listen to her.

They had been living in Dalesford for a year nearly, when hard work and exposure brought the woman down to bed with pneumonia.[4] They were very poor—too poor even to call in a doctor, so there was nothing to do but to call in the city physician. Now this medical man had too frequent calls into Little Africa, and he did not like to go there. So he was very gruff when any of its denizens called him, and it was even said that he was careless of his patients.

Patsy's heart bled as he heard the doctor talking to his mother:

"Now, there can't be any foolishness about this," he said. "You've got to stay in bed and not get yourself damp."

"How long you think I got to lay hyeah, doctah?" she asked.

"I'm a doctor, not a fortune-teller," was the

---

2. **livery** (liv′ ər ē) **stable** n.: Place where horses are kept and fed.
3. **paddocks** (pad′ əks) n.: Enclosed areas near a stable in which horses are exercised.

---

4. **pneumonia** (noo mōn′ yə) n.: Inflammation of the lungs.

◆ **Build Vocabulary**

compulsory (kəm pul′ sə rē) adj.: Enforced; required

meager (mē′ gər) adj.: Lacking in some way; inadequate

The Finish of Patsy Barnes ◆ 581

❺ Ask students to retell, in their own words, how the author is describing Patsy and his mother. *Students may note that school officials complain about Patsy to his hard-working mother. She cleans houses every day to support the family. Despite the fact that Patsy's behavior disappoints her, she never shows him anything but love and affection.*

Thematic Focus

❻ **Conflicts and Challenges** Conflicts between parents and children and between racial groups are frequent themes in literature. Ask students to note the conflicts in this selection and to think about and discuss the kinds of challenges that might arise from such conflicts.

◆ **Reading Strategy**

❼ **Ask Questions** Have students ask a question that might help them to better understand Patsy: *What is unusual about Patsy's reaction to his father's death?* Guide them to read the rest of the story to answer this and other questions they may have.

◆ **Literary Focus**

❽ **Setting** Ask students to describe the setting of the story. *Little Africa, Douglass Street in Dalesford, Ohio.* Point out to students that Dalesford is a setting that Dunbar used for several short stories and he usually referred to it as "Little Africa."

Customize for
Verbal/Linguistic Learners
Point out to students that Dunbar is best known for his poetry. Suggest that students look for examples of alliteration such as "bleeding body bruised and broken" and other poetic devices the author uses in the short story.

 Beyond the Classroom

Career Connection

Part Time Jobs In "The Finish of Patsy Barnes," young Patsy spends as much time as possible around horse stables. In so doing, he learns a great deal about caring for horses and even earns some money. Because he learns from skilled workers, his experience in the stables is much like that of an apprentice. An apprentice works for someone else in order to gain experience and to learn a trade.

Initiate a class discussion about part-time work as not only a way to make spending money, but

also as a way for students to learn skills that might help them in future jobs. Part-time jobs and summer jobs are an opportunity for students to explore career interests. Without investing a great deal of time and money in education or training for a career, a job may provide experience that helps a person decide whether they are interested in pursuing the career as life work.

Ask students to choose careers that interest them, and then work in groups to brainstorm the kinds of part-time jobs that might be available to them in those fields.

❶ Draw Conclusions Suggest that students look up the definition of *obdurate* in the dictionary. *Students may say that the boy appears to be intensely focused on something important to him while he does his chores, but that it is not clear that he is obdurate.*

◆ **Literary Focus**

❷ Setting *The doctor is prejudiced against the African Americans who have come north, implying that they bring poverty and crime into northern communities.*

◆ **Critical Thinking**

❸ Analyze Ask students to explain the conflicting feelings Patsy is experiencing and what he plans to do. *Patsy is furious with the doctor's racism and demeaning behavior toward his mother and ashamed that he can do nothing about it. He plans to work hard and earn money in order to pay for another doctor's care.*

◆ **LITERATURE AND YOUR LIFE**

❹ Ask students to reread the description of Patsy's request for a job from McCarthy, the liveryman. If students were giving advice to a friend who needed a job to earn extra money, what suggestions would they make for applying for a job?

Customize for
Verbal/Linguistic Learners
Dunbar is well known for his use of African American dialect in his writing. Beginning at the bottom of this page, he recreates the grammar and pronunciation Eliza would have used—that of an African American woman raised in the South. Invite volunteers to read excerpts from the dialogue. Alternatively, students may wish to listen to the audio tapes of the selection in order to appreciate the use of language.

Listening to Literature Audiocassettes

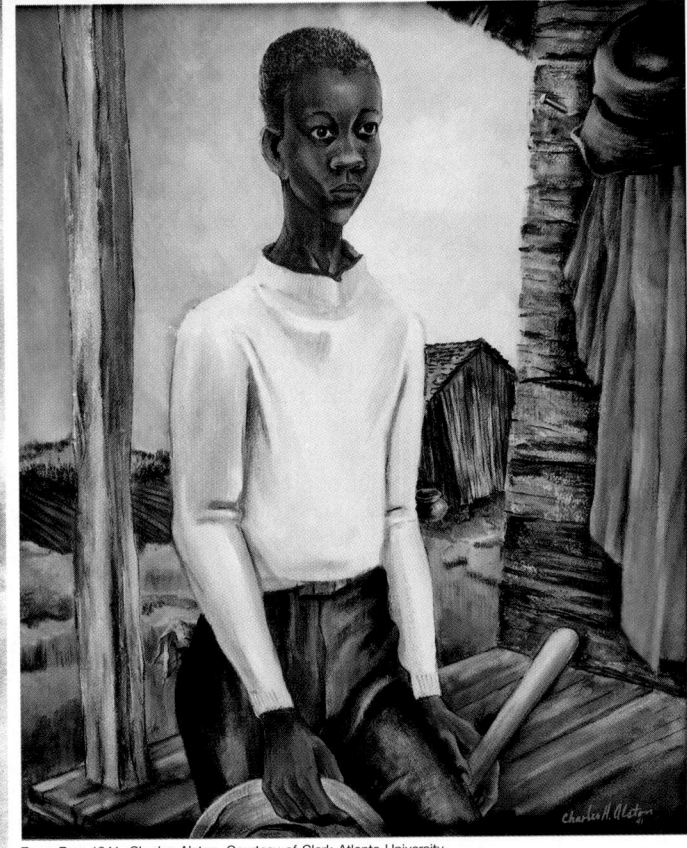
Farm Boy, 1941, Charles Alston, Courtesy of Clark Atlanta University

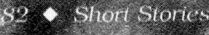
❶ ▲ Critical Viewing Would you describe the boy in this painting as "obdurate"? Why or why not? [Draw Conclusions]

reply. "You'll lie there as long as the disease holds you."

"But I can't lay hyeah long, doctah, case I ain't got nuffin' to go on."

"Well, take your choice: the bed or the boneyard."

Eliza began to cry.

"You needn't sniffle," said the doctor; "I don't see what you people want to come up here for anyhow. Why don't you stay down South where you belong? You come up here and you're just a burden and a trouble to the city. The South deals with all of you better, both in poverty and crime."

❷ ◆ Literary Focus People's attitudes are part of the setting. What prejudice does the doctor express?

He knew that these people did not understand him, but he wanted an outlet for the heat within him.

There was another angry being in the room, and that was Patsy. His eyes were full of tears that scorched him and would not fall. The memory of many beautiful and appropriate oaths came to him; but he dared not let his mother hear him swear. Oh! to have a stone—to be across the street from that man!

When the physician walked out, Patsy went to the bed, took his mother's hand, and bent over shame-facedly to kiss her. The little mark of affection comforted Eliza unspeakably. The mother-feeling overwhelmed her in one burst of tears. Then she dried her eyes and smiled at him.

"Honey," she said; "mammy ain' gwine lay hyeah long. She be all right putty soon."

"Nevah you min'," said Patsy with a choke in his voice. "I can do somep'n', an' we'll have an-othah doctah."

"La, listen at de chile; what kin you do?"

"I'm goin' down to McCarthy's stable and see if I kin git some horses to exercise."

A sad look came into Eliza's eyes as she said: "You'd bettah not go, Patsy; dem hosses'll kill you yit, des lak dey did yo' pappy."

But the boy, used to doing pretty much as he pleased, was <u>obdurate</u>, and even while she was talking, put on his ragged jacket and left the room.

Patsy was not wise enough to be <u>diplomatic</u>. He went right to the point with McCarthy, the liveryman.

The big red-faced fellow slapped him until he spun round and round. Then he said, "Ye little devil, ye, I've a mind to knock the whole head off o' ye. Ye want harses to exercise, do ye? Well git on that 'un, an' see what ye kin do with him."

The boy's honest desire to be helpful had tickled the big, generous Irishman's peculiar

❸

❹

🎵 **Humanities: Art**

Farm Boy (1941), by Charles Alston
The African American painter Charles Alston, born in 1907, studied and worked in New York City. His paintings, which influenced the work of celebrated artists Romare Bearden and Jacob Lawrence, carried the message to all Americans that the African American experience was a rich subject. *Farm Boy* is done in Alston's "primitive" style. The melancholy expression on the boy's face may reflect the injustices suffered by African Americans in the rural South. Use these questions for discussion:

1. What does the boy in the painting seem to have in common with Patsy Barnes? *Students may cite the boy's determined, serious expression and faraway look, both of which Patsy might exhibit.*

2. If you were to paint Patsy's portrait, how might his expression and pose differ from those of this boy? *Some students might say that they wouldn't differ; others might say that since Patsy loved his work in the stables and took it seriously, his expression would not be as melancholy as the boy's, despite his worries for his mother. Others might include a horse in the picture.*

sense of humor, and from now on, instead of giving Patsy a horse to ride now and then as he had formerly done, he put into his charge all the animals that needed exercise.

It was with a king's pride that Patsy marched home with his first considerable earnings.

They were small yet, and would go for food rather than a doctor, but Eliza was inordinately proud, and it was this pride that gave her strength and the desire of life to carry her through the days approaching the crisis of her disease.

⑤ As Patsy saw his mother growing worse, saw her gasping for breath, heard the rattling as she drew in the little air that kept going her clogged lungs, felt the heat of her burning hands, and saw the pitiful appeal in her poor eyes, he became convinced that the city doctor

⑥ was not helping her. She must have another. But the money?

That afternoon, after his work with McCarthy, found him at the Fair-grounds. The spring races were on, and he thought he might get a job warming up the horse of some independent jockey. He hung around the stables, listening to the talk of men he knew and some he had never seen before. Among the latter was a tall, lanky man, holding forth to a group of men.

"No, suh," he was saying to them generally, "I'm goin' to withdraw my hoss, because thaih ain't nobody to ride him as he ought to be rode. I haven't brought a jockey along with me, so I've got to depend on pickups. Now, the talent's set again my hoss, Black Boy, because he's been losin' regular, but that hoss has lost for the want of ridin', that's all."

The crowd looked in at the slim-legged, raw-boned horse, and walked away laughing.

"The fools!" muttered the stranger. "If I could ride myself I'd show 'em!"

Patsy was gazing into the stall at the horse.

"What are you doing thaih?" called the owner to him.

⑦ "Look hyeah, mistah," said Patsy, "ain't that a bluegrass hoss?"

"Of co'se it is, an' one o' the fastest that

evah grazed."

"I'll ride that hoss, mistah."

"What do you know bout ridin'?"

"I used to gin'ally be' roun' Mistah Boone's paddock in Lexington, an'—"

"Aroun' Boone's paddock—what! Look here, if you can ride that hoss to a winnin' I'll give you more money than you ever seen before."

"I'll ride him."

Patsy's heart was beating very wildly beneath his jacket. That horse. He knew that glossy coat. He knew that raw-boned frame and those flashing nostrils. That black horse there owed something to the orphan he had made.

The horse was to ride in the race before the last. Somehow out of odds and ends, his owner scraped together a suit and colors for Patsy. The colors were maroon and green, a curious combination. But then it was a curious horse, a curious rider, and a more curious combination that brought the two together.

Long before the time for the race Patsy went into the stall to become better acquainted with his horse. The animal turned its wild eyes upon him and neighed. He patted the long, slender head, and grinned as the horse stepped aside as gently as a lady.

"He sholy is full o' ginger," he said to the owner, whose name he had found to be Brackett.

⑩ "He'll show 'em a thing or two," laughed Brackett.

"His dam[5] was a fast one," said Patsy, unconsciously.

Brackett whirled on him in a flash. "What do you know about his dam?" he asked.

The boy would have retracted, but it was too late. Stammeringly he told the story of his

---

5. **dam** (dam) *n.*: Female parent of a four-legged animal.

◆ Reading Strategy

Why does the black horse owe something to Patsy?

◆ Build Vocabulary

obdurate (äb´ dŏŏr it) *adj.*: Stubbornly persistent

diplomatic (dip´ lə mat´ ik) *adj.*: Tactful; showing skill in dealing with people

---

The Finish of Patsy Barnes ◆ 583

◆**Reading Strategy**

⑤ Ask Questions Have students suggest a question that will require them to read further in order to answer. *Will Eliza recover and will Patsy's efforts be successful?*

Comprehension Check ☑

⑥ What does Patsy realize that he must do? *Students can understand that Patsy recognizes that he must do even more to make a significant impact on his mother's condition and help her recover. He knows that his mother is very sick and that he has limited resources to call upon.*

◆**Literary Focus**

⑦ Setting Tell students that Kentucky, the "Bluegrass State," is known for the breeding of thoroughbred horses and for horse racing. What does Patsy think when he asks if the animal is a "bluegrass hoss"? *He is suspecting that it is from Kentucky, from where his family came.*

◆**Reading Strategy**

⑧ Ask Questions *The black horse is the one that killed his father.*

Clarification

⑨ Each race horse owner has special colors which are draped over the horse and which make up the jockey's outfit. Spectators can identify each horse in a race not only by its number, but by its distinctive colors.

◆**Critical Thinking**

⑩ Infer Is Patsy afraid to ride the black horse? *Students will probably say that Patsy is afraid to ride the horse because it killed his father and is a wild and unpredictable animal, but he is also determined to prove himself and win.*

 Beyond the Classroom

Workplace Skills

Restraint Young Patsy Barnes exhibited a great deal of determination, but he also was capable of restraint, which he showed on several occasions. First of all, he showed self-control and restraint by not running back to Kentucky. Then he showed it by not confronting the racism of the doctor. Finally, he showed restraint in the way he masterfully handled his horse in the race.

Discuss with students that on the job it is often very important to be able to exhibit self-control

and restraint, to consider all aspects of a situation before acting. Guide them to appreciate that impulsive behavior can easily be counter-productive. Have groups of students discuss hypothetical and real situations they have experienced or witnessed, in which restraint and patience proved to be the best course of action, or in which impulsive behavior proved to be the worst. After all, Patsy got exactly the results he wanted not only because of his skills with horses, but also because he was able to show self-control.

Comprehension Check ☑

❶ How did the black horse come into the possession of the current owner, Bracket? *The owner won him in a poker game.*

◆ **LITERATURE AND YOUR LIFE**

❷ *Students may say they had similar feelings of self-confidence at times when they were doing something they knew they were good at, and at which they expected to achieve success.*

▶ **Critical Viewing** ◀

❸ **Infer** *Students may say that Patsy would take pride in the symbols, as they imply a mastery in the handling of horses.*

◆ **Reading Strategy**

❹ **Ask Questions** Have students share what questions they ask themselves as they read this passage. *Students may say they asked themselves whether Patsy will win the race and whether the race will indeed make a difference in Patsy's and his mother's life.*

Customize for
Visual/Spatial Learners

Visualizing a thrilling event like a close race can aid in comprehension and enjoyment. Encourage students to reread the second-by-second account of the race more slowly to visualize it as if they were watching it in person from the stands or on television.

Customize for
Musical/Rhythmic Learners

Suggest that interested students watch a movie or television program that contains a race or competition and note the kind of musical background that often accompanies the race. Challenge students to locate appropriate music to use as a background for Patsy's horse race. Suggest that they work with a group to read the description with selected musical accompaniment and perform for the class.

father's death and the horse's connection therewith.

"Well," said Bracket, "if you don't turn out a hoodoo,[6] you're a winner, sure. But I'll be blessed if this don't sound like a story! But I've heard that story before.

❶ The man I got Black Boy from, no matter how I got him, you're too young to understand the ins and outs of poker, told it to me."

When the bell sounded and Patsy went out to warm up, he felt as if he were riding on air. Some of the jockeys laughed at

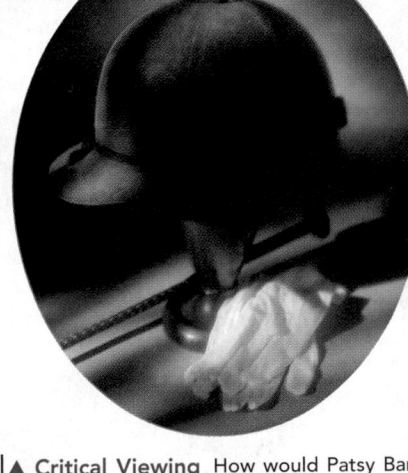

his getup, but there was something in him—or under him, maybe—that made him scorn their derision. He saw a sea of faces

❸ ▲ **Critical Viewing** How would Patsy Barnes feel about these symbols of a jockey? **[Infer]**

about him, then saw no more. Only a shining white track loomed ahead of him, and a rest-

❹ less steed[7] was cantering with him around the curve. Then the bell called him back to the stand.

They did not get away at first, and back they trooped. A second trial was a failure. But at the third they were off in a line as straight as a chalk-mark. There were Essex and Firefly, Queen Bess and Mosquito, galloping away side by side, and Black Boy a neck ahead. Patsy knew the family reputation of his horse for endurance as well as fire, and began riding the race from the first. Black Boy came of blood that would not be passed, and to this his rider trusted. At the eighth the line was hardly broken, but as the quarter was reached Black

---

6. **hoodoo** (hoō' doō) *n.*: Here, someone or something that causes bad luck.
7. **steed** (stēd) *n.*: High-spirited riding horse.

Boy had forged a length ahead, and Mosquito was at his flank. Then, like a flash, Essex shot out ahead under whip and spur, his jockey standing straight in the stirrups.

The crowd in the stand screamed; but Patsy smiled as he lay low over his horse's neck. He saw that Essex had made his best spurt. His only fear was for Mosquito, who hugged and hugged his flank. They were nearing the three-quarter post, and he was tightening his grip on the black. Essex fell back; his spurt was over. The whip fell unheeded on his sides. The spurs dug him in vain.

Black Boy's breath touches the leader's ear. They are neck and neck—nose to nose. The black stallion passes him.

Another cheer from the stand, and again Patsy smiles as they turn into the stretch. Mosquito has gained a head. The colored boy flashes one glance at the horse and rider who are so surely gaining upon him, and his lips close in a grim line. They are half-way down the stretch, and Mosquito's head is at the stallion's neck.

For a single moment Patsy thinks of the sick woman at home and what that race will mean to her, and then his knees close against the horse's sides with a firmer dig. The spurs shoot deeper into the steaming flanks. Black Boy shall win; he must win. The horse that has taken away his father shall give him back his mother. The stallion leaps away like a flash, and goes under the wire—a length ahead.

Then the band thundered, and Patsy was off his horse, very warm and very happy, following his mount to the stable. There, a little later, Brackett found him. He rushed to him, and flung his arms around him.

"You little devil," he cried, "you rode like you

Pneumonia Patsy's mother suffers from pneumonia, a lung infection. Before Louis Pasteur, Joseph Lister, and others revolutionized medicine through their study of bacteriology, pneumonia was often a killer. The disease is an inflammation of the lungs caused by a variety of bacteria, fungi, viruses, and other kinds of organisms. Pneumonia occurs when germs manage to evade the body's defenses in the upper respiratory tract, or enter through the mouth.

Invite students to find out more about the diagnosis and treatment of pneumonia by

answering questions such as these:

• How do doctors diagnose pneumonia?
• What are the symptoms? Are they always the same?
• Which are the most frequent infecting agents?
• Who gets pneumonia?
• How is pneumonia treated?
• Are there vaccinations?

Encourage students to consult a science teacher or school nurse. Have them share their findings with classmates in a report or visual display.

⑤ were kin to that hoss! We've won! We've won!" And he began sticking banknotes[8] at the boy. At first Patsy's eyes bulged, and then he seized the money and got into his clothes.

"Goin' out to spend it?" asked Brackett.

"I'm goin' for a doctah fu' my mother," said Patsy, "she's sick."

"Don't let me lose sight of you."

"Oh, I'll see you again. So long," said the boy.

An hour later he walked into his mother's room with a very big doctor, the greatest the druggist could direct him to. The doctor left his medicines and his orders, but, when Patsy told his story, it was Eliza's pride that started her on the road to recovery. Patsy did not tell his horse's name.

---

8. **banknotes** (baŋkʹ nōts) *n.*: Form of paper money.

Beyond Literature

Career Connection

Horse Trainer A horse trainer deals firmly but gently as he or she teaches a horse to respond to certain commands or situations. The trainer begins soon after the horse's birth, getting it used to being handled by humans. When the horse is a year old, the trainer slowly accustoms it to having a saddle on its back. Eventually, the horse is mounted and ridden for a few steps, then a few more, until it is used to having a rider. Once that is accomplished, the horse is taught to obey the signals used by riders and drivers. Finally, the trainer teaches the horse to fulfill the job or compete in the sport he's been trained to do.

Cross-Curricular Activity
Choosing Your Own Career Learn what it takes to become a horse trainer. Then, create a chart, showing the training and skills necessary to become successful at that career.

Guide for Responding

◆ LITERATURE AND YOUR LIFE

Reader's Response What do you think will happen to Patsy and his mother?

Thematic Focus What conflict inspires Patsy to take the risk of riding Black Boy?

Journal Writing In your journal, jot down a play-by-play description of Patsy's race.

☑ Check Your Comprehension

1. Instead of going to school, how does Patsy spend his time?
2. What happens to Patsy's mother that keeps her from working?
3. Why is Black Boy not a stranger to Patsy?
4. What does Patsy do with his earnings from the race?

◆ Critical Thinking

INTERPRET
1. What is similar about Patsy's reaction to his father's death and his reaction to the prejudiced doctor? **[Compare and Contrast]**
2. Explain the meaning of this statement: "That black horse there owed something to the orphan he had made." **[Interpret]**
3. How does Patsy show intelligence and judgment during the race? **[Support]**
4. In what way is Patsy's triumph a victory for both his father and mother? **[Infer]**

EVALUATE
5. Was Patsy's decision not to tell his mother the horse's name a good one? Why or why not? **[Make a Judgment]**

EXTEND
6. What does this story reveal about the problems African Americans faced when they moved from the South to the North? **[Social Studies Link]**

The Finish of Patsy Barnes ◆ 585

◆ Critical Thinking

❺ **Draw Conclusions** Ask students whether they believe Patsy won the race because of his riding skill. *Most students will believe that Patsy won not only because of his skill but because he was so determined and needed very much to win in order to help his mother.*

Beyond Literature

Have students brainstorm a list of techniques common to the training of different kinds of animals—from large mammals like elephants and bears, to small pets like parrots and poodles. Ask students to discuss the character traits and skills animal trainers need for success. Then, invite students to share their own experiences, both successful and not so successful, with training pets.

Answers
◆ LITERATURE AND YOUR LIFE

Reader's Response Students may say that Patsy's determination and his mother's love will cause things to turn out all right for them.

Thematic Focus Because Patsy needs to earn money to get his mother good medical care and he wants to master the horse that killed his father, he takes this risky money-making opportunity.

☑ Check Your Comprehension
1. He works at a stable.
2. She becomes ill with pneumonia.
3. Black Boy is the horse that killed Patsy's father.
4. With his earnings, he finds his mother a good doctor.

◆ Critical Thinking
1. In each case, he simmers helplessly with grief and anger.
2. A victory on the horse that made him an orphan could save his mother.
3. Patsy uses his knowledge of horses and of the horse he is riding to win the race.
4. He honors his father's life and saves his mother's.
5. Students may agree that bringing up the tragedy could upset his mother.
6. When African Americans moved north they did not leave prejudice behind.

Cross-Curricular Connection: Social Studies

Place Names Patsy Barnes lived on Douglass Street, a street named for the famous abolitionist Frederick Douglass. Many towns, cities, streets, parks and schools are named for people. Have students use an atlas or map to find locations such as:

- Madisonville, Kentucky
- Jeffersonville, Indiana
- Franklin, Kansas
- Washington, D.C.
- Roosevelt, Texas
- Churchill, Idaho
- Lincoln, Nebraska
- Monroe, Michigan

Ask students what all of these places have in common. Help them realize that all but Churchill are named for presidents of the United States. Challenge students to find place names in your community that honor famous people—more than 2 dozen U. S. schools are named for Carl Sandburg. Some names may be locally famous people. Have students research the name of your school or a local park. They can find who it was named for, when it was named or renamed, and what the person it was named for did that caused them to be honored with the place name. Point out to students that it is a great and lasting honor to be remembered with a place name.

Tears of Autumn

Yoshiko Uchida

▲ **Critical Viewing** What kinds of emotions do you see on the faces of the newly arrived immigrants pictured here? **[Interpret]**

❶

Hana Omiya stood at the railing of the small ship that shuddered toward America in a turbulent November sea. She shivered as she pulled the folds of her silk kimono close to her throat and tightened the wool shawl about her shoulders.

She was thin and small, her dark eyes shadowed in her pale face, her black hair piled high in a pompadour that seemed too heavy for so slight a woman. She clung to the moist rail and breathed the damp salt air deep into her lungs. Her body seemed leaden and lifeless, as though it were simply the vehicle transporting her soul to a strange new life, and she longed with childlike intensity to be home again in Oka Village.

She longed to see the bright persimmon dotting the barren trees beside the thatched roofs, to see the fields of golden rice stretching to the mountains where only last fall she had gathered plum white mushrooms, and to see once more the maple trees lacing their flaming colors through the green pine. If only she could see a familiar face, eat a meal without retching, walk on solid ground, and stretch out at night on a *tatami* mat[1] instead of in a hard narrow bunk. She thought now of seeking the warm shelter of her bunk but could

---

1. *tatami* (tə tä′ mē) **mat** *n.*: Floor mat woven of rice straw, traditionally used in Japanese homes.

586 ◆ Short Stories

Cultural Connection

Mail-Order or Picture Brides Hana and Taro did not know each other at all, yet Hana arrives from Japan to marry and live with Taro. The immigrant experience has been documented in print, photographs, paintings, cartoons, and films. Other movies focus on the custom of mail-order brides, or arranging marriages by long distance. They tell stories that explore issues faced by participants in these marriages between strangers.

Invite students to view movies such as *Sarah Plain and Tall*, *Heartland*, and *Seven Brides for Seven*

Brothers. Ask them to compare and discuss the experiences of these women and men and Hana and Taro with questions such as:

- Why would women and men choose this method of matchmaking?
- What do the women feel as they leave to meet their husbands?
- What are their expectations?
- What are the first encounters like?
- How do the marriages seem to work out?

not bear to face the relentless smell of fish that penetrated the lower decks.

Why did I ever leave Japan? she wondered bitterly. Why did I ever listen to my uncle? And yet she knew it was she herself who had begun the chain of events that placed her on this heaving ship. It was she who had first planted in her uncle's mind the thought that she would make a good wife for Taro Takeda, the lonely man who had gone to America to make his fortune in Oakland, California.

It all began one day when her uncle had come to visit her mother.

⑤ "I must find a nice young bride," he had said, startling Hana with this blunt talk of marriage in her presence. She blushed and was ready to leave the room when her uncle quickly added, "My good friend Takeda has a son in America. I must find someone willing to travel to that far land."

This last remark was intended to indicate to Hana and her mother that he didn't consider this a suitable prospect for Hana, who was the youngest daughter of what once had been a fine family. Her father, until his death fifteen years ago, had been the largest landholder of the village and one of its last samurai.[2] They had once had many servants and field hands, but now all that was changed. Their money was gone. Hana's three older sisters had made good marriages, and the eldest remained in their home with her husband to carry on the Omiya name and perpetuate the homestead. Her other sisters had married merchants in Osaka and Nagoya and were living comfortably.

◆ Literary Focus
What attitudes toward marriage are part of the setting of this story?

⑥

⑦ Now that Hana was twenty-one, finding a proper husband for her had taken on an urgency that produced an embarrassing secretive air over the entire matter. Usually, her mother didn't speak of it until they were lying side by side on their quilts at night. Then,

---

2. **samurai** (sam´ ə ri´) n.: Japanese army officer or member of the military class.

under the protective cover of darkness, she would suggest one name and then another, hoping that Hana would indicate an interest in one of them.

Her uncle spoke freely of Taro Takeda only because he was so sure Hana would never consider him. "He is a conscientious, hard-working man who has been in the United States for almost ten years. He is thirty-one, operates a small shop, and rents some rooms above the shop where he lives." Her uncle rubbed his chin thoughtfully. "He could provide well for a wife," he added.

"Ah," Hana's mother said softly.

"You say he is successful in this business?" Hana's sister inquired.

"His father tells me he sells many things in his shop—clothing, stockings, needles, thread, and buttons—such things as that. He also sells bean paste, pickled radish, bean cake, and soy sauce. A wife of his would not go cold or hungry."

⑧

They all nodded, each of them picturing this merchant in varying degrees of success and affluence. There were many Japanese emigrating to America these days, and Hana had heard of the picture brides who went with nothing more than an exchange of photographs to bind them to a strange man.

⑨

◆ Build Vocabulary
turbulent (tur´ byoo lənt) adj.: Full of commotion; wild
affluence (af´ loo əns) n.: Wealth; abundance

Tears of Autumn ◆ 587

Cultural Connection

Food In his shop, Taro Takeda sells many traditional Japanese food products, such as bean paste, bean cake, pickled radish, and soy sauce. Food commonly served in the United States might have seemed quite foreign to Japanese immigrants such as Hana. Although immigrants leave much behind, when they arrive in America they long for their favorite foods from their homelands.

Rice is a staple food in Japanese diets—cooked and eaten with vegetables at almost every meal. One of the main sources of protein is fish, which is not surprising as Japan is an island country

with easy access to the ocean and fishing industries. Other important sources of protein are soybean products such as tofu, miso paste, and soy sauce, a flavoring. Fresh fruits and fresh ingredients are also an important element in Japanese cuisine, as foods are not heavily spiced and covered with sauces, but natural flavors are enhanced. Hot tea is a popular drink. Food is eaten with chopsticks and arranged artistically on beautiful dishes whenever possible. Students may wish to study recipes to find out how Japanese food is commonly prepared and served.

"Taro San[3] is lonely," her uncle continued. "I want to find for him a fine young woman who is strong and brave enough to cross the ocean alone."

"It would certainly be a different kind of life," Hana's sister ventured, and for a moment, Hana thought she glimpsed a longing ordinarily concealed behind her quiet, obedient face. In that same instant, Hana knew she wanted more for herself than her sisters had in their proper, arranged, and loveless marriages. She wanted to escape the smothering strictures of life in her village. She certainly was not going to marry a farmer and spend her life working beside him planting, weeding, and harvesting in the rice paddies until her back became bent from too many years of stooping and her skin was turned to brown leather by the sun and wind. Neither did she particularly relish the idea of marrying a merchant in a big city as her two sisters had done. Since her mother objected to her going to Tokyo to seek employment as a teacher, perhaps she would consent to a flight to America for what seemed a proper and respectable marriage.

Almost before she realized what she was doing, she spoke to her uncle. "Oji San, perhaps I should go to America to make this lonely man a good wife."

---

3. San (sän): Japanese term added to names, indicating respect.

"You, Hana Chan?"[4] Her uncle observed her with startled curiosity. "You would go all alone to a foreign land so far away from your mother and family?"

"I would not allow it." Her mother spoke fiercely. Hana was her youngest and she had lavished upon her the attention and latitude that often befall the last child. How could she permit her to travel so far, even to marry the son of Takeda who was known to her brother?

But now, a notion that had seemed quite impossible a moment before was lodged in his receptive mind, and Hana's uncle grasped it with the pleasure that comes from an unexpected discovery.

"You know," he said looking at Hana, "it might be a very good life in America."

Hana felt a faint fluttering in her heart. Perhaps this lonely man in America was her means of escaping both the village and the encirclement of her family.

Her uncle spoke with increasing enthusiasm of sending Hana to become Taro's wife. And the husband of Hana's sister, who was head of their household, spoke with equal eagerness. Although he never said so, Hana guessed he would be pleased to be rid of her, the spirited younger sister who stirred up his placid life with what he considered radical ideas about life and the role of women. He often claimed

---

4. Chan (chän): Japanese term added to children's names.

588 ◆ *Short Stories*

 Speaking and Listening Mini-Lesson

Monologue

This mini-lesson supports the Speaking and Listening activity in the Idea Bank on p. 593.

Introduce Tell students that a monologue is a speech by one character. Discuss how it can reveal a character's inner thoughts and feelings.

Develop Have students form groups to discuss what they know about Patsy and Hana. Tell them to talk about what makes each character unique. Students should consider the influences of setting and other characters when they discuss Patsy's and Hana's personalities, beliefs, and goals.

Apply Have students write, edit, and practice their monologues. Encourage them to rehearse with another classmate for feedback before presenting to the entire class. You may wish to have students perform the monologues privately, tape them, and then play the tapes for the class.

Assess Evaluate students' monologues according to how accurately they express the views and personalities of the characters, as well as the quality of the dramatic presentations. Or, use the Peer Assessment: Dramatic Performance form, p. 116, in **Alternative Assessment.**

that Hana had too much schooling for a girl. She had graduated from Women's High School in Kyoto, which gave her five more years of schooling than her older sister.

"It has addled her brain—all that learning from those books," he said when he tired of arguing with Hana.

A man's word carried much weight for Hana's mother. Pressed by the two men, she consulted her other daughters and their husbands. She discussed the matter carefully with her brother and asked the village priest. Finally, she agreed to an exchange of family histories and an investigation was begun into Taro Takeda's family, his education, and his health, so they would be assured there was no insanity or tuberculosis or police records concealed in his family's past. Soon Hana's uncle was devoting his energies entirely to serving as go-between for Hana's mother and Taro Takeda's father.

◆ **Literary Focus**
For a Japanese family living at this time, what was necessary before a marriage could be approved?

❺

When at last an agreement to the marriage was almost reached, Taro wrote his first letter to Hana. It was brief and proper and gave no more clue to his character than the stiff formal portrait taken at his graduation from middle school. Hana's uncle had given her the picture with apologies from his parents, because it was the only photo they had of him and it was not a flattering likeness.

❻

Hana hid the letter and photograph in the sleeve of her kimono and took them to the outhouse to study in private. Squinting in the dim light and trying to ignore the foul odor, she read and reread Taro's letter, trying to find the real man somewhere in the sparse unbending prose.

By the time he sent her money for her steamship tickets, she had received ten more letters, but none revealed much more of the man than the first. In none did he disclose his loneliness or his need, but Hana understood this. In fact, she would have recoiled from a man who bared his intimate thoughts to her so soon. After all, they would have a lifetime together to get to know one another.

So it was that Hana had left her family and sailed alone to America with a small hope trembling inside of her. Tomorrow, at last, the ship would dock in San Francisco and she would meet face to face the man she was soon to marry. Hana was overcome with excitement at the thought of being in America, and terrified of the meeting about to take place. What would she say to Taro Takeda when they first met, and for all the days and years after?

Hana wondered about the flat above the shop. Perhaps it would be luxuriously furnished with the finest of brocades and lacquers,[5] and perhaps there would be a servant, although he had not mentioned it. She worried whether she would be able to manage on the meager English she had learned at Women's High School. The overwhelming anxiety for the day to come and the violent rolling of the ship were more than Hana could bear. Shuddering in the face of the wind, she leaned over the railing and became violently and wretchedly ill.

By five the next morning, Hana was up and dressed in her finest purple silk kimono and coat. She could not eat the bean soup and rice that appeared for breakfast and took only a few bites of the yellow pickled radish. Her bags, which had scarcely been touched since she boarded the ship, were easily packed, for all they contained were her kimonos and some of her favorite books. The large willow basket, tightly secured by a rope, remained under the bunk, untouched since her uncle had placed it there.

She had not befriended the other women in her cabin, for they had lain in their bunks for most of the voyage, too sick to be company to anyone. Each morning Hana had fled the closeness of the sleeping quarters and spent most of the day huddled in a corner of the deck, listening to the lonely songs of some Russians also traveling to an alien land.

As the ship approached land, Hana hurried up to the deck to look out at the gray expanse

❻
❼
❽

---

5. **brocades** (brō′ kādz′) **and lacquers** (lak′ ərz) n.: Brocades are rich cloths with raised designs; lacquers are highly polished, decorative pieces of wood.

Tears of Autumn ◆ 589

◆ **Literary Focus**
❺ **Setting** *Before a marriage could be approved, it had to have the blessing of the elders in both families and of the village religious leader. The families had to approve of one another and of the suitability, in terms of health, education, and prospects, of each prospective partner.*

◆ **Critical Thinking**
❻ **Compare and Contrast** Have students compare the nature of Hana's and Taro's "courtship" with today's customs. *Students may note that intimate feelings are kept private and that Hana and Taro need to read between the lines to try to understand who the other is. They can infer that people do not marry for love in Hana's culture, but that marriages are more like long-term financial arrangements.*

◆ **LITERATURE AND YOUR LIFE**
❼ Have students think about how they would feel if they were in Hana's place on the ship. Discuss Hana's excited and terrified frame of mind during her voyage toward the unknown. Ask students to share some of the things they think they themselves would be wondering about or dreaming about whether they were the ones on that ship.

◆ **Critical Thinking**
❽ **Infer** Ask students to tell why Hana is worrying more about what her home will be like and how she'll fare with her limited English than she is about what her new husband will be like. *Students may suggest that Hana is in a sense running away in coming to America. Her marriage is but a secondary concern to her main consideration—escape from the constraints of her family and village.*

Customize for
Interpersonal Learners
When interpreting Hana's decision to come to America and marry Taro, students should keep in mind the role of women in Japanese society at that time. They should judge Hana's decisions in light of the prevailing attitudes to best appreciate her independence and bravery, as well as her concerns and apprehensions.

Cross-Curricular Connection: Social Studies

Angel Island Generally speaking, European immigrants entered the United States through the immigration center at Ellis Island in the New York Harbor. Those who arrived here from Asia during the years 1910–1940 were held at Angel Island, in California, where they were examined and where they awaited their citizenship papers.

Have students research more about Angel Island and the Asian immigrant experience there. Have them find out what has happened to Angel Island since the immigration station closed, and what it is used for today. Encourage them to use the Internet and other sources to dig up first-hand information, if possible. Invite students to share their findings and to read aloud some of the descriptions of individual experiences.

In addition, students may wish to research and find out what kind of immigration restrictions are placed on prospective immigrants by the United States government today.

Enoshima. Island at left with cluster of buildings among trees. Fuji in distance at right, c. 1823, (detail), Katsusika Hokusai, The Newark Museum

of ocean and sky, eager for a first glimpse of her new homeland.

"We won't be docking until almost noon," one of the deckhands told her.

Hana nodded, "I can wait," she answered, but the last hours seemed the longest.

When she set foot on American soil at last, it was not in the city of San Francisco as she had expected, but on Angel Island, where all third-class passengers were taken. She spent two miserable days and nights waiting, as the immigrants were questioned by officials, examined for trachoma[6] and tuberculosis, and tested for hookworm.[7] It was a bewildering, degrading beginning, and Hana was sick with anxiety, wondering if she would ever be released.

On the third day, a Japanese messenger from San Francisco appeared with a letter for her from Taro. He had written it the day of her arrival, but it had not reached her for two days.

Taro welcomed her to America, and told her that the bearer of the letter would inform Taro

---

6. trachoma (trə kō´ mə) *n*.: Contagious infection of the eyes.
7. hookworm (hŏŏk´ wʉrm´) *n*.: Disease caused by hookworms, small worms that attach themselves to the intestines.

590 ◆ *Short Stories*

▲ **Critical Viewing** This painting depicts a Japanese village like the one Hana left. Why would her arrival at Angel Island cause her confusion and worry? [Infer] **②**

when she was to be released so he could be at the pier to meet her.

The letter eased her anxiety for a while, but as soon as she was released and boarded the launch for San Francisco, new fears rose up to smother her with a feeling almost of dread. **③**

The early morning mist had become a light chilling rain, and on the pier black umbrellas bobbed here and there, making the task of recognition even harder. Hana searched desperately for a face that resembled the photo she had studied so long and hard. Suppose he hadn't come. What would she do then? **④**

Hana took a deep breath, lifted her head and walked slowly from the launch. The moment she was on the pier, a man in a black coat, wearing a derby and carrying an umbrella, came quickly to her side. He was of slight build, not much taller than she, and his

◆ **Build Vocabulary**

degrading (dē grād´ iŋ) *adj*.: Insulting; dishonorable

 Humanities: Art

Enoshima. Island at left with cluster of buildings among trees. Fuji in distance at right (c. 1823), by Katsusika Hokusai

Katsusika Hokusai (1760–1849) was a Japanese wood engraver. Refer students to "Hokusai: The Old Man Mad About Drawing," by Stephen Longstreet, which appears on pp. 654–655 of this book. The landscape shown on this page can be found in Hokusai's collection known as Thirty-Six Views of Mount Fuji.

Use these questions for discussion:

1. What can you infer about life in the village in this painting? *Students may respond that life appears to be communal, pre-industrial, simple, and based on fishing and perhaps some agriculture.*

2. How do you think life in this village differs from life in the San Francisco Hana found when she arrived there? *By the time Hana arrived in San Francisco, it was a large, growing, bustling port city. Its inhabitants were rich, poor, and from all over the world.*

face was sallow and pale. He bowed stiffly and murmured, "You have had a long trip, Miss Omiya. I hope you are well."

Hana caught her breath. "You are Takeda San?" she asked.

He removed his hat and Hana was further startled to see that he was already turning bald. "You are Takeda San?" she asked again. He looked older than thirty-one.

"I am afraid I no longer resemble the early photo my parents gave you. I am sorry."

Hana had not meant to begin like this. It was not going well.

"No, no," she said quickly. "It is just that I . . . that is, I am terribly nervous. . . ." Hana stopped abruptly, too flustered to go on.

"I understand," Taro said gently. "You will feel better when you meet my friends and have some tea. Mr. and Mrs. Toda are expecting you in Oakland. You will be staying with them until . . ." He couldn't bring himself to

mention the marriage just yet and Hana was grateful he hadn't.

He quickly made arrangements to have her baggage sent to Oakland, then led her carefully along the rain-slick pier toward the streetcar that would take them to the ferry.

Hana shuddered at the sight of another boat, and as they climbed to its upper deck she felt a queasy tightening of her stomach.

"I hope it will not rock too much," she said anxiously. "Is it many hours to your city?"

Taro laughed for the first time since their meeting, revealing the gold fillings of his teeth. "Oakland is just across the bay," he explained. "We will be there in twenty minutes."

Raising a hand to cover her mouth, Hana laughed with him and suddenly felt better. I am in America now, she thought, and this is the man I came to marry. Then she sat down carefully beside Taro, so no part of their clothing touched.

❺

❺

Guide for Responding

◆ LITERATURE AND YOUR LIFE

Reader's Response If you were Hana, would you feel you had made a mistake in coming to the United States?

Thematic Focus What is courageous about Hana's journey?

Journal Writing As Hana, write a brief diary entry to record your first impressions of Taro.

☑ Check Your Comprehension

1. What problems at home make Hana willing to go to the United States?
2. Why does her mother change her mind about the marriage?
3. What keeps Hana from befriending the other women on the ship?
4. Summarize what happens when she meets Taro.

◆ Critical Thinking

INTERPRET

1. How does a phrase like "the small ship that shuddered" reflect Hana's feelings about her voyage? **[Connect]**
2. In what way does the description of her life in Japan reveal that she is "spirited"? **[Support]**
3. What does Taro's behavior toward Hana suggest about his personality? **[Infer]**
4. What does the end of the story suggest about Hana's future happiness? Explain. **[Draw Conclusions]**

EXTEND

5. What do you think ended the custom of arranged marriages in modern societies? **[Social Studies Link]**

COMPARE LITERARY WORKS

6. In which of these stories does the main character face greater obstacles? Why? **[Compare and Contrast]**

Tears of Autumn ◆ 591

Beyond the Selection

FURTHER READING
Other Works by Paul Laurence Dunbar
Lyrics of a Lowly Life
Complete Poems
Other Works by Yoshiko Uchida
Journey to Topaz
Desert Exile
Picture Bride

INTERNET
We suggest the following sites on the Internet (all Web sites are subject to change).

For biographical information about Paul Laurence Dunbar, and to see some of his poems:
http://members.aol.com/bonvibre/pldunbar.html

For more information on Katsusika Hokusai:
http://netspot.city.unisa.edu.au/wm/paint/auth/hokusai/

We *strongly recommend* that you preview the sites before you send students to them.

◆ LITERATURE AND YOUR LIFE

❺ The events leading up to the story of Hana's marriage to Taro are told as Hana sees them. Students may wonder what is going through Taro's mind. Invite them to reread the passages about Taro. Have them talk about what his concerns might be. Ask them to explain what they might feel if they were in his place.

Reinforce and Extend

Answers
◆ LITERATURE AND YOUR LIFE

Reader's Response Students' responses will vary, but most are likely to say that she made the right choice.

Thematic Focus She undertakes a journey not only to a new land with its new customs, but to meet a husband she has never seen.

☑ Check Your Comprehension
1. Options for her life in Japan were limited.
2. She is persuaded by her brother and the local priest.
3. She spent her time on deck, while the other women were sick in their bunks.
4. When they meet, she and Taro are polite, but reserved and nervous with one another.

◆ Critical Thinking
1. Hana herself was like a small ship—both fearful and excited, her emotions tossed about by her bold undertaking.
2. She has a plan to go to the big city and work, which is rejected by her mother. Her sister's husband accuses her of being "addled" by her education.
3. Taro's letters to her and his polite and appropriate behavior when they meet indicate that he is reserved, traditional, and seemingly reliable.
4. Hana's laughter implies that she will be happy in America.
5. Students may say that both men and women have become more independent and more interested in making their own life choices.
6. Responses will vary; have students support their views with details from the stories.

Answers

◆ Reading Strategy

1. Have students explain whether they found the answer to their questions by rereading, by reading ahead, or by doing research.
2. Students probably will want to know more about Patsy's life as he grew up and about Hana's life with Taro in America. Invite them to make predictions.

◆ Build Vocabulary

Using the Word Root: -flu-

1. *Influence* refers to an effect on actions or characters of people.
2. *Fluent* relates to something that flows or moves easily. Someone fluent in a language speaks with ease.
3. *Affluence* is a flowing toward, as in the way riches flow.
4. *Fluid* means "able to move and change shape." For example, *fluid assets* are available as cash or for other financial purposes.

Spelling Strategy
1. read; 2. lead

Using the Word Bank
1. d 2. f 3. a 4. g 5. b 6. c 7. e

◆ Literary Focus

1. The first story takes place in a town in Ohio in the late 19th century. The second takes place in Japan, on an ocean voyage, and in the San Francisco area during the first quarter of the 20th century.
2. The doctor's prejudice caused Patsy to make an effort to earn the money needed for better medical care for his mother.
3. The accepted ways to behave during the premarital period affect actions of both Hana and Taro. They are polite and cordial, but not intimate in their letters and their meeting.

◆ Build Grammar Skills

Practice
1. <u>She wanted him to go to school.</u> (Simple)
2. <u>The little mark of affection comforted Eliza unspeakably.</u> (Simple)
3. <u>The boy would have retracted</u> but <u>it was too late.</u> (Compound)
4. <u>He knew that raw-boned frame and those flashing nostrils.</u> (Simple)
5. <u>They were nearing the three-quarter post,</u> and <u>he was tightening his grip on the black.</u> (Compound)

Guide for Responding (continued)

◆ Reading Strategy

ASK QUESTIONS

By **asking questions** and answering them, you come to a more thorough understanding of the fictional worlds in "The Finish of Patsy Barnes" and "Tears of Autumn."

1. For each story, jot down a question you asked about a passage or phrase. Then, explain how you answered it or found the answer.
2. Identify a question you have about either of these stories that is still unanswered. Explain how you will answer it.

◆ Build Vocabulary

USING THE WORD ROOT -flu-

Explain how each of these -flu- words relates to the idea of flowing or movement. Use a dictionary if you need help.

1. influence   3. affluence
2. fluent   4. fluid

SPELLING STRATEGY

The long e sound in words such as *meager, peas,* and *league* is spelled *ea* rather than *ee.*

On your paper, write the answers to the following clues. Each answer is a word containing the *ea* spelling of the long e sound:

1. What you do as you look at the words on a page: ___?___.
2. What you do as you get in front and show the way: ___?___.

USING THE WORD BANK

On your paper, match each Word Bank word in the first column with the word or phrase closest in meaning in the second column.

1. compulsory   **a.** stubborn
2. meager   **b.** disturbed and wild
3. obdurate   **c.** wealth
4. diplomatic   **d.** required
5. turbulent   **e.** making one feel worthless
6. affluence   **f.** scanty; skimpy
7. degrading   **g.** polite in dealing with people

◆ Literary Focus

SETTING

The **setting** of these stories—where and when they take place—affects what happens in them. If Patsy Barnes hadn't grown up around horses, he wouldn't have learned how to ride. Also, if the city to which he moved didn't have a racetrack, he might have had no way to earn money.

1. Tell where and when each story takes place.
2. Attitudes are also part of the setting. Show how the doctor's prejudice influences Patsy.
3. Explain how a detail from the setting—including a belief or custom—influences Hana in "Tears of Autumn."

◆ Build Grammar Skills

SIMPLE AND COMPOUND SENTENCES

A **simple sentence** is one independent clause, and a **compound sentence** is two or more independent clauses joined by a coordinating conjunction or a semicolon.

Simple Sentence: Patsy was incorrigible.

Compound Sentence: His name was Patsy Barnes, and he was a denizen of Little Africa.

Practice On your paper, indicate which sentences are simple and which are compound. Underline each independent clause.

1. She wanted him to go to school.
2. The little mark of affection comforted Eliza unspeakably.
3. The boy would have retracted, but it was too late.
4. He knew that raw-boned frame and those flashing nostrils.
5. They were nearing the three-quarter post, and he was tightening his grip on the black.

Writing Application Choose one of these stories, and write a prediction about what will become of its main character. Use two simple and three compound sentences.

Writing Application
Possible response:
Hana will marry Taro and she will live in San Francisco. At first, she will work at the store until her English improves. It will improve, and then she will leave that job and begin teaching. She will have success as a teacher. Girls will look up to her. She will teach them to think for themselves, and they will respond to her guidance.

 **Writer's Solution**

For additional instruction and practice, use the lesson in the *Writer's Solution Language Lab CD-ROM* on Simple and Compound Sentences. You may also use the Classifying Sentences by Structure page, p. 59, in the *Writer's Solution Grammar Practice Book.*

Build Your Portfolio

 Idea Bank

Writing

1. **Description** Find a passage in one of these stories that describes the setting. Then, write a paragraph of your own, continuing the description. Be sure that the details you make up are in keeping with the ones the author uses.

2. **Personal Letter** Write a letter home as Hana, telling about your first week in the United States. As an alternative, write as Patsy to a friend in Kentucky, telling him about the race.

3. **Critical Review** Write a review of either story, exploring in detail the use of setting within it. Use details from the story to support your views.

Speaking and Listening

4. **Monologue** Write a monologue—a speech revealing a character's inner thoughts—for Hana or Patsy. Rehearse your monologue, and perform it for the class. Tape-record your performance if possible. **[Performing Arts Link]**

5. **Sportscast** Reread the account of the race in "The Finish of Patsy Barnes." Then, adapt it as a script for a radio broadcast, and read it aloud to the class. **[Media Link]**

Projects

6. **Museum Display [Group Activity]** With a few classmates, create a museum display on immigration. Using history books and Web sites, research the emigration of African Americans from the South to the North or the emigration of Japanese to California. In a display, show what you've learned. **[Art Link; Social Studies Link]**

7. **Set Design** Design a set for a play based on one of these stories. Figure out how to suggest the story's setting on a stage. Sketch out your ideas, including notes on the set's dimensions and building materials. **[Art Link]**

 Writing Mini-Lesson

Comparison and Contrast

It's natural to compare these stories, which are set at about the same time. For example, both Patsy and Hana have to fight prejudice and take risks. Write a comparison-and-contrast essay about the stories, showing how they're alike and different.

Writing Skills Focus: Clear and Logical Organization

Readers will follow your comparison more easily if it has a **clear and logical organization.** There are two basic types of organization that work well for a comparison-and-contrast paper. In subject-by-subject organization, you discuss one story first and then the next. In point-by-point organization, you discuss each point of comparison in turn.

Prewriting Decide which element of the stories you will compare and contrast—for example, the risks that the main characters take or the prejudices they face. Then, jot down ways in which this element is similar and different in both stories.

Drafting Choose a clear and logical organization, like one of those suggested in the Writing Skills Focus. Refer to your notes about similarities and differences as you write.

> ◆ **Grammar Application**
>
> For variety, use both simple and compound sentences in your essay.

Revising Check that your organization is consistent. For example, if you included ideas about Hana in a paragraph devoted to Patsy, move these ideas to where they belong. If you forgot a summary, stating your conclusion, add it now.

The Finish of Patsy Barnes/Tears of Autumn ◆ 593

 Idea Bank

Following are suggestions for matching the Idea Bank topics with your students' performance levels and learning modalities:

Customize for
Performance Levels
Less Advanced Students: 1, 4, 5
Average Students: 2, 4, 5, 6, 7
More Advanced Students: 3, 4, 6, 7

Customize for
Learning Modalities
Verbal/Linguistic: 1, 2, 3, 4, 5, 6, 7
Visual/Spatial: 5, 6, 7
Bodily/Kinesthetic: 6, 7
Logical/Mathematical: 3, 6, 7
Interpersonal: 2, 6, 7
Intrapersonal: 1, 3, 4

 Writing Mini-Lesson

Refer students to the Writing Handbook in the back of the book for instruction on the writing process and for further information on comparison/contrast essays. Have students use the Venn Diagram in **Writing and Language Transparencies,** p. 77, to organize their ideas.

 **Writer's Solution**

Writers at Work Videodisc
Use the segment on drafting an expository work (Ch. 5), featuring Bruce Brooks, to show students how he describes his method for writing.

Play frames 46111 to 47767

Writing Lab CD-ROM
Have students complete the tutorial on Exposition: Making Connections. Follow these steps:

1. Have students use the Interactive Writing Hint in which they choose from among the five Ws (*who, what, when, where, and why*) to find hints for gathering details.
2. Have students use organization models for comparison and contrast.
3. Have students draft on computer.
4. Have students use Self-Evaluation Checklists when revising.

Writer's Solution Sourcebook
Have students use Chapter 5, "Exposition: Making Connections," pp. 136–165, for additional support.

✓ **ASSESSMENT OPTIONS**

Formal Assessment, Selection Test, pp. 168–170, and Assessment Resources Software. The selection test is designed so that it can be easily customized to the performance levels of your students.

Alternative Assessment, p. 40, includes options for less advanced students, more advanced students, verbal/linguistic learners, musical/rhythmic learners, bodily/kinesthetic learners, interpersonal learners, and logical/mathematical learners.

PORTFOLIO ASSESSMENT
Use the following rubrics in the **Alternative Assessment** booklet to assess student writing:
Description: Description, p. 93
Personal Letter: Expression, p. 90
Critical Review: Critical Review, p. 107
Writing Mini-Lesson: Comparison/Contrast, p. 99

OBJECTIVES

1. To read, comprehend, and interpret two short stories
2. To relate short stories to personal experience
3. To make inferences
4. To recognize theme
5. To build vocabulary in context and learn the suffix *-less*
6. To identify complex sentences
7. To create a book jacket that provides supporting details
8. To respond to stories through writing, speaking and listening, and projects

SKILLS INSTRUCTION

Vocabulary:
Suffixes:
-less
Spelling:
Final *ur* Sound as
-or
Grammar:
Complex Sentences
Reading Strategy:
Make Inferences
Literary Focus:
Theme
Writing:
Supporting Details

Speaking and Listening:
Storytelling
(Teacher Edition)
Viewing and Representing:
Remembering an Elder (Teacher Edition)
Critical Viewing:
Draw Conclusions; Contrast; Infer; Connect

PORTFOLIO OPPORTUNITIES

Writing: List; Compare and Contrast; Analysis and Evaluation
Writing Mini-Lesson: Book Jacket
Speaking and Listening: Storytelling; DJ's Rap
Projects: Space Capsule; Travel Itinerary

More About the Authors
Hector Hugh Munro, or Saki loved the outrageous. He used his glib wit to satirize social situations, cruelty, and lack of understanding. The character of the aunt in "The Story-Teller" may have been inspired by the aunts who raised him. Munro took his pen name from the *Rubaiyat of Omar Khayyam,* a book of twelfth-century Persian poetry.

Virginia Driving Hawk Sneve (whose last name rhymes with gravy) has not only written for children and adults, but has also taught music, English, speech, and drama; has been a guidance counselor, a TV producer, and consultant. With her husband, she owns and runs an antiques shop.

Guide for Reading

Meet the Authors:

Saki (H. H. Munro) (1870–1916)

Long before today's celebrities started using single names, H. H. Munro became famous under the pen name of Saki. Born to British parents in Burma (Myanmar), Saki was sent to England to be raised by two aunts after his mother died.

A Writing Career Plagued by illness for most of his life, Saki was unable to follow his father in a career as a Burmese police-man. However, Saki made his name as a witty newspaper writer in London. He also became famous for his humorous short stories, which often had surprise endings.

A Soldier's End Saki's own life ended with a surprise twist. After surviving all the illnesses in his life, he died a soldier in World War I.

Virginia Driving Hawk Sneve (1933–   )

Virginia Driving Hawk Sneve (snā vē) grew up on the Sioux Reserva-tion in South Dakota. A writer and teacher, she has won many awards for her fiction. In novels like *Jimmy Yellow Hawk* and *High Elk's Treasure,* she draws on her inti-mate knowledge of Sioux life. Her Sioux heritage also plays an important role in "The Medicine Bag."

594 ◆ Short Stories

◆ LITERATURE AND YOUR LIFE

CONNECT YOUR EXPERIENCE

You've probably received gifts from older friends and family members. Some you can touch—for example, a ring passed down from a great-grandparent. Other gifts, just as valuable, touch your heart but cannot be physi-cally touched—for example, a wise or funny story.

These two stories deal with the gifts that adults give to young people, in a casual way or with great ceremony.

THEMATIC FOCUS: Appreciating Others

In what ways do the characters in these stories earn the gratitude of others?

◆ Background for Understanding

SOCIAL STUDIES

In "The Medicine Bag," you'll read about a young boy who receives his grandfather's medicine bag. For Native American groups living on the Great Plains, medicine bags were sacred gifts. A personal medicine bag would contain symbolic items that were suggested to an indi-vidual by a supernatural power. A tribal medicine bundle would contain items given to the group in ancient times.

◆ Build Vocabulary

SUFFIXES: *-less*

The suffix *-less* means "without." In "The Story-Teller," Saki writes that children moved *listlessly.* The word part *list-* means "to wish or desire," and *-less,* which acts as a "minus sign," changes the meaning to "without desire."

WORD BANK

Which of these words from the list describes someone who is not married? Check the Build Vocabulary box on page 597 to see if you chose correctly.

bachelor
resolute
listlessly
authentic
procession

Prentice Hall Literature Program Resources

REINFORCE / RETEACH / EXTEND
Selection Support Pages
Build Vocabulary: Suffixes: *-less,* p. 219
Build Spelling Skills, p. 220
Build Grammar Skills: Complex Sentences, p. 221
Reading Strategy: Make Inferences, p. 222
Literary Focus: Theme, p. 223
Strategies for Diverse Student Needs, pp. 81–82
Beyond Literature Community Connection: Parks, p. 41

Formal Assessment Selection Test, pp. 173–175, Assessment Resources Software
Alternative Assessment, p. 41
Writing and Language Transparencies Sensory Language Chart, p. 69; Sunburst Organizer, p. 85
Resource Pro CD-ROM
"The Story-Teller"; "The Medicine Bag"—includes all resource material and customizable lesson plan

 Listening to Literature Audiocassettes
"The Story-Teller"; "The Medicine Bag"

The Story-Teller
◆ The Medicine Bag ◆

Story Teller, Velino "Shije" Herrera, National Museum of American Art, Washington, D.C.

◆ Literary Focus

THEME

The **theme** of a story—its insight into life—is a gift of meaning that the author gives you. Usually, you can sum up a story's theme in a sentence or two about people or life. Sometimes, an author hands you the gift of meaning and **states the theme** directly in the story. Other times, an author **implies the theme,** asking you to figure it out for yourself.

In each of these stories, the author implies the theme.

◆ Reading Strategy

MAKE INFERENCES

You must **make inferences,** reach conclusions based on evidence, to figure out an implied theme as you read. The evidence you use may include the way in which events develop, the contrasts between characters, and the changes in a character. Reflecting on these details, you decide what message they suggest about life and human relationships.

Use a flowchart like the one below to make inferences about these stories:

Detail		Reflection		Inference
The bachelor's frown turns to a scowl.	→	He is not happy.	→	The bachelor is annoyed with the children.

Guide for Reading ◆ 595

Write the following statement on the board: "A good storyteller can make any tale worth hearing." Let students free-write for a moment to react to this statement. Then have volunteers share some of their opinions of good stories and good story-telling. Guide students to "The Story-Teller" by telling them that they will read about storytellers who may or may not match their ideals.

◆ Build Grammar Skills

Complex Sentences If you wish to introduce the grammar concept for this selection before students read, refer to the instruction on p. 610.

Customize for
Less Proficient Readers
Good stories, and storytellers, include details that appeal to all the senses. Students can use the Sensory Language Chart, **Writing and Language Transparencies,** p. 69, to keep track of the variety of sensory details in the stories, and then use the information to evaluate the stories.

Customize for
More Advanced Students
Both stories in this selection use objects as symbols to represent ideas. For example, in "The Story-Teller," the wolf is a symbol of evil. Challenge students to identify at least two symbols in each story and tell how each one helps the author express the theme.

 Humanities: Art

Story Teller, ca. 1925–1935, by Velina "Shije" Herrera
Velina Shije Herrera (1902–1973) was a member of the Zia people of New Mexico. His Zia name was *Ma Pe Wi* (Oriole, or Red Bird). A well-known artist, he spent much of his life working as a rancher and cowboy. Discuss with students the universal elements he illustrates in this scene. *In any culture, people might gather to hear the stories of an elder. They might sit in a circle near him and listen intently.*

 Preparing for Standardized Tests

Vocabulary The vocabulary-building skill for this selection will help students as they read in general, and as they answer certain items on standardized tests. Standardized tests may ask questions about a passage whose meaning depends on students' interpretation of a word with the suffix *-less*. Knowing what the suffix means can help students interpret the word, and thus grasp the meaning of the passage. Present the following sample question, based on "The Story-Teller":

The aunt might have told the bachelor that telling stories to children was a *thankless* task

because the children—

(A) never liked unhappy endings
(B) did not appreciate her stories
(C) never remembered to say "please"
(D) did not possess full hearing

Students who know that the suffix *-less* means "without" can determine that a *thankless* task is one without thanks, or one that does not evoke gratitude. So, *(B)* is the best choice. For further practice, use Build Vocabulary: Suffixes, p. 219 in **Selection Support.**

One-Minute Insight With a setting on a train, "The Story-Teller" relates how a bachelor becomes an unlikely hero to a trio of bored children and their frazzled aunt when he concocts an irreverent story that calms and entertains them.

The Story-Teller
Saki

Stirling Station, 1887, William Kennedy, Collection of Andrew McIntosh Patrick, UK

◆ **Literary Focus**

❶ Theme Challenge students to predict what the theme of this story may be, based on the title and the visuals that accompany it. Who is the storyteller? Will the story be about that person or about the story he or she tells? *Students may predict that this selection is about a storyteller on a train.*

▶**Critical Viewing**◀

❷ Draw Conclusions *Platforms were outdoors, giving little shelter from the weather. The crowd at the station suggests that trains were an important means of transportation.*

Customize for
English Language Learners
Students may not understand the setting of the close quarters of a crowded passenger train. Help them envision the conditions by setting up a mock train compartment. Arrange six chairs in two rows facing each other, with little leg room separating the rows. Have students sit on the chairs and ask how they might feel sitting in such a cramped space with a group of strangers.

Customize for
Verbal/Linguistic Learners
This story would be a good selection to perform in the Readers Theatre format. Assign parts, including one or more narrators. Encourage readers to use expressive voices that fit the characters and tone of the situation.

▲ **Critical Viewing** Basing your answer on the details in this painting, describe what rail travel was like in the early 1900's in England. [Draw Conclusions]

596 ◆ *Short Stories*

Block Scheduling Strategies

Consider these suggestions to take advantage of extended class time:

• Focus on the role of storytellers and story-telling in this selection with the Interest Grabber, p. 595. To expand on these concepts, present the Community Connection, p. 600, and the Speaking and Listening Mini-Lesson, p. 601.

• Before having students read the stories, discuss the Reading Strategy, p. 595. Then, have students read independently or in groups and answer the Guide for Responding questions on p. 601 and p. 609.

• To prepare students for the Writing Mini-Lesson, discuss the Literary Focus feature on p. 595.

• Have students spend class time working on the Projects in the Idea Bank, p. 611, or the Cultural Connection in Beyond Literature, p. 609. Extend instruction by presenting the Cross-Curricular Connections in Social Studies, p. 602, and Math, p. 604.

• Conclude instruction of these selections by teaching the Viewing and Representing Mini-Lesson, p. 605, and allowing students several days to complete their tribute to an elder.

It was a hot afternoon, and the railway carriage was correspondingly sultry, and the next stop was at Templecombe, nearly an hour ahead. The occupants of the carriage were a small girl, and a smaller girl, and a small boy. An aunt belonging to the children occupied one corner seat, and the further corner seat on the opposite side was occupied by a <u>bachelor</u> who was a stranger to their party, but the small girls and the small boy emphatically occupied the compartment. Both the aunt and the children were conversational in a limited, persistent way, reminding one of the attentions of a housefly that refused to be discouraged. Most of the aunt's remarks seemed to begin with "Don't," and nearly all of the children's remarks began with "Why?" The bachelor said nothing out loud.

"Don't, Cyril, don't," exclaimed the aunt, as the small boy began smacking the cushions of the seat, producing a cloud of dust at each blow.

"Come and look out of the window," she added.

The child moved reluctantly to the window. "Why are those sheep being driven out of that field?" he asked.

"I expect they are being driven to another field where there is more grass," said the aunt weakly.

"But there is lots of grass in that field," protested the boy; "there's nothing else but grass there. Aunt, there's lots of grass in that field."

"Perhaps the grass in the other field is better," suggested the aunt fatuously.[1]

"Why is it better?" came the swift, inevitable question.

"Oh, look at those cows!" exclaimed the aunt. Nearly every field along the line had contained cows or bullocks, but she spoke as

---

1. **fatuously** (fach´ oo wəs lē) *adv.*: In a foolish way.

though she were drawing attention to a rarity.

"Why is the grass in the other field better?" persisted Cyril.

The frown on the bachelor's face was deepening to a scowl. He was a hard, unsympathetic man, the aunt decided in her mind. She was utterly unable to come to any satisfactory decision about the grass in the other field.

The smaller girl created a diversion by beginning to recite "On the Road to Mandalay."[2] She only knew the first line, but she put her limited knowledge to the fullest possible use. She repeated the line over and over again in a dreamy but <u>resolute</u> and very audible voice; it seemed to the bachelor as though someone had had a bet with her that she could not repeat the line aloud two thousand times without stopping. Whoever it was who had made the wager was likely to lose his bet.

> ◆ **Reading Strategy**
> What inference can you make about the aunt based on the children's misbehavior?

"Come over here and listen to a story," said the aunt, when the bachelor had looked twice at her and once at the communication cord.

The children moved <u>listlessly</u> toward the aunt's end of the carriage. Evidently her reputation as a story-teller did not rank high in their estimation.

In a low, confidential voice, interrupted at frequent intervals by loud, petulant[3] questions

---

2. **"On the Road to Mandalay"**: Poem by Rudyard Kipling.
3. **petulant** (pech´ oo lənt) *adj.*: Impatient.

◆ **Build Vocabulary**

bachelor (bach´ ə lər) *n.*: A man who has not married

resolute (rez´ ə loot´) *adj.*: Fixed in purpose; resolved

listlessly (list´ lis lē) *adv.*: Without interest; spiritlessly

The Story-Teller ◆ 597

Viewing and Representing

Stirling Station, 1887, by William Kennedy
Scottish painter William Kennedy (1859–1918) was best known for his landscapes. He worked and lived in Stirling, northeast of Glasgow. Encourage students to note how the fragile nature of the painting and its age are apparent through the cracks, chips, and blurriness on the painting's surface. Tell students that -scape means a kind of view or scene.

Have students study the painting's subject details. Then discuss these questions:

1. Why might a landscape artist paint a railway station? *The artist can show the broad, flat land and smoke-filled gray skies. He also might wish to portray the view of excited people, waiting for the arrival of a train. A traveler might be looking forward to the pleasure of a vacation or trip.*
2. What inferences can you make about the importance of this station? *Students may say that a long, crowded platform suggests that Stirling is a travel hub. People seem to watch for the next train, so perhaps trains arrive often.*

Comprehension Check ☑

❶ What is the younger girl doing? *She is so bored that she has gone back to reciting the first line of "On the Road to Mandalay," as she did before.*

◆ **Literary Focus**

❷ **Theme** Discuss with students what theme the author intends for this story. *Students may suggest the theme that an outside observer can make a difference, or that bored children can respond to a new situation.*

◆ **Reading Strategy**

❸ **Make Inferences** Guide students to notice that Saki always describes this man as a "bachelor," not a traveler, a man, a stranger, or a gentleman. Discuss what inference might be made from this descriptive choice. *Students may say that Saki wants readers to assume that a bachelor would have no experience dealing with young children.*

◆ **Critical Thinking**

❹ **Speculate** Ask students to predict whether the bachelor will succeed at telling a story that will grab the children's interest. *Students may say that his strong story introduction suggests that he will make a fine storyteller; others may expect him to fail, as the aunt did, in the face of so many questions and interruptions from the children.*

Thematic Focus

❺ **Appreciating Others** Have students describe what they think the aunt expects to happen and what surprises her and causes her to take a new view of the bachelor. *She smiles because she thinks the children will hound the bachelor with impossible questions, just as they did to her. But when she hears the bachelor's original and amusing answer, the aunt is surprised by his cleverness.*

---

from her listeners, she began an unenterprising and deplorably uninteresting story about a little girl who was good, and made friends with everyone on account of her goodness, and was finally saved from a mad bull by a number of rescuers who admired her moral character.

"Wouldn't they have saved her if she hadn't been good?" demanded the bigger of the small girls. It was exactly the question that the bachelor had wanted to ask.

"Well, yes," admitted the aunt lamely, "but I don't think they would have run quite so fast to her help if they had not liked her so much."

"It's the stupidest story I've ever heard," said the bigger of the small girls, with immense conviction.

"I didn't listen after the first bit, it was so stupid," said Cyril.

The smaller girl made no actual comment on the story, but she had long ago recommenced a murmured repetition of her favorite line.

❶ "You don't seem to be a success as a storyteller," said the bachelor suddenly from his corner.

The aunt bristled in instant defense at this unexpected attack.

❷ "It's a very difficult thing to tell stories that children can both understand and appreciate," she said stiffly.

"I don't agree with you," said the bachelor.

"Perhaps *you* would like to tell them a story," was the aunt's retort.

"Tell us a story," demanded the bigger of the small girls.

"Once upon a time," began the bachelor, "there was a little girl called Bertha, who was extraordinarily good."

❸ The children's momentarily aroused interest began at once to flicker; all stories seemed dreadfully alike, no matter who told them.

"She did all that she was told, she was always truthful, she kept her clothes clean, ate milk puddings as though they were jam tarts, learned her lessons perfectly, and was polite in her manners."

"Was she pretty?" asked the bigger of the small girls.

"Not as pretty as any of you," said the bachelor, "but she was horribly good."

There was a wave of reaction in favor of the story; the word horrible in connection with goodness was a novelty that commended itself. It seemed to introduce a ring of truth that was absent from the aunt's tales of infant life.

❹ "She was so good," continued the bachelor, "that she won several medals for goodness, which she always wore, pinned on to her dress. There was a medal for obedience, another medal for punctuality, and a third for good behavior. They were large metal medals and they clinked against one another as she walked. No other child in town where she lived had as many as three medals, so everybody knew that she must be an extra good child."

"Horribly good," quoted Cyril.

"Everybody talked about her goodness, and the Prince of the country got to hear about it, and he said that as she was so very good she might be allowed once a week to walk in his park, which was just outside the town. It was a beautiful park, and no children were ever allowed in it, so it was a great honor for Bertha to be allowed to go there."

"Were there any sheep in the park?" demanded Cyril.

"No," said the bachelor, "there were no sheep."

"Why weren't there any sheep?" came the inevitable question arising out of that answer.

The aunt permitted herself a smile, which might almost have been described as a grin.

❺ "There were no sheep in the park," said the bachelor, "because the Prince's mother had once had a dream that her son would either be killed by a sheep or else by a clock falling on him. For that reason the Prince never kept a sheep in his park or a clock in his palace."

The aunt suppressed a gasp of admiration.

"Was the Prince killed by a sheep or by a clock?" asked Cyril.

598 ◆ Short Stories

 Viewing and Representing

Untitled illustration, by John Wolcott Adams
   John Wolcott Adams (1874–1925) was an illustrator whose work was characterized by flickering pen strokes. He had a talent for vignettes that captured the energy, mood, or action of a situation. Use these questions for discussion about the illustration:

1. In what ways might you see some of these people as characters from the story? *They sit close together in a train compartment with windows. The older woman on the left might look like the children's aunt.*

2. What mood does the scene evoke? *Students may say that it shows boredom and distance. The women seem lost in thought; the men lose themselves in newspapers. There is no interaction among them.*

3. What might interest a storyteller about this group? *A storyteller might be inclined to make up relationships among the characters, imagine what's in the box the young woman holds, or invent something in the newspaper that could create conflict in the compartment.*

"He is still alive, so we can't tell whether the dream will come true," said the bachelor unconcernedly; "anyway, there were no sheep in the park, but there were lots of little pigs running all over the place."

"What color were they?"

"Black with white faces, white with black spots, black all over, gray with white patches, and some were white all over."

The story-teller paused to let a full idea of the park's treasures sink into the children's imaginations; then he resumed:

6 "Bertha was rather sorry to find that there were no flowers in the park. She had promised her aunts, with tears in her eyes, that she would not pick any of the kind Prince's flowers, and she had meant to keep her promise, so of course it made her feel silly to find that there were no flowers to pick."

"Why weren't there any flowers?"

"Because the pigs had eaten them all," said the bachelor promptly. "The gardeners had told the Prince that you couldn't have pigs and flowers, so he decided to have pigs and no flowers."

There was a murmur of approval at the excellence of the Prince's decision; so many people would have decided the other way.

"There were lots of other delightful things in the park. There were ponds with gold and blue and green fish in them, and trees with beautiful parrots that said clever things at a moment's notice, and hummingbirds that hummed all the popular tunes of the day. Bertha walked up and down and enjoyed herself immensely, and thought to herself: 'If I were not so extraordinarily good, I should not have been allowed to come into this beautiful park and enjoy all that **7** there is to be seen in it,' and her three medals clinked against one another as she walked and helped to remind her how very good she really was. Just then an enormous wolf came prowling into the park to see if it could catch a fat little pig for its supper."

"What color was it?" asked the children, amid an immediate quickening of interest.

"Mud color all over, with a black tongue and pale gray eyes that gleamed with unspeakable ferocity. The first thing that it saw in the park was Bertha; her pinafore[4] was so spotlessly white and clean that it could be seen from a great distance. Bertha saw the wolf and saw that it was stealing toward her, and she began to wish that she had never been allowed to come into the park. She ran as hard as she could, and the wolf came after her with huge leaps and bounds. She managed to reach a shrubbery of myrtle bushes, and she hid herself in one of the thickest of the bushes. The wolf came sniffing among the branches, its black tongue lolling out of its mouth and its pale gray eyes glaring with rage. Bertha was terribly frightened, and thought to herself: 'If I had not been so extraordinarily good, I should have been safe in the town at this moment.' However, the scent of the myrtle was so strong that the wolf could not sniff out where Bertha was hiding, and the bushes were so thick that he might have hunted about in them for a long time without catching sight of her, so he thought he might as well go off and catch a little pig instead. Bertha was trembling very much at having the wolf prowling and sniffing so near her, and as she trembled the medal for obedience clinked against the medals for good conduct and punctuality. The wolf was just moving away when he heard the sound of the medals clinking and stopped to listen; they clinked again in a bush quite near him. He dashed into the bush, his pale gray eyes gleaming with ferocity and triumph, and dragged Bertha out **9** and devoured her to the last morsel. All that was left of her were her shoes, bits of clothing, and the three medals for goodness."

"Were any of the little pigs killed?"

8

---

4. **pinafore** (pĭn′ ə fôr′) *n.*: An apronlike garment worn over a dress.

◆ **Critical Thinking**

6 Analyze Why did the children begin to enjoy the bachelor's story so much? *As a good storyteller will do, he used a strong introduction and a number of colorful descriptions to capture the children's imaginations and keep them interested in listening to the details of the story he was telling.*

◆ **Critical Thinking**

7 Draw Conclusions Have students explain what the children appreciate in the bachelor's storytelling. *They like that the story he tells is irreverent, funny, original, and does not force a moral lesson upon them.*

◆ **Reading Strategy**

8 Make Inferences The bachelor has revealed some of his personality and philosophy through the story he tells the children. Have students infer what sort of man he is. *Students may say that he is good-natured, fun-loving, irreverent, and creative.*

 Cross-Curricular Connection: Language Arts

Oxymoron An oxymoron is a figure of speech in which contradictory or opposing ideas or terms are combined for dramatic effect. Brainstorm with students to think of some examples, such as "thundering silence" or "sweet sorrow." Point out that oxymorons can be humorous, understated, or just plain silly, such as "jumbo shrimp."

Have students look through the Saki story for examples of the author's use of oxymorons. For example, the bachelor charms the children when he describes Bertha as being "horribly good." They seem to recognize a truthfulness from the bachelor that was totally lacking in their aunt's unoriginal story line.

Challenge students to create original oxymorons for a bulletin board display. Suggest that they think of colorful or interesting words and then combine them with descriptive words that seem to contradict.

◆ Literary Focus

❶ Theme Ask students to express the theme of the story the bachelor has told the children. *Students might say that it's fine to be good, but not too good!*

◆ Literary Focus

❷ Theme *A story can teach a better lesson if children are motivated to listen to it; children are entertained by things that poke fun at the rules; a good story should entertain, not preach.*

Reinforce and Extend

Answers
◆ LITERATURE AND YOUR LIFE

Reader's Response Most students will enjoy the outrageous humor of the bachelor's story.

Thematic Focus It teaches them that it's fine to be good, but it's unwise to boast about it.

☑ Check Your Comprehension

1. They annoy those around them in the train compartment because they won't sit quietly.
2. She hopes a story will distract them.
3. They interrupt her with questions and squirm with boredom.
4. (a) He tells a story about a little girl who earns medals and favors for being very good, but she gets devoured by a hungry wolf.
(b) He amuses and entertains the children and captures their imaginations.

◆ Critical Thinking

1. They sense that she doesn't take them seriously, and they know that the questions irritate her.
2. It attempts to preach a dull lesson about perfection.
3. They enjoy the use of a word that usually has negative associations with something so entertaining; they like the contrast between good and horrible.
4. It is creative and irreverent; he stays in charge of the situation by not letting the children's foolish questions annoy him, using them in the story instead.
5. Students may say that children need to learn lessons about life one way or another. If a story can entertain and convey a message, it is good.
6. Adults want children to learn lessons about life, and hope that stories can illustrate moral choices.

600

---

❶ "No, they all escaped."

"The story began badly," said the smaller of the small girls, "but it had a beautiful ending."

"It is the most beautiful story that I ever heard," said the bigger of the small girls, with immense decision.

"It is the *only* beautiful story I have ever heard," said Cyril.

A dissentient⁵ opinion came from the aunt.

"A most improper story to tell to young children! You have undermined the effect of years of careful teaching."

"At any rate," said the bachelor, collecting his belongings preparatory to leaving the carriage, "I kept them quiet for ten minutes, which was more than you were able to do."

"Unhappy woman!" he observed to himself as he walked down the platform of Templecombe station; "for the next six months or so those children will assail her in public with demands for an improper story!"

> ◆ **Literary Focus**
> What does the contrast between the two stories suggest about this story's theme?
> ❷

---

5. **dissentient** (di sen′ shənt) *adj.*: Differing from the majority.

Guide for Responding

◆ LITERATURE AND YOUR LIFE

Reader's Response Did you like the bachelor's story? Why or why not?

Thematic Focus In addition to quieting the children, what message or moral does the bachelor's story teach them?

Story Guidelines [Group Activity] With several classmates, use the bachelor's tale to list some guidelines for children's stories. Jot down the qualities that make such stories effective.

☑ Check Your Comprehension

1. Describe the children's behavior at the start of the trip.
2. Why does the aunt decide to tell them a story?
3. How do the children react to her story?
4. (a) Summarize the story that the bachelor tells the children. (b) What is he able to accomplish that the aunt could not?

600 ◆ Short Stories

◆ Critical Thinking

INTERPRET
1. Why are the children unsatisfied by the aunt's answers to their questions? **[Infer]**
2. What makes the aunt's story "deplorably uninteresting"? **[Analyze]**
3. Why do you think the children like the use of the word "horribly" and the ending of the bachelor's story? **[Interpret]**
4. In general, what makes the bachelor's story more effective than the aunt's? **[Draw Conclusions]**
5. Are stories like the one the bachelor tells helpful to children? Why or why not? **[Evaluate]**

APPLY
6. Why do you think adults tell children stories that teach moral lessons? **[Speculate]**

Speaking and Listening Mini-Lesson

Storytelling

This mini-lesson supports the Speaking and Listening activity in the Idea Bank on p. 611.

Introduce Ask students to think about being small children. Have them brainstorm for a list of favorite childhood stories. Elicit the qualities that make these stories memorable, such as colorful characters, humor, suspense, exaggeration, fantasy.

Develop Have students work independently to create an original story they think would appeal to young listeners. Have students decide whether they wish to write the story, or create an outline

to use for an oral telling of their tale. Have students practice delivering the story to classmates, so they can revise it to make it more appealing and interesting.

Apply Have students tell their stories to groups of young children. The audiences' reactions will be useful to gauge the story's effectiveness.

Assess Evaluate students on how well they present their story and on how well they respond to questions or comments. Or use the Peer Assessment: Oral Interpretation form, p. 115, in **Alternative Assessment.**

CONNECTIONS TO TODAY'S WORLD

Saki's storyteller continues an age-old tradition: enthralling an audience through the magic of words and ideas. To this day, storytelling continues to be an important part of life, and it can take many forms—from a friend recounting a true-life event to a formal storytelling presentation, complete with costumes and props. The following article contains some storytelling tips that will help you to capture and hold the interest of your audience successfully.

How to Tell a Good Story
Chris Granstorm

Whether you're a grandmother with a lapful of youngsters, or a new parent tucking the kids into bed, whether you're telling stories about your own life, or spinning yarns about life in outer space, you'll need the same techniques for performing the story.

1. Select a story that's appropriate for you and your audience. Younger audiences like more action; older students and adults will enjoy more complex characters and humor.

2. Take time to memorize your story, and to practice it. But don't recite it verbatim. Allow it to develop itself each time you tell it. Visualize the scenes as you learn it and retell it. Stories with repetitive phrases are easier to remember. Practice telling the story to anyone who will listen.

3. Try to assure a favorable storytelling environment. Select a quiet location where your listeners can sit comfortably in a semicircle close to you.

4. Vary the pitch, tone and rhythm of your story. (You can learn this by watching good storytellers.) Except with young children, keep your gestures to a minimum—enrich the story with your eyes and facial expressions instead. Build to a climax, and when you get to the end, stop. Don't trail off.

5. Your voice can help listeners keep track of your characters, and it can convey moods and emotions. You can whisper, yell, moan, sigh and laugh. You can also select a different tone for each character. This is perhaps the most effective technique, but don't do it unless you're good at it.

6. Make eye contact. Look at your listeners directly. If you have a large crowd, pick a few faces around the audience, and beam the story to them.

7. Go slowly. Take your time and move gradually through the material. Vary the cadence of your voice, allow dramatic pauses. And, if you lose track of your place momentarily, don't get flustered, just take your time. You'll remember.

8. Use body language. Move around. Act out the scenes a little. But don't distract your audience. Find a comfortable level of theatrics.

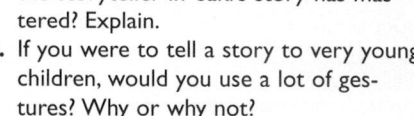

1. Of these tips, which do you imagine the storyteller in Saki's story has mastered? Explain.
2. If you were to tell a story to very young children, would you use a lot of gestures? Why or why not?
3. Which of the tips listed come to you naturally? Which would you have to work on?

The Story-Teller ◆ 601

Develop Understanding

One-Minute Insight

"The Medicine Bag" tells the story of Martin, a suburban boy from Iowa, and how his life changes when his great-grandfather, Joe Iron Shell, pays an unexpected visit. Joe teaches Martin about traditional Sioux ways and gives him an object of great spiritual and sentimental value. Martin, both embarrassed and at the same time touched by the old man and his tales, grows to respect and embrace his family traditions.

◆ Reading Strategy

❶ Make Inferences Ask students to explain why they think Cheryl and Martin exaggerated when they told about their times on the reservation. *As people often do, they got carried away in the telling and an exaggerated tale is more fun to relate. Some may point out that most listeners were unlikely ever to be able to verify whether or not the stories were accurate.*

Comprehension Check ☑

❷ What about Joe Iron Shell's appearance makes Martin reluctant to show his picture around? *In real life, Joe did not look much like the TV stereotype of an Indian and he didn't look very much like the exaggerated stories they had told their friends.*

▶Critical Viewing◀

❸ Infer *Some students may say that the embroidery and irregular hand-stitching along the left side and bottom make the bag look handmade. Others may notice that the leather thong is like a manufactured shoelace, and that other stitching seems to be done by machine.*

Customize for
English Language Learners
Obtain photographs, illustrations, or artifacts for students to examine that can help them visualize the Native American items they will encounter in this story, such as moccasins, tepee, or bolo tie.

602

The Medicine Bag
Virginia Driving Hawk Sneve

❶ My kid sister Cheryl and I always bragged about our Sioux[1] grandpa, Joe Iron Shell. Our friends, who had always lived in the city and only knew about Indians from movies and TV, were impressed by our stories. Maybe we exaggerated and made Grandpa and the reservation sound glamorous, but when we'd return home to Iowa after our yearly summer visit to Grandpa, we always had some exciting tale to tell.

We always had some <u>authentic</u> Sioux article to show our listeners. One year Cheryl had new moccasins[2] that Grandpa had made. On another visit he gave me a small, round, flat, rawhide drum that was decorated with a painting of a warrior riding a horse. He taught me a real Sioux chant to sing while I beat the drum with a leather-covered stick that had a feather on the end. Man that really made an impression.

❷ We never showed our friends Grandpa's picture. Not that we were ashamed of him, but because we knew that the glamorous tales we told didn't go with the real thing. Our friends would have laughed at the picture because Grandpa wasn't tall and stately like TV Indians. His hair wasn't in braids but hung in stringy, gray strands on his neck, and he was old. He was our great-grandfather, and he didn't live in a tepee,[3] but all by himself in a part log, part tar-paper shack on the Rosebud Reservation[4]

---

1. **Sioux** (sōō) *n.*: Native American tribes of the northern plains of the United States and nearby southern Canada.
2. **moccasins** (mäk´ ə sənz) *n.*: Heelless slippers of soft, flexible leather.
3. **tepee** (tē´ pē) *n.*: Cone-shaped tent of animal skins; used by the Plains Indians.

▲ **Critical Viewing** Do you think the medicine bag pictured was manufactured or handmade? How can you tell? [Infer] **❸**

602 ◆ *Short Stories*

Cross-Curricular Connection: Social Studies

Displacement In the 19th century, it was the policy of the United States government to remove Native Americans, often forcibly, from their traditional homelands and resettle them on isolated reservation lands. The westward movement of American settlers displaced many of the Americans who were native to the land. Often people were placed in regions where continuing their lifestyles was not possible—even if they were permitted to retain their language and religion. Often these forced relocations led to disease and depression.

Have students find out more about this governmental policy—why did our government decide to do it and what did they expect would happen? Students may wish to focus on the struggles of one particular Native American group to discover what changes they were forced to endure and where they stand today. Suggest that they investigate the laws concerning Native American reservation land and its uses that are in effect at the present time, and how they have been changed and modified over the years.

4 Make Inferences *Students may recognize typical teenage attitudes in his behavior, such as boasting to impress friends, or feeling ashamed if a family member is different. He is torn between love and respect for his great-grandfather and his need for approval from his friends.*

Comprehension Check ☑

5 Why does Grandpa keep looking down at something in his hand as he walks? *He's probably checking a note that contains Martin's address, or maybe he has a photograph of their house to help him find it.*

◆ **Reading Strategy**

6 Make Inferences Ask students to explain why Joe Iron Shell, who can speak English, would greet his great-grandson formally in the Sioux language. *Students may say that he believes in keeping up traditions and passing them along, and that he feels pride in his Sioux heritage. He wants Martin to understand and respect the Sioux language.*

◆ **LITERATURE AND YOUR LIFE**

7 Invite students to share any similar experiences they have had in which they felt embarrassed by a family member who acted in an embarrassing way in front of their friends, or who just drew unwelcome attention by looking or being different. Students who can recall such moments can appreciate the conflict that Martin feels.

Customize for
Verbal/Linguistic Learners
Students may enjoy learning words in the Sioux language. Suggest that they use research materials to facilitate their interest and, if possible, to locate an audio source so that they can hear the words pronounced properly.

◆ Reading Strategy
What inferences can you make about the narrator based on his conflicting attitudes toward his great-grandfather?

4

in South Dakota. So when Grandpa came to visit us, I was so ashamed and embarrassed I could've died.

There are a lot of yippy poodles and other fancy little dogs in our neighborhood, but they usually barked singly at the mailman from the safety of their own yards. Now it sounded as if a whole pack of mutts were barking together in one place.

I got up and walked to the curb to see what the commotion was. About a block away I saw a crowd of little kids yelling, with the dogs yipping and growling around someone who was walking down the middle of the street.

5

I watched the group as it slowly came closer and saw that in the center of the strange procession was a man wearing a tall black hat. He'd pause now and then to peer at something in his hand and then at the houses on either side of the street. I felt cold and hot at the same time as I recognized the man. "Oh, no!" I whispered. "It's Grandpa!"

I stood on the curb, unable to move even though I wanted to run and hide. Then I got mad when I saw how the yippy dogs were growling and nipping at the old man's baggy pant legs and how wearily he poked them away with his cane. "Stupid mutts," I said as I ran to rescue Grandpa.

When I kicked and hollered at the dogs to get away, they put their tails between their legs and scattered. The kids ran to the curb where they watched me and the old man.

---

4. **Rosebud Reservation:** Small Indian reservation in southcentral South Dakota.

"Grandpa," I said and felt pretty dumb when my voice cracked. I reached for his beat-up old tin suitcase, which was tied shut with a rope. But he set it down right in the street and shook my hand.

"*Hau, Takoza*, Grandchild," he greeted me formally in Sioux.

6

All I could do was stand there with the whole neighborhood watching and shake the hand of the leather-brown old man. I saw how his gray hair straggled from under his big black hat, which had a drooping feather in its crown. His rumpled black suit hung like a sack over his stooped frame. As he shook my hand, his coat fell open to expose a bright red satin shirt with a beaded bolo tie[5] under the collar. His get-up wasn't out of place on the reservation, but it sure was here, and I wanted to sink right through the pavement.

7

"Hi," I muttered with my head down. I tried to pull my hand away when I felt his bony hand trembling, and looked up to see fatigue in his face. I felt like crying. I couldn't think of anything to say so I picked up Grandpa's suitcase, took his arm, and guided him up the driveway to our house.

Mom was standing on the steps. I don't know how long she'd been watching, but her hand was over her mouth and she looked as if she couldn't believe what she saw. Then she ran to us.

---

5. **bolo** (bō′ lō) **tie** *n.*: String tie held together with a decorated sliding device.

◆ **Build Vocabulary**
authentic (ô then′ tik) *adj.*: Genuine; real
procession (prō sesh′ ən) *n.*: A group of people or things moving forward

---

Cultural Connection

Language and Greetings Martin's grandfather greets him formally with the Sioux words *Hau, Takoza*. Discuss with students the differences and similarities between American formal and informal greetings. Guide them to compare and contrast greeting someone with, "Hi, how are you?" and "Good afternoon," or "How do you do?" Then, point out Martin's simple, informal response to his grandfather: "Hi."

Have students conduct an unofficial survey of greetings that they use, have met with, or overheard. Challenge them to categorize the greetings

by the people that use them. Do older people tend to greet others formally? Do people in your school or community use "Hi" or "Hello?" Hold a class discussion for students to pool the results of their observations about greetings.

Encourage students to extend their research into language and greetings by exploring the languages and greetings of other cultures. They might look to find who uses *Hau, Takoza* as a typical Sioux greeting—whether it is used by people of Martin's age or Grandpa's age; if there is a literal translation; and so forth.

◆ **Critical Thinking**

❶ Analyze Explain that to "check" a move, as Marie did when she greeted Grandpa means to restrain or stop. Ask students to explain why they think Marie didn't hug him, although it is likely that she customarily hugs other family members. *Students can infer that Marie holds back out of respect for Grandpa's traditional ways.*

◆ **Reading Strategy**

❷ Make Inferences Ask students to infer why Joe Iron Shell has money stuffed into his boots, and why he would have brought so much cash along. *Although students may not be able to guess Joe's plans for the money, they may say that he keeps it in his boots because it is safe there from pickpockets, or that he is old-fashioned and ill-at-ease with banks.*

Comprehension Check ☑

❸ Why is Grandpa angry? *He is angry because he dislikes being fussed over, or is frustrated with being so helpless.*

◆ **Critical Thinking**

❹ Interpret Grandpa simply takes a bus and arrives in the city to visit his family unannounced. Ask students to explain why he didn't alert his family about his visit. *Students may say that he does not have a phone, or dislikes using one if it is available; others may suggest that he's not used to sharing his plans with others or didn't think it was necessary.*

Customize for
Bodily/Kinesthetic Learners
Ask volunteers to demonstrate or role-play the arrival of Grandpa at Martin's home, how he and his family greeted him, and what happened.

604

---

❶ "Grandpa," she gasped. "How in the world did you get here?"

She checked her move to embrace Grandpa and I remembered that such a display of affection is unseemly to the Sioux and would embarrass him.

"*Hau*, Marie," he said as he shook Mom's hand. She smiled and took his other arm.

As we supported him up the steps, the door banged open and Cheryl came bursting out of the house. She was all smiles and was so obviously glad to see Grandpa that I was ashamed of how I felt.

"Grandpa!" she yelled happily. "You came to see us!"

Grandpa smiled, and Mom and I let go of him as he stretched out his arms to my ten-year-old sister, who was still young enough to be hugged.

"*Wicincala*, little girl," he greeted her and then collapsed.

He had fainted. Mom and I carried him into her sewing room, where we had a spare bed.

After we had Grandpa on the bed, Mom stood there helplessly patting his shoulder.

"Shouldn't we call the doctor, Mom?" I suggested, since she didn't seem to know what to do.

"Yes," she agreed with a sigh. "You make Grandpa comfortable, Martin."

I reluctantly moved to the bed. I knew Grandpa wouldn't want to have Mom undress him, but I didn't want to, either. He was so skinny and frail that his coat slipped off easily. When I loosened his tie and opened his shirt collar, I felt a small leather pouch that hung from a thong[6] around his neck. I left it alone and moved to remove his boots. The scuffed old cowboy boots were tight, and he moaned as I put pressure on his legs to jerk them off.

6. **thong** *n.*: Narrow strip of leather.

I put the boots on the floor and saw why ❷ they fit so tight. Each one was stuffed with money. I looked at the bills that lined the boots and started to ask about them, but Grandpa's eyes were closed again.

Mom came back with a basin of water. "The doctor thinks Grandpa is suffering from heat exhaustion," she explained as she bathed Grandpa's face. Mom gave a big sigh, "Oh, *hinh*, Martin. How do you suppose he got here?"

We found out after the doctor's visit. ❸ Grandpa was angrily sitting up in bed while Mom tried to feed him some soup.

"Tonight you let Marie feed you, Grandpa," spoke my dad, who had gotten home from work just as the doctor was leaving. "You're not really sick," he said as he gently pushed Grandpa back against the pillows. "The doctor said you just got too tired and hot after your long trip."

Grandpa relaxed, and between sips of soup, he told us of his journey. Soon after our visit to him, Grandpa decided that he would like to see where his only living descendants lived and what our home was like. Besides, he admitted sheepishly, he was lonesome after we left.

I knew that everybody felt as guilty as I did—especially Mom. Mom was all Grandpa had left. So even after she married my dad, who's a white man and teaches in the college in our city, and after Cheryl and I were born, Mom made sure that every summer we spent a week with Grandpa.

I never thought that Grandpa would be lonely after our visits, and none of us noticed how old and weak he had become. But ❹ Grandpa knew, and so he came to us. He had ridden on buses for two and a half days. When he arrived in the city, tired and stiff from sitting for so long, he set out, walking, to find us.

He had stopped to rest on the steps of

604 ◆ *Short Stories*

📖 **Cross-Curricular Connection: Social Studies**

Geography In "The Medicine Bag," old Joe Iron Shell makes an arduous journey from his home on the Rosebud Reservation in South Dakota to visit his relatives in Iowa. Help students gain a better sense of his efforts by challenging them to plan a similar trip. Present these conditions:

• Travel may begin at any Indian reservation in the United States that is located in a state other than your own.

• Plan a trip using public transportation only (or footpower) to get from the reservation to your house.

• If choices exist, select the best route. Formulate a complete itinerary for this trip that evaluates its cost, distance, and time. Include other likely factors such as overnight stays, meals (Where? How many? Cost?), layovers to change transportation, and possible delays or cancellations due to weather or traffic conditions.

After students complete their research and planning, have them present the itineraries to classmates. They may want to use maps or charts to show the route and itinerary and verbally describe any difficulties they expect to encounter.

some building downtown, and a policeman found him. The cop, according to Grandpa, was a good man who took him to the bus stop and waited until the bus came and told the driver to let Grandpa out at Bell View Drive. After Grandpa got off the bus, he started walking again. But he couldn't see the house numbers on the other side when he walked on the sidewalk, so he walked in the middle of the street. That's when all the little kids and dogs followed him.

5 I knew everybody felt as bad as I did. Yet I was so proud of this eighty-six-year-old man, who had never been away from the reservation, having the courage to travel so far alone.

"You found the money in my boots?" he asked Mom.

"Martin did," she answered, and roused herself to scold. "Grandpa, you shouldn't have carried so much money. What if someone had stolen it from you?"

Grandpa laughed. "I would've known if anyone tried to take the boots off my feet. The money is what I've saved for a long time—a hundred dollars—for my funeral. But you take it now to buy groceries so that I won't be a burden to you while I am here."

"That won't be necessary, Grandpa," Dad said. "We are honored to have you with us, and you will never be a burden. I am only sorry that we never thought to bring you home with us this summer and spare you the discomfort of a long trip."

Grandpa was pleased. "Thank you," he answered. "But do not feel bad that you didn't bring me with you, for I would not have come then. It was not time." He said this in such **6** a way that no one could argue with him. To Grandpa and the Sioux, he once told me, a thing would be done when it was the right time to do it, and that's the way it was.

"Also," Grandpa went on, looking at me, "I have come because it is soon time for Martin to have the medicine bag."

We all knew what that meant. Grandpa thought he was going to die, and he had to follow the tradition of his family to pass the medicine bag, along with its history, to the oldest male child. **7**

"Even though the boy," he said still looking at me, "bears a white man's name, the medicine bag will be his."

I didn't know what to say. I had the same hot and cold feeling that I had when I first saw Grandpa in the street. The medicine bag was the dirty leather pouch I had found around his neck. "I could never wear such a thing," I almost said aloud. I thought of having my friends see it in gym class or at the swimming pool and could imagine the smart things they would say. But I just swallowed hard and took a step toward the bed. I knew I would have to take it.

But Grandpa was tired. "Not now, Martin," he said, waving his hand in dismissal. "It is not time. Now I will sleep."

So that's how Grandpa came to be with us for two months. My friends kept asking to come see the old man, but I put them off. I told myself that I didn't want them laughing **9** at Grandpa. But even as I made excuses, I knew it wasn't Grandpa that I was afraid they'd laugh at.

Nothing bothered Cheryl about bringing her friends to see Grandpa. Every day after school started, there'd be a crew of giggling little girls or round-eyed little boys crowded around the old man on the patio, where he'd gotten in the habit of sitting every afternoon.

Grandpa would smile in his gentle way and patiently answer their questions, or he'd tell them stories of brave warriors, ghosts, animals; and the kids listened in awed silence. Those little guys thought Grandpa was great.

> *"I have come because it is soon time for Martin to have the medicine bag."*

◆ **Literary Focus**
What does Martin's reaction to the medicine bag reveal about his attitude toward his Sioux heritage?

The Medicine Bag ◆ 605

Comprehension Check ☑

5 Martin says that he and everyone else felt bad for Joe Iron Shell. Why do they feel bad? Why is Martin also proud of Grandpa? *They feel bad that Grandpa had such an exhausting journey. Martin is proud that this old man, who had never been off the reservation, managed to plan a trip and arrive at his destination.*

◆ **Critical Thinking**

6 Infer Grandpa says that he didn't come sooner because "it was not time." Ask students to infer what it is time for now. *Students may guess that the old man believes that it is time for him to die; he has come to Iowa so that he will be with family when he dies.*

Thematic Focus

7 Appreciating Others Grandpa takes great pains to come all the way to his family's home in Iowa to give the medicine bag to Martin. Ask students to explain why Grandpa didn't just mail the bag to him. *Students may say that passing on the medicine bag is an important personal event for both the giver and receiver, and that such a solemn transfer should be done face to face.*

◆ **Literary Focus**

8 *Martin is a modern boy with modern interests, experiences, and friends. With deep doubts about taking and wearing that "dirty leather pouch," Martin still approaches Grandpa respectfully to receive whatever the elder is about to give to him.*

◆ **Critical Thinking**

9 Connect Ask students to explain why Martin hesitates to have friends over. *Martin tells himself that he's afraid his friends will laugh at Grandpa, but he secretly fears that they will laugh at him.*

Viewing and Representing Mini-Lesson

Remembering an Elder
This mini-lesson supports the story's theme and guides students to think about acknowledgment of elders.

Introduce Martin's great-grandfather gives Martin something meaningful that he can use to remember the honor of his grandfather. Have students think of an elder who has passed away, such as a family member or mentor; a famous figure, such as a performer or political leader; or a fictional character. Challenge them to design and present a visual display to honor this person.

Develop A display can take any form, such as a collage, sculpture, quilt, or scrapbook. Students should think of representations of values and traditions, or what the people meant to them. Have students prepare plans, gather materials, and create their visual displays.

Apply Allow time for students to create the representations. Provide display space in the classroom. Invite students to stand by their work and answer questions as classmates pass by.

Assess Evaluate the visual displays on the qualities discussed above.

❶ **Make Inferences** Martin is surprised and amused by how polite his friends are toward Grandpa. Ask students to explain why he might find their behavior so comical. *Martin might find it amusing that someone who is just a relative to him comes across as such an imposing figure to his friends. Also, it might amuse Martin to see his friends behave in such unexpected ways.*

Comprehension Check ☑

❷ What do Martin's friends think is the real reason Martin has kept them away from Grandpa? *The friends believe that Martin kept them away because he didn't want to share Grandpa.*

◆ **Critical Thinking**

❸ **Assess** Why don't Martin's friends suspect the real reason he hasn't invited them to visit earlier? *They don't find the old man to be laughable, so they don't guess that Martin had felt ashamed of him.*

◆ **Critical Thinking**

❹ **Draw Conclusions** What did Martin learn from his friends' visit with his Grandpa? *He learned that his Grandpa had a lot of information to share and that the fact that he looked and acted differently was not important to his friends.*

Customize for
Verbal/Linguistic Learners
Some students may want to interview an older adult and find out interesting facts about his or her life and memories. Challenge students to visit with a family member or an adult at a senior center or nursing home who might have interesting stories to tell. Suggest that students prepare a list of questions about childhood, holidays, or job experiences that might elicit memories from the adult.

Finally, one day after school, my friends came home with me because nothing I said stopped them. "We're going to see the great Indian of Bell View Drive," said Hank, who was supposed to be my best friend. "My brother has seen him three times so he oughta be well enough to see us."

When we got to my house, Grandpa was sitting on the patio. He had on his red shirt, but today he also wore a fringed leather vest that was decorated with beads. Instead of his usual cowboy boots, he had solidly beaded moccasins on his feet that stuck out of his black trousers. Of course, he had his old black hat on—he was seldom without it. But it had been brushed, and the feather in the beaded headband was proudly erect, its tip a brighter white. His hair lay in silver strands over the red shirt collar.

I stared just as my friends did, and I heard one of them murmur, "Wow!"

Grandpa looked up, and, when his eyes met mine, they twinkled as if he were laughing inside. He nodded to me, and my face got all hot. I could tell that he had known all ❶ along I was afraid he'd embarrass me in front of my friends.

"*Hau, hoksilas,* boys," he greeted and held out his hand.

My buddies passed in a single file and shook his hand as I introduced them. They were so polite I almost laughed. "How, there, Grandpa," and even a "How-do-you-do, sir."

"You look fine, Grandpa," I said as the guys sat on the lawn chairs or on the patio floor.

"*Hanh,* yes," he agreed. "When I woke up this morning, it seemed the right time to dress in the good clothes. I knew that my grandson would be bringing his friends."

"You guys want some lemonade or something?" I offered. No one answered. They were listening to Grandpa as he ❷ started telling how he'd killed the deer from which his vest was made.

Grandpa did most of the talking while my friends were there. I was so proud of him and amazed at how respectfully quiet my buddies were. Mom had to chase them home at supper time. As they left, they shook Grandpa's hand ❸ again and said to me,

"Martin, he's really great!"

"Yeah, man! Don't blame you for keeping him to yourself."

❹ "Can we come back?"

But after they left, Mom said, "No more visitors for a while, Martin. Grandpa won't admit it, but his strength hasn't returned. He likes having company, but it tires him."

That evening Grandpa called me to his room before he

 Beyond the Classroom

Career Connection
Ethnologist People who enjoy hearing stories about cultural traditions may be able to turn this interest into a career. Ethnology is the study of contemporary or recent societies or cultures and their related language. It is a branch of the field of anthropology, or the study of humanity. One way ethnologists gather information for their research is by interviewing people, often elders of a society or culture, to learn about their ways. The tape recorder and video camera are two useful tools for this kind of work.

Invite interested students to learn more about anthropology and ethnology by browsing through high school or college catalogs to see the kinds of courses people who go into this field take. Or they can educate themselves by interviewing a museum worker or field anthropologist. Have students prepare a visual display with the information they gather.

◆ **Reading Strategy**

5 Make Inferences Ask students to guess what Martin might be thinking about and what so frightens him. *Receiving the medicine bag is a rite of passage, and Martin is excited at the thought of being regarded as an adult, but he is also scared by the responsibilities. Martin worries that he will have to wear the medicine bag and his friends will laugh at him. He fears that Grandpa is dying.*

◆ **Critical Thinking**

6 Analyze Ask students what they think Martin's dream may mean. *Students may say he is thinking about the importance of what Grandpa is going to give him and tell him, so he dreams about thunder and lightning and drumbeats.*

▶ **Critical Viewing** ◀

7 Connect *As in the description, a boy is alone atop a butte. He reaches upwards, as if he is praying, searching for answers, or offering praise for newly gained insights.*

◆ **Literary Focus**

8 Theme The importance of passing on traditions is a key theme in this story. How does the author set the tone for this moment in Martin's life? *She evokes the importance of this event by describing Martin as feeling shivers down his back.*

went to sleep. "Tomorrow," he said, "when you come home, it will be time to give you the medicine bag."

5 I felt a hard squeeze from where my heart is supposed to be and was scared, but I answered, "OK, Grandpa."

6 All night I had weird dreams about thunder and lightning on a high hill. From a distance I heard the slow beat of a drum. When I woke up in the morning, I felt as if I hadn't slept at all. At school it seemed as if the day would never end and, when it finally did, I ran home.

Grandpa was in his room, sitting on the bed.

▲ **Critical Viewing** How does this scene fit the image of a vision quest as described on page 608? Explain. **[Connect]** **7**

The shades were down, and the place was dim and cool. I sat on the floor in front of Grandpa, but he didn't even look at me. After what seemed a long time he spoke.

"I sent your mother and sister away. What you will hear today is only for a man's ears. What you will receive is only for a man's hands." **8** He fell silent, and I felt shivers down my back.

"My father in his early manhood," Grandpa

The Medicine Bag ◆ 607

◈ **Beyond the Classroom**

Workplace Skills

Appreciating Differences As Martin comes to know his grandfather, he learns about his Sioux heritage and how it differs from his typical American upbringing. Many of Grandpa's mannerisms and traits, which initially embarrass or bother Martin, become endearing to him. Learning about others' cultures and individuality is the key to appreciating their differences. This process is a valuable life skill that applies in all workplace settings.

Discuss with students the reactions that Martin has to his grandfather throughout the story.

Encourage them to compare these reactions to those of his sister, parents, and friends. What does Martin learn about Grandpa? How does he come to appreciate Grandpa? What differs between the two of them? What similar traits do they share and/or come to share? How does Martin feel about Grandpa after he has gotten to know him better?

Point out to students that it is much easier to get along with others when there is mutual appreciation and respect for cultures, ages, lifestyles, and individual personalities.

607

1 Using the Suffix *-less* The suffix *-less* means "without." Point out the word "hopeless," and ask students to explain what it means, both from the suffix and from the contextual clues in the passage. *It means without hope. The young men lacked hope that a vision quest would help them in any way, because so many old ways had already been lost.*

Clarification

2 Tell students that it was once a United States government policy to take young Native Americans off their reservations and send them to boarding schools to "civilize" them. To do so, they removed children, usually boys, from their traditional cultures and educated them away from home. The great Native American athlete Jim Thorpe (1888–1953) gained fame at one such place, the Carlisle Indian School in Pennsylvania.

◆ Reading Strategy

3 Make Inferences Ask students to explain what Grandpa means by making a connection between the medicine bag and his son. *Grandpa believes that his son, Martin's grandfather, had died because he did not take the medicine bag when he went to war; without its power to protect him, he was killed.*

Comprehension Check ☑

4 Why doesn't Grandpa believe that his son's daughter should have the leather pouch? *In his tradition, it is not proper for women to learn of such things.*

---

began, "made a vision quest[7] to find a spirit guide for his life. You cannot understand how it was in that time, when the great Teton Sioux were first made to stay on the reservation. There was a strong need for guidance from *Wakantanka*,[8] the Great Spirit. But too many of the young men were filled with despair and hatred. They thought **1** it was hopeless to search for a vision when the glorious life was gone and only the hated confines of a reservation lay ahead. But my father held to the old ways.

"He carefully prepared for his quest with a purifying sweat bath, and then he went alone to a high butte top[9] to fast and pray. After three days he received his sacred dream—in which he found, after long searching, the white man's iron. He did not understand his vision of finding something belonging to the white people, for in that time they were the enemy. When he came down from the butte to cleanse himself at the stream below, he found the remains of a campfire and the broken shell of an iron kettle. This was a sign that reinforced his dream. He took a piece of the iron for his medicine bag, which he had made of elk skin years before, to prepare for his quest.

"He returned to his village, where he told his dream to the wise old men of the tribe. They gave him the name *Iron Shell*, but neither did they understand the meaning of the dream. The first Iron Shell kept the piece of iron with him at all times and believed it gave him protection from the evils of those unhappy days.

"Then a terrible thing happened to Iron Shell. He and several other young men were taken from their homes by the soldiers and **2** sent far away to a white man's boarding school. He was angry and lonesome for his parents and the young girl he had wed before

---

7. **vision quest:** A search for a revelation that would aid understanding.
8. **Wakantanka** (wä´ kən tank´ ə) *n.*: The Sioux religion's most important spirit—the creator of the world.
9. **butte** (byōōt) **top** *n.*: Top of a steep hill standing alone in a plain.

---

he was taken away. At first Iron Shell resisted the teacher's attempts to change him, and he did not try to learn. One day it was his turn to work in the school's blacksmith **2** shop. As he walked into the place, he knew that his medicine had brought him there to learn and work with the white man's iron.

"Iron Shell became a blacksmith and worked at the trade when he returned to the reservation. All of his life he treasured the medicine bag. When he was old, and I was a man, he gave it to me, for no one made the vision quest any more."

Grandpa quit talking, and I stared in disbelief as he covered his face with his hands. His shoulders were shaking with quiet sobs, and I looked away until he began to speak again.

"I kept the bag until my son, your mother's father, was a man and had to leave us to fight in the war across the ocean. I gave him the bag, for I believed it would protect him in bat- **3** tle, but he did not take it with him. He was afraid that he would lose it. He died in a faraway place."

Again Grandpa was still, and I felt his grief around me.

"My son," he went on after clearing his throat, "had only a daughter, and it is not **4** proper for her to know of these things."

He unbuttoned his shirt, pulled out the leather pouch, and lifted it over his head. He held it in his hand, turning it over and over as if memorizing how it looked.

"In the bag," he said as he opened it and removed two objects, "is the broken shell of the iron kettle, a pebble from the butte, and a piece of the sacred sage."[10] He held the pouch upside down and dust drifted down.

"After the bag is yours you must put a piece of prairie sage within and never open it again until you pass it on to your son." He replaced the pebble and the piece of iron, and tied the bag.

I stood up, somehow knowing I should. **5** Grandpa slowly rose from the bed and stood

---

10. **sage:** (sāj) *n.*: Plant belonging to the mint family.

 Cultural Connection

Ceremonies In "The Medicine Bag," Joe Iron Shell describes his vision quest as a sacred rite of passage that marked his leap from boyhood to adulthood. Most cultures have ceremonies, events, celebrations, or other traditions that mark various rites of passage into adulthood or into a new stage of life. In the Jewish tradition, the Bar or Bat Mitzvah is a ceremony that welcomes thirteen-year-old boys or girls as adults in the Jewish community. In Japan, September 15 is a national holiday called Old People's Day, designed to honor the elders of the community. Graduation from high school or college becomes a big celebration in many families.

Invite students to select a culture, and then investigate some of its rites of passage. The rites can be religious or cultural, and can focus on milestones of life for children or adults. Encourage students to share their findings orally or in a bulletin board display.

upright in front of me holding the bag before my face. I closed my eyes and waited for him to slip it over my head. But he spoke.

"No, you need not wear it." He placed the soft leather bag in my right hand and closed my other hand over it. "It would not be right to wear it in this time and place where no one will understand. Put it safely away until you are again on the reservation. Wear it then, when you replace the sacred sage."

Grandpa turned and sat again on the bed. Wearily he leaned his head against the pillow. "Go," he said. "I will sleep now."

"Thank you, Grandpa," I said softly and left with the bag in my hands.

That night Mom and Dad took Grandpa to the hospital. Two weeks later I stood alone on the lonely prairie of the reservation and put the sacred sage in my medicine bag.

Beyond Literature

Cultural Connection

The Sioux Grandpa Joe lived on a Sioux reservation. The Sioux used to live throughout the northern plains of North America, and they were famous for their bravery and fighting ability.

Tension developed and increased between the Sioux and the United States in the mid-1800's. The two main reasons for this friction were settlers' slaughtering of the buffalo and gold prospectors' violating the sacred Black Hills. The United States decided to settle the conflict by forcing the Sioux onto reservations. Many Sioux decided to fight, led by the famous chiefs Sitting Bull and Crazy Horse. They were eventually defeated, but not before inflicting a major defeat on the United States Army by killing the celebrated Civil War hero George Custer and his troops at Little Big Horn.

Cross-Curricular Activity
Research the Battle of Little Big Horn, and create an illustrated map showing the opposing forces and areas of battle. Post your map in the classroom.

Guide for Responding

◆ LITERATURE AND YOUR LIFE

Reader's Response What items do you own that have a special meaning for you? Explain.

Thematic Focus In what way does Martin come to appreciate his grandfather?

☑ Check Your Comprehension

1. Describe how each family member welcomes Grandpa.
2. What three reasons for coming does Grandpa give?
3. How does Martin's attitude toward the medicine bag change after his friends visit Grandpa?
4. What does Martin do at the very end of the story?

◆ Critical Thinking

INTERPRET

1. What causes Martin to feel ashamed when his Grandpa suddenly appears? **[Analyze]**
2. How do the events of the story support Grandpa's idea that things will be done when it's "the right time"? **[Support]**
3. In what way does the Sioux heritage Martin brags about differ at first from the Sioux heritage Grandpa describes to him? **[Compare and Contrast]**
4. What does Martin's final action in the story reveal about his relationship to his heritage? **[Draw Conclusions]**

COMPARE LITERARY WORKS

5. In what way do both the bachelor in "The Story-Teller" and Grandpa in "The Medicine Bag" influence the lives of others? **[Compare and Contrast]**

The Medicine Bag ◆ 609

Beyond the Selection

FURTHER READING
Other Works by the Authors
Reginald in Russia, Saki
Beasts and Super-Beasts, Saki
Betrayed, Virginia Driving Hawk Sneve
When Thunder Spoke, Virginia Driving Hawk Sneve
Other Works on Appreciating Others
Christmas Day in the Morning, Pearl S. Buck
For My Sister Molly Who in the Fifties, Alice Walker
I Know Why the Caged Bird Sings, Maya Angelou

INTERNET
We suggest the following sites on the Internet (all Web sites are subject to change).
For more information about H. H. Munro (Saki):
http://www.crl.com/~subir/saki/index.html
For information on Virginia Driving Hawk Sneve:
http://English.cla.umn.edu/lkd/vfg/authors/VirginiaDrivingHawkSneve
We *strongly recommend* that you preview the sites before you send students to them.

Thematic Focus

❺ **Appreciating Others** Ask students to explain how the old man shows understanding for a changed world even as he holds to ancient traditions. *Grandpa realizes that his great-grandson may not feel at ease wearing the old pouch when most people around him won't understand its significance. But he still wants Martin to have it, to treasure it, and to bring it with him when he visits the reservation.*

Beyond Literature

Interested students might read all or part of a history of the events leading up to the battle of the Little Big Horn and its aftermath: *Son of the Morning Star* by Evan S. Connell.

Reinforce and Extend

Answers
◆ LITERATURE AND YOUR LIFE

Reader's Response Guide students to focus on items that provide a link with tradition or culture.

Thematic Focus He comes to appreciate how much he loves and values his traditions.

☑ Check Your Comprehension

1. Martin greets Grandpa with an informal "Hi," Cheryl hugs him, Marie keeps a proper distance and Martin's father tells him that he is welcome in their home.
2. He wants to see where his only living descendants live, he misses them, he knows he is dying and has a tradition to pass on.
3. He develops new respect for the powerful traditions it represents.
4. He goes to Rosebud Reservation to get some of the sacred sage.

◆ Critical Thinking

1. He is embarrassed that his grandfather doesn't look the way he thinks he should.
2. Grandpa passes the medicine bag to a boy who is ready to accept it. Grandpa dies shortly thereafter.
3. Martin creates a romanticized version of the family heritage to impress his pals; but Grandpa's true stories, ordinary and tinged with regret, convey a sadness that Martin hadn't understood.
4. He carries out a tradition.
5. Each influences the lives and attitudes of younger people.

Answers

◆ Reading Strategy

1. He seems to know that such a surprising description would intrigue the children.
2. Seeing how much awe his friends have for Grandpa helps Martin appreciate the power of his traditions.

◆ Build Vocabulary

Using the Suffix *-less*

1. Careless means unthinking.
2. Faithless means disloyal.
3. Helpless means unable to help oneself.
4. Mindless means dull or idiotic.
5. Restless means impatient or fidgety.

Spelling Strategy

1. collector; 2. director;
3. connector; 4. calculator;
5. processor

Using the Word Bank

1. resolute; 2. listlessly; 3. bachelor;
4. authentic; 5. procession

◆ Literary Focus

1. . . . can tell the difference between a story told simply to teach a lesson and one that is told to entertain.
2. A young person who is able to open his or her mind and heart to the power of long-standing tradition can gain insights into life.

◆ Build Grammar Skills

Practice

IC: independent clause
SC: subordinate clause

1. **IC:** "Wouldn't they have saved her **SC:** if she hadn't been good?"
2. **IC:** "It is a very difficult thing to tell stories **SC:** that children can both understand and appreciate."
3. **IC:** "I kept them quiet for ten minutes, **SC:** which was more than you were able to do."
4. **IC:** Our friends would have laughed at the picture **SC:** because Grandpa wasn't tall and stately like TV Indians.
5. **IC:** Mom and I carried him into her sewing room, **SC:** where we had a spare bed.

610

Guide for Responding (continued)

◆ Reading Strategy

MAKE INFERENCES

Making inferences involves formulating ideas based on evidence. Making inferences while you read helps you build toward an understanding of the theme. For example, you may have inferred that Martin's "glamorous tales" about his Sioux heritage in "The Medicine Bag" show his insecurity.

1. In "The Story-Teller," what does the term "horribly good" suggest about the bachelor's knowledge of children?
2. How does Grandpa's success with Martin's friends relate to Martin's agreement to receive the medicine bag?

◆ Build Vocabulary

USING THE SUFFIX *-less*

The suffix *-less* in *listless* means "without." Explain how adding the suffix *-less* to each of these good qualities turns them into negative ones:

1. care   2. faith   3. help   4. mind   5. rest

SPELLING STRATEGY

When a noun refers to a person or thing that does something, spell the final *ur* sound *or*:

direct + or = director   confess + or = confessor

On your paper, write the noun that corresponds to each verb:

1. collect   3. connect   5. process
2. direct   4. calculate

USING THE WORD BANK

On your paper, fill in each blank with a suitable word from the Word Bank.

1. Despite problems, Grandpa is ____?____ in locating his family.
2. The children approached ____?____ to hear the boring story.
3. The ____?____ had never met a woman he wanted to marry.
4. The museum displayed an ____?____ medicine bag.
5. The ____?____ consisted of three kids, a dog, and Grandpa.

610 ◆ Short Stories

◆ Literary Focus

THEME

Some stories have **themes**—insights into life—that are **stated** directly. However, these two stories have **implied** themes, so you must figure out the author's message. In "The Story-Teller," the contrast between the aunt's dull story and the bachelor's lively tale leads you to the theme.

1. State the theme of "The Story-Teller" by completing this sentence in your notebook: The contrast between the stories shows that children ____?____.
2. Reflecting on Martin's change of heart in "The Medicine Bag," state an insight about the importance of heritage.

◆ Build Grammar Skills

COMPLEX SENTENCES

A **complex sentence** contains one independent clause and one or more subordinate clauses. Here is an example of a complex sentence from "The Medicine Bag":

> ⌐———— independent clause ————⌐
> One year Cheryl had new moccasins

> ⌐——— subordinate clause ———⌐
> that Grandpa had made.

Practice On your paper, identify the independent and subordinate clauses in the following complex sentences.

1. "Wouldn't they have saved her if she hadn't been good?"
2. "It is a very difficult thing to tell stories that children can both understand and appreciate."
3. "I kept them quiet for ten minutes, which was more than you were able to do."
4. Our friends would have laughed at the picture because Grandpa wasn't tall and stately like TV Indians.
5. Mom and I carried him into her sewing room, where we had a spare bed.

Writing Application Using five complex sentences, describe a gift you have received from an older friend or family member.

Writing Application
Possible response:
My Aunt Shirley gave me an old locket that belonged to her. It is inscribed with the date 1909, which makes it nearly a century old. My aunt told me that the locket was solid gold. In it, she kept tiny pictures of my cousins, who are her children. I'll pass the locket to my children someday, if I have any.

✒ Writer's Solution

For additional instruction and practice, use the lessons in the *Writer's Solution Language Lab CD-ROM* on Complex Sentences. You may also use the Classifying Sentences by Structures page, p. 60, in the *Writer's Solution Grammar Practice Book*.

Build Your Portfolio

Idea Bank

Writing

1. List Write a list of items you'd like to put in your own medicine bag.

2. Compare and Contrast Compare and contrast the aunt's ideas about the upbringing of children with the bachelor's. Use details from "The Story-Teller" to support your points.

3. Analysis and Evaluation In a brief essay, analyze the importance of the title for either story. Make inferences about why the author chose it and how it relates to the theme. Then, after considering alternative titles, decide whether the original is the best choice.

Speaking and Listening

4. Storytelling Like the bachelor in "The Story-Teller," write a story that is sure to interest young children. Practice reading your story aloud, and then tell it to your classmates. **[Performing Arts Link]**

5. DJ's Rap Brainstorm for a group of songs that deal with a similar theme—for example, the trials and tribulations of love. Then, play the songs for the class, introducing each one with a speech that links it to the other songs. **[Music Link; Career Link]**

Projects

6. Space Capsule [Group Activity] A space capsule is like a medicine bag for our planet. With two classmates, choose five items that convey the theme of friendship to include in a capsule aimed at a distant star. Write a brief explanation to go with each item. **[Science Link]**

7. Travel Itinerary Using travel guides and other resources, create a one-week automobile tour of Sioux sites in South Dakota. Indicate mileage, travel time, and hotels or motels. Also, summarize the historical importance of each site on the tour. **[Social Studies Link]**

Writing Mini-Lesson

Book Jacket

Like the tale of Bertha in "The Story-Teller," a book jacket tries to be lively and engaging. It gives you a taste of the plot, characters, setting, and theme of a story—just enough to make you want to buy it. Write a book jacket for one of these stories that will have readers reaching for their wallets.

Writing Skills Focus: Supporting Details

Make your book jacket engaging by providing **supporting details** from the story—brief quotations, summaries, or descriptions. This passage from the jacket of Amy Tan's *The Kitchen God's Wife* entices you with a summary of the plot and details of the characters and setting:

Model of Real-World Writing
"Thus begins an unfolding of secrets that takes mother and daughter back to a small island outside Shanghai in the 1920s. . . ."

Prewriting Decide how much of the story's plot you can summarize without giving away the ending. Also, review the story for details that will illustrate the characters, setting, and theme in a lively way.

Drafting Imagine that you're facing the customer, trying to sell the book. Give a partial summary of the plot, breaking off at a suspenseful point. Also, use details from the story to support what you say about plot, characters, setting, or theme.

> ◆ **Grammar Application**
> When you use complex sentences in your book jacket, put a main idea in the independent clause and a less important idea in the subordinate clause.

Revising Have a few classmates read your book jacket. If it doesn't interest them in the story, use livelier details to support your descriptions of the story's elements.

Idea Bank

Following are suggestions for matching the Idea Bank topics with your students' performance levels and learning modalities:

Customize for
Performance Levels
Less Advanced Students: 1, 4, 5, 6
Average Students: 2, 4, 5, 6, 7
More Advanced Students: 3, 4, 5, 7

Customize for
Learning Modalities
Verbal/Linguistic: 1, 2, 3, 4, 5, 6, 7
Visual/Spatial: 6, 7
Bodily/Kinesthetic: 4, 5
Logical/Mathematical: 7
Musical/Rhythmic: 5
Interpersonal: 4, 5, 6
Intrapersonal: 1, 2, 3, 7

Writing Mini-Lesson

Refer students to the Writing Handbook in the back of the book for instruction on the writing process and for further information on providing supporting details. Have students use the Sunburst Organizer in **Writing and Language Transparencies,** p. 85, to organize their supporting details.

Writer's Solution

Writing Lab CD-ROM
Have students complete the tutorial on Description. Follow these steps:
1. Have students view the About Description introduction.
2. Guide students to the Interactive Instruction on Ordering Details.
3. Have students draft on computer.
4. Have students revise with the Descriptive Word Bin.

Writer's Solution Sourcebook
Have students use Chapter 2, "Description," pp. 32–69, for further support. The chapter includes in-depth instruction on focusing a description, p. 53.

✓ ASSESSMENT OPTIONS

Formal Assessment, Selection Test, pp. 173–175, and Assessment Resources Software. The selection test is designed so that it can be easily customized to the performance levels of your students.

Alternative Assessment, p. 41, includes options for less advanced students, more advanced students, interpersonal learners, visual/spatial learners, verbal/linguistic learners, and musical/rhythmic learners.

PORTFOLIO ASSESSMENT
Use the following rubrics in the **Alternative Assessment** booklet to assess student writing:
List: Description, p. 93
Compare and Contrast: Comparison/Contrast, p. 99
Analysis and Evaluation: Evaluation/Review, p. 100
Writing Mini-Lesson: Response to Literature, p. 106

Establish Writing Guidelines
Review the following key characteristics of a literary analysis:

- A literary analysis is a written response to a piece of literature in which the writer closely examines the piece.

- A literary analysis goes beyond reporting and describing the work by helping to interpret it for readers.

- A literary analysis focuses on a main point to support with evidence taken from the work.

You may want to distribute the scoring rubric for Literary Analysis/Interpretation, p. 108 in **Alternative Assessment,** to make students aware of the criteria on which they will be evaluated. See the suggestions on p. 614 for customizing the rubric to this workshop.

Refer students to the Writing Handbook in the back of the book for instruction on the writing process and further information on response to literature.

 Writer's Solution

Writers at Work Videodisc
To show students how writer Marilyn Stasio answers the question *What kind of writing is used to respond to literature?*, play the videodisc segment on Response to Literature (Ch. 9).

Play frames 30102 to 39013

Writing Lab CD-ROM
If your students have access to computers, they might work in the tutorial on Response to Literature to complete all or part of their literary analyses. Follow these steps:

1. Have students use the Writing Hint for choosing literature to come up with topic ideas.
2. Suggest that students view the audio-annotated models in the Prewriting section for examples of details on various elements of literature.
3. Allow students to draft on computer.
4. When revising, have students use the Revision Checker for language variety.

Writer's Solution Sourcebook
Students can find additional support in the chapter on Response to Literature, pp. 266–295.

612

Response to Literature

Literary Analysis

Writing Process Workshop

Have you ever discussed a book with a friend and traded opinions on the best and worst parts of it? If you have, you were doing a literary analysis. A literary analysis is a response to a work of literature in which you closely examine the work by taking it apart and discussing its various elements.

Write a literary analysis of one of the short stories in this section. Use the following skills, introduced in the Writing Mini-lessons in this section, to help you:

Writing Skills Focus

▶ **Use supporting details** to back up your ideas about the work. Use quotations and specific examples from the literature. (See p. 611.)

▶ **Use a clear organization.** Include an introduction, body, and conclusion. Organize details in a logical way, such as from the least important to the most important or vice versa. (See p. 593.)

▶ **Be accurate** when referring to titles, author's names, dates, or when using exact quotations.

The following excerpt from a student's literary analysis shows these skills:

MODEL FROM LITERATURE

"The Finish of Patsy Barnes" by Paul Laurence Dunbar

"The Finish of Patsy Barnes" by Paul Laurence Dunbar illustrates a young boy's determination to help a sick parent. ① He plans to win enough money racing a horse to get a good doctor for his mother. The determination is evident in Dunbar's description of Patsy's motivation: "For a single moment Patsy thinks of the sick woman at home and what that race will mean to her, and then his knees close against the horse's sides with a firmer dig." ② Barnes wins the race and helps his mother, but the real story lies in the many incidents that lead up to the race. First, ... ③

① The title and author are spelled and punctuated correctly.

② A quotation supports the writer's analysis of the author's purpose.

③ The writer plans to organize the paper by listing the events that lead to the climax of the story. The transition word *first* indicates that he will explain events in order.

612 ◆ *Short Stories*

 Beyond the Classroom

Community Connection
Literary Magazines and Literary Discussion Groups Explain to students that there are many literary magazines published in this country which provide readers with literature, analyses and reviews of contemporary and classical literature. These publications can range from weekly magazines, such as *The New Yorker* and *Atlantic Monthly,* to smaller journals which may appear monthly or quarterly. Suggest that students investigate literary magazines that may be published in their community, by local colleges, or in their own schools.

Students might look into literary discussion groups, in which groups of people of all ages come together to discuss books, poetry, or short stories. Usually, the group chooses a work to discuss and then the individuals read on their own. When the group meets again, they discuss each other's ideas and opinions about the literary work. Meeting in a literary group is a good way of connecting with people about literature and finding common interests with other members of the community. You might supervise as students browse online literary magazines or literary discussion groups.

Prewriting

Focus Your Topic Explore your reactions to the work you've chosen. You won't be able to include everything you think and feel about the work, so concentrate on one of its literary elements, such as setting, character, plot, or theme.

Interview Yourself Answer the following questions about the story you've chosen to analyze:

► What were the most enjoyable and interesting parts of the story? Why?

► What was especially memorable about the story? Explain.

► Which characters came to life in an especially vivid way? How did the writer achieve this effect?

► What was unique about the setting?

► Would you recommend this book to others?

Use your answers to provide content for your paper.

Gather Supporting Details Make a list of the key points you are going to address in your literary analysis. Then, find specific examples from the short story that support each point. For example:

Tears of Autumn

Key Point: The author uses vivid descriptions of the settings; she includes details that help you visualize the places Hana describes.

Supporting Example: "She longed to see the bright persimmon dotting the barren trees beside the thatched roofs, to see the fields of golden rice stretching to the mountains where only last fall she had gathered plum white mushrooms, and to see once more the maple trees lacing their flaming colors through the green pine."

Drafting

Grab Your Readers Write an introduction that grabs your readers' attention. Use a quotation from the story, a startling fact, or a thought-provoking question to begin your paper.

Include Key Points The body of your paper includes the key points that you have already listed. Choose a logical organization for your points, such as order of importance. Incorporate quotations from the story to support your points.

Summarize Complete your analysis with a brief summary of your main points. Restate your main idea, and make a final compelling point.

Writing Process Workshop

DRAFTING/REVISING

APPLYING LANGUAGE SKILLS: Avoiding Wordiness

Clean up your writing by getting rid of words that aren't necessary to the meaning:

Wordy: *Although Patsy Barnes has never been a jockey who rode a horse before, he rides the black stallion named Black Boy in a race and even wins.*

Clean: *Although Patsy has never been a jockey, he rides Black Boy and wins.*

Practice Rewrite these sentences to eliminate wordiness:

1. Patsy's mother needs a good doctor who can take care of her because she is sick with pneumonia and can't really get out of bed.

2. Patsy is a stubborn boy who won't listen to his mother when she tells him not to go to the racetrack.

3. Mr. Brackett, the owner of the horse that wins the race, is very happy when Patsy wins the race.

Writing Application In your paper, create sentences that are clear and concise.

Writer's Solution Connection Language Lab

For practice eliminating unnecessary words, complete the lesson Eliminating Unnecessary Words.

613

Revising

When revising, students may want to consider their paper's title and whether paragraphs and ideas connect with smooth transitions.

 Writer's Solution

Writing Lab CD-ROM

In the tutorial on Response to Literature, have students use the proofreading checklist to find errors in spelling, mechanics, and grammar.

Publishing

Students might submit their literary analyses to a school literary magazine. If none exist, suggest that students create their own, and ask for submissions from other students.

Reinforce and Extend

Review the Writing Guidelines After students have completed their papers, review the characteristics of a literary analysis.

Applying Language Skills

Writing Titles Correctly Tell students that when they use a word processing program, italics take the place of underlining. Underlining should only be used on a handwritten paper.

Answers

1. The novel *War and Peace* has over 1,000 pages!
2. The short story "The Tell-Tale Heart" scared me.
3. Is "The Bat" a poem about baseball?

 Writer's Solution

For additional instruction, have students use the practice pages on Capitals for Titles of Things, p. 98, and Underlining and Other Uses of the Quotation Marks, p. 113, in the *Writer's Solution Grammar Practice Book*.

Writing Process Workshop

EDITING/PROOFREADING

Applying Language Skills: Writing Titles Correctly

Different titles are punctuated differently. In general, if a work is short, its title goes in quotation marks. If a work is long, its title is underlined or written in italics.

Underline or italicize a novel or full-length play:
Black Beauty or *Black Beauty*

Enclose a short story, poem, or essay in quotation marks:
"January"

Practice Copy the following sentences, punctuating the titles correctly.

1. The novel "War and Peace" has over 1,000 pages!
2. The short story <u>The Tell-Tale Heart</u> scared me.
3. Is <u>The Bat</u> a poem about baseball?

Writing Application In your literary analysis, punctuate titles correctly.

Writer's Solution Connection Writing Lab

To check whether your organization is clear and logical, use the Revision Checker for Unity and Coherence in the Revising and Editing section of the Response to Literature tutorial.

614 ◆ *Short Stories*

Revising

Use a Checklist Use the following checklist to help you revise your literary analysis.

▶ Are there enough supporting details to make key points understandable? *If not, find additional examples from the story to support points you are making about the work of literature.*

▶ Does the analysis have a clear introduction, body, and conclusion? *Make sure that you state your main idea in your introduction, discuss it in the body, and refer to it in your conclusion.*

▶ Are details organized in a logical way? *If not, reorganize them in a way that will help your readers follow your points, such as order of importance.*

▶ Do you refer to titles and use quotations accurately? *Double-check against the text all quotations taken from the story. Also, make sure you have punctuated titles correctly.*

REVISION MODEL

① Imagine reading an action story and not knowing where it took place or the time period in which it occurred?
A story is incomplete without a description of the setting.
② "
The settings in Tears of Autumn by Yoshiko Uchida help "
the reader visualize the scenes that the main character,
③ Uchida uses such phrases as "plum white mushrooms" and "maple trees lacing their flaming colors through the green pine" to help us visualize the scenes.
Hana, describes.

① The writer adds to the introduction to grab the readers' attention.
② A short-story title must be enclosed in quotation marks.
③ These quotations from the story support the writer's point that Uchida describes settings beautifully.

Publishing and Presenting

Classroom Use a camcorder to tape a 20-minute program that analyzes several stories, poems, and essays for a young audience. With several classmates, take turns reading your analyses in front of the camera. Share your program with other students.

Library Combine your essays into a class literary magazine, and give the magazine a table of contents and an introduction. Display it in your school library.

Real-World Reading Skills Workshop

Recognizing Bias

Strategies for Success

Short stories, poems, and personal essays are shaped by the writer's personal beliefs and opinions. Other types of writing, such as news articles or informative articles in a magazine, are meant to be objective but sometimes show a bias—a leaning toward a certain position. Use the following strategies to help you recognize bias:

Look for Loaded Words Writers often use words loaded with emotional meanings. For example, calling someone *self-confident* gives a positive slant to a person's actions. The same actions could be described as *arrogant* or *conceited*, which have negative connotations. Words like these might reflect the writer's bias.

Be Aware of Stereotypes Stereotypes unfairly suggest that all members of a group are exactly the same. A stereotype creates a label that ignores each person's individual differences. Statements like "all teenagers watch too much television" are misleading and show a bias against teenagers.

Examine Slanted Arguments A slanted argument promotes only one side of an issue and omits information that goes against that side. For example, a candidate for student government might tell students that he has attended every student government meeting in the last three months—but leave out that he had missed all the previous meetings. This misinformation is biased. It may lead people to believe an untruth.

Apply the Strategies

Read this article from the *Marston News*, and answer the questions that follow.

New Leash Law in Marston

Proponents of a stricter leash law have finally scared the town leaders into accepting a new leash law. Citing the many individuals (seven reported cases) who have been mauled by crazed dogs, these people have gotten their way. Dogs can no longer be off their leashes any place in Marston, including the back field at Cold Creek Park, for years an accepted and safe place for dogs to run. Now all these dangerous tiny toy poodles and Chihuahuas will be controlled.

1. What words in this article have negative meanings?

2. Has the writer used stereotypes to describe anyone in the article? Explain.

3. Point out the writer's slanted arguments.

4. Do you think the writer of this news article has a bias? If so, describe it.

✔ Watch for bias in these places:
▶ Editorials
▶ Letters to the editor
▶ Regular feature columns in the newspaper
▶ Petitions

Reviewing Sentence Structure

The selections in Part 2 include instruction on the following:

- Simple and Compound Sentences
- Complex Sentences

This instruction is reinforced with the Build Grammar Skills practice pages in **Selection Support,** pp. 216 and 221.

As you review sentence structure, you may wish to include the following:

- Compound-Complex Sentences
Explain to students that a compound-complex sentence contains two or more independent clauses and one or more subordinate clause. Examples include:

She went to the store, which was closing soon, and then she walked home.

In this sentence, the two independent clauses are *She went to the store* and *and then she walked home.* The subordinate clause is *which was closing soon.*

- Compound Subjects and Predicates in Simple Sentences

Tell students that although a sentence may have a compound subject and/or predicate, the sentence itself may still be simple if it consists of a single independent clause.

| *The dog and I walked to the park.* | Simple sentence with a compound subject (dog and I) |
| *She sat and drank a soda after the game.* | Simple sentence with a compound predicate (sat and drank) |

Sentence Structure — Grammar Review

Sentences can be classified according to the number and kinds of clauses they contain. Sentences are either simple, compound, or complex.

Simple Sentences Simple sentences consist of one independent clause. (See page 592.) A simple sentence may have a compound subject or a compound verb, as well as modifiers and complements, but it does not contain a subordinate clause.

S   V   V
"She clung to the moist rail and breathed the damp salt air deep into her lungs."

Compound Sentences A compound sentence contains two or more independent clauses. The independent clauses are joined by a comma and a coordinating conjunction (*and, but, for, nor, or, so, yet*) or sometimes by a semicolon. Compound sentences do not contain subordinate clauses:

S   V   S   V
His name was Patsy Barnes, and he was a denizen of Little Africa.

Complex Sentences A complex sentence contains one independent clause and one or more subordinate clauses. (See page 610.)

Independent Clause	Subordinate Clause
S V	S V
It all began one day	when her uncle had come

to visit her mother.

Practice 1 In your notebook, identify the following sentences as simple, compound, or complex.

1. Her uncle spoke freely of Taro Takedao only because he was so sure Hana . . .

2. A man's word carried much weight for Hana's mother.

complex sentence *n.* a sentence made up of a main clause and one or more dependent clauses (Examples: After I cleaned the kitchen, I did the bathroom. He didn't know whether they were staying.)

3. In none did he disclose his loneliness or his need, but Hana understood this.

4. The horse that has taken away his father shall give him back his mother.

5. We are honored to have you with us, and you will never be a burden.

Practice 2 Combine the following pairs of sentences into one sentence as indicated.

1. There are a lot of yippy little dogs in our neighborhood. They usually bark at the mailman from the safety of their own yards. (compound sentence)

2. Bertha was sad. There were no flowers in the park. (complex sentence using the subordinating conjunction *because*)

3. Cheryl and her brother adored their grandfather. He was a Sioux Indian. (complex sentence using the relative pronoun *who*)

4. An agreement to the marriage was almost reached. Taro wrote his first letter to Hana. (complex sentence using the subordinating conjunction *when*)

Grammar in Writing

✔ *Do not join independent clauses with a comma. If you do, you create a run-on sentence—an error to be avoided. If you use a comma between independent clauses, you must also use a coordinating conjunction.*

Answers
Practice 1
1. Her uncle spoke freely of Taro Takedao only because he was so sure Hana . . . (complex)
2. A man's word carried much weight for Hana's mother. (simple)
3. In none did he disclose his loneliness or his need, but Hana understood this. (compound)
4. The horse that has taken away his father shall give him back his mother. (simple)
5. We are honored to have you with us, and you will never be a burden. (compound)

Practice 2
Possible responses:
1. There are a lot of yippy little dogs in our neighborhood, but they usually bark at the mailman from the safety of their own yards.
2. Bertha was sad because there were no flowers in the park.
3. Cheryl and her brother adored their grandfather who was a Sioux Indian.
4. An agreement to the marriage was almost reached when Taro wrote his first letter to Hana.

Speaking, Listening, and Viewing Workshop

Interviewing

Conducting interviews is a great way to gather information. Whether you use the telephone or meet person to person, interviewing provides you with firsthand information about your subject.

Plan Your Questions Before you begin, research your topic so you can ask appropriate questions. List specific things you want to find out in the interview. Ask questions that cannot be answered with a simple yes or no but that require elaboration or explanation.

Prepare for Responses As an interviewer, you must be ready to record information quickly. If you conduct an interview in person, ask your subject for permission to tape-record the interview. If you are not using a tape recorder, jot down key words and phrases that will help you remember the entire answer later. If you missed part of an answer, politely ask the speaker to repeat it.

Strategies for Interviewing

✔ *To conduct a successful interview, follow these strategies:*

▶ *For an in-person interview, dress appropriately and arrive promptly.*
▶ *Be respectful when the speaker is answering your questions. Pay attention, and do not interrupt.*
▶ *Be polite. Begin and end the interview by thanking the person for his or her time.*

Apply the Strategies

Practice interviewing strategies by doing the following activities:

1. Ask a peer about his or her last vacation. Before interviewing, find out where he or she visited and gather information about the vacation spot. Then, develop questions that will get firsthand descriptions and opinions of the vacation spot.

2. Interview an older family member about a period of history that he or she experienced. Research that period of time, and construct intelligent questions before the interview.

3. Conduct a telephone interview about a product or service that interests you. Before getting on the phone, have a list of questions ready, along with a pen and paper to jot down notes.

Introduce the Strategies

Ask students to volunteer any experiences they may have had conducting interviews. Explain that some interviews can be quite informal, such as asking a relative for information about their life growing up in a different country, or asking a friend about a book he or she had just read.

Customize for
Bodily/Kinesthetic Learners

Ask volunteers to act out their interviews with a partner in front of the class. Explain to the students watching how the interviewers use body language to show interest to the interviewee. Encourage students to suggest ways eye contact, body language, and hand gestures can help the interview go smoothly.

Apply the Strategies

Suggest to students that they write out a list of questions to ask the person they are going to interview. Remind them to ask questions that will allow the interviewee to do more than answer "yes" or "no." For example, instead of asking "Is the Grand Canyon really big?" ask "Can you compare the size of the Grand Canyon to anything else you've ever seen?"

 Beyond the Classroom

Workplace Skills

Interviewing One of the most essential parts in obtaining a new job is the interview. Most employers review resumes or applications for an open job position and then contact appropriate applicants for an interview. In the interview, the employer will usually ask the applicant for more information about qualifications for the job, work experience, and why the person is interested in the position. The employer will usually ask the applicant if he/she has any questions about the position or the company. One way to be prepared

for an interview is to do some preliminary research on the company or its workfield to know what kinds of questions to ask.

Have students form groups and choose a career. Then, have one or two students act as employers advertising for an open position, and another one or two students act as prospective applicants. Have the employers make up a list of questions for the applicant, and the applicant a list of questions for the employer. Then, have students conduct interviews. Suggest that groups volunteer to conduct their interviews for the rest of the class.

What's Behind the Words

Ask students to discuss any phobia terms with which they are already familiar. Then have students come up with a list of common fears that people are known to have, such as fear of crowds, fear of heights, or fear of insects. Explain that each of these fears can be described by a phobia word.

Answers

Activity 1

1. d	4. e
2. b	5. c
3. a	6. f

Activity 2

Examples:

malodorophobia (fear of bad smells)

itchaphobia (fear of itching)

photophobia (fear of photographs)

danceaphobia (fear of dancing)

What's Behind the Words

Vocabulary Adventures With Richard Lederer

Phobia Words

Do you have a pet fear? No? Think again. Does your stomach want to scream when it and you arrive at the zenith of a Ferris wheel? Does your head retract turtlelike into your body when lightning flashes and thunder cracks? Does a snake send your mind into a spin cycle?

Fearsome Phobias

Excessive fears are called phobias. In ancient Greek mythology, Phobos was the son of the god of war. The names of our deepest dreads generally include the Greek root *phobia*, meaning "fear" or "hatred." The two most common human phobias are *acrophobia*, a fear of heights, and *claustrophobia*, a fear of enclosed spaces. By giving names to these terrors, you may be taking the first step in overcoming them.

What's Your Phobia?

The charts below list some of people's most persistent fears, along with the names we have assigned to them.

Fears of Animals	
1. bees	apiphobia
2. cats	ailurophobia
3. dogs	cynophobia
4. sharks	galeophobia
5. spiders	arachnophobia

Fears of Nature	
1. comets	cometophobia
2. darkness	nyctophobia
3. fire	pyrophobia
4. the sea	thalassophobia
5. water	hydrophobia

Fearless About Phobias

Enough people fear the number thirteen that many buildings pretend not to have a thirteenth floor. Still, we assign this dread a name—*triskaidekaphobia*, from *tris*, "three," *kai*, "and," *deka*, "ten," and *phobia*, "fear." Incredible as it may seem, there is even a label for the fear of getting peanut butter stuck to the roof of the mouth. It's called *arachibutyrophobia*.

When President Franklin Delano Roosevelt said, in his 1933 inaugural address, "The only thing we have to fear is fear itself," he was warning us against *phobophobia*, the fear of being afraid. Now that you know that all your phobias have names, you may experience less fear about your fears—and about fear itself.

ACTIVITY 1 Here's a quiz about other psychological fears. Match each fear in the left column with its corresponding phobia in the right column.

1. fear of numbers		a. agoraphobia
2. fear of spirits or goblins		b. bogyphobia
3. fear of open spaces		c. chronophobia
4. fear of speaking in public		d. numerophobia
5. fear of time		e. phonophobia
6. fear of strangers		f. xenophobia

ACTIVITY 2 Make up three original phobias and a name for each. Example: *malohumorophobia*, a fear of bad jokes.

Extended Reading Opportunities

Throughout time, people have told stories in an attempt to share the human experience. While Poe's collection of short stories explores the darker side of humanity, the other collections celebrate the diversity of the American experience.

Suggested Titles

18 Best Stories by Edgar Allan Poe
Vincent Price and Chandler Brossard, Editors

Poe's most terrifying and hair-raising stories can be found in this collection. Introduced by co-editor and master of movie horror Vincent Price, the reader begins a journey into the most bone-chilling and suspenseful stories ever written. The collection includes his best-loved tales, among them, "The Black Cat," "The Masque of the Red Death," "The Murders in the Rue Morgue," "The Tell-Tale Heart," and "The Cask of Amontillado."

America Street
Anne Mazer, Editor

America's diversity is celebrated in this collection of fourteen short stories by renowned authors. Story themes range from Lesley Namioka's "The All-American Slurp," a comical story of an Asian family's introduction to American table manners, to Francisco Jimenez's sober account of a migrant child laborer in "The Circuit." The stories are unified in their depiction of common themes and experiences across cultures.

A Gathering of Flowers: Stories About Being Young in America
Joyce Carol Thomas, Editor

Focusing on the rich cultural heritage of America, Thomas collects eleven stories by such distinguished authors as Maxine Hong Kingston and Gary Soto. The settings of these stories range from rural Oklahoma to a Chicago Latino barrio to a Chippewa Indian reservation. As the reader explores these different places, he or she experiences the fantasies, fables, and stories that address what it means to be young and American.

Other Possibilities

100 Selected Stories   O. Henry

*Sixteen: Short Stories by
    Outstanding Young Adult Writers*   Donald Gallo, Editor

El Bronx Remembered   Nicholasa Mohr

(L) ©1965 by Vincent Price and Chandler Brossard, Dell Publishing (C) Cover collage; A detail from The Block II(1972) by Romare Bearden, ©1993. by Anne Mazer, Persea Books, NY (R) Cover ©1992 by HarperCollins Publishers, ©1990 by Joyce Carol Oates, Harper Trophy, HarperCollins Publishers

---

Planning Students' Extended Reading

All of the works listed on this page are good choices for extending reading of short stories. Following is some information that may help you choose which to teach:

Customize for
Varying Student Needs

When assigning the selections in this part to your students, keep in mind the following factors:

• *18 Best Stories by Edgar Allan Poe* is edited by Vincent Price and Chandler Brossard and includes other Poe classics such as "The Fall of the House of Usher," "The Gold Bug," "The Purloined Letter," and "The Pit and the Pendulum."

• *America Street* is a multicultural anthology of short stories, which may stimulate class discussion about immigrant and minority experiences of American childhood.

• *A Gathering of Flowers: Stories About Being Young in America* is a collection of eleven stories focusing on the range of cultural experiences of kids in America. Through its focus on love and hope and compassion, students may learn what draws together the different cultures and settings which make up this country.

Planning Instruction and Assessment

Unit Objectives

1. To read nonfiction selections
2. To apply a variety of reading strategies, particularly strategies for reading nonfiction, appropriate for reading these selections
3. To recognize literary elements used in these selections
4. To increase vocabulary
5. To learn elements of grammar and usage
6. To write in a variety of modes about situations based on the selections
7. To develop speaking and listening skills, by completing activities
8. To view images critically and create visual representations

Meeting the Objectives Each selection provides instructional material and portfolio opportunities by which students can meet unit objectives. You will find additional practice pages for reading strategies, literary elements, vocabulary, and grammar in the **Selection Support** booklet in the **Teaching Resources** box.

Setting Goals Work with your students to set goals for unit outcomes. Plan what skills and concepts you wish students to acquire. Match instruction and activities to students' performance levels or learning modalities.

Portfolios Students may keep portfolios of their completed work or of their work in progress. The Build Your Portfolio page of each selection provides opportunities for students to apply the concepts presented.

Humanities: Art

Still Life #31, 1963, by Tom Wesselmann

Tom Wesselmann (born 1931) is an American painter known for his ties to Abstract Expressionism, a popular 1960's art movement. Wesselmann's art moved from small, abstract collages using everyday objects to paintings of objects and landscapes.

What elements of this painting are symbols of real people, events and places, and culture? *Students may say that the TV represents media, the portrait of George Washington represents the historical aspects of the birth of the nation, the landscape outside the window represents the geography of the United States, and so forth.*

Still Life #31, 1963, Tom Wesselmann, Frederick P. Weisman Art Foundation, ©Tom Wesselmann/Licensed by VAGA, New York, NY

Art Transparencies

The **Art Transparencies** booklet in the **Teaching Resources** box offers fine art to help students make connections to other curriculum areas and high-interest topics.

To connect to the art on this page, and to the nonfiction selections that address symbols in American life in Unit 7, use Art Transparency 1, p. 9, *Lotto: The American Dream* by Luis Cruz Azaceta. Like Wesselmann's painting, this painting presents American symbols. Use one of the booklet's activities to help students explore the art through discussion, a writing activity, or taking a poll.

Beyond Literature

Each unit presents Beyond Literature features that lead students into an exploration of careers, communities, and other subject areas. In this unit, students will learn about the Nobel Prize, and make a sports connection to baseball and a social studies connection that combines history and geography. In addition, the **Teaching Resources** box contains a **Beyond Literature** booklet of activities. Using literature as a springboard, these activity pages offer students opportunities to connect literature to other curriculum areas and to the workplace and careers, community, media, and humanities.

Nonfiction

Nonfiction writing tells about real people, events, places, and objects. Nonfiction falls into several categories, which you'll encounter in this unit:

- An **autobiography** is the writer's own story of his or her life.

- A **biography** is the story of someone's life written by another person.

- An **essay** is a short nonfiction work about a particular subject. A **reflective essay** shares the writer's inner thoughts and feelings. A **narrative essay** tells a story about an actual event. A **descriptive essay** brings to life an event, a person, or a thing. An **expository essay** explains something about a subject. A **persuasive essay** attempts to convince the reader to think or act in a certain way.

- A **speech** is an oral presentation of facts and insights.

◆ 621

Assessing Student Progress

The tools that are available to measure the degree to which students meet the unit objectives are listed below.

Informal Assessment

The questions in the Guide for Responding sections are a first level of response to the concepts and skills presented with the selection. As a brief, informal measure of students' grasp of the material, these responses indicate where further instruction and practice are needed. The practice pages in the **Selection Support** booklet provide for this type of instruction and practice.

You will also find literature and reading guides in the **Alternative Assessment** booklet, which students can use for informal assessment of their individual performances.

Formal Assessment

The **Formal Assessment** booklet contains Selection Tests and Unit Tests.

Selection Tests measure comprehension and skills acquisition for each selection or group of selections.

Each Unit Test provides students with 30 multiple-choice questions and 5 essay questions designed to assess students' knowledge of the literature and skills taught in the unit.

Each Alternative Unit Test: Standardized-Test Practice provides 15 multiple-choice questions and 3 essay questions based on two new literature selections not contained in the student book. The questions on the Alternative Unit Test are designed to assess students' ability to compare and contrast selections, applying skills taught in the unit.

Alternative Assessment

For portfolio and alternative assessment, the **Alternative Assessment** booklet contains Scoring Rubrics, Assessment sheets, and Learning Modalities activities.

Scoring Rubrics provide writing modes that can be applied to Writing activities, Writing Mini-Lessons, and Writing Process Workshop lessons.

Assessment sheets for speaking and listening activities provide peer and self-assessment direction.

Learning Modalities activities appeal to different learning styles. Use these as an alternative measurement of students' growth.

Connections

Within this unit, you will find selections and activities that make connections beyond literature. Use these selections to connect students' understanding and appreciation of literature beyond the traditional literature and language arts curriculum.

Encourage students to connect literature to other curriculum areas. You may wish to coordinate with teachers in other curriculum areas to determine ways to team teach and further extend instruction.

Connections to Today's World

Use these selections to guide students to recognize the relevance of literature to contemporary writings. In this unit, students will make connections and further explore the concept of hard questions by reading an excerpt from Colin Powell's speech, *Sharing the American Dream.*

Connecting Literature to Social Studies

Each unit contains a selection that connects literature to social studies. In this unit, students will read about the Suffragist Movement in an excerpt from *The United States* vs. *Susan B. Anthony.*

Guide for Reading

OBJECTIVES

1. To read, comprehend, and interpret an essay
2. To relate an essay to personal experience
3. To learn strategies for reading nonfiction
4. To understand a reflective essay
5. To build vocabulary in context and learn forms of *habitable*
6. To develop skill in using subjective case pronouns
7. To write an article for the school newspaper with appropriate tone
8. To respond to a reflective essay through writing, speaking and listening, and projects

SKILLS INSTRUCTION

Vocabulary:
Forms of *habitable*

Spelling:
Silent *b*

Grammar:
Subjective Case Pronouns

Reading for Success:
Strategies for Reading Nonfiction

Literary Focus:
Reflective Essay

Writing:
Appropriate Tone

Speaking and Listening:
Discussion (Teacher Edition)

Critical Viewing:
Connect; Evaluate

PORTFOLIO OPPORTUNITIES

Writing: Fan Letter; Nature Poem; Essay
Writing Mini-Lesson: Article for the School Newspaper
Speaking and Listening: Discussion; Dramatic Reading
Projects: Animal Poster; Mud Wasps' Nest

More About the Author
Bruce Brooks spent much of his childhood in North Carolina, although he was born in Washington, D.C. In addition to his work as a writer, he has also been a printer, a newspaper and magazine reporter, and a teacher. Brooks says that a terrific thing about being a writer "is that you have an excuse to be interested in a lot of different things."

Meet the Author:

Bruce Brooks (1950–)

"I have an affinity for independence, for loners, for smart people who are watchers," says Bruce Brooks. It's not surprising, then, that Brooks displays these characteristics as he studies the nest-building techniques of wasps in "Animal Craftsmen."

Honors and Awards
Brooks has shown his versatility as a writer. His first novel, *The Moves Make the Man,* was a Newbery Honor book. More recently, his novel *What Hearts* also won a Newbery Honor. His first nonfiction book, *On the Wing,* was an American Library Association Best Book for young adults.

THE STORY BEHIND THE STORY

Bruce Brooks hadn't originally planned to introduce his book on animal architecture with "Animal Craftsmen." When he finished the book, however, he realized that he needed to tell the reader why he had chosen this topic in the first place. "It seemed that I had forgotten to begin with a beginning," he says. "So I went back to the incident that had started my interest, and I simply told that story, hoping my readers would get a similar sense of starting up."

◆ LITERATURE AND YOUR LIFE

CONNECT YOUR EXPERIENCE

As you walk down the street, out in the park, or in your back yard, you discover something miraculous. You wonder how that flower can bloom in a concrete crack, or you speculate about a tiny nest resting in the branch of a tree. You're not alone in your feelings of awe and amazement. The wonders of nature have intrigued many people, including Bruce Brooks.

THEMATIC FOCUS: Respecting Nature

As you read this essay, look for evidence of Brooks's awe and respect for the world around him.

◆ Background for Understanding

SCIENCE

In "Animal Craftsmen," Bruce Brooks marvels at the skill of mud wasps as they build their incredible nests. Your experience with wasps, like most people's, is probably limited: Many people avoid wasps for fear of being stung. Yet wasps play an important role in the ecology of their territory and provide a beneficial service to humans. Once the mud wasp's nest is built, the female paralyzes spiders or insects with a sting and places them alongside eggs that she has laid. This provides food for the developing wasps and rids an area of insects that would otherwise damage crops or trees.

Prentice Hall Literature Program Resources

REINFORCE / RETEACH / EXTEND

Selection Support Pages
Build Vocabulary: Forms of *habitable*, p. 224
Build Spelling Skills, p. 225
Build Grammar Skills: Subjective Case Pronouns, p. 226
Reading for Success: Strategies for Reading Nonfiction, pp. 227–228
Literary Focus: Reflective Essay, p. 229

Strategies for Diverse Student Needs, pp. 83–84

Beyond Literature Cross-Curricular Connection: Science, p. 42
Formal Assessment Selection Test, pp. 184–186, Assessment Resources Software
Alternative Assessment, p. 42
Writing and Language Transparencies Open Mind Organizer, p. 81; Sunburst Organizer, p. 85
Resource Pro CD-R⊘M "Animal Craftsmen"
 Listening to Literature Audiocassettes "Animal Craftsmen"
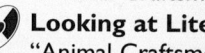 **Looking at Literature Videodisc/Videotape** "Animal Craftsmen"

◆ Animal Craftsmen ◆

◆ Literary Focus

REFLECTIVE ESSAY

In this reflective essay, Bruce Brooks expresses his appreciation of animals' skills at designing and engineering their homes. A **reflective essay** is a work of nonfiction that communicates a writer's thoughts about a topic of personal interest. In presenting his or her thoughts, the writer may re-create and evaluate personal experiences to make a point.

◆ Build Vocabulary

RELATED WORDS: FORMS OF *habitable*

In "Animal Craftsmen," mud wasps make a hive *habitable,* which means "fit to be lived in." Words related to *habitable* include *habitat,* meaning "native environment," *inhabitant,* meaning "resident," and *inhabit,* meaning "to live in."

WORD BANK

Which word from the list shares a root with the verb *sympathy*? Check the Build Vocabulary box on page 627 to see if you chose correctly.

subtle
infusion
habitable
empathy

Guide for Reading ◆ 623

Preparing for Standardized Tests

Vocabulary The related words vocabulary feature in this selection (forms of *habitable*) will help students understand the concept of answering certain types of reading comprehension items on standardized tests. Students may be asked to select the word that best fits the meaning of a sentence. This task may require students to interpret forms of known words to fit a new situation. Use the following sample test question:

Most people would decide that an old tobacco barn is _____ because it provides little protection from wind, rain, and cold.

(A) inexpensive (C) unfixable
(B) infrequent (D) uninhabitable

To decide which answer is correct, students should determine the root word of each answer choice (*expensive, frequent, fixable,* and *habitable*). Being familiar with the definition of *habitable* ("fit to be lived in") and related forms of the word, will lead students to the conclusion that a barn that provides little protection from weather elements would be *(D) uninhabitable,* or "not fit to be lived in." For further practice, use Build Vocabulary in **Selection Support,** p. 224.

Interest Grabber Write the phrase "wonders of nature" on the board as the central concept of an idea web.

```
    plants              animals
   _____          _____

          ⟨ wonders of nature ⟩

   ‾‾‾‾‾‾‾‾          ‾‾‾‾‾‾‾‾‾
```

Have students freewrite for a few minutes on the wonders of nature to fill out the web—you might suggest that they use subtopics, such as plants and animals for their web ideas. Then introduce the selection by explaining that it is an essay in which the writer reflects on his own thoughts and feelings about nature.

◆ Build Grammar Skills

Subjective Case Pronouns If you wish to introduce the grammar skill for this selection before students read, refer to instruction on p. 629.

Customize for
Less Proficient Readers

In a reflective essay, an author attempts to convey his or her own thoughts and feelings on a topic of personal interest. As students read, they can note examples of the author's personal opinions, and jot them down in the Open Mind Organizer, p. 81 of **Writing and Language Transparencies.**

Customize for
More Advanced Students

Challenge students to create a character profile of Bruce Brooks based on the observations, feelings, and impressions he reveals in this reflective essay. Students can use copies of the Sunburst Organizer, p. 85 of **Writing and Language Transparencies,** to collect details for this profile.

Customize for
English Language Learners

Display examples or pictures of animal architecture: wasps' nests, spider webs, beaver dams, and so on, to help students better visualize the objects and imagine the sense of wonder a small boy might bring to the discovery of such a marvel.

623

The Reading for Success page in each unit presents a set of problem-solving strategies to help readers understand authors' words and ideas on multiple levels. Good readers develop a bank of strategies from which they can draw as needed.

Unit 7 introduces strategies for reading nonfiction. Students must be able to read nonfiction before they can apply higher-level critical thinking strategies. These strategies for reading nonfiction give readers an array of approaches for mastering a text: set a purpose for reading, identify the author's main points, and understand the author's purpose.

These strategies for reading nonfiction are modeled with "Animal Craftsmen." Each green box shows an example of the thinking process involved in applying one of these strategies. Additional notes provide support for applying these strategies throughout the selection.

How to Use the Reading for Success Page

- Introduce the strategies for reading nonfiction, presenting each as a problem-solving procedure.

- Before students read the selection, have them preview it, looking at the annotations in the green boxes that model the strategies.

- To reinforce these strategies, have students use Reading for Success, pp. 227–228, in **Selection Support.** These pages give students an opportunity to read a selection and practice strategies for reading nonfiction by writing their own annotations.

Reading Strategies: Support and Reinforcement

Using Boxed Annotations and Prompts

Throughout the unit, the notes in green, red, and maroon are intended to help students apply reading strategies, understand the literary focus, and make connections with their lives. Use boxed material in these ways:

- Have students pause at each box and respond to its prompt before they continue reading.

- Urge students to read through the selection, ignoring the boxes. After they complete the selection, they may go back and review the text, responding to the prompts.

Reading for Success

Strategies for Reading Nonfiction

Nonfiction is prose that presents and explains ideas or tells about real people, places, things, and events. Your school books, newspapers, magazines, encyclopedias, and certain information on the Internet are all examples of nonfiction. So are biographies, autobiographies, and essays. Although the writing is nonfiction, that doesn't mean that you should accept everything the writer tells you. Instead, judge the facts for yourself, and form your own opinions. The following strategies will help you read nonfiction effectively:

Set a purpose for reading.

Before you begin, set a goal for reading a work of nonfiction. Your goal may be to find facts, to analyze a writer's theory, to understand an opinion, or simply to be entertained. Keep your purpose in mind, and look for details in your reading that support that purpose.

Identify the author's main points.

Ask yourself what the author wants you to learn or think as a result of reading his or her nonfiction work. These main points are the most important ideas in the piece. Bruce Brooks makes the following point early in "Animal Craftsmen."

> I *did* find something under the eaves—something very strange.

As he continues the essay, Brooks makes points about the strange and extraordinary "homes" that animals build for themselves.

Understand the author's purpose.

Authors of nonfiction have a reason, or a purpose, for writing. Their details and information support their purpose. They also adopt a tone, or attitude, toward their topic and the reader that indicates their purpose.

▶ Consider the details that the author includes or does not include. Also, consider the author's tone: Is it friendly? Warning? Serious? Think about what the choices of details and tone reveal about the writer's beliefs and purpose for writing.

▶ Once you recognize the author's purpose, decide whether you will accept the writer's ideas or whether you should question them.

As you read "Animal Craftsmen" by Bruce Brooks, notice the notes along the sides. The notes demonstrate how to apply these strategies to your reading.

Model a Reading Strategy: Set a Purpose for Reading

Tell students that as they are reading a nonfiction selection, it will help to set a purpose or goal for their reading. Have students read the Guide for Reading information on pp. 622–623, then demonstrate for students how to set a goal for reading "Animal Craftsmen."

Before I read, I look at the title and photographs to decide whether I know the author's writings, and I read information on the book cover or book jacket. In this case, I read the information on the Guide for Reading pages. Because I find that the textbook contains science background information about wasps, and talks about respecting nature, I decide that my purpose for reading this selection is to find out scientific information about wasps.

As I read the essay, I revise my purpose to include finding out about wasps' homes. Point out to students that setting a purpose for their reading directs their reading, helping them look for specific ideas and details. In turn, the information gained helps clarify their understanding of the author's meanings.

MODEL

Animal Craftsmen

Bruce Brooks

1 One evening, when I was about five, I climbed up a ladder on the outside of a rickety old tobacco barn at sunset. The barn was part

> Your **purpose for reading** may be to learn about the "animal craftsmen" of the essay's title.

of a small farm near the home of a country relative my mother and I visited periodically; though we did not really know the farm's family, I was allowed to roam, poke around, and conduct sudden studies of anything small and harmless. On this evening, as on most of my jaunts, I was not looking for anything; I was simply climbing with an open mind. But as I balanced on the next-to-the-top rung and inhaled the

2 spicy stink of the tobacco drying inside, I *did* find something under the eaves[1] —something very strange.

It appeared to be a kind of gray paper sphere, suspended from the dark planks by a thin stalk, like an apple made of ashes hanging on its stem. I studied it closely in the clear light. I saw that the bottom was a little ragged,

3 and open. I could not tell if it had been torn, or if it had been made that way on purpose—for it was clear to me, as I studied it, that this thing had been *made*. This was no fruit or fungus.[2] Its shape, rough but trim; its intricately[3] colored surface with <u>subtle</u> swirls of gray and tan; and most of all the uncanny adhesiveness with

---

1. **eaves** (ēvz) *n*.: Lower edges of a roof.
2. **fungus** (fuŋ´ gəs) *n*.: Growth caused by parasites living on organisms.
3. **intricately** (in´ tri kit lē) *adv*.: In a complex, highly detailed way.

◆ **Build Vocabulary**

subtle (sut´ əl) *adj*.: Delicate; fine

---

which the perfectly tapered stem stuck against the rotten old pine boards—all of these features gave evidence of some intentional design. **3** The troubling thing was figuring out who had designed it, and why.

I assumed the designer was a human being: someone from the farm, someone wise and skilled in a craft that had so far escaped my curiosity. Even when I saw wasps entering and leaving the thing (during a vigil I kept every evening for two weeks), it did not occur to me that the wasps might have fashioned it for themselves. I assumed it was a man-made "wasp house" placed there expressly for the purpose of attracting a family of wasps, much as the "martin hotel," a giant birdhouse on a pole near the farmhouse, was maintained to shelter migrant[4] purple martins who returned every spring. I didn't ask myself why anyone would want to give wasps a bivouac;[5] it seemed no more odd than attracting birds.

> From this paragraph and what you have already read, you know that at least part of the **author's purpose** is to explain his discovery.

As I grew less wary of the wasps (and they grew less wary of me), and as my confidence on the ladder improved, I moved to the upper rung and peered through the sphere's bottom. I could see that the paper swirled in layers around some secret center the wasps inhabited, and I marveled at the delicate hands of the craftsman who had devised such tiny apertures[6] for their protection.

I left the area in the late summer, and in my ↓

---

4. **migrant** (mī´ grənt) *adj*.: Moving from one region to another with the changing seasons.
5. **bivouac** (biv´ wak´) *n*.: Temporary shelter.
6. **apertures** (ap´ ər chərz) *n*.: Openings.

Animal Craftsmen ◆ 625

Develop Understanding

One-Minute Insight "Animal Craftsmen" is an essay from Bruce Brooks's book, *Nature by Design*. In his essay, the author shares an experience from his youth that inspired him to respect animal architects. He uses his awe of a wasp nest as a way to explain the admiration with which he still regards the wonders of the natural world.

Clarification

1 Tobacco barns, used for drying tobacco leaves prior to marketing, are usually wooden structures with numerous openings for ventilation. Their open structure makes them more rickety than other barns.

*R*eading for Success

2 **Understand the Author's Purpose** Discuss with students what the author hopes to get readers to do by including this passage. *He hopes to draw readers to the subject by putting them in his place, by motivating them with his own deep curiosity and fascination.*

◆ Literary Focus

3 **Reflective Essay** Ask students to explain what this passage reveals about young Brooks and his interest in nature. *Even at the early age of five, he was so fascinated by the mysterious nest that he kept a two-week vigil, thought about the structure, and tried to make sense of it from what he already knew.*

Looking at Literature Videodisc/Videotape

To provide background and insight into the author of "Animal Craftsmen," play Chapter 7 of the videodisc. In this interview, Brooks discusses how his curiosity about the world around him and his appreciation of nature influence his writing. Ask students to discuss which of their interests might make good topics for writing.

Chapter 7

⊕ **Block Scheduling Strategies**

Consider these suggestions to take advantage of extended class time:

- Present the Reading for Success strategies, p. 624, before students read the essay. Then, as a class, review the annotations in the side notes as they read aloud. Students can work on their own to apply the strategies as they annotate the Reading for Success practice essay in **Selection Support**, pp. 227–228.
- Structure class time by having students alternate between working on their own and with partners. Have them read the essay and then answer the

Check Your Comprehension and Critical Thinking questions independently, p. 628. Following each of these activities, allow students to meet briefly with partners to discuss Reader's Response and Thematic Focus, p. 628.

- Interest students in this essay with a science theme by showing Chapter 7 of the videodisc. After students have read the essay, have them work in groups to research the Cross-Curricular Connection: Science activity, p. 626 (Teacher Edition).

 Looking at Literature Videodisc/ Videotape

◆Literary Focus

❶ **Reflective Essay** Ask students what role imagination plays in a reflective essay. *Students may say that imagination plays a large role. Brooks shares his thoughts as he reflects on the event he reveals to readers. It is his imagination that raises questions and guides him to dig deeper into his discovery.*

Clarification

❷ This particular kind of wasp house is often called a hornet's nest. Wasps die after the first hard freeze, leaving an unprotected nest with its unhatched larvae. Certain birds who feed on these morsels often shred the nest.

Reading for Success

❸ **Identify the Author's Main Points** Have students summarize the main point the author conveys about the importance of his discovery and interest in the wasp nest. *In addition to the curiosity it sparked in him, it set the tone for a life of observation and respect for nature.*

Reading for Success

❹ **Set a Purpose for Reading** Students have set general purposes for reading this essay. Regardless of their chosen purposes, students' purposes may change as they read. Ask how this paragraph may motivate them to establish a new purpose for reading. *Students may say that they will want to read on to find out what Brooks did with the nest when he got it home, or how studying the nest led to other things.*

▶Critical Viewing◀

❺ **Connect** *Like an apple, it hangs from a "stem," attracts insects, and has a curved shape.*

---

❶ imagination I took the strange structure with me. I envisioned unwrapping it, and in the middle finding—what? A tiny room full of bits of wool for sleeping, and countless manufactured pellets of scientifically determined wasp food? A glowing blue jewel that drew the wasps at twilight, and gave them a cool infusion of energy as they clung to it overnight? My most definite idea was that the wasps lived in a small block of fine cedar the craftsman had drilled full of holes, into which they slipped snugly, rather like the bunks aboard submarines in World War II movies.

As it turned out, I got the chance to discover that my idea of the cedar block had not been wrong by much. We visited our relative again in the winter. We arrived at night, but first thing in the morning I made straight for the farm and its barn. The shadows under the eaves were too dense to let me spot the sphere from far off. I stepped on the bottom rung of the ladder—slick with frost—and climbed ❷ carefully up. My hands and feet kept slipping, so my eyes stayed on the rung ahead, and it was not until I was secure at the top that I could look up. The sphere was gone.

❸ I was crushed. That object had fascinated me like nothing I had come across in my life; I had even grown to love wasps because of it. I sagged on the ladder and watched my breath eddy[7] around the blank eaves. I'm afraid I pitied myself more than the apparently homeless wasps.

But then something snapped me out of my sense of loss: I recalled that I had watched the farmer taking in the purple martin hotel every November, after the birds left. From its spruce appearance when he brought it out in March, it was clear he had cleaned it and repainted it and kept it out of the weather. Of course he would do the same thing for *this* house, which was even more fragile. I had never mentioned the wasp dwelling to anyone, but now I decided I would go to the farm, introduce myself, and inquire about it. Perhaps I would even be permitted to handle it, or, best of all, learn how to make one myself.

I scrambled down the ladder, leaping from the third rung and landing in the frosty salad of tobacco leaves and windswept grass that collected at the foot of the barn wall. I looked down and saw that my left boot had, by no more than an inch, just missed crushing the very thing I was rushing off to seek. There, lying dry and separate on the leaves, was the wasp house.

I looked up. Yes. I was standing directly beneath the spot where the sphere had hung—it was a straight fall. I picked up the wasp house, gave it a shake to see if any insects were inside, and, discovering none, took it home. ❹

My awe of the craftsman grew as I unwrapped the layers of the nest. Such beautiful paper! It was much tougher than any I had encountered, and it held a curve (something my experimental paper airplanes never did), but it was very light, too. The secret at the center of the swirl turned out to be a neatly made fan of tiny cells, all of the same size and shape, reminding me of the heart of a sunflower that had lost its seeds to birds. The fan hung from the sphere's ceiling by a stem the thickness of a pencil lead.

---

7. **eddy** (ed´ ē) *v.*: Move in a circular motion.

◀ **Critical Viewing** In what way does this wasps' nest look like "an apple made of ashes hanging on its stem"? **[Connect]** ❺

Cross-Curricular Connection: Science

Wasps' Nests In this essay, students learn how the author as a young boy becomes fascinated by a wasp nest. Wasps are a group of insects similar to bees and ants that usually have wings and can fly. Solitary wasps often dig in the ground or use abandoned insect holes or hollow sticks as nesting sites. Social wasps live and work as an organized group to build a large nest of a paperlike material. To build the nest, female wasps chew up old wood or sticks and spread this paper pulp in a thin layer on which to lay eggs.

Brainstorm with students for a list of other natural animal structures that fascinate them, such as: ant hills, prairie dog burrows, eagle aeries, or beaver lodges. Have students select a particular animal structure to research. Have them learn where it is built, how it is made, who lives in it, what materials are used, and how long the structure usually lasts. Invite students to share their findings with classmates in a brief oral or written report, accompanied by photographs, diagrams, or sketches.

The rest of the story is a little embarrassing. More impressed than ever, I decided to pay homage to the creator of this <u>habitable</u> sculpture. I went boldly to the farmhouse. The farmer's wife answered my knock. I showed her the nest and asked to speak with the person in the house who had made it. She blinked and frowned. I had to repeat my question twice before she understood what I believed my mission to be; then, with a gentle laugh, she dispelled my illusion about an ingenious old papersmith fond of wasps. The nest, she explained, had been made entirely by the insects themselves, and wasn't that amazing?

Well, of course it was. It still is. I needn't have been so embarrassed—the structures that animals build, and the sense of design they display, *should* always astound us. On my way home from the farmhouse, in my own defense I kept thinking, "But *I* couldn't build anything like this! Nobody could!"

> Brooks presents a **main point** here: Ordinary animals that we take for granted can do extraordinary things.

The most natural thing in the world for us to do, when we are confronted with a piece of animal architecture, is to figure out if we could possibly make it or live in it. Who hasn't peered into the dark end of a mysterious hole in the woods and thought, "It must be pretty weird to live in there!" or looked up at a hawk's nest atop a huge sycamore and shuddered at the thought of waking up every morning with nothing but a few twigs preventing a hundred-foot fall. How, we wonder, do those twigs stay together, and withstand the wind so high?

> Another **main point** is that people tend to find similarities between animal behavior and human behavior.

It is a human tendency always to regard animals first in terms of ourselves. Seeing the defensive courage of a mother bear whose cubs are threatened, or the cooperative determination of a string of ants dismantling a stray chunk of cake, we naturally use our own behavior as reference for our <u>empathy</u>. We put ourselves in the same situation and express the animal's action in

▲ **Critical Viewing** What about this spiderweb do you find "awesome"? Explain. [Evaluate] ❽

feelings—and words—that apply to the way people do things.

Sometimes this is useful. But sometimes it is misleading. Attributing human-like intentions to an animal can keep us from looking at the *animal's* sense of itself in its surroundings—its immediate and future needs, its physical and mental capabilities, its genetic[8] instincts. Most animals, for example, use their five senses in ways that human beings cannot possibly understand or express. How can a forty-two-year-old nearsighted biologist have any real idea what a two-week-old barn owl sees in the dark? How can a sixteen-year-old who lives in the Arizona desert identify with ❾

---

8. **genetic** (jə net′ ik) *adj.*: Inherited biologically.

◆ **Build Vocabulary**

infusion (in fyo͞o′ zhən) *n.*: The act of putting one thing into another

habitable (hab′ ə tə bəl) *adj.*: Fit to live in

empathy (em′ pə thē) *n.*: Ability to share another's emotions, thoughts, or feelings

Animal Craftsmen ◆ 627

Reading for Success

❻ **Understand the Author's Purpose** Discuss with students why the author would reveal a childhood embarrassment to make a larger point. *He wants readers to know that although the nest fascinated him in the first place, once he discovered that it had been built by insects, he developed more appreciation for it and a new type of fascination.*

◆**LITERATURE AND YOUR LIFE**

❼ Ask students to think of a time when they had questions about something that they didn't know about and really wanted to understand. Did they have a friend, teacher, or adult they were not too ashamed and embarrassed to ask questions of, or did they try to find out the answers by themselves to keep their lack of knowledge a secret? Have volunteers share their experiences with the class.

▶**Critical Viewing**◀

❽ **Evaluate** *Students may cite the regular architecture of its spirals, the logic and strength of its support "beams," the delicate beauty of the structure, and how it can be created by a spider from its own body fluids.*

Thematic Focus

❾ **Respecting Nature** Ask students to explain how this passage reflects the respect the author feels toward nature. *The author expresses awe that animals are motivated by their own internal senses and instincts. He respects animals for what they do, not for how much humans may be impressed by them. He accepts them on their own terms.*

 Speaking and Listening Mini-Lesson

Discussion This mini-lesson supports the Speaking and Listening activity in the Idea Bank on p. 630.

Introduce Remind students that they frequently participate in discussions. Explain that they will conduct their own group discussions, and record and share information generated during them.

Develop Divide the class into discussion groups of 6–8 students. Have each group assign a moderator and a recorder. Review general rules of productive speaking and respectful listening, and encourage participation. Set a time limit, and at

various points in the activity, signal the remaining time. Present the topic and have groups proceed with their own discussions.

Apply As groups discuss the topic, monitor their discussions, asking and answering occasional questions, or challenging points that are raised.

Assess Evaluate students on their participation, whether they demonstrate effective speaking and respectful listening, and how well they record and share the examples they discussed. Or use the Self-Assessment Speaking and Listening Progress forms, pp. 118–119 in **Alternative Assessment.**

❶ Identify the Author's Main Points Have students rephrase the author's point in this passage. *Animals may be amazing, but humans must remember that they have animal instincts and responses, not human ones. Humans can understand nature better if we can learn about the entire environment and each creature's place in the web of life.*

◆**LITERATURE AND YOUR LIFE**

❷ Invite students to share similar examples of creative natural wonder they have experienced in their own lives.

Reinforce and Extend

Answers
◆**LITERATURE AND YOUR LIFE**

Reader's Response Most students will agree with Brooks, though not all may share his degree of fascination with the natural world.

Thematic Focus Answers will vary, but students should give examples and explain their choices.

☑ **Check Your Comprehension**

1. He assumes that it was made by humans, as a bird house is.
2. He discovers its strength and its intricate interior structures.
3. We wonder if we could make the structures and if we could live in them.

◆**Critical Thinking**

1. He thinks of the nest as a "wasp house," which is a human term.
2. He has already developed a sense of awe and respect for the nest's creator.
3. The more we understand about animals' instincts and intelligence, the more we appreciate them.
4. Students may say that humans have the abilities to imagine and empathize, which enable them to envision things they have neither seen nor experienced.

---

❶ the muscular jumps improvised by a waterfall-leaping salmon in Alaska? There's nothing wrong with trying to empathize with an animal, but we shouldn't forget that ultimately animals live *animal* lives.

Animal structures let us have it both ways—we can be struck with a strange wonder, and we can empathize right away, too. Seeing a vast spiderweb, taut and glistening between two bushes, it's easy to think, "I have no idea how that is done; the engineering is awesome." But it is just as easy to imagine **❷** climbing across the bright strands, springing from one to the next as if the web were a new Epcot attraction, the Invisible Flying Flexible Space Orb. That a clear artifact of an animal's wits and agility[9] stands right there in front of us—that we can touch it, look at it from different angles, sometimes take it home—inspires our imagination as only a strange reality can. We needn't move into a molehill to experience a life of darkness and digging; our creative wonder takes us down there in a second, without even getting our hands dirty.

---

9. **agility** (ə jil′ ə tē) *n.*: Ability to move quickly and easily.

But what if we discover some of the mechanics of how the web is made? Once we see how the spider works (or the humming bird, or the bee), is the engineering no longer awesome? This would be too bad: we don't want to lose our sense of wonder just because we gain understanding.

And we certainly do *not* lose it. In fact, seeing how an animal makes its nest or egg case or food storage vaults has the effect of increasing our amazement. The builder's energy, concentration, and athletic adroitness are qualities we can readily admire and envy. Even more startling is the recognition that the animal is working from a precise design in its head, a design that is exactly replicated time after time. This knowledge of architecture—knowing where to build, what materials to use, how to put them together—remains one of the most intriguing mysteries of animal behavior. And the more *we* develop that same knowledge, the more we appreciate the instincts and intelligence of the animals.

> Brooks indicates his **purpose:** He wants you to understand that animal behavior is mysterious and deserving of appreciation.

Guide for Responding

◆ **LITERATURE AND YOUR LIFE**

Reader's Response Do you agree with the author that animal behavior and nature itself are fascinating? Explain.

Thematic Focus What aspects of nature inspire your respect? Explain.

Natural Art Sketch something from nature that you find extraordinary.

☑ **Check Your Comprehension**

1. As the child in the essay, what assumptions does Brooks make about the nest he finds?
2. What does Brooks discover as he unwraps layers of the wasps' nest?
3. According to Brooks, what are two natural reactions to seeing animal structures?

◆ **Critical Thinking**

INTERPRET

1. What evidence in the essay indicates that as a child, Brooks showed a tendency to regard animals in human terms? **[Analyze]**
2. What do you learn about Brooks when he says, "Perhaps I would even be permitted to handle [the nest], or, best of all, learn how to make one myself." **[Infer]**
3. What is the theme or central message of the essay? **[Interpret]**

EVALUATE

4. Brooks states that it is not necessary to move into a molehill to experience a life underground. Do you agree? Why or why not? **[Evaluate]**

📖 **Beyond the Selection**

FURTHER READING
Other Works by Bruce Brooks
Moves Make the Man
Asylum for Nightface
Nature by Design
Other Works on the Theme of Respecting Nature
Beneath the Oceans, Penny Clarke
Discovering Endangered Species, Nancy Field and Sally MacHlis
How Nature Works, David A. Burnie

INTERNET
We suggest the following sites on the Internet (all Web sites are subject to change).
For more information on Bruce Brooks:
http://www.scils.rutgers.edu/special/kay/brooks.html
For more information on nature and the environment, visit:
http://www.epa.gov/kids/
We *strongly recommend* that you preview these sites before you send students to them.

Guide for Responding (continued)

◆ Reading for Success

STRATEGIES FOR READING NONFICTION

Review the reading strategies and the notes showing how to read nonfiction. Then, apply the strategies to answer the following:

1. What purpose did you set when you began reading this essay? Explain how you fulfilled your purpose.
2. (a) State the author's purpose for writing "Animal Craftsmen." (b) How does his attitude reflect his purpose?
3. List the author's main points, and explain how they support his purpose.

◆ Build Vocabulary

USING FORMS OF *habitable*

The word *habitable* means "suitable for living in." Write the following sentences, completing each with one of these words related to *habitable*:

    habitat   inhabit   inhabitant

1. The starlings _____?_____ a bird house.
2. The polar bear's _____?_____ is very cold.
3. The wasp was an _____?_____ of the hive.

SPELLING STRATEGY

The *b* in *subtle* is silent. Several other common English words contain a silent *b*. On your paper, answer each clue with a word that contains a silent *b*.

1. This person fixes water-supply pipes.
2. You use this to untangle your hair.
3. This is another word for a tree bough.

USING THE WORD BANK

On your paper, match the Word Bank word in Column A with the word or phrase closest in meaning in Column B.

Column A	Column B
1. subtle	a. shared feeling
2. infusion	b. injection
3. habitable	c. livable
4. empathy	d. delicate

◆ Literary Focus

REFLECTIVE ESSAY

The goal of a **reflective essay** is to present a writer's ideas about a topic of personal interest. In a reflective essay, a writer may share how his or her life has been affected by his or her experience. In "Animal Craftsmen," Brooks recalls how a childhood experience—finding a wasps' nest—fascinated him and led to a lifelong love of nature's wonders.

1. List two statements in which Brooks shares his thoughts, feelings, and opinions.
2. Explain how Brooks uses the tale of the nest to lead to a broader subject.
3. In what way was Brooks's life changed by the experience described in the essay?

◆ Build Grammar Skills

SUBJECTIVE CASE PRONOUNS

Personal pronouns change form based on their grammatical use in a sentence. This form is called its *case*. When a pronoun is a subject or a predicate pronoun (following a linking verb), use the **subjective case.** These are the subjective case pronouns: *I, we, you, he, she, it, they.*

Subject: *I* climbed up a ladder.
Predicate Pronoun: It was *I* who discovered the nest.

Practice On your paper, identify the subjective case pronoun in each sentence.

1. I was not looking for anything.
2. We visited our relative again in the winter.
3. It was he who unwrapped the wasps' nest.
4. She blinked and frowned.
5. It seems they built the nests themselves.

Writing Application On your paper, use each of the following pronouns in a sentence according to the instructions in parentheses.

1. They (as a subject)
2. She (as a predicate pronoun)
3. I (as a predicate pronoun)
4. He (as a subject)
5. They (as a predicate pronoun)

Answers
Reading for Success

1. Students may say that their purpose for reading was to find out about the meaning of the title, or to learn why the author had an interest in this topic.
2. (a) He wants to convey his sense of wonder at and respect for the marvels of nature, and encourage readers to share his views. (b) By sharing his own sense of wonder as a five-year-old boy, he helps his readers look at nature with fresh eyes.
3. The more we understand about animals' abilities and intelligence, the more we can appreciate them.

◆ Build Vocabulary

Using Forms of *habitable*
1. inhabit; 2. habitat; 3. inhabitant

Spelling Strategy
1. plumber; 2. comb; 3. limb

Using the Word Bank
1. d   2. b   3. c   4. a

◆ Literary Focus

1. "I marveled at the delicate hands of the craftsman who had devised such tiny apertures. . . ." "That object had fascinated me like nothing I had come across in my life; I had even grown to love wasps because of it."
2. He leads readers through the steps of his own discovery, allowing us to experience the same awe and wonder he did, and explaining how he developed a respect for nature.
3. His life has embraced experiences of exploration, imagination, and understanding.

◆ Build Grammar Skills

Practice:
1. I;   2. we;   3. It;   4. She;   5. It

Writing Application
Possible responses:
1. They are hard-working creatures.
2. It was she who taught me Latin.
3. It is I playing the trumpet.
4. He was adventurous in the barn.
5. It seems they were all exhausted.

 Writer's Solution

For additional instruction and practice, use the lesson in the *Writer's Solution Language Lab CD-ROM* on pronouns.

629

Idea Bank

Following are suggestions for matching the Idea Bank topics with your students' performance levels and learning modalities:

Customize for
Performance Levels

Less Advanced Students: 1, 4, 6
Average Students: 3, 4, 5, 6, 7
More Advanced Students: 2, 4, 6, 7

Customize for
Learning Modalities

Verbal/Linguistic: 1, 2, 3, 4, 5, 6, 7
Visual/Spatial: 6, 7
Bodily/Kinesthetic: 4, 5
Logical/Mathematical: 7
Musical/Rhythmic: 5
Interpersonal: 4
Intrapersonal: 1, 2, 3, 6

 Writing Mini-Lesson

Refer students to the Writing Handbook in the back of the book for instruction on the writing process and for more information on nonfiction articles.

 Writer's Solution

Writers at Work Videodisc

Have students view the videodisc segment featuring Bruce Brooks, to learn his views on expository writing. Have students discuss his use of his own curiosity to find topics for nonfiction writing.

Play frames 43069 to 51462

Writing Lab CD-ROM

Have students complete the tutorial on Exposition: Making Connections.

1. Have students view the opening segment to learn about writing to make connections.
2. Have students use the Audience Profile to establish tone.
3. Have students draft on computer.
4. Have students use the Transition Word Bin and interactive revision models on sentence structure.

Writer's Solution Sourcebook

Have students use Chapter 5, "Exposition: Making Connections," pp. 136–165, for further support. The chapter includes an essay by Bruce Brooks entitled "Are Animals Smart?" pp. 164–165.

Build Your Portfolio

 Idea Bank

Writing

1. **Fan Letter** Compose a fan letter to the builders of the wasps' nest, telling how much you admire their work. Use the correct form for a friendly letter.

2. **Nature Poem** Think about something in nature that fascinates you. Then, write a poem in which you convey its appearance and essence.

3. **Essay** Write an essay about "Animal Craftsmen," explaining what you learn about the author from reading about his childhood experience.

Speaking and Listening

4. **Discussion [Group Activity]** As a class, discuss examples of animal instinct and animal intelligence that seem to be similar to that of humans. Cite personal observations and experiences as examples. Create a chart, listing your examples.

5. **Dramatic Reading** Prepare and present a dramatic reading of a section of "Animal Craftsmen." Consider turning some of the narrative into dialogue or adding a narrator or other characters. **[Performing Arts Link]**

Projects

6. **Animal Poster** Choose an animal that interests you. Research its habits and behavior, paying special attention to any humanlike actions or exceptional skills. Present your findings on a poster entitled, "The Extraordinary ____?____." **[Science Link]**

7. **Mud Wasps' Nest** Brooks becomes fascinated with a mud wasps' nest in "Animal Craftsmen." Research the type of nest that mud wasps build. Then, draw a diagram of the nest, labeling its parts. One diagram should show the interior of the nest. **[Science Link; Art Link]**

Writing Mini-Lesson

Article for the School Newspaper

In "Animal Craftsmen," Brooks chose the form of a reflective essay to describe the amazing ability of animals to engineer and build their habitats. Using the form of a newspaper article—another type of nonfiction—write an article for your school paper about a scientific discovery or an extraordinary animal.

Writing Focus: Appropriate Tone

In your article, create an **appropriate tone,** or attitude, toward your subject and audience by choosing your words carefully. Notice how Brooks created a tone of wonder in these lines:

Model From the Essay
It appeared to be a kind of gray paper sphere, suspended from the dark planks by a thin stalk, like an apple made of ashes hanging on its stem.

Prewriting Research your subject, and jot down notes. With your audience and subject in mind, decide on the appropriate tone for your article.

Drafting Use your notes to draft your newspaper article. In the first paragraph, introduce your subject and hook your readers' interest. Then, develop your main points in the body of the article. Conclude by restating your main points and summing up your ideas.

Revising Reread your article, revising your word choice, where necessary, to create a consistent tone. Delete any unnecessary details.

◆ **Grammar Application**
You may want to replace some proper nouns with subjective case pronouns in your article.

☑ **ASSESSMENT OPTIONS**

Formal Assessment, Selection Test, pp. 184–186, and Assessment Resources Software. The selection test is designed so that it can be customized easily to the performance levels of your students.

Alternative Assessment, p. 42, includes options for less advanced students, more advanced students, interpersonal learners, visual/spatial learners, logical/mathematical learners, verbal/linguistic learners, and bodily/kinesthetic learners.

PORTFOLIO ASSESSMENT
Use the following rubrics in the **Alternative Assessment** booklet to assess student writing:
Fan Letter: Expression, p. 90
Nature Poem: Poetry, p. 104
Essay: Literary Analysis/Interpretation, p. 108
Writing Mini-Lesson: Research Report/Paper, p. 102

PART 1

Personal Accounts and Biographies

Portrait of Joseph Roulin, 1889, Vincent Van Gogh, Museum of Modern Art, New York, NY

Personal Accounts and Biographies ◆ 631

One-Minute
Planning Guide

The selections in this section are all examples of personal essays and biographies and autobiographies. The first selection is a reflective essay of the writer's observations about animals. An excerpt from her autobiography *One Writer's Beginnings* details Eudora Welty's early childhood observations about the moon. "Baseball" relates Lionel García's adaptation of the game to the circumstances of his neighborhood. *The United States* vs. *Susan B. Anthony* is a biographical sketch of the famous suffragist. "Hokusai: The Old Man Mad About Drawing" is a brief biography of the Japanese painter. "Not to Go With the Other," is a true story of one man's escape from a Nazi prison camp during World War II.

Customize for
Varying Student Needs

When assigning the selections in this section to your students, keep in mind the following factors:

from *One Writer's Beginnings*
- Excerpt from Eudora Welty's biography
- Students may need help with the theme

"Baseball"
- Autobiographical account of Lionel García's youth
- Includes a Beyond Literature Sports Connection

The United States vs. *Susan B. Anthony*
- Biographical essay by Margaret Truman
- Provides an opportunity for connecting literature to social studies

"Hokusai: The Old Man Mad About Drawing"
- Short biography of Japanese painter
- May be of special interest to students with interest in the arts

"Not to Go With the Others"
- True account of Frantizek Zaremski's escape from a Nazi prison camp
- Students may need help with geographical and war-related terms
- Includes a Beyond Literature Social Studies Connection

 Humanities: Art

Portrait of Joseph Roulin, 1889, Vincent van Gogh

Vincent van Gogh (1853–1890) was a Dutch painter famous for his expressionist works. His late works are characterized by heavy swirling brush strokes and vibrant color. Van Gogh was encouraged to paint by his brother Theo, who in later life, supported Vincent when he lived in Southern France. Vincent van Gogh was a hard worker but he had an unstable temperament.

Portrait of Joseph Roulin was one of six portraits done by Van Gogh of his neighbor and friend in Southern France. Van Gogh did portraits of the entire Roulin family. Joseph Roulin was a postman in southern France in the late 1800's.

1. How can you tell from the painting that this man is a postman? *Students should note the man's uniform and French word Postes on his hat.*
2. What about the painting makes Roulin look intriguing? *Students may say his long, full beard makes him look wise and his deep-set eyes make him look as if he has seen a lot of things. Perhaps, being a postman, he knows a lot about the families in the village where he lives.*

Guide for Reading

OBJECTIVES

1. To read, comprehend, and interpret an excerpt from an autobiography and an autobiographical essay
2. To relate autobiographies to personal experience
3. To understand the author's purpose
4. To appreciate autobiography
5. To build vocabulary in context and learn the Word Root: -vis-
6. To develop skill in using objective case pronouns
7. To write a clear rule book
8. To respond to autobiography through writing, speaking and listening, and projects

SKILLS INSTRUCTION

Vocabulary:
Word Root: -vis-

Spelling:
Rules for Using ie or ei

Grammar:
Objective Case Pronouns

Reading Strategy:
Understand the Author's Purpose

Literary Focus:
Autobiography

Writing:
Achieving Clarity

Speaking and Listening:
Sports Radio (Teacher Edition)

Critical Viewing:
Infer; Relate; Generalize; Support

PORTFOLIO OPPORTUNITIES

Writing: Glossary; Autobiography; Report
Writing Mini-Lesson: Rule Book
Speaking and Listening: Sports Radio; Monologue
Projects: Plan for a Baseball Field; Moon Chart

More About the Authors

Eudora Welty is a short-story writer and novelist. Her work focuses on the way of life and characteristics of people living in a small Mississippi town, much like the one in the Delta country in which she lived—she demonstrates her sharp ear for the speech patterns of that region. During the Depression, Welty worked as a photographer on the Works Progress Administration's guide to Mississippi. This experience led to a lifelong interest in photography.

Lionel G. García grew up in the years following World War II. The small town of his childhood, his family, and his neighbors, all influence his writing.

Meet the Authors:

Eudora Welty (1909–)

Eudora Welty was born and raised in Jackson, Mississippi, and this environment formed the backdrop for most of her writing. Her childhood was a happy one. Her parents filled their home with books and encouraged their children to learn.

Writing Inspiration
Following college in New York, Welty traveled around Mississippi, reporting, interviewing, and taking photographs. Her desire to become a writer grew out of this experience. In 1973, she was awarded a Pulitzer Prize for her novel *The Optimist's Daughter*.

Lionel G. García (1935–)

Lionel García chronicles the world of people of Mexican ancestry living in the United States. García was born in San Diego, Texas. As a child, he lived with his grandfather, who was a goat herder. As an adult, he became a veterinarian.

Pets and Writing
García trained himself to write at night after his day's work as a veterinarian was done. His novels and short stories tell of the joys and sorrows of people struggling to survive in a difficult world. "A writer's job is to present people as they are," he says, "usually to the surprise of the reader."

632 ◆ *Nonfiction*

◆ LITERATURE AND YOUR LIFE

CONNECT YOUR EXPERIENCE

In many ways, childhood is the most important time of your life. The things you learn, the beliefs you form, even the games you play influence your life in profound ways. In these selections, you'll learn about childhood events of two writers, Eudora Welty and Lionel García.

THEMATIC FOCUS: Living Each Day

As you read, look for ways in which a "typical day" can generate enlightenment and joy.

◆ Background for Understanding

SPORTS

In "Baseball," you'll read about an informal version of the popular game. Here are a few terms you're likely to hear when you watch a baseball game:

Strike Zone: Area from batter's armpits to knees and over home plate
Ball: A pitch outside the strike zone
Strike: When a batter swings at a pitch and misses or lets a ball go by that's within the strike zone
Count: Number of balls and strikes a batter has
Double Play: A play in which two outs are made

◆ Build Vocabulary

WORD ROOTS: -vis-

Eudora Welty describes the risen moon in the *visible* sky. The word root -vis- means "to see"; *visible* means "able to be seen."

WORD BANK

Which word from the list has to do with a stellar, or starry, arrangement? Check the Build Vocabulary box on page 634 to see if you chose correctly.

visible
reigning
respectively
constellations
eclipses
devices
evaded

Prentice Hall Literature Program Resources

REINFORCE / RETEACH / EXTEND
Selection Support Pages
Build Vocabulary: Word Root -vis-, p. 230
Build Spelling Skills, p. 231
Build Grammar Skills: Objective Case Pronouns, p. 232
Reading Strategy: Understand the Author's Perspective, p. 233
Literary Focus: Autobiography, p.234
Strategies for Diverse Student Needs, pp. 85–86
Beyond Literature Study Skills: Outlining, p. 43

Formal Assessment Selection Test, pp. 187–189, Assessment Resources Software
Alternative Assessment, p. 43
Writing and Language Transparencies Main Idea and Supporting Details Organizer, p. 61; Sensory Language Chart, p. 69; Venn Diagram, p. 77
Resource Pro CD-ROM from "One Writer's Beginnings"; "Baseball"—includes all resource material and customizable lesson plan
🎧 **Listening to Literature Audiocassettes** from "One Writer's Beginnings"; "Baseball"

from One Writer's Beginnings ◆ Baseball

◆ Literary Focus

AUTOBIOGRAPHY

An **autobiography** is the story of a writer's own life, told by the writer. Usually, the writer of an autobiography uses the first-person pronoun "I" to write about his or her experiences. In an autobiography, you meet people and learn of events through the eyes of the author. In both "One Writer's Beginnings" and "Baseball," the authors recount vivid memories of childhood events that helped shape the direction of their lives.

◆ Reading Strategy

UNDERSTAND THE AUTHOR'S PURPOSE

Authors write for a reason. They may aim to teach or to convince you about something, or they may aim to make you laugh, or cry, or think. A good way to **understand the author's purpose** is to ask yourself, "Why is he or she telling me this?" When you know the author's purpose, you can read accordingly— to learn, to be entertained, or to be alert for an attempt to persuade you of something. As you read, fill in a chart like the one below to help you determine the author's purpose.

Text From Story	How It Affects Me	Possible Purpose
"Learning stamps you with its moments."	It makes me stop and think.	To teach

Remind students that small children often have many misconceptions and unusual beliefs. Invite the class to come up with a top-10 list of the funniest misconceptions they had when they were little, for example believing the Earth is flat, or that a man actually lives in the moon, as the rhyme states. Introduce the selection by informing them that, as a child, the author Eudora Welty was no exception. They will see this for themselves when they read the excerpt, in which she admits to having had a misunderstanding about the moon.

◆ Build Grammar Skills

Objective Case Pronouns If you wish to introduce the grammar concept for this selection before students read, refer to the instruction on p. 640.

Customize for
Less Proficient Readers

Have students read this excerpt with a partner or within a small group, and discuss and clarify the points the author makes. Encourage them to use a Main Idea and Supporting Details Organizer, **Writing and Language Transparencies,** p. 61, to help them compare the formal rules of baseball with the neighborhood rules for the game described in the second selection.

Customize for
More Advanced Students

Guide students to look for evidence of originality and creativity in each writer's recollection. Have them note and discuss examples as they read.

Customize for
English Language Learners

To better understand the author's purpose in writing, have students use a Sensory Language Chart, **Writing and Language Transparencies,** p. 69, to record the words and phrases the author uses to create sensory images.

Preparing for Standardized Tests

Grammar The grammar concept for this selection is objective case pronouns. Standardized tests may include questions that test students' understanding of when to use the objective case. Point out to students that the objective case pronouns are *me, you, him, her, it, us,* and *them.* Write each on the board. Then explain that they should use this form for a pronoun when it is a direct object, an indirect object, or the object of a preposition. Use the following sample test question:

Identify the sentence that uses the objective case correctly.

(A) Me and Juan play our own special version of baseball.
(B) I began writing the minute my mother gave me paper and a pen.
(C) Carla and her are on the same team.
(D) Us and the kids from next door made up our own game with our own rules.

Discuss with students that *(B)* is the only sentence that uses the objective case correctly—the objective case pronoun *me* is an indirect object. For more practice, use Build Grammar Skills in **Selection Support,** p. 232.

from One Writer's Beginnings

Eudora Welty

Learning stamps you with its moments. Childhood's learning is made up of moments. It isn't steady. It's a pulse.

In a children's art class, we sat in a ring on kindergarten chairs and drew three daffodils that had just been picked out of the yard; and while I was drawing, my sharpened yellow pencil and the cup of the yellow daffodil gave off whiffs just alike. That the pencil doing the drawing should give off the same smell as the flower it drew seemed part of the art lesson—as shouldn't it be? Children, like animals, use all their senses to discover the world. Then artists come along and discover it the same way, all over again. Here and there, it's the same world. Or now and then we'll hear from an artist who's never lost it.

> ◆ **Literary Focus**
> ❶ How can you tell that this is the writer's own story?

▲ **Critical Viewing** Why has the moon, especially as seen here, been an object of fascination throughout the centuries? **[Infer]**

In my sensory[1] education I include my physical awareness of the *word*. Of a certain word, that is; the connection it has with what it stands for. At around age six, perhaps, I was standing by myself in our front yard waiting for supper, just at that hour in a late summer day when the sun is already below the horizon and the risen full moon in the <u>visible</u> sky stops being chalky and begins to take on light. There

---

1. **sensory** (sen´ sər ē) *adj.*: Appealing to the senses of sight, hearing, smell, taste, and touch.

◆ Build Vocabulary

visible (viz´ ə bəl) *adj.*: Able to be seen

reigning (rān´ iŋ) *adj.*: Ruling

respectively (ri spek´ tiv lē) *adv.*: In the order named

constellations (kän´ stə lā´ shəns) *n.*: Collections of stars

eclipses (i klips´ əz) *n.*: Here, lunar eclipses: when the moon is obscured by the Earth's shadow

---

comes the moment, and I saw it then, when the moon goes from flat to round. For the first time it met my eyes as a globe. The word "moon" came into my mouth as though fed to me out of a silver spoon. Held in my mouth the moon became a word. It had the roundness of a Concord grape Grandpa took off his vine and gave me to suck out of its skin and swallow whole, in Ohio.

This love did not prevent me from living for years in foolish error about the moon. The new moon just appearing in the west was the rising moon to me. The new should be rising. And in early childhood the sun and moon, those opposite reigning powers, I just as easily assumed rose in east and west respectively in their opposite sides of the sky, and like partners in a reel[2] they advanced, sun from the east, moon from the west, crossed over (when I wasn't looking) and went down on the other side. My father couldn't have known I believed that when bending behind me and guiding my

shoulder, he positioned me at our telescope in the front yard and, with careful adjustment of the focus, brought the moon close to me.

The night sky over my childhood Jackson was velvety black. I could see the full constellations in it and call their names; when I could read, I knew their myths. Though I was always waked for eclipses and indeed carried to the window as an infant in arms and shown Halley's Comet[3] in my sleep, and though I'd been taught at our diningroom table about the solar system and knew the earth revolved around the sun, and our moon around us, I never found out the moon didn't come up in the west until I was a writer and Herschel Brickell, the literary critic, told me after I misplaced it in a story. He said valuable words to me about my new profession: "Always be sure you get your moon in the right part of the sky." **⑤**

---

2. **reel** (rēl) *n*.: Lively Scottish dance.

3. **Halley's Comet:** Famous comet that reappears every 75 years.

◆ LITERATURE AND YOUR LIFE

Reader's Response Do you agree with Welty that "rising" is an appropriate image for new things, such as the new moon? Explain.

Thematic Focus In what way was Welty's day "typical"? Why did it become so memorable?

Journal Writing Jot down some childhood beliefs you once held that proved to be false.

☑ Check Your Comprehension

1. According to Welty, how are children and animals alike?
2. What did Welty realize about the moon while waiting in her front yard for supper?
3. What error does Welty believe about the moon's movement?

◆ Critical Thinking

INTERPRET

1. What does Welty mean when she says, "Learning stamps you with its moments"? **[Analyze]**
2. Compare Welty's way of learning about the moon with her father's way of teaching her. **[Compare and Contrast]**
3. What does Welty believe about the role the senses play in the development of a writer? **[Infer]**

EXTEND

4. The last sentence of the story is, "Always be sure you get your moon in the right part of the sky." Identify three professions, besides writing, for which this would be good advice. Explain why. **[Career Link]**

from *One Writer's Beginnings* ◆ 635

Cultural Connection

Pictographs Eudora Welty talks about words and what they represent. Students may never have considered that there are relationships between words and the objects or ideas to which they refer. To help make these relationships more tangible, introduce the idea of pictographs. Ancient civilizations, such as the Chinese, the Sumerian, and the Assyrian, used them—as well as Native American cultures later.

Explain that pictographs are pictures used to represent particular objects. Pictographs are not considered a type of writing because they are

pictures of, not words for, those objects. Pictographs slowly evolved into actual writing. First, they stood for the object itself; next, they were simplified so that they were easier to draw. Finally, the simplified pictures came to represent other words with the same sounds.

Invite students to design their own pictograph "alphabet" in which the pictures represent various objects, actions, or emotions. Challenge them to create messages for classmates to interpret. Post the completed alphabets and messages for all students to examine.

In "Baseball," Lionel G. García describes the unique neighborhood rules that he and his friends developed for their version of the national pastime of baseball, as well as the reactions their game got from those who watched it being played.

◆ LITERATURE AND YOUR LIFE

❶ Ask students to think about why creating unique, personalized versions of games is fun. Invite them to share descriptions of any imaginative games or renderings of games they and their friends play.

◆ Critical Thinking

❷ **Hypothesize** Ask students to explain why the game the narrator and his friends played had only one base. *Students may say that there wasn't enough room for a conventional baseball diamond, there weren't enough players to use a whole field, or they wanted to use only one base to make the game go faster.*

► Critical Viewing ◄

❸ **Relate** *It is fun and exciting to learn a new skill or game, particularly if you are good at it.*

Customize for
Less Proficient Readers

Have students use the Venn Diagram, p. 77 in **Writing and Language Transparencies,** to help them compare the formal rules of baseball with the rules for the game described in this piece.

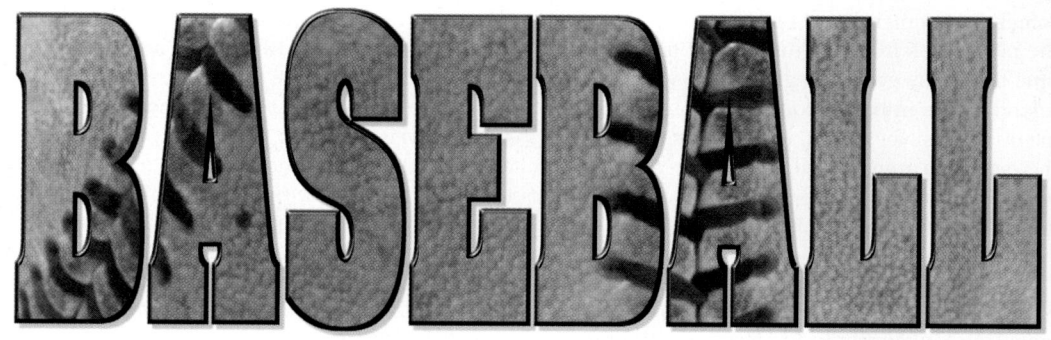

BASEBALL
Lionel G. García

We loved to play baseball. We would take the old mesquite[1] stick and the old ball across the street to the parochial[2] school grounds to play a game. Father Zavala enjoyed watching us. We could hear him laugh mightily from the screened porch at the rear of the rectory[3] where he sat.

❶ The way we played baseball was to rotate positions after every out. First ❷ base, the only base we used, was located where one would normally find second base.

---

1. **mesquite** (mes´ kēt´): Thorny shrub of North America.
2. **parochial** (pə rō´ kē əl) *adj.*: Supported by a church.
3. **rectory** (rek´ tər ē) *n.*: Residence for priests.

This made the batter have to run past the pitcher and a long way to first baseman, increasing the odds of getting thrown out. The pitcher stood in line with the batter, and with first base, and could stand as close or as far ❶ from the batter as he or she wanted. Aside from the pitcher, the batter and the first baseman, we had a catcher. All the rest of us would stand in the outfield. After an out, the catcher would come up to bat. The pitcher

◄ **Critical Viewing** What does it feel ❸ like to learn a new skill or game? [Relate]

🏴 Cross-Curricular Connection: Physical Education

Baseball Most students will be familiar with how baseball is played and with many of its basic rules. The fundamental rules of the game of baseball have not changed significantly for a century. Point out to students that the game professional teams play has changed since the 1870's, by which time it had evolved from rounders to the game they would recognize as baseball. For instance, before the 1870's, a ball caught on a bounce was an out, nobody bunted, and pitches were delivered underhand, and from a distance of only 45 feet—compared with 60 feet, 6 inches today.

Ask students to do research to find out either how and when baseball as we know it came to be played, or about how some of the rules, features, equipment, or uniforms have changed over time. One source of information students can turn to is *The Bill James Historical Baseball Abstract.* Invite students to share some of their most interesting findings with classmates.

▲ Critical Viewing How do young players adapt the game of baseball to their own neighborhood or circumstances? [Generalize] ❼

took the position of catcher, and the first baseman moved up to be the pitcher. Those in the outfield were left to their own <u>devices</u>. I don't remember ever getting to bat.

❶ There was one exception to the rotation scheme. I don't know who thought of this, but whoever caught the ball on the fly would directly to be the batter. This was not a popular ❺ thing to do. You could expect to have the ball thrown at you on the next pitch.

There was no set distance for first base.

◆ Literary Focus
❻ What does this passage reveal about García's background?

First base was wherever Matías or Juan or Cota tossed a stone. They were the law. The distance could be long or short depending on how soon we thought we were going to be called in to eat. The size of the stone marking the base mattered more than the distance from home plate ❽ to first base. If we hadn't been called in to eat

by dusk, first base was hard to find. Sometimes someone would kick the stone farther away and arguments erupted.

When the batter hit the ball in the air and it was caught that was an out. So far so good. But if the ball hit the ground, the fielder ❽ had two choices. One, in keeping with the standard rules of the game, the ball could be thrown to the first baseman and, if caught before the batter arrived at the base, that was an out. But the second, more interesting option allowed the fielder, ball in hand, to ❾ take off running after the batter. When close

◆ **Build Vocabulary**

devices (di vīs´ ez) *n.*: Technique or means for working things out

Baseball ◆ 637

◆Critical Thinking

❹ **Interpret** How could an outfield player move up to batter in the neighborhood game of baseball? *The outfielder was not in the rotation to batter unless he caught a fly ball.*

Comprehension Check ☑

❺ Ask students to explain why the batter was in danger of being hit by a pitched ball. *Because catching fly balls angers the other players, the player who makes the catch and steps up to the plate as the next batter may become the target of angry pitched balls.*

◆**Literary Focus**

❻ **Autobiography** *Students may say that he probably grew up in a neighborhood filled with kids, but short on ball fields and play areas. They may say that he had experience, from an early age, functioning with others in a group and understanding and following accepted rules.*

▶**Critical Viewing**◀

❼ **Generalize** *Students may say that young players change the rules to fit the size and shape of the space they have to play in, the number of available participants, and the sports equipment on hand.*

◆**LITERATURE AND YOUR LIFE**

❽ Ask students to consider the rules of the neighborhood baseball game and determine whether they would enjoy playing in such a chaotic game of baseball. Volunteers may wish to state their opinion of the neighborhood game and give reasons for it.

Comprehension Check ☑

❾ What option was available to the outfielder in the neighborhood baseball game that is not an option in formal baseball? *The more interesting option was to chase the batter all over the neighborhood with the ball in hand and attempt to actually hit the batter with the thrown ball to put him out.*

Beyond the Classroom

Community Connection
Although it may not have been the case in Lionel García's neighborhood, many of today's communities provide opportunities for young people to participate in organized sports—both team sports, such as soccer, basketball, and baseball, and individual sports, such as dance, gymnastics, karate, and swimming.

Have students research, as needed, what organized sports are available in your community. Have them gather data and then record the information in a community sports directory.

Students might create their own directories or work together in groups, or as a class to create one directory. Point out that directories are most useful when they contain accurate information and information is presented clearly. A person who is interested in participating in the sport would need information including location, phone number of a contact person, equipment needed, and cost to participate. Students might contribute their completed directory(ies) to the school library as a resource for interested students and parents.

1 Support *The fact that these children are smiling indicates that they are enjoying themselves. The glove, ball, and base show that it is the game of baseball that pleases them.*

◆**Reading Strategy**

2 Understand the Author's Purpose *Students may suggest that the author includes this information to show that the game is a community affair, the rules are flexible, and that players really enjoyed themselves.*

◆**Build Grammar Skills**

3 Objective Case Pronouns Discuss with students that they should use the objective case of a pronoun when that pronoun is a direct object, an indirect object, or the object of a preposition. Point out that in this sentence, the objective case pronoun *him* is used twice—each time as a direct object. For more practice, use p. 232 in **Selection Support.**

◆**Reading Strategy**

4 Understand the Author's Purpose Ask students to explain why the author includes this paragraph in his description of the game. *Students may say that he does so to contrast the active, creative play of the kids with the idle, shiftless behavior of the men.*

◆**Critical Thinking**

5 Infer Have students explain what Father Zavala loves about the game and what kind of man he appears to be. *Father Zavala loves seeing the boys occupied and enjoying themselves. He appears to be caring, supportive, and sensitive to the needs of children.*

▲ **Critical Viewing** How can you tell that these children are enjoying the game of baseball? [Support] **1**

enough, the fielder would throw the ball at the batter. If the batter was hit before reaching first base, the batter was out. But if the batter evaded being hit with the ball, he or she could either run to first base or run back to home plate. All the while, everyone was chasing the batter, picking up the ball and throwing it at him or her. To complicate matters, on the way to home plate the batter had the choice of running anywhere possible to avoid getting hit. For example, the batter could run to hide behind the hackberry trees[4] at the parochial school grounds, going from tree to tree until he or she could make it safely back to home plate. Many a time we would wind up playing the game past Father Zavala and in front of the rectory half a block away. Or we could be seen running after the batter several blocks

down the street toward town, trying to hit the batter with the ball. One time we wound up all the way across town before we cornered Juan against a fence, held him down, and hit him with the ball. Afterwards, we all fell laughing in a pile on top of each other, exhausted from the run through town.

◆ **Reading Strategy**
What is the author's purpose in providing this information? **2**

The old codgers, the old shiftless men who spent their day talking at the street corners, never caught on to what we were doing. They would halt their idle conversation just long enough to watch us run by them, hollering and throwing the old ball at the batter. **4**

It was the only kind of baseball game Father Zavala had ever seen. What a wonderful game it must have been for him to see us hit the ball, run to a rock, then run for our lives down the street. He loved the game, shouting from the screened porch at us, pushing us on. And then all of a sudden we were gone, running after the batter. What a game! In what enormous stadium would it be played to allow **5**

---

4. hackberry trees: Fruit-bearing trees of the elm family.

◆ **Build Vocabulary**

evaded (ē vād′ əd) v.: Avoided

638 ◆ *Nonfiction*

 Speaking and Listening Mini-Lesson

Sports Radio
This mini-lesson supports the Speaking and Listening activity in the Idea Bank on p. 641.

Introduce Have students talk about the kinds of things radio broadcasters need to know about sports in order to give the play-by-play description of a game that listeners cannot see, but only hear about. If possible, play a few minutes of a radio sports broadcast to help students understand the kinds of information listeners need. Generally, sports broadcasts have

one person who describes precisely what is happening in the game, and one or two others who provide additional commentary.

Develop Have students form 2–3-member broadcast teams. Teams should review the rules of the neighborhood game García and his friends play. They should recreate a brief portion of that game to analyze and report. Have students practice their broadcasts; they may find it helpful to tape-record and review their practice broadcasts to note places they want to change. Suggest that

students include an appropriate commercial announcement if they think it will add to the authenticity of their presentation.

Apply Have teams perform their broadcasts for classmates. Alternatively, you may wish to have students tape–record their broadcasts for presentation.

Assess Evaluate the broadcasts on how engagingly and effectively students describe the action in the game. Or use the Peer Assessment: Dramatic Performance form, p. 116, in **Alternative Assessment.**

5 such freedom over such an expanse of ground.

My uncle Adolfo, who had pitched for the Yankees and the Cardinals in the majors, had given us the ball several years before. Once when he returned for a visit, he saw us playing from across the street and walked over to ask us what we were doing.

6 "Playing baseball," we answered as though we thought he should know better. After all, he was the professional baseball player.

He walked away shaking his head. "What a waste of a good ball," we heard him say, marveling at our ignorance.

Beyond Literature

Sports Connection

Little League Baseball In "Baseball," Lionel García describes the street version of a baseball game he and his friends played when they were children. The game became a fond memory.

Many people have fond memories of baseball games they played in Little League. In 1939, in Williamsport, Pennsylvania, the international baseball organization for Little League began its long career of adapting America's "favorite" pastime for boys aged eight to twelve. In 1974, the league began admitting girls of the same age. The game is played on a field two thirds the size of a professional baseball diamond, and games last six innings instead of the customary nine. Each Little League consists of four to twelve teams that play a fifteen-game season climaxing with the Little League World Series.

Cross-Curricular Activity

Major league baseball is composed of two leagues, the American League and the National League, which each contain a number of teams grouped into various divisions. Research to find out how many divisions there are in each league, how many teams are in each division, and how this grouping is determined. Share your findings with your classmates.

Guide for Responding

◆ LITERATURE AND YOUR LIFE

Reader's Response Do you think Lionel García and his friends would have had more fun playing baseball by the standard rules?

Thematic Focus In what ways does reflecting on his childhood give García insights into his adult life?

Rule Book Using the rules described in the story, create a baseball rule book.

☑ Check Your Comprehension

1. How many bases did García and his friends use when they played ball?
2. How was the distance from home plate to first base determined?
3. Why would García and his friends have needed an enormous stadium to play their version of baseball?
4. (a) What did Father Zavala know about baseball? (b) What did Uncle Adolfo know about baseball?

◆ Critical Thinking

INTERPRET

1. What do you learn about the circumstances of García's childhood from his account of playing baseball? **[Infer]**
2. When García's uncle Adolfo sees the way Lionel and his friends play, he says they are wasting a good ball. Compare his attitude toward baseball with the attitude of the children. **[Compare and Contrast]**
3. García doesn't mention anyone winning or losing. Why do you think this is so? **[Speculate]**
4. García and his friends thought they were playing baseball. If they had found out how real baseball is played, do you think they would have changed their game? Explain your answer. **[Speculate]**

COMPARE LITERARY WORKS

5. What basic idea do both Welty and García convey to readers? Explain. **[Compare and Contrast]**

Baseball ◆ 639

◆ Reading Strategy

6 **Infer** Does García think the game the boys play is a "waste of a good ball"? *Students may say that he sees good in the creative game the boys play.*

Beyond Literature

Challenge students to extend their sports investigation by finding out who Nancy Lotsey is and about her connection to baseball. (She was the first girl to play in organized baseball competition with boys in 1963.) Students may also be interested in researching the Ladies Professional Baseball League, which came into existence during World War II.

Reinforce and Extend

Answers

◆ LITERATURE AND YOUR LIFE

Reader's Response Students may say that the nonstandard game they play seems to provide lots of fun.

Thematic Focus Reflecting on his childhood points out the advantages in being imaginative, flexible, and able to work and play with others.

☑ Check Your Comprehension

1. They used one base.
2. The base was located wherever one of the boys tossed a stone and sometimes moved around during the game.
3. The rules of the game were such that the chase might take players all over the neighborhood.
4. (a) This neighborhood version of baseball was the only one Father Zavala had seen. (b) Uncle Adolfo had been a professional player and was very knowledgeable about formal baseball.

◆ Critical Thinking

1. Students may infer that he grew up in a poor neighborhood where imagination made up for the lack of ball fields and equipment.
2. The children are interested in having fun rather than playing by rules that don't fit their circumstances.
3. Playing and enjoying the game is what matters most.
4. In time, they might change to the real game, because it is a good game that they would enjoy.
5. Both writers emphasize that there is much to be gained by using one's imagination and creativity.

Beyond the Selection

FURTHER READING

Other Works by the Authors
Delta Wedding, Eudora Welty
A Curtain of Green and Other Stories, Eudora Welty
Hardscrub, Lionel G. García
I Can Hear the Cowbells Ring, Lionel G. García

Other Autobiographies
An American Childhood, Annie Dillard
The Story of My Life, Helen Keller

INTERNET
We suggest the following sites on the Internet (all Web sites are subject to change).
For more information on Eudora Welty, go to:
http://members.xoom.com/eudorawelty/welty.html
For more information on Lionel García, go to:
http://www.lionelgarcia-novelist.com
We *strongly recommend* that you preview these sites before you send students to them.

Answers

◆ Reading Strategy

1. She does so to emphasize the power of words to evoke images and ideas.
2. (a) His purpose is to show the value in using one's imagination to make the most of one's surroundings, and to show what can result from people actively working together toward a common goal. (b) They may point out the delight the boys take in playing their creative version of the game and the pleasure Father Zavala derives from watching it.

◆ Build Vocabulary

Using the Word Root: -vis-
1. invisible;   2. vision

Spelling Strategy
1. received;   2. friends, reigning

Using the Word Bank
Possible answers:
1. False; sometimes first base was not visible.
2. True; she loves the expressiveness of words.
3. False; she believed that the moon rose in the west, not the east.
4. True; she knew their myths.
5. True for lunar eclipses; solar eclipses are eclipses of the sun by the moon.
6. False; her parents were involved in her education.
7. True; they tried to avoid being hit by it.

◆ Literary Focus

1. She shares the time her pencil smelled like the flower she was drawing, and the time the moon appeared to her as a globe. Both experiences emphasized the power of words to evoke images and ideas.
2. Outsiders might not understand the dynamics that created the rules and made them work. They might not appreciate how it felt to play that chaotic game.

◆ Build Grammar Skills
Practice
1. you, D.O.;   2. me, I.O.;   3. it, D.O.; him/her, O.P.;   4. us, I.O.; 5. no objective pronoun

---

Guide for Responding (continued)

◆ Reading Strategy

UNDERSTAND THE AUTHOR'S PURPOSE

These writers tell about episodes in their lives. Their **purposes** may be to teach you, charm you, convince you, or impress you. As they share what they value in life, you can relate their experiences to your own.

1. Welty describes how the word *moon* and the actual moon became one and the same in her mind. Why does she tell about this experience?
2. (a) What is García's purpose in writing "Baseball"? (b) How do you know?

◆ Build Vocabulary

USING THE WORD ROOT -vis-

The word root -vis- in *visible* means "to see." On your paper, replace each word or phrase in parentheses with a word containing -vis-.

1. The moon is usually (not able to be seen) during the day.
2. A pitcher needs good (eyesight).

SPELLING STRATEGY

Apply this useful rule when spelling *reigning*: Place *i* before *e* except after *c* or when sounded like *a* as in *neighbor* and *weigh*. Copy the following sentences. Fill in the blanks with *ie* or *ei*.

1. Welty rec_?_ved advice from a literary critic.
2. García and his fr_?_nds were the r_?_gning champions.

USING THE WORD BANK

On your paper, label each statement true or false. Then, explain your responses.

1. The important thing about first base was that it be *visible*.
2. Welty's *reigning* passion was for words.
3. Welty assumed that the sun and the moon rose in the west and the east, *respectively*.
4. Welty's approach to the *constellations* was largely literary.
5. *Eclipses* occur when the moon falls within the Earth's shadow.
6. Educationally, Welty was left to her own *devices*.
7. The boys tried to *evade* the ball.

640 ◆ Nonfiction

◆ Literary Focus

AUTOBIOGRAPHY

An **autobiography** is more than a factual account of the writer's life. It includes thoughts, feelings, and memories of incidents that only the writer could know. By revealing these things, the writer shares his or her life with the reader.

1. Identify two memories that Welty shares with readers. Explain why these memories are important to her.
2. By describing a game of baseball, García shares the world of his childhood. How could this account differ if it were told by an outside narrator instead of by García himself?

◆ Build Grammar Skills

OBJECTIVE CASE PRONOUNS

Personal pronouns change form according to their use in a sentence. When the pronoun is a direct object, an indirect object, or an object of a preposition, use the **objective case.** Objective case pronouns are *me, you, him, her, it, us,* and *them.*

> **Direct Object:** We could hear *him* laugh.
> **Indirect Object:** He gave *me* a baseball bat.
> **Object of a Preposition:** All the rest of *us* would stand in the outfield . . .

Practice Copy the following sentences. Underline the objective case pronouns. Write D.O. (direct object), I.O. (indirect object), and O.P. (object of a preposition) over each underlined pronoun.
1. Learning stamps you with its moments.
2. Grandpa gave me a grape from his vine.
3. Everyone was chasing the batter, picking up the ball and throwing it at him or her.
4. My uncle Adolfo had given us the ball several years before.
5. He hit the baseball over the building.

Writing Application Write three sentences, using objective case pronouns. Use the pronouns in the following situations: direct object, indirect object, and object of a preposition.

Writing Application
Possible responses:
1. She hit it over the fence.
2. He gave me good advice about writing.
3. Some of us knew the rules.

 **Writer's Solution**

For additional instruction and practice, use the lesson in the *Writer's Solution Language Lab CD-ROM* on Objective Case Pronouns.

Build Your Portfolio

Idea Bank

Writing

1. **Glossary** Put together a complete glossary of baseball terms that could be used to help someone read "Baseball."

2. **Autobiography** Using García's "Baseball" as a model, write an autobiographical account of one of your favorite childhood games or activities.

3. **Report** Eudora Welty had the mistaken idea that the sun and the moon rose at opposite sides of the sky and passed each other on their daily journey. Find out the real movements of the sun and moon, and write a report on your findings. **[Science Link]**

Speaking and Listening

4. **Sports Radio** Imagine that you are a radio sportscaster covering a baseball game played by Lionel García and his friends. Present a play-by-play commentary on the game to your class. **[Media Link]**

5. **Monologue** Rewrite Welty's story as a monologue. Rehearse and deliver your monologue for the class. In your performance, try to capture the young girl's sense of wonder and awe. **[Performing Arts Link]**

Projects

6. **Plan for a Baseball Field [Group Activity]** With a partner, create a diagram of a playing field for García's version of baseball. Label the various parts of the field and the positions of the players.

7. **Moon Chart** During her childhood, Eudora Welty made a magical discovery about the moon. Make your own "discovery" of the moon by researching and observing its appearance in the night sky. Then, create a moon chart in which you illustrate the various stages of the moon during its monthly cycle. Post your completed chart in the classroom. **[Science Link]**

Writing Mini-Lesson

Rule Book

Every board or computer game you play comes with a set of rules. Organizations or clubs, such as Scouts and 4-H, have rules, too. Write a short rule book for a real or an imaginary game or club. If you like, you can write a baseball rule book that Lionel García and his friends might have used or a rule book for an astronomy club that Eudora Welty might have joined.

Writing Skills Focus: Clarity

Rules have to be clear. Otherwise, people will argue about them. To achieve **clarity,** you first need to understand the rules yourself, then write them in short declarative sentences and organize them in a logical way.

Model From "Baseball"

After an out, the catcher would come up to bat. The pitcher took the position of the catcher, and the first baseman moved up to be the pitcher.

Prewriting Study the rules for a game you like to play or a club to which you belong. Notice how the rules are organized and presented. Then, make a list of all the rules you want to include in your rule book.

Drafting Decide which rules a newcomer would need to know first. Organize the rules in a logical way, and write them in short declarative sentences. You may want to number the rules or present them in outline form.

Revising Give your rule book to a classmate to read. Ask if he or she is able to understand the rules and if your writing is clear. Revise to answer any questions your classmate may have.

◆ **Grammar Application**
Underline objective case pronouns you've used in your rule book.

---

from *One Writer's Beginnings/Baseball* ◆ 641

Idea Bank

Following are suggestions for matching the Idea Bank topics with your students' performance levels and learning modalities:

Customize for
Performance Levels
Less Advanced Students: 1, 4
Average Students: 2, 4, 6, 7
More Advanced Students: 3, 5, 7

Customize for
Learning Modalities
Verbal/Linguistic: 1, 2, 3, 4, 5, 6, 7
Visual/Spatial: 4, 6, 7
Logical/Mathematical: 1, 3, 6, 7
Musical/Rhythmic: 4, 5
Interpersonal: 1, 4, 6,
Intrapersonal: 5

Writing Mini-Lesson

Refer students to the Writing Handbook in the back of the book for instruction on the writing process and for further information on exposition. Have students use the Main Idea and Supporting Details Organizer in **Writing and Language Transparencies,** p. 61, to organize their examples.

 Writer's Solution

Writing Lab CD-ROM
Have students complete the tutorial on Exposition: Giving Information. Follow these steps:
1. Have students view the video clip from the About Exposition section, in which Gary Matsumoto discusses expository writing.
2. Have students consult the interactive models on purpose to discover how to focus their rule books to meet the needs of their audience.
3. Have students draft on computer.
4. Have students use the Self-Evaluation Checklist for explanation of procedures or instructions.

Writer's Solution Sourcebook
Have students use Chapter 4, "Exposition: Giving Information," pp. 104–135, for additional support. The chapter includes in-depth instruction on organizing details, p. 124.

✓ ASSESSMENT OPTIONS

Formal Assessment, Selection Test, pp. 187–189, and Assessment Resources Software. The selection test is designed so that it can easily be customized to the performance levels of your students.

Alternative Assessment, p. 43, includes options for less advanced students, more advanced students, verbal/linguistic learners, interpersonal learners, bodily/kinesthetic learners, and musical/rhythmic learners.

PORTFOLIO ASSESSMENT
Use the following rubrics in the **Alternative Assessment** booklet to assess student writing:
Glossary: Definition/Classification, p. 95
Autobiography: Narrative Based on Personal Experience, p. 92
Report: Research Report/Paper, p. 102
Writing Mini-Lesson: Definition/Classification, p. 95

CONNECTING LITERATURE TO SOCIAL STUDIES
THE SUFFRAGIST MOVEMENT

The United States *vs.* Susan B. Anthony *by Margaret Truman*

OBJECTIVES

1. To read, comprehend, and interpret an essay that has a social studies focus
2. To relate an essay with a social studies focus to personal experience
3. To connect literature to social studies
4. To respond to social studies guiding questions
5. To respond to the essay through writing, speaking and listening, and projects

SOCIAL STUDIES GUIDING QUESTIONS

Reading an essay about women's suffrage will help students discover answers to these Social Studies Questions:

- What was it like to be part of the suffragist movement?
- Why is knowledge of how our judicial and political systems work essential to those trying to change unfair laws?

Interest Grabber Ask students the following question: Who is the first woman to have had her likeness minted on a United States coin? Discuss students' answers. Introduce the selection by telling students that the honor was given to Susan B. Anthony in 1979 and 1980 when the government produced silver dollars bearing her picture. This essay will explain how and why she earned such a high honor.

Map Study

Historical Maps The connection between geography and history is often a key to understanding people and their response to political issues. The color-coded political map on this page illustrates where women in the United States in 1919 enjoyed equal, partial, or no statewide voting privileges. By studying the map, students can make generalizations about attitudes toward women's suffrage in different regions of the country. For example, they may notice that people in the West appeared to support women's suffrage, whereas people in the South appeared more resistant to it.

The Vote for Women by 1919

- Equal suffrage (date effective)
- Partial suffrage
- No statewide suffrage

In 1920, American women gained the right to vote. Before 1920, some states allowed women to vote in certain types of elections—for example, presidential or primary elections only. This map shows the years in which states with equal rights prior to 1920 granted women the right to vote.

WOMAN SUFFRAGE *Suffrage* means "the right to vote." For more than half its history, the United States did not extend that right to women. In the early 1800's, more educational opportunities for women became available and women began to participate more openly in political reform movements. During the 1830's, women began organizing, speaking, and marching in hopes of winning the right to vote.

The Suffragist Movements By the year 1869, two major women's suffrage movements had formed. The American Woman Suffragist movement, led by Lucy Stone and her husband, Henry Blackwell, worked to win voting rights for women state by state. It was considered more conservative than the National Woman Suffrage Association, which was led by Elizabeth Cady Stanton and Susan B. Anthony. This group's main goal was to amend the United States Constitution to give women the right to vote.

The two movements joined forces in 1890 to form the American Woman Suffrage Association. In the early 1900's, the movement received a boost from dynamic new leaders Carrie Chapman Catt and Maud Wood Park. These women organized rallies and gathered support for their cause among middle-class women. It was not until 1920, however, that the Nineteenth Amendment to the Constitution was ratified, giving all women in the United States the right to vote.

Susan B. Anthony Of all the people who spoke and demonstrated for women's rights, one of the most famous is Susan B. Anthony (1820–1906). She gave speeches, organized marches, and edited a magazine called *The Revolution*. This essay by Margaret Truman shows how this memorable, dynamic woman helped change the course of history.

642 ◆ *Nonfiction*

 Prentice Hall Literature Program Resources

REINFORCE / RETEACH / EXTEND
Selection Support Pages
Build Vocabulary, p. 235
Connecting Literature to Social Studies, p. 236
Formal Assessment Selection Test, pp. 190–191
Assessment Resources Software
Readings From Social Studies
Writing and Language Transparencies Series of Events Chain, p. 57

Resource Pro CD-ROM
from *United States* vs. *Susan B. Anthony*—includes all resource material and customizable lesson plan
Listening to Literature Audiocassettes
from *United States* vs. *Susan B. Anthony*
Connection to Prentice Hall The American Nation *Independence Through 1914*—Ch. 21, "Women in the Progressive Era"

from The United States vs. Susan B. Anthony

Margaret Truman

Susan B. Anthony was a stern and single-minded woman. Like most crusaders for causes—especially unpopular causes—she had little time for fun and games. But I have a sneaky feeling that behind her severe manner and <u>unremitting</u> devotion to duty, she may actually have had a sense of humor. Let me tell you about my favorite episode in Susan B. Anthony's career, and perhaps you'll agree.

❶

It began on Friday morning, November 1, 1872. Susan was reading the morning paper at her home in Rochester. There, at the top of the editorial page of the *Democrat and Chronicle*, was an exhortation[1] to the city's residents:

Now register! Today and tomorrow are the only remaining opportunities. If you were not permitted to vote, you would fight for the right, undergo all privations for it, face death for it. You have it now at the cost of five minutes' time to be spent in seeking your place of registration and having your name entered. And yet, on election day, less than a week hence, hundreds of you are likely to lose your votes because you have not thought it worth while to give the five minutes. Today and tomorrow are your only opportunities. Register now!

Susan B. Anthony read the editorial again. Just as she thought, it said nothing about being addressed to men only. With a gleam in her eye, she put down the paper and summoned her sister Guelma, with whom she lived. The two women donned their hats and cloaks and went off to call on two other Anthony sisters who lived nearby. Together, the four women headed for the barber shop on West Street, where voters from the Eighth Ward were being registered.

For some time, Susan B. Anthony had been looking for an opportunity to test the Fourteenth Amendment to the Constitution

> **Connecting Literature to Social Studies**
> Why might this editorial have been offensive to many women in 1872?
>
> **❷**

---

1. **exhortation** (eg´ zôr tā´ shən) *n*.: Plea, sermon, or warning.

◆ **Build Vocabulary**

unremitting (un ri mit´ iŋ) *adj*.: Not stopping; persistent

from *The United States* vs. *Susan B. Anthony* ◆ 643

◆ Critical Thinking

① Infer Ask students to explain why this section of the amendment did not specifically spell out that only male citizens had the right to vote.

Students may say that the idea of women voting was inconceivable to the men who wrote the amendment, therefore, they saw no reason to include the restriction.

Ⓒ CONNECTING LITERATURE TO SOCIAL STUDIES

② *Students may say that to many men of that time, the idea of women voting was a "crackpot" idea and that women who actively campaigned for the vote were as crazy as the idea itself.*

Links Across Time

③ Explain to students that wards were units into which cities were often divided for the election of members of the city council.

Customize for
English Language Learners

This excerpt contains legal terminology such as *prosecuted* and *jurisdiction*, and terms related to voting and to government—*voter registration* and *ward*. Have students work with partners to create a glossary explaining these legal and political terms. Suggest that they extend their glossaries to include political terms they may encounter in other Extending Literature to Social Studies selections.

Customize for
Less Proficient Readers

Suggest that students make a three-column chart to keep track of the cast of characters and their point of view regarding women's suffrage and related issues.

Character	Character's Job	Character's Point of View

644

CONNECTING LITERATURE TO SOCIAL STUDIES

as a weapon to win the vote for women. Adopted in 1870, the amendment had been designed to protect the civil rights—especially the voting rights—of recently freed slaves. It stated that:

> All persons born or naturalized in the United States, and subject to the jurisdiction thereof, are citizens of the United States and of the State wherein they reside. No State shall make or enforce any law which shall <u>abridge</u> the privileges or immunities[2] of citizens of the United States, nor shall any State deprive any person of life, liberty, or property without due process of law, nor deny to any person within its jurisdiction the equal protection of the laws.

① The amendment did not say that "persons" meant only males, nor did it spell out "the privileges or immunities of citizens." Susan B. Anthony felt perfectly justified in concluding that the right to vote was among the privileges of citizenship and that it extended to women as well as men. I'm sure she must have also seen the humor of outwitting the supposedly superior males who wrote the Amendment.

It was bad enough for a bunch of women to barge into one sacred male precinct—the barber shop—but to insist on being admitted to another holy of holies—the voting booth—was absolutely outrageous. Moustaches twitched, throats were cleared, a whispered conference was held in the corner.

Susan had brought along a copy of the Fourteenth Amendment. She read it aloud, carefully pointing out to the men in charge of registration that the document failed to state that the privilege of voting extended only to males.

Only one man in the barber shop had the nerve to refuse the Anthony sisters the right to register. The rest buckled under Susan's determined <u>oratory</u> and allowed them to sign the huge, leather-bound voter registration book. If the men in the barber shop

---
2. **immunities** (im myoon′ i tēs) *n.*: Freedom from public services or duties.

644 ◆ *Nonfiction*

---

thought they were getting rid of a little band of crackpots the easy way, they were wrong. Susan urged all her followers in Rochester to register. The next day, a dozen women invaded the Eighth Ward barber shop, and another thirty-five appeared at registration sites elsewhere in the city. The *Democrat and Chronicle*, which had <u>inadvertently</u> prompted the registrations, expressed no editorial opinion on the phenomenon, but its rival, the *Union and Advertiser*, denounced the women. If they were allowed to vote, the paper declared, the poll inspectors "should be prosecuted to the full extent of the law."

The following Tuesday, November 5, was Election Day. Most of the poll inspectors in Rochester had read the editorial in the *Union and Advertiser* and were too <u>intimidated</u> to allow any of the women who had registered to vote. Only in the Eighth Ward did the males weaken. Maybe the inspectors were *Democrat and Chronicle* readers, or perhaps they were more afraid of Susan B. Anthony than they were of the law. Whatever the reason, when Susan and her sisters showed up at the polls shortly after 7 A.M., there was only a minimum of fuss. A couple of inspectors were hesitant about letting the women vote, but when Susan assured them that she would pay all their legal expenses if they were prosecuted, the men relented, and one by one, the women took their ballots and stepped into the voting booth. There were no insults or sneers, no rude remarks. They marked their ballots, dropped them into the ballot box, and returned to their homes.

Susan B. Anthony's feat quickly became the talk of the country. She was applauded

◆ Build Vocabulary

abridge (ə brij′) *v.*: Reduce in scope; shorten; lessen

oratory (ôr′ ə tôr′ ē) *n.*: Skill or eloquence in public speaking

inadvertently (in′ ad vʉrt′ ənt lē) *adv.*: Unintentionally

intimidated (in tim′ ə dāt′ əd) *v.*: Made afraid through threats and violence

Connecting Literature to Social Studies
Why would the men have thought the Anthony sisters were "crackpots"?

②

③

Block Scheduling Strategies

Consider these suggestions to take advantage of extended class time:

• Use the Interest Grabber to introduce and draw students into the story. Then look at the political map with them. Discuss what it illustrates about women's voting rights in 1919.

• Have students read the selection in small groups. Encourage groups to discuss Anthony's tactics and the judicial and political issues that arise. Guide them to refer to their social studies text, Prentice Hall *The American Nation Independence Through 1914,* or a United States

government text, to help them understand the legal and political terms used in the selection.

• Have students work on the timeline project in the Idea Bank on p. 651. Students might use computer software to generate their timelines. Provide time for groups to display, present, and explain their timelines.

• Use Prentice Hall *The American Nation: Independence Through 1914,* Chapter 21, Section 4, "Women in the Progressive Era," to team teach or to further connect literature to social studies.

in some circles, vilified[3] in others. But the day of reckoning was not long in arriving. On November 28, Deputy U.S. Marshall E. J. Keeney appeared at her door with a warrant for her arrest. She had violated Section 19 of the Enforcement Act of the Fourteenth Amendment, which held that anyone who voted illegally was to be arrested and tried on criminal charges.

Susan B. Anthony was a great believer in planning ahead. The day after she registered, she decided to get a legal opinion on whether or not she should attempt to vote. A number of lawyers turned her away, but she finally found one who agreed to ❹ consider the case. He was Henry R. Selden, a former judge of the Court of Appeals, now a partner in one of Rochester's most prestigious law firms.

On the Monday before Election Day, Henry Selden informed his new client that he agreed with her interpretation of the Fourteenth Amendment and that in his opinion, she had every right to cast her ballot. The U.S. Commissioner of Elections in Rochester, William C. Storrs, did not concur.

E. J. Keeney, the marshal dispatched to arrest Susan B. Anthony, was not at all happy with his assignment. He nervously twirled his tall felt hat while waiting for her to come to the front door. When she finally appeared, he blushed and stammered, shifted uncomfortably from one foot to the other, and finally blurted out, "The Commissioner wishes to arrest you."

Susan couldn't help being amused at Keeney's embarrassment. "Is this your usual method of serving a warrant?" she asked

---

3. **vilified** (vilʹ ə fīd) v.: Spoken of in abusive or slanderous language; defamed.

calmly. With that, the marshal recovered his official dignity, presented her with the warrant, and told her that he had come to escort her to the office of the Commissioner of Elections.

When Susan asked if she could change into a more suitable dress, the marshal saw his opportunity to escape. "Of course," he said, turning to leave. "Just come down to the Commissioner's office whenever you're ready."

"I'll do no such thing," Susan informed him curtly. "You were sent here to arrest me and take me to court. It's your duty to do so."

Keeney had no choice but to wait while his prisoner when upstairs and put on a more appropriate outfit. When she returned, she thrust out her wrists and said, "Don't you want to handcuff me, too?"

"I assure you, madam," Marshal Keeney muttered, "it isn't at all necessary."

With the U.S. Marshal at her side, Susan was brought before the Federal Commissioner of Elections, William C. Storrs. Her arrest was recorded, and she was ordered to appear the next day for a hearing. It was conducted by U.S. District Attorney Richard Crowley and his assistant, John E. Pound.

Susan answered District Attorney Crowley's questions politely. She said that she thought the Fourteenth Amendment gave her the right to vote. She admitted that she had consulted an attorney on the question but said that she would have voted even if he had not advised her to do so. When Crowley asked if she had voted deliberately to test the law, she said, "Yes, sir. I have

When she returned, she thrust out her wrists and said, "Don't you want to handcuff me, too?"

❺ **Connecting Literature to Social Studies** Why would Anthony insist on being taken in, instead of going in alone?

❻

from *The United States vs. Susan B. Anthony* ◆ 645

CONNECTING LITERATURE TO SOCIAL STUDIES

❹ **Deduce** Ask students to explain why many lawyers refused to help Anthony. Ask them to explain what it says about Selden that he did accept her as a client. *Students may say that many attorneys didn't want to risk unpopularity, or worse, by taking her as a client. Selden was a risk taker, he believed in the merits of her case, or both. Students may suggest that many women of that time, as well as men, did not think that women should have the right to vote.*

CONNECTING LITERATURE TO SOCIAL STUDIES

❺ *Students may say that she wanted to be sure to act within the law and to draw attention to herself at the same time. They may say that an arrest would be an effective way to bring publicity to her cause.*

Comprehension Check ☑

❻ Why does Susan B. Anthony request that she be handcuffed? *The picture of a well-dressed, 52-year-old woman taken away in handcuffs would evoke sympathy for her plight and negative publicity for her opponents.*

Customize for
More Advanced Students
Help students understand that by forcing the marshal to handcuff her and arrest her, Susan B. Anthony was employing tactics of civil disobedience that were later used with similar success by civil rights activists and antiwar protesters. Guide students to think about and evaluate Anthony's tactics in terms of success at forcing change without violence.

Cross-Curricular Connection: Social Studies

Voting In Susan B. Anthony's time, only men had the right to vote. Invite students to do research to find out more about who can and does vote today, by researching and answering these and other questions they formulate:

• What are the requirements or qualifications for voting in the United States today?

• How does someone register to vote?

• When, where, how, and for what do people vote?

• What is a "write-in vote," and who gets to vote this way?

• What percent of eligible voters cast their ballots in the last presidential election? In the last off-year election? How have those figures changed over time? Make a line graph to show the data.

Have students discuss these questions. Invite them to display and compare data they have found and display the graphs they have made.

645

CONNECTING LITERATURE TO SOCIAL STUDIES

❶ Deduce Ask students to explain why the District Attorney backed down. *Students may say that he chose not to keep Anthony in custody because doing so would be an embarrassment, as she posed no threat. They may say that he was aware that because many people would feel that she had committed no crime, putting her in jail might bring negative public reaction.*

Links Across Time

❷ Discuss with students that a "test case" is one in which a single, representative case is brought before the courts so that the judges can rule on its constitutionality. In this instance, what is being tested for constitutionality is whether, by voting, women are breaking the law.

CONNECTING LITERATURE TO SOCIAL STUDIES

❸ Analyze Susan B. Anthony refuses to post bond. Ask students to speculate what her reasons were. What do her actions say about her? *Students may say that time spent in jail would draw attention to her case and bring about sympathy for her and her cause. They might say that she was determined to get the right to vote for women and that she would use every means available, including self-sacrifice, to accomplish her goal.*

▶Critical Viewing◀

❹ Assess *Some students might say that although Crowley makes every effort to uphold the law, he is sensitive to Anthony's point of view. Others might say that he has one eye on the law and the other on public opinion, which would be against jailing a respected woman who has a large following.*

been determined for three years to vote the first time I happened to be at home for the required thirty days before an election."

The District Attorney's next step was to convene a grand jury to draw up a bill of indictment.[4] He and his assistant fell to wrangling over a suitable trial date. Susan interrupted them. "I have lecture dates that will take me to central Ohio," she said. "I won't be available until December 10."

"But you're supposed to be in custody until the hearing," Crowley informed her.

"Is that so?" said Susan coolly. "I didn't know that."

❶ The District Attorney backed down without an argument and scheduled the grand jury session for December 23.

❷ Sixteen women had voted in Rochester. All sixteen were arrested and taken before the grand jury, but Susan alone was brought to trial. The District Attorney had decided to single her out as a test case. The three poll inspectors who had allowed the women to vote were also arrested. The grand jury indicted them too, set bail at five hundred dollars each, and ordered their trial set for the summer term of the U.S. District Court.

Susan Anthony's case now involved nineteen other men and women. All of them—including Susan—were liable to go to prison if they were found guilty and the judge

was in a sentencing mood. Prison in the 1870s was a very unpleasant place. There were no minimum security setups where a benevolent government allowed corrupt politicians, crooked labor leaders, and political agitators to rest and rehabilitate, as we do today. Prison meant a cold cell, wretched food, the company of thieves and murderers.

❸ For a while it looked as if Susan might be behind bars even before her trial. She refused to post a bond for her five-hundred dollar bail. Henry Selden paid the money for her. "I could not see a lady I respected put in jail." he said.

It must be agonizing to sweat out the weeks before a trial. There is time to look ahead and brood about the possibility of an unfavorable verdict and time to look back, perhaps with regret, at the decision that placed you in the hands of the law. But Susan B. Anthony had no regrets. Nor did she appear to have any anxieties about her trial. She had already proven her fortitude by devoting twenty years of her life to fighting for the right to vote. If she won her case, the struggle would be over. But even if she lost, Susan was not ready to give up the fight. . . .

❺ The trial of *The United States* vs. *Susan B. Anthony* opened on the afternoon of June 17, 1873, with the tolling of the Canandaigua Courthouse bell. The presiding justice was

---

4. **bill of indictment:** A formal written accusation.

646 ◆ *Nonfiction*

▲ Critical Viewing District Attorney Richard Crowley conducted the inquiry to indict Susan B. Anthony. He also "backed down" about keeping her in custody. What kind of person do you think he was? **[Assess]** **❹**

Cross-Curricular Connection: Music

Protest Traditionally, Americans have found many laws and issues to debate and to protest. One way Americans have chosen to express dissent is through song. Protest songs have accompanied workers complaining about long hours and dangerous conditions, civil rights demonstrators protesting unfairness and racism, and antiwar protesters urging the government to stop sending young men overseas to fight. Few Americans who watched television news during Martin

Luther King's speeches would not recognize "We Shall Overcome" as a protest theme song. Play for students an assortment of protest songs that represent a range of political or social issues. Discuss common elements in these songs and the effects they can have in rallying people to a cause.

Invite interested students to write their own protest songs about an issue that interests them. Have volunteers play and sing their songs for classmates.

Ward Hunt, a prim, pale man, who owed his judgeship to the good offices of Senator Roscoe Conkling, the Republican boss of New York State. Conkling was a fierce foe of woman suffrage, and Hunt, who had no wish to offend his powerful patron, had written his decision before the trial started.

District Attorney Crowley opened the arguments for the prosecution. They didn't make much sense at the time, and in retrospect, they sound nothing short of ridiculous. The district attorney mentioned that Susan B. Anthony was a woman and therefore she had no right to vote. His principal witness was an inspector of elections for the Eighth Ward, who swore that on November 5 he had seen Miss Anthony put her ballot in the ballot box. To back up his testimony, the inspector produced the voter registration book with Susan B. Anthony's signature in it.

Henry Selden's reply for the defense was equally simple. He contended that Susan Anthony had registered and voted in good faith, believing that it was her constitutional right to do so. When he attempted to call his client to the stand, however, District Attorney Crowley announced that she was not competent to testify in her own behalf. Judge Hunt agreed, and the only thing Henry Selden could do was read excerpts from the testimony Susan had given at her previous hearings when presumably she was no less incompetent than she was right now.

Henry Selden tried to make up for this gross injustice by making his closing argument a dramatic, three-hour speech on behalf of woman suffrage. District Attorney Crowley replied with a two-hour rehash of the original charge.

By the afternoon of June 18, the case of *The United States* vs. *Susan B. Anthony* was ready to go to the jury. It was impossible to predict what their verdict might be, so Judge Hunt, determined to make it the verdict he and Roscoe Conkling wanted, took matters into his own hands. "Gentlemen of the jury," he said, "I direct that you find the defendant guilty."

Henry Selden leaped to his feet. "I object, your honor," he thundered. "The court has no power to direct the jury in a criminal case."

Judge Hunt ignored him. "Take the verdict, Mr. Clerk," he said.

The clerk of the court must have been another Conkling man. "Gentlemen of the jury," he intoned as if the whole proceeding was perfectly normal, "hearken to the verdict as the court hath recorded it. You say you find the defendant guilty of the offense charged. So say you all."

The twelve jurymen looked stunned. They had not even met to discuss the case, much

▲ **Critical Viewing** What character traits of Susan B. Anthony are evident in this photograph? [Analyze]

◆ **Build Vocabulary**
retrospect (re´ trə spekt´) *n*.: Hindsight

from *The United States* vs. *Susan B. Anthony* ◆ 647

Comprehension Check ☑
❺ Ask students to explain what the judge did and why. *Judge Hunt was beholden, for political reasons, to Senator Conkling, who was against suffrage for women. Therefore, Hunt made his prejudiced decision—against Anthony—before hearing the case and evidence before him.*

CONNECTING LITERATURE TO SOCIAL STUDIES
❻ **Interpret** Ask students to explain how the writer of this essay demonstrates her bias. *By describing Selden's closing as "dramatic" and Crowley's as a "rehash," she shows her preference for the position of the defense, and of our modern view of women's inalienable rights.*

CONNECTING LITERATURE TO SOCIAL STUDIES
❼ **Courtroom Procedures** Discuss with students that the judge generally charges the jury to go and deliberate. Instead, he directs the jury to the verdict Conkling wants. The clerk of the court concurs. Point out that it is no surprise that the attorneys and the members of the jury—all of whom were men—were stunned. Susan B. Anthony was denied her right to due process under the law.

▶Critical Viewing◀
❽ **Analyze** *The photograph shows that Anthony appears to be formal, determined, proper, intelligent, and serious.*

Speaking and Listening Mini-Lesson

Legal Arguments
This mini-lesson supports the Speaking and Listening activity in the Idea Bank on p. 651.

Introduce Have students review what was discussed before the Federal Commissioner of Elections. Talk about the responsibilities a district attorney has and the role a defense attorney plays. Discuss the importance of using precise language and acting respectfully and properly, as if the classroom were an actual courtroom.

Develop Have groups assign courtroom roles. Provide time for students to research their parts by rereading portions of the essay. Have them rehearse their legal arguments and practice the role play. One group member can act as facilitator. He or she can introduce the participants and summarize the outcome of the hearing.

Apply Have students present their arguments. You may wish to tape or videotape the performances.

Assess Evaluate students on how clearly and accurately they state the arguments for both sides and demonstrate courtroom demeanor. Or, use the Peer Assessment: Dramatic Performance form, p. 116, in **Alternative Assessment.**

CONNECTING LITERATURE TO SOCIAL STUDIES

❶ Evaluate Have students react to the judge's decision and the reasons for it. *Students may say that politics has no place in the legal system and that they feel disappointed and angry with the judge's actions. Others may note that politics and justice have gone hand in hand in our society for a long time.*

Links Across Time

❷ Discuss with students how Susan B. Anthony carefully observes all of the court's rules and procedures. She speaks her mind, but with respect for the court's authority. Students can compare her strategy with the efforts of people today who take the "test case" approach to effecting change in a law or its interpretation.

►Critical Viewing◄

❸ Speculate *Meetings like this one could be spirited and result in heated arguments. Others might point to the panel on stage and speculate that the meetings were informative, well organized, and characterized by lively intellectual debate.*

CONNECTING LITERATURE TO SOCIAL STUDIES

❹ Defend Ask students to suggest a reasonable, if opposing, response to Susan B. Anthony's claims of unfairness. *Some students may say that there is no reasonable answer to her claims. Some may say that her act of voting had been illegal according to law, that she had her trial, and that she lost. Others might suggest that she should be thankful for Hunt's politically motivated judgment, for it gives her the opportunity to take her case to a higher court.*

Customize for
Verbal/Linguistic Learners

To help students grasp the elegance of Susan B. Anthony's speech and the power of her logical ideas, invite a volunteer to read her courtroom words aloud.

A meeting of the National Woman's Suffrage Association in the 1870's, with Susan B. Anthony and Elizabeth Cady Stanton on the platform

◄ **Critical Viewing** What might it have been like to attend a woman's suffrage meeting, such as this one? [Speculate] **❸**

❶ less agree on a verdict. When Henry Selden asked if the clerk could at least poll the jury, Judge Hunt rapped his gavel sharply and declared, "That cannot be allowed. Gentlemen of the jury, you are discharged."

An enraged Henry Selden lost no time in introducing a motion for a new trial on the grounds that his client had been denied the right to a jury verdict. Judge Hunt denied the motion. He turned to Susan B. Anthony and said, "The prisoner will stand up. Has the prisoner anything to say why sentence shall not be pronounced?"

Thus far in the trial, Susan B. Anthony had remained silent. Now, she rose to her feet and said slowly, "Yes, Your Honor, I have many things to say."

❷ Without further preliminaries, she launched into a scathing denunciation of Judge Hunt's conduct of her trial. ". . . In your ordered verdict of guilty," she said, "you have trampled underfoot every vital principle of our government. My natural rights, my civil rights, my political rights, are all alike ignored. Robbed of the fundamental privilege of citizenship, I am degraded from the status of a citizen to that of a subject; and not only myself individually, but all of my sex, are, by your honor's verdict, doomed to political

subjection under this so-called Republican government."

Judge Hunt reached for his gavel, but Susan B. Anthony refused to be silent.

"May it please your honor," she continued. **❷** "Your denial of my citizen's right to vote is the denial of my right to a trial by a jury of my peers as an offender against law, therefore, the denial of my sacred rights to life, liberty, property, and—"

"The court cannot allow the prisoner to go on," Judge Hunt cried out.

Susan ignored him and continued her impassioned tirade against the court. Hunt frantically rapped his gavel and ordered her to sit down and be quiet. But Susan, who must have been taking delight in his <u>consternation</u>, kept on talking. She deplored the fact that she had been denied the right to a fair trial. Even if she had been given such a **❹** trial, she insisted, it would not have been by her peers. Jury, judges, and lawyers were not her equals, but her superiors, because they

◆ **Build Vocabulary**
consternation (kän′ stər nā′ shən) *n.*: Great shock that makes one feel helpless or bewildered
futile (fyoot′ əl) *adj.*: Ineffective

648 ◆ *Nonfiction*

 Cultural Connection

Quakers Susan B. Anthony (1820–1906) was born in Adams, Massachusetts, to a Quaker family. It is no surprise that she became a leader in the fight to achieve voting rights for women, because her family believed strongly in the rights and equality of women and men. In addition, her family worked for the movement to abolish slavery and in the temperance movement, which attempted to abolish alcoholic beverages.

The Religious Society of Friends, more commonly known as Quakers or Friends, was established in England by George Fox. The term *Quaker* was originally intended as an insult. Quakers have long been known for humanitarian activities that stress peace and equality for all persons regardless of race, religion, or sex.

William Penn, a Quaker, established the colony of Pennsylvania in 1681 to insure religious freedom and safety for persecuted English Quakers.

Interested students may wish to further research the history of the Quakers or actions and writings of other well-known Quakers.

could vote and she could not. Susan was adamant about the fact that she had been denied the justice guaranteed in the Constitution to every citizen of the United States.

Judge Hunt was sufficiently cowed by now to try to defend himself. "The prisoner has been tried according to the established forms of law," he sputtered.

"Yes, Your Honor," retorted Susan, overlooking his blatant lie, "but by forms of law all made by men, interpreted by men, administered by men, in favor of men, and against women; and hence your honor's ordered verdict of guilty, against a United States citizen for the exercise of that citizen's right to vote, simply because that citizen was a woman and not a man. But yesterday, the same manmade forms of law declared it a crime punishable with a one-thousand-dollar fine and six months imprisonment, for you, or me, or any of us, to give a cup of cold water, a crust of bread, or a night's shelter to a panting fugitive while he was tracking his way to Canada. And every man or woman in whose veins coursed a drop of human sympathy violated that wicked law, reckless of consequences, and was justified in so doing. As, then, the slaves who got their freedom must take it over, or under, or through the unjust forms of law, precisely so now must women, to get their right to a voice in this government, take it, and I have taken mine and mean to take it at every opportunity."

Judge Hunt flailed his gavel and gave the by now <u>futile</u> order for the prisoner to sit down and be quiet. Susan kept right on talking.

"When I was brought before your honor for trial," she said, "I hoped for a broad and liberal interpretation of the Constitution and its recent Amendments. One that would declare all United States citizens under its protection. But failing to get this justice—failing, even, to get a trial by a jury *not* of my peers—

I ask not leniency at your hands—but to take the full rigors of the law."

With that Susan finally obeyed Judge Hunt's orders and sat down. Now he had to reverse himself and order her to stand up so he could impose sentence. As soon as he pronounced the sentence—a fine of one hundred dollars plus the costs of prosecuting the trial—Susan spoke up again. "May it please your honor," she said, "I shall never pay a dollar of your unjust penalty. All the stock in trade I possess is a ten-thousand-dollar debt, incurred by publishing my paper—*The Revolution*—four years ago, the sole object of which was to educate all women to do precisely as I have done, rebel against your manmade, unjust, unconstitutional forms of law, that tax, fine, imprison, and hang women, while they deny them the right of representation in the government; and I shall work on with might and main to pay every dollar of that honest debt, but not a penny shall go to this unjust claim. And I shall earnestly and persistently continue to urge all women to the practical recognition of the old Revolutionary maxim, that 'Resistance to tyranny is obedience to God.'"

Judge Hunt must have had strict orders not only to see that the defendant was convicted, but to do everything he could to prevent the case from going on to a higher court. He allowed Susan to walk out of the courtroom without imposing a prison sentence in lieu of[5] her unpaid fine. If he had sent her to prison, she could have been released on a writ of habeas corpus[6] and would have

---

5. **in lieu** (loo) **of:** In place of.
6. **writ of habeas corpus** (hā′ bē əs kôr′ pəs): Legal document requiring that a detained person be brought before a court to decide the lawfulness of the imprisonment.

▲ Critical Viewing What accomplishments of Susan B. Anthony made her worthy of appearing on U.S. currency? [Connect] ❽

from *The United States* vs. *Susan B. Anthony* ◆ 649

Links Across Time

❺ Susan B. Anthony refers here to the aid abolitionists gave to fugitive slaves. In her view, this was another instance in which the laws on the books would demand punishment for an honorable, sympathetic act.

Comprehension Check ☑

❻ What is Anthony asking for? *She wants a trial by jury and would rather accept the full measure of Judge Hunt's verdict than accept any leniency. In so doing, she will bring more attention to her test case and cause.*

CONNECTING LITERATURE TO SOCIAL STUDIES

❼ **Interpret** Ask students to explain the reasons for Judge Hunt's "strict orders" to convict and to prevent the case from going further. *Conkling wanted to avoid having the case tried in higher court, where he thought Anthony might win.*

▶Critical Viewing◀

❽ **Connect** *Susan B. Anthony campaigned long and hard for equal rights for women and, in particular, for the right to vote.*

Customize for
Interpersonal Learners

Write the following statements on the board: "Individuals can make a difference," and "Individuals cannot make a difference." Then have interested students debate the point. Guide students to support their views with information and examples. Provide time for teams of students to gather their data. Choose students to be moderators. Formulate rules for speaking, including time limits, for participants to follow. Then hold the debates.

Viewing and Representing Mini-Lesson

Commemorative Coins

This mini-lesson will extend students' understanding of the honor Susan B. Anthony has received for her efforts to gain women the right to vote.

Introduce Have students look at the Susan B. Anthony silver dollar that appears on this page, and review their answers to the Critical Viewing question about why the coin was issued.

Develop Have students research the coin, to find what is on its reverse side. Challenge students to choose other Americans who have made a difference, and design a coin to honor one of them.

Guide students to examine regular and commemorative United States coins as they plan their designs, so they are aware of elements that must be included.

Apply Have students draw large pictures of their coins, front and back, or design them using clay. Students can present their coins, explaining why they chose the person, as well as their design; then create a display of commemorative coins.

Assess Evaluate students on their selection of Americans who deserve honor and their understanding of the concept of a commemorative coin.

①Infer Have students discuss what this information tells them about Susan B. Anthony. *She was a formidable advocate for her cause, not only because she had connections and a national reputation, but because she was well prepared, thorough, persuasive, demanding, and brave.*

Reinforce and Extend

Answers
◆ **LITERATURE AND YOUR LIFE**

Reader's Response Students may say that she was justified, because women were citizens deprived of equal rights.

Thematic Focus She was a hero because she put all her efforts into achieving the goal of suffrage for women, risking harassment, fines, and imprisonment to do so.

☑ **Check Your Comprehension**

1. The editorial urged people to spend five minutes using the right they once fought long and hard to earn.
2. The amendment did not specifically deny women the right to vote.
3. The District Attorney postponed the grand jury session because he did not want to send Anthony to jail.

More About the Author
Margaret Truman graduated from George Washington University in 1946, with a Bachelor of Arts degree in history. Her father, the 33rd President of the United States, gave the commencement address and presented her diploma. In addition to her skills as a writer, Truman was a singer. She made her concert debut with the Detroit Symphony Orchestra when she was sixteen. In 1949, she appeared in concert with the National Symphony Orchestra at Constitution Hall in Washington, D. C.

had the right to appeal. As it was, the case was closed.

Although she was disappointed that her case would not go to the Supreme Court as she had originally hoped, Susan knew that she had struck an important blow for woman's suffrage. Henry Selden's arguments and her own speech at the end of the trial were widely publicized, and Judge Hunt's conduct of the trial stood as proof that women were treated unjustly before the law.

① Susan did not forget the election inspectors who had allowed her to cast her ballot. The men were fined twenty-five dollars each and sent to jail when they refused to pay. In all, they spent about a week behind bars before Susan, through the influence of friends in Washington, obtained presidential pardons for each of them. In the meantime, her followers, who included some of the best cooks in Rochester, saw to it that the men were supplied with delicious hot meals and home-baked pies.

True to her promise, Susan paid the legal expenses for the three inspectors. With the help of contributions from sympathetic admirers, she paid the costs of her own trial. But she never paid that one-hundred-dollar fine. Susan B. Anthony was a woman of her word as well as a woman of courage.

Meet the Author
Margaret Truman (1924–) spent a good part of her life being known as the daughter of President Harry Truman (1945–1953). She has since become known as the author of more than twenty books. Truman has written a dozen murder mysteries, all of them set in Washington, D.C. She has also written books about each of her parents and about life in the White House. *First Ladies* is a series of essays about wives of American presidents.

650 ◆ *Nonfiction*

Guide for Responding

◆ **LITERATURE AND YOUR LIFE**

Reader's Response Was Anthony justified in using the wording of the Fourteenth Amendment to support her actions? Explain.

Thematic Focus In what ways can Susan B. Anthony be considered a hero? Explain.

☑ **Check Your Comprehension**

1. Summarize the editorial that led Anthony to register to vote.
2. What missing feature of the Fourteenth Amendment did Anthony use as support for her right to register?
3. Why did the district attorney agree to postpone Anthony's trial until late December?

◆ **Critical Thinking**

INTERPRET

1. How was the behavior of Marshal Keeney similar to and different from the behavior of the men in the barber shop? **[Compare and Contrast]**
2. Why did Anthony have trouble finding a lawyer who would defend her in court? **[Infer]**
3. What do you think the author means when she says, "I have a sneaky feeling that . . . she may actually have had a sense of humor"? **[Interpret]**

APPLY

4. What other situations do you know in which a person publicly violated a law he or she considered unjust? **[Relate]**

Beyond the Selection

FURTHER READING

Other Works by Margaret Truman
First Ladies, Women of Courage

Other Works About the Suffragist Movement
The Elisabeth Cady Stanton-Susan B. Anthony Reader: Correspondence, Writing, and Speeches, Ellen Carol Dubois (ed.)
A History of the American Suffragist Movement, Doris Weatherford

INTERNET
We suggest the following sites on the Internet (all Web sites are subject to change).

For more information about Margaret Truman:
http://www.lbjlib.utexas.edu/truman/mtd-bio.htm

For information about Susan B. Anthony:
http://www.susanbanthonyhouse.org/

For more information about suffragists:
http://www.inform.umd.edu/EdRes/Topic/Womens Studies/ReadingRoom/History/Vote/75-suffragists.html

We *strongly recommend* that you preview these sites before you send students to them.

CONNECTING LITERATURE TO SOCIAL STUDIES

In the nineteenth century, many Americans believed that a woman could not be as intelligent as a man, that a woman could not handle business affairs the way a man could, and that a "normal" woman wanted nothing more than to stay at home, raise children, and care for a husband. As a result of these beliefs, the idea of allowing women to vote was outrageous to many people. Susan B. Anthony and others decided to show how foolish these beliefs were. It took more than a century for women's groups to win the right to vote for all American women.

1. Think about the society of Susan B. Anthony's time. Explain whether or not her methods of raising the issue of woman suffrage were effective.
2. List other actions Anthony might have taken. Would they have been more effective or less effective? Explain.
3. For what other rights have Americans publicly fought? How have their methods been similar to those Anthony used?

Idea Bank

Writing

1. **Journal Entry** Write an entry that Anthony might have put into her journal after her first visit to the barber shop.
2. **Dialogue** Write a dialogue between two men who were in the barber shop when the Anthony sisters made their demand.
3. **Editorial** Write an editorial for a Rochester newspaper, either praising or condemning the Anthony sisters for trying to register to vote.

Speaking and Listening

4. **Legal Arguments [Group Activity]** With a classmate, role-play parts in the hearing before the Federal Commissioner of Elections. Decide who will be U.S. District Attorney Crowley and who will be Henry R. Selden, Anthony's defense attorney. Then, present your arguments to the class.

Project

5. **Timeline of the Woman Suffrage Movement** Do research to learn about the struggle to win voting rights for women in the United States. Create a timeline showing significant events on the road to the approval of the Nineteenth Amendment. **[Social Studies Link]**

Further Reading, Listening, and Viewing

- Margaret Truman's book *Women of Courage* (1976) contains the full story of the 1872 incident described in this essay, along with stories of other women who brought about changes.
- Susan Clinton's *The Story of Susan B. Anthony* (1986) is a biography of Susan B. Anthony.
- Kate Connell's *They Shall Be Heard* is a biography of Susan B. Anthony and Elizabeth Cady Stanton.
- The Susan B. Anthony House online at http://www.susanbanthonyhouse.org/ contains an interactive tour through this historic site.

from *The United States vs. Susan B. Anthony* ◆ 651

✓ ASSESSMENT OPTIONS

OBJECTIVES

1. To read, comprehend, and interpret two biographical essays
2. To relate biography to personal experience
3. To identify the author's main points
4. To appreciate biography
5. To build vocabulary in context and learn the prefix *en-*
6. To develop skill using *who* and *whom*
7. To write a testimonial supported with examples
8. To respond to biography through writing, speaking and listening, and projects

SKILLS INSTRUCTION

Vocabulary:
Using the Prefix *en-*

Spelling:
Words With a Silent *g*

Grammar:
Using *who* and *whom*

Reading Strategy:
Identify the Author's Main Points

Literary Focus:
Biography

Writing:
Support With Examples

Speaking and Listening:
Radio Play (Teacher Edition)

Critical Viewing:
Assess; Analyze; Speculate

PORTFOLIO OPPORTUNITIES

Writing: Advice Letters; Casting Memo; Biography

Writing Mini-Lesson: Testimonial

Speaking and Listening: Radio Play; Dialogue

Projects: Holocaust Exhibit; Art Catalog

More About the Authors
Stephen Longstreet has had a long and productive career. His diverse interests have led him to write about the Chicago jazz scene, cooking, history, and art criticism of painters as varied as Rembrandt, Dali, and Degas. Some of his own artworks are on exhibit at the Senior Eye Gallery in Long Beach, California.

John Hersey, who won the 1945 Pulitzer Prize for Literature for the novel *A Bell for Adano,* has been called "a living tape recorder." His sharp ear for the rhythms of natural speech and his keen ability to understand his subjects has helped him to write compelling profiles and character sketches of people from all walks of life, including artist Jacob Lawrence and former President Gerald Ford.

Meet the Authors:

Stephen Longstreet (1907–   )

Stephen Longstreet has written screenplays, novels, art criticism, television scripts, and detective stories. In addition to being a writer, he is an experienced artist who has studied painting in Paris, Rome, London, and Berlin. While living in Europe in the 1920's, Longstreet met such famous artists as Marc Chagall, Henri Matisse, and Pablo Picasso.

John Hersey (1914–1993)

John Hersey was born in Tientsin, China, where his parents were missionaries. After his early education in China, he attended Yale, as well as Clare College in Cambridge, England. He was an assistant to the famous author Sinclair Lewis and then worked as a journalist for several New York magazines.

THE STORY BEHIND THE STORY

"Not to Go With the Others" tells of the escape of Frantizek Zaremski from a Nazi prison camp during World War II. Hersey describes meeting Zaremski a few days after his escape: "The skin of his face was drawn tight over the bones and cartilage, and the hair on his head, which had been shaved by the Nazis, was just beginning to grow back. . . . More than once, as he told his story, he covered his eyes with his free hand, and I thought he might faint."

652 ◆ Nonfiction

◆ LITERATURE AND YOUR LIFE

CONNECT YOUR EXPERIENCE

You may admire people for many different reasons. Some have exceptional talent; some have great courage; some inspire strong emotional connections. You will meet two people in these biographies—Katsushika Hokusai and Frantizek Zaremski—who are likely to fit your definition of admirable.

THEMATIC FOCUS: Heroes

Both Hokusai and Zaremski are heroes in different ways. What makes each a hero?

◆ Background for Understanding

HISTORY

In "Not to Go With the Others," Frantizek Zaremski is put in a Gestapo prison during World War II. The Gestapo was a German military police force. Its mission was to eliminate all enemies of Nazi Germany, including Jews, Catholics, political opponents, Gypsies, and the mentally ill. The Gestapo operated outside the law. Its officers had the power to imprison people without trials. Many Gestapo prisoners were tortured, sent to concentration camps, or executed.

◆ Build Vocabulary

PREFIXES: *en-*

Longstreet describes one of Hokusai's pictures as "great waves engulfing fishermen." The prefix *en-* in *engulf* means "cover with." *Engulf* means "to swallow up" or "to cover completely."

WORD BANK

Which word from the list is related to the verb *pretend*? Check the Build Vocabulary box on page 657 to see if you chose correctly.

apprenticed
engulfing
mania
feigned
ensued
dispatched
pretense
immersed

Prentice Hall Literature Program Resources

REINFORCE / RETEACH / EXTEND

Selection Support Pages
Build Vocabulary: Prefixes: *en-,* p. 237
Build Spelling Skills, p. 238
Build Grammar Skills: Using *who* and *whom,* p. 239
Reading Strategy: Identify the Author's Main Points, p. 240
Literary Focus: Biography, p. 241

Strategies for Diverse Student Needs, pp. 87–88

Beyond Literature Media Connection: Film Documentary, p. 44

Formal Assessment Selection Test, pp. 192–194, Assessment Resources Software

Alternative Assessment, p. 44

Writing and Language Transparencies Main Idea and Supporting Details Organizer, p. 61

Resource Pro CD-ROM "Hokusai: The Old Man Mad About Drawing"; "Not to Go With the Others"

 Listening to Literature Audiocassettes "Hokusai: The Old Man Mad About Drawing"; "Not to Go With the Others"

Hokusai: The Old Man Mad About Drawing
◆ Not to Go With the Others ◆

VII, Fuji in clear weather. One of the "Thirty-six Views of Fuji." Hokusai, British Museum

◆ Literary Focus

BIOGRAPHY

Both "Hokusai: The Old Man Mad About Drawing" and "Not to Go With the Others" are biographies. A **biography** is a form of nonfiction in which a writer tells about the life of another person. Most biographies are written about famous or admirable people. Although biographies are nonfiction, many share the elements of narrative writing—settings, interesting characters and dialogue, and a theme or message.

Main Point of Selection:

Paragraph 4 – Main Point:

Paragraph 3 – Main Point:

Paragraph 2 – Main Point:

Paragraph 1 – Main Point:
Hokusai had a unique personality.

◆ Reading Strategy

IDENTIFY THE AUTHOR'S MAIN POINTS

To **identify the author's main points,** ask yourself what he or she wants you to discover or think as you read. These main points are the most important ideas. In many cases, you'll find a main point in each paragraph, as well as in the introduction and conclusion to an essay. Often, you can piece together the main points of individual paragraphs to determine the main point of the work as a whole. To help you, fill in a chart like the one at left as you read:

Preparing for Standardized Tests

Vocabulary Standardized tests may evaluate students' understanding of word affixes, such as the prefix *en-*, which is featured in this selection. Mastery of this prefix can help students to answer certain kinds of test questions.

Write this sentence on the board: "The Gestapo would *enslave* its prisoners at the camps." Ask students to identify the prefix *en-* and its base word, *slave*. Discuss how this word construction literally means "to cause to be a slave." Then present the following sample test question, based on the Hersey biography:

The Gestapo tried to *entrap prisoners in the loft.*

In the sentence above, entrap means

(A) feed   (C) snare
(B) frighten   (D) protect

Help students assess the choices. Guide them to examine the base word, *trap*, and apply the prefix *-en-*, which means to cause to be in a trap, and look for a single word that expresses this idea. *(C)* is the best answer. For more practice, use Build Vocabulary: Prefixes: *en-*, in **Selection Support,** p. 237.

◆ Build Grammar Skills

Using *Who* and *Whom* If you wish to introduce the grammar concept for this selection before students read, refer to the instruction on p. 660.

Customize for
Less Proficient Readers

To help students with the Reading Strategy, have them identify the topic sentence in each paragraph of the essays. A list of topic sentences can help them determine a flow of ideas, which can lead them to the main points of the works.

Customize for
More Advanced Students

The subjects of the two biographical essays in this set can be linked by creativity and courage. These traits manifest themselves in different ways, but are there to discover. Challenge students, as they read, to jot down examples of creativity and courage by Hokusai and by Zaremski.

Humanities: Art

VII, Fuji in clear weather, by Katsushika Hokusai

Hokusai (1760–1849) is one of the outstanding *Ukiyo-e* printmakers who created "pictures of the floating world" (everyday life). His *Thirty Six Views of Mount Fuji* were done sometime between 1826 and 1833. Discuss with students the impact of making the mountain bright red.

Students may say that the vivid color makes the sacred mountain seem surreal and more powerful and vibrant than an ordinary mountain.

653

One-Minute Insight

"Hokusai: The Old Man Mad About Drawing" is a biographical essay of the Japanese artist. The author creates a portrait of a great artist by providing brief anecdotes about Hokusai's ongoing efforts to introduce innovations into traditional art forms and test himself with difficult artistic tasks. Then he adds a quotation from Hokusai's own writings to enhance the portrait.

►Critical Viewing◄

❶ Assess *Responses will vary. Some students may respond most to the color and dramatic sense of motion in the wave. Others may appreciate the balance of line and shape.*

◆Reading Strategy

❷ Identify the Author's Main Points Have students discuss the author's main point about the personality of Hokusai, based on the opening paragraph. *He portrays Hokusai as a man who not only was artistically talented but had curiosity and drive that made him a unique character.*

Clarification

❸ A woodcut picture is made by carving an image into a block of wood. The uncut portions of the wood are coated with ink, and paper is pressed over the block to transfer the image to paper. The cutaway sections of the wood appear white.

◆Literary Focus

❹ Biography Discuss with students why Hokusai may have been a man ahead of his time, and why he might have been thought of as "mad." *He was impatient with any one style of art and was always ready to try something new, different, and challenging. He was adventurous, dramatic, creative, and outrageous.*

Customize for
English Language Learners

In these essays, students will read words from Japanese and Polish that are transliterated into English. Help students pronounce the names and words, but do not expect mastery.

654

Hokusai: The Old Man Mad About Drawing

Stephen Longstreet

The Great Wave of Kangawa, Katsushika Hokusai, The Metropolitan Museum of Art, New York, NY

► Critical Viewing
❶ What do you appreciate most about this drawing by Hokusai—its colors, sense of movement, style, or lines? **[Assess]**

Of all the great artists of Japan, the one Westerners probably like and understand best is Katsushika Hokusai. He was a restless, unpredictable man who lived in as many as a hundred different houses and changed his name at least thirty times. For a very great artist, he acted at times like P. T. Barnum[1] or a Hollywood producer with his curiosity and drive for novelty.

❷ Hokusai was born in 1760 outside the city of Edo[2] in the province of Shimofusa. He was apprenticed early in life to a mirror maker and then worked in a lending library, where he was fascinated by the woodcut illustrations of the piled-up books. At eighteen he became a pupil of Shunsho, a great artist known mainly for his prints of actors. Hokusai was soon signing his name as Shunro, and for the next fifteen years he, too, made actor prints, as well as illustrations for popular novels. By 1795 he was calling himself Sori and had begun working with the European copper etchings which had

❸

1. **P. T. Barnum:** Phineas Taylor Barnum (1810–1891); U.S. showman and circus operator.
2. **Edo** (ē′ dō): Former name of Tokyo.

become popular in Japan. Every time Hokusai changed his name, he changed his style. He drew, he designed fine surimino (greeting prints), he experimented with pure landscape.

Hokusai never stayed long with a period or style, but was always off and running to something new. A great show-off, he painted with his fingers, toothpicks, a bottle, an eggshell; he worked left-handed, from the bottom up, and from left to right. Once he painted two sparrows on a grain of rice. Commissioned by a shogun (a military ruler in 18th century Japan) to decorate a door of the Temple of Dempo-ji, he tore it off its hinges, laid it in the courtyard, and painted wavy blue lines on it to represent running water, then dipped the feet of a live rooster in red seal ink and chased the bird over the painted door. When the shogun came to see the finished job, he at once saw the river Tatsuta and the falling red maple leaves of autumn. Another time Hokusai used a large broom dipped into a vat of ink to draw the full-length figure of a god, over a hundred feet long, on the floor of a courtyard.

When he was fifty-four, Hokusai began to

❹

Block Scheduling Strategies

Consider these suggestions to take advantage of extended class time:

• Draw students to the biographical essays in this set with the Interest Grabber on p. 653. Guide them to examine the art with the Humanities notes on pp. 653, 655, 656, and 658 in the Teacher Edition.

• Use Background for Understanding and Meet the Authors on p. 652 to acquaint students with what Zaremski faced.

• Have students read the essays on their own, and then meet in small groups to discuss the Reader's Response and Thematic Focus features on pp. 655 and 659.

• To prepare students for the Writing Mini-Lesson, use the Biography writing activity in the Idea Bank on p. 661.

• Have students work on Projects in the Idea Bank on p. 661, or plan the Interview activity in Beyond Literature on p. 659.

issue books of his sketches, which he called *The Manga*. He found everything worth sketching: radish grinders, pancake women, street processions, jugglers, and wrestlers. And he was already over sixty when he began his great series, *Thirty-six Views of Fuji*, a remarkable set of woodcut prints that tell the story of the countryside around Edo: people at play or work, great waves engulfing fishermen, silks drying in the sun, lightning playing on great mountains, and always, somewhere, the ash-tipped top of Fuji.

Hokusai did thirty thousand pictures during a full and long life. When he was seventy-five he wrote:

From the age of six I had a mania for drawing the shapes of things. When I was fifty I had published a universe of designs. But all I have done before the age of seventy is not worth bothering with. At seventy-five I have learned something of the pattern of nature, of animals, of plants, of trees, birds, fish,

◆ Reading Strategy
❺ What is the main point of this passage?

and insects. When I am eighty you will see real progress. At ninety I shall have cut my way deeply into the mystery of life itself. At a hundred I shall be a marvelous artist. At a hundred and ten everything I create, a dot, a line, will jump to life as never before. To all of you who are going to live as long as I do, I promise to keep my word. I am writing this in my old age. I used to call myself Hokusai, but today I sign myself "The Old Man Mad About Drawing."

He didn't reach a hundred and ten, but he nearly reached ninety. On the day of his death, in 1849, he was cheerfully at work on a new drawing.

◆ Build Vocabulary

apprenticed (ə pren´ tist) *v.*: Contracted to learn a trade under a skilled worker

engulfing (en gulf´ iŋ) *v.*: Flowing over and swallowing

mania (mā´ nē ə) *n.*: Uncontrollable enthusiasm

◆ Reading Strategy
❺ **Identify the Author's Main Points** *Hokusai's lifelong passion kept him a busy artist; with the wisdom of age, he expected to improve more.*

Reinforce and Extend

Answers
◆ LITERATURE AND YOUR LIFE

Reader's Response Most students will admire his originality, creativity, and passion to experiment.

Thematic Focus Students may find him a hero because he was true to his lifelong passion, and worked on his art until the day he died.

☑ Check Your Comprehension

1. He was born in 1760 outside the city of Edo (ancient Tokyo).
2. He was an apprentice to a mirror maker, and worked in a library.
3. He did actor prints, illustrations for popular novels, copper etchings, greeting prints, and landscapes.
4. He created 30,000 pictures during his lifetime.
5. He was making a new drawing.
6. He lived to be 89.

◆ Critical Thinking

1. He was a restless, unpredictable, driven man who was always ready to try something new.
2. He had innovative artistic ideas.
3. He meant that he was always learning, so as he grew older, he would know more and more.
4. Students may say that as a man who liked experimentation, he would fit into today's art world. With so much in the modern world to observe and draw, he'd have no shortage of subjects.
5. Senior citizens might feel proud to know how much Hokusai accomplished late in life.

Guide for Responding

◆ LITERATURE AND YOUR LIFE

Reader's Response What do you admire most about Hokusai? Explain.

Thematic Focus In what way can Hokusai be considered a hero?

☑ Check Your Comprehension

1. Where and when was Hokusai born?
2. What kind of work did he do when he was a young man?
3. Name five styles of art that Hokusai produced.
4. How many pictures and illustrations did Hokusai create during his lifetime?
5. What was Hokusai doing the day that he died?
6. How long did Hokusai live?

◆ Critical Thinking

INTERPRET
1. What does the first paragraph tell you about Hokusai? What kind of person was he? **[Analyze]**
2. Why might Hokusai be considered a man ahead of his time? **[Speculate]**
3. What did Hokusai mean when he said, "At a hundred I shall be a marvelous artist"? **[Interpret]**

EVALUATE
4. Would Hokusai fit into the art world today? Explain. **[Make a Judgment]**

APPLY
5. Hokusai lived a very long and productive life. How would a present-day senior citizen feel after reading this essay? **[Hypothesize]**

Hokusai: The Old Man Mad About Drawing ◆ 655

Humanities: Art

The Great Wave of Kangawa, by Katsushika Hokusai

Japanese artist and printmaker Hokusai mastered the artistic philosophy of his tradition: Everything in nature has an invariable form. Within this tradition, he was able to create uniquely beautiful and powerful images. His works had a great impact on the European impressionist painters Edgar Degas, Claude Monet, and Henri de Toulouse-Lautrec. Use these questions to discuss the painting on p. 654:

1. What repetitions do you see in this picture?
Students may cite that the shape and colors of distant Fuji are repeated in the nearest wave; the curves of the waves repeat; and the long, tan boats are duplicated.

2. What emotions does this scene evoke?
Students may suggest that on the one hand it evokes fear, desperation, or determination as the sailors row for their lives beneath the big wave, or that Fuji, standing peacefully in the distance evokes a feeling of hope and security.

"Not to Go With the Others" is a biographical sketch about Frantizek Zaremski, a Polish prisoner of the Nazis during World War II. He made split-second decisions that saved his life during life-or-death situations.

◆ Critical Thinking

❶ Interpret Ask students to explain what was rebellious about the poem Zaremski carried. *It expresses hope that Hitler will sleep (or die) as Allied planes come to defeat him.*

► Critical Viewing ◄

❷ Analyze *Students may say that the faded colors make the scene look dry and hot like a desert. The bit of green in the lower part of the painting may represent life that still exists in the prison, although it is only a small part of the scene.*

Customize for
Intrapersonal Learners

Challenge students to try to imagine themselves in Zaremski's place. They can try to get a sense of the turmoil he feels and what he might be thinking during his awful ordeal.

Not to Go With the Others

John Hersey

The Watchtower, 1942, Savielly Schleifer, Musée d'Histoire Contemporaine, Paris, France

▲ **Critical Viewing** What do the colors in this painting convey about conditions within the prison camp? **[Analyze]**

❶ In the third year of the war, Frantizek Zaremski was arrested by the invaders on a charge of spreading underground literature—specifically, for carrying about his person a poem a friend from Gdynia[1] had given him, which began: *Sleep, beloved Hitler, planes will come by night . . .*

After he had spent six weeks of a three-year sentence for this crime in the Gestapo[2] prison at Inowroczon, Zaremski was sent to Kalice[3] to do carpentry. By bad luck, at the time when his term expired, the Russians had broken through at the Vistula, and his captors, instead of releasing him, took him, in their general panic, to the transfer camp for Polish political prisoners at Rodogoszcz,[4] where he was placed in Hall Number Four with nine hundred men. Altogether there were between two and three thousand men and women—no Jews, only "Aryan"[5] Poles suspected or convicted of political activity—in the prison.

---

1. **Gdynia** (gə din′ ē ə): A city in the northern region of Poland.
2. **Gestapo** (gə stä′ pō): The secret police force of the German Nazi state, notorious for its terrorism and brutality.
3. **Inowroczon** (ē nəv rô′ zôn′) . . . **Kalice** (kä′ lish): Cities in the central region of Poland.
4. **Rodogoszcz** (rô dô gôzh′): A suburb of the city of Lódź.
5. **"Aryan"** (âr′ ē ən): In Naziism, people of northern European descent who were said to possess racially superior traits and capacities for government, social organization, and civilization, while the non-Aryan peoples, such as the Jews, were seen as being inferior.

Humanities: Art

The Watchtower, 1942, by Savielly Schleifer

Nazi prison camps, like many prisons, had tall towers where guards were stationed to look down on prison grounds and buildings. This vantage point allowed the guards to keep watch over the prisoners' movements and was intended to prevent escapes. For many inmates, the towers became monuments to the monstrous evils they had to endure. Have students study the painting and consider the significance of a watchtower.

Use these questions for discussion:
1. Notice how the surface of the painting has a crackled look. Why do you think the artist made it look this way? *Students may say that the crackled look shows the cracks in humanity that prison life created.*
2. Why do you think the artist left human figures out of this work? *He may wish to convey the idea that this place is inhuman, or that life is not valued here.*

Late in the evening of Wednesday, January 17, 1945, three days before Lódź was to fall to the Russians, all the prisoners were gathered on the third and fourth floors of the main building, even those who were sick, and there they all lay down on wooden bunks and floors to try to sleep. At about two in the morning guards came and ordered the inmates to get up for roll call.

They divided the prisoners into groups of about twenty each and lined up the groups in pairs. Zaremski was in the second group. SS[6] men led it down concrete stairs in a brick-walled stairwell at one end of the building and halted it on a landing of the stairway, near a door opening into a large loft on the second floor. The first group had apparently been led down to the ground floor.

Someone gave an order that the prisoners should run in pairs into the loft as fast as they could. When the first pairs of Zaremski's group ran in, SS men with their backs to the wall inside the room began to shoot at them from behind. Zaremski's turn came. He ran in terror. A bullet burned through his trouser leg. Another grazed his thigh. He fell down and feigned death.

Others, from Zaremski's and later groups, ran into the hall and were shot and fell dead or wounded on top of Zaremski and those who had gone first. At one time Zaremski heard the Polish national anthem being sung somewhere.

Finally the running and shooting ended, and there ensued some shooting on the upper floors, perhaps of people who had refused to run downstairs.

SS men with flashlights waded among the bodies, shining lights in the faces of the prostrate victims. Any wounded who moaned or moved, or any whose eyes reacted when the shafts of light hit their faces, were dispatched with pistol shots. Somehow Zaremski passed the test of pretense.

6. **SS:** Abbreviation of the German *Schutzstaffel,* meaning "protective rank." They were a quasi-military unit of the Nazi party used as a special police force.

As dawn began to break, Zaremski heard the iron doors of the main building being locked, and he heard some sort of grenades or bombs being thrown into the lowest hall and exploding there; they seemed to him to make only smoke, but they may have been incendiaries.[7] Later, in any case, the ground floor began to burn. Perhaps benzine or petrol[8] had been poured around. Zaremski was still lying among the bodies of others.

There were several who were still alive, and they began jumping out of the burning building, some from windows on the upper stories. A few broke through a skylight to the roof, tied blankets from the prisoners' bunks into long ropes and let themselves down outside. Zaremski, now scurrying about the building, held back to see what would happen. Those who jumped or climbed down were shot at leisure in the camp enclosure by SS men in the turrets on the walls, and Zaremski decided to try to stay inside.

On the fourth floor, at the top of the reinforced concrete staircase, in the bricked stairwell at the end of the building, Zaremski found the plant's water tank, and for a time he and others poured water over the wounded lying on the wooden floors in the main rooms. Later Zaremski took all his clothes off, soaked them in the tank, and put them back on. He lay down and kept pouring water over himself. He put a soaked blanket around his head.

The tank was a tall one, separated from the main room by the stairwell's brick wall, and

7. **incendiaries** (in sen′ dē er′ ēz): Bombs made with a chemical substance that cause a large fire when exploded.
8. **benzine** (ben′ zēn′) . . . **petrol** (pet′ rəl): Clear, poisonous, highly flammable liquid fuels.

◆ **Build Vocabulary**

feigned (fānd) *v.*: Imitated; pretended

ensued (en sōod′) *v.*: Came afterward; followed immediately

dispatched (di spacht′) *v.*: Put an end to; killed

pretense (prē tens′) *n.*: False showing; pretending

Not to Go With the Others ◆ 657

◆**Literary Focus**

❸ **Biography** Clarify with students the mission of the SS forces here. The SS forces were setting up the prisoners for mass execution. As prisoners would run into the loft, they would be shot down. Those who refused to run to the loft would be gunned down anyway. How does Zaremski survive? *He is wounded, but not mortally, so he plays dead when the SS men check the bodies.*

◆**Reading Strategy**

❹ **Identify the Author's Main Points** Discuss with students ways in which Zaremski's behavior differs from that of the other prisoners. *Students may note that Zaremski seems to be more cautious and thinks of ways to avoid the deadly forces that all of the prisoners face.*

Thematic Focus

❺ **Heroes** Wars produce thousands of "unsung heroes"—people who do heroic deeds that go unremembered because there are no survivors to bear witness to their heroism. Such unsung heroes may exist among soldiers, prisoners, and civilians. Discuss with students the heroism described in this passage. Zaremski, who fears for his own life, finds the compassion to pour water over the wounded men to try to protect them from fire.

Speaking and Listening Mini-Lesson

Radio Play

This mini-lesson supports the Speaking and Listening activity in the Idea Bank on p. 661.

Introduce Tell students that long before television could bring dramas into people's homes, radio served a similar function. Radio plays, like stage or screen plays, employ professional actors who read from well-rehearsed scripts. Because radio plays only heard and not seen, they often include sound effects, musical interludes, and voice-over narration to fill in important details.

Develop Divide the class into performance groups. It is each group's task to adapt the biographical essay into a script suitable for a radio play. Emphasize that all action must be described or referred to, because it cannot be seen. Discuss whether groups can or should include sound effects and/or music to enhance the play. Allow time for groups to write and edit the script, and rehearse the delivery to make it as effective as possible.

Apply Have students present their radio plays to a "live studio audience" of their

classmates, or have them record their presentations with sound effects and then play the recordings for the class. Encourage audience members to listen for details that build suspense and capture the drama of the biographical essay.

Assess Evaluate radio plays on how accurately students adapt the biographical essay, and how effectively they present the facts and details orally. Or use the Peer Assessment: Dramatic Performance form, p. 116, in **Alternative Assessment.**

❶ **Biography** Point out to students that in this passage, the biographer omits all of Zaremski's emotions, but presents a detailed description of what he hears, sees, and does. Discuss why a biographer might use this approach. *Students may say that if a writer describes the actual events with enough detail and clarity, readers can put themselves in the subject's place without having to be told what he or she feels.*

▶ **Critical Viewing** ◀

❷ **Speculate** *He might long for freedom, safety, protection, friends and family, food, health, or peace.*

◆ **Literary Focus**

❸ **Biography** Here, and at other points in the story, Zaremski chooses not to go with the others. These decisions seem to have saved his life.

◆ **Reading Strategy**

❹ **Identify the Author's Main Points** Have students identify the traits the author wants readers to see in his portrayal of Zaremski here. *Students may say that Zaremski is resourceful and quick-thinking, and possesses a strong will to survive.*

---

❶ when the fire began to eat through the wooden floor of the fourth story and the heat in the stairwell grew unbearable, Zaremski climbed up and got right into the water in the tank. He stayed <u>immersed</u> there all day long. Every few minutes he could hear shots from the wall turrets. He heard floors of the main halls fall and heard the side walls collapse. The staircase shell and the concrete stairs remained standing.

It was evening before the shooting and the fire died down. When he felt sure both had ended, Zaremski pulled himself out of the tank and lay awhile on the cement floor beside it. Then, his strength somewhat restored, he made his way down the stairs, and on the way he found six others who were wounded but could walk.

The seven went outside. Dusk. All quiet. They thought the Germans had left, and they wanted to climb the wall and escape. The first three climbed up and dropped away in apparent safety, but then the lights flashed on in the turrets and bursts of firing broke out. Three of the remaining four decided to take their chances at climbing out after total darkness; they did not know whether the first three had been killed or

❷ ▲ **Critical Viewing** What might the prisoner depicted in this painting be longing for? [Speculate]

The Unattainable, Henri Pieck, by courtesy of Karrie Pieck, Holland, and Ineke Pieck, England

◆ **Literary Focus**
What fact about Zaremski's life may have given the author the idea for the title of this biography?

had escaped. Only Zaremski decided to stay.

The three climbed, but this time the lights came sooner, and the guards killed all three while they were still scaling the wall.

Zaremski crept into the camp's storehouse in a separate building. Finding some damp blankets, he wrapped them around himself and climbed into a big box, where he stayed all night. Once during the night he heard steps outside the building, and in the early morning he heard walking again. This time the footsteps approached the storeroom door. The door opened. The steps entered. Through the cracks of the box Zaremski sensed that the beam of a flashlight was probing the room. Zaremski could hear box tops opening and slamming and a foot kicking barrels. He held the lid of his box from the inside. Steps came near, a hand tried the lid, but Zaremski held tight, and the searcher must have decided the box was locked or nailed down. The footsteps went away.

❹

Later two others came at different times and inspected the room, but neither tried

◆ **Build Vocabulary**
immersed (im murst´) *v.:* Plunged into; submerged

658 ◆ *Nonfiction*

◆ **Humanities: Art**

The Unattainable, by Henri Pieck
The barbed wire background of this image offers a revealing clue about the location of this man. Point out the effects of the black and white shading that enhance the stark setting. Use these questions for discussion:
1. What do you think the title of this image means? *Students may say that the prisoner knows that he's unlikely to escape, so any dreams he holds for the future are unattainable: freedom, life, happiness, security, comfort, and love.*

2. Why does the artist show the prisoner from behind? *Possible response: By not giving the prisoner a face, the artist can use this figure to stand for all prisoners in any prison camp. His thin, bony fingers show that he is starving.*

3. Contrast the grid of the barbed wire with the wrinkles and folds of the prisoner's clothes. *Possible response: The rigid, regular grid of barbed wire may stand for the unyielding harshness of the prison camp. By contrast, the soft, irregular creases represent the humanity of the prisoner.*

Zaremski's box; the third hunter locked the door from the outside.

Much later Zaremski heard a car start and drive away.

Much later still—some time on the nineteenth of January in the year of victory—Zaremski heard the Polish language being spoken, even by the voices of women and children. He jumped out of the box and broke the window of the storehouse and climbed out to his countrymen.

Beyond Literature

Social Studies Connection

Axis vs. Allies World War II (1939–1945) directly involved nearly every country in the world, with fighting raging over four continents. It started when the three main Axis countries—Japan, Germany, and Italy—invaded their weaker neighbors to gain land and natural resources. The opponents of the Axis—the Allies—consisted of fifty countries, including the United States, Great Britain, and the Soviet Union. These countries fought against the nine countries comprising the Axis. The war lasted for several years, and there was a time when it looked as if the Axis might win. By the war's end, more than seventy million people had served in the armies of either side and more than seventeen million soldiers died. Civilian casualties, including the Jewish Holocaust, brought the total death figure to between twenty-five and thirty million people.

Cross-Curricular Activity
Interviewing Speak with a person old enough to remember World War II. Ask him or her what it was like to live through that period. Record the interview and your reactions to it, and share it with the rest of the class.

Guide for Responding

◆ LITERATURE AND YOUR LIFE

Reader's Response Zaremski was able to think clearly in an extremely challenging and dangerous situation. What would you have done if you had been in his position?

Thematic Focus What challenges did Zaremski face and overcome?

Journal Writing Jot down in your journal qualities or characteristics that are useful during crisis situations.

☑ Check Your Comprehension

1. For what crime was Zaremski arrested?
2. What happened to Zaremski after his term of imprisonment expired?
3. What did the SS men do to the prisoners who were running into the loft?
4. How did Zaremski save himself from the fire?
5. After the fire died out, where did Zaremski hide from the Nazi soldiers?

◆ Critical Thinking

INTERPRET
1. Why do you think the Nazis did not release the political prisoners from Rodogoszcz when the Russians were advancing? **[Infer]**
2. What would have happened to Zaremski if he had not pretended to be dead? **[Draw Conclusions]**
3. Instead of climbing the prison walls to escape, Zaremski held back. How did he know it was safer to stay? **[Infer]**

EVALUATE
4. Zaremski was the only prisoner to survive the Nazi slaughter. What characteristics did he have that enabled him to live? **[Assess]**

COMPARE LITERARY WORKS
5. In what way do both Hokusai and Zaremski triumph? Explain. **[Compare and Contrast]**

Not to Go With the Others ◆ 659

Beyond Literature

The United States Holocaust Memorial Museum in Washington, D.C., is a source of information about the Holocaust and World War II. Students can write to the museum at 100 Raoul Wallenberg Place SW, Washington, DC 20024-2150; call (202) 488-0400: or visit the Web site: **http://www.ushmm.org**

Reinforce and Extend

Answers
◆LITERATURE AND YOUR LIFE

Reader's Response Most students will respect his clearheadedness under such dire circumstances and hope they would have done the same.

Thematic Focus He faced and overcame cruel captors and harsh conditions; he overcame death by bullets, fire, and starvation.

☑ Check Your Comprehension
1. He was arrested for spreading underground literature.
2. He was taken to a transfer camp for Polish political prisoners.
3. They shot them.
4. He used water from a water tank.
5. He hid inside a large box in the camp's storehouse.

◆Critical Thinking
1. They may have hoped to use them as hostages; they may have simply panicked and brought them along; or they may have planned to kill them to prevent them from talking to the advancing Russians about the prison later and to dispose of their bodies in a place where no one would find them.
2. He would have been killed.
3. He didn't know for sure, but he had seen so many others gunned down, he decided to take his chances within the building.
4. He was a levelheaded thinker who weighed a situation and acted quickly. He was brave, compassionate, and strong, and had a deep will to live.
5. Each, in his own way, triumphs over death. Hokusai lived a long and productive life as an artist; after he died, he left a rich body of work that lives on. Zaremski survived unspeakable horrors and found a way to share his shocking ordeal with the world.

Beyond the Selection

FURTHER READING
Other Works by the Authors
Child in Art, Stephen Longstreet
Magic Trumpets, Stephen Longstreet
The Algiers Motel Incident, John Hersey
Hiroshima, John Hersey
Other Works About Heroes
The Double Life of Pocahontas, Jean Fritz
Four Perfect Pebbles: A Holocaust Story, Lila Perl
Wallenberg, Missing Hero, Kati Marton

INTERNET
We recommend the following sites on the Internet (all Web sites are subject to change).

For more information on John Hersey, go to:
http://www.encyclopedia.com/articles/05868.html
For oral histories of World War II, go to:
http://history.rutgers.edu/oralhistory/orlhom.htm
We *strongly recommend* that you preview these sites before you send students to them.

Answers

◆ Reading Strategy

1. His curiosity and inventiveness drove him to try many forms, and kept him working on art to his last day.
2. Possible responses: He read underground literature that he knew could be dangerous to him; he feigned death in order to try to survive; he helped other wounded prisoners; he hid in a water tank for hours; he hid in a box for nearly two days until he felt it was safe to emerge.

◆ Build Vocabulary

Using the Prefix en-
1. enclosed; 2. enjoy; 3. enrich

Spelling Strategy
1. gnat; 2. gnaw; 3. resign; 4. reign

Using the Word Bank
1. d 2. f 3. e 4. a 5. g 6. c 7. b 8. h

◆ Literary Focus

1. He wants readers to know that Hokusai was passionate about art, and that he devoted his life to art.
2. Possible responses: He acted like P.T. Barnum with his drive for novelty; he changed his name every time he tried different art styles; he was an innovative creator; he did 30,000 pictures during his life; he painted to the moment of his death.
3. Each led an unusual life and left something to enrich the world.

◆ Build Grammar Skills

Practice
1. who; 2. whom; 3. whom; 4. who; 5. whom

Writing Application
Possible response:
Among Japanese artists, Hokusai is the one who is most familiar to me. His beautiful works are full of energy. To whom could I write for more information about this artist?

Writer's Solution

For additional instruction and practice, use the lesson in the *Writer's Solution Language Lab CD-ROM* on the use of *who* and *whom*. You may also use the practice page on the Cases of *Who* and *Whom*, p. 80, in the *Writer's Solution Grammar Practice Book*.

660

Guide for Responding *(continued)*

◆ Reading Strategy

IDENTIFY THE AUTHOR'S MAIN POINTS

To discover the **main points** in a nonfiction work, ask yourself what the author wants you to learn or think as a result of reading.

1. What is the main point Longstreet makes about Hokusai?
2. List three examples from "Not to Go With the Others" that support Hersey's main point that Zaremski was a man of great courage.

◆ Build Vocabulary Skills

USING THE PREFIX en-

The prefix *en-* has several meanings. They include "in or into," "cover with," and "cause to be." Using these *en-* words, complete the sentences that follow.

| enrich | enjoy | enclosed |

1. The people were ___?___ in a room.
2. Following his escape, Zaremski could ___?___ his freedom.
3. Stories like this ___?___ our lives.

SPELLING STRATEGY

In some words, the letter *g* is silent—often when the *g* comes before an *n*, such as in the words *feigned* and *design*. Practice spelling words with a silent *g* by unscrambling the words in parentheses.

1. A small insect (tagn)
2. What a dog does to a bone (gawn)
3. To quit a job (sireng)
4. To rule (ernig)

USING THE WORD BANK

Match the Word Bank word in Column A with its definition or synonym in Column B.

Column A	Column B
1. apprenticed	a. pretended
2. engulfing	b. deception
3. mania	c. put to death
4. feigned	d. trained
5. ensued	e. excessive enthusiasm
6. dispatched	f. swallowing up
7. pretense	g. followed
8. immersed	h. submerged

◆ Literary Focus

BIOGRAPHY

A **biography** is an account of a person's life, written by another person. It often focuses on the individual's achievements and explains the difficulties that the subject had to overcome.

1. What do you think Longstreet wants you to know about Hokusai?
2. Find two details from "Hokusai: The Old Man Mad About Drawing" that help create a strong impression about its subject.
3. For what reasons do you think Hokusai and Zaremski are good subjects for biographies?

◆ Build Grammar Skills

USING who AND whom

Many people have problems deciding when to use *whom* instead of *who*. *Who* is in the subjective case; use it for the subject of a sentence or a clause. *Whom* is the objective case; use it for a direct object, an indirect object, or an object of a preposition.

Subject: To all of you *who* are going to live as long as I do, I promise . . .

Direct Object: Hokusai was an artist *whom* others imitated. [Others imitated *whom*.]

Object of a Preposition: At *whom* were the shots directed?

Practice On your paper, complete the following sentences with *who* or *whom*.

1. The guards, ___?___ led the prisoners to the loft, were silent.
2. From ___?___ did Hokusai learn to draw?
3. To ___?___ did the prisoner explain the escape plans?
4. ___?___ asked for a woodcut of Mt. Fuji?
5. The man ___?___ the Nazis pursued.

Writing Application Write a short description of Hokusai or Zaremski, using *who* and *whom* at least once each.

Build Your Portfolio

 Idea Bank

Writing

1. Advice Letters Write a letter asking advice about how to overcome an obstacle. Then, write the response that either Hokusai or Zaremski might offer.

2. Casting Memo Write a memo suggesting actors to play parts in a movie about Zaremski's life. Give reasons for your choices.

3. Biography Write a short biography about a person you admire. Stress the individual's admirable accomplishments and the challenges he or she faced. Include direct quotations whenever possible.

Speaking and Listening

4. Radio Play [Group Activity] With a group of classmates, adapt "Not to Go With the Others" as a radio play. Rehearse first; then perform or record the play for the class. **[Performing Arts Link]**

5. Dialogue [Group Activity] With a classmate, write and perform a dialogue that Hokusai and Zaremski might have about the importance of not giving up. Perform the dialogue for the class. **[Performing Arts Link]**

Projects

6. Holocaust Exhibit Research information about the concentration camps and political prisons run by the Nazis. Collect copies of paintings, photographs, and first-person accounts of the Holocaust. Prepare an exhibit about the Holocaust for your classmates. **[Social Studies Link]**

7. Art Catalog Research the life and works of Hokusai. Then, create an art catalog in which you give a brief biography of the artist and his works. Include photocopies of some of Hokusai's most famous drawings in your catalog. **[Art Link]**

 Writing Mini-Lesson

Testimonial

A testimonial is a short speech that expresses appreciation or gratitude for an individual. Testimonials are usually given at dinners or meetings that honor the subject of the speech. Certainly, both Hokusai and Zaremski would be worthy subjects for this kind of praise. Choose a person you admire, and write a testimonial to him or her.

Writing Skills Focus: Support With Examples

A testimonial contains main points supported by **examples** that illustrate why the subject is admirable. Notice how Longstreet supports a main point—that Hokusai was unpredictable and forever changing—with these examples:

Model From "Hokusai: . . ."
A great show-off, he painted with his fingers, toothpicks, a bottle, an eggshell; he worked left-handed, from the bottom up, and from left to right.

Prewriting Brainstorm for examples, details, facts and incidents that show your individual in the most positive light. Group your notes according to the points they make about the person. Organize your ideas in an outline.

Drafting Draft your testimonial, emphasizing your points and supporting them with examples. Include transitions to make your thoughts flow smoothly.

Revising Read your testimonial aloud to a partner. Ask whether or not you have included enough examples to show why your individual is admirable, and revise accordingly. Proofread your draft for errors in grammar.

> ◆ **Grammar Application**
> Be sure that you have used the correct forms of *who* and *whom* in your testimonial.

Hokusai: The Old Man Mad About Drawing/Not to Go With the Others ◆ 661

 Idea Bank

Following are suggestions for matching the Idea Bank topics with your students' performance levels and learning modalities:

Customize for *Performance Levels*
Less Advanced Students: 2, 6, 7
Average Students: 3, 4, 5, 6, 7
More Advanced Students: 1, 4, 5, 6, 7

Customize for *Learning Modalities*
Verbal/Linguistic: 1, 2, 3, 4, 5, 6, 7
Visual/Spatial: 6, 7
Bodily/Kinesthetic: 4, 5
Logical/Mathematical: 7
Interpersonal: 4, 5
Intrapersonal: 1, 2, 3, 6, 7

 Writing Mini-Lesson

Refer students to the Writing Handbook in the back of the book for instruction on the writing process and for further information on testimonials. Have students use the Main Idea and Supporting Details Organizer in **Writing and Language Transparencies,** p. 61, to organize their examples.

 Writer's Solution

Writers at Work Videodisc
Have students view the videodisc segment on Reports (Ch. 7), featuring biographer Virginia Hamilton, to learn how she feels about research, and how she goes about it for her own work.

Play frames 9330 to 17762

Writing Lab CD-ROM
Have students complete the tutorial on Reports. Follow these steps:
1. Have students use the interactive models on grouping ideas, writing a thesis statement, and organizing examples according to different plans.
2. Have students draft on computer.
3. Have students use the Proofreading Checklist when revising.

Writer's Solution Sourcebook
Have students use Chapter 7, "Reports," pp. 200–233, for further support. The chapter includes in-depth instruction on citing sources, p. 231.

✓ ASSESSMENT OPTIONS

Formal Assessment, Selection Test, pp. 192–194, and Assessment Resources Software. The selection test is designed so that it can be easily customized to the performance levels of your students.
Alternative Assessment, p. 44, includes options for less advanced students, more advanced students, interpersonal learners, visual/spatial learners, logical/mathematical learners, verbal/linguistic learners, and bodily/kinesthetic learners.

PORTFOLIO ASSESSMENT
Use the following rubrics in the **Alternative Assessment** booklet to assess student writing:
Advice Letters: Problem/Solution, p. 97
Casting Memo: Business Letter/Memo, p. 109
Biography: Research Report/Paper, p. 102
Writing Mini-Lesson: Expression, p. 90

Prepare and Engage

Establish Writing Guidelines

Review the following key characteristics of a public-service announcement:

- A public-service announcement is intended to educate, advise, or persuade the public to respond to an issue of public concern.

- A public-service announcement may include visuals or sound along with words, depending on whether it appears in print, or on radio or TV.

- A public-service announcement must use examples, reasons, or facts to support the position.

You may want to distribute the scoring rubric for Persuasion, p. 101 in **Alternative Assessment,** to make students aware of the criteria on which they will be evaluated. See the suggestions on p. 664 for how to customize the rubric to this workshop.

Refer students to the Writing Handbook in the back of the book for instruction on the writing process and further information on persuasion.

 Writer's Solution

Writers at Work Videodisc

To introduce students to persuasive writing, and to show them how environmentalist Kate Mitchell uses persuasion, play the videodisc segment on Persuasion (Ch. 6).

Play frames 3 to 7453

Writing Lab CD-ROM

If your students have access to computers, you may want to have them work in the tutorial on Persuasion to complete all or part of their summaries. Follow these steps:

1. Have students view the interactive model of a public-service announcement.
2. Have students use the Brainstormer activity for topic ideas.
3. Allow students to draft on computer.
4. When revising, have students use the interactive instruction on word choice.

Writer's Solution Sourcebook

Students can find additional support, including instruction on using active and passive voice, pp. 197–198, in the chapter on Persuasion, pp. 166–199.

Persuasive Writing
Public-Service Announcement

Writing Process Workshop

The writers in this section share important information with others. One way they could bring their information to a larger audience is through public-service announcements. A **public-service announcement** is a message intended to educate, advise, or persuade the public about an issue of public concern. It involves words plus visuals or sound, depending on whether the announcement appears in print, on radio, or on television.

Write a public-service announcement. Use the following writing skills, introduced in this section's Writing Mini-Lessons, to help you make your point:

Writing Skills Focus

▶ **Choose an appropriate tone** for your subject and audience. (See p. 630.)

▶ **Strive for clarity** to ensure that you get your points across. (See p. 641.)

▶ **Support your points.** Examples, reasons, and statistics will help you persuade, advise, educate, or inform. (See p. 661.)

The following excerpt is from a public-service announcement encouraging those who have the right to vote to use it.

WRITING MODEL

If you enjoy your freedom, then exercise your right to vote! ① In this country, we are entitled to choose our leaders, yet each November, millions don't bother to show up at the voting booths. In fact, almost half the eligible voters don't vote in a presidential election. ② Make sure you are not one of those people. Don't throw away your precious right to vote. ③

① The purpose behind this public-service announcement is clearly stated.

② This startling statistic supports the writer's point.

③ The writer uses a forceful tone to try to persuade readers to vote.

662 ◆ Nonfiction

 Beyond the Classroom

Community Connection

Public Information Public-service announcements serve to inform, educate, or persuade a community about issues of concern. Ask students to describe public-service announcements they have read, heard, or viewed. Create a list of topics that these announcements cover. Then create another list of public-service topics for which students have not heard an announcement. Suggest to students that they concentrate on issues within the school that may be of special concern. They may want to look at the editorial section of a local newspaper to get more topic ideas.

In groups, have students choose a topic from the list they created. Then have them consider what points they want to address in a public-service announcement. Have a member of each group explain their plan for the announcement. Encourage the rest of the class to offer advice about what will or won't work, and why.

Prewriting

State Your Purpose First, you must have something to say. What is your purpose in calling people to action? To inspire change? To get people to think about something seriously? Here are a few suggestions:

Topic Ideas

- Persuade your audience to take care of their environment
- Advise people on saving or spending money wisely
- Educate teenagers on maintaining good health
- Inform parents of issues that concern teenagers

Define Your Audience Who will hear or read your announcement? Before you begin, define your "target audience" very specifically. These questions may help:

▶ How old is your audience?
▶ What do they care about?
▶ What gender are they?
▶ Where do they live?
▶ What do they have in common?
▶ What do they already know about the topic?

Review your answers to these questions. Then, choose information that would appeal to this audience.

Choose Strong Examples Gather information or examples that will illustrate the points you are making. Statistics are often a strong way of supporting your points.

Drafting

State Your Message With Clarity Because a public-service announcement is usually brief, you must be clear about your message. Don't try to say too much, or your message may become unfocused.

Use Examples That Support Work in examples that support your main points. If your examples don't directly support your subject, people will be confused by your message.

Use an Appropriate Tone Choose words that communicate your attitude toward your subject and audience. For example, if you are scolding people for not voting, use a stern tone to let them know how serious the issue is.

DRAFTING/REVISING

Applying Language Skills: Using Appositives

An **appositive** is a noun phrase, usually set off by commas, that further identifies or defines the noun it follows:

Women's suffrage, the right to vote, was denied nationwide until 1920.

In a public-service announcement, you may identify or define something or someone using an appositive.

Practice Copy these sentences into your notebook. Combine them so one of the sentences becomes an appositive phrase.

1. Heart disease affects us all. Heart disease is the leading cause of death.
2. Clean water is everyone's business. Clean water is our most basic need.
3. Walking is a great exercise. Walking is a lot of fun.

Writing Application As you write your public-service announcement, include at least one appositive and punctuate it correctly.

Writer's Solution Connection Language Lab

For help punctuating appositives, complete the lesson on Commas in the Punctuation unit.

Applying Language Skills

Using Appositives Explain to students that the word *appositive* comes from a Latin verb meaning "to be near or next to." An appositive is placed next to another noun or pronoun to identify, rename, or explain it.

Answers
Suggested responses:
1. Heart disease, the leading cause of death, affects us all.
2. Clean water, our most basic need, is everyone's business.
3. A great exercise, walking is a lot of fun.

Writer's Solution

For additional instruction and practice, have students use the practice page on Appositives in Phrases, p. 48, in the *Writer's Solution Grammar Practice Book.*

Prewriting
Encourage students to scan headlines of local newspapers for ideas for their public-service announcements. Suggest that students look for issues that are of public concern, whether locally or nationally.

Customize for
Less Proficient Writers
Explain to students that their public-service announcement should be brief and should not try to cover more than one topic at a times. Suggest that students use the Cluster Organizer, p. 73, from **Writing and Language Transparencies** to organize their topic into subtopics and supporting details. Students may then want to consider writing their public-service announcements on one of the subtopics rather than the whole main topic.

Writer's Solution

For additional help on considering audience and purpose, suggest that students view the audio-annotated models in the Prewriting section of the tutorial on Persuasion in the *Writer's Solution Writing Lab CD-ROM.* They can see how the language and tone of the writer changes, depending on his or her purpose.

Drafting
Encourage students to think of an interesting introduction that will grab readers'/viewers'/listeners' attention. Students may want to consider beginning their announcements with a question or a brief anecdote.

Writer's Solution

Writing Lab CD-ROM
Students can develop strategies for writing their drafts by viewing the audio-annotated writing models of different kinds of organization in the Drafting section of the tutorial on Persuasion.

Revising

Have students read their public service announcements in pairs, pointing out any areas that need clarification.

 Writer's Solution

In the tutorial on Persuasion, have students use the Peer editing checklist to evaluate their partner's writing.

Publishing

Suggest that students videotape their public-service announcements. Encourage them to speak clearly and use visuals for additional support.

Reinforce and Extend

Review the Writing Guidelines After students have completed their papers, review the characteristics of a public-service announcement.

Applying Language Skills
Using *Who*, *That*, and *Which* Correctly Relative pronouns connect adjective clauses to the words they modify and act as subjects, direct objects, objects of prepositions, or adjectives in the clauses.

Answers
Possible responses:
1. Voting is a right that should be exercised.
2. My father is a man who always votes.
3. The United States is a country that depends on public opinion.

 Writer's Solution

For additional instruction, have students use Twenty Common Usage Problems in the *Writer's Solution Grammar Practice Book*, p. 92.

Writing Process Workshop

EDITING/PROOFREADING

APPLYING LANGUAGE SKILLS: Using *Who*, *That*, and *Which* Correctly

Who, *that*, and *which* are relative pronouns. They introduce clauses that add information about a person or thing. Use *that* and *which* to refer to things. Use *who* or *whom* to refer to people.

- The computer is a tool *that* changed the world.
- Baseball, *which* is played all over the world, began in the United States.
- She is a woman *who* changed the world.

Practice As you copy these sentences into your notebook, correct the use of *who*, *that*, and *which* as necessary.

1. Voting is a right who should be exercised.
2. My father is a man that always votes.
3. The United States is a country which depends on public opinion.

Writing Application As you write your public-service announcement, use *who*, *that*, and *which* correctly.

Writer's Solution Writing Lab

For more help with revising, use the Self-Evaluation Checklist in the Revising section of the Persuasion tutorial.

664 ◆ *Nonfiction*

Revising

Use a Checklist Use the Writing Skills Focus list on p. 662 as a checklist for your self-revision.

Ask a Listener Share your announcement with a partner. Read your draft to your partner, and ask these questions:
- ▶ Does my opening grab your attention?
- ▶ Are my words strong?
- ▶ Is my purpose clear?
- ▶ Is there enough information?
- ▶ Have I used an appropriate tone?
- ▶ Does the announcement hold your interest until the end?

If your partner answers no to any of these questions, make revisions that will enable your partner to answer yes.

REVISION MODEL

People all over the world are struggling for simple
① , such as the right to vote.
human rights. In April 1994, South Africans had to stand
② The polls had to stay open for four days to
accommodate everyone who wanted to vote.
in line for days to vote, and they did. In the United States,
more than half the people eligible to vote do not do so. They let
③ Don't be one of those people!
others make the choice for them. ∧

① For clarity, the writer adds the specific human right that is the subject of this announcement.
② The writer adds this information to strengthen her argument that voting is a precious right.
③ The writer ends with a forceful tone.

Publishing and Presenting

School Turn your announcement into a colorful, eye-catching poster. Choose a visual that makes sense and stands out. Display your poster somewhere in your school.

Radio Get permission to read your announcement over your school's public address system, or send it to a local radio station. If appropriate, include music or sound effects to help make your point.

✓ ASSESSMENT		4	3	2	1
PORTFOLIO ASSESSMENT Use the rubric on Summary in the **Alternative Assessment** booklet, p. 94, to assess the students' writing. Add these criteria to customize this rubric to this assignment.	**Clear Purpose**	The purpose of the announcement is clearly stated and supported with strong examples	The purpose of the announcement is not clearly stated, but examples make it clear.	The purpose of the announcement is vague, and there are few examples to support it.	The purpose of the announcement is vague, and there are no examples to support it.
	Using *Who*, *That*, and *Which*	Relative pronouns are used correctly to introduce clauses.	Relative pronouns are mostly used correctly, but sometimes are interchanged.	Relative pronouns are often interchanged.	Relative pronouns are not used correctly.

Real-World Reading Skills Workshop

Evaluating Advertisements

Strategies for Success

Every time you turn on the radio or the television or pick up a newspaper or a magazine, you encounter advertisements. Advertisers try to persuade you to buy, do, or believe something. Whatever forms these ads take, you need to decide how to respond to them.

Recognize Persuasion As you evaluate an advertisement, remember that its purpose is to persuade you. When deciding how to respond to an advertisement, try to make an informed decision. Do not simply go with your "gut reaction."

Evaluate the Message In order to make an informed decision, first examine the writer's statements. Evaluate them by answering questions like these:

▶ Are the statements true?
▶ Do the statements contain facts, or are they statements of the writer's opinions?
▶ To what feelings or beliefs is the advertisement appealing?

Make a Decision After evaluating the ad, decide whether or not you accept the

advertiser's claims. If you accept them, you will probably make the purchase or do what the advertiser wishes. If not, you will probably not make a purchase. With either choice, you will have made an informed decision.

Apply the Strategies

You are looking for a special gift for your mother, an avid baseball fan. Evaluate the claims of this advertisement before deciding whether to make a purchase.

EVERY BASEBALL FAN MUST HAVE THE SOUVENIR PRINTING PLATES OF MCGWIRE'S RECORD HOME RUNS!!!

If you love baseball, you'll have to have these beautiful metal souvenir plates from home-run history! These copies of the *Sun's* front pages capture the special moment forever. They will look perfect on the den wall, and you will be the envy of every baseball fan.

To order call 1-XXX-BASEBALL.
Don't Delay! Limited Offer!
(Plates cost $10.00 each plus $3.00 postage and handling.)

---

1. What is the writer's purpose? How do you know?
2. What does this advertisement claim the product will do?
3. What statements are written to persuade you to make a purchase?
4. Would you buy a printing plate as a gift for your mother?

✔ Here are some forms of advertising that are important to evaluate:
▶ Infomercials on television
▶ Ads for cosmetics
▶ Flyers

◆ Build Grammar Skills

Reviewing Correct Pronoun Use

The selections in Part 1 include instruction on the following:

- Subjective Case Pronouns
- Objective Case Pronouns
- Use of *who* and *whom*

This instruction is reinforced with the Build Grammar Skills practice pages in **Selection Support,** pp. 226, 232, and 239.

As you review conjunctions, you may wish to include the following:

- Subjective Case in Compound Constructions

Sometimes, using the subjective case is a problem when the pronoun is part of a compound subject. In these cases, check by mentally removing the other subject. For example:

Stephanie and *I* walked the dog.

(*I walked the dog.*) If the pronoun is part of a compound predicate nominative, the sentence must be reworded.

For example:

The teachers are Mr. Green and *she*. (*She* and Mr. Green are the teachers.)

- Using Pronouns in Elliptical Clauses

An elliptical clause is one in which some words are omitted because they are understood. Sentences with elliptical clauses are often comparisons, divided into two parts connected by *than* or *as*.

For example:

Steve is faster than she. [is]

In this sentence, the omitted word is *is*. If the words left out come after the pronoun, use a nominative pronoun, because it is the subject of an omitted verb. If the words left out come before the pronoun, use an objective pronoun, because the pronoun will be an object.

For example:

Losing the game means more to Judy than her.

In this sentence, the omitted words are *it means to*. The pronoun takes the objective case.

---

case (kās) *n.* **1** *Grammar* the form of a noun, pronoun, or adjective that shows how it is related to the other words around it (Example: in "He hit me," the subject *he* is in the nominative case and the object *me* is in the objective case)

Pronoun Case Case is the form of a personal pronoun that shows its use in a sentence. To use pronouns correctly, you must know when to use the subjective case and when to use the objective case. (See pp. 629 and 640.)

Singular		Plural	
Subjective	**Objective**	**Subjective**	**Objective**
I, you, he, she, it	me, you, him, her, it	we, you, they	us, you, them

Use the subjective case when the pronoun is a subject or a subject complement:

Subject of a Verb: ". . . *I* climbed up a ladder . . ."

Subject Complement (Predicate pronoun): The first people in the barn were *she* and *I*.

Use the objective case when the pronoun is a direct object, an indirect object, or an object of the preposition:

Direct Object: "But then something snapped *me* out of my sense of loss. . . ."

Indirect Object: Susan B. Anthony's fight gave *us* the right to vote.

Object of a Preposition: For *whom* did she vote?

Who and Whom You can use the forms of *who* either as interrogative or relative pronouns. *Who* is the subjective form; *whom* is the objective form. (See p. 660.)

Subject: *Who* can believe that wasps could create such an amazing piece of architecture?

Direct Object: I wondered about the man *whom* I had met earlier.

Object of a Preposition: With *whom* did Susan B. Anthony live?

Practice Choose the correct pronoun to complete the following sentences:

1. (We, Us) believe that everyone should explore nature.
2. We found (they, them) in the tree.
3. His uncle gave (he, him) a baseball.
4. That is (he, him) up at bat.
5. Caroline and (I, me) are thankful to (she, her) for defending our rights.
6. (Who, whom) hasn't wondered about the mysteries of nature?
7. To (who, whom) did you give your notes?

Grammar in Writing

✔ To determine which pronoun case to use in a compound structure, say the sentence to yourself without the other part of the compound construction.

My mother took Melinda and _____?_____ to see Hokusai's paintings.

Say: My mother took *me* to see Hokusai's paintings.

Correct: My mother took Melinda and *me* to see Hokusai's paintings.

Answers
Practice
1. We believe that everyone should explore nature.
2. We found them in the tree.
3. His uncle gave him a baseball.
4. That is he up at bat.
5. Caroline and I are thankful to her for defending our rights.
6. Who hasn't wondered about the mysteries of nature?
7. To whom did you give your notes?

PART 2   *Essays and Speeches*

A Social History of Missouri (detail), 1936, Thomas Hart Benton, ©T.H. Benton and R.P. Benton Testamentary Trusts/Licensed by VAGA, New York, NY

Essays and Speeches ◆ 667

The selections in this section are examples of essays and speeches. "Debbie" is a veterinarian's account of his experiences with a stray cat. "Forest Fire" presents a vivid description of a fire in California. In "How to Be Polite Online," readers learn the etiquette of being on the Internet. "The Trouble with Television" is a persuasive essay about the dangers of television in society. Finally, "The American Dream" is a speech by Martin Luther King, Jr., about the problems America faced in the struggle for civil rights.

Customize for
Varying Student Needs
When assigning the selections in this section to your students, keep in mind the following factors:

"Debbie"
• A narrative essay by James Herriot
• May be of special interest to students who like animals

"Forest Fire"
• A descriptive essay
• Students may need help with vocabulary

"How to Be Polite Online"
• An expository essay
• Will be especially informative for students who actively surf the Internet

"The Trouble with Television"
• A persuasive essay about the potential harm of watching television
• Students may need help with vocabulary

"The American Dream"
• A speech by Martin Luther King, Jr.
• Includes a Beyond Literature Social Studies connection

Humanities: Art

A Social History of Missouri (detail), 1936, by Thomas Hart Benton
    Thomas Hart Benton (1889–1975) was a leader of the regionalist field of painting. He spent many years roaming the United States, especially through the South and the Midwest. The subjects of his paintings were drawn from these trips and include mountaineers, farmers, and other characters from small town and rural life.
    This work is part of a large mural done by Benton in the 1930's, when he was one of

America's most active muralists. This mural can be seen at the Missouri State Capitol in Jefferson City.
    Have students study the painting, and then ask them to describe the action and the characters.
Most students will say the man on the platform is giving a speech, perhaps a speech about the person in the portrait that stands behind him. The other two men on the platform with the speechmaker look a little uninterested. They are probably city or town officials. It looks as if the speech is being given at a city or town hall, from the building in the background.

667

Guide for Reading

OBJECTIVES

1. To read, comprehend, and interpret three essays
2. To relate essays to personal experience
3. To set a purpose for reading
4. To recognize the characteristics of a narrative essay, a descriptive essay, and an expository essay
5. To build vocabulary in context and learn the word root -vac-
6. To use pronouns that agree with their antecedents
7. To write an interview, using quotation marks
8. To respond to essays through writing, speaking and listening, and projects

SKILLS INSTRUCTION

Vocabulary:
Using the Word Root -vac-

Spelling:
Spell the j Sound With g

Grammar:
Pronoun and Antecedent Agreement

Reading Strategy:
Set a Purpose for Reading

Literary Focus:
Essay

Writing:
Using Quotation Marks

Speaking and Listening:
Role Play (Teacher Edition)

Viewing and Representing:
Computer Symbol Imagery (Teacher Edition)

Critical Viewing:
Assess; Speculate; Deduce; Interpret; Infer

PORTFOLIO OPPORTUNITIES

Writing: Computer Checklist; Essay; Analysis

Writing Mini-Lesson: Interview

Speaking and Listening: Role Play; Oral Interpretation

Projects: Survey and Analysis; Firefighting Report

Meet the Authors:

James Herriot (1916–1995)

Born in Scotland, James Herriot wrote many memorable true stories about his fifty years as a veterinarian. The incidents Herriot describes, such as the one in "Debbie," have filled more than ten books and inspired a popular television series. Although he didn't start writing until he was fifty, he found a natural talent for describing the people and animals that made his career memorable. As Herriot told one interviewer, "I think it was the fact that I liked it so much that made the writing just come out of me automatically."

Anaïs Nin (1903–1977)

A native of France, Anaïs Nin grew up in the United States. At age eleven, she began the writing that continued throughout her life. Although she wrote novels and short stories, Nin was best known for her six diaries spanning sixty years. "Forest Fire," from the fifth diary, illustrates how Nin looked at life "as an adventure and a tale."

Virginia Shea

A widely published journalist, Virginia Shea's writing has appeared in newspapers and journals. After attending Princeton, she moved to Sunnyvale, California, with her husband and four cats. Inspired by the booming computer industry there, Shea became an expert on Internet manners and skills. Recognizing her insights into the do's and don'ts of on-line communication, the San Jose Mercury News declared Shea the "network manners guru."

668 ◆ Nonfiction

More About the Authors

James Herriot is the pen name of James Alfred Wight. After serving in World War II, he became a veterinarian in a rural area of Yorkshire. In 1966 he began writing to record his experiences as a veterinarian.

Anaïs Nin began her literary career in 1932 by publishing a critical analysis of D. H. Lawrence's works. She wrote and published books at her own expense until 1966, when the first volume of her diary earned her the literary recognition she had worked so long to achieve. Her writing reflects her interest in psychology.

◆ LITERATURE AND YOUR LIFE

CONNECT YOUR EXPERIENCE

In the course of daily life—on the bus, in a store, or at a school game—you probably observe funny, interesting, or frightening things that you relate to your family and friends. In the following essays, James Herriot, Anaïs Nin, and Virginia Shea share their observations of the world around them.

THEMATIC FOCUS: Living Each Day

Look for the surprises of everyday life as you read the essays that follow.

◆ Background for Understanding

SCIENCE

Anaïs Nin writes about a raging forest fire she witnesses while living in California. In addition to time-tested firefighting strategies like the ones Nin describes, today's firefighters use the latest technology to combat wildfires. Once a forest fire breaks out, airplanes and helicopters are often used to gather data and spray fire retardants. In NASA's Firefly system, airplanes fly an infrared scanner over a fire in progress. The information is relayed to a satellite and then to firefighters on the ground so that they can attack the fire efficiently.

◆ Build Vocabulary

WORD ROOTS: -vac-

The word evacuees contains the word root -vac-, which means "empty." An evacuee is someone who is removed from a place, leaving that place empty.

WORD BANK

Which word from the list means "things one is deprived of"? Check the Build Vocabulary box on page 673 to see if you chose correctly.

privations
evacuees
tenacious
dissolution
ravaging
implemented
encompasses

Prentice Hall Literature Program Resources

REINFORCE / RETEACH / EXTEND

Selection Support Pages
Build Vocabulary: Word Roots: -vac-, p. 242
Build Spelling Skills, p. 243
Build Grammar Skills: Pronoun and Antecedent Agreement, p. 244
Reading Strategy: Set a Purpose for Reading, p. 245
Literary Focus: Essay, p. 246

Strategies for Diverse Student Needs, pp. 89–90

Beyond Literature Workplace Skills: Acting Responsibly, p. 45

Formal Assessment Selection Test, pp. 195–197, Assessment Resources Software

Alternative Assessment, p. 45

Writing and Language Transparencies
Sensory Language Chart, p. 69

Art Transparencies Art Transparency 3, pp. 15–18

Resource Pro CD-ROM
"Debbie"; "Forest Fire"; "How to Be Polite Online"

 Listening to Literature Audiocassettes
"Debbie"; "Forest Fire"; "How to Be Polite Online"

Debbie ◆ Forest Fire ◆ How to Be Polite Online ◆

◆ Literary Focus

ESSAY

An **essay** is a short nonfiction work about a particular subject. A **narrative essay,** like "Debbie," tells a true story about real people. You learn about them the same way you learn about characters in fiction—through their actions, words, and thoughts. In a **descriptive essay,** such as "Forest Fire," the author describes events and feelings by including images and details that show how things look, sound, smell, taste, or feel. An **expository essay,** like "How to Be Polite Online," presents information, explains a process, or discusses ideas.

◆ Reading Strategy

SET A PURPOSE FOR READING

When reading nonfiction, you may become bewildered by the amount of factual information you encounter. A good way to focus your reading is to **set a purpose** before you read. Read the first paragraph of an essay, and then stop to set a purpose for reading the rest.

A KWL chart like the one below, set up for "How to Be Polite Online," can help you focus your purpose. A KWL chart can show what you **K**now about the subject, what you **W**ant to know, and what you **L**earn from your reading.

K	W	L
How to send e-mail	How to be polite online	?

Guide for Reading ◆ 669

Preparing for Standardized Tests

Grammar Understanding pronoun and antecedent agreement (the grammar skill for this selection) will help students as they speak and write and as they answer standardized test questions. Students may be asked to identify or construct sentences that are grammatically correct. Use the following sample test question, which is based on "Debbie":

Select the best replacement for the underlined portion of this sentence:

Buster was too energetic in the way <u>she</u> played with the old hounds.

(A) they   (C) he
(B) it   (D) No Change

Students should recall that Buster is a male kitten. (D) is not the correct answer because a personal pronoun must agree with its antecedent in gender and number; the sentence needs a singular, masculine personal pronoun. (A) *they* is plural and feminine; (B) *it* has no gender; therefore the correct answer is (C), which is singular and masculine. For further practice, use Build Grammar Skills in **Selection Support,** p. 244.

Interest Grabber To draw students' attention to the subject matter of the selection, use Art Transparency 3 in **Art Transparencies,** pp. 15–18. Show students *Cat and Spider.* Then ask them to think about an animal they personally know or have known in the past, or one such as Lassie from television or a movie. Ask them to freewrite for five minutes about the animal's unique personality. Then, explain that they will read a narrative essay by an author who firmly believes that animals can develop personalities that make them personal friends and beloved companions.

◆ Build Grammar Skills

Pronoun and Antecedent Agreement If you wish to introduce the grammar concept for this selection before students read, refer to the instruction on p. 682.

Customize for
Less Proficient Readers
Listening to these essays may provide an opportunity for students to increase their enjoyment of the selections and enhance comprehension. You may wish to have groups of students read the selection aloud, or make use of the audiocassette.

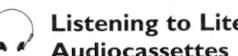 **Listening to Literature Audiocassettes**

Customize for
More Advanced Students
Ask students to consider the role of the narrator in each essay. What point of view does the narrator use? How does this choice influence the essay? How would the nature of the essay change if it were written from a different point of view? Have students write a comparison of the three essays and analyze the point of view selected in each essay.

Customize for
English Language Learners
Help students with the numerous medical and scientific terms on p. 672, such as *mucous membranes, palpated the abdomen, mass,* and *viscera.*

669

One-Minute Insight

"Debbie" is the heartwarming story of an independent and regal stray cat whose personality traits and actions intrigue both the woman who feeds her and the caring veterinarian who treats her serious illness.

◆ Literary Focus

❶ Essay Ask students to describe how Herriot begins this essay. *He does not use expository details to set the scene or provide background. He simply begins his narrative, as if he were speaking personally to his audience.*

▶ Critical Viewing ◀

❷ Assess *Some students may say that this cat looks strong, well fed, and agile. Others may say that the look in its eyes suggests fear, indicating that it may be timid.*

Thematic Focus

❸ Living Each Day Many people's daily lives involve animals. Pet owners and people who work with animals often notice unique personality traits. Ask students what they can tell about a person who notices unique animal characteristics. *The person probably takes animals seriously; such people may see aspects of themselves in the animal's behavior, or regard animals as companions.*

Customize for
Visual/Spatial Learners

"Debbie" is set in a tiny Yorkshire village that may look very different from the American towns students are familiar with. Photographs or travel brochures of the region may help students gain a sense of the essay's setting.

Debbie James Herriot

Autumn Leaves, 1994, Ditz, Private Collection

◀ **Critical Viewing**
Would you think the cat in this painting was "a timid little thing"? Why or why not? [Assess] ❷

❶ I first saw her one autumn day when I was called to see one of Mrs. Ainsworth's dogs, and I looked in some surprise at the furry black creature sitting before the fire.

"I didn't know you had a cat," I said.

The lady smiled. "We haven't, this is Debbie."

"Debbie?"

"Yes, at least that's what we call her. She's a stray. Comes here two or three times a week and we give her some food. I don't know where she lives but I believe she spends a lot of her time around one of the farms along the road."

"Do you ever get the feeling that she wants to stay with you?"

"No." Mrs. Ainsworth shook her head. "She's a timid little thing. Just creeps in, has some food then flits away. There's something so appealing about her but she doesn't seem to want to let me or anybody into her life."

I looked again at the little cat. "But she isn't just having food today."

"That's right. It's a funny thing but every now and again she slips through here into the lounge and sits by the fire for a few minutes. It's as though she was giving herself a treat."

"Yes . . . I see what you mean." There was no doubt there was something unusual in the attitude of the little animal. She was sitting bolt upright on the thick rug which lay before the fireplace in which the coals glowed and flamed. She made no effort to curl up or wash herself or do anything other than gaze quietly **❸**

670 ◆ Nonfiction

 Block Scheduling Strategies

Consider these suggestions to take advantage of extended class time:

• Review the definition of an essay, then use the Literary Focus, p. 669, to examine the three types of essays students will read in this grouping. Have students read and respond to each essay. Have them work in small groups to share and discuss answers to the Guides for Responding on pp. 674, 677, 681, and 682.

• To prepare students for the Writing Mini-Lesson, p. 683, teach the Speaking and Listening Mini-Lesson on p. 676 of the Teacher's Edition,

or use the Firefighting Report Project in the Idea Bank on p. 683.

• Use the notes for customizing for Verbal/Linguistic Learners on pp. 672 and 673 of the Teacher's Edition to engage students with a special interest in animals and further their understanding of the essay.

• Use the recordings of the essays to enhance students' enjoyment and understanding, and to extend their appreciation of the essay genre.

 Listening to Literature Audiocassettes

ahead. And there was something in the dusty black of her coat, the half-wild scrawny look of her, that gave me a clue. This was a special event in her life, a rare and wonderful thing; she was lapping up a comfort undreamed of in her daily existence.

As I watched she turned, crept soundlessly from the room and was gone.

"That's always the way with Debbie," Mrs. Ainsworth laughed. "She never stays more than ten minutes or so, then she's off."

Mrs. Ainsworth was a plumpish, pleasant-faced woman in her forties and the kind of client veterinary surgeons dream of; well off, generous, and the owner of three cosseted[1] Basset hounds. And it only needed the habitually mournful expression of one of the dogs to deepen a little and I was round there posthaste.[2] Today one of the Bassets had raised its paw and scratched its ear a couple of times and that was enough to send its mistress scurrying to the phone in great alarm.

So my visits to the Ainsworth home were frequent but undemanding, and I had ample opportunity to look out for the little cat that had intrigued me. On one occasion I spotted her nibbling daintily from a saucer at the kitchen door. As I watched she turned and almost floated on light footsteps into the hall then through the lounge door.

The three Bassets were already in residence, draped snoring on the fireside rug, but they seemed to be used to Debbie because two of them sniffed her in a bored manner and the third merely cocked a sleepy eye at her before flopping back on the rich pile.

Debbie sat among them in her usual posture; upright, intent, gazing absorbedly into the glowing coals. This time I tried to make friends with her. I approached her carefully but she leaned away as I stretched out my hand. However, by patient wheedling[3] and soft talk I managed to touch her and gently stroked her cheek with one finger. There was a moment when she responded by putting her head on one side and rubbing back against

my hand but soon she was ready to leave. Once outside the house she darted quickly along the road then through a gap in a hedge and the last I saw was the little black figure flitting over the rain-swept grass of a field.

"I wonder where she goes," I murmured half to myself.

Mrs. Ainsworth appeared at my elbow. "That's something we've never been able to find out."

It must have been nearly three months before I heard from Mrs. Ainsworth, and in fact I had begun to wonder at the Bassets' long symptomless run when she came on the phone.

It was Christmas morning and she was apologetic. "Mr. Herriot, I'm so sorry to bother you today of all days. I should think you want a rest at Christmas like anybody else." But her natural politeness could not hide the distress in her voice.

"Please don't worry about that," I said. "Which one is it this time?"

"It's not one of the dogs. It's . . . Debbie."

"Debbie? She's at your house now?"

"Yes. . . but there's something wrong. Please come quickly."

Driving through the marketplace I thought again that Darrowby on Christmas Day was like Dickens come to life; the empty square with the snow thick on the cobbles and hanging from the eaves of the fretted[4] lines of roofs; the shops closed and the colored lights of the Christmas trees winking at the windows of the clustering houses, warmly inviting against the cold white bulk of the fells[5] behind.

Mrs. Ainsworth's home was lavishly decorated with tinsel and holly, rows of drinks stood on the sideboard and the rich aroma of turkey and sage and onion stuffing wafted[6] from the kitchen. But her eyes were full of pain as she led me through to the lounge.

Debbie was there all right, but this time everything was different. She wasn't sitting upright in her usual position; she was

---

1. **cosseted** (käs´ it əd) adj.: Pampered; indulged.
2. **posthaste** (pōst´ hāst´) adv.: With great speed.
3. **wheedling** (hwēd´ liŋ) v.: Gentle, constant persuading.

4. **fretted** (fret´ əd) adj.: Decoratively arranged.
5. **fells** n.: Rocky or barren hills.
6. **wafted** (waf´ təd) v.: Moved lightly through the air.

Debbie ◆ 671

◆ **Literary Focus**

1 Essay *Debbie seemed to know that she was seriously ill, and brought her kitten to the one place where she had known comfort.*

Comprehension Check ☑

2 What has happened to Debbie? How does the veterinarian respond? *Debbie, who recently bore kittens, is dying of cancer. According to the vet, she is in a coma and dying.*

◆ **Critical Thinking**

3 Speculate Have students explain why Mrs. Ainsworth thinks that Debbie brought the kitten to her. *Mrs. Ainsworth believes that Debbie saw her home as a safe haven. When Debbie knew she was dying and would not be able to take care of her kitten, she used the last ounce of her strength to bring the kitten to Mrs. Ainsworth.*

Customize for
Verbal/Linguistic Learners
"Debbie" is told from the point of view of the veterinarian. Challenge students to use their imaginations to retell the story from the point of view of one of the animals: Debbie, Buster, or one of the dogs. Encourage them to include details that make it clear that the narrator is not human, and that reflect the kinds of concerns and observations they can imagine an animal might include in a story. Have students read their narrations to the other members of the class.

---

stretched quite motionless on her side, and huddled close to her lay a tiny black kitten.

I looked down in bewilderment. "What's happened here?"

◆ **Literary Focus**
What does Mrs. Ainsworth's story reveal about Debbie's personality?

"It's the strangest thing," Mrs. Ainsworth replied. "I haven't seen her for several weeks then she came in about two hours ago—sort of staggered into the kitchen, and she was carrying the kitten in her mouth. She took it through to the lounge and laid it on the rug and at first I was amused. But I could see all was not well because she sat as she usually does, but for a long time—over an hour—then she lay down like this and she hasn't moved."

I knelt on the rug and passed my hand over Debbie's neck and ribs. She was thinner than ever, her fur dirty and mudcaked. She did not resist as I gently opened her mouth. The tongue and mucous membranes were abnormally pale and the lips ice-cold against my fingers. When I pulled down her eyelid and saw the dead white conjunctiva[7] a knell[8] sounded in my mind.

I palpated[9] the abdomen with a grim certainty as to what I would find and there was no surprise, only a dull sadness as my fingers closed around a hard lobulated[10] mass deep among the viscera.[11] Massive lymphosarcoma.[12] Terminal and hopeless. I put my stethoscope on her heart and listened to the increasingly faint, rapid beat then I straightened up and sat on the rug looking sightlessly into the fireplace, feeling the warmth of the flames on my face.

Mrs. Ainsworth's voice seemed to come from afar. "Is she ill, Mr. Herriot?"

I hesitated. "Yes . . . yes, I'm afraid so. She has a malignant growth." I stood up. "There's absolutely nothing I can do. I'm sorry."

---

7. **conjunctiva** (kän' jəŋk tī' və) *n.*: Lining of the inner surface of the eyelids.
8. **knell** (nel) *n.*: Sound of a bell slowly ringing, as for a funeral.
9. **palpated** (pal' pāt ed) *v.*: Examined by touching.
10. **lobulated** (läb' yōō lā' təd) *adj.*: Subdivided.
11. **viscera** (vis' ər ə) *n.*: Internal organs.
12. **lymphosarcoma** (lim' fō sär kō' mə) *n.*: Malignant tumor in the tissue.

672 ◆ Nonfiction

"Oh!" Her hand went to her mouth and she looked at me wide-eyed. When at last she spoke her voice trembled. "Well, you must put her to sleep immediately. It's the only thing to do. We can't let her suffer."

"Mrs. Ainsworth," I said. "There's no need. She's dying now—in a coma—far beyond suffering."

She turned quickly away from me and was very still as she fought with her emotions. Then she gave up the struggle and dropped on her knees beside Debbie.

"Oh, poor little thing!" she sobbed and stroked the cat's head again and again as the tears fell unchecked on the matted fur. "What she must have come through. I feel I ought to have done more for her."

For a few moments I was silent, feeling her sorrow, so discordant among the bright seasonal colors of this festive room. Then I spoke gently.

"Nobody could have done more than you," I said. "Nobody could have been kinder."

"But I'd have kept her here—in comfort. It must have been terrible out there in the cold when she was so desperately ill—I daren't think about it. And having kittens, too—I . . . I wonder how many she did have?"

I shrugged. "I don't suppose we'll ever know. Maybe just this one. It happens sometimes. And she brought it to you, didn't she?"

"Yes . . . that's right . . . she did . . . she did." Mrs. Ainsworth reached out and lifted the bedraggled black morsel. She smoothed her finger along the muddy fur and the tiny mouth opened in a soundless miaow. "Isn't it strange? She was dying and she brought her kitten here. And on Christmas Day."

I bent and put my hand on Debbie's heart. There was no beat.

I looked up. "I'm afraid she's gone." I lifted the small body, almost feather light, wrapped it in the sheet which had been spread on the rug and took it out to the car.

When I came back Mrs. Ainsworth was still stroking the kitten. The tears had dried on her cheeks and she was brighteyed as she looked at me.

"I've never had a cat before," she said.

 Beyond the Classroom

Community Connection

Animal Care Most U. S. communities have public or private agencies that have been established to help animals that may be lost, unwanted, or injured. The SPCA, Society for the Prevention of Cruelty to Animals, is the name of one such organization that works to protect animals and to find adoptive homes. Humane societies such as the SPCA or local organizations may help investigate reports of cruelty to animals, work to enforce laws, and help deal with health threats that animals sometimes pose to the community. These organizations also educate children and adults about their responsibilities to animals and the advisability of animal birth control to help alleviate the problem of stray and unwanted animals. Staff may include animal health workers, veterinarians, public relations people, environmental scientists, and animal caretakers.

Have students research agencies or organizations in your area that serve the needs of animals or that deal with human health and safety issues related to animals. Interested students may wish to make a list of community contacts.

◆ **Reading Strategy**
Did you satisfy your purpose for reading? If so, set a new purpose before you finish the essay.

I smiled. "Well, it looks as though you've got one now."

And she certainly had. That kitten grew rapidly into a sleek handsome cat with a boisterous nature which earned him the name of Buster. In every way he was the opposite to his timid little mother. Not for him the privations of the

▲ **Critical Viewing** In what ways might an energetic kitten stir up the life of Basset hounds like these? [Speculate]

secret outdoor life; he stalked the rich carpets of the Ainsworth home like a king and the ornate collar he always wore added something more to his presence.

On my visits I watched his development with delight but the occasion which stays in my mind was the following Christmas Day, a year from his arrival.

I was out on my rounds as usual. I can't remember when I haven't had to work on Christmas Day because the animals have never got

◆ **Build Vocabulary**

privations (prī vā´ shənz) *n.*: Deprivation or lack of common comforts

round to recognizing it as a holiday; but with the passage of the years the vague resentment I used to feel has been replaced by philosophical acceptance. After all, as I tramped around the hillside barns in the frosty air I was working up a better appetite for my turkey than all the millions lying in bed or slumped by the fire.

I was on my way home, bathed in a rosy glow. I heard the cry as I was passing Mrs. Ainsworth's house.

"Merry Christmas, Mr. Herriot!" She was letting a visitor out of the front door and she waved at me gaily. "Come in and have a drink to warm you up."

I didn't need warming up but I pulled in to the curb without hesitation. In the house there was all the festive cheer of last year and the same glorious whiff of sage and onion which set my gastric[13] juices surging. But there was not the sorrow; there was Buster.

He was darting up to each of the dogs in turn, ears pricked, eyes blazing with devilment, dabbing a paw at them then streaking away.

Mrs. Ainsworth laughed. "You know, he plagues the life out of them. Gives them no peace."

She was right. To the Bassets, Buster's arrival was rather like the intrusion of an irreverent outsider into an exclusive London club. For a long time they had led a life of measured grace; regular sedate walks with their mistress, superb food in ample quantities and long snoring sessions on the rugs and armchairs. Their days followed one upon another in unruffled calm. And then came Buster.

He was dancing up to the youngest dog

---

13. **gastric** (gas´ trik) *adj.*: Of the stomach.

Debbie ◆ 673

◆ **Reading Strategy**

❹ **Set a Purpose for Reading** You may wish to remind students to set a new purpose for reading after Debbie dies—such as finding out what becomes of the kitten. *Students may respond that their established purpose for reading was to find out who Debbie was.*

▶**Critical Viewing**◀

❺ **Speculate** *Students may say that these Basset hounds look slow and awkward. A lively kitten might annoy them, take their food or toys, or otherwise drive them crazy and change their quiet lives.*

◆ **Literary Focus**

❻ **Essay** How does Herriot use the narrative elements of setting and character to compare Buster's rambunctious behavior to "the intrusion of an irreverent outsider into an exclusive London club"? *He describes the life that the dogs lead in the luxury of the Ainsworth home, where Buster's arrival upsets the calm and completely changes things.*

Customize for
Verbal/Linguistic Learners
In this essay, the narrator describes some of the personality traits Debbie and Buster demonstrate. Have students reread "Sancho" by Frank Dobie, pp. 400–404, which describes another animal that demonstrated surprising characteristics and actions. Challenge students to write a comparison-and-contrast essay that examines ways in which Sancho is similar to and different from Debbie and/or Buster. Students can explore how these unusual animals amaze the humans who know and love them.

Cross-Curricular Connection: Science

Cats Many people frequently choose cats as household pets. The domesticated cat that is kept as a pet today is a descendent of wildcats from long ago and a related family member of tigers, leopards, lions, and panthers. All members of the cat family are similar in that they are highly adapted to hunting. Buster's pouncing and teasing the basset hounds and retrieving a ball for Mrs. Ainsworth are examples of a cat's specialized skills that can be used to hunt prey.

Ask students if they have ever seen a cat's eyes glowing mysteriously in the dark. Explain

that cats have a substance in the back of their eyes called the *tapetum lucidum,* which reflects light like a mirror and helps a cat see better to hunt in the dark. A cat's eyes contract to a slit during the day, but open wide at night to let in light. Cats' ears move independently from each other and are very keen at hearing sounds, such as that of an electric can opener. Challenge interested students to select and research a topic related to cats—a specific breed or member of the cat family, hunting skills, or wild cats. Have them write a report to share with the class.

Reinforce and Extend

Answers

◆ **LITERATURE AND YOUR LIFE**

Reader's Response Students will probably say that they would adopt the orphaned kitten themselves or find it a good home.

Thematic Focus He brings new energy and joy to the quiet home, and entertains Mrs. Ainsworth.

☑ **Check Your Comprehension**

1. She was a wild and independent outdoor cat.
2. When she was dying, Debbie used her last strength to bring her tiny kitten to the safe home of her friend Mrs. Ainsworth.
3. Buster is bold and healthy, and torments and pesters his fellow pets.
4. They remember Debbie fondly and believe that she would be pleased with how well Buster turned out.

◆ **Critical Thinking**

1. She was a stray cat whose instinct led her to return to the wild.
2. She might have judged Mrs. Ainsworth's home as a safe place for her newborn kitten.
3. Unlike Debbie, Buster is strong, healthy, and quite comfortable being a house cat.
4. Unexpected rewards can be more valued because they offer a pleasing surprise and renew one's faith in the joys of daily life.
5. A successful vet must care about animals, be patient and kind to them and their owners, keep up on new medical procedures and treatments, and be on call at all times of day or night.

674

---

again, sideways this time, head on one side, goading him. When he started boxing with both paws it was too much even for the Basset. He dropped his dignity and rolled over with the cat in a brief wrestling match.

"I want to show you something." Mrs. Ainsworth lifted a hard rubber ball from the sideboard and went out to the garden, followed by Buster. She threw the ball across the lawn and the cat bounded after it over the frosted grass, the muscles rippling under the black sheen of his coat. He seized the ball in his teeth, brought it back to his mistress, dropped it at her feet and waited expectantly. She threw it and he brought it back again.

I gasped incredulously. A feline retriever!

The Bassets looked on disdainfully. Nothing would ever have induced them to chase a ball, but Buster did it again and again as though he would never tire of it.

Mrs. Ainsworth turned to me. "Have you ever seen anything like that?"

"No," I replied. "I never have. He is a most remarkable cat."

She snatched Buster from his play and we went back into the house where she held him close to her face, laughing as the big cat purred and arched himself ecstatically against her cheek.

Looking at him, a picture of health and contentment, my mind went back to his mother. Was it too much to think that that dying little creature with the last of her strength had carried her kitten to the only haven of comfort and warmth she had ever known in the hope that it would be cared for there? Maybe it was.

But it seemed I wasn't the only one with such fancies. Mrs. Ainsworth turned to me and though she was smiling her eyes were wistful.

"Debbie would be pleased," she said.

I nodded. "Yes, she would . . . It was just a year ago today she brought him, wasn't it?"

"That's right." She hugged Buster to her again. "The best Christmas present I ever had." ❶

Guide for Responding

◆ **LITERATURE AND YOUR LIFE**

Reader's Response How would you react if Debbie had left you her newborn kitten?

Thematic Focus Describe the ways in which Buster is a welcome surprise.

Group Activity Work with a team to create a pamphlet of advice for new pet owners.

☑ **Check Your Comprehension**

1. Describe Debbie and her life.
2. Describe how Buster came to live with Mrs. Ainsworth.
3. How did the Ainsworth household change after Buster arrived?
4. What thoughts do Herriot and Mrs. Ainsworth share at the end of the essay?

◆ **Critical Thinking**

INTERPRET

1. Why did Debbie never stay with Mrs. Ainsworth for long? **[Infer]**
2. Why might she have chosen to bring Buster to Mrs. Ainsworth's home? **[Speculate]**
3. How is Buster different from his mother? **[Compare and Contrast]**

APPLY

4. Mrs. Ainsworth receives an unexpected reward for her kindness to Debbie. Why are unexpected rewards sometimes more valued than expected ones? **[Generalize]**

EXTEND

5. What qualities and training do you think it takes to be a successful veterinarian? **[Career Link]**

Beyond the Classroom

Career Connection

Animal Caretakers Author James Herriot was a veterinarian who cared for animals in a small village. In this essay, Herriot and Mrs. Ainsworth help the stray cat Debbie when she becomes ill and her kitten is orphaned. In small towns, a veterinarian is often called upon to do the work a humane society might do in a larger community.

Veterinary medicine is a branch of medicine that deals with the illnesses and diseases of both large and small animals. Because some animal diseases such as rabies can be transmitted to humans

and can be very dangerous, the work of a veterinarian is also important to people.

Suggest that interested students work in small groups to brainstorm for a list of occupations that are related to the care of animals. In addition to veterinarians and their office assistants, students may list jobs such as humane society volunteer, animal control officer, and zoo worker. Encourage students to identify educational requirements for each job on their list. Invite them to add brief descriptions of why they might like each job, and post the list for the class in a bulletin board display.

Forest Fire
Anaïs Nin

A man rushed in to announce he had seen smoke on Monrovia Peak.[1] As I looked out of the window I saw the two mountains facing the house on fire. The entire rim burning wildly in the night. The flames, driven by hot Santa Ana winds[2] from the desert, were as tall as the tallest trees, the sky already tinted coral, and the crackling noise of burning trees, the ashes and the smoke were already increasing. The fire raced along, sometimes descending behind the mountain where I could only see the glow, sometimes descending toward us. I thought of the foresters in danger. I made coffee for the weary men who came down occasionally with horses they had led out, or with old people from the isolated cabins. They were covered with soot from their battle with the flames.

At six o'clock the fire was on our left side and rushing toward Mount Wilson. <u>Evacuees</u> from the cabins began to arrive and had to be given blankets and hot coffee. The streets were blocked with fire engines readying to fight the fire if it touched the houses. Policemen and firemen and guards turned away the sightseers. Some were relatives concerned over the fate of the foresters, or the pack station family. The policemen lighted flares, which gave the scene a theatrical, tragic air. The red lights on

▲ **Critical Viewing** Why are forest fires such dangerous occurrences? Refer to details in the photograph in your response. **[Deduce]** ❸

the police cars twinkled alarmingly. More fire engines arrived. Ashes fell, and the roar of the fire was now like thunder.

We were told to ready ourselves for evacuation. I packed the diaries. The saddest spectacle, beside that of the men fighting the fire as they would a war, were the animals, rabbits, coyotes, mountain lions, deer, driven by the fire to the edge of the mountain, taking a look at the crowd of people and panicking, choosing rather to rush back into the fire. ❹

The fire now was like a ring around Sierra Madre,[3] every mountain was burning. People living at the foot of the mountain were packing ❺

---

1. **Monrovia** (mən rō′ vē ə) **Peak**: Mountain in southwest California.
2. **Santa** (san′ tə) **Ana** (an′ ə) **winds**: Hot desert winds from the east or northeast in southern California.

3. **Sierra** (sē er′ ə) **Madre** (mä′ drā): Mountain range.

◆ **Build Vocabulary**

evacuees (ē vak′ yōō ēz′) *n.*: People who leave a place, especially because of danger

Forest Fire ◆ 675

◆ One-Minute Insight

In "Forest Fire," the author recalls a horrific fire that swept through the mountains near the community of Sierra Madre, California, threatening lives, property, and the forest itself. She describes in vivid detail what she and the firefighters, rescuers, and evacuees did during this ordeal. She reflects that one who truly loves nature must love it not only during its peaceful moments, but also during its wild and dangerous times.

◆ **Reading Strategy**

❷ **Set a Purpose for Reading**
After students read the first paragraph of this essay, have them stop and establish a purpose for reading on. *Students may say that they want to read on to learn the outcome of the fire and what the narrator does.*

▶ **Critical Viewing** ◀

❸ **Deduce** *Forest fires can destroy wilderness areas and the plants and animals that live there. Forest fires that burn out of control can threaten residential areas, homes, and people. Firefighters and rescue workers face danger from burns, collapsing trees, exhaustion, and smoke inhalation.*

◆ **Critical Thinking**

❹ **Draw Conclusions** Ask why the wild animals choose the fire over the crowds of people. *Animals instinctively fear humans, especially large numbers of them. They also fear fire, but the animals evidently heeded their most primal instinct—fear of other creatures.*

Clarification

❺ Sierra Madre names a small community located east of Pasadena, California, at the base of the San Gabriel Mountains in suburban Los Angeles.

Customize for
Less Proficient Readers
Have students use the Sensory Language Chart, p. 69, **Writing and Language Transparencies,** to record some of the sensory images Nin uses in her descriptive essay.

 Cross-Curricular Connection: Science

Forest Fires Although uncontrolled fire is a dreaded disaster in most circumstances, forest fires actually have certain benefits. For instance, some trees have coated seeds that open only during the intense heat of a fire. Some forest fires provide natural thinning of areas that are overgrown.

Challenge students to research the benefits as well as the destruction of forest fires. They can begin by finding out about the dramatic fires in Yellowstone National Park during 1988 that damaged thousands of acres of land but proved

to naturalists and environmentalists that forest fires are not necessarily a tragedy. Other students can investigate the factors that scientists and firefighters evaluate to decide when or if to attempt to bring a natural fire under control. Students may wish to study firefighting methods and the jobs related to the field. Others may wish to research the causes of fires—both natural and man-made. Students can present their findings to the class, along with a brief bibliography of books on the subject.

◆ Critical Thinking

❶ Analyze How does the narrator react to the crisis? *In contrast to the drama and chaos around her, she calmly takes care of ordinary tasks like making coffee, answering phone calls, and looking after a neighbor's children.*

◆ Literary Focus

❷ Essay What sensory details does the author use? *The author describes the fire "burning, more vivid than the sun," "spirals of smoke," "rain of ashes," "air…acid and pungent," "dragon tongues of flames," "panicked animals"—creating bold images of nature's power to be enormously violent and chaotic. The details stir up a sense of fear and uneasiness.*

Clarification

❸ Backfiring is a defensive strategy firefighters sometimes use to stop or slow an advancing forest fire. Teams start one or more separate fires ahead of the major blaze to destroy the fuel in its path.

◆ Critical Thinking

❹ Evaluate Encourage students to question the actions of the narrator and the newspaper reporter. Discuss how the reporter missed the "human interest" in a writer rescuing her diaries. *The reporter wanted to photograph something the audience would find sensational. Even though the narrator was making an important rescue of her own, the impact escaped the reporter's understanding.*

---

❶ their cars. I rushed next door to the Campion children, who had been left with a baby-sitter, and got them into the car. It was impossible to save all the horses. We parked the car on the field below us. I called up the Campions, who were out for the evening, and reassured them. The baby-sitter dressed the children warmly. I made more coffee. I answered frantic telephone calls.

All night the fire engines sprayed water over the houses. But the fire grew immense, angry, and rushing at a speed I could not believe. It would rush along and suddenly leap over a road, a trail, like a monster, devouring all in its path. The firefighters cut breaks in the heavy brush, but when the wind was strong enough, the fire leaped across them. At dawn one arm of the fire reached the back of our houses but was finally contained.

> ❷ **◆ Literary Focus**
> What effect does this vivid description have on you?

But high above and all around, the fire was burning, more vivid than the sun, throwing spirals of smoke in the air like the smoke from a volcano. Thirty-three cabins burned, and twelve thousand acres of forest still burning endangered countless homes below the fire. The fire was burning to the back of us now, and a rain of ashes began to fall and continued for days. The smell of the burn in the air, acid and pungent and <u>tenacious</u>. The dragon tongues of flames devouring, the flames leaping, the roar of destruction and <u>dissolution</u>, the eyes of the panicked animals, caught between fire and human beings, between two forms of death. They chose the fire. It was as if the fire had come from the bowels of the earth, like that of a fiery volcano, it was so powerful, so swift, and so <u>ravaging</u>. I saw trees become skeletons in one minute, I saw trees fall, I saw bushes turned to ashes in a second, I saw weary,

> **◆ Build Vocabulary**
> **tenacious** (tə nā′ shəs) *adj.*: Holding on firmly
> **dissolution** (dis′ ə loo′ shən) *n.*: The act of breaking down and crumbling
> **ravaging** (rav′ ij iŋ) *adj.*: Severely damaging

676 ◆ Nonfiction

ash-covered men, looking like men returned from war, some with burns, others overcome by smoke.

The men were rushing from one spot to another watching for recrudescence.[4] Some ❸ started backfiring up the mountain so that the ascending flames could counteract the descending ones.

As the flames reached the cities below, hundreds of roofs burst into flame at once. There was no water pressure because all the fire hydrants were turned on at the same time, and the fire departments were helpless to save more than a few of the burning homes.

The blaring loudspeakers of passing police cars warned us to prepare to evacuate in case the wind changed and drove the fire in our direction. What did I wish to save? I thought only of the diaries. I appeared on the porch carrying a huge stack of diary volumes, preparing to ❹ pack them in the car. A reporter for the Pasadena *Star News* was taking pictures of the evacuation. He came up, very annoyed with me. "Hey, lady, next time could you bring out something more important than all those old papers? Carry some clothes on the next trip. We gotta

---

4. recrudescence (rē′ kroo des′ əns) *n.*: Fresh outbreak of something that has been inactive.

Speaking and Listening Mini-Lesson

Role Play

This mini-lesson supports the Speaking and Listening activity in the Idea Bank on p. 683.

Introduce Role-play participants act and speak as the character of the person they portray. In this role play, students will need to create stories that coincide with Nin's descriptions in her essay.

Develop Divide the class into groups. Each group needs one or more "reporters" to ask questions and some "survivors" to respond. It may help to have the whole group formulate questions together so that survivors can think about reasonable

responses. Encourage reporters to include questions beyond the typical Who? What? Where? Why? and How? to draw out the emotions of people who experience a natural disaster.

Apply Have groups present their role plays for the rest of the class.

Assess Evaluate role plays on how incisive the reporters' questions are, how convincingly survivors respond, and how engaging the overall role play is. Alternatively, you may use the Peer Assessment: Dramatic Performance form, p. 116, in **Alternative Assessment.**

mountains cannot hold the rains and slide down bringing rocks and mud. One of the rangers must now take photographs and movies of the disaster. He asks if I will help by holding an umbrella over the cameras. I put on my raincoat and he lends me hip boots which look to me like seven-league boots.

We drive a little way up the road. At the third curve it is impassable. A river is rushing across the road. The ranger takes pictures while I hold the umbrella over the camera. It is terrifying to see the muddied waters and rocks, the mountain disintegrating. When we are ready to return, the road before us is covered by large rocks but the ranger pushes on as if the truck were a jeep and forces it through. The edge of the road is being carried away.

I am laughing and scared too. The ranger is at ease in nature, and without fear. It is a wild moment of danger. It is easy to love nature in its peaceful and consoling moments, but one must love it in its furies too, in its despairs and wildness, especially when the damage is caused by us. ⑥

④ have human interest in these pictures!"
A week later, the danger was over.
Gray ashy days.
In Sierra Madre, following the fire, the January rains brought floods. People are sandbagging their homes. At four A.M. the streets are covered with mud. The bare, burnt, naked

Guide for Responding

◆ LITERATURE AND YOUR LIFE

Reader's Response What would you try to save if you were caught in a fire?

Thematic Focus In what ways does life go on during the fire? In what ways is life disrupted?

☑ Check Your Comprehension

1. Describe the setting—the time and place— of the forest fire.
2. What does Nin rescue from the fire?
3. What natural disaster occurred after the fire?

◆ Critical Thinking

INTERPRET
1. How are the fire and mudslides related? [Connect]
2. What is the effect of Nin's use of figurative language, such as "the dragon tongues of flames"? [Interpret]
3. What conclusion does Nin draw from observing these disasters? [Draw Conclusions]

COMPARE LITERARY WORKS
4. Compare and contrast the messages or themes within "Debbie" and "Forest Fire." [Compare and Contrast]

Forest Fire ◆ 677

►Critical Viewing◄

⑤ **Interpret** *The fire dominates the entire scene. The brilliant red color suggests rage and fear.*

◆ LITERATURE AND YOUR LIFE

⑥ Ask students whether they agree or disagree with the author's belief that nature can be lovable in its fury. Invite students to share their responses. *Students may feel no love for nature in all its forms, especially if they have experienced losses from natural disasters firsthand. Others may possess only positive feelings about nature.*

Reinforce and Extend

Answers
◆ LITERATURE AND YOUR LIFE

Reader's Response Encourage students to give reasons for their choices.

Thematic Focus Even during a crisis, people must eat, rest, find shelter, care for children, and communicate with others. Normal life is disrupted because all sense of calm, relaxation, and safety disappear.

☑ Check Your Comprehension

1. The forest fire starts at night in the mountains around the town of Sierra Madre, California, and lasts for a week.
2. She rescues her diaries.
3. There were mudslides after the fire.

◆ Critical Thinking

1. Because the fire destroyed the natural foliage, which would have absorbed the water, the rains led to destructive slides of rock and mud.
2. She heightens readers' ability to visualize the fire.
3. She concludes that we must love nature even when it is wild and dangerous.
4. "Debbie" conveys a hopeful message about life, whose joys can offset the sadness of death. "Forest Fire" warns humans to respect nature, because our own carelessness can add to its ability to destroy.

Cross-Curricular Connection: Social Studies

Natural Disasters are certainly memorable to those people who survive them, but some are so unusual or dramatic that they linger in the memory of all of us long after. Natural disasters become the setting for novels, plays, and films. Others become benchmarks by which other similar disasters are judged.

Invite interested students to select a particular kind of natural disaster that interests them such as earthquake, flood, volcanic eruption, blizzard, or avalanche. Have them learn the characteristics of such a disaster and the conditions

that make it occur. Then have them find and research an example of that kind of disaster that people still remember and talk about to this day. Some examples might include Hurricane Mitch in 1998, the San Francisco earthquake in 1906, or the Krakatau volcanic eruption in 1883.

In addition to researching the details of the disaster, have students discuss the kinds of disaster relief that is available from the Red Cross, federal aid programs, and local community organizations and groups. Have students report their findings to others in the class in a written report.

"How to Be Polite Online" is an expository essay that offers tips and guidelines to help computer users communicate more effectively and courteously online.

◆ Critical Thinking

❶ Analyze Explain to students that Netiquette is a "portmanteau word"—a word that is a combination of two other words. Ask students to determine what two words Shea has combined and what the new word means. *The author has combined the words net (as in Internet) and etiquette (rules for manners, social conventions) to describe a set of rules and customs for Internet users.*

► Critical Viewing ◄

❷ Infer *The painting seems to show that the whole world may be connected by computers and the Internet, but people are still at the center of the cyber-universe.*

Customize for
English Language Learners
Some students may be confused by the technological computer terms used in this essay. You might de-emphasize the highly technical terms, such as ASCII (pronounced "askee"), and help them focus on the general ideas of the essay.

Customize for
Verbal/Linguistic Learners
Help students identify other "portmanteau words" in this essay, and determine their derivation. For instance, students should be able to determine that the word "emoticon" is a combination of the words *emotion* and *icon*.

Customize for
Visual/Spatial Learners
Have students refer to the image on p. 41 that accompanies the excerpt from *E-Mail From Bill Gates*. They can compare what is similar and different between that media montage and the computer illustration on this page. Interested students may wish to suggest other ways to represent the ever-changing world of computers and the cyberspace world of information in life and daily activities.

678

How to Be Polite Online
❶ *from* Netiquette

Virginia Shea

Untitled, James Yang

 ❷ ▲ **Critical Viewing** What does this painting seem to say about the relationship between people and technology? **[Infer]**

678 ◆ Nonfiction

🎼 Humanities: Art

Untitled, by James Yang

This artist represents the computer with colors such as turquoise and green, taking on the irridescent hues of a computer's motherboard circuitry. Point out the talking head to the left, which is the same shape as the large figure except that the mouth is talking—giving visual representation to e-mail communication or possibly an Internet chat room. The stylized angle of the frontal perspective visually represents an emoticon.

1. What messages does the author convey about the world's computers? *He shows that comput-* ers can be connected, but suggests that the connections may be fragile and misunderstandings are possible.

2. Why does the green computer say WWW on its display? *WWW stands for "World Wide Web," another name for part of the Internet.*

3. The artist creates an almost cartoonlike image of the central user. What is the effect of this simple figure in the midst of a technological scene? *The artist may be saying that despite technological advances, people are still the central elements of cyberspace.*

The truth is that computer networking is still in its infancy. Probably nothing illustrates this more clearly than the "ASCII[1] jail": 90% of network communications are still limited to plain old ASCII text—that is, the characters of the alphabet, the numerals 0 through 9, and the most basic punctuation marks. It's bad enough that multimedia communications have not been <u>implemented</u> in most of cyberspace.[2] Most of the time you can't even put a word in bold or italics!

Because people cannot see or hear you in cyberspace, you need to pay close attention to the style of your electronic communications if you hope to make a good impression there. The *style* of electronic communications <u>encompasses</u> everything about your correspondence except its content, from your use of network conventions like "smileys" and "sigs" to the number of characters per line in your email messages.

Style considerations are influenced by several of the rules of Netiquette, especially Rule 4, Respect other people's time, and Rule 5, Make yourself look good online. It doesn't matter how brilliant your messages are if they're formatted in such a way that no one can read them.

Tone of voice online

The fact that most network interactions are limited to written words can be the source of misunderstandings. Fortunately, clever network users have had years to deal with this. They've created a shorthand to help communicate the tone that you'd otherwise get from the other person's voice, facial expressions, and gestures. These shorthand expressions are known as smileys or emoticons. They're easy to figure out once you get the hang of it. Just remember that they're all sideways faces.

◆ **Literature and Your Life**
What expressions and gestures do you often use when conversing with others?

See Table 1 for a list of the most commonly used emoticons. There are whole books about smileys for those who are interested, including the enjoyable *Smiley Dictionary* by Seth Godin.

People also use abbreviations to express emotional states or to qualify what they're saying. See Table 2 for a list of common abbreviations.

The "FLAME ON/FLAME OFF" notifier

When you really want to run off at the keyboard—but you want your readers to know that you know that you're not expressing yourself in your usual measured, reasoned manner—you need to let them know that you know that you're flaming.[3] So before you begin your rant, simply

---

1. **ASCII:** Abbreviation of American Standard Code for Information Interchange, a standard computer code used to assist the interchange of information among various types of data-processing equipment.
2. **cyberspace:** Global communication performed through the use of computer technology.

3. **flaming:** Slang for "ranting."

◆ **Build Vocabulary**
implemented (im′ plə mənt′ əd) v.: Put into effect
encompasses (en kum′ pəs′ səz) v.: Contains; includes

How to Be Polite Online ◆ 679

Comprehension Check ☑
❸ What limitations are placed on the user of the Internet as far as the graphic capabilities of most computer software programs go? *A communication written for the Internet cannot put a word in bold letters, italics, or even underlined, which is a source of frustration to some users.*

◆ **Reading Strategy**
❹ **Set a Purpose for Reading** Ask students to describe their purpose for reading, based on this passage. *Students may say that they want to read to learn how a person's style of electronic communication can reflect his or her personality or attitude.*

◆ **Critical Thinking**
❺ **Interpret** Why does the author believe the style of electronic communication is so important? *Because the writer cannot be seen or heard, it is important to make a good impression by the style of writing, which is how what is said might be judged.*

Comprehension Check ☑
❻ Why can computer network transactions be misunderstood? *Because only written words are used, if the writer is careless, misunderstandings can occur.*

◆ **LITERATURE AND YOUR LIFE**
❼ *Students may list or demonstrate various hand gestures, such as waving, pointing, or extending the fingers outward to express frustration. Facial expressions may include arching the eyebrows, tilting the head, making faces, sticking out the tongue, and so on. Other demonstrated actions may be shrugging the shoulders, crossing your arms in front, or tapping a foot impatiently.*

Beyond the Classroom

Workplace Skills

Computer Literacy It has become hard to envision a workplace without computer technology; fax machines send data over phone lines, computer chips regulate heating and security systems, mainframe computers at banks or communications enterprises track massive amounts of data, cash registers at grocery stores count change. Computers are everywhere, and today's workers must develop computer literacy skills.

Suggest that students take an imaginary stroll through a mall, hospital, office building, school, or other multipurpose institution to think of ways that computers are used. What computer literacy skills does the typical worker need? Have students interview adults they know about computer use in their workplaces; suggest that they ask them what computer skills had to be mastered. Challenge students to think of ways that people rely on computers outside of their jobs—such as those who use a bank ATM to withdraw cash or a voice-mail system to take their phone messages. Have students create a bulletin board display illustrating computer uses in today's world.

◆ **Literary Focus**

1 Essay In an expository essay, the author may have great quantities of information to convey. In some cases, this may best be done by the use of graphic organizers, such as tables, charts, diagrams, or lists. *Students may say that the use of a table allows the writer to present a lot of information in an orderly, user-friendly way.*

◆ **Literary Focus**

2 Essay In a "bulleted" list, paragraphs are indented to stand out, and each one begins with a simple graphic character—sometimes known as a bullet—so that the reader can easily follow a group of related points. Ask students to point out the bulleted list technique that the author uses. *Students should note the bulleted text on pp. 680–681.*

◆ **Critical Thinking**

3 Solve Have students examine the table of emoticons to see which keyboard characters make up each one. Then ask them to explain how they could use emoticons to communicate with someone who is unfamiliar with them. *Students might suggest sending a chart like this to their e-mail correspondents. Others might suggest introducing one or two emoticons at a time, along with a quick explanation.*

◆ **LITERATURE AND YOUR LIFE**

4 Table 2 presents abbreviations for some of the common expressions people use when they speak or write. Challenge students to come up with additional abbreviations that would reflect their own speech patterns, habits, or recurring topics.

enter the words FLAME ON. Then rant away. When you're done, write FLAME OFF and resume normal discourse.

Looking good online

One of the neat things about computers is that they let us use all kinds of special effects in our documents that we didn't even dream of back in the days of typewriters (if you're old enough to remember those days). But when you're communicating online, in most cases it's back to the typewriter as far as effects go. Even if your mail system lets you use boldface, italics, and tabs, there's no guarantee that your correspondent's system will understand them. At worst, your communication will turn into unreadable gibberish.

What to do?

- Forget about boldface, italics, tabs, and font changes. Never use any effect you couldn't get on an old-fashioned typewriter. In fact, you can't even use all of those. Underlining won't work, for example. Nor can you use the old "required backspace" trick to put a diacritical mark[4] (a tilde or an accent mark, for example) over another character.
- Most systems won't read the diacritical marks anyway, so just leave them out. If you feel an accent mark is absolutely necessary, type an apostrophe *after* the letter the accent would have gone over.
- Use only ASCII characters. This includes all 26 letters of the alphabet

◆ **Literary Focus**
Why might a writer use tables in an expository essay?

---
4. **diacritical** (dī´ ə krit´ ik əl) **mark:** Mark added to a letter or symbol to show its pronunciation.

Table 1: Emoticons

:-)	Smile; laugh; "I'm joking"
:-(	Frown; sadness; "Bummer"
:)	Variant of :-) or "Have a nice day"
:(	Variant of :-(
;-)	Wink; denotes a pun or sly joke
:-O	Yelling or screaming; or completely shocked
:-()	Can't (or won't) stop talking
:-D	Big, delighted grin
:-P	Sticking out your tongue
:-] or :-)	Sarcastic smile
%-)	Confused but happy
%-(	Confused and unhappy
:'-(	Crying
:'-)	Crying happy tears
:-I	Can't decide how to feel; no feelings either way
:-\	Mixed but mostly happy
:-/	Mixed but mostly sad
*	Kiss
{ } or [ ]	Hug
{{{***}}}	Hugs and kisses

Table 2: Abbreviations

BTW	By the way
IMHO	In my humble opinion
IMNSHO	In my not so humble opinion
IOW	In other words
IRL	In real life
ITRW	In the real world
LOL	Laughing out loud
OTF	On the floor (laughing)
ROTFL	Rolling on the floor laughing
WRT	With regard to
YMMV	Your mileage may vary
<g> or <G>	Grin
<bg>	Big grin

Viewing and Representing Mini-Lesson

Computer Symbol Imagery

In this mini-lesson, students will expand their understanding of computer symbols and emoticons by producing a visual representation based on computer images.

Introduce Ask students to review the image on p. 678 and discuss the computer imagery the artist has used. Then have them study the table of emoticons and computer abbreviations on p. 680.

Develop Discuss with students how writers create images with words and phrases and

artists use visual effects. Have students work in pairs to discuss and come up with a visual image that uses the computer symbols on p. 680 or other computer-related symbols and images. For example, to represent the feeling of happiness, students might use the emoticon :-) and expand on it.

Apply Provide materials and equipment and have student pairs create visual representations of computer-related words or phrases that they choose. If you have access to technology, students can use computer

software to create their representations, or they can draw their representations. If possible, encourage them to use color in their representations.

Assess Have students display their visual representations for the class. Encourage the viewing audience to guess what computer-related word or phrase is being illustrated. Ask students to explain their choices of computer symbols and representations. Evaluate students on their work as pairs and their presentations to the class.

(upper and lower case), the numerals 0 through 9, and most commonly used punctuation marks. For any publishing mavens out there, however, it excludes em dashes ("—"), en dashes ("–"), and bullets.

❷
- Limit your line length to 80 characters, or better yet, 60 characters.

Otherwise, your lines may break in weird places and your readers

will have to wade through notes that look like this.

Believe me,

it gets annoying after a very short while.

- NEVER TYPE YOUR NOTES IN ALL CAPS, LIKE THIS. It's rude—like shouting constantly. And, like constant shouting, it makes people stop listening. All caps may be used, IN MODERATION, for emphasis. ❺
- To indicate *italics*, you may *surround the material to be italicized with asterisks.*

Guide for Responding

◆ LITERATURE AND YOUR LIFE

Reader's Response Which of the emoticons do you find most clever? Why?

Thematic Focus In what ways does communicating on-line provide a newness to everyday life?

Group Activity Design your own emoticons, or smileys. Display the new emoticons, and have classmates guess their meanings.

☑ Check Your Comprehension

1. What does "the *style* of electronic communications" include?
2. What is "flaming"?
3. What formatting recommendations does Shea make?
4. Why does Shea discourage the reader from typing in all caps?

◆ Critical Thinking

INTERPRET

1. Which of Shea's rules of Netiquette do you think is most important? Why? **[Support]**
2. Which of the emoticons do you think would be understood by someone who didn't have Shea's reference chart? **[Infer]**
3. How is writing online similar to and different from handwriting a note? **[Compare and Contrast]**

APPLY

4. People didn't use emoticons when they wrote with typewriters. Why do you think emoticons became popular in computer communications? **[Generalize]**

EVALUATE

5. Is electronic mail appropriate for all occasions? In what situation might a traditional letter be a better choice? **[Assess]**

How to Be Polite Online ◆ 681

Reinforce and Extend

Answers

◆ LITERATURE AND YOUR LIFE

Reader's Response Responses will vary. Encourage students to give reasons for their opinions.

Thematic Focus Students may say that on-line communication can be instant and unexpected.

☑ Check Your Comprehension

1. It includes everything but the content of the message.
2. "Flaming" means ranting.
3. She recommends using only what is possible on an old-fashioned typewriter, and sticking to 60 characters per line.
4. She says it represents shouting.

◆ Critical Thinking

1. Responses will vary; have students support their opinions.
2. Most would understand the smile and frown variants.
3. Both methods convey ideas with words. They are different because a note can be done on different kinds of stationery, and reflects one's handwriting and personality, while an online note is just plain words.
4. People became used to icons and clip art and felt that they needed more emotion in their e-mail communication.
5. Students may say that e-mail is fine for general purposes. For formal occasions, or with messages that have sentimental or historic value, a traditional letter might be a better choice.

 Beyond the Selection

FURTHER READING
Other Works by the Authors
All Creatures Great and Small, James Herriot
All Things Wise and Wonderful, James Herriot
Netiquette, Virginia Shea

INTERNET
We recommend the following sites on the Internet (all Web sites are subject to change).
  For more information on James Herriot, go to:
http://www.geocities.com/Athens/Acropolis /3907/herriot2.html
  For more information on Anaïs Nin, visit:
http://www.anaisnin.com
  For more information on Netiquette, go to:
http://www.etiquette.net/index.html
  We *strongly recommend* that you preview these sites before you send students to them.

Answers

◆ Reading Strategy

1. (a) Students may say that their purpose for reading was to grasp the meaning of the titles. (b) Most students will say that they have met each purpose.
2. Students may note that they added new purposes for reading when the essay took a surprising turn, or if the author made an unexpected statement or revelation.
3. It is helpful to change a purpose if the initial purpose is wrong or if the selection takes an unanticipated direction.

◆ Build Vocabulary

Using the Word Root -vac-
1. vacant; 2. vacuum; 3. evacuate

Spelling Strategy
1. average, endangered; 2. aging, savage; 3. surgeon, digestive

Using the Word Bank
1. a 2. c 3. c 4. b 5. a 6. c 7. c

◆ Literary Focus

1. (a) Students may say that Mrs. Ainsworth is the most fully drawn character. (b) He brought her to life by describing her home, her feelings about animals, and her strong reaction to Debbie's death and Buster's arrival.
2. (a) "...monster, devouring all in its path"; "...more vivid than the sun"; "dragon tongues of flames." (b) The first image makes the fire sound gluttonous and greedy; the next image suggests unbearable heat and light; the last suggests something that will eventually be vanquished.
3. It discusses proper online tone of voice; it gives a chart of emoticons to use; it lists useful abbreviations.

◆ Build Grammar Skills

Practice
1. Debbie/her; singular feminine
2. Ball/it; singular neuter
3. Man/he; singular masculine
4. Children/them; plural neuter
5. Marks/them; plural neuter

Guide for Responding (continued)

◆ Reading Strategy

SET A PURPOSE FOR READING

Setting a purpose helps you to focus your reading. Your purpose makes it easier to identify and remember important information.
1. (a) What was your purpose for reading each essay? (b) Was each purpose met?
2. Did you shift or extend your purpose while reading any of the essays? If so, explain how and why.
3. When do you think it is helpful to change a purpose you have set for reading?

◆ Build Vocabulary

USING THE WORD ROOT -vac-

The Latin root -vac-, as in *evacuees,* means "empty." Complete each sentence with the most appropriate word containing the word root -vac-.

vacuum   evacuate   vacant

1. After the forest fire, the town was ____?____.
2. The suction of the backdraft left a ____?____ inside the room.
3. We were forced to ____?____ when the fire reached our property line.

SPELLING STRATEGY

The *j* sound can be spelled with a *g*, as in the word *ravaging*. Rewrite these sentences, correcting misspelled words.
1. The averaje pet owner should not keep an endanjered species as a pet.
2. Some ajing animals become savaje when ill.
3. Only an experienced surjeon can operate on an animal's dijestive system.

USING THE WORD BANK

On your paper, write the letter of the word most opposite in meaning to the Word Bank word.
1. privations: (a) riches, (b) limits, (c) public
2. evacuees: (a) helpers, (b) fears, (c) inhabitants
3. tenacious: (a) wild, (b) brilliant, (c) weak
4. dissolution: (a) height, (b) growth, (c) visible
5. ravaging: (a) harmless, (b) evil, (c) sharp
6. implemented: (a) held, (b) spoken, (c) unused
7. encompasses: (a) believes, (b) refers, (c) omits

◆ Literary Focus

ESSAY

Authors write **essays** to communicate information and ideas about the real world. A **narrative essay** tells about a true event. A **descriptive essay** presents a detailed view of an incident or experience. An **expository essay** provides the reader with information, explanations, or instruction.
1. (a) Which character do you think is most fully drawn in Herriot's essay? (b) Tell how Herriot brought this character to life.
2. (a) Find three different images Nin uses to describe the fire. (b) Explain the effectiveness of each image.
3. Give three examples of ways that "How to Be Polite Online" informs the reader.

◆ Build Grammar Skills

PRONOUN AND ANTECEDENT AGREEMENT

A personal pronoun must **agree** with its antecedent in gender (masculine, feminine, or neuter) and number (singular or plural).

> *Buster* did it again and again as though *he* would never tire of it. (The pronoun *he* agrees with the singular masculine antecedent *Buster*.)

Practice On your paper, write the pronoun and antecedent in each example. Then, identify the gender and number of each pair.
1. The Bassets were used to Debbie and sniffed her in a bored way. . . .
2. Mrs. Ainsworth threw the ball across the lawn, and the cat bounded after it.
3. A man rushed in to announce he had seen smoke on Monrovia Peak.
4. I rushed next door to the Campion children . . . and got them into the car.
5. Most systems won't read the diacritical marks anyway, so just leave them out.

Writing Application Write sentences with pronouns that agree with the antecedents below:
1. Mrs. Ainsworth   3. firefighters
2. Buster   4. computer

Writing Application
Possible responses:
1. Mrs. Ainsworth pampered her pets.
2. Buster chased the ball because he enjoyed it.
3. Firefighters risk their lives.
4. A computer is expensive, but it can be worth the expense.

 **Writer's Solution**

For additional instruction and practice, use the lesson in the *Writer's Solution Language Lab CD-ROM* on pronoun and antecedent agreement. You may also use p. 85, Agreement Between Pronouns and Antecedents, in the *Writer's Solution Grammar Practice Book.*

Build Your Portfolio

 Idea Bank

Writing

1. **Computer Checklist** Write a list of hints to help others use a computer. Use ideas from "How to Be Polite Online" as well as your own experience.

2. **Essay** Choose an interesting location, and watch the area for at least thirty minutes. Write a descriptive essay to share your observations and insights.

3. **Analysis** In a brief paper, describe the ways in which "Debbie" is like a fictional short story. Then, describe the ways in which it is nonfiction.

Speaking and Listening

4. **Role Play** Imagine that you are a reporter interviewing people who survived the Santa Ana forest fire. Write a list of questions about the fire, and then conduct interviews with your classmates, who should pose as survivors.

5. **Oral Interpretation** Read one of the essays aloud, as if you were performing for a radio audience. Practice your delivery before reading the essay for the class. **[Media Link]**

Projects

6. **Survey and Analysis [Group Activity]** With a partner, conduct a survey about people's attitudes toward their pets. Write survey questions that can be statistically analyzed. For example, ask people to rate favorite pets on a scale from 1 to 10. Then, work together to graph and interpret your data. Compile the results in a report to share with the class. **[Math Link]**

7. **Firefighting Report** Visit your local fire department, and request an interview with a firefighter or with the fire chief. Ask questions about the educational requirements and the training necessary to become a firefighter. Also, ask about careers related to fire safety and prevention. Present your findings to the class. **[Career Link]**

 Writing Mini-Lesson

Interview

True stories make some of the most interesting reading. One of the best ways to get firsthand information about an exciting event is to interview someone who was there. Plan and conduct an interview with someone in your community who witnessed an exciting event.

Writing Skills Focus: Using Quotation Marks

When quoting people—whether from interviews or from their writing—always **use quotation marks** around their exact words.

Model

Although she enjoys the fame she has gained, it hasn't gone to her head. "My patients are cats and dogs," she says. "They really aren't impressed by a piece of paper."

Prewriting Choose an interview subject. Then, prepare a list of questions. If possible, bring a tape recorder to the interview. After the interview, evaluate your information and decide which information you want to include.

Drafting Write about your interview, sharing both your subject's experiences as well as your insights into his or her personality. Use quotation marks to indicate your subject's exact words.

Revising Reread your draft, and review your notes. Add interesting or relevant details that you left out. Be sure you've used quotation marks correctly.

> ◆ **Grammar Application**
> Check to be sure that your pronouns agree with their antecedents.

Debbie/Forest Fire/How to Be Polite Online ◆ 683

 Idea Bank

Following are suggestions for matching the Idea Bank topics with your students' performance levels and learning modalities:

Customize for *Performance Levels*
Less Advanced Students: 1, 4, 7
Average Students: 3, 4, 5, 6, 7
More Advanced Students: 2, 5, 6

Customize for *Learning Modalities*
Verbal/Linguistic: 1, 2, 3, 4, 5, 6, 7
Visual/Spatial: 6, 7
Bodily/Kinesthetic: 4, 5
Logical/Mathematical: 3, 6
Interpersonal: 4, 5, 6, 7
Intrapersonal: 1, 2, 3

 Writing Mini-Lesson

Refer students to the Writing Handbook in the back of the book for instruction on the writing process and for further information on interviews. Have students prepare their questions in advance to make the interview go more smoothly.

✎ Writer's Solution

Writing Lab CD-ROM
Have students complete the tutorial on Reports. Follow these steps:
1. Have students use the audio tips on conducting interviews and guidelines for taking notes.
2. Have students work through the Organizing Information section.
3. Have students draft on computer.
4. Have students apply the Proofreading Checklist.

Writer's Solution Sourcebook
Have students use Chapter 7, "Reports," pp. 200–233, for further support. The chapter includes a final draft of a student's report called "To Become a Veterinarian," p. 229.

✓ ASSESSMENT OPTIONS

Formal Assessment, Selection Test, pp. 195–197, and Assessment Resources Software. The selection test is designed so that it can be easily customized to the performance levels of your students.

Alternative Assessment, p. 45, includes options for less advanced students, more advanced students, interpersonal learners, logical/mathematical learners, verbal/linguistic learners, and visual/spatial learners.

PORTFOLIO ASSESSMENT
Use the following rubrics in the **Alternative Assessment** booklet to assess student writing:
Computer Checklist: Summary, p. 94
Essay: Description, p. 93
Analysis: Literary Analysis/Interpretation, p. 108
Writing Mini-Lesson: Research Report/Paper, p. 102

Guide for Reading

OBJECTIVES

1. To read, comprehend, and interpret a persuasive essay and speech
2. To relate a persuasive essay and speech to personal experience
3. To identify persuasive techniques
4. To understand a persuasive essay
5. To build vocabulary in context and learn the prefix *anti-*
6. To develop skill in pronoun agreement with indefinite subjects
7. To write a persuasive speech with a strong beginning and ending
8. To respond to a persuasive essay and speech through writing, speaking and listening, and projects

SKILLS INSTRUCTION

Vocabulary:
Using the Prefix *anti-*

Spelling:
Words With the *oy* Sound

Grammar:
Pronoun Agreement With Indefinite Subjects

Reading Strategy:
Identify Persuasive Techniques

Literary Focus:
Persuasive Essay

Writing:
Strong Beginning and Ending

Speaking and Listening:
Speech (Teacher Edition)

Critical Viewing:
Make a Judgment; Analyze; Interpret

PORTFOLIO OPPORTUNITIES

Writing: List; Business Letter; News Analysis

Writing Mini-Lesson: Persuasive Speech

Speaking and Listening: Speech; Dialogue

Projects: Civil Rights Exhibit; Multimedia Presentation

More About the Authors
Robert MacNeil became a journalist in 1955 and has spent most of his life working in that field. Since retiring in 1995, he has focused on writing fiction, hosting documentaries, and leading the MacDowell Colony—an artists' retreat in New Hampshire.

Martin Luther King, Jr., was raised in the tradition of the dynamic music and oratory of African American Baptist worship. He drew upon the traditional call-and-response style to inspire and engage his listeners. Consistently advocating nonviolence, King used melodious delivery of exciting phrases and literary quotations and is remembered as one of America's most powerful speakers.

Meet the Authors:

Robert MacNeil (1931–)
Born in Montreal, Canada, Robert MacNeil worked on a children's show for the Canadian Broadcasting System early in his career. After becoming a broadcast journalist, MacNeil went to public television to host his own news analysis program, which grew into the highly regarded *MacNeil/Lehrer NewsHour.* His show differed from other news programs by offering more in-depth reports on important issues.

Martin Luther King, Jr. (1929–1968)
The grandson and son of Baptist ministers, Rev. Dr. Martin Luther King, Jr., followed the family tradition and became a clergyman and an activist. King's first well-publicized venture into civil rights occurred in 1953. After Rosa Parks refused to give up her bus seat to a white person as required by the law, King led a boycott of buses in Montgomery, Alabama.

"I Have a Dream" Ten years later, King led a civil rights march in Washington, D.C. There, he delivered his famous "I Have a Dream" speech. In the spring of 1968, King was shot and killed in Memphis, Tennessee, where he had gone to support striking city workers.

◆ LITERATURE AND YOUR LIFE

CONNECT YOUR EXPERIENCE
For how many hours a day is the television on in your home? In "The Trouble with Television," you'll learn what one highly regarded journalist thinks about the amount of time some people spend watching television.

THEMATIC FOCUS: Facing Hard Questions
In the essay and speech in this group, MacNeil and King put hard questions before the American public. What are the answers?

◆ Background for Understanding

MATH
According to Robert MacNeil, Americans watch too much television. The A. C. Nielson Co., which keeps statistics about television, stated that in 1996, the average American watched more than four hours of television every day. That's over two months of nonstop TV watching per year! In a sixty-five-year life, that person will have spent nine years glued to the tube. To figure how many hours a year you watch television, multiply the number of hours you watch per day by seven, and then multiply that number by fifty-two.

◆ Build Vocabulary

PREFIXES: *anti-*
In "The American Dream," King speaks of the *antithesis* of democracy. The prefix *anti-* means "opposed to" or "opposite." Combined with *thesis,* "a statement supported by argument," *antithesis* refers to a statement that is the opposite of another.

WORD BANK
Which word from the list describes something as empty, or void? Check the Build Vocabulary box on page 690 to see if you chose correctly.

diverts
usurps
august
pervading
antithesis
paradoxes
devoid

 Prentice Hall Literature Program Resources

REINFORCE / RETEACH / EXTEND
Selection Support Pages
Build Vocabulary: Using the Prefix *anti-*, p. 247
Build Spelling Skills, p. 248
Build Grammar Skills: Pronoun Agreement With Indefinite Subjects, p. 249
Reading Strategy: Identify Persuasive Techniques, p. 250
Literary Focus: Persuasive Essay, p. 251
Strategies for Diverse Student Needs, pp. 91–92

Beyond Literature Cultural Connection: Television and Society, p. 46
Formal Assessment Selection Test, pp. 198–200, Assessment Resources Software
Alternative Assessment, p. 46
Resource Pro CD-ROM "The Trouble with Television"; "The American Dream"—includes all resource material and customizable lesson plan

 Listening to Literature Audiocassettes
"The Trouble with Television"; "The American Dream"

The Trouble with Television ◆ The American Dream

◆ Build Grammar Skills

Pronoun Agreement With Indefinite Subjects If you wish to introduce the grammar skill for this selection before students read, refer to the instruction on p. 692.

Customize for
Less Proficient Readers

The arguments and strategies used in the persuasive essay and speech in this selection may be hard for students to follow. The prose has challenging words and ideas that some students may find difficult to understand. It may help students to read with a partner, stopping after each paragraph to summarize the main idea, grasp the author's arguments, and talk about how he builds his case.

◆ Literary Focus
PERSUASIVE ESSAY

In a **persuasive essay,** a writer presents his or her views in order to convince you to accept those views or to act in a certain way. Because you may not share the opinion, the writer offers strong arguments, or reasons, to support his or her position or to propel you to act.

Use a graphic organizer like the one below to identify each writer's opinions and arguments.

MacNeil's Opinion:

Supporting Arguments:

◆ Reading Strategy
IDENTIFY PERSUASIVE TECHNIQUES

Writers like MacNeil and King use **persuasive techniques.** These techniques include supporting points with facts, statistics, and quotations; using words that have strong emotional impact; appealing to the masses by quoting popular movies and books; repeating key ideas or beliefs; and using slogans or chants that can stir an audience to action. Notice MacNeil's and King's use of these techniques in their essays.

Customize for
More Advanced Students

The author of each of these essays refers to the Declaration of Independence as part of his persuasive strategy. Challenge students to analyze how and why each author refers to this great document and to the Founding Fathers of our country to make a persuasive point.

Customize for
English Language Learners

The number of unfamiliar words in these essays will make reading a challenge for students acquiring English. It may help to prepare a glossary ahead of time that presents some of the most difficult words that are not otherwise addressed, such as *gratification, serial,* and *perpetual.* Pair students with native English speakers who can rephrase or clarify ideas as necessary.

Guide for Reading ◆ 685

Preparing for Standardized Tests

Reading Students can apply the reading strategy of identifying authors' persuasive techniques to help them answer reading comprehension items on standardized tests. These techniques include using facts or statistics to support a point, using slogans or chants to stir emotions, or appealing to people by quoting popular films or songs.

Have students evaluate the following sample test question, based on "The Trouble with Television," by Robert MacNeil:

Statistics reveal that the average American will have watched about 20,000 hours of television by the age of 20.

MacNeil tries to persuade readers that they watch too much television by

(A) making an outrageous claim.
(B) presenting a startling statistic.
(C) stating a personal opinion.
(D) using a familiar quotation.

Each choice represents a persuasive technique an author might use in an essay. Although this fact may seem outrageous, it is identified as a statistic, which makes *(B)* the best answer.

Former broadcast journalist Robert MacNeil presents a persuasive case to prove his point that television has had a negative effect on society. In his view, TV threatens to undermine our language, literacy, imagination, tolerance for effort, and particularly our ability to handle complexity.

◆ **Reading Strategy**

❶ **Identify Persuasive Techniques** Have students pinpoint the persuasive techniques MacNeil uses to open his essay. *He gives shocking statistics to grab readers' attention. He makes a bold statement to get them to read on.*

◆ **LITERATURE AND YOUR LIFE**

❷ Ask students to think about how the difficult question the author asks relates to their lives. He asks whether an activity other than watching television would not be a better use of a person's time. Challenge students to list alternative activities that would broaden and expand their lives.

◆ **Literary Focus**

❸ **Persuasive Essay** Ask students to paraphrase the thought-provoking statement the author makes. Guide them to recognize that this tactic requires the author to provide support for his statement in the rest of the paragraph. *The author believes that watching television limits a person's ability to concentrate.*

▶ **Critical Viewing** ◀

❹ **Make a Judgment** *She seems either bored, tired, or uninterested, yet she stares intently at the screen.*

The Trouble with TELEVISION

Robert MacNeil

▲ **Critical Viewing** What effect does watching television seem to be having on this girl? [Make a Judgment] ❹

❶ It is difficult to escape the influence of television. If you fit the statistical averages, by the age of 20 you will have been exposed to at least 20,000 hours of television. You can add 10,000 hours for each decade you have lived after the age of 20. The only things Americans do more than watch television are work and sleep.

❷ Calculate for a moment what could be done with even a part of those hours. Five thousand hours, I am told, are what a typical college undergraduate spends working on a bachelor's degree. In 10,000 hours you could have learned enough to become an astronomer or engineer. You could have learned several languages fluently. If it appealed to you, you could be reading Homer[1] in the original Greek or Dostoevski[2] in Russian. If it didn't, you could have walked around the world and written a book about it.

❸ The trouble with television is that it discourages concentration. Almost anything

interesting and rewarding in life requires some constructive, consistently applied effort. The dullest, the least gifted of us can achieve things that seem miraculous to those who never concentrate on anything. But television encourages us to apply no effort. It sells us instant gratification. It diverts us only to divert, to make the time pass without pain.

Television's variety becomes a narcotic,[3] not a stimulus.[4] Its serial, kaleidoscopic[5] exposures force us to follow its lead. The viewer is on a perpetual guided tour: thirty minutes at the museum, thirty at the cathedral, then back on the bus to the next attraction—except on television, typically, the spans allotted are on the order of minutes or seconds, and the chosen delights are more often car crashes and people killing one another. In short, a lot

---

1. **Homer** (hō´ mər): Greek epic poet of the eighth century B.C.
2. **Dostoevski** (dôs´ tô yef´ skē): Fyodor (fyô´ dôr) Dostoevski (1821–1881); Russian novelist.

3. **narcotic** (när kät´ ik) *n.*: Something that has a soothing effect.
4. **stimulus** (stim´ yə ləs) *n.*: Something that rouses to action.
5. **kaleidoscopic** (kə lī´ də skäp´ ik) *adj.*: Constantly changing.

686 ◆ *Nonfiction*

Block Scheduling Strategies

Consider these suggestions to take advantage of extended class time:

• Develop the Literary Focus and Reading Strategy features, p. 685. Provide reinforcement as needed with related activities from **Selection Support**, pp. 250–251.

• Pique students' curiosity about the MacNeil essay with the Interest Grabber, p. 685 of the Teacher's Edition. Then have them read the essay in groups so they can analyze and debate the issues he raises.

• Use the Speaking and Listening Mini-Lesson, Teacher Edition, p. 690, to engage students in "The American Dream." Extend the activity by having students read the Connections to Today's World feature on pp. 694–695 and answer the questions on p. 695.

• If you have access to technology, have students work on the *Writer's Solution Writing Lab CD-ROM* to complete all or part of the Writing Mini-Lesson. Follow the suggestions on p. 693 to help you structure class time.

◀ **Critical Viewing** How does this photograph support MacNeil's statement that "television encourages us to apply no effort"? [Analyze] **7**

of television <u>usurps</u> one of the most precious of all human <u>gifts</u>, the ability to focus your attention yourself, rather than just passively surrender it.

5 Capturing your attention—and holding it—is the prime motive of most television programming and enhances its role as a profitable advertising vehicle. Programmers live in constant fear of losing anyone's attention—anyone's. The surest way to avoid doing so is to keep everything brief, not to strain the attention of anyone but instead to provide constant stimulation through variety, novelty, action and movement. Quite simply, television operates on the appeal to the short attention span.

It is simply the easiest way out. But it has come to be regarded as a given, as inherent[6] in the medium[7] itself: as an imperative, as **6** though General Sarnoff, or one of the other <u>august</u> pioneers of video, had bequeathed to us tablets of stone commanding that nothing in television shall ever require more than a few moments' concentration.

In its place that is fine. Who can quarrel with a medium that so brilliantly packages escapist entertainment as a mass-marketing tool? But I see its values now <u>pervading</u> this nation and its life. It has become fashionable to think that, like fast food, fast ideas are the

---

6. **inherent** (in hir′ ənt) *adj.*: Natural.
7. **medium** (mē′ dē əm) *n.*: Means of communication.

way to get to a fast-moving, impatient public.

In the case of news, this practice, in my view, results in inefficient communication. I question how much of television's nightly news effort is really absorbable and understandable.

Much of it is what has been aptly described as "machine gunning with scraps." I **8** think its technique fights coherence.[8] I think it tends to make things ultimately boring and dismissable (unless they are accompanied by horrifying pictures) because almost anything is boring and dismissable if you know almost nothing about it.

I believe that TV's appeal to the short attention span is not only inefficient communication but decivilizing as well. Consider the casual assumptions that television tends to cultivate: that complexity must be avoided, that visual stimulation is a substitute for thought, that verbal precision is an anachronism.[9] It may be old-fashioned, but I was taught that thought is words, arranged in **9** grammatically precise ways.

There is a crisis of literacy in this country. One study estimates that some 30 million adult Americans are "functionally illiterate" and cannot read or write well enough to answer a want ad or understand the instructions on a medicine bottle.

---

8. **coherence** (kō hir′ əns) *n.*: The quality of being connected in an intelligible way.
9. **anachronism** (ə nak′ rə niz′ əm) *n.*: Anything that seems to be out of its proper place in history.

◆ **Build Vocabulary**

diverts (dī vʉrts′) *v.*: Distracts
usurps (yoo sʉrps′) *v.*: Takes over
august (ô gust′) *adj.*: Honored
pervading (pər vād′ iŋ) *v.*: Spreading throughout

The Trouble with Television ◆ 687

Comprehension Check ☑

5 Why do TV program executives fear losing viewers? *Corporate sponsors pay huge sums of money to promote their products to television viewers, so they want to reach the largest possible audience to make their investments pay. If a program does not appeal to a large enough audience on commercial television, sponsors won't support it, and the program is canceled.*

Clarification

6 David Sarnoff (1891–1971) was one of the first business executives to envision the promise of using radio and television for entertainment. In 1926, Sarnoff organized the National Broadcasting Company (NBC), the first permanent broadcast network, and in 1930, he became president of the Radio Corporation of America (RCA).

▶Critical Viewing◀

7 Analyze *The viewers lie in very relaxed positions passively watching the screen. They do not interact in any way with the television or with one another.*

◆ Critical Thinking

8 Analyze Ask students to explain what *scraps* means. *Students may say that it refers to a fast and steady stream of tidbits that television aims at viewers. He calls them "scraps" because they are incomplete and insignificant.*

Comprehension Check ☑

9 What is the "old-fashioned" belief that MacNeil holds? *He believes that words and thoughts ought to be arranged precisely and grammatically, not as they are on television.*

 Cross-Curricular Connection: Math

Time Analysis Suggest that students list a detailed timetable of the activities in which they participate each day. Then have students create a circle graph—pie chart—that displays the breakdown of time for a typical day in their life. They can begin by drawing a large circle and dividing it into 24 equal sectors—one for each hour of the day. Students can color or shade them to reflect how many hours they spend studying, sleeping, eating, commuting, watching television, and so on.

Students will need to express their data in terms of percents; assist them, as necessary. Extend the activity by having students create a second circle graph that presents an analysis of their television-viewing habits for a given day or week. Have them break it down by types of programs seen: comedies, movies, news, music, and so on. Have interested students write a brief memo indicating whether their statistical findings will affect their television-watching habits.

Clarification

❶ The phrase "inalienable human right" comes from the Declaration of Independence. It refers to the rights of "life, liberty, and the pursuit of happiness."

◆ Reading Strategy

❷ Identify Persuasive Techniques
To arouse concern, he uses a quotation in his closing argument.

◆ LITERATURE AND YOUR LIFE

Reader's Response Most students will probably say that television is important to their lives, but many will say that it provides relaxation, not information and intellectual challenge.

Thematic Focus He forces readers to question whether they spend too much time watching television, and whether television has become harmful to our society.

☑ Check Your Comprehension

1. The average viewer has watched about 20,000 hours.
2. It reduces our attention span and ability to focus on complex ideas.
3. It contributes to illiteracy.

◆ Critical Thinking

1. He means that television uses the fast-paced delivery of a machine gun to serve short bits of information, not substance.
2. He wants people to do things that require thought, demand attention, and foster literacy.
3. He might have more educational or informational programs, limit commercials, and insist on the use of good language and rich ideas.
4. Some students may agree with MacNeil, but have reason to support television as it is.
5. (a) Make programs more educational, less violent, more honest, and limit commercials. (b) Television allows a flow of culture, ideas, lifestyles, languages, and information.

---

❶ Literacy may not be an inalienable human right, but it is one that the highly literate Founding Fathers might not have found unreasonable or even unattainable. We are not only not attaining it as a nation, statistically speaking, but we are falling further and further short of attaining it. And, while I would not be so simplistic as to suggest that television is the cause, I believe it contributes and is an influence.

Everything about this nation—the structure of the society, its forms of family organization, its economy, its place in the world—has become more complex, not less. Yet its dominating communications instrument, its principal form of national linkage, is one that sells neat resolutions to human problems that usually have no neat resolutions. It is all symbolized in my mind by the hugely successful art form that television has made central to the culture, the thirty-second commercial: the tiny drama of the earnest housewife who finds happiness in choosing the right toothpaste.

When before in human history has so much humanity collectively surrendered so much of its leisure to one toy, one mass diversion? When before has virtually an entire nation surrendered itself wholesale to a medium for selling?

Some years ago Yale University law professor Charles L. Black, Jr. wrote: ". . . forced feeding on trivial fare is not itself a trivial matter." I think this society is being force fed with trivial fare, and I fear that the effects on our habits of mind, our language, our tolerance for effort, and our appetite for complexity are only dimly perceived. If I am wrong, we will have done no harm to look at the issue skeptically and critically, to consider how we should be resisting it. I hope you will join with me in doing so.

> ◆ **Reading Strategy**
> What persuasive techniques does MacNeil use in this paragraph?
>
> **❷**

Guide for Responding

◆ LITERATURE AND YOUR LIFE

Reader's Response Is television a waste of time or a valuable source of information? Explain.

Thematic Focus What hard question does MacNeil present?

Television Log For one week, keep a log of the programs you watch on television and what you learn from each.

☑ Check Your Comprehension

1. When the average viewer reaches the age of twenty, how many hours of television has he or she watched?
2. According to MacNeil, what is the major trouble with television?
3. To what growing crisis in the United States does MacNeil believe television contributes?

◆ Critical Thinking

INTERPRET
1. MacNeil writes that much of television news is "'machine gunning with scraps.'" Explain what he means. **[Interpret]**
2. What do you think MacNeil wants people to do instead of watching television? Explain. **[Draw Conclusions]**
3. If MacNeil were the president of a television network, what changes in the programming might he make? **[Speculate]**

EVALUATE
4. Are MacNeil's arguments justified? Explain. **[Evaluate]**

APPLY
5. (a) How do you think television could be improved? (b) In what ways is it a valuable tool for society? **[Generalize]**

Beyond the Classroom

Career Connection

Television Jobs Regardless of whether one approves of television or not, TV is a giant communications medium that has become a basic part of culture and is here to stay. As such, TV provides numerous job opportunities for careers in front of the cameras as well as behind them.

Divide the class into groups. Have each group brainstorm for a list of television-related jobs. Encourage them to think about supporting job opportunities in addition to high-profile jobs such as starring roles or anchor positions.

Guide students to consider everyone that is involved in bringing a program to airtime: writers, technical teams, costumers, prop crews, directors, publicity teams, station managers, camera operators, clerical staff, caterers, legal advisers, and so on. Have groups pool the results of their brainstorming sessions.

If there is a television station in your area, help students arrange to take a tour. They might interview a station worker or learn more about opportunities that may exist for internships or volunteer jobs suited to young people their age.

The American Dream

MARTIN LUTHER KING, JR.

▲ **Critical Viewing** What qualities of King does this portrait emphasize? **[Interpret]** | 4 |

The American Dream ◆ 689

One-Minute Insight In his speech "The American Dream," Dr. Martin Luther King, Jr., explores the ideal of what America was meant to be, and criticizes America's failure to make the dream available to all citizens. He concludes his speech by trying to convince his audience that everyone can be a part of the American dream if we find ways to work together to create a sense of community and mutual respect.

Thematic Focus

❸ Facing Hard Questions Dr. Martin Luther King's most enduring legacy is his relentless struggle for respect, equality, and freedom for all citizens. He poses difficult questions in this speech, and challenges his audience to think long and hard about how to answer them. Before students read, have them jot down some of the questions they know that Dr. King asked during his lifetime. Then have them read the speech to see which ones he discusses.

►Critical Viewing◄

❹ Interpret *Students may find his expression hard to interpret, but the fact that he is shown with an American flag emphasizes his patriotism, his stature as a key political figure, and his importance to American society. His face shows that he is involved in what he is talking about.*

Customize for
Verbal/Linguistic Learners

Suggest that interested students contrast the speaking style of Dr. King and other noted speakers. Have them locate recordings of various persuasive speakers, listen to the recordings, and compare the methods of persuasion used.

Cross-Curricular Connection: Social Studies

Political Representation The United States is a democracy, in which citizens vote for public servants whose job it is to represent their interests in local, state, and federal government. While eighth graders are not yet eligible to vote, they are old enough to find out who represents their interests at each level of government.

Have students work independently, or in small groups, to find out the names and positions of the federal, state, and local representatives elected, or appointed, to serve them. They can create a directory of these people and how to contact them by letter, telephone, or e-mail. Direct them to begin with the federal Congress—House of Representatives and Senate. Then they can find out about their state and local leaders.

Finally, have students identify problems on the local, state, and federal levels that they have concerns about and might like to address. Have them determine the best person to contact for each concern. Encourage students to follow through with addressing their concerns by composing letters or e-mails and contacting the appropriate political representatives.

Reading Strategy

1 Identify Persuasive Techniques What is the persuasive technique King uses here to advance his argument? *He dissects the famous quotation almost word by word to make his point.*

Critical Thinking

2 Interpret Challenge students to restate this statement in their own words to better understand the idea King wants to convey. *The American dream is that every American should be entitled to the same rights as every other. All are worthy, not just some.*

Comprehension Check ✓

3 What is King attempting to persuade his audience to believe in this passage? *He gives a warning, a call to action, and urges people to understand the seriousness of his plea.*

Critical Thinking

4 Interpret Discuss with students the meaning of "…dwarfed distance and placed time in chains." *Modern advances have brought people of the world closer together than ever, and ways to communicate instantly have made time lags less significant.*

America is essentially a dream, a dream as yet unfulfilled. It is a dream of a land where men of all races, of all nationalities and of all creeds can live together as brothers. The substance of the dream is expressed in these sublime words, words lifted to cosmic proportions: "We hold these truths to be self-evident, that all men are created equal, that they are endowed by their Creator with certain unalienable rights, that among these are life, liberty, and pursuit of happiness."[1] This is the dream.

One of the first things we notice in this dream is an amazing universalism. It does not say some men, but it says all men. It does not say all white men, but it says all men, which includes black men. It does not say all Gentiles, but it says all men, which includes Jews. It does not say all Protestants, but it says all men, which includes Catholics.

And there is another thing we see in this dream that ultimately distinguishes democracy and our form of government from all of the totalitarian regimes[2] that emerge in history. It says that each individual has certain basic rights that are neither conferred by nor derived from the state. To discover where they came from it is necessary to move back behind the dim mist of eternity, for they are God-given. Very seldom if ever in the history of the world has a sociopolitical document expressed in such profoundly eloquent and unequivocal language the dignity and the worth of human personality. The American dream reminds us that every man is heir to the legacy of worthiness.

Ever since the Founding Fathers of our nation dreamed this noble dream, America has been something of a schizophrenic[3] personality, tragically divided against herself. On the one hand we have proudly professed the principles of democracy, and on the other hand we have sadly practiced the very antithesis of those principles. Indeed slavery and segregation have been strange paradoxes in a nation founded on the principle that all men are created equal. This is what the Swedish sociologist, Gunnar Myrdal, referred to as the American dilemma.

But the shape of the world today does not permit us the luxury of an anemic democracy. The price America must pay for the continued exploitation of the Negro and other minority groups is the price of its own destruction. The hour is late; the clock of destiny is ticking out. It is trite, but urgently true, that if America is to remain a first-class nation she can no longer have second-class citizens. Now, more than ever before, America is challenged to bring her noble dream into reality, and those who are working to implement the American dream are the true saviors of democracy.

Now may I suggest some of the things we must do if we are to make the American dream a reality. First I think all of us must develop a world perspective if we are to survive. The American dream will not become a reality devoid of the larger dream of a world of brotherhood and peace and good will. The world in which we live is a world of geographical oneness and we are challenged now to make it spiritually one.

Man's specific genius and technological ingenuity has dwarfed distance and placed time in chains. Jet planes have compressed into minutes distances that once took days and months to cover. It is not common for a preacher to be quoting Bob Hope, but I think he has aptly described this jet age in which we live. If, on taking off on a nonstop flight from Los Angeles to New York City, you develop hiccups, he said, you will hic in Los Angeles and

---

1. **"We hold these . . . pursuit of happiness":** From the Declaration of Independence, which declares the American colonies free and independent of Great Britain.
2. **totalitarian** (tō tal´ ə ter´ ē ən) **regimes:** Governments or states in which one political party or group maintains complete control under a dictatorship.
3. **schizophrenic** (skit´ se fren´ ik) *adj.:* Characterized by a separation between the thought processes and emotions.

Build Vocabulary

antithesis (an tith´ ə sis) *n.:* Contrast or opposition of thought

paradoxes (par´ ə däks´ es) *n.:* Things that seem to be contradictory

devoid (di void´) *adj.:* Completely without; lacking

Speaking and Listening Mini-Lesson

Speech

This mini-lesson supports the Speaking and Listening activity in the Idea Bank on p. 693.

Introduce You may wish to begin by having students listen to a recorded excerpt from any speech given by Dr. Martin Luther King, Jr. Have students pay particular attention to the way King speaks, how he emphasizes certain words or phrases, how he pauses for effect, how he uses vocal pitch and tone to connect ideas, and how he urges the audience to participate. Tell them that King had a gift for oratory, but that his techniques can be used effectively by any public speaker.

Develop Have students reread "The American Dream" several times to be sure they understand it and can pronounce all the words. Then have them practice delivering it aloud, as if to a large audience. Urge them to speak slowly, clearly, and dramatically to keep listeners' attention, and to make their points plainly. Speakers can team up as pairs to share constructive criticism for ways to improve and enhance their oral presentations.

Apply Have students deliver King's speech to a group of classmates, or if equipment is available, record it on audio- or videotape.

Assess Evaluate speeches on how clearly and effectively students present the words, how well they hold listeners' attention, and how accurately they emphasize the key points. Or, use the Peer Assessment: Oral Interpretation form, p. 115, in **Alternative Assessment.**

cup in New York City. That is really *moving*. If you take a flight from Tokyo, Japan, on Sunday morning, you will arrive in Seattle, Washington, on the preceding Saturday night. When your friends meet you at the airport and ask you when you left Tokyo, you will have to say, "I left tomorrow." This is the kind of world in which we live. Now this is a bit humorous but I am trying to laugh a basic fact into all of us: the world in which we live has become a single neighborhood.

❺ Through our scientific genius we have made of this world a neighborhood; now through our moral and spiritual development we must make of it a brotherhood. In a real sense, we must all learn to live together as brothers, or we will all perish together as fools. We must come to see that no individual can live alone; no nation can live alone. We must all live together; we must all be concerned about each other.

Beyond Literature

Social Studies Connection

The Nobel Prize Dr. Martin Luther King, Jr., was awarded the Nobel Peace Prize in 1964. The Prize is named after the Swedish chemist Alfred Bernhard Nobel (1883–1896), who upon his death left the bulk of his fortune to establish a prize that would be annually awarded to those who have made the greatest contributions in the fields of physics, chemistry, medicine, literature, the promotion of peace, and, in 1968, economics. The first prizes were presented on December 10, 1901, five years after the death of Nobel.

Cross-Curricular Activity
Make a timeline, beginning with the year you were born, listing all the Nobel Prize winners in the field of study that you find most exciting. Share this project with your class.

◆ *Guide for Responding*

◆ LITERATURE AND YOUR LIFE

Reader's Response What is your "American Dream"?

Thematic Focus What hard question does King want America to address?

Journal Writing Jot down ideas for an inspirational speech you'd like to give.

☑ Check Your Comprehension

1. According to King, what historic document reveals "the American dream"?
2. What does King think will happen if the United States continues to exploit minority groups?
3. King talks about the impact of rapid travel on the world. What does he say has been a result of this ability to travel?

◆ Critical Thinking

INTERPRET
1. What is the significance of the lines King recites from the Declaration of Independence? **[Interpret]**
2. Explain what King means when he speaks of the "American dilemma." **[Infer]**
3. According to King, what is the difference between a neighborhood and a brotherhood? **[Analyze]**

EVALUATE
4. (a) What does King think must be done if the American dream is to become a reality?
   (b) Do you agree? Explain. **[Assess]**

COMPARE LITERARY WORKS
5. Of these two persuasive selections, which do you find more appropriate for today's audience? Explain. **[Make a Judgment]**

The American Dream ◆ 691

Thematic Focus

❺ Facing Hard Questions Ask students to summarize the questions Dr. King asks. *How can we accomplish these goals? Who can help us foster brotherhood and peace in our communities? How can people learn to accept and respect one another?*

Beyond Literature

To help students with their timelines, provide them with the following Internet address (all Web sites are subject to change).

For more information about the Nobel Foundation:
http://www.nobel.se
We *strongly recommend* that you preview the site before you send students to it.

Reinforce and Extend

Answers
◆ LITERATURE AND YOUR LIFE

Reader's Response Students may wish to record their thoughts in a reader's response log.

Thematic Focus He wants America to acknowledge that its dream is not available to all its citizens.

☑ Check Your Comprehension

1. The Declaration of Independence reveals the American dream.
2. He thinks that America will risk destruction of its democratic ideals.
3. The world is more of a "global village" than ever before.

◆ Critical Thinking

1. He argues that it never intended to exclude anyone.
2. He says that America was founded as a place where "all men are created equal," but the practices of slavery and segregation go against this ideal.
3. In a neighborhood, people are civil just because they live near one another. Brotherhood requires effort and commitment.
4. (a) He thinks people must develop true concern for one another.
   (b) Most will agree that this is the ideal.
5. Have students justify their opinions.

 Beyond the Selection

FURTHER READING
Other Works by the Authors
Breaking News, Robert MacNeil
Wordstruck: A Memoir, Robert MacNeil
A Knock at Midnight, Martin Luther King, Jr.
The Measure of a Man, Martin Luther King, Jr.
Other Essays and Speeches
I Have a Dream: Writings and Speeches That Changed the World, James Melvin Washington (ed.)
Lend Me Your Ears: Great Speeches in History, William Safire (ed.)

INTERNET
We recommend the following sites on the Internet (all Web sites are subject to change).
For an interview with Robert MacNeil:
http://web -cr05.pbs.org/newshour/ww/robin_macneil.html
For information on Martin Luther King, Jr.:
http://www.nps.gov/malu/
We *strongly recommend* that you preview all sites before sending students to them.

Answers

◆ Reading Strategy

1. MacNeil uses supporting evidence, persuasive language, and references to negative aspects of popular culture.
2. He refers to popular culture.
3. He begins each point with "We must…" He repeats the words *together* and *alone*.

◆ Build Vocabulary

Using the Prefix *anti-*
1. antislavery; opposed to slavery
2. anticlimax; disappointing ending
3. antiterrorism; against terrorism
4. antifreeze; a substance to prevent a fluid from freezing

Spelling Strategy
1. annoy;   2. avoid;   3. coil

Using the Word Bank
1. d   3. g   5. e   7. c
2. b   4. a   6. f

◆ Literary Focus

1. (a) He says TV discourages concentration; it makes us passive; and it contributes to illiteracy. (b) His comments about discouraging concentration and making people passive are less effective because they are mostly supported by his own opinions. His statement that TV contributes to illiteracy is more effective because it is supported by statistics.
2. Starting with the fundamental premise of the Declaration of Independence, King argues, point by point, that the American dream has not been extended to all Americans.

◆ Build Grammar Skills

Practice
1. its/one; 2. his or her/nobody;
3. their/many; 4. his or her/person;
5. their/several

Writing Application
1. Neither MacNeil nor King wrote his essay in a narrative style.
2. Each of the men had his own message to communicate.

 Writer's Solution

For additional instruction and practice, use the lesson in the *Writer's Solution Language Lab CD-ROM* on subject-verb agreement. You may also use the practice page on Agreement Between Pronouns and Antecedents, p. 85, in the *Writer's Solution Grammar Practice Book.*

Guide for Responding (continued)

◆ Reading Strategy

IDENTIFY PERSUASIVE TECHNIQUES

To convince readers or listeners to think or act in a certain way, writers use **persuasive techniques.** These include supporting evidence, persuasive language, references to popular culture, repetition, and slogans.

1. Which types of persuasive techniques does MacNeil use most throughout "The Trouble with Television"? Explain.
2. What technique is King employing when he quotes Bob Hope?
3. Find an example of repetition in the final paragraph of King's speech.

◆ Build Vocabulary

USING THE PREFIX *anti-*

The prefix *anti-*, as in *antithesis*, means "opposed to" or "against." Combine the following words with the prefix *anti-*, and define the new word:
1. slavery 2. climax 3. terrorism 4. freeze

SPELLING STRATEGY

The *oy* sound is spelled differently, depending on its location in a word. If the *oy* sound is in the middle of a word, it is spelled *oi*, as in the word *devoid*. At the end of a word, it is spelled *oy* as in *toy*. Choose the correct spelling of the *oy* word:
1. annoi, annoy 2. avoid, avoyd 3. coil, coyl

USING THE WORD BANK

Match each Word Bank word in Column A with the word or phrase closest in meaning in Column B:

Column A	Column B
1. diverts	a. spreading throughout
2. usurps	b. seizes power
3. august	c. empty
4. pervading	d. distracts
5. antithesis	e. something opposite of
6. paradoxes	f. seemingly contradictory statements
7. devoid	g. honored

◆ Literary Focus

PERSUASIVE ESSAY

A **persuasive essay** is a short piece of non-fiction in which the writer strives to make readers act or think in a certain way.
1. (a) List three points MacNeil makes that warn against watching television. (b) Explain why each point is or is not effective.
2. In what ways is "The American Dream" an example of persuasive writing?

◆ Build Grammar Skills

**PRONOUN AGREEMENT
WITH INDEFINITE SUBJECTS**

Pronouns must agree with their antecedents in both number and gender, even when the antecedent is indefinite.

Some antecedents may be masculine or feminine. When referring to such antecedents, use both the masculine and the feminine singular forms:

Each *person* must do what *he or she* (not *they*) thinks is right.

If the antecedent is *anybody, anyone, everybody, everyone, neither, nobody, no one, someone,* or *somebody,* use a singular pronoun to refer to it: Everyone can help in *his or her* own way.

Practice On your paper, identify the pronoun and its antecedent:
1. Not one of the programs reached (its, their) audience.
2. Nobody volunteered to give up (their, his or her) favorite television show.
3. Many spend (their, his or her) time watching television.
4. Give each person (their, his or her) civil rights.
5. Several volunteered (their, his or her) time.

Writing Application On your paper, write corrected versions of the following sentences:
1. Neither of these writers wrote their essays in a narrative style.
2. Each of the men had their own message to communicate.

Build Your Portfolio

 Idea Bank

Writing

1. List Make a list of television programs that you or your family watch regularly. You may also list the hours each family member spends watching television during an average week.

2. Business Letter Write to a television network or producer offering suggestions about programming that would make television a more worthwhile experience. Use correct business letter form.

3. News Analysis News commentators often review or critique political speeches after they're delivered. Write an analysis of King's speech, identifying its message and overall effectiveness.

Speaking and Listening

4. Speech Martin Luther King, Jr., was a powerful speaker. Practice reading "The American Dream" aloud until you can give an inspiring rendition. Then, present it to your classmates. **[Performing Arts Link]**

5. Dialogue [Group Activity] With a partner, role-play a conversation between King and MacNeil in which they discuss ways to improve American life. **[Social Studies Link]**

Projects

6. Civil Rights Exhibit Research the history of the civil rights movement, using the library and other reference materials. Create a multimedia exhibit that shows a chronological progression in the battle for civil rights. **[Media Link; Social Studies Link]**

7. Multimedia Presentation Learn about some aspect of television—how satellites work, how broadcasting stations send and receive television signals, or how your television set works. Then, develop a multimedia presentation, complete with diagrams and charts, to present to the class. **[Media Link; Science Link]**

 Writing Mini-Lesson

Persuasive Speech

A persuasive speech like Martin Luther King's "The American Dream" can inspire an audience to think in a particular way or to perform some action. Prepare a persuasive speech about how your school, community, or nation can be made better.

Writing Skills Focus: Strong Beginning and Ending

Effective speeches have **strong beginnings and endings.** Choose one of the following to begin your speech: a startling fact or surprising statistic, a quotation, a question, or an anecdote. MacNeil used the first method:

Model From the Essay
If you fit the statistical averages, by the age of 20 you will have been exposed to at least 20,000 hours of television.

Prewriting Choose a subject about which you feel strongly. Then, gather all the facts and supporting details you need to persuade your listeners. Organize your main ideas and supporting details in outline form.

Drafting From your outline, draft your speech, creating a strong beginning and ending. Use powerful words that you can stress when you deliver your speech.

Revising Read your speech to a classmate, and ask for feedback. If your beginning and ending are not effective, revise them to provide more impact. Also, proofread to correct any errors in grammar.

> **◆ Grammar Application**
> If you have used pronouns to refer to indefinite antecedents, check that your pronouns agree in number and gender.

The Trouble with Television/The American Dream ◆ 693

 Idea Bank

Following are suggestions for matching the Idea Bank topics with your students' performance levels and learning modalities:

Customize for
Performance Levels
Less Advanced Students: 1, 4, 6
Average Students: 2, 4, 5, 6, 7
More Advanced Students: 3, 4, 5, 6, 7

Customize for
Learning Modalities
Verbal/Linguistic: 1, 2, 3, 4, 5, 6
Visual/Spatial: 6, 7
Bodily/Kinesthetic: 4, 5
Interpersonal: 1, 4, 5
Intrapersonal: 2, 3, 6, 7

 Writing Mini-Lesson

Refer students to the Writing Handbook in the back of the book for instruction on the writing process and for further information on persuasion.

 **Writer's Solution**

Writers at Work Videodisc
Have students view the videodisc segment on Persuasion (Ch. 6), featuring Kate Mitchell, to see how she tries to begin a draft with a "hook." Have students discuss this approach to help them write their persuasive speeches.

Play frames 5312 to 6086

Writing Lab CD-ROM
Have students complete the tutorial on Persuasion. Follow these steps:
1. Direct students to the Evaluating Your Topic section, which will help them establish whether the topic can be supported by facts and evidence.
2. Have students use the interactive instruction in the Drafting section on avoiding faulty reasoning. Then they can draft on computer.
3. Have students revise with the Self-Evaluation Checklist.

Writer's Solution Sourcebook
Have students use Chapter 6, "Persuasion," pp. 166–199, for more support. The chapter includes in-depth instruction on developing a strong introduction, body, and conclusion, pp. 188–189.

✓ ASSESSMENT OPTIONS

Formal Assessment, Selection Test, pp. 198–200, and Assessment Resources Software. The selection test is designed so that it can be easily customized to the performance levels of your students.

Alternative Assessment, p. 46, includes options for less advanced students, more advanced students, verbal/linguistic learners, visual/spatial learners, logical/mathematical learners, interpersonal learners, and bodily/kinesthetic learners.

PORTFOLIO ASSESSMENT
Use the following rubrics in the **Alternative Assessment** booklet to assess student writing:
List: Definition/Classification, p. 95
Business Letter: Business Letter/Memo, p. 109
News Analysis: Literary Analysis/Interpretation, p. 108
Writing Mini-Lesson: Persuasion, p. 101

Politicians, writers, philosophers, and everyday people in all times and circumstances have always faced the challenge of posing and trying to answer hard questions. "Sharing the America Dream" is a persuasive speech that explores the importance of extending the ideals of the Founding Fathers to less fortunate Americans. Colin Powell reexamines the American dream by suggesting a way to make it available to more citizens.

Comprehension Check ☑

❶ What event does the author describe? *He describes the men of the Continental Congress—a group of unpaid representatives from the thirteen colonies who got together in Philadelphia in 1776 to hammer out the principles that would guide a new nation.*

Clarification

❷ Langston Hughes (1902–1967) was a prominent writer of the Harlem Renaissance.

Thematic Focus

❸ Facing Hard Questions Ask students to restate the difficult question Colin Powell poses in this passage. *He wants people to think of ways to help the less fortunate to experience the American dream.*

More About the Author

The son of Jamaican immigrants, retired U.S. Army General **Colin Powell** (born 1937) grew up in and was educated in the New York City public schools and at City College of New York. During his distinguished military career, he served as a battalion commander in Korea, did two tours of duty in Vietnam, and commanded the 2nd Brigade of the 101st Airborne Division of the U.S. Army in Europe. At age 52, Powell became the youngest-ever Chairman of the Joint Chiefs of Staff. From this post, he led the Persian Gulf War effort. When he retired from military service in 1993, many Americans hoped he would run for president, but he declined. Instead, he devotes his time to his family, to volunteering, and to speaking and writing. Powell believes that the family structure bonds people together—whether as family groups or as a broad national family.

694

CONNECTIONS TO TODAY'S WORLD

"The American Dream" is an idea that has inspired many political figures and writers. The following speech was given by General Colin Powell at the National Volunteer Summit in Philadelphia, Pennsylvania, on June 1, 1997. In the speech, he shares his vision for what America can become through volunteerism.

from

Sharing the American Dream

Colin Powell

Over 200 years ago, a group of volunteers gathered on this sacred spot to found a new nation. In perfect words, they voiced their dreams and aspirations of an imperfect world. They pledged their lives, their fortune and their sacred honor to secure inalienable rights given by God for life, liberty and pursuit of happiness—pledged that they would provide them to all who would inhabit this new nation.

They look down on us today in spirit, with pride for all we have done to keep faith with their ideals and their sacrifices. Yet, despite all we have done, this is still an imperfect world. We still live in an imperfect society. Despite more than two centuries of moral and material progress, despite all our efforts to achieve a more perfect union, there are still Americans who are not sharing in the American Dream. There are still Americans who wonder: is the journey there for them, is the dream there for them, or, whether it is, at best, a dream deferred.

The great American poet, Langston Hughes, talked about a dream deferred, and he said, "What happens to a dream deferred? Does it dry up like a raisin in the sun, or fester like a sore and then run? Does it stink like rotten meat or crust and sugar over like a syrupy sweet? Maybe it just sags, like a heavy load. Or, does it explode?" . . .

So today, we gather here today to pledge that the dream must no longer be deferred and it will never, as long as we can do anything about it, become a dream denied. That is why we are here, my friends. We gather here to pledge that those of us who are more fortunate will not forsake those who are less fortunate. We are a compassionate and caring people. We are a generous people. We will reach down, we will reach back, we will reach across to help our brothers and sisters who are in need.

Above all, we pledge to reach out to the most vulnerable members of the American family, our children. As you've heard, up to 15 million young Americans today are at risk. . . .

In terms of numbers the task may seem staggering. But if we look at the simple needs that these children have, then the task is manageable, the goal is

694 ◆ *Nonfiction*

Cross-Curricular Connection: Social Studies

Working Together Colin Powell and Martin Luther King, Jr., share an idea of people working together for a common good. In King's speech, he said " . . . the world in which we live has become a single neighborhood . . . we must all be concerned about each other." In Powell's speech, he said, "We will reach down, we will reach back, we will reach across to help our brothers and our sisters who are in need." Both men were speaking of teamwork—working together toward a common goal of helping others so that everyone's life is better.

To help students connect and extend this idea to today's world, use Art Transparency 17, pp. 71–74, in **Art Transparencies.** Show students *Les Constructeurs (The Builders),* and let them study what is happening in the painting. Invite them to suggest descriptions for the activity that is depicted, such as teamwork, working or building together, helping one another, and making a heavy load light. Point out that working together to create a common good requires the type of teamwork displayed by this workman to create a large structure such as a building.

▲ **Critical Viewing** In what ways are Powell and the volunteers in this photograph helping others to achieve "the American dream"? **[Connect]**

4

5 achievable. We know what they need. They need an adult caring person in their life, a safe place to learn and grow, a healthy start, marketable skills and an opportunity to serve so that early in their lives they learn the virtue of service so that they can reach out then and touch another young American in need.

These are basic needs that we commit ourselves today, we promise today. We are making America's promise today to provide to those children in need. This is a grand

alliance. It is an alliance between government and corporate America and nonprofit America, between our institutions of faith, but especially between individual Americans.

You heard the governors and the mayors, and you'll hear more in a little minute that says the real answer is for each and every one of us, not just here in Philadelphia, but across this land—for each and every one of us to reach out and touch someone in need.

All of us can spare 30 minutes a week or an hour a week. All of us can give an extra dollar. All of us can touch someone who doesn't look like us, who doesn't speak like us, who may not dress like us, but needs us in their lives. And that's what we all have to do to keep this going.

And so there's a spirit of Philadelphia here today. There's a spirit of Philadelphia that we saw yesterday in Germantown. There is a spirit of Philadelphia that will leave Philadelphia tomorrow afternoon and spread across this whole nation—30 governors will go back and spread it; over 100 mayors will go back and spread it, and hundreds of others, leaders around this country who are watching will go back and spread it. Corporate America will spread it, nonprofits will spread it. And each and every one of us will spread it because it has to be done, we have no choice. We cannot leave these children behind if we are going to meet the dreams of our founding fathers.

And so let us all join in this great crusade. Let us make sure that no child in America is left behind, no child in America has their dream deferred or denied. We can do it. We can do it because we are Americans.

---

1. To what group of people does Powell refer in his opening paragraph?
2. What is Powell's pledge?
3. According to Powell, what do the children of the United States need?
4. What action does Powell urge citizens to take?
5. In what ways is Powell's speech similar to King's? How does it differ?

---

from Sharing the American Dream ◆ 695

▶Critical Viewing◀

4 Connect *Powell and the volunteers are donating "muscle time" to help clean up a vacant lot or schoolyard to make it safer and more attractive for local children. Instead of just talking about the American dream, they are working to make it a reality.*

◆ Critical Thinking

5 Evaluate Discuss with students what virtue Powell sees in service, and challenge them to evaluate why it is virtuous to serve. *Service means putting one's own needs aside for the benefit of others. It is a virtue because it shows compassion and kindness, and expresses hope for making the world a better place.*

Answers

1. He refers to the Founding Fathers who signed the Declaration of Independence in Philadelphia.
2. He pledges to do what he can to help those who are less fortunate or in need so that they, too, can enjoy the American dream.
3. They need caring adults in their lives, safe places to learn and grow, good health, marketable skills, and a chance to learn the value of service to others.
4. He urges citizens to give spare time or small sums of money to reach out to help others.
5. Both men believe in the values of community and brotherhood; both are concerned that the American dream is not available to all Americans. King's speech is more intellectual, idealistic, and spiritual, while Powell's is more practical, uses simpler language, and offers a concrete suggestion.

 Beyond the Selection

FURTHER READING
Other Works by Colin Powell
My American Journey
In His Own Words, Colin Powell and Lisa Shaw (ed.)
The Golden Thirteen: Recollections of the First Black Naval Officers, Paul Stillwell (ed.)
Other Works on the Theme of the American Dream
It Doesn't Have to Take a Hero, General H. Norman Schwarzkopf
Succeeding Against the Odds, John H. Johnson

INTERNET
We recommend the following sites on the Internet (all Web sites are subject to change).
For more information on Colin Powell, go to:
http://www.mojuan.com/in2000powell/index.htm
For an interview with Colin Powell, go to:
http://www.achievement.org/autodoc/page/pow0pro-1
We *strongly recommend* that you preview all sites before sending students to them.

Establish Writing Guidelines

Review the following key characteristics of a research paper:

- A research paper provides factual information researched on a topic.
- A research paper uses information gathered from a variety of sources.
- A research paper includes a bibliography citing sources used by the writer, and may include footnotes or parenthetical citations.

You may want to distribute the scoring rubric for Research Report/Paper, p. 102 in **Alternative Assessment,** to make students aware of the criteria on which they will be evaluated. See the suggestions on page 698 for how you can customize the rubric to this workshop.

Refer students to the Writing Handbook in the back of the book for instruction on the writing process and further information on reports.

Writer's Solution

Writers at Work Videodisc

To introduce students to reports and to show them how writer Virginia Hamilton feels about doing research, play the videodisc segment on Reports (Ch. 7).

Play frames 9330 to 17762

Writing Lab CD-ROM

If your students have access to computers, you may want to have them work in the tutorial on Reports to complete all or part of their research reports. Follow these steps:

1. Have students view the interactive model of a library research report.
2. Suggest that students use the Sunburst Diagram Activity to come up with topic ideas.
3. Encourage students to use the Outliner Tool to arrange main ideas and details.
4. Have students draft on computer.

Writer's Solution Sourcebook

Students can find additional support, including in-depth instruction on developing an organization plan, p. 223, in the chapter on Reports, pp. 200–233.

Report Writing

Research Paper

Writing Process Workshop

A report based on information you've researched—such as animal behavior or the effects of television—is called a research paper. A research paper consists of an introduction that states your main idea, a body that offers information with evidence from your research, and a conclusion that sums up the main points of the paper. The body of your paper includes citations that give credit to the sources of the information and ideas you've used in your paper.

Write a research paper on a topic that interests you. These writing skills, covered in the Writing Mini-Lessons in this part, will help you:

Writing Skills Focus

▶ **Use quotation marks** around information you take directly from a source. You must acknowledge information and ideas that are not your own. (See p. 683.)

▶ **Write a strong beginning** to hook your readers and **a strong ending** to leave a lasting impression. (See p. 693.)

▶ **Maintain a clear organization** with an introduction, a body, and a conclusion.

Anaïs Nin's essay about forest fires prompted one student to write a research paper about the career of firefighting:

WRITING MODEL

Although firefighting looks exciting, it's a dangerous occupation. The chance of a firefighter's being killed on the job is thirteen times as high as it is for other workers. ① "Every week in the United States, an average of one firefighter is killed and four hundred others are injured." (Dean, p. 103) ② The physical act of fighting fires occurs in four steps—protection of uninvolved buildings and areas, confinement of a fire, ventilation of a building, and extinguishment of a fire. ③

① The writer begins strongly with a startling fact.

② Quotation marks indicate that these words come from an outside source, noted in parentheses.

③ The writer ends the introduction with a statement of the main idea that will be explored in the body of the paper.

696 ◆ Nonfiction

 Beyond the Classroom

Career Connection

Journalist A career in journalism entails writing of reports on a daily or weekly basis. Journalists are assigned stories or topic ideas, then they must research and create a finished report. Research may include interviews, analysis of statistics or other data, and using published works on the topic.

Have students review a copy of a local or national newspaper. Have them, as a class, choose a headline and summarize the information given in the article. Then, ask students to consider what type of research the journalist may have

done to write the article. Does the article contain quotations from people? Are there graphs or charts? Are there references to other articles?

Have students come up with a list of questions about journalism careers and then research to find answers. They may examine the differences between being a newspaper journalist and a television anchorperson. They may want to find out the specific requirements for being a sports journalist or a fashion journalist. Have them report their findings to the class, explaining where they found their information.

Prewriting

Choose a Topic Choose a topic that interests you. Browsing through a library can stimulate some ideas. Flipping through a news magazine or looking through your journal can generate more. Possible topics include historical figures, historical events, scientific occurrences, music, art, and sports.

Write a Main Idea Statement Write a statement of your main idea or the point you plan to make in the body of your paper. Refer to this statement as you draft.

Use a Variety of Sources Use different kinds of sources. In addition to print sources (encyclopedias, nonfiction books, and articles), you might talk to an expert or watch a documentary on your subject. Use up-to-date resources.

Take Careful Notes Be accurate when researching your paper. Assign each source a number, and use that number to identify all notes taken from the source. Use the following tips when taking notes:

Source Cards	Note Cards
• Create one card for each source, and give it a number.	• Enter only one item of information on each card.
• Include title, author, date and place of publication, etc.	• Include the page number and number of source.
	• When copying exact words, use quotation marks.

Drafting

Maintain a Clear Organization

▶ **Introduction** Start your paper by grabbing your readers' attention. Use a lively quotation, a fascinating statistic, an intriguing question, an interesting anecdote, or a vivid description to hook your readers. Then, include a statement of the main idea of your paper.

▶ **Body** In the main part of your paper, explore and develop your main idea. Incorporate quotations from your research to support the points you are making.

▶ **Strong Conclusion** End with a thought-provoking question or a strong statement of fact. Leave your reader with a strong impression about your topic.

DRAFTING/REVISING

APPLYING LANGUAGE SKILLS: Varying Sentence Structure

Vary your sentence structure to make your writing more interesting. Use simple, compound, and complex sentences:

Simple:
Many fires occur because of carelessness.

Compound:
Many fires are accidentally started at campsites, and the fires sometimes destroy entire forests.

Complex:
Although rangers remind campers to extinguish camp-fires, many still leave behind live embers.

Practice Rewrite this paragraph to vary sentence style and length:

Chemicals help fight forest fires. Borate or bentonite is usually used. The chemicals penetrate heavy foliage. They make trees resist fire longer than water alone.

Writing Application As you draft your paper, vary the structure of your sentences.

Writer's Solution Connection
Language Lab
For additional practice, complete the lesson on Varying Sentence Structure.

Writing Process Workshop ◆ 697

Prewriting

After students have finished taking notes, have them create a thesis statement that will point the report in a specific direction. Suggest that students read through all their notes and decide on the most important idea. Then, they can put that idea into a sentence that sums up the main point of the paper, the thesis statement.

Customize for
Less Proficient Writers

To help students organize their information into an outline, suggest that students fill out the Main Idea and Supporting Details Organizer, p. 61 in **Writing and Language Transparencies.** Have them list the main idea and then the supporting details. Explain to students that these supporting details may actually be subtopics of the report. If those subtopics can be supported with details, students may want to create another organizer using the subtopic as the main idea.

Writer's Solution

Writing Lab CD-ROM
Suggest that students use the Guidelines for Taking Notes in the Prewriting section. The Guidelines include Notecard Stationery, which may help students when taking notes at the library.

Drafting

Explain to students that they will want to use transitions to connect the ideas in their report smoothly. Suggest to students that as they draft they read what they write aloud, to check how the ideas flow in their drafts. If there are awkward breaks, suggest that students use a transitional word or phrase.

Writer's Solution

Writing Lab CD-ROM
Suggest that students view the audio-annotated professional and student Writing Models to help them develop effective strategies for writing the first drafts of their reports.

Applying Language Skills

Varying Sentence Structure Explain to students that another way to vary their sentences is to vary sentence beginnings. The most common way to begin sentences is with a subject followed by a verb. Suggest to students that they review their sentence openings and try to begin with a clause, phrase, or modifier.

Answers
Possible response:
Chemicals, such as borate or bentonite, are usually used to help fight forest fires. The

chemicals penetrate heavy foliage, making the trees resist fire longer than water alone.

Writer's Solution

For additional instruction and practice, have students use the practice page on Expanding Short Sentences, p. 123, in the *Writer's Solution Grammar Practice Book.* They can also use the Varying Sentence Structure lesson in the Sentence Style unit of the *Writer's Solution Language Lab CD-ROM.*

Revising

Other points to consider when revising:

1. Could you add details to make your report more interesting?
2. Is your purpose clear to readers within the introduction?
3. Have you used a variety of sources to gather information?

 Writer's Solution

Writing Lab CD-ROM

For additional help revising, suggest that students use the Revision Checker in the Revision section to help them check for coherence and unity between paragraphs.

Publishing

For other publishing ideas, suggest that students create a class display of their research reports. Have students provide their reports with a table of contents and cover page.

Reinforce and Extend

Review the Writing Guidelines
After students have completed their papers, review the characteristics of a research paper.

Applying Language Skills

Citing Your Sources Explain to students that a bibliography lists all the sources they have used in their research—both the works cited in footnotes or parentheses and the works that have been read but not specifically cited.

Writing Process Workshop

EDITING/PROOFREADING

APPLYING LANGUAGE SKILLS: Citing Your Sources

List your sources in alphabetical order in a bibliography at the end of your paper. Follow these examples:

Book:
Ragan, Bridget. *Firefighting in America.* New York: Acme Publishing, 1998.

Article:
Lin, Sam. "Fighting Fires from the Air," *Real People,* June 1997, p. 52.

Interview:
Moore, Robert. Personal Interview, Portland, Maine, April 12, 1998.

Internet:
Smoke Jumpers: http://eagle.online.discovery.com

When you use quotations from these sources within your paper, cite the author's last name and add the page number of the work in parentheses.

"Steam fire engines were used in the great fire of Chicago." (Holmes, p. 19.)

Writing Application Use the proper format to cite sources in your research paper.

> ### Writer's Solution Connection Writing Lab
>
> For help with revising, use the Self-Evaluation Checklist in the Revising section of the Reports tutorial.

Revising

Use a Checklist Use the following checklist to help you revise your research paper:

▶ Does your paper have a strong beginning?
  If not, add a startling quotation or fact, an anecdote, or a thought-provoking question.

▶ Did you quote accurately and use quotation marks to indicate material from other sources?
  Check that quotations are exact, and enclose them in quotation marks.

▶ Did you use a logical organization?
  Begin with an introduction that states your main idea, explore the subtopics of your main idea in the body, and end the paper with a conclusion.

▶ Do you end strongly?
  Use your conclusion to summarize the main points of the paper. Ending with a thought-provoking question can leave a lasting impression on your readers.

REVISION MODEL

① Firefighting is as systematic as using a computer.

The four steps of firefighting are protection of uninvolved buildings and areas, confinement of a fire, ventilation of a ② Although a firefighter uses a system, this job is much more dangerous than working at a computer.
building, and extinguishment of a fire. B. Ramelli sums up the importance of a firefighter's job. ③ " Daily, the firefighter dons heavy gear and faces nature's fury. Yet how often do we stop to thank the men and women who have placed our protection above their own lives? "

① The writer adds this statement to lead the reader to a conclusion about firefighting.
② The writer adds this sentence to introduce the quotation. Using this quotation leaves a lasting impression.
③ The writer added quotation marks around the words that were not his own.

Publishing and Presenting

▶ **Home** Present your report orally to your family and friends. Include at least one visual aid to make your presentation more appealing.

▶ **Library** Place a copy of your finished report in your school library.

✓ ASSESSMENT		4	3	2	1
PORTFOLIO ASSESSMENT Use the rubric on Research Report/Paper in the **Alternative Assessment** booklet, p. 102, to assess the students' writing. Add these criteria to customize this rubric to this assignment.	**Varying Sentence Structure**	The paper uses a variety of sentences that make the writing interesting.	The paper uses a variety of sentences; however, there are places where more variation is needed.	The paper uses mainly simple sentences, with a few compound or complex sentences.	The paper uses mostly simple sentences that sound redundant.
	Citation of Sources	All sources are thoroughly documented in correct bibliographic form.	Most sources are thoroughly documented in correct bibliographic form.	Some sources are thoroughly documented in correct bibliographic form.	There are no sources cited, or none of the sources cited are cited correctly.

Real-World Reading Skills Workshop

Evaluating Sources of Information

Strategies for Success

As you read for information, you will encounter magazines, encyclopedias, and Web sites that contain interesting information. Before using this information, you should evaluate whether or not it is credible and relevant to your needs. Use the following guidelines for evaluating sources:

Evaluate the Author Relying on the information of experts in each field is usually a good idea. Look at bibliographical information to find out whether an author is an expert or has firsthand experience in the topic being covered.

Check the Publication Date In the fields of science, technology, and politics, changes happen quickly. Use the most current sources. Information in older sources might be outdated. Check for the most recent date on the copyright page. If your topic requires current information, choose sources that have been published very recently.

Check the Web Site The Internet carries a huge amount of information—some reliable and some not reliable. Note who publishes the Web site: The United States government or *National Geographic,* for example, are reliable. If the site ends in **.edu,** it is an educational source, and its information is likely correct.

Apply the Strategies

Suppose your assignment is a paper on Dubrovnik, a city in Croatia, which declared its independence from Yugoslavia in 1991. You have found the sources shown in the left column. Answer the following questions about these sources.

1. Which encyclopedia is the better choice? Why?
2. Which of the Web sites is designed for educational purposes? How do you know that?
3. Of the three Web sites, which two would you use? Why?
4. The book on Yugoslavia probably has information on Dubrovnik. Would you use it? Why or why not?

Sources for Assignment

- **The Encyclopedia Britannica,** Vol. D, © 1960
- **The World Book,** Vol. D, © 1998
- www.FUN FACTS@pqr.letsbuy.com
- www.nationalgeographic.com
- www.smithsonianmag.si.edu (click on Dubrovnik)
- **Yugoslavia,** by Breshniv Kovacs, © 1968 by Prentice Hall

✔ Here are other situations in which it's important to evaluate sources of information:
▶ Reading a political pamphlet
▶ Reading a newspaper editorial
▶ Investigating a rumor

Introduce the Strategies

Explain to students that by doing research of different types of materials, they may find different types of useful information. For example, although one may be able to find a wealth of information on the Internet about a topic, it may be more useful to consult an encyclopedia or reference book on the topic as well, for concise, verified information. Explain to students that when viewing Web addresses, sites that end in .gov are government sites, and most likely their information is correct and up-to-date.

Customize for
Less Proficient Readers

Some students may not have as much experience on the Internet as others. When doing research on the Internet, try to pair less experienced students with Web-savvy students. This way, students can pick up tips from their partners about surfing the Web and verifying addresses of Web sites.

Apply the Strategies

Explain to students that encyclopedias are a good way to start their research. Students should make sure to find the most recently published encyclopedia to obtain a quick overview of their topic. Many encyclopedias are now available in CD-ROM or online.

Answers

1. The *World Book* is the better choice because it was published more recently than the *Encyclopedia Britannica.*
2. The web site **www.smithsonianmag.si.edu** is designed for an educational purpose, because the address contains the suffix **.edu.**
3. Students should say they would use the **www.smithsonianmag.si.edu** site and the **www. nationalgeographic.com** site. From their addresses, you can tell the sites are published by reliable sources (*Smithsonian* and *National Geographic*).
4. Students should realize that they would not want to use the book because it was published in 1968. The topic of their report is Dubrovnik, which declared its independence in 1991, so the information in the book will be invalid or out-of-date.

**Reviewing Pronoun
and Antecedent Agreement**
The selections in Part 2 include
instruction on the following:

- Pronoun and Antecedent
  Agreement
- Pronoun Agreement With Indefinite
  Antecedents

This instruction is reinforced with
the Build Grammar Skills practice
pages in **Selection Support,** pp. 244
and 249.

As you review pronoun and
antecedent agreement, you may wish
to review the following:

- Agreement With Reflexive
  Pronouns

Explain to students that reflexive
pronouns end in *-self* or *-selves* and
refer to an antecedent earlier in the
sentence. A personal pronoun requires
an antecedent that is clearly stated
or clearly understood. For example:

INCORRECT: The real estate agent gave John and myself a tour of the apartment.

CORRECT: The real estate agent gave John and me a tour of the apartment.

✒ *Writer's Solution*

For additional practice and support,
use the practice page on Agreement
Between Pronouns and Antecedents,
p. 85, in the *Writer's Solution Grammar
Practice Book.* If students have access
to technology, suggest that they use
the Pronouns and Antecedents lesson
in the Using Pronouns unit in the
*Writer's Solution Language Lab CD-
ROM.*

Pronoun and Antecedent Agreement | Grammar Review

A pronoun usually refers to another noun or
pronoun, called its **antecedent.** A personal
pronoun must agree with its antecedent in
number (singular or plural) and gender
(masculine, feminine, or neither). (See p. 682.)

Use a **singular pronoun** to refer to a
singular antecedent:

A *man* rushed in to announce *he* had seen
smoke on Monrovia Peak. (The singular
masculine pronoun *he* refers to the
singular masculine noun *man.*)

Use a **plural pronoun** to refer to a **plural
antecedent:**

The three *Bassets* were already in
residence, draped snoring on the fireside
rug, but *they* seemed to be used to
Debbie. . . . (The plural pronoun *they*
refers to the plural noun *Bassets.*)

Indefinite Pronouns Sometimes an antecedent
may be an **indefinite pronoun.** Some indefinite pronouns are singular, some are plural, and
some can be either:

Singular		Plural	Singular or Plural
another	much	both	all
anybody	neither	few	any
each	no one	many	more
either	nothing	others	most
everyone	other	several	none
everything	something		some
little			

Singular: *Neither* of the women brought *her*
pets to the picnic.

Plural: *Both* of the foresters struggled to keep
their feet on the sliding mud.

Either:
Singular: Take *all* of the food and eat *it.*
Plural: *All* of the dogs were checked by *their*
veterinarians.

ante·ced·ent (an'tə sēd'nt) 4 *Gram.* the word, phrase, or clause to
which a pronoun refers ("man" is the *antecedent* of "who" in "the
man who spoke") 5 *Logic* the part of a conditional proposition that

Agreement in Gender Some antecedents
may be either masculine or feminine. When
referring to such antecedents, use both the
masculine and the feminine forms:

The *person* who lost *his* or *her* notebook
will be looking for it.

Practice 1 Copy the following sentences into
your notebook, completing them with a
pronoun that agrees with its antecedent:

1. Mrs. Ainsworth answered the door and I
   showed _____?_____ the cat.

2. "People living at the foot of the mountain
   were packing _____?_____ cars."

3. Each student turned off _____?_____ television
   set for a week.

Practice 2 Copy the following sentences
into your notebook, correcting any errors in
pronoun and antecedent agreement:

1. Everyone packed their bags and left as
   quickly as possible.

2. Both the spectators and the reporters
   expressed his or her desire to help.

Grammar in Writing

✔ *Sometimes using* his *or* her *to refer
to an indefinite antecedent is awkward
and confusing. When that is the case,
rewrite the sentence with a plural
antecedent and pronoun.*

Awkward: Each student will copy the
sentences into his or her notebook.

Plural: Students will copy the
sentences into their notebooks.

Answers
Practice 1
1. Mrs. Ainsworth answered the door and I
   showed *her* the cat.
2. "People living at the foot of the mountain
   were packing *their* cars."
3. Each student turned off *his* or *her* television
   set for a week.

Practice 2
1. Everyone packed his or her bags and left
   as quickly as possible.
2. Both the spectators and the reporters
   expressed their desire to help.

Speaking, Listening, and Viewing Workshop

Resisting Persuasion

Are you easily persuaded? Do you ever wonder why you agreed to do something that you didn't really want to do or bought a useless item because someone convinced you to buy it? Like many people, you've probably been persuaded to do things you wish you hadn't. As a responsible listener, you should resist easy persuasion. Evaluate *what* is said as well as *how* it is said.

Listen for Loaded Language Don't be misled or trapped by language that plays on your emotions. Listen for the following devices:

Flattery: "Those sunglasses were *made* for you!"

Empty Promises: "With Perfecto, all your blemishes will disappear."

Threats: "Your grades will suffer without EZSpellCheck."

Compromise You need to keep your best interests in mind when someone is trying to persuade you. For example, a friend wants you to go rollerblading in the park, but you recently hurt your knee and would rather go to a movie. Think about how you would respond.

Friend: "I really want to go skating; your knee won't hurt. You were walking around on it all day today."

You: "I'm sorry, but I can't risk hurting it again so soon. How about going to a movie today, and as soon as I'm feeling better, we'll go skating."

Apply the Strategies

Role-play the following situations with a partner. Work out a conversation that shows how you would resist persuasion.

1. You've agreed to baby sit for your little brother on Saturday night. Your friend Max wants you to baby sit for his little brother so he can go out that same Saturday night. How does he try to persuade you? How do you resist?

2. You've gone to buy simple swimming goggles at $5.95 a pair. A new salesperson, the best diver on the high-school swim team, tries to convince you that you really need the $12.50 pair. What does she say? What do you say?

Tips for Resisting Persuasion

✔ If you want to resist persuasion and make responsible decisions, follow these guidelines:

▶ Ignore loaded words that trigger emotions.
▶ Be on the lookout for empty promises.
▶ Ask yourself what is *really being said*.

Speaking, Listening, and Viewing Workshop ◆ 701

Introduce the Strategies

Explain to students that probably most of their experiences dealing with persuasion come from advertising. Ask students to describe any experiences they might have had with resisting persuasion from advertising or salespeople. Were they successful with resisting persuasion? Or, did they buy a product only to realize later what convinced them was a false promise?

Customize for
Bodily/Kinesthetic Learners

Have volunteers role-play the situations for the rest of the class. Encourage the volunteers to be creative and use body language and gestures in their conversations.

Apply the Strategies

Suggest that students get together and script out their role plays. Have them perform the role play once, and then have them switch positions and do it again. Have students consider which attempts to persuade and which resistance attempts are the most effective.

1. Students should consider what promises they have made to their parents about baby-sitting Saturday night. Then, they could consider having Max bring his little brother to their house so they could baby-sit for both children at the same time. Students can also say that their responsibility to their family comes first.

2. The salesperson may say that she uses these goggles and they have helped her performance. The student buying the goggles can say that she needs only simple goggles, since she may go through them quickly or has a habit of losing them, so buying the expensive pair seems like a bad decision.

 Beyond the Classroom

Community Connection
Resisting Peer Pressure Explain to students that one type of persuasion they are sure to encounter is peer pressure. Peer pressure comes not from advertisers or salespeople, but from one's own friends and acquaintances who try to persuade one to act, believe, or do something. Part of every student's life will be the attempt to resist peer pressure.

Explain to students that peer pressure can be very simple and not appear as a bad thing. A friend persuading you to go for a bike ride rather than do your homework may be exerting peer pressure. Other peer pressure situations can be much more serious and dangerous, involving disobeying parental or school rules.

Ask students to freewrite about any experiences they may have had with peer pressure. Explain that no one will see what they write. Rather, by writing about an experience, they may discover how they resisted peer pressure or why they gave in. Tell students that many guidance counselors have information on how to resist peer pressure.

What's Behind the Words
To find the origins of these expressions, suggest that students first consult a dictionary or a reference book on sports or sports history.

Answers
Activity 1
1. "Dark horse" is usually a little-known contender (such as a race-horse) that makes an unexpectedly good showing.
2. "Champing at the bit" means to show impatience with delay or restraint. A bit is the usually steel part of a bridle inserted in the mouth of the horse.
3. "A shoo-in" is a certain or easy winner.

Activity 2
1. "Throw in the towel" means to abandon a struggle or contest. In boxing, a boxer's manager might throw in the towel, calling for an end to the fight if he thinks his boxer is in danger of getting hurt.
2. "Beat someone to the punch" means to come in before the other person, as in a competition. In boxing, if you beat someone to the punch, you hit the person before he or she hits you.
3. "Come out swinging" means to begin an event or activity aggressively or ferociously. In boxing, to come out swinging means to begin throwing punches as soon as the round starts.
4. "Saved by the bells" means a narrow escape. In boxing, the bell signals the end of the round.
5. A "low blow" is a nasty or inappropriate offensive action. In boxing, opponents are allowed to hit each other only above the belt.

Activity 3
up for grabs (basketball); tossing in a red herring (fishing); knuckle down (boxing); hold the line (sailing); call the shots (pool); hit the bull's-eye (darts); get the ball rolling (soccer); take the bull by the horns (bullfighting); no holds barred (wrestling); keep one jump ahead (hurdles); put the ball in the other guy's court (tennis); jumping the gun (sprinting or swimming); not up to par (golf); down and out (horse racing); behind the eight ball (pool); coming a cropper (horse racing); taking the bait hook, line, and sinker (fishing); facing a sticky wicket (croquet).

What's Behind the Words
Vocabulary Adventures With Richard Lederer

Sportspeak

Because sports occupy such a prominent place in American life and imagination, athletic expressions fill up our everyday speech and writing. The sporty metaphors that make our English language so athletic are vivid reminders of the games that we, as a people, watch and play.

Horsing Around With Politics

Take the language of politics. American political life is filled with horse racing and track metaphors that shape our thinking about campaigns and elections. Some candidates are *dark horses champing at the bit* to make a *stretch run*. Others are *front-runners* whose *track records* give them the *inside track* on the nomination. Still others are *shoo-ins* who take the whole thing *in stride*. In some campaigns, the *pacesetters* stumble, trying to *clear the initial hurdles,* and those *back in the pack* give them a good *run for the money*. Then, the contest turns into *a real horse race*—a marathon that may go right *down to the wire.*

Politics and Boxing

When candidates enter a political race, they *throw their hat in the ring*. This popular expression, dating back to the nineteenth century, springs from the custom of throwing a hat in a boxing ring to signal acceptance of a fighter's challenge. *Straight from the shoulder,* boxing metaphors *pull no punches* in our language.

ACTIVITY 1 Find out the origins of the following expressions from racing:
1. dark horse
2. champing at the bit
3. shoo-in

ACTIVITY 2 Explain the popular usage of the following expressions from boxing:
1. throw in the towel
2. beat someone to the punch
3. come out swinging
4. saved by the bell
5. a low blow

ACTIVITY 3 Okay, sports fans, how many sports and games can you find hidden in the following game plan:

When the situation is up for grabs and your opponent is tossing in a red herring, you must knuckle down, hold the line, call the shots, hit the bull's-eye, get the ball rolling, take the bull by the horns with no holds barred, keep one jump ahead, and put the ball in the other guy's court. Otherwise, you may end up jumping the gun; not up to par; down and out; out in left field; behind the eight ball; coming a cropper; taking the bait hook, line, and sinker; and facing a sticky wicket.

ACTIVITY 4 Research the origins of five of the phrases you identified in Activity 3.

Activity 4
Possible responses:

1. Call the shots: In pool, a player must call his or her shots before the balls are sunk on the table.
2. Hit the bull's-eye: In darts, the bull's-eye is the center and smallest ring on the dart board, which, in certain versions of the game, earns the thrower the most points.
3. Put the ball in the other guy's court: In tennis, the player attempts to hit the ball over the net into the opponent's court.
4. Jumping the gun: In swimming or sprinting, the race begins with the firing of a gun. A competitor who jumps the gun begins before the gun goes off, causing a false start.
5. Out in left field: The left hand part of the outfield in baseball (as viewed from the stands) is left field.

Extended Reading Opportunities

True stories—biographies, histories, essays, and articles—let us see the world around us more clearly. The following works of nonfiction will help you better understand our world.

Suggested Titles

Nonfiction Readings Across the Curriculum

This collection of nonfiction works includes essays, speeches, memoirs, book introductions, and excerpts from biographies and auto-biographies. The collection includes nonfiction works related to the major subject areas: language arts, science, social studies, math, physical education, music, and art. You are guaranteed to find a work about your favorite academic subject.

Lincoln: A Photobiography
Russell Freedman

Recipient of the Newbery Medal, the Jefferson Cup Award, and the Golden Kite Honor Book Award, this comprehensive work provides insight into the life of one of the nation's most fascinating presidents. Freedman uses drawings and photos to tell the story of an ambitious but modest man who came from humble beginnings. The interesting facts of Lincoln's boyhood and manhood, as well as his presidency, are sure to hold your attention.

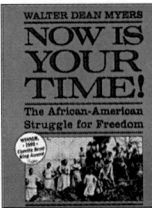

Now Is Your Time! The African-American Struggle for Freedom
Walter Dean Myers

This compelling history of African Americans is unified with the accounts of outstanding lives, such as Ibrahima, unconquerable African prince; James Forten, entrepreneur; and Ida B. Wells. Myers also describes the many contributions that African Americans have made to the United States—black soldiers fighting in the Civil War, the landmark decision of *Plessy* vs. *Ferguson,* and the civil rights movement.

Other Possibilities

Puppies, Dogs, and Blue Northers	Gary Paulsen
Ishi, Last of His Tribe	Theodora Kroebler
A Photohistory of American Women in Sports: Winning Ways	Sue Macy

(C) Houghton Mifflin Company, ©1987 by Russell Freedman; (R) ©1991 by Walter Dean Myers, HarperCollins Publishers

---

Planning Students' Extended Reading

All of the works listed on this page are good choices for students' exploration of the genre of nonfiction. Following is some information that will help you choose what to teach:

Customize for
Varying Student Needs

When assigning the selections in this part to your students keep in mind the following factors:

- *Nonfiction Readings Across the Curriculum,* an offering in the Prentice Hall Literature Library, offers a chance for students to encounter a wide range of different types of nonfiction. The pieces vary in level of difficulty.

- *Lincoln: A Photobiography* is a truly engaging biography covering the life of Abraham Lincoln, including 90 photographs.

- *Now Is Your Time! The African-American Struggle for Freedom* is a complete study of African American history. It includes photographs, an index, and a bibliography.

Planning Instruction and Assessment

Unit Objectives

1. To read nonfiction selections
2. To apply a variety of reading strategies, particularly strategies for reading legends, folk tales, and myths, appropriate for reading these selections
3. To recognize literary elements used in these selections
4. To increase vocabulary
5. To learn elements of grammar and usage
6. To write in a variety of modes about situations based on the selections
7. To develop speaking and listening skills, by completing proposed activities
8. To view images critically and create visual representations

Meeting the Objectives Each selection provides instructional material and portfolio opportunities by which students can meet unit objectives. You will find additional practice pages for reading strategies, literary elements, vocabulary, and grammar in the **Selection Support** booklet in the **Teaching Resources** box.

Setting Goals Work with your students to set goals for unit outcomes. Plan what skills and concepts you wish students to acquire. Match instruction and activities to performance levels or learning modalities.

Portfolios Students may keep portfolios of their completed work or of their work in progress. The Build Your Portfolio page of each selection provides opportunities for students to apply the concepts presented.

Humanities: Art

First Night, by Mark Baring
This painting shows an audience at a theatrical performance in progress. The title "First Night" is a term for the opening night of a performance.

1. Have you ever been to the theater? How did it resemble the one illustrated here? *Depending on students' experiences, they will note differences and similarities among theaters.*

2. What do you notice about the theater's structure? the people? *Students may note the tiered seating and private boxes, the spotlight, the performers' costumes, and the men in the audience wearing tuxedos.*

First Night, Mark Baring, Private Collection

Art Transparencies
The **Art Transparencies** booklet in the **Teaching Resources** box offers fine art to help students make connections to other curriculum areas and high-interest topics.

Beyond Literature
Each unit presents Beyond Literature features that lead students into an exploration of careers, communities and other subject areas. In this unit, students will make a connection to drama by finding out about Broadway theaters. In addition, the **Teaching Resources** box contains a **Beyond Literature** booklet of activities. Using literature as a springboard, these activity pages offer students opportunities to connect literature to other curriculum areas and to the workplace and careers, community, media, and humanities.

Drama

Drama is a form of literature that is meant to be performed on a stage. When you read a drama, you should picture in your mind how it would appear and sound to an audience. As you read the dramas in this unit, notice the following elements, which can help bring the dramas to life in your mind:

- **Stage Directions:** These notes convey information to the cast, crew, and readers of the drama about sound effects, actions, sets, and line readings.

- **Dialogue:** In drama, much of what you learn about the characters, setting, and events is revealed through dialogue—conversations among the characters.

- **Characters:** Dramatic characters are brought to life by their dialogue and actions onstage.

- **Plot:** Most dramas contain a plot in which events unfold, rise to a climax, and are resolved.

- **Theme:** A theme is the central message the playwright conveys to the audience.

◆ 705

Assessing Student Progress

The tools that are available to measure the degree to which students meet the unit objectives are listed below.

Informal Assessment

The questions in the Guide for Responding sections are a first level of response to the concepts and skills presented with the selection. As a brief, informal measure of students' grasp of the material, these responses indicate where further instruction and practice are needed. The practice pages in the **Selection Support** booklet provide for this type of instruction and practice.

You will also find literature and reading guides in the **Alternative Assessment** booklet, which students can use for informal assessment of their individual performances.

Formal Assessment

The **Formal Assessment** booklet contains Selection Tests and Unit Tests.

Selection Tests measure comprehension and skills acquisition for each selection or group of selections.

Each Unit Test provides students with 30 multiple-choice questions and 5 essay questions designed to assess students' knowledge of the literature and skills taught in the unit.

Each Alternative Unit Test: Standardized-Test Practice provides 15 multiple-choice questions and 3 essay questions based on two new literature selections not contained in the student book. The questions on the Alternative Unit Test are designed to assess students' ability to compare and contrast selections, applying skills taught in the unit.

Alternative Assessment

For portfolio and alternative assessment, the **Alternative Assessment** booklet contains Scoring Rubrics, Assessment sheets, and Learning Modalities activities.

Scoring Rubrics provide writing modes that can be applied to Writing activities, Writing Mini-Lessons, and Writing Process Workshop lessons.

Assessment sheets for speaking and listening activities provide peer and self-assessment direction.

Learning Modalities activities appeal to different learning styles. Use these as an alternative measurement of students' growth.

Connections

Within this unit, you will find selections and activities that make connections beyond literature. Use these selections to connect students' understanding and appreciation of literature beyond the traditional literature and language arts curriculum.

Encourage students to connect literature to other curriculum areas. You may wish to coordinate with teachers in other curriculum areas to determine ways to team teach and further extend instruction.

Connections to Today's World

Use these selections to guide students to recognize the relevance of literature to contemporary writings. In this unit, students will look at parts of the Playbill for the revised revival of *The Diary of Anne Frank.*

Connecting Literature to Social Studies

Each unit contains a selection that connects Literature to Social Studies. In this unit, students will read an excerpt from the play *A Walk in the Woods.* Like *The Diary of Anne Frank,* it was produced on Broadway, but it is about the Cold War.

The Reading for Success page in each unit presents a set of problem-solving strategies to help readers understand authors' words and ideas on multiple levels. Good readers develop a bank of strategies from which they can draw as needed.

Unit 8 introduces strategies for reading drama. Students must be able to "see" the drama when they read a script. These strategies for reading drama give readers an approach to understanding a playwright's intent: envision the setting, action, and characters; summarize; and be aware of historical content.

The strategies for reading drama can be applied in all of the selections of Unit 8. Annotated notes provide support for applying these strategies throughout the selections.

How to Use the Reading for Success Page

- Introduce the strategies for reading drama, presenting each as a problem-solving procedure.

- Before students read the selection, have them preview it, looking at the annotations in the green boxes that model the strategies.

- To reinforce these strategies, use Reading Strategy pages in **Selection Support,** pp. 255, 260, and 267. These pages give students an opportunity to practice strategies for reading drama.

Reading Strategies: Support and Reinforcement

Using Boxed Annotations and Prompts

Throughout the unit, the notes in green, red, and maroon boxes are intended to help students apply reading strategies, understand the literary focus, and make a connection with their lives. You may use boxed material in these ways:

- Have students pause at each box and respond to its prompt before they continue reading.

- Urge students to read through the selection, ignoring the boxes. After they complete the selection, they may go back and review the text, responding to the prompts.

Reading for Success

Strategies for Reading Drama

Although dramas have existed for thousands of years, they have remained basically the same: Actors assume roles and interact with one another. Dramas share many elements with other forms of literature: most contain a plot, build to a climax, and reveal themes. Some dramas are written entirely in poetry!

The one thing, however, that distinguishes dramas from other types of literature is that they are meant to be performed. The written script is merely a blueprint, or guide, that allows the actors and you, the reader, to understand the playwright's vision.

When you read a drama, apply the following strategies to interact with the text:

Envision the setting, action, and characters.

Use your senses to envision the setting, action, and characters.
▶ Use information in the stage directions to picture in your mind the time and place of the drama's action.
▶ Use the stage directions to understand the characters' attitudes and to picture their physical actions.
▶ Try to imagine the dialogue being spoken. You may even find it helpful to read passages aloud.

Summarize.

Most dramas are broken into acts and scenes. As you finish each scene and act, summarize what has happened. Take note of how characters change and how the action progresses during the course of the play.

Passage	Summary
Act I, Scene I	Mr. Frank and Miep return to the attic in which the Frank family hid. They find Anne's diary.

Be aware of historical context.

If a drama was written long ago, or if the drama takes place during a specific time period, be aware of the historical context in which it was written. For example, when you read *The Diary of Anne Frank,* it's necessary to know that Anne Frank's family is Jewish and that the Nazis persecuted Jews during World War II. This context enables you to understand the tension and fear in the play.

Apply these strategies as you read the dramas in this unit. They will help you to read the dramas more effectively.

706 ◆ *Drama*

Model a Reading Strategy: Set a Purpose for Reading

Tell students that as they are reading the script of a historical drama or any type of literature that takes place in the past, they should be aware of historical context. You may wish to have students read the Guide for Reading information on pp. 709–710, then model awareness of the historical context of *The Diary of Anne Frank.*

As I read about this play, I know that the characters' lives were in constant danger because of the intent of Hitler and the Nazis. The play's setting is a hiding place. Because Holland was occupied, it was very important that only a few trusted people knew about the people in the Secret Annex.

As I read the play's dialogue, I understand the characters' frustrations and hopes, because I know about the danger and political climate of the world at that time in history.

Point out to students that researching a historical period will provide more details to appreciate the context of a historical drama or other type of historical literature.

PART 1

Modern Drama

Theater poster for the 1996 season for the McCarter Theatre in Princeton, New Jersey, Wiktor Sadowski

The play *The Diary of Anne Frank* is the main component of this section. Based on *The Diary of a Young Girl* by Anne Frank, the play was written by Frances Goodrich and Albert Hackett. This dramatization brings to life Anne's daily life and struggles with growing up while she and her family hide from the Nazis in the attic of an office building in Amsterdam. Although the conditions of their hiding and the realities of their fear pervade the drama, students will relate to the moments of joy, compassion, and frustration that are part of being a young adult in an adult world. Also in this section is a brief excerpt from Lee Blessing's play about the Cold War, *A Walk in the Woods*.

Customize for
Varying Student Needs
When assigning the selections in this section to your students, keep in mind the following factors:

The Diary of Anne Frank
- Long play (56 pp.) in two acts
- Subject matter of Anne Frank's life and World War II may be familiar to some students
- Exposes students to the genre of drama with a serious theme
- Includes a Beyond Literature social studies connection
- Provides opportunities for students to relate literature to history

from *A Walk in the Woods*
- Brief (2 pp.) excerpt from a full-length drama
- Historical setting of the Cold War may be familiar to some students
- Provides an opportunity for connecting literature to social studies

Modern Drama ◆ 707

 Humanities: Art

Theater poster for the 1996 season for the McCarter Theatre in Princeton, New Jersey, by Wiktor Sadowski

Wiktor Sadowsi (born 1956) is a Polish artist, most famous for his posters and illustrations. In 1992, he won a gold medal for his exhibition at the International Art Directors Club in New York. This poster resembles the Surrealist style first made popular by René Magritte and, later, by Salvador Dali. Surrealism was an art movement attempting to distort reality and delve into the areas of dreams and the subconscious.

Use the following questions for discussion:
1. What do you think the masks in the painting represent? *Students may recognize the mask as an element of Greek drama. Masks can represent different characters or different sides of one character.*
2. Do you think this poster is a good advertisement for a theater's upcoming performances? *Some students will say yes, because the overall feeling of the picture is magical and exciting, and the masks show different types of shows. Other students will say they would rather see a poster that shows pictures of specific upcoming shows.*

707

Guide for Reading

OBJECTIVES

1. To read, comprehend, and interpret a play
2. To relate a play to personal experience
3. To be aware of historical context
4. To analyze staging in a play
5. To build vocabulary in context and use the prefixes *un-* and *in-*
6. To develop skill in using verb forms that agree in number with their subjects
7. To respond to the play through writing and speaking and listening

SKILLS INSTRUCTION

Vocabulary:
Prefixes: *un-* and *in-*
Spelling:
Words With *ie* or *ei* Combinations
Grammar:
Subject and Verb Agreement
Reading Strategy:
Be Aware of Historical Context
Literary Focus:
Staging

Speaking and Listening:
Reading (Teacher Edition)
Viewing and Representing:
Design Stage Set (Teacher Edition); Commemorative Stamps (Teacher Edition)
Critical Viewing:
Connect; Assess; Infer; Draw Conclusions; Speculate

PORTFOLIO OPPORTUNITIES

Writing: Letter; Program Notes
Speaking and Listening: Reading

More About the Authors
As part of their research for the drama *The Diary of Anne Frank,* **Frances Goodrich** and **Albert Hackett** visited with Anne's father, Otto Frank. Together, Goodrich and Hackett also wrote screenplays for such well-known films as *The Thin Man, It's a Wonderful Life,* and *Father of the Bride.* Their partnership produced thirty film scripts and four plays.

Meet the Authors:

Frances Goodrich (1890–1984) and Albert Hackett (1900–1995)

Frances Goodrich and Albert Hackett spent two years writing the drama *The Diary of Anne Frank,* which is based on the world-renowned *The Diary of a Young Girl* by Anne Frank. Their play won a Pulitzer Prize, the Drama Critics Circle award, and the Tony award for best play of the 1955–1956 season.

From Acting to Writing
Goodrich and Hackett began working together in 1927 and were married in 1931. Both had been actors. Hackett had worked in both vaudeville and silent films. Goodrich had been a stage actor who had appeared on Broadway. The couple ended their writing careers in 1962, after writing the script for the screenplay of *The Diary of Anne Frank.*

◆ LITERATURE AND YOUR LIFE

CONNECT YOUR EXPERIENCE
Can you imagine what it would be like if all your plans for life—school, career, raising a family—were cut short, and you had to change your life radically? In this drama, you'll learn of a young girl who has to put aside all her plans when she is forced into hiding with her family because of a war.

THEMATIC FOCUS: Heroes
As you read, note the heroic qualities that the young girl and her family display as they try to cope with their terrifying situation.

◆ Build Vocabulary

PREFIXES: *un-* AND *in-*
The prefix *un-* and its variation *in-* mean "not" or "without." When these prefixes are joined to a word, the meaning of the word is the opposite. For example, *insufferable* means "*not* able to be suffered or tolerated."

WORD BANK
Which word from the list describes a person who believes in fate? Check the Build Vocabulary box on page 737 to see if you chose correctly.

conspicuous
mercurial
leisure
unabashed
insufferable
meticulous
fatalist
ostentatiously

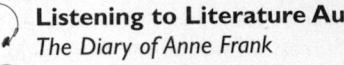

Prentice Hall Literature Program Resources

REINFORCE / RETEACH / EXTEND
Selection Support Pages
Build Vocabulary: Prefixes: *un-* and *in-*, p. 252
Build Grammar Skills: Subject and Verb Agreement, p. 254
Reading Strategy: Be Aware of Historical Context, p. 255
Literary Focus: Staging, p. 256
Strategies for Diverse Student Needs, pp. 93–94
Beyond Literature Cross-Curricular Connection: Art, p. 47

Formal Assessment Selection Test, pp. 209–211, Assessment Resources Software
Alternative Assessment, p. 47
Writing and Language Transparencies
KWL Organizer, p. 49; Timeline, p. 65; Series of Events Chain, p. 57; Venn Diagram, p. 77
Resource Pro CD-ROM The Diary of Anne Frank
Listening to Literature Audiocassettes *The Diary of Anne Frank*
Looking at Literature Videodisc/Videotape

The Diary of Anne Frank

◆ Background for Understanding

HISTORY: WORLD WAR II AND THE HOLOCAUST

Hitler and the Nazis In 1933, Adolf Hitler and the National Socialist (Nazi) party seized power in Germany. The Nazis claimed that Germans were superior to non-Germans. They blamed Jews and other minorities for all of Germany's troubles—from its defeat in World War I to the severe economic depression of the 1920's. To punish Jews for these imagined sins, the Nazis denied them the right to own property, attend schools, and serve in the professions.

The Start of World War II In foreign affairs, Hitler worked for a "Greater Germany" by occupying Austria and seizing Czechoslovakia. Then, after signing a secret treaty with the Soviet Union, he invaded Poland on September 1, 1939. Two days later, Britain and France declared war on Germany. However, they could not prevent Hitler's forces from conquering much of Europe, including Belgium and France.

The Defeat of Hitler Two events in 1941 foreshadowed Hitler's downfall. In June of that year, Hitler staged a surprise invasion of the Soviet Union, his former ally. Eventually, however, German troops would suffer great losses in this campaign. The second key development of that year was the entry of the United States into the war. American military and industrial might was important in defeating Germany. It was not until May 1945, however, that Germany surrendered to the Allies.

Guide for Reading ◆ 709

Customize for
Visual/Spatial Learners
Have volunteers describe what expressions they see on the faces of the people in the photograph. Ask students what the people shown in the photograph might be doing. *Students may say that the photograph appears to be an old one that shows a long line of people standing or walking along a city sidewalk. Many of the people are carrying objects that could be possessions. The expressions on the people's faces seem glum. Perhaps the people are being forced to move or go somewhere they don't want to go.*

Customize for
Verbal/Linguistic Learners
Before students read the Background for Understanding, *History: World War II and the Holocaust,* have them use the KWL Organizer in **Writing and Language Transparencies,** p. 49, to record the information they already know about Adolf Hitler and the Nazis' involvement in World War II. Have students write facts they already know in the first column of the organizer. Then instruct students to list additional information they would like to learn in the second column. Point out to students that the questions in the second column can be used to focus their reading. After their reading, have students write answers to their questions in the third column.

Clarification
During World War II, the Allies included Britain, France, the former Soviet Union, and the United States, as well as 45 smaller nations.

Preparing for Standardized Tests

Grammar The grammar concept for this selection is subject and verb agreement. Explain to students that a verb must agree with its subject in number, as in *The curtain rises* (singular subject, singular verb) and *The men come at about eight-thirty* (plural subject, plural verb).

Grammar, usage, and mechanics portions of standardized tests may require students to choose the verb that agrees in number with the subject of a sentence. Write this sample test item on the board:

> Mrs. Van Daan ____ a fur coat.

Choose the verb that agrees with the subject of the sentence.

(A) wearing   (C) wears
(B) wear   (D) worn

Guide students to see that *(A)* and *(D)* are incorrect choices because *wearing* and *worn* require helping verbs. Choice *(B)* does not agree with the singular subject, *Mrs. Van Daan.* Therefore, *(C)* is the only correct choice.

Clarification

In addition to being sent to ghettos, Jews were dismissed from civil service and public office. They were prohibited from working in journalism, radio, movies, or the theater and could not teach in schools or universities. Eventually, they were not allowed to practice medicine, law, or engage in any business.

Customize for
Verbal/Linguistic Learners

As students read *The Story Behind the Play,* on p. 710, suggest that they use the Timeline in **Writing and Language Transparencies,** p. 65, to make notes about the order of events described.

Customize for
Logical/Mathematical Learners

The number of Jews killed by the Nazis is estimated at six million. Have students work in pairs or in small groups to devise a way to illustrate the sheer magnitude of the number six million. For example, use your school population as a divisor. For a school population of 200, you would need thirty thousand schools to contain a total of six million students (6,000,000 ÷ 200 = 30,000). Encourage students to use visual aids such as charts or drawings to illustrate the number six million.

Customize for
Intrapersonal Learners

Encourage students to write about their reactions to the background information—*The Holocaust, Persecution of Other Peoples,* and *The Story Behind the Play.* Suggest that they imagine themselves in one of the situations described on p. 710. Have them speculate about how they might react.

Guide for Reading (continued)

◆ Background for Understanding (continued)

The Holocaust Meanwhile, during World War II, everywhere the German army went, Jews and other peoples were persecuted. The name that has been given to these events is the Holocaust, which comes from a Greek word meaning "burnt whole."

Jews were made to wear yellow stars on their clothing and were sent to ghettos—crowded, closed-off neighborhoods in cities. There, many died of starvation and disease. Those who survived were eventually transported in freight cars to special prisons known as concentration camps, where most died within a few months. Then, the Nazis thought of an even more efficient way to destroy the Jews: camps where people were gassed to death in special rooms almost as soon as they arrived.

The number of people killed by the Nazis is staggering. An estimated three million Jews died in concentration camps. Another three million were either shot or died in the ghettos of starvation and disease. By the end of the war, some six million Jews had perished, three fourths of Europe's Jewish population.

Persecution of Other Peoples Another group that nearly disappeared during the Holocaust was Europe's Gypsies. Many Gypsies had lived for centuries in Germany, but along with the Jews, they were targeted for destruction as a so-called foreign race. It is estimated that during the Holocaust, a half million Gypsies died, 80 percent of the European Gypsy population.

Millions of other people died as well, especially in Eastern Europe. In addition to losing three million Jews, Poland lost another three million citizens through slave labor, starvation, and murder. The Soviet Union lost at least seven million people—not counting the millions of prisoners of war who never returned home.

THE STORY BEHIND THE PLAY *The Diary of Anne Frank* is based on a real diary written by a young girl during the Holocaust. Anne Frank was born to a Jewish family in Frankfurt, Germany, on June 12, 1929. She had a normal, happy childhood until the Nazis took power in 1933.

That year, Anne's family left their home in Germany to escape persecution, moving to the Netherlands. In Amsterdam, Mr. Frank reestablished his business, and Mrs. Frank set up their new household. Anne and her older sister, Margot, attended school and made new friends.

In 1940, the German army invaded the Netherlands. Unfortunately, the Dutch army was unable to withstand the German army, and in May 1940, the Netherlands fell under German control. It wasn't long before Jews there were subjected to Nazi discrimination and abuse.

Even as late as 1942, however, the Frank family and many other European Jews were unaware of the dangers they faced. Most simply thought they would be temporarily imprisoned by the Nazis. To avoid this fate, the Frank family hid in the attic of a warehouse and office building that had been part of Mr. Frank's business in Amsterdam.

On her thirteenth birthday, Anne had received a diary as a gift. When her family went into hiding, she began to write regularly in this diary. The play you are about to read is based on this diary, which Mr. Frank recovered when he returned to the secret attic after the war.

710 ◆ What Matters

Block Scheduling Strategies

Consider these suggestions to take advantage of extended class time:

• Review the Literary Focus with students before they read Act I. Then instruct students to use a chart such as the one on p. 711 as they read. After students finish reading, have them discuss their charts and use the information to answer the Literary Focus questions on p. 745. For additional practice, use **Selection Support,** p. 256.

• Introduce the grammar concept, subject and verb agreement, before students read Act I. After students read this portion of the play,

have them work in groups to complete the Build Grammar Skills practice on p. 745. For additional practice, have students use **Selection Support,** p. 254.

• After students read Act I independently, have them form groups to discuss responses to Reader's Response and Thematic Focus, p. 744. Suggest that one student in each group make notes on the various responses. Then hold a class discussion in which students summarize their discussions before they answer the Critical Thinking questions.

◆ The Diary of Anne Frank, Act I ◆

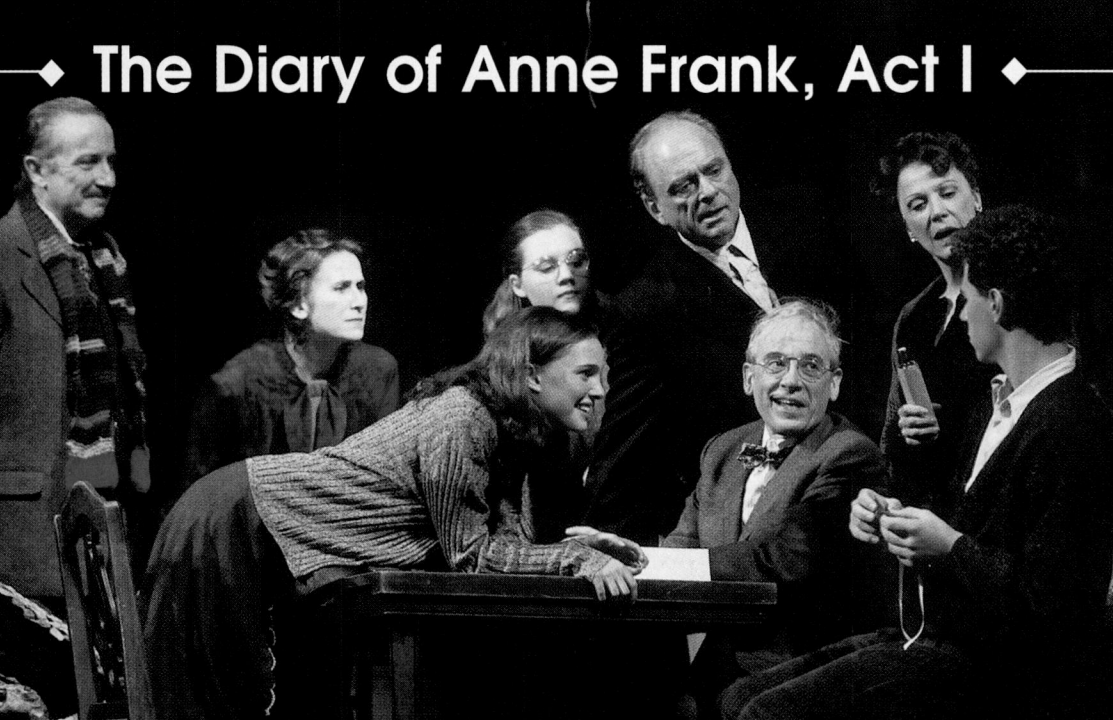

Interest Grabber Ask students to imagine that they are awakened early one morning and told that they will be leaving home to go into hiding with their family for an indefinite period of time. They can take only a few items of clothing and personal possessions, all of which they must wear or pack to fit in their school backpack. Have students consider objects they might choose to take. Provide each student with a letter- or legal-size envelope and six strips of paper. Have students think carefully and write on the paper strips the names of the items they would take, one item per strip. Then instruct students to put the strips in the envelopes. Collect the envelopes and have volunteers take turns selecting envelopes and reading aloud the contents. Use this activity as a springboard for a discussion of items that students feel are necessary for survival.

◆ Literary Focus

STAGING

Staging is a term that refers to the techniques that bring a drama to life. These techniques include scenery, costumes, lighting, and sound effects, as well as actors' movements and characters' motives. This information appears in the script within brackets. Directors use these stage directions to help them produce the drama. Readers use the information to help them to visualize the characters and action onstage.

As you read, create a chart like the one below for each scene.

◆ Reading Strategy

BE AWARE OF HISTORICAL CONTEXT

As you read any type of literature that takes place in the past, be aware of the **historical context** in which it takes place. Historical context includes the political forces, cultural beliefs and attitudes, and events of the time that affect the action and characters. For example, the characters in *The Diary of Anne Frank* lived during World War II in Holland, which had been taken over by the Nazis. Knowing the history of the Holocaust helps you to understand why the Frank family, who were Jewish, acted as they did.

Act I	Scenery	Lighting	Sound	Costumes	Actors' Movements
Scene 1:	3 small attic rooms	Dim—windows painted over	Church bells	Mr. Frank: worn and tattered suit	Mr. Frank walks slowly, as if ill.

Guide for Reading ◆ 711

◆ Build Grammar Skills

Subject and Verb Agreement If you wish to introduce the grammar concept for this selection before students read, refer to the instruction on p. 745.

Customize for
Less Proficient Readers
Because Act I of *The Diary of Anne Frank* is long, students may have more success if they read the play in small sections, stopping to review and summarize the events. You may also want to have students listen to all or some of the play on audiocassette.

🎧 **Listening to Literature Audiocassettes**

Customize for
More Advanced Students
Have students keep "diaries" of character traits of Mr. and Mrs. Frank, Mr. and Mrs. Van Daan, Peter, Margot, Anne, and Mr. Dussel. Suggest that students staple together several sheets of paper, one sheet per character, on which to record the traits as they read Act I. After students finish reading, have them compare the traits they noticed for each character with several classmates.

Humanities: Drama

The Play The American printing of *Anne Frank: The Diary of a Young Girl* was first published by Doubleday in 1952. The book was an instant success, due to excellent reviews of the importance of Anne's experiences and message, and many people wanted to produce a play version of it. The producing rights went to Kermit Bloomgarden; he hired the husband-and-wife playwriting team of Frances Goodrich and Albert Hackett, who met with Otto Frank and visited the Annex to help them with their adaptation. When the play opened, success was immediate. *The Diary*

of Anne Frank won the 1955 Pulitzer Prize for Drama and three Tony Awards. It played a total of 717 shows on Broadway, followed by numerous professional and amateur productions throughout America and the rest of the world. *The Diary of Anne Frank* not only brought to life the optimism and sensitivity of Anne Frank, but also refocused the world on the events of the Holocaust.

Audiences have always been moved by the dramatic version of Anne's story—around the world, it is met with emotional reactions and stunned silence when the curtain comes down.

One-Minute Insight In the opening scene of the play, Anne Frank's father returns to Amsterdam to say good-bye to his dear friend Miep Gies in the cramped attic above his old business. There, with the courageous help of Miep and Mr. Kraler, Otto Frank's family and three other Jews hid for two years from the Nazis. Miep gives Mr. Frank Anne's diary, which she found after the family was captured. As he holds the diary, the offstage voice of Anne reading from her diary draws us into the past as the families begin their new life hiding from the Nazis in the attic. As the months of hiding drag on, fear and lack of privacy bring increasing tension. An eighth refugee joins them. Act I ends on the first night of Hanukkah. The group's makeshift celebration is interrupted by the sounds of a thief below, who may have heard them. After the thief has gone, the group tries to resume its celebration, despite the fear that their hiding place had been discovered.

Team Teaching Strategy

The historical aspects of *The Diary of Anne Frank* offer an opportunity to coordinate instruction with a social studies teacher to enhance and extend students' knowledge about the events of World War II and the Holocaust.

Customize for
English Language Learners
Help students understand events in the play by having them listen to the audiocassette, scene by scene. After listening to a scene, have students work with proficient partners to review and summarize events in the scene, using pantomime or sketches as necessary to enhance understanding. Suggest that students complete a Series of Events Chain, p. 57 in **Writing and Language Transparencies,** for each scene.

Listening to Literature Audiocassettes

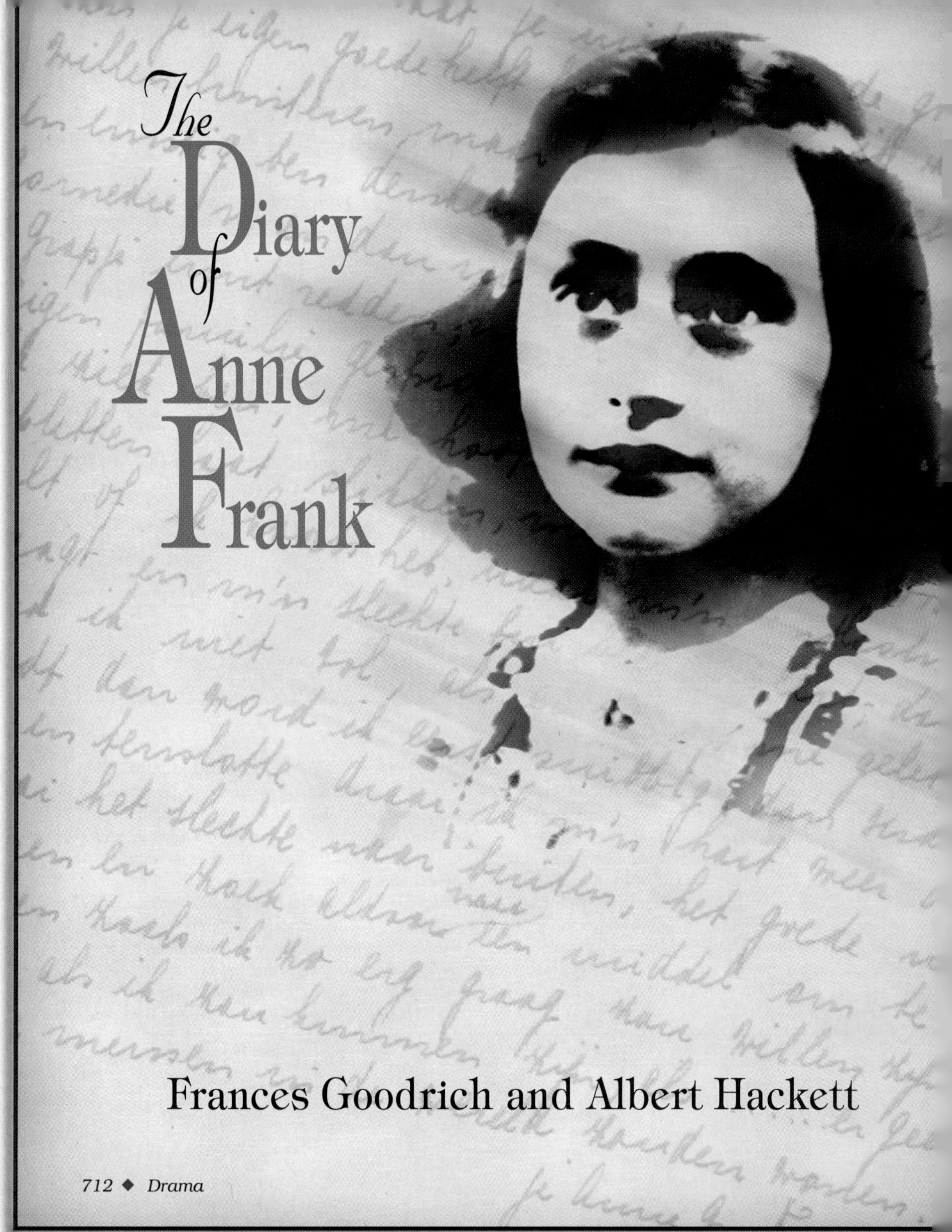

The Diary of Anne Frank

Frances Goodrich and Albert Hackett

712 ◆ Drama

Humanities: Literature

Anne Frank's Diary In 1945, when Otto Frank returned to Amsterdam, he learned that his family had not survived. Miep Gies, having carefully kept Anne's diary and papers, gave them to Mr. Frank when she knew that Anne would not be returning for them. He began translating parts of the diary into German and pressed Miep to read it—Miep refused for a long time because she could not face the painful memories.

At first, Mr. Frank resisted sharing Anne's writing with anyone but Miep. As he talked about the diary—her legacy—to others, he was persuaded to show it to a historian who subsequently wrote a newspaper article about it. With more persuasion to forgo his sense of invaded privacy in light of the importance of Anne's voice being heard, Mr. Frank allowed an edited version of the diary, *Het Achterhuis* ("The Annex"), to be published. It was not widely read; nevertheless, the diary was reprinted to reach more readers (as *Anne Frank: The Diary of a Young Girl* in America). Its audience grew. Today, Anne's diary is still being reprinted and has been translated into numerous languages, fulfilling her wish to become a famous writer.

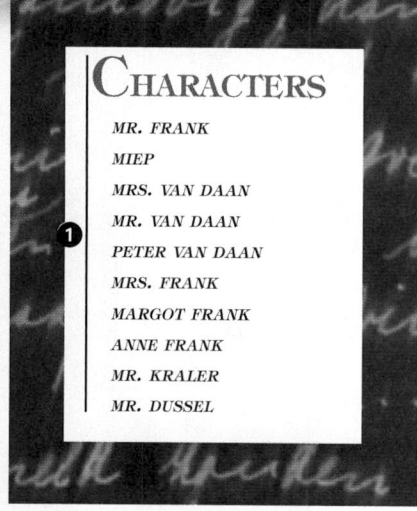

CHARACTERS

MR. FRANK

MIEP

MRS. VAN DAAN

MR. VAN DAAN

PETER VAN DAAN

MRS. FRANK

MARGOT FRANK

ANNE FRANK

MR. KRALER

MR. DUSSEL

ACT I

Scene 1

[The scene remains the same throughout the play. It is the top floor of a warehouse and office building in Amsterdam, Holland. The sharply peaked roof of the building is outlined against a sea of other rooftops, stretching away into the distance. Nearby is the belfry[1] of a church tower, the Westertoren, whose carillon[2] rings out the hours. Occasionally faint sounds float up from below: the voices of children playing in the street, the tramp of marching feet, a boat whistle from the canal.

The three rooms of the top floor and a small attic space above are exposed to our view. The largest of the rooms is in the center, with two small rooms, slightly raised, on either side. On the right is a bathroom, out of sight. A narrow steep flight of stairs at the back leads up to the attic. The rooms are sparsely furnished with a few chairs, cots, a table or two. The windows are painted over, or covered with makeshift blackout curtains.[3] In the main room there is a sink, a gas ring for cooking and a woodburning stove for warmth.

---

1. **belfry** (bel′ frē) n.: The part of a tower that holds the bells.
2. **carillon** (kar′ ə län′) n.: A set of stationary bells, each producing one note of the scale.
3. **blackout curtains:** Draperies that conceal all lights that might otherwise be visible to enemy air raiders at night.

The room on the left is hardly more than a closet. There is a skylight in the sloping ceiling. Directly under this room is a small steep stairwell, with steps leading down to a door. This is the only entrance from the building below. When the door is opened we see that it has been concealed on the outer side by a bookcase attached to it.

The curtain rises on an empty stage. It is late afternoon, November 1945.

The rooms are dusty, the curtains in rags. Chairs and tables are overturned.

The door at the foot of the small stairwell swings open. MR. FRANK comes up the steps into view. He is a gentle, cultured European in his middle years. There is still a trace of a German accent in his speech.

He stands looking slowly around, making a supreme effort at self-control. He is weak, ill. His clothes are threadbare.

After a second he drops his rucksack[4] on the couch and moves slowly about. He opens the door to one of the smaller rooms, and then abruptly closes it again, turning away. He goes to the window at the back, looking off at the Westertoren as its carillon strikes the hour of six, then he moves restlessly on.

From the street below we hear the sound of a barrel organ[5] and children's voices at play. There is a many-colored scarf hanging from a nail. MR. FRANK takes it, putting it around his neck. As he starts back for his rucksack, his eye is caught by something lying on the floor. It is a woman's white glove. He holds it in his hand and suddenly all of his self-control is gone. He breaks down, crying.

We hear footsteps on the stairs. MIEP GIES comes up, looking for MR. FRANK. MIEP is a Dutch girl of about twenty-two. She wears a coat and hat, ready to go home. She is pregnant. Her attitude toward MR. FRANK is protective, compassionate.]

MIEP. Are you all right, Mr. Frank?

MR. FRANK. [Quickly controlling himself] Yes, Miep, yes.

---

4. **rucksack** (ruk′ sak′) n.: Knapsack or backpack.
5. **barrel organ** n.: Mechanical musical instrument played by turning a crank.

The Diary of Anne Frank, Act I ◆ 713

Cross-Curricular Connection: Social Studies

Amsterdam The capital and largest city of the Netherlands, Amsterdam, was established in the early 1200's near a dam on the Amstel River as Amstelredam or *dam of the Amstel*. The architecture of the old portion of the city has changed little since the 17th century and is filled with tall slender houses built along the canals as homes for spice merchants like Mr. Frank. The city lies on marshy land almost 12 feet below sea level, therefore many buildings stand on piles or posts. There are over 63 miles of canals forming the shape of a fan in the old town with many houseboats parked along the banks. Picturesque bridges, canals, and homes give the lovely city a distinct personality.

Many of the streets in the old portion of town are narrow and congested. As a result, many of Amsterdam's inhabitants use bicycles equipped with baskets as a means of transportation for everything from groceries to children. One thing that Anne missed quite often while hiding in the Secret Annex was riding her bicycle. Interested students may wish to research additional information about the city of Amsterdam or the country of the Netherlands.

►**Critical Viewing**◄

❶ **Connect** *Everyone in the photograph seems happy. The people appear to be in a festive mood.*

◆ **Critical Thinking**

❷ **Speculate** Why do you suppose Mr. Frank refers to himself as a "bitter old man"? *Students may say that Mr. Frank has probably suffered the loss of his family and does not want to be reminded of his former life.*

◆ **LITERATURE AND YOUR LIFE**

❸ Ask students to put themselves in the place of Mr. Frank, who has returned to the scene of a difficult time in his life. Would you want to keep the papers that Miep found, or, like Mr. Frank, would you want them burned? *Some students may say they would like to look through the papers to see if there is something important among them. Others might sympathize with the desire to destroy evidence of so much sadness.*

Customize for
Interpersonal Learners
Have two students conduct a dramatic reading of the lines on p. 714. Encourage students to use varied voice tone, gestures, and facial expressions to convey the characters' emotions. Explain that Miep is pronounced "MEEP." After students give their reading, have them discuss with the class insights into Miep and Mr. Frank that they gained from the reading.

▲ **Critical Viewing** This photograph captures the Frank family out for a walk with friends. How would you describe their mood, judging from their expressions? **[Connect]**

MIEP. Everyone in the office has gone home . . . It's after six. [*Then pleading*] Don't stay up here, Mr. Frank. What's the use of torturing yourself like this?

MR. FRANK. I've come to say good-bye . . . I'm leaving here, Miep.

MIEP. What do you mean? Where are you going? Where?

MR. FRANK. I don't know yet. I haven't decided.

MIEP. Mr. Frank, you can't leave here! This is your home! Amsterdam is your home. Your business is here, waiting for you . . . You're needed here . . . Now that the war is over, there are things that . . .

MR. FRANK. I can't stay in Amsterdam, Miep. It has too many memories for me. Everywhere there's something . . . the house we lived in . . . the school . . . that street organ playing

out there . . . I'm not the person you used to know, Miep. I'm a bitter old man. [*Breaking off*] Forgive me. I shouldn't speak to you like this . . . after all that you did for us . . . the suffering . . .

MIEP. No. No. It wasn't suffering. You can't say we suffered. [*As she speaks, she straightens a chair which is overturned.*]

MR. FRANK. I know what you went through, you and Mr. Kraler. I'll remember it as long as I live. [*He gives one last look around.*] Come, Miep. [*He starts for the steps, then remembers his rucksack, going back to get it.*]

MIEP. [*Hurrying up to a cupboard*] Mr. Frank, did you see? There are some of your papers here. [*She brings a bundle of papers to him.*] We found them in a heap of rubbish on the floor after . . . after you left.

MR. FRANK. Burn them. [*He opens his rucksack to put the glove in it.*]

MIEP. But, Mr. Frank, there are letters, notes . . .

MR. FRANK. Burn them. All of them.

714 ◆ *Drama*

 Humanities: Photography

Family Photographs The photograph shows Anne Frank and her father—in the center of the photograph—with other wedding guests on the day of Miep's marriage to Jan Gies, July 16, 1941. Mrs. Frank is at home with Anne's grandmother, who is ill, and Margot does not appear in the photograph. Less than a year later, Anne would be in hiding with her family.

Use questions such as these for discussion about the photograph:
1. Based on this image, describe the relationship between Anne and her father. *Anne seems*

happy and comfortable with her father. Both Anne and her father appear to be good-natured and happy.

2. In what ways might photographs such as these have helped the playwrights as they composed the drama? *The photographs offer insights into the Franks and, along with the diary, help bring Anne to life.*

3. What historical facts can be learned from a photograph such as this? *The observer can learn about clothing styles of the period. For example, all the women are wearing hats.*

MIEP. Burn this? [*She hands him a paper-bound notebook.*]

MR. FRANK. [*quietly*] Anne's diary. [*He opens the diary and begins to read.*] "Monday, the sixth of July, nineteen forty-two." [*To* MIEP] Nineteen forty-two. Is it possible, Miep? . . . Only three years ago. [*As he continues his reading, he sits down on the couch.*] "Dear Diary, since you and I are going to be great friends, I will start by telling you about myself. My name is Anne Frank. I am thirteen years old. I was born in Germany the twelfth of June, nineteen twenty-nine. As my family is Jewish, we emigrated to Holland when Hitler came to power."

[*As* MR. FRANK *reads on, another voice joins his, as if coming from the air. It is* ANNE'S VOICE.]

MR. FRANK and **ANNE.** "My father started a business, importing spice and herbs. Things went well for us until nineteen forty. Then the war came, and the Dutch capitulation,[6] followed by the arrival of the Germans. Then things got very bad for the Jews."

[MR. FRANK'S VOICE *dies out.* ANNE'S VOICE *continues alone. The lights dim slowly to darkness. The curtain falls on the scene.*]

ANNE'S VOICE. You could not do this and you could not do that. They forced Father out of his business. We had to wear yellow stars.[7] I had to turn in my bike. I couldn't go to a Dutch school any more. I couldn't go to the movies, or ride in an automobile, or even on a streetcar, and a million other things. But somehow we children still managed to have fun. Yesterday Father told me we were going into hiding. Where, he wouldn't say. At five

---

6. **capitulation** (kə pich′ ə lā′ shən) *n*.: Surrender.
7. **yellow stars:** Stars of David, which are six-pointed stars that are symbols of Judaism. The Nazis ordered all Jews to wear them sewn to their clothing so that Jews could be easily identified.

◆ **Build Vocabulary**

conspicuous (kən spik′ yōō əs) *adj*.: Noticeable

---

o'clock this morning Mother woke me and told me to hurry and get dressed. I was to put on as many clothes as I could. It would look too suspicious if we walked along carrying suitcases. It wasn't until we were on our way that I learned where we were going. Our hiding place was to be upstairs in the building where Father used to have his business. Three other people were coming in with us . . . the Van Daans and their son Peter . . . Father knew the Van Daans but we had never met them . . .

[*During the last lines the curtain rises on the scene. The lights dim on.* ANNE'S VOICE *fades out.*]

Scene 2

[*It is early morning, July 1942. The rooms are bare, as before, but they are now clean and orderly.*

MR. VAN DAAN, *a tall, portly[8] man in his late forties, is in the main room, pacing up and down, nervously smoking a cigarette. His clothes and overcoat are expensive and well cut.*

MRS. VAN DAAN *sits on the couch, clutching her possessions, a hatbox, bags, etc. She is a pretty woman in her early forties. She wears a fur coat over her other clothes.*

PETER VAN DAAN *is standing at the window of the room on the right, looking down at the street below. He is a shy, awkward boy of sixteen. He wears a cap, a raincoat, and long Dutch trousers, like "plus fours."[9] At his feet is a black case, a carrier for his cat.*

The yellow Star of David is conspicuous *on all of their clothes.*]

MRS. VAN DAAN. [*Rising, nervous, excited*] Something's happened to them! I know it!

MR. VAN DAAN. Now, Kerli!

MRS. VAN DAAN. Mr. Frank said they'd be here at seven o'clock. He said . . .

MR. VAN DAAN. They have two miles to walk. You can't expect . . .

MRS. VAN DAAN. They've been picked up. That's what's happened. They've been taken . . .

---

8. **portly** (pôrt′ lē) *adj*.: Large, heavy, and dignified.
9. **plus fours** *n*.: Loose knickers worn for active sports.

The Diary of Anne Frank, Act I ◆ 715

Clarification

4 When Anne's parents gave her a diary, Anne decided to treat the diary as a friend. Beginning each entry "Dear Kitty," Anne recorded her thoughts, feelings, and descriptions of events that happened. Explain that the diary entries used in the play are based on translations of Anne's actual diaries but are not necessarily her exact words.

◆ Reading Strategy

5 Be Aware of Historical Context *The Frank family was worried about Hitler because he blamed Jews for Germany's problems and was intent on punishing them.*

◆ Literary Focus

6 Staging Ask students why the authors chose to have the voice of the actor portraying Anne join that of the actor portraying Mr. Frank as the diary excerpt is read. *Students may say that the authors wanted to provide a smooth and understandable transition from the present to the past.*

◆ Literary Focus

7 Staging How do these stage directions help you visualize the members of the Van Daan family? *The directions give important details about each character's physical appearance, age, and style of clothing. They also include descriptions of possessions that are probably important to each character, such as the cigarette, the fur coat, and the cat carrier.*

Comprehension Check ☑

8 What does Mrs. Van Daan fear might have happened to the Frank family? *They may have been taken away by the Nazis, perhaps to jail or to a concentration camp.*

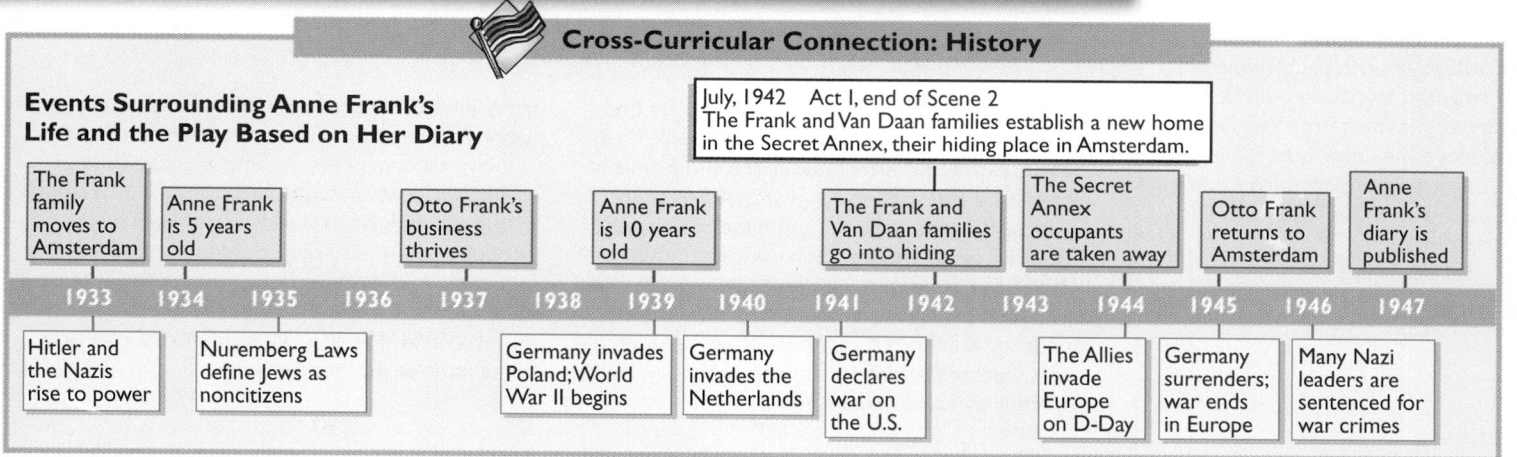

Cross-Curricular Connection: History

Events Surrounding Anne Frank's Life and the Play Based on Her Diary

July, 1942 Act I, end of Scene 2
The Frank and Van Daan families establish a new home in the Secret Annex, their hiding place in Amsterdam.

The Frank family moves to Amsterdam | Anne Frank is 5 years old | Otto Frank's business thrives | Anne Frank is 10 years old | The Frank and Van Daan families go into hiding | The Secret Annex occupants are taken away | Otto Frank returns to Amsterdam | Anne Frank's diary is published

| 1933 | 1934 | 1935 | 1936 | 1937 | 1938 | 1939 | 1940 | 1941 | 1942 | 1943 | 1944 | 1945 | 1946 | 1947 |

Hitler and the Nazis rise to power | Nuremberg Laws define Jews as noncitizens | Germany invades Poland; World War II begins | Germany invades the Netherlands | Germany declares war on the U.S. | The Allies invade Europe on D-Day | Germany surrenders; war ends in Europe | Many Nazi leaders are sentenced for war crimes

❶ **Staging** Explain that "upstage" refers to the rear of the stage. Point out that directions such as "upstage" and "downstage" tell the actors where to go. The directions "left" and "right" in stage directions are oriented from the point of view of the actors facing out towards the audience. Sketch a diagram of a stage on the board and have students point out the following areas:

THE STAGE

Upstage Right	Upstage Center	Upstage Left
Right	Center	Left
Downstage Right	Downstage Center	Downstage Left

Audience

◆ **LITERATURE AND YOUR LIFE**

❷ Discuss with students other characters from literature, movies, or television that are similar to Anne as she is described in the stage directions. Have students predict how Anne will react to her new situation. *In their predictions, some students may say that Anne's lively spirit will help her cope with living in hiding. Others may say that her emotions will cause problems.*

Clarification

❸ When food and other items became scarce during World War II, the government issued ration books with coupons or stamps in them. Every registered citizen in the Netherlands received a certain number of coupons. Since people in hiding did not have an official address, they could not receive coupons. These people had to depend on others to buy scarce items for them, or buy illegal ration books.

Customize for
Bodily/Kinesthetic Learners
Have volunteers use pantomime or body language to convey Anne's personality as she meets the Van Daans and explores her new home. Discuss what might be going through Anne's mind as she sees the hiding place for the first time.

716

[MR. VAN DAAN *indicates that he hears someone coming.*]

MR. VAN DAAN. You see?

[PETER *takes up his carrier and his schoolbag, etc., and goes into the main room as* MR. FRANK *comes up the stairwell from below.* MR. FRANK *looks much younger now. His movements are brisk, his manner confident. He wears an over-coat and carries his hat and a small cardboard box. He crosses to the* VAN DAANS, *shaking hands with each of them.*]

MR. FRANK. Mrs. Van Daan, Mr. Van Daan, Peter. [*Then, in explanation of their lateness*] There were too many of the Green Police[10] on the streets . . . we had to take the long way around.

[*Up the steps come* MARGOT FRANK, MRS. FRANK, MIEP *(not pregnant now) and* MR. KRALER. *All of them carry bags, packages, and so forth. The Star of David is conspicuous on all of the* FRANKS' *clothing.* MARGOT *is eighteen, beautiful, quiet, shy.* MRS. FRANK *is a young mother, gently bred, reserved. She, like* MR. FRANK, *has a slight German accent.* MR. KRALER *is a Dutchman, dependable, kindly.*

❶ *As* MR. KRALER *and* MIEP *go upstage to put down their parcels,* MRS. FRANK *turns back to call* ANNE.]

MRS. FRANK. Anne?

[ANNE *comes running up the stairs. She is thirteen, quick in her movements, interested in everything,* mercurial *in her emotions. She wears a cape, long wool socks and carries a schoolbag.*]

MR. FRANK. [*Introducing them*] My wife, Edith.
❷ Mr. and Mrs. Van Daan . . . their son, Peter . . . my daughters, Margot and Anne.

[MRS. FRANK *hurries over, shaking hands with them.*]

[ANNE *gives a polite little curtsy as she shakes* MR. VAN DAAN's *hand. Then she immediately starts off on a tour of investigation of her new home, going upstairs to the attic room.*]

---

10. **Green Police:** Nazi police, who wore green uniforms.

MIEP *and* MR. KRALER *are putting the various things they have brought on the shelves.*]

MR. KRALER. I'm sorry there is still so much confusion.

MR. FRANK. Please. Don't think of it. After all, we'll have plenty of leisure to arrange everything ourselves.

MIEP. [*To* MRS. FRANK] We put the stores of food you sent in here. Your drugs are here . . . soap, linen here.

MRS. FRANK. Thank you, Miep.

MIEP. I made up the beds . . . the way Mr. Frank and Mr. Kraler said. [*She starts out.*] Forgive me. I have to hurry. I've got to go to the other side of town to get some ration books[11] for you.

MRS. VAN DAAN. Ration books? If they see our names on ration books, they'll know we're here.

MR. KRALER. There isn't anything . . .

MIEP. Don't worry. Your names won't be on them. [*As she hurries out*] I'll be up later. ❸

MR. FRANK. Thank you, Miep.

MRS. FRANK. [*To* MR. KRALER] It's illegal, then, the ration books? We've never done anything illegal.

MR. FRANK. We won't be living here exactly according to regulations.

[*As* MR. KRALER *reassures* MRS. FRANK, *he takes various small things, such as matches, soap, etc., from his pockets, handing them to her.*]

MR. KRALER. This isn't the black market,[12] Mrs. Frank. This is what we call the white market . . . helping all of the hundreds

---

11. **ration books** (rash´ ən books) *n.*: Books of stamps given to ensure the even distribution of scarce items, especially in wartime. Stamps as well as money must be given to obtain an item that is scarce.

12. **black market:** Illegal way of buying scarce items without ration stamps.

◆ **Build Vocabulary**

mercurial (mər kyoor´ ē əl) *adj.*: Quick or changeable in behavior

leisure (lezh´ ər) *n.*: Free and unoccupied time

Cultural Connection

Persecution The persecution of Jews by the Nazis was not the first time Jewish people have been treated in this manner. When the Romans conquered Palestine in A.D. 135, Jews were forced to leave their homeland. They scattered throughout the Roman Empire, North Africa, and Europe, where they often met with hostility. In many cases, Jews were prohibited from owning property or becoming traders. This pattern of persecution has been repeated at different times in history. Held together by their religion and culture, however,

many Jews prospered and contributed to other nations' cultures as scholars, financiers, and doctors.

Have students research more about the persecution of Jews throughout history. You may want to suggest specific research topics such as the Exodus and the Diaspora. Students might also find out about other groups, such as the gypsies, who were persecuted and forced into hiding during World War II. Invite students to give oral presentations on their research.

and hundreds who are hiding out in Amsterdam.

[*The carillon is heard playing the quarter-hour before eight.* MR. KRALER *looks at his watch.* ANNE *stops at the window as she comes down the stairs.*]

ANNE. It's the Westertoren!

MR. KRALER. I must go. I must be out of here and downstairs in the office before the workmen get here. [*He starts for the stairs leading out.*] Miep or I, or both of us, will be up each day to bring you food and news and find out what your needs are. Tomorrow I'll get you a better bolt for the door at the foot of the stairs. It needs a bolt that you can throw yourself and open only at our signal. [*To* MR. FRANK] Oh . . . You'll tell them about the noise?

MR. FRANK. I'll tell them.

MR. KRALER. Good-bye then for the moment. I'll come up again, after the workmen leave.

MR. FRANK. Good-bye, Mr. Kraler.

MRS. FRANK. [*Shaking his hand*] How can we thank you?

[*The others murmur their good-byes.*]

MR. KRALER. I never thought I'd live to see the day when a man like Mr. Frank would have to go into hiding. When you think—

[*He breaks off, going out.* MR. FRANK *follows him down the steps, bolting the door after him. In the interval before he returns,* PETER *goes over to* MARGOT, *shaking hands with her. As* MR. FRANK *comes back up the steps,* MRS. FRANK *questions him anxiously.*]

MRS. FRANK. What did he mean, about the noise?

MR. FRANK. First let us take off some of these clothes.

▶ **Critical Viewing** The photograph shows the front view of the building in which the Franks hid. Why was this location a good one for hiding? [Assess]

◆ Critical Thinking

❹ Speculate Besides food, what might the families' needs be while they are in hiding? *Students may mention needs such as these: ways to prepare the food and keep the hiding place clean, information about what is happening on the outside, forms of entertainment and diversion, and items for maintaining health. Students may name specific items such as sheets and towels, toiletries, newspapers, books, games, paper and pens, laundry detergent, a first-aid kit, a radio.*

▶ Critical Viewing ◀

❺ Assess *As students view the photograph, they may say that the location is a good one for hiding because it appears to be a business or warehouse and seems an unlikely place for two families to be living.*

Humanities: Architecture

263 Prinsengracht Explain to students that the warehouse of Mr. Frank's business was on the ground floor of the building shown in the photograph. The door farthest to the left leads to the third and fourth floors, which were used as storage space. The next door leads to a second-floor office. Behind the building shown in the photograph and connected to it by a small corridor is another building, which is not visible from the road. This rear building, known as the "Secret Annex," is where the families hid. The families occupied two levels of the Secret Annex. They stored food in the attic of the building. In Amsterdam, the price of houses was determined by their width, thus they were built several stories tall with courtyard and annex buildings behind.

Encourage students to study the arrangement, as depicted in the photograph, to better understand the setting of the play. If possible they should try to locate information about the size of the rooms in the Secret Annex. They might compare them to the size of rooms in the school or their own home to understand the small size of the rooms into which the two families crowded.

◆ Critical Thinking

❶ Compare and Contrast
Encourage students to visualize the characters removing layer after layer of garments. Lead them to appreciate the humor in the situation. Discuss how this humorous moment contrasts with the seriousness of the families' situation. As they read, encourage students to look for other examples of humor that contrast with the gravity of the events described in the play.

◆ LITERATURE AND YOUR LIFE

❷ The characters indicate by their behavior that Mr. Frank is the leader of the group in hiding. Have students discuss reasons why the situation faced by the Franks and Van Daans demands that one person be the acknowledged leader. *The families' situation is so serious that it requires a trustworthy leader who will make decisions and plan courses of action. Without a designated leader, the group could waste time or risk discovery by arguing among themselves.*

Comprehension Check ☑

❸ Why is everyone "paralyzed with fear"? *The families know that the foot-steps might mean that the Nazis will discover their hiding place.*

◆ Critical Thinking

❹ Infer Why is Peter embarrassed by his mother's questions? *Students may say that Peter feels too old to be asked whether he might be afraid. Also, he may not want his mother fussing over him, regardless of the situation.*

Customize for
Interpersonal Learners
Ask student to imagine how they might spend their ten-hour "quiet time" while following the rules set forth by Mr. Frank. Have them make lists of ways they would pass the time.

718

---

❶ [*They all start to take off garment after garment. On each of their coats, sweaters, blouses, suits, dresses, is another yellow Star of David.* MR. *and* MRS. FRANK *are underdressed quite simply. The others wear several things, sweaters, extra dresses, bathrobes, aprons, nightgowns, etc.*]

MR. VAN DAAN. It's a wonder we weren't arrested, walking along the streets . . . Petronella with a fur coat in July . . . and that cat of Peter's crying all the way.

ANNE. A cat?

❷ [*Finally, as they have all removed their surplus clothes, they look to* MR. FRANK, *waiting for him to speak.*]

MR. FRANK. Now. About the noise. While the men are in the building below, we must have complete quiet. Every sound can be heard down there, not only in the work-rooms, but in the offices too. The men come at about eight-thirty, and leave at about five-thirty. So, to be perfectly safe, from eight in the morning until six in the evening we must move only when it is necessary, and then in stockinged feet. We must not speak above a whisper. We must not run any wa-ter. We cannot use the sink, or even, forgive me, the w.c.[13] The pipes go down through the workrooms. It would be heard. No trash . . .

❸ [MR. FRANK *stops abruptly as he hears the sound of marching feet from the street below. Everyone is motionless, paralyzed with fear.* MR. FRANK *goes quietly into the room on the right to look down out of the window.* ANNE *runs after him, peering out with him. The tramping feet pass without stopping. The tension is re-lieved.* MR. FRANK, *followed by* ANNE, *returns to the main room and resumes his instructions to the group.*]

. . . No trash must ever be thrown out which might reveal that someone is living up here . . . not even a potato paring. We must burn

---

13. **w.c.:** Water closet; bathroom.

---

everything in the stove at night. This is the way we must live until it is over, if we are to survive.

[*There is silence for a second.*]

MRS. FRANK. Until it is over.

MR. FRANK. [*Reassuringly*] After six we can move about . . . we can talk and laugh and have our supper and read and play games . . . just as we would at home. [*He looks at his watch.*] And now I think it would be wise if we all went to our rooms, and were settled before eight o'clock. Mrs. Van Daan, you and your husband will be up-stairs. I regret that there's no place up there for Peter. But he will be here, near us. This will be our common room, where we'll meet to talk and eat and read, like one family.

MR. VAN DAAN. And where do you and Mrs. Frank sleep?

MR. FRANK. This room is also our bedroom.

[*Together*] {
  MRS. VAN DAAN. That isn't right. We'll sleep here and you take the room upstairs.

  MR. VAN DAAN. It's your place.
}

MR. FRANK. Please. I've thought this out for weeks. It's the best arrangement. The only arrangement.

MRS. VAN DAAN. [*To* MR. FRANK] Never, never can we thank you. [*Then to* MRS. FRANK] I don't know what would have happened to us, if it hadn't been for Mr. Frank.

MR. FRANK. You don't know how your husband helped me when I came to this country . . . knowing no one . . . not able to speak the language. I can never repay him for that. [*Going to* VAN DAAN] May I help you with your things?

MR. VAN DAAN. No. No. [*To* MRS. VAN DAAN] Come along, *liefje.*[14]

MRS. VAN DAAN. You'll be all right, Peter? You're not afraid? **❹**

PETER. [*Embarrassed*] Please, Mother.

---

14. *liefje* (lēf´ hyə): Dutch for "little love."

Beyond the Classroom

Workplace Skills

Leadership Mr. Frank's responsibility for the members of his family and the others in the hiding place in the annex depended on his ability to exer-cise good leadership skills. The move to the hiding place relied on careful and precise planning. Supplies had to be carried in secretly by hand and he had to assess the trustworthiness of Miep and Mr. Kraler. He had to take a leadership role in designing rules that would guarantee their safety and enable them to escape capture. Their very lives depended on his leadership and planning skills.

Encourage students to make a list of jobs they are interested in and the leadership skills required for each job. For example: A teacher must not only be able to teach and explain materials, but must also be able to use leadership skills to set a good example and motivate students to learn. A lawyer provides leadership when he explains facts and attempts to convince a jury. The foreman on a work crew is responsible for the safety of his workers and must keep everyone on task. Have students work in small groups to compare their job skills lists and gain from one another's ideas.

◆ **Literary Focus**
In what ways does this staging direction help you to envision what's happening onstage?

❺

[*They start up the stairs to the attic room above.* MR. FRANK *turns to* MRS. FRANK.]

MR. FRANK. You too must have some rest, Edith. You didn't close your eyes last night. Nor you, Margot.

ANNE. I slept, Father. Wasn't that funny? I knew it was the last night in my own bed, and yet I slept soundly.

MR. FRANK. I'm glad, Anne. Now you'll be able to help me straighten things in here. [*To* MRS. FRANK *and* MARGOT] Come with me . . . You and Margot rest in this room for the time being.

[*He picks up their clothes, starting for the room on the right.*]

MRS. FRANK. You're sure . . . ? I could help . . . And Anne hasn't had her milk . . .

MR. FRANK. I'll give it to her. [*To* ANNE *and* PETER] Anne, Peter . . . it's best that you take off your shoes now, before you forget.

[*He leads the way to the room, followed by* MARGOT.]

MRS. FRANK. You're sure you're not tired, Anne?

ANNE. I feel fine. I'm going to help Father.

MRS. FRANK. Peter, I'm glad you are to be with us.

PETER. Yes, Mrs. Frank.

[MRS. FRANK *goes to join* MR. FRANK *and* MARGOT.]

❻ [*During the following scene* MR. FRANK *helps* MARGOT *and* MRS. FRANK *to hang up their clothes. Then he persuades them both to lie down and rest. The* VAN DAANS *in their room above settle themselves. In the main room* ANNE *and* PETER *remove their shoes.* PETER *takes his cat out of the carrier.*]

ANNE. What's your cat's name?

PETER. Mouschi.

ANNE. Mouschi! Mouschi! Mouschi! [*She picks up the cat, walking away with it. To* PETER] I love cats. I have one . . . a darling little cat.

But they made me leave her behind. I left some food and a note for the neighbors to take care of her . . . I'm going to miss her terribly. What is yours? A him or a her?

PETER. He's a tom. He doesn't like strangers. [*He takes the cat from her, putting it back in its carrier.*] ❼

ANNE. [*Unabashed*] Then I'll have to stop being a stranger, won't I? Where did you go to school?

PETER. Jewish Secondary.

ANNE. But that's where Margot and I go! I never saw you around.

PETER. I used to see you . . . sometimes . . .

ANNE. You did?

PETER. . . . In the school yard. You were always in the middle of a bunch of kids. [*He takes a penknife from his pocket.*]

ANNE. Why didn't you ever come over?

PETER. I'm sort of a lone wolf. [*He starts to rip off his Star of David.*]

ANNE. What are you doing?

PETER. Taking it off.

ANNE. But you can't do that. They'll arrest you if you go out without your star.

[*He tosses his knife on the table.*]

PETER. Who's going out?

ANNE. Why, of course! You're right! Of course we don't need them any more. [*She picks up his knife and starts to take her star off.*] ❽ I wonder what our friends will think when we don't show up today?

PETER. I didn't have any dates with anyone.

ANNE. Oh, I did. I had a date with Jopie to go and play ping-pong at her house. Do you know Jopie de Waal?

PETER. No.

ANNE. Jopie's my best friend. I wonder what she'll think when she telephones and there's

◆ **Build Vocabulary**
unabashed (un ə basht′) *adj.:* Unashamed

The Diary of Anne Frank, Act I ◆ 719

◆ **Literary Focus**
❺ **Staging** *Students may say that the staging direction helps them visualize the moment when the Franks and Van Daans begin the routine of their new lives.*

◆ **Literary Focus**
❻ **Staging** Review with students the description of the set from the opening of the play to help them visualize the living areas in the Secret Annex. Point out that all the areas are visible to the audience all the time. Ask students why the playwrights chose to stage the play this way. *The playwrights may have wanted the audience to be able to see, at certain moments, how everyone is passing the time in the hiding place.*

◆ **Critical Thinking**
❼ **Analyze** Ask students if they think Mouschi really doesn't like strangers. If they think the cat is not afraid, why does Peter say this to Anne? Have students give reasons for their responses. *Mouschi does not seem to be afraid of strangers. Perhaps Peter himself is fearful of strangers and is passing his own feelings off as those of his cat, or he doesn't want to share the cat's affections with Anne.*

Comprehension Check ☑
❽ Why does Anne say that they do not need the stars any more? *The families are hiding until the Germans are defeated. Once the Nazis are out of power, Jews will no longer have to identify themselves by wearing a Star of David sewn on their clothing.*

Customize for
Interpersonal Learners
Have students work with partners to list similarities and differences between Anne and Peter. Suggest that they use the Venn Diagram, p. 77 in **Writing and Language Transparencies,** to list ways in which the two are alike and ways they are different.

Viewing and Representing Mini-Lesson

Design Stage Set

Introduce Explain that the stage set for a play establishes the setting for the entire production and is very important.

Develop Ask students to reread the descriptions and stage directions that describe the setting of the play. Have small groups of students work together to list the important details.

Apply Have groups plan how they wish to represent the stage set. They may choose to draw detailed diagrams and sketches on paper or poster board, or they may prefer to build a three-

dimensional representation of the set. Remind them to include elements and details that are included in the play itself as to size, room decoration, room arrangement, and furniture.

Assess Students should display their stage set representation to the class and explain the elements they have chosen to illustrate, along with their relationship to the play's descriptions. Evaluate students on their work as a group, their research into the play details and set descriptions, and the oral presentation they make to the class.

❶ Have students compare Peter's feelings about the Star of David to those of Anne. *Peter resents the star because it is a symbol of oppression. Anne also resents having to wear the star and the persecution it represents; at the same time, though, she sees the star as an important religious symbol.*

◆ Critical Thinking

❷ **Speculate** Have students speculate about the pros and cons of Peter's keeping a cat while he is in hiding. *Having a cat might be a welcome diversion from the problems of being in hiding. A cat requires food and care, though, which may be difficult to provide while in hiding. In addition, a cat might make noise, which could lead to the discovery of the hiding place.*

▶ Critical Viewing ◀

❸ **Infer** *Jews were forced to wear the stars to identify them as targets of persecution and to isolate them from non-Jews.*

◆ Critical Thinking

❹ **Speculate** Ask students if they think Anne and Peter will become good friends. Have them give reasons for their responses. *Some students may say that Anne's friendliness may draw Peter out of his shyness, and the two will become friends. Others may say that the differences between Anne and Peter may make friendship between them difficult.*

◆ Literary Focus

❺ **Staging** Ask students why the playwrights included the sound of children playing outside. Have them describe the effect of this stage direction. *The authors may have included the sounds of children playing as a symbol of freedom, in contrast to the families' confinement in the small hiding place. The cheerful sounds outside compared with the somber tone inside add to the drama and tension of the families' situation.*

---

no answer? . . . Probably she'll go over to the house . . . I wonder what she'll think . . . we left everything as if we'd suddenly been called away . . . breakfast dishes in the sink . . . beds not made . . . [*As she pulls off her star, the cloth underneath shows clearly the color and form of the star.*] Look! It's still there!

[PETER *goes over to the stove with his star.*] What're you going to do with yours?

PETER. Burn it.

❶ **ANNE.** [*She starts to throw hers in, and cannot.*] It's funny, I can't throw mine away. I don't know why.

PETER. You can't throw . . . ? Something they branded you with . . . ? That they made you wear so they could spit on you?

ANNE. I know. I know. But after all, it is the Star of David, isn't it?

[*In the bedroom, right,* MARGOT *and* MRS. FRANK *are lying down.* MR. FRANK *starts quietly out.*]

PETER. Maybe it's different for a girl.

[MR. FRANK *comes into the main room.*]

❷ **MR. FRANK.** Forgive me, Peter. Now let me see. We must find a bed for your cat. [*He goes to a cupboard.*] I'm glad you brought your cat. Anne was feeling so badly about hers. [*Getting a used small washtub*] Here we are. Will it be comfortable in that?

PETER. [*Gathering up his things*] Thanks.

MR. FRANK. [*Opening the door of the room on the left*] And here is your room. But I warn you, Peter, you can't grow any more. Not an inch, or you'll have to sleep with your feet out of the skylight. Are you hungry?

---

❸ ▲ **Critical Viewing** Why do you think Jews were forced to wear yellow stars like this one? [Infer]

720 ◆ Drama

PETER. No.

MR. FRANK. We have some bread and butter.

PETER. No, thank you.

MR. FRANK. You can have it for luncheon then. And tonight we will have a real supper . . . our first supper together.

PETER. Thanks. Thanks. [*He goes into his room. During the following scene he arranges his possessions in his new room.*]

MR. FRANK. That's a nice boy, Peter.

ANNE. He's awfully shy, isn't he?

MR. FRANK. You'll like him, I know.

❹ **ANNE.** I certainly hope so, since he's the only boy I'm likely to see for months and months.

[MR. FRANK *sits down, taking off his shoes.*]

MR. FRANK. Annele,[15] there's a box there. Will you open it?

[*He indicates a carton on the couch.* ANNE brings it to the center table. In the street below there is the sound of children playing.*]

❺ **ANNE.** [*As she opens the carton*] You know the way I'm going to think of it here? I'm going to think of it as a boarding house. A very peculiar summer boarding house, like the one that we—[*She breaks off as she pulls out some photographs.*] Father! My movie stars! I was wondering where they were! I was looking for them this morning . . . and Queen Wilhelmina![16] How wonderful!

MR. FRANK. There's something more. Go on. Look further. [*He goes over to the sink, pouring a glass of milk from a thermos bottle.*]

ANNE. [*Pulling out a pasteboard-bound book*] A diary! [*She throws her arms around her*

---

15. **Annele** (än´ ə lə): Nickname for *Anne*.
16. **Queen Wilhelmina** (wil´ hel mē´ nə): Queen of the Netherlands from 1890 to 1948.

Cultural Connection

Star of David Symbol All Jews aged six and older were required to wear a yellow Star of David with the word "Jew" written in the center, as shown in the illustration on p. 720. The Nazis imposed this policy to identify Jews and isolate them from non-Jews.

The Star of David is also known as the Shield of David, from the Hebrew words *Magen David*. Legend claims the star was used on the shields of King David's soldiers as a symbol of God's protection. The star is a 6-pointed figure made from 2 intertwined triangles. Although the figure is ancient, it is unknown at what point in history the star became widely known and recognized as a Jewish symbol. The Star of David no longer carries the stigma that it did when the Nazis forced the Jews to wear the symbol. It is used on many Jewish symbols and has been used on the flag of Israel since 1948. Discuss with students the places where they may have seen the Star of David.

father.] I've never had a diary. And I've always longed for one. [*She looks around the room.*] Pencil, pencil, pencil, pencil. [*She starts down the stairs.*] I'm going down to the office to get a pencil.

MR. FRANK. Anne! No! [*He goes after her, catching her by the arm and pulling her back.*]

ANNE. [*Startled*] But there's no one in the building now.

MR. FRANK. It doesn't matter. I don't want you ever to go beyond that door.

ANNE. [*Sobered*] Never . . . ? Not even at night-time, when everyone is gone? Or on Sundays? Can't I go down to listen to the radio?

MR. FRANK. Never. I am sorry, Anneke.[17] It isn't safe. No, you must never go beyond that door.

[*For the first time* ANNE *realizes what "going into hiding" means.*]

ANNE. I see.

MR. FRANK. It'll be hard, I know. But always remember this, Anneke. There are no walls, there are no bolts, no locks that anyone can put on your mind. Miep will bring us books. We will read history, poetry, mythology. [*He gives her the glass of milk.*] Here's your milk. [*With his arm about her, they go over to the couch, sitting down side by side.*] As a matter of fact, between us, Anne, being here has certain advantages for you. For instance, you remember the battle you had with your mother the other day on the subject of over-shoes? You said you'd rather die than wear overshoes? But in the end you had to wear them? Well now, you see, for as long as we are here you will never have to wear over-shoes! Isn't that good? And the coat that you inherited from Margot, you won't have to wear that any more. And the piano! You won't have to practice on the piano. I tell you, this is going to be a fine life for you!

[ANNE*'s panic is gone.* PETER *appears in the doorway of his room, with a saucer in his hand. He is carrying his cat.*]

---
17. **Anneke** (än´ ə kə): Nickname for "Anne."

PETER. I . . . I . . . I thought I'd better get some water for Mouschi before . . .

MR. FRANK. Of course.

[*As he starts toward the sink the carillon begins to chime the hour of eight. He tiptoes to the window at the back and looks down at the street below. He turns to* PETER, *indicating in pantomime that it is too late.* PETER *starts back for his room. He steps on a creaking board. The three of them are frozen for a minute in fear. As* PETER *starts away again,* ANNE *tiptoes over to him and pours some of the milk from her glass into the saucer for the cat.* PETER *squats on the floor, putting the milk before the cat.* MR. FRANK *gives* ANNE *his fountain pen, and then goes into the room at the right. For a second* ANNE *watches the cat, then she goes over to the center table, and opens her diary.*

In the room at the right, MRS. FRANK *has sat up quickly at the sound of the carillon.* MR. FRANK *comes in and sits down beside her on the settee, his arm comfortingly around her.*

Upstairs, in the attic room, MR. *and* MRS. VAN DAAN *have hung their clothes in the closet and are now seated on the iron bed.* MRS. VAN DAAN *leans back exhausted.* MR. VAN DAAN *fans her with a newspaper.*

ANNE *starts to write in her diary. The lights dim out, the curtain falls.*

In the darkness ANNE'S VOICE *comes to us again, faintly at first, and then with growing strength.*]

ANNE'S VOICE. I expect I should be describing what it feels like to go into hiding. But I really don't know yet myself. I only know it's funny never to be able to go outdoors . . . never to breathe fresh air . . . never to run and shout and jump. It's the silence in the nights that frightens me most. Every time I hear a creak in the house, or a step on the street outside, I'm sure they're coming for us. The days aren't so bad. At least we know that Miep and Mr. Kraler are down there below us in the office. Our protectors, we call them. I asked Father what would happen to them if the Nazis found out they were hiding us. Pim said that they would suffer the same fate that we would . . . Imagine!

The Diary of Anne Frank, Act I ◆ 721

Cultural Connection

Nicknames Anne's father uses several nicknames for Anneliese Marie—*Annele* and *Anneke*—and she often refers to him as *Pim*. Have students look through the play to see if any other characters are referred to by nicknames.

All people, many pets, and sometimes inanimate objects such as cars are given names, and sometimes nicknames. Most names have specific meanings—sometimes names refer to places where people lived, their occupations, or ancestors' names. In some cultures, the giving of a name is a particularly important and solemn occasion.

Nicknames are names that are substituted for a person's actual name. They can be descriptive names that characterize the person (*Smiley*), derivations of a person's name (*Annele*), or abbreviations of a name (*Rick*). Occasionally, nicknames originate with a young child's inability to pronounce a name correctly. Sometimes nicknames originate with a particular event or experience.

Interested students may wish to research types of nicknames and their origins, or interesting or unique nicknames that have been used for well-known or famous people.

❶ Have students think of traits associated with being a teenager, such as the desire for more independence. Ask students if Anne's reaction to her mother's concern seems reasonable. *Mrs. Frank is probably just showing parental concern for her daughter. Many will say they can understand Anne's reaction and feel that it is reasonable, given her age and desire for independence. Others may say that Anne is overreacting to her mother's concern.*

Clarification

❷ Explain to students that Anne, Margot, and Peter are doing school-work assigned to them by Mr. Frank and Mr. Van Daan. The men are acting as teachers to help the children keep up with their studies so they will not be behind when they return to school after the war ends; the adults also want to bring a sense of normal life to the hiding place.

◆ Critical Thinking

❸ Analyze Ask students how the relationship between Anne and Peter seems to have changed since Scene 2. *Anne and Peter have moved past the awkwardness of their first conversation. While they are not necessarily friends, they seem more used to each other. Anne's teasing of Peter and his annoyance with her resemble the behavior between an adolescent girl and her older brother.*

Customize for
English Language Learners

Have students proficient in English use facial expressions and body language to demonstrate the meanings of words and terms such as "pent-up energy," "startled," "amused," "innocently," "lunge," and "self-consciously."

They know this, and yet when they come up here, they're always cheerful and gay as if there were nothing in the world to bother them . . . Friday, the twenty-first of August, nineteen forty-two. Today I'm going to tell you our general news. Mother is unbearable. She insists on treating me like a baby, which I loathe. Otherwise things are going better. The weather is . . .

[*As* ANNE'S VOICE *is fading out, the curtain rises on the scene.*]

Scene 3

[*It is a little after six o'clock in the evening, two months later.*

MARGOT *is in the bedroom at the right, studying.* MR. VAN DAAN *is lying down in the attic room above.*

The rest of the "family" is in the main room. ANNE *and* PETER *sit opposite each other at the center table, where they have been doing their lessons.* MRS. FRANK *is on the couch.* MRS. VAN DAAN *is seated with her fur coat, on which she has been sewing, in her lap. None of them are wearing their shoes.*

Their eyes are on MR. FRANK, *waiting for him to give them the signal which will release them from their day-long quiet.* MR. FRANK, *his shoes in his hand, stands looking down out of the window at the back, watching to be sure that all of the workmen have left the building below.*

After a few seconds of motionless silence, MR. FRANK *turns from the window.*]

MR. FRANK. [*Quietly, to the group*] It's safe now. The last workman has left.

[*There is an immediate stir of relief.*]

ANNE. [*Her pent-up energy explodes.*] WHEE!

MR. FRANK. [*Startled, amused*] Anne!

MRS. VAN DAAN. I'm first for the w.c.

[*She hurries off to the bathroom.* MRS. FRANK *puts on her shoes and starts up to the sink to prepare supper.* ANNE *sneaks* PETER'S *shoes from under the table and hides them behind her back.* MR. FRANK *goes in to* MARGOT'S *room.*]

MR. FRANK. [*To* MARGOT] Six o'clock. School's over.

[MARGOT *gets up, stretching.* MR. FRANK *sits down*

---

to put on his shoes. In the main room PETER *tries to find his.*]

PETER. [*To* ANNE] Have you seen my shoes?

ANNE. [*Innocently*] Your shoes?

PETER. You've taken them, haven't you?

ANNE. I don't know what you're talking about.

PETER. You're going to be sorry!

ANNE. Am I?

[PETER *goes after her.* ANNE, *with his shoes in her hand, runs from him, dodging behind her mother.*]

MRS. FRANK. [*Protesting*] Anne, dear!

PETER. Wait till I get you!

ANNE. I'm waiting!

[PETER *makes a lunge for her. They both fall to the floor.* PETER *pins her down, wrestling with her to get the shoes.*]

Don't! Don't! Peter, stop it. Ouch!

MRS. FRANK. Anne! . . . Peter!

[*Suddenly* PETER *becomes self-conscious. He grabs his shoes roughly and starts for his room.*]

ANNE. [*Following him*] Peter, where are you going? Come dance with me.

PETER. I tell you I don't know how.

ANNE. I'll teach you.

PETER. I'm going to give Mouschi his dinner.

ANNE. Can I watch?

PETER. He doesn't like people around while he eats.

ANNE. Peter, please.

PETER. No! [*He goes into his room.* ANNE *slams his door after him.*]

MRS. FRANK. Anne, dear, I think you shouldn't play like that with Peter. It's not dignified.

ANNE. Who cares if it's dignified? I don't want to be dignified.

[MR. FRANK *and* MARGOT *come from the room on the right.* MARGOT *goes to help her mother.* MR. FRANK *starts for the center table to correct* MARGOT'S *school papers.*]

MRS. FRANK. [*To* ANNE] You complain that I

Career Connections

Teachers To try to maintain normal routine in their children's lives, Mr. Frank and Mr. Van Daan acted as teachers to Margot, Anne, and Peter. Students who are interested in teaching might consider teaching opportunities other than in a standard classroom. For instance, they might think about being tutors to students in hospitals or on movie sets, or to homebound students. Discuss opportunities to teach abroad, including teaching English to students in other countries. Other teaching opportunities include teaching special skills, crafts or

hobbies to children or adults, providing technical training, camp settings, or working as a tutor in a prison or detention center.

Suggest that interested students investigate teaching opportunities that are available and report their findings to the class in the form of a visual display. Other students may wish to explore the increased interest in home-schooling by parents and families in the United States. They might be interested in finding out what requirements for education are mandated by the government and what kind of tests home-schooled children are required to take.

4 don't treat you like a grownup. But when I do, you resent it.

ANNE. I only want some fun . . . someone to laugh and clown with . . . After you've sat still all day and hardly moved, you've got to have some fun. I don't know what's the matter with that boy.

MR. FRANK. He isn't used to girls. Give him a little time.

ANNE. Time? Isn't two months time? I could cry. [*Catching hold of* MARGOT] Come on, Margot . . . dance with me. Come on, please.

MARGOT. I have to help with supper.

ANNE. You know we're going to forget how to dance . . . When we get out we won't remember a thing.

[*She starts to sing and dance by herself.* MR. FRANK *takes her in his arms, waltzing with her.* MRS. VAN DAAN *comes in from the bathroom.*]

5 **MRS. VAN DAAN.** Next? [*She looks around as she starts putting on her shoes.*] Where's Peter?

ANNE. [*As they are dancing*] Where would he be!

MRS. VAN DAAN. He hasn't finished his lessons, has he? His father'll kill him if he catches him in there with that cat and his work not done.

[MR. FRANK *and* ANNE *finish their dance. They bow to each other with extravagant formality.*]

Anne, get him out of there, will you?

ANNE. [*At* PETER's *door*] Peter? Peter?

PETER. [*Opening the door a crack*] What is it?

ANNE. Your mother says to come out.

PETER. I'm giving Mouschi his dinner.

MRS. VAN DAAN. You know what your father says. [*She sits on the couch, sewing on the lining of her fur coat.*]

PETER. For heaven's sake, I haven't even looked at him since lunch.

MRS. VAN DAAN. I'm just telling you, that's all.

ANNE. I'll feed him.

PETER. I don't want you in there.

MRS. VAN DAAN. Peter!

PETER. [*To* ANNE] Then give him his dinner and come right out, you hear?

[*He comes back to the table.* ANNE *shuts the door of* PETER's *room after her and disappears behind the curtain covering his closet.*]

MRS. VAN DAAN. [*To* PETER] Now is that any way to talk to your little girl friend?

PETER. Mother . . . for heaven's sake . . . will you please stop saying that?

MRS. VAN DAAN. Look at him blush! Look at him!

PETER. Please! I'm not . . . anyway . . . let me alone, will you?

6 **MRS. VAN DAAN.** He acts like it was something to be ashamed of. It's nothing to be ashamed of, to have a little girl friend.

PETER. You're crazy. She's only thirteen.

MRS. VAN DAAN. So what? And you're sixteen. Just perfect. Your father's ten years older than I am. [*To* MR. FRANK] I warn you, Mr. Frank, if this war lasts much longer, we're going to be related and then . . .

MR. FRANK. *Mazeltov!*[18]

MRS. FRANK. [*Deliberately changing the conversation*] I wonder where Miep is. She's usually so prompt.

[*Suddenly everything else is forgotten as they hear the sound of an automobile coming to a screeching stop in the street below. They are tense, motionless in their terror. The car starts away. A wave of relief sweeps over them. They pick up their occupations again.* ANNE *flings open the door of* PETER's *room, making a dramatic entrance. She is dressed in* PETER's *clothes.* PETER *looks at her in fury. The others are amused.*]

ANNE. Good evening, everyone. Forgive me if I don't stay. [*She jumps up on a chair.*] I have a friend waiting for me in there. My friend

---

18. **Mazeltov** (mä´ zəl tōv´): "Good luck" in Hebrew and Yiddish.

The Diary of Anne Frank, Act I ◆ 723

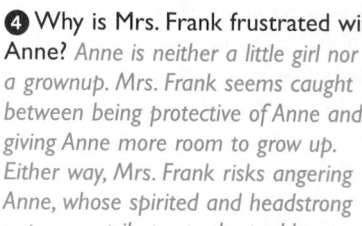

Comprehension Check ☑

4 Why is Mrs. Frank frustrated with Anne? *Anne is neither a little girl nor a grownup. Mrs. Frank seems caught between being protective of Anne and giving Anne more room to grow up. Either way, Mrs. Frank risks angering Anne, whose spirited and headstrong nature contributes to the problem.*

◆ **Critical Thinking**

5 **Interpret** Ask students what Anne's impulse to dance and Mrs. Van Daan's wish for Peter to finish his studies both reveal. *They reveal a desire to maintain a normal routine and keep up with the outside world. They also reveal a belief that life will one day return to normal.*

◆ **LITERATURE AND YOUR LIFE**

6 Have students put themselves in Peter's place. Ask them how they might feel if their mother were saying such things in front of others. *Students will probably say that they would feel embarrassed and angry by her teasing and especially by her implication of a romantic relationship.*

◆ **Reading Strategy**

7 **Be Aware of Historical Context** An automobile screeching to a stop in the street below could signal the arrival of the Green Police. When the Nazis were in power in Germany, the Netherlands, and elsewhere, Jews lived in constant fear that they would be deported to labor camps or concentration camps at any moment. The danger for a family of Jews in hiding was even greater, because the punishment for hiding would be more severe.

Customize for
Musical/Rhythmic Learners
If possible, obtain a recording of a waltz to play for students. After students listen to several of the waltzes, invite them to comment on the rhythm and flow of the music. Have them speculate as to why the playwrights included the waltzing scene.

◆ **Reading Strategy**
Why might an event like this make the attic's occupants nervous?

 Humanities: Drama

Character Adaptation Anne's descriptions of her fellow inhabitants of the Secret Annex were based on her perception of their personal qualities and traits. One reason her father was reluctant to publish the diary was her sometimes-less-than-favorable portrayal of the Secret Annex occupants.

As part of her writing style, Anne included many characterization details about her family, the Van Daans, and Mr. Dussel. Her sense of characterization was so strong that she changed the characters' names as she began revising her diary, hoping for its eventual publication.

When Goodrich and Hackett took on the task of creating dramatic characters based on the diary, they had to further distill the characters' traits in order for them to be portrayed on stage. The playwrights used Anne's pseudonyms and the general characteristics that she had described as they developed the dramatic characters. The people on the "outside" who helped the Secret Annex occupants, however, were combined into two play characters—Miep and Mr. Kraler. Having characters for each of the real people would have been too complicated in a two-hour play.

◆ Build Vocabulary

1 Using the Prefixes un- and in-
Explain that the prefixes *un-* and *in-* create opposite meanings in words to which they are added. Have students identify the words with *in-* prefixes in this passage. Ask volunteers to give the meanings of the base words and then define the words with their prefixes. Encourage students to look for other words that use the prefixes *un-* and *in-* as they read the play.

◆ Critical Thinking

2 Analyze After students read this passage, have them discuss the relationship between Anne and her mother. Encourage students to debate whether or not Mrs. Frank treats Anne like a baby. *Anne and her mother often quarrel. Some students may say that Mrs. Frank seems to be unreasonable, whereas others may say that under the circumstances, Mrs. Frank's concerns seem reasonable.*

◆ Critical Thinking

3 Infer Why does Anne's father suggest things that Anne cannot do because she is in hiding? *By suggesting that Anne would feel better if she could ride her bike or visit her friend Jopie, Mr. Frank is acknowledging that he understands Anne's needs and knows how restricted she feels and that she would feel better if she were able to do what other girls her age are free to do.*

◆ LITERATURE AND YOUR LIFE

4 Have students imagine that they are in hiding with Anne's family. Ask them to discuss how they might react to Anne's clowning, such as when she imitates Mr. Van Daan and complains about the "bean cycle." *Some may say that they would be cheered by Anne's clowning. Others might say her behavior might get on their nerves if they were confined with her for months on end.*

Tom. Tom Cat. Some people say that we look alike. But Tom has the most beautiful whiskers, and I have only a little fuzz. I am hoping . . . in time . . .

PETER. All right, Mrs. Quack Quack!

ANNE. [*Outraged—jumping down*] Peter!

PETER. I heard about you . . . How you talked so much in class they called you Mrs. Quack Quack. How Mr. Smitter made you write a composition . . . "'Quack, Quack,' said Mrs. Quack Quack."

ANNE. Well, go on. Tell them the rest. How it was so good he read it out loud to the class and then read it to all his other classes!

PETER. Quack! Quack! Quack . . . Quack . . . Quack . . .

[ANNE *pulls off the coat and trousers.*]

1 ANNE. You are the most intolerable, <u>insufferable</u> boy I've ever met!

[*She throws the clothes down the stairwell.* PETER *goes down after them.*]

PETER. Quack, Quack, Quack!

MRS. VAN DAAN. [*To* ANNE] That's right, Anneke! Give it to him!

ANNE. With all the boys in the world . . . Why I had to get locked up with one like you! . . .

PETER. Quack, Quack, Quack, and from now on stay out of my room!

[*As* PETER *passes her,* ANNE *puts out her foot, tripping him. He picks himself up, and goes on into his room.*]

MRS. FRANK. [*Quietly*] Anne, dear . . . your hair. [*She feels* ANNE'*s forehead.*] You're warm. Are you feeling all right?

ANNE. Please, Mother. [*She goes over to the center table, slipping into her shoes.*]

MRS. FRANK. [*Following her*] You haven't a fever, have you?

2 ANNE. [*Pulling away*] No. No.

MRS. FRANK. You know we can't call a doctor here, ever. There's only one thing to do . . . watch carefully. Prevent an illness before it comes. Let me see your tongue.

ANNE. Mother, this is perfectly absurd.

MRS. FRANK. Anne, dear, don't be such a baby. Let me see your tongue. [*As* ANNE *refuses,* MRS. FRANK *appeals to* MR. FRANK] Otto . . . ?

MR. FRANK. You hear your mother, Anne.

[ANNE *flicks out her tongue for a second, then turns away.*]

MRS. FRANK. Come on—open up! [*As* ANNE *opens her mouth very wide*] You seem all right . . . but perhaps an aspirin . . .

MRS. VAN DAAN. For heaven's sake, don't give that child any pills. I waited for fifteen minutes this morning for her to come out of the w.c.

ANNE. I was washing my hair!

MR. FRANK. I think there's nothing the matter with our Anne that a ride on her bike, or a visit with her friend Jopie de Waal wouldn't cure. Isn't that so, Anne?

[MR. VAN DAAN *comes down into the room. From outside we hear faint sounds of bombers going over and a burst of ack-ack.*][19]

MR. VAN DAAN. Miep not come yet?

MRS. VAN DAAN. The workmen just left, a little while ago.

MR. VAN DAAN. What's for dinner tonight?

MRS. VAN DAAN. Beans.

MR. VAN DAAN. Not again!

MRS. VAN DAAN. Poor Putti! I know. But what can we do? That's all that Miep brought us.

[MR. VAN DAAN *starts to pace, his hands behind his back.* ANNE *follows behind him, imitating him.*]

ANNE. We are now in what is known as the "bean cycle." Beans boiled, beans en casserole, beans with strings, beans without strings . . .

[PETER *has come out of his room. He slides into his place at the table, becoming immediately absorbed in his studies.*]

MR. VAN DAAN. [*To* PETER] I saw you . . . in there, playing with your cat.

---

19. ack-ack (ak' ak') *n.*: Slang for an antiaircraft gun's fire.

Cross-Curricular Connection: Health

Health Concerns Mrs. Frank often worries that Anne is running a fever. Discuss with students why she might be concerned with health issues.

Have students consider what might have happened if one of those in hiding had developed a serious illness or needed surgery—for example, a ruptured appendix or a broken bone. They would not have been able to leave the hiding place and seek help from a hospital or doctor. In the 1997 revival of the Broadway play, Mrs. Van Daan needs a tooth pulled; the group is fortunate that Dussel is a dentist and able to take care of the problem.

Food supplies became scarce, and hunger and starvation were serious concerns—without proper nutrition, the body's natural defenses against disease weaken. In the overcrowded concentration camps, typhus and communicable diseases caused many deaths due to years of poor nutrition and health care. Have students list additional health concerns that those living in hiding might have faced. Alternatively, students might list first aid supplies and general medicines they would take if they and their family were going into hiding for an undetermined length of time.

MRS. VAN DAAN. He just went in for a second, putting his coat away. He's been out here all the time, doing his lessons.

MR. FRANK. [*Looking up from the papers*] Anne, you got an excellent in your history paper today . . . and very good in Latin.

ANNE. [*Sitting beside him*] How about algebra?

MR. FRANK. I'll have to make a confession. Up until now I've managed to stay ahead of you in algebra. Today you caught up with me. We'll leave it to Margot to correct.

ANNE. Isn't algebra *vile*, Pim!

MR. FRANK. Vile!

MARGOT. [*To* MR. FRANK] How did I do?

ANNE. [*Getting up*] Excellent, excellent, excellent, excellent!

MR. FRANK. [*To* MARGOT] You should have used the subjunctive[20] here . . .

MARGOT. Should I? . . . I thought . . . look here . . . I didn't use it here . . .

[*The two become absorbed in the papers.*]

ANNE. Mrs. Van Daan, may I try on your coat?

MRS. FRANK. No, Anne.

MRS. VAN DAAN. [*Giving it to* ANNE] It's all right . . . but careful with it.
[ANNE *puts it on and struts with it.*]
My father gave me that the year before he died. He always bought the best that money could buy.

⑥ ANNE. Mrs. Van Daan, did you have a lot of boy friends before you were married?

MRS. FRANK. Anne, that's a personal question. It's not courteous to ask personal questions.

MRS. VAN DAAN. Oh I don't mind. [*To* ANNE] Our house was always swarming with boys. When I was a girl we had . . .

MR. VAN DAAN. Oh, no. Not again!

MRS. VAN DAAN. [*Good-humored*] Shut up!

---

20. **subjunctive** (səb juŋk′ tiv) *n.*: A particular form of a verb.

◆ **Build Vocabulary**

insufferable (in suf′ ər ə bəl) *adj.*: Unbearable

[*Without a pause, to* ANNE, MR. VAN DAAN *mimics* MRS. VAN DAAN, *speaking the first few words in unison with her.*] **⑦**

One summer we had a big house in Hilversum. The boys came buzzing round like bees around a jam pot. And when I was sixteen! . . . We were wearing our skirts very short those days and I had good-looking legs. [*She pulls up her skirt, going to* MR. FRANK.] I still have 'em. I may not be as pretty as I used to be, but I still have my legs. How about it, Mr. Frank?

MR. VAN DAAN. All right. All right. We see them.

MRS. VAN DAAN. I'm not asking you. I'm asking Mr. Frank.

PETER. Mother, for heaven's sake.

MRS. VAN DAAN. Oh, I embarrass you, do I? Well, I just hope the girl you marry has as good. [*Then to* ANNE] My father used to worry about me, with so many boys hanging round. He told me, if any of them gets fresh, you say to him . . . "Remember, Mr. So-and-So, remember I'm a lady."

ANNE. "Remember, Mr. So-and-So, remember I'm a lady." [*She gives* MRS. VAN DAAN *her coat.*]

MR. VAN DAAN. Look at you, talking that way in front of her! Don't you know she puts it all down in that diary? **⑧**

MRS. VAN DAAN. So, if she does? I'm only telling the truth!

[ANNE *stretches out, putting her ear to the floor, listening to what is going on below. The sound of the bombers fades away.*]

MRS. FRANK. [*Setting the table*] Would you mind, Peter, if I moved you over to the couch?

ANNE. [*Listening*] Miep must have the radio on.

[PETER *picks up his papers, going over to the couch beside* MRS. VAN DAAN.]

MR. VAN DAAN. [*Accusingly, to* PETER] Haven't you finished yet?

PETER. No.

MR. VAN DAAN. You ought to be ashamed of yourself.

 Humanities: Drama

Staging Plays Many issues must be considered and dealt with in order to produce a play. The playwright's stage directions determine where actors will move and how they will use the set and props. However, the set must first be designed with an eye to applying these stage directions. A production team typically includes the producer, director, set designer, lighting designer, and costume designer. These theater specialists use their talents best in a collaborative setting. The set designer considers the dimensions and layout of the stage and theater—the attic area of the set for *The Diary of Anne Frank* will not be useful if it is so high that the audience members in the back row cannot see the action that takes place because their view is limited. With the set design, the director can *block* scenes, telling actors where and how they should move and interact. In order to light scenes and actors properly, the lighting designer makes final decisions about lighting when the director and actors finish blocking and rehearsing. The production team continues to work together to make adjustments for individual actors and considerations that come up while the play is in rehearsal.

725

❶ Ask students what Mr. Frank means when he asks Peter if he wants to make their school "coeducational." Before students answer the question, have a volunteer define *coeducational*. *Mr. Frank is suggesting that the school be expanded to include a boy; he is inviting Peter to join Anne and Margot as his students.*

◆ Critical Thinking

❷ Interpret Ask students what the bickering between Mr. and Mrs. Van Daan reveals about their relationship, as well as about the tensions of living in hiding. *The Van Daans' bickering may mean that the two do not communicate well, or they lack respect for each other, or they are simply in the habit of treating each other that way. Their bickering may also be magnified by stressful living in cramped quarters.*

◆ Critical Thinking

❸ Infer What does Anne's comment about the grownups' quarreling reveal about the Frank household? *Anne's surprise at hearing the Van Daans quarreling suggests that in her home, her parents did not argue in front of their children.*

Customize for
Interpersonal Learners

Have students work with partners to write a description of Mrs. Van Daan. They may want to list information about Mrs. Van Daan on an organizer such as the one shown. Invite students to share their organizer with the class.

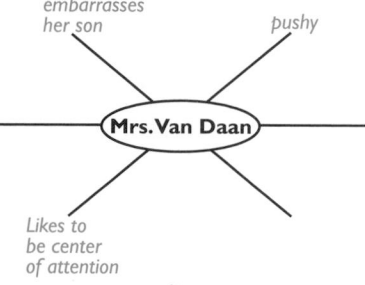

PETER. All right. All right. I'm a dunce. I'm a hopeless case. Why do I go on?

MRS. VAN DAAN. You're not hopeless. Don't talk that way. It's just that you haven't anyone to help you, like the girls have. [*To* MR. FRANK] Maybe you could help him, Mr. Frank?

MR. FRANK. I'm sure that his father . . . ?

MR. VAN DAAN. Not me. I can't do anything with him. He won't listen to me. You go ahead . . . if you want.

❶ MR. FRANK. [*Going to* PETER] What about it, Peter? Shall we make our school coeducational?

MRS. VAN DAAN. [*Kissing* MR. FRANK] You're an angel, Mr. Frank. An angel. I don't know why I didn't meet you before I met that one there. Here, sit down, Mr. Frank . . . [*She forces him down on the couch beside* PETER.] Now, Peter, you listen to Mr. Frank.

MR. FRANK. It might be better for us to go into Peter's room.

[PETER *jumps up eagerly, leading the way.*]

MRS. VAN DAAN. That's right. You go in there, Peter. You listen to Mr. Frank. Mr. Frank is a highly educated man.

[*As* MR. FRANK *is about to follow* PETER *into his room,* MRS. FRANK *stops him and wipes the lipstick from his lips. Then she closes the door after them.*]

ANNE. [*On the floor, listening*] Shh! I can hear a man's voice talking.

MR. VAN DAAN. [*To* ANNE] Isn't it bad enough here without your sprawling all over the place?

[ANNE *sits up.*]

❷ MRS. VAN DAAN. [*To* MR. VAN DAAN] If you didn't smoke so much, you wouldn't be so bad-tempered.

MR. VAN DAAN. Am I smoking? Do you see me smoking?

MRS. VAN DAAN. Don't tell me you've used up all those cigarettes.

MR. VAN DAAN. One package. Miep only brought me one package.

MRS. VAN DAAN. It's a filthy habit anyway. It's a good time to break yourself.

MR. VAN DAAN. Oh, stop it, please.

❷ MRS. VAN DAAN. You're smoking up all our money. You know that, don't you?

MR. VAN DAAN. Will you shut up?

[*During this,* MRS. FRANK *and* MARGOT *have studiously kept their eyes down. But* ANNE, *seated on the floor, has been following the discussion interestedly.* MR. VAN DAAN *turns to see her staring up at him.*]

And what are you staring at?

❸ ANNE. I never heard grownups quarrel before. I thought only children quarreled.

MR. VAN DAAN. This isn't a quarrel! It's a discussion. And I never heard children so rude before.

ANNE. [*Rising, indignantly*] I, rude!

MR. VAN DAAN. Yes!

MRS. FRANK. [*Quickly*] Anne, will you get me my knitting?

[ANNE *goes to get it.*]

I must remember, when Miep comes, to ask her to bring me some more wool.

MARGOT. [*Going to her room*] I need some hairpins and some soap. I made a list. [*She goes into her bedroom to get the list.*]

MRS. FRANK. [*To* ANNE] Have you some library books for Miep when she comes?

ANNE. It's a wonder that Miep has a life of her own, the way we make her run errands for us. Please, Miep, get me some starch. Please take my hair out and have it cut. Tell me all the latest news, Miep. [*She goes over, kneeling on the couch beside* MRS. VAN DAAN] Did you know she was engaged? His name is Dirk, and Miep's afraid the Nazis will ship him off to Germany to work in one of their war plants. That's what they're doing with some of the young Dutchmen . . . they pick them up off the streets—

MR. VAN DAAN. [*Interrupting*] Don't you ever get tired of talking? Suppose you try keeping still for five minutes. Just five minutes.

 Beyond the Classroom

Community Connections

Manners Because of the close living quarters and Anne's boisterous nature, Mrs. Frank often reminds her daughter to mind her manners. People have customs that dictate what is considered polite or rude behavior. These manners are taught to young children as a way of ensuring polite behavior.

Rules of etiquette and polite manners differ among cultures and change as a society changes. As women in the U. S. have asserted their rights in the voting booth and work place, manners have changed as well—many women no longer expect to have a door held open for them, carry their own packages, and shake hands as an equal with a male associate. Good manners apply when making introductions, eating, speaking on the telephone, extending invitations, and driving. Courtesy is the most important aspect of good manners. Have students review the play for examples of reminders about manners given to Anne and decide whether these rules would apply to them. Students may be interested in researching manners and etiquette in our society. Suggest that they post a list of "Good Manners" for the class.

[*He starts to pace again. Again* ANNE *follows him, mimicking him.* MRS. FRANK *jumps up and takes her by the arm up to the sink, and gives her a glass of milk.*]

❹

MRS. FRANK. Come here, Anne. It's time for your glass of milk.

MR. VAN DAAN. Talk, talk, talk. I never heard such a child. Where is my . . . ? Every evening it's the same talk, talk, talk. [*He looks around.*] Where is my . . . ?

MRS. VAN DAAN. What're you looking for?

MR. VAN DAAN. My pipe. Have you seen my pipe?

MRS. VAN DAAN. What good's a pipe? You haven't got any tobacco.

MR. VAN DAAN. At least I'll have something to hold in my mouth! [*Opening* MARGOT's *bedroom door*] Margot, have you seen my pipe?

MARGOT. It was on the table last night.

[ANNE *puts her glass of milk on the table and picks up his pipe, hiding it behind her back.*]

MR. VAN DAAN. I know. I know. Anne, did you see my pipe? . . . Anne!

MRS. FRANK. Anne, Mr. Van Daan is speaking to you.

ANNE. Am I allowed to talk now?

MR. VAN DAAN. You're the most aggravating . . . The trouble with you is, you've been spoiled. What you need is a good old-fashioned spanking.

ANNE. [*Mimicking* MRS. VAN DAAN] "Remember, Mr. So-and-So, remember I'm a lady." [*She thrusts the pipe into his mouth, then picks up her glass of milk.*]

❺

MR. VAN DAAN. [*Restraining himself with difficulty*] Why aren't you nice and quiet like your sister Margot? Why do you have to show off all the time? Let me give you a little advice, young lady. Men don't like that kind of thing in a girl. You know that? A man likes a girl who'll listen to him once in a while . . . a domestic girl, who'll keep her house shining for her husband . . . who loves to cook and sew and . . .

ANNE. I'd cut my throat first! I'd open my veins! I'm going to be remarkable! I'm going to Paris . . .

MR. VAN DAAN. [*Scoffingly*] Paris!

ANNE. . . . to study music and art.

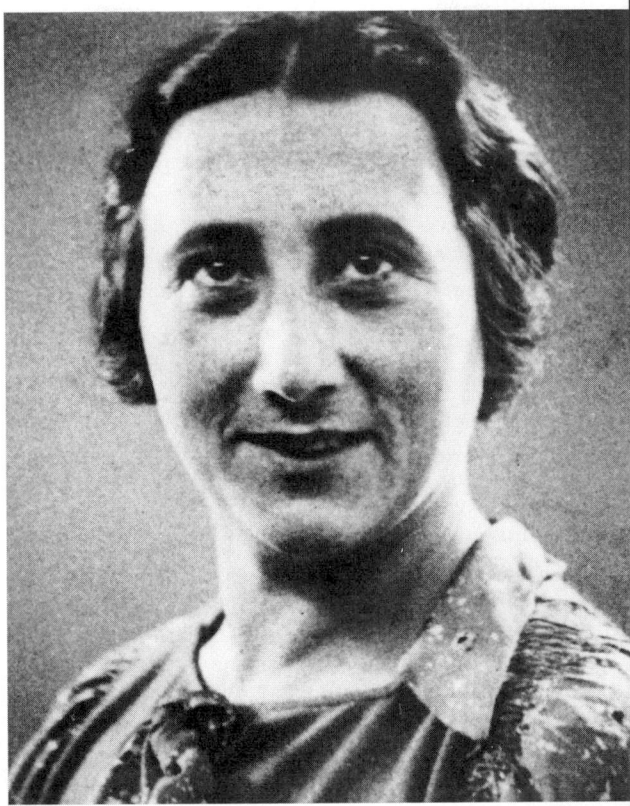

▲ **Critical Viewing** What kind of personality would you say Mrs. Frank had, based on details in this photograph? [Infer] ❻

MR. VAN DAAN. Yeah! Yeah!

ANNE. I'm going to be a famous dancer or singer . . . or something wonderful.

[*She makes a wide gesture, spilling the glass of milk on the fur coat in* MRS. VAN DAAN's *lap.* MARGOT *rushes quickly over with a towel.* ANNE *tries to brush the milk off with her skirt.*] ❼

The Diary of Anne Frank, Act I ◆ 727

Comprehension Check ☑

❹ In what ways does Mrs. Frank defuse the tension when Anne is mimicking Mr. Van Daan? Have students note a similar example on p. 726. Encourage students to note other examples of ways that Mrs. Frank subtly manages the tension among the families. *Mrs. Frank leads Anne away, telling her that it is time for her milk. Earlier, Mrs. Frank asked Anne to get her knitting.*

◆ **LITERATURE AND YOUR LIFE**

❺ Ask students how they might react if Mr. Van Daan were saying these things to them. Have students discuss whether they agree or disagree with Mr. Van Daan's comments about a woman's role. *Students may say that they would resent Margot for being so good and resent Mr. Van Daan for being so critical. Some may completely disagree with his view of a woman's role at home.*

▶ **Critical Viewing** ◀

❻ **Infer** *Students may say that, based on Mrs. Frank's expression—her eyes and smile—she seems to be shy and kind.*

◆ **Critical Thinking**

❼ **Predict** Have students predict how Mrs. Van Daan will react to Anne's spilling milk on her fur coat. *Mrs. Van Daan will be furious with Anne, because she values the coat and her possessions so highly.*

Beyond the Classroom

Career Connection
Exploring Options Even though Anne is trapped in the Secret Annex with no escape in sight, she dreams of her future—studying music and art in Paris and someday doing "something wonderful."

Challenge students to dream of their future. Ask them to freewrite about "something wonderful" that they would like to become one day. Exploring job opportunities, options, and educational requirements is an important career-planning tool. Many schools, communities, and colleges or universities plan "Job Fairs" to acquaint students with employment opportunities. Part-time employment and summer jobs help students try out jobs and decide if they wish to pursue a career in that field. Early commitment to career goals is important if the job requires extensive training and education. For example, a young person wishing to be a dancer needs to understand the level of commitment necessary; a student interested in medicine needs to understand the education requirements. It is never too late to dream, or change career directions, but exploring options may make the career path easier.

◆ Critical Thinking

❶ Compare and Contrast Have students compare Mrs. Van Daan's attitude toward Anne earlier in the scene to her attitude after Anne accidentally spills milk on the fur coat. *Earlier, Mrs. Van Daan was friendly and accommodating when Anne wanted to try on the coat. Now she is furious with Anne, ignoring Anne's apologies and accusing her of ruining the coat on purpose.*

◆ LITERATURE AND YOUR LIFE

❷ Have students discuss the pros and cons of being "self-willed," as Anne is. Ask students if they think that Anne is capable of becoming more like Margot. *Anne's temperament may offend some people, but she is likely to get what she wants in life by standing up for herself. Students may speculate that it would be impossible for Anne to try to be like Margot, since her personality is so completely different.*

◆ Critical Thinking

❸ Infer Why does Anne think that her mother is against her more than the others? *Anne feels this way because her mother often tries to control or change her behavior.*

◆ Critical Thinking

❹ Predict Ask students whether they agree or disagree with Margot's prediction. *Anne's optimistic nature prevents her from remaining upset for very long. Others may say that since Anne has been severely criticized by the Van Daans, perhaps it will be a while before she is "laughing and joking" again.*

Customize for
Interpersonal Learners

Have students meet in small groups to discuss how they might counsel the families to reduce the tension of living together in a small area.

---

❶ MRS. VAN DAAN. Now look what you've done . . . you clumsy little fool! My beautiful fur coat my father gave me . . .

ANNE. I'm so sorry.

MRS. VAN DAAN. What do you care? It isn't yours . . . So go on, ruin it! Do you know what that coat cost? Do you? And now look at it! Look at it!

ANNE. I'm very, very sorry.

MRS. VAN DAAN. I could kill you for this. I could just kill you!

[MRS. VAN DAAN *goes up the stairs, clutching the coat.* MR. VAN DAAN *starts after her.*]

MR. VAN DAAN. Petronella . . . *Liefje! Liefje!* . . . Come back . . . the supper . . . come back!

MRS. FRANK. Anne, you must not behave in that way.

ANNE. It was an accident. Anyone can have an accident.

MRS. FRANK. I don't mean that. I mean the answering back. You must not answer back. They are our guests. We must always show the greatest courtesy to them. We're all living under terrible tension.

[*She stops as* MARGOT *indicates that* VAN DAAN *can hear. When he is gone, she continues.*]

That's why we must control ourselves . . . You don't hear Margot getting into arguments with them, do you? Watch Margot. She's always courteous with them. Never familiar. She keeps her distance. And they respect her for it. Try to be like Margot.

ANNE. And have them walk all over me, the way they do her? No, thanks!

MRS. FRANK. I'm not afraid that anyone is going to walk all over you, Anne. I'm afraid for other people, that you'll walk on them. I don't know what happens to you, Anne. You **❷** are wild, self-willed. If I had ever talked to my mother as you talk to me . . .

ANNE. Things have changed. People aren't like that any more. "Yes, Mother." "No, Mother." "Anything you say, Mother." I've got to fight things out for myself! Make something of myself!

MRS. FRANK. It isn't necessary to fight to do it. Margot doesn't fight, and isn't she . . . ?

ANNE. [*Violently rebellious*] Margot! Margot! Margot! That's all I hear from everyone . . . how wonderful Margot is . . . "Why aren't you like Margot?"

MARGOT. [*Protesting*] Oh, come on, Anne, don't be so . . .

ANNE. [*Paying no attention*] Everything she does is right, and everything I do is wrong! I'm the goat around here! . . . You're all **❸** against me! . . . And you worst of all!

[*She rushes off into her room and throws herself down on the settee, stifling her sobs.* MRS. FRANK *sighs and starts toward the stove.*]

MRS. FRANK. [*To* MARGOT] Let's put the soup on the stove . . . if there's anyone who cares to eat. Margot, will you take the bread out?

[MARGOT *gets the bread from the cupboard.*]

I don't know how we can go on living this way . . . I can't say a word to Anne . . . she flies at me . . .

MARGOT. You know Anne. In half an hour she'll **❹** be out here, laughing and joking.

MRS. FRANK. And . . . [*She makes a motion upwards, indicating the* VAN DAANS.] . . . I told your father it wouldn't work . . . but no . . . no . . . he had to ask them, he said . . . he owed it to him, he said. Well, he knows now that I was right! These quarrels! . . . This bickering!

MARGOT. [*With a warning look*] Shush. Shush.

[*The buzzer for the door sounds.* MRS. FRANK *gasps, startled.*]

MRS. FRANK. Every time I hear that sound, my heart stops!

MARGOT. [*Starting for* PETER'*s door*] It's Miep. [*She knocks at the door.*] Father?

[MR. FRANK *comes quickly from* PETER'*s room.*]

MR. FRANK. Thank you, Margot. [*As he goes down the steps to open the outer door*] Has everyone his list?

MARGOT. I'll get my books. [*Giving her mother a list*] Here's your list.

Cross-Curricular Connection: Social Studies

The Nazi Party After World War I, several political parties were established in Germany. Among these was the German National Socialist Labor Party, established in 1920 and later known as the Nazi Party (based on the German word *NAtionalsoZIalistische*). As with other extremist groups, the Nazi Party appealed to people who were discontented—idealists, defeated soldiers, unemployed workers, business and property owners fearful of a Communist takeover, criminals, and outcasts of all kinds. The Nazi program promised to restore Germany's former power,

redistribute the national wealth, and provide jobs for everyone.

Adolf Hitler, an Austrian-born former house painter, became leader, or Führer, of the Nazi party in 1921. Hitler was a shrewd leader who often used lies and force to get his way. Shortly after he became Chancellor of Germany, in 1933, Hitler demanded and won the power to rule by decree.

Have interested students conduct research to learn more about the Nazi Party and Adolph Hitler. Invite volunteers to share their findings with the class.

⑤ [MARGOT *goes into her and* ANNE's *bedroom on the right.* ANNE *sits up, hiding her tears, as* MARGOT *comes in.*]

Miep's here.

[MARGOT *picks up her books and goes back.* ANNE *hurries over to the mirror, smoothing her hair.*]

MR. VAN DAAN. [*Coming down the stairs*] Is it Miep?

MARGOT. Yes. Father's gone down to let her in.

MR. VAN DAAN. At last I'll have some cigarettes!

MRS. FRANK. [*To* MR. VAN DAAN] I can't tell you how unhappy I am about Mrs. Van Daan's coat. Anne should never have touched it.

MR. VAN DAAN. She'll be all right.

MRS. FRANK. Is there anything I can do?

MR. VAN DAAN. Don't worry.

[*He turns to meet* MIEP. *But it is not* MIEP *who comes up the steps. It is* MR. KRALER, *followed by* MR. FRANK. *Their faces are grave.* ANNE *comes from the bedroom.* PETER *comes from his room.*]

⑥ MRS. FRANK. Mr. Kraler!

MR. VAN DAAN. How are you, Mr. Kraler?

MARGOT. This is a surprise.

MRS. FRANK. When Mr. Kraler comes, the sun begins to shine.

MR. VAN DAAN. Miep is coming?

MR. KRALER. Not tonight.

[KRALER *goes to* MARGOT *and* MRS. FRANK *and* ANNE, *shaking hands with them.*]

MRS. FRANK. Wouldn't you like a cup of coffee? . . . Or, better still, will you have supper with us?

MR. FRANK. Mr. Kraler has something to talk over with us. Something has happened, he says, which demands an immediate decision.

MRS. FRANK. [*Fearful*] What is it?

[MR. KRALER *sits down on the couch. As he talks he takes bread, cabbages, milk, etc., from his briefcase, giving them to* MARGOT *and* ANNE *to put away.*]

MR. KRALER. Usually, when I come up here, I try to bring you some bit of good news. What's the use of telling you the bad news when there's nothing that you can do about it? But today something has happened . . . Dirk . . . Miep's Dirk, you know, came to me just now. He tells me that he has a Jewish friend living near him. A dentist. He says he's in trouble. He begged me, could I do anything for this man? Could I find him a hiding place? . . . So I've come to you . . . I know it's a terrible thing to ask of you, living as you are, but would you take him in with you?

⑦

MR. FRANK. Of course we will.

MR. KRALER. [*Rising*] It'll be just for a night or two . . . until I find some other place. This happened so suddenly that I didn't know where to turn.

MR. FRANK. Where is he?

MR. KRALER. Downstairs in the office.

MR. FRANK. Good. Bring him up.

MR. KRALER. His name is Dussel . . . Jan Dussel.

MR. FRANK. Dussel . . . I think I know him.

MR. KRALER. I'll get him.

[*He goes quickly down the steps and out.* MR. FRANK *suddenly becomes conscious of the others.*]

MR. FRANK. Forgive me. I spoke without consulting you. But I knew you'd feel as I do.

MR. VAN DAAN. There's no reason for you to consult anyone. This is your place. You have a right to do exactly as you please. The only thing I feel . . . there's so little food as it is . . . and to take in another person . . .

[PETER *turns away, ashamed of his father.*]

MR. FRANK. We can stretch the food a little. It's only for a few days.

MR. VAN DAAN. You want to make a bet?

MRS. FRANK. I think it's fine to have him. But, Otto, where are you going to put him? Where?

The Diary of Anne Frank, Act I ◆ 729

◆ **Critical Thinking**

⑤ Infer Why does Anne hide her tears as Margot comes into the room? *Anne does not want to show Margot how badly her feelings are hurt. Perhaps Anne thinks that crying in front of others is a sign of weakness.*

◆ **Literary Focus**

⑥ Staging Have students identify the contradiction between the stage directions and the dialogue in the passage that describes Mr. Kraler's arrival. *In the stage directions, the arrival of Mr. Kraler indicates a serious, possibly dangerous, matter. His face—as well as that of Mr. Frank—is described as grave. To Mrs. Frank, Mr. Kraler's arrival brings happiness.*

◆ **Critical Thinking**

⑦ Predict Have students predict how each of the characters will react to Mr. Kraler's request. Encourage students to support their predictions by citing traits they have observed in the characters. *Mr. and Mrs. Frank will accept the dentist, since they are both kind and generous. Mr. and Mrs. Van Daan tend to be more selfish, so they may not want to share with another person. Because he is uncomfortable with strangers, Peter may feel uneasy about having another person join them. Margot will probably not object as she has an accepting nature. Because of her sociable, friendly nature and natural curiosity, Anne will welcome another person into the group.*

Customize for
English Language Learners
Point out to students that many English words have more than one meaning. Have students proficient in English help English language learners identify multiple-meaning words on p. 729, such as *down, grave, steps,* and *fine.* Suggest that partners use a dictionary to explore the words' multiple meanings.

Beyond the Classroom

Community Connections
Helping Others Of the 140,000 Jews living in the Netherlands when World War II began, about 25,000 went into hiding. The Dutch word for hiding is *onderduiken,* which literally means "diving underwater." Those in hiding were often called *divers.* Jews who went into hiding depended on the help of non-Jews, such as Miep and Mr. Kraler. Helping Jews find secret homes and obtaining provisions were difficult and dangerous tasks. Punishment for helping to hide Jews was often as severe as that for the Jews themselves. Helpers provided food, toiletries, news, and books, as well as encouragement and reassurance, for those in hiding.

Not only Jews were hidden by the Dutch people; young Dutch men who were called up for work service in Germany and identified members of the resistance also went underground—hiding in barns, cellars, attics, and cupboards. By 1944, it is estimated that 15,000 volunteers were helping over 300,000 people to hide from the Nazis. Have students write about the courage of—and the immense risks taken by—volunteers who helped the "divers."

◆ Critical Thinking

① Interpret What do Peter, Anne, and Margot reveal about themselves in this passage? *All three show that they are generous and selfless, even in trying circumstances.*

◆ Critical Thinking

② Analyze Have students contrast the reactions of Mr. and Mrs. Frank and Mr. and Mrs. Van Daan to having Dussel join them in hiding. Ask students which viewpoint they agree with and how they might respond in that situation. *Mr. and Mrs. Frank are accepting of Mr. Dussel—eager to make him feel welcome. The Van Daans, used to an extravagant lifestyle and plenty of space, are unhappy at the prospect of sharing their hiding place with yet another person. Students may say that in spite of the additional hardship, they would welcome Mr. Dussel because his life is in grave danger.*

◆ Literary Focus

③ Staging Based on the information in these stage directions, how do you think Mr. Dussel will adjust to his life in hiding with the Franks and Van Daans? Explain. *The description of Mr. Dussel as meticulous and finicky indicates that he may have trouble adjusting to life in cramped quarters with seven other people. He may be used to a quiet, orderly life and may find sharing a room with boisterous Anne difficult because of her lively, uninhibited nature.*

◆ Reading Strategy

④ Be Aware of Historical Context Explain to students that the Dutch people resented the anti-Semitic laws that Hitler enacted. You may wish to give students more context and discuss the occupation of Holland (see the Cross-Curricular Connection: Social Studies information below).

PETER. He can have my bed. I can sleep on the floor. I wouldn't mind.

MR. FRANK. That's good of you, Peter. But your room's too small . . . even for *you.*

① ANNE. I have a much better idea. I'll come in here with you and Mother, and Margot can take Peter's room and Peter can go in our room with Mr. Dussel.

MARGOT. That's right. We could do that.

MR. FRANK. No, Margot. You mustn't sleep in that room . . . neither you nor Anne. Mouschi has caught some rats in there. Peter's brave. He doesn't mind.

ANNE. Then how about *this?* I'll come in here with you and Mother, and Mr. Dussel can have my bed.

MRS. FRANK. No. No. *No!* Margot will come in here with us and he can have her bed. It's the only way. Margot, bring your things in here. Help her, Anne.

[MARGOT *hurries into her room to get her things.*]

ANNE. [*To her mother*] Why Margot? Why can't I come in here?

MRS. FRANK. Because it wouldn't be proper for Margot to sleep with a . . . Please, Anne. Don't argue. Please.

[ANNE *starts slowly away.*]

MR. FRANK. [*To* ANNE] You don't mind sharing your room with Mr. Dussel, do you, Anne?

ANNE. No. No, of course not.

MR. FRANK. Good.

[ANNE *goes off into her bedroom, helping* MARGOT. MR. FRANK *starts to search in the cupboards.*]

Where's the cognac?

MRS. FRANK. It's there. But, Otto, I was saving it in case of illness.

MR. FRANK. I think we couldn't find a better time to use it. Peter, will you get five glasses for me?

[PETER *goes for the glasses.* MARGOT *comes out of her bedroom, carrying her possessions, which she hangs behind a curtain in the main room.* MR. FRANK *finds the cognac and pours it into the*

---

five glasses that PETER *brings him.* MR. VAN DAAN *stands looking on sourly.* MRS. VAN DAAN *comes downstairs and looks around at all the bustle.*]

MRS. VAN DAAN. What's happening? What's going on?

MR. VAN DAAN. Someone's moving in with us.

MRS. VAN DAAN. In here? You're joking.

MARGOT. It's only for a night or two . . . until Mr. Kraler finds him another place. **②**

MR. VAN DAAN. Yeah! Yeah!

[MR. FRANK *hurries over as* MR. KRALER *and* DUSSEL *come up.* DUSSEL *is a man in his late fifties,* <u>meticulous</u>, *finicky . . . bewildered now.* **③** *He wears a raincoat. He carries a briefcase, stuffed full, and a small medicine case.*]

MR. FRANK. Come in, Mr. Dussel.

MR. KRALER. This is Mr. Frank.

DUSSEL. Mr. Otto Frank?

MR. FRANK. Yes. Let me take your things. [*He takes the hat and briefcase, but* DUSSEL *clings to his medicine case.*] This is my wife Edith . . . Mr. and Mrs. Van Daan . . . their son, Peter . . . and my daughters, Margot and Anne.

[DUSSEL *shakes hands with everyone.*]

MR. KRALER. Thank you, Mr. Frank. Thank you all. Mr. Dussel, I leave you in good hands. Oh . . . Dirk's coat.

[DUSSEL *hurriedly takes off the raincoat, giving it to* MR. KRALER. *Underneath is his white dentist's jacket, with a yellow Star of David on it.*]

DUSSEL. [*To* MR. KRALER] What can I say to thank you . . . ?

MRS. FRANK. [*To* DUSSEL] Mr. Kraler and Miep . . . They're our life line. Without them we couldn't live.

MR. KRALER. Please. Please. You make us seem very heroic. It isn't that at all. We simply don't like the Nazis. [*To* MR. FRANK, *who offers him a drink*] No, thanks. [*Then going on*] We don't like their methods. We don't like . . .

MR. FRANK. [*Smiling*] I know. I know. "No one's going to tell us Dutchmen what to do with our Jews!" **④**

MR. KRALER. [*To* DUSSEL] Pay no attention to Mr.

Cross-Curricular Connection: Social Studies

Occupied Holland The Germans invaded Holland in 1940. Queen Wilhelmina and her cabinet escaped to England, where they formed a government in exile. A German high commissioner, Arthur Seyss-Inquart, ruled occupied Holland. As they did in other conquered countries, the Germans suppressed political parties and the press, banned listening to Allied broadcasts, and closed the universities. Whether they were Jewish or not, many of the country's military, political, and intellectual leaders were imprisoned.

As was happening in occupied countries across Europe, harsh anti-Jewish measures were imposed in Holland. The Nazis launched a roundup of Jews in Amsterdam in February, 1941. Those who were arrested were deported and sent to labor camps in Germany. Aware of the situation and his family's vulnerability, Otto Frank made plans for the family to go into hiding. Anne's sister, Margot, received a deportation notice on July 5, 1942. The next morning, the Frank family left their house to go into hiding.

Have students research more about Germany's occupation of the Netherlands. The Dutch people were particularly resentful of the anti-Semitic laws that Hitler enacted and at first sought to defy them by open opposition such as workers' strikes. Resistance fighters were forced underground, where they secretly worked to destroy the occupation forces. Despite the efforts of Dutch religious and political groups to hide Jews, 75 percent of the country's 140,000 Jews were dead by the end of the war.

Frank. I'll be up tomorrow to see that they're treating you right. [*To* MR. FRANK] Don't trouble to come down again. Peter will bolt the door after me, won't you, Peter?

PETER. Yes, sir.

MR. FRANK. Thank you, Peter. I'll do it.

MR. KRALER. Good night. Good night.

❺ GROUP. Good night, Mr. Kraler. We'll see you tomorrow, etc., etc.

[MR. KRALER *goes out with* MR. FRANK, MRS. FRANK *gives each one of the "grownups" a glass of cognac.*]

MRS. FRANK. Please, Mr. Dussel, sit down.

[MR. DUSSEL *sinks into a chair.* MRS. FRANK *gives him a glass of cognac.*]

DUSSEL. I'm dreaming. I know it. I can't believe my eyes. Mr. Otto Frank here! [*To* MRS. FRANK] You're not in Switzerland then? A woman told me . . . She said she'd gone to your house . . . the door was open, everything was in disorder, dishes in the sink. She said she found a piece of paper in the wastebasket with an address scribbled on it . . . an address in Zurich. She said you must have escaped to Zurich.

ANNE. Father put that there purposely . . . just so people would think that very thing!

DUSSEL. And you've been *here* all the time?

MRS. FRANK. All the time . . . ever since July.

[ANNE *speaks to her father as he comes back.*]

ANNE. It worked, Pim . . . the address you left! Mr. Dussel says that people believe we escaped to Switzerland.

MR. FRANK. I'm glad. . . . And now let's have a little drink to welcome Mr. Dussel.

[*Before they can drink,* MR. DUSSEL *bolts his drink.* MR. FRANK *smiles and raises his glass.*]

To Mr. Dussel. Welcome. We're very honored to have you with us.

MRS. FRANK. To Mr. Dussel, welcome.

◆ Build Vocabulary

meticulous (mə tik′ yōō ləs) *adj.*: Extremely careful about details

[*The* VAN DAANS *murmur a welcome. The "grownups" drink.*]

MRS. VAN DAAN. Um. That was good.

MR. VAN DAAN. Did Mr. Kraler warn you that you won't get much to eat here? You can imagine . . . three ration books among the seven of us . . . and now you make eight. **❻**

[PETER *walks away, humiliated. Outside a street organ is heard dimly.*]

DUSSEL. [*Rising*] Mr. Van Daan, you don't realize what is happening outside that you should warn me of a thing like that. You don't realize what's going on . . .

[*As* MR. VAN DAAN *starts his characteristic pacing,* DUSSEL *turns to speak to the others.*]

Right here in Amsterdam every day hundreds of Jews disappear . . . They surround a block and search house by house. Children come home from school to find their parents gone. Hundreds are being deported . . . people that you and I know . . . the Hallensteins . . . the Wessels . . .

MRS. FRANK. [*In tears*] Oh, no. No! **❼**

DUSSEL. They get their call-up notice . . . come to the Jewish theater on such and such a day and hour . . . bring only what you can carry in a rucksack. And if you refuse the call-up notice, then they come and drag you from your home and ship you off to Mauthausen.[21] The death camp!

MRS. FRANK. We didn't know that things had got so much worse.

DUSSEL. Forgive me for speaking so.

ANNE. [*Coming to* DUSSEL] Do you know the de Waals? . . . What's become of them? Their daughter Jopie and I are in the same class. Jopie's my best friend.

DUSSEL. They are gone.

ANNE. Gone?

DUSSEL. With all the others.

ANNE. Oh, no. Not Jopie!

---

21. **Mauthausen** (mou tou′ zən): Village in Austria that was the site of a Nazi concentration camp.

The Diary of Anne Frank, Act I ◆ 731

◆ Literary Focus

❺ Staging Point out to students that "etc., etc." is not meant to be spoken. This is the playwrights' cue to the actors to ad lib, or make up, words that fit the situation. Explain that in cases such as this, when members of a group speak at once, playwrights need not write every word that is spoken; rather, they trust the actors to stay in character and speak naturally. Have students name situations other than the one in this scene in which the characters might all speak at once. *Students may suggest times when the characters are greeting Miep and Mr. Kraler or when they are complimenting Mrs. Frank on a particularly good dinner.*

◆ Critical Thinking

❻ Interpret Have students paraphrase the events in this passage. Ask them why the playwrights included the sound of a street organ at this moment. *Mr. Van Daan "welcomes" Mr. Dussel by expressing dismay that they will now have to share their food with eight rather than seven people. Peter is ashamed of his father's rudeness. The playwrights probably included the street organ as a symbol of gaiety and freedom, in contrast to the difficulties faced by the group in hiding.*

◆ Reading Strategy

❼ Be Aware of Historical Context Up to this point, Miep and Mr. Kraler have tried to bring only good news to the group. Now, Mr. Dussel paints a terrifying picture of life for Jews in Amsterdam. Have students imagine how they might react to the news that Mr. Dussel brings. *Students may predict that the group would be even more fearful about being caught and saddened to learn that friends have been deported.*

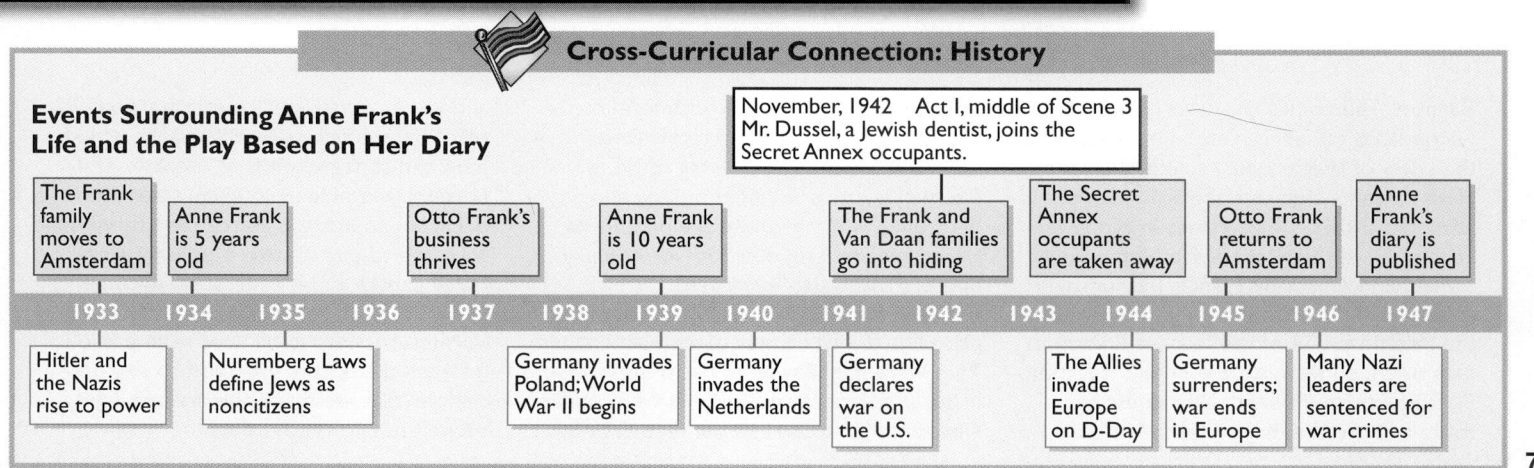

Cross-Curricular Connection: History

Events Surrounding Anne Frank's Life and the Play Based on Her Diary

November, 1942 Act I, middle of Scene 3 Mr. Dussel, a Jewish dentist, joins the Secret Annex occupants.

| The Frank family moves to Amsterdam | Anne Frank is 5 years old | | Otto Frank's business thrives | | Anne Frank is 10 years old | | The Frank and Van Daan families go into hiding | | The Secret Annex occupants are taken away | Otto Frank returns to Amsterdam | | Anne Frank's diary is published |

| 1933 | 1934 | 1935 | 1936 | 1937 | 1938 | 1939 | 1940 | 1941 | 1942 | 1943 | 1944 | 1945 | 1946 | 1947 |

| Hitler and the Nazis rise to power | Nuremberg Laws define Jews as noncitizens | | | | Germany invades Poland; World War II begins | Germany invades the Netherlands | | Germany declares war on the U.S. | | | The Allies invade Europe on D-Day | Germany surrenders; war ends in Europe | Many Nazi leaders are sentenced for war crimes |

◆ Critical Thinking

❶ Infer Why does Mr. Frank interrupt Mrs. Van Daan to suggest that they continue the topic later? *He thinks that Anne has heard enough upsetting news already.*

Clarification

❷ Explain that Mr. Dussel is Jewish by lineage but that he identifies more strongly with his Dutch nationality. Nonetheless, he is in as much danger as the Franks and other Jews in the Netherlands.

◆ Build Grammar Skills

❸ Subject and Verb Agreement Remind students that a verb must agree with its subject in number (singular or plural). Have students identify four singular verbs that agree with singular subjects in this passage. *Students should name these verbs and subjects: gives (Dussel), hurries (Dussel), looks (Dussel), speaks (Margot).*

◆ LITERATURE AND YOUR LIFE

❹ Mr. Kraler has chosen not to tell the families about the worsening situation for Jews on the outside. Have students put themselves in Mr. Kraler's place. Would they protect the families from the truth or tell them the bad news? Encourage students to give reasons for their responses. *Some students may say that if they were Mr. Kraler, they would want to shield the families from bad news because there is nothing the families could do about the situation and no reason to add to their worries. Others may say they would feel the need to be truthful with the families in order to prepare them for the time they are freed.*

[*She turns away, in tears.* MRS. FRANK *motions to* MARGOT *to comfort her.* MARGOT *goes to* ANNE, *putting her arms comfortingly around her.*]

MRS. VAN DAAN. There were some people called Wagner. They lived near us . . . ?

❶ MR. FRANK. [*Interrupting, with a glance at* ANNE] I think we should put this off until later. We all have many questions we want to ask . . . But I'm sure that Mr. Dussel would like to get settled before supper.

DUSSEL. Thank you. I would. I brought very little with me.

MR. FRANK. [*Giving him his hat and briefcase*] I'm sorry we can't give you a room alone. But I hope you won't be too uncomfortable. We've had to make strict rules here . . . a schedule of hours . . . We'll tell you after supper. Anne, would you like to take Mr. Dussel to his room?

ANNE. [*Controlling her tears*] If you'll come with me, Mr. Dussel? [*She starts for her room.*]

❷ DUSSEL. [*Shaking hands with each in turn*] Forgive me if I haven't really expressed my gratitude to all of you. This has been such a shock to me. I'd always thought of myself as Dutch. I was born in Holland. My father was born in Holland, and my grandfather. And now . . . after all these years . . . [*He breaks off.*] If you'll excuse me.

[DUSSEL *gives a little bow and hurries off after* ANNE. MR. FRANK *and the others are subdued.*]

❸ ANNE. [*Turning on the light*] Well, here we are.

[DUSSEL *looks around the room. In the main room* MARGOT *speaks to her mother.*]

MARGOT. The news sounds pretty bad, doesn't it? It's so different from what Mr. Kraler tells us. Mr. Kraler says things are improving.

❹ MR. VAN DAAN. I like it better the way Kraler tells it.

[*They resume their occupations, quietly.* PETER *goes off into his room. In* ANNE's *room,* ANNE *turns to* DUSSEL.]

ANNE. You're going to share the room with me.

DUSSEL. I'm a man who's always lived alone. I haven't had to adjust myself to others. I

hope you'll bear with me until I learn.

ANNE. Let me help you. [*She takes his briefcase.*] Do you always live all alone? Have you no family at all?

DUSSEL. No one. [*He opens his medicine case and spreads his bottles on the dressing table.*]

ANNE. How dreadful. You must be terribly lonely.

DUSSEL. I'm used to it.

ANNE. I don't think I could ever get used to it. Didn't you even have a pet? A cat, or a dog?

DUSSEL. I have an allergy for fur-bearing animals. They give me asthma.

ANNE. Oh, dear. Peter has a cat.

DUSSEL. Here? He has it here?

ANNE. Yes. But we hardly ever see it. He keeps it in his room all the time. I'm sure it will be all right.

DUSSEL. Let us hope so. [*He takes some pills to fortify himself.*]

ANNE. That's Margot's bed, where you're going to sleep. I sleep on the sofa there. [*Indicating the clothes hooks on the wall*] We cleared these off for your things. [*She goes over to the window.*] The best part about this room . . . you can look down and see a bit of the street and the canal. There's a houseboat . . . you can see the end of it . . . a bargeman lives there with his family . . . They have a baby and he's just beginning to walk and I'm so afraid he's going to fall into the canal some day. I watch him. . . . **❺**

DUSSEL. [*Interrupting*] Your father spoke of a schedule.

ANNE. [*Coming away from the window*] Oh, yes. It's mostly about the times we have to be quiet. And times for the w.c. You can use it now if you like.

DUSSEL. [*Stiffly*] No, thank you.

ANNE. I suppose you think it's awful, my talking about a thing like that. But you don't know how important it can get to be, especially when you're frightened . . . About this room, the way Margot and I did . . . she

---

Cross-Curricular Connection: Geography

Escape The Franks chose to hide in the Netherlands rather than attempt to escape to the safety of Switzerland—a neutral country. Have students study a classroom map or atlas that shows the countries in Northern Europe. Have them locate the Netherlands, Switzerland, Germany, France, Belgium, and the city of Amsterdam. You may wish to use the map on p. 733 of the Teacher Edition to help orient students to the Franks' location.

Suggest that students plot an escape route and use the map distance scale or

mileage chart in the atlas to determine the distance from Amsterdam to Switzerland by the most direct cross-country route, avoiding German borders. In addition, they should determine whether there are mountains, rivers, geographical obstacles, or country borders that must be crossed.

Remind students of the travel restriction placed on Jewish citizens of the Netherlands. They were not allowed to use transportation. In addition, France and Belgium were under German occupation like the Netherlands

and were controlled by German troops. To reach Switzerland safely, the Franks would have had to travel on foot, cross several borders, and hide from enemy troops in the occupied countries. Alternatively, they would have had to pay someone to forge illegal travel papers and identification documents in an attempt to reach Switzerland. Each border crossing would have been perilous. Interested students may wish to explore options that were available to Jews trying desperately to reach safety.

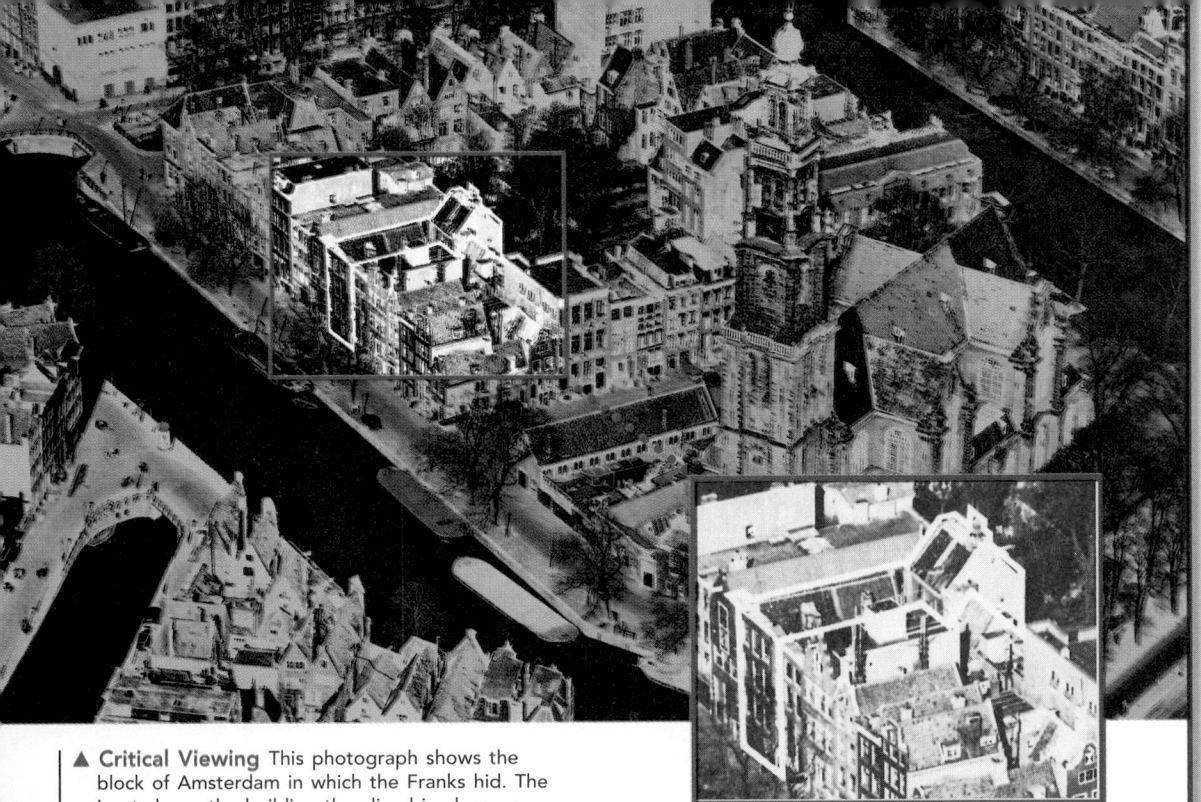

◆ **Critical Thinking**

5 Infer What does Anne's description of the room and its view tell you about her character? *She is optimistic and takes pleasure in even the smallest advantage.*

▶**Critical Viewing**◀

6 Draw Conclusions *Some students may say that perhaps the Franks believed that the war would soon end and they would be able to return to their normal lives in Amsterdam rather than settle in a new country. Others may say that the risk of trying to escape with a family to another country through occupied territory was too great.*

◆ **Critical Thinking**

7 Speculate Ask students how they think Anne and Mr. Dussel will get along. *Given what students already know about Anne and Mr. Dussel, they are likely to predict that the two will not get along well. Anne is lively and outgoing, whereas Mr. Dussel seems quiet and introverted. Anne will probably get on Mr. Dussel's nerves.*

Customize for
Verbal/Linguistic Learners
Have two volunteers give a dramatic reading of the exchange between Anne and Dussel on this page. Encourage students to use voice tone and facial expressions to convey meaning. After the reading, have students suggest possible alternative interpretations of the lines. For example, Dussel's line, "I'm not at my best in the morning," could be read with an assertive tone or with an apologetic tone.

6 ▲ **Critical Viewing** This photograph shows the block of Amsterdam in which the Franks hid. The inset shows the building they lived in close up. Why do you think the Franks chose to remain in Amsterdam, in hiding, rather than flee to Switzerland? [Draw Conclusions]

had it to herself in the afternoons for studying, reading . . . lessons, you know . . . and I took the mornings. Would that be all right with you?

DUSSEL. I'm not at my best in the morning.

ANNE. You stay here in the mornings then. I'll take the room in the afternoons.

DUSSEL. Tell me, when you're in here, what happens to me? Where am I spending my time? In there, with all the people?

ANNE. Yes.

DUSSEL. I see. I see.

ANNE. We have supper at half past six.

DUSSEL. [*Going over to the sofa*] Then, if you don't mind . . . I like to lie down quietly for ten minutes before eating. I find it helps the digestion.

ANNE. Of course. I hope I'm not going to be too much of a bother to you. I seem to be able to get everyone's back up.

[DUSSEL *lies down on the sofa, curled up, his back to her.*]

DUSSEL. I always get along very well with children. My patients all bring their children to me, because they know I get on well with them. So don't you worry about that.

[ANNE *leans over him, taking his hand and shaking it gratefully.*]

ANNE. Thank you. Thank you, Mr. Dussel.

[*The lights dim to darkness. The curtain falls on the scene.* ANNE'S VOICE *comes to us faintly at first, and then with increasing power.*]

ANNE'S VOICE. . . . And yesterday I finished Cissy Van Marxvelt's latest book. I think she is a first-class writer. I shall definitely let my children read her. Monday the twenty-first of September, nineteen forty-two. Mr. Dussel

7

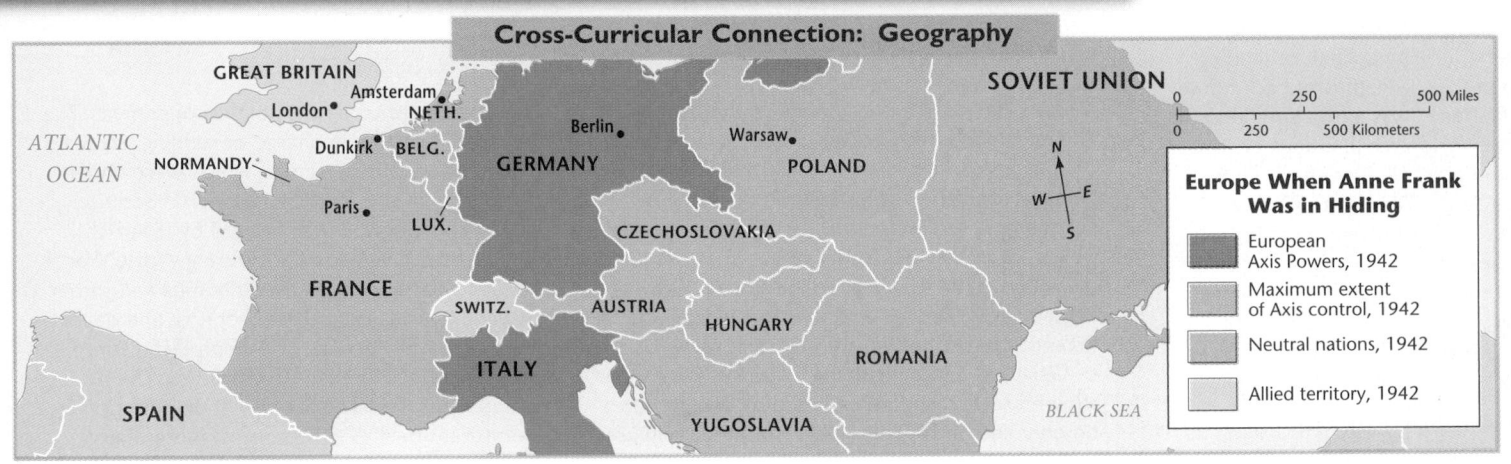

Cross-Curricular Connection: Geography

GREAT BRITAIN

London •

ATLANTIC OCEAN

NORMANDY

FRANCE

Paris •

Dunkirk

Amsterdam •

NETH.

BELG.

LUX.

SWITZ.

SPAIN

ITALY

GERMANY

Berlin •

AUSTRIA

HUNGARY

CZECHOSLOVAKIA

Warsaw •

POLAND

SOVIET UNION

ROMANIA

YUGOSLAVIA

BLACK SEA

N
W   E
S

0   250   500 Miles
0   250   500 Kilometers

Europe When Anne Frank Was in Hiding

■ European Axis Powers, 1942
■ Maximum extent of Axis control, 1942
■ Neutral nations, 1942
□ Allied territory, 1942

and I had another battle yesterday. Yes, Mr. Dussel! According to him, nothing, I repeat . . . nothing, is right about me . . . my appearance, my character, my manners. While he was going on at me I thought . . . sometime I'll give you such a smack that you'll fly right up to the ceiling! Why is it that every grownup thinks he knows the way to bring up children? Particularly the grownups that never had any. I keep wishing that Peter was a girl instead of a boy. Then I would have someone to talk to. Margot's a darling, but she takes everything too seriously. To pause for a moment on the subject of Mrs. Van Daan. I must tell you that her attempts to flirt with father are getting her nowhere. Pim, thank goodness, won't play.

[*As she is saying the last lines, the curtain rises on the darkened scene.* ANNE'S VOICE *fades out.*]

Scene 4

[*It is the middle of the night, several months later. The stage is dark except for a little light which comes through the skylight in* PETER'S *room.*

Everyone is in bed. MR. *and* MRS. FRANK *lie on the couch in the main room, which has been pulled out to serve as a makeshift double bed.*

MARGOT *is sleeping on a mattress on the floor in the main room, behind a curtain stretched across for privacy. The others are all in their accustomed rooms.*

From outside we hear two drunken soldiers singing "Lili Marlene." A girl's high giggle is heard. The sound of running feet is heard coming closer and then fading in the distance. Throughout the scene there is the distant sound of airplanes passing overhead.

A match suddenly flares up in the attic. We dimly see MR. VAN DAAN. *He is getting his bearings. He comes quickly down the stairs, and goes to the cupboard where the food is stored. Again the match flares up, and is as quickly blown out. The dim figure is seen to steal back up the stairs.*

There is quiet for a second or two, broken

only by the sound of airplanes, and running feet on the street below.

Suddenly, out of the silence and the dark, we hear ANNE *scream.*]

ANNE. [*Screaming*] No! No! Don't . . . don't take me!

[*She moans, tossing and crying in her sleep. The other people wake, terrified.* DUSSEL *sits up in bed, furious.*]

> ◆ **Reading Strategy**
> Why is it so dangerous for everyone when Anne screams in her sleep?

DUSSEL. Shush! Anne! Shush!

ANNE. [*Still in her nightmare*] Save me! Save me!

[*She screams and screams.* DUSSEL *gets out of bed, going over to her, trying to wake her.*]

DUSSEL. Quiet! Quiet! You want someone to hear?

[*In the main room* MRS. FRANK *grabs a shawl and pulls it around her. She rushes in to* ANNE, *taking her in her arms.* MR. FRANK *hurriedly gets up, putting on his overcoat.* MARGOT *sits up, terrified.* PETER'S *light goes on in his room.*]

MRS. FRANK. [*To* ANNE, *in her room*] Hush, darling, hush. It's all right. It's all right. [*Over her shoulder to* DUSSEL] Will you be kind enough to turn on the light, Mr. Dussel? [*Back to* ANNE] It's nothing, my darling. It was just a dream.

[DUSSEL *turns on the light in the bedroom.* MRS. FRANK *holds* ANNE *in her arms. Gradually* ANNE *comes out of her nightmare still trembling with horror.* MR. FRANK *comes into the room, and goes quickly to the window, looking out to be sure that no one outside has heard* ANNE's *screams.* MRS. FRANK *holds* ANNE, *talking softly to her. In the main room* MARGOT *stands on a chair, turning on the center hanging lamp. A light goes on in the* VAN DAANS' *room overhead.* PETER *puts his robe on, coming out of his room.*]

DUSSEL. [*To* MRS. FRANK, *blowing his nose*] Something must be done about that child, Mrs. Frank. Yelling like that! Who knows but there's somebody on the streets? She's endangering all our lives.

734 ◆ Drama

MRS. FRANK. Anne, darling.

DUSSEL. Every night she twists and turns. I don't sleep. I spend half my night shushing her. And now it's nightmares!

[MARGOT *comes to the door of* ANNE's *room, followed by* PETER. MR. FRANK *goes to them, indicating that everything is all right.* PETER *takes* MARGOT *back.*]

MRS. FRANK. [*To* ANNE] You're here, safe, you see? Nothing has happened. [*To* DUSSEL] Please, Mr. Dussel, go back to bed. She'll be herself in a minute or two. Won't you, Anne?

DUSSEL. [*Picking up a book and a pillow*] Thank you, but I'm going to the w.c. The one place where there's peace!

[*He stalks out.* MR. VAN DAAN, *in underwear and trousers, comes down the stairs.*]

MR. VAN DAAN. [*To* DUSSEL] What is it? What happened?

DUSSEL. A nightmare. She was having a nightmare!

MR. VAN DAAN. I thought someone was murdering her.

DUSSEL. Unfortunately, no.

[*He goes into the bathroom.* MR. VAN DAAN *goes back up the stairs.* MR. FRANK, *in the main room, sends* PETER *back to his own bedroom.*]

MR. FRANK. Thank you, Peter. Go back to bed.

[PETER *goes back to his room.* MR. FRANK *follows him, turning out the light and looking out the window. Then he goes back to the main room, and gets up on a chair, turning out the center hanging lamp.*]

MRS. FRANK. [*To* ANNE] Would you like some water? [ANNE *shakes her head.*] Was it a very bad dream? Perhaps if you told me . . . ?

ANNE. I'd rather not talk about it.

❻ **MRS. FRANK.** Poor darling. Try to sleep then. I'll sit right here beside you until you fall asleep. [*She brings a stool over, sitting there.*]

ANNE. You don't have to.

MRS. FRANK. But I'd like to stay with you . . . very much. Really.

ANNE. I'd rather you didn't.

MRS. FRANK. Good night, then.

[*She leans down to kiss* ANNE. ANNE *throws her arm up over her face, turning away.* MRS. FRANK, *hiding her hurt, kisses* ANNE's *arm.*]

You'll be all right? There's nothing that you want? **❻**

ANNE. Will you please ask Father to come.

MRS. FRANK. [*After a second*] Of course, Anne dear.

[*She hurries out into the other room.* MR. FRANK *comes to her as she comes in.*]

Sie verlangt nach Dir! [22]

MR. FRANK. [*Sensing her hurt*] Edith, *Liebe, schau . . .* [23] **❼**

MRS. FRANK. *Es macht nichts! Ich danke dem lieben Herrgott, dass sie sich wenigstens an Dich wendet, wenn sie Trost braucht! Geh hinein, Otto, sie ist ganz hysterisch vor Angst.* [24] [*As* MR. FRANK *hesitates*] *Geh zu ihr.* [25]

[*He looks at her for a second and then goes to get a cup of water for* ANNE. MRS. FRANK *sinks down on the bed, her face in her hands, trying to keep from sobbing aloud.* MARGOT *comes over to her, putting her arms around her.*]

She wants nothing of me. She pulled away when I leaned down to kiss her.

MARGOT. It's a phase . . . You heard Father . . . Most girls go through it . . . they turn to their fathers at this age . . . they give all their love to their fathers.

MRS. FRANK. You weren't like this. You didn't shut me out.

MARGOT. She'll get over it . . .

[*She smooths the bed for* MRS. FRANK *and sits beside her a moment as* MRS. FRANK *lies down. In* ANNE's *room* MR. FRANK *comes in, sitting down*

---

22. *Sie verlangt nach Dir* (sē fer´ laŋt´ näk dir): German for "She is asking for you."
23. *Liebe, schau* (lē´ bə shou): German for "Dear, look."
24. *Es macht . . . vor Angst* (es mäkt nichts ich dän´ kə dəm lē´ bən här´ gôt däs sē sich ven´ ig stəns än dish ven´ dət ven sē träst broukt gē hē nīn ät´ tō sē ist gänz hi ste rik fär äŋst): German for "It's all right. I thank dear God that at least she turns to you when she needs comfort. Go in, Otto, she is hysterical because of fear."
25. *Geh zu ihr* (gē tsoo ēr): German for "Go to her."

The Diary of Anne Frank, Act I ◆ **735**

◆ **Critical Thinking**

❻ Speculate Have students summarize Anne's reaction to her mother's attempts to comfort her. Ask them to describe Mrs. Frank's reaction to Anne's rejection. *Anne refuses her mother's offer of comfort several times and asks for her father. Mrs. Frank stays calm and supportive, hiding her hurt feelings at Anne's rejection of her.*

Clarification

❼ Mr. and Mrs. Frank have been living in the Netherlands for several years, but German, rather than Dutch, is their native language. They speak Dutch with their daughters and the others in hiding, but they speak German for privacy. Ask students why Mrs. Frank speaks to Mr. Frank in German in this scene. *Mrs. Frank shows how upset she is by speaking her native language. Also, the playwrights may have had Mr. and Mrs. Frank speak German to remind the audience that the Franks are immigrants.*

Customize for
Interpersonal Learners
After students read p. 735, have them work with partners to identify four examples in which people comfort or reassure each other. Mrs. Frank tries to comfort and reassure Anne after Anne's bad dream; Mr. Frank reassures Peter and Margot that everything is all right; Mr. Frank comforts Mrs. Frank when she is hurt over Anne's rejection of her; Margot comforts and reassures Mrs. Frank.

Cross-Curricular Connection: Foreign Language

German is the language spoken by Mr. and Mrs. Frank in the Secret Annex when they wish to have a few moments of "privacy" in the crowded space. Ask students to look at the German phrases on p. 735 and try to interpret what they mean before reading the translation at the bottom of the page. They may be able to infer the meaning from the context of what is probably being said, or even to decode some words.

The official language spoken in Germany, Austria, and Liechtenstein is German. The Dutch language spoken in the Netherlands and by the occupants of the Secret Annex is a language related to German, developed from the same roots. English and German are also related because they were both developed from an old Germanic language, and both languages have some closely related vocabulary words, such as *house/haus*. The word *kindergarten* is a German word that was adopted into the English language. Challenge interested students to construct an English-German vocabulary list of words that might be recognized by English speaking students without translation.

◆ Critical Thinking

❶ Analyze Have students discuss insights that Anne has about herself in this passage. Ask them whether they agree or disagree with Anne's assessment of herself. *Anne thinks that she is a coward because she calls on her father whenever she is upset. Students may disagree with Anne, because it is not cowardly to depend on a parent in times of trouble. Another insight Anne has is that she treats her mother badly. Some students may agree that Anne is cruel to her mother.*

◆ LITERATURE AND YOUR LIFE

❷ Ask students if Anne's struggle to understand herself seems normal for a teenager. *Students may say that no matter what situations teenagers find themselves in, they are likely to go through periods of confusion and self doubt, as Anne is doing.*

◆ Reading Strategy

❸ Be Aware of Historical Context Ask students to identify a line of dialogue in the play that indicates a change in the war situation. *Anne discusses how the air raids are more frequent, which probably means the fighting is getting closer to Amsterdam and perhaps the end of the war is closer.*

Customize for
Intrapersonal Learners

Have students imagine themselves in Anne's place, forced to live in hiding with seven other people and separated from ordinary routines of daily life. Ask students to write a brief essay in which they describe several things they would dream about doing when they were finally free.

---

by ANNE. ANNE *flings her arms around him, clinging to him. In the distance we hear the sound of ack-ack.*]

ANNE. Oh, Pim. I dreamed that they came to get us! The Green Police! They broke down the door and grabbed me and started to drag me out the way they did Jopie.

MR. FRANK. I want you to take this pill.

ANNE. What is it?

MR. FRANK. Something to quiet you.

[*She takes it and drinks the water. In the main room* MARGOT *turns out the light and goes back to her bed.*]

MR. FRANK. [*To* ANNE] Do you want me to read to you for a while?

ANNE. No. Just sit with me for a minute. Was I awful? Did I yell terribly loud? Do you think anyone outside could have heard?

MR. FRANK. No. No. Lie quietly now. Try to sleep.

ANNE. I'm a terrible coward. I'm so disappointed in myself. I think I've conquered my fear . . . I think I'm really grown-up . . . and then something happens . . . and I run to you like a baby . . . I love you, Father. I don't love anyone but you.

MR. FRANK. [*Reproachfully*] Annele!

ANNE. It's true. I've been thinking about it for a long time. You're the only one I love.

MR. FRANK. It's fine to hear you tell me that you love me. But I'd be happier if you said you loved your mother as well . . . She needs your help so much . . . your love . . .

ANNE. We have nothing in common. She doesn't understand me. Whenever I try to explain my views on life to her she asks me if I'm constipated.

MR. FRANK. You hurt her very much just now. She's crying. She's in there crying.

ANNE. I can't help it. I only told the truth. I didn't want her here . . . [*Then, with sudden change*] Oh, Pim, I was horrible, wasn't I? And the worst of it is, I can stand off and look at myself doing it and know it's cruel and yet I can't stop doing it. What's the

matter with me? Tell me. Don't say it's just a phase! Help me.

MR. FRANK. There is so little that we parents can do to help our children. We can only try to set a good example . . . point the way. The rest you must do yourself. You must build your own character.

ANNE. I'm trying. Really I am. Every night I think back over all of the things I did that day that were wrong . . . like putting the wet mop in Mr. Dussel's bed . . . and this thing now with Mother. I say to myself, that was wrong. I make up my mind, I'm never going to do that again. Never! Of course I may do something worse . . . but at least I'll never do *that* again! . . . I have a nicer side, Father . . . a sweeter, nicer side. But I'm scared to show it. I'm afraid that people are going to laugh at me if I'm serious. So the mean Anne comes to the outside and the good Anne stays on the inside, and I keep on trying to switch them around and have the good Anne outside and the bad Anne inside and be what I'd like to be . . . and might be . . . if only . . . only . . .

[*She is asleep.* MR. FRANK *watches her for a moment and then turns off the light, and starts out. The lights dim out. The curtain falls on the scene.* ANNE'*s voice is heard dimly at first, and then with growing strength.*]

ANNE'S VOICE. . . . The air raids are getting worse. They come over day and night. The noise is terrifying. Pim says it should be music to our ears. The more planes, the sooner will come the end of the war. Mrs. Van Daan pretends to be a <u>fatalist</u>. What will be, will be. But when the planes come over, who is the most frightened? No one else but Petronella! . . . Monday, the ninth of November, nineteen forty-two. Wonderful news! The Allies have landed in Africa. Pim says that we can look for an early finish to the war. Just for fun he asked each of us what was the first thing we wanted to do when we got out of here. Mrs. Van Daan longs to be home with her own things, her needle-point chairs, the Beckstein piano her father gave her . . . the best that money could buy. Peter

---

 Cross-Curricular Connection: History

Air Raids The air raids that Anne mentions were raids by Allied troops on German cities. The airfare war against Germany was played out on four fronts: over England, over North Africa, over the Soviet Union, and over Germany. British and, later, American troops were mostly responsible for the raids on German cities. These air raids succeeded in destroying key points of operation, including railway yards, factories, and major cities. In September 1942, British and American troops agreed to mount a major military offensive against Germany, with American planes bombing during the day and British planes bombing at night. At this time, Hitler's air force *(Luftwaffe)* was not strong enough to strike back. Anne and the others listened for reports of the bombings on the radio, and expected the war to end quickly.

would like to go to a movie. Mr. Dussel wants to get back to his dentist's drill. He's afraid he is losing his touch. For myself, there are so many things . . . to ride a bike again . . . to laugh till my belly aches . . . to have new clothes from the skin out . . . to have a hot tub filled to overflowing and wallow in it for hours . . . to be back in school with my friends . . .

[*As the last lines are being said, the curtain rises on the scene. The lights dim on as* ANNE'S VOICE *fades away.*]

Scene 5

[*It is the first night of the Hanukkah*[26] *celebration.* MR. FRANK *is standing at the head of the table on which is the Menorah.*[27] *He lights the Shamos,*[28] *or servant candle, and holds it as he says the blessing. Seated listening is all of the "family," dressed in their best. The men wear hats,* PETER *wears his cap.*]

MR. FRANK. [*Reading from a prayer book*] "Praised be Thou, oh Lord our God, Ruler of the universe, who has sanctified us with Thy commandments and bidden us kindle the Hanukkah lights. Praised be Thou, oh Lord our God, Ruler of the universe, who has wrought wondrous deliverances for our fathers in days of old. Praised be Thou, oh Lord our God, Ruler of the universe, that Thou has given us life and sustenance and brought us to this happy season." [MR. FRANK *lights the one candle of the Menorah as he continues.*] "We kindle this Hanukkah light to celebrate the great and wonderful deeds wrought through the zeal with which God filled the hearts of the heroic Maccabees, two thousand years ago. They fought against indifference, against tyranny and oppression, and they restored our Temple to us. May these lights remind us that we should ever look to God, whence cometh our help." Amen.

❹

---

26. Hanukkah (khä´ nōō kä´) *n.*: Jewish celebration that lasts eight days.
27. menorah (mə nō´ rə) *n.*: A candle holder with nine candles, used during Hanukkah.
28. shamos (shä´ məs) *n.*: The candle used to light the others in a menorah.

ALL. Amen.

[MR. FRANK *hands* MRS. FRANK *the prayer book.*]

MRS. FRANK. [*Reading*] "I lift up mine eyes unto the mountains, from whence cometh my help. My help cometh from the Lord who made heaven and earth. He will not suffer thy foot to be moved. He that keepeth thee will not slumber. He that keepeth Israel doth neither slumber nor sleep. The Lord is thy keeper. The Lord is thy shade upon thy right hand. The sun shall not smite thee by day, nor the moon by night. The Lord shall keep thee from all evil. He shall keep thy soul. The Lord shall guard thy going out and thy coming in, from this time forth and forevermore." Amen.

❺

ALL. Amen.

[MRS. FRANK *puts down the prayer book and goes to get the food and wine.* MARGOT *helps her.* MR. FRANK *takes the men's hats and puts them aside.*]

DUSSEL. [*Rising*] That was very moving.

ANNE. [*Pulling him back*] It isn't over yet! **❻**

MRS. VAN DAAN. Sit down! Sit down!

ANNE. There's a lot more, songs and presents.

DUSSEL. Presents?

MRS. FRANK. Not this year, unfortunately.

MRS. VAN DAAN. But always on Hanukkah everyone gives presents . . . everyone!

DUSSEL. Like our St. Nicholas' Day.[29]

[*There is a chorus of "no's" from the group.*]

MRS. VAN DAAN. No! Not like St. Nicholas! What kind of a Jew are you that you don't know Hanukkah?

MRS. FRANK. [*As she brings the food*] I remember particularly the candles . . . First one, as we have tonight. Then the

---

29. St. Nicholas' Day: December 6, the day Christian children in Holland receive gifts.

◆ **Build Vocabulary**

fatalist (fā´ tə list) *n.*: One who believes that all events are determined by fate and cannot be changed

---

The Diary of Anne Frank, Act I ◆ 737

◆ **Critical Thinking**

❹ Analyze Causes and Effects Ask students to describe the effects on the group of celebrating an important religious holiday even though they are in hiding. *Students may say that celebrating Hanukkah gives the "family" a connection to Jews all over the world. The celebration lifts them above the daily stresses of their dangerous situation, if only momentarily.*

Clarification

❺ Explain that the words in this passage are from the Bible, Psalm 121. The most familiar English version of the Bible was published in 1611, using the language of the time, in which the second-person familiar pronoun *(thou)* and verb tenses (such as *cometh*) were formed differently from the way they are formed today.

◆ **Critical Thinking**

❻ Infer What does Mr. Dussel's remark and Anne's reaction to it reveal about Dussel? *He is unfamiliar with the rituals associated with the Jewish celebration of Hanukkah and instead is more familiar with St. Nicholas' Day, celebrated by the Dutch.*

Customize for
English Language Learners
Have students proficient in English work with English language learners to make a chart of words from the prayer book that may be unfamiliar, such as *Thou, sanctified, Thy, wrought, sustenance, cometh, whence.* Students can list unfamiliar words in one column of the chart and define the words in a second column. Instruct one student in each pair to look up the unfamiliar word in a dictionary and dictate its meaning to the other student, who can record the meaning on the chart.

Cultural Connection

Hanukkah is a Jewish holiday that commemorates victory over oppression and dedication to God. In 165 B.C., a small Jewish army defeated a much larger Syrian army in a battle for religious freedom. After the victory, the Jews reclaimed their temple in Jerusalem from the Syrians, who had filled it with pagan idols. The Jews removed the idols and rededicated the temple to God. According to legend, they could find only one tiny flask of oil with which to light the holy lamps. Miraculously, the oil lasted for eight days, which is why Jews celebrate the holiday for eight days.

Have students work in pairs to learn more about Hanukkah and traditions associated with it, such as lighting the menorah. Jewish students might wish to share memories of their own Hanukkah celebrations. Invite students to give a presentation in which they explain an aspect of the holiday that especially interests them. Alternatively, some students may wish to find out more about the Dutch celebration of St. Nicholas' Day that Dussel suggested. They might compare and contrast holidays celebrated in December.

Clarification

❶ Explain to students that *latkes* is the Yiddish word for potato pancakes. Latkes are a traditional food served at Hanukkah celebrations. Invite students who have eaten latkes to describe their taste.

◆ Critical Thinking

❷ **Interpret** What common hope are Mr. and Mrs. Frank and Mrs. Van Daan expressing in their remarks? *They are hoping that the Germans will be defeated and that their lives will have returned to normal by this time next year.*

▶Critical Viewing◀

❸ **Connect** Have a volunteer describe Anne's appearance from details in the photograph. Then have students name those details that reveal Anne's personality. *Students may say that Anne's smile and her direct gaze show her exuberant personality.*

◆ Critical Thinking

❹ **Analyze** Ask students why it is important to Anne that everyone have Hanukkah presents. *Anne wants to give everyone presents in order to create a happy moment for herself and for the others in the midst of their difficult lives. Also, making presents gives Anne an outlet for her creative energy. Finally, in giving presents, Anne may be trying to make amends for having been difficult.*

Customize for
Visual/Spatial Learners

Have students discuss why photographs such as these help make Anne Frank more vivid in their minds as they read the play.

◀ **Critical Viewing** What evidence in this photograph of Anne Frank can you find that reveals Anne's exuberant personality? [Connect] ❸

second night you light two candles, the next night three . . . and so on until you have eight candles burning. When there are eight candles it is truly beautiful.

MRS. VAN DAAN. And the potato pancakes.

MR. VAN DAAN. Don't talk about them!

❶ **MRS. VAN DAAN.** I make the best *latkes* you ever tasted!

❷ **MRS. FRANK.** Invite us all next year . . . in your own home.

MR. FRANK. God willing!

MRS. VAN DAAN. God willing.

MARGOT. What I remember best is the presents we used to get when we were little . . . eight days of presents . . . and each day they got better and better.

MRS. FRANK. [*Sitting down*] We are all here, alive. That is present enough.

ANNE. No, it isn't. I've got something . . . [*She rushes into her room, hurriedly puts on a little hat improvised from the lamp shade, grabs a satchel bulging with parcels and comes running back.*] ❹

MRS. FRANK. What is it?

ANNE. Presents!

738 ◆ *Drama*

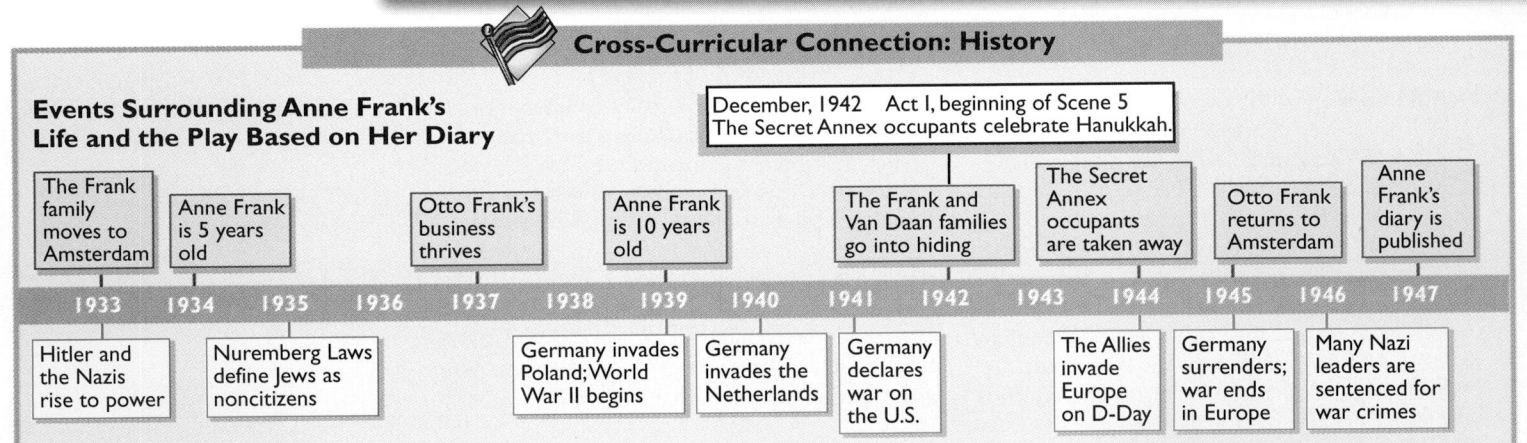

Cross-Curricular Connection: History

Events Surrounding Anne Frank's Life and the Play Based on Her Diary

December, 1942   Act I, beginning of Scene 5
The Secret Annex occupants celebrate Hanukkah.

The Frank family moves to Amsterdam	Anne Frank is 5 years old		Otto Frank's business thrives		Anne Frank is 10 years old		The Frank and Van Daan families go into hiding		The Secret Annex occupants are taken away	Otto Frank returns to Amsterdam	Anne Frank's diary is published

1933	1934	1935	1936	1937	1938	1939	1940	1941	1942	1943	1944	1945	1946	1947

Hitler and the Nazis rise to power	Nuremberg Laws define Jews as noncitizens			Germany invades Poland; World War II begins	Germany invades the Netherlands	Germany declares war on the U.S.		The Allies invade Europe on D-Day	Germany surrenders; war ends in Europe	Many Nazi leaders are sentenced for war crimes

738

MRS. VAN DAAN. Presents!

DUSSEL. Look!

MR. VAN DAAN. What's she got on her head?

PETER. A lamp shade!

ANNE. [*She picks out one at random.*] This is for Margot. [*She hands it to* MARGOT, *pulling her to her feet.*] Read it out loud.

MARGOT. [*Reading*]
"You have never lost your temper.
You never will, I fear,
You are so good.
But if you should,
Put all your cross words here."

[*She tears open the package.*] A new crossword puzzle book! Where did you get it?

ANNE. It isn't new. It's one that you've done. But I rubbed it all out, and if you wait a little and forget, you can do it all over again.

MARGOT. [*Sitting*] It's wonderful, Anne. Thank you. You'd never know it wasn't new.

④ [*From outside we hear the sound of a streetcar passing.*]

⑤ **ANNE.** [*With another gift*] Mrs. Van Daan.

⑥ **MRS. VAN DAAN.** [*Taking it*] This is awful . . . I haven't anything for anyone . . . I never thought . . .

MR. FRANK. This is all Anne's idea.

MRS. VAN DAAN. [*Holding up a bottle*] What is it?

ANNE. It's hair shampoo. I took all the odds and ends of soap and mixed them with the last of my toilet water.

MRS. VAN DAAN. Oh, Anneke!

ANNE. I wanted to write a poem for all of them, but I didn't have time. [*Offering a large box to* MR. VAN DAAN] Yours, Mr. Van Daan, is *really* something . . . something you want more than anything. [*As she waits for him to open it*] Look! Cigarettes!

MR. VAN DAAN. Cigarettes!

ANNE. Two of them! Pim found some old pipe tobacco in the pocket lining of his coat . . . and we made them . . . or rather, Pim did.

MRS. VAN DAAN. Let me see . . . Well, look at that! Light it, Putti! Light it.

[MR. VAN DAAN *hesitates.*]

ANNE. It's tobacco, really it is! There's a little fluff in it, but not much.

[*Everyone watches intently as* MR. VAN DAAN *cautiously lights it. The cigarette flares up. Everyone laughs.*]

PETER. It works!

MRS. VAN DAAN. Look at him.

MR. VAN DAAN. [*Spluttering*] Thank you, Anne. Thank you.

[ANNE *rushes back to her satchel for another present.*]

ANNE. [*Handing her mother a piece of paper*] For Mother, Hanukkah greeting.

[*She pulls her mother to her feet.*]

MRS. FRANK. [*She reads*] "Here's an I.O.U. that I promise to pay. Ten hours of doing whatever you say. Signed, Anne Frank." [MRS. FRANK, *touched, takes* ANNE *in her arms, holding her close.*]

DUSSEL. [*To* ANNE] Ten hours of doing what you're told? *Anything* you're told?

ANNE. That's right.

⑦ **DUSSEL.** You wouldn't want to sell that, Mrs. Frank?

MRS. FRANK. Never! This is the most precious gift I've ever had!

[*She sits, showing her present to the others.* ANNE *hurries back to the satchel and pulls out a scarf, the scarf that* MR. FRANK *found in the first scene.*]

ANNE. [*Offering it to her father*] For Pim.

MR. FRANK. Anneke . . . I wasn't supposed to have a present! [*He takes it, unfolding it and showing it to the others.*]

⑧ **ANNE.** It's a muffler . . . to put round your neck . . . like an ascot, you know. I made it myself out of odds and ends . . . I knitted it in the dark each night, after I'd gone to bed. I'm afraid it looks better in the dark!

MR. FRANK. [*Putting it on*] It's fine. It fits me perfectly. Thank you, Annele.

[ANNE *hands* PETER *a ball of paper with a string attached to it.*]

The Diary of Anne Frank, Act I ◆ 739

◆ **Literary Focus**

⑤ Staging Why do you think the playwrights included the sound of a streetcar passing at this moment in the play? *Students may say that while the Franks, Van Daans, and Mr. Dussel are in a sense "frozen" in time in their hiding place, the sound of the streetcar is a reminder that another kind of life is passing in the world outside.*

◆ **Critical Thinking**

⑥ Compare and Contrast Have students compare the reaction of Margot to receiving a gift from Anne to that of Mrs. Van Daan. *Margot is touched and appreciative. She calls Anne's gesture "wonderful." Mrs. Van Daan responds with guilt for not having presents for the others. As she receives her gift from Anne, she refers to the moment as "awful."*

Comprehension Check ☑

⑦ What does Dussel mean when he asks Mrs. Frank if she would be willing to sell Anne's IOU? *Dussel would probably like to own the IOU in order to have Anne under his control for ten hours, during which time he would probably command her to be still and quiet.*

◆ **Critical Thinking**

⑧ Connect/Speculate Have students review the first scene of the play, in which Mr. Frank finds the scarf and puts it around his neck. Ask students to speculate about what may have happened in the hiding place for the scarf to be left behind and discovered three years later. *Students may speculate that the families were taken away from the hiding place suddenly, leaving behind items such as the scarf. This probably means that they were discovered by the Green Police and deported.*

Cultural Connection

Gift-giving Anne uses a great deal of creativity and imagination to plan and make inexpensive gifts to give the other occupants of the Secret Annex to celebrate Hanukkah.

Ask students to brainstorm a list of occasions on which gifts are often given or received:
• birthdays
• new baby
• marriage
• anniversary celebrations
• holidays such as Hanukkah, Christmas, Kwanzaa, Valentine's Day

Have students suggest reasons why these occasions have become associated with gift-giving. As Anne lovingly planned each gift for her family and friends, she thought of things they enjoyed or needed. Most of her gifts were handmade. Challenge students to write a list of alternative, yet creative, gifts they might give to family or friends on the next gift-giving occasion, such as the IOU Anne's mother was so pleased to receive. Interested students may wish to research more about the history and origins of gift-giving, or how commercialism has become a part of major holidays.

739

1 Infer Why is Peter afraid that something in the gift will jump out and hit him? *He is used to being teased by Anne and suspects that her gift may be a trick in disguise.*

◆ **Literary Focus**

2 Staging Why do the stage directions call for the sound of a dog persistently barking? *Students may say that the sound of the barking dog, following the references to Mouschi the cat, is a symbol of the Nazi pursuit of the Jews, as a dog would chase a cat. They may also say that the sound of the dog barking in the midst of a celebration foreshadows danger for the group, because dogs often bark to signal danger.*

◆ **Critical Thinking**

3 Connect In what way do Anne's Hanukkah gifts illustrate the saying "It's the thought that counts"? *None of the gifts are particularly valuable in and of themselves, but each one reflects care and thought on Anne's part.*

◆ **LITERATURE AND YOUR LIFE**

4 Ask students whether they think that it is appropriate to sing a song of rejoicing, considering the circumstances. *Some students may say that singing such a song can lift everyone's spirits. Others may say that the song will sadden members of the group, perhaps reminding them of how little they have to rejoice about.*

ANNE. That's for Mouschi.

PETER. [*Rising to bow*] On behalf of Mouschi, I thank you.

ANNE. [*Hesitant, handing him a gift*] And . . . this is yours . . . from Mrs. Quack Quack. [*As he holds it gingerly in his hands*] Well . . . open it . . . Aren't you going to open it?

1 PETER. I'm scared to. I know something's going to jump out and hit me.

ANNE. No. It's nothing like that, really.

MRS. VAN DAAN. [*As he is opening it*] What is it, Peter? Go on. Show it.

ANNE. [*Excitedly*] It's a safety razor!

DUSSEL. A what?

ANNE. A razor!

MRS. VAN DAAN. [*Looking at it*] You didn't make that out of odds and ends.

ANNE. [*To* PETER] Miep got it for me. It's not new. It's second-hand. But you really do need a razor now.

DUSSEL. For what?

ANNE. Look on his upper lip . . . you can see the beginning of a mustache.

DUSSEL. He wants to get rid of that? Put a little milk on it and let the cat lick it off.

PETER. [*Starting for his room*] Think you're funny, don't you.

DUSSEL. Look! He can't wait! He's going in to try it!

PETER. I'm going to give Mouschi his present!

[*He goes into his room, slamming the door behind him.*]

MR. VAN DAAN. [*Disgustedly*] Mouschi, Mouschi, Mouschi.

2 [*In the distance we hear a dog persistently barking.* ANNE *brings a gift to* DUSSEL.]

ANNE. And last but never least, my roommate, Mr. Dussel.

DUSSEL. For me? You have something for me?

[*He opens the small box she gives him.*]

ANNE. I made them myself.

DUSSEL. [*Puzzled*] Capsules! Two capsules!

ANNE. They're ear-plugs!

DUSSEL. Ear-plugs?

ANNE. To put in your ears so you won't hear me when I thrash around at night. I saw them advertised in a magazine. They're not real ones . . . I made them out of cotton and candle wax. Try them . . . See if they don't work . . . see if you can hear me talk . . .

DUSSEL. [*Putting them in his ears*] Wait now until I get them in . . . so.

ANNE. Are you ready?

DUSSEL. Huh?

ANNE. Are you ready?

DUSSEL. Oh! They've gone inside! I can't get them out! [*They laugh as* MR. DUSSEL *jumps about, trying to shake the plugs out of his ears. Finally he gets them out. Putting them away*] Thank you, Anne! Thank you!

[*Together*]
> MR. VAN DAAN. A real Hanukkah!
> MRS. VAN DAAN. Wasn't it cute of her?
> MRS. FRANK. I don't know when she did it.
> MARGOT. I love my present.

3

ANNE. [*Sitting at the table*] And now let's have the song, Father . . . please . . . [*To* DUSSEL] Have you heard the Hanukkah song, Mr. Dussel? The song is the whole thing! [*She sings.*] "Oh, Hanukkah! Oh, Hanukkah! The sweet celebration . . ."

MR. FRANK. [*Quieting her*] I'm afraid, Anne, we shouldn't sing that song tonight. [*To* DUSSEL] It's a song of jubilation, of rejoicing. One is apt to become too enthusiastic.

4

ANNE. Oh, please, please. Let's sing the song. I promise not to shout!

MR. FRANK. Very well. But quietly now . . . I'll keep an eye on you and when . . .

[*As* ANNE *starts to sing, she is interrupted by*

◆ **Build Vocabulary**

ostentatiously (äs´ tən tā´ shəs lē) *adv.*: In a showy way

Cross-Curricular Connection: History

World War II Today, historians often see World War II as an effort to revise the 1919 Treaty of Versailles, which had divided Europe into two camps—those who were satisfied with its terms and those who were not. Germany, Italy, Japan, and the Soviet Union all felt betrayed or excluded by the settlement and wanted to change it. World War I had ended in November, 1918, and the Paris Peace Conference and the League of Nations were attempts to establish world peace. Political and economic difficulties and a lack

of strong European leaders, however, encouraged people to turn to dictators.

Since 1939, when World War II began, people have debated why the western democracies did not respond forcefully to the Nazi Threat and whether they could have stopped Hitler had they done so. Dreading war, the democracies hoped that diplomacy and compromise would right old wrongs and prevent further aggression. They were distracted by political and economic problems and misread Hitler's intentions.

Many historians today think that Hitler could have been stopped in 1936, before Germany was fully rearmed. If Britain and France had taken military action then, they argue, Hitler would have had to retreat. But the French and British were unwilling to risk war. The experience of World War I and awareness of the destructive power of modern technology made the idea of renewed fighting unbearable. Unfortunately, when war came, it proved to be even more horrendous than anyone had imagined.

DUSSEL, *who is snorting and wheezing.*]

DUSSEL. [*Pointing to* PETER] You . . . You!

[PETER *is coming from his bedroom, ostentatiously holding a bulge in his coat as if he were holding his cat, and dangling* ANNE's *present before it.*]

How many times . . . I told you . . . Out! Out!

MR. VAN DAAN. [*Going to* PETER] What's the matter with you? Haven't you any sense? Get that cat out of here.

PETER. [*Innocently*] Cat?

MR. VAN DAAN. You heard me. Get it out of here!

PETER. I have no cat. [*Delighted with his joke, he opens his coat and pulls out a bath towel. The group at the table laugh, enjoying the joke.*]

❺ **DUSSEL.** [*Still wheezing*] It doesn't need to be the cat . . . his clothes are enough . . . when he comes out of that room . . .

MR. VAN DAAN. Don't worry. You won't be bothered any more. We're getting rid of it.

DUSSEL. At last you listen to me. [*He goes off into his bedroom.*]

MR. VAN DAAN. [*Calling after him*] I'm not doing it for you. That's all in your mind . . . all of it! [*He starts back to his place at the table.*] I'm doing it because I'm sick of seeing that cat eat all our food.

PETER. That's not true! I only give him bones . . . scraps . . .

MR. VAN DAAN. Don't tell me! He gets fatter every day! Damn cat looks better than any of us. Out he goes tonight!

PETER. No! No!

ANNE. Mr. Van Daan, you can't do that! That's Peter's cat. Peter loves that cat.

MRS. FRANK. [*Quietly*] Anne.

PETER. [*To* MR. VAN DAAN] If he goes, I go.

MR. VAN DAAN. Go! Go!

MRS. VAN DAAN. You're not going and the cat's not going! Now please . . . this is Hanukkah . . . Hanukkah . . . this is the

time to celebrate . . . What's the matter with all of you? Come on, Anne. Let's have the song.

ANNE. [*Singing*]

"Oh, Hanukkah! Oh, Hanukkah! The sweet celebration."

MR. FRANK. [*Rising*] I think we should first blow out the candle . . . then we'll have something for tomorrow night.

MARGOT. But, Father, you're supposed to let it burn itself out.

MR. FRANK. I'm sure that God understands shortages. [*Before blowing it out*] "Praised be Thou, oh Lord our God, who hast sustained us and permitted us to celebrate this joyous festival."

[*He is about to blow out the candle when suddenly there is a crash of something falling below. They all freeze in horror, motionless. For a few seconds there is complete silence.* MR. FRANK *slips off his shoes. The others noiselessly follow his example.* MR. FRANK *turns out a light near him. He motions to* PETER *to turn off the center lamp.* PETER *tries to reach it, realizes he cannot and gets up on a chair. Just as he is touching the lamp he loses his balance. The chair goes out from under him. He falls. The iron lamp shade crashes to the floor. There is a sound of feet below, running down the stairs.*] ❻

MR. VAN DAAN. [*Under his breath*] Oh, oh!

[*The only light left comes from the Hanukkah candle.* DUSSEL *comes from his room.* MR. FRANK *creeps over to the stairwell and stands listening. The dog is heard barking excitedly.*]

Do you hear anything?

MR. FRANK. [*In a whisper*] No. I think they've gone.

MRS. VAN DAAN. It's the Green Police. They've found us.

MR. FRANK. If they had, they wouldn't have left. They'd be up here by now.

MRS. VAN DAAN. I know it's the Green Police. They've gone to get help. That's all. They'll be back!

The Diary of Anne Frank, Act I ◆ 741

Comprehension Check ☑

❺ What has Peter demonstrated by pretending to have the cat? *He has shown that Mr. Dussel is highly suggestible. Judging from Dussel's store of medicines and his seemingly delicate nature, he may be a hypochondriac.*

◆ **Critical Thinking**

❻ **Speculate** After students read these stage directions, have a volunteer summarize the sequence of events. Then have students speculate about what is happening below and what Peter's fall might mean. *Students may summarize the events in this way: The group hears the sound of something falling below. They immediately grow quiet. Peter falls as he is trying to turn off the lamp. The lamp shade crashes to the floor. The group then hears the sound of someone below running down the stairs. Students may say that the noise from below indicates that the families have been discovered.*

Customize for
Musical/Rhythmic Learners
Explain that the song Anne wants to sing is "O Hanukkah!" This song is customarily sung on the first night of Hanukkah. The words vary from translation to translation, but it is generally included in most anthologies of traditional Jewish holiday songs. Ask a student who knows the song to sing it for the class, or play a recording of it.

Customize for
Bodily/Kinesthetic Learners
Have a group of students pantomime the action as a volunteer reads aloud the events on p. 741. After the pantomime, have students discuss insights into the play or the characters by observing the pantomime as they listen to the lines and stage directions.

Speaking and Listening Mini-Lesson

Reading

This mini-lesson supports the Speaking and Listening activity in the Idea Bank on p. 745.

Introduce Have students reread pp. 741–744 (the group's reaction to noises downstairs). As a class, list the events of the scene and discuss the significance of the dialogue and actions.

Develop Divide the class into small groups of students to prepare and tape-record a dramatic reading of these suspenseful pages. As students prepare their readings have them think about the following suggestions:

• As they read, they should speak clearly and precisely, using careful diction.
• They should vary the speed and tone of their voice to represent different emotions.

Have students practice their readings several times.

Apply After students rehearse, provide them with an opportunity to tape-record their readings.

Assess Play the recorded readings to the class. Discuss variations among the recordings. Have students evaluate each other's work with the Peer Assessment Dramatic Performance form, p. 116, in **Alternative Assessment.**

❶ Why does Mr. Van Daan not want Margot to get water for Anne? *He fears that if there is anyone below, they will hear the water flowing through the pipes.*

◆ Critical Thinking

❷ Speculate Have students discuss the dangers that Mr. Frank faces if he goes downstairs to investigate what happened. *The Green Police could be hiding downstairs in wait for the families. Also, Mr. Frank risks being seen by someone passing by the building.*

◆ Literary Focus

❸ Staging Explain that the stage directions that accompany the dialogue on pp. 742 and 743 reveal the characters' reactions to the possibility that their hiding place has been discovered. Have students discuss what is revealed about Peter and his father in these stage directions. Have students speculate about whether the relationship between Peter and his father will change as a result. *Peter's father shows that even in the worst moment, he has no sympathy for his son. Peter's intense anger at his father is understandable. Peter shows more self control than his father when he prevents himself from hitting his father with the chair. Peter's father is not likely to change his manner toward his son.*

MRS. VAN DAAN. Or it may have been the Gestapo,[30] looking for papers . . .

MR. FRANK. [*Interrupting*] Or a thief, looking for money.

MRS. VAN DAAN. We've got to do something . . . Quick! Quick! Before they come back.

MR. VAN DAAN. There isn't anything to do. Just wait.

[MR. FRANK *holds up his hand for them to be quiet. He is listening intently. There is complete silence as they all strain to hear any sound from below. Suddenly* ANNE *begins to sway. With a low cry she falls to the floor in a faint.* MRS. FRANK *goes to her quickly, sitting beside her on the floor and taking her in her arms.*]

MRS. FRANK. Get some water, please! Get some water!

❶ [MARGOT *starts for the sink.*]

MR. VAN DAAN. [*Grabbing* MARGOT] No! No! No one's going to run water!

MR. FRANK. If they've found us, they've found us. Get the water. [MARGOT *starts again for the sink.* MR. FRANK, *getting a flashlight*] I'm going down.

[MARGOT *rushes to him, clinging to him.* ANNE *struggles to consciousness.*]

MARGOT. No, Father, no! There may be someone there, waiting . . . It may be a trap!

❷ **MR. FRANK.** This is Saturday. There is no way for us to know what has happened until Miep or Mr. Kraler comes on Monday morning. We cannot live with this uncertainty.

MARGOT. Don't go, Father!

MRS. FRANK. Hush, darling, hush.

[MR. FRANK *slips quietly out, down the steps and out through the door below.*]

Margot! Stay close to me.

[MARGOT *goes to her mother.*]

MR. VAN DAAN. Shush! Shush!

[MRS. FRANK *whispers to* MARGOT *to get the water.* MARGOT *goes for it.*]

---

30. Gestapo (gə stä′ pō) *n.:* The secret police force of the German Nazi state, known for its terrorism and atrocities.

MRS. VAN DAAN. Putti, where's our money? Get our money. I hear you can buy the Green Police off, so much a head. Go upstairs quick! Get the money!

MR. VAN DAAN. Keep still!

MRS. VAN DAAN. [*Kneeling before him, pleading*] Do you want to be dragged off to a concentration camp? Are you going to stand there and wait for them to come up and get you? Do something, I tell you!

MR. VAN DAAN. [*Pushing her aside*] Will you keep still!

[*He goes over to the stairwell to listen.* PETER *goes to his mother, helping her up onto the sofa. There is a second of silence, then* ANNE *can stand it no longer.*]

ANNE. Someone go after Father! Make Father come back!

PETER. [*Starting for the door*] I'll go.

MR. VAN DAAN. Haven't you done enough?

[*He pushes* PETER *roughly away. In his anger against his father* PETER *grabs a chair as if to hit him with it, then puts it down, burying his face in his hands.* MRS. FRANK *begins to pray softly.*] **❸**

ANNE. Please, please, Mr. Van Daan. Get Father.

MR. VAN DAAN. Quiet! Quiet!

[ANNE *is shocked into silence.* MRS. FRANK *pulls her closer, holding her protectively in her arms.*]

MRS. FRANK. [*Softly, praying*] "I lift up mine eyes unto the mountains, from whence cometh my help. My help cometh from the Lord who made heaven and earth. He will not suffer thy foot to be moved . . . He that keepeth thee will not slumber . . ."

[*She stops as she hears someone coming. They all watch the door tensely.* MR. FRANK *comes quietly in.* ANNE *rushes to him, holding him tight.*]

MR. FRANK. It was a thief. That noise must have scared him away.

MRS. VAN DAAN. Thank goodness!

MR. FRANK. He took the cash box. And the radio. He ran away in such a hurry that he didn't stop to shut the street door. It was

---

Cultural Connection

Commemorative Stamps The first commemorative stamp appeared on a British postcard issued in 1890. Commemorative stamps differ from regular decorative postage stamps in that they are issued in smaller quantities and usually remain on sale only for a limited amount of time. In addition, they may be larger than regular stamps. Most commemorative stamps seek to remember a specific person or memorable event in history. Since the mid-20th century, more commemorative stamps have been issued than regular stamps. Commemorative stamps can become the start of a stamp collection because of their decorative pictures of characters, such as movie stars and political figures, or of historical events.

swinging wide open. [*A breath of relief sweeps over them.*] I think it would be good to have some light.

MARGOT. Are you sure it's all right?

MR. FRANK. The danger has passed.

[MARGOT *goes to light the small lamp.*]

❹ Don't be so terrified, Anne. We're safe.

DUSSEL. Who says the danger has passed? Don't you realize we are in greater danger than ever?

MR. FRANK. Mr. Dussel, will you be still!

[MR. FRANK *takes* ANNE *back to the table, making her sit down with him, trying to calm her.*]

❺ **DUSSEL.** [*Pointing to* PETER] Thanks to this clumsy fool, there's someone now who knows we're up here! Someone now knows we're up here, hiding!

MRS. VAN DAAN. [*Going to* DUSSEL] Someone knows we're here, yes. But who is the someone? A thief! A thief! You think a thief is going to go to the Green Police and say . . . I was robbing a place the other night and I heard a noise up over my head? You think a thief is going to do that?

❻ **DUSSEL.** Yes. I think he will.

MRS. VAN DAAN. [*Hysterically*] You're crazy!

[*She stumbles back to her seat at the table.* PETER *follows protectively, pushing* DUSSEL *aside.*]

DUSSEL. I think some day he'll be caught and then he'll make a bargain with the Green Police . . . if they'll let him off, he'll tell them where some Jews are hiding!

[*He goes off into the bedroom. There is a second of appalled silence.*]

MR. VAN DAAN. He's right.

ANNE. Father, let's get out of here! We can't stay here now . . . Let's go . . .

MR. VAN DAAN. Go! Where?

MRS. FRANK. [*Sinking into her chair at the table*] Yes. Where?

MR. FRANK. [*Rising, to them all*] Have we lost all faith? All courage? A moment ago we thought that they'd come for us. We were

▲ **Critical Viewing** Why might the designers of this stamp have chosen such a happy photograph of Anne? [**Speculate**] ❼

sure it was the end. But it wasn't the end. We're alive, safe.

[MR. VAN DAAN *goes to the table and sits.* MR. FRANK *prays.*]

"We thank Thee, oh Lord our God, that in Thy infinite mercy Thou hast again seen fit to spare us." [*He blows out the candle, then turns to* ANNE.] Come on, Anne. The song! Let's have the song!

[*He starts to sing.* ANNE *finally starts falteringly to sing, as* MR. FRANK *urges her on. Her voice is hardly audible at first.*]

ANNE. [*Singing*] "Oh, Hanukkah! Oh, Hanukkah! The sweet . . . celebration . . ."

[*As she goes on singing, the others gradually join in, their voices still shaking with fear.* MRS. VAN DAAN *sobs as she sings.*]

GROUP. "Around the feast . . . we . . . gather
In complete . . . jubilation . . .
Happiest of sea . . . sons
Now is here.
Many are the reasons for good cheer."

[DUSSEL *comes from the bedroom. He comes over to the table, standing beside* MARGOT, *listening to them as they sing.*]

"Together/We'll weather/Whatever tomorrow may bring."

The Diary of Anne Frank, Act I ◆ 743

◆ **Critical Thinking**

❹ **Analyze** Why is it important for everyone in the group to calm down and gain their composure? *Everyone must calm down in order to think clearly about what has just happened and what to do next.*

◆ **LITERATURE AND YOUR LIFE**

❺ Have students put themselves in Peter's place. Ask them how they might feel at hearing Mr. Dussel's accusation. *Students may say they would feel a mixture of guilt for causing the noise, anger for being blamed so mercilessly by Mr. Dussel, and anguish over the whole episode.*

◆ **Critical Thinking**

❻ **Predict** Have students predict whether they think the thief will reveal the families' hiding place in the Secret Annex. *Students may realize that he probably will not volunteer the information to the police, but if he is caught he may use the information to bargain with.*

▶ **Critical Viewing** ◀

❼ **Speculate** *Students may say that the designers wanted people to remember Anne for her joyful spirit, lively intelligence, and ability to look for the good in a situation, no matter how bad or how hopeless it was.*

Customize for
Interpersonal Learners
Have students work in small groups to prepare charts or other types of graphic organizers on which to record the reactions of each character to the noise below the hiding place.

 Viewing and Representing Mini-Lesson

Commemorative Stamps
In this mini-lesson students will extend their understanding of commemorative stamps and how they are used to honor individuals and events.

Introduce Students can study the illustrations on pp. 743 and 767 of stamps from the United States and Germany that honor Anne Frank. Invite students to compare and contrast the two stamps. You also might have a stamp collector or student hobbyist show a collection of stamps.

Develop Divide the class into small groups to work together to plan and formulate a commem-

orative stamp in honor of a person of their choice. Have students select a person they know or have read about that they believe would be worthy of such a great honor.

Apply Provide art materials, such as poster board, markers, pencils, and construction paper for students to use to illustrate the commemorative stamp they have planned.

Assess Evaluate students' work based on how well they worked as a group, and whether they planned the concept of their stamp and carried out their representation effectively and creatively.

LITERATURE AND YOUR LIFE

1 Ask students to describe how they would respond as audience members viewing the end of Act I. *Students may say they would feel a mixture of fear for the families' safety and admiration for their courage.*

Beyond Literature

Before students begin their research, encourage those who have seen or are familiar with Broadway plays or musicals to describe the productions.

Reinforce and Extend

Answers
LITERATURE AND YOUR LIFE

Reader's Response Possible response: Having to stay quiet for ten hours during the day would be the hardest rule to follow.

Thematic Focus Miep is a hero because she risks her own life.

☑ Check Your Comprehension

1. At first, Anne is excited by the challenges of her new surroundings.
2. Anne understands when her father explains that she can never go beyond the door to the office.
3. Anne, Margot, and Peter continue their studies and the group engages in normal daily activities. They can't go outside, and must maintain a strict regimen to protect the secrecy of their hiding place.
4. She says that she is going to Paris to study music and art.
5. The celebration is a reminder of their faith.

◆ Critical Thinking

1. (a) Anne is lively and outgoing, while Margot is quiet and even-tempered. (b) Anne's independent nature annoys her mother, while Margot's gentle nature pleases her.
2. She is terrified of being taken away by the Green Police.
3. (a) The gifts show that Anne is generous and resourceful. (b) Anne's family is touched by her thoughtfulness.
4. There is a feeling of foreboding because a thief hears Peter fall, and probably knows that someone is hiding in the building.
5. Anne's creative gifts and insightful diary entries prove that her father's assertion is true.

744

[*As they sing on with growing courage, the lights start to dim.*]

"So hear us rejoicing/And merrily voicing/The Hanukkah song that we sing./Hoy!"

[*The lights are out. The curtain starts slowly to fall.*]

1 "Hear us rejoicing/And merrily voicing/The Hanukkah song that we sing."

[*They are still singing, as the curtain falls.*]

Beyond Literature

Social Studies Connection

Broadway Theaters Goodrich and Hackett's award-winning play first appeared on the Broadway stage in 1955. The Broadway theater district consists of the thirty-five or so theaters located in a small section of New York City between Sixth and Eighth avenues. Broadway gained its status as an important theater district in the mid-nineteenth century, attracting various staging companies through its central location and fashionable reputation. The term "Broadway" also refers to the size, scale, and type of production. A Broadway show is a large-scaled project with a tremendous budget whose purpose is to showcase commercial entertainment. An Off-Broadway show is usually produced on a smaller budget, in a smaller theater, and the content is generally more experimental.

Cross-Curricular Activity
In the 1927–1928 season, there were 280 new productions on Broadway—a record number. There are significantly fewer productions in these times. Do some research to find out the current number of Broadway productions and how many years each has been running.

744 ◆ Drama

Guide for Responding

◆ LITERATURE AND YOUR LIFE

Reader's Response The families live by strict rules in order to prevent discovery. Which of these rules would be hardest for you to follow? Why?

Thematic Focus Would you describe Miep as a hero? Explain.

Journal Writing In your journal, write down the activities that you could, or could not, continue if you had to live silently with eight other people in a three-room attic.

☑ Check Your Comprehension

1. How does going into hiding affect Anne at first?
2. When does Anne realize what going into hiding really means?
3. In what ways do the families try to live their lives normally? Which events remind them that their lives are not normal?
4. What are Anne's hopes for her future?
5. What special meaning does Hanukkah have for the families?

◆ Critical Thinking

INTERPRET
1. (a) How are Margot and Anne different? (b) How does the difference between the two sisters account for their relationship with Mrs. Frank? **[Compare and Contrast]**
2. What do Anne's dreams at night reveal? **[Analyze Cause and Effect]**
3. (a) What do Anne's Hanukkah presents reveal about her? (b) How do you think the presents affect her family? **[Deduce]**
4. Describe the feeling at the end of Act I. What event causes this feeling? **[Interpret]**

APPLY
5. Anne's father tells her, "There are no walls, there are no bolts, no locks that anyone can put on your mind." How does Anne prove that this is true? **[Generalize]**

🎵 Humanities: Drama

Broadway Theater Experience It is possible to see live theater every day of the week in New York City. Broadway shows perform as often as 8 times a week and run for as long as tickets are sold. The anticipation and excitement in a theater just before a show begins is universal. When the house lights dim and the curtain rises on a lighted stage, the thrill of a live performance is felt in community theaters as well as Broadway theaters.

The experience of seeing live theater is interactive. An actor on stage receives immediate feedback from the audience and can react to it, while a movie actor may never hear the roar of laughter or see the tears. Audience members respond to what they see by laughing, clapping, and even coughing and fidgeting. Seeing a movie 3 times enables viewers to pick up new details, but they see exactly the same performance each time. Seeing a play 3 times gives viewers different experiences—performances are similar, but not exactly the same. Each audience brings new perspectives and life experiences to a performance. Live theater, whether it is performed and watched in a local community or on Broadway, is a unique experience.

Guide for Responding (continued)

◆ Reading Strategy

BE AWARE OF HISTORICAL CONTEXT

When you know the **historical context** of a story, you can more fully understand why characters act and think as they do.

1. List three details from Act I that place *The Diary of Anne Frank* into its historical context.
2. What outside force determines which characters can come and go from the attic?
3. Could the events in this play have taken place at a different time in history? Why or why not?

◆ Build Vocabulary

USING THE PREFIXES *un-* AND *in-*

The prefixes *un-* and *in-* create opposite meanings of the words to which they are added. On your paper, complete the second sentence by adding *un-* or *in-* to the word in italics in the first sentence.

1. Before the war, the Frank family felt *secure*. After the war began, they felt _____?_____.
2. Anne's lack of freedom was *bearable* when she forgot about the past. It was _____?_____ if she remembered all the fun she used to have.

SPELLING STRATEGY

Most words with *ie* or *ei* combinations follow the rule, "Put *i* before *e* except after *c* or when sounded like *a* as in *neighbor* and *weigh*." A few words that do not follow this rule include *either, leisure, seize, height, weird,* and *their*. On your paper, alphabetize the *ei* words that do not follow the rule.

USING THE WORD BANK

On your paper, replace each word or phrase in italics with the Word Bank word closest in meaning.

1. He was a *person who believed that there was nothing one could do to change one's destiny.*
2. Her temper was so *changeable* people never knew what she would do next.
3. She dressed *in a showy manner.*
4. He was *not shy* about telling his secrets.
5. Her handwriting was *extremely careful.*
6. The heat in the room became *unbearable.*
7. The yellow star made her *very visible.*
8. Her busy schedule allowed for no *rest* time.

◆ Literary Focus

STAGING

Throughout *The Diary of Anne Frank,* **staging**— the scenery, lighting, sounds, costumes, and stage directions—helps bring the drama vividly to life.

1. Explain why the scenery is crucial in conveying the Franks' situation.
2. Why is the staging information about costumes and actors' movements helpful for the reader?

◆ Build Grammar Skills

SUBJECT AND VERB AGREEMENT

A **verb** must agree with its **subject** in number (singular or plural). Verbs change form to **agree** with their subjects. Notice that the singular form of the verb ends in *s,* but the plural form does not:

Singular: The *scene remains* the same. . . .
Plural: The *lights dim* slowly to darkness.

Practice On your paper, write the form of the verb in parentheses that agrees with the subject.

1. The curtain (fall, falls) on the scene.
2. There is complete silence as they all (strain, strains) to hear any sound from below.
3. Mrs. Frank (begin, begins) to pray softly.
4. Anne and Peter (remove, removes) their shoes.
5. A narrow flight of stairs (lead, leads) up to the attic.

Idea Bank

Writing

1. **Letter** Imagine that you are Anne or Peter. Write a letter to a friend about what life in hiding is like.
2. **Program Notes** To introduce each of the play's characters, write several sentences that could be included in the audience's program notes.

Speaking and Listening

3. **Reading [Group Activity]** With a small group, tape-record a dramatic reading of the last half of Act I, Scene 5, to play for the class.

The Diary of Anne Frank, Act I ◆ 745

 Beyond the Selection

FURTHER READING
Other Works About Anne Frank
Anne Frank: The Diary of a Young Girl, Anne Frank
Anne Frank: Beyond the Diary: A Photographic Remembrance, Ruud Van Der Pol
Anne Frank in the World: Essays and Reflections, Carol Rittner (ed.)
Memories of Anne Frank, Alison Leslie Gold
Anne Frank: A Portrait in Courage, Ernst Schnabel
Anne Frank: The Biography, Melissa Muller
The Last Seven Months of Anne Frank, Willy Lindwer
Anne Frank Remembered, Miep Gies

INTERNET
We suggest the following sites on the Internet (all Web sites are subject to change).
For more about the 1998 Broadway production of *The Diary of Anne Frank:*
http://www.annefrankonbroadway.com
For more information on Anne Frank, go to:
http://www.annefrank.com
For more on the Anne Frank house, visit:
http://www.annefrank.nl
We *strongly recommend* that you preview these sites before you send students to them.

Answers
◆ Reading Strategy

1. Anne's diary begins on July 6, 1942; food is rationed; Anne mentions the sounds of air raids.
2. Discrimination against Jews allows only Miep and Mr. Kraler to come and go, because they are not Jewish.
3. The events could have taken place at times in history when persecuted people's lives were in danger.

◆ Build Vocabulary

Using the Prefixes *un-* and *in-*
1. insecure; 2. unbearable

Spelling Strategy
either; height; leisure; seize; their; weird

Using the Word Bank
1. fatalist	5. meticulous
2. mercurial	6. insufferable
3. ostentatiously	7. conspicuous
4. unabashed	8. leisure

◆ Literary Focus

1. Scenery shows the cramped surroundings and meager furnishings that cause tension in the group.
2. This information helps the characters come alive for the reader.

◆ Build Grammar Skills

Practice
1. falls; 2. strain; 3. begins; 4. remove
5. leads

 Writer's Solution

For more instruction, use p. 81 in the *Writer's Solution Grammar Practice Book.*

 Idea Bank

Following are suggestions for matching Idea Bank topics with students' performance levels and learning modalities:

Customize for
Performance Levels
Less Advanced Students: 1
Average Students: 3
More Advanced Students: 2

Customize for
Learning Modalities
Verbal/Linguistic: 1, 2, 3
Intrapersonal: 1

ASSESSMENT OPTIONS

Formal Assessment, pp. 209–211
Alternative Assessment, p. 47

PORTFOLIO ASSESSMENT
Use **Alternative Assessment** rubrics: Letter: Expression, p. 90; Program Notes: Description, p. 93

745

The original production of *The Diary of Anne Frank* opened at the Cort Theater in New York City on October 5, 1955. After its initial success on Broadway, the play opened simultaneously in seven German cities on October 1, 1956. It opened in Amsterdam the following month. Many Netherlanders who had lost family members and friends in the Holocaust were in the audience. After the curtain went down at the end of the performance, the audience sat in silence for several minutes before rising to leave the theater.

Thematic Connection

❶ Ask students if they think teenage audiences of today might react differently to the play than did teenage audiences of the 1950's. *Teenagers in the 1950's, who might have been directly affected by the events of World War II or lost relatives in the Holocaust, might have related more easily to the drama's historical context. For today's teenagers, the historical events may seem somewhat remote, but the drama's powerful story can still be appreciated.*

◆ Critical Thinking

❷ **Speculate** Remind students that Anne Frank wrote her diary in Dutch. Refer them to the photograph on p. 712. Ask students why they think the diary excerpt on the playbill is written in English. *The excerpt is translated into English to make the diary more accessible to English speakers who may have come to see the play.*

Answers

1. Portman was born in Jerusalem, a city in Israel, and she dedicates her performance to "children who are victims of war."

2. Some students may say they would expect the 1997 production to remain true to the original drama because the original play is powerful. Others may say that Wendy Kesselman may have changed some aspects of the drama based on new information or on a different or more updated interpretation of some of the events described in the diary.

746

CONNECTIONS TO TODAY'S WORLD

The Diary of Anne Frank was first produced on Broadway in 1955. Since then, the play has been produced time and again, touching countless audiences through the years. Below are pages from a Playbill that gives information about a 1998 production.

❶ **Anne Frank . . . on Broadway**

PLAYBILL®

THE MUSIC BOX

❷

THE DIARY OF ANNE FRANK

NATALIE PORTMAN
GEORGE HEARN   LINDA LAVIN
HARRIS YULIN   AUSTIN PENDLETON

THE DIARY OF
AnneFrank

A PLAY BY
FRANCES GOODRICH AND ALBERT HACKETT
NEWLY ADAPTED BY
WENDY KESSELMAN
ALSO STARRING
SOPHIE HAYDEN

...ID GOODWIN   JESSICA WALLING

WHO'S WHO IN

NATALIE PORTMAN (*Anne Frank*). *The Diary of Anne Frank* marks Natalie's Broadway debut. She made her feature film debut in Luc Besson's *The Professional*. Other films include Ted Demme's *Beautiful Girls* and Michael Mann's *Heat*, as well as last year's Woody Allen musical, *Everyone Says I Love You*, and Tim Burton's *Mars Attacks!*. She will next be seen on the big screen in the first prequel to George Lucas' *Star Wars* series. Born in Jerusalem and raised on the East Coast, Natalie is a high school student. She would like to dedicate her performance to children who are victims of war.

GEORGE HEARN (*Otto Frank*) last appeared on Broadway in *Sunset Boulevard*, winning his second Tony Award...

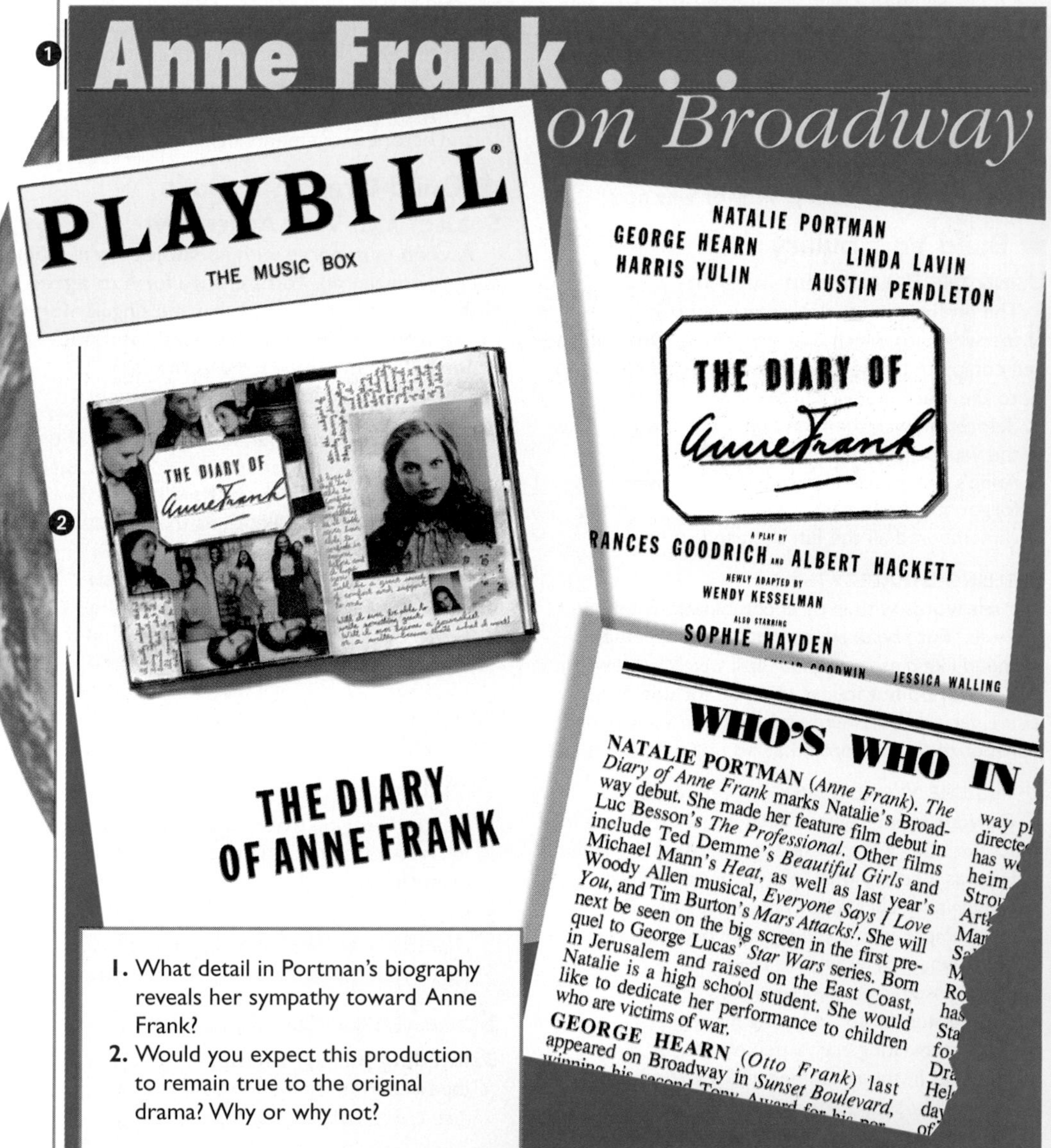

1. What detail in Portman's biography reveals her sympathy toward Anne Frank?
2. Would you expect this production to remain true to the original drama? Why or why not?

746 ◆ Drama

 Humanities: Drama

Anne Frank on Broadway A new adaptation of *The Diary of Anne Frank* opened on Broadway in 1997. This script adaptation was based on the publication of the Definitive Edition of *Anne Frank: The Diary of a Young Girl,* published in 1995. The Definitive Edition restored diary entries which had been omitted in the first edition by Otto Frank due to their sensitive nature involving Anne's negative feelings toward her mother and her feelings towards the events of the Holocaust. Theater producers David Stone and Amy Nederlander-Case analyzed the new edition of the diary in light of the 1955 play and saw an opportunity to create a new production. They hired Wendy Kesselman, a writer who had previously written about World War II and the Holocaust, to adapt the original script for the play that would be seen by audiences in the 1990's. Kesselman consulted with Miep Gies, one of the Dutch office workers who helped hide the Franks. The resulting script is more suited to audiences that are not familiar with the details of the Holocaust. The new script, however, still dramatically presents Anne Frank's powerful message—"lest we forget."

Guide for Reading, Act II

OBJECTIVES

1. To read, comprehend, and interpret a play
2. To relate a play to personal experience
3. To envision characters, setting, and action in a play
4. To understand characterization and theme in drama
5. To build vocabulary in context and use forms of *effect*
6. To recognize correct verb agreement with indefinite pronouns
7. To write a dramatic scene with dialogue by using script format
8. To respond to the play through writing, speaking and listening, and projects

SKILLS INSTRUCTION

Vocabulary:
Using Forms of *effect*

Spelling:
Words That Contain the *choo* Sound Spelled *tu*

Grammar:
Verb Agreement With Indefinite Pronouns

Reading Strategy:
Envision

Literary Focus:
Characterization and Theme in Drama

Speaking and Listening:
Dramatic Monologue (Teacher Edition)

Viewing and Representing:
Decorated Wall (Teacher Edition)

Critical Viewing:
Relate; Assess; Deduce; Connect

PORTFOLIO OPPORTUNITIES

Writing: Timeline; Diary Entry; Essay
Writing Mini-Lesson: Scene With Dialogue
Speaking and Listening: Scene; Dramatic Monologue
Projects: Book Club; Holocaust Research

◆ Review and Anticipate

In Act I, Anne Frank's family, along with the Van Daans and Mr. Dussel, are hiding from the Nazis in the attic of a house in Amsterdam. As Act I closes, they are keeping up their courage and celebrating the Jewish holiday Hanukkah. Just as they begin the ceremony, they are frightened by a thief in the building. At first, they think the thief is a member of the Green Police. How does this scare hint at what might occur in Act II?

◆ Literary Focus

CHARACTERIZATION AND THEME IN DRAMA

Playwrights reveal characters' personalities through **characterization**—what characters say, their actions, and what others say about them. Observing the growth and changes in characters in the course of a drama can lead you to understand the theme of the work.

The **theme** of a literary work is the general message about life that it communicates. As the characters struggle with their situation, they reveal how humans can behave in difficult circumstances.

◆ Reading Strategy

ENVISION

When you see a live performance of a drama, the characters are brought to life by the actors who portray them. It takes a little more work to bring the characters to life when you read a drama. However, you can do so by envisioning, or picturing in your mind, the characters, setting, and action. Use the stage directions to help you do this. Look carefully for details that describe how the characters and setting look, and rely on your imagination to fill in any gaps.

◆ Build Vocabulary

RELATED WORDS: FORMS OF *effect*

The word *effect* means "result." You can use your knowledge of the prefix *in-*, meaning "not," to help you figure out that *ineffectually* means "without results" or "uselessly."

WORD BANK

Which word on the list means "secretly"? Check the Build Vocabulary Box on page 761 to see if you chose correctly.

inarticulate
apprehension
intuition
sarcastic
indignant
stealthily
ineffectually

Guide for Reading ◆ 747

Prentice Hall Literature Program Resources

REINFORCE / RETEACH / EXTEND

Selection Support Pages
Build Vocabulary: Related Words: Forms of *effect*, p. 257
Build Spelling Skills, p. 258
Build Grammar Skills: Verb Agreement With Indefinite Pronouns, p. 259
Reading Strategy: Envision, p. 260
Literary Focus: Characterization and Theme in Drama, p. 261
Strategies for Diverse Student Needs, pp. 93–94

Beyond Literature Humanities Connection: Philosophy, p. 48
Formal Assessment Selection Test, pp. 212–214, Assessment Resources Software
Alternative Assessment, p. 48
Writing and Language Transparencies
KWL Organizer, p. 49; Open Mind Organizer, p. 81
Daily Language Practice, p. 26
Resource Pro CD-ROM *The Diary of Anne Frank*

Listening to Literature Audiocassettes
The Diary of Anne Frank

Interest Grabber Have students think about "helpful hints" that might appear in a booklet for teenagers entitled "How to Survive in Times of Trouble." Ask them to make suggestions to help others cope. Explain that their tips could apply to different situations, including Anne Frank's difficult circumstances. Write their suggestions on the board or a chart and keep them posted as students read Act II.

One-Minute Insight The Franks, Van Daans, and Mr. Dussel have been in hiding for a year and a half. They are buoyed by news of the long-awaited Allied invasion, but tension among the group is high. Food is scarce and fear is ever-present. In the midst of these problems, Anne and Peter have formed a close friendship that sustains them through the difficult days. The most difficult day of all comes when the Nazis discover the group's hiding place. As the families are taken away, we hear Anne's last diary entry. The play then returns to 1945, when Otto Frank revisits the hiding place and reveals the others' fates. The drama concludes with Anne's often quoted words: "In spite of everything, I still believe that people are really good at heart."

◆ Build Grammar Skills

Verb Agreement With Indefinite Pronouns If you wish to introduce the grammar concept for this act of the play before students read, refer to the instruction on p. 770.

Customize for
Less Proficient Readers

Before students read Act II, have them use the KWL Organizer, p. 49 in **Writing and Language Transparencies,** to write facts learned about characters and situations in Act I of the play and questions about what might happen in Act II. Invite students to share their questions. Then as they read, have students record answers to their questions in the third column of the organizer.

Customize for
More Advanced Students

As students read, have them make a visual representation of what two of the characters in the play are thinking or feeling at critical moments in the drama. Students may choose any two characters they wish. Suggest that students use the Open Mind Organizer, p. 81 in **Writing and Language Transparencies,** on which to record their impressions of each character's thoughts and feelings.

Humanities: Photography

The Secret Annex Explain that the bookcase "door" that is ajar in this photo had not been built when the Franks moved into the Secret Annex. A single door led to the Annex rooms. Anne wrote in her diary that no one would guess that there are so many rooms hidden behind the plain gray door. In order to protect the families' hiding place, the movable bookcase that opened like a door was built to conceal the entrance.

Anne wrote in her diary about looking onto a courtyard with a large chestnut tree from an attic window at the rear of the hiding place.

Have students discuss how their point of view might change if they could not come and go freely and could see only a small portion of the outside world. Ask them to speculate about what Anne might and might not see with her limited view—encourage them to think about how her observations might be more detailed because of the restrictions. To help students better understand Anne's restricted view, suggest that they narrow their field of vision to a small window size, using their hands, and describe in detail what they are able to see through the classroom window.

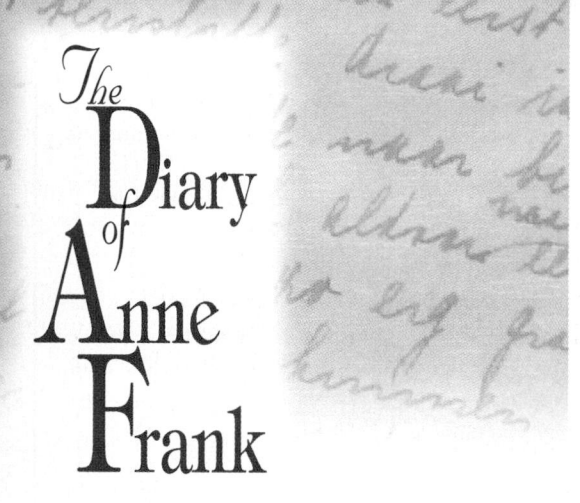

The Diary of Anne Frank

ACT II

Scene 1

[*In the darkness we hear* ANNE'S VOICE, *again reading from the diary.*]

❶ ANNE'S VOICE. Saturday, the first of January, nineteen forty-four. Another new year has begun and we find ourselves still in our hiding place. We have been here now for one year, five months and twenty-five days. It seems that our life is at a standstill.

[*The curtain rises on the scene. It is late afternoon. Everyone is bundled up against the cold. In the main room* MRS. FRANK *is taking down the laundry which is hung across the back.* MR. FRANK *sits in the chair down left, reading.* MARGOT *is lying on the couch with a blanket over her and the many-colored knitted scarf around her throat.* ANNE *is seated at the center table, writing in her diary.* PETER, MR. *and* MRS. VAN DAAN *and* DUSSEL *are all in their own rooms, reading or lying down.*

As the lights dim on, ANNE'S VOICE *continues, without a break.*]

❷ ANNE'S VOICE. We are all a little thinner. The Van Daans' "discussions" are as violent as ever. Mother still does not understand me.

◀ **Critical Viewing** Behind the bookcase is the staircase leading to the attic in which the Franks hid. How does this photograph of the setting contribute to your understanding of the suspense and tension in the play? [Relate]

❸

But then I don't understand her either. There is one great change, however. A change in myself. I read somewhere that girls of my age don't feel quite certain of themselves. . . . ❷

[*We hear the chimes and then a hymn being played on the carillon outside. The buzzer of the door below suddenly sounds. Everyone is startled.* MR. FRANK *tiptoes cautiously to the top of the steps and listens. Again the buzzer sounds, in* MIEP's *V-for-Victory signal.*][1]

MR. FRANK. It's Miep!

[*He goes quickly down the steps to unbolt the door.* MRS. FRANK *calls upstairs to the* VAN DAANS *and then to* PETER.]

MRS. FRANK. Wake up, everyone! Miep is here!

[ANNE *quickly puts her diary away.* MARGOT *sits up, pulling the blanket around her shoulders.* MR. DUSSEL *sits on the edge of his bed, listening, disgruntled.* MIEP *comes up the steps, followed by* MR. KRALER. *They bring flowers, books, newspapers, etc.* ANNE *rushes to* MIEP, *throwing her arms affectionately around her.*]

Miep . . . and Mr. Kraler . . . What a delightful surprise!

MR. KRALER. We came to bring you New Year's greetings.

MRS. FRANK. You shouldn't . . . you should have at least one day to yourselves. [*She goes quickly to the stove and brings down teacups and tea for all of them.*]

ANNE. Don't say that, it's so wonderful to see them! [*Sniffing at* MIEP's *coat*] I can smell the wind and the cold on your clothes.

MIEP. [*Giving her the flowers*] There you are. [*Then to* MARGOT, *feeling her forehead*] How are you, Margot? . . . Feeling any better?

MARGOT. I'm all right.

ANNE. We filled her full of every kind of pill so she won't cough and make a noise.[*She runs into her room to put the flowers in water.* MR. *and* MRS. VAN DAAN *come from upstairs. Outside there is the sound of a band playing.*]

---

1. **V-for-Victory signal:** Three short rings and one long one (the letter *V* in Morse code).

The Diary of Anne Frank, Act II ◆ 749

◆ Critical Thinking

1 Speculate Ask students what might have happened to Mouschi. *Some students may say that perhaps Mouschi escaped when Miep or Mr. Kraler came to visit. Others may say that perhaps Mr. Dussel let the cat out, since he is allergic to cats. Others may speculate that Peter's father let the cat escape because it ate too much food.*

◆ LITERATURE AND YOUR LIFE

2 Discuss with students how excited the families are to have a cake. Explain that for people not in hiding or subject to rationing, having a cake might not be such a remarkable event. Have students speculate about other foods or items that the families and Mr. Dussel might be pleased to have brought to them by Miep. *Students may name foods such as meat or sweets and items such as new clothes, shampoo, or cologne.*

◆ Literary Focus

3 Characterization and Theme in Drama Have students summarize each character based on her or his behavior as the cake is being cut. *Mr. Van Daan is greedy; Dussel is short-tempered; Anne is indignant; Mrs. Frank is pleasant; Mrs. Van Daan is argumentative; and Mr. Frank is conciliatory.*

Comprehension Check ☑

4 Why does Mr. Frank apologize to Miep that sugar is going to everyone's head? *After all Miep has risked to take care of them, Mr. Frank is embarrassed to have the group arguing and quarreling in front of her.*

750

MRS. VAN DAAN. Well, hello, Miep. Mr. Kraler.

MR. KRALER. [*Giving a bouquet of flowers to* MRS. VAN DAAN] With my hope for peace in the New Year.

PETER. [*Anxiously*] Miep, have you seen Mouschi? Have you seen him anywhere around?

❶ MIEP. I'm sorry, Peter. I asked everyone in the neighborhood had they seen a gray cat. But they said no.

[MRS. FRANK *gives* MIEP *a cup of tea.* MR. FRANK *comes up the steps, carrying a small cake on a plate.*]

MR. FRANK. Look what Miep's brought for us!

MRS. FRANK. [*Taking it*] A cake!

MR. VAN DAAN. A cake! [*He pinches* MIEP's *cheeks gaily and hurries up to the cupboard.*] I'll get some plates.

[DUSSEL, *in his room, hastily puts a coat on and starts out to join the others.*]

MRS. FRANK. Thank you, Miepia. You shouldn't have done it. You must have used all of your sugar ration for weeks. [*Giving it to* MRS. VAN DAAN] It's beautiful, isn't it?

❷ MRS. VAN DAAN. It's been ages since I even saw a cake. Not since you brought us one last year. [*Without looking at the cake, to* MIEP] Remember? Don't you remember, you gave us one on New Year's Day? Just this time last year? I'll never forget it because you had "Peace in nineteen forty-three" on it. [*She looks at the cake and reads*] "Peace in nineteen forty-four!"

MIEP. Well, it has to come sometime, you know. [*As* DUSSEL *comes from his room*] Hello, Mr. Dussel.

MR. KRALER. How are you?

MR. VAN DAAN. [*Bringing plates and a knife*] Here's the knife, *liefje.* Now, how many of us are there?

MIEP. None for me, thank you.

MR. FRANK. Oh, please. You must.

MIEP. I couldn't.

MR. VAN DAAN. Good! That leaves one . . . two . . . three . . . seven of us.

DUSSEL. Eight! Eight! It's the same number as it always is!

MR. VAN DAAN. I left Margot out. I take it for granted Margot won't eat any.

ANNE. Why wouldn't she!

MRS. FRANK. I think it won't harm her.

MR. VAN DAAN. All right! All right! I just didn't want her to start coughing again, that's all.

DUSSEL. And please, Mrs. Frank should cut the cake.

[*Together*] {
MR. VAN DAAN. What's the difference?

MRS. VAN DAAN. It's not Mrs. Frank's cake, is it, Miep? It's for all of us.
}

DUSSEL. Mrs. Frank divides things better.

❸ [*Together*] {
MRS. VAN DAAN. [*Going to* DUSSEL] What are you trying to say?

MR. VAN DAAN. Oh, come on! Stop wasting time!
}

MRS. VAN DAAN. [*To* DUSSEL] Don't I always give everybody exactly the same? Don't I?

MR. VAN DAAN. Forget it, Kerli.

MRS. VAN DAAN. No. I want an answer! Don't I?

DUSSEL. Yes. Yes. Everybody gets exactly the same . . . except Mr. Van Daan always gets a little bit more.

[VAN DAAN *advances on* DUSSEL, *the knife still in his hand.*]

MR. VAN DAAN. That's a lie!

[DUSSEL *retreats before the onslaught of the* VAN DAANS.]

❹ MR. FRANK. Please, please! [*Then to* MIEP] You see what a little sugar cake does to us? It goes right to our heads!

◆ Build Vocabulary

inarticulate (in′ är tik′ yə lit) *adj.*: Speechless or unable to express oneself

---

Block Scheduling Strategies

Consider these suggestions to take advantage of extended class time:

• Introduce the Reading Strategy on p. 747. Then have students read Act II or listen to the audio-cassette of this act of the play, noting ways that the playwrights give clues to help them envision the characters and setting of the drama (written or demonstrated by the readers). When students have finished reading, have them work with partners to answer the Reading Strategy questions on p. 770. For additional practice, have students use **Selection Support**, p. 260.

• After students read the selection, have them form groups and answer the Critical Thinking questions on p. 769.

• Have students form small groups to research various topics for the Holocaust Research project in the Idea Bank on p. 771.

• Before students read Act II, have them use **Daily Language Practice**, p. 26.

• Have students use the *Writer's Solution Writing Lab CD-ROM* to complete all or part of the Writing Mini-Lesson.

MR. VAN DAAN. [*Handing* MRS. FRANK *the knife*] Here you are, Mrs. Frank.

MRS. FRANK. Thank you. [*Then to* MIEP *as she goes to the table to cut the cake*] Are you sure you won't have some?

MIEP. [*Drinking her tea*] No, really, I have to go in a minute.

[*The sound of the band fades out in the distance.*]

PETER. [*To* MIEP] Maybe Mouschi went back to our house . . . they say that cats . . . Do you ever get over there . . . ? I mean . . . do you suppose you could . . . ?

MIEP. I'll try, Peter. The first minute I get I'll try. But I'm afraid, with him gone a week . . .

DUSSEL. Make up your mind, already someone has had a nice big dinner from that cat!

[PETER *is furious,* <u>inarticulate</u>. *He starts toward* DUSSEL *as if to hit him.* MR. FRANK *stops him.* MRS. FRANK *speaks quickly to ease the situation.*]

MRS. FRANK. [*To* MIEP] This is delicious, Miep!

MRS. VAN DAAN. [*Eating hers*] Delicious!

MR. VAN DAAN. [*Finishing it in one gulp*] Dirk's in luck to get a girl who can bake like this!

MIEP. [*Putting down her empty teacup*] I have to run. Dirk's taking me to a party tonight.

ANNE. How heavenly! Remember now what everyone is wearing, and what you have to eat and everything, so you can tell us tomorrow.

MIEP. I'll give you a full report! Good-bye, everyone!

MR. VAN DAAN. [*To* MIEP] Just a minute. There's something I'd like you to do for me.

[*He hurries off up the stairs to his room.*]

MRS. VAN DAAN. [*Sharply*] Putti, where are you going? [*She rushes up the stairs after him, calling hysterically.*] What do you want? Putti, what are you going to do?

MIEP. [*To* PETER] What's wrong?

PETER. [*His sympathy is with his mother.*] Father says he's going to sell her fur coat. She's crazy about that old fur coat.

DUSSEL. Is it possible? Is it possible that anyone is so silly as to worry about a fur coat in times like this?

PETER. It's none of your darn business . . . and if you say one more thing . . . I'll, I'll take you and I'll . . . I mean it . . . I'll . . .

[*There is a piercing scream from* MRS. VAN DAAN *above. She grabs at the fur coat as* MR. VAN DAAN *is starting downstairs with it.*]

MRS. VAN DAAN. No! No! No! Don't you dare take that! You hear? It's mine!

[*Downstairs* PETER *turns away, embarrassed, miserable.*]

My father gave me that! You didn't give it to me. You have no right. Let go of it . . . you hear?

[MR. VAN DAAN *pulls the coat from her hands and hurries downstairs.* MRS. VAN DAAN *sinks to the floor, sobbing. As* MR. VAN DAAN *comes into the main room the others look away, embarrassed for him.*]

MR. VAN DAAN. [*To* MR. KRALER] Just a little—discussion over the advisability of selling this coat. As I have often reminded Mrs. Van Daan, it's very selfish of her to keep it when people outside are in such desperate need of clothing . . . [*He gives the coat to* MIEP.] So if you will please to sell it for us? It should fetch a good price. And by the way, will you get me cigarettes. I don't care what kind they are . . . get all you can.

MIEP. It's terribly difficult to get them, Mr. Van Daan. But I'll try. Good-bye.

[*She goes.* MR. FRANK *follows her down the steps to bolt the door after her.* MRS. FRANK *gives* MR. KRALER *a cup of tea.*]

MRS. FRANK. Are you sure you won't have some cake, Mr. Kraler?

MR. KRALER. I'd better not.

MR. VAN DAAN. You're still feeling badly? What does your doctor say?

MR. KRALER. I haven't been to him.

MRS. FRANK. Now, Mr. Kraler! . . .

Cross-Curricular Connection: Health

Nutrition One important aspect of good health is nutrition. Healthy eating habits prevent many illnesses and build strong bones and bodies. Because Anne was still growing, Mrs. Frank often reminded her to drink her milk. Even though the Secret Annex occupants worked hard to prepare nutritious meals from the limited ingredients that Miep was able to supply, they often went hungry. Fresh produce, meat, and many other foods that we take for granted were unavailable, not only to those in hiding but also to the Dutch people in general. Miep had to spend many hours each day searching for food. During the winter of 1944–1945, food was so scarce in the Netherlands that many people dug their tulip bulbs and ate them because they were starving.

Experts recommend that a healthy diet consist of selections from each food group daily: (1) fruits; (2) vegetables; (3) breads, cereals, rice, and pastas; (4) cheese, milk, and yogurt; and (5) meat, poultry, fish, dried beans, and eggs. Challenge students to reread the play, analyzing the foods described and determining which food groups Anne's family were unable to eat from while they were in hiding.

◆ **Critical Thinking**

❶ **Speculate** What gives Margot the sudden sense that something has happened? *It is unusual for Mr. Kraler and Mr. Frank to go downstairs to talk, which arouses Margot's suspicions. Others may say that the tension and fear may have caused Margot to become more sensitive or intuitive about matters that concern the group's safety.*

◆ **LITERATURE AND YOUR LIFE**

❷ Discuss with students whether they agree or disagree with Mr. Frank's comment that what Margot, Anne, and Peter would imagine would be worse than the actual situation. Have volunteers relate the comment to their own experiences of imagining that things were worse than they actually were. *Some students may say that the "children" aren't so young any more; they have had to grow up fast during the terrible circumstances of war. Any news, no matter how bad, will affect the three, so they have a right to hear it.*

◆ **Critical Thinking**

❸ **Speculate** Have students predict what Mr. Kraler wants to discuss. *Students may say that Mr. Kraler wants to warn the group of the increasing threat of discovery, perhaps because of the thief who may have heard Peter fall.*

Clarification

❹ Explain that a war plant is a factory for the manufacture of wartime supplies or materials.

◆ **Literary Focus**

❺ **Characterization and Theme in Drama** Students may say that Mr. Frank is thoughtful, reserved, intelligent, and sincere. Dussel is selfish, miserly, headstrong, and rude.

MR. KRALER. [*Sitting at the table*] Oh, I tried. But you can't get near a doctor these days . . . they're so busy. After weeks I finally managed to get one on the telephone. I told him I'd like an appointment . . . I wasn't feeling very well. You know what he answers . . . over the telephone . . . Stick out your tongue! [*They laugh. He turns to* MR. FRANK *as* MR. FRANK *comes back.*] I have some contracts here . . . I wonder if you'd look over them with me . . .

MR. FRANK. [*Putting out his hand*] Of course.

MR. KRALER. [*He rises*] If we could go downstairs . . . [MR. FRANK *starts ahead;* MR. KRALER *speaks to the others.*] Will you forgive us? I won't keep him but a minute. [*He starts to follow* MR. FRANK *down the steps.*]

MARGOT. [*With sudden foreboding*] What's happened? Something's happened! Hasn't it, Mr. Kraler?

[MR. KRALER *stops and comes back, trying to reassure* MARGOT *with a pretense of casualness.*]

MR. KRALER. No, really. I want your father's advice . . .

MARGOT. Something's gone wrong! I know it!

MR. FRANK. [*Coming back, to* MR. KRALER] If it's something that concerns us here, it's better that we all hear it.

MR. KRALER. [*Turning to him, quietly*] But . . . the children . . . ?

MR. FRANK. What they'd imagine would be worse than any reality.

[*As* MR. KRALER *speaks, they all listen with intense apprehension.* MRS. VAN DAAN *comes down the stairs and sits on the bottom step.*]

MR. KRALER. It's a man in the storeroom . . . I don't know whether or not you remember him . . . Carl, about fifty, heavy-set, near-sighted . . . He came with us just before you left.

MR. FRANK. He was from Utrecht?

◆ **Build Vocabulary**

apprehension (ap′ rə hen′ shən) *n.:* A fearful feeling about the future; dread

---

MR. KRALER. That's the man. A couple of weeks ago, when I was in the storeroom, he closed the door and asked me . . . how's Mr. Frank? What do you hear from Mr. Frank? I told him I only knew there was a rumor that you were in Switzerland. He said he'd heard that rumor too, but he thought I might know something more. I didn't pay any attention to it . . . but then a thing happened yesterday . . . He'd brought some invoices to the office for me to sign. As I was going through them, I looked up. He was standing staring at the bookcase . . . your bookcase. He said he thought he remembered a door there . . . Wasn't there a door there that used to go up to the loft? Then he told me he wanted more money. Twenty guilders[2] more a week.

MR. VAN DAAN. Blackmail!

MR. FRANK. Twenty guilders? Very modest blackmail.

MR. VAN DAAN. That's just the beginning.

DUSSEL. [*Coming to* MR. FRANK] You know what I think? He was the thief who was down there that night. That's how he knows we're here.

MR. FRANK. [*To* MR. KRALER] How was it left? What did you tell him?

MR. KRALER. I said I had to think about it. What shall I do? Pay him the money? . . . Take a chance on firing him . . . or what? I don't know.

DUSSEL. [*Frantic*] Don't fire him! Pay him what he asks . . . keep him here where you can have your eye on him.

MR. FRANK. Is it so much that he's asking? What are they paying nowadays?

MR. KRALER. He could get it in a war plant. But this isn't a war plant. Mind you, I don't know if he really knows . . . or if he doesn't know.

MR. FRANK. Offer him half. Then we'll soon find out if it's blackmail or not.

DUSSEL. And if it is? We've got to pay it, haven't we?

◆ **Literary Focus**
In what ways do the characters of Mr. Frank and Dussel differ?

---

2. **guilders** (gil′ dərz) *n.:* Monetary units of the Netherlands.

Cross-Curricular Connection: History

Challenges to World Peace Challenges to peace followed a pattern throughout the 1930's. Despite the League of Nations, dictators took aggressive action and encountered only verbal protests and pleas for peace. Mussolini and Hitler viewed that desire for peace as weakness and responded with new acts of aggression. With hindsight, the democracies' policies were an insufficient response to the aggressive actions that were taking place. At the time, however, people strongly believed that the policies would work.

At the end of World War II, the Allies set up an international organization to secure the peace, just as they had done after World War I. In April, 1945 delegates from 50 nations met in San Francisco to draft a Charter for the United Nations. The UN would last longer and play a greater role in world affairs than its predecessor, the League of Nations. The goal of creating the Security Council—the U. S., the Soviet Union (now Russia), Britain, France, and China—was to allow power to ensure the peace.

The UN's work would go far beyond peacekeeping, taking on many world problems—from preventing disease and improving education to protecting refugees and aiding nations to develop economically.

Encourage students to research the UN and the League of Nations and compare the two organizations. Suggest that they find out which world leaders were instrumental in the establishment of both organizations and how each organization affected world events and world peace.

Anything he asks we've got to pay!

MR. FRANK. Let's decide that when the time comes.

MR. KRALER. This may be all my imagination. You get to a point, these days, where you suspect everyone and everything. Again and again . . . on some simple look or word, I've found myself . . .

[*The telephone rings in the office below.*]

MRS. VAN DAAN. [*Hurrying to* MR. KRALER] There's the telephone! What does that mean, the telephone ringing on a holiday?

MR. KRALER. That's my wife. I told her I had to go over some papers in my office . . . to call me there when she got out of church. [*He starts out.*] I'll offer him half then. Goodbye . . . we'll hope for the best!

[*The group calls their good-byes halfheartedly.* MR. FRANK *follows* MR. KRALER *to bolt the door below. During the following scene,* MR. FRANK *comes back up and stands listening, disturbed.*]

DUSSEL. [*To* MR. VAN DAAN] You can thank your son for this . . . smashing the light! I tell you, it's just a question of time now.

[*He goes to the window at the back and stands looking out.*]

MARGOT. Sometimes I wish the end would come . . . whatever it is.

MRS. FRANK. [*Shocked*] Margot!

[ANNE *goes to* MARGOT, *sitting beside her on the couch with her arms around her.*]

MARGOT. Then at least we'd know where we were.

MRS. FRANK. You should be ashamed of yourself! Talking that way! Think how lucky we are! Think of the thousands dying in the war, every day. Think of the people in concentration camps.

ANNE. [*Interrupting*] What's the good of that? What's the good of thinking of misery when you're already miserable? That's stupid!

MRS. FRANK. Anne!

[*As* ANNE *goes on raging at her mother,* MRS. FRANK *tries to break in, in an effort to quiet her.*]

ANNE. We're young, Margot and Peter and I! You grownups have had your chance! But look at us . . . If we begin thinking of all the horror in the world, we're lost! We're trying to hold onto some kind of ideals . . . when everything . . . ideals, hopes . . . everything, are being destroyed! It isn't our fault that the world is in such a mess! We weren't around when all this started! So don't try to take it out on us! [*She rushes off to her room, slamming the door after her. She picks up a brush from the chest and hurls it to the floor. Then she sits on the settee, trying to control her anger.*]

MR. VAN DAAN. She talks as if we started the war! Did we start the war?

[*He spots* ANNE's *cake. As he starts to take it,* PETER *anticipates him.*]

PETER. She left her cake.

[*He starts for* ANNE's *room with the cake. There is silence in the main room.* MRS. VAN DAAN *goes up to her room, followed by* VAN DAAN. DUSSEL *stays looking out the window.* MR. FRANK *brings* MRS. FRANK *her cake. She eats it slowly, without relish.* MR. FRANK *takes his cake to* MARGOT *and sits quietly on the sofa beside her.* PETER *stands in the doorway of* ANNE's *darkened room, looking at her, then makes a little movement to let her know he is there.* ANNE *sits up, quickly, trying to hide the signs of her tears.* PETER *holds out the cake to her.*]

You left this.

ANNE. [*Dully*] Thanks.

[PETER *starts to go out, then comes back.*]

PETER. I thought you were fine just now. You know just how to talk to them. You know just how to say it. I'm no good . . . I never can think . . . especially when I'm mad . . . That Dussel . . . when he said that about Mouschi . . . someone eating him . . . all I could think is . . . I wanted to hit him. I wanted to give him such a . . . a . . . that he'd . . . That's what I used to do when there was an argument at school . . . That's the

◆ **Reading Strategy**
How do you envision the scene described in this stage direction?

❽

Comprehension Check ☑

❻ What is Mr. Kraler trying to explain to the group about his suspicions? *He is saying that tensions among people in Amsterdam as a result of the German occupation have intensified and that he is uncertain about whom he can trust. He fears that he may be misinterpreting someone's look or words.*

◆ **Critical Thinking**

❼ Analyze Remind students that up to now in the play, Margot has said little. Have students analyze her comments to determine what she is thinking and feeling and possible reasons why. *Students may say that Margot is showing a sense of despair that she has not revealed up to now, possibly because of the months of tension and fear. They may also speculate that being sick may have weakened Margot's defenses against despair or depression.*

◆ **Reading Strategy**

❽ Envision *Students may say that the specific details in this stage direction appeal to their senses of sight, sound, and even taste. These details allow them to picture each person's actions and gain a sense of the somber mood in the wake of Mr. Kraler's visit.*

◆ **Critical Thinking**

❾ Analyze What does Peter reveal about himself in this passage? *He shows his admiration for Anne and for her ability to express herself in words—a trait he claims he lacks. He also admits that when he is frustrated and angry, he tends to want to use his fists rather than words.*

The Diary of Anne Frank, Act II ◆ 753

Cross-Curricular Connection: History

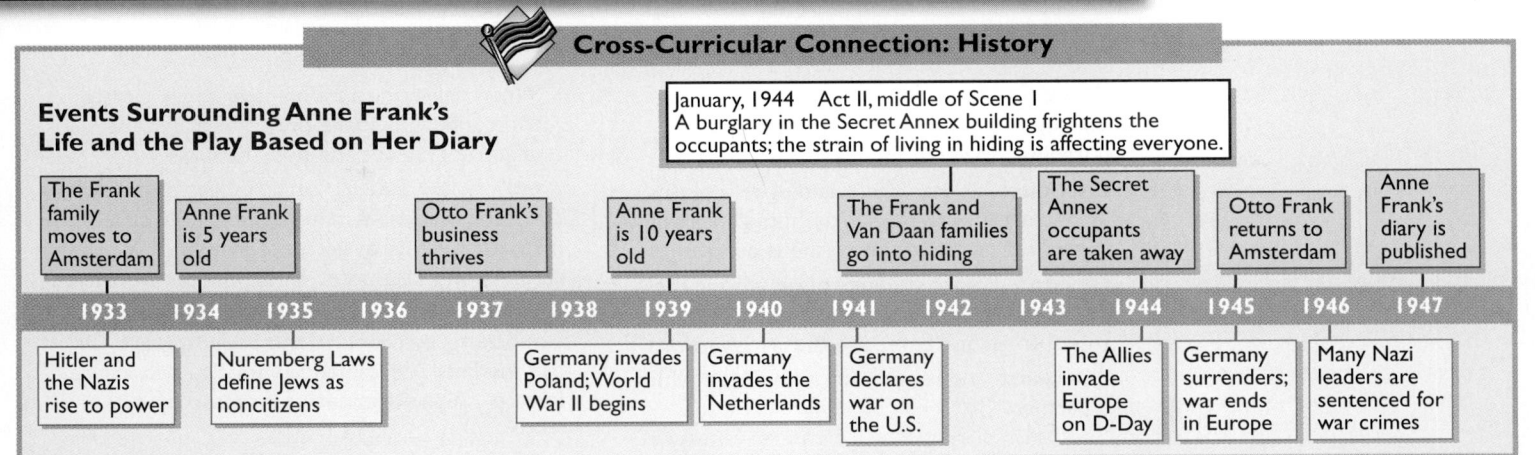

Events Surrounding Anne Frank's Life and the Play Based on Her Diary

January, 1944   Act II, middle of Scene 1
A burglary in the Secret Annex building frightens the occupants; the strain of living in hiding is affecting everyone.

| The Frank family moves to Amsterdam | Anne Frank is 5 years old | | Otto Frank's business thrives | | Anne Frank is 10 years old | | The Frank and Van Daan families go into hiding | | The Secret Annex occupants are taken away | Otto Frank returns to Amsterdam | Anne Frank's diary is published |

| 1933 | 1934 | 1935 | 1936 | 1937 | 1938 | 1939 | 1940 | 1941 | 1942 | 1943 | 1944 | 1945 | 1946 | 1947 |

| Hitler and the Nazis rise to power | Nuremberg Laws define Jews as noncitizens | | | | Germany invades Poland; World War II begins | Germany invades the Netherlands | Germany declares war on the U.S. | | | | The Allies invade Europe on D-Day | Germany surrenders; war ends in Europe | Many Nazi leaders are sentenced for war crimes |

753

Literary Focus

❶ Characterization and Theme in Drama Have students explore this interaction between Anne and Peter and compare it with their earlier interactions. Ask students how Anne and Peter's friendship seems to have changed in their year and a half of living in hiding. *Students may say that this interaction seems more mature and open, with both Anne and Peter confessing to shortcomings in dealing with others. Peter expresses his feelings honestly and directly, and Anne no longer teases Peter.*

◆ LITERATURE AND YOUR LIFE

❷ Of these statements by Anne, which could be made by teenagers today? Have students explain their responses. *All of Anne's statements could be made by today's teenagers. All teens, regardless of their personal situations, struggle to establish their identities and form their own opinions. Even though they are not facing the horrors of a war, today's teenagers face challenges and problems that are unique to their generation. Anne's last statement, about new problems cropping up, is one that most teenagers would also agree and identify with.*

◆ Critical Thinking

❸ Infer Ask students why Anne's father won't discuss Mrs. Frank with Anne. *Mr. Frank probably feels that it would be disrespectful and a violation of confidence to discuss his wife with his daughter. Also, Mr. Frank may feel that Anne is old enough to work through her problems with her mother.*

ANNE. You're making a big mistake about me. I do it all wrong. I say too much. I go too far. I hurt people's feelings . . .

[DUSSEL *leaves the window, going to his room.*]

PETER. I think you're just fine . . . What I want to say . . . if it wasn't for you around here, I don't know. What I mean . . .

❶ [PETER *is interrupted by* DUSSEL'*s turning on the light.* DUSSEL *stands in the doorway, startled to see* PETER. PETER *advances toward him forbiddingly.* DUSSEL *backs out of the room.* PETER *closes the door on him.*]

ANNE. Do you mean it, Peter? Do you really mean it?

PETER. I said it, didn't I?

ANNE. Thank you, Peter!

[*In the main room* MR. *and* MRS. FRANK *collect the dishes and take them to the sink, washing them.* MARGOT *lies down again on the couch.* DUSSEL, *lost, wanders into* PETER'*s room and takes up a book, starting to read.*]

PETER. [*Looking at the photographs on the wall*] You've got quite a collection.

ANNE. Wouldn't you like some in your room? I could give you some. Heaven knows you spend enough time in there . . . doing heaven knows what . . .

PETER. It's easier. A fight starts, or an argument . . . I duck in there.

ANNE. You're lucky, having a room to go to. His lordship is always here . . . I hardly ever get a minute alone. When they start in on me, I can't duck away. I have to stand there and take it.

PETER. You gave some of it back just now.

❷ ANNE. I get so mad. They've formed their opinions . . . about everything . . . but we . . . we're still trying to find out . . . We have problems here that no other people our age have ever had. And just as you think you've solved them, something comes along and bang! You have to start all over again.

PETER. At least you've got someone you can talk to.

ANNE. Not really. Mother . . . I never discuss anything serious with her. She doesn't understand. Father's all right. We can talk about everything . . . everything but one thing. Mother. He simply won't talk about her. I don't think you can be really intimate with anyone if he holds something back, do you?

PETER. I think your father's fine.

ANNE. Oh, he is, Peter! He is! He's the only one who's ever given me the feeling that I have any sense. But anyway, nothing can take the place of school and play and friends of your own age . . . or near your age . . . can it?

PETER. I suppose you miss your friends and all.

ANNE. It isn't just . . . [*She breaks off, staring up at him for a second.*] Isn't it funny, you and I? Here we've been seeing each other every minute for almost a year and a half, and this is the first time we've ever really talked. It helps a lot to

Speaking and Listening Mini-Lesson

Dramatic Monologue

This mini-lesson supports the Speaking and Listening activity in the Idea Bank, p. 771.

Introduce A dramatic monologue is performed by one actor who reveals the thoughts and feelings of the character he or she is portraying.

Develop Before students begin writing their monologues, discuss ways to make a monologue appeal to an audience. Use these suggestions:

• Rehearse and revise your monologue with a partner.

• When delivering a monologue, speak clearly and confidently, make eye contact, and use effective gestures and body language.

Apply Allow time for each student to develop and perform a brief monologue for the class. Instruct students, as audience members, to listen carefully and take notes during the performances.

Assess Evaluate students' preparation, speaking, composure, eye contact, and body language. Or, use the Peer Assessment: Dramatic Performance form, p. 116 in **Alternative Assessment.**

◆ Critical Thinking

❹ Speculate Why do you think it took so long for Anne and Peter to have a serious talk? *Students may say that Peter's shyness prevented him from talking to Anne. Also, because Peter is constantly criticized and embarrassed by his parents, he tends to withdraw into himself, preferring to spend time alone rather than developing a friendship with Anne or Margot.*

▶ Critical Viewing ◀

❺ Relate *Teenagers often decorate their bedroom walls with photographs, pictures, and posters of things they like or enjoy, particularly of celebrities, such as Anne has done.*

Customize for
Verbal/Linguistic Learners
Have pairs of students take turns giving dramatic readings of the dialogue between Anne and Peter on pp. 754 and 755. Encourage students to rehearse their readings at least once before they perform in front of the class. Encourage students to explore variations in voice tone and inflection in lines such as "Father's all right." After each reading, lead a discussion of new insights into the characters of Anne and Peter that students gained from giving the readings or from listening to them being performed.

❹ have someone to talk to, don't you think? It helps you to let off steam.

PETER. [*Going to the door*] Well, any time you want to let off steam, you can come into my room.

ANNE. [*Following him*] I can get up an awful lot

▲ **Critical Viewing** This photograph shows a wall in Anne Frank's room. In what ways does Anne's room resemble a typical teenager's room today? [Relate] **❺**

of steam. You'll have to be careful how you say that.

The Diary of Anne Frank, Act II ◆ 755

Viewing and Representing Mini-Lesson

Decorated Wall

Introduce Anne's collection of movie-star photos and picture postcards were important to her during her time in hiding. Have students create a "celebrity wall" of their own, with magazine pictures pasted or taped onto poster board.

Develop Discuss with students reasons for collecting and displaying pictures of movie stars and sports figures. As students consider pictures for their celebrity walls, have them also consider what their choices reveal about themselves.

Apply Provide students with poster board to represent a wall such as Anne's. Using magazines that feature photographs of movie stars, singers, musicians, sports figures, and other well-known persons, have students select photos and arrange them on their poster board "walls." Students may want to refer to the photo on p. 755.

Assess Have students display their work. Assess students' celebrity walls on how well they reflect thoughtful planning and arrangement. Encourage students to discuss their choices of photos.

◆ Reading Strategy

❶ Envision Have students summarize what they envision in the scene described in the stage directions following Anne and Peter's first serious talk. *Peter leaves Anne's room. He and Anne gaze at each other for a moment before both enter their rooms. Dussel leaves Peter's room and walks toward his and Anne's room. Both Peter and Anne shut their doors, leaving Dussel perplexed and "roomless."*

◆ Critical Thinking

❷ Analyze As students read Anne's diary entry, have them organize her information into categories such as Good News and Bad News. Suggest that students create tables with two or three columns and summarize Anne's information under the appropriate headings. *Under Good News, students might list "The Americans landed in Italy," "The war may end soon," "Spring may be coming." For Bad News, they might list "There is less food," "Mr. Kraler is in the hospital," "Anne feels confused."*

◆ LITERATURE AND YOUR LIFE

❸ Peter and Anne are trying to act as naturally as they can in their unnatural world. As students read this stage direction, encourage them to discuss ways in which Peter and Anne are behaving like most teenagers. *They are grooming themselves and dressing as if they were going to a party. Peter is carefully preparing his clothes, and Anne is trying new ways of wearing her hair, both of which represent common teenage behavior.*

Customize for
English Language Learners
Help students understand the meaning of idiomatic expressions such as "Stop fishing." Explain that when Margot tells Anne to stop fishing, the word *fish* means to try to get something in an indirect way. Margot thinks that Anne is fishing for a compliment. Have students proficient in English offer additional examples of fishing for information or for compliments.

PETER. It's all right with me.

ANNE. Do you mean it?

PETER. I said it, didn't I?

[*He goes out.* ANNE *stands in her doorway looking after him. As* PETER *gets to his door he stands for a minute looking back at her. Then he goes into his room.* DUSSEL *rises as he comes in, and quickly passes him, going out. He starts across for his room.* ANNE *sees him coming, and pulls her door shut.* DUSSEL *turns back toward* PETER's *room.* PETER *pulls his door shut.* DUSSEL *stands there, bewildered, forlorn.*

The scene slowly dims out. The curtain falls on the scene. ANNE'S VOICE *comes over in the darkness . . . faintly at first, and then with growing strength.*]

ANNE'S VOICE. We've had bad news. The people from whom Miep got our ration books have been arrested. So we have had to cut down on our food. Our stomachs are so empty that they rumble and make strange noises, all in different keys. Mr. Van Daan's is deep and low, like a bass fiddle. Mine is high, whistling like a flute. As we all sit around waiting for supper, it's like an orchestra tuning up. It only needs Toscanini[3] to raise his baton and we'd be off in the Ride of the Valkyries.[4] Monday, the sixth of March, nineteen forty-four. Mr. Kraler is in the hospital. It seems he has ulcers. Pim says we are his ulcers. Miep has to run the business and us too. The Americans have landed on the southern tip of Italy. Father looks for a quick finish to the war. Mr. Dussel is waiting every day for the warehouse man to demand more money. Have I been skipping too much from one subject to another? I can't help it. I feel that spring is coming. I feel it in my whole body and soul. I feel utterly confused. I am longing . . . so longing . . . for everything . . . for friends . . . for someone to talk to . . . someone who understands . . . someone young, who feels as I do . . .

---

3. Toscanini (täs′ kə nē′ nē): Arturo Toscanini, a famous Italian American orchestra conductor.
4. Ride of the Valkyries (val′ kir′ ēz): A stirring selection from an opera by Richard Wagner, a German composer.

[*As these last lines are being said, the curtain rises on the scene. The lights dim on.* ANNE'S VOICE *fades out.*]

Scene 2

[*It is evening, after supper. From outside we hear the sound of children playing. The "grownups," with the exception of* MR. VAN DAAN, *are all in the main room.* MRS. FRANK *is doing some mending,* MRS. VAN DAAN *is reading a fashion magazine.* MR. FRANK *is going over business accounts.* DUSSEL, *in his dentist's jacket, is pacing up and down, impatient to get into his bedroom.* MR. VAN DAAN *is upstairs working on a piece of embroidery in an embroidery frame.*

In his room PETER *is sitting before the mirror, smoothing his hair. As the scene goes on, he puts on his tie, brushes his coat and puts it on, preparing himself meticulously for a visit from* ANNE. *On his wall are now hung some of* ANNE's *motion picture stars.*

In her room ANNE *too is getting dressed. She stands before the mirror in her slip, trying various ways of dressing her hair.* MARGOT *is seated on the sofa, hemming a skirt for* ANNE *to wear.*

In the main room DUSSEL *can stand it no longer. He comes over, rapping sharply on the door of his and* ANNE's *bedroom.*]

ANNE. [*Calling to him*] No, no, Mr. Dussel! I am not dressed yet.

[DUSSEL *walks away, furious, sitting down and burying his head in his hands.* ANNE *turns to* MARGOT.]

How is that? How does that look?

MARGOT. [*Glancing at her briefly*] Fine.

ANNE. You didn't even look.

MARGOT. Of course I did. It's fine.

ANNE. Margot, tell me, am I terribly ugly?

MARGOT. Oh, stop fishing.

ANNE. No. No. Tell me.

MARGOT. Of course you're not. You've got nice eyes . . . and a lot of animation, and . . .

ANNE. A little vague, aren't you?

[*Outside,* MRS. FRANK, *feeling sorry for* DUSSEL, *comes over, knocking at the girls' door.*]

◆ Cross-Curricular Connection: History

Rationing All citizens in Germany and occupied countries were given ration books to exchange for food and other items, such as clothing, tobacco, and fuel. The members of the Secret Annex relied on Miep Gies to supply them with food and supplies. She used ration coupons that were secretly provided for the Secret Annex occupants, but eventually their providers were caught. Since ration coupons had to be bought on the black market, they were forced to give up one clothing ration for each food ration. Miep recalls her struggles to find any food and her attempts to go from shop to shop to find food that was not rotting. Rationing existed in the Polish ghettos as well, where Jews were allotted 2 pounds of bread, 9 ounces of sugar, 3½ ounces of jam, and 1½ ounces of fat per month. Meat and cheese were virtually impossible to get, whether in the ghettos or on the outside.

Anne remarked in her diary when their rations were "cut back." For example, on December 22, 1942, she wrote that they had exceeded their ration for electricity and, therefore, had to spend the next two weeks without light.

MRS. FRANK. [*Outside*] May I come in?

MARGOT. Come in, Mother.

MRS. FRANK. [*Shutting the door behind her*] Mr. Dussel's impatient to get in here.

ANNE. Heavens, he takes the room for himself the entire day.

MRS. FRANK. [*Gently*] Anne, dear, you're not going in again tonight to see Peter?

ANNE. [*Dignified*] That is my intention.

MRS. FRANK. But you've already spent a great deal of time in there today.

ANNE. I was in there exactly twice. Once to get the dictionary, and then three-quarters of an hour before supper.

MRS. FRANK. Aren't you afraid you're disturbing him?

❹ **ANNE.** Mother, I have some <u>intuition</u>.

MRS. FRANK. Then may I ask you this much, Anne. Please don't shut the door when you go in.

ANNE. You sound like Mrs. Van Daan! [*She picks up her blouse, putting it on.*]

MRS. FRANK. No. No. I don't mean to suggest anything wrong. I only wish that you wouldn't expose yourself to criticism . . . that you wouldn't give Mrs. Van Daan the opportunity to be unpleasant.

ANNE. Mrs. Van Daan doesn't need an opportunity to be unpleasant!

MRS. FRANK. Everyone's on edge, worried about Mr. Kraler. This is one more thing . . .

ANNE. I'm sorry, Mother. I'm going to Peter's room. I'm not going to let Petronella Van Daan spoil our friendship.

[*MRS. FRANK hesitates for a second, then goes out, closing the door after her. She gets a pack of playing cards and sits at the center table, playing solitaire. In ANNE's room MARGOT hands the finished skirt to ANNE. As ANNE is putting it on, MARGOT takes off her high-heeled shoes*

◆ **Build Vocabulary**

intuition (in′ tōō wish′ ən) *n.*: Ability to know immediately, without reasoning

---

and stuffs paper in the toes so that ANNE *can wear them.*]

MARGOT. [*To* ANNE] Why don't you two talk in the main room? It'd save a lot of trouble. It's hard on Mother, having to listen to those remarks from Mrs. Van Daan and not say a word.

ANNE. Why doesn't she say a word? I think it's ridiculous to take it and take it.

MARGOT. You don't understand Mother at all, do you? She can't talk back. She's not like you. It's just not in her nature to fight back. ❺

ANNE. Anyway . . . the only one I worry about is you. I feel awfully guilty about you. [*She sits on the stool near* MARGOT, *putting on* MARGOT's *high-heeled shoes.*]

MARGOT. What about?

ANNE. I mean, every time I go into Peter's room, I have a feeling I may be hurting you. [MARGOT *shakes her head.*] I know if it were me, I'd be wild. I'd be desperately jealous, if it were me.

MARGOT. Well, I'm not.

ANNE. You don't feel badly? Really? Truly? You're not jealous?

MARGOT. Of course I'm jealous . . . jealous that you've got something to get up in the morning for . . . But jealous of you and Peter? No.

[ANNE *goes back to the mirror.*]

ANNE. Maybe there's nothing to be jealous of. Maybe he doesn't really like me. Maybe I'm just taking the place of his cat . . . [*She picks up a pair of short white gloves, putting them on.*] Wouldn't you like to come in with us? ❻

MARGOT. I have a book.

[*The sound of the children playing outside fades out. In the main room* DUSSEL *can stand it no longer. He jumps up, going to the bedroom door and knocking sharply.*]

DUSSEL. Will you please let me in my room!

ANNE. Just a minute, dear, dear Mr. Dussel. [*She picks up her mother's pink stole and adjusts it elegantly over her shoulders, then*

The Diary of Anne Frank, Act II ◆ 757

◆ **Literary Focus**

❹ **Characterization and Theme in Drama** Anne's mother feels uneasy about Anne and Peter spending so much unchaperoned time together. Have students give examples from this passage that illustrate how Mrs. Frank goes to great lengths to avoid a conflict with Anne over this issue. *Mrs. Frank introduces the subject gently, according to the stage direction, and she uses the phrase "may I ask you this much," instead of stating her wishes more directly.*

◆ **Critical Thinking**

❺ **Compare and Contrast** Does Margot seem more like Anne or more like Mrs. Frank? Explain. *Margot seems more like Mrs. Frank, because she tends to be quiet and avoids confrontation.*

◆ **Critical Thinking**

❻ **Connect** Ask students to describe another passage in the play in which white gloves are mentioned. *In Act I, at the beginning of the play, Otto Frank finds a white glove on the floor of the Secret Annex, which causes him to cry.*

Customize for
Intrapersonal Learners
Explain to students that Margot also kept a diary during her time in hiding, but the diary was lost. Have students imagine a diary entry that Margot might have written on this night. Ask them to write about helping Anne prepare for seeing Peter and about Margot and Anne's discussion about jealousy.

Cross-Curricular Connection: History

Winter of Starvation in the Netherlands
In September 1944, British and Polish airborne troops attempted to stop the German control of the port of Antwerp in Belgium with an airborne bombing in the Battle of Arnhem. Their defeat led to the isolation of the northern part of the Netherlands. As the German armies continued to maintain military pressure on all fronts, they also used up vital supplies of food and fuel. The people of the Netherlands began to starve during the winter of 1944–1945. Many residents of Amsterdam resorted to tearing apart abandoned buildings to use the wood as fuel for cooking. People regularly formed long lines to wait for food rations—meager portions of endives or beans. Survivors of the winter recall trying to make food out of sugar beets and frying tulip bulbs. Eventually, in the late spring of 1945, Canadian air troops flew low enough to drop supplies of food to the people. For ten days, ending with the German surrender on May 8, 1945, Canadian and American Air Force troops dropped over 11,000 tons of food. Unfortunately, 20,000 people had already died of starvation.

gives a last look in the mirror.] Well, here I go . . . to run the gauntlet.[5]

[*She starts out, followed by* MARGOT.]

❶ DUSSEL. [*As she appears—sarcastic*] Thank you so much.

[DUSSEL *goes into his room.* ANNE *goes toward* PETER's *room, passing* MRS. VAN DAAN *and her parents at the center table.*]

MRS. VAN DAAN. My God, look at her!

[ANNE *pays no attention. She knocks at* PETER's *door.*]

❷ I don't know what good it is to have a son. I never see him. He wouldn't care if I killed myself.

[PETER *opens the door and stands aside for* ANNE *to come in.*]

Just a minute, Anne. [*She goes to them at the door.*] I'd like to say a few words to my son. Do you mind?

[PETER *and* ANNE *stand waiting.*]

Peter, I don't want you staying up till all hours tonight. You've got to have your sleep. You're a growing boy. You hear?

MRS. FRANK. Anne won't stay late. She's going to bed promptly at nine. Aren't you, Anne?

ANNE. Yes, Mother . . . [*To* MRS. VAN DAAN] May we go now?

MRS. VAN DAAN. Are you asking me? I didn't know I had anything to say about it.

MRS. FRANK. Listen for the chimes, Anne dear.

[*The two young people go off into* PETER's *room, shutting the door after them.*]

MRS. VAN DAAN. [*To* MRS. FRANK] In my day it was the boys who called on the girls. Not the girls on the boys.

MRS. FRANK. You know how young people like to feel that they have secrets. Peter's room is the only place where they can talk.

MRS. VAN DAAN. Talk! That's not what they called it when I was young.

---

5. **to run the gauntlet** (gônt´ lit): Formerly, to pass between two rows of men who struck at the offender with clubs as he passed; here, a series of troubles or difficulties.

[MRS. VAN DAAN *goes off to the bathroom.* MARGOT *settles down to read her book.* MR. FRANK *puts his papers away and brings a chess game to the center table. He and* MRS. FRANK *start to play. In* PETER's *room,* ANNE *speaks to* PETER, *indignant, humiliated.*]

❸

ANNE. Aren't they awful? Aren't they impossible? Treating us as if we were still in the nursery.

[*She sits on the cot.* PETER *gets a bottle of pop and two glasses.*]

PETER. Don't let it bother you. It doesn't bother me.

ANNE. I suppose you can't really blame them . . . they think back to what *they* were like at our age. They don't realize how much more advanced we are . . . When you think what wonderful discussions we've had! . . . Oh, I forgot. I was going to bring you some more pictures.

PETER. Oh, these are fine, thanks.

ANNE. Don't you want some more? Miep just brought me some new ones.

PETER. Maybe later. [*He gives her a glass of pop and, taking some for himself, sits down facing her.*]

ANNE. [*Looking up at one of the photographs*] I remember when I got that . . . I won it. I bet Jopie that I could eat five ice-cream cones. We'd all been playing ping-pong . . . We used to have heavenly times . . . we'd finish up with ice cream at the Delphi, or the Oasis, where Jews were allowed . . . there'd always be a lot of boys . . . we'd laugh and joke . . . I'd like to go back to it for a few days or a week. But after that I know I'd be bored to

◆ Build Vocabulary

sarcastic (sär kas´ tik) *adj.:* Speaking with sharp mockery intended to hurt another

indignant (in dig´ nənt) *adj.:* Filled with anger over some meanness or injustice

---

 Cultural Connection

Remembering Anne Frank The diary that Anne Frank kept in the few months before she went into hiding and during the 25 months that she lived in the Secret Annex has been widely read, and her story is well known. The original 1955 play based on the diary and the 1997 updated revival of the play, based on a new version of the diary, were seen by many.

Anne Frank's legacy goes beyond her own writing. Ernst Schnabel's book, *Anne Frank: A Portrait in Courage,* published in 1958, extended her story— he interviewed 42 people who had known Anne or

had come in contact with her after she left the Secret Annex and before she died. Miep Gies's compelling book, *Anne Frank Remembered,* details Anne's story from the perspective of someone outside the Annex who cared deeply about Anne.

Many schools are named for Anne Frank, and in Israel, a forest of 10,000 trees has been planted in her name. Artists have memorialized Anne in many art forms. Amsterdam's Anne Frank House allows visitors to see the Secret Annex, and Holland's Anne Frank Foundation fights racism of every kind and fosters understanding.

death. I think more seriously about life now. I want to be a journalist . . . or something. I love to write. What do you want to do?

PETER. I thought I might go off some place . . . work on a farm or something . . . some job that doesn't take much brains.

ANNE. You shouldn't talk that way. You've got the most awful inferiority complex.

PETER. I know I'm not smart.

ANNE. That isn't true. You're much better than I am in dozens of things . . . arithmetic and algebra and . . . well, you're a million times better than I am in algebra. [*With sudden directness*] You like Margot, don't you? Right from the start you liked her, liked her much better than me.

PETER. [*Uncomfortably*] Oh, I don't know.

[*In the main room* MRS. VAN DAAN *comes from the bathroom and goes over to the sink, polishing a coffee pot.*]

ANNE. It's all right. Everyone feels that way. Margot's so good. She's sweet and bright and beautiful and I'm not.

PETER. I wouldn't say that.

ANNE. Oh, no, I'm not. I know that. I know quite well that I'm not a beauty. I never have been and never shall be.

PETER. I don't agree at all. I think you're pretty.

ANNE. That's not true!

PETER. And another thing. You've changed . . . from at first, I mean.

ANNE. I have?

PETER. I used to think you were awful noisy.

ANNE. And what do you think now, Peter? How have I changed?

PETER. Well . . . er . . . you're . . . quieter.

[*In his room* DUSSEL *takes his pajamas and toilet articles and goes into the bathroom to change.*]

ANNE. I'm glad you don't just hate me.

PETER. I never said that.

ANNE. I bet when you get out of here you'll never think of me again.

PETER. That's crazy.

ANNE. When you get back with all of your friends, you're going to say . . . now what did I ever see in that Mrs. Quack Quack.

PETER. I haven't got any friends.

ANNE. Oh, Peter, of course you have. Everyone has friends.

PETER. Not me. I don't want any. I get along all right without them.

ANNE. Does that mean you can get along without me? I think of myself as your friend.

PETER. No. If they were all like you, it'd be different.

[*He takes the glasses and the bottle and puts them away. There is a second's silence and then* ANNE *speaks, hesitantly, shyly.*]

ANNE. Peter, did you ever kiss a girl?

PETER. Yes. Once.

ANNE. [*To cover her feelings*] That picture's crooked.

[PETER *goes over, straightening the photograph.*] Was she pretty?

PETER. Huh?

ANNE. The girl that you kissed.

PETER. I don't know. I was blindfolded. [*He comes back and sits down again.*] It was at a party. One of those kissing games.

ANNE. [*Relieved*] Oh. I don't suppose that really counts, does it?

PETER. It didn't with me.

ANNE. I've been kissed twice. Once a man I'd never seen before kissed me on the cheek when he picked me up off the ice and I was crying. And the other was Mr. Koophuis, a friend of Father's who kissed my hand. You wouldn't say those counted, would you?

PETER. I wouldn't say so.

ANNE. I know almost for certain that Margot would never kiss anyone unless she was engaged to them. And I'm sure too that Mother never touched a man before Pim. But I don't know . . . things are so different now . . . What do you think? Do you think a girl

---

Clarification

6 An inferiority complex is a state of mind characterized by feelings of low self-esteem and a nagging belief that everyone else is more capable or more intelligent.

◆ Critical Thinking

7 Interpret Do you think Anne is "fishing" for compliments as she did with Margot? Explain. *Students may say that Anne is so insistent that she is not "sweet and bright and beautiful" that she seems to be fishing for compliments from Peter. Anne may not think that she is pretty, but she knows that she is bright.*

◆ LITERATURE AND YOUR LIFE

8 Both Peter and Anne have changed as a result of their long months in hiding. Lead a discussion of changes that students have noticed in themselves and in friends over time. Explore the reasons for the changes, such as a change of environment, newly developed talents or skills, or a new appreciation for traits once taken for granted.

◆ Critical Thinking

9 Connect In what way does Peter resemble Dussel when he says that he doesn't want any friends? *When Anne first met Dussel, he told her that he was someone "who's always lived alone" and had not adjusted himself to others. Both Peter and Dussel seem to find getting along with others difficult.*

The Diary of Anne Frank, Act II ◆ 759

 Cultural Connection

Dating Customs Trapped in the Secret Annex, Anne, Peter, and Margot have no way to participate in social activities enjoyed by young people. When Anne and Peter become good friends and want to have an evening "date," it is an event that piques the interest of all inhabitants of the hiding place. Mrs. Van Daan and Mrs. Frank worry about the unchaperoned visit and its length, while Anne and Margot fuss over her hair and clothing.

Most adolescent boys and girls participate in group activities at school or church and get acquainted with groups of friends. Occasional

dating follows, then later many teenagers begin to date one person exclusively. Different societies encourage or even restrict the age at which young people can marry without parental permission. In most of the United States, both young people must be 18 years old to marry without permission.

Interested students may wish to use research materials to investigate and compare dating and marriage customs in other cultures with those followed in the United States. Suggest that they share their findings in a written report.

759

1 Assess Guide students to note the tilt of Peter's head, his wary eyes, and his pleasant smile. *Students may say that the photograph seems to capture Peter's shy personality because of his pose and his expression.*

◆ Reading Strategy

2 Envision Guide students to notice how the interruption of the carillon bells adds dramatic tension by causing Peter to stop in the middle of an important sentence. Ask students why the playwrights chose to add the sound of the bells at this moment in the play. Have them explain how the stage direction and lines spoken by Anne and Peter help them envision the moment. *Students may say that perhaps the playwrights wanted to suspend this moment and leave the audience wondering how Anne and Peter's date will end. Students may say that they can envision Anne and Peter were "saved by the bell" at an awkward moment for them.*

◆ Critical Thinking

3 Infer Why does Anne remain seated even though she has said good night to Peter? *Anne may be "fishing" for a kiss from Peter, or she may not want the pleasure of the evening to end.*

Comprehension Check ☑

4 Why does Anne kiss Mrs. Van Daan? What suspicion does Anne's kiss confirm for Mrs. Van Daan? *Students may say that Anne kisses Mrs. Van Daan as a way to communicate that she and Peter have grown closer. Others may say that Anne's kiss is one of gratitude—to thank her for her son. Because of Anne's unusual gesture, Mrs. Van Daan knows that Anne has probably been kissed by her son and that Anne and Peter are becoming closer friends.*

▲ **Critical Viewing** Does this photograph of Peter Van Daan seem to capture his personality? Explain. **1** [Assess]

shouldn't kiss anyone except if she's engaged or something? It's so hard to try to think what to do, when here we are with the whole world falling around our ears and you think . . . well . . . you don't know what's going to happen tomorrow and . . . What do you think?

760 ◆ Drama

PETER. I suppose it'd depend on the girl. Some girls, anything they do's wrong. But others . . . well . . . it wouldn't necessarily be wrong with them.

[*The carillon starts to strike nine o'clock.*]

I've always thought that when two people . . . **2**

ANNE. Nine o'clock. I have to go.

PETER. That's right.

ANNE. [*Without moving*] Good night. **3**

[*There is a second's pause, then* PETER *gets up and moves toward the door.*]

PETER. You won't let them stop you coming?

ANNE. No. [*She rises and starts for the door.*] Sometimes I might bring my diary. There are so many things in it that I want to talk over with you. There's a lot about you.

PETER. What kind of thing?

ANNE. I wouldn't want you to see some of it. I thought you were a nothing, just the way you thought about me.

PETER. Did you change your mind, the way I changed my mind about you?

ANNE. Well . . . You'll see . . .

[*For a second* ANNE *stands looking up at* PETER, *longing for him to kiss her. As he makes no move she turns away. Then suddenly* PETER *grabs her awkwardly in his arms, kissing her on the cheek.* ANNE *walks out dazed. She stands for a minute, her back to the people in the main room. As she regains her poise she goes to her mother and father and* MARGOT, *silently kissing them. They murmur their good nights to her. As she is about to open her bedroom door, she catches sight of* MRS. VAN DAAN. *She goes quickly* **4**

Cross-Curricular Connection: History

Axis Powers During the 1920's, the western democracies tried to strengthen the framework for peace. In the 1930's, it crumbled. Dictators in Italy and Germany and militarists in Japan pursued ambitious goals for empire. They scorned peace and glorified war.

Unlike these dictators, leaders of the western democracies tried to use diplomacy to avoid conflict—the two sides tested each other. As war clouds gathered over Europe in the mid-1930's, the fundamental goal of American policy was to avoid involvement.

In pursuit of more power, Japan seized Manchuria and began invading eastern China. From Italy, Mussolini invaded and conquered Ethiopia. By this time, Hitler had violated the terms of the Versailles treaty and sent troops into the Rhineland—the area belonged to Germany, but lay on the frontier with France and was considered a "demilitarized" zone, off-limits to German troops. France was being threatened by Hitler, but they needed British support to move against him; the British had no desire to confront the German dictator.

In the face of the democracies' apparent weakness, Germany, Italy, and Japan formed the Rome-Berlin-Tokyo Axis, agreeing not to interfere with one another's plans for expansion. The agreement cleared the way for these anti-democratic, aggressor powers to bring other nations under their sway.

World War II, lasting for six devastating years, pitted the Axis powers against the Allied powers, which eventually included Britain, France, the Soviet Union, China, the United States, and 45 other nations.

❹ to her, taking her face in her hands and kissing her first on one cheek and then on the other. Then she hurries off into her room. MRS. VAN DAAN looks after her, and then looks over at PETER's room. Her suspicions are confirmed.]

MRS. VAN DAAN. [She knows.] Ah hah!

[The lights dim out. The curtain falls on the scene. In the darkness ANNE'S VOICE comes faintly at first and then with growing strength.]

ANNE'S VOICE. By this time we all know each other so well that if anyone starts to tell a story, the rest can finish it for him. We're having to cut down still further on our meals. What makes it worse, the rats have been at work again. They've carried off some of our precious food. Even Mr. Dussel wishes now that Mouschi was here. Thurs-**❺** day, the twentieth of April, nineteen forty-four. Invasion fever is mounting every day. Miep tells us that people outside talk of nothing else. For myself, life has become much more pleasant. I often go to Peter's room after supper. Oh, don't think I'm in love, because I'm not. But it does make life more bearable to have someone with whom you can exchange views. No more tonight. P.S. . . . I must be honest. I must confess that I actually live for the next meeting. Is there anything lovelier than to sit under the skylight and feel the sun on your cheeks and have a darling boy in your arms? I admit now that I'm glad the Van Daans had a son and not a daughter. I've outgrown another dress. That's the third. I'm having to wear Margot's clothes after all. I'm working hard on my French and am now reading *La Belle Nivernaise*.[6]

[As she is saying the last lines—the curtain rises on the scene. The lights dim on, as ANNE'S VOICE fades out.]

Scene 3

❻ [It is night, a few weeks later. Everyone is in bed. There is complete quiet. In the VAN DAANS' room a match flares up for a moment and then

---

6. *La Belle Nivernaise:* A story by Alphonse Daudet, a French author.

---

is quickly put out. MR. VAN DAAN, in bare feet, dressed in underwear and trousers, is dimly seen coming <u>stealthily</u> down the stairs and into the main room, where MR. and MRS. FRANK and MARGOT are sleeping. He goes to the food safe and again lights a match. Then he cautiously opens the safe, taking out a half-loaf of bread. As he closes the safe, it creaks. He stands rigid. MRS. FRANK sits up in bed. She sees him.] **❻**

MRS. FRANK. [Screaming] Otto! Otto! *Komme schnell!*[7]

[The rest of the people wake, hurriedly getting up.]

MR. FRANK. *Was ist los? Was ist passiert?*[8] **❼**

[DUSSEL, followed by ANNE, comes from his room.]

MRS. FRANK. [As she rushes over to MR. VAN DAAN] *Er stiehlt das Essen!*[9]

DUSSEL. [Grabbing MR. VAN DAAN] You! You! Give me that.

MRS. VAN DAAN. [Coming down the stairs] Putti . . . Putti . . . what is it?

DUSSEL. [His hands on VAN DAAN's neck] You dirty thief . . . stealing food . . . you good-for-nothing . . .

MR. FRANK. Mr. Dussel! Oh! Help me, Peter!

[PETER comes over, trying, with MR. FRANK, to separate the two struggling men.]

PETER. Let him go! Let go!

[DUSSEL drops MR. VAN DAAN, pushing him away. He shows them the end of a loaf of bread that he has taken from VAN DAAN.]

DUSSEL. You greedy, selfish . . . !

[MARGOT turns on the lights.]

MRS. VAN DAAN. Putti . . . what is it?

[All of MRS. FRANK's gentleness, her self-control,

---

7. *Komme schnell!* (käm´ ə shnel): German for "Come quick!"
8. *Was ist los? Was ist passiert?* (väs ist los väs ist päs´ ērt): German for "What's the matter? What happened?"
9. *Er stiehlt das Essen!* (er stēlt däs es´ ən): German for "He steals food!"

◆ **Build Vocabulary**

stealthily (stel´ thi lē) *adv.*: In a secretive or sneaky way

---

The Diary of Anne Frank, Act II ◆ 761

Clarification

❺ People were hoping for an Allied invasion of German-occupied countries, which would end Hitler's stranglehold on Europe. Less than two months after Anne's diary entry, on June 6, 1944, the Allies invaded Normandy, France. The event marked an important turning point in the war.

◆ Reading Strategy

❻ Envision Have students summarize what they envision happening at the beginning of Scene 3, based on the stage directions. *All is quiet. The light from a match flares in the Van Daans' room. Mr. Van Daan creeps downstairs. He goes to the food safe and lights another match. Quietly, he removes a half-loaf of bread. The safe door creaks as he is closing it, which awakens Mrs. Frank, who finally catches Mr. Van Daan stealing the bread.*

◆ Critical Thinking

❼ Interpret As students read the lines in which Mr. and Mrs. Frank speak to each other in German, have them try to guess what they are saying, before referring to the footnotes. After students make their guesses, have them check the footnotes. Students may be surprised at how well they interpret the dialogue based on the similarities between some of the German words and the same words in English *(Komme/come and stiehlt/steals)* and based on the context.

Customize for
Interpersonal Learners

Point out to students that not only has Mr. Van Daan stolen food, he has betrayed the trust of the group. Have students meet in small groups to discuss the importance of trust for people who are dependent on one another. Ask them to work together to list situations in which group trust is especially important. Have them list responsibilities of individuals to maintain that trust.

Cross-Curricular Connection: History

Invasion Fever Several steps led up to the invasion of Western Europe by the Allies. In late 1942, American and British troops engaged in air raids to bomb German cities. Subsequently, in January 1943, the Casablanca Conference was held, during which world leaders French General Henri Giraud, Franklin Delano Roosevelt, Charles de Gaulle, and Winston Churchill met and announced that the Allies would fight for the "unconditional surrender" of the Axis Powers.

Another important conference was held in Teheran, Iran, in November 1943. Here, Churchill and Roosevelt met with Russian leader Josef Stalin and confirmed a plan to invade Western Europe in the spring of 1944. To prepare for this invasion, British and American troops went through a massive buildup—3.5 million troops were concentrated in England. General Dwight D. Eisenhower organized a strategic bombing of German sites to destroy the German military and economic system by attacking the German air force, rail communications, and transportation systems. Finally, on June 6, 1944, American and British troops landed on the beach at Normandy, France.

◆ Literary Focus

❶ Characterization and Theme in Drama In what way is Mrs. Van Daan's defense of her husband consistent with her character? *Mrs. Van Daan excuses her husband's wrongdoing rather than standing up for what is right. As in the scene in which the cake is cut, Mrs. Van Daan ignores the group's interests in favor of those of her husband.*

◆ Critical Thinking

❷ Speculate Ask students how Mr. Van Daan feels as he moves to sit on the couch. *Students may say that he feels guilty and embarrassed, particularly since Mrs. Frank accuses him of stealing food from the children.*

Comprehension Check ☑

❸ What does Mrs. Frank mean when she accuses Mrs. Van Daan of sacrificing her child to "this man"? *Mrs. Frank is saying that Mrs. Van Daan allows her own son to go hungry, while condoning Mr. Van Daan's theft of food. Students may say that Mrs. Frank is also referring to Mrs. Van Daan's tendency to do nothing to defend Peter from Mr. Van Daan's harsh and unfair criticism of him.*

◆ Critical Thinking

❹ Analyze Discuss why Mrs. Frank's rage seems out of character for her. Have students debate whether her anger is justified. *Students may say that Mrs. Frank's anger is justified, because Mr. Van Daan has been selfish and greedy from the first, particularly toward his son. Mrs. Frank has tried for months to be kind and understanding.*

◆ Critical Thinking

❺ Interpret Why does Mr. Frank say "We're destroying ourselves"? *He sees that greed, selfishness, mistrust, fear, and anger are destroying the group by turning them against one another.*

---

is gone. She is outraged, in a frenzy of indignation.]

MRS. FRANK. The bread! He was stealing the bread!

DUSSEL. It was you, and all the time we thought it was the rats!

MR. FRANK. Mr. Van Daan, how could you!

MR. VAN DAAN. I'm hungry.

MRS. FRANK. We're all of us hungry! I see the children getting thinner and thinner. Your own son Peter . . . I've heard him moan in his sleep, he's so hungry. And you come in the night and steal food that should go to them . . . to the children!

❶ MRS. VAN DAAN. [*Going to* MR. VAN DAAN *protectively*] He needs more food than the rest of us. He's used to more. He's a big man.

❷ [MR. VAN DAAN *breaks away, going over and sitting on the couch.*]

❸ MRS. FRANK. [*Turning on* MRS. VAN DAAN] And you . . . you're worse than he is! You're a mother, and yet you sacrifice your child to this man . . . this . . . this . . .

MR. FRANK. Edith! Edith!

[MARGOT *picks up the pink woolen stole, putting it over her mother's shoulders.*]

MRS. FRANK. [*Paying no attention, going on to* MRS. VAN DAAN] Don't think I haven't seen you! Always saving the choicest bits for him! I've watched you day after day and I've held my tongue. But not any longer! Not after this! Now I want him to go! I want him to get out of here!

❹ [*Together*]
MR. FRANK. Edith!
MR. VAN DAAN. Get out of here?
MRS. VAN DAAN. What do you mean?

MRS. FRANK. Just that! Take your things and get out!

MR. FRANK. [*To* MRS. FRANK] You're speaking in anger. You cannot mean what you are saying.

MRS. FRANK. I mean exactly that!

[MRS. VAN DAAN *takes a cover from the* FRANKS' *bed, pulling it about her.*]

MR. FRANK. For two long years we have lived here, side by side. We have respected each other's rights . . . we have managed to live in peace. Are we now going to throw it all away? I know this will never happen again, will it, Mr. Van Daan?

MR. VAN DAAN. No. No.

MRS. FRANK. He steals once! He'll steal again!

[MR. VAN DAAN, *holding his stomach, starts for the bathroom.* ANNE *puts her arms around him, helping him up the step.*]

MR. FRANK. Edith, please. Let us be calm. We'll all go to our rooms . . . and afterwards we'll sit down quietly and talk this out . . . we'll find some way . . .

MRS. FRANK. No! No! No more talk! I want them to leave!

MRS. VAN DAAN. You'd put us out, on the streets?

MRS. FRANK. There are other hiding places.

MRS. VAN DAAN. A cellar . . . a closet. I know. And we have no money left even to pay for that.

MRS. FRANK. I'll give you money. Out of my own pocket I'll give it gladly. [*She gets her purse from a shelf and comes back with it.*]

MRS. VAN DAAN. Mr. Frank, you told Putti you'd never forget what he'd done for you when you came to Amsterdam. You said you could never repay him, that you . . .

MRS. FRANK. [*Counting out money*] If my husband had any obligation to you, he's paid it, over and over.

MR. FRANK. Edith, I've never seen you like this before. I don't know you.

MRS. FRANK. I should have spoken out long ago.

DUSSEL. You can't be nice to some people.

MRS. VAN DAAN. [*Turning on* DUSSEL] There would have been plenty for all of us, if *you* hadn't come in here!

❺ MR. FRANK. We don't need the Nazis to destroy us. We're destroying ourselves.

762 ◆ *Drama*

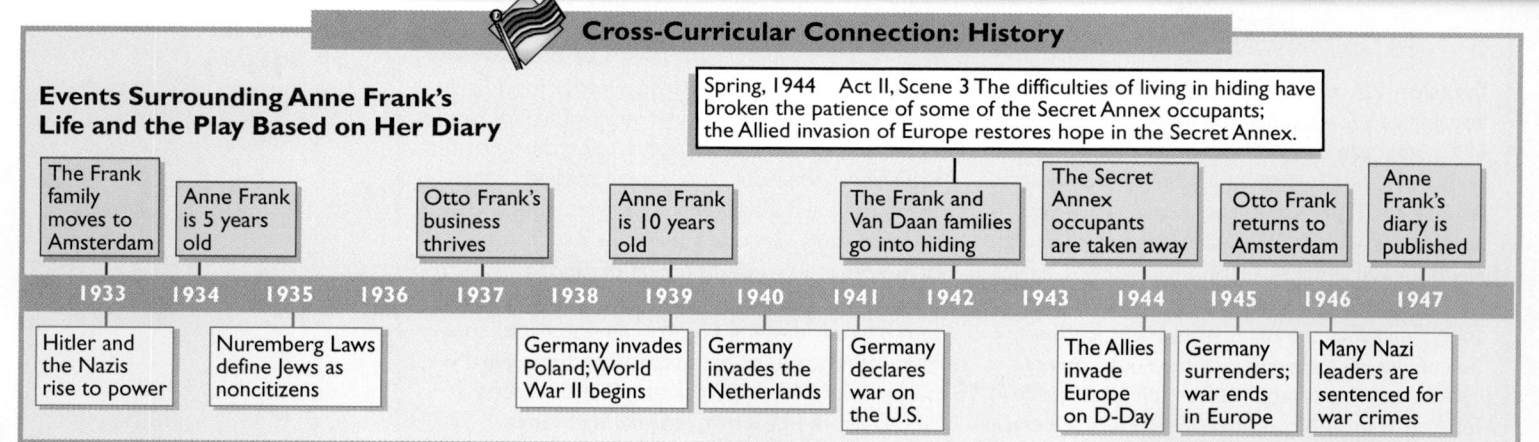

Cross-Curricular Connection: History

Events Surrounding Anne Frank's Life and the Play Based on Her Diary

Spring, 1944 Act II, Scene 3 The difficulties of living in hiding have broken the patience of some of the Secret Annex occupants; the Allied invasion of Europe restores hope in the Secret Annex.

The Frank family moves to Amsterdam | Anne Frank is 5 years old | Otto Frank's business thrives | Anne Frank is 10 years old | The Frank and Van Daan families go into hiding | The Secret Annex occupants are taken away | Otto Frank returns to Amsterdam | Anne Frank's diary is published

1933 1934 1935 1936 1937 1938 1939 1940 1941 1942 1943 1944 1945 1946 1947

Hitler and the Nazis rise to power | Nuremberg Laws define Jews as noncitizens | Germany invades Poland; World War II begins | Germany invades the Netherlands | Germany declares war on the U.S. | The Allies invade Europe on D-Day | Germany surrenders; war ends in Europe | Many Nazi leaders are sentenced for war crimes

[*He sits down, with his head in his hands.* MRS. FRANK *goes to* MRS. VAN DAAN.]

MRS. FRANK. [*Giving* MRS. VAN DAAN *some money*] Give this to Miep. She'll find you a place.

ANNE. Mother, you're not putting *Peter* out. Peter hasn't done anything.

MRS. FRANK. He'll stay, of course. When I say I must protect the children, I mean Peter too.

[PETER *rises from the steps where he has been sitting.*]

PETER. I'd have to go if Father goes.

[MR. VAN DAAN *comes from the bathroom.* MRS. VAN DAAN *hurries to him and takes him to the couch. Then she gets water from the sink to bathe his face.*]

❻ **MRS. FRANK.** [*While this is going on*] He's no father to you . . . that man! He doesn't know what it is to be a father!

PETER. [*Starting for his room*] I wouldn't feel right. I couldn't stay.

MRS. FRANK. Very well, then. I'm sorry.

ANNE. [*Rushing over to* PETER] No, Peter! No!

[PETER *goes into his room, closing the door after him.* ANNE *turns back to her mother, crying.*]

❼ I don't care about the food. They can have mine! I don't want it! Only don't send them away. It'll be daylight soon. They'll be caught . . .

MARGOT. [*Putting her arms comfortingly around* ANNE] Please, Mother!

MRS. FRANK. They're not going now. They'll stay here until Miep finds them a place. [*To* MRS. VAN DAAN] But one thing I insist on! He must never come down here again! He must never come to this room where the food is stored! We'll divide what we have . . . an equal share for each!

[DUSSEL *hurries over to get a sack of potatoes from the food safe.* MRS. FRANK *goes on, to* MRS. VAN DAAN]

You can cook it here and take it up to him.

[DUSSEL *brings the sack of potatoes back to the center table.*]

MARGOT. Oh, no. No. We haven't sunk so far

that we're going to fight over a handful of rotten potatoes.

DUSSEL. [*Dividing the potatoes into piles*] Mrs. Frank, Mr. Frank, Margot, Anne, Peter, Mrs. Van Daan, Mr. Van Daan, myself . . . Mrs. Frank . . .

[*The buzzer sounds in* MIEP'*s signal.*]

MR. FRANK. It's Miep! [*He hurries over, getting his overcoat and putting it on.*] **❽**

MARGOT. At this hour?

MRS. FRANK. It is trouble.

MR. FRANK. [*As he starts down to unbolt the door*] I beg you, don't let her see a thing like this!

MR. DUSSEL. [*Counting without stopping*] . . . Anne, Peter, Mrs. Van Daan, Mr. Van Daan, myself . . .

MARGOT. [*To* DUSSEL] Stop it! Stop it!

DUSSEL. . . . Mr. Frank, Margot, Anne, Peter, Mrs. Van Daan, Mr. Van Daan, myself, Mrs. Frank . . .

MRS. VAN DAAN. You're keeping the big ones for yourself! All the big ones . . . Look at the size of that! . . . And that! . . .

[DUSSEL *continues on with his dividing.* PETER, *with his shirt and trousers on, comes from his room.*]

MARGOT. Stop it! Stop it!

[*We hear* MIEP'*s excited voice speaking to* MR. FRANK *below.*]

MIEP. Mr. Frank . . . the most wonderful news! . . . The invasion has begun!

MR. FRANK. Go on, tell them! Tell them!

[MIEP *comes running up the steps ahead of* MR. FRANK. *She has a man's raincoat on over her nightclothes and a bunch of orange-colored flowers in her hand.*]

MIEP. Did you hear that, everybody? Did you hear what I said? The invasion has begun! The invasion!

[*They all stare at* MIEP, *unable to grasp what she is telling them.* PETER *is the first to recover his wits.*] **❾**

PETER. Where?

◆ **Literary Focus**

❻ Characterization and Theme in Drama Remind students that up to this point, Peter has felt embarrassment and shame at his father's actions. Ask students how Peter reveals a different side of his character when Mrs. Frank orders Mr. Van Daan to leave. *In spite of how he feels about his father's actions, Peter shows that he is loyal to his family by saying that he could not stay if his father had to leave.*

◆ **Critical Thinking**

❼ Infer At this moment, what does Anne value more than she values food? *She values friendship more than food. As she said in her earlier diary entry, " . . . it does make life more bearable to have someone with whom you can exchange views."*

◆ **Critical Thinking**

❽ Speculate Have students predict what Miep may be coming to tell the group. *Students may say that she is coming to warn them that the Nazis have learned of the hiding place. Others may hope that she is coming to tell them good news.*

◆ **LITERATURE AND YOUR LIFE**

❾ The group is unable to grasp what Miep has just told them. Perhaps they are still stunned by the discovery that Mr. Van Daan has been stealing food and by Mrs. Frank's rage. Also, they have been living under such strained conditions that good news seems impossible to believe. Encourage students to discuss times when they have been shocked or surprised into silence by important news.

Cross-Curricular Connection: Social Studies

D-Day The Allied invasion of German-occupied France during World War II occurred on D-Day, a code name for the first day of a military attack. On June 6, 1944, Allied forces launched an invasion of German-held Normandy, a province in northern France (see p. 733 of the Teacher Edition for a map that shows Normandy). The difficult, but successful, invasion was the beginning of the Allied victory in Europe. Less than a year later, Germany surrendered to the Allies.

Have students work in groups to learn more about D-Day and its significance. Use questions such as these to help students choose a topic for research: Who led the invasion of Normandy on D-Day? What are some important facts about the planning and strategy of the invasion? How many troops landed at Normandy? Why was the invasion of Normandy so important? Challenge students to interview adults who can provide personal recollections and information about D-Day.

Reading Strategy

1 Envision Have students explain how these stage directions help them picture the scene of celebration. *Students may say that references to embraces, parades, weaves, and pandemonium make it easy to picture the action because these words describe the actions of the characters.*

Clarification

2 Normandy is a region in north-west France that faces the English Channel. The region is known for its dairy products, fruit, brandy, wheat, and flax. The main industries of Normandy are shipbuilding, steel, iron, and textiles. Use a map to point out Normandy and help students understand where the invasion took place in relation to other areas of Europe (see p. 733 of the Teacher Edition).

Literary Focus

3 Characterization and Theme in Drama Have students describe how the news about D-Day affects each person. Then guide students to discover key themes in this passage, such as the need to remain optimistic in spite of trouble, the importance of unity and forgiveness, and the terrible effects of constant fear and pressure on people. *Everyone is excited at first. Mr. Van Daan feels ashamed for stealing, Margot dismisses the matter, Mrs. Frank is forgiving and then remorseful for her anger, Anne is regretful of her behavior toward her mother, Dussel wants everyone to be happy, and Mr. Frank is in a festive mood.*

MRS. VAN DAAN. When? When, Miep?

MIEP. It began early this morning . . .

[*As she talks on, the realization of what she has said begins to dawn on them. Everyone goes crazy. A wild demonstration takes place.* MRS. FRANK *hugs* MR. VAN DAAN.]

MRS. FRANK. Oh, Mr. Van Daan, did you hear that?

[DUSSEL *embraces* MRS. VAN DAAN. PETER *grabs a frying pan and parades around the room, beating on it, singing the Dutch National Anthem.* ANNE *and* MARGOT *follow him, singing, weaving in and out among the excited grown-ups.* MARGOT *breaks away to take the flowers from* MIEP *and distribute them to everyone. While this pandemonium is going on* MRS. FRANK *tries to make herself heard above the excitement.*]

MRS. FRANK. [*To* MIEP] How do you know?

MIEP. The radio . . . The B.B.C.![10] They said they landed on the coast of Normandy![11]

PETER. The British?

MIEP. British, Americans, French, Dutch, Poles, Norwegians . . . all of them! More than four thousand ships! Churchill spoke, and General Eisenhower! D-Day they call it!

MR. FRANK. Thank God, it's come!

MRS. VAN DAAN. At last!

MIEP. [*Starting out*] I'm going to tell Mr. Kraler. This'll be better than any blood transfusion.

MR. FRANK. [*Stopping her*] What part of Normandy did they land, did they say?

MIEP. Normandy . . . that's all I know now . . . I'll be up the minute I hear some more! [*She goes hurriedly out.*]

MR. FRANK. [*To* MRS. FRANK] What did I tell you? What did I tell you?

[MRS. FRANK *indicates that he has forgotten to bolt the door after* MIEP. *He hurries down the steps.* MR. VAN DAAN, *sitting on the couch, suddenly breaks into a convulsive[12] sob. Everybody looks at him, bewildered.*]

---

10. **B.B.C.:** British Broadcasting Corporation.
11. **Normandy** (nôr′mən dē): A region in northwest France, on the English Channel.
12. **convulsive** (kən vul′ siv) *adj.*: Having an involuntary contraction or spasm of the muscles; shuddering.

764 ◆ *Drama*

MRS. VAN DAAN. [*Hurrying to him*] Putti! Putti! What is it? What happened?

MR. VAN DAAN. Please, I'm so ashamed.

[MR. FRANK *comes back up the steps.*]

DUSSEL. Oh!

MRS. VAN DAAN. Don't, Putti.

MARGOT. It doesn't matter now!

MR. FRANK. [*Going to* MR. VAN DAAN] Didn't you hear what Miep said? The invasion has come! We're going to be liberated! This is a time to celebrate! [*He embraces* MRS. FRANK *and then hurries to the cupboard and gets the cognac and a glass.*]

MR. VAN DAAN. To steal bread from children!

MRS. FRANK. We've all done things that we're ashamed of.

ANNE. Look at me, the way I've treated Mother . . . so mean and horrid to her.

MRS. FRANK. No, Anneke, no.

[ANNE *runs to her mother, putting her arms around her.*]

ANNE. Oh, Mother, I was. I was awful.

MR. VAN DAAN. Not like me. No one is as bad as me!

DUSSEL. [*To* MR. VAN DAAN] Stop it now! Let's be happy!

MR. FRANK. [*Giving* MR. VAN DAAN *a glass of cognac*] Here! Here! *Schnapps! L'chaim!*[13]

[VAN DAAN *takes the cognac. They all watch him. He gives them a feeble smile.* ANNE *puts up her fingers in a V-for-Victory sign. As* VAN DAAN *gives an answering V-sign, they are startled to hear a loud sob from behind them. It is* MRS. FRANK, *stricken with remorse. She is sitting on the other side of the room.*]

MRS. FRANK. [*Through her sobs*] When I think of the terrible things I said . . .

[MR. FRANK, ANNE *and* MARGOT *hurry to her, trying to comfort her.* MR. VAN DAAN *brings her his glass of cognac.*]

MR. VAN DAAN. No! No! You were right!

---

13. *Schnapps! L'chaim!* (shnäps lə khä′ yim): German for "a drink," and a Hebrew toast meaning "To life."

Cross-Curricular Connection: Social Studies

Radio Broadcasting During World War II
When Mr. Dussel arrived in the Secret Annex, he was handed a preliminary list of rules created by the Van Daans. In it was a special section about listening to radio broadcasts. Members of the Annex were allowed to listen to the radio only after 6 P.M., so as not to create excess noise. In addition, they were required to listen only to non-German news broadcasts. German broadcasting had been taken over by Hitler when he became Chancellor of Germany in 1933, and was mainly used as a propaganda system for anti-Semitic beliefs. Anne and the others relied on broadcasts from the BBC for information on the progress of the war and the Allied invasion. The radio broadcasts were so important to the members of the Secret Annex that they arranged their dinner time around them. Another popular broadcasting station was the Dutch Radio Oranj, which provided listeners with information on the extermination of Jews in Poland and the occupation of Europe by Nazi forces. Through radio broadcasts such as these, the rest of the world was alerted to the crisis faced by the Jews in Europe.

MRS. FRANK. That I should speak that way to you! . . . Our friends! . . . Our guests! [*She starts to cry again.*]

4

DUSSEL. Stop it, you're spoiling the whole invasion!

[*As they are comforting her, the lights dim out. The curtain falls.*]

ANNE'S VOICE. [*Faintly at first and then with growing strength*] We're all in much better spirits these days.

◆ **Literary Focus**
What does this passage reveal about Anne's character?
5

There's still excellent news of the invasion. The best part about it is that I have a feeling that friends are coming. Who knows? Maybe I'll be back in school by fall. Ha, ha! The joke is on us! The warehouse man doesn't know a thing and we are paying him all that money! . . . Wednesday, the second of July, nineteen forty-four. The invasion seems temporarily to be bogged down. Mr. Kraler has to have an operation, which looks bad. The Gestapo have found the radio that was stolen. Mr. Dussel says they'll trace it back and back to the thief, and then, it's just a matter of time till they get to us. Everyone is low. Even poor Pim can't raise their spirits. I have often been downcast myself . . . but never in despair. I can shake off everything if I write. But . . . and that is the great question . . . will I ever be able to write well? I want to so much. I want to go on living even after my death. Another birthday has gone by, so now I am fifteen. Already I know what I want. I have a goal, an opinion.

[*As this is being said—the curtain rises on the scene, the lights dim on, and ANNE'S VOICE fades out.*]

Scene 4

[*It is an afternoon a few weeks later . . . Everyone but MARGOT is in the main room. There is a sense of great tension.*

Both MRS. FRANK and MR. VAN DAAN are nervously pacing back and forth, DUSSEL is

▲ **Critical Viewing** This is a page of Anne Frank's diary. Judging from its appearance, was Anne a careful writer or a careless one? Explain. [**Deduce**] **6**

standing at the window, looking down fixedly at the street below. PETER *is at the center table, trying to do his lessons.* ANNE *sits opposite him, writing in her diary.* MRS. VAN DAAN *is seated on the couch, her eyes on* MR. FRANK *as he sits reading.*

The sound of a telephone ringing comes from the office below. They all are rigid, listening tensely. DUSSEL *rushes down to* MR. FRANK.]

DUSSEL. There it goes again, the telephone! Mr. Frank, do you hear?

MR. FRANK. [*Quietly*] Yes. I hear.

DUSSEL. [*Pleading, insistent*] But this is the third time, Mr. Frank! The third time in quick succession! It's a signal! I tell you it's Miep, trying to get us! For some reason she can't come to us and she's trying to warn us of something!

7

The Diary of Anne Frank, Act II ◆ 765

Comprehension Check ☑

4 What does Dussel mean by his remark to Mrs. Frank that she is "spoiling the whole invasion"? *Dussel is trying to lighten the mood and tease Mrs. Frank out of her tears.*

◆ **Literary Focus**

5 **Characterization and Theme in Drama** *Anne shows that she is always the optimist, in spite of the turmoil she feels in the face of ever-changing news. She refuses to give in to despair and is sustained by her writing, through which she hopes to continue living, even after her death. She is more self-assured than ever and proud of the fact that she now has a goal.*

▶ **Critical Viewing** ◀

6 **Deduce** *The diary page shows that Anne was a careful writer because the lines of writing are even and neat, and the letters are well-formed and graceful.*

◆ **Critical Thinking**

7 **Speculate** *Ask students what the tension between the families and Mr. Dussel and the incessant ringing of the telephone might mean. Students may say that it foreshadows the discovery of the group's hiding place.*

Humanities: Art

Anne Frank's Writing Anne's diary recorded her keen observations for a few months when they still lived in their home in Amsterdam and during their extended stay in the Secret Annex. Before the Franks went into hiding, her father had enjoyed photographing the family, visually recording observations similar to the ones Anne wrote down with detail and insight.

In the spring of 1944, Anne heard a radio announcement that the Dutch government would be publishing diaries and letters after the war. With a publication goal in mind, she began to edit her diary, although she continued to write new entries on a regular basis.

When Otto Frank prepared the diary manuscript for publication, he drew on both the original diary and Anne's revision. He left all of the written materials to the State of the Netherlands when he died. To dispel arguments that the diary was a fake—no 15-year-old could have written so well—the diary was scientifically examined and authenticated. Subsequent editions of the diary include the results of the examination, and newer versions include more of the original entries.

◆ Critical Thinking

❶ Analyze Ask students if they agree or disagree with Dussel's assessment of what has happened.

Students may say that it is possible that Mr. Kraler has died and that the office has closed out of respect for him. They may also say, though, that Miep is not likely to phone the group, because she knows how careful they are. Others may think that the hiding place has been discovered and a trap was set for the group by the ringing telephone.

◆ LITERATURE AND YOUR LIFE

❷ Ask students what they might do under these circumstances. Have them support their views with details from the play. *Students may say that they would not do anything extraordinary that might expose the group's hiding place, since the group has no proof that they are safe.*

◆ Literary Focus

❸ Characterization and Theme in Drama Have students describe how Anne tries to comfort Peter.

Anne notes the clouds through the sky-light in Peter's room and points out what a beautiful day it is. She tells Peter how she uses her imagination to escape the imprisonment of the Secret Annex, hoping that Peter can do the same.

MR. FRANK. Please. Please.

MR. VAN DAAN. [*To* DUSSEL] You're wasting your breath.

DUSSEL. Something has happened, Mr. Frank. For three days now Miep hasn't been to see us! And today not a man has come to work. There hasn't been a sound in the building!

MRS. FRANK. Perhaps it's Sunday. We may have lost track of the days.

MR. VAN DAAN. [*To* ANNE] You with the diary there. What day is it?

❶ DUSSEL. [*Going to* MRS. FRANK] I don't lose track of the days! I know exactly what day it is! It's Friday, the fourth of August. Friday, and not a man at work. [*He rushes back to* MR. FRANK, *pleading with him, almost in tears.*] I tell you Mr. Kraler's dead. That's the only explanation. He's dead and they've closed down the building, and Miep's trying to tell us!

MR. FRANK. She'd never telephone us.

DUSSEL. [*Frantic*] Mr. Frank, answer that! I beg you, answer it!

MR. FRANK. No.

MR. VAN DAAN. Just pick it up and listen. You don't have to speak. Just listen and see if it's Miep.

DUSSEL. [*Speaking at the same time*] Please . . . I ask you.

MR. FRANK. No. I've told you, no. I'll do nothing that might let anyone know we're in the building.

PETER. Mr. Frank's right.

MR. VAN DAAN. There's no need to tell us what side you're on.

❷ MR. FRANK. If we wait patiently, quietly, I believe that help will come.

[*There is silence for a minute as they all listen to the telephone ringing.*]

DUSSEL. I'm going down.

◆ Build Vocabulary

ineffectually (in´ e fek´ choo ə lē) *adv.*: Without producing the desired effect

---

[*He rushes down the steps.* MR. FRANK *tries ineffectually to hold him.* DUSSEL *runs to the lower door, unbolting it. The telephone stops ringing.* DUSSEL *bolts the door and comes slowly back up the steps.*]

Too late.

[MR. FRANK *goes to* MARGOT *in* ANNE*'s bedroom.*]

MR. VAN DAAN. So we just wait here until we die.

MRS. VAN DAAN. [*Hysterically*] I can't stand it! I'll kill myself! I'll kill myself!

MR. VAN DAAN. Stop it!

[*In the distance, a German military band is heard playing a Viennese waltz.*]

MRS. VAN DAAN. I think you'd be glad if I did! I think you want me to die!

MR. VAN DAAN. Whose fault is it we're here?

[MRS. VAN DAAN *starts for her room. He follows, talking at her.*]

We could've been safe somewhere . . . in America or Switzerland. But no! No! You wouldn't leave when I wanted to. You couldn't leave your things. You couldn't leave your precious furniture.

MRS. VAN DAAN. Don't touch me!

[*She hurries up the stairs, followed by* MR. VAN DAAN. PETER, *unable to bear it, goes to his room.* ANNE *looks after him, deeply concerned.* DUSSEL *returns to his post at the window.* MR. FRANK *comes back into the main room and takes a book, trying to read.* MRS. FRANK *sits near the sink, starting to peel some potatoes.* ANNE *quietly goes to* PETER*'s room, closing the door after her.* PETER *is lying face down on the cot.* ANNE *leans over him, holding him in her arms, trying to bring him out of his despair.*]

❸ ANNE. Look, Peter, the sky. [*She looks up through the skylight.*] What a lovely, lovely day! Aren't the clouds beautiful? You know what I do when it seems as if I couldn't stand being cooped up for one more minute? I *think* myself out. I think myself on a walk in the park where I used to go with Pim. Where the jonquils and the crocus and the violets grow down the slopes. You know the

---

Cross-Curricular Connection: Social Studies

Those Who Helped In the prologue to her book, *Anne Frank Remembered*, Miep Gies denies being a hero, claiming that she only did what thousands of her fellow Dutch countrymen also tried to do. From the vendors who gave her bits of extra food to those who actually hid desperate Jews, many people tried to counter the hatred and persecution that were prevalent during World War II with support and compassion. As the Franks, the Van Daans, and Dussel knew, the efforts of people like Miep Gies were life-saving.

Having grown up in Vienna, Austria, during World War I, Miep was not unfamiliar with the harsh realities of war. When Otto Frank asked her to help hide his family, she never hesitated and worked tirelessly to provide them with food, supplies, and encouragement. Fortunately, when the occupants of the Secret Annex were arrested, Miep was questioned only briefly and was left free to continue running the business for Mr. Frank. In addition, she bravely, but unsuccessfully, attempted to bribe Gestapo officials to release her friends.

She was able to safeguard Anne's treasured diary, and gave it to Mr. Frank when he returned—the only survivor among the Secret Annex occupants. Interested students may wish to read about Miep Gies's memories in *Anne Frank Remembered*. Or, they may wish to research other heroes from the occupation, such as Mrs. Helen Theodora Kuipers-Rietberg, a non-Jew who helped but died at Ravensbruck, a concentration camp, or Pastor Frits Slomp, who helped found the National Organization for Help to People in Hiding.

DEUTSCHE BUNDESPOST
60
ANNE FRANK · 12.6.1929 · 31.3.1945
1979

▲ Critical Viewing In what ways is Anne Frank deserving of being honored on a postage stamp? [Connect]

❹

most wonderful part about *thinking* yourself out? You can have it any way you like. You can have roses and violets and chrysanthemums all blooming at the same time . . . It's funny . . . I used to take it all for granted . . . and now I've gone crazy about everything to do with nature. Haven't you?

❸

PETER. I've just gone crazy. I think if something doesn't happen soon . . . if we don't get out of here . . . I can't stand much more of it!

ANNE. [*Softly*] I wish you had a religion, Peter.

PETER. No, thanks! Not me!

ANNE. Oh, I don't mean you have to be Orthodox[14] . . . or believe in heaven and hell and purgatory[15] and things . . . I just mean some religion . . . it doesn't matter what. Just to believe in something! When I think of all

---

14. **Orthodox** (ôr´ thə däks´) *adj.*: Strictly observing the rites and traditions of Judaism.
15. **purgatory** (pʉr´gə tôr´ ē) *n.*: A state or place of temporary punishment.

---

that's out there . . . the trees . . . and flowers . . . and seagulls . . . when I think of the dearness of you, Peter . . . and the goodness of the people we know . . . Mr. Kraler, Miep, Dirk, the vegetable man, all risking their lives for us every day . . . When I think of these good things, I'm not afraid any more . . . I find myself, and God, and I . . .

[PETER *interrupts, getting up and walking away.*]

PETER. That's fine! But when I begin to think, I get mad! Look at us, hiding out for two years. Not able to move! Caught here like . . . waiting for them to come and get us . . . and all for what?

ANNE. We're not the only people that've had to suffer. There've always been people that've had to . . . sometimes one race . . . sometimes another . . . and yet . . .

PETER. That doesn't make me feel any better!

ANNE. [*Going to him*] I know it's terrible, trying to have any faith . . . when people are doing such horrible . . . But you know what I sometimes think? I think the world may be going through a phase, the way I was with Mother. It'll pass, maybe not for hundreds of years, but some day . . . I still believe, in spite of everything, that people are really good at heart.

PETER. I want to see something now . . . Not a thousand years from now! [*He goes over, sitting down again on the cot.*]

ANNE. But, Peter, if you'd only look at it as part of a great pattern . . . that we're just a little minute in the life . . . [*She breaks off.*] Listen to us, going at each other like a couple of stupid grownups! Look at the sky now. Isn't it lovely?

[*She holds out her hand to him.* PETER *takes it and rises, standing with her at the window looking out, his arms around her.*]

Some day, when we're outside again, I'm going to . . .

◆ Literary Focus
What do you learn about the play's theme in this passage?

❺

❻

❼

The Diary of Anne Frank, Act II ◆ 767

Cultural Connection

Lest We Forget From 1930 until mid-1942, the Axis ran up a string of successes. During that time, the conquerors blasted villages and towns and divided up the spoils. Then the Allies won some key victories and the tide slowly began to turn. World War II was fought on a larger scale and in more places than any other war in history. It was also more costly in human life than any earlier conflict. Civilians were targeted as often as soldiers.

Hitler's "new order" grew out of his racial obsessions. The most savage policy was his program to kill Jews and others he judged "racially inferior," such as Slavs, Gypsies, and the mentally ill. The scale and savagery of the Holocaust has been unequaled in history. The Nazis deliberately set out to destroy the Jews for no other reason than their religious and ethnic heritage. Today, the record of that slaughter is a vivid reminder of the monstrous results of racism and intolerance.

"Lest we forget" is a phrase that reminds people today of the atrocities that took place. Anne Frank's diary is the voice of one person who suffered and died and serves as a reminder not to forget—in order that it may never happen again.

◆ Literary Focus

❶ Characterization and Theme in Drama In the course of the play, Anne has grown from an immature thirteen-year-old girl to a serious young woman. Have students name ways in which Anne has shown a maturity beyond her years. *Anne endures the terrible conditions of two years in hiding, all the while holding on to her creativity, humanity, and optimism. She is no doubt afraid of her fate but faces it with courage and dignity.*

◆ Critical Thinking

❷ Interpret What does Mr. Frank's closing line mean? *Students may say that it means that he is awed and moved by the deep faith his daughter was able to maintain even in the face of terrible circumstances.*

Clarification

What Happened to the Real People Behind the Characters

Anne Frank died of typhus shortly after her sister Margot in March of 1945.

Margot Frank died of typhus at Auschwitz in March of 1945.

Mr. Frank (Otto) survived at Auschwitz until the Russian Army liberated the camp in January of 1945; arrived in Amsterdam in June of 1945; the only survivor of the Secret Annex; died in Switzerland in 1980 at the age of 91.

Mrs. Frank (Edith) died of starvation and exhaustion at Birkenau, the women's sub-camp of Auschwitz, in January of 1945.

Mrs. Van Daan (Auguste van Pels) died at Theresienstadt in Czechoslovakia in the spring of 1945.

Mr. Van Daan (Hermann van Pels) died at Auschwitz shortly after his arrival in September of 1944.

Peter Van Daan (Peter van Pels) survived the "death march" from Auschwitz to Mauthausen; died in May of 1945.

Mr. Dussel (Fritz Pfeffer) died at Neuengamme in December of 1944.

Miep Gies continues to live in Amsterdam.

[*She breaks off as she hears the sound of a car, its brakes squealing as it comes to a sudden stop. The people in the other rooms also become aware of the sound. They listen tensely. Another car roars up to a screeching stop.* ANNE *and* PETER *come from* PETER'S *room.* MR. *and* MRS. VAN DAAN *creep down the stairs.* DUSSEL *comes out from his room. Everyone is listening, hardly breathing. A doorbell clangs again and again in the building below.* MR. FRANK *starts quietly down the steps to the door.* DUSSEL *and* PETER *follow him. The others stand rigid, waiting, terrified.*]

In a few seconds DUSSEL *comes stumbling back up the steps. He shakes off* PETER'S *help and goes to his room.* MR. FRANK *bolts the door below, and comes slowly back up the steps. Their eyes are all on him as he stands there for a minute. They realize that what they feared has happened.* MRS. VAN DAAN *starts to whimper.* MR. VAN DAAN *puts her gently in a chair, and then hurries off up the stairs to their room to collect their things.* PETER *goes to comfort his mother. There is a sound of violent pounding on a door below.*]

MR. FRANK. [*Quietly*] For the past two years we have lived in fear. Now we can live in hope.

[*The pounding below becomes more insistent. There are muffled sounds of voices, shouting commands.*]

MEN'S VOICES. *Auf machen! Da drinnen! Auf machen! Schnell! Schnell! Schnell!*[16] *etc., etc.*

[*The street door below is forced open. We hear the heavy tread of footsteps coming up.* MR. FRANK *gets two school bags from the shelves, and gives one to* ANNE *and the other to* MARGOT. *He goes to get a bag for* MRS. FRANK. *The sound of feet coming up grows louder.* PETER *comes to* ANNE, *kissing her good-bye, then he goes to his room to collect his things. The buzzer of their door starts to ring.* MR. FRANK *brings* MRS. FRANK *a bag. They stand together, waiting. We hear the thud of gun butts on the door, trying to break it down.*]

---

16. *Auf machen! . . . Schnell!* (ou̇f mäk´ ən dä drĭ´ nən ou̇f mäk´ ən shnel shnel shnel): German for "Open up, you in there, open up, quick, quick, quick."

ANNE *stands, holding her school satchel, looking over at her father and mother with a soft, reassuring smile. She is no longer a child, but a woman with courage to meet whatever lies ahead.*

The lights dim out. The curtain falls on the scene. We hear a mighty crash as the door is shattered. After a second ANNE'S VOICE *is heard.*]

ANNE'S VOICE. And so it seems our stay here is over. They are waiting for us now. They've allowed us five minutes to get our things. We can each take a bag and whatever it will hold of clothing. Nothing else. So, dear Diary, that means I must leave you behind. Good-bye for a while. P.S. Please, please, Miep, or Mr. Kraler, or anyone else. If you should find this diary, will you please keep it safe for me, because some day I hope . . .

[*Her voice stops abruptly. There is silence. After a second the curtain rises.*]

Scene 5

[*It is again the afternoon in November, 1945. The rooms are as we saw them in the first scene.* MR. KRALER *has joined* MIEP *and* MR. FRANK. *There are coffee cups on the table. We see a great change in* MR. FRANK. *He is calm now. His bitterness is gone. He slowly turns a few pages of the diary. They are blank.*]

MR. FRANK. No more. [*He closes the diary and puts it down on the couch beside him.*]

MIEP. I'd gone to the country to find food. When I got back the block was surrounded by police . . .

MR. KRALER. We made it our business to learn how they knew. It was the thief . . . the thief who told them.

[MIEP *goes up to the gas burner, bringing back a pot of coffee.*]

MR. FRANK. [*After a pause*] It seems strange to say this, that anyone could be happy in a concentration camp. But Anne was happy in the camp in Holland where they first took us. After two years of being shut up in these rooms, she could be out . . . out in the sunshine and the fresh air that she loved.

Cultural Connection

Holocaust Memorials and Museums An important mission for Jews who survived the Holocaust is to remember and to remind people of its devastation. The United States Holocaust Memorial Museum in Washington, D.C., was chartered by an Act of Congress in 1980. The museum collects evidence and material from the Holocaust, deepens the public's understanding of the history of the Holocaust through exhibitions and publications, and distributes educational materials and teacher resources. Other Holocaust Memorials in the United States can be found in Tampa, Houston, Detroit, and El Paso. Another major Holocaust museum is the Simon Wiesenthal Center and Museum of Tolerance in Los Angeles, California. Wiesenthal was a Jew who survived the Nazi concentration camps. The Museum of Tolerance has a multimedia learning center: **http://motlc.wiesenthal.org**

To visit the Web site of the United States Holocaust Memorial Museum: **http://www.ushmm.org**

We *strongly recommend* you preview all Web sites before sending students to them.

MIEP. [*Offering the coffee to* MR. FRANK] A little more?

MR. FRANK. [*Holding out his cup to her*] The news of the war was good. The British and Americans were sweeping through France. We felt sure that they would get to us in time. In September we were told that we were to be shipped to Poland . . . The men to one camp. The women to another. I was sent to Auschwitz.[17] They went to Belsen.[18] In January we were freed, the few of us who were left. The war wasn't yet over, so it took us a long time to get home. We'd be sent here and there behind the lines where we'd be safe. Each time our train would stop . . . at a siding, or a crossing . . . we'd all get out and go from group to group . . . Where were you? Were you at Belsen? At Buchenwald?[19] At Mauthausen? Is it possible that you knew my wife? Did you ever see my husband? My son? My daughter? That's how I found out about my wife's death . . . of Margot, the Van Daans . . . Dussel. But Anne . . . I still hoped . . . Yesterday I went to Rotterdam. I'd heard of a woman there . . . She'd been in Belsen with Anne . . . I know now.

[*He picks up the diary again, and turns the pages back to find a certain passage. As he finds it we hear* ANNE'S VOICE.]

ANNE'S VOICE. In spite of everything, I still believe that people are really good at heart. [MR. FRANK *slowly closes the diary.*]

❷ **MR. FRANK.** She puts me to shame.

[*They are silent.*]

---

17. **Auschwitz** (oush´ vits): Nazi concentration camp in Poland notorious as an extermination center.
18. **Belsen** (bel´ zən): Village in Germany that with the village of Bergen was the site of Bergen-Belsen, a Nazi concentration camp and extermination center.
19. **Buchenwald** (bōō´ kən wôld´): Notorious Nazi concentration camp and extermination center in central Germany.

Guide for Responding

◆ LITERATURE AND YOUR LIFE

Reader's Response What do you like best about Anne Frank? In what way was she an ordinary teenager?

Thematic Focus What did the world learn from Anne Frank's diary?

Journal Writing Jot down in your journal your reactions to the drama's ending.

☑ Check Your Comprehension

1. When does Act II take place?
2. How does the relationship between Anne and Peter change during Act II?
3. Why does Mrs. Frank want to make the Van Daans leave the attic?
4. What happens to the families at the end of the play?

◆ Critical Thinking

INTERPRET

1. In Act I, Anne explains to her father that she worries about the bad things she does and that she is afraid people will laugh at her if she is serious. How do we know that a year later, in Act II, she has changed? **[Support]**
2. In what way does Anne's friendship with Peter help her live through a difficult time? **[Infer]**
3. How can Anne believe that "in spite of everything, . . . people are really good at heart"? **[Draw Conclusions]**
4. Scene 5 occurs several years after Scene 4 closes. Explain what Mr. Frank might mean by his last line: "She puts me to shame." **[Interpret]**

APPLY

5. How might Anne's speech on page 754 beginning "I get so mad" express the attitudes of other young people toward their parents' generation? **[Relate]**

EVALUATE

6. Does the fact the Anne Frank was a real person make this play more meaningful for you? Explain. **[Assess]**

The Diary of Anne Frank, Act II ◆ 769

Reinforce and Extend

Answers
◆ LITERATURE AND YOUR LIFE

Reader's Response Students may respond that they liked Anne's courage in the face of danger and her zest for life. She was an ordinary teenager who occasionally rebelled against her mother.

Thematic Focus The world learned about the anguish and stress faced by those in hiding and the terrible consequences of persecution.

☑ Check Your Comprehension

1. Act II begins in January of 1944 and ends with the raid on the Secret Annex and Mr. Frank's visit after the war ends.
2. Anne and Peter become close friends.
3. Mrs. Frank is angry because Mr. Van Daan steals food from the cupboard and breaks trust with the group.
4. The families are captured by the German soldiers.

◆ Critical Thinking

1. As they are eating New Year's Day cake, she talks seriously about her ideals and hopes for life being destroyed.
2. Anne is a very sociable person and being friends with Peter gives her someone to confide in.
3. She still believes that there is hope that the world is only going through a phase and the evil of persecution will pass.
4. Anne still maintained hope, even at the end, and because Mr. Frank could not, he was ashamed.
5. Anne was upset because her parents had already formed their opinions and did not think she should be allowed the same adult choices.
6. The problems Anne faced were real and very serious and it makes it easier to understand and believe what she says.

Beyond the Selection

FURTHER READING
Other Works About Facing Challenges
North to Freedom, Anne Holm
The Tulips Are Red, Leesha Rose
Letters from Westerbork, Etty Hillesum
Farewell to Manzanar, Jeanne W. Houston and James D. Houston

Other Works About the Holocaust
Rescue: The Story of How Gentiles Saved the Jews in the Holocaust, Milton Meltzer
We Are Witnesses: Diaries of Five Teenagers Who Died in the Holocaust, Jacob Boas (ed.)

INTERNET
We suggest the following site on the Internet (all Web sites are subject to change).
For information about World War II:
http://www.grolier.com/wwii/wwii_mainpage.html
For examples of World War II materials such as letters, diaries, and ration coupons:
http://www.fsu.edu/~ww2/pictures.htm
For information about the Dutch Resistance:
http://www.hi.nl/musea/verzetmu.htm
We *strongly recommend* that you preview these sites before you send students to them.

◆ Reading Strategy

1. (a) The vivid descriptions of each person's activity offer a clear visual image of the evening scene. (b) The sound of children playing outside and the pacing of Dussel appeal to the sense of hearing.

2. Mr. Frank calmly reads pages of Anne's diary. He then explains to Miep and Mr. Kraler what happened to his wife and daughters and the others. Once again, he picks up the diary, turns back to a particular passage, and remarks that Anne's deep faith puts him to shame.

◆ Build Vocabulary

Using Forms of *effect*
1. ineffective
2. effective
3. effectiveness

Spelling Strategy
1. fortune
2. actual

Using the Word Bank
1. apprehension
2. stealthily
3. inarticulate
4. sarcastic
5. intuition
6. indignant
7. ineffectually

◆ Literary Focus

1. Anne is lively, bright, teasing, and sensitive.
2. Some people are able to rise to a crisis, remaining strong and optimistic; others are unable to cope.
3. The play reveals that hope and courage can see people through the worst of times.

◆ Build Grammar Skills

Practice
1. makes
2. is
3. know
4. is
5. are

Writing Application
Students' reviews should contain the listed indefinite pronouns and reveal an understanding of the play.

Guide for Responding (continued)

◆ Reading Strategy

ENVISION
As you read a play, the stage directions and your imagination enable you to **envision** the characters, setting, and action. View the play in your mind just as you would on the stage.
1. (a) Which details at the beginning of Act II, Scene 2 call to mind visual images? (b) Which details appeal to your sense of hearing?
2. Describe Mr. Frank's actions throughout Act II, Scene 5.

◆ Build Vocabulary

USING FORMS OF *effect*
Knowing that the word *effect* means "result," define the following words. Then, copy the sentences on your paper. Complete each sentence by writing the correct word.

> effective   effectiveness   ineffective

1. The fever remained because the medicine was _____?_____.
2. She learned her lessons well because her method of studying was _____?_____.
3. The _____?_____ of the play was proved by the audience's enthusiastic applause.

SPELLING STRATEGY
The *choo* sound is sometimes spelled *tu* when the sound occurs in the middle of a word, as in *ineffectual* and *situation*. Unscramble the letters in parentheses to find a word that contains the *choo* sound spelled *tu* that answers each clue. Write the words on your paper.
1. a great amount of money (routfen)
2. something that is real (ltacua)

USING THE WORD BANK
Write the word from the Word Bank that is closest in meaning to the following:
1. fear
2. secretly
3. unintelligible
4. cutting; mocking
5. hunch; inner knowledge
6. resentful
7. uselessly

◆ Literary Focus

CHARACTERIZATION AND THEME IN DRAMA
You learn about the personalities of dramatic characters through **characterization**—what a character says and does, as well as what others say about the characters. Often, a character's thoughts and actions will lead you to the **theme** of the drama, the insight into life revealed by the work.
1. What do you learn about Anne's personality through dialogue?
2. What do the changes in the characters reveal about people's ability to deal with a crisis?
3. What does the play reveal about the nature of hope and courage?

◆ Build Grammar Skills

VERB AGREEMENT WITH INDEFINITE PRONOUNS
A verb must agree with its subject in number. One type of subject that can cause confusion is an **indefinite pronoun,** a pronoun that does not refer to any particular person, place, or thing. The following indefinite pronouns are always singular and, therefore, always take a singular verb: *anybody, anyone, everybody, everyone, nobody, somebody, someone.* The following indefinite pronouns are always plural: *both, few, many, others, several.*

> Everyone is bundled up.... (The singular pronoun *everyone* requires a singular verb form.)

Practice Copy the following sentences, choosing the correct form of the verb to agree with the indefinite pronoun subject.
1. Someone (make, makes) a noise downstairs.
2. Everyone (is, are) on edge, worried about Mr. Kraler.
3. Few (know, knows) about the Franks' place of hiding.
4. Is it possible that anyone (is, are) so silly as to worry . . .
5. Many (is, are) touched by Anne Frank's story.

Writing Application Write a brief review of this play. Use the indefinite pronouns *everyone, someone,* and *anyone* in your paragraph, making sure the subjects and verbs agree.

Writer's Solution

For additional instruction and practice, use the practice page on Special Problems With Subject-Verb Agreement, p. 84, in the *Writer's Solution Grammar Practice Book.* If students have access to technology, have them use the lesson on Agreement With Indefinite Pronouns in the unit on Subject-Verb Agreement on the *Writer's Solution Language Lab CD-ROM.*

Build Your Portfolio

 Idea Bank

Writing

1. **Timeline** Make a timeline of the major events in the play. Write a few sentences that explain what occurs at each of the important points.

2. **Diary Entry** Imagine that you are Miep. Write a diary entry about helping to hide the people in the attic.

3. **Essay** Write an essay telling what important lessons the play offers that people today can apply to their daily lives. Support your points with passages from the play.

Speaking and Listening

4. **Scene [Group Activity]** With classmates, choose a scene from *The Diary of Anne Frank* to perform for the class. Rehearse the scene, and have it videotaped as you perform it. **[Performing Arts Link]**

5. **Dramatic Monologue** Imagine that you are Anne Frank on the day of the fight over the cake. Use passages from the play to help you write and perform a monologue—a dramatic speech—expressing her feelings about the arguments taking place in the attic. **[Performing Arts Link]**

Projects

6. **Book Club** From the library, get a copy of Anne Frank's *The Diary of a Young Girl*. With a group of classmates, hold several book club meetings for the purpose of discussing the diary. Take meeting notes that detail the group's responses. **[Literature Link]**

7. **Holocaust Research [Group Activity]** Working with a group, research information about the Holocaust that occurred during World War II. Find articles, books, maps, and Web sites that will help you. You may wish to write to the National Holocaust Museum in Washington, D.C., for free materials. Present your findings to the class. **[Social Studies Link]**

 Writing Mini-Lesson

Scene With Dialogue

The words that the characters speak in a drama are called **dialogue.** In *The Diary of Anne Frank,* the dialogue reveals characters' personalities and advances the action of the play. Write a dramatic scene that develops a conflict through dialogue.

Writing Skills Focus: Script Format

The **format** of a play script—the way it appears on the page—makes it easier for everyone working on a play to do his or her job. Actors find their lines by looking for the name of their character printed in boldface. Stage directions, which tell about the actors' actions and give important information about the setting, are written in brackets and printed in italics.

Model From the Play
MR. FRANK. Good-bye, Mr. Kraler.
MRS. FRANK. [*Shaking his hand*] How can we thank you?

Prewriting Decide on the subject of your scene, and jot down notes about the characters, the conflict they face, and the setting.

Drafting Draft the scene, introducing the characters and conflict. Weave stage directions into the script. Let your characters reveal themselves through dialogue.

Revising Review your script for correct script format. Then, review your dialogue to make sure it's realistic and that it furthers the audience's knowledge of the characters or furthers the play's action.

> ◆ **Grammar Application**
> If you use any indefinite pronouns, be sure you have used the correct verb form to agree with them.

The Diary of Anne Frank, Act II ◆ 771

 Idea Bank

Following are suggestions for matching the Idea Bank topics with your students' performance levels and learning modalities:

Customize for *Performance Levels*
Less Advanced Students: 2, 4, 7
Average Students: 1, 4, 7
More Advanced Students: 3, 5, 6, 7

Customize for *Learning Modalities:*
Verbal/Linguistic: 2, 3, 4, 5
Visual/Spatial: 1, 7
Logical/Mathematical: 1
Interpersonal: 4, 6, 7
Intrapersonal: 3

 Writing Mini-Lesson

Refer students to the Writing Handbook in the back of the book for instruction on the writing process and for further information on script format.

✐ **Writer's Solution**

Writing Lab CD-ROM
Have students complete the tutorial on Creative Writing. Follow these steps:
1. Have students view the interactive model of a dialogue.
2. Suggest that students use the Emotion Word Bin activity to select words and phrases which correspond with a character's emotions.
3. Have students draft on computer.
4. Encourage students to use the interactive revision dialogue models for examples of how to revise dialogue.

Writer's Solution Sourcebook
Have students use Chapter 8, "Creative Writing," pp. 234–265, for additional support. The chapter includes in-depth instruction on punctuation and formatting dialogue, p. 263.

✓ **ASSESSMENT OPTIONS**

Formal Assessment, Selection Test, pp. 212–214, and Assessment Resources Software. The selection test is designed so that it can be easily customized to the performance levels of your students.
Alternative Assessment, p. 48, includes options for less advanced students, more advanced students, interpersonal learners, visual/spatial learners, and verbal/linguistic learners.

PORTFOLIO ASSESSMENT
Use the following rubrics in the **Alternative Assessment** booklet to assess student writing:
Timeline: Summary, p. 94
Diary Entry: Expression, p. 90
Essay: Literary Analysis/Interpretation, p. 108
Writing Mini-Lesson: Drama, p. 105

OBJECTIVES

1. To read, comprehend, and interpret a drama that has a social studies focus
2. To relate a drama with a social studies focus to personal experience
3. To connect literature to social studies
4. To respond to Social Studies Guiding Questions
5. To respond to the drama through writing, speaking and listening, and projects

SOCIAL STUDIES GUIDING QUESTIONS

Reading about the tensions of the Cold War will help students discover answers to these Guiding Questions:

- What can we learn from events during the Cold War about the dangers of nuclear weapons?
- How can treaties help avoid the threat of a nuclear war?

Ask students to think of how two children react to each other when they want to play with the same toy at the same time. Have students freewrite for five minutes describing the actions and reactions each child might have and the negotiations they might use in order to play with the same toy. Encourage students to examine the action a parent of one of the children might take. Ask students to consider how the negotiations might change if one of the children picks up a large stick. Have students predict whether or not the children will fight. Introduce the drama by explaining that *A Walk in the Woods* portrays Cold War treaty and arms negotiations between representatives of the U. S. and the Soviet Union.

Map Study

Political Maps Students gain a better understanding of events and places when they are able to make connections between geography and historical events. With the help of the map on this page, students can determine which countries were allies of the U. S. and which were allies of the Soviet Union during the Cold War. Have students read the information about alliances on this page.

CONNECTING LITERATURE TO SOCIAL STUDIES
THE COLD WAR

from *A Walk in the Woods* by Lee Blessing

The Cold War in Europe

NATO, 1955	Warsaw Pact, 1955	Nonaligned nations	Areas added to the Soviet Union after World War II

THE COLD WAR During World War II, the United States and the Soviet Union were allies. After the war, however, tension developed between the two countries over governmental philosophies and practices. Before long, the two countries were threatening each other with nuclear weapons that could kill millions of people.

Nuclear Weapons The atomic bomb was developed during World War II. The first atomic bomb was dropped on Hiroshima, Japan, in August 1945. The destruction was horrifying. After the war, the Soviet Union announced that it, too, had developed an atomic bomb. This was the beginning of the "arms race," as each country tried to make more bombs than its enemy.

Opposing Alliances Countries in Europe aligned themselves with either the Soviet Union or the United States. The map on this page shows which countries were part of the North Atlantic Treaty Organization (NATO), aligned with the United States; which were part of the Warsaw Pact, aligned with the Soviet Union; and which were unaligned.

A Timely Play When *A Walk in the Woods* was first produced, in 1987, the Cold War had been going on for decades, and the arms race was still raging. The two characters in the play represent the governments of the Soviet Union and the United States. They have been meeting off and on for years to try to negotiate an arms reduction treaty, which would lessen the threat of a nuclear war.

772 ◆ *Drama*

 Prentice Hall Literature Program Resources

REINFORCE / RETEACH / EXTEND
Selection Support Pages
Build Vocabulary, p. 262
Connecting Literature to Social Studies, p. 263
Formal Assessment Selection Test, pp. 215–216, Assessment Resources Software
Readings From Social Studies
Writing and Language Transparencies
Series of Events Chain, p. 57
Resource Pro CD-ROM "The Cold War" from *A Walk in the Woods*

 Listening to Literature Audiocassettes
"The Cold War" from *A Walk in the Woods*

Connection to Prentice Hall World Explorer
Eastern Hemisphere
Ch. 7, "Europe and Russia Shaped by History," pp. 191–192
Ch. 9, "Exploring Western Europe," pp. 257–259
Western Hemisphere
Ch. 7, "The United States and Canada: Shaped by History," p. 176

from A Walk in the Woods

Lee Blessing

HONEYMAN. Why did your government delay so long? What was it about the proposal you objected to? . . .

* * *

BOTVINNIK. Nothing. We liked the whole proposal.

HONEYMAN. I don't understand. You liked it?

BOTVINNIK. Very much.

HONEYMAN. Then why did you delay so long?

BOTVINNIK. Because your proposal was . . . too good.

HONEYMAN. Too good?

BOTVINNIK. It could have led to real arms reductions. Serious ones.

HONEYMAN. Don't you want that?

BOTVINNIK. Of course. But . . . also we are afraid of it.

HONEYMAN. Why? It's a treaty. We've made treaties before.

BOTVINNIK. Look at those treaties, John. They aren't treaties—they're blueprints. We determine what weapons we'll build in the next few years, then agree to let each other build them. We get rid of small systems so that we can keep bigger ones. We trade obsolete technology for state-of-the-art, we take weapons out of Europe so we can put up new ones in space. Then we say to the world, "See? We are capable of restraint. Here is a small step forward." It is laughable.

HONEYMAN. But it is a step forward. Every treaty is. Each time we come—stumbling—to some sort of agreement, even if it's self-serving, even if it's flawed . . . that's progress.

BOTVINNIK. It is not progress to take a step and slide back three. Every ten years we wake up and say, "It is time to take the first step." But meanwhile we have spent a decade creating bargaining chips—new weapons built expressly so they can be bargained away later. And what is the result? We build and get rid of bargaining chips. Nothing more. The real arsenals remain untouched. In fact, they grow.

HONEYMAN. You're right. Each year, each month, each day someone is proposing a new weapons system. Someone is securing a grant for more research, dreaming up a new technology that will do God-knows-what destruction—to our economies, if nothing else. How, knowing that, can we let any opportunity slip through our fingers? Especially this opportunity, this treaty, these comprehensive reductions. These *real* reductions.

BOTVINNIK. I know, I know. But we have problems with reductions such as these.

HONEYMAN. What are they?

BOTVINNIK. We don't trust you.

HONEYMAN. You don't trust us?

BOTVINNIK. Do you trust *us*?

HONEYMAN. Yes. Well—we try to. But whether we trust each other or not, the proposal has provisions. It has safeguards.

BOTVINNIK. We don't trust the safeguards.

> **Connecting Literature to Social Studies**
> What role does "trust" play in negotiations between nations? ➊

from *A Walk in the Woods* ◆ 773

Preparing for Standardized Tests

Punctuation As students prepare for standardized tests, they must be able to punctuate and recognize correctly punctuated paragraphs and sentences that contain dialogue. Challenge students to change the first four lines of dramatic dialogue in "The Cold War" from *A Walk in the Woods* to paragraph format. Remind students that they must properly use quotation marks, end punctuation, and capital letters, and remember to add *he said* clarifying words to the paragraph in order to maintain precision. The following is an example of how students might write the paragraph.

Honeyman asked Botvinnik, "Why did your government delay so long? What was it about the proposal you objected to?" Botvinnik replied, "Nothing. We liked the whole proposal." "I don't understand," Honeyman said. "You liked it?" Botvinnik replied, "Very much."

Point out to students that they may choose to divide lengthy dialogue comments with a *he said* addition in the middle, but it must be punctuated differently if they choose to do so.

Clarification

① Star Wars, more properly known as SDI or Strategic Defense Initiative, is a U. S. plan to devise a high-technology satellite-based system that can defend against nuclear missile threat.

Links Across Time

② During the Cold War, the U. S. built underground "silos" for missiles deep below the states of Arizona, Kansas, and Arkansas. After the SALT treaty called for removal of the missiles, the Air Force removed the warheads and sold the silos. Some silos were filled, or used to store crops and other materials. One Kansas county turned a silo into a school. In 1984, a family bought a silo and built a home inside. The family paid $40,000 for the silo. Originally, it had cost the American people $4 million to build. A silo in Green Valley, Arizona, has been opened to the public as a museum. Visitors wearing hard hats can tour the silo, see a deactivated missile capsule, and learn about the history of the Titan missile program and the tensions of the Cold War.

Reinforce and Extend

Answers

◆ LITERATURE AND YOUR LIFE

Reader's Response Many students will agree with Botvinnik that a lasting treaty preventing nuclear arms races will never become a reality.

Thematic Focus They faced a serious lack of trust as well as the threat of aggression from other countries.

☑ Check Your Comprehension

1. He complains that the country's leaders want only the appearance of hope for lasting peace, not an actual workable treaty.
2. His country is afraid that the U. S. might be secretly designing new technology that is not covered by the treaty proposal; therefore, they cannot trust an agreement.

More About the Author

Lee Blessing has written a number of plays, beginning with *Independence,* written in 1983. His play *Fortinbras,* a commissioned work written in 1991, was highly praised by critics as a "wicked comedy" that picked up William Shakespeare's *Hamlet* characters and continued the story.

HONEYMAN. There are checks on the safeguards. Verifications.

BOTVINNIK. We don't trust them.

HONEYMAN. Andrey . . .

BOTVINNIK. Even if there were checks on the checks on the checks, we wouldn't trust them.

HONEYMAN. Why not?

BOTVINNIK. Because we don't trust *you.* Who knows what you are making right now that lies outside this proposal?

HONEYMAN. We're not making any . . .

BOTVINNIK. Multiple warheads, Star Wars—these things came *after* treaties were signed, not before.

HONEYMAN. We can control new technologies. Together.

BOTVINNIK. Can we? How can you be sure of what's going on in your own country right now? Do you think they tell you everything? Face it, John—you can't even completely trust *your* side. And you want to trust ours?

HONEYMAN. We *can* work . . .

BOTVINNIK. Suppose we sign an agreement, and the next day you—or we—suddenly unveil a new weapon. What happens? Immediately, a new arms race.

HONEYMAN. Even if you're right—you're not, but even if you were . . .

BOTVINNIK. I am right. I am always right. And how do we appear to the rest of the world? As two warmongers who can't keep a treaty. If, however, we have never agreed to a treaty, then when a new technology comes along, we are simply two nations who are trying to make a treaty, but who must remain prepared for war. It creates a much better impression.

HONEYMAN. Looking for peace, and purposely never finding it?

BOTVINNIK. [*Taking out his eyedrops, applying them.*] It is better for everyone. Broken treaties make people too nervous, yes?

HONEYMAN. So this makes your job and my job—what? Sort of a nuclear night light? Providing no real hope, just . . .

BOTVINNIK. The appearance. Yes.

HONEYMAN. This is what you truly think is preferable?

BOTVINNIK. Not I. My leaders. Your leaders.

HONEYMAN. How long do you—do they—think this is supposed to go on?

BOTVINNIK. [*Shrugging, putting away his eyedrops.*] Until the world ends.

Meet the Author

Lee Blessing (1949–   ) has been writing plays since he was in college. *A Walk in the Woods* was first performed at Yale University. In 1987, it became the first of Blessing's plays to be produced on Broadway.

Guide for Responding

◆ LITERATURE AND YOUR LIFE

Reader's Response Is Botvinnik's pessimistic view of his job justified? Explain.

Thematic Focus What kind of conflicts and challenges did diplomats like Botvinnik and Honeyman face during the Cold War?

☑ Check Your Comprehension

1. What fault did the Soviets find with the treaty proposal?
2. What reason does Botvinnik give for not trusting any promises made by Americans?

774 ◆ *Drama*

Block Scheduling Strategies

Consider these suggestions to take advantage of extended class time:

• Before reading the dramatic selection, discuss with students the information about the Cold War on p. 772—as an introduction and to provide background for understanding the arms race and the development of deadly nuclear weapons—as well as the dialogue of the scene.

• Have students read the map information on p. 772 and study the political map that appears on that page, detailing the alliances between countries during the Cold War.

• Students can use a Series of Events Chain, p. 57, **Writing and Language Transparencies,** to organize the events of the Cold War, detailing what led to it and what has happened since.

• Have students read the selection independently and answer the Guide for Responding questions on pp. 774–775, then discuss their answers in small groups.

• Have students prepare and rehearse the Dramatic Reading activity from Speaking and Listening on p. 775 and present their reading to the class.

◆ Critical Thinking

INTERPRET

1. What is each man's goal in the ongoing negotiations? **[Compare and Contrast]**
2. What feature would a plan need in order to satisfy Botvinnik and his superiors? **[Deduce]**
3. What do you think Botvinnik means by the last line? **[Interpret]**

EVALUATE

4. How well does Blessing convey the personalities of the two characters? **[Assess]**

EXTEND

5. What sort of relationship do the United States and Russia (formerly a part of the Soviet Union) share today? **[Social Studies Link]**

CONNECTING LITERATURE TO SOCIAL STUDIES

This play provides a "behind-the-scenes" look at how governments work. At the same time, it puts a human face on those diplomats who negotiate with their counterparts in "enemy" countries. Lastly, *A Walk in the Woods* is full of ironic humor, as the efforts of Botvinnik and Honeyman to create a workable treaty are defeated time and time again.

1. Why might the Soviet government be "afraid" of arms reductions?
2. Why doesn't Botvinnik feel the treaties are useful?
3. Why does neither government trust the other?
4. Why do you think it was important for it to "appear" as if the United States and the Soviet Union were working toward a treaty?

Idea Bank

Writing

1. **Description** Based on this scene, write a description of either Honeyman or Botvinnik.
2. **Reporter's Questions** Imagine that Botvinnik and Honeyman will hold a press conference after their walk in the woods. As a reporter, write a series of questions you might ask either or both of them.
3. **Official Report** Write a summary of the conversation that either Botvinnik or Honeyman might submit to his superiors about the progress they've made.

Speaking and Listening

4. **Dramatic Reading [Group Activity]** With a partner, rehearse this scene and perform it for the class. Videotape the performance, and view it afterwards. **[Performing Arts Link]**

Project

5. **Maps** Since the time of the Cold War, the Soviet Union has disbanded. Do research and create a map that shows the Soviet Union as it was in 1980. Then, create a map showing the nations of the former Soviet Union today.

Further Reading, Listening, and Viewing

- Lee Blessing's *A Walk in the Woods* is the full-length play from which this excerpt was taken.
- Victoria Sherrow's *Joseph McCarthy and the Cold War* shows how the Cold War sparked a "witch hunt" for communists.
- *The Cold War* is a television documentary originally aired in 1998.

from *A Walk in the Woods* ◆ 775

 Idea Bank

Following are suggestions for matching the Idea Bank topics with your students' performance levels and learning modalities:

Customize for *Performance Levels*

Less Advanced Students: 1, 4, 5
Average Students: 2, 4, 5
More Advanced Students: 1, 3, 5

Customize for *Learning Modalities*

Verbal/Linguistic: 1, 2, 3, 4
Visual/Spatial: 5
Logical/Mathematical: 5
Intrapersonal: 1, 3, 5
Interpersonal: 2, 4

Answers (continued)

◆ Critical Thinking

1. Each man wants to negotiate the best treaty for his country.
2. It would need guarantees that new technology wasn't being developed.
3. He is pessimistic and thinks that the world will end in a nuclear war.
4. Students will probably think each character portrays his country's beliefs and fears realistically.
5. The relationship between Russia and the United States continues to change as leadership and politics change.

CONNECTING LITERATURE TO SOCIAL STUDIES

1. They might be afraid because of the threat from other countries; they don't trust the United States not to develop weapon technology outside of the treaty terms.
2. Broken treaties make people nervous; the countries look untrustworthy to the world community.
3. Each country thinks the other might do something dishonest.
4. They appear to be trying to create peace so the rest of the world doesn't think they are warmongers.

Establish Writing Guidelines

Review the following key characteristics of a video script:

- A video script is a script for a performance on film rather than before a live audience.
- A video script includes realistic dialogue, stage directions, and technical directions for camera work.
- A video script should follow an appropriate script format.

You may want to distribute the scoring rubric for Drama, p. 105 in **Alternative Assessment,** to make students aware of the criteria on which they will be evaluated. See the suggestions on p. 778 for how to customize the rubric to this workshop.

Refer students to the Writing Handbook in the back of the book for instruction on the writing process and further information on creative writing.

 Writer's Solution

Writers at Work Videodisc

To introduce students to creative writing and to show them how writer Julia Alvarez gets her ideas for creative writing, play the videodisc segment on Creative Writing (Ch. 8). Ask students to listen for how Alvarez answers the question "What is creative writing?"

Play frames 19343 to 27848

Writing Lab CD-ROM

If your students have access to computers, you may have them work in the tutorial on Creative Writing to complete all or part of their video scripts. Follow these steps:

1. Have students view the interactive model of a screenplay to see a basic script format.
2. Suggest that students view the interactive dialogue models to see examples of dialogue a character might use in a scene.
3. Allow students to draft on computer.
4. When revising, have students use the Proofreading Checklist for plays.

Writer's Solution Sourcebook

Students can find additional support, including in-depth instruction on drafting a play, p. 258, in the chapter on Creative Writing, pp. 234–265.

Plays are written to be performed on stage. When you read a play, you are reading the script that actors and directors use to create a performance. Some performances are done for film rather than for a live audience. Actors in those performances use a video script. A video script includes dialogue and instructions to actors, but it is meant to be performed in front of a camera. Write a one-scene video script of an eventful day in your life. In addition to dialogue, include the directions for actors' movements, sound, lighting, and camera angles.

The following skills will help you write a video script:

Writing Skills Focus

▶ **Use a script format.** To show that a character is speaking, write the character's name followed by a colon or period. Write directions for lights, sound, camera angles, and actors' movements in italics, if you are writing with a computer, and enclose them in brackets. (See p. 771.)

▶ **Use realistic dialogue** to create believable characters.

The following excerpt from *The Diary of Anne Frank* shows some features found in video scripts.

MODEL FROM LITERATURE

from The Diary of Anne Frank

MR. FRANK. ① [*Quietly*] Anne's diary. [*He opens the diary and begins to read.*] "Monday, the sixth of July, nineteen forty-two." [*To* MIEP] Nineteen forty-two. Is it possible, Miep? . . . Only three years ago. ② [*As he continues his reading, he sits down on the couch.*] ③ "Dear Diary, since you and I are going to be great friends, I will start by telling you about myself. My name is Anne Frank. I am thirteen years old. . . ."

① The character's name precedes the words he speaks.

② Mr. Frank's remarks reveal his shock that so many terrible things have happened in just three years.

③ Directions appear in italics and brackets.

776 ◆ Drama

 Humanities: Drama

Screenplays Explain to students that most of the entertainment they watch begins with an idea that is turned into a script. TV programs and movies are written in script format, called screenplays. Screenplays can be written exclusively for filming, or they can be adapted from other media, such as plays or novels. A good screenplay should include realistic dialogue, as well as essential information on settings, props, and movement. The decisions for lighting and camera angles are usually made by the director, the person in charge of the artistic production of the film.

Have students research screenplays. Scripts of current and classic movies often are available in bookstores or through the Internet. Suggest to students that they view a scene from a TV program or film more than once and write a screenplay for that scene. Remind them to include information on props, movement, and settings, as well as the dialogue the characters speak.

Prewriting

Choose the Scene For your scene, choose a day in your life that was memorable. It could be a winning game, a day trip taken with your family, the program where you won an award, the first time you went to a large city, and so on. Write down answers to *who, when,* and *where.* You can fictionalize events and add new characters to make the scene interesting.

Develop Each Character In a dramatic scene, you reveal the personalities of characters through their dialogue and actions, as well as through the comments and behavior of other characters. Fill out a chart like the one below for each character, choosing details that help you imagine how your characters will look, sound, and act.

CHARACTER'S NAME: _____	
Male or female:	Age:
Hair and eyes:	Physical type:
Clothes:	Personality:
Favorite foods:	Favorite activities:
What he/she wants:	What he/she dislikes:

Use this information to guide you in writing appropriate dialogue and coming up with actions and events that would be performed by a person with these characteristics. For example, a character's heroism can be revealed to the audience when he or she helps an elderly person or takes responsibility for a mistake. A character's personality can also be revealed when other characters discuss the heroic or brave act.

Drafting

Create Realistic Dialogue Review the format of dialogue in *The Diary of Anne Frank* and *A Walk in the Woods.* Use it as a model for formatting your dialogue. As you develop your dialogue, keep in mind how people actually speak. Conversational language may include slang, contractions, and incomplete sentences.

Include Stage and Camera Directions Provide instructions that describe the actors' delivery, settings, costumes, and movements. Also, include directions that indicate camera shots, such as INT for an interior shot (filmed indoors) and EXT for an exterior shot (filmed outdoors).

Writing Process Workshop

APPLYING LANGUAGE SKILLS: Using Pronouns Correctly

Directions in a video script often include pronouns. Personal pronouns have different forms, or cases, that reflect how they are used in a sentence.

Subjective case:
[*He answers the phone. It is she.*]

Objective Case:
[*The phone call is for him. He then gives her the phone. The caller tells her about the meeting.*]

Practice On your paper, write the following stage directions, choosing the correct pronoun.

[EXT. VERONA PARK. *Sean runs across the field to (she, her). (She, Her) then turns to pick (he, him) up. After (he, him) kisses (she, her), the little boy and his mother leave holding hands.*]

Writing Application As you write your video script, make sure that all your personal pronouns are in the correct case.

Writer's Solution Connection Writing Lab

For help with a topic, use the Inspirations Browser in the Creative Writing tutorial.

Develop Student Writing

Prewriting

Tell students that when writing a short scene for a video script, they may want to concentrate on a small number of characters, rather than a large group of characters. The fewer characters there are, the more chances each character has to speak or act, thereby revealing his or her true nature.

Customize for *Less Proficient Writers*

Some students may do better working in pairs on a video script. Have students pair up with another student and work as a script-writing team. Before they begin drafting, they should discuss the action that will take place in their scenes and the characters who will perform that action. As they write their drafts, have partners confer with each other about different dialogue options for each character.

Drafting

Explain to students that they probably want to include specific instructions for their settings, where different actions take place. For example, rather than just writing [INT] for an interior shot, they may want to write [INT-KITCHEN-NIGHT] to explain that this scene takes place at night in a kitchen.

Writer's Solution

Writing Lab CD-ROM

In the drafting section on the tutorial for Creative Writing, suggest that students view the video clip and annotated model on setting and stage directions. Students will see how stage directions can explain the setting, the lights, the camera, and the movement of the characters.

Applying Language Skills

Using Pronouns Correctly Explain to students that pronouns also have a possessive case, which shows ownership. For example, in the following sentence *his* is a possessive pronoun: Tom lost *his* mittens. The pronoun *his* shows that the mittens belong to Tom.

Answers
[EXT. VERONA PARK. *Sean runs across the field to her. She then turns to pick him up. After he kisses her, the little boy and his mother leave holding hands.*]

Writer's Solution

For additional instruction and practice, have students use the practice page on Cases of Personal Pronouns, pp. 77–79, in the *Writer's Solution Grammar Practice Book.* If students have access to technology, they can use the lesson on Pronoun Case in the Pronouns unit on the *Writer's Solution Language Lab CD-ROM.*

Revising

Partners might read their dialogue aloud to note where it needs work.

 Writer's Solution

Writing Lab CD-ROM
In the revising section of the tutorial on Creative Writing, students can use the annotated model from literature on formatting and punctuation in plays.

Publishing

Suggest that students publish an anthology of video scripts. Encourage them to add illustrations or other visuals, as appropriate.

Reinforce and Extend

Review the Writing Guidelines
After students have completed their writing, review the characteristics of a video script.

Applying Language Skills
Avoiding Double Negatives
Explain to students that negative words also include the words *barely, hardly,* and *scarcely.* When these words are used in a sentence, the sentence should not contain any other negative words.

Answers
1. The detective couldn't find any proof.
2. You shouldn't go anywhere in this storm.
3. I don't want to hear any of your excuses.

 Writer's Solution

For more instruction, use the page on Double Negatives, p. 91, in the *Writer's Solution Grammar Practice Book.*

WRITING PROCESS WORKSHOP

EDITING/PROOFREADING

APPLYING LANGUAGE SKILLS: Avoiding Double Negatives

In math, two negatives make a positive. In writing, if you want to express a negative idea, use only one negative word.

Negative Words: *not, never, no, none, nothing, nowhere*

Contractions including *not* are also negative, such as *didn't, wouldn't, don't,* and *can't.*

Double Negative:
I *don't* want *no* popcorn.

Revised:
I *don't* want *any* popcorn.

Practice Write the following sentences, correcting the double negatives.

1. The detective couldn't find no proof.
2. You shouldn't go nowhere in this storm.
3. I don't want to hear none of your excuses.

Writing Application As you write, avoid double negatives unless you want to show a character speaking in non-standard English.

Writer's Solution Connection
Language Lab

For more practice identifying and correcting double negatives, complete the Using Modifiers lesson, in the Using Modifiers unit.

778 ◆ *Drama*

Revising

Read It Aloud When you have completed your draft, read the dialogue aloud. Then, ask yourself whether it sounds realistic. Does this sound like something this character would say? If the dialogue sounds too stiff, revise it to include aspects of everyday speech, such as contractions or incomplete sentences. If your dialogue does not sound appropriate to your characters, review your character chart. Then, choose words that indicate your character's personality.

Make a Test Run Ask a few classmates to act out your scene. If they are confused by camera directions or perform the scene differently than you intended, revise the problem areas to clearly and concisely communicate your vision.

REVISION MODEL

① [INT. LIVING ROOM.]

② I'm
LARA. ~~I am~~ so excited about going to see *Phantom of the* ② How did you ever get these tickets? *Opera.*

③ [*Winks and smiles*]
GARY. I have my ways.

① The writer adds this camera direction so that the crew will know where to shoot the scene.
② The writer changes *I am* to the contraction *I'm* to make the dialogue sound more conversational.
③ This stage direction, which appears in italics in brackets, helps reveal Gary's good-natured personality.

Publishing and Presenting

Videotape Share your work with an audience by capturing it on videotape. Follow these suggestions to record your production:
▶ Use the directions to guide actors, set designers, and camera operators.
▶ Have your cast rehearse the scene. Plan and practice where actors will stand, how they will move, and where the camera will be in each scene. Run through the action a few times before filming.
▶ Don't take technology for granted. Make sure that the camera operator is skilled in using the equipment.

Real-World Reading Skills Workshop

Reading Visuals

Introduce the Strategies

Ask students to describe any experiences they have had with reading visuals. Students may have had workshops in their social studies classes about interpreting timelines, charts, and graphs. Ask them how a visual can help a reader more fully understand a text.

Strategies for Success

Illustrations, photographs, maps, charts, and graphs are types of visuals that support the written text of the article, story, poem, play, or chapter in which they appear. Learn to use visuals to improve your reading performance:

Preview the Visuals Before reading, examine the visuals. Ask yourself:

▶ What information do they provide?

▶ How do they relate to the title of the work?

▶ Does information in the captions explain the visuals?

▶ What mood does a piece of art set?

Previewing the visuals will help you understand what you are about to read.

Make the Connections Think of visuals as extensions of the text rather than something separate. As you read, refer to the visuals, and make connections between what you are reading and the visual information. After you have finished reading, ask yourself: What do the visuals add to what I have read?

A visual can add humor, set a mood, give background on a period of history, provide statistical information, give the geographical location, or illustrate something in the text.

Apply the Strategies

Examine the visuals on the page at right from an American history textbook. Then, answer the questions that follow.

✔ Here are other texts in which visual clues might provide additional information:

▶ Cookbooks

▶ Instruction manuals

▶ Magazine articles

A Search for Peace and Prosperity 10

(1919–1928)

Chapter Outline   Readings, page 503

1 The Rocky Road to Peacetime

2 The Politics of Normalcy

3 Calvin Coolidge and the Business of America

When the World War ended on November 11, 1918, Americans jubilantly looked forward to better times. After a period of fighting abroad and new government regulations at home, many yearned for calmer, more familiar times. Instead, they entered a decade of startling, bewildering change. The 1920s opened with labor unrest, social turmoil, and widespread panic about the possible effect of the Russian Revolution on the United States.

In such turbulent times, voters turned to politicians who promised calm and a return to prewar order. Business became the symbol of that order. Americans seemed worn out by crusades for peace abroad and reform at home. Many were far more concerned with gaining a bigger share of the "good life" for themselves.

Yet while newspapers wrote of rich movie stars and fancy new cars, many Americans struggled just to earn enough to eat. The prosperity of the Roaring Twenties masked underlying economic problems.

Flag Day by Childe Hassam

Politics of "normalcy"

1918	1920	1922	1924	1926	1928
1919 Labor unrest; Red Scare begins	**1920** Warren G. Harding elected President	**1923** Calvin Coolidge succeeds Harding	**1924** Immigration Act passed	**1926** Revenue Act passed	**1928** Coolidge vetoes McNary-Haugen bill

196

1. What does the painting suggest about the outcome of American involvement in World War I? What mood does it set?

2. How does the timeline support the chapter outline?

3. Which presidents were in office during the time period the chapter covers?

4. What important acts were passed between 1918 and 1928?

5. Why might a writer provide these visuals with the written text?

Customize for
Visual/Spatial Learners

Students who are aware of their capacity as visual/spatial learners may want to volunteer their experiences reading visuals. Encourage students to explain how they may use sketches or illustrations to understand texts or study for tests.

Customize for
English Language Learners

Explain to students that often, seeing a picture of something is easier to understand than reading an elaborate description of it. Find an entry in the dictionary that has an accompanying picture. First, read the definition to students. Then, show students the picture. Ask students to explain which they found more helpful—the picture or the worded definition.

Apply the Strategies

Have students look at the visuals on the page, and then have them read the accompanying text to get a better idea of what the page describes.

Answers

Possible responses:

1. The painting suggests that the Americans triumphed in the outcome of World War I. The painting suggests a joyous mood, one of celebration and victory because of the multitudes of hanging flags.

2. The timeline supports the chapter outline by placing the major events of the nine years in a linear form. The timeline gives precise dates in years and shows a visual representation of how long each event lasted.

3. Warren G. Harding and Calvin Coolidge were the two presidents in office during the time of 1919–1928.

4. Important acts passed between 1918 and 1928 include the Immigrations Act and the Revenue Act.

5. A writer might provide these visuals to strike a mood, to provide additional information, or to explain the information in a given way.

◆ Build Grammar Skills

Reviewing Complements

The selections in Part I include instruction on the following:

- Subject and Verb Agreement
- Verb Agreement With Indefinite Pronouns

This instruction is reinforced with the Build Grammar Skills practice pages in **Selection Support**, pp. 254 and 259.

As you review subject and verb agreement, you may wish to include the following:

- Agreement With Compound Subjects

There are four rules to remember when dealing with subject and verb agreement with compound subjects.

1. If both parts of a compound subject are singular and are joined by *or* or *nor,* a singular verb must be used. For example: A dog or a cat is a great companion.
2. If both parts of a compound subject are plural and are connected by *or* or *nor,* a plural verb must be used. For example: Neither the daisies nor the tulips are to be watered tomorrow.
3. If one part of a compound subject is plural and the other part is singular, and they are joined by *or* or *nor,* the verb must agree with the subject nearest to it in the sentence. For example: Neither Joey nor the twins are coming.
4. All compound subjects joined by *and* take a plural verb. For example: Both the car and the truck fit in the garage.

- Agreement With Collective Nouns

If a collective noun names a group acting as a single unit, use a singular verb. For example:
The team wins the meet.
If a collective noun names a group acting as individuals with different points of view, use a plural verb. For example:
The family are in agreement on where to eat dinner.

Subject and Verb Agreement

Grammar Review

The **verb** in a sentence or clause must **agree** with its subject in number (singular or plural). Verbs in the present tense change form to agree with a singular or plural subject. (See p. 745.) Notice how the verbs change in the following examples to agree with a singular or a plural subject:

Singular: "The *curtain falls* on the scene."

Plural: "The *curtains fall* on the scene"

Verbs that end in -s or -es agree with singular subjects. Verbs that do not end with -s or -es agree with plural subjects.

A **subject** may be an indefinite pronoun, which is a pronoun that does not refer to any particular person, place, or thing. Some indefinite pronouns are always singular, some are always plural, and some can be either. The verb in a sentence must agree in number with the number of the indefinite pronoun. (See p. 770.) The following chart lists the indefinite pronouns that are singular, plural, or either:

Singular:	another, anybody, anyone, each, either, everybody, everyone, everything, much, neither, nobody, no one, nothing, one, somebody, something "*Everyone watches* intently. . . ."
Plural:	both, few, many, others, several *Both* of the men *remain* quiet.
Singular or Plural:	all, any, more, most, none, some **Singular:** *Most* of the day *is spent* studying. **Plural:** *Most* of the children *miss* their "old life."

Practice 1 Write the following sentences, choosing the verb that agrees with the subject.

1. Mr. Frank (look, looks) around the rooms where they hid.
2. Anne's diary (record, records) the days spent in hiding.
3. The police (search, searches) house by house.
4. Margot and Anne (dance, dances) to the music.
5. The ration cards (fall, falls) to the ground.

Practice 2 Write the following sentences, choosing the verb that agrees with the subject.

1. Neither of the two cats (like, likes) Mr. Dussel.
2. Most of the food (was, were) eaten.
3. Someone (know, knows) we're up here, hiding!
4. Each of the girls (listen, listens) for noises.
5. Others (seem, seems) too frightened to live silently in an attic.

Grammar in Writing

✔ To make verbs agree, identify the subject and the verb of the sentence. Be sure the verb agrees with the subject, not with another word in the sentence.

Answers
Practice I

1. Mr. Frank *looks* around the rooms where they hid.
2. Anne's diary *records* the days spent in hiding.
3. The police *search* house by house.
4. Margot and Anne *dance* to the music.
5. The ration cards *fall* to the ground.

Practice 2

1. Neither of the two cats *likes* Mr. Dussel.
2. Most of the food *was* eaten.
3. Someone *knows* we're up here, hiding!
4. Each of the girls *listens* for noises.
5. Others *seem* too frightened to live silently in an attic.

PART **2**   *Scenes and Soliloquies*

The Singer Faure as Hamlet, Edouard Manet, Kunsthalle, Hamburg, Germany/A.K.G., Berlin

Scenes and Soliloquies ◆ 781

The Singer Faure as Hamlet, by Edouard Manet

Edouard Manet (1832–1883) was a French painter, often thought of as a founder of modern painting. Born in Paris, he joined the navy and spent two months in Rio de Janeiro, where he made innumerable sketches. His early formal studies included copying the old masters from museums in Europe.

Some of Manet's works caused scandal within the formalized artistic society in France at the time. Manet mostly painted

the human figure in accurately realistic settings, but his treatment of some of these figures caused some disturbances.

The Singer Faure as Hamlet is a portrait of the baritone singer Jean-Baptiste Faure (1830–1914), painted by Manet as a remembrance of his last performance in the opera in 1880. The opera was *Hamlet*, based on the William Shakespeare play, by Ambroise Thomas. Faure was an avid supporter of the arts, whose art collection at one time included works by Manet, Degas, Sisley, and Renoir.

1. What do you think the man is doing in the painting? *Students may say his posture indicates he is addressing the audience. Or, they may say that because of the way he holds his sword to the ground and the hand away from him, he is preparing to fight.*

2. Would you rather hear an opera or see a play? Why? *Students who think they would prefer opera may say so because of the added interest level of the music. Others may feel that plays, such as Shakespeare's, should not be set to music.*

The selections in this section are examples of scenes and soliloquies from plays by William Shakespeare. The scene from *A Midsummer Night's Dream* details the bewitchment of Demetrius and Lysander and the confusion it presents for their past and present loves, Hermia and Helena. The soliloquy from *Much Ado About Nothing* is given by Benedick and explains his conflicting feelings toward love. The soliloquy from *The Life and Death of King Richard III* is a well-known speech in which King Richard plots to overthrow the throne.

Customize for
Varying Student Needs

When assigning the selections in this section to your students, keep in mind the following factors:

from *A Midsummer Night's Dream*

from *Much Ado About Nothing*

from *The Life and Death of King Richard III*

- Introduction to the dramatic style of Shakespeare
- The vocabulary and language will be difficult for all but the most advanced students
- Students may benefit from a line-by-line reading or performance
- The theme of relationships in all three pieces may be accessible to students

 Guide for Reading

Meet the Author:

William Shakespeare (1564–1616)

Widely regarded as one of the best writers of all time, William Shakespeare wrote plays and poems that are among the best in the English language. They endure through the years because of his insight into human nature, his ability to lighten the tragic with the humorous, and his portrayal of kings and scoundrels with equal understanding.

A Life in the Theater Shakespeare was a part owner of the Lord Chamberlain's Men of London, a theater company that built and then performed in the Globe theater, located on the south bank of the Thames River. He sometimes performed in the plays, but it was as a playwright that he became famous. His thirty-seven plays continue to be performed throughout the world.

THE STORY BEHIND THE PLAYS
In *A Midsummer Night's Dream,* Shakespeare added new inventions to tales that would have been familiar to his audiences. The lovesick quartet, who serve as the play's main characters, may have been inspired by Geoffrey Chaucer's "Knight's Tale" from *The Canterbury Tales.*

The Life and Death of King Richard III is based loosely on the reign of this king of England.

Much Ado About Nothing is a romantic comedy whose plot echoes Edmund Spenser's *Faerie Queene,* Book II, Canto 4.

782 ◆ *Drama*

◆ LITERATURE AND YOUR LIFE

CONNECT YOUR EXPERIENCE

In recent years, Shakespeare's *Romeo and Juliet, Hamlet,* and *Much Ado About Nothing* have been made into major motion pictures, inspiring a new generation of fans. If you were to make a movie based on a Shakespearean tale, how would you attract a modern audience?

THEMATIC FOCUS: Relationships

As you read these scenes from Shakespeare's plays, look for his insights into human relationships.

◆ Background for Understanding

CULTURE

Shakespeare's plays were performed in open-air theaters in London. The most famous theater was the Globe, a three-tiered circle of seats surrounding a central area called the pit. The audience stood in the pit or sat on benches in the gallery. The arrangement was somewhat like a modern stadium, only much smaller.

Plays were staged with very little scenery, and, because they were performed in daylight, no lighting was used. To provide this kind of information for the audience, playwrights revealed the place, time of day, and weather conditions through dialogue.

◆ Build Vocabulary

SUFFIX: -OUS

The suffix -ous means "full of." When -ous is added to the noun *office,* meaning "an important position, job, or duty," it creates the word *officious,* an adjective meaning "excessively full of the sense of one's office."

WORD BANK

Which word means "enemies"? Check the Build Vocabulary box on page 793 to see if you chose correctly.

apprehension
confederacy
officious
discourse
censured
adversaries

from A Midsummer Night's Dream
◆ from Much Ado About Nothing ◆
from The Life and Death of King Richard III

Interest Grabber Have students think about skills or activities that seemed difficult to them initially but turned out to be very enjoyable—for example, mastery of a computer program or a new sport. It may have taken a long time to reach proficiency and to develop the necessary skills. Explain to students that they are about to read short selections from three of Shakespeare's plays and that even adults find his language challenging. The reward of knowing Shakepeare, however, can provide a lifetime of pleasure and enlightenment.

◆ **Build Grammar Skills**

Subject and Verb Agreement in Inverted Sentences If you wish to introduce the grammar concept for this selection before students read, refer to the instruction on p. 794.

Customize for
Less Proficient Readers
Shakespeare's vocabulary will be a challenging problem for less proficient readers. Point out that many of the unfamiliar words occur often, such as the pronouns *thou* or *thee* for *you* and *thy* or *thine* for *your* and *yours*. Point out familiar verbs that appear in unfamiliar forms ending in *t, st,* or *th*. Examples: are = *art;* can = *canst;* do or does = *dost;* has = *hast* or *hath;* were = *wert*. Suggest that students keep a list of these words with their modern counterparts.

Customize for
More Advanced Students
Remind students that Shakespeare's audience could hear the words and see the action as the play progressed; they were not relying on just written words. They probably didn't understand or even hear every word, but they could follow the development of the plot. Have students read through several speeches or a whole page before going back to reread challenging sections. Then have them check the meanings of words that are still unclear to them.

◆ **Literary Focus**

SCENES AND SOLILOQUIES

Like most plays, Shakespeare's plays are divided into acts and scenes. A **scene** is a unified series of action that takes place between two or more characters. The scenes linked together tell the story of the drama.

A **soliloquy** is a speech that reveals the inner thoughts of a character. Soliloquies can be delivered either directly to the audience or as internal monologues, as though the character were speaking to himself or herself. The speeches from *Much Ado About Nothing* and *The Life and Death of King Richard III* are both soliloquies.

◆ **Reading Strategy**

SUMMARIZE

When you **summarize** a soliloquy or a scene, you tell its key ideas or events in your own words. Summarizing passages and scenes of a Shakespeare play will help you keep track of what's happening.

Practice this technique as you read the following sections from Shakespeare's plays. Keep a chart like the one below to summarize.

Shakespeare's Version	Summary
A Midsummer Night's Dream: Act III, scene ii, lines 1–7	Hermia asks Lysander why he's left her.

Preparing for Standardized Tests

Grammar The grammar skill for this selection is subject and verb agreement in inverted sentences. Standardized tests may require students to recognize sentences in which subjects and verbs agree in number and person.

Write the sample test question and sentence choices on the board. Ask students to choose the sentence in which the subject and verb agree in number and person.

(A) Only after a time was the lovers brought together.

(B) Unhappy be a man whose brother is king.
(C) Married was he, in spite of his objections.
(D) Wherefore speak he this to her he hates?

Guide students to see that (C) is the only correct response in which the subject and verb agree in number and person. The subject, *he,* is a singular noun in the third person; the verb, *was married,* agrees with *he* in number and person. For additional practice with subject-verb agreement, use **Selection Support,** p. 266.

One-Minute Insight

In this scene from *A Midsummer Night's Dream,* four young lovers' lives are made very complicated by the interference of fairies in an enchanted forest. When the four young people arrive in the forest, Hermia has been promised in marriage to Demetrius by her father, but she is in love with Lysander. Demetrius, who loves Hermia, is loved by Helena. As this scene begins, the love of both men has been transferred by fairy magic from Hermia to Helena. Although the women are friends from childhood, neither of them is pleased with the turn of events, and they blame each other.

◆ Critical Thinking

❶ Distinguish Have students read the first four lines carefully and identify the subject of the sentence. Then have them explain how lines 3 and 4 complement lines 1 and 2. *Students should identify the subject of the sentence as "night," which is also the antecedent of "it" in lines three and four. Lines 1 and 2 describe how the dark diminishes sight but improves hearing; lines 3 and 4 assert that the dark makes one's hearing twice as good.*

►Critical Viewing◄

❷ Infer *Students may say that an argument between the two men, Demetrius and Lysander, seems to be going on around Helena. Helena looks frightened and unhappy, and Hermia is staring furiously at all of them.*

Customize for
English Language Learners

As English Language Learners read the scene, they may be particularly challenged by unfamiliar words and expressions, as well as by long, complex sentences. Support these students by pausing often to paraphrase and discuss various passages. For example, paraphrase "Dark night, that from the eye his function takes" as "Dark night that makes it hard to see."

from

A Midsummer Night's Dream

William Shakespeare

In this lighthearted comedy, fairies place a spell on four young people, and succeed in transferring the love of Lysander and Demetrius for Hermia to Helena, her friend. In the following scene, the mixed-up lovers meet in a nearby forest, and express their feelings of love, anger, and confusion.

from *Act III, scene ii.* *Another part of the wood.*

[*Enter* HERMIA.]

❶ **HERMIA.** Dark night, that from the eye his function takes,
The ear more quick of <u>apprehension</u> makes;
Wherein it doth impair the seeing sense,

▲ **Critical Viewing**
Judging from the characters' expressions, what is happening in this scene? [Infer] **❷**

Block Scheduling Strategies

Consider these suggestions to take advantage of extended class time:

- Review the Reading Strategy with students before they read the scene from *A Midsummer Night's Dream.* Have students fill in the chart on p. 783 as they read. Then have groups of students compare and discuss their charts and use the information in them to answer the Reading Strategy questions on p. 794. For additional practice, use **Selection Support,** p. 267.
- To aid comprehension, suggest that students use Series of Events Chain, p. 57 in **Writing**

and Language Transparencies, to take notes on the events in each selection.

- Introduce the grammar concept before students read the scenes. After students read, have them work in groups to complete the Build Grammar Skills practice and writing application on p. 794. For additional practice, have students use **Selection Support,** p. 266.
- Have students prepare for the Writing Mini-Lesson by working on the *Writer's Solution Language Lab CD-ROM* and *Writer's Solution Writing Lab CD-ROM.*

① It pays the hearing double recompense.[1]

5 Thou art not by mine eye, Lysander, found;
Mine ear, I thank it, brought me to thy sound.
But why unkindly didst thou leave me so?

LYSANDER. Why should he stay, whom love doth press to go?

HERMIA. What love could press Lysander from my side?

10 **LYSANDER.** Lysander's love, that would not let him bide,[2]
③ Fair Helena, who more engilds[3] the night
Than all yon fiery oes[4] and eyes of light.
Why seek'st thou me? Could not this make thee know,
The hate I bare thee made me leave thee so?

15 **HERMIA.** You speak not as you think: it cannot be.

HELENA. Lo, she is one of this confederacy!
Now I perceive they have conjoined all three
To fashion this false sport, in spite of me.
Injurious Hermia! Most ungrateful maid!

20 Have you conspired, have you with these contrived
To bait me with this foul derision?
Is all the counsel[5] that we two have shared,
The sisters' vows, the hours that we have spent,
When we have chid[6] the hasty-footed time

25 For parting us—O, is all forgot?
All school days friendship, childhood innocence?
We, Hermia, like two artificial gods,
Have with our needles created both one flower,
Both on one sampler,[7] sitting on one cushion,

30 Both warbling of one song, both in one key;
As if our hands, our sides, voices, and minds
Had been incorporate.[8] So we grew together,
Like to a double cherry, seeming parted,
But yet an union in partition;[9]

35 Two lovely berries moulded on one stem;
So, with two seeming bodies, but one heart;
Two of the first, like coats in heraldry,
Due but to one, and crownèd with one crest.[10]
And will you rent our ancient love asunder,

40 To join with men in scorning your poor friend?
It is not friendly, 'tis not maidenly.
Our sex, as well as I, may chide you for it,
Though I alone do feel the injury.

HERMIA. I am amazèd at your passionate words.

45 I scorn you not. It seems that you scorn me.

HELENA. Have you not sent Lysander, as in scorn,
To follow me and praise my eyes and face?
And made your other love, Demetrius
(Who even but now did spurn me with his foot),

---

1. **recompense** (rek´ əm pens´): Something given in return for something lost.

2. **bide:** Remain.
3. **engilds:** Brightens ornately.
4. **oes** (ōz): Any of the celestial spheres, such as the sun, moon, and other stars.

◆ **Reading Strategy**
Summarize lines 16–44? **④**

5. **counsel:** Discussion.

6. **chid:** Scolded; reprimanded.

7. **sampler:** Work of embroidery.

8. **incorporate** (in kôr´ pər it): One body.

9. **partition:** Separation.
10. **Two of . . . one crest:** Helena imagines a shield on which the coat of arms appears twice but which has a single crest; Helena and Hermia have two bodies but a single heart.

◆ **Build Vocabulary**

apprehension (ap´ rə hen´ shən) *n.*: Mental grasp; perception or understanding

confederacy (kən fed´ ər ə sē) *n.*: Conspiracy

from A Midsummer Night's Dream ◆ 785

Humanities: Drama

Elizabethan Theater Theater was an important aspect of life in England during the Elizabethan and early Stuart periods. The plays of the period illustrate the unique way in which the theater can combine various viewpoints on life and introduce memorable characters. Dramatic performances were inexpensive entertainment, performed in the afternoon for all professions and for royalty in the evening.

The English have always had a taste and talent for pageantry. This pageantry is noticed today in various government ceremonies, such as the opening of Parliament, state funerals, and the many ceremonies associated with royalty. This love for pageantry carried over into their drama. In Elizabethan times, codes of dress were rigid, and they defined rank and status. Shakespeare's audiences instantly knew a great deal about a character, just from his costume.

Shakespeare's plays reflect the turbulent period in which he lived and wrote. Characters expressed ideas on stage that even today seem revolutionary to many people. The language used by Shakespeare and his contemporaries reflects an excitement and joy in the spoken word that has all but vanished in modern English.

Interested students may wish to find out more about Shakespeare's plays, the Globe Theater where his plays were performed, and life in England during that time period. Have them report findings to the class in a written report.

50   To call me goddess, nymph, divine and rare,
    Precious, celestial? Wherefore speaks he this
    To her he hates? And wherefore doth Lysander
    Deny your love, so rich within his soul,
    And tender me (forsooth)[11] affection,
55   But by your setting on, by your consent?
    What though I be not so in grace as you,
    So hung upon with love, so fortunate,
    But miserable most, to love unloved?
    This you should pity rather than despise.

60 **HERMIA.** I understand not what you mean by this.

    HELENA. Ay, do! Persever,[12] counterfeit sad looks,
    Make mouths[13] upon me when I turn my back;
    Wink each at other; hold the sweet jest up.
    This sport, well carried, shall be chronicled.

11. forsooth (fôr sooth´): In truth.

12. persever (pʉr´ sə vir´): Continue in some effort.

13. Make mouths: Make mocking faces.

◄ Critical Viewing Which characters are depicted in each of these photographs? How can you tell? [Deduce] ❶

65   If you have any pity, grace, or manners,
    You would not make me such an argument.[14]
    But fare ye well. 'Tis partly my own fault,
    Which death or absence soon shall remedy.

    LYSANDER. Stay, gentle Helena; hear my excuse:
70   My love, my life, my soul, fair Helena!

    HELENA. O excellent!

    HERMIA.   Sweet, do not scorn her so.

    DEMETRIUS. If she cannot entreat, I can compel.

    LYSANDER. Thou canst compel no more than she entreat.
75   Thy threats have no more strength than her weak prayers.
    Helen, I love thee; by my life I do!
    I swear by that which I will lose for thee,
    To prove him false that says I love thee not.

    DEMETRIUS. I say I love thee more than he can do.

14. argument: Subject of scorn and ridicule.

786 ◆ Drama

 Beyond the Classroom

Career Connection
Costume Design The professional production of a play such as *A Midsummer Night's Dream* requires artistic decisions by costume designers as well as other specialists. Costume designers help communicate the mood, period, and meaning of a play. If the play is set in a specific region, country, or historical period, costume designers must conduct research to learn about authentic designs and materials.

The costumes on this page are modeled on costumes of Shakespeare's own day. Other productions have had costumes inspired by Greek attire, as well as Pop Art and even spacesuits.

Costume designers who work on large and expensive theatrical productions must develop management skills in order to oversee budgets and supervise other professionals.

Have interested students list industries and organizations, such as movies, television, theater, and dance companies, that employ costume designers and other costume support help, such as seamstresses, wardrobe supervisors, and dressers. Others might explore requirements for study of costume design.

80 **LYSANDER.** If thou say so, withdraw and prove it too.

DEMETRIUS. Quick, come!

HERMIA. Lysander, whereto tends all this?

LYSANDER. Away, you Ethiope!¹⁵

DEMETRIUS. No, no; he'll
85 Seem to break loose; take on as you would follow,¹⁶
But yet come not: you are a tame man, go!

❷ **LYSANDER.** Hang off, thou cat, thou burr! Vile thing, let loose,
Or I will shake thee from me like a serpent!

HERMIA. Why are you grown so rude! What change is this,
90 Sweet love?

LYSANDER. Thy love! Out, tawny Tartar,¹⁷ out!
Out, loathèd med'cine! O hated potion, hence!

HERMIA. Do you not jest?

HELENA. Yes, sooth;¹⁸ and so do you.

95 **LYSANDER.** Demetrius, I will keep my word with thee.

DEMETRIUS. I would I had your bond; for I perceive
A weak bond holds you. I'll not trust your word.

LYSANDER. What, should I hurt her, strike her, kill her dead?
Although I hate her, I'll not harm her so.

100 **HERMIA.** What, can you do me greater harm than hate?
Hate me! wherefore? O me! What news, my love!
Am not I Hermia? Are not you Lysander?
I am as fair now as I was erewhile.¹⁹
Since night²⁰ you loved me; yet since night you left me.
105 Why, then, you left me—O, the gods forbid!—
In earnest, shall I say?

LYSANDER. Ay, by my life!
And never did desire to see thee more.
Therefore be out of hope, of question, of doubt;
110 Be certain, nothing truer. 'Tis no jest
That I do hate thee, and love Helena.

❸ **HERMIA.** O me! You juggler! You canker blossom!
❹ You thief of love! What, have you come by night
And stol'n my love's heart from him?

115 **HELENA.** Fine, i' faith!
Have you no modesty, no maiden shame,
No touch of bashfulness? What, will you tear
Impatient answers from my gentle tongue?
Fie, fie! You counterfeit, you puppet, you!

120 **HERMIA.** Puppet? Why so? Ay, that way goes the game.
Now I perceive that she hath made compare²¹
Between our statures; she hath urged her height,
And with her personage, her tall personage,

15. Ethiope
(ē′ thē ōp′): Here,
a brunette.

**16. take on as you
would follow:** Act as
if you (Hermia) will
pursue him (Lysander).

17. Tartar (tär′ tər):
Irritable person.

18. sooth: Truly.

19. erewhile (er′
hwīl′): A short time
ago.

20. Since night:
Since the beginning of
this night.

21. compare:
Comparison.

from *A Midsummer Night's Dream* ◆ 787

◆ **Critical Thinking**

❷ **Assess** Remind students that before the intervention of the fairies, Lysander was in love with Hermia. Now, he seems intent on offending her as much as possible. Have students suggest reasons why he is being so unpleasant to her. *He is trying to demonstrate to Helena and Demetrius how much he now loves Helena. A more subtle interpretation is the view that when strong love turns to hatred, the hatred is stronger still.*

Thematic Focus

❸ **Relationships** Hermia has already accused Helena of joining with Demetrius and Lysander to tease her and make fun of her. Ask students what she thinks now. *Students will say that now she thinks that Helena has deliberately stolen Lysander's love.*

Clarification

❹ A canker blossom is a flower or flower bud that has been destroyed from the inside by a worm or caterpillar. Hermia is being insulting by saying that Helena may look like a flower from the outside but is rotten inside.

Customize for
Bodily/Kinesthetic Learners
Have students reread the scene on this page, paying particular attention to lines 84 through 88. Discuss with students what is happening here. Hermia seems to be clutching Lysander to prevent him from fighting, and Demetrius is taunting him. Invite four volunteers to pantomime the action. Make sure the action doesn't become too violent.

Humanities: Music

Music and Dance Adaptations The intricate romantic misadventures in *A Midsummer Night's Dream,* as well as its variety of characters, have always attracted musicians and dancers to the plot of the play.

Although many famous composers, including Henry Purcell, have written music for the play, the best-known music is by Felix Mendelssohn. His musical score was written for a production of the play in 1843, but it was used in a lavish production by

Charles Kean in London in 1856. The "Wedding March" from Mendelssohn's composition still is often used during wedding ceremonies.

Mendelssohn's score is so popular that two ballet versions have been choreographed to the music and are almost as well known today as Shakespeare's text of the play. They are Frederick Ashton's *The Dream* and George Balanchine's *A Midsummer Night's Dream.*

Suggest that interested students listen to Mendelssohn's *A Midsummer Night's Dream.* They might check with your school's music teacher or at the local library for a recording. Have them select those parts of the music that they like best, describe the parts of the play they were written for, and play them for the class. Or, students may wish to explore other musical and dance adaptations of Shakespeare's plays, such as the many versions of *Romeo and Juliet.*

◆ Critical Thinking

❶ Make a Judgment Ask students what they think of the way that Hermia describes herself and Helena. Would anyone talk like this to a friend today? *Students may be surprised that Hermia is so insulting both to herself and to Helena. Apparently, Hermia is self-conscious about her height. She asks if she is "so dwarfish and low" and refers to Helena as a "painted maypole." Perhaps she is trying to understand why the two men have rejected her for Helena. Students may say that they would not talk to a friend that way.*

◆ LITERATURE AND YOUR LIFE

❷ *Students may say that Helena displays more sensitivity than any of the others at this point and that Hermia should forgive her. Other students will recognize that Hermia is not being reasonable at this point, having been rejected by two men who used to love her.*

Thematic Focus

❸ Relationships This is the first time that either Demetrius or Lysander has referred to the other as "Sir." Ask students what this might mean. *Either Demetrius is being sarcastic or he is trying to introduce some formality into the bickering. To Shakespeare's audience, this sudden formality of address would have signaled the end of the two men's friendship.*

Her height, forsooth, she hath prevailed with him.

125 And are you grown so high in his esteem,

❶ Because I am so dwarfish and so low?

How low am I, thou painted maypole? Speak!

How low am I? I am not yet so low

But that my nails can reach unto thine eyes.

130 HELENA. I pray you, though you mock me, gentlemen,

Let her not hurt me. I was not curst;[22]

I have no gift at all in shrewishness;[23]

I am a right maid[24] for my cowardice.

Let her not strike me. You perhaps may think,

135 Because she's something lower than myself,

That I can match her.

HERMIA.   Lower! Hark, again!

HELENA. Good Hermia, do not be so bitter with me.

I evermore did love you, Hermia,

140 Did ever keep your counsels, never wronged you;

Save that, in love unto Demetrius,

I told him of your stealth unto this wood.

He followed you; for love I followed him.

But he hath chid me hence, and threatened me

145 To strike me, spurn me, nay, to kill me too.

And now, so you will let me quiet go,

To Athens will I bear my folly back,

And follow you no further. Let me go.

You see how simple and how fond[25] I am.

150 HERMIA. Why, get you gone. Who is't that hinders you?

HELENA. A foolish heart, that I leave here behind.

HERMIA. What! with Lysander?

HELENA.   With Demetrius.

LYSANDER. Be not afraid. She shall not harm thee, Helena.

❸ 155 DEMETRIUS. No sir, she shall not, though you take her part.

HELENA. O, when she's angry, she is keen and shrewd![26]

She was a vixen[27] when she went to school;

And though she be but little, she is fierce.

HERMIA. "Little" again! Nothing but "low" and "little"!

160 Why will you suffer her to flout[28] me thus?

Let me come to her.

LYSANDER.   Get you gone, you dwarf;

You minimus,[29] of hind'ring knotgrass[30] made;

You bead, you acorn!

165 DEMETRIUS.   You are too officious

In her behalf that scorns your services.

Let her alone. Speak not of Helena;

788 ◆ Drama

---

22. **curst:** Quarrelsome.

23. **shrewishness** (shrōō´ ish nəs´): Having a scolding, evil temperament.

24. **right maid:** Young virtuous woman.

◆ Literature and Your Life

❷ If you were in Hermia's place, would you forgive Helena at this point? Why or why not?

25. **fond:** Foolish.

26. **keen and shrewd:** Sharp-tongued and overbearing.

27. **vixen:** Malicious woman.

28. **flout** (flout): Show scorn and contempt for; to mock.

29. **minimus** (min´ ə mus): Smallest thing.

30. **knotgrass:** A weed that allegedly stunted one's growth.

Speaking and Listening Mini-Lesson

Radio Drama

This mini-lesson supports the Speaking and Listening activity in the Idea Bank on p. 795.

Introduce A radio drama is a form of oral interpretation that relies completely on the lines read aloud and the expressiveness of the voice to communicate the ideas and mood of the writing.

Develop Arrange students in small groups to reread the excerpt from *A Midsummer Night's Dream* and select a portion to portray in their radio drama. Instruct students to choose roles and decide how best to use their voices to convey meaning.

Apply Give students an opportunity to rehearse before they tape-record their drama. Encourage them to explore different interpretations to provide the most creative drama. Play the recorded dramas for the class.

Assess After the presentations, lead a class discussion about the dramatic interpretations. Evaluate students' work based on the interpretive quality, their group effort, and the total effectiveness of their presentation. Or use the Peer Assessment: Dramatic Performance form, p. 116 in **Alternative Assessment.**

Take not her part; for if thou dost intend
Never so little show of love to her,
170 Thou shalt aby[31] it.

LYSANDER.   Now she holds me not.
Now follow, if thou dar'st, to try whose right,
Or thine or mine, is most in Helena.

DEMETRIUS. Follow! Nay, I'll go with thee, cheek by jowl.[32]

[*Exeunt* LYSANDER *and* DEMETRIUS.]

175 **HERMIA.** You, mistress, all this coil is 'long of you:[33]
Nay, go not back.

HELENA.   I will not trust you, I,
Nor longer stay in your curst company.
Your hands than mine are quicker for a fray,[34]
180 My legs are longer though, to run away.

HERMIA. I am amazed, and know not what to say.

[*Exeunt* HELENA *and* HERMIA.]

---

31. **aby** (ə bī'): Pay for.
32. **cheek by jowl:** Close together.

33. **all this coil is 'long of you:** All this turmoil is brought about by you.

34. **fray:** Fight; brawl.

◆ **Build Vocabulary**

officious (ə fish' əs) *adj.*: Overly eager to serve; excessively obliging

---

Guide for Responding

◆ LITERATURE AND YOUR LIFE

Reader's Response Which parts of the scene did you find funny? Did you find any parts sad or moving?

Thematic Focus In what ways do the relationships among the four people become confused?

☑ Check Your Comprehension

1. Why is Hermia surprised by Lysander's actions?
2. What do Lysander and Demetrius have in common?
3. (a) How do Helena and Hermia feel about each other at the beginning of the scene? (b) How do their feelings change by the scene's end?

◆ Critical Thinking

INTERPRET
1. How does Helena describe her childhood with Hermia? **[Interpret]**
2. How does this description contrast with later events in the scene? **[Compare and Contrast]**
3. (a) Which characters are given more focus in this scene: the women or the men? (b) Why do you think Shakespeare wrote the scene with this emphasis? **[Draw Conclusions]**

EVALUATE
4. Whom would you rather have as a friend—Helena or Hermia? Why? **[Make a Judgment]**

APPLY
5. What advice would you give Hermia and Helena to help them resolve their conflict? **[Solve]**

from A Midsummer Night's Dream ◆ 789

Humanities: Literature

Shakespeare's Influence Although Shakespeare's plays were written many years ago, they still influence culture today. Point out to students how many quotations, characters, and Shakespearean events they have encountered—for example, the quotation, "To be, or not to be: that is the question."

Actual Shakespeare plays have been produced on film many times through the years. Actors such as Mel Gibson (*Hamlet*) and Leonardo di Caprio (*Romeo and Juliet*) consider their performances in Shakespeare's plays or films based on the plays to be important career achievements.

In addition to the musical and dance interpretations of Shakespeare (discussed on p. 787 of the Teacher Edition), many authors and playwrights use Shakespeare's characters and plots as a catalyst in their own creative process. Books have been written modeling Shakespeare plots. New plays have been written that take Shakespeare's characters and expand their roles in a new work, such as Tom Stoppard's *Rosencrantz and Guildenstern Are Dead* and Lee Blessing's *Fortinbras*.

Students might research current films and literature that have been influenced by Shakespeare.

---

4 Ask students what Lysander means by "Now follow, if thou dar'st, to try whose right,/Or thine or mine, is most in Helena." *Students may recognize that Lysander is challenging Demetrius to a duel over Helena.*

◆ Literary Focus

5 **Scenes** Tell students that the stage direction *exeunt,* Latin for "they go out," is used to specify that all or certain named characters leave the stage. In this case, it is Helena and Hermia. The stage direction *exit* refers to one person leaving the stage.

Reinforce and Extend

Answers
◆ LITERATURE AND YOUR LIFE

Reader's Response Depending on their appreciation of funny insults and misunderstandings, most students will find the scene funny.

Thematic Focus Because of the fairies and misunderstandings, the two young couples become hopelessly confused.

☑ Check Your Comprehension

1. She thought he was in love with her.
2. In this scene, they are both in love with Helena.
3. (a) Helena thinks Hermia has joined the two men in ridiculing her. (b) They are hostile and angry toward each other.

◆ Critical Thinking

1. She describes it as a perfect friendship.
2. Helena talks at the beginning about how much alike they were. They end up pointing out their differences and attacking each other.
3. (a) The women are given more focus. (b) The women were more likely to argue and insult each other than the men, who go off to fight.
4. Students may say that Helena seems kinder, more reflective and thoughtful, and less hotheaded than Hermia.
5. They should all go home, think things over, and try to resolve their differences.

One-Minute Insight

Beatrice and Benedick are not the main characters in *Much Ado About Nothing*. The lead characters are Hero, a girl from a noble Italian family, and Claudio, her soldier fiancé. In these two soliloquies, we see two sides of Benedick's personality. In the first, he complains about how love has altered the manly behavior of his friend Claudio and decides that only the perfect woman could make him fall in love. Because he believes Beatrice loves him, in the second, he finds that he resolves to behave differently and to seriously consider marriage.

▶Critical Viewing◀

❶ Draw Conclusions *Students may conclude that these characters are very much in love with each other. Their faces have intense expressions, and they seem relaxed and at ease in each other's company.*

Clarification

❷ Students will notice that the text here is different from that in *A Midsummer Night's Dream;* it is in prose rather than blank verse. In his early plays, Shakespeare used prose for the speech of clowns, servants, and people from the country. His noble characters spoke blank verse. In his later plays, this distinction is not as clear. Three fourths of *Much Ado About Nothing* is written in prose.

◆ Reading Strategy

❸ Summarize Have students summarize lines 1–15. *Benedick wonders how a man like Claudio, who has believed other men foolish when they fall in love, can then fall in love himself and behave the same way. He contrasts Claudio's former interests with his new preoccupations: formerly he liked martial music and now he likes dance music; formerly suits of armor, now fancy clothes; and formerly direct speech, now flowery language.*

from **Much Ado About Nothing**

William Shakespeare

❶ ▶ **Critical Viewing** What do the characters' facial expressions and posture reveal about their relationship? [Draw Conclusions]

Benedick and Beatrice have for years had a barbed friendship, trading insults and witticisms whenever they meet. Benedick, who rejoices in being single, reveals his attitude toward love in this soliloquy.

from *Act II, scene iii.* *Leonato's garden.*

BENEDICK. . . . I do much wonder
that one man, seeing how much another man is a
fool when he dedicates his behaviors to love, will,
after he hath laughed at such shallow follies in
5 others, become the argument[1] of his own scorn by
falling in love; and such a man is Claudio. I have
known when there was no music with him but the
drum and the fife;[2] and now had he rather hear the
tabor and the pipe.[3] I have known when he would
10 have walked ten mile afoot to see a good armor; and
now will he lie ten nights awake carving the fashion
of a new doublet.[4] He was wont[5] to speak plain and
to the purpose, like an honest man and a soldier;
and now is he turned orthography;[6] his words are
15 a very fantastical banquet—just so many strange
dishes. May I be so converted and see with these
eyes? I cannot tell; I think not. I will not be sworn[7]
but love may transform me to an oyster;[8] but I'll take

1. **argument:** Subject matter.
2. **drum and the fife:** Instruments associated with war.
3. **tabor** (tā´ bər) **and the pipe:** Music associated with dancing.
4. **doublet** (dub´ lit): A close-fitting jacket.
5. **wont:** Accustomed.
6. **turned orthography** (ôr thäg´ rə fē): Begun speaking in an affected manner.
7. **sworn:** Bound by an oath.
8. **oyster:** Someone who can be taken advantage of.

Beyond the Classroom

Career Connection

Acting When the actors shown on this page, Emma Thompson and Kenneth Branagh, appeared as Beatrice and Benedick in the film version of *Much Ado About Nothing* (1993), they were established British actors. Most students are aware of movie actors, but many actors, particularly British actors such as Thompson and Branagh, learn to act on stage before they appear in films.

Although many people are exposed to acting through the stage and screen, people in the theater business know what a difficult profession it can be. The old notion of actors with "natural" talent making it big in acting without any formal training is largely fantasy.

Students interested in a theatrical career might start with theater groups in your school or local community theater to explore acting. Most universities and colleges have theater departments to train students in all facets of play production.

Suggest that students research the requirements for a theater degree, actors union membership requirements, and possibilities for participation in community theater productions.

my oath on it, till he have made an oyster of me he
shall never make me such a fool. One woman is fair,
yet I am well; another is wise, yet I am well; another
virtuous, yet I am well. But till all graces be in one
woman, one woman shall not come in my grace.
Rich she shall be, that's certain; wise, or I'll none;
virtuous, or I'll never cheapen⁹ her; fair, or I'll never
look on her; mild, or come not near me; noble, or
not I for an angel; of good <u>discourse</u>, an excellent
musician, and her hair shall be of what color it
please God. Ha, the Prince and Monsieur Love!
[*Retiring*] I will hide me in the arbor. . . .¹⁰

---

*Benedick's friends play a trick on him, causing him
to think that Beatrice is secretly in love with him. In this
soliloquy, Benedick shows another side of himself, one
that welcomes Beatrice's love.*

BENEDICK. . . . [*Advancing*] This can be no trick; the conference was sadly borne.¹¹ They have the truth of
this from Hero. They seem to pity the lady; it seems
her affections have their full bent.¹² Love me? Why,
it must be requited.¹³ I hear how I am <u>censured</u>. They
say I will bear myself proudly if I perceive the love
come from her. They say too that she will rather die
than give any sign of affection. I did never think to
marry; I must not seem proud. Happy are they that
hear their detractions and can put them to mending.
They say the lady is fair—'tis a truth, I can bear
them witness; and virtuous—'tis so, I cannot reprove¹⁴
it; and wise, but for loving me; by my troth,¹⁵ it is
no addition to her wit, nor no great argument of her
folly; for I will be horribly in love with her. I may
chance have some odd quirks and remnants of wit
broken on me because I have railed so long against
marriage; but doth not the appetite alter? A man
loves the meat in his youth that he cannot endure
in his age. Shall quips and sentences¹⁶ and these
paper bullets of the brain awe a man from the
career of his humor?¹⁷ No, the world must be peo–
pled. When I said I would die a bachelor, I did not
think I should live till I were married. . . .

9. **cheapen:** Bargain
for (court her against
other suitors).

10. **arbor:** Garden.

11. **sadly borne:**
Seriously carried out.
12. **affections have
their full bent:** Emo-
tions are tightly
stretched (like a bent
bow).
13. **requited** (ri kwit´
əd): Returned.

14. **reprove:** Refute;
disprove.
15. **troth** (trôth):
Faithfulness; loyalty.
16. **sentences:** Max-
ims or moral sayings.
17. **humor:** Disposi-
tion; temperament.

♦ **Build Vocabulary**

discourse (dis´ kôrs) *n.*: Reasoning or
rationality

censured (sen´ shərd) *v.*: Condemned
as wrong; criticized

from Much Ado About Nothing ♦ 791

791

Richard, Duke of Gloucester, later Richard III, King of England, is a Shakespearean villain you love to hate. In the opening soliloquy of the play, he wastes no time in letting the audience know that he is unscrupulous and evil. To secure the throne for himself, he plans the murder of his older brother, George, Duke of Clarence. When his younger brother, King Edward IV, dies, Richard has his two young sons imprisoned and murdered. He justifies his ruthless behavior in this soliloquy by explaining that since his physical deformity deprives him of love, he must get pleasure from satisfying his ambition.

►Critical Viewing◄

❶ Make a Judgment *Students may say that the king shown here looks very serious, if not discontented. His knitted eyebrows express concern.*

Clarification

❷ Explain to students that the word *sun* in line 2 is a pun. A pun can have two meanings—both meanings are intended to be understood and appreciated. Here, the word means the sun, literally, and son of York, Richard's brother, King Edward IV, whose emblem was three shining suns.

◆ Critical Thinking

❸ Connect Ask students if this selection is in blank verse or prose. *Students will recognize that this selection is in the same form as the scene from A Midsummer Night's Dream—blank verse.*

Customize for
Verbal/Linguistic Learners

For better comprehension of Shakespeare's speeches, have students locate and rearrange words into basic sentences. Suggest that students analyze the long sentence beginning with line 14 and ending with line 27. Have students locate the subject, or subjects, the verb, and the direct object. Have them discuss why Shakespeare arranges the sentence this way.

---

from The Life and Death of King Richard III
William Shakespeare

❶ ► Critical Viewing Does the king in the photograph appear to be "discontented"? Explain. [**Make a Judgment**]

This soliloquy is one of Shakespeare's most famous. In it, you are introduced to Richard, Duke of Gloucester, King Edward's brother, who has recently triumphed in battle along with his brothers in the Wars of the Roses. Richard is an unhappy man who resents his place in life and begins plotting to seize the throne of England for himself.

Act I, scene i. *London. A street.*
[*Enter* RICHARD, DUKE OF GLOUCESTER, *alone.*]

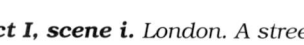

> **RICHARD.** Now is the winter of our discontent
> Made glorious summer by this sun[1] of York;
> And all the clouds that loured[2] upon our house
> In the deep bosom of the ocean buried.
> 5 Now are our brows bound with victorious wreaths,
> Our bruisèd arms hung up for monuments,
> Our stern alarums chang'd to merry meetings,
> Our dreadful marches to delightful measures.
> Grim-visaged War hath smooth'd his wrinkled front,[3]
> 10 And now, instead of mounting barbèd steeds
> To fright the souls of fearful adversaries,
> He capers[4] nimbly in a lady's chamber
> To the lascivious[5] pleasing of a lute.
> But I, that am not shaped for sportive tricks
> 15 Nor made to court an amorous looking glass;
> I, that am rudely stamped, and want[6] love's majesty
> To strut before a wanton[7] ambling nymph;
> I, that am curtailed[8] of this fair proportion,
> Cheated of feature[9] by dissembling Nature,

1. **sun:** (1) Emblem of King Edward. (2) Son.
2. **loured** (lou´ ərd): Lowered.

3. **front:** Forehead.
4. **capers** (kā´ pərz): Skips or jumps about in a playful way.

5. **lascivious** (lə siv´ ē əs): Unrestrained.
6. **want:** Lack.
7. **wanton:** Unreserved; playful.
8. **curtailed:** Reduced; cut short.
9. **feature:** Good shape and pleasing appearance.

Cross-Curricular Connection: Social Studies

The Wars of the Roses Richard III was the last king to rule England during the Wars of the Roses—a series of battles and confrontations between the noble houses of York and Lancaster. The period of wartime takes its name from the roses because the opposing forces had roses as their emblems—white for York, red for Lancaster. The main reason for the wars was competition between the two houses for the throne, but there were social problems that contributed to strife as well. The decline of the feudal order and the rise of the middle class continued from the 1300's. The 1400's in England are generally thought of as a period of cultural decline, and constant warfare did not help. Both Yorks and Lancasters were descended from Edward III (1327–1377), and both families wished to claim the throne. The first battle was in 1455, and the Battle of Bosworth in 1485 was the last. Richard III was defeated and killed in battle, and Henry Tudor, the victor, was proclaimed king (Henry VII).

Interested students may wish to research further details about the Wars of the Roses and report back to the class.

❹ The prophecy is that someone whose name begins with *G* will kill King Edward IV and his heirs. The King believes that his brother George will be the murderer. Richard thinks that perhaps he, the Duke of Gloucester, will be the murderer.

Customize for
Verbal/Linguistic Learners
The photograph on p. 792 shows Al Pacino as Richard III in the documentary film *Looking for Richard* (1996). This film includes analyses of scenes and informal discussions among the actors about what Shakespeare's lines mean. Pacino offers a particularly helpful explanation and performance of this soliloquy. Interested students may wish to watch the film and share what they learn with the class.

---

20 Deformed, unfinished, sent before my time
    Into this breathing world scarce half made up,
    And that so lamely and unfashionable
    That dogs bark at me as I halt by them;
    Why, I, in this weak piping time[10] of peace,
25 Have no delight to pass away the time,
    Unless to spy my shadow in the sun
    And descant[11] on mine own deformity.
    And therefore, since I cannot prove a lover
    To entertain these fair well-spoken days,
30 I am determinèd to prove a villain
    And hate the idle pleasures of these days.
    Plots have I laid, inductions[12] dangerous,
    By drunken prophecies, libels, and dreams,
    To set my brother Clarence and the King
35 In deadly hate the one against the other;
    And if King Edward be as true and just
    As I am subtle, false, and treacherous,
    This day should Clarence closely be mewed up[13]
    About a prophecy which says that G
40 ❹ Of Edward's heirs the murderer shall be.
    Dive, thoughts, down to my soul. . . .

10. **piping time:** Of a pleasing and simple time where shepherds play flutes; idyllic; pastoral.
11. **descant** (des kant´): Comment.

12. **inductions:** First steps.
13. **mewed up:** Confined or caged in prison.

◆ **Build Vocabulary**
adversaries (ad´ vər ser´ ēz) *n.*: Enemies; opponents

Guide for Responding

◆ LITERATURE AND YOUR LIFE

Reader's Response Do you find Benedick or Richard III more likeable? Explain.

Thematic Focus What kind of relationship does Richard III have with his relatives?

☑ Check Your Comprehension

1. In *Much Ado About Nothing*, why does Benedick say he scorns Claudio?
2. How does Benedick describe the perfect woman in the first soliloquy?
3. Why do the dogs bark at Richard?
4. Whom does Richard plan to set against each other? Why?
5. (a) In the second soliloquy, whom does Benedick believe to be in love with him? (b) How does he feel about that?

◆ Critical Thinking

INTERPRET
1. Whom does Benedick view as "oysters" in *Much Ado About Nothing*? **[Connect]**
2. Describe the ways in which Benedick has changed from the first to the second soliloquy. **[Compare and Contrast]**
3. In lines 5 through 13, what does Richard III reveal about the setting of the play? **[Interpret]**
4. What comparison does Richard make between himself and King Edward? **[Compare and Contrast]**

COMPARE LITERARY WORKS
5. Which soliloquy do you think would be more effective if read in an aggressive tone? Why? **[Speculate]**

from The Life and Death of King Richard III ◆ 793

Reader's Response Students will probably find Benedick more likeable because he is sweet-natured. Few will find Richard likeable.

Thematic Focus Richard's relatives underestimate him, and he cares nothing for them.

☑ Check Your Comprehension

1. Benedick scorns the way love has changed Claudio's behavior.
2. He describes her as beautiful, virtuous, intelligent, rich, gentle, noble, a good conversationalist, and an accomplished musician.
3. He's ugly, so dogs bark at him.
4. He plans conflict between his older brother, Clarence, and his younger brother, King Edward IV.
5. (a) He believes Beatrice is in love with him. (b) He is surprised and touched.

◆ Critical Thinking

1. He views men who are taken in by women as "oysters."
2. He finds that he likes the idea of having a woman love him.
3. He describes the setting in the royal palace in London.
4. Richard describes King Edward as an aggressive ladies' man and himself as deformed and undesirable.
5. Students may choose Richard's, because he is resentful.

Beyond the Selection

FURTHER READING
Other Plays by William Shakespeare
As You Like It
The Merry Wives of Windsor
Henry IV, Parts One and Two
Books About Shakespeare
Shakespeare's Life: A Biographical Handbook, G. E. Bentley
Young Shakespeare, Russell Fraser
Books About Shakespeare's Language
Shakespeare's Language: An Introduction, Norman Blake

Other Drama Works
Center Stage: One Act Plays for Teenage Readers and Actors, Donald R. Gallo (ed.)
Monologues for Kids, Ruth Mae Roddy
INTERNET
We suggest the following sites on the Internet (all Web sites are subject to change).
  For more on William Shakespeare, go to:
http://the-tech.mit.edu/Shakepeare/works.html
  Or, visit:
http://www2.pbs.org/wgbh/pages/frontline/shakespeare/index.html

◆ Reading Strategy

1. Students might emphasize the breakdown in the relationship between Lysander and Hermia, the friendship of Helena and Hermia, and finally the argument between the two women.

2. Since Richard is deformed and ugly and cannot attract lovers like his brother King Edward IV, he decides to use his intelligence to destroy his brothers and take the throne.

3. (a) Benedick's friend Claudio has fallen in love, and Benedick reflects on how his friend has changed from sensible soldier to fatuous lover. He says that only a perfect woman could make him change in this way, and he suggests humorously that such a woman doesn't exist and he will never marry. (b) Benedick is informed that Beatrice is in love with him. He suddenly finds her appealing and attractive and likes the idea of being in love. As for marriage, he now thinks it's a good idea. (c) The opinions expressed are totally opposite.

◆ Build Vocabulary

Using the Suffix -ous
1. deserving ridicule
2. full of virtue
3. full of self-importance
4. having victory

Spelling Strategy
1. malicious; 2. delicious

Using the Word Bank
1. a   2. a   3. b   4. b   5. a   6. b

◆ Literary Focus

1. Students learn that all four feel very strongly about being in love. Hermia is impulsive and combative. Helena is thoughtful and easily hurt. (b) The four people argue with one another. Lysander and Demetrius pursue Helena and attack Hermia, and Hermia attacks Helena.

2. (a) Benedick is cynical about love, is not interested in marriage, and is very witty. (b) He is really tender-hearted and enjoys the thought of love.

3. Possible response: Shakespeare wants the audience to understand Richard's evil plots and his villainy, so he has the villain confide in the audience.

Guide for Responding (continued)

◆ Reading Strategy

SUMMARIZE
Summarizing is retelling key events and ideas in your own words. Summarizing can help you focus on a play's main events.
1. Imagine that you were summarizing the lovers' quarrel from *A Midsummer Night's Dream* to an audience of fifth graders. Which events would you emphasize?
2. How would you summarize Richard III's soliloquy?
3. (a) Summarize the first soliloquy of Benedick in *Much Ado About Nothing*. (b) Summarize the second soliloquy. (c) How do they differ?

◆ Build Vocabulary

USING THE SUFFIX -ous
The suffix *-ous,* meaning "full of," creates an adjective from a noun. On your paper, define these adjectives containing the suffix *-ous*.

1. ridiculous
2. virtuous
3. pompous
4. victorious

SPELLING STRATEGY
The *shus* sound can be spelled *cious,* as in *officious.* On your paper, correct the misspelled word in each sentence.
1. King Richard III was a malishous man.
2. *Much Ado About Nothing* was especially delishous.

USING THE WORD BANK
On your paper, write the letter of the word or phrase closest in meaning to the Word Bank word.
1. apprehension: (a) understanding, (b) catch, (c) arrest
2. confederacy: (a) union, (b) friendship, (c) antigovernment
3. officious: (a) correct, (b) overly eager, (c) vain
4. discourse: (a) silence, (b) conversation, (c) track
5. censured: (a) disapproved, (b) counted, (c) estimated
6. adversaries: (a) sayings, (b) opponents, (c) camels

◆ Literary Focus

SCENES AND SOLILOQUIES
Scenes are divisions of plays that show action and dialogue between characters. **Soliloquies** are speeches that reveal a character's inner thoughts. The sequence of scenes moves the dramatic action of a play forward. Soliloquies can indicate important plot turning points by drawing attention to a character's feelings and motives for action.
1. (a) What do you learn about the characters in the scene from *A Midsummer Night's Dream?* (b) What action occurs?
2. (a) What do you learn about Benedick in the first soliloquy from *Much Ado About Nothing?* (b) What do you learn about him in the second soliloquy?
3. Richard's soliloquy opens *The Life and Death of King Richard III.* Why do you think Shakespeare chose to start the play with a soliloquy?

◆ Build Grammar Skills

SUBJECT AND VERB AGREEMENT IN INVERTED SENTENCES
In an **inverted sentence,** the subject follows the verb. Most sentences beginning with *here* and *there* are inverted. When a sentence is inverted, identify the subject and make the verb agree with it.

Singular Verb and Subject: Now *is* the *winter* of our discontent / Made glorious summer . . .
Plural Verb and Subject: Happy *are they* that hear their detractions. . . .

Practice Identify the subjects and verbs in the following inverted passages. Tell whether the subject and verb are singular or plural.
1. Now are our brows bound . . .
2. Wherefore speaks he this to her he hates?
3. And wherefore doth Lysander deny your love . . .
4. Plots have I laid, inductions dangerous . . .
5. Here are comedies to keep you amused.

Writing Application Write *is* or *are* to complete each inverted sentence.
1. Here _____?_____ a few more lines for your play.
2. There _____?_____ an exciting scene in Act II.
3. Now, _____?_____ we ready to begin rehearsal?

◆ Build Grammar Skills

Practice
1. subject: brows; verb: are; plural
2. subject: he; verb: speaks; singular
3. subject: Lysander; verb: doth deny; singular
4. subject: I; verb: have laid; singular
5. subject: comedies; verb: are; plural

Writing Application
1. are; 2. is; 3. are

✎ Writer's Solution

For additional instruction and practice, use the practice page on Special Problems With Subject-Verb Agreement, p. 84, in the *Writer's Solution Grammar Practice Book.* If students have access to technology, have them use the lesson on Special Problems in Agreement 1 and 2 in the unit on Subject-Verb Agreement on the *Writer's Solution Language Lab CD-ROM.*

Build Your Portfolio

 Idea Bank

Writing

1. **Summary** Choose one of Shakespeare's soliloquies, and write a summary in your own words. Include the main ideas in your retelling.

2. **Casting Advice** Choose one of these scenes or soliloquies and cast the parts with famous actors. In a note to the play's director, give reasons why you think each actor will suit his or her role so well.

3. **Comparison-and-Contrast Essay** In an essay, compare and contrast either Helena and Hermia or Demetrius and Lysander from *A Midsummer Night's Dream*. Use details from the play to support your points.

Speaking and Listening

4. **Shakespeare Recitation** Memorize 5 to 10 lines from one of the plays. Choose lines that you like and would like to study closely. Practice saying them aloud. When you are ready, recite your lines for the class. **[Performing Arts Link]**

5. **Radio Drama [Group Activity]** With a group, rehearse and tape-record one of the Shakespearean scenes or soliloquies for a radio show. Play the finished product for the class. **[Media Link]**

Projects

6. **Comic Book [Group Activity]** Create a comic book based on one of these selections. You may wish to use some of the original Shakespearean lines in your character's speech balloons. Divide the jobs required to create your comic. You might need a writer, an artist, an editor, and a layout director. Hold team meetings to keep your project on course. **[Art Link]**

7. **Historical Soliloquy** *The Life and Death of King Richard III* is about an English king. Choose a well-known political figure of the twentieth century, and write a soliloquy for that character to begin a play about his or her life. **[History Link]**

 Writing Mini-Lesson

Biographical Report

Knowing about an author's life can help you appreciate his or her writing. Even though William Shakespeare lived more than 400 years ago, much is known about his life. Write a biographical report about Shakespeare to help others come to appreciate his accomplishments.

Writing Skills Focus: Narrowing Your Topic

The topic of Shakespeare is too large for a brief biographical report. Choose a **narrower topic** that is manageable and interesting. For example, instead of writing about Shakespeare's entire life, you might write about one part of it, such as his childhood.

Model

Although no written evidence of Shakespeare's boyhood exists, it is likely that he attended the Stratford Grammar School. As part of his schooling there, he would have learned Latin and other subjects.

Prewriting Research Shakespeare's life using various sources. Jot down ideas for specific topics you might write about. Choose one, and gather information for your report.

Drafting Begin your report with a sentence that tells what aspect of Shakespeare's life your report will discuss. Develop the body of your report by arranging details in a logical order.

Revising Read your report aloud to a team of classmates. Ask them to identify sections that could be written more clearly or could be elaborated. Follow their suggestions for revision.

◆ **Grammar Application**

Make sure that your subjects and verbs agree, even in sentences in which the verb comes before the subject.

---

from A Midsummer Night's Dream/from Much Ado. . . /from . . . King Richard III ◆ 795

✓ **ASSESSMENT OPTIONS**

Prepare and Engage

Establish Writing Guidelines

Review the following key characteristics of a critical review:

- A critical review is an evaluation of a subject.
- A critical review must include information on the subject being critiqued.
- The opinions of the writer are backed up by specific details from the subject being reviewed.

You may want to distribute the scoring rubric for Evaluation/Review, p. 100 in **Alternative Assessment,** to make students aware of the criteria on which they will be evaluated. See the suggestions on p. 798 for how you can customize the rubric to this workshop.

Refer students to the Writing Handbook in the back of the book for instruction on the writing process and further information on response to literature.

 **Writer's Solution**

Writers at Work Videodisc

To introduce students to responding to literature and to show them what reviewer Marilyn Stasio says about writing reviews, play the videodisc segment on Response to Literature (Ch. 9). Ask students to consider what Stasio says about making her review clear and accurate.

Play frames 30102 to 39013

Writing Lab CD-ROM

If your students have access to computers, you may want to have them work in the tutorial on Response to Literature to complete all or part of their critical reviews. Follow these steps:

1. Have students view the interactive model of a critical review.
2. Suggest that students view the writing hints on focusing topics to help narrow their topic ideas.
3. Allow students to draft on computer.
4. Have students use the interactive guide to using quotations when revising.

Writer's Solution Sourcebook

Students can find additional support, including in-depth instruction on using quotations, p. 292, in the chapter on Responding to Literature, pp. 266–295.

796

Response to Literature
Critical Review

Writing Process Workshop

We often determine whether to read a book or go to a movie based on other people's evaluations. Critical reviews provide this type of evaluation. As a writer of a critical evaluation, it's important to give specific reasons to support your opinions.

Write a critical review of your favorite book, play, or movie. The following writing skills will help you:

Writing Skills Focus

▶ **Narrow your topic** to focus on a specific aspect of your topic. (See p. 795.)

▶ **Be accurate** with titles, authors, dates, and other vital information so your evaluation seems credible.

▶ **Support** your opinions with passages from the work.

After reading the scenes and soliloquies from Shakespeare's plays, one writer wrote a critical review of a scene from *The Life and Death of King Richard III:*

WRITING MODEL

I am amazed that the issues that Shakespeare writes about are as relevant today as they were in his time. ① For example, in *The Life and Death of King Richard III,* ② Shakespeare shows how Richard, an evil man, is caught up in wanting more. Because he feels slighted, he is "determined to prove a villain." ③ Like Richard, many people today are unable to appreciate what they have and want more at any cost.

① In this sentence, the writer gives her purpose for writing about the soliloquy. She feels its topic is still relevant.

② The writer uses the complete and accurate title of the play.

③ This quotation from the play supports the writer's point.

796 ◆ Drama

 Beyond the Classroom

Career Connection

Critic Have students look through local and national newspapers to find examples of critical reviews. Explain to students that a critic must have a wealth of knowledge on the area being reviewed, such as dance, film, and books, as well as have good writing skills to make the review interesting. For example, a book critic probably has experience in literature and composition; a movie critic probably has experience in film appreciation and film history; and an art critic probably has experience in art history and art theory.

If possible, have students find more than one review of the same film, book, or performance. Then discuss with students which review they think is best, based on the writing and the quality of the supporting evidence. Ask students to note where reviewers have compared the item reviewed to a similar work. Explain that reviewers who have a vast knowledge of their general field, may review more accurately because they know more about their subject.

Prewriting

Choose a Topic Think about a book you read or a play or movie you saw that has had a lasting impression. A topic that you feel strongly about will make the best subject for your critical review.

Clarify Your Opinions Once you've chosen your topic, collect your thoughts about it. Create a chart like the one below. List what you liked about the selection and what you didn't like about it.

What I Liked	What I Disliked
_____	_____
_____	_____
_____	_____

Look at Some Models Look in a newspaper for models of reviews. In a big-city Sunday newspaper, for example, you should be able to find reviews of plays and books. Notice what points they focus on, what language they use to indicate positive or negative opinions, and how they use details to support opinions.

Identify Your Purpose Review your list of likes and dislikes. Decide whether you will or will not recommend the work to others.

Collect Supporting Details Jot down your opinions about various aspects of the book, play, or movie you have chosen. Finally, list specific details that support each opinion.

Drafting

Follow a Format Using your Prewriting notes and lists, draft your evaluation. Start with a paragraph that states your general opinion. Then, elaborate on your opinion of the work, providing examples and details for support. End with a recommendation to the readers.

Use Descriptive Language Choose words that convey your positive or negative evaluations. Look at the following examples:

Negative Language
unfocused, awful, confusing, vague, boring

Positive Language
imaginative, hilarious, original, expressive, stimulating

Get the Facts Right Check your facts to make sure they're accurate. Be sure to capitalize and punctuate titles correctly, spell names correctly, quote lines exactly, and enclose quotations in quotation marks.

APPLYING LANGUAGE SKILLS: Direct and Indirect Quotations

Direct quotations represent a person's exact spoken or written words. Enclose them in quotation marks, and give credit to the owner of the words. **Indirect quotations** report the general meaning of what a person says. They don't require quotation marks.

Direct: The goal of Richard's plan is "To set my brother Clarence and the King/ In deadly hate the one against the other."

Indirect: Shakespeare describes the goal of Richard's plan as getting his brother Clarence and the King to hate each other.

Practice On your paper, cite the following two ways: as a direct quotation and as an indirect quotation.

Dr. Fried said "Shakespeare is a writer for all time."

Writing Application In your critical review, use direct quotations when the speaker's words are especially powerful. Use indirect quotations to summarize information.

Writer's Solution Connection Language Lab

For more practice, complete the Quotation Marks lesson in the Punctuation unit.

Prewriting

Encourage students to choose something recent to review—for example, a book or movie that has just come out. Explain to students that most reviews come out at or about the same time as the movie, novel, or play. Alternatively, students may want to review an older movie that has just come out on video or was aired on television.

Customize for *Less Proficient Writers*

To help students organize their ideas in their reviews, have them use the Main Idea and Supporting Details Organizer, p. 61 in **Writing and Language Transparencies.** In the space for Main Idea they should write their general recommendation for the subject reviewed. In the spaces for supporting details, they should provide examples that support the main idea.

Drafting

Tell students that they may want to organize their reviews by listing the most important points first and ending with the least important points. Encourage students to experiment with the organization of details.

Writer's Solution

Writing Lab CD-ROM
In the drafting section of the tutorial on Response to Literature, suggest that students view the audio-annotated models of an introduction, a body, and a conclusion. They can select words or passages from the models and hear the writer's comments.

Applying Language Skills

Direct and Indirect Quotations Explain to students that writers use indirect quotations when they wish to summarize or rephrase what a person has said. A direct quotation is used when a writer wants to use the speaker's exact words.

Writer's Solution

For additional instruction and support, have students use the practice page on Quotation Marks With Direct Quotations, pp. 111–112, in the *Writer's Solution Grammar Practice Book.*

Answers
Possible responses:
1. Direct quotation: Dr. Fried said, "Shakespeare is a writer for all time."
2. Indirect quotation: Dr. Fried said that Shakespeare's writing is timeless.

Revising

Remind students, when revising, to check for the following:

- The title and author of the work, as well as any other relevant information, are included in the introduction.
- The review is organized well enough for the reader to have a clear idea of the writer's opinion of the subject.
- The writer has used transitions to connect ideas between sentences and paragraphs smoothly.

 Writer's Solution

Writing Lab CD-ROM
In the tutorial on Response to Literature, have students use the Proofreading Checklist to find possible errors in grammar, mechanics, or spelling.

Publishing
For other publishing ideas, suggest that students send their reviews to local newspapers or publish them in the school newspaper.

Reinforce and Extend

Review the Writing Guidelines
After students have completed their papers, review the characteristics of a critical review.

Applying Language Skills
Using *good* and *well* Correctly
Tell students that adjectives and adverbs that form their comparative and superlative degrees in unpredictable ways (like *good* and *well*) must be memorized.

Answers
1. *Hamlet* is written well.
2. They performed well.
3. The food at the restaurant was cooked well.

Writing Process Workshop

EDITING/PROOFREADING

APPLYING LANGUAGE SKILLS: Using *good* and *well* Correctly

Good (like *bad*) is an adjective. It cannot be used as an adverb after an action verb. It can, however, be used as a predicate adjective (after a linking verb). *Well* (like *badly*) is an adverb. It should be used after an action verb.

Incorrect:
The band played *good*.
Correct:
The band played *well*. (adverb describing *played*)
Correct:
It was a *good* movie. (adjective describing *movie*)

Practice Rewrite the following sentences, choosing *good* or *well*.
1. *Hamlet* is written (good, well).
2. They performed (good, well).
3. The food at the restaurant was cooked (good, well).

Writing Application *Good* and *well* convey a positive attitude. Use them correctly in your critical review.

Writer's Solution Connection Writing Lab

To add precise words to your review, use the Descriptive Word Bin in the Revising section of the Description tutorial.

Revising

Use a Checklist Use the following checklist to help you revise your critical review.

▶ Have you clearly expressed your opinion of the work? *Ask a friend to read your paper and state your opinion. If what your friend gets out of your paper is different from what you meant to convey, add language and details that make your opinion clear.*

▶ Does your language express the appropriate degree of praise or disappointment? *List words in your paper that convey your feelings. Then, decide whether you have enough and whether they are strong enough. If not, add more or stronger words.*

▶ Is your information accurate? *Check all quotations, titles, and references to Shakespeare to make sure they are spelled and punctuated correctly.*

REVISION MODEL

① from *The Life and Death of King Richard III*
The soliloquy provides a chilling look into Richard's mind.
② In it, he contemplates his reasons for committing an evil deed.
Satisfied that he is justified in his evil desire, he devises a
③ well-crafted
treacherous plan. This soliloquy helps the reader determine
his or her own feelings toward Richard.

① For accuracy, the writer adds the full title of the play.
② This point was added to support the writer's point.
③ The writer adds positive language to indicate her feelings about the soliloquy.

Publishing and Presenting

Library With classmates, create a class magazine of critical reviews. Post the magazine in the school library.

Talk Show Television and radio talk shows often include critical reviews. With a partner, imagine that you are a guest and a host. Using a question-and-answer format, the host should quiz the guest about his or her critical evaluation. If you can, videotape your talk show.

✓ ASSESSMENT		4	3	2	1
PORTFOLIO ASSESSMENT Use the rubric on Evaluation/Review in the **Alternative Assessment** booklet, p. 100, to assess the students' writing. Add these criteria to customize this rubric to this assignment.	**Opinions and Support**	The review contains clear opinions about the topic and supports every opinion with details.	The review contains clear opinions about the topic, but not all opinions are supported.	The review contains opinions that are not always clearly expressed, and some are not supported.	The review contains opinions that are unclear and not supported with details.
	Direct and Indirect Quotations	The writer uses direct and indirect quotations effectively and correctly throughout the review.	The writer uses direct and indirect quotations effectively, although there may be punctuation errors.	There are one or two points in the review where the writer uses an indirect quotation incorrectly.	The writer uses only indirect quotations in the review, although direct quotations would be more effective.

Real-World Reading Skills Workshop

Distinguishing Between Important and Unimportant Details

Strategies for Success

Have you ever watched a movie and become so absorbed with some unimportant detail that you missed important dialogue? The same thing can happen in reading. It is also important to stay focused on the details that will help you follow and understand what you are reading. Don't be distracted by unimportant and unrelated details.

Set Your Purpose First, determine your purpose for reading. You may be reading to find facts for a report, to get information about a club you want to join, or to be entertained. Setting your purpose before you read will enable you to focus on details that will help you accomplish your goal.

Look for Key Points As you read, determine which information is central, or key, to understanding. For example, if you are reading a mystery in which a gem is stolen, the movements and whereabouts of *all* the characters are very important. If you are reading a biography about a man who solves mysteries, the only movements and whereabouts that are important are those of the man.

✔ *Here are other texts in which it's important to distinguish between important and unimportant information:*
▶ *Newspaper articles*
▶ *Textbooks*
▶ *Magazine articles*
▶ *Camp brochures*

RARE BEAUTIES MAY SOON BE GONE

Many people know of endangered animal species—such as the gray wolf, the bald eagle, and the white leopard—but few know about endangered plant species. Actually, there are now almost 700 plants listed as endangered, or threatened. Hawaii is home to 263 of them! Most plants are endangered because their habitat is being destroyed by new construction and the elimination of open spaces. Aside from losing the beauty of the plants, scientists worry about losing the possibility of their life-saving medical properties.

Endangered Wildflowers

Northern wild monkshood
Large-flowered fiddleneck
Western prairie fringed orchid
Silversword
Rough-leaf loosestrife
Addison's leatherflower

Apply the Strategies

Scan the article above. Then, answer the following questions:

1. What might be your purpose for reading this article?
2. Just by skimming this article, tell what it's about.
3. List three key points.
4. Which sentence could be deleted from this article without changing its meaning?
5. How does the special boxed section help you determine what's important in this article?

Real-World Reading Skills Workshop ◆ 799

Reviewing Subject and Verb Agreement

The selection in Part 2 includes instruction on the following:

- Verb Agreement in Inverted Sentences

This instruction is reinforced with the Build Grammar Skills practice page in **Selection Support,** p. 256.

As you review subject and verb agreement, you may wish to include the following:

- Subjects of Linking Verbs

In some sentences with a subject and a predicate nominative, they may not agree in number. In these cases, the linking verb must agree with the number of the subject, regardless of the number of its predicate nominative. For example:

Heavy rains are a reason for extreme caution.

In this sentence, the verb is plural because the subject *rains* is plural. However, if the sentence is reworded, the subject is now singular, so the verb is singular:

A reason for extreme caution is heavy rains.

Writer's Solution

For additional practice and support, use the practice pages on Agreement Between Subjects and Verbs, pp. 81–85 in the *Writer's Solution Grammar Practice Book.* If students have access to technology, they can use the lessons in the unit on Subject-Verb Agreement in the *Writer's Solution Language Lab CD-ROM.*

Subject and Verb Agreement

Grammar Review

in·vert (ĭn vûrt') **v. 1** to turn upside down *[The image that falls on the film in a camera is inverted.]* **2** to reverse the order, position, or direction of *[to invert the subject and predicate of a sentence]*

The subject and verb of a sentence must **agree** in number (singular or plural). (See p. 794.) In most sentences, the subject comes before the verb. Sometimes, however, the normal word order of the sentence is inverted, and the subject comes after the verb. Even though the subject comes after the verb, the verb must still agree with the subject in number:

               V

"Moving across the stage were two

  S

actors."

Sentences beginning with *here* or *there* are almost always in inverted word order.

        V   S

Here are Shakespeare's most famous lines.

Many questions are also in inverted word order:

          V   S

"Wherefore speaks he this to her he hates?"

Practice 1 On your paper, write the following sentences with the correct verb. Then, underline the subject.

1. Beyond London (is, are) someone who knows of Richard's plot.

2. Here (come, comes) the two lovers, Beatrice and Benedick.

3. What (make, makes) Lysander profess his love to her?

4. How wickedly (do, does) Richard plan against the King!

5. There (is, are) many Shakespearean plays and sonnets to read.

Practice 2
Rewrite the following sentences, making the change indicated in parentheses and any other changes necessary.

1. Where is my book? (Change *book* to *books*.)

2. Here comes Hermia. (Change *Hermia* to *Hermia and Helena*.)

3. What is the meaning of Benedick's statement? (change *meaning* to *meanings*.)

4. There are flowers growing along the fence. (Change *flowers* to *a flower*.)

5. There seems no plan crueler than Richard's. (Change *plan* to *plans*.)

Grammar in Writing

✔ Be careful not to use the contractions *there's (there is), here's (here is),* and *where's (where is),* which contain the singular verb *is* with plural subjects.

Incorrect: Here's the plays of Shakespeare.

Correct: Here are the plays of Shakespeare.

Answers
Practice 1
1. Beyond London is <u>someone</u> who knows of Richard's plot.
2. Here come the two <u>lovers</u>, Beatrice and Benedick.
3. <u>What</u> makes Lysander profess his love to her?
4. How wickedly does <u>Richard</u> plan against the King!
5. There are many Shakespearean <u>plays</u> and <u>sonnets</u> to read.

Practice 2
1. Where are my books?
2. Here come Hermia and Helena.
3. What are the meanings of Benedick's statement?
4. There is a flower growing along the fence.
5. There seem no plans crueler than Richard's.

Speaking, Listening, and Viewing Workshop

Debating

Debates are conducted in Congress, as well as in middle schools, high schools, and universities. A debate is a formal argument in which two people or teams prepare and present arguments on opposing sides of an issue. The issue or question is a stated proposition, such as: "Should all students be required to take swimming?" The debaters either *defend* or *attack* the stated proposition.

Know the Rules In most debates, the affirmative side argues first. Then, the opposing side presents its arguments. Each side has an opportunity for rebuttal, in which they may challenge or question the other side's arguments. Each speech is timed. At the conclusion, a judge or panel decides the winner.

Be Prepared To prepare for a debate, decide whether you are "for" (affirmative) or "against" (negative) the proposition. Then, prepare your argument—the points you will make to prove your side of the proposition. If necessary, do research to find information to support your argument. In your opening, include the points that most strongly support your position. Also, acknowledge any weaknesses that your argument may have. By dealing with possible weaknesses, you can make them sound insignificant, and your opponent cannot use them against you. Your research can provide background knowledge that will help you defend your points.

After you have presented your argument, be prepared to defend your position. Think of any possible points your opponent might make, and practice how you will respond. Speak loudly, clearly, and directly to your audience.

Apply the Strategies

With a classmate, practice debating one of the following propositions:

1. Students should wear uniforms to school.
2. The privilege of voting should be revoked if not used in two consecutive presidential elections.
3. School should be in session twelve months a year.
4. Television programs should be censored.

Debating Tips

▶ Prepare a strong factual opening.
▶ Speak loudly and clearly.
▶ Be prepared to refute your opponent's points and to defend your own.

Ask students if they have ever seen a Congressional debate on television, or perhaps a debate between political candidates. Explain that in many political races, a debate between two opposing candidates allows the viewers to see more clearly the contrasting positions of the candidates.

Customize for
Interpersonal Learners

Some students may do better working in a group in a debate. Have students form groups, and each group can choose a side to the issue. Then have each group prepare their arguments, by discussing the issue and collaborating on research to find support for their positions. When presenting the argument, groups can elect one speaker or take turns in speaking.

Apply the Strategies

To gather research for their debates, suggest that students use a newspaper or periodical database in the library. Explain to students that they will need to use key words to search for articles about their topics. For example, for the first proposition, "Students should wear uniforms to school," students will want to search under the key words *school uniforms*.

Cross-Curricular Connection: Social Studies

History of Debating Explain to students that debating has been popular since pre-classical times. One of the first historical references to a debate is in Homer's *Iliad*. Both the Greeks and the Romans debated cases in law courts. One of the first publicly recognized debaters was Cicero.

With the advent of parliamentary and congressional government, debating became popular in England and then in the United States. In the U.S., debating in the Senate is more important than debating in the House of Representatives, because of the time allowed for the debate to be concluded. Some great debates in history include the Webster-Hayne debate of 1830, the Webster-Calhoun debate of 1833, and debates over the Compromise of 1850 and the Kansas-Nebraska bill of 1854.

In the twentieth century, political debates were made more accessible through radio and television. In 1960, presidential candidates Richard Nixon and John Kennedy held a series of four televised debates on political issues, which, analysts said, greatly influenced the more than 80 million viewers.

Have students research the history of debating. They may choose to focus on a specific debate or on debating within a specific historical era. Encourage students to write a brief summary of their findings and share it with the rest of the class.

◆ Build Vocabulary

What's Behind the Words

Explain to students that they can find definitions for film terms by looking in a dictionary or a reference book on filmmaking. Many words that are used in reference to film began as a general term, whose meaning was modified specifically for film.

Answers
Activity 1

1. actor = one who represents a character in a dramatic production
2. angle = the precise viewpoint from which something is observed or considered (as in a camera angle)
3. credits = names shown on a cinema or TV screen of persons responsible for the acting, direction, production, and so on.
4. cut = make an abrupt transition from one sound or image to another in motion picture, radio, TV
5. director = person who supervises and instructs the actors and actresses, the camera crew, and so on.
6. dissolve = a gradual superimposing of one motion picture or television shot upon another on a screen
7. frame = single exposure on a roll of photographic film
8. pan(orama) = rotate (as a motion picture camera) to keep an object in the picture or to secure a panoramic effect
9. screen = a flat surface on which a picture, or a series of pictures, is projected or reflected
10. shot = a single sequence of a motion picture or a television program shot by one camera without interruption

Activity 2

1. gaffer = a lighting electrician on a television or movie set
2. best boy = chief assistant to the gaffer
3. key grip = technician in charge of moving and setting up camera tracks and scenery in motion picture or television production

---

What's Behind the Words
Vocabulary Adventures With Richard Lederer

Movie Vocabulary

For more than a century, people around the globe have drawn many of their hopes and dreams and their images of life from the cinema. *Cinema* itself is a word that was coined from the Greek *kinematos,* or "motion," to describe the movies.

Movie is a shortening of *moving* or *motion picture*. Movies don't really "move" at all. What we see is a series of still pictures flashed on the screen one after the other. They seem to move because each is just a little different from the one before, and we see each image for just a fraction of a second.

The Language of Film

Most words having to do with movies existed long before the motion picture was invented. Many of them have old and fascinating origins:

In Latin, *camera* meant "chamber" or "room." Our picture-taking camera gets its name from the small dark "room" inside that holds the film.

Our word *film* comes from the Old English *filmen,* or "thin skin." The idea of a thin coating is expressed in "a film of dust on the furniture." Modern camera film is coated with a thin skin of light-sensitive chemicals.

A Flourishing Root

Film stars work from a movie *script*. The Latin roots *script* and *scribe* mean "write." These roots flourish in words such as *ascribe, conscript, describe, inscribe, manuscript, nondescript, postscript, prescribe, proscribe, scribble, scripture,* and *transcribe*.

Film and stage actors also *rehearse*. The origins of the word *rehearse* differ greatly from its meaning today. The root of *rehearse* grows out of the Old French *hercer,* "to harrow; to cultivate the soil for farming." The Middle English *rehersen* meant "to harrow over again," that is, to go over the same ground. This idea of a repeated action is seen in our modern use of the word. When actors rehearse a film script, they go over the same lines many times.

Chasing a Phrase

An expression that is quite popular these days is *cut to the chase*. Here, the reference is to the movies. The idea is that we should get past the boring stuff, such as a mushy love scene, and cut to the chase scene for more excitement. Since its birth in the movies, *cut to the chase* has broadened to mean "stop wasting time and get to the point!"

ACTIVITY 1 Look up and explain the following film terms:

1. actor	5. director	9. producer
2. angle	6. dissolve	10. projector
3. credits	7. frame	11. screen
4. cut	8. pan(orama)	12. shot

ACTIVITY 2 Discover the meanings of three specialized movie terms that you see in the credits that follow the movie:

1. gaffer	2. best boy	3. key grip

802 ◆ Drama

Extended Reading Opportunities

Envisioning the action of a play will help you bring the drama to life. Following are just a few possibilities for extending your exploration of drama.

Suggested Titles

Tales From Shakespeare
Charles Lamb and Mary Lamb

This book provides an excellent introduction to the exciting plots and beautiful language of Shakespeare's plays. This brother-and-sister team turn the plays into short narratives that make the stories of Shakespeare's plays understandable to a young audience. Written in 1807, it is as easy to read today as it was when it was written. Before tackling the plays of Shakespeare, use this book to familiarize yourself with the plots, settings, and characters of his works.

Nothing But The Truth
Ronn Smith

This play is based on a novel by Avi. When ninth-grader Philip Malloy hums along with a tape of "The Star-Spangled Banner" during homeroom, he is told he is breaking school rules. What happens next stirs a national controversy. Now everyone has a different story and no one except the reader knows the truth. As you read, you will be amazed at how the versions of what happened continue to change until no one seems to know the truth.

Let Me Hear You Whisper
Paul Zindel

A new cleaning lady is hired at a laboratory. The supervisor instructs her not to touch anything—especially a dolphin that the scientists have been unsuccessful in getting to speak. Helen is happy to mind her own business, but when the dolphin decides to speak to her, she feels compelled to become involved. After a confrontation with her supervisor and the scientists, she makes a bold protest against the misuse of animals.

Other Possibilities

It's a Wonderful Life   Frances Goodrich

Invasion of the Body Snatchers   Al LaValley

I Remember Mama   John Van Druten

Planning Instruction and Assessment

Unit Objectives

1. To read poetry
2. To apply a variety of reading strategies, particularly strategies for reading poetry, appropriate for reading these selections
3. To recognize literary elements used in these selections
4. To increase vocabulary
5. To learn elements of grammar and usage
6. To write in a variety of modes about situations based on the selections
7. To develop speaking and listening skills, by completing activities
8. To view images critically and create visual representations

Meeting the Objectives Each selection provides instructional material and portfolio opportunities by which students can meet unit objectives. You will find additional practice pages for reading strategies, literary elements, vocabulary, and grammar in the **Selection Support** booklet in the **Teaching Resources box.**

Setting Goals Work with your students to set goals for unit outcomes. Plan skills and concepts you wish them to acquire. Match instruction and activities according to students' performance levels or learning modalities.

Portfolios Students may keep portfolios of their completed work or of their work in progress. The Build Your Portfolio page of each selection provides opportunities for students to apply the concepts presented.

 Humanities: Art

Man at the Edge of Paradise, 1994, by Adam Straus
Adam Straus is an American painter, born in Florida but currently residing in New York City. His work often involves a fine balance between formalism and romance.

1. What images in the painting are symbols of paradise? *Students may say the parrot, the butterfly, and the hummingbird are symbols of a tropical paradise.*

2. What elements of this painting seem realistic to you? unrealistic? *The birds and the flowers may seem like the most realistic parts of the painting. Students may note that the background seems unrealistic.*

Man at the Edge of Paradise, 1994, Adam Straus, Courtesy Nohra Haime Gallery

Art Transparencies

The **Art Transparencies** booklet in the **Teaching Resources** box offers fine art to help students make connections to other curriculum areas and high-interest topics.

To extend the concept of symbols in painting as exemplified by the art on these pages, use Art Transparency 18, p. 75, *Dog Barking at the Moon* by Joan Miró. The booklet's Responding to Art section on Appreciation can be used to spark a discussion on symbolism.

Beyond Literature

Each unit presents Beyond Literature features that lead students into an exploration of careers, communities, and other subject areas. In this unit, students will make humanities and sports connections. In addition, the **Teaching Resources** box contains a **Beyond Literature** booklet of activities. Using literature as a springboard, these activity pages offer students opportunities to connect literature to other curriculum areas and to the workplace and careers, community, media, and humanities.

Poetry

In poetry, language is used in special ways to create vivid, memorable, and sometimes musical impressions. Poems may capture a single moment in time, take you into a world of make-believe, or tell the story of a person's life. As you explore the poems in this unit, you will encounter the following terms:

- **Lyric poetry** is poetry that expresses vivid thoughts and feelings.

- **Narrative poetry** tells a story.

- **Poetic form** refers to the structure of a poem—its stanzas and its pattern of rhymes and rhythms.

- **Sound devices** are such elements as *rhyme, rhythm, alliteration,* and *onomatopoeia* that give poems a musical quality.

- **Figurative language** refers to the use of figures of speech—such as *simile, metaphor,* and *personification*—which present a fresh and unusual way of looking at things.

♦ 805

Connections

Within this unit, you will find selections and activities that make connections beyond literature. Use these selections to connect students' understanding and appreciation of literature beyond the traditional literature and language arts curriculum.

Encourage students to connect literature to other curriculum areas. You may wish to coordinate with teachers in other curriculum areas to determine ways to team teach and further extend instruction.

Connections to Today's World

Use these selections to guide students to recognize the relevance of literature to contemporary writings. In this unit, the lyrics of "The Wind Beneath My Wings" connects poetry to contemporary songs.

Connecting Literature to Social Studies

Each unit contains a selection that connects literature to social studies. In this unit, students will read a poem about the Vietnam War, "Wahbegan."

Assessing Student Progress

The tools that are available to measure the degree to which students meet the unit objectives are listed below.

Informal Assessment

The questions in the Guide for Responding sections are a first level of response to the concepts and skills presented with the selection. As a brief, informal measure of students' grasp of the material, these responses indicate where further instruction and practice are needed. The practice pages in the **Selection Support** booklet provide for this type of instruction and practice.

You will also find literature and reading guides in the **Alternative Assessment** booklet, which students can use for informal assessment of their individual performances.

Formal Assessment

The **Formal Assessment** booklet contains Selection Tests and Unit Tests.

Selection Tests measure comprehension and skills acquisition for each selection or group of selections.

Each Unit Test provides students with 30 multiple-choice questions and 5 essay questions designed to assess students' knowledge of the literature and skills taught in the unit.

Each Alternative Unit Test: Standardized-Test Practice provides 15 multiple-choice questions and 3 essay questions based on two new literature selections not contained in the student book. The questions on the Alternative Unit Test are designed to assess students' ability to compare and contrast selections, applying skills taught in the unit.

Alternative Assessment

For portfolio and alternative assessment, the **Alternative Assessment** booklet contains Scoring Rubrics, Assessment sheets, and Learning Modalities activities.

Scoring Rubrics provide writing modes that can be applied to Writing activities, Writing Mini-Lessons, and Writing Process Workshop lessons.

Assessment sheets for speaking and listening activities provide peer and self-assessment direction.

Learning Modalities activities appeal to different learning styles. Use these as an alternative measurement of students' growth.

Guide for Reading

OBJECTIVES

1. To read, comprehend, and interpret a poem
2. To relate a poem to personal experience
3. To apply strategies for reading poetry
4. To identify and analyze symbols in a poem
5. To build vocabulary in context and learn the word root -semble-
6. To identify comparative forms of modifiers
7. To write an explanation of a symbol, justified with reasons
8. To respond to the poem through writing, speaking and listening, and projects

SKILLS INSTRUCTION

Vocabulary:
Word Roots:
-semble-

Spelling:
Words Ending With
the *uhl* Sound
Spelled *le*

Grammar:
Comparison of
Modifiers

**Reading
for Success:**
Strategies for
Reading Poetry

Literary Focus:
Symbols

Writing:
Give Reasons

**Speaking
and Listening:**
Poetry Reading
(Teacher Edition)

Critical Viewing:
Interpret

PORTFOLIO OPPORTUNITIES

Writing: List; Poem; Essay
Writing Mini-Lesson: Explanation
of a Symbol
Speaking and Listening: Love Song;
Poetry Reading
Projects: Salute to the Poet; Musical
Archives

Meet the Author:
Robert P. Tristram Coffin
(1892–1955)

Robert P. Tristram Coffin grew up on a farm in Brunswick, Maine. He attended Bowdoin College and Oxford University, where he was a Rhodes scholar. After serving in World War I, he became a professor at Wells College. Later, he returned to his alma mater, Bowdoin, where he was a professor of English from 1934 until his death.

Literature and Art Coffin published thirty-seven books of poetry, prose, essays, and biographies during his lifetime. He won the Pulitzer Prize in Poetry in 1936 for his book *Strange Holiness.* Besides all these accomplishments, Coffin was an artist who created etchings and sketches. His artistic imagination served his poetry well, as is shown in the poem "The Secret Heart."

◆ LITERATURE AND YOUR LIFE

CONNECT YOUR EXPERIENCE

How would you complete the sentence, "I'll never forget . . . ?" Our minds hold thousands of memories, but some stand out as vividly as if they happened only yesterday. These memories are almost like short films that we can run before our eyes at will, with all their colors, smells, and characters. In this poem, Robert Coffin describes such a memory.

THEMATIC FOCUS: Appreciating Others

How might evidence of a father's unspoken love for his child form a cherished memory?

◆ Background for Understanding

CULTURE

"The Secret Heart" contains an unusual image of a heart. Traditionally, the heart is used to symbolize love. For instance, valentines and other love tokens are often decorated with hearts, and Cupid, the Roman god of love, is often depicted shooting his arrow through a heart. Further examples of the heart as a symbol of love include the phrases "dear to my heart," "sweetheart," and "heartache."

More About the Author
Much of **Robert P. Tristram Coffin's** writing deals with his love for New England and its people. He has said that he was "a New Englander by birth, by bringing up, by spirit." Throughout the latter part of his career, Coffin gave numerous lectures and readings of his work. He often used these occasions to display his watercolors and pen-and-ink sketches. In a reference to "The Secret Heart," Coffin explained that the poem describes a time when, as a small child, he was ill. He awoke in the night and saw his father leaning over him, illuminating the area with a lighted match held between his hands.

 Prentice Hall Literature Program Resources

REINFORCE / RETEACH / EXTEND
Selection Support Pages
Build Vocabulary: Word Roots: -semble-, p. 269
Build Spelling Skills: p. 270
Building Grammar Skills: Comparison of Modifiers, p. 271
Reading for Success: Strategies for Reading Poetry, p. 272
Literary Focus: Symbols, p. 273
Strategies for Diverse Student Needs, pp. 99–100

Beyond Literature Cross-Curricular Connection: Science, p. 50
Formal Assessment Selection Test, pp. 228–229, Assessment Resources Software
Alternative Assessment, p. 50
Writing and Language Transparencies Cluster Organizer, p. 85
Resource Pro CD-R⦶M "The Secret Heart"
 Listening to Literature Audiocassettes "The Secret Heart"

◆ The Secret Heart ◆

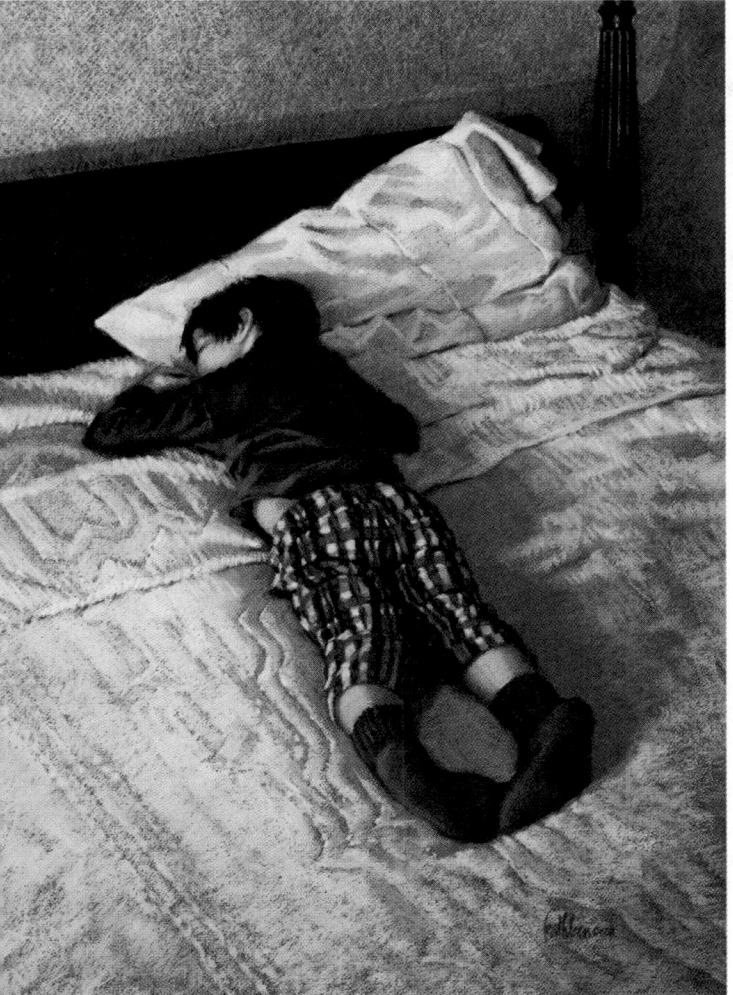

Nap in the Afternoon, Kathleen Cook, Courtesy of the artist

◆ Literary Focus

SYMBOLS

A **symbol** is an object, person, or idea that stands for something beyond itself. For example, the heart is a universal symbol of love and affection. Writers use symbols as a kind of poetic shorthand in order to make a point, create a mood, or reinforce a theme. Depending on the subject of a poem or story, practically anything may serve as a symbol—an egg may represent a beginning, a horse may stand for nature, or a grandmother may represent history.

◆ Build Vocabulary

WORD ROOTS: *-semble-*

In "The Secret Heart," you will read: "His two hands were curved apart / In the semblance of a heart." *Semblance* includes the word root *-semble-,* which means "to seem or appear." *Semblance* means "appearance" or "likeness."

WORD BANK

Kindling means "small twigs used to start a fire." Use the definition to help you guess at the meaning of *kindled.* See the Build Vocabulary box on page 810 to see if you guessed correctly.

> kindled
> semblance

 Interest Grabber Write the following words on the board: *friendship, education, United States of America.* Ask students to work in groups to brainstorm for a list of symbols that represent each of these—for example, joined hands to symbolize friendship, a book to represent education, and the U. S. flag to represent the United States of America. Discuss the variety of symbols students thought of for each concept. Encourage them to consider what the poet expresses with a symbol as they read "The Secret Heart."

◆ Build Grammar Skills

Comparison of Modifiers If you wish to introduce the grammar concept for this selection before students read, refer to the instruction on p. 811.

Customize for
Less Proficient Readers
Have students listen to the recording of the poem prior to reading. Then have them read the poem aloud, stopping to restate each sentence in their own words.

🎧 **Listening to Literature Audiocassettes**

Customize for
More Advanced Students
Explain that poets sometimes use homophones (words that sound the same but are spelled differently and have different meanings) in hopes that the reader will attach a double meaning to a line. Have students identify homophones in the poem. Challenge them to write a paragraph explaining the double meaning the poet may have intended by using the word *sun* in the last line of the poem.

🎵 **Humanities: Art**

Nap in the Afternoon, by Kathleen Cook
In this painting, the artist uses dark colors to emphasize the child's shape against the white background. Use these questions for discussion:
1. How can you tell the child is napping and not in bed for the night? *He is wearing his socks; he is not tucked in.*
2. How do you think parents feel when they see their sleeping children? *They feel protective and loving.*

Preparing for Standardized Tests

Grammar The grammar skill for this selection is comparison of modifiers. Grammar sections of standardized tests may require students to select the correct comparative form of a modifier in a given sentence. Discuss comparative forms (used when two things are compared) and superlative forms (used when more than two things are compared) of adjectives and adverbs. Invite volunteers to give examples of sentences using each form. Give students the following sample test question:

> The heart was _____ than any other heart the boy had ever seen.

(A) sweeter   (C) sweetest
(B) more sweet   (D) most sweet

Explain that *more* and *most* are generally used before adjectives with more than two syllables. Since the adjective *sweet* is a one-syllable word, the comparative and superlative forms end with *-er* and *-est,* and neither (B) nor (D) would be correct. Although the heart may be the sweetest the boy had ever seen, the writer compares one heart with all the other hearts the boy had ever seen; therefore the answer is (A). The word *than* is the tip-off that the comparative form is correct.

The Reading for Success page in each unit presents a set of problem-solving strategies to help readers understand authors' words and ideas on multiple levels. Good readers develop a bank of strategies from which they can draw as needed.

Unit 9 introduces strategies for reading poetry. Poems differ structurally from prose and they may condense meaning. Strategies for reading poetry encourage students to pay attention to punctuation, identify the poem's speaker, use their senses by identifying sensory images, and paraphrase lines to help understand meaning.

These strategies for reading poetry are modeled with "The Secret Heart." Each green box shows an example of the thinking process involved in applying one of these strategies. Additional notes provide support for applying these strategies throughout the selection.

How to Use the Reading for Success Page

- Introduce the strategies for reading poetry, presenting each as a problem-solving procedure.

- Before students read the poem, have them preview it, looking at the annotations in the green boxes that model the strategies.

- To reinforce these strategies after students read the poem, have them do the Reading for Success page, p. 272, in **Selection Support.** These pages give students an opportunity to read a selection and practice critical reading strategies by writing their own annotations.

Reading Strategies: Support and Reinforcement
Using Boxed Annotations and Prompts

Throughout the unit, the notes in green, red, and maroon boxes are intended to help students apply reading strategies, understand the literary focus, and make a connection with their lives. You may use boxed material in these ways:

- Have students pause at each box and respond to its prompt before they continue reading.

- Urge students to read through the selection, ignoring the boxes. After they complete the selection, they may go back and review the text, responding to the prompts.

808

*R*eading for Success

Strategies for Reading Poetry

Poetry is unlike other types of literature. Poets use language imaginatively to create images, tell stories, explore feelings and experiences, and suggest meanings. They choose and combine words carefully to enable you to see your world in a new and fresh way. They may also use rhythm and rhyme to create musical effects in a poem. To appreciate and enjoy poetry fully, use the following reading strategies:

Read the lines according to punctuation.

Punctuation marks are like traffic signals to the reader of poetry. They tell you when to pause, for how long to pause, and when to stop. Look for sentences or complete thoughts in a poem. If there is no punctuation mark at the end of a line, read on without pausing or stopping.

For example, the first line of "The Secret Heart" contains no end punctuation. Therefore, you would read on without pausing until you get to the period at the end of the second line: "Across the years he could recall / His father one way best of all."

Identify the speaker.

The speaker in poetry is the voice that the poet creates to communicate his or her message. Sometimes the speaker is identified; sometimes the speaker is a nameless voice; and sometimes the speaker is the poet him- or herself.

Use your senses.

Poetry is full of images that appeal to your senses of sight, hearing, taste, smell, and touch. Identify those images as you read, and pause to experience and appreciate their appeal.

Paraphrase the lines.

When reading poetry, periodically pause to restate in your own words the poet's ideas. Paraphrasing in this way ensures that you understand the basic meaning of the poem.

Lines From Poem:	Paraphrase:
In the stillest hour of the night The boy awakened to a light.	A light woke the boy in the middle of the night.

As you read "The Secret Heart," look at the notes along the sides of the pages. They will demonstrate how to apply these strategies to a poem.

Model a Reading Strategy: Use Your Senses
Good readers know that one of the pleasures of poetry is a full appreciation of the poet's images and the sensory details he uses to create them. Demonstrate how to fully recognize how the poet uses words by modeling your thinking about lines 11–16 in the poem.

The boy sees his father's hands cupped around a lighted match as a heart. If I cup my own hands, I can see something similar. The light would increase the redness of the father's hands, further intensifying the image. The poet then uses this visual image, and imagines that this is a heart he can see—"a bare heart"—that represents the father's real heart.

If I continue to think about it, I can understand that the poet combines the glowing, visual heart made of the father's hands with the father's real heart which glows with love.

By following the poet's imagination through his visual images, I can understand the feelings of the father and the boy.

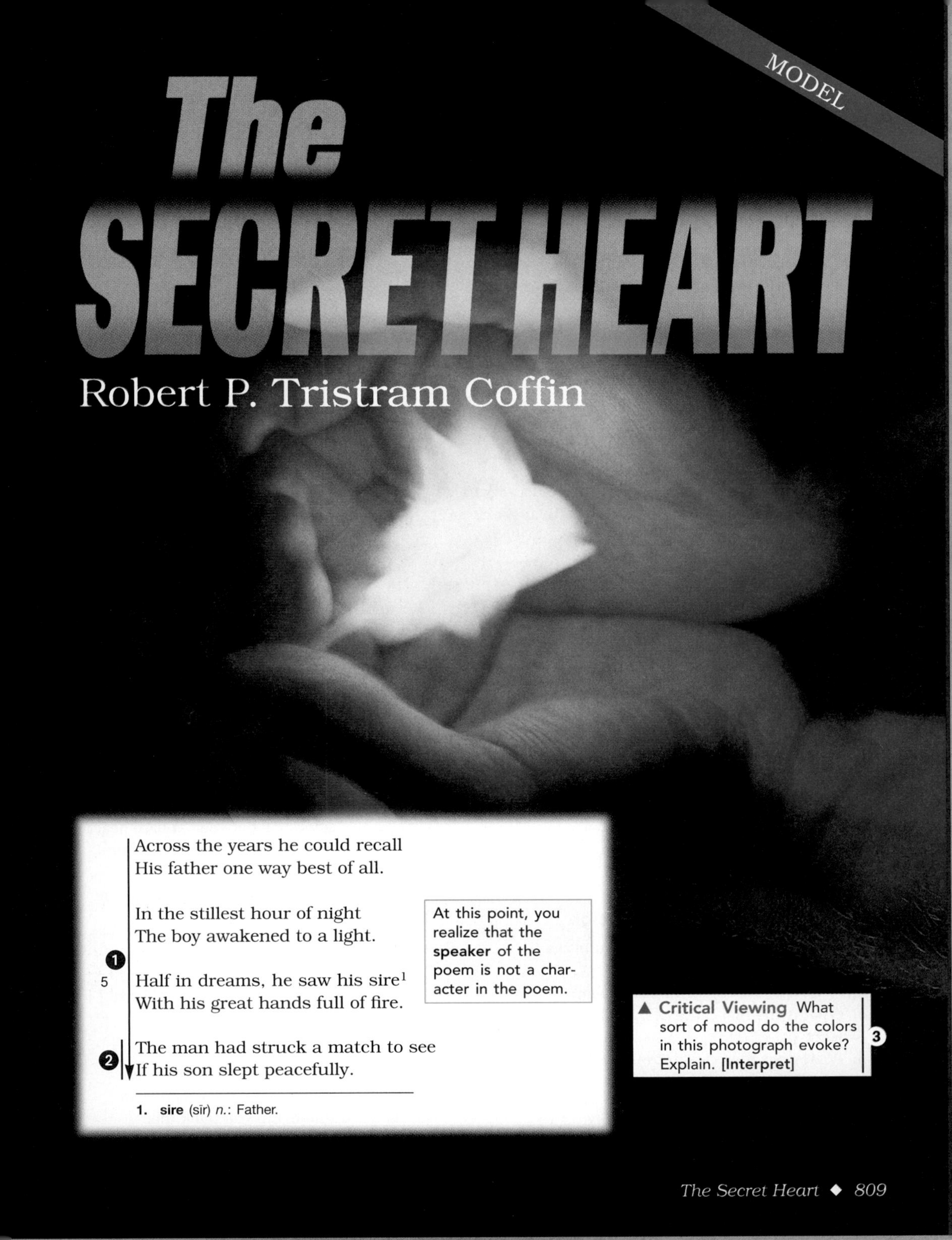

MODEL

The SECRET HEART

Robert P. Tristram Coffin

Across the years he could recall
His father one way best of all.

In the stillest hour of night
The boy awakened to a light.

❶ Half in dreams, he saw his sire[1]
With his great hands full of fire.

❷ The man had struck a match to see
If his son slept peacefully.

At this point, you realize that the **speaker** of the poem is not a character in the poem.

▲ Critical Viewing What sort of mood do the colors in this photograph evoke? Explain. **[Interpret]** ❸

1. **sire** (sīr) *n.*: Father.

Develop Understanding

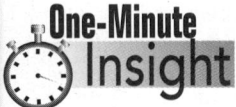

One-Minute Insight

In "The Secret Heart," Robert P. Tristram Coffin describes a simple event from childhood. The speaker recalls waking in the night to see his father standing over his bed. The father is holding a lit match in his cupped hands to help him see his sleeping child. The speaker recalls the love and tenderness apparent on his father's face and recognizes that the feelings are so strong and personal they would never be shared intentionally. The boy appreciates the gift his father unknowingly gives him—the shared secret of this parent's boundless love for his child.

◆ Literary Focus

❶ **Speaker** Ask students how they can tell the speaker is not in the poem. *No first-person pronouns are used. The people described are a boy and his father.*

Reading for Success

❷ **Read the Lines According to Punctuation** Read this stanza aloud, first pausing after *see*. Then read it again without pausing. Discuss how the natural flow of the sentence makes it easier to listen to and understand.

▶Critical Viewing◀

❸ **Interpret** *Possible answer: The warm reds and yellows surrounded by black create a mood of warmth, security, and closeness.*

Customize for
English Language Learners
Help students understand the poem as they read by pantomiming various actions and expressions. For example, you can act out sleepily awakening and partially opening your eyes; striking and holding a match in your hands; or looking down lovingly, as if at a sleeping child.

Block Scheduling Strategies

Consider these suggestions to take advantage of extended class time:

- Discuss the strategies for reading poetry. Then have students read the poem independently. Have them meet with learning buddies to discuss the Reader's Response and Thematic Focus. Then ask pairs of students to complete the Reading for Success and Literary Focus questions on p. 811.
- Alternatively, read the poem aloud with the class. Then have students work in small groups to answer the Check Your Comprehension and Critical Thinking questions on p. 810.
- To reinforce the strategies for reading poetry, have students complete the Reading for Success pages in **Selection Support,** p. 272.
- Have students prepare for the Writing Mini-Lesson by working on the *Writer's Solution Language Lab CD-ROM* and *Writer's Solution Writing Lab CD-ROM.* Refer to the teaching suggestions on p. 812 to guide students through the process.

◆ Literary Focus

❶ Symbol Ask students what the heart mentioned here and elsewhere in the poem, as well as in the title, symbolizes. *It symbolizes the love the father feels for his son.*

◆ Critical Thinking

❷ Draw Conclusions What does the boy mean when he says his father's hands held up the sun? *Possible answer: By understanding his father's love and care for him, he feels secure, and this feeling of security extends to his whole being and his view of everything.*

Reinforce and Extend

Answers

◆ LITERATURE AND YOUR LIFE

Reader's Response Some students may say that a father's love should not be a secret; others may say that the secret makes it special.

Thematic Focus Possible answer: The boy appreciates his father because he has seen proof of his father's love.

☑ Check Your Comprehension

1. The boy's point of view is reflected.
2. The boy recalls his father checking on him during the night.
3. The glowing heart is a lit match cupped in the father's hands.
4. The boy discovers how much his father loves him.

◆ Critical Thinking

1. He might not be seeing things quite clearly, so that the hands take on the appearance of a heart.
2. The "bare heart" is the one the boy sees—this could mean the cupped hands or the expression of love on his father's face. The "hidden one" is the heart inside his father's chest—it could also be the deeper and more personal feelings that are not seen on the father's face.
3. The "secret heart" is the match-lit hands; it is also the feelings of love the boy saw on his father's face.
4. Yes. Coffin created a visual image of the heart-shaped hands and created the feelings of a secret heart in the description of the father's loving expression.
5. No. The son says that he saw his father's love expressed just long enough to know that he was secure in that love.

810

---

10 He held his palms each side the spark
His love had <u>kindled</u> in the dark.

His two hands were curved apart
In the <u>semblance</u> of a heart.

❶ He wore, it seemed to his small son,
A bare heart on his hidden one.

15 A heart that gave out such a glow
No son awake could bear to know.

It showed a look upon a face
Too tender for the day to trace.

One instant, it lit all about,
20 And then the secret heart went out.

❷ But it shone long enough for one
To know that hands held up the sun.

> You might **para-phrase** these lines as, "He cupped his hands around the flame of the match."

> **Use the punctuation** to aid your understanding. Pause at the commas, and stop at the period.

> This image in line 18, which describes the father's facial expression, appeals to your **sense** of sight.

◆ Build Vocabulary

kindled (kin´ dəld) *v.*: Stirred up; awakened

semblance (sem´ bləns) *n.*: Look or appearance

Guide for Responding

◆ LITERATURE AND YOUR LIFE

Reader's Response Should the father have been less secretive about his love? Why or why not?

Thematic Focus Why does the son come to appreciate his father?

Sketch Capture the essence of this poem in a drawing or a sketch.

☑ Check Your Comprehension

1. Whose point of view is reflected in the poem?
2. What event is recalled in the poem?
3. What is the real cause of the "glowing heart"?
4. What does the boy discover about his father?

◆ Critical Thinking

INTERPRET

1. The son is "half in dreams" when he sees his father. How might being half asleep affect the boy's impressions? **[Infer]**
2. What is the difference between "a bare heart" and "his hidden one" in line 14? What does each one mean? **[Draw Conclusions]**
3. Give two meanings of what Coffin means by "the secret heart." **[Interpret]**

EVALUATE

4. Do you think Coffin succeeds in creating a strong central image in "The Secret Heart"? Explain. **[Assess]**

APPLY

5. Coffin implies that the love between father and son was not expressed the same way during the daytime. Do you think this bothered the son? Explain. **[Speculate]**

810 ◆ Poetry

  Speaking and Listening Mini-Lesson

Poetry Reading

This mini-lesson supports the Speaking and Listening activity in the Idea Bank on p. 812.

Introduce Discuss how poets choose words to express ideas and to create rhythms and sounds. Reading poetry aloud provides opportunities to understand and enjoy what the poet intended.

Develop Have pairs of students reread and discuss the poem, paraphrasing to understand each line. Have them pay attention to punctuation—pausing at commas and stopping at periods—so that their phrasing is what the poet intended.

Apply Pairs can decide whether to read the poem together, alternate lines, or take turns reading sections. Have them practice reading expressively, varying the tone and pitch of their voices to create a mood.

Assess Have students present their readings and discuss with the class how various interpretations affected their appreciation of the poem. Evaluate readings based on expressiveness and clarity of presentation. You may also have students evaluate the readings by completing the Oral Interpretation form, p. 115, in **Alternative Assessment.**

Guide for Responding (continued)

◆ Reading for Success

STRATEGIES FOR READING POETRY

Review the reading strategies and the notes showing how to read poetry. Then, apply those strategies to answer the following questions:

1. Where would you pause when reading lines 19 and 20? Where would you stop?
2. Is the poem's speaker identified? Explain.
3. To which sense does this poem appeal most? Give two examples.
4. How would you paraphrase lines 15 and 16?

◆ Build Vocabulary

USING THE WORD ROOT -semble-

The word root -semble- means "to seem" or "to appear." Complete each sentence with one of these words containing -semble-:

resemblance   resembling   resemble

1. When he cupped his hands around the burning match, he made a shape ____?____ a fiery heart.
2. The ____?____ between the twin boys was almost startling.
3. The child hoped that he would ____?____ his father when he grew up.

SPELLING STRATEGY

Most English words that end in the *uhl* sound are spelled *le*, as in the word *resemble*. The *uhl* sound occurs most often in an unaccented syllable:

apple   candle   mingle   trouble

Some common exceptions to the *le* spelling are *nickel* and *panel*. On your paper, write the word that matches the definition and ends in *le*.

1. a silly type of laugh
2. a squirming movement
3. not complicated

WORD BANK

On a piece of paper, complete each sentence with the correct word from the Word Bank.

1. The boy's drawing had the ____?____ of a boat, but he had added some odd details.
2. The description of the villain ____?____ the young boy's interest in the story.

◆ Literary Focus

SYMBOLS

A **symbol** is anything that stands for or represents something else. An object that serves as a symbol has its own meaning, but it also represents an idea or a quality. For example, a dawn is a dawn, but as a symbol, *dawn* may mean a new start or a discovery.

1. (a) What is the main symbol of "The Secret Heart"? (b) How do you know it's a symbol?
2. What words in the poem reinforce the meaning of the symbol?

◆ Build Grammar Skills

COMPARISON OF MODIFIERS

Adjectives modify or describe nouns or pronouns. Adverbs modify verbs, adjectives, or other adverbs. Both adjectives and adverbs have different forms, which can be used to compare people, places, and things.

The comparative form of adjectives and adverbs compares two items. The superlative form compares more than two items.

Positive	Comparative	Superlative
fast	faster	fastest
speedy	speedier	speediest
sadly	more sadly	most sadly

Practice On your paper, underline each modifier, and indicate whether it is comparative or superlative. Then, circle the word that it modifies.

1. In the stillest hour of the night . . .
2. His father loved him more dearly than anything else.
3. The boy was happier than he had been before.
4. It was his most cherished memory.
5. Of the two, it is the harder poem.

Writing Application Write each sentence, using the correct form of the modifier.

1. The guidebook never mentioned the ____?____ part of the two-week trip. (exciting)
2. She was ____?____ than her friend Yolanda. (healthy)

The Secret Heart ◆ 811

Answers
Reading for Success

1. I would pause after *instant* and *about* and stop after *out*.
2. The poem's speaker is not identified. The speaker refers to a boy and his father but never refers to himself or herself.
3. The poem appeals mostly to sight. Examples: "great hands full of fire," "He held his palms each side the spark," "curved apart in the semblance of a heart."
4. Possible answer: It would be hard for a child to see so much love on his father's face during their daily routine.

◆ Build Vocabulary

Using the Word Root -semble-
1. resembling
2. resemblance
3. resemble

Spelling Strategy
1. giggle
2. wiggle
3. simple

Using the Word Bank
1. semblance
2. kindled

◆ Literary Focus
1. (a) A heart is the main symbol. (b) It is used in the poem to represent the father's love for his son.
2. Possible answers: semblance, glow, tender, shone

◆ Build Grammar Skills

Comparison of Modifiers
1. stillest; superlative (hour)
2. more dearly; comparative (loved)
3. happier; comparative (boy)
4. most cherished; superlative (memory)
5. harder; comparative (poem)

Writing Application
1. most exciting
2. healthier

Writer's Solution

For additional instruction and practice, use the Using Adverbs unit in the *Writer's Solution Language Lab CD-ROM*. You may also use the practice pages on adjectives and adverbs, pp. 86–89, in the *Writer's Solution Grammar Practice Book*.

Idea Bank

Following are suggestions for matching the Idea Bank topics with your students' performance levels and learning modalities:

Customize for
Performance Levels
Less Advanced Students: 1, 5, 7
Average Students: 2, 5, 6, 7
More Advanced Students: 3, 4, 6

Customize for
Learning Modalities
Verbal/Linguistic: 1, 2, 3, 4, 5
Musical/Rhythmic: 5, 7
Visual/Spatial: 2, 6
Interpersonal: 5, 6, 7
Intrapersonal: 1, 2, 3, 4

Writing Mini-Lesson

Refer students to the Writing Handbook in the back of the book for instruction on the writing process and for further information on literary analysis and symbols. Have students use the Cluster Organizer in **Writing and Language Transparencies,** p. 73, to arrange their prewriting examples.

Writer's Solution

Writing Lab CD-ROM
Have students complete the tutorial on Response to Literature. Follow these steps:
1. Have students use the Group Discussion on sharing impressions of a poem.
2. Students can use the annotated model on purpose to find out how the writer explains a work according to its literary elements.
3. Have students use the audio-annotated model to hear a writer's comments on details that state and support an opinion.
4. Have students use Writing Hints to help them begin drafting their explanations of a symbol.
5. Students can use the Self-Evaluation Checklist to help them revise their explanations.

Writer's Solution Sourcebook
Have students use Chapter 9, "Response to Literature," pp. 266–295, for additional support. The chapter includes in-depth instruction on writing about literature; p. 286 will help them gather details about the meaning of a poem.

Build Your Portfolio

Idea Bank

Writing

1. **List** Make a list of memories that would be suitable for sharing in a poem.

2. **Poem** Write a poem about a child's memory. Include vivid details that will show the "picture" of the memory.

3. **Essay** Write an essay to explain how Robert P. Tristram Coffin used symbols in "The Secret Heart." Support your ideas with examples from the poem.

Speaking and Listening

4. **Love Song** Write a song about love using the word *heart.* You may want to write a rap, a ballad, or a pop song. Read or perform the song for your class. **[Performing Arts Link]**

5. **Poetry Reading [Group Activity]** With a partner, rehearse and perform "The Secret Heart" for your classmates. You may want to alternate lines or divide the poem in half, with each of you reading one section. **[Performing Arts Link]**

Projects

6. **Salute to the Poet [Group Activity]** With a partner, find more poems by Robert P. Tristram Coffin. Choose your five favorites, and create a classroom display that includes photocopies of the poems and original artwork you create to accompany each. **[Literature Link; Art Link]**

7. **Musical Archives [Group Activity]** Love is one of the most popular subjects in song, and the heart as a symbol is used in love songs very often. With a small group of classmates, find songs about love. Then, collect the lyrics for five songs that include the word *heart.* Next, make a display that includes lyric sheets and lists the lyricist and performing artist. If possible, play some of the songs for your classmates. **[Music Link]**

Writing Mini-Lesson

Explanation of a Symbol

"The Secret Heart" contains a symbol of a heart, which stands for the love of a father for his son. Choose a familiar symbol, such as a dove, a flag, a heart, a turtle, the peace sign, or a lion. Then, write an explanation that reveals what the symbol means.

Writing Skills Focus: Give Reasons

As you write your explanation, **give reasons** or information to justify your conclusions about the meaning of a symbol. A reason may be a fact, an opinion, a situation, or an example. For example, in an explanation of the heart symbol, you could include the following lines as an example:

Model From the Poem
He wore, it seemed to his small son,
A bare heart on his hidden one.

Prewriting Start by choosing a symbol. Then, try out several definitions of its meaning. List some reasons why the symbol is recognized as standing for another idea. If necessary, do some research to find examples of how that symbol has been used in literature.

Drafting Begin your paper by identifying the symbol you plan to explain. Give your explanation, and organize your reasons in logical order in the body. For example, you might list facts and examples in one paragraph and include your opinions in a separate paragraph.

Revising Read your explanation to a partner, and ask for feedback. Make revisions according to his or her comments. Also, check that you've given enough reasons to support your ideas. Proofread carefully to correct errors in grammar, punctuation, and spelling.

◆ **Grammar Application**
If you've used comparisons in your explanation, check to be sure you've chosen the correct form of the modifying words.

✓ ASSESSMENT OPTIONS

Formal Assessment, Selection Test, pp. 228–229, and Assessment Resources Software. The selection test is designed so that it can easily be customized to the performance levels of your students.
Alternative Assessment, p. 50, includes options for less advanced students, more advanced students, verbal/linguistic learners, visual/spatial learners, interpersonal learners, and musical/rhythmic learners.

PORTFOLIO ASSESSMENT
Use the following rubrics in the **Alternative Assessment** booklet to assess student writing:
Poem: Poetry, p. 104
Essay: Literary Analysis/Interpretation, p. 108
Love Song: Poetry, p. 104
Writing Mini-Lesson: Technical Description/Explanation, p. 111

PART **1**

Types of Poetry

Birds of the Bagaduce, 1939, Marsden Hartley, The Butler Institute of American Art, Youngstown, Ohio

Types of Poetry ◆ 813

One-Minute
Planning Guide

The selections in this section focus on different types of poetry. "The Wreck of the Hesperus" and "The Centaur" are narrative poems. "Harlem Night Song," "Blow Blow, Thou Winter Wind," "love is a place," and "The Freedom of the Moon" are examples of lyric poetry. "January" is another lyric poem in four stanzas. Two Haiku are examples of haiku by Bashō and Moritake. "Identity" is a free verse poem and "400-Meter Free Style" is a concrete poem written to show the movements of a swimmer. "Wahbegan" is a lyric poem that expresses vivid and painful memories.

Customize for
Varying Student Needs

When assigning the selections in this section to your students, keep in mind the following factors:

"The Wreck of the Hesperus" and "The Centaur"
• Two narrative poems
• Students may find the vocabulary difficult
• "The Centaur" includes a Beyond Literature Humanities connection
• Both poems challenge students to read poetry according to punctuation

"Harlem Night Song," "Blow, Blow, Thou Winter Wind," "love is a place," "The Freedom of the Moon"
• Four lyric poems exploring the theme of respecting nature
• Varying styles of poets
• Students may need help with Shakespeare's language in "Blow, Blow, Thou Winter Wind"

"January," Two Haiku, "Identity," "400-Meter Free Style"
• Four poems which represent different poetic structures, including haiku, free verse, and concrete poetry
• "400-Meter Free Style" includes a Beyond Literature Science connection

"Wahbegan"
• Short poem about Vietnam's effects on a veteran
• Provides an opportunity for connecting literature to social studies

 Humanities: Art

Birds of the Bagaduce, 1939, by Marsden Hartley

Marsden Hartley (1877–1943) was an American painter sometimes referred to as the founder of modern art. He was born in Maine and studied in Cleveland and New York, where he had his first show with Alfred Stieglitz, the famous modernist photographer. Later, he went to Europe where he was influenced by the abstract expressionists. *Birds of the Bagaduce* was created when Hartley returned to America and stayed with friends in Brooksville, Maine.

Have students study the painting and then ask the following questions:
1. What is the dominant image in the painting? *Students should recognize that although the painting is of boats and birds, the space given to the sky and clouds dominates the painting.*
2. Why do you think the artist painted the boats smaller than the birds and the clouds? *Students may say that the painter has tried to represent the power of nature by painting those objects larger than the manmade ships.*

Guide for Reading

OBJECTIVES

1. To read, comprehend, and interpret two narrative poems
2. To relate two narrative poems to personal experience
3. To read lines according to punctuation
4. To identify a narrative poem
5. To build vocabulary in context and learn the suffix *-ful*
6. To make comparisons with *more* or *most*
7. To write a response to a poem, with supporting points
8. To respond to the poem through writing, speaking and listening, and projects

SKILLS INSTRUCTION

Vocabulary:
Suffixes: *-ful*

Spelling:
Words That End in *-ful*

Grammar:
Comparisons With *more* and *most*

Reading Strategy:
Read Lines According to Punctuation

Literary Focus:
Narrative Poetry

Writing:
Support Points

Speaking and Listening:
Anecdotes (Teacher Edition)

Viewing and Representing:
Imagery (Teacher Edition)

Critical Viewing:
Connect; Compare and Contrast; Interpret

PORTFOLIO OPPORTUNITIES

Writing: Continue the Poem; News Story; Character Study

Writing Mini-Lesson: Response to a Poem

Speaking and Listening: "Fireside" Reading; Anecdotes

Projects: Weather Report; Mythical Creatures Poster

More About the Authors
Henry Wadsworth Longfellow
saw his poetry as a way to express ideas about topics of common interest, such as historical figures, newsworthy events, patriotism, and nature. He was so popular and respected that his 75th birthday was recognized in classrooms across the U. S.

May Swenson's poems reflect her love of words and optimism about life. She enjoyed observing the world around her. Swenson experimented with various forms of poetry, including riddle poems and concrete poems.

Meet the Authors:

Henry Wadsworth Longfellow
(1807–1882)

Longfellow was the most popular poet of his time. When he entered a room, people stood up and gentlemen took off their hats. He published his first poem when he was thirteen. At fifteen, he entered Bowdoin College, where he excelled as a student. His poem *The Song of Hiawatha* sold over a million copies in his lifetime. [For more on Longfellow, see page 304.]

THE STORY BEHIND THE POEM
Longfellow's journal entry of December 17, 1839, tells of his horror on reading about a schooner called the *Hesperus*, which had been wrecked off Norman's Reef near Gloucester, Massachusetts. Twenty bodies were washed ashore, one of them tied to a piece of the wreckage. A few weeks later, Longfellow wrote this poem.

May Swenson (1919–1989)
May Swenson was born in Ogden, Utah, and later attended Utah State University. After working for a while as a newspaper reporter, she moved to New York City, where she worked as an editor and as a college lecturer. Her poems were published in such magazines as *The New Yorker*, *Harper's*, and *The Nation*. [For more on May Swenson, see page 464.]

814 ◆ Poetry

◆ LITERATURE AND YOUR LIFE

CONNECT YOUR EXPERIENCE
Certain moments in time seem to be etched forever on our memories. Whether the memories are horrific or sweetly nostalgic, they form part of who we are. "The Wreck of the Hesperus" was inspired by a real-life disaster at sea, and "The Centaur" was inspired by memories of a child's play.

THEMATIC FOCUS: Respecting Nature
In "The Wreck of the Hesperus," look for the poet's message about respecting the forces of nature.

◆ Background for Understanding

LITERATURE
In Longfellow's day, the fireside was the focal point of the home. During the long, cold, dark evenings, most families sat around the fire, knitting, reading, and talking. During this era, four poets—Longfellow, Oliver Wendell Holmes, James Russell Lowell, and John Greenleaf Whitter—came to be known as the Fireside Poets. They emerged as literary giants whose poems were read time and time again by countless families around the fireside.

◆ Build Vocabulary

SUFFIXES: *-ful*
The skipper of the *Hesperus* "laughed a scornful laugh." Knowing that the suffix *-ful* means "full of" or "having the qualities of," you can figure out that *scornful* means "full of scorn or contempt."

WORD BANK
Which word names waves that break as they reach the shore? Check the Build Vocabulary box on page 818 to see if you chose correctly.

Word Bank
scornful
gale
breakers
cinched
canter
negligent

Prentice Hall Literature Program Resources

REINFORCE / RETEACH / EXTEND
Selection Support Pages
Build Vocabulary: Suffixes: *-ful,* p. 274
Building Spelling Skills: p. 275
Building Grammar Skills: Comparisons With *more* and *most,* p. 276
Reading Strategy: Read Lines According to Punctuation, p. 277
Literary Focus: Narrative Poetry, p. 278
Strategies for Diverse Student Needs, pp. 101–102

Beyond Literature Study Skills: Reading Graphic Organizers, p. 51
Formal Assessment Selection Test, pp. 231–233, Assessment Resources Software
Alternative Assessment, p. 51
Writing and Language Transparencies Sunburst Organizer, p. 85
Resource Pro CD-ROM "Wreck of the Hesperus"; "The Centaur"
Listening to Literature Audiocassettes "Wreck of the Hesperus"; "The Centaur"

The Wreck of the Hesperus
◆ The Centaur ◆

Benares, Marshall Johnson, Courtesy, Peabody Essex Museum, Salem, Mass. Photo by Mark Sexton.

◆ Literary Focus
NARRATIVE POETRY

A poem that tells a story is called a **narrative poem.** Like short stories, narrative poems have a plot, setting, characters, dialogue, and a theme. Unlike stories, however, narrative poems rely on rhyme and rhythm and are broken into stanzas rather than paragraphs. Such a poem can be simple or complex, long or short. It can be based on a true story or a fictional story.

As you read these narrative poems, keep track of story events by filling in a plot diagram such as this one:

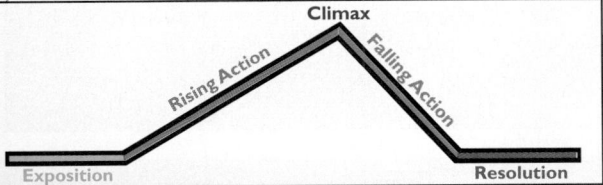

Climax

Rising Action

Falling Action

Exposition

Resolution

◆ Reading Strategy
READ LINES ACCORDING TO PUNCTUATION

Just as a driver follows road signs that tell when to stop, slow down, or go, so too does the reader of a poem follow "signs." In poetry, these signs are the punctuation marks. **Read lines of poetry according to punctuation.** If there is no mark of punctuation at the end of a line of poetry, keep going until you get to a punctuation mark. A comma tells you to slow down; a period tells you to stop. Exclamation marks, question marks, and dashes give you other signals to help in your reading.

Guide for Reading ◆ 815

Preparing for Standardized Tests

Grammar Standardized tests may require students to select correct forms of comparison (the grammar skill for this selection). Both adjectives and adverbs have comparative forms (used when two things are compared) and superlative forms (used when more than two things are compared). Use this sample test question: Supply the correct form of comparison for the word in parentheses.

In 1839, there was a shipwreck even (deadly) than that of the Hesperus.

(A) most deadly   (C) deadly
(B) deadlier   (D) deadliest

More than one shipwreck are being discussed, and *(C)* does not compare; there are only 2 shipwrecks being compared, so the superlative forms *(D)* and *(A)* are incorrect. Therefore, *(B)* is correct.

Although *-er* and *-est* are usually added to one-syllable words and *more* and *most* are generally used before modifiers with more than two syllables, some two-syllable words can be compared either way—most modern dictionaries give *-er* and *-est* as the preferred forms for two-syllable words.

Develop Understanding

One-Minute Insight

In "The Wreck of the *Hesperus*," Henry Wadsworth Longfellow describes the events leading up to the sinking of the schooner *Hesperus*. The skipper has brought his beautiful young daughter along to keep him company on this particular voyage. When the weather begins to change, an old sailor begs the skipper to put into port, fearing that a hurricane is brewing. The skipper brushes off the old sailor's warning. Soon a cold wind is blowing and waves are crashing over the schooner. The skipper wraps his daughter in his warmest coat and ties her to the mast to keep her from being swept overboard. The daughter cries out with questions for her father, who has frozen to death at the helm of the ship. Finally, the storm-tossed *Hesperus* breaks up on the rocks, and everyone is swept overboard. The next day, a fisherman finds the daughter's body floating in the water, still tied to the mast. The last verse is a plea that others might be spared a fate like the one caused by the skipper's refusal to respect nature's power.

Customize for
English Language Learners

English language learners may have difficulty understanding this poem because of unfamiliar terms and the formal literary style. Help them through the poem by letting them follow along in their books as they listen to the audiocassette of the selection.

Listening to Literature Audiocassettes

Customize for
Logical/Mathematical Learners

Have students use atlases, an encyclopedia, books on meteorology, and the World Wide Web to research conditions that cause storms. Ask them to focus on why different kinds of storms occur in different seasons of the year. Invite volunteers to share their findings with the class.

The Lookout — "All's Well," Winslow Homer, Courtesy, Museum of Fine Arts, Boston, MA

816 ◆ *Poetry*

 Block Scheduling Strategies

Consider these suggestions to take advantage of extended class time:

- For project-oriented instruction, have students read independently and then meet with a partner to discuss the poems. Have them answer the Guide for Responding questions on pp. 819 and 823. Then allow pairs to choose and complete either the Weather Report project or the Mythical Creatures Poster project on p. 825.

- Have students write a response to a poem by using the *Writer's Solution Writing Lab CD-ROM.* Refer to the teaching suggestions on p. 825.

- Before students read, use the reading strategy feature on p. 815. Then have them listen to the recordings of the poems, noting how each poem is read according to punctuation. Then have pairs of students read the poems aloud, paying particular attention to punctuation as they read. To reinforce the reading strategy, have pairs complete Reading Strategy: Read Lines According to Punctuation, p. 277 in **Selection Support.**

Listening to Literature Audiocassettes

The Wreck of the Hesperus

Henry Wadsworth Longfellow

❶ It was the schooner[1] Hesperus,
    That sailed the wintry sea;
And the skipper had taken his little daughter,
    To bear him company.

5 Blue were her eyes as the fairy-flax,[2]
    Her cheeks like the dawn of day,
And her bosom white as the hawthorn buds
❷   That ope in the month of May.

The skipper he stood beside the helm,
10   His pipe was in his mouth,
❸ And he watched how the veering flaw[3] did blow
    The smoke now West, now South.

❹ Then up and spake an old sailor,
    Had sailed to the Spanish Main,[4]
15 "I pray thee, put into yonder port,
    For I fear a hurricane.

❺ "Last night the moon had a golden ring,
    And tonight no moon we see!"
The skipper he blew a whiff from his pipe,
20   And a <u>scornful</u> laugh laughed he.

Colder and colder blew the wind,
    A <u>gale</u> from the Northeast,
The snow fell hissing in the brine,
    And the billows frothed like yeast.

25 Down came the storm, and smote amain,[5]
    The vessel in its strength;
She shuddered and paused, like a frighted steed,
    Then leaped her cable's length.

1. **schooner** (skōōn′ ər) *n.*: Ship with two or more masts.

2. **fairy-flax:** Slender plant with delicate blue flowers.

3. **veering flaw:** Gust of wind that changes direction.
4. **Spanish Main:** Coastal region bordering the Caribbean Sea.
5. **smote** (smōt) **amain** (ə mān′): Struck with great, vigorous force.

◀ **Critical Viewing** What details in this painting convey the roughness of the sea? [Connect] **❻**

◆ **Build Vocabulary**
scornful (skôrn′ fəl) *adj.*: Full of contempt or disdain
gale (gāl) *n.*: Strong wind

The Wreck of the Hesperus ◆ 817

◆ **Literary Focus**

❶ Narrative Poem Discuss with students the elements of a narrative that are introduced in the first verse. *The setting is described as the deck of a schooner on a wintry sea; two characters, the skipper and his daughter, are introduced.*

Clarification

❷ Lead students to see that the poet uses *ope* to mean *open* in this line. Discuss how a two-syllable word would have thrown off the established rhythm pattern.

◆ **Reading Strategy**

❸ Read Lines According to Punctuation Invite a volunteer to read lines 11 and 12 aloud. Ask students what clues the reader used to decide on phrasing. *Since there was no comma after blow, the reader did not pause at the end of that line, but rather paused after West and stopped at the period following South.*

Clarification

❹ Explain that *spake* is an archaic, or old-fashioned, way of saying *spoke.* Point out that, although *who* would follow *sailor* in common usage, it is omitted here to preserve the rhythm pattern.

Comprehension Check ☑

❺ Ask students who is speaking here and how they know. *The old sailor is still speaking, since there is no ending quotation mark at the end of line 16.*

▶ **Critical Viewing** ◀

❻ Connect *The man seems to be surprised and thrown off balance. The bell's clapper is swinging, showing how the boat is rolling on the rough water. There are whitecaps on the waves.*

Humanities: Art

The Lookout—"All's Well," by Winslow Homer
  Born in Boston, Massachusetts, Winslow Homer (1826–1910) spent the early years of his career illustrating newsworthy events, such as Lincoln's inauguration and Civil War battles for *Harper's Weekly*. As a painter, Homer used his vision of the interaction between people and nature to create artworks filled with drama and excitement.

1. How does this painting help you imagine the story's setting? *The clothes the man is wearing and the ship details help me imagine life onboard a ship in the 1800's.*

2. Which character from the poem might be shown in this painting? *The man in the painting might be the skipper or the old sailor.*

Literary Focus

1 Narrative Poetry Discuss how the dialogue compares to that found in stories. *As in stories, the dialogue shows what a character thinks and feels, but in this poem, the lines rhyme and do not sound like everyday speech.*

Critical Thinking

2 Infer Tell students that a mast is a large pole that rises from the deck of a ship to support the rigging. Ask students why the father bound his daughter to the mast. *He wanted to keep her from being thrown overboard as the ship tossed in the storm.*

Comprehension Check ☑

3 Ask students why the skipper steered to the open sea, instead of toward the shore. *He knew that the ship would be torn apart by the rocks near the shore.*

Reading Strategy

4 Read Lines According to Punctuation Point out the stress mark over the second syllable in *saved* in line 54. Explain that this mark tells the reader to read the word in two syllables (sa-ved). Then ask a volunteer to read aloud lines 53 and 54, using punctuation to guide the phrasing. Emphasize that there should be no pause at the end of line 53.

Literary Focus

5 Narrative Poetry Review with students how, in a narrative, events build to a climax, or high point. Discuss how the events described in these verses create suspense and build toward a climax. *These verses describe how the ship is being blown closer and closer to the shore, where it will almost surely be torn apart by the rocks and waves.*

Critical Thinking

6 Interpret Ask students what is being described in this verse. *The ship has been wrecked, and a large wave has swept the crew overboard.*

---

1 30 "Come hither! come hither! my little daughter,
　　　　And do not tremble so;
　　　For I can weather the roughest gale,
　　　　That ever wind did blow."

2 35 He wrapped her warm in his seaman's coat
　　　　Against the stinging blast;
　　　He cut a rope from a broken spar,[6]
　　　　And bound her to the mast.

3　　"O father! I hear the church-bells ring,
　　　　O say, what may it be?"
　　　"'Tis a fog-bell on a rock-bound coast!—"
　　40　　And he steered for the open sea.

　　　"O father! I hear the sound of guns,
　　　　O say, what may it be?"
　　　"Some ship in distress, that cannot live
　　　　In such an angry sea!"

　　45　"O father! I see a gleaming light,
　　　　O say, what may it be?"
　　　But the father answered never a word,
　　　　A frozen corpse was he.

　　　Lashed to the helm, all stiff and stark,
　　50　　With his face turned to the skies,
　　　The lantern gleamed through the gleaming snow
　　　　On his fixed and glassy eyes.

4　　Then the maiden clasped her hands and prayed
　　　　That savèd she might be;
　　55　And she thought of Christ, who stilled the wave,
　　　　On the Lake of Galilee.[7]

　　　And fast through the midnight dark and drear
　　　　Through the whistling sleet and snow,
　　　Like a sheeted ghost, the vessel swept
　　60　　Towards the reef of Norman's Woe.
5

　　　And ever the fitful gusts between
　　　　A sound came from the land;
　　　It was the sound of the trampling surf,
　　　　On the rocks and the hard sea-sand.

6 65 The <u>breakers</u> were right beneath her bows,
　　　　She drifted a dreary wreck,
　　　And a whooping billow swept the crew
　　　　Like icicles from her deck.

---

6. spar (spär) *n.*: Pole supporting the sail of a ship.

7. Lake of Galilee (gal′ ə lē′): Lake in northeastern Israel.

◆ **Build Vocabulary**

breakers (brāk′ ərz) *n.*: Waves that break into foam

818 ◆ *Poetry*

Cross-Curricular Connection: Science

Weather Prediction at Sea Throughout history, navigators have feared running into storms at sea because of the difficulties and dangers of navigating through strong winds and waves. Early sailors became experts at reading signs in the clouds and winds to determine what kind of weather the future held in store for them. Sayings such as "Red sky at morning, sailor take warning" and "Wind from the east carries the beast" helped seafarers remember the rules of weather forecasting that had been tried and tested over the years.

Modern-day sailors benefit from technological advances that provide weather data to those who need it. Radar and satellite images alert sailors days in advance of dangerous storms that might be brewing over the ocean. Ships' routes can be altered to avoid potential weather problems. Most ships today have onboard computers that supply current weather information to the crew.

Invite interested students to learn more about present-day or historical weather forecasting methods used by sailors and to share their findings with the class.

She struck where the white and fleecy waves
   Looked soft as carded[8] wool,
But the cruel rocks, they gored[9] her side
   Like the horns of an angry bull.

❼ Her rattling shrouds,[10] all sheathed in ice,
   With the masts went by the board;
Like a vessel of glass, she stove[11] and sank,
   Ho! ho! the breakers roared!

At daybreak, on the bleak sea-beach,
   A fisherman stood aghast,[12]
To see the form of a maiden fair,
   Lashed close to a drifting mast.

The salt sea was frozen on her breast,
   The salt tears in her eyes;
And he saw her hair, like the brown sea-weed,
   On the billows fall and rise.

Such was the wreck of the Hesperus,
   In the midnight and the snow!
Christ save us all from a death like this,
   On the reef of Norman's Woe!

70

75

80

85

8. **carded:** Combed.
9. **gored:** Pierced.

10. **shrouds:** Ropes or wires stretched from the ship's side to the mast.
11. **stove:** Broke.

12. **aghast** (ə gäst') *adj.*: In horror; terrified.

◆ **Literary Focus**

❼ **Narrative Poetry** Ask students to identify the climax of the narrative poem. *The climax occurs when the ship strikes the rocks and then sinks.*

Reinforce and Extend

Answers
◆ **LITERATURE AND YOUR LIFE**

Reader's Response Possible answer: You should have listened to the old sailor. Because you thought you knew best, you caused the death of your daughter and your crew and lost your own life.

Thematic Focus Possible answers: Some of nature's forces are so strong that no human can survive when pitted against them. A healthy respect for nature can save your life.

☑ **Check Your Comprehension**

1. The old sailor warned that there might be a hurricane.
2. He heads toward the open sea to keep away from the rocks along the shore.
3. The schooner is dashed against the rocks and sinks.
4. Everyone on board freezes to death or is drowned.

◆ **Critical Thinking**

1. Possible answer: The skipper's stubbornness and feelings of superiority lead to the shipwreck.
2. The old sailor respects the powers of the sea and does not want to test them. The skipper does not respect nature's powers, feeling he can overcome them.
3. The old sailor may have been in similar storms, causing him to worry about what was in store for them.
4. (a) People should respect the powers of nature. (b) By not respecting the power of the storm at sea, the skipper loses his daughter, his crew, his ship, and his life.
5. Possible answer: Nature provides for humans in many ways, but if its power is not respected, it can cause terrible problems.

Guide for Responding

◆ **LITERATURE AND YOUR LIFE**

Reader's Response What would you say to the skipper about his decision not to listen to the old sailor's advice?

Thematic Focus What does this poem have to say about the power of nature?

☑ **Check Your Comprehension**

1. What warning does the old sailor give?
2. Why does the skipper head for the open sea instead of toward land?
3. What finally happens to the schooner?
4. What happens to everyone on board, including the skipper's daughter?

◆ **Critical Thinking**

INTERPRET
1. What character trait in the skipper leads to the shipwreck? **[Infer]**
2. Compare and contrast the attitudes of the skipper and the old sailor about the sea and its dangers. **[Compare and Contrast]**
3. Why do you think the old sailor is afraid of what might happen? **[Deduce]**
4. (a) What is the message or theme of this poem? (b) How do you know? **[Interpret]**

APPLY
5. What lesson about the relationship between human beings and nature can you draw from this poem? **[Generalize]**

The Wreck of the Hesperus ◆ 819

Beyond the Classroom

Career Connection
Working on a Ship Explain that the shipwreck described in "The Wreck of the Hesperus" occurred in the 19th century, and that ships today have many safety features that prevent such accidents from happening. Point out that there are many types of jobs available on ships. Merchant seafarers work on ships that transport raw materials and products from one place to another. Their jobs can include painting and maintaining the surfaces of the ship, working on the ship's engines, steering the ship, communicating with shore and with other ships, and so forth. Cruise ships hire employees to operate and maintain the ship, as well as to serve and entertain guests. Some ships are designed to help companies drill for oil in deep-sea locations. These ships hire petroleum engineers and oil-drilling technicians to establish drilling sites and platforms.

Invite interested students to learn more about job opportunities on ships. Have them note which jobs are common to all ships and which are specific to certain types of ships. Ask students to report what they find to the class.

In "The Centaur," the 10-year-old speaker goes to her imaginary stable, a willow grove, and cuts a limb that becomes a horse. On the limb, she trots along a path, pretending in various ways to act the part of both horse and rider. Finally, back at the house, she leaves the "horse" by the door and goes inside. She answers her mother's questions about her whereabouts and appearance, revealing that her mouth is green because her horse, Rob Roy, ate clover in the field. The poem illustrates the magical qualities that can result from combining a child's imagination and a natural setting. (Note: It is not revealed that the speaker in the poem is a girl until line 51.)

◆ Reading Strategy

❶ Read Lines According to Punctuation Have students identify punctuation clues they can use while reading this section. *Stop at dash after ten; raise voice in a question after second ten; stop at dash after then; read straight to period after canal and stop.*

◆ Literary Focus

❷ Narrative Poetry Identify the setting and the character who has been introduced at this point. *The setting is a willow grove near a canal; the character is a 10-year-old child.*

Comprehension Check ☑

❸ Ask students what kind of horse is described here. *It is a stick horse cut from a willow branch.*

Customize for
English Language Learners
Students may benefit from seeing a volunteer pantomime certain action words in the poem, such as *cinched, trot, jouncing, arched, snorted, shied, reared,* and *quivered.*

The Centaur[1]

May Swenson

The summer that I was ten—
Can it be there was only one
summer that I was ten? It must

❶ have been a long one then—
5   each day I'd go out to choose
❷ a fresh horse from my stable

which was a willow grove
down by the old canal.
I'd go on my two bare feet.

10   But when, with my brother's jack-knife,
I had cut me a long limber horse
with a good thick knob for a head,

❸ and peeled him slick and clean
except a few leaves for the tail,
15   and <u>cinched</u> my brother's belt

around his head for a rein,
❹ I'd straddle and <u>canter</u> him fast
up the grass bank to the path,

820 ◆ Poetry

1. Centaur (sen´ tôr´): Mythological creature with a man's head, trunk, and arms, and a horse's body and legs.

◆ Build Vocabulary

cinched (sincht) *v.*: Bound firmly; tightly fastened

canter (kan´ tər) *v.*: Ride at a smooth, gentle pace

Speaking and Listening Mini-Lesson

Anecdotes
This mini-lesson supports the Speaking and Listening activity in the Idea Bank on p. 825.

Introduce An anecdote is a short, often amusing, narrative that people tell about themselves or others. Stress to students that a long anecdote or a wandering, indirect telling loses listeners' interest.

Develop Have groups discuss the summer when they were 10—recalling popular movies that were popular, songs people were listening to, and who they spent time with. Ask each group member to select a specific event to describe.

Apply Have groups practice their anecdotes for one another, timing each member to make sure the group stays within the allotted time. Ask group members to tell what they like about each anecdote. Then have groups present their anecdotes for the class.

Assess Tape-record students' anecdote presentations. Assess each student's performance based on its entertainment quality. You may want to have students assess each other's performance by completing the Peer Assessment: Speaker/Speech form, p. 114, in **Alternative Assessment.**

◆ **Critical Thinking**

❹ **Infer** Discuss with students how the dust on the child's feet turned the horse's feet to "swift half-moons." *The child imagines himself/herself as both the rider and the horse.*

◆ **Literary Focus**

❺ **Narrative Poetry** Ask students how the cast of characters has changed since the opening of the poem. *The speaker has introduced an imaginary horse, and sometimes the speaker and horse seem to be one combined character.*

◆ **Critical Thinking**

❻ **Interpret** Ask students why the poet uses the personal pronouns *my* and *I* in these lines. *The 10-year-old speaker is pretending to be the horse rather than the rider.*

▶**Critical Viewing**◀

❼ **Compare and Contrast** *Possible answers: The girl is skipping along, as the girl in the poem might have; both girls have hair that swings like a horse's mane as they run; the girl in the picture does not have a stick horse, while the girl in the poem does.*

20   trot along in the lovely dust
     that talcumed² over his hoofs,
❹   hiding my toes, and turning

     his feet to swift half–moons.
     The willow knob with the strap
     jouncing between my thighs

25   was the pommel³ and yet the poll⁴
     of my nickering pony's head.
     My head and my neck were mine,

     yet they were shaped like a horse.
     My hair flopped to the side
30   like the mane of a horse in the wind.

❺   My forelock swung in my eyes,
❻   my neck arched and I snorted.
     I shied and skittered and reared,

     stopped and raised my knees,
35   pawed at the ground and quivered.
     My teeth bared as we wheeled

2. talcumed (tal´ kəmd´) *v.*: Blew like fine powder.

3. pommel (päm´ əl) *n.*: The rounded knob on the front part of a saddle.
4. poll: Head or mane (the long hair growing from the top of a horse).

▲ **Critical Viewing** How do the actions of the girl in the photograph compare with the actions of the poem's speaker? [Compare and Contrast] ❼

The Centaur ◆ 821

 Viewing and Representing Mini-Lesson

Imagery
In this mini-lesson, students will extend their understanding of imagery by creating a visual replica of an image described in the poem.

Introduce Tell students that poets and other writers often create clear visual images by using carefully chosen descriptive words.

Develop Lead students to identify passages in the poem that create clear mental pictures of what is being described (for example, "peeled him slick and clean except a few leaves for the tail"; "talcumed over his hoofs"; "My hair flopped

to the side like the mane of a horse in the wind"; etc.). Invite students to use art materials of their choice to illustrate one of the poem's images.

Apply As students create, have them consider the mood and feeling of the poem, and choose materials, colors, and shapes that reflect that mood. Students may want to illustrate a scene, or show just one or two details.

Assess Have students display their work. Discuss how the illustrated imagery portrays verbal descriptions. Evaluate each student's work based on originality and representational creativity.

5. **paling** (pāl´ iŋ) *n.*: Fence.

◆ Reading Strategy

❶ Read Lines According to Punctuation Explain to students that they should not pause, even at the end of a verse, if lack of punctuation guides them to continue reading. Ask a volunteer to illustrate this by reading aloud lines 38–40, pausing only after *rider* and stopping after *behind*.

Clarification

❷ Point out that the speaker has only two feet, and so these would have to be doubled to create four horse's hooves.

◆ Literary Focus

❸ Narrative Poetry Discuss how the speaker assumes the character of the horse, and then that of the rider. Help students identify the horse as the character in lines 43–44 and the rider as the character in lines 45–46.

◆ Critical Thinking

❹ Connect The child's mention of her skirt in line 51 is the first hint we have that the speaker is a girl. Ask students why they may have assumed this all along. *Students may say they assumed this because the poet is a woman. Or they may have been influenced by the illustration on p. 821.*

►Critical Viewing◄

❺ Interpret Help students identify the red horse in the foreground of the painting as they consider answers to the question. *Possible answer: The artist created a colorful landscape in which he placed a bright red horse. Horses like this one do not exist in real life, and so this animal was the product of the artist's imagination. In the poem, the speaker imagines that she is both riding a horse and becoming a horse.*

and swished through the dust again.
I was the horse and the rider,
❶ and the leather I slapped to his rump
40 spanked my own behind.
❷ Doubled, my two hoofs beat—
a gallop along the bank,

the wind twanged in my mane,
❸ my mouth squared to the bit.
45 And yet I sat on my steed

quiet, <u>negligent</u> riding,
my toes standing the stirrups,
my thighs hugging his ribs.

At a walk we drew up to the porch.
50 I tethered him to a paling.[5]
❹ Dismounting, I smoothed my skirt

◆ Build Vocabulary

negligent (neg´ lə jənt) *adj.*: Without care or attention; indifferent

Horse in the Countryside, 1910, Franz Marc, Museum Folkwang Essen, Essen, Germany

❺ ▲ **Critical Viewing** How does this painting reflect the magic of the speaker's imaginary world? [Interpret]

822 ◆ *Poetry*

🎼 Humanities: Art

Horse in the Countryside, 1910, by Franz Marc
    Franz Marc (1880–1916) belonged to a group of German Expressionist painters known as the Blue Riders. These artists used bold colors in unusual ways to express their feelings about a painting's subject. Animals were common subjects in Marc's paintings, because he felt that animals represented harmony with nature—a harmony that he found lacking among people in pre-World War I Europe. Ironically, Marc was called to serve in the German army and was killed in battle.

Help students connect the painting to the poem by asking questions such as these:
1. How do the shapes and colors in this painting make you feel? *Possible answer: The curved shapes and lines make me feel peaceful and relaxed, but the colors give an energetic and exciting feeling.*
2. How would you compare the mood of the painting with the mood of the poem? *Both the poem and the painting have a lively, dreamlike mood.*

and entered the dusky hall.
6 My feet on the clean linoleum
left ghostly toes in the hall.

55 *Where have you been?* said my mother.
Been riding, I said from the sink,
and filled me a glass of water.

What's that in your pocket? she said.
Just my knife. It weighted my pocket
7 and stretched my dress awry.

Go tie back your hair, said my mother,
and *Why is your mouth all green?*
Rob Roy, he pulled some clover
as we crossed the field, I told her.

Beyond Literature

Humanities Connection

The Centaur The speaker in this poem
imagines herself to be a Centaur. This mythical creature of Greek origin generally is represented as having the upper body and head
of a man attached to the lower half and
hindlegs of a horse. Centaurs were thought
to inhabit the mountains and forests of
Thessaly and Arcadia. In Greek mythology,
they are chiefly known for conducting
countless battles with their neighbors, the
Lapiths, which resulted from the Centaurs'
attempts to abduct the princess of that kingdom. In later Greek times, they were often
depicted as drawing the chariot of Dionysus
or being ridden by Eros, the god of love.
Centaurs are typically regarded as being
wild, lawless, and vulgar characters, with
little control of their animal instincts.

Cross-Curricular Activity
Draw your own version of a mythological
creature that is part human and part beast.
In a caption to the drawing, name your
creature and describe its characteristics.

Guide for Responding

◆ LITERATURE AND YOUR LIFE

Reader's Response If you could have
a conversation with the narrator in "The
Centaur," what would you want to talk
about? Why?

Thematic Focus In what way does the
natural world enhance the speaker's life?

Journal Writing Rewrite "The Centaur" as if
it were a diary entry written by the speaker.

☑ Check Your Comprehension

1. The speaker says she got a fresh horse from
   her stable. What was the "stable"?
2. Describe the speaker's horse.
3. What does the speaker use for reins?
4. Why is the speaker's mouth green at the end
   of the poem?

◆ Critical Thinking

INTERPRET
1. What kind of relationship do you think
   the narrator in "The Centaur" has with
   her brother? Explain. **[Speculate]**
2. According to the speaker, how are she
   and a real horse alike? **[Connect]**
3. How does the speaker's mother think a
   ten-year-old girl should behave? **[Infer]**

EVALUATE
4. Do you think "The Centaur" is an appropriate
   title for this poem? Why? **[Evaluate]**

COMPARE LITERARY WORKS
5. "The Wreck of the Hesperus" and "The
   Centaur" are both examples of narrative
   poetry, yet they are very different from each
   other. Contrast the formats and themes of
   the poems. **[Compare and Contrast]**

The Centaur ◆ 823

◆ Critical Thinking

6 Connect Ask students to recall
what happened earlier to guess why
the speaker's feet left "ghostly toes
in the hall." *The girl had been running
along a dusty trail; the dust from her
feet left tracks on the clean linoleum.*

◆ Literary Focus

7 Narrative Poetry Remind students that dialogue is one element of
narrative writing. Ask them how the
dialogue in this poem is different from
other dialogue they have seen. *It is set
in italics instead of using quotation marks.*

Reinforce and Extend

Answers
◆ LITERATURE AND YOUR LIFE

Reader's Response Students might
say they'd want to talk about what
she imagined and felt as a horse.

Thematic Focus Students may note
that the natural world offers props
and a stage for the speaker to use
as she acts out her imaginary plays.

☑ Check Your Comprehension

1. The stable was the willow grove.
2. The horse was a stripped branch
   with a few leaves left for the tail.
3. She uses her brother's belt for
   reins.
4. Her mouth is green because she
   has been eating clover.

◆ Critical Thinking

1. The relationship with her brother
   is good, since he lets her use his
   knife and belt.
2. Her head and neck are shaped like
   a horse's, and her hair is like a
   mane and forelock.
3. The girl's mother thinks she
   should behave more calmly and
   engage in clean, quiet play.
4. Possible answer: Yes, "The Centaur"
   is an appropriate title, since the
   speaker imagines herself as a combination of a person and a horse.
5. "The Wreck of the Hesperus" is
   traditional, with 4-line stanzas,
   strong meter, and the 2nd and 4th
   lines rhyming. "The Centaur" has
   irregular 3-line stanzas in free
   verse. The theme of "The Wreck
   of the Hesperus" is that of
   respecting nature's fury; the theme
   of "The Centaur" deals with
   enjoying what nature has to offer
   through the imagination.

Beyond the Selection

FURTHER READING
**Other Works by Henry Wadsworth
Longfellow**
Evangeline
The Song of Hiawatha
Other Works by May Swenson
"Ornamental Sketch With Verbs"
"Painting the Gate"
Other Poems About Respecting Nature
"The Runaway," Robert Frost
"Nature" is what we see—," Emily Dickinson
"Big Wind," Theodore Roethke

INTERNET
We suggest the following sites on the Internet
(all Web sites are subject to change).
   For more information about and selected poetry
by Henry Wadsworth Longfellow:
**http://www.library.utoronto.ca/www/utel/RP/
authors/longfel.html**
   For more information about May Swenson:
**http://www.poets.org/poets/LIT/POET/
mswenson.htm**
   We *strongly recommend* that you preview
these sites before you send students to them.

Answers

◆ Reading Strategy

1. Students should pause following each comma, change tone at the beginning of the quote at line 15, and stop at the period at the end of line 16.
2. There are 13 lines before a full stop, since the thought concludes with a period at the end of line 22.

◆ Build Vocabulary

Using the Suffix *-ful*
1. successful   4. cheerful
2. fearful   5. peaceful
3. beautiful

Spelling Strategy
1. masterful   4. playful
2. eventful   5. useful
3. joyful   6. hopeful

Using the Word Bank
1. c   3. a   5. a
2. b   4. b   6. b

◆ Literary Focus

1. The skipper takes his daughter to sea; he is warned of an approaching storm; he disregards the warning; he ties his daughter to the mast; the storm freezes the skipper; the ship is dashed against the rocks and sinks; all aboard are lost; the dead daughter is found still tied to the mast.
2. The theme is that people must have a fearful respect for nature's forces.
3. (a) A girl goes out to play on a make-believe horse. (b) The ten-year-old girl is the main character. (c) Dialogue is indicated by italics.

◆ Build Grammar Skills

Comparisons With *more* and *most*
1. more
2. most
3. most
4. more
5. most

Writing Application
Sample answer:
It was the most ferocious wind I had ever experienced. Each gust was more frigid than the one before. I was more frightened than my sister. It was definitely the most dangerous situation we had ever been in.

Guide for Responding *(continued)*

◆ Reading Strategy

READ LINES ACCORDING TO PUNCTUATION

When you **read according to punctuation,** you use the commas, dashes, quotation marks, semicolons, and end marks in these poems as guides to pauses, breaks, changes of tone, and stops.
1. Explain where you would pause, change tone, and stop in lines 13–16 of "The Wreck of the Hesperus."
2. Begin at line 10 of "The Centaur," and count the lines until you come to a full stop. How many lines is it? Explain how you know to stop there.

◆ Build Vocabulary

USING THE SUFFIX *-ful*

The suffix *-ful*, as in *scornful*, can mean "full of" or "having the qualities of." On your paper, complete each sentence with the most appropriate word from this list: *beautiful, cheerful, fearful, successful, peaceful.*
1. Work hard, and you'll be ____?____.
2. Don't be ____?____; the dog won't bite.
3. The painting of the sunset was ____?____.
4. The tune she whistled was quite ____?____.
5. The sleeping baby had a ____?____ look.

SPELLING STRATEGY

When you write words with the suffix *-ful*, do not double the final *l*.

On your paper, complete the following words by adding *-ful*.
1. master____?____   4. play____?____
2. event____?____   5. use____?____
3. joy____?____   6. hope____?____

USING THE WORD BANK

On your paper, write the letter of the word that is closest in meaning to the Word Bank word.
1. breakers: (a) lights, (b) repairs, (c) waves
2. canter: (a) scold, (b) run, (c) crawl
3. cinched: (a) tied, (b) cut, (c) cheated
4. gale: (a) valley, (b) wind, (c) innocence
5. negligent: (a) careless, (b) fast, (c) slow
6. scornful: (a) respectful, (b) sneering, (c) lucky

◆ Literary Focus

NARRATIVE POETRY

Like a work of fiction, **narrative poetry** has certain elements that you can count on. Those elements are character, plot, setting, and theme. If a poem has a story with a beginning, a middle, and an end, you can be sure it is narrative poetry.
1. What are the plot highlights of "The Wreck of the Hesperus"?
2. In "The Wreck of the Hesperus," what theme or message is revealed?
3. (a) What happens in "The Centaur"? (b) Who is the main character? (c) How is dialogue indicated?

◆ Build Grammar Skills

COMPARISONS WITH *more* AND *most*

With longer adjectives and adverbs, you make comparisons by adding *more* or *most*. If you are comparing two things, use *more*. If you are comparing three or more things, use *most*.

Comparative: Of the two poems, which is *more interesting*? (comparing two poems)
Superlative: It was the *most dangerous* storm in years. (comparing all the storms ever)

Practice On your paper, write *more* or *most* to complete each sentence.
1. Of the two nights, this is ____?____ ominous.
2. He is the ____?____ fearful sailor ever.
3. This is the ____?____ useful type of wood for carving.
4. This daughter is ____?____ adventurous than the other.
5. She thinks that the centaur is the ____?____ fascinating mythological figure.

Writing Application Write a paragraph about a fierce storm like the one in "The Wreck of the Hesperus." In the paragraph, use *more* or *most* with the following adjectives: *ferocious, frigid, frightened,* and *dangerous.* Be sure to use the comparative and superlative forms correctly.

 Writer's Solution

For additional instruction and practice, use the Using Modifiers unit in the *Writer's Solution Language Lab CD-ROM.* You may also use the practice page on using comparative and superlative degrees, p. 88, in the *Writer's Solution Grammar Practice Book.*

Build Your Portfolio

 Idea Bank

Writing

1. **Continue the Poem** Write another stanza (grouping of lines) for "The Centaur," continuing the story.

2. **News Story** Imagine that there was a survivor of the shipwreck in "The Wreck of the Hesperus." Write the newspaper story that might have resulted from an interview with the survivor. Don't forget to reveal the five W's: *who, what, when, where,* and *why.* **[Media Link]**

3. **Character Study** Why is the skipper of the *Hesperus* so determined to sail? Write a character sketch in which you describe the skipper's personality and reasons for his actions. Use details from the poem to support your points.

Speaking and Listening

4. **"Fireside" Reading** Perform for the class "The Wreck of the Hesperus" as it may have been read by a family member sitting by the fireside on a cold New England night. If you like, ask a classmate to work with you, and divide up the reading of the poem. **[Performing Arts Link]**

5. **Anecdotes [Group Activity]** With a group of classmates, prepare anecdotes that tell of something that happened to you the summer you were ten. Rehearse your anecdotes before presenting them to the class. Tape-record your presentation to review afterward. **[Performing Arts Link]**

Projects

6. **Weather Report** Find out about the weather conditions that may have caused the fierce storm that sank the *Hesperus.* Prepare a chart that reveals the information you find. **[Science Link]**

7. **Mythical Creatures Poster** Create a poster about mythical creatures, such as centaurs, unicorns, sphinxes, and phoenixes. Include drawings and captions describing each creature and its characteristics. **[Art Link]**

 Writing Mini-Lesson

Response to a Poem

When you finish reading a poem, you have a certain response to it. You might say to yourself, "I really enjoyed the rhyme and rhythm in that poem," or you might say, "I could really picture what the poet was describing in that poem." Capture your response to either "The Wreck of the Hesperus" or "The Centaur" in written form.

Writing Skills Focus: Support Points

Your response will have greater impact if you **support your points** with examples from the poem. For example, if you enjoyed the vivid descriptions in a poem, you would quote the lines that were especially effective.

Model

The visual images in the lines "Lashed to the helm, all stiff and stark, / With his face turned to the skies, . . ." impressed me the most.

Prewriting Decide whether or not you like the poem, and jot down the poem's strengths or weaknesses. For example, you could comment on the use of language, vivid descriptions, memorable characters, and rhyme scheme (if any).

Drafting Open your response with a general statement about your reaction to the poem. In the body, develop your opening statement with examples that support your opinion.

> ◆ **Grammar Application**
> As you write, use comparisons with *more* and *most* if they will help you make your points.

Revising Look for places where you could use more examples to support your points. Then, proofread your writing to correct errors in grammar, punctuation, and spelling.

The Wreck of the Hesperus/The Centaur ◆ 825

 Idea Bank

Following are suggestions for matching the Idea Bank topics with your students' performance levels and learning modalities:

Customize for
Performance Levels
Less Advanced Students: 1, 5, 7
Average Students: 2, 4, 5, 7
More Advanced Students: 3, 4, 6

Customize for
Learning Modalities
Verbal/Linguistic: 1, 2, 3, 4, 5
Visual/Spatial: 6, 7
Logical/Mathematical: 6
Interpersonal: 4, 5
Intrapersonal: 1, 2, 3, 6, 7

 Writing Mini-Lesson

Refer students to the Writing Handbook in the back of the book for instruction on the writing process and for further information on responding to literature. Have students use the Sunburst Organizer in **Writing and Language Transparencies,** p. 85, to arrange their prewriting examples.

 **Writer's Solution**

Writers at Work Videodisc
Use the Response to Literature section of the videodisc featuring Marilyn Stasio to help students become acquainted with the concept of responding to a piece of literature.

Play frames 30102 to 39013

Writing Lab CD-ROM
Have students complete the tutorial on Response to Literature. Follow these steps:

1. Have students review the Response to a Poem section of the Models From Literature.
2. Students can use the audio–annotated models to explore two passages written about the same poem for different audiences.
3. Have students listen to the audio–annotated model from literature on sound details in poems.
4. Have students draft on computer.

Writer's Solution Sourcebook
Have students use Chapter 9, "Response to Literature," pp. 266–295, for additional support. This chapter includes in-depth instruction on responding to poetry.

✓ ASSESSMENT OPTIONS

Formal Assessment, Selection Test, pp. 231–233, and Assessment Resources Software. The selection test is designed so that it can easily be customized to the performance levels of your students.

Alternative Assessment, p. 51, includes options for less advanced students, more advanced students, verbal/linguistic learners, musical/rhythmic learners, interpersonal learners, and visual/spatial learners.

PORTFOLIO ASSESSMENT
Use the following rubrics in the **Alternative Assessment** booklet to assess student writing:
Continue the Poem: Poetry, p. 104
New Story: Description, p. 93
Character Study: Literary Analysis/ Interpretation, p. 108
Writing Mini-Lesson: Response to Literature, p. 106

Guide for Reading

OBJECTIVES

1. To read, comprehend, and interpret four lyric poems
2. To relate four lyric poems to personal experience
3. To identify the speaker in a poem
4. To recognize lyric poetry
5. To build vocabulary in context and learn the word root *-lus-*
6. To use irregular comparisons of modifiers
7. To retell a poem in prose, using an appropriate tone
8. To respond to the poems through writing, speaking and listening, and projects

SKILLS INSTRUCTION

Vocabulary:
Word Roots: *-lus-*

Spelling:
Words With *ei* and *ie*

Grammar:
Irregular Comparisons of Modifiers

Reading Strategy:
Identify the Speaker

Literary Focus:
Lyric Poetry

Writing:
Use an Appropriate Tone

Speaking and Listening:
Monologue (Teacher Edition)

Critical Viewing:
Interpret; Make a Judgment

PORTFOLIO OPPORTUNITIES

Writing: Invitation; Paraphrase; Essay
Writing Mini-Lesson: Retelling of a Poem in Prose
Speaking and Listening: Monologue; Discussion
Projects: Music of the 1920's; Constellations Poster

More About the Authors
Langston Hughes was a key figure in the 1920's Harlem Renaissance. He was one of the first poets to express in writing the spirit of blues music. His poems deal with the trials and joys of African Americans.

William Shakespeare's plays often included lyric songs which are sung by actors during performances. "Blow, Blow, Thou Winter Wind" is from *As You Like It.* Its original tune is unknown.

E. E. Cummings was a fine artist, playwright, and novelist, as well as a poet. His poems reveal clever wit and childlike love of fun, as well as satire.

Robert Frost often used descriptions of nature to create poetry with profound insights into life. He found an eager audience during a time when poetry had lost its general appeal.

826

Meet the Authors:

Langston Hughes (1902–1967)

Langston Hughes wrote poems, stories, plays, essays, histories, and songs. As a songwriter, he wrote the lyrics for Kurt Weill's music for *Street Scene*, a successful 1947 Broadway musical. [For more on Langston Hughes, see pages 88 and 184.]

William Shakespeare (1564–1616)

Probably the most famous author in English literature, William Shakespeare was born in Stratford-on-Avon, a small town in England. In addition to writing thirty-seven plays, he also wrote poems and songs. [For more on William Shakespeare, see page 782.]

E. E. Cummings (1894–1962)

Best known for the playful, experimental nature of his poetry, E. E. Cummings once said that poetry is "the only thing that matters." In his poems, he celebrates families, parents, children, and fun.

Robert Frost (1874–1963)

Although identified with New England, Robert Frost was born in San Francisco. He is recognized as one of the best-known American poets, winning the Pulitzer Prize four times. [For more on Robert Frost, see page 32.]

826 ◆ Poetry

◆ LITERATURE AND YOUR LIFE

CONNECT YOUR EXPERIENCE

The beauty of the world can sometimes take your breath away. You can be walking along, having an ordinary day, when suddenly a flock of birds, a field of flowers, or the moon awakens you to the wonders around you. These poems celebrate such moments in the lives of the poets.

THEMATIC FOCUS: Respecting Nature

In what ways does the world around them inspire these poets?

◆ Background for Understanding

SCIENCE

Poets frequently refer to the light of the moon. The moon, however, does not shine with its own light: It reflects the light of the sun. From Earth, the moon appears to change throughout the month, although it does not. We always see the same side of the moon, but the amount of illumination on that side varies, depending on the moon's position in relation to the Earth and the sun. When Robert Frost speaks of the "new moon," he refers to the moon seen as a thin crescent with the hollow side on the left. At this stage, the moon's dark side is toward the Earth, making the moon appear almost invisible.

◆ Build Vocabulary

WORD ROOTS: *-lus-*

The word root *-lus-* comes from a Latin word that means "to light." The word *luster*, which contains this root, means "shine."

WORD BANK

Which word on the list means "faking"? Check the Build Vocabulary box on page 828 to see if you chose correctly.

roam
keen
feigning
breadth
luster

Prentice Hall Literature Program Resources

REINFORCE / RETEACH / EXTEND
Selection Support Pages
Build Vocabulary: Word Roots: *-lus-*, p. 279
Building Spelling Skills, p. 280
Building Grammar Skills: Irregular Comparisons of Modifiers, p. 281
Reading Strategy: Identify the Speaker, p. 282
Literary Focus: Lyric Poetry, p. 283
Strategies for Diverse Student Needs, pp. 103–104
Beyond Literature Career Connection: Meteorologist, p. 52

Formal Assessment Selection Test, pp. 234–236, Assessment Resources Software
Alternative Assessment, p. 52
Writing and Language Transparencies Venn Diagram, p. 77; Sensory Language Chart, p. 69
Resource Pro CD-ROM "Harlem Night Song"; "Blow, Blow, Thou Winter Wind"; "love is a place"; "The Freedom of the Moon"
 Listening to Literature Audiocassettes "Harlem Night Song"; "Blow, Blow, Thou Winter Wind"; "love is a place"; "The Freedom of the Moon"

Harlem Night Song
◆ Blow, Blow, Thou Winter Wind ◆
love is a place ◆ The Freedom of the Moon

Tell students that the famous English poet Alexander Pope wrote the following short verse, which you may want to write on the board: "I am his Highness' dog at Kew; Pray tell me, sire, whose dog are you?" Ask students to identify the speaker in the verse. Point out that, even though the pronoun *I* is used, it is not the poet, but rather a dog who is speaking. Ask students to watch for clues that can help them identify the speaker in the following poems.

◆ Build Grammar Skills

Irregular Comparisons of Modifiers If you wish to introduce the grammar concept for this selection before students read, refer to the instruction on p. 832.

Customize for
Less Proficient Readers
To help less proficient readers understand the poems, define and discuss the vocabulary words before reading. Then have small groups follow along in their books as they listen to the audiocassette of the poems. After they listen to each poem, help students paraphrase lines or phrases that contain vocabulary words. For example, paraphrase "Let us roam the night together" as "Let's go out tonight and wander around."

Listening to Literature Audiocassettes

Customize for
More Advanced Students
Invite students to write a short poem that uses words to help the reader "see" or "hear" the image described. Encourage them to think of an image that is vivid in their memory or one that they can imagine in detail. Have volunteers read their poems aloud for the class.

◆ Literary Focus

LYRIC POETRY

Lyric poetry expresses the poet's thoughts and feelings, creating a mood through vivid images, descriptive words, and the musical quality of the lines. In lyric poetry, you can almost "see" or "hear" the images the poet presents. Lyric poems may be made up of regular stanzas, like "Blow, Blow, Thou Winter Wind," or they may have uneven stanzas, like "Harlem Night Song."

Keep track of your favorite images from these poems by completing a chart like this one:

Poem	Image
"Harlem Night Song"	A band is playing.

◆ Reading Strategy

IDENTIFY THE SPEAKER

The **speaker** in a poem is the imaginary voice assumed by the poet. Sometimes the speaker is the poet; sometimes the speaker is a character created by the poet. When a poet uses the pronoun "I," it does not necessarily mean that the speaker represents the poet. The "I" could be an imaginary character, such as another person, an animal, or an inanimate object.

Guide for Reading ◆ 827

Customize for
English Language Learners
To help students hear the lyrical quality of the words and phrases, read the poems aloud for them. Then reread the poems with students, drawing pictures as necessary to help students understand the images described.

Preparing for Standardized Tests

Spelling Spelling sections of standardized tests may contain questions that require students to recognize incorrectly spelled words in the context of phrases. The spelling skill for this selection is understanding the correct usage of *ie* and *ei* and correctly choosing between the two spellings. Review that *i* comes before *e* except after *c* or when sounded like *ay*, as in *weight.* Write the following sample test question on the board:

Find the phrase containing an underlined word that is *not* spelled correctly.

(A) <u>fierce</u> wind
(B) purchase <u>reciept</u>
(C) <u>deceitful</u> <u>neighbor</u>
(D) <u>piece</u> of <u>cake</u>

Point out to students that with this question, they must evaluate the spelling of each word in the underlined phrase. The correct answer is (B), because the *c* in *receipt* indicates that the spelling should be *ei*. (C) is correct because *ei* makes the *ay* sound in *neighbor*, and *ei* in *deceitful* follows *c*. For more practice spelling words with *ei* and *ie*, use **Selection Support,** p. 280.

One-Minute Insight

In "Harlem Nights," the speaker invites a loved one to come along so the two can wander together, listening to music and enjoying the natural beauty of the night sky. The moon and stars are natural wonders that are apparent even in the heart of the city.

◆ Reading Strategy

❶ Speaker Have students discuss who the speaker might be and whom he or she is addressing. *The speaker is not identified, but it might be the poet. The speaker is addressing a person whom he or she loves.*

◆ Literary Focus

❷ Lyric Poetry Ask students what mood these descriptive phrases help establish. *The descriptions help to create an exciting, magical mood.*

◆ Critical Thinking

❸ Infer Point out the word *singing* at the end of the first and last verses. Ask students why the speaker might want to sing. *The speaker enjoys music and is in love. When people are happy and in love, they might feel like singing.*

►Critical Viewing◄

❹ Interpret *Possible answer: Streetlights, car lights, and lit windows brighten the darkness. The couple walks closely together and seem to have somewhere to go. The man in the doorway may have just closed his business for the night.*

HARLEM NIGHT SONG
Langston Hughes

Relics, Martin Lewis, Philadelphia Museum of Art, Philadelphia, PA

Come,
Let us <u>roam</u> the night together
❶ Singing.

I love you.

5　Across
The Harlem[1] roof-tops
❷ Moon is shining.
Night sky is blue.
Stars are great drops
10　Of golden dew.

Down the street
A band is playing.

I love you.

Come,
15　Let us roam the night together
❸ Singing.

---

1. **Harlem** (här´ ləm) *n.*: Section of New York City in the northern part of Manhattan.

▲ **Critical Viewing** In what ways has the artist captured the spirit of the night in this drawing? [Interpret]

◆ Build Vocabulary

roam (rōm) *v.*: Go aimlessly; wander

keen (kēn) *adj.*: Having a sharp cutting edge

feigning (fān´ iŋ) *v.*: Pretending

Block Scheduling Strategies

Consider these suggestions to take advantage of extended class time:

• Review the Literary Focus before students read. Then have them complete a chart like the one on p. 827 as they read the poems independently. Have groups of students compare and discuss their charts prior to answering the Literary Focus questions on p. 832. For additional practice, use **Selection Support,** p. 283.

• Have students prepare for the Writing Mini-Lesson by working on the *Writer's Solution*

Language Lab CD-ROM and *Writer's Solution Writing Lab CD-ROM.* Refer to the teaching suggestions on p. 833 to guide students through the process.

• Have students listen to the recordings of the poems, noting how the words and rhythms help to create certain moods. Then have students read the poems aloud in small groups and answer the Guide for Responding questions on pp. 829 and 831.

Listening to Literature Audiocassettes

Blow, Blow, Thou Winter Wind
William Shakespeare

Blow, blow, thou winter wind.
Thou art not so unkind
   As man's ingratitude.
Thy tooth is not so <u>keen</u>,
5 Because thou art not seen,
   Although thy breath be rude.[1]
Heigh-ho! Sing, heigh-ho! unto the green holly.
Most friendship is <u>feigning</u>, most loving mere folly.
   Then, heigh-ho, the holly!
10   This life is most jolly.

Freeze, freeze, thou bitter sky,
That dost not bite so nigh
   As benefits forgot.
Though thou the waters warp,[2]
15 Thy sting is not so sharp
   As friend remembered not.
Heigh-ho! Sing, heigh-ho! unto the green holly.
Most friendship is feigning, most loving mere folly.
   Then, heigh-ho, the holly!
20   This life is most jolly.

1. **rude** *adj.*: Rough; harsh.
2. **warp** *v.*: Freeze.

◆ Guide for Responding

◆ LITERATURE AND YOUR LIFE

Reader's Response Do you share the view toward friendship expressed by the speaker in "Blow, Blow, Thou Winter Wind"? Explain.

Thematic Focus Explain how each poem celebrates the physical world.

☑ Check Your Comprehension

1. (a) To whom is the speaker of "Harlem Night Song" speaking? (b) What does the speaker want the listener to do?
2. (a) In "Blow, Blow, Thou Winter Wind," what does the speaker say is more unkind than the winter wind? (b) What is sharper than the sting of the bitter sky?

◆ Critical Thinking

INTERPRET

1. In "Harlem Night Song," why does the speaker feel so full of life? **[Infer]**
2. Explain what "Blow, Blow, Thou Winter Wind" suggests about the harshness of nature compared to the pain of human relationships. **[Interpret]**

COMPARE LITERARY WORKS

3. Compare and contrast the attitudes toward love and friendship of the speakers in "Harlem Night Song" and in "Blow, Blow, Thou Winter Wind." **[Compare and Contrast]**

Harlem Night Song/Blow, Blow, Thou Winter Wind ◆ 829

 Humanities: Art

Relics, by Martin Lewis
   Australian-born Martin Lewis (1883–1962) was a painter, printmaker, and draftsman. He made his reputation by capturing the energy and excitement of street life in 1920's Manhattan. In *Relics*, the viewer can see Lewis's skill with the drypoint technique and his ability to capture the mood of a certain time and place in New York City.
1. What feelings do you have when you look at this drawing? *Students may say that the drawing*
gives them a feeling of being alone in the middle of a large city. The couple in the lamplight seem isolated from the rest of the world. The man coming out of the store seems lonely.
2. How does the drawing relate to the poem? *Both provide images of a city street at night. When couples are in love, they can feel as if they are alone, even in a crowd. The couple in the drawing seem to be in their own world, created by the circle of light from the streetlamp.*

829

One-Minute Insight

E. E. Cummings begins each stanza of "love is a place" with a metaphor. He compares love with a state of mind that anyone can "visit" and the word *yes* with an ideal world where a person can do anything she or he dreams, since *no* is never heard. In this poem, the world around the poet is not the natural world but rather a state of mind extended to the rest of the world.

◆ Literary Focus

❶ Lyric Poetry Ask students what mood is created by this poem. *The images described create a peaceful, calm mood, while the use of ampersands, parentheses, and the lack of punctuation create a playful, offbeat mood.*

◆ Reading Strategy

❷ Speaker Discuss who the speaker might be. *The speaker is not identified, and may or may not be the poet.*

►Critical Viewing◄

❸ Interpret *The peaceful setting is brightened by colorful flowers and the bright faces of the woman and the baby birds.*

Customize for
Logical/Mathematical Learners

Have students use the Venn Diagram, p. 77 of **Writing and Language Transparencies,** to compare and contrast the world described by E. E. Cummings in "love is a place" with the natural world. For example, they might write "filled with possibilities" in the center section of the diagram, "possibilities always realized" under "love is a place," and "possibilities not always realized" under "natural world."

🎼 Humanities: Art

The Nest, 1893, by Constant Montald

Belgian Impressionist Constant Montald uses light and color to create an idealized image of the natural world. Ask students why this painting is an appropriate illustration for the poem. *The painting shows a tranquil scene filled with possibilities and showing an expression of love.*

830

---

love is a place
E.E. Cummings

The Nest, 1893, Constant Montald, Musées Royaux des Beaux-Arts de Belgique, Bruxelles-Koninklijke Musea voor Schone Kunsten van Belgie, Brussels, Belgium

▲ **Critical Viewing** In what ways does this painting bring to life the phrase "brightness of peace"? [Interpret] ❸

830 ◆ Poetry

```
   love is a place
   & through this place of
   love move
   (with brightness of peace)
 5 all places                        ❶
                                     ❷
   yes is a world
   & in this world of
   yes live
   (skillfully curled)
10 all worlds
```

🎤 Speaking and Listening Mini-Lesson

Monologue

This mini-lesson supports the Speaking and Listening activity in the Idea Bank on p. 833.

Introduce Tell students that a monologue is a speech that usually reveals something about the character or personality of the speaker.

Develop Have students reread "Blow, Blow, Thou Winter Wind" and discuss what the poem reveals about the speaker. Then have students think of a force of nature they might address in a monologue. Stimulate students' imagination by having them name forces of nature, such as thunderstorms, snowfall, ocean waves, earthquakes, gentle rain, and so forth.

Apply Have students write a rough draft. Then have them practice performing their monologues with partners, suggesting ways their partners can make the monologues more interesting or entertaining. After students revise, have them practice making clear and effective oral presentations.

Assess Evaluate students' work based on the level of preparation and effectiveness of presentation. Or, use the Peer Assessment: Dramatic Performance, p. 110, in **Alternative Assessment.**

The Freedom of the Moon

Robert Frost

I've tried the new moon tilted in the air
Above a hazy tree-and-farmhouse cluster
As you might try a jewel in your hair.
I've tried it fine with little <u>breadth</u> of <u>luster</u>,
5   Alone, or in one ornament combining
With one first-water star almost as shining.

I put it shining anywhere I please.
By walking slowly on some evening later,
I've pulled it from a crate of crooked trees
10 And brought it over glossy water, greater,
And dropped it in, and seen the image wallow,
The color run, all sorts of wonder follow.

❹
❺

◆ **Build Vocabulary**

breadth (bredth) *n.*: Width
luster (lus´ tər) *n.*: Brightness; radiance

▲ **Critical Viewing** Which line from the poem does this photograph best illustrate? [Make a Judgment] **❻**

Develop Understanding

One-Minute Insight In "The Freedom of the Moon," Robert Frost describes ways he viewed the moon and was inspired by its beauty.

◆ **Reading Strategy**

❹ Speaker Discuss who the poem's speaker might be. *The speaker could be the poet—he uses the pronoun I, implying that the moon is his inspiration.*

◆ **Literary Focus**

❺ Lyric Poetry Ask students how these lines help them identify this as a lyric poem. *The words and phrases help the reader "see" the images.*

▶**Critical Viewing**◀

❻ Make a Judgment *Possible answer:"I've pulled it from a crate of crooked trees" (line 9).*

Reinforce and Extend

Answers

◆ **LITERATURE AND YOUR LIFE**

Reader's Response Students may say they enjoy looking at the moon in different stages, but have never been inspired to write a poem about it.

Thematic Focus Cummings celebrates a natural but interior world. Frost celebrates the moon and its beauty in natural settings.

☑ **Check Your Comprehension**

1. (a) The speaker says all places move through the place of love; (b) all worlds live in a world of yes.
2. The speaker is occupied with looking at the moon.

◆ **Critical Thinking**

1. In a world of yes, everything would fit together perfectly.
2. Even a bright star does not shine as brightly as the moon.
3. It creates a musical sense and a connection between the words.
4. Students may answer that both speakers seem satisfied with the world as it is, but the speaker in "love is a place" is perhaps most satisfied. She or he finds the natural world to be filled with love and positive possibilities.

Guide for Responding

◆ **LITERATURE AND YOUR LIFE**

Reader's Response Are you inspired by the moon, as the speaker is in "The Freedom of the Moon"? Why or why not?

Thematic Focus In what ways do both Frost and Cummings celebrate nature?

Sketch Sketch the moon as described in the second stanza of Frost's poem.

☑ **Check Your Comprehension**

1. (a) In "love is a place," what does the speaker say moves through the place of love? (b) Where does the speaker say all worlds live?
2. With what activity is the speaker in "The Freedom of the Moon" occupied?

◆ **Critical Thinking**

INTERPRET

1. In "love is a place," what do you think the speaker means when he describes "all worlds" in the "world of yes" as being "skillfully curled"? **[Interpret]**
2. "First-water" describes gems of the highest luster. Explain its meaning as used in "The Freedom of the Moon." **[Connect]**
3. How does alliteration—repetition of beginning consonant sounds—in "The Freedom of the Moon" add to the poem's effect? **[Analyze]**

COMPARING LITERARY WORKS

4. Which speaker seems more satisfied with the world as it is—the one in "love is a place" or the one in "The Freedom of the Moon"? Explain. **[Assess]**

love is a place/The Freedom of the Moon ◆ 831

Beyond the Selection

FURTHER READING
Other Works by the Authors
"Dream Variations," Langston Hughes
"Sigh No More Ladies," William Shakespeare
"maggie and milly and molly and may," E. E. Cummings
"The Pasture," Robert Frost
Other Examples of Lyric Poetry
"A Red, Red Rose," Robert Burns
"The Tropics of New York," Claude McKay
"Guitarreros," Américo Paredes

INTERNET
We suggest the following sites on the Internet (all Web sites are subject to change).
For more information about Langston Hughes:
http://www.technoir.net/Jazz/hughes.html
For an Internet guide to William Shakespeare:
http://daphne.palomar.edu/shakespeare/
For more information about Robert Frost:
http://www.pro-net.co.uk/home/catalyst/RF/body.html
We *strongly recommend* that you preview these sites before you send students to them.

Answers

◆ Reading Strategy

1. (a) Possible answer: The speaker believes that enjoying the moment with a loved one is worthwhile. (b) The speaker invites a loved one to enjoy with him or her the music and the night.
2. (a) The speaker values friendship and love. (b) The speaker says that those who treat love and friendship lightly are colder and more unkind than the bitterest cold wind.
3. Students may say that the speaker in "The Freedom of the Moon" is a person who seeks to experience all of the natural world's beauty and wonder and describe it in poetry.

◆ Build Vocabulary

Word Roots: -lus-
1. illustrious; 2. illustrate; 3. lustrous

Spelling Strategy
1. sleigh   3. friend   5. receive
2. ceiling   4. niece   6. beige

Using the Word Bank
1. Feigning
2. breadth
3. keen
4. luster
5. roam

◆ Literary Focus

1. Students may say the emotion expressed is love, exhilaration, or anticipation.
2. "Then, heigh-ho, the holly!" "This life is most jolly." "Heigh-ho! Sing, heigh-ho! unto the green holly."
3. The speaker's favorite words might be *love* and *yes*.
4. Students may say that it leaves them with the image of the moon's reflection on rippling water.

◆ Build Grammar Skills

Practice
1. Most, most; superlative
2. least; superlative
3. More; comparative
4. less; comparative—more; comparative
5. better; comparative

Writing Application
Possible answers:
1. but you could see it better last night.
2. but there were more colors reflected in the diamond.
3. and she will feel better tomorrow.
4. but last year was the worst season I can remember.
5. but it stings less when I wear this parka.

Guide for Responding (continued)

◆ Reading Strategy

IDENTIFY THE SPEAKER

When you read poetry, be aware of the **speaker,** the character or voice assumed by the poet. Even if the poet uses the pronoun "I," that doesn't always mean that the speaker is the poet.
1. (a) In "Harlem Night Song," what can you infer about the speaker's attitude concerning what is worthwhile in life? (b) What makes you think so?
2. (a) In "Blow, Blow, Thou Winter Wind," what does the speaker value in life? (b) How do you know?
3. How would you describe the speaker of "The Freedom of the Moon"?

◆ Build Vocabulary

USING THE WORD ROOT -lus-

The word root -lus-, as in *luster,* means "light." On your paper, complete each sentence with the correct word from this list:

illustrate: to make clear by giving an example
illustrious: brilliantly outstanding
lustrous: reflecting light evenly without sparkle
1. Our _____?_____ guest of honor will now speak.
2. Let me _____?_____ what I mean.
3. The opal in her ring was _____?_____.

SPELLING STRATEGY

When choosing between *ei* and *ie,* follow this rule: Put *i* before *e* except after *c* or when sounded like *ay* as in *neighbor* and *weigh.*

On your paper, complete the following words by adding *ei* or *ie.*
1. sl_?_gh   3. fr_?_nd   5. rec_?_ve
2. c_?_ling   4. n_?_ce   6. b_?_ge

USING THE WORD BANK

On your paper, write the Word Bank word that best completes each sentence.
1. _____?_____ sleep, the child kept her eyes closed.
2. We toured the length and _____?_____ of the country by train.
3. David has a _____?_____ interest in science.
4. This conditioner will restore the _____?_____ in your hair.
5. Be careful when you _____?_____ the streets at night.

◆ Literary Focus

LYRIC POETRY

To determine whether a poem is a **lyric poem,** ask yourself these questions: Is it a personal expression of feeling? Is it emotional? Is it musical? Does it create a single impression on the reader? If you can answer yes to all these questions, it is an example of lyric poetry.
1. What is the emotion expressed by the speaker in "Harlem Night Song"?
2. Give three examples of lines with musical quality in "Blow, Blow, Thou Winter Wind."
3. What might be two favorite words of the speaker of "love is a place"?
4. With what single impression does "The Freedom of the Moon" leave you?

◆ Build Grammar Skills

IRREGULAR COMPARISONS OF MODIFIERS

Some modifiers have **irregular forms for comparisons:**

Positive	Comparative	Superlative
bad	worse	worst
good	better	best
well	better	best
little	less	least
many, much	more	most

Practice Write these sentences, underlining the modifiers and labeling them as comparative or superlative.
1. Most friendship is feigning, most loving mere folly.
2. Winter is the least friendly season.
3. More stars are visible tonight.
4. Give me less war and more peace.
5. The moon looked better over the water.

Writing Application To each sentence, add a second part, in which you use a different form of comparison of the italicized modifier.
1. You can see the moon *well* tonight.
2. I saw *many* colors reflected in the water.
3. She felt *good* today.
4. It's a *bad* season for skiing.
5. The wind stings a *little.*

 Writer's Solution

For additional instruction and practice, use the lesson in the *Writer's Solution Language Lab CD-ROM* on Troublesome Adjectives and Adverbs in the Using Modifiers unit. You may also use the practice page on irregular adjectives and adverbs, p. 87, in the *Writer's Solution Grammar Practice Book.*

Build Your Portfolio

Idea Bank

Writing

1. **Invitation** The speaker in "Harlem Night Song" invites the listener to join him on a walk through the night. Write your own invitation to someone, asking him or her to join you for an outing.

2. **Paraphrase** Shakespeare's "Blow, Blow, Thou Winter Wind" was written about four hundred years ago. Write a line-by-line paraphrase—restatement in your own words—to put the poem's essence in modern English.

3. **Essay** Write an essay on "The Freedom of the Moon." In it, examine Frost's use of rhyme and repetition. Also, explore the images he creates, and comment on their effectiveness.

Speaking and Listening

4. **Monologue** The speaker of "Blow, Blow, Thou Winter Wind" speaks to the wind as if it were a person. Write and perform for the class a monologue, which is a dramatic speech in which the speaker addresses some force of nature.

5. **Discussion [Group Activity]** Suppose that the speaker of "Harlem Night Song" and the speaker of "The Freedom of the Moon" are discussing the best night scenes. One likes the country; the other likes the city. With a classmate, stage for the class the discussion they might have. **[Performing Arts Link]**

Projects

6. **Music of the 1920's [Group Activity]** With a small group, research the music that might have been playing "down the street" in "Harlem Night Song." Prepare a presentation for the class about music in Harlem in the 1920's. Play recordings of the songs, and include information about the composers and performers. **[Music Link]**

7. **Constellations Poster** Two of these poems mention stars. Create a poster about constellations—configurations of stars. Include captions that tell about each one. **[Science Link]**

Writing Mini-Lesson

Retelling of a Poem in Prose

Poems contain highly charged, emotional language that is unlike ordinary, conversational language. Choose one poem from this grouping to retell in prose—in ordinary language. In your retelling, capture the original essence of the poem.

Writing Skills Focus: Use an Appropriate Tone

When you write a prose retelling of a poem, it is important to **use an appropriate tone.** Once you figure out what the tone of the poem is—serious, playful, ironic, bitter—you should use that same tone in the prose retelling.

Model Based on "The Freedom of the Moon"

Original: I've tried the new moon tilted in the air / Above a hazy tree-and-farmhouse cluster / As you might try a jewel in your hair.

Prose Retelling: While walking by a farmhouse that had trees near it, I saw the new moon. It seemed like a jewel that you might fasten in your hair. . . .

Prewriting Paraphrase the poem you want to retell. You may have to look up some words in a dictionary to make sure you understand their exact meaning. Also, pinpoint the tone of the poem, and plan how you'll capture that tone in the retelling.

Drafting Rewrite the poem as prose. You will find that it takes more words to tell the same thing in prose than it does in poetry.

Revising Check your retelling against the original to be sure you've included all the poet's ideas. Replace words wherever the tone does not match that of the poem.

> ◆ **Grammar Application**
>
> If you used irregular modifiers in your retelling, be sure you've used the correct form.

Harlem Night Song/Blow, Blow. . ./love is a place/The Freedom of the Moon ◆ 833

Idea Bank

Following are suggestions for matching the Idea Bank topics with your students' performance levels and learning modalities:

Customize for
Performance Levels
Less Advanced Students: 1, 5, 6
Average Students: 2, 4, 5, 6
More Advanced Students: 3, 4, 7

Customize for
Learning Modalities
Verbal/Linguistic: 1, 2, 3, 4, 5
Visual/Spatial: 7
Musical/Rhythmic: 6
Logical/Mathematical: 7
Interpersonal: 5, 6
Intrapersonal: 1, 2, 3, 4, 7

Writing Mini-Lesson

Refer students to the Writing Handbook in the back of the book for instruction on the writing process and for further information on prose. Have students use the Sensory Language Chart in **Writing and Language Transparencies,** p. 69, to arrange their prewriting examples.

✎ Writer's Solution

Writing Lab CD-ROM
Have students complete the tutorial on Creative Writing. Follow these steps:

1. Have students use Writing Hints on Audience to help them picture their audience in order to develop language that is appropriate for their choice.

2. Students can use the Emotion Word Bin activity to explore words and phrases that communicate emotions.

3. Have students draft on computer.

4. Students can use the audio-annotated Student Models to explore replacing abstract words with more vivid, specific words.

Writer's Solution Sourcebook
Have students use Chapter 8, "Creative Writing," pp. 234–265, for additional support. This chapter includes instruction on choosing words and conveying ideas.

✓ ASSESSMENT OPTIONS

Formal Assessment, Selection Test, pp. 234–236, and Assessment Resources Software. The selection test is designed so that it can easily be customized to the performance levels of your students.

Alternative Assessment, p. 52, includes options for less advanced students, more advanced students, verbal/linguistic learners, musical/rhythmic learners, interpersonal learners, logical/mathematical learners, and visual/spatial learners.

PORTFOLIO ASSESSMENT
Use the following rubrics in the **Alternative Assessment** booklet to assess student writing:
Invitation: Expression, p. 90
Paraphrase: Summary, p. 94
Essay: Literary Analysis/Interpretation, p. 108
Writing Mini-Lesson: Summary, p. 94

OBJECTIVES

1. To read, comprehend, and interpret five poems
2. To relate five poems to personal experience
3. To paraphrase lines in a poem
4. To recognize four poetic forms
5. To build vocabulary in context and learn the forms of *fertile*
6. To use coordinate adjectives
7. To write a self-description with a comparison, elaborating with supporting details
8. To respond to the poems through writing, speaking and listening, and projects

SKILLS INSTRUCTION

Vocabulary:
Related Words:
Forms of *fertile*

Spelling:
Using *y* to Spell the Short *i* Sound

Grammar:
Coordinate Adjectives

Reading Strategy:
Paraphrase Lines

Writing:
Elaborate With Supporting Details

Literary Focus:
Poetic Form

Speaking and Listening:
Dramatic Reading (Teacher Edition)

Viewing and Representing:
Swimming Poem (Teacher Edition)

Critical Viewing:
Compare and Contrast; Extend; Interpret

PORTFOLIO OPPORTUNITIES

Writing: Glossary; Concrete Poem; Essay
Writing Mini-Lesson: Description of Yourself With a Comparison
Speaking and Listening: Rebuttal; Dramatic Reading
Projects: Multimedia Presentation; Glossary of Terms

More About the Authors
John Updike uses scenes from his childhood as the background for much of his writing.

Matsuo Bashō was born a Samurai warrior but devoted himself to writing poems inspired by nature.

Moritake found inspiration for his writing in Shinto, a religion in which the gods are believed to live in natural surroundings.

Julio Noboa Polanco writes poetry in English and Spanish and runs a dropout prevention program.

Maxine Kumin has served as Poet Laureate of New Hampshire. She is a Chancellor of The Academy of American Poets.

Guide for Reading

Meet the Authors:

John Updike (1932–)

Best known as a Pulitzer Prize-winning novelist, John Updike is also an essayist, poet, and editor. Updike's quartet of novels—*Rabbit Run, Rabbit Redux, Rabbit Is Rich,* and *Rabbit at Rest*—is considered to be one of the great chronicles of modern life.

Matsuo Bashō (1644–1694)

Japanese poet Matsuo Bashō is widely regarded as the greatest of haiku poets. He began writing poetry at age nine, and at the age of thirty, he founded a school for the study of haiku.

Moritake (1452–1540)

A priest as well as a poet, Moritake is considered one of the leading Japanese poets of the sixteenth century.

Julio Noboa Polanco (1949–)

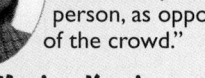

Bilingual poet Julio Noboa Polanco was an eighth-grader at the time he wrote "Identity." Of "Identity," the poet says, "The whole poem is essentially a search for my individuality—finding myself as a person, as opposed to being one of the crowd."

Maxine Kumin (1925–)

In addition to poetry, Maxine Kumin has written novels, essays, and children's books. In Kumin's poems, the reader hears the music of nature and is sometimes given a warm glimpse of Kumin's family and her New Hampshire farm.

834 ◆ Poetry

◆ LITERATURE AND YOUR LIFE

CONNECT YOUR EXPERIENCE

When was the last time you saw or experienced a bitterly cold day, flowers, lightning, a magnificent weed, or a swimming competition? These sights and experiences inspired the poems that follow.

THEMATIC FOCUS: Respecting Nature

How does the environment contribute to the subject matter of these poems?

◆ Background for Understanding

SCIENCE

In "January," Updike mentions the shortness of the winter days, which is caused by the twenty-four-hour rotation of the Earth on its axis. The part of the Earth facing the sun has day. However, the Earth's axis is permanently tilted about twenty-three degrees off-center. So, as the Earth travels on its 365-day orbit around the sun, the part that is tilted toward the sun has the longer days. The Northern Hemisphere tilts away from the sun in winter and receives fewer hours of sunlight then than it does in summer.

◆ Build Vocabulary

RELATED WORDS: FORMS OF *fertile*

In "Identity," Polanco writes that he'd rather be unseen than grow in a "fertile" valley. The adjective *fertile* means "rich or productive." Knowing the definition of *fertile* will help you understand the meaning of related words, such as *fertilizer* and *fertilization*.

WORD BANK

Which word from the poems means "done in a sly or cunning way"? Check the Build Vocabulary box on page 840 to see if you chose correctly.

harnessed
abyss
shunned
fertile
catapults
cunningly
extravagance
nurtures

Prentice Hall Literature Program Resources

REINFORCE / RETEACH / EXTEND
Selection Support Pages
Build Vocabulary: Related Words: Forms of *fertile*, p. 284
Building Spelling Skills: Using *y* to Spell the Short *i* Sound, p. 285
Building Grammar Skills: Coordinate Adjectives, p. 286
Reading Strategy: Paraphrase Lines, p. 287
Literary Focus: Poetic Form, p. 288
Strategies for Diverse Student Needs, pp. 105–106

Beyond Literature Cross-Curricular Connection: Science, p. 53
Formal Assessment Selection Test, pp. 237–239, Assessment Resources Software
Alternative Assessment, p. 53
Daily Language Practice, p. 56 and p. 58
Resource Pro CD-ROM "January"; Two Haiku; "Identity"; "400-Meter Free Style"

 Listening to Literature Audiocassettes "January"; Two Haiku; "Identity"; "400-Meter Free Style"

January ◆ Two Haiku ◆ Identity
◆ 400-Meter Free Style ◆

View to Orchard, Winter, Cerney House, Charles Neal

◆ Literary Focus

POETIC FORM

Poetic form is the structure of a poem. Updike's "January" is a lyric poem that captures a single image. This particular poem contains four stanzas of four lines each. The Japanese **haiku** is a form that consists of three lines of verse whose subject is nature. The first and third lines have five syllables each. The second line has seven syllables. Polanco's "Identity" is written in **free verse**, which means that the poet created its line breaks and stanzas where he wanted them. Kumin's poem is an example of **concrete poetry**, which uses the shape of the poem on the page to symbolize an idea or image within the poem.

◆ Reading Strategy

PARAPHRASE LINES

When you **paraphrase,** you restate in your own words what someone else has written. You can paraphrase lines of a poem to express the thought or image in your own words. The following example shows how paraphrasing helps you to identify the basic meaning of a line.

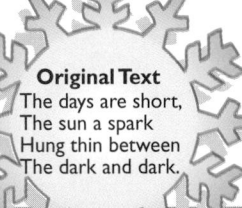

Original Text
The days are short,
The sun a spark
Hung thin between
The dark and dark.

Paraphrase
The sun shines only briefly between dawn and dusk on short winter days.

Guide for Reading ◆ 835

One-Minute Insight

In "January," John Updike describes images that he connects with during the first month of the year. The length of the lines and stanzas are as descriptive of days in January as are the word choices he makes for the poem.

In his haiku, Bashō captures a moment in nature during which a flash of lightning is transformed into a night heron's screech.

Moritake's haiku describes a moment during which something thought to be a falling flower is recognized as a butterfly.

◆ **Critical Thinking**

❶ **Analyze** Ask students what else is short besides "the days." *The lines of the poem are very short.*

◆ **Literary Focus**

❷ **Poetic Form** Help students identify "January" as a lyric poem. Then ask them what elements of lyric poetry they find in these lines. *The poet uses descriptive language to help create a mood and capture the image of days in January.*

◆ **Reading Strategy**

❸ **Paraphrase Lines** Have students paraphrase these lines to illustrate their understanding. *The frozen river is motionless beneath the ice- and snow-covered trees.*

◆ **Critical Thinking**

❹ **Compare and Contrast** Discuss how this image contrasts with the other images in the poem. *The purring radiator is a warm image, whereas all the other images are cold ones.*

▶ **Critical Viewing** ◀

❺ **Compare and Contrast** *Both the poem and the painting describe a winter day with a low, gray sky and trees covered in ice and snow. There is a river in the poem but not in the painting. There is a bird in the painting but not in the poem.*

836

JANUARY
John Updike

The Magpie, 1869, Claude Monet, Musée d'Orsay, Paris, France

❶ The days are short,
   The sun a spark
Hung thin between
   The dark and dark.

5 Fat snowy footsteps
   Track the floor,
And parkas pile up
   Near the door.

❷
   The river is
10   A frozen place
❸ Held still beneath
   The trees' black lace.

The sky is low.
   The wind is gray.
15 The radiator
   Purrs all day.

836 ◆ Poetry

❺ ▲ **Critical Viewing** Compare and contrast the artist's concept of winter with Updike's. **[Compare and Contrast]**

 Block Scheduling Strategies

Consider these suggestions to take advantage of extended class time:

• Have students read the poems silently. Prior to discussing each poem, have a volunteer read it aloud for the class. Have pairs of students discuss the Literary Focus questions on p. 842.

• To separate instructional activities, use the **Daily Language Practice** tasks on p. 56 and p. 58.

• Arrange students in small groups to complete the cross-curricular activity on p. 841. Students can apply their research to the Glossary of Terms Project from the Idea Bank on p. 843.

• Have students prepare for the Writing Mini-Lesson by working on the *Writer's Solution Language Lab CD-ROM* and *Writer's Solution Writing Lab CD-ROM*. Refer to the teaching suggestions on p. 843 to guide students through the writing process.

• Review the literary focus with students. To help them hear the differences among the various poetic forms, have students listen to the poems on audiocassette.

 Listening to Literature Audiocassettes

Two Haiku

The lightning flashes!
And slashing through the darkness,
A night-heron's[1] screech.

Bashō

5 The falling flower
I saw drift back to the branch
Was a butterfly.

Moritake

---

1. **night-heron** (nīt´ her´ ən) *n.*: A large wading bird with a long neck and long legs that is active at night.

► **Critical Viewing** Bashō's haiku has images of sight and sound. To what senses does this painting of herons appeal? [Extend]

Herons and Reeds, Japanese, Asian Art Museum of San Francisco, CA

Guide for Responding

◆ LITERATURE AND YOUR LIFE

Reader's Response Which image in "January" best conveys to you the essence of that month? Why?

Thematic Focus Describe the ways in which these poets celebrate the wonders of nature.

☑ **Check Your Comprehension**

1. (a) In "January," how does Updike describe the sun? (b) What sound fills the air at the end of the poem?
2. (a) What is the subject in the haiku by Bashō? (b) What is the subject in the haiku by Moritake?

◆ Critical Thinking

INTERPRET

1. Explain the image "dark and dark" in line 4 of "January." [Interpret]
2. In "January," why do the trees appear to be made of lace? [Interpret]
3. How does the image in Bashō's haiku change by the third line? [Interpret]
4. To what does Moritake compare the falling flower? [Connect]

APPLY

5. Updike uses the color gray to describe wind in winter. What colors do you associate with the other seasons? Explain. [Relate]

which appears on p. 836,

◆ **Literary Focus**

❻ **Poetic Form** Ask students how they can identify this poem as haiku. *It has three lines; the first and third lines have five syllables each; the second line has seven syllables; the subject is nature.*

► **Critical Viewing** ◄

❼ **Extend** *It appeals to the sense of sight, since you can see the herons. It appeals to the sense of touch, because you can imagine how the water and the grasses might feel if you touched them. It appeals to the sense of hearing, since you can imagine how the wind sounds blowing through the grasses and how the birds might sound.*

Reinforce and Extend

Answers

◆ LITERATURE AND YOUR LIFE

Reader's Response Possible answer: "The days are short," because it rarely snows and the rivers never freeze where I live, but short days help me know it is winter.

Thematic Focus John Updike celebrates winter. Bashō celebrates a storm, and Moritake celebrates the delicate beauty of a butterfly.

☑ **Check Your Comprehension**

1. (a) He describes the sun as a spark. (b) The purring of the radiator fills the air.
2. (a) The subject of Bashō's haiku is a storm. (b) The subject of Moritake's haiku is a butterfly.

◆ Critical Thinking

1. The image refers to the dark before sunrise and the dark following sunset.
2. The coating of ice and snow gives the trees a lacy appearance.
3. It changes from lightning, which is seen, to the bird's screech, which is heard.
4. He compares it to a butterfly.
5. Students may suggest associations such as spring with many shades of green, because of new grass and leaves; summer with yellow, because of the hot, yellow sun; fall with the gold, brown, and orange of autumn leaves and pumpkins.

 Humanities: Art

The Magpie, 1869, by Claude Monet
French Impressionist Claude Monet (1840–1926) is perhaps best known for his landscapes. He often painted the same scene again and again, showing how it looked at different times of day and in different seasons of the year. In *The Magpie,* which appears on p. 836, Monet shows a wintry scene with the sun casting long shadows on the snow. A magpie is perched on the gate, the only living creature in the frozen setting. Footprints in the snow, however, indicate someone has recently passed by.

Have students study the style and subject matter of the painting, then use these questions for discussion:
1. How would you feel if you were in this painting? *I would feel cold; I would want to go out and play in the snow.*
2. If there were a line about the magpie in Updike's poem, what might it say? *"The magpie perched."* Help students recognize that the description would need to be short—only four or five syllables—to match the style of the poem.

One-Minute Insight

In "Identity," Julio Noboa Polanco uses images from nature to express his desire for freedom and independence. He compares the life he seeks to that of a weed growing in high, jagged rocks. Polanco then contrasts this image with that of carefully tended flowers—people who live comfortably but without a sense of personal freedom.

◆ Critical Thinking

1 Infer Ask students to whom the speaker refers when he writes, "Let them be as flowers." *He is referring to people who do not share his independent views about life.*

◆ Literary Focus

2 Poetic Form Discuss the lack of rhyme or set rhythm pattern in these lines. Ask students what this helps them know about the form of this poem. *It is an example of free verse.*

◆ Critical Thinking

3 Interpret Ask students what the poet means when he says he would rather be exposed to the "madness" of the sky? *He is willing to take his chances with the unpredictability that comes with freedom.*

◆ Reading Strategy

4 Paraphrase Lines Have students restate these lines in their own words. *Possible answers: I would choose to be unappealing, like a smelly weed, instead of attractive, like a fragrant flower, if it means I can enjoy my freedom.*

▶ Critical Viewing ◀

5 Compare and Contrast *Neither the speaker nor the person in the painting mind being alone; both express an independent attitude—the speaker through his words and the subject through his stance.*

Customize for *Visual/Spatial Learners*

Prior to reading each poem, have students preview the illustrations and make predictions about the poem's content. After reading, discuss with students the ways the illustrations affected their responses to the poems.

Identity

Julio Noboa Polanco

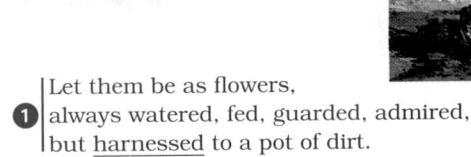

Seashore at Palavas, 1854, Gustave Courbet, Musée Fabre, Montpellier, France

1 Let them be as flowers,
always watered, fed, guarded, admired,
but <u>harnessed</u> to a pot of dirt.

2 I'd rather be a tall, ugly weed,
5   clinging on cliffs, like an eagle
wind-wavering above high, jagged rocks.

To have broken through the surface
of stone,
3 to live, to feel exposed to the madness
of the vast, eternal sky.
10   To be swayed by the breezes of an
ancient sea,
carrying my soul, my seed, beyond
the mountains of time
or into the <u>abyss</u> of the bizarre.

4 I'd rather be unseen, and if
then <u>shunned</u> by everyone,
15   than to be a pleasant-smelling flower,
growing in clusters in the <u>fertile</u> valley,
where they're praised, handled, and
plucked
by greedy, human hands.

I'd rather smell of musty, green stench
20   than of sweet, fragrant lilac.
If I could stand alone, strong and free,
I'd rather be a tall, ugly weed.

5 ▲ **Critical Viewing** What qualities do the speaker of the poem and the subject of the painting share? [Compare and Contrast]

◆ Build Vocabulary

harnessed (här′ nist) *v.*: Tied; bound
abyss (ə bis′) *n.*: Great depth
shunned (shund) *v.*: Avoided
fertile (fur′ təl) *adj.*: Rich; fruitful
catapults (kat′ ə pults′) *v.*: Launches; leaps

838 ◆ *Poetry*

Humanities: Art

Seashore at Palavas, 1854, by Gustave Courbet
Gustave Courbet (1819–1877) would have had much in common with the speaker in "Identity." He chose to go against mainstream ideas of art and aesthetics by painting realistic images from ordinary life—images that most people of Courbet's time found offensive (impressionism was the predominant style of the time). In *Seashore at Palavas*, Courbet shows a solitary figure standing on the shore, striking a pose that can be interpreted in a variety of ways by viewers.

1. What is the person in the painting doing? *The person is waving to someone out at sea; the person is showing a feeling of exhilaration at being in such a pretty spot; the person is giving a salute to the sea or the sky.*

2. Based on what you read in the poem, what kind of plant would this person be? Why do you think so? *Like the speaker in the poem, this person would probably be a weed, since he is alone on the shore. His pose indicates that he feels independent and quite happy to be alone.*

400-Meter Free Style

Maxine Kumin

6 | The gun full swing the swimmer <u>catapults</u> and cracks
s
i
x

▼ **Critical Viewing** What words would you choose to describe the swimmer pictured here? [Interpret] **7**

Identity/400-Meter Free Style ◆ *839*

One-Minute Insight In "400-Meter Free Style," a concrete poem, Maxine Kumin verbally and graphically portrays one swimmer's performance in a competitive swimming event. The poem begins when the starting gun fires; progresses with the swimmer's racing movements through the water; and ends with the display of the swimmer's time, which registers as he touches the end of the pool following the last lap.

◆ Literary Focus

6 Poetic Form Ask students what they can tell about the form of this poem from the first line. *It is not a haiku, because the line is too long. It is probably not a lyric poem since this line seems to introduce an event rather than state the speaker's thoughts or feelings. The word six printed vertically at the end of the line indicates it might be a concrete poem, which creates a shape to symbolize an idea or image within the poem.*

▶ Critical Viewing ◀

7 Interpret *The swimmer appears skilled, confident, physically fit, and well-trained as a swimmer.*

Customize for *Visual/Spatial Learners*

Invite groups of students to brainstorm other subjects for concrete poems and then sketch examples of the outlines the poems might take. For example, if the subject were a chess game, the sketch might show a large square with text appearing in smaller, alternating black and white squares.

Speaking and Listening Mini-Lesson

Dramatic Reading

This mini-lesson supports the Speaking and Listening activity in the Idea Bank on p. 843.

Introduce Explain that dramatic readings are expressive, oral presentations of literature.

Develop As students prepare for their dramatic readings, encourage them to consider these points:

• What mood is expressed by the poem?

• What marks of punctuation indicate how the poem should be read?

• How can I vary my voice to express the drama and excitement of the poem in my reading?

Apply Have students write out the poem, marking pauses and vocal changes. You may want to have students work in pairs, practicing their readings and providing ideas for improving their partner's performance.

Assess Evaluate dramatic readings based on vocal effects, overall delivery, and attention to punctuation. You may also want to have students complete the Peer Assessment: Oral Interpretation form, p. 115, in **Alternative Assessment.**

❶ feet away onto that perfect glass he catches at
a
n
d

throws behind him scoop¹ after scoop cunningly moving
t
h
e

water back to move him forward. Thrift is his wonderful
s
e
❷ c
5 ret; he has schooled out all extravagance. No muscle
r
i
p
ples without compensation wrist cock² to heel snap to
h
i
s
mobile mouth that siphons³ in the air that nurtures
h
❸ i
m
❹ at half an inch above sea level so to speak.
T
h
e
astonishing whites of the soles of his feet rise
a
n
d
10 salute us on the turns. He flips, converts, and is gone
a
l
l
in one. We watch him for signs. His arms are steady at
t
h
❺ e
catch, his cadent⁴ feet tick in the stretch, they know
t
h
e

1. **scoop** (skōōp) *n.*: The amount taken up; in this case, with a cupped hand.

2. **wrist cock**: The tilted position of the wrist.

3. **siphons** (sī´fənz) *v.*: Draws; pulls.

4. **cadent** (kā´dənt) *adj.*: Rhythmic beating.

◆ **Build Vocabulary**
cunningly (kun´ iŋ lē) *adv.*: Skillfully
extravagance (ik strav´ ə gəns) *n.*: Wastefulness
nurtures (nʉr´ chərz) *v.*: Nourishes

🔍 Viewing and Representing Mini-Lesson

Swimming Poem

In this mini-lesson students will extend their understanding of how various cultures have developed different uses for swimming and other water skills by visually representing their research in a concrete poem.

Introduce Synchronized swimming, or water ballet, is a popular dance-like sport among American women. Endurance swimming, or long-distance swimming, in Western Europe has produced many well-publicized attempts to cross the English Channel. Competitive cliff diving remains an internationally popular sport for many daring thrill seekers. Pearl cultivation in Asia and some Pacific Islands once relied on divers to harvest pearl-bearing oysters.

Develop Have students research swimming, diving, or other water-related activities, in other countries and cultures and select a topic.

Apply Have students write a concrete poem, like Kumin's, in which form mirrors content. Explain that the poem's content will stem from their imagination and world view, as well as from what they have learned about the culture and type of water activity they chose. For example: lines in a poem about Japanese pearl divers might dip up and down across a page, whereas a poem about long-distance swimming might appear as a straight, unbroken line over several pages.

Assess Display students' poetry in a bulletin board classroom display. Evaluate students on their research and the visual representation they use in the poem.

lesson well. Lungs know, too; he does not list[5] for
       a
       i
       r

6

he drives along on little sips carefully expended
b
u
t

15   that plum[6] red heart pumps hard cries hurt how soon
                                     i
                                     t
                                     s

near one more and makes its final surge   TIME 4:25:9

5. list (list) v.: Tilt to one side.

6. plum (plum) adj.: Here, first class.

Guide for Responding

◆ LITERATURE AND YOUR LIFE

Reader's Response How does the shape of "400-Meter Free Style" affect your reading?

Thematic Focus In what way does Kumin's poem celebrate the swimming environment?

☑ Check Your Comprehension

1. According to the speaker in "Identity," what benefits and drawbacks do flowers have?
2. In "400-Meter Free Style," what pattern do the poem's lines make?

◆ Critical Thinking

INTERPRET

1. (a) What is the speaker really choosing between in "Identity?" **[Interpret]**
2. How can you tell that Maxine Kumin admires the swimmer? **[Infer]**
3. Why did Kumin end "400-Meter Free Style" with the swimmer's racing time? **[Interpret]**

COMPARE LITERARY WORKS

4. Describe the similarities between the swimmer and the speaker in these poems. **[Compare and Contrast]**

Beyond Literature

Sports Connection

Freestyle Swimming In "400-Meter Free Style," Maxine Kumin depicts the body movements of a swimmer in competition. The stroke described in the poem is the free style, or crawl. It is the fastest of all strokes used in swimming competition and is executed through alternate arm movements, timed so that one arm will start pulling water just before the other has finished giving continuous motion to the swimmer.

Other kinds of strokes most often used in competitive swimming are the breaststroke, the butterfly, and the backstroke.

Cross-Curricular Activity

Do some research to learn how to perform each of the swimming strokes mentioned above. Then, create a how-to manual, illustrating each.

400-Meter Free Style ◆ 841

Comprehension Check

6 Ask students to explain what the swimmer is sipping. *He is sipping small gulps of air as he turns his head out of the water.*

Customize for
Logical/Mathematical Learners
Point out the swimmer's time, printed at the end of the last line of the poem. Challenge students to determine the average lap time, including turns, for this swimmer during the race.

Reinforce and Extend

Answers

◆ LITERATURE AND YOUR LIFE

Reader's Response It makes the poem harder to read at first, but the shape helps the reader imagine the race that is being described.

Thematic Focus She celebrates the skill and strength required to swim quickly for long distances.

☑ Check Your Comprehension

1. They have the benefit of being fed, guarded, and admired, but they are harnessed to a pot of dirt.
2. The lines make the shape of a swimmer's path during a 400-meter race.

◆ Critical Thinking

1. The speaker is choosing between an easy life that has strings attached to it and a less conventional life that offers more personal freedom.
2. The detail she uses to describe the swimmer's skill and physical ability shows her admiration.
3. The exact time of the race that has been described completes the description.
4. The speaker in "Identity" has the courage to live life on his or her own terms; the swimmer must be courageous to compete in a sport that requires so much energy and endurance.

Beyond the Selection

FURTHER READING

Other Works by the Authors
A Helpful Alphabet of Friendly Objects, John Updike
A Haiku Journey, Matsuo Bashō
Connecting the Dots: Poems, Maxine Kumin

Other Works on the Theme of Respecting Nature
The Earth Under Sky Bear's Feet: Native American Poems of the Land, Joseph Bruchac
The Beauty of the Beast: Poems from the Animal Kingdom, Jack Prelutsky (ed.)

INTERNET

We suggest the following sites on the Internet (all Web sites are subject to change).

For more information on John Updike, go to:
http://www.users.fast.net/~joyerkes

For more on Matsuo Bashō, visit:
http://www.lsi.usp.br/usp/rod/poet/sumie/bashoimg.html

For more information on Maxine Kumin, go to:
http://www.poets.org/poets/lit/poet/mkumin.htm

We *strongly recommend* that you preview these sites before you send students to them.

Answers

◆ Reading Strategy

1. There is not a lot of time between sunrise and sunset.
2. (a) I would rather be unnoticed than be an attention-drawing flower that is praised but then used by people for their own purposes. (b) It helps the reader understand that the speaker is willing to make sacrifices to be independent.
3. The artistic format of the poem can make it difficult to read. Paraphrasing lines can make it easier to understand what is happening.

◆ Build Vocabulary

Related Words: Forms of *fertile*
1. fertilizer; 2. fertilization

Spelling Strategy
1. typical; 2. mystery

Using the Word Bank
1. extravagance, fertile
2. catapults, abyss
3. shunned, cunningly
4. harnessed
5. nurtures

◆ Literary Focus

1. Haiku has only three lines and the subject always relates to nature.
2. Free verse is appropriate for "Identity," since the speaker longs for freedom.
3. The lines of "400-Meter Free Style" illustrate the path a swimmer would take while swimming a 400-meter race.

◆ Build Grammar Skills

1. I'd rather be a tall, ugly weed . . .
2. to feel exposed to the madness/of a vast, eternal sky, . . .
3. The stubborn, unsightly weeds grew wild.
4. Polanco is an effective, creative poet.
5. His vivid, colorful word choice is memorable.

Writing Application
Possible answers:
1. delicate, lacy
2. wet, heavy
3. colorful, fragrant
4. fragrant, appealing

◆ Guide for Responding *(continued)*

◆ Reading Strategy

PARAPHRASE LINES

When you **paraphrase** lines of a poem, you express the meaning of the lines in your own words. Paraphrasing lines helps you understand the key ideas, which in turn will help you discover the meaning of the whole poem.

1. Paraphrase lines 1–4 of "January."
2. (a) Paraphrase lines 13–18 of "Identity." (b) How does your paraphrase enable you to understand the meaning of that passage?
3. Explain why paraphrasing a poem like "400-Meter Free Style" is especially useful.

◆ Build Vocabulary

USING FORMS OF *fertile*

On your paper, complete the following sentences with the appropriate form of the word *fertile*.
1. Every farmer or gardener seeks the best ____?____ for the crops they cultivate.
2. On a large farm, ____?____ is a big expense.

SPELLING STRATEGY

Some words spell the short sound of *i* with the letter *y*, as in *abyss, lynch,* and *myth*.

On your paper, choose the correct spelling of the word in each sentence. Check a dictionary if you are unsure how to spell a word.
1. Bashō's poem is (tipical, typical) of haiku.
2. How the rules for writing a haiku came to be is a (mystery, mistery) to me.

USING THE WORD BANK

On your paper, fill in the blanks with the appropriate Word Bank word or form of the word.
1. Because of our ____?____, our once ____?____ farmland is now barren.
2. We used ____?____ to get us out of the ____?____.
3. The ____?____ business woman ____?____ won back her clients.
4. The horse was ____?____ to a post.
5. A healthy diet ____?____ growing children.

◆ Literary Focus

POETIC FORM

Poetic form is the structure of a poem. It is the framework on which the poem is built. Some forms, like haiku, have strict rules. Other forms, like concrete poetry and lyric poetry, have more general rules. Free verse has no rules about the number of lines or rhythmic pattern; however, most free-verse poets attempt to capture the rhythms of speech using everyday language.

1. How can you tell whether a poem is a haiku?
2. Why is free verse an appropriate form for "Identity"?
3. Explain how "400-Meter Free Style" illustrates its subject.

◆ Build Grammar Skills

COORDINATE ADJECTIVES

Adjectives that modify the same noun separately and equally are **coordinate.**

Example: wind-wavering above *high, jagged* rocks

Use a comma to separate coordinate adjectives. To test whether two adjectives are coordinate, switch the order of the adjectives. If the new order still makes sense, the adjectives are coordinate. Do not use a comma between adjectives whose order cannot be reversed.

Practice Write the following passages on your paper. Punctuate the coordinate adjectives correctly.
1. I'd rather be a tall ugly weed . . .
2. to feel exposed to the madness/of a vast eternal sky, . . .
3. The stubborn unsightly weeds grew wild.
4. Polanco is an effective creative poet.
5. His vivid colorful word choice is memorable.

Writing Application On your paper, write coordinate adjectives for the following sentences.
1. The ____?____ snowflakes fell all night.
2. Shoveling the ____?____ snow took all day.
3. The garden will burst with ____?____ flowers.
4. The ____?____ smells of herbs will fill the air.

✎ Writer's Solution

For additional instruction and practice, use the Using Modifiers unit in the *Writer's Solution Language Lab CD-ROM.*

Build Your Portfolio

 Idea Bank

Writing

1. **Glossary** Write glossary entries in which you define and give examples of various poetic forms.

2. **Concrete Poem** Write a concrete poem using an image, such as a key, that you could illustrate with word placement and line breaks.

3. **Essay** Free verse has no strict form, but it does attempt to capture the rhythms and sounds of everyday speech. Write an essay in which you examine how effectively "Identity" meets these criteria. Use details from the poem to support your points.

Speaking and Listening

4. **Rebuttal** In "Identity," Polanco argues that it's better to be ugly but free than to be beautiful and pampered. Take the opposing view, and deliver a short speech to the class in which you support your views.

5. **Dramatic Reading** Choose one of the poems in this section to read aloud. Practice reading it, paying attention to its rhythms but avoiding a singsong effect. Then, read the poem to the class. Tape-record your presentation to listen to afterward. **[Performing Arts Link]**

Projects

6. **Multimedia Presentation [Group Activity]** With a small group of classmates, conduct research to learn more about the Japanese haiku and how it fits into Japanese culture. Collect information about Japanese music, art, and architecture, and explain how haiku fits into Japanese society's views of art and beauty. Present your findings to the class. **[Social Studies Link]**

7. **Glossary of Terms** "400-Meter Free Style" is full of swimming terms. Choose a sport you admire, and create a glossary in which you define terms that are used in that sport. **[Sports Link]**

 Writing Mini-Lesson

Description of Yourself With a Comparison

Making a comparison is a way of describing something. In "Identity," Julio Polanco gives his reasons for preferring to be like a weed. Write a description of yourself that includes insights into your personality, appearance, or beliefs. Choose an idea, object, or even another person, to which you can compare yourself as you write your description.

Writing Skills Focus: Elaborate With Supporting Details

Once you present an idea, **elaborate** with vivid, precise details that give the reader a full-color picture rather than a sketch. In the following example, Polanco elaborates on why he would rather be a weed than a flower by comparing a weed to an eagle:

> **Model From the Poem**
> I'd rather be a tall, ugly weed,
> clinging on cliffs, like an eagle

Prewriting Decide on the main comparison you will make in your description of yourself. Then, create a list of details that are related to the description of yourself or to the comparison.

Drafting Give your self-description a memorable beginning. As you write, include comparisons that describe you.

Revising Revise by further elaborating with supporting details. Check to be sure that your comparison contains no errors in spelling, grammar, or punctuation.

> ◆ **Grammar Application**
> Look for places where you have used coordinate adjectives. Make sure you've used a comma to separate them.

 Idea Bank

Following are suggestions for matching the Idea Bank topics with your students' performance levels and learning modalities:

Customize for *Performance Levels*
Less Advanced Students: 1, 6, 7
Average Students: 2, 5, 6, 7
More Advanced Students: 3, 4, 6

Customize for *Learning Modalities*
Verbal/Linguistic: 1, 2, 3, 4, 5, 7
Visual/Spatial: 2, 6
Musical/Rhythmic: 6
Interpersonal: 5, 6
Intrapersonal: 1, 2, 3, 4, 7

 Writing Mini-Lesson

Refer students to the Writing Handbook in the back of the book for instruction on the writing process and for further information on description. Have students use the Venn Diagram in **Writing and Language Transparencies,** p. 77, to arrange their prewriting examples.

 Writer's Solution

Writing Lab CD-ROM
Have students complete the tutorial on Description. Follow these steps:
1. Have students use the Considering Your Purpose section to explore how different purposes affect the choice of details.
2. Students can use the audio-annotated Student Model to learn how to establish and develop a main impression.
3. Have students draft on computer.
4. Students can use the Interactive Models of Revision to explore examples that show how vague language can be replaced with precise language.

Writer's Solution Sourcebook
Have students use Chapter 2, "Description," pp. 32–69, or Chapter 5, "Exposition: Making Connections," pp. 136–165, for additional support. Chapter 5 includes instruction on making comparisons.

✓ ASSESSMENT OPTIONS

Formal Assessment, Selection Test, pp. 237–239, and Assessment Resources Software. The selection test is designed so that it can easily be customized to the performance levels of your students.

Alternative Assessment, p. 53, includes options for less advanced students, more advanced students, bodily/kinesthetic learners, visual/spatial learners, interpersonal learners, verbal/linguistic learners, and musical/rhythmic learners.

PORTFOLIO ASSESSMENT

Use the following rubrics in the **Alternative Assessment** booklet to assess student writing:
Glossary: Definition/Classification, p. 95
Concrete Poem: Poetry, p. 104
Essay: Literary Analysis/Interpretation, p. 108
Writing Mini-Lesson: Comparison/Contrast, p. 99

OBJECTIVES

1. To read, comprehend, and interpret a poem that has a social studies focus
2. To relate a poem with a social studies focus to personal experience
3. To connect literature to social studies
4. To respond to Social Studies Guiding Questions
5. To respond to the poem through writing, speaking and listening, and projects

SOCIAL STUDIES GUIDING QUESTIONS

Reading a poem about a Vietnam War veteran will help students explore these Social Studies Guiding Questions:

• What lasting effects did the Vietnam War have on some of those involved in the fighting?

• How does war affect the families of those who fight?

Interest Grabber In several paper bags, place fragrant or heavily scented items such as a small piece of evergreen, cinnamon sticks, and moth balls. (Warn students who are allergic or sensitive to strong odors not to participate in this activity.) Without looking, have students sniff the contents of each bag. Discuss what memories each particular smell evokes. For example, evergreen might make students think of the holiday season, and moth balls might remind them of cleaning a closet. Tell students that in the poem they are about to read, smells, tastes, and sounds bring back memories of Vietnam to a soldier who fought in the war there.

Map Study

Political Maps Connecting geography to history can help students understand that conflicts often arise among countries who share common borders. The map on this page shows the countries involved—directly or indirectly—in the Vietnam War. The red lines show routes by which Viet Cong soldiers traveled to invade South Vietnam. Studying this map may help students recognize the threat U.S. soldiers felt, not knowing from which direction attacks might come.

CONNECTING LITERATURE TO SOCIAL STUDIES
THE VIETNAM WAR

Wahbegan by Jim Northrup

War in Southeast Asia

(map legend)
0   200   400   600 Miles
0   200   400   600 Kilometers

844 ◆ Poetry

TWO NATIONS COLLIDE Following Vietnam's independence from France, an agreement was signed at Geneva, Switzerland, in 1954 that divided Vietnam into two nations. Communist-led North Vietnam received aid from the Soviet Union, and South Vietnam was supported by the United States. During the next few years, the aggressive activities of the Viet Cong—North Vietnamese guerrillas—and pro-Communist rebels in South Vietnam led the United States to take a stand. The result was the Vietnam War.

The Challenge of War From 1961 to 1973, more than a half million American soldiers fought in Vietnam. The troops would patrol the steamy jungles of a countryside in search of the Viet Cong, who could be hiding anywhere. No matter how carefully soldiers kept watch, they were often ambushed. In conditions that proved to be so uncertain and dangerous, it was difficult to win clear victories.

An Unpleasant Return In the United States, disapproval about United States' participation in the war rose steadily. Politicians and citizens questioned the success and legitimacy of the war effort, and by 1973, almost all American troops had been withdrawn. Since many people had been against the war, Vietnam veterans were not honored as veterans of other wars had been. In addition, many veterans suffered mentally from the memory of their traumatic experiences in the war and would reexperience these events in nightmares and daytime hallucinations.

In "Wahbegan," the poet describes the tragic, emotionally numbing effects that the Vietnam War had on a veteran.

Prentice Hall Literature Program Resources

REINFORCE / RETEACH / EXTEND
Selection Support Pages
Build Vocabulary, p. 289
Connecting Literature to Social Studies, p. 290
Formal Assessment Selection Test, pp. 240–241, Assessment Resources Software
Readings From Social Studies
Writing and Language Transparencies
Main Idea and Supporting Details, p. 61
Resource Pro CD-ROM "Wahbegan"

Listening to Literature Audiocassettes
"Wahbegan"

Connection to Prentice Hall World Explorer
Eastern Hemisphere: Ch. 3, "Earth's Human Geography," Section 3: "Why People Migrate," pp. 64–66; Ch. 21, "South and Southeast Asia: Cultures and History," Section 5: "Vietnam: A Reunited Nation," pp. 583–587

Wahbegan[1]

Jim Northrup

❶ Didja ever hear a sound
   smell something
   taste something
   that brought you back
5 to Vietnam, instantly?
❷ Didja ever wonder
   when it would end?
   It ended for my brother.

---

1. **Wahbegan:** Ojibwe name.

---

❸ ▲ **Critical Viewing** What can you infer about
this soldier from the details in the photograph?
[Infer]

---

❶ **Interpret** Ask students what the poet means by these lines. *Even though his body continued to function, the soldier's spirit died and he lost his will to live during the war.*

Links Across Time

❷ In 1980, Congress approved a site near the Lincoln Memorial in Washington, D.C., for the Vietnam Veterans Memorial. Of the more than 1400 designs submitted, the planning committee selected the one created by 21-year-old Maya Ying Lin, a student at Yale University. The completed memorial was dedicated in November 1982 and lists the names of all Americans killed or missing during the Vietnam War.

Comprehension Check ☑

❸ Ask students who the speaker believes should be remembered. *He would like to see those soldiers memorialized who died as a result of the war, even though the deaths occurred after the war had ended.*

Reinforce and Extend

Answers
◆ LITERATURE AND YOUR LIFE

Reader's Response It might be hard to accept everyday life after witnessing death and destruction.

Thematic Focus People fight not only the enemy but also the memories of the horrors of war.

☑ Check Your Comprehension

1. Sound, smell, and taste could bring a person back.
2. He lived for fifteen tortured years.
3. The smell of flowers provided no comfort.

More About the Author
In addition to being a writer, **Jim Northrup** is a radio commentator and a filmmaker. His film, *Jim Northrup: With Reservations,* was recognized with an award at the Dreamspeakers Native Film Festival in 1997.

846

CONNECTING LITERATURE TO SOCIAL STUDIES

He died in the war
10 but didn't fall down
❶ for fifteen tortured years.
His flashbacks[2] are over,
another <u>casualty</u> whose name
❷ will never be on the Wall.[3]
15 Some can find peace
only in death.
The sound of his
family crying hurt.
The smell of the flowers
20 didn't comfort us.
The bitter taste
in my mouth
still sours me.
How about a memorial
25 for those who made it
❸ through the war
but still died
before their time?

---

2. **flashbacks:** Past incidents recurring in the mind.
3. **Wall:** Vietnam Veterans Memorial, which is inscribed with the names of all Americans who died or who remained classified as missing in action in the Vietnam War.

◆ Build Vocabulary

casualty (kazh′ ōō əl tē) *n.*: Loss resulting from some unfortunate or unseen happening

---

Meet the Author

Jim Northrup (1943–   ) is a Native American short-story writer, poet, and syndicated columnist who presents in his writings the rich and singular lives of Native Americans. For six years, he served in the Marine Corps and made a tour of duty through Vietnam. In poems such as "Wahbegan," he relates the experience of Vietnam and its aftermath. With his wife and family, he currently lives the traditional life of the Chippewa on the Fond du Lac Reservation in northern Minnesota.

846 ◆ *Poetry*

Guide for Responding

◆ LITERATURE AND YOUR LIFE

Reader's Response Why might veterans of war have difficulty coping with postwar living?

Thematic Focus What does the poem suggest about the conflicts and challenges faced by those in combat?

☑ Check Your Comprehension

1. What three senses does the poet say could bring a man back to Vietnam?
2. How many years of the man's life are said to be "tortured"?
3. What scent provided no comfort?

◆ Critical Thinking

INTERPRET
1. How does the repetition of the senses of sound, smell, and taste add meaning to the poem? **[Interpret]**
2. Explain the message or main idea of the poem. **[Analyze]**
3. What do you think is the cause of the man's "flashbacks"? **[Infer]**
4. Why do some "find peace only in death"? **[Draw Conclusions]**

APPLY
5. What perspective can be gained from this poem by someone who has never experienced war? **[Relate]**

Block Scheduling Strategies

Consider these suggestions to take advantage of extended class time:

• Begin by using the information about the Vietnam War and the return of the veterans on p. 844. Then, have students read the poem aloud in small groups and answer the Guide for Responding questions on p. 846. Group students to work on the Speaking and Listening activity in the Idea Bank on p. 847.
• Have pairs of students select one of the projects from the Idea Bank on p. 847, and allow class time for students to work.

• Suggest that students use the Main Idea and Supporting Details Organizer, p. 61, in **Writing and Language Transparencies** to help them organize their ideas for the Response to a Poem in the Idea Bank, p. 847.
• Introduce the selection and build background by reading and discussing the information about the Vietnam War on p. 844 with the class. Following the discussion, have students listen to the audiocassette of "Wahbegan."

 Listening to Literature Audiocassettes

CONNECTING LITERATURE TO SOCIAL STUDIES

In "Wahbegan," Northrup gives insights into the life of a war veteran. He describes how the veteran's experience of the war has resulted in flashbacks that cripple him emotionally. The United States has tried to eliminate the stress of war on its armed forces through such practices as frequent troop rotations, regular hot meals, increased rest and recreation, and the use of psychiatric techniques. Also, many studies have been done to determine whether the stressful conditions and hardships of battle have lasting harmful consequences.

1. Which lines of the poem tell you that the man has suffered since the war?
2. Why would the poet suggest that a memorial be built for those who made it through the war?
3. What evidence does the poem give to suggest that war does have lasting consequences?

Idea Bank

Writing

1. **Letter Home** Imagine that you are a soldier in the Vietnam War. Write a letter home describing the conditions there.
2. **Response to a Poem** What is the poem's central idea? What images and details does Northrup use to express this idea effectively? Explain.
3. **Persuasive Essay** Write an essay either in favor of or against the building of a memorial or some other kind of public display honoring those who fought and lived through the Vietnam War.

Speaking and Listening

4. **Discussion** With a group of classmates, discuss under what conditions, if any, war is justified. Share your conclusions with classmates.

Projects

5. **Art** Make an illustrated map of Vietnam during the war, and outline the different regions, plains, and rivers in which the soldiers patrolled and fought.
6. **Encyclopedia Entry** With a group of students, do some research on the Ho Chi Minh Trail. What purpose did it serve throughout the Vietnam War? Report your findings to the class.

Further Reading, Listening, and Viewing

- Frederick Porter and Walter Dean Myers's book *A Place Called Heartbreak: A Story of Vietnam* describes the ordeal of Major Fred Cherry, who was shot down in combat over Vietnam.
- "Goodnight Saigon" is a song by Billy Joel about the Vietnam War.
- *In Country* is a motion picture based on a novel by Bobbie Ann Mason about a young girl's coming to terms with her father's death in Vietnam.
- Barry Denenberg's book *Voices from Vietnam* contains personal narratives of people who experienced the war firsthand—from presidents and generals to soldiers, nurses, and Vietnamese citizens.

 Beyond the Selection

FURTHER READING
Other Works by Jim Northrup
The Rez Road Follies: Canoes, Casinos, Computers, and Birch Bark Baskets
Walking the Rez Road
Other Works on Vietnam
And One for All, Theresa Nelson
Goodbye, Vietnam, Gloria Whelan
A Multicultural Portrait of the War in Vietnam, David K. Wright

INTERNET
We suggest the following sites on the Internet (all Web sites are subject to change).
For information about Jim Northrup:
http://team.liu.edu/eev-web2/NativeAmerican/jim_northrup.htm
For pictures, stories, and information about Vietnam Veterans memorials around the world:
http://www.vietvet.org/vietmems.htm
We *strongly recommend* that you preview these sites before you send your students to them.

 Idea Bank

Following are suggestions for matching the Idea Bank topics with your students' performance levels and learning modalities.

Customize for
Performance Levels
Less Advanced Students: 1, 4
Average Students: 2, 4, 5, 6
More Advanced Students: 3, 4, 5, 6

Customize for
Learning Modalities
Verbal/Linguistic: 1, 2, 3, 4, 6
Visual/Spatial: 5
Interpersonal: 4, 6

Answers (continued)
◆ Critical Thinking

1. The repetition emphasizes that the simple experiences of everyday life can bring back memories of the horror of war.
2. Not all of a war's victims are killed on the battleground.
3. His "flashbacks" might be caused by the horrible nature of what he witnessed during the war.
4. Some are tormented while awake and even when they dream by memories of the horrors they experienced.
5. They can imagine how much pain is caused by a war.

CONNECTING LITERATURE TO SOCIAL STUDIES

1. Lines 9–11 tell that the man has suffered since the war.
2. He would like to memorialize the pain and suffering of the survivors.
3. Lasting consequences include the veteran's flashbacks and his family's pain at his death, which they blamed on the war.

ASSESSMENT OPTIONS

Formal Assessment Selection Test, pp. 240–241, and Assessment Resources Software. The selection test is designed so that it can be easily customized to the performance levels of your students.

PORTFOLIO ASSESSMENT
Use the following rubrics in the **Alternative Assessment** booklet to assess student writing:
Letter Home: Expression, p. 90
Response to a Poem: Response to Literature, p. 106
Persuasive Essay: Persuasion, p. 101

Establish Writing Guidelines
Review the following key characteristics of a comparison-and-contrast essay:

- Comparison-and-contrast essays point out similarities and differences between two subjects.

- A comparison-and-contrast essay demonstrates the writer's knowledge of the subject as well as his/her ability to analyze.

You may want to distribute the scoring rubric for Comparison/Contrast, p. 99 in **Alternative Assessment,** to make students aware of the criteria on which they will be evaluated. See the suggestions on p. 850 for how you can customize the rubric to this workshop.

Refer students to the Writing Handbook in the back of the book for instruction on the writing process and further information on expository writing.

Writer's Solution

Writers at Work Videodisc
To show students how writer Bruce Brooks uses expository writing, play the videodisc segment on Exposition: Making Connections (Ch. 5.)

Play frames 43069 to 51462

Writing Lab CD-ROM
If your students have access to computers, you may want to have them work in the tutorial on Exposition: Making Connections to complete all or part of their comparison-and-contrast essays. Follow these steps:

1. Have students view the interactive model of a comparison-and-contrast essay.
2. Suggest that students use the interactive models of organization for comparison and contrast to learn about different ways to organize their essays.
3. Allow students to draft on computer.
4. Have students use the Revision checker for sentence length.

Writer's Solution Sourcebook
Students can find additional support, including in-depth instruction on unity and coherence in paragraphs, p. 162, in the chapter on Exposition: Making Connections, pp. 136–165.

848

Expository Writing
Comparison-and-Contrast Essay

Writing Process Workshop

While reading the poems in this section, you probably noticed the similarities and differences in form, rhyme, and subject.

A **comparison-and-contrast essay** is a brief written exploration of the similarities and differences between two or more things. Using the Writing Skills introduced in this section's Writing Mini-Lessons, compare and contrast two poems.

Writing Skills Focus

▶ **Give reasons** for your choice of poems. Also, give reasons for your ideas and evaluations. (See p. 812.)

▶ **Support your points** by using examples from both poems. (See p. 825.)

▶ **Choose an appropriate tone.** For a formal comparison-and-contrast essay, an objective or neutral tone is most effective. (See p. 833.)

▶ **Elaborate with supporting details** to make your points clear. (See p. 843.)

One writer who loves sports and enjoyed "400-Meter Free Style" found another sports poem to compare and contrast with "400-Meter Free Style." Here is the introductory paragraph to his essay:

WRITING MODEL

Maxine Kumin's "400-Meter Free Style" and Edwin Hoey's "Foul Shot" are both concrete poems about sports—swimming and basketball. ① Both poets describe an athletic event but in very different ways. ② While Kumin's poem uses form to express its meaning, Hoey's poem depends more on the words. The words in Kumin's poem stretch across the page, resembling the stroke of a swimmer. ③

① The writer gives the reasons for choosing these two poems.
② The tone of the essay is formal. The writer shows no preference for either poem.
③ Here, the writer provides a supporting detail to elaborate on the differences in form.

848 ◆ Poetry

 Beyond the Classroom

Career Connection
Reviewer Critics who write reviews of new books, films, or albums often use comparing/contrasting skills. Sometimes reviewers may review two items at once and compare and contrast the two items to save space as well as to give the reader an opinion as to which of the two is better. For example, a movie reviewer may write a single review on two new movies because they are both about space. The reviewer may compare and contrast the two movies and end with a recommendation of which movie readers should see.

Have students scan local and national newspapers or magazines for examples of a movie, book, or album review which compares and contrasts two items. Then have them analyze the review by listing the different points being compared and contrasted. Suggest that students make a Venn Diagram to illustrate the similarities and differences discussed in the review. Then, encourage students to write their own reviews of similar items. They may want to review two songs from the same album, or two movies about the same topic, or two books from the same series.

Prewriting

Choose the Poems Choose two poems to examine in your comparison-and-contrast essay. Following are some ideas about types of poems to compare:

> ### Topic Ideas
> - Two poems by the same poet
> - Two poems about the same subject
> - Two poems that have the same form (for example, a sonnet or a haiku)

Organize Details Before you begin writing, use a Venn diagram like the one below to help organize your details. Write the similarities in the space where the circles overlap, and write the differences in the outer sections of the circles.

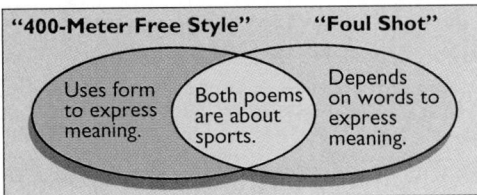

"400-Meter Free Style"   "Foul Shot"

Uses form to express meaning. Both poems are about sports. Depends on words to express meaning.

Locate Passages Locate passages from the poems you're comparing to use as support for your ideas. Make sure you copy the passages accurately.

Drafting

Choose an Organization There are two basic ways to organize a comparison-and-contrast essay: the point-by-point method and the subject-by-subject method. Choose the one that works best for your subject and ideas.

POINT BY POINT	SUBJECT BY SUBJECT
• Moves back and forth between the two subjects	• Covers one subject completely, then the other subject completely
• Each paragraph is about a different point of comparison as it applies to both subjects.	• Each paragraph is all about one subject.

Use a Consistent Tone The tone of your essay should be consistent throughout. To achieve an objective tone, avoid words with positive or negative connotations. Use long straightforward sentences. They often lend a more serious, objective tone than short sentences do. Stick to the facts, and steer clear of opinions.

DRAFTING/REVISING

APPLYING LANGUAGE SKILLS: Varying Sentence Beginnings

Effective writers vary their sentence beginnings to make their work lively and interesting.

Subject: *The flower in the meadow gently swayed in the wind.*

Adverb: *Gently, the flower in the meadow swayed in the wind.*

Prepositional Phrase: *In the meadow, the flower gently swayed in the wind.*

Practice Rewrite this paragraph, shifting a part of each sentence to the beginning to add variety:

> The poem about nature with unusual examples of figurative language conveys an important message. The poet obviously spent a lot of time choosing words that convey a specific mood. The poem stands up well when you compare it against others of its kind.

Writing Application As you write your comparison-and-contrast essay, vary your sentence beginnings.

> ### Writer's Solution Connection
> ### Writing Lab
> For help organizing your essay, see the Organizing section of the Exposition: Making Connections tutorial.

Writing Process Workshop ◆ 849

Prewriting

Explain to students that when choosing poems to compare and contrast, they will want to analyze each poem for different elements on which to base their essay. They may want to consider such poetic elements as structure, figurative language, or sound devices. Suggest that students review the literary focus sections of the Guide for Reading pages in this section to come up with a list of criteria for which to analyze the poems.

Customize for
Less Proficient Learners
Students may have difficulty dividing their topic into points by which to compare and contrast. Suggest that students use the Cluster Organizer from **Writing and Language Transparencies**, p. 73. Have them write the title of the poem in the space for the central subject and then fill the spaces around it with reactions to or details about the poem. Have students fill out a separate organizer for their second poem. They can then use the organizers to find points on which to compare and contrast their poems.

Drafting

Explain to students that in addition to choosing a way to organize their drafts, they will also want to include an introduction which clearly states the two items which are to be compared and contrasted. They can then proceed to the body of the paper and end with a conclusion which will restate the main idea of the introduction.

Writer's Solution

Writing Lab CD-ROM
Suggest that students use the Venn Diagram activity for comparison and contrast to help them discover the similarities and differences between their two poems.

Applying Language Skills
Varying Sentence Beginnings Explain to students that varying sentence beginnings achieves a variety of sentence structures for more enjoyable reading.

Answers
Possible response:

With unusual examples of figurative language, the poem about nature conveys an important message. Obviously, the poet spent a lot of time choosing words that convey a specific mood. When you compare it against others of its own kind, the poem stands up well.

Writer's Solution

For additional instruction and practice, have students use the practice page on Using a Variety of Sentences, p. 125, in the *Writer's Solution Grammar Practice Book.* If students have access to technology, they can use the lesson Varying Sentence Structure in the Sentence Style Unit of the *Writer's Solution Language Lab CD-ROM.*

Revising

Have students consider whether the details in the essay clearly show similarities or differences between the poems and whether the details are arranged in the same order for each subject.

Writing Lab CD-ROM

In the tutorial on Exposition: Making Connections, have students use the Transition Word Bin to select transitional words and phrases to connect their ideas.

Publishing

Students can submit their essays, along with copies of the two poems being compared and contrasted, to create a class anthology.

Reinforce and Extend

Review the Writing Guidelines
After students have completed their papers, review the characteristics of a comparison-and-contrast essay.

Applying Language Skills
Avoid Double Comparisons
Explain to students that when they try to overstate their position, they may make errors with double comparisons.

Answers
1. The poems of Robert Frost are better than mine.
2. Writing poetry is the most pleasant hobby.
3. Shakespeare's poems are harder to read than Robert Frost's.

Writing Process Workshop

EDITING/PROOFREADING

Applying Language Skills: Avoiding Double Comparisons

A double comparison is an error caused by using both *-er* or *-est* and *more* or *most* to form the comparative and superlative degrees. It can also be caused by adding any of these endings or words to an irregular modifier:

Incorrect: It was *the most happiest* day of my life.

Correct: It was the *happiest* day of my life.

Incorrect: It was *more better* than I thought it could be.

Correct: It was *better* than I thought it could be.

Practice On your paper, correct any double comparisons:

1. The poems of Robert Frost are more better than mine.
2. Writing poetry is the most pleasantest hobby.
3. Shakespeare's poems are more harder to read than Robert Frost's.

Writing Application As you write your essay, avoid double comparisons.

Writer's Solution Connection Language Lab

For more help, complete the Problems With Modifiers lesson in the Using Modifiers unit.

Revising

Use a Checklist Refer to the Writing Skills Focus points on page 848 as you revise your comparison-and-contrast essay.

Write Clear Paragraphs Review your paragraphs. Make sure each paragraph has a clear, distinct purpose and a good topic sentence.

Be Specific Replace any vague, general words with concrete, specific ones. As with any expository writing, the more specific your examples and support, the better your essay will be.

Ask a Peer Read your essay aloud to a peer. Ask the following, and revise accordingly:
- Is my conclusion clear?
- Are any sections of the essay confusing?
- Is the tone consistent throughout?
- Should I add supporting points?

REVISION MODEL

① had striking similarities in form and content.
The two haiku I read ~~were alike.~~ They were both about
② For example, Bashō's is about a night-heron's cry, ③ "The lightning and Moritake's is about a butterfly. flashes! . . ."
nature. Bashō's begins with a reference to lightning. ~~I liked~~
④ Both poems were satisfying because they manage
to capture vivid images in nature in three short lines.
~~both poems.~~

① This sentence was revised to make it more formal and to provide a reason for the essay.
② This line was added to support the first sentence.
③ Citing a passage from the work is stronger than referring to a passage.
④ This line was changed to match the tone of the essay and to support the writer's idea.

Publishing and Presenting

Classroom Hold a special "Pairs of Poems" session in which pairs of students read pairs of poems and lead the class in discussions about their similarities and differences. Use ideas from your essay to guide the discussion. How many of your points do your classmates observe?

Library Print out or copy the two poems you've chosen. Display them on a poster along with your essay. Include illustrations or drawings to make your display visually appealing. Ask a librarian if you can hang your poster in the poetry section of your school library.

✓ ASSESSMENT		4	3	2	1
PORTFOLIO ASSESSMENT Use the rubric on Comparison/Contrast in the **Alternative Assessment** booklet, p. 99, to assess the students' writing. Add these criteria to customize this rubric to this assignment.	**Clear Comparisons**	The writer consistently makes clear comparisons.	The writer mostly makes clear comparisons.	The writer makes only some clear comparisons.	The writer makes unclear comparisons.
	Varying Sentence Beginnings	The writer varies sentence beginnings throughout the essay, making it easier to read.	The writer varies sentence beginnings through most of the essay.	The writer varies sentence beginnings for some of the essay; more variation is needed.	The writer does not vary sentence beginnings.

Real-World Reading Skills Workshop

Reading to Extend Cultural Understanding

Strategies for Success

When reading about people with backgrounds different from your own, you may make interesting discoveries about the way people all over the world live. For example, when reading a story about another culture, you notice that a teenager bows her head when speaking with her elders. You learn that not looking an elder in the eye is a sign of respect in her culture. A person's culture is his or her ideas, traditions, and way of life.

Identify Cultural Characteristics When you read about another culture, notice the characteristics of that culture. Pay attention to the way people interact with each other, their clothing, modes of transportation, food, education, celebration of holidays, and aspects of daily life. Make a list of these characteristics.

Make Connections Make connections as you read to learn about different cultures. For example, a boy in the novel you are reading lives on an island and goes fishing with his father every day after school. You do your homework every day after school. From your reading, you learn that the father supports his family by fishing. By making connections, you can understand why it is important for the boy to fish everyday and finish his homework later.

Explore Common Elements All cultures share common elements. Respect the distinctions between cultures, and look for similarities. Although approaches may be different, the experiences and emotions are similar. You may not bow to your elders, but you treat them with respect; you may not fish with your father every day, but you help your parents in other ways.

Apply the Strategies

Read this brief description of *Dogsong* by Gary Paulsen, and answer the following questions:

1. What do you learn about the Inuits?
2. What common experience does this description suggest?
3. How does this passage increase your understanding of the Inuit culture?

Come, see my dogs.
With them I ran,
ran north to the sea.
I stand by the sea and I sing.
I sing of my hunts
and of Oogruk.

This is the "Dogsong" of Russel Suskitt, a fourteen-year-old Inuit who undertakes the demanding journey of his ancestors. Unhappy with the modern life of his village—the awful sounds of the snow-machines and the cramped "boxed" government houses of the village, he follows the stories of the old shaman Oogruk to take the dog team and sled and travel to the sea—across ice floes, tundra, and mountains—to find himself and his own "song." Russel discovers the pride of his people and the strength of human and dog working together as a team.

✔ *Here are other types of reading through which you can extend your cultural understanding:*
▶ News and specialty magazines
▶ Novels
▶ Newspapers
▶ Nonfiction

Real-World Reading Skills Workshop ◆ *851*

◆ Build Grammar Skills

Reviewing Correct Use of Modifiers

The selections in Part 1 include instruction on the following:

- Comparison of Modifiers
- Comparisons with *more* and *most*
- Irregular Comparisons of Modifiers
- Coordinate Adjectives

This instruction is reinforced with the Build Grammar Skills practice pages in **Selection Support,** pp. 266, 272, 277, and 282.

As you review modifiers you may wish to review the following:

- Double Comparisons
Explain to students that they should use only one form of comparison between items. They should not add both -*er* and *more* or -*est* and *most* to a regular modifier, or any of these endings or words to an irregular modifier. Double comparisons only overstate the reason for the comparison.

Writer's Solution

For additional practice and support with using modifiers, use the practice pages on Using Modifiers, pp. 86–90 in the *Writer's Solution Grammar Practice Book.* If students have access to technology, they can use the Using Modifiers unit on the *Writer's Solution Language Lab CD-ROM.*

Answers
Practice 1
1. The train moved <u>faster</u> than the horses that ran alongside it.
2. The sky was full of gray clouds. The <u>darkest</u> clouds seemed to hover over the ship.
3. Langston Hughes's poetry is <u>easier</u> to read than Shakespeare's poetry.
4. Swimming is a <u>more competitive</u> sport than volleyball.
5. The <u>best</u> poem I have ever read is "The Wreck of Hesperus."

Correct Use of Modifiers

Grammar Review

Adjectives and adverbs are modifiers—they describe or limit the meaning of another word. Most adjectives and adverbs change form to show degrees of comparison. The three degrees of comparison are the positive, comparative, and superlative (see p. 811).

The **positive** degree is the basic form of an adjective or an adverb. It is used when no comparison is being made:

The **comparative** degree is used when two things are being compared. For most one- and two-syllable modifiers, the comparative degree is formed by adding -*er.* For longer words, use *more* with the positive form:

The **superlative** degree is used when more than two things are being compared. For most one- and two-syllable modifiers, the superlative degree is formed by adding -*est.* For longer words, use *most* with the positive form:

Positive	Comparative	Superlative
small	smaller	smallest
distant	more distant	most distant
eagerly	more eagerly	most eagerly

Irregular Comparisons Some adjectives and adverbs are irregular in form (see p. 832). Memorize the comparative and superlative forms of these modifiers.

Positive	Comparative	Superlative
bad, badly	worse	worst
little	less	least
good, well	better	best
many, much	more	most

Coordinate Adjectives When you use more than one adjective to modify the same noun separately and equally, the adjectives are coordinate (see p. 842). Use commas to separate

coordinate adjectives: "I'd rather smell of *musty, green* stench/ than of *sweet, fragrant* lilac."

Practice 1 Write each sentence, using the correct form of the modifier given.

1. The train moved _____?_____ than the horses that ran alongside it. (fast)
2. The sky was full of gray clouds. The _____?_____ clouds seemed to hover over the ship. (dark)
3. Langston Hughes's poetry is _____?_____ to read than Shakespeare's poetry. (easy)
4. Swimming is a _____?_____ sport than volleyball. (competitive)
5. The _____?_____ poem I have ever read is "The Wreck of the Hesperus." (good)

Practice 2 Write the following paragraph, punctuating any coordinate adjectives:

The vivid interesting poems in this section represent different types of poetry. The storylike suspenseful elements of the narrative poem are evident in "The Wreck of the Hesperus." Lyric poems, such as the musical rhythmic "Blow, Blow, Thou Winter Wind," are meant to be read aloud.

Grammar in Writing

✔ *Avoid double comparisons, which use -er or -est as well as more or most.*

Incorrect: The poem was *more funnier* than the one we read last week.

Correct: The poem was *funnier* than the one we read last week.

PART **2** $\quad$ *Elements of Poetry*

Black Hat on a Yellow Chair, 1952, Fernand Leger, University of Iowa Museum of Art, Iowa City, IA

Elements of Poetry ◆ 853

The selections in this section focus on elements of poetry. "Silver," "Forgotten Language," "Drum Song," and "If I can stop one Heart from breaking" use sound devices such as rhyme, repetition, and alliteration. "New World," "One Time," "Lyric 17," and "For My Sister Molly Who in the Fifties" are poems with powerful imagery. "The Dark Hills," "Solar," and "An Incident in a Rose Garden" include elements of figurative language.

Customize for
Varying Student Needs
When assigning the selections in this section to your students, keep in mind the following factors:

"Silver"; "Forgotten Language"; "Drum Song"; "If I can stop one Heart from breaking"
• Reading these poems aloud will help students understand the poets' use of sound devices such as alliteration, rhyme, and repetition

"New World"; "One Time"; "Lyric 17"; "For My Sister Molly Who in the Fifties"
• Imagery in these poems may be difficult for some students to understand
• "One Time" includes a Beyond Literature Science connection

"The Dark Hills"; "Solar"; "An Incident in a Rose Garden"
• Three poems that use elements of figurative language such as similes, metaphors, and personification
• Students may need help with vocabulary

 Humanities: Art

Black Hat on a Yellow Chair, 1952, by Fernand Leger

Fernand Leger (1881–1955) was a French painter who also did design work for theater sets, murals, posters, and stained glass. His work is often referred to as a predecessor to Pop Art. Leger first studied architecture at the Ecole des Arts Decoratifs and then went on to study art at the Ecole des Beaux Arts. He served in WWI, where his attention was drawn to the beauty of machinery. Influenced by Cubism and Cezanne, many of Leger's paintings show a strong relation-ship between form and color; draw students' attention to this relationship as it is portrayed in *Black Hat on a Yellow Chair*.

Have students study the painting, and then ask the following questions:
1. Do you like the style of the painting? *Some students will like the style because it is like a cartoon; others may dislike it because of its simplicity.*
2. What strikes you as unreal about the painting? *Some students will say the bold black lines seem forced, or the bird perched on the cactus seems out of place.*

OBJECTIVES

1. To read, comprehend, and interpret four poems
2. To relate four poems to personal experience
3. To make inferences
4. To recognize sound devices
5. To build vocabulary in context and use word pairs
6. To use adjectives and adverbs correctly
7. To write song lyrics, using effective repetition
8. To respond to the poems through writing, speaking and listening, and projects

SKILLS INSTRUCTION

Vocabulary:
Word Pairs

Spelling:
Spelling the Long o Sound as *ow*

Grammar:
Correct Use of Adjectives and Adverbs

Reading Strategy:
Make Inferences

Literary Focus:
Sound Devices

Writing:
Use Effective Repetition

Speaking and Listening:
Reading (Teacher's Edition)

Critical Viewing:
Analyze; Connect

PORTFOLIO OPPORTUNITIES

Writing: Stanza of Poetry; Public-Service Announcement; Inference About an Author

Writing Mini-Lesson: Song Lyrics

Speaking and Listening: Reading; Poem With Drums

Projects: Sound Devices in Speeches; Report on Animal Communication

---

More About the Authors

Walter de la Mare began his literary career by writing and publishing a high school magazine. His writings reflect his belief that the world is best understood through the imagination.

Shel Silverstein spends much of his time traveling around the world. Youngsters enjoy his poems' images, while older readers appreciate his observations about growing up.

Wendy Rose manages a museum bookstore and lectures at the University of California in addition to writing poetry. Also a visual artist, she designs posters and postcards.

Emily Dickinson lived almost her whole life in her parents' home, in close companionship with her sister and brother, "like friendly monarchs, each in his own domain."

Guide for Reading

Meet the Authors:

Walter de la Mare (1873–1956)

For years, this British poet worked in the statistics department of a big oil company. At night, however, his imagination roamed freely as he wrote poems about the magic and mystery of life. These poems, found in books like *The Listeners*, delight children and adults alike. [For more on Walter de la Mare, see page 32.]

Shel Silverstein (1932–)

Silverstein is a poet, a writer of children's books, a cartoonist, a folk singer, and a composer. The critic William Cole has called Silverstein's poems "tender, funny, sentimental, philosophical, and ridiculous in turn . . ."

Wendy Rose (1948–)

The work of this award-winning poet reflects her Native American ancestry. However, she wants readers to view her poems not only as Native American but as human.

Emily Dickinson (1830–1886)

Dickinson led a quiet life in Amherst, Massachusetts. She published only a few poems in her lifetime. However, she secretly wrote the 1,775 lyric poems that made her one of the founders of American poetry. Sparkling with thought and feeling, these poems show how active her inner life really was. [For more on Emily Dickinson, see page 192.]

854 ◆ Poetry

◆ LITERATURE AND YOUR LIFE

CONNECT YOUR EXPERIENCE

Sometimes, with a friend or a family member, you just need to share a look or a single word. Then, both of you nod or burst into laughter. You don't need to spell things out because you share a secret language. As these poems show, poetry is also a kind of secret language. It begins with a child's wisdom, speaks in the rhythm of a heartbeat, and offers words to save a breaking heart.

THEMATIC FOCUS: Relationships

How does each of these poems speak to you as a friend, telling you something secret or surprising?

◆ Background for Understanding

CULTURE

In Native American cultures, as Wendy Rose reveals in "Drum Song," poetry and dance were accompanied by drums. These instruments usually consisted of a hide stretched on a frame. Drums came in all shapes and sizes—from the small water drum of the Iroquois to the large Great Plains drum that was beaten by four men together.

◆ Build Vocabulary

WORD PAIRS

Because some words occur in pairs, as opposites, it's useful to learn them together. The word *vertical*, from "Drum Song" is part of such a pair: vertical/horizontal. *Vertical* means "upright," while *horizontal* means "flat."

WORD BANK

Which word from these poems is related to the word *vertex*, a mathematical term meaning "the highest point of a triangle"? Check the Build Vocabulary box on page 858 to see if you chose correctly.

vertical
burrow
gourds

 Prentice Hall Literature Program Resources

REINFORCE / RETEACH / EXTEND
Selection Support Pages
Build Vocabulary: Word Pairs, p. 291
Build Spelling Skills, p. 292
Build Grammar Skills: Correct Use of Adjectives and Adverbs, p. 293
Reading Strategy: Make Inferences, p. 294
Literary Focus: Sound Devices, p. 295
Strategies for Diverse Student Needs, pp. 107–108
Beyond Literature Study Skills: Using a Graphic Organizer, p. 54

Formal Assessment Selection Test, pp. 242–244, Assessment Resources Software
Alternative Assessment, p. 54
Resource Pro CD-ROM "Silver," "Forgotten Language," "Drum Song," "If I can stop one Heart from breaking"

 Listening to Literature Audiocassettes
"Silver," "Forgotten Language," "Drum Song," "If I can stop one Heart from breaking"

Silver ◆ Forgotten Language ◆ Drum Song
◆ If I can stop one Heart from breaking ◆

Egrets in Summer, 1940–45, N.C. Wyeth, Courtesy of Metropolitan Life Insurance Company, New York, NY

◆ Literary Focus

SOUND DEVICES

Poets use **sound devices** to create musical effects in poems. The most familiar of these devices is **rhyme**, identical sounds at the ends of words: "... *sees* / ... *trees*" ("Silver"). Another device is **repetition**, repeated words or grammatical structures: "Once I ... / Once I ... ("Forgotten Language"). Still another is **alliteration**, repeated vowel sounds at the beginning of words or stressed syllables near each other: "*bush* to *burrow*" ("Drum Song").

Read the poems aloud to hear these sound devices. Also, think about the effect of these devices on each poem.

◆ Reading Strategy

MAKE INFERENCES

To get at the sense of a poem, you can **make inferences,** or reach conclusions based on evidence in the poems. First, notice details like sound devices, pictures the poem creates, and the thoughts or feelings it expresses. Then, compare these details, and think about what meanings they suggest.

Use a chart like the one below to record your inferences (a sample is filled in):

Detail	Inference
The poet repeats sentences beginning with "Once I ..."	Repetition of the word *once* as in "Once upon a time" calls to mind a fairy tale or a situation that is magical.

Guide for Reading ◆ 855

Have students look at the artwork on p. 855 and imagine themselves standing beside a pond. Ask them what sounds they might hear—flapping of wings, rustle of wind in the grasses, water lapping against the shore, bird calls, fish splashing, and insect noises. Imagining these sounds can help them appreciate the painting. In a similar way, poets often use sound devices in their poetry to help the reader understand and enjoy the message of the words. Invite students to listen for a variety of sounds as they read aloud or listen to the following poems.

◆ Build Grammar Skills

Correct Use of Adjectives and Adverbs If you wish to introduce the grammar concept for this selection before students read, refer to the instruction on p. 860.

Customize for
Less Proficient Readers
To help students understand the literary focus, read aloud the first stanza of each poem, emphasizing a sound device used by the poet. Have students read aloud the same stanza, following your example. Continue by having students work with partners to read the poems aloud.

Customize for
More Advanced Students
Invite students to look through books of poetry for examples of poems that include sound devices. Have students select poems that they find appealing. Then have students write an essay describing the sound device used by the author and explain its effect on the poem.

 Humanities: Art

Egrets in Summer, 1940–45, by N. C. Wyeth
N. C. Wyeth was the patriarch of a family of artists—father of Andrew Wyeth, grandfather of Jamie Wyeth. He spent his career working as a successful illustrator. Ask students what other poems they have read that might be illustrated using this same artwork. *Possible answers:* "love is a place," Bashō's haiku.

 Preparing for Standardized Tests

Grammar The grammar skill for this lesson is the correct use of adjectives and adverbs. Remind students that adjectives modify nouns and adverbs modify verbs, adjectives, and other adverbs. Have volunteers give examples of each usage. The editing portion of standardized tests may include questions that test students' knowledge of correct usage. Write the following sample question on the board:

Which sentence includes a modifier that is <u>not</u> used correctly?

(A) The clouds raced swiftly across the moon.
(B) The blossoms were real fragrant.
(C) Silent birds settled in their nests.
(D) We slept well in our comfortable tent.

First, have students identify the modifiers in each sentence *(A) swiftly; (B) real, fragrant; (C) Silent; (D) well, comfortable.* All modifiers are used correctly, except for *(B).* Because an adverb is needed to modify the adjective *fragrant,* the modifier should be *really.* For additional practice, use p. 293 in **Selection Support.**

One-Minute Insight In "Silver," Walter de la Mare describes the effects of silvery moonlight on the landscape and creatures below. Rather than expressing a particular idea, the images in the poem create a mood of magical peacefulness.

◆ Literary Focus

❶ Sound Devices Ask students to identify and point out two examples of a sound device. *The poet uses alliteration in the repetition of beginning s sounds, as in* slowly, silently, silver shoon, she, sees, silver, silver *(lines 1–4); and in the repetition of beginning c sounds, as in* casements catch, couched, kennel *(lines 5–8).*

◆ Reading Strategy

❷ Make Inferences How do you think the poet feels about the moonlight, and why do you think so? *The repetition of the word* silver *leads the reader to believe that the poet feels that a moonlit night is lovely.*

►Critical Viewing◄

❸ Analyze *The scene evokes a mood of peacefulness, magic, or mystery.*

Customize for
English Language Learners
Arrange students in small groups and discuss the literary focus, giving several examples of each sound device. Then have students listen to the audiocassettes of the poems while they follow along in their books. Have students point to lines in each poem where they hear a sound device used.

Listening to Literature Audiocassettes

Customize for
Musical/Rhythmic Learners
Ask volunteers to read the poems aloud in small groups, emphasizing the sound devices. Encourage them to use the tone and level of their voices to convey the mood of each poem, almost as if it had a musical accompaniment.

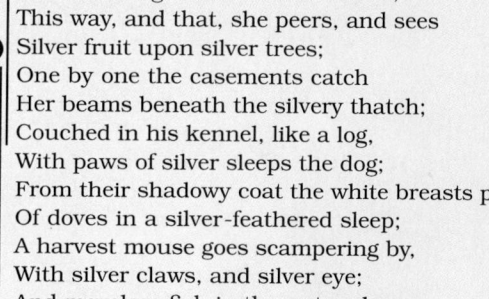

Silver
Walter de la Mare

Slowly, silently, now the moon
Walks the night in her silver shoon;[1]
This way, and that, she peers, and sees
❶ Silver fruit upon silver trees;
5   One by one the casements catch
Her beams beneath the silvery thatch;
Couched in his kennel, like a log,
❷ With paws of silver sleeps the dog;
From their shadowy coat the white breasts peep
10   Of doves in a silver-feathered sleep;
A harvest mouse goes scampering by,
With silver claws, and silver eye;
And moveless fish in the water gleam,
By silver reeds in a silver stream.

1. **shoon** (shōōn) *n.*: Old-fashioned word for "shoes."

❸ ▼ Critical Viewing What mood does this silvery scene evoke? [Analyze]

Block Scheduling Strategies

Consider these suggestions to take advantage of extended class time:

• Have groups of students discuss the Critical Thinking questions on pp. 857 and 859 and the Literary Focus and Reading Strategy questions on p. 860. To reinforce the Reading Strategy, use **Selection Support,** p. 294.

• Have students prepare for the Writing Mini-Lesson by working on the *Writer's Solution Language Lab CD-ROM* and *Writer's Solution Writing Lab CD-ROM.* Refer to the teaching suggestions on p. 861 to guide students through

the process. Students might use the Sensory Language Chart in **Writing and Language Transparencies,** p. 69, to gather lyric ideas.

• Read and discuss the Literary Focus on p. 855. Then have students listen to the audiocassettes of the poems. Next, have students read the poems silently. Follow with a discussion of how an oral performance allows the listener to better understand and appreciate the sound devices used.

 Listening to Literature Audiocassettes

Forgotten Language

Shel Silverstein

Once I spoke the language of the flowers,
Once I understood each word the caterpillar said,
Once I smiled in secret at the gossip of the starlings,¹ **4**
And shared a conversation with the housefly
    in my bed.
5 Once I heard and answered all the questions
    of the crickets,
And joined the crying of each falling dying
    flake of snow,
Once I spoke the language of the flowers . . .
      How did it go? **5**
      How did it go?

---

1. **starlings** (stär′ liŋz) *n.*: Dark-colored birds with a short tail, long wings, and a sharp, pointed bill.

Guide for Responding

◆ LITERATURE AND YOUR LIFE

Reader's Response Describe a time when something in nature "spoke" to you.

Thematic Focus Do you think it's possible to remember the "Forgotten Language" that Silverstein describes? Why or why not?

☑ Check Your Comprehension

1. What kind of night does De la Mare describe in "Silver"?
2. (a) Name the only creature that moves in "Silver." (b) What are the other animals doing?
3. Name six things from nature that speak a "Forgotten Language" in Silverstein's poem.
4. What does he ask at the end of "Forgotten Language"?

◆ Critical Thinking

INTERPRET

1. Describe the effects of the moon's walk in "Silver." **[Analyze Cause and Effect]**
2. Which details in "Silver" contribute to the poem's sense of magic? Explain. **[Support]**
3. When do you think Silverstein understood the "Forgotten Language" he describes? Explain. **[Infer]**
4. How does the language to which Silverstein refers differ from a language like English or Spanish? **[Draw Conclusions]**

COMPARE LITERARY WORKS

5. Does "Silver" use the "Forgotten Language" Silverstein mentions? Explain. **[Connect]**

One-Minute Insight

In "Forgotten Language," Shel Silverstein describes a magical time during which he could do amazing things such as speak to flowers and understand the feelings of snowflakes. Silverstein reminds readers of the limitless possibilities of a world when it is seen through the eyes of a small child.

◆ Literary Focus

4 Sound Devices Have students identify and discuss the effect of the sound devices used. *Repetition emphasizes that things happened long ago, rhyme emphasizes particular ideas.*

◆ Reading Strategy

5 Make Inferences What can students infer about the poet based on the last two lines of the poem? *Now that he is grown, he has lost the ability to communicate with nature.*

Reinforce and Extend

Answers

◆ LITERATURE AND YOUR LIFE

Reader's Response Student answers will vary.

Thematic Focus No, as we get older other things demand our attention.

☑ Check Your Comprehension

1. He describes a moonlit night.
2. (a) The only creature that moves is a harvest mouse. (b) The other animals are sleeping.
3. Flowers, the caterpillar, starlings, a housefly, crickets, and a snowflake speak a forgotten language.
4. "How did that language go?"

◆ Critical Thinking

1. It casts silvery light on the earth.
2. The repetition of the word *silver* creates the effect of a magical landscape gleaming with items made of precious metal.
3. He understood it when he was a small child.
4. It is an unspoken language of the heart.
5. Yes; the description includes the speaker's feelings about the beauty of the night.

Speaking and Listening Mini-Lesson

Reading

This mini-lesson supports the Speaking and Listening activity in the Idea Bank on p. 861.

Introduce Review how punctuation in poems often indicates where a reader should pause or stop. Point out that sound devices and changes in tone of voice help communicate a poem's mood.

Develop As students develop their poetry readings, have them consider these questions:

• What mood or idea does the poem express?
• How can I use sound devices to express both

the mood and the ideas in the poem?
• How can punctuation help me?

Apply Ask students to create a script that includes notations for phrasing and vocal changes. Have them work in pairs to practice and improve their reading. Then invite students to perform their readings for the class.

Assess Evaluate readings based on attention to phrasing and vocal effects, and on overall delivery. You may want to have students use Peer Assessment: Oral Interpretation form, p. 115, in **Alternative Assessment.**

One-Minute Insight

In "Drum Song", poet Wendy Rose describes the actions necessary for survival of the turtle, woodpecker, snowhare, and humans. Set to the rhythm of an imaginary beating drum, the poem expresses the idea that all animals, even humans, must follow nature's rhythms in order to survive.

◆ Literary Focus

1 Sound Devices Point out the repetition of the word *Listen* at the beginning of each stanza. Ask students why the poet might have used this sound device and what effect it has on the poem. *The poet wants the reader to listen for the rhythm of life described in each stanza. The repetition of the word emphasizes the importance of the message.*

◆ Critical Thinking

2 Interpret Ask students why the snowhare would look up to where owls hunt. *The snowhare would do this to protect itself from the owl who hunts small animals.*

►Critical Viewing◄

3 Connect *The turtle's flat, round feet with claws help it walk on the land and rocks and also to swim in the water.*

DRUM SONG
Wendy Rose

Listen. Turtle
    your flat round feet
    of four claws each
    go slow, go steady,
5   from rock to water
    to land to rock to
water.

Listen. Woodpecker
    you lift your red head
10   on wind, perch
    on <u>vertical</u> earth
    of tree bark and
branch.

Listen. Snowhare[1]
15   your belly drags,
    your whiskers dance
    bush to <u>burrow</u>
    your eyes turn up
    to where owls
20 hunt.

Listen. Women
    your tongues melt,
    your seeds are planted
    mesa[2] to mesa a shake
25   of <u>gourds</u>,
    a line of mountains
    with blankets
    on their
hips.

1. **Snowhare** (snō′ her) *n.*: Snoeshoe hare, a large rabbitlike animal whose color changes from brown in summer to white in winter and whose broad feet resemble snowshoes.
2. **mesa** (mā′ sə) *n.*: Small, high plateau with steep sides.

Crawling Turtle II, Barry Wilson

3 ▲ Critical Viewing What physical characteristics of the turtle allow it to go from "land to rock to water"? [Connect]

◆ Build Vocabulary

vertical (vʉr′ ti kəl) *adj.*: Straight up and down; upright

burrow (bʉr′ ō) *n.*: Passage or hole for shelter

gourds (gôrdz) *n.*: Dried, hollowed-out shell of fruits such as melons and pumpkins

---

 Humanities: Art

Crawling Turtle II, by Barry Wilson
    Barry Wilson (born 1952) is a Haisla from the Henaaksiala branch. He was born in Kitamaat Village in British Columbia, Canada, and began carving at age 5, learning from his grandfather, a Henaaksiala chief and carver. After graduating from school, Wilson began working as an artist and teaching young people to carve through a program sponsored by the Vancouver Indian Center. Although today he concentrates mainly on jewelry making, Wilson also creates carvings, screen prints, drums, and bentwood boxes. Draw students' attention to the texture of this image.
    Relate the artwork to the poem by asking the following discussion questions:
1. What details in the artwork reflect the words in the poem? *The turtle has claws that are clearly visible on the right rear foot.*
2. What rhythm would the steps of the turtle create? *Students can illustrate the rhythm by clapping out a slow, steady rhythm with their hands.*

If I can stop one Heart from breaking

Emily Dickinson

If I can stop one Heart from breaking
I shall not live in vain
If I can ease one Life the Aching
Or cool one Pain   ❹

5   Or help one fainting Robin
Unto his Nest again
I shall not live in Vain. ❺

Guide for Responding

◆ LITERATURE AND YOUR LIFE

Reader's Response What makes you feel that you haven't lived "in vain"?

Thematic Focus In what way can performing or hearing "Drum Song" help you better understand the natural world?

Journal Writing Jot down ways in which you could help others, as Dickinson does with her poetry.

☑ Check Your Comprehension

1. (a) What is each of the animals in "Drum Song" doing? (b) What are the women in the last stanza doing?
2. In "If I can stop one Heart . . . ," what four things will keep the speaker from living in vain?

◆ Critical Thinking

INTERPRET
1. In "Drum Song," to whom is the word *listen* addressed in each stanza? Explain. **[Infer]**
2. Find details that support this description of "Drum Song": It tells how living things go about their business, and the drum is like the pulse of daily rhythms. **[Support]**
3. Judging by "If I can stop one Heart . . . ," what do you think Dickinson wanted poetry to do? Explain. **[Draw Conclusions]**

COMPARE LITERARY WORKS
4. If a drum goes best with "Drum Song," what instrument would you use with "If I can stop one Heart . . ."? Why? **[Compare and Contrast]**

Drum Song/If I can stop one Heart from breaking ◆ 859

Beyond the Selection

FURTHER READING
Other Works by the Authors
The Listeners and Other Poems, Walter de la Mare
Where the Sidewalk Ends, Shel Silverstein
Now Poof She Is Gone: Poetry, Wendy Rose
Final Harvest: Emily Dickinson's Poems, T. H. Johnson (ed.)
Other Works About Relationships
Out of the Dust, Karen Hesse
The Dream Keeper and Other Poems, Langston Hughes

INTERNET
We suggest the following sites on the Internet (all Web sites are subject to change).
    For more on Walter de la Mare, go to:
http://www.columbia.edu/acis/bartleby/mbp/48.html
    For more on Shel Silverstein, visit:
http://www.harpercollins.com/authors/pages/silverstein_shel.htm
    For more on Wendy Rose, go to:
http://www.ipl.org/cgi/ref/native/browse.pl/A74
    For more on Emily Dickinson, visit:
http://www.planet.net/pkrisxle/emily/dickinson.html

One-Minute Insight In "If I can stop one Heart from breaking," Emily Dickinson expresses the idea that life is made worthwhile by the things people do to help others. By her example, she offers the reader ways to reach out to others.

◆ Literary Focus

❹ **Sound Devices** Ask students what sound device Dickinson uses in these lines. *She uses rhyme. The words at the end of every other line, have the same ending sound.*

◆ Reading Strategy

❺ **Make Inferences** Ask students what they can infer about the poet from this line, which she used twice in the poem. *The poet wanted her life to mean something, she wanted to make a difference.*

Reinforce and Extend

Answers
◆ LITERATURE AND YOUR LIFE

Reader's Response Doing things that touch other lives in positive ways makes people feel as though they haven't "lived in vain."

Thematic Focus Performing or hearing the poem helps you understand the rhythms and patterns of life.

☑ Check Your Comprehension

1. (a) The turtle is crawling out of the water and back; the woodpecker is perching on a tree; the snowhare is dashing to its burrow. (b) The women are planting seeds.
2. The four things are: stop one heart from breaking, ease one life the aching, cool one pain, help one fainting robin.

◆ Critical Thinking

1. The word *listen* is addressed to the reader.
2. Details include "from rock to water to land to rock to water"; "bush to burrow"; "mesa to mesa."
3. She wanted her poetry to touch the lives of others and help them.
4. A strumming guitar might be a nice accompaniment, because the poem is similar in style to song lyrics.

859

Answers

◆ Reading Strategy

1. De la Mare is fascinated by the moon and thinks it is beautiful. He describes the moon's light only in the most positive terms.
2. The speaker imagined conversations in which he or she spoke to crickets and they answered back.
3. The women were responsible for growing the food crops and raising children.

◆ Build Vocabulary

Using Word Pairs
1. curving inward
2. a measure of north-south distance using lines drawn parallel to the equator.

Spelling Strategy
1. furrows; 2. sorrow

Using the Word Bank
1. False. A vertical direction would be up and down; to cross a street would be horizontal.
2. True. A burrow is a hole in the ground.
3. True. A gourd can be used as a container.

◆ Literary Focus

1. "Silver" includes alliteration: "Slowly, silently.... in her silver shoon." "Drum Song" includes alliteration: "flat round feet of four claws." "Forgotten Language" includes repetition: "Once..." and "How did it go? How did it go?"
2. (a) Repetition is more apparent in "Drum Song." (b) It reinforces the basic rhythms of the natural world, such as the progression of seasons and the rhythm of life cycles.

◆ Build Grammar Skills

1. awkwardly—You use an adverb to modify a verb (drags).
2. well—You use an adverb to modify a verb (spoke).
3. deeply—You use an adverb to modify a verb (were sleeping).
4. soft—You use an adjective to modify a noun (word).
5. sad—You use an adjective to modify a noun (crying).

Guide for Responding (continued)

◆ Reading Strategy

MAKE INFERENCES

Making inferences—using evidence to reach conclusions—helps you appreciate these poems. For example, the repetition of the ending question in "Forgotten Language" hints at its importance. Further thought reveals that the lines pose a dual question: *What was that language?* and *How did it vanish?*

1. What can you infer about De la Mare's attitude toward the moon in "Silver"? What evidence helped you make your inference?
2. What can you infer about the speaker of "Forgotten Language" from the line: "Once I heard and answered all the questions of the crickets"?
3. What inference can you make about women's place in the world, according to "Drum Song"?

◆ Build Vocabulary

USING WORD PAIRS

Some words with opposite or complementary meanings are often used in pairs, like *vertical* and *horizontal*. On your paper, use your knowledge of word pairs to fill in the blanks.

1. If *convex* means "curving outward," *concave* means _____?.
2. If *longitude* is "a measure of east-west distance using lines drawn through the Earth's poles and at right angles to the equator," *latitude* is _____?_____.

SPELLING STRATEGY

The long o sound in words may be spelled *ow*, as in *low* and *burrow*. On your paper, write these sentences, filling in the blanks with the correct spelling for the long o sound.

1. Look at the furr_ _s on the poet's forehead.
2. He feels sorr_ _ because he's forgotten a magical language.

USING THE WORD BANK

On your paper, answer each question true or false. Then, explain your answer.

1. To cross a street, you'd go in a *vertical* direction.
2. Animals that like to *burrow* can be found in the ground.
3. You might use *gourds* to carry water in a desert.

860 ◆ Poetry

◆ Literary Focus

SOUND DEVICES

In these poems and others, **sound devices** that add to the music of the poems also add to the meaning. Think about what "Silver" would lose without its **rhymes**—chiming sounds at the ends of lines. Imagine "Drum Song" without the drumming **repetition** of "Listen" or "Forgotten Language" without whispering **alliteration** like "smiled in secret."

1. Within these poems, find another example of each sound device.
2. (a) Which sound device is more apparent in "Drum Song"? (b) How does use of the sound device enhance the poem's meaning?

◆ Build Grammar Skills

CORRECT USE OF ADJECTIVES AND ADVERBS

Don't confuse the use of **adjectives** and **adverbs**. Adjectives modify nouns, and adverbs modify verbs, adjectives, and other adverbs. A common mistake is the use of an adjective, rather than an adverb, to modify a verb. In "Silver," for example, using the adjectives *slow* and *silent* to modify "Walks" would be an error: "Slowly, silently, now the moon / Walks . . ." However, expressions like "go slow" in "Drum Song" are generally acceptable in informal speech.

Practice On your paper, write the correct modifier for each sentence. Then, explain your choice.

1. The snowhare drags its belly (awkward, awkwardly).
2. I spoke the language of flowers really (good, well).
3. The doves in their nests were sleeping (deep, deeply).
4. She spoke a (softly, soft) word to him to calm his heart.
5. I joined the (sad, sadly) crying of each falling flake.

Writing Application Write five sentences about a moonlit night in which you correctly use these adjectives and adverbs: *bright, brightly; silent, silently; quiet, quietly.*

Writing Application
Sample answer:
When I shut off the bright porch light, I could see the moon shining brightly on the field. I sat silently for a moment, enjoying the silent stillness of the night. In the quiet hush of the darkness I saw a deer walking quietly into the woods.

✎ **Writer's Solution**

For additional instruction and practice, use the lesson in the Using Modifiers unit of *Writer's Solution Language Lab CD-ROM* on Problems With Modifiers and Troublesome Adjectives and Adverbs. You may also use the pages on Adjectives and Adverbs, pp. 16–23, in the *Writer's Solution Grammar Practice Book.*

Build Your Portfolio

 ## Idea Bank

Writing

1. **Stanza of Poetry** Choose an animal that is familiar to you, and write a stanza of poetry about it. Imitate the form of the stanzas in "Drum Song." Also, use alliteration and repetition to make your stanza sound musical.

2. **Public-Service Announcement** Write a public-service announcement in which you encourage people to volunteer their time helping others. You may want to model your announcement on Dickinson's "If I can stop one Heart from breaking."

3. **Inference About an Author** Using details from "Silver," make inferences about the ideas and feelings that De la Mare associates with the moon. Consider such details as rhythm, sound devices, and pictures created by the words.

Speaking and Listening

4. **Reading** Choose one of these poems to read aloud. Note on a copy of the poem where you will pause, stop, or stress repeated words. Don't pause at the ends of lines where there is no punctuation. **[Performing Arts Link]**

5. **Poem With Drums** Recite Wendy Rose's "Drum Song" and use a drum to accompany your reading. Tape-record your performance to listen to afterward. **[Music Link]**

Projects

6. **Sound Devices in Speeches [Group Activity]** With a few classmates, point out the use of sound devices in famous American political speeches. Use live readings, recordings, and video clips to demonstrate examples. **[Social Studies Link]**

7. **Report on Animal Communication** Using inference, summarize Silverstein's ideas about animal communication in "Forgotten Language." Then, compare and contrast his ideas with scientists' views on the subject. **[Science Link]**

 ## Writing Mini-Lesson

Song Lyrics

Shel Silverstein is a songwriter as well as a poet, so you can imagine hearing his "Forgotten Language" set to music. Using his poems and your favorite songs as a source of inspiration, write your own song lyrics. Write in any style that feels comfortable—rock, folk, rap, or romantic ballad.

Writing Skills Focus: Use Effective Repetition

As you know, song lyrics use **effective repetition.** A catchy phrase or verse, called a refrain, usually appears after every verse of the song. In fact, when you start to memorize the lyrics of a song, the refrain is often what you recall first. In adapting "Forgotten Language" as a song, Silverstein might use the last two lines as a refrain, repeating them after each verse:

> *Model From the Poem*
> How did it go?
> How did it go?

Prewriting Jot down some of the thoughts and feelings that you'd like to express in your song lyrics. Think about which ideas you'd like to emphasize through repetition.

Drafting Refer to your prewriting notes as you draft the song lyrics. The phrase or verse you repeat—the refrain—should sum up the main thoughts and feelings you'd like to convey. Also, use devices like alliteration to make the refrain memorable.

Revising Read your lyrics to a classmate. If he or she doesn't find the refrain memorable, spice it up with alliteration, rhyme, or rhythms.

> ◆ **Grammar Application**
> Be sure that you haven't used an adjective to modify a verb, an adverb, or another adjective.

Silver/Forgotten Language/Drum Song/If I can stop one Heart from breaking ◆ 861

 ## Idea Bank

Following are suggestions for matching the Idea Bank topics with your students' performance levels and learning modalities:

Customize for *Performance Levels*
Less Advanced Students: 1, 5
Average Students: 2, 4, 5, 6
More Advanced Students: 3, 4, 6, 7

Customize for *Learning Modalities*
Verbal/Linguistic: 1, 2, 3, 4, 5, 6, 7
Musical/Rhythmic: 1, 3, 5
Logical/Mathematical: 7
Interpersonal: 6
Intrapersonal: 1, 2, 3, 5, 7

 ## Writing Mini-Lesson

Refer students to the Writing Handbook in the back of the book for instruction on the writing process and for further information on poetry. Have students use the Sensory Language Chart in **Writing and Language Transparencies,** p. 69, to arrange their prewriting examples.

✒ Writer's Solution

Writing Lab CD-ROM
Have students complete the tutorial on Creative Writing. Follow these steps:
1. Have students use Creative Writing Models From Literature.
2. The Inspirations for Creative Writing will allow possible topics for their song lyrics.
3. Have students use Models From Literature to explore a model of a lyric poem and a narrative poem.
4. To revise, students can use writing hints and models for revising poems to check all the words in their poems against a central image.

Writer's Solution Sourcebook
Have students use Chapter 8, "Creative Writing," pp. 234–265, for additional support. This chapter include instruction on song lyrics, pp. 240, 246, 250, and 255.

✓ ASSESSMENT OPTIONS

Formal Assessment, Selection Test, pp. 242–244, and Assessment Resources Software. The selection test is designed so that it can easily be customized to the performance levels of your students.

Alternative Assessment, p. 54, includes options for less advanced students, more advanced students, verbal/linguistic learners, visual/spatial learners, musical/rhythmic learners, and interpersonal learners.

PORTFOLIO ASSESSMENT
Use the following rubrics in the **Alternative Assessment** booklet to assess student writing:
Stanza of Poetry: Poetry, p. 104
Public-Service Announcement: Persuasion, p. 101
Inference About an Author: Response to Literature, p. 106
Writing Mini-Lesson: Poetry, p. 104

OBJECTIVES

1. To read, comprehend, and interpret four poems
2. To relate four poems to personal experience
3. To make inferences
4. To recognize sound devices
5. To build vocabulary in context and use word pairs
6. To use adjectives and adverbs correctly
7. To write song lyrics, using effective repetition
8. To respond to the poems through writing, speaking and listening, and projects

SKILLS INSTRUCTION

Vocabulary:
Word Pairs

Spelling:
Spelling the Long o Sound as ow

Grammar:
Correct Use of Adjectives and Adverbs

Reading Strategy:
Make Inferences

Literary Focus:
Sound Devices

Writing:
Use Effective Repetition

Speaking and Listening:
Reading (Teacher's Edition)

Critical Viewing:
Analyze; Connect

PORTFOLIO OPPORTUNITIES

Writing: Stanza of Poetry; Public-Service Announcement; Inference About an Author
Writing Mini-Lesson: Song Lyrics
Speaking and Listening: Reading; Poem With Drums
Projects: Sound Devices in Speeches; Report on Animal Communication

---

More About the Authors
Walter de la Mare began his literary career by writing and publishing a high school magazine. His writings reflect his belief that the world is best understood through the imagination.

Shel Silverstein spends much of his time traveling around the world. Youngsters enjoy his poems' images, while older readers appreciate his observations about growing up.

Wendy Rose manages a museum bookstore and lectures at the University of California in addition to writing poetry. Also a visual artist, she designs posters and postcards.

Emily Dickinson lived almost her whole life in her parents' home, in close companionship with her sister and brother, "like friendly monarchs, each in his own domain."

Guide for Reading

Meet the Authors:

Walter de la Mare (1873–1956)

For years, this British poet worked in the statistics department of a big oil company. At night, however, his imagination roamed freely as he wrote poems about the magic and mystery of life. These poems, found in books like *The Listeners,* delight children and adults alike. [For more on Walter de la Mare, see page 32.]

Shel Silverstein (1932–   )

Silverstein is a poet, a writer of children's books, a cartoonist, a folk singer, and a composer. The critic William Cole has called Silverstein's poems "tender, funny, sentimental, philosophical, and ridiculous in turn . . ."

Wendy Rose (1948–   )

The work of this award-winning poet reflects her Native American ancestry. However, she wants readers to view her poems not only as Native American but as human.

Emily Dickinson (1830–1886)

Dickinson led a quiet life in Amherst, Massachusetts. She published only a few poems in her lifetime. However, she secretly wrote the 1,775 lyric poems that made her one of the founders of American poetry. Sparkling with thought and feeling, these poems show how active her inner life really was. [For more on Emily Dickinson, see page 192.]

◆ LITERATURE AND YOUR LIFE

CONNECT YOUR EXPERIENCE

Sometimes, with a friend or a family member, you just need to share a look or a single word. Then, both of you nod or burst into laughter. You don't need to spell things out because you share a secret language. As these poems show, poetry is also a kind of secret language. It begins with a child's wisdom, speaks in the rhythm of a heartbeat, and offers words to save a breaking heart.

THEMATIC FOCUS: Relationships

How does each of these poems speak to you as a friend, telling you something secret or surprising?

◆ Background for Understanding

CULTURE

In Native American cultures, as Wendy Rose reveals in "Drum Song," poetry and dance were accompanied by drums. These instruments usually consisted of a hide stretched on a frame. Drums came in all shapes and sizes—from the small water drum of the Iroquois to the large Great Plains drum that was beaten by four men together.

◆ Build Vocabulary

WORD PAIRS

Because some words occur in pairs, as opposites, it's useful to learn them together. The word *vertical,* from "Drum Song" is part of such a pair: vertical/horizontal. *Vertical* means "upright," while *horizontal* means "flat."

WORD BANK

Which word from these poems is related to the word *vertex,* a mathematical term meaning "the highest point of a triangle"? Check the Build Vocabulary box on page 858 to see if you chose correctly.

vertical
burrow
gourds

 Prentice Hall Literature Program Resources

REINFORCE / RETEACH / EXTEND

Selection Support Pages
Build Vocabulary: Word Pairs, p. 291
Build Spelling Skills, p. 292
Build Grammar Skills: Correct Use of Adjectives and Adverbs, p. 293
Reading Strategy: Make Inferences, p. 294
Literary Focus: Sound Devices, p. 295
Strategies for Diverse Student Needs, pp. 107–108
Beyond Literature Study Skills: Using a Graphic Organizer, p. 54

Formal Assessment Selection Test, pp. 242–244, Assessment Resources Software
Alternative Assessment, p. 54
Resource Pro CD-ROM "Silver," "Forgotten Language," "Drum Song," "If I can stop one Heart from breaking"

 Listening to Literature Audiocassettes
"Silver," "Forgotten Language," "Drum Song," "If I can stop one Heart from breaking"

854

New World ◆ One Time ◆ Lyric 17
For My Sister Molly Who in the Fifties

Have students remember back to the first day of school years ago, when they were younger. Remind them of the smell of a fresh new box of crayons, the stiff, itchiness of new jeans, the prickliness of a fresh hair-cut, the smoothness of new note-books, the promise of unsharpened pencils, and the fluttery feeling of excitement when facing a new teacher. Challenge students to list words that appeal to the senses to describe their memories of that long–ago first day of school. Tell students that the poems they are about to read contain many such examples of sensory imagery. As they read, invite them to be aware of the way in which the words reach out and touch their senses.

◆ Build Grammar Skills

Pronouns in Comparisons With *than* or *as* If you wish to introduce the grammar concept for this selection before students read, refer to the instruction on p. 870.

Customize for
Less Proficient Readers
To help students recognize the imagery in the poems, as they read have them complete a chart like the one below.

Image	sight	sound	taste	smell	touch
warm, dark loam	X				X

Customize for
More Advanced Students
Invite students to restate passages from the poems as ordinary conver-sational speech. Then have groups of students discuss why the descriptive language used by poets has more impact than the expression of the same idea in everyday speech.

Customize for
English Language Learners
Read each poem aloud with students, helping them paraphrase the meaning of each stanza. Then discuss the meaning of the entire poem, making sure that students understand it on a literal level.

◆ Literary Focus
IMAGERY

Scientists use models to help you visualize the Earth's rotation and other phenomena. In a dif-ferent way, poets help you see a scene by using **imagery,** language that appeals to your senses. Often an image is a visual description of color, shape, or movement. However, it can also appeal to senses other than sight.

Find images by looking for words that speak to your senses. In "New World," for example, you will find this image, which speaks to your sense of sight: "the earth/*glitters*/with leaves."

◆ Reading Strategy
USE YOUR SENSES

It's not enough to find the words that create an image. That would be reading with your mind alone, and poets want you to **use your senses** to experience imagery. They want you to call on your own sense memories to see, hear, taste, smell, and touch what the words are describing.

Use a chart like the one below to bring your senses into play as you read (one example is done for you):

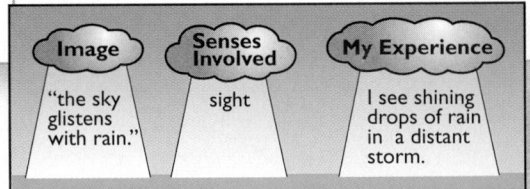

Image	Senses Involved	My Experience
"the sky glistens with rain."	sight	I see shining drops of rain in a distant storm.

Guide for Reading ◆ 863

Preparing for Standardized Tests

Writing Explain that writers often choose not to use commonly accepted rules of sentence structure in poetry. Students should be cautioned to recognize examples of poetic license so they do not model incorrect usage in their own writ-ing. As an example, write the following sentence from "New World" on the board: "Cedars black-en the slopes—and pines." Discuss how the more direct way to state the sentence would be "Cedars and pines blacken the slopes." Write the following sample standardized test item on the board:

Which of the following is <u>not</u> an example of standard sentence structure?

(A) First, a poem must be magical.
(B) And over all I would like to hover God.
(C) Rivers follow the moon.
(D) Meadows recede through planes of heat.

Lead students to see that *(A)*, *(C)*, and *(D)* are all arranged in standard order. Item *(B)* would be more precisely restated as "And over all I would like God to hover."

One-Minute Insight

"New World" describes the beginning of a new world or the progression of a new day. The first verse describes the setting in vivid but general terms. The remaining three verses present images of the world at dawn, noon, and dusk. Using the words of the poem, the author, N. Scott Momaday, communicates his respect for the beauty and balance of nature.

◆ **Critical Thinking**

❶ **Infer** Ask students whom the speaker is addressing in the poem. *He is addressing the first human—"First Man."*

▶**Critical Viewing**◀

❷ **Interpret** *Everything appears fresh, clean, and untouched.*

◆ **Literary Focus**

❸ **Imagery** Discuss the sense or senses appealed to in this passage. *The description of eagles flying and the plain below appeals to the sense of sight.*

▶**Critical Viewing**◀

❹ **Connect** *This painting best illustrates the second stanza, which describes the dawn. Grasses are shimmering, light is gathering on the plain, and shadows are withdrawing.*

Customize for
Musical/Rhythmic Learners

Have students select one of the poems and illustrate it with music. Ask them to choose a piece of music that reflects something about the poem. Then have students read the poem aloud using the music as background.

New World

N. Scott Momaday

1.

❶ First Man,
behold:
the earth
glitters
5   with leaves;
the sky
glistens
with rain.
Pollen[1]
10   is <u>borne</u>
on winds
that <u>low</u>
and lean
upon
15   mountains.
Cedars
blacken
the slopes—
and pines.

Wallowa Lake, Harley, Abby Aldrich Rockefeller Folk Art Center, Williamsburg, VA

---

1.   **pollen** (päl′ ən) *n.*: Yellow, powderlike male cells formed in the stamen of a flower.

▲ **Critical Viewing** What aspects of this painting convey the idea of a "new world"? [Interpret]

Jack's Fireplace, Jack Palance

2.

20   At dawn
eagles
hie[2] and
<u>hover</u>
above   ❸
25   the plain
where light
gathers
in pools.
Grasses
30   shimmer
and shine.
Shadows
withdraw
and lie
35   away
like smoke.

---

2.   **hie** (hī) *v.*: Hurry or hasten.

◀ **Critical Viewing** Which stanza of the poem does this painting best illustrate? Explain. [Connect]

⬥ **Block Scheduling Strategies**

Consider these suggestions to take advantage of extended class time:

• Read and discuss Literary Focus and Reading Strategy on p. 863. Then have students read the poems in small groups. Ask them to set up a sensory image chart like the one on p. 863 and to fill in the chart as they read the poems.

• Instruct students to preview the words in the Word Bank and complete the Build Vocabulary lesson on p. 870. Encourage students to look through a dictionary to find other words that contain the word root *-cede-*. For additional

practice, assign the Build Vocabulary page in **Selection Support,** p. 296.

• Following reading, arrange students in pairs and have them answer the Literature and Your Life and Critical Thinking questions on pp. 865, 867, and 869.

• Have students prepare for the Writing Mini-Lesson by working on the *Writer's Solution Language Lab CD-ROM* and *Writer's Solution Writing Lab CD-ROM.* Refer to the teaching suggestions on p. 871 to guide students through the process.

3.

At noon
turtles
enter

40 slowly
into
the warm
dark loam.[3]

45 Bees hold
the swarm.
Meadows
recede ❺
through planes
of heat

50 and pure
distance.

4.

At dusk
the gray
foxes

55 stiffen
in cold;
blackbirds
are fixed
in the

60 branches.
Rivers
follow
the moon,
the long

65 white track
of the
full moon.

---

3. loam (lōm) *n.*:
Rich, dark soil.

◆ **Build Vocabulary**

glistens (glis´ ənz) *v.*: Shines; sparkles

borne (bôrn) *v.*: Carried

low (lō) *v.*: Make the typical sound that a cow makes; moo

hover (huv´ ər) *v.*: Flutter in the air

recede (ri sēd´) *v.*: Move away

Guide for Responding

◆ LITERATURE AND YOUR LIFE

Reader's Response How is the world you live in different from and similar to the one described in the poem?

Thematic Focus In what ways are different aspects of nature interrelated?

Sketch Using pencil or pen, quickly sketch one of the images from "New World."

☑ Check Your Comprehension

1. Whom does Momaday address at the start of the poem?
2. What are the main features in the landscape that Momaday describes?
3. Summarize the progression of time in the poem.

◆ Critical Thinking

INTERPRET

1. Who is "First Man"? **[Infer]**
2. What do you think Momaday wants "First Man" to feel as he beholds his world? Why? **[Infer]**
3. What meaning or meanings does the title of the poem suggest? Explain. **[Connect]**
4. How is the poem's title related to its central message? **[Draw Conclusions]**

EVALUATE

5. Would this poem work better with long lines? Why or why not? **[Assess]**

APPLY

6. In what way is the world new every day? **[Speculate]**

New World ◆ 865

♪ Humanities: Art

Wallowa Lake, by Harley
This colorful painting is an example of folk art—art created by artists who have not been formally trained or educated. The subject is Wallowa Lake in northeast Oregon. The surrounding mountains and a soaring eagle are reflected in the lake's still surface.

Jack's Fireplace, by Jack Palance
Academy Award-winning actor Jack Palance painted this brightly colored impression of a rising or setting sun casting a yellow glow over an idealized landscape.

Have students study the paintings and reread the poem. Then, connect the paintings to the poem by asking questions such as these:

1. How are the two paintings similar? How are they different? *They both illustrate mountains, bodies of water, trees, and birds; the paintings use different styles of applying color.*
2. How do the paintings illustrate the poem? *Both the paintings and the poem provide fresh, beautiful images of nature. Details of mountains, tree-covered slopes, pools, and rivers, are included in both paintings and in the poem.*

The speaker in William Stafford's "One Time" recalls a single, memorable event from childhood. Daylight is fading as the speaker finds Hilary's blind sister, Tina, alone outside. Just as the sun is setting, the speaker leads Tina safely home. The poet paints the image of a warm and innocent relationship between the two.

◆ Literary Focus

❶ Imagery Ask students what senses the poet addresses in this passage. *The description of the evening flowing between houses and pausing on the schoolground appeals to the sense of sight. The description of the "gray smooth railing still warm from the sun" appeals to the sense of touch.*

◆ Reading Strategy

❷ Use Your Senses Have students recall times they have seen or heard an outdoor lawn sprinkler or come across a flock of pigeons. Ask them to use the memory of those experiences to imagine and describe the sounds in this passage. *The sprinkler makes a rhythmic clicking sound, and the water drops splash quietly on the lawn and more loudly on the pavement. The pigeons make soft, cooing noises.*

◆ Critical Thinking

❸ Speculate Ask students if they think Tina knew it was getting dark and, if she did, how she knew. *She probably knew it was getting dark because, even though she couldn't see, she could feel that the sun was no longer shining as warmly on her.*

►Critical Viewing◄

❹ Assess *Most students will note the two children holding hands and relate it to the interaction of the poem's characters.*

Beyond Literature

In addition to Braille, suggest that interested students research other tools that blind people might find useful. For example, they may wish to find out about guide dogs, the use of a white cane, talking books and optical scanners.

One Time

William Stafford

❶ When evening had flowed between houses
and paused on the schoolground, I met
Hilary's blind little sister following
the gray smooth railing still warm from the sun
5   with her hand; and she stood by the edge
holding her face upward waiting
while the last light found her cheek
and her hair, and then on over the trees.

10 **❷** You could hear the great sprinkler arm
of water find and then leave the pavement,
and pigeons telling each other their dreams
or the dreams they would have. We were
deep in the well of shadow by then, and I
held out my hand, saying, "Tina, it's me—
15   Hilary says I should tell you it's dark,
and, oh, Tina, it is. Together now—"

❸ And I reached, our hands touched,
and we found our way home.

▲ Critical Viewing Do the children in this photograph seem to share a relationship like the one described in the poem? Explain. [Assess]

Beyond Literature

Science Connection

Braille The girl in "One Time" is blind, and the poem's speaker helps guide her home at sundown. The lives of the blind, however, are not wholly dependent on others, partly because of Louis Braille. Braille (1809–1852) was a Frenchman who became blind at the age of three. At the age of fifteen, he developed a system of writing for the blind.

Braille is a code of small, raised dots that are read by touch. Various arrangements of six dots stand for letters, numbers, and punctuation. Although Braille was developed in 1824, it is still widely used today.

Cross-Curricular Activity
Research the Braille system, and create a chart showing the arrangements of dots and what they stand for. Then, spell out your name and address using Braille.

Cross-Curricular Connection: Science

Blindness The partial or total inability to see is considered blindness. Tina, in the poem, is blind and must enjoy the outdoor world by using her other senses. Some of the causes of blindness are congenital defects, disease, and injury.

There are many agencies and schools that provide training for people who either are born unable to see or become blind from disease or injury later in life. They are able to learn many specialized skills, become quite self-reliant and independent, and are able to hold jobs in a number of fields.

In addition to Braille, many devices and aids help blind people function in a seeing world. Scanners and talking books enable reading, and guide dogs allow independence and mobility. Paris established the first school for the blind in 1784 and Perkins School for the Blind opened in Boston in 1832. More than 60 percent of blind children today go to school in a regular school setting.

Good health habits and protection from injury are important in the prevention of blindness. Have interested students research and then prepare a

Lyric 17

José Garcia Villa

First, a poem must be magical,
Then musical as a sea-gull.
It must be a brightness moving
And hold secret a bird's flowering.
5   It must be slender as a bell,
And it must hold fire as well.
It must have the wisdom of bows
And it must kneel like a rose.
It must be able to hear
10   The luminance of dove and deer.
It must be able to hide
What it seeks, like a bride.
And over all I would like to hover
God, smiling from the poem's cover.

⑤

◆ **Build Vocabulary**

luminance (lōō´ mə nəns) *n.*: Brightness; brilliance

Guide for Responding

◆ LITERATURE AND YOUR LIFE

Reader's Response In answer to "Lyric 17," tell what you think "a poem must be."

Thematic Focus In what way is the relationship described in "One Time" special?

Journal Writing Thinking of "One Time," describe a quiet but meaningful moment that you once experienced.

☑ **Check Your Comprehension**

1. (a) Who takes part in the moment described in "One Time"? (b) At what time of day does this moment take place?
2. Briefly describe what happens in the poem.
3. According to "Lyric 17," what are three of the qualities a poem must have?

◆ Critical Thinking

INTERPRET

1. Find a detail in "One Time" that creates a sense of mystery. Then, explain your choice. **[Support]**
2. What makes the moment described in "One Time" so memorable? Explain. **[Analyze]**
3. In what ways does "Lyric 17" make poetry seem mysterious? Explain. **[Connect]**

EVALUATE

4. Is "Lyric 17" effective as a definition of poetry? Why or why not? **[Evaluate]**

COMPARE LITERARY WORKS

5. Compare and contrast the descriptions of dusk in "One Time" and stanza 4 of "New World." **[Compare and Contrast]**

One Time/Lyric 17 ◆ 867

Speaking and Listening Mini-Lesson

Choral Reading

This mini-lesson supports the Speaking and Listening activity in the Idea Bank on p. 871.

Introduce Discuss ways in which choral reading is similar to a choral musical performance; several voices perform together or in solos, and voices are sometimes arranged in varying groups by pitch. Through choral readings, readers can express the mood as well as the words of a poem.

Develop Have students decide on the type of choral group they want to form—all female or all male voices, or mixed voices. After groups are

formed, have them select poems and decide whether to read in unison or with solo and group parts. Encourage groups to rehearse, using varied vocal tone and pitch to express the poem's mood. Remind them to speak loudly and clearly so that the words are easily understood by the audience.

Apply Have students perform their choral readings for the class.

Assess To evaluate the choral readings, have students complete the Peer Assessment: Oral Interpretation form, p. 115, in **Alternative Assessment.**

867

In "For My Sister Molly Who in the Fifties," the speaker lists things she has learned from her older sister. She also expresses the many things about her sister that she respects and admires.

Clarification

❶ Help students understand the title by explaining that the word *Fifties* refers to the decade of the 1950's and not to Molly's age.

◆ Literary Focus

❷ Imagery Ask students what senses are appealed to in these lines. *The food descriptions appeal to the senses of sight, taste, and smell.*

◆ Critical Thinking

❸ Interpret Discuss what the speaker means in these lines. *She learned to use the pronouns* we *and* us *correctly; Molly must have argued that Sonny, who was probably a friend, did not use them properly.*

◆ Reading Strategy

❹ Use Your Senses Have students use memories from their own experiences to describe what they imagine as they read these lines. *Students may mention the fragrant smoke from the fireplace and the vision of a tree draped with soft angel hair, glowing brightly with lights.*

► Critical Viewing ◄

❺ Infer The girls appear to have a warm, close relationship. They might be sisters, aunt and niece, or good friends.

---

❶ # For My Sister Molly Who in the Fifties
Alice Walker

For my Sister Molly Who in the Fifties
Once made a fairy rooster from
Mashed potatoes
❷ Whose eyes I forget
5   But green onions were his tail
And his two legs were carrot sticks
A tomato slice his crown.
Who came home on vacation
When the sun was hot
10   and cooked
and cleaned
And minded least of all
The children's questions
A million or more
15   Pouring in on her
Who had been to school
And knew (and told us too) that certain
Words were no longer good
❸ And taught me not to say us for we
20   No matter what "Sonny said" up the road.

FOR MY SISTER MOLLY WHO IN THE FIFTIES
Knew Hamlet well and read into the night
And coached me in my songs of Africa
25   A continent I never knew
But learned to love
Because "they" she said could carry
A tune
And spoke in accents never heard
30   In Eatonton.[1]
Who read from *Prose and Poetry*
And loved to read "Sam McGee from Tennessee"
On nights the fire was burning low
❹ And Christmas wrapped in angel hair[2]
35   And I for one prayed for snow.

---

1. **Eatonton** (ēt′ ən tən): Town in Georgia.
2. **angel hair:** Fine, white, filmy Christmas tree decoration.

❺ ▲ Critical Viewing How would you describe the relationship between the girls in the photograph? [Infer]

Viewing and Representing Mini-Lesson

Class Bulletin Board Display
In this mini-lesson, students will create a "Who Am I?" bulletin board display.

Introduce Review how poets use imagery to help them describe an object or idea in a poem. Discuss how students can use images in a similar way to describe something about themselves.

Develop Have students think of images that might represent them, such as a color, a picture of a sporting event, a flower, an animal, or a computer. Ask each student to select the one image that best represents her or him.

Apply Have students create a representation of their chosen image to place on the bulletin board. They may want to draw a picture; create a collage of shapes, colors, or magazine photographs; or use their imaginations to produce a representative image. Have students write a brief explanation of the image on an index card and place this beneath the image on the bulletin board.

Assess Challenge students to tie each image to the person it represents. Invite volunteers to explain their image choices. Evaluate students' work based on the quality of preparation and creativity.

WHO IN THE FIFTIES
Knew all the written things that made
Us laugh and stories by
The hour   Waking up the story buds

❻

40 Like fruit. Who walked among the flowers
And brought them inside the house
And smelled as good as they
And looked as bright.
Who made dresses, braided

45 Hair. Moved chairs about
Hung things from walls
Ordered baths
Frowned on wasp bites
And seemed to know the endings

50 Of all the tales
I had forgot.

◆ Reading Strategy

❻ Use Your Senses Ask students what they see as they read these lines. *Students may see the potential to become a writer as a bud that blossoms and finally becomes fruit—all as a result of the attention paid to the "bud" by the older sister.*

Reinforce and Extend

Answers
◆ LITERATURE AND YOUR LIFE

Reader's Response Answers should provide details that explain why students looked up to another person.

Thematic Focus They have a close relationship in which the younger sister looks up to her older sister.

☑ **Check Your Comprehension**
1. Molly cooks and cleans.
2. Molly made dresses, braided hair, ordered baths, and frowned on wasp bites.
3. The speaker was taught that certain words were no longer good, learned not to say *us* for *we*, and was coached in songs of Africa.

◆ Critical Thinking
1. The speaker is young enough to pose a child's questions, so she may be 9 or 10 years old. The sister has been away to school so she is probably at least 18 or 19 years old.
2. (a) She makes a fairy rooster from food. (b) She sings and reads to them.
3. She introduces ideas and works of literature her sister had never experienced before.
4. Yes, the speaker points out the many things she learned from her sister.
5. "For My Sister Molly..." includes details of many events in the lives of the speaker and her sister Molly. "One Time" describes a single evening for the speaker and Tina.

*G*uide for Responding

◆ LITERATURE AND YOUR LIFE

Reader's Response Have you looked up to someone the way the speaker looked up to her sister? Explain.

Thematic Focus How would you describe the relationship between the speaker and her sister?

Personality Profile Using the poem as evidence, jot down a brief profile of Molly.

☑ **Check Your Comprehension**
1. How does Molly help take care of the house?
2. Name three ways in which Molly takes physical care of the younger children.
3. List three things that the speaker learned from Molly.

◆ Critical Thinking

INTERPRET
1. What do you think is the difference in age between the speaker and Molly? Explain. **[Infer]**
2. (a) How does Molly reveal her creative spirit? (b) How does Molly awaken the creative spirit in the children? **[Analyze]**
3. In what ways does Molly bring home the world to her little sister? **[Support]**

EVALUATE
4. Is the speaker successful in expressing her appreciation for her sister? Why or why not? **[Make a Judgment]**

COMPARE LITERARY WORKS
5. In what way is "For My Sister Molly ..." a poem of many moments while "One Time" is a poem of a single moment? **[Compare and Contrast]**

For My Sister Molly Who in the Fifties ◆ 869

 Beyond the Selection

FURTHER READING
Other Works by N. Scott Momaday
House Made of Dawn
In the Presence of the Sun: Stories and Poems
Other Works by William Stafford
Methow River Poems
Other Works by José Garcia Villa
Parlement of Giraffes: Poems for the World's Children
Other Works by Alice Walker
Her Blue Body Everything We Know: Earthling Poems 1965–1990

INTERNET
We recommend the following sites on the Internet.
    For more information on N. Scott Momaday:
http://www.angstgrrl.com/intelligensia/authors/momaday/momaday.html
    For more information on William Stafford:
http://www.poems.com/~poems/wayitsta.htm
    For more information on Alice Walker:
http://www.public.asu.edu/~metro/aflit/walker/bio.html
    We *strongly recommend* that you preview these sites before you send students to them.

Answers

◆ Reading Strategy

Possible answers for each question:
1. I could feel the "warm dark loam."
2. I could hear the cooing of the pigeons.
3. I could see a bird opening its wings, like a flower blooming.
4. I could smell the fire burning at Christmas.

◆ Build Vocabulary

Using the Word Root -cede

1. c 2. a 3. b

Spelling Strategy

2. precede 5. succeed

Using the Word Bank

1. The lake glistens in the moonlight.
2. The kite was borne upward on the warm air.
3. I heard the cows low softly in the barn.
4. The hawk would hover like a kite over the green meadow.
5. It took centuries for the glacier to recede, leaving bare, scrapped land behind.
6. The firefly's luminance was softer than that of a flashlight.

◆ Literary Focus

Possible answers:
1. In "New World," "winds that low" appeals to hearing; "eagles hie and hover" appeals to sight. In "One Time," "railing still warm" appeals to touch; "deep in the well of shadow" appeals to sight. In "Lyric 17," "musical as a sea-gull" appeals to hearing; "slender as a bell" appeals to sight." In "For My Sister Molly Who in the Fifties" "spoke in accents never heard" appeals to hearing and "the sun was hot" appeals to touch.
2. In "For My Sister Molly...," the poet wants the reader to experience what it was like to have a special sister like Molly, and she uses imagery to capture and communicate the feeling of love for her sister.

◆ Build Grammar Skills

1. he (sensed)
2. they (loved)
3. he (defines)
4. we (learned)
5. they (looked)

Guide for Responding (continued)

◆ Reading Strategy

USE YOUR SENSES

By using **your senses,** you saw, heard, touched, tasted, and smelled what these poems described. Reading "New World," for example, you heard the winds "low" like cows and saw "Grasses/shimmer."

Tell how the sense listed next to each poem helped you experience one description in it:
1. "New World"— touch
2. "One Time"—hearing
3. "Lyric 17"—sight
4. "For My Sister Molly Who . . ."—smell

◆ Build Vocabulary

USING THE WORD ROOT -cede

Sometimes the root -cede- is spelled -ceed. Match the -cede or -ceed ("to go") words in the first column with their meanings in the second column:

1. recede   **a.** to go apart
2. secede   **b.** to go forward
3. proceed   **c.** to go back

SPELLING STRATEGY

Only three words ending in the *seed* sound are spelled *ceed: exceed, succeed,* and *proceed*. In all other words, this ending sound is spelled *cede*. On your paper, identify and correct the misspelled words:

1. secede   3. recede   5. succede
2. preceed   4. exceed

USING THE WORD BANK

On your paper, write a sentence that is a response to each direction:
1. Use the word *glistens* to describe a lake.
2. Describe a flying kite using the word *borne*.
3. Use the word *low* in a description of barnyard sounds.
4. Paint a word picture of a hawk using the word *hover*.
5. Using the word *recede,* describe a glacier's movement.
6. Use the word *luminance* to compare a flashlight and a firefly.

◆ Literary Focus

IMAGERY

In addition to giving you ideas to think about and emotions to feel, each of these poems gives you a world to experience. It does this by using **imagery,** or language that appeals to your senses. "New World," for example, has sensory words like "*shimmer/*and *shine,*" which help you see an image.

As in many poems, the imagery of "New World" also supports the theme. Momaday wants you to feel the wonder of nature, so he uses images that capture the beauty of the natural world.
1. Identify two images in each of these poems. Then, explain why they are images.
2. Choose a poem other than "New World," and show how its imagery supports its message or overall feeling.

◆ Build Grammar Skills

PRONOUNS IN COMPARISONS WITH *than* OR *as*

In some **comparisons using *than* or *as,*** one or more words are implied rather than stated. If you mentally supply the missing words, you can easily select the pronoun form to use. Here's an example from "For My Sister Molly . . .":

> And smelled as good as *they* [smelled]
> (*They* is the correct pronoun, not *them*.)

Practice On your paper, fill in the missing word or words for each comparison. Then, choose the right pronoun form.
1. Hilary's sister sensed the light as well as (him, he).
2. No one loved the evening better than (they, them).
3. Who defines poetry better than (he, him)?
4. No one learned grammar as well as (us, we).
5. Her sister looked as bright as (they, them).

Writing Application Use three *than* or *as* comparisons with pronouns to discuss the performances of athletes. Be sure you choose the correct form of each pronoun.

Writing Application

Sample answers:
Our team was more excited than they.
No relay team ran faster than we.
The first gymnast scored higher than she.

 Writer's Solution

For additional instruction and practice, use the lessons in the Using Pronouns unit of the *Writer's Solution Language Lab CD-ROM.* Or, have students use the practice pages on Using Pronouns, pp. 77–80, in the *Writer's Solution Grammar Practice Book.*

Build Your Portfolio

 Idea Bank

Writing

1. **Description** Support Momaday's theme about the wonder of nature with an image of your own. Appealing to one or more senses, describe a scene from the natural world.

2. **License-Plate Proposal** Suggest an image to appear on the automobile license plates of your state. Describe your image, and explain why it suggests the values or beauty of your region. **[Career Link]**

3. **Essay** Choose one of the poems in this section, and write an essay in which you explore its imagery. Give examples from the work to support your views.

Speaking and Listening

4. **Choral Reading [Group Activity]** With several classmates, give a group reading of "New World" or one of the other poems. Divide the poem into sections, and have one or more readers perform each section. **[Performing Arts Link]**

5. **Tribute** Publicly thank someone who has positively influenced your life with an oral tribute. Deliver the tribute to your classmates. Tape-record your tribute to analyze afterward.

Projects

6. **Presentation** Research events in space that create morning, noon, and night. Make a model or poster that illustrates the process. Then, present your findings to the class. **[Science Link; Career Link]**

7. **Captioned Picture** Illustrate an image from one of these poems with a collage, oil painting, or watercolor. Use the words of the poem's image as a caption for your illustration. Display your finished picture in the classroom. **[Art Link]**

 Writing Mini-Lesson

Free-Verse Poem

Except for "Lyric 17," the poems in this group are in free verse. They are unrhymed and do not make use of regular rhythms. Imitate them by writing your own free-verse poem. Use line lengths and rhythms that seem right for the subject you choose. Also, focus on creating a single, vivid image.

Writing Skills Focus: Dominant Image

By using a **dominant image** that runs through your whole poem, you can create a powerful effect. In "One Time," for instance, the disappearing light of day is such an image:

Model From the Poem

"When evening had flowed between houses . . ."

"while the last light found her cheek . . ."

"deep in the well of shadow . . ."

Prewriting Write about something you can experience or imagine experiencing. Then, freewrite about your subject, letting the lines break wherever you like. Scan your freewriting to find a dominant image you'll use.

Drafting Let your prewriting notes suggest the best line lengths and rhythms for your subject. Momaday, for example, uses short lines to stress each word. Also, focus on your dominant image throughout the poem.

Revising Have several classmates read your poem, and ask them to describe the dominant image. If they get it wrong, add sensory language throughout the poem to help you better convey that image.

> ◆ **Grammar Application**
>
> In comparisons with *than* or *as,* be sure you have used the right form of the pronoun.

New World/One Time/Lyric 17/For My Sister Molly Who in the Fifties ◆ 871

 Idea Bank

Following are suggestions for matching the Idea Bank topics with your students' performance levels and learning modalities:

Customize for *Performance Levels*
Less Advanced Students: 1, 4, 7
Average Students: 2, 4, 5, 7
More Advanced Students: 3, 5, 6

Customize for *Learning Modalities*
Verbal/Linguistic: 1, 2, 3, 4, 5
Musical/Rhythmic: 1, 4
Logical/Mathematical: 6
Visual/Spatial: 2, 7
Interpersonal: 4
Intrapersonal: 1, 2, 3, 6, 7

 Writing Mini-Lesson

Refer students to the Writing Handbook in the back of the book for instruction on the writing process and for further information on poetry.

 **Writer's Solution**

Writers at Work Videodisc
To have students hear about creative writing techniques from writer Julia Alvarez, play the videodisc segment on Creative Writing (Ch. 8).

Play frames 19343 to 27848

Writing Lab CD-ROM
Have students complete the tutorial on Creative Writing. Follow these steps:

1. Have students view the interactive model of a free-verse poem, "Concrete Mixers," by Patricia Hubbell.
2. Suggest that students use the Emotion Word Bin activity to help them select words and phrases that express different emotions.
3. Have students draft on computer.
4. When revising, have students use the Self-Evaluation Checklist for poetry.

Writer's Solution Sourcebook
Have students use Chapter 9, "Creative Writing," pp. 234–265 for additional support. The chapter includes in-depth instruction on using figurative language, p. 264.

✓ ASSESSMENT OPTIONS

Formal Assessment, Selection Test, pp. 245–247, and Assessment Resources Software. The selection test is designed so that it can easily be customized to the performance levels of your students.

Alternative Assessment, p. 55, includes options for less advanced students, more advanced students, intrapersonal learners, verbal/linguistic learners, and interpersonal learners.

PORTFOLIO ASSESSMENT
Use the following rubrics in the **Alternative Assessment** booklet to assess student writing:
Description: Description, p. 93
License-Plate Proposal: Description, p. 93
Essay: Literary Analysis/Interpretation, p. 108
Writing Mini-Lesson: Poetry, p. 104

Connections to Today's World

The four poems in this section use imagery to appeal to the readers' senses and help them imagine what the poet is describing. In a similar way, these song lyrics provide vivid images to help the listener understand the nature of the special relationship between the singer and a loved one.

Customize for
Less Proficient Readers
Arrange students in groups and have them listen to a recording of "The Wind Beneath My Wings." Then have volunteers read the lyrics aloud for the group. Encourage students to point out and discuss the effects of imagery used in the lyrics.

Customize for
More Advanced Students
Ask students to write an essay comparing and contrasting the relationship described in these lyrics to a relationship described in one of the poems in this lesson. Invite volunteers to read their essays aloud for the class.

Customize for
Musical/Rhythmic Learners
Allow interested students to work together to practice and then perform this song for the class. Students who play musical instruments might find sheet music in a music library. Vocalists may choose to sing the lyrics in unison, in harmony, or as a progression of solos, verse by verse.

CONNECTIONS TO TODAY'S WORLD

In "For My Sister Molly Who in the Fifties," the speaker pays tribute to her sister, Molly, who had a great influence on her life. This poetic "thank you" details Molly's generosity and caring qualities. In the popular song "The Wind Beneath My Wings," a similar tribute is paid to a person who provides the speaker with love and encouragement, enabling her to achieve success and fame. Originally written for the motion picture "Beaches," the sentiment in the song has touched a wide audience and become a modern classic.

The Wind Beneath My Wings

Larry Henley and Jeff Silbar

872 ◆ Poetry

Cross-Curricular Connection: Science

Airborne Effects Discuss with students how airplanes, like the eagle in the photographs on these pages, use air beneath their wings to keep them airborne. The shape of an airplane's wing (curved on top and straight on the bottom) is what helps to lift it off the ground and keep it in the air. Air flows faster over the curved portion of the wing than it does under the straight portion. This causes the air pressure beneath the wing to be greater than that above the wing. The suction effect created by this difference in pressure lifts the wing upward.

Invite interested students to use library resources or the Internet to explore other areas of flight. For example, they may want to learn how the flight of a bird differs from airplane flight. They may research the history of flight, pioneers in aviation history, and changes through the years in the design of airplanes. They may wish to compare hot-air balloon flights with airplane flights. Interested students may also find references and stories about flight in ancient mythology. Ask students to share what they learn with the class in a written report using illustrations.

It must have been cold there in my shadow,
To never have sunlight on your face.
You were content to let me shine, that's your way,
You always walked a step behind.
So, I was the one with all the glory,
While you were the one with all the strength.
A beautiful face without a name for so long,
A beautiful smile to hide the pain.

Did you ever know that you're my hero,
And everything I would like to be?
I can fly higher than an eagle,
'Cause you are the wind beneath my wings.

It might have appeared to go unnoticed,
But I've got it all here in my heart.
I want you to know I know the truth,
Of course I know it,
I would be nothing without you.

Did you ever know that you're my hero,
And everything I would like to be?
I can fly higher than an eagle,
'Cause you are the wind beneath my wings.

Fly, fly, fly away,
You let me fly so high.
Oh, fly, fly,
So high against the sky,
So high I almost touch the sky.
Thank you, thank you, thank God for you,
The wind beneath my wings.

1. Explain the meaning of the phrase "wind beneath my wings."
2. Name three things the speaker appreciates about her "hero."
3. In what ways are "For My Sister Molly . . ." and "The Wind Beneath My Wings" similar and different?

The Wind Beneath My Wings ◆ 873

◆ **Literary Focus**

❶ **Imagery** To what senses do the lyrics of this passage appeal? *The senses appealed to are feeling— cold there in my shadow, and sight—sunlight on your face.*

Thematic Connection

❷ Discuss what these lines reveal about the relationship between the speaker and the person being addressed. *The speaker is grateful to a loved one who provided unacknowledged support while the speaker was busy gaining success.*

◆ **Reading Strategy**

❸ **Use Your Senses** Ask students what they imagine when they read these lines and how the image helps them understand the relationship. *Students may see a bird like the one in the photograph soaring in the sky. They will probably recognize that, even though the air is not seen, it is the thing that makes the bird's flight possible.*

Answers

1. The phrase "wind beneath my wings" refers to the support that someone gives to a friend or loved one.
2. The speaker appreciates the "hero's" strength, support for him or her, and ability to let him or her "shine."
3. Both the poem and the song describe a caring, supportive person; the song differs from the poem because the person being described is not especially noticeable and is content to be in the shadows; Molly, in the poem, seems to be very high profile in a number of people's lives.

 Humanities: Music

Songs as Symbols Just as "The Wind Beneath My Wings" has become associated with the movie "Beaches," many other songs have become symbols and have come to be associated with an idea, a person, or a movie. Sometimes, songs become closely associated with a performer, such as "Somewhere Over the Rainbow," sung by Judy Garland in the unforgettable *Wizard of Oz*. The song has been performed many times since by many other singers, but it is associated with its original. Alternatively, songs like "The Star-Spangled Banner" have come to represent a nation and all it stands for. However, many students will also recall the shouted addition to the end of the song, "Play ball!" because it is often performed at the beginning of a ball game. Some songs have become symbols for holidays, such as "Come Ye Thankful People Come" (Thanksgiving), or places, such as "I Left My Heart in San Francisco."

Challenge students to list songs and the symbols they have come to represent. Interested students may wish to share recordings of their listed songs in a multimedia report.

OBJECTIVES

1. To read, comprehend, and interpret three poems
2. To relate three poems to personal experience
3. To respond to poetry
4. To recognize figurative language
5. To build vocabulary in context and learn commonly confused words
6. To use *like* and *as* correctly
7. To write a dialogue using figurative language
8. To respond to the poems through writing, speaking and listening, and projects

SKILLS INSTRUCTION

Vocabulary:
Commonly Confused Words: *continuously* and *continually*

Spelling:
Using *o* to Spell the *uh* Sound

Grammar:
Correct Use of *like* and *as*

Reading Strategy:
Respond

Literary Focus:
Figurative Language

Writing:
Use Figurative Language

Speaking and Listening:
Readers Theatre (Teacher Edition)

Critical Viewing:
Assess; Connect

PORTFOLIO OPPORTUNITIES

Writing: Personification; Report on Hidden Figures of Speech; Figurative Definition

Writing Mini-Lesson: Dialogue

Speaking and Listening: Readers Theatre; Oral Interpretation

Projects: Presentation and Discussion; Personification in Art

---

More About the Authors

Edwin Arlington Robinson won the Pulitzer Prize for several of his works. Though his poetry revealed a dark pessimism, Robinson retained the belief in a divine spark within all humans and nature.

Philip Larkin was the leading voice in a group of young English writers called "The Movement" who rejected the neo-Romantic writing style of Yeats and Thomas, focusing instead on pure, unsentimental emotion.

Donald Justice has held teaching positions at a number of prestigious universities during his career. In 1997, he was elected a Chancellor of The Academy of American Poets.

Guide for Reading

Meet the Authors:

Edwin Arlington Robinson (1869–1935)

Robinson was raised in Gardiner, Maine. This small town served as the model for Tilbury Town, the fictional setting of his finest poems. Many of his poems grew out of his childhood observations of Gardiner and focus on people's inner struggles.

Philip Larkin (1922–1985)

Larkin was a British poet whose clear-eyed, honest writing won him international fame. His poetry speaks of everyday realities, sometimes discouragingly, but is quietly haunted by realities beyond everyday life. In "Solar," he focuses on one of these greater realities: the sun.

Donald Justice (1925–   )

Donald Justice was awarded the Pulitzer Prize for his *Selected Poems* and the Bollingen Prize for his lifetime achievement in poetry.

THE STORY BEHIND THE POEM

Justice's poem was inspired by this traditional story set in southwestern Asia: A servant meets Death, a female, in the marketplace of Baghdad. Believing that Death has threatened him, the servant flees to the city of Samarra. The servant's employer asks Death why she threatened his servant. Death explains that she didn't threaten the servant: She was surprised to see him in Baghdad because she knew she had an appointment with him that night in Samarra!

874 ◆ Poetry

◆ **LITERATURE AND YOUR LIFE**

CONNECT YOUR EXPERIENCE

A movie *star,* a *jackknifed* tractor-trailer, a *bookworm*: These phrases are so common that you're often unaware they are comparisons. However, you can't miss the unusual and lively comparisons in these poems.

THEMATIC FOCUS: Respecting Nature

As you read, notice how the natural world inspires these poets.

◆ **Background for Understanding**

SCIENCE

In "Solar," Larkin uses a poetic language of comparison to describe the sun. Scientifically speaking, our sun is classified as a yellow star. It is 93 million miles from Earth. Basically a ball of gases, the sun provides the heat and light necessary to sustain life on Earth.

◆ **Build Vocabulary**

COMMONLY CONFUSED WORDS: *continuously* AND *continually*

Larkin writes in "Solar" that the sun is "Continuously exploding." Don't confuse *continuously*, which means "without interruption," with *continually*, which means "occurring again and again."

WORD BANK

Which of these words from the poems comes from the old word *becen*, meaning "a beacon or sign"? Check the Build Vocabulary Box on page 879 to see if you chose correctly.

hovers
legions
unrecompensed
continuously
scythe
beckoned
gestures

Prentice Hall Literature Program Resources

REINFORCE / RETEACH / EXTEND
Selection Support Pages
Build Vocabulary: Commonly Confused Words: *continuously* and *continually*, p. 301
Build Spelling Skills, p. 302
Building Grammar Skills: Correct Use of *like* and *as,* p. 303
Reading Strategy: Respond, p. 304
Literary Focus: Figurative Language, p. 305
Strategies for Diverse Student Needs, pp. 111–112

Beyond Literature Study Skills: Using an Outline, p. 56
Formal Assessment Selection Test, pp. 248–250, Assessment Resources Software
Alternative Assessment, p. 56
Writing and Language Transparencies, p. 57
Resource Pro CD-ROM "The Dark Hills"; "Solar"; "Incident in a Rose Garden"

 Listening to Literature Audiocassettes "The Dark Hills"; "Solar"; "Incident in a Rose Garden"

The Dark Hills ◆ Solar
◆ Incident in a Rose Garden ◆

Focus students' attention on the photograph on this page. Write the following on the board: *The hills are like _____.* Ask volunteers to complete the sentence in ways that describe the hills by comparing them to something else. For example, *The hills are like dark waves on a stormy sea.* Explain that the poems students are about to read use unlikely comparisons to describe objects or ideas. Encourage students to be aware of these unusual comparisons as they read the poems.

◆ Build Grammar Skills

Correct Use of *like* and *as* If you wish to introduce the grammar concept for this selection before students read, refer to the instruction on p. 880.

Customize for
Less Proficient Readers
Have students read along as they listen to the recordings of the poems. Then have them reread the poems silently by themselves or aloud to a partner.

Listening to Literature Audiocassettes

Customize for
More Advanced Students
Have students select one of the poems and write a literary analysis explaining the poem's meaning and mood. Encourage them to include references to figurative language used in the poem.

Customize for
English Language Learners
The poems in this group may be difficult for students to read and understand in English. Allow them to translate the poems into their first languages, getting help from class members as necessary. Tell them the poems need not rhyme but should follow the line pattern used by the poet. Then have groups discuss the poems in their first language. Volunteers may wish to share their translated poems with others in the class.

◆ Literary Focus
FIGURATIVE LANGUAGE
Based on comparisons, **figurative language** is an imaginative use of words that goes beyond dictionary meanings. A **simile** is a comparison of two apparently unlike items that uses the words *like* or *as*. A **metaphor** is a description of one item as if it were another, without using *like* or *as*. **Personification** is a description of something nonhuman as if it were human.

Use a chart like the one below to identify the figures of speech as you read:

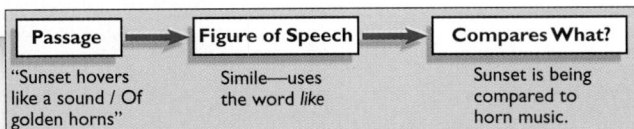

Passage	Figure of Speech	Compares What?
"Sunset hovers like a sound / Of golden horns"	Simile—uses the word *like*	Sunset is being compared to horn music.

◆ Reading Strategy
RESPOND
Poetry will sleep on a page unless you **respond** to it, bringing your own experience to the words. Use your memory and senses to picture what the poet describes. Feel the beat of the rhythm, just as you do when you listen to a song.

When reading these poems, focus your response on the figurative language. Picture the items being compared. No matter how different they are, search for the hidden similarities that the poet has found.

Preparing for Standardized Tests

Vocabulary Standardized tests may test students' ability to correctly use commonly confused words. Review the following pairs of commonly confused words—*continuously/continually, besides/beside, infer/imply*—and have volunteers demonstrate the words' correct usage in sentences. Then write the following sample question on the board:

Find the sentence that contains an underlined word that is not used correctly.

(A) The clock ticked <u>continually</u> and kept me awake.

(B) She placed a candle <u>beside</u> the vase of flowers.

(C) I did not mean to <u>imply</u> that you were wrong.

(D) No mistake.

Lead students to see that the answer is *(A)*, as *continually* means "frequently repeated" rather than "without interruption." Both *(B)* and *(C)* are correct, as the candle was placed "next to" the flowers and *suggest* could be used in place of *imply*. For more practice, use Build Vocabulary in **Selection Support,** p. 301

Develop Understanding

One-Minute Insight

In "The Dark Hills," Edwin Arlington Robinson compares a warrior burial ground to a bright, flag-bordered street filled with marching legions. He uses these phrases to describe the ending of a day. Then he addresses the sun directly, saying it seemed as if it were the end of time.

◆ Literary Focus

❶ Figurative Language Ask students to identify the type of figurative language used in this passage and to tell what two things are being compared. *A simile is used to compare the sunset to the sound of golden horns.*

◆ Reading Strategy

❷ Respond Have students describe what they imagine when they read these lines. *Students may say they see soldiers marching down a street lined with banners and flags on a bright, sunny day.*

►Critical Viewing◄

❸ Assess *They look forbidding. The dark red color and lack of vegetation make the hills look very hot and dangerous.*

THE DARK HILLS

Edwin Arlington Robinson

> Dark hills at evening in the west,
> Where sunset <u>hovers</u> like a sound
> ❶ Of golden horns that sang to rest
> Old bones of warriors under ground,
> 5 Far now from all the bannered ways
> ❷ Where flash the <u>legions</u> of the sun,
> You fade—as if the last of days
> Were fading, and all wars were done.

◆ Build Vocabulary

hovers (huv´ ərz) v.: Suspends; lingers

legions (lē´ jənz) n.: Large number; multitude

unrecompensed (un rek´ əm penst´) v.: Unrewarded

continuously (kən tin´ yo͞o əs lē) adv.: Extending without interruption

❸ ▼ **Critical Viewing** Are the dark hills in this painting inviting or forbidding? Explain. [Assess]

Red Hills, Lake George, 1927, Georgia O'Keeffe, The Phillips Collection, Washington, DC

876 ◆ *Poetry*

Block Scheduling Strategies

Consider these suggestions to take advantage of extended class time:

- Review the Literary Focus before students read. As they read the poems, have them fill in a chart like the one on p. 875. Then have groups of students compare and discuss their charts as they answer the Literary Focus questions on p. 880. For additional support, use **Selection Support,** p. 305.

- Alternatively, have groups of students read the poems aloud and discuss the Guide for

Responding questions on pp. 877 and 879. Then have the group prepare and present the Readers Theatre from the Idea Bank on p. 881.

- Have students use the Series of Events Chain, p. 57, in the **Writing and Language Transparencies** to organize details for their Dialogues in the Writing Mini-Lesson, p. 881. You may also want to have students work in small groups using the *Writer's Solution Writing Lab CD-ROM* to complete the Writing Mini-Lesson.

SOLAR[1]

PHILIP LARKIN

Suspended lion face
Spilling at the centre[2]
Of an unfurnished sky
How still you stand,
5 And how unaided
Single stalkless flower
You pour unrecompensed. **④**

The eye sees you
Simplified by distance
10 Into an origin,
Your petalled head of flames
Continuously exploding.
Heat is the echo of your **⑤**
Gold.

15 Coined there among
Lonely horizontals
You exist openly.
Our needs hourly
Climb and return like angels.
20 Unclosing like a hand,
You give for ever.

---

1. **solar:** Of or having to do with the sun.
2. **centre:** British spelling of *center*.

Develop Understanding

One-Minute Insight In "Solar" Philip Larkin speaks to the sun. He uses figurative language and other vivid descriptions to express admiration and respect. The poem emphasizes the importance of the sun to all life.

◆ Reading Strategy

④ Responding Ask students how their experiences with the sun help them understand this description. *You can't really look directly at the sun overhead, but pictures of the sun in a cloudless sky reflect the poet's comparisons.*

◆ Literary Focus

⑤ Figurative Language Have students identify and discuss the figurative language in these lines. *The sun's heat is described metaphorically as an echo of its gold—the heat is secondary to the sun's gold light.*

Reinforce and Extend

Answers

◆ LITERATURE AND YOUR LIFE

Reader's Response Students might describe the sun setting into the ocean; a desert sunrise; or hot, noonday sun.

Thematic Focus The sun is common to both these poems.

☑ **Check Your Comprehension**

1. He compares the setting sun to the sound of golden horns.
2. He compares the sun to a lion face, a stalkless flower, and a petalled head of flames.

◆ Critical Thinking

1. "Hovers like ..." describes the golden rays of the sun before it sets. "You fade" describes the fading light as the sun sets.
2. The details give a feeling of something beautiful that once was but is now lost forever.
3. The poem is a series of descriptions. There is no story line.
4. They show that Larkin recognizes the need all living things have for the gifts from the sun.
5. Like its title, the mood of "The Dark Hills" is dark, like the night. The mood of "Solar" is as hopeful and bright as the sun it describes.

Guide for Responding

◆ LITERATURE AND YOUR LIFE

Reader's Response Briefly describe a time when you saw the sun in a fresh way—whether at dawn, midday, or sunset.

Thematic Focus Describe the element of nature common to both these poems.

Monologue Write and deliver a brief speech the sun might make in response to "Solar."

☑ **Check Your Comprehension**

1. To what does Robinson compare the sunset in "The Dark Hills"?
2. List three things to which Larkin compares the sun in "Solar."

Critical Thinking

INTERPRET

1. Find two phrases in "The Dark Hills" that help you experience the sunset. Explain. **[Analyze]**
2. What overall feeling do the details in "The Dark Hills" create? Why? **[Interpret]**
3. Does Larkin organize "Solar" as a story or as a series of descriptions? Explain. **[Analyze]**
4. How do the last four lines of "Solar" reveal Larkin's attitude toward the sun? **[Infer]**

COMPARE LITERARY WORKS

5. In what way do these two poems communicate opposite moods? **[Compare and Contrast]**

 Humanities: Art

Red Hills, Lake George, 1927, by Georgia O'Keeffe

Wisconsin-born Georgia O'Keeffe (1887–1986) decided to become an artist at age 10. After studying at the Art Institute of Chicago, she spent a number of years teaching art in public schools. While teaching in rural north Texas, O'Keeffe became fascinated with the stark beauty of the plains and rolling hills. Later, after achieving success in New York art circles, O'Keeffe moved permanently to New Mexico, where she created many of the works for which she is best known.

1. Lake George is in Wisconsin. Do these hills look like your impression of a Wisconsin landscape? Why or why not? *I think of Wisconsin as having green rolling hills in the summer and snow-covered land in the winter.*
2. Why do you think the artist chose to show the hills in this way? *She shows her vision of the landscape rather than showing it as it actually exists.*
3. Why is this a good illustration for this poem? *The dark hills in the painting look as if they are being colored red by the sun setting behind them, similar to the scene described in the poem.*

One-Minute Insight In "Incident in a Rose Garden," Donald Justice tells the story of a gardener who encounters Death. Thinking Death has come for him, the gardener tells his master he is quitting so he can see his sons once more before he dies. The master confronts Death and tells him he is not welcome. Death responds that he had not meant to threaten the gardener, because he had actually come for the master.

Listening to Literature Videodisc/Videotape

To capture students' interest and motivate them to read "Incident in a Rose Garden," play Chapter 9 of the videodisc. The segment begins with a presentation of "Incident in a Rose Garden," followed by one student's response to the poem. Ask students to compare and contrast the student's response to the poem with their own responses.

Chapter 9

▶Critical Viewing◀

❶ Connect *The setting is so beautiful and so alive with flowers and birds that a dark presence like Death would seem out of place.*

Humanities: Art

China Roses, Broadway, by Alfred William Parsons

This decorative, realistic painting shows a rose garden in full bloom. A flock of birds adds interest to the inviting space. Discuss the painting using questions such as these:

1. What would you smell, hear, and feel if you were in this garden?
   You would smell the flowers and grass, hear the birds and the garden door creaking open; feel the warmth of the sun or a soft breeze.
2. What is the mood of the painting?
   It has a calm, peaceful mood.

Incident in a Rose Garden
Donald Justice

China Roses, Broadway, Alfred William Parsons, Christopher Wood Gallery, London, UK

878 ◆ Poetry

◀ **Critical Viewing** Why would a figure like Death be so startling to encounter in a setting such as this? **[Connect]** ❶

Speaking and Listening Mini-Lesson

Readers Theatre
This mini-lesson supports the Speaking and Listening activity in the Idea Bank on p. 881.

Introduce Explain that Readers Theatre is a dramatic reading of a piece of literature, in which participants take parts and read aloud in expressive voices. Unlike actors in a play, readers do not memorize lines or use costumes or props, and usually remain seated during the performance.

Develop Arrange students in groups of three, and have them decide who will read each of the three parts. Instruct students to decide how they

will use their voices, gestures, and facial expressions to convey the poem's meaning and mood.

Apply Provide time for groups to rehearse. Encourage them to explore different interpretations. Then have each group present its Readers Theatre for the class.

Assess After the readings, lead a class discussion about variations among the presentations. Evaluate students' work based on the interpretive quality of their presentations, or use the Peer Assessment: Dramatic Performance form, p. 116, **in Alternative Assessment.**

◆ **Reading Strategy**

❸ **Respond** Have students discuss what they imagine when they read these lines. *Students may picture skeletons, whose mouths look wide and filled with teeth, and imagine one of these dressed all in black.*

Gardener:	Sir, I encountered Death Just now among our roses. Thin as a <u>scythe</u> he stood there.

5
I knew him by his pictures.
He had his black coat on,
Black gloves, a broad black hat.

❸

I think he would have spoken.
Seeing his mouth stood open.
Big it was, with white teeth.

❷

10
As soon as he <u>beckoned</u>, I ran.
I ran until I found you.
Sir, I am quitting my job.

I want to see my sons
Once more before I die.
15
I want to see California.

Master: Sir, you must be that stranger
Who threatened my gardener.
This is my property, sir.

I welcome only friends here.
20 **Death:** Sir, I knew your father.
And we were friends at the end.

As for your gardener,
I did not threaten him.
Old men mistake my <u>gestures</u>.

25
I only meant to ask him
To show me to his master.
I take it you are he?

Guide for Responding

◆ **LITERATURE AND YOUR LIFE**

Reader's Response Do you find this poem amusing or alarming? Explain.

Thematic Focus What message about nature does this poem convey?

Journal Writing As the Gardener, write a diary entry describing your encounter with Death.

☑ **Check Your Comprehension**

1. Describe Death as he appears in the poem.
2. What does Death do to make the Gardener run away?
3. Paraphrase what the Master says to Death.
4. Whom does Death really want?

◆ **Critical Thinking**

1. In what way do lines 25–27 give you a surprising view of the Gardener's flight? **[Connect]**
2. What does Death mean when he tells the Master, "I knew your father. / And we were friends at the end"? **[Interpret]**
3. Why do you think old men "mistake" Death's "gestures"? **[Interpret]**
4. What do you think Death wants from the Master? **[Infer]**
5. The Master is full of pride. What lesson does he learn? **[Draw Conclusions]**

APPLY
6. Is there a lesson about life that you can take from this poem? Explain. **[Apply]**

COMPARE LITERARY WORKS
7. Compare "Incident . . ." with the traditional story that inspired it (see The Story Behind the Poem, p. 874). **[Compare and Contrast]**

Incident in a Rose Garden ◆ 879

Reinforce and Extend

Answers
◆ **LITERATURE AND YOUR LIFE**

Reader's Response Students may say they find it alarming, because they don't like to think about a scary person calling on people to die.

Thematic Focus Even in a beautiful setting like a rose garden, there is a cycle of life, which includes death.

☑ **Check Your Comprehension**
1. He is dressed all in black and has a wide mouth with obvious teeth.
2. He beckons the gardener.
3. You have no right to be on my property frightening my gardener. You are not welcome here.
4. Death really wants the master.

◆ **Critical Thinking**
1. The gardener did not have to leave because Death was not coming for him.
2. He means that the Master's father has already died.
3. They expect that Death will be coming for them, since they are near the end of their lives.
4. Death wants the Master to go with him and die.
5. He learns that his pride cannot help him escape from Death.
6. We never know when our lives might end.
7. In the original story, Death is a female, not a male as in the poem; she threatens a servant in a marketplace instead of a gardener in a rose garden. The idea of Death coming to get someone is the same.

◆ **Build Vocabulary**

scythe (sīth) *n.*: Long tool with a single-edged blade used in cutting tall grass

beckoned (bek′ ənd) *v.*: Summoned by a silent motion; called

gestures (jes′ chərz) *n.*: Movements used to convey an idea, emotion, or intention

Beyond the Selection

FURTHER READING
Other Works by the Authors
Selected Poems, Edward Arlington Robinson
The Essential Robinson, Edward Arlington Robinson
Collected Poems: Philip Larkin, Philip Larkin
A Girl in Winter, Philip Larkin
New and Selected Poems, Donald Justice

INTERNET
We suggest the following sites on the Internet (all Web sites are subject to change).
For more on Edward Arlington Robinson:
http://www.accd.edu/Sac/english/bailey/robinson.htm
For more poems by Philip Larkin:
http://redfrog.norconnect.no/poems/poetpage?author=Philip+Larkin
For more on Donald Justice:
http://www.poems.com/~poems/selecjus.htm
We *strongly recommend* that you preview these sites before you send students to them.

◆ Reading Strategy

Possible Responses:
1. "Far now from all the bannered ways/Where flash the legions of the sun" created an image of the bright and glorious day that preceded the sunset.
2. I did not like the image of Death. I think the image would have been more frightening in a more sinister setting.

◆ Build Vocabulary

Using Commonly Confused Words

implies should be *infers*. The gardener deduces something about the stranger's behavior.

besides should be *beside*. Death stood next to the Master.

Spelling Strategy
1. lovers; 2. brother; 3. above

Using the Word Bank
1. Something that hovers remains in one place; while something that soars travels through the sky.
2. *Legions* means many; while *several* means only a few.
3. *Unrecompensed* is the opposite of *paid.*
4. *Continuously* means "without stopping," while *continually* means "frequently repeated."
5. A scythe has a long blade and is used for cutting grass; an ax has a short blade and is used for chopping wood.
6. To beckon means to call forward; to dismiss is to let go.

◆ Literary Focus

1. "Solar" includes comparisons to living things, such as a lion and a flower to describe the sun. It compares the sun to an open hand to describe the way in which the sun is giving.
2. No, Death must be a character if the story is to make sense.

◆ Build Grammar Skills

1. Like
2. as if
3. like
4. as though
5. As

◆ Guide for Responding (continued)

◆ Reading Strategy

RESPOND

You **responded** to the figurative language in these poems by thinking about the comparisons the poets made. For example, you may have responded to Larkin's comparison of the sun to a "lion face."
1. Which image or phrase in "The Dark Hills" provoked the strongest response in you? Explain.
2. How did you respond to the image of Death in a rose garden? Would your response have been different if Death had appeared in a more sinister setting? Why or why not?

◆ Build Vocabulary

USING COMMONLY CONFUSED WORDS

Note these commonly confused words: *continuously* ("without interruption") and *continually* ("frequently repeated"); *beside* ("next to") and *besides* ("in addition to"); and *imply* ("suggest") and *infer* ("deduce"). On your paper, correct any misused italicized words, and explain your changes:

The Gardener *implies* from the stranger's behavior that danger threatens. Death then stands *besides* the Master, saying that old men *continually* mistake his gestures.

SPELLING STRATEGY

The *uh* sound is sometimes spelled with an *o* rather than a *u*, as in *hovers* and *other*. Working on your own paper, correct any of the following words that are misspelled.
1. of   2. luvers   3. bruther   4. abuve   5. mother

USING THE WORD BANK

On your paper, answer each question:
1. What's the difference between *hovers* and *soars*?
2. What's the difference between *legions* and *several*?
3. What's the difference between *unrecompensed* and *paid*?
4. What's the difference between *continuously* and *continually*?
5. What's the difference between *scythe* and *ax*?
6. What's the difference between *beckoned* and *dismissed*?

◆ Literary Focus

FIGURATIVE LANGUAGE

These poets enable you to see the world in a fresh way by using **figurative language,** such as **simile** (comparison with *like* or *as*), **metaphor** (comparison without *like* or *as*), and **personification** (giving human qualities to the nonhuman). If "The Dark Hills" didn't use comparisons to describe a sunset, you'd think only of a day's end. Through simile ("sunset hovers like a sound") and metaphor ("legions of the sun"), the poem suggests the end of "all wars."
1. Show how "Solar" uses metaphor and simile to suggest that the sun is living and giving.
2. Without personification, could "Incident in a Rose Garden" effectively convey its message about death? Explain.

◆ Build Grammar Skills

CORRECT USE OF *like* AND *as*

Like and **as** are sometimes confused. *Like* is a preposition introducing a prepositional phrase. *As* may be a preposition, but *as* (or *as if* or *as though*) is also a subordinating conjunction in a clause with a noun and a verb. Don't use *like* as a conjunction.

Like: Where sunset hovers *like* a sound/Of golden horns . . . (prepositional phrase: like a sound)

As: You fade—*as if* [not *like*] the last of days/Were fading . . . (subordinating conjunction)

Practice On your paper, choose *like* or a form of *as* for each sentence. Then, explain your choice.
1. (Like, As) Larkin, I feel strongly about the sun.
2. The Master acts (like, as if) he doesn't recognize Death.
3. Robinson's poem is itself (as, like) a horn melody.
4. Larkin addresses the sun (like, as though) it were a person.
5. (Like, As) I was telling you, Robinson is a great poet.

Writing Application On your paper, write a description of the moon using two sentences with *like* and two with *as*.

Writing Application

Sample answer: The moon looked like a large ball in the sky. It seemed as if it would not be able to rise above the trees. Moonlight fell like silver across the lawn. It looked as bright as day.

✒ Writer's Solution

For additional practice and instruction on usage problems, have students use the practice page on Twenty Common Usage Problems, p. 92, in the *Writer's Solution Grammar Practice Book.* If students have access to technology, have them use the lesson on Special Problems With Pronouns in the Using Pronouns unit of the *Writer's Solution Language Lab CD-ROM.*

Build Your Portfolio

Idea Bank

Writing

1. **Personification** Create a cartoon character based on the personification of a natural phenomenon, like a hurricane. Describe what the character would look like, wear, and carry. Also, think of an appropriate name for the character.

2. **Report on Hidden Figures of Speech** Find five similes or metaphors that are hidden in common words and phrases, like *skyscraper*. Then, explain how each of your choices is a simile, metaphor, or personification.

3. **Figurative Definition** Write a definition of a word or a concept, like justice, using similes and metaphors rather than synonyms.

Speaking and Listening

4. **Readers Theatre [Group Activity]** With a few classmates, give a dramatic reading of "Incident in a Rose Garden." You can remain seated, but you should read your parts with expression. **[Performing Arts Link]**

5. **Oral Interpretation** Read one of these poems aloud for the class. Remember to pause briefly for commas and longer for end marks. Don't automatically stop at the ends of lines where there is no punctuation. **[Performing Arts Link]**

Projects

6. **Presentation and Discussion** Describe a natural phenomenon using both scientific terms and figures of speech. Then, present both descriptions to the class, and invite questions from the class. **[Science Link]**

7. **Personification in Art** Find paintings in which Death is personified, as in Albert Pinkham Ryder's *The Race Track* or *Death on a Pale Horse*. Display copies of these for the class, and write captions comparing the personifications. **[Art Link]**

Writing Mini-Lesson

Dialogue

"Incident in a Rose Garden" is a dialogue in the form of a poem. Write your own dialogue, using two or more characters. Imitate "Incident in a Rose Garden" by making your dialogue into a complete scene in which characters face and solve a problem. You can have your characters speak in prose rather than poetry. However, they should sometimes use figurative language.

Writing Skills Focus: Use Figurative Language

When characters use **figurative language,** they add to the drama and interest of what they're saying. For example, the Gardener in "Incident . . ." uses a simile, a comparison with *like* or *as*, to describe Death:

> ##### Model From the Poem
> Sir, I encountered Death/Just now among our roses./*Thin* as a *scythe* he stood there.

Prewriting Invent two or three characters, and give them a problem to solve. Plan how the problem will build to a climax and be resolved.

Drafting Have the characters engage with each other to solve the problem you have given them. Step into the shoes of each character as you write his or her words. The more you identify with the characters and get excited with them, the more naturally they'll "speak" in figurative language.

Revising Be sure that your dialogue introduces and resolves a problem. Also, check that your characters use some figurative language—metaphors as well as similes.

> ◆ **Grammar Application**
> Check your dialogue to be sure you've used *like* and *as* correctly.

Idea Bank

Following are suggestions for matching the Idea Bank topics with your students' performance levels and learning modalities:

Customize for *Performance Levels*
Less Advanced Students: 1, 4, 7
Average Students: 2, 4, 5, 7
More Advanced Students: 3, 5, 6

Customize for *Learning Modalities*
Verbal/Linguistic: 1, 2, 3, 4, 5, 6
Logical/Mathematical: 6
Visual/Spatial: 1, 7
Interpersonal: 4
Intrapersonal: 1, 2, 3, 6, 7

Writing Mini-Lesson

Refer students to the Writing Handbook in the back of the book for instruction on the writing process and for further information on dialogue.

Writer's Solution

Writing Lab CD-ROM
Have students complete the tutorial on Creative Writing. Follow these steps:

1. Have students view the interactive model of a dialogue.
2. Suggest that students view the Interactive dialogue models to see how different characters might use different kinds of dialogue.
3. Allow students to draft on computer.
4. To help in revising, have students view the interactive revision dialogue models.

Writer's Solution Sourcebook
Have students use Chapter 9, "Creative Writing," pp. 234–265 for additional support. This chapter includes in-depth instruction on writing dialogue for a play, p. 258.

✓ ASSESSMENT OPTIONS

Formal Assessment, Selection Test, pp. 248–250, and Assessment Resources Software. The selection test is designed so that it can easily be customized to the performance levels of your students.

Alternative Assessment, p. 56, includes options for less advanced students, more advanced students, logical/mathematical learners, interpersonal learners, verbal/linguistic learners, and visual/spatial learners.

PORTFOLIO ASSESSMENT
Use the following rubrics in the **Alternative Assessment** booklet to assess student writing:
Personification: Description, p. 93
Report on Hidden Figures of Speech: Technical Description/Explanation, p. 111
Figurative Definition: Definition/Classification, p. 95
Writing Mini-Lesson: Fictional Narrative, p. 91

Establish Writing Guidelines
Review the following key characteristics of a poem:

- A poem expresses a writer's thoughts or feelings on a subject.

- Poems can use sound devices such as alliteration, rhyme, repetition, and figurative language, including similes and metaphors.

- Poems are often written in lines grouped into stanzas.

You may want to distribute the scoring rubric for Poetry, p. 104 in **Alternative Assessment,** to make students aware of the criteria on which they will be evaluated. See the suggestions on p. 884 for how you can customize the rubric to this workshop.

Refer students to the Writing Handbook in the back of the book for instruction on the writing process and further information on creative writing.

Writer's Solution

Writers at Work Videodisc
To introduce students to creative writing and to show them what writer Julia Alvarez says about creative writing, play the videodisc segment on Creative Writing (Ch. 8). Ask students to consider what Alvarez says she learns about herself through writing.

Play frames 19343 to 27848

Writing Lab CD-ROM
If your students have access to computers, you may want to have them work in the tutorial on Creative Writing to complete all or part of their poems. Follow these steps:

1. Have students view the interactive model of a poem.
2. Suggest that students use the Concrete Image Bin Activity to gather sensory words.
3. Allow students to draft on computer.
4. Have students use the Self-Evaluation Checklist for poetry when revising.

Writer's Solution Sourcebook
Students can find additional support, including in-depth instruction on using figurative language, pp. 264–265, in the chapter on Creative Writing, pp. 234–265.

Creative Writing
Poem

Writing Process Workshop

As you can see from this unit, just about anything can become a poet's subject: memories, sports, sounds, or love. Now it's time to try your hand at writing a poem. Choose a moment of your own experience that was important to you—something that was especially fun, exciting, sad, frustrating, or beautiful. You might write a lyric poem or a narrative poem. It might rhyme or it might not. The important part is that no one else could have written it—just you.

Use these Writing Skills, covered in the Writing Mini-Lessons in this part, to help you:

Writing Skills Focus

▶ **Use repetition** of a key word, phrase, or line for emphasis and rhythm. (See p. 861.)

▶ **Create a dominant image** that guides your writing and your readers' reading. (See p. 871.)

▶ **Use figurative language** to give your poem interest and variety. (See p. 881.)

One young poet wrote this lyric poem after a weekend camping trip:

MODEL

Northern Lights

Someone took a paint box ① and a black
   velvet night,
Blended pinks and turquoise until she got
   it right.
She brushed and she studied and stood
   back very far,
Then threw glitter—and each piece
   became a star. ②
She watercolored streaks of yellow, gold,
   and red,
Then put away her paint box ③ and
   snuggled back in bed.

① The image of a painter painting dominates this poem.

② The metaphor "each piece became a star" provides an interesting comparison.

③ Repeating *paint box* emphasizes the dominant image and brings the poem full circle.

 Beyond the Classroom

Community Connection
Poetry Readings and Poetry Slams Explain to students that popular events in many cafes, bookstores, and community centers are poetry readings and poetry slams. In a poetry reading, one or several poets may recite poems they have written. Sometimes, the poets are chosen to represent their ideas on a specific topic or to commemorate a special event. In poetry slams, poets compete with one another in a recital rivalry. The first poetry slam was organized by Marc Smith

and held in the Green Mill in Chicago. The event became popular, and other people started similar slams in Boston, San Francisco, and New York. Today, there are virtual slams on the World Wide Web.

Have students research poetry readings and poetry slams in their community or on the World Wide Web. Encourage them to compile a list of rules for a poetry slam. Then, suggest that students stage their own poetry readings and poetry slams.

Prewriting

Choose a Topic Choose a subject or a topic for your poem. You may want to choose a topic that is unique and meaningful, startling, frightening, hilarious, or lovely. Here are a few suggestions to spark your imagination:

> ## Topic Ideas
> - A person's face
> - An animal you've loved
> - A delicious food
> - A machine you think is cool

Make a Sensory Chart Don't just rely on your sense of sight. Include sounds (and sound words), tastes—even smells. Appeal to the sense of touch. Make your poem as rich as the experience itself.

Decide on a Dominant Image What is the main idea you want to convey? For example, is your dog funny, sad, clumsy, old, crazy, or lazy? Is he your best friend or a big pest? Once you settle on a dominant impression, make the details of your poem contribute to it.

Drafting

Use Figurative Language Compare the subject of your poem to various things, people, or places. To create a simile, connect the image with *like* or *as*. To create a metaphor, describe your subject as if it were the thing to which you're comparing it. Other forms of figurative language include personification—investing your subject with humanlike qualities—and hyperbole—greatly exaggerating your subject's qualities or abilities.

Repeat for Effect If you've got a great line—or a great word—repeat it for emphasis and rhythm.

Make Every Word Count Since poems are short, take the time to make every word ring with truth. For example, in the model poem about the Northern Lights, the poet chose *turquoise* instead of just *blue, brushed* and *watercolored* instead of just *painted,* and *threw* instead of just *put.* Use a dictionary or thesaurus to discover wonderfully rich words.

DRAFTING/REVISING

APPLYING LANGUAGE SKILLS: Avoiding Clichés

A cliché is an expression that is overused. Avoid clichés in your writing. Instead, rephrase your ideas or create new, fresh comparisons.

Cliché: As happy as a clam

New comparison: As happy as a playful puppy

Newly phrased: Radiating happiness

Cliché: Raining cats and dogs

Newly phrased: Wall to wall rain

Personification: The rain viciously pelted the houses.

Practice Rewrite these clichés to convey original ideas:

1. Quiet as a mouse
2. A deafening silence
3. Like a ton of bricks
4. Bubbling over with enthusiasm
5. Mother Nature

Writing Application Avoid using clichés in your poetry. Rephrase or create new comparisons.

Writer's Solution Connection Language Lab

For help with figurative language, complete the lessons on Simile and Metaphor in the Choosing Words unit.

Writing Process Workshop ◆ 883

Prewriting

To help gather topic ideas, suggest to students that they reread any old journals or letters they may have for a special moment. Or, have them browse through photo albums to stir up ideas for a poem.

Customize for
Musical/Rhythmic Learners
Students who have an appreciation for music may be able to come up with ideas for a poem by listening to a favorite song or album. As they listen, have students jot down words or phrases about how the music affects them. Then encourage students to use these words and phrases as a starting point for their poems.

 **Writer's Solution**

Writing Lab CD-ROM
For more topic ideas, suggest that students browse through the Inspirations for Creative Writing in the Prewriting section of the tutorial on Creative Writing.

Drafting

When drafting, have students consider what their poem is about and then choose an appropriate form for the poem. A poem that tells a story, for example, is a narrative poem and may be grouped into stanzas that show the progression of the action. A lyric poem expresses a feeling or mood and may have lines of irregular length that create a musical rhythm.

Writer's Solution

Writing Lab CD-ROM
In the drafting section of the tutorial on Creative Writing, suggest that students view the Annotated Student Models of drafts of poems. Students can view different types of poems and learn about the decisions the authors made in their drafts.

Applying Language Skills

Avoiding Clichés Explain to students that clichés are sometimes called dead metaphors, meaning they have lost their power to create a strong image or feeling.

Answers
Possible responses:
1. Quiet as snow falling
2. A heart-wrenching silence
3. Like carrying a dead cow
4. Giggling wildly with enthusiasm
5. Natura

Revising

Encourage students, when revising, to look for vague words that can be replaced with more specific and lively words. In addition, suggest that students look for places where they can add sound devices, such as alliteration, repetition, or onomatopoeia.

 Writer's Solution

Writing Lab CD-ROM

In the Revising and Editing section of the tutorial on Creative Writing, have students view the writing hints and models for revising poems.

Publishing

For other publishing ideas, suggest that students post their poems on a class Web site.

Reinforce and Extend

Review the Writing Guidelines
After students have completed their papers, review the characteristics of a poem.

Applying Language Skills
Choosing the Correct
Homophone Other examples of homophones include *bail* and *bale*; *stair* and *stare*; *knew* and *new*; and *ware* and *wear*.

Answers
1. Two children wanted to go, too.
2. They're doing their homework now.
3. How can I bear life without you?
4. Whose papers are these?
5. Night fell over the town.

884

EDITING/PROOFREADING

Applying Language Skills: Choosing the Correct Homophone

Words that sound alike but have different meanings and spellings are called homophones. Check to be sure that you've selected the correct homophone in your writing.

Examples:

to, two, too

their, they're, there

threw, through

so, sew, sow

Practice On your paper, write the correct homophone for each passage.

1. (To, Too, Two) children wanted to go, (to, too, two).
2. (They're, Their) doing (they're, their) homework now.
3. How can I (bare, bear) life without you?
4. (Who's, Whose) papers are these?
5. (Night, knight) fell over the town.

Writing Application In your poem, be sure you've chosen the correct homophones.

Writer's Solution Connection Writing Lab

For help revising, use the Proofreading Checklist for Poetry in the Creative Writing tutorial.

884 ◆ Poetry

Revising

Use a Checklist Use the Writing Skills Focus points on page 882 as a revision checklist. An effective poem usually contains these elements.

Read It Aloud Read your poem aloud to yourself or to a peer. Consider adding repetition to emphasize ideas. Be sure the figurative language you've used is fresh and original; if not, delete it. Lastly, delete or revise details that do not support the dominant image you've created.

Keep It Short The delete key can be the poet's best friend. If some lines in your poem are weak or not really working, don't be afraid to cross them out. Your poem will be better for it.

REVISION MODEL

① It is Twilight

② Like a purple cloud

Soft purple hazy

End of day

Sleeping

③ dwindling dwindling

Dwindling fading ebbing

Night

① To make the image more dominant, the writer deleted "It is."
② This simile lends interest to the poem.
③ Repetition makes this line more memorable and to the point.

Publishing and Presenting

Classroom Collect poems into a class anthology in which everyone contributes one poem. Together, choose a title. Have volunteers design a cover, create a table of contents, and even write a brief introduction. If possible, make sure each contributor gets one copy to keep.

Podium With classmates, hold a poetry reading in your class or school. Take turns reading your poetry.

Real-World Reading Skills Workshop

Breaking Down Difficult Texts

Strategies for Success

Occasionally you have to read something that appears difficult, such as a technical manual or a research article. The sentence structure and vocabulary can look overwhelming. The following strategies can help you break down difficult texts so that you can get what you need from them:

Preview the Selection First, get an overall sense of the work. Note its title, which provides you with clues to its content. Then, look at the organization of the piece, its length, its chapters or sections, and its use of study questions. If there are subtitles, read them for clues to the content.

Break It Into Sections Tackle only one section at a time. Use captions, highlighted words, footnotes, and sidenotes. These aids offer additional information to help you understand the text. Next, go through the text sentence by sentence. If a sentence is long, break it into parts where commas appear. Read the text once for general meaning. Then, go back and reread those parts you didn't understand fully.

Decipher the Vocabulary As you read, note any words that are unfamiliar. Try to figure out a word's meaning from its context—how it's used in the passage. If this doesn't work, look up the word in a dictionary before rereading.

✔ Here are situations in which you might use these strategies for breaking down difficult texts:
▶ Reading Shakespearean plays and sonnets
▶ Reading school texts
▶ Reading a contract

Apply the Strategies

Answer the following questions about the passage below. Use the strategies from this lesson to help you.

1. Scan the passage, and break it into sections.
2. Use context clues to determine the meaning of *pedagogy, valor, amaranthine.*
3. What is *Crispin Crispian?* How do you know?
4. What is the general meaning of Prince Hal's speech?

The Use of Shakespeare's Speeches in Military Leadership

For many years, Shakespeare's speeches have been part of the pedagogy of military academies as examples of inspiration, leadership, and valor.

The Inspirational Speech

Prince Hal inspires his men with his own bravery and promises them not only unending, amaranthine glory but brotherhood with him—their noble and extraordinary king and leader:

This story shall the good man teach his son:
And Crispin Crispian[1] shall ne'er go by,
From this day to the ending of the world,
But we in it shall be remembered—
We few, we happy few, we band of brothers.

Henry V: 4.3

1. The feast day of St. Crispin, October 25.

Introduce the Strategies

Have students discuss different types of texts they have read for their different classes. Ask them to consider which reading they find the most difficult and why. Explain that by learning how to break down difficult texts, students can improve their overall reading ability.

Customize for
Less Proficient Readers

Some students may do best taking notes while reading difficult texts. They can first mark down the title of the text and a note about what they think that title means. As they read the text, encourage them to jot down unfamiliar words and phrases. After they look up the meanings of these words, have them reread the text for a better understanding.

Apply the Strategies

Remind students that when reading difficult texts, they should read slowly and try to understand each sentence rather than read for speed.

Answers

1. The passage can be broken down into the introduction about Shakespeare's speeches used in the military, information on the use of a speech as inspiration, and an example from Shakespeare of an inspirational speech.
2. *Pedagogy* means schooling or instruction; *valor* means courage; *amaranthine* means never-ending
3. Crispin Crispian is the feast day of St. Crispin on October 25. You know this from the footnote.
4. The general meaning of Prince Hal's speech is that his men will be remembered for the glory and courage, and also will establish ties of brotherhood with him and with one another.

◆ Build Grammar Skills

Reviewing Usage Problems

The selections in Part 2 include instruction on the following:

- Correct Use of Adjectives and Adverbs
- Pronouns in Comparison with *than* or *as*
- Correct Use of *as* and *like*

This instruction is reinforced with the Build Grammar Skills practice pages in **Selection Support,** pp. 289, 294, and 299.

As you review subject and verb agreement, you may wish to include the following:

- Double Negatives

Explain to students that a double negative is the use of two negative words in a sentence when only one is needed. Negatives include such words as *no one, not, nothing, none, never, hardly,* and *barely.*

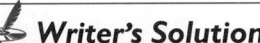

Writer's Solution

For additional practice and support, use the practice pages on Double Negatives and Twenty Common Usage Problems, pp. 91–92 in the *Writer's Solution Grammar Practice Book.*

Usage Problems — Grammar Review

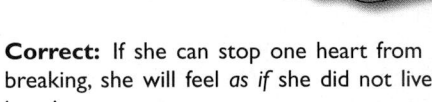

Correct Use of Adjectives and Adverbs

Do not confuse the use of adjectives and adverbs (see p. 860). Use adjectives to modify nouns and pronouns; use adverbs to modify verbs, adjectives, and adverbs. A common mistake is to use an adjective instead of an adverb to modify a verb.

> **Incorrect:** The turtle addressed in "Drum Song" probably didn't move very *quick.* (adjective)

> **Correct:** The turtle addressed in "Drum Song" probably didn't move very *quickly.* (adverb modifying the verb *move*)

Pronouns in Comparisons Sometimes it is difficult to know which pronouns to use in a comparison using *than* or *as* (see p. 870). In these comparisons, one or more words are implied instead of stated. In order to select the correct pronoun, mentally fill in the missing words, and use the pronoun you would use if the comparison were complete.

> **Incorrect:** Molly was a better sister than *her.*

> **Correct:** Molly was a better sister than *she* [was].

When you supply the missing words, you can see that you need a pronoun in the subjective case to complete the comparison.

Correct Use of *Like* and *As* The word *like* is commonly misused (see p. 880). *Like* is a preposition that introduces a prepositional phrase. *As* can be used as a preposition and as a subordinating conjunction (or *as if* or *as though*) that introduces a subordinate clause. Do not use *like* to begin a subordinate clause.

> **Incorrect:** If she can stop one heart from breaking, she will feel *like* she did not live in vain.

> **Correct:** If she can stop one heart from breaking, she will feel *as if* she did not live in vain.

Practice 1 Choose the adjective or adverb to complete these sentences correctly:

1. The language of the flowers was (delicate, delicately).
2. The moon rose (slow, slowly) in the night.
3. The animals described in "Drum Song" are all (real, really) small.
4. The Robin did not move (quick, quickly) enough to catch the worm.
5. Molly took care of her siblings very (careful, carefully).

Practice 2 Write the following sentences in your notebook. Complete each sentence with the correct word in parentheses.

1. My brother is a better poet than (he, him).
2. It seemed (like, as if) night came quickly after school ended.
3. The gardener was more frightened by the visitor than (he, him).
4. No one is as bold as (she, her).

Grammar in Writing

✔ When deciding between like or as, look for a subject and a verb following the word. If both appear, then the subordinating conjunction as is needed. Like is never a conjunction.

886 ◆ Poetry

Answers
Practice 1
1. The language of the flowers was delicate.
2. The moon rose slowly in the night.
3. The animals described in "Drum Song" are all really small.
4. The Robin did not move quickly enough to catch the worm.
5. Molly took care of her siblings very carefully.

Practice 2
1. My brother is a better poet than he.
2. It seemed as if night came quickly after school ended.
3. The gardener was more frightened by the visitor than he.
4. No one is as bold as she.

Speaking, Listening, and Viewing Workshop

Critically Viewing TV Messages

Television offers you all kinds of variety. You can view drama and comedy programs, commercials, newscasts, news bulletins, public-service announcements, advertisements, and infomercials. Whatever kinds of programs you watch, look for the messages in them, and evaluate the messages before you accept them.

Identify the Purpose Identify the message of a program and the goal of the program. The purpose of an advertisement or infomercial is to get you to make a purchase or to take some action. The claims made about a product or a service or a candidate include only information that the advertiser wants you to know. For example, a toothpaste might claim "Dentists recommend this toothpaste." What you are not told is that only fifty dentists recommend it. Listen carefully, and question claims made by advertisers. Ask yourself, "Are they telling me everything?"

Consider the Source With advertisements, it's easy to figure out the purpose of the message. With news reports, it is often difficult to know what is fact and what is opinion or what is simply a guess. Objective news programs, such as nightly news reports, are better sources for factual information. Television "magazines" may include reporting that entertains more than it informs, and it can be misleading. To keep an audience's interest, they may make assumptions about people and report those assumptions as fact. Before accepting a television message as fact, evaluate the source.

Consider Bias Bias is the tendency to think in a certain way. As you watch television programs, consider whether the information is being presented in a one-sided way or whether it takes into account all points of view.

Apply the Strategies

Complete one or both of the following activities.

1. Watch a television "magazine" show, and write a report in which you critically evaluate its messages.

2. Tape a commercial or infomercial. With your class, determine its purpose, question its claims, and evaluate its message.

Tips for Viewing TV Messages Critically

▶ Be aware of the kind of program you're watching and its purpose.
▶ Listen for bias.
▶ Remember that there is often another point of view to a public-service announcement or a station editorial.
▶ Infomercials are designed to sell something.

Introduce the Strategies

Have students brainstorm for a list of different kinds of television programs. Ask them to consider which programs they watch the most. Explain that some television stations may have certain biases in their programming, which is reflected in the choice of programs they broadcast.

Customize for *More Advanced Students*

Suggest to students that they watch a television "magazine" show and pick one issue to analyze. Have students create a list of information that the program has not considered. Explain to students that many times programs say they tried to reach someone for a comment, but the person was unavailable. Have students consider how this affects the information given in the program.

Apply the Strategies

Explain to students that most television "magazine" shows report on several issues in one program. Have students analyze only one issue. When they choose a commercial to evaluate, suggest that students choose one that actually makes claims about a product, rather than a more artistic one.

 Beyond the Classroom

Career Connection

Advertising Advertisers "sell" products. A successful advertiser combines a sense of creativity with a solid business knowledge to create an original and effective "ad" campaign.

Within the field of advertising, there are several different types of work to be done. The account manager correlates the work of the advertising agency with the desires and needs of the client. People who work in the creative department come up with general ideas for campaigns and then write copy and create art work. The media department studies demographics and decides which kind of media— print, radio, or TV—the client needs, based on potential customers and the client's budget. Many advertising agencies also have a research department whose primary function is to gather and analyze information on the product to be advertised.

Encourage students to find a specific job within an advertising agency that appeals to them. Have them research and write a brief essay explaining why they think they would be good at that particular job.

Explain to students that many verbal portions of standardized tests include analogy questions. Understanding the different kinds of relationship used in analogies will help these students on their tests.

Customize for
Less Proficient Learners
Some students will do better working in pairs on analogy questions. Encourage students to choose a partner and discuss each analogy as they come to it. Students may benefit from hearing how the partner verbalizes the relationship between a pair of words. Explain to students that when analyzing a relationship between two words it may be helpful to switch the order of the words to come up with a statement that explains that relationship.

Answers
Activity 1
Possible responses:
1. *Clumsy* is the same as *Awkward*
2. *Heavy* is a characteristic of *Lead*
3. A *Bear* lives in a *Den*
4. A *Human Being* is a type of *Mammal*
5. An *Incision* will cause a *Scar*
6. An *Automobile* is a vehicle used for *Travel*

Activity 2
1. (b) gosling: goose
2. (a) cheddar: cheese
3. (b) high: low

What's Behind the
Words
Vocabulary Adventures With Richard Lederer

Analogies

An analogy, derived from the Greek *analogia,* "relation," is a relationship between one idea and another. When you take analogies tests, you will usually be asked to demonstrate your understanding of how one word relates to another.

Typically, you will be given one pair of words that are capitalized and four or five other uncapitalized pairs. You must identify the relationship between the two capitalized terms and then find another pair of words with the same relationship. Often, colons are used to suggest "is to," as shown in the following examples:

EAGER:LAZY:: (a) angry:mad, (b) enthusiastic:bored, (c) energetic:vigorous, (d) intelligent:curious (e) brilliant:genius.

DAWN:DAY:: (a) star:heavens, (b) curtain:play, (c) beginning:end, (d) moon:night, (e) birth:life

Making Connections

When you encounter analogies tests, try to find the exact connection between the capitalized words. Before examining the choices for the answer, state the relationship as clearly as you can in a sentence, as "EAGER is the opposite of LAZY" and "DAWN is the beginning of DAY."

Such a statement will be a powerful aid in your arriving at a correct answer: "EAGER is the opposite of LAZY, and *enthusiastic* is the opposite of *bored*"; "DAWN is the beginning of DAY, and *birth* is the beginning of *life*."

The Most Common Relationships
Practice recognizing the most common relationships used in analogies:

Relationship	Examples
synonyms	rich:wealthy; mammoth:colossal
antonyms	pleasure:pain; patience:intolerance
part of the whole	tree:woods; song:repertoire
one of a group	pear:fruit; giraffe:animal
characteristic of	light:feather; hard:diamond
degree of intensity	warm:boiling; breeze:gale
lack of	food:starvation; generosity:miser
purpose of	school:learning; sandbox:play
sign of	applause:approval; blush:shyness

From a study of related words, you will become more accurate in recognizing shades of meaning.

ACTIVITY 1. State clearly the relationship between each of the following pairs:
1. clumsy:awkward
2. lead:heavy
3. bear:den
4. human being:mammal
5. incision:scar
6. automobile:travel

ACTIVITY 2. Choose the pair that shows the same relationship as the first pair.
1. KITTEN:CAT:: (a) modem:computer, (b) gosling:goose, (c) cat:lion
2. CARROT:VEGETABLE:: (a) cheddar:cheese, (b) car:automobile, (c) crayon:pen
3. HAPPY:SAD:: (a) noisy:loud, (b) high:low, (c) smart:intelligent

Extended Reading Opportunities

The musical language of poetry, along with form and theme, can present a rewarding reading experience. Following are a few possibilities for further exploration of poetry.

Suggested Titles

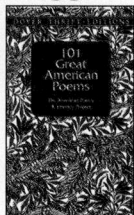

101 Great American Poems
The American Poetry & Literacy Project

This collection of poetry was assembled by the American Poetry & Literacy Project. Its aim is to provide poetry to the American public free of charge. Collections like this one are distributed free at hospitals, train stations, libraries, and other public places. This collection of well-loved works from various classic poets provides an opportunity to appreciate the magical and musical language of poetry.

Poem-Making: Ways to Begin Writing Poetry
Myra Cohn Livingston

This book is an excellent handbook for the budding poet. Basing the work on the formal terminology of poetic techniques, Livingston makes the mechanics of writing a poem understandable. She invites young people to "make the image, the thought, even the sound, come alive" and to enjoy the experience of writing a poem.

The Complete Poems of Emily Dickinson
Thomas H. Johnson, Editor

All 1,775 of Dickinson's poems are available in this collection exactly as she first wrote them. The brief poems express her ideas on nature and life. The comprehensive collection includes poems from her youth to the end of her career—even valentines she wrote during the 1850's. The editor also includes an introduction that outlines Dickinson's career.

Other Possibilities

American Sports Poems	R. R. Knudson
101 Famous Poems	Roy J. Cook, Editor
Poetry After Lunch: Poems to Read Aloud	Joyce Armstrong Carroll and Edward E. Wilson

Planning Students' Extended Reading

All of the works listed on this page are good choices for extending the genre of poetry. The following information may help you choose which to teach.

Customize for *Varying Student Needs*

When assigning these extended reading selections to your students, keep in mind the following factors:

- *101 Great American Poems* is free of charge but not available in bookstores. The American Poetry and Literacy Project, created by Joseph Brodsky and Andrew Carroll, seeks to provide poetry to the public for free. Another project they are working on is collaborating with Yellow Pages publishers to intersperse poetry through the telephone directories.

- *Poem-Making: Ways to Begin Writing Poetry* is written by poet and teacher Myra Cohn Livingston. She focuses on the formal structure of poetry and encourages readers to appreciate and create their own ballads, haiku, limericks, and poems in free verse.

- *The Complete Poems of Emily Dickinson* is the only edition that contains all of her poems. The poems are arranged by Thomas Johnson in chronological order.

Planning Instruction and Assessment

Unit Objectives

1. To read folk literature
2. To apply a variety of reading strategies, particularly strategies for reading folk literature, appropriate for reading these selections
3. To recognize literary elements used in these selections
4. To increase vocabulary
5. To learn elements of grammar and usage
6. To write in a variety of modes about situations based on the selections
7. To develop speaking and listening skills, by completing activities
8. To view images critically and create visual representations

Meeting the Objectives Each selection provides instructional material and portfolio opportunities by which students can meet unit objectives. You will find additional practice pages for reading strategies, literary elements, vocabulary, and grammar in the **Selection Support** booklet in the **Teaching Resources** box.

Setting Goals Work with your students to set goals for unit outcomes. Plan what skills and concepts you wish students to acquire. Match instruction and activities to students' performance levels or learning modalities.

Portfolios Students may keep portfolios of their completed work or of their work in progress. The Build Your Portfolio page of each selection provides opportunities for students to apply the concepts presented.

 Humanities: Art

Woodcutter, 1891, by Winslow Homer.

Winslow Homer (1836–1910) was an American painter and graphic artist best known for his naturalistic works. Winslow did not start painting until 1862, focusing on happy scenes from country life. Discuss with students whether they think this painting is a good visual representation of the American folk tradition. *Some students will say yes—the man in the painting looks like a hardworking American; other students will say no, because the painting shows only one man looking over a specific area of America—the painting doesn't represent the diversity of Americans.*

Woodcutter, 1891, Winslow Homer, Private Collection

Art Transparencies
The **Art Transparencies** booklet in the **Teaching Resources** box offers fine art to help students make connections to other curriculum areas and high-interest topics.

Beyond Literature
Each unit presents Beyond Literature features that lead students into an exploration of careers, communities and other subject areas. In this unit, students will delve into the concept of the Coyote Trickster, learn about the Mexican-American War, and make a science connection. In addition, the **Teaching Resources** box contains a **Beyond Literature** booklet of activities. Using literature as a springboard, these activity pages offer students opportunities to connect literature to other curriculum areas and to the workplace and careers, community, media, and humanities.

10

The American Folk Tradition

The American folk tradition is a rich collection of literature that grew out of the oral tradition. These stories amaze, explain, teach, and amuse the reader of today just as they did the listener of generations ago. Following are the types of folk literature you'll encounter in this unit:

- **Myths** are ancient tales that explain or summarize the beliefs of a culture.

- **Folk Tales** are stories of a region that are passed down through the generations to teach a lesson or to entertain.

- **Tall Tales,** written in the language of the common people, often tell of life on the American frontier and contain larger-than-life characters who take part in or witness fantastic events.

◆ *891*

Assessing Student Progress

The tools that are available to measure the degree to which students meet the unit objectives are listed below.

Informal Assessment

The questions in the Guide for Responding sections are a first level of response to the concepts and skills presented with the selection. As a brief, informal measure of students' grasp of the material, these responses indicate where further instruction and practice are needed. The practice pages in the **Selection Support** booklet provide for this type of instruction and practice.

You will also find literature and reading guides in the **Alternative Assessment** booklet, which students can use for informal assessment of their individual performances.

Formal Assessment

The **Formal Assessment** booklet contains Selection Tests and Unit Tests.

Selection Tests measure comprehension and skills acquisition for each selection or group of selections.

Each Unit Test provides students with 30 multiple-choice questions and 5 essay questions designed to assess students' knowledge of the literature and skills taught in the unit.

Each Alternative Unit Test: Standardized-Test Practice provides 15 multiple-choice questions and 3 essay questions based on two new literature selections not contained in the student book. The questions on the Alternative Unit Test are designed to assess students' ability to compare and contrast selections, applying skills taught in the unit.

Alternative Assessment

For portfolio and alternative assessment, the **Alternative Assessment** booklet contains Scoring Rubrics, Assessment sheets, and Learning Modalities activities.

Scoring Rubrics provide writing modes that can be applied to Writing activities, Writing Mini-Lessons, and Writing Process Workshop lessons.

Assessment sheets for speaking and listening activities provide peer and self-assessment direction.

Learning Modalities activities appeal to different learning styles. Use these as an alternative measurement of students' growth.

Connections

Within this unit, you will find selections and activities that make connections beyond literature. Use these selections to connect students' understanding and appreciation of literature beyond the traditional literature and language arts curriculum.

Encourage students to connect literature to other curriculum areas. You may wish to coordinate with teachers in other curriculum areas to determine ways to team teach and further extend instruction.

Connections to Today's World

Use these selections to guide students to recognize the relevance of literature to contemporary writings. In this unit, students will study an Internet Home Page, "Superman Online."

Connecting Literature to Social Studies

Each unit contains a selection that connects literature to social studies. In this unit, students will read about the heroic astronaut, Alan Shepard, in an excerpt from *The Right Stuff.*

Guide for Reading

OBJECTIVES

1. To read, comprehend, and interpret a poem about a folk hero
2. To relate a poem about a folk hero to personal experience
3. To apply strategies for reading folk literature
4. To analyze writings based on oral tradition
5. To build vocabulary in context and learn words using forms of *encumber*
6. To recognize unnecessary commas
7. To write a legendary story using details that show the character
8. To respond to the poem through writing, speaking and listening, and projects

SKILLS INSTRUCTION

Vocabulary:
Forms of *encumber*

Spelling:
Words With *ai* and *ia*

Grammar:
Unnecessary Commas

Literary Focus:
Oral Tradition

Reading for Success:
Strategies for Reading Folk Literature

Writing:
Show, Don't Tell

Critical Viewing:
Deduce

PORTFOLIO OPPORTUNITIES

Writing: Epitaph; Folk Ballad; Essay
Writing Mini-Lesson: Legendary Story
Speaking and Listening: Interview; Musical Setting
Projects: Apple Poster; How-to Booklet

More About the Author
Rosemary Carr Benét and her husband Stephen Vincent Benét co-wrote *A Book of Americans,* which contains poems describing a variety of well-known Americans from Jesse James and P.T. Barnum to Woodrow Wilson. Rosemary Carr Benét was a contributor to the *New Yorker* magazine and also worked as an editor. Her poem about Johnny Appleseed joins with many stories, novels, and poems written about this folklore hero.

Meet the Author:

Rosemary Carr Benét (1898–1962)

Many of Rosemary Carr Benét's poems were inspired by historical events and legends. She often wrote poems with her husband, Stephen Vincent Benét. Their close friends called them "the last of the romantics" because of their close bond and love of poetry.

Poetry for Young People After their children were born, the Benéts started to write poetry for young people. In 1933, they published *A Book of Americans,* a collection of verses that expand on United States history and American personalities.

THE STORY BEHIND THE STORY

Johnny Appleseed (1774–1845) was a frontiersman whose real name was John Chapman. Born in Leominster, Massachusetts, Chapman's life was so extraordinary that he became a folk hero. In stories about him, which blend truth and fantasy, he collected apple seeds from Pennsylvania cider mills and planted them in fertile spots throughout Ohio, Indiana, and Illinois. He received no pay for his work, but he was often given a meal or a cast-off piece of clothing by those who appreciated his efforts.

◆ LITERATURE AND YOUR LIFE

CONNECT YOUR EXPERIENCE

Perhaps you've planted or tended flowers in your home or garden; perhaps you've grown sea monkeys or tended newborn kittens. Think about the rewards that come from watching something grow and thrive. In "Johnny Appleseed," you'll learn of a special person who devoted his life to planting apple trees.

THEMATIC FOCUS: Heroes

Johnny Appleseed is an unusual folk hero. As you read about him in this poem, look for the qualities that make him heroic.

◆ Background for Understanding

GEOGRAPHY

Johnny Appleseed is a folk hero who planted apple trees throughout the midwestern United States. Apples have been grown in many regions of the world since the earliest human cultures flourished. They are mentioned in the earliest writings of China, Babylon, and Egypt. Charred apples have been discovered in the mud of prehistoric cave homes. They even show up in some early stone carvings.

Today, China is the world's largest producer of apples, followed by the United States, France, Italy, and Turkey. In the United States, the Pacific Northwest produces the most apples, led by Washington State. California, New York, Michigan, and Virginia are also major apple producers. Three varieties make up about two thirds of all apples grown in the United States: Delicious, Golden Delicious, and Granny Smith.

 Prentice Hall Literature Program Resources

REINFORCE / RETEACH / EXTEND
Selection Support Pages
Build Vocabulary: Forms of *encumber*, p. 306
Build Spelling Skills, p. 307
Build Grammar Skills: Unnecessary Commas, p. 308
Reading for Success: Strategies for Reading Folk Literature, pp. 309–310
Literary Focus: Oral Tradition, p. 311
Strategies for Diverse Student Needs, pp. 113–114
Beyond Literature Media Connection: Interview, p. 57

Formal Assessment Selection Test, pp. 259–261, Assessment Resources Software
Alternative Assessment, p. 57
Writing and Language Transparencies
KWL Organizer, p. 49; Series of Events Chain, p. 57
Resource Pro CD-ROM
"Johnny Appleseed"—includes all resource material and customizable lesson plan

 Listening to Literature Audiocassettes
"Johnny Appleseed"

◆ Johnny Appleseed ◆

John Chapman, known as Johnny Appleseed (1775–1845)

◆ Literary Focus

ORAL TRADITION

The **oral tradition** is the passing of stories, beliefs, and customs from generation to generation by word of mouth. Many folk stories and tales were originally sung as ballads. Only after years of being heard, remembered, and loved were they written down.

Modern writers often return to the powerful and engaging stories kept alive by the oral tradition. Rosemary Carr Benét's poem was inspired by the vibrant body of American folk tales and songs about Johnny Appleseed.

◆ Build Vocabulary

RELATED WORDS: FORMS OF *encumber*

The verb *encumber* means "to weigh down." Words related to encumber include *cumbersome, encumbrance,* and *unencumbered.*

WORD BANK

Which word from the poem might mean "having a healthy red color"? Check the Build Vocabulary box on page 895 to see if you chose correctly.

gnarled
ruddy
encumber
tendril
stalking
lair

Guide for Reading ◆ 893

◆ Build Grammar Skills

Unnecessary Commas If you wish to introduce the grammar concept for this selection before students read, refer to the instruction on p. 897.

Customize for
Less Proficient Readers
Point out that most verses of the poem contain either one or two sentences. Most verses with one sentence have a comma at the end of the second line, while many of those with two sentences have a period at the end of the second line. Tell students to watch for these punctuation signals, reminding them to pause at commas and stop at periods as they read to help them "hear" the sentences.

Customize for
More Advanced Students
Discuss with students that stories that become part of the oral tradition of a culture must appeal to many people. After students read the poem, have them work with a partner to define the special qualities of this tale by answering this question: *Why do so many people enjoy the story of Johnny Appleseed?* Have partners share their insights in a small group.

Customize for
English Language Learners
Understanding the process of growing apples will assist comprehension of the poem about Johnny Appleseed and his activities. Students may benefit from studying pictures of apples, apple trees, and apple trees in bloom.

 Humanities: Art

Have students make predictions about the poem based on the illustration on p. 893. *Students may conclude that the story is about a man who likes to plant trees. They may recognize the title of the illustration and be familiar with the story of Johnny Appleseed.*

Preparing for Standardized Tests

Listening Students must interpret what they read, and sometimes they must interpret what they hear. Standardized tests may evaluate their ability to listen to and interpret text. Read aloud the following passage and question:

Even though he wasn't a doctor, many people considered Johnny Appleseed to be a healer. He planted apple orchards wherever he went and sometimes he planted herbs near the orchards. People used these herbs to treat common ailments such as headaches and colds.

What is the main idea of this paragraph?

(A) Johnny Appleseed planted apple orchards.
(B) Johnny Appleseed wasn't a doctor.
(C) Many people considered Johnny Appleseed to be a healer.
(D) People used Johnny Appleseed's herbs for headaches.

Ask students to briefly restate the passage in their own words, leading them to conclude that (C) is the correct answer. For more practice with listening and interpreting text, have students work in pairs to read aloud paragraphs and summarize the main ideas of the passages that they hear.

Reading for Success

The Reading for Success page in each unit presents a set of problem-solving strategies to help readers understand authors' words and ideas on multiple levels. Good readers develop a bank of strategies from which they can draw as needed.

Unit 10 introduces strategies for reading folk literature. Students must be able to read and understand folk literature before they apply higher-level critical thinking strategies. These strategies for reading folk literature give readers an array of approaches for mastering a text: understand the cultural context, recognize the storyteller's purpose, and predict.

Strategies for reading folk literature are modeled with the poem, "Johnny Appleseed." Each green box shows an example of the thinking process involved in applying one of these strategies. Additional notes provide support for applying these strategies throughout the selection.

How to Use the Reading for Success Page

- Introduce the strategies for reading folk literature, presenting each as a problem-solving procedure.

- Before students read the selection, have them preview it, looking at the annotations in the green boxes that model the strategies.

- To reinforce these strategies after students read the selection, use Reading for Success, pp. 309–310, in **Selection Support.** These pages give students an opportunity to read a selection and practice strategies for reading folk literature by writing their own annotations.

Reading Strategies: Support and Reinforcement

Using Boxed Annotations and Prompts

Throughout the unit, the notes in green, red, and maroon are intended to help students apply reading strategies, understand the literary focus, and make connections with their lives. You may use boxed material in these ways:

- Have students pause at each box and respond to its prompt before they continue reading.

- Urge students to read through the selection, ignoring the boxes. After they complete the selection, they may go back and review the text, responding to the prompts.

894

Reading for Success

Strategies for Reading Folk Literature

Folk literature is older than recorded history: Its tales, stories, legends, and myths have been passed down for many generations. Because these tales were told orally, they often contain repetition (making them easier to remember) and dialect (specialized vocabulary and grammar of a region). As you read the folk literature in this unit, use the following strategies to guide your reading:

Understand the cultural context.

You will better understand the action and characters of a story if you know the culture from which it comes. For example, a southwestern tale—a *cuento*—would reveal different beliefs or customs from a Native American tale or a pioneer tale. Look at the following example based on "Johnny Appleseed."

> **Poem Passage:** For fifty years over/ Of harvest and dew,/ He planted his apples/ Where no apples grew.
>
> **Cultural Context:** The pioneers admired rugged individualism.

Recognize the storyteller's purpose.

Folk literature often amuses the reader at the same time that it teaches a lesson or conveys a message. Storytellers often used folk tales to transmit beliefs or values. Some tales serve to explain scientific mysteries or natural occurrences. As you read, consider what message the story might be conveying to listeners.

▶ Examine the details of the tale for clues to the storyteller's purpose.

▶ Look for a stated message or moral near the story's end.

Predict.

Folk literature is predictable. Good characters and deeds are rewarded; bad characters are either banished or reformed. This pattern makes it easy for you to predict the instructional message.

> **Story Event:** Chicoria makes a bet with someone.
>
> **What I Know:** Chicoria is the "good" character.
>
> **Prediction:** He will probably win the bet.

As you read "Johnny Appleseed," look at the notes in the boxes. The notes demonstrate how to apply these strategies to your reading.

Model a Reading Strategy: Recognize the Storyteller's Purpose

Good readers use the storyteller's purpose to guide their reading and better understand the author's meaning. Demonstrate this strategy by modeling your thinking for students. Ask students to read Lines 41–44 from "Johnny Appleseed":

First I think about what the storyteller's purpose may be. As I try to interpret the meaning of this verse from the poem, I realize that it reflects the author's purpose in writing the poem. I ask myself why the storyteller chose to tell this story about a gentle, nature-loving man. I think the poet admires Johnny Appleseed, and believes his legacy will live as long as apple trees continue to grow and flourish. He left a living memorial behind, which is more important than any stone monument. The storyteller wants me to be inspired by his perseverance in sharing his love for apple trees with his friends and neighbors.

Point out to students that recognizing the storyteller's purpose as they read will help clarify the author's meaning and increase their enjoyment of what they read.

Johnny Appleseed

Rosemary Carr Benét

John Chapman, known as Johnny Appleseed (1775–1845)

▲ **Critical Viewing** What does Johnny Appleseed appear to be doing in this illustration? Support your answer. [Deduce]

 Build Vocabulary

gnarled (närld) *adj.*: Knotty and twisted, as the trunk of an old tree

ruddy (rud´ē) *adj.*: Having a healthy red color

encumber (in kum´ bər) *v.*: Weigh down

tendril (ten´ drəl) *n.*: Thin shoot from a plant

Of Jonathan Chapman
Two things are known,
That he loved apples,
That he walked alone.

> You can recognize that the story-teller's purpose is to tell of Jonathan Chapman.

5 At seventy-odd
He was gnarled as could be,
But ruddy and sound
As a good apple tree.

For fifty years over
10 Of harvest and dew,
He planted his apples
Where no apples grew.

The winds of the prairie
Might blow through his rags,
15 But he carried his seeds
In the best deerskin bags.

From old Ashtabula
To frontier Fort Wayne,
He planted and pruned
20 And he planted again.

He had not a hat
To encumber his head.
He wore a tin pan
On his white hair instead. ❸

25 He nested with owl,
And with bear-cub and possum,
And knew all his orchards
Root, tendril and blossom. ❹

Johnny Appleseed ◆ 895

Develop Understanding

One-Minute Insight

"Johnny Appleseed" describes the life of folk hero John Chapman, who spent over fifty years traveling in the Ohio River valley planting and tending apple orchards for other people to enjoy.

▶Critical Viewing◀

❶ **Deduce** *Students may say that the man appears to be preparing the ground so that he can plant seeds from the bag on the ground. This idea is supported by details in the poem.*

◆ Literary Focus

❷ **Oral Tradition** Have students identify the main idea of this verse. *John Chapman planted apple seeds for fifty years, which is important because it meant that many people knew Chapman and told stories about him for many years. These stories were the basis for the oral tradition of Johnny Appleseed stories.*

◆ Critical Thinking

❸ **Defend** Remind students that as stories are passed down orally from one generation to the next, they often become embellished with details that may not be factual. Ask students if they think that John Chapman actually wore a tin pan as a hat. *Some students will not believe Chapman really wore such an uncomfortable hat, while others may point out that a tin pan was a cooking necessity and carrying it on his head was an easy way to transport it.*

Reading for Success

❹ **Understand the Cultural Context** The animals in this verse actually live in the Ohio River valley where John Chapman traveled. Why is this important? *The realistic details bring to life the setting of the folk tale.*

Humanities: Art

John Chapman
This colored engraving, *John Chapman,* was created a quarter-century after Chapman's death. Challenge students to think of a person living today who might become an artist's subject twenty-five years from now.

Block Scheduling Strategies

Consider these suggestions to take advantage of extended class time:

- Before students read the selection, introduce the Reading for Success strategies, p. 894. Then read the selection as a class, reviewing the annotations. After discussing with students the Reading for Success questions on p. 897, have them apply the strategies they have learned as they annotate the Reading for Success practice selection, pp. 309–310, in **Selection Support.**

- Students who select the Essay activity in the Idea Bank, p. 898, might use the Main Idea and Supporting Details Organizer in **Writing and Language Transparencies,** p. 61. Students who choose the How-to Booklet might use the KWL Organizer, p. 49, as a prewriting activity.

- Introduce the literary focus, Oral Tradition. Have students listen to the audiocassette and then reread the poem. Have pairs of students answer the Literary Focus questions on p. 897 and then plan the Interview activity in the Idea Bank, p. 898.

 Listening to Literature Audiocassettes

◆ Literacy Focus

❶ Oral Tradition This verse demonstrates that people did not always understand why Johnny Appleseed did what he did. Why is this important? *Many people simply did not understand Johnny Appleseed's lifelong commitment to his dream of spreading apple orchards throughout the Ohio River valley. It was not only his commitment to his work, but people's lack of understanding that helped to fuel the legends and stories about him.*

Reinforce and Extend

Answers

◆ LITERATURE AND YOUR LIFE

Reader's Response Most students will probably say that Johnny Appleseed's work would be appreciated today because it provides food and natural beauty.

Thematic Focus He was committed to his dream of spreading apple orchards across the land.

☑ Check Your Comprehension

1. He is better known as Johnny Appleseed.
2. He was gnarled, ruddy, and sound.
3. He lived with nature, dressed in rags, and carried his seeds in a deerskin bag.

◆ Critical Thinking

1. His most important possession is his deerskin bag of apple seeds.
2. He loves nature; he spends his life planting trees that bear delicious fruit and beautiful blossoms.
3. The speaker admires Johnny Appleseed and his accomplishments.
4. Students may identify areas such as Russia or countries in Africa, where there is a shortage of food. They may say that these places need people who will organize and implement an agricultural program.
5. A scientist might discover a new species of apple that is resistant to insects, drought, and diseases.

        A fine old man,
30   As ripe as a pippin,[1]
        His heart still light,
        And his step still skipping.

        The stalking Indian,
        The beast in its lair
35   Did no hurt
        While he was there.

        For they could tell,
        As wild things can,
        That Jonathan
            Chapman
40   Was God's own man.

❶
        Why did he do it?
        We do not know.
        He wished that apples
        Might root and grow.

45   He has no statue.
        He has no tomb.
        He has his apple trees
        Still in bloom.

        Consider, consider,
50   Think well upon
        The marvelous story
        Of Appleseed John.

---

1. **pippin** (pip´ in) *n.*: A type of apple.

> When you put this poem in **cultural context**, you'll realize that at the time this poem was written, many people of European ancestry misunderstood Native Americans.

> You can **predict** that Chapman will be remembered, despite the lack of memorials.

◆ Build Vocabulary

stalking (stôk´ iŋ) *adj.*: Secretly approaching

lair (ler) *n.*: Den of a wild animal

Guide for Responding

◆ LITERATURE AND YOUR LIFE

Reader's Response Would the work of Johnny Appleseed be appreciated today? Why or why not?

Thematic Focus What heroic qualities does Johnny Appleseed display?

Journal Writing What modern figures remind you of Johnny Appleseed? Jot down a list in your journal.

☑ Check Your Comprehension

1. By what name is Jonathan Chapman better known?
2. List three physical details that Benét uses to describe Chapman.
3. Describe Chapman's life on the frontier.

◆ Critical Thinking

INTERPRET

1. What is Chapman's most important possession? **[Infer]**
2. How does Chapman feel about nature? **[Infer]**
3. How would you describe the speaker's attitude toward the person who became known as Johnny Appleseed? **[Analyze]**

APPLY

4. What areas in today's world would benefit from having someone provide help in growing food? Explain what those areas most need. **[Relate]**

EXTEND

5. How might a scientist in a laboratory today carry on Johnny Appleseed's legacy? **[Science Link]**

Beyond the Selection

FURTHER READING
Other Works by Rosemary Carr Benét
A Book of Americans
Other Works About Johnny Appleseed
Johnny Appleseed, Stephen Kellogg
Johnny Appleseed (American Heroes and Legends), Garrison Keillor (VHS videotape)

INTERNET
Additional information about Johnny Appleseed can be found on the Internet. We suggest the following site on the Internet (all Web sites are subject to change).
http://www.appleseed.org/johnny.html
    We *strongly recommend* that you preview this site before you send students to it.

Guide for Responding (continued)

◆ Reading for Success

STRATEGIES FOR READING FOLK LITERATURE

Review the reading strategies and the notes showing how to read folk literature. Then, apply the strategies to answer the following:

1. How does knowing about prairie life help you to understand "Johnny Appleseed"?
2. What is the storyteller's purpose in telling "Johnny Appleseed"? What details helped you to identify the purpose?

◆ Build Vocabulary

USING FORMS OF *encumber*

The verb *encumber* means "to weigh down." Related words convey a similar meaning. Complete the following sentences with these related words: *cumbersome, unencumbered, encumbrance*. Then state each sentence in your own words.

1. The heavy bags of grass seed are ____?____.
2. A weighty ____?____ can make it hard to walk.
3. When his sack of seed was empty, Johnny felt ____?____.

SPELLING STRATEGY

Words containing the letter combinations of *ai* and *ia* are often mistakenly or carelessly misspelled. For example, *lair* and *liar* are often confused, as are *trail* and *trial*. Rewrite the following sentences, correcting any misspelled words.

1. The liar of the wolf was deep inside a cave.
2. The trial led through the prairie to an orchard.

USING THE WORD BANK

On your paper, write the Word Bank word that completes each sentence.

1. Stay away from the ____?____ of a bear family.
2. She watered the knotty and ____?____ old tree.
3. After planting the seedlings, her face was glowing and ____?____.
4. A young ____?____ from the tree wrapped around stones and clay.
5. A ____?____ cat hid in the branches.
6. In a short time, the bushels of apples will ____?____ the orchard's fruit pickers.

◆ Literary Focus

ORAL TRADITION

The **oral tradition** is the passing of songs, stories, and poems from generation to generation by word of mouth. Songs, myths, legends, and tall tales are all products of the oral tradition.

1. Why do you think Benét chose a poetic form for her retelling of a legend about a folk hero?
2. In a song, a catchy melody or memorable phrase is called a "hook" because it catches a listener's attention. (a) Does Benét's poem include any hooks? (b) How can a strong hook help a song or poem become part of the oral tradition?

◆ Build Grammar Skills

UNNECESSARY COMMAS

Commas are supposed to help readers, not confuse them. **Unnecessary commas** can cause confusion. One place where a comma is unnecessary is before a coordinating conjunction that links words or groups that are *not* independent clauses. Notice that Rosemary Carr Benét does not use a comma when she joins two adjectives or two verbs:

> But ruddy and sound / as a good apple tree.
> (*Not:* ruddy, and sound)
> He wished that apples might root and grow.
> (*Not:* might root, and grow)

Practice Copy the following sentences, leaving out unnecessary commas.

1. In song, and story, Johnny Appleseed planted healthy, and robust apples.
2. For more than fifty years, he planted, and pruned his trees.
3. Many ballads describe, and praise his gentle, and heroic deeds.
4. In addition to seeding apples, Chapman also sowed herbs, and other plants.
5. Tales describe his life in vivid, and sharp details, although some are certainly exaggerated.

Writing Application Use each of the following phrases in a sentence. Avoid unnecessary commas.

1. apples and pears
2. slowly and steadily

Johnny Appleseed ◆ 897

Idea Bank

Following are suggestions for matching the Idea Bank topics with your students' performance levels and learning modalities:

Customize for
Performance Levels
Less Advanced Students: 1, 5, 6
Average Students: 2, 4, 5, 6
More Advanced Students: 3, 7

Customize for
Learning Modalities
Verbal/Linguistic: 1, 2, 3, 4
Interpersonal: 4, 6, 7
Visual/Spatial: 6, 7
Logical/Mathematical: 6, 7
Musical/Rhythmic: 2, 5
Intrapersonal: 1, 2, 3

 Writing Mini-Lesson

Refer students to the Writing Handbook in the back of the book for instructions on the writing process and for further information on writing stories. Have students adapt the Series of Events Chain, p. 57 in **Writing and Language Transparencies,** to arrange their prewriting examples.

 Writer's Solution

Writing Lab CD-ROM
Have students complete the tutorial on Creative Writing. Follow these steps:
1. Have students use the Character Trait Word Bin activity.
2. Students can use the Writing Hints on dialogue to help them write believable, interesting dialogue that shows instead of telling.
3. Have students draft on computer.
4. Students can use the audio-annotated Student Models to explore replacing abstract words with more vivid, specific words.

Writer's Solution Sourcebook
Have students use Chapter 8, "Creative Writing," pp. 234–265, for additional support. This chapter includes instruction on choosing words and conveying ideas.

Build Your Portfolio

 Idea Bank

Writing

1. **Epitaph** Write a three- or four-line epitaph— an inscription for a gravestone—that might have been carved on John Chapman's memorial. Your epitaph can be written in prose or in verse.
2. **Folk Ballad** Write a poem about a modern folk hero. Use Rosemary Carr Benét's rhyming pattern, and give your poem a strong beat.
3. **Essay** Write an essay in which you tell what made Johnny Appleseed a folk hero. Use details from the poem and other sources to support your ideas.

Speaking and Listening

4. **Interview** Imagine what would happen if Johnny Appleseed were suddenly transported to the present day. How would he react to modern life in your community? Role-play an interview between a local news commentator and the newly modernized folk hero. **[Performing Arts Link]**
5. **Musical Setting** Set "Johnny Appleseed" to music. Choose a simple, catchy tune that's easy to sing. If you play an instrument, create an instrumental accompaniment. Teach the song to your class, and sing it together. **[Music Link]**

Projects

6. **Apple Poster [Group Activity]** With a group of classmates, create a poster illustrating various types of apples. Include information that lists differences between varieties, regions in which they are grown, and popular recipes. Display your poster in the classroom. **[Science Link]**
7. **How-to Booklet** Work with a team to create a how-to booklet for growing apples. Research how and where to plant trees, kinds of fertilizer to use, and methods of harvesting. Your finished brochure can include diagrams, articles, and sources of additional information. **[Science Link]**

 Writing Mini-Lesson

Legendary Story

Modern writers often retell stories of legendary characters to bring them to life for contemporary readers. Choose a favorite legendary tale, and write your own version.

Writing Skills Focus: Show, Don't Tell

One of the best pieces of advice you'll hear about writing is **"show, don't tell."** This means that you should avoid simply *telling* readers what a character is like; instead, *show* the character doing something that reveals what the character is like. For example, Benét doesn't just tell readers that Chapman loved nature; instead, she shows him in action.

Model From the Poem
For fifty years over
Of harvest and dew,
He planted his apples
Where no apples grew.

Prewriting Choose a legendary tale you'd like to retell. Make a story map to jot down the basic story elements. Think about story details you want to emphasize in your version.

Drafting Write the story events chronologically. Don't worry about including every little detail in your first draft. It's more important to get the main events clearly stated.

Revising Apply the rule "show, don't tell." Look for spots where you've *told* the reader directly about a character. Replace those sentences with scenes that show the character in action.

> **Grammar Application**
> Check your writing to eliminate unnecessary commas.

✓ **ASSESSMENT OPTIONS**

Formal Assessment, Selection Test, pp. 259–261, and Assessment Resources Software. The selection test is designed so that it can easily be customized to the performance levels of your students.

Alternative Assessment, p. 57, includes options for less advanced students, more advanced students, verbal/linguistic learners, musical/rhythmic learners, interpersonal learners, and visual/spatial learners.

PORTFOLIO ASSESSMENT
Use the following rubrics in the **Alternative Assessment** booklet to assess student writing:
Epitaph: Expression, p. 90
Folk Ballad: Poetry, p. 104
Essay: Research Report/Paper, p. 102
Writing Mini-Lesson: Fictional Narrative, p. 91

PART **1** *A Sampling of Stories*

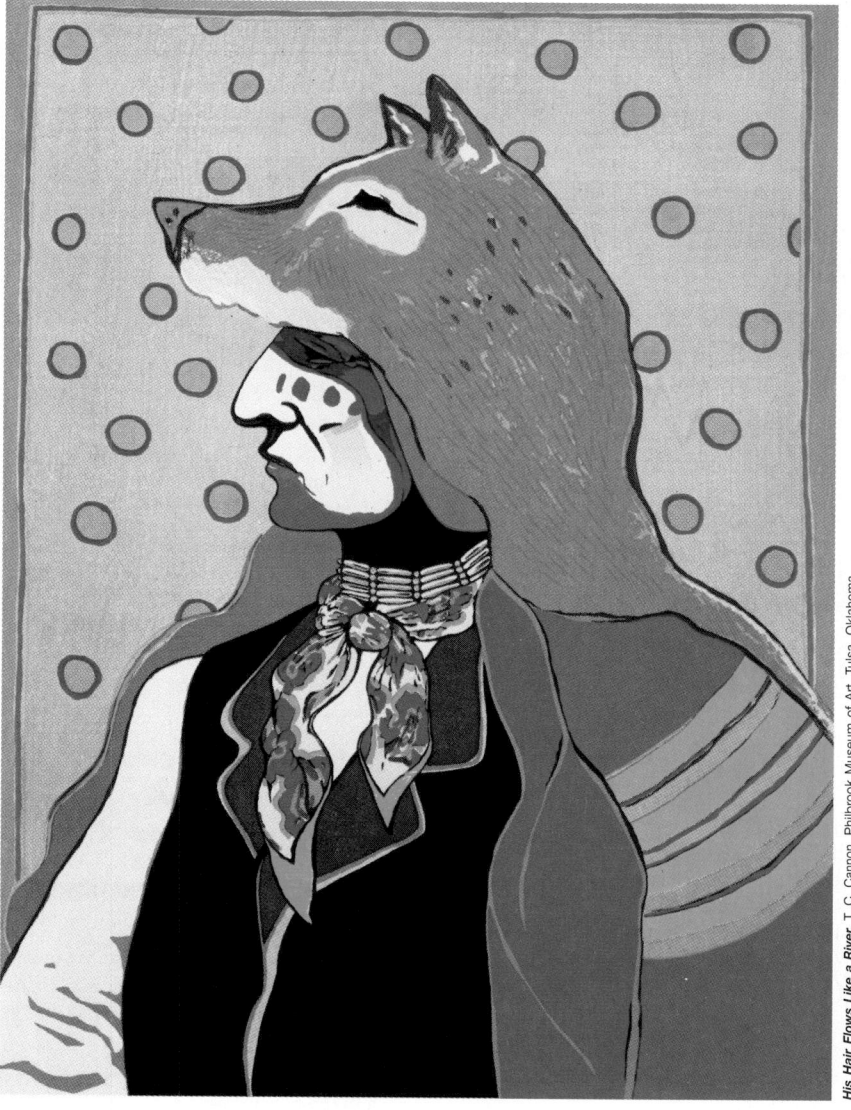

His Hair Flows Like a River, T. C. Cannon, Philbrook Museum of Art, Tulsa, Oklahoma

A Sampling of Stories ◆ 899

One-Minute Planning Guide

The selections in this section focus on a sampling of stories. "Coyote Steals the Sun and the Moon" and "The Spirit Chief Names the Animal People" are two Native American myths. "Chicoria," "Brer Possum's Dilemma," and "Why the Waves Have Whitecaps" are three folk tales; one is New Mexican; the other two are African American. An excerpt from *The Right Stuff* allows students to read about a modern-day American hero.

Customize for
Varying Student Needs
When assigning the selections in this section to your students, keep in mind the following factors:

"Coyote Steals the Sun and Moon," "The Spirit Chief Names the Animal People"
- Two Native American myths that introduce the character of the coyote
- "The Spirit Chief Names the Animal People" provides an opportunity for a Beyond Literature cultural connection

"Chicoria," "Brer Possum's Dilemma," "Why the Waves Have Whitecaps"
- Three folk tales, including one New Mexican and two African American
- Students may need help with pronunciation of Spanish vocabulary and understanding dialect
- "Chicoria" includes a Beyond Literature social studies connection

from *The Right Stuff*
- An excerpt from a novel by Tom Wolfe about Alan Shepard
- Provides an opportunity for connecting literature to social studies

---

Humanities: Art

His Hair Flows Like a River, by T. C. Cannon
T. C. Cannon was born in Oklahoma in 1946. He was an avid reader as well as an artist, and his work focused on an interest in both world art and literature. A Native American, Cannon explored the difficulty of maintaining cultural ties to one's heritage while at the same time creating an independent identity. His contemporary treatment of classic Native American themes drove Native American art in a new, modern direction, with a popular following.

Have students study the painting, and then ask the following questions:
1. What elements of Native American culture do you see in this painting? *Students should note the hat made from a fox, the paint on the man's face, and the beaded necklace.*
2. What modern elements do you see in the painting? *Students may note that the man seems to be wearing a classic suit and flowered handkerchief. The background of the painting, also, seems modern.*

899

OBJECTIVES

1. To read, comprehend, and interpret two myths
2. To relate two myths to personal experience
3. To understand the cultural context of a myth
4. To analyze a myth
5. To build vocabulary in context and learn the suffix -ify
6. To develop skill in using commas in compound sentences
7. To report on an animal, using visual support
8. To respond to the myths through writing, speaking and listening, and projects

SKILLS INSTRUCTION

Vocabulary:
Suffixes: -ify
Spelling:
Adding -ify to Words Ending in e or y
Grammar:
Commas in Compound Sentences
Literary Focus:
Myth
Writing:
Give Visual Support

Reading Strategy:
Understand the Cultural Context
Speaking and Listening:
Coyote's Trial (Teacher Edition)
Viewing and Representing:
Myths (Teacher Edition)
Critical Viewing:
Infer; Connect

PORTFOLIO OPPORTUNITIES

Writing: Letter; Newspaper Story; Essay
Writing Mini-Lesson: Report on an Animal
Speaking and Listening: Coyote's Trial; Dramatic Reading
Projects: Multimedia Report; Collection of Story Summaries

More About the Authors
Richard Erdoes is an artist, photographer, and author of more than 20 books about the American West. He lives in Santa Fé, New Mexico.

Alfonso Ortiz described his pilgrimage to the ancient homeland of his Tewa people; on the way, he recognized mountains and other geographical features from Tewa tales. Ortiz, who died in 1997, taught anthropology at the University of New Mexico.

Mourning Dove was an Okanogan Indian, from the state of Washington. Her pen name commemorated the faithful wife of Salmon, who welcomes his wife's return each spring.

Guide for Reading

Meet the Authors:

Richard Erdoes (1912–   )
Alfonso Ortiz (1939–   )

For their book *American Indian Myths and Legends*, Richard Erdoes and Alfonso Ortiz collected many stories over a period of twenty-five years. Some of the stories in that book "were jotted down at powwows, around campfires, even inside a moving car." Richard Erdoes (top) was born in Frankfurt, Germany.
Alfonso Ortiz (bottom) was born in San Juan, a Tewa pueblo in New Mexico.

Mourning Dove (1884?–1936)

Mourning Dove is the pen name of Christine Quintasket. While earning her living as a migrant worker, Quintasket became a writer and political activist. Always interested in the stories she had heard all her life from relatives and visitors, she collected and recorded the folklore of her people to preserve it for posterity. This story is from her collection *Coyote Stories*, originally published in 1933.

◆ **LITERATURE AND YOUR LIFE**

CONNECT YOUR EXPERIENCE
Imagine if you didn't understand or couldn't explain why things are as they are. Every people since the beginning of time has created stories to explain the world around them. The stories in this section are creation myths invented by Native Americans.

THEMATIC FOCUS: Respecting Nature
As you read these myths, notice how they explain and highlight the wonders of nature.

◆ **Background for Understanding**

SCIENCE
Coyote is a common character in many Native American stories. The coyote is a smaller cousin of the wolf. Its habitat is most of North America. Usually a solitary animal, it has been known to hunt in pairs and sometimes in an odd partnership with the badger. The Coyote of Native American tales is a combination of godlike, human, and animal characteristics. He symbolizes the balance of qualities within us all, including wisdom and foolishness, generosity and greed, honesty and deception.

◆ **Build Vocabulary**

SUFFIXES: -ify
The suffix -ify, meaning "to make," changes a noun or adjective into a verb. It appears in the Word Bank word *purify*, which means "to make pure."

WORD BANK
Which word from the list means "to awaken" or "to stir or rouse"? Check the Build Vocabulary box on page 906 to see if you chose correctly.

shriveled
pursuit
arouse
purify

900 ◆ *The American Folk Tradition*

 Prentice Hall Literature Program Resources

REINFORCE / RETEACH / EXTEND
Selection Support Pages
Build Vocabulary: Suffixes: -ify, p. 312
Build Grammar Skills: Commas in Compound Sentences, p. 314
Reading Strategy: Understand the Cultural Context, p. 315
Literary Focus: Myth, p. 316
Strategies for Diverse Student Needs, pp. 115–116
Beyond Literature Workplace Skills: Qualities of Leadership, p. 57

Formal Assessment Selection Test, pp. 262–264, Assessment Resources Software
Alternative Assessment, p. 58
Art Transparencies, pp. 11–14
Resource Pro CD-ROM
 Listening to Literature Audiocassettes "Coyote Steals the Sun and Moon" and "The Spirit Chief Names the Animal People"
 **Looking at Literature Videodisc/ Videotape**

◆ Coyote Steals the Sun and Moon ◆
The Spirit Chief Names the Animal People

Sunset in Memoriam (detail), 1946, Woody (Woodrow Wilson) Crumbo, Philbrook Museum of Art, Tulsa, Oklahoma

◆ Literary Focus

MYTH

A **myth** is an ancient tale having its roots in the beliefs of a particular group or nation. Just as science and history teach and explain about the world, mythology develops certain common themes, such as creation, the origin of the universe, the meaning of existence and death, and natural occurrences. Myths often tell about the adventures of great heroes who possess special powers.

◆ Reading Strategy

UNDERSTAND THE CULTURAL CONTEXT

As you read, look for details within the myth to help you **understand the cultural context** of the story. For example, in these works, details about animal behavior, the weather, and the change of seasons may lead you to understand that, like all peoples of centuries ago, the culture originating these tales was agricultural, depending on aspects of nature for survival.

As you read, keep track of the details that reveal the cultural context. You might want to use a chart like the one below to help you.

Detail	What It Shows
Coyote steals the sun and moon	
The Spirit Chief names the Animal People	

Guide for Reading ◆ 901

◆ Build Grammar Skills

Commas in Compound Sentences If you wish to introduce the grammar concept for this selection before students read, refer to the instruction on p. 908.

Customize for
Less Proficient Readers

Students may have difficulty understanding the cultural context of these myths. Encourage them to fill in the table on p. 901 as they read. Have them look for specific details about the culture each myth comes from. For example, they might note the human characteristics that Coyote and Eagle exhibit or consider the human qualities of the animals who want to receive proud names and do powerful work in "The Spirit Chief Names the Animal People."

Customize for
More Advanced Students

Encourage students to consider the characters other than Coyote. How do they behave? Is Coyote the only character with good and bad traits? Have students select another character and write a short explanation of his contradictory behavior.

Customize for
English Language Learners

As they read "Coyote Steals the Sun and Moon," ask students to think about the story-teller's purpose—to explain why the sun and moon are in the sky and why winter comes each year. This myth also describes Coyote, a character common to Native American tales. Ask students if they know any myths from their own culture that explain a natural phenomenon or introduce a folk character such as Coyote.

Preparing for Standardized Tests

Punctuation Standardized tests may ask students to identify correct punctuation. Review the grammar skill on p. 908. Then, use this sample question:

Which sentence has correct punctuation?

(A) Myths are ancient tales that explain, or summarize the beliefs of a culture, and folk tales are regional stories that are told to teach a lesson, or entertain.

(B) Myths are ancient tales that explain, or summarize the beliefs of a culture and folk tales are regional stories that are told to teach a lesson, or entertain.

(C) Myths are ancient tales that explain or summarize the beliefs of a culture, and folk tales are regional stories that are told to teach a lesson or entertain.

(D) Myths are ancient tales that explain or summarize the beliefs of a culture and folk tales are regional stories that are told to teach a lesson or entertain.

Help students understand that *or* is not a coordinating conjunction in these sentences. The correct answer, *(C),* has the comma placed before the coordinating conjunction *and*.

In the dark time before the sun and the moon are in the sky providing light, Coyote and Eagle team up and go searching for a light source. They find the Kachinas, who keep the sun and the moon in two boxes. They steal the sun and moon, and Eagle flies off, carrying a box containing both the sun and moon, with Coyote running below. After Coyote begs to be allowed to carry the box, Eagle finally lets him. Unfortunately, Coyote curiously opens the box and allows the sun and moon to escape into the sky, causing fall and winter to come to the land.

Team Teaching Strategy

These myths offer an opportunity for team teaching with a social studies teacher, creating a cross-curricular unit on Native American culture and stories.

Customize for
Visual/Spatial Learners

Before students read the myth, have them study the illustration. Ask students what they think the coyote is doing. Is he howling at the moon, calling to it, or singing? Have students write a journal entry about the coyote. After reading the myth, students can write another journal entry, explaining what they think the coyote is doing based on what they read.

Coyote Steals the Sun and Moon

Zuñi Myth

Retold by Richard Erdoes and Alfonso Ortiz

Cosmic Canine, John Nieto, Courtesy of the artist

902 ◆ *The American Folk Tradition*

Block Scheduling Strategies

Consider these suggestions to take advantage of extended class time:

- Introduce the first selection with the background information on p. 900, or use **Daily Language Practice,** p. 64. Then have students read independently and answer the questions on p. 904. After completing the Beyond Literature activity on p. 904, have students read the second selection in small groups and discuss the questions on p. 907.
- Allow students class time to prepare for the Speaking and Listening activity Coyote's Trial

from the Idea Bank, p. 909, and the Teacher's Edition, p. 904.

- Have each student retell a story selected from the Collection of Story Summaries in the Idea Bank activity on p. 909 in his or her own speaking style, using the summary as a reference tool.
- If you have access to technology, have students use the *Writer's Solution Writing Lab CD-ROM* tutorial to help them complete their reports. Have students exchange drafts and help each other revise the reports. Allow time for students to present their reports with visual aids.

Coyote is a bad hunter who never kills anything. Once he watched Eagle hunting rabbits, catching one after another—more rabbits than he could eat. Coyote thought, "I'll team up with Eagle so I can have enough meat." Coyote is always up to something.

"Friend," Coyote said to Eagle, "we should hunt together. Two can catch more than one."

"Why not?" Eagle said, and so they began to hunt in partnership. Eagle caught many rabbits, but all Coyote caught was some little bugs.

At this time the world was still dark; the sun and moon had not yet been put in the sky. "Friend," Coyote said to Eagle, "no wonder I can't catch anything; I can't see. Do you know where we can get some light?"

"You're right, friend, there should be some light," Eagle said. "I think there's a little toward the west. Let's try and find it."

And so they went looking for the sun and moon. They came to a big river, which Eagle flew over. Coyote swam, and swallowed so much water that he almost drowned. He crawled out with his fur full of mud, and Eagle asked, "Why don't you fly like me?"

"You have wings; I just have hair," Coyote said. "I can't fly without feathers."

At last they came to a pueblo,[1] where the Kachinas[2] happened to be dancing. The people invited Eagle and Coyote to sit down and have something to eat while they watched the sacred dances. Seeing the power of the Kachinas, Eagle said, "I believe these are the people who have light."

Coyote, who had been looking all around, pointed out two boxes, one large and one small, that the people opened whenever they wanted light. To produce a lot of light, they opened the lid of the big box, which contained the sun. For less light they opened the small box, which held the moon.

---

1. **pueblo** (pweb´ lō): Native American village in the southwestern United States.
2. **Kachinas** (kə chē´ nəz): Masked dancers who imitate gods or the spirits of their ancestors.

◀ Critical Viewing Why might the artist have chosen to depict Coyote as multicolored? [Infer]

Coyote nudged Eagle. "Friend, did you see that? They have all the light we need in the big box. Let's steal it."

"You always want to steal and rob. I say we should just borrow it."

"They won't lend it to us."

"You may be right," said Eagle. "Let's wait till they finish dancing and then steal it."

After a while the Kachinas went home to sleep, and Eagle scooped up the large box and flew off. Coyote ran along trying to keep up, panting, his tongue hanging out. Soon he yelled up to Eagle, "Ho, friend, let me carry the box a little way."

"No, no," said Eagle, "you never do anything right."

He flew on, and Coyote ran after him. After a while Coyote shouted again: "Friend, you're my chief, and it's not right for you to carry the box; people will call me lazy. Let me have it."

"No, no, you always mess everything up." And Eagle flew on and Coyote ran along.

So it went for a stretch, and then Coyote started again. "Ho, friend, it isn't right for you to do this. What will people think of you and me?"

"I don't care what people think. I'm going to carry this box."

Again Eagle flew on and again Coyote ran after him. Finally Coyote begged for the fourth time: "Let me carry it. You're the chief, and I'm just Coyote. Let me carry it."

Eagle couldn't stand any more pestering. Also, Coyote had asked him four times, and if someone asks four times, you'd better give him what he wants. Eagle said, "Since you won't let up on me, go ahead and carry the box for a while. But promise not to open it."

"Oh, sure, oh yes, I promise." They went on as before, but now Coyote had the box. Soon Eagle was far ahead, and Coyote lagged behind a hill where Eagle couldn't see him. "I wonder what the light looks like, inside there," he said to himself. "Why shouldn't I take a peek? Probably there's something extra in the box, something good that Eagle wants to keep to himself."

And Coyote opened the lid. Now, not only was the sun inside, but the moon also. Eagle had put them both together, thinking that it would be easier to carry one box than two.

Coyote Steals the Sun and Moon ◆ 903

◆ **Reading Strategy**

❶ **Understand the Cultural Context** What do you learn about how the Zuñi people view Coyote and Eagle? *Coyote is considered a bad hunter who is always scheming. Eagle is a good hunter who seems willing to cooperate with Coyote.*

Comprehension Check ☑

❷ Why does Coyote have more trouble hunting than Eagle? *Coyote seems to have a hard time and only catches bugs, because the world is dark and he cannot see very well.*

▶**Critical Viewing**◀

❸ **Infer** *Students may notice that Coyote has many different character traits, both good and bad. The artist may have illustrated Coyote as multicolored to reveal his many different qualities.*

Comprehension Check ☑

❹ Does Coyote steal the sun and the moon from the Kachinas by himself? *No, Eagle helps with the theft.*

◆ **Critical Thinking**

❺ **Draw Conclusions** Why does Coyote pester and beg the Eagle for a chance to carry the box? *Because Coyote is sneaky and tricks other people, he is afraid that Eagle might be going do the same thing to him and keep something extra out of the box for himself.*

◆ **Critical Thinking**

❻ **Predict** What do you think will happen when Coyote opens the box? *The Coyote is a character who is always up to something and seems to be unlucky. Also, Eagle asks him not to open the box, so he hides from Eagle in order to open it. Probably something bad will happen when he opens it.*

Cross-Curricular Connection: Social Studies

Zuñi The Zuñi live in the southwestern part of the United States in desert and mesa country. Like other Pueblo people of this area, the Zuñi build homes of sandstone on bluffs or of adobe on the banks of the Rio Grande. The villages blend with their surroundings because of the people's belief that all things, living and nonliving, have a place.

The Kachina culture is at least 600 years old. The Zuñi celebrate the Kachinas' coming in December and February to bring rain, award gifts, and enforce discipline. Villagers watch the Kachinas dance to songs and drums by firelight at night—like the event that Coyote and Eagle encounter at a pueblo and join at the people's invitation.

Suggest that students research the Kachina. They can locate photographs of Kachina figures, or if possible, visit a museum where Kachina figures are displayed.

◆ Literary Focus

1 Myth *The myth explains how the sun and moon came to be in the sky, and why there is winter.*

Beyond Literature

As students research to learn about the coyote's habitat, eating habits, and life span, ask them to think about why Native American tales may have depicted coyote as a trickster character.

Reinforce and Extend

Answers
◆ LITERATURE AND YOUR LIFE

Reader's Response Students may advise Eagle to ask the Kachinas to share the light, or at least not to let the curious Coyote carry the important box.

Thematic Focus The message might be to not try to change the natural course of events.

☑ Check Your Comprehension

1. (a) Eagle is a better hunter.
   (b) They search for light.
2. They find light in a pueblo where Kachinas are dancing.
3. (a) Coyote begs and asks four times, which means Eagle should give him what he wants. Eagle was also very tired of being pestered.
   (b) He curiously opens the box and lets the sun and moon escape into the sky.

◆ Critical Thinking

1. Eagle can fly, is a good hunter, and, though he steals, he is cautious. Coyote is a bad hunter, must swim or run rather than fly, likes to steal, and is sneaky.
2. Coyote is determined.
3. Eagle's hunting and flying abilities are real, as is Coyote's willingness to steal. Containing the sun and moon in a box is not possible.
4. The revolution of the earth around the sun and the tilt of the earth on its axis causes the seasons.

904

As soon as Coyote opened the lid, the moon escaped, flying high into the sky. At once all the plants <u>shriveled</u> up and turned brown. Just as quickly, all the leaves fell off the trees,

> ◆ **Literary Focus**
> **1** What event in nature does this story explain?

and it was winter. Trying to catch the moon and put it back in the box, Coyote ran in <u>pursuit</u> as it skipped away from him. Meanwhile the sun flew out and rose into the sky. It drifted far away, and the peaches, squashes, and melons shriveled up with cold.

Eagle turned and flew back to see what had delayed Coyote. "You fool! Look what you've done!" he said. "You let the sun and moon escape, and now it's cold." Indeed, it began to snow, and Coyote shivered. "Now your teeth are chattering," Eagle said, "and it's your fault that cold has come into the world."

It's true. If it weren't for Coyote's curiosity and mischief making, we wouldn't have winter; we could enjoy summer all the time.

◆ Build Vocabulary

shriveled (shriv´ əld) *v.:* Dried up; withered
pursuit (pər soot´) *n.:* Following in order to overtake and capture

---

Beyond Literature

Cultural Connection

Coyote the Trickster Tales of tricks and pranks and those who play them on others have amused people from the dawn of time to the present day. Among Native Americans, the greatest trickster is Coyote. The character of Coyote the Trickster had the form of a coyote but exhibited human qualities. Tales of Coyote's exploits have been told from Alaska to the southern deserts and from coast to coast. These stories tell of Coyote's cleverness and foolishness, his ability to cheat his enemies, and his never-ending appetite. They also tell of those who manage to play tricks on Coyote.

Cross-Curricular Activity

Report Use a variety of sources to learn about coyotes—where they live, what they eat, how long they live, and so on. Reveal your findings in a report.

Guide for Responding

◆ LITERATURE AND YOUR LIFE

Reader's Response What advice would you like to give to Eagle?

Thematic Focus In what way does "Coyote Steals the Sun and Moon" caution the reader to respect nature?

☑ Check Your Comprehension

1. (a) Why does Coyote want to team up with Eagle? (b) What do they decide to search for?
2. Where do Coyote and Eagle find what they have been searching for?
3. (a) Why does Eagle finally let Coyote carry the box? (b) What happens once Coyote gets it?

◆ Critical Thinking

INTERPRET
1. Contrast the characters of Eagle and Coyote in terms of their appearance, their abilities, and their attitudes. **[Compare and Contrast]**
2. What can you tell about Coyote from the fact that he pesters Eagle until he gets the box? **[Infer]**
3. Which details in this story are based on fact, and which ones are invented? **[Distinguish]**

EXTEND
4. This story offers one explanation for why we have summer and winter. What are the scientific reasons? **[Science Link]**

904 ◆ The American Folk Tradition

Speaking and Listening Mini-Lesson

Coyote's Trial
This mini-lesson supports the Speaking and Listening activity in the Idea Bank on p. 909.

Introduce Tell students they will be acting out a trial in which the Kachinas take Eagle and Coyote to court for stealing the sun and the moon.

Develop Ask students to work in groups to list the participants of a trial. Make sure they include members of the jury, the judge, witnesses, and the prosecuting and defense attorneys. Students should cast the roles and work as a group to write a script for the trial.

Apply After rehearsing, have students perform the trial for another class that is studying a related topic. Students may wish to let the audience act as the jury. If they choose this performance method, they will want to leave the ending unscripted and let the jury members actually vote on the verdict.

Assess Evaluate students' work based on the effectiveness of their preparation, group work, and ability to engage the audience. Or, have students use the Peer Assessment: Dramatic Performance form, p. 116, in **Alternative Assessment**.

The Spirit Chief Names the Animal People
Mourning Dove

Hah-ah' Eel-me'-whem, the great Spirit Chief,[1] called the Animal People together. They came from all parts of the world. Then the Spirit Chief told them there was to be a change, that a new kind of people was coming to live on the earth.

"All of you *Chip-chap-tiqulk*—Animal People—must have names," the Spirit Chief said. "Some of you have names now, some of you haven't. But tomorrow all will have names that shall be kept by you and your descendants forever. In the morning, as the first light of day shows in the sky, come to my lodge and choose your names. The first to come may choose any name that he or she wants. The next person may take any other name. That is the way it will go until all the names are taken. And to each person I will give work to do."

That talk made the Animal People very excited. Each wanted a proud name and the power to rule some tribe or some part of the world, and everyone determined to get up early and hurry to the Spirit Chief's lodge.

Sin-ka-lip'—Coyote—boasted that no one would be ahead of him. He walked among the people and told them that he would be the first. Coyote did not like his name; he wanted another. Nobody respected his name, Imitator, but it fitted him. He was called *Sin-ka-lip'* because he liked to imitate people. He thought that he could do anything that other persons

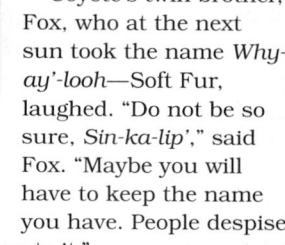

Thunder Knives, 1957, Pablita Velarde, Museum of Indian Arts & Culture/Laboratory of Anthropology Collections, Museum of New Mexico, Santa Fe, NM

▲ **Critical Viewing** What animals can you identify in this painting? **[Connect]**

did, and he pretended to know everything. He would ask a question, and when the answer was given he would say:

"I knew that before. I did not have to be told."

Such smart talk did not make friends for Coyote. Nor did he make friends by the foolish things he did and the rude tricks he played on people.

"I shall have my choice of the three biggest names," he boasted. "Those names are: *Kee-lau-naw*, the Mountain Person—Grizzly Bear, who will rule the four-footed people; *Milka-noups*—Eagle, who will rule the birds; and *En-tee-tee-ueh*, the Good Swimmer—Salmon. Salmon will be the chief of all the fish that the New People use for food."

Coyote's twin brother, Fox, who at the next sun took the name *Why-ay'-looh*—Soft Fur, laughed. "Do not be so sure, *Sin-ka-lip'*," said Fox. "Maybe you will have to keep the name you have. People despise that name. No one wants it."

"I am tired of that name," Coyote said in an angry voice. "Let someone else carry it. Let some old person take it—someone who cannot win in war. I am going to be a great warrior. My smart brother, I will make you beg of me when I am called Grizzly Bear, Eagle, or Salmon."

"Your strong words mean nothing," scoffed Fox. "Better go to your *swool'-hu* (tepee) and get some sleep, or you will not wake up in time to choose any name."

---

1. **Spirit Chief:** Many Native American groups believe in a Spirit Chief, an all-powerful god.

The Spirit Chief Names the Animal People ◆ 905

Cultural Connection

Name Giving The giving of names to people, places, and animals is very important for many Native Americans.

In the League of the Iroquois in the northeast, the names of the tribes indicated their power. The Mohawk were the "Keepers of the Eastern Door," meaning they protected the eastern boundary of the league. The Seneca were the "Keepers of the Western Door," and the powerful Onondaga were "Keepers of the Central Fire."

The Creek, who now live in Oklahoma but originally lived in Georgia and Alabama, have a name-giving ritual as part of the Green Corn Ceremony. This ritual names and installs young men as full members of the tribe. The boys purify themselves before the ceremony, just as warriors once did before going to battle. As part of the ritual, women and girls perform a ribbon dance.

In the northwest, the Haida chiefs gave their houses names like "The Clouds Sound Against It As They Pass Over."

Suggest that interested students research the origins of other Native American names and report their findings in a visual display.

◆ Critical Thinking

❶ Interpret From reading the selection, what do you think the qualities of a good wife were considered to be in this culture? *Mole was considered a good wife because she was loyal to Coyote, was never jealous, and did not talk back to him even when he was unkind to her and didn't bring the children any food.*

◆ Reading Strategy

❷ Understand the Cultural Context To cook, people heated stones on the fire, and then dropped them into a cooking-basket filled with water. The stones made the water boil, cooking the food in the water.

◆ Critical Thinking

❸ Infer Do you think Coyote is being paid back for boasting and for being rude to his wife? *Students may say that he is, since Mole did not wake him up early enough to get a new name.*

◆ Literary Focus

❹ Myth What can you learn from the conversation between the Spirit Chief and Coyote? *The Spirit Chief seems to understand Coyote, and to have arranged everything to happen just as it has. Perhaps Coyote can't change because the Spirit Chief doesn't want him to and wants him to learn a lesson.*

Looking at Literature Videodisc/Videotape

To capture students' interest and motivate them to read "The Spirit Chief Names the Animal People," play Chapter 10 of the videodisc. In this chapter, Native American Tone Kei discusses the importance of balance in nature and retells a Native American myth. Discuss why balance in nature, and in our lives, is so important.

Chapter 10

Customize for
Interpersonal Learners

Have students work in groups to compare and contrast Coyote in "Coyote Steals the Sun and Moon" and "The Spirit Chief Names the Animal People." In which myth do they learn more about Coyote's character? Have students write a brief explanation of how Coyote is a trickster.

906

Coyote stalked off to his tepee. He told himself that he would not sleep any that night; he would stay wide awake. He entered the lodge, and his three sons called as if with one voice:

"Le-ee'-oo!" ("Father!")

They were hungry, but Coyote had brought them nothing to eat. Their mother, who after the naming day was known as *Pul'-laqu-whu*—Mole, the Mound Digger—sat on her foot at one side of the doorway. Mole was a good woman, always loyal to her husband in spite of his mean ways, his mischief-making, and his foolishness. She never was jealous, never talked back, never replied to his words of abuse. She looked up and said:

"Have you no food for the children? They are starving. I can find no roots to dig."

"Eh-ha!" Coyote grunted. "I am no common person to be addressed in that manner. I am going to be a great chief tomorrow. Did you know that? I will have a new name. I will be Grizzly Bear. Then I can devour my enemies with ease. And I shall need you no longer. You are growing too old and homely to be the wife of a great warrior and chief."

Mole said nothing. She turned to her corner of the lodge and collected a few old bones, which she put into a *klek'-chin* (cooking-basket). With two sticks she lifted hot stones from the fire and dropped them into the basket. Soon the water boiled, and there was weak soup for the hungry children.

◆ Reading Strategy
What does Mole's action tell about how the people cooked their food?

"Gather plenty of wood for the fire," Coyote ordered. "I am going to sit up all night."

Mole obeyed. Then she and the children went to bed.

Coyote sat watching the fire. Half of the night passed. He got sleepy. His eyes grew heavy. So he picked up two little sticks and braced his eyelids apart. "Now I can stay awake," he thought, but before long he was fast asleep, although his eyes were wide open.

The sun was high in the sky when Coyote awoke. But for Mole he would not have wakened then. Mole called him. She called him

906 ◆ The American Folk Tradition

---

after she returned with her name from the Spirit Chief's lodge. Mole loved her husband. She did not want him to have a big name and be a powerful chief. For then, she feared, he would leave her. That was why she did not <u>arouse</u> him at daybreak. Of this she said nothing.

Only half-awake and thinking it was early morning, Coyote jumped at the sound of Mole's voice and ran to the lodge of the Spirit Chief. None of the other *Chip-chap-tiqulk* were there. Coyote laughed. Blinking his sleepy eyes, he walked into the lodge. "I am going to be *Kee-lau-naw*, " he announced in a strong voice. "That shall be my name."

"The name Grizzly Bear was taken at dawn," the Spirit Chief answered.

"Then I shall be *Milka-noups*," said Coyote, and his voice was not so loud.

"Eagle flew away at sunup," the other replied.

"Well, I shall be called *En-tee-tee-ueh*," Coyote said in a voice that was not loud at all.

"The name Salmon also has been taken," explained the Spirit Chief. "All the names except your own have been taken. No one wished to steal your name."

Poor Coyote's knees grew weak. He sank down beside the fire that blazed in the great tepee, and the heart of *Hah-ah' Eel-me'-whem* was touched.

"Sin-ka-lip',*"* said that Person, "you must keep your name. It is a good name for you. You slept long because I wanted you to be the last one here. I have important work for you, much for you to do before the New People come. You are to be chief of all the tribes.

"Many bad creatures inhabit the earth. They bother and kill people, and the tribes cannot increase as I wish. These *En-alt-na Skil-ten*—People-Devouring Monsters—cannot keep on like that. They must be stopped. It is for you to conquer them. For doing that, for all the good things you do, you will be honored and

◆ Build Vocabulary
arouse (ə rouz´) *v.*: Awaken, as from sleep
purify (pyoor´ ə fī) *v.*: To rid of impurities

Viewing and Representing Mini-Lesson

Myths

This mini-lesson will extend students' understanding of mythological explanations.

Introduce Discuss with students that there are stories from different cultures that are similar, and use a story format to explain things about nature that we can now explain or do scientifically.

Develop Have students work in small groups to select an event of nature such as lightning or comets. The group may choose to explain a more unnatural event such as flying to the moon, but something that is scientifically possible—if not

now, in the future. Groups should do research and study photographs. For example, to write a story about a comet, or an animal riding to the stars on a comet, they should study the scientific facts and visual representations available to us at the present time before they begin writing their fictionalized explanation.

Apply Have one of the group members orally present the story to the class by reading it dramatically, or storytelling the details from notes.

Assess Evaluate students on their group interaction, research, and storytelling skills.

praised by the people that are here now and that come afterward. But, for the foolish and mean things you do, you will be laughed at and despised. That you cannot help. It is your way.

"To make your work easier, I give you *squas-tenk'*. It is your own special magic power. No one else ever shall have it. When you are in danger, whenever you need help, call to your power. It will do much for you, and with it you can change yourself into any form, into anything you wish.

"To your twin brother, *Why-ay'-looh*, and to others I have given *shoo'-mesh*.[2] It is strong power. With that power Fox can restore your life should you be killed. Your bones may be scattered but, if there is one hair of your body left, Fox can make you live again. Others of the people can do the same with their *shoo'-mesh*. Now, go, *Sin-ka-lip'*! Do well the work laid for your trail!"

Well, Coyote was a chief after all, and he felt good again. After that day his eyes were different. They grew slant from being propped

open that night while he sat by his fire. The New People, the Indians, got their slightly slant eyes from Coyote.

After Coyote had gone, the Spirit Chief thought it would be nice for the Animal People and the coming New People to have the benefit of the spiritual sweat-house.[3] But all of the Animal People had names, and there was no one to take the name of Sweathouse—*Quil'-sten*, the Warmer. So the wife of the Spirit Chief took the name. She wanted the people to have the sweat-house, for she pitied them. She wanted them to have a place to go to <u>purify</u> themselves, a place where they could pray for strength and good luck and strong medicine-power, and where they could fight sickness and get relief from their troubles.

The ribs, the frame poles, of the sweathouse represent the wife of *Hah-ah, Eel-me'-whem*. As she is a spirit, she cannot be seen, but she always is near. Songs to her are sung by the present generation. She hears them. She hears what her people say, and in her heart there is love and pity.

---

2. **shoo'-mesh** (shoo´ mesh) *n.*: Medicine, or strong magic power, provided by the Spirit Chief.

3. **sweat-house:** A mound-shaped lodge where bathers cleanse themselves physically and spiritually.

Guide for Responding

◆ LITERATURE AND YOUR LIFE

Reader's Response Did you want Coyote to get a new name? Why or why not?

Thematic Focus What aspect of nature does this story explain?

☑ Check Your Comprehension

1. Why does the Spirit Chief convene a council of the Animal People?
2. Why does Coyote want to change his name?
3. What happens to prevent Coyote from getting a new name?
4. What physical characteristic of Coyote is passed on to the New People, the Indians?

◆ Critical Thinking

INTERPRET

1. Why does Coyote want to be named Grizzly Bear, Eagle, or Salmon? **[Connect]**
2. How does Coyote's behavior lead to his misfortune? **[Interpret]**
3. Why does the Spirit Chief give Fox powers to restore Coyote's life? **[Draw Conclusions]**

COMPARE LITERARY WORKS

4. In "The Spirit Chief Names the Animal People," Coyote is given a very important job: to conquer the People-Devouring Monsters. Based on what you learn about Coyote in "Coyote Steals the Sun and Moon," do you think Coyote will succeed at this? **[Assess]**

The Spirit Chief Names the Animal People ◆ 907

Beyond the Selection

FURTHER READING
Other Works by Richard Erdoes
Legends of the American West
American Indian Trickster Tales (with Alfonso Ortiz)
Other Works by Alfonso Ortiz
The Tewa World
Other Works by Mourning Dove
Cowegea
Other Native American Literature
Anpao: An American Indian Odyssey, Jamake Highwater
Earthmaker's Tales, Star Tales, Gretchen Will Mayo

INTERNET
We suggest the following site on the Internet (all Web sites are subject to change).
For coyote stories and poems:
http://www.indians.org/welker/coyote.htm
We *strongly recommend* that you preview this site before you send students to it.

◆ Reading Strategy

1. The people who told this myth probably suffered during winter because of cold and lack of food.

2. The sweat house is important because there people can purify themselves, pray for strength and good luck, fight sickness, and get relief from their troubles.

◆ Build Vocabulary

Using the Suffix -ify

1. to make solid
2. to make stronger or more intense
3. to involve in mystery; to puzzle or perplex

Spelling Strategy

1. simplify; 2. beautify; 3. codify

Using the Word Bank

1. b   2. d   3. c   4. a

◆ Literary Focus

1. (a) The location of the sun and moon and the coming of winter are explained. (b) The sun and moon escaped to the sky when Coyote let them out of the box. Because the sun and moon went so far away, the earth became cold, causing first fall, then winter.

2. The New People got their slanted eyes from Coyote, whose eyes became slanted because he propped them open with sticks.

◆ Build Grammar Skills

Practice

1. After a while, the Kachinas went home to sleep, and Eagle scooped up the large box and flew off.
2. You're the chief, and I'm just Coyote.
3. They went on as before, but now Coyote had the box.
4. They were hungry, but Coyote had brought them nothing to eat.
5. Soon the water boiled, and there was weak soup for the hungry children.

Writing Application

1. The Kachinas left, and Eagle took the box.
2. Eagle flew on, and Coyote ran after him.
3. Coyote's sons were hungry, but Coyote had brought them nothing to eat.

◆ Guide for Responding (continued)

◆ Reading Strategy

UNDERSTAND THE CULTURAL CONTEXT

When reading myths, it is useful to **understand the cultural context** from which they came. For example, if you know that a myth is Native American in origin, you would understand the importance of animals in main character roles.

1. In "Coyote Steals the Sun and Moon," the snows of winter come when Coyote loses the sun, and this occurrence causes great suffering. What does this tell you about the people's way of life?

2. The importance of the sweat-house is explained in "The Spirit Chief Names the Animal People." What does this explanation reveal about the culture?

◆ Build Vocabulary

USING THE SUFFIX -ify

The suffix -ify, which means "to make," changes a noun or an adjective to a verb. Sometimes the noun or adjective form changes slightly when -ify is added. On your paper, write a definition for the following words:

1. solidify   2. intensify   3. mystify

SPELLING STRATEGY

When adding -ify to words ending in e or y, drop the e or y:

pure + -ify = purify   glory + -ify = glorify

Add -ify to the following words. Write the new words on your paper.

1. simple   2. beauty   3. code

USING THE WORD BANK

On your paper, write the letter of the definition that matches each Word Bank word.

1. shriveled   a. to make clean
2. pursuit   b. dried up
3. arouse   c. awaken
4. purify   d. chase

◆ Literary Focus

MYTH

A **myth** is a story handed down through the generations by word of mouth. Myths often explain something about nature. These explanations often involve an interaction between gods, humans, and forces of nature.

1. (a) What forces of nature are explained in "Coyote Steals the Sun and Moon"? (b) Summarize the explanations.

2. What human physical characteristic is explained in "The Spirit Chief Names the Animal People"?

◆ Build Grammar Skills

COMMAS IN COMPOUND SENTENCES

These stories have many examples of compound sentences, which contain two independent clauses joined by a coordinating conjunction (and, but, or, or nor). Use a **comma** in a compound sentence before the coordinating conjunction. Notice the comma before and in this example of a compound sentence:

independent   coordinating   independent
clause   conjunction   clause
[He flew on,] and [Coyote ran after him.]

Practice On your paper, write these compound sentences, placing commas correctly.

1. After a while, the Kachinas went home to sleep and Eagle scooped up the large box and flew off.
2. You're the chief and I'm just Coyote.
3. They went on as before but now Coyote had the box.
4. They were hungry but Coyote had brought them nothing to eat.
5. Soon the water boiled and there was weak soup for the hungry children.

Writing Application. On your paper, write each pair of sentences as a compound sentence. Place commas correctly.

1. The Kachinas left. Eagle took the box.
2. Eagle flew on. Coyote ran after him.
3. Coyote's sons were hungry. Coyote had brought them nothing to eat.

✎ Writer's Solution

For additional instruction and practice, use the commas lesson in the Punctuation unit of the *Writer's Solution Language Lab CD-ROM.*

Build Your Portfolio

 ## Idea Bank

Writing

1. **Letter** Take the part of Mole in "The Spirit Chief Names the Animal People," and think about how you'd feel about Coyote's treatment of you. Write a letter to your best friend, telling how you feel and what you plan to do.

2. **Newspaper Story** Write a newspaper story based on the day the Spirit Chief named the animals. **[Media Link]**

3. **Essay** Write an essay in which you identify the theme or message of "Coyote Steals the Sun and Moon." Explain whether or not it is effectively presented. Use details from the story to support your ideas. **[Literature Link]**

Speaking and Listening

4. **Coyote's Trial [Group Activity]** Imagine that the Kachinas are taking Coyote and Eagle to court for the crime of stealing the sun and the moon. With a group, assume the roles of judge, prosecuting attorney, defense attorney, witnesses, Coyote, Eagle, and the jury. Act out the trial for the class.

5. **Dramatic Reading** "The Spirit Chief Names the Animal People" was originally told orally. Read the story dramatically, and tape-record your performance. Play the finished tape for the class. **[Performing Arts Link]**

Projects

6. **Multimedia Report [Group Activity]** Work with a group of classmates to create a multimedia presentation about Zuñi culture—past or present. Include photographs, recordings, and drawings of artifacts. **[Social Studies Link]**

7. **Collection of Story Summaries [Group Activity]** With a group, find and read more stories about Coyote. Write the title and a summary of each on an index card. Put the cards in a box labeled "Coyote Stories," and make them available for others to read. **[Literature Link]**

 ## Writing Mini-Lesson

Report on an Animal

Many animals are mentioned in these myths—coyotes, eagles, and foxes, to name a few. Choose one animal that holds special interest for you, and write a report on it.

Writing Skills Focus: Give Visual Support

Give visual support to help your readers understand what you are saying. Among the types of visual support you can use are maps, graphs, pictures, diagrams, and charts.

Model

Coyote	
Length	approx. 4 ft., including tail
Height	approx. 2 ft.
Weight	from 25 to 30 lbs.

Prewriting Conduct research on your animal before creating your visual aids. You could create a timeline of the animal's life span, a chart giving physical statistics, or a diagram of the animal's anatomy. You can also photocopy appropriate maps, photographs, and illustrations.

Drafting Using the information gathered in your research, write a draft of your report. Place visual aids where they'll be most effective.

◆ **Grammar Application**
For variety, use some compound sentences. Be sure that you use a comma before the coordinating conjunction.

Revising Look for places where visual aids will make the information clearer. Be sure the data in your report is accurate and provable. Proofread your report to correct errors in grammar, spelling, and punctuation.

Coyote Steals the Sun and Moon/The Spirit Chief Names the Animal People ◆ 909

 ## Idea Bank

Following are suggestions for matching the Idea Bank topics with your students' performance levels and learning modalities:

Customize for
Performance Levels
Less Advanced Students: 1, 4
Average Students: 2, 4, 6, 7
More Advanced Students: 3, 4, 5, 6, 7

Customize for
Learning Modalities
Verbal/Linguistic: 1, 2, 3, 4, 5, 6, 7
Logical/Mathematical: 4
Visual/Spatial: 6
Bodily/Kinesthetic: 4
Interpersonal: 4, 6
Intrapersonal: 1, 2, 3, 5, 7

 ## Writing Mini-Lesson

Refer students to the Writing Handbook at the back of the book for instruction on the writing process and for further information on reports.

 ### Writer's Solution

Writers at Work Videodisc
Play the videodisc segment in which Virginia Hamilton talks about how she focuses her topic, knowing when the topic is narrow enough to manage.

Play frames 18484 to 19340

Writing Lab CD-ROM
Have students complete the tutorial on Reports. Follow these steps:
1. Have students use the audio-annotated Writing models and interactive activities about purpose.
2. Students can use the annotated instruction on using library resources to help find information for creating visual support for their reports.
3. Students can view the video demonstrating how to add visuals to a report to see examples of reports enhanced by maps, diagrams, photographs, drawings, or charts.
4. Have students draft on computer.
5. As students revise, they can use the strategies for improving the content of a report.

Writer's Solution Sourcebook
Have students use Chapter 7, "Reports," pp. 200–233, for additional support. This chapter includes in-depth instruction on writing reports.

✓ ASSESSMENT OPTIONS

Formal Assessment, Selection Test, pp. 262–264, and Assessment Resources Software. The selection test is designed so that it can easily be customized to the performance levels of your students.

Alternative Assessment, p. 58, includes options for less advanced students, more advanced students, musical/rhythmic learners, visual/spatial learners, verbal/linguistic learners, and logical/mathematical learners.

PORTFOLIO ASSESSMENT
Use the following rubrics in the **Alternative Assessment** booklet to assess student writing:
Letter: Expression, p. 90
Newspaper Story: Description, p. 93
Essay: Literary Analysis/Interpretation, p. 108
Writing Mini-Lesson: Multimedia Report, p. 103

OBJECTIVES

1. To read, comprehend, and interpret three folk tales
2. To relate folk tales to personal experience
3. To recognize the storyteller's purpose
4. To appreciate a folk tale
5. To build vocabulary in context and learn about synonyms
6. To develop skill using commas in a series
7. To write a persuasive advertisement using an effective format
8. To respond to folk tales through writing, speaking and listening, and projects

SKILLS INSTRUCTION

Vocabulary:
Synonyms
Spelling:
Words With the *aw* Sound
Grammar:
Commas in a Series
Reading Strategy:
Recognize the Storyteller's Purpose

Literary Focus:
Folk Tale
Writing:
Effective Format
Speaking and Listening:
Oral Tale (Teacher Edition)
Critical Viewing:
Draw Conclusions; Interpret; Make a Judgment

PORTFOLIO OPPORTUNITIES

Writing: List; Retelling; Essay
Writing Mini-Lesson: Persuasive Advertisement
Speaking and Listening: Skit; Oral Tale
Projects: Folk-Tale Collection; Illustration of a Story

More About the Authors
José Griego y Maestas is interested in tales of New Mexico and all of the Hispanic Southwest. His tales include folk tales from Colorado.

Rudolfo A. Anaya had a swimming accident as a teenager and nearly died. During his long convalescence, he became determined to live life fully and to try to become the best writer his talents would allow.

Jackie Torrence heard many tales from her grandfather, Jim Carson, an ex-slave. She would repeat these tales to her grandmother, who would counter with new tales.

Zora Neale Hurston was an anthropologist, dramatist, essayist, novelist, short story writer, and autobiographer, but folk lore and the preservation of African American folk stories were her passion.

Guide for Reading

Meet the Authors:

José Griego y Maestas

José Griego y Maestas received a master's degree from the University of New Mexico. An expert in bilingual education, he became the director of the Guadalupe Historic Foundation in Santa Fe, New Mexico.

Rudolfo A. Anaya (1937–)

New Mexico resident Rudolfo Anaya, an acclaimed writer of short stories and novels that evoke the culture of the Hispanic people, translated the folk tales collected by José Griego y Maestas into English.

Jackie Torrence (1944–)
Widely known to audiences as "the Story Lady," Jackie Torrence has written several collections of folk tales and stories for children, including *The Accidental Angel, My Grandmother's Treasure,* and *Classic Children's Tales.* A popular and entertaining reader, Torrence has recorded many of her stories on compact disks.

Zora Neale Hurston (1901–1960)
Zora Neale Hurston was the first American to collect and publish African American folklore. She re-created and interpreted the folk tales that she had heard while growing up in Eatonville, Florida, and used the local dialect in her tales. She also wrote novels, short stories, and magazine articles.

910 ◆ The American Folk Tradition

◆ LITERATURE AND YOUR LIFE

CONNECT YOUR EXPERIENCE
Folk tales often provide insights into human nature. In observing how characters think or act in certain situations, these folk tales point out how they *should* act. As you read these folk tales, decide which of their lessons you could apply to your own life.

THEMATIC FOCUS: **Relationships**
What do these folk tales teach you about relationships?

◆ Background for Understanding

SCIENCE
In "Why the Waves Have Whitecaps," you'll find a folk explanation for what causes whitecaps—waves with white-foam tops. Scientifically, this is what really happens: Wind pushes the water, making waves on the water's surface. As the wave nears the shore, where the water is shallower, the height of the wave increases. When the wind has driven the wave to its highest possible point, the crest of the wave breaks up into water droplets. The droplets reflect light and appear to be white. People call these waves either *whitecaps* or *breakers.*

◆ Build Vocabulary

SYNONYMS
Synonyms are words that have nearly the same meaning. In "Chicoria," the author uses the word *haughty,* meaning "full of disdainful pride" to describe a rancher. You may be more familiar with its synonyms: *conceited, arrogant, snobbish, egotistical.*

WORD BANK
Which word from the list means "inspiring pity"? Check the Build Vocabulary box on page 917 to see if you chose correctly.

cordially
haughty
commenced
pitiful

Prentice Hall Literature Program Resources

REINFORCE / RETEACH / EXTEND
Selection Support Pages
Build Vocabulary: Synonyms, p. 317
Build Spelling Skills, p. 318
Build Grammar Skills: Commas in a Series, p. 319
Reading Strategy: Recognize the Storyteller's Purpose, p. 320
Literary Focus: Folk Tales, p. 321
Strategies for Diverse Student Needs, pp. 117–118
Beyond Literature Cross-Curricular Connection: Science, p. 59

Formal Assessment Selection Test, pp. 265–267, Assessment Resources Software
Alternative Assessment, p. 59
Writing and Language Transparencies, Series of Events Chain, p. 57; Sensory Language Chart, p. 69
Resource Pro CD-ROM "Chicoria"; "Brer Possum's Dilemma"; "Why the Waves Have Whitecaps"
 Listening to Literature Audiocassettes "Chicoria"; "Brer Possum's Dilemma"; "Why the Waves Have Whitecaps"

Breakers at Floodtide, 1909, Frederick Judd Waugh, The Butler Institute of American Art, Youngstown, Ohio

Chicoria ◆ Brer Possum's Dilemma ◆ Why the Waves Have Whitecaps ◆

◆ Literary Focus

FOLK TALE

Folk tales were composed orally and passed by word of mouth from generation to generation. Many folk tales have been collected and written down for all to enjoy. These stories often express a belief or a custom of the culture that creates them. Folk tales usually entertain, explain something in nature, or teach a lesson. Look for the lessons in the New Mexican tale "Chicoria" and the African American tales "Brer Possum's Dilemma" and "Why the Waves Have Whitecaps."

◆ Reading Strategy

RECOGNIZE THE STORYTELLER'S PURPOSE

It is storytellers who carry on the oral tradition. Storytellers want to entertain their audience, of course, but they have an additional purpose: They must communicate the message of the tale they are telling. For example, they may instruct listeners about why things are as they are or about how to behave.

Fill in a chart like the one below to help you **recognize the storyteller's purpose.**

Chicoria		
Purpose		**Details From the Tale**
to entertain		Chicoria makes a bet.
to teach		
to model behavior		
to explain		

Guide for Reading ◆ 911

Preparing for Standardized Tests

Grammar Students who punctuate sentences correctly tend to write with greater precision. When used incorrectly, commas in a series can give a sentence an unintended meaning. Standardized tests may evaluate students' accurate use of commas in a series. Use this sample test question:

In which sentence are commas in a series correctly used?

(A) Chicoria recited a wonderful, new, poem for the guests.

(B) Chicoria was a proud, intelligent and gifted poet.

(C) The poet made a bet, told a little story and then proved his point.

(D) In the end, he received his dinner, respect, and twenty dollars.

Lead students to see that *(D)* is the only sentence in which the commas in a series are used correctly. The commas in *(A)* are unnecessary because the adjectives express one idea made up of two closely related ideas; when reading the sentence, you would not pause between the words. Both *(B)* and *(C)* contain Dhree elements in a series and require a comma after the final conjunction *and*.

911

In "Chicoria," a wealthy ranch owner in California is gently taught some manners by a clever poet from New Mexico. The rancher asks his hired workers from New Mexico to bring a poet from home to compete with their celebrated California poet, Gracia. The workers return with a well-known poet named Chicoria. When Chicoria is told that he will have to eat dinner in the kitchen after he performs, he bets a servant that he will receive an invitation to eat at the master's table. Chicoria tells a New Mexican story that tests the master's courtesy to guests and gets Chicoria invited to eat in the dining room with the rich ranchers.

▶Critical Viewing◀

❶ Draw Conclusions *Students will probably say that the men on horseback are welcomed. The man and little girl on the left seem quite calm, and the woman at the door shows interest but not alarm. Some of the riders are playing musical instruments and smiling.*

Customize for
English Language Learners
English language learners may have difficulty understanding what is happening in this folk tale because it has so much action concentrated into less than two pages. As a further complication, there is a story within a story. You may want to have proficient English speakers in the class help these students organize the story events on a Series of Events Chain, p. 57, in **Writing and Language Transparencies.**

CHICORIA[1]

Adapted in Spanish by José Griego y Maestas
Retold in English by Rudolfo A. Anaya

Invitation to the Dance (el convite), Theodore Gentilz, The Daughters of the Republic of Texas Library, San Antonio, Texas

 ▲ **Critical Viewing** Are the men on horseback welcomed or feared? Explain. [Draw Conclusions]

1. **Chicoria** (chē kō´ rē ä)

 Block Scheduling Strategies

Consider these suggestions to take advantage of extended class time:

• Use the Literary Focus: Folk Tales, p. 911, to stimulate discussion and to introduce the three folk tales. Augment this with **Selection Support,** p. 321.

• Have students read the folk tales and work in peer groups to discuss the Guide for Responding questions, pp. 914, 917, and 919, before completing written responses.

• After they have read the three tales, have students think about Reader's Response in

Literature and your Life, p. 910. Have groups discuss what these folk tales teach about relationships between people.

• To prepare students for the Writing Mini-Lesson, have students use the *Writer's Solution Writing Lab CD-ROM* tutorial on Persuasion.

• Teach the Speaking and Listening Mini-lesson on p. 916 (Teacher Edition), allowing students time to decide on the subject of their oral tales and then to develop the tales.

• Have individuals or small groups select a Project from the Idea Bank, p. 921.

There were once many big ranches in California, and many New Mexicans went to work there. One day one of the big ranch owners asked his workers if there were any poets in New Mexico.

"Of course, we have many fine poets," they replied. "We have old Vilmas,[2] Chicoria, Cinfuegos,[3] to say nothing of the poets of Cebolleta[4] and the Black Poet."

"Well, when you return next season, why don't you bring one of your poets to compete with Gracia[5]—here none can compare with him!"

When the harvest was done the New Mexicans returned home. The following season when they returned to California they took with them the poet Chicoria, knowing well that in spinning a rhyme or in weaving wit there was no *Californio*[6] who could beat him.

As soon as the rancher found out that the workers had brought Chicoria with them, he sent his servants to invite his good neighbor and friend to come and hear the new poet. Meanwhile, the cooks set about preparing a big meal. When the maids began to dish up the plates of food, Chicoria turned to one of the servers and said, "Ah, my friends, it looks like they are going to feed us well tonight!"

The servant was surprised. "No, my friend," he explained, "the food is for *them*. We don't eat at the master's table. It is not permitted. We eat in the kitchen."

"Well, I'll bet I can sit down and eat with them," Chicoria boasted.

"If you beg or if you ask, perhaps, but if you don't ask they won't invite you," replied the servant.

"I never beg," the New Mexican answered.

◆ Reading Strategy
What might the storyteller want readers to know about the relationship between New Mexicans and *Californios*?

---

2. **Vilmas** (vēl' mäs)
3. **Cinfuegos** (sin fwä' gōs)
4. **Cebolleta** (sā bō' yā tä)
5. **Gracia** (grä' sē ä)
6. **Californio** (kä lē fôr' nyō) *n.*: Spanish for "person from California."

"The master will invite me of his own accord, and I'll bet you twenty-dollars he will!"

So they made a twenty-dollar bet and they instructed the serving maid to watch if this self-confident New Mexican had to ask the master for a place at the table. Then the maid took Chicoria into the dining room. Chicoria greeted the rancher cordially, but the rancher appeared haughty and did not invite Chicoria to sit with him and his guest at the table. Instead, he asked that a chair be brought and placed by the wall where Chicoria was to sit. The rich ranchers began to eat without inviting Chicoria.

So it is just as the servant predicted, Chicoria thought. The poor are not invited to share the rich man's food!

Then the master spoke: "Tell us about the country where you live. What are some of the customs of New Mexico?"

"Well, in New Mexico when a family sits down to eat each member uses one spoon for each biteful of food," Chicoria said with a twinkle in his eyes.

The ranchers were amazed that the New Mexicans ate in that manner, but what Chicoria hadn't told them was that each spoon was a piece of tortilla:[7] one fold and it became a spoon with which to scoop up the meal.

"Furthermore," he continued, "our goats are not like yours."

"How are they different?" the rancher asked.

"Here your nannies[8] give birth to two kids, in New Mexico they give birth to three!"

"What a strange thing!" the master said.

---

7. **tortilla** (tôr tē' yə) *n.*: Thin, round pancake of cornmeal or flour.
8. **nannies** (nan' ēz) *n.*: Female goats.

◆ **Build Vocabulary**

cordially (kôr' jəl lē) *adv.*: Warm and friendly
haughty (hôt' ē) *adj.*: Proud of oneself and scornful of others

Chicoria ◆ 913

◆ **Literary Focus**

❷ **Folk Tale** Have students speculate about why the storyteller has the rancher assert that no poet can compare with Gracia. *Students may say that the workers returning to New Mexico will almost certainly return with a poet to challenge the rancher's favorite poet and perhaps teach the rancher a lesson.*

◆ **Reading Strategy**

❸ **Recognize the Storyteller's Purpose** *Students may say the storyteller wants the readers to know that the Californios consider the New Mexicans to be their social inferiors. By creating conflict, he advances the plot of the story.*

◆ **Critical Thinking**

❹ **Speculate** Have students speculate about which will be more important, the quality of Chicoria's poetry or where he sits during dinner? *Students may notice that the argument over poetry has almost disappeared. Where Chicoria sits has become a central issue in the tale.*

◆ **LITERATURE AND YOUR LIFE**

❺ Have students think about Chicoria's opinion that he is worthy to sit at the table with the master and the other rich ranchers, and his belief that the rancher placed him elsewhere because he is poor. Have students think about how they might feel in a similar situation.

◆ **Critical Thinking**

❻ **Deduce** Ask students why Chicoria tells the story about New Mexicans using a different spoon for every bite of food. *He tells the ranchers an unbelievable story to get their attention and set them up for a lesson.*

Clarification

❼ Nanny goats sometimes do give birth to three kids—and even four—rather than two. This is another of Chicoria's half-truths like the story about the spoons.

♪ **Humanities: Art**

Invitation to the Dance (el convite), by Theodore Gentilz

Born in France, Theodore Jean Gentilz (1819–1906) studied art in Paris and emigrated to Texas in 1843. Gentilz became a surveyor and draftsman and served as a journalist. Later, Gentilz moved to San Antonio and taught art at St. Mary's College in San Antonio—living and painting in San Antonio during the last half of the 19th century. His paintings provide a unique and invaluable record of the customs and daily life of Mexican Americans during this period. Most of his paint-

ings are relatively small, with clear detail and vivid colors. The painting shown here is only 9 by 12 inches. Some art historians consider his most beautiful works to be his botanical studies of the native wildflowers of southern Texas.

1. What details indicate that this painting is set on a ranch? *Students may note that the men are dressed as cowboys, riding horses.*
2. Based on the title of the painting, and the activity depicted, what do you think is happening? *Students should infer that the men are asking the women to go to a dance with them.*

Reading Strategy

❶ Recognize the Storyteller's Purpose Have students identify the lesson that Chicoria's story teaches. *Chicoria's story, and indeed the entire folk tale, teaches a lesson about how to behave. The text of the story is about a poetry contest; the subtext is about treating people with proper respect.*

Beyond Literature

You may want to show students part or all of the documentary film *The U.S.–Mexican War (1846–1848)*, produced in 1998 by PBS station KERA. Videocassettes of this film are available in English or Spanish versions. There is also a curriculum kit for the film designed for use in middle schools, available by calling PBS Video at 1-800-344-3337. For discussions of the film and related materials, you may wish to visit the following Web site: **http;//www.pbs.org/dera/ usmexicanwar/**

Reinforce and Extend

Answers
◆ LITERATURE AND YOUR LIFE

Reader's Response Most students will say they thought Chicoria would win the bet because he is so smart.

Thematic Focus It is not uncommon for one group of people to view another as inferior.

☑ Check Your Comprehension

1. Chicoria is a well-known poet and storyteller from New Mexico.
2. They want to prove that they are just as cultured as the Californios.
3. He bets the servants twenty dollars that their master will invite him to eat at the dinner table with his guests.
4. He tells a story that makes the rancher realize that he needs to show respect and hospitality.

◆ Critical Thinking

1. He knows he can appeal to the rancher's cultural sense of courtesy.
2. He is smart and can get what he wants in ways other than begging.
3. The rancher's guests at the table are determined by social class.

"But tell us, how can the female nurse three kids?"

"Well, they do it exactly as you're doing it now: While two of them are eating the third one looks on."

❶ The rancher then realized his lack of manners and took Chicoria's hint. He apologized and invited his New Mexico guest to dine at the table. After dinner, Chicoria sang and recited his poetry, putting Gracia to shame. And he won his bet as well.

Beyond Literature

Social Studies Connection

The Mexican-American War "Chicoria" subtly portrays the relationship and history of the states of California and New Mexico, both of which were the territory of the independent Republic of Mexico until 1848. The first American settlers traveled by wagon to these areas during the early 1800's. During the next few decades, the relationship between the United States and Mexico deteriorated over boundary disputes. After many failed negotiations, the countries severed all ties with each other. Hostilities increased between the two countries and provoked the Mexican-American War, which began in 1846. The war was marked by a series of United States victories and ended in 1848 with the signing of the treaty of Guadelupe. According to the treaty, Mexico ceded, among other land, the territory now included in the states of California and New Mexico. California became the thirty-first state in 1850, and New Mexico became the forty-seventh state in 1912.

Cross-Curricular Activity
The central conflict of the Mexican-American War was the disagreement over which territories were claimed by which country and how far these territories expanded. Do research, and draw a map showing the territory under dispute between the United States and Mexico during this war.

4. By equating himself with the kid who looks on while the others are nursing, Chicoria shames the ranchers at the table.
5. The story is imaginative and funny and enables the rancher to do the right thing without too much embarrassment.
6. The rancher would have kicked him out.

Guide for Responding

◆ LITERATURE AND YOUR LIFE

Reader's Response Whom did you think would win the bet—the servants or Chicoria?

Thematic Focus What did you learn about relationships from reading this tale?

Journal Writing Jot down other ways in which Chicoria might have taught the rancher a lesson.

☑ Check Your Comprehension
1. Who is Chicoria?
2. Why do the New Mexicans bring Chicoria to California?
3. What bet does Chicoria make with the servants on the ranch?
4. How does Chicoria win the bet?

◆ Critical Thinking
INTERPRET
1. Why does Chicoria assume that he will eat at the rancher's table? **[Analyze]**
2. Chicoria states that "I never beg," and then makes a bet with the servants. What does this show about his character? **[Interpret]**
3. What determines who sits with the rancher at dinner and who does not? **[Connect]**
4. How does Chicoria's story about the goats mirror the situation in the dining room? **[Compare and Contrast]**

EVALUATE
5. Explain why telling the story about the goats was a good way to get the rancher to invite Chicoria to the table. **[Evaluate]**

APPLY
6. What might have happened if Chicoria had been so insulted that he started a confrontation with the rancher? **[Speculate]**

BRER POSSUM'S DILEMMA

JACKIE TORRENCE

Back in the days when the animals could talk, there lived ol' Brer[1] Possum. He was a fine feller. Why, he never liked to see no critters[2] in trouble. He was always helpin' out, a-doin' somethin' for others.

Ever' night, ol' Brer Possum climbed into a persimmon tree, hung by his tail, and slept all night long. And each mornin', he climbed outa the tree and walked down the road to sun 'imself.

One mornin', as he walked, he come to a big hole in the middle of the road. Now, ol' Brer Possum was kind and gentle, but he was also nosy, so he went over to the hole and looked in. All at once, he stepped back, 'cause layin'

in the bottom of that hole was ol' Brer Snake with a brick on his back.

Brer Possum said to 'imself, "I best git on outa here, 'cause ol' Brer Snake is mean and evil and lowdown, and if I git to stayin' around 'im, he jist might git to bitin' me."

So Brer Possum went on down the road.

But Brer Snake had seen Brer Possum, and he <u>commenced</u> to callin' for 'im.

---

1. Brer (brʉr): Dialect for "brother," used before a name.
2. critters: Dialect for "creatures"; animals.

◆ **Build Vocabulary**

commenced (kə menst′) v.: Started; began

◀ **Critical Viewing** What human characteristics does the snake exhibit in this illustration? [Interpret]

Brer Possum's Dilemma ◆ 915

Humanities: Literature

African American Folk Tales The first American to write down numerous African American folk tales was Joel Chandler Harris (1848–1908). His animal stories, told by the fictional storyteller Uncle Remus, are famous for their gentle humor and the lively use of African American dialect. His tales are still considered by many to be the greatest in this genre.

Harris was born in a small town in Georgia. He spent much time on an antebellum plantation, Ironwold, and the owner encouraged his literary gifts. After working on newspapers in Macon, New

Orleans, and Savannah, he joined the editorial staff of the Atlanta *Constitution*. The first Uncle Remus story appeared in 1879. Harris published nine collections of stories, most of which appeared first in the newspaper. "The Tar Baby Story," about Brer Rabbit, is probably the most famous.

The 1946 Walt Disney film, *Song of the South*, is based on the Uncle Remus stories. It was one of the earliest films to combine live action with animation. Among the animated figures included in the stories told by Uncle Remus in this film are Brer Rabbit, Brer Fox, and Brer Bear.

915

❶ Recognize the Storyteller's Purpose *The message of the story will somehow derive from the contrasting characters of Brer Possum and Brer Snake.*

◆ **LITERATURE AND YOUR LIFE**

❷ Ask students if there is anything familiar to them about the developing relationship between Brer Possum and Brer Rabbit. *Students may say that they recognize a relationship in which one person asks the other for numerous favors to see just how far he or she can take advantage of the other's generosity.*

◆ **Critical Thinking**

❸ Speculate Have students make suggestions about why Brer Snake always gives Brer Possum the same answer when he is asked if he will bite him. *The exact repetition of the words "Maybe not. Maybe not. Maaaaaaaybe not" alerts the reader, if not Brer Possum, that it is almost inevitable that Brer Snake plans to strike. The repetition of the words also increases the tension and the reader's curiosity about what will happen.*

◆ **Build Grammar Skills**

❹ Tell students that writers use commas to separate three or more words, phrases, or elements in a series, with a comma before the final conjunction. Ask them why there are no commas after *mean* and *evil* in this sentence. *The presence of conjunctions between all the words eliminates the need for any commas.*

Customize for
Interpersonal Learners

This folk tale well suits interpersonal learners because the two animals have distinct personalities, and they behave in ways that can be predicted by people interested in human behavior patterns. Suggest that students identify Brer Possum's character traits and predict how he will deal with Brer Snake. Have interested students think of other pairs of animals that might be good characters in stories dealing with conflicting personalities.

916

"Help me, Brer Possum."

Brer Possum stopped and turned around. He said to 'imself, "That's ol' Brer Snake a-callin' me. What do you reckon he wants?"

Well, ol' Brer Possum was kindhearted, so he went back down the road to the hole, stood at the edge, and looked down at Brer Snake.

"Was that you a-callin' me? What do you want?"

Brer Snake looked up and said, "I've been down here in this hole for a mighty long time with this brick on my back. Won't you help git it offa me?"

Brer Possum thought.

> ◆ **Reading Strategy**
> Why does the story-teller point out the contrast between the characters of Brer Possum and Brer Snake at the beginning of the story?

"Now listen here, Brer Snake. I knows you. You's mean and evil and lowdown, and if'n I was to git down in that hole and git to liftin' that brick offa your back, you wouldn't do nothin' but bite me."

Ol' Brer Snake just hissed.

"Maybe not. Maybe not. Maaaaaaaybe not."

Brer Possum said, "I ain't sure 'bout you at all. I jist don't know. You're a-goin' to have to let me think about it."

So ol' Brer Possum thought—he thought high, and he thought low—and jist as he was thinkin', he looked up into a tree and saw a dead limb a-hangin' down. He climbed into the tree, broke off the limb, and with that ol' stick, pushed that brick offa Brer Snake's back. Then he took off down the road.

Brer Possum thought he was away from ol' Brer Snake when all at once he heard somethin'.

"Help me, Brer Possum."

Brer Possum said, "Oh, no, that's him agin."

But bein' so kindhearted, Brer Possum turned around, went back to the hole, and stood at the edge.

"Brer Snake, was that you a-callin' me? What do you want now?"

Ol' Brer Snake looked up outa the hole and hissed.

"I've been down here for a mighty long time, and I've gotten a little weak, and the sides of this ol' hole are too slick for me to climb. Do you think you can lift me outa here?"

Brer Possum thought.

"Now, you jist wait a minute. If'n I was to git down into that hole and lift you outa there, you wouldn't do nothin' but bite me."

Brer Snake hissed.

"Maybe not. Maybe not. Maaaaaaaybe not." ❸

Brer Possum said, "I jist don't know. You're a-goin' to have to give me time to think about this."

So ol' Brer Possum thought.

And as he thought, he jist happened to look down there in that hole and see that ol' dead limb. So he pushed the limb underneath ol' Brer Snake and he lifted 'im outa the hole, way up into the air, and throwed 'im into the high grass.

Brer Possum took off a-runnin' down the road.

Well, he thought he was away from ol' Brer Snake when all at once he heard somethin'.

"Help me, Brer Possum."

Brer Possum thought, "That's him agin."

But bein' so kindhearted, he turned around, went back to the hole, and stood there a-lookin' for Brer Snake. Brer Snake crawled outa the high grass just as slow as he could, stretched 'imself out across the road, rared up,[3] and looked at ol' Brer Possum.

Then he hissed. "I've been down there in that ol' hole for a mighty long time, and I've gotten a little cold 'cause the sun didn't shine. Do you think you could put me in your pocket and git me warm?"

Brer Possum said, "Now you listen here, Brer Snake. I knows you. You's mean and evil and lowdown, and if'n I put you in my pocket you wouldn't do nothin' but bite me." ❹

Brer Snake hissed.

"Maybe not. Maybe not. Maaaaaaaybe not."

"No sireee. Brer Snake. I knows you. I jist ain't a-goin' to do it."

---

3. **rared up:** Dialect for "reared up."

Speaking and Listening Mini-Lesson

Oral Tale

This mini-lesson supports the Speaking and Listening activity in the Idea Bank on p. 921.

Introduce Have students brainstorm for situations from which a moral or lesson can be derived.

Develop Encourage students to develop their tales by planning a chronological narrative. A Series of Events Chain from **Writing and Language Transparencies,** p. 57, might be useful to students for organizational purposes. Encourage them to update their tales with modern innovations such as computers or appliances that talk. Students

should not use written material in the final presentation. The final tale must be delivered orally.

Apply Have students tell the tale to a classmate, who in turn will retell the story to the entire class. Encourage the second student to improvise if he or she forgets a detail or event in the story.

Assess Have the original creator of the folk tale critique the retelling, and the other students can discuss the changes from creator to storyteller. Or, use the Peer Assessment: Speaker/Speech form, p. 114, or Oral Interpretation, p. 115, in **Alternative Assessment.**

But jist as Brer Possum was talkin' to Brer Snake, he happened to git a real good look at 'im. He was a-layin' there lookin' so <u>pitiful</u>, and Brer Possum's great big heart began to feel sorry for ol' Brer Snake.

"All right," said Brer Possum. "You must be cold. So jist this once I'm a-goin' to put you in my pocket."

So ol' Brer Snake coiled up jist as little as he could, and Brer Possum picked 'im up and put 'im in his pocket.

Brer Snake laid quiet and still—so quiet and still that Brer Possum even forgot that he was a-carryin' 'im around. But all of a sudden, Brer Snake commenced to crawlin' out, and he turned and faced Brer Possum and hissed.

"I'm a-goin' to bite you."

But Brer Possum said, "Now wait a minute. Why are you a-goin' to bite me? I done took that brick offa your back, I got you outa that hole, and I put you in my pocket to git you warm. Why are you a-goin' to bite me?"

Brer Snake hissed.

"You knowed I was a snake before you put me in you pocket." **⑤**

And when you're mindin' your own business and you spot trouble, don't never trouble trouble 'til trouble troubles you.

> ◆ **Literary Focus**
> How does stating the message of the tale contribute to the humor of this story?

⑥

◆ **Build Vocabulary**

pitiful (pit´ i fəl) *adj.*: Deserving compassion or sympathy

◇ Guide for Responding

◆ **LITERATURE AND YOUR LIFE**

Reader's Response Is Brer Snake to be blamed for his behavior? Why or why not?

Thematic Focus What does this tale reveal about the relationship between opossums and snakes?

Journal Writing If you were to defend Brer Snake's actions in a courtroom, what would you say? Jot down your ideas in your journal.

☑ **Check Your Comprehension**

1. What is Brer Possum's dilemma?
2. What does Brer Possum do every time Brer Snake asks for help?
3. Why does Brer Possum keep helping Brer Snake?
4. Why does Brer Snake bite Brer Possum?

◆ **Critical Thinking**

INTERPRET

1. In what ways are Brer Possum and Brer Snake different? **[Compare and Contrast]**
2. Why might Brer Possum think it was safe to put Brer Snake in his pocket even though he says the snake is mean and evil? **[Deduce]**
3. Is Brer Possum meant to look foolish or simply big-hearted? Explain. **[Infer]**

APPLY

4. How does the action of Brer Snake reveal the difficulty of changing an animal's or a person's basic nature? **[Relate]**

EXTEND

5. What do you know about opossum behavior that suits the character of Brer Possum in the story? **[Science Link]**

Brer Possum's Dilemma ◆ 917

◆ **Critical Thinking**

⑤ Draw Conclusions Ask students why they think the author does not have Brer Snake actually bite Brer Possum. *Students may say that this would kill the humor of the story along with Brer Possum. Other, more optimistic readers may say that there's always the possibility that Brer Possum gets away.*

◆ **Literary Focus**

⑥ Folk Tale *The repetition of the word* trouble, *used both as a noun and a verb, shows the storyteller's versatility and lets the reader know that the storyteller has been "setting the reader up" for this all along.*

Reinforce and Extend

Answers

◆ **LITERATURE AND YOUR LIFE**

Reader's Response Some students may think that Brer Snake's behavior is instinctive and he should not be blamed.

Thematic Focus An opossum's innocence will always make him a victim of the snake's predatory nature.

☑ **Check Your Comprehension**

1. Brer Possum's dilemma is that he knows he can't trust Brer Snake, but he has a simple and obliging nature.
2. Brer Possum tells Brer Snake that he won't help him, and then he helps anyway.
3. Brer Possum is the sort of animal who is always helping others.
4. It is Brer Snake's nature.

◆ **Critical Thinking**

1. Brer Possum is trusting, helpful, and generous. Brer Snake is sneaky, selfish, and manipulative.
2. Brer Possum thinks that his kindness and generosity will set a good example.
3. Brer Possum is meant to look both foolish and big-hearted.
4. When it is a snake's nature to kill, another animal's kindness won't necessarily change anything.
5. Opossums don't see very well and blunder onto highways and into other animals' nests. Also, they are practically defenseless.

One-Minute Insight

In "Why the Waves Have Whitecaps," both the wind and the water are women who spend a lot of time talking to each other. Mrs. Wind brags constantly to Mrs. Water about her children. Her children are breezes, gales, and other kinds of winds. Mrs. Water gets tired of listening to the bragging. When Mrs. Wind sends her children to Mrs. Water for a drink, Mrs. Water drowns them. When Mrs. Wind passes over the ocean calling for her lost children, white feathers come up to the top of the water. That explains why waves have whitecaps, and storms at sea are the wind and the water fighting over the children.

◆ Reading Strategy

❶ Recognize the Storyteller's Purpose What kind of folk tale does the title indicate this story will be? *It explains something in nature.*

Thematic Focus

❷ Relationships How does the storyteller humanize Mrs. Wind and Mrs. Water and make them sympathetic? *The storyteller has given the two forces of nature polite married names—"Mrs."—and their conversations about their children are typical of mothers who are friends and spend time together.*

◆ Critical Thinking

❸ Infer Who or what are Mrs. Wind's children? *Students may say that her children are the various kinds of winds and the visual effects of the winds, such as trees bending, clouds moving, and things being blown around.*

►Critical Viewing◄

❹ Make a Judgment *The painting is well balanced to show the equal strength of the wind and the water. The power of the wind is seen in the bending tree and the clouds, and the power of the water is suggested by the stylized foam of the wave and the dark, rising mass of the ocean.*

Why the Waves Have WHITECAPS

ZORA NEALE HURSTON

Wind and Geometry, 1978, David True, Courtesy of the artist

De wind is a woman, and de water is a woman too. They useter[1] talk together a whole heap. Mrs. Wind useter go set down by de ocean and talk and patch and crochet.

They was jus' like all lady people. They loved to talk about their chillun, and brag on 'em.

Mrs. Water useter say, "Look at *my* chillun! Ah[2] got de biggest and de littlest in de world.

All kinds of chillun. Every color in de world, and every shape!"

De wind lady bragged louder than de water woman:

"Oh, but Ah got mo' different chilluns than anybody in de world. They flies, they walks, they swims, they sings, they talks, they cries. They got all de colors from de sun. Lawd, my

---

1. **useter** (yoō´ stə) *v.*: Dialect for "used to."
2. **Ah** *pron.*: Dialect for "I."

▲ **Critical Viewing** In this painting, which force would you say is stronger—the wind or the water? Explain. **[Make a Judgment]**

918 ◆ *The American Folk Tradition*

Beyond the Classroom

Workplace Skills

Oceanographer About 71 percent of the Earth's surface is covered by oceans, and more than 98 percent of the water on Earth is contained in the oceans. For people interested in the oceans, there are many opportunities for employment.

Oceanography is divided into four major areas of research: physical, chemical, biological, and geological. Physical oceanographers are concerned with the comparison of different oceans and weather patterns over oceans. Chemical oceanographers study the chemical makeup of the water in the sea.

This field is becoming increasingly important as pollution from land sources increases. Biological oceanographers study the sea's plant and animal life, and geological oceanographers study the structure and mineral content of the ocean floor.

With the increased use of the sea as a source of food, petroleum, and minerals, the field of oceanography is expanding rapidly. A research oceanographer needs a college degree in a related field and specialized graduate courses. Marine farming of seafood is one job opportunity that requires less educational training.

chillun sho is a pleasure. 'Tain't nobody got no babies like mine."

Mrs. Water got tired of hearin' 'bout Mrs. Wind's chillun so she got so she hated 'em.

One day a whole passle³ of her chillun come to Mrs. Wind and says: "Mama, wese thirsty. Kin we go git us a cool drink of water?"

She says, "Yeah chillun. Run on over to Mrs. Water and hurry right back soon."

5 When them chillun went to squinch they thirst Mrs. Water grabbed 'em all and drowned 'em.

When her chillun didn't come home, de wind woman got worried. So she went on

down to de water and ast for her babies.

"Good evenin' Mis' Water, you see my chillun today?"

De water woman tole her, "No-oo-oo."

Mrs. Wind knew her chillun had come down to Mrs. Water's house, so she passed over de ocean callin' her chillun, and every time she call de white feathers would come up on top of de water. And dat's how come we got white caps on waves. It's de feathers comin' up when de wind woman calls her lost babies.

When you see a storm on de water, it's de wind and de water fightin' over dem chillun.

---
3. **passle** *n.*: Dialect for "parcel."

◆ **Reading Strategy**
What is the story-teller's purpose in this tale?
6

Guide for Responding

◆ LITERATURE AND YOUR LIFE

Reader's Response What did you enjoy most about "Why the Waves Have Whitecaps"?

Thematic Focus How would you describe the relationship between Mrs. Wind and Mrs. Water?

Role Play With a classmate, role-play the scene between Mrs. Wind and Mrs. Water.

☑ Check Your Comprehension

1. Who are the main characters in this tale?
2. What do the characters brag about?
3. Why are the children drowned?
4. According to this tale, what are the white-caps on the waves?

◆ Critical Thinking

INTERPRET

1. In what ways are Mrs. Wind's and Mrs. Water's activities like those of ordinary women? **[Analyze]**
2. What negative human traits are shown by Mrs. Water and Mrs. Wind? **[Compare and Contrast]**
3. What is the moral of this story? **[Draw Conclusions]**

EXTEND

4. In what sense are whitecaps truly the result of a "dialogue" between wind and water? **[Science Link]**

COMPARE LITERARY WORKS

5. What do "Chicoria," "Brer Possum's Dilemma," and "Why the Waves Have Whitecaps" have in common? **[Connect]**

Why the Waves Have Whitecaps ◆ 919

Beyond the Selection

FURTHER READING
Other Works by Rudolfo A. Anaya
The Anaya Reader, Bless Me, Ultima
Other Works by Jackie Torrence
Jackie Tales: The Magic of Creating Stories and the Art of Telling Them
Other Works by Zora Neale Hurston
Tell My Horse, Mules and Men, Jonah's Gourd Vine

INTERNET
We suggest the following sites on the Internet (all Web sites are subject to change).

For more on Rudolfo A. Anayo: **http://www.pathfinder.com/ twep/warner_books/authors/rudolfo_anaya/index.html**

For more on Jackie Torrence:
http://www.ntn-storytelling.com/jackie.htm

For more on Zora Heale Hurston:
http://pages.prodigy.com/zora/

For more North American folk tales: **http://www. ipl.org/youth/cquest/northamerica/usa/folk.html**

We *strongly recommend* that you preview the sites before you send students to them.

◆ Literary Focus

5 Folk Tale Discuss with students the fact that Mrs. Water drowns Mrs. Wind's children and then denies having ever seen them. Why has the sto-ryteller included this incident in a humorous, lighthearted story?
Although the story is humorous, folk tales often explain the destructive power of nature. The storyteller acknowledges this force here.

◆ Reading Strategy

6 Recognize the Storyteller's Purpose *The storyteller's purpose is to explain why whitecaps form on the water when the wind is high.*

Reinforce and Extend

Answers

◆ LITERATURE AND YOUR LIFE

Reader's Response Students may say they appreciated the imaginative explanation of whitecaps in the ocean.

Thematic Focus Students might describe their relationship as cordial but combative.

☑ Check Your Comprehension

1. The main characters are Mrs. Water and Mrs. Wind.
2. They brag about their children.
3. The children are drowned because Mrs. Water is tired of hearing Mrs. Wind brag.
4. The whitecaps are white feathers from Mrs. Wind's drowned children.

◆ Critical Thinking

1. They spend time together, talking, sewing, and bragging about their children.
2. Mrs. Wind is excessively proud of her children and talks about them too much. Mrs. Water is murder-ous and deceitful.
3. Students may say that the moral of the story is: Spend your time taking care of your children, not bragging about them.
4. Waves and their whitecaps are the result of the water pushing one way and the wind pushing the other way.
5. All three tales are humorous and teach a lesson. Each tale has a character that outsmarts another, and the tales are told in an infor-mal style.

◆ Reading Strategy

1. (a) The storyteller's purpose is to demonstrate that poor people are the equal of rich people. (b) Students may say that they recognize the purpose when Chicoria makes his bet.
2. The message is mind your own business and don't ask for trouble.
3. The title reveals that the storyteller is explaining something in nature.

◆ Build Vocabulary

Using Synonyms
1. snobbish
2. haughty

Spelling Strategy
1. audience
2. sought
3. loss
4. haughty

Using the Word Bank
commenced; pitiful; haughty; cordially

◆ Literary Focus

1. Students may say that the Hispanic Americans of the time valued poetry, storytelling, wit, and the oral tradition. They were very conscious of class distinctions but valued courtesy.
2. These words are not standard written English, and they have a singsong, rhythmic quality that sounds like poetic speech.
3. (a) The story shows the ruthlessness of nature and the wisdom of not bragging too much. (b) It gives an imaginative, nonscientific explanation for the natural occurrence of whitecaps or waves.

◆ Build Grammar Skills

Practice
1. The waves can talk, sing, and cry.
2. When Mrs. Water got angry, she grabbed the children, drowned them, and lied to Mrs. Wind.
3. Mrs. Water had children of every color, all shapes, and different sizes.
4. The women used to chat, sew, brag, and crochet.
5. The wind never found her children, her happiness, or her peace of mind.

Guide for Responding (continued)

◆ Reading Strategy

RECOGNIZE THE STORYTELLER'S PURPOSE

Storytellers have a **purpose** in sharing folk tales. They pass on beliefs, customs, and instruction.
1. (a) What is the storyteller's purpose in "Chicoria"? (b) At what point do you recognize this purpose?
2. In "Brer Possum's Dilemma," the storyteller directly states the message. What is the message?
3. What does the title "Why the Waves Have Whitecaps" reveal about the storyteller's purpose?

◆ Build Vocabulary

USING SYNONYMS

Synonyms are words with the same basic meaning but different connotations—associations or slight variations in meaning. On your paper, choose the synonym that fits best in each sentence.
1. The lady of the manor was ____?____. (snobbish, haughty)
2. The ____?____ man shunned people he considered lower class. (haughty, snobbish)

SPELLING STRATEGY

One way to spell the *aw* sound is *au*, as in *haughty* and the words *caught, taught,* and *taut*. The *aw* sound can also be spelled *ou, o, a,* or *aw*, like *thought, toss, tall,* and *dawn*. Consult your dictionary, if necessary, to find the correct spelling.

On your paper, write the correct spelling of each of these misspelled words:
1. oudience 2. soght 3. lauss 4. hawghty

USING THE WORD BANK

On your paper, write the word from the Word Bank that best completes each sentence.

The entertainment ____?____ with a parade of magnificently clothed riders. In contrast, my own plain clothes and old horse seemed ____?____. The king and queen's ____?____ appearance was in keeping with the stately procession, although they waved ____?____ at the passersby.

◆ Literary Focus

FOLK TALES

Part of the oral tradition, **folk tales** were passed on for many generations before finally being written down. Folk tales often use humor to engage listeners while they pass on cultural information, explain mysteries of nature, or teach a lesson.
1. What can you learn about life in the Southwest by reading "Chicoria"?
2. In "Brer Possum's Dilemma," how do words like *a-callin'* and *a-lookin'* indicate that this tale came from the oral tradition?
3. (a) In what ways does "Why the Waves Have Whitecaps" teach a lesson? (b) In what ways does it explain a natural occurrence?

◆ Build Grammar Skills

COMMAS IN A SERIES

Writers use **commas** to separate three or more words, phrases, or elements in a series. Include a comma before the final conjunction. The following example has a series of three phrases:

Ever' night, ol' Brer Possum *climbed into a persimmon tree, hung by his tail,* and *slept all night long.*

Practice On your paper, copy the sentences, adding commas in the series.
1. The waves can talk sing and cry.
2. When Mrs. Water got angry, she grabbed the children drowned them and lied to Mrs. Wind.
3. Mrs. Water had children of every color all shapes and different sizes.
4. The women used to chat sew brag and crochet.
5. The wind never found her children her happiness or her peace of mind.

Writing Application Write the following sentences, adding another item to create a series, and placing commas where they are needed.
1. When Chicoria began telling his fantastic tale, the servants and the rancher listened.
2. Brer Snake is mean and evil.
3. Folk tales amuse and teach their listeners.

Writing Application
Possible responses:
1. When Chicoria began telling his fantastic tale, the servants, the rancher, and the other guests listened.
2. Brer Snake is mean, evil, and sneaky.
3. Folk tales amuse, teach, and explain things to their listeners.

✎ **Writer's Solution**

For further instruction and practice, use the commas lesson in the Punctuation unit in the *Writer's Solution Language Lab CD-ROM.* You may also use the practice page on commas that separate basic elements, p. 105, in the *Writer's Solution Grammar Practice Book.*

Build Your Portfolio

 Idea Bank

Writing

1. **List** Create a list of details from "Chicoria" that reveal its cultural setting.

2. **Retelling** Update "Chicoria" by writing a modern version of the tale. Maintain the lesson taught in the original tale.

3. **Essay** Could Brer Snake have overcome his natural inclinations and refrained from biting Brer Possum? In a brief essay, examine the characters of Brer Possum and Brer Snake, and come to a conclusion about their natures. Use details from the story to support your points.

Speaking and Listening

4. **Skit [Group Activity]** With a group of classmates, present a skit based on one of the folk tales in this group. First, prepare a written script that includes dialogue and stage notes. Then, create costumes. Finally, perform your skit for your class. **[Performing Arts Link]**

5. **Oral Tale [Group Activity]** Without ever writing it down, make up a new folk tale. After the tale is firm in your mind, practice telling it aloud. Then, tell your tale to a classmate. Have your classmate tell your tale to the class. Finally, discuss the subtle changes that occurred from one telling to the next.

Projects

6. **Folk-Tale Collection [Group Activity]** With a small group of classmates, find folk tales from different parts of the world. Compile a collection of folk tales to share with the class. **[Literature Link]**

7. **Illustration of a Story** Choose a story from this group to illustrate. Use paints, pastels, or whatever art materials you prefer. Display your artwork for the class. **[Art Link]**

 Writing Mini-Lesson

Persuasive Advertisement

A persuasive advertisement attempts to convince you to accept an idea or buy a product. In order to be convincing, the ad makes claims about or offers reasons why the product or idea is important or superior to another one. Write an advertisement that persuades your audience to buy a copy of one of the stories in this group.

Writing Skills Focus: Use an Effective Format

Advertisements are not written in paragraph form because they aim to capture readers' attention quickly and easily. **Use an effective format,** like bulleted lists, numbered lists, and boldface headings, to make your ideas stand out.

Model
"A Thrilling Read!" *New Britain Daily Journal*

- Adventure
- Romance
- Suspense

Prewriting Choose the story you will advertise. Write catchy phrases you could use as headlines, and list the details you will include in your ad.

Drafting As you draft, include the persuasive details you thought of while prewriting. Experiment with different formats. When you find a format you like, such as a bulleted list, make another draft that keeps to that format.

Revising Make sure you have a strong opening line and that you include details that will persuade your audience to buy the story. Then, check to make sure that your format is clear and effective.

> ◆ **Grammar Application**
> Insert commas between words or phrases in a series of three or more.

Chicoria/Brer Possum's Dilemma/Why the Waves Have Whitecaps ◆ *921*

 Idea Bank

Following are suggestions for matching the Idea Bank topics with your students' performance levels and learning modalities:

Customize for
Performance Levels
Less Advanced Students: 1, 7
Average Students: 2, 4, 5, 6, 7
More Advanced Students: 3, 4, 5, 6

Customize for
Learning Modalities
Verbal/Linguistic: 1, 2, 3, 4, 5, 6
Visual/Spatial: 1, 7
Bodily/Kinesthetic: 4, 5
Logical/Mathematical: 3, 4, 5
Interpersonal: 4, 5, 6
Intrapersonal: 1, 2, 3, 7

Writing Mini-Lesson

Refer students to the Writing Handbook in the back of the book for instruction on the writing process and for further information on persuasion. Use the Sensory Language Chart, p. 69, in **Writing and Language Transparencies,** to help students develop catchy phrases.

 **Writer's Solution**

Writers at Work Videodisc
To see how environmental writer Kate Mitchell develops persuasive arguments, have students view the videodisc segment on persuasion (Ch. 6).

Play frames 3 to 7453

Writing Lab CD-ROM
Have students complete the tutorial on Persuasion. Follow these steps:
1. Have students browse through the Inspirations for Persuasion to select a topic.
2. Have students draft on computer, paying particular attention to how they organize the evidence they have gathered for the piece.
3. Have students use the revision checker for sentence openers.

Writer's Solution Sourcebook
Have students use Chapter 6, "Persuasion," pp. 166–199, for more support. The chapter includes an annotated literature model of a persuasive essay on an environmental topic, p. 199.

✓ ASSESSMENT OPTIONS

Formal Assessment, Selection Test, pp. 265–267, and Assessment Resources Software. The selection test is designed so that it can be easily customized to the performance levels of your students.

Alternative Assessment, p. 59, includes options for less advanced students, more advanced students, verbal/linguistic learners, musical/rhythmic learners, interpersonal learners, and visual/spatial learners.

PORTFOLIO ASSESSMENT
Use the following rubrics in the **Alternative Assessment** booklet to assess student writing:
List: Description, p. 93
Retelling: Fictional Narrative, p. 91
Essay: Comparison/Contrast, p. 99
Writing Mini-Lesson: Persuasion, p. 101

Have students think of stories, myths, folk tales, and tall tales related to the moon, the sky, and outer space. For example, students might suggest the "Man in the Moon," the moon being made of green cheese, or a myth that explains a star constellation. Compile a list on the board, and discuss reasons why each tale might have been told—to explain an unknown or frightening phenomenon, or something extraordinary or unusual. Introduce the selection by explaining that Alan Shepard accomplished an extraordinary and heroic true-life feat on May 5, 1961, when he became the first United States astronaut to travel in space—a story more fantastic than any tall tale could ever be.

Map Study

Topographical Maps Students gain a better understanding of events and places when they are able to make connections between geography and historical events. To help students picture what an astronaut in orbit might actually see, have them compare photographs of the Earth taken from outer space with topographical maps of the same areas, looking at physical features such as mountains and bodies of water.

CONNECTING LITERATURE TO SOCIAL STUDIES

THE SPACE AGE: PUSHING THE FRONTIER

from **The Right Stuff** *by* Tom Wolfe

Shepard's Flight
Altitude: 116.5 statute miles
Duration: 15 min., 12 sec.
Distance: 303 statute miles
Velocity: 5,134 m.p.h.

THE FRONTIER IN AMERICAN HISTORY

Throughout most of American history, there was a far-off land that was unsettled or unexplored. This area was known as "the frontier." In the minds of many people, the frontier was what made the United States different from most European countries. Americans—at least in their imaginations—could embark on adventure by heading for the frontier.

The New Frontier By the middle of the twentieth century, virtually all large tracts of land in the United States had been developed and populated. Many people felt they no longer had an unexplored place to dream about. When John F. Kennedy was elected President in 1960, he began using the term "The New Frontier." He said Americans needed to think of ways to replace the frontier that no longer existed. As one replacement, Kennedy suggested Americans begin thinking about exploring the last frontier—the moon.

"The Right Stuff" One of the biggest news topics of the 1960's was the preparation for a trip to the moon. Tom Wolfe later wrote a book about the former test pilots who were selected and the rigorous training they underwent for the trip into space. It was a difficult and very dangerous job, requiring levels of ability and courage that few people had. The outstanding qualifications needed to be an astronaut were known as "the right stuff." Wolfe used this expression as the title of his book about these men.

The following excerpt from *The Right Stuff* tells how Alan Shepard was elevated to hero status following a groundbreaking rocket flight.

922 ◆ *The American Folk Tradition*

Prentice Hall Literature Program Resources

REINFORCE / RETEACH / EXTEND
Selection Support Pages
Build Vocabulary, p. 322
Connecting Literature to Social Studies, p. 323
Formal Assessment Selection Test, pp. 268–269, Assessment Resources Software
Readings From Social Studies
Writing and Language Transparencies
Series of Events Chain, p. 57

Resource Pro CD-ROM "The Space Age: Pushing the Frontier"—includes all resource material and customizable lesson plan

 Listening to Literature Audiocassettes "The Space Age: Pushing the Frontier"

from THE
RIGHT STUFF

Tom Wolfe

Glenn[1] and the others now watched from the sidelines as Al Shepard[2] was hoisted out of their midst and installed as a national hero on the order of a Lindbergh.[3] That was the way it looked. As soon as his technical debriefings[4] had been completed, Shepard was flown straight from Grand Bahama Island to Washington. The next day the six also-rans[5] joined him there. They stood by as President Kennedy gave Al the Distinguished Service Medal in a ceremony in the Rose Garden of the White House. Then they followed in his wake as Al sat up on the back of an open limousine waving to the crowds along Constitution Avenue. Tens of thousands of people had turned out to watch the motorcade, even though it had been arranged with barely twenty-four hours' notice. They were screaming to Al, reaching out,

> **Connecting Literature to Social Studies**
> ❶ Why would the spectators feel gratitude toward Shepard?

---

1. **Glenn:** John Herschel Glenn, Jr. (b. 1921); First American to orbit the Earth (1962).
2. **Shepard:** Alan B. Shepard, Jr. (1923–1998); on May 5, 1961, he became the first U.S. astronaut to travel in space.
3. **Lindbergh** (lind′ bərg): Charles Augustus Lindbergh (1902–1974); U.S. navigator who made the first nonstop flight from New York to Paris in 1927.
4. **debriefings:** Information given concerning a flight or mission just completed.
5. **also-rans:** Nonwinners in a race, competition, or election.

▲ **Critical Viewing** This photograph captures Alan Shepard being honored in a parade. What evidence shows that he had become a hero of the people? [Connect]

The Right Stuff ◆ 923

❶ One of Alan Shepard's legacies to the American people and the space program was his unforgettable golf shot on the moon. He intrigued television-viewing Americans when he attached a golf club to the lunar soil scoop during the Apollo 14 moon landing mission in 1971 and proceeded to hit a golf ball into a small moon crater, calling it a "hole-in-one" shot. While still on Earth prior to blast-off, he had practiced the shot suited up in his space gear.

Reinforce and Extend

Answers

◆ LITERATURE AND YOUR LIFE

Reader's Response Astronaut space explorers were courageous and performed dangerous missions, so Americans did not overreact when they arrived home safely.

Thematic Focus Heroes are courageous and willing to attempt new things.

☑ Check Your Comprehension

1. They watched from the sidelines.
2. Shepard was usually quite calm, but this time he was excited and moved.
3. His hometown had a parade in his honor.

◆ Critical Thinking

1. Wolfe describes them as "also-rans" and "they followed in his [Shepard's] wake."
2. The public adoration continued to grow and grow.
3. Wolfe seems to imply that Shepard belongs to the American people by referring to him familiarly.
4. Winning athletes and teams are sometimes honored with parades and ceremonies. Students may think Shepard's accomplishments were more important because they were more dangerous.

More About the Author

Tom Wolfe grew up in Richmond, Virginia, graduated from Washington and Lee University, and received a doctorate from Yale University. In addition to working as a reporter, he has authored many books. *The Right Stuff,* published in 1979, was awarded the American Book Award for general nonfiction.

CONNECTING LITERATURE TO SOCIAL STUDIES

crying, awash with awe and gratitude. It took the motorcade half an hour to travel the one mile from the White House to the Capitol. Al sometimes seemed to have transistors in his solar plexus.[6] But not now; now he seemed truly moved. They adored him. He was on . . . the Pope's balcony . . . Thirty minutes of it . . . The next day New York City gave Al a ticker-tape parade up Broadway. There was Al on the back ledge of the limousine, with all that paper snow and confetti coming down, just the way you used to see it in the Movietone News in the theaters. Al's hometown, Derry, New Hampshire, which was not much more than a village, gave Al a parade, and it drew the biggest crowd the state had ever seen. Army, Navy, Marine, Air Force, and National Guard troops from all over New England marched down Main Street, and <u>aerobatic</u> teams of jet fighters flew overhead. The politicians thought New Hampshire was entering Metro Heaven and came close to renaming Derry "Spacetown U.S.A." before they got hold of themselves. In the town of Deerfield, Illinois, a new school was named for Al, overnight, just like that. Then Al started getting tons of greeting cards in the mail, cards saying "Congratulations to Alan ❶ Shepard, Our First Man in Space!" That was already printed on the cards, along with NASA's address. All the buyers had to do was sign them and mail them. The card companies were cranking these things out. Al was that much of a hero.

---

6. **seemed to have transistors in his solar plexus:** Showed little or no emotion.

◆ Build Vocabulary

aerobatic (er´ ə bat´ ik) *adj.*: Performing loops, rolls, etc., with an airplane; stuntlike

---

Meet the Author

Tom Wolfe (1931–) began his career as a reporter for the *Washington Post* in 1959 and then worked for the *New York Herald Tribune* in 1962. His first collection of articles, published in 1965, was entitled *The Kandy-Kolored Tangerine-Flake Streamline Baby.* He has since published eight books of nonfiction and three novels. He is best known for his style of humorously criticizing some of the more foolish things that Americans do.

Guide for Responding

◆ LITERATURE AND YOUR LIFE

Reader's Response Do you think the crowd overreacted to Shepard's accomplishment? Explain.

Thematic Focus What does this selection suggest about heroism and how heroes are made?

☑ Check Your Comprehension

1. What did the other astronauts do while Shepard was being honored by President Kennedy and the crowds of people?
2. How was Shepard's reaction to the crowds different from his usual reaction to things?
3. How did the town of Deerfield, Illinois, honor Alan Shepard?

◆ Critical Thinking

INTERPRET

1. Wolfe refers to "Glenn and the others," the astronauts who were not chosen to take that first flight into space. What phrases does he use to suggest that they were not happy with their situation? **[Infer]**
2. As the days pass, does the public become more appreciative or less appreciative of Shepard? Explain. **[Analyze]**
3. Wolfe continually refers to Shepard as "Al." What can you conclude about Wolfe's attitude toward Shepard from this reference? **[Draw Conclusions]**

APPLY

4. In what other situations have you seen one or more people treated as Alan Shepard was treated after his flight? How do their accomplishments compare with Shepard's? **[Relate]**

⊕ Block Scheduling Strategies

Consider these suggestions to take advantage of extended class time:

- Discuss the information about the Frontier in American History on p. 922 with students as an introduction and background for understanding the admiration the American people had for the astronaut heroes of the space program.
- Have pairs of students work on a list of space-related stories, myths, and tall tales for the Interest Grabber activity on p. 922.
- Locate photographs of the Earth taken from space and topographical maps. Use these materials to guide students through the map study on p. 922 of the Teacher's Edition.
- Suggest that students use the Series of Events Chain, p. 57 in **Writing and Language Transparencies,** to organize the events of Alan Shepard's extraordinary and historical trip into outer space and his hero's welcome at home in the United States.
- Have students read the selection independently and answer the Guide for Responding questions on p. 924. Then they can discuss their answers in small groups.

CONNECTING LITERATURE TO SOCIAL STUDIES

In *The Right Stuff*, Tom Wolfe shows that the work done by test pilots and astronauts was both difficult and dangerous. But he also shows that the American people were more than ready to celebrate new American heroes. This need for heroes was perhaps due to political unrest during the Vietnam War and the ever-present threat of Soviet aggression during the Cold War.

1. What qualities and achievements do Alan Shepard and Charles Lindbergh share?
2. List the details in the selection that make Alan Shepard seem like a heroic figure.
3. According to Tom Wolfe, is Shepard truly deserving of the adoration of the public? Why or why not?

Idea Bank

Writing

1. **Journal Entry** Write an entry that Alan Shepard might have put into his journal after the events described in the selection.
2. **News Article** Write a newspaper article describing the parade honoring Shepard. You may want to "interview" parade watchers and get their reactions to Shepard's accomplishments.
3. **Essay** In an essay, describe the qualities that an astronaut must have in order to be successful. You may also want to include information about the training and education necessary to qualify for the job.

Speaking and Listening

4. **Dialogue [Group Activity]** With a classmate, pretend you are at one of the parades given for Alan Shepard. Discuss your feelings about what he accomplished. **[Performing Arts Link]**
5. **Speech** Write a speech for Alan Shepard to make at one of the parades honoring him. Deliver the speech to your class.

Projects

6. **Report** Use an encyclopedia and other sources to learn about the accomplishments of Alan Shepard and other early astronauts. Report to the class on what you learn.
7. **Illustration** Use reference works to learn about the rocket ship that Shepard rode on his first flight into space. Create a detailed illustration of the ship, and place it on the classroom bulletin board. **[Art Link; Science Link]**

Further Reading, Listening, and Viewing

- *The Right Stuff*, a feature film based on Tom Wolfe's book, tells the story of the group of pilots selected to be trained as astronauts for America's first flight to the moon.
- Paul Westman's *Alan Shepard, The First American in Space* (1979) covers the life of Shepard from his boyhood in New England to his walk on the moon.
- Carolyn Blacknall's *Sally Ride* (1984) is a biography of the first American woman in space.

from *The Right Stuff* ◆ 925

 Beyond the Selection

FURTHER READING
Other Works About Space Exploration
NASA and the Exploration of Space, Mary Kalamaras, Bertram Ulrich, Roger D. Launius; introduction by John Glenn
Flying to the Moon: An Astronaut's Story, Michael Collins
The Greatest Adventure/Apollo 13 and Other Space Adventures by Those Who Flew Them! Edward Gibson, James A. Michener; Ed Gibson, editor
Books of Space Photographs
Orbit: NASA Astronauts Photograph the Earth, Jay Apt, Michael Helfert, Justin Wilkinson, Roger Ressmeyer

INTERNET
We suggest the following sites on the Internet (all Web sites are subject to change).
    For information about NASA:
http://www.nasa.gov/hqpao/nasa_centers.html
    For information about Alan Shepard:
http://chabot.cosc.org/eas/r0898-7.htm
    For information about space exploration:
http://www.imagine5.com/
    We *strongly recommend* that you preview these sites before you send students to them.

 Idea Bank

Following are suggestions for matching the Idea Bank topics with your students' performance levels and learning modalities:

Customize for
Performance Levels
Less Advanced Students: 1, 4
Average Students: 2, 4, 7
More Advanced Students: 3, 5, 6, 7

Customize for
Learning Modalities
Verbal/Linguistic: 1, 2, 3, 4, 5, 6
Visual/Spatial: 7
Logical/Mathematical: 6, 7
Intrapersonal: 1, 6, 7
Interpersonal: 2, 4, 5

Answers (continued)
CONNECTING LITERATURE TO SOCIAL STUDIES

1. They were both brave and willing to try something new and dangerous.
2. The people were screaming, crying, and reaching out to him; he received tons of congratulatory mail; and thousands of people attended welcome-home parades.
3. Students will probably think Wolfe believes he was a hero because the final line of the selection is "Al was that much of a hero."

ASSESSMENT OPTIONS

Formal Assessment, Selection Test, pp. 268–269, and Assessment Resources Software. The selection test is designed so that it can be easily customized to the performance levels of your students.

PORTFOLIO ASSESSMENT
Use the following rubrics in the **Alternative Assessment** booklet to assess student writing:
Journal Entry: Narrative Based on Personal Experience, p. 92
News Article: Description, p. 93
Essay: Description, p. 93

Establish Writing Guidelines

Review the following key characteristics of a multimedia presentation:

- Multimedia presentations provide textual and visual information on a subject.

- A multimedia presentation may use a variety of media to present information such as slides, videos, music, photos, and drawings.

You may want to distribute the scoring rubric for Multimedia Report, p. 103 in **Alternative Assessment,** to make students aware of the criteria on which they will be evaluated. See the suggestions on p. 928 for how you can customize the rubric to this workshop.

Refer students to the Writing Handbook in the back of the book for instruction on the writing process and further information on reports.

Writer's Solution

Writers at Work Videodisc

To introduce students to writing reports and to show them how writer Virginia Hamilton uses report-writing techniques, play the videodisc segment on Reports (Ch. 7).

Play frames 9330 to 17762

Writing Lab CD-ROM

If your students have access to computers, you may want to have them work in the tutorial on Reports to complete all or part of their multimedia presentations. Follow these steps:

1. Have students use the Topic Web activity to help them divide and subdivide their topics.
2. Suggest that students use the annotated instruction on using library resources.
3. Allow students to draft on computer.
4. Have students use the Strategies for improving the content of a report when revising.

Writer's Solution Sourcebook

Students can find additional support, including in-depth instruction on organizing information, pp. 222–223, in the chapter on Reports, pp. 200–233.

Report Writing

Multimedia Presentation

Writing Process Workshop

Storytellers and writers have brought folk tales to life for centuries through their dynamic presentations of the tales. In the contemporary age, you have other resources for creating a dynamic presentation. You can create a multimedia presentation, which supplies information through a variety of media, such as written materials, slides, videos, music, audio, maps, charts, graphs, photos, drawings, and fine art reproductions.

Create a multimedia presentation of or about folk tales. The following skills from this section's Writing Mini-Lessons will help you make an interesting multimedia presentation:

Writing Skills Focus

▶ Use vivid descriptions to **show, not just tell,** information. (See p. 898.)

▶ **Use visual support** to portray a character, event, or description. (See p. 909.)

▶ **Use an effective format.** Choose a method of presenting that is manageable and suits your audience. (See p. 921.)

After reading "Coyote Steals the Sun and Moon," one student created a multimedia presentation about the Zuñi.

MODEL FROM LITERATURE

"Coyote Steals the Sun and Moon" comes from the Zuñi culture. The Zuñi live in New Mexico on the Arizona border. [Show map of southwestern United States.] ① Zuñi Pueblo—a village including modern and traditional dwellings, mostly made of adobe bricks and wood— ② is still home to many of the Zuñi people. This is what a pueblo looks like. [Show picture of pueblo.] ③

① A map of the southwestern United States visually supports the writer's point.

② This description of a pueblo helps the audience visualize it.

③ Directions placed in brackets remind the presenter when to introduce the media.

926 ◆ American Folk Tradition

 Cross-Curricular Connection: Science

Multimedia Technology Have students consider different types of multimedia and technology that they use. Explain that the range of multimedia material has grown significantly in the last part of the twentieth century. Make a list on the chalkboard that roughly charts the introduction of various forms of multimedia technology: radio, television, phonographs, 8-track cassette players, portable stereos, CD players, DVD players, videodisc players, and so on. Also elicit from students types of telecommunications technology they've used: fax machines, cell phones, the Internet.

Ask students to consider the different types of technology and research the invention or scientific advances of various forms of technology. You may want to have students create an annotated list of multimedia resources that they use, identifying the reasons for their use. Have students share their lists with their classmates to increase the technology awareness of your students.

Prewriting

Choose a Topic For your topic, you may want to use one of the folk tales in this unit, find a new folk tale (see p. 963 for Extended Reading Opportunities), or write about the culture or history related to a folk tale. You may decide, however, to use one of the topic ideas suggested below:

> **Other Topic Ideas**
> - Cyclones and tornadoes
> - Transcontinental railroads of the 1800's
> - Heroes of our time

Find Multimedia Support Visual aids and other types of media will significantly enliven your presentation. Indicate how the media will enhance your audience's understanding of the folk tale. For instance, your written report may indicate when readers should press Play. If you are giving an oral presentation, explain why you are showing a visual.
- ▶ **Maps** can clarify historical or geographical information.
- ▶ **Graphs and charts** can make complicated information easier to understand.
- ▶ **Pictures or drawings** illustrate objects, scenes, and other details.
- ▶ **Audio and video** provide visual and auditory support for your points.

Plan Your Organization Make an outline of the organization for your presentation. On the outline, note the points during which you plan to present audio and visual aspects of your presentation.

> I. **Cyclones**
>> A. [Show photograph of cyclone]
>>> 1. [Post chart of statistics]

Drafting

Show, Don't Tell Use visual support to back up your vivid descriptions. When incorporating media, make sure you introduce the pieces and explain why you are using them.

Use an Effective Format As you draft, use an effective format to make the information within your multimedia presentation easy to find. You may want to use bulleted lists, numbered lists, boldface, italics, and other visual clues to call out important information.

DRAFTING/REVISING

APPLYING LANGUAGE SKILLS: Creating Unity

When every detail in a piece of writing supports one idea, that writing has **unity.** In a multi-media presentation, all the media used should relate to the main point. Use the following strategies to achieve unity:

- **Identify your main idea,** and choose details that support it.
- **Delete ideas** that are unrelated to the main point.

Practice Identify the main idea, and eliminate any details that do not belong.

In 1977, a spacecraft named *Voyager 2* was launched on a mission to the outer edge of the solar system. The solar system, as you know, has nine planets. Using radio signals, *Voyager 2* sent back thousands of photographs. *Voyager 2* has provided crucial clues to the origins of our solar system. It has also given humans a vivid sense of the vastness of space.

Writing Application In your presentation, create unity by deleting details that do not support your main point.

> ### Writer's Solution Connection Writing Lab
>
> For help finding sources, see the instruction on library resources in the Prewriting section of the Reports tutorial.

Develop Student Writing

Prewriting

Suggest that students, when gathering visual support for their topics, refer to the art accompanying the folk tales in this unit. Suggest that they find information on the artist whose work accompanies the folk tale they have chosen. They can then do further research to see if the artist has more work relating to their particular topic.

Writer's Solution

Writing Lab CD-ROM

Suggest to students that they view the guidelines for taking notes in the Prewriting section of the tutorial on Reports before starting their research.

Customize for
Less Proficient Writers
Some students may do better working in pairs on their multimedia presentations. Suggest that students pair up and select a folk tale on which to find more information. Students can do their research independently and then share the information they have found. In terms of organizing the report, suggest that students take turns presenting information.

Drafting

Have students note in the model from literature, on p. 926, where the writer has left bracketed directions for providing visual support. Encourage students to think of their presentations as a chronological process and to include notes to themselves on where and when to provide visuals.

Applying Language Skills

Creating Unity Explain to students that creating unity depends on narrowing a topic and selecting only the best and most important information to use in the presentation. Encourage students to keep all textual material and visual support focused on the main point of their presentations.

Writer's Solution

For additional instruction and practice, have students use the practice page on Recognizing Unity, p. 128, in the *Writer's Solution Grammar Practice Book*. If students have access to technology, they can use the lesson on Unity in Paragraphs in the Building Paragraphs unit of the *Writer's Solution Language Lab CD-ROM*.

Answers

The main idea is that in 1977, the *Voyager 2* launched a mission to the edge of the solar system. Eliminate these details: The solar system has nine planets, and *Voyager* used radio signals.

Revising

Encourage students to work with a peer reviewer when revising. Have the reviewer consider which visuals provide the most information and where more information may be needed.

Writer's Solution

Writing Lab CD-ROM

In the Revising and Editing section of the tutorial on Reports, suggest that students use the Proofreading Checklist to find errors in grammar, spelling, and punctuation.

Publishing

Students might use videotape to document their multimedia presentations, including their development and creation.

Reinforce and Extend

Review the Writing Guidelines
After students have completed their papers, review the characteristics of a multimedia presentation.

Applying Language Skills

Using Commas in Compound Sentences Explain to students that coordinating conjunctions can also join compound subjects, verbs, prepositional phrases, and clauses. Remind students that in these cases, no comma is required.

Answers

1. The Zuñi girl is learning French, but she already speaks three languages.
2. The Zuñi raise corn and wheat, and they engage in sheep herding on a large scale.
3. You could watch the masked dancers, or you could attend a Zuñi feast.

Writing Process Workshop

EDITING/PROOFREADING

APPLYING LANGUAGE SKILLS: Using Commas in Compound Sentences

A **compound sentence** combines two or more independent clauses with a comma and a coordinating conjunction (*and, or, but, for, nor, yet, so*). Following are examples:

Cleopatra was born in 69 B.C., **and** she died in 30 B.C.

Cleopatra was not beautiful, **but** she attracted some of the greatest Romans of her time.

Practice Write these sentences with correct punctuation:

1. This Zuñi girl is learning French but she already speaks three languages.
2. The Zuñi raise corn and wheat and they engage in sheep herding on a large scale.
3. You could watch the masked dancers or you could attend a Zuñi feast.

Writing Application As you write your multimedia presentation, use commas in compound sentences correctly.

Writer's Solution Connection Language Lab

For more help with commas, complete the Commas lesson in the Punctuation unit.

Revising

Use a Checklist Use the following checklist to help you evaluate and revise your presentation:

▶ Do my descriptions show, not just tell, information? *Read descriptive passages to a partner. Ask him or her to describe what type of visual picture the description gives. If he or she comes up with a picture that doesn't resemble your description, revise by deleting or adding descriptive details to create the impression you want.*

▶ Did I use appropriate visual support? *Review your choice of visuals. Ask yourself whether they really support your points. If a visual is not strong support, don't use it. It will only confuse your audience.*

▶ Did I use an effective format? *Review your placement of media to make sure they clearly support the points they accompany. Make sure media are manageable. If you have to use audio, television, and several pictures one after another, it might distract your audience. Spread the media throughout your presentation.*

REVISION MODEL

① [Press cassette for audio of fireworks]
Cyclone Bill invented the Fourth of July. The holiday
② [Play video of cyclone]
celebrated with fireworks and picnics angered the cyclone.
② twisting and turning
As you can see, the cyclone is dangerous, but Pecos Bill

[Show drawing of Bill] was not afraid.

① Since this presentation will be read by the teacher, the writer made the format more effective by including directions for using the media.

② The writer included the video of the cyclone because not everyone knows what one is and how powerful it is.

③ The writer adds these words to make his description more vivid.

Publishing and Presenting

Live Audience Find a live audience who will appreciate your presentation: an elementary-school class, a local organization, or a group or club in your school. Encourage questions following your presentation.

Internet Publish your work on a site devoted to your topic.

928 ◆ *The American Folk Tradition*

✓ ASSESSMENT		4	3	2	1
PORTFOLIO ASSESSMENT Use the rubric on Multimedia Presentation in the **Alternative Assessment** booklet, p. 103, to assess the students' writing. Add these criteria to customize this rubric to this assignment.	**Unity**	The presentation has a distinct unity, with all details supporting the main idea.	The presentation is mostly unified, with only a few details that do not support the main idea.	The presentation has a sense of unity in some parts, but doesn't always support the main idea.	The presentation is not unified, making it difficult to determine the main idea.
	Avoid Double Negatives	The writer consistently avoids using double negatives.	The writer uses one double negative in the script.	The writer uses a few double negatives in the script.	The writer uses several double negatives in the script.

Real-World Reading Skills Workshop

Using Headings and Text Structure

Strategies for Success

By working with the text and the layout—or overall design—of a page, editors and designers create pages that are attractive and easy to use. To make different sections of text stand out, they use some of these features:

- ▶ Heads in different colors or fonts
- ▶ Text in **bold** or *italic* typeface
- ▶ Bulleted/or numbered lists
- ▶ Boxed sections

Learn to take advantage of the structure of text on a page.

Scan the Headings Often the main topics of a chapter or an article are printed in larger or darker headings. If you scan these headings, you can gain an overview of the entire article before you read it. The overview will provide a context for the information in the article.

Determine Text Functions As you read, you'll soon find a pattern in the use of headings and **boldface** and *italic* type. Usually, headings of the same size and style indicate equal importance; for example, a large heading would be the main topic and four equally smaller subheads would indicate supporting sections. **Boldface** is often used to draw attention to important terms. *Italics* are often used for glossary or vocabulary terms.

Look for Set-off Items Significant terms, related concepts, formulas, dates, and summaries may be set apart in a box, a sidebar, or with special shading.

Apply the Strategies

Use the headings and text structure in the article at left to answer the following questions.

1. Scan the headings and provide an overview of this article.

2. Locate three technical terms. How are they printed?

3. Why is the information on summer protection presented in a box?

THE SUN'S EFFECT ON THE SKIN

The largest and most visible organ of your body, the skin is greatly affected by the sun.

THE ROLE OF MELANIN

Melanin is the dark, protective coloring in the skin. The amount of melanin determines whether a person tans or burns in the sun. . . .

SEVERE SUN BURN

Sunburn can be a serious problem, causing fever, chills, and first- and second-degree burn damage to the skin.
Sun blisters are one defense the body raises against serious burns. . . .

THE WORK OF SWEAT

Without the sweat glands in the skin, the body would overheat and expire. Sweat glands produce about a pint of sweat daily, but in the hot summer, they can produce up to four pints.

Summer Protection Plan
* Always wear sunscreen outdoors
* Wear a hat when the sun is highest
* Wear sunglasses
* Drink plenty of water
* If you begin to burn, get out of the sun

✔ *Use headings and text structure to read the following texts more efficiently:*

- ▶ *Newspaper feature articles*
- ▶ *Textbooks*
- ▶ *Long encyclopedia entries*
- ▶ *World Wide Web pages*

Reviewing Commas

The selections in Part 1 include instruction on the following:

- Unnecessary Commas
- Commas in Compound Sentences
- Commas in Series

This instruction is reinforced with the Build Grammar Skills practice pages in **Selection Support**, pp. 304, 310, and 315.

As you review commas, you may wish to review the following:

- Commas With Introductory Elements

Explain to students that they should use a comma after an introductory word, phrase, or clause to separate it from the rest of the sentence.

Kinds of Introductory Material	
Introductory Words	No, I do not play pranks.
Nouns of Direct Address	Brer Possum, will you help me?
Common Expressions	Of course, the story was true.
Introductory Adverbs	Obviously, Coyote opened the lid. Hurriedly, he closed it.
Prepositional Phrases (of four or more words)	In the early light of morning, they chose their names.
Participal Phrases	Flying high, Eagle left Coyote behind.
Infinitive Phrases	To help Brer Snake, Brer Possum lifted him out of the hole.
Adverb Clauses	When Brer Snake was free, he bit Brer Possum.

✒ Writer's Solution

For additional practice and support with using commas, use the practice pages on Commas That Separate Basic Elements and Commas That Set Off Added Elements, pp. 105–108, in the *Writer's Solution Grammar Practice Book.* If students have access to technology, they can use the lesson on commas in the Punctuation unit on the *Writer's Solution Language Lab CD-ROM.*

Commas | Grammar Review

Commas are used to create pauses in sentences that help readers follow ideas.

Commas in Compound Sentences A comma is used in a compound sentence to separate two independent clauses that are joined by a comma and a coordinating conjunction (*and, but, for, nor, or, so,* and *yet*). (See p. 908.) An independent clause has a subject and a verb and expresses a complete thought. In the following example, the comma before the conjunction *but* separates independent clauses:

Nobody respected his name, Imitator, *but* it fit him.

Commas in a Series When listing three or more items in a series, use commas to separate them. The items may be words, phrases, or other elements. Include a comma before the conjunction preceding the final item. In the following example, commas separate the three things that Chicoria did:

Chicoria *sang, recited poetry,* and *put Gracia to shame.*

Unnecessary Commas Using unnecessary commas can mislead the reader. (See p. 897.) A comma is not necessary before a coordinating conjunction when it links words or groups of words that are *not* independent clauses.

Unnecessary: Of Johnny Appleseed, two things are known: he loved apples, *and* walking alone.

Correct: Of Johnny Appleseed, two things are known: he loved apples *and* walking alone.

Practice 1 In your notebook, write these sentences, adding commas where necessary and eliminating unnecessary commas:

1. "They bother and kill people and the tribes cannot increase as I wish."
2. They fly, and walk, and sing and cry.

3. "Well, Coyote was a chief after all and he felt good again."
4. For fifty years, Johnny Appleseed planted nurtured and harvested apple trees.
5. He lived with owl, and bear-cub, and possum.

Practice 2 Revise the following sentences according to the directions in parentheses. Place commas correctly.

1. The master will invite me of his own accord. I'll sit at the master's table. (Make compound sentence)
2. You can beg or ask but they won't invite you. (Add one item to make a series)
3. Chicoria greeted the rancher. The rancher replied haughtily. (Make a compound sentence)
4. Johnny Appleseed wished trees would root and blossom. (Add one item to make a series)
5. Coyote is often a troublemaker. Other animals distrusted him because he stole a box and the sun. (Make compound sentence, and add one item to make a series)

Grammar in Writing

✔ Be careful not to write run-on sentences when you are writing compound sentences. A run-on sentence is one that omits the comma and conjunction between two independent clauses or has only a comma between the two clauses.

Answers
Practice 1

1. "They bother and kill people, and the tribes cannot increase as I wish."
2. They fly and walk and sing and cry.
3. "Well, Coyote was a chief after all, and he felt good again."
4. For fifty years, Johnny Appleseed planted, nurtured, and harvested apple trees.
5. He lived with owl and bear-cub and possum.

Practice 2
Possible responses:

1. The master will invite me of his own accord, and I'll sit at the master's table.
2. You can beg, ask, or plead, but they won't invite you.
3. Chicoria greeted the rancher, and the rancher replied haughtily.
4. Johnny Appleseed wished trees would root, grow, and blossom.
5. Coyote is often a troublemaker, and other animals distrusted him because he stole a box, the moon, and the sun.

PART 2 *Tales of American Heroes*

The Giant, 1923, N.C. Wyeth, Brandywine River Museum, Chadds Ford, PA

The selections in this section focus on tales of American heroes. "Hammerman" and "John Henry" focus on the legendary man, John Henry. "Paul Bunyan of the North Woods" tells several short tales about this legendary character. "Pecos Bill: The Cyclone" is a tall tale about a Texas cowpuncher. "Davy Crockett's Dream" tells the tale of another legendary man, Davy Crockett.

Customize for
Varying Student Needs

When assigning the selections in this section to your students, keep in mind the following factors:

"Hammerman," "John Henry," "Paul Bunyan of the North Woods," "Pecos Bill: The Cyclone," "Davy Crockett's Dream"

- Five tall tales about legendary American characters
- "John Henry" includes a Beyond Literature science connection
- Students may need help with vocabulary in "Paul Bunyan of the North Woods"
- Students may need help with unfamiliar spellings and language in "Davy Crockett's Dream"
- John Henry and Davy Crockett were real men who became legendary as tales about them were told over the years

 Humanities: Art

The Giant, 1923, by N. C. Wyeth

N. C. Wyeth (1882–1945) was an American painter and also one of America's most celebrated illustrators. He created illustrations for many juvenile classics such as *Treasure Island, Robin Hood,* and *The Yearling.* He also did murals for several churches. His son, Andrew Wyeth, was also his pupil and a noted painter.

Wyeth's paintings were usually done with egg tempera. The subject matter was rural scenes. He painted many landscapes of New England and Pennsylvania.

Have students study the painting, and then ask the following questions:

1. This painting is titled *The Giant.* Do you think it represents an American hero? *Some students will say yes, because the giant is a classic figure in folklore. Others will say no, because there is nothing inherently American about the giant.*

2. What do the positions of the children tell you? *Students should note that the children are looking up at the giant in awe. It looks as if they had been playing in the sand and stopped in the middle of what they were doing to stare at this giant.*

OBJECTIVES

1. To read, comprehend, and interpret four tall tales and a poem about folk heroes
2. To relate these works to personal experience
3. To predict
4. To analyze tall tales
5. To build vocabulary in context and use forms of *skeptic*
6. To develop skill in varying sentence beginnings
7. To write a nomination using only important details
8. To respond to the tall tales and poem through writing, speaking and listening, and projects

SKILLS INSTRUCTION

Vocabulary:
Forms of *skeptic*
Spelling:
Multi-syllable Words With the *m* Sound in the Middle
Grammar:
Variety in Sentence Beginnings
Reading Strategy:
Predict
Literary Focus:
Tall Tale
Writing:
Important Details

Speaking and Listening:
Oral Storytelling (Teacher Edition)
Viewing and Representing:
Folk Hero Illustration (Teacher Edition)
Critical Viewing:
Connect; Infer; Analyze; Evaluate; Summarize; Assess

PORTFOLIO OPPORTUNITIES

Writing: Journal Entry; Tall Tale; Analysis
Writing Mini-Lesson: Nomination
Speaking and Listening: Performance; Oral Storytelling
Projects: Collage; Report

More About the Authors

Adrien Stoutenburg is best known for her stories about folk heroes, but she also wrote books with nonfiction subjects, such as endangered bird species, and the life of Walt Whitman.

Carl Sandburg's "Rootabaga" stories were published after his death. One reviewer claimed that the stories were written for the eternal child.

Harold W. Felton enjoyed writing about the dangers and excitement of the West. His favorite folk hero was Pecos Bill, the timeless superhero.

Davy Crockett was known as a devoted family man and a politician with integrity. His autobiography has been called "clever fiction."

Guide for Reading

Meet the Authors:

Adrien Stoutenburg (1916–1982)

A poet, biographer, and writer, Adrien Stoutenburg wrote close to forty books. In addition to writing, Stoutenburg worked as a librarian and a political reporter. "Hammerman" was taken from her book *American Tall Tales.*

Carl Sandburg (1878–1976)

Carl Sandburg is best known for his poetry, but he was also a journalist, an author of children's books, and a historian. Sandburg received two Pulitzer Prizes—one in 1940 for his biography of Abraham Lincoln and one in 1950 for his *Complete Poems.* [For more on Carl Sandburg, see page 344.]

Harold W. Felton (1902–   )

Harold William Felton practiced law and worked for the Internal Revenue Service, yet he became increasingly interested in the legends and folklore of the United States. He has published collections of stories about folk heroes and the cowboys of the West.

Davy Crockett (1786–1836)

Davy Crockett was a celebrated frontiersman, soldier in the United States Army, and Tennessee congressman. His tall tales strongly influenced the comic tradition and legendary history of the western frontier. He fought at the Alamo for Texan independence and was killed there by Mexican troops.

932 ◆ The American Folk Tradition

◆ LITERATURE AND YOUR LIFE

CONNECT YOUR EXPERIENCE

Think about people from real life and fiction who perform heroic deeds that amaze and surprise you. The tales in this group are about several such larger-than-life heroes.

THEMATIC FOCUS: Heroes

What qualities and actions elevate these characters to folk-hero status?

◆ Background for Understanding

SOCIAL STUDIES

John Henry was an actual person who was employed by the Chesapeake and Ohio Railroad. Railroad companies boomed during the 1870's. The Central Pacific Railroad began building tracks west from Omaha, Nebraska, and the Union Pacific Railroad began building tracks east from Sacramento, California. The tracks met and joined to create the first transcontinental railroad. By the end of the decade, more than 70,000 miles of railroad track crisscrossed the United States.

◆ Build Vocabulary

RELATED WORDS: FORMS OF *skeptic*

Skeptic is a noun meaning "a person who questions matters that are generally accepted." Words related to *skeptic* include the adjective *skeptical* and the adverb *skeptically.*

WORD BANK

Which word from the selections means "unexplainable"? Check the Build Vocabulary box on page 949 to see if you chose correctly.

hefted
granite
commotion
usurped
invincible
futile
inexplicable
skeptics

Prentice Hall Literature Program Resources

REINFORCE / RETEACH / EXTEND
Selection Support Pages
Build Vocabulary: Forms of *skeptic*, p. 324
Build Spelling Skills, p. 325
Build Grammar Skills: Varying Sentence Beginnings, p. 326
Reading Strategy: Predict, p. 327
Literary Focus: Tall Tales, p. 328
Strategies for Diverse Student Needs, pp. 119–120
Beyond Literature, Workplace Skills: Goal Setting, p. 60

Formal Assessment Selection Test, pp. 270–272, Assessment Resources Software
Alternative Assessment, p. 60
Writing and Language Transparencies
Series of Events Chain, p. 57; Cluster Organizer, p. 73
Daily Language Practice, pp. 68–72
Resource Pro CD-ROM

Listening to Literature Audiocassettes
"Hammerman"; "John Henry"; "Paul Bunyan"; "Pecos Bill: The Cyclone"; "Davy Crockett's Dream"

Hammerman ◆ John Henry
◆ Paul Bunyan of the North Woods ◆
Pecos Bill: The Cyclone ◆ Davy Crockett's Dream

Hammer in His Hand, Palmer C. Hayden, Museum of African American Art, Los Angeles, CA

◆ Literary Focus

TALL TALE

A **tall tale** is a humorous story that recounts exaggerated events in a matter-of-fact way, using the everyday speech of the common people. Tall tales are often associated with life on the American frontier. They are considered to be part of the oral tradition because they have been handed down from generation to generation by word of mouth.

◆ Reading Strategy

PREDICT

Tall tales, like other folk tales, develop in predictable patterns. You can **predict** that the characters will perform exaggerated or even impossible feats. Once you learn the character's traits, you can predict the kinds of events that will occur. For example, John Henry is known for his strength, so you can predict that he will perform some amazing feat of strength.

Use a chart like the one below to predict the kinds of events the stories will tell.

Character	Trait	Prediction
John Henry	Strength	

Guide for Reading ◆ 933

Preparing for Standardized Tests

Vocabulary The vocabulary skill for this lesson helps students see the relationships between words. Write the following analogy on the board.

John Henry : Hammerman :: Davy Crockett : Frontiersman

The object of an analogy question is to determine the relationships between words. In the example, guide students to see the relationship between people and descriptions. Most standardized tests offer a choice of words to answer an analogy question. Have students complete the following analogy with words that might be used to describe John Henry's contest with the steam engine.

futile : useless :: skeptical : _____

(A) fearful   (C) careful
(B) doubtful   (D) none of the above

Remind students that more than one answer may complete an analogy, but they should choose the best answer. In the first pair, the words are synonyms. *Fearful* and *careful* are not synonyms for *skeptical,* but *doubtful* is. Therefore, *(B)* is the best answer.

Interest Grabber
Divide the class into groups and have them discuss the details of the Cinderella story. Have each group select a narrator and decide on the details they wish to emphasize in a 3-minute tape-recorded retelling of the story. The details may include exaggeration, but the story should be told in a matter-of-fact style. Have the entire class listen to the recordings and compare and contrast the details that the groups chose to tell. Explain that the tall tales in the selections they are about to read have been told and retold through the years with changes and exaggerations.

◆ Build Grammar Skills

Variety in Sentence Beginnings
If you wish to introduce the grammar concept for this selection before students read, refer to the instruction on p. 954.

Customize for
Less Proficient Readers
As students read each tall tale, have them complete the details in a chart like the one below, evaluating how the characters' traits make them seem like heroes.

Character	Thoughts/Words	Actions

Customize for
More Advanced Students
In these stories, characters resolve conflicts between themselves and external forces. Ask students to note the primary conflict faced by the main character in each selection. Discuss how each conflict is resolved and what the outcomes reveal about the people who first told the tales.

Humanities: Art

Hammer in His Hand, 1944–1947, by Palmer C. Hayden

For information about Palmer C. Hayden, see p. 935 of the Teacher Edition. Ask students how they would describe John Henry as shown in this image. *John Henry appears confident, strong, and happy.*

One-Minute Insight

In "Hammerman," John Henry builds railroad tracks with a twenty-pound hammer in each hand. One day he accepts a challenge to complete in a race with a steam drill. Soon, man and machine are driving a hole into the side of a mountain to create a tunnel. After a grueling battle, John Henry wins the contest, only to die a few minutes later. The story of this hero with amazing strength and determination proves that humans, not machines, have hearts and souls. The tale quickly spread to become part of the American folk tradition.

◆ Literary Focus

❶ Tall Tale Ask students how a person who did not know that the story of John Henry is a tall tale might recognize it as one from reading the first sentence. *The sentence says that a person could "hear thunder behind" a hammer swung by John Henry. This is an obvious exaggeration.*

Clarification

❷ The Civil War began in 1861.

◆ Critical Thinking

❸ Infer Ask students what inferences they can make about John Henry from these sentences. *Although John Henry possesses unusual strength, he views himself as being like everyone else.*

◆ Reading Strategy

❹ Predict Invite students to describe sounds that have evoked a specific feeling for them as the wail of the train whistle did for John Henry. Then ask them to predict what John Henry might do next. *John Henry will probably go to work for a railroad.*

HAMMERMAN
Adrien Stoutenburg

❶ People down South still tell stories about John Henry, how strong he was, and how he could whirl a big sledge[1] so lightning-fast you could hear thunder behind it. They even say he was born with a hammer in his hand. John Henry himself said it, but he probably didn't mean it exactly as it sounded.

The story seems to be that when John Henry was a baby, the first thing he reached out for was a hammer, which was hung nearby on the cabin wall.

John Henry's father put his arm around his wife's shoulder. "He's going to grow up to be a steel-driving man. I can see it plain as rows of cotton running uphill."

As John Henry grew a bit older, he practiced swinging the hammer, not hitting at things, but just enjoying the feel of it whooshing against the air. When he was old enough to talk, he told everyone, "I was born with a hammer in my hand."

❷ ❸ John Henry was still a boy when the Civil War started, but he was a big, hard-muscled boy, and he could outwork and outplay all the other boys on the plantation.

---

1. **sledge** (slej) *n.*: Heavy hammer, usually swung with both hands.

934 ◆ *The American Folk Tradition*

❸ "You're going to be a mighty man, John Henry," his father told him.

"A man ain't nothing but a man," young John Henry said. "And I'm a natural man, born to swing a hammer in my hand."

❹ At night, lying on a straw bed on the floor, John Henry listened to a far-off train whistling through the darkness. Railroad tracks had been laid to carry trainloads of Southern soldiers to fight against the armies of the North. The trains had a lonesome, longing sound that made John Henry want to go wherever they were going.

When the war ended, a man from the North came to John Henry where he was working in the field. He said, "The slaves are free now. You can pack up and go wherever you want, young fellow."

"I'm craving to go where the trains go," said John Henry.

The man shook his head. "There are too many young fellows trailing the trains around now. You better settle down to doing what you know, like handling a cotton hook or driving a mule team."

John Henry thought to himself, there's a big hammer waiting for me somewhere, because I know I'm a steel-driving man. All I have to do is

---

Block Scheduling Strategies

Consider these suggestions to take advantage of extended class time:

- Review the Literary Focus of Tall Tales before students read the selections. After they read, discuss as a group their answers to the Literary Focus questions on p. 954. For additional activities, use the **Daily Language Practice,** pp. 68–72, as they read the tall tales.

- Have students prepare a performance or an oral storytelling from the Speaking and Listening activities in the Idea Bank on p. 955.

- Have students work in small groups, using the *Writer's Solution Writing Lab CD-ROM* to complete the Writing Mini-Lesson on p. 955.

- Alternatively, suggest that students listen to the recording of each tall tale, while filling in a prediction chart such as the one shown on p. 933. Instruct groups of students to compare and discuss their charts and to answer the Reading Strategy questions on p. 954.

🎧 **Listening to Literature Audiocassettes**

hunt 'til I find it.

That night, he told his folks about a dream he had had.

"I dreamed I was working on a railroad somewhere," he said, "a big, new railroad called the C.& O., and I had a mighty hammer in my hand. Every time I swung it, it made a whirling flash around my shoulder. And every time my hammer hit a spike,[2] the sky lit up from the sparks."

"I believe it," his father said. "You were born to drive steel."

"That ain't all of the dream," John Henry said. "I dreamed that the railroad was going to be the end of me and I'd die with the hammer in my hand."

◆ Reading Strategy
Do you predict John Henry's dream will come true? Why or why not?

The next morning, John Henry bundled up some food in a red bandanna handkerchief, told his parents good-bye, and set off into the world. He walked until he heard the clang-clang of hammers in the distance. He followed the sound to a place where gangs of men were building a railroad. John Henry watched the men driving steel spikes down into the crossties[3] to hold the rails in place. Three men would stand around a spike, then each, in turn, would swing a long hammer.

2. **spike** (spīk) *n.*: Long, thick metal nail used for splitting rock.
3. **crossties** (krôs´ tīz) *n.*: Beams laid crosswise under railroad tracks to support them.

John Henry on the Right, Steam Drill on the Left, Palmer Hayden, Collection of The Museum of African American Art, Los Angeles, CA

▲ Critical Viewing What story event does this painting illustrate? Point out the details that reflect details in the story. [Connect]

John Henry's heart beat in rhythm with the falling hammers. His fingers ached for the feel of a hammer in his own hands. He walked over to the foreman.

"I'm a natural steel-driving man," he said. "And I'm looking for a job."

"How much steel-driving have you done?" the foreman asked.

"I was born knowing how," John Henry said.

The foreman shook his head. "That ain't good enough, boy. I can't take any chances. Steel-driving's dangerous work, and you might hit somebody."

"I wouldn't hit anybody," John Henry said, "because I can drive one of those spikes all by myself."

The foreman said sharply, "The one kind of man I don't need in this outfit is a bragger. Stop wasting my time."

John Henry didn't move. He got a stubborn look around his jaw. "You loan me a hammer, mister, and if somebody will hold the spike for me, I'll prove what I can do."

The three men who had just finished driving in a spike looked toward him and laughed. One of them said, "Anybody who would hold a spike for a greenhorn[4] don't want to live long."

"I'll hold it," a fourth man said.

John Henry saw that the speaker was a small, dark-skinned fellow about his own age.

The foreman asked the small man, "D'you aim to get yourself killed, Li'l Willie?"

Li'l Willie didn't answer. He knelt and set a

4. **greenhorn** (grēn´ hôrn) *n.*: Inexperienced person; a beginner.

Hammerman ◆ 935

▶Critical Viewing◀

❺ **Connect** *It shows John Henry and his opponent, the man holding a steam engine, preparing for the contest. It also shows the crowd gathered around, the gleaming steam engine, a man in "city clothes," and John Henry with Li'l Willie.*

◆ **Reading Strategy**

❻ **Predict** *Students may base their predictions on what they already know about John Henry and his great strength. They may predict that he will perform some amazing feat of strength but somehow die in the process.*

◆ **Literary Focus**

❼ **Tall Tale** Point out that despite the danger and difficulty involved, John Henry knows he has the strength and skill to drive steel even before he tries. How did John Henry's father know this as well? How does this help to glorify his deeds? *Students should recognize that these details help to embellish the story of John Henry by making him seem different from other humans.*

◆ **LITERATURE AND YOUR LIFE**

❽ Ask students to think of people they know who like to brag. How does the foreman's statement support what they know about this type of person? *Students may say that people who brag a lot sometimes also take unnecessary chances to prove themselves. Even though John Henry was stating the facts and not bragging, the foreman did not know that and may have been trying to keep his workers safe.*

Customize for
Less Proficient Readers
Play a segment of the audiocassette recording to help students focus on the dialogue and the exaggerated details of the story.

Listening to Literature Audiocassettes

Humanities: Art

John Henry on the Right, Steam Drill on the Left, 1944–1947, by Palmer C. Hayden
African American painter Palmer Hayden (1890–1973) was a leading artist of the Harlem Renaissance during the 1920's. This painting is one in a series of twelve paintings about John Henry. The series helped awaken America's awareness of the value of African American myth and legend.
John Henry on the Right, Steam Drill on the Left captures the excitement surrounding the contest between John Henry and the steam drill. Have stu-

dents compare this painting with the one on p. 933. Use the following questions for class discussion.
1. How does the artist portray John Henry in both paintings? *In the painting on p. 933, John Henry is smiling and confidently striding along the railroad tracks. Both paintings portray him as a handsome and strong young man.*
2. How would you describe the mood of the two teams in the contest? *The friendly, human interaction between John Henry and L'il Willie is more relaxed than the worried expressions on the faces of the men near the steam engine.*

1 Infer Ask students what they can infer from the foreman's quick response. *His response indicates that he was impressed that John Henry's strength required far fewer strokes than most men would need to drive in the spike.*

◆ **Literary Focus**

2 Tall Tale *The exaggerated details show that John Henry accomplishes much more than a normal man would.*

◆ **Critical Thinking**

3 Interpret This is the second time the strange dream is mentioned in this tall tale and is an example of repetition, a common feature of tall tales. Ask students to interpret what John Henry's strange dream might mean. *Students may think that the dream means John Henry may be going to die while working for the railroad.*

◆ **Reading Strategy**

4 Predict Ask students what a black cloud often symbolizes in literature. What predictions can students make about John Henry? *Black clouds often represent danger for the characters in a story. In this case, the cloud reinforces earlier predictions that John Henry may die.*

Customize for
English Language Learners
Students will encounter several words with multiple meanings in this selection that look and sound familiar but are used in a new context. On this page, they will find *light, lean, spike, head, smoking, driving, drive,* and *sized.* Ask students to use context clues to try to determine an approximate meaning. Then have a student who is proficient in English read aloud the passage in which the word appears to check the suggested meaning. Encourage students to search this story and the other tall tales for examples of words with more than one meaning.

spike down through the rail on the crosstie. "Come on, big boy," he said.

John Henry picked up one of the sheepnose hammers lying in the cinders. He <u>hefted</u> it and decided it was too light. He picked up a larger one which weighed twelve pounds. The handle was lean and limber and greased with tallow[5] to make it smooth.

Everyone was quiet, watching, as he stepped over to the spike.

John Henry swung the hammer over his shoulder so far that the hammer head hung down against the back of his knees. He felt a thrill run through his arms and chest.

"Tap it down gentle, first," said Li'l Willie.

But John Henry had already started to swing. He brought the hammer flashing down, banging the spike squarely on the head. Before the other men could draw a breath of surprise, the hammer flashed again, whirring through the air like a giant hummingbird. One more swing, and the spike was down, its steel head smoking from the force of the blow.

1 The foreman blinked, swallowed, and blinked again. "Man," he told John Henry, "you're hired!"

That's the way John Henry started steel driving. From then on, Li'l Willie was always with him, setting the spikes, or placing the drills[6] that John Henry drove with his hammer. There wasn't another steel-driving man in the world who could touch John Henry for speed and power. He could hammer every which way, up or down or sidewise. He could drive for ten hours at a stretch and never miss a stroke.

After he'd been at the work for a few years, he started using a twenty-pound hammer in each hand. It took six men, working fast, to carry fresh drills to him. People would come for miles around to watch John Henry.

> Whenever John Henry worked, he sang. Li'l Willie sang with him, chanting the rhythm of the clanging hammer strokes.

2
◆ **Literary Focus**
What element of tall tales is evident here?

---

5. **tallow** (tal′ ō) *n.*: Solid fat obtained from sheep or cattle.
6. **drills** (drilz) *n.*: Pointed tools used for making holes in hard substances.

936 ◆ *The American Folk Tradition*

Those were happy days for John Henry. One of the happiest days came when he met a black-eyed, curly-haired girl called Polly Ann. And, on the day that Polly Ann said she would marry him, John Henry almost burst his throat with singing.

Every now and then, John Henry would remember the strange dream he had had years before, about the C.& O. Railroad and dying with a hammer in his hand. One night, he had the dream again. The next morning, when he went to work, the steel gang gathered round him, hopping with excitement. **3**

"The Chesapeake and Ohio Railroad wants men to drive a tunnel through a mountain in West Virginia!" they said.

"The C. & O. wants the best hammermen there are!" they said. "And they'll pay twice as much as anybody else."

Li'l Willie looked at John Henry. "If they want the best, John Henry, they're goin' to need you."

John Henry looked back at his friend. "They're going to need you, too, Li'l Willie. I ain't going without you." He stood a minute, looking at the sky. There was a black thundercloud way off, with sunlight flashing behind it. John **4** Henry felt a small chill between his shoulder blades. He shook himself, put his hammer on his shoulder, and said, "Let's go, Willie!"

When they reached Summers County where the Big Bend Tunnel was to be built, John Henry sized up the mountain standing in the way. It was almost solid rock.

"Looks soft," said John Henry. "Hold a drill up there, Li'l Willie."

Li'l Willie did. John Henry took a seventy-pound hammer and drove the drill in with one mountain-cracking stroke. Then he settled down to working the regular way, pounding in the drills with four or five strokes of a twenty-pound sledge. He worked so fast that his helpers had to keep buckets of water ready to pour on his hammers so they wouldn't catch fire.

◆ **Build Vocabulary**

hefted (hef′ tid) *v.*: Lifted; tested the weight of

Cross-Curricular Connection: Social Studies

The Man Behind the Hammer John Henry was an actual person—an African American laborer who helped to build the Big Bend Tunnel on the Chesapeake and Ohio Railroad in the early 1870's. He was a huge man, capable of extraordinary deeds of strength. His unusual feats formed the basis for his legendary and sometimes exaggerated reputation. At that period in history, railroad workers used long-handled hammers to pound steel drills into rocks. One day a man arrived with a steam-powered drill, claiming it could drill faster than twenty men

using hammers. John Henry successfully raced the drill, disproving the man's claim.

The differences between the tall tale about John Henry—sometimes called Hammerman—and the actual contest events were the length of the race and the way he died. The contest was to last only 35 minutes rather than the entire day, and the real John Henry was said to have been killed by a falling rock after he beat the engine.

Have students consider why these particular details may have changed as the story was told and retold about this real man.

Polly Ann, who had come along to West Virginia, sat and watched and cheered him on. She sang along with him, clapping her hands to the rhythm of his hammer, and the sound echoed around the mountains. The songs blended with the rumble of dynamite where the blasting crews were at work. For every time John Henry drilled a hole in the mountain's face, other men poked dynamite and black powder into the hole and then lighted a fuse to blow the rock apart.

One day the tunnel boss Cap'n Tommy Walters was standing watching John Henry, when a stranger in city clothes walked up to him.

"Howdy, Cap'n Tommy," said the stranger. "I'd like to talk to you about a steam engine[7] I've got for sale. My engine can drive a drill through rock so fast that not even a crew of your best men can keep up with it."

"I don't need any machine," Cap'n Tommy said proudly. "My man John Henry can out-drill any machine ever built."

"I'll place a bet with you, Cap'n," said the salesman. "You race your man against my machine for a full day. If he wins, I'll give you the steam engine free."

Cap'n Tommy thought it over. "That sounds fair enough, but I'll have to talk to John Henry first." He told John Henry what the stranger had said. "Are you willing to race a steam drill?" Cap'n Tommy asked.

John Henry ran his big hands over the handle of his hammer, feeling the strength in the

7. **steam engine:** Here, a machine that drives a drill by means of steam power.

It's Wrote on the Rock, Palmer C. Hayden, Museum of African American Art, Los Angeles, CA

▲ **Critical Viewing** What do the couple in this painting appear to be doing? Support your answer. [Infer] **⑤**

wood and in his own great muscles.

"A man's a man," he said, "but a machine ain't nothing but a machine. I'll beat that steam drill, or I'll die with my hammer in my hand!" **⑥**

"All right, then," said Cap'n Tommy. "We'll set a day for the contest."

Polly Ann looked worried when John Henry told her what he had promised to do.

"Don't you worry, honey," John Henry said. It was the end of the workday, with the sunset burning across the mountain, and the sky shining like copper. He tapped his chest. "I've got a man's heart in here. All a machine has is a metal engine." He smiled and picked Polly Ann up in his arms, as if she were no heavier than a blade of grass.

On the morning of the contest, the slopes around the tunnel were crowded with people. At one side stood the steam engine, its gears and valves and mechanical drill gleaming. Its operators rushed around, giving it final spurts of grease and oil and shoving fresh pine knots into the fire that fed the steam boiler. **⑦**

Hammerman ◆ 937

►**Critical Viewing**◄

⑤ Infer *Students may say that the man on the right is talking while pointing to a rock with John Henry's name on it that may be a tombstone. Two people listen to the man's story, while a train disappears into a train tunnel, which may be the one that John Henry helped to build.*

◆**Literary Focus**

⑥ Tall Tale Invite volunteers to give their interpretations of John Henry's statement. *Some students may say that his statement means that humans are superior to machines because humans understand determination and commitment.*

◆**LITERATURE AND YOUR LIFE**

⑦ Have students describe times that they have gathered for an exciting sports event, or another type of event, in which some of the participants were known to be unusually talented. How does this experience help them relate to the description of John Henry?

Customize for
Verbal/Linguistic Learners
Guide students to note the author's use of words that help the reader "hear" the sounds of this scene. Polly Ann "cheered" and "sang" to the rhythm of the booming hammer. As these sounds "echo" around the mountains, they blend with the "rumble of dynamite." Suggest that students look for additional descriptive words the author uses.

Customize for
Interpersonal Learners
Students may enjoy reading the dialogue on this page as a group, with one reader for each character. Encourage students to discuss how this exercise helps them better understand details such as John Henry's self-assurance, Cap'n Tommy's confidence in him, and the build-up of suspense as the day for the contest nears.

 Humanities: Art

It's Wrote on the Rock, by Palmer C. Hayden
John Henry left home immediately following the Civil War. At the same time, many newly freed African Americans began searching for jobs. It is possible that John Henry's story quickly became a legend because his strength and courage came to represent this African American journey.

This painting is another in the series about John Henry's life created by Palmer C. Hayden. Use the following questions for discussion.
1. What do you see in this image? *The painting shows people looking at a rock with John Henry's*

name on it, perhaps his tombstone. In the distance, a train chugs toward a tunnel.
2. How would you describe the clothing of the couple in the painting? *The man is wearing a suit and the woman a skirt, blouse, fancy hat, and earrings.*
3. What do you think is the message of this painting? *The painting makes a connection between people today and people who lived during John Henry's time. The painting shows that the story of John Henry is not just a legend, but part of the heritage of real people.*

❶ **Tall Tale** The image of John Henry standing "as still as a mountain rock" heightens the impression of his being extraordinary or larger than life. Ask students what they visualize when they read this description. *Students may say that they imagine a large, strong man who appears confident and eager to begin the contest.*

◆ **Reading Strategy**

❷ **Predict** Invite students to make a prediction about the outcome of the contest. *Most students will predict that John Henry will win. They may guess that the machine will need to be repaired, and they may point out that because the story is about his strength, the outcome is obvious.*

◆ **Critical Thinking**

❸ **Analyze** Ask students how the author builds suspense. *She builds suspense by describing Li'l Willie's words, actions, and appearance.*

◆ **Critical Thinking**

❹ **Interpret** The story of John Henry is about the effects of technology on humans. Ask them what the contest in the story represents. *It demonstrates the superiority of humans over machines. When machines break, only humans can repair them.*

Customize for
Less Proficient Readers
Reading about the contest between John Henry and the steam engine may be confusing because the focus moves quickly back and forth from John Henry to the steam engine. To help students keep track of the events of the contest, you may want to suggest that they fill in a chart such as this as they read these pages.

John Henry	Steam Engine
1.	1.
2.	2.
3.	3.

938

❶ John Henry stood leaning on his hammer, as still as the mountain rock, his shoulders shining like hard coal in the rising sun.

"How do you feel, John Henry?" asked Li'l Willie. Li'l Willie's hands trembled a bit as he held the drill ready.

"I feel like a bird ready to bust out of a nest egg," John Henry said. "I feel like a rooster ready to crow. I feel pride hammering at my heart, and I can hardly wait to get started against that machine." He sucked in the mountain air. "I feel powerful free, Li'l Willie."

❷ Cap'n Tommy held up the starting gun. For a second everything was as silent as the dust in a drill hole. Then the gun barked, making a yelp that bounced against mountain and sky.

John Henry swung his hammer, and it rang against the drill.

At the same time, the steam engine gave a roar and a hiss. Steam whistled through its escape valve. Its drill crashed down, gnawing into the granite.

John Henry paid no attention to anything except his hammer, nor to any sound except the steady pumping of his heart. At the end of an hour, he paused long enough to ask, "How are we doing, Li'l Willie?"

❸ Willie licked his lips. His face was pale with rock dust and with fear. "The machine's ahead, John Henry."

John Henry tossed his smoking hammer aside and called to another helper, "Bring me two hammers! I'm only getting warmed up."

He began swinging a hammer in each hand. Sparks flew so fast and hot they singed his face. The hammers heated up until they glowed like torches.

"How're we doing now, Li'l Willie?" John Henry asked at the end of another hour.

❹ Li'l Willie grinned. "The machine's drill busted. They have to take time to fix up a new one. You're almost even now, John Henry! How're you feeling?"

"I'm feeling like sunrise," John Henry took time to say before he flashed one of his hammers down against the drill. "Clean out the hole, Willie, and we'll drive right down to China."

Above the clash of his hammers, he heard the chug and hiss of the steam engine starting up again and the whine of its rotary drill biting into rock. The sound hurt John Henry's ears.

❺ "Sing me a song, Li'l Willie!" he gasped. "Sing me a natural song for my hammers to sing along with."

Li'l Willie sang, and John Henry kept his hammers going in time. Hour after hour, he kept driving, sweat sliding from his forehead and chest.

The sun rolled past noon and toward the west.

"How're you feeling, John Henry?" Li'l Willie asked.

"I ain't tired yet," said John Henry and stood back, gasping, while Willie put a freshly sharpened drill into the rock wall. "Only, I have a kind of roaring in my ears." ❻

"That's only the steam engine," Li'l Willie said, but he wet his lips again. "You're gaining on it, John Henry. I reckon you're at least two inches ahead."

John Henry coughed and slung his hammer back. "I'll beat it by a mile, before the sun sets."

At the end of another hour, Li'l Willie called out, his eyes sparkling, "You're going to win, John Henry, if you can keep on drivin'!"

John Henry ground his teeth together and tried not to hear the roar in his ears or the racing thunder of his heart. "I'll go until I drop," he gasped. "I'm a steel-driving man and I'm bound to win, because a machine ain't nothing but a machine."

The sun slid lower. The shadows of the crowd grew long and purple.

"John Henry can't keep it up," someone said.

"The machine can't keep it up," another said.

Polly Ann twisted her hands together and waited for Cap'n Tommy to fire the gun to mark the end of the contest.

"Who's winning?" a voice cried.

"Wait and see," another voice answered. There were only ten minutes left.

"How're you feeling, John Henry?" Li'l Willie whispered, sweat dripping down his own face.

938 ◆ *The American Folk Tradition*

Beyond the Classroom

Career Connections

Workers Versus Technology The development of the steam engine changed not only manual labor jobs, but transportation and travel as well. The legend of John Henry represents the theme of a struggle between workers and new-and-improved machines designed not only to save time but eventually to replace workers. This theme is just as applicable today as it was during the late 1800's.

Ask students to think of current employment situations in which the use of machines and tech-nology threatens the jobs of people. For example, you might discuss the introduction of robots to factory assembly lines that build cars or airplanes, unmanned space flights monitored by technology, or lightning-fast computers doing specific jobs that people once did, such as answering the phones or telemarketing.

Students might explore whether computers and technology are responsible for creating new employment opportunities. Suggest that they make a poster comparing the advantages and disadvantages of technological advances.

John Henry didn't answer. He just kept slamming his hammers against the drill, his mouth open.

Li'l Willie tried to go on singing. "Flash that hammer—uh! Wham that drill—uh!" he croaked.

Out beside the railroad tracks, Polly beat her hands together in time, until they were numb.

The sun flared an instant, then died behind the mountain. Cap'n Tommy's gun cracked. The judges ran forward to measure the depth of the holes drilled by the steam engine and by John Henry. At last, the judges came walking back and said something to Cap'n Tommy before they turned to announce their findings to the crowd.

Cap'n Tommy walked over to John Henry, who stood leaning against the face of the mountain.

"John Henry," he said, "you beat that steam engine by four feet!" He held out his hand and smiled.

John Henry heard a distant cheering. He held his own hand out, and then he staggered.

He fell and lay on his back, staring up at the mountain and the sky, and then he saw Polly Ann and Li'l Willie leaning over him.

"Oh, how do you feel, John Henry?" Polly Ann asked.

"I feel a bit tuckered out," said John Henry.

"Do you want me to sing to you?" Li'l Willie asked.

"I got a song in my own heart, thank you, Li'l Willie," John Henry said. He raised up on his elbow and looked at all the people and the last sunset light gleaming like the edge of a golden trumpet. "I was a steel-driving man," he said, and lay back and closed his eyes forever.   ❼

Down South, and in the North, too, people still talk about John Henry and how he beat the steam engine at the Big Bend Tunnel. They say, if John Henry were alive today, he could beat almost every other kind of machine, too.

Maybe so. At least, John Henry would die trying.

◆Guide for Responding

◆ LITERATURE AND YOUR LIFE

Reader's Response Describe your reactions as you read about the contest between John Henry and the steam engine. Who did you think would win and why?

Thematic Focus What does "Hammerman" reveal about people's resistance to technology?

Journal Writing What modern hero reminds you of John Henry? Write your response in your journal.

☑ Check Your Comprehension

1. According to legend, what did John Henry have in his hand when he was born?
2. Describe John Henry's dream.
3. (a) Against what does John Henry compete? (b) Who wins the contest?

◆ Critical Thinking

INTERPRET

1. How does the prophetic dream contribute to John Henry's status as a hero? **[Connect]**
2. Why is Li'l Willie willing to hold the spike for John Henry even though the others refuse? **[Interpret]**
3. (a) What does John Henry believe his purpose in life to be? (b) Why is it important to him that he follow this purpose even when others disapprove? **[Speculate]**

EVALUATE

4. (a) Do you think that John Henry would have won the contest if the machine had not temporarily broken down? (b) What would be the effect of this story if John Henry had lost? **[Modify]**

Hammerman ◆ 939

"John Henry," a larger-than-life African American hero, battles a steam drill to dig a railroad tunnel. After showing that he can beat the drill, the hero dies. This ballad-style tale of John Henry's story captures the oral tradition of story-telling, the basis of much of American literature.

Clarification

❶ This version of the story of the folk hero, John Henry, shares many details with the tall tale "Hammerman." However, the ballad uses dialogue and repetition with little description to sing its story. Point out that the last two lines are repeated in each verse, which helped storytellers or singers in the past remember and retell the ballad.

▶Critical Viewing◀

❷ Analyze *Students may say that the message of the painting is that the story of John Henry will live on in people's memories.*

◆ Reading Strategy

❸ Predict Ask students to make predictions based on this first verse. *After reading "Hammerman," students will probably predict that John Henry's dream comes true.* Discuss with students that in this ballad, the reader learns about the dream at the very beginning of the story, while in the tall tale, they first learn about the character of John Henry. Invite volunteers to comment on this difference.

◆ Critical Thinking

❹ Infer Ask students what they can infer about John Henry from the way he responds to the captain. *Students might infer that John Henry is a proud man.*

❶ # JOHN HENRY
Traditional

Big Bend Tunnel, Palmer Hayden, Collection of The Museum of African American Art, Los Angeles, CA

 ▲ Critical Viewing What message does this painting convey? [Analyze]

> John Henry was a lil baby,
> Sittin' on his mama's knee,
> **❸** Said: 'The Big Bend Tunnel on the C. & O. road
> Gonna cause the death of me,
> 5 Lawd, Lawd, gonna cause the death of me.'
>
> Cap'n says to John Henry,
> 'Gonna bring me a steam drill 'round,
> Gonna take that steam drill out on the job,
> Gonna whop that steel on down,
> 10 Lawd, Lawd, gonna whop that steel on down.'
>
> John Henry tol' his cap'n,
> Lightnin' was in his eye:
> **❹** 'Cap'n, bet yo' las', red cent on me,
> Fo' I'll beat it to the bottom or I'll die,
> 15 Lawd, Lawd, I'll beat it to the bottom or I'll die.'

940 ◆ The American Folk Tradition

✦ Humanities: Art

Big Bend Tunnel, 1944–1945, by Palmer C. Hayden

This image is another in Palmer C. Hayden's series of paintings depicting stages in the life of John Henry. In this image, four men standing next to the railroad tracks by the Big Bend Tunnel look toward a cloud of blue containing a ghost-like image of John Henry swinging his hammer. Discuss with students that the blue cloud is a visual representation of the thoughts or words of the men, much as thought bubbles in a cartoon contain the thoughts of its characters. Viewers might assume that the men are talking about John Henry and the legend that surrounds him.

Have students study the painting, and then use the following questions for discussion.

1. What details in the painting symbolize John Henry's death? *The skull of an animal lying beside the tracks and the dark entrance to the tunnel may be symbols of his death.*

2. What do you think the telegraph pole represents? *Students may say that it represents technology, which plays an important role in the story of John Henry.*

Sun shine hot an' burnin',
Wer'n't no breeze a-tall,
Sweat ran down like water down a hill,
That day John Henry let his hammer fall,
20   Lawd, Lawd, that day John Henry let his hammer fall.

John Henry went to the tunnel,
An' they put him in the lead to drive,
The rock so tall an' John Henry so small,
That he lied down his hammer an' he cried,
25   Lawd, Lawd, that he lied down his hammer an' he cried.

John Henry started on the right hand,
The steam drill started on the lef'—
'Before I'd let this steam drill beat me down,
I'd hammer my fool self to death,
30   Lawd, Lawd, I'd hammer my fool self to death.' **❺**

John Henry had a lil woman,
Her name were Polly Ann,
John Henry took sick an' had to go to bed,
Polly Ann drove steel like a man,
35   Lawd, Lawd, Polly Ann drove steel like a man. **❻**

John Henry said to his shaker,[1]
'Shaker, why don' you sing?
I'm throwin' twelve poun's from my hips on down, **❼**
Jes' listen to the col' steel ring,
40   Lawd, Lawd, jes' listen to the col' steel ring.'

Oh, the captain said to John Henry,
'I b'lieve this mountain's sinkin' in.'
John Henry said to his captain, oh my! **❽**
'Ain' nothin' but my hammer suckin' win',
45   Lawd, Lawd, ain' nothin' but my hammer suckin' win'.'

John Henry tol' his shaker,
'Shaker, you better pray,
For, if I miss this six-foot steel,
Tomorrow'll be yo' buryin' day,
50   Lawd, Lawd, tomorrow'll be yo' buryin' day.'

John Henry tol' his captain,
'Look yonder what I see—
Yo' drill's done broke an' yo' hole's done choke,
An' you cain' drive steel like me,
55   Lawd, Lawd, an' you cain' drive steel like me.'

1. shaker (shā´ kər) *n.*: Person who sets the spikes and places the drills for a steel-driver to hammer.

John Henry ◆ *941*

◆ **Reading Strategy**

❺ Predict Reinforce the concept that making predictions is an active process in which the reader continually engages while reading. Discuss with students that even though they know the outcome of this ballad, they can look for clues that help readers make predictions. Invite volunteers to identify the clues in these lines. *The lines represent the second time the main character has discussed his own death.*

◆ **Critical Thinking**

❻ Infer Ask students what they can infer about Polly Ann from these lines and how her role in the ballad compares with her role in "Hammerman." *Polly Ann is strong and courageous, and she loves John Henry. She has a more active role in the ballad version of the story.*

Comprehension Check

❼ What does John Henry mean when he says that he is "throwin' twelve poun's from my hips on down"? *He is using a 12-pound hammer.*

◆ **Literary Focus**

❽ Tall Tale Ask students how this description is similar to the one in the tall tale about John Henry. *Both versions use exaggeration to demonstrate John Henry's superior strength. In this example, John Henry implies that his hammer is moving so fast that it is sucking in air, causing the mountain to rumble.*

Customize for
English Language Learners
Students may have difficulty with the use of dialect in the ballad. Explain that many words are simply missing a letter, and that this is indicated by an apostrophe. Others are variations of familiar words. Point out examples of each.

burnin'	poun's
'round	Cap'n
don'	lil
throwin'	jes'

 Cross-Curricular Connection: Music

Ballads Poems or folk music that tell a dramatic story are called ballads. Many ballads have a romantic theme or tell of heroic deeds. They follow a pattern of verses with a refrain that is repeated. A typical ballad stanza has four lines, with rhyming second and fourth lines.

The ballad style of poetry and music is thousands of years old and was originally used by people who could not read or write. Just as folk tales were passed down orally, ballads and folk songs were sung and passed down from one generation to the next.

Interested students may want to check your school or local library for an audio recording of "John Henry," a copy of Carl Sandburg's *American Songbook* and *American Ballads and Folk Songs,* or other folk song materials. You may want to enlist the help of your school's music teacher to guide students' research.

Suggest that students compare the stories in the selections or other folk tales they may know to the stories in the ballads. Individual students or groups may wish to perform a ballad or share one of the recordings with the class.

1 Who is ahead in the race, and by how much? *John Henry is ahead by six feet.*

◆ Critical Thinking

2 **Interpret** Ask students if they feel that John Henry would have become a folk hero if he hadn't died. *His death is important to the story because it confirms that the battle against the steam drill was very dangerous and that John Henry showed courage when he agreed to participate in the contest.*

◆ Critical Thinking

3 **Speculate** Ask students to speculate why the author changes the weather from sunny and bright to rain. *The gloomy weather reinforces the change of mood from exciting to sad.*

►Critical Viewing◄

4 **Evaluate** *Students may say that it depicts him as both superhero and man. Although he is a very strong man, he is crying.*

Customize for
Musical/Rhythmic Learners
"John Henry" provides an excellent opportunity for choral reading. Have students work in small groups to assign different lines of the ballad for individual or group recitation. Allow them time to practice the reading before presenting it to the class.

He Layed Down His Hammer and Cried, 1944–47, Palmer C. Hayden, Museum of African American Art, Los Angeles, CA

◄ **Critical Viewing** Does this painting depict John Henry as a superhero or as a man? Explain. [Evaluate] **4**

The man that invented the steam drill,
Thought he was mighty fine.
John Henry drove his fifteen feet,
1 An' the steam drill only made nine,
60 Lawd, Lawd, an' the steam drill only made nine.

The hammer that John Henry swung,
It weighed over nine pound;
He broke a rib in his lef'-han' side,
2 An' his intrels[2] fell on the groun',
65 Lawd, Lawd, an' his intrels fell on the groun'.

All the womens in the Wes',
When they heared of John Henry's death,
3 Stood in the rain, flagged the eas'-boun' train,
Goin' where John Henry fell dead,
70 Lawd, Lawd, goin' where John Henry fell dead.

2. intrels (en´ trālz) *n.*: Entrails; inner organs.

 Humanities: Art

He Layed Down His Hammer and Cried,
1944–1947, by Palmer C. Hayden

This painting is another of Hayden's series of twelve paintings about the life of John Henry. Hayden wanted the John Henry paintings to capture the economic struggle of African Americans as they moved from life on the farm to life in the industrialized city. He hoped that the series reminded them of their greatness even in the face of their struggle for survival. This painting depicts the effects of John Henry's hard work.

1. What can be inferred about the economic conditions in which Hayden's subjects lived? *They were poor people who worked at jobs that required hard physical labor.*
2. What details convey John Henry's weariness? *His hand rests on his knee in a limp position, he is slumped, and he wipes his brow.*
3. Why do you think that the artist shows mules working in the background? *The mules may symbolize the back-breaking labor that John Henry must do to support himself.*

John Henry's lil mother,
She was all dressed in red,
She jumped in bed, covered up her head,
Said she didn' know her son was dead,
75 Lawd, Lawd, didn' know her son was
   dead.

Dey took John Henry to the graveyard,
An' they buried him in the san',
An' every locomotive come roarin' by,
Says, 'There lays a steel-drivin' man,
80 ❺ Lawd, Lawd, there lays a steel-drivin'
   man.'

Beyond Literature

Science Connection

Development of the Locomotive
Although the first reported locomotive, or steam-driven vehicle, was built in the late seventeenth century, it was not until 1823, when George Stephenson constructed the first railway system and locomotive built for both freight and passengers, that the railroad era really began. The steam locomotive became the dominant form of railway transportation for more than a century. At the turn of the century, however, the steam locomotive began to be replaced by the electric locomotive and the improved diesel-electric locomotive, in part because they were powered by cheap electricity instead of expensive coal and produced no hazardous smoke or fumes.

   Today, high-speed electrified trains travel on major routes at speeds over 100 miles per hour. Magnetically levitated trains (maglev) in Europe and Japan travel at speeds approaching 200 miles per hour.

Cross-Curricular Activity
Learn more about maglev technology, and create a diagram showing how these trains operate.

Guide for Responding

◆ LITERATURE AND YOUR LIFE

Reader's Response Do you admire John Henry's decision to challenge the steam engine in a drilling match? Explain.

Thematic Focus Did John Henry display heroism or foolishness? Explain.

Journal Writing Jot down in your journal other instances in which a human pitted his or her strength against that of a machine.

☑ Check Your Comprehension

1. At what stage in his life does John Henry predict his own death?
2. What tribute do the people in the trains give John Henry when they pass by his grave?

◆ Critical Thinking

INTERPRET
1. In the first few stanzas, how do descriptions of nature intensify the drama of the contest? **[Analyze]**
2. How important is it to John Henry to beat the steam engine? Explain. **[Infer]**
3. (a) Why do you think people pay tribute to John Henry? (b) What do their tributes tell you about his character? **[Speculate]**
4. What qualities of John Henry make him a folk hero? **[Interpret]**

EVALUATE
5. Do you think the tribute to John Henry in lines 78–80 accurately sums up his character? **[Make a Judgment]**

COMPARE LITERARY WORKS
6. "John Henry" is a ballad, a sentimental song that tells a story in short stanzas with the repetition of lines, while "Hammerman" is written in prose. (a) Which form do you find more enjoyable to read? (b) Which one is more effective in relating the tale of John Henry? **[Evaluate]**

John Henry ◆ 943

◆ Literary Focus

❺ **Tall Tale** Ask students to turn to p. 939 and reread the last paragraphs of the tall tale. What is similar about the endings of the two stories? *Both reflect the oral tradition of the story by stating that long after John Henry died, people continued to tell his story.*

Beyond Literature

Before students begin their research, show them examples of well-designed diagrams. Guide students to note the important role that the captions and title play in understanding a diagram.

   Suggest that students sketch the diagram to work out placement of the captions and title before they begin drawing the final version.

Reinforce and Extend

Answers
◆ LITERATURE AND YOUR LIFE

Reader's Response Some students may admire the self-confidence that was shown by John Henry's willingness to compete with a machine.

Thematic Focus Students who say John Henry is a hero may point out that he accepts a challenge. Students who say he was foolish may point out that he dies in a vain effort.

☑ Check Your Comprehension

1. He makes the prediction when he is a baby.
2. They say, "There lays a steel-drivin' man."

◆ Critical Thinking

1. It is a hot, still day that makes John Henry's work even more difficult.
2. It is so important that he will accept the challenge knowing that he may die.
3. (a) People pay tribute because they have heard John Henry's story. (b) Their tributes reflect his abilities as a steel driver.
4. Students may say that his courage and strength make him a hero.
5. Students who agree may cite lines that reflect what John Henry would have wanted people to say about him. Those who do not agree may point out that the lines do not provide details about his unique abilities.
6. Students' answers to (a) and (b) should contain details from the tall tale or ballad to support their evaluation.

Cross-Curricular Connection: Science

Human Against Machine—A Modern Contest In May of 1997, after playing six games, a computer named Deep Blue beat the most skilled chess player in the world. Before the game, Garry Kasparov predicted that a win by Deep Blue would be a "very important and frightening milestone in the history of mankind."

   Like the contest between John Henry and the steam drill, people followed the chess contest with eager anticipation, most of them rooting for the human contestant. Like John Henry's contest, from the beginning it was a close race. Kasparov won the first game, Deep Blue the second; the next three games were draws. Kasparov was tired and out of sorts when he began the sixth game on May 11. In the early moments of the game, he made a mistake. Nineteen moves later, he resigned the game, giving Deep Blue the win. Deep Blue won $700,000, which was given to the computer's development team. A discouraged Kasparov took home $400,000.

   Ask students to discuss whether they think that this story might some day be told as a tall tale or ballad, even though the machine won.

943

◆ Critical Thinking

❶ Analyze The first written references to Paul Bunyan may have been written by James McGillivray for a Detroit newspaper in 1910. The stories were based on tales he had heard from Michigan lumberjacks. Have students identify the audience for stories about Paul Bunyan as described in this passage. *The audience consists of the pioneers who had few books and struggled to create new homes for themselves and their families.*

▶Critical Viewing◀

❷ Summarize *The illustration conveys an impression of the subject's great size and strength.*

◆ Literary Focus

❸ Tall Tale Ask students to identify exaggerated events in this story. What natural event is described? *Seven men dancing with Paul Bunyan cause an earthquake, which is a natural event that is exaggerated. The earthquake causes a river to create a new course.*

PAUL BUNYAN OF THE NORTH WOODS

Carl Sandburg

Who made Paul Bunyan, who gave him birth as a myth, who joked him into life as the Master Lumberjack, who fashioned him forth as an apparition[1] easing the hours of men amid axes and trees, saws and lumber? The people, the bookless people, they made Paul and had him alive long before he got into the books for those who read. He grew up in shanties, around the hot stoves of winter, among socks and mittens drying, in the smell of tobacco smoke and the roar of laughter mocking the outside weather. And some of Paul came overseas in wooden bunks below decks in sailing vessels. And some of Paul is old as the hills, young as the alphabet.

Paul Bunyan Carrying a Tree on His Shoulder and an Ax in His Hand

▲ **Critical Viewing** What impression of Paul Bunyan does this illustration convey? [Summarize]

The Pacific Ocean froze over in the winter of the Blue Snow and Paul Bunyan had long teams of oxen hauling regular white snow over from China. This was the winter Paul gave a party to the Seven Axmen. Paul fixed a granite floor sunk two hundred feet deep for them to dance on. Still, it tipped and tilted as the dance went on. And because the Seven Axmen refused to take off their hobnailed boots, the sparks from the nails of their dancing feet lit up the place so that Paul didn't light the kerosene lamps. No women being on the Big Onion river at that time the Seven Axmen had to dance with each other, the one left over in each set taking Paul as a partner. The commotion of the dancing that night brought on an earthquake and the Big Onion river moved over three counties to the east.

One year when it rained from St. Patrick's Day till the Fourth of July, Paul Bunyan got disgusted because his celebration on the Fourth was spoiled. He dived into Lake Superior and swam to where a solid pillar of water was coming down. He dived under this pillar, swam up into it and climbed with

---

1. **apparition** (ap´ ə rish´ ən) *n.*: A strange figure appearing suddenly or in an extraordinary way.

Humanities: Art

Paul Bunyan Carrying a Tree on His Shoulder and an Ax in His Hand, artist unknown

For years, artists have created their own interpretations of the American hero, Paul Bunyan, and the stories surrounding his legendary feats. Use the following questions for discussion:

1. How do the perspective and lighting of the illustration contribute to the impression of Bunyan's great size? *Paul Bunyan is illustrated as if the viewer is standing below him, looking up at his great height. The horizontal beam of light across his shoulders makes them appear very broad and strong and also emphasizes the large size of the tree that he is easily holding.*

2. What is the mood of this artwork? *Paul Bunyan is happy and has a smile on his face, which gives the artwork a cheerful mood.*

3. What details in this artwork reinforce the perceptions you have of Paul Bunyan? *The ax, tree, boots, jeans, and patterned shirt show that Paul Bunyan is a lumberjack.*

powerful swimming strokes, was gone about an hour, came splashing down, and as the rain stopped, he explained, "I turned the darn thing off." This is told in the Big North Woods and on the Great Lakes, with many particulars.

Two mosquitoes lighted on one of Paul Bunyan's oxen, killed it, ate it, cleaned the bones, and sat on a grub shanty picking their teeth as Paul came along. Paul sent to Australia for two special bumblebees to kill these mosquitoes. But the bees and the mosquitoes intermarried; their children had stingers on both ends. And things kept getting worse till Paul brought a big boatload of sorghum[2] up from Louisiana and while all the bee-mosquitoes were eating at the sweet sorghum he floated them down to the Gulf of Mexico. They got so fat that it was easy to drown them all between New Orleans and Galveston.

Paul logged on the Little Gimlet in Oregon one winter. The cookstove at that camp covered an acre of ground. They fastened the side of a hog on each snowshoe and four men used to skate on the griddle while the cook flipped the pancakes. The eating table was three miles long; elevators carried the cakes to the ends of the table where boys on bicycles rode back and forth on a path down the center of the table dropping the cakes where called for.

Benny, the Little Blue Ox of Paul Bunyan, grew two feet every time Paul looked at him, when a youngster. The barn was gone one morning and they found it on Benny's back; he grew out of it in a night. One night he kept pawing and bellowing for more pancakes, till there were two hundred men at the cookshanty stove trying to keep him fed. About breakfast time Benny broke loose, tore down the cookshanty, ate all the pancakes piled up for the loggers' breakfast. And after that Benny made his mistake; he ate the red hot stove; and that finished him. This is only one of the hot-stove stories told in the North Woods.

◆ LITERARY FOCUS
Explain how the tone of this passage fits the tall-tale tradition.

2. **sorghum** (sôr′ gəm) *n.*: Tropical grasses bearing flowers and seeds, grown for use as grain or syrup.

◆ Build Vocabulary

granite (gran′ it) *adj.*: Made of granite, a very hard rock

commotion (kə mō′ shən) *n.*: Noisy movement

Guide for Responding

◆ LITERATURE AND YOUR LIFE

Reader's Response Which tall tale about Paul Bunyan is your favorite? Why?

Thematic Focus In what ways does Paul Bunyan display heroic qualities?

☑ Check Your Comprehension

1. What is Paul Bunyan's occupation?
2. What natural occurrence is caused by the dancing of the Axmen?
3. (a) What is the name of Paul Bunyan's Little Blue Ox? (b) How did the ox die?

◆ Critical Thinking

INTERPRET
1. What qualities and abilities are valued in this tale? **[Interpret]**
2. Interpret the following statement: "And some of Paul is old as the hills, young as the alphabet." **[Interpret]**
3. Explain how Bunyan combines cleverness with strength to achieve his purpose. **[Support]**

APPLY
4. What generalization can you make about folk tales based on your reading of "Paul Bunyan of the North Woods"? **[Generalize]**

Paul Bunyan of the North Woods ◆ 945

Cultural Connection

The Original Story The Paul Bunyan legend may have originated with tales of giants told by French-Canadian lumberjacks. Stories about Bunyan spread quickly and were often told by diverse groups of immigrant settlers in many territories. In the state of Washington, once populated by Russian fur traders, Paul Bunyan was credited with scooping out Puget Sound. Settlers in North and South Dakota—Germans, Norwegians, and Russians—claimed that he cleared their land of trees. German, Norwegian, and Swedish iron miners in Minnesota's early days said that when Babe the ox needed new shoes, Paul's friend Bill Ole had to open a new iron mine. Because he embodied the spirit of independence and determination shared by all early settlers, the Paul Bunyan character was later popularized in booklets and magazines by an advertising agency trying to boost the logging industry.

Ask students to name sports celebrities whose strength, skill, independence, and determination have caught the eye of advertisers. Challenge students to think of stories about these people that could be exaggerated and told as tall tales.

One-Minute Insight

Pecos Bill's plans to enjoy a fine Fourth of July celebration are ruined when a cyclone arrives. Bill is determined not to let the cyclone ruin the fun, so he leaps onto the back of the cyclone and rides it like a bucking bronco. The cyclone tries all sorts of tricks, but cannot dislodge the folk hero until its strength is dissipated. When Bill jumps from the cyclone onto a streak of lightning and falls to the ground, Death Valley is created.

Clarification

① Pecos Bill, a cowboy hero of Texas, was created in 1923 by journalist Edward Reilly in *Century* magazine. According to the legend, Pecos Bill was born in 1832 and raised by coyotes after his parents lost him. He works as a cowboy and train robber in Texas, and then travels to Arizona, where he finds his famous horse, Widow Maker. Pecos Bill's greatest feat is riding a cyclone bareback, which this selection describes.

◆ Literary Focus

② **Tall Tale** Ask students to describe an example of exaggeration. *The story claims that Pecos Bill invented the Fourth of July.*

◆ Critical Thinking

③ **Compare** Ask students what this comparison tells them about the character of this tall tale. *He is big and strong, like a cyclone.*

◆ Critical Thinking

④ **Analyze** Ask students what is humorous about this idea. *Students should recognize that the humor lies in the nonsensical idea of shipping empty space.*

Customize for
English Language Learners

Students might keep a list of words, definitions, and illustrations that relate to life in the West. Have peers who are proficient in English help English language learners define words by using gestures and drawings. Students can add words to the list as they read the next selection. Suggested words include: *posthole, well, prairie dog, badger, mountain lion, bucking horse, trot, mustang, rattlesnake, quirt.*

① Pecos Bill: THE CYCLONE

Harold W. Felton

② One of Bill's greatest feats, if not the greatest feat of all time, occurred unexpectedly one Fourth of July. He had invented the Fourth of July some years before. It was a great day for the cowpunchers.[1] They had taken to it right off like the real Americans they were. But the celebration had always ended on a dismal note. Somehow it seemed to be spoiled by a cyclone.

Bill had never minded the cyclone much. The truth is he rather liked it. But the other celebrants ran into caves for safety. He invented cyclone cellars for them. He even named the cellars. He called them "'fraid holes." Pecos wouldn't even say the word "afraid." **③** The cyclone was something like he was. It was big and strong too. He always stood by musing[2] pleasantly as he watched it.

The cyclone caused Bill some trouble, though. Usually it would destroy a few hundred miles of fence by blowing the postholes away. But it wasn't much trouble for him to fix it. All he had to do was to go and get the postholes and then take them back and put the fence posts in them. The holes were rarely ever blown more than twenty or thirty miles.

In one respect Bill even welcomed the cyclone, for it blew so hard it blew the earth away from his wells. The first time this happened, he thought the wells would be a total loss. There they were, sticking up several hundred feet out of the ground. As wells they were useless. But he found he could cut them up into lengths and sell them for postholes to farmers in Iowa and Nebraska. It was very profitable, especially after he invented a special posthole saw to cut them with. He didn't use that type of posthole himself. He got the prairie dogs to dig his for him. He simply caught a few gross[3] of prairie dogs and set them down at proper intervals. The prairie dog would dig a hole. Then Bill would put a post in it. The prairie dog would get disgusted and go down the row ahead of the others and dig another hole. Bill fenced all of Texas and parts of New Mexico and Arizona in this manner. He took a few contracts and fenced most of the Southern Pacific right of way too. That's the reason it is so crooked. He had trouble getting the prairie dogs to run a straight fence.

As for his wells, the badgers dug them. The system was the same as with the prairie dogs. The labor was cheap so it didn't make much difference if the cyclone did spoil some of the wells. The badgers were digging all of the time anyway. They didn't seem to care whether they dug wells or just badger holes.

④ One year he tried shipping the prairie dog holes up north, too, for postholes. It was not successful. They didn't keep in storage and they couldn't stand the handling in shipping. After they were installed they seemed to wear out quickly. Bill always thought the difference in climate had something to do with it.

It should be said that in those days there

---

1. **cowpunchers** (kou´ pun chərz) *n.*: Cowboys.
2. **musing** (my$\overline{oo}$z´ ing) *adj.*: Thinking deeply.

3. **gross** (grōs) *n.*: Twelve dozen.

946 ◆ *The American Folk Tradition*

Speaking and Listening Mini-Lesson

Oral Storytelling

This mini-lesson supports the Speaking and Listening activity in the Idea Bank on p. 955.

Introduce Have students discuss stories they have told or heard in the past. What are the elements of the stories they remember that make them memorable and exciting to hear and retell?

Develop Suggest that students base the tall tale they will write on people they know or have read about. They may wish to combine characteristics of several people they know. Although they may exaggerate certain details and personality traits,

the story should be somewhat believable. Have students write and revise their stories, then practice and prepare to tell the stories from memory.

Apply As students present their stories to the class, remind them to use these strategies:

• Look directly at the audience.
• Speak clearly and with emotion.
• Use facial expressions and body language.

Assess Have each student self-assess a recording of his or her story, listening for one good thing and one thing to improve.

▲ Critical Viewing Does this cyclone seem capable of destroying "a few hundred miles of fence"? Explain. [Assess]

5

was only one cyclone. It was the first and original cyclone, bigger and more terrible by far than the small cyclones of today. It usually stayed by itself up north around Kansas and Oklahoma and didn't bother anyone much. But it was attracted by the noise of the Fourth of July celebration and without fail managed to put in an appearance before the close of the day.

On this particular Fourth of July, the celebration had gone off fine. The speeches were loud and long. The contests and games were hard fought. The high point of the day was Bill's exhibition with Widow Maker, which came right after he showed off Scat and Rat. People seemed never to tire of seeing them in action. The mountain lion was almost useless as a work animal after his accident, and the snake had grown old and somewhat infirm, and was troubled with rheumatism in his rattles. But they too enjoyed the Fourth of July and liked to make a public appearance. They relived the old days.

Widow Maker had put on a good show, bucking as no ordinary horse could ever buck. Then Bill undertook to show the gaits[4] he had taught the palomino.[5] Other mustangs[6] at that time had only two gaits. Walking and running. Only Widow Maker could pace. But now Bill had developed and taught him other gaits. Twenty-seven in all. Twenty-three forward and three reverse. He was very proud of the achievement. He showed off the slow gaits and the crowd was eager for more.

He showed the walk, trot, canter, lope, jog, slow rack, fast rack, single foot, pace, stepping pace, fox trot, running walk and the others now known. Both men and horses confuse the various gaits nowadays. Some of the gaits are now thought to be the same, such as the rack and the single foot. But with Widow Maker and Pecos Bill, each one was different. Each was precise and to be distinguished from the others. No one had ever imagined such a thing.

Then the cyclone came! All of the people except Bill ran into the 'fraid holes. Bill was

---

4. **gaits** (gāts) *n*.: Foot movements of a horse.
5. **palomino** (pal′ ə mē′ nō) *n*.: A light-tan or golden-brown horse with a cream-colored mane and tail.
6. **mustangs** (mus′ taŋz) *n*.: Wild horses.

Pecos Bill: The Cyclone ◆ 947

6
7
8

▶Critical Viewing◀
5 Assess *Students may say that the cyclone appears to be very powerful because it is coming from an area of very dark clouds.*

Clarification
6 Widow Maker is Pecos Bill's horse. Scat is his mountain lion and Rat is his rattlesnake.

◆ **Critical Thinking**
7 Infer Ask students why they think that Pecos Bill's horse is named Widow Maker. *The name implies that the horse is so dangerous to ride that it could kill a man—making his wife a widow.*

◆ **Reading Strategy**
8 Predict Have students predict what might happen next. *Students may say that they have already learned that Pecos Bill has remarkable abilities. They may conclude that because this is a tall tale and Pecos Bill is a folk hero, Pecos Bill and the cyclone will have a struggle of some type and Pecos Bill will win.*

 Humanities: Photography

Cyclone This photograph shows a large cyclone, or tornado, moving toward a field. Several neatly rolled bales of hay in the field contrast sharply with the destructive turbulence of the approaching storm. The image is divided horizontally. Dark, swirling clouds and a well-defined funnel cloud make up the top two-thirds of the image, while the field, which is drenched in sunlight coming from behind the viewer, takes up the bottom third.

1. How would you feel if you were standing in this field? *Students may say that they would be frightened and awed by the approaching storm.*

2. What important role do the neatly rolled bales of hay play in the photograph? *The compact and neat bales of hay contrast with the violent, turbulent motion of the approaching storm. The images are like a prediction in a story. The viewer knows that the terrific force of the wind will destroy everything in its path, including the neat bales of hay.*

3. How does the photograph support the tall tale about Pecos Bill? *It shows a powerful and destructive force that no real human can possibly control.*

◆ Critical Thinking

① Generalize Discuss with students that the author describes the cyclone with human qualities. Ask students how these traits are like the traits of "villains" in other stories they have read. *Like many villains, the cyclone is jealous of people who are having fun, and it uses its power for destructive purposes.*

◆ Literary Focus

② Tall Tale Ask students why the cyclone is so angry with Pecos Bill. What does this say about the folk hero? *The cyclone feels that its power has been threatened. Because the very strong cyclone feels threatened by Pecos Bill, the reader assumes that Pecos Bill must indeed be quite powerful.*

◆ Literary Focus

③ Tall Tale *Examples of exaggeration might include green clouds dripping from the cyclone's jaws, lightning flashing from its eyes, Widow Maker turning on a dime, Pecos Bill having the foresight to throw down a dime, and the cyclone meeting itself coming back.*

Customize for
Less Proficient Readers

Point out that the story has been written as if someone were telling it aloud. Because of this, the speaker occasionally gets off the subject. Suggest that students keep track of the most important story events by filling in a Series of Events Chain, p. 57, in **Writing and Language Transparencies,** as they read.

---

annoyed. He stopped the performance. The remaining gaits were not shown. From that day to this horses have used no more than the gaits Widow Maker exhibited that day. It is unfortunate that the really fast gaits were not shown. If they were, horses might be much faster today than they are.

Bill glanced up at the cyclone and the quiet smile on his face faded into a frown. He saw the cyclone was angry. Very, very angry indeed.

The cyclone had always been the center of attention. Everywhere it went people would look up in wonder, fear and amazement. It had been the undisputed master of the country. It had observed Bill's rapid climb to fame and had seen the Fourth of July celebration grow. It had been keeping an eye on things all right.

In the beginning, the Fourth of July crowd had aroused its curiosity. It liked nothing more than to show its superiority and power by breaking the crowd up sometime during the day. But every year the crowd was larger. This preyed on the cyclone's mind. This year it did not come to watch. It deliberately came to spoil the celebration. Jealous of Bill and of his success, it resolved to do away with the whole institution of the Fourth of July once and for all. So much havoc and destruction would be wrought that there would never be another Independence Day Celebration. On that day, in future years, it would circle around the horizon leering[7] and gloating. At least, so it thought.

The cyclone was resolved, also, to do away with this bold fellow who did not hold it in awe and run for the 'fraid hole at its approach. For untold years it had been the most powerful thing in the land. And now, here was a mere man who threatened its position. More! Who had usurped its position!

When Bill looked at the horizon and saw the cyclone coming, he recognized the anger and rage. While a cyclone does not often smile, Bill had felt from the beginning that it was just a grouchy fellow who never had a pleasant word for anyone. But now, instead of merely an un-

pleasant character, Bill saw all the viciousness of which an angry cyclone is capable. He had no way of knowing that the cyclone saw its kingship tottering and was determined to stop this man who threatened its supremacy.

But Bill understood the violence of the onslaught even as the monster came into view. He knew he must meet it. The center of the cyclone was larger than ever before. The fact is, the cyclone had been training for this fight all winter and spring. It was in best form and at top weight. It headed straight for Bill intent on his destruction. In an instant it was upon him. Bill had sat quietly and silently on the great pacing mustang. But his mind was working rapidly. In the split second between his first sight of the monster and the time for action he had made his plans. Pecos Bill was ready! Ready and waiting!

Green clouds were dripping from the cyclone's jaws. Lightning flashed from its eyes as it swept down upon him. Its plan was to envelop Bill in one mighty grasp. Just as

> ◆ Literary Focus
> Find five examples of exaggeration in this paragraph.

it was upon him, Bill turned Widow Maker to its left. This was a clever move for the cyclone was right-handed, and while it had been training hard to get its left in shape, that was not its best side. Bill gave rein to his mount. Widow Maker wheeled and turned on a dime which Pecos had, with great foresight[8] and accuracy, thrown to the ground to mark the exact spot for this maneuver. It was the first time that anyone had thought of turning on a dime. Then he urged the great horse forward. The cyclone, filled with surprise, lost its balance and rushed forward at an increased speed. It went so fast that it met itself coming back. This confused the cyclone, but it did not confuse Pecos Bill. He had expected that to happen. Widow Maker went into his twenty-first gait and edged up close to the whirlwind. Soon they were running neck and neck.

At the proper instant Bill grabbed the cyclone's ears, kicked himself free of the stirrups and pulled himself lightly on its back.

---

7. **leering** (lir´ ing) *adj.*: Looking with malicious triumph.

8. **foresight** (fôr´ sit) *n.*: The act of seeing beforehand.

Viewing and Representing Mini-Lesson

Folk Hero Illustration
In this mini-lesson, students will create an exaggerated illustration or cartoon strip portraying a folk hero.

Introduce Discuss with students that folk heroes are "larger than life" characters. Stories and illustrations about them are often humorous and contain exaggeration.

Develop Invite students to visit the library to find stories and illustrations of familiar folk heroes. Discuss the main accomplishment that each character is known for. For

example, Johnny Appleseed is known for planting apple trees and is often illustrated with a pan on his head. Have students study the drawing of Paul Bunyan on p. 944 or the illustration on p. 347 and note how the artist uses exaggeration to convey the "larger than life" essence of Bunyan's personality and activities.

Apply Have students select a folk hero to illustrate and decide what details about the character they wish to include. They may prefer to portray a specific occasion or

story event such as Pecos Bill riding the cyclone, or simply to depict Paul Bunyan with Babe. Provide art materials for students to use to create a cartoon strip or drawing. If you have access to technology, students might create their folk hero with computer software. Have students make an oral presentation of their representation for the class.

Assess Evaluate students' illustrations on how well they identify and portray characteristics or accomplishments of the folk hero they have chosen.

Bill never used spurs on Widow Maker. Sometimes he wore them for show and because he liked the jingling sound they made. They made a nice accompaniment for his cowboy songs. But he had not been singing, so he had no spurs. He did not have his rattlesnake for a quirt.[9] Of course there was no bridle. It was man against monster! There he was! Pecos Bill astride a raging cyclone, slick heeled and without a saddle!

The cyclone was taken by surprise at this sudden turn of events. But it was undaunted. It was sure of itself. Months of training had given it a conviction that it was <u>invincible</u>. With a mighty heave, it twisted to its full height. Then it fell back suddenly, twisting and turning violently, so that before it came back to earth, it had turned around a thousand times. Surely no rider could ever withstand such an attack. No rider ever had. Little wonder. No one had ever ridden a cyclone before. But Pecos Bill did! He fanned the tornado's ears with his hat and dug his heels into the demon's flanks and yelled, "Yipee-ee!"

The people who had run for shelter began to come out. The audience further enraged the cyclone. It was bad enough to be disgraced by having a man astride it. It was unbearable not to have thrown him. To have all the people see the failure was too much! It got down flat on the ground and rolled over and over. Bill retained his seat throughout this ruse.[10] Evidence of this desperate but <u>futile</u> stratagem[11] remains today. The great Staked Plains, or as the Mexicans call it, *Llano Estacado* is the result. Its small, rugged mountains were covered with trees at the time. The rolling of the cyclone destroyed the mountains, the trees, and almost everything else in the area. The destruction was so complete, that part of the country is flat and treeless to this day. When the settlers came, there were no landmarks to guide them across the vast unmarked space, so they drove stakes in the ground to mark the trails. That is the reason it is called "Staked Plains." Here is an example of the proof of the events of history by careful and painstaking research. It is also an example of how seemingly <u>inexplicable</u> geographical facts can be explained.

It was far more dangerous for the rider when the cyclone shot straight up to the sky. Once there, the twister tried the same thing it had tried on the ground. It rolled on the sky. It was no use. Bill could not be unseated. He kept his place, and he didn't have a sky hook with him either.

As for Bill, he was having the time of his life, shouting at the top of his voice, kicking his opponent in the ribs and jabbing his thumb in its flanks. It responded and went on a wild bucking rampage over the entire West. It used all the bucking tricks known to the wildest broncos as well as those known only to cyclones. The wind howled furiously and beat against the fearless rider. The rain poured. The lightning flashed around his ears. The fight went on and on. Bill enjoyed himself immensely. In spite of the elements he easily kept his place. . . .

The raging cyclone saw this out of the corner of its eye. It knew then who the victor was. It was twisting far above the Rocky Mountains when the awful truth came to it. In a horrible heave it disintegrated! Small pieces of cyclone flew in all directions. Bill still kept his seat on the main central portion until that rained out from under him. Then he jumped to a nearby streak of lightning and slid down it toward earth. But it was raining so hard that the rain put out the lightning. When it fizzled out from under him, Bill dropped the rest of the way. He lit in what is now called Death Valley. He hit quite hard, as is apparent from the fact that he so compressed the place that it is still two hundred and seventy-six feet below sea level.

◆ Build Vocabulary

usurped (yoo surpt´) *v.*: Took power or authority away from

invincible (in vin´ sə bəl) *adj.*: Unbeatable

futile (fyoot´ əl) *adj.*: Useless; hopeless

inexplicable (in eks´ pli kə bəl) *adj.*: Unexplainable

---

9. **quirt** (kwurt) *n.*: Short-handled riding whip with a braided rawhide lash.
10. **ruse** (rooz) *n.*: Trick.
11. **stratagem** (strat´ ə jəm) *n.*: Plan for defeating an opponent.

Pecos Bill: The Cyclone ◆ 949

 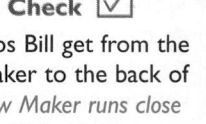
❹ How does Pecos Bill get from the back of Widow Maker to the back of the cyclone? *Widow Maker runs close to the cyclone; Pecos Bill grabs its ears and jumps on its back. He is not able to use a bridle or saddle.*

◆ Literary Focus

❺ **Tall Tale** Point out that Pecos Bill is not only riding the cyclone but also digging his heels into its side and yelling, "Yippee!" What does this show about him? *This may show that Pecos Bill is brave, that he likes to torment and tease his enemies, and that he has fun while taking risks.*

Clarification

❻ The Staked Plain, or Llano Estacado in Spanish, stretches on both sides of the Texas and New Mexico border. About 4,000 feet in elevation, it is a flat-topped, featureless plateau. Some people believe that the area was named by Francisco Vasquez de Coronado in 1541. As mentioned in the story, some say it is so named because, with no other markers to guide them, explorers had to place stakes in the ground. Others say the explorers simply placed stakes in the ground as a place to tie their horses.

◆ Critical Thinking

❼ **Speculate** Ask students what element of the story might have remained the same even if the cyclone had thrown Pecos Bill from its back. *Students may say that the folk hero still could have fallen to earth and created Death Valley.*

Cross-Curricular Connection: Social Studies

Geography After students have read this tale, suggest that they study the geography of the land that forms the setting for the story. Have students look at detailed maps of the western part of the United States. Challenge them to find the actual locations of the places that Pecos Bill mentions such as the Llano Estacado, the Rocky Mountains, Death Valley, and the Grand Canyon.

After students have located each place on the map, have them use the distance scale on the map to calculate how far Pecos Bill traveled. Students may wish to draw a map for display that marks the story locations.

Interested students may also want to learn more about these natural features of the Western landscape. Suggest that teams of students conduct research using library and Internet resources. Have them create a poster that combines text and graphics, giving information about each location.

① Connect Discuss with students that the story mentions Paul Bunyan, another American folk hero. Ask students if this reference supports what they already learned about him. *Like the stories in "Paul Bunyan of the North Woods," this incident relates to Paul Bunyan's enormous size.*

◆ Critical Thinking

② Make a Judgment Discuss with students the "hidden" humor in this example of exaggeration. (The twenty-dollar coin not only shrank in size but also in value.) Ask them if they think the author was successful in his attempt to make his audience laugh. *Students should support their opinions.*

◆ Literary Focus

③ Tall Tale Ask students if they think Death Valley is a fitting monument to the folk hero of Pecos Bill. *Students may point out that Death Valley is sometimes the setting in other stories about cowboys, cattle drives, and ranching. They may conclude that both Pecos Bill and Death Valley are part of the culture of the West and because of this, it is a fitting monument for him.*

Customize for
Bodily/Kinesthetic Learners
Students who are interested in movement and dance might like to choreograph an interpretive dance showing Pecos Bill riding the cyclone. Some students may want to have a narrator read the story aloud as they perform; others may wish to use musical accompaniment.

---

① The Grand Canyon was washed out by the rain, though it must be understood that this happened after Paul Bunyan had given it a good start by carelessly dragging his ax behind him when he went west a short time before.

The cyclones and the hurricanes and the tornadoes nowadays are the small pieces that broke off of the big cyclone Pecos Bill rode. In fact, the rainstorms of the present day came into being in the same way. There are always skeptics, but even they will recognize the logic of the proof of this event. They will recall that even now it almost always rains on the Fourth of July. That is because the rainstorms of to-day still retain some of the characteristics of the giant cyclone that met its comeuppance at the hands of Pecos Bill.

Bill lay where he landed and looked up at the sky, but he could see no sign of the cyclone. Then he laughed softly as he felt the warm sand of Death Valley on his back. . . .

② It was a rough ride though, and Bill had resisted unusual tensions and pressures. When he got on the cyclone he had a twenty-dollar gold piece and a bowie knife[12] in his pocket. The tremendous force of the cyclone was such that when he finished the ride he found that his pocket contained a plugged nickel[13] and a little pearl-handled penknife. His two giant six-shooters were compressed and transformed into a small water pistol and a popgun. **②**

It is a strange circumstance that lesser men have monuments raised in their honor. Death Valley is Bill's monument. Sort of a monument in reverse. Sunk in his honor, you might say. Perhaps that is as it should be. After all, Bill was different. He made his own monument. He made it with his hips, as is evident from the great depth of the valley. That is the hard way. **③**

---

12. **bowie** (bōʹ ē) **knife:** A strong, single-edged hunting knife named after James Bowie (1799–1836), a soldier.
13. **plugged nickel:** Fake nickel.

◆ Build Vocabulary
skeptics (skepʹ tiks) *n.*: People who frequently doubt and question matters generally accepted

---

*G*uide for Responding

◆ LITERATURE AND YOUR LIFE

Reader's Response Which parts of the story did you find humorous? Explain.

Thematic Focus Describe the qualities of Pecos Bill that are heroic.

☑ Check Your Comprehension

1. Which two animals does Pecos Bill employ to help him dig holes?
2. (a) What is the name of Pecos Bill's horse? (b) Name some of the gaits, or foot movements, that Pecos Bill taught him.
3. Why is the cyclone angry with Pecos Bill?
4. What happens to the cyclone when it realizes that Pecos Bill is the victor?

◆ Critical Thinking

INTERPRET
1. In what ways does the cyclone resemble Pecos Bill? **[Infer]**
2. What do you learn about the character of Pecos Bill from his refusal to join the others in the caves? **[Interpret]**
3. Explain the meaning of these sentences: "Death Valley is Bill's monument. Sort of a monument in reverse." **[Analyze]**
4. How does Pecos Bill's resolution never to say the word "afraid" explain why he is a folk hero? **[Draw Conclusions]**

COMPARE LITERARY WORKS
5. Who possesses greater qualities and abilities—Paul Bunyan or Pecos Bill? Explain. **[Make a Judgment]**

Reinforce and Extend

Answers
◆ LITERATURE AND YOUR LIFE

Reader's Response Students should support their examples with details from the story.

Thematic Focus Pecos Bill did not back down when the terrifying cyclone approached, and he enjoyed fighting it.

☑ Check Your Comprehension
1. He uses a badger and a prairie dog.
2. (a) His horse is named Widow Maker. (b) Gaits the horse learned include the trot, single foot, fox trot, and running walk.
3. It is angry because it is jealous of Pecos Bill.
4. It disintegrates into the cyclones, hurricanes, and tornadoes that we have today.

◆ Critical Thinking
1. They are both bold, strong, and powerful.
2. He is not easily frightened.
3. It is a monument in reverse because it goes down into the ground rather than rising from it.
4. Pecos Bill will stand up to anything.
5. Students should use the folk heroes' specific traits and accomplishments to support their opinions.

CONNECTIONS TO TODAY'S WORLD

John Henry, Pecos Bill, and Davy Crockett all possessed extraordinary abilities that made them folk heroes. The twentieth century has its own special folk hero: Superman. Following is a portion of a Web site dedicated to fans of Superman, the superhero.

Netscape: DC Comics

Netsite: http://www.dccomics.com/

SUPERMAN on line...

1. Name three extraordinary talents or abilities of Superman.
2. Which hero in this section does Superman remind you of most? Why?

Netscape: DC Comics

Netsite: http://www.dccomics.com/

Superman

- Super-strength, super-speed, super-invulnerability, and the power of flight. An arsenal of super-senses, including X-ray vision, telescopic vision, microscopic vision, heat vision, and super-hearing.

- He is especially vulnerable to Kryptonite radiation.

Real Name: Clark Kent, Kal-El
Occupation: Journalist, novelist
Base of Operations: Metropolis
Marital Status: Married
Height: 6'3"
Weight: 225 lbs.
Eyes: Blue
Hair: Black
First Appearance: Historical, ACTION COMICS #1 (JUNE, 1938); canonical, MAN OF STEEL #1 (June, 1986)

Though genetically an alien conceived on the late planet Krypton, Superman is an American by birth, born in a Kansas corn field. Living by the moral values instilled in him by his Earthly parents, Superman's high ideals are sometimes mistaken for naivete, his steadfast determination for unrealistic optimism, by those who cannot or will not understand him.

Through his deeds, Superman has become Earth's preeminent super hero. Time and again, through all adversity, he has proven himself a true hero, capable of whatever bravery and self-sacrifice is necessary to right a wrong or save a life.

Superman has actually been worshipped by some of his many admirers, but he is not a god. Though slow to anger, he does not suffer villains gladly. Superman is, at heart, a warm, compassionate, courageous man with powers and abilities far beyond those of mortal men. He has devoted his life to the promotion of truth, justice, and the great ideals of the American way.

Pecos Bill: The Cyclone/Superman ◆ 951

Connections to Today's World

Today, one of the best sources for finding up-to-the-minute information on almost any topic is the Internet. This page illustrates an example of a site that might be found on a part of the Internet called the World Wide Web. Direct students' attention to the inset computer screen page on the left. Tell students that if a person were looking at that screen and used a computer mouse to click on the underlined word *Superman*, the written page of information on the right would appear. Explain that information on the Internet is linked in the same way and that a topic on one page might even be linked to information at another Web site. Explain that students could easily use the Internet to do research for a project about a superhero such as Superman, or an American folk hero like those in this unit.

◆ Critical Thinking

❹ **Make a Judgment** Is Superman a man or a superhero? *Students may say that he is both because he can bruise and bleed, might be killed by a bomb, and is weakened by Kryptonite, but he has extraordinary powers that no normal man can hope to have.*

Answers

1. He has x-ray vision; he has superior strength and is nearly invulnerable; and he can easily fly around skyscrapers.
2. Students' answers will vary. Remind them to support their responses with details from the tall tales and from the Internet page shown.

Beyond the Classroom

Career Connection

Creating the Internet Discuss with students that it takes many people to create and maintain an Internet site. Explain that people must create the graphics for the site, do the research and write the text that is seen on the screen, and insert codes for the words and graphics so that they can be read and displayed by a variety of browsers and computers. In addition, many companies hire a Web master to maintain the site and revise its contents so that the information is up to date. Tell students that many companies have people on staff to do these jobs. Other companies hire consultants whose business it is to create and maintain Web sites for many different companies.

Have interested students gather further information about the design of Web pages and share their findings with the class. They may enjoy creating a mock-up of an Internet site that tells about folk heroes. Have students create a design for their Web page and write a summary of the text for each linked page.

One-Minute Insight

As Davy Crockett hunts for food in cold weather, he stops for a break and falls asleep in an abandoned cabin. He dreams that he is stuck in a log and asks Oak Wing, a man who lives nearby, to pull him out. Instead, Oak Wing decides to push him out with a pole. As Crockett dreams that his head is being rammed between his shoulders, he is awakened by his wife. Angry, Davy finds Oak Wing and tells him of the dream. They agree that Oak Wing will apologize to Crockett in his next dream.

◆ Literary Focus

❶ Tall Tale Ask how they might identify these sentences as being characteristic of a tall tale. *The sentences contain examples of exaggeration: Davy Crockett's hat freezes to his head; when he sneezes icicles crackle inside his nose.*

▶Critical Viewing◀

❷ Assess Tell students that a chestnut bur is a hard, spiny shell that contains chestnuts. *Students may point out that Davy Crockett is outdoors wearing deerskin clothing. They may say that he appears tough enough to use chestnut burs for a pillow.*

◆ Reading Strategy

❸ Predict Tell students that Crockett falls asleep and has a dream. Have them predict what he will dream about. *Students may predict that the dream is about an incident in which the events are exaggerated.*

Check Comprehension ☑

❹ How does Davy Crockett plan to keep an eye on the time? *He sleeps with his head in the fireplace so that he will know when the sun is overhead at noon.*

Davy Crockett's Dream

Davy Crockett

One day when it was so cold that I was afeard to open my mouth, lest I should freeze my tongue, I took my little dog named Grizzle and cut out for Salt River Bay to kill something for dinner. I got a good ways from home afore I knowed where I was, and as I had swetted some before I left the house my hat froze fast to my head, and I like to have put my neck out of joint in trying to pull it off. When I sneezed the icicles crackled all up and down the inside of my nose, like when you walk over a bog in winter time. The varmints was so scarce that I couldn't find one, and so when I come to an old log hut that had belonged to some squatter that had ben reformed out by the nabors, I stood my rifle up agin one of the door posts and went in. I kindled up a little fire and told Grizzle I was going to take a nap. I piled up a heap of chestnut burs for a pillow and straitened myself out on the ground, for I can curl closer than a rattlesnake and lay straiter than a log. I laid with the back of my head agin the hearth, and my eyes looking up chimney so that I could see when it was noon by the sun, for Mrs. Crockett was always rantankerous[1] when I staid out over the time. I got to sleep before Grizzle had done warming the eend of his nose, and I had swallowed so much cold wind that it laid hard on my stomach, and as I laid gulping and belching the wind went out of me and roared up chimney like a young whirlwind. So I had a pesky dream, and kinder thought, till I waked up, that I was floating down the Massassippy in a holler tree, and I hadn't room to stir my legs and arms no more than they were withed together with young saplings. While I was there and want able to help myself a feller called Oak Wing that lived about twenty miles

▲ **Critical Viewing** Does Davy Crockett, pictured here, look as if he might use "a heap of chestnut burs" for a pillow? Explain. [Assess]

---

1. **rantankerous** (ran tan´ kər əs) *adj.*: Dialect for *cantankerous*, meaning "wildly and noisily upset."

Humanities: Art

Illustration Artists who illustrate a well-known American folk hero must use visual representation to tell the story of a character who is larger than life and who represents a specific region of America. In this image of Davy Crockett, the artist shows Crockett hunting with his dogs. Crockett wears deerskin pants, shirt, and moccasins—clothing most likely adapted from that used by Native Americans in the region. He carries a rifle and pouch. Crockett is a sturdily built man, who seems at home in nature. His dogs appear anxious as if they are ready for the hunt.

Use the following questions for discussion:

1. How does the artist use color in this interpretation of Davy Crockett? *The neutral colors of Crockett's clothing seem to blend with the environment, which makes the subject appear to be a part of nature.*

2. Why would the artist choose to have Davy Crockett wear clothing that blends with nature? *Because he appears to be going hunting, the clothing and colors might be used as hunters today wear camouflage clothing to hide from the animals they are hunting.*

off, and that I had give a most almighty licking once, cum and looked in with his blind

♦ Literary Focus

Explain how Crockett's use of language is appropriate for a tall tale.

eye that I had gouged out five years before, and I saw him looking in one end of the hollow log, and he axed me if I wanted to get out. I told him to tie a rope to one of my legs and draw me out as soon as God would let him and as much sooner as he was a mind to. But he said he wouldn't do it that way, he would ram me out with a pole. So he took a long pole and rammed it down agin my head as if he was ramming home the cattridge in a cannon. This didn't make me budge an inch, but it pounded my head down in between my shoulders till I look'd like a turcle with his head drawn in. This started my temper a trifle, and I ript and swore till the breath boiled out of the end of the log like the steam out of the funnel pipe of a steemboat. Jest then I woke up, and seed my wife pulling my leg, for it was enermost sundown and she had cum arter me. There was a long icicle hanging to her nose, and when she tried to kiss me, she run it right into my eye. I told her my dreem, and sed I would have revenge on Oak Wing for pounding my head. She said it was all a dreem and that Oak was not to blame; but I had a very diffrent idee of the matter. So I went and talked to him, and told him what he had done to me in a dreem, and it was settled that he should make me an apology in his next dreem, and that wood make us square,[2] for I don't like to be run upon when I'm asleep, any more than I do when I'm awake.

2. **square:** Even.

Guide for Responding

◆ LITERATURE AND YOUR LIFE

Reader's Response Do you think you would like Davy Crockett if you met him? Why or why not?

Thematic Focus Do you find Crockett heroic? Why or why not?

☑ Check Your Comprehension

1. Name three instances in which Davy Crockett exaggerates events.
2. Describe Davy Crockett's dream.
3. Where does Davy Crockett take his nap?
4. What is the arrangement made at the end of the tale between Davy Crockett and Oak Wing?

◆ Critical Thinking

INTERPRET
1. Describe ways in which exaggeration adds humor to this tale. **[Connect]**
2. How does the absurd and humorous settlement between Crockett and Oak Wing indicate that this is a tall tale? **[Draw Conclusions]**
3. (a) Do you think that Davy Crockett's descriptions are meant to be taken literally? (b) How does your answer explain Crockett's anger toward Oak Wing? **[Interpret]**

APPLY
4. (a) How does Crockett's dialect affect the narration of the tale? (b) How would the story be different if it had been written in standard English? **[Modify]**
5. What agreement would you suggest to Davy Crockett and Oak Wing to settle the conflict? **[Solve]**

COMPARE LITERARY WORKS
6. Characters in these tall tales generally achieve their goals through a combination of reason and strength. Find examples in the stories that illustrate this point. **[Analyze]**

Davy Crockett's Dream ◆ 953

◆ Literary Focus

❺ **Tall Tale** Review with students that tall tales are written in the language of the common people and tell of life on the American frontier. Have students point out examples that show that Davy Crockett's story is a tall tale told by a "common" person. *The language is informal and grammatically incorrect in places, and the story is about his experiences in a rural area.*

Reinforce and Extend

Answers
◆ LITERATURE AND YOUR LIFE

Reader's Response Students should support their examples with details from the story.

Thematic Focus Some may say he is not heroic because he does not show unusual characteristics or do great deeds.

☑ Check Your Comprehension
1. His hat freezes to his head; he uses chestnut burs for a pillow; his wife sticks him in the eye with an icicle hanging from her nose.
2. He dreams that he is stuck in a log. Oak Wing tries to push him out of the log by ramming his head with a pole until his head is between his shoulders like a turtle.
3. He takes a nap with his head in the fireplace.
4. They agree that Oak Wing will apologize in his next dream.

◆ Critical Thinking
1. The visual clues of the exaggeration help readers picture the humorous events described.
2. It shows that the story is a tall tale because the men agree to do something that is impossible.
3. (a) Students should recognize the humorous intent of the descriptions. (b) The fact that Crockett is angry at Oak Wing for something that Oak Wing did in Crockett's own dream shows it isn't serious.
4. (a) The dialect adds authenticity to the tall tale because it sounds like the conversation of a real person. (b) The story would not be as life-like if it were written in formal English.
5. Students may like the agreement that Crockett and Oak Wing make.
6. Students' ideas should include examples from the tall tales.

Beyond the Selection

FURTHER READING
Other Works by Adrien Stoutenburg
American Tall Tales
Greenwich Mean Time

Other Works by Carl Sandburg
The Complete Poems of Carl Sandburg
Billy Sunday and Other Poems

Other Works by Harold W. Felton
Big Mose, Hero Fireman
Cowboy Jamboree: Western Songs and Lore

Other Works by Davy Crockett
A Narrative of the Life of Davy Crockett

INTERNET
We suggest the following sites on the Internet (all Web sites are subject to change).

For more on Carl Sandburg, go to:
http://educeth.ethz.ch/english/readinglist/sandburg

For more information on American folklore, visit:
http://www.seanet.com/~eldrbarry/roos/books/amer.htm

For more information on Davy Crockett, go to:
http://www.americanwest.com/pages/davycroc.htm

We *strongly recommend* that you preview these sites before you send students to them.

953

Answers

◆ Reading Strategy

1. Most students will say that they predicted that he would die while working on the railroad.
2. Students may say that they predicted that Pecos Bill's fearlessness would lead to some sort of fight with the cyclone.
3. Most students will say that they predicted he would fall asleep.

◆ Build Vocabulary

Forms of *skeptic*
1. skeptical
2. skeptically

Spelling Strategy
1. commitment
2. commander
3. accommodate

Using the Word Bank
1. c   3. h   5. g   7. e
2. f   4. d   6. b   8. a

◆ Literary Focus

1. (a) John Henry was a real man who worked for the railroad; he was very large and strong; he entered a contest with a steam drill. (b) Details such as working with two hammers at once, and having people pour water over his hammers to keep them cool are exaggerations.
2. (a) Pecos Bill believes in never saying the word *afraid;* he rides a horse named Widow Maker. (b) Pecos Bill has a rattlesnake and mountain lion for pets; he rides a cyclone; he creates Death Valley.
3. It is difficult to find game on a cold day; a cartridge is rammed into a cannon for firing.

◆ Build Grammar Skills

Practice
1. adverb clause
2. subject
3. adverb
4. adverb
5. prepositional phrase

Writing Application
Sample:
Tall tales are full of exaggeration. Sometimes they tell about life on the American frontier. While sitting around the campfire at night, cowboys often told tall tales.

Guide for Responding (continued)

◆ Reading Strategy

PREDICT

Because tall tales have very predictable patterns, you can easily **predict** the types of events that will occur once you discover the character's traits or qualities.

1. In "Hammerman," John Henry says that he would "die with a hammer in my hand." What did you predict based on that statement?
2. Which quality or trait of Pecos Bill helped you to predict what would happen?
3. When Davy Crockett says that he "piled up a heap of chestnut burs for a pillow," what might you predict about his future actions?

◆ Build Vocabulary

USING FORMS OF *skeptic*

Knowing that *skeptics* means "people who doubt what others accept as true," you can figure out the meaning of related words. Complete the sentences that follow with words related to *skeptic*:

skeptically   skeptical

1. Although several people assured her that bungee jumping was safe, she remained _____?_____.
2. Before signing the standard lease, the lawyer _____?_____ reviewed the contract again.

SPELLING STRATEGY

Most multi-syllable words with the *m* sound in the middle, like *commotion*, are spelled with two *m*s, not one. Practice this rule by correcting the spelling of the following words:

1. comitment   2. comander   3. accomodate

USING THE WORD BANK

On your paper, match the Word Bank word with its definition.

1. hefted   a. doubters
2. granite   b. useless
3. commotion   c. lifted or heaved
4. usurped   d. took power
5. invincible   e. unexplainable
6. futile   f. hard stone
7. inexplicable g. unbeatable
8. skeptics   h. disturbance

◆ Literary Focus

TALL TALES

Tall tales are stories that are highly exaggerated. Because many tall tales originally were told by western pioneers, they often reveal aspects of the settling of the American West.

1. (a) Which elements of "Hammerman" are based on fact? (b) Which elements are exaggerated?
2. (a) What aspects of Peco Bill's character are believable? (b) What aspects are highly exaggerated?
3. What can you learn about frontier life from "Davy Crockett's Dream"?

◆ Build Grammar Skills

VARIETY IN SENTENCE BEGINNINGS

Writers use a **variety of sentence beginnings** to keep their stories interesting. Look at these possible ways to begin sentences:

Subject: *People down South* still tell stories about John Henry. . . .
Adverb: *The next morning,* John Henry bundled up some food. . . .
Adverb Clause: *As John Henry grew a bit older,* he practiced swinging the hammer. . . .
Prepositional Phrase: *At night,* . . . John Henry listened to a far-off train . . .

Practice On your paper, identify the type of sentence element that begins each of the following:

1. When the war ended, a man from the North came to John Henry. . . .
2. The cyclone caused Bill some trouble, though.
3. One year, he tried shipping the prairie dog holes up north. . . .
4. Usually it would destroy a few hundred miles of fence. . . .
5. In the beginning, the Fourth of July crowd had aroused its curiosity.

Writing Application Rewrite the following, varying the sentence beginnings to add variety:

Tall tales are full of exaggeration. Tall tales often tell about life on the American frontier. Cowboys on the frontier liked to tell tall tales at night by the campfire.

✎ Writer's Solution

For additional instruction and practice, use the Varying Sentence Structure lesson in the Styling Sentences unit on the *Writer's Solution Language Lab CD-ROM.* You may also use Using a Variety of Sentences, p. 125 in the *Writer's Solution Grammar Practice Book.*

Build Your Portfolio

 ## Idea Bank

Writing

1. **Journal Entry** Imagine that you are one of the spectators watching the contest in "Hammerman" or watching Pecos Bill ride the cyclone. Write a journal entry describing the fantastic event and your reactions to it.

2. **Tall Tale** Write about a daily occurrence in your life, but make it a tall tale by exaggerating the events or your abilities.

3. **Analysis** Analyze the qualities of the tall tale character using examples from the stories. Write an essay outlining these qualities and how they account for the hero's actions.

Speaking and Listening

4. **Performance** "John Henry" is a ballad. Ballads are usually sung long before they are ever put into writing. Rehearse and recite this ballad for your classmates. You may wish to accompany yourself on the piano or the guitar if you are able to. **[Performing Arts Link]**

5. **Oral Storytelling** Continue the oral tradition by making up a tall tale and telling it to the class. Tape-record your recitation to evaluate it afterwards. **[Performing Arts Link]**

Projects

6. **Collage** Reread "Paul Bunyan of the North Woods," and draw pictures illustrating the adventures and merriment of Paul Bunyan and his friends. Then, combine your work into a collage, and display it for your classmates. **[Art Link]**

7. **Report [Group Activity]** In "Pecos Bill: The Cyclone," the hero is said to have caused many of the natural wonders in the United States. With a small group of classmates, research the scientific explanations of the origins of the Great Plains, Death Valley, and the Grand Canyon. Share your findings with the class. **[Science Link]**

 ## Writing Mini-Lesson

Nomination for Hero of the Year

Many of the characters in tall tales display heroic qualities: They seem to be larger than life, displaying amazing abilities of strength and courage. Choose a person, real or fictional, who exhibits heroic qualities, to nominate for hero of the year. In your nomination, explain why that person deserves the honor.

Writing Skills Focus:
Use Only Important Details

Because an effective nomination is brief and to the point, **use only important details** within it.

Model
Sassie Betty displays all the qualities that a hero should have: She's kind, strong, generous, and selfless.

Prewriting Choose a candidate for hero of the year, and list all the positive qualities that your hero possesses. For each quality, list an important point that supports it.

Drafting Draft an introduction in which you present your nominee to the audience. Then, in the body, explain why your nominee deserves to be hero of the year. Conclude by summarizing your most important ideas.

Revising Read your nomination to a classmate, and ask whether or not your points are convincing. Delete any points that are unimportant, and add details where needed to support your views.

> ◆ **Grammar Application**
> Review your sentence beginnings. Vary them, where necessary, to avoid monotony and dullness in your writing.

 ## Idea Bank

Following are suggestions for matching the Idea Bank topics with your students' performance levels and learning modalities:

Customize for
Performance Levels
Less Advanced Students: 1, 4
Average Students: 2, 5, 6
More Advanced Students: 3, 5, 7

Customize for
Learning Modalities
Verbal/Linguistic: 1, 2, 3, 4, 5
Interpersonal: 7
Visual/Spatial: 6, 7
Musical/Rhythmic: 4
Logical/Mathematical: 7
Intrapersonal: 6

 ## Writing Mini-Lesson

Refer students to the Writing Handbook in the back of the book for instructions on the writing process and for further information on persuasion. Have students use the Cluster Organizer in **Writing and Language Transparencies,** p. 73, to arrange their prewriting examples.

Have students complete the tutorial on Persuasion. Follow these steps:
1. Have students view the interactive model of a persuasive essay.
2. Suggest that students use the Audio-annotated Writing Models to see different ways of organizing their drafts.
3. Have students draft on computer.
4. When revising, have students use the Revision checker for sentence openers.

✒ Writer's Solution

Writer's Solution Sourcebook Have students use Chapter 6, "Persuasion," pp. 166–199 for additional support. The chapter includes in-depth instruction eliminating unnecessary words, pp. 195–196.

✓ ASSESSMENT OPTIONS

Formal Assessment, Selection Test, pp. 270–272, and Assessment Resources Software. The selection test is designed so that it can easily be customized to the performance levels of your students.

Alternative Assessment, p. 60, includes options for less advanced students, more advanced students, interpersonal learners, visual/spatial learners, logical/mathematical learners, and verbal/linguistic learners.

PORTFOLIO ASSESSMENT
Use the following rubrics in the **Alternative Assessment** booklet to assess student writing:
Journal Entry: Expression, p. 90
Tall Tale: Fictional Narrative, p. 91
Analysis: Research Report/Paper, p. 102
Writing Mini-Lesson: Persuasion, p. 101

Prepare and Engage

Establish Writing Guidelines
Review the following key characteristics of an Internet Web page:

- An Internet Web page contains information on a range of subjects and may include hyperlinks to other sites.

- An Internet Web page is written using a computer language called HTML, which uses codes to format information as it appears on screen.

- An Internet Web page uses visual support to add interest to a topic.

You may want to distribute the scoring rubric for Multimedia Report, p. 103 in **Alternative Assessment,** to make students aware of the criteria on which they will be evaluated. See the suggestions on p. 958 for customizing the rubric to this workshop.

Refer students to the Writing Handbook in the back of the book for instruction on the writing process and information on technical writing.

✒ Writer's Solution

Writers at Work Videodisc
Explain to students that reporting factual information is expository writing. Play the videodisc segment on Exposition: Giving Information (Ch. 4) to introduce students to expository writing and show them what professional journalist Gary Matsumoto says about communicating information.

Play frames 33108 to 41558

Writing Lab CD-ROM
If your students have access to computers, they can work in the tutorial on Exposition: Giving Information to complete all or part of their Web pages. Follow these steps:

1. Have students view the interactive models of different types of expository writing.
2. Suggest that students use the Cluster Diagram to think about details related to their topic.
3. Have students use the Notecard Activity to help develop an order for the details of their topics.
4. Students can draft on computer.

Writers Solution Sourcebook
Students can find in-depth instruction on gathering information, pp. 123–124, in the chapter on Exposition: Giving Information, pp. 104–135.

Technical Writing

Internet Web Page

Writing Process Workshop

The information superhighway—the Internet—is quickly becoming the fastest way to acquire information on any topic. One reason that the Internet is so popular is that anyone from anywhere in the world can share expertise through his or her own Web site. Web sites on the Internet contain a Home Page that provides information and often includes media as well as links to other sites. Each Web site has its own address.

Create a plan for your own Web page through which you can communicate your knowledge to the world. This workshop will help you design an **Internet Web page.** The following writing skills will help you get started:

Writing Skills Focus

▶ **Use only important details** on your Web Home Page. Too much text onscreen is difficult to read. (See p. 955.)

▶ **Include an explanation of your purpose.** Introduce your Web page by explaining why you created it.

▶ **Give visual support.** Drawing, photos, and video that support the topic of your Web page can be included.

▶ **Choose an organization** that is visually appealing and easy to follow.

Following is a plan for a Web page on superheroes:

WRITING MODEL

The Mighty Heroes of the Comics

The superheroes of the comics have long been saving the world from doom. This page is dedicated to their selfless adventures. ① I chose three superheroes—Xena, Superman, and Batman—to feature on this page. ② Click on each picture, and you will learn all I have learned about each superhero.
[Image of Xena, Warrior Princess]
[Image of Superman]
[Image of Batman] ③

① This sentence explains the writer's purpose for creating this Web page.
② Here, the writer explains the organization of the Home Page.
③ These visuals help support the content of the Web page.

956 ◆ The American Folk Tradition

🏳 Cross-Curricular Connection: Science

Internet Explain to students that the Internet is the largest computer network in the world. Since 1990, the number of computers participating in the Internet has doubled each year. The Internet began in 1962 as a project by the United States government to come up with a communications system that would be able to survive nuclear war. The main consideration of such a system was that it would have to be free of a central control that could be attacked or bombed. The result of the project was called ARPANET after the United States Department of Defense's Advanced

Projects Research Agency.

Have students research the history of the Internet. Suggest that students gather statistics about how many current users are on the Internet and projected rates for expansion. In addition, students may want to come up with a brief summary of different uses for the Internet. To start them off, suggest they visit the Internet Society Home Page at:
http://www.isoc.org
This site provides current and historical information about the Internet.

Prewriting

Choose a Subject Create an informative Web page on a hobby or an interest that you have, or select one of the following topics:

> ### Topic Ideas
> - An animal
> - A favorite author
> - A sports player
> - Cultural traditions

Research the Links Browse the Internet for sites related to your topic. Then, choose those that best support your topic. You can use these links for your Web page.

Create a Plan Before writing the text, create a plan for the appearance of your page. Consider how many headings you want on a page, how many links, what will be highlighted as "hot text," and what type of media you will include.

The following chart shows the codes you'll need to format a page:

FORMATTING A PAGE

HTML codes:	
<title></title>	Title
<h1></h1> through <h5></h5>	Heading sizes
<center></center>	Centers text
<hr>	Inserts rule (a straight line)
<p></p>	Paragraph
<li>	Bulleted list item
 	Break between lines
<img src="name of graphic file">	Graphic or image tag
<a href="address of Internet site"></a>	Hyperlink

Drafting

Maintain a Consistent Purpose Introduce your Web page by stating your purpose. Make sure that all text, media, and links relate to that purpose.

Introduce Media When you place media on your site, introduce each piece by explaining what it is and why it is on your Web page.

DRAFTING/REVISING

Applying Language Skills: Commonly Confused Words

The following are a few commonly confused word pairs:

accept, except: *Accept is a verb meaning "to receive" or "to agree with." Except is a preposition meaning "not including"; it is also sometimes a verb meaning "to leave out."*

affect, effect: *Affect is a verb meaning "to influence." Effect is a noun meaning "result" or a verb meaning "to bring about."*

than, then: *Than introduces the second part of a comparison. Then means "next" or "after that."*

Practice Choose the correct word to complete the sentence:

1. Harvey plays ball better _____?_____ Abe does. (than, then)
2. The story had a strange _____?_____ on the listeners. (affect, effect)
3. No one _____?_____ Wilma is allowed to enter that room. (accept, except)

Writing Application As you write, refer to the above definitions to choose the correct word.

> ### Writer's Solution Connection Writing Lab
> For help organizing your Web page, use the Outliner in the Organizing section of the Writer's Toolkit.

Develop Student Writing

Prewriting

Suggest that students do searches on the Internet for already existing Web sites that include information on their topic. Have students consider how the information is presented and if there seems to be any information that is missing or unreliable. Explain to students that they should aim to create a Web page that links the best sites.

✎ Writer's Solution

Writing Lab CD-ROM

For more topic ideas, suggest that students browse through the Inspirations for Exposition in the Prewriting section of the tutorial on Exposition: Giving Information.

Customize for *Logical/Mathematical Learners*

Some students may be familiar with HTML or other programming languages. Encourage these students to pair up with others in the class who are less experienced with technical writing or computer skills.

Customize for *Less Proficient Writers*

Some students may benefit from group work when coming up with ideas for their topics. Suggest that students pair up with one or two other students and analyze the same piece of literature. After students have read the piece a few times, have them hold a group discussion on the different literary elements in the piece. This discussion may spark ideas for possible topics.

Drafting

Explain to students that one of the easiest ways to learn how to create Web pages is to see how other people have done it. Tell students that they can find the coding for any Web page by clicking the button called "View Document Source" on their Internet browser. A new window will open up that contains the source, or HTML coding, for the Web page they are currently viewing. Suggest that students begin by finding a rather simple page and viewing its source.

Applying Language Skills

Commonly Confused Words Explain to students that these words are commonly confused because of their similarities in spelling and sound.

Answers

Suggested responses:
1. Harvey plays ball better <u>than</u> Abe does.
2. The story had a strange <u>effect</u> on the listeners.
3. No one <u>except</u> Wilma is allowed to enter that room.

✎ Writer's Solution

For additional instruction, have students use the practice page on Twenty Common Usage Problems, p. 92, in the *Writer's Solution Grammar Practice Book*.

Revising

When they revise, have students share their Internet Web pages with a partner. Encourage the students to comment on what they like and don't like about the Web page. Have them consider the amount and type of information given as well as the corresponding visuals.

Publishing

For other publishing ideas, suggest that students print out a copy of their document source or coding for their Web pages and share them with the rest of the class.

Review the Writing Guidelines
After students have completed their papers, review the characteristics of a Web page.

Applying Language Skills

Capitalization of Proper Nouns
Explain to students that capitalization of proper nouns helps readers understand that the noun names a specific person, place, or thing.

Answers

1. My favorite players are Babe Ruth and Jackie Robinson.
2. I've been to ballparks in Houston, Toronto, and Cleveland.
3. Sometimes, it's chilly to watch baseball in April and October.

EDITING/PROOFREADING

Applying Language Skills:
Capitalization of Proper Nouns

Nouns are either common or proper. A common noun names any one of a class of people, places, or things. A proper noun names a specific person, place, or thing. Proper nouns are capitalized.

Common Nouns	Proper Nouns
computer	Macintosh, Compaq
city	Dallas, Honolulu
language	Danish, Spanish

Practice Write these sentences, capitalizing all proper nouns:

1. My favorite players are babe ruth and jackie robinson.
2. I've been to ballparks in houston, toronto, and cleveland.
3. Sometimes, it's chilly to watch baseball in april and october.

Writing Application As you revise your Internet Web page, make sure all proper nouns are capitalized.

**Writer's Solution Connection
Language Lab**

For more help with capitalization, see the Capitalization in Sentences lesson in the Capitalization unit.

Revising

Use a Checklist Review the Writing Skills Focus on page 956. Use the items as a checklist to evaluate and revise your Web page.

Check Links Make sure you have the correct addresses for links you have chosen for your Web page.

Get More Advice Here are some on-line resources for your Web author toolbox:
- ▶ A beginner's guide to HTML: http://www.ncsa.uiuc.edu/General/Internet/WWW/HTMLPrimer.html
- ▶ A list of software that provides the HTML codes (HTML editors): info@classroom.net
- ▶ Free textures, clip art, and images: http://www.itw.com:80/~imagesys/Ftpto:ftp.classroom.net

REVISION MODEL

① I designed this Web page so I could share my knowledge of comic books.

Comic books are a hobby and an obsession of mine. ② and the following text of Superman to learn more about his first comic book. Click on this image.

① The writer added this statement to make clear his purpose for creating the Web page.
② This statement introduces the media and lets the reader know why it's there.

Publishing and Presenting

On-line To mount or launch your Web page onto the Internet so that other Internet users can visit it, you must copy the folder or directory onto a Web server. The server lets anyone connected to the Net access your pages with a Web browser. Once you've found a server, you can send your page to your host (the server you've chosen) via diskette, by e-mail, or by uploading it via ftp (file transfer protocol).

Visitors Ask visitors to your Web site to give you feedback. You might want to use their suggestions when you update your page.

958 ◆ *The American Folk Tradition*

✓ ASSESSMENT		4	3	2	1
PORTFOLIO ASSESSMENT Use the rubric on Multimedia Report in the **Alternative Assessment** booklet, p. 103, to assess students' writing. Add these criteria to customize this rubric to this assignment.	**Web Page Format**	The Web page is in a simple, easy-to-follow format and includes well-researched links to other sites.	The Web page is in an easy-to-follow format and includes at least two well-researched links to related sites.	The Web page is organized but not easy to follow; it includes at least one researched link to a related site.	The Web page is not organized or formatted adequately, and links are improper or missing.
	Capitalization of Proper Nouns	All of the text on the Web page includes correctly capitalized proper nouns.	Most of the text on the Web page includes correctly capitalized proper nouns.	Some of the text on the Web page includes correctly capitalized proper nouns.	None of the text on the Web page includes correctly capitalized proper nouns.

Real-World Reading Skills Workshop

Using an Internet Web Page

Strategies for Success

Using the Internet means using Web pages. Each Web page contains information on a specific topic, as well as media and links to other pages. The following information will help you use a Web page effectively:

Click on the Highlighted Text The text that is highlighted is called hot text. It leads you to more information. When you click on a highlighted term, it will take you to another page that offers information about the topic.

Use the Links A link on a Web site is hot text that takes you directly to another Web site. Instead of locating a Web page by using an address, you can get there by clicking on the link provided by the Web sponsor—the person who created the Web site.

Evaluate the Web Site Don't get caught up in the colors and graphics of a Web site. Remember that you're after reliable information—for a school report or your personal life—and you want current, accurate facts. Check the site's sponsor: Government or education sites are usually the most reliable.

Guides exist that review and evaluate Web sites for their reliability. For practice, look up a Web site you have recently used in these two guides:

▶ **Argus Clearinghouse**
http://www.clearinghouse.net/chhome.html
▶ **Mining Company**
http://miningco.com

Superhero Central

Welcome to my collection of superhero trivia. I am a middle-school student at Rock Middle School Rock, SC. I am a lover of comic books and all superheroes.

- Xena
- Superman
- Batman
- Hercules

Other cool superhero sites:
http://www.thebat.com
http://www.histsupher.edu

Apply the Strategies

Using the Internet page above, answer the following questions:

1. Which words are hot text? What happens if you click on them?
2. Is there a list of links available? Where can you find them?
3. Would you consider this site a reliable source? Why or why not?

> ✔ Here are situations in which you may use an Internet Web page for information:
> ▶ Reading the daily news
> ▶ Finding weather reports for a vacation destination

◆ Build Grammar Skills

Reviewing Variety in Sentence Beginnings

The selections in Part 2 include instruction on the following:

• Variety in Sentence Beginnings

This instruction is reinforced with the Build Grammar Skills practice pages in **Selection Support,** p. 322.

Writer's Solution

For additional practice and support, use the practice page on Using a Variety of Sentences, p. 125 in the *Writer's Solution Grammar Practice Book.* If students have access to technology, have them use the lesson on Varying Sentence Structure in the Sentence Style unit of the *Writer's Solution Language Lab CD-ROM.*

Variety in Sentence Beginnings — Grammar Review

To keep their writing interesting, writers **vary the beginnings of their sentences** (see p. 954). You need not always begin a sentence with the subject. Sometimes you can place other sentence elements at the beginning of the sentence.

The following chart shows different ways that you may begin a sentence:

phrase (frāz) *n.* 1 a group of words that is not a complete sentence, but that gives a single idea, usually as a separate part of a sentence ["Drinking fresh milk," "with meals," and "to be healthy" are phrases.]

Sentence Beginnings	Examples
Subject:	*John Henry's father put his arm around her shoulder.*
Adverb:	*Still, it tipped and tilted as the dance went on.*
Phrases: Prepositional Phrases:	*On the morning of the contest, the slopes around the tunnel were loaded with people.*
Participial Phrase:	*Lying in bed at night, young John Henry listened to far-off train whistles.*
Adverb Clause:	*As John Henry grew a bit older, he practiced swinging his hammer. . . .*

Practice 1 Write the following sentences in your notebook. Then, underline each sentence beginning and identify what type it is.

1. At night, lying on a straw bed on the floor, John Henry listened to a far-off train whistling through the darkness.

2. Whenever John Henry worked, he sang.

3. The cookstove at that camp covered an acre of ground.

4. Usually, it would destroy a few hundred miles of fence by blowing the postholes away.

5. Raging toward the town, the cyclone twisted in the air a thousand times.

Practice 2 Write each of the following sentences using the type of sentence beginning specified.

1. The cyclone was strong and fierce, frightening most people. (participial phrase)

2. Everyone knew that Pecos Bill had defeated the cyclone when it disintegrated. (adverb clause)

3. Paul Bunyan, angered by the bad weather, stopped the rain. (participial phrase)

4. John Henry collapsed suddenly from exhaustion after the race. (adverb)

5. John Henry dreamed during the night of driving steel. (prepositional phrase)

Grammar in Writing

✔ *When you begin a sentence with an adverb, a phrase, or a clause, use a comma to separate it from the rest of the sentence.*

960 ◆ *The American Folk Tradition*

Answers
Practice 1

1. At night, lying on a straw bed on the floor, John Henry listened to a far-off train whistling through the darkness. Begins with a prepositional phrase and a participial phrase.
2. Whenever John Henry worked, he sang. Begins with an adverb clause.
3. The cookstove at that camp covered an acre of ground. Begins with a subject.
4. Usually, it would destroy a few hundred miles of fence by blowing the postholes away. Begins with an adverb.
5. Raging toward the town, the cyclone twisted in the air a thousand times. Begins with a participial phrase.

Practice 2

1. Frightening most people, the cyclone was strong and fierce.
2. When it disintegrated, everyone knew that Pecos Bill had defeated the cyclone.
3. Angered by the bad weather, Paul Bunyan stopped the rain.
4. Suddenly, John Henry collapsed from exhaustion after the race.
5. During the night, John Henry dreamed of driving steel.

Speaking, Listening, and Viewing Workshop

Conducting Business

Conducting business is a part of life. You need business skills to order items from a catalog, to open and/or use a savings account, to request product information, to find and keep a job, to return a defective item, to correct a mistake (yours or the business's), or to praise a job well done.

Always Be Courteous "Please" and "thank you" are part of a business vocabulary. Be polite and respectful—whether you are ordering an item, complaining about a defect or problem, or requesting information. Everyone likes and deserves to be treated with respect.

Be Direct and Specific Know exactly what you want and ask for it. If you are ordering an item, know your size and the item number. If you are returning something, decide whether you want a replacement or a refund.

Be Responsible; Do Your Math Check the prices of items you're buying. Check your change. Keep your receipts in case you want to exchange something. If you're offering services or looking for a job, have a fee or wage in mind.

Follow Up If someone has done something particularly nice for you, such as helping you get a job or training you in a helpful, cheerful way, thank him or her with a note or a call. If something you've ordered is late in coming, check on it. Complete the warranty application for your new items.

Apply the Strategies

With a partner, role-play these situations, following the strategies in this lesson. Switch roles with your partner.

1. You received a shirt as a gift, but you need it in a larger size. The sales clerk has asked you for a receipt, but you don't have it.

2. You ordered a three-dimensional puzzle from a catalog and the puzzle is missing several pieces. You did not lose them.

3. You are answering an ad for someone to water plants and bring in mail. You want to know the hours and the wages. Your parents want some information about the person for whom you'd be working.

Tips for Conducting Business

▶ Be polite and respectful.
▶ Be organized, direct, and specific.
▶ Follow up.

961

What's Behind the Words

Ask students what kinds of dialects they have heard or read in books. Explain that writers who write dialect use variant spellings and apostrophes to make the reader hear how the character speaks.

Customize for
More Advanced Students

Explain to students that sometimes groups of friends make up their own vocabulary without even knowing it. This vocabulary may consist of nicknames for members of the group, abbreviations for commonly used words, and different ways of pronouncing certain words. Encourage students to write down a list of words or dialects that they use or have used. Or, have students work in groups to come up with new terms to express the names of familiar things.

Activity

Encourage students to begin their research into regional dialects on the Internet. One site that includes over a hundred links to other dialect-oriented sites is the American Dialect Home Page at:

http://www.netaxs.com/~salvucci/ AmDialhome.html

Another Web site with information on regional dialects is the Linguistic Atlas of the United States, at:

http://hyde.park.uga.edu/matlas/ main_atlas.html

Remember, all Web sites are subject to change, and we *strongly recommend* that you preview any sites before sending students to them.

What's Behind the Words

Vocabulary Adventures With Richard Lederer

Regional Vocabulary

Midway through John Steinbeck's novel *The Grapes of Wrath,* young Ivy observes, "Ever'body says words different. Arkansas folks says 'em different, and Oklahomy folks says 'em different. And we seen a lady from Massachusetts, an' she said 'em differentest of all. Couldn't hardly make out what she was sayin'."

One aspect of our sprawling American language is that not all of us say the same word in the same way. Sometimes we don't even use the same name for the same object. These vocabulary and pronunciation differences create dialects, the form of speech used in a particular region.

Food for Thought

You probably enjoy eating a certain sandwich made with cold cuts, cheese, tomatoes, pickles, and onions stuffed into a long, hard-crusted Italian bread. That sandwich was invented in the Italian section of Philadelphia known as Hog Island. Some language experts claim that from *Hog Island* came the word *hoagie.* Others contend that *hoagie* arose because only a hog had the appetite or the technique to eat one properly.

In New England, the same sandwich is called a *grinder*—you need a good set of *grinders,* or teeth, to chew it. Around the United States, the *hoagie* or *grinder* is called at least a dozen other names—a *bomber, Cuban sandwich, Garibaldi, hero, Italian sandwich, rocket, sub, submarine, torpedo, wedge, wedgie,* and, in the deep South, a *poor-boy* (usually pronounced "poh-boy").

In Philadelphia, people wash their *hoagies* down with *soda.* In New England, they wash *grinders* down with *tonic. Soda* and *tonic* in other areas are known as *pop, soda pop, a soft drink,* or *Coke.*

All-American Dialects

Clear—Or is it clean? Or is it plumb?—across the nation, Americans sure do talk "different." Is that simple strip of grass between the street and the sidewalk a *berm, boulevard, boulevard strip, city strip, green belt, the parking, the parking strip, parkway, sidewalk plot, strip, swale, tree bank,* or *tree lawn?* Is the part of the highway that separates the northbound lanes from the southbound lanes the *centerline, center strip, mall, medial strip, median strip, medium strip,* or *neutral ground?* It depends where you live and to whom you're speaking.

Everyone—including you—speaks a dialect. *Dialect* isn't a label for careless, uneducated, incorrect speech or something to be avoided or cured. Each language is a great pie. Each slice of that pie is a dialect, and no single slice is the language. Be proud of your slice of the pie.

ACTIVITY With a partner, learn about the dialect of another region of the country. Make a list comparing the words you use for lining up for something (*on line, in line*), the sandwich you eat (*hoagie, sub, grinder, hero*), the soft drink (*soda* or *pop*) you prefer. Then, write a skit in which two characters from different regions have difficulty communicating because of language differences. Perform the skit for the class.

Extended Reading Opportunities

The people of the United States, with their diverse backgrounds, have contributed stories and songs to the national folk literature. This literature reveals something of the culture from which it originated. For further exploration of American folklore, consider the following.

Suggested Titles

From Sea to Shining Sea: A Treasury of American Folklore and Folk Songs
Amy Cohn, Editor

This anthology includes 140 folk songs and stories illustrated by award-winning artists. A collection for all ages, the book begins with Native American stories and ends with the folklore of this century. It includes such diverse material as classic tall tales to Abbott and Costello's famous skit "Who's on First?" Each piece includes an introduction and end-notes. The collection reflects the richness of American diversity.

Big Men, Big Country: A Collection of American Tall Tales
Paul Robert Walker and James Bernardin

This collection includes episodes of tall-tale heroes like the mythical Paul Bunyan, Pecos Bill, and New York City's Big Mose as well as real historical figures like Gib Morgan, John Darling, and Jim Bridger. Walker bases each tale on the earliest printed version of the story. A note at the end of each story gives information about the tale's origin and, for tales based on historical figures, it includes information on each man's life.

Native American Literature

This anthology includes Native American origin stories, legends, and songs. The works show Native American culture as the foundation for American literature. Following the trail of Coyote the trickster, we are led on a journey through the magical, beautiful world of America's first people.

Other Possibilities

Cut From the Same Cloth: American Women of Myth, Legend, and Tall Tale — Robert D. San Souci

Her Stories: African American Folktales, Fairy Tales, and True Tales — Virginia Hamilton

Come Go With Me: Old Timers From the Southern Mountains — Roy Edwin Thomas

---

Planning Students' Extended Reading

All of the works listed on this page are good choices for extending the American folklore genre. The following information may help you choose which to teach.

Customize for
Varying Student Needs

When assigning these extended reading selections to your students, keep in mind the following factors:

- *From Sea to Shining Sea: A Treasury of American Folklore and Folk Songs* includes a subject guide for easy access to songs from different regions, ethnicities, and historical periods. The book is organized chronologically in subsections, with a different award-winning artist's illustrations for each subsection.

- *Big Men, Big Country: A Collection of American Tall Tales* includes nine tall tales with accompanying illustrations. Each tale includes details of its historical and cultural context. This book is appropriate for less proficient readers.

- *Native American Literature* is an offering from the Prentice Hall Library. It offers a chance for students to encounter a wide range of Native American literature. The pieces vary in level of difficulty.

ACCESS GUIDE TO VOCABULARY

This Access Guide lists all words presented in the Word Banks. The Guide refers you to the pages where the words are used and defined in context.

abhorrence, 321
abridge, 644
abyss, 838
accustomed, 403
acquiescent, 68
acquire, 508
acute, 543
adversaries, 793
aerobatic, 924
affluence, 587
aggregation, 553
aghast, 309
alienate, 263
amendments, 322
amiss, 511
ancestors, 197
ancestral, 369
anguish, 257
anonymously, 329
antithesis, 690
anxiously, 416
apprehension, 369, 752, 785
apprenticed, 655
arouse, 906
arresting, 536
ascent, 158, 444
assent, 194
assiduously, 253
august, 687
austere, 424
authentic, 603
availed, 379
bachelor, 597
bafflement, 180
banked, 424

bargain, 411
barren, 189
beckoned, 879
bedraggled, 51
benediction, 5
benign, 27
bitter, 175
blunders, 36, 385
borne, 865
brandishing, 279
breadth, 831
breakers, 818
brisk, 67
brittle, 562
broached, 275
burrow, 858
cajoling, 137
camouflage, 459
canter, 820
capricious, 460
casualty, 846
catapults, 838
celestial, 358
censured, 791
chronic, 424
cinched, 820
coincidental, 446
colossal, 372
commenced, 915
commotion, 945
compensate, 263
competent, 125
compounded, 7
compulsory, 581
conceivably, 446
conception, 331

confederacy, 785
configuration, 515
conscience, 372
conspicuous, 715
constellation, 82, 416
constellations, 634
consternation, 648
contiguous, 444
continuously, 876
convulsed, 479
cordially, 913
couched, 28
countenance, 455
credibility, 415
crevice, 544
criteria, 328
cunningly, 840
decisive, 265
defray, 477
degrading, 590
deliberating, 245
derision, 546
descended, 85
descent, 158
devices, 637
devoid, 690
devoured, 53
diagnostic, 355
diffused, 507
diligent, 243
diplomatic, 583
discerning, 194
discharged, 178
discourse, 791
discreet, 415
discreetly, 508

discrepancies, 176
disheveled, 135
dispatched, 657
dissimulation, 543
dissolution, 676
diverged, 34
diverts, 687
eclipses, 634
elongate, 446
eloquent, 329
elusive, 241
emancipated, 116
eminence, 517
empathy, 627
encompasses, 679
encumber, 895
engulfing, 655
ensued, 657
envelop, 411
equestrian, 517
etiquette, 43
evacuees, 675
evade, 194
evaded, 638
exertion, 156
exhausted, 155
extravagance, 85, 840
exulting, 267
fastidious, 139
fatalist, 737
feigned, 657
feigning, 828
fertile, 838
fiscal, 25
flue, 347
forsaken, 560

friction, 82
fugitives, 133
furrows, 76
furtive, 110
futile, 648, 949
gale, 817
galore, 469
gesticulations, 546
gestures, 879
glistens, 865
gnarled, 273, 895
gourds, 858
granite, 945
gratification, 455
guffawed, 457
guileless, 180
guttural, 135
habitable, 627
harmonious, 328
harnessed, 838
haughty, 913
heedless, 125
hefted, 936
hemisphere, 125
horde, 311
hover, 865, 876
humiliating, 265
illiteracy, 219
immersed, 369, 658
immigrate, 369
imperturbably, 482
impetuous, 309, 519
implemented, 679
implications, 125
inadvertently, 644
inarticulate, 750
incentive, 135
incredulously, 17
indicative, 90
indignant, 758
indomitable, 137
indulgent, 114
ineffectually, 766
inexplicable, 356, 949
inferior, 176
infinite, 65
infuse, 27
infusion, 627
innumerable, 273
inquiry, 356
inscription, 322
inscrutable, 553
insolently, 15
insufferable, 725
intangible, 245
interaction, 43
intimate, 43
intimation, 114
intimidated, 644

intolerant, 28
introspective, 220
intuition, 757
invincible, 949
ire, 321
judicious, 114
keen, 828
kindled, 810
lair, 896
languor, 517
latching, 189
lavish, 565
legions, 876
leisure, 716
lilting, 36
listlessly, 597
literally, 372
loitering, 67
looming, 126
low, 865
luminance, 867
luminous, 444
luster, 831
macabre, 459
mandate, 519
maneuver, 158, 356
mania, 655
manifestly, 156
manifold, 477
mantle, 51
meager, 581
melancholy, 569
membrane, 444
mercurial, 716
meticulous, 731
microbes, 125
misinterpret, 43
mistrusted, 189
molding, 425
morose, 477
mosquitoes, 347
mutineers, 347
mutinous, 137, 144
naturalist, 535
negligent, 822
negotiation, 273
nurtures, 840
obdurate, 583
obscure, 220, 377
officious, 789
oppressed, 245
orators, 90
oratory, 644
orbit, 82
ostentatiously, 740
pandemonium, 560
paradoxes, 690
peril, 263
peripatetic, 356,

periscope, 297
persistent, 403
pervading, 687
petition, 279
pitiful, 917
placidly, 67
precipitate, 553
predisposed, 459
predominantly, 241
presentable, 189
pretense, 657
pretext, 113
prevail, 194
privations, 673
procession, 603
procured, 49
prodigy, 295
profound, 543
prominent, 331
psychology, 212
purify, 906
pursuit, 904
quake, 427
radial, 125
ravaging, 676
recede, 865
receding, 122
refugees, 569
refute, 216
registrants, 328
reigning, 634
renounced, 15
resolute, 7, 597
respectively, 634
retribution, 255
retrospect, 647
revelation, 419
reverie, 487
rigorous, 356
riveted, 5
rivulets, 76
roam, 828
romp, 469
ruddy, 895
runt, 347
sagacity, 543
sarcastic, 758
sauntering, 90
scolded, 75
scornful, 817
scythe, 879
semblance, 810
sentinel, 517
shackles, 263
shriveled, 904
shunned, 838
signify, 295
simultaneously, 16, 257
sinew, 51

singular, 457
skeptics, 950
smoldering, 36
sobers, 536
somber, 307
specter, 216
spectral, 309
spirited, 535
spontaneously, 44
stalking, 896
stalwart, 148
stealthily, 761
stealthy, 307
stilted, 379
stoic, 76
strictures, 321
strife, 92
sturdy, 75
sublimity, 519
subtle, 625
supple, 76
surveyed, 411
swagger, 379
swarthy, 144
syndromes, 220
tangible, 216, 487
taut, 27
tenacious, 676
tendril, 895
tenement, 425
thoroughly, 155
timidly, 175
tranquil, 309
transparent, 466
tread, 267
tropical, 469
turbulent, 587
unabashed, 719
unanimous, 329
unconstitutional, 245
unfurled, 144
unobtrusively, 255
unrecompensed, 876
unremitting, 643
unwonted, 51
usurped, 949
usurps, 687
ventriloquist, 295
vertical, 858
vigorous, 401
virtuous, 253
visible, 634
voracious, 53
wan, 144
wizened, 279
worthily, 194
yearling, 401

Access Guide to Vocabulary ◆ 965

LITERARY TERMS HANDBOOK

ALLITERATION *Alliteration* is the repetition of initial consonant sounds. Writers use alliteration to draw attention to certain words or ideas, to imitate sounds, and to create musical effects. In the opening lines from "Silver," on page 856, notice how Walter de la Mare includes alliteration to create a sense of musical enchantment in the moonlit night:

> Slowly, silently, now the moon
> Walks the night in her silver shoon;

See *Repetition.*

ALLUSION An *allusion* is a reference to a well-known person, place, event, literary work, or work of art. Understanding what a writer is saying often depends on recognizing allusions. Walt Whitman's "O Captain! My Captain!" on page 266, contains allusions to the Civil War.

ANECDOTE An *anecdote* is a brief story about an interesting, amusing, or strange event. Writers tell anecdotes to entertain or to make a point. In "Animal Craftsmen," on page 625, Bruce Brooks relates an anecdote from his childhood.

ANTAGONIST An *antagonist* is a character or force in conflict with a main character, or protagonist. In "The Girl Who Hunted Rabbits," on page 49, both the Demon and the weather are antagonists to the young maiden. See *Conflict* and *Protagonist.*

ATMOSPHERE See *Mood.*

AUTOBIOGRAPHY An *autobiography* is a form of nonfiction in which the writer tells the story of his or her own life. An autobiography may tell about the person's whole life or only a part of it. Lionel García tells about his childhood neighborhood and activities in "Baseball," on page 636.

See *Biography* and *Nonfiction.*

BALLAD A *ballad* is a songlike poem that tells a story, often one dealing with adventure and romance. Most ballads are written in four- to six-line stanzas and have regular rhythms and rhyme schemes. A ballad often features a refrain—a regularly repeated line or group of lines. "John Henry," on page 940, is an example of a *folk ballad.*

See *Oral Tradition* and *Refrain.*

BIOGRAPHY A *biography* is a form of nonfiction in which a writer tells the life story of another person. Most biographies are written about famous or admirable people. Although biographies are nonfiction, the most effective ones share the qualities of good narrative writing. Stephen Longstreet's "Hokusai: The Old Man Mad About Drawing," on page 654, is a biography.

See *Autobiography* and *Nonfiction.*

BLANK VERSE *Blank verse* is poetry written in unrhymed iambic pentameter lines. William Shakespeare wrote many of his plays in blank verse. The following example is from King Richard's soliloquy, on page 792:

> Now is the winter of our discontent
> Made glorious summer by this sun of York;
> And all the clouds that loured upon our house
> In the deep bosom of the ocean buried.

See *Meter.*

CHARACTER A *character* is a person or an animal that takes part in the action of a literary work. A *main,* or *major, character* is the most important character in a story, poem, or play. A *minor character* plays a lesser role but is necessary for the story to develop. In "Raymond's Run," on page 292, the major character, Squeaky, tells the story.

Characters are sometimes classified as flat or round. A *flat character* is one-sided and often stereotypical. A *round character,* on the other hand, is fully developed and exhibits many traits. Characters can also be classified as dynamic or static. A *dynamic character* is one who changes or grows during the course of the work. A *static character* is one who does not change.

See *Characterization, Hero/Heroine,* and *Motivation.*

CHARACTERIZATION *Characterization* is the process by which authors create memorable characters. Authors use two major methods of characterization—*direct* and *indirect.* When using *direct characterization,* an author tells what a character is like. In "The Day I Got Lost," on page 558, Isaac Bashevis Singer directly tells about Professor Shlemiel—what he looks like and what he does.

When using *indirect characterization,* a writer reveals a character's personality through his or her appearance, words, actions, and effects on others. Sometimes the writer describes what other participants in the story say and think about the character. The reader then draws his or her own conclusions.

See *Character* and *Motivation.*

CLIMAX See *Conflict* and *Plot.*

CONCRETE POEM A *concrete poem* is one with a shape that suggests its subject. The poet arranges the letters, punctuation, and lines to create an image, or picture, on the page. Maxine Kumin's poem "400-Meter Free Style," on page 839, is an example of a concrete poem.

CONFLICT A *conflict* is a struggle between opposing forces. Conflict is one of the most important elements of stories, novels, and plays because it causes the action. Conflict can be external or internal. *External conflict* may be between two characters and may be caused by a difference in ideas or personalities. In "Cub Pilot on the Mississippi," on page 109, Mark Twain describes the conflict between himself and the steamboat pilot. Another type of external conflict may take place between a character and some force in nature. For example, in "Up the Slide," on page 154, the conflict is between a character and the cold, icy Yukon. An *internal conflict* takes place within the mind of a character, as in "A Retrieved Reformation," on page 252.

See *Plot.*

DESCRIPTION A *description* is a portrait, in words, of a person, place, or object. Descriptive writing uses images that appeal to the five senses—sight, hearing, touch, taste, and smell.

See *Image.*

DEVELOPMENT See *Plot.*

DIALECT *Dialect* is the form of a language spoken by people in a particular region or group. Dialects differ in pronunciation, grammar, and word choice.

Writers use dialect to make their characters seem realistic. For example, in Paul Laurence Dunbar's "The Finish of Patsy Barnes," on page 580, notice the dialect spoken by Patsy and his mother:

"Honey," she said; "mammy ain' gwine lay hyeah long. She be all right putty soon."

"Nevah you min'," said Patsy with a choke in his voice. "I can do somep'n', an' we'll have anothah doctah."

DIALOGUE A *dialogue* is a conversation between characters. In poems, novels, and short stories, dialogue is usually set off by quotation marks to indicate a speaker's exact words. In a play, dialogue follows the names of the characters, and no quotation marks are used. The following example is from *A Walk in the Woods,* on page 773.

HONEYMAN.   I don't understand. You liked it?
BOTVINNIK.   Very much.
HONEYMAN.   Then why did you delay so long?
BOTVINNIK.   Because your proposal was . . . too good.

See *Drama.*

DRAMA A *drama* is a story written to be performed. Although a drama is meant to be performed, one can also read the *script,* or written version, and imagine the action. The script of a drama is made up of dialogue and stage directions. The *dialogue* is the words spoken by the actors. The *stage directions,* usually printed in italics, tell how the actors should look, move, and speak. They also describe the setting, sound effects, and lighting.

Dramas are often divided into parts called *acts.* The acts are often divided into smaller parts called *scenes.*

DYNAMIC CHARACTER See *Character.*

ESSAY An *essay* is a short nonfiction work about a particular subject. Most essays have a single major focus and a clear introduction, body, and conclusion.

There are many types of essays. A *narrative essay,* like "Debbie," on page 670, tells a true story about real people. An *expository essay,* like "Netiquette," on page 678, presents information, discusses ideas, or explains a process. A *persuasive essay,* like "The Trouble with Television," on page 686, presents and supports an opinion with strong arguments, or reasons. A *descriptive essay,* such as "Forest Fire," on page 675, describes events and feelings by including images and details. A *reflective essay,* like "Animal Craftsmen," on page 625, communicates a writer's thoughts about a topic of personal interest.

See *Description, Exposition, Narration,* and *Persuasion.*

EXPOSITION *Exposition* is writing or speech that explains a process or presents information. This Literary Terms Handbook and the introductions to the selections in this text are both examples of exposition. In the plot of a story or drama, the exposition, or introduction, is the part of the work that introduces the characters, setting, and basic situation.

See *Plot.*

EXTENDED METAPHOR In an *extended metaphor,* as in a regular metaphor, a subject is spoken of, or written, as though it were something else. However, an extended metaphor differs from a regular metaphor in that several comparisons are made. In her poem "Mushrooms," on page 508, Sylvia Plath uses extended metaphors to creatively describe mushrooms.

See *Metaphor.*

FABLE A *fable* is a brief story or poem, usually with animal characters, that teaches a lesson, or moral. The moral is usually stated at the end of the fable.

The fable is an ancient literary form found in many cultures. The fables written by Aesop, a Greek slave who lived in the sixth century B.C., are still popular with children today. Many familiar expressions, such as "crying wolf," "sour grapes," and "crying over spilt milk," come from Aesop's fables.

See *Moral.*

FANTASY A *fantasy* is highly imaginative writing that contains elements not found in real life. Examples of fantasy include stories that involve supernatural elements, stories that resemble fairy tales, stories that deal with imaginary places and creatures, and science-fiction stories.

See *Science Fiction.*

FICTION *Fiction* is prose writing that tells about imaginary characters and events. Short stories and novels are works of fiction. Some writers base their fiction on actual events and people, adding invented characters, dialogue, settings, and plots. Other writers of fiction rely on imagination alone to provide their materials.

See *Narration, Nonfiction,* and *Prose.*

FIGURATIVE LANGUAGE *Figurative language* is writing or speech that is not meant to be taken literally. The many types of figurative language are known as *figures of speech.* Common figures of speech include metaphor, simile, and personification. Writers use figurative language to state ideas in vivid and imaginative ways.

See *Metaphor, Personification, Simile,* and *Symbol.*

FIGURE OF SPEECH See *Figurative Language.*

FLASHBACK A *flashback* is a scene within a story that interrupts the sequence of events to relate events that occurred in the past. "Christmas Day in the Morning," on page 64, contains flashback.

FLAT CHARACTER See *Character.*

FOLK TALE A *folk tale* is a story composed orally and then passed from person to person by word of mouth. Most folk tales are highly entertaining, with plots featuring heroes, adventure, magic, or romance. The folk tales in this text tell of legendary heroes such as Pecos Bill, Paul Bunyan, and Davy Crockett.

See *Fable, Legend, Myth,* and *Oral Tradition.*

FORESHADOWING *Foreshadowing* is the author's use of clues to hint at what might happen later in the story. Writers use foreshadowing to build their readers' expectations and to create suspense. In "Flowers for Algernon," on page 204, the death of Algernon foreshadows Charlie's fate.

FREE VERSE *Free verse* is poetry not written in a regular rhythmical pattern, or meter. Free verse poems may contain lines of any length or with any number of stresses, or beats. Julio Noboa Polanco's "Identity," on page 838, is an example of free verse.

See *Meter.*

GENRE A *genre* is a division or type of literature. Literature is commonly divided into three major genres: poetry, prose, and drama. Each major genre is in turn divided into lesser genres, as follows:

1. *Poetry:* lyric poetry, concrete poetry, dramatic poetry, narrative poetry, epic poetry
2. *Prose:* fiction (novels and short stories) and nonfiction (biography, autobiography, letters, essays, and reports)
3. *Drama:* serious drama and tragedy, comic drama, melodrama, and farce

See *Drama, Poetry,* and *Prose.*

HAIKU The *haiku* is a three-line Japanese verse form. The first and third lines of a haiku each have five syllables. The second line has seven syllables. A writer of haiku uses images to create a single, vivid picture, generally of a scene from nature. See the examples of haiku by Bashō and Moritake on page 837.

HERO/HEROINE A *hero* or *heroine* is a character whose actions are inspiring or noble. Often, heroes and heroines struggle mightily to overcome the obstacles and problems that stand in their way. Some examples of heroic characters are the title characters in "Paul Revere's Ride," "Barbara Frietchie," and "Elizabeth Blackwell." The most obvious examples of heroes and heroines are the larger-than-life characters in myths and legends, like John Henry and Pecos Bill.

The term *heroes* was originally used only for male characters, while heroic female characters were always called *heroines.* However, it is now acceptable to use the word *hero* to refer to females as well as to males.

HUBRIS *Hubris* is excessive pride, and it is often the downfall of literary characters.

IAMB See *Meter.*

IMAGE An *image* is a word or a phrase that appeals to one or more of the five senses. Writers use images to describe how their subjects look, sound, feel, taste, and smell. "This We Know," on page 196, includes images that appeal to the senses of sight, sound, and smell.

IRONY *Irony* is the general name given to literary techniques that involve surprising, interesting, or amusing contradictions. In *verbal irony,* words are used to suggest the opposite of their usual meanings. In *dramatic irony,* there is a contradiction between what a character thinks and what the reader or audience knows to be true. In *irony of situation,* an event occurs that directly contradicts the expectations of the characters, the reader, or the audience. For example, in "A Retrieved Reformation," on page 252, Jimmy Valentine has to resume safecracking in order to earn the respect of a policeman.

LEGEND A *legend* is a widely told story about the past, one that may or may not have a foundation in fact. Every culture has its own legends—its familiar, traditional stories. "The Girl Who Hunted Rabbits," on page 49, is a legend that originated with the Zuñi culture.

See *Oral Tradition.*

LYRIC POEM A *lyric poem* is a short, highly musical poem that expresses the observations and feelings of a single speaker. "Harlem Night Song," on page 828, is an example of a lyric poem.

MAIN CHARACTER See *Character.*

MEMOIR A *memoir* is a form of autobiographical writing that deals with the writer's memory of someone or of a significant event. Often, the writing is very personal, as in the excerpt from *I Know Why the Caged Bird Sings,* on page 24.

See *Autobiography.*

METAPHOR A *metaphor* is a figure of speech in which something is described as though it were something else. A metaphor, like a simile, works by pointing out a similarity between two unlike things. For example, in Robert Frost's "The Road Not Taken," on page 34, the diverging roads are a metaphor for the major choices that people must make in their lives.

See *Extended Metaphor* and *Simile.*

METER The *meter* of a poem is its rhythmical pattern. This pattern is determined by the number of stresses, or beats, in each line. To describe the meter of a poem, you must *scan* its lines. *Scanning* involves marking the stressed and unstressed syllables, as follows:

Most | friendship is | feigning, most | loving mere | folly

Each stress is marked with a slanted line (´) and each unstressed syllable with a horseshoe symbol (˘). The stressed and unstressed syllables are then divided by vertical lines (|) into groups called feet. The following types of feet are common in English poetry:

1. *Iamb:* a foot with one unstressed syllable followed by one stressed syllable, as in the word "begin"
2. *Trochee:* a foot with one stressed syllable followed by one unstressed syllable, as in the word "people"
3. *Anapest:* a foot with two unstressed syllables followed by one stressed syllable, as in the phrase "on the sea"
4. *Dactyl:* a foot with one stressed syllable followed by two unstressed syllables, as in the word "happiness"
5. *Spondee:* a foot with two stressed syllables, as in the word "downtown"

Depending on the type of foot that is most common in them, lines of poetry are described as *iambic, trochaic, anapestic,* or *dactylic.*

Lines are also described in terms of the number of feet that occur in them, as follows:

1. *Monometer:* verse written in one-foot lines:
   First Man,
   behold:
   　　　　　—N. Scott Momaday, "New World"

2. *Dimeter:* verse written in two-foot lines:
   The days | are short
   　The sun | a spark
   Hung thin | between
   　The dark | and dark.
   　　　　　—John Updike, "January"

3. *Trimeter:* verse written in three-foot lines:
   My mother | taught me | purple
   　Although | she never | wore it
   　　　　　—Evelyn Tooley Hunt, "Taught Me Purple"

4. *Tetrameter:* verse written in four-foot lines:
   O Captain! | My Captain! | our fearful trip | is done,
   The ship has weathered | every rack, | the prize we sought | is won,
   　　　　　—Walt Whitman, "O Captain! My Captain!"

5. *Pentameter:* verse written in five-foot lines:
   All things | within | this fad | ing world | hath end,
   Adver | sity | doth still | our joys | attend;
   No ties | so strong, | no friends | so dear | and sweet,
   But with | death's part | ing blow | is sure | to meet.
   　　　　　—Anne Bradstreet,
   　　"Before the Birth of One of Her Children"

A six-foot line is called a *hexameter.* A seven-foot line is called a *heptameter.* A complete description of the meter of a line tells the kinds of feet each line contains, as well as how many feet of each kind. Thus, the lines from Anne Bradstreet's poem would be described as *iambic pentameter. Blank verse* is poetry written in unrhymed iambic pentameter. Poetry that does not have a regular meter is called *free verse.*

See *Blank Verse* and *Free Verse.*

MINOR CHARACTER See *Character.*

MOOD *Mood,* or *atmosphere,* is the feeling created in

the reader by a literary work or passage. Writers use many devices to create mood, including images, dialogue, setting, and plot. Often, a writer creates a mood at the beginning of a work and then sustains this mood throughout. Sometimes, however, the mood of the work changes dramatically. For example, the mood of "The Finish of Patsy Barnes," on page 580, changes from one of tension and despair to one of success and hope as Patsy wins the race and then finds a caring doctor for his mother.

MORAL A *moral* is a lesson taught by a literary work. A fable usually ends with a moral that is directly stated. For example, the concluding words of "Brer Possum's Dilemma" are, "And when you're mindin' your own business and you spot trouble, don't never trouble trouble 'til trouble troubles you." A poem, novel, short story, or essay often suggests a moral that is not directly stated. The moral must be drawn by the reader, based on other elements in the work.

See *Fable*.

MOTIVATION A *motivation* is a reason that explains, or partially explains, a character's thoughts, feelings, actions, or speech. Writers try to make their characters' motivations, or motives, as clear as possible. If the motives of a main character are not clear, then the character will not be believable.

Characters are often motivated by needs, such as food and shelter. They are also motivated by feelings, such as fear, love, and pride. For example, in "The Adventure of the Speckled Band," on page 474, fear motivates Miss Stoner to seek the help of Sherlock Holmes.

MYTH A *myth* is a fictional tale that explains the actions of gods or heroes or the origins of elements of nature. Myths are part of the oral tradition. They are composed orally and then passed from generation to generation by word of mouth. Every ancient culture has its own mythology, or collection of myths. The Zuñi myth "Coyote Steals the Sun and Moon," on page 902, explains the origins of winter and gives insight into Zuñi beliefs.

See *Oral Tradition*.

NARRATION *Narration* is writing that tells a story. The act of telling a story is also called narration. Fictional works, such as novels and short stories, are examples of *narration*, as are poems that tell stories, such as "Elizabeth Blackwell," on page 314. Narration can also be found in many kinds of nonfiction, including autobiographies, biographies, and newspaper reports. A story told in fiction, nonfiction, poetry, or even in drama is called a narrative.

See *Narrative Poem* and *Narrator*.

NARRATIVE See *Narration*.

NARRATIVE POEM A *narrative poem* is a story told in verse. Narrative poems often have all the elements of short stories, including characters, conflict, and plot. An example of a narrative poem is John Greenleaf Whittier's "Barbara Frietchie," on page 311.

NARRATOR A *narrator* is a speaker or character who tells a story. A *third-person narrator* is one who stands outside the action and speaks about it. A *first-person narrator* is one who tells a story and participates in its action.

In some dramas, there is a separate character called "The Narrator" who introduces, comments on, and concludes the play.

See *Point of View*.

NONFICTION *Nonfiction* is prose writing that presents and explains ideas or that tells about real people, places, objects, or events. Autobiographies, biographies, essays, reports, letters, memos, and newspaper articles are all types of nonfiction.

See *Fiction*.

NOVEL A *novel* is a long work of fiction. Novels contain such elements as characters, plot, conflict, and setting. The writer of novels, or novelist, develops these elements in the story. A novel may have several themes, and in addition to its main plot, a novel may contain one or more subplots, or independent, related stories.

See *Fiction*.

ONOMATOPOEIA *Onomatopoeia* is the use of words that imitate sounds. *Crash, buzz, screech, hiss, neigh, jingle,* and *cluck* are examples of onomatopoeia. In the following line from Bashō's "The falling flower," on page 837, the word *screech* is an example of onomatopoeia: "A night-heron's screech."

ORAL TRADITION *Oral tradition* is the passing of songs, stories, and poems from generation to generation by word of mouth. Folk songs, folk tales, legends, and myths all come from the oral tradition. No one knows who first created these stories and poems. In the selection from "The People, Yes," on page 347, Carl Sandburg pulls together stories from the oral tradition.

See *Folk Tale, Legend,* and *Myth*.

PERSONIFICATION *Personification* is a type of figurative language in which a nonhuman subject is given human characteristics. In "Incident in a Rose Garden," on page 878, Donald Justice personifies death as a walking, talking, questioning being.

PERSUASION *Persuasion* is used in writing or in speech that attempts to convince the reader or listener to adopt a particular opinion or course of action. Newspaper editorials and letters to the editor use persuasion. So do advertisements and campaign speeches given by political candidates. Robert MacNeil's essay "The Trouble with Television," on page 686, is an example of a persuasive essay.

PLOT *Plot* is the sequence of events in which each event results from a previous one and causes the next. In most novels, dramas, short stories, and narrative poems, the plot involves both characters and a central conflict. The plot usually begins with an *exposition* that introduces the setting, the characters, and the basic situation. This is followed by the *rising action,* in which the central conflict is introduced and developed. The conflict then increases until it reaches a high point of interest or suspense, the *climax.* The climax is followed by the *falling action,* or end, of the central conflict. Any events that occur during the falling action make up the *resolution.*

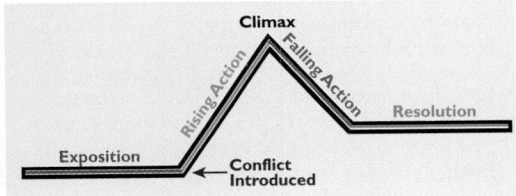

Some plots do not contain all of these elements. For example, some stories begin in the midst of a conflict and end with the resolution.

See *Conflict.*

POETRY *Poetry* is one of the three major types of literature, the others being prose and drama. Defining poetry more precisely isn't easy, for there is no single, unique characteristic that all poems share. Poems are often divided into lines and stanzas and often employ regular rhythmical patterns, or meters. However, some poems are written out just like prose, and some are written in free verse. Most poems make use of highly concise, musical, and emotionally charged language. Many also make use of imagery, figurative language, and special devices of sound such as rhyme.

Major types of poetry include *lyric poetry, narrative poetry,* and *concrete poetry.*

Other forms of poetry include *dramatic poetry,* in which characters speak in their own voices, and *epic poetry,* in which the poet tells a long, involved tale about gods or heroes.

See *Concrete Poem, Genre, Lyric Poem,* and *Narrative Poem.*

POINT OF VIEW *Point of view* is the perspective, or vantage point, from which a story is told. Three commonly used points of view are first person, omniscient third person, and limited third person.

First-person point of view is told by a character who uses the first-person pronoun "I." "Flowers for Algernon," on page 204, is told in the first person by the subject of the experiment.

"Charles," on page 14, is told from the *third-person limited point of view*—the point of view of the main character's mother. The narrator uses third-person pronouns such as "he" and "she" to refer to the characters.

In stories told from the *omniscient third-person point of view,* the narrator knows and tells about what each character feels and thinks. Jack London's "Up the Slide," on page 154, is written from the omniscient third-person point of view.

See *Narrator.*

PROSE *Prose* is the ordinary form of written language. Most writing that is not poetry, drama, or song is considered prose. Prose is one of the major genres of literature and occurs in two forms, fiction and nonfiction.

See *Fiction, Genre,* and *Nonfiction.*

PROTAGONIST The *protagonist* is the main character in a literary work. In "A Ribbon for Baldy," on page 410, the protagonist, or main character, is the boy who plants the corn and has the best science project.

See *Antagonist* and *Character.*

REFRAIN A *refrain* is a regularly repeated line or group of lines in a poem or a song. In the following passage from "Columbus," on page 144, the refrain has been italicized:

> Brave Adm'r'l, say but one good word:
> What shall we do when hope is gone?
> The words leapt like a leaping sword:
> *"Sail on! sail on! sail on! and on!"*

REPETITION *Repetition* is the use, more than once, of any element of language—a sound, word, phrase, clause, or sentence. Repetition is used in both prose and poetry. In prose fiction, a plot may be repeated, with variations, in a subplot; or a minor character may be similar to a major character in important ways. In poetry, repetition often involves the recurring use of certain words, images, structures, and devices. *Rhyme, alliteration,* and *rhythm* are all repetitions of sounds or sound patterns. A *refrain* is a repeated line or group of lines.

See *Alliteration, Meter, Plot, Rhyme,* and *Rhyme Scheme.*

RESOLUTION See *Plot.*

RHYME *Rhyme* is the repetition of sounds at the ends

of words. Poets use rhyme to lend a songlike quality to their verses and to emphasize certain words and ideas. Many traditional-style poems contain *end rhymes,* or rhyming words at the ends of lines. Alfred, Lord Tennyson, uses end rhyme in "Ring Out, Wild Bells," on page 92:

> Ring out, wild bells, to the wild *sky,*
>> The flying cloud, the frosty *light:*
>> The year is dying in the *night;*
> Ring out, wild bells, and let him *die.*

Another common device is the use of *internal rhymes,* or rhyming words within lines. Notice, for example, the internal rhymes in this passage of "Annabel Lee," by Edgar Allan Poe: "For the moon never *beams* without bringing me *dreams* / Of the beautiful Annabel Lee."
See *Rhyme Scheme.*

RHYME SCHEME A *rhyme scheme* is a regular pattern of rhyming words in a poem. The rhyme scheme of a poem is indicated by lowercase letters. Each rhyme is assigned a different letter, as follows, in the poem "Dark Hills," by Edwin Arlington Robinson:

Dark hills at evening in the west,	*a*
Where sunset hovers like a sound	*b*
Of golden horns that sang to rest	*a*
Old bones of warriors under ground,	*b*
Far now from all the bannered ways	*c*
Where flash the legions of the sun,	*d*
You fade—as if the last of days	*c*
Were fading, and all wars were done.	*d*

Thus, this poem has the rhyme scheme *ababcdcd.*

RHYTHM *Rhythm* is the pattern of beats, or stresses, in spoken or written language.
See *Meter.*

ROUND CHARACTER See *Character.*

SCIENCE FICTION *Science fiction* combines elements of fiction and fantasy with scientific fact. This type of writing is most effective when the writer creates a believable setting and characters, and balances new ideas with familiar details. "The Secret," on page 122, is a science-fiction story with elements that are "possible" and "impossible." Many science-fiction stories are set in the future.

SENSORY LANGUAGE *Sensory language* is writing or speech that appeals to one or more of the five senses.
See *Image.*

SETTING The *setting* of a literary work is the time and place of the action. The setting includes *all* the details of a place and time—the year, the time of day, even the weather. The place may be a specific country, state, region, community, neighborhood, building, institution, or home. Details such as dialect, clothing, customs, and modes of transportation are often used to establish setting.

In most stories, the setting serves as a backdrop—a context in which the characters interact. The setting of Ray Bradbury's "The Drummer Boy of Shiloh," on page 5, is an April night in 1862 during the Civil War, at a place named Shiloh near the Tennessee River, close to a church.

The setting of a story often helps to create a particular mood, or feeling. The mood of Ray Bradbury's story is one of nervous expectation—of fear mingled with resolve.
See *Mood.*

SHORT STORY A *short story* is a brief work of fiction. Like a novel, a short story presents a sequence of events, or plot. The plot usually deals with a central conflict faced by a main character, or protagonist. Like a lyric poem, a short story is concise and creates a single effect, or dominant impression, on its reader. The events in a short story usually communicate a message about life or human nature. This message, or central idea, is the story's theme.
See *Conflict, Plot,* and *Theme.*

SIMILE A *simile* is a figure of speech that uses *like* or *as* to make a direct comparison between two unlike ideas. Everyday speech often contains similes, such as "pale as a ghost," "good as gold," "spread like wildfire," and "clever as a fox."

Writers use similes to describe people, places, and things vividly. Poets, especially, create similes to point out new and interesting ways of viewing the world. José García Villa's poem "Lyric 17," on page 867, contains several similes to describe poetry, such as "musical as a sea-gull," "slender as a bell," and "it must kneel like a rose."

SOLILOQUY A soliloquy is a long speech in a play or in a prose work made by a character who is alone. The character reveals his or her private thoughts and feelings to the audience or reader. In William Shakespeare's *Much Ado About Nothing,* Act II, scene iii, on page 790, Benedick speaks a soliloquy.

SPEAKER The *speaker* is the imaginary voice assumed by the writer of a poem. In other words, the speaker is the character who tells the poem. This character, or voice, is often not identified by name. In Robert Frost's poem "The Road Not Taken," on page 34, the speaker is contemplative, and even a bit sad, as he tells the poem.
See *Narrator.*

STAGE DIRECTIONS *Stage directions* are notes included in a drama to describe how the work is to be performed or staged. Stage directions are usually printed in italics and enclosed within parentheses or brackets. Some stage directions describe the movements and costumes, as well as the emotional states and ways of speaking of the characters. The following lines are from *The Diary of Anne Frank*:

ANNE. [*Screaming*] No! No! Don't . . . don't take me!
[*She moans, tossing and crying in her sleep. The other people wake, terrified.* DUSSEL *sits up in bed, furious.*]
DUSSEL. Shush! Anne! Shush!

See *Drama*.

STANZA A *stanza* is a formal division of lines in a poem, considered as a unit. Many poems are divided into stanzas that are separated by spaces. Stanzas often function just like paragraphs in prose. Each stanza states and develops a single main idea.

Stanzas are commonly named according to the number of lines found in them, as follows:

1. *Couplet:* two-line stanza
2. *Tercet:* three-line stanza
3. *Quatrain:* four-line stanza
4. *Cinquain:* five-line stanza
5. *Sestet:* six-line stanza
6. *Heptastich:* seven-line stanza
7. *Octave:* eight-line stanza

Evelyn Tooley Hunt's "Taught Me Purple" is written in quatrains:

My mother taught me purple
   Although she never wore it.
Wash-gray was her circle,
   The tenement her orbit.

Division into stanzas is common in traditional poetry and is often accompanied by rhyme. Notice, for example, that in the stanza above from "Taught Me Purple," the first and third lines and the second and fourth lines rhyme. That is, it follows the rhyme scheme *abab*. The remaining stanzas of the poem also have the rhyme scheme *abab*. However, some rhyming poems are not divided into stanzas, and some poems divided into stanzas do not contain rhyme.

STATIC CHARACTER See *Character*.

SURPRISE ENDING A *surprise ending* is a conclusion that is unexpected. Sometimes a surprise ending follows a false resolution. The reader thinks that the conflict has already been resolved but then is confronted with a new twist that changes the outcome of the plot. Often a surprise ending is *foreshadowed*, or subtly hinted at, in the course of the work. O. Henry's "A Retrieved Reformation," on page 252, contains a surprise ending for both the reader and the main character.

See *Foreshadowing* and *Plot*.

SUSPENSE *Suspense* is a feeling of anxious uncertainty about the outcome of events in a literary work. Writers create suspense by raising questions in the minds of their readers. For example, in "The Tell-Tale Heart," on page 542, Edgar Allan Poe uses the intensity of the narrator to create suspense.

SYMBOL A *symbol* is anything that stands for or represents something else. Symbols are common in everyday life. A dove with an olive branch in its beak is a symbol of peace, and a blindfolded woman holding a balanced scale is a symbol of justice.

TALL TALE Most *tall tales* come out of the oral tradition of the American frontier. They typically involve characters with highly exaggerated abilities and qualities. "Paul Bunyan of the North Woods," on page 944, and "Pecos Bill: The Cyclone," on page 946, are both examples of tall tales.

See *Legend, Myth,* and *Oral Tradition*.

THEME The *theme* of a literary work is its central message, concern, or purpose. A theme can usually be expressed as a generalization, or general statement, about people or life.

The theme may be stated directly by the writer, although it is more often presented indirectly. When the theme is stated indirectly, the reader must figure out the theme by looking carefully at what the work reveals about people or about life.

TONE The *tone* is the writer's attitude toward the readers and toward the subject, conveyed by the language and rhythm of the speaker. For example, the tone of Edgar Allan Poe's "The Tell-Tale Heart," on page 542, is frantic and sinister. In contrast, the tone of John Updike's poem "January," on page 836, is light and humorous.

See *Mood*.

*W*RITING *H*ANDBOOK

THE WRITING PROCESS

The writing process can be roughly divided into a series of stages: prewriting, drafting, revising, editing, proofreading, and publishing. It is important to remember that the writing process is one that moves backward as well as forward. Even while you are moving forward in the creation of your composition, you may still return to a previous stage—to rethink or to rewrite.

Following are stages of the writing process, with key points to address during each stage.

Prewriting

In this stage, you plan out the work to be done. You prepare to write by exploring ideas, gathering information, and working out an organization plan. Following are the key steps to take at this stage:

Step 1: Analyze the writing situation. Before writing, analyze or study the parts of the writing assignment. To do this, ask yourself the following questions:

- *Topic (the subject you will be writing about):* What will you write about? Can you state your subject in a sentence? Is your subject too broad or too narrow?
- *Purpose (what you want your writing to accomplish):* Do you want your writing to explain? To describe? To persuade? To tell a story? To entertain? What do you want your audience to learn or to understand?
- *Audience (the people who will read or listen to your writing):* Who is your audience? What might they already know about your subject? What basic facts will you have to provide for them?

Step 2: Gather ideas and information. After thinking about the writing situation, you may find that you need more information. If so, you must decide how to gather this information. On the other hand, you may find that you already have too much information—that your topic is too broad. If this is the case, then you must decide how to narrow your topic. If you have the right amount of information but don't know how to present it clearly, you will have to choose a way to organize your information.

There are many ways to gather information, to narrow a topic, and to organize ideas. Following are some ways:

- *Brainstorm:* Discuss the topic with a group of people. Try to generate as many ideas as possible. Not all of your ideas will be useful or suitable. You'll need to evaluate them later.
- *Consult other people about your topic:* Speaking with others may suggest an idea or approach you did not think about.
- *Make a list of questions about your topic:* Begin your

questions with words like *who, what, where, when, why,* and *how.* Then, find answers to your questions.
- *Do research:* Your topic may require you to go to other sources to find information. Read relevant books, pamphlets, newspapers, magazines, and reference works.

Step 3: Organize your notes. Once you have gathered enough information, organize it. Sort your ideas and notes; decide which points are most important. You can make an outline to show the order of ideas, or you can use some other organizing plan.

There are many ways to organize and develop your material. Careful organization will make your writing easy to read and understand. The following are common methods of organizing information:

- *Time Order or Chronological Order:* Events are organized in order of occurrence (from earliest to latest, for example).
- *Spatial Order:* Details are organized by position in space (from left to right, for example).
- *Degree Order:* This order is organization by size, amount, or intensity (from coldest to warmest, for example).
- *Priority Order:* This is organization by importance, value, usefulness, or familiarity (from worst to best, for example).

Drafting

Drafting follows prewriting and is the second stage in the writing process. Working from your prewriting notes and your outline or plan, you develop and present your ideas in sentences and paragraphs. The following are important points to remember about drafting:

- Write your rough draft in whichever way works best for you. Some writers like to develop each paragraph carefully and thoughtfully, writing very slowly, correcting and polishing as they write. Others prefer to write their rough drafts very quickly—putting down all their ideas without stopping to evaluate them.
- Do not try to make your rough draft perfect. Concentrate on getting your ideas on paper. Once this is done, you can make improvements in the revision and proofreading stages.
- Keep your audience and purpose in mind as you write. This will help you determine what you say and how you say it.
- Don't be afraid to set aside earlier ideas if later ones work better. Some of the best ideas are those that were not planned at the beginning. After you have written one draft, you might review it and realize that

you need to add more information, to change your purpose, or to narrow your focus.

Most papers, regardless of the topic, are developed with an introduction, a body, and a conclusion. Here are tips for developing these parts of a paper:

Introduction In the introduction to a paper, you want to engage your readers' attention and let them know the purpose of your paper. You may use the following strategies in your introduction:

- State your main idea.
- Take a stand.
- Use an anecdote.
- Quote someone.
- Startle your readers.

Body of the paper In the body of your paper, you present your information and make your points. Your organization is an important factor in leading readers through your ideas. Your elaboration on your main ideas is also important. Elaboration is the development of ideas to make your written work precise and complete. You can use the following to elaborate your main ideas:

- Facts and statistics
- Anecdotes
- Sensory details
- Examples
- Explanation and definition
- Quotations

Conclusion The ending of your paper is the final impression you leave with your readers. It should give readers the sense that you have pulled everything together. Following are some effective ways to end your paper:

- Summarize and restate.
- Ask a question.
- State an opinion.
- Call for action.
- Tell an anecdote.

Revising

Once you have a draft, you can look at it critically or have others review it. This is the time to make changes on many levels. Revising is the process of reworking what you have written to make it as good as it can be. You may change some details so that your ideas flow smoothly and are clearly supported. You may discover that some details don't work, and you'll need to discard them. Two strategies may help you start the revising process:

- Read your work aloud. This is an excellent way to catch any ideas or details that have been left out and to notice errors in logic.
- Ask someone else to read your work. Choose someone who can point out how to improve it.

How do you know what to look for and what to change? Here is a checklist of major writing issues. If the answer to any of these questions is no, then that is an area that needs revision.

1. Does the writing achieve my purpose?
2. Does the paper have unity—a single focus, with all details and information contributing to that focus?
3. Is the arrangement of information clear and logical?
4. Have I elaborated enough to give my audience adequate information?

Editing

When you edit, you refine your language to express your ideas in the most effective way possible.

- Replace dull language with vivid, precise words.
- Cut or change unnecessary repetition.
- Cut empty words and phrases, (those that do not add anything to the writing).
- Check passive voice; active voice is more effective.
- Replace wordy expressions with shorter, more precise ones.

Proofreading

When you have completed your final draft, proofread it to make it accurate for the reader. You may do this on your own or with the help of a partner. Refer to a dictionary, writing textbook, or style handbook as necessary.

- Correct errors in grammar and usage.
- Correct errors in punctuation and capitalization.
- Correct errors in spelling.

Publishing and Presenting

These are some of the many ways in which you can share your work:

- Share your writing in a small group by reading it aloud or by passing it around for others to read.
- Read your work aloud to the class.
- Display your work on a classroom bulletin board.
- Save your writing in a folder for later publication. At the end of the year, choose the best pieces from your folder and bind them together. Share the collection with your relatives and friends.
- Submit your writing to the school literary magazine, or start a literary magazine for your school or class.
- Submit your writing to your school or community newspaper.
- Enter your writing in literary contests for student writers.
- Submit your writing to a magazine that publishes work by young people.

THE MODES OF WRITING

Expression

Expression is any writing that conveys your personal thoughts, feelings, or experiences. Some expressive writing is private, written only for you to read. Some is written to be shared with an audience—friends, family, or other interested readers. Through expressive writing, you can capture on paper what is most meaningful to you. Expressive writing takes many forms. Here are a few of them:

Anecdote An anecdote is a brief, entertaining account of one specific, true event. Most anecdotes contain an observation about life or human nature, often in a humorous way.

Personal Journal A journal, or diary, is a record of a

person's experiences and feelings over a period of time. Most personal journals are kept private because they are very personal, although some journals have been published to be read by the public.

Personal Letter Writing a personal letter is a good way to reveal your thoughts, attitudes, opinions, and experiences about many different subjects.

Personal Memoir In a memoir, you write about significant events from your past, including your thoughts and experiences about those experiences. A memoir can be brief and focus on a single event or it can describe a larger part of your life.

Description

Description is writing that creates a vivid picture for readers, draws readers into a scene, and makes readers feel as if they are meeting a character or experiencing an event firsthand. A description may stand on its own or be part of a longer work, such as a short story.

When you write a description, bring it to life with sensory details that tell you how your subject looks, smells, sounds, tastes, or feels. You'll want to choose your details carefully so that you create a single main impression of your subject. Here are a few types of description:

Remembrance When you write a remembrance, you use vivid, descriptive details to convey your impressions of people or places from your past. When writing a remembrance of a person, include details that capture both the person's personality and physical appearance.

Observation In an observation, you describe an event or occurrence that you have witnessed firsthand, often over an extended period of time. An observation may focus on an aspect of daily life or on a scientific phenomenon, such as a storm or a change of season.

Travelogue A travelogue is descriptive writing that takes the reader to the place being described. It is a record of a writer's journey. Travelogues often include information about a locale's climate, geography, foods, and tourist attractions, as well as your experiences.

Narration

Whenever writers tell any type of story, they are using *narration.* While there are many kinds of narration, most narratives share certain elements—characters, a setting, a sequence of events (or plot, in fiction), and, often, a theme. You might be asked to write one of these types of narration:

Personal Narrative A personal narrative is a story based on the writer's real-life experiences. In a personal narrative, past events are brought to life through dialogue, action, and description. The first-person point of view is used to tell a personal narrative.

Autobiographical Incident An autobiographical incident tells a true story about a specific event in the writer's life. It contains characters, a plot, and a theme, but it reveals more about the writer than it does about the other characters.

Firsthand Biography In a firsthand biography, you tell about the entire life, or a period in the life, of a person whom you know or knew personally. In firsthand biography, the writer usually plays a part, but he or she is not the main character. The writer's firsthand knowledge of the subject gives the reader an unusual perspective on the subject.

Short Story A short story is a brief fictional narrative with a beginning, in which we meet the characters; a middle, in which problems arise between characters; and an end, in which the problems are resolved. A short story usually has a theme, or message, to convey to the reader. In a short story, dialogue reveals the thoughts and feelings of the characters. Details help the reader understand the world in which the story takes place.

Exposition: Giving Information

Exposition to give information is writing that informs or explains. In this type of writing, include factual information to clarify or explain your topic. Here are some examples of exposition that give information:

Classification Classification is writing that puts a subject into a category or a class. Classification is used when you explain several parts of a single subject. In classification, you organize your information by grouping facts and examples into categories and then showing the similarities and/or differences among the various categories. For example, to classify types of motorcycles, break the topic down into categories of dirt bikes, street bikes, and a combination of dirt and street bikes.

Summary To write a summary of a true or fictional event, include the main characters in the event, the time period, and present the most important details as factually as possible. Avoid giving personal opinions and observations about the events.

How-to Composition A how-to composition, or a set of instructions, tells the reader how to do or to make something. In writing how-to instructions, it is important to anticipate and answer questions the reader may have about why a particular procedure or direction is included.

Exposition: Making Connections

Exposition can *make connections* for readers by comparing and contrasting two subjects, by examining a problem and its solution, or by connecting information to an opinion about something. Here are some types of exposition that makes connections:

Comparison-and-Contrast Essay A comparison-and-contrast essay explores the similarities and differences between two or more people, places, events, or ideas. When writing this type of essay, organize your point of comparison subject by subject or point by point.

Problem-and-Solution Essay A problem-and-solution essay focuses on a problem and offers one or more possible solutions to it. The solutions presented should be supported by facts and examples. When writing a problem-and-solution essay, first identify the problem. Then, present all possible solutions by describing the steps necessary to achieve the goal.

Persuasion

Persuasion is writing or speaking that attempts to convince people to agree with you about something or to urge them to take a certain kind of action. When used effectively, persuasive writing has the power to change people's lives. As a reader and a writer, you will find yourself engaged in many forms of persuasion. Here are a few:

Letter to the Editor A letter to the editor is a reader's response to an article or an editorial in a newspaper or magazine. When writing a letter to an editor, present clear, organized reasons to support your opinion.

Advertisement An advertisement tries to persuade people to buy something, accept an idea, vote for a candidate, or support a cause. When you write an advertisement, present your information in an appealing way to make your product or service seem desirable.

Persuasive Essay A persuasive essay is a short piece of writing that aims to convince an audience to take action or to accept a position on an issue. In writing a persuasive essay, you build an argument and support your opinions with a variety of evidence: facts, statistics, examples, and statements from experts. You also anticipate and develop counter-arguments to opposing opinions.

Persuasive Speech A persuasive speech is a persuasive essay that's presented orally instead of in writing. As a persuasive speaker, address the audience directly and with enthusiasm, use vivid language, repeat key points, and include facts and statistics to support your argument.

Reports

A *report* is any writing based on outside research. People write reports to present information and ideas, to share findings and research, and to explain subjects they have studied. To write reports, you will have to research, organize, and present information. The following are some types of reports:

Biographical Report A biographical report gives information about a person's life and achievements. When you write a biographical report, include the dates and details of the main events in the person's life, presenting the information in chronological order beginning with childhood.

I-Search Report An I-search report is a personal, in-depth exploration of a topic that especially interests you. In the report, you tell how you became interested in the topic, how you explored it, and what you learned.

Library Research Report A library research report can be about any topic for which information can be researched in the library. When you write a library research report, you put together information from books and other sources. You must credit source materials and authors in footnotes and bibliographies.

Creative Writing

Creative writing blends imagination, experience, ideas, and emotions. It allows you to present your own unique view of the world. Poems, plays, short stories, and dramas are examples of creative writing. Following are some types of creative writing:

Poem Writing a poem is a way to express thoughts and feelings about a subject. In writing poems, use figurative language and sensory images to create a strong impact. Also, consider using rhyme, rhythm, and repetition within your poem to create a musical quality.

Monologue A monologue is a dramatic speech written to be spoken by a single character to another character or directly to an audience. In writing a monologue, choose a subject and write the details from the point of view of your subject or from your own point of view.

Dialogue A dialogue is a conversation between characters in a drama. Use realistic language to develop characters, explain the setting, and advance the plot.

Short Video or Play Script A script for a video or stage play includes dialogue and stage directions. A video script also includes technical directions in capital letters for the camera person.

Response to Literature

In a *response to literature,* you express your thoughts and feelings about the work. Often, in so doing, you gain a better understanding of the work. Your response to literature can take many forms—oral or written, formal or informal. Following are a few examples:

Reader's Response Journal Entry Your reader's response journal is a record of your thoughts and feelings about works you have read. Use it to remind yourself of writers and works that you particularly liked or disliked or to provide a source of writing ideas.

Response to a Literary Work When you respond to a literary work, you analyze one or more of the following aspects: its theme, characters, setting, form, timeliness, and originality. Use details from the work in your response to support the point you make.

Critical Review When you write a review of a literary work, you offer an opinion of the work and give specific details and quotes from the book to support that opinion.

GRAMMAR AND MECHANICS HANDBOOK

Nouns A **noun** is the name of a person, place, or thing. A **common noun** names any one of a class of people, places, or things. A **proper noun** names a specific person, place, or thing.

Common Nouns	Proper Nouns
writer	Edgar Allan Poe
city	Fort Worth

Pronouns A **pronoun** is a word that stands for a noun or for a word that takes the place of a noun.

A **personal pronoun** refers to (1) the person speaking, (2) the person spoken to, or (3) the person, place, or thing spoken about.

	Singular	Plural
First Person	I, me, my, mine	we, us, our, ours
Second Person	you, your, yours	you, your, yours
Third Person	he, him, his, she, her, hers, it, its	they, them, their, theirs

He took them downstairs into the living room.
— "Christmas Day in the Morning," Buck, p. 68

A **demonstrative pronoun** directs attention to a specific person, place, or thing.

this lamp   *these* rugs   *that* chair   *those* tables

An **interrogative pronoun** is used to begin a question.

What did all of this mean to Andy?
— "Saving the Wetlands," Lewis, p. 280
Who is the author of "Space Oddity"?

An **indefinite pronoun** refers to a person, place, or thing, often without specifying which one.

Many of the students participated.
Everyone arrived early.

Verbs A **verb** is a word that expresses time while showing an action, a condition, or the fact that something exists.

An **action verb** indicates the action of someone or something.

I *loved* the old man.
— "The Tell-Tale Heart," Poe, p. 542

A **linking verb** connects the subject of a sentence with a noun or a pronoun that renames or describes the subject.

There *were* others who proffered assistance.
— "An Episode of War," Crane, p. 552

A **helping verb** can be added to another verb to make a single verb phrase.

They *had been* living in Dalesford for a year nearly, . . .
— "The Finish of Patsy Barnes," Dunbar, p. 581

Adjectives An **adjective** describes a noun or a pronoun or gives a noun or a pronoun a more specific meaning. Adjectives answer these questions:

What kind?	*big* cyclone, *pink* petunia
Which one?	*this* land, *those* people
How many?	*two* cats, *many* flies
How much?	*some* snow, *little* effort

The articles *the, a,* and *an* are adjectives. *An* is used before a word beginning with a vowel sound.

A noun may sometimes be used as an adjective.

family home   *science* fiction

Adverbs An **adverb** modifies a verb, an adjective, or another adverb. Adverbs answer the questions *where, when, in what way,* or *to what extent.*

He ran *outside.* (modifies verb *ran*)
She *never* wrote us. (modifies verb *wrote*)
Close the window *quickly.* (modifies verb *close*)
We were *very* sad. (modifies adjective *sad*)
They left *too* suddenly. (modifies adverb *suddenly*)

Prepositions A **preposition** relates a noun or a pronoun following it to another word in the sentence.

across the road	*near* the corner
except me	*during* the show
at school	*with* them

Conjunctions A **conjunction** connects other words or groups of words.

A **coordinating conjunction** connects similar kinds or groups of words.

lions *and* tigers   small *but* strong

Correlative conjunctions are used in pairs to connect similar words or groups of words.

both Jonah *and* Elias   *neither* they *nor* I

Interjections An **interjection** is a word that expresses feeling or emotion and functions independently of a sentence.

"*Oh, no!*" I whispered.
— "Medicine Bag," Sneve, p. 603

Sentences A **sentence** is a group of words with two main parts: a complete subject and a complete predicate. Together, these parts express a complete thought.

The rest of the story is a little embarrassing.
— "Animal Craftsmen," p. 627

A **fragment** is a group of words that does not contain a subject or a verb and does not express a complete thought.

With the others.
Left suddenly.

Subject-Verb Agreement To make a **subject** and a **verb agree,** make sure that both are singular or both are plural. Two or more singular subjects joined by *or* or *nor* must have a singular verb. When singular and plural subjects are joined by *or* or *nor,* the verb must agree with the closest subject.

He *is* at the door.
They *drive* home every day.
Jeff or *Sam is* absent.
Both *pets are* hungry.
Either the *chairs* or the *table is* on sale.
Neither the *tree* nor the *shrubs were* in bloom.

Phrases A **phrase** is a group of words, without a subject and a verb, that functions in a sentence as one part of speech.

A **prepositional phrase** is a group of words that includes a preposition and a noun or a pronoun that is the object of the preposition.

near the town   with them
inside our house   beneath the floor

An **adjective phrase** is a prepositional phrase that modifies a noun or a pronoun by telling *what kind* or *which one.*

The left arm *of your jacket* is spattered with mud. . . .
— The Adventure of the Speckled Band, Doyle, p. 475

An **adverb phrase** is a prepositional phrase that modifies a verb, an adjective, or an adverb by pointing out *where, when, in what way,* or *to what extent.*

The lady gave a violent start and stared in *bewilderment* at my companion.
— "The Adventure of the Speckled Band," Doyle, p. 475

An **appositive phrase** is a noun or a pronoun with modifiers that is placed next to a noun or a pronoun to add information and details.

When Dr. Roylott was in India he married my mother, *Mrs. Stoner, the young widow of Major-General Stoner,* of the Bengal Artillery.
— "The Adventure of the Speckled Band," Doyle, p. 476

A **participial phrase** is a participle with its modifiers and complements. The entire phrase acts as an adjective.

Turning his eyes from the hostile wood, he looked at the sword as he held it there. . . .
— "An Episode of War," Crane, p. 551

An **infinitive phrase** is an infinitive with modifiers, complements, or a subject, all acting together as a single part of speech.

I was about *to enter the store* when I realized I had left my briefcase behind.
— "The Day I Got Lost," Singer, p. 559

Clauses A **clause** is a group of words with a subject and verb.

An **independent clause** can stand by itself as a complete sentence.

A **subordinate clause** has a subject and a verb, but it cannot stand by itself as a complete sentence; it can only be part of a sentence.

An **adjective clause** is a subordinate clause that modifies a noun or a pronoun by telling *what kind* or *which one.*

He wore the look of one *who knows he is the victim of a terrible disease and understands his helplessness.*
— "An Episode of War," Crane, p. 552

An **adverb clause** modifies a verb, an adjective, or an adverb by telling *where, when, in what way, to what extent, under what condition,* or *why.*

As I stood in the street wondering what to do, it began to rain.
— "The Day I Got Lost," Singer, p. 560

Summary of Capitalization and Punctuation

Capitalization

Capitalize the first word of a sentence.

The light had an eerie green-yellow glow.

— *A Glow in the Dark*, Paulsen, p. 506

Capitalize all proper nouns and adjectives.

Amy Ling	Amazon River	Thanksgiving Day
Florida	October	Italian

Capitalize a person's title when it is followed by the person's name or when it is used in direct address.

Congressman Brooks Hays   Professor Shlemiel
King Edward

Capitalize titles showing family relationships when they refer to a specific person unless they are preceded by a possessive noun or a pronoun.

Uncle Charlie   my aunt   Susan's father

Capitalize the first word and all other key words in the titles of books, periodicals, poems, stories, plays, paintings, and other works of art.

The Diary of Anne Frank
"Drum Song"

Capitalize the first word and all nouns in letter salutations and the first word in letter closings.

Dear Fred,   Yours truly,

Punctuation

End Marks Use a **period** to end a declarative sentence, an imperative sentence, and most abbreviations.

There are half a dozen meteor showers each year.

— "Shooting Stars," Borland, p. 82

Take this book of poems and memorize one for me.

— from *I Know Why the Caged Bird Sings*, Maya Angelou, p. 28

Use a **question mark** to end a direct question or an incomplete question in which the rest of the question is understood.

"Was I bothering *you* when I turned that corner?" asked the woman.

— "Thank You, M'am," Hughes, p. 187

"You're sure ...?"

— *The Diary of Anne Frank*, Goodrich and Hackett, p. 719

Use an **exclamation mark** after a statement showing strong emotion, an urgent imperative sentence, or an interjection expressing strong emotion.

When he heard these words, something in him woke: his father loved him!

— "Christmas Day in the Morning," Buck, p. 67

"Hold up your foot!"

— "Cub Pilot on the Mississippi," Twain, p. 111

Commas Use a **comma** before the coordinating conjunction to separate two independent clauses in a compound sentence.

The door was standing half open, and at last one old jay happened to go and light on it and look in.

— "What Stumped the Blue Jays," Twain, p. 456

Use commas to separate three or more words, phrases, or clauses in a series.

He twisted himself over on his stomach, thrust both hands out to one side, and pressed them heavily against the flying surface.

— "Up the Slide," London, p. 157

Use commas to separate adjectives of equal rank. Do not use commas to separate adjectives that must stay in a specific order.

The clerks were pleased to be greeted by the good-looking, agreeable young man ...

— "A Retrieved Reformation," Henry, p. 255

Use a comma after an introductory word, phrase, or clause.

"Mom, you've got to take me to the library," Andy insisted.

— "Saving the Wetlands," Lewis, p. 276

Even on this trip, she suddenly fell asleep in the woods.

— "Harriet Tubman: Guide to Freedom" Petry, p. 137

Use commas to set off parenthetical and nonessential expressions.

Animals talk to teach other, of course.

— "What Stumped the Blue Jays," Twain, p. 453

Use commas with places and dates made up of two or more parts.

Ray Bradbury was born in Waukegan, Illinois.

On May 17, 1954, after deliberating for nearly a year and a half, the Supreme Court made its ruling.

— "Brown vs. Board of Education,"
Myers, p. 245

Use commas after items in addresses, after the salutation in a personal letter, after the closing in all letters, and in numbers of more than three digits.

Linden Lane, Durham, N.C.   My dear Cal,
Sincerely yours,   1,372,597

Use a comma to set off a direct quotation.

"All right, Charlie," he said, "you've seen these cards before, remember?"

— "Flowers for Algernon," Keyes, p. 213

Semicolons Use a **semicolon** to join independent clauses that are not already joined by a conjunction.

But nature guards her greatest secrets well; to such places men must come to find them.

— "The Secret," Clarke, p. 124

Use a semicolon to join independent clauses or items in a series that already contain commas.

I could see the door whiten at its touch; I could see the blue wall turn pale where it raced over it, and see the maple headboard of Amy's bed glow.

— from "An American Childhood," Dillard, p. 444

Colons Use a **colon** before a list of items following an independent clause.

The following words are examples of onomatopoeia: *buzz, hiss, jingle,* and *cluck.*

Use a colon in numbers giving the time, in salutations in business letters, and in labels used to signal important ideas.

4:30 A.M.   Dear Dr. Strauss:
Danger: Landslide Area Ahead

Quotation Marks A **direct quotation** represents a person's exact speech or thoughts and is enclosed in quotation marks.

"Good morning, madam," said Holmes cheerily.

— "The Adventure of the Speckled Band,"
Doyle, p. 475

An **indirect quotation** reports only the general meaning of what a person said or thought and does not require quotation marks.

He tells us that your land extends across the river and that you own almost twice as much as you thought.

— "Gentleman of Río en Medio," Sedillo, p. 273

Always place a comma or a period inside the final quotation mark of a direct quotation.

He pressed my hand and said, "Bless you! Tell me their names," and he pointed to the stars on the flag.

— "The Man Without a Country," Hale, p. 388

Place a question mark or an exclamation mark inside the final quotation mark if the end mark is part of the quotation; if it is not part of the quotation, place it outside the final quotation mark.

"Then we shall both come. What are you going to do yourself?"

— "The Adventure of the Speckled Band,"
Doyle p. 481

Does the poem by Robert Frost start with the line, "Two roads diverged in a yellow wood"?

Underline or italicize the titles of long written works, movies, television and radio shows, lengthy works of music, paintings, and sculptures.

The Diary of Anne Frank   *Star Trek*   The Mona Lisa

Use quotation marks around the titles of short written works, episodes in a series, songs, and titles of works mentioned as parts of collections.

"The Road Not Taken"   "Something From the Sixties"
"Space Oddity"   "January"

Hyphens Use a **hyphen** with certain numbers, after certain prefixes, with two or more words used as one word, and with a compound modifier that comes before a noun.

fifty-four   self-employed
daughter-in-law   happy-go-lucky friend

Apostrophes Add an **apostrophe** and -s to show the possessive case of most singular nouns.

Simon's plays   the author's story
Hughes's poems

Add an apostrophe to show the possessive case of plural nouns ending in -s and -es.

the bats' squeaks   the Robertses' home

Add an apostrophe and -s to show the possessive case of plural nouns that do not end in -s or -es.

the women's hats   the mice's whiskers

Use an apostrophe in a contraction to indicate the position of the missing letter or letters.

"I would've known if anyone tried to take the boots off my feet."

— "Medicine Bag," Sneve, p. 605

GLOSSARY OF COMMON USAGE

accept, except
Accept is a verb that means "to receive" or "to agree to." *Except* is a preposition that means "other than" or "leaving out." Do not confuse these two words.

The dinner party *accepted* the challenge to sit still for five minutes.

Every person *except* Philip Nolan has a country.

affect, effect
Affect is normally a verb meaning "to influence" or "to bring about a change in." *Effect* is usually a noun meaning "result."

Rob's special Christmas gift deeply *affected* his father.

Shooting his father may have a lasting *effect* on Carter Druse.

among, between
Among is usually used with three or more items. *Between* is generally used with only two items.

"Charles" was *among* the stories I liked best.

There is tension *between* Squeaky and Gretchen in "Raymond's Run."

amount, number
Amount refers to a mass or a unit, whereas *number* refers to individual items that can be counted. Therefore, *amount* generally appears with singular nouns, and *number* appears with plural nouns.

To remain calm while in danger, Clay Dilham needed a huge *amount* of determination.

In "The White Umbrella," the narrator makes a *number* of excuses about her mother's activities.

bad, badly
Use the predicate adjective *bad* after linking verbs such as *feel, look,* and *seem.* Use *badly* whenever an adverb is required.

Knowing how much his father loves him, Rob feels *bad* about getting him only a necktie for Christmas.

When the blue jay does not hear the acorn fall to the bottom of the hole, he is *badly* confused.

because of, due to
Use *due to* if it can logically replace the phrase *caused by.* In introductory phrases, however, *because of* is better usage than *due to.*

O. Henry's popularity was largely *due to* the intriguing endings of his stories.

Because of Philip Nolan's brashness, the judge gave him a unique sentence.

beside, besides
Do not confuse these two prepositions, which have different meanings. *Beside* means "at the side of" or "close to." *Besides* means "in addition to."

Martin sits *beside* his Grandfather's bed when it is time to receive the medicine bag.

No one *besides* me wrote a paper on Amy Ling's poem "Grandma."

can, may
The verb *can* generally refers to the ability to do something. The verb *may* generally refers to permission to do something.

The bachelor *may* tell a story if he believes he *can* captivate the children.

compare, contrast
The verb *compare* can involve both similarities and differences. The verb *contrast* always involves differences. Use *to* or *with* after *compare.* Use *with* after *contrast.*

Stan *compared* King Richard's soliloquy *with* Benedick's.

Joaquin Miller's tribute to Christopher Columbus *contrasts with* many people's opinions.

different from, different than
Different from is generally preferred over *different than.*

Similes are *different from* metaphors because similes use the words *like* or *as* to make comparisons.

farther, further
Use *farther* when you refer to distance. Use *further* when you mean "to a greater degree or extent" or "additional."

As he races *farther* down the track, Patsy knows his horse still has plenty of energy.

The singing of his dogs *further* unsettles the narrator in "A Glow in the Dark."

fewer, less

Use *fewer* for things that can be counted. Use *less* for amounts or quantities that cannot be counted.

Which animals have *fewer* legs: spiders or ladybugs?

The Sioux grandfather is *less* willing to let some of the customs die than are many of the younger Sioux.

good, well

Use the predicate adjective *good* after linking verbs such as *feel, look, smell, taste,* and *seem.* Use *well* whenever you need an adverb.

The narrator in "A Ribbon for Baldy" feels *good* about his science project idea.

Jack London describes the Yukon *well.*

hopefully

You should not loosely attach this adverb to a sentence, as in "*Hopefully,* the rain will stop by noon." Rewrite the sentence so *hopefully* modifies a specific verb. Other possible ways of revising such sentences include using the adjective *hopeful* or a phrase like "everyone *hopes* that."

Robert MacNeil writes *hopefully* that the American public will be skeptical about what they see and hear on television.

Laurie's parents were *hopeful* that Charles's mother would come to the PTA meeting.

its, it's

Do not confuse the possessive pronoun *its* with the contraction *it's,* standing for "it is" or "it has."

If a rattler thinks *it's* not seen, it will lie quietly without revealing *its* location.

lay, lie

Do not confuse these verbs. *Lay* is a transitive verb meaning "to set or put something down." Its principal parts are *lay, laying, laid, laid. Lie* is an intransitive verb meaning "to recline." Its principal parts are *lie, lying, lay, lain.*

The soldiers *lay* down their guns.

Debbie likes to *lie* down in front of the fireplace.

leave, let

Be careful not to confuse these verbs. *Leave* means "to go away" or "to allow to remain." *Let* means "to permit."

Carter Druse *left* his parents to fight for the Union army in the war.

Clay Dilham did not *let* challenging circumstances defeat him.

like

Like is a preposition that usually means "similar to" or "in the same way as." *Like* should always be followed by an object. Do not use *like* before a subject and a verb. Use *as* or *that* instead.

A story *like* "The Tell-Tale Heart" by Edgar Allan Poe uses suspense to hold the reader's interest.

Jimmy Valentine's final meeting with Ben Price did not end *as* he expected.

loose, lose

Loose can be either an adjective (meaning "unattached") or a verb (meaning "to untie"). *Lose* is always a verb (meaning "to fail to keep, have, or win").

There is often only a *loose* connection between the speaker of a poem and the poem's author; sometimes there is no link whatsoever between the two.

Professor Shlemiel continually *loses* anything he has in his hands.

many, much

Use *many* to refer to a specific quantity. Use *much* for an indefinite amount or for an abstract concept.

Mark Twain wrote *many* humorous stories.

Maya Angelou has won *much* praise for her writing.

of, have

Do not use *of* in place of *have* after auxiliary verbs like *would, could, should, may, might,* or *must.*

Jimmy Valentine's heroic decision to open the safe and reveal himself *must have* distressed him greatly.

raise, rise

Raise is a transitive verb that usually takes a direct object. *Rise* is intransitive and never takes a direct object.

The purpose of Colin Powell's speech is to *raise* the consciousness of all Americans to help America's children at risk.

Squeaky listens for the starting gun, then *rises* from the ground and becomes weightless as she flies past the other runners.

Grammar and Mechanics Handbook ◆ 983

set, sit

Do not confuse these verbs. *Set* is a transitive verb meaning "to put (something) in a certain place." Its principal parts are *set, setting, set, set. Sit* is an intransitive verb meaning "to be seated." Its principal parts are *sit, sitting, sat, sat.*

> The speaker *sets* the planks in the furnace.
>
> Every now and then, Debbie would *sit* by the fire for a few minutes.

than, then

The conjunction *than* is used to connect the two parts of a comparison. Do not confuse *than* with the adverb *then,* which usually refers to time.

> Gina liked "The Ninny" more *than* "The Governess."
>
> Mark Twain worked on a riverboat and *then* moved to California to search for gold.

that, which, who

Use the relative pronoun *that* to refer to things or people. Use *which* only for things and *who* only for people.

> The season *that* Langston Hughes describes is winter.
>
> Lyric poems, *which* express personal emotions, are often brief.
>
> One writer *who* has vividly captured the experiences of African Americans is Alice Walker.

their, there, they're

Do not confuse the spelling of these three words. *Their* is a possessive adjective and always modifies a noun. *There* is usually used either at the beginning of a sentence or as an adverb. *They're* is a contraction for "they are."

> Todd and his parents are very happy about *their* new pet.
>
> For most people, *there* are few creatures more terrifying than sharks.
>
> Tim and Nina are in the class production of *The Diary of Anne Frank,* and *they're* rehearsing right now in the auditorium.

to, too, two

Do not confuse the spelling of these words. *To* is a preposition that begins a prepositional phrase or an infinitive. *Too,* with two *o*'s, is an adverb and modifies adjectives and other adverbs. *Two* is a number.

> Mrs. Frank wants Anne *to* show courtesy *to* their guests.
>
> Josh thought that his paper on the Civil War was *too* short, so he added another paragraph.
>
> *Two* poems that Helen especially liked were Walt Whitman's "O Captain! My Captain!" and John Greenleaf Whittier's "Barbara Frietchie."

unique

Because *unique* means "one of a kind," you should not use it carelessly to mean "interesting" or "unusual." Avoid such illogical expressions as *most unique, very unique,* and *extremely unique.*

> Mark Twain's experiences in California gave him a *unique* insight into the gold-mining camps.

when, where, why

Do not use *when, where,* or *why* directly after a linking verb such as *is.* Reword the sentence.

> **Faulty:** Suspense is *when* an author increases the reader's tension.
>
> **Revised:** An author uses suspense to increase the reader's tension.
>
> **Faulty:** Holland is *where* the drama *The Diary of Anne Frank* takes place.
>
> **Revised:** *The Diary of Anne Frank* takes place in Holland.

who, whom

In formal writing, remember to use *who* only as a subject in clauses and sentences and *whom* only as an object.

> Amy Ling, *who* is Chinese American, writes about a meeting with her grandmother.
>
> Langston Hughes, *whom* we discussed yesterday, was a leader in an important cultural movement during the 1920's called the Harlem Renaissance.

SPEAKING, LISTENING, AND VIEWING HANDBOOK

Communication is the way in which people convey their ideas and interact with one another. The literature in this book is written, which is one form of communication, but much of your personal communication is probably oral or visual. Oral communication involves both speaking and listening. Visual communication involves both conveying messages through physical expression or pictorial representations and interpreting images. Developing strong communication skills can benefit your school life and your life outside of school.

Many of the assignments accompanying the literature in this textbook involve speaking, listening, viewing, and representing. This handbook identifies some of the terminology related to the oral and visual communication you experience every day and the assignments you may do in conjunction with the literature in this book.

Communication

You use many different kinds of communication every day. When you communicate with your friends, your teachers, or your parents, or when you interact with a cashier in a store, you are communicating orally. In addition to ordinary conversation, oral communication includes class discussions, speeches, interviews, presentations, and debates. When you communicate face to face, you usually use more than your voice to get your message across. If you communicate by telephone, however, you must rely solely on your verbal skills. At times, you may use more visual communication than any other kind. For example, when you paint a picture, participate in a dance recital, or prepare a multimedia presentation, you use strategies of visual communication.

The following terms will give you a better understanding of the many elements that are a part of oral and visual communication:

BODY LANGUAGE refers to the use of facial expressions, eye contact, gestures, posture, and movement to communicate a feeling or an idea.

CONNOTATION is the set of associations a word calls to mind. The connotations of the words you choose influence the message you send. For example, most people respond more favorably to being described as "slim" rather than as "skinny." The connotation of *slim* is more appealing than that of *skinny*.

EYE CONTACT is direct visual contact with another person's eyes.

FEEDBACK is the set of verbal and nonverbal reactions that indicate to a speaker that a message has been received and understood.

GESTURES are the movements made with arms, hands, face, and fingers to communicate.

LISTENING is understanding and interpreting sound in a meaningful way. You listen differently for different purposes.
Listening for key information: For example, when a teacher gives an assignment, or when someone gives you directions to a place, you listen for key information.
Listening for main points: In a classroom exchange of ideas or information, or while watching a television documentary, you listen for main points.
Listening critically: When you evaluate a performance, a song, or a persuasive or political speech, you listen critically, questioning and judging the speaker's message.

MEDIUM is the material or technique used to present a visual image. Common media include paint, clay, and film.

NONVERBAL COMMUNICATION is communication without the use of words. People communicate nonverbally through gestures, facial expressions, posture, and body movements. Sign language is an entire language based on nonverbal communication.

VIEWING is observing, understanding, analyzing, and evaluating information presented through visual means. You might use the following questions to help you interpret what you view:
- What subject is presented?
- What is communicated about the subject?
- Which parts are factual? Which are opinion?
- What mood, attitude, or opinion is conveyed?
- What is your emotional response?

VOCAL DELIVERY is the way in which you present a message. Your vocal delivery involves all of the following elements:
Volume: the loudness or quietness of your voice
Pitch: the high or low quality of your voice
Rate: the speed at which you speak; also called pace
Stress: the amount of emphasis placed on different syllables in a word or on different words in a sentence

All of these elements individually, and the way in which they are combined, contribute to the meaning of a spoken message.

Speaking, Listening, and Viewing Handbook ◆ *985*

Speaking, Listening, and Viewing Situations

Here are some of the many types of situations in which you apply speaking, listening, and viewing skills:

AUDIENCE Your audience in any situation refers to the person or people to whom you direct your message. An audience can be a group of people sitting in a classroom or auditorium observing a performance or just one person to whom you address a question or a comment. When preparing for any speaking situation, it's useful to analyze your audience, learning what you can about their backgrounds, interests, and attitudes so that you can tailor your message to them.

CHARTS AND GRAPHS are visual representations of statistical information. For example, a pie chart might indicate how the average dollar is spent by government, and a bar graph might compare populations in cities over time.

DEBATE A debate is a formal public-speaking situation in which participants prepare and present arguments on opposing sides of a question, stated as a **proposition.**

The two sides in a debate are the *affirmative* (pro) and the *negative* (con). The affirmative side argues in favor of the proposition, while the negative side argues against it. The affirmative side begins the debate, since it is seeking a change in belief or policy. The opposing sides take turns presenting their arguments, and each side has an opportunity for *rebuttal,* in which they may challenge or question the other side's argument.

DOCUMENTARIES are nonfiction films that analyze news events or other focused subjects. You can watch a documentary for the information on its subject.

GROUP DISCUSSION results when three or more people meet to solve a common problem, arrive at a decision, or answer a question of mutual interest. Group discussion is one of the most widely used forms of interpersonal communication in modern society.

INTERVIEW An interview is a form of interaction in which one person, the interviewer, asks questions of another person, the interviewee. Interviews may take place for many purposes: to obtain information, to discover a person's suitability for a job or a college, or to inform the public of a notable person's opinions.

MAPS are visual representations of the Earth's surface. Maps may show political boundaries or physical features. They can also provide information on a variety of other topics. A map's title and its key identify the content of the map.

ORAL INTERPRETATION is the reading or speaking of a work of literature aloud for an audience. Oral interpretation involves giving expression to the ideas, meaning, or even the structure of a work of literature. The speaker interprets the work through his or her vocal delivery. **Storytelling,** in which a speaker reads or tells a story expressively, is a form of oral interpretation.

PANEL DISCUSSION is a group discussion on a topic of interest common to all members of a panel and to a listening audience. A panel is usually composed of four to six experts on a particular topic who are brought together to share information and opinions.

PANTOMIME is a form of nonverbal communication in which an idea or a story is communicated completely through the use of gesture, body language, and facial expressions, without any words at all.

POLITICAL CARTOONS are drawings that comment on important political or social issues. Often, these cartoons use humor to convey a message about their subject. Viewers use their own knowledge of events to evaluate the cartoonist's opinion.

READERS THEATRE is a dramatic reading of a work of literature in which participants take parts from a story or a play and read them aloud in expressive voices. Unlike a play, however, sets and costumes are not part of the performance, and the participants remain seated as they deliver their lines.

ROLE PLAY To role-play is to take the role of a person or character and, as that character, act out a given situation, speaking, acting, and responding in the manner of the character.

SPEECH A speech is a talk or an address given to an audience. A speech may be **impromptu**—delivered on the spur of the moment with no preparation—or formally prepared and delivered for a specific purpose or occasion.
- *Purposes:* The most common purposes of speeches are to persuade (for example, political speeches), to entertain, to explain, and to inform.
- *Occasions:* Different occasions call for different types of speeches. Speeches given on these occasions could be persuasive, entertaining, or informative, as appropriate. The following are common occasions for speeches:

Introduction: Introducing a speaker at a meeting
Presentation: Giving an award or acknowledging the contributions of someone
Acceptance: Accepting an award or a tribute
Keynote: Giving an inspirational address at a large meeting or convention
Commencement: Honoring the graduates of a school

Test Preparation Handbook

Contents

Test Preparation Workshops

Test Preparation Workshop 1   Reading Comprehension: Context Clues and Prefixes/Suffixes

Test Preparation Workshop 2   Reading Comprehension: Following Written Directions

Test Preparation Workshop 3   Reading Comprehension: Identify Main Idea; Identify Best Summary

Test Preparation Workshop 4   Reading Comprehension: Analyzing Information and Making Judgments

Test Preparation Workshop 5   Reading Comprehension: Interpreting Diagrams, Graphs, and Statistical Illustrations

Test Preparation Workshop 6   Reading Comprehension: Cause and Effect

Test Preparation Workshop 7   Reading Comprehension: Fact and Opinion; Propaganda and Persuasive Language

Test Preparation Workshop 8   Writing Skills: Sentence Construction

Test Preparation Workshop 9   Writing Skills: Appropriate Usage

Test Preparation Workshop 10   Writing Skills: Spelling, Capitalization, and Punctuation

Test Preparation Workshop 11   Research Skills: Using Information Resources

Test Preparation Workshop 12   Writing Skills: Proofreading

Test Preparation Workshop 13   Writing Skills: Responding to Writing Prompts

Test Practice Bank

Correlations to Standardized Tests

The reading comprehension skills reviewed in this workshop correspond to the following standardized test sections:

SAT 9   Reading Vocabulary

SAT   Critical Reading

ACT   Reading

TerraNova Reading

Answers

1. (C) related to cooking
2. (D) signing up ahead of time

Test Preparation Workshop 1

Reading Comprehension — Context Clues and Prefixes/Suffixes

Strategies for Success

The reading sections of standardized tests ask you to read a passage and answer questions about word meanings. Some questions require you to determine the meanings of words by using context clues, prefixes, and suffixes. Use the following strategies to help you answer this type of test question:

Use Context Clues The words or phrases near an unfamiliar word are context clues that can help you figure out the word's meaning. A context clue may be a synonym (word with the same meaning) or an antonym (word with the opposite meaning) for the unfamiliar word. Sometimes the passage contains a definition or an explanation of the unfamiliar word or a description with details or examples that can help you figure out the word's meaning. Even if the unfamiliar word is part of the technical vocabulary of people who share a particular activity or interest, context clues can help you determine its meaning. Look at this example:

> The town's first Amateur Scientists Night was a huge success. The most popular participant was a local **ornithologist,** who showed slides of birds he had studied all over the world.

The word **ornithologist** in this passage means—
- **A** worldwide traveler
- **B** person who studies birds
- **C** photographer
- **D** endangered species

The context tells you that the correct answer has to be an amateur scientist, so **A** and **C** are incorrect. **D** does not make sense because humans are not an endangered species. **B** is correct.

Use Prefixes and Suffixes Knowing the meanings of prefixes and suffixes—such as *circum-* (around), *pre-* (before), *re-* (again), *un-* (not), *-ful* (full of), *-ness* (condition of, state of), *-logy* (study of), and *-less* (without)—can help you determine the meanings of unfamiliar words. Look at this example:

> In a few hours we were able to **circumnavigate** the small island.

In this passage, **circumnavigate** means—
- **A** cross over
- **C** sail around
- **B** map
- **D** explore thoroughly

The prefix *circum-* means around. *Navigate* comes from the Latin word meaning "to sail." So the correct answer is **C**.

Apply the Strategies

Answer these test questions based on the passage.

> On her way home from work, Janice saw the sign in the storefront: Cooking Classes Start Tonight at 8 P.M. She imagined herself surprising her family with one **culinary** treat after another. Promptly at eight, she returned to the store, only to discover that **preregistration** was required.

1 In this passage, the word **culinary** means—
- **A** related to school
- **C** related to cooking
- **B** related to money
- **D** related to dessert

2 The word **preregistration** in this passage means—
- **A** wearing specialized clothing
- **B** bringing supplies
- **C** paying cash
- **D** signing up ahead of time

Additional Text-Taking Tip

Substituting the Answer

Explain to students that vocabulary items on the TAAS, SAT 9, SAT, and ACT are tested in a multiple-choice format. One way to help determine whether a possible answer makes sense in context is by rereading the sentence with each answer choice in place of the word to be defined. Often this will eliminate several if not all of the wrong answers. Advise students to look at all the possible answers and then choose the one that makes the most sense in the context of the paragraph.

For example, if students substitute answers for the first question in place of culinary, it becomes clear that *related to school* and *related to money* do not make sense in context. Although *related to dessert* might make sense, the classes are in cooking in general, not dessert making. By eliminating the other choices, students can arrive at the correct answer, *related to cooking*.

Test Preparation Workshop 2

Reading Comprehension — Following Written Directions

Correlations to Standardized Tests

The reading comprehension skills reviewed in this workshop correspond to the following standardized test sections:

SAT 9 Reading Comprehension

ACT Reading

Strategies for Success

The reading sections of standardized tests require you to read a passage and answer multiple-choice questions about directions. Use the following strategies to help you answer test questions about directions:

Notice the Details In written directions, every detail is important. Read the question carefully and notice what detail you are being asked to recall. Then, skim the passage quickly to locate the specific detail. Look at the following example:

Follow these directions to make a melted cheese sandwich using only the sun for heat:

Find an empty shoebox, discard the cover, and cut off one of the long sides. On each short side, draw a diagonal line from the corner where the short and long sides are connected to the opposite corner. Next, cut along the two diagonal lines you have drawn until you have removed a triangle from each short side. Tape a piece of black construction paper to the bottom of the shoebox. Tape aluminum foil to the three sides. Tape plastic wrap tightly over the opening, leaving one corner loose. Place a thin slice of cheese on a piece of bread, and put the bread in the box. Finally, put the box outside in the sun. In a while, you will have a melted cheese sandwich.

With what do you cover the bottom of the shoebox?

A shiny black paper   **C** plastic wrap
B black construction paper   **D** aluminum foil

A is not mentioned in the passage. **C** covers the opening. **D** covers the three sides. **B** is correct.

Notice the Sequence of Steps Test questions about directions require you to understand the order in which steps should be taken. Words such as *first, next, then, after, before, finally,* and *last* give you clues to the correct sequence of steps. Look at the following question based on the passage:

What should you do immediately before cutting a triangle from each short side?

A Line the bottom with black construction paper
B Cut off one long side
C Tape aluminum foil to three sides
D Draw a diagonal line on each short side

A and **C** are done after the triangles are cut off. **B** is done before the triangles are cut off but not immediately before. **D** is correct.

Apply the Strategies

Answer the questions based on this passage.

Everyone should know what to do in case of a burn. Here are the basic steps. First, put cool water on the burn. If you cannot apply running water to the burn, soak clean cloths in cool water and apply them. Keep adding cool water to the cloths. After you have cooled the burn for several minutes, cover it loosely with a clean dry cloth. This helps prevent infection. Get the burn victim medical attention as soon as possible. For minor burns that do not require medical attention, wash the burned area with soap and water, pat it dry gently, and apply antibiotic ointment.

1 What should be applied first to a burn?
A clean dry cloths   **C** cool water
B ice   **D** lukewarm water

2 For minor burns, what should you do after washing the burn?
A Apply antibiotic ointment
B Apply a loose bandage
C Call a doctor
D Check for infection

Answers

1. (C) cool water
2. (A) Apply antibiotic ointment

Additional Test-Taking Tip

Using Signal Words

Point out to students that standardized test questions often include transition words that are clues to meaning. Some words indicate chronological order. Spotting *first, then, after,* or *before* in a passage will help students to determine a sequence of events or steps. Other signal words that may help with comprehension are those that signal comparison (*like, similar to*), contrast (*unlike, different from, in contrast*), and summary statements (*in conclusion, finally*).

For example, in the selection about first aid for a burn, the passage uses the terms *first* and *after*. These words help the student to answer the question about what should be applied first to a burn. The signal word *first* leads the student to the answer, C (cool water).

The reading comprehension skills
reviewed in this workshop correspond
to the following standardized test
sections:

ACT	Reading
SAT 9	Reading Comprehension
ITBS	Reading Comprehension
TerraNova	Reading

Answers

1. (A) Students held a car wash and bake sale to benefit the Tiny Tots Preschool.
2. (B) When a local preschool was damaged in a fire, students held a bake sale and car wash.

Test Preparation Workshop 3

Reading Comprehension — Identify Main Idea; Identify Best Summary

Strategies for Success

The reading sections of both national and Texas standardized tests require you to read a passage and answer multiple-choice questions about main ideas and summaries. Use the following strategies to help you answer such questions:

Identify the Main Idea Sometimes the main idea of a passage is stated in a topic sentence, which may appear anywhere in the passage. Sometimes the main idea is not stated directly but is implied, or suggested, by the details in the passage. Look at the following passage and find the answer choice that summarizes the author's message:

> The platypus lives in the lakes and streams of eastern Australia. It looks like a duck-billed seal and acts like a lizard. Being a mammal, the platypus is warm-blooded and has fur. However, it also has some characteristics of a reptile. For example, instead of bearing live young, it lays eggs. Like a lizard, its legs are attached to the side of its body rather than underneath it.

What is the main idea of this passage?

A The platypus lives in Australia.
B Although it is a mammal, the platypus shares some characteristics with reptiles.
C The platypus looks like a duck-billed seal.
D The platypus is a graceful swimmer.

A and **C** are details. **D** is not mentioned in the passage. **B** is the implied main idea of the passage.

Identify the Best Summary A summary briefly restates the most important information or ideas in a passage. A good summary describes the most important information of the passage as a whole, not just the beginning or end. Look at this question based on the passage above:

What is the best summary of this passage?

A The platypus is a mammal that shares characteristics with reptiles.
B The platypus is found in eastern Australia.
C The platypus, found in Australia, is a mammal who lays eggs and has legs attached to its sides like a reptile.
D Found in streams and lakes, the platypus is warm-blooded, fur-bearing, and egg-laying.

A states the main idea but is not a summary. **B** and **D** don't include all the important information. **C** is correct.

Apply the Strategies

Answer the questions based on this passage:

> On Saturday, at 7:30 A.M., students began gathering in the school parking lot. Many carried home-baked goodies. Others brought pails, soap, sponges, and clothes. The students had formed a committee to raise money for the Tiny Tots Preschool, which has been severely damaged in a fire. With the car wash and bake sale, they hoped to raise funds to replace most of the school's books. By one o'clock, the students were counting their hard-earned money.

1 What is the main idea of the passage?
  A Students held a car wash and bake sale to benefit the Tiny Tots Preschool.
  B The Tiny Tots Preschool had fire damage.
  C Students like to help out in a crisis.
  D The students worked hard to earn money.

2 What is the best summary of the passage?
  A Students brought food and cleaning supplies to the car wash and bake sale.
  B When a local preschool was damaged in a fire, students held a bake sale and car wash.
  C Students counted their money.
  D The Tiny Tots Preschool lost all of its books.

Additional Test-Taking Tip

True Statements and Correct Answers

Tell students that when they take a standardized test, it is important to read all answer choices carefully and critically. Caution students against being confused by distractors, or answer choices, that are true statements. The fact that a statement is true in relation to a passage does not mean that it is the correct answer. In many cases, all of the distractors may be true statements. Only one of them, however, answers the specific question that was asked. Test-takers must read questions carefully, and reread them if necessary, to make sure they know what they are looking for.

Test Preparation Workshop 4

Reading Comprehension
Analyzing Information and Making Judgments

Correlations to Standardized Tests

The reading comprehension skills reviewed in this workshop correspond to the following standardized test sections:

ACT   Reading
ITBS   Reading Comprehension
TerraNova Reading

Answers

1. (C) 4
2. (B) the price range she can afford

Strategies for Success

The reading sections of both national and Texas standardized tests require you to read a passage and answer multiple-choice questions by analyzing information and making judgments. Use the following strategies to answer such questions:

Analyze Information Some test questions require you not only to locate information in a passage but also to apply it. You may have to put information in categories, compare and contrast things, or determine causes and effects. Think about what the question is asking you to do, and analyze the information you need in order to do it. Look at this example:

> Mr. and Mrs. Alvarez had left the babysitter a list of instructions:
> 1. Feed the children at 5:30. Warm up the soup in the refrigerator.
> 2. They can watch half an hour of TV.
> 3. Be sure they brush their teeth and wash their faces and hands.
> 4. Read them a story of their choice.
> 5. They should be in bed by 8:00.
> Martin fed the children on time. At 6:00, while cleaning up, he heard the TV. At 7:30, the children were still watching TV. Martin hurried them off to the bathroom and tucked them into bed. Then he started his homework.

Which of the guidelines did Martin not follow?
A 1 and 2   **C** 2 and 3
B 2 and 4   **D** 3 and 5

Comparing the list with the description of what Martin did, you see that he did 1, 3, and 5. He didn't do 2 and 4, so **B** is correct.

Make Judgments When you make judgments, you evaluate a thing or an action based on a standard. The first step is deciding what the standard is. The second step is asking yourself how the thing or action measures up to it. Look at the following question:

Martin would have been a better babysitter if he had—
> **A** not brought his homework
> **B** given the children supper earlier
> **C** limited the children's TV viewing
> **D** cleaned the house

The standard for a good babysitter is to follow the parents' instructions. Martin let the children watch TV one hour longer than the parents wanted, so **C** is correct.

Apply the Strategies

Answer the questions based on this passage:
> Erica made a list of the features she wanted in a new binder:
> 1. zipper closure
> 2. inside pockets for ruler and calculator
> 3. inside pouch for pens and pencils
> 4. subject dividers
> 5. inside pocket for loose papers.
> Then she saw this ad:

> **STUDY AID 3-RING BINDER**
> - Zips closed to keep paper from falling out
> - Full-sized pockets inside back and front
> - Inside pouch
> - Available in a variety of colors
> - Only $15.95!

1 Which of Erica's requirements is not mentioned in the ad?
    A 2   **B** 3   **C** 4   **D** 5

2 Erica's list would be more helpful to her process of choosing a new binder if it specified—
    A the brand she bought last year
    B the price range she can afford
    C the colors she likes

Additional Test-Taking Tip

Read Word by Word
Remind students that working efficiently when taking a standardized test is important. However, they should not work so quickly that they skim instructions, passages, questions, or choices. Missing or misreading even one word in the instructions may cause students to waste time doing the wrong thing. Misreading or skipping over words in a passage or in a question may lead students to answer incorrectly.

Emphasize to students that reading word by word the first time will save them time in the long run. To make sure they are reading carefully, students may self-question, identify signal words, or summarize as they read instructions, a passage, or a question.

Challenge students to read the sample passage on p. 437 so carefully that they don't have to refer to Erica's list to answer the questions.

Correlations to Standardized Tests

The reading comprehension skills reviewed in this workshop correspond to the following standardized test section:

ACT   Reading

Answers

1. (C) Alan's

2. (D) astronomy

Test Preparation Workshop 5

Reading Comprehension

Interpreting Diagrams, Graphs, and Statistical Illustrations

Strategies for Success

The reading sections of both national and Texas standardized tests require you to read a passage and answer multiple-choice questions about visual aids. Use the following strategies to help you answer such questions:

Study the Key Diagrams, graphs, and statistical illustrations present information visually with a minimum of words. A key tells you what the visual symbols represent. Study the key to learn what each symbol stands for or what each axis of a graph measures.

Interpret the Visual Questions of this nature may ask you to locate information, to compare two items of information, or to make calculations using the information. Read the questions carefully. Look at this example:

As treasurer of Student Council, Tony prepared a bar graph to show how many boxes of greeting cards each class sold for the school fund-raiser. Here is his graph on the fourth day of the sale.

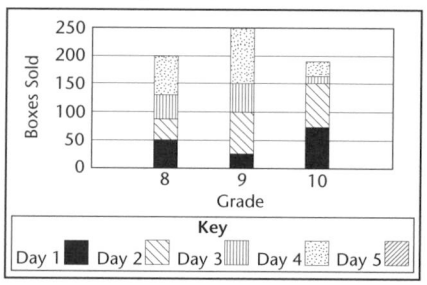

1 How many boxes did the eighth grade sell on Day 2?

A 25   **B** 50   **C** 75   **D** 100

On Day 1, eighth-graders sold 50. On Day 2 the number went from 50 to 75, so 25 were sold.

A is correct.

2 By Day 4, how many classes had sold 200 or more boxes of cards?

A 0   **B** 1   **C** 2   **D** 3

At the end of Day 4, the eighth grade had sold 200; the seventh grade had sold over 200; the sixth grade had sold fewer than 200. Since the question asks how may classes had sold 200 or more boxes, **C** is correct.

Apply the Strategies

Answer the questions based on the passage.

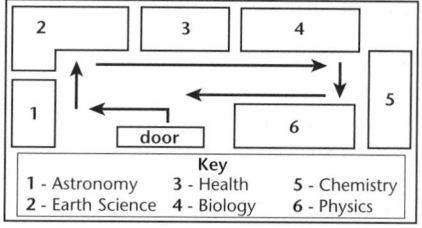

At the school science fair, Tanya, Alan, Dominic, and Gloria wanted to look at all four of their projects before looking at any other projects. Tanya's project was on the earth science table; Alan's was an astronomy project; Gloria did a physics experiment; and Dominic reported on a health issue.

1 If the four students follow the suggested flow of traffic, whose project will they see first?

A Tanya's   **C** Alan's

B Dominic's   **D** Gloria's

2 After looking at Gloria's physics experiment, the friends wanted to look at all of the earth science projects. Which table did they pass on their way to the earth science table?

A health   **C** biology

B chemistry   **D** astronomy

Additional Test-Taking Tip

Previewing the Questions

Many passages on standardized tests are long and contain a large amount of information. Students may find it helpful to preview the questions they will have to answer about a passage before reading the passage. Then, instead of having to take in a lot of information at once, they can look for the specific information they know they will need.

The same strategy can be applied to questions with visual aids. For example, students answering the questions in "Apply the Strategies" might take an unnecessarily long time examining and decoding the map if they did not know what to look for. By previewing the questions, they can see that the first question asks which project the four students in the passage will see first. Test takers can then find Table 1 on the map, look at the key to see that this is the astronomy table, and look at the passage to see that Alan's project will be on that table.

Test Preparation Workshop 6

Reading Comprehension — Cause and Effect

Correlations to Standardized Tests

The reading comprehension skills reviewed in this workshop correspond to the following standardized test sections:

ACT Reading

SAT 9 Reading Comprehension

Answers

1. (C) extra practice each day
2. (A) the director's comment

Strategies for Success

The reading sections of both national and Texas standardized tests require you to read a passage and answer multiple-choice questions about cause-and-effect relationships. Use the following strategies to answer such questions:

Notice Cause-and-Effect Relationships A cause is an event or condition that makes something else happen. What happens is the effect or result. In the sentence, *Because we got lost, we were an hour late,* our getting lost is the cause, and our being late is the effect. One cause may have several effects, and one effect may have multiple causes. However, do not confuse time sequence with cause and effect. Even if one event follows another, the first event does not necessarily cause the second one.

Look for Signal Words Certain words or phrases in a passage may signal cause-and-effect relationships. These words and phrases include *because, why, the reason for, as a result of,* and *in order to.* When you see these words or phrases, read carefully. Consider this sentence: *As a result of poor playing, they lost the game.* The words that follow the phrase, *as a result of,* describe the cause, not the effect. Look at the following passage and questions:

Tigers are an endangered species. In 1999 there were fewer than seven thousand of them living in the wild. These few are dying off fast as a result of illegal hunting and loss of habitat. When land is cleared to make room for a growing human population, tigers have less land on which to hunt and raise their young. To save wild tigers, governments need to protect tiger habitats and impose stricter hunting penalties.

1 What are two reasons that tigers are an endangered species?
A hunting and limitations on development
B loss of habitat and illegal hunting
C new habitats and stricter hunting penalties
D growing human population

The phrase "as a result of illegal hunting and loss of habitat" tells you that **B** is correct.

2 In order to prevent tigers from dying out, governments need to—
A clear land   **C** protect habitats
B encourage hunters   **D** place tigers in zoos

A and **B** are not causes that will have the effect of protecting tigers. **D** is not mentioned in the passage. **C** is correct.

Apply the Strategies

Answer the questions based on this passage.

The extra half-hour of practice each day had paid off. Maya could hear the improvement in her violin playing. She was sure that her new-found confidence would result in her being more relaxed at the audition for Senior Orchestra. Just as she was about to raise her bow for the first note, she heard a ping. One of her strings had snapped. Maya's face fell. "Don't worry," smiled the director. "I always bring an extra set of strings to auditions. We'll have your violin restrung in a jiffy."

1 Maya's new confidence was a result of—
A being more relaxed at the audition
B getting a new string
C extra practice each day
D the director's friendly attitude

2 What caused Maya's face to fall?
A the snap of her violin string
B the director's comment
C the sound of a wrong note
D her lack of confidence

Additional Test-Taking Tip

Set a Purpose

Explain to students that they should always set a purpose for reading the passages that appear on standardized tests, generally to grasp the main idea. Often it is helpful to glance at the questions before reading and thus get an idea of what to look for. They may also want to identify the pattern of organization used by the writer.

Thinking visually about organization may be useful. Visualizing a timeline or flowchart while reading a passage can improve students' comprehension of the text as well as reduce the time needed to reread the passage to answer the questions.

Answers

1. (B) My dog has never been in a fight.
2. (D) It was passed by dog-haters!

Test Preparation Workshop 7

Reading Comprehension | Fact and Opinion; Propaganda and Persuasive Language

Strategies for Success

The reading sections of standardized tests require you to read a passage and answer multiple-choice questions about fact and opinion, propaganda, and persuasive language. Use the following strategies to help you answer such questions:

Recognize Facts and Opinions A fact can be proven true by a reliable source, such as an unbiased book or an expert. An opinion is a statement of belief. A writer may use facts to support opinions, but that does not make the opinions true. Look at this example:

Bob Giles *for* Student Council President

Why vote for Bob?
- ✔ Bob was SC treasurer last year.
- ✔ Bob is captain of the football team.
- ✔ Bob is well liked by everyone.
- ● Bob's opponent has no school spirit.
- ● Bob's opponent is a one-issue candidate.
- ● Bob's opponent is new to the school.

Bob Giles will put this school on the map!

Which of the following is an OPINION?

A Bob is captain of the football team.
B His opponent has no school spirit.
C His opponent is new to the school.
D Bob was SC treasurer last year.

Research can prove that **A**, **C**, and **D** are true. **B** is an opinion.

Recognize Propaganda and Persuasive Language When writers want to influence you to think or act in a certain way, they often use words that appeal to your emotions rather than to your thinking. Propaganda is meant to influence the way you respond. Propaganda techniques include loaded words (words that appeal to emotions), sweeping generalizations (statements too general to be meaningful), and empty promises (promises that cannot be kept). Look at this question based on the passage above:

Which of the following is a sweeping generalization?

A Bob's opponent is a one-issue candidate.
B Bob is captain of the football team.
C Bob will put this school on the map.
D Bob is well liked by everyone.

A is not a generalization. **B** is a fact. **C** is an empty promise. **D** is correct.

Apply the Strategies

Read the passage and answer the questions.

Dear Editor:

I am writing to protest the new city law that dogs must be on leashes at all times. Everyone knows dogs deserve to run free. They can't enjoy running at a human's pace. I know the law is designed to keep dogs from annoying people and fighting with other dogs. However, my dog is obedient and has never been in a fight. The leash law is unfair to well-behaved dogs. It was passed by dog haters!

A Dog Lover

1 Which of these statements is a FACT?
   A The leash law is unfair to well-behaved dogs.
   B My dog has never been in a fight.
   C Everyone knows dogs deserve to run free.
   D Dogs can't enjoy running at a human's pace.

2 Which statement is an example of propaganda?
   A The law is designed to keep dogs from annoying people.
   B I'm writing to protest the new city law.
   C My dog has never been in a fight.
   D It was passed by dog haters!

Additional Test-Taking Tip

Plan Your Time

Tell students that on a timed test, it is a good idea to work through the questions in sequence, answering as many as possible. If they cannot figure out an answer in a reasonable amount of time or if they are unsure of the correct response, they should leave a blank, make a note of it, and move on to the next question. After completing all of the questions that they are able to answer with confidence, tell students to go back and work on those questions that posed more of a challenge.

Test Preparation Workshop 8

Writing Skills — Sentence Construction

Correlations to Standardized Tests

The writing skills reviewed in this workshop correspond to the following standardized test sections:

SAT 9	Language
ACT	English
ITBS	Usage and Expression
TerraNova	Language Arts

Strategies for Success

The writing sections of standardized tests require you to read a passage and answer multiple-choice questions about sentence construction. Use the following strategies to help you answer such questions:

Recognize Incomplete Sentences and Run-on Sentences An incomplete sentence does not express a complete thought. Correct an incomplete sentence by making sure it has a subject and a verb. A run-on sentence is made up of two or more sentences without the proper punctuation between them. Correct a run-on sentence by adding the correct punctuation and, if necessary, a conjunction.

Combine Sentences Sometimes two short sentences sound better if they are combined. When you join two short sentences on a test, make sure that they are closely related in subject matter. Look at the following example:

Over the years, numerous animals have spent time in the White House. (1) Abraham Lincoln rescued a turkey. It was supposed to be killed for Thanksgiving. It became a family pet. (2) Theodore Roosevelt's children had a pony. They once took it up in a service elevator.

Choose the best way to rewrite each underlined passage. If it needs no change, choose "Correct as is."

1 **A** Abraham Lincoln rescued a turkey. That was supposed to be killed for Thanksgiving.
  B Abraham Lincoln rescued a turkey that was supposed to be killed for Thanksgiving.
  C Abraham Lincoln rescued a turkey it was supposed to be killed for Thanksgiving.
  D Correct as is

The second part of **A** is an incomplete sentence. **C** is a run-on sentence. **B** is correct because it combines two short, related sentences.

2 **A** Theodore Roosevelt's children taking a pony up in a service elevator.
  B Theodore Roosevelt's children had a pony that they once took up in a service elevator.
  C Theodore Roosevelt's children took a pony. Up in a service elevator.
  D Correct as is

A is an incomplete sentence. The second half of **C** is an incomplete sentence. **B** combines two short sentences correctly.

Apply the Strategies

Choose the best way to rewrite each underlined passage. If it needs no change, choose "Correct as is."

An animal's tongue can be very useful. (1) A gecko wipes its eyelids with its tongue a giraffe's tongue strips leaves from a tree. (2) Some lizards scare their enemies with their tongues. The tongues are blue.

1 **A** A gecko wipes its eyelids with its tongue, a giraffe's tongue strips leaves from trees.
  B A gecko wipes its eyelids with its tongue but a giraffe's tongue strips leaves from trees.
  C A gecko wipes its eyelids with its tongue. A giraffe's tongue strips leaves from trees.
  D Correct as is

2 **A** Some lizards scare enemies with their blue tongues.
  B Some lizards. Scare enemies with their blue tongues.
  C Some lizards scaring enemies with their blue tongues.
  D Correct as is

Answers

1. (C) A gecko wipes its eyelids with its tongue. A giraffe's tongue strips leaves from a tree.

2. (A) Some lizards scare enemies with their blue tongues.

Additional Test-Taking Tip

Process of Elimination

Tell students that before deciding on an answer, they should look carefully at all the choices. They will be able to eliminate some choices as obviously wrong. For example, in a question testing sentence construction, there will be some sentences that are grammatically incorrect or have other apparent inaccuracies. When they have narrowed down their choices, they should look again at the passage before making a final decision. They should then pick the answer that correctly expresses the intended meaning of the passage and provides the necessary details.

Test Preparation Workshop 9

Writing Skills   Appropriate Usage

Strategies for Success

The writing sections of both national and Texas standardized tests require you to read a passage and answer multiple-choice questions about appropriate usage. Use the following strategies to help you answer such questions:

Use the Correct Form of a Word Some test questions will ask you to choose the correct part of speech, the appropriate form or correct case of a word, or a way to express a negative. Look at these examples:

1 The directions were very—
   A confusion   **C** confused
   B confusing   **D** confuse

An adjective is needed. **B** and **C** are both adjectives, but *confused* would mean the directions experienced confusion. **B** is correct.

2 This book encourages readers to think—
   A creative   **C** creatively
   B more creative   **D** most creatively

An adverb is needed to modify the verb *think*. **C** and **D** are both adverbs, but **D** is the superlative form, used only in comparisons. **C** is correct.

3 The Wilsons and _____ took a vacation.
   A us   **B** we   **C** ourselves   **D** ourself

The type of pronoun required in this sentence is part of a compound subject, so the answer is **B**.

4 It was so dark, I _____ see nothing.
   A couldn't hardly   **C** couldn't
   B could   **D** couldn't barely

A, **C**, and **D** make double negatives when combined with *nothing*. **B** is correct.

Use Correct Agreement A verb agrees with its subject in number. Don't be misled by singular indefinite pronouns like *anyone* and *everyone*.

A pronoun agrees with its antecedent in person, number, and gender. Look at these examples:

5 Everyone who _____ to go on this trip must have a signed permission slip.
   A want   **C** wants
   B are wanting   **D** have wanted

The verb must agree with the singular subject *everyone*. **C** is correct.

6 Students have not turned in _____ reports.
   A her   **B** their   **C** your   **D** our

The antecedent, *students,* is third person plural, so **B** is correct.

Use Correct Verb Tense and Form Some test questions will require you to choose the correct tense of a verb or the correct form of an irregular verb. Look at this example:

7 We _____ to the rodeo every June.
   A have gone **B** have went **C** is going **D** gone

The verb describes past action continuing in the present, so the present perfect tense is needed. *Gone* is the past participle of *go*. **A** is correct.

Apply the Strategies

Read the passage and choose the word or words that belong in each space.

Everyone I know __(1)__ Helen Keller was an __(2)__ person. Although she __(3)__ her sight and hearing at the age of nineteen months, __(4)__ learned to communicate with the whole world. With the help of __(5)__ teacher, Anne Sullivan, Keller went to college.

1 A think **B** thinks **C** thinking **D** have thought

2 A amaze **B** amazement **C** amazed **D** amazing

3 A has losed **B** losed **C** will lost **D** lost

4 A her **B** she **C** hers **D** herself

5 A its **B** their **C** his **D** her

Additional Test-Taking Tip

Reread the Question with the Answer in Place
Explain to students the importance of checking their answers on standardized tests. One effective way to check answers on fill-in-the-blank questions is to reread the question or statement with the answer in place. This is particularly effective because students can "hear" an incorrect word choice when it is read in context. Have students practice this test-taking strategy by checking their answers to the sample test questions on this page.

Test Preparation Workshop 10

Writing Skills
Spelling, Capitalization, and Punctuation

Strategies for Success

The writing sections of standardized tests require you to read a passage and answer multiple-choice questions about spelling, capitalization, and punctuation. Use the following strategies to help you answer such questions:

Recognize Spelling Errors Check the spelling of each word in the passage. Pay special attention to homophones (*there, their, they're*), vowel sounds (*moan* not *mone*), double consonants (*worry* not *wory*), irregular verbs (*dealt*, not *dealed*), and words containing -ie- or -ei-.

Recognize Capitalization Errors Make sure that the first word in a sentence or a quotation is capitalized, that proper nouns are capitalized, and that no words are capitalized unnecessarily. All the words in a compound proper noun should be capitalized (Texas Education Agency).

Recognize Punctuation Errors Check end punctuation. Determine if commas are missing, misplaced, or unnecessary. Check for opening and closing quotation marks. Look at this example:

Read the passage and decide which type of error, if any, appears in each underlined section.

(1) Windmills are old and new. (2) The first ones were used more then a thousand years ago in Persia. (3) Modern windmills called wind turbines convert wind energy into electricity. (4) some are powered by the wind produced by speeding cars.

1	**A** Spelling error	**C** Punctuation error
	B Capitalization error	**D** No error
2	**A** Spelling error	**C** Punctuation error
	B Capitalization error	**D** No error
3	**A** Spelling error	**C** Punctuation error
	B Capitalization error	**D** No error
4	**A** Spelling error	**C** Punctuation error
	B Capitalization error	**D** No error

For question 1, there are no errors, so **D** is correct. For question 2, *then* should be *than,* so **A** is correct. For question 3, "called wind turbines" should be set off with commas, so **C** is correct. For question 4, *some* should be capitalized, so **B** is correct.

Apply the Strategies

Read the passage and decide which type of error, if any, appears in each underlined section.

(1) Yellowstone national Park has something for everyone. (2) Hikers, boaters, skiers campers and photographers can all find lots of ways to have fun. (3) In 1872, Yellowstone became the country's first national park. (4) More than one hundred years later, it is still impresing visitors.

1	**A** Spelling error	**C** Punctuation error
	B Capitalization error	**D** No error
2	**A** Spelling error	**C** Punctuation error
	B Capitalization error	**D** No error
3	**A** Spelling error	**C** Punctuation error
	B Capitalization error	**D** No error
4	**A** Spelling error	**C** Punctuation error
	B Capitalization error	**D** No error

Answers

1. (B) Capitalization error
2. (C) Punctuation error
3. (D) No error
4. (A) Spelling error

Additional Test-Taking Tip

Look at Each Word

When analyzing an underlined passage for spelling, capitalization, and punctuation errors, remind students to read slowly and look at each word and sentence. It is easy, when reading for sense, to skim past a misspelled word or a missing comma. Students should pretend that they are proofreading their own writing when they respond to the type of standardized test question featured on p. 963.

Test Preparation Workshop 11

Research Skills | Using Information Resources

Strategies for Success

Some tests require you to review a packet of information resources and to respond to questions about how you would use these resources to gather information and plan a report on a given subject. Use these strategies:

Review the Packet of Information Skim through the packet to see what types of material are included, such as articles from encyclopedias and computer information.

Scan the Questions Look through the questions to see which types of information are required to answer the questions. Focus on each question separately. The questions are not necessarily related to each other. Locate the best example or piece of information in the packet to answer each question.

Use Correct Sentence Form Write responses to the short-answer questions in complete sentences and include key words. Look at these examples:.

Directions: Suppose that you are writing a report on the life and times of Thomas Alva Edison (1847–1931). Edison is one of the world's most important inventors.
This packet includes several information resources about Thomas Alva Edison:

- an excerpt from an encyclopedia article, "Inventions of the Nineteenth Century"
- a biographical dictionary entry
- *Thomas Alva Edison*, a biography of the inventor: a short excerpt, table of contents, and a list of key dates in Edison's life and career
- Computer screen: on-line index of library books about Thomas Edison

Excerpt from encyclopedia article: "Inventions of the Nineteenth Century"

A flood of inventions swept the United States in the late 1800's. By the 1890's Americans were patenting 21,000 new inventions a year. These inventions helped industry to grow and become more efficient. New devices also made daily life easier in many American homes.

Advanced Communication Some remarkable new devices filled the need for faster communication. The telegraph speeded communication within the United States. It still took weeks, however, for news from Europe to arrive by boat. In 1866, Cyrus Field ran an underwater telegraph cable across the Atlantic Ocean, bringing the United States and Europe closer together.

Thomas Edison In an age of invention, Thomas Edison was right at home. In 1876, he opened a research laboratory in Menlo Park, New Jersey. There, Edison boasted that he and his 15 co-workers set out to create "minor" inventions every 10 days and "a big thing every 6 months or so."

Biographical Dictionary

Edison, Thomas Alva A poor student, Thomas Edison grew up to invent the light bulb, the phonograph, and dozens of other devises. Edison once went without sleep for three days working on his phonograph. At last, he heard his own voice reciting "Mary Had a Little Lamb." Edison said, "Genius is one percent inspiration and ninety-nine percent perspiration."

Table of Contents from *Thomas Alva Edison*

List of Key Dates 1
Introduction 2
Early Years 3
Menlo Park 45
The Light Bulb 57

Test Preparation Workshop 11

Research Skills — Using Information Resources (cont.)

The Phonograph 69
Later Years. 83
Bibliography 112

Short Excerpt from *Thomas Alva Edison*

The key to Edison's success was his approach. He turned inventing into a system. Teams of experts refined Edison's ideas and turned them into practical inventions. Menlo Park became an "invention factory." The results were amazing. Edison became knows as the "Wizard of Menlo Park" for inventing the light bulb, the phonograph, and hundreds of other devices.

Lists of Key Dates
from *Thomas Alva Edison*

1847: Born in Milan, Ohio
1852: Moved to Port Huron, Michigan
1869: Was paid $40,000 for improvements to the stock ticker. Opened his first workshop in Newark, New Jersey
1874: Improved the typewriter
1877: Invented the phonograph
1879: Perfected the electric light
1887: Moved to West Orange, New Jersey. Worked on such inventions as the motion picture, a storage battery, a cement mixer, the Dictaphone, and a duplicating machine.
1931: Died at 84 in West Orange, New Jersey

Computer Screen

Library Online Catalog
Subject Search: Thomas Alva Edison

Line	Titles	Subjects
1	2	Edison, Thomas: Early Life
2	4	Edison, Thomas: Bibliography
3	1	Edison, Thomas: Biography

Sample Questions and Explanations

1 Which information given in the encyclopedia article would be LEAST useful for your report?
  A the number of patents in the 1890's
  B the date Edison opened his laboratory
  C Cyrus Field's contributions to communication
  D the description of Edison's workshop

The correct answer is **C**. Cyrus Field's contributions are not important to a report on Edison.

2 In which chapter of *Thomas Alva Edison* would you find information about Edison's schooling? ("Early Years" would provide the information.)

3 Which of these sources would you use to find books written about Thomas Alva Edison?
  A the encyclopedia article
  B the biographical dictionary article
  C computer screen
  D the biography Thomas Alva Edison

The correct answer is **C**. The other sources do not reference other books about Edition.

Apply the Strategies

4 Suppose you are going to write an outline of your report on the life of Thomas Alva Edison. What three main topics would you include?

5 State the main idea of your report.

6 In which source would you find detailed information about Edison's marriage?
  A the encyclopedia article
  B the biographical dictionary entry
  C the main body of the biography
  D the list of key dates from the biography

Answers

4. Two possible topic lists are: Edison's Early Years; Edison's Most Famous Inventions; Edison's Later Years; Edison's Childhood; Nineteenth Century Inventions; Edison's Inventions.

5. Students' answers should relate to Edison's importance as an inventor.

6. (C) The most detailed information would appear in the main body of the biography.

Correlations to Standardized Tests

The writing skills reviewed in this workshop correspond to the following standardized test sections:

SAT 9   Language

ACT   English Usage

ITBS   Usage and Expression

TerraNova   Language Arts

Answers

1. (A) Secretary of State Seward bought Alaska from Russia. The deal was mocked as "Seward's Folly."

2. (A) Delete sentence 3

Test Preparation Workshop 12

Writing Skills   Proofreading

Strategies for Success

The writing sections of some standardized tests assess your ability to edit, proofread, and use other writing processes. You are required to look for mistakes in passages and then to choose the best way to correct them.

Check for Incorrect Verb Tense and Errors in Subject-Verb Agreement Check to see that the correct verb tense is used and make the verb agree in number with its subject. If the parts of the subject name more than one thing, use a plural verb. If the parts of the subject refer to the same thing, use a singular verb.

Correct Run-on Sentences Use an end mark and a capital letter to separate main clauses. Use a semicolon between clauses.

Correct Sentence Fragments Add a subject or verb to make a sentence fragment a complete sentence.

Use Supporting Details Effectively Avoid the use of details that interrupt the flow of the passage and that do not support the main idea.

Sample Passage and Questions:

Directions: A student wrote a paper about Alaska. There are mistakes that need correcting.

(1) Susan Butcher win the Iditarod dog-sled race several times. (2) A large strip of mountains cross Alaska. (3) Despite its challenges, the race attracts more and more racers every year. (4) In the years ahead, racers may come from such far-off countries as Sweden Norway and Denmark.

1 Select the best way to write sentence 1.

  A Susan Butcher won the Iditarod dog-sled race several times.

  B Susan Butcher will win the Iditarod dog-sled race several times.

  C Susan Butcher would have won the Iditarod dog-sled race several times.

  D Best as it is

The correct answer is **A.** *Won* is the past tense of the irregular verb *win*.

2 Select the best way to write sentence 2.

  A A large strip of mountains crosses Alaska.

  B A large strip of mountains do cross Alaska.

  C A mountainous strip crosses Alaska.

  D Best as it is.

The correct answer is **A.** A large strip of mountains crosses Alaska. The subject is singular and requires a singular verb.

Apply the Strategies

(1) Secretary of State Seward bought Alaska from Russia the deal was mocked as "Seward's Folly." (2) Seward's $7.2 million purchase proved to be a bargain; gold deposits were discovered there three decades later. (3) My uncle told me about a trip he took to Alaska when he was only 12 years old. (4) Prospectors first struck gold in 1889.

1 Which is the best way to write the underlined section in sentence one?

  A Secretary of State Seward bought Alaska from Russia. The deal was mocked as "Seward's Folly."

  B Secretary of State Seward bought Alaska from Russia, and the deal was mocked.

  C Secretary of State Seward bought Alaska. The deal was "Seward's Folly."

  D Best as it is

2 Which is the correct way to fix the flow of the passage?

  A Delete sentence 3

  B Move sentence 4 to the beginning.

  C Switch sentences 1 and 2

  D Move sentence 1 to the end.

Test Preparation Workshop 13

Writing Skills — Responding to Writing Prompts

Strategies for Success

The writing sections of many standardized tests require you to write an essay based on a writing prompt. Your essay usually is evaluated as a whole, on a 1–6 point scale from *outstanding* to *deficient,* and assessed for focus, content, organization, grammar, usage, and mechanics. Use the following strategies to help you with a writing assessment.

Read the Writing Prompt The writing prompt consists of two parts. The first part explains the topic you are asked to write about, or the writing situation. The second part provides specific instructions on how to respond to the prompt.

Look for Key Words As you examine the writing prompt, look for key words such as *define, explain, classify,* and *contrast.* These words indicate the purpose of your essay. It is essential that you keep these key words in mind as you develop your essay.

Budget Your Time When writing for a test, you need to be aware of how much time you have. Allow one quarter of your time for gathering ideas, half your time for writing your first draft, and one quarter of your time for revising.

Collect Your Ideas Before you begin writing, jot down key ideas and details that you plan to include. Then, review your ideas and decide on the best organization.

Draft Carefully Because you'll have less time to revise then you might in other writing situations, take care in the words and sentences you use as you draft your essay. Begin with an introduction that presents your main point. Follow with body paragraphs, each focusing on a single subtopic. End with a conclusion restating your point.

Use Transitions As you draft, use transitional words to indicate the connections between ideas. The following words show comparison-and-contrast relationships: *however, nevertheless, yet, likewise, in like manner, on the contrary, similarly, instead,* and *nonetheless.*

Proofread Make sure your descriptions are clear. Check that there are no errors in spelling, grammar, usage, or mechanics.

Key Strategies:

- Focus on the topic and do not include unnecessary information.
- Present the material in an organized manner.
- Provide supporting ideas.
- Write with sentence variety.
- Proofread your work.

Apply the Strategies

Practice the preceding strategies by writing an essay in response to the following prompt.

Sample Writing Prompt

Everyone looks forward to weekends and a break from the weekday routine. Think about one thing that you like to do on weekends and why. It could be a community activity, an opportunity to be by yourself to play video games or watch television, or sharing time with family members and friends.

Now explain in an essay why this event or activity is important to you. Support your ideas with examples and details.

Using the Test Practice Bank

These tests provide practice test items in reading comprehension and writing skills. For each Test Preparation Workshop that appears in the book, you will find here a page of extra test items that focus on the same skill. In addition, several tests provide practice in a combination of skills, along with writing prompts.

You may choose to have your students use this practice bank from time to time in conjunction with the Test Preparation Workshops; alternatively, you may want students to spend a block of time working on the entire practice bank during a standardized test preparation period.

Correlations to Standardized Tests

The reading comprehension practice items on this page correspond to the following standardized test sections:

ACT	Reading
SAT 9	Reading Vocabulary
SAT	Critical Reading
TerraNova	Reading

Answers

1 (B) The words "food preparation" provide a context clue indicating that *cuisine* means "cooking."
2 (J) The suffix *-age* indicates that *spoilage* means "the act of spoiling."
3 (C) The words "more than 1,000" and "kinds of hot peppers" provide a context indicating that *discrete* means "separate."
4 (F) The words "enough to make a person sweat" provide a context suggesting that *piquant* means "spicy."
5 (D) The words "the habañero is about 1000 times hotter" provide a context indicating that *jalapeño* means "a kind of pepper."
6 (G) The prefix *dis-*, meaning "not," indicates that *disinclined* means "not inclined," or "hesitant."

Test Practice Bank

Reading Comprehension

Using Context Clues and Prefixes/Suffixes

Read the passage, and then answer the questions that follow. Mark the letter of your answer on a bubble sheet if your teacher provides one; otherwise, number from 1 to 6 on a separate sheet of paper, and write the letter of the correct answer next to each number.

> Cuisine in most hot climates features hot peppers because they cool people who eat them by making them perspire. Using peppers in food preparation can also delay spoilage. Peppers come in many varieties. Worldwide, there are more than 1,000 discrete kinds of hot peppers, although not all are piquant enough to make a person sweat. Peppers come in many degrees of hotness; for instance, the habañero (Scotch bonnet) is about 1,000 times hotter than the jalapeño. If you serve these peppers to guests without warning them, they will be disinclined to try your cooking again.

1 In this passage, the word *cuisine* means—
A sweating
B cooking
C gardening
D measuring

2 The word *spoilage* in this passage means—
F the prevention of spoiling
G the prevention of using peppers
H the act of using peppers
J the act of spoiling

3 In this passage, the word *discrete* means—
A similar
B popular
C separate
D unknown

4 In this passage, the word *piquant* means—
F spicy
G mild
H unpleasant
J widespread

5 From this passage, you can tell that a jalapeño is—
A a Scotch bonnet
B another word for habañero
C a person who likes spicy food
D a kind of pepper

6 The word *disinclined* in this passage means—
F happy
G hesitant
H eager
J able

1002 ◆ Test Practice Bank

Reading Comprehension

Following Written Directions

Read the passage, and then answer the questions that follow. Mark the letter of your answer on a bubble sheet if your teacher provides one; otherwise, number from 1 to 6 on a separate sheet of paper, and write the letter of the correct answer next to each number.

When you're making a personal or professional telephone call, begin by introducing yourself and stating your purpose. "Hello. My name is Lakota Sandford. I'm calling in response to your advertisement for a baby sitter." "Hi, Mrs. Martinez. This is Dave. Is Nick home?"

When calling for information or to order a product, it is not necessary to introduce yourself. If you're ordering something, you will be asked for personal information at the appropriate time.

If your listener keeps asking you to repeat yourself, you may need to speak more slowly and distinctly.

Repeating information ensures that you have heard the other person correctly. When you are receiving information, repeat it to verify its accuracy.

Be courteous on the phone. Say "please" and "thank you." Confirm any future contact. "Thanks for calling, Lakota. I'll meet with you Tuesday."

---

1 What is the first thing you should do when making a personal or professional phone call?
   A Repeat information.
   B Confirm future contact.
   C Introduce yourself.
   D Say "please" and "thank you."

2 It is NOT necessary to introduce yourself —
   F when calling a friend
   G when calling a professional
   H when ordering a product
   J when talking on the phone

3 How should you verify that your information is accurate?
   A Repeat the information.
   B Speak slowly and clearly.
   C Introduce yourself.
   D Call for information.

4 You should be courteous—
   F when requesting information
   G when on the phone
   H when repeating yourself
   J when making a professional call

5 Why is it important to speak clearly?
   A to verify the accuracy of your information
   B to keep from repeating yourself
   C so your listener will not ask for your personal information.
   D so your listener can understand

6 If your listener asks you to repeat yourself, you may—
   F not have spoken clearly enough
   G not have heard correctly
   H not have introduced yourself
   J not have confirmed future plans

Answers

1 (C) The first sentence states that when making a personal or professional telephone call, you should begin by introducing yourself.

2 (H) The first sentence of the second paragraph states that you do not have to introduce yourself when ordering a product.

3 (A) The second sentence in the fourth paragraph advises you to repeat information to verify its accuracy.

4 (G) The first sentence in the last paragraph advises that you should be courteous on the phone.

5 (D) You can infer from the context of the third paragraph that you need to speak clearly so the listener can understand.

6 (F) The third paragraph states that you may need to speak more slowly and distinctly if the listener keeps asking you to repeat yourself.

Correlations to Standardized Tests

The reading comprehension practice items on this page correspond to the following standardized test sections:

ACT Reading

SAT 9 Reading Comprehension

ITBS Reading Comprehension

TerraNova Reading

Answers

1 (A) The first sentence in the passage states the main idea that is supported by the sentences that follow.

2 (J) The answer includes the main idea and all the other important points in the passage. The other choices omit some important points.

Reading Comprehension

Identifying Main Idea; Identifying Best Summary

Read the passage, and then answer the questions that follow. Mark the letter of your answer on a bubble sheet if your teacher provides one; otherwise, number 1 and 2 on a separate sheet of paper, and write the letter of the correct answer next to each number.

> Wetlands are areas of land where the water level remains near or above the surface of the ground for most of the year. Types of wetlands include bogs, fens, marshes, and swamps. Wetlands are home to many types of plants and animals, including several endangered species. They also help control flooding by holding large amounts of water. Although wetlands in the United States are protected by the Federal Clean Water Act and by various state and local laws, many environmentalists are asking for stronger laws to protect them.

1 What is the main idea of this passage?
   A Wetlands are land areas in which water remains near or above the surface of the ground for most of the year.
   B Wetlands are areas that are important for plants, animals, and people, and they may need special protection.
   C Environmentalists are asking for stronger laws to protect wetlands.
   D Wetlands are home to many plants and animals, including endangered species.

2 What is the best summary of this passage?
   F Wetlands are important because they help control flooding.
   G Wetlands are areas where the water is near or above the surface for most of the year, and they provide homes for endangered species.
   H Wetlands are land areas where the water remains near or above the ground surface for most of the year. They provide homes for many plants and animals, some of which are endangered. Wetlands help control flooding. Although wetlands are currently protected by laws, stronger laws may be needed.
   J Wetlands are areas where the water remains near or above the surface most of the year; wetlands can be bogs, fens, marshes, or swamps; wetlands are protected by the Federal Clean Water Act and by state and local laws, but many environmentalists want stronger laws.

Reading Comprehension

Arranging Details in Sequential Order

Read the passage, and then answer the questions that follow. Mark the letter of your answer on a bubble sheet if your teacher provides one; otherwise, number from 1 to 6 on a separate sheet of paper, and write the letter of the correct answer next to each number.

> Born in Galesburg, Illinois, in 1878, Carl Sandburg became one of the best-known American poets. Sandburg enlisted in the 6th Illinois Infantry when the Spanish-American War broke out in 1898. From 1910 to 1912, he was secretary to the mayor of Milwaukee. Sandburg moved to Chicago in 1913, where he became an editor of a business magazine and later became a staff member of the *Chicago Daily News. Poetry* magazine published a number of his poems in 1914, and his first collection, *Chicago Poems,* came out in 1916.
>
> Sandburg's epic poem, *The People, Yes,* was published in 1936. At that time, the United States was experiencing the Great Depression, a time of economic struggle that began in 1929 and continued into World War II (1939–1945). *The People, Yes* celebrates the common people and their courage in hard times.
>
> Sandburg won the Pulitzer Prize three times: in 1918, for his poetry collection, *Cornhuskers*; in 1940, for his biography of Abraham Lincoln; and in 1951, for his *Complete Poems.*

1 Carl Sandburg first won the Pulitzer Prize in—
A 1936 **B** 1918 **C** 1940 **D** 1951

2 Sandburg published *Chicago Poems*—
F during the Great Depression
G after World War II
H before publishing *The People, Yes*
J before *Poetry* magazine published some of his poems

3 Which of the following happened during World War II?
A *The People, Yes* was published.
B Sandburg won a Pulitzer Prize for his biography of Lincoln.
C Sandburg's poems were published in *Poetry* magazine.
D Sandburg won a Pulitzer Prize for his *Complete Poems.*

4 Sandburg moved to Chicago AFTER—
F working for Milwaukee's mayor
G publishing in *Poetry* magazine
H working at the *Chicago Daily News*
J publishing his first collection of poems

5 BEFORE becoming an editor, Sandburg had—
A won a Pulitzer Prize
B worked at the *Chicago Daily News*
C published his first poetry collection
D been in the 6th Illinois Infantry

6 The Great Depression began—
F after World War II
G after Sandburg moved to Chicago
H before the Spanish-American War
J before Sandburg was an editor

Correlations to Standardized Tests

The reading comprehension practice items on this page correspond to the following standardized test sections:

ACT   Reading
SAT 9   Reading Comprehension

Answers

1 (B) In 1918, Sandburg won the first of his three Pulitzer Prizes.
2 (H) Sandburg's first collection, *Chicago Poems,* came out in 1916. *The People, Yes* was published in 1936.
3 (B) Sandburg won the Pulitzer Prize in 1940, during World War II, which lasted from 1939 until 1945.
4 (F) Sandburg worked for the mayor of Milwaukee from 1910 to 1912. He moved to Chicago in 1913.
5 (D) Sandburg joined the 6th Illinois infantry in 1898. He did not become an editor until *after* his arrival in Chicago in 1913.
6 (G) Sandburg moved to Chicago in 1913, long before the Great Depression, which began in 1929.

Answers

1 (C) Because he could not find the timer, Enrique skipped steps 3 and 4.

2 (G) Enrique decided to watch TV because he finished his tasks earlier than he had expected.

3 (D) It's most probable that by setting the timer and removing the casserole from the oven when the timer went off, Enrique would have cooked dinner successfully.

4 (F) Since the timer was so important to the success of the meal, it was critical Enrique know where it was.

5 (B) It is likely that if Enrique had not spent a half hour watching TV, he would have completed his homework.

6 (H) The third sentence of the second paragraph confirms that Enrique did the vacuuming (step 6) before washing the dishes (step 5).

Reading Comprehension

Analyzing Information and Making Judgments

Read the passage, and then answer the questions that follow. Mark the letter of your answer on a bubble sheet if your teacher provides one; otherwise, number from 1 to 6 on a separate sheet of paper, and write the letter of the correct answer next to each number.

Enrique got home from school to find a list of instructions from his father.

1. Heat the oven to 350 degrees.
2. Take the casserole out of the refrigerator and put it in the oven.
3. Set the timer for 45 minutes.
4. When the timer goes off, remove the casserole and put it aside to cool.
5. Wash the breakfast dishes.
6. Vacuum the carpet in your room.
7. Do your homework.

Enrique heated the oven and put in the casserole. He looked for the timer but could not find it. Enrique vacuumed his room and then washed the breakfast dishes. He finished earlier than he thought he would, so he watched TV. After half an hour, he sat down at his desk to do his homework. After an hour, he smelled something burning. He ran to the kitchen and opened the oven door. The casserole was badly burned. Enrique turned off the oven and looked at the clock. His father would be home in a few minutes, and Enrique had burned dinner and had not finished his homework.

---

1 Which things did Enrique not do?
  A 1 and 3   **C** 3 and 4
  B 2 and 6   **D** 4 and 5

2 What did Enrique do that was not on the list?
  F remove the casserole
  G watch TV
  H wash the breakfast dishes
  J heat the oven

3 Enrique might have cooked dinner successfully if he had—
  A not watched TV
  B finished his homework earlier
  C washed the dishes first
  D set the timer

4 Enrique's father's instructions would have been more useful if they had included—

  F the location of the timer
  G instructions not to watch TV
  H a description of the casserole
  J vacuuming instructions

5 What would have helped Enrique complete his homework?
  A setting the timer
  B not watching TV
  C not vacuuming
  D removing the casserole

6 Which two tasks did Enrique perform in reverse order?
  F Heating the oven and putting in the casserole
  G Setting the timer and doing homework
  H Vacuuming and washing dishes
  J Doing homework and vacuuming

Reading Comprehension

Interpreting Diagrams, Graphs, and Statistical Illustrations

Read the passage, and then answer the questions that follow. Mark the letter of your answer on a bubble sheet if your teacher provides one; otherwise, number from 1 to 4 on a separate sheet of paper, and write the letter of the correct answer next to each number.

Charles Elder is taking a trip with his fourteen-year-old daughter, Melinda. The Elders live in a city called Cleaver and have decided to spend the weekend visiting historic places in Brady, a town located 200 miles away. Mr. Elder thought it would be a special treat if they could take the train instead of driving. It is summer, so Melinda is out of school, but Mr. Elder has to work Monday through Friday from 8:00 until 4:30 P.M. He is very busy, and so he has given Melinda the job of finding infor-mation about the train schedule and hotels. Melinda has received the following information from the Brady Chamber of Commerce.

TRAIN SCHEDULE

Train	Days	Departs Cleaver	Arrives in Nelsonville	Arrives in Brady
BRADY COMMUTER	Monday through Friday	7:00 A.M		10:00 A.M.
BRADY BULLET	Sunday through Friday	5:00 P.M.	6:30 P.M.	9:00 P.M.
BRADY EXPRESS	Monday through Saturday	7:30 P.M.		10:30 P.M.
BRADY FLYER	Daily	6:30 P.M.	8:00 P.M. (stays in Nelsonville for 30 minutes)	11:00 P.M.

1 If Mr. Elder works his normal day on Friday, which train would they have to take to arrive in Brady before the stores close at 10:00 P.M.?
A Brady Commuter
B Brady Bullet
C Brady Express
D Brady Flyer

2 If the Elders decided to spend the night in Nelsonville, how many trains could they take that would get them there in time to do some shopping before the stores close at 7:30 P.M.?
F One
G Two
H Three
J Four

3 If Mr. Elder has a meeting on Friday night that lasts until 9:00 P.M., what is the first train they could take the next day?
A Brady Commuter
B Brady Bullet
C Brady Express
D Brady Flyer

4 If the Elders waited until Saturday to leave, how many trains would they have to choose from?
F One
G Two
H Three
J Four

Correlations to Standardized Tests

The reading comprehension practice items on this page correspond to the following standardized test section:

ACT   Reading

Answers

1   (B) If Mr. Elder hurries, he can catch the 5:00 P. M. train, the Brady Bullet, which is due to arrive in Brady at 9:00 P. M., allowing one hour for shopping.

2   (F) The 5:00 P. M. Brady Bullet, which is due to arrive at Nelsonville at 6:30 P. M., is the only train that would get them to Nelsonville before the stores close.

3   (D) The first train to Brady on Saturday is the Brady Flyer, which departs at 6:30 P. M.

4   (G) On Saturday two trains to Brady are available: the Brady Flyer, departing at 6:30 P. M., and the Brady Express, departing at 7:30 P. M.

Answers

1 (B) Because the narrator perceives that his accomplishments were negated by his riding a mule to school, you can infer that he needs to prove his worth to his classmates.

2 (J) Since the narrator claims he is very excited about his project and wants it to be outstanding, you can conclude that he is enthusiastic and determined.

3 (B) Because the narrator wants his project to be greater and more unusual than anyone else's, he will probably design an elaborate project.

4 (G) Since the author includes details that create a strong impression of the narrator, you can infer that the passage was probably written to introduce the narrator.

5 (C) Because the narrator rode a mule to school, you can conclude that the setting is in the country, sometime in the past before the advent of school buses.

6 (F) The generalization that the narrator is competitive grows out of the third sentence of the first paragraph.

Reading Comprehension

Drawing Inferences and Conclusions; Making Generalizations

Read the passage, and then answer the questions that follow. Mark the letter of your answer on a bubble sheet if your teacher provides one; otherwise, number from 1 to 6 on a separate sheet of paper, and write the letter of the correct answer next to each number.

> The day Professor Herbert started talking about a project for each member of our General Science class, I was more excited than I had ever been. I wanted to have an outstanding project. I wanted it to be greater, to be more unusual than those of my classmates. I wanted to do something worthwhile, and something to make them respect me.
>
> I'd made the best grade in my class in General Science. I'd made more yardage, more tackles and carried the football across the goal line more times than any player on my team. But making good grades and playing rugged football hadn't made them forget that I rode a mule to school. . . .
>
> —"A Ribbon for Baldy"
> by Jesse Stuart

1 You can infer from the passage that the narrator wishes to—
  A become a great scientist some day
  B prove his worth to his classmates
  C become as good at science as he is at football
  D gain the confidence he needs to reach his goals

2 Which words best describe the narrator's feelings?
  F doubtful and afraid
  G depressed and hopeless
  H quick-tempered and fiery
  J determined and enthusiastic

3 You can conclude from the passage that the narrator will probably—
  A quit the football team
  B design an elaborate project
  C try to change science classes
  D let his classmates ride his mule

4 This passage was probably written to—
  F create a suspenseful mood
  G introduce the story's narrator
  H tell how a problem was solved
  J explain the effects of a decision

5 You can conclude from the passage that the setting is—
  A an imaginary place, in the future
  B a city, in the present
  C the country, in the past
  D a city, in the past

6 Which of these statements is a generalization based on the passage?
  F The narrator is competitive.
  G The narrator has never failed at anything.
  H The narrator prefers playing sports to studying.
  J The narrator has never been afraid of being teased.

Reading Comprehension

Identifying Cause and Effect

Read the passage, and then answer the questions that follow. Mark the letter of your answer on a bubble sheet if your teacher provides one; otherwise, number from 1 to 6 on a separate sheet of paper, and write the letter of the correct answer next to each number.

> "Last week he hurled the local blacksmith over a parapet into a stream, and it was only by paying over all the money which I could gather together that I was able to avert another public exposure. He had no friends at all save the wandering gypsies, and he would give these vagabonds leave to encamp upon the few acres of bramble-covered land which represent the family estate, and would accept in return the hospitality of their tents, wandering away with them sometimes for weeks on end. He has a passion also for Indian animals, which are sent over to him by a correspondent, and he has at this moment a cheetah and a baboon, which wander freely over his grounds and are feared by the villagers almost as much as is their master."
> —"The Adventure of the Speckled Band" by Arthur Conan Doyle

1 The man described in this passage is able to acquire Indian animals because of his friendship with—
   A nearby villagers
   B a local blacksmith
   C a group of gypsies
   D a correspondent

2 The man has left himself open to public attack because he has—
   F assaulted a blacksmith
   G purchased a large estate
   H misspent a friend's money
   J expressed fear of the villagers

3 What effect does the man's behavior have on the villagers?
   A They are afraid of him.
   B They feel pity for him.
   C They return his kindness.
   D They admire his generosity.

4 Why do the gypsies offer their tents to the man described in the passage?

F He lets them camp on his estate.
G He often guides them during their travels.
H He shares their passion for Indian animals.
J He gives them money.

5 Why is the man often absent from his estate?
   A He is arrested for his behavior.
   B He takes trips with the gypsies.
   C He travels overseas to purchase animals.
   D He has arguments with villagers.

6 How did the narrator prevent the man's assault on the blacksmith from being revealed?
   F by contacting a correspondent
   G by paying a large sum of money
   H by gaining the gypsies' cooperation
   J by appealing to the villagers' generosity

The reading comprehension practice items on this page correspond to the following standardized test sections:

ACT   Reading

SAT 9   Reading Comprehension

Answers

1 (D) The third sentence in the passage states that a correspondent sent the animals over to the man.

2 (F) Because the man assaulted a blacksmith, you can predict that the latter might tell some of his customers about the incident. They, in turn, could react negatively to the man.

3 (A) The villagers fear the man, undoubtedly because he has no friends, behaves poorly, and keeps animals that terrify them.

4 (F) Since the man permits the gypsies to stay on his land, they respond with hospitality.

5 (B) The second sentence states that the man joins the gypsies and wanders with them for weeks at a time.

6 (G) The first sentence in the passage corroborates that the narrator spent money to avoid another public exposure.

Answers

1 (D) The writer's opinion that there is no such thing as a typical human being cannot be proved.

2 (H) That teenagers take part in after-school activities is a fact that can be proved.

3 (D) That Hanover Middle School eighth graders conducted a survey is a fact that can be proved.

4 (F) That 65% of the students participated in an after-school club or on a sports team is a fact that can be proved.

5 (A) This statement is the opinion of the writer of the article, not of the writer of the letter.

6 (G) The statement that there is no typical teenager, just as there is no typical adult, is an opinion because it cannot be proved.

Reading Comprehension

Distinguishing Fact and Opinion

Read each passage, and then answer the questions that follow. Mark the letter of your answer on a bubble sheet if your teacher provides one; otherwise, number from 1 to 6 on a separate sheet of paper, and write the letter of the correct answer next to each number.

> Dear Editor:
>
> Don't call me lazy! In a May 19 article titled "The Trouble with Teens," the writer states that "typical teenagers do nothing but skateboard and hang out at the mall." I strongly disagree, and here's why. In a survey conducted by eighth graders at Hanover Middle School, 65 percent of the students said that they participate in an after-school club or play on a sports team. More important, though, there is no typical teenager, just as there is no typical adult. We are all individual and unique.
>
> Sincerely,
> 13 and Proud of It

1 Which of the following expresses the writer's opinion?
  A Sixty-five percent of students participate in after-school activities.
  B A survey was conducted at Hanover Middle School.
  C An article concerning teens appeared on May 19.
  D There is no such thing as a typical human being.

2 In this passage, the writer states the fact that teenagers—
  F are typical
  G are unlike adults
  H do after-school activities
  J spend time at malls

3 The writer uses facts to support claims about—
  A typical teenagers
  B typical adults
  C unique persons
  D eighth graders

4 The writer uses a fact to support the opinion that—
  F local teens are not typically lazy
  G the writer is not typically lazy
  H local adults are not typically lazy
  J typical people do not exist

5 Which of the following does NOT express the writer's opinion?
  A Typical teenagers do nothing.
  B Every adult and teenager is unique.
  C There are no typical teenagers.
  D The article misrepresents teenagers.

6 In this passage, the writer's comparison of adults and teenagers is based on—
  F fact
  G opinion
  H research
  J surveys

Reading Comprehension

Recognizing Author's Point of View and Purpose

Read the passage, and then answer the questions that follow. Mark the letter of your answer on a bubble sheet if your teacher provides one; otherwise, number from 1 to 6 on a separate sheet of paper, and write the letter of the correct answer next to each number.

> There are people who I have corresponded with on email for months before actually meeting them—people at work and otherwise. If someone isn't saying something of interest it's easier to not respond to their mail than it is not to answer the phone. In fact I give out my home phone number to almost no one but my email address is known very broadly. I am the only person who reads my email so no one has to worry about embarrassing themselves or going around people when they send a message. Our email is completely secure. . . .
>
> —from "E-Mail from Bill Gates" by John Seabrook

1 How does the author of this passage feel about e-mail?
   A annoyed
   B cautious
   C enthusiastic
   D indifferent

2 The author's main purpose is to—
   F explain the process of sending e-mail
   G inform readers of the history of e-mail
   H describe a past experience sending e-mail
   J convince readers of the advantages of e-mail

3 What secondary purpose might the author have for writing this passage?
   A to convince readers that he is easy to contact
   B to entertain readers with a humorous incident
   C to describe his life before the development of e-mail
   D to present his own role in the development of e-mail

4 The author includes the first sentence of the passage to show that e-mail is—
   F convenient
   G inexpensive
   H problematic
   J time-consuming

5 The author says that people do not have to "worry about embarrassing themselves" while using e-mail in order to convince readers that e-mail—
   A can be sent anonymously
   B is used by almost everyone
   C cannot be secretly read by others
   D can prevent unintended mistakes

6 The author believes that communicating by telephone is—
   F more costly than using e-mail
   G more private than using e-mail
   H more personal than using e-mail
   J more adaptable than using e-mail

Correlations to Standardized Tests

The reading comprehension practice items on this page correspond to the following standardized test sections:

ACT — Reading
SAT — Critical Reading
ITBS — Reading Comprehension
TerraNova — Reading

Answers

1 (C) In discussing the convenience and privacy of e-mail, the author indicates that he is enthusiastic about it.

2 (J) The author's emphasis on the positive aspects of e-mail, such as its convenience and privacy, indicate that his purpose is to convince readers of the advantages of e-mail.

3 (A) By indicating that his e-mail address is known broadly, a secondary purpose might be to convince readers that the author is easy to contact.

4 (F) It is convenient to correspond with people even though you have not met them, or have no time to meet them.

5 (C) The author's statement that his e-mail is secure is intended to reassure.

6 (H) The author states that he rarely gives out his home phone number while his e-mail address is available to many. You can conclude that his point of view is that the phone is for more personal communications than e-mail is.

Correlations to Standardized Tests

The reading comprehension practice items on these two pages correspond to the following standardized test sections:

ACT   Reading
SAT   Critical Reading
ITBS   Reading Comprehension
TerraNova Reading

Answers

1 (D) The context of *implemented* indicates that the word means "put into effect."

2 (G) The context of *encompasses* indicates that the word means "includes."

3 (C) The second sentence describing ASCII text clearly identifies it as belonging to the early age of computer networking.

4 (F) The author does not state that computing has many basic problems, but the irritated tone of the paragraph implies this.

Combined Reading and Literary Skills

Read the passage, and then answer the questions that follow. Mark your answers to questions 1–9 on a bubble sheet if your teacher provides one; otherwise, number from 1 to 9 on a separate sheet of paper, and write the letter of the correct answer next to each number. Answer number 10 on a separate sheet of paper.

The truth is that computer networking is still in its infancy. Probably nothing illustrates this more clearly than the "ASCII[1] jail": 90% of network communications are still limited to plain old ASCII text—that is, the characters of the alphabet, the numerals 0 through 9, and the most basic punctuation marks. It's bad enough that multimedia communications have not been implemented in most of cyberspace.[2] Most of the time you can't even put a word in bold or italics!

Because people cannot see or hear you in cyberspace, you need to pay close attention to the style of your electronic communications if you hope to make a good impression there. The *style* of electronic communications encompasses everything about your correspondence except its content, from your use of network conventions like "smileys" and "sigs" to the number of characters per line in your email messages.

Style considerations are influenced by several rules of Netiquette, especially Rule 4, Respect other people's time, and Rule 5, Make yourself look good online. It doesn't matter how brilliant your messages are if they're formatted in such a way that no one can read them.

—"How to Be Polite Online"
from *Netiquette* by Virginia Shea

1. **ASCII:** Abbreviation of American Standard Code for Information Interchange, a standard computer code used to assist the interchange of information among various types of data-processing equipment.
2. **cyberspace:** Global communication performed through the use of computer technology.

1 In this passage, the word *implemented* means—
A outlawed
B recognized
C reasoned with
D put into effect

2 The word *encompasses* in this passage means—
F imitates
G includes
H precedes
J reverses

3 What example shows that computer networking remains in its early stages of development?
A network conventions
B multimedia style
C ASCII text
D Netiquette

4 What is the implied main idea of the first paragraph?
F Network communication still has many basic problems.
G Multimedia communications have

revolutionized cyberspace.

H People fear the use of ASCII text because it's so new.

J The use of ASCII text for networking was always a bad idea.

5 Why does the author refer to ASCII text as a "jail"?

A It is used by many people.

B It has very limited features.

C It is a relatively new method.

D It cannot be used in cyberspace.

6 The author believes that the style of an electronic message is—

F not limited by conventions

G enhanced by ASCII text

H as important as content

J of little consequence

7 Which of these is a FACT from the passage?

A Respecting others' time is an important rule of Netiquette.

B Ninety percent of network communications use ASCII text.

C Paying attention to style makes a good impression.

D Electronic messages should be clearly formatted.

8 The author's main purpose is to—

F protest rude behavior in cyberspace

G relate stories about cyberspace

H predict the future of network communication

J give advice about network communication

9 Based on the article, what is likely to happen to network communications in the future?

A The need for style guidelines will decrease.

B The use of bold and italic text will decrease.

C The use of multimedia in cyberspace will increase.

D The percentage of messages using ASCII will increase.

10 Why should style be an important consideration when you create an electronic message? Support your answer with evidence from the text.

Answers (Continued)

5 (B) The author is irritated and feels imprisoned by the limited features of ASCII text.

6 (H) The second sentence of the second paragraph states that the style of an electronic message encompasses everything *but* content, a fact which concerns the author.

7 (B) Choice B is a fact because it can be proved.

8 (J) Since the second and third paragraphs contain advice, you can conclude that the author's main purpose is to give advice about network communication.

9 (C) This author offers a convincing argument showing why the use of multimedia in cyberspace must increase.

10 *Possible response:*
The whole point of communicating is to be understood. The author's premise is that ASCII text is not the best medium of communication in cyberspace because its features are so limited. Virginia Shea wants multimedia communications to be implemented in cyberspace. She advises that in order to make a good impression in cyberspace, you must pay close attention to the style of your electronic communications. She urges people to pay attention to Rule 4 and respect other people's time. You should also follow Rule 5 and make yourself look good online. It doesn't matter how brilliant your remarks are if no one can read or understand them.

Rubric for Evaluating Responses to Writing Prompts				
0	**1**	**2**	**3**	**4**
Off topic Blank paper Foreign language Illegible, incoherent Not enough content to score	Incorrect purpose, mode, or audience Brief, vague Unelaborated Rambling	Lack of language control Poor organization Correct purpose, mode, audience Some elaboration Some details	Gaps in organization Limited language control Correct purpose, mode, audience Moderately well elaborated Clear, effective language	Organized (perhaps with brief digressions) Correct purpose, mode, audience Effective elaboration Consistent organization Sense of completeness, fluency

Answers

1 (B) The period after *reservation* corrects the comma splice between two complete sentences.

2 (H) This choice is correct because it eliminates the sentence fragment, *And their fighting skills.*

3 (C) The sentence is correct without the colon after *between* and the comma after *U.S.*

4 (H) This sentence is correct because a comma should not appear between a subject and a verb.

5 (A) The clause *which is Poland's capital* is nonrestrictive and needs a comma before *which.*

6 (J)

Writing Skills
Sentence Construction

Read each passage, and then answer the questions that follow. Mark the letter of the answer on a bubble sheet if your teacher provides one; otherwise, number 1 to 6 on a separate sheet of paper, and write the letter of the correct answer next to each number.

---

(1) Grandpa lived on a Sioux reservation, the Sioux once lived on the northern plains of North America.
(2) They were famous for their bravery.
(3) And their fighting skills. (4) Tension developed between: the Sioux and the U.S., in the 1800's.

---

1 How would you correct the underlined portion of sentence 1?
   A Grandpa lived on a Sioux reservation the Sioux once lived
   B Grandpa lived on a Sioux reservation. The Sioux once lived
   C Grandpa lived on a Sioux reservation: the Sioux once lived
   D Correct as is

2 How would you correct the structure of sentences 2 and 3?
   F They were famous for their bravery, And their fighting skills.
   G They were famous for their bravery, and their fighting skills.
   H They were famous for their bravery and their fighting skills.
   J Correct as is

3 How would you correct the structure of sentence 4?
   A Tension developed between, the Sioux and the U.S., in the 1800's.
   B Tension developed between the Sioux, and the U.S. in the 1800's.
   C Tension developed between the Sioux and the U.S. in the 1800's.
   D Correct as is

---

(1) Isaac Bashevis Singer, came from a family of Jewish religious leaders. (2) He grew up in Warsaw which is Poland's capital. (3) Singer received a Jewish education before he decided to become a writer.

---

4 How would you correct the structure of sentence 1?
   F Isaac Bashevis Singer, came from, a family of Jewish religious leaders.
   G Isaac Bashevis Singer came from: a family of Jewish religious leaders.
   H Isaac Bashevis Singer came from a family of Jewish religious leaders.
   J Correct as is

5 How would you correct the underlined portion of sentence 2?
   A Warsaw, which is Poland's capital.
   B Warsaw; which is Poland's capital.
   C Warsaw. Which is Poland's capital.
   D Correct as is

6 How would you correct the structure of sentence 3?
   F Singer received a Jewish education; before he decided, to become a writer.
   G Singer received a Jewish education, before; He decided to become a writer.
   H Singer received a Jewish education; before, he decided to become a writer.
   J Correct as is

Writing Skills

Appropriate Usage

Read the passage, and choose the word or group of words that belongs in each space. Mark the letter of the answer on a bubble sheet if your teacher provides one; otherwise, number 1 to 6 on a separate sheet of paper, and write the letter of the correct answer next to each number.

John Steinbeck described the Badlands in South Dakota as "sculptured hills and ravines." The geologic formation of areas like this __(1)__ by water erosion, __(2)__ creates steep hills and deep valleys. __(3)__ geological areas are often found in very dry regions, where occasional flash floods __(4)__ gushing streams of water __(5)__ the surrounding rock and soil layers. Visitors __(6)__ come to the Badlands enjoy a variety of rock formations.

1   **A** caused
    B are caused
    C is caused
    D causes

2   **F** which
    G while
    H where
    J but

3   **A** What
    B This
    C That
    D These

4   **F** cause
    G causes
    H will causes
    J was caused

5   **A** erode
    B eroding
    C to erode
    D have eroded

6   **F** what
    G they
    H which
    J who

The writing skills items on this page correspond to the following standardized test sections:

ACT English Usage

SAT 9 Language

ITBS Usage and Expression

Answers

1   (C) The singular verb *is caused* agrees in number with its singular subject, *formation*.

2   (F) The relative pronoun *which* introduces the adjective clause that follows and modifies *erosion*.

3   (D) The plural demonstrative adjective *these* modifies the plural subject, *areas*.

4   (F) In the adjective clause, the plural verb *cause* agrees in number with its plural subject, *floods*.

5   (C) The infinitive phrase *gushing streams to erode the surrounding rock and soil layers* is the direct object of the verb *cause* in the adjective clause.

6   (J) The relative pronoun *who* introduces the adjective clause *who come to the Badlands,* which modifies the subject of the sentence, *visitors*.

Answers

1 (C) A comma should not be used after the word *sports*.
2 (F) *Biographies* is misspelled.
3 (D)
4 (H) A comma is needed after an introductory infinitive. Therefore, a comma belongs after the word *involve*.
5 (D)
6 (G) The word *Or* should not be capitalized; it introduces the rest of a compound sentence.

Writing

Spelling, Capitalization, and Punctuation

Read the passage, and decide which type of error, if any, appears in each underlined section. Mark the letter of your answer on a bubble sheet if your teacher provides one; otherwise, number from 1 to 6 on a separate sheet of paper, and write the letter of the correct answer next to each number.

Sporting events are big news. <u>People with a love of sports, and a</u>
                                                    (1)
flair for public speaking may want to pursue careers in sports reporting. <u>Some</u>

<u>sports reporter careers started with an interest in TV sports commentary,</u>
                                                                        (2)
newspaper sports articles, or biographys of great athletes. <u>Still others began by</u>

<u>following player and team statistics.</u> <u>To understand what sports reporting</u>
                (3)   (4)
<u>might involve focus on local sports activities.</u> <u>Write an article about</u>

<u>a football game or a track meet,</u> <u>and submit it to your school newspaper;</u>
                (5)   (6)
<u>Or consider writing a profile of an athlete.</u>

---

1 **A** Spelling error
  B Capitalization error
  C Punctuation error
  D No error

2 **F** Spelling error
  G Capitalization error
  H Punctuation error
  J No error

3 **A** Spelling error
  B Capitalization error
  C Punctuation error
  D No error

4 **F** Spelling error
  G Capitalization error
  H Punctuation error
  J No error

5 **A** Spelling error
  B Capitalization error
  C Punctuation error
  D No error

6 **F** Spelling error
  G Capitalization error
  H Punctuation error
  J No error

Writing Tasks

The following activity is designed to assess your writing ability. The prompts will ask you to explain something. You may think of your audience as being any reader other than yourself.

Think of a game you enjoy playing. The game could be a board game, such as chess; a word game, such as twenty questions; or a physical game, such as charades or soccer. Write an essay explaining how to play the game or sport. Describe any special equipment that's needed to play. Explain in detail the rules and instructions of the game, so that the reader can clearly understand how to play it.

Recently technicians have found a way to use computers to manipulate a photograph by changing its color, size, shape, brightness, and clarity. Computer experts can even add, move, or delete parts of a photograph. Manipulated photographs can be informative and entertaining. However, altering photographs can also be deceptive and misleading; for example, a piece of evidence might be removed from the photograph of a crime scene. Some people think that laws should be passed to prevent photograph manipulation; others think that people should be free to express themselves. Still others suggest that all altered photographs should be labeled. As editor of your school newspaper, take a position for or against including a manipulated photograph in a news story. Explain your position.

There are advantages and disadvantages to being an only child, just as there are to having brothers and sisters. Choose one situation to describe. Either write an essay explaining the advantages and disadvantages of having brothers and sisters, or write about the pros and cons of being an only child. Support your personal essay with specific details and examples from your own experience, books, movies, or television shows.

Rubric for Evaluating Responses to Writing Prompts				
0	**1**	**2**	**3**	**4**
Off topic Blank paper Foreign language Illegible, incoherent Not enough content to score	Incorrect purpose, mode, or audience Brief, vague Unelaborated Rambling	Lack of language control Poor organization Correct purpose, mode, audience Some elaboration Some details	Gaps in organization Limited language control Correct purpose, mode, audience Moderately well elaborated Clear, effective language	Organized (perhaps with brief digressions) Correct purpose, mode, audience Effective elaboration Consistent organization Sense of completeness, fluency

Scoring Rubric

Use this scoring rubric to assess the composition you write in response to the prompts on the previous page. The scale runs from **0** (the poorest) to **4** (the best).

0	1	2	3	4
Blank paper	Vague or brief	Correct purpose, audience, and mode	Correct purpose, audience, and mode	Correct purpose, audience, and mode
In a foreign language	Poorly organized			
Unreadable because of incoherence or illegibility	Wrong purpose, audience, or mode	Organization has lapses	Fair organization	Full, appropriate elaboration
On wrong topic	Loses focus; rambles	Some elaboration and detail	Moderate elaboration and detail	Logical, effective organization
Content too scant to score	Lacks elaboration, detail, language control	Language control is limited	Clear, effective language	Fluent, clear, effective language

INDEX OF AUTHORS AND TITLES

Page numbers in *italics* refer to biographical information.

A

Achieving the American Dream, 368
Ackerman, Diane, *450, 458*
Adventure of the Speckled Band, The, 474
All But Blind, 36
Always to Remember: The Vision of Maya Ying Lin, 326
American Childhood, An, 443
American Dream, The, 689
Anaya, Rudolfo A., *910, 912*
Angelou, Maya, *22, 24*
Animal Craftsmen, 625
Anne Frank . . . On Broadway, 746
Ashabranner, Brent, *324, 326*

B

Bambara, Toni Cade, *290, 292*
Barbara Frietchie, 311
Baseball, 636
Bashō Matsuo, *834, 837*
Bat, The, 511
Benét, Rosemary Carr, *892, 895*
Benét, Stephen Vincent, *142, 146*
Bierce, Ambrose, 515, *520*
Blessing, Lee, 773, *774*
Blow, Blow, Thou Winter Wind, 829
Bontemps, Arna, *502, 510*
Borland, Hal, *80, 82*
Bowie, David, 127
Bradbury, Ray, 2, *5*
Bradford, William, 163
Brer Possum's Dilemma, 915
Brooks, Bruce, *622, 625*
Brown vs. Board of Education, 241
Bruchac, Joseph, *364, 367*
Buck, Pearl S., *62, 64*

C

Calvin and Hobbes, 19
Centaur, The, 820
Charles, 14
Chekhov, Anton, *172, 174*
Chicoria, 912
Choice: A Tribute to Dr. Martin Luther King, Jr., 370
Choice, The, 37
Christmas Day in the Morning, 64
City Is So Big, The, 426
Clarke, Arthur C., *120, 122*
Closing of the Rodeo, The, 405
Coffin, Robert P. Tristram, *806, 809*
Columbus, 144
Coyote Steals the Sun and Moon, 902

Crane, Stephen, 551, *554*
Crime-Solving Procedures for the Modern Detective, 494
Crockett, Davy, *932, 952*
Cruz, Victor Hernández, *464, 468*
Cub Pilot on the Mississippi, 109
Cummings, E. E., *826, 830*
Cuomo, Mario, *364, 368*

D

Dark Hills, The, 876
Davy Crockett's Dream, 952
Day I Got Lost, The, 558
De la Mare, Walter, *32, 36, 854, 856*
Debbie, 670
Diary of Anne Frank, The, 712
Dickinson, Emily, *192, 195, 854, 859*
Dillard, Annie, *440, 443*
Dinner Party, The, 535
Dobie, J. Frank, *398, 400*
Doyle, Sir Arthur Conan, *472, 474*
Drum Song, 858
Drummer Boy of Shiloh, The, 5
Dunbar, Paul Laurence, *578, 580*

E

Elizabeth Blackwell, 314
Ellis Island, 367
E-Mail from Bill Gates, from, 42
Emancipation, 262
Episode of War, An, 551
Erdoes, Richard, *900, 902*

F

Felton, Harold W., *932, 946*
Finish of Patsy Barnes, The, 580
Flowers for Algernon, 204
For My Sister Molly Who in the Fifties, 868
Forest Fire, 675
Forgotten Language, 857
400-Meter Free Style, 839
Freedman, Russell, *260, 262*
Freedom of the Moon, The, 831
Frost, Robert, *32, 34, 826, 831*

G

García, Lionel G., *632, 636*
García, Richard, *422, 426*
Garcia Villa, José, *862, 867*
Gardner, Mona, *532, 535*
Gentleman of Río en Medio, 272
Girl Who Hunted Rabbits, The, 49
Glow in the Dark, A, 504
Goodrich, Frances, *708, 712*
Governess, The, 176
Grandma, 75

Granstrom, Chris, 601
Griego y Maestas, José, *910, 912*

H

Hackett, Albert, *708, 712*
Hale, Edward Everett, 377, *390*
Hamadi, 562
Hammerman, 934
Hard Questions, 198
Harlem Night Song, 828
Harriet Tubman: Guide to Freedom, 132
Hayden, Robert, *422, 424*
Henley, Larry, 872
Henry, O., *250, 252*
Herriot, James, *668, 670*
Hersey, John, *652, 656*
Hokusai: The Old Man Mad About Drawing, 654
Horseman in the Sky, A, 515
How to Be Polite Online, 678
How to Tell a Good Story, 601
Hughes, Langston, *88, 91, 184, 186, 826, 828*
Hunt, Evelyn Tooley, *422, 425*
Hurston, Zora Neale, *910, 918*

I

I Know Why the Caged Bird Sings, from, 24
Identity, 838
If I can stop one Heart from breaking, 859
Incident in a Rose Garden, 878

J

Jackson, Shirley, *12, 14*
January, 836
Jefferson, Thomas, 321, *323*
Jen, Gish, *408, 414*
Jensen, Jamie, 361
John Henry, 940
Johnny Appleseed, 895
Justice, Donald, *874, 878*

K

Keillor, Garrison, *80, 84*
Keyes, Daniel, *202, 204*
King, Martin Luther, Jr., *684, 689*
Kumin, Maxine, *834, 839*

L

Larkin, Philip, *874, 877*
Lazarus, Emma, *364, 366*
Lewis, Barbara A., *270, 276*
Life and Death of King Richard III, The, from, 792
Lights in the Night, 443

Lincoln: A Photobiography, 262
Ling, Amy, 72, 75
London, Jack, 152, 154
Longfellow, Henry Wadsworth, 304, 306,
   814, 817
Longstreet, Stephen, 652, 654
love is a place, 830
Lyric 17, 867

M

MacNeil, Robert, 684, 686
Man Without a Country, The, 377
Medicine Bag, The, 602
Merriam, Eve, 304, 314
Midsummer Night's Dream, A, from, 784
Miller, Joaquin, 142, 144
Momaday, N. Scott, 862, 864
Moritake, 834, 837
Mourning Dove, 900, 905
Much Ado About Nothing, from, 790
Much Madness is divinest Sense—, 195
Munro, H. H. (Saki), 594, 596
Mushrooms, 508
Myers, Walter Dean, 238, 241

N

New Colossus, The, 366
New World, 864
New Yorks, Los, 468
Nin, Anaïs, 668, 675
Ninny, The, 174
Northrup, Jim, 845, 846
Not to Go With the Others, 656
Nye, Naomi Shihab, 556, 562

O

O Captain! My Captain!, 266
Old Grandfather and His Little Grandson,
   The, 74
Old Man, 76
One Time, 866
One Writer's Beginnings, from, 634
Ortiz, Alfonso, 900, 902
Other Pioneers, The, 148

P

Parker, Dorothy, 32, 37
Paul Bunyan of the North Woods, 944
Paul Revere's Ride, 306
Paulsen, Gary, 502, 504
Payne, Robert, 174
Pecos Bill: The Cyclone, 946
People, Yes, The, from, 347
Petry, Ann, 130, 132
Pilgrims' Landing and First Winter, The, from,
   163
Plath, Sylvia, 502, 508

Poe, Edgar Allan, 540, 542
Poets to Come, 90
Polanco, Julio Noboa, 834, 838
Powell, Colin, 694
Prospective Immigrants Please Note, 194

R

Raymond's Run, 292
Retrieved Reformation, A, 252
Ribbon for Baldy, A, 410
Rich, Adrienne, 192, 194
Right Stuff, The, from, 923
Ring Out, Wild Bells, 92
Road Not Taken, The, 34
Road Trip U.S.A., from, 361
Robinson, Edwin Arlington, 874, 876
Roethke, Theodore, 502, 511
Rose, Wendy, 854, 858

S

Saki (H. H. Munro), 594, 596
Salazar, Roberto Félix, 142, 148
Sánchez, Ricardo, 72, 76
Sancho, 400
Sandburg, Carl, 344, 347, 932, 944
Saving the Wetlands, 276
Seabrook, John, 40, 42
Seattle, Chief, 192, 196
Secret, The, 122
Secret Heart, The, 809
Sedillo, Juan A. A., 270, 272
Shakespeare, William, 782, 784, 790, 792,
   826, 829
Sharing the American Dream, from, 694
Shea, Virginia, 668, 678
Shooting Stars, 82
Silbar, Jeff, 872
Silver, 856
Silverstein, Shel, 854, 857
Simon, Neil, 172, 176
Singer, Isaac Bashevis, 556, 558
Smith, William Jay, 398, 405
Sneve, Virginia Driving Hawk, 594, 602
Solar, 877
Something From the Sixties, 84
Southbound on the Freeway, 466
Southern Mansion, 510
Space Oddity, 127
Special Olympics, 302
Spirit Chief Names the Animal People, The,
   905
Stafford, William, 862, 866
Steinbeck, John, 352, 354
Story-Teller, The, (poem), 467
Story-Teller, The, (story), 596
Stoutenburg, Adrien, 932, 934
Stuart, Jesse, 408, 410
Superman Online, 951

Swenson, May, 464, 466, 814, 820

T

Taught Me Purple, 425
Tears of Autumn, 586
Tell-Tale Heart, The, 542
Tennyson, Alfred, Lord, 88, 92
Thank You, M'am, 186
There Is No Off-Season, 302
This We Know, 196
Those Winter Sundays, 424
Tolstoy, Leo, 72, 74
Torrence, Jackie, 910, 915
Travels with Charley, from, 354
Trouble with Television, The, 686
Truman, Margaret, 643, 650
Tsuda, Margaret, 192, 198
Twain, Mark, 106, 109, 450, 452
Two Haiku, 837

U

Uchida, Yoshiko, 578, 586
United States vs. Susan B. Anthony, from,
   643
Up the Slide, 154
Updike, John, 834, 836

V

Van Doren, Mark, 464, 467

W

Wahbegan, 845
Walk in the Woods, A, from, 773
Walker, Alice, 364, 370, 862, 868
Watterson, Bill, 19
Welty, Eudora, 632, 634
Western Wagons, 146
What Stumped the Blue Jays, 452
White Umbrella, The, 414
Whitman, Walt, 88, 90, 260, 266
Whittier, John Greenleaf, 304, 311
Why Leaves Turn Color in the Fall, 458
Why the Waves Have Whitecaps, 918
Wind Beneath My Wings, The, 872
Winter Moon, 91
Wolfe, Tom, 923, 924
Woodsong, from 504
Wreck of the Hesperus, The, 817

Y

Young Jefferson Gets Some Advice From Ben
   Franklin, 321

Z

Zuñi, 48, 49, 902

INDEX OF SKILLS

LITERARY TERMS

Alliteration, 855, 860, 966
Antagonist, 966
Autobiography, 621, 633, 640, 966
Biographical profile, 325, 332
Biography, 621, 653, 660, 966
Character traits, 409, 420
Characterization, 557, 570, 966
  in drama, 747, 770
Characters, 291, 300, 531, 705, 966
Characters' motives, 173, 182
Climax, 533
Concrete poetry, 835, 842, 967
Conflict, 271, 282, 533, 967
  between characters, 107, 117
  with nature, 153, 160
Descriptive essay, 621, 669, 682
Dialect, 967
Dialogue, 705, 967
Direct characterization, 557, 570, 966
Drama, 705, 747, 770, 967
Epithet, 365, 374
Essay, 239, 247, 353, 362, 621, 623, 629,
  669, 682, 685, 692, 967
Exposition, 533, 967
Expository essay, 621, 669, 682
Extended metaphor, 967
Fable, 967
Falling action, 533
Fantasy, 968
Fiction, 968
Figurative language, 805, 875, 880, 968
First-person narrative, 81, 86
First-person point of view, 203, 226
Flashback, 63, 70, 968
Folk tales, 891, 911, 920, 968
Free verse, 465, 470, 835, 968
Genre, 968
Haiku, 835, 968
Heroic characters, 305, 318, 968
Historical context, 261, 268
Historical setting, 3, 9
Hubris, 968
Image, 863, 968
Imagery, 193, 200, 863, 870
Implied theme, 610
Indirect characterization, 557, 570, 966
Informative essay, 239, 247
Irony, 968
Legend, 969
Lyric poetry, 805, 827, 832, 969
Magazine article, 41, 46
Major characters, 291, 300
Memoir, 23, 30, 969
Metaphor, 875, 880, 969
Meter, 969
Minor characters, 291, 300
Mood, 969
Motives of characters, 173, 182, 970
Mystery story, 473, 492
Myth, 891, 901, 908, 970
Narrative
  first-person, 81, 86
  third-person, 131, 140
Narrative essay, 621, 669, 682

Narrative poetry, 805, 815, 824, 970
Narrator, 970
Nonfiction, 621, 624, 629, 970
Novel, 970
Observation, 451, 462
Onomatopoeia, 970
Oral tradition, 345, 349, 893, 897, 970
Personification, 875, 880, 970
Persuasive essay, 621, 685, 692, 970
Plot, 531, 533, 537, 541, 548, 705, 971
Poetic form, 805, 835, 842
Poetry, 805, 824, 971
  concrete, 835, 967
  lyric, 827, 832, 969
  narrative, 815, 824, 970
  repetition in, 89, 94
  stanzas in, 143, 150
Point of view, 13, 20, 203, 226, 971
Reflective essay, 621, 623, 629
Refrain, 971
Repetition, 855, 860, 971
  in poetry, 89, 94
Resolution, 271, 282, 533
Rhyme, 855, 860, 971
Rhyme scheme, 972
Rising action, 533
Scenes, 783, 794
Science fiction, 121, 128, 972
Sensory language, 73, 78, 972
Setting, 399, 406, 531, 579, 592, 705, 972
Short stories, 531, 972
Simile, 875, 880, 972
Soliloquy, 783, 794, 972
Sound devices, 805, 855, 860
Speaker in a poem, 33, 38, 972
Speech, 621
Stage directions, 705, 973
Staging, 711, 745
Stanzas, 143, 150, 973
Stated theme, 595, 610
Surprise ending, 251, 258, 973
Suspense, 541, 548, 973
Symbol, 807, 811, 973
Tall tale, 891, 933, 954, 973
Theme, 185, 190, 531, 595, 610, 705, 973
  in drama, 747, 770
Third-person narrative, 131, 140
Tone, 503, 512, 973
Travel essay, 353, 362
Vignette, 441, 447
Word choice, 423, 428

READING STRATEGIES

Adjusting your reading rate, 99
Advertisements, 59, 665
Analyzing a position, 287
Author's bias, 287, 442, 465, 470
Author's main points, 624, 629, 653, 660
Author's message, 442, 447
Author's purpose, 59, 442, 447, 451, 462,
  624, 629, 633, 640
Bias, 287, 442, 465, 470
Boldface, 929
Breaking down difficult texts, 885
Breaking down long sentences, 4, 9, 13, 20
Brochures, 59

Captions, 99
Catalogs, 59
Cause, 240, 261, 268
Challenging the text, 231
Characters
  envisioning, 706
  identifying, 534, 537, 557, 570
  questioning actions, 173, 182
  responding to, 185, 190
Clarifying, 346, 349, 353, 362
Common sense, 231
Conflict, 117
Constructing meaning, 240, 247
Context clues, 4, 9, 41, 43, 46
Critical reading, 442, 447
Cultural context, 894, 901, 908
Cultural understanding, 851
Details, 353, 362, 575, 799
Drama, 706
Drawing conclusions, 433
Editorial, 287
Effect, 240, 261, 268
End of the article, 395
Envisioning, 346, 399, 406, 706, 747, 770
Evaluating the author, 699
Evaluating advertisements, 665
Evaluating persuasive techniques, 337
Evaluating sources of information, 699
Evidence, 473, 492
Facts, 287
Fiction, 534, 537
Flyers, 59
Folk literature, 894, 897
Goals, 99
Headings, 99, 929
Historical context, 706, 711, 745
Ideas
  important, 240, 247, 325, 332
  main, 395
Identifying main ideas, 395
Identifying reality, 337
Identifying the speaker, 808
Identifying with a character, 534, 537,
  557, 570
Identifying your response, 337
Index, 169
Inferences, 240, 247, 271, 282, 433, 442,
  447, 503, 512, 534, 537, 595, 610, 855,
  860
Information
  sources of, 699
  specific, 169
Informed decision, 337
Interactive reading strategies, 108, 117,
  346, 349
Internet web page, 699, 959
Interpretation, 240, 247, 305, 318
Key points, 799
Lead sentence, 395
Literal comprehension strategies, 4, 9
Loaded words, 615
Magazine articles, 41, 46, 59
Making inferences, 433
Manuals, 525
Maps, 169

Menus, 59
Motivation, 231
News articles, 59
Nonfiction, 629
Novels, 575
Opinions, 287
Original lines, 33, 38
Overview, 575
Paraphrasing, 4, 9, 33, 38, 808, 835, 842
Pause, 575
Persuasive techniques, 337, 685, 692
Plan, 575
Poetry, 808, 811
    paraphrasing lines of, 835, 842
    and punctuation, 89
    responding to, 875, 880
Positions, opposing, 287
Posters, 59
Predicting, 153, 160, 291, 300, 409, 420,
    534, 537, 541, 548, 894, 933, 954
Prior knowledge, 108, 346, 349
Product labels, 499
Publication date, 699
Punctuation, reading according to, 89, 94,
    808, 815, 824
Purpose
    author's, 59, 442, 447, 451, 462, 624,
        629, 633, 640
    storyteller's, 894, 911, 920
Purpose for reading, 108, 117, 131, 140,
    624, 629, 669, 682, 799
Questioning, 108, 121, 128, 251, 258,
    433, 537, 579, 592
Questioning characters' actions, 173,
    182, 534
Reading ahead, 4, 23, 30
Reading between the lines, 433
Reading manuals, 525
Reading novels, 575
Reading product labels, 499
Reading visuals, 779
Real message, 337
Reality, identifying, 337
Recognizing bias, 615
References, 231
Reflect, 575
Related topics, 169
Relating to what you know, 73, 78, 143,
    150
Repetition, 861
Rereading, 4, 23, 30
Responding, 108, 346, 349, 423, 428
    to characters' actions, 185, 190
    to poetry, 875, 880
Response, identifying your, 337
Senses, using your, 193, 200, 808, 863,
    870
Sequence of events, 63, 70
Set-off items, 929
Skimming a text for difficulty, 99
Slanted arguments, 615
Sources of information, 699
Speaker, 827, 832
Specific information, 169
Stereotypes, 615
Storyteller's purpose, 894, 911, 920
Subheads, 169
Summarizing, 203, 226, 365, 374, 706,
    783, 794
Table of contents, 169
Text structure, 929
Using your senses, 193, 200, 808, 863, 870

Web page, 699, 959
Word identification, 81, 86
Writer's position, 287

**GRAMMAR, USAGE,
AND MECHANICS**
Abstract noun, 46, 60
Action verbs, 128, 170
Active voice, 160, 168, 170
Adjective clauses, 570, 576
Adjectives, 247, 258, 288, 338, 860, 978
    coordinate, 286, 842
    precise, 431
    predicate, 470, 500
    prepositional phrases as, 332
Adverb clause, 548, 576
Adverbs, 268, 282, 288, 332, 335, 338,
    860, 954, 978
Agreement
    pronoun and antecedent, 682, 700
    pronoun and subject, 692
    pronoun and verb, 770
    subject and verb, 745, 780, 794, 800,
        979
Animal, 9
Antecedents, 70, 100, 682, 692, 700
Appositive, 663
Appositive phrase, 512, 526
Base form of verb, 182
Bibliography, 698
Case, 629, 640, 777
Citing your sources, 698
Clauses
    adjective, 570, 576, 979
    adverbs, 548, 576, 979
    independent, 537, 576, 610, 979
    subordinate, 537, 576, 610, 979
Clichés, 883
Combining sentences, 230
Commas
    in compound sentences, 908, 928
    and coordinate adjectives, 286
    and introductory transitions, 524
    in a series, 336, 920
    unnecessary, 897
Common nouns, 20, 58, 60
Commonly confused words, 957
    lie and lay, 150
Company names, 498
Comparative form, 285, 824, 832
Comparative modifiers, 811
Comparison, degrees of, 285
Comparisons using
    more and most, 824
    than or as, 870
Complement, 500
Complete thought, 98
Complex sentence, 610, 616
Compound sentence, 592, 616, 908
Compound subject, 420, 434
Compound verb, 420, 434
Concrete noun, 46, 60
Conjunctions, 396, 978
    coordinating, 362, 978
    correlative, 374, 978
    subordinating, 349, 576
Coordinate adjectives, 286, 842
Coordinating conjunctions, 362, 396
Correct use of
    good and well, 798
    as and like, 880
    than or as, 870

who, that, and which, 664
    who and whom, 660
Correlative conjunctions, 374, 396
Dialogue, 57
Direct object, 447, 500, 640, 660
Direct quotations, 797
Double comparisons, 850
Double negatives, 778
English, formal and informal, 497
First-person pronoun, 78, 100
Formal English, 497
Formal phrasing, 57
Fragments, 98, 979
Future perfect, 226
Future perfect tense, 232
Future tense, 200, 232
Gender, 700
General nouns, 38
Helping verbs, 117
Homophones, 884
How?, 288
How many?, 288
How much?, 288
Idea, 9, 60
Indefinite pronouns, 86, 100, 700, 770
Independent clause, 537, 576, 610
Indirect object, 462, 500, 640
Indirect quotations, 797
Informal English, 497
Intensive pronouns, 94, 100
Interjections, 979
Intransitive verbs, 140, 170
Inverted order, 434
Inverted sentences, 428, 794
Irregular comparisons of modifiers, 832
Irregular verb, 190
Jargon, 432
Linking verb, 128, 170, 258
Modified words, 258
Modifiers, 811, 832
Negatives, double, 778
Neutral words, 97
Nouns, 9, 60, 978
    common and proper, 20, 58, 978
    concrete and abstract, 46
    general and specific, 38
    plural and possessive, 30
    predicate, 492, 500, 629
Object of a preposition, 640, 660
Objective case, 640, 777
Objects, 447, 462, 500, 640
Participial phrase, 526
Passive verbs, 170
Passive voice, 160, 168, 170
Past form of verb, 182, 190, 232
Past participle form of verb, 182, 190,
    232
Past perfect, 226
Past perfect tense, 232
Past tense, 200
Perfect tense, 226
Person, 9, 60
Personal pronouns, 78, 100
Phrases, 526, 979
    adjective, 979
    adverb, 979
    appositive, 512, 526, 979
    infinitive, 979
    participial, 526, 979
    prepositional, 318, 332, 338, 954, 979
    series of, 336
    verb, 117, 170, 393

Place, 9, 60
Plural, 780, 794
Plural noun, 30, 60
Plural possessive, 30
Plural pronoun, 700
Possessive noun, 30
Possessive plural, 60
Possessive singular, 60
Precise adjectives, 431
Predicate, 406, 434
Predicate adjectives, 470, 500
Predicate nouns, 492, 500, 629
Preposition, 300, 338, 978
  object of, 640, 660
Prepositional phrase, 318, 332, 338, 954
Present form of verb, 190, 232
Present participle, 182, 232
Present perfect, 226
Present perfect tense, 232
Present tense, 200
Principal part of verbs, 182, 190, 232
Pronouns, 70, 100, 777, 978
  agreement with indefinite subjects, 692
  and antecedent agreement, 682, 700
  in comparison with *than* or *as*, 870
  indefinite, 86, 100, 700, 770, 978
  intensive, 94
  interrogative, 978
  objective case, 640
  personal, 78, 978
  relative, 576
  subjective case, 629
Proper nouns, 20, 58, 60, 958
Quality, 60
Quotations, 797
Realistic dialogue, 57
Regular verb, 182
Relative pronouns, 576
Run-on sentences, 229, 394
Second-person pronoun, 78, 100
Sensory words, 97
Sentence beginnings, 849, 954, 960
Sentence structure, 697
Sentences, 592, 616, 979
  combining, 230
  complex, 610
  inverted, 428
Series
  of commas, 336, 920
  of phrases, 336
  of words, 336
Simple predicate, 406, 434
Simple sentence, 592, 616
Simple subject, 406, 434
Singular, 780, 794
Singular possessive, 30
Singular pronouns, 700
Sources, citing your, 698
Specific nouns, 38
Subject, 406, 434, 629, 660, 954
  compound, 420, 434
  and verb agreement, 745, 780, 794, 800
Subjective case, 629, 777
Subordinate clause, 537, 576, 610, 954
Subordinating conjunctions, 349, 396
Superlative form, 285, 824, 832
Tag words, 573
Tenses, 200, 226, 232, 574
Thing, 9, 60
Third-person pronoun, 78, 100
Titles, 614
Transitions, 523, 524

Transitive verbs, 140, 170
Unity, 927
Usage problems, 886
Verb phrase, 117, 170, 393
Verb tenses, 200, 226, 232, 574
Verbs, 117, 170, 232, 978
  action and linking, 128, 978
  agreement with pronouns, 770
  compound, 420, 434
  correct forms of, 167
  helping, 978
  irregular, 190
  linking, 128, 170, 258, 978
  regular, 182
  and subject agreement, 745, 780, 794, 800
  transitive and intransitive, 140, 170
Voice, 160, 168, 170
To what extent?, 288
What kind?, 288
When?, 288
Where?, 288
Which?, 288
Who, That, and *Which,* 664
Wordiness, 613

VOCABULARY
Address, 375
Analogies, 888
Antonyms
  wan and *swarthy,* 142, 150
Calendar words, 102
Commonly confused words, 880
  continuously and *continually,* 874
Detective, 528
Dramatization, 375
Government, 340
Journalistic words, 436
Latin plural forms, 324, 332
Magazine vocabulary, 436
Movie vocabulary, 802
Mystery vocabulary, 528
Native American vocabulary, 234
Newspaper and magazine vocabulary, 436
Phobia words, 618
Politics, 340, 702
Prefixes
  a-, 502, 512
  anti-, 684, 692
  en-, 652, 660
  extra-, 80, 86
  in-, 239, 247
  inter-, 40, 46
  trans-, 464, 470
  un- and *in-,* 708, 745
Regional vocabulary, 962
Related words
  forms of *convulse,* 472, 492
  forms of *effect,* 747, 770
  forms of *encumber,* 893, 897
  forms of *evade,* 192, 200
  forms of *exhaust,* 152, 160
  forms of *fertile,* 834, 842
  forms of *finite,* 62, 70
  forms of *habitable,* 623, 629
  forms of *judge,* 107, 117
  forms of *migrate,* 364, 374
  forms of *skeptic,* 932, 954
  forms of *tolerate,* 22, 30
Sportspeak, 702
Suffixes

  -able, 184, 190
  -ate, 260, 268
  -eer, 345, 349
  -ent and *-ant,* 398, 406
  -ful, 814, 824
  -ic, 352, 362
  -ify, 900, 908
  -less, 594, 610
  -ment, 172, 182
  -or, 88, 94
  -ous, 782, 794
Synonyms, 910, 920
  rivulets, 72, 78
Word pairs, 854, 860
Word parts
  bene-, 3, 9
  micro, 120, 128
  scope, 290, 300
Word roots
  -cede-, 862, 870
  -chol-, 556, 570
  -chron-, 422, 428
  -cred-, 12, 20, 408, 420
  -flu-, 578, 592
  -found-, 540, 548
  -fug-, 130, 140
  -grat-, 450, 462
  -lum-, 441, 447
  -lus-, 826, 832
  -num-, 270, 282
  -psych-, 202, 226
  -semble-, 807, 811
  -simul-, 250, 258
  -spec-, 304, 318
  -spir-, 532, 537
  -vac-, 668, 682
  -verg-, 32, 38
  -vis-, 632, 640

CRITICAL THINKING AND VIEWING
Analyze, 35, 45, 67, 77, 83, 109, 110, 139, 145, 149, 163, 181, 189, 218, 246, 275, 281, 299, 307, 310, 313, 317, 328, 359, 366, 369, 373, 390, 402, 413, 419, 427, 446, 457, 467, 491, 507, 520, 547, 569, 600, 609, 628, 635, 647, 655, 656, 687, 691, 831, 846, 856, 867, 869, 877, 896, 914, 919, 924, 940, 943, 953
Analyze cause and effect, 195, 744, 857
Apply, 8, 35, 181, 225, 246, 317, 322, 331, 367, 427, 509, 520, 878
Assess, 6, 27, 112, 126, 149, 159, 181, 299, 311, 313, 317, 404, 468, 545, 552, 559, 561, 646, 654, 659, 670, 681, 691, 717, 760, 769, 775, 810, 831, 865, 876, 907, 947, 952
Classify, 175, 281, 405, 508
Compare, 425
Compare and contrast, 8, 19, 69, 75, 77, 93, 145, 147, 181, 195, 207, 211, 225, 267, 275, 278, 310, 313, 360, 367, 373, 404, 419, 446, 455, 467, 469, 491, 511, 554, 567, 569, 585, 591, 609, 635, 639, 650, 659, 674, 677, 681, 744, 775, 789, 793, 819, 821, 823, 829, 836, 838, 841, 859, 869, 877, 879, 904, 917, 919
Connect, 17, 35, 54, 69, 91, 126, 158, 199, 242, 243, 252, 256, 262, 281, 309, 331, 348, 373, 382, 404, 427, 460, 461, 477, 507, 511, 520, 535, 536, 543, 551, 561, 591, 607, 626, 649, 677, 695, 714, 738,

767, 793, 817, 823, 831, 837, 857, 858, 864, 865, 867, 878, 879, 905, 907, 914, 919, 923, 935, 939, 953
Contrast, 598
Criticize, 69, 91
Deduce, 116, 159, 189, 254, 314, 368, 369, 412, 481, 509, 510, 518, 675, 744, 765, 775, 786, 819, 895, 917
Defend, 264, 329, 419
Define, 69, 297
Distinguish, 457, 904
Draw conclusions, 8, 19, 29, 45, 54, 69, 77, 85, 91, 93, 116, 133, 139, 147, 165, 174, 257, 277, 327, 331, 360, 386, 390, 400, 411, 413, 419, 425, 446, 453, 457, 461, 469, 484, 520, 561, 562, 569, 582, 591, 597, 600, 609, 659, 677, 688, 733, 769, 789, 790, 810, 846, 857, 859, 865, 879, 907, 912, 919, 924, 953
Evaluate, 8, 116, 145, 274, 360, 419, 427, 461, 467, 479, 600, 627, 628, 688, 823, 867, 914, 942, 943
Extend, 837
Generalize, 126, 149, 159, 175, 189, 293, 369, 461, 637, 674, 681, 688, 744, 819, 945
Hypothesize, 19, 37, 85, 199, 281, 404, 413, 655
Infer, 8, 19, 29, 35, 37, 85, 93, 116, 126, 136, 147, 149, 159, 165, 175, 181, 189, 205, 225, 257, 265, 273, 275, 321, 322, 348, 367, 369, 370, 413, 414, 419, 425, 446, 457, 466, 475, 509, 516, 536, 547, 569, 584, 590, 591, 600, 602, 628, 634, 635, 639, 650, 659, 674, 678, 681, 691, 720, 727, 769, 810, 819, 823, 829, 841, 845, 846, 857, 859, 865, 868, 869, 877, 879, 896, 903, 904, 917, 924, 937, 943
Interpret, 8, 29, 35, 37, 52, 54, 65, 69, 74, 77, 83, 84, 85, 91, 93, 126, 139, 145, 147, 149, 175, 177, 179, 189, 195, 199, 215, 244, 246, 257, 266, 267, 299, 310, 313, 317, 347, 348, 360, 367, 373, 385, 390, 404, 425, 427, 443, 467, 469, 507, 509, 511, 547, 561, 569, 585, 586, 600, 628, 650, 655, 677, 688, 691, 744, 769, 775, 789, 793, 809, 810, 819, 822, 828, 829, 830, 831, 837, 839, 841, 864, 877, 879, 907, 914, 915, 939, 943, 945, 953
Make a decision, 580
Make a judgment, 19, 35, 45, 54, 76, 77, 93, 139, 147, 165, 175, 187, 189, 195, 225, 246, 263, 267, 310, 378, 390, 413, 417, 424, 489, 507, 547, 564, 585, 655, 686, 691, 789, 792, 831, 869, 918, 943
Modify, 159, 939, 953
Relate, 29, 275, 299, 355, 390, 427, 444, 467, 491, 504, 536, 636, 650, 749, 755, 769, 837, 846, 896, 917, 924
Solve, 789, 953
Speculate, 25, 37, 54, 83, 126, 147, 159, 181, 194, 195, 246, 265, 276, 294, 298, 313, 315, 317, 330, 348, 373, 381, 388, 405, 457, 461, 491, 506, 547, 554, 568, 600, 639, 648, 655, 658, 673, 674, 688, 743, 793, 810, 823, 865, 914, 939, 943
Summarize, 558, 944
Support, 116, 199, 223, 257, 317, 469, 554, 561, 585, 591, 609, 638, 681, 769, 857, 859, 867, 869, 945
Synthesize, 257

WRITING OPPORTUNITIES
Action plan, 493
Advertisement, 47, 129, 183, 283, 471, 493, 921
Advice letter, 661
Analysis, 31, 471, 611, 683, 955
Anecdote, 118, 549
Annotated list, 448
Article, 10, 129, 227, 323, 421, 630, 925
Autobiography, 641
Award plaque, 227
Biographical description, 141
Biographical profile, 333
Biographical report, 323, 795
Biography, 248, 661
Book jacket, 71, 429, 611
Business letter, 496, 693
Casting advice, 795
Casting memo, 661
Cause-and-effect essay, 47, 55, 166
Character profile, 269, 407
Character sketch, 118, 319
Character study, 825
Childhood remembrance, 448
City poem, 471
Clues, list of, 55
Comparative essay, 549
Compare and contrast, 39, 421, 593, 611
Comparison
  description of yourself, 843
  of forms of communication, 47
  of poems, 429
  of stories, 183
Comparison-and-contrast essay, 151, 795
Computer checklist, 683
Concrete poem, 843
Consumer report, 430
Continue the poem, 825
Critical interpretation, 95
Critical response, 129
Critical review, 593, 796
Definition, 881
Description, 21, 95, 96, 593, 775, 871
  of an older person, 79
  of yourself, 843
Descriptive close-up, 79
Descriptive letter, 463
Dialogue, 39, 151, 571, 651, 771, 881
Diary entry, 10, 141, 161, 421, 521, 538, 771
Dramatization, 141
Editorial, 248, 651
Editor's foreword, 463
Episode, 571
Epitaph, 269, 898
Essay, 71, 87, 259, 301, 350, 363, 375, 513, 555, 630, 683, 771, 812, 833, 843, 871, 898, 921, 925
  cause-and-effect, 47, 55, 166
  comparative, 549
  comparison-and-contrast, 151, 795
  how-to, 522
  on humor, 118
  observational, 463
  personal, 248
  persuasive, 39, 334, 391, 407
  problem-and-solution, 21, 228
  reflective, 521
  on theme, 909
Evaluation, 611
Explanation, 227
"Eyewitness" speech, 319

Family reunion, 79
Fan letter, 630
Fictional narrative, 572
  with flashback, 71
Figurative definition, 881
Figures of speech, 881
Flashback, 71
Folk ballad, 898
Folk tale, 79
Formula, 283
Free-verse poem, 871
Glossary, 641, 843
Guidebook description, 363
Hero-of-the-year nomination, 955
Historical cause-and-effect essay, 166
How-to essay, 522
Humorous description, 21
Inference about an author, 861
Interior monologue, 183, 538
Interview, 683
Introduction, 141
Invitation, 833
I-Search paper, 513
Job description, 161
Job manual, 10
Journal, 227, 363, 375
Journal article, 227
Journal entry, 31, 118, 201, 333, 555, 651, 925, 955
Legendary figure, 350
Legendary story, 898
Letter, 21, 55, 151, 165, 191, 201, 248, 269, 301, 323, 333, 391, 407, 448, 745, 909
  of advice, 661
  to the author, 47
  business, 693
  descriptive, 463
  to the editor, 283, 284
  fan, 630
  of guidance, 191
  personal, 593
  of recommendation, 493
  of resignation, 183
Letter from Billy, 259
Letter from Robert, 71
Letter home, 847
Letter home from a soldier, 10
License-plate proposal, 871
List, 39, 513, 611, 693, 812, 921
List of clues, 55
Literary analysis, 612
Memoir poem, 31
Missing-person bulletin, 571
Modified story, 161
Monologue, 183, 538, 877
Movie summary, 319
Nature poem, 630
News analysis, 693
News article, 10, 129, 925
News story, 513, 825
Newspaper account, 391
Newspaper article, 421, 630
Newspaper story, 909
Nomination for hero of the year, 955
Observation journal, 227
Observational essay, 463
Official report, 555, 775
Paraphrase, 833
Pattern poem, 95
Personal essay, 248, 493
Personal letter, 593

Personal memoir about a turning point, 31
Personal narrative, 56
Personal response, 350
Personification, 881
Persuasive advertisement, 921
Persuasive appeal, 201
Persuasive essay, 39, 334, 391, 407, 847
Persuasive speech, 693
Poem, 87, 269, 812, 882
  about a person or place, 471
  city, 471
  comparison, 429
  concrete, 843
  continue the, 825
  free-verse, 871
  memoir, 31
  nature, 630
  pattern, 95
  response to, 429, 825, 847
  stanza of, 861
Police report, 549
Postcard, 375
Prediction, 549
Prequel, 521
Problem-and-solution essay, 21, 228
Profile of a legendary figure, 350
Program notes, 745
Proposal for a reunion, 79
Public-service announcement, 662, 861
Recommendation, 421
Reflective essay, 521
Regulations, 165
Report, 319, 407, 641
  on an animal, 909
  on hidden figures of speech, 881
  on the Yukon, 161
Reporter's questions, 775
Research paper, 696
Research plan, 538
Responding
  to poems, 429, 825, 847
  to the story, 259
Retelling, 921
Rule book, 641
Science magazine, 463
Script, 165
  for a sportscaster, 301
  for a time-capsule video, 95
Self-portrait, 571
Sequel, 191, 301, 538
Song lyrics, 861
Speech, 151, 191
  "eyewitness," 319
  persuasive, 693
  supporting the environment, 283
Speech analysis, 201
Spoken introduction, 141
Sportscaster, 301
Stanza of poetry, 861
Stories, comparison of, 183
Story, responding to the, 259
Story continuation, 129
Summary, 392, 448, 795
Surprise ending, 259
Suspenseful anecdote, 549
Symbol, 812
Testimonial, 661
Thank-you note, 87
Timeline, 771
Tourist brochure, 333
Travel advertisement, 471

Travel journal entry, 363
Tribute, 375, 871
Video script, 95, 776
Word analysis, 429
Yarn, 350

WRITING SKILLS
Accurate references, 612
Appropriate tone, 471, 496, 630, 662, 833
Audience, 87, 96, 319, 334, 463, 496
Author's purpose, 201, 448, 496
Background information, 191, 228, 301, 334
Beginning, 284, 693, 696
Body, 118, 166
Character details, 538, 572
Clarity, 641, 662
Clear and logical organization, 593, 612
Compare-and-contrast organization, 429, 430
Conclusion, 118, 166
Critical reviews, 796
Descriptive details, 269, 284
Details
  descriptive, 269, 284
  elaborating with, 407, 430, 843
  important, 955
  persuasive, 333, 334
  to support your points, 227, 228, 363, 392, 611, 612, 843
  that reveal character, 538, 572
Dialogue, realistic, 571, 572
Dominant image, 871, 882
Dramatic reading, 745
Elaborating
  with details, 407, 430, 843
  to make writing personal, 31, 56
Ending, 693, 696
Examples, 141, 259
Figurative language, 881, 882
Format, 95, 921
  of script, 771, 776
General writing, 141
Humorous tone, 21
Important details, 955
Introduction, 118, 166, 248
Main points, 513
Narrowing a topic, 161, 166, 795
Necessary background, 191, 228
Neutral tone, 21
Organization, 183, 696
  clear and logical, 593, 612
  compare-and-contrast, 429, 430
Organizational strategy, 228
Persuasive details, 333, 334
Persuasive tone, 283, 284
Precise language, 79, 96, 350, 392
Quotation marks, 683, 696
Reasons, 151, 166, 812
References, accurate, 612
Relevant background, 334
Repetition, 882
Script format, 771, 776
Sequence of events, 129, 166
Show, don't tell, 10, 898
Specific examples, 141
Stating your main points, 513
Strong beginning, 284, 693, 696
Strong ending, 696
Supporting details, 227, 228, 363, 392,

611, 612, 843
Supporting your argument, 39
Supporting your ideas with examples, 259
Supporting your points, 227, 228, 284, 421, 430, 493, 496, 661, 662, 825
Supporting your statements with reasons, 151, 166
Suspense, 549, 572
Tone, 21, 56
  appropriate, 471, 496, 630, 662, 833
  persuasive, 283, 284
Transitions, 47, 56, 71, 96, 375, 392
Visual support, 909

SPEAKING, LISTENING, AND VIEWING
Advisory panel, 21
Agreement, 233
Anecdotes, 825
Audience, 527, 986
Author's chat, 463
Casting proposal, 161
Choral reading, 429, 871
Commencement address, 333
Committee discussion, 201
Common sense and facts, 233
Compromise, 701
Conducting business, 961
Contributing, 101
Conversation, 391
Coyote's trial, 909
Critically viewing TV messages, 887
Debate, 10, 45, 87, 141, 227, 259, 283, 521, 801, 986
Detective skills, 491
Dialogue, 47, 269, 661, 693, 925
Dialogue with yourself, 79
Dinner speech, 538
Disagreement, 233
Discussion, 165, 630, 833, 847, 986
DJ's rap, 611
Drama, 248
Dramatic monologue, 771
Dramatic reading, 118, 269, 319, 630, 775, 843, 909
Dramatic scene, 39, 71, 421
Dramatization, 183, 201, 227
Eye contact, 985
Feedback, 985
"Fireside" reading, 825
Group participation, 101
Group story, 350
Group's purpose, 101
Hearing everyone, 101
Interview, 47, 617, 898
  job, 183
  news, 549
  talk-show, 118
Job interview, 183
Legal arguments, 651
Listening, 985
Listening thoughtfully, 233
Loaded language, 701
Love song, 812
Making a contribution, 101
Memorized reading, 350
Modern scene, 71
Monologue, 87, 259, 513, 571, 593, 641, 771, 833
Music connection, 55
Musical setting, 898

New Year's speech, 95
News interview, 549
Nonverbal communication, 985
Opening argument, 549
Oral history, 333
Oral interpretation, 31, 161, 448, 463,
    683, 881, 986
Oral presentation, 151, 407, 513
Oral report, 391
Oral storytelling, 955
Oral tale, 921
Oral tribute, 31
Panel discussion, 248, 363, 986
Performance, 955
Persuasion, 339, 701
Poetry reading, 95, 812
Radio commentary, 363
Radio drama, 795
Radio monologue, 87
Radio play, 493, 661
Radio review, 129
Radio sportscast, 641
Rap song, 191
Readers Theatre, 191, 881, 986
Rebuttal, 843
Recording ideas, 101
Responding to others, 101
Retelling, 10, 21, 319, 521
Role play, 323, 448, 555, 571, 683, 986
Scene, 301, 538, 771
Scene, modern, 71
Shakespeare reading, 795
Skit, 151, 921
Speaking slowly, 233
Speech, 39, 71, 95, 141, 283, 407, 527,
    538, 693, 925, 986
Sportscast, 593
    radio, 641
Storyteller, 471
Storytelling, 79, 611, 955
Taking turns speaking, 101
Talk show, 118, 471, 493
Telephone call, 129, 301, 429, 435
Thinking before you speak, 233
Tour guide speech, 407
Vocal delivery, 985
Work song, 421

LIFE AND WORK SKILLS
Advice for professions, 635
Architects, 331
Childhood experiences, 446
Community action, 283
Computer career, 45
DJ's rap, 611
Firefighting report, 683
Horse trainer, 585
Job description, 161
Job interview, 183
Job manual, 10
License-plate proposal, 871
News article, 10
News interview, 549
Opening argument, 549
Radio sportscast, 641
Reading manuals, 525
Reading product labels, 499
Reading visuals, 779
Recognizing bias, 615
Riverboat navigation, 116
Scientific image presentation, 871

Tour guide speech, 407
Travel advertisement, 471
Travel writer, 360
Using an Internet Web page, 959
Veterinarian, 674
Wetlands campaign, 281
Women in medicine, 317

PROJECTS
Advertisement, 31
Analysis, 683
Animal poster, 630
Apple poster, 898
Art, 55, 847
    personification in, 881
Art catalog, 661
Artwork, 283
Audiovisual interviews, 227
Author research, 161
Baseball field plan, 641
Bibliography, 301
Book club, 771
Book cover, 151
Botanical drawings, 463
Brochure, 118, 898
Caption, 448
Captioned picture, 871
City life magazine, 429
Civil rights exhibit, 693
Classroom mystery, 493
Collage, 248, 493, 955
Collection
    of folk tales, 350
    of story summaries, 909
Comic book, 129, 259, 795
Comic strip, 21, 71
Community action, 283
Community-service project, 79
Constellations poster, 833
Dance, 79
Diagram, 47, 448
Documentary script, 363
Drawing, 191, 350, 463, 555
Encyclopedia entry, 55, 847
Essay, photo, 31
Farm report, 421
Film script, 363
Film treatment, 538
Final words, 39
Firefighting report, 683
Folk ballad, 319
Folk tales, 350, 571, 921
Fugitive slave laws, 141
Glossary of terms, 843
Grower's brochure, 898
Historic newspaper, 407
Historical soliloquy, 795
History
    living, 151
    of the piano, 421
Holiday spirit, 71
Holocaust exhibit, 661
Holocaust research, 771
Illustrated scene, 391
Illustration, 39, 513, 921, 925
Internet exploration, 47
Kentucky farm report, 421
Life dance, 79
Literary panel, 549
Living history, 151
Magazine, 429

Map, 319, 363, 775
    of the setting, 301
Mayflower illustration, 165
Memorial budget, 333
Meteor presentation, 87
Monument, 375
Moon chart, 641
Movie review, 549
Mud wasps' nest, 630
Multimedia display, 21
Multimedia presentation, 95, 191, 269,
    333, 521, 693, 843
Multimedia report, 161, 375, 471, 909
Museum display, 593
Music of the 1920's, 833
Musical archives, 812
Mystery, 493
Mythical creature poster, 825
Newspaper, historic, 407
Obituary notices, 39
Opinion poll, 183
Oral report, 165
Painting, 191, 350, 471
Personification in art, 881
Photo essay, 31
Piano, history of, 421
Picture book, 269
Plan for baseball field, 641
Poet, salute to the, 812
Poetry display, 429
Poster, 407, 630, 825, 833, 898
Presentation of a scientific image, 871
Production plan, 183
Reality check, 538
Report, 555, 925, 955
    on animal communication, 861
    on the Civil War, 10
    on Kahlil Gibran, 571
    on phases of the moon, 95
Research, 141, 323, 463
Research report, 227, 259, 448
Salute to the poet, 812
Science article, 513
Scientific image, 871
Scientific vs. poetic language, 881
Sculpture, 201
Set design, 593
Social research, 87
Soliloquy, 795
Sound devices in speeches, 861
Space capsule, 611
Space settlement, 129
Story illustration, 513
Summaries, collection of, 909
Survey, 683
Time capsule, 10
Timeline, 118, 201, 248, 651
Track and running bibliography, 301
Transportation brochure, 118
Travel itinerary, 611
Weather report, 825
Wise fools and tricksters, 571
Woman suffrage timeline, 651

STAFF CREDITS

The people who made up the *Prentice Hall Literature: Timeless Voices, Timeless Themes* team—representing design services, editorial, editorial services, managing editor, manufacturing and inventory planning, market research, marketing services, on-line services/multimedia development, permissions, product marketing, production services, and publishing processes—are listed below. Bold type denotes core team members.

Laura Bird, Betsy Bostwick, Pam Cardiff, **Megan Chill,** Rhett Conklin, Carlos Crespo, Gabriella Della Corte, Ed de Leon, Donna C. DiCuffa, **Amy E. Fleming, Holly Gordon, Rebecca Z. Graziano, William J. Hanna, Rick Hickox,** Jim Jeglikowski, John Kingston, **Perrin Moriarty,** James O'Neill, **Jim O'Shea, Maureen Raymond,** Rob Richman, Doris Robinson, Gerry Schrenck, Ann Shea, Melissa Shustyk, Annette Simmons, **Rita M. Sullivan, Elizabeth Torjussen**

ADDITIONAL CREDITS

Ernie Albanese, Robert H. Aleman, Diane Alimena, Michele Angelucci, Rosalyn Arcilla, Penny Baker, Anthony Barone, Rui Camarinha, Tara Campbell, Amy Capetta, Lorena Cerisano, Kam Cheng, Elizabeth Crawford, Mark Cryan, Paul Delsignore, Robert Dobaczewski, Irene Ehrmann, Kathryn Foot, Joe Galka, Catalina Gavilanes, Elaine Goldman, Joe Graci, Stacey Hosid, Leanne Korszoloski, Jan Kraus, Gregory Lynch, Mary Luthi, Vickie Menanteaux, John McClure, Frances Medico, Omni-Photo Communications, Inc., Photosearch, Inc., Linda Punskovsky, David Rosenthal, Laura Ross, Rose Sievers, Gillian Speeth/Picture This, Cindy Talocci, Mark Taylor, Lashonda Williams, Jeff Zoda

ACKNOWLEDGMENTS (continued)

Harcourt Brace & Company Excerpts from *The People, Yes* by Carl Sandburg, copyright 1936 by Harcourt Brace & Company and renewed 1964 by Carl Sandburg. "Choice: A Tribute to Dr. Martin Luther King, Jr." from *In Search of Our Mothers' Gardens: Womanist Prose,* copyright © 1983 by Alice Walker. "Forest Fire" from *The Diary of Anaïs Nin 1947–1955,* Volume V, copyright © 1974 by Anaïs Nin. From "For My Sister Molly Who in the Fifties" from *Revolutionary Petunias & Other Poems,* copyright © 1972 by Alice Walker. "Paul Bunyan of the North Woods" is excerpted from *The People, Yes* by Carl Sandburg, copyright 1936 by Harcourt Brace & Company and renewed 1964 by Carl Sandburg. Reprinted by permission of the publisher, Harcourt Brace & Company.

HarperCollins Publishers "Forgotten Language" from *Where the Sidewalk Ends* by Shel Silverstein. Copyright © 1974 by Evil Eye Music, Inc. "Brown vs. Board of Education" from *Now Is Your Time: The African-American Struggle for Freedom* by Walter Dean Myers. Copyright © 1991 by Walter Dean Myers. 3 lines from "The Falling Flower" by Moritake from *Poetry Handbook: A Dictionary of Terms* by Babette Deutsch. Copyright © 1974, 1969, 1962, 1957 by Babette Deutsch. "Why the Waves Have Whitecaps" from *Mules and Men* by Zora Neale Hurston. Copyright 1935 by Zora Neale Hurston. Copyright renewed 1963 by John C. Hurston and Joel Hurston. "Lights in the Night" from *An American Childhood* by Annie Dillard. Copyright © 1987 by Annie Dillard. Used by permission of HarperCollins Publishers.

Harvard University Press "Much Madness is divinest Sense—" (#835) and "If I can stop one Heart from breaking" by Emily Dickinson are reprinted by permission of the publishers and the Trustees of Amherst College from *The Poems of Emily Dickinson,* Thomas H. Johnson, editor, Cambridge, Mass.: The Belknap Press of Harvard University Press, Copyright © 1951, 1955, 1979, 1983 by the President and Fellows of Harvard College. "The Tell-Tale Heart" is reprinted by permission of the publisher from *The Collected Works of Edgar Allen Poe,* edited by Thomas Olive Mabbott, Cambridge, Mass.: Harvard University Press, Copyright © 1978 by the President and Fellows of Harvard College. Reprinted by permission of the publisher from *One Writer's Beginnings* by

Eudora Welty, Cambridge, Mass.: Harvard University Press, Copyright © 1983, 1984 by Eudora Welty.

Brook Hersey for the Estate of John Hersey "Not to Go With the Others" from *Here to Stay,* Copyright © 1962, 1987 by John Hersey, published by Alfred A. Knopf. Used by permission of Brook Hersey for the Estate of John Hersey.

Hill and Wang, a division of Farrar, Straus & Giroux, Inc. "Thank You M'am" from *Short Stories* by Langston Hughes, edited by Akiba Sullivan. Copyright © 1996 by Romana Bass and Arnold Rampersad. "The Story-Teller" from *Collected and New Poems 1924–1963* by Mark Van Doren. Copyright © 1963 by Mark Van Doren. Copyright renewed © 1997 by Dorothy G. Van Doren. Reprinted by permission of Hill and Wang, a division of Farrar, Straus & Giroux, Inc.

Holiday House, Inc. "January" from *A Child's Calendar* by John Updike. Copyright © 1965, 1999 by John Updike. All rights reserved. Reprinted by permission of Holiday House, Inc.

Henry Holt and Company, Inc. "The Road Not Taken" copyright 1916, 1923 by Holt, Rinehart and Winston, Inc. and renewed 1944, 1951 by Robert Frost from *The Poetry of Robert Frost,* edited by Edward Connery Lathem. "The Freedom of the Moon" from *The Poetry of Robert Frost,* edited by Edward Connery Lathem, Copyright 1956 by Robert Frost. Copyright 1928, © 1969 by Henry Holt & Company, reprinted by permission of Henry Holt and Company, Inc.

Evelyn Tooley Hunt and Negro Digest "Taught Me Purple" by Evelyn Tooley Hunt from *Negro Digest,* February 1964, © 1964 by Johnson Publishing Company, Inc. Reprinted by permission of Evelyn Tooley Hunt and *Negro Digest.*

Gish Jen "The White Umbrella" by Gish Jen. Copyright © 1984 by Gish Jen. All rights reserved. First published in *The Yale Review.* Reprinted by permission of the author.

Garrison Keillor "Something from the Sixties" by Garrison Keillor, from *The Talk of the Town,* published in *The New Yorker.* Used by permission of the author.

Daniel Keyes "Flowers for Algernon" (short story version) by Daniel Keyes. Copyright © 1959, 1987 by Daniel Keyes. Expanded story published in paperback by Bantam Books. Reprinted by permission of the author.

The Heirs to the Estate of Martin Luther King, Jr., c/o Writers House, Inc. as agent for the proprietor "The American Dream" by Martin Luther King, Jr. Copyright 1968 by Martin Luther King, Jr., copyright renewed 1996 by The Estate of Martin Luther King, Jr. Reprinted by arrangement with The Heirs to the Estate of Martin Luther King, Jr., c/o Writers House, Inc. as agent for the proprietor.

Alfred A. Knopf, Inc. "The Ninny" from *The Image of Chekhov,* Robert Payne, translator. Copyright © 1963 and renewed 1991 by Alfred A. Knopf Inc. "Mushrooms" from *The Colossus and Other Poems* by Sylvia Plath. Copyright © 1960 by Sylvia Plath. "Incident in a Rose Garden" from *New and Selected Poems* by Donald Justice. Copyright © 1995 by Donald Justice. "Harlem Night Song" and "Winter Moon" from *Selected Poems of Langston Hughes* by Langston Hughes. Copyright 1926 by Alfred A. Knopf, Inc. and renewed 1954 by Langston Hughes. "The Cyclone" from *Pecos Bill: Texas Cowpuncher* by Harold W. Felton. Copyright 1949 by Alfred A. Knopf, Inc. Reprinted by permission of the publisher, Alfred A. Knopf, Inc.

Barbara S. Kouts for Joseph Bruchac "Ellis Island" by Joseph Bruchac from *This Remembered Earth,* Geary Hobson, Editor, Red Earth Press, 1979. Used by permission of Barbara S. Kouts for Joseph Bruchac.

Acknowledgments ◆ *1027*

Amy Ling "Grandma Ling" by Amy Ling, originally published as "Grandma" in *Bridge: An Asian American Perspective*, Vol. 7, no. 3 (1980) by Amy Ling. Copyright © 1980 by Amy Ling. Used by permission of the author.

Little, Brown and Company "Sancho" from *The Longhorns* by J. Frank Dobie. Copyright © 1941 by J. Frank Dobie; © renewed 1969 by J. Frank Dobie. Reprinted by permission of Little, Brown and Company. Excerpt from *The Man Without a Country* by Edward Everett Hale (Little, Brown & Company).

Liveright Publishing Corporation "Those Winter Sundays," copyright © 1966 by Robert Hayden, from *Collected Poems of Robert Hayden* by Frederick Glaysher, editor. "love is a place," copyright 1935, © 1963, 1991 by the Trustees for the E.E. Cummings Trust. Copyright © 1978 by George James Firmage, from *Complete Poems: 1904–1962* by E.E. Cummings. Edited by George J. Firmage. Reprinted by permission of Liveright Publishing Corporation.

The LULAC National "The Other Pioneers" by Roberto Félix Salazar, published in *The LULAC News*, July 1939. Reprinted by permission of LULAC National.

Literary Trustees of Walter de la Mare, and the Society of Authors as their representative "Silver" from *Collected Poems 1901–1918* by Walter de la Mare. "All But Blind" by Walter de la Mare, from *The Complete Poems of Walter de la Mare*, Copyright 1969, 1970. Used by permission of the Literary Trustees of Walter de la Mare, and the Society of Authors as their representative.

N. Scott Momaday "New World" from *The Gourd Dancers* by N. Scott Momaday, copyright © 1976 by N. Scott Momaday. Reprinted by permission of the author.

Moon Publications Inc. From *Road Trip USA* by Jamie Jensen. Published by Moon Travel Handbooks. Text copyright © Jamie Jensen 1996. All rights reserved. Used by permission of Moon Publications Inc.

William Morris Literary Agency "Achieving the American Dream" by Mario M. Cuomo, Introduction from *The Italian Family Album*. Copyright © 1994 by Mario M. Cuomo. Reprinted by permission of William Morris Agency, Inc., on behalf of the author.

William Morrow and Company, Inc. "The United States *vs.* Susan B. Anthony" from *Women of Courage* by Margaret Truman. Copyright © 1976 by Margaret Truman Daniel. Reprinted by permission of William Morrow and Company, Inc.

Museum of New Mexico Press "Chicoria," translated by Rudolfo Anaya, is reprinted with permission of the Museum of New Mexico Press, from *Cuentos: Tales From the Hispanic Southwest* by José Griego y Maestas and Rudolfo A. Anaya, copyright 1980.

W. W. Norton & Company, Inc. "400-Meter Free Style" from *Selected Poems 1960–1990* by Maxine Kumin. Copyright © 1959 and renewed 1987 by Maxine Kumin. Originally published in *The Hudson Review*, Summer 1959. Reprinted by permission of W. W. Norton & Company, Inc.

W. W. Norton & Company, Inc., and Adrienne Rich "Prospective Immigrants Please Note," copyright © 1993, 1967, 1963 by Adrienne Rich, from *Collected Early Poems: 1950–1970* by Adrienne Rich. Reprinted by permission of the author and W. W. Norton & Company, Inc.

Naomi Shihab Nye "Hamadi" by Naomi Shihab Nye, copyright © 1993 by Naomi Shihab Nye. First published in *American Street*. Reprinted by permission of the author.

Harold Ober Associates Incorporated "Southern Mansion" by Arna Bontemps, published in *Personals*. Copyright 1949 by Arna Bontemps and Langston Hughes. Copyright renewed 1976 by Alberta Bontemps and George Houston Bass. "Christmas Day in the Morning" by Pearl S. Buck. Copyright © 1955 by Pearl S. Buck. Copyright renewed 1983 by Pearl S. Buck. Reprinted by permission of Harold Ober Associates Incorporated.

Pantheon Books, a division of Random House, Inc. "Coyote Steals the Sun and Moon" from *American Indian Myths and Legends* by Richard Erdoes and Alfonso Ortiz, editors. Copyright © 1984 by Richard Erdoes and Alfonso Ortiz. Reprinted by permission of Pantheon Books, a division of Random House, Inc.

Julio Noboa Polanco "Identity" by Julio Noboa Polanco from *The Rican, Journal of Contemporary Puerto Rican Thought*, copyright 1973. Reprinted by permission of the author.

Putnam Publishing Group "The Girl Who Hunted Rabbits" from *Zuñi Folk Tales*, translated by Frank H. Cushing with an introduction by J. W. Powell.

Random House, Inc. From *I Know Why the Caged Bird Sings* by Maya Angelou. Copyright © 1969 and renewed 1997 by Maya Angelou. "Raymond's Run" from *Gorilla My Love* by Toni Cade Bambara. Copyright © 1971 by Toni Cade Bambara. "Why Leaves Turn Color in the Fall" from *A Natural History of the Sense* by Diane Ackerman. Copyright © 1990. "Los New Yorks" from *Mainland* by Victor Hernández Cruz. Copyright © 1973 by Victor Hernández Cruz. Reprinted by permission of Random House, Inc. From *The Diary of Anne Frank* by Frances Goodrich and Albert Hackett. Copyright 1954, 1956 as an unpublished work. Copyright © 1956 by Albert Hackett, Frances Goodrich, and Otto Frank. Reprinted by permission of Random House, Inc. CAUTION: *The Diary of Anne Frank* is the sole property of the dramatists and is fully protected by copyright. It may not be acted by professionals or amateurs without written permission and the payment of a royalty. All rights, including professional, amateur, stock, radio broadcasting, television, motion picture, recitation, lecturing, public reading, and the rights of translation into foreign languages are reserved.

Reader's Digest and Robert MacNeil "The Trouble with Television" by Robert MacNeil (condensed from a speech delivered November 13, 1984, at the President's Leadership Forum, State University of New York at Purchase). Reprinted with permission from the March 1985 *Reader's Digest* and the author.

Marian Reiner "Elizabeth Blackwell" by Eve Merriam, from *Independent Voices* by Eve Merriam. Copyright © 1968 Eve Merriam. © Renewed 1996 Guy Michel and Dee Michel. Reprinted by permission of Marian Reiner.

Andrea Reynolds "The Adventure of the Speckled Band" from *The Complete Sherlock Holmes* by Sir Arthur Conan Doyle.

Wendy Rose "Drum Song" from *The Halfbreed Chronicles and Other Poems* by Wendy Rose. Copyright © 1985 by Wendy Rose. Reprinted by permission of the author.

Russell & Volkening as agents for the author "Harriet Tubman: Guide to Freedom" from *Harriet Tubman: Conductor on the Underground Railroad* by Ann Petry. Copyright © 1955 by Ann Petry, renewed 1983 by Ann Petry. Reprinted by the permission of Russell & Volkening as agents for the author.

St. Martin's Press, Inc., and Harold Ober Associates Inc. "Debbie" from *All Things Wise and Wonderful* by James Herriot.

Copyright © 1976, 1977 by James Herriot. Used by permission of St. Martin's Press, Inc., and Harold Ober Associates Incorporated.

Scovil Chichak Galen Literary Agency, Inc., and the author "The Secret" by Arthur C. Clarke from *The Wind from the Sun: Stories of the Space Age,* published by Victor Gollancz Ltd. Copyright © 1962, 1963, 1964 1965, 1967, 1970, 1971, 1972 by Arthur C. Clarke. Reprinted by permission of the author and the author's agent, Scovil Chichak Galen Literary Agency, Inc.

John Seabrook From "E-Mail from Bill" from *Deeper: Adventures on the Net* by John Seabrook, first published in *The New Yorker,* January 1994. Copyright John Seabrook. Used by permission of the author.

Simon & Schuster "The Secret Heart" is reprinted with the permission of Simon & Schuster from *Collected Poems* by Robert P. Tristram Coffin. Copyright 1939 by Macmillan Publishing Company; copyright renewed © 1967 by Margaret Coffin Halvosa.

Simon & Schuster Books for Young Readers, an imprint of Simon & Schuster Children's Publishing Division "The Old Grandfather and His Little Grandson" from *Twenty-Two Russian Tales for Young Children* by Leo Tolstoy, selected, translated, and with an afterword by Miriam Morton. Translation copyright © 1969 Miriam Morton. "The Centaur" by May Swenson from *The Complete Poems to Solve* by May Swenson. Copyright © 1956 by May Swenson; copyright renewed 1984 by May Swenson. "A Glow in the Dark" from *Woodsong* by Gary Paulsen. Text copyright © 1990 Gary Paulsen. "Southbound on the Freeway" by May Swenson from *The Complete Poems to Solve* by May Swenson. Text copyright © 1993 by The Literary Estate of May Swenson. (Originally appeared in *The New Yorker,* 1963). Reprinted with the permission of Simon & Schuster Books for Young Readers, an imprint of Simon & Schuster Children's Publishing Division.

Virginia Driving Hawk Sneve "The Medicine Bag" by Virginia Driving Hawk Sneve, published in *Boy's Life,* March 1975. Reprinted by permission of the author.

Jesse Stuart Foundation "A Ribbon for Baldy" by Jesse Stuart from *A Jesse Stuart Reader,* selected and introduced by Jesse Stuart. Copyright 1956 Esquire, Inc. © 1963 McGraw-Hill Book Company. © Renewed 1984, 1991 Jesse Stuart and the Jesse Stuart Foundation. Reprinted by permission of the Jesse Stuart Foundation, P.O. Box #391, Ashland, KY 41114.

Jackie Torrence "Brer Possum's Dilemma" by Jackie Torrence, copyright © 1988 by Jackie Torrence, published in *Homespun: Tales from America's Favorite Storytellers* by Jimmy Neil Smith. Reprinted by permission of the author.

TRO-Essex Music International, Inc., New York "Space Oddity," words and music by David Bowie. © Copyright 1969 (Renewed), Onward Music Ltd., London, England. TRO-Essex Music International, Inc., New York, New York controls all publication rights for the U.S.A. and Canada. Used by permission.

Margaret Tsuda "Hard Questions" from *Cry Love Aloud* by Margaret Tsuda. Copyright © 1972 by Margaret Tsuda. Published by Discovery Books. Reprinted by permission of the author.

University of Tennessee "Davy Crockett's Dream" by Davy Crockett from *The Tall Tales of Davy Crockett: The Second Nashville Series of Crockett Almanacs, 1839–1841.* An enlarged facsimile edition, with an introduction by Michael A. Lobaro. Copyright © 1987 by the University of Tennessee Press. Reprinted by permission.

Viking Penguin, a division of Penguin Putnam Inc. "The Choice" by Dorothy Parker, copyright 1926, copyright renewed 1954 by Dorothy Parker, from *The Portable Dorothy Parker* by Dorothy Parker. From *Travels With Charley* by John Steinbeck. Copyright © 1961, 1962 by The Curtis Publishing Co., © 1962 by John Steinbeck, renewed © 1990 by Elaine Steinbeck, Thom Steinbeck, and John Steinbeck IV. "Hammerman" by Adrien Stoutenburg, from *American Tall Tales* by Adrien Stoutenburg, illustrated by Richard M. Powers. Copyright © 1968 by Adrien Stoutenburg. Used by permission of Viking Penguin, a division of Penguin Putnam Inc.

José Garcia Villa "Lyric 17" from *Have Come, Am Here* by José Garcia Villa. Copyright 1942 by José Garcia Villa, copyright renewed © 1969 by José Garcia Villa. Reprinted by permission of the author.

Vital Speeches From "Sharing in the American Dream" by Colin Powell from *Vital Speeches,* June 1, 1967, v. 63, no. 16. Reprinted by permission of *Vital Speeches of the Day,* June 1, 1997.

Voyageur Press, Inc. "Wahbegan" from *Walking the Rez Road,* © 1993 by Jim Northrup, reprinted with permission of Publisher, Voyageur Press, Inc., 123 North Second Street, Stillwater, Minnesota 55082 USA, 1-800-888-9653.

Warner Bros. Publications U.S. Inc. "The Wind Beneath My Wings" by Larry Henley and Jeff Silbar, © 1982 Warner House of Gold Music Corp. All Rights Reserved. Used by permission of Warner Bros. Publications U.S. Inc., Miami, FL 33014.

Note: Every effort has been made to locate the copyright owner of material reprinted in this book. Omissions brought to our attention will be corrected in subsequent editions.

ART CREDITS

Cover: Super Stock; **vii:** SuperStock; **viii:** *Woman Standing at Highboy,* John Collier, Courtesy of the artist; **ix: t.** Dr. E.R. Degginger; **b.** James Lemass/Liaison International; **x:** Will Faller; **xi: t.** *Where to? What for? #3* ©1998 Nancie B. Warner, Courtesy of the artist; **b.** Merlin Tuttle/Photo Reseachers, Inc. **xii:** *Farm Boy,* 1941, Charles Alston, Courtesy of Clark Atlanta University; **xiii: t.** Mel DiGiacomo/The Image Bank; **b.** ©James Yang/Stock Illustration Source, Inc.; **xiv: t.** The Granger Collection, New York; **b.** Photofest; **xv:** *The Nest,* 1893, Constant Montald, Musees Royaux des Beaux-Arts de Belgique, Bruxelles-Koninklijke Musea voor Schone Kunsten van Belgie, Brussels, Belgium (photo Speltdom); **xvi:** UPI/Corbis-Bettmann; **1:** *The Cat,* Robert Vickrey, egg tempera, 36" x 48 ⅛", ©Robert Vickrey/Licensed by VAGA, New York; **2:** Thomas Victor; **3:** *Drummer Boy,* Julian Scott, N.S. Mayer; **5:** UPI/CORBIS-BETTMANN; **6:** Courtesy National Archives; **11:** *Untitled,* Jim Lang, Stockworks; **12:** AP/Wide World Photos; **13:** Bill Tucker/International Stock Photography, Ltd. **14:** SuperStock; **17:** Courtesy of the Library of Congress; **19:** CALVIN AND HOBBES ©Watterson. Dist. by UNIVERSAL PRESS SYNDICATE. Reprinted with permission. All rights reserved.; **22:** Henry McGee/Globe Photos; **23:** ©FPG International Corp.; **25:** *Parkville, Main Street (Missouri),* 1933, Gale Stockwell, National Museum of American Art, Washington, DC/Art Resource, NY; **27:** *Woman in Calico,* 1944, William Johnson, National Museum of American Art, Washington DC/Art Resource, NY; **32 t.:** Dimitri Kessel/Life Magazine; **m.:** ©Faber & Faber Ltd; **b.:** The Granger Collection, New York; **33:** ©The Stock Market/Alan Goldsmith; **34-37:** Corel Professional Photos CD-ROM™;

(Art Credits continue on page 1030.)

ART CREDITS (CONTINUED)

40: The New Yorker; **41:** Michael Agliolo/International Stock Photography, Ltd.; **49-51:** Corel Professional Photos CD-ROM™; **52:** *Indian Girl,* Robert Henri, © 1989 Indianapolis Museum of Art, Gift of Mrs. John N. Carey; **52-54:** Corel Professional Photos CD-ROM™; **56:** Bernard Wolf/Monkmeyer; **61:** *Late September Afternoon, Viola's Field,* 1997, 24" x 22", pastel by Jim Schantz. Courtesy of Pucker Gallery, Boston, photography by Andy Abrahamson; **62:** *Pearl S. Buck* (detail), Vita Solomon, National Portrait Gallery, Smithsonian Institution, Washington, D.C./Art Resource, New York; **63:** Chuck Schmeiser/New England Stock Photo; **64–65:** *Christmas Snow,* 1984, David Armstrong, watercolor, 15" x 20", North Mountain Press, Inc.; **66:** *Albert's Son,* Andrew Wyeth, Nasjonalgalleriet; **72 t.:** L. N. Tolstoi, I. E. Repin, Sovfoto/Eastfoto; **72 m.:** Photo by Catherine Ling Hinds; **b.:** Arte Publico Press/University of Houston; **73:** *Second Circle Dance,* Phoebe Beasley, 36" x 36" collage; **74:** *Remembrance (Erinnerung),* ca. 1918, Marc Chagall, Solomon R. Guggenheim Museum, New York, Gift, Solomon R. Guggenheim Museum, 1941, Photograph by David Heald © Solomon R. Guggenheim Foundation, New York (FN 41.440). (C) 2000 Artists Rights Society (ARS), New York/ADAGP, Paris.; **75:** *Woman with White Kerchief (Uygur),* Painting by Lunda Hoyle Gill; **76:** *El Pan Nuestro (Our Daily Bread),* Ramon Frade, oil on canvas, 60 ¼" x 38 ¼", Instituto de Cultura Puertorriquena, San Juan, Photo courtesy Squibb Galleries, New Jersey; **80 t.:** Les Line; **b.:** Minnesota Public Radio, photo by Carmen Quesada; **81:** Pekka Parviainen/Science Photo Library/Photo Research-ers, Inc.; **84:** ©Popperfoto/ Archive Photos; **88 t.:** Library of Congress; **m:** New York Public Library **b.:** *Alfred Lord Tennyson,* c.1840, S. Laurence, By courtesy of the National Portrait Gallery, London; **89 & 91:** Corel Professional Photos CD-ROM™; **92–93:** Vail Resorts; **96:** Tom Miner/ The Image Works; **101:** Mary Kate Denny/PhotoEdit; **104–105:** *The Idleness of Sisyphus,* 1981, Sandro Chia, oil on canvas, in two parts, overall, 10' 2" x 12' 8 ¼" (307 x 386.7 cm); top panel: 6' 9" x 12' 1 ¼" (104.5 x 386.7 cm). The Museum of Modern Art, New York. Acquired through the Carter Burden, Barbara Jakobson, and Saidie A. May funds and purchase. Photograph ©1998 The Museum of Modern Art, New York; **106:** *Samuel Longhorne Clemens (Mark Twain),* (detail), 1935, Frank Edwin Larson, National Portrait Gallery, Smithsonian Institution, Washington, D.C./Art Resource, New York; **107:** *The Champions of the Mississippi,* Currier & Ives, Scala/Art Resource, New York; **109:** *The Great Mississippi Steamboat Race,* 1870, Currier & Ives, The Granger Collection, New York; **110–111:** *Looking down the Mississippi River at Hannibal,* MO, George L. Crosby, Mark Twain Home and Museum; **112:** from "The Book of the Great South" by Edward King, 1875. Photo by Silver Burdett Ginn; **119:** *The Parkman Outfit - Henry Chatillon, Guide and Hunter,* c. 1925, N.C. Wyeth, The Oregon Trail by Francis Parkman, Little Brown and Company, 1925, oil on canvas, 40 ½" x 29 ⅛" (104 x 75 cm), Courtesy of Wells Fargo & Co.; **120:** Corbis-Bettmann; **121–127:** NASA; **130:** AP/Wide World Photos; **131–132:** Harriet Tubman Quilt made by the Negro History Club of Marin City and Sausalito, CA, 1951, 120" x 96", cotton appliqued. Designed by Ben Irvin. Gift of the Howard Thurman Educational Trust to the permanent collection of the Robert W. Woodruff Library, University Center, Atlanta, GA; **133:** *Harriet Tubman Series, #16,* Jacob Lawrence, Hampton University Museum, Hampton, Virginia; **136:** *Harriet Tubman Series, #20,* Jacob Lawrence, Hampton University Museum, Hampton, Virginia; **142 t.:** The Granger Collection, New York; **m.:** AP/Wide World Photos; **b.:** Juan Guzman/LIFE Magazine ©TIME Inc.; **145:** *The Landing of Columbus,* 1876, Currier & Ives, The Harry T. Peters Collection, Museum of the City of New York; **147:** *A New Beginning,* oil 24" x 36", Duane Bryers, Courtesy of the artist; **149:** *East Side Main Plaza, San Antonio, Texas,* 1844, William G. M. Samuel, Courtesy of Bexar County and the Witte Museum, San Antonio, Texas; **152:** Corbis-Bettmann; **153:** Corel Professional Photos CD-ROM™; **154–155:** ©Anchorage Museum/Alaska Stock Images; **156:** Shelley Rotner/Omni-Photo Communications, Inc.; **158:** ©Anchorage Museum/Alaska Stock Images; **163:** *Pilgrims Going to Church,* George Henry Boughton, oil on canvas, 1867, accession number S-117, Collection of The New York Historical Society; **166:** *Harrriet Tubman Series #28,* Hampton University Museum, Hampton, Virginia; **171:** *The Letter,* oil, Tim Solliday, Courtesy of the artist; **172 t.:** Corbis-Bettmann; **b.:** ©Peter Iovino/SAGA/Archive Photos; **173:** *The Rev. and Mrs. Palmer-Lovell with their daughters Georgina and Christina,* Augustus Egg (1816–1863), Phillips, the International Fine Art Auctioneers, UK/The Bridgeman Art Library International Ltd., London/New York; **174 t.:** image©Copyright 1997 PhotoDisc, Inc.; **b.:** *The Governess,* 1844 (detail), Richard Redgrave (1804–88), Victoria & Albert

Museum, London, UK/The Bridgeman Art Library International Ltd., London/New York; **177:** *Woman in Chair,* John Collier, Courtesy of the artist; **179:** *Woman Standing at Highboy,* John Collier, Courtesy of the artist; **184:** New York Public Library; **185:** *Empire State,* Tom Christopher, Vicki Morgan Associates; **187:** *Minnie,* 1930, William Johnson, National Museum of American Art, Washington, DC/Art Resource, NY; **192 t.:** Thomas Victor; **m.t.:** The Granger Collection, New York; **m.b.:** The Granger Collection, New York; **b.:** From Urban River by Margaret Tsuda. Discovery Books, HCR 01 Box 343, Owls Head, NY 12969; **193:** *Rind,* 1955, M.C. Escher, ©1998 Cordon Art B.V. - Baarn-Holland. All rights reserved; **194:** The Granger Collection, New York; **196-197:** Corel Professional Photos CD-ROM™; **198:** Kenneth W. Fink/Photo Researchers, Inc.; **202:** Harry Snaveley; **203:** © 1997, Telegraph Color Library/FPG International Corp.; **204–205:** ©Cinerama/ Archive Photos; **207:** Photofest; **211:** Photofest; **215:** ©Cinerama/ Archive Photos; **218:** Photofest; **223:** Photofest; **228:** Corel Professional Photos CD-ROM™; **233:** Tony Freeman/PhotoEdit; **236–237:** *Trial by Jury,* 1964, Thomas Hart Benton, oil on canvas; 30" x 40" (76.0 x 1010.7cm), The Nelson-Atkins Museum of Art, Kansas City, Missouri, bequest of the artist. ©T. H. Benton and R. P. Benton Testamentary Trusts/Licensed by VAGA, New York, NY; **238:** John Craig Photo; **239:** AP/Wide World Photos; **242:** Lass/Archive Photos; **243:** UPI/Corbis-Bettmann; **244:** Library of Congress; **249:** Joe Jones, *We Demand,* 1934, Oil on canvas, 48" x 36", The Butler Institute of American Art, Youngstown, Ohio; **250:** Corbis-Bettmann; **251:** *Young of the Town,* 1933, oil on board, Gerrit V. Sinclair, Williams American Art Galleries, Tennessee; **252:** New York State Historical Association, Cooperstown, New York; **254:** Culver Pictures, Inc.; **256:** New York State Historical Association, Cooperstown, New York; **260 t.:** Photograph by Charles Osgood, Copyrighted 5/23/88, Chicago Tribune Company, All rights reserved. Used with permission.; **b.:** Library of Congress; **261:** *Abraham Lincoln,* George Peter Alexander Healy, In the Collection of The Corcoran Gallery of Art, Washington, DC, Museum Purchase, Gallery Fund, 79.19; **262:** Collection of The New-York Historical Society; **263:** Library of Congress; **264:** *The First reading of the Emancipation Proclamation before the Cabinet,* Courtesy of the Library of Congress; **266:** Courtesy National Archives **270 t.:** Courtesy Raul Sedillo; **b.:** Free Spirit Publishing; **271:** Paul Fusco/Magnum Photos, Inc.; **272:** *The Sacristan of Trampas* (detail), ca. 1915, Paul Burlin, Collection of the Museum of Fine Arts, Museum of New Mexico, 1922; **274:** *Springtime,* c. 1928–29, oil on canvas, 24" x 20", Victor Higgins, Private collection, photo courtesy of the Gerald Peters Gallery, Santa Fe, NM; **276 inset:** Dr. E.R. Degginger; **276–277 background:** ©The Stock Market/Randy Ury; **277 inset:** Dr. E. R. Degginger; **278 t.:** Dr. E. R. Degginger; **b.:** Dr. E. R. Degginger; **278–279 border:** ©The Stock Market/Randy Ury; **279 & 280:** Dr. E. R. Degginger; **280– 281 border:** ©The Stock Market/Randy Ury; **284:** Esbin/Anderson/ Omni-Photo Communications, Inc.; **289:** *Lightning Bolt,* Paul Colon, Vicki Morgan Associates; **290:** Nikky Finney; **291:** ©Otto Greule/Allsport; **292:** *Shoe Series, #2,* Private Collection/Marilee Whitehouse-Holm, SuperStock; **294:** Rogers/Monkmeyer; **296–297:** Audrey Gottlieb/Monkmeyer; **298:** Steven E. Sutton/ Duomo Photography, Inc.; **302–303** Special Olympics; **304 t.:** *Henry Wadsworth Longfellow* (detail), Thomas B. Read, The National Portrait Gallery, Smithsonian Institution, Washington, D.C./Art Resource, New York; **m.:** *John Greenleaf Whittier* (detail), 1881, William Notman, The National Portrait Gallery, Smithsonian Institution, Washington, D.C./Art Resource, New York; **b.:** Photo by Bachrach; **305:** James Lemass/Gamma Liaison; **306:** *The Midnight Ride of Paul Revere,* 1931, Grant Wood, Copyright © 1988 Metropolitan Museum of Art. Arthur Hoppock Hearn Fund, 1950. (50.117), ©1996 Estate of Grant Wood /Licensed by VAGA, New York NY; **308–309:** David Binder/Stock, Boston; **311:** *The Battle of Fredericksburg,* 1862, Frederic Cavada, The Historical Society of Pennsylvania; **314:** Brown Brothers; **315:** Photograph courtesy of the American Medical Women's Association, photograph by Silver Burdett Ginn; **321 l.:** *Thomas Jefferson,* 3rd President of the United States, Publisher: N. Currier, undated, Museum of the City of New York, The Harry T. Peters Collection, 56.300.1044; **r.:** The Granger Collection, New York; **324:** Photo by Jennifer Ashabranner; **325:** Steve Weber/Stock, Boston; **326–327:** Catherine Ursillo/Photo Researchers, Inc.; **327 inset:** Richard Howard/Black Star; **328:** Paul Conklin/PhotoEdit; **329:** Lea/ Omni-Photo Communications, Inc.; **330:** Corbis; **334:** ©Otto Greule/Allsport; **339:** David Young-Wolff/ PhotoEdit; **342–343:** *From Sea to Shining Sea,* 1990, Jacqueline Paton, From the Permanent Collection of The Museum of American Folk Art, New York, NY;

668 t.: John Wyand; **b.:** AP/Wide World Photos; **669:** AP/Wide World Photos; **670:** *Autumn Leaves,* 1994 by Ditz, Private Collection/Bridgeman Art Library International Ltd., London/New York; **673:** ©Robert Pearcy/ Animals Animals; **675:** AP/Wide World Photos; **676–677:** Nathan Beck/Omni-Photo Communications, Inc.; **678:** *Untitled,* ©James Yang /Stock Illustration Source, Inc.; **684 t.:** Corbis-Bettmann; **b:** Library of Congress; **685:** Hazel Carew/Monkmeyer; **686:** Richard Hutchings/ Photo Researchers, Inc.; **687:** Bob Daemmrich/Stock, Boston; **689:** Corbis-Bettmann; **695:** Reuters/Jay Gorodetzer/Archive Photos; **696:** Donna & Kent Dannen/ Photo Researchers, Inc.; **701:** Billy E. Barnes/PhotoEdit; **704–705:** *First Night,* oil on board, Mark Baring, Private Collection/The Bridgeman Art Library International Ltd., London/ New York; **707:** Theatre poster for the 1996 season for the McCarter Theatre in Princeton, NJ. Howard Levine/ David Meyhew, Art Directors, 7 x 11 acrylic, Wiktor Sadowski, Marlena agency; **708 t.:** UPI/Corbis-Bettmann; **711:** Joan Marcus Photography; **712:** UPI/Corbis-Bettmann; **714:** Copyright ANNE FRANK-Fonds, Basle/Switzerland; **717:** Copyright ANNE FRANK-Fonds, Basle/Switzerland; **720:** Jewish Historical Museum, Amsterdam; **727:** Copyright ANNE FRANK-Fonds, Basle/Switzerland; **733:** UPI/Corbis-Bettmann; **738:** The Granger Collection, New York; **743:** The Granger Collection, New York; **746:** Courtesy of Playbill; **747:** Joan Marcus Photography; **748–760:** Copyright ANNE FRANK-Fonds, Basle/Switzerland; **765 & 767:** The Granger Collection, New York; **773:** Peter Cunningham; **776:** Copyright ANNE FRANK-Fonds, Basle/Switzerland; **781:** *The Singer Faure as Hamlet,* Edouard Manet, Kunsthalle, Hamburg, Germany/ A.K.G., Berlin/SuperStock; **782:** *William Shakespeare,* (detail), Artist unknown, by courtesy of the National Portrait Gallery, London; **783:** Bonnie Kamin/ PhotoEdit; **784:** Photofest; **786 l. & r.:** Photo by M. Marigold/ Photofest; **790 & 792:** Photofest; **796:** Title Page with a Portrait of Shakespeare, from Mr. William Shakespeare's Comedies, Histories and Tragedies, edited by J. Heminge and H. Condell, engraved by Droeshurt, 1623, British Library, London, UK/Bridgeman Art Library, London/New York; **801:** Tony Freeman PhotoEdit; **804–805:** *Man at the Edge of Paradise,* 1994, oil on canvas encased in lead, 60" x 84" x 2 ½", Adam Straus, Private Collection, Courtesy Nohra Haime Gallery; **806:** AP/Wide World Photos; **807:** *Nap in the Afternoon,* Kathleen Cook, Courtesy of the artist; **809 & 810:** Ken Karp; **813:** Marsden Hartley, *Birds of the Bagaduce,* 1939, oil on board, 28 x 22". The Butler Institute of American Art, Youngstown, Ohio; **814 t.:** *Henry Wadsworth Longfellow* (detail), Thomas B. Read, The National Portrait Gallery, Smithsonian Institution, Washington, D.C./Art Resource, New York; **b.:** Photo by Dorothy Alexander; **815:** *Benares,* Marshall Johnson, Courtesy, Peabody Essex Museum, Salem, Mass. Photo by Mark Sexton; **816:** *The Lookout—"All's Well,"* 1896, oil on canvas, 39 ⅞ x 30 ⅛" (101.3 x 76.5 cm.), Winslow Homer, Courtesy, Museum of Fine Arts, Boston, MA, Warren Collection; **820–821:** Shelley Rotner/Omni-Photo Communications, Inc.; **822:** *Horse in the Countryside,* 1910, canvas 33 ½ x 44 ½, Franz Marc, Museum Folkwang Essen, Essen, Germany; **826 t.:** New York Public Library; **m.t.:** *William Shakespeare,* (detail), Artist unknown, by courtesy of the National Portrait Gallery, London; **m.b.:** *E. E. Cummings* (detail), 1958, Self Portrait, The National Portrait Gallery, Smithsonian Institution, Washington, D.C./Art Resource, New York; **b.:** Dimitri Kessel/ Life Magazine; **827:** Bruce M. Esbin/Omni-Photo Communications, Inc.; **828:** *Relics,* Martin Lewis, Philadelphia Museum of Art: Bequest of Staunton B. Peck; **829:** Paul Hermansen/Tony Stone Images; **830:** *The Nest,* 1893, Constant Montald, Musées Royaux des Beaux-Arts de Belgique, Bruxelles-Koninklijke Musea voor Schone Kunsten van Belgie, Brussels, Belgium (photo Speltdom); **831:** Amos Zezmer/Omni-Photo Communications, Inc.; **834 t.:** Thomas Victor; **m.t.:** The Granger Collection, New York; **b.:** Photo by Victor Kumin; **835:** *View to Orchard,* Winter, Cerney House, Charles Neal, SuperStock; **836:** *The Magpie,* 1869, Claude Monet, Musée d'Orsay, Paris, ©Photo RMN; **837:** *Herons and Reeds,* hanging scroll, Japan, Asian Art Museum of San Francisco, The Avery Brunkage Collection, B65 D14, photo copyright © 1992 Asian Art Museum of San Francisco, CA. All Rights Reserved.; **838:** *Seashore at Palavas,* 1854, Gustave Courbet, Musée Fabre, Montpellier, France; **839:** Peter Terry/ Tony Stone Images; **845:** Hulton Gutty/Liaison Agency; **848:** Simon Battensby/Tony Stone Images; **853:** *Black Hat on a Yellow Chair,* 1952, Fernand Leger, University of Iowa Museum of Art, Iowa City, IA, Gift of Owen and Leone Elliott, ©2000 Artists Rights Society (ARS), New York/ADAGP, Paris; **854 t.:** ©Faber & Faber Ltd; **m.t.:** AP/Wide World Photos; **m.b.:** Pat Allen-Wolk; **b.:** The Granger Collection, New York; **855:** *Egrets in Summer,* 1940–45, oil on canvas, 82 ⅞ x 159", N. C. Wyeth, Courtesy of Metropolitan Life Insurance Company, Photograph © Malcolm Varon, New York, NY; **856:** Aram Gesar/The Image Bank; **858:** *Crawling Turtle II,* Barry Wilson, SuperStock; **859:** Jeff Greenberg/Omni-Photo Communications, Inc.; **862 t.:** Thomas Victor; **m.t.:** Photo by Kit Stafford; **m.b.:** NYT Pictures; **b.:** Thomas Victor; **863:** Liz Hymans/Tony Stone Images; **864 t.:** *Wallowa Lake,* Harley, Abby Aldrich Rockefeller Folk Art Center, Williamsburg, VA; **b.:** *Jack's Fireplace,* Jack Palance, 29" x 30", oil, photo©Ralph Merlino/ Shooting Star; **866:** ©Telegraph Colour Library/FPG International Corp.; **867:** David Young-Wolff/PhotoEdit; **868:** Mary Kate Denny/Tony Stone Images; **872 & 873:** Corel Professional Photos CD-ROM™; **874 t.:** Corbis-Bettmann; **m.:** *Philip Larkin* (detail), Humphrey Ocean, by Courtesy of the National Portrait Gallery, London; **b.:** Thomas Victor; **875:** Nathan Beck/Omni-Photo Communications, Inc.; **876:** *Red Hills, Lake George,* 1927, oil on canvas, Georgia O'Keeffe, Acquired 1945, The Phillips Collection, Washington, DC, ©2000 The Georgia O'Keeffe Foundation/ Artists Rights Society (ARS), New York; **878:** *China Roses, Broadway,* Alfred William Parsons, watercolor on paper, Christopher Wood Gallery, London, UK/The Bridgeman Art Library International Ltd., London/New York; **882:** Jack Finch/Photo Researchers, Inc.; **887:** David Young-Wolff/ PhotoEdit; **890–891:** *Woodcutter,* 1891, Winslow Homer, Private Collection; **892:** Courtesy of Thomas Benét; **893 & 895:** The Granger Collection, New York; **899:** *His Hair Flows Like a River,* T.C. Cannon, Philbrook Museum of Art, Tulsa, Oklahoma; **900 t.:** © Peter Basch; **m.:** AP/Wide World Photos; **b.:** Mourning Dove (Humishuma) photo by John Lei/Omni-Photo Communications, Inc.; **901:** *Sunset in Memoriam* (detail), 1946, watercolor, 16 ⅞ x 23 ¹⁵⁄₁₆", Woody (Woodrow Wilson) Crumbo, Philbrook Museum of Art, Tulsa, Oklahoma, Gift of Clark Field (1946.45.5); **902:** *Cosmic Canine,* John Nieto, Courtesy of the artist; **905:** *Thunder Knives,* 1957, Pablita Velarde, Santa Clara, Museum of Indian Arts & Culture/Laboratory of Anthropology Collections, Museum of New Mexico, photographer: Blair Clark; **910 t.:** Chuck Slade; **m.t.:** Courtesy of the author; **m.b.:** Jackie Torrence from "Jackie Tales," (detail), published by Avon Books, 1998, Photograph by Michael Pateman; **b.:** Courtesy of the Estate of Carl Van Vechten, Joseph Solomon, Executor, The National Portrait Gallery, Smithsonian Institution, Washington, D.C./Art Resource, New York; **911:** Frederick Judd Waugh, *Breakers at Floodtide,* 1909, 35" x 40", The Butler Institute of American Art, Youngstown, Ohio; **912:** *Invitation to the Dance (el convite),* Theodore Gentilz, Gift, Yanaguana Society in memory of Frederick C. Chabot, Daughters of the Republic of Texas Library; **918:** *Wind and Geometry,* 1978, David True, Courtesy of the artist; **922:** NASA; **923:** AP/Wide World Photos; **926:** Tom Bean/Tony Stone Images; **931:** Collection of Westtown School, Westtown Pennsylvania 19395. Photograph courtesy of the Brandywine River Museum, Chadds Ford, PA; **932: t.** Carl Sandburg, Miriam Svet, The National Portrait Gallery, Smithsonian Institution, Washington, D.C./Art Resource, New York; **m.** Falls Village–Canaan Historical Society; **b.** Davey Crockett, Artist Unknown, The Granger Collection, New York; **933:** *Hammer in His Hand,* Palmer C. Hayden, Museum of African American Art, Palmer C. Hayden Collection, Gift of Miriam A. Hayden, Photograph by Armando Solis; Los Angeles, CA; **935:** *John Henry on the Right, Steam Drill on the Left,* 1944–47, Palmer Hayden, oil on canvas, 30 x 40", Collection of The Museum of African American Art, Los Angeles, CA, Palmer C. Hayden Collection, Gift of Miriam A. Hayden; **937:** *It's Wrote on the Rock,* Palmer C. Hayden, oil on canvas, 25 x 31 ⅞", Collection of The Museum of African American Art, Los Angeles, CA, Palmer C. Hayden Collection, Gift of Miriam A. Hayden; **940:** *Big Bend Tunnel,* 1944–45, Palmer Hayden, oil on canvas, 30 x 40", Collection of The Museum of African American Art, Los Angeles, CA, Palmer C. Hayden Collection, Gift of Miriam A. Hayden; **942:** *He Laid Down his Hammer and Cried,* 1944–47, Palmer C. Hayden, Museum of African American Art, Los Angeles, CA; **944:** UPI/Corbis-Bettmann; **947:** Eric Meola/The Image Bank; **951:** Superman and all related elements are trademarks of DC Comics ©1998. All rights reserved. Used with permission. **952:** Culver Pictures, Inc.; **956:** Photofest; **961:** Will & Deni McIntyre/Photo Researchers, Inc.

344: *Carl Sandburg,* Miriam Svet, The National Portrait Gallery, Smithsonian Institution, Washington, D.C./Art Resource, New York; **345:** Will Faller; **347:** *Paul Bunyan,* Rockwell Kent, The Granger Collection, New York; **351:** *July Hay,* Thomas Hart Benton, oil and egg tempera on composition board, 38" x 26 ¾", Signed and dated (lower left): Benton '43. The Metropolitan Museum of Art, George A. Hearn Fund, 1943. (43.159.1) Photograph copyright ©1982 By the Metropolitan Museum of Art/ ©T.H.Benton and R.P. Benton Testamentary Trusts/Licensed by VAGA, New York, NY; **352:** UPI/Corbis-Bettmann; **353:** Corel Professional Photos CD-ROM™; **354:** Corel Professional Photos CD-ROM™; **356–357 border:** ©The Stock Market/Jeff Gnass; **358–359 border:** Stephen J. Kraseman/DRK Photo; **361 l.:** Photo by South Dakota Tourism; **r.:** Photo courtesy of Jamie Jensen **364 t.:** Archive Photos; **m.t.:** Prentice Hall; **m.b.:** AP/Wide World Photos; **b.:** Thomas Victor; **365:** Corbis-Bettmann; **366:** Corel Professional Photos CD-ROM™; **368 t.:** Courtesy of the Governor; **b.:** Corel Professional Photos CD-ROM™; **371:** AP/Wide World Photos; **378:** Library of Congress; **380–381:** *USS* Constitution *and HMS* Guerriere (Aug. 19, 1812), Thomas Birch, U. S. Naval Academy Museum; **382–383:** *Prisoners,* from Iconographic Encylcopedia, Vol. 2, Div. VI, Naval Sciences, pl. 25, drawn by G. Heck, eng. by Henry Winkles, negative n. 72095, © Collection of the New–York Historical Society; **384–385:** *Row of Cannon,* from Iconographic Encylcopedia, Vol. 2, Div. VI, Naval Sciences, pl. 21 (detail), drawn by G. Heck, eng. by Henry Winkles, negative n. 72094, © Collection of the New–York Historical Society; **386–387:** *Officer of the Watch on the Horseblock,* Heck's Iconographic Encyclopedia, 1851, Collection of The New–York Historical Society; **388–389:** *Ship Plans,* from Iconographic Encylcopedia, Vol. 2, Div. VI, Naval Sciences, pl. 20 (detail), drawn by G. Heck, eng. by Henry Winkles, negative #. 72092, © Collection of the New York Historical Society; **392:** Chapman Billies Inc., Sandwich, MA; **397:** Chen Chi, *High Noon, New York,* 1986. Watercolor, 38" x 35", The Butler Institute of American Art, Youngstown, Ohio; **398 t.:** Russel Lee Photograph Collection, CN #03126, The Center for American History, The University of Texas at Austin; **b.:** Sonja H. Smith; **399–402:** Corel Professional Photos CD-ROM™; **405:** Renee Lynn/Photo Researchers, Inc.; **408 t.:** Jesse Stuart Foundation; **b.:** Prentice Hall; **409 t.:** ©The Stock Market/Gabe Palmer; **m.:** Richard Hutchings/PhotoEdit; **b.:** Bob Daemmrich/Stock, Boston; **411:** Jeff Greenberg/Omni-Photo Communications, Inc.; **412:** Fotopic/ Omni-Photo Communications, Inc.; **414:** *Girl in Car Window,* Winson Trang, Courtesy of the artist; **417:** Will Faller; **422 t.:** Pach/Corbis-Bettmann; **423:** Annie Griffiths/DRK Photo; **424:** *Hearth,* 1957, Loren MacIver, oil and plaster on masonite, H. 49 ⅝" W. 34 ⅝" The Metropolitan Museum of Art, Purchase, Maria-Gaetana Matisse Gift, 1993. (1993.280). Photograph copyright © 1994 by the Metropolitan Museum of Art **426–427:** image©Copyright 1997 PhotoDisc, Inc. **430:** Robert Brennan/PhotoEdit; **435:** Bruce Forster/Tony Stone Images; **438–439:** *Les Memoires d'un saint, (The Memories of a Saint),* 1960, René Magritte, oil on canvas, 31 ½" x 39 ¼", Menil Collection, Houston, photographer: Hickey-Robertson, Houston, ©1998 C. Herscovici/Artists Rights Sociey (ARS), New York; **440:** Thomas Victor; **441:** Edward Holub/Photonica; **443:** Eric Perry/ Photonica; **445:** Joe Squillante/Photonica; **449:** *Spring,* ©1922, Georgia O'Keeffe, oil on canvas, 35 ½" x 30 ⅜", Frances Lehman Loeb Art Center, Vassar College, Poughkeepsie, New York, Bequest of Mrs. Arthur Schwab (Edna Bryner, class of 1907) 1967.31.15, ©2000 The Georgia O'Keeffe Foundation/Artists Rights Society (ARS), New York; **450 t.:** The Mark Twain House, Hartford, CT; **b.:** Janklow & Nesbit Associates, Photograph © by Jill Krementz; **451:** Steve & Dave Maslowski/Photo Researchers, Inc.; **452:** ©1994, Stan Osolinski/FPG International Corp.; **453:** image© Copyright 1997 PhotoDisc, Inc.; **454–455:** Martin and Sally Fox; **455:** image©Copyright 1997 PhotoDisc, Inc.; **456:** image©Copyright 1997 PhotoDisc, Inc.; **458–459 border:** L. West/ Photo Researchers, Inc.; **460:** The Image Bank; **460–461 border:** L. West/Photo Researchers, Inc.; **464 t.:** Photo by Dorothy Alexander; **m.:** ©Archive Photos; **b.:** Photo by William Lewis; **465:** Esbin Anderson/Omni-Photo Communications, Inc.; **466:** *Where to? What For? #3* ©1998 Nancie B. Warner, Courtesy of the artist; **467:** *Inspiration,* Daniel Nevins, SuperStock; **468:** *New York City—Bird's Eye View,* 1920, Joaquin Torres-Garcia, Yale University Art Gallery, Gift of Collection Societe Anonyme, ©1998 Artists Rights Society (ARS), New York/ADAGP, Paris; **472:** *Sir Arthur Conan Doyle* (detail), H. L. Gates, The National Portrait Gallery, London; **473:** Photofest; **475–489:** from *The Complete Adventures of Sherlock Holmes,* illustration by Sidney Paget; **496:** Kurt Wittman/Omni-Photo Communications, Inc.; **501:** *The Blank Signature (Carte Blanche),* 1965, René Magritte, oil on canvas, ©Board of Trustees, National Gallery of Art, Washington, D.C., Collection of Mr. and Mrs. Paul Mellon, ©2000 C. Herscovici/Artists Rights Sociey (ARS), New York; **502 t.:** Flannery Literary, photo © Ruth Wright Paulsen 1993; **m.t.:** AP/Wide World Photos; **m.b.:** Corbis-Bettmann; **b.:** AP/Wide World Photos; **503 b.l.:** Phil Dotson/Photo Researchers, Inc.; **r.:** *Brittle Willow, Brooklyn,* 1992, Anders Knutsson, 37"x 48", acrylic on linen (in the dark), Courtesy of the artist; **t.r.:** Merlin Tuttle/Photo Researchers, Inc.; **504–505:** *Brittle Willow, Brooklyn,* 1992, Anders Knutsson, 37" x 48", acrylic on linen (in the dark), Courtesy of the artist; **506:** Steve Kraseman/DRK Photo; **508–509:** Phil Dotson/ Photo Researchers, Inc.; **510:** Billy E. Barnes/PhotoEdit; **511:** Merlin Tuttle/Photo Researchers, Inc.; **516:** *Album of Virginia "Rockfish Gap and Mountain House,"* Edward Beyer, State Capitol, Commonwealth of Virginia. Courtesy The Library of Virginia; **518:** Culver Pictures, Inc.; **522:** *Variation IV,* Wassily Kandinsky, Russian Bauhaus Archive/SuperStock, **527:** Jonathan Nourok/PhotoEdit; **530–531:** *Mrs. Cushman's House,* 1942, N.C. Wyeth, Harriet Russell Stanley Fund, New Britain Museum of American Art, Conneticut, Photo by E. Irving Blomstrann; **533:** *Dinner at Haddo House,* Alfred Edward Emslie, National Portrait Gallery, London/SuperStock; **535:** Tim Flach/Tony Stone Images; **539:** *Fisherman's Family,* 1916, color woodcut with graphite, B.J.O. Nordfeldt, Amon Carter Museum, Fort Worth, Texas; **540:** Corbis-Bettmann; **541:** M. C. Escher "Self-Portrait" © 1998 Cordon Art B.V. Baarn-Holland. All rights reserved; **543–546:** Culver Pictures, Inc.; **551:** Courtesy National Archives; **552:** Library of Congress; **556 t.:** Thomas Victor; **b.:** Photo by Michael Nye; **557:** *Transfer to the #6,* Kathy Ruttenberg, Gallery Henoch; **558:** *Windows,* 1952, oil on canvas, 32" x 20 ¼", Charles Sheeler, Collection, Hirschl & Adler Galleries; **559:** Ken Karp; **562:** ©Ulf Sjostedt/FPG International Corp.; **564:** "The Prophet" a book by Kahlil Gibran; **567–568:** Bob Daemmrich/Stock, Boston; **572:** *The Tell-Tale Heart,* 1883, Odilon Redon, Charcoal on paper, 15 ¾" x 13 ⅛", Santa Barbara Museum of Art, Museum Purchase; **577:** *Moonwalk,* 1987, serigraph on paper, Andy Warhol, ©1999 Andy Warhol Foundation for the Visual Arts/Ronald Feldman Fine Arts, photograph by D. James Dee/ARS, NY; **578 t.:** *Paul Laurence Dunbar,* The Granger Collection, New York; **b.:** Prentice Hall; **579:** Corel Professional Photos CD-ROM™; **580:** Alan D. Carey/Photo Researchers, Inc.; **582:** *Farm Boy,* 1941, Charles Alston, Courtesy of Clark Atlanta University; **584:** image©Copyright 1997 PhotoDisc, Inc.; **586 b.:** UPI/Corbis-Bettmann **586–588:** Corel Professional Photos CD-ROM™; **590:** *Enoshima. Island at left with cluster of buildings among trees. Fuji in distance at right,* c. 1823. (detail), Katsusika Hokusai, The Newark Museum/Art Resource, NY; **594 t.:** The Granger Collection, New York; **b.:** Courtesy of the author; **595:** *Story Teller,* Velino "Shije" Herrera, National Museum of American Art, Washington, D.C./Art Resource, NY; **596:** *Stirling Station,* 1887, William Kennedy, Collection of Andrew McIntosh Patrick, UK/The Bridgeman Art Library International Ltd., London/New York; **601:** Lawrence Migdale; **602:** Courtesy of D. Alimena; **606–607:** ©The Stock Market/Tom Bean; **612:** Alan D. Carey/Photo Researchers, Inc.; **617:** David Young-Wolff/PhotoEdit; **620–621:** *Still Life #31,* 1963, mixed media construction with television, 48 x 60 x 10 ¾", Tom Wesselmann, Frederick P. Weisman Art Foundation, Los Angeles, CA., ©Tom Wesselmann/ Licensed by VAGA, New York, NY; **622:** Courtesy of the author; **623:** Pat & Tom Leeson/Photo Researchers, Inc.; **626:** Mike Mazzaschi/Stock, Boston; **627:** Tim Flach/Tony Stone Images; **631:** Vincent Van Gogh, *Portrait of Joseph Roulin,* (April 1889), Oil on canvas, 25 ⅜ x 21 ¾" (64.6 x 55.2 cm). The Museum of Modern Art, New York. Gift of Mr. and Mrs. William A. M. Burden, Mr. and Mrs. Paul Rosenberg, Nelson A. Rockefeller, Mr. and Mrs. Armand Bartos, Sidney and Harriet Janis, Mr. and Mrs. Werner E. Josten, and Loula D. Laskar Bequest (by exchange). Photograph ©2000 The Museum of Modern Art, New York; **632 t.:** Thomas Victor; **b.:** Arte Publico Press. Photo by Georgia McInnis; **633:** AP/Wide World Photos; **634:** Jean Paul Nacivet/Leo De Wys, Inc.; **636:** Mel Di Giacomo/ The Image Bank; **637:** Gottlieb/Monkmeyer; **638:** Michael Newman/ PhotoEdit; **646:** The Granger Collection, New York; **647:** Brown Brothers; **648:** The Granger Collection, New York; **649:** Courtesy of D. Alimena; **652 t.:** AP/Wide World Photos; **b.:** ©Archive Photos; **653:** *VII. Fuji in clear weather. One of the "Thirty-six Views of Fuji,"* Hokusai, © Copyright British Museum; **654:** *The Great Wave Off Kanagawa,* Katsushika Hokusai, From the series of Thirty-six views of Fuji, The Metropolitan Museum of Art, The H. O. Havemeyer Collection, Bequest of Mrs. H. O. Havemeyer, 1929, (JP 1847) Photograph © 1978 The Metropolitan Museum of Art; **656:** *The Watchtower,* 1942, watercolor on eggshell lacquered to wood, 5 ½ x 4", Savielly Schleifer, Musée d'Histoire Contemporaine, B.D.I.C., photo courtesy of ARCHIPEL; **658:** *The Unattainable,* Henri Pieck, by courtesy of Karrie Pieck, Holland, and Ineke Pieck, England; **662:** Capece/Monkmeyer Press; **665:** AP/Wide World Photos; **667:** *A Social History of Missouri,* (detail) 1936, Thomas Hart Benton, Courtesy Missouri Department of Natural Resources, photo by Greg Leech/©T. H. Benton and R. P. Benton Testamentary Trusts/Licensed by VAGA, New York, NY;